BUTTERWORTHS
COMMERCIAL AND CONSUMER LAW
HANDBOOK

MEMBERS OF THE LEXISNEXIS GROUP WORLDWIDE

United Kingdom	LexisNexis, a Division of Reed Elsevier (UK) Ltd, Halsbury House, 35 Chancery Lane, London, WC2A 1EL, and London House, 20–22 East London Street, Edinburgh EH7 4BQ
Australia	LexisNexis Butterworths, Chatswood, New South Wales
Austria	LexisNexis Verlag ARD Orac GmbH & Co KG, Vienna
Benelux	LexisNexis Benelux, Amsterdam
Canada	LexisNexis Canada, Markham, Ontario
China	LexisNexis China, Beijing and Shanghai
France	LexisNexis SA, Paris
Germany	LexisNexis Deutschland GmbH Munster
Hong Kong	LexisNexis Hong Kong, Hong Kong
India	LexisNexis India, New Delhi
Italy	Giuffrè Editore, Milan
Japan	LexisNexis Japan, Tokyo
Malaysia	Malayan Law Journal Sdn Bhd, Kuala Lumpur
New Zealand	LexisNexis NZ Ltd, Wellington
Poland	Wydawnictwo Prawnicze LexisNexis Sp, Warsaw
Singapore	LexisNexis Singapore, Singapore
South Africa	LexisNexis Butterworths, Durban
USA	LexisNexis, Dayton, Ohio

© Reed Elsevier (UK) Ltd 2010

Published by LexisNexis

This is a Butterworths title

A CIP Catalogue record for this book is available from the British Library.

ISBN 978 1 4057 5589 4

Typeset by Columns Design Ltd, Reading, England
Printed in the UK by CPI William Clowes Beccles NR34 7TL
Visit LexisNexis at www.lexisnexis.co.uk

BUTTERWORTHS
COMMERCIAL AND CONSUMER LAW
HANDBOOK

Sixth Edition

Consultant Editors

RICHARD B MAWREY QC
Barrister, Henderson Chambers

TOBIAS RILEY-SMITH
Barrister, Henderson Chambers

PREFACE

The last (5th) edition of this Handbook took statute law down to 1 June 2008. The cut-off date for its predecessor, the 4th edition, was 16 May 2003. The astute reader will immediately notice that the interval between editions has dropped dramatically from five years to two. The reason for this was that the legislative fervour which gripped the Labour Government throughout its time in office did not abate as the prospect of a General Election approached – indeed, if anything, it increased. In mitigation, it could be said that much of the legislation involved implementation of EU Directives.

In the preface to the 5th edition we spoke of the 'fundamental changes in the Consumer Credit Act 1974 and its attendant statutory instruments' brought about by the series of new consumer credit regulations in 2004 and the Consumer Credit Act 2006. Shortly after the publication of that edition, the Business Department realised that both the Act and the Regulations were seriously flawed and carried out major changes just before the final implementation dates in October 2008.

Consumer credit practitioners would have been foolish if they had paused to draw breath at this point. The final material in the 5th edition was the Consumer Credit Directive 2008 (2008/48/EC). The implementation of this Directive by the prescribed date of 11 June 2010 proved impossible for the UK Government and most of the legislation will come into force on 1 February 2011. Unusually for legislation, however, some credit-providers are given an option to 'contract into' the new legislation between 30 April 2010 and 31 January 2011. Even after 1 February 2011, some creditors who would otherwise be outside the scope of the changes brought about by the Directive will be able to contract into them if they wish.

Implementation of the Directive has necessarily meant major amendments to the Consumer Credit Act 1974 and a raft of new regulations. These changes will sit alongside the earlier law and the applicable law will depend on the type of agreement. It has thus been necessary to include a new Appendix which shows the Consumer Credit Act 1974 as it stood on 15 June 2006, before any amendments made by the 2006 Act entered into force. The Act as it currently reads and as it will read after 1 February 2011 can be ascertained from the version in the main body of this Handbook (as to the formatting of amendments, see below). It will take many years for even the earliest of these to pass through the system.

On other fronts the major new legislation has been Third Parties (Rights against Insurers) Act 2010 and the (EU derived) Payment Services Regulations 2009 (SI 2009/209). The breathing space afforded by the accession of the Coalition Government seemed a good moment to present the law as at 29 July 2010.

Amendments made by new legislation are incorporated into the text of existing legislation and the notes which follow a provision detail the changes that have been made to the text. In the text:

- an ellipsis (...) indicates that text has been repealed or revoked (or is outside the scope of this Handbook);

- square brackets denote new text which has been inserted or substituted (and which is in force);

- italicised text is prospectively repealed or substituted, or repealed subject to savings;

- underlining denotes text which has been prospectively inserted or substituted (thus where words are prospectively substituted, the existing words will appear in italics followed by the new words underlined and in square brackets).

As on the last occasion, we acknowledge that the law covered by a Handbook of this kind must necessarily overlap with the law relating to financial services, although this overlap has been kept to a minimum, and readers are directed to its companion volume *Butterworths Securities and Financial Services Law Handbook*. Nonetheless, the editorial team will be very grateful for any reader's comments as to material which might usefully have been included in this edition but was not.

As always, the real credit for this edition must go to the in-house team at LexisNexis who do virtually all the work of sourcing the material and putting it into attractive and manageable form. They do all this with no fuss and the utmost efficiency.

The contents of this edition of the Handbook take into account materials available as at 29 July 2010 (although later amendments have been noted where possible).

Richard B. Mawrey QC

Tobias Riley-Smith

July 2010

CONTENTS

PART 2 STATUTORY INSTRUMENTS

PART 3 EU AND INTERNATIONAL MATERIALS

APPENDIX

Consumer Credit Act 1974 (pre CCA 2006) .... **[A1]**

ALPHABETICAL LIST OF CONTENTS

PART 1
STATUTES

STATUTE OF FRAUDS (1677)

(29 Car 2 c 3)

An Act for prevention of Frauds and Perjuryes

NOTES

The short title was given to this Act by the Short Titles Act 1896.

1–3   (*Repealed by the Law of Property Act 1925, s 207, Sch 7.*)

4 No action against executors, etc, upon a special promise, or upon any agreement, or contract for sale of lands, etc, unless agreement, etc, be in writing, and signed

… noe action shall be brought … whereby to charge the defendant upon any speciall promise to answere for the debt default or miscarriages of another person … unlesse the agreement upon which such action shall be brought or some memorandum or note thereof shall be in writeing and signed by the partie to be charged therewith or some other person thereunto by him lawfully authorized.

[1]

NOTES

Words omitted in the first place repealed by the Statute Law Revision Act 1883 and the Statute Law Revision Act 1948; words omitted in the second place repealed by the Law Reform (Enforcement of Contracts) Act 1954, s 1; words omitted in the third place repealed by the Law of Property Act 1925, s 207, Sch 7, and the Law Reform (Enforcement of Contracts) Act 1954, s 1.

5–24   (*Ss 5, 6, 12, 18–21, 22 repealed by the Wills Act 1837, s 2; ss 7–9 repealed by the Law of Property Act 1925, s 207, Sch 7; ss 10, 11, 23 repealed by the Administration of Estates Act 1925, s 56, Sch 2; ss 13, 14 repealed by the Civil Procedure Acts Repeal Act 1879, s 2, Schedule, Pt I; ss 15, 16 repealed by the Sale of Goods Act 1893, s 60, Schedule, s 17 repealed by the Statute Law Revision and Civil Procedure Act 1881; s 24 repealed by the Law of Property Act 1925, s 207, Sch 7 and by the Administration of Estates Act 1925, s 56, Sch 2.*)

LIFE ASSURANCE ACT 1774

(14 Geo 3 c 48)

An Act for regulating Insurances upon Lives, and for prohibiting all such Insurances except in cases where the Persons insuring shall have an Interest in the Life or Death of the Persons insured

NOTES

The short title was given to this Act by the Short Titles Act 1896. It is also known as the Gambling Act 1774.

Exemptions: this Act is excluded in relation to insurance by local authorities against accidents to their members and voluntary assistants by the Local Government Act 1972, ss 140(3), 140C(3), and in relation to insurance by internal drainage boards against accidents to their members by the Land Drainage Act 1991, s 1, Sch 2, para 1(3).

Whereas it hath been found by experience that the making insurances on lives or other events wherein the assured shall have no interest hath introduced a mischievous kind of gaming:

[2]

1 No insurance to be made on lives, etc, by persons having no interest etc

From and after the passing of this Act no insurance shall be made by any person or persons, bodies politick or corporate, on the life or lives of any person or persons, or on any other event or events whatsoever, wherein the person or persons for whose use, benefit, or on whose account such policy or policies shall be made, shall have no interest, or by way of gaming or wagering; and that every assurance made contrary to the true intent and meaning hereof shall be null and void to all intents and purposes whatsoever.

[3]

2 No policies on lives without inserting the names of persons interested, etc

And … it shall not be lawful to make any policy or policies on the life or lives of any person or persons, or other event or events, without inserting in such policy or policies the person or persons name or names interested therein, or for whose use, benefit, or on whose account such policy is so made or underwrote.

[4]

NOTES
Words omitted repealed by the Statute Law Revision Act 1888.
Validation of certain group policies: certain group policies are excluded from the effect of this section with retrospective effect, by the Insurance Companies Amendment Act 1973, s 50.

3 How much may be recovered where the insured hath interest in lives

And ... in all cases where the insured hath interest in such life or lives, event or events, no greater sum shall be recovered or received from the insurer or insurers than the amount of value of the interest of the insured in such life or lives, or other event or events.

[5]

NOTES
Words omitted repealed by the Statute Law Revision Act 1888.

4 Not to extend to insurances on ships, goods, etc

Provided, always, that nothing herein contained shall extend or be construed to extend to insurances bona fide made by any person or persons on ships, goods, or merchandises, but every such insurance shall be as valid and effectual in the law as if this Act had not been made.

[6]

FIRES PREVENTION (METROPOLIS) ACT 1774

(14 Geo 3 c 78)

An Act ... for the more effectually preventing Mischiefs by Fire within the Cities of London and Westminster and the Liberties thereof, and other the Parishes, Precincts, and Places within the Weekly Bills of Mortality, the Parishes of Saint Mary-le-bon, Paddington, Saint Pancras and Saint Luke at Chelsea, in the County of Middlesex ...

NOTES
Short title: given to this Act by the Short Titles Act 1896.
Long title: words omitted repealed by the Statute Law Revision Act 1887. This Act applies to the whole of England.

(Whole Act, except ss 83, 86, repealed by the Metropolitan Fire Brigade Act 1865, s 34.)

83 Money insured on houses burnt how to be applied

And in order to deter and hinder ill-minded persons from wilfully setting their house or houses or other buildings on fire with a view of gaining to themselves the insurance money, whereby the lives and fortunes of many families may be lost or endangered: Be it further enacted by the authority aforesaid, that it shall and may be lawful to and for the respective governors or directors of the several insurance offices for insuring houses or other buildings against loss by fire, and they are hereby authorised and required, upon the request of any person or persons interested in or intitled unto any house or houses or other buildings which may hereafter be burnt down, demolished or damaged by fire, or upon any grounds of suspicion that the owner or owners, occupier or occupiers, or other person or persons who shall have insured such house or houses or other buildings have been guilty of fraud, or of wilfully setting their house or houses or other buildings on fire, to cause the insurance money to be laid out and expended, as far as the same will go, towards rebuilding, reinstating or repairing such house or houses or other buildings so burnt down, demolished or damaged by fire, unless the party or parties claiming such insurance money shall, within sixty days next after his, her or their claim is adjusted, give a sufficient security to the governors or directors of the insurance office where such house or houses or other buildings are insured, that the same insurance money shall be laid out and expended as aforesaid, or unless the said insurance money shall be in that time settled and disposed of to and amongst all the contending parties, to the satisfaction and approbation of such governors or directors of such insurance office respectively.

[7]

86 No action to lie against a person where the fire accidentally begins

And ... no action, suit or process whatever shall be had, maintained or prosecuted against any person in whose house, chamber, stable, barn or other building, or on whose estate any fire shall ... accidentally begin, nor shall any recompence be made by such person for any damage suffered thereby, any law, usage or custom to the contrary notwithstanding: ... provided that no contract or agreement made between landlord and tenant shall be hereby defeated or made void.

[8]

NOTES
   Words omitted in the first place repealed by the Statute Law Revision Act 1888; words omitted in the second place repealed by the Statute Law Revision Act 1948; words omitted in the final place repealed by the Statute Law Revision Act 1958 and by virtue of the Statute Law Revision Act 1861.

STATUTE OF FRAUDS AMENDMENT ACT 1828

(9 Geo 4 c 14)

An Act for rendering a written Memorandum necessary to the Validity of certain Promises and Engagements

[9 May 1828]

NOTES
   The short title was given to this Act by the Short Titles Act 1896. It is also known as Lord Tenterden's Act.

1–5   (*Ss 1, 3, 4 repealed by the Limitation Act 1939, s 34, Schedule, and the Statute of Limitations Act (Northern Ireland) 1958, s 75, Schedule; s 2 repealed by the Statute Law Revision Act 1890; s 5 repealed by the Statute Law Revision Act 1875.*)

6 Action not maintainable on representations of character, etc, unless they be in writing signed by the party chargeable

No action shall be brought whereby to charge any person upon or by reason of any representation or assurance made or given concerning or relating to the character, conduct, credit, ability, trade, or dealings of any other person, to the intent or purpose that such other person may obtain credit, money, or goods upon, unless such representation or assurance be made in writing, signed by the party to be charged therewith.

[9]

7, 8   (*S 7 repealed by the Sale of Goods Act 1893, s 60, Schedule; s 8 repealed by the Limitation Act 1939, s 34, Schedule, and the Statute of Limitations Act (Northern Ireland) 1958, s 75, Schedule.*)

9 Act not to extend to Scotland

Nothing in this Act contained shall extend to Scotland.

[10]

10   (*Repealed by the Statute Law Revision Act 1873.*)

AUCTIONEERS ACT 1845

(8 & 9 Vict c 15)

An Act ... to impose a new Duty on the Licence to be taken out by all Auctioneers in the United Kingdom

[8 May 1845]

NOTES
   The short title was given to this Act by the Short Titles Act 1896. Words omitted repealed by the Statute Law Revision Act 1891.

1–6   (*S 1 repealed by the Statute Law Revision Act 1875; ss 2–6 repealed retrospectively by the Finance Act 1949, ss 14, 52(9), (10), Sch 11, Pt I.*)

7 Auctioneer, before commencing any sale, shall affix or suspend a ticket or board containing his full christian and surname and place of residence

... Every auctioneer, before beginning any auction, shall affix or suspend, or cause to be affixed or suspended, a ticket or board, containing his true and full christian and surname and residence painted, printed, or written in large letters publicly visible and legible, in some conspicuous part of the room or place where the auction is held, so that all persons may easily read the same, and shall also keep such ticket or board so affixed or suspended during the whole time of such auction being held; and if any auctioneer begins any auction, or acts as auctioneer at any auction, in any room or place where his name and residence is not so painted or written on a ticket or board so affixed or suspended, and kept affixed or suspended as aforesaid, he shall forfeit for every such offence the sum of twenty pounds.

[11]–[12]

NOTES
Words omitted repealed by the Statute Law Revision Act 1891.
The sum of twenty pounds: this Act does not state whether this offence is to be tried summarily or on indictment. In the case of an offence that is triable on indictment only, there is now no limit to the fine that may be imposed; see the Criminal Law Act 1977, s 32.
The particulars which under this section must be displayed in some conspicuous part of the room, etc, where the auction is held include a copy of the Auctions (Bidding Agreements) Act 1927 and the Auctions (Bidding Agreements) Act 1969; see s 3 of the 1927 Act at **[355]** and s 4 of the 1969 Act at **[479]**.

8, 9   (*S 8 repealed retrospectively by the Finance Act 1949, ss 14, 52(9), (10), Sch 11, Pt I; s 9 repealed by the Statute Law Revision Act 1875.*)

COMMON LAW PROCEDURE ACT 1854

(17 & 18 Vict c 125)

An Act for the further Amendment of the Process, Practice, and Mode of Pleading in and enlarging the Jurisdiction of the Superior Courts of Common Law at Westminster, and of the Superior Courts of Common Law of the Counties Palatine of Lancaster and Durham ...

[12 August 1854]

NOTES
Long title: words omitted repealed by the Statute Law Revision and Civil Procedure Act 1883, s 3, Schedule, and the Statute Law Revision Act 1892. Repeals by those Acts were, however, subject to savings of jurisdiction established by the repealed enactments and savings of the application of the repealed enactments to local courts.

1–86   (*Ss 1, 2, 18, 19, 31–58, 60–86 repealed by the Statute Law Revision and Civil Procedure Act 1883, s 3, Schedule and ss 21–27, 30 repealed by the Statute Law Revision Act 1892, all subject to the savings mentioned in the Introductory Note to this Act; ss 3–17 repealed by the Arbitration Act 1889, s 26, Sch 2; s 20 repealed by the Oaths Act 1888, s 6, Schedule; ss 28, 29 repealed by the Inland Revenue Repeal Act 1870, s 2, Schedule; s 59 repealed by the Courts Act 1971, s 56, Sch 11, Pt I.*)

87   Actions on lost negotiable instruments

In case of any action founded upon a ... negotiable instrument, it shall be lawful for the court or a judge to order that the loss of such instrument shall not be set up, provided an indemnity is given, to the satisfaction of the court or judge, or a master, against the claims of any other person upon such negotiable instrument.

[13]

NOTES
Words omitted, which related to bills of exchange, repealed by the Statute Law Revision Act 1892.

88–98   (*S 88 repealed by the Common Law Procedure Act 1860, s 35; s 89 repealed by the Statute Law Revision Act 1892 and ss 90–96 repealed by the Statute Law Revision and Civil Procedure Act 1883, s 3, Schedule, subject to the savings mentioned in the Introductory Note to this Act; ss 97, 98 repealed by the Supreme Court of Judicature (Officers) Act 1879, s 29, Sch 2.*)

99   Interpretation of terms

In the construction of this Act the word "court" shall be understood to mean any one of the Superior Courts of Common Law at Westminster: and the word "judge" shall be understood to mean a judge or baron of any of the said courts; and the word "master" shall be understood to mean a master of any of the said courts; and the word "action" shall be understood to mean any personal action in any of the said courts.

[14]

NOTES
Repealed by the Statute Law Revision and Civil Procedure Act 1883, s 3, Schedule, subject to the savings mentioned in the Introductory Note to this Act.

Superior Courts of Common Law: the jurisdiction of the former Courts of Common Law was vested in the High Court by the Supreme Court of Judicature (Consolidation) Act 1925, ss 18, 224 (repealed), see now the Senior Courts Act 1981, s 19, Sch 4, para 1.

100–105   (*Ss 100–102, 104, 105 repealed by the Statute Law Revision and Civil Procedure Act 1883, s 3, Schedule, and s 103 repealed by the Statute Law Revision Act 1892, subject to the savings mentioned in the Introductory Note to this Act.*)

106   Short title of Act

In citing this Act in any instrument, document, or proceeding, it shall be sufficient to use the expression, "The Common Law Procedure Act 1854."

[15]

107   Act not to extend to Ireland or Scotland

Nothing in this Act shall extend to Ireland or Scotland …

[16]

NOTES

Words omitted repealed by the Statute Law Revision Act 1875.

MERCANTILE LAW AMENDMENT ACT 1856

(19 & 20 Vict c 97)

An Act to amend the Laws of England and Ireland affecting Trade and Commerce
[29 July 1856]

1, 2   (*Repealed by the Sale of Goods Act 1893, s 60, Schedule.*)

3   Written guarantee not to be invalid by reason that the consideration does not appear in writing

No special promise to be made by any person … to answer for the debt default, or miscarriage of another person, being in writing, and signed by the party to be charged therewith, or some other person by him thereunto lawfully authorised, shall be deemed invalid to support an action, suit, or other proceeding to charge the person by whom such promise shall have been made, by reason only that the consideration for such promise does not appear in writing or by necessary inference from a written document.

[17]

NOTES

Words omitted repealed by the Statute Law Revision Act 1892.

4   (*Repealed by the Partnership Act 1890, s 48, Schedule.*)

5   Surety who discharges the liability to be entitled to assignment of all securities held by the creditor, and to stand in the place of the creditor

Every person who, being surety for the debt or duty of another, or being liable with another for any debt or duty, shall pay such debt or perform such duty, shall be entitled to have assigned to him, or to a trustee for him, every judgment specialty, or other security which shall be held by the creditor in respect of such debt or duty, whether such judgment, specialty, or other security shall or shall not be deemed at law to have been satisfied by the payment of the debt or performance of the duty, and such person shall be entitled to stand in the place of the creditor, and to use all the remedies, and, if need be, and upon a proper indemnity, to use the name of the creditor, in any action or other proceeding, at law or in equity, in order to obtain from the principal debtor, or any co-surety, co-contractor, or co-debtor, as the case may be, indemnification for the advances made and loss sustained by the person who shall have so paid such debt or performed such duty, and such payment or performance so made by such surety shall not be pleadable in bar of any such action or other proceeding by him: Provided always, that no co-surety, cocontractor, or codebtor shall be entitled to recover from any other co-surety, cocontractor, or codebtor, by the means aforesaid, more than the just proportion to which, as between those parties themselves, such last-mentioned person shall be justly liable.

[18]

6, 7   (*Ss 6, 7 repealed by the Bills of Exchange Act 1882, s 96, Sch 2.*)

8 Definition of home port

In relation to the rights and remedies of persons having claims for repairs done to or supplies furnished to or for, ships, every port within the United Kingdom of Great Britain and Ireland, the Islands of Man, Guernsey, Jersey, Alderney, and Sark, and the islands adjacent to any of them, being part of the dominions of Her Majesty, shall be deemed a home port.

[19]

9–15 (*Ss 9–14 repealed by the Limitation Act 1939, s 34, Schedule, and the Statute of Limitations Act (Northern Ireland) 1958, s 75, Schedule; s 15 repealed by the Statute Law Revision Act 1894.*)

16 Short title

In citing this Act, it shall be sufficient to use the expression "The Mercantile Law Amendment Act 1856."

[20]

17 Extent

Nothing in this Act shall extend to Scotland.

[21]

POLICIES OF ASSURANCE ACT 1867

(30 & 31 Vict c 144)

ARRANGEMENT OF SECTIONS

An Act to enable Assignees of Policies of Life Assurance to sue thereon in their own names

[20 August 1867]

(*Preamble repealed by the Statute Law Revision Act 1893.*)

1 Assignees of life policies, empowered to sue

Any person or corporation now being or hereafter becoming entitled, by assignment or other derivative title, to a policy of life assurance, and possessing at the time of action brought the right in equity to receive and the right to give an effectual discharge to the assurance company liable under such policy for monies thereby assured or secured, shall be at liberty to sue at law in the name of such person or corporation to recover such monies.

[22]

2 Defence or reply on equitable grounds

In any action on a policy of life assurance, a defence on equitable grounds, or a reply to such defence on similar grounds, may be respectively pleaded and relied upon in the same manner and to the same extent as in any other personal action.

[23]

3 Notice of assignment

No assignment made after the passing of this Act of a policy of life assurance shall confer on the assignee therein named, his executors, administrators, or assigns, any right to sue for the amount of such policy, or the monies assured or secured thereby, until a written notice of the date and purport of such assignment shall have been given to the assurance company liable under such policy at their principal place of business for the time being, or in case they have two or more principal places of business, then at some one of such principal places of business, either in England or Scotland or Ireland; and the date on which such notice shall be received shall regulate the priority of all claims under any assignment; and a payment bona fide made in respect of any policy by any assurance company before the date on which such notice shall have been received shall be as valid against the assignee giving such notice as if this Act had not been passed.

[24]

4 Principal place of business to be specified on policies

Every assurance company shall, on every policy issued by them after the thirtieth day of September one thousand eight hundred and sixty-seven, specify their principal place or principal places of business at which notices of assignment may be given in pursuance of this Act.

[25]

5 Mode of assignment

Any such assignment may be made either by endorsement on the policy or by a separate instrument in the words or to the effect set forth in the schedule hereto, such endorsement or separate instrument being duly stamped.

[26]

6 Receipt of notice of assignment

Every assurance company to whom notice shall have been duly given of the assignment of any policy under which they are liable shall, upon the request in writing of any person by whom any such notice was given or signed, or of his executors or administrators, and upon payment in each case of a fee not exceeding [25p] deliver an acknowledgment in writing, under the hand of the manager, secretary, treasurer, or other principal officer of the assurance company, of their receipt of such notice; and every such written acknowledgment, if signed by a person being de jure or de facto the manager, secretary, treasurer, or other principal officer of the assurance company whose acknowledgment the same purports to be, shall be conclusive evidence as against such assurance company of their having duly received the notice to which such acknowledgment relates.

[27]

NOTES
Sum in square brackets substituted by virtue of the Decimal Currency Act 1969, s 10(1).

7 Interpretation

In the construction and for the purposes of this Act the expression "policy of life assurance" or "policy" shall mean any instrument by which the payment of monies by or out of the funds of an assurance company, on the happening of any contingency depending on the duration of human life, is assured or secured; and the expression "assurance company" shall mean and include every corporation, association, society, or company now or hereafter carrying on the business of assuring lives, or survivorships, either alone or in conjunction with any other object or objects.

[28]

8 Saving of contracts under 16 & 17 Vict c 45, or 27 & 28 Vict c 43, and of engagements by friendly societies

Provided always, that this Act shall not apply to any policy of assurance granted or to be granted or to any contract for a payment on death entered into or to be entered into in pursuance of the provisions of the Government Annuities Act 1853, and the Government Annuities Act 1864, or either of those Acts, or to any engagement for payment on death by any friendly society.

[29]

NOTES
Government Annuities Act 1853 and Government Annuities Act 1864: repealed with savings by the Government Annuities Act 1929, s 66, Sch 2, Pt II, see now Pt II of that Act.

9 Short title

For all purposes this Act may be cited as "The Policies of Assurance Act 1867."

[30]

SCHEDULE

Section 5

I *A.B.*, of, &c, in consideration of, &c, do hereby assign unto *C.D.*, of, &c, his executors, administrators, and assigns, the [within] policy of assurance granted, &c [*here describe the policy*].

In witness, &c

[31]

BILLS OF SALE ACT 1878

(41 & 42 Vict c 31)

ARRANGEMENT OF SECTIONS

An Act to consolidate and amend the Law for preventing Frauds upon Creditors by secret Bills of Sale of Personal Chattels

[22 July 1878]

NOTES

Bills of Sale Acts 1878 and 1882: by the Bills of Sale Act (1878) Amendment Act 1882, s 1, that Act and this Act may be cited together as the Bills of Sale Acts 1878 and 1882; see **[57]**.

1 Short title

This Act may be cited for all purposes as the Bills of Sale Act 1878.

[32]

2 Commencement

… the first day of January one thousand eight hundred and seventy-nine, … is in this Act referred to as the commencement of this Act.

[33]

NOTES

Words omitted repealed by the Statute Law Revision Act 1894.

3 Application

This Act shall apply to every bill of sale executed on or after the first day of January one thousand eight hundred and seventy-nine (whether the same be absolute, or subject or not subject to any trust) whereby the holder or grantee has power, either with or without notice, and either immediately or at any future time, to seize or take possession of any personal chattels comprised in or made subject to such bill of sale.

[34]

NOTES

Application, construction and partial repeal of this Act: this Act remains in force so far as it relates to absolute bills of sale executed after its commencement; as to bills of sale given as security for the payment of money it is to be construed as one with the Bills of Sale Act (1878) Amendment Act 1882 (by virtue of s 3 of the 1882 Act at **[59]**), but as to such bills of sale only, this Act is repealed as far as it is inconsistent with the 1882 Act (by virtue of s 15 of the 1882 Act at **[72]**).

4   Interpretation of terms

In this Act the following words and expressions shall have the meanings in this section assigned to them respectively, unless there be something in the subject or context repugnant to such construction; (that is to say),

    The expression "bill of sale" shall include bills of sale, assignments, transfers, declarations of trust without transfer, inventories of goods with receipt thereto attached, or receipts for purchase moneys of goods, and other assurances of personal chattels, and also powers of attorney, authorities, or licenses to take possession of personal chattels as security for any debt, and also any agreement, whether intended or not to be followed by the execution of any other instrument, by which a right in equity to any personal chattels, or to any charge or security thereon, shall be conferred, but shall not include the following documents; that is to say, assignments for the benefit of the creditors of the person making or giving the same, marriage settlements, transfers or assignments of any ship or vessel or any share thereof, transfers of goods in the ordinary course of business of any trade or calling, bills of sale of goods in foreign parts or at sea, bills of lading, India warrants, warehouse-keepers' certificates, warrants or orders for the delivery of goods, or any other documents used in the ordinary course of business as proof of the possession or control of goods, or authorising or purporting to authorise, either by indorsement or by delivery, the possessor of such document to transfer or receive goods thereby represented:

    The expression "personal chattels" shall mean goods, furniture, and other articles capable of complete transfer by delivery, and (when separately assigned or charged) fixtures and growing crops, but shall not include chattel interests in real estate, nor fixtures (except trade machinery as herein-after defined), when assigned together with a freehold or leasehold interest in any land or building to which they are affixed, nor growing crops when assigned together with any interest in the land on which they grow, nor shares or interests in the stock, funds, or securities of any government, or in the capital or property of incorporated or joint stock companies, nor choses in action, nor any stock or produce upon any farm or lands which by virtue of any covenant or agreement or of the custom of the country ought not to be removed from any farm where the same are at the time of making or giving of such bill of sale:

    Personal chattels shall be deemed to be in the "apparent possession" of the person making or giving a bill of sale, so long as they remain or are in or upon any house, mill, warehouse, building, works, yard, land, or other premises occupied by him, or are used and enjoyed by him in any place whatsoever, notwithstanding that formal possession thereof may have been taken by or given to any other person:

    "Prescribed" means prescribed by rules made under the provisions of this Act.

[35]

5   Application of Act to trade machinery

From and after the commencement of this Act trade machinery shall, for the purposes of this Act, be deemed to be personal chattels, and any mode of disposition of trade machinery by the owner thereof which would be a bill of sale as to any other personal chattels shall be deemed to be a bill of sale within the meaning of this Act.

    For the purposes of this Act—

        "Trade machinery" means the machinery used in or attached to any factory or workshop;

1st	Exclusive of the fixed motive-powers, such as the water-wheels and steam-engines, and the steam-boilers, donkey-engines, and other fixed appurtenances of the said motive-powers; and,
2nd	Exclusive of the fixed power machinery, such as the shafts, wheels, drums, and their fixed appurtenances, which transmit the action of the motive-powers to the other machinery, fixed and loose, and
3rd	Exclusive of the pipes for steam gas and water in the factory or workshop.

        The machinery or effects excluded by this section from the definition of trade machinery shall not be deemed to be personal chattels within the meaning of this Act.

        "Factory or workshop" means any premises on which any manual labour is exercised by way of trade, or for purposes of gain, in or incidental to the following purposes or any of them; that is to say,

(a)	In or incidental to the making any article or part of an article; or
(b)	In or incidental to the altering, repairing, ornamenting, finishing, of any article; or
(c)	In or incidental to the adapting for sale any article.

[36]

6   Certain instruments giving powers of distress to be subject to this Act

Every attornment instrument or agreement, not being a mining lease, whereby a power of distress is given or agreed to be given by any person to any other person by way of security for any present future or contingent debt or advance, and whereby any rent is reserved or made payable as a mode of providing for the payment of interest on such debt or advance, or otherwise for the purpose of such security only, shall be deemed to be a bill of sale, within the meaning of this Act, of any personal chattels which may be seized or taken under such power of distress.

Provided, that nothing in this section shall extend to any mortgage of any estate or interest in any land tenement or hereditament which the mortgagee, being in possession, shall have demised to the mortgagor as his tenant at a fair and reasonable rent.

[37]

7 Fixtures or growing crops not to be deemed separately assigned when the land passes by the same instrument

No fixtures or growing crops shall be deemed, under this Act, to be separately assigned or charged by reason only that they are assigned by separate words, or that power is given to sever them from the land or building to which they are affixed, or from the land on which they grow, without otherwise taking possession of or dealing with such land or building, or land, if by the same instrument any freehold or leasehold interest in the land or building to which such fixtures are affixed, or in the land on which such crops grow, is also conveyed or assigned to the same persons or person.

The same rule of construction shall be applied to all deeds or instruments, including fixtures or growing crops, executed before the commencement of this Act, and then subsisting and in force, in all questions arising under any bankruptcy liquidation assignment for the benefit of creditors, or execution of any process of any court, which shall take place or be issued after the commencement of this Act.

[38]

8 Avoidance of unregistered bill of sale in certain cases

Every bill of sale to which this Act applies shall be duly attested and shall be registered under this Act, within seven days after the making or giving thereof, and shall set forth the consideration for which such bill of sale was given, otherwise such bill of sale, as against all trustees or assignees of the estate of the person whose chattels, or any of them, are comprised in such bill of sale under the law relating to bankruptcy or liquidation, or under any assignment for the benefit of the creditors of such person, and also as against all sheriffs officers and other persons seizing any chattels comprised in such bill of sale, in the execution of any process of any court authorising the seizure of the chattels of the person by whom or of whose chattels such bill has been made, and also as against every person on whose behalf such process shall have been issued, shall be deemed fraudulent and void so far as regards the property in or right to the possession of any chattels comprised in such bill of sale which, at or after the time of filing the petition for bankruptcy or liquidation, or of the execution of such assignment, or of executing such process (as the case may be), and after the expiration of such seven days are in the possession or apparent possession of the person making such bill of sale (or of any person against whom the process has issued under or in the execution of which such bill has been made or given, as the case may be).

[39]

NOTES

This section is in terms repealed by the Bills of Sale Act (1878) Amendment Act 1882, s 15 at [72], but notwithstanding that, the effect of the Bills of Sale Act (1878) Amendment Act 1882, s 3 at [59], is that the repeal applies only to bills of sale to which the later Act applies, so that this section remains in force so far as regards bills of sale not given as a security for money (ie, absolute bills of sale).

9 Avoidance of certain duplicate bills of sale

Where a subsequent bill of sale is executed within or on the expiration of seven days after the execution of a prior unregistered bill of sale, and comprises all or any part of the personal chattels comprised in such prior bill of sale, then, if such subsequent bill of sale is given as a security for the same debt as is secured by the prior bill of sale, or for any part of such debt, it shall, to the extent to which it is a security for the same debt or part thereof, and so far as respects the personal chattels or part thereof comprised in the prior bill, be absolutely void, unless it is proved to the satisfaction of the court having cognizance of the case that the subsequent bill of sale was bona fide given for the purpose of correcting some material error in the prior bill of sale, and not for the purpose of evading this Act.

[40]

10 Mode of registering bills of sale

A bill of sale shall be attested and registered under this Act in the following manner—
   (1)   The execution of every bill of sale shall be attested by a solicitor of the [Senior Courts], and the attestation shall state that before the execution of the bill of sale the effect thereof has been explained to the grantor by the attesting solicitor.
   (2)   Such bill, with every schedule or inventory thereto annexed or therein referred to, and also a true copy of such bill and of every such schedule or inventory, and of every attestation of the execution of such bill of sale, together with an affidavit of the time of

such bill of sale being made or given, and of its due execution and attestation, and a description of the residence and occupation of the person making or giving the same (or in case the same is made or given by any person under or in the execution of any process, then a description of the residence and occupation of the person against whom such process issued), and of every attesting witness to such bill of sale, shall be presented to and the said copy and affidavit shall be filed with the registrar within seven clear days after the making or giving of such bill of sale, in like manner as a warrant of attorney in any personal action given by a trader is now by law required to be filed:

(3)   If the bill of sale is made or given subject to any defeasance or condition, or declaration of trust not contained in the body thereof such defeasance, condition, or declaration shall be deemed to be part of the bill, and shall be written on the same paper or parchment therewith before the registration, and shall be truly set forth in the copy filed under this Act therewith and as part thereof, otherwise the registration shall be void.

In case two or more bills of sale are given, comprising in whole or in part any of the same chattels, they shall have priority in the order of the date of their registration respectively as regards such chattels.

A transfer or assignment of a registered bill of sale need not be registered.

[41]

NOTES

Sub-s (1): as regards absolute bills of sale the requirements of sub-s (1) must still be observed, for, although repealed by the Bills of Sale Act (1878) Amendment Act 1882, s 10, it remains in force so far as absolute bills are concerned by virtue of s 3 of that Act at **[59]**; words in square brackets substituted by the Constitutional Reform Act 2005, s 59(5), Sch 11, Pt 2, para 4(1), (3).

Local registration: see the Bills of Sale Act (1878) Amendment Act 1882, s 11 at **[68]**, and the Bills of Sale (Local Registration) Rules 1960, SI 1960/2326.

11   Renewal of registration

The registration of a bill of sale, whether executed before or after the commencement of this Act, must be renewed once at least every five years, and if a period of five years elapses from the registration or renewed registration of a bill of sale without a renewal or further renewal (as the case may be), the registration shall become void.

The renewal of a registration shall be effected by filing with the registrar an affidavit stating the date of the bill of sale and of the last registration thereof, and the names, residences, and occupations of the parties thereto as stated therein, and that the bill of sale is still a subsisting security.

Every such affidavit may be in the form set forth in the schedule (A.) to this Act annexed.

A renewal of registration shall not become necessary by reason only of a transfer or assignment of a bill of sale.

[42]

12   Form of register

The registrar shall keep a book (in this Act called "the register") for the purposes of this Act, and shall, upon the filing of any bill of sale or copy under this Act, enter therein in the form set forth in the second schedule (B) to this Act annexed, or in any other prescribed form, the name, residence and occupation of the person by whom the bill was made or given (or in case the same was made or given by any person under or in the execution of process, then the name residence and occupation of the person against whom such process was issued, and also the name of the person or persons to whom or in whose favour the bill was given), and the other particulars shown in the said schedule or to be prescribed under this Act, and shall number all such bills registered in each year consecutively, according to the respective dates of their registration.

Upon the registration of any affidavit of renewal the like entry shall be made, with the addition of the date and number of the last previous entry relating to the same bill, and the bill of sale or copy originally filed shall be thereupon marked with the number affixed to such affidavit of renewal.

The registrar shall also keep an index of the names of the grantors of registered bills of sale with reference to entries in the register of the bills of sale given by each such grantor.

Such index shall be arranged in divisions corresponding with the letters of the alphabet, so that all grantors whose surnames begin with the same letter (and no others) shall be comprised in one division, but the arrangement within each such division need not be strictly alphabetical.

[43]

13   The registrar

The masters of the [Senior Courts] attached to the Queen's Bench Division of the High Court of Justice, or such other officers as may for the time being be assigned for this purpose under the provisions of the Supreme Court of Judicature Acts, 1873 and 1875, shall be the registrar for the purposes of this Act, and any one of the said masters may perform all or any of the duties of the registrar.

[44]

NOTES
Words in square brackets substituted by the Constitutional Reform Act 2005, s 59(5), Sch 11, Pt 2, para 4(1), (3).
Supreme Court of Judicature Acts 1873 and 1875: repealed by the Supreme Court of Judicature (Consolidation) Act 1925, s 226, Sch 6 (repealed).

14 Rectification of register

Any judge of the High Court of Justice on being satisfied that the omission to register a bill of sale or an affidavit or renewal thereof within the time prescribed by this Act, or the omission or mis-statement of the name residence or occupation of any person, was accidental or due to inadvertence, may in his discretion order such omission or mis-statement to be rectified by the insertion in the register of the true name residence or occupation, or by extending the time for such registration on such terms and conditions (if any) as to security, notice by advertisement or otherwise, or as to any other matter, as he thinks fit to direct.

[45]

15 Entry of satisfaction

Subject to and in accordance with any rules to be made under and for the purposes of this Act, the registrar may order a memorandum of satisfaction to be written upon any registered copy of a bill of sale, upon the prescribed evidence being given that the debt (if any) for which such bill of sale was made or given has been satisfied or discharged.

[46]

16 Copies may be taken, etc

Any person shall be entitled to have an office copy or extract of any registered bill of sale, and affidavit of execution filed therewith, or copy thereof, and of any affidavit filed therewith, if any, or registered affidavit of renewal, upon paying for the same at the like rate as for office copies of judgments of the High Court of Justice, and any copy of a registered bill of sale, and affidavit purporting to be an office copy thereof, shall in all courts and before all arbitrators or other persons, be admitted as prima facie evidence thereof, and of the fact and date of registration as shown thereon …

[47]

NOTES
Words omitted repealed by the Bills of Sale Act (1878) Amendment Act 1882, s 16.

17 Affidavits

Every affidavit required by or for the purposes of this Act may be sworn before a master of any division of the High Court of Justice, or before any commissioner empowered to take affidavits in the [Senior Courts] …

[48]

NOTES
Words in square brackets substituted by the Constitutional Reform Act 2005, s 59(5), Sch 11, Pt 2, para 4(1), (3); words omitted repealed by the Perjury Act 1911, s 17 (repealed), see now s 2(2) of that Act.

18   (*Repealed by the Statute Law Revision Act 1950.*)

19 Collection of fees under 38 & 39 Vict c 77 s 26

Section twenty-six of the Supreme Court of Judicature Act 1875, and any enactments for the time being in force amending or substituted for that section shall apply to fees under this Act, and an order under that section may, if need be, be made in relation to such fees accordingly.

[49]

NOTES
Supreme Court of Judicature 1875, s 26: repealed by the Supreme Court of Judicature (Consolidation) Act 1925, s 226, Sch 6 (repealed).

20   Order and disposition

Chattels comprised in a bill of sale which has been and continues to be duly registered under this Act shall not be deemed to be in the possession, order, or disposition of the grantor of the bill of sale within the meaning of the Bankruptcy Act 1869.

[50]

NOTES

The provisions of this section are not affected, so far as regards absolute bills of sale, by the repeal of the section by the Bills of Sale Act (1878) Amendment Act 1882, s 15 at **[72]**, the effect of s 3 of the 1882 Act at **[59]** being that the repeal only applies to bills which are within the latter Act (ie, bills given as security for the payment of money).

Bankruptcy Act 1869: repealed by the Bankruptcy Act 1883, s 169, Sch 5 (repealed). See now the Insolvency Act 1986, s 283 and c f ss 307–309, 338 of that Act.

21   Rules

Rules for the purposes of this Act may be made and altered from time to time by the like persons and in the like manner in which rules and regulations may be made under and for the purposes of the Supreme Court of Judicature Acts 1873 and 1875.

[51]

NOTES

Supreme Court of Judicature Acts 1873 and 1875: repealed as to the relevant provisions for the purposes of this section by the Supreme Court of Judicature (Consolidation) Act 1925, s 226, Sch 6 (repealed).

Rules: the Bills of Sale (Local Registration) Rules 1960, SI 1960/2326.

22   Time for registration

When the time for registering a bill of sale expires on a Sunday, or other day on which the registrar's office is closed, the registration shall be valid if made on the next following day on which the office is open.

[52]

23   As to bills of sale and under repealed Acts

… Except as is herein expressly mentioned with respect to construction and with respect to renewal of registration, nothing in this Act shall affect any bill of sale executed before the commencement of this Act, and as regards bills of sale so executed the Acts hereby repealed shall continue in force.

Any renewal after the commencement of this Act of the registration of a bill of sale executed before the commencement of this Act, and registered under the Acts hereby repealed, shall be made under this Act in the same manner as the renewal of a registration made under this Act.

[53]

NOTES

Words omitted repealed the Bills of Sale Act 1854 and the Bills of Sale Act 1866 and were themselves repealed by the Statute Law Revision Act 1894.

24   Extent of Act

This Act shall not extend to Scotland or to Ireland.

[54]

SCHEDULES

SCHEDULE A

Section 11

I [*AB*] of do swear that a bill of sale, bearing date the day of 18 [*insert the date of the bill,*] and made between [*insert the names and descriptions of the parties in the original bill of sale*] and which said bill of sale [*or, and a copy of which said bill of sale, as the case may be*] was registered on the day of 18 [*insert date of registration*], is still a subsisting security.

Sworn, & c.

[55]

SCHEDULE B

Section 12

Satis-faction entered	No	By whom given (or against whom process issued)			To whom given	Nature of Instru-ment	Date	Date of Regist-ration	Date of Regist-ration of affidavit of renewal
		Name	Resid-ence	Occu-pation					

[56]

BILLS OF SALE ACT (1878) AMENDMENT ACT 1882

(45 & 46 Vict c 43)

ARRANGEMENT OF SECTIONS

An Act to amend the Bills of Sale Act 1878

[18 August 1882]

1 Short title

This Act may be cited for all purposes as the Bills of Sale Act (1878) Amendment Act 1882; and this Act and the Bills of Sale Act 1878 may be cited together as the Bills of Sale Acts 1878 and 1882.

[57]

2 Commencement of Act

This Act shall come into operation on the first day of November one thousand eight hundred and eighty-two, which date is herein-after referred to as the commencement of this Act.

[58]

3 Construction of Act

The Bills of Sale Act 1878 is herein-after referred to as "the principal Act," and this Act shall, so far as is consistent with the tenor thereof, be construed as one with the principal Act; but unless the context otherwise requires shall not apply to any bill of sale duly registered before the commencement of this Act so long as the registration thereof is not avoided by non-renewal or otherwise.

The expression "bill of sale," and other expressions in this Act, have the same meaning as in the principal Act, except as to bills of sale or other documents mentioned in section four of the principal

Act, which may be given otherwise than by way of security for the payment of money, to which last-mentioned bills of sale and other documents this Act shall not apply.

[59]

4 Bill of sale to have schedule of property attached thereto

Every bill of sale shall have annexed thereto or written thereon a schedule containing an inventory of the personal chattels comprised in the bill of sale; and such bill of sale, save as herein-after mentioned, shall have effect only in respect of the personal chattels specifically described in the said schedule; and shall be void, except as against the grantor, in respect of any personal chattels not so specifically described.

[60]

5 Bill of sale not to affect after acquired property

Save as herein-after mentioned, a bill of sale shall be void, except as against the grantor, in respect of any personal chattels specifically described in the schedule thereto of which the grantor was not the true owner at the time of the execution of the bill of sale.

[61]

6 Exception as to certain things

Nothing contained in the foregoing sections of this Act shall render a bill of sale void in respect of any of the following things; (that is to say,)
(1)   Any growing crops separately assigned or charged where such crops were actually growing at the time when the bill of sale was executed.
(2)   Any fixtures separately assigned or charged, and any plant, or trade machinery where such fixtures, plant, or trade machinery are used in, attached to, or brought upon any land, farm, factory, workshop, shop, house, warehouse, or other place in substitution for any of the like fixtures, plant, or trade machinery specifically described in the schedule to such bill of sale.

[62]

7 Bill of sale with power to seize except in certain events to be void

Personal chattels assigned under a bill of sale shall not be liable to be seized or taken possession of by the grantee for any other than the following causes:—
(1)   If the grantor shall make default in payment of the sum or sums of money thereby secured at the time therein provided for payment, or in the performance of any covenant or agreement contained in the bill of sale and necessary for maintaining the security;
(2)   If the grantor shall become a bankrupt, or suffer the said goods or any of them to be distrained[, or taken control of using the power in Schedule 12 to the Tribunals, Courts and Enforcement Act 2007,] for rent, rates, or taxes;
(3)   If the grantor shall fraudulently either remove or suffer the said goods, or any of them, to be removed from the premises;
(4)   If the grantor shall not, without reasonable excuse, upon demand in writing by the grantee, produce to him his last receipts for rent, rates, and taxes;
(5)   If execution shall have been levied against the goods of the grantor under any judgment at law:
  Provided that the grantor may within five days from the seizure or taking possession of any chattels on account of any of the above-mentioned causes, apply to the High Court, or to a judge thereof in chambers, and such court or judge, if satisfied that by payment of money or otherwise the said cause of seizure no longer exists, may restrain the grantee from removing or selling the said chattels, or may make such other order as may seem just.

[63]

NOTES
  Sub-s (2): words in square brackets inserted by the Tribunals, Courts and Enforcement Act 2007, s 62(3), Sch 13, paras 17, 18, as from a day to be appointed.

[7A Defaults under consumer credit agreements

  (1)   Paragraph (1) of section 7 of this Act does not apply to a default relating to a bill of sale given by way of security for the payment of money under a regulated agreement to which section 87(1) of the Consumer Credit Act 1974 applies—
    (a)   unless the restriction imposed by section 88(2) of that Act has ceased to apply to the bill of sale; or
    (b)   if, by virtue of section 89 of that Act, the default is to be treated as not having occurred.
  (2)   Where paragraph (1) of section 7 of this Act does apply in relation to a bill of sale such as is mentioned in subsection (1) of this section, the proviso to that section shall have effect with the substitution of "county court" for "High Court".]

[64]

NOTES
  Inserted by the Consumer Credit Act 1974, s 192(3)(a), Sch 4, para 1.

8 Bill of sale to be void unless attested and registered

Every bill of sale shall be duly attested, and shall be registered under the principal Act within seven clear days after the execution thereof, or if it is executed in any place out of England then within seven clear days after the time at which it would in the ordinary course of post arrive in England if posted immediately after the execution thereof; and shall truly set forth the consideration for which it was given; otherwise such bill of sale shall be void in respect of the personal chattels comprised therein.

[65]

NOTES
  Principal Act: ie, the Bills of Sale Act 1878.

9 Form of bill of sale

A bill of sale made or given by way of security for the payment of money by the grantor thereof shall be void unless made in accordance with the form in the schedule to this Act annexed.

[66]

10 Attestation

The execution of every bill of sale by the grantor shall be attested by one or more credible witness or witnesses, not being a party or parties thereto ...

[67]

NOTES
  Words omitted repealed by the Statute Law Revision Act 1898.

11 Local registration of contents of bills of sale

Where the affidavit (which under section ten of the principal Act is required to accompany a bill of sale when presented for registration) describes the residence of the person making or giving the same or of the person against whom the process is issued to be in some place outside [the London insolvency district] or where the bill of sale describes the chattels enumerated therein as being in some place outside [the London insolvency district], the registrar under the principal Act shall forthwith and within three clear days after registration in the principal registry, and in accordance with the prescribed directions, transmit an abstract in the prescribed form of the contents of such bill of sale to the [district judge] in whose district such places are situate, and if such places are in the districts of different [district judges] to each such [district judge].

Every abstract so transmitted shall be filed, kept, and indexed by the [district judge] of the county court in the prescribed manner, and any person may search, inspect, make extracts from, and obtain copies of the abstract so registered in the like manner, and upon the like terms as to payment or otherwise as near as may be as in the case of bills of sale registered by the registrar under the principal Act.

[68]

NOTES
  Words in first and second pairs of square brackets substituted by the Insolvency Act 1985, s 235(1), Sch 8, para 1; for savings, see the Insolvency Act 1986, s 437, Sch 11, Pt II para 10; words in third, fourth, fifth and sixth pairs of square brackets substituted by the Courts and Legal Services Act 1990, s 74(1)(a), (3).
  Registration: the Bills of Sale (Local Registration) Rules 1960, SI 1960/2326, regulate the local registration of bills of sale.
  Principal Act: ie, the Bills of Sale Act 1878.

12 Bill of sale under £30 to be void

Every bill of sale made or given in consideration of any sum under thirty pounds shall be void.

[69]

13 Chattels not to be removed or sold

All personal chattels seized or of which possession is taken ... under or by virtue of any bill of sale (whether registered before or after the commencement of this Act), shall remain on the premises where they were so seized or so taken possession of, and shall not be removed or sold until after the expiration of five clear days from the day they were so seized or so taken possession of.

[70]

NOTES
  Words omitted repealed by the Statute Law Revision Act 1898.

14   Bill of sale not to protect chattels against poor and parochial rates

A bill of sale to which this Act applies shall be no protection in respect of personal chattels included in such bill of sale which but for such bill of sale would have been liable to distress under a warrant[, or subject to a warrant of control,] for the recovery of taxes and poor and other parochial rates.

[71]

NOTES
   Words in square brackets inserted by the Tribunals, Courts and Enforcement Act 2007, s 62(3), Sch 13, paras 17, 19, as from a day to be appointed.

15   Repeal of part of Bills of Sale Act 1878

... all ... enactments contained in the principal Act which are inconsistent with this Act are repealed ...

[72]

NOTES
   Words omitted repealed by the Statute Law Revision Act 1898.
   Principal Act: ie, the Bills of Sale Act 1878.

16   Inspection of registered bills of sale

... any person shall be entitled at all reasonable times to search the register on payment of a fee of [five pence], or such other fee as may be prescribed, and subject to such regulations as may be prescribed, and shall be entitled at all reasonable times to inspect, examine, and make extracts from any and every registered bill of sale without being required to make a written application, or to specify any particulars in reference thereto, upon payment of [five pence] for each bill of sale inspected, and such payment shall be made by a judicature stamp: Provided that the said extracts shall be limited to the dates of execution registration, renewal of registration, and satisfaction, to the names, addresses, and occupations of the parties, to the amount of the consideration, and to any further prescribed particulars.

[73]

NOTES
   Words omitted repealed by the Statute Law Revision Act 1898; words in square brackets substituted by virtue of the Decimal Currency Act 1969, s 10(1).

17   Debentures to which Act not to apply

Nothing in this Act shall apply to any debentures issued by any mortgage, loan or other incorporated company [or by any limited liability partnership], and secured upon the capital stock or goods, chattels, and effects of such company [or a limited liability partnership].

[74]

NOTES
   Words in square brackets inserted and added by the Limited Liability Partnerships Regulations 2001, SI 2001/1090, reg 9, Sch 5, para 1.

18   Extent of Act

This Act shall not extend to Scotland or Ireland.

[75]

SCHEDULE
FORM OF BILL OF SALE

Section 9

This Indenture made the day of, between *AB* of the one part, and *CD* of the other part, witnesseth that in consideration of the sum of £ now paid to *AB* by *CD* the receipt of which the said *AB* hereby acknowledges [*or whatever else the consideration may be*], he the said *AB* doth hereby assign unto *CD*, his executors, administrators, and assigns, all and singular the several chattels and things specifically described in the schedule hereto annexed by way of security for the payment of the sum of £   , and interest thereon at the rate of per cent per annum [*or whatever else may be the rate*]. And the said *AB* doth further agree and declare that he will duly pay to the said *CD* the principal sum aforesaid, together with the interest then due, by equal payments of £   on the day of [*or whatever else may be the stipulated times or time of payment*]. And the said *AB* doth also agree with the said *CD* that he will [*here insert terms as to insurance, payment of rent or otherwise, which the parties may agree to for the maintenance or defeasance of the security*].

   Provided always, that the chattels hereby assigned shall not be liable to seizure or to be taken possession of by the said *CD* for any cause other than those specified in section seven of the Bills of Sale Act (1878) Amendment Act 1882.

In Witness, &c.

Signed and sealed by the said *AB* in the presence of me *EF* [*add witness' name, address, and description*].

[76]

BILLS OF EXCHANGE ACT 1882

(45 & 46 Vict c 61)

ARRANGEMENT OF SECTIONS

PART I
PRELIMINARY

PART II
BILLS OF EXCHANGE

Form and interpretation

Capacity and authority of parties

The consideration for a bill

Negotiation of bills

General duties of the holder

An Act to codify the law relating to Bills of Exchange, Cheques, and Promissory Notes

[18 August 1882]

NOTES

By the Bills of Exchange (Time of Noting) Act 1917, s 2, the Bills cf Exchange Act 1882 and the 1917 Act may be cited by the collective title of the Bills of Exchange Acts 1882 to 1917.

PART I
PRELIMINARY

1   Short title

This Act may be cited as the Bills of Exchange Act, 1882.

[77]

2   Interpretation of terms

In this Act, unless the context otherwise requires,—

"Acceptance" means an acceptance completed by delivery or notification.

"Action" includes counter claim and set off.

"Banker" includes a body of persons whether incorporated or not who carry on the business of banking.

"Bankrupt" includes any person whose estate is vested in a trustee or assignee under the law for the time being in force relating to bankruptcy.

"Bearer" means the person in possession of a bill or note which is payable to bearer.

"Bill" means bill of exchange, and "note" means promissory note.

"Delivery" means transfer of possession, actual or constructive, from one person to another.

"Holder" means the payee or indorsee of a bill or note who is in possession of it, or the bearer thereof.

"Indorsement" means an indorsement completed by delivery.

"Issue" means the first delivery of a bill or note, complete in form to a person who takes it as a holder.

"Person" includes a body of persons whether incorporated or not.

["postal operator" has the meaning given by section 125(1) of the Postal Services Act 2000.]

"Value" means valuable consideration.

"Written" includes printed, and "writing" includes print.

[78]

NOTES

Definition "postal operator" inserted by the Postal Services Act 2000 (Consequential Modifications No 1) Order 2001, SI 2001/1149, art 3(1), Sch 1, para 4(1), (2).

PART II
BILLS OF EXCHANGE

Form and interpretation

3   Bill of exchange defined

(1)   A bill of exchange is an unconditional order in writing, addressed by one person to another, signed by the person giving it, requiring the person to whom it is addressed to pay on demand or at a fixed or determinable future time a sum certain in money to or to the order of a specified person, or to bearer.

(2)   An instrument which does not comply with these conditions, or which orders any act to be done in addition to the payment of money, is not a bill of exchange.

(3)   An order to pay out of a particular fund is not unconditional within the meaning of this section; but an unqualified order to pay, coupled with (a) an indication of a particular fund out of which the drawee is to re-imburse himself or a particular account to be debited with the amount, or (b) a statement of the transaction which gives rise to the bill, is unconditional.

(4)   A bill is not invalid by reason—
   (a)   That it is not dated;
   (b)   That it does not specify the value given, or that any value has been given therefor;
   (c)   That it does not specify the place where it is drawn or the place where it is payable.

[79]

NOTES

Bill of exchange: a bill of exchange drawn on or after 15 February 1971 is invalid if the sum payable is an amount of money wholly or partly in shillings or pence, see the Decimal Currency Act 1969, s 2(1).

---

4   Inland and foreign bills

(1)   An inland bill is a bill which is or on the face of it purports to be (a) both drawn and payable within the British Islands, or (b) drawn within the British Islands upon some person resident therein. Any other bill is a foreign bill.

For the purposes of this Act "British Islands" mean any part of the United Kingdom of Great Britain and Ireland the islands of Man, Guernsey, Jersey Alderney, and Sark, and the islands adjacent to any of them being part of the dominions of Her Majesty.

(2)   Unless the contrary appear on the face of the bill the holder may treat it as an inland bill.

[80]

5   Effect where different parties to bill are the same person

(1)   A bill may be drawn payable to, or to the order of, the drawer; or it may be drawn payable to, or to the order of, the drawee.

(2)   Where in a bill drawer and drawee are the same person, or where the drawee is a fictitious person or a person not having capacity to contract, the holder may treat the instrument, at his option, either as a bill of exchange or as a promissory note.

[81]

6   Address to drawee

(1)   The drawee must be named or otherwise indicated in a bill with reasonable certainty.

(2)   A bill may be addressed to two or more drawees whether they are partners or not, but an order addressed to two drawees in the alternative or to two or more drawees in succession is not a bill of exchange.

[82]

7   Certainty required as to payee

(1)   Where a bill is not payable to bearer, the payee must be named or otherwise indicated therein with reasonable certainty.

(2)   A bill may be made payable to two or more payees jointly, or it may be made payable in the alternative to one of two, or one or some of several payees. A bill may also be made payable to the holder of an office for the time being.

(3)   Where the payee is a fictitious or non-existing person the bill may be treated as payable to bearer.

[83]

8   What bills are negotiable

(1)   When a bill contains words prohibiting transfer, or indicating an intention that it should not be transferable, it is valid as between the parties thereto, but is not negotiable.

(2)   A negotiable bill may be payable either to order or to bearer.

(3)   A bill is payable to bearer which is expressed to be so payable, or on which the only or last indorsement is an indorsement in blank.

(4)   A bill is payable to order which is expressed to be so payable, or which is expressed to be payable to a particular person, and does not contain words prohibiting transfer or indicating an intention that it should not be transferable.

(5)   Where a bill, either originally or by indorsement, is expressed to be payable to the order of a specified person, and not to him or his order, it is nevertheless payable to him or his order at his option.

[84]

9 Sum payable

(1) The sum payable by a bill is a sum certain within the meaning of this Act, although it was required to be paid—
  (a) With interest.
  (b) By stated instalments.
  (c) By stated instalments, with a provision that upon default in payment of any instalment the whole shall become due.
  (d) According to an indicated rate of exchange or according to a rate of exchange to be ascertained as directed by the bill.

(2) Where the sum payable is expressed in words and also in figures, and there is a discrepancy between the two, the sum denoted by the words is the amount payable.

(3) Where a bill is expressed to be payable with interest, unless the instrument otherwise provides, interest runs from the date of the bill, and if the bill is undated from the issue thereof.

[85]

10 Bill payable on demand

(1) A bill is payable on demand—
  (a) Which is expressed to be payable on demand, or at sight, or on presentation; or
  (b) In which no time for payment was expressed.

(2) Where a bill is accepted or indorsed when it is overdue, it shall, as regards the acceptor who so accepts, or any indorser who so indorses it, be deemed a bill payable on demand.

[86]

11 Bill payable at a future time

A bill is payable at a determinable future time within the meaning of this Act which is expressed to be payable—
  (1) At a fixed period after date or sight.
  (2) On or at a fixed period after the occurrence of a specified event which is certain to happen, though the time of happening may be uncertain.

An instrument expressed to be payable on a contingency is not a bill, and the happening of the event does not cure the defect.

[87]

12 Omission of date in bill payable after date

Where a bill expressed to be payable at a fixed period after date is issued undated, or where the acceptance of a bill payable at a fixed period after sight is undated, any holder may insert therein the true date of issue or acceptance, and the bill shall be payable accordingly.

Provided that (1) where the holder in good faith and by mistake inserts a wrong date, and (2) in every case where a wrong date is inserted, if the bill subsequently comes into the hands of a holder in due course the bill shall not be avoided thereby, but shall operate and be payable as if the date so inserted had been the true date.

[88]

13 Ante-dating and post-dating

(1) Where a bill or an acceptance or any indorsement on a bill is dated, the date shall, unless the contrary be proved, be deemed to be the true date of the drawing, acceptance, or indorsement, as the case may be.

(2) A bill is not invalid by reason only that it is ante-dated or post-dated, or that it bears date on a Sunday.

[89]

14 Computation of time of payment

Where a bill is not payable on demand the day on which it falls due is determined as follows—
  [(1) The bill is due and payable in all cases on the last day of the time of payment as fixed by the bill or, if that is a non-business day, on the succeeding business day.]
  (2) Where a bill is payable at a fixed period after date, after sight, or after the happening of a specified event, the time of payment is determined by excluding the day from which the time is to begin to run and by including the day of payment.
  (3) Where a bill is payable at a fixed period after sight, the time begins to run from the date of the acceptance if the bill be accepted, and from the date of noting or protest if the bill be noted or protested for non-acceptance, or for non-delivery.
  (4) The term "month" in a bill means calendar month.

[90]

NOTES

Sub-s (1): substituted by the Banking and Financial Dealings Act 1971, s 3(2).

15   Case of need

The drawer of a bill and any indorser may insert therein the name of a person to whom the holder may resort in case of need, that is to say, in case the bill is dishonoured by non-acceptance or non-payment. Such person is called the referee in case of need. It is in the option of the holder to resort to the referee in case of need or not as he may think fit.

[91]

16   Optional stipulations by drawer or indorser

The drawer of a bill, and any indorser, may insert therein an express stipulation—

    (1)   Negativing or limiting his own liability to the holder.

    (2)   Waiving as regards himself some or all of the holder's duties.

[92]

17   Definition and requisites of acceptance

    (1)   The acceptance of a bill is the signification by the drawee of his assent to the order of the drawer.

    (2)   An acceptance is invalid unless it complies with the following conditions, namely—

    (a)   It must be written on the bill and be signed by the drawee. The mere signature of the drawee without additional words is sufficient.

    (b)   It must not express that the drawee will perform his promise by any other means than the payment of money.

[93]

18   Time for acceptance

A bill may be accepted—

    (1)   Before it has been signed by the drawer, or while otherwise incomplete:

    (2)   When it is overdue, or after it has been dishonoured by a previous refusal to accept, or by non-payment:

    (3)   When a bill payable after sight is dishonoured by non-acceptance, and the drawee subsequently accepts it, the holder, in the absence of any different agreement, is entitled to have the bill accepted as of the date of first presentment to the drawee for acceptance.

[94]

19   General and qualified acceptances

    (1)   An acceptance is either (a) general or (b) qualified.

    (2)   A general acceptance assents without qualification to the order of the drawer. A qualified acceptance in expressed terms varies the effect of the bill as drawn.

In particular an acceptance is qualified which is—

    (a)   conditional, that is to say, which makes payment by the acceptor dependent on the fulfilment of a condition therein stated:

    (b)   partial, that is to say, an acceptance to pay part only of the amount for which the bill is drawn:

    (c)   local, that is to say, an acceptance to pay only at a particular specified place:

    An acceptance to pay at a particular place is a general acceptance, unless it expressly states that the bill is to be paid there only and not elsewhere:

    (d)   qualified as to time:

    (e)   the acceptance of some one or more of the drawees, but not of all.

[95]

20   Inchoate instruments

    (1)   Where a simple signature on a blank ... paper is delivered by the signer in order that it may be converted into a bill, it operates as a prima facie authority to fill it up as a complete bill for any amount ... , using the signature for that of the drawer, or the acceptor, or an indorser; and, in like manner, when a bill is wanting in any material particular, the person in possession of it has a prima facie authority to fill up the omission in any way he thinks fit.

    (2)   In order that any such instrument when completed may be enforceable against any person who became a party thereto prior to its completion, it must be filled up within a reasonable time, and strictly in accordance with the authority given. Reasonable time for this purpose is a question of fact.

Provided that if any such instrument after completion is negotiated to a holder in due course it shall be valid and effectual for all purposes in his hands, and he may enforce it as if it had been filled up within a reasonable time and strictly in accordance with the authority given.

[96]

NOTES
Sub-s (1): words omitted repealed by the Finance Act 1970, s 36(8), Sch 8, Pt V and the Finance Act (Northern Ireland) 1970, s 19, Sch 3, Pt III.

21 Delivery

(1)   Every contract on a bill, whether it be the drawer's, the acceptor's, or an indorser's, is incomplete and revocable, until delivery of the instrument in order to give effect thereto.

Provided that where an acceptance is written on a bill, and the drawee gives notice to or according to the directions of the person entitled to the bill that he has accepted it, the acceptance then becomes complete and irrevocable.

(2)   As between immediate parties, and as regards a remote party other than a holder in due course, the delivery—

(a)   in order to be effectual must be made either by or under the authority of the party drawing, accepting, or indorsing, as the case may be:

(b)   may be shown to have been conditional or for a special purpose only, and not for the purpose of transferring the property in the bill.

But if the bill be in the hands of a holder in due course a valid delivery of the bill by all parties prior to him so as to make them liable to him is conclusively presumed.

(3)   Where a bill is no longer in the possession of a party who has signed it as drawer, acceptor, or indorser, a valid and unconditional delivery by him is presumed until the contrary is proved.

[97]

Capacity and authority of parties

22 Capacity of parties

(1)   Capacity to incur liability as a party to a bill is co-extensive with capacity to contract.

Provided that nothing in this section shall enable a corporation to make itself liable as drawer, acceptor, or indorser of a bill unless it is competent to it so to do under the law for the time being in force relating to corporations.

(2)   Where a bill is drawn or indorsed by an infant, minor, or corporation having no capacity or power to incur liability on a bill, the drawing or indorsement entitles the holder to receive payment of the bill, and to enforce it against any other party thereto.

[98]

23 Signature essential to liability

No person is liable as drawer, indorser, or acceptor of a bill who has not signed it as such: Provided that

(1)   Where a person signs a bill in a trade or assumed name, he is liable thereon as if he had signed it in his own name:

(2)   The signature of the name of a firm is equivalent to the signature by the person so signing of the names of all persons liable as partners in that firm.

[99]

24 Forged or unauthorised signature

Subject to the provisions of this Act, where a signature on a bill is forged or placed thereon without the authority of the person whose signature it purports to be, the forged or unauthorised signature is wholly inoperative, and no right to retain the bill or to give a discharge therefor or to enforce payment thereof against any party thereto can be acquired through or under that signature, unless the party against whom it is sought to retain or enforce payment of the bill is precluded from setting up the forgery or want of authority.

Provided that nothing in this section shall affect the ratification of an unauthorised signature not amounting to a forgery.

[100]

25 Procuration signatures

A signature by procuration operates as notice that the agent has but a limited authority to sign, and the principal is only bound by such signature if the agent in so signing was acting within the actual limits of his authority.

[101]

26 Person signing as agent or in representative capacity

(1)   Where a person signs a bill as drawer, indorser, or acceptor, and adds words to his signature, indicating that he signs for or on behalf of a principal, or in a representative character, he is not personally liable thereon; but the mere addition to his signature of words describing him as an agent, or as filling a representative character, does not exempt him from personal liability.

(2)   In determining whether a signature on a bill is that of the principal or that of the agent by whose hand it is written, the construction most favourable to the validity of the instrument shall be adopted.

[102]

The consideration for a bill

27   Value and holder for value

(1)   Valuable consideration for a bill may be constituted by,—
(a)   Any consideration sufficient to support a simple contract;
(b)   An antecedent debt or liability. Such a debt or liability is deemed valuable consideration whether the bill is payable on demand or at a future time.

(2)   Where value has at any time been given for a bill the holder is deemed to be a holder for value as regards the acceptor and all parties to the bill who became parties prior to such time.

(3)   Where the holder of a bill has a lien on it arising either from contract or by implication of law, he is deemed to be a holder for value to the extent of the sum for which he has a lien.

[103]

28   Accommodation bill or party

(1)   An accommodation party to a bill is a person who has signed a bill as drawer, acceptor, or indorser, without receiving value therefor, and for the purpose of lending his name to some other person.

(2)   An accommodation party is liable on the bill to a holder for value; and it is immaterial whether, when such holder took the bill, he knew such party to be an accommodation party or not.

[104]

29   Holder in due course

(1)   A holder in due course is a holder who has taken a bill, complete and regular on the face of it, under the following conditions; namely,
(a)   That he became the holder of it before it was overdue, and without notice that it had been previously dishonoured, if such was the fact:
(b)   That he took the bill in good faith and for value, and that at the time the bill was negotiated to him he had no notice of any defect in the title of the person who negotiated it.

(2)   In particular the title of a person who negotiates a bill is defective within the meaning of this Act when he obtained the bill, or the acceptance thereof, by fraud, duress, or force and fear, or other unlawful means, or an illegal consideration, or when he negotiates it in breach of faith, or under such circumstances as amount to a fraud.

(3)   A holder (whether for value or not), who derives his title to a bill through a holder in due course, and who is not himself a party to any fraud or illegality affecting it, has all the rights of that holder in due course as regards the acceptor and all parties to the bill prior to that holder.

[105]

30   Presumption of value and good faith

(1)   Every party whose signature appears on a bill is prima facie deemed to have become a party thereto for value.

(2)   Every holder of a bill is prima facie deemed to be a holder in due course; but if in an action on a bill it is admitted or proved that the acceptance, issue, or subsequent negotiation of the bill is affected with fraud, duress, or force and fear, or illegality, the burden of proof is shifted, unless and until the holder proves that, subsequent to the alleged fraud or illegality, value has in good faith been given for the bill.

[106]

Negotiation of bills

31   Negotiation of bill

(1)   A bill is negotiated when it is transferred from one person to another in such a manner as to constitute the transferee the holder of the bill.

(2)   A bill payable to bearer is negotiated by delivery.

(3)   A bill payable to order is negotiated by the indorsement of the holder completed by delivery.

(4)   Where the holder of a bill payable to his order transfers it for value without indorsing it, the transfer gives the transferee such title as the transferor had in the bill, and the transferee in addition acquires the right to have the indorsement of the transferor.

(5)   Where any person is under obligation to indorse a bill in a representative capacity, he may indorse the bill in such terms as to negative personal liability.

[107]

32   Requisites of a valid indorsement

An indorsement in order to operate as a negotiation must comply with the following conditions, namely,—

(1)   It must be written on the bill itself and be signed by the indorser. The simple signature of the indorser on the bill, without additional words, is sufficient.

An indorsement written on an allonge, or on a "copy" of a bill issued or negotiated in a country where "copies" are recognised, is deemed to be written on the bill itself.

(2)   It must be an indorsement of the entire bill. A partial indorsement, that is to say, an indorsement which purports to transfer to the indorsee a part only of the amount payable, or which purports to transfer the bill to two or more indorsees severally, does not operate as a negotiation of the bill.

(3)   Where a bill is payable to the order of two or more payees or indorsees who are not partners all must indorse, unless the one indorsing has authority to indorse for the others.

(4)   Where, in a bill payable to order, the payee or indorsee is wrongly designated, or his name is mis-spelt, he may indorse the bill as therein described, adding, if he think fit, his proper signature.

(5)   Where there are two or more indorsements on a bill, each indorsement is deemed to have been made in the order in which it appears on the bill, until the contrary is proved.

(6)   An indorsement may be made in blank or special. It may also contain terms making it restrictive.

[108]

33   Conditional indorsement

Where a bill purports to be indorsed conditionally the condition may be disregarded by the payer, and payment to the indorsee is valid whether the condition has been fulfilled or not.

[109]

34   Indorsement in blank and special indorsement

(1)   An indorsement in blank specifies no indorsee, and a bill so indorsed becomes payable to bearer.

(2)   A special indorsement specifies the person to whom, or to whose order, the bill is to be payable.

(3)   The provisions of this Act relating to a payee apply with the necessary modifications to an indorsee under a special indorsement.

(4)   When a bill has been indorsed in blank, any holder may convert the blank indorsement into a special indorsement by writing above the indorser's signature a direction to pay the bill to or to the order of himself or some other person.

[110]

35   Restrictive indorsement

(1)   An indorsement is restrictive which prohibits the further negotiation of the bill or which expresses that it is a mere authority to deal with the bill as thereby directed and not a transfer of the ownership thereof, as, for example, if a bill be indorsed "Pay D only," or "Pay D for the account of X," or "Pay D or order for collection."

(2)   A restrictive indorsement gives the indorsee the right to receive payment of the bill and to sue any party thereto that his indorser could have sued, but gives him no power to transfer his rights as indorsee unless it expressly authorise him to do so.

(3)   Where a restrictive indorsement authorises further transfer, all subsequent indorsees take the bill with the same rights and subject to the same liabilities as the first indorsee under the restrictive indorsement.

[111]

36   Negotiation of overdue or dishonoured bill

(1)   Where a bill is negotiable in its origin it continues to be negotiable until it has been (a) restrictively indorsed or (b) discharged by payment or otherwise.

(2)   Where an overdue bill is negotiated, it can only be negotiated subject to any defect of title affecting it at its maturity, and thenceforward no person who takes it can acquire or give a better title than that which the person from whom he took it had.

(3)   A bill payable on demand is deemed to be overdue within the meaning and for the purposes of this section, when it appears on the face of it to have been in circulation for an unreasonable length of time. What is an unreasonable length of time for this purpose is a question of fact.

(4)   Except where an indorsement bears date after the maturity of the bill, every negotiation is prima facie deemed to have been effected before the bill was overdue.

(5)   Where a bill which is not overdue has been dishonoured any person who takes it with notice of the dishonour takes it subject to any defect of title attaching thereto at the time of dishonour, but nothing in this sub-section shall affect the rights of a holder in due course.

[112]

37 Negotiation of bill to party already liable thereon

Where a bill is negotiated back to the drawer, or to a prior indorser or to the acceptor, such party may, subject to the provisions of this Act, re-issue and further negotiate the bill, but he is not entitled to enforce payment of the bill against any intervening party to whom he was previously liable.

[113]

38 Rights of the holder

The rights and powers of the holder of a bill are as follows—
  (1)   He may sue on the bill in his own name:
  (2)   Where he is a holder in due course, he holds the bill free from any defect of title of prior parties, as well as from mere personal defences available to prior parties among themselves, and may enforce payment against all parties liable on the bill:
  (3)   Where his title is defective (a) if he negotiates the bill to a holder in due course, that holder obtains a good and complete title to the bill, and (b) if he obtains payment of the bill the person who pays him in due course gets a valid discharge for the bill.

[114]

General duties of the holder

39 When presentment for acceptance is necessary

  (1)   Where a bill is payable after sight, presentment for acceptance is necessary in order to fix the maturity of the instrument.

  (2)   Where a bill expressly stipulates that it shall be presented for acceptance, or where a bill is drawn payable elsewhere than at the residence or place of business of the drawee, it must be presented for acceptance before it can be presented for payment.

  (3)   In no other case is presentment for acceptance necessary in order to render liable any party to the bill.

  (4)   Where the holder of a bill, drawn payable elsewhere than at the place of business or residence of the drawee, has not time, with the exercise of reasonable diligence, to present the bill for acceptance before presenting it for payment on the day that it falls due, the delay caused by presenting the bill for acceptance before presenting it for payment is excused, and does not discharge the drawer and indorsers.

[115]

40 Time for presenting bill payable after sight

  (1)   Subject to the provisions of this Act, when a bill payable after sight is negotiated, the holder must either present it for acceptance or negotiate it within a reasonable time.

  (2)   If he do not do so, the drawer and all indorsers prior to that holder are discharged.

  (3)   In determining what is a reasonable time within the meaning of this section, regard shall be had to the nature of the bill, the usage of trade with respect to similar bills, and the facts of the particular case.

[116]

41 Rules as to presentment for acceptance, and excuses for non-presentment

  (1)   A bill is duly presented for acceptance which is presented in accordance with the following rules—
  (a)   The presentment must be made by or on behalf of the holder to the drawee or to some person authorised to accept or refuse acceptance on his behalf at a reasonable hour on a business day and before the bill is overdue:
  (b)   Where a bill is addressed to two or more drawees, who are not partners, presentment must be made to them all, unless one has authority to accept for all, then presentment may be made to him only:
  (c)   Where the drawee is dead presentment may be made to his personal representative:
  (d)   Where the drawee is bankrupt, presentment may be made to him or to his trustee:
  (e)   Where authorised by agreement or usage, a presentment through [a postal operator] is sufficient.

  (2)   Presentment in accordance with these rules is excused, and a bill may be treated as dishonoured by non-acceptance—

(a)   Where the drawee is dead or bankrupt, or is a fictitious person or a person not having capacity to contract by bill:
(b)   Where, after the exercise of reasonable diligence, such presentment cannot be effected:
(c)   Where, although the presentment has been irregular, acceptance has been refused on some other ground.

(3)   The fact that the holder has reason to believe that the bill, on presentment, will be dishonoured does not excuse presentment.

[117]

NOTES

Sub-s (1): words in square brackets in para (e) substituted by the Postal Services Act 2000 (Consequential Modifications No 1) Order 2001, SI 2001/1149, art 3(1), Sch 1, para 4(1), (3).

42   Non-acceptance

When a bill is duly presented for acceptance and is not accepted within the customary time, the person presenting it must treat it as dishonoured by non-acceptance. If he do not, the holder shall lose his right of recourse against the drawer and indorsers.

[118]

43   Dishonour by non-acceptance and its consequences

(1)   A bill is dishonoured by non-acceptance—
   (a)   when it is duly presented for acceptance, and such an acceptance as is prescribed by this Act is refused or cannot be obtained; or
   (b)   when presentment for acceptance is excused and the bill is not accepted.

(2)   Subject to the provisions of this Act when a bill is dishonoured by nonacceptance, an immediate right of recourse against the drawer and indorsers accrues to the holder, and no presentment for payment is necessary.

[119]

44   Duties as to qualified acceptances

(1)   The holder of a bill may refuse to take a qualified acceptance, and if he does not obtain an unqualified acceptance may treat the bill as dishonoured by non-acceptance.

(2)   Where a qualified acceptance is taken, and the drawer or an indorser has not expressly or impliedly authorised the holder to take a qualified acceptance, or does not subsequently assent thereto, such drawer or indorser is discharged from his liability on the bill.

The provisions of this subsection do not apply to a partial acceptance, whereof due notice has been given. Where a foreign bill has been accepted as to part, it must be protested as to the balance.

(3)   When the drawer or indorser of a bill receives notice of a qualified acceptance, and does not within a reasonable time express his dissent to the holder he shall be deemed to have assented thereto.

[120]

45   Rules as to presentment for payment

Subject to the provisions of this Act a bill must be duly presented for payment. If it be not so presented the drawer and indorsers shall be discharged.

A bill is duly presented for payment which is presented in accordance with the following rules:—
   (1)   Where the bill is not payable on demand, presentment must be made on the day it falls due.
   (2)   Where the bill is payable on demand, then, subject to the provisions of this Act, presentment must be made within a reasonable time after its issue in order to render the drawer liable, and within a reasonable time after its indorsement, in order to render the indorser liable.
          In determining what is a reasonable time, regard shall be had to the nature of the bill, the usage of trade with regard to similar bills, and the facts of the particular case.
   (3)   Presentment must be made by the holder or by some person authorised to receive payment on his behalf at a reasonable hour on a business day, at the proper place as herein-after defined, either to the person designated by the bill as payer, or to some person authorised to pay or refuse payment on his behalf if with the exercise of reasonable diligence such person can there be found.
   (4)   A bill is presented at the proper place:—
          (a)   Where a place of payment is specified in the bill and the bill is there presented.
          (b)   Where no place of payment is specified, but the address of the drawee or acceptor is given in the bill, and the bill is there presented.
          (c)   Where no place of payment is specified and no address given, and the bill is presented at the drawee's or acceptor's place of business if known, and if not, at his ordinary residence if known.

(d)　　In any other case if presented to the drawee or acceptor wherever he can be found, or if presented at his last known place of business or residence.

(5)　Where a bill is presented at the proper place, and after the exercise of reasonable diligence no person authorised to pay or refuse payment can be found there, no further presentment to the drawee or acceptor is required.

(6)　Where a bill is drawn upon, or accepted by two or more persons who are not partners, and no place of payment is specified, presentment must be made to them all.

(7)　Where the drawee or acceptor of a bill is dead, and no place of payment is specified, presentment must be made to a personal representative, if such there be, and with the exercise of reasonable diligence he can be found.

(8)　Where authorised by agreement or usage a presentment through [a postal operator] is sufficient.

[121]

NOTES

Rule (8): words in square brackets substituted by the Postal Services Act 2000 (Consequential Modifications No 1) Order 2001, SI 2001/1149, art 3(1), Sch 1, para 4(1), (4).

46　Excuses for delay or non-presentment for payment

(1)　Delay in making presentment for payment is excused when the delay is caused by circumstances beyond the control of the holder, and not imputable to his default, misconduct, or negligence. When the cause of delay ceases to operate presentment must be made with reasonable diligence.

(2)　Presentment for payment is dispensed with,—

(a)　Where, after the exercise of reasonable diligence presentment, as required by this Act, cannot be effected.
The fact that the holder has reason to believe that the bill will, on presentment, be dishonoured, does not dispense with the necessity for presentment.

(b)　Where the drawee is a fictitious person.

(c)　As regards the drawer where the drawee or acceptor is not bound as between himself and the drawer, to accept or pay the bill, and the drawer has no reason to believe that the bill would be paid if presented.

(d)　As regards an indorser, where the bill was accepted or made for the accommodation of that indorser, and he has no reason to expect that the bill would be paid if presented.

(e)　By waiver of presentment, express or implied.

[122]

47　Dishonour by non-payment

(1)　A bill is dishonoured by non-payment (a) when it is duly presented for payment and payment is refused or cannot be obtained, or (b) when presentment is excused and the bill is overdue and unpaid.

(2)　Subject to the provisions of this Act, when a bill is dishonoured by non-payment, an immediate right of recourse against the drawer and indorsers accrues to the holder.

[123]

48　Notice of dishonour and effect of non-notice

Subject to the provisions of this Act, when a bill has been dishonoured by nonacceptance or by non-payment, notice of dishonour must be given to the drawer and each indorser, and any drawer or indorser to whom such notice is not given is discharged: Provided that—

(1)　Where a bill is dishonoured by non-acceptance, and notice of dishonour is not given, the rights of a holder in due course, subsequent to the omission, shall not be prejudiced by the omission.

(2)　Where a bill is dishonoured by non-acceptance, and due notice of dishonour is given, it shall not be necessary to give notice of a subsequent dishonour by non-payment unless the bill shall in the meantime have been accepted.

[124]

49　Rules as to notice of dishonour

Notice of dishonour in order to be valid and effectual must be given in accordance with the following rules:—

(1)　The notice must be given by or on behalf of the holder, or by or on behalf of an indorser who, at the time of giving it, is himself liable on the bill.

(2)　Notice of dishonour may be given by an agent either in his own name, or in the name of any party entitled to give notice whether that party be his principal or not.

(3)　Where the notice is given by or on behalf of the holder, it enures for the benefit of all subsequent holders and all prior indorsers who have a right of recourse against the party to whom it is given.

(4)   Where notice is given by or on behalf of an indorser entitled to give notice as herein-before provided, it enures for the benefit of the holder and all indorsers subsequent to the party to whom notice is given.

(5)   The notice may be given in writing or by personal communication, and may be given in any terms which sufficiently identify the bill, and intimate that the bill has been dishonoured by non-acceptance or non-payment.

(6)   The return of a dishonoured bill to the drawer or an indorser is, in point of form, deemed a sufficient notice of dishonour.

(7)   A written notice need not be signed, and an insufficient written notice may be supplemented and validated by verbal communication. A misdescription of the bill shall not vitiate the notice unless the party to whom the notice is given is in fact misled thereby.

(8)   Where notice of dishonour is required to be given to any person, it may be given either to the party himself, or to his agent in that behalf.

(9)   Where the drawer or indorser is dead, and the party giving notice knows it, the notice must be given to a personal representative if such there be, and with the exercise of reasonable diligence he can be found.

(10)   Where the drawer or indorser is bankrupt, notice may be given either to the party himself or to the trustee.

(11)   Where there are two or more drawers or indorsers who are not partners, notice must be given to each of them, unless one of them has authority to receive such notice for the others.

(12)   The notice may be given as soon as the bill is dishonoured and must be given within a reasonable time thereafter.

In the absence of special circumstances notice is not deemed to have been given within a reasonable time, unless—

(a)   where the person giving and the person to receive notice reside in the same place, the notice is given or sent off in time to reach the latter on the day after the dishonour of the bill;

(b)   where the person giving and the person to receive notice reside in different places, the notice is sent off on the day after the dishonour of the bill, if there be a post at a convenient hour on that day, and if there be no post on that day then by the next post thereafter.

(13)   Where a bill when dishonoured is in the hands of an agent, he may either himself give notice to the parties liable on the bill, or he may give notice to his principal. If he give notice to his principal, he must do so within the same time as if he were the holder, and the principal upon receipt of such notice has himself the same time for giving notice as if the agent had been an independent holder.

(14)   Where a party to a bill receives due notice of dishonour, he has after the receipt of such notice the same period of time for giving notice to antecedent parties that the holder has after the dishonour.

(15)   Where a notice of dishonour is duly addressed and posted, the sender is deemed to have given due notice of dishonour, notwithstanding any miscarriage by [a postal operator].

[125]

NOTES

Rule (15): words in square brackets substituted by the Postal Services Act 2000 (Consequential Modifications No 1) Order 2001, SI 2001/1149, art 3(1), Sch 1, para 4(1), (5).

50   Excuses for non-notice and delay

(1)   Delay in giving notice of dishonour is excused where the delay is caused by circumstances beyond the control of the party giving notice, and not imputable to his default, misconduct, or negligence. When the cause of delay ceases to operate the notice must be given with reasonable diligence.

(2)   Notice of dishonour is dispensed with—

(a)   When, after the exercise of reasonable diligence, notice as required by this Act cannot be given to or does not reach the drawer or indorser sought to be charged:

(b)   By waiver express or implied. Notice of dishonour may be waived before the time of giving notice has arrived, or after the omission to give due notice:

(c)   As regards the drawer in the following cases, namely, (1) where drawer and drawee are the same person, (2) where the drawee is a fictitious person or a person not having capacity to contract, (3) where the drawer is the person to whom the bill is presented for payment, (4) where the drawee or acceptor is as between himself and the drawer under no obligation to accept or pay the bill, (5) where the drawer has countermanded payment:

(d)   As regards the indorser in the following cases, namely, (1) where the drawee is a fictitious person or a person not having capacity to contract, and the indorser was aware of the fact at the time he indorsed the bill, (2) where the indorser is the person to whom the bill is presented for payment, (3) where the bill was accepted or made for his accommodation.

[126]

51   Noting or protest of bill

(1)   Where an inland bill has been dishonoured it may, if the holder think fit, be noted for non-acceptance or non-payment, as the case may be; but it shall not be necessary to note or protest any such bill in order to preserve the recourse against the drawer or indorser.

(2)   Where a foreign bill, appearing on the face of it to be such, has been dishonoured by non-acceptance it must be duly protested for non-acceptance, and where such a bill, which has not been previously dishonoured by non-acceptance, is dishonoured by non-payment it must be duly protested for non-payment. If it be not so protested the drawer and indorsers are discharged. Where a bill does not appear on the face of it to be a foreign bill, protest thereof in case of dishonour is unnecessary.

(3)   A bill which has been protested for non-acceptance may be subsequently protested for non-payment.

(4)   Subject to the provisions of this Act, when a bill is noted or protested, [it may be noted on the day of its dishonour and must be noted not later than the next succeeding business day]. When a bill has been duly noted, the protest may be subsequently extended as of the date of the noting.

(5)   Where the acceptor of a bill becomes bankrupt or insolvent or suspends payment before it matures, the holder may cause the bill to be protested for better security against the drawer and indorsers.

(6)   A bill must be protested at the place where it is dishonoured: Provided that—
   (a)   When a bill is presented through [a postal operator], and returned by post dishonoured, it may be protested at the place to which it is returned and on the day of its return if received during business hours, and if not received during business hours, then not later than the next business day:
   (b)   When a bill drawn payable at the place of business or residence of some person other than the drawee has been dishonoured by non-acceptance, it must be protested for non-payment at the place where it is expressed to be payable, and no further presentment for payment to, or demand on, the drawee is necessary.

(7)   A protest must contain a copy of the bill, and must be signed by the notary making it, and must specify—
   (a)   The person at whose request the bill is protested:
   (b)   The place and date of protest, the cause or reason for protesting the bill, the demand made, and the answer given, if any, or the fact that the drawee or acceptor could not be found.

[(7A)   In subsection (7) "notary" includes a person who, for the purposes of the Legal Services Act 2007, is an authorised person in relation to any activity which constitutes a notarial activity (within the meaning of that Act).]

(8)   Where a bill is lost or destroyed, or is wrongly detained from the person entitled to hold it, protest may be made on a copy or written particulars thereof.

(9)   Protest is dispensed with by any circumstance which would dispense with notice of dishonour. Delay in noting or protesting is excused when the delay is caused by circumstances beyond the control of the holder, and not imputable to his default, misconduct, or negligence. When the cause of delay ceases to operate the bill must be noted or protested with reasonable diligence.

[127]

NOTES
Sub-s (4): words in square brackets substituted by the Bills of Exchange (Time of Noting) Act 1917, s 1.
Sub-s (6): words in square brackets in para (a) substituted by the Postal Services Act 2000 (Consequential Modifications No 1) Order 2001, SI 2001/1149, art 3(1), Sch 1, para 4(1), (6).
Sub-s (7A): inserted by the Legal Services Act 2007, s 208(1), Sch 21, paras 8, 9.

52   Duties of holder as regards drawee or acceptor

(1)   When a bill is accepted generally presentment for payment is not necessary in order to render the acceptor liable.

(2)   When by the terms of a qualified acceptance presentment for payment is required, the acceptor, in the absence of an express stipulation to that effect, is not discharged by the omission to present the bill for payment on the day that it matures.

(3)   In order to render the acceptor of a bill liable it is not necessary to protest it, or that notice of dishonour should be given to him.

(4)   Where the holder of a bill presents it for payment, he shall exhibit the bill to the person from whom he demands payment, and when a bill is paid the holder shall forthwith deliver it up to the party paying it.

[128]

Liabilities of parties

53   Funds in hands of drawee

(1)   A bill, of itself, does not operate as an assignment of funds in the hands of the drawee available for the payment thereof, and the drawee of a bill who does not accept as required by this Act is not liable on the instrument. This sub-section shall not extend to Scotland.

(2)   (*Applies to Scotland only.*)

[129]

54   Liability of acceptor

The acceptor of a bill, by accepting it—

(1)   Engages that he will pay it according to the tenor of his acceptance:
(2)   Is precluded from denying to a holder in due course:
   (a)   The existence of the drawer, the genuineness of his signature, and his capacity and authority to draw the bill;
   (b)   In the case of a bill payable to drawer's order, the then capacity of the drawer to indorse, but not the genuineness or validity of his indorsement;
   (c)   In the case of a bill payable to the order of a third person, the existence of the payee and his then capacity to indorse, but not the genuineness or validity of his indorsement.

[130]

55   Liability of drawer or indorser

(1)   The drawer of a bill by drawing it—
   (a)   Engages that on due presentment it shall be accepted and paid according to its tenor, and that if it be dishonoured he will compensate the holder or any indorser who is compelled to pay it, provided that the requisite proceedings on dishonour be duly taken;
   (b)   Is precluded from denying to a holder in due course the existence of the payee and his then capacity to indorse.

(2)   The indorser of a bill by indorsing it—
   (a)   Engages that on due presentment it shall be accepted and paid according to its tenor, and that if it be dishonoured he will compensate the holder or a subsequent indorser who is compelled to pay it, provided that the requisite proceedings on dishonour be duly taken;
   (b)   Is precluded from denying to a holder in due course the genuineness and regularity in all respects of the drawer's signature and all previous indorsements;
   (c)   Is precluded from denying to his immediate or a subsequent indorsee that the bill was at the time of his indorsement a valid and subsisting bill, and that he had then a good title thereto.

[131]

56   Stranger signing bill liable as indorser

Where a person signs a bill otherwise than as drawer or acceptor, he thereby incurs the liabilities of an indorser to a holder in due course.

[132]

57   Measure of damages against parties to dishonoured bill

Where a bill is dishonoured, the measure of damages, which shall be deemed to be liquidated damages, shall be as follows—

(1)   The holder may recover from any party liable on the bill, and the drawer who has been compelled to pay the bill may recover from the acceptor, and an indorser who has been compelled to pay the bill may recover from the acceptor or from the drawer, or from a prior indorser—
   (a)   The amount of the bill:
   (b)   Interest thereon from the time of presentment for payment if the bill is payable on demand, and from the maturity of the bill in any other case:
   (c)   The expenses of noting, or, when protest is necessary, and the protest has been extended, the expenses of protest.

(2)   ...

(3)   Where by this Act interest may be recovered as damages, such interest may, if justice require it, be withheld wholly or in part, and where a bill is expressed to be payable with interest at a given rate, interest as damages may or may not be given at the same rate as interest proper.

[133]

PART 1
STATUTES

NOTES

Sub-s (2): repealed by the Administration of Justice Act 1977, ss 4, 32(4), Sch 5, Pt I, except in relation to bills drawn before 29 August 1977.

58   Transferor by delivery and transferee

(1)   Where the holder of a bill payable to bearer negotiates it by delivery without indorsing it he is called a "transferor by delivery."

(2)   A transferor by delivery is not liable on the instrument.

(3)   A transferor by delivery who negotiates a bill thereby warrants to his immediate transferee being a holder for value that the bill is what it purports to be, that he has a right to transfer it, and that at the time of transfer he is not aware of any fact which renders it valueless.

[134]

Discharge of bill

59   Payment in due course

(1)   A bill is discharged by payment in due course by or on behalf of the drawee or acceptor. "Payment in due course" means payment made at or after the maturity of the bill to the holder thereof in good faith and without notice that his title to the bill is defective.

(2)   Subject to the provisions herein-after contained, when a bill is paid by the drawer or an indorser it is not discharged; but

   (a)   Where a bill payable to, or to the order of, a third party is paid by the drawer, the drawer may enforce payment thereof against the acceptor, but may not re-issue the bill.

   (b)   Where a bill is paid by an indorser, or where a bill payable to drawer's order is paid by the drawer, the party paying it is remitted to his former rights as regards the acceptor or antecedent parties and he may, if he thinks fit, strike out his own subsequent indorsements, and again negotiate the bill.

(3)   Where an accommodation bill is paid in due course by the party accommodated the bill is discharged.

[135]

NOTES

Sub-s (2): the word "and" appears to be needed between "own" and "subsequent", but does not appear in the Queen's Printer's copy of the Act.

60   Banker paying demand draft whereon indorsement is forged

When a bill payable to order on demand is drawn on a banker, and the banker on whom it is drawn pays the bill in good faith and in the ordinary course of business, it is not incumbent on the banker to show that the indorsement of the payee or any subsequent indorsement was made by or under the authority of the person whose indorsement it purports to be, and the banker is deemed to have paid the bill in due course, although such indorsement has been forged or made without authority.

[136]

61   Acceptor the holder at maturity

When the acceptor of a bill is or becomes the holder of it at or after its maturity, in his own right, the bill is discharged.

[137]

62   Express waiver

(1)   When the holder of a bill at or after its maturity absolutely and unconditionally renounces his rights against the acceptor the bill is discharged.

The renunciation must be in writing, unless the bill is delivered up to the acceptor.

(2)   The liabilities of any party to a bill may in like manner be renounced by the holder before, at, or after its maturity; but nothing in this section shall affect the rights of a holder in due course without notice of the renunciation.

[138]

63   Cancellation

(1)   Where a bill is intentionally cancelled by the holder or his agent, and the cancellation is apparent thereon, the bill is discharged.

(2)   In like manner any party liable on a bill may be discharged by the intentional cancellation of his signature by the holder or his agent. In such case any indorser who would have had a right of recourse against the party whose signature is cancelled is also discharged.

(3)   A cancellation made unintentionally, or under a mistake, or without the authority of the holder is inoperative; but where a bill or any signature thereon appears to have been cancelled the burden of proof lies on the party who alleges that the cancellation was made unintentionally, or under a mistake, or without authority.

[139]

64   Alteration of bill

(1)   Where a bill or acceptance is materially altered without the assent of all parties liable on the bill, the bill is avoided except as against a party who has himself made, authorised, or assented to the alteration, and subsequent indorsers.

Provided that,
> Where a bill has been materially altered, but the alteration is not apparent, and the bill is in the hands of a holder in due course, such holder may avail himself of the bill as if it had not been altered, and may enforce payment of it according to its original tenour.

(2)   In particular the following alterations are material, namely, any alteration of the date, the sum payable, the time of payment, the place of payment and, where a bill has been accepted generally, the addition of a place of payment without the acceptor's assent.

[140]

Acceptance and payment for honour

65   Acceptance for honour suprà protest

(1)   Where a bill of exchange has been protested for dishonour by non-acceptance, or protested for better security, and is not overdue, any person, not being a party already liable thereon, may, with the consent of the holder, intervene and accept the bill *suprà protest*, for the honour of any party liable thereon, or for the honour of the person for whose account the bill is drawn.

(2)   A bill may be accepted for honour for part only of the sum for which it is drawn.

(3)   An acceptance for honour *suprà protest* in order to be valid must—
(a)   be written on the bill, and indicate that it is an acceptance for honour:
(b)   be signed by the acceptor for honour.

(4)   Where an acceptance for honour does not expressly state for whose honour it is made, it is deemed to be an acceptance for the honour of the drawer.

(5)   Where a bill payable after sight is accepted for honour, its maturity is calculated from the date of the noting for non-acceptance, and not from the date of the acceptance for honour.

[141]

66   Liability of acceptor for honour

(1)   The acceptor for honour of a bill by accepting it engages that he will, on due presentment, pay the bill according to the tenor of his acceptance, if it is not paid by the drawee, provided it has been duly presented for payment, and protested for non-payment, and that he receives notice of these facts.

(2)   The acceptor for honour is liable to the holder and to all parties to the bill subsequent to the party for whose honour he has accepted.

[142]

67   Presentment to acceptor for honour

(1)   Where a dishonoured bill has been accepted for honour *suprà protest*, or contains a reference in case of need, it must be protested for non-payment before it is presented for payment to the acceptor for honour, or referee in case of need.

(2)   Where the address of the acceptor for honour is in the same place where the bill is protested for non-payment, the bill must be presented to him not later than the day following its maturity; and where the address of the acceptor for honour is in some place other than the place where it was protested for non-payment, the bill must be forwarded not later than the day following its maturity for presentment to him.

(3)   Delay in presentment or non-presentment is excused by any circumstance which would excuse delay in presentment for payment or non-presentment for payment.

(4)   When a bill of exchange is dishonoured by the acceptor for honour it must be protested for non-payment by him.

[143]

68   Payment for honour suprà protest

(1)   Where a bill has been protested for non-payment, any person may intervene and pay it *suprà protest* for the honour of any party liable thereon, or for the honour of the person for whose account the bill is drawn.

(2)   Where two or more persons offer to pay a bill for the honour of different parties, the person whose payment will discharge most parties to the bill shall have the preference.

(3)   Payment for honour *suprà protest*, in order to operate as such and not as a mere voluntary payment, must be attested by a notarial act of honour which may be appended to the protest or form an extension of it.

(4)   The notarial act of honour must be founded on a declaration made by the payer for honour, or his agent in that behalf, declaring his intention to pay the bill for honour, and for whose honour he pays.

(5)   Where a bill has been paid for honour, all parties subsequent to the party for whose honour it is paid are discharged, but the payer for honour is subrogated for, and succeeds to both the rights and duties of, the holder as regards the party for whose honour he pays, and all parties liable to that party.

(6)   The payer for honour on paying to the holder the amount of the bill and the notarial expenses incidental to its dishonour is entitled to receive both the bill itself and the protest. If the holder do not on demand deliver them up he shall be liable to the payer for honour in damages.

(7)   Where the holder of a bill refuses to receive payment *suprà protest* he shall lose his right of recourse against any party who would have been discharged by such payment.

[144]

Lost instruments

69   Holder's right to duplicate of lost bill

Where a bill has been lost before it is overdue the person who was the holder of it may apply to the drawer to give him another bill of the same tenor, giving security to the drawer if required to indemnify him against all persons whatever in case the bill alleged to have been lost shall be found again.

If the drawer on request as aforesaid refuses to give such duplicate bill he may be compelled to do so.

[145]

70   Action on lost bill

In any action or proceeding upon a bill, the court or a judge may order that the loss of the instrument shall not be set up, provided an indemnity be given to the satisfaction of the court or judge against the claims of any other person upon the instrument in question.

[146]

NOTES

Repealed in relation to Northern Ireland by the Judicature (Northern Ireland) Act 1978, s 122, Sch 7, Pt I.

Bill in a set

71   Rules as to sets

(1)   Where a bill is drawn in a set, each part of the set being numbered, and containing a reference to the other parts the whole of the parts constitute one bill.

(2)   Where the holder of a set indorses two or more parts to different persons, he is liable on every such part, and every indorser subsequent to him is liable on the part he has himself indorsed as if the said parts were separate bills.

(3)   Where two or more parts of a set are negotiated to different holders in due course, the holder whose title first accrues is as between such holders deemed the true owner of the bill; but nothing in this sub-section shall affect the rights of a person who in due course accepts or pays the part first presented to him.

(4)   The acceptance may be written on any part, and it must be written on one part only.

If the drawee accepts more than one part, and such accepted parts get into the hands of different holders in due course, he is liable on every such part as if it were a separate bill.

(5)   When the acceptor of a bill drawn in a set pays it without requiring the part bearing his acceptance to be delivered up to him, and that part at maturity is outstanding in the hands of a holder in due course, he is liable to the holder thereof.

(6)   Subject to the preceding rules, where any one part of a bill drawn in a set is discharged by payment or otherwise, the whole bill is discharged.

[147]

Conflict of laws

72 Rules where laws conflict

Where a bill drawn in one country is negotiated, accepted, or payable in another, the rights, duties, and liabilities of the parties thereto are determined as follows—

(1) The validity of a bill as regards requisites in form is determined by the law of the place of issue, and the validity as regards requisites in form of the supervening contracts, such as acceptance, or indorsement, or acceptance *suprà protest*, is determined by the law of the place where such contract was made.

Provided that—

(a) Where a bill is issued out of the United Kingdom it is not invalid by reason only that it is not stamped in accordance with the law of the place of issue:

(b) Where a bill, issued out of the United Kingdom, conforms, as regards requisites in form, to the law of the United Kingdom, it may, for the purpose of enforcing payment thereof, be treated as valid as between all persons who negotiate, hold, or become parties to it in the United Kingdom.

(2) Subject to the provisions of this Act, the interpretation of the drawing, indorsement, acceptance, or acceptance *suprà protest* of a bill, is determined by the law of the place where such contract is made.

Provided that where an inland bill is indorsed in a foreign country the indorsement shall as regards the payer be interpreted according to the law of the United Kingdom.

(3) The duties of the holder with respect to presentment for acceptance or payment and the necessity for or sufficiency of a protest or notice of dishonour, or otherwise, are determined by the law of the place where the act is done or the bill is dishonoured.

(4) …

(5) Where a bill is drawn in one country and is payable in another, the due date thereof is determined according to the law of the place where it is payable.

[148]

NOTES

Sub-s (4): repealed by the Administration of Justice Act 1977, ss 4, 32(4), Sch 5, Pt I, except in relation to bills drawn before 29 August 1977.

PART III
CHEQUES ON A BANKER

73 Cheque defined

A cheque is a bill of exchange drawn on a banker payable on demand.

Except as otherwise provided in this Part, the provisions of this Act applicable to a bill of exchange payable on demand apply to a cheque.

[149]

NOTES

Cheque: certain warrants are deemed cheques by virtue of the National Loans Act 1968, s 14(7).

74 Presentment of cheque for payment

Subject to the provisions of this Act—

(1) Where a cheque is not presented for payment within a reasonable time of its issue, and the drawer or the person on whose account it is drawn had the right at the time of such presentment as between him and the banker to have the cheque paid and suffers actual damage through the delay, he is discharged to the extent of such damage, that is to say, to the extent to which such drawer or person is a creditor of such banker to a larger amount than he would have been had such cheque been paid.

(2) In determining what is a reasonable time regard shall be had to the nature of the instrument, the usage of trade and of bankers, and the facts of the particular case.

(3) The holder of such cheque as to which such drawer or person is discharged shall be a creditor, in lieu of such drawer or person, of such banker to the extent of such discharge, and entitled to recover the amount from him.

[150]

[74A Presentment of cheque for payment: alternative place of presentment

Where the banker on whom a cheque is drawn—

(a) has by notice published in the London, Edinburgh and Belfast Gazettes specified an address at which cheques drawn on him may be presented, and

(b) has not by notice so published cancelled the specification of that address, the cheque is also presented at the proper place if it is presented there.]

[151]

NOTES
Inserted by the Deregulation (Bills of Exchange) Order 1996, SI 1996/2993, art 3.

[74B Presentment of cheque for payment: alternative means of presentment by banker

(1)　A banker may present a cheque for payment to the banker on whom it is drawn by notifying him of its essential features by electronic means or otherwise, instead of by presenting the cheque itself.

(2)　If a cheque is presented for payment under this section, presentment need not be made at the proper place or at a reasonable hour on a business day.

(3)　If, before the close of business on the next business day following presentment of a cheque under this section, the banker on whom the cheque is drawn requests the banker by whom the cheque was presented to present the cheque itself—
(a)　the presentment under this section shall be disregarded, and
(b)　this section shall not apply in relation to the subsequent presentment of the cheque.

(4)　A request under subsection (3) above for the presentment of a cheque shall not constitute dishonour of the cheque by non-payment.

(5)　Where presentment of a cheque is made under this section, the banker who presented the cheque and the banker on whom it is drawn shall be subject to the same duties in relation to the collection and payment of the cheque as if the cheque itself had been presented for payment.

(6)　For the purposes of this section, the essential features of a cheque are—
(a)　the serial number of the cheque,
(b)　the code which identifies the banker on whom the cheque is drawn,
(c)　the account number of the drawer of the cheque, and
(d)　the amount of the cheque is entered by the drawer of the cheque.]

[152]

NOTES
Inserted, together with s 74C, by the Deregulation (Bills of Exchange) Order 1996, SI 1996/2993, art 4(1), in relation to cheques drawn on or after 28 November 1996.

[74C　Cheques presented for payment under section 74B: disapplication of section 52(4)
Section 52(4) above—
(a)　so far as relating to presenting a bill for payment, shall not apply to presenting a cheque for payment under section 74B above, and
(b)　so far as relating to a bill which is paid, shall not apply to a cheque which is paid following presentment under that section.]

[153]

NOTES
Inserted as noted to s 74B at **[152]**.

75　Revocation of banker's authority
The duty and authority of a banker to pay a cheque drawn on him by his customer are determined by—
(1)　Countermand of payment:
(2)　Notice of the customer's death.

[154]

75A　*(Inserted, in relation to Scotland only, by the Law Reform (Miscellaneous Provisions) (Scotland) Act 1985, s 11(b) and repealed by the Banking Act 2009, s 254(4)(b).)*

Crossed cheques

76　General and special crossings defined
(1)　Where a cheque bears across its face an addition of—
(a)　The words "and company" or any abbreviation thereof between two parallel transverse lines, either with or without the words "not negotiable"; or
(b)　Two parallel transverse lines simply, either with or without the words "not negotiable"; that addition constitutes a crossing, and the cheque is crossed generally.

(2)　Where a cheque bears across its face an addition of the name of a banker, either with or without the words "not negotiable," that addition constitutes a crossing, and the cheque is crossed specially and to that banker.

[155]

NOTES
Application: the provisions of this Act relating to crossed cheques are applied to dividend warrants by s 95 of this Act at **[174]**, and to instruments (other than cheques) to which the Cheques Act 1957, s 4 applies (see s 5 of the 1957 Act at **[378]**).

77 Crossing by drawer or after issue

(1) A cheque may be crossed generally or specially by the drawer.

(2) Where a cheque is uncrossed, the holder may cross it generally or specially.

(3) Where a cheque is crossed generally the holder may cross it specially.

(4) Where a cheque is crossed generally or specially, the holder may add the words "not negotiable."

(5) Where a cheque is crossed specially, the banker to whom it is crossed may again cross it specially to another banker for collection.

(6) Where an uncrossed cheque, or a cheque crossed generally, is sent to a banker for collection, he may cross it specially to himself.

[156]

NOTES
Application: see the note to s 76 at **[155]**.

78 Crossing a material part of cheque

A crossing authorised by this Act is a material part of the cheque; it shall not be lawful for any person to obliterate or, except as authorised by this Act, to add to or alter the crossing.

[157]

NOTES
Application: see the note to s 76 at **[155]**.

79 Duties of banker as to crossed cheques

(1) Where a cheque is crossed specially to more than one banker except when crossed to an agent for collection being a banker, the banker on whom it is drawn shall refuse payment thereof.

(2) Where the banker on whom a cheque is drawn which is so crossed nevertheless pays the same, or pays a cheque crossed generally otherwise than to a banker, or if crossed specially otherwise than to the banker to whom it is crossed, or his agent for collection being a banker, he is liable to the true owner of the cheque for any loss he may sustain owing to the cheque having been so paid.

Provided that where a cheque is presented for payment which does not at the time of presentment appear to be crossed, or to have had a crossing which has been obliterated, or to have been added to or altered otherwise than as authorised by this Act, the banker paying the cheque in good faith and without negligence shall not be responsible or incur any liability, nor shall the payment be questioned by reason of the cheque having been crossed, or of the crossing having been obliterated or having been added to or altered otherwise than as authorised by this Act, and of payment having been made otherwise than to a banker or to the banker to whom the cheque is or was crossed, or to his agent for collection being a banker, as the case may be.

[158]

NOTES
Application: see the note to s 76 at **[155]**.

80 Protection to banker and drawer where cheque is crossed

Where the banker, on whom a crossed cheque [(including a cheque which under section 81A below or otherwise is not transferable)] is drawn, in good faith and without negligence pays it, if crossed generally, to a banker, and if crossed specially, to the banker to whom it is crossed, or his agent for collection being a banker, the banker paying the cheque, and, if the cheque has come into the hands of the payee, the drawer, shall respectively be entitled to the same rights and be placed in the same position as if payment of the cheque had been made to the true owner thereof.

[159]

NOTES
Words in square brackets inserted by the Cheques Act 1992, s 2.
Application: see the note to s 76 at **[155]**.

81 Effect of crossing on holder

Where a person takes a crossed cheque which bears on it the words "not negotiable," he shall not have and shall not be capable of giving a better title to the cheque than that which the person from whom he took it had.

[160]

NOTES

Application: see the note to s 76 at **[155]**.

[81A Non-transferable cheques

(1) Where a cheque is crossed and bears across its face the words "account payee" or "a/c payee", either with or without the word "only", the cheque shall not be transferable, but shall only be valid as between the parties thereto.

(2) A banker is not to be treated for the purposes of section 80 above as having been negligent by reason only of his failure to concern himself with any purported indorsement of a cheque which under subsection (1) above or otherwise is not transferable.]

[161]

NOTES

Inserted by the Cheques Act 1992, s 1.
Application: see the note to s 76 at **[155]**.

82 (*Repealed by the Cheques Act 1957, s 6(3), Schedule; see now s 4 of that Act at* **[377]**.)

PART IV
PROMISSORY NOTES

83 Promissory note defined

(1) A promissory note is an unconditional promise in writing made by one person to another signed by the maker, engaging to pay, on demand or at a fixed or determinable future time, a sum certain in money, to, or to the order of, a specified person or to bearer.

(2) An instrument in the form of a note payable to maker's order is not a note within the meaning of this section unless and until it is indorsed by the maker.

(3) A note is not invalid by reason only that it contains also a pledge of collateral security with authority to sell or dispose thereof.

(4) A note which is, or on the face of it purports to be, both made and payable within the British Islands is an inland note. Any other note is a foreign note.

[162]

84 Delivery necessary

A promissory note is inchoate and incomplete until delivery thereof to the payee or bearer.

[163]

85 Joint and several notes

(1) A promissory note may be made by two or more makers, and they may be liable thereon jointly, or jointly and severally according to its tenour.

(2) Where a note runs "I promise to pay" and is signed by two or more persons it is deemed to be their joint and several note.

[164]

86 Note payable on demand

(1) Where a note payable on demand has been indorsed, it must be presented for payment within a reasonable time of the indorsement. If it be not so presented the indorser is discharged.

(2) In determining what is reasonable time, regard shall be had to the nature of the instrument, the usage of trade, and the facts of the particular case.

(3) Where a note payable on demand is negotiated, it is not deemed to be overdue, for the purpose of affecting the holder with defects of title of which he had no notice, by reason that it appears that a reasonable time for presenting it for payment has elapsed since its issue.

[165]

87 Presentment of note for payment

(1) Where a promissory note is in the body of it made payable at a particular place, it must be presented for payment at that place in order to render the maker liable. In any other case, presentment for payment is not necessary in order to render the maker liable.

(2)   Presentment for payment is necessary in order to render the indorser of a note liable.

(3)   Where a note is in the body of it made payable at a particular place, presentment at that place is necessary in order to render an indorser liable; but when a place of payment is indicated by way of memorandum only, presentment at that place is sufficient to render the indorser liable, but a presentment to the maker elsewhere, if sufficient in other respects, shall also suffice.

[166]

88   Liability of maker

The maker of a promissory note by making it—
  (1)   Engages that he will pay it according to its tenour;
  (2)   Is precluded from denying to a holder in due course the existence of the payee and his then capacity to indorse.

[167]

89   Application of Part II to notes

(1)   Subject to the provisions in this part, and except as by this section provided, the provisions of this Act relating to bills of exchange apply, with the necessary modifications, to promissory notes.

(2)   In applying those provisions the maker of a note shall be deemed to correspond with the acceptor of a bill, and the first indorser of a note shall be deemed to correspond with the drawer of an accepted bill payable to drawer's order.

(3)   The following provisions as to bills do not apply to notes; namely, provisions relating to—
  (a)   Presentment for acceptance;
  (b)   Acceptance;
  (c)   Acceptance *suprà protest*;
  (d)   Bills in a set.

(4)   Where a foreign note is dishonoured, protest thereof is unnecessary.

[168]

PART V
SUPPLEMENTARY

90   Good faith

A thing is deemed to be done in good faith, within the meaning of this Act where it is in fact done honestly, whether it is done negligently or not.

[169]

91   Signature

(1)   Where, by this Act, any instrument or writing is required to be signed by any person it is not necessary that he should sign it with his own hand, but it is sufficient if his signature is written thereon by some other person by or under his authority.

(2)   In the case of a corporation, where, by this Act, any instrument or writing is required to be signed, it is sufficient if the instrument or writing be sealed with the corporate seal.

But nothing in this section shall be construed as requiring the bill or note of a corporation to be under seal.

[170]

92   Computation of time

Where, by this Act, the time limited for doing any act or thing is less than three days, in reckoning time, non-business days are excluded.
  "Non-business days" for the purposes of this Act mean—
  (a)   [Saturday] Sunday, Good Friday, Christmas Day:
  (b)   A bank holiday under [the Banking and Financial Dealings Act 1971]:
  (c)   A day appointed by Royal proclamation as a public fast or thanksgiving day:
  [(d)   a day declared by an order under section 2 of the Banking and Financial Dealings Act 1971 to be a non-business day].
  Any other day is a business day.

[171]

NOTES
  Words in square brackets in para (a) and the whole of para (d) inserted, and words in square brackets in para (b) substituted, by the Banking and Financial Dealings Act 1971, ss 3(1), (3), 4(4).

93   When noting equivalent to protest

For the purposes of this Act, where a bill or note is required to be protested within a specified time or before some further proceeding is taken, it is sufficient that the bill has been noted for protest before the expiration of the specified time or the taking of the proceeding; and the formal protest may be extended at any time thereafter as of the date of the noting.

[172]

94   Protest when notary not accessible

[(1)]   Where a dishonoured bill or note is authorised or required to be protested, and the services of a notary cannot be obtained at the place where the bill is dishonoured, any householder or substantial resident of the place may, in the presence of two witnesses, give a certificate, signed by them, attesting the dishonour of the bill, and the certificate shall in all respects operate as if it were a formal protest of the bill.

The form given in Schedule 1 to this Act may be used with necessary modifications, and if used shall be sufficient.

[(2)   In subsection (1), "notary" includes a person who, for the purposes of the Legal Services Act 2007, is an authorised person in relation to any activity which constitutes a notarial activity (within the meaning of that Act).]

[173]

NOTES
Sub-s (1): numbered as such by the Legal Services Act 2007, s 208(1), Sch 21, paras 8, 10(a).
Sub-s (2): added by the Legal Services Act 2007, s 208(1), Sch 21, paras 8, 10(b).

95   Dividend warrants may be crossed

The provisions of this Act as to crossed cheques shall apply to a warrant for payment of dividend.

[174]

96   *(Repealed by the Statute Law Revision Act 1898.)*

97   Savings

(1)   The rules in bankruptcy relating to bills of exchange, promissory notes, and cheques, shall continue to apply thereto notwithstanding anything in this Act contained.

(2)   The rules of common law including the law merchant, save in so far as they are inconsistent with the express provisions of this Act, shall continue to apply to bills of exchange, promissory notes, and cheques.

(3)   Nothing in this Act or in any repeal effected thereby shall affect—
    (a)   … any law or enactment for the time being in force relating to the revenue:
    (b)   The provisions of the Companies Act, 1862, or Acts amending it, or any Act relating to joint stock banks or companies:
    (c)   The provisions of any Act relating to or confirming the privileges of the Bank of England or the Bank of Ireland respectively:
    (d)   The validity of any usage relating to dividend warrants, or the indorsements thereof.

[175]

NOTES
Sub-s (3): words omitted from para (a) repealed by the Statute Law Revision Act 1898.
Companies Act 1862: repealed by the Companies Consolidation Act 1908.

98   *(Applies to Scotland only.)*

99   Construction with other Acts, etc

Where any Act or document refers to any enactment repealed by this Act, the Act or document shall be construed, and shall operate, as if it referred to the corresponding provisions of this Act.

[176]

100   *(Applies to Scotland only.)*

SCHEDULES

FIRST SCHEDULE

Section 94

Form of protest which may be used when the services of a notary cannot be obtained.

Know all men that I, *AB* [householder], of in the county of in the United Kingdom, at the request of *CD*, there being no notary public available, did on the day of 188 at demand payment [*or* acceptance] of the bill of exchange hereunder written, from *EF*, to which demand he made answer [state answer, if any] wherefore I now, in the presence of *GH* and *JK* do protest the said bill of exchange.

(Signed) *AB*

GH Witnesses.

JK

NB—The bill itself should be annexed, or a copy of the bill and all that is written thereon should be underwritten.

[177]

(*Second Schedule repealed by the Statute Law Revision Act 1898.*)

FACTORS ACT 1889

(52 & 53 Vict c 45)

ARRANGEMENT OF SECTIONS

Preliminary

An Act to amend and consolidate the Factors Acts

[26 August 1889]

Preliminary

1 Definitions

For the purposes of this Act—
- (1)   The expression "mercantile agent" shall mean a mercantile agent having in the customary course of his business as such agent authority either to sell goods, or to consign goods for the purpose of sale, or to buy goods, or to raise money on the security of goods:
- (2)   A person shall be deemed to be in possession of goods or of the documents of title to goods, where the goods or documents are in his actual custody or are held by any other person subject to his control or for him or on his behalf:
- (3)   The expression "goods" shall include wares and merchandise:
- (4)   The expression "document of title" shall include any bill of lading, dock warrant, warehouse-keeper's certificate, and warrant or order for the delivery of goods, and any other document used in the ordinary course of business as proof of the possession or control of goods, or authorising or purporting to authorise, either by endorsement or by delivery, the possessor of the document to transfer or receive goods thereby represented:
- (5)   The expression "pledge" shall include any contract pledging, or giving a lien or security on, goods, whether in consideration of an original advance or of any further or continuing advance or of any pecuniary liability:
- (6)   The expression "person" shall include any body of persons corporate or unincorporate.

[178]

Dispositions by mercantile agents

2   Powers of mercantile agent with respect to disposition of goods

(1)   Where a mercantile agent is, with the consent of the owner, in possession of goods or of the documents of title to goods, any sale, pledge, or other disposition of the goods, made by him when acting in the ordinary course of business of a mercantile agent, shall, subject to the provisions of this Act, be as valid as if he were expressly authorised by the owner of the goods to make the same, provided that the person taking under the disposition acts in good faith, and has not at the time of the disposition notice that the person making the disposition has not authority to make the same.

(2)   Where a mercantile agent has, with the consent of the owner, been in possession of goods or of the documents of title to goods, any sale, pledge, or other disposition, which would have been valid if the consent had continued shall be valid notwithstanding the determination of the consent: provided that the person taking under the disposition has not at the time thereof notice that the consent has been determined.

(3)   Where a mercantile agent has obtained possession of any documents of title to goods by reason of his being or having been, with the consent of the owner, in possession of the goods represented thereby, or of any other documents of title to the goods, his possession of the first-mentioned documents shall, for the purposes of this Act, be deemed to be with the consent of the owner.

(4)   For the purposes of this Act the consent of the owner shall be presumed in the absence of evidence to the contrary.

[179]

3   Effect of pledges of documents of title

A pledge of the documents of title to goods shall be deemed to be a pledge of the goods.

[180]

4   Pledge for antecedent debt

Where a mercantile agent pledges goods as security for a debt or liability due from the pledgor to the pledgee before the time of the pledge, the pledgee shall acquire no further right to the goods than could have been enforced by the pledgor at the time of the pledge.

[181]

5   Rights acquired by exchange of goods or documents

The consideration necessary for the validity of a sale, pledge, or other disposition, of goods, in pursuance of this Act, may be either a payment in cash, or the delivery or transfer of other goods, or of a document of title to goods, or of a negotiable security, or any other valuable consideration; but where goods are pledged by a mercantile agent in consideration of the delivery or transfer of other goods, or of a document of title to goods, or of a negotiable security, the pledgee shall acquire no right or interest in the goods so pledged in excess of the value of the goods, documents, or security when so delivered or transferred in exchange.

[182]

6   Agreements through clerks, etc

For the purposes of this Act an agreement made with a mercantile agent through a clerk or other person authorised in the ordinary course of business to make contracts of sale or pledge on his behalf shall be deemed to be an agreement with the agent.

[183]

7   Provisions as to consignors and consignees

(1)   Where the owner of goods has given possession of the goods to another person for the purpose of consignment or sale, or has shipped the goods in the name of another person, and the consignee of the goods has not had notice that such person is not the owner of the goods, the consignee shall, in respect of advances made to or for the use of such person, have the same lien on the goods as if such person were the owner of the goods, and may transfer any such lien to another person.

(2)   Nothing in this section shall limit or effect the validity of any sale, pledge, or disposition, by a mercantile agent.

[184]

Dispositions by sellers and buyers of goods

8   Disposition by seller remaining in possession

Where a person, having sold goods, continues, or is, in possession of the goods or of the documents of title to the goods, the delivery or transfer by that person, or by a mercantile agent acting for him, of the goods or documents of title under any sale, pledge, or other disposition thereof, or under any agreement for sale pledge, or other disposition thereof, to any person receiving the same in good faith and without notice of the previous sale, shall have the same effect as if the person making the delivery or transfer were expressly authorised by the owner of the goods to make the same.

[185]

9 Disposition by buyer obtaining possession

Where a person, having bought or agreed to buy goods, obtains with the consent of the seller possession of the goods or the documents of title to the goods, the delivery or transfer, by that person or by a mercantile agent acting for him, of the goods or documents of title, under any sale, pledge, or other disposition thereof, or under any agreement for sale, pledge, or other disposition thereof, to any person receiving the same in good faith and without notice of any lien or other right of the original seller in respect of the goods, shall have the same effect as if the person making the delivery or transfer were a mercantile agent in possession of the goods or documents of title with the consent of the owner.

[For the purposes of this section—
(i) the buyer under a conditional sale agreement shall be deemed not to be a person who has bought or agreed to buy goods, and
(ii) "conditional sale agreement" means an agreement for the sale of goods which is a consumer credit agreement within the meaning of the Consumer Credit Act 1974 under which the purchase price or part of it is payable by instalments, and the property in the goods is to remain in the seller (notwithstanding that the buyer is to be in possession of the goods) until such conditions as to the payment of instalments or otherwise as may be specified in the agreement are fulfilled.]

[186]

NOTES
Words in square brackets added by the Consumer Credit Act 1974, s 192(3)(a), Sch 4, Pt I, para 2.

10 Effect of transfer of documents on vendor's lien or right of stoppage in transitu

Where a document of title to goods has been lawfully transferred to a person as a buyer or owner of the goods, and that person transfers the document to a person who takes the document in good faith and for valuable consideration, the last-mentioned transfer shall have the same effect for defeating any vendor's lien or right of stoppage in transitu as the transfer of a bill of lading has for defeating the right of stoppage in transitu.

[187]

Supplemental

11 Mode of transferring documents

For the purposes of this Act, the transfer of a document may be by endorsement, or, where the document is by custom or by its express terms transferable by delivery, or makes the goods deliverable to the bearer, then by delivery.

[188]

12 Saving for rights of true owner

(1) Nothing in this Act shall authorise an agent to exceed or depart from his authority as between himself and his principal, or exempt him from any liability, civil or criminal, for so doing.

(2) Nothing in this Act shall prevent the owner of goods from recovering the goods from an agent or his trustee in bankruptcy at any time before the sale or pledge thereof, or shall prevent the owner of goods pledged by an agent from having the right to redeem the goods at any time before the sale thereof, on satisfying the claim for which the goods were pledged, and paying to the agent, if by him required, any money in respect of which the agent would by law be entitled to retain the goods or the documents of title thereto, or any of them, by way of lien as against the owner, or from recovering from any person with whom the goods have been pledged any balance of money remaining in his hands as the produce of the sale of the goods after deducting the amount of his lien.

(3) Nothing in this Act shall prevent the owner of goods sold by an agent from recovering from the buyer the price agreed to be paid for the same, or any part of that price, subject to any right of set off on the part of the buyer against the agent.

[189]

13 Saving for common law powers of agent

The provisions of this Act shall be construed in amplification and not in derogation of the powers exercisable by an agent independently of this Act.

[190]

14, 15   (*Repealed by the Statute Law Revision Act 1908.*)

16   Extent of Act

This Act shall not extend to Scotland.

[191]

NOTES

The Factors (Scotland) Act 1890 extended this Act to Scotland, subject to certain provisions. This section should, therefore, be regarded as spent.

17   Short title

This Act may be cited as the Factors Act 1889.

[192]

(Schedule repealed by virtue of the Statute Law Revision Act 1908.)

BILLS OF SALE ACT 1890

(53 & 54 Vict c 53)

An Act to exempt certain letters of hypothecation from the operation of the Bills of Sale Act 1882
[10 August 1890]

1   Exemption of letters of hypothecation of imported goods from 41 & 42 Vict c 31, and 45 & 46 Vict c 43, s 9

[An instrument charging or creating any security on or declaring trusts of imported goods given or executed at any time prior to their deposit in a warehouse, factory, or store, or to their being reshipped for export, or delivered to a purchaser not being the person giving or executing such instrument shall not be deemed a bill of sale within the meaning of the Bills of Sale Acts 1878 and 1882.]

[193]

NOTES

Substituted by the Bills of Sale Act 1891, s 1.

2   Savings of 46 & 47 Vict c 52, s 44

Nothing in this Act shall affect the operation of section forty-four of the Bankruptcy Act 1883 in respect of any goods comprised in any such instrument as is hereinbefore described, if such goods would but for this Act be goods within the meaning of sub-section three of that section.

[194]

NOTES

Bankruptcy Act 1883, s 44: repealed by the Bankruptcy Act 1914, s 168, Sch 6 (repealed). See now the Insolvency Act 1986, s 283, and c f ss 307–309, 338 of that Act.

3   Short title

This Act may be cited as the Bills of Sale Act 1890.

[195]

PARTNERSHIP ACT 1890

(53 & 54 Vict c 39)

ARRANGEMENT OF SECTIONS

Nature of Partnership

Relations of Partners to persons dealing with them

Relations of Partners to one another

Dissolution of Partnership, and its consequences

Supplemental

An Act to declare and amend the Law of Partnership

[14 August 1890]

Nature of Partnership

1   Definition of Partnership

(1)   Partnership is the relation which subsists between persons carrying on a business in common with a view of profit.

(2)   But the relation between members of any company or association which is—
   [(a)   registered under the Companies Act 2006, or]
   (b)   Formed or incorporated by or in pursuance of any other Act of Parliament or letters patent, or Royal Charter; ...
   (c)   ...
is not a partnership within the meaning of this Act.

[196]

NOTES

Sub-s (2): para (a) substituted by the Companies Act 2006 (Consequential Amendments, Transitional Provisions and Savings) Order 2009, SI 2009/1941, art 2(1), Sch 1, para 2; para (c) and word immediately preceding it repealed by the Statute Law (Repeals) Act 1998.

2   Rules for determining existence of partnership

In determining whether a partnership does or does not exist, regard shall be had to the following rules:

(1)   Joint tenancy, tenancy in common, joint property, common property, or part ownership does not of itself create a partnership as to anything so held or owned, whether the tenants or owners do or do not share any profits made by the use thereof.

(2)   The sharing of gross returns does not of itself create a partnership, whether the persons sharing such returns have or have not a joint or common right or interest in any property from which or from the use of which the returns are derived.

(3)   The receipt by a person of a share of the profits of a business is prima facie evidence that he is a partner in the business, but receipt of such a share, or of a payment contingent on or varying with the profits of a business, does not of itself make him a partner in the business; and in particular—

(a)   The receipt by a person of a debt or other liquidated amount by instalments or otherwise out of the accruing profits of a business does not of itself make him a partner in the business or liable as such:

(b)   A contract for the remuneration of a servant or agent of a person engaged in a business by a share of the profits of the business does not of itself make the servant or agent a partner in the business or liable as such:

(c)   A person being the widow[, widower, surviving civil partner] or child of a deceased partner, and receiving by way of annuity a portion of the profits made in the business in which the deceased person was a partner, is not by reason only of such receipt a partner in the business or liable as such:

(d)   The advance of money by way of loan to a person engaged or about to engage in any business on a contract with that person that the lender shall receive a rate of interest varying with the profits, or shall receive a share of the profits arising from carrying on the business, does not of itself make the lender a partner with the person or persons carrying on the business or liable as such. Provided that the contract is in writing, and signed by or on behalf of all the parties thereto:

(e)   A person receiving by way of annuity or otherwise a portion of the profits of a business in consideration of the sale by him of the goodwill of the business is not by reason only of such receipt a partner in the business or liable as such.

[197]

NOTES

Sub-s (3): words in square brackets in para (c) inserted by the Civil Partnership Act 2004, s 261(1), Sch 27, para 2.

3   Postponement of rights of person lending or selling in consideration of share of profits in case of insolvency

In the event of any person to whom money has been advanced by way of loan upon such a contract as is mentioned in the last foregoing section, or of any buyer of a goodwill in consideration of a share of the profits of the business, being adjudged a bankrupt, entering into an arrangement to pay his creditors less than [100p] in the pound, or dying in insolvent circumstances, the lender of the loan shall not be entitled to recover anything in respect of his loan, and the seller of the goodwill shall not be entitled to recover anything in respect of the share of profits contracted for, until the claims of the other creditors of the borrower or buyer for valuable consideration in money or money's worth have been satisfied.

[198]

NOTES

Sum in square brackets substituted by virtue of the Decimal Currency Act 1969, s 10(1).

4   Meaning of firm

(1)   Persons who have entered into partnership with one another are for the purposes of this Act called collectively a firm, and the name under which their business is carried on is called the firm-name.

(2)   (*Applies to Scotland only*.)

[199]

Relations of Partners to persons dealing with them

5   Power of partner to bind the firm

Every partner is an agent of the firm and his other partners for the purpose of the business of the partnership; and the acts of every partner who does any act for carrying on in the usual way business of the kind carried on by the firm of which he is a member bind the firm and his partners, unless the partner so acting has in fact no authority to act for the firm in the particular matter, and the person with whom he is dealing either knows that he has no authority, or does not know or believe him to be a partner.

[200]

6 Partners bound by acts on behalf of firm

An act or instrument relating to the business of the firm done or executed in the firm-name, or in any other manner showing an intention to bind the firm, by any person thereto authorised, whether a partner or not, is binding on the firm and all the partners.

Provided that this section shall not affect any general rule of law relating to the execution of deeds or negotiable instruments.

[201]

7 Partner using credit of firm for private purposes

Where one partner pledges the credit of the firm for a purpose apparently not connected with the firm's ordinary course of business, the firm is not bound, unless he is in fact specially authorised by the other partners; but this section does not affect any personal liability incurred by an individual partner.

[202]

8 Effect of notice that firm will not be bound by acts of partner

If it has been agreed between the partners that any restriction shall be placed on the power of any one or more of them to bind the firm, no act done in contravention of the agreement is binding on the firm with respect to persons having notice of the agreement.

[203]

9 Liability of partners

Every partner in a firm is liable jointly with the other partners, and in Scotland severally also, for all debts and obligations of the firm incurred while he is a partner; and after his death his estate is also severally liable in a due course of administration for such debts and obligations, so far as they remain unsatisfied, but subject in England or Ireland to the prior payment of his separate debts.

[204]

10 Liability of the firm for wrongs

Where, by any wrongful act or omission of any partner acting in the ordinary course of the business of the firm, or with the authority of his co-partners, loss or injury is caused to any person not being a partner in the firm, or any penalty is incurred, the firm is liable therefor to the same extent as the partner so acting or omitting to act.

[205]

11 Misapplication of money or property received for or in custody of the firm

In the following cases; namely—
    (a)   Where one partner acting within the scope of his apparent authority receives the money or property of a third person and misapplies it; and
    (b)   Where a firm in the course of its business receives money or property of a third person, and the money or property so received is misapplied by one or more of the partners while it is in the custody of the firm;
the firm is liable to make good the loss.

[206]

12 Liability for wrongs joint and several

Every partner is liable jointly with his co-partners and also severally for everything for which the firm while he is a partner therein becomes liable under either of the two last preceding sections.

[207]

13 Improper employment of trust-property for partnership purposes

If a partner, being a trustee, improperly employs trust-property in the business or on the account of the partnership, no other partner is liable for the trust property to the persons beneficially interested therein:

Provided as follows:—
    (1)   This section shall not affect any liability incurred by any partner by reason of his having notice of a breach of trust; and
    (2)   Nothing in this section shall prevent trust money from being followed and recovered from the firm if still in its possession or under its control.

[208]

14   Persons liable by "holding out"

(1)   Every one who by words spoken or written or by conduct represents himself, or who knowingly suffers himself to be represented, as a partner in a particular firm, is liable as a partner to any one who has on the faith of any such representation given credit to the firm, whether the representation has or has not been made or communicated to the person so giving credit by or with the knowledge of the apparent partner making the representation or suffering it to be made.

(2)   Provided that where after a partner's death the partnership business is continued in the old firm's name, the continued use of that name or of the deceased partner's name as part thereof shall not of itself make his executors or administrators estate or effects liable for any partnership debts contracted after his death.

[209]

15   Admissions and representations of partners

An admission or representation made by any partner concerning the partnership affairs, and in the ordinary course of its business, is evidence against the firm.

[210]

16   Notice to acting partner to be notice to the firm

Notice to any partner who habitually acts in the partnership business of any matter relating to partnership affairs operates as notice to the firm, except in the case of a fraud on the firm committed by or with the consent of that partner.

[211]

17   Liabilities of incoming and outgoing partners

(1)   A person who is admitted as a partner into an existing firm does not thereby become liable to the creditors of the firm for anything done before he became a partner.

(2)   A partner who retires from a firm does not thereby cease to be liable for partnership debts or obligations incurred before his retirement.

(3)   A retiring partner may be discharged from any existing liabilities, by an agreement to that effect between himself and the members of the firm as newly constituted and the creditors, and this agreement may be either expressed or inferred as a fact from the course of dealing between the creditors and the firm as newly constituted.

[212]

18   Revocation of continuing guaranty by change in firm

A continuing guaranty or cautionary obligation given either to a firm or to a third person in respect of the transactions of a firm is, in the absence of agreement to the contrary, revoked as to future transactions by any change in the constitution of the firm to which, or of the firm in respect of the transactions of which, the guaranty or obligation was given.

[213]

Relations of Partners to one another

19   Variation by consent of terms of partnership

The mutual rights and duties of partners, whether ascertained by agreement or defined by this Act, may be varied by the consent of all the partners, and such consent may be either express or inferred from a course of dealing.

[214]

20   Partnership property

(1)   All property and rights and interests in property originally brought into the partnership stock or acquired, whether by purchase or otherwise, on account of the firm, or for the purposes and in the course of the partnership business, are called in this Act partnership property, and must be held and applied by the partners exclusively for the purposes of the partnership and in accordance with the partnership agreement.

(2)   Provided that the legal estate or interest in any land, or in Scotland the title to and interest in any heritable estate, which belongs to the partnership shall devolve according to the nature and tenure thereof, and the general rules of law thereto applicable, but in trust, so far as necessary, for the persons beneficially interested in the land under this section.

(3)   Where co-owners of an estate or interest in any land, or in Scotland of any heritable estate, not being itself partnership property, are partners as to profits made by the use of that land or estate, and purchase other land or estate out of the profits to be used in like manner, the land or estate so purchased belongs to them, in the absence of an agreement to the contrary, not as partners, but as co-owners for the same respective estates and interests as are held by them in the land or estate first mentioned at the date of the purchase.

[215]

21 Property bought with partnership money

Unless the contrary intention appears, property bought with money belonging to the firm is deemed to have been bought on account of the firm.

[216]

22 (*Repealed by the Trusts of Land and Appointment of Trustees Act 1996, s 25(2), Sch 4, subject to savings contained in s 25(4), (5) thereof.*)

23 Procedure against partnership property for a partner's separate judgment debt

(1)   ... A writ of execution shall not issue against any partnership property except on a judgment against the firm.

(2)   The High Court, or a judge thereof, ... , or a county court, may, on the application by summons of any judgment creditor of a partner, make an order charging that partner's interest in the partnership property and profits with payment of the amount of the judgment debt and interest thereon, and may by the same or a subsequent order appoint a receiver of that partner's share of profits (whether already declared or accruing), and of any other money which may be coming to him in respect of the partnership, and direct all accounts and inquiries, and give all other orders and directions which might have been directed or given if the charge had been made in favour of the judgment creditor by the partner, or which the circumstances of the case may require.

(3)   The other partner or partners shall be at liberty at any time to redeem the interest charged, or in case of a sale being directed, to purchase the same.

(4)   ...

(5)   This section shall not apply to Scotland.

[217]

NOTES

Sub-s (1): words omitted repealed by the Statute Law Revision Act 1908.
Sub-s (2): words omitted repealed by the Courts Act 1971, s 56(4), Sch 11, Pt II.
Sub-s (4): repealed by the Statute Law (Repeals) Act 1998.

24 Rules as to interests and duties of partners subject to special agreement

The interests of partners in the partnership property and their rights and duties in relation to the partnership shall be determined, subject to any agreement express or implied between the partners, by the following rules:—

(1)   All the partners are entitled to share equally in the capital and profits of the business, and must contribute equally towards the losses whether of capital or otherwise sustained by the firm.

(2)   The firm must indemnify every partner in respect of payments made and personal liabilities incurred by him—

(a)   In the ordinary and proper conduct of the business of the firm; or,

(b)   In or about anything necessarily done for the preservation of the business or property of the firm.

(3)   A partner making, for the purpose of the partnership, any actual payment or advance beyond the amount of capital which he has agreed to subscribe, is entitled to interest at the rate of five per cent per annum from the date of the payment or advance.

(4)   A partner is not entitled, before the ascertainment of profits, to interest on the capital subscribed by him.

(5)   Every partner may take part in the management of the partnership business.

(6)   No partner shall be entitled to remuneration for acting in the partnership business.

(7)   No person may be introduced as a partner without the consent of all existing partners.

(8)   Any difference arising as to ordinary matters connected with the partnership business may be decided by a majority of the partners, but no change may be made in the nature of the partnership business without the consent of all existing partners.

(9)   The partnership books are to be kept at the place of business of the partnership (or the principal place, if there is more than one), and every partner may, when he thinks fit, have access to and inspect and copy any of them.

[218]

25 Expulsion of partner

No majority of the partners can expel any partner unless a power to do so has been conferred by express agreement between the partners.

[219]

26 Retirement from partnership at will

(1) Where no fixed term has been agreed upon for the duration of the partnership, any partner may determine the partnership at any time on giving notice of his intention so to do to all the other partners.

(2) Where the partnership has originally been constituted by deed, a notice in writing, signed by the partner giving it, shall be sufficient for this purpose.

[220]

27 Where partnership for term is continued over, continuance on old terms presumed

(1) Where a partnership entered into for a fixed term is continued after the term has expired, and without any express new agreement, the rights and duties of the partners remain the same as they were at the expiration of the term, so far as is consistent with the incidents of a partnership at will.

(2) A continuance of the business by the partners or such of them as habitually acted therein during the term, without any settlement or liquidation of the partnership affairs, is presumed to be a continuance of the partnership.

[221]

28 Duty of partners to render accounts, etc

Partners are bound to render true accounts and full information of all things affecting the partnership to any partner or his legal representatives.

[222]

29 Accountability of partners for private profits

(1) Every partner must account to the firm for any benefit derived by him without the consent of the other partners from any transaction concerning the partnership, or from any use by him of the partnership property name or business connexion.

(2) This section applies also to transactions undertaken after a partnership has been dissolved by the death of a partner, and before the affairs thereof have been completely wound up, either by any surviving partner or by the representatives of the deceased partner.

[223]

30 Duty of partner not to compete with firm

If a partner, without the consent of the other partners, carries on any business of the same nature as and competing with that of the firm, he must account for and pay over to the firm all profits made by him in that business.

[224]

31 Rights of assignee of share in partnership

(1) An assignment by any partner of his share in the partnership, either absolute or by way of mortgage or redeemable charge, does not, as against the other partners, entitle the assignee, during the continuance of the partnership, to interfere in the management or administration of the partnership business or affairs, or to require any accounts of the partnership transactions, or to inspect the partnership books, but entitles the assignee only to receive the share of profits to which the assigning partner would otherwise be entitled, and the assignee must accept the account of profits agreed to by the partners.

(2) In case of a dissolution of the partnership, whether as respects all the partners or as respects the assigning partner, the assignee is entitled to receive the share of the partnership assets to which the assigning partner is entitled as between himself and the other partners, and, for the purpose of ascertaining that share, to an account as from the date of the dissolution.

[225]

Dissolution of Partnership, and its consequences

32 Dissolution by expiration or notice

Subject to any agreement between the partners, a partnership is dissolved—

    (a) If entered into for a fixed term, by the expiration of that term:

    (b) If entered into for a single adventure or undertaking, by the termination of that adventure or undertaking:

    (c) If entered into for an undefined time, by any partner giving notice to the other or others of his intention to dissolve the partnership.

In the last-mentioned case the partnership is dissolved as from the date mentioned in the notice as the date of dissolution, or, if no date is so mentioned, as from the date of the communication of the notice.

[226]

33 Dissolution by bankruptcy, death or charge

(1) Subject to any agreement between the partners, every partnership is dissolved as regards all the partners by the death or bankruptcy of any partner.

(2) A partnership may, at the option of the other partners, be dissolved if any partner suffers his share of the partnership property to be charged under this Act for his separate debt.

[227]

34 Dissolution by illegality of partnership

A partnership is in every case dissolved by the happening of any event which makes it unlawful for the business of the firm to be carried on or for the members of the firm to carry it on in partnership.

[228]

35 Dissolution by the Court

On application by a partner the Court may decree a dissolution of the partnership in any of the following cases:

(a) ...
(b) When a partner, other than the partner suing, becomes in any other way permanently incapable of performing his part of the partnership contract:
(c) When a partner, other than the partner suing, has been guilty of such conduct as, in the opinion of the Court, regard being had to the nature of the business, is calculated to prejudicially affect the carrying on of the business:
(d) When a partner, other than the partner suing, wilfully or persistently commits a breach of the partnership agreement, or otherwise so conducts himself in matters relating to the partnership business that it is not reasonably practicable for the other partner or partners to carry on the business in partnership with him:
(e) When the business of the partnership can only be carried on at a loss:
(f) Whenever in any case circumstances have arisen which, in the opinion of the Court, render it just and equitable that the partnership be dissolved.

[229]

NOTES

Para (a) repealed by the Mental Health Act 1959, s 149(2), Sch 8.

36 Rights of persons dealing with firm against apparent members of firm

(1) Where a person deals with a firm after a change in its constitution he is entitled to treat all apparent members of the old firm as still being members of the firm until he has notice of the change.

(2) An advertisement in the London Gazette as to a firm whose principal place of business is in England or Wales, in the Edinburgh Gazette as to a firm whose principal place of business is in Scotland, and in the [Belfast] Gazette as to a firm whose principal place of business is in Ireland, shall be notice as to persons who had not dealings with the firm before the date of the dissolution or change so advertised.

(3) The estate of a partner who dies, or who becomes bankrupt, or of a partner who, not having been known to the person dealing with the firm to be a partner, retires from the firm, is not liable for partnership debts contracted after the date of the death, bankruptcy, or retirement respectively.

[230]

NOTES

Sub-s (2): word in square brackets substituted by virtue of the General Adaptation of Enactments (Northern Ireland) Order 1921, SR & O 1921/1804, art 7.

37 Right of partners to notify dissolution

On the dissolution of a partnership or retirement of a partner any partner may publicly notify the same, and may require the other partner or partners to concur for that purpose in all necessary or proper acts, if any, which cannot be done without his or their concurrence.

[231]

38 Continuing authority of partners for purposes of winding up

After the dissolution of a partnership the authority of each partner to bind the firm, and the other rights and obligations of the partners, continue notwithstanding the dissolution so far as may be necessary to wind up the affairs of the partnership, and to complete transactions begun but unfinished at the time of the dissolution, but not otherwise.

Provided that the firm is in no case bound by the acts of a partner who has become bankrupt; but this proviso does not affect the liability of any person who has after the bankruptcy represented himself or knowingly suffered himself to be represented as a partner of the bankrupt.

[232]

39 Rights of partners as to application of partnership property

On the dissolution of a partnership every partner is entitled, as against the other partners in the firm, and all persons claiming through them in respect of their interests as partners, to have the property of the partnership applied in payment of the debts and liabilities of the firm, and to have the surplus assets after such payment applied in payment of what may be due to the partners respectively after deducting what may be due from them as partners to the firm; and for that purpose any partner or his representatives may on the termination of the partnership apply to the Court to wind up the business and affairs of the firm.

[233]

40 Apportionment of premium where partnership prematurely dissolved

Where one partner has paid a premium to another on entering into a partnership for a fixed term, and the partnership is dissolved before the expiration of that term otherwise than by the death of a partner, the Court may order the repayment of the premium, or of such part thereof as it thinks just, having regard to the terms of the partnership contract and to the length of time during which the partnership has continued; unless

  (a)   the dissolution is, in the judgment of the Court, wholly or chiefly due to the misconduct of the partner who paid the premium; or

  (b)   the partnership has been dissolved by an agreement containing no provision for a return of any part of the premium.

[234]

41 Rights where partnership dissolved for fraud or misrepresentation

Where a partnership contract is rescinded on the ground of the fraud or misrepresentation of one of the parties thereto, the party entitled to rescind is, without prejudice to any other right, entitled—

  (a)   to a lien on, or right of retention of, the surplus of the partnership assets, after satisfying the partnership liabilities, for any sum of money paid by him for the purchase of a share in the partnership and for any capital contributed by him, and is

  (b)   to stand in the place of the creditors of the firm for any payments made by him in respect of the partnership liabilities, and

  (c)   to be indemnified by the person guilty of the fraud or making the representation against all the debts and liabilities of the firm.

[235]

42 Right of outgoing partner in certain cases to share profits made after dissolution

(1)   Where any member of a firm has died or otherwise ceased to be a partner, and the surviving or continuing partners carry on the business of the firm with its capital or assets without any final settlement of accounts as between the firm and the outgoing partner or his estate, then, in the absence of any agreement to the contrary, the outgoing partner or his estate is entitled at the option of himself or his representatives to such share of the profits made since the dissolution as the Court may find to be attributable to the use of his share of the partnership assets, or to interest at the rate of five per cent per annum on the amount of his share of the partnership assets.

(2)   Provided that where by the partnership contract an option is given to surviving or continuing partners to purchase the interest of a deceased or outgoing partner, and that option is duly exercised, the estate of the deceased partner, or the outgoing partner or his estate, as the case may be, is not entitled to any further or other share of profits; but if any partner assuming to act in exercise of the option does not in all material respects comply with the terms thereof, he is liable to account under the foregoing provisions of this section.

[236]

43 Retiring or deceased partner's share to be a debt

Subject to any agreement between the partners, the amount due from surviving or continuing partners to an outgoing partner or the representatives of a deceased partner in respect of the outgoing or deceased partner's share is a debt accruing at the date of the dissolution or death.

[237]

44 Rule for distribution of assets on final settlement of accounts

In settling accounts between the partners after a dissolution of partnership, the following rules shall, subject to any agreement, be observed:

  (a)   Losses, including losses and deficiencies of capital, shall be paid first out of profits, next out of capital, and lastly, if necessary, by the partners individually in the proportion in which they were entitled to share profits:

  (b)   The assets of the firm including the sums, if any, contributed by the partners to make up losses or deficiencies of capital, shall be applied in the following manner and order:

    1.   In paying the debts and liabilities of the firm to persons who are not partners therein:

    2.   In paying to each partner rateably what is due from the firm to him for advances as distinguished from capital:

3. In paying to each partner rateably what is due from the firm to him in respect of capital:
4. The ultimate residue, if any, shall be divided among the partners in the proportion in which profits are divisible.

[238]

Supplemental

45 Definitions of "court" and "business"

In this Act, unless the contrary intention appears,—
The expression "court" includes every court and judge having jurisdiction in the case:
The expression "business" includes every trade, occupation, or profession.

[239]

46 Saving for rules of equity and common law

The rules of equity and of common law applicable to partnership shall continue in force except so far as they are inconsistent with the express provisions of this Act.

[240]

47–49 *(S 47 applies to Scotland only; ss 48, 49 repealed by the Statute Law Revision Act 1908.)*

50 Short title

This Act may be cited as the Partnership Act 1890.

[241]

(Schedule repealed by the Statute Law Revision Act 1908.)

MARINE INSURANCE ACT 1906

(6 Edw 7 c 41)

ARRANGEMENT OF SECTIONS

An Act to codify the Law relating to Marine Insurance

[21 December 1906]

NOTES

Marine Insurance Acts 1906 and 1909. By the Marine Insurance (Gambling Policies) Act 1909, s 2, at **[350]**, that Act and this Act may be cited together by this collective title.

Hovercraft: references in this Act to ships, vessels and boats (in whatever terms) and activities, etc, connected therewith, are extended to include hovercraft, by the Hovercraft (Application of Enactments) Order 1972, SI 1972/971.

Marine Insurance

1   Marine insurance defined

A contract of marine insurance is a contract whereby the insurer undertakes to indemnify the assured, in manner and to the extent thereby agreed, against marine losses, that is to say, the losses incident to marine adventure.

[242]

2   Mixed sea and land risks

(1)   A contract of marine insurance may, by its express terms, or by usage of trade, be extended so as to protect the assured against losses on inland waters or on any land risk which may be incidental to any sea voyage.

(2)   Where a ship in course of building, or the launch of a ship, or any adventure analogous to a marine adventure, is covered by a policy in the form of a marine policy, the provisions of this Act, in so far as applicable, shall apply thereto; but, except as by this section provided, nothing in this Act shall alter or affect any rule of law applicable to any contract of insurance other than a contract of marine insurance as by this Act defined.

[243]

3   Marine adventure and maritime perils defined

(1)   Subject to the provisions of this Act, every lawful marine adventure may be the subject of a contract of marine insurance.

(2)   In particular there is a marine adventure where—
    (a)   Any ship goods or other moveables are exposed to maritime perils. Such property is in this Act referred to as "insurable property";
    (b)   The earning or acquisition of any freight, passage money, commission, profit, or other pecuniary benefit, or the security for any advances, loan, or disbursements, is endangered by the exposure of insurable property to maritime perils;

(c) Any liability to a third party may be incurred by the owner of, or other person interested in or responsible for, insurable property, by reason of maritime perils.

"Maritime perils" means the perils consequent on, or incidental to, the navigation of the sea, that is to say, perils of the seas, fire, war perils, pirates, rovers, thieves, captures, seisures, restraints, and detainments of princes and peoples, jettisons, barratry, and any other perils, either of the like kind or which may be designated by the policy.

[244]

Insurable Interest

4 Avoidance of wagering or gaming contracts

(1) Every contract of marine insurance by way of gaming or wagering is void.

(2) A contract of marine insurance is deemed to be a gaming or wagering contract—
  (a) Where the assured has not an insurable interest as defined by this Act, and the contract is entered into with no expectation of acquiring such an interest; or
  (b) Where the policy is made "interest or no interest," or "without further proof of interest than the policy itself," or "without benefit of salvage to the insurer," or subject to any other like term:

Provided that, where there is no possibility of salvage, a policy may be effected without benefit of salvage to the insurer.

[245]

5 Insurable interest defined

(1) Subject to the provisions of this Act, every person has an insurable interest who is interested in a marine adventure.

(2) In particular a person is interested in a marine adventure where he stands in any legal or equitable relation to the adventure or to any insurable property at risk therein, in consequence of which he may benefit by the safety or due arrival of insurable property, or may be prejudiced by its loss, or damage thereto, or by the detention thereof, or may incur liability in respect thereof.

[246]

6 When interest must attach

(1) The assured must be interested in the subject-matter insured at the time of the loss though he need not be interested when the insurance is effected:

Provided that where the subject-matter is insured "lost or not lost," the assured may recover although he may not have acquired his interest until after the loss, unless at the time of effecting the contract of insurance the assured was aware of the loss, and the insurer was not.

(2) Where the assured has no interest at the time of the loss, he cannot acquire interest by any act or election after he is aware of the loss.

[247]

7 Defeasible or contingent interest

(1) A defeasible interest is insurable, as also is a contingent interest.

(2) In particular, where the buyer of goods has insured them, he has an insurable interest, notwithstanding that he might, at his election, have rejected the goods, or have treated them as at the seller's risk, by reason of the latter's delay in making delivery or otherwise.

[248]

8 Partial interest

A partial interest of any nature is insurable.

[249]

9 Re-insurance

(1) The insurer under a contract of marine insurance has an insurable interest in his risk, and may re-insure in respect of it.

(2) Unless the policy otherwise provides, the original assured has no right or interest in respect of such re-insurance.

[250]

10 Bottomry

The lender of money on bottomry or respondentia has an insurable interest in respect of the loan.

[251]

11 Master's and seamen's wages

The master or any member of the crew of a ship has an insurable interest in respect of his wages.

[252]

12 Advance freight

In the case of advance freight, the person advancing the freight has an insurable interest, in so far as such freight is not repayable in case of loss.

[253]

13 Charges of insurance

The assured has an insurable interest in the charges of any insurance which he may effect.

[254]

14 Quantum of interest

(1) Where the subject-matter insured is mortgaged, the mortgagor has an insurable interest in the full value thereof, and the mortgagee has an insurable interest in respect of any sum due or to become due under the mortgage.

(2) A mortgagee, consignee, or other person having an interest in the subject matter insured may insure on behalf and for the benefit of other persons interested as well as for his own benefit.

(3) The owner of insurable property has an insurable interest in respect of the full value thereof, notwithstanding that some third person may have agreed, or be liable, to indemnify him in case of loss.

[255]

15 Assignment of interest

Where the assured assigns or otherwise parts with his interest in the subject-matter insured, he does not thereby transfer to the assignee his rights under the contract of insurance, unless there be an express or implied agreement with the assignee to that effect.

But the provisions of this section do not affect a transmission of interest by operation of law.

[256]

Insurable Value

16 Measure of insurable value

Subject to any express provision or valuation in the policy, the insurable value of the subject-matter insured must be ascertained as follows:—

(1) In insurance on ship, the insurable value is the value, at the commencement of the risk, of the ship, including her outfit, provisions and stores for the officers and crew, money advanced for seamen's wages, and other disbursements (if any) incurred to make the ship fit for the voyage or adventure contemplated by the policy, plus the charges of insurance upon the whole:
The insurable value, in the case of a steamship, includes also the machinery, boilers, and coals and engine stores if owned by the assured, and, in the case of a ship engaged in a special trade, the ordinary fittings requisite for that trade:

(2) In insurance on freight, whether paid in advance or otherwise, the insurable value is the gross amount of the freight at the risk of the assured, plus the charges of insurance:

(3) In insurance on goods or merchandise, the insurable value is the prime cost of the property insured, plus the expenses of and incidental to shipping and the charges of insurance upon the whole:

(4) In insurance on any other subject-matter, the insurable value is the amount at the risk of the assured when the policy attaches, plus the charges of insurance.

[257]

Disclosure and Representations

17 Insurance is uberrimae fidei

A contract of marine insurance is a contract based upon the utmost good faith, and, if the utmost good faith be not observed by either party, the contract may be avoided by the other party.

[258]

18 Disclosure by assured

(1) Subject to the provisions of this section, the assured must disclose to the insurer, before the contract is concluded, every material circumstance which is known to the assured, and the assured is deemed to know every circumstance which, in the ordinary course of business, ought to be known by him. If the assured fails to make such disclosure, the insurer may avoid the contract.

(2) Every circumstance is material which would influence the judgment of a prudent insurer in fixing the premium, or determining whether he will take the risk.

(3) In the absence of inquiry the following circumstances need not be disclosed, namely—

(a) Any circumstance which diminishes the risk;

   (b)   Any circumstance which is known or presumed to be known to the insurer. The insurer is presumed to know matters of common notoriety or knowledge, and matters which an insurer in the ordinary course of his business, as such, ought to know;

   (c)   Any circumstance as to which information is waived by the insurer;

   (d)   Any circumstance which it is superfluous to disclose by reason of any express or implied warranty.

(4)   Whether any particular circumstance, which is not disclosed, be material or not is, in each case, a question of fact.

(5)   The term "circumstance" includes any communication made to, or information received by, the assured.

[259]

19   Disclosure by agent effecting insurance

Subject to the provisions of the preceding section as to circumstances which need not be disclosed, where an insurance is effected for the assured by an agent, the agent must disclose to the insurer—

   (a)   Every material circumstance which is known to himself, and an agent to insure is deemed to know every circumstance which in the ordinary course of business ought to be known by, or to have been communicated to, him; and

   (b)   Every material circumstance which the assured is bound to disclose, unless it come to his knowledge too late to communicate it to the agent.

[260]

20   Representations pending negotiation of contract

(1)   Every material representation made by the assured or his agent to the insurer during the negotiations for the contract, and before the contract is concluded, must be true. If it be untrue the insurer may avoid the contract.

(2)   A representation is material which would influence the judgment of a prudent insurer in fixing the premium, or determining whether he will take the risk.

(3)   A representation may be either a representation as to a matter of fact, or as to a matter of expectation or belief.

(4)   A representation as to matter of fact is true, if it be substantially correct, that is to say, if the difference between what is represented and what is actually correct would not be considered material by a prudent insurer.

(5)   A representation as to a matter of expectation or belief is true if it be made in good faith.

(6)   A representation may be withdrawn or corrected before the contract is concluded.

(7)   Whether a particular representation be material or not is, in each case, a question of fact.

[261]

21   When contract is deemed to be concluded

A contract of marine insurance is deemed to be concluded when the proposal of the assured is accepted by the insurer, whether the policy be then issued or not; and, for the purpose of showing when the proposal was accepted, reference may be made to the slip or covering note or other customary memorandum of the contract, …

[262]

NOTES

   Words omitted repealed by the Finance Act 1959, s 37(5), Sch 8, Pt II, and the Finance Act (Northern Ireland) 1959, s 17(2), Sch 3, Pt II.

The Policy

22   Contract must be embodied in policy

Subject to the provisions of any statute, a contract of marine insurance is inadmissible in evidence unless it is embodied in a marine policy in accordance with this Act. The policy may be executed and issued either at the time when the contract is concluded, or afterwards.

[263]

23   What policy must specify

A marine policy must specify—

   (1)   The name of the assured, or of some person who effects the insurance on his behalf:

   (2)–(5)   …

[264]

24 Signature of insurer

(1)   A marine policy must be signed by or on behalf of the insurer, provided that in the case of a corporation the corporate seal may be sufficient, but nothing in this section shall be construed as requiring the subscription of a corporation to be under seal.

(2)   Where a policy is subscribed by or on behalf of two or more insurers, each subscription, unless the contrary be expressed, constitutes a distinct contract with the assured.

[265]

25 Voyage and time policies

(1)   Where the contract is to insure the subject-matter "at and from", or from one place to another or others, the policy is called a "voyage policy", and where the contract is to insure the subject-matter for a definite period of time the policy is called a "time policy". A contract for both voyage and time may be included in the same policy.

(2)   …

[266]

26 Designation of subject-matter

(1)   The subject-matter insured must be designated in a marine policy with reasonable certainty.

(2)   The nature and extent of the interest of the assured in the subject-matter insured need not be specified in the policy.

(3)   Where the policy designates the subject-matter insured in general terms, it shall be construed to apply to the interest intended by the assured to be covered.

(4)   In the application of this section regard shall be had to any usage regulating the designation of the subject-matter insured.

[267]

27 Valued policy

(1)   A policy may be either valued or unvalued.

(2)   A valued policy is a policy which specifies the agreed value of the subject matter insured.

(3)   Subject to the provisions of this Act, and in the absence of fraud, the value fixed by the policy is, as between the insurer and assured, conclusive of the insurable value of the subject intended to be insured, whether the loss be total or partial.

(4)   Unless the policy otherwise provides, the value fixed by the policy is not conclusive for the purpose of determining whether there has been a constructive total loss.

[268]

28 Unvalued policy

An unvalued policy is a policy which does not specify the value of the subject-matter insured, but, subject to the limit of the sum insured, leaves the insurable value to be subsequently ascertained, in the manner herein-before specified.

[269]

29 Floating policy by ship or ships

(1)   A floating policy is a policy which describes the insurance in general terms, and leaves the name of the ship or ships and other particulars to be defined by subsequent declaration.

(2)   The subsequent declaration or declarations may be made by indorsement on the policy, or in other customary manner.

(3)   Unless the policy otherwise provides, the declarations must be made in the order of dispatch or shipment. They must, in the case of goods, comprise all consignments within the terms of the policy, and the value of the goods or other property must be honestly stated, but an omission or erroneous declaration may be rectified even after loss or arrival, provided the omission or declaration was made in good faith.

(4) Unless the policy otherwise provides, where a declaration of value is not made until after notice of loss or arrival, the policy must be treated as an unvalued policy as regards the subject-matter of that declaration.

[270]

30 Construction of terms in policy

(1) A policy may be in the form in the First Schedule to this Act.

(2) Subject to the provisions of this Act, and unless the context of the policy otherwise requires, the terms and expressions mentioned in the First Schedule to this Act shall be construed as having the scope and meaning in that schedule assigned to them.

[271]

31 Premium to be arranged

(1) Where an insurance is effected at a premium to be arranged, and no arrangement is made, a reasonable premium is payable.

(2) Where an insurance is effected on the terms that an additional premium is to be arranged in a given event, and that event happens but no arrangement is made, then a reasonable additional premium is payable.

[272]

Double Insurance

32 Double insurance

(1) Where two or more policies are effected by or on behalf of the assured on the same adventure and interest or any part thereof, and the sums insured exceed the indemnity allowed by this Act, the assured is said to be over-insured by double insurance.

(2) Where the assured is over-insured by double insurance—
(a) The assured, unless the policy otherwise provides, may claim payment from the insurers in such order as he may think fit, provided that he is not entitled to receive any sum in excess of the indemnity allowed by this Act;
(b) Where the policy under which the assured claims is a valued policy, the assured must give credit as against the valuation for any sum received by him under any other policy without regard to the actual value of the subject-matter insured;
(c) Where the policy under which the assured claims is an unvalued policy he must give credit, as against the full insurable value, for any sum received by him under any other policy;
(d) Where the assured receives any sum in excess of the indemnity allowed by this Act, he is deemed to hold such sum in trust for the insurers, according to their right of contribution among themselves.

[273]

Warranties, etc

33 Nature of warranty

(1) A warranty, in the following sections relating to warranties, means a promissory warranty, that is to say, a warranty by which the assured undertakes that some particular thing shall or shall not be done, or that some condition shall be fulfilled, or whereby he affirms or negatives the existence of a particular state of facts.

(2) A warranty may be express or implied.

(3) A warranty, as above defined, is a condition which must be exactly complied with, whether it be material to the risk or not. If it be not so complied with, then, subject to any express provision in the policy, the insurer is discharged from liability as from the date of the breach of warranty, but without prejudice to any liability incurred by him before that date.

[274]

34 When breach of warranty excused

(1) Non-compliance with a warranty is excused when, by reason of a change of circumstances, the warranty ceases to be applicable to the circumstances of the contract, or when compliance with the warranty is rendered unlawful by any subsequent law.

(2) Where a warranty is broken, the assured cannot avail himself of the defence that the breach has been remedied, and the warranty complied with, before loss.

(3) A breach of warranty may be waived by the insurer.

[275]

PART 1
STATUTES

35 Express warranties

(1)   An express warranty may be in any form of words from which the intention to warrant is to be inferred.

(2)   An express warranty must be included in, or written upon, the policy, or must be contained in some document incorporated by reference into the policy.

(3)   An express warranty does not exclude an implied warranty, unless it be inconsistent therewith.

[276]

36 Warranty of neutrality

(1)   Where insurable property, whether ship or goods, is expressly warranted neutral, there is an implied condition that the property shall have a neutral character at the commencement of the risk, and that, so far as the assured can control the matter, its neutral character shall be preserved during the risk.

(2)   Where a ship is expressly warranted "neutral" there is also an implied condition that, so far as the assured can control the matter, she shall be properly documented, that is to say, that she shall carry the necessary papers to establish her neutrality, and that she shall not falsify or suppress her papers, or use simulated papers. If any loss occurs through breach of this condition, the insurer may avoid the contract.

[277]

37 No implied warranty of nationality

There is no implied warranty as to the nationality of a ship, or that her nationality shall not be changed during the risk.

[278]

38 Warranty of good safety

Where the subject-matter insured is warranted "well" or "in good safety" on a particular day, it is sufficient if it be safe at any time during that day.

[279]

39 Warranty of seaworthiness of ship

(1)   In a voyage policy there is an implied warranty that at the commencement of the voyage the ship shall be seaworthy for the purpose of the particular adventure insured.

(2)   Where the policy attaches while the ship is in port, there is also an implied warranty that she shall, at the commencement of the risk, be reasonably fit to encounter the ordinary perils of the port.

(3)   Where the policy relates to a voyage which is performed in different stages, during which the ship requires different kinds of or further preparation or equipment, there is an implied warranty that at the commencement of each stage the ship is seaworthy in respect of such preparation or equipment for the purposes of that stage.

(4)   A ship is deemed to be seaworthy when she is reasonably fit in all respects to encounter the ordinary perils of the seas of the adventure insured.

(5)   In a time policy there is no implied warranty that the ship shall be seaworthy at any stage of the adventure, but where, with the privity of the assured, the ship is sent to sea in an unseaworthy state, the insurer is not liable for any loss attributable to unseaworthiness.

[280]

40 No implied warranty that goods are seaworthy

(1)   In a policy on goods or other moveables there is no implied warranty that the goods or moveables are seaworthy.

(2)   In a voyage policy on goods or other moveables there is an implied warranty that at the commencement of the voyage the ship is not only seaworthy as a ship, but also that she is reasonably fit to carry the goods or other moveables to the destination contemplated by the policy.

[281]

41 Warranty of legality

There is an implied warranty that the adventure insured is a lawful one, and that, so far as the assured can control the matter, the adventure shall be carried out in a lawful manner.

[282]

The Voyage

42 Implied condition as to commencement of risk

(1)   Where the subject-matter is insured by a voyage policy "at and from" or "from" a particular place, it is not necessary that the ship should be at that place when the contract is concluded, but

there is an implied condition that the adventure shall be commenced within a reasonable time, and that if the adventure be not so commenced the insurer may avoid the contract.

(2)   The implied condition may be negatived by showing that the delay was caused by circumstances known to the insurer before the contract was concluded, or by showing that he waived the condition.

[283]

43   Alteration of port of departure

Where the place of departure is specified by the policy, and the ship instead of sailing from that place sails from any other place, the risk does not attach.

[284]

44   Sailing for different destination

Where the destination is specified in the policy, and the ship, instead of sailing for that destination, sails for any other destination, the risk does not attach.

[285]

45   Change of voyage

(1)   Where, after the commencement of the risk, the destination of the ship is voluntarily changed from the destination contemplated by the policy, there is said to be a change of voyage.

(2)   Unless the policy otherwise provides, where there is a change of voyage, the insurer is discharged from liability as from the time of change, that is to say, as from the time when the determination to change it is manifested; and it is immaterial that the ship may not in fact have left the course of voyage contemplated by the policy when the loss occurs.

[286]

46   Deviation

(1)   Where a ship, without lawful excuse, deviates from the voyage contemplated by the policy, the insurer is discharged from liability as from the time of deviation, and it is immaterial that the ship may have regained her route before any loss occurs.

(2)   There is a deviation from the voyage contemplated by the policy—
  (a)   Where the course of the voyage is specifically designated by the policy, and that course is departed from; or
  (b)   Where the course of the voyage is not specifically designated by the policy, but the usual and customary course is departed from.

(3)   The intention to deviate is immaterial; there must be a deviation in fact to discharge the insurer from his liability under the contract.

[287]

47   Several ports of discharge

(1)   Where several ports of discharge are specified by the policy, the ship may proceed to all or any of them, but, in the absence of any usage or sufficient cause to the contrary, she must proceed to them, or such of them as she goes to, in the order designated by the policy. If she does not there is a deviation.

(2)   Where the policy is to "ports of discharge", within a given area, which are not named, the ship must, in the absence of any usage or sufficient cause to the contrary, proceed to them, or such of them as she goes to, in their geographical order. If she does not there is a deviation.

[288]

48   Delay in voyage

In the case of a voyage policy, the adventure insured must be prosecuted throughout its course with reasonable dispatch, and, if without lawful excuse it is not so prosecuted, the insurer is discharged from liability as from the time when the delay became unreasonable.

[289]

49   Excuses for deviation or delay

(1)   Deviation or delay in prosecuting the voyage contemplated by the policy is excused—
  (a)   Where authorised by any special term in the policy; or
  (b)   Where caused by circumstances beyond the control of the master and his employer; or
  (c)   Where reasonably necessary in order to comply with an express or implied warranty; or
  (d)   Where reasonably necessary for the safety of the ship or subject-matter insured; or
  (e)   For the purpose of saving human life, or aiding a ship in distress where human life may be in danger; or
  (f)   Where reasonably necessary for the purpose of obtaining medical or surgical aid for any person on board the ship; or

(g) Where caused by the barratrous conduct of the master or crew, if barratry be one of the perils insured against.

(2) When the cause excusing the deviation or delay ceases to operate, the ship must resume her course, and prosecute her voyage, with reasonable dispatch.

[290]

Assignment of Policy

50 When and how policy is assignable

(1) A marine policy is assignable unless it contains terms expressly prohibiting assignment. It may be assigned either before or after loss.

(2) Where a marine policy has been assigned so as to pass the beneficial interest in such policy, the assignee of the policy is entitled to sue thereon in his own name; and the defendant is entitled to make any defence arising out of the contract which he would have been entitled to make if the action had been brought in the name of the person by or on behalf of whom the policy was effected.

(3) A marine policy may be assigned by indorsement thereon or in other customary manner.

[291]

51 Assured who has no interest cannot assign

Where the assured has parted with or lost his interest in the subject-matter insured, and has not, before or at the time of so doing, expressly or impliedly agreed to assign the policy, any subsequent assignment of the policy is inoperative:

Provided that nothing in this section affects the assignment of a policy after loss.

[292]

The Premium

52 When premium payable

Unless otherwise agreed, the duty of the assured or his agent to pay the premium, and the duty of the insurer to issue the policy to the assured or his agent, are concurrent conditions, and the insurer is not bound to issue the policy until payment or tender of the premium.

[293]

53 Policy effected through broker

(1) Unless otherwise agreed, where a marine policy is effected on behalf of the assured by a broker, the broker is directly responsible to the insurer for the premium, and the insurer is directly responsible to the assured for the amount which may be payable in respect of losses, or in respect of returnable premium.

(2) Unless otherwise agreed, the broker has, as against the assured, a lien upon the policy for the amount of the premium and his charges in respect of effecting the policy; and, where he has dealt with the person who employs him as a principal, he has also a lien on the policy in respect of any balance on any insurance account which may be due to him from such person, unless when the debt was incurred he had reason to believe that such person was only an agent.

[294]

54 Effect of receipt on policy

Where a marine policy effected on behalf of the assured by a broker acknowledges the receipt of the premium, such acknowledgment is, in the absence of fraud, conclusive as between the insurer and the assured, but not as between the insurer and broker.

[295]

Loss and Abandonment

55 Included and excluded losses

(1) Subject to the provisions of this Act, and unless the policy otherwise provides, the insurer is liable for any loss proximately caused by a peril insured against, but, subject as aforesaid, he is not liable for any loss which is not proximately caused by a peril insured against.

(2) In particular,—
   (a) The insurer is not liable for any loss attributable to the wilful misconduct of the assured, but, unless the policy otherwise provides, he is liable for any loss proximately caused by a peril insured against, even though the loss would not have happened but for the misconduct or negligence of the master or crew;
   (b) Unless the policy otherwise provides, the insurer on ship or goods is not liable for any loss proximately caused by delay, although the delay be caused by a peril insured against;

(c)   Unless the policy otherwise provides, the insurer is not liable for ordinary wear and tear, ordinary leakage and breakage, inherent vice or nature of the subject-matter insured, or for any loss proximately caused by rats or vermin, or for any injury to machinery not proximately caused by maritime perils.

[296]

56   Partial and total loss

(1)   A loss may be either total or partial. Any loss other than a total loss, as herein-after defined, is a partial loss.

(2)   A total loss may be either an actual total loss, or a constructive total loss.

(3)   Unless a different intention appears from the terms of the policy, an insurance against total loss includes a constructive, as well as an actual, total loss.

(4)   Where the assured brings an action for a total loss and the evidence proves only a partial loss, he may, unless the policy otherwise provides, recover for a partial loss.

(5)   Where goods reach their destination in specie, but by reason of obliteration of marks, or otherwise, they are incapable of identification, the loss, if any, is partial, and not total.

[297]

57   Actual total loss

(1)   Where the subject-matter insured is destroyed, or so damaged as to cease to be a thing of the kind insured, or where the assured is irretrievably deprived thereof, there is an actual total loss.

(2)   In the case of an actual total loss no notice of abandonment need be given.

[298]

58   Missing ship

Where the ship concerned in the adventure is missing, and after the lapse of a reasonable time no news of her has been received, an actual total loss may be presumed.

[299]

59   Effect of transhipment, etc

Where, by a peril insured against, the voyage is interrupted at an intermediate port or place, under such circumstances as, apart from any special stipulation in the contract of affreightment, to justify the master in landing and re-shipping the goods or other moveables, or in transhipping them, and sending them on to their destination, the liability of the insurer continues, notwithstanding the landing or transhipment.

[300]

60   Constructive total loss defined

(1)   Subject to any express provision in the policy, there is a constructive total loss where the subject-matter insured is reasonably abandoned on account of its actual total loss appearing to be unavoidable, or because it could not be preserved from actual total loss without an expenditure which would exceed its value when the expenditure had been incurred.

(2)   In particular, there is a constructive total loss—
   (i)   Where the assured is deprived of the possession of his ship or goods by a peril insured against, and (a) it is unlikely that he can recover the ship or goods, as the case may be, or (b) the cost of recovering the ship or goods, as the case may be, would exceed their value when recovered; or
   (ii) In the case of damage to a ship, where she is so damaged by a peril insured against that the cost of repairing the damage would exceed the value of the ship when repaired.
         In estimating the cost of repairs, no deduction is to be made in respect of general average contributions to those repairs payable by other interests, but account is to be taken of the expense of future salvage operations and of any future general average contributions to which the ship would be liable if repaired; or
   (iii) In the case of damage to goods, where the cost of repairing the damage and forwarding the goods to their destination would exceed their value on arrival.

[301]

61   Effect of constructive total loss

Where there is a constructive total loss the assured may either treat the loss as a partial loss, or abandon the subject-matter insured to the insurer and treat the loss as if it were an actual total loss.

[302]

62   Notice of abandonment

(1)   Subject to the provisions of this section, where the assured elects to abandon the subject-matter insured to the insurer, he must give notice of abandonment. If he fails to do so the loss can only be treated as a partial loss.

(2)   Notice of abandonment may be given in writing, or by word of mouth, or partly in writing and partly by word of mouth, and may be given in terms which indicate the intention of the assured to abandon his insured interest in the subject matter insured unconditionally to the insurer.

(3)   Notice of abandonment must be given with reasonable diligence after the receipt of reliable information of the loss, but where the information is of a doubtful character the assured is entitled to a reasonable time to make inquiry.

(4)   Where notice of abandonment is properly given, the rights of the assured are not prejudiced by the fact that the insurer refuses to accept the abandonment.

(5)   The acceptance of an abandonment may be either express or implied from the conduct of the insurer. The mere silence of the insurer after notice is not an acceptance.

(6)   Where a notice of abandonment is accepted the abandonment is irrevocable. The acceptance of the notice conclusively admits liability for the loss and the sufficiency of the notice.

(7)   Notice of abandonment is unnecessary where, at the time when the assured receives information of the loss, there would be no possibility of benefit to the insurer if notice were given to him.

(8)   Notice of abandonment may be waived by the insurer.

(9)   Where an insurer has re-insured his risk, no notice of abandonment need be given by him.

[303]

63   Effect of abandonment

(1)   Where there is a valid abandonment the insurer is entitled to take over the interest of the assured in whatever may remain of the subject-matter insured, and all proprietary rights incidental thereto.

(2)   Upon the abandonment of a ship, the insurer thereof is entitled to any freight in course of being earned, and which is earned by her subsequent to the casualty causing the loss, less the expenses of earning it incurred after the casualty; and, where the ship is carrying the owner's goods, the insurer is entitled to a reasonable remuneration for the carriage of them subsequent to the casualty causing the loss.

[304]

Partial Losses (including Salvage and General Average and Particular Charges)

64   Particular average loss

(1)   A particular average loss is a partial loss of the subject-matter insured, caused by a peril insured against, and which is not a general average loss.

(2)   Expenses incurred by or on behalf of the assured for the safety or preservation of the subject-matter insured, other than general average and salvage charges, are called particular charges. Particular charges are not included in particular average.

[305]

65   Salvage charges

(1)   Subject to any express provision in the policy, salvage charges incurred in preventing a loss by perils insured against may be recovered as a loss by those perils.

(2)   "Salvage charges" means the charges recoverable under maritime law by a salvor independently of contract. They do not include the expenses of services in the nature of salvage rendered by the assured or his agents, or any person employed for hire by them, for the purpose of averting a peril insured against. Such expenses, where properly incurred, may be recovered as particular charges or as a general average loss, according to the circumstances under which they were incurred.

[306]

66   General average loss

(1)   A general average loss is a loss caused by or directly consequential on a general average act. It includes a general average expenditure as well as a general average sacrifice.

(2)   There is a general average act where any extraordinary sacrifice or expenditure is voluntarily and reasonably made or incurred in time of peril for the purpose of preserving the property imperilled in the common adventure.

(3)   Where there is a general average loss, the party on whom it falls is entitled, subject to the conditions imposed by maritime law, to a rateable contribution from the other parties interested, and such contribution is called a general average contribution.

(4)   Subject to any express provision in the policy, where the assured has incurred a general average expenditure, he may recover from the insurer in respect of the proportion of the loss which

falls upon him; and, in the case of a general average sacrifice, he may recover from the insurer in respect of the whole loss without having enforced his right of contribution from the other parties liable to contribute.

(5)　Subject to any express provision in the policy, where the assured has paid, or is liable to pay, a general average contribution in respect of the subject insured, he may recover therefor from the insurer.

(6)　In the absence of express stipulation, the insurer is not liable for any general average loss or contribution where the loss was not incurred for the purpose of avoiding, or in connexion with the avoidance of, a peril insured against.

(7)　Where ship, freight, and cargo, or any two of those interests, are owned by the same assured, the liability of the insurer in respect of general average losses or contributions is to be determined as if those subjects were owned by different persons.

[307]

Measure of Indemnity

67　Extent of liability of insurer for loss

(1)　The sum which the assured can recover in respect of a loss on a policy by which he is insured, in the case of an unvalued policy to the full extent of the insurable value, or, in the case of a valued policy to the full extent of the value fixed by the policy, is called the measure of indemnity.

(2)　Where there is a loss recoverable under the policy, the insurer, or each insurer if there be more than one, is liable for such proportion of the measure of indemnity as the amount of his subscription bears to the value fixed by the policy in the case of a valued policy, or to the insurable value in the case of an unvalued policy.

[308]

68　Total loss

Subject to the provisions of this Act and to any express provision in the policy, where there is a total loss of the subject-matter insured,—

    (1)　If the policy be a valued policy, the measure of indemnity is the sum fixed by the policy:

    (2)　If the policy be an unvalued policy, the measure of indemnity is the insurable value of the subject-matter insured.

[309]

69　Partial loss of ship

Where a ship is damaged, but is not totally lost, the measure of indemnity, subject to any express provision in the policy, is as follows:—

    (1)　Where the ship has been repaired, the assured is entitled to the reasonable cost of the repairs, less the customary deductions, but not exceeding the sum insured in respect of any one casualty:

    (2)　Where the ship has been only partially repaired, the assured is entitled to the reasonable cost of such repairs, computed as above, and also to be indemnified for the reasonable depreciation, if any, arising from the unrepaired damage, provided that the aggregate amount shall not exceed the cost of repairing the whole damage, computed as above:

    (3)　Where the ship has not been repaired, and has not been sold in her damaged state during the risk, the assured is entitled to be indemnified for the reasonable depreciation arising from the unrepaired damage, but not exceeding the reasonable cost of repairing such damage, computed as above.

[310]

70　Partial loss of freight

Subject to any express provision in the policy, where there is a partial loss of freight, the measure of indemnity is such proportion of the sum fixed by the policy in the case of a valued policy, or of the insurable value in the case of an unvalued policy, as the proportion of freight lost by the assured bears to the whole freight at the risk of the assured under the policy.

[311]

71　Partial loss of goods, merchandise, etc

Where there is a partial loss of goods, merchandise, or other moveables, the measure of indemnity, subject to any express provision in the policy, is as follows:—

    (1)　Where part of the goods, merchandise or other moveables insured by a valued policy is totally lost, the measure of indemnity is such proportion of the sum fixed by the policy as the insurable value of the part lost bears to the insurable value of the whole, ascertained as in the case of an unvalued policy:

    (2)　Where part of the goods, merchandise, or other moveables insured by an unvalued policy is totally lost, the measure of indemnity is the insurable value of the part lost, ascertained as in case of total loss:

PART 1
STATUTES

(3)   Where the whole or any part of the goods or merchandise insured has been delivered damaged at its destination, the measure of indemnity is such proportion of the sum fixed by the policy in the case of a valued policy, or of the insurable value in the case of an unvalued policy, as the difference between the gross sound and damaged values at the place of arrival bears to the gross sound value:

(4)   "Gross value" means the wholesale price or, if there be no such price, the estimated value, with, in either case, freight, landing charges, and duty paid beforehand; provided that, in the case of goods or merchandise customarily sold in bond, the bonded price is deemed to be the gross value. "Gross proceeds" means the actual price obtained at a sale where all charges on sale are paid by the sellers.

[312]

72   Apportionment of valuation

(1)   Where different species of property are insured under a single valuation, the valuation must be apportioned over the different species in proportion to their respective insurable values, as in the case of an unvalued policy. The insured value of any part of a species is such proportion of the total insured value of the same as the insurable value of the part bears to the insurable value of the whole, ascertained in both cases as provided by this Act.

(2)   Where a valuation has to be apportioned, and particulars of the prime cost of each separate species, quality, or description of goods cannot be ascertained, the division of the valuation may be made over the net arrived sound values of the different species, qualities, or descriptions of goods.

[313]

73   General average contributions and salvage charges

(1)   Subject to any express provision in the policy, where the assured has paid, or is liable for, any general average contribution, the measure of indemnity is the full amount of such contribution, if the subject-matter liable to contribution is insured for its full contributory value; but, if such subject-matter be not insured for its full contributory value, or if only part of it be insured, the indemnity payable by the insurer must be reduced in proportion to the under insurance, and where there has been a particular average loss which constitutes a deduction from the contributory value, and for which the insurer is liable, that amount must be deducted from the insured value in order to ascertain what the insurer is liable to contribute.

(2)   Where the insurer is liable for salvage charges the extent of his liability must be determined on the like principle.

[314]

74   Liabilities to third parties

Where the assured has effected an insurance in express terms against any liability to a third party, the measure of indemnity, subject to any express provision in the policy, is the amount paid or payable by him to such third party in respect of such liability.

[315]

75   General provisions as to measure of indemnity

(1)   Where there has been a loss in respect of any subject-matter not expressly provided for in the foregoing provisions of this Act, the measure of indemnity shall be ascertained, as nearly as may be, in accordance with those provisions, in so far as applicable to the particular case.

(2)   Nothing in the provisions of this Act relating to the measure of indemnity shall affect the rules relating to double insurance, or prohibit the insurer from disproving interest wholly or in part, or from showing that at the time of the loss the whole or any part of the subject-matter insured was not at risk under the policy.

[316]

76   Particular average warranties

(1)   Where the subject-matter insured is warranted free from particular average, the assured cannot recover for a loss of part, other than a loss incurred by a general average sacrifice unless the contract contained in the policy be apportionable; but, if the contract be apportionable, the assured may recover for a total loss of any apportionable part.

(2)   Where the subject-matter insured is warranted free from particular average, either wholly or under a certain percentage, the insurer is nevertheless liable for salvage charges, and for particular charges and other expenses properly incurred pursuant to the provisions of the suing and labouring clause in order to avert a loss insured against.

(3)   Unless the policy otherwise provides, where the subject-matter insured is warranted free from particular average under a specified percentage, a general average loss cannot be added to a particular average loss to make up the specified percentage.

(4)   For the purpose of ascertaining whether the specified percentage has been reached, regard shall be had only to the actual loss suffered by the subject-matter insured. Particular charges and the expenses of and incidental to ascertaining and proving the loss must be excluded.

[317]

77 Successive losses

(1)   Unless the policy otherwise provides, and subject to the provisions of this Act, the insurer is liable for successive losses, even though the total amount of such losses may exceed the sum insured.

(2)   Where, under the same policy, a partial loss, which has not been repaired or otherwise made good, is followed by a total loss, the assured can only recover in respect of the total loss:

Provided that nothing in this section shall affect the liability of the insurer under the suing and labouring clause.

[318]

78 Suing and labouring clause

(1)   Where the policy contains a suing and labouring clause, the engagement thereby entered into is deemed to be supplementary to the contract of insurance, and the assured may recover from the insurer any expenses properly incurred pursuant to the clause, notwithstanding that the insurer may have paid for a total loss, or that the subject-matter may have been warranted free from particular average, either wholly or under a certain percentage.

(2)   General average losses and contributions and salvage charges, as defined by this Act, are not recoverable under the suing and labouring clause.

(3)   Expenses incurred for the purpose of averting or diminishing any loss not covered by the policy are not recoverable under the suing and labouring clause.

(4)   It is the duty of the assured and his agents, in all cases, to take such measures as may be reasonable for the purpose of averting or minimising a loss.

[319]

Rights of Insurer on Payment

79 Right of subrogation

(1)   Where the insurer pays for a total loss, either of the whole, or in the case of goods of any apportionable part, of the subject-matter insured, he thereupon becomes entitled to take over the interest of the assured in whatever may remain of the subject-matter so paid for, and he is thereby subrogated to all the rights and remedies of the assured in and in respect of that subject-matter as from the time of the casualty causing the loss.

(2)   Subject to the foregoing provisions, where the insurer pays for a partial loss, he acquires no title to the subject-matter insured, or such part of it as may remain, but he is thereupon subrogated to all rights and remedies of the assured in and in respect of the subject-matter insured as from the time of the casualty causing the loss, in so far as the assured has been indemnified, according to this Act, by such payment for the loss.

[320]

80 Right of contribution

(1)   Where the assured is over-insured by double insurance, each insurer is bound, as between himself and the other insurers, to contribute rateably to the loss in proportion to the amount for which he is liable under his contract.

(2)   If any insurer pays more than his proportion of the loss, he is entitled to maintain an action for contribution against the other insurers, and is entitled to the like remedies as a surety who has paid more than his proportion of the debt.

[321]

81 Effect of under insurance

Where the assured is insured for an amount less than the insurable value or, in the case of a valued policy, for an amount less than the policy valuation, he is deemed to be his own insurer in respect of the uninsured balance.

[322]

Return of Premium

82 Enforcement of return

Where the premium or a proportionate part thereof is, by this Act, declared to be returnable,—
    (a)   If already paid, it may be recovered by the assured from the insurer; and
    (b)   If unpaid, it may be retained by the assured or his agent.

[323]

PART I
STATUTES

83 Return by agreement

Where the policy contains a stipulation for the return of the premium, or a proportionate part thereof, on the happening of a certain event, and that event happens, the premium, or, as the case may be, the proportionate part thereof, is thereupon returnable to the assured.

[324]

84 Return for failure of consideration

(1)   Where the consideration for the payment of the premium totally fails, and there has been no fraud or illegality on the part of the assured or his agents, the premium is thereupon returnable to the assured.

(2)   Where the consideration for the payment of the premium is apportionable and there is a total failure of any apportionable part of the consideration, a proportionate part of the premium is, under the like conditions, thereupon returnable to the assured.

(3)   In particular—
　(a)　Where the policy is void, or is avoided by the insurer as from the commencement of the risk, the premium is returnable, provided that there has been no fraud or illegality on the part of the assured; but if the risk is not apportionable, and has once attached, the premium is not returnable;
　(b)　Where the subject-matter insured, or part thereof, has never been imperilled, the premium, or, as the case may be, a proportionate part thereof, is returnable:
　　Provided that where the subject-matter has been insured "lost or not lost" and has arrived in safety at the time when the contract is concluded, the premium is not returnable unless, at such time, the insurer knew of the safe arrival.
　(c)　Where the assured has no insurable interest throughout the currency of the risk, the premium is returnable, provided that this rule does not apply to a policy effected by way of gaming or wagering;
　(d)　Where the assured has a defeasible interest which is terminated during the currency of the risk, the premium is not returnable;
　(e)　Where the assured has over-insured under an unvalued policy, a proportionate part of the premium is returnable;
　(f)　Subject to the foregoing provisions, where the assured has over-insured by double insurance, a proportionate part of the several premiums is returnable:
　　Provided that, if the policies are effected at different times, and any earlier policy has at any time borne the entire risk, or if a claim has been paid on the policy in respect of the full sum insured thereby, no premium is returnable in respect of that policy, and when the double insurance is effected knowingly by the assured no premium is returnable.

[325]

Mutual Insurance

85 Modification of Act in case of mutual insurance

(1)   Where two or more persons mutually agree to insure each other against marine losses there is said to be a mutual insurance.

(2)   The provisions of this Act relating to the premium do not apply to mutual insurance, but a guarantee, or such other arrangement as may be agreed upon, may be substituted for the premium.

(3)   The provisions of this Act, in so far as they may be modified by the agreement of the parties, may in the case of mutual insurance be modified by the terms of the policies issued by the association, or by the rules and regulations of the association.

(4)   Subject to the exceptions mentioned in this section, the provisions of this Act apply to a mutual insurance.

[326]

Supplemental

86 Ratification by assured

Where a contract of marine insurance is in good faith effected by one person on behalf of another, the person on whose behalf it is effected may ratify the contract even after he is aware of a loss.

[327]

87 Implied obligations varied by agreement or usage

(1)   Where any right, duty, or liability would arise under a contract of marine insurance by implication of law, it may be negatived or varied by express agreement, or by usage, if the usage be such as to bind both parties to the contract.

(2)   The provisions of this section extend to any right, duty, or liability declared by this Act which may be lawfully modified by agreement.

[328]

88   Reasonable time, etc, a question of fact

Where by this Act any reference is made to reasonable time, reasonable premium, or reasonable diligence, the question what is reasonable is a question of fact.

[329]

89   Slip as evidence

Where there is a duly stamped policy, reference may be made, as heretofore, to the slip or covering note, in any legal proceeding.

[330]

90   Interpretation of terms

In this Act, unless the context or subject-matter otherwise requires,—
   "Action" includes counter-claim and set off:
   "Freight" includes the profit derivable by a shipowner from the employment of his ship to
      carry his own goods or moveables, as well as freight payable by a third party, but does not
      include passage money:
   "Moveables" means any moveable tangible property, other than the ship, and includes money,
      valuable securities, and other documents:
   "Policy" means a marine policy.

[331]

91   Savings

(1)   Nothing in this Act, or in any repeal effected thereby, shall affect—
   (a)   The provisions of the Stamp Act 1891, or any enactment for the time being in force
         relating to the revenue;
   (b)   The provisions of the Companies Act 1862, or any enactment amending or substituted
         for the same;
   (c)   The provisions of any statute not expressly repealed by this Act.

(2)   The rules of the common law including the law merchant, save in so far as they are inconsistent with the express provisions of this Act, shall continue to apply to contracts of marine insurance.

[332]

NOTES
   Companies Act 1862: repealed by the Companies (Consolidation) Act 1908.

92, 93   *(Repealed by the Statute Law Revision Act 1927.)*

94   Short title

This Act may be cited as the Marine Insurance Act 1906.

[333]

SCHEDULES
Section 30

FIRST SCHEDULE
FORM OF POLICY

Be it known that   as well in   own name as for and in the name and names of all and every other person or persons to whom the same doth, may, or shall appertain, in part or in all doth make assurance and cause   and them, and every of them, to be insured lost or not lost, at and from

Upon any kind of goods and merchandise, and also upon the body, tackle, apparel, ordnance, munition, artillery, boat, and other furniture, of and in the good ship or vessel called the whereof is master under God, for this present voyage,   or whosoever else shall go for master in the said ship, or by whatsoever other name or names the said ship, or the master thereof, is or shall be named or called; beginning the adventure upon the said goods and merchandises from the loading thereof aboard the said ship.

upon the said ship, etc

and so shall continue and endure, during her abode there, upon the said ship, etc

And further, until the said ship, with all her ordnance, tackle, apparel, etc, and goods and merchandises whatsoever shall be arrived at upon the said ship, etc, until she hath moored at anchor twenty-four hours in good safety; and upon the goods and merchandises, until the same be there discharged and safely landed. And it shall be lawful for the said ship, etc, in this voyage to proceed and sail to and touch and stay at any ports or places whatsoever

without prejudice to this insurance. The said ship, etc, goods and merchandises, etc, for so much as concerns the assured by agreement between the assured and assurers in this policy, are and shall be valued at

Touching the adventures and perils which we the assurers are contented to bear and do take upon us in this voyage: they are of the seas, men of war, fire, enemies, pirates, rovers, thieves, jettisons, letters of mart and countermart, surprisals, takings at sea, arrests, restraints, and detainments of all kings, princes, and people, of what nation, condition, or quality soever, barratry of the master and mariners, and of all other perils, losses, and misfortunes, that have or shall come to the hurt, detriment, or damage of the said goods and merchandises, and ship, etc, or any part thereof. And in case of any loss or misfortune it shall be lawful to the assured, their factors, servants and assigns, to sue, labour, and travel for, in and about the defence, safeguards, and recovery of the said goods and merchandises, and ship, etc, or any part thereof, without prejudice to this insurance; to the charges whereof we, the assurers, will contribute each one according to the rate and quantity of his sum herein assured. And it is especially declared and agreed that no acts of the insurer or insured in recovering, saving, or preserving the property insured shall be considered as a waiver, or acceptance of abandonment. And it is agreed by us, the insurers, that this writing or policy of assurance shall be of as much force and effect as the surest writing or policy of assurance heretofore made in Lombard Street, or in the Royal Exchange, or elsewhere in London. And so we, the assurers, are contented, and do hereby promise and bind ourselves, each one for his own part, our heirs, executors, and goods to the assured, their executors, administrators, and assigns, for the true performance of the premises, confessing ourselves paid the consideration due unto us for this assurance by the assured, at and after the rate of

IN WITNESS whereof we, the assurers, have subscribed our names and sums assured in London.

N.B.—Corn, fish, salt, fruit, flour, and seed are warranted free from average, unless general, or the ship be stranded—sugar, tobacco, hemp, flax, hides and skins are warranted free from average, under five pounds per cent., and all other goods, also the ship and freight, are warranted free from average, under three pounds per cent. unless general, or the ship be stranded.

RULES FOR CONSTRUCTION OF POLICY

The following are the rules referred to by this Act for the construction of a policy in the above or other like form, where the context does not otherwise require:—

1.   Where the subject-matter is insured "lost or not lost," and the loss has occurred before the contract is concluded, the risk attaches, unless at such time the assured was aware of the loss, and the insurer was not.

2.   Where the subject-matter is insured "from" a particular place, the risk does not attach until the ship starts on the voyage insured.

3.—
   (a)   Where a ship is insured "at and from" a particular place, and she is at that place in good safety when the contract is concluded, the risk attaches immediately.
   (b)   If she be not at that place when the contract is concluded, the risk attaches as soon as she arrives there in good safety, and, unless the policy otherwise provides, it is immaterial that she is covered by another policy for a specified time after arrival.
   (c)   Where chartered freight is insured "at and from" a particular place, and the ship is at that place in good safety when the contract is concluded the risk attaches immediately. If she be not there when the contract is concluded, the risk attaches as soon as she arrives there in good safety.
   (d)   Where freight, other than chartered freight, is payable without special conditions and is insured "at and from" a particular place, the risk attaches pro rata as the goods or merchandise are shipped; provided that if there be cargo in readiness which belongs to the shipowner, or which some other person has contracted with him to ship, the risk attaches as soon as the ship is ready to receive such cargo.

4.   Where goods or other moveables are insured "from the loading thereof," the risk does not attach until such goods or moveables are actually on board, and the insurer is not liable for them while in transit from the shore to ship.

5.   Where the risk on goods or other moveables continues until they are "safely landed," they must be landed in the customary manner and within a reasonable time after arrival at the port of discharge, and if they are not so landed the risk ceases.

6.   In the absence of any further license or usage, the liberty to touch and stay "at any port or place whatsoever" does not authorise the ship to depart from the course of her voyage from the port of departure to the port of destination.

7. The term "perils of the seas" refers only to fortuitous accidents or casualties of the seas. It does not include the ordinary action of the winds and waves.

8. The term "pirates" includes passengers who mutiny and rioters who attack the ship from the shore.

9. The term "thieves" does not cover clandestine theft or a theft committed by any one of the ship's company, whether crew or passengers.

10. The term "arrests, etc, of kings, princes, and people" refers to political or executive acts, and does not include a loss caused by riot or by ordinary judicial process.

11. The term "barratry" includes every wrongful act wilfully committed by the master or crew to the prejudice of the owner, or, as the case may be, the charterer.

12. The term "all other perils" includes only perils similar in kind to the perils specifically mentioned in the policy.

13. The term "average unless general" means a partial loss of the subject-matter insured other than a general average loss, and does not include "particular charges."

14. Where the ship has stranded, the insurer is liable for the excepted losses, although the loss is not attributable to the stranding, provided that when the stranding takes place the risk has attached and, if the policy be on goods, that the damaged goods are on board.

15. The term "ship" includes the hull, materials and outfit, stores and provisions for the officers and crew, and, in the case of vessels engaged in a special trade, the ordinary fittings requisite for the trade, and also, in the case of a steamship, the machinery, boilers, and coals and engine stores, if owned by the assured.

16. The term "freight" includes the profit derivable by a shipowner from the employment of his ship to carry his own goods or moveables, as well as freight payable by a third party, but does not include passage money.

17. The term "goods" means goods in the nature of merchandise, and does not include personal effects or provisions and stores for use on board.

In the absence of any usage to the contrary, deck cargo and living animals must be insured specifically, and not under the general denomination of goods.

[334]

NOTES
The form of policy contained in this Schedule is the same as the model policy called "the Lloyd's policy" which was in common use for marine insurances in the UK for about 200 years. This has largely been superseded by a modern standard form of marine policy issued by Lloyd's.

(Second Schedule repealed by the Statute Law Revision Act 1927.)

LIMITED PARTNERSHIPS ACT 1907

(1907 c 24)

ARRANGEMENT OF SECTIONS

An Act to establish Limited Partnership

[28 August 1907]

1 Short title

This Act may be cited for all purposes as the Limited Partnerships Act 1907.

[335]

NOTES
Whole Act repealed, in relation to Northern Ireland, by the Companies Act 2006, s 1286(2)(b). See also the Companies Act 2006, s 1286(1)(b), which extends the enactments in force in Great Britain relating to limited partnerships to Northern Ireland.

2 (Repealed by the Statute Law Revision Act 1927.)

3 Interpretation of terms

In the construction of this Act the following words and expressions shall have the meanings respectively assigned to them in this section, unless there be something in the subject or context repugnant to such construction—

"Firm," "firm name," and "business" have the same meanings as in the Partnership Act 1890;

"General partner" shall mean any partner who is not a limited partner as defined by this Act.

[336]

NOTES
Repealed (in relation to Northern Ireland) as noted to s 1 at [335].

4 Definition and constitution of limited partnership

(1) … Limited partnerships may be formed in the manner and subject to the conditions by this Act provided.

(2) A limited partnership … must consist of one or more persons called general partners, who shall be liable for all debts and obligations of the firm, and one or more persons to be called limited partners, who shall at the time of entering into such partnership contribute thereto a sum or sums as capital or property valued at a stated amount, and who shall not be liable for the debts or obligations of the firm beyond the amount so contributed.

(3) A limited partner shall not during the continuance of the partnership, either directly or indirectly, draw out or receive back any part of his contribution, and if he does so draw out or receive back any such part shall be liable for the debts and obligations of the firm up to the amount so drawn out or received back.

(4) A body corporate may be a limited partner.

[337]

NOTES
Repealed (in relation to Northern Ireland) as noted to s 1 at [335].
Sub-s (1): words omitted repealed by the Statute Law Revision Act 1927.
Sub-s (2): words omitted repealed by the Banking Act 1979, ss 46(b), 51(2), Sch 7, and by the Regulatory Reform (Removal of 20 Member Limit in Partnerships etc) Order 2002, SI 2002/3203, art 3, and in relation to Northern Ireland, by the Partnerships etc (Removal of Twenty Member Limit) (Northern Ireland) Order 2003, SI 2003/2904, arts 3(1), 4, Schedule.

5 Registration of limited partnership required

Every limited partnership must be registered as such in accordance with the provisions of this Act …

[338]

NOTES
Repealed (in relation to Northern Ireland) as noted to s 1 at [335]; words omitted repealed by the Legislative Reform (Limited Partnerships) Order 2009, SI 2009/1940, art 8, in relation to limited partnerships for which registration applications are received on or after 1 October 2009.

6 Modifications of general law in case of limited partnerships

(1) A limited partner shall not take part in the management of the partnership business, and shall not have power to bind the firm—

Provided that a limited partner may by himself or his agent at any time inspect the books of the firm and examine into the state and prospects of the partnership business, and may advise with the partners thereon.

If a limited partner takes part in the management of the partnership business he shall be liable for all debts and obligations of the firm incurred while he so takes part in the management as though he were a general partner.

(2)   A limited partnership shall not be dissolved by the death or bankruptcy of a limited partner, and the lunacy of a limited partner shall not be a ground for dissolution of the partnership by the court unless the lunatic's share cannot be otherwise ascertained and realised.

(3)   In the event of the dissolution of a limited partnership its affairs shall be wound up by the general partners unless the court otherwise orders.

(4)   ...

(5)   Subject to any agreement expressed or implied between the partners—
    (a)   Any difference arising as to ordinary matters connected with the partnership business may be decided by a majority of the general partners;
    (b)   A limited partner may, with the consent of the general partners, assign his share in the partnership, and upon such an assignment the assignee shall become a limited partner with all the rights of the assignor;
    (c)   The other partners shall not be entitled to dissolve the partnership by reason of any limited partner suffering his share to be charged for his separate debt;
    (d)   A person may be introduced as a partner without the consent of the existing limited partners;
    (e)   A limited partner shall not be entitled to dissolve the partnership by notice.

[339]

NOTES
Repealed (in relation to Northern Ireland) as noted to s 1 at **[335]**.
Sub-s (4): repealed by the Companies (Consolidation) Act 1908, s 286, Sch 6, Pt I.

7   Law as to private partnerships to apply where not excluded by this Act

Subject to the provisions of this Act, the Partnership Act 1890 and the rules of equity and of common law applicable to partnerships, except so far as they are inconsistent with the express provisions of the last-mentioned Act, shall apply to limited partnerships.

[340]

NOTES
Repealed (in relation to Northern Ireland) as noted to s 1 at **[335]**.

[8   Duty to register

The registrar shall register a limited partnership if an application is made to the registrar in accordance with section 8A.]

[341]

NOTES
Commencement: 1 October 2009.
Substituted by the Legislative Reform (Limited Partnerships) Order 2009, SI 2009/1940, arts 3(2), 4, in relation to limited partnerships for which registration applications are received on or after 1 October 2009.
Repealed (in relation to Northern Ireland) as noted to s 1 at **[335]**.

[8A   Application for registration

(1)   An application for registration must—
    (a)   specify the firm name, complying with section 8B, under which the limited partnership is to be registered,
    (b)   contain the details listed in subsection (2),
    (c)   be signed or otherwise authenticated by or on behalf of each partner, and
    (d)   be made to the registrar for the part of the United Kingdom in which the principal place of business of the limited partnership is to be situated.

(2)   The required details are—
    (a)   the general nature of the partnership business,
    (b)   the name of each general partner,
    (c)   the name of each limited partner,
    (d)   the amount of the capital contribution of each limited partner (and whether the contribution is paid in cash or in another specified form),
    (e)   the address of the proposed principal place of business of the limited partnership, and
    (f)   the term (if any) for which the limited partnership is to be entered into (beginning with the date of registration).]

[341A]

NOTES
Commencement: 1 October 2009.
Inserted by the Legislative Reform (Limited Partnerships) Order 2009, SI 2009/1940, arts 3(2), 5, in relation to limited partnerships for which registration applications are received on or after 1 October 2009.
Repealed (in relation to Northern Ireland) as noted to s 1 at **[335]**.

[8B Name of limited partnership

(1) This section sets out conditions which must be satisfied by the firm name of a limited partnership as specified in the application for registration.

(2) The name must end with—
    (a)   the words "limited partnership" (upper or lower case, or any combination), or
    (b)   the abbreviation "LP" (upper or lower case, or any combination, with or without punctuation).

(3) But if the principal place of business of a limited partnership is to be in Wales, its firm name may end with—
    (a)   the words "partneriaeth cyfyngedig" (upper or lower case, or any combination), or
    (b)   the abbreviation "PC" (upper or lower case, or any combination, with or without punctuation).]

[341B]

NOTES
Commencement: 1 October 2009.
Inserted by the Legislative Reform (Limited Partnerships) Order 2009, SI 2009/1940, arts 3(2), 6, in relation to limited partnerships for which registration applications are received on or after 1 October 2009.
Repealed (in relation to Northern Ireland) as noted to s 1 at **[335]**.

[8C Certificate of registration

(1) On registering a limited partnership the registrar shall issue a certificate of registration.

(2) The certificate must be—
    (a)   signed by the registrar, or
    (b)   authenticated with the registrar's seal.

(3) The certificate must state—
    (a)   the firm name of the limited partnership given in the application for registration,
    (b)   the limited partnership's registration number,
    (c)   the date of registration, and
    (d)   that the limited partnership is registered as a limited partnership under this Act.

(4) The certificate is conclusive evidence that a limited partnership came into existence on the date of registration.]

[341C]

NOTES
Commencement: 1 October 2009.
Inserted by the Legislative Reform (Limited Partnerships) Order 2009, SI 2009/1940, arts 3(2), 7, in relation to limited partnerships for which registration applications are received on or after 1 October 2009.
Repealed (in relation to Northern Ireland) as noted to s 1 at **[335]**.

9 Registration of changes in partnerships

(1) If during the continuance of a limited partnership any change is made or occurs in—
    (a)   the firm name,
    (b)   the general nature of the business,
    (c)   the principal place of business,
    (d)   the partners or the name of any partner,
    (e)   the term or character of the partnership,
    (f)   the sum contributed by any limited partner,
    (g)   the liability of any partner by reason of his becoming a limited instead of a general partner or a general instead of a limited partner,
a statement, signed by the firm, specifying the nature of the change shall within seven days be sent by post or delivered to the registrar …

(2) If default is made in compliance with the requirements of this section each of the general partners shall, on conviction under the Summary Jurisdiction Acts, be liable to a fine not exceeding one pound for each day during which the default continues.

[342]

NOTES
Repealed (in relation to Northern Ireland) as noted to s 1 at **[335]**.
Sub-s (1): words omitted repealed by the Companies Act 2006 (Consequential Amendments, Transitional Provisions and Savings) Order 2009, SI 2009/1941, art 2(1), Sch 1, para 3(1), (2).

10 Advertisement in Gazette of statement of general partner becoming a limited partner and of assignment of share of limited partner

(1)   Notice of any arrangement or transaction under which any person will cease to be a general partner in any firm, and will become a limited partner in that firm, or under which the share of a limited partner in a firm will be assigned to any person, shall be forthwith advertised in the Gazette, and until notice of the arrangement or transaction is so advertised the arrangement or transaction shall, for the purposes of this Act, be deemed to be of no effect.

(2)   For the purposes of this section, the expression "the Gazette" means—
In the case of a limited partnership registered in England, the London Gazette.
In the case of a limited partnership registered in Scotland, the Edinburgh Gazette.
In the case of a limited partnership registered in [Northern Ireland], the [Belfast] Gazette.

[343]

NOTES
Repealed (in relation to Northern Ireland) as noted to s 1 at **[335]**.
Sub-s (2): words in square brackets substituted by the Companies Act 2006 (Consequential Amendments, Transitional Provisions and Savings) Order 2009, SI 2009/1941, art 2(1), Sch 1, para 3(1), (3).

11, 12   (*S 11 repealed by the Finance Act 1973, s 59(7), Sch 22, Pt V and the Finance (Miscellaneous Provisions) (Northern Ireland) Order 1973, SI 1973/1323, art 10(1), Sch 4; s 12 repealed by the Perjury Act 1911, s 17, Schedule and the Perjury Act (Northern Ireland) 1946, s 16(3), Schedule.*)

13 Registrar to file statement and issue certificate of registration
On receiving any statement made in pursuance of this Act the registrar shall cause the same to be filed, and he shall send by post to the firm from whom such statement shall have been received a certificate of the registration thereof.

[344]

NOTES
Repealed (in relation to Northern Ireland) as noted to s 1 at **[335]**.

14 Register and index to be kept
... The registrar shall keep ... a register and an index of all the limited partnerships registered as aforesaid, and of all the statements registered in relation to such partnerships.

[345]

NOTES
Repealed (in relation to Northern Ireland) as noted to s 1 at **[335]**.
Words omitted repealed by the Companies Act 2006 (Consequential Amendments, Transitional Provisions and Savings) Order 2009, SI 2009/1941, art 2(1), Sch 1, para 3(1), (4).

[15 The registrar
[(1)   The registrar of companies is the registrar of limited partnerships.

(2)   In this Act—
(a)   references to the registrar in relation to the registration of a limited partnership are to the registrar to whom the application for registration is to be made (see section 8A(1)(d));
(b)   references to registration in a particular part of the United Kingdom are to registration by the registrar for that part of the United Kingdom;
(c)   references to the registrar in relation to any other matter relating to a limited partnership are to the registrar for the part of the United Kingdom in which the partnership is registered.]

[346]

NOTES
Commencement: 1 October 2009.
Substituted by the Companies Act 2006 (Consequential Amendments, Transitional Provisions and Savings) Order 2009, SI 2009/1941, art 2(1), Sch 1, para 3(1), (5).
Repealed (in relation to Northern Ireland) as noted to s 1 at **[335]**.

16 Inspection of statements registered

(1)   Any person may inspect the statements filed by the registrar ... ; and any person may require a certificate of the registration of any limited partnership, or a copy of or extract from any registered statement, to be certified by the registrar, ...

(2) A certificate of registration or a copy of or extract from any statement registered under this Act, if duly certified to be a true copy under the hand of the registrar ... (whom it shall not be necessary to prove to be the registrar ...) shall, in all legal proceedings, civil or criminal, and in all cases whatsoever be received in evidence.

[347]

NOTES

Repealed (in relation to Northern Ireland) as noted to s 1 at **[335]**.

Sub-s (1): words omitted repealed by the Companies Act 2006, ss 1063(7)(a), 1295, Sch 16 and the Companies Act 2006 (Consequential Amendments, Transitional Provisions and Savings) Order 2009, SI 2009/1941, art 2(1), Sch 1, para 3(1), (6)(a).

Sub-s (2): words omitted repealed by SI 2009/1941, art 2(1), Sch 1, para 3(1), (6)(b).

17 Power to Board of Trade to make rules

The Board of Trade may make rules ... concerning any of the following matters—

(a) ...

(b) The duties or additional duties to be performed by the registrar for the purposes of this Act;

(c) The performance by assistant registrars and other officers of acts by this Act required to be done by the registrar;

(d) The forms to be used for the purposes of this Act;

(e) Generally, the conduct and regulation of registration under this Act and any matters incidental thereto.

[348]

NOTES

Repealed (in relation to Northern Ireland) as noted to s 1 at **[335]**.

Words omitted repealed by the Companies Act 2006, ss 1063(7)(b), 1295, Sch 16.

Rules: the Limited Partnerships (Forms) Rules 2009, SI 2009/2160.

MARINE INSURANCE (GAMBLING POLICIES) ACT 1909

(9 Edw 7 c 12)

An Act to prohibit Gambling on Loss by Maritime Perils

[20 October 1909]

1 Prohibition of gambling on loss by maritime perils

(1) If—

(a) any person effects a contract of marine insurance without having any bona fide interest, direct or indirect, either in the safe arrival of the ship in relation to which the contract is made or in the safety or preservation of the subject-matter insured, or a bona fide expectation of acquiring such an interest; or

(b) any person in the employment of the owner of a ship, not being a part owner of the ship, effects a contract of marine insurance in relation to the ship, and the contract is made "interest or no interest," or "without further proof of interest than the policy itself," or "without benefit of salvage to the insurer," or subject to any other like term,

the contract shall be deemed to be a contract by way of gambling on loss by maritime perils, and the person effecting it shall be guilty of an offence, and shall be liable, on summary conviction, to imprisonment ... for a term not exceeding six months or to a fine not exceeding [level 3 on the standard scale], and in either case to forfeit to the Crown any money he may receive under the contract.

(2) Any broker or other person through whom, and any insurer with whom, any such contract is effected shall be guilty of an offence and liable on summary conviction to the like penalties if he acted knowing that the contract was by way of gambling on loss by maritime perils within the meaning of this Act.

(3) Proceedings under this Act shall not be instituted without the consent in England of the Attorney-General, in Scotland of the Lord Advocate, and in Ireland of the Attorney-General for Ireland.

(4) Proceedings shall not be instituted under this Act against a person (other than a person in the employment of the owner of the ship in relation to which the contract was made) alleged to have effected a contract by way of gambling on loss by maritime perils until an opportunity has been

afforded him of showing that the contract was not such a contract as aforesaid, and any information given by that person for that purpose shall not be admissible in evidence against him in any prosecution under this Act.

(5)　If proceedings under this Act are taken against any person (other than a person in the employment of the owner of the ship in relation to which the contract was made) for effecting such a contract, and the contract was made "interest or no interest," or "without further proof of interest than the policy itself," or "without benefit of salvage to the insurer," or subject to any other like term, the contract shall be deemed to be a contract by way of gambling on loss by maritime perils unless the contrary is proved.

(6)　For the purpose of giving jurisdiction under this Act, every offence shall be deemed to have been committed either in the place in which the same actually was committed or in any place in which the offender may be.

(7)　Any person aggrieved by an order or decision of a court of summary jurisdiction under this Act, may appeal to [the Crown Court].

(8)　For the purposes of this Act the expression "owner" includes charterer.

(9)　Subsection (7) of this section shall not apply to Scotland.

[349]

NOTES
Sub-s (1): words omitted repealed by virtue of the Criminal Justice Act 1948, s 1(2); reference to a level on the standard scale substituted by virtue of the Criminal Justice Act 1982, ss 38, 46.
Sub-s (7): words in square brackets substituted by the Courts Act 1971, s 56, Sch 9, Pt I.

2　Short title
This Act may be cited as the Marine Insurance (Gambling Policies) Act 1909, and the Marine Insurance Act 1906 and this Act may be cited together as the Marine Insurance Acts 1906 and 1909.

[350]

ADMINISTRATION OF JUSTICE ACT 1925

(15 & 16 Geo 5 c 28)

An Act to amend the law with respect to the jurisdiction and business of the Supreme Court in England and with respect to the judges, officers and offices thereof and otherwise with respect to the administration of justice

[7 May 1925]

1–21　(*Ss 1–18, 21 repealed by the Supreme Court of Judicature (Consolidation) Act 1925, s 226(1), Sch 6; s 19 repealed by the Courts Act 1971, s 56(4), Sch 11, Pt IV; s 20 repealed by the County Courts Act 1934, s 193, Sch 5.*)

Miscellaneous

22　Registration of deeds of arrangement
(1)　The office for the registration of deeds of arrangement under the Deeds of Arrangement Act 1914 (in this section referred to as "the Act of 1914"), shall be transferred to the Board of Trade, and the registrar for the purposes of the Act of 1914 shall be appointed by the Board of Trade, and references in that Act to the registrar of bills of sale or to the registrar for the purposes of that Act shall be construed as references to the registrar so appointed.

(2)　Subsection (1) of section five of the Act of 1914 (which provides that a copy of every deed to be registered shall be presented to the registrar) shall have effect as if it provided that there shall be presented to the registrar such number of copies of the deed and of every schedule or inventory annexed thereto or referred to therein as he may deem to be necessary for the purpose of carrying out the requirements of the Act of 1914 as amended by this section.

(3)　...

(4)　... all ... fees whatsoever to be taken under the Act of 1914 shall be prescribed by order made by the Lord Chancellor with the concurrence of the Treasury and not otherwise, and all such ... fees shall be paid into such account as the Treasury may direct.

(5)　Subject to the provisions of subsection (4) of this section, rules for carrying into effect the provisions of the Act of 1914, as amended by this section, other than the provisions of section seven thereof, may be made [by the Lord Chief Justice with the concurrence of the Lord Chancellor and] of the President of the Board of Trade, and, subject as aforesaid, the expression "prescribed" in the Act of 1914 shall mean prescribed by rules made under this subsection.

[(5A) The Lord Chief Justice may nominate a judicial office holder (as defined in section 109(4) of the Constitutional Reform Act 2005) to exercise his functions under subsection (5).]

(6) This section shall be construed as one with the Act of 1914.

[351]

NOTES
Sub-s (3): repealed by the Statute Law (Repeals) Act 1989.
Sub-s (4): words omitted repealed by the Statute Law (Repeals) Act 1989.
Sub-s (5): words in square brackets substituted by the Constitutional Reform Act 2005, s 15(1), Sch 4, Pt 1, para 19(1), (2).
Sub-s (5A): inserted by the Constitutional Reform Act 2005, s 15(1), Sch 4, Pt 1, para 19(1), (3).
Rules: the Deeds of Arrangement Rules 1925, SR & O 1925/795; the Deeds of Arrangement Rules 1941, SI 1941/1253.
Order: the Deeds of Arrangement Fees Order 1984, SI 1984/887.

23 Local registration of bills of sale under Bills of Sale Acts 1878 and 1882

(1) Section eleven of the Bills of Sale Act (1878) Amendment Act 1882 (which makes provision for the local registration of the contents of bills of sale), shall have effect as if it required the registrar of bills of sale to transmit to county court registrars copies of the bills instead of abstracts of the contents of the bills, and references in that section to the abstract transmitted and the abstract registered shall be construed accordingly.

(2) Section ten of the Bills of Sale Act 1878 shall have effect as though it required the presentation to the registrar on the registration of a bill of sale, in addition to the copy of the bill of sale mentioned in paragraph (2) of that section, of such number of copies of the bill and every schedule and inventory annexed thereto as the registrar may deem to be necessary for the purpose of carrying out the requirements of the said section eleven as amended by this section.

[352]

24–28 (*Ss 24–26 repealed by the Supreme Court of Judicature (Consolidation) Act 1925, s 226(1), Sch 6; s 27 repealed by the Statute Law Revision Act 1950; s 28 spent.*)

29 Short title, interpretation and extent

(1) This Act may be cited as the Administration of Justice Act 1925.

(2) ...

(3) This Act shall not extend to Scotland or Northern Ireland.

(4), (5) ...

[353]

NOTES
Sub-s (2): repealed by the Statute Law (Repeals) Act 1973.
Sub-ss (4), (5): repealed by the Statute Law Revision Act 1950.

(*Schs 1–3 repealed by the Supreme Court of Judicature (Consolidation) Act 1925, s 226(1), Sch 6; Schs 4, 5 repealed by the Statute Law Revision Act 1950.*)

AUCTIONS (BIDDING AGREEMENTS) ACT 1927

(17 & 18 Geo 5 c 12)

An Act to render illegal certain agreements and transactions affecting bidding at auctions
[29 July 1927]

1 Certain bidding agreements to be illegal

(1) If any dealer agrees to give, or gives, or offers any gift or consideration to any other person as an inducement or reward for abstaining, or for having abstained, from bidding at a sale by auction either generally or for any particular lot, or if any person agrees to accept, or accepts, or attempts to obtain from any dealer any such gift or consideration as aforesaid, he shall be guilty of an offence under this Act, and shall be liable on summary conviction to a fine not exceeding one hundred pounds, or to a term of imprisonment for any period not exceeding six months, or to both such fine and such imprisonment:

Provided that, where it is proved that a dealer has previously to an auction entered into an agreement in writing with one or more persons to purchase goods at the auction bona fide on a joint account and has before the goods were purchased at the auction deposited a copy of the agreement with the auctioneer, such an agreement shall not be treated as an agreement made in contravention of this section.

(2)   For the purposes of this section the expression "dealer" means a person who in the normal course of his business attends sales by auction for the purpose of purchasing goods with a view to reselling them.

(3)   In England and Wales a prosecution for an offence under this section shall not be instituted without the consent of the Attorney-General …

[354]

PART 1
STATUTES

NOTES

Sub-s (3): words omitted repealed by the Law Officers Act 1997, s 3(2), Schedule.

Shall be liable on summary conviction: by virtue of the Auctions (Bidding Agreements) Act 1969, s 1(1) at **[477]**, this offence is now triable either way, and the penalty that may be imposed upon conviction on indictment is a fine or imprisonment for a short term not exceeding two years, or both. By virtue of the Magistrates' Courts Act 1980, s 32(2), the penalty that may be imposed on summary conviction for an offence triable either way is imprisonment for a term not exceeding six months or a fine not exceeding the "prescribed sum", or both. By s 32(9) of the 1980 Act, the prescribed sum is currently £5,000.

2   *(Repealed by the Statute Law (Repeals) Act 2004.)*

3 **Copy of Act to be exhibited at sale**

The particulars which under section seven of the Auctioneers Act 1845, are required to be affixed or suspended in some conspicuous part of the room or place where the auction is held shall include a copy of this Act, and that section shall have effect accordingly.

[355]

4 **Short title, commencement and extent**

(1)   This Act may be cited as the Auctions (Bidding Agreements) Act 1927 …

(2)   This Act shall not extend to Northern Ireland.

[356]

NOTES

Sub-s (1): words omitted repealed by the Statute Law Revision Act 1950.

THIRD PARTIES (RIGHTS AGAINST INSURERS) ACT 1930

(20 & 21 Geo 5 c 25)

An Act to confer on third parties rights against insurers of third-party risks in the event of the insured becoming insolvent, and in certain other events

[10 July 1930]

NOTES

This Act does not apply in relation to any contract of insurance to which such a certificate as is mentioned in the Merchant Shipping Act 1995, s 163 relates, by s 165(5) of that Act.

Whole Act repealed by the Third Parties (Rights against Insurers) Act 2010, s 20(3), Sch 4, as from a day to be appointed and subject to transitional provisions and savings in s 20(2) of, and Sch 3, para 3 to, the 2010 Act at **[2201]**, **[2204]**.

1 **Rights of third parties against insurers on bankruptcy, etc, of the insured**

(1)   Where under any contract of insurance a person (hereinafter referred to as the insured) is insured against liabilities to third parties which he may incur, then—

(a)   *in the event of the insured becoming bankrupt or making a composition or arrangement with his creditors; or*

(b)   *in the case of the insured being a company, in the event of a winding-up order […] being made, or a resolution for a voluntary winding-up being passed, with respect to the company, [or of the company entering administration,] or of a receiver or manager of the company's business or undertaking being duly appointed, or of possession being taken, by or on behalf of the holders of any debentures secured by a floating charge, of any property comprised in or subject to the charge [or of [a voluntary arrangement proposed for the purposes of Part I of the Insolvency Act 1986 being approved under that Part]];*

if, either before or after that event, any such liability as aforesaid is incurred by the insured, his rights against the insurer under the contract in respect of the liability shall, notwithstanding anything in any Act or rule of law to the contrary, be transferred to and vest in the third party to whom the liability was so incurred.

(2)   *Where [the estate of any person falls to be administered in accordance with an order under section [421 of the Insolvency Act 1986]], then, if any debt provable in bankruptcy [in Scotland, any claim accepted in the sequestration] is owing by the deceased in respect of a liability against which he was insured under a contract of insurance as being a liability to a third party, the deceased debtor's rights against the insurer under the contract in respect of that liability shall, notwithstanding anything in [any such order], be transferred to and vest in the person to whom the debt is owing.*

(3)   *In so far as any contract of insurance made after the commencement of this Act in respect of any liability of the insured to third parties purports, whether directly or indirectly, to avoid the contract or to alter the rights of the parties thereunder upon the happening to the insured of any of the events specified in paragraph (a) or paragraph (b) of subsection (1) of this section or upon the [estate of any person falling to be administered in accordance with an order under section [421 of the Insolvency Act 1986]], the contract shall be of no effect.*

(4)   *Upon a transfer under subsection (1) or subsection (2) of this section, the insurer shall, subject to the provisions of section three of this Act, be under the same liability to the third party as he would have been under to the insured, but—*

(a)   *if the liability of the insurer to the insured exceeds the liability of the insured to the third party, nothing in this Act shall affect the rights of the insured against the insurer in respect of the excess; and*

(b)   *if the liability of the insurer to the insured is less than the liability of the insured to the third party, nothing in this Act shall affect the rights of the third party against the insured in respect of the balance.*

(5)   *For the purposes of this Act, the expression "liabilities to third parties", in relation to a person insured under any contract of insurance, shall not include any liability of that person in the capacity of insurer under some other contract of insurance.*

(6)   *This Act shall not apply—*

(a)   *where a company is wound up voluntarily merely for the purposes of reconstruction or of amalgamation with another company; or*

(b)   *to any case to which subsections (1) and (2) of section seven of the Workmen's Compensation Act 1925 applies.*

[357]

NOTES

Repealed as noted at the beginning of this Act.

Sub-s (1): words omitted from first pair of square brackets and words in third (outer) pair of square brackets inserted by the Insolvency Act 1985, s 235, Sch 8, para 7(2); words omitted from first pair of square brackets repealed and words in second pair of square brackets inserted by the Enterprise Act 2002 (Insolvency) Order 2003, SI 2003/2096, art 4, Schedule, Pt 1, paras 1, 2, except in relation to any case where a petition for an administration order was presented before 15 September 2003; words in fourth (inner) pair of square brackets substituted by the Insolvency Act 1986, s 439(2), Sch 14.

Sub-s (2): words in first (outer) and final pairs of square brackets substituted by the Insolvency Act 1985, s 235, Sch 8, para 7(2); words in second (inner) pair of square brackets substituted by the Insolvency Act 1986, s 439(2), Sch 14; words in third pair of square brackets inserted by the Bankruptcy (Scotland) Act 1985, s 75(1), Sch 7, Pt I, para 6(1).

Sub-s (3): words in first (outer) pair of square brackets substituted by the Insolvency Act 1985, s 235, Sch 8, para 7(2); words in second (inner) pair of square brackets substituted by the Insolvency Act 1986, s 439(2), Sch 14.

Workman's Compensation Act 1925: repealed, subject to savings, by the National Insurance (Industrial Injuries) Act 1946, now itself repealed by the Social Security Act 1973, ss 100, 101, Schs 26, 28, Pt I and the Social Security (Consequential Provisions) Act 1975, s 1(2), (5), Sch 1, Pt I.

---

2   Duty to give necessary information to third parties

(1)   *In the event of any person becoming bankrupt or making a composition or arrangement with his creditors, or in the event of [the estate of any person falling to be administered in accordance with an order under section [421 of the Insolvency Act 1986]], or in the event of a winding-up order [...] being made, or a resolution for a voluntary winding-up being passed, with respect to any company [or of the company entering administration] or of a receiver or manager of the company's business or undertaking being duly appointed or of possession being taken by or on behalf of the holders of any debentures secured by a floating charge of any property comprised in or subject to the charge it shall be the duty of the bankrupt, debtor, personal representative of the deceased debtor or company, and, as the case may be, of the trustee in bankruptcy, trustee, liquidator, [administrator,] receiver, or manager, or person in possession of the property to give at the request of any person claiming that the bankrupt, debtor, deceased debtor, or company is under*

a liability to him such information as may reasonably be required by him for the purpose of ascertaining whether any rights have been transferred to and vested in him by this Act and for the purpose of enforcing such rights, if any, and any contract of insurance, in so far as it purports, whether directly or indirectly, to avoid the contract or to alter the rights of the parties thereunder upon the giving of any such information in the events aforesaid or otherwise to prohibit or prevent the giving thereof in the said events shall be of no effect.

[(1A)   The reference in subsection (1) of this section to a trustee includes a reference to the supervisor of a [voluntary arrangement proposed for the purposes of, and approved under, Part I or Part VIII of the Insolvency Act 1986].]

(2)   If the information given to any person in pursuance of subsection (1) of this section discloses reasonable ground for supposing that there have or may have been transferred to him under this Act rights against any particular insurer, that insurer shall be subject to the same duty as is imposed by the said subsection on the persons therein mentioned.

(3)   The duty to give information imposed by this section shall include a duty to allow all contracts of insurance, receipts for premiums, and other relevant documents in the possession or power of the person on whom the duty is so imposed to be inspected and copies thereof to be taken.

[358]

NOTES
Repealed as noted at the beginning of this Act.
Sub-s (1): words in first (outer) pair of square brackets substituted, words omitted from third pair of square brackets and word in final pairs of square brackets inserted, by the Insolvency Act 1985, s 235, Sch 8, para 7(3)(a); words omitted from third pair of square brackets repealed and words in fourth pair of square brackets inserted by the Enterprise Act 2002 (Insolvency) Order 2003, SI 2003/2096, art 4, Schedule, Pt 1, paras 1, 3, except in relation to any case where a petition for an administration order was presented before 15 September 2003; words in second (inner) pair of square brackets substituted by the Insolvency Act 1986, s 439(2), Sch 14.
Sub-s (1A): inserted by the Insolvency Act 1985, s 235, Sch 8, para 7(3)(b); words in square brackets substituted by the Insolvency Act 1986, s 439(2), Sch 14.

3   Settlement between insurers and insured persons

Where the insured has become bankrupt or where in the case of the insured being a company, a winding-up order [or an administration order] has been made or a resolution for a voluntary winding-up has been passed, with respect to the company, no agreement made between the insurer and the insured after liability has been incurred to a third party and after the commencement of the bankruptcy or winding-up [or the day of the making of the administration order], as the case may be, nor any waiver, assignment, or other disposition made by, or payment made to the insured after the commencement [or day] aforesaid shall be effective to defeat or affect the rights transferred to the third party under this Act, but those rights shall be the same as if no such agreement, waiver, assignment, disposition or payment had been made.

[359]

NOTES
Repealed as noted at the beginning of this Act; words in square brackets inserted by the Insolvency Act 1985, s 235, Sch 8, para 7.

[3A   Application to limited liability partnerships

(1)   This Act applies to limited liability partnerships as it applies to companies.

(2)   In its application to limited liability partnerships, references to a resolution for a voluntary winding-up being passed are references to a determination for a voluntary winding-up being made.]

[360]

NOTES
Inserted by the Limited Liability Partnerships Regulations 2001, SI 2001/1090, reg 9(1), Sch 5, para 2 and repealed as noted at the beginning of this Act.

4   (*Applies to Scotland only.*)

5   Short title

This Act may be cited as the Third Parties (Rights Against Insurers) Act 1930.

[361]

NOTES
Repealed as noted at the beginning of this Act.

LAW REFORM (FRUSTRATED CONTRACTS) ACT 1943

(6 & 7 Geo 6 c 40)

An Act to amend the law relating to the frustration of contracts

[5 August 1943]

1 Adjustment of rights and liabilities of parties to frustrated contracts

(1) Where a contract governed by English law has become impossible of performance or been otherwise frustrated, and the parties thereto have for that reason been discharged from the further performance of the contract, the following provisions of this section shall, subject to the provisions of section two of this Act, have effect in relation thereto.

(2) All sums paid or payable to any party in pursuance of the contract before the time when the parties were so discharged (in this Act referred to as "the time of discharge") shall, in the case of sums so paid, be recoverable from him as money received by him for the use of the party by whom the sums were paid, and, in the case of sums so payable, cease to be so payable:

Provided that, if the party to whom the sums were so paid or payable incurred expenses before the time of discharge in, or for the purpose of, the performance of the contract, the court may, if it considers it just to do so having regard to all the circumstances of the case, allow him to retain or, as the case may be, recover the whole or any part of the sums so paid or payable, not being an amount in excess of the expenses so incurred.

(3) Where any party to the contract has, by reason of anything done by any other party thereto in, or for the purpose of, the performance of the contract, obtained a valuable benefit (other than a payment of money to which the last foregoing subsection applies) before the time of discharge, there shall be recoverable from him by the said other party such sum (if any), not exceeding the value of the said benefit to the party obtaining it, as the court considers just, having regard to all the circumstances of the case and, in particular,—

    (a)   the amount of any expenses incurred before the time of discharge by the benefited party in, or for the purpose of, the performance of the contract, including any sums paid or payable by him to any other party in pursuance of the contract and retained or recoverable by that party under the last foregoing subsection, and

    (b)   the effect, in relation to the said benefit, of the circumstances giving rise to the frustration of the contract.

(4) In estimating, for the purposes of the foregoing provisions of this section, the amount of any expenses incurred by any party to the contract, the court may, without prejudice to the generality of the said provisions, include such sum as appears to be reasonable in respect of overhead expenses and in respect of any work or services performed personally by the said party.

(5) In considering whether any sum ought to be recovered or retained under the foregoing provisions of this section by any party to the contract, the court shall not take into account any sums which have, by reason of the circumstances giving rise to the frustration of the contract, become payable to that party under any contract of insurance unless there was an obligation to insure imposed by an express term of the frustrated contract or by or under any enactment.

(6) Where any person has assumed obligations under the contract in consideration of the conferring of a benefit by any other party to the contract upon any other person, whether a party to the contract or not, the court may, if in all the circumstances of the case it considers it just to do so, treat for the purposes of subsection (3) of this section any benefit so conferred as a benefit obtained by the person who has assumed the obligations as aforesaid.

[362]

2 Provision as to application of this Act

(1) This Act shall apply to contracts, whether made before or after the commencement of this Act, as respects which the time of discharge is on or after the first day of July, nineteen hundred and forty-three, but not to contracts as respects which the time of discharge is before the said date.

(2) This Act shall apply to contracts to which the Crown is a party in like manner as to contracts between subjects.

(3) Where any contract to which this Act applies contains any provision which, upon the true construction of the contract, is intended to have effect in the event of circumstances arising which operate, or would but for the said provision operate, to frustrate the contract, or is intended to have effect whether such circumstances arise or not, the court shall give effect to the said provision and shall only give effect to the foregoing section of this Act to such extent, if any, as appears to the court to be consistent with the said provision.

(4) Where it appears to the court that a part of any contract to which this Act applies can properly be severed from the remainder of the contract, being a part wholly performed before the time of discharge, or so performed except for the payment in respect of that part of the contract of

sums which are or can be ascertained under the contract, the court shall treat that part of the contract as if it were a separate contract and had not been frustrated and shall treat the foregoing section of this Act as only applicable to the remainder of that contract.

(5)   This Act shall not apply—

(a)   to any charterparty, except a time charterparty or a charterparty by way of demise, or to any contract (other than a charterparty) for the carriage of goods by sea; or

(b)   to any contract of insurance, save as is provided by subsection (5) of the foregoing section; or

(c)   to any contract to which [section 7 of the Sale of Goods Act 1979] (which avoids contracts for the sale of specific goods which perish before the risk has passed to the buyer) applies, or to any other contract for the sale, or for the sale and delivery, of specific goods, where the contract is frustrated by reason of the fact that the goods have perished.

[363]

NOTES

Sub-s (5): words in square brackets in para (c) substituted by the Sale of Goods Act 1979, s 63, Sch 2, para 2.

3   Short title and interpretation

(1)   This Act may be cited as the Law Reform (Frustrated Contracts) Act 1943.

(2)   In this Act the expression "court" means, in relation to any matter, the court or arbitrator by or before whom the matter falls to be determined.

[364]

ARBITRATION ACT 1950

(14 Geo 6 c 27)

ARRANGEMENT OF SECTIONS

PART II
ENFORCEMENT OF CERTAIN FOREIGN AWARDS

An Act to consolidate the Arbitration Acts 1889 to 1934

[28 July 1950]

1–34   (*Ss 1–20, 22–34 repealed by the Arbitration Act 1996, s 107(2), Sch 4; s 21 repealed by the Arbitration Act 1979, ss 1(1), 8(3).*)

PART II
ENFORCEMENT OF CERTAIN FOREIGN AWARDS

35   Awards to which Part II applies

(1)   This Part of this Act applies to any award made after the twenty-eighth day of July, nineteen hundred and twenty-four—

(a)   in pursuance of an agreement for arbitration to which the protocol set out in the First Schedule to this Act applies; and

(b)   between persons of whom one is subject to the jurisdiction of some one of such Powers as His Majesty, being satisfied that reciprocal provisions have been made, may by Order in Council declare to be parties to the convention set out in the Second Schedule to this Act, and of whom the other is subject to the jurisdiction of some other of the Powers aforesaid; and

(c)   in one of such territories as His Majesty, being satisfied that reciprocal provisions have been made, may by Order in Council declare to be territories to which the said convention applies;

and an award to which this Part of this Act applies is in this Part of this Act referred to as "a foreign award".

(2)   His Majesty may by a subsequent Order in Council vary or revoke any Order previously made under this section.

(3)   Any Order in Council under section one of the Arbitration (Foreign Awards) Act 1930, which is in force at the commencement of this Act shall have effect as if it had been made under this section.

[365]

NOTES
Orders in Council: the Arbitration (Foreign Awards) Order 1984, SI 1984/1168. In addition, the following orders also have effect by virtue of sub-s (3) above, as if made under this section: the Arbitration (Foreign Awards) No 1 Order 1930, SR & O 1930/674; the Arbitration (Foreign Awards) No 2 Order 1930, SR & O 1930/1096; the Arbitration (Foreign Awards) No 1 Order 1931, SR & O 1931/166; the Arbitration (Foreign Awards) No 2 Order 1931, SR & O 1931/669; the Arbitration (Foreign Awards) No 3 Order 1931, SR & O 1931/898; the Arbitration (Foreign Awards) No 1 Order 1933, SR & O 1933/42; the Arbitration (Foreign Awards) No 1 Order 1935, SR & O 1935/133; the Arbitration (Foreign Awards) No 2 Order 1938, SR & O 1938/1360; the Arbitration (Foreign Awards) No 1 Order 1939, SR & O 1939/152. Note, although none of these Orders have been revoked, they have been largely superseded by SI 1984/1168 or have become obsolete following political and other changes in the countries concerned.

36   Effect of foreign awards

(1)   A foreign award shall, subject to the provisions of this Part of this Act, be enforceable in England either by action or in the same manner as the award of an arbitrator is enforceable by virtue of [section 66 of the Arbitration Act 1996].

(2)   Any foreign award which would be enforceable under this Part of this Act shall be treated as binding for all purposes on the persons as between whom it was made, and may accordingly be relied on by any of those persons by way of defence, set off or otherwise in any legal proceedings in England, and any references in this Part of this Act to enforcing a foreign award shall be construed as including references to relying on an award.

[366]

NOTES
Sub-s (1): words in square brackets substituted by the Arbitration Act 1996, s 107(1), Sch 3, para 10.

37   Conditions for enforcement of foreign awards

(1)   In order that a foreign award may be enforceable under this Part of this Act it must have—
(a)   been made in pursuance of an agreement for arbitration which was valid under the law by which it is governed;
(b)   been made by the tribunal provided for in the agreement or constituted in manner agreed upon by the parties;
(c)   been made in conformity with the law governing the arbitration procedure;
(d)   become final in the country in which it was made;
(e)   been in respect of a matter which may lawfully be referred to arbitration under the law of England;

and the enforcement thereof must not be contrary to the public policy or the law of England.

(2)   Subject to the provisions of this subsection, a foreign award shall not be enforceable under this Part of this Act if the court dealing with the case is satisfied that—
(a)   the award has been annulled in the country in which it was made; or
(b)   the party against whom it is sought to enforce the award was not given notice of the arbitration proceedings in sufficient time to enable him to present his case, or was under some legal incapacity and was not properly represented; or
(c)   the award does not deal with all the questions referred or contains decisions on matters beyond the scope of the agreement for arbitration:

Provided that, if the award does not deal with all the questions referred, the court may, if it thinks fit, either postpone the enforcement of the award or order its enforcement subject to the giving of such security by the person seeking to enforce it as the court may think fit.

(3)   If a party seeking to resist the enforcement of a foreign award proves that there is any ground other than the non-existence of the conditions specified in paragraphs (a), (b) and (c) of subsection (1) of this section, or the existence of the conditions specified in paragraphs (b) and (c) of subsection (2) of this section, entitling him to contest the validity of the award, the court may, if it thinks fit, either refuse to enforce the award or adjourn the hearing until after the expiration of such

period as appears to the court to be reasonably sufficient to enable that party to take the necessary steps to have the award annulled by the competent tribunal.

[367]

38   Evidence

(1)   The party seeking to enforce a foreign award must produce—
- (a)   the original award or a copy thereof duly authenticated in manner required by the law of the country in which it was made; and
- (b)   evidence proving that the award has become final; and
- (c)   such evidence as may be necessary to prove that the award is a foreign award and that the conditions mentioned in paragraphs (a), (b) and (c) of subsection (1) of the last foregoing section are satisfied.

(2)   In any case where any document required to be produced under subsection (1) of this section is in a foreign language, it shall be the duty of the party seeking to enforce the award to produce a translation certified as correct by a diplomatic or consular agent of the country to which that party belongs, or certified as correct in such other manner as may be sufficient according to the law of England.

(3)   Subject to the provisions of this section, rules of court may be made under section [84 of the [Senior Courts Act 1981]], with respect to the evidence which must be furnished by a party seeking to enforce an award under this Part of this Act.

[368]

NOTES

Sub-s (3): words in first (outer) pair of square brackets substituted by the Senior Courts Act 1981, s 152(1), Sch 5; words in second (inner) pair of square brackets substituted by the Constitutional Reform Act 2005, s 59(5), Sch 11, Pt 1, para 1(2).

39   Meaning of "final award"

For the purposes of this Part of this Act, an award shall not be deemed final if any proceedings for the purpose of contesting the validity of the award are pending in the country in which it was made.

[369]

40   Saving for other rights, etc

Nothing in this Part of this Act shall—
- (a)   prejudice any rights which any person would have had of enforcing in England any award or of availing himself in England of any award if neither this Part of this Act nor Part I of the Arbitration (Foreign Awards) Act 1930, had been enacted; or
- (b)   apply to any award made on an arbitration agreement governed by the law of England.

[370]

41–43   *(S 41 applies to Scotland only; s 42(1), (2) apply to Northern Ireland only; s 42(3) repealed with savings by the Arbitration Act 1996, s 107(2), Sch 4; s 42(4) repealed by the Judicature (Northern Ireland) Act 1978, s 122(2), Sch 7, Pt I; s 43 repealed by the Statute Law (Repeals) Act 1978.)*

PART III
GENERAL

44   Short title, commencement and repeal

(1)   This Act may be cited as the Arbitration Act 1950.

(2)   This Act shall come into operation on the first day of September, nineteen hundred and fifty.

(3)   The Arbitration Act 1889, the Arbitration Clauses (Protocol) Act 1924, and the Arbitration Act 1934 are hereby repealed except in relation to arbitrations commenced (within the meaning of subsection (2) of section twenty-nine of this Act) before the commencement of this Act, and the Arbitration (Foreign Awards) Act 1930 is hereby repealed; and any reference in any Act or other document to any enactment hereby repealed shall be construed as including a reference to the corresponding provision of this Act.

[371]

(Sch 1 (Protocol on Arbitration Clauses signed on behalf of His Majesty at a meeting of the Assembly of the League of Nations held on 24 September 1923) and Sch 2 (Convention on the Exclusion of Foreign Arbitral Awards signed at Geneva on behalf of His Majesty on 26 September 1927) outside the scope of this work.)

ACCOMMODATION AGENCIES ACT 1953

(1 & 2 Eliz 2 c 23)

An Act to prohibit the taking of certain commissions in dealings with persons seeking houses or flats to let and the unauthorised advertisement for letting of houses and flats

[14 July 1953]

1 Illegal commissions and advertisements

(1) Subject to the provisions of this section, any person who, ... —

    (a) demands or accepts payment of any sum of money in consideration of registering, or undertaking to register, the name or requirements of any person seeking the tenancy of a house;

    (b) demands or accepts payment of any sum of money in consideration of supplying, or undertaking to supply, to any person addresses or other particulars of houses to let; or

    (c) issues any advertisement, list or other document describing any house as being to let without the authority of the owner of the house or his agent,

shall be guilty of an offence.

(2) A person shall not be guilty of an offence under this section by reason of his demanding or accepting payment from the owner of a house of any remuneration payable to him as agent for the said owner.

(3) A person being a solicitor [or an authorised person] shall not be guilty of an offence under this section by reason of his demanding or accepting payment of any remuneration in respect of business done by him as such.

(4) A person shall not be guilty of an offence under this section by reason of his demanding or accepting any payment in consideration of the display in a shop, or of the publication in a newspaper, of any advertisement or notice, or by reason of the display or publication as aforesaid of an advertisement or notice received for the purpose in the ordinary course of business.

(5) Any person guilty of an offence under this section shall be liable on summary conviction to a fine not exceeding [level 3 on the standard scale] *or to imprisonment for a term not exceeding three months, or to both such fine and imprisonment.*

(6) In this section the following expressions have the meanings hereby assigned to them that is to say:—

    ["authorised person" means a person (other than a solicitor) who, for the purposes of the Legal Services Act 2007, is an authorised person in relation to an activity which is a reserved legal activity (within the meaning of that Act);]

    "house" includes any part of a building which is occupied or intended to be occupied as a dwelling;

    "newspaper" includes any periodical or magazine;

    "owner", in relation to a house, means the person having power to grant a lease of the house.

[372]

NOTES

Sub-s (1): words omitted repealed by the Expiring Laws Act 1969.

Sub-s (3): words in square brackets inserted by the Legal Services Act 2007, s 208(1), Sch 21, para 22(a).

Sub-s (5): reference to a level on the standard scale substituted by virtue of the Criminal Justice Act 1982, ss 38, 46; words in italics repealed by the Criminal Justice Act 2003, s 332, Sch 37, Pt 9, as from a day to be appointed.

Sub-s (6): definition "authorised person" inserted by the Legal Services Act 2007, s 208(1), Sch 21, para 22(b).

Solicitors: references to solicitors are modified so as to include references to recognised bodies within the meaning of the Administration of Justice Act 1985, s 9, by the Solicitors' Incorporated Practices Order 1991, SI 1991/2684, arts 3–5, Sch 1.

2 Short title, extent, commencement and duration

(1) This Act may be cited as the Accommodation Agencies Act 1953.

(2) This Act shall not extend to Northern Ireland.

(3) This Act shall come into operation one month after the date on which it is passed.

(4) ...

[373]

NOTES

Sub-s (4): repealed by the Expiring Laws Act 1969, s 1.

CHEQUES ACT 1957

(5 & 6 Eliz 2 c 36)

ARRANGEMENT OF SECTIONS

An Act to amend the law relating to cheques and certain other instruments

[17 July 1957]

1   Protection of bankers paying unindorsed or irregularly indorsed cheques, etc

(1)   Where a banker in good faith and in the ordinary course of business pays a cheque drawn on him which is not indorsed or is irregularly indorsed, he does not, in doing so, incur any liability by reason only of the absence of, or irregularity in, indorsement, and he is deemed to have paid it in due course.

(2)   Where a banker in good faith and in the ordinary course of business pays any such instrument as the following, namely,—
   (a)   a document issued by a customer of his which, though not a bill of exchange, is intended to enable a person to obtain payment from him of the sum mentioned in the document;
   (b)   a draft payable on demand drawn by him upon himself, whether payable at the head office or some other office of his bank;

he does not, in doing so, incur any liability by reason only of the absence of, or irregularity in, indorsement, and the payment discharges the instrument.

[374]

2   Rights of bankers collecting cheques not indorsed by holders

A banker who gives value for, or has a lien on, a cheque payable to order which the holder delivers to him for collection without indorsing it, has such (if any) rights as he would have had if, upon delivery, the holder had indorsed it in blank.

[375]

3   Unindorsed cheques as evidence of payment

[(1)]   An unindorsed cheque which appears to have been paid by the banker on whom it is drawn is evidence of the receipt by the payee of the sum payable by the cheque.

[(2)   For the purposes of subsection (1) above, a copy of a cheque to which that subsection applies is evidence of the cheque if—
   (a)   the copy is made by the banker in whose possession the cheque is after presentment and,
   (b)   it is certified by him to be a true copy of the original.]

[376]

NOTES
   Sub-s (1): numbered as such by the Deregulation (Bills of Exchange) Order 1996, SI 1996/2993, art 5.
   Sub-s (2): added by SI 1996/2993, art 5.

---

4   Protection of bankers collecting payment of cheques, etc

(1)   Where a banker, in good faith and without negligence,—
   (a)   receives payment for a customer of an instrument to which this section applies; or
   (b)   having credited a customer's account with the amount of such an instrument, receives payment thereof for himself;

and the customer has no title, or a defective title, to the instrument, the banker does not incur any liability to the true owner of the instrument by reason only of having received payment thereof.

(2)   This section applies to the following instruments, namely,—
   (a)   cheques [(including cheques which under section 81A(1) of the Bills of Exchange Act 1882 or otherwise are not transferable)];
   (b)   any document issued by a customer of a banker which, though not a bill of exchange, is intended to enable a person to obtain payment from that banker of the sum mentioned in the document;

(c)   any document issued by a public officer which is intended to enable a person to obtain payment from the Paymaster General or the Queen's and Lord Treasurer's Remembrancer of the sum mentioned in the document but is not a bill of exchange;

(d)   any draft payable on demand drawn by a banker upon himself, whether payable at the head office or some other office of his bank.

(3)   A banker is not to be treated for the purposes of this section as having been negligent by reason only of his failure to concern himself with absence of, or irregularity in, indorsement of an instrument.

[377]

NOTES

Sub-s (2): words in square brackets in para (a) inserted by the Cheques Act 1992, s 3.

5   Application of certain provisions of Bills of Exchange Act, 1882, to instruments not being bills of exchange

The provisions of the Bills of Exchange Act, 1882, relating to crossed cheques shall, so far as applicable, have effect in relation to instruments (other than cheques) to which the last foregoing section applies as they have effect in relation to cheques.

[378]

6   Construction, saving and repeal

(1)   This Act shall be construed as one with the Bills of Exchange Act, 1882.

(2)   The foregoing provisions of this Act do not make negotiable any instrument which, apart from them, is not negotiable.

(3)   ...

[379]

NOTES

Sub-s (3): repealed by the Statute Law (Repeals) Act 1974.

7   Provisions as to Northern Ireland

This Act extends to Northern Ireland, ...

[380]

NOTES

Words omitted repealed by the Northern Ireland Constitution Act 1973, s 41(1), Sch 6, Pt I.

8   Short title and commencement

(1)   This Act may be cited as the Cheques Act 1957.

(2)   This Act shall come into operation at the expiration of a period of three months beginning with the day on which it is passed.

[381]

(*Schedule repealed by the Statutes Law (Repeals) Act 1974.*)

CORPORATE BODIES' CONTRACTS ACT 1960

(8 & 9 Eliz 2 c 46)

An Act to amend the law governing the making of contracts by or on behalf of bodies corporate; and for connected purposes

[29 July 1960]

1   Cases where contracts need not be under seal

(1)   Contracts may be made on behalf of any body corporate, wherever incorporated, as follows:—

(a)   a contract which if made between private persons would be by law required to be in writing, signed by the parties to be charged there-with, may be made on behalf of the body corporate in writing signed by any person acting under its authority, express or implied, and

(b)   a contract which if made between private persons would by law be valid although made by parol only, and not reduced into writing, may be made by parol on behalf of the body corporate by any person acting under its authority, express or implied.

(2) A contract made according to this section shall be effectual in law, and shall bind the body corporate and its successors and all other parties thereto.

(3) A contract made according to this section may be varied or discharged in the same manner in which it is authorised by this section to be made.

(4) Nothing in this section shall be taken as preventing a contract under seal from being made by or on behalf of a body corporate.

(5) This section shall not apply to the making, variation or discharge of a contract before the commencement of this Act but shall apply whether the body corporate gave its authority before or after the commencement of this Act.

[382]

[2   Exclusion of companies etc

This Act does not apply to—
  (a)   a company registered under the Companies Act 2006,
  (b)   a company incorporated outside the United Kingdom, or
  (c)   a limited liability partnership.]

[383]

NOTES
  Commencement: 1 October 2009.
  Substituted by the Companies Act 2006 (Consequential Amendments, Transitional Provisions and Savings) Order 2009, SI 2009/1941, art 2(1), Sch 1, para 8.

3   (*Repealed by the Northern Ireland Constitution Act 1973, s 41, Sch 6, Pt I.*)

4   Short title, repeal and extent

  (1)   This Act may be cited as the Corporate Bodies' Contracts Act 1960.
  (2)   …
  (3)   This Act shall not affect the law of Scotland or … of Northern Ireland.

[384]–[388]

NOTES
  Sub-s (2): repealed by the Statute Law (Repeals) Act 1974.
  Sub-s (3): words omitted repealed by the Northern Ireland Constitution Act 1973, s 41(1), Sch 6, Pt I.

(*Schedule repealed by the Statute Law (Repeals) Act 1974.*)

HIRE-PURCHASE ACT 1964

(1964 c 53)

An Act to amend the law relating to hire-purchase and credit-sale, and, in relation thereto, to amend the enactments relating to the sale of goods; to make provision with respect to dispositions of motor vehicles which have been let or agreed to be sold by way of hire-purchase or conditional sale; to amend the Advertisements (Hire-Purchase) Act 1957; and for purposes connected with the matters aforesaid

[16 July 1964]

1–26   (*Ss 1–24 (Pt I) repealed by the Hire-Purchase Act 1965, s 59, Sch 6; ss 25, 26 (Pt II) repealed by the Hire-Purchase (Scotland) Act 1965, s 55, Sch 6.*)

[PART III
TITLE TO MOTOR VEHICLES ON HIRE-PURCHASE OR CONDITIONAL SALE

27   Protection of purchasers of motor vehicles

  (1)   This section applies where a motor vehicle has been bailed or (in Scotland) hired under a hire-purchase agreement, or has been agreed to be sold under a conditional sale agreement, and, before the property in the vehicle has become vested in the debtor, he disposes of the vehicle to another person.

  (2)   Where the disposition referred to in subsection (1) above is to a private purchaser, and he is a purchaser of the motor vehicle in good faith, without notice of the hire-purchase or conditional sale agreement (the "relevant agreement") that disposition shall have effect as if the creditor's title to the vehicle has been vested in the debtor immediately before that disposition.

(3)   Where the person to whom the disposition referred to in subsection (1) above is made (the "original purchaser") is a trade or finance purchaser, then if the person who is the first private purchaser of the motor vehicle after that disposition (the "first private purchaser") is a purchaser of the vehicle in good faith without notice of the relevant agreement, the disposition of the vehicle to the first private purchaser shall have effect as if the title of the creditor to the vehicle had been vested in the debtor immediately before he disposed of it to the original purchaser.

(4)   Where, in a case within subsection (3) above—

(a)   the disposition by which the first private purchaser becomes a purchaser of the motor vehicle in good faith without notice of the relevant agreement is itself a bailment or hiring under a hire-purchase agreement, and

(b)   the person who is the creditor in relation to that agreement disposes of the vehicle to the first private purchaser, or a person claiming under him, by transferring to him the property in the vehicle in pursuance of a provision in the agreement in that behalf,

the disposition referred to in paragraph (b) above (whether or not the person to whom it is made is a purchaser in good faith without notice of the relevant agreement) shall as well as the disposition referred to in paragraph (a) above, have effect as mentioned in subsection (3) above.

(5)   The preceding provisions of this section apply—

(a)   notwithstanding anything in [section 21 of the Sale of Goods Act 1979] (sale of goods by a person not the owner), but

(b)   without prejudice to the provisions of the Factors Act (as defined by [section 61(1) of the said Act of 1979]) or of any other enactment enabling the apparent owner of goods to dispose of them as if he were the true owner.

(6)   Nothing in this section shall exonerate the debtor from any liability (whether criminal or civil) to which he would be subject apart from this section; and, in a case where the debtor disposes of the motor vehicle to a trade or finance purchaser, nothing in this section shall exonerate—

(a)   that trade or finance purchaser; or

(b)   any other trade or finance purchaser who becomes a purchaser of the vehicle and is not a person claiming under the first private purchaser,

from any liability (whether criminal or civil) to which he would be subject apart from this section.]

[389]

NOTES

Part III (ss 27–29) substituted by the Consumer Credit Act 1974, s 192(3)(a), Sch 4, para 22.

Sub-s (5): words in square brackets substituted by the Sale of Goods Act 1979, s 63, Sch 2, para 4.

[28   Presumptions relating to dealings with motor vehicles

(1)   Where in any proceedings (whether criminal or civil) relating to a motor vehicle it is proved—

(a)   that the vehicle was bailed or (in Scotland) hired under a hire-purchase agreement, or was agreed to be sold under a conditional sale agreement and

(b)   that a person (whether a party to the proceedings or not) became a private purchaser of the vehicle in good faith without notice of the hire-purchase or conditional sale agreement (the "relevant agreement"),

this section shall have effect for the purposes of the operation of section 27 of this Act in relation to those proceedings.

(2)   It shall be presumed for those purposes, unless the contrary is proved, that the disposition of the vehicle to the person referred to in subsection (1)(b) above (the "relevant purchaser") was made by the debtor.

(3)   If it is proved that that disposition was not made by the debtor, then it shall be presumed for those purposes, unless the contrary is proved—

(a)   that the debtor disposed of the vehicle to a private purchaser purchasing in good faith without notice of the relevant agreement, and

(b)   that the relevant purchaser is or was a person claiming under the person to whom the debtor so disposed of the vehicle.

(4)   If it is proved that the disposition of the vehicle to the relevant purchaser was not made by the debtor, and that the person to whom the debtor disposed of the vehicle (the "original purchaser") was a trade or finance purchaser, then it shall be presumed for those purposes, unless the contrary is proved,—

(a)   that the person who, after the disposition of the vehicle to the original purchaser, first became a private purchaser of the vehicle was a purchaser in good faith without notice of the relevant agreement, and

(b)   that the relevant purchaser is or was a person claiming under the original purchaser.

(5)   Without prejudice to any other method of proof, where in any proceedings a party thereto admits a fact, that fact shall, for the purposes of this section, be taken as against him to be proved in relation to those proceedings.]

[390]

NOTES

Substituted as noted to s 27 at **[389]**.

[29   Interpretation of Part III

(1)   In this Part of this Act—

"conditional sale agreement" means an agreement for the sale of goods under which the purchase price or part of it is payable by instalments, and the property in the goods is to remain in the seller (notwithstanding that the buyer is to be in possession of the goods) until such conditions as to the payment of instalments or otherwise as may be specified in the agreement are fulfilled;

"creditor" means the person by whom goods are bailed or (in Scotland) hired under a hire-purchase agreement or as the case may be, the seller under a conditional sale agreement, or the person to whom his rights and duties have passed by assignment or operation of law;

"disposition" means any sale or contract of sale (including a conditional sale agreement), any bailment or (in Scotland) hiring under a hire-purchase agreement and any transfer of the property in goods in pursuance of a provision in that behalf contained in a hire-purchase agreement, and includes, any transaction purporting to be a disposition (as so defined), and "dispose of" shall be construed accordingly;

"hire-purchase agreement" means an agreement, other than a conditional sale agreement, under which—

    (a)   goods are bailed or (in Scotland) hired in return for periodical payments by the person to whom they are bailed or hired, and

    (b)   the property in the goods will pass to that person if the terms of the agreement are complied with and one or more of the following occurs—

        (i)   the exercise of an option to purchase by that person,

        (ii)   the doing of any other specified act by any party to the agreement,

        (iii)   the happening of any other specified events; and

"motor vehicle" means a mechanically propelled vehicle intended or adapted for use on roads to which the public has access.

(2)   In this Part of this Act, "trade or finance purchaser" means a purchaser who, at the time of the disposition made to him, carries on a business which consists, wholly or partly,—

    (a)   of purchasing motor vehicles for the purpose of offering or exposing them for sale, or

    (b)   of providing finance by purchasing motor vehicles for the purpose of bailing or (in Scotland) hiring them under hire-purchase agreements or agreeing to sell them under conditional sale agreements,

and "private purchaser" means a purchaser who, at the time of the disposition made to him, does not carry on any such business.

(3)   For the purposes of this Part of this Act a person becomes a purchaser of a motor vehicle if, and at the time when, a disposition of the vehicle is made to him; and a person shall be taken to be a purchaser of a motor vehicle without notice of a hire-purchase agreement or conditional sale agreement if, at the time of the disposition made to him, he has no actual notice that the vehicle is or was the subject of any such agreement.

(4)   In this Part of this Act the "debtor" in relation to a motor vehicle which has been bailed or hired under a hire-purchase agreement, or, as the case may be, agreed to be sold under a conditional sale agreement, means the person who at the material time (whether the agreement has before that time been terminated or not) is either—

    (a)   the person to whom the vehicle is bailed or hired under that agreement, or

    (b)   is, in relation to the agreement, the buyer, including a person who at the time is, by virtue of section 130(4) of the Consumer Credit Act 1974 treated as a bailee or (in Scotland) a custodier of the vehicle.

(5)   In this Part of this Act any reference to the title of the creditor to a motor vehicle which has been bailed or (in Scotland) hired under a hire-purchase agreement, or agreed to be sold under a conditional sale agreement, and is disposed of by the debtor, is a reference to such title (if any) to the vehicle as, immediately before that disposition, was vested in the person who then was the creditor in relation to the agreement.]

[391]

NOTES

Substituted as noted to s 27 at **[389]**.

30–32 *((Pt IV) repealed by the Advertisements (Hire-Purchase) Act 1967, s 8(2), Sch 2.)*

PART V
SUPPLEMENTARY PROVISIONS

33–36 *(S 33 repealed by the Hire-Purchase Act 1965, s 59, Sch 6; ss 34–36 repealed by the Consumer Credit Act 1974, s 192(3)(b), Sch 5.)*

37 Short title, citation and extent

(1) This Act may be cited as the Hire-Purchase Act 1964.

(2)–(4) …

(5) This Act shall not extend to Northern Ireland.

[392]–[403]

NOTES
Sub-s (2): repealed by the Hire-Purchase Act 1965, s 59, Sch 6.
Sub-s (3): repealed by the Hire-Purchase (Scotland) Act 1965, s 55, Sch 6.
Sub-s (4): repealed by the Hire-Purchase Act 1965, s 55, Sch 6, and the Hire-Purchase (Scotland) Act 1965, s 55, Sch 6.

(Schs 1, 4 (in part), 5, 6, repealed by the Hire-Purchase Act 1965, s 55, Sch 6; Schs 2, 3, 7 repealed by the Hire-Purchase (Scotland) Act 1965, s 55, Sch 6; Schs 3, 4 (remainder) repealed by the Advertisements (Hire-Purchase) Act 1967, s 8(2), Sch 2.)

CARRIAGE OF GOODS BY ROAD ACT 1965

(1965 c 37)

ARRANGEMENT OF SECTIONS

An Act to give effect to the Convention on the Contract for the International Carriage of Goods by Road signed at Geneva on 19th May 1956; and for purposes connected therewith

[5 August 1965]

1 Convention to have force of law

Subject to the following provisions of this Act, the provisions of the Convention on the Contract for the International Carriage of Goods by Road (in this Act referred to as "the Convention"), as set out in the Schedule to this Act, shall have the force of law in the United Kingdom so far as they relate to the rights and liabilities of persons concerned in the carriage of goods by road under a contract to which the Convention applies.

[404]

NOTES
Convention on the Contract for the International Carriage of Goods by Road: signed at Geneva on 19 May 1956; see Cmnd 2260.

2 Designation of High Contracting Parties

(1) Her Majesty may by Order in Council from time to time certify who are the High Contracting Parties to the Convention and in respect of what territories they are respectively parties.

(2)   An Order in Council under this section shall, except so far as it has been superseded by a subsequent Order, be conclusive evidence of the matters so certified.

[405]

NOTES
Orders in Council: the Carriage of Goods by Road (Parties to Convention) Order 1967, SI 1967/1683.

3 Power of court to take account of other proceedings

(1)   A court before which proceedings are brought to enforce a liability which is limited by article 23 in the Schedule to this Act may at any stage of the proceedings make any such order as appears to the court to be just and equitable in view of the provisions of the said article 23 and of any other proceedings which have been, or are likely to be, commenced in the United Kingdom or elsewhere to enforce the liability in whole or in part.

(2)   Without prejudice to the preceding subsection, a court before which proceedings are brought to enforce a liability which is limited by the said article 23 shall, where the liability is, or may be, partly enforceable in other proceedings in the United Kingdom or elsewhere, have jurisdiction to award an amount less than the court would have awarded if the limitation applied solely to the proceedings before the court, or to make any part of its award conditional on the result of any other proceedings.

[406]

4 Registration of foreign judgments

(1)   Subject to the next following subsection, Part I of the Foreign Judgments (Reciprocal Enforcement) Act 1933 (in this section referred to as "the Act of 1933") shall apply, whether or not it would otherwise have so applied, to any judgment which—
  (a)   has been given in any such action as is referred to in paragraph 1 of article 31 in the Schedule to this Act, and
  (b)   has been so given by any court or tribunal of a territory in respect of which one of the High Contracting Parties, other than the United Kingdom, is a party to the Convention, and
  (c)   has become enforceable in that territory.

(2)   In the application of Part I of the Act of 1933 in relation to any such judgment as is referred to in the preceding subsection, section 4 of that Act shall have effect with the omission of subsections (2) and (3).

(3)   The registration, in accordance with Part I of the Act of 1933, of any such judgment as is referred to in subsection (1) of this section shall constitute, in relation to that judgment, compliance with the formalities for the purposes of paragraph 3 of article 31 in the Schedule to this Act.

[407]

5 Contribution between carriers

(1)   Where a carrier under a contract to which the Convention applies is liable in respect of any loss or damage for which compensation is payable under the Convention, nothing in [section 1 of the Civil Liability (Contribution) Act 1978], or section 3(2) of the Law Reform (Miscellaneous Provisions) (Scotland) Act 1940 shall confer on him any right to recover contribution in respect of that loss or damage from any other carrier who, in accordance with article 34 in the Schedule to this Act, is a party to the contract of carriage.

(2)   The preceding subsection shall be without prejudice to the operation of article 37 in the Schedule to this Act.

[408]

NOTES
Sub-s (1): words in square brackets substituted by the Civil Liability (Contribution) Act 1978, s 9(1), Sch 1, para 7.

6 Actions against High Contracting Parties

Every High Contracting Party to the Convention shall, for the purposes of any proceedings brought in a court in the United Kingdom in accordance with the provisions of article 31 in the Schedule to this Act to enforce a claim in respect of carriage undertaken by that Party, be deemed to have submitted to the jurisdiction of that court, and accordingly rules of court may provide for the manner in which any such action is to be commenced and carried on; but nothing in this section shall authorise the issue of execution, or in Scotland the execution of diligence, against the property of any High Contracting Party.

[409]

7 Arbitrations

(1) Any reference in the preceding provisions of this Act to a court includes a reference to an arbitration tribunal acting by virtue of article 33 in the Schedule to this Act.

(2) For the purposes of article 32 in the Schedule to this Act, as it has effect (by virtue of the said article 33) in relation to arbitrations,—

[(a) as respects England and Wales and Northern Ireland, the provisions of section 14(3) to (5) of the Arbitration Act 1996 (which determine the time at which an arbitration is commenced) apply;]

(c) (*applies to Scotland only*.)

[410]

NOTES

Sub-s (2): para (a) substituted, for original paras (a), (b), by the Arbitration Act 1996, s 107, Sch 3, para 21, Sch 4.

8 Resolution of conflicts between Conventions on carriage of goods

(1) If it appears to Her Majesty in Council that there is any conflict between the provisions of this Act (including the provisions of the Convention as set out in the Schedule to this Act) and any provisions relating to the carriage of goods for reward by land, sea or air contained in—

(a) any other Convention which has been signed or ratified by or on behalf of Her Majesty's Government in the United Kingdom before the passing of this Act, or

(b) any enactment of the Parliament of the United Kingdom giving effect to such a Convention,

Her Majesty may by Order in Council make such provision as may seem to Her to be appropriate for resolving that conflict by amending or modifying this Act or any such enactment.

(2) Any statutory instrument made by virtue of this section shall be subject to annulment in pursuance of a resolution of either House of Parliament.

[411]

[8A Amendments consequential on revision of Convention

(1) If at any time it appears to Her Majesty in Council that Her Majesty's Government in the United Kingdom have agreed to any revision of the Convention, Her Majesty may by Order in Council make such amendment of—

[(a) this Act; and]

(c) section 5(1) of the Carriage by Air and Road Act 1979,

as appear to Her to be appropriate in consequence of the revision.

(2) In the preceding subsection "revision" means an omission from, addition to or alteration of the Convention and includes replacement of the Convention or part of it by another convention.

(3) An Order in Council under this section shall not be made unless a draft of the Order has been laid before Parliament and approved by a resolution of each House of Parliament.]

[412]

NOTES

Inserted by the Carriage by Air and Road Act 1979, s 3(3).

Sub-s (1): para (a) substituted, for original paras (a), (b), by the International Transport Conventions Act 1983, s 9, Sch 2, para 2.

9 Application to British possessions, etc

Her Majesty may by Order in Council direct that this Act shall extend, subject to such exceptions, adaptations and modifications as may be specified in the Order, to—

(a) the Isle of Man;

(b) any of the Channel Islands;

(c) any colony;

(d) ...

[413]

NOTES

Para (d) repealed by the Statute Law (Repeals) Act 1993.

Orders in Council: the Carriage of Goods by Road (Gibraltar) Order 1967, SI 1967/820; the Carriage of Goods by Road (Isle of Man) Order 1981, SI 1981/1543; the Carriage of Goods by Road (Guernsey) Order 1986, SI 1986/1882.

10, 11   (*S 10 applies to Scotland only; s 11 applies to Northern Ireland only.*)

12   Orders in Council

An Order in Council made under any of the preceding provisions of this Act may contain such transitional and supplementary provisions as appear to Her Majesty to be expedient and may be varied or revoked by a subsequent Order in Council made under that provision.

[414]

13   Application to Crown

This Act shall bind the Crown.

[415]

14   Short title, interpretation and commencement

    (1)   This Act may be cited as the Carriage of Goods by Road Act 1965.

    (2)   The persons who, for the purposes of this Act, are persons concerned in the carriage of goods by road under a contract to which the Convention applies are—

        (a)   the sender,

        (b)   the consignee,

        (c)   any carrier who, in accordance with article 34 in the Schedule to this Act or otherwise, is a party to the contract of carriage,

        (d)   any person for whom such a carrier is responsible by virtue of article 3 in the Schedule to this Act,

        (e)   any person to whom the rights and liabilities of any of the persons referred to in paragraphs (a) to (d) to this subsection have passed (whether by assignment or assignation or by operation of law).

    (3)   Except in so far as the context otherwise requires, any reference in this Act to an enactment shall be construed as a reference to that enactment as amended or extended by or under any other enactment.

    (4)   This Act shall come into operation on such day as Her Majesty may by Order in Council appoint; but nothing in this Act shall apply in relation to any contract or the carriage of goods by road made before the day so appointed.

[416]

NOTES

   Orders in Council: the Carriage of Goods by Road Act 1965 (Commencement) Order 1967, SI 1967/819.

<hr>

SCHEDULE

CONVENTION ON THE CONTRACT FOR THE INTERNATIONAL CARRIAGE OF GOODS BY ROAD

Section 1

CHAPTER I
SCOPE OF APPLICATION

Article 1

1.   This Convention shall apply to every contract for the carriage of goods by road in vehicles for reward, when the place of taking over of the goods and the place designated for delivery, as specified in the contract, are situated in two different countries, of which at least one is a Contracting country, irrespective of the place of residence and the nationality of the parties.

2.   For the purposes of this Convention, "vehicles" means motor vehicles, articulated vehicles, trailers and semi-trailers as defined in article 4 of the Convention on Road Traffic dated 19th September 1949.

3.   This Convention shall apply also where carriage coming within its scope is carried out by States or by governmental institutions or organizations.

4.   This Convention shall not apply:

        (a)   to carriage performed under the terms of any international postal convention;

        (b)   to funeral consignments;

        (c)   to furniture removal.

5.   The Contracting Parties agree not to vary any of the provisions of this Convention by special agreements between two or more of them, except to make it inapplicable to their frontier traffic or to authorise the use in transport operations entirely confined to their territory of consignment notes representing a title to the goods.

Article 2

1.   Where the vehicle containing the goods is carried over part of the journey by sea, rail, inland waterways or air, and, except where the provisions of article 14 are applicable, the goods are not unloaded from the vehicle, this Convention shall nevertheless apply to the whole of the carriage.

Provided that to the extent that it is proved that any loss, damage or delay in delivery of the goods which occurs during the carriage by the other means of transport was not caused by an act or omission of the carrier by road, but by some event which could only have occurred in the course of and by reason of the carriage by that other means of transport, the liability of the carrier by road shall be determined not by this Convention but in the manner in which the liability of the carrier by the other means of transport would have been determined if a contract for the carriage of the goods alone had been made by the sender with the carrier by the other means of transport in accordance with the conditions prescribed by law for the carriage of goods by that means of transport. If, however, there are no such prescribed conditions, the liability of the carrier by road shall be determined by this Convention.

2. If the carrier by road is also himself the carrier by the other means of transport, his liability shall also be determined in accordance with the provisions of paragraph 1 of this article, but as if, in his capacities as carrier by road and as carrier by the other means of transport, he were two separate persons.

CHAPTER II
PERSONS FOR WHOM THE CARRIER IS RESPONSIBLE

Article 3

For the purposes of this Convention the carrier shall be responsible for the acts and omissions of his agents and servants and of any other persons of whose services he makes use for the performance of the carriage, when such agents, servants or other persons are acting within the scope of their employment, as if such acts or omissions were his own.

CHAPTER III
CONCLUSION AND PERFORMANCE OF THE CONTRACT OF CARRIAGE

Article 4

The contract of carriage shall be confirmed by the making out of a consignment note. The absence, irregularity or loss of the consignment note shall not affect the existence or the validity of the contract of carriage which shall remain subject to the provisions of this Convention.

Article 5

1. The consignment note shall be made out in three original copies signed by the sender and by the carrier. These signatures may be printed or replaced by the stamps of the sender and the carrier if the law of the country in which the consignment note has been made out so permits. The first copy shall be handed to the sender, the second shall accompany the goods and the third shall be retained by the carrier.

2. When the goods which are to be carried have to be loaded in different vehicles, or are of different kinds or are divided into different lots, the sender or the carrier shall have the right to require a separate consignment note to be made out for each vehicle used, or for each kind or lot of goods.

Article 6

1. The consignment note shall contain the following particulars:
    (a) the date of the consignment note and the place at which it is made out;
    (b) the name and address of the sender;
    (c) the name and address of the carrier;
    (d) the place and the date of taking over of the goods and the place designated for delivery;
    (e) the name and address of the consignee;
    (f) the description in common use of the nature of the goods and the method of packing, and, in the case of dangerous goods, their generally recognised description;
    (g) the number of packages and their special marks and numbers;
    (h) the gross weight of the goods or their quantity otherwise expressed;
    (i) charges relating to the carriage (carriage charges, supplementary charges, customs duties and other charges incurred from the making of the contract to the time of delivery);
    (j) the requisite instructions for Customs and other formalities;
    (k) a statement that the carriage is subject, notwithstanding any clause to the contrary, to the provisions of this Convention.

2. Where applicable, the consignment note shall also contain the following particulars:
    (a) a statement that transhipment is not allowed;
    (b) the charges which the sender undertakes to pay;
    (c) the amount of "cash on delivery" charges;
    (d) a declaration of the value of the goods and the amount representing special interest in delivery;
    (e) the sender's instructions to the carrier regarding insurance of the goods;

(f)   the agreed time-limit within which the carriage is to be carried out;

(g)   a list of the documents handed to the carrier.

3.   The parties may enter in the consignment note any other particulars which they may deem useful.

Article 7

1.   The sender shall be responsible for all expenses, loss and damage sustained by the carrier by reason of the inaccuracy or inadequacy of:

(a)   the particulars specified in article 6, paragraph 1(b), (d), (e), (f), (g), (h) and (j);

(b)   the particulars specified in article 6, paragraph 2;

(c)   any other particulars or instructions given by him to enable the consignment note to be made out or for the purpose of their being entered therein.

2.   If, at the request of the sender, the carrier enters in the consignment note the particulars referred to in paragraph 1 of this article, he shall be deemed, unless the contrary is proved, to have done so on behalf of the sender.

3.   If the consignment note does not contain the statement specified in article 6, paragraph 1(k), the carrier shall be liable for all expenses, loss and damage sustained through such omission by the person entitled to dispose of the goods.

Article 8

1.   On taking over the goods, the carrier shall check:

(a)   the accuracy of the statements in the consignment note as to the number of packages and their marks and numbers, and

(b)   the apparent condition of the goods and their packaging.

2.   Where the carrier has no reasonable means of checking the accuracy of the statements referred to in paragraph 1(a) of this article, he shall enter his reservations in the consignment note together with the grounds on which they are based. He shall likewise specify the grounds for any reservations which he makes with regard to the apparent condition of the goods and their packaging. Such reservations shall not bind the sender unless he has expressly agreed to be bound by them in the consignment note.

3.   The sender shall be entitled to require the carrier to check the gross weight of the goods or their quantity otherwise expressed. He may also require the contents of the packages to be checked. The carrier shall be entitled to claim the cost of such checking. The result of the checks shall be entered in the consignment note.

Article 9

1.   The consignment note shall be *prima facie* evidence of the making of the contract of carriage, the conditions of the contract and the receipt of the goods by the carrier.

2.   If the consignment note contains no specific reservations by the carrier, it shall be presumed, unless the contrary is proved, that the goods and their packaging appeared to be in good condition when the carrier took them over and that the number of packages, their marks and numbers corresponded with the statements in the consignment note.

Article 10

The sender shall be liable to the carrier for damage to persons, equipment or other goods, and for any expenses due to defective packing of the goods, unless the defect was apparent or known to the carrier at the time when he took over the goods and he made no reservations concerning it.

Article 11

1.   For the purposes of the Customs or other formalities which have to be completed before delivery of the goods, the sender shall attach the necessary documents to the consignment note or place them at the disposal of the carrier and shall furnish him with all the information which he requires.

2.   The carrier shall not be under any duty to enquire into either the accuracy or the adequacy of such documents and information. The sender shall be liable to the carrier for any damage caused by the absence, inadequacy or irregularity of such documents and information, except in the case of some wrongful act or neglect on the part of the carrier.

3.   The liability of the carrier for the consequences arising from the loss or incorrect use of the documents specified in and accompanying the consignment note or deposited with the carrier shall be that of an agent, provided that the compensation payable by the carrier shall not exceed that payable in the event of loss of the goods.

Article 12

1.   The sender has the right to dispose of the goods, in particular by asking the carrier to stop the goods in transit, to change the place at which delivery is to take place or to deliver the goods to a consignee other than the consignee indicated in the consignment note.

2.   This right shall cease to exist when the second copy of the consignment note is handed to the consignee or when the consignee exercises his right under article 13, paragraph 1; from that time onwards the carrier shall obey the orders of the consignee.

3.   The consignee shall, however, have the right of disposal from the time when the consignment note is drawn up, if the sender makes an entry to that effect in the consignment note.

4.   If in exercising his right of disposal the consignee has ordered the delivery of the goods to another person, that other person shall not be entitled to name other consignees.

5.   The exercise of the right of disposal shall be subject to the following conditions:
   (a)   that the sender or, in the case referred to in paragraph 3 of this article, the consignee who wishes to exercise the right produces the first copy of the consignment note on which the new instructions to the carrier have been entered and indemnifies the carrier against all expenses, loss and damage involved in carrying out such instructions;
   (b)   that the carrying out of such instructions is possible at the time when the instructions reach the person who is to carry them out and does not either interfere with the normal working of the carrier's undertaking or prejudice the senders or consignees of other consignments;
   (c)   that the instructions do not result in a division of the consignment.

6.   When, by reason of the provisions of paragraph 5(b) of this article, the carrier cannot carry out the instructions which he receives, he shall immediately notify the person who gave him such instructions.

7.   A carrier who has not carried out the instructions given under the conditions provided for in this article, or who has carried them out without requiring the first copy of the consignment note to be produced, shall be liable to the person entitled to make a claim for any loss or damage caused thereby.

Article 13

1.   After arrival of the goods at the place designated for delivery, the consignee shall be entitled to require the carrier to deliver to him, against a receipt, the second copy of the consignment note and the goods. If the loss of the goods is established or if the goods have not arrived after the expiry of the period provided for in article 19, the consignee shall be entitled to enforce in his own name against the carrier any rights arising from the contract of carriage.

2.   The consignee who avails himself of the rights granted to him under paragraph 1 of this article shall pay the charges shown to be due on the consignment note, but in the event of dispute on this matter the carrier shall not be required to deliver the goods unless security has been furnished by the consignee.

Article 14

1.   If for any reason it is or becomes impossible to carry out the contract in accordance with the terms laid down in the consignment note before the goods reach the place designated for delivery, the carrier shall ask for instructions from the person entitled to dispose of the goods in accordance with the provisions of article 12.

2.   Nevertheless, if circumstances are such as to allow the carriage to be carried out under conditions differing from those laid down in the consignment note and if the carrier has been unable to obtain instructions in reasonable time from the person entitled to dispose of the goods in accordance with the provisions of article 12, he shall take such steps as seem to him to be in the best interests of the person entitled to dispose of the goods.

Article 15

1.   Where circumstances prevent delivery of the goods after their arrival at the place designated for delivery, the carrier shall ask the sender for his instructions. If the consignee refuses the goods the sender shall be entitled to dispose of them without being obliged to produce the first copy of the consignment note.

2.   Even if he has refused the goods, the consignee may nevertheless require delivery so long as the carrier has not received instructions to the contrary from the sender.

3.   When circumstances preventing delivery of the goods arise after the consignee, in exercise of his rights under article 12, paragraph 3, has given an order for the goods to be delivered to another person, paragraphs 1 and 2 of this article shall apply as if the consignee were the sender and that other person were the consignee.

Article 16

1.   The carrier shall be entitled to recover the cost of his request for instructions, and any expenses entailed in carrying out such instructions, unless such expenses were caused by the wrongful act or neglect of the carrier.

2.   In the cases referred to in article 14, paragraph 1, and in article 15, the carrier may immediately unload the goods for account of the person entitled to dispose of them and thereupon the carriage shall be deemed to be at an end. The carrier shall then hold the goods on behalf of the person so entitled. He may however entrust them to a third party, and in that case he shall not be under any liability except for the exercise of reasonable care in the choice of such third party. The charges due under the consignment note and all other expenses shall remain chargeable against the goods.

3.   The carrier may sell the goods, without awaiting instructions from the person entitled to dispose of them, if the goods are perishable or their condition warrants such a course, or when the storage expenses would be out of proportion to the value of the goods. He may also proceed to the sale of the goods in other cases if after the expiry of a reasonable period he has not received from the person entitled to dispose of the goods instructions to the contrary which he may reasonably be required to carry out.

4.   If the goods have been sold pursuant to this article, the proceeds of sale, after deduction of the expenses chargeable against the goods, shall be placed at the disposal of the person entitled to dispose of the goods. If these charges exceed the proceeds of sale, the carrier shall be entitled to the difference.

5.   The procedure in the case of sale shall be determined by the law or custom of the place where the goods are situated.

CHAPTER IV
LIABILITY OF THE CARRIER

Article 17

1.   The carrier shall be liable for the total or partial loss of the goods and for damage thereto occurring between the time when he takes over the goods and the time of delivery, as well as for any delay in delivery.

2.   The carrier shall however be relieved of liability if the loss, damage or delay was caused by the wrongful act or neglect of the claimant, by the instructions of the claimant given otherwise than as the result of a wrongful act or neglect on the part of the carrier, by inherent vice of the goods or through circumstances which the carrier could not avoid and the consequences of which he was unable to prevent.

3.   The carrier shall not be relieved of liability by reason of the defective condition of the vehicle used by him in order to perform the carriage, or by reason of the wrongful act or neglect of the person from whom he may have hired the vehicle or of the agents or servants of the latter.

4.   Subject to article 18, paragraphs 2 to 5, the carrier shall be relieved of liability when the loss or damage arises from the special risks inherent in one or more of the following circumstances:
    (a)   use of open unsheeted vehicles, when their use has been expressly agreed and specified in the consignment note;
    (b)   the lack of, or defective condition of packing in the case of goods which, by their nature, are liable to wastage or to be damaged when not packed or when not properly packed;
    (c)   handling, loading, stowage or unloading of the goods by the sender, the consignee or persons acting on behalf of the sender or the consignee;
    (d)   the nature of certain kinds of goods which particularly exposes them to total or partial loss or to damage, especially through breakage, rust, decay, desiccation, leakage, normal wastage, or the action of moth or vermin;
    (e)   insufficiency or inadequacy of marks or numbers on the packages;
    (f)   the carriage of livestock.

5.   Where under this article the carrier is not under any liability in respect of some of the factors causing the loss, damage or delay, he shall only be liable to the extent that those factors for which he is liable under this article have contributed to the loss, damage or delay.

Article 18

1.   The burden of proving that loss, damage or delay was due to one of the causes specified in article 17, paragraph 2, shall rest upon the carrier.

2.   When the carrier establishes that in the circumstances of the case, the loss or damage could be attributed to one or more of the special risks referred to in article 17, paragraph 4, it shall be presumed that it was so caused. The claimant shall however be entitled to prove that the loss or damage was not, in fact, attributable either wholly or partly to one of these risks.

3.   This presumption shall not apply in the circumstances set out in article 17, paragraph 4(a), if there has been an abnormal shortage, or a loss of any package.

4. If the carriage is performed in vehicles specially equipped to protect the goods from the effects of heat, cold, variations in temperature or the humidity of the air, the carrier shall not be entitled to claim the benefit of article 17, paragraph 4(d), unless he proves that all steps incumbent on him in the circumstances with respect to the choice, maintenance and use of such equipment were taken and that he complied with any special instructions issued to him.

5. The carrier shall not be entitled to claim the benefit of article 17, paragraph 4(f), unless he proves that all steps normally incumbent on him in the circumstances were taken and that he complied with any special instructions issued to him.

Article 19

Delay in delivery shall be said to occur when the goods have not been delivered within the agreed time-limit or when, failing an agreed time-limit, the actual duration of the carriage having regard to the circumstances of the case, and in particular, in the case of partial loads, the time required for making up a complete load in the normal way, exceeds the time it would be reasonable to allow a diligent carrier.

Article 20

1. The fact that goods have not been delivered within thirty days following the expiry of the agreed time-limit, or, if there is no agreed time-limit, within sixty days from the time when the carrier took over the goods, shall be conclusive evidence of the loss of the goods, and the person entitled to make a claim may thereupon treat them as lost.

2. The person so entitled may, on receipt of compensation for the missing goods, request in writing that he shall be notified immediately should the goods be recovered in the course of the year following the payment of compensation. He shall be given a written acknowledgment of such request.

3. Within the thirty days following receipt of such notification, the person entitled as aforesaid may require the goods to be delivered to him against payment of the charges shown to be due on the consignment note and also against refund of the compensation he received less any charges included therein but without prejudice to any claims to compensation for delay in delivery under article 23 and, where applicable, article 26.

4. In the absence of the request mentioned in paragraph 2 or of any instructions given within the period of thirty days specified in paragraph 3, or if the goods are not recovered until more than one year after the payment of compensation, the carrier shall be entitled to deal with them in accordance with the law of the place where the goods are situated.

Article 21

Should the goods have been delivered to the consignee without collection of the "cash on delivery" charge which should have been collected by the carrier under the terms of the contract of carriage, the carrier shall be liable to the sender for compensation not exceeding the amount of such charge without prejudice to his right of action against the consignee.

Article 22

1. When the sender hands goods of a dangerous nature to the carrier, he shall inform the carrier of the exact nature of the danger and indicate, if necessary, the precautions to be taken. If this information has not been entered in the consignment note, the burden of proving, by some other means, that the carrier knew the exact nature of the danger constituted by the carriage of the said goods shall rest upon the sender or the consignee.

2. Goods of a dangerous nature which, in the circumstances referred to in paragraph 1 of this article, the carrier did not know were dangerous, may, at any time or place, be unloaded, destroyed or rendered harmless by the carrier without compensation; further, the sender shall be liable for all expenses, loss or damage arising out of their handing over for carriage or of their carriage.

Article 23

1. When, under the provisions of this Convention, a carrier is liable for compensation in respect of total or partial loss of goods, such compensation shall be calculated by reference to the value of the goods at the place and time at which they were accepted for carriage.

2. The value of the goods shall be fixed according to the commodity exchange price or, if there is no such price, according to the current market price or, if there is no commodity exchange price or current market price, by reference to the normal value of goods of the same kind and quality.

[3. Compensation shall not, however, exceed 8.33 units of account per kilogram of gross weight short.]

4. In addition, the carriage charges, Customs duties and other charges incurred in respect of the carriage of the goods shall be refunded in full in case of total loss and in proportion to the loss sustained in case of partial loss, but no further damages shall be payable.

5. In the case of delay, if the claimant proves that damage has resulted therefrom the carrier shall pay compensation for such damage not exceeding the carriage charges.

6. Higher compensation may only be claimed where the value of the goods or a special interest in delivery has been declared in accordance with articles 24 and 26.

[7. The unit of account mentioned in this Convention is the Special Drawing Right as defined by the International Monetary Fund. The amount mentioned in paragraph 3 of this article shall be converted into the national currency of the State of the Court seised of the case on the basis of the value of that currency on the date of the judgment or the date agreed upon by the Parties.]

Article 24

The sender may, against payment of a surcharge to be agreed upon, declare in the consignment note a value for the goods exceeding the limit laid down in article 23, paragraph 3, and in that case the amount of the declared value shall be substituted for that limit.

Article 25

1. In case of damage, the carrier shall be liable for the amount by which the goods have diminished in value, calculated by reference to the value of the goods fixed in accordance with article 23, paragraphs 1, 2 and 4.

2. The compensation may not, however, exceed:
   (a) if the whole consignment has been damaged, the amount payable in the case of total loss;
   (b) if part only of the consignment has been damaged, the amount payable in the case of loss of the part affected.

Article 26

1. The sender may, against payment of a surcharge to be agreed upon, fix the amount of a special interest in delivery in the case of loss or damage or of the agreed time-limit being exceeded, by entering such amount in the consignment note.

2. If a declaration of a special interest in delivery has been made, compensation for the additional loss or damage proved may be claimed, up to the total amount of the interest declared, independently of the compensation provided for in articles 23, 24 and 25.

Article 27

1. The claimant shall be entitled to claim interest on compensation payable. Such interest, calculated at five per centum per annum, shall accrue from the date on which the claim was sent in writing to the carrier or, if no such claim has been made, from the date on which legal proceedings were instituted.

2. When the amounts on which the calculation of the compensation is based are not expressed in the currency of the country in which payment is claimed, conversion shall be at the rate of exchange applicable on the day and at the place of payment of compensation.

Article 28

1. In cases where, under the law applicable, loss, damage or delay arising out of carriage under this Convention gives rise to an extra-contractual claim, the carrier may avail himself of the provisions of this Convention which exclude his liability or which fix or limit the compensation due.

2. In cases where the extra-contractual liability for loss, damage or delay of one of the persons for whom the carrier is responsible under the terms of article 3 is in issue, such person may also avail himself of the provisions of this Convention which exclude the liability of the carrier or which fix or limit the compensation due.

Article 29

1. The carrier shall not be entitled to avail himself of the provisions of this chapter which exclude or limit his liability or which shift the burden of proof if the damage was caused by his wilful misconduct or by such default on his part as, in accordance with the law of the court or tribunal seised of the case, is considered as equivalent to wilful misconduct.

2. The same provision shall apply if the wilful misconduct or default is committed by the agents or servants of the carrier or by any other persons of whose services he makes use for the performance of the carriage, when such agents, servants or other persons are acting within the scope

of their employment. Furthermore, in such a case such agents, servants or other persons shall not be entitled to avail themselves, with regard to their personal liability, of the provisions of this chapter referred to in paragraph 1.

CHAPTER V
CLAIMS AND ACTIONS

Article 30

1. If the consignee takes delivery of the goods without duly checking their condition with the carrier or without sending him reservations giving a general indication of the loss or damage, not later than the time of delivery in the case of apparent loss or damage and within seven days of delivery, Sundays and public holidays excepted, in the case of loss or damage which is not apparent, the fact of his taking delivery shall be *prima facie* evidence that he has received the goods in the condition described in the consignment note. In the case of loss or damage which is not apparent the reservations referred to shall be made in writing.

2. When the condition of the goods has been duly checked by the consignee and the carrier, evidence contradicting the result of this checking shall only be admissible in the case of loss or damage which is not apparent and provided that the consignee has duly sent reservations in writing to the carrier within seven days, Sundays and public holidays excepted, from the date of checking.

3. No compensation shall be payable for delay in delivery unless a reservation has been sent in writing to the carrier, within twenty-one days from the time that the goods were placed at the disposal of the consignee.

4. In calculating the time-limits provided for in this Article the date of delivery, or the date of checking, or the date when the goods were placed at the disposal of the consignee, as the case may be, shall not be included.

5. The carrier and the consignee shall give each other every reasonable facility for making the requisite investigations and checks.

Article 31

1. In legal proceedings arising out of carriage under this Convention, the plaintiff may bring an action in any court or tribunal of a contracting country designated by agreement between the parties and, in addition, in the courts or tribunals of a country within whose territory
    (a)   the defendant is ordinarily resident, or has his principal place of business, or the branch or agency through which the contract of carriage was made, or
    (b)   the place where the goods were taken over by the carrier or the place designated for delivery is situated,
and in no other courts or tribunals.

2. Where in respect of a claim referred to in paragraph 1 of this article an action is pending before a court or tribunal competent under that paragraph, or where in respect of such a claim a judgment has been entered by such a court or tribunal no new action shall be started between the same parties on the same grounds unless the judgment of the court or tribunal before which the first action was brought is not enforceable in the country in which the fresh proceedings are brought.

3. When a judgment entered by a court or tribunal of a contracting country in any such action as is referred to in paragraph 1 of this article has become enforceable in that country, it shall also become enforceable in each of the other contracting States, as soon as the formalities required in the country concerned have been complied with. The formalities shall not permit the merits of the case to be re-opened.

4. The provisions of paragraph 3 of this article shall apply to judgments after trial, judgments by default and settlements confirmed by an order of the court, but shall not apply to interim judgments or to awards of damages, in addition to costs against a plaintiff who wholly or partly fails in his action.

5. Security for costs shall not be required in proceedings arising out of carriage under this Convention from nationals of contracting countries resident or having their place of business in one of those countries.

Article 32

1. The period of limitation for an action arising out of carriage under this Convention shall be one year. Nevertheless, in the case of wilful misconduct, or such default as in accordance with the law of the court or tribunal seised of the case, is considered as equivalent to wilful misconduct, the period of limitation shall be three years. The period of limitation shall begin to run:
    (a)   in the case of partial loss, damage or delay in delivery, from the date of delivery;
    (b)   in the case of total loss, from the thirtieth day after the expiry of the agreed time-limit or where there is no agreed time-limit from the sixtieth day from the date on which the goods were taken over by the carrier;

(c)   in all other cases, on the expiry of a period of three months after the making of the contract of carriage.

The day on which the period of limitation begins to run shall not be included in the period.

2.   A written claim shall suspend the period of limitation until such date as the carrier rejects the claim by notification in writing and returns the documents attached thereto. If a part of the claim is admitted the period of limitation shall start to run again only in respect of that part of the claim still in dispute. The burden of proof of the receipt of the claim, or of the reply and of the return of the documents, shall rest with the party relying upon these facts. The running of the period of limitation shall not be suspended by further claims having the same object.

3.   Subject to the provisions of paragraph 2 above, the extension of the period of limitation shall be governed by the law of the court or tribunal seised of the case. That law shall also govern the fresh accrual of rights of action.

4.   A right of action which has become barred by lapse of time may not be exercised by way of counter-claim or set-off.

PART 1
STATUTES

Article 33

The contract of carriage may contain a clause conferring competence on an arbitration tribunal if the clause conferring competence on the tribunal provides that the tribunal shall apply this Convention.

CHAPTER VI
PROVISIONS RELATING TO CARRIAGE PERFORMED BY SUCCESSIVE CARRIERS

Article 34

If carriage governed by a single contract is performed by successive road carriers, each of them shall be responsible for the performance of the whole operation, the second carrier and each succeeding carrier becoming a party to the contract of carriage, under the terms of the consignment note, by reason of his acceptance of the goods and the consignment note.

Article 35

1.   A carrier accepting the goods from a previous carrier shall give the latter a dated and signed receipt. He shall enter his name and address on the second copy of the consignment note. Where applicable, he shall enter on the second copy of the consignment note and on the receipt reservations of the kind provided for in article 8, paragraph 2.

2.   The provisions of article 9 shall apply to the relations between successive carriers.

Article 36

Except in the case of a counter-claim or a set-off raised in an action concerning a claim based on the same contract of carriage, legal proceedings in respect of liability for loss, damage or delay may only be brought against the first carrier, the last carrier or the carrier who was performing that portion of the carriage during which the event causing the loss, damage or delay occurred; an action may be brought at the same time against several of these carriers.

Article 37

A carrier who has paid compensation in compliance with the provisions of this Convention, shall be entitled to recover such compensation, together with interest thereon and all costs and expenses incurred by reason of the claim, from the other carriers who have taken part in the carriage, subject to the following provisions:

(a)   the carrier responsible for the loss or damage shall be solely liable for the compensation whether paid by himself or by another carrier;

(b)   when the loss or damage has been caused by the action of two or more carriers, each of them shall pay an amount proportionate to his share of liability; should it be impossible to apportion the liability, each carrier shall be liable in proportion to the share of the payment for the carriage which is due to him;

(c)   if it cannot be ascertained to which carriers liability is attributable for the loss or damage, the amount of the compensation shall be apportioned between all the carriers as laid down in (b) above.

Article 38

If one of the carriers is insolvent, the share of the compensation due from him and unpaid by him shall be divided among the other carriers in proportion to the share of the payment for the carriage due to them.

Article 39

1. No carrier against whom a claim is made under articles 37 and 38 shall be entitled to dispute the validity of the payment made by the carrier making the claim if the amount of the compensation was determined by judicial authority after the first mentioned carrier had been given due notice of the proceedings and afforded an opportunity of entering an appearance.

2. A carrier wishing to take proceedings to enforce his right of recovery may make his claim before the competent court or tribunal of the country in which one of the carriers concerned is ordinarily resident, or has his principal place of business or the branch or agency through which the contract of carriage was made. All the carriers concerned may be made defendants in the same action.

3. The provisions of article 31, paragraphs 3 and 4, shall apply to judgments entered in the proceedings referred to in articles 37 and 38.

4. The provisions of article 32 shall apply to claims between carriers. The period of limitation shall, however, begin to run either on the date of the final judicial decision fixing the amount of compensation payable under the provisions of this Convention, or, if there is no such judicial decision, from the actual date of payment.

Article 40

Carriers shall be free to agree among themselves on provisions other than those laid down in articles 37 and 38.

CHAPTER VII
NULLITY OF STIPULATIONS CONTRARY TO THE CONVENTION

Article 41

1. Subject to the provisions of Article 40, any stipulation which would directly or indirectly derogate from the provisions of this Convention shall be null and void. The nullity of such a stipulation shall not involve the nullity of the other provisions of the contract.

2. In particular, a benefit of insurance in favour of the carrier or any other similar clause, or any clause shifting the burden of proof shall be null and void.

[Chapter VIII of the Convention is not reproduced. This deals with the coming into force of the Convention, the settlement of disputes between the High Contracting Parties and related matters.]

PROTOCOL OF SIGNATURE

1. This Convention shall not apply to traffic between the United Kingdom of Great Britain and Northern Ireland and the Republic of Ireland.

[417]

NOTES

Article 23: para 3 substituted and para 7 added by the Carriage by Air and Road Act 1979, s 4(2).

ARBITRATION (INTERNATIONAL INVESTMENT DISPUTES) ACT 1966

(1966 c 41)

ARRANGEMENT OF SECTIONS

An Act to implement an international Convention on the settlement of investment disputes between States and nationals of other States

[13 December 1966]

Enforcement of Convention Awards

1 Registration of Convention awards

(1)   This section has effect as respects awards rendered pursuant to the Convention on the settlement of investment disputes between States and nationals of other States which was opened for signature in Washington on 18th March 1965.

That Convention is in this Act called "the Convention", and its text is set out in the Schedule to this Act.

(2)   A person seeking recognition or enforcement of such an award shall be entitled to have the award registered in the High Court subject to proof of the prescribed matters and to the other provisions of this Act.

(3) ...

(4)   In addition to the pecuniary obligations imposed by the award, the award shall be registered for the reasonable costs of and incidental to registration.

(5)   If at the date of the application for registration the pecuniary obligations imposed by the award have been partly satisfied, the award shall be registered only in respect of the balance, and accordingly if those obligations have then been wholly satisfied, the award shall not be registered.

(6)   The power to make rules of court under section [84 of the [Senior Courts Act 1981]] shall include power—

    (a)   to prescribe the procedure for applying for registration under this section, and to require an applicant to give prior notice of his intention to other parties,

    (b)   to prescribe the matters to be proved on the application and the manner of proof, and in particular to require the applicant to furnish a copy of the award certified pursuant to the Convention,

    (c)   to provide for the service of notice of registration of the award by the applicant on other parties,

and in this and the next following section "prescribed" means prescribed by rules of court.

(7)   For the purposes of this and the next following section—

    (a)   "award" shall include any decision interpreting, revising or annulling an award, being a decision pursuant to the Convention, and any decision as to costs which under the Convention is to form part of the award,

    (b)   an award shall be deemed to have been rendered pursuant to the Convention on the date on which certified copies of the award were pursuant to the Convention dispatched to the parties.

(8)   This and the next following section shall bind the Crown (but not so as to make an award enforceable against the Crown in a manner in which a judgment would not be enforceable against the Crown).

[418]

NOTES

Sub-s (3): repealed by the Administration of Justice Act 1977, ss 4(1), (2), (4), 32(4), Sch 5, Pt I, except in relation to awards registered before 29 August 1977.

Sub-s (6): words in first (outer) pair of square brackets substituted by the Senior Courts Act 1981, s 152(1), Sch 5; words in second (inner) pair of square brackets substituted by the Constitutional Reform Act 2005, s 59(5), Sch 11, Pt 1, para 1(2).

2 Effect of registration

(1)   Subject to the provisions of this Act, an award registered under section 1 above shall, as respects the pecuniary obligations which it imposes, be of the same force and effect for the purposes of execution as if it had been a judgment of the High Court given when the award was rendered pursuant to the Convention and entered on the date of registration under this Act, and, so far as relates to such pecuniary obligations—

    (a)   proceedings may be taken on the award,

    (b)   the sum for which the award is registered shall carry interest,

    (c)   the High Court shall have the same control over the execution of the award,

as if the award had been such a judgment of the High Court.

(2)   Rules of court under section [84 of the [Senior Courts Act 1981]] may contain provisions requiring the court on proof of the prescribed matters to stay execution of any award registered under this Act so as to take account of cases where enforcement of the award has been stayed (whether provisionally or otherwise) pursuant to the Convention, and may provide for the provisional stay of execution of the award where an application is made pursuant to the Convention which, if granted, might result in a stay of enforcement of the award.

[419]

NOTES
Sub-s (2): words in first (outer) pair of square brackets substituted by the Senior Courts Act 1981, s 152(1), Sch 5; words in second (inner) pair of square brackets substituted by the Constitutional Reform Act 2005, s 59(5), Sch 11, Pt 1, para 1(2).

Procedural Provisions

[3   Application of provisions of Arbitration Act 1996
(1)   The Lord Chancellor may by order direct that any of the provisions contained in sections 36 and 38 to 44 of the Arbitration Act 1996 (provisions concerning the conduct of arbitral proceedings, &c) shall apply to such proceedings pursuant to the Convention as are specified in the order with or without any modifications or exceptions specified in the order.

(2)   Subject to subsection (1), the Arbitration Act 1996 shall not apply to proceedings pursuant to the Convention, but this subsection shall not be taken as affecting section 9 of that Act (stay of legal proceedings in respect of matter subject to arbitration).

(3)   An order made under this section—
   (a)   may be varied or revoked by a subsequent order so made, and
   (b)   shall be contained in a statutory instrument.]

[420]

NOTES
Substituted by the Arbitration Act 1996, s 107(1), Sch 3, para 24.

Immunities and Privileges

4   Status, immunities and privileges conferred by the Convention
(1)   In Section 6 of Chapter I of the Convention (which governs the status, immunities and privileges of the International Centre for Settlements of Investment Disputes established by the Convention, of members of its Council and Secretariat and of persons concerned with conciliation or arbitration under the Convention) Articles 18 to 20, Article 21 (a) (with Article 22 as it applies Article 21 (a)), Article 23 (1) and Article 24 shall have the force of law.

(2)   Nothing in Article 24 (1) of the Convention as given the force of law by this section shall be construed as—
   (a)   entitling the said Centre to import goods free of customs duty without any restriction on their subsequent sale in the country to which they were imported, or
   (b)   conferring on that Centre any exemption from duties or taxes which form part of the price of goods sold, or
   (c)   conferring on that Centre any exemption from duties or taxes which are no more than charges for services rendered.

(3)   For the purposes of Article 20 and Article 21 (a) of the Convention as given the force of law by this section, a statement to the effect that the said Centre has waived an immunity in the circumstances specified in the statement, being a statement certified by the Secretary-General of the said Centre (or by the person acting as Secretary-General), shall be conclusive evidence.

[421]

Supplemental

5   Government contribution to expenses under the Convention
The Treasury may discharge any obligations of Her Majesty's Government in the United Kingdom arising under Article 17 of the Convention (which obliges the Contracting States to meet any deficit of the International Centre for Settlement of Investment Disputes established under the Convention), and any sums required for that purpose shall be met out of money provided by Parliament.

[422]

6   Application to British possessions, etc
(1)   Her Majesty may by Order in Council direct that the provisions of this Act shall extend, with such exceptions, adaptations and modifications as may be specified in the Order, to—
   (a)   the Isle of Man,

(b)   any of the Channel Islands,
(c)   any colony, or any country or place outside Her Majesty's dominions in which for the time being Her Majesty has jurisdiction, or any territory consisting partly of one or more colonies and partly of one or more such countries or places.

(2)   An Order in Council under this section—
(a)   may contain such transitional and other supplemental provisions as appear to Her Majesty to be expedient;
(b)   may be varied or revoked by a subsequent Order in Council under this section.

[423]

NOTES
    Orders in Council: the Arbitration (International Investment Disputes) Act 1966 (Application to Colonies etc) Order 1967, SI 1967/159; the Arbitration (International Investment Disputes) Act 1966 (Application to Tonga) Order 1967, SI 1967/585; the Arbitration (International Investment Disputes) (Guernsey) Order 1968, SI 1968/1199; the Arbitration (International Investment Disputes) (Jersey) Order 1979, SI 1979/572.

7, 8   (*S 7 applies to Scotland only; s 8 applies to Northern Ireland only.*)

9   Short title and commencement

(1)   This Act may be cited as the Arbitration (International Investment Disputes) Act 1966.

(2)   This Act shall come into force on such day as Her Majesty may by Order in Council certify to be the day on which the Convention comes into force as regards the United Kingdom.

[424]

NOTES
    Order in Council: the Arbitration (International Investment Disputes) Act 1966 (Commencement) Order 1966, SI 1966/1597.

SCHEDULE
TEXT OF CONVENTION
Section 1

CONVENTION ON THE SETTLEMENT OF INVESTMENT DISPUTES BETWEEN STATES AND NATIONALS OF OTHER STATES

PREAMBLE

The Contracting States

Considering the need for international co-operation for economic development, and the role of private international investment therein;

Bearing in mind the possibility that from time to time disputes may arise in connection with such investment between Contracting States and nationals of other Contracting States;

Recognizing that while such disputes would usually be subject to national legal processes, international methods of settlement may be appropriate in certain cases;

Attaching particular importance to the availability of facilities for international conciliation or arbitration to which Contracting States and nationals of other Contracting States may submit such disputes if they so desire;

Desiring to establish such facilities under the auspices of the International Bank for Reconstruction and Development;

Recognizing that mutual consent by the parties to submit such disputes to conciliation or to arbitration through such facilities constitutes a binding agreement which requires in particular that due consideration be given to any recommendation of conciliators, and that any arbitral award be complied with; and

Declaring that no Contracting State shall by the mere fact of its ratification acceptance or approval of this Convention and without its consent be deemed to be under any obligation to submit any particular dispute to conciliation or arbitration.

Have agreed as follows:

CHAPTER I
INTERNATIONAL CENTRE FOR SETTLEMENT OF INVESTMENT DISPUTES

SECTION 1
ESTABLISHMENT AND ORGANIZATION

Article 1

(1)   There is hereby established the International Centre for Settlement of Investment Disputes (hereinafter called the Centre).

(2)   The purpose of the Centre shall be to provide facilities for conciliation and arbitration of investment disputes between Contracting States and nationals of other Contracting States in accordance with the provisions of this Convention.

Article 2

The seat of the Centre shall be at the principal office of the International Bank for Reconstruction and Development (hereinafter called the Bank).

The seat may be moved to another place by decision of the Administrative Council adopted by a majority of two-thirds of its members.

Article 3

The Centre shall have an Administrative Council and a Secretariat and shall maintain a Panel of Conciliators and a Panel of Arbitrators.

SECTION 2
THE ADMINISTRATIVE COUNCIL

Article 4

(1)   The Administrative Council shall be composed of one representative of each Contracting State. An alternate may act as representative in case of his principal's absence from a meeting or inability to act.

(2)   In the absence of a contrary designation, each governor and alternate governor of the Bank appointed by a Contracting State shall be *ex officio* its representative and its alternate respectively.

Article 5

The President of the Bank shall be ex officio Chairman of the Administrative Council (hereinafter called the Chairman) but shall have no vote. During his absence or inability to act and during any vacancy in the office of President of the Bank, the person for the time being acting as President shall act as Chairman of the Administrative Council.

Article 6

(1)   Without prejudice to the powers and functions vested in it by other provisions of this Convention, the Administrative Council shall
  (a)   adopt the administrative and financial regulations of the Centre;
  (b)   adopt the rules of procedure for the institution of conciliation and arbitration proceedings;
  (c)   adopt the rules of procedure for conciliation and arbitration proceedings (hereinafter called the Conciliation Rules and the Arbitration Rules);
  (d)   approve arrangements with the Bank for the use of the Bank's administrative facilities and services;
  (e)   determine the conditions of service of the Secretary-General and of any Deputy Secretary-General;
  (f)   adopt the annual budget of revenues and expenditures of the Centre;
  (g)   approve the annual report on the operation of the Centre.
The decisions referred to in sub-paragraphs (a), (b), (c) and (f) above shall be adopted by a majority of two-thirds of the members of the Administrative Council.

(2)   The Administrative Council may appoint such committees as it considers necessary.

(3)   The Administrative Council shall also exercise such other powers and perform such other functions as it shall determine to be necessary for the implementation of the provisions of this Convention.

Article 7

(1)   The Administrative Council shall hold an annual meeting and such other meetings as may be determined by the Council, or convened by the Chairman, or convened by the Secretary-General at the request of not less than five members of the Council.

(2)   Each member of the Administrative Council shall have one vote and, except as otherwise herein provided, all matters before the Council shall be decided by a majority of the votes cast.

(3)   A quorum for any meeting of the Administrative Council shall be a majority of its members.

(4)   The Administrative Council may establish, by a majority of two-thirds of its members, a procedure whereby the Chairman may seek a vote of the Council without convening a meeting of the Council. The vote shall be considered valid only if the majority of the members of the Council cast their votes within the time limit by the said procedure.

Article 8

Members of the Administrative Council and the Chairman shall serve without remuneration from the Centre.

SECTION 3
THE SECRETARIAT

Article 9

The Secretariat shall consist of a Secretary-General, one or more Deputy Secretaries-General and staff.

Article 10

(1)   The Secretary-General and any Deputy Secretary-General shall be elected by the Administrative Council by a majority of two-thirds of its members upon the nomination of the Chairman for a term of service not exceeding six years and shall be eligible for re-election. After consulting the members of the Administrative Council, the Chairman shall propose one or more candidates for each such office.

(2)   The offices of Secretary-General and Deputy Secretary-General shall be incompatible with the exercise of any political function. Neither the Secretary-General nor any Deputy Secretary-General may hold any other employment or engage in any other occupation except with the approval of the Administrative Council.

(3)   During the Secretary-General's absence or inability to act, and during any vacancy of the office of Secretary-General, the Deputy Secretary-General shall act as Secretary-General. If there shall be more than one Deputy Secretary-General, the Administrative Council shall determine in advance the order in which they shall act as Secretary-General.

Article 11

The Secretary-General shall be the legal representative and the principal officer of the Centre and shall be responsible for its administration, including the appointment of staff, in accordance with the provisions of this Convention and the rules adopted by the Administrative Council. He shall perform the function of registrar and shall have the power to authenticate arbitral awards rendered pursuant to this Convention, and to certify copies thereof.

SECTION 4
THE PANELS

Article 12

The Panel of Conciliators and the Panel of Arbitrators shall each consist of qualified persons, designated as hereinafter provided, who are willing to serve thereon.

Article 13

(1)   Each Contracting State may designate to each Panel four persons who may but need not be its nationals.

(2)   The Chairman may designate ten persons to each Panel. The persons so designated to a Panel shall each have a different nationality.

Article 14

(1)   Persons designated to serve on the Panels shall be persons of high moral character and recognized competence in the fields of law, commerce, industry or finance, who may be relied upon to exercise independent judgment. Competence in the field of law shall be of particular importance in the case of persons on the Panel of Arbitrators.

(2)   The Chairman, in designating persons to serve on the Panels, shall in addition pay due regard to the importance of assuring representation on the Panels of the principal legal systems of the world and of the main forms of economic activity.

PART 1
STATUTES

Article 15

(1)   Panel members shall serve for renewable periods of six years.

(2)   In case of death or resignation of a member of a Panel, the authority which designated the member shall have the right to designate another person to serve for the remainder of that member's term.

(3)   Panel members shall continue in office until their successors have been designated.

Article 16

(1)   A person may serve on both Panels.

(2)   If a person shall have been designated to serve on the same Panel by more than one Contracting State, or by one or more Contracting States and the Chairman, he shall be deemed to have been designated by the authority which first designated him or, if one such authority is the State of which he is a national, by that State.

(3)   All designations shall be notified to the Secretary-General and shall take effect from the date on which the notification is received.

SECTION 5
FINANCING THE CENTRE

Article 17

If the expenditure of the Centre cannot be met out of charges for the use of its facilities, or out of other receipts, the excess shall be borne by Contracting States which are members of the Bank in proportion to their respective subscriptions to the capital stock of the Bank, and by Contracting States which are not members of the Bank in accordance with rules adopted by the Administrative Council.

SECTION 6
STATUS, IMMUNITIES AND PRIVILEGES

Article 18

The Centre shall have full international legal personality. The legal capacity of the Centre shall include the capacity
  (a)   to contract;
  (b)   to acquire and dispose of movable and immovable property;
  (c)   to institute legal proceedings.

Article 19

To enable the Centre to fulfil its functions, it shall enjoy in the territories of each Contracting State the immunities and privileges set forth in this Section.

Article 20

The Centre, its property and assets shall enjoy immunity from all legal process, except when the Centre waives this immunity.

Article 21

The Chairman, the members of the Administrative Council, persons acting as conciliators or arbitrators or members of a Committee appointed pursuant to paragraph (3) of Article 52, and the officers and employees of the Secretariat
  (a)   shall enjoy immunity from legal process with respect to acts performed by them in the exercise of their functions, except when the Centre waives this immunity;
  (b)   not being local nationals, shall enjoy the same immunities from immigration restrictions, alien registration requirements and national service obligations, the same facilities as regards exchange restrictions and the same treatment in respect of travelling facilities as are accorded by Contracting States to the representatives, officials and employees of comparable rank of other Contracting States.

Article 22

The provisions of Article 21 shall apply to persons appearing in proceedings under this Convention as parties, agents, counsel, advocates, witnesses or experts; provided, however, that sub-paragraph (b) thereof shall apply only in connection with their travel to and from, and their stay at, the place where the proceedings are held.

Article 23

(1)   The archives of the Centre shall be inviolable, wherever they may be.

(2)   With regard to its official communications, the Centre shall be accorded by each Contracting State treatment not less favourable than that accorded to other international organizations.

Article 24

(1)   The Centre, its assets, property and income, and its operations and transactions authorized by this Convention shall be exempt from all taxation and customs duties. The Centre shall also be exempt from liability for the collection or payment of any taxes or customs duties.

(2)   Except in the case of local nationals, no tax shall be levied on or in respect of expense allowances paid by the Centre to the Chairman or members of the Administrative Council, or on or in respect of salaries, expense allowances or other emoluments paid by the Centre to officials or employees of the Secretariat.

(3)   No tax shall be levied on or in respect of fees or expense allowances received by persons acting as conciliators, or arbitrators, or members of a Committee appointed pursuant to paragraph (3) of Article 52, in proceedings under this Convention, if the sole jurisdictional basis for such tax is the location of the Centre or the place where such proceedings are conducted or the place where such fees or allowances are paid.

CHAPTER II
JURISDICTION OF THE CENTRE

Article 25

(1)   The jurisdiction of the Centre shall extend to any legal dispute arising directly out of an investment, between a Contracting State (or any constituent subdivision or agency of a Contracting State designated to the Centre by that State) and a national of another Contracting State, which the parties to the dispute consent in writing to submit to the Centre. When the parties have given their consent, no party may withdraw its consent unilaterally.

(2)   "National of another Contracting State" means:
  (a)   any natural person who had the nationality of a Contracting State other than the State party to the dispute on the date on which the parties consented to submit such dispute to conciliation or arbitration as well as on the date on which the request was registered pursuant to paragraph (3) of Article 28 or paragraph (3) of Article 36, but does not include any person who on either date also had the nationality of the Contracting State party to the dispute; and
  (b)   any juridical person which had the nationality of a Contracting State other than the State party to the dispute on the date on which the parties consented to submit such dispute to conciliation or arbitration and any juridical person which had the nationality of the Contracting State party to the dispute on that date and which, because of foreign control, the parties have agreed should be treated as a national of another Contracting State for the purposes of this Convention.

(3)   Consent by a constituent subdivision or agency of a Contracting State shall require the approval of that State unless that State notifies the Centre that no such approval is required.

(4)   Any Contracting State may, at the time of ratification, acceptance or approval of this Convention or at any time thereafter, notify the Centre of the class or classes of disputes which it would or would not consider submitting to the jurisdiction of the Centre. The Secretary-General shall forthwith transmit such notification to all Contracting States. Such notification shall not constitute the consent required by paragraph (1).

Article 26

Consent of the parties to arbitration under this Convention shall, unless otherwise stated, be deemed consent to such arbitration to the exclusion of any other remedy. A Contracting State may require the exhaustion of local administrative or judicial remedies as a condition of its consent to arbitration under this Convention.

Article 27

(1)   No Contracting State shall give diplomatic protection, or bring an international claim, in respect of a dispute which one of its nationals and another Contracting State shall have consented to submit or shall have submitted to arbitration under this Convention, unless such other Contracting State shall have failed to abide by and comply with the award rendered in such dispute.

(2)   Diplomatic protection, for the purposes of paragraph (1), shall not include informal diplomatic exchanges for the sole purpose of facilitating a settlement of the dispute.

CHAPTER III
CONCILIATION

SECTION 1
REQUEST FOR CONCILIATION

Article 28

(1)   Any Contracting State or any national of a Contracting State wishing to institute conciliation proceedings shall address a request to that effect in writing to the Secretary-General who shall send a copy of the request to the other party.

(2)   The request shall contain information concerning the issues in dispute, the identity of the parties and their consent to conciliation in accordance with the rules of procedure for the institution of conciliation and arbitration proceedings.

(3)   The Secretary-General shall register the request unless he finds, on the basis of the information contained in the request, that the dispute is manifestly outside the jurisdiction of the Centre. He shall forthwith notify the parties of registration or refusal to register.

SECTION 2
CONSTITUTION OF THE CONCILIATION COMMISSION

Article 29

(1)   The Conciliation Commission (hereinafter called the Commission) shall be constituted as soon as possible after registration of a request pursuant to Article 28.

(2)
  (a)   The Commission shall consist of a sole conciliator or any uneven number of conciliators appointed as the parties shall agree.
  (b)   Where the parties do not agree upon the number of conciliators and the method of their appointment, the Commission shall consist of three conciliators, one conciliator appointed by each party and the third, who shall be the president of the Commission, appointed by agreement of the parties.

Article 30

If the Commission shall not have been constituted within 90 days after notice of registration of the request has been dispatched by the Secretary-General in accordance with paragraph (3) of Article 28, or such other period as the parties may agree, the Chairman shall, at the request of either party and after consulting both parties as far as possible, appoint the conciliator or conciliators not yet appointed.

Article 31

(1)   Conciliators may be appointed from outside the Panel of Conciliators, except in the case of appointments by the Chairman pursuant to Article 30.

(2)   Conciliators appointed from outside the Panel of Conciliators shall possess the qualities stated in paragraph (1) of Article 14.

SECTION 3
CONCILIATION PROCEEDINGS

Article 32

(1)   The Commission shall be the judge of its own competence.

(2)   Any objection by a party to the dispute that that dispute is not within the jurisdiction of the Centre, or for other reasons is not within the competence of the Commission, shall be considered by the Commission which shall determine whether to deal with it as a preliminary question or to join it to the merits of the dispute.

Article 33

Any conciliation proceeding shall be conducted in accordance with the provisions of this Section and, except as the parties otherwise agree, in accordance with the Conciliation Rules in effect on the date on which the parties consented to conciliation. If any question of procedure arises which is not covered by this Section or the Conciliation Rules or any rules agreed by the parties, the Commission shall decide the question.

Article 34

(1)   It shall be the duty of the Commission to clarify the issues in dispute between the parties and to endeavour to bring about agreement between them upon mutually acceptable terms. To that

end, the Commission may at any stage of the proceedings and from time to time recommend terms of settlement to the parties. The parties shall cooperate in good faith with the Commission in order to enable the Commission to carry out its functions, and shall give their most serious consideration to its recommendations.

(2)   If the parties reach agreement, the Commission shall draw up a report noting the issues in dispute and recording that the parties have reached agreement. If, at any stage of the proceedings, it appears to the Commission that there is no likelihood of agreement between the parties, it shall close the proceedings and shall draw up a report noting the submission of the dispute and recording the failure of the parties to reach agreement. If one party fails to appear or participate in the proceedings, the Commission shall close the proceedings and shall draw up a report noting that party's failure to appear or participate.

Article 35

Except as the parties to the dispute shall otherwise agree, neither party to a conciliation proceeding shall be entitled in any other proceeding, whether before arbitrators or in a court of law or otherwise, to invoke or rely on any views expressed or statements or admissions or offers of settlement made by the other party in the conciliation proceedings, or the report or any recommendations made by the Commission.

CHAPTER IV
ARBITRATION

SECTION 1
REQUEST FOR ARBITRATION

Article 36

(1)   Any Contracting State or any national of a Contracting State wishing to institute arbitration proceedings shall address a request to that effect in writing to the Secretary-General who shall send a copy of the request to the other party.

(2)   The request shall contain information concerning the issues in dispute, the identity of the parties and their consent to arbitration in accordance with the rules of procedure for the institution of conciliation and arbitration proceedings.

(3)   The Secretary-General shall register the request unless he finds, on the basis of the information contained in the request, that the dispute is manifestly outside the jurisdiction of the Centre. He shall forthwith notify the parties of registration or refusal to register.

SECTION 2
CONSTITUTION OF THE TRIBUNAL

Article 37

(1)   The Arbitral Tribunal (hereinafter called the Tribunal) shall be constituted as soon as possible after registration of a request pursuant to Article 36.

(2)
- (a)   The Tribunal shall consist of a sole arbitrator or any uneven number of arbitrators appointed as the parties shall agree.
- (b)   Where the parties do not agree upon the number of arbitrators and the method of their appointment, the Tribunal shall consist of three arbitrators, one arbitrator appointed by each party and the third, who shall be the president of the Tribunal, appointed by agreement of the parties.

Article 38

If the Tribunal shall not have been constituted within 90 days after notice of registration of the request has been dispatched by the Secretary-General in accordance with paragraph (3) of Article 36, or such other period as the parties may agree, the Chairman shall, at the request of either party and after consulting both parties as far as possible, appoint the arbitrator or arbitrators not yet appointed. Arbitrators appointed by the Chairman pursuant to this Article shall not be nationals of the Contracting State party to the dispute or of the Contracting State whose national is a party to the dispute.

Article 39

The majority of the arbitrators shall be nationals of States other than the Contracting State party to the dispute and the Contracting State whose national is a party to the dispute; provided, however, that the foregoing provisions of this Article shall not apply if the sole arbitrator or each individual member of the Tribunal has been appointed by agreement of the parties.

Article 40

(1)   Arbitrators may be appointed from outside the Panel of Arbitrators, except in the case of appointments by the Chairman pursuant to Article 38.

(2)   Arbitrators appointed from outside the Panel of Arbitrators shall possess the qualities stated in paragraph (1) of Article 14.

SECTION 3
POWERS AND FUNCTIONS OF THE TRIBUNAL

Article 41

(1)   The Tribunal shall be the judge of its own competence.

(2)   Any objection by a party to the dispute that that dispute is not within the jurisdiction of the Centre, or for other reasons is not within the competence of the Tribunal, shall be considered by the Tribunal which shall determine whether to deal with it as a preliminary question or to join it to the merits of the dispute.

Article 42

(1)   The Tribunal shall decide a dispute in accordance with such rules of law as may be agreed by the parties. In the absence of such agreement, the Tribunal shall apply the law of the Contracting State party to the dispute (including its rules on the conflict of laws) and such rules of international law as may be applicable.

(2)   The Tribunal may not bring in a finding of *non liquet* on the ground of silence or obscurity of the law.

(3)   The provisions of paragraphs (1) and (2) shall not prejudice the power of the Tribunal to decide a dispute *ex aequo et bono* if the parties so agree.

Article 43

Except as the parties otherwise agree, the Tribunal may, if it deems it necessary at any stage of the proceedings,
    (a)   call upon the parties to produce documents or other evidence, and
    (b)   visit the scene connected with the dispute, and conduct such enquiries there as it may deem appropriate.

Article 44

Any arbitration proceeding shall be conducted in accordance with the provisions of this Section and, except as the parties otherwise agree, in accordance with the Arbitration Rules in effect on the date on which the parties consented to arbitration. If any question of procedure arises which is not covered by this Section or the Arbitration Rules or any rules agreed by the parties, the Tribunal shall decide the question.

Article 45

(1)   Failure of a party to appear or to present his case shall not be deemed an admission of the other party's assertions.

(2)   If a party fails to appear or to present his case at any stage of the proceedings the other party may request the Tribunal to deal with the questions submitted to it and to render an award. Before rendering an award, the Tribunal shall notify, and grant a period of grace to, the party failing to appear or to present its case, unless it is satisfied that that party does not intend to do so.

Article 46

Except as the parties otherwise agree, the Tribunal shall, if requested by a party, determine any incidental or additional claims or counter-claims arising directly out of the subject-matter of the dispute provided that they are within the scope of the consent of the parties and are otherwise within the jurisdiction of the Centre.

Article 47

Except as the parties otherwise agree, the Tribunal may, if it considers that the circumstances so require, recommend any provisional measures which should be taken to preserve the respective rights of either party.

SECTION 4
THE AWARD

Article 48

(1)   The Tribunal shall decide questions by a majority of the votes of all its members.

(2)   The award of the Tribunal shall be in writing and shall be signed by the members of the Tribunal who voted for it.

(3)   The award shall deal with every question submitted to the Tribunal, and shall state the reasons upon which it is based.

(4)   Any member of the Tribunal may attach his individual opinion to the award, whether he dissents from the majority or not, or a statement of his dissent.

(5)   The Centre shall not publish the award without the consent of the parties.

Article 49

(1)   The Secretary-General shall promptly dispatch certified copies of the award to the parties. The award shall be deemed to have been rendered on the date on which the certified copies were dispatched.

(2)   The Tribunal upon the request of a party made within 45 days after the date on which the award was rendered may after notice to the other party decide any question which it had omitted to decide in the award, and shall rectify any clerical, arithmetical or similar error in the award. Its decision shall become part of the award and shall be notified to the parties in the same manner as the award. The periods of time provided for under paragraph (2) of Article 51 and paragraph (2) of Article 52 shall run from the date on which the decision was rendered.

SECTION 5
INTERPRETATION, REVISION AND ANNULMENT OF THE AWARD

Article 50

(1)   If any dispute shall arise between the parties as to the meaning or scope of an award, either party may request interpretation of the award by an application in writing addressed to the Secretary-General.

(2)   The request shall, if possible, be submitted to the Tribunal which rendered the award. If this shall not be possible, a new Tribunal shall be constituted in accordance with Section 2 of this Chapter. The Tribunal may, if it considers that the circumstances so require, stay enforcement of the award pending its decision.

Article 51

(1)   Either party may request revision of the award by an application in writing addressed to the Secretary-General on the ground of discovery of some fact of such a nature as decisively to affect the award, provided that when the award was rendered that fact was unknown to the Tribunal and to the applicant and that the applicant's ignorance of that fact was not due to negligence.

(2)   The application shall be made within 90 days after the discovery of such fact and in any event within three years after the date on which the award was rendered.

(3)   The request shall, if possible, be submitted to the Tribunal which rendered the award. If this shall not be possible, a new Tribunal shall be constituted in accordance with Section 2 of this Chapter.

(4)   The Tribunal may, if it considers that the circumstances so require, stay enforcement of the award pending its decision. If the applicant requests stay of enforcement of the award in his application, enforcement shall be stayed provisionally until the Tribunal rules on such request.

Article 52

(1)   Either party may request annulment of the award by an application in writing addressed to the Secretary-General on one or more of the following grounds:
    (a)   that the Tribunal was not properly constituted;
    (b)   that the Tribunal has manifestly exceeded its powers;
    (c)   that there was corruption on the part of a member of the Tribunal;
    (d)   that there has been a serious departure from a fundamental rule of procedure; or
    (e)   that the award has failed to state the reasons on which it is based.

(2)   The application shall be made within 120 days after the date on which the award was rendered except that when annulment is requested on the ground of corruption such application shall be made within 120 days after discovery of the corruption and in any event within three years after the date on which the award was rendered.

(3)   On receipt of the request the Chairman shall forthwith appoint from the Panel of Arbitrators an *ad hoc* Committee of three persons. None of the members of the Committee shall have been a member of the Tribunal which rendered the award, shall be of the same nationality as any such member, shall be a national of the State party to the dispute or of the State whose national is a party to the dispute, shall have been designated to the Panel of Arbitrators by either of those States, or shall have acted as a conciliator in the same dispute. The Committee shall have the authority to annul the award or any part thereof on any of the grounds set forth in paragraph (1).

(4)   The provisions of Articles 41–45, 48, 49, 53 and 54, and of Chapters VI and VII shall apply *mutatis mutandis* to proceedings before the Committee.

(5)   The Committee may, if it considers that circumstances so require, stay enforcement of the award pending its decision. If the applicant requests a stay of enforcement of the award in his application, enforcement shall be stayed provisionally until the Committee rules on such request.

(6)   If the award is annulled the dispute shall, at the request of either party, be submitted to a new Tribunal constituted in accordance with Section 2 of this Chapter.

SECTION 6
RECOGNITION AND ENFORCEMENT OF THE AWARD

Article 53

(1)   The award shall be binding on the parties and shall not be subject to any appeal or to any other remedy except those provided for in this Convention. Each party shall abide by and comply with the terms of the award except to the extent that enforcement shall have been stayed pursuant to the relevant provisions of this Convention.

(2)   For the purposes of this Section, "award" shall include any decision interpreting, revising or annulling such award pursuant to Articles 50, 51 or 52.

Article 54

(1)   Each Contracting State shall recognize an award rendered pursuant to this Convention as binding and enforce the pecuniary obligations imposed by that award within its territories as if it were a final judgment of a court in that State. A Contracting State with a federal constitution may enforce such an award in or through its federal courts and may provide that such courts shall treat the award as if it were a final judgment of the courts of a constituent state.

(2)   A party seeking recognition or enforcement in the territories of a Contracting State shall furnish to a competent court or other authority which such State shall have designated for this purpose a copy of the award certified by the Secretary-General. Each Contracting State shall notify the Secretary-General of the designation of the competent court or other authority for this purpose and of any subsequent change in such designation.

(3)   Execution of the award shall be governed by the laws concerning the execution of judgments in force in the State in whose territories such execution is sought.

Article 55

Nothing in Article 54 shall be construed as derogating from the law in force in any Contracting State relating to immunity of that State or of any foreign State from execution.

CHAPTER V
REPLACEMENT AND DISQUALIFICATION OF CONCILIATORS AND ARBITRATORS

Article 56

(1)   After a Commission or a Tribunal has been constituted and proceedings have begun, its composition shall remain unchanged; provided, however, that if a conciliator or an arbitrator should die, become incapacitated, or resign, the resulting vacancy shall be filled in accordance with the provisions of Section 2 of Chapter III or Section 2 of Chapter IV.

(2)   A member of the Commission or Tribunal shall continue to serve in that capacity notwithstanding that he shall have ceased to be a member of the Panel.

(3)   If a conciliator or arbitrator appointed by a party shall have resigned without the consent of the Commission or Tribunal of which he was a member, the Chairman shall appoint a person from the appropriate Panel to fill the resulting vacancy.

Article 57

A party may propose to a Commission or Tribunal the disqualification of any of its members on account of any fact indicating a manifest lack of the qualities required by paragraph (1) of

Article 14. A party to arbitration proceedings may, in addition, propose the disqualification of an arbitrator on the ground that he was ineligible for appointment to the Tribunal under Section 2 of Chapter IV.

Article 58

The decision on any proposal to disqualify a conciliator or arbitrator shall be taken by the other members of the Commission or Tribunal as the case may be, provided that where those members are equally divided, or in the case of a proposal to disqualify a sole conciliator or arbitrator, or a majority of the conciliators or arbitrators, the Chairman shall take that decision. If it is decided that the proposal is well-founded the conciliator or arbitrator to whom the decision relates shall be replaced in accordance with the provisions of Section 2 of Chapter III or Section 2 of Chapter IV.

CHAPTER VI
COST OF PROCEEDINGS

Article 59

The charges payable by the parties for the use of the facilities of the Centre shall be determined by the Secretary-General in accordance with the regulations adopted by the Administrative Council.

Article 60

(1)   Each Commission and each Tribunal shall determine the fees and expenses of its members within limits established from time to time by the Administrative Council and after consultation with the Secretary-General.

(2)   Nothing in paragraph (1) of this Article shall preclude the parties from agreeing in advance with the Commission or Tribunal concerned upon the fees and expenses of its members.

Article 61

(1)   In the case of conciliation proceedings the fees and expenses of members of the Commission as well as the charges for the use of the facilities of the Centre, shall be borne equally by the parties. Each party shall bear any other expenses it incurs in connection with the proceedings.

(2)   In the case of arbitration proceedings the Tribunal shall, except as the parties otherwise agree, assess the expenses incurred by the parties in connection with the proceedings, and shall decide how and by whom those expenses, the fees and expenses of the members of the Tribunal and the charges for the use of the facilities of the Centre shall be paid. Such decision shall form part of the award.

CHAPTER VII
PLACE OF PROCEEDINGS

Article 62

Conciliation and arbitration proceedings shall be held at the seat of the Centre except as hereinafter provided.

Article 63

Conciliation and arbitration proceedings may be held, if the parties so agree,
  (a)   at the seat of the Permanent Court of Arbitration or of any other appropriate institution, whether private or public, with which the Centre may make arrangements for that purpose; or
  (b)   at any other place approved by the Commission or Tribunal after consultation with the Secretary-General.

CHAPTER VIII
DISPUTES BETWEEN CONTRACTING STATES

Article 64

Any dispute arising between Contracting States concerning the interpretation or application of this Convention which is not settled by negotiation shall be referred to the International Court of Justice by the application of any party to such dispute, unless the States concerned agree to another method of settlement.

CHAPTER IX
AMENDMENT

Article 65

Any Contracting State may propose amendment of this Convention. The text of a proposed amendment shall be communicated to the Secretary-General not less than 90 days prior to the meeting of the Administrative Council at which such amendment is to be considered and shall forthwith be transmitted by him to all the members of the Administrative Council.

Article 66

(1)   If the Administrative Council shall so decide by a majority of two-thirds of its members, the proposed amendment shall be circulated to all Contracting States for ratification, acceptance or approval. Each amendment shall enter into force 30 days after dispatch by the depositary of this Convention of a notification to Contracting States that all Contracting States have ratified, accepted or approved the amendment.

(2)   No amendment shall affect the rights and obligations under this Convention of any Contracting State or of any of its constituent subdivisions or agencies, or of any national of such State arising out of consent to the jurisdiction of the Centre given before the date of entry into force of the amendment.

CHAPTER X
FINAL PROVISIONS

Article 67

This Convention shall be open for signature on behalf of States members of the Bank. It shall also be open for signature on behalf of any other State which is a party to the Statute of the International Court of Justice and which the Administrative Council, by a vote of two-thirds of its members, shall have invited to sign the Convention.

Article 68

(1)   This Convention shall be subject to ratification, acceptance or approval by the signatory States in accordance with their respective constitutional procedures.

(2)   This Convention shall enter into force 30 days after the date of deposit of the twentieth instrument of ratification, acceptance or approval. It shall enter into force for each State which subsequently deposits its instrument of ratification, acceptance or approval 30 days after the date of such deposit.

Article 69

Each Contracting State shall take legislative or other measures as may be necessary for making the provisions of this Convention effective in its territories.

Article 70

This Convention shall apply to all territories for whose international relations a Contracting State is responsible, except those which are excluded by such State by written notice to the depositary of this Convention either at the time of ratification, acceptance or approval or subsequently.

Article 71

Any Contracting State may denounce this Convention by written notice to the depositary of this Convention. The denunciation shall take effect six months after receipt of such notice.

Article 72

Notice by a Contracting State pursuant to Article 70 or 71 shall not affect the rights or obligations under this Convention of that State or of any of its constituent subdivisions or agencies or of any national of that State arising out of consent to the jurisdiction of the Centre given by one of them before such notice was received by the depositary.

Article 73

Instruments of ratification, acceptance or approval of this Convention and of amendments thereto shall be deposited with the Bank which shall act as the depositary of this Convention. The depositary shall transmit certified copies of this Convention to States members of the Bank and to any other State invited to sign the Convention.

Article 74

The depositary shall register this Convention with the Secretariat of the United Nations in accordance with Article 102 of the Charter of the United Nations and the Regulations thereunder adopted by the General Assembly.

Article 75

The depositary shall notify all signatory States of the following:

(a) signatures in accordance with Article 67;
(b) deposits of instruments of ratification, acceptance and approval in accordance with Article 73;
(c) the date on which this Convention enters into force in accordance with Article 68;
(d) exclusions from territorial application pursuant to Article 70;
(e) the date on which any amendment of this Convention enters into force in accordance with Article 66; and
(f) denunciations in accordance with Article 71.

DONE at Washington in the English, French and Spanish languages, all three texts being equally authentic, in a single copy which shall remain deposited in the archives of the International Bank for Reconstruction and Development, which has indicated by its signature below its agreement to fulfil the functions with which it is charged under this Convention.

(Here follow the signatures)

[425]

MISREPRESENTATION ACT 1967

(1967 c 7)

An Act to amend the law relating to innocent misrepresentations and to amend sections 11 and 35 of the Sale of Goods Act 1893

[22 March 1967]

1 Removal of certain bars to rescission for innocent misrepresentation

Where a person has entered into a contract after a misrepresentation has been made to him, and—

(a) the misrepresentation has become a term of the contract; or
(b) the contract has been performed;

or both, then, if otherwise he would be entitled to rescind the contract with-out alleging fraud, he shall be so entitled, subject to the provisions of this Act, notwithstanding the matters mentioned in paragraphs (a) and (b) of this section.

[426]

2 Damages for misrepresentation

(1) Where a person has entered into a contract after a misrepresentation has been made to him by another party thereto and as a result thereof he has suffered loss, then, if the person making the misrepresentation would be liable to damages in respect thereof had the misrepresentation been made fraudulently, that person shall be so liable notwithstanding that the misrepresentation was not made fraudulently, unless he proves that he had reasonable ground to believe and did believe up to the time the contract was made that the facts represented were true.

(2) Where a person has entered into a contract after a misrepresentation has been made to him otherwise than fraudulently, and he would be entitled, by reason of the misrepresentation, to rescind the contract, then, if it is claimed, in any proceedings arising out of the contract, that the contract ought to be or has been rescinded, the court or arbitrator may declare the contract subsisting and award damages in lieu of rescission, if of opinion that it would be equitable to do so, having regard to the nature of the misrepresentation and the loss that would be caused by it if the contract were upheld, as well as to the loss that rescission would cause to the other party.

(3) Damages may be awarded against a person under subsection (2) of this section whether or not he is liable to damages under subsection (1) thereof, but where he is so liable any award under the said subsection (2) shall be taken into account in assessing his liability under the said subsection (1).

[427]

[3 Avoidance of provision excluding liability for misrepresentation

If a contract contains a term which would exclude or restrict—

(a) any liability to which a party to a contract may be subject by reason of any misrepresentation made by him before the contract was made; or

(b)   any remedy available to another party to the contract by reason of such a misrepresentation,

that term shall be of no effect except in so far as it satisfies the requirement of reasonableness as stated in section 11(1) of the Unfair Contract Terms Act 1977; and it is for those claiming that the term satisfies that requirement to show that it does.]

[428]

NOTES

Substituted by the Unfair Contract Terms Act 1977, s 8(1).

4   *(Repealed by the Sale of Goods Act 1979, s 63(2), Sch 3.)*

5   Saving for past transactions

Nothing in this Act shall apply in relation to any misrepresentation or contract of sale which is made before the commencement of this Act.

[429]

6   Short title, commencement and extent

(1)   This Act may be cited as the Misrepresentation Act 1967.

(2)   This Act shall come into operation at the expiration of the period of one month beginning with the date on which it is passed.

(3)   This Act ... does not extend to Scotland.

(4)   This Act does not extend to Northern Ireland.

[430]

NOTES

Sub-s (3): words omitted repealed by the Sale of Goods Act 1979, ss 62, 63, Sch 3.

UNIFORM LAWS ON INTERNATIONAL SALES ACT 1967

(1967 c 45)

ARRANGEMENT OF SECTIONS

An Act to give effect to two Conventions with respect to the international sale of goods; and for purposes connected therewith

[14 July 1967]

1   Application of Uniform Law on the International Sale of Goods

(1)   In this Act "the Uniform Law on Sales" means the Uniform Law on the International Sale of Goods forming the Annex to the First Convention and set out, with the modification provided for by Article III of that Convention, in Schedule 1 to this Act; and "the First Convention" means the Convention relating to a Uniform Law on the International Sale of Goods done at The Hague on 1st July 1964.

(2)   The Uniform Law on Sales shall, subject to the following provisions of this section, have the force of law in the United Kingdom.

(3)   While an Order of Her Majesty in Council is in force declaring that a declaration by the United Kingdom under Article V of the First Convention (application only by choice of parties) has been made and not withdrawn the Uniform Law on Sales shall apply to a contract of sale only if it has been chosen by the parties to the contract as the law of the contract.

[(4)   In determining the extent of the application of the Uniform Law on Sales by virtue of Article 4 thereof (choice of parties)—

(a)   in relation to a contract made before 18th May 1973, no provision of the law of any part of the United Kingdom shall be regarded as a mandatory provision within the meaning of that Article;

(b)   in relation to a contract made on or after 18th May 1973 and before 1st February 1978, no provision of that law shall be so regarded except sections 12 to 15, 55 and 56 of the Sale of Goods Act 1979;

(c)   in relation to a contract made on or after 1st February 1978, no provision of that law shall be so regarded except sections [12 to 15B] of the Sale of Goods Act 1979.]

(5)   If Her Majesty by Order in Council declares what States are Contracting States and in respect of what territories or what declarations under Article II of the First Convention are for the time being in force, the Order shall, while in force, be conclusive for the purposes of paragraph 1 or, as the case may be, paragraph 5 of Article 1 of the Uniform Law on Sales; but any Order in Council under this subsection may be varied or revoked by a subsequent Order in Council.

(6)   The Uniform Law on Sales shall not apply to contracts concluded before such date as Her Majesty may by Order in Council declare to be the date on which the First Convention comes into force in respect of the United Kingdom.

(7)   Any Order in Council under the preceding provisions of this section shall be laid before Parliament after being made.

(8)   An Order in Council made under subsection (3) of this section may be revoked by a subsequent Order in Council; but no recommendation shall be made to Her Majesty in Council to make an Order under this subsection unless a draft thereof has been laid before and approved by each House of Parliament.

[431]

NOTES

Sub-s (4): substituted by the Sale of Goods Act 1979, s 63, Sch 2, para 15; words in square brackets substituted by the Sale and Supply of Goods Act 1994, s 7(1), Sch 2 para 3.

Orders in Council: the Uniform Laws on International Sales Order 1972, SI 1972/973; the Uniform Laws on International Sales Order 1987, SI 1987/2061.

2 Application of Uniform Law on the Formation of Contracts for the International Sale of Goods

(1)   In this Act "the Uniform Law on Formation" means the Law forming Annex I to the Second Convention as set out, with the modifications provided for by paragraph 3 of Article I of that Convention, in Schedule 2 to this Act; and "the Second Convention" means the Convention relating to a Uniform Law on the Formation of Contracts for the International Sale of Goods done at the Hague on 1st July 1964.

(2)   Subject to subsection (3) of this section the Uniform Law on Formation shall have the force of law in the United Kingdom.

(3)   The Uniform Law on Formation shall not apply to offers, replies and acceptances made before such date as Her Majesty may by Order in Council declare to be the date on which the Second Convention comes into force in respect of the United Kingdom.

(4)   An Order in Council under this section shall be laid before Parliament after being made.

[432]

NOTES

Order in Council: the Uniform Laws on International Sales Order 1972, SI 1972/973.

3 Revision of Uniform Laws

(1)   If by any international Convention the Uniform Law on Sales or the Uniform Law on Formation is amended Her Majesty may by Order in Council modify the Schedules to this Act in such manner as appears to Her necessary for the purpose of giving effect to the Convention.

(2)   No recommendation shall be made to Her Majesty in Council to make an Order under this section unless a draft thereof has been laid before and approved by each House of Parliament.

[433]

4 Application to Isle of Man and Channel Islands

Her Majesty may by Order in Council direct that the provisions of this Act shall extend, with such exceptions, adaptations and modifications as may be specified in the Order, to the Isle of Man or any of the Channel Islands; and an Order in Council under this section may be varied or revoked by a subsequent Order in Council.

[434]

5 Short title

This Act may be cited as the Uniform Laws on International Sales Act 1967.

[435]

SCHEDULES

SCHEDULE 1
THE UNIFORM LAW ON THE INTERNATIONAL SALE OF GOODS

Section 1

CHAPTER I—SPHERE OF APPLICATION OF THE LAW

Article 1

1.   The present Law shall apply to contracts of sale of goods entered into by parties whose places of business are in the territories of different Contracting States, in each of the following cases:

(a)   where the contract involves the sale of goods which are at the time of the conclusion of the contract in the course of carriage or will be carried from the territory of one State to the territory of another;

(b)   where the acts constituting the offer and the acceptance have been effected in the territories of different States;

(c)   where delivery of the goods is to be made in the territory of a State other than that within whose territory the acts constituting the offer and the acceptance have been effected.

2.   Where a party to the contract does not have a place of business, reference shall be made to his habitual residence.

3.   The application of the present Law shall not depend on the nationality of the parties.

4.   In the case of contracts by correspondence, offer and acceptance shall be considered to have been effected in the territory of the same State only if the letters, telegrams or other documentary communications which contain them have been sent and received in the territory of that State.

5.   For the purpose of determining whether the parties have their places of business or habitual residences in "different States", any two or more States shall not be considered to be "different States" if a valid declaration to that effect made under Article II of the Convention dated the 1st day of July 1964 relating to a Uniform Law on the International Sale of Goods is in force in respect of them.

Article 2

Rules of private international law shall be excluded for the purposes of the application of the present Law, subject to any provision to the contrary in the said Law.

Article 3

The parties to a contract of sale shall be free to exclude the application thereto of the present Law either entirely or partially. Such exclusion may be express or implied.

Article 4

The present Law shall also apply where it has been chosen as the law of the contract by the parties, whether or not their places of business or their habitual residences are in different States and whether or not such States are Parties to the Convention dated the 1st day of July 1964 relating to the Uniform Law on the International Sale of Goods, to the extent that it does not affect the application of any mandatory provisions of law which would have been applicable if the parties had not chosen the Uniform Law.

Article 5

1.   The present Law shall not apply to sales:

(a)   of stocks, shares, investment securities, negotiable instruments or money;

(b)   of any ship, vessel or aircraft, which is or will be subject to registration;

(c)   of electricity;

(d)   by authority of law or on execution or distress.

2.   The present Law shall not affect the application of any mandatory provision of national law for the protection of a party to a contract which contemplates the purchase of goods by that party by payment of the price by instalments.

Article 6

Contracts for the supply of goods to be manufactured or produced shall be considered to be sales within the meaning of the present Law, unless the party who orders the goods undertakes to supply an essential and substantial part of the materials necessary for such manufacture or production.

Article 7

The present Law shall apply to sales regardless of the commercial or civil character of the parties or of the contracts.

Article 8

The present Law shall govern only the obligations of the seller and the buyer arising from a contract of sale. In particular, the present Law shall not, except as otherwise expressly provided therein, be concerned with the formation of the contract, nor with the effect which the contract may have on the property in the goods sold, nor with the validity of the contract or of any of its provisions or of any usage.

CHAPTER II—GENERAL PROVISIONS

Article 9

1.   The parties shall be bound by any usage which they have expressly or impliedly made applicable to their contract and by any practices which they have established between themselves.

2.   They shall also be bound by usages which reasonable persons in the same situation as the parties usually consider to be applicable to their contract. In the event of conflict with the present Law, the usages shall prevail unless otherwise agreed by the parties.

3.   Where expressions, provisions or forms of contract commonly used in commercial practice are employed, they shall be interpreted according to the meaning usually given to them in the trade concerned.

Article 10

For the purposes of the present Law, a breach of contract shall be regarded as fundamental wherever the party in breach knew, or ought to have known, at the time of the conclusion of the contract, that a reasonable person in the same situation as the other party would not have entered into the contract if he had foreseen the breach and its effects.

Article 11

Where under the present Law an act is required to be performed "promptly", it shall be performed within as short a period as possible, in the circumstances, from the moment when the act could reasonably be performed.

Article 12

For the purposes of the present Law, the expression "current price" means a price based upon an official market quotation, or, in the absence of such a quotation, upon those factors which, according to the usage of the market, serve to determine the price.

Article 13

For the purposes of the present Law, the expression "a party knew or ought to have known", or any similar expression, refers to what should have been known to a reasonable person in the same situation.

Article 14

Communications provided for by the present Law shall be made by the means usual in the circumstances.

Article 15

A contract of sale need not be evidenced by writing and shall not be subject to any other requirements as to form. In particular, it may be proved by means of witnesses.

Article 16

Where under the provisions of the present Law one party to a contract of sale is entitled to require performance of any obligation by the other party, a court shall not be bound to enter or enforce a judgment providing for specific performance except in accordance with the provisions of Article VII of the Convention dated the 1st day of July 1964 relating to a Uniform Law on the International Sale of Goods.

Article 17

Questions concerning matters governed by the present Law which are not expressly settled therein shall be settled in conformity with the general principles on which the present Law is based.

PART 1
STATUTES

CHAPTER III—OBLIGATIONS OF THE SELLER

Article 18

The seller shall effect delivery of the goods, hand over any documents relating thereto and transfer the property in the goods, as required by the contract and the present Law.

SECTION I.—DELIVERY OF THE GOODS

Article 19

1. Delivery consists in the handing over of goods which conform with the contract.

2. Where the contract of sale involves carriage of the goods and no other place for delivery has been agreed upon, delivery shall be effected by handing over the goods to the carrier for transmission to the buyer.

3. Where the goods handed over to the carrier are not clearly appropriated to performance of the contract by being marked with an address or by some other means, the seller shall, in addition to handing over the goods, send to the buyer notice of the consignment and, if necessary, some document specifying the goods.

SUB-SECTION 1.—OBLIGATIONS OF THE SELLER AS REGARDS THE DATE AND PLACE OF DELIVERY

A.—*Date of Delivery*

Article 20

Where the parties have agreed upon a date for delivery or where such date is fixed by usage, the seller shall, without the need for any other formality, be bound to deliver the goods at that date, provided that the date thus fixed is determined or determinable by the calendar or is fixed in relation to a definite event, the date of which can be ascertained by the parties.

Article 21

Where by agreement of the parties or by usage delivery shall be effected within a certain period (such as a particular month or season), the seller may fix the precise date of delivery, unless the circumstances indicate that the fixing of the date was reserved to the buyer.

Article 22

Where the date of delivery has not been determined in accordance with the provisions of Articles 20 or 21, the seller shall be bound to deliver the goods within a reasonable time after the conclusion of the contract, regard being had to the nature of the goods and to the circumstances.

B.—*Place of Delivery*

Article 23

1. Where the contract of sale does not involve carriage of the goods, the seller shall deliver the goods at the place where he carried on business at the time of the conclusion of the contract, or, in the absence of a place of business, at his habitual residence.

2. If the sale relates to specific goods and the parties knew that the goods were at a certain place at the time of the conclusion of the contract, the seller shall deliver the goods at that place. The same rule shall apply if the goods sold are unascertained goods to be taken from a specified stock or if they are to be manufactured or produced at a place known to the parties at the time of the conclusion of the contract.

C.—*Remedies for the seller's failure to perform his obligations as regards the date and place of delivery*

Article 24

1. Where the seller fails to perform his obligations as regards the date or the place of delivery, the buyer may, as provided in Articles 25 to 32:
    (a)   require performance of the contract by the seller;
    (b)   declare the contract avoided.

2. The buyer may also claim damages as provided in Article 82 or in Articles 84 to 87.

3. In no case shall the seller be entitled to apply to a court or arbitral tribunal to grant him a period of grace.

PART 1
STATUTES

Article 25

The buyer shall not be entitled to require performance of the contract by the seller, if it is in conformity with usage and reasonably possible for the buyer to purchase goods to replace those to which the contract relates. In this case the contract shall be ipso facto avoided as from the time when such purchase should be effected.

(a) Remedies as regards the date of delivery

Article 26

1.   Where the failure to deliver the goods at the date fixed amounts to a fundamental breach of the contract, the buyer may either require performance by the seller or declare the contract avoided. He shall inform the seller of his decision within a reasonable time; otherwise the contract shall be ipso facto avoided.

2.   If the seller requests the buyer to make known his decision under paragraph 1 of this Article and the buyer does not comply promptly, the contract shall be ipso facto avoided.

3.   If the seller has effected delivery before the buyer has made known his decision under paragraph 1 of this Article and the buyer does not exercise promptly his right to declare the contract avoided, the contract cannot be avoided.

4.   Where the buyer has chosen performance of the contract and does not obtain it within a reasonable time, he may declare the contract avoided.

Article 27

1.   Where failure to deliver the goods at the date fixed does not amount to a fundamental breach of the contract, the seller shall retain the right to effect delivery and the buyer shall retain the right to require performance of the contract by the seller.

2.   The buyer may however grant the seller an additional period of time of reasonable length. Failure to deliver within this period shall amount to a fundamental breach of the contract.

Article 28

Failure to deliver the goods at the date fixed shall amount to a fundamental breach of the contract whenever a price for such goods is quoted on a market where the buyer can obtain them.

Article 29

Where the seller tenders delivery of the goods before the date fixed, the buyer may accept or reject delivery; if he accepts, he may reserve the right to claim damages in accordance with Article 82.

(b) Remedies as regards the place of delivery

Article 30

1.   Where failure to deliver the goods at the place fixed amounts to a fundamental breach of the contract, and failure to deliver the goods at the date fixed would also amount to a fundamental breach, the buyer may either require performance of the contract by the seller or declare the contract avoided. The buyer shall inform the seller of his decision within a reasonable time; otherwise the contract shall be ipso facto avoided.

2.   If the seller requests the buyer to make known his decision under paragraph 1 of this Article and the buyer does not comply promptly, the contract shall be ipso facto avoided.

3.   If the seller has transported the goods to the place fixed before the buyer has made known his decision under paragraph 1 of this Article and the buyer does not exercise promptly his right to declare the contract avoided, the contract cannot be avoided.

Article 31

1.   In cases not provided for in Article 30, the seller shall retain the right to effect delivery at the place fixed and the buyer shall retain the right to require performance of the contract by the seller.

2.   The buyer may however grant the seller an additional period of time of reasonable length. Failure to deliver within this period at the place fixed shall amount to a fundamental breach of the contract.

Article 32

1.   If delivery is to be effected by handing over the goods to a carrier and the goods have been handed over at a place other than that fixed, the buyer may declare the contract avoided, whenever the failure to deliver the goods at the place fixed amounts to a fundamental breach of the contract. He shall lose this right if he has not promptly declared the contract avoided.

2.   The buyer shall have the same right, in the circumstances and on the conditions provided in paragraph 1 of this Article, if the goods have been despatched to some place other than that fixed.

3.   If despatch from a place or to a place other than that fixed does not amount to a fundamental breach of the contract, the buyer may only claim damages in accordance with Article 82.

SUB-SECTION 2.—OBLIGATIONS OF THE SELLER AS REGARDS THE CONFORMITY OF THE GOODS

A.—Lack of conformity

Article 33

1.   The seller shall not have fulfilled his obligation to deliver the goods, where he has handed over:
- (a)   part only of the goods sold or a larger or a smaller quantity of the goods than he contracted to sell;
- (b)   goods which are not those to which the contract relates or goods of a different kind;
- (c)   goods which lack the qualities of a sample or model which the seller has handed over or sent to the buyer, unless the seller has submitted it without any express or implied undertaking that the goods would conform therewith;
- (d)   goods which do not possess the qualities necessary for their ordinary or commercial use;
- (e)   goods which do not possess the qualities for some particular purpose expressly or impliedly contemplated by the contract;
- (f)   in general, goods which do not possess the qualities and characteristics expressly or impliedly contemplated by the contract.

2.   No difference in quantity, lack of part of the goods or absence of any quality or characteristic shall be taken into consideration where it is not material.

Article 34

In the cases to which Article 33 relates, the rights conferred on the buyer by the present Law exclude all other remedies based on lack of conformity of the goods.

Article 35

1.   Whether the goods are in conformity with the contract shall be determined by their conditions at the time when risk passes. However, if risk does not pass because of a declaration of avoidance of the contract or of a demand for other goods in replacement, the conformity of the goods with the contract shall be determined by their condition at the time when risk would have passed had they been in conformity with the contract.

2.   The seller shall be liable for the consequences of any lack of conformity occurring after the time fixed in paragraph 1 of this Article if it was due to an act of the seller or of a person for whose conduct he is responsible.

Article 36

The seller shall not be liable for the consequences of any lack of conformity of the kind referred to in sub-paragraphs (d), (e) or (f) of paragraph 1 of Article 33, if at the time of the conclusion of the contract the buyer knew, or could not have been unaware of, such lack of conformity.

Article 37

If the seller has handed over goods before the date fixed for delivery he may, up to that date, deliver any missing part or quantity of the goods or deliver other goods which are in conformity with the contract or remedy any defects in the goods handed over, provided that the exercise of this right does not cause the buyer either unreasonable inconvenience or unreasonable expense.

B.—Ascertainment and notification of lack of conformity

Article 38

1.   The buyer shall examine the goods, or cause them to be examined, promptly.

2.   In case of carriage of the goods the buyer shall examine them at the place of destination.

3.   If the goods are redespatched by the buyer without transhipment and the seller knew or ought to have known, at the time when the contract was concluded, of the possibility of such redespatch, examination of the goods may be deferred until they arrive at the new destination.

4.   The methods of examination shall be governed by the agreement of the parties or, in the absence of such agreement, by the law or usage of the place where the examination is to be effected.

Article 39

1.　The buyer shall lose the right to rely on a lack of conformity of the goods if he has not given the seller notice thereof promptly after he has discovered the lack of conformity or ought to have discovered it. If a defect which could not have been revealed by the examination of the goods provided for in Article 38 is found later, the buyer may nonetheless rely on that defect, provided that he gives the seller notice thereof promptly after its discovery. In any event, the buyer shall lose the right to rely on a lack of conformity of the goods if he has not given notice thereof to the seller within a period of two years from the date on which the goods were handed over, unless the lack of conformity constituted a breach of a guarantee covering a longer period.

2.　In giving notice to the seller of any lack of conformity, the buyer shall specify its nature and invite the seller to examine the goods or to cause them to be examined by his agent.

3.　Where any notice referred to in paragraph 1 of this Article has been sent by letter, telegram or other appropriate means, the fact that such notice is delayed or fails to arrive at its destination shall not deprive the buyer of the right to rely thereon.

Article 40

The seller shall not be entitled to rely on the provisions of Articles 38 and 39 if the lack of conformity relates to facts of which he knew, or of which he could not have been unaware, and which he did not disclose.

C.—Remedies for lack of conformity

Article 41

1.　Where the buyer has given due notice to the seller of the failure of the goods to conform with the contract, the buyer may, as provided in Articles 42 to 46:
    (a)　require performance of the contract by the seller;
    (b)　declare the contract avoided;
    (c)　reduce the price.

2.　The buyer may also claim damages as provided in Article 82 or in Articles 84 to 87.

Article 42

1.　The buyer may require the seller to perform the contract:
    (a)　if the sale relates to goods to be produced or manufactured by the seller, by remedying defects in the goods, provided the seller is in a position to remedy the defects;
    (b)　if the sale relates to specific goods, by delivering the goods to which the contract refers or the missing part thereof;
    (c)　if the sale relates to unascertained goods, by delivering other goods which are in conformity with the contract or by delivering the missing part or quantity, except where the purchase of goods in replacement is in conformity with usage and reasonably possible.

2.　If the buyer does not obtain performance of the contract by the seller within a reasonable time, he shall retain the rights provided in Articles 43 to 46.

Article 43

The buyer may declare the contract avoided if the failure of the goods to conform to the contract and also the failure to deliver on the date fixed amount to fundamental breaches of the contract. The buyer shall lose his right to declare the contract avoided if he does not exercise it promptly after giving the seller notice of the lack of conformity or, in the case to which paragraph 2 of Article 42 applies, after the expiration of the period referred to in that paragraph.

Article 44

1.　In cases not provided for in Article 43, the seller shall retain, after the date fixed for the delivery of the goods, the right to deliver any missing part or quantity of the goods or to deliver other goods which are in conformity with the contract or to remedy any defect in the goods handed over, provided that the exercise of this right does not cause the buyer either unreasonable inconvenience or unreasonable expense.

2.　The buyer may however fix an additional period of time of reasonable length for the further delivery or for the remedying of the defect. If at the expiration of the additional period the seller has not delivered the goods or remedied the defect, the buyer may choose between requiring the performance of the contract or reducing the price in accordance with Article 46 or, provided that he does so promptly, declare the contract avoided.

Article 45

1.   Where the seller has handed over part only of the goods or an insufficient quantity or where part only of the goods handed over is in conformity with the contract, the provisions of Articles 43 and 44 shall apply in respect of the part or quantity which is missing or which does not conform with the contract.

2.   The buyer may declare the contract avoided in its entirety only if the failure to effect delivery completely and in conformity with the contract amounts to a fundamental breach of the contract.

Article 46

Where the buyer has neither obtained performance of the contract by the seller nor declared the contract avoided, the buyer may reduce the price in the same proportion as the value of the goods at the time of the conclusion of the contract has been diminished because of their lack of conformity with the contract.

Article 47

Where the seller has proffered to the buyer a quantity of unascertained goods greater than that provided for in the contract, the buyer may reject or accept the excess quantity. If the buyer rejects the excess quantity, the seller shall be liable only for damages in accordance with Article 82. If the buyer accepts the whole or part of the excess quantity, he shall pay for it at the contract rate.

Article 48

The buyer may exercise the rights provided in Articles 43 to 46, even before the time fixed for delivery, if it is clear that goods which would be handed over would not be in conformity with the contract.

Article 49

1.   The buyer shall lose his right to rely on lack of conformity with the contract at the expiration of a period of one year after he has given notice as provided in Article 39, unless he has been prevented from exercising his right because of fraud on the part of the seller.

2.   After the expiration of this period, the buyer shall not be entitled to rely on the lack of conformity, even by way of defence to an action. Nevertheless, if the buyer has not paid for the goods and provided that he has given due notice of the lack of conformity promptly, as provided in Article 39, he may advance as a defence to a claim for payment of the price a claim for a reduction in the price or for damages.

SECTION II.—HANDING OVER OF DOCUMENTS

Article 50

Where the seller is bound to hand over to the buyer any documents relating to the goods, he shall do so at the time and place fixed by the contract or by usage.

Article 51

If the seller fails to hand over documents as provided in Article 50 at the time and place fixed or if he hands over documents which are not in conformity with those which he was bound to hand over, the buyer shall have the same rights as those provided under Articles 24 to 32 or under Articles 41 to 49, as the case may be.

SECTION III.—TRANSFER OF PROPERTY

Article 52

1.   Where the goods are subject to a right or claim of a third person, the buyer, unless he agreed to take the goods subject to such right or claim, shall notify the seller of such right or claim, unless the seller already knows thereof, and request that the goods should be freed therefrom within reasonable time or that other goods free from all rights and claims of third persons be delivered to him by the seller.

2.   If the seller complies with a request made under paragraph 1 of this Article and the buyer nevertheless suffers a loss, the buyer may claim damages in accordance with Article 82.

3.   If the seller fails to comply with a request made under paragraph 1 of this Article and a fundamental breach of the contract results thereby, the buyer may declare the contract avoided and claim damages in accordance with Articles 84 to 87. If the buyer does not declare the contract avoided or if there is no fundamental breach of the contract, the buyer shall have the right to claim damages in accordance with Article 82.

4.   The buyer shall lose his right to declare the contract avoided if he fails to act in accordance with paragraph 1 of this Article within a reasonable time from the moment when he became aware or ought to have become aware of the right or claim of the third person in respect of the goods.

Article 53

The rights conferred on the buyer by Article 52 exclude all other remedies based on the fact that the seller has failed to perform his obligation to transfer the property in the goods or that the goods are subject to a right or claim of a third person.

SECTION IV.—OTHER OBLIGATIONS OF THE SELLER

Article 54

1.   If the seller is bound to despatch the goods to the buyer, he shall make, in the usual way and on the usual terms, such contracts as are necessary for the carriage of the goods to the place fixed.

2.   If the seller is not bound by the contract to effect insurance in respect of the carriage of the goods, he shall provide the buyer, at his request, with all information necessary to enable him to effect such insurance.

Article 55

1.   If the seller fails to perform any obligation other than those referred to in Articles 20 to 53, the buyer may:
   - (a)   where such failure amounts to a fundamental breach of the contract, declare the contract avoided, provided that he does so promptly, and claim damages in accordance with Articles 84 to 87, or
   - (b)   in any other case, claim damages in accordance with Article 82.

2.   The buyer may also require performance by the seller of his obligation, unless the contract is avoided.

CHAPTER IV—OBLIGATIONS OF THE BUYER

Article 56

The buyer shall pay the price for the goods and take delivery of them, as required by the contract and the present law.

SECTION I.—PAYMENT OF THE PRICE

A.—Fixing the price

Article 57

Where a contract has been concluded but does not state a price or make provision for the determination of the price, the buyer shall be bound to pay the price generally charged by the seller at the time of the conclusion of the contract.

Article 58

Where the price is fixed according to the weight of the goods, it shall, in case of doubt, be determined by the net weight.

B.—Place and date of payment

Article 59

1.   The buyer shall pay the price to the seller at the seller's place of business or, if he does not have a place of business, at his habitual residence, or, where the payment is to be made against the handing over of the goods or of documents, at the place where such handing over takes place.

2.   Where, in consequence of a change in the place of business or habitual residence of the seller subsequent to the conclusion of the contract, the expenses incidental to payment are increased, such increase shall be borne by the seller.

Article 60

Where the parties have agreed upon a date for the payment of the price or where such date is fixed by usage, the buyer shall, without the need for any other formality, pay the price at that date.

C.—Remedies for non-payment

Article 61

1.   If the buyer fails to pay the price in accordance with the contract and with the present law, the seller may require the buyer to perform his obligation.

2.   The seller shall not be entitled to require payment of the price by the buyer if it is in conformity with usage and reasonably possible for the seller to resell the goods. In that case the contract shall be ipso facto avoided as from the time when such resale should be effected.

Article 62

1.   Where the failure to pay the price at the date fixed amounts to a fundamental breach of the contract, the seller may either require the buyer to pay the price or declare the contract avoided. He shall inform the buyer of his decision within a reasonable time; otherwise the contract shall be ipso facto avoided.

2.   Where the failure to pay the price at the date fixed does not amount to a fundamental breach of the contract, the seller may grant to the buyer an additional period of time of reasonable length. If the buyer has not paid the price at the expiration of the additional period, the seller may either require the payment of the price by the buyer or, provided that he does so promptly, declare the contract avoided.

Article 63

1.   Where the contract is avoided because of failure to pay the price, the seller shall have the right to claim damages in accordance with Articles 84 to 87.

2.   Where the contract is not avoided, the seller shall have the right to claim damages in accordance with Articles 82 and 83.

Article 64

In no case shall the buyer be entitled to apply to a court or arbitral tribunal to grant him a period of grace for the payment of the price.

SECTION II.—TAKING DELIVERY

Article 65

Taking delivery consists in the buyer's doing all such acts as are necessary in order to enable the seller to hand over the goods and actually taking them over.

Article 66

1.   Where the buyer's failure to take delivery of the goods in accordance with the contract amounts to a fundamental breach of the contract or gives the seller good grounds for fearing that the buyer will not pay the price, the seller may declare the contract avoided.

2.   Where the failure to take delivery of the goods does not amount to a fundamental breach of the contract, the seller may grant to the buyer an additional period of time of reasonable length. If the buyer has not taken delivery of the goods at the expiration of the additional period, the seller may declare the contract avoided, provided that he does so promptly.

Article 67

1.   If the contract reserves to the buyer the right subsequently to determine the form, measurement or other features of the goods (sale by specification) and he fails to make such specification either on the date expressly or impliedly agreed upon or within a reasonable time after receipt of a request from the seller, the seller may declare the contract avoided, provided that he does so promptly, or make the specification himself in accordance with the requirements of the buyer in so far as these are known to him.

2.   If the seller makes the specification himself, he shall inform the buyer of the details thereof and shall fix a reasonable period of time within which the buyer may submit a different specification. If the buyer fails to do so the specification made by the seller shall be binding.

Article 68

1.   Where the contract is avoided because of the failure of the buyer to accept delivery of the goods or to make a specification, the seller shall have the right to claim damages in accordance with Articles 84 to 87.

2.   Where the contract is not avoided, the seller shall have the right to claim damages in accordance with Article 82.

SECTION III.—OTHER OBLIGATIONS OF THE BUYER

Article 69

The buyer shall take the steps provided for in the contract, by usage or by laws and regulations in force, for the purpose of making provision for or guaranteeing payment of the price, such as the acceptance of a bill of exchange, the opening of a documentary credit or the giving of a banker's guarantee.

Article 70

1. If the buyer fails to perform any obligation other than those referred to in Sections I and II of this Chapter, the seller may:
    (a) where such failure amounts to a fundamental breach of the contract, declare the contract avoided, provided that he does so promptly, and claim damages in accordance with Articles 84 to 87; or
    (b) in any other case, claim damages in accordance with Article 82.

2. The seller may also require performance by the buyer of his obligation, unless the contract is avoided.

CHAPTER V
PROVISIONS COMMON TO THE OBLIGATIONS OF THE SELLER AND OF THE BUYER

SECTION I.—CONCURRENCE BETWEEN DELIVERY OF THE GOODS AND PAYMENT OF THE PRICE

Article 71

Except as otherwise provided in Article 72, delivery of the goods and payment of the price shall be concurrent conditions. Nevertheless, the buyer shall not be obliged to pay the price until he has had an opportunity to examine the goods.

Article 72

1. Where the contract involves carriage of the goods and where delivery is, by virtue of paragraph 2 of Article 19, effected by handing over the goods to the carrier, the seller may either postpone despatch of the goods until he receives payment or proceed to despatch them on terms that reserve to himself the right of disposal of the goods during transit. In the latter case, he may require that the goods shall not be handed over to the buyer at the place of destination except against payment of the price and the buyer shall not be bound to pay the price until he has had an opportunity to examine the goods.

2. Nevertheless, when the contract requires payment against documents, the buyer shall not be entitled to refuse payment of the price on the ground that he has not had the opportunity to examine the goods.

Article 73

1. Each party may suspend the performance of his obligations whenever, after the conclusion of the contract, the economic situation of the other party appears to have become so difficult that there is good reason to fear that he will not perform a material part of his obligations.

2. If the seller has already despatched the goods before the economic situation of the buyer described in paragraph 1 of this Article becomes evident, he may prevent the handing over of the goods to the buyer even if the latter holds a document which entitles him to obtain them.

3. Nevertheless, the seller shall not be entitled to prevent the handing over of the goods if they are claimed by a third person who is a lawful holder of a document which entitles him to obtain the goods, unless the document contains a reservation concerning the effects of its transfer or unless the seller can prove that the holder of the document, when he acquired it, knowingly acted to the detriment of the seller.

SECTION II.—EXEMPTIONS

Article 74

1. Where one of the parties has not performed one of his obligations, he shall not be liable for such non-performance if he can prove that it was due to circumstances which, according to the intention of the parties at the time of the conclusion of the contract, he was not bound to take into account or to avoid or to overcome; in the absence of any expression of the intention of the parties, regard shall be had to what reasonable persons in the same situation would have intended.

2. Where the circumstances which gave rise to the non-performance of the obligation constituted only a temporary impediment to performance, the party in default shall nevertheless be permanently

relieved of his obligation if, by reason of the delay, performance would be so radically changed as to amount to the performance of an obligation quite different from that contemplated by the contract.

3. The relief provided by this Article for one of the parties shall not include the avoidance of the contract under some other provision of the present Law or deprive the other party of any right which he has under the present Law to reduce the price, unless the circumstances which entitled the first party to relief were caused by the act of the other party or of some person for whose conduct he was responsible.

SECTION III.—SUPPLEMENTARY RULES CONCERNING THE AVOIDANCE OF THE CONTRACT

A.—*Supplementary grounds for avoidance*

Article 75

1. Where, in the case of contracts for delivery of goods by instalments, by reason of any failure by one party to perform any of his obligations under the contract in respect of any instalment, the other party has good reason to fear failure of performance in respect of future instalments, he may declare the contract avoided for the future, provided that he does so promptly.

2. The buyer may also, provided that he does so promptly, declare the contract avoided in respect of future deliveries or in respect of deliveries already made or both, if by reason of their interdependence such deliveries would be worthless to him.

Article 76

Where prior to the date fixed for performance of the contract it is clear that one of the parties will commit a fundamental breach of the contract, the other party shall have the right to declare the contract avoided.

Article 77

Where the contract has been avoided under Article 75 or Article 76, the party declaring the contract avoided may claim damages in accordance with Articles 84 to 87.

B.—*Effects of avoidance*

Article 78

1. Avoidance of the contract releases both parties from their obligations thereunder, subject to any damages which may be due.

2. If one party has performed the contract either wholly or in part, he may claim the return of whatever he has supplied or paid under the contract. If both parties are required to make restitution, they shall do so concurrently.

Article 79

1. The buyer shall lose his right to declare the contract avoided where it is impossible for him to return the goods in the condition in which he received them.

2. Nevertheless, the buyer may declare the contract avoided:
   (a) if the goods or part of the goods have perished or deteriorated as a result of the defect which justifies the avoidance;
   (b) if the goods or part of the goods have perished or deteriorated as a result of the examination prescribed in Article 38;
   (c) if part of the goods have been consumed or transformed by the buyer in the course of normal use before the lack of conformity with the contract was discovered;
   (d) if the impossibility of returning the goods or of returning them in the condition in which they were received is not due to the act of the buyer or of some other person for whose conduct he is responsible;
   (e) if the deterioration or transformation of the goods is unimportant.

Article 80

The buyer who has lost the right to declare the contract avoided by virtue of Article 79 shall retain all the other rights conferred on him by the present Law.

Article 81

1. Where the seller is under an obligation to refund the price, he shall also be liable for the interest thereon at the rate fixed by Article 83, as from the date of payment.

2.   The buyer shall be liable to account to the seller for all benefits which he has derived from the goods or part of them, as the case may be:
- (a)   where he is under an obligation to return the goods or part of them,
- (b)   where it is impossible for him to return the goods or part of them, but the contract is nevertheless avoided.

SECTION IV.—SUPPLEMENTARY RULES CONCERNING DAMAGES

A.—Damages where the contract is not avoided

Article 82

Where the contract is not avoided, damages for a breach of contract by one party shall consist of a sum equal to the loss, including loss of profit, suffered by the other party. Such damages shall not exceed the loss which the party in breach ought to have foreseen at the time of the conclusion of the contract, in the light of the facts and matters which then were known or ought to have been known to him, as a possible consequence of the breach of the contract.

Article 83

Where the breach of contract consists of delay in the payment of the price, the seller shall in any event be entitled to interest on such sum as is in arrear at a rate equal to the official discount rate in the country where he has his place of business or, if he has no place of business, his habitual residence, plus 1 per cent.

B.—Damages where the contract is avoided

Article 84

1.   In case of avoidance of the contract, where there is a current price for the goods, damages shall be equal to the difference between the price fixed by the contract and the current price on the date on which the contract is avoided.

2.   In calculating the amount of damages under paragraph 1 of this Article, the current price to be taken into account shall be that prevailing in the market in which the transaction took place or, if there is no such current price or if its application is inappropriate, the price in a market which serves as a reasonable substitute, making due allowance for differences in the cost of transporting the goods.

Article 85

If the buyer has bought goods in replacement or the seller has resold goods in a reasonable manner, he may recover the difference between the contract price and the price paid for the goods bought in replacement or that obtained by the resale.

Article 86

The damages referred to in Articles 84 and 85 may be increased by the amount of any reasonable expenses incurred as a result of the breach or up to the amount of any loss, including loss of profit, which should have been foreseen by the party in breach, at the time of the conclusion of the contract, in the light of the facts and matters which were known or ought to have been known to him, as a possible consequence of the breach of the contract.

Article 87

If there is no current price for the goods, damages shall be calculated on the same basis as that provided in Article 82.

C.—General provisions concerning damages

Article 88

The party who relies on a breach of the contract shall adopt all reasonable measures to mitigate the loss resulting from the breach. If he fails to adopt such measures, the party in breach may claim a reduction in the damages.

Article 89

In case of fraud, damages shall be determined by the rules applicable in respect of contracts of sale not governed by the present law.

SECTION V.—EXPENSES

Article 90

The expenses of delivery shall be borne by the seller; all expenses after delivery shall be borne by the buyer.

SECTION VI.—PRESERVATION OF THE GOODS

Article 91

Where the buyer is in delay in taking delivery of the goods or in paying the price, the seller shall take reasonable steps to preserve the goods; he shall have the right to retain them until he has been reimbursed his reasonable expenses by the buyer.

Article 92

1.   Where the goods have been received by the buyer, he shall take reasonable steps to preserve them if he intends to reject them; he shall have the right to retain them until he has been reimbursed his reasonable expenses by the seller.

2.   Where goods despatched to the buyer have been put at his disposal at their place of destination and he exercises the right to reject them, he shall be bound to take possession of them on behalf of the seller, provided that this may be done without payment of the price and without unreasonable inconvenience or unreasonable expense. This provision shall not apply where the seller or a person authorised to take charge of the goods on his behalf is present at such destination.

Article 93

The party who is under an obligation to take steps to preserve the goods may deposit them in the warehouse of a third person at the expense of the other party provided that the expense incurred is not unreasonable.

Article 94

1.   The party who, in the cases to which Articles 91 and 92 apply, is under an obligation to take steps to preserve the goods may sell them by any appropriate means, provided that there has been unreasonable delay by the other party in accepting them or taking them back or in paying the costs of preservation and provided that due notice has been given to the other party of the intention to sell.

2.   The party selling the goods shall have the right to retain out of the proceeds of sale an amount equal to the reasonable costs of preserving the goods and of selling them and shall transmit the balance to the other party.

Article 95

Where, in the cases to which Articles 91 and 92 apply, the goods are subject to loss or rapid deterioration or their preservation would involve unreasonable expense, the party under the duty to preserve them is bound to sell them in accordance with Article 94.

CHAPTER VI—PASSING OF THE RISK

Article 96

Where the risk has passed to the buyer, he shall pay the price notwithstanding the loss or deterioration of the goods, unless this is due to the act of the seller or of some other person for whose conduct the seller is responsible.

Article 97

1.   The risk shall pass to the buyer when delivery of the goods is effected in accordance with the provisions of the contract and the present Law.

2.   In the case of the handing over of goods which are not in conformity with the contract, the risk shall pass to the buyer from the moment when the handing over has, apart from the lack of conformity, been effected in accordance with the provisions of the contract and of the present Law, where the buyer has neither declared the contract avoided nor required goods in replacement.

Article 98

1.   Where the handing over of the goods is delayed owing to the breach of an obligation of the buyer, the risk shall pass to the buyer as from the last date when, apart from such breach, the handing over could have been made in accordance with the contract.

2.   Where the contract relates to a sale of unascertained goods, delay on the part of the buyer shall cause the risk to pass only when the seller has set aside goods manifestly appropriated to the contract and has notified the buyer that this has been done.

3.   Where unascertained goods are of such a kind that the seller cannot set aside a part of them until the buyer takes delivery, it shall be sufficient for the seller to do all acts necessary to enable the buyer to take delivery.

Article 99

1.   Where the sale is of goods in transit by sea, the risk shall be borne by the buyer as from the time at which the goods were handed over to the carrier.

2.   Where the seller, at the time of the conclusion of the contract, knew or ought to have known that the goods had been lost or had deteriorated, the risk shall remain with him until the time of the conclusion of the contract.

Article 100

If, in a case to which paragraph 3 of Article 19 applies, the seller, at the time of sending the notice or other document referred to in that paragraph knew or ought to have known that the goods had been lost or had deteriorated after they were handed over to the carrier, the risk shall remain with the seller until the time of sending such notice or document.

Article 101

The passing of the risk shall not necessarily be determined by the provisions of the contract concerning expenses.

[436]

SCHEDULE 2
THE UNIFORM LAW ON THE FORMATION OF CONTRACTS FOR THE INTERNATIONAL SALE OF GOODS

Section 2

Article 1

The present Law shall apply to the formation of contracts of sale of goods which, if they were concluded, would be governed by the Uniform Law on the International Sale of Goods.

Article 2

1.   The provisions of the following Articles shall apply except to the extent that it appears from the preliminary negotiations, the offer, the reply, the practices which the parties have established between themselves or usage, that other rules apply.

2.   However, a term of the offer stipulating that silence shall amount to acceptance is invalid.

Article 3

An offer or an acceptance need not be evidenced by writing and shall not be subject to any other requirement as to form. In particular, they may be proved by means of witnesses.

Article 4

1.   The communication which one person addresses to one or more specific persons with the object of, concluding a contract of sale shall not constitute an offer unless it is sufficiently definite to permit the conclusion of the contract by acceptance and indicates the intention of the offeror to be bound.

2.   This communication may be interpreted by reference to and supplemented by the preliminary negotiations, any practices which the parties have established between themselves, usage and the provisions of the Uniform Law on the International Sale of Goods.

Article 5

1.   The offer shall not bind the offeror until it has been communicated to the offeree; it shall lapse if its withdrawal is communicated to the offeree before or at the same time as the offer.

2.   After an offer has been communicated to the offeree it can be revoked unless the revocation is not made in good faith or in conformity with fair dealing or unless the offer states a fixed time for acceptance or otherwise indicates that it is firm or irrevocable.

3.   An indication that the offer is firm or irrevocable may be express or implied from the circumstances, the preliminary negotiations, any practices which the parties have established between themselves or usage.

4.   A revocation of an offer shall only have effect if it has been communicated to the offeree before he has despatched his acceptance or has done any act treated as acceptance under paragraph 2 of Article 6.

Article 6

1.   Acceptance of an offer consists of a declaration by any means whatsoever to the offeror.

2.   Acceptance may also consist of the despatch of the goods or of the price or of any other act which may be considered to be equivalent to the declaration referred to in paragraph 1 of this Article either by virtue of the offer or as a result of practices which the parties have established between themselves or usage.

Article 7

1.   An acceptance containing additions, limitations or other modifications shall be a rejection of the offer and shall constitute a counter-offer.

2.   However, a reply to an offer which purports to be an acceptance but which contains additional or different terms which do not materially alter the terms of the offer shall constitute an acceptance unless the offeror promptly objects to the discrepancy; if he does not so object, the terms of the contract shall be the terms of the offer with the modifications contained in the acceptance.

Article 8

1.   A declaration of acceptance of an offer shall have effect only if it is communicated to the offeror within the time he has fixed or, if no such time is fixed, within a reasonable time, due account being taken of the circumstances of the transaction, including the rapidity of the means of communication employed by the offeror, and usage. In the case of an oral offer, the acceptance shall be immediate, if the circumstances do not show that the offeree shall have time for reflection.

2.   If a time for acceptance is fixed by an offeror in a letter or in a telegram, it shall be presumed to begin to run from the day the letter was dated or the hour of the day the telegram was handed in for despatch.

3.   If an acceptance consists of an act referred to in paragraph 2 of Article 6, the act shall have effect only if it is done within the period laid down in paragraph 1 of the present Article.

Article 9

1.   If the acceptance is late, the offeror may nevertheless consider it to have arrived in due time on condition that he promptly so informs the acceptor orally or by despatch of a notice.

2.   If however the acceptance is communicated late, it shall be considered to have been communicated in due time, if the letter or document which contains the acceptance shows that it has been sent in such circumstances that if its transmission had been normal it would have been communicated in due time; this provision shall not however apply if the offeror has promptly informed the acceptor orally or by despatch of a notice that he considers his offer as having lapsed.

Article 10

An acceptance cannot be revoked except by a revocation which is communicated to the offeror before or at the same time as the acceptance.

Article 11

The formation of the contract is not affected by the death of one of the parties or by his becoming incapable of contracting before acceptance unless the contrary results from the intention of the parties, usage or the nature of the transaction.

Article 12

1.   For the purposes of the present Law, the expression "to be communicated" means to be delivered at the address of the person to whom the communication is directed.

2.   Communications provided for by the present Law shall be made by the means usual in the circumstances.

Article 13

1.   "Usage" means any practice or method of dealing which reasonable persons in the same situation as the parties usually consider to be applicable to the formation of their contract.

2.   Where expressions, provisions or forms of contract commonly used in commercial practice are employed, they shall be interpreted according to the meaning usually given to them in the trade concerned.

[437]

TRADE DESCRIPTIONS ACT 1968

(1968 c 29)

ARRANGEMENT OF SECTIONS

An Act to replace the Merchandise Marks Acts 1887 to 1953 by fresh provisions prohibiting misdescriptions of goods, services, accommodation and facilities provided in the course of trade; to prohibit false or misleading indications as to the price of goods; to confer power to require information or instructions relating to goods to be marked on or to accompany the goods or to be included in advertisements; to prohibit the unauthorised use of devices or emblems signifying royal awards; to enable the Parliament of Northern Ireland to make laws relating to merchandise marks; and for purposes connected with those matters

[30 May 1968]

Prohibition of false trade descriptions

1 Prohibition of false trade descriptions

(1) ...

[(2) Sections 2 to 4 shall have effect for the interpretation of expressions used in this Act.]

[438]

NOTES

Sub-s (1): repealed by the Consumer Protection from Unfair Trading Regulations 2008, SI 2008/1277, reg 30(1), (3), Sch 2, Pt 1, paras 7, 8(a), Sch 4.

Sub-s (2): substituted by SI 2008/1277, reg 30(1), Sch 2, Pt 1, paras 7, 9.

2 Trade description

(1)   A trade description is an indication, direct or indirect, and by whatever means given of any of the following matters with respect to any goods or parts of goods, that is to say—

(a)   quantity, size or gauge;
(b)   method of manufacture, production, processing or reconditioning;
(c)   composition;
(d)   fitness for purpose, strength, performance, behaviour or accuracy;
(e)   any physical characteristics not included in the preceding paragraphs;
(f)   testing by any person and results thereof;
(g)   approval by any person or conformity with a type approved by any person;
(h)   place or date of manufacture, production, processing or reconditioning;
(i)   person by whom manufactured, produced, processed or reconditioned;
(j)   other history, including previous ownership or use.

(2)   The matters specified in subsection (1) of this section shall be taken—

(a)   in relation to any animal, to include sex, breed or cross, fertility and soundness;
(b)   in relation to any semen, to include the identity and characteristics of the animal from which it was taken and measure of dilution.

(3)   In this section "quantity" includes length, width, height, area, volume, capacity, weight and number.

(4)   Notwithstanding anything in the preceding provisions of this section, the following shall be deemed not to be trade descriptions, that is to say, any description or mark applied in pursuance of—

(a)   ...
(b)   section 2 of the Agricultural Produce (Grading and Marking) Act 1928 (as amended by the Agricultural Produce (Grading and Marking) Amendment Act 1931) or any corresponding enactment of the Parliament of Northern Ireland;
(c)   the Plant Varieties and Seeds Act 1964;
(d)   the Agriculture and Horticulture Act 1964 [or any Community grading rules within the meaning of Part III of that Act];
(e)   the Seeds Act (Northern Ireland) 1965;
(f)   the Horticulture Act (Northern Ireland) 1966;
[(g)   the Consumer Protection Act 1987;]
[(h)   the Plant Varieties Act 1997;]

[any statement made in respect of, or mark applied to, any material in pursuance of Part IV of the Agriculture Act 1970, any name or expression to which a meaning has been assigned under section 70 of that Act when applied to any material in the circumstances specified in that section] ... any mark prescribed by a system of classification compiled under section 5 of the Agriculture Act 1967 [and any designation, mark or description applied in pursuance of a scheme brought into force under section 6(1) or an order made under section 25(1) of the Agriculture Act 1970].

(5)   Notwithstanding anything in the preceding provisions of this section,

[(a)]   where provision is made under [the Food Safety Act 1990] or the [Food Safety (Northern Ireland) Order 1991] [or the Consumer Protection Act 1987] prohibiting the application of a description except to goods in the case of which the requirements specified in that provision are complied with, that description, when applied to such goods, shall be deemed not to be a trade description;

[(b)]   where by virtue of any provision made under Part V of the Medicines Act 1968 (or made under any provisions of the said Part V as applied by an order made under section 104 or section 105 of that Act) anything which, in accordance with this Act, constitutes the application of a trade description to goods is subject to any requirements or restrictions imposed by that provision, any particular description specified in that provision, when applied to goods in circumstances to which those requirements or restrictions are applicable, shall be deemed not to be a trade description]

[(c)]   where any description of a veterinary medicinal product is required to be applied to the product by an authorisation for the product granted under the Veterinary Medicines Regulations 2006, that description, when applied to the product, shall be deemed not to be a trade description.]

[439]

NOTES

Sub-s (4): para (a) repealed, and words in square brackets in para (d) added, by the European Communities Act 1972, s 4, Sch 3, Pt II, Sch 4, para 4(2); para (g) inserted by the Consumer Safety Act 1978, s 7(8), substituted by the Consumer Protection Act 1987, s 48(1), Sch 4, para 2(1); para (h) inserted by the Plant Varieties Act 1997, s 51(4); other words in square brackets substituted or added and second words omitted repealed by the Agriculture Act 1970, ss 6(4), 87(3), 113(3), Sch 5, Pt V.

Sub-s (5): the letter "(a)" and para (b) added by the Medicines Act 1968, s 135(1), Sch 5, para 16; in para (a), words in first pair of square brackets substituted by the Food Safety Act 1990, s 59(1), Sch 3, para 6, words in second pair of square brackets substituted by the Food Safety (Northern Ireland) Order 1991, SI 1991/762, art 51(1), Sch 2, para 8, and words in third pair of square brackets substituted by the Consumer Protection Act 1987, s 48(1), Sch 4, para 2(1); para (c) added by the Veterinary Medicines Regulations 2006, SI 2006/2407, reg 44(3), Sch 9, Pt 1, para 2.

3   False trade description

(1)   A false trade description is a trade description which is false to a material degree.

(2)   A trade description which, though not false, is misleading, that is to say, likely to be taken for such an indication of any of the matters specified in section 2 of this Act as would be false to a material degree, shall be deemed to be a false trade description.

(3)   Anything which, though not a trade description, is likely to be taken for an indication of any of those matters and, as such an indication, would be false to a material degree, shall be deemed to be a false trade description.

(4)   A false indication, or anything likely to be taken as an indication which would be false, that any goods comply with a standard specified or recognised by any person or implied by the approval of any person shall be deemed to be a false trade description, if there is no such person or no standard so specified, recognised or implied.

[440]

4   Applying a trade description to goods

(1)   A person applies a trade description to goods if he—
    (a)   affixes or annexes it to or in any manner marks it on or incorporates it with—
        (i)   the goods themselves, or
        (ii)   anything in, on or with which the goods are supplied; or
    (b)   places the goods in, on or with anything which the trade description has been affixed or annexed to, marked on or incorporated with, or places any such thing with the goods; or
    (c)   uses the trade description in any manner likely to be taken as referring to the goods.

(2)   An oral statement may amount to the use of a trade description.

(3)   Where goods are supplied in pursuance of a request in which a trade description is used and circumstances are such as to make it reasonable to infer that the goods are supplied as goods corresponding to that trade description, the person supplying the goods shall be deemed to have applied that trade description to the goods.

[441]

5   Trade descriptions used in advertisements

(1)   The following provisions of this section shall have effect where in an advertisement a trade description is used in relation to any class of goods.

(2)   The trade description shall be taken as referring to all goods of the class, whether or not in existence at the time the advertisement is published—
    (a)   for the purpose of determining whether an offence has been committed under paragraph (a) of section 1(1) of this Act; and
    (b)   where goods of the class are supplied or offered to be supplied by a person publishing or displaying the advertisement, also for the purpose of determining whether an offence has been committed under paragraph (b) of the said section 1(1).

(3)   In determining for the purposes of this section whether any goods are of a class to which a trade description used in an advertisement relates regard shall be had not only to the form and content of the advertisement but also to the time, place, manner and frequency of its publication and all other matters making it likely or unlikely that a person to whom the goods are supplied would think of the goods as belonging to the class in relation to which the trade description is used in the advertisement.

[442]–[447]

NOTES
Repealed by the Consumer Protection from Unfair Trading Regulations 2008, SI 2008/1277, reg 30(1), (3), Sch 2, Pt 1, paras 7, 8(b), Sch 4, subject to transitional provisions and savings in reg 30(2) of, and Sch 3, para 1 to, those Regulations at **[3702]**, **[3704]**.

6–10   *(Repealed by the Consumer Protection from Unfair Trading Regulations 2008, SI 2008/1277, reg 30(1), (3), Sch 2, Pt 1, paras 7, 8(c), (d), Sch 4.)*

Misstatements other than false trade descriptions

11   *(Repealed by the Consumer Protection Act 1987, s 48(3), Sch 5.)*

12 False representations as to royal approval or award, etc

(1) If any person, in the course of any trade or business, gives, by whatever means, any false indication, direct or indirect, that any goods or services supplied by him or any methods adopted by him are or are of a kind supplied to or approved by Her Majesty or any member of the Royal Family, he shall, subject to the provisions of this Act, be guilty of an offence.

(2) If any person, in the course of any trade or business, uses, without the authority of Her Majesty, any device or emblem signifying the Queen's Award to Industry or anything so nearly resembling such a device or emblem as to be likely to deceive, he shall, subject to the provisions of this Act, be guilty of an offence.

[(3) A person shall not be guilty of an offence under subsection (1) or (2) by reason of doing anything that is a commercial practice unless the commercial practice is unfair.

In this subsection "commercial practice" and "unfair" have the same meaning as in the Consumer Protection from Unfair Trading Regulations 2008.]

[448]–[451]

NOTES

Sub-s (3): added by the Consumer Protection from Unfair Trading Regulations 2008, SI 2008/1277, reg 30(1), Sch 2, Pt 1, paras 7, 10.

13–15 *(Repealed by the Consumer Protection from Unfair Trading Regulations 2008, SI 2008/1277, reg 30(1), (3), Sch 2, Pt 1, paras 7, 8(e), Sch 4.)*

Prohibition of importation of certain goods

16 Prohibition of importation of goods bearing false indication of origin

Where a false trade description is applied to any goods outside the United Kingdom and the false indication, or one of the false indications, given, or likely to be taken as given, thereby is an indication of the place of manufacture, production, processing or reconditioning of the goods or any part thereof, the goods shall not be imported into the United Kingdom.

[452]

17 *(Inserted the Trade Marks Act 1938, s 64A (repealed).)*

Provisions as to offences

18 Penalty for offences

A person guilty of an offence under this Act for which no other penalty is specified shall be liable—
  (a) on summary conviction, to a fine not exceeding [the prescribed sum] and
  (b) on conviction on indictment, to a fine or imprisonment for a term not exceeding two years or both.

[453]

NOTES

Reference to the prescribed sum in para (a) substituted by virtue of the Magistrates' Courts Act 1980, s 32(2).

19 Time limit for prosecutions

(1) No prosecution for an offence under this Act shall be commenced after the expiration of three years from the commission of the offence or one year from its discovery by the prosecutor, whichever is the earlier.

(2) Notwithstanding anything in [section 127(1) of the Magistrates' Courts Act 1980], a magistrates' court may try an information for an offence under this Act if the information was laid at any time within twelve months from the commission of the offence.

(3) *(Applies to Scotland only.)*

(4) Subsections (2) and (3) of this section do not apply where—
  (a) the offence was committed by the making of an oral statement; or
  (b) *the offence was one of supplying goods to which a false trade description is applied, and the trade description was applied by an oral statement; or*
  (c) *the offence was one where a false trade description is deemed to have been applied to goods by virtue of section 4(3) of this Act and the goods were supplied in pursuance of an oral request.*

[454]

NOTES

Sub-s (2): words in square brackets substituted by the Magistrates' Courts Act 1980, s 154, Sch 7, para 75.

Sub-s (4): paras (b), (c) repealed by the Consumer Protection from Unfair Trading Regulations 2008, SI 2008/1277, reg 30(3), Sch 4, subject to transitional provisions and savings in reg 30(2) of, and Sch 3, para 2 to, those Regulations at **[3702]**, **[3704]**.

20 Offences by corporations

(1)   Where an offence under this Act which has been committed by a body corporate is proved to have been committed with the consent and connivance of, or to be attributable to any neglect on the part of, any director, manager, secretary or other similar officer of the body corporate, or any person who was purporting to act in any such capacity, he as well as the body corporate shall be guilty of that offence and shall be liable to be proceeded against and punished accordingly.

(2)   In this section "director", in relation to any body corporate established by or under any enactment for the purpose of carrying on under national ownership any industry or part of an industry or undertaking, being a body corporate whose affairs are managed by the members thereof, means a member of that body corporate.

[455]

21 Accessories to offences committed abroad

(1), (2)   ...

(3)   Any person who, in the United Kingdom, assists in or induces the commission outside the United Kingdom of an act which, if committed in the United Kingdom, would be an offence under section 12 of this Act shall be guilty of an offence.

[456]–[457]

NOTES
Sub-ss (1), (2): repealed by the Consumer Protection from Unfair Trading Regulations 2008, SI 2008/1277, reg 30(1), (3), Sch 2, Pt 1, paras 7, 8(f), Sch 4.

22   *(Repealed by the Consumer Protection from Unfair Trading Regulations 2008, SI 2008/1277, reg 30(1), (3), Sch 2, Pt 1, paras 7, 8(g), Sch 4.)*

23 Offences due to fault of other person

Where the commission by any person of an offence under this Act is due to the act or default of some other person that other person shall be guilty of the offence, and a person may be charged with and convicted of the offence by virtue of this section whether or not proceedings are taken against the first-mentioned person.

[458]

Defences

24 Defence of mistake, accident, etc

(1)   In any proceedings for an offence under this Act it shall, subject to subsection (2) of this section, be a defence for the person charged to prove—

    (a)   that the commission of the offence was due to a mistake or to reliance on information supplied to him or to the act or default of another person, an accident or some other cause beyond his control; and

    (b)   that he took all reasonable precautions and exercised all due diligence to avoid the commission of such an offence by himself or any person under his control.

(2)   If in any case the defence provided by the last foregoing subsection involves the allegation that the commission of the offence was due to the act or default of another person or to reliance on information supplied by another person, the person charged shall not, without leave of the court, be entitled to rely on that defence unless, within a period ending seven clear days before the hearing, he has served on the prosecutor a notice in writing giving such information identifying or assisting in the identification of that other person as was then in his possession.

(3)   *In any proceedings for an offence under this Act of supplying or offering to supply goods to which a false trade description is applied it shall be a defence for the person charged to prove that he did not know, and could not with reasonable diligence have ascertained, that the goods did not conform to the description or that the description had been applied to the goods.*

[459]

NOTES
Sub-s (3): repealed by the Consumer Protection from Unfair Trading Regulations 2008, SI 2008/1277, reg 30(3), Sch 4, subject to transitional provisions and savings in reg 30(2) of, and Sch 3, para 3 to, those Regulations at **[3702]**, **[3704]**.

PART 1
STATUTES

25 Innocent publication of advertisement

In proceedings for an offence under this Act committed by the publication of an advertisement it shall be a defence for the person charged to prove that he is a person whose business it is to publish or arrange for the publication of advertisements and that he received the advertisement for publication in the ordinary course of business and did not know and had no reason to suspect that its publication would amount to an offence under this Act.

[460]

Enforcement

26 Enforcing authorities

(1)   It shall be the duty of every local weights and measures authority to enforce within their area the provisions of this Act and of any order made under this Act; ...

(2)   Every local weights and measures authority shall, whenever the Board of Trade so direct, make to the Board a report on the exercise of their functions under this Act in such form and containing such particulars as the Board may direct.

(3), (4)   ...

(5)   (*Applies to Scotland only.*)

[461]

NOTES
Sub-s (1): words omitted repealed by the Weights and Measures Act 1985, ss 96(1), 98(1), Sch 11, para 18(2), Sch 13, Pt I.
Sub-ss (3), (4): repealed by the Local Government, Planning and Land Act 1980, ss 1(4), 194, Sch 4, para 10(a), Sch 34, Pt IV.

27 Power to make test purchases

A local weights and measures authority shall have power to make, or to authorise any of their officers to make on their behalf, such purchases of goods, and to authorise any of their officers to secure the provision of such services, accommodation or facilities, as may appear expedient for the purpose of determining whether or not the provisions of this Act and any order made thereunder are being complied with.

[462]

28 Power to enter premises and inspect and seize goods and documents

(1)   A duly authorised officer of a local weights and measures authority or of a Government department may, at all reasonable hours and on production, if required, of his credentials, exercise the following powers, that is to say,—

    (a)   he may, for the purpose of ascertaining whether any offence under this Act has been committed, inspect any goods and enter any premises other than premises used only as a dwelling;

    (b)   if he has reasonable cause to suspect that an offence under this Act has been committed, he may, for the purpose of ascertaining whether it has been committed, require any person carrying on a trade or business or employed in connection with a trade or business to produce any books or documents relating to the trade or business and may take copies of, or of any entry in, any such book or document;

    (c)   if he has reasonable cause to believe that an offence under this Act has been committed, he may seize and detain any goods for the purpose of ascertaining, by testing or otherwise, whether the offence has been committed;

    (d)   he may seize and detain any goods or documents which he has reason to believe may be required as evidence in proceedings for an offence under this Act;

    (e)   he may, for the purpose of exercising his powers under this subsection to seize goods, but only if and to the extent that it is reasonably necessary in order to secure that the provisions of this Act and of any order made thereunder are duly observed, require any person having authority to do so to break open any container or open any vending machine and, if that person does not comply with the requirement, he may do so himself.

(2)   An officer seizing any goods or documents in the exercise of his powers under this section shall inform the person from whom they are seized and, in the case of goods seized from a vending machine, the person whose name and address are stated on the machine as being the proprietor's or, if no name and address are so stated, the occupier of the premises on which the machine stands or to which it is affixed.

(3)   If a justice of the peace, on sworn information in writing—

    (a)   is satisfied that there is reasonable ground to believe either—

        (i)   that any goods, books or documents which a duly authorised officer has power under this section to inspect are on any premises and that their inspection is likely to disclose evidence of the commission of an offence under this Act; or

(ii)   that any offence under this Act has been, is being or is about to be committed on any premises; and

(b)   is also satisfied either—

    (i)   that admission to the premises has been or is likely to be refused and that notice of intention to apply for a warrant under this subsection has been given to the occupier; or

    (ii)   that an application for admission, or the giving of such a notice, would defeat the object of the entry or that the premises are unoccupied or that the occupier is temporarily absent and it might defeat the object of the entry to await his return,

the justice may by warrant under his hand, which shall continue in force for a period of one month, authorise an officer of a local weights and measures authority or of a Government department to enter the premises, if need be by force.

(Applies to Scotland only.)

(4)   An officer entering any premises by virtue of this section may take with him such other persons and such equipment as may appear to him necessary; and on leaving any premises which he has entered by virtue of a warrant under the preceding subsection he shall, if the premises are unoccupied or the occupier is temporarily absent, leave them as effectively secured against trespassers as he found them.

(5)   ...

[(5A)   ...]

(6)   If any person who is not a duly authorised officer of a local weights and measures authority or of a Government department purports to act as such under this section he shall be guilty of an offence.

(7)   Nothing in this section shall be taken to compel the production by a solicitor of a document containing a privileged communication made by or to him in that capacity or to authorise the taking of possession of any such document which is in his possession.

[463]

NOTES

Sub-s (5): repealed by the Enterprise Act 2002, ss 247(a), 278(2), Sch 26.

Sub-s (5A): inserted by the Consumer Credit Act 1974, s 192(3)(a), Sch 4, Pt I, para 28; repealed by the Enterprise Act 2002, ss 247(a), 278(2), Sch 26.

Seize and detain goods: the powers of seizure conferred by sub-s (1)(c), (d) are powers of seizure to which the Criminal Justice and Police Act 2001, s 50 apply (additional powers of seizure from premises); see s 50 of, and Sch 1, Pt 1, para 9 to, that Act.

29   Obstruction of authorised officers

(1)   Any person who—

(a)   wilfully obstructs an officer of a local weights and measures authority or of a Government department acting in pursuance of this Act; or

(b)   wilfully fails to comply with any requirement properly made to him by such an officer under section 28 of this Act; or

(c)   without reasonable cause fails to give such an officer so acting any other assistance or information which he may reasonably require of him for the purpose of the performance of his functions under this Act,

shall be guilty of an offence and liable, on summary conviction, to a fine not exceeding [level 3 on the standard scale].

(2)   If any person, in giving any such information as is mentioned in the preceding subsection, makes any statement which he knows to be false, he shall be guilty of an offence.

(3)   Nothing in this section shall be construed as requiring a person to answer any question or give any information if to do so might incriminate him.

[464]

NOTES

Sub-s (1): reference to a level on the standard scale substituted by virtue of the Criminal Justice Act 1982, ss 38, 46.

30   Notice of test and intended prosecution

(1)   Where any goods seized or purchased by an officer in pursuance of this Act are submitted to a test, then—

(a)   if the goods were seized, the officer shall inform the person mentioned in section 28(2) of this Act of the result of the test;

(b)   if the goods were purchased and the test leads to the institution of proceedings for an offence under this Act, the officer shall inform the person from whom the goods were

PART 1
STATUTES

purchased, or, in the case of goods sold through a vending machine, the person mentioned in section 28(2) of this Act, of the result of the test;

and shall, where as a result of the test proceedings for an offence under this Act are instituted against any person, allow him to have the goods tested on his behalf if it is reasonably practicable to do so.

(2)–(4) ...

[465]

NOTES
Sub-ss (2)–(4): repealed by the Fair Trading Act 1973, s 139, Sch 13.

31 Evidence by certificate

(1) The Board of Trade may by regulations provide that certificates issued by such persons as may be specified by the regulations in relation to such matters as may be so specified shall, subject to the provisions of this section, be received in evidence of those matters in any proceedings under this Act.

(2) Such a certificate shall not be received in evidence—
   (a) unless the party against whom it is to be given in evidence has been served with a copy thereof not less than seven days before the hearing; or
   (b) if that party has, not less than three days before the hearing, served on the other party a notice requiring the attendance of the person issuing the certificate.

(3) *(Applies to Scotland only.)*

(4) For the purposes of this section any document purporting to be such a certificate as is mentioned in this section shall be deemed to be such a certificate unless the contrary is shown.

(5) Regulations under this section shall be made by statutory instrument which shall be subject to annulment in pursuance of a resolution of either House of Parliament.

[466]–[467]

Miscellaneous and supplemental

32 *(Repealed by the Consumer Protection from Unfair Trading Regulations 2008, SI 2008/1277, reg 30(1), (3), Sch 2, Pt 1, paras 7, 8(h), Sch 4.)*

33 Compensation for loss, etc of goods seized under s 28

(1) Where, in the exercise of his powers under section 28 of this Act, an officer of a local weights and measures authority or of a Government department seizes and detains any goods and their owner suffers loss by reason thereof or by reason that the goods, during the detention, are lost or damaged or deteriorate, then, unless the owner is convicted of an offence under this Act committed in relation to the goods, the authority or department shall be liable to compensate him for the loss so suffered.

(2) Any disputed question as to the right to or the amount of any compensation payable under this section shall be determined by arbitration and, in Scotland, by a single arbiter appointed, failing agreement between the parties, by the sheriff.

[468]

34 Trade marks containing trade descriptions

The fact that a trade description is a trade mark, or part of a trade mark, ... does not prevent it from being a false trade description when applied to any goods, except where the following conditions are satisfied, that is to say—
   (a) that it could have been lawfully applied to the goods if this Act had not been passed; and
   (b) that on the day this Act is passed the trade mark either is registered under the Trade Marks Act 1938 or is in use to indicate a connection in the course of trade between such goods and the proprietor of the trade mark; and
   (c) that the trade mark as applied is used to indicate such a connection between the goods and the proprietor of the trade mark or[, in the case of a registered trade mark, a person licensed to use it]; and
   (d) that the person who is the proprietor of the trade mark is the same person as, or a successor in title of, the proprietor on the day this Act is passed.

[469]

NOTES
Words omitted repealed, and words in square brackets substituted, by the Trade Marks Act 1994, s 106(1), Sch 4, para 4.
Modification: references to trade marks or registered trade marks within the meaning of the Trade Marks Act 1938 shall, unless the context otherwise requires, be construed as references to trade marks or registered trade marks within the meaning of the Trade Marks Act 1994; see the Trade Marks Act 1994, Sch 4, para 1.
Trade Marks Act 1938: repealed and replaced by the Trade Marks Act 1994.

35 Saving for civil rights

A contract for the supply of any goods shall not be void or unenforceable by reason only of a contravention of any provision of this Act.

[470]

36 Country of origin

(1) For the purposes of this Act goods shall be deemed to have been manufactured or produced in the country in which they last underwent a treatment or process resulting in a substantial change.

(2) The Board of Trade may by order specify—

    (a) in relation to any description of goods, what treatment or process is to be regarded for the purposes of this section as resulting or not resulting in a substantial change;

    (b) in relation to any description of goods different parts of which were manufactured or produced in different countries, or of goods assembled in a country different from that in which their parts were manufactured or produced, in which of those countries the goods are to be regarded for the purposes of this Act as having been manufactured or produced.

[471]–[472]

NOTES

    Order: the Trade Descriptions (Country of Origin) (Cutlery) Order 1981, SI 1981/122.

37   *(Repealed by the Consumer Protection from Unfair Trading Regulations 2008, SI 2008/1277, reg 30(1), (3), Sch 2, Pt 1, paras 7, 8(i), Sch 4.)*

38 Orders

(1) Any power to make an order under the preceding provisions of this Act shall be exercisable by statutory instrument, which shall be subject to annulment in pursuance of a resolution of either House of Parliament, and includes power to vary or revoke such an order by a subsequent order.

(2) Any order under the preceding provisions of this Act which relates to any ... fertilisers or any goods used as pesticides or for similar purposes shall be made by the Board of Trade acting jointly with the following Ministers, that is to say, if the order extends to England and Wales, the Minister of Agriculture, Fisheries and Food, and if it extends to Scotland or Northern Ireland, the Secretary of State concerned.

[(2A) Any order under the preceding provisions of this Act which relates to any agricultural, horticultural or fishery produce, whether processed or not, food, feeding stuffs or the ingredients of food or feeding stuffs shall be made by the Board of Trade acting jointly with the following Ministers, that is to say, if the order extends to England and Wales, the Secretary of State concerned with health and if it extends to Scotland or Northern Ireland, the Secretary of State concerned.

(2B) Before making an order to which subsection (2) or (2A) of this section applies the Board of Trade shall consult the Food Standards Agency.]

(3) The following provisions shall apply to the making of an order under [section 36 of this Act], that is to say—

    (a) before making the order the Board of Trade shall consult with such organisations as appear to them to be representative of interests substantially affected by it and shall publish, in such manner as the Board think appropriate, notice of their intention to make the order and of the place where copies of the proposed order may be obtained; and

    (b) the order shall not be made until the expiration of a period of twenty-eight days from the publication of the notice and may then be made with such modifications (if any) as the Board of Trade think appropriate having regard to any representations received by them.

[473]

NOTES

    Sub-s (2): words omitted repealed by the Food Standards Act 1999, s 40(1), (4), Sch 5, para 4(1), (2), Sch 6.

    Sub-ss (2A), (2B): inserted by the Food Standards Act 1999, s 40(1), Sch 5, para 4(1), (3).

    Sub-s (3): words in square brackets substituted by the Consumer Protection from Unfair Trading Regulations 2008, SI 2008/1277, reg 30(1), Sch 2, Pt 1, paras 7, 11.

    Minister of Agriculture, Fisheries and Food: now the Secretary of State for Environment, Food and Rural Affairs; see the Secretaries of State for Transport, Local Government and the Regions and for Environment, Food and Rural Affairs Order 2001, SI 2001/2568.

    Transfer of functions in relation to Wales: as to the transfer of functions under this section to the National Assembly for Wales, see the National Assembly for Wales (Transfer of Functions) Order 1999, SI 1999/672.

39 Interpretation

(1) The following provisions shall have effect, in addition to sections [2 to 4] of this Act, for the interpretation in this Act of expressions used therein, that is to say,—

    "advertisement" includes a catalogue, a circular and a price list;

    "goods" includes ships and aircraft, things attached to land and growing crops;

PART 1 STATUTES

"premises" includes any place and any stall, vehicle, ship or aircraft; and
"ship" includes any boat and any other description of vessel used in navigation.

(2)   *For the purposes of this Act, a trade description or statement published in any newspaper,
book or periodical or in any film or sound or television broadcast [or in any programme included in
any programme service (within the meaning of the Broadcasting Act 1990) other than a sound or
television broadcasting service] shall not be deemed to be a trade description applied or statement
made in the course of a trade or business unless it is or forms part of an advertisement.*

[474]

NOTES
Sub-s (1): words in square brackets substituted by the Consumer Protection from Unfair Trading
Regulations 2008, SI 2008/1277, reg 30(1), Sch 2, Pt 1, paras 7, 12.
Sub-s (2): repealed by SI 2008/1277, reg 30(1), (3), Sch 2, Pt 1, paras 7, 8(j), Sch 4, subject to transitional
provisions and savings in reg 30(2) of, and Sch 3, para 4 to, those Regulations at **[3702]**, **[3704]**; words in square
brackets originally inserted by the Cable and Broadcasting Act 1984, s 57(1), Sch 5, para 19, substituted by the
Broadcasting Act 1990, s 203(1), Sch 20, para 11.

40   Provisions as to Northern Ireland

(1)   This Act shall apply to Northern Ireland subject to the following modifications, that is to
say—
   (a)   section 19(2) shall apply as if for the references to [section 127(1) of the Magistrates'
          Courts Act 1980] and the trial and laying of an information there were substituted
          respectively references to [Article 19(1) of the Magistrates' Courts (Northern Ireland)
          Order 1981] and the hearing and determination and making of a complaint [and as if for
          the word "under" there were substituted the words "under section 29(1) of"];
   (b)   section 26 and subsections (2) to (4) of section 30 shall not apply but it shall be the duty
          of the Ministry of Commerce for Northern Ireland to enforce the provisions of this Act
          and of any order made under it (other than the provisions of section 42 of this Act);
   (c)   sections 27 to 29 and 33 shall apply as if for references to a local weights and measures
          authority and any officer of such an authority there were substituted respectively
          references to the said Ministry and any of its officers.

(2)–(5)   ...

(6)   Nothing in this Act shall authorise any department of the Government of Northern Ireland
to incur any expenses attributable to the provisions of this Act until provision has been made by the
Parliament of Northern Ireland for those expenses to be defrayed out of moneys provided by that
Parliament.

(7)   ...

[475]

NOTES
Sub-s (1): words in first pair of square brackets substituted by the Magistrates' Courts Act 1980, s 154, Sch 7,
para 74; words in second pair of square brackets substituted by the Magistrates' Courts (Northern Ireland)
Order 1981, SI 1981/1675, art 170(2), Sch 6, Pt 1, para 13; words in third pair of square brackets inserted by the
Criminal Justice (Northern Ireland) Order 1980, SI 1980/704, art 12, Sch 1, Pt II, para 43.
Sub-ss (2)–(4), (7): repealed by the Northern Ireland Constitution Act 1973, s 41(1), Sch 6, Pt I.
Sub-s (5): repealed by the Northern Ireland (Modification of Enactments—No 1) Order 1973, SI 1973/2163,
art 14(2), Sch 6.

41, 42   (*S 41 outside the scope of this work; s 42 repealed by the Statute Law (Repeals) Act 1975.*)

43   Short title and commencement

(1)   This Act may be cited as the Trade Descriptions Act 1968.

(2)   This Act shall come into force on the expiration of the period of six months beginning with
the day on which it is passed.

[476]

(*Sch 1 repealed in part by the Road Traffic Act 1972, s 205(1), Sch 9, Pt I; remainder amends the
Anglo-Portuguese Commercial Treaty Act 1914, s 1, the Anglo-Portuguese Commercial Treaty
Act 1916, s 1(1), and the Agricultural Produce (Grading and Marking Act) 1928, s 4(2); Sch 2
repealed by the Statute Law (Repeals) Act 1975.*)

AUCTIONS (BIDDING AGREEMENTS) ACT 1969

(1969 c 56)

An Act to amend the law with respect to proceedings for offences under the Auctions (Bidding Agreements) Act 1927; to make fresh provision as to the rights of a seller of goods by auction where an agreement subsists that a person or persons shall abstain from bidding for the goods; and for connected purposes

[22 October 1969]

1   Offences under Auctions (Bidding Agreements) Act 1927 to be indictable as well as triable summarily, and extension of time for bringing summary proceedings

(1)   Offences under section 1 of the Auctions (Bidding Agreements) Act 1927 (which, as amended by the Criminal Justice Act 1967, renders a dealer who agrees to give, or gives, or offers a gift or consideration to another as an inducement or reward for abstaining, or for having abstained, from bidding at a sale by auction punishable on summary conviction with a fine not exceeding £400 or imprisonment for a term not exceeding six months, or both, and renders similarly punishable a person who agrees to accept, or accepts, or attempts to obtain from a dealer any such gift or consideration as aforesaid) shall be triable on indictment as well as summarily; and the penalty that may be imposed on a person on conviction on indictment of an offence under that section shall be imprisonment for a term not exceeding two years or a fine or both.

(2)–(4)   (*Apply to Scotland only.*)

(5)   This section applies only to offences committed after the commencement of this Act.

[477]

NOTES

Sub-ss (2), (4): repealed, in relation to England and Wales, by the Criminal Law Act 1977, s 65(5), Sch 13.

2   Persons convicted not to attend or participate in auctions

(1)   On any such summary conviction or conviction on indictment as is mentioned in section 1 above, the court may order that the person so convicted or that person and any representative of him shall not (without leave of the court) for a period from the date of such conviction—

    (a)   in the case of a summary conviction, of not more than one year, or

    (b)   in the case of a conviction on indictment, of not more than three years,

enter upon any premises where goods intended for sale by auction are on display or to attend or participate in any way in any sale by auction.

(2)   In the event of a contravention of an order under this section, the person who contravenes it (and, if he is the representative of another, that other also) shall be guilty of an offence and liable—

    (a)   on summary conviction, to a fine not exceeding [the prescribed sum];

    (b)   on conviction on indictment, to imprisonment for a term not exceeding two years or to a fine or to both.

(3)   In any proceedings against a person in respect of a contravention of an order under this section consisting in the entry upon premises where goods intended for sale by auction were on display, it shall be a defence for him to prove that he did not know, and had no reason to suspect, that goods so intended were on display on the premises, and in any proceedings against a person in respect of a contravention of such an order consisting in his having done something as the representative of another, it shall be a defence for him to prove that he did not know, and had no reason to suspect, that that other was the subject of such an order.

(4)   A person shall not be guilty of an offence under this section by reason only of his selling property by auction or causing it to be so sold.

[478]

NOTES

Sub-s (2): reference to the prescribed sum substituted by virtue of the Magistrates' Courts Act 1980, s 32(7).

3   Rights of seller of goods by auction where agreement subsists that some person shall abstain from bidding for the goods

(1)   Where goods are purchased at an auction by a person who has entered into an agreement with another or others that the other or the others (or some of them) shall abstain from bidding for the goods (not being an agreement to purchase the goods bona fide on a joint account) and he or the other party, or one of the other parties, to the agreement is a dealer, the seller may avoid the contract under which the goods are purchased.

(2)   Where a contract is avoided by virtue of the foregoing subsection, then, if the purchaser has obtained possession of the goods and restitution thereof is not made, the persons who were parties to

the agreement that one or some of them should abstain from bidding for the goods the subject of the contract shall be jointly and severally liable to make good to the seller the loss (if any) he sustained by reason of the operation of the agreement.

(3), (4) …

(5) In this section, "dealer" has the meaning assigned to it by section 1(2) of the Auctions (Bidding Agreements) Act 1927.

[479]

NOTES

Sub-ss (3), (4): repealed by the Statute Law (Repeals) Act 2004.

4 Copy of Act to be exhibited at sale

Section 3 of the Auctions (Bidding Agreements) Act 1927 (copy of Act to be exhibited at sale) shall have effect as if the reference to that Act included a reference to this Act.

[480]

5 Short title, commencement and extent

(1) This Act may be cited as the Auctions (Bidding Agreements) Act 1969.

(2) …

(3) This Act shall not extend to Northern Ireland.

[481]

NOTES

Sub-s (2): repealed by the Statute Law (Repeals) Act 2004.

ADMINISTRATION OF JUSTICE ACT 1970

(1970 c 31)

An Act to make further provision about the courts (including assizes), their business, jurisdiction and procedure; to enable a High Court judge to accept appointment as arbitrator or umpire under an arbitration agreement; to amend the law respecting the enforcement of debt and other liabilities; to amend section 106 of the Rent Act 1968; and for miscellaneous purposes connected with the administration of justice

[29 May 1970]

1–39 *((Pts I–IV) outside the scope of this work.)*

PART V

MISCELLANEOUS PROVISIONS

40 Punishment for unlawful harassment of debtors

(1) A person commits an offence if, with the object of coercing another person to pay money claimed from the other as a debt due under a contract, he—

  (a) harasses the other with demands for payment which, in respect of their frequency or the manner or occasion of making any such demand, or of any threat or publicity by which any demand is accompanied, are calculated to subject him or members of his family or household to alarm, distress or humiliation;

  (b) falsely represents, in relation to the money claimed, that criminal proceedings lie for failure to pay it;

  (c) falsely represents himself to be authorised in some official capacity to claim or enforce payment; or

  (d) utters a document falsely represented by him to have some official character or purporting to have some official character which he knows it has not.

(2) A person may be guilty of an offence by virtue of subsection (1)(a) above if he concerts with others in the taking of such action as is described in that paragraph, notwithstanding that his own course of conduct does not by itself amount to harassment.

(3) Subsection (1)(a) above does not apply to anything done by a person which is reasonable (and otherwise permissible in law) for the purpose—

  (a) of securing the discharge of an obligation due, or believed by him to be due, to himself or to persons for whom he acts, or protecting himself or them from future loss; or

  (b) of the enforcement of any liability by legal process.

[(3A)   Subsection (1) above does not apply to anything done by a person to another in circumstances where what is done is a commercial practice within the meaning of the Consumer Protection from Unfair Trading Regulations 2008 and the other is a consumer in relation to that practice.]

(4)   A person guilty of an offence under this section shall be liable on summary conviction to a fine of not more than [level 5 on the standard scale].

[482]

NOTES

Sub-s (3A): inserted by the Consumer Protection from Unfair Trading Regulations 2008, SI 2008/1277, reg 30(1), Sch 2, Pt 1, para 13.

Sub-s (4): reference to a level on the standard scale substituted by virtue of the Criminal Justice Act 1982, ss 35, 38, 46.

41–51   (*Ss 41, 44, 44A, 48, 51(2), (3) outside the scope of this work; ss 42, 50, 51(1) repealed by the Magistrates' Courts Act 1980, s 154, Sch 9; s 43 repealed by the Legal Aid Act 1974, s 42(1), Sch 5, Pt I; s 45(1) repealed by the Courts Act 1971, s 56(4), Sch 11, Pt IV; s 45(2) repealed by the County Courts Act 1984, s 148(3), Sch 4; s 45(3) repealed by the Senior Courts Act 1981, s 52(4), Sch 7; s 46 repealed by the Administration of Justice Act 1973, s 19(1), Sch 5, Pt VI; s 47 repealed by the Rent Act 1977, s 155(5), Sch 25; s 49 repealed by the Guardianship of Minors Act 1971, s 18(2), Sch 2.*)

PART VI

GENERAL

52, 53   (*S 52 outside the scope of this work; s 53 repealed by the Northern Ireland Constitution Act 1973, s 41(1), Sch 6, Pt I.*)

54   Citation, interpretation, repeals, commencement and extent

(1)   This Act may be cited as the Administration of Justice Act 1970.

(2)   References in this Act to any enactment include references to that enactment as amended or extended by or under any other enactment, including this Act.

(3)–(6)   …

[483]

NOTES

Sub-ss (3), (5), (6): outside the scope of this work.

Sub-s (4): repealed by the Statute Law (Repeals) Act 2004.

Orders: the Administration of Justice Act 1970 (Commencement No 1) Order 1970, SI 1970/886; the Administration of Justice Act 1970 (Commencement No 2) Order 1970, SI 1970/1207; the Administration of Justice Act 1970 (Commencement No 3) Order 1970, SI 1970/1962; the Administration of Justice Act 1970 (Commencement No 4) Order 1970, SI 1971/834; the Administration of Justice Act 1970 (Commencement No 5) Order 1970, SI 1971/1244.

(*Schs 1–11 outside the scope of this work.*)

CARRIAGE OF GOODS BY SEA ACT 1971

(1971 c 19)

ARRANGEMENT OF SECTIONS

An Act to amend the law with respect to the carriage of goods by sea

[8 April 1971]

NOTES
Hovercraft: by the Hovercraft (Civil Liability) Order 1986, SI 1986/1305, arts 4, 5, 10, Sch 2, Sch 4, this Act
applies, with modifications, in relation to the carriage of goods by hovercraft (other than passengers' baggage) as
it applies in relation to goods on board or carried by ship.

1 Application of Hague Rules as amended

(1)   In this Act, "the Rules" means the International Convention for the unification of certain
rules of law relating to bills of lading signed at Brussels on 25th August 1924, as amended by the
Protocol signed at Brussels on 23rd February 1968 [and by the Protocol signed at Brussels on 21st
December 1979].

(2)   The provisions of the Rules, as set out in the Schedule to this Act, shall have the force of
law.

(3)   Without prejudice to subsection (2) above, the said provisions shall have effect (and have
the force of law) in relation to and in connection with the carriage of goods by sea in ships where the
port of shipment is a port in the United Kingdom, whether or not the carriage is between ports in
two different States within the meaning of Article X of the Rules.

(4)   Subject to subsection (6) below, nothing in this section shall be taken as applying anything
in the Rules to any contract for the carriage of goods by sea, unless the contract expressly or by
implication provides for the issue of a bill of lading or any similar document of title.

(5)   …

(6)   Without prejudice to Article X(c) of the Rules, the Rules shall have the force of law in
relation to—
     (a)   any bill of lading if the contract contained in or evidenced by it expressly provides that
         the Rules shall govern the contract, and
     (b)   any receipt which is a non-negotiable document marked as such if the contract contained
         in or evidenced by it is a contract for the carriage of goods by sea which expressly
         provides that the Rules are to govern the contract as if the receipt were a bill of lading,
but subject, where paragraph (b) applies, to any necessary modifications and in particular with the
omission in Article III of the Rules of the second sentence of paragraph 4 and of paragraph 7.

(7)   If and so far as the contract contained in or evidenced by a bill of lading or receipt within
paragraph (a) or (b) of subsection (6) above applies to deck cargo or live animals, the Rules as given
the force of law by that subsection shall have effect as if Article I(c) did not exclude deck cargo and
live animals.

In this subsection "deck cargo" means cargo which by the contract of carriage is stated as being
carried on deck and is so carried.

[484]

NOTES
Sub-s (1): words in square brackets inserted by the Merchant Shipping Act 1981, s 2(1); this amendment
continues to have effect by virtue of the Merchant Shipping Act 1995, s 314(2), Sch 13, para 45(1), (2).
Sub-s (5): repealed by the Merchant Shipping Act 1981, s 5(3), Schedule.

[1A Conversion of special drawing rights into sterling

(1)   For the purposes of Article IV of the Rules the value on a particular day of one special
drawing right shall be treated as equal to such a sum in sterling as the International Monetary Fund
have fixed as being the equivalent of one special drawing right—
     (a)   for that day; or
     (b)   if no sum has been so fixed for that day, for the last day before that day for which a sum
         has been so fixed.

(2)   A certificate given by or on behalf of the Treasury stating—
     (a)   that a particular sum in sterling has been fixed as aforesaid for a particular day; or
     (b)   that no sum has been so fixed for a particular day and that a particular sum in sterling
         has been so fixed for a day which is the last day for which a sum has been so fixed
         before the particular day,
shall be conclusive evidence of those matters for the purposes of subsection (1) above; and a
document purporting to be such a certificate shall in any proceedings be received in evidence and,
unless the contrary is proved, be deemed to be such a certificate.

(3)   The Treasury may charge a reasonable fee for any certificate given in pursuance of
subsection (2) above, and any fee received by the Treasury by virtue of this subsection shall be paid
into the Consolidated Fund.]

[485]

NOTES

Inserted by the Merchant Shipping Act 1995, s 314(2), Sch 13, para 45(1), (3).

2 Contracting States, etc

(1) If Her Majesty by Order in Council certifies to the following effect, that is to say, that for the purposes of the Rules—

(a)   a State specified in the Order is a contracting State, or is a contracting State in respect of any place or territory so specified; or

(b)   any place or territory specified in the Order forms part of a State so specified (whether a contracting State or not),

the Order shall, except so far as it has been superseded by a subsequent Order, be conclusive evidence of the matters so certified.

(2) An Order in Council under this section may be varied or revoked by a subsequent Order in Council.

[486]

NOTES

Order in Council: the Carriage of Goods by Sea (Parties to Convention) Order 1985, SI 1985/443.

3 Absolute warranty of seaworthiness not to be implied in contracts to which Rules apply

There shall not be implied in any contract for the carriage of goods by sea to which the Rules apply by virtue of this Act any absolute undertaking by the carrier of the goods to provide a seaworthy ship.

[487]

4 Application of Act to British possessions, etc

(1) Her Majesty may by Order in Council direct that this Act shall extend, subject to such exceptions, adaptations and modifications as may be specified in the Order, to all or any of the following territories, that is—

(a)   any colony (not being a colony for whose external relations a country other than the United Kingdom is responsible),

(b)   any country outside Her Majesty's dominions in which Her Majesty has jurisdiction in right of Her Majesty's Government of the United Kingdom.

(2) An Order in Council under this section may contain such transitional and other consequential and incidental provisions as appear to Her Majesty to be expedient, including provisions amending or repealing any legislation about the carriage of goods by sea forming part of the law of any of the territories mentioned in paragraphs (a) and (b) above.

(3) An Order in Council under this section may be varied or revoked by a subsequent Order in Council.

[488]

NOTES

Orders in Council: the Carriage of Goods by Sea (Bermuda) Order 1980, SI 1980/1507; the Carriage of Goods by Sea (Overseas Territories) Order 1982, SI 1982/1664; the Merchant Shipping (Revocation) (Bermuda) Order 2002, SI 2002/3147.

5 Extension of application of Rules to carriage from ports in British possessions, etc

(1) Her Majesty may by Order in Council provide that section 1(3) of this Act shall have effect as if the reference therein to the United Kingdom included a reference to all or any of the following territories, that is—

(a)   the Isle of Man;

(b)   any of the Channel Islands specified in the Order;

(c)   any colony specified in the Order (not being a colony for whose external relations a country other than the United Kingdom is responsible);

(d)   …

(e)   any country specified in the Order, being a country outside Her Majesty's dominions in which Her Majesty has jurisdiction in right of Her Majesty's Government of the United Kingdom.

(2) An Order in Council under this section may be varied or revoked by a subsequent Order in Council.

[489]

NOTES

Sub-s (1): para (d) repealed by the Statute Law (Repeals) Act 1989.

6 Supplemental

(1) This Act may be cited as the Carriage of Goods by Sea Act 1971.

(2) It is hereby declared that this Act extends to Northern Ireland.

(3) The following enactments shall be repealed, that is—
  (a) the Carriage of Goods by Sea Act 1924,
  (b) section 12(4)(a) of the Nuclear Installations Act 1965,

and without prejudice to section 38(1) of the Interpretation Act 1889, the reference to the said Act of 1924 in section 1(1)(i)(ii) of the Hovercraft Act 1968 shall include a reference to this Act.

[(4) It is hereby declared that for the purposes of Article VIII of the Rules section 186 of the Merchant Shipping Act 1995 (which entirely exempts shipowners and others in certain circumstances or loss of, or damage to, goods) is a provision relating to limitation of liability.]

(5) This Act shall come into force on such day as Her Majesty may by Order in Council appoint, and, for the purposes of the transition from the law in force immediately before the day appointed under this subsection to the provisions of this Act, the Order appointing the day may provide that those provisions shall have effect subject to such transitional provisions as may be contained in the Order.

[490]

NOTES

Sub-s (4): substituted by the Merchant Shipping Act 1995, s 314(3), Sch 13, para 45(1), (4).
Interpretation Act 1889, s 38(1): repealed by the Interpretation Act 1978, s 25, Sch 3; see now s 17(2)(a) of, and Sch 2, para 3 to, the 1978 Act.
Orders in Council: the Carriage of Goods by Sea Act 1971 (Commencement) Order 1977, SI 1977/981.

SCHEDULE
THE HAGUE RULES AS AMENDED BY THE BRUSSELS PROTOCOL 1968
Section 3

Article I

In these Rules the following words are employed, with the meanings set out below:—
  (a) "Carrier" includes the owner or the charterer who enters into a contract of carriage with a shipper.
  (b) "Contract of carriage" applies only to contracts of carriage covered by a bill of lading or any similar document of title, in so far as such document relates to the carriage of goods by sea, including any bill of lading or any similar document as aforesaid issued under or pursuant to a charter party from the moment at which such bill of lading or similar document of title regulates the relations between a carrier and a holder of the same.
  (c) "Goods" includes goods, wares, merchandise, and articles of every kind whatsoever except live animals and cargo which by the contract of carriage is stated as being carried on deck and is so carried.
  (d) "Ship" means any vessel used for the carriage of goods by sea.
  (e) "Carriage of goods" covers the period from the time when the goods are loaded on to the time they are discharged from the ship.

Article II

Subject to the provisions of Article VI, under every contract of carriage of goods by sea the carrier, in relation to the loading, handling, stowage, carriage, custody, care and discharge of such goods, shall be subject to the responsibilities and liabilities, and entitled to the rights and immunities hereinafter set forth.

Article III

1. The carrier shall be bound before and at the beginning of the voyage to exercise due diligence to—
  (a) Make the ship seaworthy.
  (b) Properly man, equip and supply the ship.
  (c) Make the holds, refrigerating and cool chambers, and all other parts of the ship in which goods are carried, fit and safe for their reception, carriage and preservation.

2. Subject to the provisions of Article IV, the carrier shall properly and carefully load, handle, stow, carry, keep, care for, and discharge the goods carried.

3. After receiving the goods into his charge the carrier or the master or agent of the carrier shall, on demand of the shipper, issue to the shipper a bill of lading showing among other things—
  (a) The leading marks necessary for identification of the goods as the same are furnished in writing by the shipper before the loading of such goods starts, provided such marks are

stamped or otherwise shown clearly upon the goods if uncovered, or on the cases or coverings in which such goods are contained, in such a manner as should ordinarily remain legible until the end of the voyage.

    (b)   Either the number of packages or pieces, or the quantity, or weight, as the case may be, as furnished in writing by the shipper.

    (c)   The apparent order and condition of the goods.

Provided that no carrier, master or agent of the carrier shall be bound to state or show in the bill of lading any marks, number, quantity, or weight which he has reasonable ground for suspecting not accurately to represent the goods actually received, or which he has had no reasonable means of checking.

4.   Such a bill of lading shall be prima facie evidence of the receipt by the carrier of the goods as therein described in accordance with paragraph 3 (a), (b) and (c). However, proof to the contrary shall not be admissible when the bill of lading has been transferred to a third party acting in good faith.

5.   The shipper shall be deemed to have guaranteed to the carrier the accuracy at the time of shipment of the marks, number, quantity and weight, as furnished by him, and the shipper shall indemnify the carrier against all loss, damages and expenses arising or resulting from inaccuracies in such particulars. The right of the carrier to such indemnity shall in no way limit his responsibility and liability under the contract of carriage to any person other than the shipper.

6.   Unless notice of loss or damage and the general nature of such loss or damage be given in writing to the carrier or his agent at the port of discharge before or at the time of the removal of the goods into the custody of the person entitled to delivery thereof under the contract of carriage, or, if the loss or damage be not apparent, within three days, such removal shall be prima facie evidence of the delivery by the carrier of the goods as described in the bill of lading.

The notice in writing need not be given if the state of the goods has, at the time of their receipt, been the subject of joint survey or inspection.

Subject to paragraph 6*bis* the carrier and the ship shall in any event be discharged from all liability whatsoever in respect of the goods, unless suit is brought within one year of their delivery or of the date when they should have been delivered. This period may, however, be extended if the parties so agree after the cause of action has arisen.

In the case of any actual or apprehended loss or damage the carrier and the receiver shall give all reasonable facilities to each other for inspecting and tallying the goods.

6*bis*.   An action for indemnity against a third person may be brought even after the expiration of the year provided for in the preceding paragraph if brought within the time allowed by the law of the Court seized of the case. However, the time allowed shall be not less than three months, commencing from the day when the person bringing such action for indemnity has settled the claim or has been served with process in the action against himself.

7.   After the goods are loaded the bill of lading to be issued by the carrier, master, or agent of the carrier, to the shipper shall, if the shipper so demands, be a "shipped" bill of lading, provided that if the shipper shall have previously taken up any document of title to such goods, he shall surrender the same as against the issue of the "shipped" bill of lading, but at the option of the carrier such document of title may be noted at the port of shipment by the carrier, master, or agent with the name or names of the ship or ships upon which the goods have been shipped and the date or dates of shipment, and when so noted, if it shows the particulars mentioned in paragraph 3 of Article III, shall for the purpose of this article be deemed to constitute a "shipped" bill of lading.

8.   Any clause, covenant, or agreement in a contract of carriage relieving the carrier or the ship from liability for loss or damage to, or in connection with, goods arising from negligence, fault, or failure in the duties and obligations provided in this article or lessening such liability otherwise than as provided in these Rules, shall be null and void and of no effect. A benefit of insurance in favour of the carrier or similar clause shall be deemed to be a clause relieving the carrier from liability.

Article IV

1.   Neither the carrier nor the ship shall be liable for loss or damage arising or resulting from unseaworthiness unless caused by want of due diligence on the part of the carrier to make the ship seaworthy, and to secure that the ship is properly manned, equipped and supplied, and to make the holds, refrigerating and cool chambers and all other parts of the ship in which goods are carried fit and safe for their reception, carriage and preservation in accordance with the provisions of paragraph 1 of Article III. Whenever loss or damage has resulted from unseaworthiness the burden of proving the exercise of due diligence shall be on the carrier or other person claiming exemption under this article.

2.   Neither the carrier nor the ship shall be responsible for loss or damage arising or resulting from—

    (a)   Act, neglect, or default of the master, mariner, pilot, or the servants of the carrier in the navigation or in the management of the ship.

(b) Fire, unless caused by the actual fault or privity of the carrier.
(c) Perils, dangers and accidents of the sea or other navigable waters.
(d) Act of God.
(e) Act of war.
(f) Act of public enemies.
(g) Arrest or restraint of princes, rulers or people, or seizure under legal process.
(h) Quarantine restrictions.
(i) Act or omission of the shipper or owner of the goods, his agent or representative.
(j) Strikes or lockouts or stoppage or restraint of labour from whatever cause, whether partial or general.
(k) Riots and civil commotions.
(l) Saving or attempting to save life or property at sea.
(m) Wastage in bulk or weight or any other loss or damage arising from inherent defect, quality or vice of the goods.
(n) Insufficiency of packing.
(o) Insufficiency or inadequacy of marks.
(p) Latent defects not discoverable by due diligence.
(q) Any other cause arising without the actual fault or privity of the carrier, or without the fault or neglect of the agents or servants of the carrier, but the burden of proof shall be on the person claiming the benefit of this exception to show that neither the actual fault or privity of the carrier nor the fault or neglect of the agents or servants of the carrier contributed to the loss or damage.

3.   The shipper shall not be responsible for loss or damage sustained by the carrier or the ship arising or resulting from any cause without the act, fault or neglect of the shipper, his agents or his servants.

4.   Any deviation in saving or attempting to save life or property at sea or any reasonable deviation shall not be deemed to be an infringement or breach of these Rules or of the contract of carriage, and the carrier shall not be liable for any loss or damage resulting therefrom.

5.—(a) Unless the nature and value of such goods have been declared by the shipper before shipment and inserted in the bill of lading, neither the carrier nor the ship shall in any event be or become liable for any loss or damage to or in connection with the goods in an amount exceeding [666.67 units of account] per package or unit or [2 units of account per kilogramme] of gross weight of the goods lost or damaged, whichever is the higher.
(b) The total amount recoverable shall be calculated by reference to the value of such goods at the place and time at which the goods are discharged from the ship in accordance with the contract or should have been so discharged.
The value of the goods shall be fixed according to the commodity exchange price, or, if there be no such price, according to the current market price, or, if there be no commodity exchange price or current market price, by reference to the normal value of goods of the same kind and quality.
(c) Where a container, pallet or similar article of transport is used to consolidate goods, the number of packages or units enumerated in the bill of lading as packed in such article of transport shall be deemed the number of packages or units for the purpose of this paragraph as far as these packages or units are concerned. Except as aforesaid such article of transport shall be considered the package or unit.
[(d) The unit of account mentioned in this Article is the special drawing right as defined by the International Monetary Fund. The amounts mentioned in sub-paragraph (a) of this paragraph shall be converted into national currency on the basis of the value of that currency on a date to be determined by the law of the Court seized of the case.]
(e) Neither the carrier nor the ship shall be entitled to the benefit of the limitation of liability provided for in this paragraph if it is proved that the damage resulted from an act or omission of the carrier done with intent to cause damage, or recklessly and with knowledge that damage would probably result.
(f) The declaration mentioned in sub-paragraph (a) of this paragraph, if embodied in the bill of lading, shall be prima facie evidence, but shall not be binding or conclusive on the carrier.
(g) By agreement between the carrier, master or agent of the carrier and the shipper other maximum amounts than those mentioned in sub-paragraph (a) of this paragraph may be fixed, provided that no maximum amount so fixed shall be less than the appropriate maximum mentioned in that sub-paragraph.
(h) Neither the carrier nor the ship shall be responsible in any event for loss or damage to, or in connection with, goods if the nature or value thereof has been knowingly mis-stated by the shipper in the bill of lading.

6.   Goods of an inflammable, explosive or dangerous nature to the shipment whereof the carrier, master or agent of the carrier has not consented with knowledge of their nature and character, may at any time before discharge be landed at any place, or destroyed or rendered innocuous by the carrier without compensation and the shipper of such goods shall be liable for all damages and expenses

directly or indirectly arising out of or resulting from such shipment. If any such goods shipped with such knowledge and consent shall become a danger to the ship or cargo, they may in like manner be landed at any place, or destroyed or rendered innocuous by the carrier without liability on the part of the carrier except to general average, if any.

Article IV bis

1.   The defences and limits of liability provided for in these Rules shall apply in any action against the carrier in respect of loss or damage to goods covered by a contract of carriage whether the action be founded in contract or in tort.

2.   If such an action is brought against a servant or agent of the carrier (such servant or agent not being an independent contractor), such servant or agent shall be entitled to avail himself of the defences and limits of liability which the carrier is entitled to invoke under these Rules.

3.   The aggregate of the amounts recoverable from the carrier, and such servants and agents, shall in no case exceed the limit provided for in these Rules.

4.   Nevertheless, a servant or agent of the carrier shall not be entitled to avail himself of the provisions of this article, if it is proved that the damage resulted from an act or omission of the servant or agent done with intent to cause damage or recklessly and with knowledge that damage would probably result.

Article V

A carrier shall be at liberty to surrender in whole or in part all or any of his rights and immunities or to increase any of his responsibilities and obligations under these Rules, provided such surrender or increase shall be embodied in the bill of lading issued to the shipper. The provisions of these Rules shall not be applicable to charter parties, but if bills of lading are issued in the case of a ship under a charter party they shall comply with the terms of these Rules.

Nothing in these Rules shall be held to prevent the insertion in a bill of lading of any lawful provision regarding general average.

Article VI

Notwithstanding the provisions of the preceding articles, a carrier, master or agent of the carrier and a shipper shall in regard to any particular goods be at liberty to enter into any agreement in any terms as to the responsibility and liability of the carrier for such goods, and as to the rights and immunities of the carrier in respect of such goods, or his obligation as to seaworthiness, so far as this stipulation is not contrary to public policy, or the care or diligence of his servants or agents in regard to the loading, handling, stowage, carriage, custody, care and discharge of the goods carried by sea, provided that in this case no bill of lading has been or shall be issued and that the terms agreed shall be embodied in a receipt which shall be a non-negotiable document and shall be marked as such.

Any agreement so entered into shall have full legal effect.

Provided that this article shall not apply to ordinary commercial shipments made in the ordinary course of trade, but only to other shipments where the character or condition of the property to be carried or the circumstances, terms and conditions under which the carriage is to be performed are such as reasonably to justify a special agreement.

Article VII

Nothing herein contained shall prevent a carrier or a shipper from entering into any agreement, stipulation, condition, reservation or exemption as to the responsibility and liability of the carrier or the ship for the loss or damage to, or in connection with, the custody and care and handling of goods prior to the loading on, and subsequent to the discharge from, the ship on which the goods are carried by sea.

Article VIII

The provisions of these Rules shall not affect the rights and obligations of the carrier under any statute for the time being in force relating to the limitation of the liability of owners of sea-going vessels.

Article IX

These Rules shall not affect the provisions of any international Convention or national law governing liability for nuclear damage.

Article X

The provisions of these Rules shall apply to every bill of lading relating to the carriage of goods between ports in two different States if:

   (a)   the bill of lading is issued in a contracting State, or
   (b)   the carriage is from a port in a contracting State, or
   (c)   the contract contained in or evidenced by the bill of lading provides that these Rules or
       legislation of any State giving effect to them are to govern the contract,

whatever may be the nationality of the ship, the carrier, the shipper, the consignee, or any other interested person.

[The last two paragraphs of this article are not reproduced. They require contracting States to apply the Rules to bills of lading mentioned in the article and authorise them to apply the Rules to other bills of lading.]

[Articles 11 to 16 of the International Convention for the unification of certain rules of law relating to bills of lading signed at Brussels on 25th August 1924 are not reproduced. They deal with the coming into force of the Convention, procedure for ratification, accession and denunciation, and the right to call for a fresh conference to consider amendments to the Rules contained in the Convention.]

[491]

NOTES

Article IV: words in square brackets in para 5 substituted by the Merchant Shipping Act 1981, s 2(3), (4); this amendment continues to have effect by virtue of the Merchant Shipping Act 1995, s 314(2), Sch 13, para 45(2).

Words in italics in square brackets at the end of the Schedule are as set out in the Queen's Printer's version of the Act.

POWERS OF ATTORNEY ACT 1971

(1971 c 27)

ARRANGEMENT OF SECTIONS

An Act to make new provision in relation to powers of attorney and the delegation by trustees of their trusts, powers and discretions

[12 May 1971]

1 Execution of powers of attorney

(1)   An instrument creating a power of attorney shall be [executed as a deed by] the donor of the power.

(2)   ...

(3)   This section is without prejudice to any requirement in, or having effect under, any other Act as to the witnessing of instruments creating powers of attorney and does not affect the rules relating to the execution of instruments by bodies corporate.

[492]

NOTES

Sub-s (1): words in square brackets substituted by the Law of Property (Miscellaneous Provisions) Act 1989, ss 1(8), Sch 1, para 6(a).

Sub-s (2): repealed by the Law of Property (Miscellaneous Provisions) Act 1989, ss 1, 4, Sch 1, para 6(b), Sch 2.

2   *(Repealed by the Senior Courts Act 1981, s 152(4), Sch 7.)*

3 Proof of instruments creating powers of attorney

(1)   The contents of an instrument creating a power of attorney may be proved by means of a copy which—

   (a)   is a reproduction of the original made with a photographic or other device for reproducing documents in facsimile; and

(b)   contains the following certificate or certificates signed by the donor of the power or by a
        solicitor[, authorised person] or stockbroker, that is to say—
    (i)   a certificate at the end to the effect that the copy is a true and complete copy of the
            original; and
    (ii)   if the original consists of two or more pages, a certificate at the end of each page
            of the copy to the effect that it is a true and complete copy of the corresponding
            page of the original.

(2)   Where a copy of an instrument creating a power of attorney has been made which complies
with subsection (t) of this section, the contents of the instrument may also be proved by means of a
copy of that copy if the further copy itself complies with that subsection, taking references in it to
the original as references to the copy from which the further copy is made.

(3)   In this section ["authorised person" means a person (other than a solicitor) who, for the
purposes of the Legal Services Act 2007, is an authorised person in relation to any activity which
constitutes a notarial activity (within the meaning of that Act) and] "stockbroker" means a member
of any stock exchange within the meaning of the Stock Transfer Act 1963 or the Stock Transfer Act
(Northern Ireland) 1963.

(4)   This section is without prejudice to section 4 of the Evidence and Powers of Attorney
Act 1940 (proof of deposited instruments by office copy) and to any other method of proof
authorised by law.

(5)   For the avoidance of doubt, in relation to an instrument made in Scotland the references to
a power of attorney in this section and in section 4 of the Evidence and Powers of Attorney Act 1940
include references to a factory and commission.

[493]

NOTES
    Sub-s (1): words in square brackets (as originally inserted by the Courts and Legal Services Act 1990,
s 125(2), Sch 17, para 4(a)) substituted by the Legal Services Act 2007, s 208(1), Sch 21, para 26(a).
    Sub-s (3): words in square brackets (as originally inserted by the Courts and Legal Services Act 1990,
s 125(2), Sch 17, para 4(b)) substituted by the Legal Services Act 2007, s 208(1), Sch 21, para 26(b).
    Solicitors' incorporated practices: the provisions of sub-s (1)(b) of this section are applied, with modifications,
in relation to a "recognised body" under the Administration of Justice Act 1985, s 9, by the Solicitors'
Incorporated Practices Order 1991, SI 1991/2684, arts 2–5, Sch 1.

4   Powers of attorney given as security

(1)   Where a power of attorney is expressed to be irrevocable and is given to secure—
    (a)   a proprietary interest of the donee of the power; or
    (b)   the performance of an obligation owed to the donee,
then, so long as the donee has that interest or the obligation remains undischarged, the power shall
not be revoked—
    (i)   by the donor without the consent of the donee; or
    (ii)   by the death, incapacity or bankruptcy of the donor or, if the donor is a body corporate,
            by its winding up or dissolution.

(2)   A power of attorney given to secure a proprietary interest may be given to the person
entitled to the interest and persons deriving title under him to that interest, and those persons shall be
duly constituted donees of the power for all purposes of the power but without prejudice to any right
to appoint substitutes given by the power.

(3)   This section applies to powers of attorney whenever created.

[494]

5   Protection of donee and third persons where power of attorney is revoked

(1)   A donee of a power of attorney who acts in pursuance of the power at a time when it has
been revoked shall not, by reason of the revocation, incur any liability (either to the donor or to any
other person) if at that time he did not know that the power had been revoked.

(2)   Where a power of attorney has been revoked and a person, without knowledge of the
revocation, deals with the donee of the power, the transaction between them shall, in favour of that
person, be as valid as if the power had then been in existence.

(3)   Where the power is expressed in the instrument creating it to be irrevocable and to be given
by way of security then, unless the person dealing with the donee knows that it was not in fact given
by way of security, he shall be entitled to assume that the power is incapable of revocation except by
the donor acting with the consent of the donee and shall accordingly be treated for the purposes of
subsection (2) of this section as having knowledge of the revocation only if he knows that it has been
revoked in that manner.

(4)   Where the interest of a purchaser depends on whether a transaction between the donee of a power of attorney and another person was valid by virtue of subsection (2) of this section, it shall be conclusively presumed in favour of the purchaser that that person did not at the material time know of the revocation of the power if—

    (a)   the transaction between that person and the donee was completed within twelve months of the date on which the power came into operation; or

    (b)   that person makes a statutory declaration, before or within three months after the completion of the purchase, that he did not at the material time know of the revocation of the power.

(5)   Without prejudice to subsection (3) of this section, for the purposes of this section knowledge of the revocation of a power of attorney includes knowledge of the occurrence of any event (such as the death of the donor) which has the effect of revoking the power.

(6)   In this section "purchaser" and "purchase" have the meanings specified in section 205(1) of the Law of Property Act 1925.

(7)   This section applies whenever the power of attorney was created but only to acts and transactions after the commencement of this Act.

[495]

6   Additional protection for transferees under stock exchange transactions

(1)   Without prejudice to section 5 of this Act, where—

    (a)   the donee of a power of attorney executes, as transferor, an instrument transferring registered securities; and

    (b)   the instrument is executed for the purposes of a stock exchange transaction,

it shall be conclusively presumed in favour of the transferee that the power had not been revoked at the date of the instrument if a statutory declaration to that effect is made by the donee of the power on or within three months after that date.

(2)   In this section "registered securities" and "stock exchange transaction" have the same meanings as in the Stock Transfer Act 1963.

[496]

7   Execution of instruments etc by donee of power of attorney

[(1)   If the donee of a power of attorney is an individual, he may, if he thinks fit—

    (a)   execute any instrument with his own signature, and]

    (b)   do any other thing in his own name,

by the authority of the donor of the power; and any [instrument executed or thing done in that manner shall, subject to subsection (1A) of this section, be as effective as if executed by the donee in any manner which would constitute due execution of that instrument by the donor or, as the case may be, as if done by the donee in the name of the donor].

[(1A)   Where an instrument is executed by the donee as a deed, it shall be as effective as if executed by the donee in a manner which would constitute due execution of it as a deed by the donor only if it is executed in accordance with section 1(3)(a) of the Law of Property (Miscellaneous Provisions) Act 1989.]

(2)   For the avoidance of doubt it is hereby declared that an instrument to which subsection (3) … of section 74 of the Law of Property Act 1925 applies may be executed either as provided in [that subsection] or as provided in this section.

(3)   …

(4)   This section applies whenever the power of attorney was created.

[497]

NOTES

Sub-s (1): words in first pair of square brackets substituted by the Law of Property (Miscellaneous Provisions) Act 1989, s 1(8), Sch 1, para 7; words in second pair of square brackets substituted by the Regulatory Reform (Execution of Deeds and Documents) Order 2005, SI 2005/1906, art 10(1), Sch 1, paras 5, 6, except in relation to any instrument executed before 15 September 2005.

Sub-s (1A): inserted by SI 2005/1906, art 10(1), Sch 1, paras 5, 7, except in relation to any instrument executed before 15 September 2005.

Sub-s (2): words in square brackets substituted, and words omitted repealed, by the Law of Property (Miscellaneous Provisions) Act 1989, ss 1(8), 4, Sch 1, para 7, Sch 2.

Sub-s (3): repealed by SI 2005/1906, art 10, Sch 1, paras 5, 8, Sch 2, except in relation to any instrument executed before 15 September 2005.

8, 9   (*S 8 repealed by the Statute Law (Repeals) Act 2004; s 9 repealed by the Trustee Delegation Act 1999, s 12, Schedule.*)

10 Effect of general power of attorney in specified form

(1) Subject to subsection (2) of this section, a general power of attorney in the form set out in Schedule 1 to this Act, or in a form to the like effect but expressed to be made under this Act, shall operate to confer—

(a) on the donee of the power; or

(b) if there is more than one donee, on the donees acting jointly or acting jointly or severally, as the case may be,

authority to do on behalf of the donor anything which he can lawfully do by an attorney.

(2) [Subject to section 1 of the Trustee Delegation Act 1999, this section] does not apply to functions which the donor has as a trustee or personal representative or as a tenant for life or statutory owner within the meaning of the Settled Land Act 1925.

[498]

NOTES

Sub-s (2): words in square brackets substituted by the Trustee Delegation Act 1999, s 3.

11 Short title, repeals, consequential amendments, commencement and extent

(1) This Act may be cited as the Powers of Attorney Act 1971.

(2) The enactments specified in Schedule 2 to this Act are hereby repealed to the extent specified in the third column of that Schedule.

(3), (4) ...

(5) Section 3 of this Act extends to Scotland and Northern Ireland but, save as aforesaid, this Act extends to England and Wales only.

[499]

NOTES

Sub-s (3): in part amends the Law of Property Act 1925, s 125(2); remainder repealed by the Senior Courts Act 1981, s 152(4), Sch 7.

Sub-s (4): repealed by the Statute Law (Repeals) Act 2004.

SCHEDULES

SCHEDULE 1
FORM OF GENERAL POWER OF ATTORNEY FOR PURPOSES OF SECTION 10

Section 10

THIS GENERAL POWER OF ATTORNEY is made this   day of   19   by AB of

I appoint CD of [*or* CD of   and EF

of   jointly *or* jointly and severally] to be my attorney[s]

in accordance with section 10 of the Powers of Attorney Act 1971.

IN WITNESS etc,

[500]

NOTES

Prescribed form: for a Welsh language form, see the Powers of Attorney (Welsh Language Forms) Order 2000, SI 2000/215.

(*Sch 2 (Repeals)* outside the scope of this work.)

UNSOLICITED GOODS AND SERVICES ACT 1971

(1971 c 30)

ARRANGEMENT OF SECTIONS

An Act to make provision for the greater protection of persons receiving unsolicited goods, and to amend the law with respect to charges for entries in directories

[12 May 1971]

NOTES

Unsolicited Goods and Services Acts 1971 and 1975: by the Unsolicited Goods and Services (Amendment) Act 1975, s 4(1), see **[840]**, that Act and this Act may be cited together by this collective title.

1 (*Repealed by the Consumer Protection (Distance Selling) Regulations 2000, SI 2000/2334, reg 22(4)).*

2 Demands and threats regarding payment

(1) A person who, not having reasonable cause to believe there is a right to payment, in the course of any trade or business makes a demand for payment, or asserts a present or prospective right to payment, for what he knows are unsolicited goods sent (after the commencement of this Act) to another person with a view to his acquiring them [for the purposes of his trade or business], shall be guilty of an offence and on summary conviction shall be liable to a fine not exceeding [level 4 on the standard scale].

(2) A person who, not having reasonable cause to believe there is a right to payment, in the course of any trade or business and with a view to obtaining any payment for what he knows are unsolicited goods sent as aforesaid—

  (a) threatens to bring any legal proceedings; or

  (b) places or causes to be placed the name of any person on a list of defaulters or debtors or threatens to do so; or

  (c) invokes or causes to be invoked any other collection procedure or threatens to do so,

shall be guilty of an offence and shall be liable on summary conviction to a fine not exceeding [level 5 on the standard scale].

[501]

NOTES

Sub-s (1): words in first pair of square brackets inserted by the Consumer Protection (Distance Selling) Regulations 2000, SI 2000/2334, reg 22(1), (3), in relation to goods sent after 31 October 2000; reference to a level on the standard scale substituted by virtue of the Criminal Justice Act 1982, ss 38, 46.

Sub-s (2): references to a level on the standard scale substituted by virtue of the Criminal Justice Act 1982, ss 38, 46.

3 Directory entries

[(1) A person ("the purchaser") shall not be liable to make any payment, and shall be entitled to recover any payment made by him, by way of charge for including or arranging for the inclusion in a directory of an entry relating to that person or his trade or business, unless—

  (a) there has been signed by the purchaser or on his behalf an order complying with this section,

  (b) there has been signed by the purchaser or on his behalf a note complying with this section of his agreement to the charge and before the note was signed, a copy of it was supplied, for retention by him, to him or a person acting on his behalf, ...

  (c) there has been transmitted by the purchaser or a person acting on his behalf an electronic communication which includes a statement that the purchaser agrees to the charge and the relevant condition is satisfied in relation to that communication[, or

  (d) the charge arises under a contract in relation to which the conditions in section 3B(1) (renewed and extended contracts) are met.]

(2) A person shall be guilty of an offence punishable on summary conviction with a fine not exceeding [the prescribed sum] if, in a case where a payment in respect of a charge would ... be recoverable from him in accordance with the terms of subsection (1) above, he demands payment, or asserts a present or prospective right to payment, of the charge or any part of it, without knowing or having reasonable cause to believe [that—

  (a) the entry to which the charge relates was ordered in accordance with this section,

  (b) a proper note of the agreement has been duly signed, or

  (c) the requirements set out in subsection (1)(c) [or (d)] above have been met].

(3) For the purposes of [this section—

  (a)] an order for an entry in a directory must be made by means of an order form or other stationery belonging to the [purchaser[,which may be sent electronically but which must bear] his name and address (or one or more of his addresses);] and

  [(b)] the note [of a person's agreement to a charge must—

    (i) specify the particulars set out in Part 1 of the Schedule to the Regulatory Reform (Unsolicited Goods and Services Act 1971) (Directory Entries and Demands for Payment) Order 2005, and

    (ii)   give reasonable particulars of the entry in respect of which the charge would be payable.]

[(3A)   In relation to an electronic communication which includes a statement that the purchaser agrees to a charge for including or arranging the inclusion in a directory of any entry, the relevant condition is that—

    (a)   before the electronic communication was transmitted the information referred to in subsection (3B) below was communicated to the purchaser, and

    (b)   the electronic communication can readily be produced and retained in a visible and legible form.

(3B)   That information is—

    (a)   the following particulars—

        (i)   the amount of the charge;

        (ii)   the name of the directory or proposed directory;

        (iii)   the name of the person producing the directory;

        (iv)   the geographic address at which that person is established;

        (v)   if the directory is or is to be available in printed form, the proposed date of publication of the directory or of the issue in which the entry is to be included;

        (vi)   if the directory or the issue in which the entry is to be included is to be put on sale, the price at which it is to be offered for sale and the minimum number of copies which are to be available for sale;

        (vii)   if the directory or the issue in which the entry is to be included is to be distributed free of charge (whether or not it is also to be put on sale), the minimum number of copies which are to be so distributed;

        (viii)   if the directory is or is to be available in a form other than in printed form, adequate details of how it may be accessed; and

    (b)   reasonable particulars of the entry in respect of which the charge would be payable.

(3C)   In this section "electronic communication" has the same meaning as in the Electronic Communications Act 2000.]

(4)   Nothing in this section shall apply to a payment due under a contract entered into before the commencement of this Act, or entered into by the acceptance of an offer made before that commencement.

                                                        [502]

NOTES

    Sub-s (1): substituted by the Unsolicited Goods and Services Act 1971 (Electronic Communications) Order 2001, SI 2001/2778, arts 2, 3; word omitted repealed and words in square brackets added by the Regulatory Reform (Unsolicited Goods and Services Act 1971) (Directory Entries and Demands for Payment) Order 2005, SI 2005/55, art 2(1)–(3).

    Sub-s (2): reference to the prescribed sum substituted by virtue of the Magistrates' Courts Act 1980, s 32(2); words omitted repealed and words in third (inner) pair of square brackets inserted by SI 2005/55, art 2(1), (4); words in second (outer) pair of square brackets substituted, by SI 2001/2778, arts 2, 4(b).

    Sub-s (3): words in first pair of square brackets substituted, para (b) numbered as such, and words in final pair of square brackets substituted by SI 2005/55, art 2(1), (5); words in second (outer) pair of square brackets substituted by SI 2001/2778, art 5; words in third (inner) pair of square brackets substituted by the Unsolicited Goods and Services Act 1971 (Electronic Commerce) (Amendment) Regulations 2005, SI 2005/148, reg 2.

    Sub-ss (3A)–(3C): inserted by SI 2001/2778, art 6.

    Summary conviction: see the Unsolicited Goods and Services (Amendment) Act 1975, s 3 at **[839]**, which provides that the offence under sub-s (2) may be prosecuted on indictment.

3A   *(Inserted by the Unsolicited Goods and Services (Amendment) Act 1975, s 1; repealed by the Regulatory Reform (Unsolicited Goods and Services Act 1971) (Directory Entries and Demands for Payment) Order 2005, SI 2005/55, art 2(1), (6).)*

[3B   Renewed and extended contracts

    (1)   The conditions referred to in section 3(1)(d) above are met in relation to a contract ("the new contract") if—

    (a)   a person ("the purchaser") has entered into an earlier contract ("the earlier contract") for including or arranging for the inclusion in a particular issue or version of a directory ("the earlier directory") of an entry ("the earlier entry") relating to him or his trade or business;

    (b)   the purchaser was liable to make a payment by way of a charge arising under the earlier contract for including or arranging for the inclusion of the earlier entry in the earlier directory;

    (c)   the new contract is a contract for including or arranging for the inclusion in a later issue or version of a directory ("the later directory") of an entry ("the later entry") relating to the purchaser or his trade or business;

(d)   the form, content and distribution of the later directory is materially the same as the form, content and distribution of the earlier directory;

(e)   the form and content of the later entry is materially the same as the form and content of the earlier entry;

(f)   if the later directory is published other than in electronic form—

    (i)   the earlier directory was the last, or the last but one, issue or version of the directory to be published before the later directory, and

    (ii)   the date of publication of the later directory is not more than 13 months after the date of publication of the earlier directory;

(g)   if the later directory is published in electronic form, the first date on which the new contract requires the later entry to be published is not more than the relevant period after the last date on which the earlier contract required the earlier entry to be published;

(h)   if it was a term of the earlier contract that the purchaser renew or extend the contract—

    (i)   before the start of the new contract the relevant publisher has given notice in writing to the purchaser containing the information set out in Part 3 of the Schedule to the Regulatory Reform (Unsolicited Goods and Services Act 1971) (Directory Entries and Demands for Payment) Order 2005; and

    (ii)   the purchaser has not written to the relevant publisher withdrawing his agreement to the renewal or extension of the earlier contract within the period of 21 days starting when he receives the notice referred to in sub-paragraph (i); and

(i)   if the parties to the earlier contract and the new contract are different—

    (i)   the parties to both contracts have entered into a novation agreement in respect of the earlier contract; or

    (ii)   the relevant publisher has given the purchaser the information set out in Part 4 of the Schedule to the Regulatory Reform (Unsolicited Goods and Services Act 1971) (Directory Entries and Demands for Payment) Order 2005.

(2)   For the purposes of subsection (1)(d) and (e), the form, content or distribution of the later directory, or the form or content of the later entry, shall be taken to be materially the same as that of the earlier directory or the earlier entry (as the case may be), if a reasonable person in the position of the purchaser would—

(a)   view the two as being materially the same; or

(b)   view that of the later directory or the later entry as being an improvement on that of the earlier directory or the earlier entry.

(3)   For the purposes of subsection (1)(g) "the relevant period" means the period of 13 months or (if shorter) the period of time between the first and last dates on which the earlier contract required the earlier entry to be published.

(4)   For the purposes of subsection (1)(h) and (i) "the relevant publisher" is the person with whom the purchaser has entered into the new contract.

(5)   The information referred to in subsection (1)(i)(ii) must be given to the purchaser prior to the conclusion of the new contract.]

[503]

NOTES

Inserted by the Regulatory Reform (Unsolicited Goods and Services Act 1971) (Directory Entries and Demands for Payment) Order 2005, SI 2005/55, art 2(1), (7).

4 Unsolicited publications

(1)   A person shall be guilty of an offence if he sends or causes to be sent to another person any book, magazine or leaflet (or advertising material for any such publication) which he knows or ought reasonably to know is unsolicited and which describes or illustrates human sexual techniques.

(2)   A person found guilty of an offence under this section shall be liable on summary conviction to a fine not exceeding [level 5 on the standard scale].

(3)   A prosecution for an offence under this section shall not in England and Wales be instituted except by, or with the consent of, the Director of Public Prosecutions.

[504]

NOTES

Sub-s (2): reference to a level on the standard scale substituted by virtue of the Criminal Justice Act 1982, ss 38, 46.

5 Offences by corporations

(1)   Where an offence under this Act which has been committed by a body corporate is proved to have been committed with the consent or connivance of, or to be attributable to any neglect on the part of, any director, manager, secretary, or other similar officer of the body corporate, or of any

person who was purporting to act in any such capacity, he as well as the body corporate shall be guilty of that offence and shall be liable to be proceeded against and punished accordingly.

(2)　Where the affairs of a body corporate are managed by its members, this section shall apply in relation to the acts or defaults of a member in connection with his functions of management as if he were a director of the body corporate.

[505]

6　Interpretation

(1)　In this Act, unless the context or subject matter otherwise requires,—
"acquire" includes hire;
"send" includes deliver, and "sender" shall be construed accordingly;
"unsolicited" means, in relation to goods sent to any person, that they are sent without any prior request made by him or on his behalf.

[(2)　For the purposes of this Act, any invoice or similar document stating the amount of any payment shall be regarded as asserting a right to the payment unless it complies with the conditions set out in Part 2 of the Schedule to the Regulatory Reform (Unsolicited Goods and Services Act 1971) (Directory Entries and Demands for Payment) Order 2005.]

[(3)　Nothing in sections 3 or 3B shall affect the rights of any consumer under the Consumer Protection (Distance Selling) Regulations 2000.]

[506]

NOTES
Sub-s (2): substituted by the Regulatory Reform (Unsolicited Goods and Services Act 1971) (Directory Entries and Demands for Payment) Order 2005, SI 2005/55, art 2(1), (8)(a).
Sub-s (3): added by SI 2005/55, art 2(1), (8)(b).

7　Citation, commencement and extent

(1)　This Act may be cited as the Unsolicited Goods and Services Act 1971.

(2)　This Act shall come into force at the expiration of three months beginning with the day on which it is passed.

(3)　This Act does not extend to Northern Ireland.

[507]

SUPPLY OF GOODS (IMPLIED TERMS) ACT 1973

(1973 c 13)

ARRANGEMENT OF SECTIONS

Hire-purchase agreements

An Act to amend the law with respect to the terms to be implied in contracts of sale of goods and hire-purchase agreements and on the exchange of goods for trading stamps, and with respect to the terms of conditional sale agreements: and for connected purposes

[18 April 1973]

1–7　(*Repealed by the Sale of Goods Act 1979, s 63(2), Sch 3.*)

Hire-purchase agreements

[8　Implied terms as to title

(1)　In every hire-purchase agreement, other than one to which subsection (2) below applies, there is—

(a)   an implied [term] on the part of the creditor that he will have a right to sell the goods at the time when the property is to pass; and

(b)   an implied [term] that—

    (i)   the goods are free, and will remain free until the time when the property is to pass, from any charge or encumbrance not disclosed or known to the person to whom the goods are bailed or (in Scotland) hired before the agreement is made, and

    (ii)   that person will enjoy quiet possession of the goods except so far as it may be disturbed by any person entitled to the benefit of any charge or encumbrance so disclosed or known.

(2)   In a hire-purchase agreement, in the case of which there appears from the agreement or is to be inferred from the circumstances of the agreement an intention that the creditor should transfer only such title as he or a third person may have, there is—

(a)   an implied [term] that all charges or encumbrances known to the creditor and not known to the person to whom the goods are bailed or hired have been disclosed to that person before the agreement is made; and

(b)   an implied [term] that neither—

    (i)   the creditor; nor

    (ii)   in a case where the parties to the agreement intend that any title which may be transferred shall be only such title as a third person may have, that person; nor

    (iii)   anyone claiming through or under the creditor or that third person otherwise than under a charge or encumbrance disclosed or known to the person to whom the goods are bailed or hired, before the agreement is made;

will disturb the quiet possession of the person to whom the goods are bailed or hired.

[(3)   As regards England and Wales and Northern Ireland, the term implied by subsection (1)(a) above is a condition and the terms implied by subsections (1)(b), (2)(a) and (2)(b) above are warranties.]]

[508]

NOTES

Substituted, together with ss 9–11, 12, by the Consumer Credit Act 1974, s 192(3)(a), Sch 4, para 35.

Sub-ss (1), (2): words in square brackets substituted by the Sale and Supply of Goods Act 1994, s 7(1), Sch 2 para 4(1), (2)(a).

Sub-s (3): added by the Sale and Supply of Goods Act 1994, s 7(1), Sch 2 para 4(1), (2)(b).

[9   Bailing or hiring by description

(1)   Where under a hire-purchase agreement goods are bailed or (in Scotland) hired by description, there is an implied [term] that the goods will correspond with the description, and if under the agreement the goods are bailed or hired by reference to a sample as well as a description, it is not sufficient that the bulk of the goods corresponds with the sample if the goods do not also correspond with the description.

[(1A)   As regards England and Wales and Northern Ireland, the term implied by subsection (1) above is a condition.]

(2)   Goods shall not be prevented from being bailed or hired by description by reason only that, being exposed for sale, bailment or hire, they are selected by the person to whom they are bailed or hired.]

[509]

NOTES

Substituted as noted to s 8 at **[508]**.

Sub-s (1): word in square brackets substituted by the Sale and Supply of Goods Act 1994, s 7(1), Sch 2, para 4(1), (3)(a).

Sub-s (1A): inserted by the Sale and Supply of Goods Act 1994, s 7(1), Sch 2, para 4(1), (3)(b).

[10   Implied undertakings as to quality or fitness

(1)   Except as provided by this section and section 11 below and subject to the provisions of any other enactment, including any enactment of the Parliament of Northern Ireland, or the Northern Ireland Assembly, there is no implied [term] as to the quality or fitness for any particular purpose of goods bailed or (in Scotland) hired under a hire-purchase agreement.

[(2)   Where the creditor bails or hires goods under a hire purchase agreement in the course of a business, there is an implied term that the goods supplied under the agreement are of satisfactory quality.

(2A)   For the purposes of this Act, goods are of satisfactory quality if they meet the standard that a reasonable person would regard as satisfactory, taking account of any description of the goods, the price (if relevant) and all the other relevant circumstances.

(2B)   For the purposes of this Act, the quality of goods includes their state and condition and the following (among others) are in appropriate cases aspects of the quality of goods—

    (a)   fitness for all the purposes for which goods of the kind in question are commonly supplied,

    (b)   appearance and finish,

    (c)   freedom from minor defects,

    (d)   safety, and

    (e)   durability.

(2C)   The term implied by subsection (2) above does not extend to any matter making the quality of goods unsatisfactory—

    (a)   which is specifically drawn to the attention of the person to whom the goods are bailed or hired before the agreement is made,

    (b)   where that person examines the goods before the agreement is made, which that examination ought to reveal, or

    (c)   where the goods are bailed or hired by reference to a sample, which would have been apparent on a reasonable examination of the sample]

[(2D)   If the person to whom the goods are bailed or hired deals as consumer or, in Scotland, if the goods are hired to a person under a consumer contract, the relevant circumstances mentioned in subsection (2A) above include any public statements on the specific characteristics of the goods made about them by the creditor, the producer or his representative, particularly in advertising or on labelling.

(2E)   A public statement is not by virtue of subsection (2D) above a relevant circumstance for the purposes of subsection (2A) above in the case of a contract of hire-purchase, if the creditor shows that—

    (a)   at the time the contract was made, he was not, and could not reasonably have been, aware of the statement,

    (b)   before the contract was made, the statement had been withdrawn in public or, to the extent that it contained anything which was incorrect or misleading, it had been corrected in public, or

    (c)   the decision to acquire the goods could not have been influenced by the statement.

(2F)   Subsections (2D) and (2E) above do not prevent any public statement from being a relevant circumstance for the purposes of subsection (2A) above (whether or not the person to whom the goods are bailed or hired deals as consumer or, in Scotland, whether or not the goods are hired to a person under a consumer contract) if the statement would have been such a circumstance apart from those subsections.]

(3)   Where the creditor bails or hires goods under a hire-purchase agreement in the course of a business and the person to whom the goods are bailed or hired, expressly or by implication, makes known—

    (a)   to the creditor in the course of negotiations conducted by the creditor in relation to the making of the hire-purchase agreement, or

    (b)   to a credit-broker in the course of negotiations conducted by that broker in relation to goods sold by him to the creditor before forming the subject matter of the hire-purchase agreement,

any particular purpose for which the goods are being bailed or hired, there is an implied [term] that the goods supplied under the agreement are reasonably fit for that purpose, whether or not that is a purpose for which such goods are commonly supplied, except where the circumstances show that the person to whom the goods are bailed or hired does not rely, or that it is unreasonable for him to rely, on the skill or judgment of the creditor or credit-broker.

(4)   An implied [term] as to quality or fitness for a particular purpose may be annexed to a hire-purchase agreement by usage.

(5)   The preceding provisions of this section apply to a hire-purchase agreement made by a person who in the course of a business is acting as agent for the creditor as they apply to an agreement made by the creditor in the course of a business, except where the creditor is not bailing or hiring in the course of a business and either the person to whom the goods are bailed or hired knows that fact or reasonable steps are taken to bring it to the notice of that person before the agreement is made.

(6)   In subsection (3) above and this subsection—

    (a)   "credit-broker" means a person acting in the course of a business of credit brokerage.

    (b)   "credit brokerage" means the effecting of introductions of individuals desiring to obtain credit—

        (i)   to persons carrying on any business so far as it relates to the provision of credit, or

        (ii)   to other persons engaged in credit brokerage.]

[(7)   As regards England and Wales and Northern Ireland, the terms implied by subsections (2) and (3) above are conditions.]

[(8)   ...]

NOTES

Substituted as noted to s 8 at **[508]**.

Sub-ss (1), (3), (4): words in square brackets substituted by the Sale and Supply of Goods Act 1994, s 7(1), Sch 2, para 4(1), (4)(b).

Sub-ss (2), (2A), (2B), (2C): substituted, for original sub-s (2), by the Sale and Supply of Goods Act 1994, s 7(1), Sch 2, para 4(1), (4)(a).

Sub-ss (2D)–(2F): inserted by the Sale and Supply of Goods to Consumers Regulations 2002, SI 2002/3045, reg 13(1), (2).

Sub-s (7): added by the Sale and Supply of Goods Act 1994, s 7(1), Sch 2, para 4(1), (4)(c).

Sub-s (8): added by SI 2002/3045, art 13(1), (3); applies to Scotland only.

[11 Samples

[(1)] Where under a hire-purchase agreement goods are bailed or (in Scotland) hired by reference to a sample, there is an implied [term]—

(a) that the bulk will correspond with the sample in quality; and

(b) that the person to whom the goods are bailed or hired will have a reasonable opportunity of comparing the bulk with the sample; and

(c) that the goods will be free from any defect, [making their quality unsatisfactory], which would not be apparent on reasonable examination of the sample.

[(2) As regards England and Wales and Northern Ireland, the term implied by subsection (1) above is a condition.]]

[511]

NOTES

Substituted as noted to s 8 at **[508]**.

Sub-s (1): numbered as such, and words in square brackets substituted, by the Sale and Supply of Goods Act 1994, s 7(1), Sch 2, para 4(1), (5)(a)–(c).

Sub-s (2): added by the Sale and Supply of Goods Act 1994, s 7(1), Sch 2, para 4(1), (5)(d).

[11A Modification of remedies for breach of statutory condition in non-consumer cases

(1) Where in the case of a hire purchase agreement—

(a) the person to whom goods are bailed would, apart from this subsection, have the right to reject them by reason of a breach on the part of the creditor of a term implied by section 9, 10 or 11(1)(a) or (c) above, but

(b) the breach is so slight that it would be unreasonable for him to reject them,

then, if the person to whom the goods are bailed does not deal as consumer, the breach is not to be treated as a breach of condition but may be treated as a breach of warranty.

(2) This section applies unless a contrary intention appears in, or is to be implied from, the agreement.

(3) It is for the creditor to show—

(a) that a breach fell within subsection (1)(b) above, and

(b) that the person to whom the goods were bailed did not deal as consumer.

(4) The references in this section to dealing as consumer are to be construed in accordance with Part I of the Unfair Contract Terms Act 1977.

(5) This section does not apply to Scotland.]

[512]

NOTES

Inserted by the Sale and Supply of Goods Act 1994, s 7(1), Sch 2, para 4(1), (6).

[12 Exclusion of implied terms

An express term does not negative a term implied by this Act unless inconsistent with it.]

[513]

NOTES

Substituted as noted to s 8 at **[508]**; further substituted by the Sale and Supply of Goods Act 1994, s 7(1), Sch 2 para 4(1), (7).

12A, 13 (*S 12A inserted by the Sale and Supply of Goods Act 1994, s 7(1), Sch 2 para 4(1), (8), applies to Scotland only; s 13 repealed by the Unfair Contract Terms Act 1977, s 31(4), Sch 4.*)

[14   Special provisions as to conditional sale agreements

(1)   [Section 11(4) of the Sale of Goods Act 1979] (whereby in certain circumstances a breach of a condition in a contract of sale is treated only as a breach of warranty) shall not apply to [a conditional sale agreement where the buyer deals as consumer within Part I of the Unfair Contract Terms Act 1977 ...].

(2)   In England and Wales and Northern Ireland a breach of a condition (whether express or implied) to be fulfilled by the seller under any such agreement shall be treated as a breach of warranty, and not as grounds for rejecting the goods and treating the agreement as repudiated, if (but only if) it would have fallen to be so treated had the condition been contained or implied in a corresponding hire-purchase agreement as a condition to be fulfilled by the creditor.]

[514]

NOTES

Substituted, together with s 15, by the Consumer Credit Act 1974, s 192(3)(a), Sch 4, para 36.

Sub-s (1): words in first pair of square brackets substituted by the Sale of Goods Act 1979, s 63, Sch 2, para 16; words in second pair of square brackets substituted by the Unfair Contract Terms Act 1977, s 31(3), Sch 3; words omitted repealed by the Statute Law (Repeals) Act 1981.

[15   Supplementary

(1)   In sections 8 to 14 above and this section—

"business" includes a profession and the activities of any government department (including a Northern Ireland department), [or local or public authority];

"buyer" and "seller" includes a person to whom rights and duties under a conditional sale agreement have passed by assignment or operation of law;

.....

"conditional sale agreement" means an agreement for the sale of goods under which the purchase price or part of it is payable by instalments, and the property in the goods is to remain in the seller (notwithstanding that the buyer is to be in possession of the goods) until such conditions as to the payment of instalments or otherwise as may be specified in the agreement are fulfilled;

.....

"creditor" means the person by whom the goods are bailed or (in Scotland) hired under a hire-purchase agreement or the person to whom his rights and duties under the agreement have passed by assignment or operation of law; and

"hire-purchase agreement" means an agreement, other than a conditional sale agreement, under which—

(a)   goods are bailed or (in Scotland) hired in return for periodical payments by the person to whom they are bailed or hired, and

(b)   the property in the goods will pass to that person if the terms of the agreements are complied with and one or more of the following occurs—

(i)   the exercise of an option to purchase by that person,

(ii)   the doing of any other specified act by any party to the agreement,

(iii)   the happening of any other specified event.

["producer" means the manufacturer of goods, the importer of goods into the European Economic Area or any person purporting to be a producer by placing his name, trade mark or other distinctive sign on the goods;]

(2)   ...

(3)   In section 14(2) above "corresponding hire-purchase agreement" means, in relation to a conditional sale agreement, a hire-purchase agreement relating to the same goods as the conditional sale agreement and made between the same parties and at the same time and in the same circumstances and, as nearly as may be, in the same terms as the conditional sale agreement.

(4)   Nothing in sections 8 to 13 above shall prejudice the operation of any other enactment including any enactment of the Parliament of Northern Ireland or the Northern Ireland Assembly or any rule of law whereby any [term], other than one relating to quality or fitness, is to be implied in any hire-purchase agreement.]

[515]

NOTES

Substituted as noted to s 14 at **[514]**.

Sub-s (1): in definition "business" words in square brackets substituted, and second definition omitted repealed, by the Unfair Contract Terms Act 1977, s 31(3), (4), Schs 3, 4; first definition omitted repealed by the Sale and Supply of Goods Act 1994, s 7(1), Sch 2 para 4(1), (9)(a), Sch 3; definition "producer": inserted by the Sale and Supply of Goods to Consumers Regulations 2002, SI 2002/3045, art 13(1), (4).

Sub-s (2): repealed by the Sale and Supply of Goods Act 1994, s 7(1), Sch 2 para 4(1), (9)(b), Sch 3.

Sub-s (4): word in square brackets substituted by the Sale and Supply of Goods Act 1994, s 7(1), Sch 2 para 4(1), (9)(c).

16 *(Repealed in relation to England, Wales and Scotland by the Regulatory Reform (Trading Stamps) Order 2005, SI 2005/871, art 6, Schedule and in relation to Northern Ireland by the Law Reform (Miscellaneous Provisions) (Northern Ireland) Order 2005, SI 2005/1452, art 24, Sch 2.)*

Miscellaneous

17 Northern Ireland

(1)   It is hereby declared that this Act extends to Northern Ireland.

(2)   ...

[516]

NOTES
Sub-s (2): repealed by the Northern Ireland Constitution Act 1973, s 41(1), Sch 6, Part I.

18 Short title, citation, interpretation, commencement, repeal and saving

(1)   This Act may be cited as the Supply of Goods (Implied Terms) Act 1973.

(2)   ...

(3)   This Act shall come into operation at the expiration of a period of one month beginning with the date on which it is passed.

(4)   ...

(5)   This Act does not apply to contracts of sale or hire-purchase agreements made before its commencement.

[517]–[525]

NOTES
Sub-s (2): repealed by the Sale of Goods Act 1979, s 63(2), Sch 3.
Sub-s (4): repeals the Hire-Purchase Act 1965, ss 17–20, 29(3)(c), the Hire-Purchase (Scotland) Act 1965, ss 17–20, 29(3)(c), and the Hire-Purchase Act (Northern Ireland) 1966, ss 17–20, 29(3)(c).

FAIR TRADING ACT 1973

(1973 c 41)

ARRANGEMENT OF SECTIONS

PART II
REFERENCES TO CONSUMER PROTECTION ADVISORY COMMITTEE

Order in pursuance of report of Advisory Committee

Enforcement of orders

PART VIII
ADDITIONAL PROVISIONS RELATING TO REFERENCES TO COMMISSION

PART IX
AMENDMENTS OF RESTRICTIVE TRADE PRACTICES ACTS

PART XI
PYRAMID SELLING AND SIMILAR TRADING SCHEMES

PART XII
MISCELLANEOUS AND SUPPLEMENTARY PROVISIONS

An Act to provide for the appointment of a Director General of Fair Trading and of a Consumer Protection Advisory Committee, and to confer on the Director General and the Committee so appointed, on the Secretary of State, on the Restrictive Practices Court and on certain other courts new functions for the protection of consumers; to make provisions, in substitution for the Monopolies and Restrictive Practices (Inquiry and Control) Act 1948 and the Monopolies and Mergers Act 1965, for the matters dealt with in those Acts and related matters, including restrictive labour practices; to amend the Restrictive Trade Practices Act 1956 and the Restrictive Trade Practices Act 1968, to make provision for extending the said Act of 1956 to agreements relating to services, and to transfer to the Director General of Fair Trading the functions of the Registrar of Restrictive Trading Agreements; to make provision with respect to pyramid selling and similar trading schemes; to make new provision in place of section 30(2) to (4) of the Trade Descriptions Act 1968; and for purposes connected with those matters

[25 July 1973]

NOTES

Director General of Fair Trading: the Enterprise Act 2002, s 2(1), at **[1860]**, provides that, as from the coming into force of that section (on 1 April 2003, see the Enterprise Act 2002 (Commencement No 2, Transitional and Transitory Provisions) Order 2003, SI 2003/766), the functions of the Director General of Fair Trading, his property, rights and liabilities are transferred to the Office of Fair Trading. Accordingly, (by virtue of s 2(2), (3) of the 2002 Act) the office of the Director is abolished, and any reference to the Director in any enactment, instrument or other document passed or made before the commencement of s 2(1) shall have effect as if it were a reference to the Office of Fair Trading. For transitional provisions in connection with the transfer, see s 276(1) of, and Sch 24, para 6 to, the 2002 Act.

Note also that certain functions of the Director under this Act are transferred, partly transferred, or are to be exercised concurrently, or after consultation with, specific industry regulators; ie, the Director General of Telecommunications, the Director General of Water Services, the Gas and Electricity Markets Authority, the Rail Regulator, and the Civil Aviation Authority. See the Telecommunications Act 1984, the Water Industry Act 1991, the Gas Act 1986, the Electricity Act 1989, the Railways Act 1993, and the Transport Act 2000.

1–12 (*Ss 1, 2, 6–11 repealed by the Enterprise Act 2002, s 278(2), Sch 26; s 3 repealed by ss 10(1)(a), 278(2) of, and Sch 26 to, the 2002 Act; s 4 repealed by the Competition Act 1998, s 74(1), (3), Sch 12, para 1(1), (2), Sch 14, Pt I; s 5 repealed by the Enterprise Act 2002 and Media Mergers (Consequential Amendments) Order 2003, SI 2003/3180, art 2, Schedule, para 1(1), (2); s 12 repealed by ss 9, 278(2) of, and Sch 26 to, the 2002 Act.*)

PART II
REFERENCES TO CONSUMER PROTECTION ADVISORY COMMITTEE

13–21 (*Repealed by the Enterprise Act 2002, ss 10(1)(b), 278(2), Sch 26.*)

Order in pursuance of report of Advisory Committee

22 (*Repealed by the Enterprise Act 2002, ss 10(1)(b), 278(2), Sch 26, subject to savings in relation to any Orders made under that section and its continued operation in so far as applying to the revocation of any such Order (see s 10(2)–(4) of the 2002 Act at* **[1867]**).)

23 Penalties for contravention of order under s 22

Subject to the following provisions of this Part of this Act, any person who contravenes a prohibition imposed by an order under section 22 of this Act, or who does not comply with a requirement imposed by such an order which applies to him, shall be guilty of an offence and shall be liable—
    (*a*)   *on summary conviction, to a fine not exceeding [the prescribed sum];*

(b)   on conviction on indictment, to a fine or to imprisonment for a term not exceeding two
         years or both.

[526]

NOTES
Repealed, together with ss 24–28, by the Consumer Protection from Unfair Trading Regulations 2008,
SI 2008/1277, reg 30(3), Sch 4, subject to savings in reg 30(2) of and Sch 3, para 15 to, those Regulations at
[3702], **[3704]**.
Reference to the prescribed sum substituted by virtue of the Magistrates' Courts Act 1980, s 32(2).

24   Offences due to default of other person
*Where the commission by any person of an offence under section 23 of this Act is due to the act or
default of some other person, that other person shall be guilty of the offence, and a person may be
charged with and convicted of the offence by virtue of this section whether or not proceedings are
taken against the first-mentioned person.*

[527]

NOTES
Repealed as noted to s 23 at **[526]**.

25   Defences in proceedings under s 23
*(1)   In any proceedings for an offence under section 23 of this Act it shall, subject to
subsection (2) of this section, be a defence for the person charged to prove—*
(a)   *that the commission of the offence was due to a mistake, or to reliance on information
        supplied to him, or to the act or default of another person, an accident or some other
        cause beyond his control, and*
(b)   *that he took all reasonable precautions and exercised all due diligence to avoid the
        commission of such an offence by himself or any person under his control.*

*(2)   If in any case the defence provided by the preceding subsection involves the allegation that
the commission of the offence was due to the act or default of another person or to reliance on
information supplied by another person, the person charged shall not, without leave of the court, be
entitled to rely on that defence unless, within a period ending seven clear days before the hearing,
he has served on the prosecutor a notice in writing, giving such information identifying or assisting
in the identification of that other person as was then in his possession.*

*(3)   In proceedings for an offence under section 23 of this Act committed by the publication of
an advertisement, it shall be a defence for the person charged to prove that he is a person whose
business it is to publish or arrange for the publication of advertisements, and that he received the
advertisement for publication in the ordinary course of business and did not know and had no
reason to suspect that its publication would amount to an offence under section 23 of this Act.*

[528]

NOTES
Repealed as noted to s 23 at **[526]**.

26   Limitation of effect of orders under s 22
*A contract for the supply of goods or services shall not be void or unenforceable by reason only of
a contravention of an order made under section 22 of this Act; and, subject to the provisions of
section 33 of the Interpretation Act 1889 (which relates to offences under two or more laws), the
provisions of this Part of this Act shall not be construed as—*
(a)   *conferring a right of action in any civil proceedings (other than proceedings for the
        recovery of a fine) in respect of any contravention of such an order, or*
(b)   *affecting any restriction imposed by or under any other enactment, whether public, local
        or private, or*
(c)   *derogating from any right of action or other remedy (whether civil or criminal) in
        proceedings instituted otherwise than under this Part of this Act.*

[529]

NOTES
Repealed as noted to s 23 at **[526]**.
Interpretation Act 1889, s 33: repealed by the Interpretation Act 1978, s 25(1), Sch 3; see now s 18 of, and
Sch 2, para 1 to, that Act.

Enforcement of orders

27   Enforcing authorities
*(1)   It shall be the duty of every local weights and measures authority to enforce within their
area the provisions of any order made under section 22 of this Act ...*
(2)   *(Applies to Scotland only.)*

[530]

PART 1
STATUTES

NOTES
Repealed as noted to s 23 at **[526]**.
Sub-s (1): words omitted repealed by the Weights and Measures Act 1985, s 98(1), Sch 13, Pt I.

28 Power to make test purchases

A local weights and measures authority may make, or may authorise any of their officers to make on their behalf, such purchases of goods, and may authorise any of their officers to obtain such services, as may be expedient for the purpose of determining whether or not the provisions of any order made under section 22 of this Act are being complied with.

[531]

NOTES
Repealed as noted to s 23 at **[526]**.

29 Power to enter premises and inspect and seize goods and documents

(1)   A duly authorised officer of a local weights and measures authority, or a person duly authorised in writing by the Secretary of State, may at all reasonable hours, and on production, if required, of his credentials, exercise the following powers, that is to say—

(a)   he may, for the purpose of ascertaining whether any offence under section 23 of this Act has been committed, inspect any goods and enter any premises other than premises used only as a dwelling;

(b)   if he has reasonable cause to suspect that an offence under that section has been committed, he may, for the purpose of ascertaining whether it has been committed, require any person carrying on a business or employed in connection with a business to produce any books or documents relating to the business and may take copies of, or of any entry in, any such book or document;

(c)   if he has reasonable cause to believe that such an offence has been committed, he may seize and detain any goods for the purpose of ascertaining, by testing or otherwise, whether the offence has been committed;

(d)   he may seize and detain any goods or documents which he has reason to believe may be required as evidence in proceedings for such an offence;

(e)   he may, for the purpose of exercising his powers under this subsection to seize goods, but only if and to the extent that it is reasonably necessary in order to secure that the provisions of an order made under section 22 of this Act are duly observed, require any person having authority to do so to break open any container or open any vending machine and, if that person does not comply with the requirement, he may do so himself.

(2)   A person seizing any goods or documents in the exercise of his powers under this section shall inform the person from whom they are seized and, in the case of goods seized from a vending machine, the person whose name and address are stated on the machine as being the proprietor's or, if no name and address are so stated, the occupier of the premises on which the machine stands or to which it is affixed.

(3)   If a justice of the peace, on sworn information in writing,—

(a)   is satisfied that there is reasonable ground to believe either—

(i)   that any goods, books or documents which a person has power under this section to inspect are on any premises and that their inspection is likely to disclose evidence of the commission of an offence under section 23 of this Act, or

(ii)   that any offence under section 23 has been, is being or is about to be committed on any premises, and

(b)   is also satisfied either—

(i)   that admission to the premises has been or is likely to be refused and that notice of intention to apply for a warrant under this subsection has been given to the occupier, or

(ii)   that an application for admission, or the giving of such a notice, would defeat the object of the entry or that the premises are unoccupied or that the occupier is temporarily absent, and it might defeat the object of the entry to await his return,

the justice may by warrant under his hand, which shall continue in force for a period of one month, authorise any such officer or other person as is mentioned in subsection (1) of this section to enter the premises, if need be by force.

In the application of this subsection to Scotland, "justice of the peace" shall be construed as including a sheriff and a magistrate.

(4)   A person entering any premises by virtue of this section may take with him such other persons and such equipment as may appear to him necessary; and on leaving any premises which he

has entered by virtue of a warrant under subsection (3) of this section he shall, if the premises are unoccupied or the occupier is temporarily absent, leave them as effectively secured against trespassers as he found them.

(5)   *Nothing in this section shall be taken to compel the production by a [relevant lawyer] of a document containing a privileged communication made by or to him in that capacity or to authorise the taking of possession of any such document which is in his possession.*

[(6)   *"Relevant lawyer" means a barrister, advocate, solicitor, or other legal representative communications with whom may be the subject of a claim to privilege.]*

[532]

NOTES

Repealed, together with ss 30–33, except in so far as those sections are applied by section 123 of this Act, by the Consumer Protection from Unfair Trading Regulations 2008, SI 2008/1277, reg 30(1), (3), Sch 2, Pt 1, para 15, Sch 4, subject to further savings in reg 30(2) of, and Sch 3, para 15 to, those Regulations at **[3702]**, **[3704]**.

Sub-s (5): words in square brackets substituted by the Legal Services Act 2007, s 208(1), Sch 21, para 30(a).
Sub-s (6): added by the Legal Services Act 2007, s 208(1), Sch 21, para 30(b).
Seize and detain goods: the powers of seizure conferred by sub-s (1)(c), (d) are powers to which the Criminal Justice and Police Act 2001, s 50 applies (additional powers of seizure from premises); see s 50 of, and Sch 1, Pt 1, para 16 to, that Act.

---

30   Offences in connection with exercise of powers under s 29

(1)   *Subject to subsection (6) of this section, any person who—*

   (a)   *wilfully obstructs any such officer or person as is mentioned in subsection (1) of section 29 of this Act acting in the exercise of any powers conferred on him by or under that section, or*

   (b)   *wilfully fails to comply with any requirement properly made to him by such an officer or person under that section, or*

   (c)   *without reasonable cause fails to give such an officer or person so acting any other assistance or information which he may reasonably require of him for the purpose of the performance of his functions under this Part of this Act,*

shall be guilty of an offence.

(2)   *If any person, in giving any such information as is mentioned in subsection (1)(c) of this section, makes any statement which he knows to be false, he shall be guilty of an offence.*

(3)   *…*

(4)   *If any person who is neither a duly authorised officer of a weights and measures authority nor a person duly authorised in that behalf by the Secretary of State purports to act as such under section 29 of this Act or under this section, he shall be guilty of an offence.*

(5)   *Any person guilty of an offence under subsection (1) of this section shall be liable on summary conviction to a fine not exceeding [level 3 on the standard scale]; and any person guilty of an offence under subsection (2) … or subsection (4) of this section shall be liable—*

   (a)   *on summary conviction, to a fine not exceeding [the prescribed sum];*

   (b)   *on conviction on indictment, to a fine or to imprisonment for a term not exceeding two years or to both.*

(6)   *Nothing in this section shall be construed as requiring a person to answer any question or give any information if to do so might incriminate that person or (where that person is [married or a civil partner) the spouse or civil partner] of that person.*

[533]

NOTES

Repealed as noted to s 29 at **[532]**.
Sub-s (3): repealed by the Enterprise Act 2002, ss 247(b), 278(2), Sch 26.
Sub-s (5): reference to level 3 on the standard scale substituted by virtue of the Criminal Justice Act 1982, ss 38, 46; words omitted repealed by the Enterprise Act 2002, s 278(2), Sch 26; reference to the prescribed sum in para (a) substituted by virtue of the Magistrates' Courts Act 1980, s 32(2).
Sub-s (6): words in square brackets substituted by the Civil Partnership Act 2004, s 261(1), Sch 27, para 47.

---

31   Notice of test

Where any goods seized or purchased by a person in pursuance of this Part of this Act are submitted to a test, then—

   (a)   *if the goods were seized, he shall inform any such person as is mentioned in section 29(2) of this Act of the result of the test;*

   (b)   *if the goods were purchased and the test leads to the institution of proceedings for an offence under section 23 of this Act, he shall inform the person from whom the goods were purchased, or, in the case of goods sold through a vending machine, the person mentioned in relation to such goods in section 29(2) of this Act, of the result of the test;*

and where, as a result of the test, proceedings for an offence under section 23 of this Act are instituted against any person, he shall allow that person to have the goods tested on his behalf if it is reasonably practicable to do so.

[534]

NOTES
Repealed as noted to s 29 at **[532]**.

32   Compensation for loss in respect of goods seized under s 29

(*1*)   *Where in the exercise of his powers under section 29 of this Act a person seizes and detains any goods, and their owner suffers loss by reason of their being seized or by reason that the goods, during the detention, are lost or damaged or deteriorate, unless the owner is convicted of an offence under section 23 of this Act committed in relation to the goods, the appropriate authority shall be liable to compensate him for the loss so suffered.*

(*2*)   *Any disputed question as to the right to or the amount of any compensation payable under this section shall be determined by arbitration and, in Scotland, by a single arbiter appointed, failing agreement between the parties, by the sheriff.*

(*3*)   *In this section "the appropriate authority"—*
   (*a*)   *in relation to goods seized by an officer of a local weights and measures authority, means that authority, and*
   (*b*)   *in any other case, means the Secretary of State.*

NOTES
Repealed as noted to s 29 at **[532]**.
Sub-s (3): repealed by the Enterprise Act 2002, ss 247(b), 278(2), Sch 26.
Sub-s (5): reference to level 3 on the standard scale substituted by virtue of the Criminal Justice Act 1982, ss 38, 46; words omitted repealed by the Enterprise Act 2002, s 278(2), Sch 26; reference to the prescribed sum in para (a) substituted by virtue of the Magistrates' Courts Act 1980, s 32(2).
Sub-s (6): words in square brackets substituted by the Civil Partnership Act 2004, s 261(1), Sch 27, para 47.

[535]–[613]

33–83   (*S 33 applies to Northern Ireland only; ss 34–83 (Pts III–VII) in so far as unrepealed outside the scope of this work.*)

PART VIII
ADDITIONAL PROVISIONS RELATING TO REFERENCES TO COMMISSION

84–93A   (*Ss 84, 86, 88–93 repealed by the Enterprise Act 2002, s 278(2), Sch 26; ss 85, 87 repealed by the Enterprise Act 2002 and Media Mergers (Consequential Amendments) Order 2003, SI 2003/3180, art 2, Schedule, para 1(1), (6), (7); s 93A inserted by the Companies Act 1989, s 148, repealed by the Enterprise Act 2002, s 278(2), Sch 26.*)

[93B   False or misleading information

(1)   If a person furnishes any information—
   (a)   ...
   (b)   to the Commission in connection with the functions of the Commission under ... the Airports Act 1986,
and either he knows the information to be false or misleading in a material particular, or he furnishes the information recklessly and it is false or misleading in a material particular, he is guilty of an offence.

(2)   A person who—
   (a)   furnishes any information to another which he knows to be false or misleading in a material particular, or
   (b)   recklessly furnishes any information to another which is false or misleading in a material particular,
knowing that the information is to be used for the purpose of furnishing information as mentioned in subsection (1)(a) or (b) of this section, is guilty of an offence.

(3)   A person guilty of an offence under subsection (1) or (2) of this section is liable—
   (a)   on summary conviction, to a fine not exceeding the statutory maximum, and
   (b)   on conviction on indictment, to imprisonment for a term not exceeding two years or to a fine or to both.

(4)   Section 129(1) of this Act does not apply to an offence under this section.

[(5) This section shall not have effect in relation to the furnishing of information to the Commission in connection with its functions under any provision of the Enterprise Act 2002 as applied by virtue of ... section 44B of the Airports Act 1986.]]

[614]

NOTES
Inserted by the Companies Act 1989, s 151.
Sub-s (1): para (a) repealed by the Enterprise Act 2002 and Media Mergers (Consequential Amendments) Order 2003, SI 2003/3180, art 2, Schedule, para 1(1), (8); words omitted from para (b) repealed by the Communications Act 2003, s 406(7), Sch 19(1).
Sub-s (5): added by the Enterprise Act 2002, s 278(1), Sch 25, para 5(4)(b); words omitted repealed by the Communications Act 2003, s 406(7), Sch 19(1).

PART IX
AMENDMENTS OF RESTRICTIVE TRADE PRACTICES ACTS

94   Transfer of functions of Registrar to Director

(1)   Subject to the transitional provisions having effect by virtue of section 139 of this Act, the functions of the Registrar of Restrictive Trading Agreements are hereby transferred to the Director, ...

(2)   ...

[615]

NOTES
Sub-s (1): words omitted repealed by the Statute Law (Repeals) Act 2004.
Sub-s (2): repealed by the Resale Prices Act 1976, s 29, Sch 3, Pt I.
The Director: see the note "Director General of Fair Trading" at the beginning of this Act.

95–117   (*Ss 95–106, ss 107–117 (Pt X) repealed by the Restrictive Trade Practices Act 1976.*)

PART XI
PYRAMID SELLING AND SIMILAR TRADING SCHEMES

[118   Trading schemes to which Part XI applies

(1)   This Part of this Act applies to any trading scheme if—
   (a)   the prospect is held out to participants of receiving payments or other benefits in respect of any of the matters specified in subsection (2) of this section; and
   (b)   (subject to subsection (7) of this section) either or both of the conditions in subsections (3) and (4) of this section are fulfilled in relation to the scheme.

(2)   The matters referred to in paragraph (a) of subsection (1) of this section are—
   (a)   the introduction by any person of other persons who become participants in a trading scheme;
   (b)   the continued participation of participants in a trading scheme;
   (c)   the promotion, transfer or other change of status of participants within a trading scheme;
   (d)   the supply of goods or services by any person to or for other persons;
   (e)   the acquisition of goods or services by any person.

(3)   The condition in this subsection is that—
   (a)   goods or services, or both, are to be provided by the person promoting the scheme (in this Part of this Act referred to as "the promoter") or, in the case of a scheme promoted by two or more persons acting in concert (in this Part of this Act referred to as "the promoters"), by one or more of those persons; and
   (b)   the goods or services so provided—
      (i)   are to be supplied to or for other persons under transactions effected by participants (whether in the capacity of agents of the promoter or of one of the promoters or in any other capacity), or
      (ii)   are to be used for the purposes of the supply of goods or services to or for other persons under such transactions.

(4)   The condition in this subsection is that goods or services, or both, are to be supplied by the promoter or any of the promoters to or for persons introduced to him or any of the other promoters (or an employee or agent of his or theirs) by participants.

(5)   For the purposes of this Part of this Act a prospect of a kind mentioned in paragraph (a) of subsection (1) of this section shall be treated as being held out to a participant whether it is held out so as to confer on him a legally enforceable right or not.

(6)   This Part of this Act does not apply to any trading scheme—

[(a)   under which the promoter or any of the promoters or participants is to carry on, or to purport to carry on, a relevant regulated activity;] or
(b)   which otherwise falls within a description prescribed by regulations made by the Secretary of State by statutory instrument.

[(6A)   For the purposes of subsection (6)(a), "relevant regulated activity" means—
(a)   dealing in investments as principal or agent;
(b)   arranging deals in investments;
[(ba)   operating a multilateral trading facility;]
(c)   managing investments;
(d)   safeguarding and administering investments;
(e)   sending dematerialised instructions;
(f)   establishing etc a collective investment scheme;
(g)   advising on investments,
and paragraphs (a) to (g) must be read with section 22 of the Financial Services and Markets Act 2000, any relevant order under that section, and Schedule 2 to that Act.]

(7)   The Secretary of State may by order made by statutory instrument—
(a)   disapply paragraph (b) of Subsection (1) of this section in relation to a trading scheme of a kind specified in the order; or
(b)   amend or repeal paragraph (a) of subsection (6) of this section;
and no such order, and no order varying or revoking any such order, shall be made under this subsection unless a draft of the order has been laid before Parliament and approved by a resolution of each House of Parliament.

(8)   In this Part of this Act—
"goods" includes property of any description and a right to, or interest in, property;
"participant" means, in relation to a trading scheme, a person (other than the promoter or any of the promoters) participating in the scheme;
"trading scheme" includes any arrangements made in connection with the carrying on of a business, whether those arrangements are made or recorded wholly or partly in writing or not;
and any reference to the provision or supply of goods shall be construed as including a reference to the grant or transfer of a right or interest.

(9)   In this section any reference to the provision or supply of goods or services by a person shall be construed as including a reference to the provision or supply of goods or services under arrangements to which that person is a party.]

[616]

NOTES
Substituted by the Trading Schemes Act 1996, s 1.
Sub-s (6): para (a) substituted by the Financial Services and Markets Act 2000 (Consequential Amendments and Repeals) Order 2001, SI 2001/3649, art 284(1), (2).
Sub-s (6A): inserted by SI 2001/3649, art 284(1), (3); para (ba) inserted by the Financial Services and Markets Act 2000 (Regulated Activities) (Amendment No 3) Order 2006, SI 2006/3384, art 31.
Regulations: the Trading Schemes (Exclusion) Regulations 1997, SI 1997/31 at **[3225]**.

119   Regulations relating to such trading schemes

(1)   Regulations made by the Secretary of State by statutory instrument may make provision with respect to the issue, circulation or distribution of [any form of advertisement, prospectus, circular or notice which contains any information] calculated to lead directly or indirectly to persons becoming participants in such a trading scheme, and may prohibit any such [advertisement, prospectus, circular or notice] from being issued, circulated or distributed unless it complies with such requirements as to the matters to be included or not included in it as may be prescribed by the regulations.

(2)   Regulations made by the Secretary of State by statutory instrument may prohibit the promoter or any of the promoters of, or any participant in, a trading scheme to which this Part of this Act applies from—
(a)   supplying any goods to a participant in the trading scheme, or
(b)   supplying any training facilities or other services for such a participant, or
(c)   providing any goods or services under a transaction effected by such a participant, or
(d)   being a party to any arrangements under which goods or services are supplied or provided as mentioned in any of the preceding paragraphs, or
(e)   accepting from any such participant any payment, or any undertaking to make a payment, in respect of any goods or services supplied or provided as mentioned in any of paragraphs (a) to (d) of this subsection or in respect of any goods or services to be so supplied or provided,
unless (in any such case) such requirements as are prescribed by the regulations are complied with.

(3)   Any requirements prescribed by regulations under subsection (2) of this section shall be such as the Secretary of State considers necessary or expedient for the purpose of preventing participants in trading schemes to which this Part of this Act applies from being unfairly treated; and, without prejudice to the generality of this subsection, any such requirements may include provisions—

(a)   requiring the rights and obligations of every participant under such a trading scheme to be set out in full in an agreement in writing made between the participant and the promoter or (if more than one) each of the promoters;

(b)   specifying rights required to be conferred on every such participant, and obligations required to be assumed by the promoter or promoters, under any such trading scheme; or

(c)   imposing restrictions on the liabilities to be incurred by such a participant in respect of any of the matters mentioned in paragraphs (a) to (e) of subsection (2) of this section.

(4)   Regulations made under subsection (2) of this section—

(a)   may include provision for enabling a person who has made a payment as a participant in a trading scheme to which this Part of this Act applies, in circumstances where any of the requirements prescribed by the regulations were not complied with, to recover the whole or part of that payment from any person to whom or for whose benefit it was paid, and

(b)   subject to any provision made in accordance with the preceding paragraph, may prescribe the degree to which anything done in contravention of the regulations is to be treated as valid or invalid for the purposes of any civil proceedings.

(5)   The power to make regulations under this section may be exercised so as to make different provision—

(a)   in relation to different descriptions of trading schemes to which this Part of this Act applies, or

(b)   in relation to trading schemes which are or were in operation on a date specified in the regulations and trading schemes which are or were not in operation on that date,

or in relation to different descriptions of participants in such trading schemes.

[617]

NOTES

Sub-s (1): words in square brackets substituted by the Trading Schemes Act 1996, s 2(1).
Regulations: the Trading Schemes Regulations 1997, SI 1997/30 at [3212].

---

120   Offences under Part XI

(1)   Subject to the next following section, any person who issues, circulates or distributes, or causes another person to issue, circulate or distribute, a [advertisement, prospectus, circular or notice] in contravention of any regulations made under subsection (1) of section 119 of this Act shall be guilty of an offence.

(2)   Any person who contravenes any regulations made under subsection (2) of that section shall be guilty of an offence.

(3)   If any person who is a participant in a trading scheme to which this Part of this Act applies, or has applied or been invited to become a participant in such a trading scheme,—

(a)   makes any payment to or for the benefit of the promoter or (if there is more than one) any of the promoters, or to or for the benefit of a participant in the trading scheme, and

(b)   is induced to make that payment by reason that the prospect is held out to him of receiving payments or other benefits in respect of the introduction of other persons who become participants in the trading scheme,

any person to whom or for whose benefit that payment is made shall be guilty of an offence.

(4)   If the promoter or any of the promoters of a trading scheme to which this Part of this Act applies, or any other person acting in accordance with such a trading scheme, by holding out to any person such a prospect as is mentioned in subsection (3)(b) of this section, attempts to induce him—

(a)   if he is already a participant in the trading scheme, to make any payment to or for the benefit of the promoter or any of the promoters or to or for the benefit of a participant in the trading scheme, or

(b)   if he is not already a participant in the trading scheme, to become such a participant and to make any such payment as is mentioned in the preceding paragraph,

the person attempting to induce him to make that payment shall be guilty of an offence.

(5)   In determining, for the purposes of subsection (3) or subsection (4) of this section, whether an inducement or attempt to induce is made by holding out such a prospect as is therein mentioned, it shall be sufficient if such a prospect constitutes or would constitute a substantial part of the inducement.

(6)   Where the person by whom an offence is committed under subsection (3) or subsection (4) of this section is not the sole promoter of the trading scheme in question, any other person who is

the promoter or (as the case may be) one of the promoters of the trading scheme shall, subject to the next following section, also be guilty of that offence.

(7) Nothing in subsections (3) to (6) of this section shall be construed as limiting the circumstances in which the commission of any act may constitute an offence under subsection (1) or subsection (2) of this section.

(8) In this section any reference to the making of a payment to or for the benefit of a person shall be construed as including the making of a payment partly to or for the benefit of that person and partly to or for the benefit of one or more other persons.

[618]

NOTES

Sub-s (1): words in square brackets substituted by the Trading Schemes Act 1996, s 2(2).

121 Defences in certain proceedings under Part XI

(1) Where a person is charged with an offence under subsection (1) of section 120 of this Act in respect of an advertisement, it shall be a defence for him to prove that he is a person whose business it is to publish or arrange for the publication of advertisements, and that he received the advertisement for publication in the ordinary course of business and did not know, and had no reason to suspect, that its publication would amount to an offence under that subsection.

(2) Where a person is charged with an offence by virtue of subsection (6) of section 120 of this Act, it shall be a defence for him to prove—
    (a) that the trading scheme to which the charge relates was in operation before the commencement of this Act, and
    (b) that the act constituting the offence was committed without his consent or connivance.

[619]

122 Penalties for offences under Part XI

A person guilty of an offence under this Part of this Act shall be liable—
    (a) on summary conviction, to a fine not exceeding [the prescribed sum] or to imprisonment for a term not exceeding three months or to both;
    (b) on conviction on indictment, to a fine or to imprisonment for a term not exceeding two years or to both.

[620]

NOTES

Reference to the prescribed sum substituted by virtue of the Magistrates' Courts Act 1980, s 32(2).

123 Enforcement provisions

(1) The provisions of sections 29 to 32 of this Act shall have effect for the purposes of this Part of this Act as if in those provisions—
    (a) references to a weights and measures authority or a duly authorised officer of such an authority were omitted, and
    (b) any reference to an offence under section 23 of this Act were a reference to an offence under this Part of this Act.

(2) For the purposes of the application to Northern Ireland of those provisions as applied by the preceding subsection—
    (a) any reference to the Secretary of State shall be construed as a reference to the Ministry of Commerce for Northern Ireland, and
    (b) paragraphs (c) and (d) of section 33(2) of this Act shall have effect for the purposes of the application of Part II of this Act to Northern Ireland.

[621]–[623]

PART XII
MISCELLANEOUS AND SUPPLEMENTARY PROVISIONS

124–128 (*Ss 124, 125 repealed by the Enterprise Act 2002, s 278(2), Sch 26; s 126 repealed by the Patents Act 1977, s 132(7), Sch 6; s 127 outside the scope of this work; s 128 repealed by the Restrictive Trade Practices Act 1976, s 44, Sch 6.*)

129 Time-limit for prosecutions

(1) No prosecution for an offence under this Act shall be commenced after the expiration of three years from the commission of the offence or one year from its discovery by the prosecutor, whichever is the earlier.

(2)   Notwithstanding anything in [section 127(1) of the Magistrates' Courts Act 1980], a magistrates' court may try an information for an offence under this Act if the information was laid within twelve months from the commission of the offence.

(3)   (*Applies to Scotland only.*)

(4)   In the application of this section to Northern Ireland, for the references in subsection (2) to [section 127(1) of the Magistrates' Courts Act 1980], and to the trial and laying of an information there shall be substituted respectively references to [Article 19(1) of the Magistrates' Courts (Northern Ireland) Order 1981] and to the hearing and determination and making of a complaint [and as if in that subsection for the words "an offence under this Act" there were substituted the words "an offence under section 30(1) ... of this Act"].

[624]–[626]

NOTES
Sub-s (2): words in square brackets substituted by the Magistrates' Courts Act 1980, s 154, Sch 7, para 118.
Sub-s (4): words in first pair of square brackets substituted by the Magistrates' Courts Act 1980, s 154, Sch 7, para 118; words in second pair of square brackets substituted by the Magistrates' Courts (Northern Ireland) Order 1981, SI 1981/1675, art 170(2), Sch 6, Pt I; words in final pair of square brackets added by the Criminal Justice (Northern Ireland) Order 1980, SI 1980/704, art 12, Sch 1, Pt II; words omitted repealed by the Enterprise Act 2002, s 278(2), Sch 26.

130, 131   (*Repealed by the Enterprise Act 2002, s 278(2), Sch 26.*)

132   Offences by bodies corporate

(1)   Where an offence under ... , ... , ... [section 93B] or Part XI of this Act, which has been committed by a body corporate, is proved to have been committed with the consent or connivance of, or to be attributable to any neglect on the part of, any director, manager, secretary or other similar officer of the body corporate, or any person who was purporting to act in any such capacity, he as well as the body corporate shall be guilty of that offence and be liable to be proceeded against and punished accordingly.

(2)   Where the affairs of a body corporate are managed by its members, subsection (1) of this section shall apply in relation to the acts and defaults of a member in connection with his functions of management as if he were a director of the body corporate.

[627]–[628]

NOTES
Sub-s (1): words omitted in the first place repealed by the Consumer Protection from Unfair Trading Regulations 2008, SI 2008/1277, reg 30(3), Sch 4; words omitted in the second place repealed by the Enterprise Act 2002, s 278(2), Sch 26; words omitted in the third place repealed by the Enterprise Act 2002 and Media Mergers (Consequential Amendments) Order 2003, SI 2003/3180, art 2, Schedule, para 1(1), (9); words in square brackets inserted by the Companies Act 1989, s 153, Sch 20, para 17.

133   (*Repealed by the Enterprise Act 2002, ss 247(b), 278(2), Sch 26.*)

134   Provisions as to orders

(1)   Any statutory instrument whereby any order is made under any of the preceding provisions of this Act, other than a provision which requires a draft of the order to be laid before Parliament before making the order, or whereby any regulations are made under this Act, shall be subject to annulment in pursuance of a resolution of either House of Parliament.

(2)   Any power conferred by any provision of this Act to make an order by statutory instrument shall include power to revoke or vary the order by a subsequent order made under that provision.

[629]

135   Financial provisions

(1)   The Secretary of State shall pay all remuneration, allowances or other sums payable under this Act to or in respect of persons who are or have been members of the Advisory Committee ... and shall defray—

   (a)   ...

   (b)   to such amount as the Secretary of State with the approval of the Minister for the Civil Service may determine, all other expenses duly incurred by the Advisory Committee ...

(2)   There shall be defrayed out of moneys provided by Parliament—

   (a)   all expenses incurred by the Secretary of State in consequence of the provisions of this Act;

   (b)   any expenses incurred in consequence of those provisions by any other Minister of the Crown or government department, not being a Minister or department of the Government of Northern Ireland;

   (c)   the remuneration of, and any travelling or other allowances payable under this Act to, the

Director and any staff of the Director, any other sums payable under this Act to or in respect of the Director, and any expenses duly incurred by the Director or by any of his staff in consequence of the provisions [of this or any other Act];

(d)   any increase attributable to this Act in the sums payable out of moneys so provided under the Superannuation Act 1972.

(3)   ...

[630]

NOTES

Sub-s (1): words omitted repealed by the Competition Act 1998, s 74(1), (3), Sch 12, para 1(1), (15), Sch 14, Pt I.

Sub-s (2): words in square brackets in para (c) inserted by the Competition Act 1980, s 32(2).

Sub-s (3): repealed by the Northern Ireland (Modification of Enactments—No 1) Order 1973, SI 1973/2163, art 14(2), Sch 6.

Minister for the Civil Service: now the Treasury, by virtue of the Transfer of Functions (Civil Service and Treasury) Order 1981, SI 1981/1670.

The Director: see the note "Director General of Fair Trading" at the beginning of this Act.

136   *(Repealed by the Statute Law (Repeals) Act 1977.)*

137   General interpretation provisions

(1)   In this Act—

"the Act of 1948" means the Monopolies and Restrictive Practices (Inquiry and Control) Act 1948;

.....

"the Act of 1965" means the Monopolies and Mergers Act 1965;

.....

"contract of employment" means a contract of service or of apprenticeship, whether it is express or implied, and (if it is express) whether it is oral or in writing;

"scale" (where the reference is to the scale on which any services are, or are to be, made available, supplied or obtained) means scale measured in terms of money or money's worth or in any other manner.

(2)   Except in so far as the context otherwise requires, in this Act, ... , the following expressions have the meanings hereby assigned to them respectively, that is to say—

.....

"agreement" means any agreement or arrangement, in whatever way and in whatever form it is made, and whether it is, or is intended to be, legally enforceable or not;

"business" includes a professional practice and includes any other undertaking which is carried on for gain or reward or which is an undertaking in the course of which goods or services are supplied otherwise than free of charge;

.....

"the Commission" means the [Competition] Commission;

.....

"consumer" (subject to subsection (6) of this section) means any person who is either—

(a)   a person to whom goods are or are sought to be supplied (whether by way of sale or otherwise) in the course of a business carried on by the person supplying or seeking to supply them, or

(b)   a person for whom services are or are sought to be supplied in the course of a business carried on by the person supplying or seeking to supply them,

and who does not receive or seek to receive the goods or services in the course of a business carried on by him;

.....

"enactment" includes an enactment of the Parliament of Northern Ireland;

"goods" includes buildings and other structures, and also includes ships, aircraft and hovercraft, ... ;

.....

"merger situation qualifying for investigation" has the meaning assigned to it by section 64(8) of this Act;

"Minister" includes a government department but shall not by virtue of this provision be taken to include the establishment consisting of the Director and his staff, and, except where the contrary is expressly provided, does not include any Minister or department of the Government of Northern Ireland;

.....

"practice" means any practice, whether adopted in pursuance of an agreement or otherwise;

.....

"supply", in relation to the supply of goods, includes supply by way of sale, lease, hire or hire-purchase, and, in relation to buildings or other structures, includes the construction of them by a person for another person;

.....

(3) In the provisions of this Act ... "the supply of services" does not include the rendering of any services under a contract of employment but, ...

(a) includes the undertaking and performance for gain or reward of engagements (whether professional or other) for any matter other than the supply of goods, and

(b) includes both the rendering of services to order and the provision of services by making them available to potential users; [and

(c) includes the making of arrangements for a person to put or keep on land a caravan (within the meaning of Part I of the Caravan Sites and Control of Development Act 1960) other than arrangements by virtue of which the person may occupy the caravan as his only or main residence] [and

(d) includes the making of arrangements for the use by public service vehicles (within the meaning of the Public Passenger Vehicles Act 1981) of a parking place which is used as a point at which passengers on services provided by means of such vehicles may be taken up or set down] [and

(e) includes the making of arrangements permitting use of the tunnel system (within the meaning of the Channel Tunnel Act 1987) by a person operating services for the carriage of passengers or goods by rail] [and

[(f) includes the making of arrangements, by means of such an agreement as is mentioned in paragraph 29 of Schedule 2 to the Telecommunications Act 1984, for the sharing of the use of any electronic communications apparatus, and]]

[(g) includes the supply of network services and station services, within the meaning of Part I of the Railways Act 1993;]

and any reference in those provisions to services supplied or to be supplied, or to services provided or to be provided, shall be construed accordingly.

[(3A) The Secretary of State may by order made by statutory instrument—

(a) provide that "the supply of services" in the provisions of this Act is to include, or to cease to include, any activity specified in the order which consists in, or in making arrangements in connection with, permitting the use of land; and

(b) for that purpose, amend or repeal any of paragraphs (c), (d), (e) or (g) of subsection (3) above.

(3B) No order under subsection (3A) above is to be made unless a draft of the order has been laid before Parliament and approved by a resolution of each House of Parliament.

(3C) The provisions of Schedule 9 to this Act apply in the case of a draft of any such order as they apply in the case of a draft of an order to which section 91(1) above applies.]

(4) ...

(5) For the purposes of the provisions of this Act ... , any two bodies corporate are to be treated as interconnected if one of them is a body corporate of which the other is a subsidiary (within the meaning of [section 1159 of the Companies Act 2006]) or if both of them are subsidiaries (within the meaning of that section) of one and the same body corporate; and in those provisions "interconnected bodies corporate" shall be construed accordingly, and "group of interconnected bodies corporate" means a group consisting of two or more bodies corporate all of whom are interconnected with each other.

(6) For the purposes of the application of any provision of this Act in relation to goods or services of a particular description or to which a particular practice applies, "consumers" means persons who are consumers (as defined by subsection (2) of this section) in relation to goods or services of that description or in relation to goods or services to which that practice applies.

(7) ...

(8) Except in so far as the context otherwise requires, any reference in this Act to an enactment shall be construed as a reference to that enactment as amended or extended by or under any other enactment, including this Act.

[631]

NOTES

Sub-s (1): definition "the Act of 1976" (omitted) repealed by the Resale Prices Act 1976, s 29, Sch 3, Pt I; definition "the Act of 1964" (omitted) repealed by the Competition Act 1998 (Transitional, Consequential and Supplemental Provisions) Order 2000, SI 2000/311, art 9(1), (6); definition "the Act of 1968" (omitted) repealed by the Restrictive Trade Practices Act 1976, s 44, Sch 6; definition "assignment" (omitted) repealed by the Enterprise Act 2002 and Media Mergers (Consequential Amendments) Order 2003, SI 2003/3180, art 2, Schedule, para 1(1), (10)(a).

Sub-s (2): words omitted in the first place repealed by the Restrictive Trade Practices Act 1976, s 44, Sch 6; definitions "the Advisory Committee" and "the Director" (both omitted) repealed by the Enterprise Act 2002, s 278(2), Sch 26; definitions "commercial activities in the United Kingdom", "complex monopoly situation", "group", "merger reference", "monopoly reference", "newspaper merger reference", "price", "produce", "uncompetitive practices", "worker" (all omitted) repealed by SI 2003/3180, art 2, Schedule, para 1(1), (10)(b); in definition "the Commission" word in square brackets substituted by the Competition Act 1998 (Competition Commission) Transitional, Consequential and Supplemental Provisions Order 1999, SI 1999/506, art 14; words omitted from definition "goods" repealed by the Electricity Act 1989, s 112(4), Sch 18.

Sub-s (3): words omitted repealed by the Restrictive Trade Practices Act 1976, s 44, Sch 6; para (c) and word immediately preceding it inserted by the Competition Act 1980, s 23; para (d) and word immediately preceding it inserted by the Transport Act 1985, s 116(1); para (e) and word immediately preceding it inserted by the Channel Tunnel Act 1987, s 33(10); para (f) and word immediately preceding it inserted by the Broadcasting Act 1990, s 192(1), para (f) and word immediately following it substituted by the Communications Act 2003, s 406(1), Sch 17, para 44; para (g) and word immediately preceding it inserted by the Railways Act 1993, s 66(4).

Sub-ss (3A)–(3C): inserted by the Competition Act 1998, s 68.

Sub-s (4): repealed by the Electricity Act 1989, s 112(4), Sch 18.

Sub-s (5): words omitted repealed by the Restrictive Trade Practices Act 1976, s 44, Sch 6; words in square brackets substituted by the Companies Act 2006 (Consequential Amendments, Transitional Provisions and Savings) Order 2009, SI 2009/1941, art 2(1), Sch 1, para 26.

Sub-s (7): repealed by SI 2003/3180, art 2, Schedule, para 1(1), (10)(c).

---

138 Supplementary interpretation provisions

(1)   This section applies to the following provisions of this Act, that is to say, section 2(4), … section 137(6), and the definition of "consumer" contained in section 137(2).

(2)   For the purposes of any provisions to which this section applies it is immaterial whether any person supplying goods or services has a place of business in the United Kingdom or not.

(3)   For the purposes of any provisions to which this section applies any goods or services supplied wholly or partly outside the United Kingdom, if they are supplied in accordance with arrangements made in the United Kingdom, whether made orally or by one or more documents delivered in the United Kingdom or by correspondence posted from and to addresses in the United Kingdom, shall be treated as goods supplied to, or services supplied for, persons in the United Kingdom.

(4)   In relation to the supply of goods under a hire-purchase agreement, a credit-sale agreement or a conditional sale agreement, the person conducting any antecedent negotiations, as well as the owner or seller, shall for the purposes of any provisions to which this section applies be treated as a person supplying or seeking to supply the goods.

[(5)   In subsection (4) of this section, the following expressions have the meanings given by, or referred to in, section 189 of the Consumer Credit Act 1974—

"antecedent negotiations",
"conditional sale agreement",
"credit-sale agreement",
"hire-purchase agreement".]

(6)   In any provisions to which this section applies—
(a)   any reference to a person to or for whom goods or services are supplied shall be construed as including a reference to any guarantor of such a person, and
(b)   any reference to the terms or conditions on or subject to which goods or services are supplied shall be construed as including a reference to the terms or conditions on or subject to which any person undertakes to act as such a guarantor;

and in this subsection "guarantor", in relation to a person to or for whom goods or services are supplied, includes a person who undertakes to indemnify the supplier of the goods or services against any loss which he may incur in respect of the supply of the goods or services to or for that person.

(7)   For the purposes of any provisions to which this section applies goods or services supplied by a person carrying on a business shall be taken to be supplied in the course of that business if payment for the supply of the goods or services is made or (whether under a contract or by virtue of an enactment or otherwise) is required to be made.

[632]

NOTES
Sub-s (1): words omitted repealed by the Enterprise Act 2002, s 278(2), Sch 26.
Sub-s (5): substituted by the Consumer Credit Act 1974, s 192(3)(a), Sch 4, Pt I, para 37.

---

139 Amendments, repeals and transitional provisions

(1)   Subject to the transitional provisions and savings contained in Schedule 11 to this Act—
(a)   the enactments specified in Schedule 12 to this Act shall have effect subject to the amendments specified in that Schedule (being minor amendments or amendments consequential upon the preceding provisions of this Act), and

    (b)   the enactments specified in Schedule 13 to this Act are hereby repealed to the extent specified in the third column of that Schedule.

(2)   The provisions of Schedule 11 to this Act shall have effect for the purposes of this Act.

[633]

140   Short title, citation, commencement and extent

(1)   This Act may be cited as the Fair Trading Act 1973.

(2), (3) ...

(4)   Where any provision of this Act, other than a provision contained in Schedule 11, refers to the commencement of this Act, it shall be construed as referring to the day appointed under this section for the coming into operation of that provision.

(5)   This Act extends to Northern Ireland.

[634]–[644]

NOTES

Sub-s (2): repealed by the Restrictive Trade Practices Act 1976, s 44, Sch 6.
Sub-s (3): repealed by the Statute Law (Repeals) Act 2004.
Orders: the Fair Trading Act 1973 (Commencement No 1) Order 1973, SI 1973/1545; the Fair Trading Act 1973 (Commencement No 2) Order 1973, SI 1973/1652.

(Schs 1, 2 repealed by the Enterprise Act 2002, ss 10(1)(a), 278(2), Sch 26; Sch 3 repealed by the Competition Act 1998, s 74(1), (3), Sch 12, para 1(1), (2), Sch 14, Pt I; Schs 4–9 repealed by the Enterprise Act 2002, s 278, Sch 26; Sch 10 repealed by the Restrictive Trade Practices Act 1976, s 44, Sch 6; Sch 11 (Transitional Provisions and Savings) outside the scope of this work; Sch 12, in so far as unrepealed, contains miscellaneous amendments; Sch 13 contains repeals.)

PRICES ACT 1974

(1974 c 24)

ARRANGEMENT OF SECTIONS

An Act to authorise the payment of food subsidies; to confer on the Secretary of State power to regulate the price of food and certain other goods and on the Price Commission additional powers for preventing or restricting increases in prices and charges; to make provision for requiring prices to be indicated on or in relation to goods offered or exposed for sale by retail and for requiring information as to the range within which food and certain other goods are commonly being sold by retail within the United Kingdom to be displayed by retailers dealing in those goods; to confer power to abolish the Pay Board; and for purposes connected with those matters

[9 July 1974]

1–3   *(S 1 repealed by the Statute Law (Repeals) Act 1989; s 2 repealed by the Statute Law (Repeals) Act 2004; s 3 repealed by the Price Commission Act 1977, ss 16(4), 22(7), Sch 3.)*

4 Price marking

[(1)   The Secretary of State may by order make provision for securing—
    (a)   that prices are indicated on or in relation to goods which a person indicates are or may be for sale by retail, whether or not the goods are in existence when he does so;
    (b)   that charges are indicated for services which a person indicates are or may be provided, except services which he indicates are or may be provided only for the purposes of business carried on by other persons;
    (c)   that prices of such goods or charges for such services are not indicated in a manner which the Secretary of State considers inappropriate and that no part of a penny except one half-penny is specified in the amount of an indicated price or charge.]

(2)   Without prejudice to the generality of subsection (1) above, an order under this section [may specify the kinds of goods or services to which and the circumstances in which the order applies and]

(a)   may make provision as to the manner in which any price [or charge] is to be indicated;
(b)   may require that the price [or charge] to be indicated on or in relation to any goods [or services] shall be, or shall include, a price [or charge] expressed by reference to such unit or units of measurement as may be specified in the order;
(c)   may, in relation to goods [or services] subject to value added tax, make provision as to the circumstances in which the price [or charge] to be indicated may or may not be exclusive of the tax and as to the indication to be given of the tax included in, or payable in addition to, the price [or charge];
(d)   may make different provision in relation to different circumstances and may contain such supplementary provisions as the Secretary of State thinks necessary or expedient.

[(3)   Before making an order under this section the Secretary of State shall consult, in such manner as appears to him to be appropriate having regard to the subject-matter and urgency of the order, with such organisations representative of interests substantially affected by the order as appear to him, having regard to those matters, to be appropriate.]

(4)   The power to make an order under this section shall be exercisable by statutory instrument and includes power to vary or revoke a previous order; and a statutory instrument containing an order under this section shall be subject to annulment in pursuance of a resolution of either House of Parliament.

(5)   In the application of this section to Northern Ireland for any reference to the Secretary of State there shall be substituted a reference to the Department of Commerce for Northern Ireland and any order made by the Department under this section shall be [a statutory rule for the purposes of the Statutory Rules Act (Northern Ireland) 1958 and be] subject to negative resolution within the meaning of section 41(6) of the Interpretation Act (Northern Ireland) 1954 as if it were a statutory instrument within the meaning of that Act; and subsection (4) above shall not apply to any such order except in so far as that subsection confers a power to vary or revoke a previous order.

[645]–[646]

NOTES
Sub-s (1): substituted by the Price Commission Act 1977, s 16(1).
Sub-ss (2), (5): words in square brackets inserted by the Price Commission Act 1977, s 16(2)(a), (3).
Sub-s (3): substituted by the Statute Law (Repeals) Act 2004, s 1(2), Sch 2, para 11.
Orders: the Indication of Prices (Beds) Order 1978, SI 1978/1716; the Price Marking Order 2004, SI 2004/102 at **[3369]**.

5, 6   (*S 5 repealed by the Statute Law (Repeals) Act 2004; s 6 repealed by the Statute Law (Repeals) Act 1989.*)

7   Enforcement
The Schedule to this Act shall have effect ... for the enforcement of orders under section ... 4 ... above.

[647]

NOTES
Words omitted repealed by the Statute Law (Repeals) Act 2004.

8   Financial provisions
(1)   There shall be paid out of moneys provided by Parliament—
(a)   the expenses of any government department in respect of the administration of this Act;
(b)   any increase attributable to this Act in the sums so payable under any other Act.
(2)   ...

[648]

NOTES
Sub-s (2): repealed by the Statute Law (Repeals) Act 1989.

9   Short title and interpretation
(1)   This Act may be cited as the Prices Act 1974.
(2)   In this Act "food" means food and drink for human consumption.
(3)   In this Act any reference to any enactment is a reference to that enactment as amended by or under any subsequent enactment.
(4)   ...

[649]

SCHEDULE
ENFORCEMENT

Section 7

Food subsidies

1, 2. ...

3.—*(1)   A duly authorised officer of the Secretary of State or the Minister of Agriculture, Fisheries and Food may, at all reasonable hours and on production, if required, of his credentials, exercise the powers specified in sub-paragraph (2) below for the purpose of determining—*
  (a)   *whether any payment is to be, or has been, properly made under any scheme under section 1 of this Act or falls to be repaid in accordance with any conditions subject to which it was made or falls to be made to the Secretary of State by virtue of any order under subsection (7) of that section; or*
  (b)   *whether any condition required to be observed under paragraph 2 above has been contravened.*

  (2)   *The said powers are—*
  (a)   *a power to inspect and take samples of any goods and to enter any land or any premises other than premises used only as a dwelling; and*
  (b)   *a power to require any person carrying on business, or employed in connection with a business, to produce any documents relating to the business, and a power of making extracts from, or making copies of, the documents.*

  (3)   *Any person who—*
  (a)   *wilfully obstructs an officer acting under this paragraph; or*
  (b)   *wilfully fails to comply with a requirement imposed under this paragraph,*
shall be guilty of an offence and liable on summary conviction to a fine not exceeding [level 5 on the standard scale].

  (4)   *Any person who, with intent to deceive, produces, in compliance with a requirement under this paragraph, a document which to his knowledge is or may be misleading, false or deceptive in a material particular shall be guilty of an offence and liable on summary conviction to a fine not exceeding [level 5 on the standard scale].*

  (5)   *Nothing in this paragraph shall be construed as compelling the production by a barrister, advocate or solicitor of a document containing a privileged communication made by or to him in that capacity.*

  (6)   *In this paragraph "premises" include any stall, vehicle or vessel.*

4. ...

Price regulation, price marking and price range notices

5.—(1)   Any person who contravenes an order under section ... 4 ... of this Act shall be guilty of an offence and liable—
  (a)   on conviction on indictment, to a fine;
  (b)   on summary conviction, to a fine not exceeding [the prescribed sum].

  (2)   ...

  (3)   Section 23 of the Trade Descriptions Act 1968 (offences due to fault of other person) and section 24(1) and (2) of that Act (defence of mistake, accident etc.) shall have effect in relation to an offence in respect of an order under section 4 of this Act as they have effect in relation to an offence under that Act.

6.   It shall be the duty of every local weights and measures authority to enforce within their area any such order as is mentioned in paragraph 5(1) above.

7.   A local weights and measures authority may make, or may authorise any of their officers to make, any purchases of goods [and any contracts for services] for the purpose of determining whether any such order is being complied with.

8.—(1)   Proceedings for an offence under paragraph 5 above shall not be instituted except by or on behalf of a local weights and measures authority.

  (2)   Proceedings for any such offence shall not be instituted—
  (a)   unless there has been served on the person charged a notice in writing of the date and nature of the offence alleged, being (except where he is a street trader) a notice served before the expiration of the period of thirty days beginning with that date; or
  (b)   after the expiration of the period of three months beginning with that date.

(3)   Such a notice as is mentioned in sub-paragraph (2)(a) above may be served on any person either by serving it on him personally or by sending it to him by post at his usual or last known residence or place of business in the United Kingdom or, in the case of a company, at the company's registered office.

(4)   Sub-paragraph (1) above does not apply to Scotland.

9.—(1)   A duly authorised officer of a local weights and measures authority may, at all reasonable hours and on production, if required, of his credentials, exercise any of the powers specified in paragraph 3(2) above and any of the powers specified in sub-paragraph (2) below for the purpose of determining whether an offence under paragraph 5 above has been committed.

(2)   The said powers are—
    (a)   a power to seize and detain any document or goods which the officer has reason to believe may be required as evidence in proceedings for such an offence; and
    (b)   a power to seize and detain any goods if the officer has reason to believe that their examination is likely to produce evidence of the commission of any such offence.

(3)   Any person who—
    (a)   wilfully obstructs an officer acting under this paragraph; or
    (b)   wilfully fails to comply with a requirement imposed under this paragraph; or
    (c)   without reasonable cause fails to give to any officer acting under this paragraph any other assistance or information which the officer may reasonably require for the performance by the officer of his functions under this Schedule,
shall be guilty of an offence and liable on summary conviction to a fine not exceeding [level 5 on the standard scale].

(4)   Any person who, with intent to deceive, produces or gives, in compliance with a requirement under this paragraph, a document or information which to his knowledge is or may be misleading, false or deceptive in a material particular shall be guilty of an offence and liable on summary conviction to a fine not exceeding [level 5 on the standard scale].

(5)   Nothing in this paragraph shall be construed as requiring a person to answer any question or give any information if to do so might incriminate him or as authorising the taking of possession of any such document as is mentioned in paragraph 3(5) above which is in the possession of a barrister, advocate or solicitor.

10.   Where a local weights and measures authority have made arrangements for the discharge of any of their functions as such by another local authority, the powers conferred by paragraph 9 above shall also be exercisable by a duly authorised officer of that other local authority.

11, 12.   …

Offences by bodies corporate

13.   Where an offence under this Schedule committed by a body corporate is proved to have been committed with the consent or connivance of, or to be attributable to any neglect on the part of, any director, manager, secretary or other similar officer of the body corporate or any person who was purporting to act in any such capacity, he as well as the body corporate shall be guilty of the offence and shall be liable to be proceeded against and punished accordingly.

14.   (*Outside the scope of this work.*)

[650]

NOTES
    Paras 1, 2, 4: repealed by the Statute Law (Repeals) Act 1989.
    Para 3: repealed, except as it has effect for the purposes of para 9 by the Statute Law (Repeals) Act 1989; references to a level on the standard scale in sub-paras (3), (4) substituted by virtue of the Criminal Justice Act 1982, ss 38, 46.
    Para 5: words omitted repealed by the Statute Law (Repeals) Act 2004; reference to the prescribed sum substituted by virtue of the Magistrates' Courts Act 1980, s 32(2).
    Para 7: words in square brackets inserted by the Price Commission Act 1977, s 16(2)(b).
    Para 9: references to a level on the standard scale in sub-paras (3), (4) substituted by virtue of the Criminal Justice Act 1982, ss 38, 46.
    Para 11: repealed by the Statute Law (Repeals) Act 2004.
    Para 12: repealed by the Enterprise Act 2002, ss 247(c), 278(2), Sch 26.
    Minister of Agriculture, Fisheries and Food: now the Secretary of State for Environment, Food and Rural Affairs; see the Secretaries of State for Transport, Local Government and the Regions and for Environment, Food and Rural Affairs Order 2001, SI 2001/2568.
    Seize and detain documents, etc: the powers of seizure conferred by para 9(2) are powers to which the Criminal Justice and Police Act 2001, s 50 apply (additional powers of seizure from premises); see s 50 of, and Sch 1, Pt 1, para 18 to, that Act.

CONSUMER CREDIT ACT 1974

(1974 c 39)

ARRANGEMENT OF SECTIONS

PART IV
SEEKING BUSINESS

PART V
ENTRY INTO CREDIT OR HIRE AGREEMENTS

PART VA
CURRENT ACCOUNT OVERDRAFTS

PART VI
MATTERS ARISING DURING CURRENCY OF CREDIT OR HIRE AGREEMENTS

PART VII
DEFAULT AND TERMINATION

Information sheets

Sums in arrears and default sums

Default notices

Further restriction of remedies for default

PART XII
SUPPLEMENTAL

General

Regulations, orders, etc

Interpretation

Miscellaneous

An Act to establish for the protection of consumers a new system, administered by the Director General of Fair Trading, of licensing and other control of traders concerned with the provision of credit, or the supply of goods on hire or hire-purchase, and their transactions, in place of the present enactments regulating moneylenders, pawnbrokers and hire-purchase traders and their transactions, and for related matters

[31st July 1974]

NOTES
    The text of the Consumer Credit Act 1974 reproduced here includes all amendments to the Act, including prospective amendments, as at 29 July 2010. Commencement dates for amendments are shown in the notes to each provision. Text which is prospectively inserted as at 29 July 2010 is shown as underlined, and text which is prospectively repealed appears in italics.
    For the text of the 1974 Act as it had effect on 15 June 2006, prior to amendments made by the Consumer Credit Act 2006, and subsequent amendments, see the Appendix at [A1] and notes to individual provisions affected below.
    Substitution of references to the Director General of Fair Trading: the Enterprise Act 2002, s 2(1), at **[1860]**, provides that, as from the coming into force of that section (on 1 April 2003, see the Enterprise Act 2002 (Commencement No 2, Transitional and Transitory Provisions) Order 2003, SI 2003/766), the functions of the Director General of Fair Trading, his property, rights and liabilities are transferred to the Office of Fair Trading. Accordingly, (by virtue of s 2(2), (3) of the 2002 Act) the office of the Director is abolished, and amendments are made to this Act by the 2002 Act to take account of this (see Sch 25, para 6). Consequently, throughout this Act, unless noted otherwise, the words "OFT", "OFT's", "it", "it" and "its" are substituted for the original words "Director", "Director's", "he", "him" and "his" respectively. For transitional provisions in connection with the transfer, see s 276(1) of, and Sch 24, para 6 to, the 2002 Act.

PART I
[OFFICE OF FAIR TRADING]

NOTES

Part heading: words in square brackets substituted by the Enterprise Act 2002, s 278(1), Sch 25, para 6(1), (2), as from 1 April 2003.

1   General functions of [OFT]

(1)   It is the duty of the [Office of Fair Trading ("the OFT")]—

(a)   to administer the licensing system set up by this Act,

(b)   to exercise the adjudicating functions conferred on [it] by this Act in relation to the issue, renewal, variation, suspension and revocation of licences, and other matters,

[(ba)   to monitor, as it sees fit, businesses being carried on under licences;]

(c)   generally to superintend the working and enforcement of this Act, and regulations made under it, and

(d)   where necessary or expedient, [itself] to take steps to enforce this Act, and regulations so made.

(2)   It is the duty of the [OFT], so far as appears to [it] to be practicable and having regard both to the national interest and the interests of persons carrying on businesses to which this Act applies and their customers, to keep under review and from time to time advise the Secretary of State about—

(a)   social and commercial developments in the United Kingdom and elsewhere relating to the provision of credit or bailment or (in Scotland) hiring of goods to individuals, and related activities; and

(b)   the working and enforcement of this Act and orders and regulations made under it.

[651]

NOTES

For the text of this section as it had effect on 15 June 2006, prior to amendments made by the Consumer Credit Act 2006 and subsequent amendments, see the Appendix at [A1].

Sub-s (1): words in first pair of square brackets and words in square brackets in para (d) substituted by the Enterprise Act 2002, s 278(1), Sch 25, para 6(1), (2)(a)(i), (iii), as from 1 April 2003; para (ba) inserted by the Consumer Credit Act 2006, s 62, as from 6 April 2008.

References to the OFT, etc: as to the abolition of the office of the Director General of Fair Trading and the substitution of the original references to the Director (and related expressions), see the note preceding this section.

2   Powers of Secretary of State

(1)   The Secretary of State may by order—

(a)   confer on the [OFT] additional functions concerning the provision of credit or bailment or (in Scotland) hiring of goods to individuals, and related activities, and

(b)   regulate the carrying out by the [OFT] of [its] functions under this Act.

(2)   The Secretary of State may give general directions indicating considerations to which the [OFT] should have particular regard in carrying out [its] functions under this Act, and may give specific directions on any matter connected with the carrying out by the [OFT] of those functions.

(3)   The Secretary of State, on giving any directions under subsection (2), shall arrange for them to be published in such manner as he thinks most suitable for drawing them to the attention of interested persons.

(4)   With the approval of the Secretary of State and the Treasury, the [OFT] may charge, for any service or facility provided by [it] under this Act, a fee of an amount specified by general notice (the "specified fee").

(5)   Provision may be made under subsection (4) for reduced fees, or no fees at all, to be paid for certain services or facilities by persons of a specified description, and references in this Act to the specified fee shall, in such cases, be construed accordingly.

(6)   An order under subsection (1)(a) shall be made by statutory instrument and shall be of no effect unless a draft of the order has been laid before and approved by each House of Parliament.

(7)   References in subsection (2) to the functions of the [OFT] under this Act do not include the making of a determination to which section 41 … (appeals from [OFT] to [the [First-tier Tribunal]]) applies.

[652]

NOTES

For the text of this section as it had effect on 15 June 2006, prior to amendments made by the Consumer Credit Act 2006 and subsequent amendments, see the Appendix at [A2].

Sub-s (7): words omitted repealed and words in third (outer) pair of square brackets substituted by the Consumer Credit Act 2006, ss 58(1), 70, Sch 4, as from 6 April 2008, except in relation to determinations made by the OFT before that date; words in fourth (inner) pair of square brackets substituted for word "Tribunal" by the Transfer of Functions of the Consumer Credit Appeals Tribunal Order 2009, SI 2009/1835, art 4(1), Sch 1, paras 1, 2, as from 1 September 2009, subject to transitional provisions and savings in Sch 4 thereto at **[3908]**.

References to the OFT, etc: as to the abolition of the office of the Director General of Fair Trading and the substitution of the original references to the Director (and related expressions), see the note preceding s 1 at **[651]**.

Order: the Consumer Credit Licensing (Representations) Order 1976, SI 1976/191.

---

3 *(Repealed by the Tribunals and Inquiries Act 1992, s 18(2), Sch 4, Pt I, as from 1 October 1992.)*

4 Dissemination of information and advice

The [OFT] shall arrange for the dissemination, in such form and manner as [it] considers appropriate, of such information and advice as it may appear to [it] expedient to give to the public in the United Kingdom about the operation of this Act, [the consumer credit jurisdiction under Part 16 of the Financial Services and Markets Act 2000,] the credit facilities available to them, and other matters within the scope of [its] functions under this Act.

[653]

NOTES
 For the text of this section as it had effect on 15 June 2006, prior to amendments made by the Consumer Credit Act 2006 and subsequent amendments, see the Appendix at [A3].
 Words in fourth pair of square brackets inserted by the Consumer Credit Act 2006, s 61(1), as from 16 June 2006.
 References to the OFT, etc: as to the abolition of the office of the Director General of Fair Trading and the substitution of the original references to the Director (and related expressions), see the note preceding s 1 at **[651]**.

---

5 *(Repealed by the Enterprise Act 2002, s 278(2), Sch 26, as from 20 June 2003.)*

6 Form etc of application

 (1) An application to the [OFT] under this Act is of no effect unless the requirements of this section are satisfied.

 (2) The application must be in writing, and in such form, and accompanied by such [information and documents], as the [OFT] may specify [or describe in a] general notice …

 [(2A) The application must also be accompanied—
   (a) in the case of an application for a licence or for the renewal of a licence, by the charge payable by virtue of section 6A;
   (b) in any other case, by the specified fee.]

 [(3) Where the OFT receives an application, it may by notice to the applicant at any time before the determination of the application require him to provide such information or documents relevant to the application as may be specified or described in the notice.]

 (4) The [OFT] may by notice require the applicant to publish details of his application at a time or times and in a manner specified in the notice.

 [(5) Subsection (6) applies where a general notice under subsection (2) comes into effect—
   (a) after an application has been made; but
   (b) before its determination.

 (6) The applicant shall, within such period as may be specified in the general notice, provide the OFT with any information or document—
   (a) which he has not previously provided in relation to the application by virtue of this section;
   (b) which he would have been required to provide with his application had it been made after the general notice came into effect; and
   (c) which the general notice requires to be provided for the purposes of this subsection.

 (7) An applicant shall notify the OFT, giving details, if before his application is determined—
   (a) any information or document provided by him in relation to the application by virtue of this section is, to any extent, superseded or otherwise affected by a change in circumstances; or
   (b) he becomes aware of an error in or omission from any such information or document.

 (8) A notification for the purposes of subsection (7) shall be given within the period of 28 days beginning with the day on which (as the case may be)—
   (a) the information or document is superseded;
   (b) the change in circumstances occurs; or
   (c) the applicant becomes aware of the error or omission.

 (9) Subsection (7) does not require an applicant to notify the OFT about—

(a)   anything of which he is required to notify it under section 36; or

(b)   an error in or omission from any information or document which is a clerical error or omission not affecting the substance of the information or document.]

[654]

NOTES

For the text of this section as it had effect on 15 June 2006, prior to amendments made by the Consumer Credit Act 2006 and subsequent amendments, see the Appendix at [A4].

Sub-s (2): words in first and third pairs of square brackets substituted and words omitted repealed by the Consumer Credit Act 2006, ss 44(1), 70, Sch 2, as from 1 December 2007 (except in relation to applications made before that date).

Sub-s (2A): inserted by the Consumer Credit Act 2006, s 27(2), as from 6 April 2008, subject to transitional provisions in s 69(1) of, and Sch 3, paras 1, 18(2) to, that Act at **[2077]**, **[2079]**.

Sub-s (3): substituted by the Consumer Credit Act 2006, s 44(2), as from 6 April 2008, except in relation to applications made before that date: see the Consumer Credit Act 2006 (Commencement No 3) Order 2007, SI 2007/3300, art 3(2), Sch 2 and s 69(1) of, and Sch 3, paras 1, 23(1) to, the 2006 Act at **[2077]**, **[2079]**.

Sub-ss (5)–(9): added by the Consumer Credit Act 2006, s 44(3), as from 6 April 2008 (except in relation to applications made before that date); for effect see the Consumer Credit Act 2006 (Commencement No 3) Order 2007, SI 2007/3300, art 3(2), Sch 2 and s 69(1) of, and Sch 3, paras 1, 23(1) to, the 2006 Act at **[2077]**, **[2079]**.

References to the OFT, etc: as to the abolition of the office of the Director General of Fair Trading and the substitution of the original references to the Director (and related expressions), see the note preceding s 1 at **[651]**.

[6A   Charge on applicants for licences etc

(1)   An applicant for a licence, or for the renewal of a licence, shall pay the OFT a charge towards the costs of carrying out its functions under this Act.

(2)   The amount of the charge payable by an applicant shall be determined in accordance with provision made by the OFT by general notice.

(3)   The provision that may be made by the OFT under subsection (2) includes—

(a)   different provision in relation to persons of different descriptions;

(b)   provision for no charge at all to be payable by persons of specified descriptions.

(4)   The approval of the Secretary of State and the Treasury is required for a general notice under subsection (2).]

[654A]

NOTES

Commencement: 16 June 2006 (sub-ss (2)–(4)); 6 April 2008 (sub-s (1)).

Inserted by the Consumer Credit Act 2006, s 27(1), as from dates as noted above.

[7   Penalty for false information

A person commits an offence if, for the purposes of, or in connection with, any requirement imposed or other provision made by or under this Act, he knowingly or recklessly gives information to the OFT, or to an officer of the OFT, which, in a material particular, is false or misleading.]

[655]

NOTES

For the text of this section as it had effect on 15 June 2006, prior to amendments made by the Consumer Credit Act 2006 and subsequent amendments, see the Appendix at [A5].

Commencement: 6 April 2008.

Substituted by the Consumer Credit Act 2006, s 51(1), as from 6 April 2008.

PART II

CREDIT AGREEMENTS, HIRE AGREEMENTS AND LINKED TRANSACTIONS

8   Consumer credit agreements

(1)   A [consumer] credit agreement is an agreement between an individual ("the debtor") and any other person ("the creditor") by which the creditor provides the debtor with credit of any amount.

(2)   ...

(3)   A consumer credit agreement is a regulated agreement within the meaning of this Act if it is not an agreement (an "exempt agreement") specified in or under section 16[, 16A[, 16B or 16C]].

[656]

NOTES

For the text of this section as it had effect on 15 June 2006, prior to amendments made by the Consumer Credit Act 2006 and subsequent amendments, see the Appendix at [A6].

Sub-s (1): word in square brackets substituted by the Consumer Credit Act 2006, s 2(1)(a), as from 31 October 2008: for effect and transitional provisions, see the Consumer Credit Act 2006 (Commencement No 4 and Transitional Provisions) Order 2008, SI 2008/831, arts 2(1), 4, Sch 1.

Sub-s (2): repealed by the Consumer Credit Act 2006, ss 2(1)(b), 70, Sch 4, as from 31 October 2008; for effect and transitional provisions, see SI 2008/831, arts 2(1), 4, Sch 1.

Sub-s (3): words in first (outer) pair of square brackets added by the Consumer Credit Act 2006, s 5(1), as from 6 April 2008; words in second (inner) pair of square brackets substituted by the Legislative Reform (Consumer Credit) Order 2008, SI 2008/2826, art 3(2), as from 31 October 2008.

9 Meaning of credit

(1) In this Act "credit" includes a cash loan, and any other form of financial accommodation.

(2) Where credit is provided otherwise than in sterling, it shall be treated for the purposes of this Act as provided in sterling of an equivalent amount.

(3) Without prejudice to the generality of subsection (1), the person by whom goods are bailed or (in Scotland) hired to an individual under a hire-purchase agreement shall be taken to provide him with fixed-sum credit to finance the transaction of an amount equal to the total price of the goods less the aggregate of the deposit (if any) and the total charge for credit.

(4) For the purposes of this Act, an item entering into the total charge for credit shall not be treated as credit even though time is allowed for its payment.

[657]

10 Running-account credit and fixed-sum credit

(1) For the purposes of this Act—
  (a) running-account credit is a facility under a [consumer] credit agreement whereby the debtor is enabled to receive from time to time (whether in his own person, or by another person) from the creditor or a third party cash, goods and services (or any of them) to an amount or value such that, taking into account payments made by or to the credit of the debtor, the credit limit (if any) is not at any time exceeded; and
  (b) fixed-sum credit is any other facility under a [consumer] credit agreement whereby the debtor is enabled to receive credit (whether in one amount or by instalments).

(2) In relation to running-account credit, "credit limit" means, as respects any period, the maximum debit balance which, under the credit agreement, is allowed to stand on the account during that period, disregarding any term of the agreement allowing that maximum to be exceeded merely temporarily.

(3) For the purposes of *[paragraph (a) of section 16B(1)]*, [any provision of this Act that specifies an amount of credit (except section 17(1)(a))] running-account credit shall be taken not to exceed the amount specified in *that [paragraph]* [that provision] ("the specified amount") if—
  (a) the credit limit does not exceed the specified amount; or
  (b) whether or not there is a credit limit, and if there is, notwithstanding that it exceeds the specified amount,—
    (i) the debtor is not enabled to draw at any one time an amount which, so far as (having regard to section 9(4)) it represents credit, exceeds the specified amount, or
    (ii) the agreement provides that, if the debit balance rises above a given amount (not exceeding the specified amount), the rate of the total charge for credit increases or any other condition favouring the creditor or his associate comes into operation, or
    (iii) at the time the agreement is made it is probable, having regard to the terms of the agreement and any other relevant considerations, that the debit balance will not at any time rise above the specified amount.

[658]

NOTES

For the text of this section as it had effect on 15 June 2006, prior to amendments made by the Consumer Credit Act 2006 and subsequent amendments, see the Appendix at [A8].

Sub-s (1): words in square brackets substituted by the Consumer Credit Act 2006, s 5(2)(a), as from 6 April 2008.

Sub-s (3): words in first and third pairs of square brackets substituted by the Consumer Credit Act 2006, s 5(2)(b), as from 6 April 2008; words in italics in both places substituted by subsequent words in second and fourth pairs of square brackets by the Consumer Credit (EU Directive) Regulations 2010, SI 2010/1010, regs 2, 44, as from 1 February 2011, with effect in relation to certain agreements before that date, as provided for in regs 101, 101A of the 2010 Regulations at **[3942]**, **[3942A]**.

11 Restricted-use credit and unrestricted-use credit

(1) A restricted-use credit agreement is a regulated consumer credit agreement—
  (a) to finance a transaction between the debtor and the creditor, whether forming part of that agreement or not, or

(b) to finance a transaction between the debtor and a person (the "supplier") other than the creditor, or

(c) to refinance any existing indebtedness of the debtor's, whether to the creditor or another person,

and "restricted-use credit" shall be construed accordingly.

(2) An unrestricted-use credit agreement is a regulated consumer credit agreement not falling within subsection (1), and "unrestricted-use credit" shall be construed accordingly.

(3) An agreement does not fall within subsection (1) if the credit is in fact provided in such a way as to leave the debtor free to use it as he chooses, even though certain uses would contravene that or any other agreement.

(4) An agreement may fall within subsection (1)(b) although the identity of the supplier is unknown at the time the agreement is made.

[659]

12 Debtor-creditor-supplier agreements

A debtor-creditor-supplier agreement is a regulated consumer credit agreement being—

(a) a restricted-use credit agreement which falls within section 11(1)(a), or

(b) a restricted-use credit agreement which falls within section 11(1)(b) and is made by the creditor under pre-existing arrangements, or in contemplation of future arrangements, between himself and the supplier, or

(c) an unrestricted-use credit agreement which is made by the creditor under pre-existing arrangements between himself and a person (the "supplier") other than the debtor in the knowledge that the credit is to be used to finance a transaction between the debtor and the supplier.

[660]

13 Debtor-creditor agreements

A debtor-creditor agreement is a regulated consumer credit agreement being—

(a) a restricted-use credit agreement which falls within section 11(1)(b) but is not made by the creditor under pre-existing arrangements, or in contemplation of future arrangements, between himself and the supplier, or

(b) a restricted-use credit agreement which falls within section 11(1)(c), or

(c) an unrestricted-use credit agreement which is not made by the creditor under pre-existing arrangements between himself and a person (the "supplier") other than the debtor in the knowledge that the credit is to be used to finance a transaction between the debtor and the supplier.

[661]

14 Credit-token agreements

(1) A credit-token is a card, check, voucher, coupon, stamp, form, booklet or other document or thing given to an individual by a person carrying on a consumer credit business, who undertakes—

(a) that on the production of it (whether or not some other action is also required) he will supply cash, goods and services (or any of them) on credit, or

(b) that where, on the production of it to a third party (whether or not any other action is also required), the third party supplies cash, goods and services (or any of them), he will pay the third party for them (whether or not deducting any discount or commission), in return for payment to him by the individual.

(2) A credit-token agreement is a regulated agreement for the provision of credit in connection with the use of a credit-token.

(3) Without prejudice to the generality of section 9(1), the person who gives to an individual an undertaking falling within subsection (1)(b) shall be taken to provide him with credit drawn on whenever a third party supplies him with cash, goods or services.

(4) For the purposes of subsection (1), use of an object to operate a machine provided by the person giving the object or a third party shall be treated as the production of the object to him.

[662]

15 Consumer hire agreements

(1) A consumer hire agreement is an agreement made by a person with an individual (the "hirer") for the bailment or (in Scotland) the hiring of goods to the hirer, being an agreement which—

(a) is not a hire-purchase agreement, and

(b) is capable of subsisting for more than three months, ...

(c) ...

(2) A consumer hire agreement is a regulated agreement if it is not an exempt agreement.

[663]

NOTES
   For the text of this section as it had effect on 15 June 2006, prior to amendments made by the Consumer Credit Act 2006 and subsequent amendments, see the Appendix at [A13].
   Sub-s (1): para (c) and word "and" immediately preceding it repealed by the Consumer Credit Act 2006, ss 2(2), 70, Sch 4, as from 6 April 2008.

16   Exempt agreements

   (1)   This Act does not regulate a consumer credit agreement where the creditor is a local authority ... , or a body specified, or of a description specified, in an order made by the Secretary of State, being—

     [(a)   an insurer,]
     (b)   a friendly society,
     (c)   an organisation of employers or organisation of workers,
     (d)   a charity,
     (e)   a land improvement company, ...
     (f)   a body corporate named or specifically referred to in any public general Act
     [(ff)   a body corporate named or specifically referred to in an order made under—
          section 156(4), *444(1)* or 447(2)(a) of the Housing Act 1985,
          [section 156(4) of that Act as it has effect by virtue of section 17 of the Housing Act 1996 (the right to acquire),]
          (applies to Scotland only.)
          Article 154(1)(a) or 156AA of the Housing (Northern Ireland) Order 1981 or Article 10(6A) of the Housing (Northern Ireland) Order 1983; or]
     [(g)   a building society][, or
     [(h)   a deposit-taker]].

   (2)   Subsection (1) applies only where the agreement is—
     (a)   a debtor-creditor-supplier agreement financing—
         (i)   the purchase of land, or
         (ii)   the provision of dwellings on any land,
          and secured by a land mortgage on that land, or
     (b)   a debtor-creditor agreement secured by any land mortgage; or
     (c)   a debtor-creditor-supplier agreement financing a transaction which is a linked transaction in relation to—
         (i)   an agreement falling within paragraph (a), or
         (ii)   an agreement falling within paragraph (b) financing—

             (aa)   the purchase of any land, or

             (bb)   the provision of dwellings on any land,
          and secured by a land mortgage on the land referred to in paragraph (a) or, as the case may be, the land referred to in sub-paragraph (ii).

   [(3)   Before he makes, varies or revokes an order under subsection (1), the Secretary of State must undertake the necessary consultation.

   (3A)   The necessary consultation means consultation with the bodies mentioned in the following table in relation to the provision under which the order is to be made, varied or revoked:

Table

Provision of subsection (1)	*Consultee*
Paragraph (a) or (b)	The Financial Services Authority
Paragraph (d)	[Charity Commission]
Paragraph (e), (f) or (ff)	Any Minister of the Crown with responsibilities in relation to the body in question
Paragraph (g) or (h)	The Treasury and the Financial Services Authority]

   (4)   An order under subsection (1) relating to a body may be limited so as to apply only to agreements by that body of a description specified in the order.

   (5)   The Secretary of State may by order provide that this Act shall not regulate other consumer credit agreements where—
     (a)   the number of payments to be made by the debtor does not exceed the number specified for that purpose in the order, or
     (b)   the rate of the total charge for credit does not exceed the rate so specified, or
     (c)   an agreement has a connection with a country outside the United Kingdom.

PART 1
STATUTES

(6)   The Secretary of State may by order provide that this Act shall not regulate consumer hire agreements of a description specified in the order where—

    (a)   the owner is a body corporate authorised by or under any enactment to supply electricity, gas or water, and

    (b)   the subject of the agreement is a meter or metering equipment,

[or where the owner is a [provider of a public electronic communications service who is specified in the order]].

[(6A)   This Act does not regulate a consumer credit agreement where the creditor is a housing authority and the agreement is secured by a land mortgage of a dwelling.

(6B)   In subsection (6A) "housing authority" means—

    (a)   as regards England and Wales, [the Regulator of Social Housing and] an authority or body within section 80(1) of the Housing Act 1985 (the landlord condition for secure tenancies), other than a housing association or a housing trust which is a charity;

    (b)   *(applies to Scotland only)*;

    (c)   as regards Northern Ireland, the Northern Ireland Housing Executive.]

[[(6C)   This Act does not regulate a consumer credit agreement if—

    (a)   it is secured by a land mortgage and entering into the agreement as lender is a regulated activity for the purposes of the Financial Services and Markets Act 2000; or

    (b)   it is or forms part of a regulated home purchase plan and entering into the agreement as home purchase provider is a regulated activity for the purposes of that Act.]

(6D)   But section 126, and any other provision so far as it relates to section 126, applies to an agreement which would (but for [subsection (6C)(a)]) be a regulated agreement.

(6E)   Subsection (6C) must be read with—

    (a)   section 22 of the Financial Services and Markets Act 2000 (regulated activities: power to specify classes of activity and categories of investment);

    (b)   any order for the time being in force under that section; and

    (c)   Schedule 2 to that Act.]

(7)   ...

[(7A)   Nothing in this section affects the application of sections 140A to 140C.]

(8)   *(Applies to Scotland only.)*

(9)   In the application of this section to Northern Ireland [subsection (3A)] shall have effect as if any reference to a Minister of the Crown were a reference to a Northern Ireland department, ... and any reference to the [Charity Commission] were a reference to the Department of Finance for Northern Ireland.

[(10)   In this section—

    (a)   "deposit-taker" means—

        (i)   a person who has permission under Part 4 of the Financial Services and Markets Act 2000 to accept deposits,

        (ii)   an EEA firm of the kind mentioned in paragraph 5(b) of Schedule 3 to that Act which has permission under paragraph 15 of that Schedule (as a result of qualifying for authorisation under paragraph 12 of that Schedule) to accept deposits,

        (iii)   any wholly owned subsidiary (within the meaning of [the Companies Acts (see section 1159 of the Companies Act 2006)]) of a person mentioned in sub-paragraph (i), or

        (iv)   any undertaking which, in relation to a person mentioned in sub-paragraph (ii), is a subsidiary undertaking within the meaning of any rule of law in force in the EEA State in question for purposes connected with the implementation of the European Council Seventh Company Law Directive of 13 June 1983 on consolidated accounts (No 83/349/EEC), and which has no members other than that person;

    (b)   "insurer" means—

        (i)   a person who has permission under Part 4 of the Financial Services and Markets Act 2000 to effect or carry out contracts of insurance, or

        (ii)   an EEA firm of the kind mentioned in paragraph 5(d) of Schedule 3 to that Act, which has permission under paragraph 15 of that Schedule (as a result of qualifying for authorisation under paragraph 12 of that Schedule) to effect or carry out contracts of insurance,

    but does not include a friendly society or an organisation of workers or of employers.

(11)   Subsection (10) must be read with—

    (a)   section 22 of the Financial Services and Markets Act 2000;

    (b)   any relevant order under that section; and

    (c)   Schedule 2 to that Act.]

NOTES
For the text of this section as it had effect on 15 June 2006, prior to amendments made by the Consumer Credit Act 2006 and subsequent amendments, see the Appendix at [A14].
Sub-s (1): first words omitted repealed, and para (g) added, by the Building Societies Act 1986, s 120, Sch 18, Pt I, para 10(2), Sch 19, Pt I, as from 1 January 1987; para (a) substituted by the Financial Services and Markets Act 2000 (Consequential Amendments and Repeals) Order 2001, SI 2001/3649, art 165(1), (2)(a), as from 1 December 2001; para (ff) inserted by the Housing and Planning Act 1986, s 22(2), (4), as from 7 January 1987 with respect to agreements made after that date, number in italics repealed by the Housing Act 1996, s 227, Sch 19, Pt XIV, as from a day to be appointed, and words in square brackets inserted by the Housing Act 1996 (Consequential Amendments) (No 2) Order 1997, SI 1997/627, art 2, Schedule, para 2, as from 1 April 1997; para (h) added by the Banking Act 1987, s 88 as from 1 October 1987, and substituted by SI 2001/3649, art 165(1), (2)(b), as from 1 December 2001.
Sub-s (3): substituted, together with sub-s (3A), for original sub-s (3), by SI 2001/3649, art 165(1), (3), as from 1 December 2001.
Sub-s (3A): substituted as noted to sub-s (3); in table in entry relating to "Paragraph (d)" words in square brackets substituted by the Charities Act 2006, s 75(1), Sch 8, para 56, as from 27 February 2007.
Sub-s (6): words in first (outer) pair of square brackets substituted by the Telecommunications Act 1984, s 109, Sch 4, para 60(1), as from 5 August 1984; words in second (inner) pair of square brackets substituted by the Communications Act 2003, s 406(1), Sch 17, para 47, as from 29 December 2003.
Sub-s (6A): inserted, together with sub-s (6B), by the Housing and Planning Act 1986, s 22(3), (4), as from 7 January 1987 with respect to agreements made after that date.
Sub-s (6B): inserted as noted to sub-s (6A); words in square brackets substituted by the Housing and Regeneration Act 2008 (Consequential Provisions) Order 2010, SI 2010/866, art 5, Sch 2, para 7, as from 1 April 2010.
Sub-s (6C): inserted, together with sub-ss (6D), (6E), by the Financial Services and Markets Act 2000 (Regulated Activities) Order 2001, SI 2001/544, art 90(1), (2), as from 31 October 2004; substituted by the Financial Services and Markets Act 2000 (Regulated Activities) (Amendment) (No 2) Order 2006, SI 2006/2383, art 25(1), (2)(a), as from 6 April 2007.
Sub-s (6D): inserted as noted to sub-s (6C); words in square brackets substituted by SI 2006/2383, art 25(1), (2)(b), as from 6 April 2007, subject to transitional provisions in arts 37–39 of that Order.
Sub-s (6E): inserted as noted to sub-s (6C).
Sub-s (7): repealed by the Consumer Credit Act 2006, s 70, Sch 4, as from 6 April 2007, subject to transitional provisions and savings in s 69(1) of, and Sch 3, paras 1, 15(5)(a), (7) to, the 2006 Act at **[2077]**, **[2079]**.
Sub-s (7A): inserted by the Consumer Credit Act 2006, s 22(2), as from 6 April 2007.
Sub-s (9): words in first pair of square brackets substituted, and words omitted repealed, by SI 2001/3649, art 165(1), (5), as from 1 December 2001; words in second pair of square brackets substituted by the Charities Act 2006, s 75(1), Sch 8, para 56, as from 27 February 2007.
Sub-s (10): added by SI 2001/3649, art 165(1), (6), as from 1 December 2001; words in square brackets substituted by the Companies Act 2006 (Consequential Amendments, Transitional Provisions and Savings) Order 2009, SI 2009/1941, art 2(1), Sch 1, para 28, as from 1 October 2009.
Sub-s (11): added by SI 2001/3649, art 165(1), (6), as from 1 December 2001.
Order: the Consumer Credit (Exempt Agreements) Order 1989, SI 1989/869 at **[3080]**.

[16A   Exemption relating to high net worth debtors and hirers

(1)   The Secretary of State may by order provide that this Act shall not regulate a consumer credit agreement or a consumer hire agreement where—
  (a)   the debtor or hirer is a natural person;
  (b)   the agreement includes a declaration made by him to the effect that he agrees to forgo the protection and remedies that would be available to him under this Act if the agreement were a regulated agreement;
  (c)   a statement of high net worth has been made in relation to him; and
  (d)   that statement is current in relation to the agreement and a copy of it was provided to the creditor or owner before the agreement was made.

(2)   For the purposes of this section a statement of high net worth is a statement to the effect that, in the opinion of the person making it, the natural person in relation to whom it is made—
  (a)   received during the previous financial year income of a specified description totalling an amount of not less than the specified amount; or
  (b)   had throughout that year net assets of a specified description with a total value of not less than the specified value.

(3)   Such a statement—
  (a)   may not be made by the person in relation to whom it is made;
  (b)   must be made by a person of a specified description; and
  (c)   is current in relation to an agreement if it was made during the period of one year ending with the day on which the agreement is made.

(4)   An order under this section may make provision about—
  (a)   how amounts of income and values of net assets are to be determined for the purposes of subsection (2)(a) and (b);
  (b)   the form, content and signing of—
    (i)   statements of high net worth;
    (ii)   declarations for the purposes of subsection (1)(b).

(5)   Where an agreement has two or more debtors or hirers, for the purposes of paragraph (c) of subsection (1) a separate statement of high net worth must have been made in relation to each of them; and paragraph (d) of that subsection shall have effect accordingly.

(6)   In this section—

"previous financial year" means, in relation to a statement of high net worth, the financial year immediately preceding the financial year during which the statement is made;

"specified" means specified in an order under this section.

(7)   In subsection (6) "financial year" means a period of one year ending with 31st March.

(8)   Nothing in this section affects the application of sections 140A to 140C.]

[664A]

NOTES

Commencement: 16 June 2006 (sub-ss (1)–(7)); 6 April 2008 (sub-s (8)).

Inserted by the Consumer Credit Act 2006, s 3, as from dates as noted above and subject to transitional provisions in s 69(1) of, and Sch 3, paras 1, 15(4) to, that Act at **[2077]**, **[2079]**.

Order: the Consumer Credit (Exempt Agreements) Order 2007, SI 2007/1168 at **[3550]**.

[16B   Exemption relating to businesses

(1)   This Act does not regulate—

(a)   a consumer credit agreement by which the creditor provides the debtor with credit exceeding £25,000, or

(b)   a consumer hire agreement that requires the hirer to make payments exceeding £25,000, if the agreement is entered into by the debtor or hirer wholly or predominantly for the purposes of a business carried on, or intended to be carried on, by him.

(2)   If an agreement includes a declaration made by the debtor or hirer to the effect that the agreement is entered into by him wholly or predominantly for the purposes of a business carried on, or intended to be carried on, by him, the agreement shall be presumed to have been entered into by him wholly or predominantly for such purposes.

(3)   But that presumption does not apply if, when the agreement is entered into—

(a)   the creditor or owner, or

(b)   any person who has acted on his behalf in connection with the entering into of the agreement, knows, or has reasonable cause to suspect, that the agreement is not entered into by the debtor or hirer wholly or predominantly for the purposes of a business carried on, or intended to be carried on, by him.

(4)   The Secretary of State may by order make provision about the form, content and signing of declarations for the purposes of subsection (2).

(5)   Where an agreement has two or more creditors or owners, in subsection (3) references to the creditor or owner are references to any one or more of them.

(6)   Nothing in this section affects the application of sections 140A to 140C.]

[664B]

NOTES

Commencement: 16 June 2006 (sub-s (4)); 6 April 2008 (sub-ss (1)–(3), (5), (6)).

Inserted by the Consumer Credit Act 2006, s 4, as from dates as noted above and subject to transitional provisions in s 69(1) of, and Sch 3, paras 1, 15(4) to, that Act at **[2077]**, **[2079]**.

Order: the Consumer Credit (Exempt Agreements) Order 2007, SI 2007/1168 at **[3550]**.

[16C   Exemption relating to investment properties

(1)   This Act does not regulate a consumer credit agreement if, at the time the agreement is entered into, any sums due under it are secured by a land mortgage on land where the condition in subsection (2) is satisfied.

(2)   The condition is that less than 40% of the land is used, or is intended to be used, as or in connection with a dwelling—

(a)   by the debtor or a person connected with the debtor, or

(b)   in the case of credit provided to trustees, by an individual who is the beneficiary of the trust or a person connected with such an individual.

(3)   For the purposes of subsection (2) the area of any land which comprises a building or other structure containing two or more storeys is to be taken to be the aggregate of the floor areas of each of those storeys.

(4)   For the purposes of subsection (2) a person is "connected with" the debtor or an individual who is the beneficiary of a trust if he is—

(a)   that person's spouse or civil partner;

(b)   a person (whether or not of the opposite sex) whose relationship with that person has the characteristics of the relationship between husband and wife; or

(c)   that person's parent, brother, sister, child, grandparent or grandchild.

(5)   Section 126 (enforcement of land mortgages) applies to an agreement which would but for this section be a regulated agreement.

(6)   Nothing in this section affects the application of sections 140A to 140C.]

[664C]

NOTES
Commencement: 31 October 2008.
Inserted by the Legislative Reform (Consumer Credit) Order 2008, SI 2008/2826, art 3(1), as from 31 October 2008.

17   Small agreements

(1)   A small agreement is—
  (a)   a regulated consumer credit agreement for credit not exceeding [£50], other than a hire-purchase or conditional sale agreement; or
  (b)   a regulated consumer hire agreement which does not require the hirer to make payments exceeding [£50],

being an agreement which is either unsecured or secured by a guarantee or indemnity only (whether or not the guarantee or indemnity is itself secured).

(2)   *Section 10(3)(a) applies for the purposes of subsection (1) as it applies for the purposes of section [16B(1)(a)].*

[(2)   For the purposes of paragraph (a) of subsection (1), running-account credit shall be taken not to exceed the amount specified in that paragraph if the credit limit does not exceed that amount.]

(3)   Where—
  (a)   two or more small agreements are made at or about the same time between the same parties, and
  (b)   it appears probable that they would instead have been made as a single agreement but for the desire to avoid the operation of provisions of this Act which would have applied to that single agreement but, apart from this subsection, are not applicable to the small agreements,

this Act applies to the small agreements as if they were regulated agreements other than small agreements.

(4)   If, apart from this subsection, subsection (3) does not apply to any agreements but would apply if, for any party or parties to any of the agreements, there were substituted an associate of that party, or associates of each of those parties, as the case may be, then subsection (3) shall apply to the agreements.

[665]

NOTES
For the text of this section as it had effect on 15 June 2006, prior to amendments made by the Consumer Credit Act 2006 and subsequent amendments, see the Appendix at [A15].
Sub-s (1): sums in square brackets substituted by the Consumer Credit (Increase of Monetary Limits) Order 1983, SI 1983/1878, art 3, Schedule, Pt I, as from 1 January 1984.
Sub-s (2): reference in square brackets substituted by the Consumer Credit Act 2006, s 5(3), as from 6 April 2008; sub-s (2) in italics substituted by subsequent sub-s (2) in square brackets, by the Consumer Credit (EU Directive) Regulations 2010, SI 2010/1010, regs 2, 45, as from 1 February 2011, with effect in relation to certain agreements before that date, as provided for in regs 101, 101A of the 2010 Regulations at **[3942]**, **[3942A]**.

18   Multiple agreements

(1)   This section applies to an agreement (a "multiple agreement") if its terms are such as—
  (a)   to place a part of it within one category of agreement mentioned in this Act, and another part of it within a different category of agreements so mentioned, or within a category of agreement not so mentioned, or
  (b)   to place it, or a part of it, within two or more categories of agreement so mentioned.

(2)   Where a part of an agreement falls within subsection (1), that part shall be treated for the purposes of this Act as a separate agreement.

(3)   Where an agreement falls within subsection (1)(b), it shall be treated as an agreement in each of the categories in question, and this Act shall apply to it accordingly.

(4)   Where under subsection (2) a part of a multiple agreement is to be treated as a separate agreement, the multiple agreement shall (with any necessary modifications) be construed accordingly; and any sum payable under the multiple agreement, if not apportioned by the parties, shall for the purposes of proceedings in any court relating to the multiple agreement be apportioned by the court as may be requisite.

(5)   In the case of an agreement for running-account credit, a term of the agreement allowing the credit limit to be exceeded merely temporarily shall not be treated as a separate agreement or as providing fixed-sum credit in respect of the excess.

(6)   This Act does not apply to a multiple agreement so far as the agreement relates to goods if under the agreement payments are to be made in respect of the goods in the form of rent (other than a rent-charge) issuing out of land.

[666]

19   Linked transactions

(1)   A transaction entered into by the debtor or hirer, or a relative of his, with any other person ("the other party"), except one for the provision of security, is a linked transaction in relation to an actual or prospective regulated agreement (the "principal agreement") of which it does not form part if—

   (a)   the transaction is entered into in compliance with a term of the principal agreement; or

   (b)   the principal agreement is a debtor-creditor-supplier agreement and the transaction is financed, or to be financed, by the principal agreement; or

   (c)   the other party is a person mentioned in subsection (2), and a person so mentioned initiated the transaction by suggesting it to the debtor or hirer, or his relative, who enters into it—

      (i)   to induce the creditor or owner to enter into the principal agreement, or

      (ii)   for another purpose related to the principal agreement, or

      (iii)   where the principal agreement is a restricted-use credit agreement, for a purpose related to a transaction financed, or to be financed, by the principal agreement.

(2)   The persons referred to in subsection (1)(c) are—

   (a)   the creditor or owner, or his associate;

   (b)   a person who, in the negotiation of the transaction, is represented by a credit-broker who is also a negotiator in antecedent negotiations for the principal agreement;

   (c)   a person who, at the time the transaction is initiated, knows that the principal agreement has been made or contemplates that it might be made.

(3)   A linked transaction entered into before the making of the principal agreement has no effect until such time (if any) as that agreement is made.

(4)   Regulations may exclude linked transactions of the prescribed description from the operation of subsection (3).

[667]

NOTES

Regulations: the Consumer Credit (Linked Transactions) (Exemptions) Regulations 1983, SI 1983/1560 at **[3031]**.

20   Total charge for credit

(1)   The Secretary of State shall make regulations containing such provisions as appear to him appropriate for determining the true cost to the debtor of the credit provided or to be provided under an actual or prospective consumer credit agreement (the "total charge for credit"), and regulations so made shall prescribe—

   (a)   what items are to be treated as entering into the total charge for credit, and how their amount is to be ascertained;

   (b)   the method of calculating the rate of the total charge for credit.

(2)   Regulations under subsection (1) may provide for the whole or part of the amount payable by the debtor or his relative under any linked transaction to be included in the total charge for credit, whether or not the creditor is a party to the transaction or derives benefit from it.

[668]

NOTES

Regulations: the Consumer Credit (Total Charge for Credit) Regulations 1980, SI 1980/51 at **[3010]**; the Consumer Credit (Total Charge for Credit) Regulations 2010, SI 2010/1011 at **[3944]**.

PART III
LICENSING OF CREDIT AND HIRE BUSINESSES

Licensing principles

21   Businesses needing a licence

(1)   Subject to this section, a licence is required to carry on a consumer credit business or [a consumer hire business or an ancillary credit business].

(2)   A local authority does not need a licence to carry on a business.

(3)   A body corporate empowered by a public general Act naming it to carry on a business does not need a licence to do so.

NOTES
For the text of this section as it had effect on 15 June 2006, prior to amendments made by the Consumer Credit Act 2006 and subsequent amendments, see the Appendix at [A19].
Sub-s (1): words in square brackets substituted by the Consumer Credit Act 2006, s 33(1), as from 6 April 2008.

22   Standard and group licences

(1)   A licence may be—
  (a)   a standard licence, that is a licence, issued by the [OFT] to a person named in the licence on an application made by him, which, [whilst the licence is in effect], covers such activities as are described in the licence, or
  (b)   a group licence, that is a licence, issued by the [OFT] (whether on the application of any person or of [its] own motion), which, [whilst the licence is in effect], covers such persons and activities as are described in the licence.

[(1A)   The terms of a licence shall specify—
  (a)   whether it has effect indefinitely or only for a limited period; and
  (b)   if it has effect for a limited period, that period.

(1B)   For the purposes of subsection (1A)(b) the period specified shall be such period not exceeding the prescribed period as the OFT thinks fit (subject to subsection (1E)).

(1C)   A standard licence shall have effect indefinitely unless—
  (a)   the application for its issue requests that it have effect for a limited period only; or
  (b)   the OFT otherwise thinks there is good reason why it should have effect for such a period only.

(1D)   A group licence shall have effect for a limited period only unless the OFT thinks there is good reason why it should have effect indefinitely.

(1E)   Where a licence which has effect indefinitely is to be varied under section 30 or 31 for the purpose of limiting the licence's duration, the variation shall provide for the licence to expire—
  (a)   in the case of a variation under section 30, at the end of such period from the time of the variation as is set out in the application for the variation; or
  (b)   in the case of a variation under section 31, at the end of such period from the time of the variation as the OFT thinks fit;
but a period mentioned in paragraph (a) or (b) shall not exceed the prescribed period.]

(2)   A licence is not assignable or, subject to section 37, transmissible on death or in any other way.

(3)   Except in the case of a partnership or an unincorporated body of persons, a standard licence shall not be issued to more than one person.

(4)   A standard licence issued to a partnership or an unincorporated body of persons shall be issued in the name of the partnership or body.

(5)   The [OFT] may issue a group licence only if it appears to [it] that the public interest is better served by doing so than by obliging the persons concerned to apply separately for standard licences.

[(5A)   A group licence to carry on a business may limit the activities it covers in any way the OFT thinks fit.]

(6)   The persons covered by a group licence may be described by general words, whether or not coupled with the exclusion of named persons, or in any other way the [OFT] thinks fit.

(7)   The fact that a person is covered by a group licence in respect of certain activities does not prevent a standard licence being issued to him in respect of those activities or any of them.

(8)   A group licence issued on the application of any person shall be issued to that person, and general notice shall be given of the issue of any group licence (whether on application or not).

[(9), (10)   ...]

NOTES
For the text of this section as it had effect on 15 June 2006, prior to amendments made by the Consumer Credit Act 2006 and subsequent amendments, see the Appendix at [A20].
Sub-s (1): words in second pair of square brackets in para (a) and words in third pair of square brackets in para (b) substituted by the Consumer Credit Act 2006, s 34(1), as from 6 April 2008.
Sub-ss (1A)–(1E): inserted by the Consumer Credit Act 2006, s 34(2), as from 16 June 2006 (in so far as relating to sub-ss (1B), (1E) for certain purposes) and 6 April 2008 (for remaining purposes).
Sub-s (5A): inserted by the Consumer Credit Act 2006, s 33(2), as from 6 April 2008.

PART 1 STATUTES

Sub-ss (9), (10): added by the Financial Services and Markets Act 2000 (Consequential Amendments and Repeals) Order 2001, SI 2001/3649, art 166, as from 1 December 2001; repealed by the Consumer Credit Act 2006, s 70, Sch 4, as from 6 April 2008.

References to the OFT, etc: as to the abolition of the office of the Director General of Fair Trading and the substitution of the original references to the Director (and related expressions), see the note preceding s 1 at **[651]**.

Regulations: the Consumer Credit (Termination of Licences) Regulations 1976, SI 1976/1002; the Consumer Credit (Information Requirements and Duration of Licences and Charges) Regulations 2007, SI 2007/1167 at **[3488]**.

23 Authorisation of specific activities

(1)   Subject to [the terms of the licence], a licence to carry on a business covers all lawful activities done in the course of that business, whether by the licensee or other persons on his behalf.

(2)   ...

(3)   A licence covers the canvassing off trade premises of debtor-creditor-supplier agreements or regulated consumer hire agreements only if, and to the extent that, the licence specifically so provides; and such provision shall not be included in a group licence.

(4)   [The OFT may by general notice specify] other activities which, if engaged in by or on behalf of the person carrying on a business, require to be covered by an express term in his licence.

[671]

NOTES

For the text of this section as it had effect on 15 June 2006, prior to amendments made by the Consumer Credit Act 2006 and subsequent amendments, see the Appendix at [A21].

Sub-s (1): words in square brackets substituted by the Consumer Credit Act 2006, s 33(3), as from 6 April 2008.

Sub-s (2): repealed by the Consumer Credit Act 2006, s 70, Sch 4, as from 6 April 2008.

Sub-s (4): words in square brackets substituted by the Consumer Credit Act 2006, s 33(4), as from 1 December 2007.

24 Control of name of business

A standard licence authorises the licensee to carry on a business under the name or names specified in the licence, but not under any other name.

[672]

[24A Applications for standard licences

(1)   An application for a standard licence shall, in relation to each type of business which is covered by the application, state whether the applicant is applying—
  (a)   for the licence to cover the carrying on of that type of business with no limitation; or
  (b)   for the licence to cover the carrying on of that type of business only so far as it falls within one or more descriptions of business.

(2)   An application within subsection (1)(b) in relation to a type of business shall set out the description or descriptions of business in question.

(3)   References in this Part to a type of business are references to a type of business within subsection (4).

(4)   The types of business within this subsection are—
  (a)   a consumer credit business;
  (b)   a consumer hire business;
  (c)   a business so far as it comprises or relates to credit brokerage;
  (d)   a business so far as it comprises or relates to debt-adjusting;
  (e)   a business so far as it comprises or relates to debt-counselling;
  (f)   a business so far as it comprises or relates to debt-collecting;
  (g)   a business so far as it comprises or relates to debt administration;
  (h)   a business so far as it comprises or relates to the provision of credit information services;
  (i)   a business so far as it comprises or relates to the operation of a credit reference agency.

(5)   The OFT—
  (a)   shall by general notice specify the descriptions of business which can be set out in an application for the purposes of subsection (2) in relation to a type of business;
  (b)   may by general notice provide that applications within subsection (1)(b) cannot be made in relation to one or more of the types of business within subsection (4)(c) to (i).

(6)   The power of the OFT under subsection (5) includes power to make different provision for different cases or classes of case.]

[672A]

NOTES

Commencement: 16 June 2006 (sub-ss (5), (6)); 6 April 2008 (sub-ss (1)–(4)).
Inserted by the Consumer Credit Act 2006, s 28, as from dates as noted above.

25   Licensee to be a fit person

[(1)   If an applicant for a standard licence—

    (a)   makes an application within section 24A(1)(a) in relation to a type of business, and

    (b)   satisfies the OFT that he is a fit person to carry on that type of business with no limitation,

he shall be entitled to be issued with a standard licence covering the carrying on of that type of business with no limitation.

(1AA)   If such an applicant—

    (a)   makes an application within subsection (1)(b) of section 24A in relation to a type of business, and

    (b)   satisfies the OFT that he is a fit person to carry on that type of business so far as it falls within the description or descriptions of business set out in his application in accordance with subsection (2) of that section,

he shall be entitled to be issued with a standard licence covering the carrying on of that type of business so far as it falls within the description or descriptions in question.

(1AB)   If such an applicant makes an application within section 24A(1)(a) or (b) in relation to a type of business but fails to satisfy the OFT as mentioned in subsection (1) or (1AA) (as the case may be), he shall nevertheless be entitled to be issued with a standard licence covering the carrying on of that type of business so far as it falls within one or more descriptions of business if—

    (a)   he satisfies the OFT that he is a fit person to carry on that type of business so far as it falls within the description or descriptions in question;

    (b)   he could have applied for the licence to be limited in that way; and

    (c)   the licence would not cover any activity which was not covered by his application.

(1AC)   In this section "description of business" means, in relation to a type of business, a description of business specified in a general notice under section 24A(5)(a).

(1AD)   An applicant shall not, by virtue of this section, be issued with a licence unless he satisfies the OFT that the name or names under which he would be licensed is or are not misleading or otherwise undesirable.]

[(1A) …

(1B)   If an application for the grant of a standard licence—

    (a)   is made by a person with permission under Part 4 of the Financial Services and Markets Act 2000 to accept deposits, and

    (b)   relates to a listed activity,

the Financial Services Authority may, if it considers that the [OFT] ought to refuse the application, notify him of that fact.

(1C)   In subsection (1B) "listed activity" means an activity listed in [Annex 1 to Directive 2006/48/EC of the European Parliament and of the Council of 14 June 2006 relating to the taking up and pursuit of the business of credit institutions] or in [Annex I to the markets in financial instruments directive (2004/39/EC)] and references to deposits and to their acceptance must be read with—

    (a)   section 22 of the Financial Services and Markets Act 2000;

    (b)   any relevant order under that section; and

    (c)   Schedule 2 to that Act.]

[(2)   In determining whether an applicant for a licence is a fit person for the purposes of this section the OFT shall have regard to any matters appearing to it to be relevant including (amongst other things)—

    (a)   the applicant's skills, knowledge and experience in relation to consumer credit businesses, consumer hire businesses or ancillary credit businesses;

    (b)   such skills, knowledge and experience of other persons who the applicant proposes will participate in any business that would be carried on by him under the licence;

    (c)   practices and procedures that the applicant proposes to implement in connection with any such business;

    (d)   evidence of the kind mentioned in subsection (2A).

(2A)   That evidence is evidence tending to show that the applicant, or any of the applicant's employees, agents or associates (whether past or present) or, where the applicant is a body corporate, any person appearing to the OFT to be a controller of the body corporate or an associate of any such person, has—

    (a)   committed any offence involving fraud or other dishonesty or violence;

    (b)   contravened any provision made by or under—

PART 1
STATUTES

    (i)   this Act;

[(ia)   paragraph 13 of Schedule 1A to the Financial Services and Markets Act 2000;]

    (ii)   Part 16 of the Financial Services and Markets Act 2000 so far as it relates to the consumer credit jurisdiction under that Part;

    (iii)   any other enactment regulating the provision of credit to individuals or other transactions with individuals;

  (c)   contravened any provision in force in an EEA State which corresponds to a provision of the kind mentioned in paragraph (b);

  (d)   practised discrimination on grounds of sex, colour, race or ethnic or national origins in, or in connection with, the carrying on of any business; or

  (e)   engaged in business practices appearing to the OFT to be deceitful or oppressive or otherwise unfair or improper (whether unlawful or not).

(2B)   For the purposes of subsection (2A)(e), the business practices which the OFT may consider to be deceitful or oppressive or otherwise unfair or improper include practices in the carrying on of a consumer credit business that appear to the OFT to involve irresponsible lending.]

(3)   In subsection [(2A)], "associate", in addition to the persons specified in section 184, includes a business associate.

                                                                           [673]

NOTES

For the text of this section as it had effect on 15 June 2006, prior to amendments made by the Consumer Credit Act 2006 and subsequent amendments, see the Appendix at [A23].

Sub-ss (1), (1AA)–(1AD): substituted for original sub-s (1) by the Consumer Credit Act 2006, s 29(1), as from 6 April 2008.

Sub-s (1A): inserted, together with sub-ss (1B), (1C) by the Financial Services and Markets Act 2000 (Consequential Amendments and Repeals) Order 2001, SI 2001/3649, art 167(1), (2), as from 1 December 2001; repealed by the Consumer Credit Act 2006, s 70, Sch 4, as from 6 April 2008.

Sub-s (1B): inserted as noted to sub-s (1A) above.

Sub-s (1C): inserted as noted to sub-s (1A) above; words in first pair of square brackets substituted by the Capital Requirements Regulations 2006, SI 2006/3221, reg 29(2), Sch 4, para 1, as from 1 January 2007; words in second pair of square brackets substituted by the Financial Services and Markets Act 2000 (Markets in Financial Instruments) Regulations 2007, SI 2007/126, reg 3(6), Sch 6, Pt 1, para 5, as from 1 November 2007.

Sub-s (2): substituted, together with sub-ss (2A), (2B), for original sub-s (2) by the Consumer Credit Act 2006, s 29(2), as from 6 April 2008.

Sub-s (2A): substituted as noted to sub-s (2) above; para (b)(ia) inserted by the Financial Services Act 2010, s 24(1), (2), Sch 2, Pt 2, para 36, as from a day to be appointed.

Sub-s (2B): substituted as noted to sub-s (2) above.

Sub-s (3): reference in square brackets substituted by the Consumer Credit Act 2006, s 29(3), as from 6 April 2008.

References to the OFT, etc: as to the abolition of the office of the Director General of Fair Trading and the substitution of the original references to the Director (and related expressions), see the note preceding s 1 at **[651]**.

[25A Guidance on fitness test

(1)   The OFT shall prepare and publish guidance in relation to how it determines, or how it proposes to determine, whether persons are fit persons as mentioned in section 25.

(2)   If the OFT revises the guidance at any time after it has been published, the OFT shall publish it as revised.

(3)   The guidance shall be published in such manner as the OFT thinks fit for the purpose of bringing it to the attention of those likely to be affected by it.

(4)   In preparing or revising the guidance the OFT shall consult such persons as it thinks fit.

(5)   In carrying out its functions under this Part the OFT shall have regard to the guidance as most recently published.]

                                                                           [673A]

NOTES

Commencement: 1 December 2007.

Inserted by the Consumer Credit Act 2006, s 30, as from 1 December 2007, subject to transitional provisions in s 69(1) of, and Sch 3, paras 1, 19 to, that Act at **[2077]**, **[2079]**.

[26 Conduct of business

(1)   Regulations may be made as to—

  (a)   the conduct by a licensee of his business; and

  (b)   the conduct by a consumer credit EEA firm of its business in the United Kingdom.

(2)   The regulations may in particular specify—

  (a)   the books or other records to be kept by any person to whom the regulations apply;

  (b)   the information to be furnished by such a person to those persons with whom—

    (i)   that person does business, or

(ii)   that person seeks to do business,
and the way in which that information is to be furnished.]

[674]

NOTES
   Substituted by the Financial Services and Markets Act 2000 (Consequential Amendments and Repeals) Order 2001, SI 2001/3649, art 168, as from 1 December 2001.
   Regulations: the Consumer Credit (Conduct of Business) (Credit References) Regulations 1977, SI 1977/330; the Consumer Credit (Conduct of Business) (Pawn Records) Regulations 1983, SI 1983/1565.

Issue of licences

27   Determination of applications

   (1)   Unless the [OFT] determines to issue a licence in accordance with an application [it] shall, before determining the application, by notice—
   (a)   inform the applicant, giving [its] reasons, that, as the case may be, [it] is minded to refuse the application, or to grant it in terms different from those applied for, describing them, and
   (b)   invite the applicant to submit to the [OFT] representations in support of his application in accordance with section 34.

   (2)   If the [OFT] grants the application in terms different from those applied for then, whether or not the applicant appeals, the [OFT] shall issue the licence in the terms approved by [it] unless the applicant by notice informs [it] that he does not desire a licence in those terms.

[675]

NOTES
   References to the OFT, etc: as to the abolition of the office of the Director General of Fair Trading and the substitution of the original references to the Director (and related expressions), see the note preceding s 1 at **[651]**.

[27A   Consumer credit EEA firms

   (1)   Where—
   (a)   a consumer credit EEA firm makes an application for a standard licence, and
   (b)   the activities covered by the application are all permitted activities,
the OFT shall refuse the application.

   (2)   Subsection (3) applies where—
   (a)   a consumer credit EEA firm makes an application for a standard licence; and
   (b)   some (but not all) of the activities covered by the application are permitted activities.

   (3)   In order to be entitled to be issued with a standard licence in accordance with section 25(1) to (1AB) in relation to a type of business, the firm need not satisfy the OFT that it is a fit person to carry on that type of business so far as it would involve any of the permitted activities covered by the application.

   (4)   A standard licence held by a consumer credit EEA firm does not at any time authorise the carrying on of an activity which is a permitted activity at that time.

   (5)   In this section "permitted activity" means, in relation to a consumer credit EEA firm, an activity for which the firm has, or could obtain, permission under paragraph 15 of Schedule 3 to the Financial Services and Markets Act 2000.]

[675A]

NOTES
   Commencement: 6 April 2008.
   Inserted by the Consumer Credit Act 2006, s 33(5), as from 6 April 2008.

28   Exclusion from group licence

Where the [OFT] is minded to issue a group licence (whether on the application of any person or not), and in doing so to exclude any person from the group by name, [it] shall, before determining the matter,—
   (a)   give notice of that fact to the person proposed to be excluded, giving [its] reasons, and
   (b)   invite that person to submit to the [OFT] representations against his exclusion in accordance with section 34.

[676]

NOTES
   References to the OFT, etc: as to the abolition of the office of the Director General of Fair Trading and the substitution of the original references to the Director (and related expressions), see the note preceding s 1 at **[651]**.

[Charges for indefinite licences

28A Charges to be paid by licensees etc before end of payment periods

(1)   The licensee under a standard licence which has effect indefinitely shall, before the end of each payment period of his, pay the OFT a charge towards the costs of carrying out its functions under this Act.

(2)   The original applicant for a group licence which has effect indefinitely shall, before the end of each payment period of his, pay the OFT such a charge.

(3)   The amount of the charge payable by a person under subsection (1) or (2) before the end of a payment period shall be determined in accordance with provision which—
   (a)   is made by the OFT by general notice; and
   (b)   is current on such day as may be determined in accordance with provision made by regulations.

(4)   The provision that may be made by the OFT under subsection (3)(a) includes—
   (a)   different provision in relation to persons of different descriptions (including persons whose payment periods end at different times);
   (b)   provision for no charge at all to be payable by persons of specified descriptions.

(5)   The approval of the Secretary of State and the Treasury is required for a general notice under subsection (3)(a).

(6)   For the purposes of this section a person's payment periods are to be determined in accordance with provision made by regulations.]

[676A]

NOTES

Commencement: 16 June 2006 (sub-ss (3)–(6)); 6 April 2008 (sub-ss (1), (2)).
Inserted, together with preceding cross-heading, by the Consumer Credit Act 2006, s 35, as from dates as noted above.
Regulations: the Consumer Credit (Information Requirements and Duration of Licences and Charges) Regulations 2007, SI 2007/1167 at **[3488]**.

[28B   Extension of period to pay charge under s 28A

(1)   A person who is required under section 28A to pay a charge before the end of a period may apply once to the OFT for that period to be extended.

(2)   The application shall be made before such day as may be determined in accordance with provision made by the OFT by general notice.

(3)   If the OFT is satisfied that there is a good reason—
   (a)   why the applicant has not paid that charge prior to his making of the application, and
   (b)   why he cannot pay that charge before the end of that period,

it may, if it thinks fit, by notice to him extend that period by such time as it thinks fit having regard to that reason.

(4)   The power of the OFT under this section to extend a period in relation to a charge—
   (a)   includes the power to extend the period in relation to a part of the charge only;
   (b)   may be exercised even though the period has ended.]

[676B]

NOTES

Commencement: 16 June 2006 (sub-s (2) for the purpose of determining the day before which an application under s 28B(1) may be made); 6 April 2008 (sub-ss (1), (3), (4), sub-s (2) otherwise).
Inserted by the Consumer Credit Act 2006, s 36, as from dates as noted above.

[28C   Failure to pay charge under s 28A

(1)   This section applies if a person (the "defaulter") fails to pay a charge—
   (a)   before the end of a period (the "payment period") as required under section 28A; or
   (b)   where the payment period is extended under section 28B, before the end of the payment period as extended (subject to subsection (2)).

(2)   Where the payment period is extended under section 28B in relation to a part of the charge only, this section applies if the defaulter fails—
   (a)   to pay so much of the charge as is not covered by the extension before the end of the payment period disregarding the extension; or
   (b)   to pay so much of the charge as is covered by the extension before the end of the payment period as extended.

(3)   Subject to subsection (4), if the charge is a charge under section 28A(1), the defaulter's licence terminates.

(4)   If the defaulter has applied to the OFT under section 28B for the payment period to be extended and that application has not been determined—

(a)   his licence shall not terminate before the application has been determined and the OFT has notified him of the determination; and

(b)   if the OFT extends the payment period on that application, this section shall have effect accordingly.

(5)   If the charge is a charge under section 28A(2), the charge shall be recoverable by the OFT.]

[676C]

NOTES
Commencement: 6 April 2008.
Inserted by the Consumer Credit Act 2006, s 37(1), as from 6 April 2008.

Renewal, variation, suspension and revocation of licences

29   Renewal

(1)   If the licensee under a standard licence [of limited duration], or the original applicant for, or any licensee under, a group licence of limited duration, wishes the [OFT] to renew the licence, whether on the same terms (except as to expiry) or on varied terms, he must, during the period specified by the [OFT] by general notice or such longer period as the [OFT] may allow, make an application to the [OFT] for its renewal.

(2)   The [OFT] may of [its] own motion renew any group licence.

(3)   The preceding provisions of this Part apply to the renewal of a licence as they apply to the issue of a licence, except that section 28 does not apply to a person who was already excluded in the licence up for renewal.

[(3A)   In its application to the renewal of standard licences by virtue of subsection (3) of this section, section 27(1) shall have effect as if for paragraph (b) there were substituted—

"(b)   invite the applicant to submit to the OFT in accordance with section 34 representations—

(i)   in support of his application; and

(ii)   about the provision (if any) that should be included under section 34A as part of the determination were the OFT to refuse the application or grant it in terms different from those applied for."]

(4)   Until the determination of an application under subsection (1) and, where an appeal lies from the determination, until the end of the appeal period, the licence shall continue [to have effect], notwithstanding that apart from this subsection it would expire earlier.

(5)   …

(6)   General notice shall be given of the renewal of a group licence.

[677]

NOTES
For the text of this section as it had effect on 15 June 2006, prior to amendments made by the Consumer Credit Act 2006 and subsequent amendments, see the Appendix at [A27].
Sub-s (1): words in first pair of square brackets inserted by the Consumer Credit Act 2006, s 34(3)(a), as from 6 April 2008.
Sub-s (3A): inserted by the Consumer Credit Act 2006, s 32(2), as from 6 April 2008.
Sub-s (4): words in square brackets substituted by the Consumer Credit Act 2006, s 34(3)(b), as from 6 April 2008.
Sub-s (5): repealed by the Consumer Credit Act 2006, ss 32(3), 70, Sch 4, as from 6 April 2008.
References to the OFT, etc: as to the abolition of the office of the Director General of Fair Trading and the substitution of the original references to the Director (and related expressions), see the note preceding s 1 at **[651]**.

30   Variation by request

[(1)   If it thinks fit, the OFT may by notice to the licensee under a standard licence—

(a)   in the case of a licence which covers the carrying on of a type of business only so far as it falls within one or more descriptions of business, vary the licence by—

(i)   removing that limitation;

(ii)   adding a description of business to that limitation; or

(iii)   removing a description of business from that limitation;

(b)   in the case of a licence which covers the carrying on of a type of business with no limitation, vary the licence so that it covers the carrying on of that type of business only so far as it falls within one or more descriptions of business;

(c)   vary the licence so that it no longer covers the carrying on of a type of business at all;

(d)   vary the licence so that a type of business the carrying on of which is not covered at all by the licence is covered either—

       (i)   with no limitation; or

       (ii)   only so far as it falls within one or more descriptions of business; or

  (e)   vary the licence in any other way except for the purpose of varying the descriptions of activities covered by the licence.

(1A)   The OFT may vary a licence under subsection (1) only in accordance with an application made by the licensee.

(1B)   References in this section to a description of business in relation to a type of business—

  (a)   are references to a description of business specified in a general notice under section 24A(5)(a); and

  (b)   in subsection (1)(a) (apart from sub-paragraph (ii)) include references to a description of business that was, but is no longer, so specified.]

(2)   In the case of a group licence issued on the application of any person, the [OFT], on an application made by that person, may if [it] thinks fit by notice to that person vary the terms of the licence in accordance with the application; but the [OFT] shall not vary a group licence under this subsection by excluding a named person, other than the person making the request, unless that named person consents in writing to his exclusion.

(3)   In the case of a group licence from which (whether by name or description) a person is excluded, the [OFT], on an application made by that person, may if [it] thinks fit, by notice to that person, vary the terms of the licence so as to remove the exclusion.

(4)   Unless the [OFT] determines to vary a licence in accordance with an application [it] shall, before determining the application, by notice—

  (a)   inform the applicant, giving [its] reasons, that [it] is minded to refuse the application, and

  (b)   invite the applicant to submit to the [OFT] representations in support of his application in accordance with section 34.

(5)   General notice shall be given that a variation of a group licence has been made under this section.

[678]

NOTES

For the text of this section as it had effect on 15 June 2006, prior to amendments made by the Consumer Credit Act 2006 and subsequent amendments, see the Appendix at [A28].

Sub-ss (1), (1A), (1B): substituted for original sub-s (1) by the Consumer Credit Act 2006, s 31(1), as from 6 April 2008.

References to the OFT, etc: as to the abolition of the office of the Director General of Fair Trading and the substitution of the original references to the Director (and related expressions), see the note preceding s 1 at [651].

31 Compulsory variation

(1)   Where at a time during the currency of a licence the [OFT] is of the opinion that, if the licence had expired at that time [(assuming, in the case of a licence which has effect indefinitely, that it were a licence of limited duration)], [it] would, on an application for its renewal or further renewal on the same terms (except as to expiry), have been minded to grant the application but on different terms, and that therefore [it should take steps mentioned in subsection (1A)], [it] shall proceed as follows.

[(1A)   Those steps are—

  (a)   in the case of a standard licence, steps mentioned in section 30(1)(a)(ii) and (iii), (b), (c) and (e);

  (b)   in the case of a group licence, the varying of terms of the licence.]

[(1B)   The OFT shall also proceed as follows if, having regard to section 22(1B) to (1E), it is of the opinion—

  (a)   that a licence which has effect indefinitely should have its duration limited; or

  (b)   in the case of a licence of limited duration, that the period during which it has effect should be shortened.]

(2)   In the case of a standard licence the [OFT] shall, by notice—

  (a)   inform the licensee of the variations the [OFT] is minded to make in the terms of the licence, stating [its] reasons, and

  [(b)   invite him to submit to the OFT in accordance with section 34 representations—

      (i)   as to the proposed variations; and

      (ii)   about the provision (if any) that should be included under section 34A as part of the determination were the OFT to vary the licence.]

(3)   In the case of a group licence the [OFT] shall—

  (a)   give general notice of the variations [it] is minded to make in the terms of the licence, stating [its] reasons, and

(b) in the notice invite any licensee to submit to [it] representations as to the proposed variations in accordance with section 34.

(4) In the case of a group licence issued on application the [OFT] shall also—
  (a) inform the original applicant of the variations the [OFT] is minded to make in the terms of the licence, stating [its] reasons, and
  (b) invite him to submit to the [OFT] representations as to the proposed variations in accordance with section 34.

(5) If the [OFT] is minded to vary a group licence by excluding any person (other than the original applicant) from the group by name the [OFT] shall, in addition, take the like steps under section 28 as are required in the case mentioned in that section.

(6) General notice shall be given that a variation of any group licence has been made under this section.

(7) A variation under this section shall not take effect before the end of the appeal period.

[(8) Subsection (1) shall have effect in relation to a standard licence as if an application could be made for the renewal or further renewal of the licence on the same terms (except as to expiry) even if such an application could not be made because of provision made in a general notice under section 24A(5).

(9) Accordingly, in applying subsection (1AA) of section 25 in relation to the licence for the purposes of this section, the OFT shall treat references in that subsection to the description or descriptions of business in relation to a type of business as references to the description or descriptions of business included in the licence in relation to that type of business, notwithstanding that provision under section 24A(5).]

[679]

NOTES
  For the text of this section as it had effect on 15 June 2006, prior to amendments made by the Consumer Credit Act 2006 and subsequent amendments, see the Appendix at [A29].
  Sub-s (1): words in second pair of square brackets inserted and words in fourth pair of square brackets substituted by the Consumer Credit Act 2006, ss 31(2), 34(4), as from 6 April 2008.
  Sub-ss (1A), (1B): inserted by the Consumer Credit Act 2006, ss 31(3), 34(5), as from 6 April 2008.
  Sub-s (2): para (b) substituted by the Consumer Credit Act 2006, s 32(4), as from 6 April 2008.
  Sub-ss (8), (9): added by the Consumer Credit Act 2006, s 31(4), as from 6 April 2008.
  References to the OFT, etc: as to the abolition of the office of the Director General of Fair Trading and the substitution of the original references to the Director (and related expressions), see the note preceding s 1 at **[651]**.

---

32 Suspension and revocation

(1) Where at a time during the currency of a licence the [OFT] is of the opinion that if the licence had expired at that time [(assuming, in the case of a licence which has effect indefinitely, that it were a licence of limited duration)] [it] would have been minded not to renew it, and that therefore it should be revoked or suspended, [it] shall proceed as follows.

(2) In the case of a standard licence the [OFT] shall, by notice—
  (a) inform the licensee that, as the case may be, the [OFT] is minded to revoke the licence, or suspend it until a specified date or indefinitely, stating [its] reasons, and
  [(b) invite him to submit to the OFT in accordance with section 34 representations—
    (i) as to the proposed revocation or suspension; and
    (ii) about the provision (if any) that should be included under section 34A as part of the determination were the OFT to revoke or suspend the licence.]

(3) In the case of a group licence the [OFT] shall—
  (a) give general notice that, as the case may be, [it] is minded to revoke the licence, or suspend it until a specified date or indefinitely, stating [its] reasons, and
  (b) in the notice invite any licensee to submit to [it] representations as to the proposed revocation or suspension in accordance with section 34.

(4) In the case of a group licence issued on application the [OFT] shall also—
  (a) inform the original applicant that, as the case may be, the [OFT] is minded to revoke the licence, or suspend it until a specified date or indefinitely, stating [its] reasons, and
  (b) invite him to submit representations as to the proposed revocation or suspension in accordance with section 34.

(5) …

(6) General notice shall be given of the revocation or suspension of a group licence.

(7) A revocation or suspension under this section shall not take effect before the end of the appeal period.

(8) Except for the purposes of section 29, a licensee under a suspended licence shall be treated, in respect of the period of suspension, as if the licence had not been issued; and where the

suspension is not expressed to end on a specified date it may, if the [OFT] thinks fit, be ended by notice given by [it] to the licensee or, in the case of a group licence, by general notice.

[(9) The OFT has no power to revoke or to suspend a standard licence simply because, by virtue of provision made in a general notice under section 24A(5), a person cannot apply for the renewal of such a licence on terms which are the same as the terms of the licence in question.]

[680]

NOTES

For the text of this section as it had effect on 15 June 2006, prior to amendments made by the Consumer Credit Act 2006 and subsequent amendments, see the Appendix at [A30].

Sub-s (1): words in second pair of square brackets inserted by the Consumer Credit Act 2006, s 34(6), as from 6 April 2008.

Sub-s (2): para (b) substituted by the Consumer Credit Act 2006, s 32(5), as from 6 April 2008.

Sub-s (5): repealed by the Consumer Credit Act 2006, ss 32(6), 70, Sch 4, as from 6 April 2008.

Sub-s (9): added by the Consumer Credit Act 2006, s 31(5), as from 6 April 2008.

References to the OFT, etc: as to the abolition of the office of the Director General of Fair Trading and the substitution of the original references to the Director (and related expressions), see the note preceding s 1 at [651].

33 Application to end suspension

(1) On an application made by a licensee the [OFT] may, if [it] thinks fit, by notice to the licensee end the suspension of a licence, whether the suspension was for a fixed or indefinite period.

(2) Unless the [OFT] determines to end the suspension in accordance with the application [it] shall, before determining the application, by notice—

    (a) inform the applicant, giving [its] reasons, that [it] is minded to refuse the application, and

    (b) invite the applicant to submit to the [OFT] representations in support of his application in accordance with section 34.

(3) General notice shall be given that a suspension of a group licence has been ended under this section.

(4) In the case of a group licence issued on application—

    (a) the references in subsection (1) to a licensee include the original applicant;

    (b) the [OFT] shall inform the original applicant that a suspension of a group licence has been ended under this section.

[681]

NOTES

References to the OFT, etc: as to the abolition of the office of the Director General of Fair Trading and the substitution of the original references to the Director (and related expressions), see the note preceding s 1 at [651].

[Further powers of OFT to regulate conduct of licensees etc

33A Power of OFT to impose requirements on licensees

(1) This section applies where the OFT is dissatisfied with any matter in connection with—

    (a) a business being carried on, or which has been carried on, by a licensee or by an associate or a former associate of a licensee;

    (b) a proposal to carry on a business which has been made by a licensee or by an associate or a former associate of a licensee; or

    (c) any conduct not covered by paragraph (a) or (b) of a licensee or of an associate or a former associate of a licensee.

(2) The OFT may by notice to the licensee require him to do or not to do (or to cease doing) anything specified in the notice for purposes connected with—

    (a) addressing the matter with which the OFT is dissatisfied; or

    (b) securing that matters of the same or a similar kind do not arise.

(3) A requirement imposed under this section on a licensee shall only relate to a business which the licensee is carrying on, or is proposing to carry on, under the licence under which he is a licensee.

(4) Such a requirement may be framed by reference to a named person other than the licensee.

(5) For the purposes of subsection (1) it is immaterial whether the matter with which the OFT is dissatisfied arose before or after the licensee became a licensee.

(6) If—

    (a) a person makes an application for a standard licence, and

    (b) while dealing with that application the OFT forms the opinion that, if such a licence were to be issued to that person, it would be minded to impose on him a requirement under this section, the OFT may, before issuing such a licence to that person, do (in whole or in part) anything that it must do under section 33D or 34(1) or (2) in relation to the imposing of the requirement.

(7)   In this section "associate", in addition to the persons specified in section 184, includes a business associate.]

[681A]

NOTES
  Commencement: 6 April 2008.
  Inserted by the Consumer Credit Act 2006, s 38, as from 6 April 2008, subject to transitional provisions in s 69(1) of, and Sch 3, paras 1, 20 to, that Act at **[2077]**, **[2079]**.

[33B   Power of OFT to impose requirements on supervisory bodies

(1)   This section applies where the OFT is dissatisfied with the way in which a responsible person in relation to a group licence—
  (a)   is regulating or otherwise supervising, or has regulated or otherwise supervised, persons who are licensees under that licence; or
  (b)   is proposing to regulate or otherwise to supervise such persons.

(2)   The OFT may by notice to the responsible person require him to do or not to do (or to cease doing) anything specified in the notice for purposes connected with—
  (a)   addressing the matters giving rise to the OFT's dissatisfaction; or
  (b)   securing that matters of the same or a similar kind do not arise.

(3)   A requirement imposed under this section on a responsible person in relation to a group licence shall only relate to practices and procedures for regulating or otherwise supervising licensees under the licence in connection with their carrying on of businesses under the licence.

(4)   For the purposes of subsection (1) it is immaterial whether the matters giving rise to the OFT's dissatisfaction arose before or after the issue of the group licence in question.

(5)   If—
  (a)   a person makes an application for a group licence, and
  (b)   while dealing with that application the OFT forms the opinion that, if such a licence were to be issued to that person, it would be minded to impose on him a requirement under this section,
the OFT may, before issuing such a licence to that person, do (in whole or in part) anything that it must do under section 33D or 34(1) or (2) in relation to the imposing of the requirement.

(6)   For the purposes of this Part a person is a responsible person in relation to a group licence if—
  (a)   he is the original applicant for it; and
  (b)   he has a responsibility (whether by virtue of an enactment, an agreement or otherwise) for regulating or otherwise supervising persons who are licensees under the licence.]

[681B]

NOTES
  Commencement: 6 April 2008.
  Inserted by the Consumer Credit Act 2006, s 39, as from 6 April 2008, subject to transitional provisions in s 69(1) of, and Sch 3, paras 1, 21 to, that Act at **[2077]**, **[2079]**.

[33C   Supplementary provision relating to requirements

(1)   A notice imposing a requirement under section 33A or 33B may include provision about the time at or by which, or the period during which, the requirement is to be complied with.

(2)   A requirement imposed under section 33A or 33B shall not have effect after the licence by reference to which it is imposed has itself ceased to have effect.

(3)   A person shall not be required under section 33A or 33B to compensate, or otherwise to make amends to, another person.

(4)   The OFT may by notice to the person on whom a requirement has been imposed under section 33A or 33B vary or revoke the requirement (including any provision made under subsection (1) of this section in relation to it) with effect from such date as may be specified in the notice.

(5)   The OFT may exercise its power under subsection (4) in relation to a requirement either on its own motion or on the application of a person falling within subsection (6) or (7) in relation to the requirement.

(6)   A person falls within this subsection in relation to a requirement if he is the person on whom the requirement is imposed.

(7)   A person falls within this subsection in relation to a requirement if—
  (a)   the requirement is imposed under section 33A;

    (b)   he is not the person on whom the requirement is imposed;

    (c)   the requirement is framed by reference to him by name; and

    (d)   the effect of the requirement is—

        (i)   to prevent him being an employee of the person on whom the requirement is imposed;

        (ii)   to restrict the activities that he may engage in as an employee of that person; or

        (iii)   otherwise to prevent him from doing something, or to restrict his doing something, in connection with a business being carried on by that person.]

[681C]

NOTES
Commencement: 6 April 2008.
Inserted by the Consumer Credit Act 2006, s 40, as from 6 April 2008.

[33D Procedure in relation to requirements

    (1)   Before making a determination—

    (a)   to impose a requirement on a person under section 33A or 33B,

    (b)   to refuse an application under section 33C(5) in relation to a requirement imposed under either of those sections, or

    (c)   to vary or to revoke a requirement so imposed,

the OFT shall proceed as follows.

    (2)   The OFT shall give a notice to every person to whom subsection (3) applies in relation to the determination—

    (a)   informing him, with reasons, that it is minded to make the determination; and

    (b)   inviting him to submit to it representations as to the determination under section 34.

    (3)   This subsection applies to a person in relation to the determination if he falls within, or as a consequence of the determination would fall within, section 33C(6) or (7) in relation to the requirement in question.

    (4)   This section does not require the OFT to give a notice to a person if the determination in question is in the same terms as a proposal made to the OFT by that person (whether as part of an application under this Part or otherwise).]

[681D]

NOTES
Commencement: 6 April 2008.
Inserted by the Consumer Credit Act 2006, s 41, as from 6 April 2008.

[33E Guidance on requirements

    (1)   The OFT shall prepare and publish guidance in relation to how it exercises, or how it proposes to exercise, its powers under sections 33A to 33C

    (2)   If the OFT revises the guidance at any time after it has been published, the OFT shall publish it as revised.

    (3)   The guidance shall be published in such manner as the OFT thinks fit for the purpose of bringing it to the attention of those likely to be affected by it.

    (4)   In preparing or revising the guidance the OFT shall consult such persons as it thinks fit.

    (5)   In exercising its powers under sections 33A to 33C the OFT shall have regard to the guidance as most recently published.]

[681E]

NOTES
Commencement: 1 December 2007.
Inserted by the Consumer Credit Act 2006, s 42, as from 1 December 2007, subject to transitional provisions in s 69(1) of, and Sch 3, paras 1, 22 to, that Act at **[2077]**, **[2079]**.

Miscellaneous

34 Representations to [OFT]

    (1)   Where this section applies to an invitation by the [OFT] to any person to submit representations, the [OFT] shall invite that person, within 21 days after the notice containing the invitation is given to him or published, or such longer period as the [OFT] may allow,—

    (a)   to submit his representations in writing to the [OFT], and

    (b)   to give notice to the [OFT], if he thinks fit, that he wishes to make representations orally,

and where notice is given under paragraph (b) the [OFT] shall arrange for the oral representations to be heard.

(2)   In reaching [its] determination the [OFT] shall take into account any representations submitted or made under this section.

(3)   The [OFT] shall give notice of [its] determination to the persons who were required to be invited to submit representations about it or, where the invitation to submit representations was required to be given by general notice, shall give general notice of the determination.

[682]

NOTES
References to the OFT, etc: as to the abolition of the office of the Director General of Fair Trading and the substitution of the original references to the Director (and related expressions), see the note preceding s 1 at **[651]**.

[34A   Winding-up of standard licensee's business

(1)   If it thinks fit, the OFT may, for the purpose of enabling the licensee's business, or any part of his business, to be transferred or wound up, include as part of a determination to which subsection (2) applies provision authorising the licensee to carry on for a specified period—
   (a)   specified activities, or
   (b)   activities of specified descriptions,
which, because of that determination, the licensee will no longer be licensed to carry on.

(2)   This subsection applies to the following determinations—
   (a)   a determination to refuse to renew a standard licence in accordance with the terms of the application for its renewal;
   (b)   a determination to vary such a licence under section 31;
   (c)   a determination to suspend or revoke such a licence.

(3)   Such provision—
   (a)   may specify different periods for different activities or activities of different descriptions;
   (b)   may provide for persons other than the licensee to carry on activities under the authorisation;
   (c)   may specify requirements which must be complied with by a person carrying on activities under the authorisation in relation to those activities;
and, if a requirement specified under paragraph (c) is not complied with, the OFT may by notice to a person carrying on activities under the authorisation terminate the authorisation (in whole or in part) from a specified date.

(4)   Without prejudice to the generality of paragraph (c) of subsection (3), a requirement specified under that paragraph may have the effect of—
   (a)   preventing a named person from being an employee of a person carrying on activities under the authorisation, or restricting the activities he may engage in as an employee of such a person;
   (b)   preventing a named person from doing something, or restricting his doing something, in connection with activities being carried on by a person under the authorisation;
   (c)   securing that access to premises is given to officers of the OFT for the purpose of enabling them to inspect documents or to observe the carrying on of activities.

(5)   Activities carried on under an authorisation shall be treated for the purposes of sections 39(1), 40, 148 and 149 as if carried on under a standard licence.]

[682A]

NOTES
Commencement: 6 April 2008.
Inserted by the Consumer Credit Act 2006, s 32(1), as from 6 April 2008.

35   The register

(1)   The [OFT] shall establish and maintain a register, in which [it] shall cause to be kept particulars of—
   (a)   applications not yet determined for the issue, variation or renewal of licences, or for ending the suspension of a licence;
   (b)   licences which are in [effect], or have at any time been suspended or revoked [or terminated by section 28C], with details of any variation of the terms of a licence;
   [(ba)   requirements imposed under section 33A or 33B which are in effect or which have been in effect, with details of any variation of such a requirement;]
   (c)   decisions given by [it] under this Act, and any appeal from those decisions; and
   (d)   such other matters (if any) as [it] thinks fit.

[(1A)   The [OFT] shall also cause to be kept in the register any copy of any notice or other document relating to a consumer credit EEA firm which is given to the [OFT] by the Financial Services Authority for inclusion in the register.]

(2) The [OFT] shall give general notice of the various matters required to be entered in the register, and of any change in them made under subsection (1)(d).

(3) Any person shall be entitled, on payment of the specified fee—
  (a) to inspect the register during ordinary office hours and take copies of any entry, or
  (b) to obtain from the [OFT] a copy, certified by the [OFT] to be correct, of any entry in the register.

(4) The [OFT] may, if [it] thinks fit, determine that the right conferred by subsection (3)(a) shall be exercisable in relation to a copy of the register instead of, or in addition to, the original.

(5) The [OFT] shall give general notice of the place or places where, and times when, the register or a copy of it may be inspected.

[683]

NOTES
  For the text of this section as it had effect on 15 June 2006, prior to amendments made by the Consumer Credit Act 2006 and subsequent amendments, see the Appendix at [A33].
  Sub-s (1): in para (b) word in first pair of square brackets substituted, and words in second pair of square brackets inserted, and para (ba) inserted, by the Consumer Credit Act 2006, ss 34(7), 37(2), 43(1), as from 6 April 2008.
  Sub-s (1A): inserted by the Financial Services and Markets Act 2000 (Consequential Amendments and Repeals) Order 2001, SI 2001/3649, art 169, as from 1 December 2001.
  References to the OFT, etc: as to the abolition of the office of the Director General of Fair Trading and the substitution of the original references to the Director (and related expressions), see the note preceding s 1 at [651].

36 Duty to notify changes

(1) Within 21 working days after a change takes place in any particulars entered in the register in respect of a standard licence or the licensee under section 35(1)(d) (not being a change resulting from action taken by the [OFT]), the licensee shall give the [OFT] notice of the change; and the [OFT] shall cause any necessary amendment to be made in the register.

(2) Within 21 working days after—
  (a) any change takes place in the officers of—
    (i) a body corporate, or an unincorporated body of persons, which is the licensee under a standard licence, or
    (ii) a body corporate which is a controller of a body corporate which is such a licensee, or
  (b) a body corporate which is such a licensee becomes aware that a person has become or ceased to be a controller of the body corporate, or
  (c) any change takes place in the members of a partnership which is such a licensee (including a change on the amalgamation of the partnership with another firm, or a change whereby the number of partners is reduced to one),
the licensee shall give the [OFT] notice of the change.

(3) Within 14 working days after any change takes place in the officers of a body corporate which is a controller of another body corporate which is a licensee under a standard licence, the controller shall give the licensee notice of the change.

(4) Within 14 working days after a person becomes or ceases to be a controller of a body corporate which is a licensee under a standard licence, that person shall give the licensee notice of the fact.

(5) Where a change in a partnership has the result that the business ceases be carried on under the name, or any of the names, specified in a standard licence the licence shall cease to have effect.

(6) ...

[684]

NOTES
  For the text of this section as it had effect on 15 June 2006, prior to amendments made by the Consumer Credit Act 2006 and subsequent amendments, see the Appendix at [A34].
  Sub-s (6): repealed by the Consumer Credit Act 2006, s 70, Sch 4, as from 6 April 2008.
  References to the OFT, etc: as to the abolition of the office of the Director General of Fair Trading and the substitution of the original references to the Director (and related expressions), see the note preceding s 1 at [651].

[36A Further duties to notify changes etc

(1) Subsections (2) to (4) apply where a general notice under section 6(2) comes into effect.

(2) A person who is the licensee under a standard licence or who is the original applicant for a group licence shall, in relation to each relevant application which he has made and which was determined before the general notice came into effect, provide the OFT with any information or document—

(a) which he would have been required to provide with the application had the application been made after the general notice came into effect; and

(b) which the general notice requires to be provided for the purposes of this subsection.

(3) Any such information or document shall be provided within such period as may be specified in the general notice.

(4) Subsection (2) does not require a person to provide any information or document—

(a) which he provided in relation to the application by virtue of section 6;

(b) which he has previously provided in relation to the application by virtue of this section; or

(c) which he would have been required to provide in relation to the application by virtue of subsection (5) but for subsection (6).

(5) A person who is the licensee under a standard licence or who is the original applicant for a group licence shall, in relation to each relevant application which he has made, notify the OFT giving details if, after the application is determined, any information or document which he—

(a) provided in relation to the application by virtue of section 6, or

(b) has so provided by virtue of this section,

is, to any extent, superseded or otherwise affected by a change in circumstances.

(6) Subsection (5) does not require a person to notify the OFT about a matter unless it falls within a description of matters specified by the OFT in a general notice.

(7) A description may be specified for the purposes of subsection (6) only if the OFT is satisfied that the matters which would fall within that description are matters which would be relevant to the question of—

(a) whether, having regard to section 25(2), a person is a fit person to carry on a business under a standard licence; or

(b) whether the public interest is better served by a group licence remaining in effect than by obliging the licensees under it to apply separately for standard licences.

(8) A person who is the licensee under a standard licence or who is the original applicant for a group licence shall, in relation to each relevant application which he has made, notify the OFT about every error or omission—

(a) in or from any information or document which he provided by virtue of section 6, or which he has provided by virtue of this section, in relation to the application; and

(b) of which he becomes aware after the determination of the application.

(9) A notification for the purposes of subsection (5) or (8) shall be given within the period of 28 days beginning with the day on which (as the case may be)—

(a) the information or document is superseded;

(b) the change in circumstances occurs; or

(c) the licensee or the original applicant becomes aware of the error or omission.

(10) This section does not require a person to notify the OFT about—

(a) anything of which he is required to notify it under section 36; or

(b) an error in or omission from any information or document which is a clerical error or omission not affecting the substance of the information or document.

(11) In this section "relevant application" means, in relation to a person who is the licensee under a standard licence or who is the original applicant for a group licence—

(a) the original application for the licence; or

(b) an application for its renewal or for its variation.]

[684A]

NOTES

Commencement: 1 December 2007 (sub-ss (6), (7)); 6 April 2008 (sub-ss (1)–(5), (8)–(11)).

Inserted by the Consumer Credit Act 2006, s 45, as from dates as noted above and subject to transitional provisions in s 69(1) of, and Sch 3, paras 1, 24 to, that Act at **[2077]**, **[2079]**.

[36B Power of OFT to require information generally

(1) The OFT may by notice to a person require him—

(a) to provide such information as may be specified or described in the notice; or

(b) to produce such documents as may be so specified or described.

(2) The notice shall set out the reasons why the OFT requires the information or documents to be provided or produced.

(3) The information or documents shall be provided or produced—

(a)   before the end of such reasonable period as may be specified in the notice; and

(b)   at such place as may be so specified.

(4)   A requirement may be imposed under subsection (1) on a person who is—

(a)   the licensee under a standard licence, or

(b)   the original applicant for a group licence,

only if the provision or production of the information or documents in question is reasonably required for purposes connected with the OFT's functions under this Act.

(5)   A requirement may be imposed under subsection (1) on any other person only if—

(a)   an act or omission mentioned in subsection (6) has occurred or the OFT has reason to suspect that such an act or omission has occurred; and

(b)   the provision or production of the information or documents in question is reasonably required for purposes connected with—

   (i)   the taking by the OFT of steps under this Part as a consequence; or

   (ii)   its consideration of whether to take such steps as a consequence.

(6)   Those acts or omissions are acts or omissions which—

(a)   cast doubt on whether, having regard to section 25(2), a person is a fit person to carry on a business under a standard licence;

(b)   cast doubt on whether the public interest is better served by a group licence remaining in effect, or being issued, than by obliging the persons who are licensees under it, or who would be licensees under it, to apply separately for standard licences;

(c)   give rise, or are likely to give rise, to dissatisfaction for the purposes of section 33A(1) or 33B(1); or

(d)   constitute or give rise to a failure of the kind mentioned in section 39A(1).]

[684B]

NOTES

Commencement: 6 April 2008.

Inserted by the Consumer Credit Act 2006, s 46, as from 6 April 2008.

[36C   Power of OFT to require access to premises

(1)   The OFT may by notice to a licensee under a licence require him to secure that access to the premises specified or described in the notice is given to an officer of an enforcement authority in order for the officer—

(a)   to observe the carrying on of a business under the licence by the licensee; or

(b)   to inspect such documents of the licensee relating to such a business as are—

   (i)   specified or described in the notice; and

   (ii)   situated on the premises.

(2)   The notice shall set out the reasons why the access is required.

(3)   The premises which may be specified or described in the notice—

(a)   include premises which are not premises of the licensee if they are premises from which he carries on activities in connection with the business in question; but

(b)   do not include premises which are used only as a dwelling.

(4)   The licensee shall secure that the required access is given at such times as the OFT reasonably requires.

(5)   The OFT shall give reasonable notice of those times.

(6)   Where an officer is given access to any premises by virtue of this section, the licensee shall also secure that persons on the premises give the officer such assistance or information as he may reasonably require in connection with his observation or inspection of documents (as the case may be).

(7)   The assistance that may be required under subsection (6) includes (amongst other things) the giving to the officer of an explanation of a document which he is inspecting.

(8)   A requirement may be imposed under subsection (1) on a person who is—

(a)   the licensee under a standard licence, or

(b)   the original applicant for a group licence,

only if the observation or inspection in question is reasonably required for purposes connected with the OFT's functions under this Act.

(9)   A requirement may be imposed under subsection (1) on any other person only if—

(a)   an act or omission mentioned in section 36B(6) has occurred or the OFT has reason to suspect that such an act or omission has occurred; and

(b)   the observation or inspection in question is reasonably required for purposes connected with—

   (i)   the taking by the OFT of steps under this Part as a consequence; or

   (ii)   its consideration of whether to take such steps as a consequence.

(10)   In this section—
    (a)   references to a licensee under a licence include, in relation to a group licence issued on application, references to the original applicant; and
    (b)   references to a business being carried on under a licence by a licensee include, in relation to the original applicant for a group licence, activities being carried on by him for the purpose of regulating or otherwise supervising (whether by virtue of an enactment, an agreement or otherwise) licensees under that licence in connection with their carrying on of businesses under that licence.]

[684C]

NOTES
Commencement: 6 April 2008.
Inserted by the Consumer Credit Act 2006, s 47, as from 6 April 2008.

[36D   Entry to premises under warrant

(1)   A justice of the peace may issue a warrant under this section if satisfied on information on oath given on behalf of the OFT that there are reasonable grounds for believing that the following conditions are satisfied.

(2)   Those conditions are—
    (a)   that there is on the premises specified in the warrant information or documents in relation to which a requirement could be imposed under section 36B; and
    (b)   that if such a requirement were to be imposed in relation to the information or documents—
        (i)   it would not be complied with; or
        (ii)   the information or documents would be tampered with.

(3)   A warrant under this section shall authorise an officer of an enforcement authority—
    (a)   to enter the premises specified in the warrant;
    (b)   to search the premises and to seize and detain any information or documents appearing to be information or documents specified in the warrant or information or documents of a description so specified;
    (c)   to take any other steps which may appear to be reasonably necessary for preserving such information or documents or preventing interference with them; and
    (d)   to use such force as may be reasonably necessary.

(4)   An officer entering premises by virtue of this section may take such persons and equipment with him as he thinks necessary.

(5)   In the application of this section to Scotland—
    (a)   the reference to a justice of the peace includes a reference to a sheriff;
    (b)   for "information on oath" there is substituted "evidence on oath".

(6)   In the application of this section to Northern Ireland the reference to a justice of the peace shall be construed as a reference to a lay magistrate.]

[684D]

NOTES
Commencement: 6 April 2008.
Inserted by the Consumer Credit Act 2006, s 48, as from 6 April 2008.

[36E   Failure to comply with information requirement

(1)   If on an application made by the OFT it appears to the court that a person (the "information defaulter") has failed to do something that he was required to do by virtue of section 36B or 36C, the court may make an order under this section.

(2)   An order under this section may require the information defaulter—
    (a)   to do the thing that it appears he failed to do within such period as may be specified in the order;
    (b)   otherwise to take such steps to remedy the consequences of the failure as may be so specified.

(3)   If the information defaulter is a body corporate, a partnership or an unincorporated body of persons which is not a partnership, the order may require any officer who is (wholly or partly) responsible for the failure to meet such costs of the application as are specified in the order.

(4)   In this section—
    "court" means—
        (a)   in England and Wales and Northern Ireland, the High Court or the county court;
        (b)   in Scotland, the Court of Session or the sheriff;
    "officer" means—

(a) in relation to a body corporate, a person holding a position of director, manager or secretary of the body or any similar position;

(b) in relation to a partnership or to an unincorporated body of persons, a member of the partnership or body.

(5) In subsection (4) "director" means, in relation to a body corporate whose affairs are managed by its members, a member of the body.]

[684E]

NOTES
Commencement: 6 April 2008.
Inserted by the Consumer Credit Act 2006, s 49, as from 6 April 2008.

[36F Officers of enforcement authorities other than OFT

(1) A relevant officer may only exercise powers by virtue of section 36C or 36D in pursuance of arrangements made with the OFT by or on behalf of the enforcement authority of which he is an officer.

(2) Anything done or omitted to be done by, or in relation to, a relevant officer in the exercise or purported exercise of a power by virtue of section 36C or 36D shall be treated for all purposes as having been done or omitted to be done by, or in relation to, an officer of the OFT.

(3) Subsection (2) does not apply for the purposes of any criminal proceedings brought against the officer, the enforcement authority of which he is an officer or the OFT in respect of anything done or omitted to be done by the officer.

(4) A relevant officer shall not disclose to a person other than the OFT information obtained by his exercise of a power by virtue of section 36C or 36D unless—
(a) he has the approval of the OFT to do so; or
(b) he is under a duty to make the disclosure.

(5) In this section "relevant officer" means an officer of an enforcement authority other than the OFT.]

[684F]

NOTES
Commencement: 6 April 2008.
Inserted by the Consumer Credit Act 2006, s 50, as from 6 April 2008.

37 Death, bankruptcy etc of licensee

(1) A licence held by one individual terminates if he—
(a) dies, or
(b) is adjudged bankrupt, or
[(c) becomes a person who lacks capacity (within the meaning of the Mental Capacity Act 2005) to carry on the activities covered by the licence.]

[(1A) A licence terminates if the licensee gives the OFT a notice under subsection (1B).

(1B) A notice under this subsection shall—
(a) be in such form as the OFT may by general notice specify;
(b) contain such information as may be so specified;
(c) be accompanied by the licence or give reasons as to why it is not accompanied by the licence; and
(d) be signed by or on behalf of the licensee.]

(2) In relation to a licence held by one individual, or a partnership or other unincorporated body of persons, or a body corporate, regulations may specify other events relating to the licensee on the occurrence of which the licence is to terminate.

(3) Regulations may—
(a) provide for the termination of a licence by subsection (1) [or (1A)], or under subsection (2), to be deferred for a period not exceeding 12 months, and
(b) authorise the business of the licensee to be carried on under the licence by some other person during the period of deferment, subject to such conditions as may be prescribed.

(4) This section does not apply to group licences.

[685]

NOTES
For the text of this section as it had effect on 15 June 2006, prior to amendments made by the Consumer Credit Act 2006 and subsequent amendments, see the Appendix at [A35].
Sub-s (1): para (c) substituted by the Mental Capacity Act 2005, s 67(1), Sch 6, para 21, as from 1 October 2007.
Sub-ss (1A), (1B): inserted by the Consumer Credit Act 2006, s 34(8), as from 16 June 2006 (sub-s (1B)(a), (b) for certain purposes) and 6 April 2008 (for remaining purposes).

Sub-s (3): words in square brackets inserted by the Consumer Credit Act 2006, s 34(9), as from 6 April 2008.
Regulations: the Consumer Credit (Termination of Licences) Regulations 1976, SI 1976/1002.

38 (*Application of s 37 to Northern Ireland and Scotland; outside the scope of this work.*)

39 Offences against Part III

(1)   A person who engages in any activities for which a licence is required when he is not a licensee under a licence covering those activities commits an offence.

(2)   A licensee under a standard licence who carries on business under a name not specified in the licence commits an offence.

(3)   A person who fails to give the [OFT] or a licensee notice under section 36 within the period required commits an offence.

[686]

NOTES

References to the OFT, etc: as to the abolition of the office of the Director General of Fair Trading and the substitution of the original references to the Director (and related expressions), see the note preceding s 1 at **[651]**.

[39A Power of OFT to impose civil penalties

(1)   Where the OFT is satisfied that a person (the "defaulter") has failed or is failing to comply with a requirement imposed on him by virtue of section 33A, 33B or 36A, it may by notice to him (a "penalty notice") impose on him a penalty of such amount as it thinks fit.

(2)   The penalty notice shall—
- (a)   specify the amount of the penalty that is being imposed;
- (b)   set out the OFT's reasons for imposing a penalty and for specifying that amount;
- (c)   specify how the payment of the penalty may be made to the OFT; and
- (d)   specify the period within which the penalty is required to be paid.

(3)   The amount of the penalty shall not exceed £50,000.

(4)   The period specified in the penalty notice for the purposes of subsection (2)(d) shall not end earlier than the end of the period during which an appeal may be brought against the imposition of the penalty under section 41.

(5)   If the defaulter does not pay the penalty to the OFT within the period so specified—
- (a)   the unpaid balance from time to time shall carry interest at the rate for the time being specified in section 17 of the Judgments Act 1838; and
- (b)   the penalty and any interest payable on it shall be recoverable by the OFT.]

[686A]

NOTES

Commencement: 6 April 2008.
Inserted by the Consumer Credit Act 2006, s 52, as from 6 April 2008.

[39B Further provision relating to civil penalties

(1)   Before determining to impose a penalty on a person under section 39A the OFT shall give a notice to that person—
- (a)   informing him that it is minded to impose a penalty on him;
- (b)   stating the proposed amount of the penalty;
- (c)   setting out its reasons for being minded to impose a penalty on him and for proposing that amount;
- (d)   setting out the proposed period for the payment of the penalty; and
- (e)   inviting him to submit representations to it about the matters mentioned in the preceding paragraphs in accordance with section 34.

(2)   In determining whether and how to exercise its powers under section 39A in relation to a person's failure, the OFT shall have regard to (amongst other things)—
- (a)   any penalty or fine that has been imposed on that person by another body in relation to the conduct giving rise to the failure;
- (b)   other steps that the OFT has taken or might take under this Part in relation to that conduct.

(3)   General notice shall be given of the imposition of a penalty under section 39A on a person who is a responsible person in relation to a group licence.

(4)   That notice shall include the matters set out in the notice imposing the penalty in accordance with section 39A(2)(a) and (b).]

[686B]

NOTES
Commencement: 6 April 2008.
Inserted by the Consumer Credit Act 2006, s 53(1), as from 6 April 2008.

[39C Statement of policy in relation to civil penalties

(1) The OFT shall prepare and publish a statement of policy in relation to how it exercises, or how it proposes to exercise, its powers under section 39A.

(2) If the OFT revises the statement of policy at any time after it has been published, the OFT shall publish it as revised.

(3) No statement of policy shall be published without the approval of the Secretary of State.

(4) The statement of policy shall be published in such manner as the OFT thinks fit for the purpose of bringing it to the attention of those likely to be affected by it.

(5) In preparing or revising the statement of policy the OFT shall consult such persons as it thinks fit.

(6) In determining whether and how to exercise its powers under section 39A in relation to a person's failure, the OFT shall have regard to the statement of policy as most recently published at the time the failure occurred.

(7) The OFT shall not impose a penalty on a person under section 39A in relation to a failure occurring before it has published a statement of policy.]

[686C]

NOTES
Commencement: 1 December 2007.
Inserted by the Consumer Credit Act 2006, s 54, as from 1 December 2007, subject to transitional provisions in s 69(1) of, and Sch 3, paras 1, 25 to, that Act at **[2077]**, **[2079]**.

40 Enforcement of agreements made by unlicensed trader

[(1) A regulated agreement is not enforceable against the debtor or hirer by a person acting in the course of a consumer credit business or a consumer hire business (as the case may be) if that person is not licensed to carry on a consumer credit business or a consumer hire business (as the case may be) of a description which covers the enforcement of the agreement.

(1A) Unless the OFT has made an order under subsection (2) which applies to the agreement, a regulated agreement is not enforceable against the debtor or hirer if—
   (a) it was made by the creditor or owner in the course of a consumer credit business or a consumer hire business (as the case may be); and
   (b) at the time the agreement was made he was not licensed to carry on a consumer credit business or a consumer hire business (as the case may be) of a description which covered the making of the agreement.

(2) Where—
   (a) during any period a person (the "trader" has made regulated agreements in the course of a consumer credit business or a consumer hire business (as the case may be), and
   (b) during that period he was not licensed to carry on a consumer credit business or a consumer hire business (as the case may be) of a description which covered the making of those agreements,
he or his successor in title may apply to the OFT for an order that the agreements are to be treated for the purposes of subsection (1A) as if he had been licensed as required.]

(3) Unless the [OFT] determines to make an order under subsection (2) in accordance with the application, [it] shall, before determining the application, by notice—
   (a) inform the applicant, giving his reasons, that, as the case may be, [it] is minded to refuse the application, or to grant it in terms different from those applied for, describing them, and
   (b) invite the applicant to submit to the [OFT] representations in support of [its] application in accordance with section 34.

(4) In determining whether or not to make an order under subsection (2) in respect of any period the [OFT] shall consider, in addition to any other relevant factors—
   (a) how far, if at all, debtors or hirers under [the regulated agreements in question] were prejudiced by the trader's conduct,
   (b) whether or not the [OFT] would have been likely to grant a licence covering [the making of those agreements during] that period on an application by the trader, and
   (c) the degree of culpability for the failure to [be licensed as required].

(5) If the [OFT] thinks fit, [it] may in an order under subsection (2)—

(a)   limit the order to specified agreements, or agreements of a specified description or made at a specified time;

(b)   make the order conditional on the doing of specified acts by the applicant.

[(6)   This section [(apart from subsection (1))] does not apply to a regulated agreement ... made by a consumer credit EEA firm unless at the time it was made that firm was precluded from entering into it as a result of

(a)   a consumer credit prohibition imposed under section 203 of the Financial Services and Markets Act 2000; or

(b)   a restriction imposed on the firm under section 204 of that Act.]

[(7)   Subsection (1) does not apply to the enforcement of a regulated agreement by a consumer credit EEA firm unless that firm is precluded from enforcing it as a result of a prohibition or restriction mentioned in subsection (6)(a) or (b).

(8)   This section (apart from subsection (1)) does not apply to a regulated agreement made by a person if by virtue of section 21(2) or (3) he was not required to be licensed to make the agreement.

(9)   Subsection (1) does not apply to the enforcement of a regulated agreement by a person if by virtue of section 21(2) or (3) he is not required to be licensed to enforce the agreement.]

[687]

NOTES
    For the text of this section as it had effect on 15 June 2006, prior to amendments made by the Consumer Credit Act 2006 and subsequent amendments, see the Appendix at [A37].
    Sub-ss (1), (1A), (2): substituted for original sub-ss (1), (2) by the Consumer Credit Act 2006, s 26(1), as from 6 April 2008.
    Sub-s (4): in paras (a), (c) words in square brackets substituted and in para (b) words in second pair of square brackets inserted by the Consumer Credit Act 2006, s 26(2), as from 6 April 2008.
    Sub-s (6): added by the Financial Services and Markets Act 2000 (Consequential Amendments and Repeals) Order 2001, SI 2001/3649, art 170, as from 1 December 2001; words in square brackets inserted and words omitted repealed by the Consumer Credit Act 2006, ss 26(3), 70, Sch 4, as from 6 April 2008.
    Sub-ss (7)–(9): added by the Consumer Credit Act 2006, s 26(4), as from 6 April 2008.
    References to the OFT, etc: as to the abolition of the office of the Director General of Fair Trading and the substitution of the original references to the Director (and related expressions), see the note preceding s 1 at **[651]**.

[Appeals]

NOTES
    Cross heading inserted, together with s 40A, by the Consumer Credit Act 2006, s 55(1), as from 6 April 2008, subject to transitional provisions in s 69(1) of, and Sch 3, paras 1, 26 to, that Act at **[2077]**, **[2079]**.

[40A   The Consumer Credit Appeals Tribunal

    (1)   There shall be a tribunal known as the Consumer Credit Appeals Tribunal ("the Tribunal").

    (2)   The Tribunal shall have the functions conferred on it by or under this Part.

    (3)   The Lord Chancellor may by rules make such provision as he thinks fit for regulating the conduct and disposal of appeals before the Tribunal.

    (4)   Schedule A1 (which makes provision about the Tribunal and proceedings before it) shall have effect.

    (5)   But that Schedule does not limit the Lord Chancellor's powers under subsection (3).]

[687A]

NOTES
    Commencement: 1 December 2007 (sub-ss (3), (5), sub-s (4) in so far as it relates to Sch A1, paras 9(2), 10, (5)); 6 April 2008 (sub-ss (1), (2), sub-s (4) otherwise).
    Inserted, together with preceding cross-heading, by the Consumer Credit Act 2006, s 55(1), subject to transitional provisions in s 69(1) of, and Sch 3, paras 1, 26 to, that Act at **[2077]**, **[2079]**; repealed by the Transfer of Functions of the Consumer Credit Appeals Tribunal Order 2009, SI 2009/1835, art 4(1), Sch 1, paras 1, 3, as from 1 September 2009 subject to transitional provisions and savings in Sch 4 thereto at **[3908]**.
    Rules: the Consumer Credit Appeals Tribunal Rules 2008, SI 2008/668 at **[3616]**.

41   Appeals to [First-tier Tribunal] under Part III

    (1)   If, in the case of a determination by the [OFT] such as is mentioned in column 1 of the table set out at the end of this section, a person mentioned in relation to that determination in column 2 of the table is aggrieved by the determination he may, within the [specified period, appeal to the [First-tier Tribunal]].

    [(1A)   The means for making an appeal is by sending the Tribunal a notice of appeal.

    (1B)   The notice of appeal shall—
        (a)   be in the specified form;

PART 1
STATUTES

(b)   set out the grounds of appeal in the specified manner; and

(c)   include the specified information and documents.

(1C)   An appeal to the Tribunal is to be by way of a rehearing of the determination appealed against.

(1D)   In this section "specified" means specified by rules under section 40A(3).]

(2)–(5)   ...

Table

Determination	Appellant
Refusal to issue, renew or vary licence in accordance with terms of application.	The applicant.
Exclusion of person from group licence.	The person excluded.
...	...
Compulsory variation, or suspension or revocation, of standard licence.	The licensee.
Compulsory variation, or suspension or revocation, of group licence.	The original applicant or any licensee.
Refusal to end suspension of licence in accordance with terms of application.	The applicant.
[Determination— (a) to impose a requirement under section 33A or 33B; (b) to refuse an application under section 33C(5) in relation to a requirement imposed under either of those sections; or (c) to vary or revoke a requirement so imposed.	A person who falls within section 33C(6) or (7) in relation to the requirement unless the OFT was not required to give a notice to him in relation to the determination by virtue of section 33D(4).]
[Imposition of penalty under section 39A.	The person on whom the penalty is imposed.]
Refusal to make order under section 40(2)[, 148(2) or 149(2)] in accordance with terms of application.	The applicant.
[Imposition of, or refusal to withdraw, consumer credit prohibition under section 203 of the Financial Services and Markets Act 2000.	The consumer credit EEA firm concerned.
Imposition of, or refusal to withdraw, a restriction under section 204 of the Financial Services and Markets Act 2000.	The consumer credit EEA firm concerned.]

[688]

NOTES

For the text of this section as it had effect on 15 June 2006, prior to amendments made by the Consumer Credit Act 2006 and subsequent amendments, see the Appendix at [A38].

References to the OFT, etc: as to the abolition of the office of the Director General of Fair Trading and the substitution of the original references to the Director (and related expressions), see the note preceding s 1 at [651].

Section heading: words in square brackets substituted for original words "Secretary of State" by the Transfer of Functions of the Consumer Credit Appeals Tribunal Order 2009, SI 2009/1835, art 4(1), Sch 1, paras 1, 4(a), as from 1 September 2009, subject to transitional provisions and savings in Sch 4 thereto at [3908].

Sub-s (1): words in second (outer) pair of square brackets substituted by the Consumer Credit Act 2006, s 56(1), as from 6 April 2008 except in relation to determinations made by the OFT before that date, and subject to transitional provisions in s 69(1) of, and Sch 3, paras 1, 27(1)(a) to, that Act at [2077], [2079]; words in third (inner) pair of square brackets substituted for word "Tribunal" by SI 2009/1835, art 4(1), Sch 1, paras 1, 4(b), as from 1 September 2009, subject to transitional provisions and savings in Sch 4 thereto at [3908].

Sub-ss (1A)–(1D): inserted by the Consumer Credit Act 2006, s 56(2), (as from 1 December 2007 (sub-s (1D)) and 6 April 2008 (sub-ss (1A)–(1C)) and subject to transitional provisions in s 69(1) of, and Sch 3, paras 1, 27(1)(a) to, that Act at [2077], [2079]; repealed by SI 2009/1835, art 4(1), Sch 1, paras 1, 4(c), as from 1 September 2009, subject to transitional provisions and savings in Sch 4 thereto at [3908].

Sub-ss (2)–(5): repealed by the Consumer Credit Act 2006, ss 56(3), 70, Sch 4, as from 6 April 2008 (except in relation to determinations made by the OFT before that date) and subject to transitional provisions in s 69(1) of, and Sch 3, paras 1, 27(1)(b) to, that Act at **[2077]**, **[2079]**.

Table: entry omitted repealed, entries relating to ss 33A–33D and s 39A inserted, and in entry relating to s 40(2), words in square brackets inserted by the Consumer Credit Act 2006, ss 33(6), 43(2), 53(2), 70, Sch 4, as from 6 April 2008; entries relating to the Financial Services and Markets Act 2000, ss 203, 204 added by the Financial Services and Markets Act 2000 (Consequential Amendments and Repeals) Order 2001, SI 2001/3649, art 171, as from 1 December 2001.

Regulations: the Consumer Credit Licensing (Appeals) Regulations 1998, SI 1998/1203.

[41ZA Tribunal Procedure Rules: suspension of OFT determinations

In the case of appeals to the First-tier Tribunal under section 41, Tribunal Procedure Rules may make provision for the suspension of determinations of the OFT.]

[688ZA]

NOTES
Commencement: 1 September 2009.
Inserted, together with s 41ZB, by the Transfer of Functions of the Consumer Credit Appeals Tribunal Order 2009, SI 2009/1835, art 4(1), Sch 1, paras 1, 5, as from 1 September 2009, subject to transitional provisions and savings in Sch 4 thereto at **[3908]**.

[41ZB Disposal of appeals

(1) The First-tier Tribunal shall decide an appeal under section 41 by way of a rehearing of the determination appealed against.

(2) In disposing of an appeal under section 41 the First-tier Tribunal may do one or more of the following—
    (a) confirm the determination appealed against;
    (b) quash that determination;
    (c) vary that determination;
    (d) remit the matter to the OFT for reconsideration and determination in accordance with the directions (if any) given to it by the tribunal;
    (e) give the OFT directions for the purpose of giving effect to its decision.

(3) In the case of an appeal under section 41 against a determination to impose a penalty, the First-tier Tribunal—
    (a) has no power by virtue of subsection (2)(c) to increase the penalty;
    (b) may extend the period within which the penalty is to be paid (including in cases where that period has already ended).

(4) Subsection (3) does not affect—
    (a) the tribunal's power to give directions to the OFT under subsection (2)(d); or
    (b) what the OFT can do where a matter is remitted to it under subsection (2)(d).

(5) Where the First-tier Tribunal remits a matter to the OFT, it may direct that the requirements of section 34 of this Act are not to apply, or are only to apply to a specified extent, in relation to the OFT's reconsideration of the matter.

(6) Subject to subsections (7) and (8), where the First-tier Tribunal remits an application to the OFT, section 6(1) and (3) to (9) of this Act shall apply as if the application had not been previously determined by the OFT.

(7) In the case of a general notice which came into effect after the determination appealed against was made but before the application was remitted, the applicant shall provide any information or document which he is required to provide under section 6(6) within—
    (a) the period of 28 days beginning with the day on which the application was remitted; or
    (b) such longer period as the OFT may allow.

(8) In the case of—
    (a) any information or document which was superseded,
    (b) any change in circumstances which occurred, or
    (c) any error or omission of which the applicant became aware,
after the determination appealed against was made but before the application was remitted, any notification that is required to be given by the applicant under section 6(7) shall be given within the period of 28 days beginning with the day on which the application was remitted.]

[688ZB]

NOTES
Commencement: 1 September 2009.
Inserted as noted to s 41ZA at **[688ZA]**.

[41A Appeals from the Consumer Credit Appeals Tribunal

(1) A party to an appeal to the Tribunal may with leave appeal—
* (a) in England and Wales and Northern Ireland, to the Court of Appeal, or*
* (b) in Scotland, to the Court of Session,*

on a point of law arising from a decision of the Tribunal.

(2) For the purposes of subsection (1) leave to appeal may be given by—
* (a) the Tribunal; or*
* (b) the Court of Appeal or the Court of Session.*

(3) An application for leave to appeal may be made to the Court of Appeal or the Court of Session only if the Tribunal has refused such leave.

(4) If on an appeal under this section the court considers that the decision of the Tribunal was wrong in law, it may do one or more of the following—
* (a) quash or vary that decision;*
* (b) substitute for that decision a decision of its own;*
* (c) remit the matter to the Tribunal for rehearing and determination in accordance with the directions (if any) given to it by the court.*

(5) An appeal may be brought from a decision of the Court of Appeal under this section only if leave to do so is given by the Court of Appeal or the House of Lords.

(6) Rules under section 40A(3) may make provision for regulating or prescribing any matters incidental to or consequential on an appeal under this section.

(7) In this section "party" means, in relation to an appeal to the Tribunal, the appellant or the OFT.]

[688A]

___

NOTES

Commencement: 1 December 2007 (sub-s (6)); 6 April 2008 (sub-ss (1)–(5), (7)).

Inserted by the Consumer Credit Act 2006, s 57, as from dates as noted above; repealed by the Transfer of Functions of the Consumer Credit Appeals Tribunal Order 2009, SI 2009/1835, art 4(1), Sch 1, paras 1, 6, as from 1 September 2009, subject to transitional provisions and savings in Sch 4 thereto at **[3908]**.

Rules: the Consumer Credit Appeals Tribunal Rules 2008, SI 2008/668 at **[3616]**.

42 *(Repealed by the Tribunals and Inquiries Act 1992, s 18(2), Sch 4, Pt I, as from 1 October 1992.)*

PART IV
SEEKING BUSINESS

Advertising

43 Advertisements to which Part IV applies

(1) This Part applies to any advertisement, published for the purposes of a business carried on by the advertiser, indicating that he is willing—
* (a) to provide credit, or
* (b) to enter into an agreement for the bailment or (in Scotland) the hiring of goods by him.

(2) An advertisement does not fall within subsection (1) if the advertiser does not carry on—
* (a) a consumer credit business or consumer hire business, or
* (b) a business in the course of which he provides credit to individuals secured on land, or
* (c) a business which comprises or relates to unregulated agreements where—
* (i) the [law applicable to] the agreement is the law of a country outside the United Kingdom, and
* (ii) if the [law applicable to] the agreement were the law of a part of the United Kingdom it would be a regulated agreement.

(3) An advertisement does not fall within subsection (1)(a) if it indicates—
* (a) ...
* (b) that the credit is available only to a body corporate.

[(3A) An advertisement does not fall within subsection (1)(a) in so far as it is a communication of an invitation or inducement to engage in investment activity within the meaning of section 21 of the Financial Services and Markets Act 2000, other than an exempt generic communication.

(3B) An "exempt generic communication" is a communication to which subsection (1) of section 21 of the Financial Services and Markets Act 2000 does not apply, as a result of an order under subsection (5) of that section, because it does not identify a person as providing an investment or as carrying on an activity to which the communication relates.]

(4) An advertisement does not fall within subsection (1)(b) if it indicates that the advertiser is not willing to enter into a consumer hire agreement.

(5)   The Secretary of State may by order provide that this Part shall not apply to other advertisements of a description specified in the order.

[689]

NOTES
    For the text of this section as it had effect on 15 June 2006, prior to amendments made by the Consumer Credit Act 2006 and subsequent amendments, see the Appendix at [A39].
    Sub-s (2): words in square brackets substituted by the Contracts (Applicable Law) Act 1990, s 5, Sch 4, para 2, as from 1 April 1991.
    Sub-s (3): para (a) repealed by the Consumer Credit Act 2006, ss 2(3), 70, Sch 4, as from 6 April 2008.
    Sub-ss (3A), (3B): inserted by the Financial Services and Markets Act 2000 (Regulated Activities) Order 2001, SI 2001/544, art 90(1), (3), as from 31 October 2004.
    Order: the Consumer Credit (Exempt Advertisements) Order 1985, SI 1985/621.

44   Form and content of advertisements

(1)   The Secretary of State shall make regulations as to the form and content of advertisements to which this Part applies, and the regulations shall contain such provisions as appear to him appropriate with a view to ensuring that, having regard to its subject-matter and the amount of detail included in it, an advertisement conveys a fair and reasonably comprehensive indication of the nature of the credit or hire facilities offered by the advertiser and of their true cost to persons using them.

(2)   Regulations under subsection (1) may in particular—
    (a)   require specified information to be included in the prescribed manner in advertisements, and other specified material to be excluded;
    (b)   contain requirements to ensure that specified information is clearly brought to the attention of persons to whom advertisements are directed, and that one part of an advertisement is not given insufficient or excessive prominence compared with another.

[690]

NOTES
    Regulations: the Consumer Credit (Advertisements) Regulations 2004, SI 2004/1484 at **[3400]**; the Consumer Credit (Advertisements) Regulations 2010, SI 2010/1970 at **[3991]**.

45   Prohibition of advertisement where goods etc not sold for cash
If an advertisement to which this Part applies indicates that the advertiser is willing to provide credit under a restricted-use credit agreement relating to goods or services to be supplied by any person, but at the time when the advertisement is published that person is not holding himself out as prepared to sell the goods or provide the services (as the case may be) for cash, the advertiser commits an offence.

[691]–[692]

46   *(Repealed by the Consumer Protection from Unfair Trading Regulations 2008, SI 2008/1277, reg 30(1), (3), Sch 2, Pt 1, paras 17, 18, Sch 4, as from 26 May 2008. For the text of this section as it had effect on 15 June 2006, prior to amendments made by the Consumer Credit Act 2006 and subsequent amendments, see the Appendix at [A42].)*

47   Advertising infringements

(1)   Where an advertiser commits an offence against regulations made under section 44 or against section 45 … , or would be taken to commit such an offence but for the defence provided by section 168, a like offence is committed by—
    (a)   the publisher of the advertisement, and
    (b)   any person who, in the course of a business carried on by him, devised the advertisement, or a part of it relevant to the first-mentioned offence, and
    (c)   where the advertiser did not procure the publication of the advertisement, the person who did procure it.

(2)   In proceedings for an offence under subsection (1)(a) it is a defence for the person charged to prove that—
    (a)   the advertisement was published in the course of a business carried on by him, and
    (b)   he received the advertisement in the course of that business, and did not know and had no reason to suspect that its publication would be an offence under this Part.

[693]

NOTES
    For the text of this section as it had effect on 15 June 2006, prior to amendments made by the Consumer Credit Act 2006 and subsequent amendments, see the Appendix at [A43].
    Sub-s (1): words omitted repealed by the Consumer Protection from Unfair Trading Regulations 2008, SI 2008/1277, reg 30(3), Sch 4, as from 26 May 2008.

Canvassing etc

48 Definition of canvassing off trade premises (regulated agreements)

(1)   An individual (the "canvasser") canvasses a regulated agreement off trade premises if he solicits the entry (as debtor or hirer) of another individual (the "consumer") into the agreement by making oral representations to the consumer, or any other individual, during a visit by the canvasser to any place (not excluded by subsection (2)) where the consumer, or that other individual, as the case may be, is, being a visit—

(a)   carried out for the purpose of making such oral representations to individuals who are at that place, but

(b)   not carried out in response to a request made on a previous occasion.

(2)   A place is excluded from subsection (1) if it is a place where a business is carried on (whether on a permanent or temporary basis) by—

(a)   the creditor or owner, or

(b)   a supplier, or

(c)   the canvasser, or the person whose employee or agent the canvasser is, or

(d)   the consumer.

[694]

49 Prohibition of canvassing debtor-creditor agreements off trade premises

(1)   It is an offence to canvass debtor-creditor agreements off trade premises.

(2)   It is also an offence to solicit the entry of an individual (as debtor) into a debtor-creditor agreement during a visit carried out in response to a request made on a previous occasion, where—

(a)   the request was not in writing signed by or on behalf of the person making it, and

(b)   if no request for the visit had been made, the soliciting would have constituted the canvassing of a debtor-creditor agreement off trade premises.

(3)   Subsections (1) and (2) do not apply to any soliciting for an agreement enabling the debtor to overdraw on a current account of any description kept with the creditor, where—

(a)   the [OFT] has determined that current accounts of that description kept with the creditor are excluded from subsections (1) and (2), and

(b)   the debtor already keeps an account with the creditor (whether a current account or not).

(4)   A determination under subsection (3)(a)—

(a)   may be made subject to such conditions as the [OFT] thinks fit, and

(b)   shall be made only where the [OFT] is of opinion that it is not against the interests of debtors.

(5)   If soliciting is done in breach of a condition imposed under subsection (4)(a), the determination under subsection (3)(a) does not apply to it.

[695]

NOTES

References to the OFT, etc: as to the abolition of the office of the Director General of Fair Trading and the substitution of the original references to the Director (and related expressions), see the note preceding s 1 at **[651]**.

50 Circulars to minors

(1)   A person commits an offence who, with a view to financial gain, sends to a minor any document inviting him to—

(a)   borrow money, or

(b)   obtain goods on credit or hire, or

(c)   obtain services on credit, or

(d)   apply for information or advice on borrowing money or otherwise obtaining credit, or hiring goods.

(2)   In proceedings under subsection (1) in respect of the sending of a document to a minor, it is a defence for the person charged to prove that he did not know, and had no reasonable cause to suspect, that he was a minor.

(3)   Where a document is received by a minor at any school or educational establishment for minors, a person sending it to him at that establishment knowing or suspecting it to be such an establishment shall be taken to have reasonable cause to suspect that he is a minor.

[696]

51 Prohibition of unsolicited credit-tokens

(1)   It is an offence to give a person a credit-token if he has not asked for it.

(2)   To comply with subsection (1) a request must be contained in a document signed by the person making the request, unless the credit-token agreement is a small debtor-creditor-supplier agreement.

(3)   Subsection (1) does not apply to the giving of a credit-token to a person—

   (a)   for use under a credit-token agreement already made, or

   (b)   in renewal or replacement of a credit-token previously accepted by him under a credit-token agreement which continues in force, whether or not varied.

[697]

[51A   Restrictions on provision of credit card cheques

(1)   A person who provides credit card cheques otherwise than in accordance with this section commits an offence.

(2)   Credit card cheques may be provided only to a person who has asked for them.

(3)   They may be provided only on a single occasion in respect of each request that is made.

(4)   The number of cheques provided in respect of a request must not exceed three (or, if less, the number requested).

(5)   Where a single request is made for the provision of credit card cheques in connection with more than one credit-token agreement, subsections (3) and (4) apply as if a separate request had been made in relation to each agreement.

(6)   Where more than one request for the provision of cheques is made in the same document or at the same time—

   (a)   they may be provided in respect of only one of the requests, but

   (b)   if the requests relate to more than one credit-token agreement, in relation to each agreement they may be provided only in respect of one of the requests made in relation to that agreement.

(7)   "Credit card cheque" means a cheque (whether or not drawn on a banker) which, whenever used, will result in the provision of credit under a credit-token agreement.

(8)   Accordingly, "credit card cheque" does not include a cheque to be used only in connection with a current account.]

[697A]

NOTES

Commencement: to be appointed.

Inserted, together with s 51B, by the Financial Services Act 2010, s 15(1), (2), as from a day to be appointed.

[51B   Section 51A: exemption for business

(1)   Section 51A does not apply to credit card cheques provided in connection with a credit-token agreement that is entered into by the debtor wholly or predominantly for the purposes of a business carried on, or intended to be carried on, by the debtor.

(2)   If a credit-token agreement includes a declaration made by the debtor to the effect that the agreement is entered into as mentioned in subsection (1), the agreement is treated for the purposes of that subsection as having been so entered into.

(3)   Subsection (2) does not apply if, when the agreement is entered into—

   (a)   the creditor, or

   (b)   any person who has acted on behalf of the creditor in connection with the entering into of the agreement,

knows, or has reasonable cause to suspect, that the agreement is not entered into as mentioned in subsection (1).

(4)   The Secretary of State may by order make provision about the form, content and signing of declarations for the purposes of subsection (2).

(5)   Where an agreement has two or more creditors, references in subsection (3) to the creditor are to any one or more of them.]

[697B]

NOTES

Commencement: to be appointed.

Inserted as noted to s 51A at **[697A]**.

Miscellaneous

52   Quotations

(1)   Regulations may be made—

   (a)   as to the form and content of any document (a "quotation") by which a person who carries on a consumer credit business or consumer hire business, or a business in the course of which he provides credit to individuals secured on land, gives prospective customers information about the terms on which he is prepared to do business;

(b) requiring a person carrying on such a business to provide quotations to such persons and in such circumstances as are prescribed.

(2) Regulations under subsection (1)(a) may in particular contain provisions relating to quotations such as are set out in relation to advertisements in section 44.

[(3) In this section, "quotation" does not include—
(a) any document which is a communication of an invitation or inducement to engage in investment activity within the meaning of section 21 of the Financial Services and Markets Act 2000; or
(b) any document (other than one falling within paragraph (a)) provided by an authorised person (within the meaning of that Act) in connection with an agreement which would or might be an exempt agreement as a result of section 16(6C).]

[698]

NOTES
Sub-s (3): added by the Financial Services and Markets Act 2000 (Regulated Activities) Order 2001, SI 2001/544, art 90(1), (4), as from 31 October 2004.
Regulations: the Consumer Credit (Quotations) (Revocation) Regulations 1997, SI 1997/211.

53 Duty to display information

Regulations may require a person who carries on a consumer credit business or consumer hire business, or a business in the course of which he provides credit to individuals secured on land [(other than credit provided under an agreement which is an exempt agreement as a result of [section16(6C)(a)])], to display in the prescribed manner, at any premises where the business is carried on to which the public have access, prescribed information about the business.

[699]

NOTES
For the text of this section as it had effect on 15 June 2006, prior to amendments made by the Consumer Credit Act 2006 and subsequent amendments, see the Appendix at [A49].
Words in first (outer) pair of square brackets inserted by the Financial Services and Markets Act 2000 (Regulated Activities) Order 2001, SI 2001/544, art 90(1), (5), as from 31 October 2004; words in second (inner) pair of square brackets substituted by the Financial Services and Markets Act 2000 (Regulated Activities) (Amendment) (No 2) Order 2006, SI 2006/2383, art 25(1), (3), as from 6 April 2007, subject to transitional provisions in arts 37–39 of that Order.

54 Conduct of business regulations

Without prejudice to the generality of section 26, regulations under that section may include provisions further regulating the seeking of business by [a person to whom the regulations apply] who carries on a consumer credit business or a consumer hire business.

[700]

NOTES
Words in square brackets substituted by the Financial Services and Markets Act 2000 (Consequential Amendments and Repeals) Order 2001, SI 2001/3649, art 172, as from 1 December 2001.

PART V
ENTRY INTO CREDIT OR HIRE AGREEMENTS

Preliminary matters

55 Disclosure of information

(1) Regulations may require specified information to be disclosed in the prescribed manner to the debtor or hirer before a regulated agreement is made.

(2) *A regulated agreement is not properly executed unless regulations under subsection (1) were complied with before the making of the agreement.*

[(2) If regulations under subsection (1) are not complied with, the agreement is enforceable against the debtor or hirer on an order of the court only (and for these purposes a retaking of goods or land to which the agreement relates is an enforcement of the agreement).]

[701]

NOTES
For the text of this section as it had effect on 15 June 2006, prior to amendments made by the Consumer Credit Act 2006 and subsequent amendments, see the Appendix at [A51].
Sub-s (2): sub-s (2) in italics substituted by subsequent sub-s (2) in square brackets, by the Consumer Credit (EU Directive) Regulations 2010, SI 2010/1010, regs 2, 16, as from 1 February 2011, with effect in relation to certain agreements before that date, as provided for in regs 101, 101A of the 2010 Regulations at **[3942]**, **[3942A]**.

Regulations: the Consumer Credit (Disclosure of Information) Regulations 2004, SI 2004/1481 at **[3385]**; the Consumer Credit (Disclosure of Information) Regulations 2010, SI 2010/1013 at **[3964]**.

[55A Pre-contractual explanations etc

(1) Before a regulated consumer credit agreement, other than an excluded agreement, is made, the creditor must—

    (a) provide the debtor with an adequate explanation of the matters referred to in subsection (2) in order to place him in a position enabling him to assess whether the agreement is adapted to his needs and his financial situation,

    (b) advise the debtor—

        (i) to consider the information which is required to be disclosed under section 55(1), and

        (ii) where this information is disclosed in person to the debtor, that the debtor is able to take it away,

    (c) provide the debtor with an opportunity to ask questions about the agreement, and

    (d) advise the debtor how to ask the creditor for further information and explanation.

(2) The matters referred to in subsection (1)(a) are—

    (a) the features of the agreement which may make the credit to be provided under the agreement unsuitable for particular types of use,

    (b) how much the debtor will have to pay periodically and, where the amount can be determined, in total under the agreement,

    (c) the features of the agreement which may operate in a manner which would have a significant adverse effect on the debtor in a way which the debtor is unlikely to foresee,

    (d) the principal consequences for the debtor arising from a failure to make payments under the agreement at the times required by the agreement including legal proceedings and, where this is a possibility, repossession of the debtor's home, and

    (e) the effect of the exercise of any right to withdraw from the agreement and how and when this right may be exercised.

(3) The advice and explanation may be given orally or in writing except as provided in subsection (4).

(4) Where the explanation of the matters specified in paragraphs (a), (b) or (e) of subsection (2) is given orally or in person to a debtor, the explanation of the matters specified in paragraphs (c) and (d) of that subsection, and the advice required to be given by subsection (1)(b), must be given orally to him.

(5) Subsections (1) to (4) do not apply to a creditor if a credit intermediary (see section 160A) has complied with those subsections in respect of the agreement.

(6) For the purposes of this section an agreement is an excluded agreement if it is—

    (a) an agreement under which the creditor provides the debtor with credit which exceeds £60, 260, or

    (b) an agreement secured on land.

(7) Where the regulated consumer credit agreement is an agreement under which a person takes an article in pawn—

    (a) the obligation in subsection (1)(a) only relates to the matters listed in paragraphs (d) and (e) of subsection (2), and

    (b) the obligations in subsection (1)(b) and (d) do not apply.]

[701A]

NOTES

Commencement: 1 February 2011.

Inserted by the Consumer Credit (EU Directive) Regulations 2010, SI 2010/1010, regs 2, 3 (as amended by the Consumer Credit (Amendment) Regulations 2010, SI 2010/1969, regs 4, 6), as from 1 February 2011, with effect in relation to certain agreements before that date, as provided for in regs 101, 101A of the 2010 Regulations at **[3942]**, **[3942A]**.

[55B Assessment of creditworthiness

(1) Before making a regulated consumer credit agreement, other than an excluded agreement, the creditor must undertake an assessment of the creditworthiness of the debtor.

(2) Before significantly increasing—

    (a) the amount of credit to be provided under a regulated consumer credit agreement, other than an excluded agreement, or

    (b) a credit limit for running-account credit under a regulated consumer credit agreement, other than an excluded agreement,

the creditor must undertake an assessment of the debtor's creditworthiness.

(3) A creditworthiness assessment must be based on sufficient information obtained from—

    (a)   the debtor, where appropriate, and
    (b)   a credit reference agency, where necessary.

  (4)   For the purposes of this section an agreement is an excluded agreement if it is—
    (a)   an agreement secured on land, or
    (b)   an agreement under which a person takes an article in pawn.]

[701B]

NOTES
Commencement: 1 February 2011.
Inserted by the Consumer Credit (EU Directive) Regulations 2010, SI 2010/1010, regs 2, 5, as from 1 February 2011, with effect in relation to certain agreements before that date, as provided for in regs 101, 101A of the 2010 Regulations at **[3942]**, **[3942A]**.

[55C   Copy of draft consumer credit agreement

  (1)   Before a regulated consumer credit agreement, other than an excluded agreement, is made, the creditor must, if requested, give to the debtor without delay a copy of the prospective agreement (or such of its terms as have at that time been reduced to writing).

  (2)   Subsection (1) does not apply if at the time the request is made, the creditor is unwilling to proceed with the agreement.

  (3)   A breach of the duty imposed by subsection (1) is actionable as a breach of statutory duty.

  (4)   For the purposes of this section an agreement is an excluded agreement if it is—
    (a)   an agreement secured on land,
    (b)   an agreement under which a person takes an article in pawn,
    (c)   an agreement under which the creditor provides the debtor with credit which exceeds £60,260, or
    (d)   an agreement entered into by the debtor wholly or predominantly for the purposes of a business carried on, or intended to be carried on, by him.

  (5)   Subsections (2) to (5) of section 16B (declaration by the debtor as to the purposes of the agreement) apply for the purposes of subsection (4)(d).]

[701C]

NOTES
Commencement: 1 February 2011.
Inserted by the Consumer Credit (EU Directive) Regulations 2010, SI 2010/1010, regs 2, 6, as from 1 February 2011, with effect in relation to certain agreements before that date, as provided for in regs 101, 101A of the 2010 Regulations at **[3942]**, **[3942A]**.

56 Antecedent negotiations

  (1)   In this Act "antecedent negotiations" means any negotiations with the debtor or hirer—
    (a)   conducted by the creditor or owner in relation to the making of any regulated agreement, or
    (b)   conducted by a credit-broker in relation to goods sold or proposed to be sold by the credit-broker to the creditor before forming the subject-matter of a debtor-creditor-supplier agreement within section 12(a), or
    (c)   conducted by the supplier in relation to a transaction financed or proposed to be financed by a debtor-creditor-supplier agreement within section 12(b) or (c),
and "negotiator" means the person by whom negotiations are so conducted with the debtor or hirer.

  (2)   Negotiations with the debtor in a case falling within subsection (1)(b) or (c) shall be deemed to be conducted by the negotiator in the capacity of agent of the creditor as well as in his actual capacity.

  (3)   An agreement is void if, and to the extent that, it purports in relation to an actual or prospective regulated agreement—
    (a)   to provide that a person acting as, or on behalf of, a negotiator is to be treated as the agent of the debtor or hirer, or
    (b)   to relieve a person from liability for acts or omissions of any person acting as, or on behalf of, a negotiator.

  (4)   For the purposes of this Act, antecedent negotiations shall be taken to begin when the negotiator and the debtor or hirer first enter into communication (including communication by advertisement), and to include any representations made by the negotiator to the debtor or hirer and any other dealings between them.

[702]

57 Withdrawal from prospective agreement

(1) The withdrawal of a party from a prospective regulated agreement shall operate to apply this Part to the agreement, any linked transaction and any other thing done in anticipation of the making of the agreement as it would apply if the agreement were made and then cancelled under section 69.

(2) The giving to a party of a written or oral notice which, however expressed, indicates the intention of the other party to withdraw from a prospective regulated agreement operates as a withdrawal from it.

(3) Each of the following shall be deemed to be the agent of the creditor or owner for the purpose of receiving a notice under subsection (2)—
    (a)   a credit-broker or supplier who is the negotiator in antecedent negotiations, and
    (b)   any person who, in the course of a business carried on by him, acts on behalf of the debtor or hirer in any negotiations for the agreement.

(4) Where the agreement, if made, would not be a cancellable agreement, subsection (1) shall nevertheless apply as if the contrary were the case.

[703]

NOTES
Regulations: the Consumer Credit (Repayment of Credit on Cancellation) Regulations 1983, SI 1983/1559.

58 Opportunity for withdrawal from prospective land mortgage

(1) Before sending to the debtor or hirer, for his signature, an unexecuted agreement in a case where the prospective regulated agreement is to be secured on land (the "mortgaged land"), the creditor or owner shall give the debtor or hirer a copy of the unexecuted agreement which contains a notice in the prescribed form indicating the right of the debtor or hirer to withdraw from the prospective agreement, and how and when the right is exercisable, together with a copy of any other document referred to in the unexecuted agreement.

(2) Subsection (1) does not apply to—
    (a)   a restricted-use credit agreement to finance the purchase of the mortgaged land, or
    (b)   an agreement for a bridging loan in connection with the purchase of the mortgaged land or other land.

[704]

NOTES
Regulations: the Consumer Credit (Cancellation Notices and Copies of Documents) Regulations 1983, SI 1983/1557.

59 Agreement to enter future agreement void

(1) An agreement is void if, and to the extent that, it purports to bind a person to enter as debtor or hirer into a prospective regulated agreement.

(2) Regulations may exclude from the operation of subsection (1) agreements such as are described in the regulations.

[705]

NOTES
Regulations: the Consumer Credit (Agreements to Enter Prospective Agreements) (Exemptions) Regulations 1983, SI 1983/1552.

Making the agreement

60 Form and content of agreements

(1) The Secretary of State shall make regulations as to the form and content of documents embodying regulated agreements, and the regulations shall contain such provisions as appear to him appropriate with a view to ensuring that the debtor or hirer is made aware of—
    (a)   the rights and duties conferred or imposed on him by the agreement,
    (b)   the amount and rate of the total charge for credit (in the case of a consumer credit agreement),
    (c)   the protection and remedies available to him under this Act, and
    (d)   any other matters which, in the opinion of the Secretary of State, it is desirable for him to know about in connection with the agreement.

(2) Regulations under subsection (1) may in particular—
    (a)   require specified information to be included in the prescribed manner in documents, and other specified material to be excluded;
    (b)   contain requirements to ensure that specified information is clearly brought to the

attention of the debtor or hirer, and that one part of a document is not given insufficient or excessive prominence compared with another.

(3) If, on an application made to the [OFT] by a person carrying on a consumer credit business or a consumer hire business, it appears to the [OFT] impracticable for the applicant to comply with any requirement of regulations under subsection (1) in a particular case, [it] may, by notice to the applicant, direct that the requirement be waived or varied in relation to such agreements, and subject to such conditions (if any), as [it] may specify, and this Act and the regulations shall have effect accordingly.

(4) The [OFT] shall give a notice under subsection (3) only if [it] is satisfied that to do so would not prejudice the interests of debtors or hirers.

[(5) An application may be made under subsection (3) only if it relates to—
    (a)   a consumer credit agreement secured on land,
    (b)   a consumer credit agreement under which a person takes an article in pawn,
    (c)   a consumer credit agreement under which the creditor provides the debtor with credit which exceeds £60,260,
    (d)   a consumer credit agreement entered into by the debtor wholly or predominantly for the purposes of a business carried on, or intended to be carried on, by him, or
    (e)   a consumer hire agreement.

(6) Subsections (2) to (5) of section 16B (declaration by the debtor as to the purposes of the agreement) apply for the purposes of subsection (5)(d).]

[706]

NOTES
    For the text of this section as it had effect on 15 June 2006, prior to amendments made by the Consumer Credit Act 2006 and subsequent amendments, see the Appendix at [A56].
    Sub-ss (5), (6): added by the Consumer Credit (EU Directive) Regulations 2010, SI 2010/1010, regs 2, 7, as from 1 February 2011, with effect in relation to certain agreements before that date, as provided for in regs 101, 101A of the 2010 Regulations at **[3942]**, **[3942A]**.
    References to the OFT, etc: as to the abolition of the office of the Director General of Fair Trading and the substitution of the original references to the Director (and related expressions), see the note preceding s 1 at **[651]**.
    Regulations: the Consumer Credit (Agreements) Regulations 1983, SI 1983/1553; the Consumer Credit (Agreements) Regulations 2010, SI 2010/1014 at **[3979]**.

61 Signing of agreement

(1) A regulated agreement is not properly executed unless—
    (a)   a document in the prescribed form itself containing all the prescribed terms and conforming to regulations under section 60(1) is signed in the prescribed manner both by the debtor or hirer and by or on behalf of the creditor or owner, and
    (b)   the document embodies all the terms of the agreement, other than implied terms, and
    (c)   the document is, when presented or sent to the debtor or hirer for signature, in such a state that all its terms are readily legible.

(2) In addition, where the agreement is one to which section 58(1) applies, it is not properly executed unless—
    (a)   the requirements of section 58(1) were complied with, and
    (b)   the unexecuted agreement was sent, for his signature, to the debtor or hirer [by an appropriate method] not less than seven days after a copy of it was given to him under section 58(1), and
    (c)   during the consideration period, the creditor or owner refrained from approaching the debtor or hirer (whether in person, by telephone or letter, or in any other way) except in response to a specific request made by the debtor or hirer after the beginning of the consideration period, and
    (d)   no notice of withdrawal by the debtor or hirer was received by the creditor or owner before the sending of the unexecuted agreement.

(3) In subsection (2)(c), "the consideration period" means the period beginning with the giving of the copy under section 58(1) and ending—
    (a)   at the expiry of seven days after the day on which the unexecuted agreement is sent, for his signature, to the debtor or hirer, or
    (b)   on its return by the debtor or hirer after signature by him,
whichever first occurs.

(4) Where the debtor or hirer is a partnership or an unincorporated body of persons, subsection (1)(a) shall apply with the substitution for "by the debtor or hirer" of "by or on behalf of the debtor or hirer".

[707]

PART I
STATUTES

NOTES

Sub-s (2): in para (b) words in square brackets substituted by the Consumer Credit Act 1974 (Electronic Communications) Order 2004, SI 2004/3236, art 2(1), (2), as from 31 December 2004.

Regulations: the Consumer Credit (Agreements) Regulations 1983, SI 1983/1553; the Consumer Credit (Agreements) Regulations 2010, SI 2010/1014 at **[3979]**.

[61A   Duty to supply copy of executed consumer credit agreement

(1)   Where a regulated consumer credit agreement, other than an excluded agreement, has been made, the creditor must give a copy of the executed agreement, and any other document referred to in it, to the debtor.

(2)   Subsection (1) does not apply if—

(a)   a copy of the unexecuted agreement (and of any other document referred to in it) has already been given to the debtor, and

(b)   the unexecuted agreement is in identical terms to the executed agreement.

(3)   In a case referred to in subsection (2), the creditor must inform the debtor in writing—

(a)   that the agreement has been executed,

(b)   that the executed agreement is in identical terms to the unexecuted agreement a copy of which has already been given to the debtor, and

(c)   that the debtor has the right to receive a copy of the executed agreement if the debtor makes a request for it at any time before the end of the period referred to in section 66A(2).

(4)   Where a request is made under subsection (3)(c) the creditor must give a copy of the executed agreement to the debtor without delay.

(5)   If the requirements of this section are not observed, the agreement is not properly executed.

(6)   For the purposes of this section, an agreement is an excluded agreement if it is—

(a)   a cancellable agreement, or

(b)   an agreement—

(i)   secured on land,

(ii)   under which the creditor provides the debtor with credit which exceeds £60,260, or

(iii)   entered into by the debtor wholly or predominantly for the purposes of a business carried on, or intended to be carried on, by him,

unless the creditor or a credit intermediary has complied with or purported to comply with regulation 3(2) of the Consumer Credit (Disclosure of Information) Regulations 2010.

(7)   Subsections (2) to (5) of section 16B (declaration by the debtor as to the purposes of the agreement) apply for the purposes of subsection (6)(b)(iii).]

[707A]

NOTES

Commencement: 1 February 2011.

Inserted by the Consumer Credit (EU Directive) Regulations 2010, SI 2010/1010, regs 2, 8, as from 1 February 2011, with effect in relation to certain agreements before that date, as provided for in regs 101, 101A of the 2010 Regulations at **[3942]**, **[3942A]**.

[61B   Duty to supply copy of overdraft agreement

(1)   Where an authorised business overdraft agreement or an authorised non-business overdraft agreement has been made, a document containing the terms of the agreement must be given to the debtor.

(2)   The creditor must provide the document referred to in subsection (1) to the debtor before or at the time the agreement is made unless—

(a)   the creditor has provided the debtor with the information referred to in regulation 10(3) of the Consumer Credit (Disclosure of Information) Regulations 2010, in which case it may be provided after the agreement is made,

(b)   the creditor has provided the debtor with the information referred to in regulation 10(3)(c), (e), (f), (h) and (k) of those Regulations, in which case it must be provided immediately after the agreement is made, or

(c)   the agreement is an agreement of a description referred to in regulation 10(4)(b) of those Regulations, in which case it must be provided immediately after the agreement is made.

(3)   If the requirements of this section are not observed, the agreement is enforceable against the debtor on an order of the court only (and for these purposes a retaking of goods or land to which the agreement relates is an enforcement of the agreement).]

[707B]

NOTES
   Commencement: 1 February 2011.
   Inserted by the Consumer Credit (EU Directive) Regulations 2010, SI 2010/1010, regs 2, 9 (as amended by the
Consumer Credit (Amendment) Regulations 2010, SI 2010/1969, regs 4, 7), as from 1 February 2011, with effect
in relation to certain agreements before that date, as provided for in regs 101, 101A of the 2010 Regulations at
[3942], **[3942A]**.

62   Duty to supply copy of unexecuted agreement[: excluded agreements]

   (1)   If [in the case of a regulated agreement which is an excluded agreement] the unexecuted
agreement is presented personally to the debtor or hirer for his signature, but on the occasion when
he signs it the document does not become an executed agreement, a copy of it, and of any other
document referred to in it, must be there and then delivered to him.

   (2)   If the unexecuted agreement is sent to the debtor or hirer for his signature, a copy of it, and
of any other document referred to in it, must be sent to him at the same time.

   (3)   A regulated agreement [which is an excluded agreement] is not properly executed if the
requirements of this section are not observed.

   [(4)   In this section, "excluded agreement" has the same meaning as in section 61A.]

                                                                                                    [708]

NOTES
   **For the text of this section as it had effect on 15 June 2006, prior to amendments made by the Consumer
Credit Act 2006 and subsequent amendments, see the Appendix at [A58].**
   Section heading: words in square brackets inserted by the Consumer Credit (EU Directive) Regulations 2010,
SI 2010/1010, regs 2, 10(a), as from 1 February 2011, with effect in relation to certain agreements before that
date, as provided for in regs 101, 101A of the 2010 Regulations at **[3942]**, **[3942A]**.
   Sub-ss (1), (3): words in square brackets inserted by SI 2010/1010, regs 2, 10(b), (c), as from 1 February 2011,
with effect in relation to certain agreements before that date, as provided for in regs 101, 101A of the 2010
Regulations at **[3942]**, **[3942A]**.
   Sub-s (4): added by SI 2010/1010, regs 2, 10(d), as from 1 February 2011, with effect in relation to certain
agreements before that date, as provided for in regs 101, 101A of the 2010 Regulations at **[3942]**, **[3942A]**.

63   Duty to supply copy of executed agreement[: excluded agreements]

   (1)   If [in the case of a regulated agreement which is an excluded agreement] the unexecuted
agreement is presented personally to the debtor or hirer for his signature, and on the occasion when
he signs it the document becomes an executed agreement, a copy of the executed agreement, and of
any other document referred to in it, must be there and then delivered to him.

   (2)   A copy of the executed agreement, and of any other document referred to in it, must be
given to the debtor or hirer within the seven days following the making of the agreement unless—
       (a)   subsection (1) applies, or
       (b)   the unexecuted agreement was sent to the debtor or hirer for his signature and, on the
             occasion of his signing it, the document became an executed agreement.

   (3)   In the case of a cancellable agreement, a copy under subsection (2) must be sent [by an
appropriate method].

   (4)   In the case of a credit-token agreement, a copy under subsection (2) need not be given
within the seven days following the making of the agreement if it is given before or at the time when
the credit-token is given to the debtor.

   (5)   A regulated agreement [which is an excluded agreement] is not properly executed if the
requirements of this section are not observed.

   [(6)   In this section, "excluded agreement" has the same meaning as in section 61A.]

                                                                                                    [709]

NOTES
   **For the text of this section as it had effect on 15 June 2006, prior to amendments made by the Consumer
Credit Act 2006 and subsequent amendments, see the Appendix at [A59].**
   Section heading: words in square brackets inserted by the Consumer Credit (EU Directive) Regulations 2010,
SI 2010/1010, regs 2, 11(a), as from 1 February 2011, with effect in relation to certain agreements before that
date, as provided for in regs 101, 101A of the 2010 Regulations at **[3942]**, **[3942A]**.
   Sub-s (1): words in square brackets inserted by SI 2010/1010, regs 2, 11(b), as from 1 February 2011, with
effect in relation to certain agreements before that date, as provided for in regs 101, 101A of the 2010
Regulations at **[3942]**, **[3942A]**.
   Sub-s (3): words in square brackets substituted by the Consumer Credit Act 1974 (Electronic
Communications) Order 2004, SI 2004/3236, art 2(1), (3), as from 31 December 2004.
   Sub-s (5): words in square brackets inserted by SI 2010/1010, regs 2, 11(c), as from 1 February 2011, with
effect in relation to certain agreements before that date, as provided for in regs 101, 101A of the 2010
Regulations at **[3942]**, **[3942A]**.

Sub-s (6): added by SI 2010/1010, regs 2, 11(d), as from 1 February 2011, with effect in relation to certain agreements before that date, as provided for in regs 101, 101A of the 2010 Regulations at **[3942]**, **[3942A]**.

64 Duty to give notice of cancellation rights

(1)   In the case of a cancellable agreement, a notice in the prescribed form indicating the right of the debtor or hirer to cancel the agreement, how and when that right is exercisable, and the name and address of a person to whom notice of cancellation may be given,—

(a)   must be included in every copy given to the debtor or hirer under section 62 or 63, and

(b)   except where section 63(2) applied, must also be sent [by an appropriate method] to the debtor or hirer within the seven days following the making of the agreement.

(2)   In the case of a credit-token agreement, a notice under subsection (1)(b) need not be sent [by an appropriate method] within the seven days following the making of the agreement if either—

(a)   it is sent [by an appropriate method] to the debtor or hirer before the credit-token is given to him, or

(b)   it is sent [by an appropriate method] to him together with the credit-token.

(3)   Regulations may provide that except where section 63(2) applied a notice sent under subsection (1)(b) shall be accompanied by a further copy of the executed agreement, and of any other document referred to in it.

(4)   Regulations may provide that subsection (1)(b) is not to apply in the case of agreements such as are described in the regulations, being agreements made by a particular person, if—

(a)   on an application by that person to the [OFT], the [OFT] has determined that, having regard to—

(i)   the manner in which antecedent negotiations for agreements with the applicant of that description are conducted, and

(ii)   the information provided to debtors or hirers before such agreements are made, the requirement imposed by subsection (1)(b) can be dispensed with without prejudicing the interests of debtors or hirers; and

(b)   any conditions imposed by the [OFT] in making the determination are complied with.

(5)   A cancellable agreement is not properly executed if the requirements of this section are not observed.

[710]

NOTES
Sub-ss (1), (2): words in square brackets substituted by the Consumer Credit Act 1974 (Electronic Communications) Order 2004, SI 2004/3236, art 2(1), (4), as from 31 December 2004.

References to the OFT, etc: as to the abolition of the office of the Director General of Fair Trading and the substitution of the original references to the Director (and related expressions), see the note preceding s 1 at **[651]**.

Regulations: the Consumer Credit (Cancellation Notices and Copies of Documents) Regulations 1983, SI 1983/1557; the Consumer Credit (Notice of Cancellation Rights) (Exemptions) Regulations 1983, SI 1983/1558.

65 Consequences of improper execution

(1)   An improperly-executed regulated agreement is enforceable against the debtor or hirer on an order of the court only.

(2)   A retaking of goods or land to which a regulated agreement relates is an enforcement of the agreement.

[711]

66 Acceptance of credit-tokens

(1)   The debtor shall not be liable under a credit-token agreement for use made of the credit-token by any person unless the debtor had previously accepted the credit-token, or the use constituted an acceptance of it by him.

(2)   The debtor accepts a credit-token when—

(a)   it is signed, or

(b)   a receipt for it is signed, or

(c)   it is first used,

either by the debtor himself or by a person who, pursuant to the agreement, is authorised by him to use it.

[712]

[Withdrawal from certain agreements

66A   Withdrawal from consumer credit agreement

(1)   The debtor under a regulated consumer credit agreement, other than an excluded agreement, may withdraw from the agreement, without giving any reason, in accordance with this section.

(2)   To withdraw from an agreement under this section the debtor must give oral or written notice of the withdrawal to the creditor before the end of the period of 14 days beginning with the day after the relevant day.

(3)   For the purposes of subsection (2) the relevant day is whichever is the latest of the following—

    (a)   the day on which the agreement is made;

    (b)   where the creditor is required to inform the debtor of the credit limit under the agreement, the day on which the creditor first does so;

    (c)   in the case of an agreement to which section 61A (duty to supply copy of executed consumer credit agreement) applies, the day on which the debtor receives a copy of the agreement under that section or on which the debtor is informed as specified in subsection (3) of that section;

    (d)   in the case of an agreement to which section 63 (duty to supply copy of executed agreement: excluded agreements) applies, the day on which the debtor receives a copy of the agreement under that section.

(4)   Where oral notice under this section is given to the creditor it must be given in a manner specified in the agreement.

(5)   Where written notice under this section is given by facsimile transmission or electronically—

    (a)   it must be sent to the number or electronic address specified for the purpose in the agreement, and

    (b)   where it is so sent, it is to be regarded as having been received by the creditor at the time it is sent (and section 176A does not apply).

(6)   Where written notice under this section is given in any other form—

    (a)   it must be sent by post to, or left at, the postal address specified for the purpose in the agreement, and

    (b)   where it is sent by post to that address, it is to be regarded as having been received by the creditor at the time of posting (and section 176 does not apply).

(7)   Subject as follows, where the debtor withdraws from a regulated consumer credit agreement under this section—

    (a)   the agreement shall be treated as if it had never been entered into, and

    (b)   where an ancillary service relating to the agreement is or is to be provided by the creditor, or by a third party on the basis of an agreement between the third party and the creditor, the ancillary service contract shall be treated as if it had never been entered into.

(8)   In the case referred to in subsection (7)(b) the creditor must without delay notify any third party of the fact that the debtor has withdrawn from the agreement.

(9)   Where the debtor withdraws from an agreement under this section—

    (a)   the debtor must repay to the creditor any credit provided and the interest accrued on it (at the rate provided for under the agreement), but

    (b)   the debtor is not liable to pay to the creditor any compensation, fees or charges except any non-returnable charges paid by the creditor to a public administrative body.

(10)   An amount payable under subsection (9) must be paid without undue delay and no later than the end of the period of 30 days beginning with the day after the day on which the notice of withdrawal was given (and if not paid by the end of that period may be recovered by the creditor as a debt).

(11)   Where a regulated consumer credit agreement is a conditional sale, hire-purchase or credit-sale agreement and—

    (a)   the debtor withdraws from the agreement under this section after the credit has been provided, and

    (b)   the sum payable under subsection (9)(a) is paid in full by the debtor,

title to the goods purchased or supplied under the agreement is to pass to the debtor on the same terms as would have applied had the debtor not withdrawn from the agreement.

(12)   In subsections (2), (4), (5), (6) and (9)(a) references to the creditor include a person specified by the creditor in the agreement.

(13)   In subsection (7)(b) the reference to an ancillary service means a service that relates to the provision of credit under the agreement and includes in particular an insurance or payment protection policy.

(14)   For the purposes of this section, an agreement is an excluded agreement if it is—

    (a)   an agreement for credit exceeding £60, 260,

    (b)   an agreement secured on land,

    (c)   a restricted-use credit agreement to finance the purchase of land, or

    (d)   an agreement for a bridging loan in connection with the purchase of land.]

[712A]

PART 1
STATUTES

NOTES

Commencement: 1 February 2011.

Inserted, together with preceding cross-heading, by the Consumer Credit (EU Directive) Regulations 2010, SI 2010/1010, regs 2, 13 (as amended by the Consumer Credit (Amendment) Regulations 2010, SI 2010/1969, regs 4, 8), as from 1 February 2011, with effect in relation to certain agreements before that date, as provided for in regs 101, 101A of the 2010 Regulations at **[3942]**, **[3942A]**.

Transitional provision: SI 2010/1969, regs 4, 8 amended SI 2010/1010, reg 13 so as to include the words "the day after" in the text of sub-s (2) reproduced above. SI 2010/1969, reg 46 provides that the insertion of these words does not apply to an agreement to which the Consumer Credit Act 1974, s 66A applies if the relevant day in relation to the agreement falls on or before 26 August 2010.

Cancellation of certain agreements within cooling-off period

67 Cancellable agreements

[(1)] [Subject to subsection (2)] A regulated agreement may be cancelled by the debtor or hirer in accordance with this Part if the antecedent negotiations included oral representations made when in the presence of the debtor or hirer by an individual acting as, or on behalf of, the negotiator, unless—

(a) the agreement is secured on land, or is a restricted-use credit agreement to finance the purchase of land or is an agreement for a bridging loan in connection with the purchase of land, or

(b) the unexecuted agreement is signed by the debtor or hirer at premises at which any of the following is carrying on any business (whether on a permanent or temporary basis)—

    (i) the creditor or owner;

    (ii) any party to a linked transaction (other than the debtor or hirer or a relative of his);

    (iii) the negotiator in any antecedent negotiations.

[(2) This section does not apply where section 66A applies.]

[713]

NOTES

For the text of this section as it had effect on 15 June 2006, prior to amendments made by the Consumer Credit Act 2006 and subsequent amendments, see the Appendix at [A63].

Sub-s (1): original provision renumbered as such and words in square brackets inserted by the Consumer Credit (EU Directive) Regulations 2010, SI 2010/1010, regs 2, 14(a), as from 1 February 2011, with effect in relation to certain agreements before that date, as provided for in regs 101, 101A of the 2010 Regulations at **[3942]**, **[3942A]**.

Sub-s (2): added by SI 2010/1010, regs 2, 14(b), as from 1 February 2011, with effect in relation to certain agreements before that date, as provided for in regs 101, 101A of the 2010 Regulations at **[3942]**, **[3942A]**.

68 Cooling-off period

The debtor or hirer may serve notice of cancellation of a cancellable agreement between his signing of the unexecuted agreement and—

(a) the end of the fifth day following the day on which he received a copy under section 63(2) or a notice under section 64(1)(b), or

(b) if (by virtue of regulations made under section 64(4)) section 64(1)(b) does not apply, the end of the fourteenth day following the day on which he signed the unexecuted agreement.

[714]

69 Notice of cancellation

(1) If within the period specified in section 68 the debtor or hirer under a cancellable agreement serves on—

(a) the creditor or owner, or

(b) the person specified in the notice under section 64(1), or

(c) a person who (whether by virtue of subsection (6) or otherwise) is the agent of the creditor or owner,

a notice (a "notice of cancellation") which, however expressed and whether or not conforming to the notice given under section 64(1), indicates the intention of the debtor or hirer to withdraw from the agreement, the notice shall operate—

    (i) to cancel the agreement, and any linked transaction, and

    (ii) to withdraw any offer by the debtor or hirer, or his relative, to enter into a linked transaction.

(2) In the case of a debtor-creditor-supplier agreement for restricted-use credit financing—

(a) the doing of work or supply of goods to meet an emergency, or

(b)   the supply of goods which, before service of the notice of cancellation, had by the act of the debtor or his relative become incorporated in any land or thing not comprised in the agreement or any linked transaction,

subsection (1) shall apply with the substitution of the following for paragraph (i)—

"(i)   to cancel only such provisions of the agreement and any linked transaction as—

(aa)   relate to the provision of credit, or

(bb)   require the debtor to pay an item in the total charge for credit, or

(cc)   subject the debtor to any obligation other than to pay for the doing of the said work, or the supply of the said goods".

(3)   Except so far as is otherwise provided, references in this Act to the cancellation of an agreement or transaction do not include a case within subsection (2).

(4)   Except as otherwise provided by or under this Act, an agreement or transaction cancelled under subsection (1) shall be treated as if it had never been entered into.

(5)   Regulations may exclude linked transactions of the prescribed description from subsection (1)(i) or (ii).

(6)   Each of the following shall be deemed to be the agent of the creditor or owner for the purpose of receiving a notice of cancellation—

(a)   a credit-broker or supplier who is the negotiator in antecedent negotiations, and

(b)   any person who, in the course of a business carried on by him, acts on behalf of the debtor or hirer in any negotiations for the agreement.

[(7)   Whether or not it is actually received by him, a notice of cancellation sent to a person shall be deemed to be served on him—.

(a)   in the case of a notice sent by post, at the time of posting, and

(b)   in the case of a notice transmitted in the form of an electronic communication in accordance with section 176A(1), at the time of the transmission.]

[715]

NOTES

Sub-s (7): substituted by the Consumer Credit Act 1974 (Electronic Communications) Order 2004, SI 2004/3236, art 2(1), (5), as from 31 December 2004.

Regulations: the Consumer Credit (Linked Transactions) (Exemptions) Regulations 1983, SI 1983/1560 at [3031].

70   Cancellation: recovery of money paid by debtor or hirer

(1)   On the cancellation of a regulated agreement, and of any linked transaction,—

(a)   any sum paid by the debtor or hirer, or his relative, under or in contemplation of the agreement or transaction, including any item in the total charge for credit, shall become repayable, and

(b)   any sum, including any item in the total charge for credit, which but for the cancellation is, or would or might become, payable by the debtor or hirer, or his relative, under the agreement or transaction shall cease to be, or shall not become, so payable, and

(c)   in the case of a debtor-creditor-supplier agreement falling within section 12(b) any sum paid on the debtor's behalf by the creditor to the supplier shall become repayable to the creditor.

(2)   If, under the terms of a cancelled agreement or transaction, the debtor or hirer, or his relative, is in possession of any goods, he shall have a lien on them for any sum repayable to him under subsection (1) in respect of that agreement or transaction, or any other linked transaction.

(3)   A sum repayable under subsection (1) is repayable by the person to whom it was originally paid, but in the case of a debtor-creditor-supplier agreement falling within section 12(b) the creditor and the supplier shall be under a joint and several liability to repay sums paid by the debtor, or his relative, under the agreement or under a linked transaction falling within section 19(1)(b) and accordingly, in such a case, the creditor shall be entitled, in accordance with rules of court, to have the supplier made a party to any proceedings brought against the creditor to recover any such sums.

(4)   Subject to any agreement between them, the creditor shall be entitled to be indemnified by the supplier for loss suffered by the creditor in satisfying his liability under subsection (3), including costs reasonably incurred by him in defending proceedings instituted by the debtor.

(5)   Subsection (1) does not apply to any sum which, if not paid by a debtor, would be payable by virtue of section 71, and applies to a sum paid or payable by a debtor for the issue of a credit-token only where the credit-token has been returned to the creditor or surrendered to a supplier.

(6)   If the total charge for credit includes an item in respect of a fee or commission charged by a credit-broker, the amount repayable under subsection (1) in respect of that item shall be the excess over [£5] of the fee or commission.

(7)   If the total charge for credit includes any sum payable or paid by the debtor to a credit-broker otherwise than in respect of a fee or commission charged by him, that sum shall for the purposes of subsection (6) be treated as if it were such a fee or commission.

(8)   So far only as is necessary to give effect to section 69(2), this section applies to an agreement or transaction within that subsection as it applies to a cancelled agreement or transaction.

[716]

NOTES
   Sub-s (6): sum in square brackets substituted by the Consumer Credit (Further Increase of Monetary Amounts) Order 1998, SI 1998/997, art 3, Schedule, as from 1 May 1998.

71   Cancellation: repayment of credit

(1)   Notwithstanding the cancellation of a regulated consumer credit agreement, other than a debtor-creditor-supplier agreement for restricted-use credit, the agreement shall continue in force so far as it relates to repayment of credit and payment of interest.

(2)   If, following the cancellation of a regulated consumer credit agreement, the debtor repays the whole or a portion of a credit—
   (a)   before the expiry of one month following service of the notice of cancellation, or
   (b)   in the case of a credit repayable by instalments, before the date on which the first instalment is due,
no interest shall be payable on the amount repaid.

(3)   If the whole of a credit repayable by instalments is not repaid on or before the date specified in subsection (2) (b), the debtor shall not be liable to repay any of the credit except on receipt of a request in writing in the prescribed form, signed by or on behalf of the creditor, stating the amounts of the remaining instalments (recalculated by the creditor as nearly as may be in accordance with the agreement and without extending the repayment period), but excluding any sum other than principal and interest.

(4)   Repayment of a credit, or payment of interest, under a cancelled agreement shall be treated as duly made if it is made to any person on whom, under section 69, a notice of cancellation could have been served, other than a person referred to in section 69(6)(b).

[717]

NOTES
   Regulations: the Consumer Credit (Repayment of Credit on Cancellation) Regulations 1983, SI 1983/1559.

72   Cancellation: return of goods

(1)   This section applies where any agreement or transaction relating to goods, being—
   (a)   a restricted-use debtor-creditor-supplier agreement, a consumer hire agreement, or a linked transaction to which the debtor or hirer under any regulated agreement is a party, or
   (b)   a linked transaction to which a relative of the debtor or hirer under any regulated agreement is a party,
is cancelled after the debtor or hirer (in a case within paragraph (a)) or the relative (in a case within paragraph (b)) has acquired possession of the goods by virtue of the agreement or transaction.

(2)   In this section—
   (a)   "the possessor" means the person who has acquired possession of the goods as mentioned in subsection (1),
   (b)   "the other party" means the person from whom the possessor acquired possession, and
   (c)   "the pre-cancellation period" means the period beginning when the possessor acquired possession and ending with the cancellation.

(3)   The possessor shall be treated as having been under a duty throughout the pre-cancellation period—
   (a)   to retain possession of the goods, and
   (b)   to take reasonable care of them.

(4)   On the cancellation, the possessor shall be under a duty, subject to any lien, to restore the goods to the other party in accordance with this section, and meanwhile to retain possession of the goods and take reasonable care of them.

(5)   The possessor shall not be under any duty to deliver the goods except at his own premises and in pursuance of a request in writing signed by or on behalf of the other party and served on the possessor either before, or at the time when, the goods are collected from those premises.

(6)   If the possessor—

(a) delivers the goods (whether at his own premises or elsewhere) to any person on whom, under section 69, a notice of cancellation could have been served (other than a person referred to in section 69(6)(b)), or

(b) sends the goods at his own expense to such a person,

he shall be discharged from any duty to retain the goods or deliver them to any person.

(7) Where the possessor delivers the goods as mentioned in subsection (6)(a) his obligation to take care of the goods shall cease; and if he sends the goods as mentioned in subsection (6)(b), he shall be under a duty to take reasonable care to see that they are received by the other party and not damaged in transit, but in other respects his duty to take care of the goods shall cease.

(8) Where, at any time during the period of 21 days following the cancellation, the possessor receives such a request as is mentioned in subsection (5), and unreasonably refuses or unreasonably fails to comply with it, his duty to take reasonable care of the goods shall continue until he delivers or sends the goods as mentioned in subsection (6), but if within that period he does not receive such a request his duty to take reasonable care of the goods shall cease at the end of that period.

(9) The preceding provisions of this section do not apply to—

(a) perishable goods, or

(b) goods which by their nature are consumed by use and which, before the cancellation, were so consumed, or

(c) goods supplied to meet an emergency, or

(d) goods which, before the cancellation, had become incorporated in any land or thing not comprised in the cancelled agreement or a linked transaction.

(10) Where the address of the possessor is specified in the executed agreement, references in this section to his own premises are to that address and no other.

(11) Breach of a duty imposed by this section is actionable as a breach of statutory duty.

[718]

73 Cancellation: goods given in part-exchange

(1) This section applies on the cancellation of a regulated agreement where, in antecedent negotiations, the negotiator agreed to take goods in part-exchange (the "part-exchange goods") and those goods have been delivered to him.

(2) Unless, before the end of the period of ten days beginning with the date of cancellation, the part-exchange goods are returned to the debtor or hirer in a condition substantially as good as when they were delivered to the negotiator, the debtor or hirer shall be entitled to recover from the negotiator a sum equal to the part-exchange allowance (as defined in subsection (7)(b)).

(3) In the case of a debtor-creditor-supplier agreement within section 12(b), the negotiator and the creditor shall be under a joint and several liability to pay to the debtor a sum recoverable under subsection (2).

(4) Subject to any agreement between them, the creditor shall be entitled to be indemnified by the negotiator for loss suffered by the creditor in satisfying his liability under subsection (3), including costs reasonably incurred by him in defending proceedings instituted by the debtor.

(5) During the period of ten days beginning with the date of cancellation, the debtor or hirer, if he is in possession of goods to which the cancelled agreement relates, shall have a lien on them for—

(a) delivery of the part-exchange goods, in a condition substantially as good as when they were delivered to the negotiator, or

(b) a sum equal to the part-exchange allowance;

and if the lien continues to the end of that period it shall thereafter subsist only as a lien for a sum equal to the part-exchange allowance.

(6) Where the debtor or hirer recovers from the negotiator or creditor, or both of them jointly, a sum equal to the part-exchange allowance, then, if the title of the debtor or hirer to the part-exchange goods has not vested in the negotiator, it shall so vest on the recovery of that sum.

(7) For the purposes of this section—

(a) the negotiator shall be treated as having agreed to take goods in part-exchange if, in pursuance of the antecedent negotiations, he either purchased or agreed to purchase those goods or accepted or agreed to accept them as part of the consideration for the cancelled agreement, and

(b) the part-exchange allowance shall be the sum agreed as such in the antecedent negotiations or, if no such agreement was arrived at, such sum as it would have been reasonable to allow in respect of the part-exchange goods if no notice of cancellation had been served.

(8)　In an action brought against the creditor for a sum recoverable under subsection (2), he shall be entitled, in accordance with rules of court, to have the negotiator made a party to the proceedings.

[719]

Exclusion of certain agreements from Part V

74　Exclusion of certain agreements from Part V

(*1*)　*This Part (except section 56) does not apply to—*
　(*a*)　*a non-commercial agreement, or*
　(*b*)　*a debtor-creditor agreement enabling the debtor to overdraw on a current account, or*
　(*c*)　*a debtor-creditor agreement to finance the making of such payments arising on, or connected with, the death of a person as may be prescribed.*

(*2*)　*This Part (except sections 55 and 56) does not apply to a small debtor-creditor-supplier agreement for restricted-use credit.*

[(1)　Except as provided in subsections (1A) to (2), this Part does not apply to—
　(a)　a non-commercial agreement,
　(b)　a debtor-creditor agreement enabling the debtor to overdraw on a current account,
　(c)　a debtor-creditor agreement to finance the making of such payments arising on, or connected with, the death of a person as may be prescribed, or
　(d)　a small debtor-creditor-supplier agreement for restricted-use credit.

(1A)　Section 56 (antecedent negotiations) applies to a non-commercial agreement.

(1B)　Where an agreement that falls within subsection (1)(b) is an authorised business overdraft agreement the following provisions apply—
　(a)　section 55B (assessment of creditworthiness);
　(b)　section 56 (antecedent negotiations);
　(c)　section 60 (regulations on form and content of agreements);
　(d)　section 61B (duty to supply copy of overdraft agreement).

(1C)　Where an agreement that falls within subsection (1)(b) is an authorised non-business overdraft agreement the following provisions apply—
　(a)　section 55 (regulations on disclosure of information);
　(b)　section 55B (assessment of creditworthiness);
　(c)　section 55C (copy of draft consumer credit agreement);
　(d)　section 56 (antecedent negotiations);
　(e)　section 60 (regulations on form and content of agreements);
　(f)　section 61B (duty to supply copy of overdraft agreement).

(1D)　Where an agreement that falls within subsection (1)(b) would be an authorised non-business overdraft agreement but for the fact that the credit is not repayable on demand or within three months the following provisions apply—
　(a)　section 55 (regulations on disclosure of information);
　(b)　section 55A (adequate explanations);
　(c)　section 55B (credit assessment);
　(d)　section 55C (copy of draft consumer credit agreement);
　(e)　section 56 (antecedent negotiations);
　(f)　section 60 (regulations on form and content of agreements);
　(g)　section 61 (signing of agreement);
　(h)　section 61A (duty to supply copy of executed agreement);
　(i)　section 66A (withdrawal from consumer credit agreement).

(1E)　In the case of an agreement that falls within subsection (1)(b) but does not fall within subsection (1B), (1C) or (1D), section 56 (antecedent negotiations) applies.

(1F)　The following provisions apply to a debtor-creditor agreement to finance the making of such payments arising on, or connected with, the death of a person as may be prescribed—
　(a)　section 55 (regulations on disclosure of information);
　(b)　section 55A (adequate explanations);
　(c)　section 55B (assessment of creditworthiness);
　(d)　section 55C (copy of draft consumer credit agreement);
　(e)　section 56 (antecedent negotiations);
　(f)　section 60 (regulations on form and content of agreements);
　(g)　section 61 (signing of agreement);
　(h)　section 61A (duty to supply copy of executed agreement);
　(i)　section 66A (withdrawal from consumer credit agreement).

(2)　The following provisions apply to a small debtor-creditor-supplier agreement for restricted-use credit—
　(a)　section 55 (regulations on disclosure of information);
　(b)　section 56 (antecedent negotiations);

(c) section 66A (withdrawal from consumer credit agreement).]

[(2A) In the case of an agreement to which the [Cancellation of Contracts made in a Consumer's Home or Place of Work etc Regulations 2008] apply the reference in subsection (2) to a small agreement shall be construed as if in section 17(1)(a) and (b) "£35" were substituted for "£50".]

(3) *Subsection (1)(b) or (c) applies* [Subsection (1)(c) applies] only where the [OFT] so determines, and such a determination—
    (a) may be made subject to such conditions as the [OFT] thinks fit, and
    (b) shall be made only if the [OFT] is of opinion that it is not against the interests of debtors.

[(3A) Notwithstanding anything in subsection (3)(b) above, in relation to a debtor-creditor agreement under which the creditor is the Bank of England or a bank within the meaning of the Bankers' Books Evidence Act 1879, the [OFT] shall make a determination that subsection (1)(b) above applies unless [it] considers that it would be against the public interest to do so.]

(4) If any term of an agreement falling within subsection *[(1)(c)] or (2)* [(1)(d)] is expressed in writing, regulations under section 60(1) shall apply to that term (subject to section 60(3)) as if the agreement was a regulated agreement not falling within subsection *[(1)(c)] or (2)* [(1)(d)].

[720]

NOTES
    For the text of this section as it had effect on 15 June 2006, prior to amendments made by the Consumer Credit Act 2006 and subsequent amendments, see the Appendix at [A70].
    Sub-ss (1), (2): sub-ss (1) and (2) in italics substituted by subsequent sub-ss (1), (1A)–(1F), (2), in square brackets, by the Consumer Credit (EU Directive) Regulations 2010, SI 2010/1010, regs 2, 17(1), (2), as from 1 February 2011, with effect in relation to certain agreements before that date, as provided for in regs 101, 101A of the 2010 Regulations at **[3942]**, **[3942A]**.
    Sub-s (2A): inserted by the Consumer Protection (Cancellation of Contracts Concluded away from Business Premises) Regulations 1987, SI 1987/2117, reg 9, as from as from 1 July 1988; words in square brackets substituted by the Cancellation of Contracts made in a Consumer's Home or Place of Work etc Regulations 2008, SI 2008/1816, reg 3, Sch 1, para 1, as from 1 October 2008.
    Sub-s (3): words in italics substituted by subsequent words in square brackets by SI 2010/1010, regs 2, 17(1), (3), as from 1 February 2011, with effect in relation to certain agreements before that date, as provided for in regs 101, 101A of the 2010 Regulations at **[3942]**, **[3942A]**.
    Sub-s (3A): added by the Banking Act 1979, s 38(1), as from 1 October 1979, and repealed by SI 2010/1010, regs 2, 17(1), (4), as from 1 February 2011, with effect in relation to certain agreements before that date, as provided for in regs 101, 101A of the 2010 Regulations at **[3942]**, **[3942A]**.
    Sub-s (4): reference "(1)(c)" in square brackets in both places substituted by the Banking Act 1979, s 38(1), as from 1 October 1979; words in italics in both places substituted by subsequent references in square brackets by SI 2010/1010, regs 2, 17(1), (5), as from 1 February 2011, with effect in relation to certain agreements before that date, as provided for in regs 101, 101A of the 2010 Regulations at **[3942]**, **[3942A]**.
    References to the OFT, etc: as to the abolition of the office of the Director General of Fair Trading and the substitution of the original references to the Director (and related expressions), see the note preceding s 1 at **[651]**.
    Regulations: the Consumer Credit (Payments Arising on Death) Regulations 1983, SI 1983/1554.

[PART VA
CURRENT ACCOUNT OVERDRAFTS

74A Information to be provided on a current account agreement

(1) This section applies to a current account agreement where—
    (a) there is the possibility that the account-holder may be allowed to overdraw on the current account without a pre-arranged overdraft or exceed a pre-arranged overdraft limit, and
    (b) if the account-holder did so, this would be a regulated consumer credit agreement.

(2) The current account agreement must include the following information at the time it is made—
    (a) the rate of interest charged on the amount by which an account-holder overdraws on the current account or exceeds the pre-arranged overdraft limit,
    (b) any conditions applicable to that rate,
    (c) any reference rate on which that rate is based,
    (d) information on any changes to the rate of interest (including the periods that the rate applies and any conditions or procedure applicable to changing that rate), and
    (e) any other charges payable by the debtor under the agreement (and the conditions under which those charges may be varied).

(3) The account-holder must be informed in writing at least annually of the information in subsection (2).

(4) For the purposes of subsections (2) and (3) where different rates of interest are charged in different circumstances, the creditor must provide the information in subsection (2)(a) to (d) in respect of each rate.

(5) Subsection (3) does not apply where the overdraft or excess would be secured on land.]

[720A]

NOTES
    Commencement: 1 February 2011.
    Inserted, together with preceding Part heading, by the Consumer Credit (EU Directive) Regulations 2010, SI 2010/1010, regs 2, 21 (as amended by the Consumer Credit (Amendment) Regulations 2010, SI 2010/1969, regs 4, 9), as from 1 February 2011, with effect in relation to certain agreements before that date, as provided for in regs 101, 101A of the 2010 Regulations at **[3942]**, **[3942A]**.

[74B   Information to be provided on significant overdrawing without prior arrangement

    (1)   Where—
        (a)   the holder of a current account overdraws on the account without a pre-arranged overdraft, or exceeds a pre-arranged overdraft limit, for a period exceeding one month,
        (b)   the amount of that overdraft or excess is significant throughout that period,
        (c)   that overdraft or excess is a regulated consumer credit agreement, and
        (d)   the account-holder has not been informed in writing of the matters mentioned in subsection (2) within that period,
the account-holder must be informed in writing of those matters without delay.

    (2)   The matters referred to in subsection (1) are—
        (a)   the fact that the current account is overdrawn or the overdraft limit has been exceeded,
        (b)   the amount of that overdraft or excess,
        (c)   the rate of interest charged on it, and
        (d)   any other charges payable by the debtor in relation to it (including any penalties and any interest on those charges).

    (3)   For the purposes of subsection (1)(b) the amount of the overdraft or excess is to be treated as significant if—
        (a)   the account-holder is liable to pay a charge for which he would not otherwise be liable,
        (b)   the overdraft or excess is likely to have an adverse effect on the debtor's ability to receive further credit (including any effect on the information about the debtor held by a credit reference agency), or
        (c)   it otherwise appears significant, having regard to all the circumstances.

    (4)   Where the overdraft or excess is secured on land, subsection (1)(a) is to be read as if the reference to one month were a reference to three months.]

                                                                                [720B]

NOTES
    Commencement: 1 February 2011.
    Inserted by the Consumer Credit (EU Directive) Regulations 2010, SI 2010/1010, regs 2, 22 (as amended by the Consumer Credit (Amendment) Regulations 2010, SI 2010/1969, regs 4, 10(1), (3)), as from 1 February 2011, with effect in relation to certain agreements before that date, as provided for in regs 100–101A of the 2010 Regulations at **[3941]–[3942A]**.

PART VI
MATTERS ARISING DURING CURRENCY OF CREDIT OR HIRE AGREEMENTS

75   Liability of creditor for breaches by supplier

    (1)   If the debtor under a debtor-creditor-supplier agreement falling within section 12(b) or (c) has, in relation to a transaction financed by the agreement, any claim against the supplier in respect of a misrepresentation or breach of contract, he shall have a like claim against the creditor, who, with the supplier, shall accordingly be jointly and severally liable to the debtor.

    (2)   Subject to any agreement between them, the creditor shall be entitled to be indemnified by the supplier for loss suffered by the creditor in satisfying his liability under subsection (1), including costs reasonably incurred by him in defending proceedings instituted by the debtor.

    (3)   Subsection (1) does not apply to a claim—
        (a)   under a non-commercial agreement, *or*
        (b)   so far as the claim relates to any single item to which the supplier has attached a cash price not exceeding [£100] or more than [£30,000][, or
        (c)   under a debtor-creditor-supplier agreement for running-account credit—
            (i)   which provides for the making of payments by the debtor in relation to specified periods which, in the case of an agreement which is not secured on land, do not exceed three months, and
            (ii)   which requires that the number of payments to be made by the debtor in repayments of the whole amount of the credit provided in each such period shall not exceed one.]

    (4)   This section applies notwithstanding that the debtor, in entering into the transaction, exceeded the credit limit or otherwise contravened any term of the agreement.

(5)   In an action brought against the creditor under subsection (1) he shall be entitled, in accordance with rules of court, to have the supplier made a party to the proceedings.

[721]

NOTES
   For the text of this section as it had effect on 15 June 2006, prior to amendments made by the Consumer Credit Act 2006 and subsequent amendments, see the Appendix at [A71].
   Sub-s (3): word in italics in para (a) repealed and para (c) and word preceding it inserted by the Consumer Credit (EU Directive) Regulations 2010, SI 2010/1010, regs 2, 24, as from 1 February 2011, with effect in relation to certain agreements before that date, as provided for in regs 101, 101A of the 2010 Regulations at [3942], [3942A]; sums in square brackets in para (b) substituted by the Consumer Credit (Increase of Monetary Limits) Order 1983, SI 1983/1878, arts 3, 4, Schedule, Pts I, II, as from 1 May 1998.

[75A   Further provision for liability of creditor for breaches by supplier

   (1)   If the debtor under a linked credit agreement has a claim against the supplier in respect of a breach of contract the debtor may pursue that claim against the creditor where any of the conditions in subsection (2) are met.

   (2)   The conditions in subsection (1) are—
   (a)   that the supplier cannot be traced,
   (b)   that the debtor has contacted the supplier but the supplier has not responded,
   (c)   that the supplier is insolvent, or
   (d)   that the debtor has taken reasonable steps to pursue his claim against the supplier but has not obtained satisfaction for his claim.

   (3)   The steps referred to in subsection (2)(d) need not include litigation.

   (4)   For the purposes of subsection (2)(d) a debtor is to be deemed to have obtained satisfaction where he has accepted a replacement product or service or other compensation from the supplier in settlement of his claim.

   (5)   In this section "linked credit agreement" means a regulated consumer credit agreement which serves exclusively to finance an agreement for the supply of specific goods or the provision of a specific service and where—
   (a)   the creditor uses the services of the supplier in connection with the preparation or making of the credit agreement, or
   (b)   the specific goods or provision of a specific service are explicitly specified in the credit agreement.

   (6)   This section does not apply where—
   (a)   the cash value of the goods or service is £30, 000 or less,
   (b)   the linked credit agreement is for credit which exceeds £60, 260, or
   (c)   the linked credit agreement is entered into by the debtor wholly or predominantly for the purposes of a business carried on, or intended to be carried on, by him.

   (7)   Subsections (2) to (5) of section 16B (declaration by the debtor as to the purposes of the agreement) apply for the purposes of subsection (6)(c).

   (8)   This section does not apply to an agreement secured on land.]

[721A]

NOTES
   Commencement: 1 February 2011.
   Inserted by the Consumer Credit (EU Directive) Regulations 2010, SI 2010/1010, regs 2, 25 (as amended by the Consumer Credit (Amendment) Regulations 2010, SI 2010/1969, regs 4, 11), as from 1 February 2011, with effect in relation to certain agreements before that date, as provided for in regs 100–101A of the 2010 Regulations at [3941]–[3942A].

76   Duty to give notice before taking certain action

   (1)   The creditor or owner is not entitled to enforce a term of a regulated agreement by—
   (a)   demanding earlier payment of any sum, or
   (b)   recovering possession of any goods or land, or
   (c)   treating any right conferred on the debtor or hirer by the agreement as terminated, restricted or deferred,
except by or after giving the debtor or hirer not less than seven days' notice of intention to do so.

   (2)   Subsection (1) applies only where—
   (a)   a period for the duration of the agreement is specified in the agreement, and
   (b)   that period has not ended when the creditor or owner does an act mentioned in subsection (1),
but so applies notwithstanding that, under the agreement, any party is entitled to terminate it before the end of the period so specified.

   (3)   A notice under subsection (1) is ineffective if not in the prescribed form.

(4)   Subsection (1) does not prevent a creditor from treating the right to draw on any credit as restricted or deferred and taking such steps as may be necessary to make the restriction or deferment effective.

(5)   Regulations may provide that subsection (1) is not to apply to agreements described by the regulations.

(6)   Subsection (1) does not apply to a right of enforcement arising by reason of any breach by the debtor or hirer of the regulated agreement.

[722]

NOTES

Regulations: the Consumer Credit (Enforcement, Default and Termination Notices) Regulations 1983, SI 1983/1561.

77   Duty to give information to debtor under fixed-sum credit agreement

(1)   The creditor under a regulated agreement for fixed-sum credit, within the prescribed period after receiving a request in writing to that effect from the debtor and payment of a fee of [£1], shall give the debtor a copy of the executed agreement (if any) and of any other document referred to in it, together with a statement signed by or on behalf of the creditor showing, according to the information to which it is practicable for him to refer,—

  (a)   the total sum paid under the agreement by the debtor;

  (b)   the total sum which has become payable under the agreement by the debtor but remains unpaid, and the various amounts comprised in that total sum, with the date when each became due; and

  (c)   the total sum which is to become payable under the agreement by the debtor, and the various amounts comprised in that total sum, with the date, or mode of determining the date, when each becomes due.

(2)   If the creditor possesses insufficient information to enable him to ascertain the amounts and dates mentioned in subsection (1)(c), he shall be taken to comply with that paragraph if his statement under subsection (1) gives the basis on which, under the regulated agreement, they would fall to be ascertained.

(3)   Subsection (1) does not apply to—

  (a)   an agreement under which no sum is, or will or may become, payable by the debtor, or

  (b)   a request made less than one month after a previous request under that subsection relating to the same agreement was complied with.

(4)   If the creditor under an agreement fails to comply with subsection (1)—

  (a)   he is not entitled, while the default continues, to enforce the agreement; ...

  (b)   ...

(5)   This section does not apply to a non-commercial agreement.

[723]

NOTES

For the text of this section as it had effect on 15 June 2006, prior to amendments made by the Consumer Credit Act 2006 and subsequent amendments, see the Appendix at [A73].

Sub-s (1): sum in square brackets substituted by the Consumer Credit (Further Increase in Monetary Amounts) Order 1998, SI 1998/997, art 3, Schedule, as from 1 May 1998.

Sub-s (4): words omitted repealed by the Consumer Protection from Unfair Trading Regulations 2008, SI 2008/1277, reg 30(1), (3), Sch 2, Pt 1, paras 17, 19, Sch 4, as from 26 May 2008.

Regulations: the Consumer Credit (Prescribed Periods for Giving Information) Regulations 1983, SI 1983/1569.

[77A   Statements to be provided in relation to fixed-sum credit agreements

[(1)   The creditor under a regulated agreement for fixed-sum credit must give the debtor statements under this section.

(1A)   The statements must relate to consecutive periods.

(1B)   The first such period must begin with either—

  (a)   the day on which the agreement is made, or

  (b)   the day the first movement occurs on the debtor's account with the creditor relating to the agreement.

(1C)   No such period may exceed a year.

(1D)   For the purposes of subsection (1C), a period of a year which expires on a non-working day may be regarded as expiring on the next working day.

(1E)   Each statement under this section must be given to the debtor before the end of the period of thirty days beginning with the day after the end of the period to which the statement relates.]

(2)   Regulations may make provision about the form and content of statements under this section.

(3)   The debtor shall have no liability to pay any sum in connection with the preparation or the giving to him of a statement under this section.

(4)   The creditor is not required to give the debtor any statement under this section once the following conditions are satisfied—
  (a)   that there is no sum payable under the agreement by the debtor; and
  (b)   that there is no sum which will or may become so payable.

(5)   Subsection (6) applies if at a time before the conditions mentioned in subsection (4) are satisfied the creditor fails to give the debtor—
  (a)   a statement under this section within the period mentioned in subsection [(1E)]; ...
  (b)   ...

(6)   Where this subsection applies in relation to a failure to give a statement under this section to the debtor—
  (a)   the creditor shall not be entitled to enforce the agreement during the period of non-compliance;
  (b)   the debtor shall have no liability to pay any sum of interest to the extent calculated by reference to the period of non-compliance or to any part of it; and
  (c)   the debtor shall have no liability to pay any default sum which (apart from this paragraph)—
    (i)   would have become payable during the period of non-compliance; or
    (ii)   would have become payable after the end of that period in connection with a breach of the agreement which occurs during that period (whether or not the breach continues after the end of that period).

(7)   In this section "the period of non-compliance" means, in relation to a failure to give a statement under this section to the debtor, the period which—
  (a)   begins immediately after the end of the period mentioned in ... subsection (5); and
  (b)   ends at the end of the day on which the statement is given to the debtor or on which the conditions mentioned in subsection (4) are satisfied, whichever is earlier.

(8)   This section does not apply in relation to a non-commercial agreement or to a small agreement.]

[(9)   This section does not apply where the holder of a current account overdraws on the account without a pre-arranged overdraft or exceeds a pre-arranged overdraft limit.]

[723A]

NOTES
  Commencement: 16 June 2006 (sub-s (2)); 1 October 2008 (sub-ss (1), (3)–(8)).
  Inserted by the Consumer Credit Act 2006, s 6, as from dates as noted above and subject to transitional provisions in s 69(1) of, and Sch 3, paras 1, 2 to, that Act at **[2077]**, **[2079]**.
  Sub-ss (1), (1A)–(1E): substituted for original sub-s (1) by the Legislative Reform (Consumer Credit) Order 2008, SI 2008/2826, art 4(a), as from 31 October 2008; for transitional provisions see the note below.
  Sub-s (5): reference in square brackets substituted and words omitted repealed by SI 2008/2826, art 4(b), as from 31 October 2008; for transitional provisions see the note below.
  Sub-s (7): words omitted repealed by SI 2008/2826, art 4(c), as from 31 October 2008; for transitional provisions see the note below.
  Sub-s (9): added by the Consumer Credit (EU Directive) Regulations 2010, SI 2010/1010, regs 2, 23, as from 1 February 2011, with effect in relation to certain agreements before that date, as provided for in regs 101, 101A of the 2010 Regulations at **[3942]**, **[3942A]**.
  Transitional provisions: the Legislative Reform (Consumer Credit) Order 2008, SI 2008/2826, art 5, provides that this section as amended by SI 2008/2826, art 4 (as noted above), applies to agreements whenever made and that it has effect in relation to agreements made before 1 October 2008, as if the period mentioned in sub-s (1B) were a period beginning no later than 1 October 2008 and ending no later than 30 September 2009; and sub-s (1C) did not apply. Accordingly, s 77A prior to the amendments made by SI 2008/2826, art 4, read as follows:

"[77A   Statements to be provided in relation to fixed-sum credit agreements
  (1)   The creditor under a regulated agreement for fixed-sum credit—
    (a)   shall, within the period of one year beginning with the day after the day on which the agreement is made, give the debtor a statement under this section; and
    (b)   after the giving of that statement, shall give the debtor further statements under this section at intervals of not more than one year.

  (2)   Regulations may make provision about the form and content of statements under this section.

  (3)   The debtor shall have no liability to pay any sum in connection with the preparation or the giving to him of a statement under this section.

  (4)   The creditor is not required to give the debtor any statement under this section once the following conditions are satisfied—
    (a)   that there is no sum payable under the agreement by the debtor; and
    (b)   that there is no sum which will or may become so payable.

(5)   Subsection (6) applies if at a time before the conditions mentioned in subsection (4) are satisfied the creditor fails to give the debtor—

(a)   a statement under this section within the period mentioned in subsection (1)(a); or

(b)   such a statement within the period of one year beginning with the day after the day on which such a statement was last given to him.

(6)   Where this subsection applies in relation to a failure to give a statement under this section to the debtor—

(a)   the creditor shall not be entitled to enforce the agreement during the period of non-compliance;

(b)   the debtor shall have no liability to pay any sum of interest to the extent calculated by reference to the period of non-compliance or to any part of it; and

(c)   the debtor shall have no liability to pay any default sum which (apart from this paragraph)—

  (i)   would have become payable during the period of non-compliance; or

  (ii)   would have become payable after the end of that period in connection with a breach of the agreement which occurs during that period (whether or not the breach continues after the end of that period).

(7)   In this section "the period of non-compliance" means, in relation to a failure to give a statement under this section to the debtor, the period which—

(a)   begins immediately after the end of the period mentioned in paragraph (a) or (as the case may be) paragraph (b) of subsection (5); and

(b)   ends at the end of the day on which the statement is given to the debtor or on which the conditions mentioned in subsection (4) are satisfied, whichever is earlier.

(8)   This section does not apply in relation to a non-commercial agreement or to a small agreement.]".

Regulations: the Consumer Credit (Information Requirements and Duration of Licences and Charges) Regulations 2007, SI 2007/1167 at **[3488]**.

***

[77B   Fixed-sum credit agreement: statement of account to be provided on request

(1)   This section applies to a regulated consumer credit agreement—

(a)   which is for fixed-sum credit,

(b)   which is of fixed duration,

(c)   where the credit is repayable in instalments by the debtor, and

(d)   which is not an excluded agreement.

(2)   Upon a request from the debtor, the creditor must as soon as reasonably practicable give to the debtor a statement in writing which complies with subsections (3) to (5).

(3)   The statement must include a table showing the details of each instalment owing under the agreement as at the date of the request.

(4)   Details to be provided under subsection (3) must include—

(a)   the date on which the instalment is due,

(b)   the amount of the instalment,

(c)   any conditions relating to payment of the instalment, and

(d)   a breakdown of the instalment showing how much of it is made up of capital repayment, interest payment and other charges.

(5)   Where the rate of interest is variable or the charges under the agreement may be varied, the statement must also indicate clearly and concisely that the information in the table is valid only until the rate of interest or charges are varied.

(6)   The debtor may make a request under subsection (2) at any time that the agreement is in force unless a previous request has been made less than a month before and has been complied with.

(7)   The debtor shall have no liability to pay any sum in connection with the preparation or the giving of a statement under this section.

(8)   A breach of the duty imposed by this section is actionable as a breach of statutory duty.

(9)   For the purposes of this section, an agreement is an excluded agreement if it is—

(a)   an agreement secured on land,

(b)   an agreement under which a person takes an article in pawn,

(c)   an agreement under which the creditor provides the debtor with credit which exceeds £60, 260, or

(d)   an agreement entered into by the debtor wholly or predominantly for the purpose of a business carried on, or intended to be carried on, by him.

(10)   Subsections (2) to (5) of section 16B (declaration by the debtor as to the purposes of the agreement) apply for the purposes of subsection (9)(d).]

[723B]

***

NOTES

Commencement: 1 February 2011.

Inserted by the Consumer Credit (EU Directive) Regulations 2010, SI 2010/1010, regs 2, 26, as from 1 February 2011, with effect in relation to certain agreements before that date, as provided for in regs 100–101A of the 2010 Regulations at **[3941]**–**[3942A]**.

78 Duty to give information to debtor under running-account credit agreement

(1)   The creditor under a regulated agreement for running-account credit, within the prescribed period after receiving a request in writing to that effect from the debtor and payment of a fee of [£1], shall give the debtor a copy of the executed agreement (if any) and of any other document referred to in it, together with a statement signed by or on behalf of the creditor showing, according to the information to which it is practicable for him to refer,—

(a)   the state of the account, and

(b)   the amount, if any, currently payable under the agreement by the debtor to the creditor, and

(c)   the amounts and due dates of any payments which, if the debtor does not draw further on the account, will later become payable under the agreement by the debtor to the creditor.

(2)   If the creditor possesses insufficient information to enable him to ascertain the amounts and dates mentioned in subsection (1)(c), he shall be taken to comply with that paragraph if his statement under subsection (1) gives the basis on which, under the regulated agreement, they would fall to be ascertained.

(3)   Subsection (1) does not apply to—

(a)   an agreement under which no sum is, or will or may become, payable by the debtor, or

(b)   a request made less than one month after a previous request under that subsection relating to the same agreement was complied with.

(4)   Where running-account credit is provided under a regulated agreement, the creditor shall give the debtor statements in the prescribed form, and with the prescribed contents—

(a)   showing according to the information to which it is practicable for him to refer, the state of the account at regular intervals of not more than twelve months, and

(b)   where the agreement provides, in relation to specified periods, for the making of payments by the debtor, or the charging against him of interest or any other sum, showing according to the information to which it is practicable for him to refer the state of the account at the end of each of those periods during which there is any movement in the account.

[(4A)   Regulations may require a statement under subsection (4) to contain also information in the prescribed terms about the consequences of the debtor—

(a)   failing to make payments as required by the agreement; or

(b)   only making payments of a prescribed description in prescribed circumstances.]

(5)   A statement under subsection (4) shall be given within the prescribed period after the end of the period to which the statement relates.

(6)   If the creditor under an agreement fails to comply with subsection (1)—

(a)   he is not entitled, while the default continues, to enforce the agreement; ...

(b)   ...

(7)   This section does not apply to a non-commercial agreement, and subsections [(4) to (5)] do not apply to a small agreement.

[724]

NOTES

For the text of this section as it had effect on 15 June 2006, prior to amendments made by the Consumer Credit Act 2006 and subsequent amendments, see the Appendix at [A74].

Sub-s (1): sum in square brackets substituted by the Consumer Credit (Further Increase in Monetary Amounts) Order 1998, SI 1998/997, art 3, Schedule, as from 1 May 1998.

Sub-s (4A): inserted by the Consumer Credit Act 2006, s 7(1), as from 16 June 2006, subject to transitional provisions in s 69(1) of, and Sch 3, paras 1, 3 to, that Act at [2077], [2079].

Sub-s (6): words omitted repealed by the Consumer Protection from Unfair Trading Regulations 2008, SI 2008/1277, reg 30(1), (3), Sch 2, Pt 1, paras 17, 20, Sch 4, as from 26 May 2008.

Sub-s (7): words in square brackets substituted by the Consumer Credit Act 2006, s 7(2), as from 16 June 2006.

Regulations: the Consumer Credit (Prescribed Periods for Giving Information) Regulations 1983, SI 1983/1569; the Consumer Credit (Running-Account Credit) Information Regulations 1983, SI 1983/1570; the Consumer Credit (Information Requirements and Duration of Licences and Charges) Regulations 2007, SI 2007/1167 at [3488].

[78A Duty to give information to debtor on change of rate of interest

(1)   Where the rate of interest charged under a regulated consumer credit agreement, other than an excluded agreement, is to be varied, the creditor must inform the debtor in writing of the matters mentioned in subsection (3) before the variation can take effect.

(2)   But subsection (1) does not apply where—

(a)   the agreement provides that the creditor is to inform the debtor in writing periodically of the matters mentioned in subsection (3) in relation to any variation, at such times as may be provided for in the agreement,

(b)   the agreement provides that the rate of interest is to vary according to a reference rate,

(c) the reference rate is publicly available,
(d) information about the reference rate is available on the premises of the creditor, and
(e) the variation of the rate of interest results from a change to the reference rate.

(3) The matters referred to in subsections (1) and (2)(a) are—
(a) the variation in the rate of interest,
(b) the amount of any payments that are to be made after the variation has effect, if different, expressed as a sum of money where practicable, and
(c) if the number or frequency of payments changes as a result of the variation, the new number or frequency.

(4) In the case of an agreement mentioned in subsection (5) this section applies as follows—
(a) the obligation in subsection (1) only applies if the rate of interest increases, and
(b) subsection (3) is to be read as if paragraphs (b) and (c) were omitted.

(5) The agreements referred to in subsection (4) are—
(a) an authorised business overdraft agreement,
(b) an authorised non-business overdraft agreement, or
(c) an agreement which would be an authorised non-business overdraft agreement but for the fact that the credit is not repayable on demand or within three months.

(6) For the purposes of this section an agreement is an excluded agreement if it is—
(a) a debtor-creditor agreement arising where the holder of a current account overdraws on the account without a pre-arranged overdraft or exceeds a pre-arranged overdraft limit, or
(b) an agreement secured on land.]

[724A]

NOTES
Commencement: 1 February 2011.
Inserted by the Consumer Credit (EU Directive) Regulations 2010, SI 2010/1010, regs 2, 27, as from 1 February 2011, with effect in relation to certain agreements before that date, as provided for in regs 100–101A of the 2010 Regulations at **[3941]**–**[3942A]**.

79 Duty to give hirer information

(1) The owner under a regulated consumer hire agreement, within the prescribed period after receiving a request in writing to that effect from the hirer and payment of a fee of [£1], shall give to the hirer a copy of the executed agreement and of any other document referred to in it, together with a statement signed by or on behalf of the owner showing, according to the information to which it is practicable for him to refer, the total sum which has become payable under the agreement by the hirer but remains unpaid and the various amounts comprised in that total sum, with the date when each became due.

(2) Subsection (1) does not apply to—
(a) an agreement under which no sum is, or will or may become, payable by the hirer, or
(b) a request made less than one month after a previous request under that subsection relating to the same agreement was complied with.

(3) If the owner under an agreement fails to comply with subsection (1)—
(a) he is not entitled, while the default continues, to enforce the agreement; ...
(b) ...

(4) This section does not apply to a non-commercial agreement.

[725]

NOTES
For the text of this section as it had effect on 15 June 2006, prior to amendments made by the Consumer Credit Act 2006 and subsequent amendments, see the Appendix at **[A75]**.
Sub-s (1): sum in square brackets substituted by the Consumer Credit (Further Increase in Monetary Amounts) Order 1998, SI 1998/997, art 3, Schedule, as from 1 May 1998.
Sub-s (3): words omitted repealed by the Consumer Protection from Unfair Trading Regulations 2008, SI 2008/1277, reg 30(1), (3), Sch 2, Pt 1, paras 17, 21, Sch 4, as from 26 May 2008.
Regulations: the Consumer Credit (Prescribed Periods for Giving Information) Regulations 1983, SI 1983/1569.

80 Debtor or hirer to give information about goods

(1) Where a regulated agreement, other than a non-commercial agreement, requires the debtor or hirer to keep goods to which the agreement relates in his possession or control, he shall, within seven working days after he has received a request in writing to that effect from the creditor or owner, tell the creditor or owner where the goods are.

(2)   If the debtor or hirer fails to comply with subsection (1), and the default continues for 14 days, he commits an offence.

[726]

81 Appropriation of payments

(1)   Where a debtor or hirer is liable to make to the same person payments in respect of two or more regulated agreements, he shall be entitled, on making any payment in respect of the agreements which is not sufficient to discharge the total amount then due under all the agreements, to appropriate the sum so paid by him—

    (a)   in or towards the satisfaction of the sum due under any one of the agreements, or

    (b)   in or towards the satisfaction of the sums due under any two or more of the agreements in such proportions as he thinks fit.

(2)   If the debtor or hirer fails to make any such appropriation where one or more of the agreements is—

    (a)   a hire-purchase agreement or conditional sale agreement, or

    (b)   a consumer hire agreement, or

    (c)   an agreement in relation to which any security is provided,

the payment shall be appropriated towards the satisfaction of the sums due under the several agreements respectively in the proportions which those sums bear to one another.

[727]

82 Variation of agreements

(1)   Where, under a power contained in a regulated agreement, the creditor or owner varies the agreement, the variation shall not take effect before notice of it is given to the debtor or hirer in the prescribed manner.

[(1A)   Subsection (1) does not apply to a variation in the rate of interest charged under an agreement not secured on land (see section 78A).

(1B)   Subsection (1) does not apply to a variation in the rate of interest charged under an agreement secured on land if—

    (a)   the agreement falls within subsection (1D), and

    (b)   the variation is a reduction in the rate.

(1C)   Subsection (1) does not apply to a variation in any other charge under an agreement if—

    (a)   the agreement falls within subsection (1D), and

    (b)   the variation is a reduction in the charge.

(1D)   The agreements referred to in subsections (1B) and (1C) are—

    (a)   an authorised business overdraft agreement,

    (b)   an authorised non-business overdraft agreement, or

    (c)   an agreement which would be an authorised non-business overdraft agreement but for the fact that the credit is not repayable on demand or within three months.

(1E)   Subsection (1) does not apply to a debtor-creditor agreement arising where the holder of a current account overdraws on the account without a pre-arranged overdraft or exceeds a pre-arranged overdraft limit.]

(2)   Where an agreement (a "modifying agreement") varies or supplements an earlier agreement, the modifying agreement shall for the purposes of this Act be treated as—

    (a)   revoking the earlier agreement, and

    (b)   containing provisions reproducing the combined effect of the two agreements,

and obligations outstanding in relation to the earlier agreement shall accordingly be treated as outstanding instead in relation to the modifying agreement.

[(2A)   Subsection (2) does not apply if [the earlier agreement or] the modifying agreement is an exempt agreement as a result of section 16(6C) [or 16C].]

[(2B)   Subsection (2) does not apply if the modifying agreement varies—

    (a)   the amount of the repayment to be made under the earlier agreement, or

    (b)   the duration of the agreement,

as a result of the discharge of part of the debtor's indebtedness under the earlier agreement by virtue of section 94(3).]

(3)   If the earlier agreement is a regulated agreement but (apart from this subsection) the modifying agreement is not then, [unless the modifying agreement is—

    (a)   for running account credit; or

    (b)   an exempt agreement as a result of section 16(6C) [or 16C],

it shall be treated as a regulated agreement.]

(4)   If the earlier agreement is a regulated agreement for running-account credit, and by the modifying agreement the creditor allows the credit limit to be exceeded but intends the excess to be merely temporary, Part V (except section 56) shall not apply to the modifying agreement.

(5)   If—

    (a)   the earlier agreement is a cancellable agreement, and

    (b)   the modifying agreement is made within the period applicable under section 68 to the earlier agreement,

then, whether or not the modifying agreement would, apart from this subsection, be a cancellable agreement, it shall be treated as a cancellable agreement in respect of which a notice may be served under section 68 not later than the end of the period applicable under that section to the earlier agreement.

    [(5A)   Subsection (5) does not apply where the modifying agreement is an exempt agreement as a result of section 16(6C) [or 16C].]

    (6)   Except under subsection (5), a modifying agreement shall not be treated as a cancellable agreement.

    [(6A)   If—

    (a)   the earlier agreement is an agreement to which section 66A (right of withdrawal) applies, and

    (b)   the modifying agreement is made within the period during which the debtor may give notice of withdrawal from the earlier agreement (see section 66A(2)),

then, whether or not the modifying agreement would, apart from this subsection, be an agreement to which section 66A applies, it shall be treated as such an agreement in respect of which notice may be given under subsection (2) of that section within the period referred to in paragraph (b) above.

    (6B)   Except as provided for under subsection (6A) section 66A does not apply to a modifying agreement.]

    (7)   This section does not apply to a non-commercial agreement.

[728]

NOTES

    For the text of this section as it had effect on 15 June 2006, prior to amendments made by the Consumer Credit Act 2006 and subsequent amendments, see the Appendix at [A78].

    Sub-ss (1A)–(1E): inserted by the Consumer Credit (EU Directive) Regulations 2010, SI 2010/1010, regs 2, 28, as from 1 February 2011, with effect in relation to certain agreements before that date, as provided for in regs 100–101A of the 2010 Regulations at **[3941]**–**[3942A]**.

    Sub-s (2A): inserted by the Financial Services and Markets Act 2000 (Consequential Amendments) Order 2005, SI 2005/2967, art 2(1), (2), as from 16 November 2005; words in first pair of square brackets inserted by the Financial Services and Markets Act 2000 (Consequential Amendments) Order 2008, SI 2008/733, art 2, as from 6 April 2008; words in second pair of square brackets inserted by the Legislative Reform (Consumer Credit) Order 2008, SI 2008/2826, art 3(3), as from 31 October 2008.

    Sub-s (2B): inserted by SI 2010/1010, regs 2, 29, as from 1 February 2011, with effect in relation to certain agreements before that date, as provided for in regs 100–101A of the 2010 Regulations at **[3941]**–**[3942A]**.

    Sub-s (3): words in first (outer) pair of square brackets substituted by SI 2005/2967, art 2(1), (3), as from 16 November 2005; words in second (inner) pair of square brackets inserted by SI 2008/2826, art 3(3), as from 31 October 2008.

    Sub-s (5A): inserted by SI 2005/2967, art 2(1), (4), as from 16 November 2005; words in square brackets inserted by SI 2008/2826, art 3(3), as from 31 October 2008.

    Sub-ss (6A), (6B): inserted by SI 2010/1010, regs 2, 15, as from 1 February 2011, with effect in relation to certain agreements before that date, as provided for in regs 101, 101A of the 2010 Regulations at **[3942]**, **[3942A]**.

    Regulations: the Consumer Credit (Notice of Variation of Agreements) Regulations 1977, SI 1977/328.

[82A   Assignment of rights

    (1)   Where rights of a creditor under a regulated consumer credit agreement are assigned to a third party, the assignee must arrange for notice of the assignment to be given to the debtor—

    (a)   as soon as reasonably possible, or

    (b)   if, after the assignment, the arrangements for servicing the credit under the agreement do not change as far as the debtor is concerned, on or before the first occasion that they do.

    (2)   This section does not apply to an agreement secured on land.]

[728A]

NOTES

    Commencement: 1 February 2011.

    Inserted by the Consumer Credit (EU Directive) Regulations 2010, SI 2010/1010, regs 2, 36, as from 1 February 2011, with effect in relation to certain agreements before that date, as provided for in regs 100–101A of the 2010 Regulations at **[3941]**–**[3942A]**.

83   Liability for misuse of credit facilities

    (1)   The debtor under a regulated consumer credit agreement shall not be liable to the creditor for any loss arising from use of the credit facility by another person not acting, or to be treated as acting, as the debtor's agent.

(2)   This section does not apply to a non-commercial agreement, or to any loss in so far as it arises from misuse of an instrument to which section 4 of the Cheques Act 1957 applies.

[729]

84   Misuse of credit-tokens

(1)   Section 83 does not prevent the debtor under a credit-token agreement from being made liable to the extent of [£50] (or the credit limit if lower) for loss to the creditor arising from use of the credit-token by other persons during a period beginning when the credit-token ceases to be in the possession of any authorised person and ending when the credit-token is once more in the possession of an authorised person.

(2)   Section 83 does not prevent the debtor under a credit-token agreement from being made liable to any extent for loss to the creditor from use of the credit-token by a person who acquired possession of it with the debtor's consent.

(3)   Subsections (1) and (2) shall not apply to any use of the credit-token after the creditor has been given oral or written notice that it is lost or stolen, or is for any other reason liable to misuse.

[(3A), (3B)   ...]

[(3C)   ...]

(4)   Subsections (1) and (2) shall not apply unless there are contained in the credit-token agreement in the prescribed manner particulars of the name, address and telephone number of a person stated to be the person to whom notice is to be given under subsection (3).

(5)   Notice under subsection (3) takes effect when received, but where it is given orally, and the agreement so requires, it shall be treated as not taking effect if not confirmed in writing within seven days.

(6)   Any sum paid by the debtor for the issue of the credit-token, to the extent (if any) that it has not been previously offset by use made of the credit token, shall be treated as paid towards satisfaction of any liability under subsection (1) or (2).

(7)   The debtor, the creditor, and any person authorised by the debtor to use the credit-token, shall be authorised persons for the purposes of subsection (1).

(8)   Where two or more credit-tokens are given under one credit-token agreement, the preceding provisions of this section apply to each credit-token separately.

[730]

NOTES
   For the text of this section as it had effect on 15 June 2006, prior to amendments made by the Consumer Credit Act 2006 and subsequent amendments, see the Appendix at [A80].
   Sub-s (1): sum in square brackets substituted by the Consumer Credit (Further Increase in Monetary Amounts) Order 1998, SI 1998/997, art 3, Schedule, as from 1 May 1998.
   Sub-ss (3A), (3B): inserted by the Consumer Protection (Distance Selling) Regulations 2000, SI 2000/2334, reg 21(5), as from 31 October 2000 and repealed by virtue of the Payment Services Regulations 2009, SI 2009/209, reg 126, Sch 6, Pt 2, para 3, as from 1 November 2009.
   Sub-s (3C): inserted by the Financial Services (Distance Marketing) Regulations 2004, SI 2004/2095, reg 14(4), as from 31 October 2004 (in relation to distance contracts made on or after that date) and repealed by virtue of the Payment Services Regulations 2009, SI 2009/209, reg 126, Sch 6, Pt 2, para 5(c), as from 1 November 2009.
   Regulations: the Consumer Credit (Credit-Token Agreements) Regulations 1983, SI 1983/1555.

85   Duty on issue of new credit-tokens

(1)   Whenever, in connection with a credit-token agreement, a credit-token (other than the first) is given by the creditor to the debtor, the creditor shall give the debtor a copy of the executed agreement (if any) and of any other document referred to in it.

(2)   If the creditor fails to comply with this section—
   (a)   he is not entitled, while the default continues, to enforce the agreement; ...
   (b)   ...

(3)   This section does not apply to a small agreement.

[731]

NOTES
   For the text of this section as it had effect on 15 June 2006, prior to amendments made by the Consumer Credit Act 2006 and subsequent amendments, see the Appendix at [A81].
   Sub-s (2): words omitted repealed by the Consumer Protection from Unfair Trading Regulations 2008, SI 2008/1277, reg 30(1), (3), Sch 2, Pt 1, paras 17, 22, Sch 4, as from 26 May 2008.

86   Death of debtor or hirer

(1)   The creditor or owner under a regulated agreement is not entitled, by reason of the death of the debtor or hirer, to do an act specified in paragraphs (a) to (e) of section 87(1) if at the death the agreement is fully secured.

(2)   If at the death of the debtor or hirer a regulated agreement is only partly secured or is unsecured, the creditor or owner is entitled, by reason of the death of the debtor or hirer, to do an act specified in paragraphs (a) to (e) of section 87(1) on an order of the court only.

(3)   This section applies in relation to the termination of an agreement only where—
    (a)   a period for its duration is specified in the agreement, and
    (b)   that period has not ended when the creditor or owner purports to terminate the agreement,
but so applies notwithstanding that, under the agreement, any party is entitled to terminate it before the end of the period so specified.

(4)   This section does not prevent the creditor from treating the right to draw on any credit as restricted or deferred, and taking such steps as may be necessary to make the restriction or deferment effective.

(5)   This section does not affect the operation of any agreement providing for payment of sums—
    (a)   due under the regulated agreement, or
    (b)   becoming due under it on the death of the debtor or hirer,
out of the proceeds of a policy of assurance on his life.

(6)   For the purposes of this section an act is done by reason of the death of the debtor or hirer if it is done under a power conferred by the agreement which is—
    (a)   exercisable on his death, or
    (b)   exercisable at will and exercised at any time after his death.

[732]

PART VII
DEFAULT AND TERMINATION

[Information sheets

86A   OFT to prepare information sheets on arrears and default

(1)   The OFT shall prepare, and give general notice of, an arrears information sheet and a default information sheet.

(2)   The arrears information sheet shall include information to help debtors and hirers who receive notices under section 86B or 86C

(3)   The default information sheet shall include information to help debtors and hirers who receive default notices.

(4)   Regulations may make provision about the information to be included in an information sheet.

(5)   An information sheet takes effect for the purposes of this Part at the end of the period of three months beginning with the day on which general notice of it is given.

(6)   If the OFT revises an information sheet after general notice of it has been given, it shall give general notice of the information sheet as revised.

(7)   A revised information sheet takes effect for the purposes of this Part at the end of the period of three months beginning with the day on which general notice of it is given.]

[732A]

NOTES
Commencement: 31 January 2007.
Inserted, together with preceding cross-heading, by the Consumer Credit Act 2006, s 8, as from 31 January 2007, subject to transitional provisions in s 69(1) of, and Sch 3, paras 1, 5 to, that Act at **[2077]**, **[2079]**.

[Sums in arrears and default sums

86B   Notice of sums in arrears under fixed-sum credit agreements etc

(1)   This section applies where at any time the following conditions are satisfied—
    (a)   that the debtor or hirer under an applicable agreement is required to have made at least two payments under the agreement before that time;
    (b)   that the total sum paid under the agreement by him is less than the total sum which he is required to have paid before that time;
    (c)   that the amount of the shortfall is no less than the sum of the last two payments which he is required to have made before that time;

PART 1
STATUTES

(d) that the creditor or owner is not already under a duty to give him notices under this section in relation to the agreement; and

(e) if a judgment has been given in relation to the agreement before that time, that there is no sum still to be paid under the judgment by the debtor or hirer.

(2) The creditor or owner—

(a) shall, within the period of 14 days beginning with the day on which the conditions mentioned in subsection (1) are satisfied, give the debtor or hirer a notice under this section; and

(b) after the giving of that notice, shall give him further notices under this section at intervals of not more than six months.

(3) The duty of the creditor or owner to give the debtor or hirer notices under this section shall cease when either of the conditions mentioned in subsection (4) is satisfied; but if either of those conditions is satisfied before the notice required by subsection (2)(a) is given, the duty shall not cease until that notice is given.

(4) The conditions referred to in subsection (3) are—

(a) that the debtor or hirer ceases to be in arrears;

(b) that a judgment is given in relation to the agreement under which a sum is required to be paid by the debtor or hirer.

(5) For the purposes of subsection (4)(a) the debtor or hirer ceases to be in arrears when—

(a) no [payments], which he has ever failed to [make] under the agreement when required, [are] still owing;

(b) no default sum, which has ever become payable under the agreement in connection with his failure to pay any sum under the agreement when required, is still owing;

(c) no sum of interest, which has ever become payable under the agreement in connection with such a default sum, is still owing; and

(d) no other sum of interest, which has ever become payable under the agreement in connection with his failure to pay any sum under the agreement when required, is still owing.

(6) A notice under this section shall include a copy of the current arrears information sheet under section 86A.

(7) The debtor or hirer shall have no liability to pay any sum in connection with the preparation or the giving to him of a notice under this section.

(8) Regulations may make provision about the form and content of notices under this section.

(9) In the case of an applicable agreement under which the debtor or hirer must make all payments he is required to make at intervals of one week or less, this section shall have effect as if in subsection (1)(a) and (c) for "two" there were substituted "four".

(10) If an agreement mentioned in subsection (9) was made before the beginning of the relevant period, only amounts resulting from failures by the debtor or hirer to make payments he is required to have made during that period shall be taken into account in determining any shortfall for the purposes of subsection (1)(c).

(11) In subsection (10) "relevant period" means the period of 20 weeks ending with the day on which the debtor or hirer is required to have made the most recent payment under the agreement.

(12) In this section "applicable agreement" means an agreement which—

(a) is a regulated agreement for fixed-sum credit or a regulated consumer hire agreement; and

(b) is neither a non-commercial agreement nor a small agreement.

[(13) In this section—

(a) "payments" in relation to an applicable agreement which is a regulated agreement for fixed-sum credit means payments to be made at predetermined intervals provided for under the terms of the agreement; and

(b) "payments" in relation to an applicable agreement which is a regulated consumer hire agreement means any payments to be made by the hirer in relation to any period in consideration of the bailment or hiring to him of goods under the agreement.]]

[732B]

NOTES

Commencement: 16 June 2006 (sub-s (8)); 1 October 2008 (sub-ss (1)–(7), (9)–(12)).

Inserted, together with preceding cross-heading, by the Consumer Credit Act 2006, s 9, as from dates as noted above and subject to transitional provisions in s 69(1) of, and Sch 3, paras 1, 6 to, that Act at **[2077]**, **[2079]**.

Sub-s (5): words in square brackets substituted by the Legislative Reform (Consumer Credit) Order 2008, SI 2008/2826, art 8(a), as from 31 October 2008.

Sub-s (13): added by SI 2008/2826, art 8(b), as from 31 October 2008.

Regulations: the Consumer Credit (Information Requirements and Duration of Licences and Charges) Regulations 2007, SI 2007/1167 at **[3488]**.

[86C Notice of sums in arrears under running-account credit agreements

(1)   This section applies where at any time the following conditions are satisfied—

(a)   that the debtor under an applicable agreement is required to have made at least two payments under the agreement before that time;

(b)   that the last two payments which he is required to have made before that time have not been made;

(c)   that the creditor has not already been required to give a notice under this section in relation to either of those payments; and

(d)   if a judgment has been given in relation to the agreement before that time, that there is no sum still to be paid under the judgment by the debtor.

(2)   The creditor shall, no later than the end of the period within which he is next required to give a statement under section 78(4) in relation to the agreement, give the debtor a notice under this section.

(3)   The notice shall include a copy of the current arrears information sheet under section 86A.

(4)   The notice may be incorporated in a statement or other notice which the creditor gives the debtor in relation to the agreement by virtue of another provision of this Act.

(5)   The debtor shall have no liability to pay any sum in connection with the preparation or the giving to him of the notice.

(6)   Regulations may make provision about the form and content of notices under this section.

(7)   In this section "applicable agreement" means an agreement which—

(a)   is a regulated agreement for running-account credit; and

(b)   is neither a non-commercial agreement nor a small agreement.

[(8)   In this section "payments" means payments to be made at predetermined intervals provided for under the terms of the agreement.]]

[732C]

NOTES

Commencement: 16 June 2006 (sub-s (6)); 1 October 2008 (sub-ss (1)–(5), (7)).

Inserted by the Consumer Credit Act 2006, s 10, as from dates as noted above and subject to transitional provisions in s 69(1) of, and Sch 3, paras 1, 7 to, that Act at **[2077]**, **[2079]**.

Sub-s (8): added by the Legislative Reform (Consumer Credit) Order 2008, SI 2008/2826, art 9, as from 31 October 2008.

Regulations: the Consumer Credit (Information Requirements and Duration of Licences and Charges) Regulations 2007, SI 2007/1167 at **[3488]**.

[86D   Failure to give notice of sums in arrears

(1)   This section applies where the creditor or owner under an agreement is under a duty to give the debtor or hirer notices under section 86B but fails to give him such a notice—

(a)   within the period mentioned in subsection (2)(a) of that section; or

(b)   within the period of six months beginning with the day after the day on which such a notice was last given to him.

(2)   This section also applies where the creditor under an agreement is under a duty to give the debtor a notice under section 86C but fails to do so before the end of the period mentioned in subsection (2) of that section.

(3)   The creditor or owner shall not be entitled to enforce the agreement during the period of non-compliance.

(4)   The debtor or hirer shall have no liability to pay—

(a)   any sum of interest to the extent calculated by reference to the period of non-compliance or to any part of it; or

(b)   any default sum which (apart from this paragraph)—

(i)   would have become payable during the period of non-compliance; or

(ii)   would have become payable after the end of that period in connection with a breach of the agreement which occurs during that period (whether or not the breach continues after the end of that period).

(5)   In this section "the period of non-compliance" means, in relation to a failure to give a notice under section 86B or 86C to the debtor or hirer, the period which—

(a)   begins immediately after the end of the period mentioned in (as the case may be) subsection (1)(a) or (b) or (2); and

(b)   ends at the end of the day mentioned in subsection (6).

(6)   That day is—

(a)   in the case of a failure to give a notice under section 86B as mentioned in subsection (1)(a) of this section, the day on which the notice is given to the debtor or hirer;

(b)   in the case of a failure to give a notice under that section as mentioned in subsection (1)(b) of this section, the earlier of the following—
    (i)   the day on which the notice is given to the debtor or hirer;
    (ii)   the day on which the condition mentioned in subsection (4)(a) of that section is satisfied;

(c)   in the case of a failure to give a notice under section 86C, the day on which the notice is given to the debtor.]

[732D]

NOTES
Commencement: 1 October 2008.
Inserted by the Consumer Credit Act 2006, s 11, as from 1 October 2008.

[86E Notice of default sums

(1)   This section applies where a default sum becomes payable under a regulated agreement by the debtor or hirer.

(2)   The creditor or owner shall, within the prescribed period after the default sum becomes payable, give the debtor or hirer a notice under this section.

(3)   The notice under this section may be incorporated in a statement or other notice which the creditor or owner gives the debtor or hirer in relation to the agreement by virtue of another provision of this Act.

(4)   The debtor or hirer shall have no liability to pay interest in connection with the default sum to the extent that the interest is calculated by reference to a period occurring before the 29th day after the day on which the debtor or hirer is given the notice under this section.

(5)   If the creditor or owner fails to give the debtor or hirer the notice under this section within the period mentioned in subsection (2), he shall not be entitled to enforce the agreement until the notice is given to the debtor or hirer.

(6)   The debtor or hirer shall have no liability to pay any sum in connection with the preparation or the giving to him of the notice under this section.

(7)   Regulations may—
    (a)   provide that this section does not apply in relation to a default sum which is less than a prescribed amount;
    (b)   make provision about the form and content of notices under this section.

(8)   This section does not apply in relation to a non-commercial agreement or to a small agreement.]

[732E]

NOTES
Commencement: 16 June 2006 (sub-s (2) for the purpose of prescribing the period referred to therein, sub-s (7)); 1 October 2008 (sub-ss (1), (3)–(6), (8), sub-s (2) otherwise).
Inserted by the Consumer Credit Act 2006, s 12, as from dates as noted above and subject to transitional provisions in s 69(1) of, and Sch 3, paras 1, 8 to, that Act at **[2077]**, **[2079]**.
Regulations: the Consumer Credit (Information Requirements and Duration of Licences and Charges) Regulations 2007, SI 2007/1167 at **[3488]**.

[86F Interest on default sums

(1)   This section applies where a default sum becomes payable under a regulated agreement by the debtor or hirer.

(2)   The debtor or hirer shall only be liable to pay interest in connection with the default sum if the interest is simple interest.]

[732F]

NOTES
Commencement: 1 October 2008.
Inserted by the Consumer Credit Act 2006, s 13, as from 1 October 2008, subject to transitional provisions in s 69(1) of, and Sch 3, paras 1, 9 to, that Act at **[2077]**, **[2079]**.

Default notices

87 Need for default notice

(1)   Service of a notice on the debtor or hirer in accordance with section 88 (a "default notice") is necessary before the creditor or owner can become entitled, by reason of any breach by the debtor or hirer of a regulated agreement,—
    (a)   to terminate the agreement, or
    (b)   to demand earlier payment of any sum, or

(c)   to recover possession of any goods or land, or
(d)   to treat any right conferred on the debtor or hirer by the agreement as terminated, restricted or deferred, or
(e)   to enforce any security.

(2)   Subsection (1) does not prevent the creditor from treating the right to draw upon any credit as restricted or deferred, and taking such steps as may be necessary to make the restriction or deferment effective.

(3)   The doing of an act by which a floating charge becomes fixed is not enforcement of a security.

(4)   Regulations may provide that subsection (1) is not to apply to agreements described by the regulations.

[(5)   Subsection (1)(d) does not apply in a case referred to in section 98A(4) (termination or suspension of debtor's right to draw on credit under open-end agreement).]

[733]

NOTES
    For the text of this section as it had effect on 15 June 2006, prior to amendments made by the Consumer Credit Act 2006 and subsequent amendments, see the Appendix at [A83].
    Sub-s (5): added by the Consumer Credit (EU Directive) Regulations 2010, SI 2010/1010, regs 2, 37, as from 1 February 2011, with effect in relation to certain agreements before that date, as provided for in regs 100–101A of the 2010 Regulations at **[3941]–[3942A]**.
    Regulations: the Consumer Credit (Enforcement, Default and Termination Notices) Regulations 1983, SI 1983/1561.

88   Contents and effect of default notice

(1)   The default notice must be in the prescribed form and specify—
    (a)   the nature of the alleged breach;
    (b)   if the breach is capable of remedy, what action is required to remedy it and the date before which that action is to be taken;
    (c)   if the breach is not capable of remedy, the sum (if any) required to be paid as compensation for the breach, and the date before which it is to be paid.

(2)   A date specified under subsection (1) must not be less than [14] days after the date of service of the default notice, and the creditor or owner shall not take action such as is mentioned in section 87(1) before the date so specified or (if no requirement is made under subsection (1)) before those [14] days have elapsed.

(3)   The default notice must not treat as a breach failure to comply with a provision of the agreement which becomes operative only on breach of some other provision, but if the breach of that other provision is not duly remedied or compensation demanded under subsection (1) is not duly paid, or (where no requirement is made under subsection (1)) if the [14] days mentioned in subsection (2) have elapsed, the creditor or owner may treat the failure as a breach and section 87(1) shall not apply to it.

(4)   The default notice must contain information in the prescribed terms about the consequences of failure to comply with it [and any other prescribed matters relating to the agreement].

[(4A)   The default notice must also include a copy of the current default information sheet under section 86A.]

(5)   A default notice making a requirement under subsection (1) may include a provision for the taking of action such as is mentioned in section 87(1) at any time after the restriction imposed by subsection (2) will cease, together with a statement that the provision will be ineffective if the breach is duly remedied or the compensation duly paid.

[734]

NOTES
    For the text of this section as it had effect on 15 June 2006, prior to amendments made by the Consumer Credit Act 2006 and subsequent amendments, see the Appendix at [A84].
    Sub-ss (2), (3): number in square brackets in each place it appears substituted by the Consumer Credit Act 2006, s 14(1), as from 1 October 2006, subject to transitional provisions in s 69(1) of, and Sch 3, paras 1, 10 to, that Act at **[2077]**, **[2079]**.
    Sub-s (4): words in square brackets added by the Consumer Credit Act 2006, s 14(2), as from 16 June 2006, subject to transitional provisions in s 69(1) of, and Sch 3, paras 1, 2 to, that Act at **[2077]**, **[2079]**.
    Sub-s (4A): inserted by the Consumer Credit Act 2006, s 14(3), as from 1 October 2008, subject to transitional provisions in s 69(1) of, and Sch 3, paras 1, 10 to, that Act at **[2077]**, **[2079]**.
    Regulations: the Consumer Credit (Enforcement, Default and Termination Notices) Regulations 1983, SI 1983/1561; the Consumer Credit (Information Requirements and Duration of Licences and Charges) Regulations 2007, SI 2007/1167 at **[3488]**.

89   Compliance with default notice

If before the date specified for that purpose in the default notice the debtor or hirer takes the action specified under section 88(1)(b) or (c) the breach shall be treated as not having occurred.

[735]

Further restriction of remedies for default

90   Retaking of protected hire-purchase etc goods

(1)   At any time when—
   (a)   the debtor is in breach of a regulated hire-purchase or a regulated conditional sale agreement relating to goods, and
   (b)   the debtor has paid to the creditor one-third or more of the total price of the goods, and
   (c)   the property in the goods remains in the creditor,
the creditor is not entitled to recover possession of the goods from the debtor except on an order of the court.

(2)   Where under a hire-purchase or conditional sale agreement the creditor is required to carry out any installation and the agreement specifies, as part of the total price, the amount to be paid in respect of the installation (the "installation charge") the reference in subsection (1)(b) to one third of the total price shall be construed as a reference to the aggregate of the installation charge and one third of the remainder of the total price.

(3)   In a case where—
   (a)   subsection (1)(a) is satisfied, but not subsection (1)(b), and
   (b)   subsection (1)(b) was satisfied on a previous occasion in relation to an earlier agreement, being a regulated hire-purchase or regulated conditional sale agreement, between the same parties, and relating to any of the goods comprised in the later agreement (whether or not other goods were also included),
subsection (1) shall apply to the later agreement with the omission of paragraph (b).

(4)   If the later agreement is a modifying agreement, subsection (3) shall apply with the substitution, for the second reference to the later agreement, of a reference to the modifying agreement.

(5)   Subsection (1) shall not apply, or shall cease to apply, to an agreement if the debtor has terminated, or terminates, the agreement.

(6)   Where subsection (1) applies to an agreement at the death of the debtor, it shall continue to apply (in relation to the possessor of the goods) until the grant of probate or administration, or (in Scotland) confirmation (on which the personal representative would fall to be treated as the debtor).

(7)   Goods falling within this section are in this Act referred to as "protected goods".

[736]

91   Consequences of breach of s 90

If goods are recovered by the creditor in contravention of section 90—
   (a)   the regulated agreement, if not previously terminated, shall terminate, and
   (b)   the debtor shall be released from all liability under the agreement, and shall be entitled to recover from the creditor all sums paid by the debtor under the agreement.

[737]

92   Recovery of possession of goods or land

(1)   Except under an order of the court, the creditor or owner shall not be entitled to enter any premises to take possession of goods subject to a regulated hire-purchase agreement, regulated conditional sale agreement or regulated consumer hire agreement.

(2)   At any time when the debtor is in breach of a regulated conditional sale agreement relating to land, the creditor is entitled to recover possession of the land from the debtor, or any person claiming under him, on an order of the court only.

(3)   An entry in contravention of subsection (1) or (2) is actionable as a breach of statutory duty.

[738]

93   Interest not to be increased on default

The debtor under a regulated consumer credit agreement shall not be obliged to pay interest on sums which, in breach of the agreement, are unpaid by him at a rate—
   (a)   where the total charge for credit includes an item in respect of interest, exceeding the rate of that interest, or
   (b)   in any other case, exceeding what would be the rate of the total charge for credit if any items included in the total charge for credit by virtue of section 20(2) were disregarded.

[739]

93A   *(Applies to Scotland only.)*

Early payment by debtor

94 Right to complete payments ahead of time

(1) The debtor under a regulated consumer credit agreement is entitled at any time, by notice to the creditor and the payment to the creditor of all amounts payable by the debtor to him under the agreement [and any amount which the creditor claims under section 95A(2)] (less any rebate allowable under section 95), to discharge the debtor's indebtedness under the agreement.

(2) A notice under subsection (1) may embody the exercise by the debtor of any option to purchase goods conferred on him by the agreement, and deal with any other matter arising on, or in relation to, the termination of the agreement.

[(3) The debtor under a regulated consumer credit agreement, other than an agreement secured on land, is entitled at any time to discharge part of his indebtedness by taking the steps in subsection (4).

(4) The steps referred to in subsection (3) are as follows—
  (a) he provides notice to the creditor,
  (b) he pays to the creditor some of the amount payable by him to the creditor under the agreement before the time fixed by the agreement, and
  (c) he makes the payment—
    (i) before the end of the period of 28 days beginning with the day following that on which notice under paragraph (a) was received by the creditor, or
    (ii) on or before any later date specified in the notice.

(5) Where a debtor takes the steps in subsection (4) his indebtedness shall be discharged by an amount equal to the sum of the amount paid and any rebate allowable under section 95 less any amount which the creditor claims under section 95A(2).

(6) A notice—
  (a) under subsection (1), other than a notice relating to a regulated consumer credit agreement secured on land, or
  (b) under subsection (4)(a),
need not be in writing.]

[740]

NOTES

For the text of this section as it had effect on 15 June 2006, prior to amendments made by the Consumer Credit Act 2006 and subsequent amendments, see the Appendix at [A90].

Sub-s (1): words in square brackets inserted by the Consumer Credit (EU Directive) Regulations 2010, SI 2010/1010, regs 2, 30(a), as from 1 February 2011, with effect in relation to certain agreements before that date, as provided for in regs 100–101A of the 2010 Regulations at **[3941]–[3942A]**.

Sub-ss (3)–(6): added by SI 2010/1010, regs 2, 30(b), as from 1 February 2011, with effect in relation to certain agreements before that date, as provided for in regs 100–101A of the 2010 Regulations at **[3941]–[3942A]**.

---

95 Rebate on early settlement

(1) Regulations may provide for the allowance of a rebate of charges for credit to the debtor under a regulated consumer credit agreement where, under section 94, on refinancing, on breach of the agreement, or for any other reason, his indebtedness is discharged [or is discharged in part] or becomes payable before the time fixed by the agreement, or any sum becomes payable by him before the time so fixed.

(2) Regulations under subsection (1) may provide for calculation of the rebate by reference to any sums paid or payable by the debtor or his relative under or in connection with the agreement (whether to the creditor or some other person), including sums under linked transactions and other items in the total charge for credit.

[741]

NOTES

For the text of this section as it had effect on 15 June 2006, prior to amendments made by the Consumer Credit Act 2006 and subsequent amendments, see the Appendix at [A91].

Sub-s (1): words in square brackets inserted by the Consumer Credit (EU Directive) Regulations 2010, SI 2010/1010, regs 2, 31, as from 1 February 2011, with effect in relation to certain agreements before that date, as provided for in regs 100–101A of the 2010 Regulations at **[3941]–[3942A]**.

Regulations: the Consumer Credit (Early Settlement) Regulations 2004, SI 2004/1483 at **[3389]**.

[95A Compensatory amount

(1) This section applies where—
  (a) a regulated consumer credit agreement, other than an agreement secured on land, provides for the rate of interest on the credit to be fixed for a period of time, and
  (b) under section 94 the debtor discharges all or part of his indebtedness during that period.

(2)   The creditor may claim an amount equal to the cost which the creditor has incurred as a result only of the debtor's indebtedness being discharged during that period if—

    (a)   the amount of the payment under section 94 exceeds £8,000 or, where more than one such payment is made in any 12 month period, the total of those payments exceeds £8,000,

    (b)   the agreement is not a debtor-creditor agreement enabling the debtor to overdraw on a current account, and

    (c)   the amount of the payment under section 94 is not paid from the proceeds of a contract of payment protection insurance.

(3)   The amount in subsection (2)—

    (a)   must be fair,

    (b)   must be objectively justified, and

    (c)   must not exceed whichever is the higher of—

        (i)   the relevant percentage of the amount of the payment under section 94, and

        (ii)   the total amount of interest that would have been paid by the debtor under the agreement in the period from the date on which the debtor makes the payment under section 94 to the date fixed by the agreement for the discharge of the indebtedness of the debtor.

(4)   In subsection (3)(c)(i) "relevant percentage" means—

    (a)   1%, where the period from the date on which the debtor makes the payment under section 94 to the date fixed by the agreement for the discharge of the indebtedness of the debtor is more than one year, or

    (b)   0.5%, where that period is equal to or less than one year.]

[741A]

NOTES

Commencement: 1 February 2011.

Inserted by the Consumer Credit (EU Directive) Regulations 2010, SI 2010/1010, regs 2, 32, as from 1 February 2011, with effect in relation to certain agreements before that date, as provided for in regs 100–101A of the 2010 Regulations at **[3941]–[3942A]**.

96   Effect on linked transactions

(1)   Where for any reason the indebtedness of the debtor under a regulated consumer credit agreement is discharged before the time fixed by the agreement, he, and any relative of his, shall at the same time be discharged from any liability under a linked transaction, other than a debt which has already become payable.

(2)   Subsection (1) does not apply to a linked transaction which is itself an agreement providing the debtor or his relative with credit.

(3)   Regulations may exclude linked transactions of the prescribed description from the operation of subsection (1).

[742]

NOTES

Regulations: the Consumer Credit (Enforcement, Default and Termination Notices) Regulations 1983, SI 1983/1561.

97   Duty to give information

(1)   The creditor under a regulated consumer credit agreement, within the prescribed period after he has received a request *in writing* to that effect from the debtor, shall give the debtor a statement in the prescribed form indicating, according to the information to which it is practicable for him to refer, the amount of the payment required to discharge the debtor's indebtedness under the agreement, together with the prescribed particulars showing how the amount is arrived at.

(2)   Subsection (1) does not apply to a request made less than one month after a previous request under that subsection relating to the same agreement was complied with.

[(2A)   A request under subsection (1) need not be in writing unless the agreement is secured on land.]

(3)   If the creditor fails to comply with subsection (1)—

    (a)   he is not entitled, while the default continues, to enforce the agreement; ...

    (b)   ...

[743]

NOTES

For the text of this section as it had effect on 15 June 2006, prior to amendments made by the Consumer Credit Act 2006 and subsequent amendments, see the Appendix at **[A93]**.

Sub-s (1): words in italics repealed by the Consumer Credit (EU Directive) Regulations 2010, SI 2010/1010, regs 2, 33(a), as from 1 February 2011, with effect in relation to certain agreements before that date, as provided for in regs 100–101A of the 2010 Regulations at **[3941]–[3942A]**.

Sub-s (2A): inserted by SI 2010/1010, regs 2, 33(b), as from 1 February 2011, with effect in relation to certain agreements before that date, as provided for in regs 100–101A of the 2010 Regulations at **[3941]–[3942A]**.

Sub-s (3): words omitted repealed by the Consumer Protection from Unfair Trading Regulations 2008, SI 2008/1277, reg 30(1), (3), Sch 2, Pt 1, paras 17, 23, Sch 4, as from 26 May 2008.

Regulations: the Consumer Credit (Settlement Information) Regulations 1983, SI 1983/1564; the Consumer Credit (Early Settlement) Regulations 2004, SI 2004/1483 at **[3389]**.

[97A Duty to give information on partial repayment

(1)   Where a debtor under a regulated consumer credit agreement—
 (a)   makes a payment by virtue of which part of his indebtedness is discharged under section 94, and
 (b)   at the same time or subsequently requests the creditor to give him a statement concerning the effect of the payment on the debtor's indebtedness,
the creditor must give the statement to the debtor before the end of the period of seven working days beginning with the day following that on which the creditor receives the request.

(2)   The statement shall be in writing and shall contain the following particulars—
 (a)   a description of the agreement sufficient to identify it,
 (b)   the name, postal address and, where appropriate, any other address of the creditor and the debtor,
 (c)   where the creditor is claiming an amount under section 95A(2), that amount and the method used to determine it,
 (d)   the amount of any rebate to which the debtor is entitled—
  (i)   under the agreement, or
  (ii)   by virtue of section 95 where that is higher,
 (e)   where the amount of the rebate mentioned in paragraph (d)(ii) is given, a statement indicating that this amount has been calculated having regard to the Consumer Credit (Early Settlement) Regulations 2004,
 (f)   where the debtor is not entitled to any rebate, a statement to this effect,
 (g)   any change to—
  (i)   the number, timing or amount of repayments to be made under the agreement, or
  (ii)   the duration of the agreement,
  which results from the partial discharge of the indebtedness of the debtor, and
 (h)   the amount of the debtor's indebtedness remaining under the agreement at the date the creditor gives the statement.]

[743A]

NOTES
Commencement: 1 February 2011.
Inserted by the Consumer Credit (EU Directive) Regulations 2010, SI 2010/1010, regs 2, 34, as from 1 February 2011, with effect in relation to certain agreements before that date, as provided for in regs 100–101A of the 2010 Regulations at **[3941]–[3942A]**.

Termination of agreements

98   Duty to give notice of termination (non-default cases)

(1)   The creditor or owner is not entitled to terminate a regulated agreement except by or after giving the debtor or hirer not less than seven days' notice of the termination.

(2)   Subsection (1) applies only where—
 (a)   a period for the duration of the agreement is specified in the agreement, and
 (b)   that period has not ended when the creditor or owner does an act mentioned in subsection (1),
but so applies notwithstanding that, under the agreement, any party is entitled to terminate it before the end of the period so specified.

(3)   A notice under subsection (1) is ineffective if not in the prescribed form.

(4)   Subsection (1) does not prevent a creditor from treating the right to draw on any credit as restricted or deferred and taking such steps as may be necessary to make the restriction or deferment effective.

(5)   Regulations may provide that subsection (1) is not to apply to agreements described by the regulations.

(6)   Subsection (1) does not apply to the termination of a regulated agreement by reason of any breach by the debtor or hirer of the agreement.

[744]

NOTES

Regulations: the Consumer Credit (Enforcement, Default and Termination Notices) Regulations 1983, SI 1983/1561.

[98A Termination etc of open-end consumer credit agreements

(1) The debtor under a regulated open-end consumer credit agreement, other than an excluded agreement, may by notice terminate the agreement, free of charge, at any time, subject to any period of notice not exceeding one month provided for by the agreement.

(2) Notice under subsection (1) need not be in writing unless the creditor so requires.

(3) Where a regulated open-end consumer credit agreement, other than an excluded agreement, provides for termination of the agreement by the creditor—

    (a) the termination must be by notice served on the debtor, and

    (b) the termination may not take effect until after the end of the period of two months, or such longer period as the agreement may provide, beginning with the day after the day on which notice is served.

(4) Where a regulated open-end consumer credit agreement, other than an excluded agreement, provides for termination or suspension by the creditor of the debtor's right to draw on credit—

    (a) to terminate or suspend the right to draw on credit the creditor must serve a notice on the debtor before the termination or suspension or, if that is not practicable, immediately afterwards,

    (b) the notice must give reasons for the termination or suspension, and

    (c) the reasons must be objectively justified.

(5) Subsection (4)(a) and (b) does not apply where giving the notice—

    (a) is prohibited by an EU obligation, or

    (b) would, or would be likely to, prejudice—

        (i) the prevention or detection of crime,

        (ii) the apprehension or prosecution of offenders, or

        (iii) the administration of justice.

(6) An objectively justified reason under subsection (4)(c) may, for example, relate to—

    (a) the unauthorised or fraudulent use of credit, or

    (b) a significantly increased risk of the debtor being unable to fulfil his obligation to repay the credit.

(7) Subsections (1) and (3) do not affect any right to terminate an agreement for breach of contract.

(8) For the purposes of this section an agreement is an excluded agreement if it is—

    (a) an authorised non-business overdraft agreement,

    (b) an authorised business overdraft agreement,

    (c) a debtor-creditor agreement arising where the holder of a current account overdraws on the account without a pre-arranged overdraft or exceeds a pre-arranged overdraft limit, or

    (d) an agreement secured on land.]

[744A]

NOTES

Commencement: 1 February 2011.

Inserted by the Consumer Credit (EU Directive) Regulations 2010, SI 2010/1010, regs 2, 38, as from 1 February 2011, with effect in relation to certain agreements before that date, as provided for in regs 100–101A of the 2010 Regulations at **[3941]–[3942A]**.

99 Right to terminate hire-purchase etc agreements

(1) At any time before the final payment by the debtor under a regulated hire-purchase or regulated conditional sale agreement falls due, the debtor shall be entitled to terminate the agreement by giving notice to any person entitled or authorised to receive the sums payable under the agreement.

(2) Termination of an agreement under subsection (1) does not affect any liability under the agreement which has accrued before the termination.

(3) Subsection (1) does not apply to a conditional sale agreement relating to land after the title to the land has passed to the debtor.

(4) In the case of a conditional sale agreement relating to goods, where the property in the goods, having become vested in the debtor, is transferred to a person who does not become the debtor under the agreement, the debtor shall not thereafter be entitled to terminate the agreement under subsection (1).

(5)   Subject to subsection (4), where a debtor under a conditional sale agreement relating to goods, terminates the agreement under this section after the property in the goods has become vested in him, the property in the goods shall thereupon vest in the person (the "previous owner") in whom it was vested immediately before it became vested in the debtor:

Provided that if the previous owner has died, or any other event has occurred whereby that property, if vested in him immediately before that event, would thereupon have vested in some other person, the property shall be treated as having devolved as if it had been vested in the previous owner immediately before his death or immediately before that event, as the case may be.

[745]

100   Liability of debtor on termination of hire-purchase etc agreement

(1)   Where a regulated hire-purchase or regulated conditional sale agreement is terminated under section 99 the debtor shall be liable, unless the agreement provides for a smaller payment, or does not provide for any payment, to pay to the creditor the amount (if any) by which one-half of the total price exceeds the aggregate of the sums paid and the sums due in respect of the total price immediately before the termination.

(2)   Where under a hire-purchase or conditional sale agreement the creditor is required to carry out any installation and the agreement specifies, as part of the total price, the amount to be paid in respect of the installation (the "installation charge") the reference in subsection (1) to one-half of the total price shall be construed as a reference to the aggregate of the installation charge and one-half of the remainder of the total price.

(3)   If in any action the court is satisfied that a sum less than the amount specified in subsection (1) would be equal to the loss sustained by the creditor in consequence of the termination of the agreement by the debtor, the court may make an order for the payment of that sum in lieu of the amount specified in subsection (1).

(4)   If the debtor has contravened an obligation to take reasonable care of the goods or land, the amount arrived at under subsection (1) shall be increased by the sum required to recompense the creditor for that contravention, and subsection (2) shall have effect accordingly.

(5)   Where the debtor, on the termination of the agreement, wrongfully retains possession of goods to which the agreement relates, then, in any action brought by the creditor to recover possession of the goods from the debtor, the court, unless it is satisfied that having regard to the circumstances it would not be just to do so, shall order the goods to be delivered to the creditor without giving the debtor an option to pay the value of the goods.

[746]

101   Right to terminate hire agreement

(1)   The hirer under a regulated consumer hire agreement is entitled to terminate the agreement by giving notice to any person entitled or authorised to receive the sums payable under the agreement.

(2)   Termination of an agreement under subsection (1) does not affect any liability under the agreement which has accrued before the termination.

(3)   A notice under subsection (1) shall not expire earlier than eighteen months after the making of the agreement, but apart from that the minimum period of notice to be given under subsection (1), unless the agreement provides for a shorter period, is as follows.

(4)   If the agreement provides for the making of payments by the hirer to the owner at equal intervals, the minimum period of notice is the length of one interval or three months, whichever is less.

(5)   If the agreement provides for the making of such payments at differing intervals, the minimum period of notice is the length of the shortest interval or three months, whichever is less.

(6)   In any other case, the minimum period of notice is three months.

(7)   This section does not apply to—

     (a)   any agreement which provides for the making by the hirer of payments which in total (and without breach of the agreement) exceed [£1,500] in any year, or

     (b)   any agreement where—

         (i)   goods are bailed or (in Scotland) hired to the hirer for the purposes of a business carried on by him, or the hirer holds himself out as requiring the goods for those purposes, and

         (ii)   the goods are selected by the hirer, and acquired by the owner for the purposes of the agreement at the request of the hirer from any person other than the owner's associate, or

     (c)   any agreement where the hirer requires, or holds himself out as requiring, the goods for the purpose of bailing or hiring them to other persons in the course of a business carried on by him.

(8)   If, on an application made to the [OFT] by a person carrying on a consumer hire business, it appears to the [OFT] that it would be in the interest of hirers to do so, [it] may by notice to the applicant direct that[, subject to such conditions (if any) as it may specify, this section shall not apply to consumer hire agreements made by the applicant; and this Act shall have effect accordingly].

[(8A)   If it appears to the OFT that it would be in the interests of hirers to do so, it may by general notice direct that, subject to such conditions (if any) as it may specify, this section shall not apply to a consumer hire agreement if the agreement falls within a specified description; and this Act shall have effect accordingly.]

(9)   In the case of a modifying agreement subsection (3) shall apply with the substitution, for "the making of the agreement" of "the making of the original agreement".

[747]

NOTES
    For the text of this section as it had effect on 15 June 2006, prior to amendments made by the Consumer Credit Act 2006 and subsequent amendments, see the Appendix at [A97].
    References to the OFT, etc: as to the abolition of the office of the Director General of Fair Trading and the substitution of the original references to the Director (and related expressions), see the note preceding s 1 at [651].
    Sub-s (7): sum in square brackets substituted by the Consumer Credit (Further Increase in Monetary Amounts) Order 1998, SI 1998/997, art 3, Schedule, as from 1 May 1998.
    Sub-s (8): words in fourth pair of square brackets substituted by the Consumer Credit Act 2006, s 63(2), as from 16 June 2006.
    Sub-s (8A): inserted by the Consumer Credit Act 2006, s 63(1), as from 16 June 2006.

102   Agency for receiving notice of rescission

(1)   Where the debtor or hirer under a regulated agreement claims to have a right to rescind the agreement, each of the following shall be deemed to be the agent of the creditor or owner for the purpose of receiving any notice rescinding the agreement which is served by the debtor or hirer—
    (a)   a credit-broker or supplier who was the negotiator in antecedent negotiations, and
    (b)   any person who, in the course of a business carried on by him, acted on behalf of the debtor or hirer in any negotiations for the agreement.

(2)   In subsection (1) "rescind" does not include—
    (a)   service of a notice of cancellation, or
    (b)   termination of an agreement under section 99 or 101, or by the exercise of a right or power in that behalf expressly conferred by the agreement.

[748]

103   Termination statements

(1)   If an individual (the "customer") serves on any person (the "trader") a notice—
    (a)   stating that—
        (i)   the customer was the debtor or hirer under a regulated agreement described in the notice, and the trader was the creditor or owner under the agreement, and
        (ii)   the customer has discharged his indebtedness to the trader under the agreement, and
        (iii)   the agreement has ceased to have any operation; and
    (b)   requiring the trader to give the customer a notice, signed by or on behalf of the trader, confirming that those statements are correct,
the trader shall, within the prescribed period after receiving the notice, either comply with it or serve on the customer a counter-notice stating that, as the case may be, he disputes the correctness of the notice or asserts that the customer is not indebted to him under the agreement.

(2)   Where the trader disputes the correctness of the notice he shall give particulars of the way in which he alleges it to be wrong.

(3)   Subsection (1) does not apply in relation to any agreement if the trader has previously complied with that subsection on the service of a notice under it with respect to that agreement.

(4)   Subsection (1) does not apply to a non-commercial agreement.

(5)   ...

[(6)   A breach of the duty imposed by subsection (1) is actionable as a breach of statutory duty.]

[749]

NOTES
    For the text of this section as it had effect on 15 June 2006, prior to amendments made by the Consumer Credit Act 2006 and subsequent amendments, see the Appendix at [A99].
    Sub-s (5): repealed by the Consumer Protection from Unfair Trading Regulations 2008, SI 2008/1277, reg 30(1), (3), Sch 2, Pt 1, paras 17, 24(a), Sch 4, as from 26 May 2008.
    Sub-s (6): added by SI 2008/1277, reg 30(1), Sch 2, Pt 1, paras 17, 24(b), as from 26 May 2008.

Regulations: the Consumer Credit (Prescribed Periods for Giving Information) Regulations 1983, SI 1983/1569.

104   (*Applies to Scotland only.*)

PART VIII
SECURITY

General

105 Form and content of securities

(1)   Any security provided in relation to a regulated agreement shall be expressed in writing.

(2)   Regulations may prescribe the form and content of documents ("security instruments") to be made in compliance with subsection (1).

(3)   Regulations under subsection (2) may in particular—
    (a)   require specified information to be included in the prescribed manner in documents, and other specified material to be excluded;
    (b)   contain requirements to ensure that specified information is clearly brought to the attention of the surety, and that one part of a document is not given insufficient or excessive prominence compared with another.

(4)   A security instrument is not properly executed unless—
    (a)   a document in the prescribed form, itself containing all the prescribed terms and conforming to regulations under subsection (2), is signed in the prescribed manner by or on behalf of the surety, and
    (b)   the document embodies all the terms of the security, other than implied terms, and
    (c)   the document, when presented or sent for the purpose of being signed by or on behalf of the surety, is in such a state that its terms are readily legible, and
    (d)   when the document is presented or sent for the purpose of being signed by or on behalf of the surety there is also presented or sent a copy of the document.

(5)   A security instrument is not properly executed unless—
    (a)   where the security is provided after, or at the time when, the regulated agreement is made, a copy of the executed agreement, together with a copy of any other document referred to in it, is given to the surety at the time the security is provided, or
    (b)   where the security is provided before the regulated agreement is made, a copy of the executed agreement, together with a copy of any other document referred to in it, is given to the surety within seven days after the regulated agreement is made.

(6)   Subsection (1) does not apply to a security provided by the debtor or hirer.

(7)   If—
    (a)   in contravention of subsection (1) a security is not expressed in writing, or
    (b)   a security instrument is improperly executed,
the security (so far as provided in relation to a regulated agreement) is enforceable against the surety on an order of the court only.

(8)   If an application for an order under subsection (7) is dismissed (except on technical grounds only) section 106 (ineffective securities) shall apply to the security.

(9)   Regulations under section 60(1) shall include provision requiring documents embodying regulated agreements also to embody any security provided in relation to a regulated agreement by the debtor or hirer.

[750]

NOTES
    Regulations: the Consumer Credit (Agreements) Regulations 1983, SI 1983/1553; the Consumer Credit (Guarantees and Indemnities) Regulations 1983, SI 1983/1556; the Consumer Credit (Agreements) Regulations 2010, SI 2010/1014 at **[3979]**.

106 Ineffective securities

Where, under any provision of this Act, this section is applied to any security provided in relation to a regulated agreement, then, subject to section 177 (saving for registered charges),—
    (a)   the security, so far as it is so provided, shall be treated as never having effect;
    (b)   any property lodged with the creditor or owner solely for the purposes of the security as so provided shall be returned by him forthwith;
    (c)   the creditor or owner shall take any necessary action to remove or cancel an entry in any register, so far as the entry relates to the security as so provided; and

(d) any amount received by the creditor or owner on realisation of the security shall, so far as it is referable to the agreement, be repaid to the surety.

[751]

107 Duty to give information to surety under fixed-sum credit agreement

(1) The creditor under a regulated agreement for fixed-sum credit in relation to which security is provided, within the prescribed period after receiving a request in writing to that effect from the surety and payment of a fee of [£1], shall give to the surety (if a different person from the debtor)—
(a) a copy of the executed agreement (if any) and of any other document referred to in it;
(b) a copy of the security instrument (if any); and
(c) a statement signed by or on behalf of the creditor showing, according to the information to which it is practicable for him to refer,—
    (i) the total sum paid under the agreement by the debtor,
    (ii) the total sum which has become payable under the agreement by the debtor but remains unpaid, and the various amounts comprised in that total sum, with the date when each became due, and
    (iii) the total sum which is to become payable under the agreement by the debtor, and the various amounts comprised in that total sum, with the date, or mode of determining the date, when each becomes due.

(2) If the creditor possesses insufficient information to enable him to ascertain the amount and dates mentioned in subsection (1)(c) (iii), he shall be taken to comply with that sub-paragraph if his statement under subsection (1)(c) gives the basis on which, under the regulated agreement, they would fall to be ascertained.

(3) Subsection (1) does not apply to—
(a) an agreement under which no sum is, or will or may become, payable by the debtor, or
(b) a request made less than one month after a previous request under that subsection relating to the same agreement was complied with.

(4) If the creditor under an agreement fails to comply with subsection (1)—
(a) he is not entitled, while the default continues, to enforce the security, so far as provided in relation to the agreement; ...
(b) ...

(5) This section does not apply to a non-commercial agreement.

[752]

NOTES
For the text of this section as it had effect on 15 June 2006, prior to amendments made by the Consumer Credit Act 2006 and subsequent amendments, see the Appendix at [A102].
Sub-s (1): sum in square brackets substituted by the Consumer Credit (Further Increase in Monetary Amounts) Order 1998, SI 1998/997, art 3, Schedule, as from 1 May 1998.
Sub-s (4): words omitted repealed by the Consumer Protection from Unfair Trading Regulations 2008, SI 2008/1277, reg 30(1), (3), Sch 2, Pt 1, paras 17, 25, Sch 4, as from 26 May 2008.
Regulations: the Consumer Credit (Prescribed Periods for Giving Information) Regulations 1983, SI 1983/1569.

108 Duty to give information to surety under running-account credit agreement

(1) The creditor under a regulated agreement for running-account credit in relation to which security is provided, within the prescribed period after receiving a request in writing to that effect from the surety and payment of a fee of [£1], shall give to the surety (if a different person from the debtor)—
(a) a copy of the executed agreement (if any) and of any other document referred to in it;
(b) a copy of the security instrument (if any); and
(c) a statement signed by or on behalf of the creditor showing, according to the information to which it is practicable for him to refer,—
    (i) the state of the account, and
    (ii) the amount, if any, currently payable under the agreement by the debtor to the creditor, and
    (iii) the amounts and due dates of any payments which, if the debtor does not draw further on the account, will later become payable under the agreement by the debtor to the creditor.

(2) If the creditor possesses insufficient information to enable him to ascertain the amounts and dates mentioned in subsection (1)(c)(iii), he shall be taken to comply with that sub-paragraph if his statement under subsection (1)(c) gives basis on which, under the regulated agreement, they would fall to be ascertained.

(3) Subsection (1) does not apply to—
(a) an agreement under which no sum is, or will or may become, payable by the debtor, or

(b)   a request made less than one month after a previous request under that subsection relating to the same agreement was complied with.

(4)   If the creditor under an agreement fails to comply with subsection (1)—

    (a)   he is not entitled, while the default continues, to enforce the security, so far as provided in relation to the agreement; ...

    (b)   ...

(5)   This section does not apply to a non-commercial agreement.

[753]

NOTES

For the text of this section as it had effect on 15 June 2006, prior to amendments made by the Consumer Credit Act 2006 and subsequent amendments, see the Appendix at [A103].

Sub-s (1): sum in square brackets substituted by the Consumer Credit (Further Increase in Monetary Amounts) Order 1998, SI 1998/997, art 3, Schedule, as from 1 May 1998.

Sub-s (4): words omitted repealed by the Consumer Protection from Unfair Trading Regulations 2008, SI 2008/1277, reg 30(1), (3), Sch 2, Pt 1, paras 17, 26, Sch 4, as from 26 May 2008.

Regulations: the Consumer Credit (Prescribed Periods for Giving Information) Regulations 1983, SI 1983/1569.

109   Duty to give information to surety under consumer hire agreement

(1)   The owner under a regulated consumer hire agreement in relation to which security is provided, within the prescribed period after receiving a request in writing to that effect from the surety and payment of a fee of [£1], shall give to the surety (if a different person from the hirer)—

    (a)   a copy of the executed agreement and of any other document referred to in it;

    (b)   a copy of the security instrument (if any); and

    (c)   a statement signed by or on behalf of the owner showing, according to the information to which it is practicable for him to refer, the total sum which has become payable under the agreement by the hirer but remains unpaid and the various amounts comprised in that total sum, with the date when each became due.

(2)   Subsection (1) does not apply to—

    (a)   an agreement under which no sum is, or will or may become, payable by the hirer, or

    (b)   a request made less than one month after a previous request under that subsection relating to the same agreement was complied with.

(3)   If the owner under an agreement fails to comply with subsection (1)—

    (a)   he is not entitled, while the default continues, to enforce the security, so far as provided in relation to the agreement; ...

    (b)   ...

(4)   This section does not apply to a non-commercial agreement.

[754]

NOTES

For the text of this section as it had effect on 15 June 2006, prior to amendments made by the Consumer Credit Act 2006 and subsequent amendments, see the Appendix at [A104].

Sub-s (1): sum in square brackets substituted by the Consumer Credit (Further Increase in Monetary Amounts) Order 1998, SI 1998/997, art 3, Schedule, as from 1 May 1998.

Sub-s (3): words omitted repealed by the Consumer Protection from Unfair Trading Regulations 2008, SI 2008/1277, reg 30(1), (3), Sch 2, Pt 1, paras 17, 27, Sch 4, as from 26 May 2008.

Regulations: the Consumer Credit (Prescribed Periods for Giving Information) Regulations 1983, SI 1983/1569.

110   Duty to give information to debtor or hirer

(1)   The creditor or owner under a regulated agreement, within the prescribed period after receiving a request in writing to that effect from the debtor or hirer and payment of a fee of [£1], shall give the debtor or hirer a copy of any security instrument executed in relation to the agreement after the making of the agreement.

(2)   Subsection (1) does not apply to—

    (a)   a non-commercial agreement, or

    (b)   an agreement under which no sum is, or will or may become, payable by the debtor or hirer, or

    (c)   a request made less than one month after a previous request under subsection (1) relating to the same agreement was complied with.

(3)   If the creditor or owner under an agreement fails to comply with subsection (1)—

    (a)   he is not entitled, while the default continues, to enforce the security (so far as provided in relation to the agreement); ...

    (b)   ...

[755]

NOTES
  For the text of this section as it had effect on 15 June 2006, prior to amendments made by the Consumer Credit Act 2006 and subsequent amendments, see the Appendix at [A105].
  Sub-s (1): sum in square brackets substituted by the Consumer Credit (Further Increase in Monetary Amounts) Order 1998, SI 1998/997, art 3, Schedule, as from 1 May 1998.
  Sub-s (3): words omitted repealed by the Consumer Protection from Unfair Trading Regulations 2008, SI 2008/1277, reg 30(1), (3), Sch 2, Pt 1, paras 17, 28, Sch 4, as from 26 May 2008.
  Regulations: the Consumer Credit (Prescribed Periods for Giving Information) Regulations 1983, SI 1983/1569.

111 Duty to give surety copy of default etc notice

(1)   When a default notice or a notice under section 76(1) or 98(1) is served on a debtor or hirer, a copy of the notice shall be served by the creditor or owner on any surety (if a different person from the debtor or hirer).

(2)   If the creditor or owner fails to comply with subsection (1) in the case of any surety, the security is enforceable against the surety (in respect of the breach or other matter to which the notice relates) on an order of the court only.

[756]

112 Realisation of securities

Subject to section 121, regulations may provide for any matters relating to the sale or other realisation, by the creditor or owner, of property over which any right has been provided by way of security in relation to an actual or prospective regulated agreement, other than a non-commercial agreement.

[757]

113 Act not to be evaded by use of security

(1)   Where a security is provided in relation to an actual or prospective regulated agreement, the security shall not be enforced so as to benefit the creditor or owner, directly or indirectly, to an extent greater (whether as respects the amount of any payment or the time or manner of its being made) than would be the case if the security were not provided and any obligations of the debtor or hirer, or his relative, under or in relation to the agreement were carried out to the extent (if any) to which they would be enforced under this Act.

(2)   In accordance with subsection (1), where a regulated agreement is enforceable on an order of the court or the [OFT] only, any security provided in relation to the agreement is enforceable (so far as provided in relation to the agreement) where such an order has been made in relation to the agreement, but not otherwise.

(3)   Where—
  (a)   a regulated agreement is cancelled under section 69(1) or becomes subject to section 69(2), or
  (b)   a regulated agreement is terminated under section 91, or
  (c)   in relation to any agreement an application for an order under section 40(2), 65(1), 124(1) or 149(2) is dismissed (except on technical grounds only), or
  (d)   a declaration is made by the court under section 142(1) (refusal of enforcement order) as respects any regulated agreement,
section 106 shall apply to any security provided in relation to the agreement.

(4)   Where subsection (3)(d) applies and the declaration relates to a part only of the regulated agreement, section 106 shall apply to the security only so far as it concerns that part.

(5)   In the case of a cancelled agreement, the duty imposed on the debtor or hirer by section 71 or 72 shall not be enforceable before the creditor or owner has discharged any duty imposed on him by section 106 (as applied by subsection (3)(a)).

(6)   If the security is provided in relation to a prospective agreement or transaction, the security shall be enforceable in relation to the agreement or transaction only after the time (if any) when the agreement is made; and until that time the person providing the security shall be entitled, by notice to the creditor or owner, to require that section 106 shall thereupon apply to the security.

(7)   Where an indemnity [or guarantee] is given in a case where the debtor or hirer is a minor, or [an indemnity is given in a case where he] is otherwise not of full capacity, the reference in subsection (1) to the extent to which his obligations would be enforced shall be read in relation to the indemnity [or guarantee] as a reference to the extent to which [those obligations] would be enforced if he were of full capacity.

(8)   Subsections (1) to (3) also apply where a security is provided in relation to an actual or prospective linked transaction, and in that case—
  (a)   references to the agreement shall be read as references to the linked transaction, and

(b) references to the creditor or owner shall be read as references to any person (other than the debtor or hirer, or his relative) who is a party, or prospective party, to the linked transaction.

[758]

NOTES

Sub-s (7): words in square brackets inserted or substituted by the Minors' Contracts Act 1987, s 4(1), as from 9 June 1987.

References to the OFT, etc: as to the abolition of the office of the Director General of Fair Trading and the substitution of the original references to the Director (and related expressions), see the note preceding s 1 at [651].

Pledges

114 Pawn-receipts

(1) At the time he receives the article, a person who takes any article in pawn under a regulated agreement shall give to the person from whom he receives it a receipt in the prescribed form (a "pawn-receipt").

(2) A person who takes any article in pawn from an individual whom he knows to be, or who appears to be and is, a minor commits an offence.

(3) This section and sections 115 to 122 do not apply to—
(a) a pledge of documents of title [or of bearer bonds], or
(b) a non-commercial agreement.

[759]

NOTES

Sub-s (3): words in square brackets inserted by the Banking Act 1979, s 38(2), as from 1 October 1979.

Regulations: the Consumer Credit (Agreements) Regulations 1983, SI 1983/1553; the Consumer Credit (Pawn Receipts) Regulations 1983, SI 1983/1566; the Consumer Credit (Agreements) Regulations 2010, SI 2010/1014 at [3979].

115 Penalty for failure to supply copies of pledge agreement, etc

If the creditor under a regulated agreement to take any article in pawn fails to observe the requirements of sections 62 to 64 or 114(1) in relation to the agreement he commits an offence.

[760]

116 Redemption period

(1) A pawn is redeemable at any time within six months after it was taken.

(2) Subject to subsection (1), the period within which a pawn is redeemable shall be the same as the period fixed by the parties for the duration of the credit secured by the pledge, or such longer period as they may agree.

(3) If the pawn is not redeemed by the end of the period laid down by subsections (1) and (2) (the "redemption period"), it nevertheless remains redeemable until it is realised by the pawnee under section 121, except where under section 120(1)(a) the property in it passes to the pawnee.

(4) No special charge shall be made for redemption of a pawn after the end of the redemption period, and charges in respect of the safe keeping of the pawn shall not be at a higher rate after the end of the redemption period than before.

[761]

117 Redemption procedure

(1) On surrender of the pawn-receipt, and payment of the amount owing, at any time when the pawn is redeemable, the pawnee shall deliver the pawn to the bearer of the pawn-receipt.

(2) Subsection (1) does not apply if the pawnee knows or has reasonable cause to suspect that the bearer of the pawn-receipt is neither the owner of the pawn nor authorised by the owner to redeem it.

(3) The pawnee is not liable to any person in tort or delict for delivering the pawn where subsection (1) applies, or refusing to deliver it where the person demanding delivery does not comply with subsection (1) or, by reason of subsection (2), subsection (1) does not apply.

[762]

118 Loss etc of pawn-receipt

(1) A person (the "claimant") who is not in possession of the pawn-receipt but claims to be the owner of the pawn, or to be otherwise entitled or authorised to redeem it, may do so at any time when it is redeemable by tendering to the pawnee in place of the pawn-receipt—
(a) a statutory declaration made by the claimant in the prescribed form, and with the prescribed contents, or

(b)   where the pawn is security for fixed-sum credit not exceeding [£75] or running-account credit on which the credit limit does not exceed [£75], and the pawnee agrees, a statement in writing in the prescribed form, and with the prescribed contents, signed by the claimant.

(2)   On compliance by the claimant with subsection (1), section 117 shall apply as if the declaration or statement were the pawn-receipt, and the pawn-receipt itself shall become inoperative for the purposes of section 117.

[763]

NOTES
Sub-s (1): sums in square brackets substituted by the Consumer Credit (Further Increase in Monetary Amounts) Order 1998, SI 1998/997, art 3, Schedule, as from 1 May 1998.
Regulations: the Consumer Credit (Loss of Pawn Receipts) Regulations 1983, SI 1983/1567.

119   Unreasonable refusal to deliver pawn

(1)   If a person who has taken a pawn under a regulated agreement refuses without reasonable cause to allow the pawn to be redeemed, he commits an offence.

(2)   On the conviction in England or Wales of a pawnee under subsection (1) where the offence does not amount to theft, [section 148 of the Powers of Criminal Courts (Sentencing) Act 2000 (restitution orders)] shall apply as if the pawnee had been convicted of stealing the pawn.

(3)   On the conviction in Northern Ireland of a pawnee under subsection (1) where the offence does not amount to theft, section 27 (orders for restitution) of the Theft Act (Northern Ireland) 1969, and any provision of the Theft Act (Northern Ireland) 1969 relating to that section, shall apply as if the pawnee had been convicted of stealing the pawn.

[764]

NOTES
Sub-s (2): words in square brackets substituted by the Powers of Criminal Courts (Sentencing) Act 2000, s 165(1), Sch 9, para 45, as from 25 August 2000.

120   Consequence of failure to redeem

(1)   If at the end of the redemption period the pawn has not been redeemed—
(a)   notwithstanding anything in section 113, the property in the pawn passes to the pawnee where *the redemption period is six months and the pawn is security for fixed-sum credit not exceeding [£75] or running-account credit on which the credit limit does not exceed [£75]; or*
[(i)   the redemption period is six months,
(ii)   the pawn is security for fixed-sum credit not exceeding £75 or running-account credit on which the credit limit does not exceed £75, and
(iii)   the pawn was not immediately before the making of the regulated consumer credit agreement a pawn under another regulated consumer credit agreement in respect of which the debtor has discharged his indebtedness in part under section 94(3); or]
(b)   in any other case the pawn becomes realisable by the pawnee.

(2)   Where the debtor or hirer is entitled to apply to the court for a time order under section 129, subsection (1) shall apply with the substitution, for "at the end of the redemption period" of "after the expiry of five days following the end of the redemption period".

[765]

NOTES
For the text of this section as it had effect on 15 June 2006, prior to amendments made by the Consumer Credit Act 2006 and subsequent amendments, see the Appendix at [A115].
Sub-s (1): sums in square brackets substituted by the Consumer Credit (Further Increase in Monetary Amounts) Order 1998, SI 1998/997, art 3, Schedule, as from 1 May 1998; words in italics substituted by subsequent words in square brackets by the Consumer Credit (EU Directive) Regulations 2010, SI 2010/1010, regs 2, 35, as from 1 February 2011, with effect in relation to certain agreements before that date, as provided for in regs 100–101A of the 2010 Regulations at **[3941]–[3942A]**.

121   Realisation of pawn

(1)   When a pawn has become realisable by him, the pawnee may sell it, after giving to the pawnor (except in such cases as may be prescribed) not less than the prescribed period of notice of the intention to sell, indicating in the notice the asking price and such other particulars as may be prescribed.

(2)   Within the prescribed period after the sale takes place, the pawnee shall give the pawnor the prescribed information in writing as to the sale, its proceeds and expenses.

(3) Where the net proceeds of sale are not less than the sum which, if the pawn had been redeemed on the date of the sale, would have been payable for its redemption, the debt secured by the pawn is discharged and any surplus shall be paid by the pawnee to the pawnor.

(4) Where subsection (3) does not apply, the debt shall be treated as from the date of sale as equal to the amount by which the net proceeds of sale fall short of the sum which would have been payable for the redemption of the pawn on that date.

(5) In this section the "net proceeds of sale" is the amount realised (the "gross amount") less the expenses (if any) of the sale.

(6) If the pawnor alleges that the gross amount is less than the true market value of the pawn on the date of sale, it is for the pawnee to prove that he and any agents employed by him in the sale used reasonable care to ensure that the true market value was obtained, and if he fails to do so subsections (3) and (4) shall have effect as if the reference in subsection (5) to the gross amount were a reference to the true market value.

(7) If the pawnor alleges that the expenses of the sale were unreasonably high, it is for the pawnee to prove that they were reasonable, and if he fails to do so subsections (3) and (4) shall have effect as if the reference in subsection (5) to expenses were a reference to reasonable expenses.

[766]

NOTES

Regulations: the Consumer Credit (Realisation of Pawn) Regulations 1983, SI 1983/1568.

122 (*Applies to Scotland only.*)

Negotiable instruments

123 Restrictions on taking and negotiating instruments

(1) A creditor or owner shall not take a negotiable instrument, other than a bank note or cheque, in discharge of any sum payable—
   (a) by the debtor or hirer under a regulated agreement, or
   (b) by any person as surety in relation to the agreement.

(2) The creditor or owner shall not negotiate a cheque taken by him in discharge of a sum payable as mentioned in subsection (1), except to a banker (within the meaning of the Bills of Exchange Act 1882).

(3) The creditor or owner shall not take a negotiable instrument as security for the discharge of any sum payable as mentioned in subsection (1).

(4) A person takes a negotiable instrument as security for the discharge of a sum if the sum is intended to be paid in some other way, and the negotiable instrument is to be presented for payment only if the sum is not paid in that way.

(5) This section does not apply where the regulated agreement is a non-commercial agreement.

(6) The Secretary of State may by order provide that this section shall not apply where the regulated agreement has a connection with a country outside the United Kingdom.

[767]

NOTES

Order: the Consumer Credit (Negotiable Instruments) (Exemption) Order 1984, SI 1984/435.

124 Consequences of breach of s 123

(1) After any contravention of section 123 has occurred in relation to a sum payable as mentioned in section 123(1)(a), the agreement under which the sum is payable is enforceable against the debtor or hirer on an order of the court only.

(2) After any contravention of section 123 has occurred in relation to a sum payable by any surety, the security is enforceable on an order of the court only.

(3) Where an application for an order under subsection (2) is dismissed (except on technical grounds only) section 106 shall apply to the security.

[768]

125 Holders in due course

(1) A person who takes a negotiable instrument in contravention of section 123(1) or (3) is not a holder in due course, and is not entitled to enforce the instrument.

(2) Where a person negotiates a cheque in contravention of section 123(2), his doing so constitutes a defect in his title within the meaning of the Bills of Exchange Act 1882.

(3) If a person mentioned in section 123(1)(a) or (b) ("the protected person") becomes liable to a holder in due course of an instrument taken from the protected person in contravention of

section 123(1) or (3), or taken from the protected person and negotiated in contravention of section 123(2), the creditor or owner shall indemnify the protected person in respect of that liability.

(4) Nothing in this Act affects the rights of the holder in due course of any negotiable instrument.

[769]

Land mortgages

126 Enforcement of land mortgages

A land mortgage securing a regulated agreement is enforceable (so far as provided in relation to the agreement) on an order of the court only.

[770]

PART IX
JUDICIAL CONTROL

Enforcement of certain regulated agreements and securities

127 Enforcement orders in cases of infringement

(1) In the case of an application for an enforcement order under—
[(za) section 55(2) (disclosure of information), or]
[(zb) section 61B(3) (duty to supply copy of overdraft agreement), or]
(a) section 65(1) (improperly executed agreements), or
(b) section 105(7)(a) or (b) (improperly executed security instruments), or
(c) section 111(2) (failure to serve copy of notice on surety), or
(d) section 124(1) or (2) (taking of negotiable instrument in contravention of section 123),

the court shall dismiss the application if, but … only if, it considers it just to do so having regard to—

(i) prejudice caused to any person by the contravention in question, and the degree of culpability for it; and
(ii) the powers conferred on the court by subsection (2) and sections 135 and 136.

(2) If it appears to the court just to do so, it may in an enforcement order reduce or discharge any sum payable by the debtor or hirer, or any surety, so as to compensate him for prejudice suffered as a result of the contravention in question.

(3)–(5) …

[771]

NOTES
For the text of this section as it had effect on 15 June 2006, prior to amendments made by the Consumer Credit Act 2006 and subsequent amendments, see the Appendix at [A121].
Sub-s (1): paras (za), (zb) inserted by the Consumer Credit (EU Directive) Regulations 2010, SI 2010/1010, regs 2, 12, 18, as from 1 February 2011, with effect in relation to certain agreements before that date, as provided for in regs 101, 101A of the 2010 Regulations at **[3942]**, **[3942A]**; words omitted repealed by the Consumer Credit Act 2006, s 70, Sch 4, as from 6 April 2007, subject to transitional provisions in s 69(1) of, and Sch 3, paras 1, 11(a) to, that Act at **[2077]**, **[2079]**.
Sub-ss (3)–(5): repealed by the Consumer Credit Act 2006, ss 15, 70, Sch 4, as from 6 April 2007, subject to transitional provisions in s 69(1) of, and Sch 3, paras 1, 11(b) to, that Act at **[2077]**, **[2079]**.
Regulations: the Consumer Credit (Agreements) Regulations 1983, SI 1983/1553.

128 Enforcement orders on death of debtor or hirer

The court shall make an order under section 86(2) if, but only if, the creditor or owner proves that he has been unable to satisfy himself that the present and future obligations of the debtor or hirer under the agreement are likely to be discharged.

[772]

Extension of time

129 Time orders

(1) [Subject to subsection (3) below,] if it appears to the court just to do so—
(a) on an application for an enforcement order; or
(b) on an application made by a debtor or hirer under this paragraph after service on him of—
(i) a default notice, or
(ii) a notice under section 76(1) or 98(1); or
[(ba) on an application made by a debtor or hirer under this paragraph after he has been given a notice under section 86B or 86C; or]

(c)   in an action brought by a creditor or owner to enforce a regulated agreement or any security, or recover possession of any goods or land to which a regulated agreement relates,

the court may make an order under this section (a "time order").

(2)   A time order shall provide for one or both of the following, as the court considers just—

(a)   the payment by the debtor or hirer or any surety of any sum owed under a regulated agreement or a security by such instalments, payable at such times, as the court, having regard to the means of the debtor or hirer and any surety, considers reasonable;

(b)   the remedying by the debtor or hirer of any breach of a regulated agreement (other than the non-payment of money) within such period as the court may specify.

(3)   *(Applies to Scotland only.)*

[773]

NOTES

For the text of this section as it had effect on 15 June 2006, prior to amendments made by the Consumer Credit Act 2006 and subsequent amendments, see the Appendix at [A123].

Sub-s (1): words in first pair of square brackets inserted by Debtors (Scotland) Act 1987, s 108(1), Sch 6, para 17, in relation to Scotland only; para (ba) inserted by the Consumer Credit Act 2006, s 16(1), as from 1 October 2008, subject to transitional provisions in s 69(1) of, and Sch 3, paras 1, 12 to, that Act at **[2077]**, **[2079]**.

[129A   Debtor or hirer to give notice of intent etc to creditor or owner

(1)   A debtor or hirer may make an application under section 129(1)(ba) in relation to a regulated agreement only if—

(a)   following his being given the notice under section 86B or 86C, he gave a notice within subsection (2) to the creditor or owner; and

(b)   a period of at least 14 days has elapsed after the day on which he gave that notice to the creditor or owner.

(2)   A notice is within this subsection if it—

(a)   indicates that the debtor or hirer intends to make the application;

(b)   indicates that he wants to make a proposal to the creditor or owner in relation to his making of payments under the agreement; and

(c)   gives details of that proposal.]

[773A]

NOTES

Commencement: 1 October 2008.

Inserted by the Consumer Credit Act 2006, s 16(2), as from 1 October 2008, subject to transitional provisions in s 69(1) of, and Sch 3, paras 1, 12 to, that Act at **[2077]**, **[2079]**.

130   Supplemental provisions about time orders

(1)   Where in accordance with rules of court an offer to pay any sum by instalments is made by the debtor or hirer and accepted by the creditor or owner, the court may in accordance with rules of court make a time order under section 129(2)(a) giving effect to the offer without hearing evidence of means.

(2)   In the case of a hire-purchase or conditional sale agreement only, a time order under section 129(2)(a) may deal with sums which, although not payable by the debtor at the time the order is made, would if the agreement continued in force become payable under it subsequently.

(3)   A time order under section 129(2)(a) shall not be made where the regulated agreement is secured by a pledge if, by virtue of regulations made under section 76(5), 87(4) or 98(5), service of a notice is not necessary for enforcement of the pledge.

(4)   Where, following the making of a time order in relation to a regulated hire-purchase or conditional sale agreement or a regulated consumer hire agreement, the debtor or hirer is in possession of the goods, he shall be treated (except in the case of a debtor to whom the creditor's title has passed) as a bailee or (in Scotland) a custodier of the goods under the terms of the agreement, notwithstanding that the agreement has been terminated.

(5)   Without prejudice to anything done by the creditor or owner before the commencement of the period specified in a time order made under section 129(2)(b) ("the relevant period"),—

(a)   he shall not while the relevant period subsists take in relation to the agreement any action such as is mentioned in section 87(1);

(b)   where—

(i)   a provision of the agreement ("the secondary provision") becomes operative only on breach of another provision of the agreement ("the primary provision"), and

(ii)   the time order provides for the remedying of such a breach of the primary provision within the relevant period, he shall not treat the secondary provision as operative before the end of that period;

(c)   if while the relevant period subsists the breach to which the order relates is remedied it shall be treated as not having occurred.

(6)   On the application of any person affected by a time order, the court may vary or revoke the order.

[774]

[Interest

130A Interest payable on judgment debts etc

(1)   If the creditor or owner under a regulated agreement wants to be able to recover from the debtor or hirer post-judgment interest in connection with a sum that is required to be paid under a judgment given in relation to the agreement (the "judgment sum"), he—

(a)   after the giving of that judgment, shall give the debtor or hirer a notice under this section (the "first required notice"); and

(b)   after the giving of the first required notice, shall give the debtor or hirer further notices under this section at intervals of not more than six months.

(2)   The debtor or hirer shall have no liability to pay post-judgment interest in connection with the judgment sum to the extent that the interest is calculated by reference to a period occurring before the day on which he is given the first required notice.

(3)   If the creditor or owner fails to give the debtor or hirer a notice under this section within the period of six months beginning with the day after the day on which such a notice was last given to the debtor or hirer, the debtor or hirer shall have no liability to pay post-judgment interest in connection with the judgment sum to the extent that the interest is calculated by reference to the whole or to a part of the period which—

(a)   begins immediately after the end of that period of six months; and

(b)   ends at the end of the day on which the notice is given to the debtor or hirer.

(4)   The debtor or hirer shall have no liability to pay any sum in connection with the preparation or the giving to him of a notice under this section.

(5)   A notice under this section may be incorporated in a statement or other notice which the creditor or owner gives the debtor or hirer in relation to the agreement by virtue of another provision of this Act.

(6)   Regulations may make provision about the form and content of notices under this section.

(7)   This section does not apply in relation to post-judgment interest which is required to be paid by virtue of any of the following—

(a)   section 4 of the Administration of Justice (Scotland) Act 1972;

(b)   Article 127 of the Judgments Enforcement (Northern Ireland) Order 1981;

(c)   section 74 of the County Courts Act 1984.

(8)   This section does not apply in relation to a non-commercial agreement or to a small agreement.

(9)   In this section "post-judgment interest" means interest to the extent calculated by reference to a period occurring after the giving of the judgment under which the judgment sum is required to be paid.]

[774A]

NOTES

Commencement: 16 June 2006 (sub-ss (6), (9)); 1 October 2008 (sub-ss (1)–(5), (7), (8)).

Inserted, together with preceding cross-heading, by the Consumer Credit Act 2006, s 17, as from dates as noted above and subject to transitional provisions in s 69(1) of, and Sch 3, paras 1, 13 to, that Act at **[2077]**, **[2079]**.

Regulations: the Consumer Credit (Information Requirements and Duration of Licences and Charges) Regulations 2007, SI 2007/1167 at **[3488]**.

Protection of property pending proceedings

131 Protection orders

The court, on the application of the creditor or owner under a regulated agreement, may make such orders as it thinks just for protecting any property of the creditor or owner, or property subject to any security, from damage or depreciation pending the determination of any proceedings under this Act, including orders restricting or prohibiting use of the property or giving directions as to its custody.

[775]

Hire and hire-purchase etc agreements

132   Financial relief for hirer

(1)   Where the owner under a regulated consumer hire agreement recovers possession of goods to which the agreement relates otherwise than by action, the hirer may apply to the court for an order that—

(a)   the whole or part of any sum paid by the hirer to the owner in respect of the goods shall be repaid, and

(b)   the obligation to pay the whole or part of any sum owed by the hirer to the owner in respect of the goods shall cease,

and if it appears to the court just to do so, having regard to the extent of the enjoyment of the goods by the hirer, the court shall grant the application in full or in part.

(2)   Where in proceedings relating to a regulated consumer hire agreement the court makes an order for the delivery to the owner of goods to which the agreement relates the court may include in the order the like provision as may be made in an order under subsection (1).

[776]

133   Hire-purchase etc agreements: special powers of court

(1)   If, in relation to a regulated hire-purchase or conditional sale agreement, it appears to the court just to do so—

(a)   on an application for an enforcement order or time order; or

(b)   in an action brought by the creditor to recover possession of goods to which the agreement relates,

the court may—

(i)   make an order (a "return order") for the return to the creditor of goods to which the agreement relates,

(ii)   make an order (a "transfer order") for the transfer to the debtor of the creditor's title to certain goods to which the agreement relates ("the transferred goods"), and the return to the creditor of the remainder of the goods.

(2)   In determining for the purposes of this section how much of the total price has been paid ("the paid-up sum"), the court may—

(a)   treat any sum paid by the debtor, or owed by the creditor, in relation to the goods as part of the paid-up sum;

(b)   deduct any sum owed by the debtor in relation to the goods (otherwise than as part of the total price) from the paid-up sum,

and make corresponding reductions in amounts so owed.

(3)   Where a transfer order is made, the transferred goods shall be such of the goods to which the agreement relates as the court thinks just; but a transfer order shall be made only where the paid-up sum exceeds the part of the total price referable to the transferred goods by an amount equal to at least one-third of the unpaid balance of the total price.

(4)   Notwithstanding the making of a return order or transfer order, the debtor may at any time before the goods enter the possession of the creditor, on payment of the balance of the total price and the fulfilment of any other necessary conditions, claim the goods ordered to be returned to the creditor.

(5)   When, in pursuance of a time order or under this section, the total price of goods under a regulated hire-purchase agreement or regulated conditional sale agreement is paid and any other necessary conditions are fulfilled, the creditor's title to the goods vests in the debtor.

(6)   If, in contravention of a return order or transfer order, any goods to which the order relates are not returned to the creditor, the court, on the application of the creditor, may—

(a)   revoke so much of the order as relates to those goods, and

(b)   order the debtor to pay the creditor the unpaid portion of so much of the total price as is referable to those goods.

(7)   For the purposes of this section, the part of the total price referable to any goods is the part assigned to those goods by the agreement or (if no such assignment is made) the part determined by the court to be reasonable.

[777]

134   Evidence of adverse detention in hire-purchase etc cases

(1)   Where goods are comprised in a regulated hire-purchase agreement, regulated conditional sale agreement or regulated consumer hire agreement, and the creditor or owner—

(a)   brings an action or makes an application to enforce a right to recover possession of the goods from the debtor or hirer, and

(b)   proves that a demand for the delivery of the goods was included in the default notice under section 88(5), or that, after the right to recover possession of the goods accrued but before the action was begun or the application was made, he made a request in writing to the debtor or hirer to surrender the goods,

then, for the purposes of the claim of the creditor or owner to recover possession of the goods, the possession of them by the debtor or hirer shall be deemed to be adverse to the creditor or owner.

(2)   In subsection (1) "the debtor or hirer" includes a person in possession of the goods at any time between the debtor's or hirer's death and the grant of probate or administration, or (in Scotland) confirmation.

(3)   Nothing in this section affects a claim for damages for conversion or (in Scotland) for delict.

[778]

Supplemental provisions as to orders

135   Power to impose conditions, or suspend operation of order

(1)   If it considers it just to do so, the court may in an order made by it in relation to a regulated agreement include provisions—
- (a)   making the operation of any term of the order conditional on the doing of specified acts by any party to the proceedings;
- (b)   suspending the operation of any term of the order either—
  - (i)   until such time as the court subsequently directs, or
  - (ii)   until the occurrence of a specified act or omission.

(2)   The court shall not suspend the operation of a term requiring the delivery up of goods by any person unless satisfied that the goods are in his possession or control.

(3)   In the case of a consumer hire agreement, the court shall not so use its powers under subsection (1)(b) as to extend the period for which, under the terms of the agreement, the hirer is entitled to possession of the goods to which the agreement relates.

(4)   On the application of any person affected by a provision included under subsection (1), the court may vary the provision.

[779]

136   Power to vary agreements and securities

The court may in an order made by it under this Act include such provision as it considers just for amending any agreement or security in consequence of a term of the order.

[780]–[784]

137–140   (*Repealed by the Consumer Credit Act 2006, ss 22(3), 70, Sch 4, as from 6 April 2007, subject to transitional provisions in s 69(1) of, and Sch 3, paras 1, 15 to, that Act at* **[2077]**, **[2079]**. *For the text of these sections as they had effect on 15 June 2006, prior to amendments made by the Consumer Credit Act 2006 and subsequent amendments, see the Appendix at* **[A131]–[A134]**.)

[Unfair relationships

140A   Unfair relationships between creditors and debtors

(1)   The court may make an order under section 140B in connection with a credit agreement if it determines that the relationship between the creditor and the debtor arising out of the agreement (or the agreement taken with any related agreement) is unfair to the debtor because of one or more of the following—
- (a)   any of the terms of the agreement or of any related agreement;
- (b)   the way in which the creditor has exercised or enforced any of his rights under the agreement or any related agreement;
- (c)   any other thing done (or not done) by, or on behalf of, the creditor (either before or after the making of the agreement or any related agreement).

(2)   In deciding whether to make a determination under this section the court shall have regard to all matters it thinks relevant (including matters relating to the creditor and matters relating to the debtor).

(3)   For the purposes of this section the court shall (except to the extent that it is not appropriate to do so) treat anything done (or not done) by, or on behalf of, or in relation to, an associate or a former associate of the creditor as if done (or not done) by, or on behalf of, or in relation to, the creditor.

(4)   A determination may be made under this section in relation to a relationship notwithstanding that the relationship may have ended.

(5)   An order under section 140B shall not be made in connection with a credit agreement which is an exempt agreement by virtue of section 16(6C).]

[784A]

NOTES
Commencement: 6 April 2007.
Inserted, together with preceding cross-heading, by the Consumer Credit Act 2006, s 19, as from 6 April 2007, subject to transitional provisions in s 69(1) of, and Sch 3, paras 1, 14 to, that Act at **[2077]**, **[2079]**.

[140B   Powers of court in relation to unfair relationships

(1)   An order under this section in connection with a credit agreement may do one or more of the following—

(a)   require the creditor, or any associate or former associate of his, to repay (in whole or in part) any sum paid by the debtor or by a surety by virtue of the agreement or any related agreement (whether paid to the creditor, the associate or the former associate or to any other person);

(b)   require the creditor, or any associate or former associate of his, to do or not to do (or to cease doing) anything specified in the order in connection with the agreement or any related agreement;

(c)   reduce or discharge any sum payable by the debtor or by a surety by virtue of the agreement or any related agreement;

(d)   direct the return to a surety of any property provided by him for the purposes of a security;

(e)   otherwise set aside (in whole or in part) any duty imposed on the debtor or on a surety by virtue of the agreement or any related agreement;

(f)   alter the terms of the agreement or of any related agreement;

(g)   direct accounts to be taken, or (in Scotland) an accounting to be made, between any persons.

(2)   An order under this section may be made in connection with a credit agreement only—

(a)   on an application made by the debtor or by a surety;

(b)   at the instance of the debtor or a surety in any proceedings in any court to which the debtor and the creditor are parties, being proceedings to enforce the agreement or any related agreement; or

(c)   at the instance of the debtor or a surety in any other proceedings in any court where the amount paid or payable under the agreement or any related agreement is relevant.

(3)   An order under this section may be made notwithstanding that its effect is to place on the creditor, or any associate or former associate of his, a burden in respect of an advantage enjoyed by another person.

(4)   An application under subsection (2)(a) may only be made—

(a)   in England and Wales, to the county court;

(b)   in Scotland, to the sheriff court;

(c)   in Northern Ireland, to the High Court (subject to subsection (6)).

(5)   In Scotland such an application may be made in the sheriff court for the district in which the debtor or surety resides or carries on business.

(6)   In Northern Ireland such an application may be made to the county court if the credit agreement is an agreement under which the creditor provides the debtor with—

(a)   fixed-sum credit not exceeding £15,000; or

(b)   running-account credit on which the credit limit does not exceed £15,000.

(7)   Without prejudice to any provision which may be made by rules of court made in relation to county courts in Northern Ireland, such rules may provide that an application made by virtue of subsection (6) may be made in the county court for the division in which the debtor or surety resides or carries on business.

(8)   A party to any proceedings mentioned in subsection (2) shall be entitled, in accordance with rules of court, to have any person who might be the subject of an order under this section made a party to the proceedings.

(9)   If, in any such proceedings, the debtor or a surety alleges that the relationship between the creditor and the debtor is unfair to the debtor, it is for the creditor to prove to the contrary.]

[784B]

NOTES
Commencement: 6 April 2007.
Inserted by the Consumer Credit Act 2006, s 20, as from 6 April 2007, subject to transitional provisions in s 69(1) of, and Sch 3, paras 1, 14, 16 to, that Act at **[2077]**, **[2079]**.

[140C   Interpretation of ss 140A and 140B

(1)   In this section and in sections 140A and 140B "credit agreement" means any agreement between an individual (the "debtor") and any other person (the "creditor") by which the creditor provides the debtor with credit of any amount.

(2) References in this section and in sections 140A and 140B to the creditor or to the debtor under a credit agreement include—

(a) references to the person to whom his rights and duties under the agreement have passed by assignment or operation of law;

(b) where two or more persons are the creditor or the debtor, references to any one or more of those persons.

(3) The definition of "court" in section 189(1) does not apply for the purposes of sections 140A and 140B.

(4) References in sections 140A and 140B to an agreement related to a credit agreement (the "main agreement") are references to—

(a) a credit agreement consolidated by the main agreement;

(b) a linked transaction in relation to the main agreement or to a credit agreement within paragraph (a);

(c) a security provided in relation to the main agreement, to a credit agreement within paragraph (a) or to a linked transaction within paragraph (b).

(5) In the case of a credit agreement which is not a regulated consumer credit agreement, for the purposes of subsection (4) a transaction shall be treated as being a linked transaction in relation to that agreement if it would have been such a transaction had that agreement been a regulated consumer credit agreement.

(6) For the purposes of this section and section 140B the definitions of "security" and "surety" in section 189(1) apply (with any appropriate changes) in relation to—

(a) a credit agreement which is not a consumer credit agreement as if it were a consumer credit agreement; and

(b) a transaction which is a linked transaction by virtue of subsection (5).

(7) For the purposes of this section a credit agreement (the "earlier agreement") is consolidated by another credit agreement (the "later agreement") if—

(a) the later agreement is entered into by the debtor (in whole or in part) for purposes connected with debts owed by virtue of the earlier agreement; and

(b) at any time prior to the later agreement being entered into the parties to the earlier agreement included—

(i) the debtor under the later agreement; and

(ii) the creditor under the later agreement or an associate or a former associate of his.

(8) Further, if the later agreement is itself consolidated by another credit agreement (whether by virtue of this subsection or subsection (7)), then the earlier agreement is consolidated by that other agreement as well.]

[784C]

NOTES

Commencement: 6 April 2007.

Inserted by the Consumer Credit Act 2006, s 21, as from 6 April 2007, subject to transitional provisions in s 69(1) of, and Sch 3, paras 1, 16, 17 to, that Act at **[2077]**, **[2079]**.

[140D Advice and information

The advice and information published by the OFT under section 229 of the Enterprise Act 2002 shall indicate how the OFT expects sections 140A to 140C of this Act to interact with Part 8 of that Act.]

[784D]

NOTES

Commencement: 6 April 2007.

Inserted by the Consumer Credit Act 2006, s 22(1), as from 6 April 2007.

Miscellaneous

141 Jurisdiction and parties

(1) In England and Wales, the county court shall have jurisdiction to hear and determine—

(a) any action by the creditor or owner to enforce a regulated agreement or any security relating to it;

(b) any action to enforce any linked transaction against the debtor or hirer or his relative;

and such an action shall not be brought in any other court.

(2) Where an action or application is brought in the High Court which, by virtue of this Act, ought to have been brought in the county court it shall not be treated as improperly brought, but shall be transferred to the county court.

(3)–(3B) *(Apply to Scotland only.)*

(4)　In Northern Ireland the county court shall have jurisdiction to hear and determine any action or application falling within subsection (1).

(5)　Except as may be provided by rules of court, all the parties to a regulated agreement, and any surety, shall be made parties to any proceedings relating to the agreement.

[785]

142　Power to declare rights of parties

(1)　Where under any provision of this Act a thing can be done by a creditor or owner on an enforcement order only, and either—
- (a)　the court dismisses (except on technical grounds only) an application for an enforcement order, or
- (b)　where no such application has been made or such an application has been dismissed on technical grounds only, an interested party applies to the court for a declaration under this subsection,

the court may if it thinks just make a declaration that the creditor or owner is not entitled to do that thing, and thereafter no application for an enforcement order in respect of it shall be entertained.

(2)　Where—
- (a)　a regulated agreement or linked transaction is cancelled under section 69(1), or becomes subject to section 69(2), or
- (b)　a regulated agreement is terminated under section 91, and an interested party applies to the court for a declaration under this subsection, the court may make a declaration to that effect.

[786]

143, 144　*(Apply to Northern Ireland only.)*

PART X
ANCILLARY CREDIT BUSINESS

Definitions

145　Types of ancillary credit business

(1)　An ancillary credit business is any business so far as it comprises or relates to—
- (a)　credit brokerage,
- (b)　debt-adjusting,
- (c)　debt-counselling,
- (d)　debt-collecting,
- [(da)　debt administration,]
- [(db)　the provision of credit information services, or]
- (e)　the operation of a credit reference agency.

(2)　Subject to section 146(5) [and (5A)], credit brokerage is the effecting of introductions—
- (a)　of individuals desiring to obtain credit—
  - (i)　to persons carrying on businesses to which this sub-paragraph applies, or
  - (ii)　in the case of an individual desiring to obtain credit to finance the acquisition or provision of a dwelling occupied or to be occupied by himself or his relative, to any person carrying on a business in the course of which he provides credit secured on land, or
- (b)　of individuals desiring to obtain goods on hire to persons carrying on businesses to which this paragraph applies, or
- (c)　of individuals desiring to obtain credit, or to obtain goods on hire, to other credit-brokers.

(3)　Subsection (2)(a)(i) applies to—
- (a)　a consumer credit business;
- (b)　a business which comprises or relates to consumer credit agreements being, otherwise than by virtue of section 16(5)(a), exempt agreements;
- (c)　a business which comprises or relates to unregulated agreements where—
  - (i)　the [law applicable to] the agreement is the law of a country outside the United Kingdom, and
  - (ii)　if the [law applicable to] the agreement were the law of a part of the United Kingdom it would be a regulated consumer credit agreement.

(4)　Subsection (2)(b) applies to—
- (a)　a consumer hire business;
- [(aa)　a business which comprises or relates to consumer hire agreements being, otherwise than by virtue of section 16(6), exempt agreements;]
- (b)　a business which comprises or relates to unregulated agreements where—

      (i)   the [law applicable to] the agreement is the law of a country outside the United Kingdom, and

      (ii)   if the [law applicable to] the agreement were the law of a part of the United Kingdom it would be a regulated consumer hire agreement.

  (5)   Subject to [section 146(5B) and (6)], debt-adjusting is, in relation to debts due under consumer credit agreements or consumer hire agreements,—

    (a)   negotiating with the creditor or owner, on behalf of the debtor or hirer, terms for the discharge of a debt, or

    (b)   taking over, in return for payments by the debtor or hirer, his obligation to discharge a debt, or

    (c)   any similar activity concerned with the liquidation of a debt.

  (6)   Subject to [section 146(5C) and (6)], debt-counselling is the giving of advice to debtors or hirers about the liquidation of debts due under consumer credit agreements or consumer hire agreements.

  (7)   Subject to section 146(6), debt-collecting is the taking of steps to procure payment of debts due under consumer credit agreements or consumer hire agreements.

  [(7A) Subject to section 146(7), debt administration is the taking of steps—

    (a)   to perform duties under a consumer credit agreement or a consumer hire agreement on behalf of the creditor or owner, or

    (b)   to exercise or to enforce rights under such an agreement on behalf of the creditor or owner,

so far as the taking of such steps is not debt-collecting.]

  [(7B) A person provides credit information services if—

    (a)   he takes any steps mentioned in subsection (7C) on behalf of an individual; or

    (b)   he gives advice to an individual in relation to the taking of any such steps.

  (7C) Those steps are steps taken with a view—

    (a)   to ascertaining whether a credit information agency (other than that person himself if he is one) holds information relevant to the financial standing of an individual;

    (b)   to ascertaining the contents of such information held by such an agency;

    (c)   to securing the correction of, the omission of anything from, or the making of any other kind of modification of, such information so held; or

    (d)   to securing that such an agency which holds such information—

      (i)   stops holding it; or

      (ii)   does not provide it to another person.

  (7D) In subsection (7C) "credit information agency" means—

    (a)   a person carrying on a consumer credit business or a consumer hire business;

    (b)   a person carrying on a business so far as it comprises or relates to credit brokerage, debt-adjusting, debt-counselling, debt-collecting, debt administration or the operation of a credit reference agency;

    (c)   a person carrying on a business which would be a consumer credit business except that it comprises or relates to consumer credit agreements being, otherwise than by virtue of section 16(5)(a), exempt agreements; or

    (d)   a person carrying on a business which would be a consumer hire business except that it comprises or relates to consumer hire agreements being, otherwise than by virtue of section 16(6), exempt agreements.]

  (8)   A credit reference agency is a person carrying on a business comprising the furnishing of persons with information relevant to the financial standing of individuals, being information collected by the agency for that purpose.

                                                      [787]

NOTES

   For the text of this section as it had effect on 15 June 2006, prior to amendments made by the Consumer Credit Act 2006 and subsequent amendments, see the Appendix at [A137].

   Sub-s (1): para (da) substituted (for original word "or" in para (d)) and para (db) inserted, by the Consumer Credit Act 2006, ss 24(1), 25(1), as from 1 October 2008.

   Sub-s (2): words in square brackets inserted by the Financial Services and Markets Act 2000 (Regulated Activities) (Amendment) (No 1) Order 2003, SI 2003/1475, art 21(1)(a), as from 31 October 2004.

   Sub-s (3): words in square brackets substituted by the Contracts (Applicable Law) Act 1990, s 5, Sch 4, para 2, as from 1 April 1991.

   Sub-s (4): para (aa) inserted by the Consumer Credit Act 2006, s 5(4), as from 6 April 2008; words in square brackets in para (b) substituted by the Contracts (Applicable Law) Act 1990, s 5, Sch 4, para 2, as from 1 April 1991.

   Sub-ss (5), (6): words in square brackets substituted by SI 2003/1475, art 21(1)(b), (c), as from 31 October 2004.

   Sub-ss (7A)–(7D): inserted by the Consumer Credit Act 2006, s 24(2), 25(2), as from 16 June 2006.

146   Exceptions from section 145

(1)   A barrister or advocate acting in that capacity is not to be treated as doing so in the course of any ancillary credit business.

(2)   A solicitor engaging in contentious business (as defined in [section 87(1) of the Solicitors Act 1974]) is not to be treated as doing so in the course of any ancillary credit business.

[(2A)   An authorised person (other than a barrister or solicitor) engaging in contentious business is not to be treated as doing so in the course of any ancillary credit business.

(2B)   In subsection (2A)—
   "authorised person" means a person who, for the purposes of the Legal Services Act 2007, is
      an authorised person in relation to an activity which constitutes the exercise of a right of
      audience or the conduct of litigation (within the meaning of that Act);
   "contentious business" means business done in or for the purposes of proceedings begun
      before a court or before an arbitrator, not being non-contentious or common form probate
      business (within the meaning of section 128 of the Supreme Court Act 1981).]

(3)   *(Applies to Scotland only.)*

(4)   A solicitor in Northern Ireland engaging in [contentious business (as defined in Article 3(2) of the Solicitors (Northern Ireland) Order 1976], is not to be treated as doing so in the course of any ancillary credit business.

(5)   For the purposes of section 145(2), introductions effected by an individual by canvassing off trade premises either debtor-creditor-supplier agreements falling within section 12(a) or regulated consumer hire agreements shall be disregarded if—
   (a)   the introductions are not effected by him in the capacity of an employee, and
   (b)   he does not by any other method effect introductions falling within section 145(2).

[(5A)   It is not credit brokerage for a person to effect the introduction of an individual desiring to obtain credit if the introduction is made—
   [(a)   to an authorised person, within the meaning of the 2000 Act, who has permission under
      that Act to enter into a relevant agreement as lender or home purchase provider (as the
      case may be); or]
   (b)   to a qualifying broker, with a view to that individual obtaining credit under [the relevant
      agreement].

(5B)   It is not debt-adjusting for a person to carry on an activity mentioned in paragraph (a), (b) or (c) of section 145(5) if—
   (a)   the debt in question is due under a relevant agreement; and
   (b)   that activity is a regulated activity for the purposes of the 2000 Act.

(5C)   It is not debt-counselling for a person to give advice to debtors about the liquidation of debts if—
   (a)   the debt in question is due under a relevant agreement; and
   (b)   giving that advice is a regulated activity for the purposes of the 2000 Act.

(5D)   In this section—
   "the 2000 Act" means the Financial Services and Markets Act 2000;
   ["relevant agreement" means an agreement which—
      (a)   is secured by a land mortgage, or
      (b)   is or forms part of a regulated home purchase plan,
      but only if entering into the agreement as lender or home purchase provider (as the case
      may be) is a regulated activity for the purposes of the 2000 Act.]
   "qualifying broker" means a person who may effect introductions of the kind mentioned in
      subsection (5A) without contravening the general prohibition, within the meaning of
      section 19 of the 2000 Act,
and references to "regulated activities"[, "regulated home purchase plan" and "home purchase provider"] and the definition of "qualifying broker" must be read with—
   (a)   section 22 of the 2000 Act (regulated activities: power to specify classes of activity and
      categories of investment);
   (b)   any order for the time being in force under that section; and
   (c)   Schedule 2 to that Act.]

(6)   It is not debt-adjusting, debt-counselling or debt-collecting for a person to do anything in relation to a debt arising under an agreement if [any of the following conditions is satisfied]—
   [(aa)   that he is the creditor or owner under the agreement, or]
   (c)   [that] he is the supplier in relation to the agreement, or
   (d)   [that] he is a credit-broker who has acquired the business of the person who was the
      supplier in relation to the agreement, or
   (e)   [that] he is a person prevented by subsection (5) from being treated as a credit-broker,
      and the agreement was made in consequence of an introduction (whether made by him
      or another person) which, under subsection (5), is to be disregarded.

[(7) It is not debt administration for a person to take steps to perform duties, or to exercise or enforce rights, under an agreement on behalf of the creditor or owner if any of the conditions mentioned in subsection (6)(aa) to (e) is satisfied in relation to that person.]

[788]

NOTES
For the text of this section as it had effect on 15 June 2006, prior to amendments made by the Consumer Credit Act 2006 and subsequent amendments, see the Appendix at [A138].
Sub-ss (2), (4): words in square brackets substituted by the Arbitration Act 1996, s 107(1), Sch 3, para 28, as from 31 January 1997.
Sub-ss (2A), (2B): inserted by the Legal Services Act 2007, s 208(1), Sch 21, para 31, as from 1 January 2010.
Sub-s (5A): inserted, together with sub-ss (5B)–(5D), by the Financial Services and Markets Act 2000 (Regulated Activities) (Amendment) (No 1) Order 2003, SI 2003/1475, art 21(2), as from 31 October 2004; para (a) substituted and words in square brackets in para (b) substituted by the Financial Services and Markets Act 2000 (Regulated Activities) (Amendment) (No 2) Order 2006, SI 2006/2383, art 25(1), (4)(a), as from 6 April 2007, subject to transitional provisions in arts 37–39 of that Order.
Sub-s (5B), (5C): inserted as noted to sub-s (5A).
Sub-s (5D): inserted as noted to sub-s (5A); definition "relevant agreement" substituted and words in second pair of square brackets inserted by SI 2006/2383, art 25(1), (4)(b), as from 6 April 2007, subject to transitional provisions in arts 37–39 of that Order.
Sub-s (6): words in square brackets inserted and para (aa) substituted for original paras (a), (b) by the Consumer Credit Act 2006, s 24(3), as from 1 October 2008.
Sub-s (7): added by the Consumer Credit Act 2006, s 24(4), as from 16 June 2006.
Solicitors: references to solicitors are modified so as to include references to recognised bodies within the meaning of the Administration of Justice Act 1985, s 9, by the Solicitors' Incorporated Practices Order 1991, SI 1991/2684, arts 3–5, Sch 1.

Licensing

147 Application of Part III

(1) ...

(2) Without prejudice to the generality of section 26, regulations under that section ... may include provisions regulating the collection and dissemination of information by credit reference agencies.

[789]

NOTES
For the text of this section as it had effect on 15 June 2006, prior to amendments made by the Consumer Credit Act 2006 and subsequent amendments, see the Appendix at [A139].
Sub-s (1): repealed by the Consumer Credit Act 2006, s 70, Sch 4, as from 6 April 2008.
Sub-s (2): words omitted repealed by the Consumer Credit Act 2006, s 70, Sch 4, as from 6 April 2008.
Regulations: the Consumer Credit (Termination of Licences) Regulations 1976, SI 1976/1002; the Consumer Credit (Conduct of Business) (Credit References) Regulations 1977, SI 1977/330; the Consumer Credit Licensing (Appeals) Regulations 1998, SI 1998/1203.

148 Agreement for services of unlicensed trader

(1) An agreement for the services of a person carrying on an ancillary credit business (the "trader"), if made when the trader was unlicensed, is enforceable against the other party (the "customer") only where the [OFT] has made an order under subsection (2) which applies to the agreement.

(2) The trader or his successor in title may apply to the [OFT] for an order that agreements within subsection (1) are to be treated as if made when the trader was licensed.

(3) Unless the [OFT] determines to make an order under subsection (2) in accordance with the application, [it] shall, before determining the application, by notice—
    (a) inform the trader, giving [its] reasons, that, as the case may be, [it] is minded to refuse the application, or to grant it in terms different from those applied for, describing them, and
    (b) invite the trader to submit to the [OFT] representations in support of his application in accordance with section 34.

(4) In determining whether or not to make an order under subsection (2) in respect of any period the [OFT] shall consider, in addition to any other relevant factors,—
    (a) how far, if at all, customers under agreements made by the trader during that period were prejudiced by the trader's conduct,
    (b) whether or not the [OFT] would have been likely to grant a licence covering that period on an application by the trader, and
    (c) the degree of culpability for the failure to obtain a licence.

(5) If the [OFT] thinks fit, [it] may in an order under subsection (2)—
    (a) limit the order to specified agreements, or agreements of a specified description or made at a specified time;

(b)	make the order conditional on the doing of specified acts by the trader.

[(6)	This section does not apply to an agreement made by a consumer credit EEA firm unless at the time it was made that firm was precluded from entering into it as a result of—
(a)	a consumer credit prohibition imposed under section 203 of the Financial Services and Markets Act 2000; or
(b)	a restriction imposed on the firm under section 204 of that Act.]

[790]

NOTES
Sub-s (6): added by the Financial Services and Markets Act 2000 (Consequential Amendments and Repeals) Order 2001, SI 2001/3649, art 173, as from 1 December 2001.
References to the OFT, etc: as to the abolition of the office of the Director General of Fair Trading and the substitution of the original references to the Director (and related expressions), see the note preceding s 1 at **[651]**.

### 149	Regulated agreements made on introductions by unlicensed credit-broker

(1)	A regulated agreement made by a debtor or hirer who, for the purpose of making that agreement, was introduced to the creditor or owner by an unlicensed credit-broker is enforceable against the debtor or hirer only where—
(a)	on the application of the credit-broker, the [OFT] has made an order under section 148(2) in respect of a period including the time when the introduction was made, and the order does not (whether in general terms or specifically) exclude the application of this paragraph to the regulated agreement, or
(b)	the [OFT] has made an order under subsection (2) which applies to the agreement.

(2)	Where during any period individuals were introduced to a person carrying on a consumer credit business or consumer hire business by an unlicensed credit-broker for the purpose of making regulated agreements with the person carrying on that business, that person or his successor in title may apply to the [OFT] for an order that regulated agreements so made are to be treated as if the credit-broker had been licensed at the time of the introduction.

(3)	Unless the [OFT] determines to make an order under subsection (2) in accordance with the application, [it] shall, before determining the application, by notice—
(a)	inform the applicant, giving [its] reasons, that, as the case may be, [it] is minded to refuse the application, or to grant it in terms different from those applied for, describing them, and
(b)	invite the applicant to submit to the [OFT] representations in support of his application in accordance with section 34.

(4)	In determining whether or not to make an order under subsection (2) the [OFT] shall consider, in addition to any other relevant factors—
(a)	how far, if at all, debtors or hirers under regulated agreements to which the application relates were prejudiced by the credit-broker's conduct, and
(b)	the degree of culpability of the applicant in facilitating the carrying on by the credit-broker of his business when unlicensed.

(5)	If the [OFT] thinks fit, [it] may in an order under subsection (2)—
(a)	limit the order to specified agreements, or agreements of a specified description or made at a specified time;
(b)	make the order conditional on the doing of specified acts by the applicant.

[(6)	For the purposes of this section, "unlicensed credit-broker" does not include a consumer credit EEA firm unless at the time the introduction was made that firm was precluded from making it as a result of—
(a)	a consumer credit prohibition imposed under section 203 of the Financial Services and Markets Act 2000; or
(b)	a restriction imposed on the firm under section 204 of that Act.]

[791]–[792]

NOTES
Sub-s (6): added by the Financial Services and Markets Act 2000 (Consequential Amendments and Repeals) Order 2001, SI 2001/3649, art 174, as from 1 December 2001.
References to the OFT, etc: as to the abolition of the office of the Director General of Fair Trading and the substitution of the original references to the Director (and related expressions), see the note preceding s 1 at **[651]**.

150	(*Repealed by the Consumer Credit Act 2006, s 70, Sch 4, as from 6 April 2008. For the text of this section as it had effect on 15 June 2006, prior to amendments made by the Consumer Credit Act 2006 and subsequent amendments, see the Appendix at* **[A142]**.)

Seeking business

151 Advertisements

(1) Sections 44 to 47 apply to an advertisement published for the purposes of a business of credit brokerage carried on by any person, whether it advertises the services of that person or the services of persons to whom he effects introductions, as they apply to an advertisement to which Part IV applies.

(2) Sections 44 … and 47 apply to an advertisement, published for the purposes of a business carried on by the advertiser, indicating that he is willing to advise on debts, [to] engage in transactions concerned with the liquidation of debts [or to provide credit information services], as they apply to an advertisement to which Part IV applies.

[(2A) An advertisement does not fall within subsection (1) or (2) in so far as it is a communication of an invitation or inducement to engage in investment activity within the meaning of section 21 of the Financial Services and Markets Act 2000, other than an exempt generic communication (as defined in section 43(3B)).]

(3) The Secretary of State may by order provide that an advertisement published for the purposes of a business of credit brokerage, debt-adjusting[, debt-counselling or the provision of credit information services] shall not fall within subsection (1) or (2) if it is of a description specified in the order.

(4) An advertisement [(other than one for credit information services)] does not fall within subsection (2) if it indicates that the advertiser is not willing to act in relation to consumer credit agreements and consumer hire agreements.

(5) In subsections (1) and (3) "credit brokerage" includes the effecting of introductions of individuals desiring to obtain credit to any person carrying on a business in the course of which he provides credit secured on land.

[793]

NOTES
  For the text of this section as it had effect on 15 June 2006, prior to amendments made by the Consumer Credit Act 2006 and subsequent amendments, see the Appendix at [A143].
  Sub-s (2): words omitted repealed by the Consumer Protection from Unfair Trading Regulations 2008, SI 2008/1277, reg 30(3), Sch 4, as from 26 May 2008; word in first pair of square brackets substituted and words in second pair of square brackets inserted by the Consumer Credit Act 2006, s 25(3)(a), as from 1 October 2008.
  Sub-s (2A): inserted by the Financial Services and Markets Act 2000 (Regulated Activities) Order 2001, SI 2001/544, art 90(1), (7), as from 31 October 2004.
  Sub-s (3): words in square brackets substituted by the Consumer Credit Act 2006, s 25(3)(b), as from 1 October 2008.
  Sub-s (4): words in square brackets inserted by the Consumer Credit Act 2006, s 25(3)(c), as from 1 October 2008.
  Regulations: the Consumer Credit (Advertisements) Regulations 2004, SI 2004/1484 at **[3400]**; the Consumer Credit (Advertisements) Regulations 2010, SI 2010/1970 at **[3991]**.

152 Application of sections 52 to 54 to credit brokerage etc

(1) Sections 52 to 54 apply to a business of credit brokerage, debt-adjusting[, debt-counselling or the provision of credit information services] as they apply to a consumer credit business.

(2) In their application to a business of credit brokerage, sections 52 and 53 shall apply to the giving of quotations and information about the business of any person to whom the credit-broker effects introductions as well as to the giving of quotations and information about his own business.

[794]

NOTES
  For the text of this section as it had effect on 15 June 2006, prior to amendments made by the Consumer Credit Act 2006 and subsequent amendments, see the Appendix at [A144].
  Sub-s (1): words in square brackets substituted by the Consumer Credit Act 2006, s 25(4)(a), as from 1 October 2008.

153 Definition of canvassing off trade premises (agreements for ancillary credit services)

(1) An individual (the "canvasser") canvasses off trade premises the services of a person carrying on an ancillary credit business if he solicits the entry of another individual (the "consumer") into an agreement for the provision to the consumer of those services by making oral representations to the consumer, or any other individual, during a visit by the canvasser to any place (not excluded by subsection (2)) where the consumer, or that other individual, as the case may be, is, being a visit—

  (a)   carried out for the purpose of making such oral representations to individuals who are at that place, but
  (b)   not carried out in response to a request made on a previous occasion.

(2)   A place is excluded from subsection (1) if it is a place where (whether on a permanent or temporary basis)—
    (a)   the ancillary credit business is carried on, or
    (b)   any business is carried on by the canvasser or the person whose employee or agent the canvasser is, or by the consumer.

[795]

154   Prohibition of canvassing certain ancillary credit services off trade premises

It is an offence to canvass off trade premises the services of a person carrying on a business of credit brokerage, debt-adjusting[, debt-counselling or the provision of credit information services].

[796]

NOTES
    For the text of this section as it had effect on 15 June 2006, prior to amendments made by the Consumer Credit Act 2006 and subsequent amendments, see the Appendix at [A146].
    Words in square brackets substituted by the Consumer Credit Act 2006, s 25(4)(b), as from 1 October 2008.

155   Right to recover brokerage fees

(1)   [Subject to subsection (2A),] the excess over [£5] of a fee or commission for his services charged by a credit-broker to an individual to whom this subsection applies shall cease to be payable or, as the case may be, shall be recoverable by the individual if the introduction does not result in his entering into a relevant agreement within the six months following the introduction (disregarding any agreement which is cancelled under section 69(1) or becomes subject to section 69(2)).

(2)   Subsection (1) applies to an individual who sought an introduction for a purpose which would have been fulfilled by his entry into—
    (a)   a regulated agreement, or
    (b)   in the case of an individual such as is referred to in section 145(2)(a)(ii), an agreement for credit secured on land, or
    (c)   an agreement such as is referred to in section 145(3)(b) or (c) or (4)(b).

[(2A)   But subsection (1) does not apply where—
    (a)   the fee or commission relates to the effecting of an introduction of a kind mentioned in section 146(5A); and
    (b)   the person charging that fee or commission is an authorised person or an appointed representative, within the meaning of the Financial Services and Markets Act 2000.]

(3)   An agreement is a relevant agreement for the purposes of subsection (1) in relation to an individual if it is an agreement such as is referred to in subsection (2) in relation to that individual.

(4)   In the case of an individual desiring to obtain credit under a consumer credit agreement, any sum payable or paid by him to a credit-broker otherwise than as a fee or commission for the credit-broker's services shall for the purposes of subsection (1) be treated as such a fee or commission if it enters, or would enter, into the total charge for credit.

[797]

NOTES
    Sub-s (1): words in first pair of square brackets inserted by the Financial Services and Markets Act 2000 (Regulated Activities) (Amendment) (No 1) Order 2003, SI 2003/1475, art 22(1), (2), as from 31 October 2004; sum in second pair of square brackets substituted by the Consumer Credit (Further Increase in Monetary Amounts) Order 1998, SI 1998/997, art 3, Schedule, as from 1 May 1998.
    Sub-s (2A): inserted by SI 2003/1475, art 22(1), (3), as from 31 October 2004.

Entry into agreements

156   Entry into agreements

Regulations may make provision, in relation to agreements entered into in the course of a business of credit brokerage, debt-adjusting[, debt-counselling or the provision of credit information services], corresponding, with such modifications as the Secretary of State thinks fit, to the provision which is or may be made by or under sections 55, 60, 61, 62, 63, 65, 127, 179 or 180 in relation to agreements to which those sections apply.

[798]

NOTES
    For the text of this section as it had effect on 15 June 2006, prior to amendments made by the Consumer Credit Act 2006 and subsequent amendments, see the Appendix at [A148].
    Words in square brackets substituted by the Consumer Credit Act 2006, s 25(4)(c), as from 1 October 2008.

Credit reference agencies

157 Duty to disclose name etc of agency

[(A1) Where a creditor under a prospective regulated agreement, other than an excluded agreement, decides not to proceed with it on the basis of information obtained by the creditor from a credit reference agency, the creditor must, when informing the debtor of the decision—

    (a)   inform the debtor that this decision has been reached on the basis of information from a credit reference agency, and

    (b)   provide the debtor with the particulars of the agency including its name, address and telephone number.]

(1)   [In any other case,] a creditor, owner or negotiator, within the prescribed period after receiving a request in writing to that effect from the debtor or hirer, shall give him notice of the name and address of any credit reference agency from which the creditor, owner or negotiator has, during the antecedent negotiations, applied for information about his financial standing.

(2)   Subsection (1) does not apply to a request received more than 28 days after the termination of the antecedent negotiations, whether on the making of the regulated agreement or otherwise.

[(2A)   A creditor is not required to disclose information under this section if such disclosure—

    (a)   contravenes the Data Protection Act 1998,

    (b)   is prohibited by any EU obligation,

    (c)   would create or be likely to create a serious risk that any person would be subject to violence or intimidation, or

    (d)   would, or would be likely to, prejudice—

        (i)   the prevention or detection of crime,

        (ii)   the apprehension or prosecution of offenders, or

        (iii)   the administration of justice.]

(3)   If the creditor, owner or negotiator fails to comply with subsection [(A1) or] (1) he commits an offence.

[(4)   For the purposes of subsection (A1) an agreement is an excluded agreement if it is—

    (a)   a consumer hire agreement, or

    (b)   an agreement secured on land.]

[799]

NOTES

For the text of this section as it had effect on 15 June 2006, prior to amendments made by the **Consumer Credit Act 2006 and subsequent amendments, see the Appendix at [A149].**

Sub-ss (A1), (2A): inserted by the Consumer Credit (EU Directive) Regulations 2010, SI 2010/1010, regs 2, 40(1), (2), (4), as from 1 February 2011, with effect in relation to certain agreements before that date, as provided for in regs 101, 101A of the 2010 Regulations at **[3942]**, **[3942A]**.

Sub-ss (1), (3): words in square brackets inserted by SI 2010/1010, regs 2, 40(1), (3), (5), as from 1 February 2011, with effect in relation to certain agreements before that date, as provided for in regs 101, 101A of the 2010 Regulations at **[3942]**, **[3942A]**.

Sub-s (4): added by SI 2010/1010, regs 2, 40(1), (6), as from 1 February 2011, with effect in relation to certain agreements before that date, as provided for in regs 101, 101A of the 2010 Regulations at **[3942]**, **[3942A]**.

Regulations: the Consumer Credit (Credit Reference Agency) Regulations 2000, SI 2000/290.

---

158 Duty of agency to disclose filed information

(1)   A credit reference agency, within the prescribed period after receiving,

    [(a)   a request in writing to that effect from a consumer,] and

    (b)   such particulars as the agency may reasonably require to enable them to identify the file, and

    (c)   a fee of [£2],

shall give the consumer a copy of the file relating to [it] kept by the agency.

(2)   When giving a copy of the file under subsection (1), the agency shall also give the consumer a statement in the prescribed form of [the consumer's] rights under section 159.

(3)   If the agency does not keep a file relating to the consumer it shall give [the consumer] notice of that fact, but need not return any money paid.

(4)   If the agency contravenes any provision of this section it commits an offence.

[(4A)   In this section "consumer" means—

    (a)   a partnership consisting of two or three persons not all of whom are bodies corporate; or

    (b)   an unincorporated body of persons which does not consist entirely of bodies corporate and is not a partnership.]

(5)   In this Act "file", in relation to an individual, means all the information about him kept by a credit reference agency, regardless of how the information is stored and "copy of the file", as respects information not in plain English, means a transcript reduced into plain English.

[800]

NOTES
   For the text of this section as it had effect on 15 June 2006, prior to amendments made by the Consumer Credit Act 2006 and subsequent amendments, see the Appendix at [A150].
   Sub-s (1): para (a) substituted by the Consumer Credit Act 2006, s 5(5), as from 6 April 2007; sum in square brackets in para (c) substituted by the Consumer Credit (Further Increase of Monetary Amounts) Order 1998, SI 1998/997, Schedule, para 3, as from 1 May 1998.
   Sub-ss (2), (3): words in square brackets substituted by the Data Protection Act 1998, s 62(1)(b), (c), as from 1 March 2000, subject to savings in Sch 14, para 20 to that Act.
   Sub-s (4A): inserted by the Consumer Credit Act 2006, s 5(6), as from 6 April 2007.
   Regulations: the Consumer Credit (Credit Reference Agency) Regulations 2000, SI 2000/290.

159   Correction of wrong information

   [(1)   Any individual (the "objector") given—
   (a)   information under section 7 of the Data Protection Act 1998 by a credit reference agency, or
   (b)   information under section 158,
who considers that an entry in his file is incorrect, and that if it is not corrected he is likely to be prejudiced, may give notice to the agency requiring it either to remove the entry from the file or amend it.]

   (2)   Within 28 days after receiving a notice under subsection (1), the agency shall by notice inform the [objector] that it has—
   (a)   removed the entry from the file, or
   (b)   amended the entry, or
   (c)   taken no action,
and if the notice states that the agency has amended the entry it shall include a copy of the file so far as it comprises the amended entry.

   (3)   Within 28 days after receiving a notice under subsection (2) or, where no such notice was given, within 28 days after the expiry of the period mentioned in subsection (2), the [objector] may, unless he has been informed by the agency that it has removed the entry from his file, serve a further notice on the agency requiring it to add to the file an accompanying notice of correction (not exceeding 200 words) drawn up by the [objector] and include a copy of it when furnishing information included in or based on that entry.

   (4)   Within 28 days after receiving a notice under subsection (3), the agency, unless it intends to apply to the [the relevant authority] under subsection (5), shall by notice inform the [objector] that it has received the notice under subsection (3) and intends to comply with it.

   (5)   If—
   (a)   the [objector] has not received a notice under subsection (4) within the time required, or
   (b)   it appears to the agency that it would be improper for it to publish a notice of correction because it is incorrect, or unjustly defames any person, or is frivolous or scandalous, or is for any other reason unsuitable,
the [objector] or, as the case may be, the agency may, in the prescribed manner and on payment of the specified fee, apply to the [the relevant authority], who may make such order on the application as he thinks fit.

   (6)   If a person to whom an order under this section is directed fails to comply with it within the period specified in the order he commits an offence.

   [(7)   The [Information Commissioner] may vary or revoke any order made by him under this section.

   (8)   In this section "the relevant authority" means—
   (a)   where the objector is a partnership or other unincorporated body of persons, the [OFT], and
   (b)   in any other case, the [Information Commissioner].]

[801]

NOTES
   Sub-s (1): substituted by the Data Protection Act 1998, s 62(1), (2), as from 1 March 2000; for savings see Sch 14, para 20 thereto and the Data Protection Act 1998 (Commencement) Order 2000, SI 2000/183, art 2(2).
   Sub-ss (2)–(5): words in square brackets substituted by the Data Protection Act 1998, s 62(3), as from 1 March 2000; for savings see Sch 14, para 20 thereto and SI 2000/183, art 2(2).
   Sub-s (7): added, together with sub-s (8), by the Data Protection Act 1998, s 62(4), as from 1 March 2000 (for savings see Sch 14, para 20 thereto and SI 2000/183, art 2(2)); words in square brackets substituted by the Freedom of Information Act 2000, s 18(4), Sch 2, Pt I, para 7, as from 30 January 2001.
   Sub-s (8): added as noted to sub-s (7); words in second pair of square brackets substituted by the Freedom of Information Act 2000, s 18(4), Sch 2, Pt I, para 7, as from 30 January 2001.
   References to the OFT, etc: as to the abolition of the office of the Director General of Fair Trading and the substitution of the original references to the Director (and related expressions), see the note preceding s 1 at **[651]**.
   Regulations: the Consumer Credit (Credit Reference Agency) Regulations 2000, SI 2000/290.

160 Alternative procedure for business consumers

(1)   The [OFT], on an application made by a credit reference agency, may direct that this section shall apply to the agency if [it] is satisfied—
- (a)   that compliance with section 158 in the case of consumers who carry on a business would adversely affect the service provided to its customers by the agency, and
- (b)   that, having regard to the methods employed by the agency and to any other relevant factors, it is probable that consumers carrying on a business would not be prejudiced by the making of the direction.

(2)   Where an agency to which this section applies receives a request, particulars and a fee under section 158(1) from a consumer who carries on a business, and section 158(3) does not apply, the agency, instead of complying with section 158, may elect to deal with the matter under the following subsections.

(3)   Instead of giving the consumer a copy of the file, the agency shall within the prescribed period give notice to the consumer that it is proceeding under this section, and by notice give the consumer such information included in or based on entries in the file as the [OFT] may direct, together with a statement in the prescribed form of the consumer's rights under subsections (4) and (5).

(4)   If within 28 days after receiving the information given [to the consumer] under subsection (3), or such longer period as the [OFT] may allow, the consumer—
- (a)   gives notice to the [OFT] that [the consumer] is dissatisfied with the information, and
- (b)   satisfies the [OFT] that [the consumer] has taken such steps in relation to the agency as may be reasonable with a view to removing the cause of [the consumer's] dissatisfaction, and
- (c)   pays the [OFT] the specified fee,

the [OFT] may direct the agency to give the [OFT] a copy of the file, and the [OFT] may disclose to the consumer such of the information on the file as the [OFT] thinks fit.

(5)   Section 159 applies with any necessary modifications to information given to the consumer under this section as it applies to information given under section 158.

(6)   If an agency making an election under subsection (2) fails to comply with subsection (3) or (4) it commits an offence.

[(7)   In this section "consumer" has the same meaning as in section 158.]

[802]

NOTES
Sub-s (4): words in first, fourth, sixth and seventh pairs of square brackets substituted by the Data Protection Act 1998, s 62(5)(a), as from 1 March 2000; for savings see Sch 14, para 20 thereto and the Data Protection Act 1998 (Commencement) Order 2000, SI 2000/183, art 2(2).

Sub-s (7): added by the Data Protection Act 1998, s 62(5)(b), as from 1 March 2000; for savings see Sch 14, para 20 thereto and SI 2000/183, art 2(2).

References to the OFT, etc: as to the abolition of the office of the Director General of Fair Trading and the substitution of the original references to the Director (and related expressions), see the note preceding s 1 at **[651]**.

Regulations: the Consumer Credit (Credit Reference Agency) Regulations 2000, SI 2000/290.

[160A   Credit intermediaries

(1)   In this section "credit intermediary" means a person who in the course of business—
- (a)   carries out any of the activities specified in subsection (2) for a consideration that is or includes a financial consideration, and
- (b)   does not do so as a creditor.

(2)   The activities are—
- (a)   recommending or making available prospective regulated consumer credit agreements, other than agreements secured on land, to individuals,
- (b)   assisting individuals by undertaking other preparatory work in relation to such agreements, or
- (c)   entering into regulated consumer credit agreements, other than agreements secured on land, with individuals on behalf of creditors.

(3)   A credit intermediary must in—
- (a)   advertising of his relating to an activity in subsection (2) which is intended for individuals not acting the course of a business, or
- (b)   documentation of his relating to an activity in subsection (2) which is intended for individuals,

indicate the extent to which the intermediary is acting independently and in particular whether he works exclusively with a creditor.

(4) Where a credit intermediary carries on an activity specified in subsection (2) for a debtor, the intermediary must secure that any financial consideration payable to him by the debtor for the activity is disclosed to the debtor and then agreed in writing before the regulated consumer credit agreement is concluded.

(5) Where a credit intermediary carries on an activity specified in subsection (2) for a debtor, the intermediary must disclose to the creditor the financial consideration for the activity payable by the debtor if the annual percentage rate of the total charge for credit prescribed under section 20 is to be ascertained by the creditor.

(6) A credit intermediary who fails to comply with a requirement of this section commits an offence.

(7) An offence under this section is to be treated for the purposes of the definition of "relevant offence" in section 38(1) and (2) of the Regulatory Enforcement and Sanctions Act 2008 as an offence contained in this Act immediately before the day on which that Act was passed.]

[802A]

NOTES

Commencement: 30 April 2010 (for the purpose of the definition "credit intermediary"); 1 February 2011 (otherwise).

Inserted by the Consumer Credit (EU Directive) Regulations 2010, SI 2010/1010, regs 2, 41, with effect in relation to certain agreements before 1 February 2011, as provided for in regs 101, 101A of the 2010 Regulations at **[3942]**, **[3942A]**.

PART XI
ENFORCEMENT OF ACT

161 Enforcement authorities

(1) The following authorities ("enforcement authorities") have a duty to enforce this Act and regulations made under it—

(a) the [OFT],

(b) in Great Britain, the local weights and measures authority,

(c) in Northern Ireland, the Department of Commerce for Northern Ireland.

(2) ...

(3) Every local weights and measures authority shall, whenever the [OFT] requires, report to [it] in such form and with such particulars as [it] requires on the exercise of their functions under this Act.

(4)–(6) ...

[803]

NOTES

Sub-s (2): repealed by the Enterprise Act 2002, s 278, Sch 25, para 6(1), (32)(b), Sch 26, as from 1 April 2003.

Sub-ss (4)–(6): repealed by the Local Government, Planning and Land Act 1980, ss 1(4), 194, Sch 4, para 10, Sch 34, Pt IV, as from 13 November 1980.

References to the OFT, etc: as to the abolition of the office of the Director General of Fair Trading and the substitution of the original references to the Director (and related expressions), see the note preceding s 1 at **[651]**.

162 Powers of entry and inspection

(1) A duly authorised officer of an enforcement authority, at all reasonable hours and on production, if required, of his credentials, may—

(a) in order to ascertain whether a breach of any provision of or under this Act has been committed, inspect any goods and enter any premises (other than premises used only as a dwelling);

(b) if he has reasonable cause to suspect that a breach of any provision of or under this Act has been committed, in order to ascertain whether it has been committed, require any person—

    (i) carrying on, or employed in connection with, a business to produce any ... documents relating to it; or

    (ii) having control of any information relating to a business [to provide him with that information];

(c) if he has reasonable cause to believe that a breach of any provision of or under this Act has been committed, seize and detain any goods in order to ascertain (by testing or otherwise) whether such a breach has been committed;

(d) seize and detain any goods ... or documents which he has reason to believe may be required as evidence in proceedings for an offence under this Act;

(e) for the purpose of exercising his powers under this subsection to seize goods ... or documents, but only if and to the extent that it is reasonably necessary for securing that the provisions of this Act and of any regulations made under it are duly observed, require any person having authority to do so to break open any container and, if that person does not comply, break it open himself.

(2)   An officer seizing goods ... or documents in exercise of his powers under this section shall not do so without informing the person he seizes them from.

(3)   If a justice of the peace, on sworn information in writing, or, in Scotland, a sheriff or a magistrate or justice of the peace, on evidence on oath,—

    (a)   is satisfied that there is reasonable ground to believe either—

        (i)   that any goods ... or documents which a duly authorised officer has power to inspect under this section are on any premises and their inspection is likely to disclose evidence of a breach of any provision of or under this Act; or

        (ii)   that a breach of any provision of or under this Act has been, is being or is about to be committed on any premises; and

    (b)   is also satisfied either—

        (i)   that admission to the premises has been or is likely to be refused and that notice of intention to apply for a warrant under this subsection has been given to the occupier; or

        (ii)   that an application for admission, or the giving of such a notice, would defeat the object of the entry or that the premises are unoccupied or that the occupier is temporarily absent and it might defeat the object of the entry to wait for his return,

the justice or, as the case may be, the sheriff or magistrate may by warrant under his hand, which shall continue in force for a period of one month, authorise an officer of an enforcement authority to enter the premises (by force if need be).

(4)   An officer entering premises by virtue of this section may take such other persons and equipment with him as he thinks necessary; and on leaving premises entered by virtue of a warrant under subsection (3) shall, if they are unoccupied or the occupier is temporarily absent, leave them as effectively secured against trespassers as he found them.

(5)   Regulations may provide that, in cases described by the regulations, an officer of a local weights and measures authority is not to be taken to be duly authorised for the purposes of this section unless he is authorised by the [OFT].

(6)   A person who is not a duly authorised officer of an enforcement authority, but purports to act as such under this section, commits an offence.

(7)   ...

[(8)   References in this section to a breach of any provision of or under this Act do not include references to—

    (a)   a failure to comply with a requirement imposed under section 33A or 33B;

    (b)   a failure to comply with section 36A; or

    (c)   a failure in relation to which the OFT can apply for an order under section 36E.]

[804]

NOTES

For the text of this section as it had effect on 15 June 2006, prior to amendments made by the Consumer Credit Act 2006 and subsequent amendments, see the Appendix at [A154].

Sub-s (1): words omitted repealed and words in square brackets substituted by the Consumer Credit Act 2006, ss 51(2), 70, Sch 4, as from 6 April 2008.

Sub-ss (2), (3): words omitted repealed by the Consumer Credit Act 2006, s 70, Sch 4, as from 6 April 2008.

Sub-s (7): repealed by the Consumer Credit Act 2006, s 70, Sch 4, as from 6 April 2008.

Sub-s (8): added by the Consumer Credit Act 2006, s 51(3) , as from 6 April 2008.

References to the OFT, etc: as to the abolition of the office of the Director General of Fair Trading and the substitution of the original references to the Director (and related expressions), see the note preceding s 1 at [651].

Seize and detain goods, etc: the powers of seizure conferred by sub-s (1)(c), (d) are powers to which the Criminal Justice and Police Act 2001, s 50 apply (additional powers of seizure from premises); see s 50 of, and Sch 1, Pt 1, para 19 to, that Act.

Regulations: the Consumer Credit (Entry and Inspection) Regulations 1977, SI 1977/331.

---

163   Compensation for loss

(1)   Where, in exercising his powers under section 162, an officer of an enforcement authority seizes and detains goods and their owner suffers loss by reason of—

    (a)   that seizure, or

    (b)   the loss, damage or deterioration of the goods during detention,

then, unless the owner is convicted of an offence under this Act committed in relation to the goods, the authority shall compensate him for the loss so suffered.

(2)　Any dispute as to the right to or amount of any compensation under subsection (1) shall be determined by arbitration.

[805]

164　Power to make test purchases etc

(1)　An enforcement authority may—

    (a)　make, or authorise any of their officers to make on their behalf, such purchases of goods; and

    (b)　authorise any of their officers to procure the provision of such services or facilities or to enter into such agreements or other transactions,

as may appear to them expedient for determining whether any provisions made by or under this Act are being complied with.

(2)　Any act done by an officer authorised to do it under subsection (1) shall be treated for the purposes of this Act as done by him as an individual on his own behalf.

(3)　Any goods seized by an officer under this Act may be tested, and in the event of such a test he shall inform the person mentioned in section 162(2) of the test results.

(4)　Where any test leads to proceedings under this Act, the enforcement authority shall—

    (a)　if the goods were purchased, inform the person they were purchased from of the test results, and

    (b)　allow any person against whom the proceedings are taken to have the goods tested on his behalf if it is reasonably practicable to do so.

[806]

165　Obstruction of authorised officers

(1)　Any person who—

    (a)　wilfully obstructs an officer of an enforcement authority acting in pursuance of this Act; or

    (b)　wilfully fails to comply with any requirement properly made to him by such an officer under section 162; or

    (c)　without reasonable cause fails to give such an officer (so acting) other assistance or information he may reasonably require in performing his functions under this Act,

commits an offence.

[(1A)　A failure to give assistance or information shall not constitute an offence under subsection (1)(c) if it is also—

    (a)　a failure to comply with a requirement imposed under section 33A or 33B;

    (b)　a failure to comply with section 36A; or

    (c)　a failure in relation to which the OFT can apply for an order under section 36E.]

(2)　If any person, in giving such information as is mentioned in subsection (1)(c), makes any statement which he knows to be false, he commits an offence.

(3)　Nothing in this section requires a person to answer any question or give any information if to do so might incriminate that person or (where that person is [married or a civil partner) the spouse or civil partner] of that person.

[807]

NOTES

For the text of this section as it had effect on 15 June 2006, prior to amendments made by the Consumer Credit Act 2006 and subsequent amendments, see the Appendix at [A157].

Sub-s (1A): inserted by the Consumer Credit Act 2006, s 51(4), as from 6 April 2008.

Sub-s (3): words in square brackets substituted by the Civil Partnership Act 2004, s 261(1), Sch 27, para 50, as from 5 December 2005.

166　Notification of convictions and judgments to [OFT]

Where a person is convicted of an offence or has a judgment given against him by or before any court in the United Kingdom and it appears to the court—

    (a)　having regard to the functions of the [OFT] under this Act, that the conviction or judgment should be brought to the [OFT's] attention, and

    (b)　that it may not be brought to [its] attention unless arrangements for that purpose are made by the court,

the court may make such arrangements notwithstanding that the proceedings have been finally disposed of.

[808]

167 Penalties

(1)   An offence under a provision of this Act specified in column 1 of Schedule 1 is triable in the mode or modes indicated in column 3, and on conviction is punishable as indicated in column 4 (where a period of time indicates the maximum term of imprisonment, and a monetary amount indicates the maximum fine, for the offence in question).

(2)   A person who contravenes any regulations made under section 44, 52, 53, or 112, or made under section 26 by virtue of section 54, commits an offence.

[809]

168 Defences

(1)   In any proceedings for an offence under this Act it is a defence for the person charged to prove—

(a)   that his act or omission was due to a mistake, or to reliance on information supplied to him, or to an act or omission by another person, or to an accident or some other cause beyond his control, and

(b)   that he took all reasonable precautions and exercised all due diligence to avoid such an act or omission by himself or any person under his control.

(2)   If in any case the defence provided by subsection (1) involves the allegation that the act or omission was due to an act or omission by another person or to reliance on information supplied by another person, the person charged shall not, without leave of the court, be entitled to rely on that defence unless, within a period ending seven clear days before the hearing, he has served on the prosecutor a notice giving such information identifying or assisting in the identification of that other person as was then in his possession.

[810]

169 Offences by bodies corporate

Where at any time a body corporate commits an offence under this Act with the consent or connivance of, or because of neglect by, any individual, the individual commits the like offence if at that time—

(a)   he is a director, manager, secretary or similar officer of the body corporate, or

(b)   he is purporting to act as such an officer, or

(c)   the body corporate is managed by its members, of whom he is one.

[811]

170 No further sanctions for breach of Act

(1)   A breach of any requirement made (otherwise than by any court) by or under this Act shall incur no civil or criminal sanction as being such a breach, except to the extent (if any) expressly provided by or under this Act.

(2)   In exercising [its] functions under this Act the [OFT] may take account of any matter appearing to [it] to constitute a breach of a requirement made by or under this Act, whether or not any sanction for that breach is provided by or under this Act and, if it is so provided, whether or not proceedings have been brought in respect of the breach.

(3)   Subsection (1) does not prevent the grant of an injunction, or the making of an order of certiorari, mandamus or prohibition or as respects Scotland the grant of an interdict or of an order under section 91 of the Court of Session Act 1868 (order for specific performance of statutory duty).

[812]

171 Onus of proof in various proceedings

(1)   If an agreement contains a term signifying that in the opinion of the parties section 10(3)(b)(iii) does not apply to the agreement, it shall be taken not to apply unless the contrary is proved.

(2)   It shall be assumed in any proceedings, unless the contrary is proved, that when a person initiated a transaction as mentioned in section 19(1)(c) he knew the principal agreement had been made, or contemplated that it might be made.

(3)   Regulations under section 44 or 52 may make provision as to the onus of proof in any proceedings to enforce the regulations.

(4)   In proceedings brought by the creditor under a credit-token agreement—

(a)   it is for the creditor to prove that the credit-token was lawfully supplied to the debtor, and was accepted by him, and

(b)   if the debtor alleges that any use made of the credit-token was not authorised by him, it is for the creditor to prove either—

(i)   that the use was so authorised, or

(ii)   that the use occurred before the creditor had been given notice under section 84(3).

(5)   In proceedings under section 50(1) in respect of a document received by a minor at any school or other educational establishment for minors, it is for the person sending it to him at that establishment to prove that he did not know or suspect it to be such an establishment.

(6)   In proceedings under section 119(1) it is for the pawnee to prove that he had reasonable cause to refuse to allow the pawn to be redeemed.

(7)   ...

[813]

NOTES

For the text of this section as it had effect on 15 June 2006, prior to amendments made by the Consumer Credit Act 2006 and subsequent amendments, see the Appendix at [A163].

Sub-s (7): repealed by the Consumer Credit Act 2006, s 70, Sch 4, as from 6 April 2007, subject to transitional provisions in s 69(1) of, and Sch 3, paras 1, 15(5)(c) to, that Act at **[2077]**, **[2079]**.

172   Statements by creditor or owner to be binding

(1)   A statement by a creditor or owner is binding on him if given under—

section 77(1),

section 78(1),

section 79(1),

section 97(1),

section 107(1)(c),

section 108(1)(c), or

section 109(1)(c).

(2)   Where a trader—

(a)   gives a customer a notice in compliance with section 103(1)(b), or

(b)   gives a customer a notice under section 103(1) asserting that the customer is not indebted to him under an agreement,

the notice is binding on the trader.

(3)   Where in proceedings before any court—

(a)   it is sought to rely on a statement or notice given as mentioned in subsection (1) or (2), and

(b)   the statement or notice is shown to be incorrect,

the court may direct such relief (if any) to be given to the creditor or owner from the operation of subsection (1) or (2) as appears to the court to be just.

[814]

173   Contracting-out forbidden

(1)   A term contained in a regulated agreement or linked transaction, or in any other agreement relating to an actual or prospective regulated agreement or linked transaction, is void if, and to the extent that, it is inconsistent with a provision for the protection of the debtor or hirer or his relative or any surety contained in this Act or in any regulation made under this Act.

(2)   Where a provision specifies the duty or liability of the debtor or hirer or his relative or any surety in certain circumstances, a term is inconsistent with that provision if it purports to impose, directly or indirectly, an additional duty or liability on him in those circumstances.

(3)   Notwithstanding subsection (1), a provision of this Act under which a thing may be done in relation to any person on an order of the court or the [OFT] only shall not be taken to prevent its being done at any time with that person's consent given at that time, but the refusal of such consent shall not give rise to any liability.

[815]

NOTES

References to the OFT, etc: as to the abolition of the office of the Director General of Fair Trading and the substitution of the original references to the Director (and related expressions), see the note preceding s 1 at **[651]**.

PART XII
SUPPLEMENTAL

General

174   (*Repealed by the Enterprise Act 2002, ss 247(d), 278(2), Sch 26, as from 20 June 2003.*)

[174A   Powers to require provision of information or documents etc

(1)   Every power conferred on a relevant authority by or under this Act (however expressed) to require the provision or production of information or documents includes the power—

    (a)   to require information to be provided or produced in such form as the authority may specify, including, in relation to information recorded otherwise than in a legible form, in a legible form;

    (b)   to take copies of, or extracts from, any documents provided or produced by virtue of the exercise of the power;

    (c)   to require the person who is required to provide or produce any information or document by virtue of the exercise of the power—

        (i)   to state, to the best of his knowledge and belief, where the information or document is;

        (ii)   to give an explanation of the information or document;

        (iii)   to secure that any information provided or produced, whether in a document or otherwise, is verified in such manner as may be specified by the authority;

        (iv)   to secure that any document provided or produced is authenticated in such manner as may be so specified;

    (d)   to specify a time at or by which a requirement imposed by virtue of paragraph (c) must be complied with.

(2)   Every power conferred on a relevant authority by or under this Act (however expressed) to inspect or to seize documents at any premises includes the power to take copies of, or extracts from, any documents inspected or seized by virtue of the exercise of the power.

(3)   But a relevant authority has no power under this Act—

    (a)   to require another person to provide or to produce,

    (b)   to seize from another person, or

    (c)   to require another person to give access to premises for the purposes of the inspection of, any information or document which the other person would be entitled to refuse to provide or produce in proceedings in the High Court on the grounds of legal professional privilege or (in Scotland) in proceedings in the Court of Session on the grounds of confidentiality of communications.

(4)   In subsection (3) "communications" means—

    (a)   communications between a professional legal adviser and his client;

    (b)   communications made in connection with or in contemplation of legal proceedings and for the purposes of those proceedings.

(5)   In this section "relevant authority" means—

    (a)   the OFT or an enforcement authority (other than the OFT);

    (b)   an officer of the OFT or of an enforcement authority (other than the OFT).]

[816]

NOTES

Commencement: 6 April 2008.
Inserted by the Consumer Credit Act 2006, s 51(5), as from 6 April 2008.

---

175   Duty of persons deemed to be agents

Where under this Act a person is deemed to receive a notice or payment as agent of the creditor or owner under a regulated agreement, he shall be deemed to be under a contractual duty to the creditor or owner to transmit the notice, or remit the payment, to him forthwith.

[817]

176   Service of documents

(1)   A document to be served under this Act by one person ("the server") on another person ("the subject") is to be treated as properly served on the subject if dealt with as mentioned in the following subsections.

(2)   The document may be delivered or sent [by an appropriate method] to the subject, or addressed to him by name and left at his proper address.

(3)   For the purposes of this Act, a document sent by post to, or left at, the address last known to the server as the address of a person shall be treated as sent by post to, or left at, his proper address.

PART 1
STATUTES

(4)   Where the document is to be served on the subject as being the person having any interest in land, and it is not practicable after reasonable inquiry to ascertain the subject's name or address, the document may be served by—

(a)   addressing it to the subject by the description of the person having that interest in the land (naming it), and

(b)   delivering the document to some responsible person on the land or affixing it, or a copy of it, in a conspicuous position on the land.

(5)   Where a document to be served on the subject as being a debtor, hirer or surety, or as having any other capacity relevant for the purposes of this Act, is served at any time on another person who—

(a)   is the person last known to the server as having that capacity, but

(b)   before that time had ceased to have it,

the document shall be treated as having been served at that time on the subject.

(6)   Anything done to a document in relation to a person who (whether to the knowledge of the server or not) has died shall be treated for the purposes of subsection (5) as service of the document on that person if it would have been so treated had he not died.

[(7)   The following enactments shall not be construed as authorising service on the Public Trustee (in England and Wales) or the Probate Judge (in Northern Ireland) of any document which is to be served under this Act—

section 9 of the Administration of Estates Act 1925;

section 3 of the Administration of Estates Act (Northern Ireland) 1955.]

(8)   References in the preceding subsections to the serving of a document on a person include the giving of the document to that person.

[818]

NOTES

Sub-s (2): words in square brackets substituted by the Consumer Credit Act 1974 (Electronic Communications) Order 2004, SI 2004/3236, art 2(1), (6), as from 31 December 2004.

Sub-s (7): substituted by the Law of Property (Miscellaneous Provisions) Act 1994, s 21(1), Sch 1, para 6, as from 1 July 1995.

[176A   Electronic transmission of documents

(1)   A document is transmitted in accordance with this subsection if—

(a)   the person to whom it is transmitted agrees that it may be delivered to him by being transmitted to a particular electronic address in a particular electronic form,

(b)   it is transmitted to that address in that form, and

(c)   the form in which the document is transmitted is such that any information in the document which is addressed to the person to whom the document is transmitted is capable of being stored for future reference for an appropriate period in a way which allows the information to be reproduced without change.

(2)   A document transmitted in accordance with subsection (1) shall, unless the contrary is proved, be treated for the purposes of this Act, except section 69, as having been delivered on the working day immediately following the day on which it is transmitted.

(3)   In this section, "electronic address" includes any number or address used for the purposes of receiving electronic communications.]

[818A]

NOTES

Inserted by the Consumer Credit Act 1974 (Electronic Communications) Order 2004, SI 2004/3236, art 2(1), (7), as from 31 December 2004.

177   Saving for registered charges

(1)   Nothing in this Act affects the rights of a proprietor of a registered charge (within the meaning of the [Land Registration Act 2002]), who—

(a)   became the proprietor under a transfer for valuable consideration without notice of any defect in the title arising (apart from this section) by virtue of this Act, or

(b)   derives title from such a proprietor.

(2)   Nothing in this Act affects the operation of section 104 of the Law of Property Act 1925 (protection of purchaser where mortgagee exercises power of sale).

(3)   Subsection (1) does not apply to a proprietor carrying on [a consumer credit business, a consumer hire business or a business of debt-collecting or debt administration].

(4)   Where, by virtue of subsection (1), a land mortgage is enforced which apart from this section would be treated as never having effect, the original creditor or owner shall be liable to indemnify the debtor or hirer against any loss thereby suffered by him.

(5)   (*Applies to Scotland only.*)

(6)   In the application of this section to Northern Ireland—

(a)   any reference to the proprietor of a registered charge (within the meaning of the [Land Registration Act 2002]) shall be construed as a reference to the registered owner of a charge under the Local Registration of Title (Ireland) Act 1891 or Part IV of the Land Registration Act (Northern Ireland) 1970, and

(b)   for the reference to section 104 of the Law of Property Act 1925 there shall be substituted a reference to section 21 of the Conveyancing and Law of Property Act 1881 and section 5 of the Conveyancing Act 1911.

[819]

NOTES
For the text of this section as it had effect on 15 June 2006, prior to amendments made by the Consumer Credit Act 2006 and subsequent amendments, see the Appendix at [A169].
Sub-ss (1), (6): words in square brackets substituted by the Land Registration Act 2002, s 133, Sch 11, para 11, as from 13 October 2003.
Sub-s (3): words in square brackets substituted by the Consumer Credit Act 2006, s 24(5), as from 1 October 2008.
Conveyancing and Law of Property Act 1881, s 21: repealed by the Law of Property Act 1925, s 207, Sch 7.
Conveyancing Act 1911: repealed by the Settled Land Act 1925, the Trustee Act 1925 and the Law of Property Act 1925.

178   Local Acts

The Secretary of State or the Department of Commerce for Northern Ireland may by order make such amendments or repeals of any provision of any local Act as appears to the Secretary of State or, as the case may be, the Department, necessary or expedient in consequence of the replacement by this Act of the enactments relating to pawnbrokers and moneylenders.

[820]

NOTES
Order: the Consumer Credit (Local Acts) Order 1984, SI 1984/1107.

Regulations, orders, etc

179   Power to prescribe form etc of secondary documents

(1)   Regulations may be made as to the form and content of credit-cards, trading-checks, receipts, vouchers and other documents or things issued by creditors, owners or suppliers under or in connection with regulated agreements or by other persons in connection with linked transactions, and may in particular—

(a)   require specified information to be included in the prescribed manner in documents, and other specified material to be excluded;

(b)   contain requirements to ensure that specified information is clearly brought to the attention of the debtor or hirer, or his relative, and that one part of a document is not given insufficient or excessive prominence compared with another.

(2)   If a person issues any document or thing in contravention of regulations under subsection (1) then, as from the time of the contravention but without prejudice to anything done before it, this Act shall apply as if the regulated agreement had been improperly executed by reason of a contravention of regulations under section 60(1).

[821]

180   Power to prescribe form etc of copies

(1)   Regulations may be made as to the form and content of documents to be issued as copies of any executed agreement, security instrument or other document referred to in this Act, and may in particular—

(a)   require specified information to be included in the prescribed manner in any copy, and contain requirements to ensure that such information is clearly brought to the attention of a reader of the copy;

(b)   authorise the omission from a copy of certain material contained in the original, or the inclusion of such material in condensed form.

(2)   A duty imposed by any provision of this Act (except section 35) to supply a copy of any document—

(a)   is not satisfied unless the copy supplied is in the prescribed form and conforms to the prescribed requirements;

(b)   is not infringed by the omission of any material, or its inclusion in condensed form, if that is authorised by regulations;

and references in this Act to copies shall be construed accordingly.

(3)   Regulations may provide that a duty imposed by this Act to supply a copy of a document referred to in an unexecuted agreement or an executed agreement shall not apply to documents of a kind specified in the regulations.

[822]

NOTES

Regulations: the Consumer Credit (Cancellation Notices and Copies of Documents) Regulations 1983, SI 1983/1557.

181   Power to alter monetary limits etc

(1)   The Secretary of State may by order made by statutory instrument amend, or further amend, any of the following provisions of this Act so as to reduce or increase a sum mentioned in that provision, namely, sections [16B(1)], 17(1), ... [39A(3),] 70(6), 75(3)(b), 77(1), 78(1), 79(1), 84(1), 101(7)(a), 107(1), 108(1), 109(1), 110(1), 118(1)(b), 120(1)(a), ... [140B(6),] 155(1) and 158(1).

(2)   An order under subsection (1) amending section [16B(1)], 17(1), ... [39A(3),] 75(3)(b) ... [or 140B(6)] shall be of no effect unless a draft of the order has been laid before and approved by each House of Parliament.

[823]

NOTES

For the text of this section as it had effect on 15 June 2006, prior to amendments made by the Consumer Credit Act 2006 and subsequent amendments, see the Appendix at [A173].

Sub-s (1): number in first pair of square brackets substituted, first number omitted repealed and number in second pair of square brackets inserted (as from 6 April 2008), second number omitted repealed and number in third pair of square brackets inserted (as from 6 April 2007) by the Consumer Credit Act 2006, ss 5(7), 22(4)(a), 53(3)(a), 70, Sch 4, subject to transitional provisions in s 69(1) of, and Sch 3, paras 1, 15(5)(d) to, that Act at **[2077]**, **[2079]**.

Sub-s (2): number in first pair of square brackets substituted, number in second pair of square brackets inserted and first number omitted repealed (as from 6 April 2008), second number omitted repealed and number in third pair of square brackets inserted (as from 6 April 2007) by the Consumer Credit Act 2006, ss 5(7), 22(4)(b), 53(3)(b), 70, Sch 4, subject to transitional provisions in s 69(1) of, and Sch 3, paras 1, 15(5)(e) to, that Act at **[2077]**, **[2079]**.

Orders: the Consumer Credit (Increase of Monetary Limits) Order 1983, SI 1983/1878; the Consumer Credit (Further Increase of Monetary Amounts) Order 1998, SI 1998/997.

182   Regulations and orders

(1)   Any power of the Secretary of State to make regulations or orders under this Act, except the power conferred by sections 2(1)(a), 181 and 192, shall be exercisable by statutory instrument subject to annulment in pursuance of a resolution of either House of Parliament.

[(1A)   The power of the Lord Chancellor to make rules under section 40A(3) shall be exercisable by statutory instrument subject to annulment in pursuance of a resolution of either House of Parliament.]

(2)   Where a power to make regulations or orders *[or rules]* is exercisable by the Secretary of State *[or by the Lord Chancellor]* by virtue of this Act, regulations or orders *[or rules]* made in the exercise of that power may—

(a)   make different provision in relation to different cases or classes of case, and

(b)   exclude certain cases or classes of case, and

(c)   contain such transitional provisions as the [Secretary of State] thinks fit.

(3)   Regulations may provide that specified expressions, when used as described by the regulations, are to be given the prescribed meaning, notwithstanding that another meaning is intended by the person using them.

(4)   Any power conferred on the Secretary of State by this Act to make orders includes power to vary or revoke an order so made.

[824]

NOTES

For the text of this section as it had effect on 15 June 2006, prior to amendments made by the Consumer Credit Act 2006 and subsequent amendments, see the Appendix at [A174].

Sub-s (1A): inserted by the Consumer Credit Act 2006, s 58(2), as from 1 December 2007, and repealed by the Transfer of Functions of the Consumer Credit Appeals Tribunal Order 2009, SI 2009/1835, art 4(1), Sch 1, paras 1, 7(a), as from 1 September 2009, subject to transitional provisions and savings in Sch 4 thereto at **[3908]**.

Sub-s (2): words in italics (as inserted by the Consumer Credit Act 2006, s 58(3)) repealed and words in square brackets in para (c) substituted for words "person making them" (as previously substituted by the Consumer Credit Act 2006, s 58(3)) by SI 2009/1835, art 4(1), Sch 1, paras 1, 7(b), as from 1 September 2009, subject to transitional provisions and savings in Sch 4 thereto at **[3908]**.

[183 Determinations etc by OFT

(1)   The OFT may vary or revoke any determination made, or direction given, by it under this Act.

(2)   Subsection (1) does not apply to—

(a)   a determination to issue, renew or vary a licence;

(b)   a determination to extend a period under section 28B or to refuse to extend a period under that section;

(c)   a determination to end a suspension under section 33;

(d)   a determination to make an order under section 40(2), 148(2) or 149(2);

(e)   a determination mentioned in column 1 of the Table in section 41.]

[825]

NOTES

For the text of this section as it had effect on 15 June 2006, prior to amendments made by the Consumer Credit Act 2006 and subsequent amendments, see the Appendix at [A175].

Commencement: 6 April 2008.

Substituted by the Consumer Credit Act 2006, s 64, as from 6 April 2008.

Interpretation

184   Associates

[(1)   A person is an associate of an individual if that person is—

(a)   the individual's husband or wife or civil partner,

(b)   a relative of—

(i)   the individual, or

(ii)   the individual's husband or wife or civil partner, or

(c)   the husband or wife or civil partner of a relative of—

(i)   the individual, or

(ii)   the individual's husband or wife or civil partner.]

(2)   A person is an associate of any person with whom he is in partnership, and of the husband or wife [or civil partner] or a relative of any individual with whom he is in partnership.

(3)   A body corporate is an associate of another body corporate—

(a)   if the same person is a controller of both, or a person is a controller of one and persons who are his associates, or he and persons who are his associates, are the controllers of the other; or

(b)   if a group of two or more persons is a controller of each company, and the groups either consist of the same persons or could be regarded as consisting of the same persons by treating (in one or more cases) a member of either group as replaced by a person of whom he is an associate.

(4)   A body corporate is an associate of another person if that person is a controller of it or if that person and persons who are his associates together are controllers of it.

(5)   In this section "relative" means brother, sister, uncle, aunt, nephew, niece, lineal ancestor or lineal descendant, ... references to a husband or wife include a former husband or wife and a reputed husband [or wife, and references to a civil partner include a former civil partner] [and a reputed civil partner]; and for the purposes of this subsection a relationship shall be established as if any illegitimate child, step-child or adopted child of a person [were the legitimate child of the relationship in question].

[826]

NOTES

Sub-s (1): substituted by the Civil Partnership Act 2004, s 261(1), Sch 27, para 51(1), (2), as from 5 December 2005.

Sub-s (2): words in square brackets inserted by the Civil Partnership Act 2004, s 261(1), Sch 27, para 51(1), (3), as from 5 December 2005.

Sub-s (5): word omitted repealed and words in first and third pairs of square brackets substituted by the Civil Partnership Act 2004, s 261(1), (4), Sch 27, para 51(1), (4), Sch 30, as from 5 December 2005; words in second pair of square brackets inserted by the Civil Partnership Act 2004 (Overseas Relationships and Consequential, etc Amendments) Order 2005, SI 2005/3129, art 4(4), Sch 4, para 2, as from 5 December 2005.

185   Agreement with more than one debtor or hirer

(1)   Where an actual or prospective regulated agreement has two or more debtors or hirers (not being a partnership or an unincorporated body of persons)—

(a)   anything required by or under this Act to be done to or in relation to the debtor or hirer shall be done to or in relation to each of them; and

(b)   anything done under this Act by or on behalf of one of them shall have effect as if done by or on behalf of all of them.

[(1A)   Notwithstanding subsection (1) above, subsection (4) of section 55A (pre-contractual explanations etc) does not require an oral explanation to be given to any debtor to whom an explanation of the matters referred to in subsection (2)(a), (b) and (e) of that section has not been given orally or in person.]

[(2)   Notwithstanding subsection (1)(a), where credit is provided under an agreement to two or more debtors jointly, in performing his duties—

(a)   in the case of fixed-sum credit, under section 77A, or

(b)   in the case of running-account credit, under section 78(4), the creditor need not give statements to any debtor who has signed and given to him a notice (a "dispensing notice") authorising him not to comply in the debtor's case with section 77A or (as the case may be) 78(4).

(2A)   A dispensing notice given by a debtor is operative from when it is given to the creditor until it is revoked by a further notice given to the creditor by the debtor.

(2B)   But subsection (2) does not apply if (apart from this subsection) dispensing notices would be operative in relation to all of the debtors to whom the credit is provided.

(2C)   Any dispensing notices operative in relation to an agreement shall cease to have effect if any of the debtors dies.

(2D)   A dispensing notice which is operative in relation to an agreement shall be operative also in relation to any subsequent agreement which, in relation to the earlier agreement, is a modifying agreement.]

(3)   Subsection (1)(b) does not apply for the purposes of section 61(1)(a) …

(4)   Where a regulated agreement has two or more debtors or hirers (not being a partnership or an unincorporated body of persons), section 86 applies to the death of any of them.

(5)   An agreement for the provision of credit, or the bailment or (in Scotland) the hiring of goods, to two or more persons jointly where—

(a)   one or more of those persons is an individual, and

(b)   one or more of them is a [not an individual],

is a consumer credit agreement or consumer hire agreement if it would have been one had they all been individuals; and [each person within paragraph (b)] shall accordingly be included among the debtors or hirers under the agreement.

(6)   Where subsection (5) applies, references in this Act to the signing of any document by the debtor or hirer shall be construed in relation to a body corporate as referring to a signing on behalf of the body corporate [within paragraph (b) of that subsection].

[827]

NOTES

For the text of this section as it had effect on 15 June 2006, prior to amendments made by the Consumer Credit Act 2006 and subsequent amendments, see the Appendix at **[A177]**.

Sub-s (1A): inserted by the Consumer Credit (EU Directive) Regulations 2010, SI 2010/1010, regs 2, 4, as from 1 February 2011, with effect in relation to certain agreements before that date, as provided for in regs 101, 101A of the 2010 Regulations at **[3942]**, **[3942A]**.

Sub-ss (2), (2A)–(2D): substituted for original sub-s (2) by the Consumer Credit Act 2006, s 7(3), as from 1 October 2008, subject to transitional provisions in s 69(1) of, and Sch 3, paras 1, 4 to, that Act at **[2077]**, **[2079]**.

Sub-s (3): words omitted repealed by the Consumer Credit Act 2006, s 70, Sch 42, as from 6 April 2007, subject to transitional provisions and savings in s 69(1) of, and Sch 3, paras 1, 11(c) to, that Act at **[2077]**, **[2079]**.

Sub-s (5): words in square brackets substituted by the Consumer Credit Act 2006, s 5(8), as from 6 April 2007.

Sub-s (6): words in square brackets added by the Consumer Credit Act 2006, s 5(9), as from 6 April 2007.

---

186   Agreement with more than one creditor or owner

Where an actual or prospective regulated agreement has two or more creditors or owners, anything required by or under this Act to be done to, or in relation to, or by, the creditor or owner shall be effective if done to, or in relation to, or by, any one of them.

[828]

187   Arrangements between creditor and supplier

(1)   A consumer credit agreement shall be treated as entered into under pre-existing arrangements between a creditor and a supplier if it is entered into in accordance with, or in furtherance of, arrangements previously made between persons mentioned in subsection (4)(a), (b) or (c).

(2)   A consumer credit agreement shall be treated as entered into in contemplation of future arrangements between a creditor and a supplier if it is entered into in the expectation that

arrangements will subsequently be made between persons mentioned in subsection (4)(a), (b) or (c) for the supply of cash, goods and services (or any of them) to be financed by the consumer credit agreement.

(3) Arrangements shall be disregarded for the purposes of subsection (1) or (2) if—
   (a) they are arrangements for the making, in specified circumstances, of payments to the supplier by the creditor, and
   (b) the creditor holds himself out as willing to make, in such circumstances, payments of the kind to suppliers generally.

[(3A) Arrangements shall also be disregarded for the purposes of subsections (1) and (2) if they are arrangements for the electronic transfer of funds from a current account at a bank within the meaning of the Bankers' Books Evidence Act 1879.]

(4) The persons referred to in subsections (1) and (2) are—
   (a) the creditor and the supplier;
   (b) one of them and an associate of the other's;
   (c) an associate of one and an associate of the other's.

(5) Where the creditor is an associate of the supplier's, the consumer credit agreement shall be treated, unless the contrary is proved, as entered into under pre-existing arrangements between the creditor and the supplier.

[829]

NOTES
Sub-s (3A): inserted by the Banking Act 1987, s 89, as from 1 October 1987.

[187A Definition of "default sum"

(1) In this Act "default sum" means, in relation to the debtor or hirer under a regulated agreement, a sum (other than a sum of interest) which is payable by him under the agreement in connection with a breach of the agreement by him.

(2) But a sum is not a default sum in relation to the debtor or hirer simply because, as a consequence of his breach of the agreement, he is required to pay it earlier than he would otherwise have had to.]

[829A]

NOTES
Commencement: 16 June 2006.
Inserted by the Consumer Credit Act 2006, s 18(1), as from 16 June 2006.

188 Examples of use of new terminology

(1) Schedule 2 shall have effect for illustrating the use of terminology employed in this Act.

(2) The examples given in Schedule 2 are not exhaustive.

(3) In the case of conflict between Schedule 2 and any other provision of this Act, that other provision shall prevail.

(4) The Secretary of State may by order amend Schedule 2 by adding further examples or in any other way.

[830]

189 Definitions

(1) In this Act, unless the context otherwise requires—
   "advertisement" includes every form of advertising, whether in a publication, by television or radio, by display of notices, signs, labels, showcards or goods, by distribution of samples, circulars, catalogues, price lists or other material, by exhibition of pictures, models or films, or in any other way, and references to the publishing of advertisements shall be construed accordingly;
   "advertiser" in relation to an advertisement, means any person indicated by the advertisement as willing to enter into transactions to which the advertisement relates;
   "ancillary credit business" has the meaning given by section 145(1);
   "antecedent negotiations" has the meaning given by section 56;
   "appeal period" means the period beginning on the first day on which an appeal to the [First-tier Tribunal] may be brought and ending on the last day on which it may be brought or, if it is brought, ending on its final determination, or abandonment;
   ["appropriate method" means–
      (a) post, or
      (b) transmission in the form of an electronic communication in accordance with section 176A(1);]
   "assignment", in relation to Scotland, means assignation;

"associate" shall be construed in accordance with section 184;

["authorised business overdraft agreement" means a debtor-creditor agreement which provides authorisation in advance for the debtor to overdraw on a current account, where the agreement is entered into by the debtor wholly or predominantly for the purposes of the debtor's business (see subsection (2A));

"authorised non-business overdraft agreement" means a debtor-creditor agreement which provides authorisation in advance for the debtor to overdraw on a current account where—

    (a)   the credit must be repaid on demand or within three months, and

    (b)   the agreement is not entered into by the debtor wholly or predominantly for the purposes of the debtor's business (see subsection (2A));]

[.....]

"bill of sale" has the meaning given by section 4 of the Bills of Sale Act 1878 or, for Northern Ireland, by section 4 of the Bills of Sale (Ireland) Act 1879;

["building society" means a building society within the meaning of the Building Societies Act 1986;]

"business" includes profession or trade, and references to a business apply subject to subsection (2);

"cancellable agreement" means a regulated agreement which, by virtue of section 67, may be cancelled by the debtor or hirer;

"canvass" shall be construed in accordance with sections 48 and 153;

"cash" includes money in any form;

"charity" means as respects England and Wales a charity registered under [the Charities Act 1993] or an exempt charity (within the meaning of that Act), [as respects] Northern Ireland an institution or other organisation established for charitable purposes only ("organisation" including any persons administering a trust and "charitable" being construed in the same way as if it were contained in the Income Tax Acts) [and as respects Scotland a body entered in the Scottish Charity Register];

"conditional sale agreement" means an agreement for the sale of goods or land under which the purchase price or part of it is payable by instalments, and the property in the goods or land is to remain in the seller (notwithstanding that the buyer is to be in possession of the goods or land) until such conditions as to the payment of instalments or otherwise as may be specified in the agreement are fulfilled;

"consumer credit agreement" has the meaning given by section 8, and includes a consumer credit agreement which is cancelled under section 69(1), or becomes subject to section 69(2), so far as the agreement remains in force;

["consumer credit business" means any business being carried on by a person so far as it comprises or relates to—

    (a)   the provision of credit by him, or

    (b)   otherwise his being a creditor,

under regulated consumer credit agreements;]

"consumer hire agreement" has the meaning given by section 15;

["consumer hire business" means any business being carried on by a person so far as it comprises or relates to—

    (a)   the bailment or (in Scotland) the hiring of goods by him, or

    (b)   otherwise his being an owner,

under regulated consumer hire agreements;]

"controller", in relation to a body corporate, means a person—

    (a)   in accordance with whose directions or instructions the directors of the body corporate or of another body corporate which is its controller (or any of them) are accustomed to act, or

    (b)   who, either alone or with any associate or associates, is entitled to exercise or control the exercise of, one third or more of the voting power at any general meeting of the body corporate or of another body corporate which is its controller;

"copy" shall be construed in accordance with section 180;

.....

"court" means in relation to England and Wales the county court, in relation to Scotland the sheriff court and in relation to Northern Ireland the High Court or the county court;

"credit" shall be construed in accordance with section 9;

"credit-broker" means a person carrying on a business of credit brokerage;

"credit brokerage" has the meaning given by section 145(2);

["credit information services" has the meaning given by section 145(7B);]

["credit intermediary" has the meaning given by section 160A;]

"credit limit" has the meaning given by section 10(2);

"creditor" means the person providing credit under a consumer credit agreement or the person to whom his rights and duties under the agreement have passed by assignment or operation of law, and in relation to a prospective consumer credit agreement, includes the prospective creditor;

"credit reference agency" has the meaning given by section 145(8);

"credit-sale agreement" means an agreement for the sale of goods, under which the purchase price or part of it is payable by instalments, but which is not a conditional sale agreement;

"credit-token" has the meaning given by section 14(1);

"credit-token agreement" means a regulated agreement for the provision of credit in connection with the use of a credit-token;

"debt-adjusting" has the meaning given by section 145(5);

["debt administration" has the meaning given by section 145(7A);]

"debt-collecting" has the meaning given by section 145(7);

"debt-counselling" has the meaning given by section 145(6);

"debtor" means the individual receiving credit under a consumer credit agreement or the person to whom his rights and duties under the agreement have passed by assignment or operation of law, and in relation to a prospective consumer credit agreement includes the prospective debtor;

"debtor-creditor agreement" has the meaning given by section 13;

"debtor-creditor-supplier agreement" has the meaning given by section 12;

"default notice" has the meaning given by section 87(1);

["default sum" has the meaning given by section 187A;]

"deposit" means [(except in section 16(10) and 25(1B))] any sum payable by a debtor or hirer by way of deposit or down-payment, or credited or to be credited to him on account of any deposit or down-payment, whether the sum is to be or has been paid to the creditor or owner or any other person, or is to be or has been discharged by a payment of money or a transfer or delivery of goods or by any other means;

["documents" includes information recorded in any form;]

"electric line" has the meaning given by [the Electricity Act 1989] or, for Northern Ireland, [the Electricity (Northern Ireland) Order 1992];

["electronic communication" means an electronic communication within the meaning of the Electronic Communications Act 2000 (c 7);]

"embodies" and related words shall be construed in accordance with subsection (4);

"enforcement authority" has the meaning given by section 161(1);

"enforcement order" means an order under section 65(1), 105(7)(a) or (b), 111(2) or 124(1) or (2);

"executed agreement" means a document, signed by or on behalf of the parties, embodying the terms of a regulated agreement, or such of them as have been reduced to writing;

"exempt agreement" means an agreement specified in or under section 16[, 16A[, 16B or 16C];

"finance" means to finance wholly or partly and "financed" and "refinanced" shall be construed accordingly;

"file" and "copy of the file" have the meanings given by section 158(5);

"fixed-sum credit" has the meaning given by section 10(1)(b);

"friendly society" means a society registered [or treated as registered under the Friendly Societies Act 1974 or the Friendly Societies Act 1992] ... ;

"future arrangements" shall be construed in accordance with section 187;

"general notice" means a notice published by the [OFT] at a time and in a manner appearing to [it] suitable for securing that the notice is seen within a reasonable time by persons likely to be affected by it;

"give", means, deliver or send [by an appropriate method] to;

"goods" has the meaning given by [section 61(1) of the Sale of Goods Act 1979];

"group licence" has the meaning given by section 22(1)(b);

"High Court" means Her Majesty's High Court of Justice, or the Court of Session in Scotland or the High Court of Justice in Northern Ireland;

"hire-purchase agreement" means an agreement, other than a conditional sale agreement, under which—

    (a)   goods are bailed or (in Scotland) hired in return for periodical payments by the person to whom they are bailed or hired, and

    (b)   the property in the goods will pass to that person if the terms of the agreement are complied with and one or more of the following occurs—

        (i)   the exercise of an option to purchase by that person,

        (ii)   the doing of any other specified act by any party to the agreement,

        (iii)   the happening of any other specified event;

"hirer" means the individual to whom goods are bailed or (in Scotland) hired under a consumer hire agreement, or the person to whom his rights and duties under the agreement have passed by assignment or operation of law, and in relation to a prospective consumer hire agreement includes the prospective hirer;

["individual" includes—

(a)   a partnership consisting of two or three persons not all of whom are bodies corporate; and

(b)   an unincorporated body of persons which does not consist entirely of bodies corporate and is not a partnership;]

"installation" means—

(a)   the installing of any electric line or any gas or water pipe,

(b)   the fixing of goods to the premises where they are to be used, and the alteration of premises to enable goods to be used on them,

(c)   where it is reasonably necessary that goods should be constructed or erected on the premises where they are to be used, any work carried out for the purpose of constructing or erecting them on those premises;

.....

"judgment" includes an order or decree made by any court;

"land", includes an interest in land, and in relation to Scotland includes heritable subjects of whatever description;

"land improvement company" means an improvement company as defined by section 7 of the Improvement of Land Act 1899;

"land mortgage" includes any security charged on land;

"licence" means a licence under Part III ... ;

"licensed", in relation to any act, means authorised by a licence to do the act or cause or permit another person to do it;

"licensee", in the case of a group licence, includes any person covered by the licence;

"linked transaction" has the meaning given by section 19(1);

"local authority", in relation to England ... , means ... a county council, a London borough council, a district council, the Common Council of the City of London, or the Council of Isles of Scilly, [in relation to Wales means a county council or a county borough council,] and in relation to Scotland, means a [council constituted under section 2 of the Local Government etc (Scotland) Act 1994], and, in relation to Northern Ireland, means a district council;

.....

"modifying agreement" has the meaning given by section 82(2);

"mortgage", in relation to Scotland, includes any heritable security;

"multiple agreement" has the meaning given by section 18(1);

"negotiator" has the meaning given by section 56(1);

"non-commercial agreement" means a consumer credit agreement or a consumer hire agreement not made by the creditor or owner in the course of a business carried on by him;

"notice" means notice in writing;

"notice of cancellation" has the meaning given by section 69(1);

["OFT" means the Office of Fair Trading;]

["open-end" in relation to a consumer credit agreement, means of no fixed duration;]

"owner" means a person who bails or (in Scotland) hires out goods under a consumer hire agreement or the person to whom his rights and duties under the agreement have passed by assignment or operation of law, and in relation to a prospective consumer hire agreement, includes the prospective bailor or persons from whom the goods are to be hired;

"pawn" means any article subject to a pledge;

"pawn-receipt" has the meaning given by section 114;

"pawnee" and "pawnor" include any person to whom the rights and duties of the original pawnee or the original pawnor, as the case may be, have passed by assignment or operation of law;

"payment" includes tender;

.....

"pledge" means the pawnee's rights over an article taken in pawn;

"prescribed" means prescribed by regulations made by the Secretary of State;

"pre-existing arrangements" shall be construed in accordance with section 187;

"principal agreement" has the meaning given by section 19(1);

"protected goods" has the meaning given by section 90(7);

"quotation" has the meaning given by section 52(1)(a);

"redemption period" has the meaning given by section 116(3);

"register" means the register kept by the [OFT] under section 35;

"regulated agreement" means a consumer credit agreement, or consumer hire agreement, other than an exempt agreement, and "regulated" and "unregulated" shall be construed accordingly;

"regulations" means regulations made by the Secretary of State;

"relative", except in section 184, means a person who is an associate by virtue of section 184(1);

"representation" includes any condition or warranty, and any other statement or undertaking, whether oral or in writing;

"restricted-use credit agreement" and "restricted-use credit" have the meanings given by section 11(1);

"rules of court", in relation to Northern Ireland means, in relation to the High Court, rules made under section 7 of the Northern Ireland Act 1962, and, in relation to any other court, rules made by the authority having for the time being power to make rules regulating the practice and procedure in that court;

"running-account credit" shall be construed in accordance with section 10;

"security", in relation to an actual or prospective consumer credit agreement or consumer hire agreement, or any linked transaction, means a mortgage, charge, pledge, bond, debenture, indemnity, guarantee, bill, note or other right provided by the debtor or hirer, or at his request (express or implied), to secure the carrying out of the obligations of the debtor or hirer under the agreement;

"security instrument" has the meaning given by section 105(2);

"serve on" means deliver or send [by an appropriate method] to;

"signed" shall be construed in accordance with subsection (3);

"small agreement" has the meaning given by section 17(1), and "small" in relation to an agreement within any category shall be construed accordingly;

"specified fee" shall be construed in accordance with section 2(4) and (5);

"standard licence" has the meaning given by section 22(1)(a);

"supplier" has the meaning given by section 11(1)(b) or 12(c) or 13(c) or, in relation to an agreement falling within section 11(1)(a), means the creditor, and includes a person to whom the rights and duties of a supplier (as so defined) have passed by assignment or operation of law, or (in relation to a prospective agreement) the prospective supplier;

"surety" means the person by whom any security is provided, or the person to whom his rights and duties in relation to the security have passed by assignment or operation of law;

"technical grounds" shall be construed in accordance with subsection (5);

"time order" has the meaning given by section 129(1);

"total charge for credit" means a sum calculated in accordance with regulations under section 20(1);

"total price" means the total sum payable by the debtor under a hire-purchase agreement or a conditional sale agreement, including any sum payable on the exercise of an option to purchase, but excluding any sum payable as a penalty or as compensation or damages for a breach of the agreement;

["the Tribunal" means the Consumer Credit Appeals Tribunal;]

"unexecuted agreement" means a document embodying the terms of a prospective regulated agreement, or such of them as it is intended to reduce to writing;

"unlicensed" means without a licence but applies only in relation to acts for which a licence is required;

"unrestricted-use credit agreement" and "unrestricted-use credit" have the meanings given by section 11(2);

"working day" means any day other than—

    (a)   Saturday or Sunday,

    (b)   Christmas Day or Good Friday,

    (c)   a bank holiday within the meaning given by section 1 of the Banking and Financial Dealings Act 1971.

[(1A)   In sections 36E(3), 70(4), 73(4) and 75(2) … "costs", in relation to proceedings in Scotland, means expenses.]

(2)   A person is not to be treated as carrying on a particular type of business merely because occasionally he enters into transactions belonging to a business of that type.

[(2A)   For the purpose of the definitions of "authorised business overdraft agreement" and "authorised non-business overdraft agreement" subsections (2) to (5) of section 16B (declaration by the debtor as to the purposes of the agreement) apply.]

(3)   Any provision of this Act requiring a document to be signed is complied with by a body corporate if the document is sealed by that body.

This subsection does not apply to Scotland.

(4)   A document embodies a provision if the provision is set out either in the document itself or in another document referred to in it.

(5)   An application dismissed by the court or the [OFT] shall, if the court or the [OFT] (as the case may be) so certifies, be taken to be dismissed on technical grounds only.

(6)   Except in so far as the context otherwise requires, any reference in this Act to an enactment shall be construed as a reference to that enactment as amended by or under any other enactment, including this Act.

(7)   In this Act, except where otherwise indicated—

(a)   a reference to a numbered Part, section or Schedule is a reference to the Part or section of, or the Schedule to, this Act so numbered, and

(b)   a reference in a section to a numbered subsection is a reference to the subsection of that section so numbered, and

(c)   a reference in a section, subsection or Schedule to a numbered paragraph is a reference to the paragraph of that section, subsection or Schedule so numbered.

[831]

NOTES

For the text of this section as it had effect on 15 June 2006, prior to amendments made by the Consumer Credit Act 2006 and subsequent amendments, see the Appendix at [A181].

Sub-s (1) is amended as follows:

in definition "appeal period" words in square brackets substituted (for word "Tribunal", as previously substituted by the Consumer Credit Act 2006, s 58(4)(a)) and definition "the Tribunal" (as inserted by the Consumer Credit Act 2006, s 58(4)(b)) repealed by the Transfer of Functions of the Consumer Credit Appeals Tribunal Order 2009, SI 2009/1835, art 4(1), Sch 1, paras 1, 8(a), as from 1 September 2009, subject to transitional provisions and savings in Sch 4 thereto at **[3908]**;

definitions "appropriate method", "electronic communication" inserted and in definitions "give" and "serve on", words in square brackets substituted by the Consumer Credit Act 1974 (Electronic Communications) Order 2004, SI 2004/3236, art 2(1), (8), (9), as from 31 December 2004;

definitions "authorised business overdraft agreement", "authorised non-business overdraft agreement", "credit intermediary" and "open-end" inserted by the Consumer Credit (EU Directive) Regulations 2010, SI 2010/1010, regs 2, 19(1), (2), 39, 42, as from 30 April 2010;

definition "authorised institution" inserted by the Banking Act 1987, s 88, as from 1 October 1987, and repealed by the Financial Services and Markets Act 2000 (Consequential Amendments and Repeals) Order 2001, SI 2001/3649, art 176(a), as from 1 December 2001;

definition "building society" substituted by the Building Societies Act 1986, s 120, Sch 18, Pt I, para 10(4), as from 1 January 1987;

in definition "charity" words in first pair of square brackets substituted by the Charities Act 1993, s 98(1), Sch 6, para 30, as from 1 March 1996, words in second pair of square brackets substituted and words in third pair of square brackets added by the Charities and Trustee Investment (Scotland) Act 2005 (Consequential Provisions and Modifications) Order 2006, SI 2006/242, art 5, Schedule, Pt 1, para 1, as from 1 April 2006;

definitions "consumer credit business", "consumer hire business" substituted, definition "costs" (omitted) repealed, and definition "documents" inserted, by the Consumer Credit Act 2006, ss 23(a), (b), 51(6), 70, Sch 4, as from 6 April 2008;

definitions "credit information services", "debt administration", "default sum" inserted, by the Consumer Credit Act 2006, ss 18(2), 24(6), 25(5), as from 16 June 2006;

in definition "deposit" words in square brackets inserted by SI 2001/3649, art 176(b), as from 1 December 2001;

definition "Director" (omitted) repealed by the Enterprise Act 2002, s 278, Sch 25, para 6(1), (38)(a)(i), Sch 26, as from 1 April 2003;

in definition "electric line" words in first pair of square brackets substituted by the Electricity Act 1989, s 112(1), Sch 16, para 17(1), (3), as from 31 March 1990, words in second pair of square brackets substituted by the Electricity (Northern Ireland) Order 1992, SI 1992/231, art 95(1), Sch 12, para 15;

in definition "exempt agreement" words in first (outer) pair of square brackets inserted by the Consumer Credit Act 2006, s 5(10), as from 6 April 2008, and words in second (inner) pair of square brackets substituted by the Legislative Reform (Consumer Credit) Order 2008, SI 2008/2826, art 3(4), as from 31 October 2008;

in definition "friendly society" words in square brackets substituted by SI 2001/3649, art 176(c), as from 1 December 2001, words omitted repealed by the Friendly Societies Act 1992, s 120, Sch 22, Pt I, as from 1 January 1994;

in definition "goods" words in square brackets substituted by the Sale of Goods Act 1979, s 63, Sch 2, para 18, as from 1 January 1980;

definition "individual" substituted by the Consumer Credit Act 2006, s 1, as from 6 April 2007, subject to transitional provisions and savings in the Consumer Credit Act 2006 (Commencement No 2 and Transitional Provisions and Savings) Order 2007, SI 2007/123, arts 4, 5 and s 69(1) of, and Sch 3, paras 1, 17, 29 to, the 2006 Act at **[2077]**, **[2079]**;

definition "insurance company" (omitted) repealed by SI 2001/3649, art 176(a), as from 1 December 2001;

in definition "licence" words omitted repealed by the Consumer Credit Act 2006, s, 70, Sch 4, as from 6 April 2008;

in definition "local authority" words omitted in the first place repealed, and words in first pair of square brackets inserted, by the Local Government (Wales) Act 1994, s 66(6), (8), Sch 16, para 45, Sch 18, as from 1 April 1996, words omitted in the second place repealed by the Local Government Act 1985, s 102, Sch 17, as from 16 July 1985, and words in second pair of square brackets substituted by the Local Government etc (Scotland) Act 1994, s 180(1), Sch 13, para 94, as from 1 April 1996;

definition "minor" (omitted) repealed by the Age of Legal Capacity (Scotland) Act 1991, s 10, Sch 2;

definition "OFT" inserted by the Enterprise Act 2002, s 278(1), Sch 25, para 6(1), (38)(a)(iii), as from 1 April 2003;

and definition "personal credit agreement" (omitted) repealed by the Consumer Credit Act 2006, s 70, Sch 4, as from 31 October 2008: for effect and transitional provisions, see the Consumer Credit Act 2006 (Commencement No 4 and Transitional Provisions) Order 2008, SI 2008/831, arts 2(1), 4, Sch 1.

Sub-s (1A): inserted by the Consumer Credit Act 2006, s 27(3), as from 6 April 2008; words "and paragraphs 14 and 15 of Schedule A1" (omitted) repealed by SI 2009/1835, art 4(1), Sch 1, paras 1, 8(b), as from 1 September 2009, subject to transitional provisions and savings in Sch 4 thereto at **[3908]**.

Sub-s (2A): inserted by the Consumer Credit (EU Directive) Regulations 2010, SI 2010/1010, regs 2, 19(1), (3), as from 30 April 2010.

References to the OFT, etc: as to the abolition of the office of the Director General of Fair Trading and the substitution of the original references to the Director (and related expressions), see the note preceding s 1 at **[651]**.

[189A Meaning of "consumer credit EEA firm"

In this Act "consumer credit EEA firm" means an EEA firm falling within sub-paragraph (a), (b) or (c) of paragraph 5 of Schedule 3 to the Financial Services and Markets Act 2000 carrying on, or seeking to carry on, consumer credit business, consumer hire business or ancillary credit business for which a licence would be required under this Act but for paragraph 15(3) of Schedule 3 to the Financial Services and Markets Act 2000.]

[832]

NOTES

Inserted by the Financial Services and Markets Act 2000 (Consequential Amendments and Repeals) Order 2001, SI 2001/3649, art 177, as from 1 December 2001.

Miscellaneous

190 Financial provisions

(1) There shall be defrayed out of money provided by Parliament—

    (a) all expenses incurred by the Secretary of State in consequence of the provisions of this Act;

    (b) any expenses incurred in consequence of those provisions by any other Minister of the Crown or Government department;

    (c) any increase attributable to this Act in the sums payable out of money so provided under the Superannuation Act 1972 or the Fair Trading Act 1973.

(2) Any fees[, charges, penalties or other sums] received by the [OFT] under this Act shall be paid into the Consolidated Fund.

[833]

NOTES

For the text of this section as it had effect on 15 June 2006, prior to amendments made by the Consumer Credit Act 2006 and subsequent amendments, see the Appendix at [A183].

Sub-s (2): words in first pair of square brackets inserted by the Consumer Credit Act 2006, s 65, as from 16 June 2006.

References to the OFT, etc: as to the abolition of the office of the Director General of Fair Trading and the substitution of the original references to the Director (and related expressions), see the note preceding s 1 at **[651]**.

191 *(Applies to Northern Ireland only.)*

192 Transitional and commencement provisions, amendments and repeals

(1) The provisions of Schedule 3 shall have effect for the purposes of this Act.

(2) The appointment of a day for the purposes of any provision of Schedule 3 shall be effected by an order of the Secretary of State made by statutory instrument; and any such order shall include a provision amending Schedule 3 so as to insert an express reference to the day appointed.

(3) Subject to subsection (4)—

    (a) the enactments specified in Schedule 4 shall have effect subject to the amendments specified in that Schedule (being minor amendments or amendments consequential on the preceding provisions of this Act), and

    (b) the enactments specified in Schedule 5 are hereby repealed to the extent shown in column 3 of that Schedule.

(4) The Secretary of State shall by order made by statutory instrument provide for the coming into operation of the amendments contained in Schedule 4 and the repeals contained in Schedule 5, and those amendments and repeals shall have effect only as provided by an order so made.

[834]

NOTES

Orders: the Consumer Credit Act 1974 (Commencement No 1) Order 1975, SI 1975/2123; the Consumer Credit Act 1974 (Commencement No 2) Order 1977, SI 1977/325; the Consumer Credit Act 1974 (Commencement No 3) Order 1977, SI 1977/802; the Consumer Credit Act 1974 (Commencement No 4) Order 1977, SI 1977/2163; the Consumer Credit Act 1974 (Commencement No 5) Order 1979, SI 1979/1685; the Consumer Credit Act 1974 (Commencement No 6) Order 1980, SI 1980/50; the Consumer Credit Act 1974

(Commencement No 7) Order 1981, SI 1981/280; the Consumer Credit Act 1974 (Commencement No 8) Order 1983, SI 1983/1551; the Consumer Credit Act 1974 (Commencement No 9) Order 1984, SI 1984/436; the Consumer Credit Act 1974 (Commencement No 10) Order 1989, SI 1989/1128

193   Short title and extent

(1)   This Act may be cited as the Consumer Credit Act 1974.

(2)   This Act extends to Northern Ireland.

[835]

SCHEDULES

[SCHEDULE A1
THE CONSUMER CREDIT APPEALS TRIBUNAL

PART 1
INTERPRETATION

1.   In this Schedule—
   "the Deputy President" means the Deputy President of the Consumer Credit Appeals Tribunal;
   "lay panel" means the panel established under paragraph 3(3);
   "panel of chairmen" means the panel established under paragraph 3(1);
   "party" means, in relation to an appeal, the appellant or the OFT;
   "the President" means the President of the Consumer Credit Appeals Tribunal;
   "rules" means rules under section 40A(3) of this Act;
   "specified" means specified by rules.]

[835A]

NOTES
Commencement: 6 April 2008.
   Inserted by the Consumer Credit Act 2006, s 55(2), Sch 1, subject to transitional provisions in s 69 of, and Sch 3, paras 1, 26 to, that Act at **[2077]**, **[2079]** and repealed by the Transfer of Functions of the Consumer Credit Appeals Tribunal Order 2009, SI 2009/1835, art 4(1), Sch 1, paras 1, 9, as from 1 September 2009, subject to transitional provisions and savings in Sch 4 thereto at **[3908]**.

[PART 2
THE TRIBUNAL

The President and the Deputy President

2.—(1)   The Lord Chancellor shall appoint one of the members of the panel of chairmen to preside over the discharge of the Tribunal's functions.

(2)   The person so appointed shall be known as the President of the Consumer Credit Appeals Tribunal.

(3)   The Lord Chancellor may appoint one of the members of the panel of chairmen to be the Deputy President of the Consumer Credit Appeals Tribunal.

(4)   The Deputy President shall have such functions in relation to the Tribunal as the President may assign to him.

(5)   If the President or the Deputy President ceases to be a member of the panel of chairmen, he shall also cease to be the President or (as the case may be) the Deputy President.

(6)   The functions of the President may, if he is absent or is otherwise unable to act, be discharged—
   (a)   by the Deputy President; or
   (b)   if there is no Deputy President or he too is absent or otherwise unable to act, by a person appointed for that purpose from the panel of chairmen by the Lord Chancellor.

Panels

3.—(1)   The Lord Chancellor shall appoint a panel of persons for the purpose of serving as chairmen of the Tribunal.

(2)   A person shall not be appointed to the panel of chairmen unless he—
   [(a)   satisfies the judicial-appointment eligibility condition on a 5-year basis;]
   (b)   is an advocate or solicitor in Scotland of at least [five] years' standing; or
   (c)   is a member of the Bar of Northern Ireland, or a solicitor of the Supreme Court of Northern Ireland, of at least [five] years' standing.

(*3*)   The Lord Chancellor shall also appoint a panel of persons who appear to him to be qualified by experience or otherwise to deal with appeals of the kind that may be made to the Tribunal.

Terms of office etc

4.—(*1*)   Each member of the panel of chairmen or the lay panel shall hold and vacate office in accordance with the terms of his appointment.

(*2*)   The Lord Chancellor may remove a member of either panel from office on the ground of incapacity or misbehaviour.

(*3*)   A member of either panel—
   (*a*)   may at any time resign office by notice in writing to the Lord Chancellor;
   (*b*)   is eligible for re-appointment if he ceases to hold office.

Remuneration and allowances

5.   The Lord Chancellor may pay to a person in respect of his service—
   (*a*)   as the President or the Deputy President,
   (*b*)   as a member of the Tribunal, or
   (*c*)   as a person appointed under paragraph 7(*4*),
such remuneration and allowances as the Lord Chancellor may determine.

Staff and costs

6.—(*1*)   The Lord Chancellor may appoint such staff for the Tribunal as he may determine.

(*2*)   The Lord Chancellor shall defray—
   (*a*)   the remuneration of the Tribunal's staff; and
   (*b*)   such other costs of the Tribunal as he may determine.]

[835B]

NOTES
Commencement: 6 April 2008.
Inserted and repealed as noted to Pt I at **[835A]**.
Para 3: words in square brackets substituted by the Tribunals, Courts and Enforcement Act 2007, s 50, Sch 10, Pt 1, para 11, as from 21 July 2008.

[PART 3
CONSTITUTION OF THE TRIBUNAL

7.—(*1*)   On an appeal to the Tribunal, the persons to act as members of the Tribunal for the purposes of the appeal shall be selected from the panel of chairmen or the lay panel.

(*2*)   The selection shall be in accordance with arrangements made by the President for the purposes of this paragraph.

(*3*)   Those arrangements shall provide for at least one member to be a person selected from the panel of chairmen.

(*4*)   If it appears to the Tribunal that a matter before it involves a question of fact of special difficulty, it may appoint one or more experts to provide assistance.]

[835C]

NOTES
Commencement: 6 April 2008.
Inserted and repealed as noted to Pt I at **[835A]**.

[PART 4
TRIBUNAL POWERS AND PROCEDURE

Sittings

8.   The Tribunal shall sit at such times and in such places as the Lord Chancellor may direct.

Evidence

9.—(*1*)   Subject to sub-paragraph (*2*), the Tribunal may, on an appeal, consider any evidence that it thinks relevant, whether or not it was available to the OFT at the time it made the determination appealed against.

(*2*)   Rules may make provision restricting the evidence that the Tribunal may consider on an appeal in specified circumstances.

Rules on procedure

10.   Rules may include, amongst other things, provision—
  (a)   about the withdrawal of appeals;
  (b)   about persons who may appear on behalf of a party to an appeal;
  (c)   about how an appeal is to be dealt with if a person acting as member of the Tribunal in respect of the appeal becomes unable to act;
  (d)   setting time limits in relation to anything that is to be done for the purposes of an appeal or for such limits to be set by the Tribunal or a member of the panel of chairmen;
  (e)   for time limits (including the period specified for the purposes of section 41(1) of this Act) to be extended by the Tribunal or a member of the panel of chairmen;
  (f)   conferring powers on the Tribunal or a member of the panel of chairmen to give such directions to the parties to an appeal as it or he thinks fit for purposes connected with the conduct and disposal of the appeal;
  (g)   about the holding of hearings by the Tribunal or a member of the panel of chairmen (including for such hearings to be held in private);
  (h)   placing restrictions on the disclosure of information and documents or for such restrictions to be imposed by the Tribunal or a member of the panel of chairmen;
  (i)   about the consequences of a failure to comply with a requirement imposed by or under any rule (including for the immediate dismissal or allowing of an appeal if the Tribunal or a member of the panel of chairmen thinks fit);
  (j)   for proceedings on different appeals (including appeals with different appellants) to take place concurrently;
  (k)   for the suspension of determinations of the OFT;
  (l)   for the suspension of decisions of the Tribunal;
  (m)   for the Tribunal to reconsider its decision disposing of an appeal where it has reason to believe that the decision was wrongly made because of an administrative error made by a member of its staff.

11.   …

Disposal of appeals

12.—(1)   The Tribunal shall decide an appeal by reference to the grounds of appeal set out in the notice of appeal.

  (2)   In disposing of an appeal the Tribunal may do one or more of the following—
  (a)   confirm the determination appealed against;
  (b)   quash that determination;
  (c)   vary that determination;
  (d)   remit the matter to the OFT for reconsideration and determination in accordance with the directions (if any) given to it by the Tribunal;
  (e)   give the OFT directions for the purpose of giving effect to its decision.

  (3)   In the case of an appeal against a determination to impose a penalty, the Tribunal—
  (a)   has no power by virtue of sub-paragraph (2)(c) to increase the penalty;
  (b)   may extend the period within which the penalty is to be paid (including in cases where that period has already ended).

  (4)   Sub-paragraph (3) does not affect—
  (a)   the Tribunal's power to give directions to the OFT under sub-paragraph (2)(d); or
  (b)   what the OFT can do where a matter is remitted to it under sub-paragraph (2)(d).

  (5)   Where the Tribunal remits a matter to the OFT, it may direct that the requirements of section 34 of this Act are not to apply, or are only to apply to a specified extent, in relation to the OFT's reconsideration of the matter.

  (6)   Subject to sub-paragraphs (7) and (8), where the Tribunal remits an application to the OFT, section 6(1) and (3) to (9) of this Act shall apply as if the application had not been previously determined by the OFT.

  (7)   In the case of a general notice which came into effect after the determination appealed against was made but before the application was remitted, the applicant shall provide any information or document which he is required to provide under section 6(6) within—
  (a)   the period of 28 days beginning with the day on which the application was remitted; or
  (b)   such longer period as the OFT may allow.

  (8)   In the case of—
  (a)   any information or document which was superseded,
  (b)   any change in circumstances which occurred, or
  (c)   any error or omission of which the applicant became aware,

after the determination appealed against was made but before the application was remitted, any notification that is required to be given by the applicant under section 6(7) shall be given within the period of 28 days beginning with the day on which the application was remitted.

Decisions of the Tribunal

13.—(*1*)   A decision of the Tribunal may be taken by majority.

(*2*)   A decision of the Tribunal disposing of an appeal shall—
   (*a*)   state whether it was unanimous or taken by majority; and
   (*b*)   be recorded in a document which—
      (*i*)   contains a statement of the reasons for the decision and any other specified information; and
      (*ii*)   is signed and dated by a member of the panel of chairmen.

(*3*)   Where the Tribunal disposes of an appeal it shall—
   (*a*)   send to each party to the appeal a copy of the document mentioned in sub-paragraph (2)(*b*); and
   (*b*)   publish that document in such manner as it thinks fit.

(*4*)   The Tribunal may exclude from what it publishes under sub-paragraph (3)(*b*) information of a specified description.

Costs

14.—(*1*)   Where the Tribunal disposes of an appeal and—
   (*a*)   it decides that the OFT was wrong to make the determination appealed against, or
   (*b*)   during the course of the appeal the OFT accepted that it was wrong to make that determination,

it may order the OFT to pay to the appellant the whole or a part of the costs incurred by the appellant in relation to the appeal.

(*2*)   In determining whether to make such an order, and the terms of such an order, the Tribunal shall have regard to whether it was unreasonable for the OFT to make the determination appealed against.

15.   Where—
   (*a*)   the Tribunal disposes of an appeal or an appeal is withdrawn before the Tribunal disposes of it, and
   (*b*)   the Tribunal thinks that a party to the appeal acted vexatiously, frivolously or unreasonably in bringing the appeal or otherwise in relation to the appeal,

it may order that party to pay to the other party the whole or a part of the costs incurred by the other party in relation to the appeal.

16.   An order of the Tribunal under paragraph 14 or 15 may be enforced—
   (*a*)   as if it were an order of the county court; or
   (*b*)   in Scotland, as if it were an interlocutor of the Court of Session.]

[835D]

NOTES

Commencement: 1 December 2007 (paras 9(2), 10); 6 April 2008 (paras 8, 9(1), 12–16); to be appointed (otherwise).

Inserted and repealed as noted to Pt I at **[835A]**.

Para 11: repealed by the Tribunals, Courts and Enforcement Act 2007, s 146, Sch 23, Pt 1, as from 3 November 2008.

Rules: the Consumer Credit Appeals Tribunal Rules 2008, SI 2008/668 at **[3616]**.

SCHEDULE 1
PROSECUTION AND PUNISHMENT OF OFFENCES
Section 167

1 Section	*2* Offence	*3* Mode of prosecution	*4* Imprisonment or fine
7	Knowingly or recklessly giving false information to [OFT].	(a) Summarily. (b) On indictment.	[The prescribed sum]. 2 years or a fine or both.
39(1)	Engaging in activities requiring a licence when not a licensee.	(a) Summarily. (b) On indictment.	[The prescribed sum]. 2 years or a fine or both.
39(2)	Carrying on business under a name not specified in licence.	(a) Summarily. (b) On indictment.	[The prescribed sum]. 2 years or a fine or both.

1 Section	2 Offence	3 Mode of prosecution	4 Imprisonment or fine
39(3)	Failure to notify changes in registered particulars.	(a) Summarily.	[The prescribed sum].
		(b) On indictment.	2 years or a fine or both.
45	Advertising credit where goods etc not available for cash.	(a) Summarily.	[The prescribed sum].
		(b) On indictment.	2 years or a fine or both.
...	...	...	...
47(1)	Advertising infringements.	(a) Summarily.	[The prescribed sum].
		(b) On indictment.	2 years or a fine or both.
49(1)	Canvassing debtor-creditor agreements off trade premises.	(a) Summarily.	[The prescribed sum].
		(b) On indictment.	1 year or a fine or both.
49(2)	Soliciting debtor-creditor agreements during visits made in response to previous oral requests.	(a) Summarily.	[The prescribed sum].
		(b) On indictment.	1 year or a fine or both.
50(1)	Sending circulars to minors.	(a) Summarily.	[The prescribed sum].
		(b) On indictment.	1 year or a fine or both.
51(1)	Supplying unsolicited credit-tokens.	(a) Summarily.	[The prescribed sum].
		(b) On indictment.	2 years or a fine or both.
[51A(1)	Breach of restrictions on provision of credit card cheques.	(a) Summarily.	The statutory maximum.
		(b) On indictment.	A fine.]
...	...	...	...
80(2)	Failure to tell creditor or owner whereabouts of goods.	Summarily.	[Level 3 on the standard scale.]
...	...	...	...
114(2)	Taking pledges from minors.	(a) Summarily.	[The prescribed sum].
		(b) On indictment.	1 year or a fine or both.
115	Failure to supply copies of a pledge agreement or pawn-receipt.	Summarily.	[Level 4 on the standard scale.]
119(1)	Unreasonable refusal to allow pawn to be redeemed.	Summarily.	[Level 4 on the standard scale.]
154	Canvassing ancillary credit services off trade premises.	(a) Summarily.	[The prescribed sum].
		(b) On indictment.	1 year or a fine or both.
157(3)	Refusal to give name etc of credit reference agency.	Summarily.	[Level 4 on the standard scale.]

PART 1 STATUTES

1	2	3	4
Section	Offence	Mode of prosecution	Imprisonment or fine
158(4)	Failure of credit reference agency to disclose filed information.	Summarily.	[Level 4 on the standard scale.]
159(6)	Failure of credit reference agency to correct information.	Summarily.	[Level 4 on the standard scale.]
160(6)	Failure of credit reference agency to comply with section 160(3) or (4).	Summarily.	[Level 4 on the standard scale.]
[160A	Failure of credit intermediary to comply with section 160A(3), (4) or (5).	Summarily.	Level 4 on the standard scale.]
162(6)	Impersonation of enforcement authority officers.	(a) Summarily.	[The prescribed sum].
		(b) On indictment.	2 years or a fine or both.
165(1)	Obstruction of enforcement authority officers.	Summarily.	[Level 4 on the standard scale.]
165(2)	Giving false information to enforcement authority officers.	(a) Summarily.	[The prescribed sum].
		(b) On indictment.	2 years or a fine or both.
167(2)	Contravention of regulations under section 44, 52, 53, 54 or 112.	(a) Summarily.	[The prescribed sum].
		(b) On indictment.	2 years or a fine or both.
174(5)	Wrongful disclosure of information.	(a) Summarily.	[The prescribed sum].
		(b) On indictment.	2 years or a fine or both.

[836]

NOTES

For the text of this Schedule as it had effect on 15 June 2006, prior to amendments made by the Consumer Credit Act 2006 and subsequent amendments, see the Appendix at [A186].

Entry relating to s 51A(1) inserted by the Financial Services Act 2010, s 15(1), (3), as from a day to be appointed.

Entry relating to s 160A inserted by the Consumer Credit (EU Directive) Regulations 2010, SI 2010/1010, regs 2, 43, as from 1 February 2011, with effect in relation to certain agreements before that date, as provided for in regs 101, 101A of the 2010 Regulations at **[3942]**, **[3942A]**.

Entries omitted repealed by the Consumer Protection from Unfair Trading Regulations 2008, SI 2008/1277, reg 30(3), Sch 4, as from 26 May 2008.

References to the prescribed sum substituted by virtue of the Magistrates' Courts Act 1980, s 32(2).

References to a level on the standard scale substituted by virtue of the Criminal Justice Act 1982, ss 38, 46.

References to the OFT, etc: as to the abolition of the office of the Director General of Fair Trading and the substitution of the original references to the Director (and related expressions), see the note preceding s 1 at **[651]**.

SCHEDULE 2
EXAMPLES OF USE OF NEW TERMINOLOGY

Section 188(1)

PART I
LIST OF TERMS

Term	Defined in section	Illustrated by example(s)
Advertisement	189(1)	2
Advertiser	189(1)	2
Antecedent negotiations	56	1, 2, 3, 4
Cancellable agreement	67	4
Consumer credit agreement	8	5, 6, 7, 15, 19, 21
Consumer hire agreement	15	20, 24
Credit	9	16, 19, 21
Credit-broker	189(1)	2
Credit limit	10(2)	6, 7, 19, 22, 23
Creditor	189(1)	1, 2, 3, 4
Credit-sale agreement	189(1)	5
Credit-token	14	3, 14, 16
Credit-token agreement	14	3, 14, 16, 22
Debtor-creditor agreement	13	8, 16, 17, 18
Debtor-creditor-supplier agreement	12	8, 16
Fixed-sum credit	10	9, 10, 17, 23
Hire-purchase agreement	189(1)	10
Individual	189(1)	19, 24
Linked transaction	19	11
Modifying agreement	82(2)	24
Multiple agreement	18	16, 18
Negotiator	56(1)	1, 2, 3, 4
…	…	…
Pre-existing arrangements	187	8, 21
Restricted-use credit	11	10, 12, 13, 14, 16
Running-account credit	10	15, 16, 18, 23
Small agreement	17	16, 17, 22
Supplier	189(1)	3, 14
Total charge for credit	20	5, 10
Total price	189(1)	10
Unrestricted-use credit	11	8, 12, 16, 17, 18

[837]

NOTES

For the text of this Schedule as it had effect on 15 June 2006, prior to amendments made by the **Consumer Credit Act 2006 and subsequent amendments, see the Appendix at [A187].**

Entry relating to "personal credit agreement" (omitted) repealed by the Consumer Credit Act 2006, s 70, Sch 4, as from 31 October 2008.

PART II
EXAMPLES
EXAMPLE 1

Facts. Correspondence passes between an employee of a moneylending company (writing on behalf of the company) and an individual about the terms on which the company would grant him a loan under a regulated agreement.

Analysis. The correspondence constitutes antecedent negotiations falling within section 56(1)(a), the moneylending company being both creditor and negotiator.

EXAMPLE 2

Facts. Representations are made about goods in a poster displayed by a shopkeeper near the goods, the goods being selected by a customer who has read the poster and then sold by the shopkeeper to a finance company introduced by him (with whom he has a business relationship). The goods are disposed of by the finance company to the customer under a regulated hire-purchase agreement.

Analysis. The representations in the poster constitute antecedent negotiations falling within section 56(1)(b), the shopkeeper being the credit-broker and negotiator and the finance company being the creditor. The poster is an advertisement and the shopkeeper is the advertiser.

EXAMPLE 3

Facts. Discussions take place between a shopkeeper and a customer about goods the customer wishes to buy using a credit-card issued by the D Bank under a regulated agreement.

Analysis. The discussions constitute antecedent negotiations falling within section 56(1)(c), the shopkeeper being the supplier and negotiator and the D Bank the creditor. The credit-card is a credit-token as defined in section 14(1), and the regulated agreement under which it was issued is a credit-token agreement as defined in section 14(2).

EXAMPLE 4

Facts. Discussions take place and correspondence passes between a secondhand car dealer and a customer about a car, which is then sold by the dealer to the customer under a regulated conditional sale agreement. Subsequently, on a revocation of that agreement by consent, the car is resold by the dealer to a finance company introduced by him (with whom he has a business relationship), who in turn dispose of it to the same customer under a regulated hire-purchase agreement.

Analysis. The discussions and correspondence constitute antecedent negotiations in relation both to the conditional sale agreement and the hire-purchase agreement. They fall under section 56(1)(a) in relation to the conditional sale agreement, the dealer being the creditor and the negotiator. In relation to the hire-purchase agreement they fall within section 56(1)(b), the dealer continuing to be treated as the negotiator but the finance company now being the creditor. Both agreements are cancellable if the discussions took place when the individual conducting the negotiations (whether the "negotiator" or his employee or agent) was in the presence of the debtor, unless the unexecuted agreement was signed by the debtor at trade premises (as defined in section 67(b)). If the discussions all took place by telephone however, or the unexecuted agreement was signed by the debtor on trade premises (as so defined) the agreements are not cancellable.

EXAMPLE 5

Facts. E agrees to sell to F (an individual) an item of furniture in return for 24 monthly instalments of £10 payable in arrears. The property in the goods passes to F immediately.

Analysis. This is a credit-sale agreement (see definition of "credit-sale agreement" in section 189(1)). The credit provided amounts to £240 less the amount which, according to regulations made under section 20(1), constitutes the total charge for credit. (This amount is required to be deducted by section 9(4)). Accordingly the agreement falls within section 8(2) and is a consumer credit agreement.

EXAMPLE 6

Facts. The G Bank grants H (an individual) an unlimited overdraft, with an increased rate of interest on so much of any debit balance as exceeds £2,000.

Analysis. Although the overdraft purports to be unlimited, the stipulation for increased interest above £2,000 brings the agreement within section 10(3)(b)(ii) and it is a consumer credit agreement.

EXAMPLE 7

Facts. J is an individual who owns a small shop which usually carries a stock worth about £1,000. K makes a stocking agreement under which he undertakes to provide on short-term credit the stock needed from time to time by J without any specified limit.

Analysis. Although the agreement appears to provide unlimited credit, it is probable, having regard to the stock usually carried by J, that his indebtedness to K will not at any time rise above £5,000. Accordingly the agreement falls within section 10(3)(b)(iii) and is a consumer credit agreement.

EXAMPLE 8

Facts. U, a moneylender, lends £500 to V (an individual) knowing he intends to use it to buy office equipment from W. W introduced V to U, it being his practice to introduce customers needing finance to him. Sometimes U gives W a commission for this and sometimes not. U pays the £500 direct to V.

Analysis. Although this appears to fall under section 11(1)(b), it is excluded by section 11(3) and is therefore (by section 11(2)) an unrestricted-use credit agreement. Whether it is a debtor-creditor agreement (by section 13(c)) or a debtor-creditor-supplier agreement (by section 12(c)) depends on whether the previous dealings between U and W amount to "pre-existing arrangements", that is whether the agreement can be taken to have been entered into "in accordance with, or in furtherance of" arrangements previously made between U and W, as laid down in section 187(1).

EXAMPLE 9

Facts. A agrees to lend B (an individual) £4,500 in nine monthly instalments of £500.

Analysis. This is a cash loan and is a form of credit (see section 9 and definition of "cash" in section 189(1)). Accordingly it falls within section 10(1)(b) and is fixed-sum credit amounting to £4,500.

EXAMPLE 10

Facts. C (in England) agrees to bail goods to D (an individual) in return for periodical payments. The agreement provides for the property in the goods to pass to D on payment of a total of £7,500 and the exercise by D of an option to purchase. The sum of £7,500 includes a down-payment of £1,000. It also includes an amount which, according to regulations made under section 20(1), constitutes a total charge for credit of £1,500.

Analysis. This is a hire-purchase agreement with a deposit of £1,000 and a total price of £7,500 (see definitions of "hire-purchase agreement", "deposit" and "total price" in section 189(1)). By section 9(3), it is taken to provide credit amounting to £7,500 – (£1,500 + £1,000), which equals £5,000. Under section 8(2), the agreement is therefore a consumer credit agreement, and under sections 9(3) and 11(1) it is a restricted-use credit agreement for fixed-sum credit. A similar result would follow if the agreement by C had been a hiring agreement in Scotland.

EXAMPLE 11

Facts. X (an individual) borrows £500 from Y (Finance). As a condition of the granting of the loan X is required—

(a)	to execute a second mortgage on his house in favour of Y (Finance), and
(b)	to take out a policy of insurance on his life with Y (Insurances).

In accordance with the loan agreement, the policy is charged to Y (Finance) as collateral security for the loan. The two companies are associates within the meaning of section 184(3).

Analysis. The second mortgage is a transaction for the provision of security and accordingly does not fall within section 19(1), but the taking out of the insurance policy is a linked transaction falling within section 19(1)(a). The charging of the policy is a separate transaction (made between different parties) for the provision of security and again is excluded from section 19(1). The only linked transaction is therefore the taking out of the insurance policy. If X had not been required by the loan agreement to take out the policy, but it had been done at the suggestion of Y (Finance) to induce them to enter into the loan agreement, it would have been a linked transaction under section 19(1)(c)(i) by virtue of section 19(2)(a).

EXAMPLE 12

Facts. The N Bank agrees to lend O (an individual) £2,000 to buy a car from P. To make sure the loan is used as intended, the N Bank stipulates that the money must be paid by it direct to P.

Analysis. The agreement is a consumer credit agreement by virtue of section 8(2). Since it falls within section 11(1)(b), it is a restricted-use credit agreement, P being the supplier. If the N Bank had not stipulated for direct payment to the supplier, section 11(3) would have operated and made the agreement into one for unrestricted-use credit.

EXAMPLE 13

Facts. Q, a debt-adjuster, agrees to pay off debts owed by R (an individual) to various moneylenders. For this purpose the agreement provides for the making of a loan by Q to R in return for R's agreeing to repay the loan by instalments with interest. The loan money is not paid over to R but retained by Q and used to pay off the moneylenders.

Analysis. This is an agreement to refinance existing indebtedness of the debtor's, and if the loan by Q does not exceed £5,000 is a restricted-use credit agreement falling within section 11(1)(c).

EXAMPLE 14

Facts. On payment of £1, S issues to T (an individual) a trading check under which T can spend up to £20 at any shop which has agreed, or in future agrees, to accept S's trading checks.

Analysis. The trading check is a credit-token falling within section 14(1)(b). The credit-token agreement is a restricted-use credit agreement within section 11(1)(b), any shop in which the credit-token is used being the "supplier". The fact that further shops may be added after the issue of the credit-token is irrelevant in view of section 11(4).

EXAMPLE 15

Facts. A retailer, L, agrees with M (an individual) to open an account in M's name and, in return for M's promise to pay a specified minimum sum into the account each month and to pay a monthly charge for credit, agrees to allow to be debited to the account, in respect of purchases made by M from L, such sums as will not increase the debit balance at any time beyond the credit limit, defined in the agreement as a given multiple of the specified minimum sum.

Analysis. This arrangement provides credit falling within the definition of running-account credit in section 10(1)(a). Provided the credit limit is not over £5,000, the agreement falls within section 8(2) and is a consumer credit agreement for running-account credit.

EXAMPLE 16

Facts. Under an unsecured agreement, A (Credit), an associate of the A Bank, issues to B (an individual) a credit-card for use in obtaining cash on credit from A (Credit), to be paid by branches of the A Bank (acting as agent of A (Credit)), or goods or cash from suppliers or banks who have agreed to honour credit-cards issued by A (Credit). The credit limit is £30.

Analysis. This is a credit-token agreement falling within section 14(1)(a) and (b). It is a regulated consumer credit agreement for running-account credit. Since the credit limit does not exceed £30, the agreement is a small agreement. So far as the agreement relates to goods it is a debtor-creditor-supplier agreement within section 12(b), since it provides restricted-use credit under section 11(1)(b). So far as it relates to cash it is a debtor-creditor agreement within section 13(c) and the credit it provides is unrestricted-use credit. This is therefore a multiple agreement. In that the whole agreement falls within several of the categories of agreement mentioned in this Act, it is, by section 18(3), to be treated as an agreement in each of those categories. So far as it is a debtor-creditor-supplier agreement providing restricted-use credit it is, by section 18(2), to be treated as a separate agreement; and similarly so far as it is a debtor-creditor agreement providing unrestricted-used credit. (See also Example 22.)

EXAMPLE 17

Facts. The manager of the C Bank agrees orally with D (an individual) to open a current account in D's name. Nothing is said about overdraft facilities. After maintaining the account in credit for some weeks, D draws a cheque in favour of E for an amount exceeding D's credit balance by £20. E presents the cheque and the Bank pay it.

Analysis. In drawing the cheque D, by implication, requests the Bank to grant him an overdraft of £20 on its usual terms as to interest and other charges. In deciding to honour the cheque, the Bank by implication accepts the offer. This constitutes a regulated small consumer credit agreement for unrestricted-use, fixed-sum credit. It is a debtor-creditor agreement, and falls within section 74(1)(b) *if covered by a determination under section 74(3)*. (Compare Example 18.)

EXAMPLE 18

Facts. F (an individual) has had a current account with the G Bank for many years. Although usually in credit, the account has been allowed by the Bank to become overdrawn from time to time. The maximum such overdraft has been is about £1,000. No explicit agreement has ever been made about overdraft facilities. Now, with a credit balance of £500, F draws a cheque for £1,300.

Analysis. It might well be held that the agreement with F (express or implied) under which the Bank operate his account includes an implied term giving him the right to overdraft facilities up to say £1,000. If so, the agreement is a regulated consumer credit agreement for unrestricted-use, running-account credit. It is a debtor-creditor agreement, and falls within section 74(1)(b) *if covered by a direction under section 74(3)*. It is also a multiple agreement, part of which (i.e. the part not dealing with the overdraft), as referred to in section 18(1)(a), falls within a category of agreement not mentioned in this Act. (Compare Example 17.)

EXAMPLE 19

Facts. H (a finance house) agrees with J (a partnership of individuals) to open an unsecured loan account in J's name on which the debit balance is not to exceed £7,000 (having regard to payments into the account made from time to time by J). Interest is to be payable in advance on this sum, with provision for yearly adjustments. H is entitled to debit the account with interest, a "setting-up" charge, and other charges. Before J has an opportunity to draw on the account it is initially debited with £2,250 for advance interest and other charges.

Analysis. This is a personal running-account credit agreement (see sections 8(1) and 10(1)(a), and definition of "individual" in section 189(1)). By section 10(2) the credit limit is £7,000. By section 9(4) however the initial debit of £2,250, and any other charges later debited to the account by H, are not to be treated as credit even though time is allowed for their payment. Effect is given to this by section 10(3). Although the credit limit of £7,000 exceeds the amount (£5,000) specified in section 8(2) as the maximum for a consumer credit agreement, so that the agreement is not within section 10(3)(a), it is caught by section 10(3)(b)(i). At the beginning J can effectively draw (as credit) no more than £4,750, so the agreement is a consumer credit agreement.

EXAMPLE 20

Facts. K (in England) agrees with L (an individual) to bail goods to L for a period of three years certain at £2,000 a year, payable quarterly. The agreement contains no provision for the passing of the property in the goods to L.

Analysis. This is not a hire-purchase agreement (see paragraph (b) of the definition of that term in section 189(1)) and is capable of subsisting for more than three months. Paragraphs (a) and (b) of section 15(1) are therefore satisfied, but paragraph (c) is not. The payments by L must exceed £5,000 if he conforms to the agreement. It is true that under section 101 L has a right to terminate the agreement on giving K three months' notice expiring not earlier than eighteen months after the making of the agreement, but that section applies only where the agreement is a regulated consumer hire agreement apart from the section (see subsection (1)). So the agreement is not a consumer hire agreement, though it would be if the hire charge were say £1,500 a year, or there were a "break" clause in it operable by either party before the hire charges exceeded £5,000. A similar result would follow if the agreement by K had been a hiring agreement in Scotland.

EXAMPLE 21

Facts. The P Bank decides to issue cheque cards to its customers under a scheme whereby the Bank undertakes to honour cheques of up to £30 in every case where the payee has taken the cheque in reliance on the cheque card, whether the customer has funds in his account or not. The P Bank writes to the major retailers advising them of this scheme and also publicises it by advertising. The Bank issues a cheque card to Q (an individual), who uses it to pay by cheque for goods costing £20 bought by Q from R, a major retailer. At the time, Q has £500 in his account at the P Bank.

Analysis. The agreement under which the cheque card is issued to Q is a consumer credit agreement even though at all relevant times Q has more than £30 in his account. This is because Q is free to draw out his whole balance and then use the cheque card, in which case the Bank has bound itself to honour the cheque. In other words the cheque card agreement provides Q with credit, whether he avails himself of it or not. Since the amount of the credit is not subject to any express limit, the cheque card can be used any number of times. It may be presumed however that section 10(3)(b)(iii) will apply. The agreement is an unrestricted-use debtor-creditor agreement (by section 13(c)). Although the P Bank wrote to R informing R of the P Bank's willingness to honour any cheque taken by R in reliance on a cheque card, this does not constitute pre-existing arrangements as mentioned in section 13(c) because section 187(3) operates to prevent it. The agreement is not a credit-token agreement within section 14(1)(b) because payment by the P Bank to R, would be a payment of the cheque and not a payment for the goods.

EXAMPLE 22

Facts. The facts are as in Example 16. On one occasion B uses the credit-card in a way which increases his debit balance with A (Credit) to £40. A (Credit) writes to B agreeing to allow the excess on that occasion only, but stating that it must be paid off within one month.

Analysis. In exceeding his credit limit B, by implication, requests A (Credit) to allow him a temporary excess (compare Example 17). A (Credit) is thus faced by B's action with the choice of treating it as a breach of contract or granting his implied request. He does the latter. If he had done the former, B would be treated as taking credit to which he was not entitled (section 14(3)) and, subject to the terms of his contract with A (Credit), would be liable to damages for breach of contract. As it is, the agreement to allow the excess varies the original credit-token agreement by adding a new term. Under section 10(2), the new term is to be disregarded in arriving at the credit limit, so that the credit-token agreement at no time ceases to be a small agreement. By section 82(2) the later agreement is deemed to revoke the original agreement and contain provisions reproducing the combined effect of the two agreements. By section 82(4), this later agreement is exempted from Part V (except section 56).

EXAMPLE 23

Facts. Under an oral agreement made on 10th January, X (an individual) has an overdraft on his current account at the Y Bank with a credit limit of £100. On 15th February, when his overdraft standards at £90, X draws a cheque for £25. It is the first time that X has exceeded his credit limit, and on 16th February the bank honours the cheque.

Analysis. The agreement of 10th January is a consumer credit agreement for running-account credit. The agreement of 15th–16th February varies the earlier agreement by adding a term allowing the credit limit to be exceeded merely temporarily. By section 82(2) the later agreement is deemed to revoke the earlier agreement and reproduce the combined effect of the two agreements. By section 82(4), Part V of this Act (except section 56) does not apply to the later agreement. By section 18(5), a term allowing a merely temporary excess over the credit limit is not to be treated as a separate agreement, or as providing fixed-sum credit. The whole of the £115 owed to the Bank by X on 16th February is therefore running-account credit.

EXAMPLE 24

Facts. On 1st March 1975 Z (in England) enters into an agreement with A (an unincorporated body of persons) to bail to A equipment consisting of two components (component P and component Q). The agreement is not a hire-purchase agreement and is for a fixed term of 3 years, so paragraphs (a) and (b) of section 15(1) are both satisfied. The rental is payable monthly at a rate of £2,400 a year, but the agreement provides that this is to be reduced to £1,200 a year for the remainder of the agreement if at any time during its currency A returns component Q to the owner Z. On 5th May 1976 A is incorporated as A Ltd., taking over A's assets and liabilities. On 1st March 1977, A Ltd. returns component Q. On 1st January 1978, Z and A Ltd. agree to extend the earlier agreement by one year, increasing the rental for the final year by £250 to £1,450.

Analysis. When entered into on 1st March 1975, the agreement is a consumer hire agreement. A falls within the definition of "individual" in section 189(1) and if A returns component Q before 1st May 1976 the total rental will not exceed £5,000 (see section 15(1)(c)). When this date is passed without component Q having been returned it is obvious that the total rental must now exceed £5,000. Does this mean that the agreement then ceases to be a consumer hire agreement? The answer is no, because there has been no change in the terms of the agreement, and without such a change the agreement cannot move from one category to the other. Similarly, the fact that A's rights and duties under the agreement pass to a body corporate on 5th May 1976 does not cause the agreement to cease to be a consumer hire agreement (see the definition of "hirer" in section 189(1)).

The effect of the modifying agreement of 1st January 1978 is governed by section 82(2), which requires it to be treated as containing provisions reproducing the combined effect of the two actual agreements, that is to say as providing that—

(a) obligations outstanding on 1st January 1978 are to be treated as outstanding under the modifying agreement;

(b) the modifying agreement applies at the old rate of hire for the months of January and February 1978, and

(c) for the year beginning 1st March 1978 A Ltd. will be the bailee of component P at a rental of £1,450.

The total rental under the modifying agreement is £1,850. Accordingly the modifying agreement is a regulated agreement. Even if the total rental under the modifying agreement exceeded £5,000 it would still be regulated because of the provisions of section 82(3).

[838]

NOTES

For the text of this Schedule as it had effect on 15 June 2006, prior to amendments made by the Consumer Credit Act 2006 and subsequent amendments, see the Appendix at [A188].

Examples 17, 18: words in italics repealed by the Consumer Credit (EU Directive) Regulations 2010, SI 2010/1010, regs 2, 20, as from 1 February 2011, with effect in relation to certain agreements before that date, as provided for in regs 101, 101A of the 2010 Regulations at [3942], [3942A].

(*Sch 3 (Transitional and Commencement Provisions), Sch 4 (Minor and Consequential Amendments) outside the scope of this work.*)

UNSOLICITED GOODS AND SERVICES (AMENDMENT) ACT 1975

(1975 c 13)

An Act to amend the Unsolicited Goods and Services Act 1971, to enable the Secretary of State to make regulations with respect to the contents and form of notes of agreement, invoices and similar documents and to provide for conviction on indictment in relation to an offence under s 3(2) of the said Act; and for connected matters

[20 March 1975]

NOTES

Unsolicited Goods and Services Acts 1971 and 1975: by s 4(1) of this Act, see **[840]**, that Act and this Act may be cited together by this collective title.

1, 2 (*S 1 inserts the Unsolicited Goods and Services Act 1971, s 3A (repealed); s 2 repealed in part, remainder spent.*)

3 Provision for offence under section 3(2) of the Act of 1971 to be prosecuted on indictment

(1) An offence under section 3(2) of the Act of 1971 may be prosecuted on indictment; and a person convicted on indictment of an offence under that section shall be liable to a fine.

(2) ...

[839]

NOTES

Sub-s (2): repealed by the Statute Law (Repeals) Act 2004.

4 Short title, citation, commencement, transitional provisions and extent

(1) This Act may be cited as the Unsolicited Goods and Services (Amendment) Act 1975 and the Unsolicited Goods and Services Act 1971 and this Act may be cited together as the Unsolicited Goods and Services Acts 1971 and 1975.

(2)–(4) ...

(5) This Act shall not extend to Northern Ireland.

[840]–[842]

NOTES

Sub-ss (2)–(4): repealed by the Statute Law (Repeals) Act 2004.
Order: the Unsolicited Goods and Services (Amendment) Act 1975 (Commencement No 1) Order 1975, SI 1975/731.

INDUSTRY ACT 1975

(1975 c 68)

ARRANGEMENT OF SECTIONS

PART II
POWERS IN RELATION TO TRANSFERS OF CONTROL OF IMPORTANT MANUFACTURING UNDERTAKINGS TO NON-RESIDENTS

PART IV
DISCLOSURE OF INFORMATION

Disclosure by Government

PART V
GENERAL AND SUPPLEMENTARY

An Act to establish a National Enterprise Board; to confer on the Secretary of State power to prohibit the passing to persons not resident in the United Kingdom of control of undertakings engaged in manufacturing industry, and power to acquire compulsorily the capital or assets of such undertakings where control has passed to such persons or there is a probability that it will pass; to amend the Industry Act 1972 and the Development of Inventions Act 1967; to make provision for the disclosure of information relating to manufacturing undertakings to the Secretary of State or the Minister of Agriculture, Fisheries and Food, and to trade unions; and for connected purposes

[12 November 1975]

1–10   (*(Pt I) ss 1–3, 5–10 repealed by the British Technology Group Act 1991, s 17(2), Sch 2, Pts II, III; s 4 repealed by the Industry Act 1980, ss 9, 21, Sch 2.*)

PART II
POWERS IN RELATION TO TRANSFERS OF CONTROL OF IMPORTANT MANUFACTURING UNDERTAKINGS TO NON-RESIDENTS

11 General extent of powers in relation to control of important manufacturing undertakings

(1) The powers conferred by this Part of this Act shall have effect in relation to changes of control of important manufacturing undertakings.

(2) In this Part of this Act—
"important manufacturing undertaking" means an undertaking which, in so far as it is carried on in the United Kingdom, is wholly or mainly engaged in manufacturing industry and appears to the Secretary of State to be of special importance to the United Kingdom or to any substantial part of the United Kingdom.

[843]

12 Meaning of "change of control"

(1) There is a change of control of an important manufacturing undertaking for the purposes of this Part of this Act only upon the happening of a relevant event.

(2) In subsection (1) above "relevant event" means any event as a result of which—
  (a) the person carrying on the whole or part of the undertaking ceases to be resident in the United Kingdom;
  (b) a person not resident in the United Kingdom acquires the whole or part of the undertaking;
  (c) a body corporate resident in the United Kingdom but controlled by a person not so resident acquires the whole or part of the undertaking;
  (d) a person not resident in the United Kingdom becomes able to exercise or control the exercise of the first, second or third qualifying percentage of votes in a body corporate carrying on the whole or part of the undertaking or in any other body corporate which is in control of such a body; or
  (e) a person resident in the United Kingdom and able to exercise or control the exercise of the first, second or third qualifying percentage of votes in a body corporate carrying on the whole or part of the undertaking or in any other body corporate which is in control of such a body ceases to be resident in the United Kingdom.

(3) For the purposes of subsection (2) above—
  (a) a body corporate or individual entitled to cast 30 per cent or more of the votes that may be cast at any general meeting of a body corporate, is in control of that body; and
  (b) control of a body corporate which has control of another body corporate gives control of the latter body.

(4) Any power to direct the holder of shares or stock in a body corporate as to the exercise of his votes at a general meeting of that body corporate is to be treated as entitlement to cast the votes in respect of the shares or stock in question.

(5) Two or more persons acting together in concert may be treated as a single person for the purposes of any provision of this Part of this Act relating to change of control.

(6) For the purposes of this Part of this Act—
  (a) the first qualifying percentage of votes is 30 per cent;
  (b) the second qualifying percentage is 40 per cent; and
  (c) the third qualifying percentage is 50 per cent;

and the references to votes in this subsection are references to votes that may be cast at a general meeting.

13   Power to make orders

(1)   If it appears to the Secretary of State—
    (a)   that there is a serious and immediate probability of a change of control of an important manufacturing undertaking; and
    (b)   that that change of control would be contrary to the interests of the United Kingdom, or contrary to the interests of any substantial part of the United Kingdom,

he may by order (in this Part of this Act referred to as a "prohibition order") specify the undertaking and
    (i)   prohibit that change of control; and
    (ii)   prohibit or restrict the doing of things which in his opinion would constitute or lead to it;

and may make such incidental or supplementary provision in the order as appears to him to be necessary or expedient.

(2)   Subject to subsection (3) below, if—
    (a)   the conditions specified in paragraphs (a) and (b) of subsection (1) above are satisfied, or
    (b)   a prohibition order has been made in relation to an important manufacturing undertaking, or
    (c)   the Secretary of State has learnt of circumstances which appear to him to constitute a change of control of an important manufacturing undertaking, occurring on or after 1st February 1975, and is satisfied that that change is contrary to the interests of the United Kingdom, or contrary to the interests of any substantial part of the United Kingdom,

the Secretary of State may by order made with the approval of the Treasury (in this Part of this Act referred to as a "vesting order") direct that on a day specified in the order—
    (i)   share capital and loan capital to which this subsection applies, or
    (ii)   any assets which are employed in the undertaking,

shall vest in ... in himself or in nominees for ... himself and may make such incidental or supplementary provision in the order as appears to him to be necessary or expedient.

(3)   A vesting order may only be made if the Secretary of State is satisfied that the order is necessary in the national interest and that, having regard to all the circumstances, that interest cannot, or cannot appropriately, be protected in any other way.

(4)   The share capital and loan capital to which subsection (2) above applies are—
    (a)   in any case where the Secretary of State considers that the interests mentioned in subsection (2)(c) above cannot, or cannot appropriately, be protected unless all the share capital of any relevant body corporate vests by virtue of the order, the share capital of that body corporate, together with so much (if any) of the loan capital of that body as may be specified in the order,
    (b)   in any other case, that part of the share capital of any relevant body corporate which, at the time that the draft of the order is laid before Parliament under section 15 (3) below, appears to the Secretary of State to be involved in the change of control.

(5)   In this section "relevant body corporate" means—
    (a)   a body corporate incorporated in the United Kingdom carrying on in the United Kingdom as the whole or the major part of its business there the whole or part of an important manufacturing undertaking, or
    (b)   a body corporate incorporated in the United Kingdom—
        (i)   which is the holding company of a group of companies carrying on in the United Kingdom as the whole or the major part of their business there the whole or part of an important manufacturing undertaking, and
        (ii)   as to which one of the conditions specified in subsection (6) below is satisfied.

(6)   The conditions mentioned in subsection (5) above are—
    (a)   that it appears to the Secretary of State that there is a serious and immediate probability of the happening of an event in relation to the company which would constitute a change of control of the undertaking, or
    (b)   that the Secretary of State has learnt of circumstances relating to the company which appear to him to constitute a change of control of the undertaking on or after 1st February 1975.

[(7)   In sections (1)(b) and (2)(c) "interests" means interests which relate to public policy, public security or public health.

(8)   In subsection (3) "the national interest" means the national interest in relation to public policy, public security or public health.]

NOTES

Sub-s (2): words omitted repealed by the British Technology Group Act 1991, s 17(2), Sch 2, Pt I.

Sub-ss (7), (8): added by the Industry Act 1975 (Prohibition and Vesting Order) Regulations 1998, SI 1998/3035, reg 2.

14 Notices to extend vesting orders to other holdings

(1)   Where 30 per cent or more of the share capital of the body corporate vests in the Secretary of State ... by virtue of a vesting order, the Secretary of State shall serve on the holders of all the share capital that does not so vest, and on any other persons who to his knowledge have a present or prospective right to subscribe for share capital of the body corporate, within 28 days of the making of the order, a notice informing them of the making of the order and of the right of each of them to require the order to extend to the share capital or rights held by him.

(2)   The recipient of a notice under subsection (1) above may, within three months of the date of the notice, serve on the Secretary of State a counter-notice requiring the order to extend to the share capital or rights held by the recipient in the body corporate.

(3)   A vesting order shall have effect, from the date of a counter-notice, as if the share capital or rights specified in the notice had been specified in the vesting order.

(4)   Subsections (1) to (3) above shall have the same effect in relation to share capital vesting in nominees for the Secretary of State ... as in relation to share capital vesting as mentioned in those subsections.

[846]

NOTES

Sub-ss (1), (4): words omitted repealed by the British Technology Group Act 1991, s 17(2), Sch 2, Pt I.

15 Parliamentary control of orders

(1)   A prohibition order shall be laid before Parliament after being made, and the order shall cease to have effect at the end of the period of 28 days beginning on the day on which it was made (but without prejudice to anything previously done by virtue of the order or to the making of a new order) unless during that period it is approved by resolution of each House of Parliament.

(2)   In reckoning the period mentioned in subsection (1) above no account shall be taken of any time during which Parliament is dissolved or prorogued or during which both Houses are adjourned for more than four days.

(3)   A vesting order shall not be made unless a draft of the order has been laid before and approved by resolution of each House of Parliament.

(4)   A draft of a vesting order shall not be laid before Parliament—

  (a)   in a case such as is mentioned in paragraph (a) of section 13(2) above, after the end of a period of three months from the service of a notice under section 16(7) below of the Secretary of State's intention to lay the draft before Parliament;

  (b)   in a case such as is mentioned in paragraph (b) of that subsection (2), after the end of a period of three months from the making of the prohibition order unless such circumstances as are mentioned in paragraph (a) or (c) of that subsection exist at the time when the draft of the order is laid before Parliament under subsection (3) above; and

  (c)   in a case such as is mentioned in paragraph (c) of that subsection, after the end of a period of three months from the date on which the Secretary of State learnt of circumstances such as are mentioned in that paragraph.

(5)   On the expiry of 28 days from the laying of the draft of a vesting order in a House of Parliament the order shall proceed in that House, whether or not it has been referred to a Committee under Standing Orders of that House relating to Private Bills, as if its provisions would require to be enacted by a Public Bill which cannot be referred to such a Committee.

(6)   In reckoning, for purposes of proceedings in either House of Parliament, the period mentioned in subsection (5) above, no account shall be taken of any time during which Parliament is dissolved or prorogued or during which that House is adjourned for more than four days.

[847]

16 Contents of vesting order

(1)   Without prejudice to the generality of section 13(2) above, a vesting order may contain provisions by virtue of which rights, liabilities or incumbrances to which assets or capital which will vest by virtue of the order are subject—

  (a)   will be extinguished in consideration of the payment of compensation as provided under section 19 below, or

  (b)   will be transferred to the Secretary of State ... , or

(c) will be charged on the compensation under section 19 below.

(2) A vesting order which provides for the vesting of assets employed in an undertaking may prohibit or set aside any transfer of assets so employed or of any right in respect of such assets.

(3) A vesting order may include such provisions as the Secretary of State considers necessary or expedient to safeguard—

(a) any capital which will vest by virtue of the order; and
(b) any assets—
    (i) of a body corporate whose capital will so vest, or
    (ii) of any subsidiary of such a body corporate;

and may in particular, but without prejudice to the generality of this subsection, prohibit or set aside the transfer of any such capital or assets or any right in respect of such capital or assets.

(4) A vesting order setting aside a transfer of capital or a transfer of assets such as are mentioned in subsection (2) above shall entitle the Secretary of State ... to recover the capital or assets transferred.

(5) A vesting order setting aside a transfer of assets such as are mentioned in subsection (3)(b) above shall entitle the body corporate or subsidiary to recover the assets transferred.

(6) Any vesting order setting aside a transfer shall give the person entitled to recover the capital or assets a right to be compensated in respect of the transfer.

(7) The transfers to which this section applies include transfers made before the draft of the order is laid before Parliament but after the Secretary of State has served notice on the person concerned of his intention to lay a draft order.

(8) In subsection (7) above "the person concerned" means—

(a) in the case of an order such as is mentioned in paragraph (i) of section 13(2) above, the relevant body corporate, and
(b) in the case of an order such as is mentioned in paragraph (ii) of that subsection, the person carrying on the undertaking.

(9) The Secretary of State shall publish a copy of any such notice in the London Gazette, the Edinburgh Gazette and the Belfast Gazette as soon as practicable after he has served it.

[848]

NOTES

Sub-ss (1), (4): words omitted repealed by the British Technology Group Act 1991, s 17(2), Sch 2, Pt I.

17 Remedies for contravention of prohibition orders

(1) No criminal proceedings shall lie against any person on the ground that he has committed, or aided, abetted, counselled or procured the commission of, or conspired or attempted to commit, or incited others to commit, any contravention of a prohibition order.

(2) Nothing in subsection (1) above shall limit any right of any person to bring civil proceedings in respect of any contravention or apprehended contravention of a prohibition order, and (without prejudice to the generality of the preceding words) compliance with any such order shall be enforceable by civil proceedings by the Crown for an injunction or interdict or for any other appropriate relief.

[849]

NOTES

See further, in relation to England, Wales and Northern Ireland, the Serious Crime Act 2007, s 63(1), Sch 6, Pt 1, para 3, which provides that the reference in sub-s (1) above to (or to conduct amounting to) the common law offence of inciting the commission of another offence, has effect (as from the day that offence is abolished) as a reference to (or to conduct amounting to) offences under the Serious Crime Act 2007, Pt 2.

18 Territorial scope of orders

(1) Nothing in a prohibition order shall have effect so as to apply to any person in relation to his conduct outside the United Kingdom unless he is—

(a) a citizen of the United Kingdom and Colonies or,
(b) a body corporate incorporated in the United Kingdom or,
(c) a person carrying on business in the United Kingdom either alone or in partnership with one or more other persons,

but in a case falling within paragraph (a), (b) or (c) above, any such order may extend to acts or omissions outside the United Kingdom.

(2) For the purposes of this Part of this Act a body corporate shall be deemed not to be resident in the United Kingdom if it is not incorporated in the United Kingdom.

[850]

19 Compensation orders

(1) No vesting order shall be made until there has also been laid before both Houses of Parliament an order (in this Part of this Act referred to as a "compensation order") providing for the payment of compensation for the acquisition of the capital or assets and for any extinguishment or transfer of rights, liabilities or encumbrances in question.

(2) A compensation order shall be subject to special parliamentary procedure.

(3) A compensation order—
    (a) shall identify the persons or descriptions of persons to be paid compensation and determine their rights and duties in relation to any compensation paid to them;
    (b) shall specify the manner in which compensation is to be paid;
    (c) shall provide for the payment of interest on compensation in respect of the relevant period;
    (d) may make different provision in relation to different descriptions of capital or assets and different rights, liabilities or incumbrances; and
    (e) may contain incidental and supplementary provisions;
and in paragraph (c) above "the relevant period" means—
    (i) in relation to capital or assets, the period commencing with the date on which the capital or assets vest in ... the Secretary of State or their or his nominees and ending with the date of payment of compensation; and
    (ii) in relation to rights, liabilities and incumbrances, the period commencing with the date on which they are extinguished and ending on the date of payment.

(4) Compensation may be paid out—
    (a) out of moneys provided by Parliament, or
    (b) by the issue of government stock (that is to say, stock the principal whereof and the interest whereon is charged on the National Loans Fund with recourse to the Consolidated Fund),
and the power conferred by subsection (3)(b) above is a power to provide for compensation by one or both of the means specified in this subsection.

(5) The proviso to section 6(2) of the Statutory Orders (Special Procedure) Act 1945 (power to withdraw an order or submit it to Parliament for further consideration by means of a Bill for its confirmation) shall have effect in relation to compensation orders as if for the words "may by notice given in the prescribed manner, withdraw the order or may" there were substituted the word "shall".

[851]

NOTES
Sub-s (3): words omitted repealed by the British Technology Group Act 1991, s 17(2), Sch 2, Pt I.

20 Arbitration of disputes relating to vesting and compensation orders

(1) Any dispute to which this section applies shall be determined under Schedule 3 to this Act.

(2) Where any such dispute has been submitted to a tribunal constituted under that Schedule, any other dispute to which this section applies shall be determined by the same tribunal.

(3) This section applies to a dispute which arises out of a vesting order or a compensation order and to which one of the parties is the Secretary of State ... or a body corporate the whole or part of whose share capital has vested by virtue of the order in either of them or in nominees for either of them—
    (a) if the provisions of the order require it to be submitted to arbitration; or
    (b) if one of the parties wishes it to be so submitted;
and where this section applies to a dispute which arises out of an order, it also applies to any dispute which arises out of a related order.

(4) A vesting order and a compensation order are related for the purposes of this section if they relate to the same capital or assets.

[852]

NOTES
Sub-s (3): words omitted repealed by the British Technology Group Act 1991, s 17(2), Sch 2, Pt I.

21–26 ((*Pt III*) *s 21 repealed by the Industry Act 1980, ss 19, 21, Sch 2; s 22 repealed by the Industrial Development Act 1982, s 19, Sch 3; ss 23–25 amend the Industry Act 1972, s 10, and insert s 10A of that Act; s 26 repealed by the British Technology Group Act 1991, s 17(2), Sch 2, Pt I.*)

PART IV
DISCLOSURE OF INFORMATION

Disclosure by Government

27   Disclosure of information by Government

Ministers of the Crown and the Treasury shall publish, make available and provide access to information and analysis as specified in Schedule 5 to this Act.

[853]

28–34   *(Repealed by the Industry Act 1980, ss 19, 21, Sch 2.)*

PART V
GENERAL AND SUPPLEMENTARY

35   Expenses

Any expenses of the Secretary of State or the Minister of Agriculture, Fisheries and Food incurred in consequence of the provisions of this Act, including any increase attributable to those provisions in sums payable under any other Act, shall be defrayed out of money provided by Parliament.

[854]

NOTES

Minister of Agriculture, Fisheries and Food: now the Secretary of State for Environment, Food and Rural Affairs; see the Secretaries of State for Transport, Local Government and the Regions and for Environment, Food and Rural Affairs Order 2001, SI 2001/2568.

36   Service of documents

(1)   Any notice or other document required or authorised by or by virtue of this Act to be served on any person may be served on him either by delivering it to him or by leaving it at his proper address or by sending it by post.

(2)   Any notice or other document so required or authorised to be served on a body corporate or a firm shall be duly served if it is served on the secretary or clerk of that body or a partner of that firm.

(3)   For the purposes of this section, and of section 26 of the Interpretation Act 1889 in its application to this section, the proper address of a person, in the case of a secretary or clerk of a body corporate, shall be that of the registered or principal office of that body, in the case of a partner of a firm shall be that of the principal office of the firm, and in any other case shall be the last known address of the person to be served.

[855]

NOTES

Interpretation Act 1889, s 26: repealed by the Interpretation Act 1978, s 25, Sch 3, and replaced by s 7 of, and Sch 2, para 3 to, that Act.

37   Interpretation

(1)   In this Act, unless the context otherwise requires—
.....

"enactment" includes an enactment of the Parliament of Northern Ireland or the Northern Ireland Assembly;

"holding company" means a holding company as defined by [section 1159 of the Companies Act 2006];

"industry" includes any description of commercial activity, and any section of an industry, and "industrial" has a corresponding meaning;

"manufacturing industry" means, subject to subsection (3) below, activities which are described in any of the minimum list headings in Orders III to XIX (inclusive) of the Standard Industrial Classification;
.....

["Standard Industrial Classification" means the revised edition published by Her Majesty's Stationery Office in 1968 of the publication of that name prepared by the Central Statistical Office [of the Chancellor of the Exchequer];]

"subsidiary" means a subsidiary as defined by [section 1159 of the Companies Act 2006];
.....

(2)   ...

(3)   In determining the extent to which an undertaking is engaged in manufacturing industry, the following activities shall be treated as manufacturing industry so far as they relate to products manufactured or to be manufactured by the undertaking—

research,
transport,
distribution,
repair and maintenance of machinery,
sales and marketing,
storage,
mining and quarrying,
production and distribution of energy and heating,
administration,
training of staff,
packaging.

(4) ...

(5) Except in so far as the context otherwise requires, any reference in this Act to an enactment shall be construed as a reference to that enactment as amended, applied or extended by or under any other enactment, including this Act.

[856]

NOTES
Sub-s (1): definitions "accounting year" and "wholly owned subsidiary" (omitted) repealed by the British Technology Group Act 1991, s 17(2), Sch 2, Pt I; words in square brackets in definitions "holding company" and "subsidiary" substituted by the Companies Act 2006 (Consequential Amendments, Transitional Provisions and Savings) Order 2009, SI 2009/1941, art 2(1), Sch 1, para 33; definitions "the Ministers" and "planning agreement" (omitted) repealed by the Industry Act 1980, s 21, Sch 2; definition "Standard Industrial Classification" substituted by the Co-operative Development Agency and Industrial Development Act 1984, s 5(2), Sch 1, Pt II, para 1, words in square brackets inserted by the Transfer of Functions (Economic Statistics) Order 1989, SI 1989/992, art 6(4), Sch 2, para 2(a).
Sub-ss (2), (4): repealed by the British Technology Group Act 1991, s 17(2), Sch 2, Pt I.

38 Orders

(1) Any power to make an order conferred by this Act shall be exercisable by statutory instrument.

(2) Any power to make an order conferred by any provision of this Act shall include power to make an order varying or revoking any order previously made under that provision.

(3) It is hereby declared that any power of giving directions or making determinations conferred on the Secretary of State by any provision of this Act includes power to vary or revoke directions or determinations given or made under that provision.

[857]

39 Citation etc

(1) This Act may be cited as the Industry Act 1975.

(2) ...

(3) The enactments specified in Schedule 8 to this Act are repealed to the extent mentioned in column 3 of that Schedule.

(4) It is hereby declared that this Act extends to Northern Ireland.

(5) Notwithstanding the provisions—
   (a) of section 12(3) of the Statutory Orders (Special Procedure) Act 1945, ...
   (b) ...
the former Act shall apply to any compensation order which extends to Northern Ireland, ...

(6) This Act shall come into force on such day as the Secretary of State may by order made by statutory instrument appoint.

(7) An order under subsection (6) above may appoint different days for different provisions and for different purposes.

[858]

NOTES
Sub-s (2): repealed by the Industrial Development Act 1982, s 19, Sch 3.
Sub-s (5): words omitted repealed by the Industry Act 1980, s 21, Sch 2.
Order: the Industry Act 1975 (Commencement) Order 1975, SI 1975/1881.

SCHEDULES

(Sch 1, paras 1–6, 11–17 repealed by the British Technology Group Act 1991, s 17(2), Sch 2, Pt III; Sch 1, paras 7–10, 18, 20, Sch 2, paras 1–7, 8(1), (2), (4) repealed by the British Technology Group Act 1991, s 17(2), Sch 2, Pt I; Sch 1, para 19 repealed by the Financial Services Act 1986, s 212(3),

Sch 17, Pt I and again by the British Technology Group Act 1991, s 17(2), Sch 2, Pt I; Sch 2, para 8(3) repealed by the Industry Act 1980, s 21, Sch 2 and again by the British Technology Group Act 1991, s 17(2), Sch 2, Pt I.)

SCHEDULE 3
ARBITRATION

Section 20

PART I
GENERAL

Establishment of Tribunal

1.   If a party to a dispute such as is mentioned in subsection (1) of section 20 above serves on the other party or parties to the dispute, at a time when no proceedings relating to it have been commenced in any court, a notice that he wishes the dispute to be determined by arbitration, the Secretary of State shall by order establish a tribunal to determine the dispute and any other dispute such as is mentioned in subsection (2) of that section.

2.   An order under paragraph 1 above shall be laid before each House of Parliament.

3.   A tribunal shall be a court of record and shall have an official seal which shall be judicially noticed.

4.—[(1)]   A tribunal shall, as the Lord Chancellor may[, after consulting the Lord Chief Justice of England and Wales, the Lord President of the Court of Session and the Lord Chief Justice of Northern Ireland,] direct, either sit as a single tribunal or sit in two or more divisions and, subject to paragraph 5 below, shall, for the hearing of any proceedings, consist of—

    (a)   a president who shall be—
        [[(i)   a person who satisfies the judicial-appointment eligibility condition on a 5-year basis; or]
        (ii)   a member of the Bar of Northern Ireland or [solicitor of the Court of Judicature of Northern Ireland] of at least [5] years' standing,]
        appointed by the Lord Chancellor, and
    (b)   two other members appointed by the Secretary of State, one being a person of experience in business and the other being a person of experience in finance.

[(2)   The Lord Chief Justice of England and Wales may nominate a judicial office holder (as defined in section 109(4) of the Constitutional Reform Act 2005) to exercise his functions under this paragraph.

(3)   The Lord President of the Court of Session may nominate a judge of the Court of Session who is a member of the First or Second Division of the Inner House of that Court to exercise his functions under this paragraph.

(4)   The Lord Chief Justice of Northern Ireland may nominate any of the following to exercise his functions under this paragraph—

    (a)   the holder of one of the offices listed in Schedule 1 to the Justice (Northern Ireland) Act 2002;
    (b)   a Lord Justice of Appeal (as defined in section 88 of that Act).]

5.   *(Applies to Scotland only.)*

6.—[(1)]   [Subject, in the case of the president of a tribunal, to sub-paragraph (2) below] the members of a tribunal shall hold office for such period as may be determined at the time of their respective appointments and shall be eligible for reappointment but, notwithstanding that the period for which a member was appointed has not expired—

    (a)   a member may, at any time by not less than one month's notice in writing to his appointor, resign his office;
    (b)   the appointor of a member may declare the office of that member vacant on the ground that he is unfit to continue in his office; and
    (c)   if any member [is the subject of a bankruptcy restrictions order or an interim order] or, in Scotland, if sequestration of a member's estate is awarded …, his office shall thereupon become vacant.

[(2)   No appointment of a person to be the president of a tribunal shall be such as to extend beyond the day on which he attains the age of 70 years; but this paragraph is subject to section 26(4) to (6) of the Judicial Pensions and Retirement Act 1993 (power to authorise continuance in office up to the age of 75 years).]

7.   If any member of a tribunal becomes, by reason of illness or other infirmity, temporarily incapable of performing the duties of his office, his appointor shall appoint some other fit person to discharge his duties for any period not exceeding 6 months at any one time, and the person so appointed shall during that period have the same powers as the person in whose place he was appointed.

8.   In this Part of this Schedule, "appointor", in relation to a member of a tribunal means—

(a)   in the case of a member appointed under sub-paragraph (a) of [paragraph 4(1)] above, the Lord Chancellor or, if paragraph 5 above applies, the Lord President of the Court of Session; and

(b)   in the case of any other member, the Secretary of State.

[8A.   Where the appointor is, by virtue of paragraph 8(a), the Lord Chancellor, the power conferred by paragraph 6(1)(b) may be exercised only with the concurrence of the appropriate senior judge.

8B.   The appropriate senior judge is the Lord Chief Justice of England and Wales, unless the member to be removed exercises functions wholly or mainly in Northern Ireland, in which case it is the Lord Chief Justice of Northern Ireland.]

9, 10.   ...

Staff and expenses

11.   A tribunal may appoint such officers as they consider necessary for assisting them in the proper execution of their duties.

12.—(1)   There shall be paid to members of a tribunal such remuneration (whether by way of salaries or fees) and such allowances as the Secretary of State may, with the approval of the Minister for the Civil Service, determine.

(2)   There shall be paid to any officer appointed under paragraph 11 above and any person to whom proceedings are referred by the tribunal under paragraph 27 below for inquiry and report such remuneration (whether by way of salary or fees) and such allowances as the tribunal may, with the approval of the Secretary of State given with the consent of the Minister for the Civil Service, determine.

(3)   The Secretary of State shall pay any such remuneration and allowances and any other expenses of a tribunal shall be defrayed by the Secretary of State out of money provided by Parliament.

[859]

NOTES

Para 4: sub-para (1) numbered as such, words in first pair of square brackets inserted, and sub-paras (2)–(4) added, by the Constitutional Reform Act 2005, s 15(1), Sch 4, Part 1, paras 81(1), (2); sub-para (1)(a)(i), (ii) substituted by the Courts and Legal Services Act 1990, s 71(2), Sch 10, para 39; sub-para (1)(a)(i) further substituted and number in sub-para (1)(a)(ii) substituted by the Tribunals, Courts and Enforcement Act 2007, s 50, Sch 10, Pt 1, para 12; words in square brackets in sub-para (1)(a)(ii) substituted by the Constitutional Reform Act 2005, s 59, Sch 11, Pt 3, para 5.

Para 6: sub-para (1) numbered as such, the words in square brackets in that paragraph inserted, and sub-para (2) added, by the Judicial Pensions and Retirement Act 1993, s 26(10), Sch 6, para 52; in sub-para (1)(c) words in square brackets substituted and words omitted repealed by the Enterprise Act 2002 (Disqualification from Office: General) Order 2006, SI 2006/1722, art 2(2), Sch 2, Pt 1, para 1.

Para 8: words in square brackets substituted by the Constitutional Reform Act 2005, s 15(1), Sch 4, Part 1, paras 81(1), (4).

Paras 8A, 8B: inserted by the Constitutional Reform Act 2005, s 15(1), Sch 4, Part 1, paras 81(1), (5).

Para 9: amends the House of Commons Disqualification Act 1975, Sch 1, Pt II, and the Northern Ireland Assembly Disqualification Act 1975, Sch 1, Pt II.

Para 10: repealed by the Tribunals and Inquiries Act 1992, s 18(2), Sch 4, Pt I.

Minister for the Civil Service: now the Treasury, see the Transfer of Functions (Minister for the Civil Service and Treasury) Order 1981, SI 1981/1670.

PART II
PROCEEDINGS

Proceedings other than Scottish proceedings

13.   Paragraphs 14 to 17 below shall have effect with respect to proceedings of a tribunal other than those which, by virtue of paragraph 18 below, are to be treated as Scottish proceedings.

14.   The provisions of [Part I of the Arbitration Act 1996] with respect to—

(a)   the administration of oaths and the taking of affirmations,

(b)   the correction in awards of mistakes and errors,

(c)   the summoning, attendance and examination of witnesses and the production of documents, and

(d)   the costs of the reference and award,

shall, with any necessary modifications, apply in respect of such proceedings but, except as provided by this paragraph, the provisions of [that Part] shall not apply to any such proceedings.

15.   A tribunal may, and if so ordered by the Court of Appeal shall, state in the form of a special case for determination by the Court of Appeal any question of law which may arise in such proceedings.

16.   An appeal shall lie to the Court of Appeal on any question of law or fact from any determination or order of the tribunal with respect to compensation under section 16(6) above.

17.—(1)   Subject to the provisions of this Schedule, the procedure in or in connection with any such proceedings shall be such as may be determined by rules made by the Lord Chancellor by statutory instrument.

(2)   A statutory instrument containing rules made under this paragraph shall be subject to annulment in pursuance of a resolution of either House of Parliament.

18–25.   (*Apply to Scotland only.*)

All proceedings

26.   Every order of a tribunal—
    (a)   shall be enforceable in England and Wales and Northern Ireland as if it were an order of the High Court; and
    (b)   may be recorded for execution in the books of Council and Session and may be enforced accordingly.

27.   A tribunal may, at any stage in any proceedings before them, refer to a person or persons appointed by them for the purpose any question arising in the proceedings, other than a question which in their opinion is primarily one of law, for inquiry and report, and the report of any such person or persons may be adopted wholly or partly by the tribunal and, if so adopted, may be incorporated in an order of the tribunal.

[860]

NOTES
    Para 14: words in square brackets substituted by the Arbitration Act 1996, s 107(1), Sch 3, para 30.

(*Sch 4 repealed by the Industry Act 1980, s 21, Sch 2 and the Industrial Development Act 1982, s 19, Sch 3.*)

SCHEDULE 5
DISCLOSURE OF INFORMATION BY GOVERNMENT
Section 27

1.   For the purposes of this Schedule the Treasury shall keep a macro-economic model suitable for demonstrating the likely effects on economic events in the United Kingdom of different assumptions about the following matters, namely—
    (a)   government economic policies;
    (b)   economic events outside the United Kingdom; and
    (c)   such (if any) other matters as appear to the Treasury from time to time likely to have a substantial effect on economic events in the United Kingdom.

2.   The model shall enable forecasts to be made—
    (a)   of any of the following, namely—
        (i)   the level of gross domestic product;
        (ii)   unemployment;
        (iii)   the balance of payments on current account;
        (iv)   the general index of retail prices; and
        (v)   average earnings; and
    (b)   of such (if any) other economic variables as are appropriate in the opinion of the Treasury from time to time.

3.   The references to forecasts in paragraph 2 above are references to forecasts relating to successive periods of three months and not to shorter periods.

4.   The model shall be maintained on a computer.

5.   The model shall be available to members of the public to make forecasts based on their own assumptions, using the computer during office hours upon payment of such reasonable fee as the Treasury may determine.

6.   Nor less than twice in each year commencing with a date not later than one year from the coming into force of this Act, the Treasury shall publish forecasts produced with the aid of the model as to such matters and based on such alternative assumptions as appear to them to be appropriate.

7.   Any forecast under this Schedule shall indicate, where possible, the margin of error attaching to it.

8.   The Treasury shall from time to time publish an analysis of errors in such forecasts that would have remained even if the assumptions set out in the forecasts and on which they were based had been correct.

9.   ...

NOTES
Para 9: repealed by the Industry Act 1980, s 21, Sch 2.

(*Sch 6 repealed by the Industry Act 1980, s 21, Sch 2; Sch 7 repealed by the Industrial Development Act 1982, s 19, Sch 3; Sch 8 (Repeals) outside the scope of this work.*)

TORTS (INTERFERENCE WITH GOODS) ACT 1977

(1977 c 32)

ARRANGEMENT OF SECTIONS

An Act to amend the law concerning conversion and other torts affecting goods

[22 July 1977]

Preliminary

1 Definition of "wrongful interference with goods"

In this Act "wrongful interference", or "wrongful interference with goods", means—
    (a)   conversion of goods (also called trover),
    (b)   trespass to goods,
    (c)   negligence so far as it results in damage to goods or to an interest in goods,
    (d)   subject to section 2, any other tort so far as it results in damage to goods or to an interest
            in goods

[and references in this Act (however worded) to proceedings for wrongful interference or to a claim or right to claim for wrongful interference shall include references to proceedings by virtue of Part I of the Consumer Protection Act 1987 [or Part II of the Consumer Protection (Northern Ireland) Order 1987] (product liability) in respect of any damage to goods or to an interest in goods or, as the case may be, to a claim or right to claim by virtue of that Part in respect of any such damage].

[862]

PART 1 STATUTES

NOTES
    Words in first (outer) pair of square brackets added by the Consumer Protection Act 1987, s 48, Sch 4; words in second (inner) pair of square brackets inserted by the Consumer Protection (Northern Ireland) Order 1987, SI 1987/2049, art 35(1), Sch 3, para 3.

Detention of goods

2 Abolition of detinue

(1)   Detinue is abolished.

(2)   An action lies in conversion for loss or destruction of goods which a bailee has allowed to happen in breach of his duty to his bailor (that is to say it lies in a case which is not otherwise conversion, but would have been detinue before detinue was abolished).

[863]

3 Form of judgment where goods are detained

(1)   In proceedings for wrongful interference against a person who is in possession or in control of the goods relief may be given in accordance with this section, so far as appropriate.

(2)   The relief is—
    (a)   an order for delivery of the goods, and for payment of any consequential damages, or
    (b)   an order for delivery of the goods, but giving the defendant the alternative of paying damages by reference to the value of the goods, together in either alternative with payment of any consequential damages, or
    (c)   damages.

(3)   Subject to rules of court—
    (a)   relief shall be given under only one of paragraphs (a), (b) and (c) of subsection (2),
    (b)   relief under paragraph (a) of subjection (2) is at the discretion of the court, and the claimant may choose between the others.

(4)   If it is shown to the satisfaction of the court that an order under subsection (2)(a) has not been complied with, the court may—
    (a)   revoke the order, or the relevant part of it, and
    (b)   make an order for payment of damages by reference to the value of the goods.

(5)   Where an order is made under subsection (2)(b) the defendant may satisfy the order by returning the goods at any time before execution of judgment, but without prejudice to liability to pay any consequential damages.

(6)   An order for delivery of the goods under subsection (2)(a) or (b) may impose such conditions as may be determined by the court, or pursuant to rules of court, and in particular, where damages by reference to the value of the goods would not be the whole of the value of the goods, may require an allowance to be made by the claimant to reflect the difference.

    For example, a bailor's action against the bailee may be one in which the measure of damages is not the full value of the goods, and then the court may order delivery of the goods, but require the bailor to pay the bailee a sum reflecting the difference.

(7)   Where under subjection (1) or subsection (2) of section 6 an allowance is to be made in respect of an improvement of the goods, and an order is made under subsection (2)(a) or (b), the court may assess the allowance to be made in respect of the improvement, and by the order require, as a condition for delivery of the goods, that allowance to be made by the claimant.

(8)   This section is without prejudice—
    (a)   to the remedies afforded by section 133 of the Consumer Credit Act 1974, or
    (b)   to the remedies afforded by sections 35, 42 and 44 of the Hire-Purchase Act 1965, or to those sections of the Hire-Purchase Act (Northern Ireland) 1966 (so long as those sections respectively remain in force), or
    (c)   to any jurisdiction to afford ancillary or incidental relief.

[864]

NOTES
    Hire-Purchase Act 1965, ss 35, 42, 44: repealed by the Consumer Credit Act 1974, s 192(3), (4), Sch 5, Pt I.
    Hire-Purchase Act (Northern Ireland) 1966: repealed by the Consumer Credit Act 1974, s 192(3), (4), Sch 5, Pt II.

4 Interlocutory relief where goods are detained

(1)   In this section "proceedings" means proceedings for wrongful interference.

(2)   On the application of any person in accordance with rules of court, the High Court shall, in such circumstances as may be specified in the rules, have power to make an order providing for the delivery up of any goods which are or may become the subject matter of subsequent proceedings in the court, or as to which any question may arise in proceedings.

(3)   Delivery shall be, as the order may provide, to the claimant or to a person appointed by the court for the purpose, and shall be on such terms and conditions as may be specified in the order.

(4)   The power to make rules of court under section [84 of the [Senior Courts Act 1981]] or under section 7 of the Northern Ireland Act 1962 shall include power to make rules of court as to the manner in which an application for such an order can be made, and as to the circumstances in which such an order can be made; and any such rules may include such incidental, supplementary and consequential provisions as the authority making the rules may consider necessary or expedient.

(5)   The preceding provisions of this section shall have effect in relation to county courts as they have effect in relation to the High Court, and as if in those provisions references to rules of court and to section [84] of the said Act of [1981] or section 7 of the Northern Ireland Act 1962 included references to county court rules and to [section 75 of the County Courts Act 1984] or [Article 47 of the County Courts (Northern Ireland) Order 1980].

[865]

NOTES

Sub-s (4): words in first (outer) pair of square brackets substituted by the Supreme Court Act 1981, s 152(1), Sch 5; words in second (inner) pair of square brackets substituted by the Constitutional Reform Act 2005, s 59(5), Sch 11, Pt 1, para 1(2).

Sub-s (5): words in first and second pairs of square brackets substituted by the Supreme Court Act 1981, s 152(1), Sch 5; words in third pair of square brackets substituted by the County Courts Act 1984, s 148(1), Sch 2, Pt V, para 64; words in final pair of square brackets substituted by the County Courts (Northern Ireland) Order 1980, SI 1980/397, art 68(2), Sch 1, Pt II.

Northern Ireland Act 1962, s 7: repealed by the Judicature (Northern Ireland) Act 1978, s 122, Sch 7, Pt I. By virtue of s 122(1) of, and Sch 5, Pt I, para 3 to, the 1978 Act, the reference in this section to rules made under s 7 of the 1962 Act is to be construed as a reference to rules of court made under s 55 of the 1978 Act.

County Courts Act 1984, s 75: repealed by the Civil Procedure Act 1997, s 10, Sch 2, para 2(1), (6).

Damages

5   Extinction of title on satisfaction of claim for damages

(1)   Where damages for wrongful interference are, or would fall to be, assessed on the footing that the claimant is being compensated—
  (a)   for the whole of his interest in the goods, or
  (b)   for the whole of his interest in the goods subject to a reduction for contributory negligence,
payment of the assessed damages (under all heads), or as the case may be settlement of a claim for damages for the wrong (under all heads), extinguishes the claimant's title to that interest.

(2)   In subsection (1) the reference to the settlement of the claim includes—
  (a)   where the claim is made in court proceedings, and the defendant has paid a sum into court to meet the whole claim, the taking of that sum by the claimant, and
  (b)   where the claim is made in court proceedings, and the proceedings are settled or compromised, the payment of what is due in accordance with the settlement or compromise, and
  (c)   where the claim is made out of court and is settled or compromised, the payment of what is due in accordance with the settlement or compromise.

(3)   It is hereby declared that subsection (1) does not apply where damages are assessed on the footing that the claimant is being compensated for the whole of his interest in the goods, but the damages paid are limited to some lesser amount by virtue of any enactment or rule of law.

(4)   Where under section 7(3) the claimant accounts over to another person (the "third party") so as to compensate (under all heads) the third party for the whole of his interest in the goods, the third party's title to that interest is extinguished.

(5)   This section has effect subject to any agreement varying the respective rights of the parties to the agreement, and where the claim is made in court proceedings has effect subject to any order of the court.

[866]

6   Allowance for improvement of the goods

(1)   If in proceedings for wrongful interference against a person (the "improver") who has improved the goods, it is shown that the improver acted in the mistaken but honest belief that he had a good title to them, an allowance shall be made for the extent to which, at the time as at which the goods fall to be valued in assessing damages, the value of the goods is attributable to the improvement.

(2)   If, in proceedings for wrongful interference against a person ("the purchaser") who has purported to purchase the goods—
  (a)   from the improver, or

(b)   where after such a purported sale the goods passed by a further purported sale on one or more occasions, on any such occasion,

it is shown that the purchaser acted in good faith, an allowance shall be made on the principle set out in subsection (1).

For example, where a person in good faith buys a stolen car from the improver and is sued in conversion by the true owner the damages may be reduced to reflect the improvement, but if the person who bought the stolen car from the improver sues the improver for failure of consideration, and the improver acted in good faith, subsection (3) below will ordinarily make a comparable reduction in the damages he recovers from the improver.

(3)   If in a case within subsection (2) the person purporting to sell the goods acted in good faith, then in proceedings by the purchaser for recovery of the purchase price because of failure of consideration, or in any other proceedings founded on that failure of consideration, an allowance shall, where appropriate, be made on the principle set out in subsection (1).

(4)   This section applies, with the necessary modifications, to a purported bailment or other disposition of goods as it applies to a purported sale of goods.

[867]

Liability to two or more claimants

7   Double liability

(1)   In this section "double liability" means the double liability of the wrongdoer which can arise—

     (a)   where one of two or more rights of action for wrongful interference is founded on a possessory title, or

     (b)   where the measure of damages in an action for wrongful interference founded on a proprietary title is or includes the entire value of the goods, although the interest is one of two or more interests in the goods.

(2)   In proceedings to which any two or more claimants are parties, the relief shall be such as to avoid double liability of the wrongdoer as between those claimants.

(3)   On satisfaction, in whole or in part, of any claim for an amount exceeding that recoverable if subsection (2) applied, the claimant is liable to account over to the other person having a right to claim to such extent as will avoid double liability.

(4)   Where, as the result of enforcement of a double liability, any claimant is unjustly enriched to any extent, he shall be liable to reimburse the wrongdoer to that extent.

For example, if a converter of goods pays damages first to a finder of the goods, and then to the true owner, the finder is unjustly enriched unless he accounts over to the true owner under subsection (3); and then the true owner is unjustly enriched and becomes liable to reimburse the converter of the goods.

[868]

8   Competing rights to the goods

(1)   The defendant in an action for wrongful interference shall be entitled to show, in accordance with rules of court, that a third party has a better right than the plaintiff as respects all or any part of the interest claimed by the plaintiff, or in right of which he sues, and any rule of law (sometimes called jus tertii) to the contrary is abolished.

(2)   Rules of court relating to proceedings for wrongful interference may—

     (a)   require the plaintiff to give particulars of his title,

     (b)   require the plaintiff to identify any person who, to his knowledge, has or claims any interest in the goods,

     (c)   authorise the defendant to apply for directions as to whether any person should be joined with a view to establishing whether he has a better right than the plaintiff, or has a claim as a result of which the defendant might be doubly liable,

     (d)   where a party fails to appear on an application within paragraph (c), or to comply with any direction given by the court on such an application, authorise the court to deprive him of any right of action against the defendant for the wrong either unconditionally, or subject to such terms or conditions as may be specified.

(3)   Subsection (2) is without prejudice to any other power of making rules of court.

[869]

9   Concurrent actions

(1)   This section applies where goods are the subject of two or more claims for wrongful interference (whether or not the claims are founded on the same wrongful act, and whether or not any of the claims relates also to other goods).

PART 1
STATUTES

(2)   Where goods are the subject of two or more claims under section 6 this section shall apply as if any claim under section 6(3) were a claim for wrongful interference.

(3)   If proceedings have been brought in a county court on one of those claims, county court rules may waive, or allow a court to waive, any limit (financial or territorial) on the jurisdiction of county courts in [the County Courts Act 1984] or the County Courts [(Northern Ireland) Order 1980] so as to allow another of those claims to be brought in the same county court.

(4)   If proceedings are brought on one of the claims in the High Court, and proceedings on any other are brought in a county court, whether prior to the High Court proceedings or not, the High Court may, on the application of the defendant, after notice has been given to the claimant in the county court proceedings—

    (a)   order that the county court proceedings be transferred to the High Court, and

    (b)   order security for costs or impose such other terms as the court thinks fit.

[870]

NOTES

Sub-s (3): words in first pair of square brackets substituted by the County Courts Act 1984, s 148(1), Sch 2, Pt V, para 65; words in second pair of square brackets substituted by the County Courts (Northern Ireland) Order 1980, SI 1980/397, art 68(2), Sch 1, Pt II.

Conversion and trespass to goods

10   Co-owners

(1)   Co-ownership is no defence to an action founded on conversion or trespass to goods where the defendant without the authority of the other co-owner—

    (a)   destroys the goods, or disposes of the goods in a way giving a good title to the entire property in the goods, or otherwise does anything equivalent to the destruction of the other's interest in the goods, or

    (b)   purports to dispose of the goods in a way which would give a good title to the entire property in the goods if he was acting with the authority of all co-owners of the goods.

(2)   Subsection (1) shall not effect the law concerning execution or enforcement of judgments, or concerning any form of distress.

(3)   Subsection (1)(a) is by way of restatement of existing law so far as it relates to conversion.

[871]

11   Minor amendments

(1)   Contributory negligence is no good defence in proceedings founded on conversion, or on intentional trespass to goods.

(2)   Receipt of goods by way of pledge is conversion if the delivery of the goods is conversion.

(3)   Denial of title is not of itself conversion.

[872]

Uncollected goods

12   Bailee's power of sale

(1)   This section applies to goods in the possession or under the control of a bailee where—

    (a)   the bailor is in breach of an obligation to take delivery of the goods or, if the terms of the bailment so provide, to give directions as to their delivery, or

    (b)   the bailee could impose such an obligation by giving notice to the bailor, but is unable to trace or communicate with the bailor, or

    (c)   the bailee can reasonably expect to be relieved of any duty to safeguard the goods on giving notice to the bailor, but is unable to trace or communicate with the bailor.

(2)   In the cases in Part I of Schedule 1 to this Act a bailee may, for the purposes of subsection (1), impose an obligation on the bailor to take delivery of the goods, or as the case may be to give directions as to their delivery, and in those cases the said Part I sets out the methods of notification.

(3)   If the bailee—

    (a)   has in accordance with Part II of Schedule 1 to this Act given notice to the bailor of his intention to sell the goods under this subsection, or

    (b)   has failed to trace or communicate with the bailor with a view to giving him such a notice, after having taken reasonable steps for the purpose,

and is reasonably satisfied that the bailor owns the goods, he shall be entitled, as against the bailor, to sell the goods.

(4)   Where subsection (3) applies but the bailor did not in fact own the goods, a sale under this section, or under section 13, shall not give a good title as against the owner, or as against a person claiming under the owner.

(5)   A bailee exercising his powers under subsection (3) shall be liable to account to the bailor for the proceeds of sale, less any costs of sale, and—

(a)   the account shall be taken on the footing that the bailee should have adopted the best method of sale reasonably available in the circumstances, and

(b)   where subsection (3)(a) applies, any sum payable in respect of the goods by the bailor to the bailee which accrued due before the bailee gave notice of intention to sell the goods shall be deductible from the proceeds of sale.

(6)   A sale duly made under this section gives a good title to the purchaser as against the bailor.

(7)   In this section, section 13, and Schedule 1 to this Act,

(a)   "bailor" and "bailee" include their respective successors in title, and

(b)   references to what is payable, paid or due to the bailee in respect of the goods include references to what would be payable by the bailor to the bailee as a condition of delivery of the goods at the relevant time.

(8)   This section, and Schedule 1 to this Act, have effect subject to the terms of the bailment.

(9)   This section shall not apply where the goods were bailed before the commencement of this Act.

[873]

13   Sale authorised by the court

(1)   If a bailee of the goods to which section 12 applies satisfies the court that he is entitled to sell the goods under section 12, or that he would be so entitled if he had given any notice required in accordance with Schedule 1 to this Act, the court—

(a)   may authorise the sale of the goods subject to such terms and conditions, if any, as may be specified in the order, and

(b)   may authorise the bailee to deduct from the proceeds of sale any costs of sale and any amount due from the bailor to the bailee in respect of the goods, and

(c)   may direct the payment into court of the net proceeds of sale, less any amount deducted under paragraph (b), to be held to the credit of the bailor.

(2)   A decision of the court authorising a sale under this section shall, subject to any right of appeal, be conclusive, as against the bailor, of the bailee's entitlement to sell the goods, and gives a good title to the purchaser as against the bailor.

(3)   In this section "the court" means the High Court or a county court, [and a county court shall have jurisdiction in the proceedings save that, in Northern Ireland, a county court shall only have jurisdiction in proceedings if the value of the goods does not exceed the county court limit mentioned in Article 10(1) of the County Courts (Northern Ireland) Order 1980].

[874]

NOTES

Sub-s (3): words in square brackets substituted by the High Court and County Courts Jurisdiction Order 1991, SI 1991/724, art 2(1), (8), Schedule, Pt I.

Supplemental

14   Interpretation

(1)   In this Act, unless the context otherwise requires—

.....

"enactment" includes an enactment contained in an Act of the Parliament of Northern Ireland or an Order in Council made under the Northern Ireland (Temporary Provisions) Act 1972, or in a Measure of the Northern Ireland Assembly,

"goods" includes all chattels personal other than things in action and money,

"High Court" includes the High Court of Justice in Northern Ireland.

(2)   References in this Act to any enactment include references to that enactment as amended, extended or applied by or under that or any other enactment.

[875]

NOTES

Sub-s (1): definition omitted repealed by the High Court and County Courts Jurisdiction Order 1991, SI 1991/724, art 2(8), Schedule, Pt I.

15   Repeal

(1)   The Disposal of Uncollected Goods Act 1952 is hereby repealed.

(2)   In England and Wales that repeal shall not affect goods bailed before the commencement of this Act.

(3)   *(Applies to Scotland only.)*

[876]

NOTES
  Disposal of Uncollected Goods Act 1952: replaced by ss 12, 13 at **[873]**, **[874]**, and Sch 1 at **[879]**, et seq.

16 Extent and application to the Crown

(1)   Section 15 shall extend to Scotland, but otherwise this Act shall not extend to Scotland.

(2)   This Act, except section 15, extends to Northern Ireland.

(3)   This Act shall bind the Crown, but as regards the Crown's liability in tort shall not bind the Crown further than the Crown is made liable in tort by the Crown Proceedings Act 1947.

[877]

17 Short title, etc

(1)   This Act may be cited as the Torts (Interference with Goods) Act 1977.

(2)   This Act shall come into force on such day as the Lord Chancellor may by order contained in a statutory instrument appoint, and such an order may appoint different dates for different provisions or for different purposes.

(3)   Schedule 2 to this Act contains transitional provisions.

[878]

NOTES
  Orders: the Torts (Interference with Goods) Act 1977 (Commencement No 1) Order 1977, SI 1977/1910; the Torts (Interference with Goods) Act 1977 (Commencement No 2) Order 1978, SI 1978/627; the Torts (Interference with Goods) Act 1977 (Commencement No 3) Order 1980, SI 1980/2024.

SCHEDULES

SCHEDULE 1
UNCOLLECTED GOODS
Section 12

PART I
POWER TO IMPOSE OBLIGATION TO COLLECT GOODS

1.—(1)   For the purposes of section 12(1) a bailee may, in the circumstances specified in this Part of this Schedule, by notice given to the bailor impose on him an obligation to take delivery of the goods.

(2)   The notice shall be in writing, and may be given either—
  (a)   by delivering it to the bailor, or
  (b)   by leaving it at his proper address, or
  (c)   by post.

(3)   The notice shall—
  (a)   specify the name and address of the bailee, and give sufficient particulars of the goods and the address or place where they are held, and
  (b)   state that the goods are ready for delivery to the bailor, or where combined with a notice terminating the contract of bailment, will be ready for delivery when the contract is terminated, and
  (c)   specify the amount, if any, which is payable by the bailor to the bailee in respect of the goods and which became due before the giving of the notice.

(4)   Where the notice is sent by post it may be combined with a notice under Part II of this Schedule if the notice is sent by post in a way complying with paragraph 6(4).

(5)   References in this Part of this Schedule to taking delivery of the goods include, where the terms of the bailment admit, references to giving directions as to their delivery.

(6)   This Part of this Schedule is without prejudice to the provisions of any contract requiring the bailor to take delivery of the goods.

Goods accepted for repair or other treatment

2.   If a bailee has accepted goods for repair or other treatment on the terms (expressed or implied) that they will be re-delivered to the bailor when the repair or other treatment has been carried out, the notice may be given at any time after the repair or other treatment has been carried out.

Goods accepted for valuation or appraisal

3.   If a bailee has accepted goods in order to value or appraise them, the notice may be given at any time after the bailee has carried out the valuation or appraisal.

Storage, warehousing, etc

4.—(1)   If a bailee is in possession of goods which he has held as custodian, and his obligation as custodian has come to an end, the notice may be given at any time after the ending of the obligation, or may be combined with any notice terminating his obligation as custodian.

(2)   This paragraph shall not apply to goods held by a person as mercantile agent, that is to say by a person having in the customary course of his business as a mercantile agent authority either to sell goods or to consign goods for the purpose of sale, or to buy goods, or to raise money on the security of goods.

Supplemental

5.   Paragraphs 2, 3 and 4 apply whether or not the bailor has paid any amount due to the bailee in respect of the goods, and whether or not the bailment is for reward, or in the course of business, or gratuitous.

[879]

PART II
NOTICE OF INTENTION TO SELL GOODS

6.—(1)   A notice under section 12(3) shall
  (a)   specify the name and address of the bailee, and give sufficient particulars of the goods and the address or place where they are held, and
  (b)   specify the date on or after which the bailee proposes to sell the goods, and
  (c)   specify the amount, if any, which is payable by the bailor to the bailee in respect of the goods, and which became due before the giving of the notice.

(2)   The period between giving of the notice and the date specified in the notice as that on or after which the bailee proposes to exercise the power of sale shall be such as will afford the bailor a reasonable opportunity of taking delivery of the goods.

(3)   If any amount is payable in respect of the goods by the bailor to the bailee, and became due before giving of the notice, the said period shall be not less than three months.

(4)   The notice shall be in writing and shall be sent by post in a registered letter, or by the recorded delivery service.

7.—(1)   The bailee shall not give a notice under section 12(3), or exercise his right to sell the goods pursuant to such a notice, at a time when he has notice that, because of a dispute concerning the goods, the bailor is questioning or refusing to pay all or any part of what the bailee claims to be due to him in respect of the goods.

(2)   This paragraph shall be left out of account in determining under section 13(1) whether a bailee of goods is entitled to sell the goods under section 12, or would be so entitled if he had given any notice required in accordance with this Schedule.

Supplemental

8.   For the purposes of this Schedule, and of section 26 of the Interpretation Act 1889 in its application to this Schedule, the proper address of the person to whom a notice is to be given shall be—
  (a)   in the case of a body corporate, a registered or principal office of the body corporate, and
  (b)   in any other case, the last known address of the person.

[880]

NOTES
Interpretation Act 1889, s 26: repealed by the Interpretation Act 1978, s 25, Sch 3, and replaced by s 7 of, and Sch 2, para 3 to, that Act.

(Sch 2 (Transitional) outside the scope of this work.)

UNFAIR CONTRACT TERMS ACT 1977

(1977 c 50)

ARRANGEMENT OF SECTIONS

PART I
AMENDMENT OF LAW FOR ENGLAND AND WALES
AND NORTHERN IRELAND

Introductory

An Act to impose further limits on the extent to which under the law of England and Wales and Northern Ireland civil liability for breach of contract, or for negligence or other breach of duty, can be avoided by means of contract terms and otherwise, and under the law of Scotland civil liability can be avoided by means of contract terms

[26 October 1977]

PART I
AMENDMENT OF LAW FOR ENGLAND AND WALES AND NORTHERN IRELAND
Introductory

1 Scope of Part I

(1)   For the purposes of this Part of this Act, "negligence" means the breach—
  (a)   of any obligation, arising from the express or implied terms of a contract, to take reasonable care or exercise reasonable skill in the performance of the contract;
  (b)   of any common law duty to take reasonable care or exercise reasonable skill (but not any stricter duty);
  (c)   of the common duty of care imposed by the Occupiers' Liability Act 1957 or the Occupiers' Liability Act (Northern Ireland) 1957.

(2)   This Part of this Act is subject to Part III; and in relation to contracts, the operation of sections 2 to 4 and 7 is subject to the exceptions made by Schedule 1.

(3)   In the case of both contract and tort, sections 2 to 7 apply (except where the contrary is stated in section 6(4)) only to business liability, that is liability for breach of obligations or duties arising—
  (a)   from things done or to be done by a person in the course of a business (whether his own business or another's); or
  (b)   from the occupation of premises used for business purposes of the occupier;
and references to liability are to be read accordingly [but liability of an occupier of premises for breach of an obligation or duty towards a person obtaining access to the premises for recreational or educational purposes, being liability for loss or damage suffered by reason of the dangerous state of

the premises, is not a business liability of the occupier unless granting that person such access for the purposes concerned falls within the business purposes of the occupier].

(4)   In relation to any breach of duty or obligation, it is immaterial for any purpose of this Part of this Act whether the breach was inadvertent or intentional, or whether liability for it arises directly or vicariously.

[881]

NOTES

Sub-s (3): words in square brackets added by the Occupiers' Liability Act 1984, s 2.

Avoidance of liability for negligence, breach of contract, etc

2   Negligence liability

(1)   A person cannot by reference to any contract term or to a notice given to persons generally or to particular persons exclude or restrict his liability for death or personal injury resulting from negligence.

(2)   In the case of other loss or damage, a person cannot so exclude or restrict his liability for negligence except in so far as the term or notice satisfies the requirement of reasonableness.

(3)   Where a contract term or notice purports to exclude or restrict liability for negligence a person's agreement to or awareness of it is not of itself to be taken as indicating his voluntary acceptance of any risk.

[882]

3   Liability arising in contract

(1)   This section applies as between contracting parties where one of them deals as consumer or on the other's written standard terms of business.

(2)   As against that party, the other cannot by reference to any contract term—
    (a)   when himself in breach of contract, exclude or restrict any liability of his in respect of the breach; or
    (b)   claim to be entitled—
        (i)   to render a contractual performance substantially different from that which was reasonably expected of him, or
        (ii)   in respect of the whole or any part of his contractual obligation, to render no performance at all,

except in so far as (in any of the cases mentioned above in this subsection) the contract term satisfies the requirement of reasonableness.

[883]

4   Unreasonable indemnity clauses

(1)   A person dealing as consumer cannot by reference to any contract term be made to indemnify another person (whether a party to the contract or not) in respect of liability that may be incurred by the other for negligence or breach of contract, except in so far as the contract term satisfies the requirement of reasonableness.

(2)   This section applies whether the liability in question—
    (a)   is directly that of the person to be indemnified or is incurred by him vicariously;
    (b)   is to the person dealing as consumer or to someone else.

[884]

Liability arising from sale or supply of goods

5   "Guarantee" of consumer goods

(1)   In the case of goods of a type ordinarily supplied for private use or consumption, where loss or damage—
    (a)   arises from the goods proving defective while in consumer use; and
    (b)   results from the negligence of a person concerned in the manufacture or distribution of the goods,

liability for the loss or damage cannot be excluded or restricted by reference to any contract term or notice contained in or operating by reference to a guarantee of the goods.

(2)   For these purposes—
    (a)   goods are to be regarded as "in consumer use" when a person is using them, or has them in his possession for use, otherwise than exclusively for the purposes of a business; and
    (b)   anything in writing is a guarantee if it contains or purports to contain some promise or assurance (however worded or presented) that defects will be made good by complete or partial replacement, or by repair, monetary compensation or otherwise.

(3)   This section does not apply as between the parties to a contract under or in pursuance of which possession or ownership of the goods passed.

[885]

6   Sale and hire-purchase

(1)   Liability for breach of the obligations arising from—
  (a)   section 12 of the Sale of Goods Act 1979] (seller's implied undertakings as to title, etc.);
  (b)   section 8 of the Supply of Goods (Implied Terms) Act 1973 (the corresponding thing in relation to hire-purchase),
cannot be excluded or restricted by reference to any contract term.

(2)   As against a person dealing as consumer, liability for breach of the obligations arising from—
  (a)   [section 13, 14 or 15 of the 1979 Act] (seller's implied undertakings as to conformity of goods with description or sample, or as to their quality or fitness for a particular purpose);
  (b)   section 9, 10 or 11 of the 1973 Act (the corresponding things in relation to hire-purchase),
cannot be excluded or restricted by reference to any contract term.

(3)   As against a person dealing otherwise than as consumer, the liability specified in subsection (2) above can be excluded or restricted by reference to a contract term, but only in so far as the term satisfies the requirement of reasonableness.

(4)   The liabilities referred to in this section are not only the business liabilities defined by section 1(3), but include those arising under any contract of sale of goods or hire-purchase agreement.

[886]

NOTES
Sub-ss (1), (2): words in square brackets substituted by the Sale of Goods Act 1979, s 63, Sch 2, para 19.

7   Miscellaneous contracts under which goods pass

(1)   Where the possession or ownership of goods passes under or in pursuance of a contract not governed by the law of sale of goods or hire-purchase, subsections (2) to (4) below apply as regards the effect (if any) to be given to contract terms excluding or restricting liability for breach of obligation arising by implication of law from the nature of the contract.

(2)   As against a person dealing as consumer, liability in respect of the goods' correspondence with description or sample, or their quality or fitness for any particular purpose, cannot be excluded or restricted by reference to any such term.

(3)   As against a person dealing otherwise than as consumer, that liability can be excluded or restricted by reference to such a term, but only in so far as the term satisfies the requirement of reasonableness.

[(3A)   Liability for breach of the obligations arising under section 2 of the Supply of Goods and Services Act 1982 (implied terms about title etc in certain contracts for the transfer of the property in goods) cannot be excluded or restricted by references to any such term.]

(4)   Liability in respect of—
  (a)   the right to transfer ownership of the goods, or give possession; or
  (b)   the assurance of quiet possession to a person taking goods in pursuance of the contract,
cannot [(in a case to which subsection (3A) above does not apply)] be excluded or restricted by reference to any such term except in so far as the term satisfies the requirement of reasonableness.

(5)   ...

[887]

NOTES
Sub-s (3A): inserted by the Supply of Goods and Services Act 1982, s 17(2).
Sub-s (4): words in square brackets inserted by the Supply of Goods and Services Act 1982, s 17(3).
Sub-s (5): repealed in relation to England and Wales by the Regulatory Reform (Trading Stamps) Order 2005, SI 2005/871, art 6, Schedule, and in relation to Northern Ireland by the Law Reform (Miscellaneous Provisions) (Northern Ireland) Order 2005, SI 2005/1452, art 24, Sch 2.

Other provisions about contracts

8   (*Substitutes the Misrepresentation Act 1967, s 3 at* **[428]**, *and the Misrepresentation Act (Northern Ireland) 1967, s 3.*)

9   Effect of breach

(1)   Where for reliance upon it a contract term has to satisfy the requirement of reasonableness, it may be found to do so and be given effect accordingly notwithstanding that the contract has been terminated either by breach or by a party electing to treat it as repudiated.

(2)   Where on a breach the contract is nevertheless affirmed by a party entitled to treat it as repudiated, this does not of itself exclude the requirement of reasonableness in relation to any contract term.

[888]

10   Evasion by means of secondary contract

A person is not bound by any contract term prejudicing or taking away rights of his which arise under, or in connection with the performance of, another contract, so far as those rights extend to the enforcement of another's liability which this Part of this Act prevents that other from excluding or restricting.

[889]

Explanatory provisions

11   The "reasonableness" test

(1)   In relation to a contract term, the requirement of reasonableness for the purposes of this Part of this Act, section 3 of the Misrepresentation Act 1967 and section 3 of the Misrepresentation Act (Northern Ireland) 1967 is that the term shall have been a fair and reasonable one to be included having regard to the circumstances which were, or ought reasonably to have been, known to or in the contemplation of the parties when the contract was made.

(2)   In determining for the purposes of section 6 or 7 above whether a contract term satisfies the requirement of reasonableness, regard shall be had in particular to the matters specified in Schedule 2 to this Act; but this subsection does not prevent the court or arbitrator from holding, in accordance with any rule of law, that a term which purports to exclude or restrict any relevant liability is not a term of the contract.

(3)   In relation to a notice (not being a notice having contractual effect), the requirement of reasonableness under this Act is that it should be fair and reasonable to allow reliance on it, having regard to all the circumstances obtaining when the liability arose or (but for the notice) would have arisen.

(4)   Where by reference to a contract term or notice a person seeks to restrict liability to a specified sum of money, and the question arises (under this or any other Act) whether the term or notice satisfies the requirement of reasonableness, regard shall be had in particular (but without prejudice to subsection (2) above in the case of contract terms) to—
   (a)   the resources which he could expect to be available to him for the purpose of meeting the liability should it arise; and
   (b)   how far it was open to him to cover himself by insurance.

(5)   It is for those claiming that a contract term or notice satisfies the requirement of reasonableness to show that it does.

[890]

12   "Dealing as consumer"

(1)   A party to a contract "deals as consumer" in relation to another party if—
   (a)   he neither makes the contract in the course of a business nor holds himself out as doing so; and
   (b)   the other party does make the contract in the course of a business; and
   (c)   in the case of a contract governed by the law of sale of goods or hire-purchase, or by section 7 of this Act, the goods passing under or in pursuance of the contract are of a type ordinarily supplied for private use or consumption.

[(1A)   But if the first party mentioned in subsection (1) is an individual paragraph (c) of that subsection must be ignored.]

[(2)   But the buyer is not in any circumstances to be regarded as dealing as consumer—
   (a)   if he is an individual and the goods are second hand goods sold at public auction at which individuals have the opportunity of attending the sale in person;
   (b)   if he is not an individual and the goods are sold by auction or by competitive tender.]

(3)   Subject to this, it is for those claiming that a party does not deal as consumer to show that he does not.

[891]

NOTES

Sub-s (1A): inserted by the Sale and Supply of Goods to Consumers Regulations 2002, SI 2002/3045, reg 14(1), (2).

Sub-s (2): substituted by SI 2002/3045, reg 14(1), (3).

13 Varieties of exemption clause

(1)   To the extent that this Part of this Act prevents the exclusion or restriction of any liability it also prevents—

- (a)   making the liability or its enforcement subject to restrictive or onerous conditions;
- (b)   excluding or restricting any right or remedy in respect of the liability, or subjecting a person to any prejudice in consequence of his pursuing any such right or remedy;
- (c)   excluding or restricting rules of evidence or procedure;

and (to that extent) sections 2 and 5 to 7 also prevent excluding or restricting liability by reference to terms and notices which exclude or restrict the relevant obligation or duty.

(2)   But an agreement in writing to submit present or future differences to arbitration is not to be treated under this Part of this Act as excluding or restricting any liability.

[892]

14 Interpretation of Part I

In this Part of this Act—

"business" includes a profession and the activities of any government department or local or public authority;

"goods" has the same meaning as in [the Sale of Goods Act 1979];

"hire-purchase agreement" has the same meaning as in the Consumer Credit Act 1974;

"negligence" has the meaning given by section 1(1);

"notice" includes an announcement, whether or not in writing, and any other communication or pretended communication; and

"personal injury" includes any disease and any impairment of physical or mental condition.

[893]

NOTES

In definition "goods" words in square brackets substituted by the Sale of Goods Act 1979, s 63, Sch 2, para 20.

15–25   ((*Pt II*) applies to Scotland only.)

PART III
PROVISIONS APPLYING TO WHOLE OF UNITED KINGDOM

Miscellaneous

26 International supply contracts

(1)   The limits imposed by this Act on the extent to which a person may exclude or restrict liability by reference to a contract term do not apply to liability arising under such a contract as is described in subsection (3) below.

(2)   The terms of such a contract are not subject to any requirement of reasonableness under section 3 or 4: and nothing in Part II of this Act shall require the incorporation of the terms of such a contract to be fair and reasonable for them to have effect.

(3)   Subject to subsection (4), that description of contract is one whose characteristics are the following—

- (a)   either it is a contract of sale of goods or it is one under or in pursuance of which the possession or ownership of goods passes; and
- (b)   it is made by parties whose places of business (or, if they have none, habitual residences) are in the territories of different States (the Channel Islands and the Isle of Man being treated for this purpose as different States from the United Kingdom).

(4)   A contract falls within subsection (3) above only if either—

- (a)   the goods in question are, at the time of the conclusion of the contract, in the course of carriage, or will be carried, from the territory of one State to the territory of another; or
- (b)   the acts constituting the offer and acceptance have been done in the territories of different States; or
- (c)   the contract provides for the goods to be delivered to the territory of a State other than that within whose territory those acts were done.

[894]

27 Choice of law clauses

(1)   Where the [law applicable to] a contract is the law of any part of the United Kingdom only by choice of the parties (and apart from that choice would be the law of some country outside the United Kingdom) sections 2 to 7 and 16 to 21 of this Act do not operate as part [of the law applicable to the contract].

(2)   This Act has effect notwithstanding any contract term which applies or purports to apply the law of some country outside the United Kingdom, where (either or both)—

(a) the term appears to the court, or arbitrator or arbiter to have been imposed wholly or mainly for the purpose of enabling the party imposing it to evade the operation of this Act; or

(b) in the making of the contract one of the parties dealt as consumer, and he was then habitually resident in the United Kingdom, and the essential steps necessary for the making of the contract were taken there, whether by him or by others on his behalf.

(3) (*Applies to Scotland only.*)

[895]

NOTES

Sub-s (1): words in square brackets substituted by the Contracts (Applicable Law) Act 1990, s 5, Sch 4, para 4.

28 Temporary provision for sea carriage of passengers

(1) This section applies to a contract for carriage by sea of a passenger or of a passenger and his luggage where the provisions of the Athens Convention (with or without modification) do not have, in relation to the contract, the force of law in the United Kingdom.

(2) In a case where—

(a) the contract is not made in the United Kingdom, and

(b) neither the place of departure nor the place of destination under it is in the United Kingdom,

a person is not precluded by this Act from excluding or restricting liability for loss or damage, being loss or damage for which the provisions of the Convention would, if they had the force of law in relation to the contract, impose liability on him.

(3) In any other case, a person is not precluded by this Act from excluding or restricting liability for that loss or damage—

(a) in so far as the exclusion or restriction would have been effective in that case had the provisions of the Convention had the force of law in relation to the contract; or

(b) in such circumstances and to such extent as may be prescribed, by reference to a prescribed term of the contract.

(4) For the purposes of subsection (3)(a), the values which shall be taken to be the official values in the United Kingdom of the amounts (expressed in gold francs) by reference to which liability under the provisions of the Convention is limited shall be such amounts in sterling as the Secretary of State may from time to time by order made by statutory instrument specify.

(5) In this section,—

(a) the references to excluding or restricting liability include doing any of those things in relation to the liability which are mentioned in section 13 or section 25(3) and (5); and

(b) "the Athens Convention" means the Athens Convention relating to the Carriage of Passengers and their Luggage by Sea, 1974; and

(c) "prescribed" means prescribed by the Secretary of State by regulations made by statutory instrument;

and a statutory instrument containing the regulations shall be subject to annulment in pursuance of a resolution of either House of Parliament.

[896]

NOTES

The Athens Convention: Cmnd 6326; set out in the Merchant Shipping Act 1979, Sch 3 and given the force of law by s 14 of that Act (as from 1 January 1996, replaced by the Merchant Shipping Act 1995, Sch 6 and s 183 respectively); brought fully into force on 30 April 1987 by the Merchant Shipping Act 1979 (Commencement No 11) Order 1987, SI 1987/635.

Modifications: the Merchant Shipping Act 1995, s 184(2), provides that Orders in Council made under s 184(1) of the Act may modify this section as the Secretary of State considers appropriate. By the Carriage of Passengers and their Luggage by Sea (Interim Provisions) Order 1980, SI 1980/1092 (made under s 16(1), (2) of the 1979 Act and now having effect under s 184 of the 1995 Act), this section ceased to apply to any contract to which that Order applies on 1 January 1981, but continues to apply to any contract made before that date. Contracts made after 30 April 1987 are governed by the Athens convention, subject, in the case of contracts for domestic carriage, to modifications contained in the Carriage of Passengers and their Luggage by Sea (Domestic Carriage) Order 1987, SI 1987/670.

Orders: as a result of the coming into force of the 1976 Protocol to the Athens Convention which replaced the references to gold francs in the Convention with references to special drawing rights, no equivalents for gold francs are now provided for by order under this section.

29 Saving for other relevant legislation

(1) Nothing in this Act removes or restricts the effect of, or prevents reliance upon, any contractual provision which—

(a) is authorised or required by the express terms or necessary implication of an enactment; or

    (b)   being made with a view to compliance with an international agreement to which the United Kingdom is a party, does not operate more restrictively than is contemplated by the agreement.

  (2)   A contract term is to be taken—

    (a)   for the purposes of Part I of this Act, as satisfying the requirement of reasonableness; and

    (b)   *(applies to Scotland only)*,

if it is incorporated or approved by, or incorporated pursuant to a decision or ruling of, a competent authority acting in the exercise of any statutory jurisdiction or function and is not a term in a contract to which the competent authority is itself a party.

  (3)   In this section—

"competent authority" means any court, arbitrator or arbiter, government department or public authority;

"enactment" means any legislation (including subordinate legislation) of the United Kingdom or Northern Ireland and any instrument having effect by virtue of such legislation; and

"statutory" means conferred by an enactment.

[897]

30   *(Repealed by the Consumer Safety Act 1978, s 10(1), Sch 3.)*

General

31 Commencement; amendments; repeals

  (1)   This Act comes into force on 1st February 1978.

  (2)   Nothing in this Act applies to contracts made before the date on which it comes into force, but subject to this, it applies to liability for any loss or damage which is suffered on or after that date.

  (3)   The enactments specified in Schedule 3 to this Act are amended as there shown.

  (4)   The enactments specified in Schedule 4 to this Act are repealed to the extent specified in column 3 of that Schedule.

[898]

32 Citation and extent

  (1)   This Act may be cited as the Unfair Contract Terms Act 1977.

  (2)   Part I of this Act extends to England and Wales and to Northern Ireland; but it does not extend to Scotland.

  (3)   Part II of this Act extends to Scotland only.

  (4)   This Part of this Act extends to the whole of the United Kingdom.

[899]

SCHEDULES

SCHEDULE 1
SCOPE OF SECTIONS 2 TO 4 AND 7

Section 1(2)

1.   Sections 2 to 4 of this Act do not extend to—

    (a)   any contract of insurance (including a contract to pay an annuity on human life);

    (b)   any contract so far as it relates to the creation or transfer of an interest in land, or to the termination of such an interest, whether by extinction, merger, surrender, forfeiture or otherwise;

    (c)   any contract so far as it relates to the creation or transfer of a right or interest in any patent, trade mark, copyright [or design right], registered design, technical or commercial information or other intellectual property, or relates to the termination of any such right or interest;

    (d)   any contract so far as it relates—

        (i)   to the formation or dissolution of a company (which means any body corporate or unincorporated association and includes a partnership), or

       (ii)   to its constitution or the rights or obligations of its corporators or members;

    (e)   any contract so far as it relates to the creation or transfer of securities or of any right or interest in securities.

2.   Section 2(1) extends to—

    (a)   any contract of marine salvage or towage;

    (b)   any charterparty of a ship or hovercraft; and

    (c)   any contract for the carriage of goods by ship or hovercraft;

but subject to this sections 2 to 4 and 7 do not extend to any such contract except in favour of a person dealing as consumer.

3. Where goods are carried by ship or hovercraft in pursuance of a contract which either—
    (a)   specifies that as the means of carriage over part of the journey to be covered, or
    (b)   makes no provision as to the means of carriage and does not exclude that means,

then sections 2(2), 3 and 4 do not, except in favour of a person dealing as consumer, extend to the contract as it operates for and in relation to the carriage of the goods by that means.

4. Section 2(1) and (2) do not extend to a contract of employment, except in favour of the employee.

5. Section 2(1) does not affect the validity of any discharge and indemnity given by a person, on or in connection with an award to him of compensation for pneumoconiosis attributable to employment in the coal industry, in respect of any further claim arising from his contracting that disease.

[900]

NOTES
    Para 1: words in square brackets in sub-para (c) inserted by the Copyright, Designs and Patents Act 1988, s 303(1), Sch 7, para 24.
    Modification: References to trade marks or registered trade marks within the meaning of the Trade Marks Act 1938 shall, unless the context otherwise requires, be construed as references to trade marks or registered trade marks within the meaning of the Trade Marks Act 1994; see the Trade Marks Act 1994, Sch 4, para 1.

SCHEDULE 2
"GUIDELINES" FOR APPLICATION OF REASONABLENESS TEST
Sections 11(2), 24(2)

The matters to which regard is to be had in particular for the purposes of sections 6(3), 7(3) and (4), 20 and 21 are any of the following which appear to be relevant—
    (a)   the strength of the bargaining positions of the parties relative to each other, taking into account (among other things) alternative means by which the customer's requirements could have been met;
    (b)   whether the customer received an inducement to agree to the term, or in accepting it had an opportunity of entering into a similar contract with other persons, but without having to accept a similar term;
    (c)   whether the customer knew or ought reasonably to have known of the existence and extent of the term (having regard, among other things, to any custom of the trade and any previous course of dealing between the parties);
    (d)   where the term excludes or restricts any relevant liability if some condition is not complied with, whether it was reasonable at the time of the contract to expect that compliance with that condition would be practicable;
    (e)   whether the goods were manufactured, processed or adapted to the special order of the customer.

[901]

(Sch 3, in so far as unrepealed, specifies amendments of the Supply of Goods (Implied Terms) Act 1973, ss 14, 15 (as originally enacted and as substituted by the Consumer Credit Act 1974); Sch 4 specifies certain enactments repealed by s 31(4).)

STATE IMMUNITY ACT 1978

(1978 c 33)

ARRANGEMENT OF SECTIONS

PART I
PROCEEDINGS IN UNITED KINGDOM BY OR AGAINST OTHER STATES

Immunity from jurisdiction

An Act to make new provision with respect to proceedings in the United Kingdom by or against other States; to provide for the effect of judgments given against the United Kingdom in the courts of States parties to the European Convention on State Immunity; to make new provision with respect to the immunities and privileges of heads of State; and for connected purposes

[20th July 1978]

PART I
PROCEEDINGS IN UNITED KINGDOM BY OR AGAINST OTHER STATES

Immunity from jurisdiction

1   General immunity from jurisdiction

(1)   A State is immune from the jurisdiction of the courts of the United Kingdom except as provided in the following provisions of this Part of this Act.

(2)   A court shall give effect to the immunity conferred by this section even though the State does not appear in the proceedings in question.

[901A]

Exceptions from immunity

2   Submission to jurisdiction

(1)   A State is not immune as respects proceedings in respect of which it has submitted to the jurisdiction of the courts of the United Kingdom.

(2)   A State may submit after the dispute giving rise to the proceedings has arisen or by a prior written agreement; but a provision in any agreement that it is to governed by the law of the United Kingdom is not to be regarded as a submission.

(3)   A State is deemed to have submitted—
    (a)   if it has instituted the proceedings; or
    (b)   subject to subsections (4) and (5) below, if it has intervened or taken any step in the proceedings.

(4)   Subsection (3)(b) above does not apply to intervention or any step taken for the purpose only of—
    (a)   claiming immunity; or
    (b)   asserting an interest in property in circumstances such that the State would have been entitled to immunity if the proceedings had been brought against it.

(5)   Subsection (3)(b) above does not apply to any step taken by the State in ignorance of facts entitling it to immunity if those facts could not reasonably have been ascertained and immunity is claimed as soon as reasonably practicable.

(6) A submission in respect of any proceedings extends to any appeal but not to any counter-claim unless it arises out of the same legal relationship or facts as the claim.

(7) The head of a State's diplomatic mission in the United Kingdom, or the person for the time being performing his functions, shall be deemed to have authority to submit on behalf of the State in respect of any proceedings; and any person who has entered into a contract on behalf of and with the authority of a State shall be deemed to have authority to submit on its behalf in respect of proceedings arising out of the contract.

[901B]

3 Commercial transactions and contracts to be performed in United Kingdom

(1) A State is not immune as respects proceedings relating to—
- (a) a commercial transaction, entered into by the State; or
- (b) an obligation of the State which by virtue of a contract (whether a commercial transaction or not) falls to be performed wholly or partly in the United Kingdom.

(2) This section does not apply if the parties to the dispute are States or have otherwise agreed in writing; and subsection (1)(b) above does not apply if the contract (not being a commercial transaction) was made in the territory of the State concerned and the obligation in question is governed by its administrative law.

(3) In this section "commercial transaction" means—
- (a) any contract for the supply of goods or services;
- (b) any loan or other transaction for the provision of finance and any guarantee or indemnity in respect of any such transaction or of any other financial obligation; and
- (c) any other transaction or activity (whether of a commercial, industrial, financial, professional or other similar character) into which a State enters or in which it engages otherwise than in the exercise of sovereign authority;

but neither paragraph of subsection (1) above applies to a contract of employment between a State and an individual.

[901C]

4 Contracts of employment

(1) A State is not immune as respects proceedings relating to a contract of employment between the State and an individual where the contract was made in the United Kingdom or the work is to be wholly or partly performed there.

(2) Subject to subsections (3) and (4) below, this section does not apply if—
- (a) at the time when the proceedings are brought the individual is a national of the State concerned; or
- (b) at the time when the contract was made the individual was neither a national of the United Kingdom nor habitually resident there; or
- (c) the parties to the contract have otherwise agreed in writing.

(3) Where the work is for an office, agency or establishment maintained by the State in the United Kingdom for commercial purposes, subsection (2) (a) and (b) above do not exclude the application of this section unless the individual was, at the time when the contract was made, habitually resident in that State.

(4) Subsection (2)(c) above does not exclude the application of this section where the law of the United Kingdom requires the proceedings to be brought before a court of the United Kingdom.

(5) In subsection (2)(b) above "national of the United Kingdom" [means—
- (a) a British citizen, a [British overseas territories citizen][, a British National (Overseas)] or a British Overseas citizen; or
- (b) a person who under the British Nationality Act 1981 is a British subject; or
- (c) a British protected person (within the meaning of that Act)].

(6) In this section "proceedings relating to a contract of employment" includes proceedings between the parties to such a contract in respect of any statutory rights or duties to which they are entitled or subject as employer or employee.

[901D]

NOTES

Sub-s (5): words in first (outer) pair of square brackets substituted by the British Nationality Act 1981, s 52(6), Sch 7; in para (a), words in first pair of square brackets substituted by virtue of the British Overseas Territories Act 2002, s 2(3); words in second pair of square brackets inserted by the Hong Kong (British Nationality) Order 1986, SI 1986/948, art 8, Schedule.

5 Personal injuries and damage to property

A State is not immune as respects proceedings in respect of—
- (a) death or personal injury; or

    (b)   damage or loss of tangible property,

caused by an act or omission in the United Kingdom.

[901E]

6   Ownership, possession and use of property

    (1)   A State is not immune as respects proceedings relating to—
        (a)   any interest of the State in, or its possession or use of, immovable property in the United Kingdom; or
        (b)   any obligation of the State arising out of its interest in, or its possession or use of, any such property.

    (2)   A State is not immune as respects proceedings relating to any interest of the State in movable or immovable property, being an interest arising by way of succession, gift or bona vacantia.

    (3)   The fact that a State has or claims an interest in any property shall not preclude any court from exercising in respect of it any jurisdiction relating to the estates of deceased persons or persons of unsound mind or to insolvency, the winding up of companies or the administration of trusts.

    (4)   A court may entertain proceedings against a person other than a State notwithstanding that the proceedings relate to property—
        (a)   which is in the possession or control of a State; or
        (b)   in which a State claims an interest,

if the State would not have been immune had the proceedings been brought against it or, in a case within paragraph (b) above, if the claim is neither admitted nor supported by prima facie evidence.

[901F]

7   Patents, trade-marks etc

A State is not immune as respects proceedings relating to—
    (a)   any patent, trade-mark design or plant breeders' rights belonging to the State and registered or protected in the United Kingdom or for which the State has applied in the United Kingdom;
    (b)   an alleged infringement by the State in the United Kingdom of any patent, trade-mark, design, plant breeders' rights or copyright; or
    (c)   the right to use a trade or business name in the United Kingdom.

[901G]

NOTES

  References to trade marks or registered trade marks within the meaning of the Trade Marks Act 1938 shall, unless the context otherwise requires, be construed as references to trade marks or registered trade marks within the meaning of the Trade Marks Act 1994; see the Trade Marks Act 1994, Sch 4, para 1.

---

8   Membership of bodies corporate etc

    (1)   A State is not immune as respects proceedings relating to its membership of a body corporate, an unincorporated body or a partnership which—
        (a)   has members other than States; and
        (b)   is incorporated or constituted under the law of the United Kingdom or is controlled from or has its principal place of business in the United Kingdom,

being proceedings arising between the State and the body or its other members or, as the case may be, between the State and the other partners.

    (2)   This section does not apply if provision to the contrary has been made by an agreement in writing between the parties to the dispute or by the constitution or other instrument establishing or regulating the body or partnership in question.

[901H]

9   Arbitrations

    (1)   Where a State has agreed in writing to submit a dispute which has arisen, or may arise, to arbitration, the State is not immune as respects proceedings in the courts of the United Kingdom which relate to the arbitration.

    (2)   This section has effect subject to any contrary provision in the arbitration agreement and does not apply to any arbitration agreement between States.

[901I]

10   Ships used for commercial purposes

    (1)   This section applies to—
        (a)   Admiralty proceedings; and
        (b)   proceedings on any claim which could be made the subject of Admiralty proceedings.

    (2)   A State is not immune as respects—

(a)   an action in rem against a ship belonging to that State; or

(b)   an action in personam for enforcing a claim in connection with such a ship,

if, at the time when the cause of action arose, the ship was in use or intended for use for commercial purposes.

(3)   Where an action in rem is brought against a ship belonging to a State for enforcing a claim in connection with another ship belonging to that State, subsection (2)(a) above does not apply as respects the first-mentioned ship unless, at the time when the cause of action relating to the other ship arose, both ships were in use or intended for use for commercial purposes.

(4)   A State is not immune as respects—

(a)   an action in rem against a cargo belonging to that State if both the cargo and the ship carrying it were, at the time when the cause of action arose, in use or intended for use for commercial purposes; or

(b)   an action in personam for enforcing a claim in connection with such a cargo if the ship carrying it was in use or intended for use as aforesaid.

(5)   In the foregoing provisions references to a ship or cargo belonging to a State include references to a ship or cargo in its possession or control or in which it claims an interest; and, subject to subsection (4) above, subsection (2) above applies to property other than a ship as it applies to a ship.

(6)   Sections 3 to 5 above do not apply to proceedings of the kind described in subsection (1) above if the State in question is a party to the Brussels Convention and the claim relates to the operation of a ship owned or operated by that State, the carriage of cargo or passengers on any such ship or the carriage of cargo owned by that State on any other ship.

[901J]

11   Value added tax, customs duties etc

A State is not immune as respects proceedings relating to its liability for—

(a)   value added tax, and duty of customs or excise or any agricultural levy; or

(b)   rates in respect of premises occupied by it for commercial purposes.

[901K]

Procedure

12   Service of process and judgements in default of appearance

(1)   Any writ or other document required to be served for instituting proceedings against a State shall be served by being transmitted through the Foreign and Commonwealth Office to the Ministry of Foreign Affairs of the State and service shall be deemed to have been effected when the writ or document is received at the Ministry.

(2)   Any time for entering an appearance (whether prescribed by rules of court or otherwise) shall begin to run two months after the date on which the writ or document is received as aforesaid.

(3)   A State which appears in proceedings cannot thereafter object that subsection (1) above has not been complied with in the case of those proceedings.

(4)   No judgment in default of appearance shall be given against a State except on proof that subsection (1) above has been complied with and that the time for entering an appearance as extended by subsection (2) above has expired.

(5)   A copy of any judgment given against a State in default of appearance shall be transmitted through the Foreign and Commonwealth Office to the Ministry of Foreign Affairs of that State and any time for applying to have the judgment set aside (whether prescribed by rules of court or otherwise) shall begin to run two months after the date on which the copy of the judgment is received at the Ministry.

(6)   Subsection (1) above does not prevent the service of a writ or other document in any manner to which the State has agreed and subsections (2) and (4) above do not apply where service is effected in any such manner.

(7)   This section shall not be construed as applying to proceedings against a State by way of counter-claim or to an action in rem; and subsection (1) above shall not be construed as affecting any rules of court whereby leave is required for the service of process outside the jurisdiction.

[901L]

13   Other procedural privileges

(1)   No penalty by way of committal or fine shall be imposed in respect of any failure or refusal by or on behalf of a State to disclose or produce any document or other information for the purposes of proceedings to which it is a party.

(2)   Subject to subsections (3) and (4) below—

(a)   relief shall not be given against a State by way of injunction or order for specific performance or for the recovery of land or other property; and

(b)   the property of a State shall not be subject to any process for the enforcement of a judgment or arbitration award or, in an action in rem, for its arrest, detention or sale.

(3)   Subsection (2) above does not prevent the giving of any relief or the issue of any process with the written consent of the State concerned; and any such consent (which may be contained in a prior agreement) may be expressed so as to apply to a limited extent or generally; but a provision merely submitting to the jurisdiction of the courts is not to be regarded as a consent for the purposes of this subsection.

(4)   Subsection (2)(b) above does not prevent the issue of any process in respect of property which is for the time being in use or intended for use for commercial purposes; but, in a case not falling within section 10 above, this subsection applies to property of a State party to the European Convention on State Immunity only if—

(a)   the process is for enforcing a judgment which is final within the meaning of section 18(1)(b) below and the State has made a declaration under Article 24 of the Convention; or

(b)   the process is for enforcing an arbitration award.

(5)   The head of a State's diplomatic mission in the United Kingdom, or the person for the time being performing his functions, shall be deemed to have authority to give on behalf of the State any such consent as is mentioned in subsection (3) above and, for the purposes of subsection (4) above, his certificate to the effect that any property is not in use or intended for use by or on behalf of the State for commercial purposes shall be accepted as sufficient evidence of that fact unless the contrary is proved.

(6)   *(Applies to Scotland only.)*

[901M]

Supplementary provisions

14   States entitled to immunities and privileges

(1)   The immunities and privileges conferred by this Part of this Act apply to any foreign or commonwealth State other than the United Kingdom; and references to a State include references to—

(a)   the sovereign or other head of that State in his public capacity;

(b)   the government of that State; and

(c)   any department of that government,

but not to any entity (hereafter referred to as a "separate entity") which is distinct from the executive organs of the government of the State and capable of suing or being sued.

(2)   A separate entity is immune from the jurisdiction of the courts of the United Kingdom if, and only if—

(a)   the proceedings relate to anything done by it in the exercise of sovereign authority; and

(b)   the circumstances are such that a State (or, in the case of proceedings to which section 10 above applies, a State which is not a party to the Brussels Convention) would have been so immune.

(3)   If a separate entity (not being a State's central bank or other monetary authority) submits to the jurisdiction in respect of proceedings in the case of which it is entitled to immunity by virtue of subsection (2) above, subsections (1) to (4) of section 13 above shall apply to it in respect of those proceedings as if references to a State were references to that entity.

(4)   Property of a State's central bank or other monetary authority shall not be regarded for the purposes of subsection (4) of section 13 above as in use or intended for use for commercial purposes; and where any such bank or authority is a separate entity subsections (1) to (3) of that section shall apply to it as if references to a State were references to the bank or authority.

(5)   Section 12 above applies to proceedings against the constituent territories of a federal State; and Her Majesty may by Order in Council provide for the other provisions of this Part of this Act to apply to any such constituent territory specified in the Order as they apply to a State.

(6)   Where the provisions of this Part of this Act do not apply to a constituent territory by virtue of any such Order subsections (2) and (3) above shall apply to it as if it were a separate entity.

[901N]

NOTES

Orders: the State Immunity (Federal States) Order 1979, SI 1979/457; the State Immunity (Federal States) Order 1993, SI 1993/2809.

15   Restriction and extension of immunities and privileges

(1)   If it appears to Her Majesty that the immunities and privileges conferred by this Part of this Act in relation to any State—

(a)   exceed those accorded by the law of that State in relation to the United Kingdom; or

(b)   are less than those required by any treaty, convention or other international agreement to which that State and the United Kingdom are parties,

Her Majesty may by Order in Council provide for restricting or, as the case may be, extending those immunities and privileges to such extent as appears to Her Majesty to be appropriate.

(2)   Any statutory instrument containing an Order under this section shall be subject to annulment in pursuance of a resolution of either House of Parliament.

[901O]

NOTES

Orders: the State Immunity (Merchant Shipping) (Revocation) Order 1999, SI 1999/668.

16   Excluded matters

(1)   This Part of this Act does not affect any immunity or privilege conferred by the Diplomatic Privileges Act 1964 or the Consular Relations Act 1968; and—

(a)   section 4 above does not apply to proceedings concerning the employment of the members of a mission within the meaning of the Convention scheduled to the said Act of 1964 or of the members of a consular post within the meaning of the Convention scheduled to the said Act of 1968;

(b)   section 6(1) above does not apply to proceedings concerning a State's title to or its possession of property used for the purposes of a diplomatic mission.

(2)   This Part of this Act does not apply to proceedings relating to anything done by or in relation to the armed forces of a State while present in the United Kingdom and, in particular, has effect subject to the Visiting Forces Act 1952.

(3)   This Part of this Act does not apply to proceedings to which section 17(6) of the Nuclear Installations Act 1965 applies.

(4)   This Part of this Act does not apply to criminal proceedings.

(5)   This Part of this Act does not apply to any proceedings relating to taxation other than those mentioned in section 11 above.

[901P]

17   Interpretation of Part I

(1)   In this Part of this Act—

"the Brussels Convention" means the International Convention for the Unification of Certain Rules Concerning the Immunity of State-owned Ships signed in Brussels on 10th April 1926;

"commercial purposes" means purposes of such transactions or activities as are mentioned in section 3(3) above;

"ship" includes hovercraft.

(2)   In sections 2(2) and 13(3) above references to an agreement include references to a treaty, convention or other international agreement.

(3)   For the purposes of sections 3 to 8 above the territory of the United Kingdom shall be deemed to include any [British overseas territory] in respect of which the United Kingdom is a party to the European Convention on State Immunity.

(4)   In sections 3(1), 4(1), 5 and 16(2) above references to the United Kingdom includes references to its territorial waters and any area designated under section 1(7) of the Continental Shelf Act 1964.

(5)   *(Applies to Scotland only.)*

[901Q]

NOTES

Sub-s (3): words in square brackets substituted by virtue of the British Overseas Territories Act 2002, s 1(2).

PART II
JUDGMENTS AGAINST UNITED KINGDOM IN CONVENTION STATES

18   Recognition of judgments against United Kingdom

(1)   This section applies to any judgment given against the United Kingdom by a court in another State party to the European Convention on State Immunity, being a judgment—

(a)   given in proceedings in which the United Kingdom was not entitled to immunity by virtue of provisions corresponding to those of sections 2 to 11 above; and

(b)   which is final, that is to say, which is not or is no longer subject to appeal or, if given in default of appearance, liable to be set aside.

(2) Subject to section 19 below, a judgment to which this section applies shall be recognised in any court in the United Kingdom as conclusive between the parties thereto in all proceedings founded on the same cause of action and may be relied on by way of defence or counter-claim in such proceedings.

(3) Subsection (2) above (but not section 19 below) shall have effect also in relation to any settlement entered into by the United Kingdom before a court in another State party to the Convention which under the law of that State is treated as equivalent to a judgment.

(4) In this section references to a court in a State party to the Convention include references to a court in any territory in respect of which it is a party.

[901R]

19   Exceptions to recognition

(1) A court need not give effect to section 18 above in the case of a judgment—
   (a)   if to do so would be manifestly contrary to public policy or if any party to the proceedings in which the judgment was given had no adequate opportunity to present his case; or
   (b)   if the judgment was given without provisions corresponding to those of section 12 above having been complied with and the United Kingdom has not entered an appearance or applied to have the judgment set aside.

(2) A court need not give effect to section 18 above in the case of a judgment—
   (a)   if proceedings between the same parties, based on the same facts and having the same purpose—
      (i)   are pending before a court in the United Kingdom and were the first to be instituted; or
      (ii)   are pending before a court in another State party to the Convention, were the first to be instituted and may result in a judgment to which that section will apply; or
   (b)   if the result of the judgment is inconsistent with the result of another judgment given in proceedings between the same parties and—
      (i)   the other judgment is by a court in the United Kingdom and either those proceedings were the first to be instituted or the judgment of that court was given before the first-mentioned judgment became final within the meaning of subsection (1)(b) of section 18 above; or
      (ii)   the other judgment is by a court in another State party to the Convention and that section has already become applicable to it.

(3) Where the judgment was given against the United Kingdom in proceedings in respect of which the United Kingdom was not entitled to immunity by virtue of a provision corresponding to section 6(2) above, a court need not give effect to section 18 above in respect of the judgment if the court that gave the judgment—
   (a)   would not have had jurisdiction in the matter if it had applied rules of jurisdiction corresponding to those applicable to such matters in the United Kingdom; or
   (b)   applied a law other than that indicated by the United Kingdom rules of private international law and would have reached a different conclusion if it had applied the law so indicated.

(4) In subsection (2) above references to a court in the United Kingdom include references to a court in any [British overseas territory] in respect of which the United Kingdom is a party to the Convention, and references to a court in another State party to the Convention include references to a court in any territory in respect of which it is a party.

[901S]

NOTES
Sub-s (4): words in square brackets substituted by virtue of the British Overseas Territories Act 2002, s 1(2).

PART III
MISCELLANEOUS AND SUPPLEMENTARY

20   Heads of State

(1) Subject to the provisions of this section and to any necessary modifications, the Diplomatic Privileges Act 1964 shall apply to—
   (a)   a sovereign or other head of State;
   (b)   members of his family forming part of his household; and
   (c)   his private servants,
as it applies to the head of a diplomatic mission, to members of his family forming part of his household and to his private servants.

(2)   The immunities and privileges conferred by virtue of subsection (1) (a) and (b) above shall not be subject to the restrictions by reference to nationality or residence mentioned in Article 37(1) or 38 in Schedule 1 to the said Act of 1964.

(3)   Subject to any direction to the contrary by the Secretary of State, a person on whom immunities and privileges are conferred by virtue of subsection (1) above shall be entitled to the exemption conferred by section 8 (3) of the Immigration Act 1971.

(4)   Except as respects value added tax and duties of customs or excise, this section does not affect any question whether a person is exempt from, or immune as respects proceedings relating to, taxation.

(5)   This section applies to the sovereign or other head of any State on which immunities and privileges are conferred by Part I of this Act and is without prejudice to the application of that Part to any such sovereign or head of State in his public capacity.

[901T]

21   Evidence by certificate

A certificate by or on behalf of the Secretary of State shall be conclusive evidence on any question—
  (a)   whether any country is a State for the purposes of Part I of this Act, whether any territory is a constituent territory of a federal State for those purposes or as to the person or persons to be regarded for those purposes as the head or government of a State;
  (b)   whether a State is a party to the Brussels Convention mentioned in Part I of this Act.
  (c)   whether a State is a party to the European Convention on State Immunity, whether it has made a declaration under Article 24 of that Convention or as to the territories in respect of which the United Kingdom or any other State is a party;
  (d)   whether, and if so when, a document has been served or received as mentioned in section 12(1) or (5) above.

[901U]

22   General interpretation

(1)   In this Act "court" includes any tribunal or body exercising judicial functions; and references to the courts or law of the United Kingdom include references to the courts or law of any part of the United Kingdom.

(2)   In this Act references to entry of appearance and judgments in default of appearance include references to any corresponding procedures.

(3)   In this Act "the European Convention on State Immunity" means the Convention of that name signed in Basle in 16th May 1972.

(4)   In this Act "[British overseas territory]" means—
  (a)   any of the Channel Islands;
  (b)   the Isle of Man;
  (c)   any colony other than one for whose external relations a country other than the United Kingdom is responsible; or
  (d)   any country or territory outside Her Majesty's dominions in which Her Majesty has jurisdiction in right of the government of the United Kingdom.

(5)   Any power conferred by this Act to make an Order in Council includes power to vary or revoke a previous Order.

[901V]

NOTES
  Sub-s (4): words in square brackets substituted by virtue of the British Overseas Territories Act 2002, s 1(2).

---

23   Short title, repeals commencement and extent

(1)   This Act may be cited as the State Immunity Act 1978.

(2)   …

(3)   Subject to subsection (4) below, Parts I and II of this Act do not apply to proceedings in respect of matters that occurred before the date of the coming into force of this Act and, in particular—
  (a)   sections 2(2) and 13(3) do not apply to any prior agreement, and
  (b)   sections 3, 4 and 9 do not apply to any transaction, contract or arbitration agreement, entered into before that date.

(4)   Section 12 above applies to any proceedings instituted after the coming into force of this Act.

(5)   This Act shall come into force on such date as may be specified by an order made by the Lord Chancellor by statutory instrument.

(6)   This Act extends to Northern Ireland.

(7)   Her Majesty may by Order in Council extend any of the provisions of this Act, with or without modification, to any [British overseas territory].

[901W]

NOTES
Sub-s (2): repeals the Administration of Justice (Miscellaneous Provisions) Act 1938, s 13, and the Law Reform (Miscellaneous Provisions) (Scotland) Act 1940, s 7.
Sub-s (7): words in square brackets substituted by virtue of the British Overseas Territories Act 2002, s 1(2).
Orders: the State Immunity Act 1978 (Commencement) Order 1978, SI 1978/1572 ; the State Immunity (Overseas Territories) Order 1979, SI 1979/458, the State Immunity (Guernsey) Order 1980, SI 1980/871, the State Immunity (Isle of Man) Order 1981, SI 1981/1112, the State Immunity (Jersey) Order 1985, SI 1985/1642.

CIVIL LIABILITY (CONTRIBUTION) ACT 1978

(1978 c 47)

ARRANGEMENT OF SECTIONS

Proceedings for contribution

An Act to make new provision for contribution between persons who are jointly or severally, or both jointly and severally, liable for the same damage and in certain other similar cases where two or more persons have paid or may be required to pay compensation for the same damage; and to amend the law relating to proceedings against persons jointly liable for the same debt or jointly or severally, or both jointly and severally, liable for the same damage

[31 July 1978]

Proceedings for contribution

1   Entitlement to contribution

(1)   Subject to the following provisions of this section, any person liable in respect of any damage suffered by another person may recover contribution from any other person liable in respect of the same damage (whether jointly with him or otherwise).

(2)   A person shall be entitled to recover contribution by virtue of subsection (1) above notwithstanding that he has ceased to be liable in respect of the damage in question since the time when the damage occurred, provided that he was so liable immediately before he made or was ordered or agreed to make the payment in respect of which the contribution is sought.

(3)   A person shall be liable to make contribution by virtue of subsection (1) above notwithstanding that he has ceased to be liable in respect of the damage in question since the time when the damage occurred, unless he ceased to be liable by virtue of the expiry of a period of limitation or prescription which extinguished the right on which the claim against him in respect of the damage was based.

(4)   A person who has made or agreed to make any payment in bona fide settlement or compromise of any claim made against him in respect of any damage (including a payment into court which has been accepted) shall be entitled to recover contribution in accordance with this section without regard to whether or not he himself is or ever was liable in respect of the damage, provided, however, that he would have been liable assuming that the factual basis of the claim against him could be established.

(5)   A judgment given in any action brought in any part of the United Kingdom by or on behalf of the person who suffered the damage in question against any person from whom contribution is

sought under this section shall be conclusive in the proceedings for contribution as to any issue determined by that judgment in favour of the person from whom the contribution is sought.

(6) References in this section to a person's liability in respect of any damage are references to any such liability which has been or could be established in an action brought against him in England and Wales by or on behalf of the person who suffered the damage; but it is immaterial whether any issue arising in any such action was or would be determined (in accordance with the rules of private international law) by reference to the law of a country outside England and Wales.

[902]

NOTES

Disapplication: this section and s 2 do not apply where liability for contribution between persons liable in respect of the same damage is governed by European Parliament and Council Regulation 1371/2007/EC on rail passengers' rights and obligations; see the Rail Passengers' Rights and Obligations Regulations 2010, SI 2010/1504, reg 5(1), (2).

2 Assessment of contribution

(1) Subject to subsection (3) below, in any proceedings for contribution under section 1 above the amount of the contribution recoverable from any person shall be such as may be found by the court to be just and equitable having regard to the extent of that person's responsibility for the damage in question.

(2) Subject to subsection (3) below, the court shall have power in any such proceedings to exempt any person from liability to make contribution, or to direct that the contribution to be recovered from any person shall amount to a complete indemnity.

(3) Where the amount of the damages which have or might have been awarded in respect of the damage in question in any action brought in England and Wales by or on behalf of the person who suffered it against the person from whom the contribution is sought was or would have been subject to—

    (a)   any limit imposed by or under any enactment or by any agreement made before the damage occurred;

    (b)   any reduction by virtue of section 1 of the Law Reform (Contributory Negligence) Act 1945 or section 5 of the Fatal Accidents Act 1976; or

    (c)   any corresponding limit or reduction under the law of a country outside England and Wales;

the person from whom the contribution is sought shall not by virtue of any contribution awarded under section 1 above be required to pay in respect of the damage a greater amount than the amount of those damages as so limited or reduced.

[903]

NOTES

Disapplication: see the note to s 1 at **[902]**.

Proceedings for the same debt or damage

3 Proceedings against persons jointly liable for the same debt or damage

Judgment recovered against any person liable in respect of any debt or damage shall not be a bar to an action, or to the continuance of an action, against any other person who is (apart from any such bar) jointly liable with him in respect of the same debt or damage.

[904]

4 Successive actions against persons liable (jointly or otherwise) for the same damage

If more than one action is brought in respect of any damage by or on behalf of the person by whom it was suffered against persons liable in respect of the damage (whether jointly or otherwise) the plaintiff shall not be entitled to costs in any of those actions, other than that in which judgment is first given, unless the court is of the opinion that there was reasonable ground for bringing the action.

[905]

Supplemental

5 Application to the Crown

Without prejudice to section 4(1) of the Crown Proceedings Act 1947 (indemnity and contribution), this Act shall bind the Crown, but nothing in this Act shall be construed as in any way affecting Her Majesty in Her private capacity (including in right of Her Duchy of Lancaster) or the Duchy of Cornwall.

[906]

6 Interpretation

(1) A person is liable in respect of any damage for the purposes of this Act if the person who suffered it (or anyone representing his estate or dependants) is entitled to recover compensation from him in respect of that damage (whatever the legal basis of his liability, whether tort, breach of contract, breach of trust or otherwise).

(2) References in this Act to an action brought by or on behalf of the person who suffered any damage include references to an action brought for the benefit of his estate or dependants.

(3) In this Act "dependants" has the same meaning as in the Fatal Accidents Act 1976.

(4) In this Act, except in section 1(5) above, "action" means an action brought in England and Wales.

[907]

7 Savings

(1) Nothing in this Act shall affect any case where the debt in question became due or (as the case may be) the damage in question occurred before the date on which it comes into force.

(2) A person shall not be entitled to recover contribution or liable to make contribution in accordance with section 1 above by reference to any liability based on breach of any obligation assumed by him before the date on which this Act comes into force.

(3) The right to recover contribution in accordance with section 1 above supersedes any right, other than an express contractual right, to recover contribution (as distinct from indemnity) otherwise than under this Act in corresponding circumstances; but nothing in this Act shall affect—

    (a)   any express or implied contractual or other right to indemnity; or

    (b)   any express contractual provision regulating or excluding contribution;

which would be enforceable apart from this Act (or render enforceable any agreement for indemnity or contribution which would not be enforceable apart from this Act).

[908]

8 (*Applies to Northern Ireland only.*)

9 Consequential amendments and repeals

(1) The enactments specified in Schedule 1 to this Act shall have effect subject to the amendments set out in that Schedule, being amendments consequential on the preceding provisions of this Act.

(2) The enactments specified in Schedule 2 to this Act are hereby repealed to the extent specified in column 3 of that Schedule.

[909]

10 Short title, commencement and extent

(1) This Act may be cited as the Civil Liability (Contribution) Act 1978.

(2) This Act shall come into force on 1st January next following the date on which it is passed.

(3) This Act, with the exception of paragraph 1 of Schedule 1 thereto, does not extend to Scotland.

[910]

(*Sch 1 (Consequential Amendments), Sch 2 (Repeals) outside the scope of this work.*)

BANKING ACT 1979

(1979 c 37)

An Act to regulate the acceptance of deposits in the course of a business; to confer functions on the Bank of England with respect to the control of institutions carrying on deposit-taking businesses; to give further protection to persons who are depositors with such institutions; to make provision with respect to advertisements inviting the making of deposits; to restrict the use of names and descriptions associated with banks and banking; to prohibit fraudulent inducement to make a deposit; to amend the Consumer Credit Act 1974 and the law with respect to instruments to which section 4 of the Cheques Act 1957 applies; to repeal certain enactments relating to banks and banking; and for purposes connected therewith

[4 April 1979]

1–37 ((*Pts I–III*) *repealed by the Banking Act 1987, s 108(2), Sch 7, Pt I.*)

PART IV
MISCELLANEOUS AND GENERAL

38–46   *(S 38 amends the Consumer Credit Act 1974, ss 74, 114, 185(2) at* **[720]**, **[759]**, **[827]**; *ss 39–46 repealed by the Banking Act 1987, s 108(2), Sch 7, Pt I.)*

47 Defence of contributory negligence

In any circumstances in which proof of absence of negligence on the part of a banker would be a defence in proceedings by reason of section 4 of the Cheques Act 1957, a defence of contributory negligence shall also be available to the banker notwithstanding the provisions of section 11(1) of the Torts (Interference with Goods) Act 1977.

[911]

48–51   *(Ss 48–50 repealed by the Banking Act 1987, s 108(2), Sch 7, Pt I; s 51(1) introduces Sch 6 to this Act (consequential amendments); s 51(2) repealed by the Statute Law (Repeals) Act 2004.)*

52 Short title, commencement and extent

(1)   This Act may be cited as the Banking Act 1979.

(2)   This Act extends to Northern Ireland.

(3)   …

(4)   Any reference in any provision of this Act to "the appointed day" shall be construed as a reference to the day appointed for the purposes of that provision; and any reference in this Act to the day appointed for the purposes of any provision of this Act—

   (a)   shall be construed as a reference to the day appointed under this section for the coming into operation of that provision; and

   (b)   where different days are appointed for different purposes of that provision, shall be construed, unless an order under this section otherwise provides, as a reference to the first day so appointed.

[912]

NOTES

Sub-s (3): repealed by the Statute Law (Repeals) Act 2004.

Orders: the Banking Act 1979 (Commencement No 1) Order 1979, SI 1979/938; the Banking Act 1979 (Commencement No 2) Order 1982, SI 1982/188; the Banking Act 1979 (Commencement No 3) Order 1985, SI 1985/797.

(Schs 1–5 repealed by the Banking Act 1987, s 108(2), Sch 7, Pt I; Sch 6, in so far as unrepealed, specifies consequential amendments made by s 51(1); Sch 7 repealed by the Banking Act 1987, s 108(2), Sch 7, Pt I.)

ESTATE AGENTS ACT 1979

(1979 c 38)

ARRANGEMENT OF SECTIONS

Application of Act

An Act to make provision with respect to the carrying on of and to persons who carry on, certain activities in connection with the disposal and acquisition of interests in land; and for purposes connected therewith

[4 April 1979]

Application of Act

1 Estate agency work

(1)   This Act applies, subject to subsections (2) to (4) below to things done by any person in the course of a business (including a business in which he is employed) pursuant to instructions received from another person (in this section referred to as "the client") who wishes to dispose of or acquire an interest in land—

   (a)   for the purpose of, or with a view to, effecting the introduction to the client of a third person who wishes to acquire or, as the case may be, dispose of such an interest; and

   (b)   after such an introduction has been effected in the course of that business, for the purpose of securing the disposal or, as the case may be, the acquisition of that interest;

and in this Act the expression "estate agency work" refers to things done as mentioned above to which this Act applies.

(2)   This Act does not apply to things done—

   (a)   in the course of his profession by a practising solicitor or a person employed by him [or by an incorporated practice (within the meaning of the Solicitors (Scotland) Act 1980) or a person employed by it]; or

   (b)   in the course of credit brokerage, within the meaning of the Consumer Credit Act 1974; or

(c)   ...
(d)   in the course of carrying out any survey or valuation pursuant to a contract which is distinct from that under which other things falling within subsection (1) above are done; or
(e)   in connection with applications and other matters arising under [the Town and Country Planning Act 1990, the Planning (Listed Buildings and Conservation Areas) Act 1990, the Planning (Hazardous Substances) Act 1990] or [the Town and Country Planning (Scotland) Act 1997, the Planning (Listed Buildings and Conservation Areas) (Scotland) Act 1997, the Planning (Hazardous Substances) (Scotland) Act 1997] or the Planning (Northern Ireland) [Order 1991].

(3)   This Act does not apply to things done by any person—
(a)   pursuant to instructions received by him in the course of his employment in relation to an interest in land if his employer is the person who, on his own behalf, wishes to dispose of or acquire that interest; or
(b)   in relation to any interest in any property if the property is subject to a mortgage and he is the receiver of the income of it; or
(c)   in relation to a present, prospective or former employee of his or of any person by whom he also is employed if the things are done by reason of the employment (whether past, present or future).

(4)   This Act does not apply to the publication of advertisements or the dissemination of information by a person who does no other acts which fall within subsection (1) above.

(5)   In this section—
(a)   "practising solicitor" means, except in Scotland, a solicitor who is qualified to act as such under section 1 of the Solicitors Act 1974 or Article 4 of the Solicitors (Northern Ireland) Order 1976, and in Scotland includes a firm of practising solicitors;
(b)   "mortgage" includes a debenture and any other charge on property for securing money or money's worth; and
(c)   any reference to employment is a reference to employment under a contract of employment.

[913]

NOTES
Sub-s (2): words in square brackets in para (a) inserted by the Law Reform (Miscellaneous Provisions) (Scotland) Act 1985, s 56, Sch 1, Pt I, para 40; para (c) repealed by the Financial Services and Markets Act 2000 (Dissolution of the Insurance Brokers Registration Council) (Consequential Provisions) Order 2001, SI 2001/1283, art 3(1); in para (e) words in first pair of square brackets substituted by the Planning (Consequential Provisions) Act 1990, s 4, Sch 2, para 42, words in second pair of square brackets substituted by the Planning (Consequential Provisions) (Scotland) Act 1997, s 4, Sch 2, para 28, words in third pair of square brackets substituted by the Planning (Northern Ireland) Order 1991, SI 1991/1220, art 133(1), Sch 5.
Solicitors: references to solicitors in sub-ss (2)(a), (5)(a) are modified so as to include references to recognised bodies within the meaning of the Administration of Justice Act 1985, s 9, by the Solicitors' Incorporated Practices Order 1991, SI 1991/2684, arts 3–5, Sch 1.

2   Interests in land

(1)   Subject to subsection (3) below, any reference in this Act to disposing of an interest in land is a reference to—
(a)   transferring a legal estate in fee simple absolute in possession; or
(b)   transferring or creating, elsewhere than in Scotland, a lease which, by reason of the level of the rent, the length of the term or both, has a capital value which may be lawfully realised on the open market; or
(c)   (*applies to Scotland only*);
and any reference to acquiring an interest in land shall be construed accordingly.

(2)   In subsection (1)(b) above the expression "lease" includes the rights and obligations arising under an agreement to grant a lease.

(3)   Notwithstanding anything in subsections (1) and (2) above, references in this Act to disposing of an interest in land do not extend to disposing of—
(a)   the interest of a creditor whose debt is secured by way of a mortgage or charge of any kind over land or an agreement for any such mortgage or charge; or
(b)   (*applies to Scotland only*).

[914]

Orders by [Office of Fair Trading]

3   Orders prohibiting unfit persons from doing estate agency work

(1)   The power of [the Office of Fair Trading (in this Act referred to as "the OFT")] to make an order under this section with respect to any person shall not be exercisable unless the [OFT] is satisfied that that person—

(a)   [has committed]—
       (i)   an offence involving fraud or other dishonesty or violence, or
       (ii)   an offence under any provision of this Act, other than section 10(6), section 22(3) or section 23(4), or
       (iii) any other offence which, at the time it was committed, was specified for the purposes of this section by an order made by the Secretary of State; or
(b)   has committed discrimination in the course of estate agency work; or
[(ba) has failed to comply with an undertaking accepted from him under section 217, 218 or 219 of the Enterprise Act 2002 and given in relation to estate agency work; or
(bb) has failed to comply with an enforcement order under section 217 of the Enterprise Act 2002 which was made against him in relation to estate agency work; or]
(c)   has failed to comply with any obligation imposed on him under any of sections 15 and 18 to *21* [21A] below; or
[(ca) has engaged in estate agency work in relation to residential property in breach of the duty imposed by an order under section 23A(1) below; or]
[(cb) has failed to comply with any requirement imposed on him under section 9(1) or 11(1A)(b) below; or]
(d)   has engaged in a practice which, in relation to estate agency work, has been declared undesirable by an order made by the Secretary of State;

and the provisions of Schedule 1 to the Act shall have effect for supplementing paragraphs (a) and (b) above.

(2)   Subject to subsection (1) above, if the [OFT] is satisfied that any person is unfit to carry on estate agency work generally or of a particular description [it] may make an order prohibiting that person—
(a)   from doing any estate agency work at all; or
(b)   from doing estate agency work of a description specified in the order;

and in determining whether a person is so unfit the [OFT] may, in addition to taking account of any matters falling within subsection (1) above, also take account of whether, in the course of estate agency work or any other business activity, that person has engaged in any practice which involves breaches of a duty owed by virtue of any enactment, contract or rule of law and which is material to his fitness to carry on estate agency work.

(3)   For the purposes of [paragraphs (ba) to (d)] of subsection (1) above,—
(a)   anything done by a person in the course of his employment shall be treated as done by his employer as well as by him, whether or not it was done with the employer's knowledge or approval, unless the employer shows that he took such steps as were reasonably practicable to prevent the employee from doing that act, or from doing in the course of his employment acts of that description; and
(b)   anything done by a person as agent for another person with the authority (whether express or implied, and whether precedent or subsequent) of that person shall be treated as done by that other person as well as by him; and
(c)   anything done by a business associate of a person shall be treated as done by that person as well, unless he can show that the act was done without his connivance or consent.

(4)   In an order under this section the [OFT] shall specify as the grounds for the order those matters falling within paragraphs (a) to (d) of subsection (1) above to which [it] is satisfied and on which, accordingly, [it] relies to give [it] power to make the order.

(5)   If the [OFT] considers it appropriate, [it] may in an order under this section limit the scope of the prohibition imposed by the order to a particular part of or area within the United Kingdom.

(6)   An order under paragraph (a)(iii) or paragraph (d) of subsection (1) above—
(a)   shall be made by statutory instrument;
(b)   shall be laid before Parliament after being made; and
(c)   shall cease to have effect (without prejudice to anything previously done in reliance on the order) after the expiry of the period of twenty-eight days beginning with the date on which it was made unless within that period it has been approved by a resolution of each House of Parliament.

(7)   In reckoning for the purposes of subsection (6)(c) above any period of twenty-eight days, no account shall be taken of any period during which Parliament is dissolved or prorogued or during which both Houses are adjourned for more than four days.

(8)   A person who fails without reasonable excuse to comply with an order of the [OFT] under this section shall be liable on conviction on indictment or on summary conviction to a fine which on summary conviction shall not exceed the statutory maximum.

[915]

NOTES

Cross-heading, sub-ss (2), (4), (5), (8): words in square brackets substituted by the Enterprise Act 2002, s 278(1), Sch 25, para 9(1), (2).

Sub-s (1): words in first and second pairs of square brackets substituted by the Enterprise Act 2002, s 278(1), Sch 25, para 9(1), (2); words in square brackets in para (a) substituted and paras (ba), (bb), (ca), (cb) inserted by the Consumers, Estate Agents and Redress Act 2007, ss 53(2), 55(1)–(3), 58(2), and number in italics in para (c) substituted by subsequent number in square brackets by the Consumers, Estate Agents and Redress Act 2007, s 54(2), as from a day to be appointed.

Sub-s (3): words in square brackets substituted by the Consumers, Estate Agents and Redress Act 2007, s 63(1), Sch 7, para 1.

Orders: the Estate Agents (Undesirable Practices) (No 2) Order 1991, SI 1991/1032; the Estate Agents (Specified Offences) (No 2) Order 1991, SI 1991/1091.

4   Warning orders

[(1)   If the OFT is satisfied that any of subsections (1A), (1B) or (1C) apply in relation to a person it may by order notify that person that it is satisfied of the matters mentioned in that subsection.

(1A)   This subsection applies in relation to a person if—
   (a)   in the course of estate agency work, he has engaged in conduct falling within paragraph (a), (b), (c), (ca) or (cb) of section 3(1); and
   (b)   were he to engage again in any conduct falling within that paragraph, the OFT would consider him unfit and proceed to make a prohibition order.

(1B)   This subsection applies in relation to a person if—
   (a)   in the course of estate agency work, he has engaged in conduct constituting a failure to comply with—
      (i)   an undertaking mentioned in section 3(1)(ba); or
      (ii)   an enforcement order mentioned in section 3(1)(bb); and
   (b)   were he to fail again to comply with that undertaking or order by engaging in the same or similar conduct, the OFT would consider him unfit and proceed to make a prohibition order.

(1C)   This subsection applies in relation to a person if—
   (a)   in the course of estate agency work, he has engaged in a practice mentioned in section 3(1)(d); and
   (b)   were he to engage again in that practice, the OFT would consider him unfit and proceed to make a prohibition order.]

(2)   An order under this section shall state whether, in the opinion of the [OFT], [further conduct as mentioned in subsection (1A)(b) or (1B)(b) or engaging again in the practice specified in the order, as the case may be,] would render the person to whom the order is addressed unfit to carry on estate agency work generally or estate agency work of a description specified in the order.

(3)   If, after an order has been made under this section, the person to whom it is addressed [engages in further conduct as mentioned in subsection (1A)(b) or (1B)(b) or engages again in the practice specified in the order, as the case may be,] then, for the purposes of this Act, that fact shall be treated as conclusive evidence that he is unfit to carry on estate agency work as stated in the order in accordance with subsection (2) above; and the [OFT] may proceed to make an order under section 3 above accordingly.

[(4)   In this section "unfit" means unfit as mentioned in subsection (2) of section 3 and "prohibition order" means an order under that section.]

[916]

NOTES

Sub-ss (1), (1A)–(1C): substituted for original sub-s (1) by the Consumers, Estate Agents and Redress Act 2007, s 56(1), (2).

Sub-s (2): word in first pair of square brackets substituted by the Enterprise Act 2002, s 278(1), Sch 25, para 9(1), (3)(a); words in second pair of square brackets substituted by the Consumers, Estate Agents and Redress Act 2007, s 56(1), (3).

Sub-s (3): words in first pair of square brackets substituted by the Consumers, Estate Agents and Redress Act 2007, s 56(1), (4); word in second pair of square brackets substituted by the Enterprise Act 2002, s 278(1), Sch 25, para 9(1), (3)(a).

Sub-s (4): added by the Consumers, Estate Agents and Redress Act 2007, s 56(1), (5).

5   Supplementary provisions as to orders under sections 3 and 4

(1)   The provisions of Part I of Schedule 2 to this Act shall have effect—
   (a)   with respect to the procedure to be followed before an order is made by the [OFT] under section 3 or section 4 above; and
   (b)   in connection with the making and coming into operation of any such order.

(2)   Where an order is made by the [OFT] under section 3 or section 4 above, against a partnership, it may, if the [OFT] thinks it appropriate, have effect also as an order against some or all of the partners individually, and in such a case the order shall so provide and shall specify the names of the partners affected by the order.

(3)   Nothing in section 62 of the Sex Discrimination Act 1975, section 53 of the Race Relations Act 1976 or Article 62 of the Sex Discrimination (Northern Ireland) Order 1976 [or Article 51 of the Race Relations (Northern Ireland) Order 1997] (restriction of sanctions for breaches of those Acts and [those Orders]) shall be construed as applying to the making of an order by the [OFT] under section 3 above.

(4)   ...

(5)   In any case where—
  (a)   an order of the [OFT] under section 3 above specifies as grounds for the order the fact that the person concerned committed discrimination by reason of the existence of any such finding or notice as is referred to in paragraph 2 of Schedule 1 to this Act, and
  (b)   the period expires at the end of which, by virtue of paragraph 3 of that Schedule, the person concerned would no longer be treated for the purposes of section 3(1)(b) above as having committed discrimination by reason only of that finding or notice,

then, unless the order also specifies other grounds which remain valid, the order shall cease to have effect at the end of that period.

[917]

NOTES

Sub-ss (1), (2), (5): words in square brackets substituted by the Enterprise Act 2002, s 278(1), Sch 25, para 9(1), (4).

Sub-s (3): words in first pair of square brackets inserted, and words in second pair of square brackets substituted, by the Race Relations (Northern Ireland) Order 1997, SI 1997/869, art 73, Sch 2, para 2(1); word in third pair of square brackets substituted by the Enterprise Act 2002, s 278(1), Sch 25, para 9(1), (4).

Sub-s (4): repealed by the Consumers, Estate Agents and Redress Act 2007, ss 55(1), (4), 64, Sch 8.

6   Revocation and variation of orders under sections 3 and 4

(1)   On an application made to [it] by the person in respect of whom the [OFT] has made an order under section 3 or section 4 above, the [OFT] may revoke or vary the order.

(2)   An application under subsection (1) above—
  (a)   shall state the reasons why the applicant considers that the order should be revoked or varied;
  (b)   in the case of an application for a variation, shall indicate the variation which the applicant seeks; and
  (c)   shall be accompanied by the prescribed fee.

(3)   If the [OFT] decides to accede to an application under subsection (1) above, [it] shall give notice in writing of [its] decision to the applicant and, upon the giving of that notice, the revocation or, as the case may be, the variation specified in the application shall take effect.

(4)   The [OFT] may decide to refuse an application under subsection (1) above—
  (a)   where it relates to an order under section 3 above, if [it] considers that the applicant remains unfit to carry on any estate agency work at all or, as the case may be, estate agency work of the description which is prohibited by the order; and
  (b)   where it relates to an order under section 4 above, if [it] considers that the applicant may [engage in further conduct as mentioned in subsection (1A)(b) or (1B)(b) of that section or engage again in the practice specified in the order, as the case may be].

(5)   If, on an application under subsection (1) above, the [OFT] decides that—
  (a)   [it] cannot accede to the application because [it] considers that the applicant remains unfit to carry on any estate agency work at all in a particular part of or area within the United Kingdom or remains unfit to carry on estate agency work of a particular description (either throughout the United Kingdom or in a particular part of or area within it), or, as the case may be, remains likely to fail to comply with a relevant statutory obligation or to engage in a particular practice, but
  (b)   the order to which the application relates could, without detriment to the public, be varied in favour of the applicant,

the [OFT] may make such a variation accordingly.

(6)   The provisions of Part II of Schedule 2 to this Act shall have effect in relation to any application to the [OFT] under subsection (1) above and the provisions of Part I of that Schedule shall have effect—
  (a)   with respect to the procedure to be followed before the [OFT] comes to a decision under subsection (4) or subsection (5) above; and
  (b)   in connection with the making and coming into operation of such a decision.

(7)   ...

[918]

NOTES

Sub-ss (1), (3), (5), (6): words in square brackets substituted by the Enterprise Act 2002, s 278(1), Sch 25, para 9(1), (5).

Sub-s (4): words in first, second and third pairs of square brackets substituted by the Enterprise Act 2002, s 278(1), Sch 25, para 9(1), (5); words in fourth pair of square brackets substituted by the Consumers, Estate Agents and Redress Act 2007, s 63(1), Sch 7, para 2(a).

Sub-s (7): repealed by the Consumers, Estate Agents and Redress Act 2007, ss 63(1), 64, Sch 7, para 2(b), Sch 8.

Regulations: the Estate Agents (Fees) Regulations 1982, SI 1982/637.

7 Appeals

(1) A person who receives notice under paragraph 9 of Schedule 2 to this Act of—

    (a) a decision of the [OFT] to make an order in respect of him under section 3 or section 4 above, or

    (b) a decision of the [OFT] under subsection (4) or subsection (5) of section 6 above on an application made by him,

may appeal against the decision to the [First-tier Tribunal].

(2) On an appeal under subsection (1) above the [First-tier Tribunal] may give such directions for disposing of the appeal as [it] thinks just …

    (3)–(6) …

[919]

NOTES

Sub-s (1): words in first and second pairs of square brackets substituted by the Enterprise Act 2002, s 278(1), Sch 25, para 9(1), (6); words in third pair of square brackets substituted by the Transfer of Functions (Estate Agents Appeals and Additional Scheduled Tribunal) Order 2009, SI 2009/1836, art 5(1), Sch 1, paras 2, 3(a).

Sub-s (2): words in square brackets substituted and words omitted repealed by SI 2009/1836, art 5(1), Sch 1, paras 2, 3(b).

Sub-ss (3)–(6): repealed by SI 2009/1836, art 5(1), Sch 1, paras 2, 3(c).

8 Register of orders etc

(1) The [OFT] shall establish and maintain a register on which there shall be entered particulars of every order made by [it] under section 3 or section 4 above and of [its] decision on any application for revocation or variation of such an order.

(2) The particulars referred to in subsection (1) above shall include—

    (a) the terms of the order and of any variation of it; and

    (b) the date on which the order or variation came into operation or is expected to come into operation or if an appeal against the decision is pending and the order or variation has in consequence not come into operation, a statement to that effect.

(3) The [OFT] may, of [its] own motion or on the application of any person aggrieved, rectify the register by the addition, variation or removal of any particulars; and the provisions of Part II of Schedule 2 to this Act shall have effect in relation to an application under this subsection.

(4) If it comes to the attention of the [OFT] that any order of which particulars appear in the register is no longer in operation, [it] shall remove those particulars from the register.

(5) Any person shall be entitled on payment of the prescribed fee—

    (a) to inspect the register during such office hours as may be specified by a general notice made by the [OFT] and to take copies of any entry, or

    (b) to obtain from the [OFT] a copy, certified by [it] to be correct, of any entry in the register.

(6) A certificate given by the [OFT] under subsection (5)(b) above shall be conclusive evidence of the fact that, on the date on which the certificate was given, the particulars contained in the copy to which the certificate relates were entered on the register; and particulars of any matters required to be entered on the register which are so entered shall be evidence and, in Scotland, sufficient evidence of those matters and shall be presumed, unless the contrary is proved, to be correct.

[920]

NOTES

Sub-ss (1), (3)–(6): words in square brackets substituted by the Enterprise Act 2002, s 278(1), Sch 25, para 9(1), (7).

Regulations: the Estate Agents (Fees) Regulations 1982, SI 1982/637.

Information, entry and inspection

9 Information for the [OFT]

(1) The [OFT] may, for the purpose of assisting [it]—

(a)   to determine whether to make an order under section 3 or section 4 above, and

(b)   in the exercise of any of [its] functions under sections 5, 6 and 8 above and 13 and 17 below,

by notice require any person to furnish to [it] such information as may be specified or described in the notice or to produce to [it] any documents so specified or described.

(2)   A notice under this section—

(a)   may specify the way in which and the time within which it is to be complied with and, in the case of a notice requiring the production of documents, the facilities to be afforded for making extracts, or taking copies of, the documents; and

(b)   may be varied or revoked by a subsequent notice.

(3)   Nothing in this section shall be taken to require a person who has acted as counsel or solicitor for any person to disclose any privileged communication made by or to him in that capacity.

(4)   A person who—

(a)   ...

(b)   in furnishing any information in compliance with [a notice under this section], makes any statement which he knows to be false in a material particular or recklessly makes any statement which is false in a material particular, or

(c)   with intent to deceive, produces in compliance with such a notice a document which is false in a material particular,

shall be liable on conviction on indictment or on summary conviction to a fine which, on summary conviction, shall not exceed the statutory maximum.

(5)   ...

(6)   It shall be the duty of—

[(a)   the Commission for Equality and Human Rights, and]

(b)   the Equal Opportunities Commission for Northern Ireland ...

(c)   ...

to furnish to the [OFT] such information relating to any finding, notice, injunction or order falling within paragraph 2 of Schedule 1 to this Act as is in their possession and appears to them to be relevant to the functions of the [OFT] under this Act.

[921]–[922]

NOTES

Section heading, sub-s (1): words in square brackets substituted by the Enterprise Act 2002, s 278(1), Sch 25, para 9(1), (8).

Sub-s (4): para (a) repealed and words in square brackets in para (b) substituted by the Consumers, Estate Agents and Redress Act 2007, ss 58(1), (3), 64, Sch 8.

Sub-s (5): repealed by the Enterprise Act 2002, s 278(2), Sch 26.

Sub-s (6): para (a) substituted, and para (c) and word omitted immediately preceding it repealed, by the Equality Act 2006, ss 40, 91, Sch 3, paras 36, 37, Sch 4; references to "OFT" in square brackets substituted by the Enterprise Act 2002, s 278(1), Sch 25, para 9(1), (8)(a).

---

10   *(Repealed by the Enterprise Act 2002, ss 247(e), 278(2), Sch 26; see further, in so far as this section remains in force: the Railways and Transport Safety Act 2003, s 16(5), Sch 2, Pt 2, para 19(e).)*

11   Powers of entry and inspection

[(1)   If a duly authorised officer of an enforcement authority ("an officer") has reasonable cause to suspect—

(a)   that an offence has been committed under this Act;

(b)   that a person has failed to comply with an obligation imposed on him under any of sections 15 and 18 to 21A; or

(c)   that a person has engaged in a practice mentioned in section 3(1)(d);

he may, in order to ascertain whether the offence has been committed, whether the person has failed to comply with the obligation or whether the person has engaged in the practice (as the case may be), exercise any power specified in subsection (1A).

(1A)   The powers are—

(a)   to enter any premises (other than premises used only as a dwelling);

(b)   to require—

(i)   any person carrying on, or employed in connection with, a business to produce any books or document relating to it, or

(ii)   any person having control of any information relating to a business which is stored in any electronic form to produce the information in a form in which it can be taken away and in which it is visible and legible (or from which it can readily be produced in a visible and legible form);

(c) to take copies of, or of any entry in, any books or documents produced or provided in pursuance of a requirement imposed under paragraph (b).

(1B) An officer may seize and detain any books or documents which he has reason to believe may be required as evidence—

 (a) in proceedings for an offence under this Act; or

 (b) in proceedings under any of sections 3, 4, 6 or 7 relating to an allegation—

  (i) that an offence has been committed under this Act;

  (ii) that a person has failed to comply with an obligation imposed on him under any of sections 15 and 18 to 21A; or

  (iii) that a person has engaged in a practice mentioned in section 3(1)(d).

(1C) If it is not reasonably practicable to exercise any power under subsection (1A)(c) to take a copy of, or of any entry in, a book or document, an officer may seize and detain the book or document for the purpose of inspecting it (or any entry in it).

(1D) A book or document which is seized in exercise of the power under subsection (1C) must be returned to the person from whom it was seized unless an officer has reason to believe that the book or document may be required as evidence in any proceedings mentioned in subsection (1B).

(1E) Any power conferred by subsection (1) to (1C) may be exercised at all reasonable hours.

(1F) An officer exercising any such power must, if required, produce his credentials.]

(2) An officer seizing books or documents in exercise of his powers under this section shall not do so without informing the person from whom he seizes them.

(3) If and so long as any books or documents which have been seized under this section are not required as evidence in connection with proceedings which have been begun for an offence under this Act, the enforcement authority by whose officer they were seized shall afford to the person to whom the books or documents belong and to any person authorised by him in writing reasonable facilities to inspect them and to take copies of or make extracts from them.

[(4) An appropriate judicial officer may, by warrant under his hand, authorise an officer of an enforcement authority to enter any premises, by force if need be, if on sworn information in writing or, in Scotland, on evidence on oath the appropriate judicial officer—

 (a) is satisfied that there is reasonable ground to believe that either of the conditions in subsection (4A) applies; and

 (b) is also satisfied that at least one of the conditions in subsection (4B) applies.

(4A) The conditions in this subsection are—

 (a) that any books or documents which a duly authorised officer has power to inspect under this section are on the premises and their inspection is likely to disclose evidence—

  (i) that an offence has been committed under this Act;

  (ii) that a person has failed to comply with an obligation imposed on him under any of sections 15 and 18 to 21A; or

  (iii) that a person has engaged in a practice mentioned in section 3(1)(d);

 (b) that an offence under this Act has been, is being or is about to be committed on the premises.

(4B) The conditions in this subsection are—

 (a) that admission to the premises has been or is likely to be refused and that notice of intention to apply for a warrant under subsection (4) has been given to the occupier;

 (b) that an application for admission, or the giving of such a notice of intention, would defeat the object of the entry;

 (c) that the premises are unoccupied;

 (d) that the occupier is temporarily absent and it might defeat the object of the entry to wait for his return.

(4C) A warrant issued under subsection (4) shall continue in force for a period of one month.

(4D) In subsection (4) "appropriate judicial officer" means—

 (a) in England and Wales, a justice of the peace;

 (b) in Scotland, the sheriff or a justice of the peace;

 (c) in Northern Ireland, a lay magistrate.]

(5) An officer entering premises by virtue of this section may take such other persons and equipment with him as he thinks necessary, and on leaving premises entered by virtue of a warrant under subsection (4) above shall, if the premises are unoccupied or the occupier is temporarily absent, leave them as effectively secured against trespassers as he found them.

(6) The Secretary of State may by regulations provide that, in cases specified in the regulations, an officer of a local weights and measures authority is not to be taken to be duly authorised for the purposes of this section unless he is authorised by the [OFT].

PART 1
STATUTES

(7)   The power to make regulations under subsection (6) above shall be exercisable by statutory instrument which shall be subject to annulment in pursuance of a resolution of either House of Parliament.

(8)   Nothing in this section shall be taken to require a person who has acted as [a relevant lawyer] for any person to produce a document containing a privileged communication made by or to him in that capacity or authorises the seizing of any such document in his possession.

[(9)   For the purposes of subsection (8) "relevant lawyer" means counsel, a solicitor or other legal representative communications with whom may be the subject of a claim to privilege.]

[923]

NOTES

Sub-ss (1), (1A)–(1F): substituted for original sub-s (1) by the Consumers, Estate Agents and Redress Act 2007, s 57(1), (2).

Sub-ss (4), (4A)–(4D): substituted for original sub-s (4) by the Consumers, Estate Agents and Redress Act 2007, s 57(1), (3).

Sub-s (6): word in square brackets substituted by the Enterprise Act 2002, s 278(1), Sch 25, para 9(1), (9)(a).

Sub-s (8): words in square brackets substituted by the Legal Services Act 2007, s 208(1), Sch 21, para 41(a).

Sub-s (9): added by the Legal Services Act 2007, s 208(1), Sch 21, para 41(b).

Seize and detain books or documents, etc: the powers of seizure conferred by sub-s (1B) are powers to which the Criminal Justice and Police Act 2001, s 50 apply (additional powers of seizure from premises); see s 50 of, and Sch 1, Pt 1, para 24 to, that Act.

Regulations: the Estate Agents (Entry and Inspection) Regulations 1981, SI 1981/1519.

[11A   Failure to produce information

(1)   If on an application made by a duly authorised officer of an enforcement authority it appears to the court that a person ("the defaulter") has failed to do something that he is required to do by virtue of section 9(1) or 11(1A)(b) the court may make an order under this section.

(2)   An order under this section may require the defaulter—
   (a)   to do the thing that it appears he failed to do within such period as may be specified in the order;
   (b)   otherwise to take such steps to remedy the consequences of the failure as may be so specified.

(3)   If the defaulter is a body corporate, a partnership or an unincorporated association, the order may require any officer who is (wholly or partly) responsible for the failure to meet such costs of the application as are specified in the order.

(4)   In this section—
"court" means—
   (a)   in England and Wales and Northern Ireland, the High Court or a county court;
   (b)   in Scotland, the Court of Session or the sheriff;
"officer" means—
   (a)   in relation to a body corporate, a person holding a position of director, manager or secretary of the body or any similar position;
   (b)   in relation to a partnership or an unincorporated association, a member of the partnership or association.

(5)   In subsection (4) "director" means, in relation to a body corporate whose affairs are managed by its members, a member of the body.]

[923A]

NOTES

Commencement: 1 October 2008.

Inserted by the Consumers, Estate Agents and Redress Act 2007, s 58(1).

Clients' money and accounts

12   Meaning of "clients' money" etc

(1)   In this Act "clients' money", in relation to a person engaged in estate agency work, means any money received by him in the course of that work which is a contract or pre-contract deposit—
   (a)   in respect of the acquisition of an interest in land in the United Kingdom, or
   (b)   in respect of a connected contract,
whether that money is held or received by him as agent, bailee, stakeholder or in any other capacity.

(2)   In this Act "contract deposit" means any sum paid by a purchaser—
   (a)   which in whole or in part is, or is intended to form part of, the consideration for acquiring such an interest as is referred to in subsection (1)(a) above or for a connected contract; and
   (b)   which is paid by him at or after the time at which he acquires the interest or enters into an enforceable contract to acquire it.

(3)   In this Act "pre-contract deposit" means any sum paid by any person—
  (a)   in whole or in part as an earnest of his intention to acquire such an interest as is referred to in subsection (1)(a) above, or
  (b)   in whole or in part towards meeting any liability of his in respect of the consideration for the acquisition of such an interest which will arise if he acquires or enters into an enforceable contract to acquire the interest, or
  (c)   in respect of a connected contract,

and which is paid by him at a time before he either acquires the interest or enters into an enforceable contract to acquire it.

(4)   In this Act "connected contract", in relation to the acquisition of an interest in land, means a contract which is conditional upon such an acquisition or upon entering into an enforceable contract for such an acquisition (whether or not it is also conditional on other matters).

[924]

13   Clients' money held on trust or as agent

(1)   It is hereby declared that clients' money received by any person in the course of estate agency work in England, Wales or Northern Ireland—
  (a)   is held by him on trust for the person who is entitled to call for it to be paid over to him or to be paid on his direction or to have it otherwise credited to him, or
  (b)   if it is received by him as stakeholder, is held by him on trust for the person who may become so entitled on the occurrence of the event against which the money is held.

(2)   (*Applies to Scotland only.*)

(3)   The provisions of sections 14 and 15 below as to the investment of clients' money, the keeping of accounts and records and accounting for interest shall have effect in place of the corresponding duties which would be owed by a person holding clients' money as trustee, or in Scotland as agent, under the general law.

(4)   Where an order of the [OFT] under section 3 above has the effect of prohibiting a person from holding clients' money the order may contain provision—
  (a)   appointing another person as trustee, or in Scotland as agent, in place of the person to whom the order relates to hold and deal with clients' money held by that person when the order comes into effect; and
  (b)   requiring the expenses and such reasonable remuneration of the new trustee or agent as may be specified in the order to be paid by the person to whom the order relates or, if the order so provides, out of the clients' money;

but nothing in this subsection shall affect the power conferred by section 41 of the Trustee Act 1925 or section 40 of the Trustee Act (Northern Ireland) 1958 to appoint a new trustee to hold clients' money.

(5)   For the avoidance of doubt it is hereby declared that the fact that any person has or may have a lien on clients' money held by him does not affect the operation of this section and also that nothing in this section shall prevent such a lien from being given effect.

[925]

NOTES
Sub-s (4): word in square brackets substituted by the Enterprise Act 2002, s 278(1), Sch 25, para 9(1), (9)(b).

14   Keeping of client accounts

(1)   Subject to such provision as may be made by accounts regulations, every person who receives clients' money in the course of estate agency work shall, without delay, pay the money into a client account maintained by him or by a person in whose employment he is.

(2)   In this Act a "client account" means a current or deposit account which—
  (a)   is with an institution authorised for the purposes of this section, and
  (b)   is in the name of a person who is or has been engaged in estate agency work; and
  (c)   contains in its title the word "client".

(3)   The Secretary of State may make provision by regulations (in this section referred to as "accounts regulations") as to the opening and keeping of client accounts, the keeping of accounts and records relating to clients' money and the auditing of those accounts; and such regulations shall be made by statutory instrument which shall be subject to annulment in pursuance of a resolution of either House of Parliament.

(4)   As to the opening and keeping of client accounts, accounts regulations may in particular specify—
  (a)   the institutions which are authorised for the purposes of this section;
  (b)   any persons or classes of persons to whom, or any circumstances in which, the obligation imposed by subsection (1) above does not apply;

   (c)   any circumstances in which money other than clients' money may be paid into a client account; and

   (d)   the occasions on which, and the persons to whom, money held in a client account may be paid out.

(5) As to the auditing of accounts relating to clients' money, accounts regulations may in particular make provision—

   (a)   requiring such accounts to be drawn up in respect of specified accounting periods and to be audited by a qualified auditor within a specified time after the end of each such period;

   (b)   requiring the auditor to report whether in his opinion the requirements of this Act and of the accounts regulations have been complied with or have been substantially complied with;

   (c)   as to the matters to which such a report is to relate and the circumstances in which a report of substantial compliance may be given; and

   (d)   requiring a person who maintains a client account to produce on demand to a duly authorised officer of an enforcement authority the latest auditor's report.

[(6) Subject to subsection (7) below, "qualified auditor" in subsection (5)(a) above means a person who is [eligible for appointment as a statutory auditor under Part 42 of the Companies Act 2006].

(7) A person is not a qualified auditor for the purposes of subsection (5)(a) above if, in the case of a client account maintained by a company, he is [prohibited from acting as statutory auditor of the company by virtue of section 1214 of the Companies Act 2006 (independence requirement)].]

(8) A person who—

   (a)   contravenes any provision of this Act or of accounts regulations as to the manner in which clients' money is to be dealt with or accounts and records relating to such money are to be kept, or

   (b)   fails to produce an auditor's report when required to do so by accounts regulations,

shall be liable on summary conviction to a fine not exceeding [level 4 on the standard scale].

[926]

NOTES

Sub-s (6): substituted, together with sub-s (7), by the Companies Act 1989 (Eligibility for Appointment as Company Auditor) (Consequential Amendments) Regulations 1991, SI 1991/1997, reg 2, Schedule, para 33; words in square brackets substituted by the Companies Act 2006 (Consequential Amendments etc) Order 2008, SI 2008/948, art 3(1)(a), 6, Sch 1, Pt 1, para 8(1), (2).

Sub-s (7): substituted, together with sub-s (6), by SI 1991/1997, reg 2, Schedule, para 33; words in square brackets substituted by SI 2008/948, art 3(1)(a), 6, Sch 1, Pt 1, para 8(1), (3).

Sub-s (8): reference to a level on the standard scale substituted by virtue of the Criminal Justice Act 1982, ss 38, 46.

15 Interest on clients' money

(1) Accounts regulations may make provision for requiring a person who has received any clients' money to account, in such cases as may be prescribed by the regulations, to the person who is or becomes entitled to the money for the interest which was, or could have been, earned by putting the money in a separate deposit account at an institution authorised for the purposes of section 14 above.

(2) The cases in which a person may be required by accounts regulations to account for interest as mentioned in subsection (1) above may be defined, amongst other things, by reference to the amount of the sum held or received by him or the period for which it is likely to be retained, or both.

(3) Except as provided by accounts regulations and subject to subsection (4) below, a person who maintains a client account in which he keeps clients' money generally shall not be liable to account to any person for interest received by him on money in that account.

(4) Nothing in this section or in accounts regulations shall affect any arrangement in writing, whenever made, between a person engaged in estate agency work and any other person as to the application of, or of any interest on, money in which that other person has or may have an interest.

(5) Failure of any person to comply with any provision of accounts regulations made by virtue of this section may be taken into account by the [OFT] in accordance with section 3(1)(c) above and may form the basis of a civil claim for interest which was or should have been earned on clients' money but shall not render that person liable to any criminal penalty.

(6) In this section "accounts regulations" has the same meaning as in section 14 above.

[927]

NOTES

Sub-s (5): word in square brackets substituted by the Enterprise Act 2002, s 278(1), Sch 25, para 9(1), (9)(c).

16 Insurance cover for clients' money

(1)   Subject to the provisions of this section, a person may not accept clients' money in the course of estate agency work unless there are in force authorised arrangements under which, in the event of his failing to account for such money to the person entitled to it, his liability will be made good by another.

(2)   The Secretary of State may by regulations made by statutory instrument, which shall be subject to annulment in pursuance of a resolution of either House of Parliament—

(a)   specify any persons or classes of persons to whom subsection (1) above does not apply;

(b)   specify arrangements which are authorised for the purposes of this section including arrangements to which an enforcement authority nominated for the purpose by the Secretary of State or any other person so nominated is a party;

(c)   specify the terms and conditions upon which any payment is to be made under such arrangements and any circumstances in which the right to any such payment may be excluded or modified;

(d)   provide that any limit on the amount of any such payment is to be not less than a specified amount;

(e)   require a person providing authorised arrangements covering any person carrying on estate agency work to issue a certificate in a form specified in the regulations certifying that arrangements complying with the regulations have been made with respect to that person; and

(f)   prescribe any matter required to be prescribed for the purposes of subsection (4) below.

(3)   Every guarantee entered into by a person (in this subsection referred to as "the insurer") who provides authorised arrangements covering another person (in this subsection referred to as "the agent") carrying on estate agency work shall enure for the benefit of every person from whom the agent has received clients' money as if—

(a)   the guarantee were contained in a contract made by the insurer with every such person; and

(b)   except in Scotland, that contract were under seal; and

(c)   where the guarantee is given by two or more insurers, they had bound themselves jointly and severally.

(4)   No person who carries on estate agency work may describe himself as an "estate agent" or so use any name or in any way hold himself out as to indicate or reasonably be understood to indicate that he is carrying on a business in the course of which he is prepared to act as a broker in the acquisition or disposal of interests in land unless, in such manner as may be prescribed,—

(a)   there is displayed at his place of business, and

(b)   there is included in any relevant document issued or displayed in connection with his business,

any prescribed information relating to arrangements authorised for the purposes of this section.

(5)   For the purposes of subsection (4) above—

(a)   any business premises at which a person carries on estate agency work and to which the public has access is a place of business of his; and

(b)   "relevant document" means any advertisement, notice or other written material which might reasonably induce any person to use the services of another in connection with the acquisition or disposal of an interest in land.

(6)   A person who fails to comply with any provision of subsection (1) or subsection (4) above or of regulations under subsection (2) above which is binding on him shall be liable on conviction on indictment or on summary conviction to a fine which, on summary conviction, shall not exceed the statutory maximum.

[928]

NOTES

Commencement: to be appointed.

---

17 Exemptions from section 16

(1)   If, on an application made to [it] in that behalf, the [OFT] considers that a person engaged in estate agency work may, without loss of adequate protection to consumers, be exempted from all or any of the provisions of subsection (1) of section 16 above or of regulations under subsection (2) of that section, [it] may issue to that person a certificate of exemption under this section.

(2)   An application under subsection (1) above—

(a)   shall state the reasons why the applicant considers that he should be granted a certificate of exemption; and

(b)   shall be accompanied by the prescribed fee.

(3)   A certificate of exemption under this section—

(a)   may impose conditions of exemption on the person to whom it is issued;

    (b)   may be issued to have effect for a period specified in the certificate or without limit of time.

(4) If and so long as—
    (a)   a certificate of exemption has effect, and
    (b)   the person to whom it is issued complies with any conditions of exemption specified in the certificate,

that person shall be exempt, to the extent so specified, from the provisions of subsection (1) of section 16 above and of any regulations made under subsection (2) of that section.

(5) If the [OFT] decides to refuse an application under subsection (1) above [it] shall give the applicant notice of [its] decision and of the reasons for it, including any facts which in [its] opinion justify the decision.

(6) If a person who made an application under subsection (1) above is aggrieved by a decision of the [OFT]—
    (a)   to refuse his application, or
    (b)   to grant him a certificate of exemption subject to conditions,

he may appeal against the decision to the Secretary of State; and subsections (2) to (6) of section 7 above shall apply to such an appeal as they apply to an appeal under that section.

(7) A person who fails to comply with any condition of exemption specified in a current certificate of exemption issued to him shall be liable on conviction on indictment or on summary conviction to a fine which, on summary conviction, shall not exceed the statutory maximum.

[929]

NOTES
    Commencement: to be appointed.
    Sub-ss (1), (5), (6): words in square brackets substituted by the Enterprise Act 2002, s 278(1), Sch 25, para 9(1), (10).

Regulation of other aspects of estate agency work

18 Information to clients of prospective liabilities

(1) Subject to subsection (2) below, before any person (in this section referred to as "the client") enters into a contract with another (in this section referred to as "the agent") under which the agent will engage in estate agency work on behalf of the client, the agent shall give the client—
    (a)   the information specified in subsection (2) below; and
    (b)   any additional information which may be prescribed under subsection (4) below.

(2) The following is the information to be given under subsection (1)(a) above—
    (a)   particulars of the circumstances in which the client will become liable to pay remuneration to the agent for carrying out estate agency work;
    (b)   particulars of the amount of the agent's remuneration for carrying out estate agency work or, if that amount is not ascertainable at the time the information is given, particulars of the manner in which the remuneration will be calculated;
    (c)   particulars of any payments which do not form part of the agent's remuneration for carrying out estate agency work or a contract or pre-contract deposit but which, under the contract referred to in subsection (1) above, will or may in certain circumstances be payable by the client to the agent or any other person and particulars of the circumstances in which any such payments will become payable; and
    (d)   particulars of the amount of any payment falling within paragraph (c) above or, if that amount is not ascertainable at the time the information is given, an estimate of that amount together with particulars of the manner in which it will be calculated.

(3) If, at any time after the client and the agent have entered into such a contract as is referred to in subsection (1) above, the parties are agreed that the terms of the contract should be varied so far as they relate to the carrying out of estate agency work or any payment falling within subsection (2)(c) above, the agent shall give the client details of any changes which, at the time the statement is given, fall to be made in the information which was given to the client under subsection (1) above before the contract was entered into.

(4) The Secretary of State may by regulations—
    (a)   prescribe for the purposes of subsection (1)(b) above additional information relating to any estate agency work to be performed under the contract; and
    (b)   make provision with respect to the time and the manner in which the obligation of the agent under subsection (1) or subsection (3) above is to be performed;

and the power to make regulations under this subsection shall be exercisable by statutory instrument which shall be subject to annulment in pursuance of a resolution of either House of Parliament.

(5) If any person—

(a)   fails to comply with the obligation under subsection (1) above with respect to a contract or with any provision of regulations under subsection (4) above relating to that obligation, or

(b)   fails to comply with the obligation under subsection (3) above with respect to any variation of a contract or with any provision of regulations under subsection (4) above relating to that obligation,

the contract or, as the case may be, the variation of it shall not be enforceable by him except pursuant to an order of the court under subsection (6) below.

(6)   If, in a case where subsection (5) above applies in relation to a contract or a variation of a contract, the agent concerned makes an application to the court for the enforcement of the contract or, as the case may be, of a contract as varied by the variation—

(a)   the court shall dismiss the application if, but only if, it considers it just to do so having regard to prejudice caused to the client by the agent's failure to comply with his obligation and the degree of culpability for the failure; and

(b)   where the court does not dismiss the application, it may nevertheless order that any sum payable by the client under the contract or, as the case may be, under the contract as varied shall be reduced or discharged so as to compensate the client for prejudice suffered as a result of the agent's failure to comply with his obligation.

(7)   In this section—

(a)   references to the enforcement of a contract or variation include the withholding of money in pursuance of a lien for money alleged to be due under the contract or as a result of the variation; and

(b)   "the court" means any court having jurisdiction to hear and determine matters arising out of the contract.

[930]

NOTES

Regulations: the Estate Agents (Provision of Information) Regulations 1991, SI 1991/859.

19   Regulation of pre-contract deposits outside Scotland

(1)   No person may, in the course of estate agency work in England, Wales or Northern Ireland, seek from any other person (in this section referred to as a "prospective purchaser") who wishes to acquire an interest in land in the United Kingdom, a payment which, if made, would constitute a pre-contract deposit in excess of the prescribed limit.

(2)   If, in the course of estate agency work, any person receives from a prospective purchaser a pre-contract deposit which exceeds the prescribed limit, so much of that deposit as exceeds the prescribed limit shall forthwith be either repaid to the prospective purchaser or paid to such other person as the prospective purchaser may direct.

(3)   In relation to a prospective purchaser, references in subsections (1) and (2) above to a pre-contract deposit shall be treated as references to the aggregate of all the payments which constitute pre-contract deposits in relation to his proposed acquisition of a particular interest in land in the United Kingdom.

(4)   In this section "the prescribed limit" means such limit as the Secretary of State may by regulations prescribe; and such limit may be so prescribed either as a specific amount or as a percentage or fraction of a price or other amount determined in any particular case in accordance with the regulations.

(5)   The power to make regulations under this section shall be exercisable by statutory instrument which shall be subject to annulment in pursuance of a resolution of either House of Parliament.

(6)   Failure by any person to comply with subsection (1) or subsection (2) above may be taken into account by the [OFT] in accordance with section 3(1)(c) above but shall not render that person liable to any criminal penalty nor constitute a ground for any civil claim, other than a claim for the recovery of such an excess as is referred to in subsection (2) above.

(7)   This section does not form part of the law of Scotland.

[931]

NOTES

Commencement: to be appointed.

Sub-s (6): word in square brackets substituted by the Enterprise Act 2002, s 278(1), Sch 25, para 9(1), (11)(a).

20   (*Applies to Scotland only.*)

21 Transactions in which an estate agent has a personal interest

(1)   A person who is engaged in estate agency work (in this section referred to as an "estate agent") and has a personal interest in any land shall not enter into negotiations with any person with respect to the acquisition or disposal by that person of any interest in that land until the estate agent has disclosed to that person the nature and extent of his personal interest in it.

(2)   In any case where the result of a proposed disposal of an interest in land or of such a proposed disposal and other transactions would be that an estate agent would have a personal interest in that land, the estate agent shall not enter into negotiations with any person with respect to the proposed disposal until he has disclosed to that person the nature and extent of that personal interest.

(3)   Subsections (1) and (2) above apply where an estate agent is negotiating on his own behalf as well as where he is negotiating in the course of estate agency work.

(4)   An estate agent may not seek or receive a contract or pre-contract deposit in respect of the acquisition or proposed acquisition of—
   (a)   a personal interest of his in land in the United Kingdom; or
   (b)   any other interest in any such land in which he has a personal interest.

(5)   For the purposes of this section, an estate agent has a personal interest in land if—
   (a)   he has a beneficial interest in the land or in the proceeds of sale of any interest in it; or
   (b)   he knows or might reasonably be expected to know that any of the following persons has such a beneficial interest, namely,—
      (i)   his employer or principal, or
      (ii)   any employee or agent of his, or
      (iii)   any associate of his or of any person mentioned in sub-paragraphs (i) and (ii) above.

(6)   Failure by an estate agent to comply with any of the preceding provisions of this section may be taken into account by the [OFT] in accordance with section 3(1)(c) above but shall not render the estate agent liable to any criminal penalty nor constitute a ground for any civil claim.

[932]

NOTES
   Sub-s (6): word in square brackets substituted by the Enterprise Act 2002, s 278(1), Sch 25, para 9(1), (11)(c).

[21A   Duty to keep permanent records

(1)   A person engaged in estate agency work shall—
   (a)   keep records for the purposes of this section ("the permanent records"); and
   (b)   ensure that anything required by subsection (3) to be included in the permanent records is kept for a period of at least six years beginning with the day on which it is included.

(2)   In the case of a person engaged in estate agency work in the course of employment the duties under subsection (1) are duties of the employer (and not the employee).

(3)   A person engaged in estate agency work shall ensure that a record of any information or event to which this subsection applies is included in the permanent records kept by that person or his employer (as the case may be).

(4)   Subsection (3) applies to—
   (a)   information the person concerned is required to give by section 18(1) or (3) and any prescribed information relating to the giving of that information;
   (b)   information the person concerned is required to disclose by section 21(1) or (2) and any prescribed information relating to the disclosure of that information;
   (c)   any offer of a prescribed description received by the person concerned and any prescribed information relating to the making of the offer;
   (d)   any action of a prescribed description taken by the person concerned in relation to such an offer and any prescribed information relating to that action; and
   (e)   any other information or event of a prescribed description.

(5)   If the person concerned is acting in the course of employment, it is also the duty of the employer to ensure that the record of the information or event is included in the permanent records; but the employer is not to be regarded as having breached his duty if he shows that he took such steps as were reasonably practicable to ensure that the duty under subsection (3) was complied with by his employees.

(6)   The Secretary of State may by regulations make provision as to—
   (a)   the manner in which the permanent records are to be kept;
   (b)   the place or places at which they are to be kept.

(7)   In this section "prescribed" means prescribed by regulations made by the Secretary of State.

(8)   Any power to make regulations under this section shall be exercisable by statutory instrument which shall be subject to annulment in pursuance of a resolution of either House of Parliament.]

[932A]

NOTES
Commencement: to be appointed.
Inserted by the Consumers, Estate Agents and Redress Act 2007, s 54(1), as from a day to be appointed.

22   Standards of competence

(1)   The Secretary of State may by regulations made by statutory instrument make provision for ensuring that persons engaged in estate agency work satisfy minimum standards of competence.

(2)   If the Secretary of State exercises his power to make regulations under subsection (1) above, he shall in the regulations prescribe a degree of practical experience which is to be taken as evidence of competence and, without prejudice to the generality of subsection (1) above, the regulations may, in addition,—

(a)   prescribe professional or academic qualifications which shall also be taken to be evidence of competence;

(b)   designate any body of persons as a body which may itself specify professional qualifications the holding of which is to be taken as evidence of competence;

(c)   make provision for and in connection with the establishment of a body having power to examine and inquire into the competence of persons engaged or professing to engage in estate agency work; and

(d)   delegate to a body established as mentioned in paragraph (c) above powers of the Secretary of State with respect of the matters referred to in paragraph (a) above;

and any reference in the following provisions of this section to a person who has attained the required standard of competence is a reference to a person who has that degree of practical experience which, in accordance with the regulations, is to be taken as evidence of competence or, where the regulations so provide, holds such qualifications or otherwise fulfils such conditions as, in accordance with the regulations, are to be taken to be evidence of competence.

(3)   After the day appointed for the coming into force of this subsection—

(a)   no individual may engage in estate agency work on his own account unless he has attained the required standard of competence;

(b)   no member of a partnership may engage in estate agency work on the partnership's behalf unless such number of the partners as may be prescribed have attained the required standard of competence; and

(c)   no body corporate or unincorporated association may engage in estate agency work unless such numbers and descriptions of the officers, members or employees as may be prescribed have attained the required standard of competence;

and any person who contravenes this subsection shall be liable on conviction on indictment or on summary conviction to a fine which, on summary conviction, shall not exceed the statutory maximum.

(4)   In subsection (3) above "prescribed" means prescribed by the Secretary of State by order made by statutory instrument, which shall be subject to annulment in pursuance of a resolution of either House of Parliament.

(5)   No regulations shall be made under this section unless a draft of them has been laid before Parliament and approved by a resolution of each House.

[933]

NOTES
Commencement: to be appointed.

23   Bankrupts not to engage in estate agency work

(1)   An individual who is adjudged bankrupt after the day appointed for the coming into force of this section or, in Scotland, whose estate is sequestrated after that day shall not engage in estate agency work of any description except as an employee of another person.

(2)   The prohibition imposed on an individual by subsection (1) above shall cease to have effect if and when—

(a)   the adjudication of bankruptcy against him is annulled, or, in Scotland, the sequestration of his estate is recalled [or reduced]; or

[(b)   he is discharged from bankruptcy.]

(3)   The reference in subsection (1) above to employment of an individual by another person does not include employment of him by a body corporate of which he is a director or controller.

(4)   If a person engages in estate agency work in contravention of subsection (1) above he shall be liable on conviction on indictment or on summary conviction to a fine which on summary conviction shall not exceed the statutory maximum.

[934]

NOTES

Sub-s (2): words in square brackets in para (a) inserted by the Bankruptcy (Scotland) Act 1985, s 75, Sch 7, para 17; para (b) substituted by the Insolvency Act 1985, s 235, Sch 8, para 33.

[Redress schemes

23A   Redress schemes

(1)   The Secretary of State may by order require persons who engage in estate agency work in relation to residential property ("relevant estate agency work") to be members of an approved redress scheme for dealing with complaints in connection with that work.

(2)   An order may provide for the duty to apply—
   (a)   only to specified descriptions of persons who engage in estate agency work; and
   (b)   in relation to any relevant estate agency work carried out by a person to whom the duty applies or only in relation to specified descriptions of work (which may be framed by reference to descriptions of residential property).

(3)   An order may also provide for the duty not to apply in relation to complaints of any specified description (which may be framed by reference to a description of person making a complaint).

(4)   In subsections (1) and (2)(a), the reference to persons who engage in estate agency work does not include a reference to persons who engage in that work in the course of their employment.

(5)   The power to make an order shall be exercisable by statutory instrument which shall be subject to annulment in pursuance of a resolution of either House of Parliament.

(6)   Before making an order the Secretary of State must be satisfied that all persons who are to be subject to the duty will be eligible to join a suitable approved redress scheme before the duty applies to them.

For this purpose the Secretary of State may disregard persons who cannot lawfully engage in the relevant estate agency work to which the duty applies.

(7)   Nothing in this section prevents an approved redress scheme from providing—
   (a)   for membership to be open to persons who are not subject to the duty;
   (b)   for the investigation and determination of any complaints in relation to which the duty does not apply, where the members concerned have voluntarily accepted the jurisdiction of the scheme over those complaints;
   (c)   for the exclusion from investigation and determination under the scheme of any complaint in such cases or circumstances as may be specified in or determined under the scheme.

(8)   For the purposes of this section—
   (a)   a "redress scheme" is a scheme which provides for complaints against members of the scheme to be investigated and determined by an independent person ("the ombudsman");
   (b)   a redress scheme is "approved" if—
      (i)   it is for the time being approved by the OFT under Schedule 3; or
      (ii)   it is administered by or on behalf of the Secretary of State and designated by him as an approved redress scheme for the purposes of this section;
   (c)   a "complaint" is a complaint made by a person by virtue of his being or having been a seller or buyer of residential property;
   (d)   "seller", in relation to residential property, means a person who claims that he is or may become interested in disposing of an interest in land in respect of that property (and includes a person who disposes of such an interest);
   (e)   "buyer", in relation to residential property, means a person who claims that he is or may become interested in acquiring an interest in land in respect of that property (and includes a person who acquires such an interest).

(9)   The Secretary of State may not designate a scheme as an approved redress scheme for the purposes of this section unless the Secretary of State is satisfied that the scheme is one which could be approved by the OFT in accordance with paragraphs 2 to 5 of Schedule 3.

(10)   Schedule 3 (which makes further provision in connection with the approval of redress schemes etc.) shall have effect.

(11)   In this section—
"order" means an order under subsection (1);

"the duty" means the requirement under an order to be a member of an approved redress scheme.]

[934A]

NOTES
Commencement: 12 October 2007.
Inserted, together with preceding cross-heading and ss 23B, 23C, by the Consumers, Estate Agents and Redress Act 2007, s 53(1), Sch 6, paras 1, 2.
Order: the Estate Agents (Redress Scheme) Order 2008, SI 2008/1712 at **[3645A]**.

[23B Enforcement

(1)   If a duly authorised officer of an enforcement authority other than the OFT believes that a person has engaged (or is engaging) in estate agency work in relation to residential property in breach of the duty imposed by an order under section 23A(1) he may give a penalty charge notice to that person.

(2)   A penalty charge notice may not be given after the end of the period of six months beginning with the day (or in the case of a continuing breach the last day) on which the breach of duty was committed.

(3)   Schedule 4 (which makes further provision in connection with penalty charge notices) shall have effect.

(4)   An enforcement authority other than the OFT must notify the OFT if it believes that a person has engaged (or is engaging) in estate agency work in relation to residential property in breach of the duty imposed by an order under section 23A(1).]

[934B]

NOTES
Commencement: 12 October 2007.
Inserted as noted to s 23A at **[934A]**.
See further: the Estate Agents (Redress Scheme) (Penalty Charge) Regulations 2008, SI 2008/1713 at **[3645C]** specify the amount of the penalty charge in a notice given to a person under sub-s (1) as £1000.

[23C Meaning of residential property

(1)   For the purposes of sections 23A and 23B "residential property"—
    (a)   has the meaning given by subsection (2); but
    (b)   does not include land of a description specified in an order made by the Secretary of State for the purposes of this section.

(2)   "Residential property" means any land that consists of or includes a building or part of a building—
    (a)   the whole or part of which is used as a dwelling or as more than one dwelling; or
    (b)   that is (or is to be) offered for sale on the basis that the whole or part of it is suitable for such use or is intended to be so suitable by the time the seller disposes of his interest in it.

(3)   In subsection (2), the reference to a building or part of a building (so far as relating to paragraph (b) of that subsection) includes a reference to a building or part that is being or is to be constructed.

(4)   A description of land specified by order under subsection (1)(b) may be framed by reference to the purpose or purposes for which the land (or part of it) is or is intended to be used.

(5)   The power to make an order under subsection (1)(b) shall be exercisable by statutory instrument which shall be subject to annulment in pursuance of a resolution of either House of Parliament.]

[935]

NOTES
Commencement: 12 October 2007.
Inserted as noted to s 23A at **[934A]**.

Supervision, enforcement, publicity etc

24   (*Sub-s (1) repealed by the Tribunals and Inquiries Act 1992, s 18(2), Sch 4, Pt I; sub-s (2) repealed by the Tribunals, Courts and Enforcement Act 2007, ss 48(1), 146, Sch 8, para 8, Sch 23, Pt 1.*)

25 General duties of [OFT]

(1)   Subject to section 26(3) below, it is the duty of the [OFT]—
    (a)   generally to superintend the working and enforcement of this Act, and

(b)   where necessary or expedient, [itself] to take steps to enforce this Act.

(2)   It is the duty of the [OFT], so far as appears to [it] to be practicable and having regard both to the national interest and the interests of persons engaged in estate agency work and of consumers to keep under review and from time to time advise the Secretary of State about—

   (a)   social and commercial developments in the United Kingdom and elsewhere relating to the carrying on of estate agency work and related activities; and

   (b)   the working and enforcement of this Act.

(3)   The [OFT] shall arrange for the dissemination, in such form and manner as [it] considers appropriate, of such information and advice as it may appear to [it] expedient to give the public in the United Kingdom about the operation of this Act.

[936]

NOTES

Words in square brackets substituted by the Enterprise Act 2002, s 278(1), Sch 25, para 9(1), (12).

26   Enforcement authorities

(1)   Without prejudice to section 25(1) above, the following authorities (in this Act referred to as "enforcement authorities") have a duty to enforce this Act—

   (a)   the [OFT],

   (b)   in Great Britain, a local weights and measures authority, and

   (c)   in Northern Ireland, the Department of Commerce for Northern Ireland.

(2)   ...

(3)   (*Applies to Scotland only.*)

(4)   Every local weights and measures authority shall, whenever the [OFT] requires, report to [it] in such form and with such particulars as [it] requires on the exercise of their functions under this Act.

(5)–(8)   ...

[937]

NOTES

Sub-ss (1), (4): words in square brackets substituted by the Enterprise Act 2002, s 278(1), Sch 25, para 9(1), (13)(a), (c).

Sub-s (2): repealed by the Enterprise Act 2002, s 278, Sch 25, para 9(1), (13)(b), Sch 26.

Sub-ss (5)–(8): repealed by the Local Government, Planning and Land Act 1980, ss 1(4), 194, Sch 4, para 10, Sch 34, Pt IV.

27   Obstruction and personation of authorised officers

(1)   Any person who—

   (a)   wilfully obstructs an authorised officer, or

   (b)   ...

   (c)   without reasonable cause fails to give an authorised officer [any] assistance or information he may reasonably require in performing his functions under this Act, or

   (d)   in giving information to an authorised officer, makes any statement which he knows to be false,

shall be liable on summary conviction to a fine not exceeding [level 4 on the standard scale].

[(1A)   A failure to give assistance or information shall not constitute an offence under subsection (1)(c) if it is also a failure in relation to which an authorised officer may apply for an order under section 11A above.]

(2)   A person who is not an authorised officer but purports to act as such shall be liable on summary conviction to a fine not exceeding [level 5 on the standard scale].

(3)   In this section "authorised officer" means a duly authorised officer of an enforcement authority who is acting in pursuance of this Act.

(4)   Nothing in subsection (1) above requires a person to answer any question or give any information if to do so might incriminate that person or that person's [spouse or civil partner].

[938]

NOTES

Sub-s (1): para (b) repealed and word in square brackets in para (c) substituted by the Consumers, Estate Agents and Redress Act 2007, ss 58(4)(a), 64, Sch 8; reference to a level on the standard scale substituted by virtue of the Criminal Justice Act 1982, ss 38, 46.

Sub-s (1A): inserted by the Consumers, Estate Agents and Redress Act 2007, s 58(4)(b).

Sub-s (2): reference to a level on the standard scale substituted by virtue of the Criminal Justice Act 1982, ss 38, 46.

Sub-s (4): words in square brackets substituted by the Civil Partnership Act 2004, s 261(1), Sch 27, para 62.

Supplementary

28 General provisions as to offences

(1) In any proceedings for an offence under this Act it shall be a defence for the person charged to prove that he took all reasonable precautions and exercised all due diligence to avoid the commission of an offence by himself or any person under his control.

(2) Where an offence under this Act committed by a body corporate is proved to have been committed with the consent or connivance of, or to be attributable to any neglect on the part of, any director, manager, secretary or other similar officer of the body corporate, or any person who was purporting to act in any such capacity, he as well as the body corporate shall be guilty of that offence and shall be liable to be proceeded against and punished accordingly.

[939]

29 Service of notices etc

(1) Any notice which under this Act is to be given to any person by the [OFT] shall be so given—

    (a)   by delivering it to him, or

    (b)   by leaving it at his proper address, or

    (c)   by sending it by post to him at that address.

(2) Any such notice may—

    (a)   in the case of a body corporate or unincorporated association, be given to the secretary or clerk of that body or association; and

    (b)   in the case of a partnership, be given to a partner or a person having the control or management of the partnership business.

(3) Any application or other document which under this Act may be made or given to the [OFT] may be so made or given by sending it by post to the [OFT] at such address as may be specified for the purposes of this Act by a general notice.

(4) For the purposes of subsections (1) and (2) above and section 7 of the Interpretation Act 1978 (service of documents by post) in its application to those subsections, the proper address of any person to whom a notice is to be given shall be his last-known address, except that—

    (a)   in the case of a body corporate or their secretary or clerk, it shall be the address of the registered or principal office of that body;

    (b)   in the case of an unincorporated association or their secretary or clerk, it shall be that of the principal office of that association;

    (c)   in the case of a partnership or a person having the control or management of the partnership business, it shall be that of the principal office of the partnership;

and for the purposes of this subsection the principal office of a company registered outside the United Kingdom or of an unincorporated association or partnership carrying on business outside the United Kingdom shall be their principal office within the United Kingdom.

(5) If the person to be given any notice mentioned in subsection (1) above has specified an address within the United Kingdom other than his proper address, within the meaning of subsection (4) above, as the one at which he or someone on his behalf will accept notices under this Act, that address shall also be treated for the purposes mentioned in subsection (4) above as his proper address.

[940]

NOTES

Sub-ss (1), (3): words in square brackets substituted by the Enterprise Act 2002, s 278(1), Sch 25, para 9(1), (14)(a).

30 Orders and regulations

(1) Before making any order or regulations under any provision of this Act to which this subsection applies, the Secretary of State shall consult the [OFT], such bodies representative of persons carrying on estate agency work, such bodies representative of consumers and such other persons as he thinks fit.

(2) Subsection (1) above applies to paragraphs (a)(iii) and (d) of section 3(1) above and to sections 14, 15, 16, 18, 19[, 21A] and 22 above.

(3) Any power of the Secretary of State to make orders or regulations under this Act—

    (a)   may be so exercised as to make different provision in relation to different cases or classes of cases and to exclude certain cases or classes of case; and

    (b)   includes power to make such supplemental, incidental and transitional provisions as he thinks fit.

[941]

NOTES
Sub-s (1): word in square brackets substituted by the Enterprise Act 2002, s 278(1), Sch 25, para 9(1), (14)(b).
Sub-s (2): number in square brackets inserted by the Consumers, Estate Agents and Redress Act 2007, s 63(1), Sch 7, para 3, as from a day to be appointed.
Regulations: the Estate Agents (Accounts) Regulations 1981, SI 1981/1520.

31 Meaning of "business associate" and "controller"

(1)   The provisions of this section shall have effect for determining the meaning of "business associate" and "controller" for the purposes of this Act.

(2)   As respects acts done in the course of a business carried on by a body corporate, every director and controller of that body is a business associate of it.

(3)   As respects acts done in the course of a business carried on by a partnership, each partner is a business associate of every other member of the partnership and also of the partnership itself and, in the case of a partner which is a body corporate, every person who, by virtue of subsection (2) above, is a business associate of that body is also a business associate of every other member of the partnership.

(4)   As respects acts done in the course of a business carried on by an unincorporated association, every officer of the association and any other person who has the management or control of its activities is a business associate of that association.

(5)   In relation to a body corporate "controller" means a person—
  (a)   in accordance with whose directions or instructions the directors of the body corporate or of any other body corporate which is its controller (or any of them) are accustomed to act; or
  (b)   who, either alone or with any associate or associates, is entitled to exercise, or control the exercise of, one third or more of the voting power at any general meeting of the body corporate or of another body corporate which is its controller.

[942]

32 Meaning of "associate"

(1)   In this Act "associate" includes a business associate and otherwise has the meaning given by the following provisions of this section.

(2)   A person is an associate of another if he is the spouse [or civil partner] or a relative of that other or of a business associate of that other.

(3)   In subsection (2) above "relative" means brother, sister, uncle, aunt, nephew, niece, lineal ancestor or linear descendant, ... references to a spouse include a former spouse and a [reputed spouse, and references to a civil partner include a former civil partner] [and a reputed civil partner]; and for the purposes of this subsection a relationship shall be established as if an illegitimate child or stepchild of a person [were the legitimate child of the relationship in question].

(4)   A body corporate is an associate of another body corporate—
  (a)   if the same person is a controller of both, or a person is a controller of one and persons who are his associates, or he and persons who are his associates, are controllers of the other; or
  (b)   if a group of two or more persons is a controller of each company, and the groups either consist of the same persons or could be regarded as consisting of the same persons by treating (in one or more cases) a member of either group as replaced by a person of whom he is an associate.

(5)   An unincorporated association is an associate of another unincorporated association if any person—
  (a)   is an officer of both associations;
  (b)   has the management or control of the activities of both associations; or
  (c)   is an officer of one association and has the management or control of the activities of the other association.

(6)   A partnership is an associate of another partnership if—
  (a)   any person is a member of both partnerships; or
  (b)   a person who is a member of one partnership is an associate of a member of the other partnership; or
  (c)   a member of one partnership has an associate who is also an associate of a member of the other partnership.

[943]

NOTES
Sub-s (2): words in square brackets inserted by the Civil Partnership Act 2004, s 261(1), Sch 27, para 63(1), (2).

Sub-s (3): word omitted repealed and words in first and third pairs of square brackets substituted by the Civil Partnership Act 2004, s 261(1), (4), Sch 27, para 63(1), (3), Sch 30; words in second pair of square brackets inserted by the Civil Partnership Act 2004 (Overseas Relationships and Consequential, etc Amendments) Order 2005, SI 2005/3129, art 4(4), Sch 4, para 5.

33   General interpretation provisions

(1)   In this Act, unless the context otherwise requires—

"associate" has the meaning assigned to it by section 32 above and "business associate" has the meaning assigned to it by section 31 above;

"client account" has the meaning assigned to it by section 14(2) above;

"clients' money" has the meaning assigned to it by section 12(1) above;

"connected contract", in relation to the acquisition of an interest in land, has the meaning assigned to it by section 12(4) above;

"contract deposit" has the meaning assigned to it by section 12(2) above;

"controller", in relation to a body corporate, has the meaning assigned to it by section 31(5) above;

.....

"enforcement authority" has the meaning assigned to it by section 26(1) above;

"estate agency work" has the meaning assigned to it by section 1(1) above;

"general notice" means a notice published by the [OFT] at a time and in a manner appearing to [it] suitable for securing that the notice is seen within a reasonable time by persons likely to be affected by it;

["OFT" means the Office of Fair Trading;]

"pre-contract deposit" has the meaning assigned to it by section 12(3) above;

"prescribed fee" means such fee as may be prescribed by regulations made by the Secretary of State;

.....

"unincorporated association" does not include a partnership.

(2)   The power to make regulations under subsection (1) above prescribing fees shall be exercisable by statutory instrument which shall be subject to annulment in pursuance of a resolution of either House of Parliament.

[944]

NOTES

Sub-s (1): definition "Director" (omitted) repealed, words in square brackets in definition "general notice" substituted, and definition "OFT" inserted, by the Enterprise Act 2002, s 278, Sch 25, para 9(1), (15), Sch 26; definition "the statutory maximum" (omitted) repealed by the Statute Law (Repeals) Act 1993.

34   Financial provisions

(1)   There shall be defrayed out of moneys provided by Parliament—

(a)   any expenses incurred by the Secretary of State in consequence of the provisions of this Act; and

(b)   any increase attributable to this Act in the sums payable out of moneys so provided under any other Act.

(2)   Any fees paid to the [OFT] under this Act shall be paid into the Consolidated Fund.

[945]

NOTES

Sub-s (2): word in square brackets substituted by virtue of the Enterprise Act 2002, s 2.

35   (*Repealed by the Statute Law (Repeals) Act 1981.*)

36   Short title, commencement and extent

(1)   This Act may be cited as the Estate Agents Act 1979.

(2)   This Act shall come into force on such day as the Secretary of State may by order made by statutory instrument appoint and different days may be so appointed for different provisions and for different purposes.

(3)   This Act extends to Northern Ireland.

[946]

NOTES

Order: the Estate Agents Act 1979 (Commencement No 1) Order 1981, SI 1981/1517.

SCHEDULES

SCHEDULE 1
PROVISIONS SUPPLEMENTARY TO SECTION 3(1)

Section 3(1)

[Spent convictions

1.   A person is not to be treated for the purposes of section 3(1)(a) of this Act as having committed an offence if he has been convicted of that offence and that conviction is to be treated as spent for the purposes of the Rehabilitation of Offenders Act 1974 or any corresponding enactment for the time being in force in Northern Ireland.]

Discrimination

2.   A person shall be deemed to have committed discrimination for the purposes of section 3(1)(b) of this Act in the following cases only, namely—

 (a)   where a finding of discrimination has been made against him in proceedings under section 66 of the Sex Discrimination Act 1975 (in this Schedule referred to as "the 1975 Act") and the finding has become final;

 [(b)   where he has been given an unlawful act notice under section 21 of the Equality Act 2006 and no appeal under that section is pending or can be brought;

 (c)   where he is the subject of an injunction, interdict or order under section 24 (unlawful acts) or 25 (unlawful advertising, pressure, &c) of the Equality Act 2006;

 (d)   where—

     (i)   a county court has determined in accordance with section 25 of the Equality Act 2006 that he committed an act which is unlawful under section 38, 39 or 40 of the Sex Discrimination Act 1975 or section 29, 30 or 31 of the Race Relations Act 1976 (unlawful advertising, pressure, &c), and (ii) no appeal under section 25 of the Equality Act 2006 is pending or can be brought (disregarding an appeal out of time);

     (ii)   no appeal under section 25 of the Equality Act 2006 is pending or can be brought (disregarding an appeal out of time);]

 (e)   where a finding of discrimination has been made against him in proceedings under section 57 of the Race Relations Act 1976 (in this Schedule referred to as "the 1976 Act") and the finding has become final;

 (f)–(h)   …

and the finding, notice, injunction[, interdict] or order related or relates to discrimination falling within Part III of the 1975 Act or the 1976 Act (discrimination in the fields other than employment).

3.   After the expiry of the period of five years beginning on the day on which any such finding or notice as is referred to in paragraph 2 above became final, no person shall be treated for the purposes of section 3(1)(b) of this Act as having committed discrimination by reason only of that finding or notice.

4.—(1)   So far as paragraphs 2 and 3 above relate to findings … under the 1975 Act, subsections … (4) of section 82 of that Act (general interpretation provisions) shall have effect as if those paragraphs were contained in that Act.

 (2)   So far as paragraphs 2 and 3 above relate to findings … under the 1976 Act, subsections … (4) of section 78 of that Act (general interpretation provisions) shall have effect as if those paragraphs were contained in that Act.

5.   In the application of paragraphs 2 to 4 above to Northern Ireland references to the 1975 Act shall be construed as references to the Sex Discrimination (Northern Ireland) Order 1976, and in particular—

 (a)   the references to sections 38, 39 and 40 of the 1975 Act shall be construed as references to Articles 39, 40 and 41 of that Order;

 (b)   the reference to subsections (1) and (4) of section 82 of the 1975 Act shall be construed as a reference to paragraphs (1), (2) and (5) of Article 2 of that Order; and

 (c)   other references to numbered sections of the 1975 Act shall be construed as references to the Articles of that Order bearing the same number.

[6.   In the application of paragraphs 2 to 4 above to Northern Ireland references to the 1976 Act shall be construed as references to the Race Relations (Northern Ireland) Order 1997, and in particular the references to sections 29, 30, 31, 57, 62, 63(2)(a) and (4) and 78(1) and (4) of the 1976 Act shall be construed as references to Articles 29, 30, 31, 54, 59, 60(2)(a) and (4) and 2(2) and (3) respectively of that Order.]

[947]

NOTES

   Para 1: substituted by the Consumers, Estate Agents and Redress Act 2007, s 55(1), (5).
   Para 2: sub-paras (b)–(d) substituted, paras (f)–(h) repealed, and word in final pair of square brackets inserted by the Equality Act 2006, ss 40, 91, Sch 3, paras 36, 38(1)–(4), Sch 4.

Para 4: words omitted repealed by the Equality Act 2006, ss 40, 91, Sch 3, paras 36, 38(1), (5), Sch 4.
Para 6: substituted for part of original para 5 by the Race Relations (Northern Ireland) Order 1997, SI 1997/869, art 73, Sch 2, para 2(2).

SCHEDULE 2
PROCEDURE ETC
Sections 5, 6, 8 (3)

PART I
ORDERS AND DECISIONS UNDER SECTIONS 3, 4 AND 6
Introductory

1.—(1)   In this Schedule—
  (a)   subject to sub-paragraph (2) below, references to "the person affected" are to the person in respect of whom the [OFT] proposes to make, or has made, an order under section 3 or section 4 of this Act, or who has made an application under section 6 of this Act for the variation or revocation of such an order; and
  (b)   references to the [OFT's] "proposal" are to any proposal of [its] to make such an order or to make a decision under subsection (4) or subsection (5) of section 6 of this Act on such an application.

(2)   In the case of a proposal of the [OFT] to make an order under section 3 or section 4 of this Act against a partnership where, by virtue of section 5(2) of this Act, [it] intends that the order shall have effect as an order against some or all of the partners individually, references in the following provisions of this Schedule to the person affected shall be construed, except where the contrary is provided, as references to each of the partners affected by the order, as well as to the partnership itself.

Notice of proposal

2.—(1)   The [OFT] shall give to the person affected a notice informing him of the proposal and of the [OFT's] reason for it; but paragraph 1(2) above shall not apply for the purposes of this sub-paragraph.

(2)   In the case of a proposal to make an order, the notice under sub-paragraph (1) above shall inform the person affected of the substance of the proposed order and, in the case of a proposal to make an order under section 3 of this Act, shall—
  (a)   set out those matters falling within subsection (1) of that section which the [OFT] intends should be specified as the grounds for the order, and
  (b)   specify any other matters of which the [OFT] has taken account under subsection (2) of that section, and
  (c)   if the [OFT] proposes to rely on section 4(3) of this Act to establish the unfitness of the person affected, state that fact.

(3)   The notice given under sub-paragraph (1) above shall invite the person affected, within such period of not less than twenty-one days as may be specified in the notice—
  (a)   to submit to the [OFT] his representations in writing as to why the order should not be made or, as the case may be, should be varied or revoked in accordance with the application, and
  (b)   to give notice to the [OFT], if he thinks fit, that he wishes to make such representations orally,
and where notice is given under paragraph (b) above the [OFT] shall arrange for the oral representations to be heard.

Hearing of representations

3.   Where the [OFT] receives notice under paragraph 2(3)(b) above [it] shall give the person affected not less than twenty-one days notice, or such shorter notice as the person affected may consent to accept, of the date, time and place at which representations are to be heard.

4.—(1)   In the course of hearing oral representations the [OFT] shall, at the request of the person affected, permit any other person (in addition to the person affected) to make representations on his behalf or to give evidence or to introduce documents for him.

(2)   The [OFT] shall not refuse to admit evidence solely on the grounds that it would not be admissible in a court of law.

5.   If the [OFT] adjourns the hearing [it] shall give the person affected reasonable notice of the date, time and place at which the hearing is to be resumed.

Decision

6.—(1)   The [OFT] shall take into account in deciding whether to proceed with [its] proposal any written or oral representations made in accordance with the preceding provisions of this Schedule.

(2)   If the [OFT] considers that [it] should proceed with [its] proposal but for a reason which differs, or on grounds which differ, from those set out in the notice of the proposal under paragraph 2 above, [it] shall give a further notice under that paragraph.

(3)   In any case where—
- (a)   a notice under paragraph 2 above gives more than one reason for the proposal or (in the case of a proposal to make an order under section 3 of this Act) sets out more than one matter which the [OFT] intends should be specified as the grounds for the order, and
- (b)   it appears to the [OFT] that one or more of those reasons should be abandoned or, as the case may be, that one or more of those matters should not be so specified,

the [OFT] may nevertheless decide to proceed with [its] proposal on the basis of any other reason given in the notice or, as the case may be, on any other grounds set out in the notice.

7.   If the [OFT] decides not to proceed with [its] proposal [it] shall give notice of that decision to the person affected and, in the case of a notice of a decision on an application under section 6 of this Act, such a notice shall be combined with a notice under subsection (3) of that section.

8.   If the [OFT] decides to proceed with [its] proposal [it] may, if [it] thinks fit having regard to any representations made to [it]—
- (a)   where the proposal is for the making of an order, make the order in a form which varies from that of the proposed order mentioned in the notice under paragraph 2 above, or
- (b)   where the proposal is to vary an order, make a variation other than that mentioned in the notice under paragraph 2 above, or
- (c)   where the proposal is to refuse to revoke an order, vary the order.

Notification of decision

9.—(1)   Notice of the decision to make the order, and of the terms of the order or, as the case may be, notice of the decision on the application for variation or revocation of the order, shall be given to the person affected, together with the [OFT's] reasons for [its] decision, including the facts which in [its] opinion justify the decision.

(2)   The notice referred to in sub-paragraph (1) above shall also inform the person affected of his right to appeal against the decision and of the period within which an appeal may be brought and of how notice of appeal may be given.

10.—(1)   Subject to sub-paragraph (2) below, the order to which the decision relates or, as the case may be, any variation of an order for which the decision provides shall not come into operation until any appeal under section 7(1) of this Act and any further appeal has been finally determined or the period within which such an appeal may be brought has expired.

(2)   Where the [OFT] states in the notice referred to in paragraph 9(1) above that [it] is satisfied that there are special circumstances which require it, an order shall come into operation immediately upon the giving of notice of the decision to make it.

[948]

NOTES

Word in square brackets substituted by the Enterprise Act 2002, s 278(1), Sch 25, para 9(1), (16).

PART II
APPLICATIONS UNDER SECTIONS 6(1) AND 8(3)

11.   Any reference in this Part of this Schedule to an application is a reference to an application to the [OFT] under section 6(1) or section 8(3) of this Act, and any reference to the applicant shall be construed accordingly.

12.   An application shall be in writing and be in such form and accompanied by such particulars as the [OFT] may specify by general notice.

13.   The [OFT] may by notice require the applicant to publish details of his application at a time and times and in a manner specified in the notice.

14.   If an application does not comply with paragraph 12 above or if an applicant fails to comply with a notice under section 9 of this Act requiring the furnishing of information or the production of documents in connection with the application, the [OFT] may decline to proceed with the application.

[949]

NOTES

Word in square brackets substituted by the Enterprise Act 2002, s 278(1), Sch 25, para 9(1), (16)(1)(a).

[SCHEDULE 3
REDRESS SCHEMES

Section 23A(10)

Approval of redress schemes

1. A redress scheme may be approved for the purposes of section 23A by the OFT acting in accordance with paragraphs 2 to 8.

2.—(1) A scheme may not be approved unless the OFT considers that—
  (a) the provisions of the scheme; and
  (b) the manner in which it will be operated (so far as can be judged from facts known to the authority);
are satisfactory for the purposes of section 23A.

(2) Without prejudice to the generality of sub-paragraph (1), a scheme must not be approved unless the OFT considers that it makes satisfactory provision about—
  (a) the complaints which may be made under the scheme (which may include complaints about non-compliance with the provisions of a code of practice or other document);
  (b) the ombudsman's duties and powers in relation to the investigation and determination of complaints (which may include power to decide not to investigate or determine a particular complaint);
  (c) the redress which the ombudsman may require members to provide to complainants, which must include the types of redress specified in sub-paragraph (3);
  (d) the enforcement of any requirement to provide redress imposed on a member in accordance with the scheme.

(3) The types of redress mentioned in sub-paragraph (2)(c) are—
  (a) providing an apology or explanation;
  (b) paying compensation; and
  (c) taking such other actions in the interests of the complainant as the ombudsman may specify.

3.—(1) In determining whether a scheme, or any provisions mentioned in paragraph 2(2), are satisfactory the OFT must have regard to—
  (a) the interests of members of the scheme and of sellers and buyers of residential properties; and
  (b) such principles as—
    (i) in the opinion of the OFT constitute generally accepted principles of best practice in relation to consumer redress schemes, and
    (ii) it is reasonable to regard as applicable to the scheme.

(2) In considering the interests mentioned in sub-paragraph (1)(a), the OFT may have regard to the number of other redress schemes which are (or are likely to become) approved redress schemes.

4. The OFT must not approve a scheme unless it considers that the scheme makes satisfactory provision about the provision of information by the ombudsman or the scheme administrator to—
  (a) persons exercising functions under other approved schemes;
  (b) persons exercising functions under other consumer redress schemes; and
  (c) the OFT or any other person exercising regulatory functions in relation to the activities of persons engaging in estate agency work.

5. The OFT must not approve a scheme if it considers that the scheme provides for membership to be revoked on any unfair grounds.

Applications for approval to the OFT

6. An application for approval by the OFT of a redress scheme must—
  (a) be made in such manner as the OFT may determine; and
  (b) be accompanied by such information as the OFT may require.

7. Where the OFT is proposing to refuse an application for approval it must give the applicant a notice stating—
  (a) that it is proposing to refuse the application;
  (b) the grounds for the proposed refusal; and
  (c) that representations about the proposed refusal may be made within such period of not less than 30 days as is specified in the notice.

8. If the OFT decides to refuse an application for approval, it must give the applicant a notice stating—
  (a) the OFT's decision to refuse the application; and
  (b) the reasons for the decision.

Notification of changes to an approved scheme

9.   The scheme administrator of a redress scheme which is approved by the OFT must notify the OFT of any change to the scheme before the end of the period of 14 days beginning with the day on which the change is made.

Withdrawal of approval by the OFT

10.   The OFT may withdraw approval of a redress scheme which is for the time being approved by it.

11.   Before withdrawing approval of a scheme, the OFT must give the scheme administrator a notice stating—
   (a)   that it proposes to withdraw its approval;
   (b)   the grounds for the proposed withdrawal of approval; and
   (c)   that representations about the proposed withdrawal may be made within such period of not less than 30 days as is specified in the notice.

12.   The OFT must give the scheme administrator a notice stating—
   (a)   its decision on a proposal to withdraw approval; and
   (b)   the reasons for its decision.

13.   If the OFT decides to withdraw approval of a scheme—
   (a)   the withdrawal has effect from such date as may be specified in the notice under paragraph 12;
   (b)   the scheme administrator must give a copy of the notice under paragraph 12 to every member of the scheme.

Revocation of designation by the Secretary of State

14.   If the Secretary of State decides to revoke his designation of a scheme for the purposes of section 23A, he must give every member of the scheme a notice stating—
   (a)   that he has decided to revoke the designation;
   (b)   the reasons for his decision; and
   (c)   the date from which the revocation has effect.

Defamation proceedings

15.   For the purposes of the law relating to defamation, proceedings under an approved redress scheme in relation to the investigation and determination of a complaint are to be treated in the same way as proceedings before a court.

Interpretation

16.   In this Schedule—
   "redress scheme" has the meaning given in section 23A(8)(a);
   "approved redress scheme" has the meaning given in section 23A(8)(b);
   "buyer", in relation to residential property, has the meaning given in section 23A(8)(e);
   "complaint" has the meaning given in section 23A(8)(c);
   "ombudsman" means the independent person mentioned in section 23A(8)(a);
   "residential property" has the meaning given in section 23C;
   "scheme administrator", in relation to a redress scheme, means the person who administers the scheme;
   "seller", in relation to residential property, has the meaning given by section 23A(8)(d).]

[949A]

NOTES
   Commencement: 12 October 2007.
   Inserted by the Consumers, Estate Agents and Redress Act 2007, s 53(1), Sch 6, paras 1, 3.

[SCHEDULE 4
PENALTY NOTICES UNDER SECTION 23B(1)

Section 23B(3)

1.   A penalty charge notice given to a person under section 23B(1) by a duly authorised officer of an enforcement authority other than the OFT must—
   (a)   state the officer's belief that that person has committed a breach of the duty imposed by an order under section 23A(1);
   (b)   give such other particulars of the circumstances as may be necessary to give reasonable notice of the breach of duty;
   (c)   require that person, within a period specified in the notice—
      (i)   to pay a penalty charge specified in the notice; or
      (ii)   to give notice to the enforcement authority that he wishes to review the notice;
   (d)   state the effect of paragraph 8;

(e)   specify the person to whom and the address at which the penalty charge may be paid and the method or methods by which payment may be made; and

(f)   specify the person to whom and the address at which a notice requesting a review may be sent (and to which any representations relating to the review may be addressed).

2.   The penalty charge specified in the notice shall be of such amount (not exceeding £1,000) as may be prescribed for the time being by regulations made by the Secretary of State.

3.—(1)   The period specified under paragraph 1(c) must not be less than 28 days beginning with the day after that on which the penalty charge notice was given.

(2)   The enforcement authority may extend the period for complying with the requirement mentioned in paragraph 1(c) in any particular case if they consider it appropriate to do so.

4.   The enforcement authority may, if they consider that the penalty charge notice ought not to have been given, give the recipient a notice withdrawing the penalty charge notice.

5.—(1)   If, within the period specified under paragraph 1(c) (or that period as extended under paragraph 3(2)), the recipient of the penalty charge notice gives notice to the enforcement authority requesting a review, the authority shall—

(a)   consider any representations made by the recipient and all other circumstances of the case;

(b)   decide whether to confirm or withdraw the notice; and

(c)   give notice of their decision to the recipient.

(2)   A notice under sub-paragraph (1)(c) confirming the penalty charge notice must also state the effect of paragraphs 6(1) to (3) and 8(1) and (3).

(3)   If the authority are not satisfied—

(a)   that the recipient committed the breach of duty specified in the notice;

(b)   that the notice was given within the time allowed by section 23B(2) and complies with the other requirements imposed by or under this Schedule; and

(c)   that in the circumstances of the case it was appropriate for a penalty charge notice to be given to the recipient;

they shall withdraw the penalty charge notice.

6.—(1)   If after a review the penalty charge notice is confirmed by the enforcement authority, the recipient may, within the period of 28 days beginning with the day after that on which the notice under paragraph 5(1)(c) is given, appeal to a county court or, in Scotland, to the sheriff against the penalty charge notice.

(2)   The county court or the sheriff may extend the period for appealing against the notice.

(3)   Such an appeal must be on one (or more) of the following grounds—

(a)   that the recipient did not commit the breach of duty specified in the penalty charge notice;

(b)   that the notice was not given within the time allowed by section 23B(2) or does not comply with any other requirement imposed by or under this Schedule; or

(c)   that in the circumstances of the case it was inappropriate for the notice to be given to the recipient.

(4)   An appeal against a penalty charge notice shall be by way of a rehearing; and the county court or sheriff shall either uphold the notice or quash it.

7.   If the penalty charge notice is withdrawn or quashed, the authority shall repay any amount previously paid as a penalty charge in pursuance of the notice.

8.—(1)   The amount of the penalty charge is recoverable from the recipient of the penalty charge notice as a debt owed to the authority unless—

(a)   the notice has been withdrawn or quashed; or

(b)   the charge has been paid.

(2)   Proceedings for the recovery of the penalty charge may not be commenced before the end of the period mentioned in paragraph 5(1).

(3)   And if within that period the recipient of the penalty charge notice gives notice to the authority that he wishes the authority to review the penalty charge notice, such proceedings may not be commenced—

(a)   before the end of the period mentioned in paragraph 6(1); and

(b)   where the recipient appeals against the penalty charge notice, before the end of the period of 28 days beginning with the day on which the appeal is withdrawn or determined.

9.   In proceedings for the recovery of the penalty charge, a certificate which—

(a)   purports to be signed by or on behalf of the person having responsibility for the financial affairs of the enforcement authority; and

(b)   states that payment of the penalty charge was or was not received by a date specified in the certificate;

is evidence of the facts stated.

10. Section 29 (service of notices etc) applies in relation to—
    (a) any penalty charge notice which is to be given under section 23B(1) by a duly authorised officer of an enforcement authority other than the OFT; and
    (b) any notice which is to be given under paragraph 5(1)(c) of this Schedule by such an enforcement authority;

as it applies in relation to any notice which under this Act is to be given to any person by the OFT.

11. The Secretary of State may by regulations make provision supplementary or incidental to the provisions of this Schedule, including in particular provision prescribing—
    (a) the form of penalty charge notices or of any other notice mentioned in this Schedule;
    (b) circumstances in which penalty charge notices may not be given;
    (c) the method or methods by which penalty charges may be paid.

12. Any power to make regulations under this Schedule shall be exercisable by statutory instrument which shall be subject to annulment in pursuance of a resolution of either House of Parliament.]

[949B]

NOTES
Commencement: 12 October 2007.
Inserted by the Consumers, Estate Agents and Redress Act 2007, s 53(1), Sch 6, paras 1, 4.
Regulations: the Estate Agents (Redress Scheme) (Penalty Charge) Regulations 2008, SI 2008/1713 at **[3645C]**.

SALE OF GOODS ACT 1979

(1979 c 54)

ARRANGEMENT OF SECTIONS

PART I
CONTRACTS TO WHICH ACT APPLIES

PART II
FORMATION OF THE CONTRACT

Contract of sale

Formalities of contract

Subject matter of contract

The price

Implied terms etc

Sale by sample

Miscellaneous

PART VI
ACTIONS FOR BREACH OF THE CONTRACT

Seller's remedies

Buyer's remedies

Interest, etc

PART VII
SUPPLEMENTARY

An Act to consolidate the law relating to the sale of goods

[6 December 1979]

PART I
CONTRACTS TO WHICH ACT APPLIES

1   Contracts to which Act applies

(1)   This Act applies to contracts of sale of goods made on or after (but not to those made before) 1 January 1894.

(2)   In relation to contracts made on certain dates, this Act applies subject to the modification of certain of its sections as mentioned in Schedule 1 below.

(3)   Any such modification is indicated in the section concerned by a reference to Schedule 1 below.

(4)   Accordingly, where a section does not contain such a reference, this Act applies in relation to the contract concerned without such modification of the section.

[950]

PART II
FORMATION OF THE CONTRACT

Contract of sale

2   Contract of sale

(1)   A contract of sale of goods is a contract by which the seller transfers or agrees to transfer the property in goods to the buyer for a money consideration, called the price.

(2)   There may be a contract of sale between one part owner and another.

(3)   A contract of sale may be absolute or conditional.

(4)   Where under a contract of sale the property in the goods is transferred from the seller to the buyer the contract is called a sale.

(5)   Where under a contract of sale the transfer of the property in the goods is to take place at a future time or subject to some condition later to be fulfilled the contract is called an agreement to sell.

(6)   An agreement to sell becomes a sale when the time elapses or the conditions are fulfilled subject to which the property in the goods is to be transferred.

[951]

3   Capacity to buy and sell

(1)   Capacity to buy and sell is regulated by the general law concerning capacity to contract and to transfer and acquire property.

(2)   Where necessaries are sold and delivered to a minor or to a person who by reason of ... drunkenness is incompetent to contract, he must pay a reasonable price for them.

(3)   In subsection (2) above "necessaries" means goods suitable to the condition in life of the minor or other person concerned and to his actual requirements at the time of the sale and delivery.

[952]

NOTES

Sub-s (2): words "mental incapacity or" (omitted) repealed, in relation to England and Wales, by the Mental Capacity Act 2005, s 67(1), Sch 6, para 24.

Formalities of contract

4   How contract of sale is made

(1)   Subject to this and any other Act, a contract of sale may be made in writing (either with or without seal), or by word of mouth, or partly in writing and partly by word of mouth, or may be implied from the conduct of the parties.

(2)   Nothing in this section affects the law relating to corporations.

[953]

Subject matter of contract

5   Existing or future goods

(1)   The goods which form the subject of a contract of sale may be either existing goods, owned or possessed by the seller, or goods to be manufactured or acquired by him after the making of the contract of sale, in this Act called future goods.

(2)   There may be a contract for the sale of goods the acquisition of which by the seller depends on a contingency which may or may not happen.

(3)   Where by a contract of sale the seller purports to effect a present sale of future goods, the contract operates as an agreement to sell the goods.

[954]

6   Goods which have perished

Where there is a contract for the sale of specific goods, and the goods without the knowledge of the seller have perished at the time when the contract is made, the contract is void.

[955]

7   Goods perishing before sale but after agreement to sell

Where there is an agreement to sell specific goods and subsequently the goods, without any fault on the part of the seller or buyer, perish before the risk passes to the buyer, the agreement is avoided.

[956]

The price

8   Ascertainment of price

(1)   The price in a contract of sale may be fixed by the contract, or may be left to be fixed in a manner agreed by the contract, or may be determined by the course of dealing between the parties.

(2)   Where the price is not determined as mentioned in subsection (1) above the buyer must pay a reasonable price.

(3)   What is a reasonable price is a question of fact dependent on the circumstances of each particular case.

[957]

9   Agreement to sell at valuation

(1)   Where there is an agreement to sell goods on the terms that the price is to be fixed by the valuation of a third party, and he cannot or does not make the valuation, the agreement is avoided; but if the goods or any part of them have been delivered to and appropriated by the buyer he must pay a reasonable price for them.

(2)   Where the third party is prevented from making the valuation by the fault of the seller or buyer, the party not at fault may maintain an action for damages against the party at fault.

[958]

[Implied terms etc]

10 Stipulations about time

(1)   Unless a different intention appears from the terms of the contract, stipulations as to time of payment are not of the essence of a contract of sale.

(2)   Whether any other stipulation as to time is or is not of the essence of the contract depends on the terms of the contract.

(3)   In a contract of sale "month" prima facie means calendar month.

[959]

NOTES
Cross-heading preceding this section substituted by the Sale and Supply of Goods Act 1994, s 7(1), Sch 2, para 5(1), (10).

11 When condition to be treated as warranty

[(1)   This section does not apply to Scotland.]

(2)   Where a contract of sale is subject to a condition to be fulfilled by the seller, the buyer may waive the condition, or may elect to treat the breach of the condition as a breach of warranty and not as a ground for treating the contract as repudiated.

(3)   Whether a stipulation in a contract of sale is a condition, the breach of which may give rise to a right to treat the contract as repudiated, or a warranty, the breach of which may give rise to a claim for damages but not to a right to reject the goods and treat the contract as repudiated, depends in each case on the construction of the contract; and a stipulation may be a condition, though called a warranty in the contract.

(4)   [Subject to section 35A below] where a contract of sale is not severable and the buyer has accepted the goods or part of them, the breach of a condition to be fulfilled by the seller can only be treated as a breach of warranty, and not as a ground for rejecting the goods and treating the contract as repudiated, unless there is an express or implied term of the contract to that effect.

(5)   ...

(6)   Nothing in this section affects a condition or warranty whose fulfilment is excused by law by reason of impossibility or otherwise.

(7)   Paragraph 2 of Schedule 1 below applies in relation to a contract made before 22 April 1967 or (in the application of this Act to Northern Ireland) 28 July 1967.

[960]

NOTES
Sub-s (1): substituted by the Sale and Supply of Goods Act 1994, s 7(1), Sch 2, para 5(1), (2).
Sub-s (4): words in square brackets inserted by the Sale and Supply of Goods Act 1994, s 3(2).
Sub-s (5): repealed by the Sale and Supply of Goods Act 1994, s 7, Sch 2, para 5(1), (2), Sch 3.

12 Implied terms about title, etc

(1)   In a contract of sale, other than one to which subsection (3) below applies, there is an implied [term] on the part of the seller that in the case of a sale he has a right to sell the goods, and in the case of an agreement to sell he will have such a right at the time when the property is to pass.

(2)   In a contract of sale, other than one to which subsection (3) below applies, there is also an implied [term] that—

(a)   the goods are free, and will remain free until the time when the property is to pass, from any charge or encumbrance not disclosed or known to the buyer before the contract is made, and

(b)   the buyer will enjoy quiet possession of the goods except so far as it may be disturbed by the owner or other person entitled to the benefit of any charge or encumbrance so disclosed or known.

(3)   This subsection applies to a contract of sale in the case of which there appears from the contract or is to be inferred from its circumstances an intention that the seller should transfer only such title as he or a third person may have.

(4)   In a contract to which subsection (3) above applies there is an implied [term] that all charges or encumbrances known to the seller and not known to the buyer have been disclosed to the buyer before the contract is made.

(5)   In a contract to which subsection (3) above applies there is also an implied [term] that none of the following will disturb the buyer's quiet possession of the goods, namely—

(a)   the seller;

(b)   in a case where the parties to the contract intend that the seller should transfer only such title as a third person may have, that person;

(c)   anyone claiming through or under the seller or that third person otherwise than under a charge or encumbrance disclosed or known to the buyer before the contract is made.

[(5A)   As regards England and Wales and Northern Ireland, the term implied by subsection (1) above is a condition and the terms implied by subsections (2), (4) and (5) above are warranties.]

(6)   Paragraph 3 of Schedule 1 below applies in relation to a contract made before 18 May 1973.

[961]

NOTES
Sub-ss (1), (2), (4), (5): words in square brackets substituted by the Sale and Supply of Goods Act 1994, s 7(1), Sch 2, para 5(1), (3)(a).
Sub-s (5A): inserted by the Sale and Supply of Goods Act 1994, s 7(1), Sch 2, para 5(1), (3)(b).

13   Sale by description

(1)   Where there is a contract for the sale of goods by description, there is an implied [term] that the goods will correspond with the description.

[(1A)   As regards England and Wales and Northern Ireland, the term implied by subsection (1) above is a condition.]

(2)   If the sale is by sample as well as by description it is not sufficient that the bulk of the goods corresponds with the sample if the goods do not also correspond with the description.

(3)   A sale of goods is not prevented from being a sale by description by reason only that, being exposed for sale or hire, they are selected by the buyer.

(4)   Paragraph 4 of Schedule 1 below applies in relation to a contract made before 18th May 1973.

[962]

NOTES
Sub-s (1): word in square brackets substituted by the Sale and Supply of Goods Act 1994, s 7(1), Sch 2, para 5(1), (4)(a).
Sub-s (1A): inserted by the Sale and Supply of Goods Act 1994, s 7(1), Sch 2, para 5(1), (4)(b).

14   Implied terms about quality or fitness

(1)   Except as provided by this section and section 15 below and subject to any other enactment, there is no implied [term] about the quality or fitness for any particular purpose of goods supplied under a contract of sale.

[(2)   Where the seller sells goods in the course of a business, there is an implied term that the goods supplied under the contract are of satisfactory quality.

(2A)   For the purposes of this Act, goods are of satisfactory quality if they meet the standard that a reasonable person would regard as satisfactory, taking account of any description of the goods, the price (if relevant) and all the other relevant circumstances.

(2B)   For the purposes of this Act, the quality of goods includes their state and condition and the following (among others) are in appropriate cases aspects of the quality of goods—
    (a)   fitness for all the purposes for which goods of the kind in question are commonly supplied,
    (b)   appearance and finish,
    (c)   freedom from minor defects,
    (d)   safety, and
    (e)   durability.

(2C)   The term implied by subsection (2) above does not extend to any matter making the quality of goods unsatisfactory—
    (a)   which is specifically drawn to the buyer's attention before the contract is made,
    (b)   where the buyer examines the goods before the contract is made, which that examination ought to reveal, or
    (c)   in the case of a contract for sale by sample, which would have been apparent on a reasonable examination of the sample.]

[(2D)   If the buyer deals as consumer or, in Scotland, if a contract of sale is a consumer contract, the relevant circumstances mentioned in subsection (2A) above include any public statements on the specific characteristics of the goods made about them by the seller, the producer or his representative, particularly in advertising or on labelling.

(2E)   A public statement is not by virtue of subsection (2D) above a relevant circumstance for the purposes of subsection (2A) above in the case of a contract of sale, if the seller shows that—
    (a)   at the time the contract was made, he was not, and could not reasonably have been, aware of the statement,

(b)   before the contract was made, the statement had been withdrawn in public or, to the extent that it contained anything which was incorrect or misleading, it had been corrected in public, or

(c)   the decision to buy the goods could not have been influenced by the statement.

(2F)   Subsections (2D) and (2E) above do not prevent any public statement from being a relevant circumstance for the purposes of subsection (2A) above (whether or not the buyer deals as consumer or, in Scotland, whether or not the contract of sale is a consumer contract) if the statement would have been such a circumstance apart from those subsections.]

(3)   Where the seller sells goods in the course of a business and the buyer, expressly or by implication, makes known—

(a)   to the seller, or

(b)   where the purchase price or part of it is payable by instalments and the goods were previously sold by a credit-broker to the seller, to that credit-broker,

any particular purpose for which the goods are being bought, there is an implied [term] that the goods supplied under the contract are reasonably fit for that purpose, whether or not that is a purpose for which such goods are commonly supplied, except where the circumstances show that the buyer does not rely, or that it is unreasonable for him to rely, on the skill or judgment of the seller or credit-broker.

(4)   An implied [term] about quality or fitness for a particular purpose may be annexed to a contract of sale by usage.

(5)   The preceding provisions of this section apply to a sale by a person who in the course of a business is acting as agent for another as they apply to a sale by a principal in the course of a business, except where that other is not selling in the course of a business and either the buyer knows that fact or reasonable steps are taken to bring it to the notice of the buyer before the contract is made.

[(6)   As regard England and Wales and Northern Ireland, the terms implied by subsections (2) and (3) above are conditions.]

(7)   Paragraph 5 of Schedule 1 below applies in relation to a contract made on or after 18 May 1973 and before the appointed day, and paragraph 6 in relation to one made before 18th May 1973.

(8)   In subsection (7) above and paragraph 5 of Schedule 1 below references to the appointed day are to the day appointed for the purposes of those provisions by an order of the Secretary of State made by statutory instrument.

[963]

NOTES

Sub-ss (1), (3), (4): words in square brackets substituted by the Sale and Supply of Goods Act 1994, s 7(1), Sch 2, para 5(1). (5)(a).

Sub-ss (2)–(2C): substituted, for original sub-s (2), by the Sale and Supply of Goods Act 1994, s 1(1).

Sub-ss (2D)–(2F): inserted by the Sale and Supply of Goods to Consumers Regulations 2002, SI 2002/3045, reg 3.

Sub-s (6): substituted by the Sale and Supply of Goods Act 1994, s 7(1), Sch 2, para (1), 5(5)(b).

Orders: the Sale of Goods Act 1979 (Appointed Day) Order 1983, SI 1983/1572 (appointing 19 May 1985 for the purposes of sub-s (7)).

Sale by sample

15 Sale by sample

(1)   A contract of sale is a contract for sale by sample where there is an express or implied term to that effect in the contract.

(2)   In the case of a contract for sale by sample there is an implied [term]—

(a)   that the bulk will correspond with the sample in quality;

(b)   ...

(c)   that the goods will be free from any defect, [making their quality unsatisfactory], which would not be apparent on reasonable examination of the sample.

[(3)   As regards England and Wales and Northern Ireland, the term implied by subsection (2) above is a condition.]

(4)   Paragraph 7 of Schedule 1 below applies in relation to a contract made before 18 May 1973.

[964]

NOTES

Sub-s (2): words in square brackets substituted, and para (b) repealed, by the Sale and Supply of Goods Act 1994, ss 1(2), 7, Sch 2, para 5(1), (6)(a), Sch 3.

Sub-s (3): substituted by the Sale and Supply of Goods Act 1994, s 7, Sch 2, para 5(1), (6)(b).

[Miscellaneous

15A Modifications of remedies for breach of condition in non-consumer cases

(1)   Where in the case of a contract of sale—
    (a)   the buyer would, apart from this subsection, have the right to reject goods by reason of a breach on the part of the seller of a term implied by section 13, 14 or 15 above, but
    (b)   the breach is so slight that it would be unreasonable for him to reject them,

then, if the buyer does not deal as consumer, the breach is not to be treated as a breach of condition but may be treated as a breach of warranty.

(2)   This section applies unless a contrary intention appears in, or is to be implied from, the contract.

(3)   It is for the seller to show that a breach fell within subsection (1)(b) above.

(4)   This section does not apply to Scotland.]

[965]

NOTES
Inserted, together with preceding cross-heading, by the Sale and Supply of Goods Act 1994, s 4(1).

15B   *(Inserted by the Sale and Supply of Goods Act 1994, s 5(1) and applies to Scotland only.)*

PART III
EFFECTS OF THE CONTRACT
Transfer of property as between seller and buyer

16 Goods must be ascertained

[Subject to section 20A below] where there is a contract for the sale of unascertained goods no property in the goods is transferred to the buyer unless and until the goods are ascertained.

[966]

NOTES
Words in square brackets inserted by the Sale of Goods (Amendment) Act 1995, s 1(1).

17 Property passes when intended to pass

(1)   Where there is a contract for the sale of specific or ascertained goods the property in them is transferred to the buyer at such time as the parties to the contract intend it to be transferred.

(2)   For the purpose of ascertaining the intention of the parties regard shall be had to the terms of the contract, the conduct of the parties and the circumstances of the case.

[967]

18 Rules for ascertaining intention

Unless a different intention appears, the following are rules for ascertaining the intention of the parties as to the time at which the property in the goods is to pass to the buyer.

    Rule 1.—Where there is an unconditional contract for the sale of specific goods in a deliverable state the property in the goods passes to the buyer when the contract is made, and it is immaterial whether the time of payment or the time of delivery, or both, be postponed.

    Rule 2.—Where there is a contract for the sale of specific goods and the seller is bound to do something to the goods for the purpose of putting them into a deliverable state, the property does not pass until the thing is done and the buyer has notice that it has been done.

    Rule 3.—Where there is a contract for the sale of specific goods in a deliverable state but the seller is bound to weigh, measure, test, or do some other act or thing with reference to the goods for the purpose of ascertaining the price, the property does not pass until the act or thing is done and the buyer has notice that it has been done.

    Rule 4.—When goods are delivered to the buyer on approval or on sale or return or other similar terms the property in the goods passes to the buyer:—
        (a)   when he signifies his approval or acceptance to the seller or does any other act adopting the transaction;
        (b)   if he does not signify his approval or acceptance to the seller but retains the goods without giving notice of rejection, then, if a time has been fixed for the return of the goods, on the expiration of that time, and, if no time has been fixed, on the expiration of a reasonable time.

    Rule 5.—(1) Where there is a contract for the sale of unascertained or future goods by description, and goods of that description and in a deliverable state are unconditionally appropriated to the contract, either by the seller with the assent of the buyer or by the buyer with the assent of the seller, the property in the goods then passes to the buyer; and the assent may be express or implied, and may be given either before or after the appropriation is made.

(2) Where, in pursuance of the contract, the seller delivers the goods to the buyer or to a carrier or other bailee or custodier (whether named by the buyer or not) for the purpose of transmission to the buyer, and does not reserve the right of disposal, he is to be taken to have unconditionally appropriated the goods to the contract.

[(3) Where there is a contract for the sale of a specified quantity of unascertained goods in a deliverable state forming part of a bulk which is identified either in the contract or by subsequent agreement between the parties and the bulk is reduced to (or to less than) that quantity, then, if the buyer under that contract is the only buyer to whom goods are then due out of the bulk—

(a)   the remaining goods are to be taken as appropriated to that contract at the time when the bulk is so reduced; and

(b)   the property in those goods then passes to that buyer.

(4) Paragraph (3) above applies also (with the necessary modifications) where a bulk is reduced to (or to less than) the aggregate of the quantities due to a single buyer under separate contracts relating to that bulk and he is the only buyer to whom goods are then due out of that bulk.]

[968]

NOTES

Paras (3), (4) of Rule 5 added by the Sale of Goods (Amendment) Act 1995, s 1(2).

19   Reservation of right of disposal

(1)   Where there is a contract for the sale of specific goods or where goods are subsequently appropriated to the contract, the seller may, by the terms of the contract or appropriation, reserve the right of disposal of the goods until certain conditions are fulfilled; and in such a case, notwithstanding the delivery of the goods to the buyer, or to a carrier or other bailee or custodier for the purpose of transmission to the buyer, the property in the goods does not pass to the buyer until the conditions imposed by the seller are fulfilled.

(2)   Where goods are shipped, and by the bill of lading the goods are deliverable to the order of the seller or his agent, the seller is prima facie to be taken to reserve the right of disposal.

(3)   Where the seller of goods draws on the buyer for the price, and transmits the bill of exchange and bill of lading to the buyer together to secure acceptance or payment of the bill of exchange, the buyer is bound to return the bill of lading if he does not honour the bill of exchange, and if he wrongfully retains the bill of lading the property in the goods does not pass to him.

[969]

[20   Passing of risk]

(1)   Unless otherwise agreed, the goods remain at the seller's risk until the property in them is transferred to the buyer, but when the property in them is transferred to the buyer the goods are at the buyer's risk whether delivery has been made or not.

(2)   But where delivery has been delayed through the fault of either buyer or seller the goods are at the risk of the party at fault as regards any loss which might not have occurred but for such fault.

(3)   Nothing in this section affects the duties or liabilities of either seller or buyer as a bailee or custodier of the goods of the other party.

[(4)   In a case where the buyer deals as consumer or, in Scotland, where there is a consumer contract in which the buyer is a consumer, subsections (1) to (3) above must be ignored and the goods remain at the seller's risk until they are delivered to the consumer.]

[970]

NOTES

Section heading: substituted by the Sale and Supply of Goods to Consumers Regulations 2002, SI 2002/3045, reg 4(1).

Sub-s (4): added by SI 2002/3045, reg 4(1), (2).

[20A   Undivided shares in goods forming part of a bulk

(1)   This section applies to a contract for the sale of a specified quantity of unascertained goods if the following conditions are met—

(a)   the goods or some of them form part of a bulk which is identified either in the contract or by subsequent agreement between the parties; and

(b)   the buyer has paid the price for some or all of the goods which are the subject of the contract and which form part of the bulk.

(2) Where this section applies, then (unless the parties agree otherwise), as soon as the conditions specified in paragraphs (a) and (b) of subsection (1) above are met or at such later time as the parties may agree—

    (a)   property in an undivided share in the bulk is transferred to the buyer, and

    (b)   the buyer becomes an owner in common of the bulk.

(3) Subject to subsection (4) below, for the purposes of this section, the undivided share of a buyer in a bulk at any time shall be such share as the quantity of goods paid for and due to the buyer out of the bulk bears to the quantity of goods in the bulk at that time.

(4) Where the aggregate of the undivided shares of buyers in a bulk determined under subsection (3) above would at any time exceed the whole of the bulk at that time, the undivided share in the bulk of each buyer shall be reduced proportionately so that the aggregate of the undivided shares is equal to the whole bulk.

(5) Where a buyer has paid the price for only some of the goods due to him out of a bulk, any delivery to the buyer out of the bulk shall, for the purposes of this section, be ascribed in the first place to the goods in respect of which payment has been made.

(6) For the purposes of this section payment of part of the price for any goods shall be treated as payment for a corresponding part of the goods.]

[971]

NOTES

Inserted, together with s 20B, by the Sale of Goods (Amendment) Act 1995, s 1(3).

[20B Deemed consent by co-owner to dealings in bulk goods

(1) A person who has become an owner in common of a bulk by virtue of section 20A above shall be deemed to have consented to—

    (a)   any delivery of goods out of the bulk to any other owner in common of the bulk, being goods which are due to him under his contract;

    (b)   any dealing with or removal, delivery or disposal of goods in the bulk by any other person who is an owner in common of the bulk in so far as the goods fall within that co-owner's undivided share in the bulk at the time of the dealing, removal, delivery or disposal.

(2) No cause of action shall accrue to anyone against a person by reason of that person having acted in accordance with paragraph (a) or (b) of subsection (1) above in reliance on any consent deemed to have been given under that subsection.

(3) Nothing in this section or section 20A above shall—

    (a)   impose an obligation on a buyer of goods out of a bulk to compensate any other buyer of goods out of that bulk for any shortfall in the goods received by that other buyer;

    (b)   affect any contractual arrangement between buyers of goods out of a bulk for adjustments between themselves; or

    (c)   affect the rights of any buyer under his contract.]

[972]

NOTES

Inserted as noted to s 20A at **[971]**.

Transfer of title

21 Sale by person not the owner

(1) Subject to this Act, where goods are sold by a person who is not their owner, and who does not sell them under the authority or with the consent of the owner, the buyer acquires no better title to the goods than the seller had, unless the owner of the goods is by his conduct precluded from denying the seller's authority to sell.

(2) Nothing in this Act affects—

    (a)   the provisions of the Factors Acts or any enactment enabling the apparent owner of goods to dispose of them as if he were their true owner;

    (b)   the validity of any contract of sale under any special common law or statutory power of sale or under the order of a court of competent jurisdiction.

[973]

22 Market overt

(1) ...

(2) This section does not apply to Scotland.

(3)   Paragraph 8 of Schedule 1 below applies in relation to a contract under which goods were sold before 1st January 1968 or (in the application of this Act to Northern Ireland) 29th August 1967.

[974]

NOTES
    Sub-s (1): repealed by the Sale of Goods (Amendment) Act 1994, ss 1, 3(2), in relation to any contract for sale of goods made after 3 January 1995.

23   Sale under voidable title

When the seller of goods has a voidable title to them, but his title has not been avoided at the time of the sale, the buyer acquires a good title to the goods, provided he buys them in good faith and without notice of the seller's defect of title.

[975]

24   Seller in possession after sale

Where a person having sold goods continues or is in possession of the goods, or of the documents of title to the goods, the delivery or transfer by that person, or by a mercantile agent acting for him, of the goods or documents of title under any sale, pledge, or other disposition thereof, to any person receiving the same in good faith and without notice of the previous sale, has the same effect as if the person making the delivery or transfer were expressly authorised by the owner of the goods to make the same.

[976]

25   Buyer in possession after sale

(1)   Where a person having bought or agreed to buy goods obtains, with the consent of the seller, possession of the goods or the documents of title to the goods, the delivery or transfer by that person, or by a mercantile agent acting for him, of the goods or documents of title, under any sale, pledge, or other disposition thereof, to any person receiving the same in good faith and without notice of any lien or other right of the original seller in respect of the goods, has the same effect as if the person making the delivery or transfer were a mercantile agent in possession of the goods or documents of title with the consent of the owner.

(2)   For the purposes of subsection (1) above—
    (a)   the buyer under a conditional sale agreement is to be taken not to be a person who has bought or agreed to buy goods, and
    (b)   "conditional sale agreement" means an agreement for the sale of goods which is a consumer credit agreement within the meaning of the Consumer Credit Act 1974 under which the purchase price or part of it is payable by instalments, and the property in the goods is to remain in the seller (notwithstanding that the buyer is to be in possession of the goods) until such conditions as to the payment of instalments or otherwise as may be specified in the agreement are fulfilled.

(3)   Paragraph 9 of Schedule 1 below applies in relation to a contract under which a person buys or agrees to buy goods and which is made before the appointed day.

(4)   In subsection (3) above and paragraph 9 of Schedule 1 below references to the appointed day are to the day appointed for the purposes of those provisions by an order of the Secretary of State made by statutory instrument.

[977]

NOTES
    Order: the Sale of Goods Act 1979 (Appointed Day) Order 1983, SI 1983/1572 (appointing 19 May 1985 for the purposes of sub-s (3)).

26   Supplementary to sections 24 and 25

In sections 24 and 25 above "mercantile agent" means a mercantile agent having in the customary course of his business as such agent authority either—
    (a)   to sell goods, or
    (b)   to consign goods for the purpose of sale, or
    (c)   to buy goods, or
    (d)   to raise money on the security of goods.

[978]

PART IV
PERFORMANCE OF THE CONTRACT

27 Duties of seller and buyer

It is the duty of the seller to deliver the goods, and of the buyer to accept and pay for them, in accordance with the terms of the contract of sale.

[979]

28 Payment and delivery are concurrent conditions

Unless otherwise agreed, delivery of the goods and payment of the price are concurrent conditions, that is to say, the seller must be ready and willing to give possession of the goods to the buyer in exchange for the price and the buyer must be ready and willing to pay the price in exchange for possession of the goods.

[980]

29 Rules about delivery

(1) Whether it is for the buyer to take possession of the goods or for the seller to send them to the buyer is a question depending in each case on the contract, express or implied, between the parties.

(2) Apart from any such contract, express or implied, the place of delivery is the seller's place of business if he has one, and if not, his residence; except that, if the contract is for the sale of specific goods, which to the knowledge of the parties when the contract is made are in some other place, then that place is the place of delivery.

(3) Where under the contract of sale the seller is bound to send the goods to the buyer, but no time for sending them is fixed, the seller is bound to send them within a reasonable time.

(4) Where the goods at the time of sale are in the possession of a third person, there is no delivery by seller to buyer unless and until the third person acknowledges to the buyer that he holds the goods on his behalf; but nothing in this section affects the operation of the issue or transfer of any document of title to goods.

(5) Demand or tender of delivery may be treated as ineffectual unless made at a reasonable hour; and what is a reasonable hour is a question of fact.

(6) Unless otherwise agreed, the expenses of and incidental to putting the goods into a deliverable state must be borne by the seller.

[981]

30 Delivery of wrong quantity

(1) Where the seller delivers to the buyer a quantity of goods less than he contracted to sell, the buyer may reject them, but if the buyer accepts the goods so delivered he must pay for them at the contract rate.

(2) Where the seller delivers to the buyer a quantity of goods larger than he contracted to sell, the buyer may accept the goods included in the contract and reject the rest, or he may reject the whole.

[(2A) A buyer who does not deal as consumer may not—
  (a) where the seller delivers a quantity of goods less than he contracted to sell, reject the goods under subsection (1) above, or
  (b) where the seller delivers a quantity of goods larger than he contracted to sell, reject the whole under subsection (2) above,
if the shortfall or, as the case may be, excess is so slight that it would be unreasonable for him to do so.

(2B) It is for the seller to show that a shortfall or excess fell within subsection (2A) above.

(2C) Subsections (2A) and (2B) above do not apply to Scotland.

(2D), (2E) *(Apply to Scotland only.)*]

(3) Where the seller delivers to the buyer a quantity of goods larger than he contracted to sell and the buyer accepts the whole of the goods so delivered he must pay for them at the contract rate.

(4) ...

(5) This section is subject to any usage of trade, special agreement, or course of dealing between the parties.

[982]

NOTES

Sub-ss (2A)–(2E): inserted by the Sale and Supply of Goods Act 1994, ss 4(2), 5(2).
Sub-s (4): repealed by the Sale and Supply of Goods Act 1994, ss 3(3), 7(2), Sch 3.

31   Instalment deliveries

(1)   Unless otherwise agreed, the buyer of goods is not bound to accept delivery of them by instalments.

(2)   Where there is a contract for the sale of goods to be delivered by stated instalments, which are to be separately paid for, and the seller makes defective deliveries in respect of one or more instalments, or the buyer neglects or refuses to take delivery of or pay for one or more instalments, it is a question in each case depending on the terms of the contract and the circumstances of the case whether the breach of contract is a repudiation of the whole contract or whether it is a severable breach giving rise to a claim for compensation but not to a right to treat the whole contract as repudiated.

[983]

32   Delivery to carrier

(1)   Where, in pursuance of a contract of sale, the seller is authorised or required to send the goods to the buyer, delivery of the goods to a carrier (whether named by the buyer or not) for the purpose of transmission to the buyer is prima facie deemed to be a delivery of the goods to the buyer.

(2)   Unless otherwise authorised by the buyer, the seller must make such contract with the carrier on behalf of the buyer as may be reasonable having regard to the nature of the goods and the other circumstances of the case; and if the seller omits to do so, and the goods are lost or damaged in course of transit, the buyer may decline to treat the delivery to the carrier as a delivery to himself or may hold the seller responsible in damages.

(3)   Unless otherwise agreed, where goods are sent by the seller to the buyer by a route involving sea transit, under circumstances in which it is usual to insure, the seller must give such notice to the buyer as may enable him to insure them during their sea transit; and if the seller fails to do so, the goods are at his risk during such sea transit.

[(4)   In a case where the buyer deals as consumer or, in Scotland, where there is a consumer contract in which the buyer is a consumer, subsections (1) to (3) above must be ignored, but if in pursuance of a contract of sale the seller is authorised or required to send the goods to the buyer, delivery of the goods to the carrier is not delivery of the goods to the buyer.]

[984]

NOTES

Sub-s (4): added by the Sale and Supply of Goods to Consumers Regulations 2002, SI 2002/3045, reg 4(3).

33   Risk where goods are delivered at distant place

Where the seller of goods agrees to deliver them at his own risk at a place other than that where they are when sold, the buyer must nevertheless (unless otherwise agreed) take any risk of deterioration in the goods necessarily incident to the course of transit.

[985]

34   Buyer's right of examining the goods

… Unless otherwise agreed, when the seller tenders delivery of goods to the buyer, he is bound on request to afford the buyer a reasonable opportunity of examining the goods for the purpose of ascertaining whether they are in conformity with the contract [and, in the case of a contract for sale by sample, of comparing the bulk with the sample.]

[986]

NOTES

Words omitted repealed, and words in square brackets added, by the Sale and Supply of Goods Act 1994, ss 2(2), 7(2), Sch 3.

35   Acceptance

(1)   The buyer is deemed to have accepted the goods [subject to subsection (2) below—
    (a)   when he intimates to the seller that he has accepted them, or
    (b)   when the goods have been delivered to him and he does any act in relation to them which is inconsistent with the ownership of the seller.

(2)   Where goods are delivered to the buyer, and he has not previously examined them, he is not deemed to have accepted them under subsection (1) above until he has had a reasonable opportunity of examining them for the purpose—
    (a)   of ascertaining whether they are in conformity with the contract, and
    (b)   in the case of a contract for sale by sample, of comparing the bulk with the sample.

(3)   Where the buyer deals as consumer or (in Scotland) the contract of sale is a consumer contract, the buyer cannot lose his right to rely on subsection (2) above by agreement, waiver or otherwise.

(4)   The buyer is also deemed to have accepted the goods when after the lapse of a reasonable time he retains the goods without intimating to the seller that he has rejected them.

(5)   The questions that are material in determining for the purposes of subsection (4) above whether a reasonable time has elapsed include whether the buyer has had a reasonable opportunity of examining the goods for the purpose mentioned in subsection (2) above.

(6)   The buyer is not by virtue of this section deemed to have accepted the goods merely because—
    (a)   he asks for, or agrees to, their repair by or under an arrangement with the seller, or
    (b)   the goods are delivered to another under a sub-sale or other disposition.

(7)   Where the contract is for the sale of goods making one or more commercial units, a buyer accepting any goods included in a unit is deemed to have accepted all the goods making the unit; and in this subsection "commercial unit" means a unit division of which would materially impair the value of the goods or the character of the unit.

(8)]   Paragraph 10 of Schedule 1 below applies in relation to a contract made before 22nd April 1967 or (in the application of this Act of Northern Ireland) 28th July 1967.

[987]

NOTES
Words in square brackets substituted by the Sale and Supply of Goods Act 1994, s 2(1).

[35A   Right of partial rejection

(1)   If the buyer—
    (a)   has the right to reject the goods by reason of a breach on the part of the seller that affects some or all of them, but
    (b)   accepts some of the goods, including, where there are any goods unaffected by the breach, all such goods,
he does not by accepting them lose his right to reject the rest.

(2)   In the case of a buyer having the right to reject an instalment of goods, subsection (1) above applies as if references to the goods were references to the goods comprised in the instalment.

(3)   For the purposes of subsection (1) above, goods are affected by a breach if by reason of the breach they are not in conformity with the contract.

(4)   This section applies unless a contrary intention appears in, or is to be implied from, the contract.]

[988]

NOTES
Inserted by the Sale and Supply of Goods Act 1994, s 3(1).

36   Buyer not bound to return rejected goods

Unless otherwise agreed, where goods are delivered to the buyer, and he refuses to accept them, having the right to do so, he is not bound to return them to the seller, but it is sufficient if he intimates to the seller that he refuses to accept them.

[989]

37   Buyer's liability for not taking delivery of goods

(1)   When the seller is ready and willing to deliver the goods, and requests the buyer to take delivery, and the buyer does not within a reasonable time after such request take delivery of the goods, he is liable to the seller for any loss occasioned by his neglect or refusal to take delivery, and also for a reasonable charge for the care and custody of the goods.

(2)   Nothing in this section affects the rights of the seller where the neglect or refusal of the buyer to take delivery amounts to a repudiation of the contract.

[990]

PART V
RIGHTS OF UNPAID SELLER AGAINST THE GOODS

Preliminary

38   Unpaid seller defined

(1)   The seller of goods is an unpaid seller within the meaning of this Act—
    (a)   when the whole of the price has not been paid or tendered;
    (b)   when a bill of exchange or other negotiable instrument has been received as conditional payment, and the condition on which it was received has not been fulfilled by reason of the dishonour of the instrument or otherwise.

(2)   In this Part of this Act "seller" includes any person who is in the position of a seller, as, for instance, an agent of the seller to whom the bill of lading has been indorsed, or a consignor or agent who has himself paid (or is directly responsible for) the price.

[991]

39 Unpaid seller's rights

(1)   Subject to this and any other Act, notwithstanding that the property in the goods may have passed to the buyer, the unpaid seller of goods, as such, has by implication of law—
    (a)   a lien on the goods or right to retain them for the price while he is in possession of them;
    (b)   in case of the insolvency of the buyer, a right of stopping the goods in transit after he has parted with the possession of them;
    (c)   a right of re-sale as limited by this Act.

(2)   Where the property in goods has not passed to the buyer, the unpaid seller has (in addition to his other remedies) a right of withholding delivery similar to and co-extensive with his rights of lien or retention and stoppage in transit where the property has passed to the buyer.

[992]

40   (*Repealed by the Debtors (Scotland) Act 1987, s 108(3), Sch 8.*)

Unpaid seller's lien

41 Seller's lien

(1)   Subject to this Act, the unpaid seller of goods who is in possession of them is entitled to retain possession of them until payment or tender of the price in the following cases:—
    (a)   where the goods have been sold without any stipulation as to credit;
    (b)   where the goods have been sold on credit but the term of credit has expired;
    (c)   where the buyer becomes insolvent.

(2)   The seller may exercise his lien or right of retention notwithstanding that he is in possession of the goods as agent or bailee or custodier for the buyer.

[993]

42 Part delivery

Where an unpaid seller has made part delivery of the goods, he may exercise his lien or right of retention on the remainder, unless such part delivery has been made under such circumstances as to show an agreement to waive the lien or right of retention.

[994]

43 Termination of lien

(1)   The unpaid seller of goods loses his lien or right of retention in respect of them—
    (a)   when he delivers the goods to a carrier or other bailee or custodier for the purpose of transmission to the buyer without reserving the right of disposal of the goods;
    (b)   when the buyer or his agent lawfully obtains possession of the goods;
    (c)   by waiver of the lien or right of retention.

(2)   An unpaid seller of goods who has a lien or right of retention in respect of them does not lose his lien or right of retention by reason only that he has obtained judgment or decree for the price of the goods.

[995]

Stoppage in transit

44 Right of stoppage in transit

Subject to this Act, when the buyer of goods becomes insolvent the unpaid seller who has parted with the possession of the goods has the right of stopping them in transit, that is to say, he may resume possession of the goods as long as they are in course of transit, and may retain them until payment or tender of the price.

[996]

45 Duration of transit

(1)   Goods are deemed to be in course of transit from the time when they are delivered to a carrier or other bailee or custodier for the purpose of transmission to the buyer, until the buyer or his agent in that behalf takes delivery of them from the carrier or other bailee or custodier.

(2)   If the buyer or his agent in that behalf obtains delivery of the goods before their arrival at the appointed destination, the transit is at an end.

(3)   If, after the arrival of the goods at the appointed destination, the carrier or other bailee or custodier acknowledges to the buyer or his agent that he holds the goods on his behalf and continues

in possession of them as bailee or custodier for the buyer or his agent, the transit is at an end, and it is immaterial that a further destination for the goods may have been indicated by the buyer.

(4)   If the goods are rejected by the buyer, and the carrier or other bailee or custodier continues in possession of them, the transit is not deemed to be at an end, even if the seller has refused to receive them back.

(5)   When goods are delivered to a ship chartered by the buyer it is a question depending on the circumstances of the particular case whether they are in the possession of the master as a carrier or as agent to the buyer.

(6)   Where the carrier or other bailee or custodier wrongfully refuses to deliver the goods to the buyer or his agent in that behalf, the transit is deemed to be at an end.

(7)   Where part delivery of the goods has been made to the buyer or his agent in that behalf, the remainder of the goods may be stopped in transit, unless such part delivery has been made under such circumstances as to show an agreement to give up possession of the whole of the goods.

[997]

46   How stoppage in transit is effected

(1)   The unpaid seller may exercise his right of stoppage in transit either by taking actual possession of the goods or by giving notice of his claim to the carrier or other bailee or custodier in whose possession the goods are.

(2)   The notice may be given either to the person in actual possession of the goods or to his principal.

(3)   If given to the principal, the notice is ineffective unless given at such time and under such circumstances that the principal, by the exercise of reasonable diligence, may communicate it to his servant or agent in time to prevent a delivery to the buyer.

(4)   When notice of stoppage in transit is given by the seller to the carrier or other bailee or custodier in possession of the goods, he must re-deliver the goods to, or according to the directions of, the seller; and the expenses of the re-delivery must be borne by the seller.

[998]

Re-sale etc by buyer

47   Effect of sub-sale etc by buyer

(1)   Subject to this Act, the unpaid seller's right of lien or retention or stoppage in transit is not affected by any sale or other disposition of the goods which the buyer may have made, unless the seller has assented to it.

(2)   Where a document of title to goods has been lawfully transferred to any person as buyer or owner of the goods, and that person transfers the document to a person who takes it in good faith and for valuable consideration, then—

(a)   if the last-mentioned transfer was by way of sale the unpaid seller's right of lien or retention or stoppage in transit is defeated; and

(b)   if the last-mentioned transfer was made by way of pledge or other disposition for value, the unpaid seller's right of lien or retention or stoppage in transit can only be exercised subject to the rights of the transferee.

[999]

Rescission: and re-sale by seller

48   Rescission: and re-sale by seller

(1)   Subject to this section, a contract of sale is not rescinded by the mere exercise by an unpaid seller of his right of lien or retention or stoppage in transit.

(2)   Where an unpaid seller who has exercised his right of lien or retention or stoppage in transit re-sells the goods, the buyer acquires a good title to them as against the original buyer.

(3)   Where the goods are of a perishable nature, or where the unpaid seller gives notice to the buyer of his intention to re-sell, and the buyer does not within a reasonable time pay or tender the price, the unpaid seller may re-sell the goods and recover from the original buyer damages for any loss occasioned by his breach of contract.

(4)   Where the seller expressly reserves the right of re-sale in case the buyer should make default, and on the buyer making default re-sells the goods, the original contract of sale is rescinded but without prejudice to any claim the seller may have for damages.

[1000]

[PART VA
ADDITIONAL RIGHTS OF BUYER IN CONSUMER CASES

48A Introductory

(1)   This section applies if—
  (a)   the buyer deals as consumer or, in Scotland, there is a consumer contract in which the buyer is a consumer, and
  (b)   the goods do not conform to the contract of sale at the time of delivery.

(2)   If this section applies, the buyer has the right—
  (a)   under and in accordance with section 48B below, to require the seller to repair or replace the goods, or
  (b)   under and in accordance with section 48C below—
     (i)   to require the seller to reduce the purchase price of the goods to the buyer by an appropriate amount, or
     (ii)   to rescind the contract with regard to the goods in question.

(3)   For the purposes of subsection (1)(b) above goods which do not conform to the contract of sale at any time within the period of six months starting with the date on which the goods were delivered to the buyer must be taken not to have so conformed at that date.

(4)   Subsection (3) above does not apply if—
  (a)   it is established that the goods did so conform at that date;
  (b)   its application is incompatible with the nature of the goods or the nature of the lack of conformity.]

[1001]

NOTES
Part VA (ss 48A–48F) inserted by the Sale and Supply of Goods to Consumers Regulations 2002, SI 2002/3045, reg 5.

[48B Repair or replacement of the goods

(1)   If section 48A above applies, the buyer may require the seller—
  (a)   to repair the goods, or
  (b)   to replace the goods.

(2)   If the buyer requires the seller to repair or replace the goods, the seller must—
  (a)   repair or, as the case may be, replace the goods within a reasonable time but without causing significant inconvenience to the buyer;
  (b)   bear any necessary costs incurred in doing so (including in particular the cost of any labour, materials or postage).

(3)   The buyer must not require the seller to repair or, as the case may be, replace the goods if that remedy is—
  (a)   impossible, or
  (b)   disproportionate in comparison to the other of those remedies, or
  (c)   disproportionate in comparison to an appropriate reduction in the purchase price under paragraph (a), or rescission under paragraph (b), of section 48C(1) below.

(4)   One remedy is disproportionate in comparison to the other if the one imposes costs on the seller which, in comparison to those imposed on him by the other, are unreasonable, taking into account—
  (a)   the value which the goods would have if they conformed to the contract of sale,
  (b)   the significance of the lack of conformity, and
  (c)   whether the other remedy could be effected without significant inconvenience to the buyer.

(5)   Any question as to what is a reasonable time or significant inconvenience is to be determined by reference to—
  (a)   the nature of the goods, and
  (b)   the purpose for which the goods were acquired.]

[1002]

NOTES
Inserted as noted to s 48A at **[1001]**.

[48C Reduction of purchase price or rescission of contract

(1)   If section 48A above applies, the buyer may—
  (a)   require the seller to reduce the purchase price of the goods in question to the buyer by an appropriate amount, or
  (b)   rescind the contract with regard to those goods,

if the condition in subsection (2) below is satisfied.

   (2)   The condition is that—

     (a)   by virtue of section 48B(3) above the buyer may require neither repair nor replacement of the goods; or

     (b)   the buyer has required the seller to repair or replace the goods, but the seller is in breach of the requirement of section 48B(2)(a) above to do so within a reasonable time and without significant inconvenience to the buyer.

   (3)   For the purposes of this Part, if the buyer rescinds the contract, any reimbursement to the buyer may be reduced to take account of the use he has had of the goods since they were delivered to him.]

[1003]

NOTES
   Inserted as noted to s 48A at **[1001]**.

[48D   Relation to other remedies etc

   (1)   If the buyer requires the seller to repair or replace the goods the buyer must not act under subsection (2) until he has given the seller a reasonable time in which to repair or replace (as the case may be) the goods.

   (2)   The buyer acts under this subsection if—

     (a)   in England and Wales or Northern Ireland he rejects the goods and terminates the contract for breach of condition;

     (b)   in Scotland he rejects any goods delivered under the contract and treats it as repudiated;

     (c)   he requires the goods to be replaced or repaired (as the case may be).]

[1004]

NOTES
   Inserted as noted to s 48A at **[1001]**.

[48E   Powers of the court

   (1)   In any proceedings in which a remedy is sought by virtue of this Part the court, in addition to any other power it has, may act under this section.

   (2)   On the application of the buyer the court may make an order requiring specific performance or, in Scotland, specific implement by the seller of any obligation imposed on him by virtue of section 48B above.

   (3)   Subsection (4) applies if—

     (a)   the buyer requires the seller to give effect to a remedy under section 48B or 48C above or has claims to rescind under section 48C, but

     (b)   the court decides that another remedy under section 48B or 48C is appropriate.

   (4)   The court may proceed—

     (a)   as if the buyer had required the seller to give effect to the other remedy, or if the other remedy is rescission under section 48C

     (b)   as if the buyer had claimed to rescind the contract under that section.

   (5)   If the buyer has claimed to rescind the contract the court may order that any reimbursement to the buyer is reduced to take account of the use he has had of the goods since they were delivered to him.

   (6)   The court may make an order under this section unconditionally or on such terms and conditions as to damages, payment of the price and otherwise as it thinks just.]

[1005]

NOTES
   Inserted as noted to s 48A at **[1001]**.

[48F   Conformity with the contract

For the purposes of this Part, goods do not conform to a contract of sale if there is, in relation to the goods, a breach of an express term of the contract or a term implied by section 13, 14 or 15 above.]

[1006]

NOTES
   Inserted as noted to s 48A at **[1001]**.

PART VI
ACTIONS FOR BREACH OF THE CONTRACT

Seller's remedies

49 Action for price

(1)   Where, under a contract of sale, the property in the goods has passed to the buyer and he wrongfully neglects or refuses to pay for the goods according to the terms of the contract, the seller may maintain an action against him for the price of the goods.

(2)   Where, under a contract of sale, the price is payable on a day certain irrespective of delivery and the buyer wrongfully neglects or refuses to pay such price, the seller may maintain an action for the price, although the property in the goods has not passed and the goods have not been appropriated to the contract.

(3)   (*Applies to Scotland only.*)

[1007]

50 Damages for non-acceptance

(1)   Where the buyer wrongfully neglects or refuses to accept and pay for the goods, the seller may maintain an action against him for damages for non-acceptance.

(2)   The measure of damages is the estimated loss directly and naturally resulting, in the ordinary course of events, from the buyer's breach of contract.

(3)   Where there is an available market for the goods in question the measure of damages is prima facie to be ascertained by the difference between the contract price and the market or current price at the time or times when the goods ought to have been accepted or (if no time was fixed for acceptance) at the time of the refusal to accept.

[1008]

Buyer's remedies

51 Damages for non-delivery

(1)   Where the seller wrongfully neglects or refuses to deliver the goods to the buyer, the buyer may maintain an action against the seller for damages for non-delivery.

(2)   The measure of damages is the estimated loss directly and naturally resulting, in the ordinary course of events, from the seller's breach of contract.

(3)   Where there is an available market for the goods in question the measure of damages is prima facie to be ascertained by the difference between the contract price and the market or current price of the goods at the time or times when they ought to have been delivered or (if no time was fixed) at the time of the refusal to deliver.

[1009]

52 Specific performance

(1)   In any action for breach of contract to deliver specific or ascertained goods the court may, if it thinks fit, on the plaintiff's application, by its judgment or decree direct that the contract shall be performed specifically, without giving the defendant the option of retaining the goods on payment of damages.

(2)   The plaintiff's application may be made at any time before judgment or decree.

(3)   The judgment or decree may be unconditional, or on such terms and conditions as to damages, payment of the price and otherwise as seem just to the court.

(4)   (*Applies to Scotland only.*)

[1010]

53 Remedy for breach of warranty

(1)   Where there is a breach of warranty by the seller, or where the buyer elects (or is compelled) to treat any breach of a condition on the part of the seller as a breach of warranty, the buyer is not by reason only of such breach of warranty entitled to reject the goods; but he may—

(a)   set up against the seller the breach of warranty in diminution or extinction of the price, or

(b)   maintain an action against the seller for damages for the breach of warranty.

(2)   The measure of damages for breach of warranty is the estimated loss directly and naturally resulting, in the ordinary course of events, from the breach of warranty.

(3)   In the case of breach of warranty of quality such loss is prima facie the difference between the value of the goods at the time of delivery to the buyer and the value they would have had if they had fulfilled the warranty.

(4)   The fact that the buyer has set up the breach of warranty in diminution or extinction of the price does not prevent him from maintaining an action for the same breach of warranty if he has suffered further damage.

[(5)   This section does not apply to Scotland.]

[1011]

NOTES

Sub-s (5): substituted by the Sale and Supply of Goods Act 1994, s 7(1), Sch 2, para 5(1), (7).

53A   *(Inserted by the Sale and Supply of Goods Act 1994, s 5(3) and applies to Scotland only.)*

Interest, etc

54 Interest

Nothing in this Act affects the right of the buyer or the seller to recover interest or special damages in any case where by law interest or special damages may be recoverable, or to recover money paid where the consideration for the payment of it has failed.

[1012]

PART VII
SUPPLEMENTARY

55 Exclusion of implied terms

(1)   Where a right, duty or liability would arise under a contract of sale of goods by implication of law, it may (subject to the Unfair Contract Terms Act 1977) be negatived or varied by express agreement, or by the course of dealing between the parties, or by such usage as binds both parties to the contract.

(2)   An express [term] does not negative a [term] implied by this Act unless inconsistent with it.

(3)   Paragraph 11 of Schedule 1 below applies in relation to a contract made on or after 18th May 1973 and before 1st February 1978, and paragraph 12 in relation to one made before 18th May 1973.

[1013]

NOTES

Sub-s (2): words in square brackets substituted by the Sale and Supply of Goods Act 1994, s 7(1), Sch 2, para 5(1), (8).

56 Conflict of laws

Paragraph 13 of Schedule 1 below applies in relation to a contract made on or after 18th May 1973 and before 1st February 1978, so as to make provision about conflict of laws in relation to such a contract.

[1014]

57 Auction sales

(1)   Where goods are put up for sale by auction in lots, each lot is prima facie deemed to be the subject of a separate contract of sale.

(2)   A sale by auction is complete when the auctioneer announces its completion by the fall of the hammer, or in other customary manner; and until the announcement is made any bidder may retract his bid.

(3)   A sale by auction may be notified to be subject to a reserve or upset price, and a right to bid may also be reserved expressly by or on behalf of the seller.

(4)   Where a sale by auction is not notified to be subject to a right to bid by or on behalf of the seller, it is not lawful for the seller to bid himself or to employ any person to bid at the sale, or for the auctioneer knowingly to take any bid from the seller or any such person.

(5)   A sale contravening subsection (4) above may be treated as fraudulent by the buyer.

(6)   Where, in respect of a sale by auction, a right to bid is expressly reserved (but not otherwise) the seller or any one person on his behalf may bid at the auction.

[1015]

58 *(Applies to Scotland only.)*

59 Reasonable time a question of fact

Where a reference is made in this Act to a reasonable time the question what is a reasonable time is a question of fact.

[1016]

60 Rights etc enforceable by action

Where a right, duty or liability is declared by this Act, it may (unless otherwise provided by this Act) be enforced by action.

[1017]

61 Interpretation

(1)   In this Act, unless the context or subject matter otherwise requires—

"action" includes counterclaim and set-off, and in Scotland condescendence and claim and compensation;

["bulk" means a mass or collection of goods of the same kind which—

   (a)   is contained in a defined space or area; and

   (b)   is such that any goods in the bulk are interchangeable with any other goods therein of the same number or quantity;]

"business" includes a profession and the activities of any government department (including a Northern Ireland department) or local or public authority;

"buyer" means a person who buys or agrees to buy goods;

["consumer contract" has the same meaning as in section 25(1) of the Unfair Contract Terms Act 1977; and for the purposes of this Act the onus of proving that a contract is not to be regarded as a consumer contract shall lie on the seller]

"contract of sale" includes an agreement to sell as well as a sale;

"credit-broker" means a person acting in the course of a business of credit brokerage carried on by him, that is a business of effecting introductions of individuals desiring to obtain credit—

   (a)   to persons carrying on any business so far as it relates to the provision of credit, or

   (b)   to other persons engaged in credit brokerage;

.....

"delivery" means voluntary transfer of possession from one person to another [except that in relation to sections 20A and 20B above it includes such appropriation of goods to the contract as results in property in the goods being transferred to the buyer;]

"document of title to goods" has the same meaning as it has in the Factors Acts;

"Factors Acts" means the Factors Act 1889, the Factors (Scotland) Act 1890, and any enactment amending or substituted for the same;

"fault" means wrongful act or default;

"future goods" means goods to be manufactured or acquired by the seller after the making of the contract of sale;

"goods" includes all personal chattels other than things in action and money, and in Scotland all corporeal moveables except money; and in particular "goods" includes emblements, industrial growing crops, and things attached to or forming part of the land which are agreed to be severed before sale or under the contract of sale [and includes an undivided share in goods;]

"plaintiff" includes pursuer, complainer, claimant in a multiplepoinding and defendant or defender counter-claiming;

["producer" means the manufacturer of goods, the importer of goods into the European Economic Area or any person purporting to be a producer by placing his name, trade mark or other distinctive sign on the goods;]

"property" means the general property in goods, and not merely a special property;

.....

["repair" means, in cases where there is a lack of conformity in goods for the purposes of section 48F of this Act, to bring the goods into conformity with the contract;]

"sale" includes a bargain and sale as well as a sale and delivery;

"seller" means a person who sells or agrees to sell goods;

"specific goods" means goods identified and agreed on at the time a contract of sale is made [and includes an undivided share, specified as a fraction or percentage, of goods identified and agreed on as aforesaid];

"warranty" (as regards England and Wales and Northern Ireland) means an agreement with reference to goods which are the subject of a contract of sale, but collateral to the main purpose of such contract, the breach of which gives rise to a claim for damages, but not to a right to reject the goods and treat the contract as repudiated.

(2)   ...

(3)   A thing is deemed to be done in good faith within the meaning of this Act when it is in fact done honestly, whether it is done negligently or not.

(4)   A person is deemed to be insolvent within the meaning of this Act if has either ceased to pay his debts in the ordinary course of business or he cannot pay his debts as they become due, ...

(5)   Goods are in a deliverable state within the meaning of this Act when they are in such a state that the buyer would under the contract be bound to take delivery of them.

[(5A)   References in this Act to dealing as consumer are to be construed in accordance with Part I of the Unfair Contract Terms Act 1977; and, for the purposes of this Act, it is for a seller claiming that the buyer does not deal as consumer to show that he does not.]

(6)   As regards the definition of "business" in subsection (1) above, paragraph 14 of Schedule 1 below applies in relation to a contract made on or after 18th May 1973 and before 1st February 1978, and paragraph 15 in relation to one made before 18th May 1973.

[1018]

NOTES
    Sub-s (1): definition "bulk" inserted, and words in square brackets in definitions "delivery", "goods" and "specific goods" added, by the Sale of Goods (Amendment) Act 1995, s 2; definition "consumer contract" inserted, and definition "quality" (omitted) repealed, by the Sale and Supply of Goods Act 1994, s 7, Sch 2, para 5(1), (9)(a), Sch 3; first definition omitted applies to Scotland only; definitions "producer" and "repair" inserted by the Sale and Supply of Goods to Consumers Regulations 2002, SI 2002/3045, reg 6.
    Sub-s (2): repealed by the Sale and Supply of Goods Act 1994, s 7, Sch 2, para 5(1), (9)(b), Sch 3.
    Sub-s (4): words omitted repealed by the Insolvency Act 1985, s 235, Sch 10, Pt III, the Bankruptcy (Scotland) Act 1985, s 75(2), Sch 8, and the Insolvency Act 1986, s 437, Sch 11, Pt II.
    Sub-s (5A): inserted by the Sale and Supply of Goods Act 1994, s 7, Sch 2, para 5(9)(c).

62   Savings: rules of law etc

(1)   The rules in bankruptcy relating to contracts of sale apply to those contracts, notwithstanding anything in this Act.

(2)   The rules of the common law, including the law merchant, except in so far as they are inconsistent with the provisions of this Act, and in particular the rules relating to the law of principal and agent and the effect of fraud, misrepresentation, duress or coercion, mistake, or other invalidating cause, apply to contracts for the sale of goods.

(3)   Nothing in this Act or the Sale of Goods Act 1893 affects the enactments relating to bills of sale, or any enactment relating to the sale of goods which is not expressly repealed or amended by this Act or that.

(4)   The provisions of this Act about contracts of sale do not apply to a transaction in the form of a contract of sale which is intended to operate by way of mortgage, pledge, charge, or other security.

(5)   (*Applies to Scotland only.*)

[1019]

NOTES
    Sale of Goods Act 1893: mostly repealed by s 63(2) of, Sch 3 to, this Act; remainder repealed by the Supreme Court Act 1981, s 152(4), Sch 7.

63   Consequential amendments, repeals and savings

(1)   Without prejudice to section 17 of the Interpretation Act 1978 (repeal and re-enactment), the enactments mentioned in Schedule 2 below have effect subject to the amendments there specified (being amendments consequential on this Act).

(2)   The enactments mentioned in Schedule 3 below are repealed to the extent specified in column 3, but subject to the savings in Schedule 4 below.

(3)   The savings in Schedule 4 below have effect.

[1020]

64   Short title and commencement

(1)   This Act may be cited as the Sale of Goods Act 1979.

(2)   This Act comes into force on 1 January 1980.

[1021]

(*Sch 1 (Modification of this Act for certain contracts), Sch 2 (Consequential amendments), (Sch 3 (Repeals), Sch 4 (Savings) outside the scope of this work.*)

PROTECTION OF TRADING INTERESTS ACT 1980

(1980 c 11)

ARRANGEMENT OF SECTIONS

An Act to provide protection from requirements, prohibitions and judgments imposed or given under the laws of countries outside the United Kingdom and affecting the trading or other interests of persons in the United Kingdom

[20 March 1980]

1 Overseas measures affecting United Kingdom trading interests

(1)   If it appears to the Secretary of State—

(a)   that measures have been or are proposed to be taken by or under the law of any overseas country for regulating or controlling international trade; and

(b)   that those measures, in so far as they apply or would apply to things done or to be done outside the territorial jurisdiction of that country by persons carrying on business in the United Kingdom, are damaging or threaten to damage the trading interests of the United Kingdom,

the Secretary of State may by order direct that this section shall apply to those measures either generally or in their application to such cases as may be specified in the order.

(2)   The Secretary of State may by order make provision for requiring, or enabling the Secretary of State to require, a person in the United Kingdom who carries on business there to give notice to the Secretary of State of any requirement or prohibition imposed or threatened to be imposed on that person pursuant to any measures in so far as this section applies to them by virtue of an order under subsection (1) above.

(3)   The Secretary of State may give to any person in the United Kingdom who carries on business there such directions for prohibiting compliance with any such requirement or prohibition as aforesaid as he considers appropriate for avoiding damage to the trading interests of the United Kingdom.

(4)   The power of the Secretary of State to make orders under subsection (1) or (2) above shall be exercisable by statutory instrument subject to annulment in pursuance of a resolution of either House of Parliament.

(5)   Directions under subsection (3) above may be either general or special and may prohibit compliance with any requirement or prohibition either absolutely or in such cases or subject to such conditions as to consent or otherwise as may be specified in the directions; and general directions under that subsection shall be published in such manner as appears to the Secretary of State to be appropriate.

(6)   In this section "trade" includes any activity carried on in the course of a business of any description and "trading interests" shall be construed accordingly.

[1022]

NOTES

Orders: the Protection of Trading Interests (US Re-export Control) Order 1982, SI 1982/885; the Protection of Trading Interests (US Antitrust Measures) Order 1983, SI 1983/900; the Protection of Trading Interests (US Cuban Assets Control Regulations) Order 1992, SI 1992/2449.

2 Documents and information required by overseas courts and authorities

(1)   If it appears to the Secretary of State—

(a)   that a requirement has been or may be imposed on a person or persons in the United Kingdom to produce to any court, tribunal or authority of an overseas country any commercial document which is not within the territorial jurisdiction of that country or to furnish any commercial information to any such court, tribunal or authority; or

(b)   that any such authority has imposed or may impose a requirement on a person or persons in the United Kingdom to publish any such document or information,

the Secretary of State may, if it appears to him that the requirement is inadmissible by virtue of subsection (2) or (3) below, give directions for prohibiting compliance with the requirement.

(2)   A requirement such as is mentioned in subsection (1)(a) or (b) above is inadmissible—

(a)   if it infringes the jurisdiction of the United Kingdom or is otherwise prejudicial to the sovereignty of the United Kingdom; or

(b)   if compliance with the requirement would be prejudicial to the security of the United Kingdom or to the relations of the government of the United Kingdom with the government of any other country.

(3)   A requirement such as is mentioned in subsection (1)(a) above is also inadmissible—

(a) if it is made otherwise than for the purposes of civil or criminal proceedings which have been instituted in the overseas country; or

(b) if it requires a person to state what documents relevant to any such proceedings are or have been in his possession, custody or power or to produce for the purposes of any such proceedings any documents other than particular documents specified in the requirement.

(4) Directions under subsection (1) above may be either general or special and may prohibit compliance with any requirement either absolutely or in such cases or subject to such conditions as to consent or otherwise as may be specified in the directions; and general directions under that subsection shall be published in such manner as appears to the Secretary of State to be appropriate.

(5) For the purposes of this section the making of a request or demand shall be treated as the imposition of a requirement if it is made in circumstances in which a requirement to the same effect could be or could have been imposed; and

(a) any request or demand for the supply of a document or information which, pursuant to the requirement of any court, tribunal or authority of an overseas country, is addressed to a person in the United Kingdom; or

(b) any requirement imposed by such a court, tribunal or authority to produce or furnish any document or information to a person specified in the requirement,

shall be treated as a requirement to produce or furnish that document or information to that court, tribunal or authority.

(6) In this section "commercial document" and "commercial information" mean respectively a document or information relating to a business of any description and "document" includes any record or device by means of which material is recorded or stored.

[1023]

3 Offences under ss 1 and 2

(1) Subject to subsection (2) below, any person who without reasonable excuse fails to comply with any requirement imposed under subsection (2) of section 1 above or knowingly contravenes any directions given under subsection (3) of that section or section 2(1) above shall be guilty of an offence and liable—

(a) on conviction on indictment, to a fine;

(b) on summary conviction, to a fine not exceeding the statutory maximum.

(2) A person who is neither a citizen of the United Kingdom and Colonies nor a body corporate incorporated in the United Kingdom shall not be guilty of an offence under subsection (1) above by reason of anything done or omitted outside the United Kingdom in contravention of directions under section 1(3) or 2(1) above.

(3) No proceedings for an offence under subsection (1) above shall be instituted in England, Wales or Northern Ireland except by the Secretary of State or with the consent of the Attorney General or, as the case may be, the Attorney General for Northern Ireland.

(4) Proceedings against any person for an offence under this section may be taken before the appropriate court in the United Kingdom having jurisdiction in the place where that person is for the time being.

(5) ...

[1024]

NOTES

Sub-s (5): repealed by the Statute Law (Repeals) Act 1993.

---

4 Restriction of Evidence (Proceedings in Other Jurisdictions) Act 1975

A court in the United Kingdom shall not make an order under section 2 of the Evidence (Proceedings in Other Jurisdictions) Act 1975 for giving effect to a request issued by or on behalf of a court or tribunal of an overseas country if it is shown that the request infringes the jurisdiction of the United Kingdom or is otherwise prejudicial to the sovereignty of the United Kingdom; and a certificate signed by or on behalf of the Secretary of State to the effect that it infringes that jurisdiction or is so prejudicial shall be conclusive evidence of that fact.

[1025]

5 Restriction on enforcement of certain overseas judgments

(1) A judgment to which this section applies shall not be registered under Part II of the Administration of Justice Act 1920 or Part I of the Foreign Judgments (Reciprocal Enforcement) Act 1933 and no court in the United Kingdom shall entertain proceedings at common law for the recovery of any sum payable under such a judgment.

(2) This section applies to any judgment given by a court of an overseas country, being—

(a) a judgment for multiple damages within the meaning of subsection (3) below;

(b)   a judgment based on a provision or rule of law specified or described in an order under subsection (4) below and given after the coming into force of the order; or

(c)   a judgment on a claim for contribution in respect of damages awarded by a judgment falling within paragraph (a) or (b) above.

(3)   In subsection (2)(a) above a judgment for multiple damages means a judgment for an amount arrived at by doubling, trebling or otherwise multiplying a sum assessed as compensation for the loss or damage sustained by the person in whose favour the judgment is given.

(4)   The Secretary of State may for the purposes of subsection (2)(b) above make an order in respect of any provision or rule of law which appears to him to be concerned with the prohibition or regulation of agreements, arrangements or practices designed to restrain, distort or restrict competition in the carrying on of business of any description or to be otherwise concerned with the promotion of such competition as aforesaid.

(5)   The power of the Secretary of State to make orders under subsection (4) above shall be exercisable by statutory instrument subject to annulment in pursuance of a resolution of either House of Parliament.

(6)   Subsection (2)(a) above applies to a judgement given before the date of the passing of this Act as well as to a judgment given on or after that date but this section does not affect any judgment which has been registered before that date under the provisions mentioned in subsection (1) above or in respect of which such proceedings as are there mentioned have been finally determined before that date.

[1026]

NOTES

Orders: the Protection of Trading Interests (Australian Trade Practices) Order 1988, SI 1988/569.

6 Recovery of awards of multiple damages

(1)   This section applies where a court of an overseas country has given a judgment for multiple damages with the meaning of section 5(3) above against—

(a)   a citizen of the United Kingdom and Colonies; or

(b)   a body corporate incorporated in the United Kingdom or in a territory outside the United Kingdom for whose international relations Her Majesty's Government in the United Kingdom are responsible; or

(c)   a person carrying on business in the United Kingdom,

(in this section referred to as a "qualifying defendant") and an amount on account of the damages has been paid by the qualifying defendant either to the party in whose favour the judgment was given or to another party who is entitled as against the qualifying defendant to contribution in respect of the damages.

(2)   Subject to subsections (3) and (4) below, the qualifying defendant shall be entitled to recover from the party in whose favour the judgment was given so much of the amount referred to in subsection (1) above as exceeds the part attributable to compensation; and that part shall be taken to be such part of the amount as bears to the whole of it the same proportion as the sum assessed by the court that gave the judgment as compensation for the loss or damage sustained by that party bears to the whole of the damages awarded to that party.

(3)   Subsection (2) above does not apply where the qualifying defendant is an individual who was ordinarily resident in the overseas country at the time when the proceedings in which the judgment was given were instituted or a body corporate which had its principal place of business there at that time.

(4)   Subsection (2) above does not apply where the qualifying defendant carried on business in the overseas country and the proceedings in which the judgment was given were concerned with activities exclusively carried on in that country.

(5)   A court in the United Kingdom may entertain proceedings on a claim under this section notwithstanding that the person against whom the proceedings are brought is not within the jurisdiction of the court.

(6)   The reference in subsection (1) above to an amount paid by the qualifying defendant includes a reference to an amount obtained by execution against his property or against the property of a company which (directly or indirectly) is wholly owned by him; and references in that subsection and subsection (2) above to the party in whose favour the judgment was given or to a party entitled to contribution include references to any person in whom the rights of any such party have become vested by succession or assignment or otherwise.

(7)   This section shall, with the necessary modifications, apply also in relation to any order which is made by a tribunal or authority of an overseas country and would, if that tribunal or authority were a court, be a judgment for multiple damages within the meaning of section 5(3) above.

(8)   This section does not apply to any judgment given or order made before the passing of this Act.

[1027]

7   Enforcement of overseas judgment under provision corresponding to s 6

(1)   If it appears to Her Majesty that the law of an overseas country provides or will provide for the enforcement in that country of judgments given under section 6 above, Her Majesty may by Order in Council provide for the enforcement in the United Kingdom of [judgments of any description specified in the Order which are given under any provision of the law of that country relating to the recovery of sums paid or obtained pursuant to a judgment for multiple damages within the meaning of section 5(3) above, whether or not that provision corresponds to section 6 above].

[(1A)   Such an Order in Council may, as respects judgments to which it relates—
  (a)   make different provisions for different descriptions of judgment; and
  (b)   impose conditions or restrictions on the enforcement of judgments of any description.]

(2)   An Order under this section may apply, with or without modification, any of the provisions of the Foreign Judgments (Reciprocal Enforcement) Act 1933.

[1028]

NOTES
Sub-s (1): words in square brackets substituted by the Civil Jurisdiction and Judgments Act 1982, s 38.
Sub-s (1A): inserted by the Civil Jurisdiction and Judgments Act 1982, s 38.
Orders: the Reciprocal Enforcement of Foreign Judgments (Australia) Order 1994, SI 1994/1901.

---

8   Short title, interpretation, repeals and extent

(1)   This Act may be cited as the Protection of Trading Interests Act 1980.

(2)   In this Act "overseas country" means any country or territory outside the United Kingdom other than one for whose international relations Her Majesty's Government in the United Kingdom are responsible.

(3)   References in this Act to the law or a court, tribunal or authority of an overseas country include, in the case of a federal state, references to the law or a court, tribunal or authority of any constituent part of that country.

(4)   References in this Act to a claim for, or to entitlement to, contribution are references to a claim or entitlement based on an enactment or rule of law.

(5), (6)   ...

(7)   This Act extends to Northern Ireland.

(8)   Her Majesty may by Order in Council direct that this Act shall extend with such exceptions, adaptations and modifications, if any, as may be specified in the Order to any territory outside the United Kingdom, being a territory for the international relations of which Her Majesty's Government in the United Kingdom are responsible.

[1029]

NOTES
Sub-s (5): repealed in part by the Magistrates' Courts Act 1980, s 154(3), Sch 9, remainder repeals the Shipping Contracts and Commercial Documents Act 1964, except in relation to any direction given under that Act before 20 March 1980.
Sub-s (6): repeals the Shipping Contracts and Commercial Documents Act 1964, except in relation to any direction given under that Act before 20 March 1980.
Orders in Council: the Protection of Trading Interests Act 1980 (Jersey) Order 1983, SI 1983/607; the Evidence (Proceedings in Other Jurisdictions) (Jersey) Order 1983, SI 1983/1700; the Protection of Trading Interests Act 1980 (Guernsey) Order 1983, SI 1983/1703; the Protection of Trading Interests Act 1980 (Isle of Man) Order 1983, SI 1983/1704.

COMPETITION ACT 1980

(1980 c 21)

ARRANGEMENT OF SECTIONS

Further references and investigations

An Act to abolish the Price Commission; to make provision for the control of anticompetitive practices in the supply and acquisition of goods and the supply and securing of services; to provide for references of certain public bodies and other persons to the Monopolies and Mergers Commission; to provide for the investigation of prices and charges by the Director General of Fair Trading; to provide for the making of grants to certain bodies; to amend and provide for the amendment of the Fair Trading Act 1973; to make amendments with respect to the Restrictive Trade Practices Act 1976; to repeal the remaining provisions of the Counter-Inflation Act 1973; and for purposes connected therewith

[3 April 1980]

NOTES
Monopolies and Mergers Commission: the Monopolies and Mergers Commission was dissolved by the Competition Act 1998, s 45(3) at **[1740]**, which also transferred the functions of the Monopolies and Mergers Commission to the Competition Commission.
Director General of Fair Trading: the Enterprise Act 2002, s 2(1), at **[1860]**, provides that, as from the coming into force of that section (on 1 April 2003, see the Enterprise Act 2002 (Commencement No 2, Transitional and Transitory Provisions) Order 2003, SI 2003/766), the functions of the Director General of Fair Trading, his property, rights and liabilities are transferred to the Office of Fair Trading. Accordingly, (by virtue of s 2(2), (3) of the 2002 Act) the office of the Director is abolished, and any reference to the Director in any enactment, instrument or other document passed or made before the commencement of s 2(1) shall have effect as if it were a reference to the Office of Fair Trading. For transitional provisions in connection with the transfer, see s 276(1) of, and Sch 24, para 6 to, the 2002 Act.

1–10   (*S 1 repealed by the Statute Law (Repeals) Act 1989; ss 2–10 repealed by the Competition Act 1998, ss 17, 74(3), Sch 14, Pt I.*)

Further references and investigations

11 References of public bodies and certain other persons to the Commission

(1)   The Secretary of State may at any time refer to the Commission any question relating to—
    (a)   the efficiency and costs of, [or]
    (b)   the service provided by, ...
    (c)   ...
a person falling within subsection (3) below and specified in the reference, including any question whether, in relation to a matter falling within [paragraph (a) or (b)] above, the person is pursuing a course of conduct which operates against the public interest.

(2)   ...

(3)   The persons referred to in subsection (1) above are—
    (a)   any body corporate—
        (i)   which supplies goods or services by way of business,
        (ii)   the affairs of which are managed by its members, and
        (iii)   the members of which hold office as such by virtue of their appointment to that or another office by a Minister under any enactment; or
    [(aa)   any publicly owned railway company, within the meaning of the Railways Act 1993, which supplies network services or station services, within the meaning of Part I of that Act; or]
    [(b)   any person (not falling within paragraph (a) above) who provides in Northern Ireland a bus service within the meaning of section 14 of the Finance Act (Northern Ireland) 1966; or]
    [(bb)   any person who provides a railway passenger service in pursuance of an agreement

entered into by Transport for London or any of its subsidiaries (within the meaning of the Greater London Authority Act 1999) by virtue of section 156(2) or (3) of the Greater London Authority Act 1999;]

[(c)   the [Environment Agency];] or

[(ca)   Scottish water;]

[(cc)   ...]

(d)   any board administering a scheme under the Agricultural Marketing Act 1958 [or the Agricultural Marketing (Northern Ireland) Order 1982]; or

(e)   any body corporate with a statutory duty to promote and assist the maintenance and development of the efficient supply of any goods or services by a body falling within paragraphs (a) to (d) above; or

(f)   any subsidiary, within the meaning of [section 1159 of the Companies Act 2006], of a body falling within paragraphs (a) to (e) above.

(4)   The Secretary of State may by order exclude from subsection (3)(b) [or (bb)] above persons of such descriptions as may be specified in the order.

(5)   No question concerning a person falling within subsection (3)(b) [or (bb)] above or a subsidiary of a body falling within [either of those paragraphs] may be referred to the Commission under this section unless it relates to the carriage of passengers by the person or, as the case may be, the subsidiary.

(6)   The Secretary of State may at any time by notice given to the Commission vary a reference under this section.

(7)   On making a reference under this section or on varying such a reference under subsection (6) above the Secretary of State shall arrange for the reference or, as the case may be, the variation to be published in such manner as he considers most suitable for bringing it to the attention of persons who in his opinion would be affected by it or be likely to have an interest in it.

(8)   On a reference under this section the Commission shall investigate and report on any question referred to them but shall exclude from their investigation and report consideration of—

(a)   any question relating to the appropriateness of any financial obligations or guidance as to financial objectives (however expressed) imposed on or given to the person in question by or under any enactment, or otherwise by a Minister; ...

(b)   ...

[(9), (9A)   ...]

(10)   A report of the Commission on a reference under this section shall be made to the Secretary of State and shall state, with reasons, the conclusions of the Commission with respect to any question referred to them and, where the Commission conclude that the person specified in the reference is pursuing a course of conduct which operates against the public interest, the report may include recommendations as to what action (if any) should be taken by the person for the purpose of remedying or preventing what the Commission consider are the adverse effects of that course of conduct.

(11)   In this section "Minister" includes a Northern Ireland department and the head of such a department.

[1030]

NOTES

Sub-s (1): word in square brackets in para (a) inserted, para (c) and word immediately preceding it repealed, and words in second pair of square brackets substituted by the Enterprise Act 2002, s 278, Sch 25, para 10(1), (2)(a), Sch 26; Schedule.

Sub-s (2): repealed by the Enterprise Act 2002, s 278, Sch 25, para 10(1), (2)(b), Sch 26.

Sub-s (3): para (aa) inserted by the Railways Act 1993, s 152(1), Sch 12, para 12(1); para (b) substituted by the Transport Act 1985, s 114(1); para (bb) inserted by the London Regional Transport Act 1984, s 71(3)(a), Sch 6, para 15, substituted by the Transport for London (Consequential Provisions) Order 2003, SI 2003/1615, art 2, Sch 1, Pt 1, para 6; para (c) substituted by the Water Act 1989, s 190(1), Sch 25, para 59(1), words in square brackets substituted by the Environment Act 1995 (Consequential Amendments) Regulations 1996, SI 1996/593, reg 2, Sch 1; para (ca) inserted by the Water Industry (Scotland) Act 2002 (Consequential Modifications) Order 2004, SI 2004/1822, art 2, Schedule, Pt 1, para 10; para (cc) inserted, in relation to Scotland only, by the Local Government etc (Scotland) Act 1994, s 72, repealed by the Water Industry (Scotland) Act 2002, s 71, Sch 7, para 10; words in square brackets in para (d) substituted by the Agricultural Marketing (Northern Ireland) Order 1982, SI 1982/1080, art 46, Schs 8, 9; words in square brackets in para (f) substituted by the Companies Act 2006 (Consequential Amendments, Transitional Provisions and Savings) Order 2009, SI 2009/1941, art 2(1), Sch 1, para 42(a).

Sub-s (4): words in square brackets inserted by the London Regional Transport Act 1984, s 71(3)(a), Sch 6, para 15.

Sub-s (5): words in first pair of square brackets inserted, and words in second pair of square brackets substituted, by the London Regional Transport Act 1984, s 71(3)(a), Sch 6, para 15.

Sub-s (8): words omitted repealed by the Competition Act 1998, s 74(1), (3), Sch 12, para 4(1), (2), Sch 14, Pt I, subject to savings in Sch 13, Pt V, para 40 of the 1998 Act at **[1787]**.

Sub-ss (9), (9A): substituted, for original sub-s (9), by the Competition Act 1998, s 74(1), Sch 12, para 4(1), (3); repealed by the Enterprise Act 2002, s 278, Sch 25, para 10(1), (2)(b), Sch 26.

[11A References under section 11: time-limits

(1)   Every reference under section 11 above shall specify a period (not longer than six months beginning with the date of the reference) within which a report on the reference is to be made.

(2)   A report of the Commission on a reference under section 11 above shall not have effect (and no action shall be taken in relation to it under section 12 below) unless the report is made before the end of the period specified in the reference or such further period (if any) as may be allowed by the Secretary of State under subsection (3) below.

(3)   The Secretary of State may, if he has received representations on the subject from the Commission and is satisfied that there are special reasons why the report cannot be made within the period specified in the reference, extend that period by no more than three months.

(4)   No more than one extension is possible under subsection (3) above in relation to the same reference.

(5)   The Secretary of State shall publish any extension made by him under subsection (3) above in such manner as he considers most suitable for bringing it to the attention of persons who in his opinion would be affected by it or be likely to have an interest in it.]

[1031]

NOTES
Inserted, together with ss 11B–11D, by the Enterprise Act 2002, s 278(1), Sch 25, para 10(1), (3).

[11B References under section 11: powers of investigation and penalties

(1)   The following sections of Part 3 of the Enterprise Act 2002 shall apply, with the modifications mentioned in subsections (2) and (3) below, for the purposes of references under section 11 above as they apply for the purposes of references under that Part—
- (a)   section 109 (attendance of witnesses and production of documents etc);
- (b)   section 110 (enforcement of powers under section 109: general);
- (c)   section 111 (penalties);
- (d)   section 112 (penalties: main procedural requirements);
- (e)   section 113 (payments and interest by instalments);
- (f)   section 114 (appeals in relation to penalties);
- (g)   section 115 (recovery of penalties); and
- (h)   section 116 (statement of policy).

(2)   Section 110 shall, in its application by virtue of subsection (1) above, have effect as if—
- (a)   subsection (2) were omitted;
- (b)   in subsection (4), for the word "publication" there were substituted "laying before both Houses of Parliament"; and
- (c)   in subsection (9) the words from "or section" to "section 65(3))" were omitted.

(3)   Section 111(5)(b)(ii) shall, in its application by virtue of subsection (1) above, have effect as if—
- (a)   for the words "published (or, in the case of a report under section 50 or 65, given)" there were substituted "made";
- (b)   for the words "published (or given)", in both places where they appear, there were substituted "made"; and
- (c)   the words "by this Part" were omitted.]

[1032]

NOTES
Inserted as noted to s 11A at **[1031]**.

[11C References under section 11: further supplementary provisions

(1)   Section 117 of the Enterprise Act 2002 (false or misleading information) shall apply in relation to functions under this Act as it applies in relation to functions under Part 3 of that Act but as if, in subsections (1)(a) and (2), the words ["the OFT, OFCOM,"] were omitted.

(2)   Section 125 of the Enterprise Act 2002 (offences by bodies corporate) shall apply for the purposes of this Act as it applies for the purposes of Part 3 of that Act.

(3)   For the purposes of section 12 below, a conclusion contained in a report of the Commission is to be disregarded if the conclusion is not that of at least two-thirds of the members of the group constituted in connection with the reference concerned in pursuance of paragraph 15 of Schedule 7 to the Competition Act 1998.]

[1033]

NOTES

Inserted as noted to s 11A at **[1031]**.

Sub-s (1): words in square brackets substituted by the Communications Act 2003, s 389(1), Sch 16, para 1.

[11D Interim orders

(1) Subsection (2) below applies where, in the circumstances specified in subsection (1) of section 12 below, the Secretary of State has under consideration the making of an order under subsection (5) of that section.

(2) The Secretary of State may by order, for the purpose of preventing pre-emptive action—

(a) prohibit or restrict the doing of things which the Secretary of State considers would constitute pre-emptive action;

(b) impose on any person concerned obligations as to the carrying on of any activities or the safeguarding of any assets;

(c) provide for the carrying on of any activities or the safeguarding of any assets either by the appointment of a person to conduct or supervise the conduct of any activities (on such terms and with such powers as may be specified or described in the order) or in any other manner;

(d) do anything which may be done by virtue of paragraph 19 of Schedule 8 to the Enterprise Act 2002 (information powers).

(3) An order under this section shall come into force at such time as is determined by or under the order.

(4) An order under this section shall, if it has not previously ceased to be in force, cease to be in force on the making of the order under section 12(5) below or (as the case may be) on the making of the decision not to make such an order.

(5) The Secretary of State shall publish any decision made by him not to make an order under section 12(5) below in such manner as he considers most suitable for bringing it to the attention of persons who in his opinion would be affected by it or would be likely to have an interest in it.

(6) The Secretary of State shall, as soon as reasonably practicable, consider any representations received by him in relation to varying or revoking an order under this section.

(7) The following provisions of Part 3 of the Enterprise Act 2002 shall apply in relation to orders under this section as they apply in relation to orders under paragraph 2 of Schedule 7 to that Act—

(a) section 86(2) and (3) (enforcement orders: general provisions);

(b) section 87 (delegated power of directions); and

(c) section 94(1) to (5), (8) and (9) (rights to enforce orders).

(8) In this section "pre-emptive action" means action which might impede the making of an order under section 12(5) below.]

[1034]

NOTES

Inserted as noted to s 11A at **[1031]**.

12 Orders following report under section 11

(1) This section applies where a report of the Commission on a reference under section 11 above concludes that the person specified in the reference is pursuing a course of conduct which operates against the public interest.

(2) If it appears to the Secretary of State that any other Minister has functions directly relating to the person specified in the reference or, in the case of a reference only concerning the activities of the person in a part of the United Kingdom, functions directly relating to the person in respect of his activities in that part, he shall send a copy of the report of the Commission on the reference to that Minister; and in subsection (3) below "the relevant Minister" means—

(a) in a case where it appears to the Secretary of State that any Minister (including himself) has such functions, that Minister, and

(b) in a case where it appears to the Secretary of State that no Minister has such functions, the Secretary of State.

(3) If—

(a) the relevant Minister considers it appropriate for the purpose of remedying or preventing what he considers are the adverse effects of the course of conduct specified in the report of the Commission as operating against the public interest, and

(b) the person specified in the reference does not fall within paragraph (d) of section 11(3) above and is not a subsidiary of a body falling within that paragraph,

he may by order direct the person to prepare within such time, if any, as may be specified in the order a plan for remedying or preventing such of those effects as are so specified; but where there is more than one relevant Minister no such order shall be made except by all the relevant Ministers acting jointly and where none of the relevant Ministers is the Secretary of State no such order shall be made except after consultation with him.

(4)   It shall be the duty of a person to whom a direction is given under subsection (3) above to prepare such a plan as is mentioned in that subsection and to send a copy of that plan to the Minister or Ministers by whom the order containing the direction was made who shall lay it before Parliament; and, in a case where the plan involves the use by a body of its powers in relation to any subsidiary within the meaning of [section 1159 of the Companies Act 2006], the plan shall specify the manner in which the body proposes using those powers.

(5)   Whether or not an order has been or may be made under subsection (3) above, the Secretary of State may, if he considers it appropriate for the purpose of remedying or preventing what he considers are the adverse effects of the course of conduct specified in the report of the Commission as operating against the public interest, [make an order under this subsection].

[(5A)   An order under subsection (5) above may contain anything permitted by Schedule 8 to the Enterprise Act 2002, except paragraphs 8, 13 and 14 of that Schedule.

(5B)   An order under subsection (5) above shall come into force at such time as is determined by or under the order.]

[(6)   The following provisions of Part 3 of the Enterprise Act 2002 shall apply in relation to orders under subsection (5) above as they apply in relation to orders under paragraph 11 of Schedule 7 to that Act—

    (a)   section 86(2) and (3) (enforcement orders: general provisions);

    (b)   section 87 (delegated power of directions);

    (c)   section 88 (contents of certain enforcement orders);

    (d)   section 94(1) to (5), (8) and (9) (rights to enforce orders); and

    (e)   Schedule 10 (procedural requirements for orders).

(7)   The Secretary of State shall publish any decision made by him to dispense with the requirements of Schedule 10 to the Enterprise Act 2002 as applied by subsection (6) above; and shall do so in such manner as he considers most suitable for bringing the decision to the attention of persons who in his opinion would be affected by it or be likely to have an interest in it.]

[1035]

13   *(Repealed by the Enterprise Act 2002, ss 9, 278(2), Sch 26.)*

Patents and agricultural schemes

14   *(Repealed by the Copyright, Designs and Patents Act 1988, s 303(2), Sch 8.)*

15   Agricultural schemes: special provisions

  (1)   ...

  (2)   The Secretary of State shall not—

    (a), (b)   ...

    (c)   make or vary a reference under section 11 above,

in a case where the person to whom or to whose conduct or activities the investigation or reference relates falls within section 11(3)(d) above unless he has first consulted the relevant Minister.

  (3), (4)   ...

  (5)   In this section "the relevant Minister" means—

    (a)   in the case of a board administering a scheme under the said Act of 1958, the Minister who would have power to make an order under section 19 of that Act in relation to that board or the board administering that scheme, and

    (b)   in the case of a board administering a scheme under [the said Order of 1982], the Department of Agriculture for Northern Ireland.

[1036]

Sub-ss (3), (4): repealed by the Competition Act 1998, s 74(1), (3), Sch 12, para 4(1), (5), Sch 14, Pt I.

Sub-s (5): words in square brackets substituted by the Agricultural Marketing (Northern Ireland) Order 1982, SI 1982/1080, art 46(1), Schs 8, 9.

General provisions about references and investigations

16   General provisions as to reports

(1)   ...

(2)   For the purposes of the law relating to defamation, absolute privilege shall attach to any report of the Commission ... under this Act.

[(3)   ...]

[1037]

NOTES

Sub-s (1): repealed by the Enterprise Act 2002, s 278, Sch 25, para 10(5)(a), Sch 26.

Sub-s (2): words omitted repealed by the Enterprise Act 2002, s 278, Sch 25, para 10(5)(b), Sch 26.

Sub-s (3): added by the Deregulation and Contracting Out Act 1994, s 39, Sch 11, para 4(1), (5); repealed by the Competition Act 1998, s 74(1), (3), Sch 12, para 4(1), (6), Sch 14, Pt I.

17   Laying before Parliament and publication of reports

(1)   Subject to subsection (2) below, the Secretary of State shall lay a copy of any report made to him under section ... , 11(10) ... above before each House of Parliament and shall arrange for the report to be published in such manner as appears to him appropriate.

(2)   The Secretary of State shall not lay a copy of a report made to him under section ... 11(10) above before either House of Parliament unless at least twenty-four hours before doing so he has transmitted to every person specified in the reference a copy of the report in the form in which it is laid (or by virtue of subsection (3) below is treated as being laid) before each House of Parliament.

(3)   If a report made to him under section ... , 11(10) ... above is presented by command of Her Majesty to either House of Parliament otherwise than at or during the time of a sitting of that House, the presentation of the report shall for the purposes of this section be treated as the laying of a copy of it before that House by the Secretary of State.

(4)   If it appears to the Secretary of State that the publication of any matter in a report made to him under section ... , 11(10) ... above would be [inappropriate], he shall exclude that matter from the copies of the report as laid before Parliament and from the report as published under this section.

[(5)   In deciding what is inappropriate for the purposes of subsection (4) the Secretary of State shall have regard to the considerations mentioned in section 244 of the Enterprise Act 2002.]

(6)   Any reference in [section] 12 above to a report of the Commission shall be construed as a reference to the report in the form in which copies of it are laid (or by virtue of subsection (3) of this section are treated as having been laid) before each House of Parliament under this section.

[1038]–[1043]

NOTES

Sub-ss (1), (3): words omitted in the first place repealed by the Competition Act 1998, s 74(1), (3), Sch 12, para 4(1), (7)(a), (b), Sch 14, Pt I; words omitted in the second place repealed by the Enterprise Act 2002, s 278, Sch 25, para 10(6)(a), Sch 26.

Sub-s (2): word omitted repealed by the Competition Act 1998, s 74(1), (3), Sch 12, para 4(1), (7)(b), Sch 14, Pt I.

Sub-s (4): word omitted in the first place repealed by the Competition Act 1998, s 74(1), (3), Sch 12, para 4(1), (7)(a), (b), Sch 14, Pt I; words omitted in the second place repealed, and word in square brackets substituted by the Enterprise Act 2002, s 278, Sch 25, para 10(6)(a), (b), Sch 26.

Sub-s (5): substituted by the Enterprise Act 2002, s 278(1), Sch 25, para 10(1), (6)(c).

Sub-s (6): word in square brackets substituted by the Competition Act 1998, s 74(1), Sch 12, para 4(1), (7)(c).

18–30   (*Ss 18, 19(1)–(3), (5), (6), 20, 21, 24 repealed by the Enterprise Act 2002, s 278, Sch 25, para 10(1), (7), (1), Sch 26; s 19(4) repealed in part by the Agricultural Marketing (Northern Ireland) Order 1982, SI 1982/1080, art 46(2), Sch 9, remainder repealed by ss 247(f), 278(2) of, and Sch 26 to, the 2002 Act; s 19(7) repealed by the Statute Law (Repeals) Act 1993; ss 22, 25–30 repealed by the Competition Act 1998, s 74(1), (3), Sch 12, para 4(1), (11), (13), Sch 14, Pt I.*)

Supplementary

31   Orders and regulations

(1)   Any power of the Secretary of State to make orders ... under this Act shall be exercisable by statutory instrument.

(2)   ...

(3) Any statutory instrument containing … an order under section … , 11(4)[, 11D] or 12(3) or (5) above[, or section 111(4) or (6) or 114(3)(b) or (4)(b) of the Enterprise Act 2002 as applied by section 11B(1)(c) or (f) above,] shall be subject to annulment in pursuance of a resolution of either House of Parliament.

(4) …

[(5) Any power of the Secretary of State to make an order under this Act—
    (a) may be exercised so as to make different provision for different cases or different purposes; and
    (b) includes power to make such incidental, supplementary, consequential, transitory, transitional or saving provision as the Secretary of State considers appropriate.]

[1044]

NOTES
Sub-s (1): words omitted repealed by the Enterprise Act 2002, s 278, Sch 25, para 10(8)(a), Sch 26.
Sub-s (2): repealed by the Competition Act 1998, s 74(1), (3), Sch 12, para 4(1), (14)(a), Sch 14, Pt I.
Sub-s (3): words omitted in the first place repealed, words in first pair of square brackets inserted, and words in second pair of square brackets substituted, by the Enterprise Act 2002, s 278, Sch 25, para 10(8)(b), Sch 26; words omitted in the second place repealed by the Competition Act 1998, s 74(1), (3), Sch 12, para 4(1), (14)(b), Sch 14, Pt I.
Sub-s (4): repealed by the Enterprise Act 2002, s 278, Sch 25, para 10(8)(c), Sch 26.
Sub-s (5): added by the Enterprise Act 2002, s 278(1), Sch 25, para 10(8)(d).

32 Financial provisions

(1) There shall be defrayed out of moneys provided by Parliament—
    (a) any expenses incurred by the Secretary of State in consequence of the provisions of this Act; and
    (b) any increase attributable to this Act in the sums payable out of moneys so provided under any other Act.

(2) …

[1045]

NOTES
Sub-s (2): amends the Fair Trading Act 1973, s 135(2)(c) at **[630]**.

33 Short title, interpretation, repeals, commencement and extent

(1) This Act may be cited as the Competition Act 1980.

[(2) Unless the context otherwise requires, in this Act "Minister" includes a government department and the following expressions shall have the same meanings as they have in Part 3 of the Enterprise Act 2002—
    "business"
    "the Commission"
    "enactment"
    "goods"
    "services"
    "supply (in relation to the supply of goods)"
    "the supply of services".]

(3), (4) …

(5) This Act shall come into operation on such day as the Secretary of State may by order appoint, and different days may be so appointed for different provisions and for different purposes.

(6) An order under this section appointing a day for the coming into operation of any provision of Schedule 2 to this Act may contain such savings with respect to the operation of that provision and such incidental and transitional provisions as appear to the Secretary of State to be appropriate.

(7) Any reference in any provision of this Act to the appointed day shall be construed as a reference to the day appointed or, as the case may require, first appointed under this section for the coming into operation of that provision.

(8) This Act extends to Northern Ireland.

[1046]–[1053]

NOTES
Sub-s (2): substituted by the Enterprise Act 2002, s 278(1), Sch 25, para 10(9).
Sub-ss (3), (4): repealed by the Competition Act 1998, s 74(1), (3), Sch 12, para 4(1), (15)(b), Sch 14, Pt I.
Orders: the Competition Act 1980 (Commencement No 1) Order 1980, SI 1980/497; the Competition Act 1980 (Commencement No 2) Order 1980, SI 1980/978.

(*Sch 1 repealed by the Statute Law* (*Repeals*) *Act 1989; Sch 2* (*Repeals*) *outside the scope of this work.*)

SUPPLY OF GOODS AND SERVICES ACT 1982

(1982 c 29)

ARRANGEMENT OF SECTIONS

PART I
SUPPLY OF GOODS

Contracts for the hire of goods

Exclusion of implied terms, etc

PART 1B
ADDITIONAL RIGHTS OF TRANSFEREE IN CONSUMER CASES

PART II
SUPPLY OF SERVICES

PART III
SUPPLEMENTARY

An Act to amend the law with respect to the terms to be implied in certain contracts for the transfer of the property in goods, in certain contracts for the hire of goods and in certain contracts for the supply of a service; and for connected purposes

[13 July 1982]

PART I
SUPPLY OF GOODS

1–5A   (*Outside the scope of this work.*)

Contracts for the hire of goods

6   The contracts concerned

(1)   In this Act [in its application to England and Wales and Northern Ireland] a "contract for the hire of goods" means a contract under which one person bails or agrees to bail goods to another by way of hire, other than [a hire-purchase agreement].

(2)   ...

(3) For the purposes of this Act [in its application to England and Wales and Northern Ireland] a contract is a contract for the hire of goods whether or not services are also provided or to be provided under the contract, and ... whatever is the nature of the consideration for the bailment or agreement to bail by way of hire.

[1053]

NOTES
Sub-s (1): words in first pair of square brackets substituted by the Sale and Supply of Goods Act 1994, s 7(1), Sch 2, para 6(1), (6); words in second pair of square brackets substituted in relation to England and Wales by the Regulatory Reform (Trading Stamps) Order 2005, SI 2005/871, art 5(b)(i) and in relation to Northern Ireland by the Law Reform (Miscellaneous Provisions) (Northern Ireland) Order 2005, SI 2005/1452, art 21(2)(b)(i).
Sub-s (2): repealed in relation to England and Wales by SI 2005/871, art 5(b)(ii) and in relation to Northern Ireland by SI 2005/1452, arts 21(2)(b)(ii), 24, Sch 2.
Sub-s (3): words in square brackets substituted by the Sale and Supply of Goods Act 1994, s 7(1), Sch 2, para 6(1), (6); words omitted repealed in relation to England and Wales by SI 2005/871, art 5(b)(iii) and in relation to Northern Ireland by SI 2005/1452, arts 21(2)(b)(iii), 24, Sch 2.

7 Implied terms about right to transfer possession, etc

(1) In a contract for the hire of goods there is an implied condition on the part of the bailor that in the case of a bailment he has a right to transfer possession of the goods by way of hire for the period of the bailment and in the case of an agreement to bail he will have such a right at the time of the bailment.

(2) In a contract for the hire of goods there is also an implied warranty that the bailee will enjoy quiet possession of the goods for the period of the bailment except so far as the possession may be disturbed by the owner or other person entitled to the benefit of any charge or encumbrance disclosed or known to the bailee before the contract is made.

(3) The preceding provisions of this section do not affect the right of the bailor to repossess the goods under an express or implied term of the contract.

[1054]

8 Implied terms where hire is by description

(1) This section applies where, under a contract for the hire of goods, the bailor bails or agrees to bail the goods by description.

(2) In such a case there is an implied condition that the goods will correspond with the description.

(3) If under the contract the bailor bails or agrees to bail the goods by reference to a sample as well as a description it is not sufficient that the bulk of the goods corresponds with the sample if the goods do not also correspond with the description.

(4) A contract is not prevented from falling within subsection (1) above by reason only that, being exposed for supply, the goods are selected by the bailee.

[1055]

9 Implied terms about quality or fitness

(1) Except as provided by this section and section 10 below and subject to the provisions of any other enactment, there is no implied condition or warranty about the quality or fitness for any particular purpose of goods bailed under a contract for the hire of goods.

[(2) Where, under such a contract, the bailor bails goods in the course of a business, there is an implied condition that the goods supplied under the contract are of satisfactory quality.

(2A) For the purposes of this section and section 10 below, goods are of satisfactory quality if they meet the standard that a reasonable person would regard as satisfactory, taking account of any description of the goods, the consideration for the bailment (if relevant) and all the other relevant circumstances.

[(2B) If the bailee deals as consumer, the relevant circumstances mentioned in subsection (2A) above include any public statements on the specific characteristics of the goods made about them by the bailor, the producer or his representative, particularly in advertising or on labelling.

(2C) A public statement is not by virtue of subsection (2B) above a relevant circumstance for the purposes of subsection (2A) above in the case of a contract for the hire of goods, if the bailor shows that—
   (a) at the time the contract was made, he was not, and could not reasonably have been, aware of the statement,
   (b) before the contract was made, the statement had been withdrawn in public or, to the extent that it contained anything which was incorrect or misleading, it had been corrected in public, or
   (c) the decision to acquire the goods could not have been influenced by the statement.

(2D)   Subsections (2B) and (2C) above do not prevent any public statement from being a relevant circumstance for the purposes of subsection (2A) above (whether or not the bailee deals as consumer) if the statement would have been such a circumstance apart from those subsections.]

(3)   The condition implied by subsection (2) above does not extend to any matter making the quality of goods unsatisfactory—

(a)   which is specifically drawn to the bailee's attention before the contract is made,

(b)   where the bailee examines the goods before the contract is made, which that examination ought to reveal, or

(c)   where the goods are bailed by reference to a sample, which would have been apparent on a reasonable examination of the sample.]

(4)   Subsection (5) below applies where, under a contract for the hire of goods, the bailor bails goods in the course of a business and the bailee, expressly or by implication, makes known—

(a)   to the bailor in the course of negotiations conducted by him in relation to the making of the contract, or

(b)   to a credit-broker in the course of negotiations conducted by that broker in relation to goods sold by him to the bailor before forming the subject matter of the contract,

any particular purpose for which the goods are being bailed.

(5)   In that case there is (subject to subsection (6) below) an implied condition that the goods supplied under the contract are reasonably fit for that purpose, whether or not that is a purpose for which such goods are commonly supplied.

(6)   Subsection (5) above does not apply where the circumstances show that the bailee does not rely, or that it is unreasonable for him to rely, on the skill or judgment of the bailor or credit-broker.

(7)   An implied condition or warranty about quality or fitness for a particular purpose may be annexed by usage to a contract for the hire of goods.

(8)   The preceding provisions of this section apply to a bailment by a person who in the course of a business is acting as agent for another as they apply to a bailment by a principal in the course of a business, except where that other is not bailing in the course of a business and either the bailee knows that fact or reasonable steps are taken to bring it to the bailee's notice before the contract concerned is made.

(9)   …

[1056]

NOTES

Sub-ss (2), (2A), (3): substituted, for original sub-ss (2), (3), by the Sale and Supply of Goods Act 1994, s 7(1), Sch 2, para 6(1), (7).

Sub-ss (2B)–(2D): inserted by the Sale and Supply of Goods to Consumers Regulations 2002, SI 2002/3045, reg 10(1), (2).

Sub-s (9): repealed by the Sale and Supply of Goods Act 1994, s 7, Sch 2, para 6(1), (7), Sch 3.

10   Implied terms where hire is by sample

(1)   This section applies where, under a contract for the hire of goods, the bailor bails or agrees to bail the goods by reference to a sample.

(2)   In such a case there is an implied condition—

(a)   that the bulk will correspond with the sample in quality; and

(b)   that the bailee will have a reasonable opportunity of comparing the bulk with the sample; and

(c)   that the goods will be free from any defect, [making their quality unsatisfactory], which would not be apparent on reasonable examination of the sample.

(3)   …

(4)   For the purposes of this section a bailor bails or agrees to bail goods by reference to a sample where there is an express or implied term to that effect in the contract concerned.

[1057]

NOTES

Sub-s (2): words in square brackets in para (c) substituted by the Sale and Supply of Goods Act 1994, s 7(1), Sch 2, para 6(1), (8).

Sub-s (3): repealed by the Sale and Supply of Goods Act 1994, s 7, Sch 2, para 6(1), (8), Sch 3.

[10A   Modification of remedies for breach of statutory condition in non-consumer cases

(1)   Where in the case of a contract for the hire of goods—

(a)   the bailee would, apart from this subsection, have the right to treat the contract as repudiated by reason of a breach on the part of the bailor of a term implied by section 8, 9 or 10(2)(a) or (c) above, but

(b)   the breach is so slight that it would be unreasonable for him to do so, then, if the bailee does not deal as consumer, the breach is not to be treated as a breach of condition but may be treated as a breach of warranty.

(2)   This section applies unless a contrary intention appears in, or is to be implied from, the contract.

(3)   It is for the bailor to show that a breach fell within subsection (1)(b) above.]

[1058]

NOTES
Inserted by the Sale and Supply of Goods Act 1994, s 7(1), Sch 2, para 6(1), (9).

Exclusion of implied terms, etc

11   Exclusion of implied terms, etc

(1)   Where a right, duty or liability would arise under a contract for the transfer of goods or a contract for the hire of goods by implication of law, it may (subject to subsection (2) below and the 1977 Act) be negatived or varied by express agreement, or by the course of dealing between the parties, or by such usage as binds both parties to the contract.

(2)   An express condition or warranty does not negative a condition or warranty implied by the preceding provisions of this Act unless inconsistent with it.

(3)   Nothing in the preceding provisions of this Act prejudices the operation of any other enactment or any rule of law whereby any condition or warranty (other than one relating to quality or fitness) is to be implied in a contract for the transfer of goods or a contract for the hire of goods.

[1059]

11A–11L   *(Pt IA (ss 11A–11L) inserted by the Sale and Supply of Goods Act 1994, s 6, Sch 1, para 1; applies to Scotland only.)*

[PART 1B
ADDITIONAL RIGHTS OF TRANSFEREE IN CONSUMER CASES

11M   Introductory

(1)   This section applies if—
   (a)   the transferee deals as consumer or, in Scotland, there is a consumer contract in which the transferee is a consumer, and
   (b)   the goods do not conform to the contract for the transfer of goods at the time of delivery.

(2)   If this section applies, the transferee has the right—
   (a)   under and in accordance with section 11N below, to require the transferor to repair or replace the goods, or
   (b)   under and in accordance with section 11P below—
      (i)   to require the transferor to reduce the amount to be paid for the transfer by the transferee by an appropriate amount, or
      (ii)   to rescind the contract with regard to the goods in question.

(3)   For the purposes of subsection (1)(b) above, goods which do not conform to the contract for the transfer of goods at any time within the period of six months starting with the date on which the goods were delivered to the transferee must be taken not to have so conformed at that date.

(4)   Subsection (3) above does not apply if—
   (a)   it is established that the goods did so conform at that date;
   (b)   its application is incompatible with the nature of the goods or the nature of the lack of conformity.

(5)   For the purposes of this section, "consumer contract" has the same meaning as in section 11F(3) above.]

[1059A]

NOTES
Part 1B (ss 11M–11S) inserted by the Sale and Supply of Goods to Consumers Regulations 2002, SI 2002/3045, reg 9.

[11N   Repair or replacement of the goods

(1)   If section 11M above applies, the transferee may require the transferor—
   (a)   to repair the goods, or
   (b)   to replace the goods.

(2)   If the transferee requires the transferor to repair or replace the goods, the transferor must—
   (a)   repair or, as the case may be, replace the goods within a reasonable time but without causing significant inconvenience to the transferee;

    (b)   bear any necessary costs incurred in doing so (including in particular the cost of any labour, materials or postage).

    (3)   The transferee must not require the transferor to repair or, as the case may be, replace the goods if that remedy is—

    (a)   impossible,

    (b)   disproportionate in comparison to the other of those remedies, or

    (c)   disproportionate in comparison to an appropriate reduction in the purchase price under paragraph (a), or rescission under paragraph (b), of section 11P(1) below.

    (4)   One remedy is disproportionate in comparison to the other if the one imposes costs on the transferor which, in comparison to those imposed on him by the other, are unreasonable, taking into account—

    (a)   the value which the goods would have if they conformed to the contract for the transfer of goods,

    (b)   the significance of the lack of conformity to the contract for the transfer of goods, and

    (c)   whether the other remedy could be effected without significant inconvenience to the transferee.

    (5)   Any question as to what is a reasonable time or significant inconvenience is to be determined by reference to—

    (a)   the nature of the goods, and

    (b)   the purpose for which the goods were acquired.]

[1059B]

NOTES
Inserted as noted to s 11M at **[1059A]**.

[11P Reduction of purchase price or rescission of contract

    (1)   If section 11M above applies, the transferee may—

    (a)   require the transferor to reduce the purchase price of the goods in question to the transferee by an appropriate amount, or

    (b)   rescind the contract with regard to those goods,

if the condition in subsection (2) below is satisfied.

    (2)   The condition is that—

    (a)   by virtue of section 11N(3) above the transferee may require neither repair nor replacement of the goods, or

    (b)   the transferee has required the transferor to repair or replace the goods, but the transferor is in breach of the requirement of section 11N(2)(a) above to do so within a reasonable time and without significant inconvenience to the transferee.

    (3)   If the transferee rescinds the contract, any reimbursement to the transferee may be reduced to take account of the use he has had of the goods since they were delivered to him.]

[1059C]

NOTES
Inserted as noted to s 11M at **[1059A]**.

[11Q Relation to other remedies etc

    (1)   If the transferee requires the transferor to repair or replace the goods the transferee must not act under subsection (2) until he has given the transferor a reasonable time in which to repair or replace (as the case may be) the goods.

    (2)   The transferee acts under this subsection if—

    (a)   in England and Wales or Northern Ireland he rejects the goods and terminates the contract for breach of condition;

    (b)   in Scotland he rejects any goods delivered under the contract and treats it as repudiated; or

    (c)   he requires the goods to be replaced or repaired (as the case may be).]

[1059D]

NOTES
Inserted as noted to s 11M at **[1059A]**.

[11R Powers of the court

    (1)   In any proceedings in which a remedy is sought by virtue of this Part the court, in addition to any other power it has, may act under this section.

PART 1
STATUTES

(2)   On the application of the transferee the court may make an order requiring specific performance or, in Scotland, specific implement by the transferor of any obligation imposed on him by virtue of section 11N above.

(3)   Subsection (4) applies if—
    (a)   the transferee requires the transferor to give effect to a remedy under section 11N or 11P above or has claims to rescind under section 11P, but
    (b)   the court decides that another remedy under section 11N or 11P is appropriate.

(4)   The court may proceed—
    (a)   as if the transferee had required the transferor to give effect to the other remedy, or if the other remedy is rescission under section 11P,
    (b)   as if the transferee had claimed to rescind the contract under that section.

(5)   If the transferee has claimed to rescind the contract the court may order that any reimbursement to the transferee is reduced to take account of the use he has had of the goods since they were delivered to him.

(6)   The court may make an order under this section unconditionally or on such terms and conditions as to damages, payment of the price and otherwise as it thinks just.]

[1059E]

NOTES
Inserted as noted to s 11M at **[1059A]**.

[11S   Conformity with the contract
(1)   Goods do not conform to a contract for the supply or transfer of goods if—
    (a)   there is, in relation to the goods, a breach of an express term of the contract or a term implied by section 3, 4 or 5 above or, in Scotland, by section 11C, 11D or 11E above, or
    (b)   installation of the goods forms part of the contract for the transfer of goods, and the goods were installed by the transferor, or under his responsibility, in breach of the term implied by section 13 below or (in Scotland) in breach of any term implied by any rule of law as to the manner in which the installation is carried out.]

[1059F]

NOTES
Inserted as noted to s 11M at **[1059A]**.

PART II
SUPPLY OF SERVICES

12   The contracts concerned

(1)   In this Act a "contract for the supply of a service" means, subject to subsection (2) below, a contract under which a person ("the supplier") agrees to carry out a service.

(2)   For the purposes of this Act, a contract of service or apprenticeship is not a contract for the supply of a service.

(3)   Subject to subsection (2) above, a contract is a contract for the supply of a service for the purposes of this Act whether or not goods are also—
    (a)   transferred or to be transferred, or
    (b)   bailed or to be bailed by way of hire,
under the contract, and whatever is the nature of the consideration for which the service is to be carried out.

(4)   The Secretary of State may by order provide that one or more of sections 13 to 15 below shall not apply to services of a description specified in the order, and such an order may make different provision for different circumstances.

(5)   The power to make an order under subsection (4) above shall be exercisable by statutory instrument subject to annulment in pursuance of a resolution of either House of Parliament.

[1060]

NOTES
Orders: the Supply of Services (Exclusion of Implied Terms) Order 1982, SI 1982/1771 at **[3027]**; the Supply of Services (Exclusion of Implied Terms) Order 1983, SI 1983/902 at **[3029]**; the Supply of Services (Exclusion of Implied Terms) Order 1985, SI 1985/1 at **[3047]**.

13   Implied term about care and skill

In a contract for the supply of a service where the supplier is acting in the course of a business, there is an implied term that the supplier will carry out the service with reasonable care and skill.

[1061]

14 Implied term about time for performance

(1)   Where, under a contract for the supply of a service by a supplier acting in the course of a business, the time for the service to be carried out is not fixed by the contract, left to be fixed in a manner agreed by the contract or determined by the course of dealing between the parties, there is an implied term that the supplier will carry out the service within a reasonable time.

(2)   What is a reasonable time is a question of fact.

[1062]

15 Implied term about consideration

(1)   Where, under a contract for the supply of a service, the consideration for the service is not determined by the contract, left to be determined in a manner agreed by the contract or determined by the course of dealing between the parties, there is an implied term that the party contracting with the supplier will pay a reasonable charge.

(2)   What is a reasonable charge is a question of fact.

[1063]

16 Exclusion of implied terms, etc

(1)   Where a right, duty or liability would arise under a contract for the supply of a service by virtue of this Part of this Act, it may (subject to subsection (2) below and the 1977 Act) be negatived or varied by express agreement, or by the course of dealing between the parties, or by such usage as binds both parties to the contract.

(2)   An express term does not negative a term implied by this Part of this Act unless inconsistent with it.

(3)   Nothing in this Part of this Act prejudices—
   (a)   any rule of law which imposes on the supplier a duty stricter than that imposed by section 13 or 14 above; or
   (b)   subject to paragraph (a) above, any rule of law whereby any term not inconsistent with this Part of this Act is to be implied in a contract for the supply of a service.

(4)   This Part of this Act has effect subject to any other enactment which defines or restricts the rights, duties or liabilities arising in connection with a service of any description.

[1064]

PART III
SUPPLEMENTARY

17   (*Sub-s (1) repealed by the Sale and Supply of Goods Act 1994, s 7(2), Sch 3; sub-ss (2), (3) amend the Unfair Contract Terms Act 1977, s 7 at* **[887]**.)

18 Interpretation: general

(1)   In the preceding provisions of this Act and this section—
   "bailee", in relation to a contract for the hire of goods means (depending on the context) a person to whom the goods are bailed under the contract, or a person to whom they are to be so bailed, or a person to whom the rights under the contract of either of those persons have passed;
   "bailor", in relation to a contract for the hire of goods, means (depending on the context) a person who bails the goods under the contract, or a person who agrees to do so, or a person to whom the duties under the contract of either of those persons have passed;
   "business" includes a profession and the activities of any government department or local or public authority;
   "credit-broker" means a person acting in the course of a business of credit brokerage carried on by him;
   "credit brokerage" means the effecting of introductions—
      (a)   of individuals desiring to obtain credit to persons carrying on any business so far as it relates to the provision of credit; or
      (b)   of individuals desiring to obtain goods on hire to persons carrying on a business which comprises or relates to the bailment [or as regards Scotland the hire] of goods under a contract for the hire of goods; or
      (c)   of individuals desiring to obtain credit, or to obtain goods on hire, to other credit-brokers;
   "enactment" means any legislation (including subordinate legislation) of the United Kingdom or Northern Ireland;
   "goods" [includes all personal chattels, other than things in action and money, and as regards Scotland all corporeal moveables; and in particular "goods" includes] emblements, industrial growing crops, and things attached to or forming part of the land which are agreed to be severed before the transfer [bailment or hire] concerned or under the contract concerned ... ;

"hire-purchase agreement" has the same meaning as in the 1974 Act;

["producer" means the manufacturer of goods, the importer of goods into the European Economic Area or any person purporting to be a producer by placing his name, trade mark or other distinctive sign on the goods;]

"property", in relation to goods, means the general property in them and not merely a special property;

.....

["repair" means, in cases where there is a lack of conformity in goods for the purposes of this Act, to bring the goods into conformity with the contract;]

.....

"transferee", in relation to a contract for the transfer of goods, means (depending on the context) a person to whom the property in the goods is transferred under the contract, or a person to whom the property is to be so transferred, or a person to whom the rights under the contract of either of those persons have passed;

"transferor", in relation to a contract for the transfer of goods, means (depending on the context) a person who transfers the property in the goods under the contract, or a person who agrees to do so, or a person to whom the duties under the contract of either of those persons have passed.

(2)   In subsection (1) above, in the definitions of bailee, bailor, transferee and transferor, a reference to rights or duties passing is to their passing by assignment [assignation], operation of law or otherwise.

[(3)   For the purposes of this Act, the quality of goods includes their state and condition and the following (among others) are in appropriate cases aspects of the quality of goods—

(a)   fitness for all the purposes for which goods of the kind in question are commonly supplied,

(b)   appearance and finish,

(c)   freedom from minor defects,

(d)   safety, and

(e)   durability.

(4)   References in this Act to dealing as consumer are to be construed in accordance with Part I of the Unfair Contract Terms Act 1977; and, for the purposes of this Act, it is for the transferor or bailor claiming that the transferee or bailee does not deal as consumer to show that he does not.]

[1065]

NOTES

Sub-s (1): words in square brackets in definitions "credit brokerage" and "goods" substituted, words omitted from definition "goods" and definition "quality" (omitted) repealed, by the Sale and Supply of Goods Act 1994, ss 6, 7, Sch 1, para 2, Sch 2, para 6(1), (10); definitions "producer" and "repair" inserted by the Sale and Supply of Goods to Consumers Regulations 2002, SI 2002/3045, reg 12; definitions "redemption" and "trading stamps" (omitted) repealed in relation to England and Wales by the Regulatory Reform (Trading Stamps) Order 2005, SI 2005/871, art 5(e) and in relation to Northern Ireland by the Law Reform (Miscellaneous Provisions) (Northern Ireland) Order 2005, SI 2005/1452, art 21(2)(c).

Sub-s (2): word in square brackets inserted by the Sale and Supply of Goods Act 1994, s 6, Sch 1, para 3.

Sub-ss (3), (4): added by the Sale and Supply of Goods Act 1994, s 7(1), Sch 2, para 6(1), (10).

19   Interpretation: references to Acts

In this Act—

"the 1973 Act" means the Supply of Goods (Implied Terms) Act 1973;

"the 1974 Act" means the Consumer Credit Act 1974;

"the 1977 Act" means the Unfair Contract Terms Act 1977; and

"the 1979 Act" means the Sale of Goods Act 1979.

[1066]

20   Citation, transitional provisions, commencement and extent

(1)   This Act may be cited as the Supply of Goods and Services Act 1982.

(2)   The transitional provisions in the Schedule to this Act shall have effect.

(3)   Part I of this Act together with section 17 and so much of sections 18 and 19 above as relates to that Part shall not come into operation until 4th January 1983; and Part II of this Act together with so much of sections 18 and 19 above as relates to that Part shall not come into operation until such day as may be appointed by an order made by the Secretary of State.

(4)   The power to make an order under subsection (3) above shall be exercisable by statutory instrument.

(5)   No provision of this Act applies to a contract made before the provision comes into operation.

(6)   This Act [except Part IA, which extends only to Scotland] extends to Northern Ireland [and Parts I and II do not extend] to Scotland.

[1067]–[1099]

NOTES

Sub-s (6): words in first pair of square brackets inserted, and words in second pair of square brackets substituted, by the Sale and Supply of Goods Act 1994, s 6, Sch 1, para 4.

Order: the Supply of Goods and Services Act 1982 (Commencement) Order 1982, SI 1982/1770.

(Schedule spent.)

WEIGHTS AND MEASURES ACT 1985

(1985 c 72)

ARRANGEMENT OF SECTIONS

PART IV
REGULATION OF TRANSACTIONS IN GOODS

PART VII
GENERAL

An Act to consolidate certain enactments relating to weights and measures

[30 October 1985]

1–20   ((*Pts I–III*) *outside the scope of this work.*)

PART IV
REGULATION OF TRANSACTIONS IN GOODS

Transactions in particular goods

21   Transactions in goods mentioned in Schedules 4 to 7

Schedules 4, 5, 6 and 7 to this Act (which relate to transactions in the goods mentioned in those Schedules) shall have effect.

[1100]

22   Orders relating to transactions in particular goods

(1)   The Secretary of State may by order make provision with respect to any goods specified in the order for all or any of the following purposes, that is to say, to ensure that, except in such cases or in such circumstances as may be so specified, the goods in question—

(a)   are sold only by quantity expressed in such manner as may be so specified,

(b)   are pre-packed, or are otherwise made up in or on a container for sale or for delivery after sale, only if the container is marked with such information as to the quantity of the goods as may be so specified,

(c)   are pre-packed, or are otherwise made up for sale or for delivery after sale, only in or on a container of a size or capacity so specified,

(d)   are sold, or are pre-packed, or are otherwise made up in or on a container for sale or for delivery after sale, or are made for sale, only in such quantities as may be so specified,

(e)   are not sold without the quantity sold expressed in such manner as may be so specified being made known to the buyer at or before such time as may be so specified,

(f)   are sold by means of, or are offered or exposed for sale in, a vending machine only if there is displayed on or in the machine—

(i)   such information as to the quantity of the goods in question comprised in each item for sale by means of that machine as may be so specified, and

(ii)   a statement of the name and address of the seller,

(g)   are carried for reward only in pursuance of an agreement made by reference to the quantity of the goods in question expressed in such manner as may be so specified,

(h)   in such circumstances as may be so specified, have associated with them in such manner as may be so specified a document containing a statement of the quantity of the goods in question expressed in such manner, and a statement of such other particulars, if any, as may be so specified, or

(i)   when carried on a road vehicle along a highway are accompanied by a document containing such particulars determined in such manner as may be so specified as to the weight of the vehicle and its load apart from the goods in question.

(2)   An order under subsection (1) above may be made with respect to any goods, including goods to which any of the provisions of Schedule 4, 5, 6, or 7 to this Act applies, and may—

(a)   make provision for any of the purposes mentioned in subsection (1) above in such manner, whether by means of amending, or of applying with or without modifications, or of excluding the application in whole or in part of, any of the provisions of this Act ... or of any previous order under subsection (1) or otherwise,

(b)   make such, if any, different provision for retail and other sales respectively, and

(c)   contain such consequential, incidental or supplementary provision, whether by such means as mentioned in paragraph (a) above or otherwise, as may appear to the Secretary of State to be expedient, and may in particular make provision in respect of contraventions of the order for which no penalty is provided by this Act for the imposition of penalties not exceeding those provided by section 84(6) below for an offence under this Act.

(3)   Without prejudice to the generality of the powers conferred by paragraph (c) of subsection (1) above, an order made by virtue of that paragraph—

(a)   may require a container to be marked with such information concerning it or its contents as is specified in the order, and

(b)   in order to prevent size or capacity from giving a false impression of the quantity of the goods in a container, may prescribe a minimum quantity for the goods in a container of a given capacity.

(4)   The minimum quantity referred to in subsection (3)(b) above may be expressed in the order by weight or volume, by percentage of the capacity of the container or in any other manner.

[1101]

NOTES

Sub-s (2): words omitted from para (a) repealed by the Weights and Measures (Packaged Goods) Regulations 2006, SI 2006/659, reg 1(2), Sch 1, Pt 2, paras (1), (2), subject to transitional provisions in reg 21 thereof.

Orders: the Weights and Measures (Liquid Fuel carried by Road Tanker) Order 1985, SI 1985/778; the Weights and Measures (Carriage of Solid Fuel by Rail) Order 1987, SI 1987/216; the Weights and Measures (Knitting Yarns) Order 1988, SI 1988/895; the Weights and Measures (Intoxicating Liquor) Order, SI 1988/2039; the Weights and Measures (Miscellaneous Foods) Order 1988, SI 1988/2040; the Weights and Measures (Cosmetic Products) Order 1994, SI 1994/1884. In addition, by virtue of the Interpretation Act 1978, s 17(2)(b), the following order has effect as if made under this section: the Weights and Measures Act 1963 (Cheese, Fish, Fresh Fruits and Vegetables, Meat and Poultry) Order 1984, SI 1984/1315.

---

23   Regulations as to information

(1)   The Secretary of State may make regulations—

(a)   as to the manner in which any container required by any of the provisions of Schedules 4, 5, 6 or 7 to this Act or of any other under section 22(1) above to be marked with information (including in particular information as to quantity or capacity) is to be so marked,

(b)   as to the manner in which any information required by any such provision to be displayed on or in a vending machine is to be so displayed,

(c)   as to the conditions which must be satisfied in marking with information as to the quantity of goods made up in it the container in or on which any goods are made up for sale (whether by way of pre-packing or otherwise) where those goods are goods on a sale of which (whether any sale or a sale of any particular description) the quantity of the goods sold is required by any such provision to be made known to the buyer at or before a particular time,

(d)   as to the units of measurement to be used in marking any such container or machine with any information,

(e)   for securing, in the case of pre-packed goods, that the container is so marked as to enable the packer to be identified,

(f)   as to the method by which and conditions under which quantity is to be determined in connection with any information relating to quantity required by or under section 21 or 22 above, and

(g)   permitting, in the case of such goods and in such circumstances as may be specified in the regulations, the weight of such articles used in making up the goods for sale as may be so specified to be included in the net weight of the goods for the purposes of this Part of this Act.

(2)   Any person who contravenes any regulation made under subsection (1) above otherwise than by virtue of paragraph (f) or (g) of that subsection shall be guilty of an offence.

[1102]

NOTES

Regulations: the Weights and Measures (Quantity Marking and Abbreviations of Units) Regulations 1987, SI 1987/1538. In addition, by virtue of the Interpretation Act 1978, s 17(2)(b), the following regulations have effect as if made under this section: the Weights and Measures (Solid Fuel) Regulations 1978, SI 1978/238; the Weights and Measures (Milk and Solid Fuel Vending Machines) Regulations 1980, SI 1980/246.

---

24   Exemption from requirements imposed under sections 21 to 23

(1)   The Secretary of State may by order grant, with respect to goods or sales of such descriptions as may be specified in the order, exemption, either generally or in such circumstances as may be so specified, from all or any of the requirements imposed by or under sections 21 to 23 above.

(2)   Until otherwise provided by an order under subsection (1) above, the following shall be exempted from all requirements imposed by or under sections 21 to 23 above, that is to say—

(a)   goods made up in or on a container for sale only for use by Her Majesty's forces or by a visiting force within the meaning of any of the provisions of Part I of the Visiting Forces Act 1952 and not sold or offered, exposed or in any person's possession for sale for any other use,

(b)   any sale of goods in the case of which the buyer gives notice in writing to the seller before the sale is completed that the goods are being bought—

(i)   for despatch to a destination outside Great Britain and any designated country, or

(ii)   for use as stores within the meaning of the Customs and Excise Management Act 1979 in a ship or aircraft on a voyage or flight to an eventual destination outside the United Kingdom and the Isle of Man,

(c)   any goods sold for, or offered, exposed or in any person's possession for sale only for, use or consumption at the premises of the seller, not being intoxicating liquor, and

(d)   any assortment of articles of food pre-packed together for consumption together as a meal and ready for such consumption without being cooked, heated or otherwise prepared.

[1103]

NOTES

Orders: the Weights and Measures (Liquid Fuel Carried by Road Tanker) Order 1985, SI 1985/778; the Weights and Measures (Carriage of Solid Fuel by Rail) Order 1987, SI 1987/216; the Weights and Measures (Intoxicating Liquor) Order, SI 1988/2039; the Weights and Measures (Miscellaneous Foods) Order 1988, SI 1988/2040; the Weights and Measures (Cosmetic Products) Order 1994, SI 1994/1884. In addition, by virtue of the Interpretation Act 1978, s 17(2)(b), the following orders have effect as if made under this section: the Weights and Measures Act 1963 (Cheese, Fish, Fresh Fruits and Vegetables, Meat and Poultry) Order 1984, SI 1984/1315.

25   Offences relating to transactions in particular goods

(1)   Subject to section 44 below, where any goods are required, when not pre-packed, to be sold only by quantity expressed in a particular manner or only in a particular quantity, any person shall be guilty of an offence who—

(a)   whether on his own behalf or on behalf of another person, offers or exposes for sale, sells or agrees to sell, or

(b)   causes or suffers any other person to offer or expose for sale, sell or agree to sell on his behalf,

those goods otherwise than by quantity expressed in that manner or, as the case may be, otherwise than in that quantity.

(2)   Any person shall be guilty of an offence who—

(a)   whether on his own behalf or on behalf of another person, has in his possession for sale, sells or agrees to sell,

(b)   except in the course of carriage of the goods for reward, has in his possession for delivery after sale, or

(c)   causes or suffers any other person to have in his possession for sale or for delivery after sale, sell or agree to sell on behalf of the first-mentioned person,

any goods to which subsection (3) below applies, whether the sale is or is to be, by retail or otherwise.

(3)   This subsection applies to any goods—

(a)   which are required to be pre-packed only in particular quantities but are not so pre-packed,

(b)   which are required to be otherwise made up in or on a container for sale or for delivery after sale only in particular quantities but are not so made up,

(c)   which are required to be made for sale only in particular quantities but are not so made,

(d)   which are required to be pre-packed only if the container is marked with particular information but are pre-packed otherwise than in or on a container so marked,

(e)   which are required to be otherwise made up in or on a container for sale or for delivery after sale only if the container is marked with particular information but are so made up otherwise than in or on a container so marked,

(f)   which are required to be pre-packed only in or on a container of a particular description but are not pre-packed in or on a container of that description, or

(g)   which are required to be otherwise made up in or on a container for sale or for delivery after sale only in or on a container of a particular description but are not so made up in or on a container of that description.

(4)　In the case of any sale where the quantity of the goods sold expressed in a particular manner is required to be made known to the buyer at or before a particular time and that quantity is not so made known, the person by whom, and any other person on whose behalf, the goods were sold shall be guilty of an offence.

(5)　Where any goods required to be sold by means of, or to be offered or exposed for sale in, a vending machine only if certain requirements are complied with are so sold, offered or exposed without those requirements being complied with, the seller or person causing the goods to be offered or exposed shall be guilty of an offence.

(6)　The preceding provisions of this section have effect subject to sections 33 to 37 below.

[(7)　For the purposes of this section the quantity of goods in a package, or of a loaf of bread, to which the packaged goods regulations apply shall be deemed to be the nominal quantity (within the meaning of those regulations) of the package or the loaf of bread.]

(8)　In this section "required" means required by or under this Part of this Act.

[1104]

NOTES

Sub-s (7): substituted by the Weights and Measures (Packaged Goods) Regulations 2006, SI 2006/659, reg 1(2), Sch 1, Pt 2, paras (1), (3), subject to transitional provisions in reg 21 thereof.

Quantity to be stated in writing

26　Quantity to be stated in writing in certain cases

(1)　Subject to section 27 below, the provisions of this section shall have effect on any sale of goods—

　　(a)　which is required by or under this Part of this Act to be a sale by quantity expressed in a particular manner,

　　(b)　in the case of which the quantity of the goods sold expressed in a particular manner is so required to be made known to the buyer at or before a particular time, or

　　(c)　which, being a sale by retail not falling within paragraph (a) or (b) above, is, or purports to be, a sale by quantity expressed in a particular manner other than by number.

(2)　Subject to subsections (4) to (6) below, unless the quantity of the goods sold expressed in the manner in question is made known to the buyer at the premises of the seller and the goods are delivered to the buyer at those premises on the same occasion as, and at or after the time when, that quantity is so made known to him, a statement in writing of that quantity shall be delivered to the consignee at or before delivery of the goods to him.

(3)　If subsection (2) above is contravened then, subject to sections 33 to 37 below, the person by whom, and any other person on whose behalf, the goods were sold shall be guilty of an offence.

(4)　If at the time when the goods are delivered the consignee is absent, it shall be sufficient compliance with subsection (2) above if the statement is left at some suitable place at the premises at which the goods are delivered.

(5)　Subsection (2) above shall not apply to any sale otherwise than by retail where, by agreement with the buyer, the quantity of the goods sold is to be determined after their delivery to the consignee.

(6)　Where any liquid goods are sold by capacity measurement and the quantity sold is measured at the time of delivery and elsewhere than at the premises of the seller, subsection (2) above shall not apply but, unless the quantity by capacity measurement of the goods sold is measured in the presence of the buyer, the person by whom the goods are delivered shall immediately after the delivery hand to the buyer, or if the buyer is not present leave at some suitable place at the premises at which the goods are delivered, a statement in writing of the quantity by capacity measurement delivered, and if without reasonable cause he fails so to do he shall be guilty of an offence.

[1105]

27　Exemption from requirements of section 26

(1)　The Secretary of State may by order grant, with respect to goods or sales of such descriptions as may be specified in the order, exemption, either generally or in such circumstances as may be so specified, from all or any of the requirements of section 26 above.

(2)　Until otherwise provided by an order under subsection (1) above, nothing in section 26 above shall apply to—

　　(a)　a sale by retail from a vehicle of—

　　　　(i)　any of the following in a quantity not exceeding [110 kilograms], that is to say, any solid fuel within the meaning of Schedule 5 to this Act, and wood fuel, or

　　　　(ii)　any of the following in a quantity not exceeding [25 litres], that is to say, liquid fuel, lubricating oil, and any mixture of such fuel and oil,

(b) a sale by retail of bread within the meaning of the Weights and Measures Act 1963 (Miscellaneous Foods) Order 1984,

(c) goods made up for sale (whether by way of pre-packing or otherwise) in or on a container marked with a statement in writing with respect to the quantity of the goods expressed in the manner in question, being a container which is delivered with the goods,

(d) a sale of goods in the case of which a document stating the quantity of the goods expressed in the manner in question is required to be delivered to the buyer or consignee of the goods by or under any other provision of this Part of this Act,

(e) any such goods or sales as are mentioned in section 24(2)(a) to (d) above,

(f) a sale of intoxicating liquor for consumption at the premises of the seller,

(g) a sale by means of a vending machine, or

(h) goods delivered at premises of the buyer by means of an installation providing a connection of a permanent nature between those premises and premises of the seller.

[1106]

NOTES

Sub-s (2): words in square brackets in para (a) substituted by the Units of Measurement Regulations 1994, SI 1994/2867, reg 6(1), (4).

Weights and Measures 1963 (Miscellaneous Foods) Order 1984, SI 1984/1316: revoked and replaced by the Weights and Measures (Miscellaneous Foods) Order 1988, SI 1988/2040.

General offences

28 Short weight, etc

(1) Subject to sections 33 to 37 below, any person who, in selling or purporting to sell any goods by weight or other measurement or by number, delivers or causes to be delivered to the buyer—

(a) a lesser quantity than that purported to be sold, or

(b) a lesser quantity than corresponds with the price charged,

shall be guilty of an offence.

(2) For the purposes of this section—

[(a) the quantity of goods in a package, or of a loaf of bread, to which the packaged goods regulations apply shall be deemed to be the nominal quantity (within the meaning of those regulations) of the package or the loaf of bread; and]

(b) any statement, whether oral or in writing, as to the weight of any goods shall be taken, unless otherwise expressed, to be a statement as to the net weight of the goods.

(3) Nothing in this section shall apply in relation to any such goods or sales as are mentioned in section 24(2)(a) or (b) above.

[1107]–[1108]

NOTES

Sub-s (2): para (a) substituted by the Weights and Measures (Packaged Goods) Regulations 2006, SI 2006/659, reg 1(2), Sch 1, Pt 2, paras (1), (4), subject to transitional provisions in reg 21 thereof.

29 (*Repealed by the Consumer Protection from Unfair Trading Regulations 2008, SI 2008/1277, reg 30(1), (3), Sch 2, Pt 1, para 31, Sch 4, subject to savings in reg 30(2) of, and Sch 3, paras 9, 11 to, those Regulations at* **[3702]**, **[3704]**.)

30 Quantity less than stated

(1) If, in the case of any goods pre-packed in or on a container marked with a statement in writing with respect to the quantity of the goods, the quantity of the goods is at any time found to be less than that stated, then, subject to sections 33 to 37 below—

(a) any person who has those goods in his possession for sale shall be guilty of an offence, and

(b) if it is shown that the deficiency cannot be accounted for by anything occurring after the goods had been sold by retail and delivered to, or to a person nominated in that behalf by, the buyer, any person by whom or on whose behalf those goods have been sold or agreed to be sold at any time while they were pre-packed in or on the container in question, shall be guilty of an offence.

(2) If—

(a) in the case of a sale of or agreement to sell any goods which, not being pre-packed, are made up for sale or for delivery after sale in or on a container marked with a statement in writing with respect to the quantity of the goods, or

(b) in the case of any goods which, in connection with their sale or an agreement for their sale, have associated with them a document containing such a statement, the quantity of the goods is at any time found to be less than that stated, then, if it is shown that the deficiency cannot be accounted for by anything occurring after the goods had been delivered to, or to a person nominated in that behalf by, the buyer, and subject to sections 33 to 37 below and paragraph 10 of Schedule 4 to this Act, the person by whom, and any other person on whose behalf, the goods were sold or agreed to be sold shall be guilty of an offence.

(3)   Subsections (1) and (2) above shall have effect notwithstanding that the quantity stated is expressed to be the quantity of the goods at a specified time falling before the time in question, or is expressed with some other qualification of whatever description, except where—

    (a)   that quantity is so expressed in pursuance of an express requirement of this Part of this Act or any instrument made under this Part, or

    (b)   the goods, although falling within subsection (1) or subsection (2)(a) above—

        (i)   are not required by or under this Part of this Act to be pre-packed as mentioned in subsection (1) or, as the case may be, to be made up for sale or for delivery after sale in or on a container only if the container is marked as mentioned in subsection (2)(a), and

        (ii)   are not goods on a sale of which (whether any sale or a sale of any particular description) the quantity sold is required by or under any provision of this Part of this Act other than section 26, to be made known to the buyer at or before a particular time, or

    (c)   the goods, although falling within subsection (2)(b) above, are not required by or under this Part of this Act to have associated with them such a document as is mentioned in that provision.

(4)   In any case to which, by virtue of paragraph (a), (b) or (c) of subsection (3) above, the provisions of subsection (1) or (2) above do not apply, if it is found at any time that the quantity of the goods in question is less than that stated and it is shown that the deficiency is greater than can be reasonably justified on the ground justifying the qualification in question, then, subject to sections 33 to 37 below—

    (a)   in the case of goods such as are mentioned in subsection (1) above, if it is further shown as mentioned in that subsection, then—

        (i)   where the container in question was marked in Great Britain, the person by whom, and any other person on whose behalf, the container was marked, or

        (ii)   where the container in question was marked outside Great Britain, the person by whom, and any other person on whose behalf, the goods were first sold in Great Britain,

    shall be guilty of an offence;

    (b)   in the case of goods such as are mentioned in subsection (2) above, the person by whom, and any other person on whose behalf, the goods were sold or agreed to be sold shall be guilty of an offence if, but only if, he would, but for paragraph (a), (b) or (c) of subsection (3) above have been guilty of an offence under subsection (2).

(5)   Subsection (2) of section 28 above shall have effect for the purposes of this section as it has effect for the purposes of that section.

(6)   Nothing in this section shall apply in relation to any such goods or sales as are mentioned in section 24(2)(a) or (b) above.

[1109]

31   Incorrect statements

(1)   Without prejudice to section 30(2) to (4) above, if in the case of any goods required by or under this Part of this Act to have associated with them a document containing particular statements, that document is found to contain any such statement which is materially incorrect, any person who, knowing or having reasonable cause to suspect that statement to be materially incorrect, inserted it or caused it to be inserted in the document, or used the document for the purposes of this Part of this Act while that statement was contained in the document, shall be guilty of an offence.

(2)   Subsection (2) of section 28 above shall have effect for the purposes of this section as it has effect for the purposes of that section.

(3)   Nothing in this section shall apply in relation to any such goods or sales as are mentioned in section 24(2)(a) or (b) above.

[1110]

32   Offences due to default of third person

Where the commission by any person of an offence under this Part of this Act or an instrument made under this Part is due to the act or default of some other person, the other person shall be guilty of an offence and may be charged with and convicted of the offence whether or not proceedings are taken against the first-mentioned person.

[1111]

Defences

33 Warranty

(1)   Subject to the following provisions of this section, in any proceedings for an offence under this Part of this Act or any instrument made under this Part, being an offence relating to the quantity or pre-packing of any goods, it shall be a defence for the person charged to prove—

   (a)   that he bought the goods from some other person—

        (i)   as being of the quantity which the person charged purported to sell or represented, or which was marked on any container or stated in any document to which the proceedings relate, or

        (ii)   as conforming with the statement marked on any container to which the proceedings relate, or with the requirements with respect to the pre-packing of goods of this Part of this Act or any instrument made under this Part,

       as the case may require, and

   (b)   that he so bought the goods with a written warranty from that other person that they were of that quantity or, as the case may be, did so conform, and

   (c)   that at the time of the commission of the offence he did in fact believe the statement contained in the warranty to be accurate and had no reason to believe it to be inaccurate, and

   (d)   if the warranty was given by a person who at the time he gave it was resident outside Great Britain and any designated country, that the person charged had taken reasonable steps to check the accuracy of the statement contained in the warranty, and

   (e)   in the case of proceedings relating to the quantity of any goods, that he took all reasonable steps to ensure that, while in his possession, the quantity of the goods remained unchanged and, in the case of such or any other proceedings, that apart from any change in their quantity the goods were at the time of the commission of the offence in the same state as when he bought them.

(2)   A warranty shall not be a defence in any such proceedings as are mentioned in subsection (1) above unless, not later than three days before the date of the hearing, the person charged has sent to the prosecutor a copy of the warranty with a notice stating that he intends to rely on it and specifying the name and address of the person from whom the warranty was received, and has also sent a like notice to that person.

(3)   Where the person charged is the employee of a person who, if he had been charged, would have been entitled to plead a warranty as a defence under this section, subsection (1) above shall have effect—

   (a)   with the substitution, for any reference (however expressed) in paragraphs (a), (b), (d) and (e) to the person charged, of a reference to his employer, and

   (b)   with the substitution for paragraph (c) of the following—

       "(c)   that at the time of the commission of the offence his employer did in fact believe the statement contained in the warranty to be accurate and the person charged had no reason to believe it to be inaccurate,".

(4)   The person by whom the warranty is alleged to have been given shall be entitled to appear at the hearing and to give evidence.

(5)   If the person charged in any such proceedings as are mentioned in subsection (1) above wilfully attributes to any goods a warranty given in relation to any other goods, he shall be guilty of an offence.

(6)   A person who, in respect of any goods sold by him in respect of which a warranty might be pleaded under this section, gives to the buyer a false warranty in writing shall be guilty of an offence unless he proves that when he gave the warranty he took all reasonable steps to ensure that the statements contained in it were, and would continue at all relevant times to be, accurate.

(7)   Where in any such proceedings as are mentioned in subsection (1) above ("the original proceedings") the person charged relies successfully on a warranty given to him or to his employer, any proceedings under subsection (6) above in respect of the warranty may, at the option of the prosecutor, be taken either before a court having jurisdiction in the place where the original proceedings were taken or before a court having jurisdiction in the place where the warranty was given.

(8)   For the purposes of this section, any statement with respect to any goods which is contained in any document required by or under this Part of this Act to be associated with the goods or in any invoice, and, in the case of goods made up in or on a container for sale or for delivery after sale, any statement with respect to those goods with which that container is marked, shall be taken to be a written warranty of the accuracy of that statement.

[1112]

34   Reasonable precautions and due diligence

(1)   In any proceedings for an offence under this Part of this Act or any instrument made under this Part, it shall be a defence for the person charged to prove that he took all reasonable precautions and exercised all due diligence to avoid the commission of the offence.

(2)   If in any case the defence provided by subsection (1) above involves an allegation that the commission of the offence in question was due to the act or default of another person or due to reliance on information supplied by another person, the person charged shall not, without the leave of the court, be entitled to rely on the defence unless, before the beginning of the period of seven days ending with the date when the hearing of the charge began, he served on the prosecutor a notice giving such information identifying or assisting in the identification of the other person as was then in his possession.

[1113]

35   Subsequent deficiency

(1)   This subsection applies to any proceedings for an offence under this Part of this Act, or any instrument made under this Part, by reason of the quantity—

    (a)   of any goods made up for sale or for delivery after sale (whether by way of pre-packing or otherwise) in or on a container marked with an indication of quantity,

    (b)   of any goods which, in connection with their sale or an agreement for their sale, have associated with them a document purporting to state the quantity of the goods, or

    (c)   of any goods required by or under this Part of this Act to be pre-packed, or to be otherwise made up in or on a container for sale or for delivery after sale, or to be made for sale, only in particular quantities,

being less than that marked on the container or stated in the document in question or than the relevant particular quantity, as the case may be.

(2)   In any proceedings to which subsection (1) above applies, it shall be a defence for the person charged to prove that the deficiency arose—

    (a)   in a case falling within paragraph (a) of subsection (1) above, after the making up of the goods and the marking of the container,

    (b)   in a case falling within paragraph (b) of that subsection, after the preparation of the goods for delivery in pursuance of the sale or agreement and after the completion of the document,

    (c)   in a case falling within paragraph (c) of that subsection, after the making up or making, as the case may be, of the goods for sale,

and was attributable wholly to factors for which reasonable allowance was made in stating the quantity of the goods in the marking or document or in making up or making the goods for sale, as the case may be.

(3)   In the case of a sale by retail of food, other than food pre-packed in a container which is, or is required by or under this Part of this Act to be, marked with an indication of quantity, in any proceedings for an offence under this Part of this Act or any instrument made under this Part, by reason of the quantity delivered to the buyer being less than that purported to be sold, it shall be a defence for the person charged to prove that the deficiency was due wholly to unavoidable evaporation or drainage since the sale and that due care and precaution were taken to minimise any such evaporation or drainage.

(4)   If in any proceedings for an offence under this Part of this Act or any instrument made under this Part, being an offence in respect of any deficiency in the quantity of any goods sold, it is shown that between the sale and the discovery of the deficiency the goods were with the consent of the buyer subjected to treatment which could result in a reduction in the quantity of those goods for delivery to, or to any person nominated in that behalf by, the buyer, the person charged shall not be found guilty of that offence unless it is shown that the deficiency cannot be accounted for by the subjecting of the goods to that treatment.

[1114]

36   Excess due to precautions

In any proceedings for an offence under this Part of this Act or any instrument made under this Part, being an offence in respect of any excess in the quantity of any goods, it shall be a defence for the person charged to prove that the excess was attributable to the taking of measures reasonably necessary in order to avoid the commission of an offence in respect of a deficiency in those or other goods.

[1115]

37   Provisions as to testing

(1)   If proceedings for an offence under this Part of this Act, or any instrument made under this Part, in respect of any deficiency or excess in the quantity—

    (a)   of any goods made up for sale (whether by way of pre-packing or otherwise) in or on a container marked with an indication of quantity, or

    (b)   of any goods which have been pre-packed or otherwise made up in or on a container for sale or for delivery after sale, or which have been made for sale, and which are required by or under this Part of this Act to be pre-packed, or to be otherwise so made up, or to be so made, as the case may be, only in particular quantities,

are brought with respect to any article, and it is proved that, at the time and place at which that article was tested, other articles of the same kind, being articles which, or articles containing goods which, had been sold by the person charged or were in that person's possession for sale or for delivery after sale, were available for testing, the person charged shall not be convicted of such an offence with respect to that article unless a reasonable number of those other articles was also tested.

(2)   In any proceedings for such an offence as is mentioned in subsection (1) above, the court—
    (a)   if the proceedings are with respect to one or more of a number of articles tested on the same occasion, shall have regard to the average quantity in all the articles tested,
    (b)   if the proceedings are with respect to a single article, shall disregard any inconsiderable deficiency or excess, and
    (c)   shall have regard generally to all the circumstances of the case.

(3)   Subsections (1) and (2) above shall apply with the necessary modifications to proceedings for an offence in respect of the size, capacity or contents of a container as they apply to proceedings for an offence in respect of the excess or deficiency in the quantity of certain goods.

(4)   Where by virtue of section 32 above a person is charged with an offence with which some other person might have been charged, the reference in subsection (1) above to articles or goods sold by or in the possession of the person charged shall be construed as a reference to articles or goods sold by or in the possession of that other person.

[1116]

Powers of inspectors

38 Special powers of inspectors with respect to certain goods

(1)   Subsection (2) below applies where any person—
    (a)   makes in any manner any representation as to the quantity of any goods offered or exposed for sale by him, or
    (b)   has in his possession or charge awaiting or in the course of delivery to the buyer any goods which have been sold or agreed to be sold, and the sale is, or purports to be, or is required by or under this Part of this Act to be, by quantity expressed in a particular manner, or is such that the quantity of the goods sold is required by or under any provision of this Part other than section 26 to be made known to the buyer at or before a particular time, or
    (c)   has in his possession or charge for sale, or awaiting or in the course of delivery to a buyer after they have been sold or agreed to be sold—
        (i)   any goods pre-packed or otherwise made up in or on a container for sale or for delivery after sale which are required by or under this Part of this Act to be pre-packed, or to be otherwise so made up, as the case may be, only in particular quantities or only if the container is marked with particular information, or
        (ii)   any goods pre-packed in or on a container marked with an indication of quantity, or
        (iii)   any goods required by or under this Part of this Act to be made for sale only in particular quantities, or
    (d)   has in his possession or charge for sale, or awaiting or in the course of delivery to a buyer after they have been sold or agreed to be sold, any goods subject to a requirement imposed by virtue of section 22(1)(c) above.

(2)   Where this subsection applies, the powers of an inspector under section 79 below shall, subject to subsection (4) below, include power to require the person referred to in subsection (1) above either to do in the presence of the inspector, or to permit the inspector to do, all or any of the following things, that is to say—
    (a)   weigh or otherwise measure or count the goods,
    (b)   weigh or otherwise measure any container in or on which the goods are made up,
    (c)   in the case of goods within subsection (1)(d) above, do anything else as respects the goods or container which is reasonably necessary to ascertain whether the requirement there mentioned is complied with, and which does not damage or depreciate the goods or container,
    (d)   if necessary for any of the purposes of paragraphs (a) to (c) above, break open any container of goods, or open any vending machine in which goods are offered or exposed for sale,

and, in the case of any of the goods which are not already sold, power to require that person to sell any of them to the inspector.

(3) Where any container of goods is broken open under subsection (2) above and all requirements of, and of any instrument made under, this Part of this Act which are applicable to those goods are found to have been complied with, then—

    (a)   if the container can be resealed without injury to the contents, the inspector may reseal it with a label certifying that all such requirements have been complied with, and

    (b)   if he does not reseal it or it cannot be so resealed without injury to the contents, the inspector shall at the request of the person referred to in subsection (1) above buy the goods on behalf of the local weights and measures authority.

(4) ...

[1117]

NOTES

Sub-s (4): repealed by the Food Safety Act 1990, s 59(1), (4), Sch 3, para 32, Sch 5.

39   Powers of inspectors with respect to certain documents

(1)   An inspector, subject to the production if so requested of his credentials, may require the person in charge of any document required by or under this Part of this Act to be associated with any goods to produce that document for inspection.

(2)   If the inspector has reasonable cause to believe that any document produced to him under subsection (1) above contains any inaccurate statement, he may either—

    (a)   seize and detain the document, giving in exchange a copy with an endorsement signed by him certifying that the original has been seized and giving particulars of any inaccuracy alleged, or

    (b)   without prejudice to any proceedings which may be taken by reason of any inaccuracy alleged, make on the document an endorsement signed by him giving particulars of any such inaccuracy;

and, except where the context otherwise requires, any reference in this Part of this Act to any such document includes a reference to a copy given in pursuance of paragraph (a) above.

[1118]

40   Powers of inspectors with respect to goods carried on road vehicles

(1)   Subsection (2) below applies where, in the case of any goods being carried on a road vehicle,—

    (a)   the whole of the vehicle's load is being carried for sale to, or for delivery after sale to, the same person, and

    (b)   any document produced in pursuance of section 39(1) above by the person in charge of the vehicle purports, or is required by or under this Part of this Act, to state the quantity of the goods.

(2)   Where this subsection applies, the inspector may, for the purpose of the exercise of his powers under section 38(2) above do all or any of the following things, that is to say—

    (a)   require the goods to which the document relates to be unloaded from the vehicle;

    (b)   require the vehicle to be taken to the nearest suitable and available weighing or measuring equipment;

    (c)   require the person in charge of the vehicle to have it check-weighed.

(3)   The powers conferred by subsection (2) above shall be exercised only to such extent as may appear to the inspector reasonably necessary in order to secure that the provisions of this Act ... and of any instrument made under those provisions are duly observed.

[1119]

NOTES

Sub-s (3): words omitted repealed by the Weights and Measures (Packaged Goods) Regulations 2006, SI 2006/659, reg 1(2), Sch 1, Pt 2, paras (1), (5), subject to transitional provisions in reg 21 thereof.

Miscellaneous and supplementary

41   Check-weighing of certain road vehicles

Where any road vehicle is loaded with goods for sale by weight to a single buyer of the whole of the vehicle's load, or for delivery to the buyer after they have been so sold, the buyer or seller of the goods, or any inspector who shows that he is authorised so to do by the buyer or seller of the goods, may require the person in charge of the vehicle to have it check-weighed, and if that person fails without reasonable cause to comply with any such requirement he shall be guilty of an offence.

[1120]

42   Power to make test purchases

A local weights and measures authority shall have power to make, or to authorise an inspector to make on their behalf, such purchases of goods as may appear expedient for the purpose of determining whether or not the provisions of this Part of this Act and any instrument made under this Part, and the provisions of Parts II and III of this Act and any instrument made under either of those Parts, are being complied with.

[1121]

43   (*Repealed by the Deregulation and Contracting Out Act 1994, ss 14, 81(1), Sch 17.*)

44   Selling by quantity

Where any goods are required by or under this Part of this Act to be sold only by quantity expressed in a particular manner—

(a)   it shall be a sufficient compliance with that requirement in the case of any sale of, or agreement to sell, any such goods if the quantity of the goods expressed in the manner in question is made known to the buyer before the purchase price is agreed; and

(b)   no person shall be guilty of an offence under section 25(1) above by reason of the exposing or offering for sale of such goods at any time if both the quantity of the goods expressed in the manner in question and the price at which they are exposed or offered for sale are made known at that time to any prospective buyer.

[1122]

45   Making quantity known to a person

(1)   For the purposes of this Part of this Act, without prejudice to any other method of making known to a person the quantity of any goods expressed in a particular manner, that quantity shall be taken to be made known to that person—

(a)   if the goods are weighed or otherwise measured or counted, as the case may require, in the presence of that person,

(b)   if the goods are made up in or on a container marked with a statement in writing of the quantity of the goods expressed in the manner in question and the container is readily available for inspection by that person, or

(c)   upon such a statement in writing being delivered to that person.

(2)   The Secretary of State may by order provide that subsection (3) below shall apply, in the case of such goods in such circumstances as are specified in the order, to any requirement so specified of, or of any instrument made under, this Part of this Act with respect to the making known to the buyer of the quantity by weight of such goods sold by retail.

(3)   In any case to which this subsection applies, the requirement specified in the order shall be taken to be satisfied if the goods are bought at premises at which weighing equipment of such description as may be prescribed—

(a)   is kept available by the occupier of those premises for use without charge by any prospective buyer of such goods for the purpose of weighing for himself any such goods offered or exposed for sale by retail on those premises, and

(b)   is so kept available in a position on those premises which is suitable and convenient for such use of the equipment, and

(c)   is reserved for use for that purpose at all times while those premises are open for retail transactions,

and a notice of the availability of the equipment for such use is displayed in a position on the premises where it may be readily seen by any such prospective buyer.

[1123]

46   Weighing in presence of a person

For the purposes of this Part of this Act, a person shall not be taken to weigh or otherwise measure or count any goods in the presence of any other person unless he causes any equipment used for the purpose to be so placed, and so conducts the operation of weighing or otherwise measuring or counting the goods, as to permit that other person a clear and unobstructed view of the equipment, if any, and of the operation, and of any indication of quantity given by any such equipment as the result of that operation.

[1124]–[1130]

47–78   (*Ss 47–68 (Pt V) repealed by the Weights and Measures (Packaged Goods) Regulations 2006, SI 2006/659, reg 1(2), Sch 1, Pt 2, paras (1), (2), subject to transitional provisions in reg 21 thereof; ss 69–78 (Pt VI) outside the scope of this work.*)

PART VII
GENERAL

79–85   (*Outside the scope of this work.*)

Miscellaneous and supplementary

86–98   *(Outside the scope of this work.)*

99   Short title and commencement

(1)   This Act may be cited as the Weights and Measures Act 1985.

(2)   … this Act shall come into force at the end of the period of three months beginning with the day on which it is passed.

[1131]

NOTES

Sub-s (2): words omitted repealed by the Deregulation and Contracting Out Act 1994, s 81, Sch 17.

SCHEDULES

(Schs 1–5 outside the scope of this work.)

SCHEDULE 6
MISCELLANEOUS GOODS OTHER THAN FOODS

Section 21

LPART I
LIQUID FUEL AND LUBRICANTS

1.   This Part of this Schedule applies to—
    (a)   liquid fuel, lubricating oil and any mixture of such fuel and oil, and
    (b)   lubricating grease.

2.   Subject to paragraph 3 below, goods to which this Part of this Schedule applies—
    (a)   unless pre-packed, shall be sold only by net weight or by capacity measurement,
    (b)   shall be pre-packed only if the container is marked with an indication of quantity either by net weight or by capacity measurement, and
    (c)   in the case of lubricating oil in a quantity of [one litre] or less, shall be made up in a container for sale otherwise than by way of pre-packing only if the container is marked with an indication of quantity by capacity measurement.

3.   Notwithstanding anything in paragraph 2 above, liquid fuel—
    (a)   when not pre-packed may be sold by volume, and
    (b)   may be pre-packed in a container marked with an indication of quantity by volume,

being in either case the volume of the gas which would be produced from the fuel in question at such temperature and such atmospheric pressure as are specified in regulations made by the Secretary of State with respect to fuel of the type in question or, if no such regulations are in force, as may be made known by the seller to the buyer before he pays for or takes possession of the fuel; and there shall be exempted from all requirements of paragraph 2 above goods of any description in a quantity of less than [250 grams] or of less than [250 millilitres]

[1132]

NOTES

Paras 2, 3: words in square brackets substituted by the Weights and Measures Act 1985 (Metrication) (Amendment) Order 1994, SI 1994/2866, art 3(1), (6)(a), (b).

PART II
READY-MIXED CEMENT MORTAR AND READY-MIXED CONCRETE

4.   This Part of this Schedule applies to ready-mixed cement mortar and ready-mixed concrete.

5.—[(1)   Subject to the following provisions of this Part of this Schedule, any goods to which this Part of this Schedule applies—
    (a)   if made up in advance ready for retail sale or wholesale in a securely closed container, shall be sold only by volume, and
    (b)   if not so made up, shall be sold only by volume in a multiple of 0.1 cubic metre.]

(2)   There shall be exempted from the requirements of this paragraph any goods in a quantity of less than one cubic metre.

6.   Part II of Schedule 4 to this Act, except sub-paragraph (3) of paragraph 7, shall apply for the purposes of this Part of this Schedule as if—
    (a)   any reference in the said Part II to ballast included a reference to goods to which this Part of this Schedule applies; and
    (b)   the reference in sub-paragraph (1) of paragraph 7 to paragraph 2 of Schedule 4 were a reference to paragraph 5 of this Schedule.

7.   *(Applies to Scotland only.)*

[1133]

NOTES
Para 5: sub-para (1) substituted by the Weights and Measures (Specified Quantities) (Pre-packed Products) Regulations 2009, SI 2009/663, reg 2(1), (4).

PART III
AGRICULTURAL LIMING MATERIALS, AGRICULTURAL SALT AND INORGANIC FERTILISERS

8. This Part of this Schedule applies—
    (a) to agricultural liming materials, other than calcareous sand,
    (b) to agricultural salt,
    (c) to, and to any mixture consisting mainly of, inorganic fertilisers, other than such fertilisers or such a mixture made up into pellets or other articles for use as individual items, and
    (d) to any mixture of any of the foregoing.

9.—(1) Goods to which this Part of this Schedule applies which are not pre-packed, other than liquid fertilisers, shall be sold only by quantity, being—
    (a) quantity by net weight; or
    (b) if the goods are sold in a container which does not exceed the permitted weight and the gross weight of the goods is not less than [25 kilograms], quantity either by net weight or by gross weight; or
    (c) quantity by volume.

(2) Goods to which this Part of this Schedule applies shall be pre-packed only if the container is marked with an indication of quantity, being—
    (a) in the case of liquid fertilisers, quantity by capacity measurement;
    (b) in any other case, quantity by net weight or, if the container does not exceed the permitted weight and the gross weight of the goods is not less than [25 kilograms], quantity either by net weight or by gross weight.

(3) In this paragraph, "the permitted weight" means a weight or the rate of [650 grams per 50 kilograms] of the gross weight.

(4) There shall be exempted from all requirements of this paragraph any sale of goods with a view to their industrial use.

10. Paragraphs 4 and 5 of Schedule 4 to this Act shall have effect as if any reference in those paragraphs to ballast included a reference to any goods to which this Part of this Schedule applies.

[1134]

NOTES
Para 9: words in square brackets substituted by the Weights and Measures Act 1985 (Metrication) (Amendment) Order 1994, SI 1994/2866, art 3(1), (6)(c).

PART IV
WOOD FUEL

11. Subject to paragraphs 12 and 13 below—
    (a) wood fuel which is not made up in a container for sale shall be sold by retail only by net weight;
    (b) in the case of a sale by retail of wood fuel made up in a container for sale, the quantity by net weight of the fuel sold shall be made known to the buyer before he pays for or takes possession of it.

12.—(1) Paragraph 11 above shall not have effect in any area unless the local weights and measures authority for that area so direct by byelaw.

(2) Not less than one month before making any byelaw by virtue of this paragraph, the local weights and measures authority shall give public notice of their intention to make it by advertisement in one or more newspapers circulating in the area to which the byelaw is to apply.

(3) The local weights and measures authority by whom any byelaw is made by virtue of this paragraph shall give notice of the making of the byelaw to the Secretary of State.

13. There shall be exempted from the requirements of paragraph 11 above any sale of wood fuel in a quantity which does not exceed [7.5 kilograms] or which exceeds [500 kilograms].

14. Paragraphs 9 and 10 of Schedule 5 to this Act shall have effect as if any reference in those paragraphs to solid fuel included a reference to wood fuel.

[1135]

NOTES
Para 13: words in square brackets substituted by the Weights and Measures Act 1985 (Metrication) (Amendment) Order 1994, SI 1994/2866, art 3(1), (6)(d).

[PART V
COSMETIC PRODUCTS

15.   In this Part of this Schedule, "cosmetic product" means any substance or preparation intended to be placed in contact with the various external parts of the human body (that is to say, the epidermis, hair system, nails, lips and external genital organs) or with the teeth and the mucous membranes of the oral cavity with a view exclusively or mainly to cleaning them, perfuming them, changing their appearance, correcting bodily odours, protecting them or keeping them in good condition.

16.—(1)   Subject to sub-paragraph (2) below, cosmetic products shall be pre-packed only if the container is marked with an indication of quantity either by net weight or by volume.

   (2)   There shall be exempted from the requirements of sub-paragraph (1) above—
   (a)   cosmetic products in quantities of less than 5 grams or 5 millilitres;
   (b)   cosmetic products in sachets or other containers for single use only; and
   (c)   cosmetic products normally sold as a number of items for which particulars of weight or volume are not significant if—
      (i)   the number of items is marked on the package, or
      (ii)   the number of items may readily be seen without opening the package, or
      (iii) the items are normally sold only individually.

   (3)   Cosmetic products which are not pre-packed shall be sold only by quantity expressed as net weight, volume or number.]

[1136]

NOTES
Substituted by the Weights and Measures (Cosmetics) Order 1994, SI 1994/1884, art 2.

PART VI
SOAP

[16A.   In this Part of this Schedule "soap" does not include any soap which is a cosmetic product as defined in paragraph 15 above.]

17.   Subject to paragraph 18 below—
   (a)   soap in the form of a cake, tablet or bar shall be pre-packed only if the container is marked with an indication of quantity by net weight,
   (b)   liquid soap shall be pre-packed only if the container is marked with an indication of quantity by capacity measurement, and
   (c)   soap in any other form—
      (i)   unless pre-packed, shall be sold by retail only by net weight, and
      (ii)   shall be pre-packed only if the container is marked with an indication of quantity by net weight.

18.   There shall be exempted from the requirements of this Part of this Schedule—
   (a)   liquid soap in a quantity of less than [125 millilitres], and
   (b)   soap in any other form in a quantity of less than [25 grams].

[1137]

NOTES
Para 16A: inserted by the Weights and Measures (Cosmetic Products) Order 1994, SI 1994/1884, art 3.
Para 18: words in square brackets substituted by the Weights and Measures Act 1985 (Metrication) (Amendment) Order 1994, SI 1994/2866, art 3(1), (6)(e).

PART VII
MISCELLANEOUS GOODS TO BE SOLD BY OR MARKED WITH LENGTH

19.   This Part of this Schedule applies to goods of any of the following descriptions, that is to say, bias binding, elastic, ribbon, tape and sewing thread.

20.   Subject to paragraph 21 below, goods to which this Part of this Schedule applies—
   (a)   unless pre-packed, shall be sold by retail only by length, and
   (b)   shall be pre-packed only if the container is marked with an indication of quantity by length.

21.   There shall be exempted from all requirements of paragraph 20 above goods of any description in a quantity of less than [one metre].

[1138]

NOTES
Para 21: words in square brackets substituted by the Weights and Measures Act 1985 (Metrication) (Amendment) Order 1994, SI 1994/2866, art 3(1), (6)(f).

PART VIII
MISCELLANEOUS GOODS TO BE SOLD BY OR MARKED WITH NET WEIGHT

22. This Part of this Schedule applies to—
    (a)   distemper,
    (b)   articles offered as feed for household pets, being manufactured feed or bird feed, other than animal feed in biscuit or cake form pre-packed in a quantity by number not exceeding sixteen,
    (c)   nails,
    (d)   paste paint,
    (e)   seeds, other than pea or bean seeds, and
    (f)   rolled oats.

23. Subject to paragraphs 24 and 25 below, goods to which this Part of this Schedule applies—
    (a)   unless pre-packed, shall be sold by retail only by net weight, and
    (b)   shall be pre-packed only if the container is marked with an indication of quantity by net weight.

[24. The following shall be exempted from the requirements of this Part of this Schedule—
    (a)   distemper or paste paint in a quantity of less than 250 grams,
    (b)   bird seed in a quantity of less than 125 grams, and
    (c)   any other goods in a quantity of less than 25 grams.]

25. Notwithstanding anything in paragraph 24 above, nails—
    (a)   when not pre-packed may be so sold by retail by number, and
    (b)   may be pre-packed in or on a container marked with an indication of quantity by number.

[1139]

NOTES
Para 24: substituted by the Weights and Measures Act 1985 (Metrication) (Amendment) Order 1994, SI 1994/2866, art 3(1), (6)(g).

PART IX
MISCELLANEOUS GOODS TO BE MARKED WHEN PRE-PACKED WITH NET WEIGHT

26. This Part of this Schedule applies to—
    (a)   Portland cement,
    (b)   cleansing powders and scouring powders,
    (c)   detergents, other than liquid detergents, and
    (d)   paint remover, other than liquid paint remover.

27. Subject to paragraph 28 below, goods to which this Part of this Schedule applies shall be pre-packed only if the container is marked with an indication of quantity by net weight.

28. There shall be exempted from the requirements of this Part of this Schedule goods of any description in a quantity of less than [25 grams].

[1140]

NOTES
Para 28: words in square brackets substituted by the Weights and Measures Act 1985 (Metrication) (Amendment) Order 1994, SI 1994/2866, art 3(1), (6)(h).

PART X
MISCELLANEOUS GOODS TO BE SOLD BY OR MARKED WITH
CAPACITY MEASUREMENT

29. This Part of this Schedule applies to antifreeze fluid for internal combustion engines, linseed oil, paint (other than paste paint), paint thinner, turpentine, turpentine substitute, varnish, and wood preservative fluid (including fungicides and insecticides).

30. Subject to paragraph 31 below, goods to which this Part of this Schedule applies—
    (a)   unless pre-packed, shall be sold by retail only by capacity measurement, and
    (b)   shall be pre-packed only if the container is marked with an indication of quantity by capacity measurement.

31. There shall be exempted from all requirements of this Part of this Schedule goods of any description in a quantity of less than [150 millilitres].

[1141]

PART 1
STATUTES

NOTES
   Para 31: words in square brackets substituted by the Weights and Measures Act 1985 (Metrication) (Amendment) Order 1994, SI 1994/2866, art 3(1), (6)(i).

PART XI
MISCELLANEOUS GOODS TO BE MARKED WHEN PRE-PACKED WITH CAPACITY MEASUREMENT

32.   This Part of this Schedule applies to enamel, lacquer, liquid detergents, liquid paint remover, petrifying fluid and rust remover.

33.   Subject to paragraph 34 below, goods to which this Part of this Schedule applies shall be pre-packed only if the container is marked with an indication of quantity by capacity measurement.

[34.   The following shall be exempted from the requirements of paragraph 33 above—
   (a)   liquid detergents in a quantity of less than 125 millilitres, and
   (b)   goods of any other description in a quantity of less than 150 millilitres.]

[1142]

NOTES
   Para 34: substituted by the Weights and Measures Act 1985 (Metrication) (Amendment) Order 1994, SI 1994/2866, art 3(1), (6)(j).

PART XII
MISCELLANEOUS GOODS TO BE SOLD BY OR MARKED WITH NET WEIGHT OR CAPACITY MEASUREMENT

35.   This Part of this Schedule applies to—
   (a)   polishes,
   (b)   dressings, analogous to polishes, and
   (c)   pea seeds and bean seeds.

36.   Subject to paragraph 37 below, goods to which this Part of this Schedule applies—
   (a)   unless pre-packed, shall be sold by retail only by net weight or by capacity measurement, and
   (b)   shall be pre-packed only if the container is marked with an indication of quantity either by net weight or by capacity measurement.

37.   The following shall be exempted from all the requirements of this Part of this Schedule, that is to say—
   (a)   pea or bean seeds in a quantity of less than [250 grams] or of less than [250 millilitres], and
   (b)   any other goods in a quantity of less than [30 grams] or of less than [30 millilitres].

[1143]

NOTES
   Para 37: words in square brackets substituted by the Weights and Measures Act 1985 (Metrication) (Amendment) Order 1994, SI 1994/2866, art 3(1), (6)(k).

PART XIII
MISCELLANEOUS GOODS TO BE MARKED WHEN PRE-PACKED WITH QUANTITY BY NUMBER

38.   This Part of this Schedule applies—
   (a)   to cheroots, cigarettes and cigars,
   (b)   to postal stationery, that is to say, paper or cards for use in correspondence, and envelopes,
   (b)   to, and to any mixture consisting mainly of, inorganic fertilisers, being such fertilisers or such a mixture made up into pellets or other articles for use as individual items, and
   (d)   to manufactured animal feed in biscuit or cake form pre-packed in a quantity by number of sixteen or less.

39.   Subject to paragraphs 40 and 41 below, goods to which this Part of this Schedule applies shall be pre-packed only if the container is marked with an indication of quantity by number.

40.   In relation to postal stationery, the reference to number in paragraph 39 above shall be construed as a reference to number of sheets of paper, cards or envelopes, as the case may be, in the pad, confining band or other form of container; and postal stationery shall be exempted from the requirements of that paragraph if pre-packed as part of a collection of articles made up for sale together and including any article other than postal stationery and blotting or other paper.

41. There shall be exempted from the requirements of this Part of this Schedule any goods in a quantity by number of one.

[1144]

SCHEDULE 7
COMPOSITE GOODS AND COLLECTIONS OF ARTICLES

Section 21

1.—(1) This paragraph applies to any goods which, not being pre-packed, and not themselves being goods—

    (a) required by or under Part IV of this Act, except this paragraph, to be sold (whether on any sale or on a sale of any particular description) only by quantity expressed in a particular manner, or

    (b) on a sale of which (whether any sale or a sale of any particular description) the quantity of the goods sold expressed in a particular manner is required by or under Part IV of this Act, except this paragraph, to be made known to the buyer at or before a particular time, or

    (c) expressly exempted by or under Part IV of this Act, except this paragraph, from all such requirements as mentioned in paragraph (a) or (b) above which would otherwise apply to them,

consist of a mixture constituted wholly or mainly of goods of one or more descriptions to which there applies any such requirement made by reference to any of the following (whether exclusively or otherwise), that is to say, weight, capacity measurement or volume.

(2) Subject to paragraph 5 below, goods to which this paragraph applies shall be sold only by net weight or by capacity measurement or by volume.

2.—(1) This paragraph applies to any goods which, not being aerosol products and not themselves being goods—

    (a) required by or under Part IV of this Act, except this paragraph, to be pre-packed only if the container is marked with an indication of quantity, or

    (b) in the case of which when sold pre-packed (whether on any sale or on a sale of any particular description) the quantity of the goods sold expressed in a particular manner is required by or under Part IV of this Act, except this paragraph, to be made known to the buyer at or before a particular time, or

    (c) expressly exempted by or under Part IV of this Act, except this paragraph, from all such requirements as mentioned in paragraph (a) or (b) above which would otherwise apply to them,

consist of a mixture constituted wholly or mainly of goods of one or more descriptions to which there applies any such requirement made by reference to any of the following (whether exclusively or otherwise), that is to say, capacity measurement or volume.

(2) Subject to paragraph 5 below, goods to which this paragraph applies shall be pre-packed only if the container is marked with an indication of quantity either by net weight or by capacity measurement or by volume.

3.—(1) This paragraph applies to aerosol products containing any goods required by or under Part IV of this Act, except this paragraph, to be pre-packed only if the container is marked with an indication of quantity expressed in a particular manner.

(2) Subject to paragraph 5 below, any aerosol product to which this paragraph applies shall be pre-packed only if the container is marked with—

    [(a) an indication of the total capacity of the container (indicated in such a way as to avoid giving a false impression of the quantity of goods in the container), and

    (b)] an indication of the quantity by [net volume] of the entire contents of the container.

4.—(1) This paragraph applies to any collection of two or more items which, not itself being—

    (a) required by or under Part IV of this Act, except this paragraph, to be pre-packed only if the container is marked with particular information, or

    (b) expressly exempted by or under Part IV of this Act, except this paragraph, from any such requirement which would otherwise apply to it,

contains one or more articles to which any such requirement applies.

(2) Any collection to which this paragraph applies shall be pre-packed only if—

    (a) the container in which the collection is pre-packed is marked with an indication of the quantity of each of any such articles as mentioned in sub-paragraph (1) above contained in it, or

    (b) each of any such articles contained in the container is made up in an individual container marked with an indication of quantity,

being in either case the like indication of the quantity of each respectively of those articles as would have been required if that article had itself been pre-packed.

5.   There shall be exempted from any requirement of paragraph 1, 2 or [3(2)(b)] above food of any description in a quantity of less than five grams or of less than five millilitres and goods of any other description in a quantity of less than [25 grams] or of less than [25 millilitres].

[1145]–[1382]

NOTES
   Para 3: words in first pair of square brackets inserted and words in second pair of square brackets substituted by the Weights and Measures (Specified Quantities) (Pre-packed Products) Regulations 2009, SI 2009/663, reg 2(1), (5)(a).
   Para 5: reference in first pair of square brackets substituted by SI 2009/663, reg 2(1), (5)(b); words in second and third pairs of square brackets substituted by the Weights and Measures Act 1985 (Metrication) (Amendment) Order 1994, SI 1994/2866, art 3(1), (7).

(*Schs 8–13 outside the scope of this work.*)

MINORS' CONTRACTS ACT 1987

(1987 c 13)

An Act to amend the law relating to minors' contracts

[9 April 1987]

1   Disapplication of Infants Relief Act 1874 etc
The following enactments shall not apply to any contract made by a minor after the commencement of this Act—
   (a)   the Infants Relief Act 1874 (which invalidates certain contracts made by minors and prohibits actions to enforce contracts ratified after majority), and
   (b)   section 5 of the Betting and Loans (Infants) Act 1892 (which invalidates contracts to repay loans advanced during minority).

[1383]

NOTES
   Infants Relief Act 1874, Betting and Loans (Infants) Act 1892, s 5: repealed by s 4(2) of this Act.

2   Guarantees
Where—
   (a)   a guarantee is given in respect of an obligation of a party to a contract made after the commencement of this Act, and
   (b)   the obligation is unenforceable against him (or he repudiates the contract) because he was a minor when the contract was made
the guarantee shall not for that reason alone be unenforceable against the guarantor.

[1384]

3   Restitution
   (1)   Where—
   (a)   a person ("the plaintiff") has after the commencement of this Act entered into a contract with another ("the defendant"), and
   (b)   the contract is unenforceable against the defendant (or he repudiates it) because he was a minor when the contract was made,
the court may, if it is just and equitable to do so, require the defendant to transfer to the plaintiff any property acquired by the defendant under the contract, or any property representing it.
   (2)   Nothing in this section shall be taken to prejudice any other remedy available to the plaintiff.

[1385]

4   (*Sub-s (1) amends the Consumer Credit Act 1974, s 113(7) at* **[758]**; *sub-s (2) repeals the Infants Relief Act 1874 and the Betting and Loans (Infants) Act 1892 (in accordance with s 1).*)

5   Short title, commencement and extent
   (1)   This Act may be cited as the Minors' Contracts Act 1987.
   (2)   This Act shall come into force at the end of the period of two months beginning with the date on which it is passed.
   (3)   This Act extends to England and Wales only.

[1386]

CONSUMER PROTECTION ACT 1987

(1987 c 43)

ARRANGEMENT OF SECTIONS

PART I
PRODUCT LIABILITY

PART II
CONSUMER SAFETY

PART IV
ENFORCEMENT OF PARTS II AND III

PART V
MISCELLANEOUS AND SUPPLEMENTAL

An Act to make provision with respect to the liability of persons for damage caused by defective products; to consolidate with amendments the Consumer Safety Act 1978 and the Consumer Safety (Amendment) Act 1986; to make provision with respect to the giving of price indications; to amend Part I of the Health and Safety at Work etc Act 1974 and sections 31 and 80 of the Explosives Act 1875; to repeal the Trade Descriptions Act 1972 and the Fabrics (Misdescription) Act 1913; and for connected purposes

[15 May 1987]

PART I
PRODUCT LIABILITY

1　Purpose and construction of Part I

(1)　This Part shall have effect for the purpose of making such provision as is necessary in order to comply with the product liability Directive and shall be construed accordingly.

(2)　In this Part, except in so far as the context otherwise requires—

.....

"dependant" and "relative" have the same meaning as they have in, respectively, the Fatal
　　　Accidents Act 1976 and the Damages (Scotland) Act 1976;
"producer", in relation to a product, means—
　　　(a)　the person who manufactured it;
　　　(b)　in the case of a substance which has not been manufactured but has been won or
　　　　　　abstracted, the person who won or abstracted it;
　　　(c)　in the case of a product which has not been manufactured, won or abstracted but
　　　　　　essential characteristics of which are attributable to an industrial or other process
　　　　　　having been carried out (for example, in relation to agricultural produce), the
　　　　　　person who carried out that process;
"product" means any goods or electricity and (subject to subsection (3) below) includes a
　　　product which is comprised in another product, whether by virtue of being a component
　　　part or raw material or otherwise; and
"the product liability Directive" means the Directive of the Council of the European
　　　Communities, dated 25th July 1985, (No 85/374/EEC) on the approximation of the laws,
　　　regulations and administrative provisions of the member States concerning liability for
　　　defective products.

(3)　For the purposes of this Part a person who supplies any product in which products are comprised, whether by virtue of being component parts or raw materials or otherwise, shall not be treated by reason only of his supply of that product as supplying any of the products so comprised.

[1387]

NOTES

Sub-s (1): definition "agricultural produce" (omitted) repealed in relation to England and Wales by the Consumer Protection Act 1987 (Product Liability) (Modification) Order 2000, SI 2000/2771, art 2(1), (2), and in relation to Scotland by the Consumer Protection Act 1987 (Product Liability) (Modification) (Scotland) Order 2001, SSI 2001/265, art 2(1), (2).

2　Liability for defective products

(1)　Subject to the following provisions of this Part, where any damage is caused wholly or partly by a defect in a product, every person to whom subsection (2) below applies shall be liable for the damage.

(2)　This subsection applies to—
　　　(a)　the producer of the product;
　　　(b)　any person who, by putting his name on the product or using a trade mark or other
　　　　　　distinguishing mark in relation to the product, has held himself out to be the producer of
　　　　　　the product;
　　　(c)　any person who has imported the product into a member State from a place outside the
　　　　　　member States in order, in the course of any business of his, to supply it to another.

(3)　Subject as aforesaid, where any damage is caused wholly or partly by a defect in a product, any person who supplied the product (whether to the person who suffered the damage, to the producer of any product in which the product in question is comprised or to any other person) shall be liable for the damage if—
　　　(a)　the person who suffered the damage requests the supplier to identify one or more of the
　　　　　　persons (whether still in existence or not) to whom subsection (2) above applies in
　　　　　　relation to the product;
　　　(b)　that request is made within a reasonable period after the damage occurs and at a time
　　　　　　when it is not reasonably practicable for the person making the request to identify all
　　　　　　those persons; and
　　　(c)　the supplier fails, within a reasonable period after receiving the request, either to comply
　　　　　　with the request or to identify the person who supplied the product to him.

(4)　...

(5)　Where two or more persons are liable by virtue of this Part for the same damage, their liability shall be joint and several.

(6)　This section shall be without prejudice to any liability arising otherwise than by virtue of this Part.

[1388]

NOTES

Sub-s (4): repealed in relation to England and Wales by the Consumer Protection Act 1987 (Product Liability) (Modification) Order 2000, SI 2000/2771, art 2(1), (3) and in relation to Scotland by the Consumer Protection Act 1987 (Product Liability) (Modification) (Scotland) Order 2001, SSI 2001/265, art 2(1), (3).

3 Meaning of "defect"

(1) Subject to the following provisions of this section, there is a defect in a product for the purposes of this Part if the safety of the product is not such as persons generally are entitled to expect; and for those purposes "safety", in relation to a product, shall include safety with respect to products comprised in that product and safety in the context of risks of damage to property, as well as in the context of risks of death or personal injury.

(2) In determining for the purposes of subsection (1) above what persons generally are entitled to expect in relation to a product all the circumstances shall be taken into account, including—

    (a)   the manner in which, and purposes for which, the product has been marketed, its get-up, the use of any mark in relation to the product and any instructions for, or warnings with respect to, doing or refraining from doing anything with or in relation to the product;

    (b)   what might reasonably be expected to be done with or in relation to the product; and

    (c)   the time when the product was supplied by its producer to another;

and nothing in this section shall require a defect to be inferred from the fact alone that the safety of a product which is supplied after that time is greater than the safety of the product in question.

[1389]

4 Defences

(1) In any civil proceedings by virtue of this Part against any person ("the person proceeded against") in respect of a defect in a product it shall be a defence for him to show—

    (a)   that the defect is attributable to compliance with any requirement imposed by or under any enactment or with any Community obligation; or

    (b)   that the person proceeded against did not at any time supply the product to another; or

    (c)   that the following conditions are satisfied, that is to say—

        (i)   that the only supply of the product to another by the person proceeded against was otherwise than in the course of a business of that person's; and

        (ii)   that section 2(2) above does not apply to that person or applies to him by virtue only of things done otherwise than with a view to profit; or

    (d)   that the defect did not exist in the product at the relevant time; or

    (e)   that the state of scientific and technical knowledge at the relevant time was not such that a producer of products of the same description as the product in question might be expected to have discovered the defect if it had existed in his products while they were under his control; or

    (f)   that the defect—

        (i)   constituted a defect in a product ("the subsequent product") in which the product in question had been comprised; and

        (ii)   was wholly attributable to the design of the subsequent product or to compliance by the producer of the product in question with instructions given by the producer of the subsequent product.

(2) In this section "the relevant time", in relation to electricity, means the time at which it was generated, being a time before it was transmitted or distributed, and in relation to any other product, means—

    (a)   if the person proceeded against is a person to whom subsection (2) of section 2 above applies in relation to the product, the time when he supplied the product to another;

    (b)   if that subsection does not apply to that person in relation to the product, the time when the product was last supplied by a person to whom that subsection does apply in relation to the product.

[1390]

5 Damage giving rise to liability

(1) Subject to the following provisions of this section, in this Part "damage" means death or personal injury or any loss of or damage to any property (including land).

(2) A person shall not be liable under section 2 above in respect of any defect in a product for the loss of or any damage to the product itself or for the loss of or any damage to the whole or any part of any product which has been supplied with the product in question comprised in it.

(3) A person shall not be liable under section 2 above for any loss of or damage to any property which, at the time it is lost or damaged, is not—

    (a)   of a description of property ordinarily intended for private use, occupation or consumption; and

(b)   intended by the person suffering the loss or damage mainly for his own private use, occupation or consumption.

(4)   No damages shall be awarded to any person by virtue of this Part in respect of any loss of or damage to any property if the amount which would fall to be so awarded to that person, apart from this subsection and any liability for interest, does not exceed £275.

(5)   In determining for the purposes of this Part who has suffered any loss of or damage to property and when any such loss or damage occurred, the loss or damage shall be regarded as having occurred at the earliest time at which a person with an interest in the property had knowledge of the material facts about the loss or damage.

(6)   For the purposes of subsection (5) above the material facts about any loss of or damage to any property are such facts about the loss or damage as would lead a reasonable person with an interest in the property to consider the loss or damage sufficiently serious to justify his instituting proceedings for damages against a defendant who did not dispute liability and was able to satisfy a judgment.

(7)   For the purposes of subsection (5) above a person's knowledge includes knowledge which he might reasonably have been expected to acquire—

(a)   from facts observable or ascertainable by him; or

(b)   from facts ascertainable by him with the help of appropriate expert advice which it is reasonable for him to seek;

but a person shall not be taken by virtue of this subsection to have knowledge of a fact ascertainable by him only with the help of expert advice unless he has failed to take all reasonable steps to obtain (and, where appropriate, to act on) that advice.

(8)   Subsections (5) to (7) above shall not extend to Scotland.

[1391]

6   Application of certain enactments

(1)   Any damage for which a person is liable under section 2 above shall be deemed to have been caused—

(a)   for the purposes of the Fatal Accidents Act 1976, by that person's wrongful act, neglect or default;

(b)–(d) *(apply to Scotland only.)*

(2)   Where—

(a)   a person's death is caused wholly or partly by a defect in a product, or a person dies after suffering damage which has been so caused;

(b)   a request such as mentioned in paragraph (a) of subsection (3) of section 2 above is made to a supplier of the product by that person's personal representatives or, in the case of a person whose death is caused wholly or partly by the defect, by any dependant or relative of that person; and

(c)   the conditions specified in paragraphs (b) and (c) of that subsection are satisfied in relation to that request,

this Part shall have effect for the purposes of the Law Reform (Miscellaneous Provisions) Act 1934, the Fatal Accidents Act 1976 and the Damages (Scotland) Act 1976 as if liability of the supplier to that person under that subsection did not depend on that person having requested the supplier to identify certain persons or on the said conditions having been satisfied in relation to a request made by that person.

(3)   Section 1 of the Congenital Disabilities (Civil Liability) Act 1976 shall have effect for the purposes of this Part as if—

(a)   a person were answerable to a child in respect of an occurrence caused wholly or partly by a defect in a product if he is or has been liable under section 2 above in respect of any effect of the occurrence on a parent of the child, or would be so liable if the occurrence caused a parent of the child to suffer damage;

(b)   the provisions of this Part relating to liability under section 2 above applied in relation to liability by virtue of paragraph (a) above under the said section 1; and

(c)   subsection (6) of the said section 1 (exclusion of liability) were omitted.

(4)   Where any damage is caused partly by a defect in a product and partly by the fault of the person suffering the damage, the Law Reform (Contributory Negligence) Act 1945 and section 5 of the Fatal Accidents Act 1976 (contributory negligence) shall have effect as if the defect were the fault of every person liable by virtue of this Part for the damage caused by the defect.

(5)   In subsection (4) above "fault" has the same meaning as in the said Act of 1945.

(6)   Schedule 1 to this Act shall have effect for the purpose of amending the Limitation Act 1980 and the Prescription and Limitation (Scotland) Act 1973 in their application in relation to the bringing of actions by virtue of this Part.

(7)   It is hereby declared that liability by virtue of this Part is to be treated as liability in tort for the purposes of any enactment conferring jurisdiction on any court with respect to any matter.

(8)   Nothing in this Part shall prejudice the operation of section 12 of the Nuclear Installations Act 1965 (rights to compensation for certain breaches of duties confined to rights under that Act).

[1392]

7   Prohibition on exclusions from liability

The liability of a person by virtue of this Part to a person who has suffered damage caused wholly or partly by a defect in a product, or to a dependant or relative of such a person, shall not be limited or excluded by any contract term, by any notice or by any other provision.

[1393]

8   Power to modify Part I

(1)   Her Majesty may by Order in Council make such modifications of this Part and of any other enactment (including an enactment contained in the following Parts of this Act, or in an Act passed after this Act) as appear to Her Majesty in Council to be necessary or expedient in consequence of any modification of the product liability Directive which is made at any time after the passing of this Act.

(2)   An Order in Council under subsection (1) above shall not be submitted to Her Majesty in Council unless a draft of the Order has been laid before, and approved by a resolution of, each House of Parliament.

[1394]

NOTES

Order: the Consumer Protection Act 1987 (Product Liability) (Modification) Order 2000, SI 2000/2771.

---

9   Application of Part I to Crown

(1)   Subject to subsection (2) below, this Part shall bind the Crown.

(2)   The Crown shall not, as regards the Crown's liability by virtue of this Part, be bound by this Part further than the Crown is made liable in tort or in reparation under the Crown Proceedings Act 1947, as that Act has effect from time to time.

[1395]–[1396]

PART II
CONSUMER SAFETY

10   *(Repealed by the General Product Safety Regulations 2005, SI 2005/1803, reg 46(1), (2).)*

11   Safety regulations

(1)   The Secretary of State may by regulations under this section ("safety regulations") make such provision as he considers appropriate ... and for the purpose of securing—
  (a)   that goods to which this section applies are safe;
  (b)   that goods to which this section applies which are unsafe, or would be unsafe in the hands of persons of a particular description, are not made available to persons generally or, as the case may be, to persons of that description; and
  (c)   that appropriate information is, and inappropriate information is not, provided in relation to goods to which this section applies.

(2)   Without prejudice to the generality of subsection (1) above, safety regulations may contain provision—
  (a)   with respect to the composition or contents, design, construction, finish or packing of goods to which this section applies, with respect to standards for such goods and with respect to other matters relating to such goods;
  (b)   with respect to the giving, refusal, alteration or cancellation of approvals of such goods, of descriptions of such goods or of standards for such goods;
  (c)   with respect to the conditions that may be attached to any approval given under the regulations;
  (d)   for requiring such fees as may be determined by or under the regulations to be paid on the giving or alteration of any approval under the regulations and on the making of an application for such an approval or alteration;
  (e)   with respect to appeals against refusals, alterations and cancellations of approvals given under the regulations and against the conditions contained in such approvals;
  (f)   for requiring goods to which this section applies to be approved under the regulations or to conform to the requirements of the regulations or to descriptions or standards specified in or approved by or under the regulations;

(g) with respect to the testing or inspection of goods to which this section applies (including provision for determining the standards to be applied in carrying out any test or inspection);

(h) with respect to the ways of dealing with goods of which some or all do not satisfy a test required by or under the regulations or a standard connected with a procedure so required;

(i) for requiring a mark, warning or instruction or any other information relating to goods to be put on or to accompany the goods or to be used or provided in some other manner in relation to the goods, and for securing that inappropriate information is not given in relation to goods either by means of misleading marks or otherwise;

(j) for prohibiting persons from supplying, or from offering to supply, agreeing to supply, exposing for supply or possessing for supply, goods to which this section applies and component parts and raw materials for such goods;

(k) for requiring information to be given to any such person as may be determined by or under the regulations for the purpose of enabling that person to exercise any function conferred on him by the regulations.

(3) Without prejudice as aforesaid, safety regulations may contain provision—

(a) for requiring persons on whom functions are conferred by or under section 27 below to have regard, in exercising their functions so far as relating to any provision of safety regulations, to matters specified in a direction issued by the Secretary of State with respect to that provision;

(b) for securing that a person shall not be guilty of an offence under section 12 below unless it is shown that the goods in question do not conform to a particular standard;

(c) for securing that proceedings for such an offence are not brought in England and Wales except by or with the consent of the Secretary of State or the Director of Public Prosecutions;

(d) for securing that proceedings for such an offence are not brought in Northern Ireland except by or with the consent of the Secretary of State or the Director of Public Prosecutions for Northern Ireland;

(e) for enabling a magistrates' court in England and Wales or Northern Ireland to try an information or, in Northern Ireland, a complaint in respect of such an offence if the information was laid or the complaint made within twelve months from the time when the offence was committed;

(f) *(applies to Scotland only;)*

(g) for determining the persons by whom, and the manner in which, anything required to be done by or under the regulations is to be done.

(4) Safety regulations shall not provide for any contravention of the regulations to be an offence.

(5) Where the Secretary of State proposes to make safety regulations it shall be his duty before he makes them—

(a) to consult such organisations as appear to him to be representative of interests substantially affected by the proposal;

(b) to consult such other persons as he considers appropriate; and

(c) in the case of proposed regulations relating to goods suitable for use at work, to consult [the Health and Safety Executive] in relation to the application of the proposed regulations to Great Britain;

but the preceding provisions of this subsection shall not apply in the case of regulations which provide for the regulations to cease to have effect at the end of a period of not more than twelve months beginning with the day on which they come into force and which contain a statement that it appears to the Secretary of State that the need to protect the public requires that the regulations should be made without delay.

(6) The power to make safety regulations shall be exercisable by statutory instrument subject to annulment in pursuance of a resolution of either House of Parliament and shall include power—

(a) to make different provision for different cases; and

(b) to make such supplemental, consequential and transitional provision as the Secretary of State considers appropriate.

(7) This section applies to any goods other than—

(a) growing crops and things comprised in land by virtue of being attached to it;

(b) water, food, feeding stuff and fertiliser;

(c) gas which is, is to be or has been supplied by a person authorised to supply it by or under [section 7A of the Gas Act 1986 (licensing of gas suppliers and gas shippers) *or paragraph 5 of Schedule 2A to that Act (supply to very large customers an exception to prohibition on unlicensed activities)*] [or under Article 8(1)(c) of the Gas (Northern Ireland) Order 1996];

(d) controlled drugs and licensed medicinal products.

NOTES

Sub-s (1): words omitted repealed by the General Product Safety Regulations 2005, SI 2005/1803, reg 46(1), (3).

Sub-s (5): words in square brackets substituted by the Legislative Reform (Health and Safety Executive) Order 2008, SI 2008/960, art 22, Sch 3, subject to transitional provisions in art 21 of, and Sch 2 to, that Order.

Sub-s (7): words in first pair of square brackets in para (c) substituted by the Gas Act 1995, s 16(1), Sch 4, para 15(2); words in italics in para (c) repealed by the Utilities Act 2000, s 108, Sch 8, as from a day to be appointed; words in second pair of square brackets in para (c) inserted by the Gas (Northern Ireland) Order 1996, SI 1996/275, art 71(1), Sch 6.

Regulations: the Furniture and Furnishings (Fire) (Safety) Regulations 1988, SI 1988/1324; the Babies' Dummies (Safety) (Revocation) Regulations 1989, SI 1989/141; the Gas Cooking Appliances (Safety) Regulations 1989, SI 1989/149; the Food Imitations (Safety) Regulations 1989, SI 1989/1291; the All-Terrain Motor Vehicles (Safety) Regulations 1989, SI 1989/2288; the Heating Appliances (Fireguards) (Safety) Regulations 1991, SI 1991/2693; the Oil Lamps (Safety) (Revocation) Regulations 1992, SI 1992/23; the Tobacco for Oral Use (Safety) Regulations 1992, SI 1992/3134; the Imitation Dummies (Safety) Regulations 1993, SI 1993/2923; the Plugs and Sockets etc (Safety) Regulations 1994, SI 1994/1768; the Motor Vehicle Tyres (Safety) Regulations 1994, SI 1994/3117; the Electrical Equipment (Safety) Regulations 1994, SI 1994/3260; the Toys (Safety) Regulations 1995, SI 1995/204; the Fireworks (Safety) (Revocation) Regulations 1995, SI 1995/415; the N-nitrosamines and N-nitrosatable Substances in Elastomer or Rubber Teats and Dummies (Safety) Regulations 1995, SI 1995/1012; the Gas Appliances (Safety) Regulations 1995, SI 1995/1629; the Stands for Carry-cots (Safety) (Revocation) Regulations 1996, SI 1996/2756; the Fireworks (Safety) Regulations 1997, SI 1997/2294; the Wheeled Child Conveyances (Safety) Regulations 1997, SI 1997/2866; the Pencil and Graphic Instruments (Safety) Regulations 1998, SI 1998/2406; the Cigarette Lighter Refill (Safety) Regulations 1999, SI 1999/1844; the Road Vehicles (Brake Linings Safety) Regulations 1999, SI 1999/2978; the Dangerous Substances and Preparations (Nickel) (Safety) Regulations 2000, SI 2000/1668; the Medical Devices Regulations 2002, SI 2002/618; the Tobacco Products (Manufacture, Presentation and Sale) (Safety) Regulations 2002 SI 2002/3041; the Pedal Bicycles (Safety) Regulations 2003, SI 2003/1101; the Unlicensed Medicinal Products for Human Use (Transmissible Spongiform Encephalopathies) (Safety) Regulations 2003, SI 2003/1680; the Fireworks Regulations 2004, SI 2004/1836; the Ceramic Articles in Contact with Food (England) Regulations 2006, SI 2006/1179; the Magnetic Toys (Safety) (Revocation) Regulations 2009, SI 2009/1347; the Aerosol Dispensers Regulations 2009, SI 2009/2824; the Pedal Bicycles (Safety) Regulations 2010, SI 2010/198.

By virtue of the Consumer Protection Act 1987 (Commencement No 1) Order 1987, SI 1987/1680, arts 6–9, the following regulations (which were made under the Consumer Protection Act 1961) have effect as if made under this section: the Cooking Utensils (Safety) Regulations 1972, SI 1972/1957; the Children's Clothing (Hood Cords) Regulations 1976, SI 1976/2; the Oil Heaters (Safety) Regulations 1977, SI 1977/167; the Nightwear (Safety) Regulations 1985, SI 1985/2043. Also, by virtue of the Interpretation Act 1978, s 17(2)(b), the following regulations (which were made under the Consumer Safety Act 1978, s 1) take effect under this section: the Filament Lamps for Vehicles (Safety) Regulations 1982, SI 1982/444; the Gas Catalytic Heaters (Safety) Regulations 1984, SI 1984/1802; the Asbestos Products (Safety) Regulations 1985, SI 1985/2042; the Nightwear (Safety) Regulations 1985, SI 1985/2043; the Bunk Beds (Entrapment Hazards) (Safety) Regulations 1987, SI 1987/1337.

12 Offences against the safety regulations

(1)   Where safety regulations prohibit a person from supplying or offering or agreeing to supply any goods or from exposing or possessing any goods for supply, that person shall be guilty of an offence if he contravenes the prohibition.

(2)   Where safety regulations require a person who makes or processes any goods in the course of carrying on a business—

   (a)   to carry out a particular test or use a particular procedure in connection with the making or processing of the goods with a view to ascertaining whether the goods satisfy any requirements of such regulations; or

   (b)   to deal or not to deal in a particular way with a quantity of the goods of which the whole or part does not satisfy such a test or does not satisfy standards connected with such a procedure,

that person shall be guilty of an offence if he does not comply with the requirement.

(3)   If a person contravenes a provision of safety regulations which prohibits or requires the provision, by means of a mark or otherwise, of information of a particular kind in relation to goods, he shall be guilty of an offence.

(4)   Where safety regulations require any person to give information to another for the purpose of enabling that other to exercise any function, that person shall be guilty of an offence if—

   (a)   he fails without reasonable cause to comply with the requirement; or

   (b)   in giving the information which is required of him—

      (i)   he makes any statement which he knows is false in a material particular; or

      (ii)   he recklessly makes any statement which is false in a material particular.

(5)   A person guilty of an offence under this section shall be liable on summary conviction to imprisonment for a term not exceeding six months or to a fine not exceeding level 5 on the standard scale or to both.

13 Prohibition notices and notices to warn

(1)   The Secretary of State may—

    (a)   serve on any person a notice ("a prohibition notice") prohibiting that person, except with the consent of the Secretary of State, from supplying, or from offering to supply, agreeing to supply, exposing for supply or possessing for supply, any relevant goods which the Secretary of State considers are unsafe and which are described in the notice;

    (b)   serve on any person a notice ("a notice to warn") requiring that person at his own expense to publish, in a form and manner and on occasions specified in the notice, a warning about any relevant goods which the Secretary of State considers are unsafe, which that person supplies or has supplied and which are described in the notice.

(2)   Schedule 2 to this Act shall have effect with respect to prohibition notices and notices to warn; and the Secretary of State may by regulations make provision specifying the manner in which information is to be given to any person under that Schedule.

(3)   A consent given by the Secretary of State for the purposes of a prohibition notice may impose such conditions on the doing of anything for which the consent is required as the Secretary of State considers appropriate.

(4)   A person who contravenes a prohibition notice or a notice to warn shall be guilty of an offence and liable on summary conviction to imprisonment for a term not exceeding six months or to a fine not exceeding level 5 on the standard scale or to both.

(5)   The power to make regulations under subsection (2) above shall be exercisable by statutory instrument subject to annulment in pursuance of a resolution of either House of Parliament and shall include power—

    (a)   to make different provision for different cases; and

    (b)   to make such supplemental, consequential and transitional provision as the Secretary of State considers appropriate.

(6)   In this section "relevant goods" means—

    (a)   in relation to a prohibition notice, any goods to which section 11 above applies; and

    (b)   in relation to a notice to warn, any goods to which that section applies or any growing crops or things comprised in land by virtue of being attached to it.

[(7)   A notice may not be given under this section in respect of any aspect of the safety of goods, or any risk or category of risk associated with goods, concerning which provision is contained in the General Product Safety Regulations 2005.]

[1399]

NOTES

Sub-s (7): added by the General Product Safety Regulations 2005, SI 2005/1803, reg 46(1), (4).

14 Suspension notices

(1)   Where an enforcement authority has reasonable grounds for suspecting that any safety provision has been contravened in relation to any goods, the authority may serve a notice ("a suspension notice") prohibiting the person on whom it is served, for such period ending not more than six months after the date of the notice as is specified therein, from doing any of the following things without the consent of the authority, that is to say, supplying the goods, offering to supply them, agreeing to supply them or exposing them for supply.

(2)   A suspension notice served by an enforcement authority in respect of any goods shall—

    (a)   describe the goods in a manner sufficient to identify them;

    (b)   set out the grounds on which the authority suspects that a safety provision has been contravened in relation to the goods; and

    (c)   state that, and the manner in which, the person on whom the notice is served may appeal against the notice under section 15 below.

(3)   A suspension notice served by an enforcement authority for the purpose of prohibiting a person for any period from doing the things mentioned in subsection (1) above in relation to any goods may also require that person to keep the authority informed of the whereabouts throughout that period of any of those goods in which he has an interest.

(4)   Where a suspension notice has been served on any person in respect of any goods, no further such notice shall be served on that person in respect of the same goods unless—

    (a)   proceedings against that person for an offence in respect of a contravention in relation to the goods of a safety provision (not being an offence under this section); or

    (b)   proceedings for the forfeiture of the goods under section 16 or 17 below,

are pending at the end of the period specified in the first-mentioned notice.

(5)   A consent given by an enforcement authority for the purposes of subsection (1) above may impose such conditions on the doing of anything for which the consent is required as the authority considers appropriate.

(6)   Any person who contravenes a suspension notice shall be guilty of an offence and liable on summary conviction to imprisonment for a term not exceeding six months or to a fine not exceeding level 5 on the standard scale or to both.

(7)   Where an enforcement authority serves a suspension notice in respect of any goods, the authority shall be liable to pay compensation to any person having an interest in the goods in respect of any loss or damage caused by reason of the service of the notice if—
    (a)   there has been no contravention in relation to the goods of any safety provision; and
    (b)   the exercise of the power is not attributable to any neglect or default by that person.

(8)   Any disputed question as to the right to or the amount of any compensation payable under this section shall be determined by arbitration or, in Scotland, by a single arbiter appointed, failing agreement between the parties, by the sheriff.

[1400]

NOTES
    Modification: this section is applied, with modifications, for the purposes of the enforcement of the Supply of Machinery (Safety) Regulations 2008, SI 2008/1597, by SI 2008/1597, reg 20, Sch 5, paras 11, 12, 17, 18.

15   Appeals against suspension notices

(1)   Any person having an interest in any goods in respect of which a suspension notice is for the time being in force may apply for an order setting aside the notice.

(2)   An application under this section may be made—
    (a)   to any magistrates' court in which proceedings have been brought in England and Wales or Northern Ireland—
        (i)   for an offence in respect of a contravention in relation to the goods of any safety provision; or
        (ii)   for the forfeiture of the goods under section 16 below;
    (b)   where no such proceedings have been so brought, by way of complaint to a magistrates' court; or
    (c)   (applies to Scotland only.)

(3)   On an application under this section to a magistrates' court in England and Wales or Northern Ireland the court shall make an order setting aside the suspension notice only if the court is satisfied that there has been no contravention in relation to the goods of any safety provision.

(4)   On an application under this section to the sheriff he shall make an order setting aside the suspension notice only if he is satisfied that at the date of making the order—
    (a)   proceedings for an offence in respect of a contravention in relation to the goods of any safety provision; or
    (b)   proceedings for the forfeiture of the goods under section 17 below,
have not been brought or, having been brought, have been concluded.

(5)   Any person aggrieved by an order made under this section by a magistrates' court in England and Wales or Northern Ireland, or by a decision of such a court not to make such an order, may appeal against that order or decision—
    (a)   in England and Wales, to the Crown Court;
    (b)   in Northern Ireland, to the county court;
and an order so made may contain such provision as appears to the court to be appropriate for delaying the coming into force of the order pending the making and determination of any appeal (including any application under section 111 of the Magistrates' Courts Act 1980 or Article 146 of the Magistrates' Courts (Northern Ireland) Order 1981 (statement of case)).

[1401]

NOTES
    Modification: this section is applied, with modifications, for the purposes of the enforcement of the Supply of Machinery (Safety) Regulations 2008, SI 2008/1597, by SI 2008/1597, reg 20, Sch 5, paras 11, 12, 17, 18.

16   Forfeiture: England and Wales and Northern Ireland

(1)   An enforcement authority in England and Wales or Northern Ireland may apply under this section for an order for the forfeiture of any goods on the grounds that there has been a contravention in relation to the goods of a safety provision.

(2)   An application under this section may be made—
    (a)   where proceedings have been brought in a magistrates' court for an offence in respect of a contravention in relation to some or all of the goods of any safety provision, to that court;
    (b)   where an application with respect to some or all of the goods has been made to a magistrates' court under section 15 above or section 33 below, to that court; and

 (c) where no application for the forfeiture of the goods has been made under paragraph (a) or (b) above, by way of complaint to a magistrates' court.

 (3) On an application under this section the court shall make an order for the forfeiture of any goods only if it is satisfied that there has been a contravention in relation to the goods of a safety provision.

 (4) For the avoidance of doubt it is declared that a court may infer for the purposes of this section that there has been a contravention in relation to any goods of a safety provision if it is satisfied that any such provision has been contravened in relation to goods which are representative of those goods (whether by reason of being of the same design or part of the same consignment or batch or otherwise).

 (5) Any person aggrieved by an order made under this section by a magistrates' court, or by a decision of such a court not to make such an order, may appeal against that order or decision—

  (a) in England and Wales, to the Crown Court;

  (b) in Northern Ireland, to the county court;

and an order so made may contain such provision as appears to the court to be appropriate for delaying the coming into force of the order pending the making and determination of any appeal (including any application under section 111 of the Magistrates' Courts Act 1980 or Article 146 of the Magistrates' Courts (Northern Ireland) Order 1981 (statement of case)).

 (6) Subject to subsection (7) below, where any goods are forfeited under this section they shall be destroyed in accordance with such directions as the court may give.

 (7) On making an order under this section a magistrates' court may, if it considers it appropriate to do so, direct that the goods to which the order relates shall (instead of being destroyed) be released, to such person as the court may specify, on condition that that person—

  (a) does not supply those goods to any person otherwise than as mentioned in section 46(7)(a) or (b) below; and

  (b) complies with any order to pay costs or expenses (including any order under section 35 below) which has been made against that person in the proceedings for the order for forfeiture.

                            [1402]

17 *(Applies to Scotland only.)*

18 Power to obtain information

 (1) If the Secretary of State considers that, for the purpose of deciding whether—

  (a) to make, vary or revoke any safety regulations; or

  (b) to serve, vary or revoke a prohibition notice; or

  (c) to serve or revoke a notice to warn,

he requires information which another person is likely to be able to furnish, the Secretary of State may serve on the other person a notice under this section.

 (2) A notice served on any person under this section may require that person—

  (a) to furnish to the Secretary of State, within a period specified in the notice, such information as is so specified;

  (b) to produce such records as are specified in the notice at a time and place so specified and to permit a person appointed by the Secretary of State for the purpose to take copies of the records at that time and place.

 (3) A person shall be guilty of an offence if he—

  (a) fails, without reasonable cause, to comply with a notice served on him under this section; or

  (b) in purporting to comply with a requirement which by virtue of paragraph (a) of subsection (2) above is contained in such a notice—

   (i) furnishes information which he knows is false in a material particular; or

   (ii) recklessly furnishes information which is false in a material particular.

 (4) A person guilty of an offence under subsection (3) above shall—

  (a) in the case of an offence under paragraph (a) of that subsection, be liable on summary conviction to a fine not exceeding level 5 on the standard scale; and

  (b) in the case of an offence under paragraph (b) of that subsection be liable—

   (i) on conviction on indictment, to a fine;

   (ii) on summary conviction, to a fine not exceeding the statutory maximum.

                            [1403]

19 Interpretation of Part II

 (1) In this Part—

  "controlled drug" means a controlled drug within the meaning of the Misuse of Drugs Act 1971;

"feeding stuff" and "fertiliser" have the same meanings as in Part IV of the Agriculture Act 1970;

"food" does not include anything containing tobacco but, subject to that, has the same meaning as in the [Food Safety Act 1990] or, in relation to Northern Ireland, the same meaning as in the [Food Safety (Northern Ireland) Order 1991];

"licensed medicinal product" means—

    (a)   any medicinal product within the meaning of the Medicines Act 1968 in respect of which a product licence within the meaning of that Act is for the time being in force; ...

    (b)   any other article or substance in respect of which any such licence is for the time being in force in pursuance of an order under section 104 or 105 of that Act (application of Act to other articles and substances); [or

    (c)   a veterinary medicinal product that has a marketing authorisation under the Veterinary Medicines Regulations 2006.]

"safe", in relation to any goods, means such that there is no risk, or no risk apart from one reduced to a minimum, that any of the following will (whether immediately or after a definite or indefinite period) cause the death of, or any personal injury to, any person whatsoever, that is to say—

    (a)   the goods;

    (b)   the keeping, use or consumption of the goods;

    (c)   the assembly of any of the goods which are, or are to be, supplied unassembled;

    (d)   any emission or leakage from the goods or, as a result of the keeping, use or consumption of the goods, from anything else; or

    (e)   reliance on the accuracy of any measurement, calculation or other reading made by or by means of the goods,

and ... "unsafe" shall be construed accordingly;

"tobacco" includes any tobacco product within the meaning of the Tobacco Products Duty Act 1979 and any article or substance containing tobacco and intended for oral or nasal use.

(2) In the definition of "safe" in subsection (1) above, references to the keeping, use or consumption of any goods are references to—

    (a)   the keeping, use or consumption of the goods by the persons by whom, and in all or any of the ways or circumstances in which, they might reasonably be expected to be kept, used or consumed; and

    (b)   the keeping, use or consumption of the goods either alone or in conjunction with other goods in conjunction with which they might reasonably be expected to be kept, used or consumed.

[1404]–[1411]

NOTES

Sub-s (1): in definition "food" words in first pair of square brackets substituted by the Food Safety Act 1990, s 59(1), Sch 3, para 37, words in second pair of square brackets substituted by the Food Safety (Northern Ireland) Order 1991, SI 1991/762, art 51(1), Sch 2, para 17; in definition "licensed medicinal product" word omitted repealed and words in square brackets added by the Veterinary Medicines Regulations 2006, SI 2006/2407, reg 44(3), Sch 9, Pt 1, para 7; in definition "safe" words omitted repealed by the General Product Safety Regulations 2005, SI 2005/1803, reg 46(1), (5).

20–26 (*Pt III repealed by the Consumer Protection from Unfair Trading Regulations 2008, SI 2008/1277, reg 30(1), (3), Sch 2, Pt 1, paras 33, 34, Sch 4, subject to savings in reg 30(2) of, and Sch 3, paras 5, 9, 11 to, those Regulations at* **[3702]**, **[3704]**.)

PART IV
ENFORCEMENT OF PARTS II AND III

27 Enforcement

(1) Subject to the following provisions of this section—

    (a)   it shall be the duty of every weights and measures authority in Great Britain to enforce within their area the safety provisions ... ; and

    (b)   it shall be the duty of every district council in Northern Ireland to enforce within their area the safety provisions.

(2) The Secretary of State may by regulations—

    (a)   wholly or partly transfer any duty imposed by subsection (1) above on a weights and measures authority or a district council in Northern Ireland to such other person who has agreed to the transfer as is specified in the regulations;

    (b)   relieve such an authority or council of any such duty so far as it is exercisable in relation to such goods as may be described in the regulations.

(3)   The power to make regulations under subsection (2) above shall be exercisable by statutory instrument subject to annulment in pursuance of a resolution of either House of Parliament and shall include power—
- (a)   to make different provision for different cases; and
- (b)   to make such supplemental, consequential and transitional provision as the Secretary of State considers appropriate.

(4)   Nothing in this section shall authorise any weights and measures authority, or any person on whom functions are conferred by regulations under subsection (2) above, to bring proceedings in Scotland for an offence.

[1412]

NOTES
Sub-s (1): words omitted repealed by the Consumer Protection from Unfair Trading Regulations 2008, SI 2008/1277, reg 30(3), Sch 4.
Regulations: the Medical Devices Regulations 2002, SI 2002/618; the Unlicensed Medicinal Products for Human Use (Transmissible Spongiform Encephalopathies) (Safety) Regulations 2003, SI 2003/1680; the Fireworks Regulations 2004, SI 2004/1836.

28   Test purchases

(1)   An enforcement authority shall have power, for the purpose of ascertaining whether any safety provision ... has been contravened in relation to any goods, services, accommodation or facilities—
- (a)   to make, or to authorise an officer of the authority to make, any purchase of any goods; or
- (b)   to secure, or to authorise an officer of the authority to secure, the provision of any services, accommodation or facilities.

(2)   Where—
- (a)   any goods purchased under this section by or on behalf of an enforcement authority are submitted to a test; and
- (b)   the test leads to—
  - (i)   the bringing of proceedings for an offence in respect of a contravention in relation to the goods of any safety provision ... or for the forfeiture of the goods under section 16 or 17 above; or
  - (ii)   the serving of a suspension notice in respect of any goods; and
- (c)   the authority is requested to do so and it is practicable for the authority to comply with the request,

the authority shall allow the person from whom the goods were purchased or any person who is a party to the proceedings or has an interest in any goods to which the notice relates to have the goods tested.

(3)   The Secretary of State may by regulations provide that any test of goods purchased under this section by or on behalf of an enforcement authority shall—
- (a)   be carried out at the expense of the authority in a manner and by a person prescribed by or determined under the regulations; or
- (b)   be carried out either as mentioned in paragraph (a) above or by the authority in a manner prescribed by the regulations.

(4)   The power to make regulations under subsection (3) above shall be exercisable by statutory instrument subject to annulment in pursuance of a resolution of either House of Parliament and shall include power—
- (a)   to make different provision for different cases; and
- (b)   to make such supplemental, consequential and transitional provision as the Secretary of State considers appropriate.

(5)   Nothing in this section shall authorise the acquisition by or on behalf of an enforcement authority of any interest in land.

[1413]

NOTES
Sub-ss (1), (2): words omitted repealed by the Consumer Protection from Unfair Trading Regulations 2008, SI 2008/1277, reg 30(3), Sch 4.
Modification: this section is applied, with modifications, for the purposes of the enforcement of the Supply of Machinery (Safety) Regulations 2008, SI 2008/1597, by SI 2008/1597, reg 20, Sch 5, paras 11, 12, 17, 18.

29   Powers of search etc

(1)   Subject to the following provisions of this Part, a duly authorised officer of an enforcement authority may at any reasonable hour and on production, if required, of his credentials exercise any of the powers conferred by the following provisions of this section.

PART 1
STATUTES

(2)   The officer may, for the purposes of ascertaining whether there has been any contravention of any safety provision …., inspect any goods and enter any premises other than premises occupied only as a person's residence.

(3)   The officer may, for the purpose of ascertaining whether there has been any contravention of any safety provision, examine any procedure (including any arrangements for carrying out a test) connected with the production of any goods.

(4)   If the officer has reasonable grounds for suspecting that any goods are manufactured or imported goods which have not been supplied in the United Kingdom since they were manufactured or imported he may—
- (a)   for the purpose of ascertaining whether there has been any contravention of any safety provision in relation to the goods, require any person carrying on a business, or employed in connection with a business, to produce any records relating to the business;
- (b)   for the purpose of ascertaining (by testing or otherwise) whether there has been any such contravention, seize and detain the goods;
- (c)   take copies of, or of any entry in, any records produced by virtue of paragraph (a) above.

(5)   If the officer has reasonable grounds for suspecting that there has been a contravention in relation to any goods of any safety provision … , he may—
- (a)   for the purpose of ascertaining whether there has been any such contravention, require any person carrying on a business, or employed in connection with a business, to produce any records relating to the business;
- (b)   for the purpose of ascertaining (by testing or otherwise) whether there has been any such contravention, seize and detain the goods;
- (c)   take copies of, or of any entry in, any records produced by virtue of paragraph (a) above.

(6)   The officer may seize and detain—
- (a)   any goods or records which he has reasonable grounds for believing may be required as evidence in proceedings for an offence in respect of a contravention of any safety provision … ;
- (b)   any goods which he has reasonable grounds for suspecting may be liable to be forfeited under section 16 or 17 above.

(7)   If and to the extent that it is reasonably necessary to do so to prevent a contravention of any safety provision … , the officer may, for the purpose of exercising his power under subsection (4), (5) or (6) above to seize any goods or records—
- (a)   require any person having authority to do so to open any container or to open any vending machine; and
- (b)   himself open or break open any such container or machine where a requirement made under paragraph (a) above in relation to the container or machine has not been complied with.

[1414]

NOTES

Sub-ss (2), (5)–(7): words omitted repealed by the Consumer Protection from Unfair Trading Regulations 2008, SI 2008/1277, reg 30(3), Sch 4.

Seize and detain: the powers of seizure conferred by sub-ss (4)–(6) are powers to which the Criminal Justice and Police Act 2001, s 50 apply (additional powers of seizure from premises); see s 50 of, and Sch 1, Pt 1, para 45 to, that Act.

Modification: this section is applied, with modifications, for the purposes of the enforcement of the Supply of Machinery (Safety) Regulations 2008, SI 2008/1597, by SI 2008/1597, reg 20, Sch 5, paras 11, 12, 17, 18.

30   Provisions supplemental to s 29

(1)   An officer seizing any goods or records under section 29 above shall inform the following persons that the goods or records have been so seized, that is to say—
- (a)   the person from whom they are seized; and
- (b)   in the case of imported goods seized on any premises under the control of the Commissioners of Customs and Excise, the importer of those goods (within the meaning of the Customs and Excise Management Act 1979).

(2)   If a justice of the peace—
- (a)   is satisfied by any written information on oath that there are reasonable grounds for believing either—
  - (i)   that any goods or records which any officer has power to inspect under section 29 above are on any premises and that their inspection is likely to disclose evidence that there has been a contravention of any safety provision … ; or
  - (ii)   that such a contravention has taken place, is taking place or is about to take place on any premises; and
- (b)   is also satisfied by any such information either—

    (i)   that admission to the premises has been or is likely to be refused and that notice of intention to apply for a warrant under this subsection has been given to the occupier; or

    (ii)   that an application for admission, or the giving of such a notice, would defeat the object of the entry or that the premises are unoccupied or that the occupier is temporarily absent and it might defeat the object of the entry to await his return,

the justice may by warrant under this hand, which shall continue in force for a period of one month, authorise any officer of an enforcement authority to enter the premises, if need be by force.

(3)   An officer entering any premises by virtue of section 29 above or a warrant under subsection (2) above may take with him such other persons and such equipment as may appear to him necessary.

(4)   On leaving any premises which a person is authorised to enter by a warrant under subsection (2) above, that person shall, if the premises are unoccupied or the occupier is temporarily absent, leave the premises as effectively secured against trespassers as he found them.

(5)   If any person who is not an officer of an enforcement authority purports to act as such under section 29 above or this section he shall be guilty of an offence and liable on summary conviction to a fine not exceeding level 5 on the standard scale.

(6)   Where any goods seized by an officer under section 29 above are submitted to a test, the officer shall inform the persons mentioned in subsection (1) above of the result of the test and, if—

    (a)   proceedings are brought for an offence in respect of a contravention in relation to the goods of any safety provision ... or for the forfeiture of the goods under section 16 or 17 above, or a suspension notice is served in respect of any goods; and

    (b)   the officer is requested to do so and it is practicable to comply with the request,

the officer shall allow any person who is a party to the proceedings or, as the case may be, has an interest in the goods to which the notice relates to have the goods tested.

(7)   The Secretary of State may by regulations provide that any test of goods seized under section 29 above by an officer of an enforcement authority shall—

    (a)   be carried out at the expense of the authority in a manner and by a person prescribed by or determined under the regulations; or

    (b)   be carried out either as mentioned in paragraph (a) above or by the authority in a manner prescribed by the regulations.

(8)   The power to make regulations under subsection (7) above shall be exercisable by statutory instrument subject to annulment in pursuance of a resolution of either House of Parliament and shall include power—

    (a)   to make different provision for different cases; and

    (b)   to make such supplemental, consequential and transitional provision as the Secretary of State considers appropriate.

(9)   (*Applies to Scotland only.*)

(10)   In the application of this section to Northern Ireland, the references in subsection (2) above to any information on oath shall be construed as references to any complaint on oath.

                                                    [1415]

NOTES

Sub-ss (2), (6): words omitted repealed by the Consumer Protection from Unfair Trading Regulations 2008, SI 2008/1277, reg 30(3), Sch 4.

Modification: this section is applied, with modifications, for the purposes of the enforcement of the Supply of Machinery (Safety) Regulations 2008, SI 2008/1597, by SI 2008/1597, reg 20, Sch 5, paras 11, 12, 17, 18.

31   Power of customs officer to detain goods

(1)   A customs officer may, for the purpose of facilitating the exercise by an enforcement authority or officer of such an authority of any functions conferred on the authority or officer by or under Part II of this Act, or by or under this Part in its application for the purposes of the safety provisions, seize any imported goods and detain them for not more than two working days.

(2)   Anything seized and detained under this section shall be dealt with during the period of its detention in such manner as the Commissioners of Customs and Excise may direct.

(3)   In subsection (1) above the reference to two working days is a reference to a period of forty-eight hours calculated from the time when the goods in question are seized but disregarding so much of any period as falls on a Saturday or Sunday or on Christmas Day, Good Friday or a day which is a bank holiday under the Banking and Financial Dealings Act 1971 in the part of the United Kingdom where the goods are seized.

(4)   In this section and section 32 below "customs officer" means any officer within the meaning of the Customs and Excise Management Act 1979.

                                                    [1416]

NOTES
Modification: this section is applied, with modifications, for the purposes of the enforcement of the Supply of Machinery (Safety) Regulations 2008, SI 2008/1597, by SI 2008/1597, reg 20, Sch 5, paras 11, 12, 17, 18.

32 Obstruction of authorised officer

(1)   Any person who—
  (a)   intentionally obstructs any officer of an enforcement authority who is acting in pursuance of any provision of this Part or any customs officer who is so acting; or
  (b)   intentionally fails to comply with any requirement made of him by any officer of an enforcement authority under any provision of this Part; or
  (c)   without reasonable cause fails to give any officer of an enforcement authority who is so acting any other assistance or information which the officer may reasonably require of him for the purposes of the exercise of the officer's functions under any provision of this Part,

shall be guilty of an offence and liable on summary conviction to a fine not exceeding level 5 on the standard scale.

(2)   A person shall be guilty of an offence if, in giving any information which is required of him by virtue of subsection (1)(c) above—
  (a)   he makes any statement which he knows is false in a material particular; or
  (b)   he recklessly makes a statement which is false in a material particular.

(3)   A person guilty of an offence under subsection (2) above shall be liable—
  (a)   on conviction on indictment, to a fine;
  (b)   on summary conviction, to a fine not exceeding the statutory maximum.

[1417]

NOTES
Modification: this section is applied, with modifications, for the purposes of the enforcement of the Supply of Machinery (Safety) Regulations 2008, SI 2008/1597, by SI 2008/1597, reg 20, Sch 5, paras 11, 12, 17, 18.

33 Appeals against detention of goods

(1)   Any person having an interest in any goods which are for the time being detained under any provision of this Part by an enforcement authority or by an officer of such an authority may apply for an order requiring the goods to be released to him or to another person.

(2)   An application under this section may be made—
  (a)   to any magistrates' court in which proceedings have been brought in England and Wales or Northern Ireland—
      (i)   for an offence in respect of a contravention in relation to the goods of any safety provision ... ; or
      (ii)   for the forfeiture of the goods under section 16 above;
  (b)   where no such proceedings have been so brought, by way of complaint to a magistrates' court; or
  (c)   *(applies to Scotland only.)*

(3)   On an application under this section to a magistrates' court or to the sheriff, an order requiring goods to be released shall be made only if the court or sheriff is satisfied—
  (a)   that proceedings—
      (i)   for an offence in respect of a contravention in relation to the goods of any safety provision ... ; or
      (ii)   for the forfeiture of the goods under section 16 or 17 above,
      have not been brought or, having been brought, have been concluded without the goods being forfeited; and
  (b)   where no such proceedings have been brought, that more than six months have elapsed since the goods were seized.

(4)   Any person aggrieved by an order made under this section by a magistrates' court in England and Wales or Northern Ireland, or by a decision of such a court not to make such an order, may appeal against that order or decision—
  (a)   in England and Wales, to the Crown Court;
  (b)   in Northern Ireland, to the county court;

and an order so made may contain such provision as appears to the court to be appropriate for delaying the coming into force of the order pending the making and determination of any appeal (including any application under section 111 of the Magistrates' Courts Act 1980 or Article 146 of the Magistrates' Courts (Northern Ireland) Order 1981 (statement of case)).

[1418]

NOTES

Sub-ss (2), (3): words omitted repealed by the Consumer Protection from Unfair Trading Regulations 2008, SI 2008/1277, reg 30(3), Sch 4.

Modification: this section is applied, with modifications, for the purposes of the enforcement of the Supply of Machinery (Safety) Regulations 2008, SI 2008/1597, by SI 2008/1597, reg 20, Sch 5, paras 11, 12, 17, 18.

34 Compensation for seizure and detention

(1)   Where an officer of an enforcement authority exercises any power under section 29 above to seize and detain goods, the enforcement authority shall be liable to pay compensation to any person having an interest in the goods in respect of any loss or damage caused by reason of the exercise of the power if—

(a)   there has been no contravention in relation to the goods of any safety provision … ; and

(b)   the exercise of the power is not attributable to any neglect or default by that person.

(2)   Any disputed question as to the right to or the amount of any compensation payable under this section shall be determined by arbitration or, in Scotland, by a single arbiter appointed, failing agreement between the parties, by the sheriff.

[1419]

NOTES

Sub-s (1): words omitted repealed by the Consumer Protection from Unfair Trading Regulations 2008, SI 2008/1277, reg 30(3), Sch 4.

Modification: this section is applied, with modifications, for the purposes of the enforcement of the Supply of Machinery (Safety) Regulations 2008, SI 2008/1597, by SI 2008/1597, reg 20, Sch 5, paras 11, 12, 17, 18.

35 Recovery of expenses of enforcement

(1)   This section shall apply where a court—

(a)   convicts a person of an offence in respect of a contravention in relation to any goods of any safety provision … ; or

(b)   makes an order under section 16 or 17 above for the forfeiture of any goods.

(2)   The court may (in addition to any other order it may make as to costs or expenses) order the person convicted or, as the case may be, any person having an interest in the goods to reimburse an enforcement authority for any expenditure which has been or may be incurred by that authority—

(a)   in connection with any seizure or detention of the goods by or on behalf of the authority; or

(b)   in connection with any compliance by the authority with directions given by the court for the purposes of any order for the forfeiture of the goods.

[1420]

NOTES

Sub-s (1): words omitted repealed by the Consumer Protection from Unfair Trading Regulations 2008, SI 2008/1277, reg 30(3), Sch 4.

Modification: this section is applied, with modifications, for the purposes of the enforcement of the Supply of Machinery (Safety) Regulations 2008, SI 2008/1597, by SI 2008/1597, reg 20, Sch 5, paras 11, 12, 17, 18.

PART V
MISCELLANEOUS AND SUPPLEMENTAL

36   (*Introduces Sch 3 (amendments to the Health and Safety at Work etc Act 1974, Pt I) outside the scope of this work.*)

37 [Power of Commissioners for Revenue and Customs to disclose information]

(1)   If they think it appropriate to do so for the purpose of facilitating the exercise by any person to whom subsection (2) below applies of any functions conferred on that person by or under Part II of this Act, or by or under Part IV of this Act in its application for the purposes of the safety provisions, [the Commissioners for Her Majesty's Revenue and Customs] may authorise the disclosure to that person of any information obtained [or held] for the purposes of the exercise [by Her Majesty's Revenue and Customs] of their functions in relation to imported goods.

(2)   This subsection applies to an enforcement authority and to any officer of an enforcement authority.

(3)   A disclosure of information made to any person under subsection (1) above shall be made in such manner as may be directed by [the Commissioners for Her Majesty's Revenue and Customs] and may be made through such persons acting on behalf of that person as may be so directed.

(4)   Information may be disclosed to a person under subsection (1) above whether or not the disclosure of the information has been requested by or on behalf of that person.

NOTES
Section heading: substituted by the Commissioners for Revenue and Customs Act 2005, s 50(6), Sch 4, para 36(1), (4).
Sub-s (1): words in first and third pairs of square brackets substituted and words in second pair of square brackets inserted by the Commissioners for Revenue and Customs Act 2005, s 50(6), Sch 4, para 36(1), (2).
Sub-s (3): words in square brackets substituted by the Commissioners for Revenue and Customs Act 2005, s 50(6), Sch 4, para 36(1), (3).
Modification: this section is applied, with modifications, for the purposes of the enforcement of the Supply of Machinery (Safety) Regulations 2008, SI 2008/1597, by SI 2008/1597, reg 20, Sch 5, paras 11, 12, 17, 18.

38   (*Repealed by the Enterprise Act 2002, ss 247(g), 278(2), Sch 26; see further, in so far as this section remains in force, the Railways and Transport Safety Act 2003, s 16(5), Sch 2, Pt 2, para 19(k).*)

39   Defence of due diligence

(1)   Subject to the following provisions of this section, in proceedings against any person for an offence to which this section applies it shall be a defence for that person to show that he took all reasonable steps and exercised all due diligence to avoid committing the offence.

(2)   Where in any proceedings against any person for such an offence the defence provided by subsection (1) above involves an allegation that the commission of the offence was due—

    (a)   to the act or default of another; or

    (b)   to reliance on information given by another,

that person shall not, without the leave of the court, be entitled to rely on the defence unless, not less than seven clear days before the hearing of the proceedings, he has served a notice under subsection (3) below on the person bringing the proceedings.

(3)   A notice under this subsection shall give such information identifying or assisting in the identification of the person who committed the act or default or gave the information as is in the possession of the person serving the notice at the time he serves it.

(4)   It is hereby declared that a person shall not be entitled to rely on the defence provided by subsection (1) above by reason of his reliance on information supplied by another, unless he shows that it was reasonable in all the circumstances for him to have relied on the information, having regard in particular—

    (a)   to the steps which he took, and those which might reasonably have been taken, for the purpose of verifying the information; and

    (b)   to whether he had any reason to disbelieve the information.

(5)   This section shall apply to an offence under section ... 12(1), (2) or (3), 13(4) [or 14(6)] above.

[1423]

NOTES
Sub-s (5): words omitted repealed by the General Product Safety Regulations 2005, SI 2005/1803, reg 46(1), (6); words in square brackets substituted by the Consumer Protection from Unfair Trading Regulations 2008, SI 2008/1277, reg 30(1), Sch 2, Pt 1, paras 33, 36.
Modification: this section is applied, with modifications, for the purposes of the enforcement of the Supply of Machinery (Safety) Regulations 2008, SI 2008/1597, by SI 2008/1597, reg 20, Sch 5, paras 11, 12, 17, 18.

40   Liability of persons other than principal offender

(1)   Where the commission by any person of an offence to which section 39 above applies is due to an act or default committed by some other person in the course of any business of his, the other person shall be guilty of the offence and may be proceeded against and punished by virtue of this subsection whether or not proceedings are taken against the first-mentioned person.

(2)   Where a body corporate is guilty of an offence under this Act (including where it is so guilty by virtue of subsection (1) above) in respect of any act or default which is shown to have been committed with the consent or connivance of, or to be attributable to any neglect on the part of, any director, manager, secretary or other similar officer of the body corporate or any person who was purporting to act in any such capacity he, as well as the body corporate, shall be guilty of that offence and shall be liable to be proceeded against and punished accordingly.

(3)   Where the affairs of a body corporate are managed by its members, subsection (2) above shall apply in relation to the acts and defaults of a member in connection with his functions of management as if he were a director of the body corporate.

[1424]

NOTES
Modification: this section is applied, with modifications, for the purposes of the enforcement of the Supply of Machinery (Safety) Regulations 2008, SI 2008/1597, by SI 2008/1597, reg 20, Sch 5, paras 11, 12, 17, 18.

41 Civil proceedings

(1)   An obligation imposed by safety regulations shall be a duty owed to any person who may be affected by a contravention of the obligation and, subject to any provision to the contrary in the regulations and to the defences and other incidents applying to actions for breach of statutory duty, a contravention of any such obligation shall be actionable accordingly.

(2)   This Act shall not be construed as conferring any other right of action in civil proceedings, apart from the right conferred by virtue of Part I of this Act, in respect of any loss or damage suffered in consequence of a contravention of a safety provision …

(3)   Subject to any provision to the contrary in the agreement itself, an agreement shall not be void or unenforceable by reason only of a contravention of a safety provision …

(4)   Liability by virtue of subsection (1) above shall not be limited or excluded by any contract term, by any notice or (subject to the power contained in subsection (1) above to limit or exclude it in safety regulations) by any other provision.

(5)   Nothing in subsection (1) above shall prejudice the operation of section 12 of the Nuclear Installations Act 1965 (rights to compensation for certain breaches of duties confined to rights under that Act).

(6)   In this section "damage" includes personal injury and death.

[1425]

NOTES

Sub-ss (2), (3): words omitted repealed by the Consumer Protection from Unfair Trading Regulations 2008, SI 2008/1277, reg 30(3), Sch 4.

42 Reports etc

(1)   It shall be the duty of the Secretary of State at least once in every five years to lay before each House of Parliament a report on the exercise during the period to which the report relates of the functions which under Part II of this Act, or under Part IV of this Act in its application for the purposes of the safety provisions, are exercisable by the Secretary of State, weights and measures authorities, district councils in Northern Ireland and persons on whom functions are conferred by regulations made under section 27(2) above.

(2)   The Secretary of State may from time to time prepare and lay before each House of Parliament such other reports on the exercise of those functions as he considers appropriate.

(3)   Every weights and measures authority, every district council in Northern Ireland and every person on whom functions are conferred by regulations under subsection (2) of section 27 above shall, whenever the Secretary of State so directs, make a report to the Secretary of State on the exercise of the functions exercisable by that authority or council under that section or by that person by virtue of any such regulations.

(4)   A report under subsection (3) above shall be in such form and shall contain such particulars as are specified in the direction of the Secretary of State.

(5)   The first report under subsection (1) above shall be laid before each House of Parliament not more than five years after the laying of the last report under section 8(2) of the Consumer Safety Act 1978.

[1426]

43 Financial provisions

(1)   There shall be paid out of money provided by Parliament—
   (a)   any expenses incurred or compensation payable by a Minister of the Crown or Government department in consequence of any provision of this Act; and
   (b)   any increase attributable to this Act in the sums payable out of money so provided under any other Act.

(2)   Any sums received by a Minister of the Crown or Government department by virtue of this Act shall be paid into the Consolidated Fund.

[1427]

44 Service of documents etc

(1)   Any document required or authorised by virtue of this Act to be served on a person may be so served—
   (a)   by delivering it to him or by leaving it at his proper address or by sending it by post to him at that address; or
   (b)   if the person is a body corporate, by serving it in accordance with paragraph (a) above on the secretary or clerk of that body; or
   (c)   if the person is a partnership, by serving it in accordance with that paragraph on a partner or on a person having control or management of the partnership business.

(2)   For the purposes of subsection (1) above, and for the purposes of section 7 of the Interpretation Act 1978 (which relates to the service of documents by post) in its application to that subsection, the proper address of any person on whom a document is to be served by virtue of this Act shall be his last known address except that—

(a)   in the case of service on a body corporate or its secretary or clerk, it shall be the address of the registered or principal office of the body corporate;

(b)   in the case of service on a partnership or a partner or a person having the control or management of a partnership business, it shall be the principal office of the partnership;

and for the purposes of this subsection the principal officer of a company registered outside the United Kingdom or of a partnership carrying on business outside the United Kingdom is its principal office within the United Kingdom.

(3)   The Secretary of State may by regulations make provision for the manner in which any information is to be given to any person under any provision of Part IV of this Act.

(4)   Without prejudice to the generality of subsection (3) above regulations made by the Secretary of State may prescribe the person, or manner of determining the person, who is to be treated for the purposes of section 28(2) or 30 above as the person from whom any goods were purchased or seized where the goods were purchased or seized from a vending machine.

(5)   The power to make regulations under subsection (3) or (4) above shall be exercisable by statutory instrument subject to annulment in pursuance of a resolution of either House of Parliament and shall include power—

(a)   to make different provision for different cases; and

(b)   to make such supplemental, consequential and transitional provision as the Secretary of State considers appropriate.

[1428]

NOTES

Modification: this section is applied, with modifications, for the purposes of the enforcement of the Supply of Machinery (Safety) Regulations 2008, SI 2008/1597, by SI 2008/1597, reg 20, Sch 5, paras 11, 12, 17, 18.

45   Interpretation

(1)   In this Act, except in so far as the context otherwise requires—

"aircraft" includes gliders, balloons and hovercraft;

"business" includes a trade or profession and the activities of a professional or trade association or of a local authority or other public authority;

"conditional sale agreement", "credit-sale agreement" and "hire-purchase agreement" have the same meanings as in the Consumer Credit Act 1974 but as if in the definitions in that Act "goods" had the same meaning as in this Act;

"contravention" includes a failure to comply and cognate expressions shall be construed accordingly;

"enforcement authority" means the Secretary of State, any other Minister of the Crown in charge of a Government department, any such department and any authority, council or other person on whom functions under this Act are conferred by or under section 27 above;

"gas" has the same meaning as in Part I of the Gas Act 1986;

"goods" includes substances, growing crops and things comprised in land by virtue of being attached to it and any ship, aircraft or vehicle;

"information" includes accounts, estimates and returns;

"magistrates' court", in relation to Northern Ireland, means a court of summary jurisdiction;
.....
"modifications" includes additions, alterations and omissions, and cognate expressions shall be construed accordingly;

"motor vehicle" has the same meaning as in [the Road Traffic Act 1988];

"notice" means a notice in writing;

"notice to warn" means a notice under section 13(1)(b) above;

"officer", in relation to an enforcement authority, means a person authorised in writing to assist the authority in carrying out its functions under or for the purposes of the enforcement of any of the safety provisions or of any of the provisions made by or under Part III of this Act;

"personal injury" includes any disease and any other impairment of a person's physical or mental condition;

"premises" includes any place and any ship, aircraft or vehicle;

"prohibition notice" means a notice under section 13(1)(a) above;

"records" includes any books or documents and any records in non-documentary form;

"safety provision" means ... any provision of safety regulations, a prohibition notice or a suspension notice;

"safety regulations" means regulations under section 11 above;

"ship" includes any boat and any other description of vessel used in navigation;

"subordinate legislation" has the same meaning as in the Interpretation Act 1978;

"substance" means any natural or artificial substance, whether in solid, liquid or gaseous form or in the form of a vapour, and includes substances that are comprised in or mixed with other goods;

"supply" and cognate expressions shall be construed in accordance with section 46 below;

"suspension notice" means a notice under section 14 above.

(2)   Except in so far as the context otherwise requires, references in this Act to a contravention of a safety provision shall, in relation to any goods, include references to anything which would constitute such a contravention if the goods were supplied to any person.

(3)   References in this Act to any goods in relation to which any safety provision has been or may have been contravened shall include references to any goods which it is not reasonably practicable to separate from any such goods.

(4)   ...

(5)   (*Applies to Scotland only.*)

[1429]

NOTES

Sub-s (1): definitions "mark" and "trade mark" (omitted) repealed by the Trade Marks Act 1994, s 106(2), Sch 5; words in square brackets in definition "motor vehicle" substituted by the Road Traffic (Consequential Provisions) Act 1988, s 4, Sch 3, para 35; in definition "safety provision" words omitted repealed by the General Product Safety Regulations 2005, SI 2005/1803, reg 46(1), (7).

Sub-s (4): repealed by the Trade Marks Act 1994, s 106(2), Sch 5.

---

46   Meaning of "supply"

(1)   Subject to the following provisions of this section, references in this Act to supplying goods shall be construed as references to doing any of the following, whether as principal or agent, that is to say—

(a)   selling, hiring out or lending the goods;

(b)   entering into a hire-purchase agreement to furnish the goods;

(c)   the performance of any contract for work and materials to furnish the goods;

(d)   providing the goods in exchange for any consideration ... other than money;

(e)   providing the goods in or in connection with the performance of any statutory function; or

(f)   giving the goods as a prize or otherwise making a gift of the goods;

and, in relation to gas or water, those references shall be construed as including references to providing the service by which the gas or water is made available for use.

(2)   For the purposes of any reference in this Act to supplying goods, where a person ("the ostensible supplier") supplies goods to another person ("the customer") under a hire-purchase agreement, conditional sale agreement or credit-sale agreement or under an agreement for the hiring of goods (other than a hire-purchase agreement) and the ostensible supplier—

(a)   carries on the business of financing the provision of goods for others by means of such agreements; and

(b)   in the course of that business acquired his interest in the goods supplied to the customer as a means of financing the provision of them for the customer by a further person ("the effective supplier"),

the effective supplier and not the ostensible supplier shall be treated as supplying the goods to the customer.

(3)   Subject to subsection (4) below, the performance of any contract by the erection of any building or structure on any land or by the carrying out of any other building works shall be treated for the purposes of this Act as a supply of goods in so far as, but only in so far as, it involves the provision of any goods to any person by means of their incorporation into the building, structure or works.

(4)   Except for the purposes of, and in relation to, notices to warn ..., references in this Act to supplying goods shall not include references to supplying goods comprised in land where the supply is effected by the creation or disposal of an interest in the land.

(5)   Except in Part I of this Act references in this Act to a person's supplying goods shall be confined to references to that person's supplying goods in the course of a business of his, but for the purposes of this subsection it shall be immaterial whether the business is a business of dealing in the goods.

(6)   For the purposes of subsection (5) above goods shall not be treated as supplied in the course of a business if they are supplied, in pursuance of an obligation arising under or in connection with the insurance of the goods, to the person with whom they were insured.

(7)   Except for the purposes of, and in relation to, prohibition notices or suspension notices, references in [Part 2 or Part 4] of this Act to supplying goods shall not include—

(a)   references to supplying goods where the person supplied carries on a business of buying goods of the same description as those goods and repairing or reconditioning them;

(b)   references to supplying goods by a sale of articles as scrap (that is to say, for the value of materials included in the articles rather than for the value of the articles themselves).

(8)   Where any goods have at any time been supplied by being hired out or lent to any person, neither a continuation or renewal of the hire or loan (whether on the same or different terms) nor any transaction for the transfer after that time of any interest in the goods to the person to whom they were hired or lent shall be treated for the purposes of this Act as a further supply of the goods to that person.

(9)   A ship, aircraft or motor vehicle shall not be treated for the purposes of this Act as supplied to any person by reason only that services consisting in the carriage of goods or passengers in that ship, aircraft or vehicle, or in its use for any other purpose, are provided to that person in pursuance of an agreement relating to the use of the ship, aircraft or vehicle for a particular period or for particular voyages, flights or journeys.

[1430]

NOTES

Sub-s (1): words omitted from para (d) repealed in relation to England, Wales and Scotland by the Regulatory Reform (Trading Stamps) Order 2005, SI 2005/871, art 6, Schedule, and in relation to Northern Ireland by the Law Reform (Miscellaneous Provisions) (Northern Ireland) Order 2005, SI 2005/1452, art 24, Sch 2.

Sub-s (4): words omitted repealed by the Consumer Protection from Unfair Trading Regulations 2008, SI 2008/1277, reg 30(3), Sch 4.

Sub-s (7): words in square brackets substituted by SI 2008/1277, reg 30(1), Sch 2, Pt 1, paras 33, 37.

47 Savings for certain privileges

(1)   Nothing in this Act shall be taken as requiring any person to produce any records if he would be entitled to refuse to produce those records in any proceedings in any court on the grounds that they are the subject of legal professional privilege or, in Scotland, that they contain a confidential communication made by or to an advocate or solicitor in that capacity, or as authorising any person to take possession of any records which are in the possession of a person who would be so entitled.

(2)   Nothing in this Act shall be construed as requiring a person to answer any question or give any information if to do so would incriminate that person or that person's spouse [or civil partner].

[1431]

NOTES

Sub-s (2): words in square brackets inserted by the Civil Partnership Act 2004, s 261(1), Sch 27, para 126.

48 Minor and consequential amendments and repeals

(1)   The enactments mentioned in Schedule 4 to this Act shall have effect subject to the amendments specified in that Schedule (being minor amendments and amendments consequential on the provisions of this Act).

(2)   The following Acts shall cease to have effect, that is to say—

(a)   the Trade Descriptions Act 1972; and

(b)   the Fabrics (Misdescription) Act 1913.

(3)   The enactments mentioned in Schedule 5 to this Act are hereby repealed to the extent specified in the third column of that Schedule.

[1432]

49 Northern Ireland

(1)   This Act shall extend to Northern Ireland with the exception of—

(a)   the provisions of [Part 1];

(b)   any provision amending or repealing an enactment which does not so extend; and

(c)   any other provision so far as it has effect for the purposes of, or in relation to, a provision falling within paragraph (a) or (b) above.

(2)   ...

(3)   An Order in Council under paragraph 1(1)(b) of Schedule 1 to the Northern Ireland Act 1974 (exercise of legislative functions for Northern Ireland) which states that it is made only for purposes corresponding to any of the provisions of this Act mentioned in subsection (1)(a) to (c) above—

(a)   shall not be subject to paragraph 1(4) and (5) of that Schedule (affirmative resolution procedure and procedure in cases of urgency); but

(b)   shall be subject to annulment in pursuance of a resolution of either House of Parliament.

[1433]

NOTES

Sub-s (1): words in square brackets in para (a) substituted by the Consumer Protection from Unfair Trading Regulations 2008, SI 2008/1277, reg 30(1), Sch 2, Pt 1, paras 33, 37.

Sub-s (2): repealed by the Northern Ireland Act 1998, s 100(2), Sch 15.

50 Short title, commencement and transitional provision

(1)   This Act may be cited as the Consumer Protection Act 1987.

(2)   This Act shall come into force on such day as the Secretary of State may by order made by statutory instrument appoint, and different days may be so appointed for different provisions or for different purposes.

(3)   The Secretary of State shall not make an order under subsection (2) above bringing into force the repeal of the Trade Descriptions Act 1972, a repeal of any provision of that Act or a repeal of that Act or of any provision of it for any purposes, unless a draft of the order has been laid before, and approved by a resolution of, each House of Parliament.

(4)   An order under subsection (2) above bringing a provision into force may contain such transitional provision in connection with the coming into force of that provision as the Secretary of State considers appropriate.

(5)   Without prejudice to the generality of the power conferred by subsection (4) above, the Secretary of State may by order provide for any regulations made under the Consumer Protection Act 1961 or the Consumer Protection Act (Northern Ireland) 1965 to have effect as if made under section 11 above and for any such regulations to have effect with such modifications as he considers appropriate for that purpose.

(6)   The power of the Secretary of State by order to make such provision as is mentioned in subsection (5) above, shall, in so far as it is not exercised by an order under subsection (2) above, be exercisable by statutory instrument subject to annulment in pursuance of a resolution of either House of Parliament.

(7)   Nothing in this Act or in any order under subsection (2) above shall make any person liable by virtue of Part I of this Act for any damage caused wholly or partly by a defect in a product which was supplied to any person by its producer before the coming into force of Part I of this Act.

(8)   Expressions used in subsection (7) above and in Part I of this Act have the same meanings in that subsection as in that Part.

[1434]

NOTES

Trade Descriptions Act 1972: repealed by s 48(2), (3) of, and Sch 5 to, this Act.

Orders: the Consumer Protection Act 1987 (Commencement No 1) Order 1987, SI 1987/1680; the Consumer Protection Act 1987 (Commencement No 2) Order 1988, SI 1988/2041; the Consumer Protection Act 1987 (Commencement No 3) Order 1988, SI 1988/2076.

SCHEDULES

(Sch 1: Pt I amends the Limitation Act 1980; Pt II applies to Scotland only.)

SCHEDULE 2
PROHIBITION NOTICES AND NOTICES TO WARN

Section 13

PART I
PROHIBITION NOTICES

1.   A prohibition notice in respect of any goods shall—
    (a)   state that the Secretary of State considers that the goods are unsafe;
    (b)   set out the reasons why the Secretary of State considers that the goods are unsafe;
    (c)   specify the day on which the notice is to come into force; and
    (d)   state that the trader may at any time make representations in writing to the Secretary of State for the purpose of establishing that the goods are safe.

2.—(1)   If representations in writing about a prohibition notice are made by the trader to the Secretary of State, it shall be the duty of the Secretary of State to consider whether to revoke the notice and—
    (a)   if he decides to revoke it, to do so;
    (b)   in any other case, to appoint a person to consider those representations, any further representations made (whether in writing or orally) by the trader about the notice and the statements of any witnesses examined under this Part of this Schedule.

(2)   Where the Secretary of State has appointed a person to consider representations about a prohibition notice, he shall serve a notification on the trader which—

    (a)   states that the trader may make oral representations to the appointed person for the purpose of establishing that the goods to which the notice relates are safe; and

    (b)   specifies the place and time at which the oral representations may be made.

(3)   The time specified in a notification served under sub-paragraph (2) above shall not be before the end of the period of twenty-one days beginning with the day on which the notification is served, unless the trader otherwise agrees.

(4)   A person on whom a notification has been served under sub-paragraph (2) above or his representative may, at the place and time specified in the notification—

    (a)   make oral representations to the appointed person for the purpose of establishing that the goods in question are safe; and

    (b)   call and examine witnesses in connection with the representations.

3.—(1)   Where representations in writing about a prohibition notice are made by the trader to the Secretary of State at any time after a person has been appointed to consider representations about that notice, then, whether or not the appointed person has made a report to the Secretary of State, the following provisions of this paragraph shall apply instead of paragraph 2 above.

(2)   The Secretary of State shall, before the end of the period of one month beginning with the day on which he receives the representations, serve a notification on the trader which states—

    (a)   that the Secretary of State has decided to revoke the notice, has decided to vary it or, as the case may be, has decided neither to revoke nor to vary it; or

    (b)   that, a person having been appointed to consider representations about the notice, the trader may, at a place and time specified in the notification, make oral representations to the appointed person for the purpose of establishing that the goods to which the notice relates are safe.

(3)   The time specified in a notification served for the purposes of sub-paragraph (2)(b) above shall not be before the end of the period of twenty-one days beginning with the day on which the notification is served, unless the trader otherwise agrees or the time is the time already specified for the purposes of paragraph 2(2)(b) above.

(4)   A person on whom a notification has been served for the purposes of sub-paragraph (2)(b) above or his representative may, at the place and time specified in the notification—

    (a)   make oral representations to the appointed person for the purpose of establishing that the goods in question are safe; and

    (b)   call and examine witnesses in connection with the representations.

4.—(1)   Where a person is appointed to consider representations about a prohibition notice, it shall be his duty to consider—

    (a)   any written representations made by the trader about the notice, other than those in respect of which a notification is served under paragraph 3(2)(a) above;

    (b)   any oral representations made under paragraph 2(4) or 3(4) above; and

    (c)   any statements made by witnesses in connection with the oral representations,

and, after considering any matters under this paragraph, to make a report (including recommendations) to the Secretary of State about the matters considered by him and the notice.

(2)   It shall be the duty of the Secretary of State to consider any report made to him under sub-paragraph (1) above and, after considering the report, to inform the trader of his decision with respect to the prohibition notice to which the report relates.

5.—(1)   The Secretary of State may revoke or vary a prohibition notice by serving on the trader a notification stating that the notice is revoked or, as the case may be, is varied as specified in the notification.

(2)   The Secretary of State shall not vary a prohibition notice so as to make the effect of the notice more restrictive for the trader.

(3)   Without prejudice to the power conferred by section 13(2) of this Act, the service of a notification under sub-paragraph (1) above shall be sufficient to satisfy the requirement of paragraph 4(2) above that the trader shall be informed of the Secretary of State's decision.

[1435]

PART II
NOTICES TO WARN

6.—(1)   If the Secretary of State proposes to serve a notice to warn on any person in respect of any goods, the Secretary of State, before he serves the notice, shall serve on that person a notification which—

    (a)   contains a draft of the proposed notice;

    (b)   states that the Secretary of State proposes to serve a notice in the form of the draft on that person;

    (c)   states that the Secretary of State considers that the goods described in the draft are unsafe;

(d)   sets out the reasons why the Secretary of State considers that those goods are unsafe; and

(e)   states that that person may make representations to the Secretary of State for the purpose of establishing that the goods are safe if, before the end of the period of fourteen days beginning with the day on which the notification is served, he informs the Secretary of State—

     (i)   of his intention to make representations; and

     (ii)   whether the representations will be made only in writing or both in writing and orally.

(2)   Where the Secretary of State has served a notification containing a draft of a proposed notice to warn on any person, he shall not serve a notice to warn on that person in respect of the goods to which the proposed notice relates unless—

(a)   the period of fourteen days beginning with the day on which the notification was served expires without the Secretary of State being informed as mentioned in sub-paragraph (1)(e) above;

(b)   the period of twenty-eight days beginning with that day expires without any written representations being made by that person to the Secretary of State about the proposed notice; or

(c)   the Secretary of State has considered a report about the proposed notice by a person appointed under paragraph 7(1) below.

7.—(1)   Where a person on whom a notification containing a draft of a proposed notice to warn has been served—

(a)   informs the Secretary of State as mentioned in paragraph 6(1)(e) above before the end of the period of fourteen days beginning with the day on which the notification was served; and

(b)   makes written representations to the Secretary of State about the proposed notice before the end of the period of twenty-eight days beginning with that day,

the Secretary of State shall appoint a person to consider those representations, any further representations made by that person about the draft notice and the statements of any witnesses examined under this Part of this Schedule.

(2)   Where—

(a)   the Secretary of State has appointed a person to consider representations about a proposed notice to warn; and

(b)   the person whose representations are to be considered has informed the Secretary of State for the purposes of paragraph 6(1)(e) above that the representations he intends to make will include oral representations,

the Secretary of State shall inform the person intending to make the representations of the place and time at which oral representations may be made to the appointed person.

(3)   Where a person on whom a notification containing a draft of a proposed notice to warn has been served is informed of a time for the purposes of sub-paragraph (2) above, that time shall not be—

(a)   before the end of the period of twenty-eight days beginning with the day on which the notification was served; or

(b)   before the end of the period of seven days beginning with the day on which that person is informed of the time.

(4)   A person who has been informed of a place and time for the purposes of sub-paragraph (2) above or his representative may, at that place and time—

(a)   make oral representations to the appointed person for the purpose of establishing that the goods to which the proposed notice relates are safe; and

(b)   call and examine witnesses in connection with the representations.

8.—(1)   Where a person is appointed to consider representations about a proposed notice to warn, it shall be his duty to consider—

(a)   any written representations made by the person on whom it is proposed to serve the notice; and

(b)   in a case where a place and time has been appointed under paragraph 7(2) above for oral representations to be made by that person or his representative, any representations so made and any statements made by witnesses in connection with those representations,

and, after considering those matters, to make a report (including recommendations) to the Secretary of State about the matters considered by him and the proposal to serve the notice.

(2)   It shall be the duty of the Secretary of State to consider any report made to him under sub-paragraph (1) above and, after considering the report, to inform the person on whom it was proposed that a notice to warn should be served of his decision with respect to the proposal.

(3)   If at any time after serving a notification on a person under paragraph 6 above the Secretary of State decides not to serve on that person either the proposed notice to warn or that notice with

modifications, the Secretary of State shall inform that person of the decision; and nothing done for the purposes of any of the preceding provisions of this Part of this Schedule before that person was so informed shall—

    (a)   entitle the Secretary of State subsequently to serve the proposed notice or that notice with modifications; or

    (b)   require the Secretary of State, or any person appointed to consider representations about the proposed notice, subsequently to do anything in respect of, or in consequence of, any such representations.

(4)   Where a notification containing a draft of a proposed notice to warn is served on a person in respect of any goods, a notice to warn served on him in consequence of a decision made under sub-paragraph (2) above shall either be in the form of the draft or shall be less onerous than the draft.

9.   The Secretary of State may revoke a notice to warn by serving on the person on whom the notice was served a notification stating that the notice is revoked.

[1436]

PART III
GENERAL

10.—(1)   Where in a notification served on any person under this Schedule the Secretary of State has appointed a time for the making of oral representations or the examination of witnesses, he may, by giving that person such notification as the Secretary of State considers appropriate, change that time to a later time or appoint further times at which further representations may be made or the examination of witnesses may be continued; and paragraphs 2(4), 3(4) and 7(4) above shall have effect accordingly.

(2)   For the purposes of this Schedule the Secretary of State may appoint a person (instead of the appointed person) to consider any representations or statements, if the person originally appointed, or last appointed under this sub-paragraph, to consider those representations or statements has died or appears to the Secretary of State to be otherwise unable to act.

11.   In this Schedule—

    "the appointed person" in relation to a prohibition notice or a proposal to serve a notice to warn, means the person for the time being appointed under this Schedule to consider representations about the notice or, as the case may be, about the proposed notice;

    "notification" means a notification in writing;

    "trader", in relation to a prohibition notice, means the person on whom the notice is or was served.

[1437]

(Schs 3–5 outside the scope of this work.)

LAW OF PROPERTY (MISCELLANEOUS PROVISIONS) ACT 1989

(1989 c 34)

An Act to make new provisions with respect to deeds and their execution and contracts for the sale or other disposition of interests in land; and to abolish the rule of law known as the rule in Bain v Fothergill

[27 July 1989]

ARRANGEMENT OF SECTIONS

1 Deeds and their execution

(1)   Any rule of law which—

    (a)   restricts the substances on which a deed may be written;

    (b)   requires a seal for the valid execution of an instrument as a deed by an individual; or

    (c)   requires authority by one person to another to deliver an instrument as a deed on his behalf to be given by deed,

is abolished.

(2)   An instrument shall not be a deed unless—

(a) it makes it clear on its face that it is intended to be a deed by the person making it or, as the case may be, by the parties to it (whether by describing itself as a deed or expressing itself to be executed or signed as a deed or otherwise); and

(b) it is validly executed as a deed[—

  (i) by that person or a person authorised to execute it in the name or on behalf of that person, or

  (ii) by one or more of those parties or a person authorised to execute it in the name or on behalf of one or more of those parties.]

[(2A) For the purposes of subsection (2)(a) above, an instrument shall not be taken to make it clear on its face that it is intended to be a deed merely because it is executed under seal.]

(3) An instrument is validly executed as a deed by an individual if, and only if—

(a) it is signed—

  (i) by him in the presence of a witness who attests the signature; or

  (ii) at his direction and in his presence and the presence of two witnesses who each attest the signature; and

(b) it is delivered as a deed ...

(4) In subsections (2) and (3) above "sign", in relation to an instrument, includes—

[(a) an individual signing the name of the person or party on whose behalf he executes the instrument; and

(b) making one's mark on the instrument,

and "signature" is to be construed accordingly.]

[(4A) Subsection (3) above applies in the case of an instrument executed by an individual in the name or on behalf of another person whether or not that person is also an individual.]

(5) Where [a relevant lawyer, or an agent or employee of a relevant lawyer], in the course of or in connection with a transaction ... , purports to deliver an instrument as a deed on behalf of a party to the instrument, it shall be conclusively presumed in favour of a purchaser that he is authorised so to deliver the instrument.

(6) In subsection (5) above—

["purchaser" has the same meaning] as in the Law of Property Act 1925;

["relevant lawyer" means a person who, for the purposes of the Legal Services Act 2007, is an authorised person in relation to an activity which constitutes a reserved instrument activity (within the meaning of that Act).]

(7) Where an instrument under seal that constitutes a deed is required for the purposes of an Act passed before this section comes into force, this section shall have effect as to signing, sealing or delivery of an instrument by an individual in place of any provision of that Act as to signing, sealing or delivery.

(8) The enactments mentioned in Schedule 1 to this Act (which in consequence of this section require amendments other than those provided by subsection (7) above) shall have effect with the amendments specified in that Schedule.

(9) Nothing in subsection (1)(b), (2), (3), (7) or (8) above applies in relation to deeds required or authorised to be made under—

(a) the seal of the county palatine of Lancaster;

(b) the seal of the Duchy of Lancaster; or

(c) the seal of the Duchy of Cornwall.

(10) The references in this section to the execution of a deed by an individual do not include execution by a corporation sole and the reference in subsection (7) above to signing, sealing or delivery by an individual does not include signing, sealing or delivery by such a corporation.

(11) Nothing in this section applies in relation to instruments delivered as deeds before this section comes into force.

[1438]

NOTES

Sub-s (2): in sub-para (b) words in square brackets substituted, except in relation to any instrument executed before 15 September 2005, by the Regulatory Reform (Execution of Deeds and Documents) Order 2005, SI 2005/1906, art 7(3).

Sub-ss (2A), (4A): inserted, except in relation to any instrument executed before 15 September 2005, by SI 2005/1906, arts 7(4), 8.

Sub-s (3): words omitted repealed, except in relation to any instrument executed before 15 September 2005, by SI 2005/1906, art 10(2), Sch 2.

Sub-s (4): words in square brackets substituted, except in relation to any instrument executed before 15 September 2005, by SI 2005/1906, art 10(1), Sch 1, paras 13, 14.

Sub-s (5): words in square brackets substituted by the Legal Services Act 2007, s 208(1), Sch 21, para 81(a); words omitted repealed, except in relation to any instrument executed before 15 September 2005, by SI 2005/1906, arts 9, 10(2), Sch 2.

Sub-s (6): in definition "purchaser" words in square brackets substituted, and definition "interest in land" (omitted) repealed, except in relation to any instrument executed before 15 September 2005, by SI 2005/1906, art 10, Sch 1, paras 13, 15, Sch 2; definition "relevant lawyer" substituted (for definition "duly certificated notary public" as inserted by the Courts and Legal Services Act 1990, s 125(2), Sch 17, para 20) by the Legal Services Act 2007, s 208(1), Sch 21, para 81(b).

2 Contracts for sale etc of land to be made by signed writing

(1)   A contract for the sale or other disposition of an interest in land can only be made in writing and only by incorporating all the terms which the parties have expressly agreed in one document or, where contracts are exchanged, in each.

(2)   The terms may be incorporated in a document either by being set out in it or by reference to some other document.

(3)   The document incorporating the terms or, where contracts are exchanged, one of the documents incorporating them (but not necessarily the same one) must be signed by or on behalf of each party to the contract.

(4)   Where a contract for the sale or other disposition of an interest in land satisfies the conditions of this section by reason only of the rectification of one or more documents in pursuance of an order of a court, the contract shall come into being, or be deemed to have come into being, at such time as may be specified in the order.

(5)   This section does not apply in relation to—
    (a)   a contract to grant such a lease as is mentioned in section 54(2) of the Law of Property Act 1925 (short leases);
    (b)   a contract made in the course of a public auction; or
    [(c)   a contract regulated under the Financial Services and Markets Act 2000, other than a regulated mortgage contract[, a regulated home reversion plan, a regulated home purchase plan or a regulated sale and rent back agreement];]

and nothing in this section affects the creation or operation of resulting, implied or constructive trusts.

(6)   In this section—
    "disposition" has the same meaning as in the Law of Property Act 1925;
    "interest in land" means any estate, interest or charge in or over land …
    ["regulated mortgage contract"[, "regulated home reversion plan"[, "regulated home purchase plan" and "regulated sale and rent back agreement"]] must be read with—
        (a)   section 22 of the Financial Services and Markets Act 2000,
        (b)   any relevant order under that section, and
        (c)   Schedule 22 to that Act.]

(7)   Nothing in this section shall apply in relation to contracts made before this section comes into force.

(8)   Section 40 of the Law of Property Act 1925 (which is superseded by this section) shall cease to have effect.

[1439]

NOTES

Sub-s (5): para (c) substituted by the Financial Services and Markets Act 2000 (Consequential Amendments and Repeals) Order 2001, SI 2001/3649, art 317(1), (2); words in square brackets in para (c) substituted by the Financial Services and Markets Act 2000 (Regulated Activities) (Amendment) Order 2009, SI 2009/1342, art 24(a).

Sub-s (6): words omitted from definition "interest in land" repealed by the Trusts of Land and Appointment of Trustees Act 1996, s 25(2), Sch 4, for savings in connection with the abolition of the doctrine of conversion, see ss 3, 18(3), 25(5) of the 1996 Act; definition "regulated mortgage contract" inserted by SI 2001/3649, art 317(1), (3), words in first (outer) pair of square brackets inserted by the Financial Services and Markets Act 2000 (Regulated Activities) (Amendment) (No 2) Order 2006, SI 2006/2383, art 27(b), subject to transitional provisions in arts 37–39 of that Order, words in second (inner) pair of square brackets substituted by SI 2009/1342, art 24(b).

3 Abolition of rule in Bain v Fothergill

The rule of law known as the rule in Bain v Fothergill is abolished in relation to contracts made after this section comes into force.

[1440]

4   (*Introduces Sch 2 (repeals) outside the scope of this work.*)

5 Commencement

(1)   The provisions of this Act to which this subsection applies shall come into force on such day as the Lord Chancellor may by order made by statutory instrument appoint.

(2)   The provisions to which subsection (1) above applies are—

(a)   section 1 above; and

(b)   section 4 above, except so far as it relates to section 40 of the Law of Property Act 1925.

(3)   The provisions of this Act to which this subsection applies shall come into force at the end of the period of two months beginning with the day on which this Act is passed.

(4)   The provisions of this Act to which subsection (3) above applies are—

(a)   sections 2 and 3 above; and

(b)   section 4 above, so far as it relates to section 40 of the Law of Property Act 1925.

[1441]

NOTES

Order: the Law of Property (Miscellaneous Provisions) Act 1989 (Commencement) Order 1990, SI 1990/1175.

---

6   Citation

(1)   This Act may be cited as the Law of Property (Miscellaneous Provisions) Act 1989.

(2)   This Act extends to England and Wales only.

[1442]

(Sch 1 repealed in part; remainder amends the Law of Property Act 1925, ss 52(2)(e), 74(2), 80(1), 81, and the Powers of Attorney Act 1971, ss 1, 7 at **[492]**, **[497]**; *Sch 2 (repeals) outside the scope of this work.)*

FOOD SAFETY ACT 1990

(1990 c 16)

ARRANGEMENT OF SECTIONS

PART I

PRELIMINARY

An Act to make new provision in place of the Food Act 1984 (except Parts III and V), the Food and Drugs (Scotland) Act 1956 and certain other enactments relating to food; to amend Parts III and V of the said Act of 1984 and Part I of the Food and Environment Protection Act 1985; and for connected purposes

[29 June 1990]

NOTES

The Act confers extensive powers to make subordinate legislation. Considerations of space preclude reference to all orders and regulations made under the Act. For details of orders and regulations made under the Act, and for modifications to the Act made by specific orders and regulations, specialist works on food and food safety should be consulted.

Transfer of functions in relation to Wales: as to the transfer of functions under this Act from Ministers of the Crown to the National Assembly for Wales, see the National Assembly for Wales (Transfer of Functions) Order 1999, SI 1999/672.

By the Transfer of Functions (Agriculture and Food) Order 1999, SI 1999/3141, arts 2(6), (7), 3, any function under this Act which is exercisable by the Minister of Agriculture, Fisheries and Food jointly with the Secretaries of State respectively concerned with health in England and food and health in Wales is hereby transferred to the Minister of Agriculture, Fisheries and Food and the Secretary of State acting jointly. The Minister for Agriculture, Fisheries and Food is now the Secretary of State for Environment, Food and Rural Affairs; see in general, the Secretaries of State for Transport, Local Government and the Regions and for Environment, Food and Rural Affairs Order 2001, SI 2001/2568. Note however, that by the Food Standards Act 1999, s 26(1), the functions of the Minister of Agriculture, Fisheries and Food under this Act ceased to be exercisable by that Minister on 1 April 2000. By s 26(3) of the 1999 Act, enforcement functions under directions or subordinate legislation made under this Act (or any power under this Act to confer such functions in directions or subordinate legislation) are unaffected.

PART I
PRELIMINARY

1 Meaning of "food" and other basic expressions

[(1)   In this Act "food" has the same meaning as it has in Regulation (EC) No 178/2002.

(2)   In this Act "Regulation (EC) No 178/2002" means Regulation (EC) No 178/2002 of the European Parliament and of the Council laying down the general principles and requirements of food law, establishing the European Food Safety Authority and laying down procedures in matters of food safety.]

(3)   In this Act, unless the context otherwise requires—

"business" includes the undertaking of a canteen, club, school, hospital or institution, whether carried on for profit or not, and any undertaking or activity carried on by a public or local authority;

"commercial operation", in relation to any food or contact material, means any of the following, namely—

(a)   selling, possessing for sale and offering, exposing or advertising for sale;

(b)   consigning, delivering or serving by way of sale;

(c)   preparing for sale or presenting, labelling or wrapping for the purpose of sale;

(d)   storing or transporting for the purpose of sale;

(e)   importing and exporting;

and, in relation to any food source, means deriving food from it for the purpose of sale or for purposes connected with sale;

PART 1
STATUTES

"contact material" means any article or substance which is intended to come into contact with food;

"food business" means any business in the course of which commercial operations with respect to food or food sources are carried out;

"food premises" means any premises used for the purposes of a food business;

"food source" means any growing crop or live animal, bird or fish from which food is intended to be derived (whether by harvesting, slaughtering, milking, collecting eggs or otherwise);

"premises" includes any place, any vehicle, stall or moveable structure and, for such purposes as may be specified in an order made by [the Secretary of State], any ship or aircraft of a description so specified.

(4)   The reference in subsection (3) above to preparing for sale shall be construed, in relation to any contact material, as a reference to manufacturing or producing for the purpose of sale.

[1443]

NOTES

Sub-s (1), (2): substituted by the Food Safety Act 1990 (Amendment) Regulations 2004, SI 2004/2990, regs 2, 3.

Sub-s (3): in definition "premises" words in square brackets substituted by the Food Standards Act 1999, s 40(1), Sch 5, paras 7, 8.

Orders: see note at the beginning of this Act.

2   Extended meaning of "sale" etc

(1)   For the purposes of this Act—

(a)   the supply of food, otherwise than on sale, in the course of a business; and

(b)   any other thing which is done with respect to food and is specified in an order made by [the Secretary of State],

shall be deemed to be a sale of the food, and references to purchasers and purchasing shall be construed accordingly.

(2)   This Act shall apply—

(a)   in relation to any food which is offered as a prize or reward or given away in connection with any entertainment to which the public are admitted, whether on payment of money or not, as if the food were, or had been, exposed for sale by each person concerned in the organisation of the entertainment;

(b)   in relation to any food which, for the purpose of advertisement or in furtherance of any trade or business, is offered as a prize or reward or given away, as if the food were, or had been, exposed for sale by the person offering or giving away the food; and

(c)   in relation to any food which is exposed or deposited in any premises for the purpose of being so offered or given away as mentioned in paragraph (a) or (b) above, as if the food were, or had been, exposed for sale by the occupier of the premises;

and in this subsection "entertainment" includes any social gathering, amusement, exhibition, performance, game, sport or trial of skill.

[1444]

NOTES

Sub-s (1): words in square brackets in para (b) substituted by the Food Standards Act 1999, s 40(1), Sch 5, paras 7, 8.

3   Presumptions that food intended for human consumption

(1)   The following provisions shall apply for the purposes of this Act.

(2)   Any food commonly used for human consumption shall, if sold or offered, exposed or kept for sale, be presumed, until the contrary is proved, to have been sold or, as the case may be, to have been or to be intended for sale for human consumption.

(3)   The following, namely—

(a)   any food commonly used for human consumption which is found on premises used for the preparation, storage, or sale of that food; and

(b)   any article or substance commonly used in the manufacture of food for human consumption which is found on premises used for the preparation, storage or sale of that food,

shall be presumed, until the contrary is proved, to be intended for sale, or for manufacturing food for sale, for human consumption.

(4)   Any article or substance capable of being used in the composition or preparation of any food commonly used for human consumption which is found on premises on which that food is prepared shall, until the contrary is proved, be presumed to be intended for such use.

[1445]

4–6 (*S 4 repealed by the Food Standards Act 1999, s 40(4), Sch 6; ss 5, 6 outside the scope of this work.*)

PART II
MAIN PROVISIONS
Food safety

7 Rendering food injurious to health

(1) Any person who renders any food injurious to health by means of any of the following operations, namely—

(a) adding any article or substance to the food;

(b) using any article or substance as an ingredient in the preparation of the food;

(c) abstracting any constituent from the food; and

(d) subjecting the food to any other process or treatment,

with intent that it shall be sold for human consumption, shall be guilty of an offence.

[(2) In determining for the purposes of this section whether any food is injurious to health, regard shall be had to the matters specified in sub-paragraphs (a) to (c) of Article 14(4) of Regulation (EC) No 178/2002.]

(3) ...

[1446]

NOTES

Sub-s (2): substituted by the General Food Regulations 2004, SI 2004/3279, regs 8, 9(a).
Sub-s (3): repealed by SI 2004/3279, regs 8, 9(b).

8 Selling food not complying with food safety requirements

(1) ...

[(2) For the purposes of this Part food fails to comply with food safety requirements if it is unsafe within the meaning of Article 14 of Regulation (EC) No. 178/2002 and references to food safety requirements or to food complying with such requirements shall be construed accordingly.]

(4) For the purposes of this Part, any part of, or product derived wholly or partly from, an animal—

(a) which has been slaughtered in a knacker's yard, or of which the carcase has been brought into a knacker's yard; or

(b) (*applies to Scotland only,*)

shall be deemed to be unfit for human consumption.

(5) (*Applies to Scotland only.*)

[1447]

NOTES

Sub-s (1): repealed by the General Food Regulations 2004, SI 2004/3279, regs 8, 10(a).
Sub-s (2): substituted for original sub-ss (2), (3) by SI 2004/3279, regs 8, 10(b).

9 Inspection and seizure of suspected food

(1) An authorised officer of a food authority may at all reasonable times inspect any food intended for human consumption which—

(a) has been sold or is offered or exposed for sale; ...

(b) is in the possession of, or has been deposited with or consigned to, any person for the purpose of sale or of preparation for sale; [or

(c) is otherwise placed on the market within the meaning of Regulation (EC) No 178/2002;]

and subsections (3) to (9) below shall apply where, on such an inspection, it appears to the authorised officer that any food fails to comply with food safety requirements.

(2) The following provisions shall also apply where, otherwise than on such an inspection, it appears to an authorised officer of a food authority that any food is likely to cause food poisoning or any disease communicable to human beings.

(3) The authorised officer may either—

(a) give notice to the person in charge of the food that, until the notice is withdrawn, the food or any specified portion of it—

(i) is not to be used for human consumption; and

(ii) either is not to be removed or is not to be removed except to some place specified in the notice; or

(b) seize the food and remove it in order to have it dealt with by a justice of the peace;

and any person who knowingly contravenes the requirements of a notice under paragraph (a) above shall be guilty of an offence.

(4)   Where the authorised officer exercises the powers conferred by subsection (3)(a) above, he shall, as soon as is reasonably practicable and in any event within 21 days, determine whether or not he is satisfied that the food complies with food safety requirements and—

    (a)   if he is so satisfied, shall forthwith withdraw the notice;

    (b)   if he is not so satisfied, shall seize the food and remove it in order to have it dealt with by a justice of the peace.

(5)   Where an authorised officer exercises the powers conferred by subsection (3)(b) or (4)(b) above, he shall inform the person in charge of the food of his intention to have it dealt with by a justice of the peace and—

    (a)   any person who under section 7 [or regulation 4(a) of the General Food Regulations 2004] might be liable to a prosecution in respect of the food shall, if he attends before the justice of the peace by whom the food falls to be dealt with, be entitled to be heard and to call witnesses; and

    (b)   that justice of the peace may, but need not, be a member of the court before which any person is charged with an offence under that section in relation to that food.

(6)   If it appears to a justice of the peace, on the basis of such evidence as he considers appropriate in the circumstances, that any food falling to be dealt with by him under this section fails to comply with food safety requirements, he shall condemn the food and order—

    (a)   the food to be destroyed or to be so disposed of as to prevent it from being used for human consumption; and

    (b)   any expenses reasonably incurred in connection with the destruction or disposal to be defrayed by the owner of the food.

(7)   If a notice under subsection (3)(a) above is withdrawn, or the justice of the peace by whom any food falls to be dealt with under this section refuses to condemn it, the food authority shall compensate the owner of the food for any depreciation in its value resulting from the action taken by the authorised officer.

(8)   Any disputed question as to the right to or the amount of any compensation payable under subsection (7) above shall be determined by arbitration.

(9)   *(Applies to Scotland only.)*

[1448]

NOTES

  Sub-s (1): word omitted repealed and para (c) and word "or" immediately preceding it inserted by the General Food Regulations 2004, SI 2004/3279, regs 8, 11(a).

  Sub-s (5): words in square brackets substituted by SI 2004/3279, regs 8, 11(b).

10   Improvement notices

(1)   If an authorised officer of an enforcement authority has reasonable grounds for believing that the proprietor of a food business is failing to comply with any regulations to which this section applies, he may, by a notice served on that proprietor (in this Act referred to as an "improvement notice")—

    (a)   state the officer's grounds for believing that the proprietor is failing to comply with the regulations;

    (b)   specify the matters which constitute the proprietor's failure so to comply;

    (c)   specify the measures which, in the officer's opinion, the proprietor must take in order to secure compliance; and

    (d)   require the proprietor to take those measures, or measures which are at least equivalent to them, within such period (not being less than 14 days) as may be specified in the notice.

(2)   Any person who fails to comply with an improvement notice shall be guilty of an offence.

(3)   This section and section 11 below apply to any regulations under this Part which make provision—

    (a)   for requiring, prohibiting or regulating the use of any process or treatment in the preparation of food; or

    (b)   for securing the observance of hygienic conditions and practices in connection with the carrying out of commercial operations with respect to food or food sources.

[1449]

11   Prohibition orders

(1)   If—

    (a)   the proprietor of a food business is convicted of an offence under any regulations to which this section applies; and

(b)   the court by or before which he is so convicted is satisfied that the health risk condition is fulfilled with respect to that business,

the court shall by an order impose the appropriate prohibition.

(2)   The health risk condition is fulfilled with respect to any food business if any of the following involves risk of injury to health, namely—

    (a)   the use for the purposes of the business of any process or treatment;

    (b)   the construction of any premises used for the purposes of the business, or the use for those purposes of any equipment; and

    (c)   the state or condition of any premises or equipment used for the purposes of the business.

[(2A)   In subsection (2) above and in sections 12(4) and 13(1) "injury" includes any impairment, whether permanent or temporary.]

(3)   The appropriate prohibition is—

    (a)   in a case falling within paragraph (a) of subsection (2) above, a prohibition on the use of the process or treatment for the purposes of the business;

    (b)   in a case falling within paragraph (b) of that subsection, a prohibition on the use of the premises or equipment for the purposes of the business or any other food business of the same class or description;

    (c)   in a case falling within paragraph (c) of that subsection, a prohibition on the use of the premises or equipment for the purposes of any food business.

(4)   If—

    (a)   the proprietor of a food business is convicted of an offence under any regulations to which this section applies by virtue of section 10(3)(b) above; and

    (b)   the court by or before which he is so convicted thinks it proper to do so in all the circumstances of the case,

the court may, by an order, impose a prohibition on the proprietor participating in the management of any food business, or any food business of a class or description specified in the order.

(5)   As soon as practicable after the making of an order under subsection (1) or (4) above (in this Act referred to as a "prohibition order"), the enforcement authority shall—

    (a)   serve a copy of the order on the proprietor of the business; and

    (b)   in the case of an order under subsection (1) above, affix a copy of the order in a conspicuous position on such premises used for the purposes of the business as they consider appropriate;

and any person who knowingly contravenes such an order shall be guilty of an offence.

(6)   A prohibition order shall cease to have effect—

    (a)   in the case of an order under subsection (1) above, on the issue by the enforcement authority of a certificate to the effect that they are satisfied that the proprietor has taken sufficient measures to secure that the health risk condition is no longer fulfilled with respect to the business;

    (b)   in the case of an order under subsection (4) above, on the giving by the court of a direction to that effect.

(7)   The enforcement authority shall issue a certificate under paragraph (a) of subsection (6) above within three days of their being satisfied as mentioned in that paragraph; and on an application by the proprietor for such a certificate, the authority shall—

    (a)   determine, as soon as is reasonably practicable and in any event within 14 days, whether or not they are so satisfied; and

    (b)   if they determine that they are not so satisfied, give notice to the proprietor of the reasons for that determination.

(8)   The court shall give a direction under subsection (6)(b) above if, on an application by the proprietor, the court thinks it proper to do so having regard to all the circumstances of the case, including in particular the conduct of the proprietor since the making of the order; but no such application shall be entertained if it is made—

    (a)   within six months after the making of the prohibition order; or

    (b)   within three months after the making by the proprietor of a previous application for such a direction.

(9)   Where a magistrates' court or, in Scotland, the sheriff makes an order under section 12(2) below with respect to any food business, subsection (1) above shall apply as if the proprietor of the business had been convicted by the court or sheriff of an offence under regulations to which this section applies.

(10)   Subsection (4) above shall apply in relation to a manager of a food business as it applies in relation to the proprietor of such a business; and any reference in subsection (5) or (8) above to the proprietor of the business, or to the proprietor, shall be construed accordingly.

(11)   In subsection (10) above "manager", in relation to a food business, means any person who is entrusted by the proprietor with the day to day running of the business, or any part of the business.

[1450]

12   Emergency prohibition notices and orders

(1)   If an authorised officer of an enforcement authority is satisfied that the health risk condition is fulfilled with respect to any food business, he may, by a notice served on the proprietor of the business (in this Act referred to as an "emergency prohibition notice"), impose the appropriate prohibition.

(2)   If a magistrates' court or, in Scotland, the sheriff is satisfied, on the application of such an officer, that the health risk condition is fulfilled with respect to any food business, the court or sheriff shall, by an order (in this Act referred to as an "emergency prohibition order"), impose the appropriate prohibition.

(3)   Such an officer shall not apply for an emergency prohibition order unless, at least one day before the date of the application, he has served notice on the proprietor of the business of his intention to apply for the order.

(4)   Subsections (2) and (3) of section 11 above shall apply for the purposes of this section as they apply for the purposes of that section, but as if the reference in subsection (2) to risk of injury to health were a reference to imminent risk of such injury.

(5)   As soon as practicable after the service of an emergency prohibition notice, the enforcement authority shall affix a copy of the notice in a conspicuous position on such premises used for the purposes of the business as they consider appropriate; and any person who knowingly contravenes such a notice shall be guilty of an offence.

(6)   As soon as practicable after the making of an emergency prohibition order, the enforcement authority shall—
  (a)   serve a copy of the order on the proprietor of the business; and
  (b)   affix a copy of the order in a conspicuous position on such premises used for the purposes of that business as they consider appropriate;
and any person who knowingly contravenes such an order shall be guilty of an offence.

(7)   An emergency prohibition notice shall cease to have effect—
  (a)   if no application for an emergency prohibition order is made within the period of three days beginning with the service of the notice, at the end of that period;
  (b)   if such an application is so made, on the determination or abandonment of the application.

(8)   An emergency prohibition notice or emergency prohibition order shall cease to have effect on the issue by the enforcement authority of a certificate to the effect that they are satisfied that the proprietor has taken sufficient measures to secure that the health risk condition is no longer fulfilled with respect to the business.

(9)   The enforcement authority shall issue a certificate under subsection (8) above within three days of their being satisfied as mentioned in that subsection; and on an application by the proprietor for such a certificate, the authority shall—
  (a)   determine, as soon as is reasonably practicable and in any event within 14 days, whether or not they are so satisfied; and
  (b)   if they determine that they are not so satisfied, give notice to the proprietor of the reasons for that determination.

(10)   Where an emergency prohibition notice is served on the proprietor of a business, the enforcement authority shall compensate him in respect of any loss suffered by reason of his complying with the notice unless—
  (a)   an application for an emergency prohibition order is made within the period of three days beginning with the service of the notice; and
  (b)   the court declares itself satisfied, on the hearing of the application, that the health risk condition was fulfilled with respect to the business at the time when the notice was served;
and any disputed question as to the right to or the amount of any compensation payable under this subsection shall be determined by arbitration or, in Scotland, by a single arbiter appointed, failing agreement between the parties, by the sheriff.

[1451]

13   Emergency control orders

(1)   If it appears to [the Secretary of State] that the carrying out of commercial operations with respect to food, food sources or contact materials of any class or description involves or may involve

imminent risk of injury to health, he may, by an order (in this Act referred to as an "emergency control order"), prohibit the carrying out of such operations with respect to food, food sources or contact materials of that class or description.

(2)   Any person who knowingly contravenes an emergency control order shall be guilty of an offence.

(3)   [The Secretary of State] [or the Food Standards Agency] may consent, either unconditionally or subject to any condition that [the authority giving the consent] considers appropriate, to the doing in a particular case of anything prohibited by an emergency control order.

(4)   It shall be a defence for a person charged with an offence under subsection (2) above to show—

(a)   that consent had been given under subsection (3) above to the contravention of the emergency control order; and

(b)   that any condition subject to which that consent was given was complied with.

(5)   [The Secretary of State] [or the Food Standards Agency]—

(a)   may give such directions as appear to [the authority giving the directions] to be necessary or expedient for the purpose of preventing the carrying out of commercial operations with respect to any food, food sources or contact materials which [the authority giving the directions] believes, on reasonable grounds, to be food, food sources or contact materials to which an emergency control order applies; and

(b)   may do anything which appears to [the authority giving the directions] to be necessary or expedient for that purpose.

(6)   Any person who fails to comply with a direction under this section shall be guilty of an offence.

(7)   If the [the Secretary of State] [or the Food Standards Agency] does anything by virtue of this section in consequence of any person failing to comply with an emergency control order or a direction under this section, [that authority] may recover from that person any expenses reasonably incurred by [that authority] under this section.

[1452]

NOTES

Sub-s (1): words in square brackets substituted by the Food Standards Act 1999, s 40(1), Sch 5, paras 7, 8.

Sub-s (3): words in first and third pairs of square brackets substituted, and words in second pair of square brackets inserted, by the Food Standards Act 1999, s 40(1), Sch 5, paras 7, 11(1), (2).

Sub-s (5): words in first, third, fourth and fifth pairs of square brackets substituted, and words in second pair of square brackets inserted, by the Food Standards Act 1999, s 40(1), Sch 5, paras 7, 11(1), (3).

Sub-s (7): words in first, third and fourth pairs of square brackets substituted, and words in second pair of square brackets inserted, by the Food Standards Act 1999, s 40(1), Sch 5, paras 7, 11(1), (4).

Orders: see note at the beginning of this Act.

Consumer protection

14   Selling food not of the nature or substance or quality demanded

(1)   Any person who sells to the purchaser's prejudice any food which is not of the nature or substance or quality demanded by the purchaser shall be guilty of an offence.

(2)   In subsection (1) above the reference to sale shall be construed as a reference to sale for human consumption; and in proceedings under that subsection it shall not be a defence that the purchaser was not prejudiced because he bought for analysis or examination.

[1453]

15   Falsely describing or presenting food

(1)   Any person who gives with any food sold by him, or displays with any food offered or exposed by him for sale or in his possession for the purpose of sale, a label, whether or not attached to or printed on the wrapper or container, which—

(a)   falsely describes the food; or

(b)   is likely to mislead as to the nature or substance or quality of the food,

shall be guilty of an offence.

(2)   Any person who publishes, or is a party to the publication of, an advertisement (not being such a label given or displayed by him as mentioned in subsection (1) above) which—

(a)   falsely describes any food; or

(b)   is likely to mislead as to the nature or substance or quality of any food,

shall be guilty of an offence.

(3)   Any person who sells, or offers or exposes for sale, or has in his possession for the purpose of sale, any food the presentation of which is likely to mislead as to the nature or substance or quality of the food shall be guilty of an offence.

(4)   In proceedings for an offence under subsection (1) or (2) above, the fact that a label or advertisement in respect of which the offence is alleged to have been committed contained an accurate statement of the composition of the food shall not preclude the court from finding that the offence was committed.

(5)   In this section references to sale shall be construed as references to sale for human consumption.

[1454]

Regulations

16   Food safety and consumer protection

(1)   [The Secretary of State] may by regulations make—
  (a)   provision for requiring, prohibiting or regulating the presence in food or food sources of any specified substance, or any substance of any specified class, and generally for regulating the composition of food;
  (b)   provision for securing that food is fit for human consumption and meets such microbiological standards (whether going to the fitness of the food or otherwise) as may be specified by or under the regulations;
  (c)   provision for requiring, prohibiting or regulating the use of any process or treatment in the preparation of food;
  (d)   provision for securing the observance of hygienic conditions and practices in connection with the carrying out of commercial operations with respect to food or food sources;
  (e)   provision for imposing requirements or prohibitions as to, or otherwise regulating, the labelling, marking, presenting or advertising of food, and the descriptions which may be applied to food; and
  (f)   such other provision with respect to food or food sources, including in particular provision for prohibiting or regulating the carrying out of commercial operations with respect to food or food sources, as appears to them to be necessary or expedient—
    (i)   for the purpose of securing that food complies with food safety requirements or in the interests of the public health; or
    (ii)   for the purpose of protecting or promoting the interests of consumers.

(2)   [The Secretary of State] may also by regulations make provision—
  (a)   for securing the observance of hygienic conditions and practices in connection with the carrying out of commercial operations with respect to contact materials which are intended to come into contact with food intended for human consumption;
  (b)   for imposing requirements or prohibitions as to, or otherwise regulating, the labelling, marking or advertising of such materials, and the descriptions which may be applied to them; and
  (c)   otherwise for prohibiting or regulating the carrying out of commercial operations with respect to such materials.

(3)   Without prejudice to the generality of subsection (1) above, regulations under that subsection may make any such provision as is mentioned in Schedule 1 to this Act.

(4)   In making regulations under subsection (1) above, [the Secretary of State] shall have regard to the desirability of restricting, so far as practicable, the use of substances of no nutritional value as foods or as ingredients of foods.

(5)   In subsection (1) above and Schedule 1 to this Act, unless the context otherwise requires—
  (a)   references to food shall be construed as references to food intended for sale for human consumption; and
  (b)   references to food sources shall be construed as references to food sources from which such food is intended to be derived.

[1455]

NOTES

Sub-ss (1), (2), (4): words in square brackets substituted by the Food Standards Act 1999, s 40(1), Sch 5, paras 7, 8.
Regulations: see note at the beginning of this Act.

---

17   Enforcement of Community provisions

(1)   [The Secretary of State] may by regulations make such provision with respect to food, food sources or contact materials, including in particular provision for prohibiting or regulating the carrying out of commercial operations with respect to food, food sources or contact materials, as appears to [him] to be called for by any Community obligation.

(2)   As respects any directly applicable Community provision which relates to food, food sources or contact materials and for which, in [his] opinion, it is appropriate to provide under this Act, [the Secretary of State] may by regulations—

(a) make such provision as [he considers] necessary or expedient for the purpose of securing that the Community provision is administered, executed and enforced under this Act; and

(b) apply such of the provisions of this Act as may be specified in the regulations in relation to the Community provision with such modifications, if any, as may be so specified.

(3) In subsections (1) and (2) above references to food or food sources shall be construed in accordance with section 16(5) above.

[1456]

NOTES
Sub-ss (1), (2): words in square brackets substituted by the Food Standards Act 1999, s 40(1), Sch 5, paras 7, 8, 12.
Regulations: see note at the beginning of this Act.

18 Special provisions for particular foods etc

(1) [The Secretary of State] may by regulations make provision—
  (a) for prohibiting the carrying out of commercial operations with respect to novel foods, or food sources from which such foods are intended to be derived, of any class specified in the regulations;
  (b) for prohibiting the carrying out of such operations with respect to genetically modified food sources, or foods derived from such food sources, of any class so specified; or
  (c) for prohibiting the importation of any food of a class so specified,

and (in each case) for excluding from the prohibition any food or food source which is of a description specified by or under the regulations and, in the case of a prohibition on importation, is imported at an authorised place of entry.

(2) [The Secretary of State] may also by regulations—
  (a) prescribe, in relation to milk of any description, such a designation (in this subsection referred to as a "special designation") as [the Secretary of State considers] appropriate;
  (b) provide for the issue by enforcement authorities of licences to producers and sellers of milk authorising the use of a special designation; and
  (c) prohibit, without the use of a special designation, all sales of milk for human consumption, other than sales made with [the Secretary of State's] consent.

(3) In this section—
  "authorised place of entry" means any port, aerodrome or other place of entry authorised by or under the regulations and, in relation to food in a particular consignment, includes any place of entry so authorised for the importation of that consignment;
  "description", in relation to food, includes any description of its origin or of the manner in which it is packed;
  "novel food" means any food which has not previously been used for human consumption in Great Britain, or has been so used only to a very limited extent.

(4) For the purposes of this section a food source is genetically modified if any of the genes or other genetic material in the food source—
  (a) has been modified by means of an artificial technique; or
  (b) is inherited or otherwise derived, through any number of replications, from genetic material which was so modified;

and in this subsection "artificial technique" does not include any technique which involves no more than, or no more than the assistance of, naturally occurring processes of reproduction (including selective breeding techniques or *in vitro* fertilisation).

[1457]

NOTES
Sub-ss (1), (2): words in square brackets substituted by the Food Standards Act 1999, s 40(1), Sch 5, paras 7, 8, 13.
Regulations: see note at the beginning of this Act.

19 Registration and licensing of food premises

(1) [The Secretary of State] may by regulations make provision—
  (a) for the registration by enforcement authorities of premises used or proposed to be used for the purposes of a food business, and for prohibiting the use for those purposes of any premises which are not registered in accordance with the regulations; or
  (b) subject to subsection (2) below, for the issue by such authorities of licences in respect of the use of premises for the purposes of a food business, and for prohibiting the use for those purposes of any premises except in accordance with a licence issued under the regulations.

(2)   [The Secretary of State] shall exercise the power conferred by subsection (1)(b) above only where it appears to [him] to be necessary or expedient to do so—

    (a)   for the purpose of securing that food complies with food safety requirements or in the interests of the public health; or

    (b)   for the purpose of protecting or promoting the interests of consumers.

[1458]

NOTES

Sub-ss (1), (2): words in square brackets substituted by the Food Standards Act 1999, s 40(1), Sch 5, paras 7, 8, 14.

Regulations: see note at the beginning of this Act.

Defences etc

20 Offences due to fault of another person

Where the commission by any person of an offence under any of the preceding provisions of this Part is due to an act or default of some other person, that other person shall be guilty of the offence; and a person may be charged with and convicted of the offence by virtue of this section whether or not proceedings are taken against the first-mentioned person.

[1459]

21 Defence of due diligence

(1)   In any proceedings for an offence under any of the preceding provisions of this Part (in this section referred to as "the relevant provision"), it shall, subject to subsection (5) below, be a defence for the person charged to prove that he took all reasonable precautions and exercised all due diligence to avoid the commission of the offence by himself or by a person under his control.

(2)   Without prejudice to the generality of subsection (1) above, a person charged with an offence under [section 14 or 15] above who neither—

    (a)   prepared the food in respect of which the offence is alleged to have been committed; nor

    (b)   imported it into Great Britain,

shall be taken to have established the defence provided by that subsection if he satisfies the requirements of subsection (3) or (4) below.

(3)   A person satisfies the requirements of this subsection if he proves—

    (a)   that the commission of the offence was due to an act or default of another person who was not under his control, or to reliance on information supplied by such a person;

    (b)   that he carried out all such checks of the food in question as were reasonable in all the circumstances, or that it was reasonable in all the circumstances for him to rely on checks carried out by the person who supplied the food to him; and

    (c)   that he did not know and had no reason to suspect at the time of the commission of the alleged offence that his act or omission would amount to an offence under the relevant provision.

(4)   A person satisfies the requirements of this subsection if he proves—

    (a)   that the commission of the offence was due to an act or default of another person who was not under his control, or to reliance on information supplied by such a person;

    (b)   that the sale or intended sale of which the alleged offence consisted was not a sale or intended sale under his name or mark; and

    (c)   that he did not know, and could not reasonably have been expected to know, at the time of the commission of the alleged offence that his act or omission would amount to an offence under the relevant provision.

(5)   If in any case the defence provided by subsection (1) above involves the allegation that the commission of the offence was due to an act or default of another person, or to reliance on information supplied by another person, the person charged shall not, without leave of the court, be entitled to rely on that defence unless—

    (a)   at least seven clear days before the hearing; and

    (b)   where he has previously appeared before a court in connection with the alleged offence, within one month of his first such appearance,

he has served on the prosecutor a notice in writing giving such information identifying or assisting in the identification of that other person as was then in his possession.

(6)   In subsection (5) above any reference to appearing before a court shall be construed as including a reference to being brought before a court.

[1460]

NOTES

Sub-s (2): words in square brackets substituted by the General Food Regulations 2004, SI 2004/3279, regs 8, 13.

22 Defence of publication in the course of business

In proceedings for an offence under any of the preceding provisions of this Part consisting of the advertisement for sale of any food, it shall be a defence for the person charged to prove—

(a) that he is a person whose business it is to publish or arrange for the publication of advertisements; and

(b) that he received the advertisement in the ordinary course of business and did not know and had no reason to suspect that its publication would amount to an offence under that provision.

[1461]

23–26 *(Ss 23, 24, 26 outside the scope of this work; s 25 repealed by the Food Standards Act 1999, s 40(1), (4), Sch 5, para 15, Sch 6.)*

PART III
ADMINISTRATION AND ENFORCEMENT

Administration

27 Appointment of public analysts

(1) Every authority to whom this section applies, that is to say, every food authority in England and Wales and every [council constituted under section 2 of the Local Government etc (Scotland) Act 1994] in Scotland, shall appoint in accordance with this section one or more persons (in this Act referred to as "public analysts") to act as analysts for the purposes of this Act within the authority's area.

(2) No person shall be appointed as a public analyst unless he possesses—

(a) such qualifications as may be prescribed by regulations made by [the Secretary of State]; or

(b) such other qualifications as [the Secretary of State] may approve,

and no person shall act as a public analyst for any area who is engaged directly or indirectly in any food business which is carried on in that area.

(3) An authority to whom this section applies shall pay to a public analyst such remuneration as may be agreed, which may be expressed to be payable either—

(a) in addition to any fees received by him under this Part; or

(b) on condition that any fees so received by him are paid over by him to the authority.

(4) An authority to whom this section applies who appoint only one public analyst may appoint also a deputy to act during any vacancy in the office of public analyst, or during the absence or incapacity of the holder of the office, and—

(a) the provisions of this section with respect to the qualifications, appointment, removal and remuneration of a public analyst shall apply also in relation to a deputy public analyst; and

(b) any reference in the following provisions of this Act to a public analyst shall be construed as including a reference to a deputy public analyst appointed under this subsection.

(5) In subsection (1) above "food authority" does not include the council of a non-metropolitan district [in England] [(except where the county functions have been transferred to that council …)], the Sub-Treasurer of the Inner Temple or the Under Treasurer of the Middle Temple; and in subsection (2) above the reference to being engaged directly or indirectly in a food business includes a reference to having made such arrangements with a food business as may be prescribed by regulations made by [the Secretary of State].

[1462]

NOTES

Sub-s (1): words in square brackets substituted by the Local Government etc (Scotland) Act 1994, s 180(1), Sch 13, para 163(3).

Sub-s (2): words in square brackets substituted by the Food Standards Act 1999, s 40(1), Sch 5, paras 7, 8.

Sub-s (5): words in first pair of square brackets inserted by the Local Government (Wales) Act 1994, s 22(3), Sch 9, para 16(2); words in second pair of square brackets inserted by the Local Government Changes for England Regulations 1994, SI 1994/867, reg 24; words omitted repealed by the Local Government and Public Involvement in Health Act 2007, ss 22, 241, Sch 1, Pt 2, para 17, Sch 18, Pt 1; words in third pair of square brackets substituted by the Food Standards Act 1999, s 40(1), Sch 5, paras 7, 8.

Regulations: see note at the beginning of this Act.

28 Provision of facilities for examinations

(1) A food authority, or a [council constituted under section 2 of the Local Government etc (Scotland) Act 1994] in Scotland, may provide facilities for examinations for the purposes of this Act.

(2)　In this Act "examination" means a microbiological examination and "examine" shall be construed accordingly.

[1463]

NOTES

Sub-s (1): words in square brackets substituted by the Local Government etc (Scotland) Act 1994, s 180(1), Sch 13, para 163(4).

Sampling and analysis etc

29　Procurement of samples

An authorised officer of an enforcement authority may—
- (a)　purchase a sample of any food, or any substance capable of being used in the preparation of food;
- (b)　take a sample of any food, or any such substance, which—
  - (i)　appears to him to be intended for sale, or to have been sold, for human consumption; or
  - (ii)　is found by him on or in any premises which he is authorised to enter by or under section 32 below;
- (c)　take a sample from any food source, or a sample of any contact material, which is found by him on or in any such premises;
- (d)　take a sample of any article or substance which is found by him on or in any such premises and which he has reason to believe may be required as evidence in proceedings under any of the provisions of this Act or of regulations or orders made under it.

[1464]

30　Analysis etc of samples

(1)　An authorised officer of an enforcement authority who has procured a sample under section 29 above shall—
- (a)　if he considers that the sample should be analysed, submit it to be analysed either—
  - (i)　by the public analyst for the area in which the sample was procured; or
  - (ii)　by the public analyst for the area which consists of or includes the area of the authority;
- (b)　if he considers that the sample should be examined, submit it to be examined by a food examiner.

(2)　A person, other than such an officer, who has purchased any food, or any substance capable of being used in the preparation of food, may submit a sample of it—
- (a)　to be analysed by the public analyst for the area in which the purchase was made; or
- (b)　to be examined by a food examiner.

(3)　If, in any case where a sample is proposed to be submitted for analysis under this section, the office of public analyst for the area in question is vacant, the sample shall be submitted to the public analyst for some other area.

(4)　If, in any case where a sample is proposed to be or is submitted for analysis or examination under this section, the food analyst or examiner determines that he is for any reason unable to perform the analysis or examination, the sample shall be submitted or, as the case may be, sent by him to such other food analyst or examiner as he may determine.

(5)　A food analyst or examiner shall analyse or examine as soon as practicable any sample submitted or sent to him under this section, but may, except where—
- (a)　he is the public analyst for the area in question; and
- (b)　the sample is submitted to him for analysis by an authorised officer of an enforcement authority,

demand in advance the payment of such reasonable fee as he may require.

(6)　A food analyst or examiner who has analysed or examined a sample shall give to the person by whom it was submitted a certificate specifying the result of the analysis or examination.

(7)　Any certificate given by a food analyst or examiner under subsection (6) above shall be signed by him, but the analysis or examination may be made by any person acting under his direction.

(8)　In any proceedings under this Act, the production by one of the parties—
- (a)　of a document purporting to be a certificate given by a food analyst or examiner under subsection (6) above; or
- (b)　of a document supplied to him by the other party as being a copy of such a certificate,

shall be sufficient evidence of the facts stated in it unless, in a case falling within paragraph (a) above, the other party requires that the food analyst or examiner shall be called as a witness.

(9)　In this section—

"food analyst" means a public analyst or any other person who possesses the requisite qualifications to carry out analyses for the purposes of this Act;

"food examiner" means any person who possesses the requisite qualifications to carry out examinations for the purposes of this Act;

"the requisite qualifications" means such qualifications as may be prescribed by regulations made by [the Secretary of State], or such other qualifications as [the Secretary of State] may approve;

"sample", in relation to an authorised officer of an enforcement authority, includes any part of a sample retained by him in pursuance of regulations under section 31 below;

and where two or more public analysts are appointed for any area, any reference in this section to the public analyst for that area shall be construed as a reference to either or any of them.

[1465]

NOTES

Sub-s (9): in definition "the requisite qualifications" words in square brackets substituted by the Food Standards Act 1999, s 40(1), Sch 5, paras 7, 8.

Regulations: see note at the beginning of this Act.

31 Regulation of sampling and analysis etc

(1) [The Secretary of State] may by regulations make provision for supplementing or modifying the provisions of sections 29 and 30 above.

(2) Without prejudice to the generality of subsection (1) above, regulations under that subsection may make provision with respect to—

(a) the matters to be taken into account in determining whether, and at what times, samples should be procured;

(b) the manner of procuring samples, including the steps to be taken in order to ensure that any samples procured are fair samples;

(c) the method of dealing with samples, including (where appropriate) their division into parts;

(d) the persons to whom parts of samples are to be given and the persons by whom such parts are to be retained;

(e) the notices which are to be given to, and the information which is to be furnished by, the persons in charge of any food, substance, contact material or food source of or from which samples are procured;

(f) the methods which are to be used in analysing or examining samples, or parts of samples, or in classifying the results of analyses or examinations;

(g) the circumstances in which a food analyst or examiner is to be precluded, by reason of a conflict of interest, from analysing or examining a particular sample or part of a sample; and

(h) the circumstances in which samples, or parts of samples, are to be or may be submitted for analysis or examination—

(i) to the Government Chemist, or to such other food analyst or examiner as he may direct; or

(ii) to a person determined by or under the regulations.

(3) In this section "food analyst" and "food examiner" have the same meanings as in section 30 above.

[1466]

NOTES

Sub-s (1): words in square brackets substituted by the Food Standards Act 1999, s 40(1), Sch 5, paras 7, 8.

Regulations: see note at the beginning of this Act.

Powers of entry and obstruction etc

32 Powers of entry

(1) An authorised officer of an enforcement authority shall, on producing, if so required, some duly authenticated document showing his authority, have a right at all reasonable hours—

(a) to enter any premises within the authority's area for the purpose of ascertaining whether there is or has been on the premises any contravention of the provisions of this Act, or of regulations or orders made under it; and

(b) to enter any business premises, whether within or outside the authority's area, for the purpose of ascertaining whether there is on the premises any evidence of any contravention within that area of any of such provisions; and

(c) in the case of an authorised officer of a food authority, to enter any premises for the purpose of the performance by the authority of their functions under this Act;

but admission to any premises used only as a private dwelling-house shall not be demanded as of right unless 24 hours' notice of the intended entry has been given to the occupier.

(2) If a justice of the peace, on sworn information in writing, is satisfied that there is reasonable ground for entry into any premises for any such purpose as is mentioned in subsection (1) above and either—

(a) that admission to the premises has been refused, or a refusal is apprehended, and that notice of the intention to apply for a warrant has been given to the occupier; or

(b) that an application for admission, or the giving of such a notice, would defeat the object of the entry, or that the case is one of urgency, or that the premises are unoccupied or the occupier temporarily absent,

the justice may by warrant signed by him authorise the authorised officer to enter the premises, if need be by reasonable force.

(3) Every warrant granted under this section shall continue in force for a period of one month.

(4) An authorised officer entering any premises by virtue of this section, or of a warrant issued under it, may take with him such other persons as he considers necessary, and on leaving any unoccupied premises which he has entered by virtue of such a warrant shall leave them as effectively secured against unauthorised entry as he found them.

(5) An authorised officer entering premises by virtue of this section, or of a warrant issued under it, may inspect any records (in whatever form they are held) relating to a food business and, where any such records are [stored in any electronic form]—

(a) may have access to, and inspect and check the operation of, any computer and any associated apparatus or material which is or has been in use in connection with the records; and

(b) may require any person having charge of, or otherwise concerned with the operation of, the computer, apparatus or material to afford him such assistance as he may reasonably require.

(6) Any officer exercising any power conferred by subsection (5) above may—

(a) seize and detain any records which he has reason to believe may be required as evidence in proceedings under any of the provisions of this Act or of regulations or orders made under it; and

(b) where the records are [stored in any electronic form], may require the records to be produced in a form in which they may be taken away.

(7) If any person who enters any premises by virtue of this section, or of a warrant issued under it, discloses to any person any information obtained by him in the premises with regard to any trade secret, he shall, unless the disclosure was made in the performance of his duty, be guilty of an offence.

(8) Nothing in this section authorises any person, except with the permission of the local authority under the Animal Health Act 1981, to enter any premises—

(a) in which an animal or bird affected with any disease to which that Act applies is kept; and

(b) which is situated in a place declared under that Act to be infected with such a disease.

(9) (*Applies to Scotland only.*)

[1467]

NOTES

Sub-ss (5), (6): words in square brackets substituted by the Criminal Justice and Police Act 2001, s 70, Sch 2, Pt 2, para 18.

Seize and detain: the powers of seizure conferred by sub-s (6) are powers to which the Criminal Justice and Police Act 2001, s 50 apply (additional powers of seizure from premises); see s 50 of, and Sch 1, Pt 1, para 50 to, that Act.

33 Obstruction etc of officers

(1) Any person who—

(a) intentionally obstructs any person acting in the execution of this Act; or

(b) without reasonable cause, fails to give to any person acting in the execution of this Act any assistance or information which that person may reasonably require of him for the performance of his functions under this Act,

shall be guilty of an offence.

(2) Any person who, in purported compliance with any such requirement as is mentioned in subsection (1)(b) above—

(a) furnishes information which he knows to be false or misleading in a material particular; or

(b) recklessly furnishes information which is false or misleading in a material particular,

shall be guilty of an offence.

(3)   Nothing in subsection (1)(b) above shall be construed as requiring any person to answer any question or give any information if to do so might incriminate him.

[1468]

Offences

34 Time limit for prosecutions

No prosecution for an offence under this Act which is punishable under section 35(2) below shall be begun after the expiry of—

   (a)   three years from the commission of the offence; or

   (b)   one year from its discovery by the prosecutor,

whichever is the earlier.

[1469]

35 Punishment of offences

   (1)   A person guilty of an offence under section 33(1) above shall be liable on summary conviction to a fine not exceeding level 5 on the standard scale or to imprisonment for a term not exceeding *three months* [51 weeks] or to both.

   (2)   A person guilty of any other offence under this Act shall be liable—

   (a)   on conviction on indictment, to a fine or to imprisonment for a term not exceeding two years or to both;

   (b)   on summary conviction, to a fine not exceeding the relevant amount or to imprisonment for a term not exceeding six months or to both.

   (3)   In subsection (2) above "the relevant amount" means—

   (a)   in the case of an offence under [section 7 or 14] above, £20,000;

   (b)   in any other case, the statutory maximum.

   (4)   If a person who is—

   (a)   licensed under section 1 of the Slaughterhouses Act 1974 to keep a … knacker's yard;

   (b)   … ; or

   (c)   *(applies to Scotland only)*,

is convicted of an offence under Part II of this Act, the court may, in addition to any other punishment, cancel his licence or registration.

[1470]

NOTES

Sub-s (1): words in italics substituted by subsequent words in square brackets by the Criminal Justice Act 2003, s 280(2), Sch 26, para 42, as from a day to be appointed.

Sub-s (3): words in square brackets substituted by the General Food Regulations 2004, SI 2004/3279, regs 8, 14.

Sub-s (4): words omitted repealed by the Deregulation (Slaughterhouses Act 1974 and Slaughter of Animals (Scotland) Act 1980) Order 1996, SI 1996/2235, art 11, Schedule.

---

36 Offences by bodies corporate

   (1)   Where an offence under this Act which has been committed by a body corporate is proved to have been committed with the consent or connivance of, or to be attributable to any neglect on the part of—

   (a)   any director, manager, secretary or other similar officer of the body corporate; or

   (b)   any person who was purporting to act in any such capacity,

he as well as the body corporate shall be deemed to be guilty of that offence and shall be liable to be proceeded against and punished accordingly.

   (2)   In subsection (1) above "director", in relation to any body corporate established by or under any enactment for the purpose of carrying on under national ownership any industry or part of an industry or undertaking, being a body corporate whose affairs are managed by its members, means a member of that body corporate.

[1471]

36A–39   *(Outside the scope of this work.)*

PART IV

MISCELLANEOUS AND SUPPLEMENTAL

40–52   *(Outside the scope of this work.)*

Supplemental

53–59   *(Outside the scope of this work.)*

60   Short title, commencement and extent

(1)   This Act may be cited as the Food Safety Act 1990.

(2)   The following provisions shall come into force on the day on which this Act is passed, namely—

section 13;

section 51; and

paragraphs 12 to 15 of Schedule 2 and, so far as relating to those paragraphs, section 52.

(3)   Subject to subsection (2) above, this Act shall come into force on such day as the Ministers may by order appoint, and different days may be appointed for different provisions or for different purposes.

(4)   An order under subsection (3) above may make such transitional adaptations of any of the following, namely—

(a)   the provisions of this Act then in force or brought into force by the order; and

(b)   the provisions repealed by this Act whose repeal is not then in force or so brought into force,

as appear to the Ministers to be necessary or expedient in consequence of the partial operation of this Act.

(5)   This Act, except—

this section;

section 51

section 58(2) to (4); and

paragraphs 7, 29 and 30 of Schedule 3 and, so far as relating to those paragraphs, section 59(1),

does not extend to Northern Ireland.

[1472]

NOTES

Orders: the Food Safety Act 1990 (Commencement No 1) Order 1990, SI 1990/1383; the Food Safety Act 1990 (Commencement No 2) Order 1990, SI 1990/2372; the Food Safety Act 1990 (Commencement No 3) Order 1992, SI 1992/57.

(Schs 1–5 outside the scope of this work.)

CONTRACTS (APPLICABLE LAW) ACT 1990

(1990 c 36)

ARRANGEMENT OF SECTIONS

An Act to make provision as to the law applicable to contractual obligations in the case of conflict of laws

[26 July 1990]

1   Meaning of "the Conventions"

In this Act—

(a) "the Rome Convention" means the Convention on the law applicable to contractual obligations opened for signature in Rome on 19th June 1980 and signed by the United Kingdom on 7th December 1981;

(b) "the Luxembourg Convention" means the Convention on the accession of the Hellenic Republic to the Rome Convention signed by the United Kingdom in Luxembourg on 10th April 1984; and

(c) "the Brussels Protocol" means the first Protocol on the interpretation of the Rome Convention by the European Court signed by the United Kingdom in Brussels on 19th December 1988;

[(d) "the Funchal Convention" means the Convention on the accession of the Kingdom of Spain and the Portuguese Republic to the Rome Convention and the Brussels Protocol, with adjustments made to the Rome Convention by the Luxembourg Convention, signed by the United Kingdom in Funchal on 18th May 1992;]

[(e) "the 1996 Accession Convention" means the Convention on the accession of the Republic of Austria, the Republic of Finland and the Kingdom of Sweden to the Rome Convention and the Brussels Protocol, with the adjustments made to the Rome Convention by the Luxembourg Convention and the Funchal Convention, signed by the United Kingdom in Brussels on 29th November 1996;]

and [these Conventions and this Protocol] ate together referred to as "the Conventions".

[1473]

NOTES

Para (d) added, and words in final pair of square brackets substituted, by the Contracts (Applicable Law) Act 1990 (Amendment) Order 1994, SI 1994/1900, arts 3, 4; para (e) added by the Contracts (Applicable Law) Act 1990 (Amendment) Order 2000, SI 2000/1825, art 3.

2 Conventions to have force of law

(1) Subject to subsections (2) and (3) below, the Conventions shall have the force of law in the United Kingdom.

[(1A) The internal law for the purposes of Article 1(3) of the Rome Convention is whichever of the following are applicable, namely—

(a) the provisions of Schedule 3A to the Insurance Companies Act 1982 (law applicable to certain contracts of insurance with insurance companies), and

(b) the provisions of Schedule 20 to the Friendly Societies Act 1992 as applied by subsections (1)(a) and (2)(a) of section 101 of that Act (law applicable to certain contracts of insurance with friendly societies).]

(2) Articles 7(1) and 10(1)(e) of the Rome Convention shall not have the force of law in the United Kingdom.

(3) Notwithstanding Article 19(2) of the Rome Convention, the Conventions shall apply in the case of conflicts between the laws of different parts of the United Kingdom.

(4) For ease of reference there are set out in [Schedules 1, 2, 3[, 3A and 3B]] to this Act respectively the English texts of—

(a) the Rome Convention;

(b) the Luxembourg Convention; ...

(c) the Brussels Protocol[, and

(d) the Funchal Convention; and

(e) the 1996 Accession Convention.]]

[1474]

NOTES

Sub-s (1A): inserted by the Insurance companies (Amendment) Regulations 1993, SI 1993/174, reg 9; substituted by the Friendly Societies (Amendment) Regulations 1993, SI 1993/2519, reg 6(5).

Sub-s (4): words in first (outer) pair of square brackets substituted, word omitted repealed and original para (d) and the word immediately preceding it added, by the Contracts (Applicable Law) Act 1990 (Amendment) Order 1994, SI 1994/1900, arts 5, 6; words in second (inner) pair of square brackets substituted, and paras (d), (e) substituted for para (d) by the Contracts (Applicable Law) Act 1990 (Amendment) Order 2000, SI 2000/1825, art 4.

3 Interpretation of Conventions

(1) Any question as to the meaning or effect of any provision of the Conventions shall, if not referred to the European Court in accordance with the Brussels Protocol, be determined in accordance with the principles laid down by, and any relevant decision of, the European Court.

(2) Judicial notice shall be taken of any decision of, or expression of opinion by, the European Court on any such question.

(3) Without prejudice to any practice of the courts as to the matters which may be considered apart from this subsection—

(a)　the report on the Rome Convention by Professor Mario Giuliano and Professor Paul Lagarde which is reproduced in the Official Journal of the Communities of 31st October 1980 may be considered in ascertaining the meaning or effect of any provision of that Convention; and

(b)　any report on the Brussels Protocol which is reproduced in the Official Journal of the Communities may be considered in ascertaining the meaning or effect of any provision of that Protocol.

[1475]

4 Revision of Conventions etc

(1)　If at any time it appears to Her Majesty in Council that Her Majesty's Government in the United Kingdom—

(a)　have agreed to a revision of any of the Conventions (including, in particular, any revision connected with the accession to the Rome Convention of any state); or

(b)　have given notification in accordance with Article 22(3) of the Rome Convention that either or both of the provisions mentioned in section 2(2) above shall have the force of law in the United Kingdom,

Her Majesty may by Order in Council make such consequential modifications of this Act or any other statutory provision, whenever passed or made, as Her Majesty considers appropriate.

(2)　An Order in Council under subsection (1) above shall not be made unless a draft of the Order has been laid before Parliament and approved by a resolution of each House.

(3)　In subsection (1) above—

"modifications" includes additions, omissions and alterations;

"revision" means an omission from, addition to or alteration of any of the Conventions and includes replacement of any of the Conventions to any extent by another convention, protocol or other description of international agreement; and

"statutory provision" means any provision contained in an Act, or in any Northern Ireland legislation, or in—

(a)　subordinate legislation (as defined in section 21(1) of the Interpretation Act 1978); or

(b)　any instrument of a legislative character made under any Northern Ireland legislation.

[1476]

[4A Disapplication where the rules in the Rome I Regulations apply: England and Wales and Northern Ireland

(1)　Nothing in this Act applies to affect the determination of issues relating to contractual obligations which fall to be determined under the Rome I Regulation.

(2)　In this section the "Rome I Regulation" means Regulation (EC) No 593/2008 of the European Parliament and of the Council on the law applicable to contractual obligations, including that Regulation as applied by regulation 3 of the Law Applicable to Contractual Obligations (England and Wales and Northern Ireland) Regulations 2009 (conflicts falling within Article 22(2) of Regulation (EC) No 593/2008).

(3)　This section extends to England and Wales and Northern Ireland only.]

[1476A]

NOTES

Commencement: 17 December 2009.

Inserted by the Law Applicable to Contractual Obligations (England and Wales and Northern Ireland) Regulations 2009, SI 2009/3064, reg 2.

4B, 5　(*S 4B inserted by the Law Applicable to Contractual Obligations (Scotland) Regulations 2009, SSI 2009/410, reg 2(a) and applies to Scotland only; s 5 introduces Sch 4 (consequential amendments) outside the scope of this work.*)

6 Application to Crown

This Act binds the Crown.

[1477]

7 Commencement

This Act shall come into force on such day as the Lord Chancellor and the Lord Advocate may by order made by statutory instrument appoint; and different days may be appointed for different provisions or different purposes.

[1478]

NOTES

Orders: the Contracts (Applicable Law) Act 1990 (Commencement No 1) Order 1991, SI 1991/707; the Contracts (Applicable Law) Act 1990 (Commencement No 2) Order 2004, SI 2004/3448.

8 Extent

(1)   [Except as provided by virtue of section 4B(3), this] Act extends to Northern Ireland.

(2)   Her Majesty may by Order in Council direct that all or any of the provisions of this Act shall extend to any of the following territories, namely—

  (a)   the Isle of Man;
  (b)   any of the Channel Islands;
  (c)   Gibraltar;
  (d)   the Sovereign Base Areas of Akrotiri and Dhekelia (that is to say, the areas mentioned in section 2(1) of the Cyprus Act 1960).

(3)   An Order in Council under subsection (2) above may modify this Act in its application to any of the territories mentioned in that subsection and may contain such supplementary provisions as Her Majesty considers appropriate; and in this subsection "modify" shall be construed in accordance with section 4 above.

[1479]

NOTES

Sub-s (1): words in square brackets substituted for original word "this" in relation to Scotland only by the Law Applicable to Contractual Obligations (Scotland) Regulations 2009, SSI 2009/410, reg 2(b).

9 Short title

This Act may be cited as the Contracts (Applicable Law) Act 1990.

[1480]

SCHEDULES

SCHEDULE 1
THE ROME CONVENTION

Section 2

The High Contracting Parties to the Treaty establishing the European Economic Community,

Anxious to continue in the field of private international law the work of unification of law which has already been done within the Community, in particular in the field of jurisdiction and enforcement of judgments,

Wishing to establish uniform rules concerning the law applicable to contractual obligations,

HAVE AGREED AS FOLLOWS—

TITLE I
SCOPE OF THE CONVENTION

Article 1
Scope of the Convention

1.   The rules of this Convention shall apply to contractual obligations in any situation involving a choice between the laws of different countries.

2.   They shall not apply to—

  (a)   questions involving the status or legal capacity of natural persons, without prejudice to Article 11;
  (b)   contractual obligations relating to—
    —   wills and succession,
    —   rights in property arising out of a matrimonial relationship,
    —   rights and duties arising out of a family relationship, parentage, marriage or affinity, including maintenance obligations in respect of children who are not legitimate;
  (c)   obligations arising under bills of exchange, cheques and promissory notes and other negotiable instruments to the extent that the obligations under such other negotiable instruments arise out of their negotiable character;
  (d)   arbitration agreements and agreements on the choice of court;
  (e)   questions governed by the law of companies and other bodies corporate or unincorporate such as the creation, by registration or otherwise, legal capacity, internal organisation or winding up of companies and other bodies corporate or unincorporate and the personal liability of officers and members as such for the obligations of the company or body;
  (f)   the question whether an agent is able to bind a principal, or an organ to bind a company or body corporate or unincorporate, to a third party;

    (g)   the constitution of trusts and the relationship between settlors, trustees and beneficiaries;

    (h)   evidence and procedure, without prejudice to Article 14.

3.   The rules of this Convention do not apply to contracts of insurance which cover risks situated in the territories of the Member States of the European Economic Community. In order to determine whether a risk is situated in these territories the court shall apply its internal law.

4.   The preceding paragraph does not apply to contracts of re-insurance.

Article 2
Application of law of non-contracting States

Any law specified by this Convention shall be applied whether or not it is the law of a Contracting State.

TITLE II
UNIFORM RULES

Article 3
Freedom of choice

1.   A contract shall be governed by the law chosen by the parties. The choice must be express or demonstrated with reasonable certainty by the terms of the contract or the circumstances of the case. By their choice the parties can select the law applicable to the whole or a part only of the contract.

2.   The parties may at any time agree to subject the contract to a law other than that which previously governed it, whether as a result of an earlier choice under this Article or of other provisions of this Convention. Any variation by the parties of the law to be applied made after the conclusion of the contract shall not prejudice its formal validity under Article 9 or adversely affect the rights of third parties.

3.   The fact that the parties have chosen a foreign law, whether or not accompanied by the choice of a foreign tribunal, shall not, where all the other elements relevant to the situation at the time of the choice are connected with one country only, prejudice the application of rules of the law of that country which cannot be derogated from by contract, hereinafter called "mandatory rules".

4.   The existence and validity of the consent of the parties as to the choice of the applicable law shall be determined in accordance with the provisions of Articles 8, 9 and 11.

Article 4
Applicable law in the absence of choice

1.   To the extent that the law applicable to the contract has not been chosen in accordance with Article 3, the contract shall be governed by the law of the country with which it is most closely connected. Nevertheless, a severable part of the contract which has a closer connection with another country may by way of exception be governed by the law of that other country.

2.   Subject to the provisions of paragraph 5 of this Article, it shall be presumed that the contract is most closely connected with the country where the party who is to effect the performance which is characteristic of the contract has, at the time of conclusion of the contract, his habitual residence or, in the case of a body corporate or unincorporate, its central administration. However, if the contract is entered into in the course of that party's trade or profession, that country shall be the country in which the principal place of business is situated or, where under the terms of the contract the performance is to be effected through a place of business other than the principal place of business, the country in which that other place of business is situated.

3.   Notwithstanding the provisions of paragraph 2 of this Article, to the extent that the subject matter of the contract is a right in immovable property or a right to use immovable property it shall be presumed that the contract is most closely connected with the country where the immovable property is situated.

4.   A contract for the carriage of goods shall not be subject to the presumption in paragraph 2. In such a contract if the country in which, at the time the contract is concluded, the carrier has his principal place of business is also the country in which the place of loading or the place of discharge or the principal place of business of the consignor is situated, it shall be presumed that the contract is most closely connected with that country. In applying this paragraph single voyage charter-parties and other contracts the main purpose of which is the carriage of goods shall be treated as contracts for the carriage of goods.

5.   Paragraph 2 shall not apply if the characteristic performance cannot be determined, and the presumptions in paragraphs 2, 3 and 4 shall be disregarded if it appears from the circumstances as a whole that the contract is more closely connected with another country.

Article 5
Certain consumer contracts

1.   This Article applies to a contract the object of which is the supply of goods or services to a person ("the consumer") for a purpose which can be regarded as being outside his trade or profession, or a contract for the provision of credit for that object.

2.   Notwithstanding the provisions of Article 3, a choice of law made by the parties shall not have the result of depriving the consumer of the protection afforded to him by the mandatory rules of the law of the country in which he has his habitual residence—

—   if in that country the conclusion of the contract was preceded by a specific invitation addressed to him or by advertising, and he had taken in that country all the steps necessary on his part for the conclusion of the contract, or

—   if the other party or his agent received the consumer's order in that country, or

—   if the contract is for the sale of goods and the consumer travelled from that country to another country and there gave his order, provided that the consumer's journey was arranged by the seller for the purpose of inducing the consumer to buy.

3.   Notwithstanding the provisions of Article 4, a contract to which this Article applies shall, in the absence of choice in accordance with Article 3, be governed by the law of the country in which the consumer has his habitual residence if it is entered into in the circumstances described in paragraph 2 of this Article.

4.   This Article shall not apply to—

(a)   a contract of carriage;

(b)   a contract for the supply of services where the services are to be supplied to the consumer exclusively in a country other than that in which he has his habitual residence.

5.   Notwithstanding the provisions of paragraph 4, this Article shall apply to a contract which, for an inclusive price, provides for a combination of travel and accommodation.

Article 6
Individual employment contracts

1.   Notwithstanding the provisions of Article 3, in a contract of employment a choice of law made by the parties shall not have the result of depriving the employee of the protection afforded to him by the mandatory rules of the law which would be applicable under paragraph 2 in the absence of choice.

2.   Notwithstanding the provisions of Article 4, a contract of employment shall, in the absence of choice in accordance with Article 3, be governed—

(a)   by the law of the country in which the employee habitually carries out his work in performance of the contract, even if he is temporarily employed in another country; or

(b)   if the employee does not habitually carry out his work in any one country, by the law of the country in which the place of business through which he was engaged is situated;

unless it appears from the circumstances as a whole that the contract is more closely connected with another country, in which case the contract shall be governed by the law of that country.

Article 7
Mandatory rules

1.   When applying under this Convention the law of a country, effect may be given to the mandatory rules of the law of another country with which the situation has a close connection, if and in so far as, under the law of the latter country, those rules must be applied whatever the law applicable to the contract. In considering whether to give effect to these mandatory rules, regard shall be had to their nature and purpose and to the consequences of their application or non-application.

2.   Nothing in this Convention shall restrict the application of the rules of the law of the forum in a situation where they are mandatory irrespective of the law otherwise applicable to the contract.

Article 8
Material validity

1.   The existence and validity of a contract, or of any term of a contract, shall be determined by the law which would govern it under this Convention if the contract or term were valid.

2.   Nevertheless a party may rely upon the law of the country in which he has his habitual residence to establish that he did not consent if it appears from the circumstances that it would not be reasonable to determine the effect of his conduct in accordance with the law specified in the preceding paragraph.

Article 9
Formal validity

1. A contract concluded between persons who are in the same country is formally valid if it satisfies the formal requirements of the law which governs it under this Convention or of the law of the country where it is concluded.

2. A contract concluded between persons who are in different countries is formally valid if it satisfies the formal requirements of the law which governs it under this Convention or of the law of one of those countries.

3. Where a contract is concluded by an agent, the country in which the agent acts is the relevant country for the purposes of paragraphs 1 and 2.

4. An act intended to have legal effect relating to an existing or contemplated contract is formally valid if it satisfies the formal requirements of the law which under this Convention governs or would govern the contract or of the law of the country where the act was done.

5. The provisions of the preceding paragraphs shall not apply to a contract to which Article 5 applies, concluded in the circumstances described in paragraph 2 of Article 5. The formal validity of such a contract is governed by the law of the country in which the consumer has his habitual residence.

6. Notwithstanding paragraphs 1 to 4 of this Article, a contract the subject matter of which is a right in immovable property or a right to use immovable property shall be subject to the mandatory requirements of form of the law of the country where the property is situated if by that law those requirements are imposed irrespective of the country where the contract is concluded and irrespective of the law governing the contract.

Article 10
Scope of the applicable law

1. The law applicable to a contract by virtue of Articles 3 to 6 and 12 of this Convention shall govern in particular—
    (a) interpretation;
    (b) performance;
    (c) within the limits of the powers conferred on the court by its procedural law, the consequences of breach, including the assessment of damages in so far as it is governed by rules of law;
    (d) the various ways of extinguishing obligations, and prescription and limitation of actions;
    (e) the consequences of nullity of the contract.

2. In relation to the manner of performance and the steps to be taken in the event of defective performance regard shall be had to the law of the country in which performance takes place.

Article 11
Incapacity

In a contract concluded between persons who are in the same country, a natural person who would have capacity under the law of that country may invoke his incapacity resulting from another law only if the other party to the contract was aware of this incapacity at the time of the conclusion of the contract or was not aware thereof as a result of negligence.

Article 12
Voluntary assignment

1. The mutual obligations of assignor and assignee under a voluntary assignment of a right against another person ("the debtor") shall be governed by the law which under this Convention applies to the contract between the assignor and assignee.

2. The law governing the right to which the assignment relates shall determine its assignability, the relationship between the assignee and the debtor, the conditions under which the assignment can be invoked against the debtor and any question whether the debtor's obligations have been discharged.

Article 13
Subrogation

1. Where a person ("the creditor") has a contractual claim upon another ("the debtor"), and a third person has a duty to satisfy the creditor, or has in fact satisfied the creditor in discharge of that duty, the law which governs the third person's duty to satisfy the creditor shall determine whether the third person is entitled to exercise against the debtor the rights which the creditor had against the debtor under the law governing their relationship and, if so, whether he may do so in full or only to a limited extent.

2.   The same rule applies where several persons are subject to the same contractual claim and one of them has satisfied the creditor.

Article 14
Burden of proof, etc

1.   The law governing the contract under this Convention applies to the extent that it contains, in the law of contract, rules which raise presumptions of law or determine the burden of proof.

2.   A contract or an act intended to have legal effect may be proved by any mode of proof recognised by the law of the forum or by any of the laws referred to in Article 9 under which that contract or act is formally valid, provided that such mode of proof can be administered by the forum.

Article 15
Exclusion of renvoi

The application of the law of any country specified by this Convention means the application of the rules of law in force in that country other than its rules of private international law.

Article 16
"Ordre public"

The application of a rule of the law of any country specified by this Convention may be refused only if such application is manifestly incompatible with the public policy ("ordre public") of the forum.

Article 17
No retrospective effect

This Convention shall apply in a Contracting State to contracts made after the date on which this Convention has entered into force with respect to that State.

Article 18
Uniform interpretation

In the interpretation and application of the preceding uniform rules, regard shall be had to their international character and to the desirability of achieving uniformity in their interpretation and application.

Article 19
States with more than one legal system

1.   Where a State comprises several territorial units each of which has its own rules of law in respect of contractual obligations, each territorial unit shall be considered as a country for the purposes of identifying the law applicable under this Convention.

2.   A State within which different territorial units have their own rules of law in respect of contractual obligations shall not be bound to apply this Convention to conflicts solely between the laws of such units.

Article 20
Precedence of Community Law

This Convention shall not affect the application of provisions which, in relation to particular matters, lay down choice of law rules relating to contractual obligations and which are or will be contained in acts of the institutions of the European Communities or in national laws harmonised in implementation of such acts.

Article 21
Relationship with other conventions

This Convention shall not prejudice the application of international conventions to which a Contracting State is, or becomes, a party.

Article 22
Reservations

1.   Any Contracting State may, at the time of signature, ratification, acceptance or approval, reserve the right not to apply—
    (a)   the provisions of Article 7(1);
    (b)   the provisions of Article 10(1)(e).
2.   …
3.   Any Contracting State may at any time withdraw a reservation which it has made; the reservation shall cease to have effect on the first day of the third calendar month after notification of the withdrawal.

TITLE III
FINAL PROVISIONS

Article 23

1.   If, after the date on which this Convention has entered into force for a Contracting State, that State wishes to adopt any new choice of law rule in regard to any particular category of contract within the scope of this Convention, it shall communicate its intention to the other signatory States through the Secretary-General of the Council of the European Communities.

2.   Any signatory State may, within six months from the date of the communication made to the Secretary-General, request him to arrange consultations between signatory States in order to reach agreement.

3.   If no signatory State has requested consultations within this period or if within two years following the communication made to the Secretary-General no agreement is reached in the course of consultations, the Contracting State concerned may amend its law in the manner indicated. The measures taken by that State shall be brought to the knowledge of the other signatory States through the Secretary-General of the Council of the European Communities.

Article 24

1.   If, after the date on which this Convention has entered into force with respect to a Contracting State, that State wishes to become a party to a multilateral convention whose principal aim or one of whose principal aims is to lay down rules of private international law concerning any of the matters governed by this Convention, the procedure set out in Article 23 shall apply. However, the period of two years, referred to in paragraph 3 of that Article, shall be reduced to one year.

2.   The procedure referred to in the preceding paragraph need not be followed if a Contracting State or one of the European Communities is already a party to the multilateral convention, or if its object is to revise a convention to which the State concerned is already a party, or if it is a convention concluded within the framework of the Treaties establishing the European Communities.

Article 25

If a Contracting State considers that the unification achieved by this Convention is prejudiced by the conclusion of agreements not covered by Article 24(1), that State may request the Secretary-General of the Council of the European Communities to arrange consultations between the signatory States of this Convention.

Article 26

Any Contracting State may request the revision of this Convention. In this event a revision conference shall be convened by the President of the Council of the European Communities.

Article 27

...

Article 28

1.   This Convention shall be open from 19 June 1980 for signature by the States party to the Treaty establishing the European Economic Community.

2.   This Convention shall be subject to ratification, acceptance or approval by the signatory States. The instruments of ratification, acceptance or approval shall be deposited with the Secretary-General of the Council of the European Communities.

Article 29

1.   This Convention shall enter into force on the first day of the third month following the deposit of the seventh instrument of ratification, acceptance or approval.

2.   This Convention shall enter into force for each signatory State ratifying, accepting or approving at a later date on the first day of the third month following the deposit of its instrument of ratification, acceptance or approval.

Article 30

1.   This Convention shall remain in force for 10 years from the date of its entry into force in accordance with Article 29(1), even for States for which it enters into force at a later date.

2.   If there has been no denunciation it shall be renewed tacitly every five years.

3.   A Contracting State which wishes to denounce shall, not less than six months before the expiration of the period of 10 or five years, as the case may be, give notice to the Secretary-General of the Council of the European Communities ...

4.   The denunciation shall have effect only in relation to the State which has notified it. The Convention will remain in force as between all other Contracting States.

Article 31

The Secretary-General of the Council of the European Communities shall notify the States party to the Treaty establishing the European Economic Community of—
   (a)   the signatures;
   (b)   the deposit of each instrument of ratification, acceptance or approval;
   (c)   the date of entry into force of this Convention;
   [(d)   communications made in pursuance of Articles 23, 24, 25, 26 and 30;]
   (e)   the reservations and withdrawals of reservations referred to in Article 22.

Article 32

The Protocol annexed to this Convention shall form an integral part thereof.

Article 33

This Convention, drawn up in a single original in the Danish, Dutch, English, French, German, Irish and Italian languages, these texts being equally authentic, shall be deposited in the archives of the Secretariat of the Council of the European Communities. The Secretary-General shall transmit a certified copy thereof to the Government of each signatory State.

[PROTOCOL

The High Contracting Parties have agreed upon the following provision which shall be annexed to the Convention:

Notwithstanding the provisions of the Convention, Denmark, Sweden and Finland may retain national provisions concerning the law applicable to questions relating to the carriage of goods by sea and may amend such provisions without following the procedure provided for in Article 23 of the Convention of Rome. The national provisions applicable in this respect are the following:
   —   in Denmark, paragraphs 252 and 321(3) and (4) of the "Sølov" (maritime law);
   —   in Sweden, Chapter 13, Article 2(1) and (2), and Chapter 14, Article 1(3), of "sjölagen" (maritime law);
   —   in Finland, Chapter 13, Article 2(1) and (2), and Chapter 14, Article 1(3) of "merilaki"/ "sjölagen" (maritime law).]

[1481]

NOTES

Articles 22.2, 27, and words omitted from Article 30.3 repealed, and Article 31(d) substituted, by the Contracts (Applicable Law) Act 1990 (Amendment) Order 1994, SI 1994/1900, arts 7, 8.

Protocol substituted by the Contracts (Applicable Law) Act 1990 (Amendment) Order 2000, SI 2000/1825, art 5.

SCHEDULE 2
THE LUXEMBOURG CONVENTION

Section 2

The High Contracting Parties to the Treaty establishing the European Economic Community,

Considering that the Hellenic Republic, in becoming a Member of the Community, undertook to accede to the Convention on the law applicable to contractual obligations, opened for signature in Rome on 19 June 1980,

Have decided to conclude this Convention, and to this end have designated as their plenipotentiaries—

(designation of plenipotentiaries)

Who, meeting within the Council, having exchanged their full powers, found in good and due form,

HAVE AGREED AS FOLLOWS—

Article 1

The Hellenic Republic hereby accedes to the Convention on the law applicable to contractual obligations, opened for signature in Rome on 19 June 1980.

Article 2

The Secretary-General of the Council of the European Communities shall transmit a certified copy of the Convention on the law applicable to contractual obligations in the Danish, Dutch, English, French, German, Irish and Italian languages to the Government of the Hellenic Republic.

The text of the Convention on the law applicable to contractual obligations in the Greek language is annexed hereto. The text in the Greek language shall be authentic under the same conditions as the other texts of the Convention on the law applicable to contractual obligations.

Article 3

This Convention shall be ratified by the Signatory States. The instruments of ratification shall be deposited with the Secretary-General of the Council of the European Communities.

Article 4

This Convention shall enter into force, as between the States which have ratified it, on the first day of the third month following the deposit of the last instrument of ratification by the Hellenic Republic and seven States which have ratified the Convention on the law applicable to contractual obligations.

This Convention shall enter into force for each Contracting State which subsequently ratifies it on the first day of the third month following the deposit of its instrument of ratification.

Article 5

The Secretary-General of the Council of the European Communities shall notify the Signatory States of—
  (a)   the deposit of each instrument of ratification;
  (b)   the dates of entry into force of this Convention for the Contracting States.

Article 6

This Convention, drawn up in a single original in the Danish, Dutch, English, French, German, Greek, Irish and Italian languages, all eight texts being equally authentic, shall be deposited in the archives of the General Secretariat of the Council of the European Communities. The Secretary-General shall transmit a certified copy to the Government of each Signatory State.

[1482]

SCHEDULE 3
THE BRUSSELS PROTOCOL

Section 2

The High Contracting Parties to the Treaty establishing the European Economic Community,

Having regard to the Joint Declaration annexed to the Convention on the law applicable to contractual obligations, opened for signature in Rome on 19 June 1980,

Have decided to conclude a Protocol conferring jurisdiction on the Court of Justice of the European Communities to interpret that Convention, and to this end have designated as their Plenipotentiaries—

(designation of plenipotentiaries)

Who, meeting within the Council of the European Communities, having exchanged their full powers, found in good and due form,

HAVE AGREED AS FOLLOWS—

Article 1

The Court of Justice of the European Communities shall have jurisdiction to give rulings on the interpretation of—
  (a)   the Convention on the law applicable to contractual obligations, opened for signature in Rome on 19 June 1980, hereinafter referred to as "the Rome Convention";
  (b)   the Convention on accession to the Rome Convention by the States which have become Members of the European Communities since the date on which it was opened for signature;
  (c)   this Protocol.

Article 2

Any of the courts referred to below may request the Court of Justice to give a preliminary ruling on a question raised in a case pending before it and concerning interpretation of the provisions contained in the instruments referred to in Article 1 if that court considers that a decision on the question is necessary to enable it to give judgment—
  (a)   —   in Belgium:
         la Cour de cassation (het Hof van Cassatie) and le Conseil d'Etat (de Raad van State),
         —   in Denmark:
         Højesteret,
         —   in the Federal Republic of Germany:
         die obersten Gerichtschöfe des Bundes,

— in Greece:
τα ανωτατα Δικαστηρια,
— in Spain:
el Tribunal Supremo,
— in France:
la Cour de cassation and le Conseil d'Etat,
— in Ireland:
the Supreme Court,
— in Italy:
la Corte suprema di cassazione and il Consiglio di Stato,
— in Luxembourg:
la Cour Supérieure de Justice, when sitting as Cour de cassation,
[— in Austria:
the Oberste Gerichtshof, the Verwaltungsgerichtshof and the Verfassungsgerichtshof,]
— in the Netherlands:
de Hoge Raad,
— in Portugal:
o Supremo Tribunal de Justiça and o Supremo Tribunal Administrativo,
[— in Finland:
korkein oikeus/högsta domstolen, korkein hallinto-oikeus/högsta förvaltningsdomstolen, markkinatuomioistuin/marknadsdomstolen and työtuomioistuin/arbetsdomstolen,
— Sweden:
Högsta domstolen, Regeringsrätten, Arbetsdomstolen and Marknadsdomstolen,]
— in the United Kingdom:
the House of Lords and other courts from which no further appeal is possible;
(b) the courts of the Contracting States when acting as appeal courts.

Article 3

1. The competent authority of a Contracting State may request the Court of Justice to give a ruling on a question of interpretation of the provisions contained in the instruments referred to in Article 1 if judgments given by courts of that State conflict with the interpretation given either by the Court of Justice or in a judgment of one of the courts of another Contracting State referred to in Article 2. The provisions of this paragraph shall apply only to judgments which have become res judicata.

2. The interpretation given by the Court of Justice in response to such a request shall not affect the judgments which gave rise to the request for interpretation.

3. The Procurators-General of the Supreme Courts of Appeal of the Contracting States, or any other authority designated by a Contracting State, shall be entitled to request the Court of Justice for a ruling on interpretation in accordance with paragraph 1.

4. The Registrar of the Court of Justice shall give notice of the request to the Contracting States, to the Commission and to the Council of the European Communities; they shall then be entitled within two months of the notification to submit statements of case or written observations to the Court.

5. No fees shall be levied or any costs or expenses awarded in respect of the proceedings provided for in this Article.

Article 4

1. Except where this Protocol otherwise provides, the provisions of the Treaty establishing the European Economic Community and those of the Protocol on the Statute of the Court of Justice annexed thereto, which are applicable when the Court is requested to give a preliminary ruling, shall also apply to any proceedings for the interpretation of the instruments referred to in Article 1.

2. The Rules of Procedure of the Court of Justice shall, if necessary, be adjusted and supplemented in accordance with Article 188 of the Treaty establishing the European Economic Community.

Article 5

This Protocol shall be subject to ratification by the Signatory States. The instruments of ratification shall be deposited with the Secretary-General of the Council of the European Communities.

Article 6

1. To enter into force, this Protocol must be ratified by seven States in respect of which the Rome Convention is in force. This Protocol shall enter into force on the first day of the third month following the deposit of the instrument of ratification by the last such State to take this step. If, however, the Second Protocol conferring on the Court of Justice of the European Communities certain powers to interpret the Convention on the law applicable to contractual obligations, opened

for signature in Rome on 19 June 1980, concluded in Brussels on 19 December 1988, enters into force on a later date, this Protocol shall enter into force on the date of entry into force of the Second Protocol.

2.   Any ratification subsequent to the entry into force of this Protocol shall take effect on the first day of the third month following the deposit of the instrument of ratification provided that the ratification, acceptance or approval of the Rome Convention by the State in question has become effective.

Article 7

The Secretary-General of the Council of the European Communities shall notify the Signatory States of—
    (a)   the deposit of each instrument of ratification;
    (b)   the date of entry into force of this Protocol;
    (c)   any designation communicated pursuant to Article 3(3);
    (d)   any communication made pursuant to Article 8.

Article 8

The Contracting States shall communicate to the Secretary-General of the Council of the European Communities the texts of any provisions of their laws which necessitate an amendment to the list of courts in Article 2(a).

Article 9

This Protocol shall have effect for as long as the Rome Convention remains in force under the conditions laid down in Article 30 of that Convention.

Article 10

Any Contracting State may request the revision of this Protocol. In this event, a revision conference shall be convened by the President of the Council of the European Communities.

Article 11

This Protocol, drawn up in a single original in the Danish, Dutch, English, French, German, Greek, Irish, Italian, Portuguese and Spanish languages, all 10 texts being equally authentic, shall be deposited in the archives of the General Secretariat of the Council of the European Communities. The Secretary-General shall transmit a certified copy to the Government of each Signatory State.

[1483]

NOTES

Art 2: in para (a) entries relating to Austria, Finland and Sweden inserted by the Contracts (Applicable Law) Act 1990 (Amendment) Order 2000, SI 2000/1825, art 6.

[SCHEDULE 3A
THE FUNCHAL CONVENTION

Section 2

The High Contracting Parties to the Treaty establishing the European Economic Community.

Considering that the Kingdom of Spain and the Portuguese Republic, in becoming Members of the Community, undertook to accede to the Convention on the law applicable to contractual obligations, opened for signature in Rome on 19th June 1980.

Have decided to conclude this Convention, and to this end have designated as their plenipotentiaries—

(designation of plenipotentiaries).

Who, meeting within the Council, having exchanged their full powers, found in good and due form.

HAVE AGREED AS FOLLOWS—

Article 1

The Kingdom of Spain and the Portuguese Republic hereby accede to the Convention on the law applicable to contractual obligations, opened for signature in Rome on 19th June 1980.

Article 2

The Convention on the law applicable to contractual obligations is hereby amended as follows—
    (1)   Article 22(2), Article 27 and the second sentence of Article 30(3) shall be deleted;
    (2)   The reference to Article 27 in Article 31(d) shall be deleted.

Article 3

The Secretary-General of the Council of the European Communities shall transmit a certified copy of the Convention on the law applicable to contractual obligations in the Danish, Dutch, English, French, German, Greek, Irish and Italian languages to the Governments of the Kingdom of Spain and the Portuguese Republic.

Article 4

This Convention shall be ratified by the Signatory States. The instruments of ratification shall be deposited with the Secretary-General of the Council of the European Communities.

Article 5

This Convention shall enter into force, as between the States which have ratified it, on the first day of the third month following deposit of the last instrument of ratification by the Kingdom of Spain or the Portuguese Republic and by one State which has ratified the Convention on the law applicable to contractual obligations.

This Convention shall enter into force for each Contracting State which subsequently ratifies it on the first day of the third month following that of deposit of its instrument of ratification.

Article 6

The Secretary-General of the Council of the European Communities shall notify the Signatory States of—
    (a)   the deposit of each instrument of ratification;
    (b)   the dates of entry into force of this Convention for the Contracting States.

Article 7

This Convention, drawn up in a single original in the Danish, Dutch, English, French, German, Greek, Irish, Italian, Portuguese and Spanish languages, all ten texts being equally authentic, shall be deposited in the archives of the General Secretariat of the Council of the European Communities. The Secretary-General shall transmit a certified copy to the Government of each Signatory State.]

[1484]

NOTES
  Inserted by the Contracts (Applicable Law) Act 1990 (Amendment) Order 1994, SI 1994/1900, art 9, Schedule.

[SCHEDULE 3B
THE 1996 ACCESSION CONVENTION

Section 2

The High Contracting Parties to the Treaty establishing the European Community.

Considering that the Republic of Austria, the Republic of Finland and the Kingdom of Sweden, in becoming Members of the European Union, undertook to accede to the Convention on the Law applicable to Contractual Obligations, opened for signature in Rome on 19th June 1980, and to the First and Second Protocols on its interpretation by the Court of Justice,

HAVE AGREED AS FOLLOWS—

TITLE I
GENERAL PROVISIONS

Article I

The Republic of Austria, the Republic of Finland and the Kingdom of Sweden hereby accede to—
    (a)   the Convention on the Law applicable to Contractual Obligations, opened for signature in Rome on 19th June 1980, hereinafter referred to as "the Convention of 1980", as it stands following incorporation of all the adjustments and amendments made thereto by—
        —   the Convention signed in Luxembourg on 10th April 1984, hereinafter referred to as "the Convention of 1984", on the accession of the Hellenic Republic to the Convention on the Law applicable to Contractual Obligations;
        —   the Convention signed in Funchal on 18th May 1992, hereinafter referred to as "the Convention of 1992", on the accession of the Kingdom of Spain and the Portuguese Republic to the Convention on the Law applicable to Contractual Obligations;
    (b)   the First Protocol, signed on 19th December 1988, hereinafter referred to as "the First Protocol of 1988", on the interpretation by the Court of Justice of the European Communities of the Convention on the Law applicable to Contractual Obligations;
    (c)   the Second Protocol, signed on 19th December 1988, hereinafter referred to as "the

Second Protocol of 1988", conferring on the Court of Justice of the European Communities certain powers to interpret the Convention on the Law applicable to Contractual Obligations.

TITLE II
ADJUSTMENTS TO THE PROTOCOL ANNEXED TO THE CONVENTION OF 1980

Article 2

The Protocol annexed to the Convention of 1980 is hereby replaced by the following—

"Notwithstanding the provisions of the Convention, Denmark, Sweden and Finland may retain national provisions concerning the law applicable to questions relating to the carriage of goods by sea and may amend such provisions without following the procedure provided for in Article 23 of the Convention of Rome. The national provisions applicable in this respect are the following—

    —   in Denmark, paragraphs 252 and 321(3) and (4) of the "Sølov" (maritime law);
    —   in Sweden, Chapter 13, Article 2(1) and (2), and Chapter 14, Article 1(3), of "sjölagen" (maritime law);
    —   in Finland, Chapter 13, Article 2(1) and (2), and Chapter 14, Article 1(3), of "merilaki"/"sjölagn" (maritime law)."

TITLE III
ADJUSTMENTS TO THE FIRST PROTOCOL OF 1988

Article 3

The following indents shall be inserted in Article 2(a) of the First Protocol of 1988:
  (a)   between the tenth and eleventh indents:
    "—   in Austria:
    the Oberste Gerichtshof, the Verwaltungsgerichtshof and the Verfassungsgerichtshof,"
  (b)   between the eleventh and twelfth indents:
    "—   in Finland:
    Korkein oikeus/högsta domstolen, korkein hallinto-oikeus/högsta förvaltningsdomstolen,
       markkinatuomioistuin/ marknadsdomstolen and työtuomioistuin/arbetsdomstolen,
    —   in Sweden:
    Högsta domstolen, Regeringsrätten, Arbetsdomstolen and Marknadsdomstolen,".

[TITLE IV
FINAL PROVISIONS

Article 4

1.   The Secretary-General of the Council of the European Union shall transmit a certified copy of the Convention of 1980, the Convention of 1984, the First Protocol of 1988, the Second Protocol of 1988 and the Convention of 1992 in the Danish, Dutch, English, French, German, Greek, Irish, Italian, Spanish and Portuguese languages to the Governments of the Republic of Austria, the Republic of Finland and the Kingdom of Sweden.

2.   The text of the Convention of 1980, the Convention of 1984, the First Protocol of 1988, the Second Protocol of 1988 and the Convention of 1992 in the Finnish and Swedish languages shall be authentic under the same conditions as the other texts of the Convention of 1980, the Convention of 1984, the First Protocol of 1988, the Second Protocol of 1988 and the Convention of 1992.

Article 5

This Convention shall be ratified by the Signatory States. The instruments of ratification shall be deposited with the Secretary-General of the Council of the European Union.

Article 6

1.   This Convention shall enter into force, as between the States which have ratified it, on the first day of the third month following the deposit of the last instrument of ratification by the Republic of Austria, the Republic of Finland or the Kingdom of Sweden and by one Contracting State which has ratified the Convention on the Law applicable to Contractual Obligations.

2.   This Convention shall enter into force for each Contracting State which subsequently ratifies it on the first day of the third month following the deposit of its instrument of ratification.

Article 7

The Secretary-General of the Council of the European Union shall notify the Signatory States of:
  (a)   the deposit of each instrument of ratification;
  (b)   the dates of entry into force of this Convention for the Contracting States.

Article 8

This Convention, drawn up in a single original in the Danish, Dutch, English, Finnish, French, German, Greek, Irish, Italian, Portuguese, Spanish and Swedish languages, all twelve texts being equally authentic, shall be deposited in the archives of the General Secretariat of the Council of the European Union. The Secretary-General shall transmit a certified copy to the Government of each Signatory State.]

[1485]

NOTES
Inserted by the Contracts (Applicable Law) Act 1990 (Amendment) Order 2000, SI 2000/1825, art 7, Schedule.

(Sch 4 (consequential amendments) repealed in part; remainder outside the scope of this work.)

PROPERTY MISDESCRIPTIONS ACT 1991

(1991 c 29)

ARRANGEMENT OF SECTIONS

An Act to prohibit the making of false or misleading statements about property matters in the course of estate agency business and property development business

[27 June 1991]

1   Offence of property misdescription

(1)   Where a false or misleading statement about a prescribed matter is made in the course of an estate agency business or a property development business, otherwise than in providing conveyancing services, the person by whom the business is carried on shall be guilty of an offence under this section.

(2)   Where the making of the statement is due to the act or default of an employee the employee shall be guilty of an offence under this section; and the employee may be proceeded against and punished whether or not proceedings are also taken against his employer.

(3)   A person guilty of an offence under this section shall be liable—
    (a)   on summary conviction, to a fine not exceeding the statutory maximum, and
    (b)   on conviction on indictment, to a fine.

(4)   No contract shall be void or unenforceable, and no right of action in civil proceedings in respect of any loss shall arise, by reason only of the commission of an offence under this section.

(5)   For the purposes of this section—
    (a)   "false" means false to a material degree,
    (b)   a statement is misleading if (though not false) what a reasonable person may be expected to infer from it, or from any omission from it, is false,
    (c)   a statement may be made by pictures or any other method of signifying meaning as well as by words and, if made by words, may be made orally or in writing,
    (d)   a prescribed matter is any matter relating to land which is specified in an order made by the Secretary of State,
    (e)   a statement is made in the course of an estate agency business if (but only if) the making of the statement is a thing done as mentioned in subsection (1) of section 1 of the Estate Agents Act 1979 and that Act either applies to it or would apply to it but for subsection (2)(a) of that section (exception for things done in course of profession by practising solicitor or employee),
    (f)   a statement is made in the course of a property development business if (but only if) it is made—

     (i)   in the course of a business (including a business in which the person making the statement is employed) concerned wholly or substantially with the development of land, and

     (ii)   for the purpose of, or with a view to, disposing of an interest in land consisting of or including a building, or a part of a building, constructed or renovated in the course of the business, and

  (g)   "conveyancing services" means the preparation of any transfer, conveyance, writ, contract or other document in connection with the disposal or acquisition of an interest in land, and services ancillary to that, but does not include anything done as mentioned in section 1(1)(a) of the Estate Agents Act 1979.

  (6)   For the purposes of this section any reference in this section or section 1 of the Estate Agents Act 1979 to disposing of or acquiring an interest in land—

  (a)   in England and Wales and Northern Ireland shall be construed in accordance with section 2 of that Act, and

  (b)   *(applies to Scotland only.)*

  (7)   An order under this section may—

  (a)   make different provision for different cases, and

  (b)   include such supplemental, consequential and transitional provisions as the Secretary of State considers appropriate;

and the power to make such an order shall be exercisable by statutory instrument which shall be subject to annulment in pursuance of a resolution of either House of Parliament.

[1486]

NOTES

Order: the Property Misdescriptions (Specified Matters) Order 1992, SI 1992/2834.

---

2   Due diligence defence

  (1)   In proceedings against a person for an offence under section 1 above it shall be a defence for him to show that he took all reasonable steps and exercised all due diligence to avoid committing the offence.

  (2)   A person shall not be entitled to rely on the defence provided by subsection (1) above by reason of his reliance on information given by another unless he shows that it was reasonable in all the circumstances for him to have relied on the information, having regard in particular—

  (a)   to the steps which he took, and those which might reasonably have been taken, for the purpose of verifying the information, and

  (b)   to whether he had any reason to disbelieve the information.

  (3)   Where in any proceedings against a person for an offence under section 1 above the defence provided by subsection (1) above involves an allegation that the commission of the offence was due—

  (a)   to the act or default of another, or

  (b)   to reliance on information given by another,

the person shall not, without the leave of the court, be entitled to rely on the defence unless he has served a notice under subsection (4) below on the person bringing the proceedings not less than seven clear days before the hearing of the proceedings or, in Scotland, the diet of trial.

  (4)   A notice under this subsection shall give such information identifying or assisting in the identification of the person who committed the act or default, or gave the information, as is in the possession of the person serving the notice at the time he serves it.

[1487]

3   Enforcement

The Schedule to this Act (which makes provision about the enforcement of this Act) shall have effect.

[1488]

4   Bodies corporate and Scottish partnerships

  (1)   Where an offence under this Act committed by a body corporate is proved to have been committed with the consent or connivance of, or to be attributable to neglect on the part of, a director, manager, secretary or other similar officer of the body corporate or a person who was purporting to act in such a capacity, he (as well as the body corporate) is guilty of the offence and liable to be proceeded against and punished accordingly.

  (2)   Where the affairs of a body corporate are managed by its members, subsection (1) above applies in relation to the acts and defaults of a member in connection with his functions of management as if he were a director of the body corporate.

  (3)   *(Applies to Scotland only.)*

[1489]

5   Prosecution time limit

(1)   No proceedings for an offence under section 1 above or paragraph 5(3), 6 ... of the Schedule to this Act shall be commenced after—
   (a)   the end of the period of three years beginning with the date of the commission of the offence, or
   (b)   the end of the period of one year beginning with the date of the discovery of the offence by the prosecutor,
whichever is the earlier.

(2)   For the purposes of this section a certificate signed by or on behalf of the prosecutor and stating the date on which the offence was discovered by him shall be conclusive evidence of that fact; and a certificate stating that matter and purporting to be so signed shall be treated as so signed unless the contrary is proved.

[1490]

NOTES

Sub-s (1): words omitted repealed by the Enterprise Act 2002 (Part 9 Restrictions on Disclosure of Information) (Amendment and Specification) Order 2003, SI 2003/1400, art 7, Sch 5.

6   Financial provision

There shall be paid out of money provided by Parliament any increase attributable to this Act in the sums payable out of such money under any other Act.

[1491]

7   Short title and extent

(1)   This Act may be cited as the Property Misdescriptions Act 1991.

(2)   This Act extends to Northern Ireland.

[1492]

SCHEDULE
ENFORCEMENT

Section 3

Enforcement authority

1.—(1)   Every local weights and measures authority in Great Britain shall be an enforcement authority for the purposes of this Act, and it shall be the duty of each such authority to enforce the provisions of this Act within their area.

(2)   The Department of Economic Development in Northern Ireland shall be an enforcement authority for the purposes of this Act, and it shall be the duty of the Department to enforce the provisions of this Act within Northern Ireland.

2.   ...

Powers of officers of enforcement authority

3.—(1)   If a duly authorised officer of an enforcement authority has reasonable grounds for suspecting that an offence under section 1 of this Act has been committed, he may—
   (a)   require a person carrying on or employed in a business to produce any book or document relating to the business, and take copies of it or any entry in it, or
   (b)   require such a person to produce in a visible and legible documentary form [or from which it can readily be produced in a visible and legible form] any information so relating which is [stored in any electronic form], and take copies of it,
for the purpose of ascertaining whether such an offence has been committed.

(2)   Such an officer may inspect any goods for the purpose of ascertaining whether such an offence has been committed.

(3)   If such an officer has reasonable grounds for believing that any documents or goods may be required as evidence in proceedings for such an offence, he may seize and detain them.

(4)   An offence seizing any documents or goods in the exercise of his power under sub-paragraph (3) above shall inform the person from whom they are seized.

(5)   The powers of an officer under this paragraph may be exercised by him only at a reasonable hour and on production (if required) of his credentials.

(6)   Nothing in this paragraph—
   (a)   requires a person to produce a document if he would be entitled to refuse to produce it in proceedings in a court on the ground that it is the subject of legal professional privilege or, in Scotland, that it contains a confidential communication made by or to an advocate or a solicitor in that capacity, or

 (b) authorises the taking possession of a document which is in the possession of a person who would be so entitled.

4.—(1) A duly authorised officer of an enforcement authority may, at a reasonable hour and on production (if required) of his credentials, enter any premises for the purpose of ascertaining whether an offence under section 1 of this Act has been committed.

 (2) If a justice of the peace, or in Scotland a justice of the peace or a sheriff, is satisfied—
  (a) that any relevant books, documents or goods are on, or that any relevant information contained in a computer is available from, any premises, and that production or inspection is likely to disclose the commission of an offence under section 1 of this Act, or
  (b) that such an offence has been, is being or is about to be committed on any premises,

and that any of the conditions specified in sub-paragraph (3) below is met, he may by warrant under his hand authorise an officer of an enforcement authority to enter the premises, if need be by force.

 (3) The conditions referred to in sub-paragraph (2) above are—
  (a) that admission to the premises has been or is likely to be refused and that notice of intention to apply for a warrant under that sub-paragraph has been given to the occupier,
  (b) that an application for admission, or the giving of such a notice, would defeat the object of the entry,
  (c) that the premises are unoccupied, and
  (d) that the occupier is temporarily absent and it might defeat the object of the entry to await his return.

 (4) In sub-paragraph (2) above "relevant", in relation to books, documents, goods or information, means books, documents, goods or information which, under paragraph 3 above, a duly authorised officer may require to be produced or may inspect.

 (5) A warrant under sub-paragraph (2) above may be issued only if—
  (a) in England and Wales, the justice of the peace is satisfied as required by that sub-paragraph by written information on oath,
  (b) in Scotland, the justice of the peace or sheriff is so satisfied by evidence on oath, or
  (c) in Northern Ireland, the justice of the peace is so satisfied by complaint on oath.

 (6) A warrant under sub-paragraph (2) above shall continue in force for a period of one month.

 (7) An officer entering any premises by virtue of this paragraph may take with him such other persons as may appear to him necessary.

 (8) On leaving premises which he has entered by virtue of a warrant under sub-paragraph (2) above, an officer shall, if the premises are unoccupied or the occupier is temporarily absent, leave the premises as effectively secured against trespassers as he found them.

 (9) In this paragraph "premises" includes any place (including any vehicle, ship or aircraft) except premises used only as a dwelling.

Obstruction of officers

5.—(1) A person who—
  (a) intentionally obstructs an officer of an enforcement authority acting in pursuance of this Schedule,
  (b) without reasonable excuse fails to comply with a requirement made of him by such an officer under paragraph 3(a) above, or
  (c) without reasonable excuse fails to give an officer of an enforcement authority acting in pursuance of this Schedule any other assistance or information which the officer may reasonably require of him for the purpose of the performance of the officer's functions under this Schedule,
shall be guilty of an offence.

 (2) A person guilty of an offence under sub-paragraph (1) above shall be liable on summary conviction to a fine not exceeding level 5 on the standard scale.

 (3) If a person, in giving any such information as is mentioned in sub-paragraph (1)(c) above,—
  (a) makes a statement which he knows is false in a material particular, or
  (b) recklessly makes a statement which is false in a material particular,
he shall be guilty of an offence.

 (4) A person guilty of an offence under sub-paragraph (3) above shall be liable—
  (a) on summary conviction, to a fine not exceeding the statutory maximum, and
  (b) on conviction on indictment, to a fine.

Impersonation of officers

6.—(1) If a person who is not a duly authorised officer of an enforcement authority purports to act as such under this Schedule he shall be guilty of an offence.

(2) A person guilty of an offence under sub-paragraph (1) above shall be liable—

    (a)   on summary conviction, to a fine not exceeding the statutory maximum, and

    (b)   on conviction on indictment, to a fine.

7. ...

Privilege against self-incrimination

8.   Nothing in this Schedule requires a person to answer any question or give any information if to do so might incriminate him.

[1493]

NOTES

Para 2: repealed by the Enterprise Act 2002, s 278(2), Sch 26.

Para 3: words in first pair of square brackets inserted, and words in second pair of square brackets substituted, by the Criminal Justice and Police Act 2001, s 70, Sch 2, Pt 2, para 20.

Para 7: repealed by the Enterprise Act 2002, ss 247(h), 278(2), Sch 26.

Seize and detain goods, etc: the powers of seizure conferred by para 3 are powers to which the Criminal Justice and Police Act 2001, s 50 apply (additional powers of seizure from premises); see s 50 of, and Sch 1, Pt 1, para 53 to, that Act.

EXPORT AND INVESTMENT GUARANTEES ACT 1991

(1991 c 67)

ARRANGEMENT OF SECTIONS

PART I
POWERS OF ECGD

PART II
TRANSFER OR DELEGATION OF ECGD FUNCTIONS

PART III
GENERAL

An Act to make new provision as to the functions exercisable by the Secretary of State through the Export Credits Guarantee Department; and make provision as to the delegation of any such functions and the transfer of property, rights and liabilities attributable to the exercise of any such functions

[22 October 1991]

PART I
POWERS OF ECGD

1 Assistance in connection with exports of goods and services

[(1)   The Secretary of State may make arrangements under this section in connection with supplies by persons carrying on business in the United Kingdom of goods or services to persons carrying on business outside the United Kingdom.

(1A)   Arrangements under subsection (1) may be made in connection with goods or services supplied before the arrangements are made or in connection with goods or services which are to be, or which may be, supplied.]

(2)   The Secretary of State may make arrangements under this section for the purpose of rendering economic assistance to countries outside the United Kingdom.

(3)   The Secretary of State may make arrangements under this section with a view to facilitating—

(a)   the performance of obligations created or arising, directly or indirectly, in connection with matters as to which he has exercised his powers under this section or section 2 of this Act, or

(b)   the reduction or avoidance of losses arising in connection with any failure to perform such obligations.

(4)   The arrangements that may be made under this section are arrangements for providing financial facilities or assistance for, or for the benefit of, persons carrying on business; and the facilities or assistance may be provided in any form, including guarantees, insurance, grants or loans.

[1494]

NOTES

Sub-ss (1), (1A): substituted for original sub-s (1), by the Industry and Exports (Financial Support) Act 2009, s 2(1), as from 21 May 2009, subject to s 2(2) thereof which provides that the power conferred by sub-s (1), as substituted, includes power to make arrangements in connection with goods or services supplied before that date.

2   Insurance in connection with overseas investment

(1)   The Secretary of State may make arrangements for insuring any person carrying on business in the United Kingdom against risks of losses arising—

(a)   in connection with any investment of resources by the insured in enterprises carried on outside the United Kingdom, or

(b)   in connection with guarantees given by the insured in respect of any investment of resources by others in such enterprises, being enterprises in which the insured has any interest,

being losses resulting directly or indirectly from war, expropriation, restrictions on remittances and other similar events.

(2)   The Secretary of State may make arrangements for insuring persons providing such insurance.

(3)   References in subsection (1) above to a person carrying on business in the United Kingdom and to the insured include any company controlled directly or indirectly by him.

[1495]

3   Financial management

(1)   The Secretary of State may make any arrangements which, in his opinion, are in the interests of the proper financial management of the ECGD portfolio, or any part of it.

(2)   In pursuance of arrangements under this section the Secretary of State may enter into any form of transaction, including—

(a)   lending, and

(b)   providing and taking out insurance and guarantees.

(3)   The Secretary of State may not, in pursuance of such arrangements, enter into any transaction for the purpose of borrowing money but, subject to that, he is not precluded from entering into any transaction by reason of its involving borrowing.

(4)   In pursuance of such arrangements the Secretary of State may—

(a)   alter any arrangements made under section 1 or 2 of this Act or the old law or make new arrangements in place of arrangements so made, or

(b)   make further arrangements in connection with arrangements so made.

(5)   Arrangements under this section may be made in anticipation of further rights being acquired or liabilities being incurred by the Secretary of State.

(6)   In this section the "ECGD portfolio" means the rights and liabilities to which the Secretary of State is entitled or subject by virtue of the exercise of his powers under this Act or the old law or in consequence of arrangements made in the exercise of those powers.

(7)   The Secretary of State may certify that any transaction he has entered into or is entering into has been or, as the case may be, is entered into in the exercise of the powers conferred by this section and such a certificate shall be conclusive evidence of the matters stated in it.

[1496]

4   Provisions supplementary to sections 1 to 3

(1)   Transactions entered into in pursuance of arrangements made under sections 1 to 3 of this Act may be on such terms and conditions as the Secretary of State considers appropriate.

(2)   The powers of the Secretary of State under those sections are exercisable only with the consent of the Treasury and such consent may be given in relation to particular cases or in relation to such descriptions of cases as may be specified in the consent.

(3)   In those sections—
- (a)   "business" includes a profession,
- (b)   "guarantee" includes indemnity,
- (c)   references to persons carrying on business, in relation to things done outside the United Kingdom, include persons carrying on any other activities, and
- (d)   references to things done in or outside the United Kingdom are to things done wholly or partly in or, as the case may be, outside the United Kingdom.

(4)   References in this and those sections to the United Kingdom include the Isle of Man and the Channel Islands.

[1497]

5   Provision of services and information

(1)   The Secretary of State may provide to any person—
- (a)   information relating to credit or investment insurance,
- (b)   services ancillary to the provision by that person of credit or investment insurance, and
- (c)   such other goods or services as may be specified in an order under this section,

and may make such charges for doing so as he may determine.

(2)   The power to make an order under this section is exercisable only with the consent of the Treasury.

[1498]

6   Commitment limits

(1)   The aggregate amount of the Secretary of State's commitments at any time under arrangements relating to exports and insurance shall not exceed—
- (a)   in the case of commitments in sterling, £35,000 million, and
- (b)   in the case of commitments in foreign currency, [30,000] million special drawing rights.

(2)   In subsection (1) above, "arrangements relating to exports and insurance" means—
- (a)   arrangements under section 1 or 2 of this Act, other than arrangements for giving grants or arrangements under section 1(3), and
- (b)   arrangements under the old law, other than arrangements for giving grants.

(3)   The aggregate amount of the Secretary of State's commitments at any time under section 3 of this Act shall not exceed—
- (a)   in the case of commitments in sterling, £15,000 million, and
- (b)   in the case of commitments in foreign currency, 10,000 million special drawing rights.

(4)   The Secretary of State may by order increase or further increase—
- (a)   either of the limits in subsection (1) above by a sum specified in the order not exceeding £5,000 million or, as the case may be, 5,000 million special drawing rights
- (b)   either of the limits in subsection (3) above by a sum specified in the order not exceeding £3,000 million or, as the case may be, 2,000 million special drawing rights,

but the Secretary of State shall not in respect of any limit exercise the power on more than three occasions.

(5)   For the purposes of this section and section 7 of this Act—
- (a)   the commitments of the Secretary of State under any arrangements are his rights and liabilities relating to the arrangements,
- (b)   the amount of any commitments shall be ascertained in accordance with principles determined from time to time by the Secretary of State with the consent of the Treasury,
- (c)   "foreign currency" means any currency other than sterling, including special drawing rights and any other units of account defined by reference to more than one currency
- (d)   whether any commitments are in sterling or foreign currency is to be determined by reference to the currency in which the amount of the commitments is measured (rather than the currency of payment) but, if the commitments are expressed to be subject to a sterling or foreign currency limit, the commitments are to be taken to be in sterling or, as the case may be, foreign currency, and
- (e)   the equivalent in special drawing rights of the amount of any commitments in foreign currency shall be ascertained at intervals determined from time to time by the Secretary of State with the consent of the Treasury and in accordance with principles so determined.

(6)   A determination under subsection (5)(e) above may provide for leaving out of account for the purposes of the limit in subsection (1)(b) or (3)(b) above any amount by which the limit would otherwise be exceeded to the extent that the amount is attributable to—

(a)   a revaluation of commitments under subsection (5)(e) above, or

(b)   the fulfilment of an undertaking which, had it been fulfilled when given, would not have caused the limit to be exceeded.

(7)   Any power to make an order under this section is exercisable only with the consent of the Treasury.

[1499]

NOTES

Sub-s (1): number in square brackets substituted by the Export and Investment Guarantees (Limit on Foreign Currency Commitments) Order 2000, SI 2000/2087, art 2.

Order: the Export and Investment Guarantees (Limit on Foreign Currency Commitments) Order 2000, SI 2000/2087.

7   Reports and returns

(1)   The Secretary of State shall prepare an annual report on the discharge of his functions under sections 1 to 5 of this Act.

(2)   The Secretary of State shall prepare, as soon as practicable after 31st March in each year, a return showing separately the aggregate amounts of the commitments in sterling and in foreign currency on that date for the purposes of the limits in section 6(1) and (3) of this Act.

(3)   Any return under this section may also give such further information as to the amounts of his commitments for the purposes of those limits as the Secretary of State may determine for that return.

(4)   ...

(5)   Reports and returns prepared under this section shall be laid before Parliament.

[1500]

NOTES

Sub-s (4): repealed by the Statute Law (Repeals) Act 2004.

PART II
TRANSFER OR DELEGATION OF ECGD FUNCTIONS

8   Scheme of transfer

(1)   The Secretary of State may make a scheme or schemes for the transfer to any person or persons of such property, rights and liabilities as are specified in or determined in accordance with the scheme, being property, rights or liabilities—

(a)   to which the Secretary of State (or, in the case of copyright, Her Majesty) is entitled or subject immediately before the day on which the scheme providing for the transfer comes into force, and

(b)   which then subsisted for the purposes of or in connection with or are otherwise attributable (wholly or partly) to the exercise of functions under Part I of this Act or the old law.

(2)   Without prejudice to the generality of subsection (1)(b) above, any property, rights or liabilities shall be taken to fall within that subsection if the Secretary of State issues a certificate to that effect.

(3)   A scheme under this section may apply—

(a)   to property wherever situated, and

(b)   to property, rights and liabilities whether or not otherwise capable of being transferred or assigned by the Secretary of State or, as the case may be, Her Majesty.

(4)   A scheme under this section shall come into force on such day as may be specified in, or determined in accordance with, the scheme; and on that day the property, rights and liabilities to which the scheme applies shall be transferred and vest in accordance with the scheme.

(5)   A scheme under this section may contain such supplementary, incidental, consequential or transitional provisions as appear to the Secretary of State to be necessary or expedient.

(6)   The Schedule to this Act (scheme of transfer: supplementary provisions) shall have effect.

(7)   References below in this Act to a transferee are to any person to whom anything is transferred by virtue of a scheme under this section.

[1501]

9 Transferred staff

(1)   No scheme under section 8 of this Act shall provide for the transfer of any rights or liabilities relating to a person's employment, but the [Transfer of Undertakings (Protection of Employment) Regulations 2006] shall apply to the transfer of property, rights or liabilities by virtue of such a scheme whether or not the transfer would, apart from this subsection, be a relevant transfer for the purposes of those regulations.

(2)   Where, by reason of the operation of those regulations in relation to a transfer of property, rights or liabilities by virtue of such a scheme, a person ceases to be employed in the civil service of the State and becomes employed by a transferee—

(a)   he shall not, on so ceasing, be treated for the purposes of any scheme under section 1 of the Superannuation Act 1972 as having retired on redundancy, and

(b)   his ceasing to be employed in that service shall not be regarded as an occasion of redundancy for the purposes of the agreed redundancy procedures applicable to persons employed in that service.

[1502]

NOTES

Sub-s (1): words in square brackets substituted, in relation to a relevant transfer that takes place on or after 6 April 2006, by the Transfer of Undertakings (Protection of Employment) Regulations 2006, SI 2006/246, reg 20(3), Sch 2, para 1(d), subject to transitional provisions and savings in reg 21 of those Regulations.

10   Vehicle companies

(1)   In this section "vehicle company" means a company formed or acquired for the purpose of—

(a)   becoming a transferee, or

(b)   holding shares in a company formed or acquired for that purpose.

(2)   Subject to subsections (3) and (4) below, the Secretary of State may—

(a)   subscribe for or otherwise acquire shares in or securities of a vehicle company, or acquire rights to subscribe for such shares or securities,

(b)   by a direction given to a company formed or acquired for the purpose of becoming a transferee require it, in consequence of the transfer by virtue of a scheme under section 8 of this Act of property, rights or liabilities, to issue to him, or to such other person as may be specified in the direction, such shares or securities as may be so specified,

(c)   from time to time by a direction given to a vehicle company require it to issue to him, or to such other person as may be specified in the direction, such shares or securities as may be so specified,

(d)   make loans to a vehicle company on such terms and conditions as he may determine.

(3)   A direction under subsection (2)(b) or (c) above may require any shares to which it relates to be issued as fully or partly paid up.

(4)   The Secretary of State shall not—

(a)   subscribe for or otherwise acquire shares in or securities of a vehicle company, or acquire rights to subscribe for such shares or securities, unless all the relevant shares are to be held by or on behalf of the Crown, or

(b)   at any time give a direction or make a loan to a vehicle company unless all the relevant shares are then held by or on behalf of the Crown.

(5)   For the purposes of subsection (4) above—

(a)   shares are held by or on behalf of the Crown where the Crown or any person acting on behalf of the Crown has a legal interest in them; and

(b)   "relevant shares", in relation to a vehicle company, means the issued shares of that company or, if it is a subsidiary of another vehicle company, the issued shares of that other company.

(6)   A scheme under section 8 of this Act may, as between any vehicle companies or as between a vehicle company and the Secretary of State, confer or impose rights and liabilities in connection with any of the matters as to which the Secretary of State may exercise his powers under this Act.

(7)   The Secretary of State shall not exercise any of the powers conferred by the preceding provisions of this section or dispose of any shares in or securities of a vehicle company without the consent of the Treasury.

[1503]

11   Reinsurance

(1)   The Secretary of State may make arrangements with any transferee under which the transferee insures the Secretary of State against risks of losses arising in consequence of arrangements made, before the day on which any scheme under section 8 of this Act comes into force, under Part I of this Act or the old law.

(2)   The Secretary of State shall from time to time determine, in relation to such classes of risk determined by him as might be insured by him under section 1 of this Act, whether it is expedient in the national interest for him to exercise his powers under that section to make arrangements for reinsuring persons providing insurance for risks of that class.

(3)   This section is without prejudice to any power of the Secretary of State under Part I of this Act.

[1504]

12 Delegation of assistance function

(1)   The Secretary of State may make arrangements for any of the functions to which this section applies to be exercised on his behalf by any transferee or any other person, instead of through the Export Credits Guarantee Department, on such terms and conditions as he may determine.

(2)   This section applies to the power of the Secretary of State to make arrangements under section 1 of this Act and to any functions of his under arrangements so made, or arrangements under the old law, including, so far as relating to any such arrangements, arrangements made by virtue of section 3(4) of this Act.

(3)   This section does not affect any requirement for the consent of the Treasury.

[1505]

PART III
GENERAL

13 The Export Credits Guarantee Department and the Export Guarantees Advisory Council

(1)   All the functions of the Secretary of State under Part I of this Act, except the power to make orders under section 5 or 6 of this Act, shall be exercised and performed through the Export Credits Guarantee Department, which shall continue to be a Department of the Secretary of State.

(2)   There shall continue to be an Export Guarantees Advisory Council.

(3)   The function of the Council shall be to give advice to the Secretary of State, at his request, in respect of ally matter relating to the exercise of his functions under this Act.

(4)   In exercising his duty under section 11(2) of this Act, the Secretary of State shall consult the Export Guarantees Advisory Council.

[1506]

14 Expenses

(1)   Any sums required by the Secretary of State for making payments or for defraying his administrative expenses under this Act shall be paid out of money provided by Parliament and any sums received by the Secretary of State by virtue of this Act shall be paid into the Consolidated Fund.

(2)   If any sum required by the Secretary of State for fulfilling his liabilities under this Act is not paid out of money provided by Parliament, it shall be charged on and paid out of the Consolidated Fund.

[1507]

15 Short title, interpretation, commencement, etc

(1)   This Act may be cited as the Export and Investment Guarantees Act 1991.

(2)   In this Act "the old law" means the Export Guarantees and Overseas Investment Act 1978 and any earlier enactment from which any provision of that Act was derived.

(3)   Any power to make an order under section 5 or 6 of this Act shall be exercisable by statutory instrument and no such order shall be made unless a draft of it has been laid before and approved by resolution of the House of Commons.

(4)   ...

(5)   Subsection (4) above does not affect any power exercisable by the Secretary of State in respect of arrangements made under the old law.

(6)   ...

[1508]

NOTES

Sub-s (4): repeals the Export Guarantees and Overseas Investment Act 1978.
Sub-s (6): repealed by the Statute Law (Repeals) Act 2004.
Order: the Export and Investment Guarantees Act 1991 (Commencement) Order 1991, SI 1991/2430.

SCHEDULE
SCHEME OF TRANSFER: SUPPLEMENTARY PROVISIONS
Section 8

Certificate of vesting

1.   A certificate by the Secretary of State that anything specified in the certificate has vested on any day in any person by virtue of a scheme under section 8 of this Act shall be conclusive evidence for all purposes of that fact.

Construction of agreements etc

2.—(1)   This paragraph applies to any agreement made, transaction effected or other thing (not contained in an enactment) which—

    (a)   has been made, effected or done by, to or in relation to the Secretary of State,

    (b)   relates to any property, right or liability transferred from the Secretary of State in accordance with the scheme, and

    (c)   is in force or effective immediately before the day on which the scheme comes into force.

(2)   The agreement, transaction or other thing shall have effect on and after that day as if made, effected or done by, to or in relation to the transferee.

(3)   Accordingly, references to the Secretary of State which relate to or affect any property, right or liability of the Secretary of State vesting by virtue of the scheme in the transferee and which are contained—

    (a)   in any agreement (whether or not in writing), deed, bond or instrument,

    (b)   in any process or other document issued, prepared or employed for the purpose of any proceeding before a court or other tribunal or authority, or

    (c)   in any other document whatever (other than an enactment) relating to or affecting any property, right or liability of the Secretary of State which vests by virtue of the scheme in the transferee,

shall be taken on and after that day to refer to the transferee.

[1509]

TIMESHARE ACT 1992

(1992 c 35)

ARRANGEMENT OF SECTIONS

An Act to provide for rights to cancel certain agreements about timeshare accommodation

[16 March 1992]

1 Application of Act

(1) In this Act—
  (a) "timeshare accommodation" means any living accommodation, in the United Kingdom or elsewhere, used or intended to be used, wholly or partly, for leisure purposes by a class of persons (referred to below in this section as "timeshare users") all of whom have rights to use, or participate in arrangements under which they may use, that accommodation, or accommodation within a pool of accommodation to which that accommodation belongs, for [a specified or ascertainable period of the year], and
  (b) "timeshare rights" means rights by virtue of which a person becomes or will become a timeshare user, being rights exercisable during a period of not less than three years.

(2) For the purposes of subsection (1)(a) above—
  (a) "accommodation" means accommodation in a building or in a caravan (as defined in section 29(1) of the Caravan Sites and Control of Development Act 1960), ...
  (b) ...

(3) Subsection (1)(b) above does not apply to a person's rights—
  (a) ...
  (b) under a contract of employment ([within the meaning of the Employment Rights Act 1996]) or a policy of insurance, ...
  (c) ...
or to such rights as may be prescribed.

[(3A) For the purposes of sections 1A to 1E, [2(2B) to (2E)], 3(3), 5A, 5B and 6A of this Act, subsection (1) above shall be construed as if in paragraph (b), after "become" there were inserted ", on payment of a global price,".]

(4) In this Act "timeshare agreement" means ... an agreement under which timeshare rights are conferred or purport to be conferred on any person and in this Act, in relation to a timeshare agreement—
  (a) references to the offeree are to the person on whom timeshare rights are conferred, or purport to be conferred, and
  (b) references to the offeror are to the other party to the agreement,
and, in relation to any time before the agreement is entered into, references in this Act to the offeree or the offeror are to the persons who become the offeree and offeror when it is entered into.

[(5) In this Act "timeshare credit agreement" means an agreement, not being a timeshare agreement, under which credit which fully or partly covers the price under a timeshare agreement is granted—
  (a) by the offeror, or
  (b) by another person, under an arrangement between that person and the offeror;
and a person who grants credit under a timeshare credit agreement is in this Act referred to as "the creditor".]

(6) ...

[(6A) No timeshare agreement or timeshare credit agreement to which this Act applies may be cancelled under section 67 of the Consumer Credit Act 1974.]

(7) This Act applies to any timeshare agreement or timeshare credit agreement if—
  (a) the agreement is to any extent governed by the law of the United Kingdom or of a part of the United Kingdom, or
  (b) when the agreement is entered into, one or both of the parties are in the United Kingdom.

[(7A) This Act also applies to any timeshare agreement if—
  (a) the relevant accommodation is situated in the United Kingdom, ...
  [(ab) the relevant accommodation is situated in another EEA State and the parties to the agreement are to any extent subject to the jurisdiction of any court in the United Kingdom in relation to the agreement, or]
  (b) when the agreement is entered into, the offeree is ordinarily resident in the United Kingdom and the relevant accommodation is situated in another EEA State.

(7B) For the purposes of subsection (7A) above, "the relevant accommodation" means—
  (a) the accommodation which is the subject of the agreement, or
  (b) some or all of the accommodation in the pool of accommodation which is the subject of the agreement,
  as the case may be.]

(8) In the application of this section to Northern Ireland—
  (a) for the reference in subsection (2)(a) above to section 29(1) of the Caravan Sites and Control of Development Act 1960 there is substituted a reference to section 25(1) of the Caravans Act (Northern Ireland) 1963, and

(b)   for the reference in subsection (3)(b) above to [the Employment Rights Act 1996] there
       is substituted a reference to article 2(2) of the Industrial Relations (Northern Ireland)
       Order 1976.

[1510]

NOTES
Sub-s (1): words in square brackets substituted by the Timeshare Regulations 1997, SI 1997/1081,
reg 2(1), (2).
Sub-ss (2), (4): words omitted repealed by SI 1997/1081, reg 14(1)–(3).
Sub-s (3): paras (a), (c) and word immediately preceding para (c) repealed by SI 1997/1081, reg 2(1), (3);
words in square brackets in para (b) substituted by the Employment Rights Act 1996, s 240, Sch 1, para 53.
Sub-s (3A): inserted by SI 1997/1081, reg 2(1), (4); words in square brackets substituted by the Timeshare
Act 1992 (Amendment) Regulations 2003, SI 2003/1922, reg 2, Schedule, para 1(1), (2).
Sub-s (5): substituted by SI 1997/1081, reg 2(1), (5).
Sub-s (6): repealed by SI 1997/1081, reg 2(1), (6).
Sub-s (6A): inserted by SI 1997/1081, reg 2(1), (7).
Sub-s (7A): inserted, together with sub-s (7B), by SI 1997/1081, reg 2(1), (8); word omitted repealed and
para (ab) inserted by SI 2003/1922, reg 2, Schedule, para 1(1), (3).
Sub-s (7B): inserted as noted to sub-s (7A).
Sub-s (8): words in square brackets in para (b) substituted by the Employment Rights Act 1996, s 240, Sch 1,
para 53.

[1A   Obligations to provide information

(1)   A person who proposes in the course of a business to enter into a timeshare agreement to
which this Act applies as offeror (an "operator") must provide any person who requests information
on the proposed accommodation with a document complying with subsection (2) below.

(2)   The document shall provide—
    (a)   a general description of the proposed accommodation,
    (b)   information (which may be brief) on the matters referred to in paragraphs (a) to (g) [and
           (i)] of Schedule 1 to this Act, ...
    [(ba) information (which may be brief) on the rights under this Act to cancel a timeshare
           agreement and the effect of cancellation on any related timeshare credit agreement to
           which this Act applies, and]
    (c)   information on how further information may be obtained.

[(2A)   In subsection (2)(ba) above "related timeshare credit agreement" means a timeshare
credit agreement under which credit which fully or partly covers the price under the timeshare
agreement is granted.]

(3)   Where an operator—
    (a)   provides a person with a document containing information on the proposed
           accommodation, and
    (b)   subsequently enters as offeror into a timeshare agreement to which this Act applies the
           subject of which is the proposed accommodation,
subsection (4) below applies.

(4)   If the offeree under the agreement is an individual who—
    (a)   is not acting in the course of a business, and
    (b)   has received the document mentioned in subsection (3) above,
any information contained in that document which was, or would on request have been, required to
be provided under section (2)(b) above shall be deemed to be a term of the agreement.

(5)   If, in a case where subsection (4) above applies, a change in the information contained in
the document is communicated to the offeree in writing before the timeshare agreement is entered
into, the change shall be deemed for the purposes of this Act always to have been incorporated in the
information contained in the document if—
    (a)   the change arises from circumstances beyond the offeror's control, or
    (b)   the offeror and the offeree expressly agree to the change before entering into the
           timeshare agreement,
and the change is expressly mentioned in the timeshare agreement.

(6)   A person who contravenes subsection (1) above is guilty of an offence and liable—
    (a)   on summary conviction, to a fine not exceeding the statutory maximum, and
    (b)   on conviction on indictment, to a fine.

(7)   In this section "the proposed accommodation" means—
    (a)   the accommodation which is the subject of the proposed agreement, or
    (b)   the accommodation in the pool of accommodation which is the subject of the proposed
           agreement,
as the case may be.

(8)   This section only applies if—

(a)   the accommodation which is the subject of the proposed agreement or agreement is accommodation in a building, or

(b)   some or all of the accommodation in the pool of accommodation which is the subject of the proposed agreement or agreement is accommodation in a building,

as the case may be.]

[1511]

NOTES
Inserted by the Timeshare Regulations 1997, SI 1997/1081, reg 3(1).
Sub-s (2): words in square brackets in para (b) substituted, word omitted repealed and para (ba) inserted by the Timeshare Act 1992 (Amendment) Regulations 2003, SI 2003/1922, reg 2, Schedule, para 2(1)–(3).
Sub-s (2A): inserted by SI 2003/1922, reg 2, Schedule, para 2(1), (4).

[1B   Advertising of timeshare rights

(1)   No person shall advertise timeshare rights in the course of a business unless the advertisement indicates the possibility of obtaining the document referred to in section 1A(1) of this Act and where it may be obtained.

(2)   A person who contravenes this section is guilty of an offence and liable—
(a)   on summary conviction, to a fine not exceeding the statutory maximum, and
(b)   on conviction on indictment, to a fine.

(3)   In proceedings against a person for an offence under this section it shall be a defence for that person to show that at the time when he advertised the timeshare rights—
(a)   he did not know and had no reasonable cause to suspect that he was advertising timeshare rights, or
(b)   he had reasonable cause to believe that the advertisement complied with the requirements of subsection (1) above.

(4)   This section only applies if—
(a)   the timeshare accommodation concerned is, or appears from the advertisement to be, accommodation in a building, or
(b)   some or all of the accommodation in the pool of accommodation concerned is, or appears from the advertisement to be, accommodation in a building,

as the case may be.]

[1512]

NOTES
Inserted by the Timeshare Regulations 1997, SI 1997/1081, reg 4.

[1C   Obligatory terms of timeshare agreement

(1)   A person must not in the course of a business enter into a timeshare agreement to which this Act applies as offeror unless the agreement includes, as terms set out in it, the information referred to in Schedule 1 to this Act.

(2)   If and to the extent that any information set out in an agreement in accordance with subsection (1) above is inconsistent with any term (the "deemed term") which is deemed to be included in the agreement under section 1A(4) of this Act, the agreement shall be treated for all purposes of this Act as if the deemed term, and not that information, were set out and included in the agreement.

(3)   A person who contravenes subsection (1) above is guilty of an offence and liable—
(a)   on summary conviction, to a fine not exceeding the statutory maximum, and
(b)   on conviction on indictment, to a fine.

(4)   This section only applies if the offeree—
(a)   is an individual, and
(b)   is not acting in the course of a business.

(5)   This section only applies if—
(a)   the accommodation which is the subject of the agreement is accommodation in a building, or
(b)   some or all of the accommodation in the pool of accommodation which is the subject of the agreement is accommodation in a building,

as the case may be.]

[1513]

NOTES
Inserted by the Timeshare Regulations 1997, SI 1997/1081, reg 5.

[1D Form of agreement and language of brochure and agreement

(1)   A person must not in the course of a business enter into a timeshare agreement to which this Act applies as offeror unless the agreement is in writing and complies with subsections (3) to (5) below, so far as applicable.

(2)   A person who is required to provide a document under subsection (1) of section 1A of this Act contravenes that subsection if he does not provide a document which complies with subsections (3) and (4) below, so far as applicable.

(3)   If the customer is resident in, or a national of, an EEA State, the agreement or document (as the case may be) must be drawn up in a language which is—
    (a)   the language, or one of the languages, of the EEA State in which he is resident, or
    (b)   the language, or one of the languages, of the EEA State of which he is a national,
and is an official language of an EEA State.

(4)   If, in a case falling within subsection (3) above, there are two or more languages in which the agreement or document may be drawn up in compliance with that subsection and the customer nominates one of those languages, the agreement or document must be drawn up in the language he nominates.

(5)   If the offeree is resident in the United Kingdom and the agreement would not, apart from this subsection, be required to be drawn up in English, it must be drawn up in English (in addition to any other language in which it is drawn up).

(6)   A person who contravenes subsection (1) above is guilty of an offence and liable—
    (a)   on summary conviction, to a fine not exceeding the statutory maximum, and
    (b)   on conviction on indictment, to a fine.

(7)   In this section "the customer" means—
    (a)   for the purposes of subsection (1) above, the offeree, and
    (b)   for the purposes of subsection (2) above, the person to whom the document is required to be provided.

(8)   Subsection (1) above only applies if the offeree—
    (a)   is an individual, and
    (b)   is not acting in the course of a business.

(9)   Subsection (1) above only applies if—
    (a)   the accommodation which is the subject of the agreement is accommodation in a building, or
    (b)   some or all of the accommodation in the pool of accommodation which is the subject of the agreement is accommodation in a building,
as the case may be.]

[1514]

NOTES
Inserted by the Timeshare Regulations 1997, SI 1997/1081, reg 6.

[1E Translation of agreement

(1)   A person must not in the course of a business enter into a timeshare agreement to which this Act applies as offeror unless he complies with subsection (2) below.

(2)   If the timeshare accommodation which is the subject of the agreement, or any of the accommodation in the pool of accommodation which is the subject of the agreement, is situated in an EEA State, the offeror must provide the offeree with a certified translation of the agreement in the language, or one of the languages, of that State.

(3)   The language of the translation must be an official language of an EEA State.

(4)   Subsection (1) above does not apply if the agreement is drawn up in a language in which the translation is required or permitted to be made.

(5)   A person who contravenes subsection (1) above is guilty of an offence and liable—
    (a)   on summary conviction, to a fine not exceeding the statutory maximum, and
    (b)   on conviction on indictment, to a fine.

(6)   In this section "certified translation" means a translation which is certified to be accurate by a person authorised to make or verify translations for the purposes of court proceedings.

(7)   This section only applies if the offeree—
    (a)   is an individual, and
    (b)   is not acting in the course of a business.

(8)   This section only applies if—
    (a)   the accommodation which is the subject of the agreement is accommodation in a building, or

(b)　some or all of the accommodation in the pool of accommodation which is the subject of the agreement is accommodation in a building,

as the case may be.]

[1515]

NOTES
　Inserted by the Timeshare Regulations 1997, SI 1997/1081, reg 7.

2 [Obligation for timeshare agreement to contain information on cancellation rights]

(1)　A person must not in the course of a business enter into a timeshare agreement to which this Act applies as offeror unless [the offeree has received the agreement and it complies with the following requirements].

(2)　[The agreement] must state—
　(a)　that the offeree is entitled to give notice of cancellation of the agreement to the offeror at any time on or before the date specified [in the agreement], being a day falling not less than fourteen days after the day on which the agreement is entered into, and
　(b)　that if the offeree gives such a notice to the offeror on or before that date he will [(subject to section 5(9) of this Act] have no further rights or obligations under the agreement, but will have the right to recover any sums paid under or in contemplation of the agreement.

[(2A)　If the agreement includes provision for providing credit for or in respect of the offeree, it must state that, notwithstanding the giving of notice of cancellation under section 5 or 5A of this Act, so far as the agreement relates to repayment of the credit and payment of interest, it will continue to be enforceable, subject to section 7 of this Act.

(2B)　Subsection (2C) below applies if—
　(a)　the price under the timeshare agreement is covered fully or partly by credit granted under a timeshare credit agreement to which this Act applies,
　(b)　the offeree is an individual, and
　(c)　the accommodation which is the subject of the timeshare agreement is accommodation in a building, or some or all of the accommodation in the pool of accommodation which is the subject of the agreement is accommodation in a building.

(2C)　The timeshare agreement must state that, if the offeree gives to the offeror a notice as mentioned in subsection (2)(b) above or a notice of cancellation of the agreement under section 5A of this Act which has the effect of cancelling the agreement—
　(a)　the notice will also have the effect of cancelling the timeshare credit agreement,
　(b)　so far as the timeshare credit agreement relates to repayment of credit and payment of interest, it shall have effect subject to section 7 of this Act, and
　(c)　subject to paragraph (b) above, the offeree will have no further rights or obligations under the timeshare credit agreement.

(2D)　Subsection (2E) below applies if—
　(a)　the offeree is an individual, and
　(b)　the accommodation which is the subject of the timeshare agreement is accommodation in a building, or some or all of the accommodation in the pool of accommodation which is the subject of the agreement is accommodation in a building.

(2E)　The agreement must state that the offeree may have, in addition to the rights mentioned in subsection (2) above, further rights under section 5A of this Act to cancel the timeshare agreement.

(2F)　The agreement must contain a blank notice of cancellation.]

(3)　A person who contravenes this section is guilty of an offence and liable—
　(a)　on summary conviction, to a fine not exceeding the statutory maximum, and
　(b)　on conviction on indictment, to a fine.

[(4)　...]

[1516]

NOTES
　Section heading: substituted by the Timeshare Act 1992 (Amendment) Regulations 2003, SI 2003/1922, reg 2, Schedule, para 3(1), (6).
　Sub-s (1): words in square brackets substituted by SI 2003/1922, reg 2, Schedule, para 3(1), (2).
　Sub-s (2): words in first pair of square brackets and words in square brackets in para (a) substituted and words in square brackets in para (b) inserted by SI 2003/1922, reg 2, Schedule, para 3(1), (3).
　Sub-ss (2A), (2B): inserted by the Timeshare Regulations 1997, SI 1997/1081, reg 8(1), (2); substituted, together with sub-ss (2C)–(2E), for original sub-ss (2A), (2B), by SI 2003/1922, reg 2, Schedule, para 3(1), (4).
　Sub-ss (2C)–(2E): substituted, together with sub-ss (2A), (2B), for original sub-ss (2A), (2B), by SI 2003/1922, reg 2, Schedule, para 3(1), (4).
　Sub-s (4): inserted by the Timeshare Regulations 1997, SI 1997/1081, reg 8(1), (2); repealed by SI 2003/1922, reg 2, Schedule, para 3(1), (5).

3 [Obligation for timeshare credit agreement to contain information on cancellation rights]

(1)   A person must not in the course of a business enter into a timeshare credit agreement to which this Act applies as creditor unless [the offeree has received the agreement and it complies with the following requirements].

(2)   [The agreement] must state—
  (a)   that the offeree is entitled to give notice of cancellation of the agreement to the creditor at any time on or before the date specified [in the agreement], being a day falling not less than fourteen days after the day on which the agreement is entered into, and
  (b)   that, if the offeree gives such a notice to the creditor on or before that date, then—
    (i)   so far as the agreement relates to repayment of credit and payment of interest, it shall have effect subject to section 7 of this Act, and
    (ii)   subject to sub-paragraph (i) above, the offeree will have no further rights or obligations under the agreement.

[(3)   [The agreement must state that it] is a timeshare credit agreement for the purposes of this Act.]

[(4)   Subsection (5) below applies if—
  (a)   the offeree is an individual, and
  (b)   the accommodation which is the subject of the timeshare agreement to which the timeshare credit agreement relates is accommodation in a building, or some or all of the accommodation in the pool of accommodation which is the subject of that timeshare agreement is accommodation in a building.

(5)   The timeshare credit agreement must state that, if the offeree gives a notice under section 5 or 5A of this Act of cancellation of the timeshare agreement which has the effect of cancelling it, the notice will also have the effect of cancelling the timeshare credit agreement (with the same consequences as mentioned in subsection (2)(b)(i) and (ii) above).

(6)   The agreement must contain a blank notice of cancellation.]

[1517]

NOTES
  Section heading: substituted by the Timeshare Act 1992 (Amendment) Regulations 2003, SI 2003/1922, reg 2, Schedule, para 4(1), (6).
  Sub-ss (1), (2): words in square brackets substituted by SI 2003/1922, reg 2, Schedule, para 4(1)–(3).
  Sub-s (3): added by the Timeshare Regulations 1997, SI 1997/1081, reg 8(3); words in square brackets substituted by SI 2003/1922, reg 2, Schedule, para 4(1), (4).
  Sub-ss (4)–(6): added by SI 2003/1922, reg 2, Schedule, para 4(1), (5).

4 Provisions supplementary to sections 2 and 3

(1)   Sections 2 and 3 of this Act do not apply where, in entering into the agreement, the offeree is acting in the course of a business.

(2)   [A timeshare agreement to which this Act applies and a timeshare credit agreement to which this Act applies must each—]
  (a)   be in such form as may be prescribed, and
  (b)   comply with such requirements (whether as to type, size, colour or disposition of lettering, quality or colour of paper, or otherwise) as may be prescribed for securing that [the matters required to be stated or contained in the agreement by virtue of section 2 or 3 are] prominent and easily legible.

(3)   An agreement is not invalidated by reason of a contravention of section 2 or 3.

[1518]

NOTES
  Sub-s (2): words in square brackets substituted by the Timeshare Act 1992 (Amendment) Regulations 2003, SI 2003/1922, reg 2, Schedule, para 5.
  Orders: the Timeshare (Cancellation Notices) Order 1992, SI 1992/1942; the Timeshare (Cancellation Information) Order 2003, SI 2003/2579.

5 Right to cancel timeshare agreement

(1)   Where a person—
  (a)   has entered, or proposes to enter, into a timeshare agreement to which this Act applies as offeree, and
  [(b)   the agreement complies with the requirements of sections 2 and 4 of this Act,]
the agreement may not be enforced against him on or before the date specified [in the agreement in pursuance of section 2(2)(a) above] and he may give notice of cancellation of the agreement to the offeror at any time on or before that date.

(2)   Subject to subsection (3) below, where[—
  (a)   a person enters into a timeshare agreement to which this Act applies as offeree, but

(b)   the agreement does not comply with the requirements of sections 2 and 4 of this Act,]
the agreement may not be enforced against him and he may give notice of cancellation of the agreement to the offeror at any time.

(3)   If in a case falling within subsection (2) above the offeree affirms the agreement at any time after the expiry of the period of fourteen days beginning with the day on which the agreement is entered into—

    (a)   subsection (2) above does not prevent the agreement being enforced against him, and

    (b)   he may not at any subsequent time give notice of cancellation of the agreement to the offeror [under subsection (2) above].

[(3A)   Where—

    (a)   the offeree is an individual, and

    (b)   the accommodation which is the subject of the agreement is accommodation in a building, or some or all of the accommodation in the pool of accommodation which is the subject of the agreement is accommodation in a building,

subsection (3) above applies as if for "fourteen days" there were substituted "three months and ten days".

(3B)   If in a case falling within subsection (3A) above the last day of the period of three months and ten days is a public holiday, the period shall not end until the end of the first working day after the public holiday.]

(4)   The offeree's giving, within the time allowed under this section [or section 5A of this Act], notice of cancellation of the agreement to the offeror at a time when the agreement has been entered into shall have the effect of cancelling the agreement.

(5)   The offeree's giving notice of cancellation of the agreement [under this section] to the offeror before the agreement has been entered into shall have the effect of withdrawing any offer to enter into the agreement.

(6)   Where a timeshare agreement is cancelled under this section [or section 5A of this Act], then, subject to subsection (9) below—

    (a)   the agreement shall cease to be enforceable, and

    (b)   subsection (8) below shall apply.

(7)   Subsection (8) below shall also apply where giving a notice of cancellation has the effect of withdrawing an offer to enter into a timeshare agreement.

(8)   Where this subsection applies—

    (a)   any sum which the offeree has paid under or in contemplation of the agreement to the offeror, or to any person who is the offeror's agent for the purpose of receiving that sum, shall be recoverable from the offeror by the offeree and shall be due and payable at the time the notice of cancellation is given, but

    (b)   no sum may be recovered by or on behalf of the offeror from the offeree in respect of the agreement.

(9)   Where a timeshare agreement includes provision for providing credit for or in respect of the offeree, then, notwithstanding the giving of notice of cancellation under this section [or section 5A of this Act], so far as the agreement relates to repayment of the credit and payment of interest—

    (a)   it shall continue to be enforceable, subject to section 7 of this Act, …

    (b)   …

[1519]

NOTES

Sub-s (1): para (b) and words in second pair of square brackets substituted by the Timeshare Act 1992 (Amendment) Regulations 2003, SI 2003/1922, reg 2, Schedule, para 6(1), (2).

Sub-s (2): words in square brackets substituted by SI 2003/1922, reg 2, Schedule, para 6(1), (3).

Sub-ss (3), (4)–(6): words in square brackets inserted by the Timeshare Regulations 1997, SI 1997/1081, reg 9(1)–(4).

Sub-ss (3A), (3B): inserted by SI 2003/1922, reg 2, Schedule, para 6(1), (4).

Sub-s (9): words in square brackets inserted by SI 1997/1081, reg 9(1), (5); words omitted repealed by SI 2003/1922, reg 2, Schedule, para 6(1), (5).

[5A   Additional right to cancel timeshare agreement

(1)   If a timeshare agreement to which this Act applies does not include, as terms set out in it, the information referred to in paragraph (a), (b), (c), (d)(i), (d)(ii), (h), (i), (k) [and (m)] of Schedule 1 to this Act, the agreement may not be enforced against the offeree before the end of the period of three months and ten days beginning with the day on which the agreement was entered into, and the offeree may give notice of cancellation of the agreement to the offeror at any time during that period.

(2)   If the information referred to in subsection (1) above is provided to the offeree before the end of the period of three months beginning with the day on which the agreement was entered into—

(a)   the offeree may give notice of cancellation of the agreement to the offeror at any time within the period of ten days beginning with the day on which the information is received by the offeree, but

(b)   the offeree may not at any subsequent time give notice of cancellation of the agreement to the offeror under subsection (1) above.

(3)   If the last day of the period referred to in subsection (1) above or the last day of the period of ten days referred to in subsection (2) above is a public holiday, the period concerned shall not end until the end of the first working day after the public holiday.

(4)   The reference in subsection (1) above to a timeshare agreement to which this Act applies includes a reference to a binding preliminary agreement.

(5)   This section only applies of the offeree—

(a)   is an individual, and

(b)   is not acting in the course of a business.

(6)   This section only applies if—

(a)   the accommodation which is the subject of the agreement is accommodation in a building, or

(b)   some or all of the accommodation in the pool of accommodation which is the subject of the agreement is accommodation in a building,

as the case may be.]

[1520]

NOTES

Inserted by the Timeshare Regulations 1997, SI 1997/1081, reg 9(6).
Sub-s (1): words in square brackets substituted by the Timeshare Act 1992 (Amendment) Regulations 2003, SI 2003/1922, reg 2, Schedule, para 7.

[5B   Advance payments]

(1)   A person who enters, or proposes to enter, in the course of a business into a timeshare agreement to which this Act applies as offeror must not (either in person or through another person) request or accept from the offeree or proposed offeree any advance payment before the end of the period during which notice of cancellation of the agreement may be given under section 5 or 5A of this Act.

(2)   A person who contravenes this section is guilty of an offence and liable—

(a)   on summary conviction, to a fine not exceeding the statutory maximum, and

(b)   on conviction on indictment, to a fine.

(3)   Subsection (1) above only applies if the offeree or proposed offeree—

(a)   is an individual, and

(b)   is not acting in the course of a business.

(4)   Subsection (1) above only applies if—

(a)   the accommodation which is the subject of the agreement or proposed agreement is accommodation in a building, or

(b)   some or all of the accommodation in the pool of accommodation which is the subject of the agreement or proposed agreement is accommodation in a building,

as the case may be.]

[1521]

NOTES

Inserted by the Timeshare Regulations 1997, SI 1997/1081, reg 10.

6   [Right to cancel timeshare credit agreement by giving notice]

(1)   Where a person—

(a)   has entered into a timeshare credit agreement to which this Act applies as offeree, and

[(b)   the agreement complies with the requirements of section 3 and 4 of this Act,]

he may give notice of cancellation of the agreement to the creditor at any time on or before the date specified [in the agreement in pursuance of section 3(2)(a) above].

(2)   Subject to subsection (3) below, where[—

(a)   a person enters into a timeshare credit agreement to which this Act applies as offeree, but

(b)   the agreement does not comply with the requirements of sections 3 and 4 of this Act,]

he may give notice of cancellation of the agreement to the creditor at any time.

(3)   If in a case falling within subsection (2) above the offeree affirms the agreement at any time after the expiry of the period of fourteen days beginning with the day on which the agreement is entered into, he may not at any subsequent time give notice of cancellation of the agreement to the creditor.

(4)   The offeree's giving, within the time allowed under this section, notice of cancellation of the agreement to the creditor at a time when the agreement has been entered into shall have the effect of cancelling the agreement.

(5)   Where a timeshare credit agreement is cancelled under this section [or section 6A of this Act]—
   (a)   the agreement shall continue in force, subject to section 7 of this Act, so far as it relates to repayment of the credit and payment of interest, and
   (b)   subject to paragraph (a) above, the agreement shall cease to be enforceable.

[1522]

NOTES
   Section heading: substituted by the Timeshare Regulations 1997, SI 1997/1081, reg 11(1).
   Sub-s (1): para (b) and words in second pair of square brackets substituted by the Timeshare Act 1992 (Amendment) Regulations 2003, SI 2003/1922, reg 2, Schedule, para 8(1), (2).
   Sub-s (2): words in square brackets substituted by SI 2003/1922, reg 2, Schedule, para 8(1), (3).
   Sub-s (5): words in square brackets inserted by SI 1997/1081, reg 11(2).

[6A   Automatic cancellation of timeshare credit agreement
   (1)   Where—
   (a)   a notice of cancellation of a timeshare agreement is given under section 5 or 5A of this Act, and
   (b)   the giving of the notice has the effect of cancelling the agreement,
the notice shall also have the effect of cancelling any related timeshare credit agreement to which this Act applies.

(2)   Where a timeshare credit agreement is cancelled as mentioned in subsection (1) above, the offeror shall, if he is not the same person as the creditor under the related timeshare credit agreement, forthwith on receipt of the notice inform the creditor that the notice has been given.

(3)   A timeshare credit agreement is related to a timeshare agreement for the purposes of this section if credit under the timeshare credit agreement fully or partly covers the price under the timeshare agreement.

(4)   Subsection (1) above only applies if the offeree under the timeshare agreement concerned is an individual.

(5)   Subsection (1) above only applies if—
   (a)   the accommodation which is the subject of the timeshare agreement is accommodation in a building, or
   (b)   some or all of the accommodation in the pool of accommodation which is the subject of the timeshare agreement is accommodation in a building,
as the case may be.]

[1523]

NOTES
   Inserted by the Timeshare Regulations 1997, SI 1997/1081, reg 11(3).

7   Repayment of credit and interest
   (1)   This section applies following—
   (a)   the giving of notice of cancellation of a timeshare agreement in accordance with section 5 of this Act in a case where subsection (9) of that section applies, …
   (b)   the giving of notice of cancellation of a timeshare credit agreement in accordance with section 6 of this Act, [or
   (c)   the cancellation of a timeshare credit agreement by virtue of section 6A of this Act.]
   (2)   If the offeree repays the whole or a portion of the credit—
   (a)   before the expiry of one month following the giving of the notice [or the cancellation of the timeshare credit agreement by virtue of section 6A of this Act (as the case may be)], or
   (b)   in the case of a credit repayable by instalments, before the date on which the first instalment is due,
no interest shall be payable on the amount repaid.

(3)   If the whole of a credit repayable by instalments is not repaid on or before the date specified in subsection (2)(b) above, the offeree shall not be liable to repay any of the credit except on receipt of a request in writing in such form as may be prescribed, signed by or on behalf of the offeror or (as

the case may be) creditor, stating the amounts of the remaining instalments (recalculated by the offeror or creditor as nearly as may be in accordance with the agreement and without extending the repayment period), but excluding any sum other than principal and interest.

[1524]

NOTES

Sub-s (1): word omitted from para (a) repealed, and para (c) and the word immediately preceding it inserted, by the Timeshare Regulations 1997, SI 1997/1081, reg 14(1), (4), (5).

Sub-s (2): words in square bracket inserted by SI 1997/1081, reg 14(1), (6).

Order: the Timeshare (Repayment of Credit on Cancellation) Order 1992, SI 1992/1943.

8 Defence of due diligence

(1)   In proceedings against a person for an offence under section [1A(6), 1B(2), 1C(3), 1D(6), 1E(5), 2(3) or 5B(2)] of this Act it shall be a defence for that person to show that he took all reasonable steps and exercised all due diligence to avoid committing the offence.

(2)   Where in proceedings against a person for such an offence the defence provided by subsection (1) above involves an allegation that the commission of the offence was due—
    (a)   to the act or default of another, or
    (b)   to reliance on information given by another,
that person shall not, without the leave of the court, be entitled to rely on the defence unless he has served a notice under subsection (3) below on the person bringing the proceedings not less than seven clear days before the hearing of the proceedings or, in Scotland, the diet of trial.

(3)   A notice under this subsection shall give such information identifying or assisting in the identification of the person who committed the act or default or gave the information as is in the possession of the person serving the notice at the time when he serves it.

[1525]

NOTES

Sub-s (1): words in square brackets substituted by the Timeshare Regulations 1997, SI 1997/1081, reg 13(1).

9   Liability of person other than principal offender

(1)   Where the commission by a person of an offence under section [1A(6), 1B(2), 1C(3), 1D(6), 1E(5), 2(3) or 5B(2)] of this Act is due to the act or default of some other person, that other person is guilty of the offence and may be proceeded against and punished by virtue of this section whether or not proceedings are taken against the first-mentioned person.

(2)   Where a body corporate is guilty of an offence under section [1A(6), 1B(2), 1C(3), 1D(6), 1E(5), 2(3) or 5B(2)] of this Act (including where it is so guilty by virtue of subsection (1) above) in respect of an act or default which is shown to have been committed with the consent or connivance of, or to be attributable to neglect on the part of, a director, manager, secretary or other similar officer of the body corporate or a person who was purporting to act in such a capacity, he (as well as the body corporate) is guilty of the offence and liable to be proceeded against and punished accordingly.

(3)   Where the affairs of a body corporate are managed by its members, subsection (2) above applies in relation to the acts and defaults of a member in connection with his functions of management as if he were a director of the body corporate.

(4)   (*Applies to Scotland only.*)

[1526]

NOTES

Sub-ss (1), (2): words in square brackets substituted by the Timeshare Regulations 1997, SI 1997/1081, reg 13(2).

10   Enforcement

[Schedule 2] to this Act (which makes provision about enforcement) shall have effect.

[1527]

NOTES

Words in square brackets substituted by the Timeshare Regulations 1997, SI 1997/1081, reg 14(1), (7).

[10A   Civil proceedings

(1)   The obligation to comply with subsection (1) of section 1A of this Act shall be a duty owed by the person who proposes to enter into a timeshare agreement to any person whom he is required to provide with a document under that subsection and a contravention of the obligation shall be actionable accordingly.

(2)   The obligation to comply with section 1C(1), 1D(1), [1E(1), and 2(1)] of this Act shall in each case be a duty owed by the person who enters into a timeshare agreement as offeror to the offeree and a contravention of the obligation shall be actionable accordingly.

(3)   The obligation to comply with section 6A(2) of this Act shall be a duty owed by the offeror under the timeshare agreement to the creditor under the related timeshare credit agreement and a contravention of the obligation shall be actionable accordingly.]

[1528]

NOTES

Inserted by the Timeshare Regulations 1997, SI 1997/1081, reg 12.

Sub-s (2): words in square brackets substituted by the Timeshare Act 1992 (Amendment) Regulations 2003, SI 2003/1922, reg 2, Schedule, para 9.

11   Prosecution time limit

(1)   No proceedings for an offence under section [1A(6), 1B(2), 1C(3), 1D(6), 1E(5), 2(3) or 5B(2)] of this Act or paragraph 4(3) … to this Act shall be commenced after—

  (a)   the end of the period of three years beginning with the date of the commission of the offence, or

  (b)   the end of the period of one year beginning with the date of the discovery of the offence by the prosecutor,

whichever is the earlier.

(2)   For the purposes of this section a certificate signed by or on behalf of the prosecutor and stating the date on which the offence was discovered by him shall be conclusive evidence of that fact; and a certificate stating that matter and purporting to be so signed shall be treated as so signed unless the contrary is proved.

(3)   (*Applies to Scotland only.*)

[1529]

NOTES

Sub-s (1): words in square brackets substituted by the Timeshare Regulations 1997, SI 1997/1081, regs 13(3); words omitted repealed by the Enterprise Act 2002 (Part 9 Restrictions on Disclosure of Information) (Amendment and Specification) Order 2003, SI 2003/1400, art 7, Sch 5.

12   General provisions

(1)   For the purposes of this Act, a notice of cancellation of an agreement is a notice (however expressed) showing that the offeree wishes unconditionally to cancel the agreement, whether or not it is in a prescribed form.

(2)   The rights conferred and duties imposed by sections [1A] to 7 of this Act are in addition to any rights conferred or duties imposed by or under any other Act.

(3)   For the purposes of this Act, if the offeree sends a notice by post in a properly addressed and pre-paid letter the notice is to be treated as given at the time of posting.

(4)   This Act shall have effect in relation to any timeshare agreement or timeshare credit agreement notwithstanding any agreement or notice.

(5)   …

(6)   In this Act—

  "credit" includes a cash loan and any other form of financial accommodation,

  ["EEA State" means a State which is a Contracting Party to the Agreement on the European Economic Area signed at Oporto on 2nd May 1992 as adjusted by the Protocol signed at Brussels on 17th March 1993,]

  "notice" means notice in writing,

  "order" means an order made by the Secretary of State, and

  "prescribed" means prescribed by an order.

(7)   An order under this Act may make different provision for different cases or circumstances.

(8)   Any power under this Act to make an order shall be exercisable by statutory instrument and a statutory instrument containing an order under this Act (other than an order made for the purposes of section 13(2) of this Act) shall be subject to annulment in pursuance of a resolution of either House of Parliament.

[1530]

NOTES

Sub-s (2): number in square brackets substituted by the Timeshare Regulations 1997, SI 1997/1081, reg 14(1), (9).

Sub-s (5): repealed by SI 1997/1081, reg 14(1), (10).

Sub-s (6): definition "EEA State" inserted by SI 1997/1081, reg 2(1), (9).

Orders: the Timeshare Act 1992 (Commencement) Order 1992, SI 1992/1941; the Timeshare (Cancellation Notices) Order 1992, SI 1992/1942; the Timeshare (Repayment of Credit on Cancellation) Order 1992, SI 1992/1943.

13 Short title, etc

(1) This Act may be cited as the Timeshare Act 1992.

(2) This Act shall come into force on such day as may be prescribed.

(3) This Act extends to Northern Ireland.

[1531]

NOTES

Order: the Timeshare Act 1992 (Commencement) Order 1992, SI 1992/1941.

SCHEDULES

[SCHEDULE 1

MINIMUM LIST OF ITEMS TO BE INCLUDED IN A TIMESHARE AGREEMENT TO WHICH SECTION 1C APPLIES

Regulations 1A(2), 1C(1), 5A(1)

(a) The identities and domiciles of the parties, including specific information on the offeror's legal status at the time of the conclusion of the agreement and the identity and domicile of the owner.

(b) The exact nature of the right which is the subject of the agreement and, if the accommodation concerned, or any of the accommodation in the pool of accommodation concerned, is situated in the territory of an EEA State, a clause setting out the conditions governing the exercise of that right within the territory of that State and if those conditions have been fulfilled or, if they have not, what conditions remain to be fulfilled.

(c) When the timeshare accommodation has been determined, an accurate description of that accommodation and its location.

(d) Where the timeshare accommodation is under construction—
   (i) the state of completion,
   (ii) a reasonable estimate of the deadline for completion of the timeshare accommodation,
   (iii) where it concerns specific timeshare accommodation, the number of the building permit and the name and full address of the competent authority or authorities,
   (iv) the state of completion of the services rendering the timeshare accommodation fully operational (gas, electricity, water and telephone connections),
   (v) a guarantee regarding completion of the timeshare accommodation or a guarantee regarding reimbursement of any payment made if the accommodation is not completed and, where appropriate, the conditions governing the operation of those guarantees.

(e) The services (lighting, water, maintenance, refuse collection) to which the offeree has or will have access and on what conditions.

(f) The common facilities, such as swimming pool, sauna, etc, to which the offeree has or may have access, and where appropriate, on what conditions.

(g) The principles on the basis of which the maintenance of and repairs to the timeshare accommodation and its administration and management will be arranged.

(h) The exact period within which the right which is the subject of the agreement may be exercised and, if necessary, its duration; the date on which the offeree may start to exercise that right.

(i) The price to be paid by the offeree to exercise the right under the agreement; an estimate of the amount to be paid by the offeree for the use of common facilities and services; the basis for the calculation of the amount of charges relating to occupation of the timeshare accommodation, the mandatory statutory charges (for example, taxes and fees) and the administrative overheads (for example, management, maintenance and repairs).

(j) A clause stating that acquisitions will not result in costs, charges or obligations other than those specified in the agreement.

(k) Whether or not it is possible to join a scheme for the exchange or resale of the rights under the agreement, and any costs involved should an exchange or resale scheme be organised by the offeror or by a third party designated by him in the agreement.

(l) ...

(m) The date and place of each party's signing of the agreement.]

[1532]

NOTES
  Inserted by the Timeshare Regulations 1997, SI 1997/1081, reg 3(3).
  Para (1) repealed by the Timeshare Act 1992 (Amendment) Regulations 2003, SI 2003/1922, reg 2, Schedule, para 10.

SCHEDULE [2]
ENFORCEMENT

Section 10

Enforcement authority

1.—(1) Every local weights and measures authority in Great Britain shall be an enforcement authority for the purposes of this Schedule, and it shall be the duty of each such authority to enforce the provisions of this Act within their area.

(2) The Department of Economic Development in Northern Ireland shall be an enforcement authority for the purposes of this Schedule, and it shall be the duty of the Department to enforce the provisions of this Act within Northern Ireland.

2. …

Powers of officers of enforcement authority

3.—(1) If a duly authorised officer of an enforcement authority has reasonable grounds for suspecting that an offence under [any of sections 1A to 2 or 5B] of this Act has been committed, he may—

  (a) require a person carrying on or employed in a business to produce any book or document relating to the business, and take copies of it or any entry in it, or

  (b) require such a person to produce in a visible and legible documentary form [or from which it can readily be produced in a visible and legible form] any information so relating which is [stored in any electronic form], and take copies of it,

for the purposes of ascertaining whether any such an offence has been committed.

(2) If such an officer has reasonable grounds for believing that any documents may be required as evidence in proceedings for such an offence, he may seize and detain them and shall, if he does so, inform the person from whom they are seized.

(3) The powers of an officer under this paragraph may be exercised by him only at a reasonable hour and on production (if required) of his credentials.

(4) Nothing in this paragraph requires a person to produce, or authorises the taking from a person of, a document which he could not be compelled to produce in civil proceedings before the High Court or (in Scotland) the Court of Session.

4.—(1) A person who—

  (a) intentionally obstructs an officer of an enforcement authority acting in pursuance of this Schedule,

  (b) without reasonable excuse fails to comply with a requirement made of him by such an officer under paragraph 3(1) above, or

  (c) without reasonable excuse fails to give an officer of an enforcement authority acting in pursuance of this Schedule any other assistance or information which the officer has reasonably required of him for the purpose of the performance of the officer's functions under this Schedule,

is guilty of an offence.

(2) A person guilty of an offence under sub-paragraph (1) above is liable on summary conviction to a fine not exceeding level 5 on the standard scale.

(3) If a person, in giving information to an officer of an enforcement authority who is acting in pursuance of this Schedule—

  (a) makes a statement which he knows is false in a material particular, or

  (b) recklessly makes a statement which is false in a material particular,

he is guilty of an offence.

(4) A person guilty of an offence under sub-paragraph (3) above is liable—

  (a) on summary conviction, to a fine not exceeding the statutory maximum, and

  (b) on conviction on indictment, to a fine.

5. …

Privilege against self-incrimination

6. Nothing in this Schedule requires a person to answer any question or give any information if to do so might incriminate him.

NOTES

The original Schedule to this Act was renumbered as Sch 2 by the Timeshare Regulations 1997, SI 1997/1081, reg 3(2).

Para 2: sub-para (1) repealed by the Enterprise Act 2002, s 278(2), Sch 26; sub-para (2) applies to Scotland only.

Para 3: words in first pair of square brackets substituted by SI 1997/1081, reg 13(4); words in second pair of square brackets inserted, and words in third pair of square brackets substituted, by the Criminal Justice and Police Act 2001, s 70, Sch 2, Pt 2, para 20.

Para 5: repealed by the Enterprise Act 2002, ss 247(i), 278(2), Sch 26.

Seize and detain: the powers of seizure conferred by para 3 are powers to which the Criminal Justice and Police Act 2001, s 50 apply (additional powers of seizure from premises); see s 50 of, and Sch 1, Pt 1, para 56 to, that Act.

CARRIAGE OF GOODS BY SEA ACT 1992

(1992 c 50)

ARRANGEMENT OF SECTIONS

An Act to replace the Bills of Lading Act 1855 with new provision with respect to bills of lading and certain other shipping documents

[16 July 1992]

1   Shipping documents etc to which Act applies

(1)   This Act applies to the following documents, that is to say—

    (a)   any bill of lading;

    (b)   any sea waybill; and

    (c)   any ship's delivery order.

(2)   References in this Act to a bill of lading—

    (a)   do not include references to a document which is incapable of transfer either by indorsement or, as a bearer bill, by delivery without indorsement; but

    (b)   subject to that, do include references to a received for shipment bill of lading.

(3)   References in this Act to a sea waybill are references to any document which is not a bill of lading but—

    (a)   is such a receipt for goods as contains or evidences a contract for the carriage of goods by sea; and

    (b)   identifies the person to whom delivery of the goods is to be made by the carrier in accordance with that contract.

(4)   References in this Act to a ship's delivery order are references to any document which is neither a bill of lading nor a sea waybill but contains an undertaking which—

    (a)   is given under or for the purposes of a contract for the carriage by sea of the goods to which the document relates, or of goods which include those goods; and

    (b)   is an undertaking by the carrier to a person identified in the document to deliver the goods to which the document relates to that person.

(5)   The Secretary of State may by regulations make provision for the application of this Act to cases where [an electronic communications network] or any other information technology is used for effecting transactions corresponding to—

    (a)   the issue of a document to which this Act applies;

    (b)   the indorsement, delivery or other transfer of such a document; or

    (c)   the doing of anything else in relation to such a document.

(6)   Regulations under subsection (5) above may—

    (a)   make such modifications of the following provisions of this Act as the Secretary of State considers appropriate in connection with the application of this Act to any case mentioned in that subsection; and

    (b)   contain supplemental, incidental, consequential and transitional provision;

and the power to make regulations under that subsection shall be exercisable by statutory instrument subject to annulment in pursuance of a resolution of either House of Parliament.

[1534]

NOTES

Sub-s (5): words in square brackets substituted by the Communications Act 2003, s 406(1), Sch 17, para 119.

2   Rights under shipping documents

(1)   Subject to the following provisions of this section, a person who becomes—
- (a)   the lawful holder of a bill of lading;
- (b)   the person who (without being an original party to the contract of carriage) is the person to whom delivery of the goods to which a sea waybill relates is to be made by the carrier in accordance with that contract; or
- (c)   the person to whom delivery of the goods to which a ship's delivery order relates is to be made in accordance with the undertaking contained in the order,

shall (by virtue of becoming the holder of the bill or, as the case may be, the person to whom delivery is to be made) have transferred to and vested in him all rights of suit under the contract of carriage as if he had been a party to that contract.

(2)   Where, when a person becomes the lawful holder of a bill of lading, possession of the bill no longer gives a right (as against the carrier) to possession of the goods to which the bill relates, that person shall not have any rights transferred to him by virtue of subsection (1) above unless he becomes the holder of the bill—
- (a)   by virtue of a transaction effected in pursuance of any contractual or other arrangements made before the time when such a right to possession ceased to attach to possession of the bill; or
- (b)   as a result of the rejection to that person by another person of goods or documents delivered to the other person in pursuance of any such arrangements.

(3)   The rights vested in any person by virtue of the operation of subsection (1) above in relation to a ship's delivery order—
- (a)   shall be so vested subject to the terms of the order; and
- (b)   where the goods to which the order relates form a part only of the goods to which the contract of carriage relates, shall be confined to rights in respect of the goods to which the order relates.

(4)   Where, in the case of any document to which this Act applies—
- (a)   a person with any interest or right in or in relation to goods to which the document relates sustains loss or damage in consequence of a breach of the contract of carriage; but
- (b)   subsection (1) above operates in relation to that document so that rights of suit in respect of that breach are vested in another person,

the other person shall be entitled to exercise those rights for the benefit of the person who sustained the loss or damage to the same extent as they could have been exercised if they had been vested in the person for whose benefit they are exercised.

(5)   Where rights are transferred by virtue of the operation of subsection (1) above in relation to any document, the transfer for which that subsection provides shall extinguish any entitlement to those rights which derives—
- (a)   where that document is a bill of lading, from a person's having been an original party to the contract of carriage; or
- (b)   in the case of any document to which this Act applies, from the previous operation of that subsection in relation to that document;

but the operation of that subsection shall be without prejudice to any rights which derive from a person's having been an original party to the contract contained in, or evidenced by, a sea waybill and, in relation to a ship's delivery order, shall be without prejudice to any rights deriving otherwise than from the previous operation of that subsection in relation to that order.

[1535]

3   Liabilities under shipping documents

(1)   Where subsection (1) of section 2 of this Act operates in relation to any document to which this Act applies and the person in whom rights are vested by virtue of that subsection—
- (a)   takes or demands delivery from the carrier of any of the goods to which the document relates;
- (b)   makes a claim under the contract of carriage against the carrier in respect of any of those goods; or
- (c)   is a person who, at a time before those rights were vested in him, took or demanded delivery from the carrier of any of those goods,

that person shall (by virtue of taking or demanding delivery or making the claim or, in a case falling within paragraph (c) above, of having the rights vested in him) become subject to the same liabilities under that contract as if he had been a party to that contract.

(2)   Where the goods to which a ship's delivery order relates form a part only of the goods to which the contract of carriage relates, the liabilities to which any person is subject by virtue of the operation of this section in relation to that order shall exclude liabilities in respect of any goods to which the order does not relate.

(3)   This section, so far as it imposes liabilities under any contract on any person, shall be without prejudice to the liabilities under the contract of any person as an original party to the contract.

[1536]

4   Representations in bills of lading

A bill of lading which—

(a)   represents goods to have been shipped on board a vessel or to have been received for shipment on board a vessel; and

(b)   has been signed by the master of the vessel or by a person who was not the master but had the express, implied or apparent authority of the carrier to sign bills of lading,

shall, in favour of a person who has become the lawful holder of the bill, be conclusive evidence against the carrier of the shipment of the goods or, as the case may be, of their receipt for shipment.

[1537]

5   Interpretation

(1)   In this Act—

"bill of lading", "sea waybill" and "ship's delivery order" shall be construed in accordance with section 1 above;

"the contract of carriage"—

(a)   in relation to a bill of lading or sea waybill, means the contract contained in or evidenced by that bill or waybill; and

(b)   in relation to a ship's delivery order, means the contract under or for the purposes of which the undertaking contained in the order is given;

"holder", in relation to a bill of lading, shall be construed in accordance with subsection (2) below;

"information technology" includes any computer or other technology by means of which information or other matter may be recorded or communicated without being reduced to documentary form; …

.....

(2)   References in this Act to the holder of a bill of lading are references to any of the following persons, that is to say—

(a)   a person with possession of the bill who, by virtue of being the person identified in the bill, is the consignee of the goods to which the bill relates;

(b)   a person with possession of the bill as a result of the completion, by delivery of the bill, of any indorsement of the bill or, in the case of a bearer bill, of any other transfer of the bill;

(c)   a person with possession of the bill as a result of any transaction by virtue of which he would have become a holder falling within paragraph (a) or (b) above had not the transaction been effected at a time when possession of the bill no longer gave a right (as against the carrier) to possession of the goods to which the bill relates;

and a person shall be regarded for the purposes of this Act as having become the lawful holder of a bill of lading wherever he has become the holder of the bill in good faith.

(3)   References in this Act to a person's being identified in a document include references to his being identified by a description which allows for the identity of the person in question to be varied, in accordance with the terms of the document, after its issue; and the reference in section 1(3)(b) of this Act to a document's identifying a person shall be construed accordingly.

(4)   Without prejudice to sections 2(2) and 4 above, nothing in this Act shall preclude its operation in relation to a case where the goods to which a document relates—

(a)   cease to exist after the issue of the document; or

(b)   cannot be identified (whether because they are mixed with other goods or for any other reason);

and references in this Act to the goods to which a document relates shall be construed accordingly.

(5)   The preceding provisions of this Act shall have effect without prejudice to the application, in relation to any case, of the rules (the Hague-Visby Rules) which for the time being have the force of law by virtue of section 1 of the Carriage of Goods by Sea Act 1971.

[1538]

NOTES

Sub-s (1): definition "telecommunication system" (omitted) and the word "and" immediately preceding it repealed by the Communications Act 2003, s 406(7), Sch 19(1).

6   Short title, repeal, commencement and extent

(1)   This Act may be cited as the Carriage of Goods by Sea Act 1992.

(2)   ...

(3)   This Act shall come into force at the end of the period of two months beginning with the day on which it is passed; but nothing in this Act shall have effect in relation to any document issued before the coming into force of this Act.

(4)   This Act extends to Northern Ireland.

[1539]

NOTES

Sub-s (2): repeals the Bills of Lading Act 1855.

REINSURANCE (ACTS OF TERRORISM) ACT 1993

(1993 c 18)

An Act to provide for the payment out of money provided by Parliament or into the Consolidated Fund of sums referable to reinsurance liabilities entered into by the Secretary of State in respect of loss or damage to property resulting from or consequential upon acts of terrorism and losses consequential on such loss or damage

[27 May 1993]

1   Financing of reinsurance obligations of the [Treasury]

(1)   There shall be paid out of money provided by Parliament such sums as may be necessary to enable the [Treasury] to meet [their] obligations under—

    (a)   any agreement of reinsurance which ... is entered into (whether before or after the passing of this Act) pursuant to arrangements to which this Act applies, or

    (b)   any guarantee which ... is entered into (whether before or after that passing) pursuant to any such agreement.

(2)   As soon as practicable after the passing of this Act or, if it is later, after [they enter] into the agreement or guarantee, the [Treasury] shall lay before each House of Parliament a copy of any agreement or guarantee falling within subsection (1) above.

(3)   There shall be paid into the Consolidated Fund any sums received by the [Treasury] pursuant to any arrangements to which this Act applies.

[1540]

NOTES

Words in square brackets substituted, and words omitted repealed, by the Transfer of Functions (Insurance) Order 1997, SI 1997/2781, art 8, Schedule, paras 120–122.

2   Reinsurance arrangements to which this Act applies

(1)   This Act applies to arrangements under which the [Treasury] ... [undertake] to any extent the liability of reinsuring risks against—

    (a)   loss of or damage to property in Great Britain resulting from or consequential upon acts of terrorism; and

    (b)   any loss which is consequential on loss or damage falling within paragraph (a) above;

and to the extent that the arrangements relate to events occurring before as well as after an agreement of reinsurance comes into being, the reference in section 1(1) above to the obligations of the [Treasury] shall be construed accordingly.

(2)   In this section "acts of terrorism" means acts of persons acting on behalf of, or in connection with, any organisation which carries out activities directed towards the overthrowing or influencing, by force or violence, of Her Majesty's government in the United Kingdom or any other government de jure or de facto.

(3)   In subsection (2) above "organisation" includes any association or combination of persons.

[1541]

3 Citation and extent

(1) This Act may be cited as the Reinsurance (Acts of Terrorism) Act 1993.

(2) This Act does not extend to Northern Ireland.

[1542]

SUNDAY TRADING ACT 1994

(1994 c 20)

ARRANGEMENT OF SECTIONS

An Act to reform the law of England and Wales relating to Sunday trading; to make provision as to the rights of shop workers under the law of England and Wales in relation to Sunday working; and for connected purposes

[5 July 1994]

1 Reform of law relating to Sunday trading

(1) Schedules 1 and 2 to this Act shall come into force on such day as the Secretary of State may by order made by statutory instrument appoint (in this section referred to as "the appointed day").

(2) ...

[1542A]

2 Loading and unloading at large shops on Sunday morning

(1) A local authority may by resolution designate their area as a loading control area for the purposes of this section with effect from a date specified in the resolution, which must be a date at least one month after the date on which the resolution is passed.

(2) A local authority may by resolution revoke any designation made by them under subsection (1) above.

(3) It shall be the duty of a local authority, before making or revoking any designation under subsection (1) above, to consult persons appearing to the local authority to be likely to be affected by the proposed designation or revocation (whether as the occupiers of shops or as local residents) or persons appearing to the local authority to represent such persons.

(4) Where a local authority make or revoke a designation under this section, they shall publish notice of the designation or revocation in such manner as they consider appropriate.

(5) Schedule 3 to this Act (which imposes restrictions on loading and unloading on Sunday before 9 am at large shops in loading control areas) shall have effect.

[1542B]

3 Construction of certain leases and agreements

(1)   Where any lease or agreement (however worded) entered into before the commencement of this section has the effect of requiring the occupier of a shop to keep the shop open for the serving of retail customers—

(a)   during normal business hours, or

(b)   during hours to be determined otherwise than by or with the consent of the occupier,

that lease or agreement shall not be regarded as requiring, or as enabling any person to require, the occupier to open the shop on Sunday for the serving of retail customers.

(2)   Subsection (1) above shall not affect any lease or agreement—

(a)   to the extent that it relates specifically to Sunday and would (apart from this section) have the effect of requiring Sunday trading of a kind which before the commencement of this section would have been lawful by virtue of any provision of Part IV of the Shops Act 1950, or

(b)   to the extent that it is varied by agreement after the commencement of this section.

(3)   In this section "retail customer" and "shop" have the same meaning as in Schedule 1 to this Act.

[1542C]

4 Rights of shop workers as respects Sunday working

Schedule 4 to this Act shall have effect.

[1542D]

5   *(Repealed by the Deregulation and Contracting Out Act 1994, s 81(1), Sch 17.)*

6 Consequential repeal or amendment of local Acts

(1)   The Secretary of State may by order made by statutory instrument—

(a)   repeal any provision of a local Act passed before or in the same Session as this Act if it appears to him that the provision is inconsistent with or has become unnecessary in consequence of any provision of this Act, and

(b)   amend any provision of such a local Act if it appears to him that the provision requires amendment in consequence of any provision of this Act or any repeal made by virtue of paragraph (a) above.

(2)   It shall be the duty of the Secretary of State, before he makes an order under subsection (1) above repealing or amending any provision of a local Act, to consult each local authority which he considers would be affected by the repeal or amendment of that provision.

(3)   A statutory instrument containing an order under subsection (1) above shall be subject to annulment in pursuance of a resolution of either House of Parliament.

[1542E]

7 Expenses

There shall be paid out of money provided by Parliament any increase attributable to this Act in the sums payable out of such money under any other Act.

[1542F]

8 Meaning of "local authority"

(1)   In this Act "local authority" means any unitary authority or any district council so far as they are not a unitary authority.

(2)   In subsection (1) above "unitary authority" means—

(a)   the council of any county so far as they are the council for an area for which there are no district councils,

(b)   the council of any district comprised in an area for which there is no county council,

(c)   a county borough council,

(d)   a London borough council,

(e)   the Common Council of the City of London, or

(f)   the Council of the Isles of Scilly.

(3)   Until 1st April 1996, the definition of "unitary authority" in subsection (2) above shall have effect with the omission of paragraph (c).

[1542G]

9 Short title, repeals, commencement and extent

(1)   This Act may be cited as the Sunday Trading Act 1994.

(2)   The enactments mentioned in Schedule 5 to this Act are hereby repealed to the extent specified in the third column of that Schedule.

(3)   The following provisions of this Act—

sections 2 to 5,
subsection (2) of this section, and
Schedules 3, 4 and 5,
shall not come into force until the appointed day (as defined in section 1 above).

(4)   This Act extends to England and Wales only.

[1542H]

SCHEDULE 1
RESTRICTIONS ON SUNDAY OPENING OF LARGE SHOPS
Section 1(1)

Interpretation

1.   In this Schedule—
["alcohol" has the same meaning as in the Licensing Act 2003,]
"large shop" means a shop which has a relevant floor area exceeding 280 square metres,
"medicinal product" and "registered pharmacy" have the same meaning as in the Medicines
Act 1968,
"relevant floor area", in relation to a shop, means the internal floor area of so much of the shop
as consists of or is comprised in a building, but excluding any part of the shop which,
throughout the week ending with the Sunday in question, is used neither for the serving of
customers in connection with the sale of goods nor for the display of goods,
"retail customer" means a person who purchases goods retail,
"retail sale" means any sale other than a sale for use or resale in the course of a trade or
business, and references to retail purchase shall be construed accordingly,
"sale of goods" does not include—
(a)   the sale of meals, refreshments or [alcohol] for consumption on the premises on
which they are sold, or
(b)   the sale of meals or refreshments prepared to order for immediate consumption
off those premises,
"shop" means any premises where there is carried on a trade or business consisting wholly or
mainly of the sale of goods, and
"stand", in relation to an exhibition, means any platform, structure, space or other area
provided for exhibition purposes;
["veterinary medicinal product" has the same meaning as in regulation 2 of the Veterinary
Medicines Regulations 2006].

[Restrictions on Sunday opening hours of large shops]

2.—(1)   Subject to sub-paragraphs (2) and (3) below, a large shop shall not be open on Sunday for
the serving of retail customers.

(2)   Sub-paragraph (1) above does not apply in relation to—
(a)   any of the shops mentioned in paragraph 3(1) below, or
(b)   any shop in respect of which a notice under paragraph 8(1) of Schedule 2 to this Act
(shops occupied by persons observing the Jewish Sabbath) has effect.

[(3)   Sub-paragraph (1) above does not apply in relation to the opening of a large shop during
any continuous period of six hours on a Sunday beginning no earlier than 10 am and ending no later
than 6 pm, but this sub-paragraph has effect subject to sub-paragraph (4) below.]

(4)   The exemption conferred by sub-paragraph (3) above does not apply where the Sunday is
Easter Day ...

[(5)   Nothing in this paragraph applies where the Sunday is Christmas Day (the opening of large
shops on Christmas Day being prohibited by section 1 of the Christmas Day (Trading) Act 2004).]

Exemptions

3.—(1)   The shops referred to in paragraph 2(2)(a) above are—
(a)   any shop which is at a farm and where the trade or business carried on consists wholly or
mainly of the sale of produce from that farm,
(b)   any shop where the trade or business carried on consists wholly or mainly of the sale of
[alcohol],
(c)   any shop where the trade or business carried on consists wholly or mainly of the sale of
any one or more of the following—
(i)   motor supplies and accessories, and
(ii)   cycle supplies and accessories,
(d)   any shop which—
(i)   is a registered pharmacy, and
(ii)   is not open for the retail sale of any goods other than medicinal products[,
veterinary medicinal products] and medical and surgical appliances,

(e) any shop at a designated airport which is situated in a part of the airport to which sub-paragraph (3) below applies,

(f) any shop in a railway station,

(g) any shop at a service area within the meaning of the Highways Act 1980,

(h) any petrol filling station,

(j) any shop which is not open for the retail sale of any goods other than food, stores or other necessaries required by any person for a vessel or aircraft on its arrival at, or immediately before its departure from, a port, harbour or airport, and

(k) any stand used for the retail sale of goods during the course of an exhibition.

(2) In determining whether a shop falls within sub-paragraph (1)(a), (b) or (c) above, regard shall be had to the nature of the trade or business carried on there on weekdays as well as to the nature of the trade or business carried on there on Sunday.

(3) This sub-paragraph applies to every part of a designated airport, except any part which is not ordinarily used by persons travelling by air to or from the airport.

(4) In this paragraph "designated airport" means an airport designated for the purposes of this paragraph by an order made by the Secretary of State, as being an airport at which there appears to him to be a substantial amount of international passenger traffic.

(5) The power to make an order under sub-paragraph (4) above shall be exercisable by statutory instrument.

(6) Any order made under section 1(2) of the Shops (Airports) Act 1962 and in force at the commencement of this Schedule shall, so far as it relates to England and Wales, have effect as if made also under sub-paragraph (4) above, and may be amended or revoked as it has effect for the purposes of this paragraph by an order under sub-paragraph (4) above.

4, 5. ....

Duty to display notice

6. At any time when—

(a) a large shop is open on Sunday for the serving of retail customers, and

(b) the prohibition in sub-paragraph (1) of paragraph 2 above is excluded only by sub-paragraph (3) of that paragraph,

a notice specifying [the Sunday opening hours] shall be displayed in a conspicuous position inside and outside the shop.

Offences

7.—(1) If paragraph 2(1) above is contravened in relation to a shop, the occupier of the shop shall be liable on summary conviction to a fine not exceeding £50,000.

(2) If paragraph 6 above is contravened in relation to a shop, the occupier of the shop shall be liable on summary conviction to a fine not exceeding level 2 on the standard scale.

[8. Where a person is charged with having contravened paragraph 2(1) above, in relation to a large shop which was permitted to be open for the serving of retail customers on the Sunday in question, by reason of his having served a retail customer after the end of the period during which the shop is permitted to be open by virtue of paragraph 2(3) above, it shall be a defence to prove that the customer was in the shop before the end of that period and left not later than half an hour after the end of that period.]

9. ....

NOTES

Para 1: definition "alcohol" substituted, for original definition "intoxicating liquor", and in definition "sale of goods" word in square brackets in para (a) substituted by the Licensing Act 2003, s 198(1), Sch 6, para 110(1), (2); definition "veterinary medicinal product" inserted by the Veterinary Medicines Regulations 2006, SI 2006/2407, reg 44(3), Sch 9, Pt 1, para 9(a).

Para 2: heading and sub-para (3) substituted by the Regulatory Reform (Sunday Trading) Order 2004, SI 2004/470, art 2(1), (2)(a), (b); words omitted from sub-para (4) repealed and sub-para (5) inserted by the Christmas Day (Trading) Act 2004, s 4(1), (2).

Para 3: in sub-para (1)(b) word in square brackets substituted by the Licensing Act 2003, s 198(1), Sch 6, para 110(1), (3); in sub-para (1)(d)(ii) words in square brackets inserted by SI 2006/2407, reg 44(3), Sch 9, Pt 1, para 9(b).

Paras 4, 5, 9: repealed by SI 2004/470, art 2(1), (2)(c), (f).

Para 6: words in square brackets substituted by SI 2004/470, art 2(1), (2)(d).

Para 8: substituted by SI 2004/470, art 2(1), (2)(e).

See further, in relation to the disapplication of para 2(1) above to large shops in the terminal area of the Channel Tunnel: the Channel Tunnel (Sunday Trading Act 1994) (Disapplication) Order 1994, SI 1994/3286, art 3.

See further, in relation to the application of para 3(2) above and the definition "relevant floor area" in para 1 above, with modifications, for the purposes of the Christmas Day (Trading) Act 2004, s 1: the Christmas Day (Trading) Act 2004, s 1(4), (5).

SCHEDULE 2
SUPPLEMENTARY PROVISIONS

Section 1(1)

PART I
GENERAL ENFORCEMENT PROVISIONS

Duty to enforce Act

1.   It shall be the duty of every local authority to enforce within their area the provisions of Schedules 1 and 3 to this Act and Part II of this Schedule.

Inspectors

2.   For the purposes of their duties under paragraph 1 above it shall be the duty of every local authority to appoint inspectors.

Powers of entry

3.   An inspector appointed by a local authority under paragraph 2 above shall, on producing if so required some duly authenticated document showing his authority, have a right at all reasonable hours—

(a)   to enter any premises within the area of the local authority, with or without a constable, for the purpose of ascertaining whether there is or has been on the premises any contravention of the provisions of Schedules 1 and 3 to this Act,

(b)   to require the production of, inspect and take copies of any records (in whatever form they are held) relating to any business carried on the premises which appear to him to be relevant for the purpose mentioned in paragraph (a) above,

(c)   where those records are kept by means of a computer, to require the records to be produced in a form in which they may be taken away, and

(d)   to take such measurements and photographs as he considers necessary for the purpose mentioned in paragraph (a) above.

Obstruction of inspectors

4.   Any person who intentionally obstructs an inspector appointed under paragraph 2 above acting in the execution of his duty shall be liable on summary conviction to a fine not exceeding level 3 on the standard scale.

Offences due to fault of other person

5.   Where the commission by any person of an offence under this Act is due to the act or default of some other person, that other person shall be guilty of the offence, and a person may be charged with and convicted of the offence by virtue of this paragraph whether or not proceedings are taken against the first-mentioned person.

Offences by bodies corporate

6.—(1)   Where an offence under this Act committed by a body corporate is proved to have been committed with the consent or connivance of, or to be attributable to any neglect on the part of, any director, manager, secretary or other similar officer of the body corporate, or any person who was purporting to act in any such capacity, he as well as the body corporate shall be guilty of the offence and shall be liable to be proceeded against and punished accordingly.

(2)   Where the affairs of a body corporate are managed by its members, sub-paragraph (1) above shall apply in relation to the acts and defaults of a member in connection with his functions of management as if he were a director of the body corporate.

Defence of due diligence

7.—(1)   In any proceedings for an offence under this Act it shall, subject to sub-paragraph (2) below, be a defence for the person charged to prove that he took all reasonable precautions and exercised all due diligence to avoid the commission of the offence by himself or by a person under his control.

(2)   If in any case the defence provided by sub-paragraph (1) above involves the allegation that the commission of the offence was due to the act or default of another person, the person charged shall not, without leave of the court, be entitled to rely on that defence unless, at least seven clear

days before the hearing, he has served on the prosecutor a notice in writing giving such information identifying or assisting in the identification of that other person as was then in his possession.

[1542J]

NOTES

   See further: in relation to the application of paras 3, 4 above, with modifications, for the purposes of the Christmas Day (Trading) Act 2004, s 3(2), see s 3(3) thereof at **[2038]**.

PART II

SHOPS OCCUPIED BY PERSONS OBSERVING THE JEWISH SABBATH

Shops occupied by persons of the Jewish religion

8.—(1)   A person of the Jewish religion who is the occupier of a large shop may give to the local authority for the area in which the shop is situated a notice signed by him stating—
- (a)   that he is a person of the Jewish religion, and
- (b)   that he intends to keep the shop closed for the serving of customers on the Jewish Sabbath.

   (2)   For the purposes of this paragraph, a shop occupied by a partnership or company shall be taken to be occupied by a person of the Jewish religion if, and only if, the majority of the partners or of the directors, as the case may be, are persons of that religion.

   (3)   A notice under sub-paragraph (1) above shall be accompanied by a certificate signed by an authorised person that the person giving the notice is a person of the Jewish religion.

   (4)   Where the occupier of the shop is a partnership or company—
- (a)   any notice under sub-paragraph (1) above shall be given by the majority of the partners or directors and, if not given by all of them, shall specify the names of the other partners or directors, and
- (b)   a certificate under sub-paragraph (3) above is required in relation to each of the persons by whom such a notice is given.

   (5)   Every local authority shall keep a register containing particulars of the name (if any) and address of every shop in respect of which a notice under sub-paragraph (1) above has effect.

   (6)   Any register kept under this paragraph—
- (a)   shall be open to inspection by members of the public at all reasonable times, and
- (b)   may be kept by means of a computer.

   (7)   If there is any change—
- (a)   in the occupation of a shop in respect of which a notice under sub-paragraph (1) above has effect, or
- (b)   in any partnership or among the directors of any company by which such a shop is occupied,

the notice shall be taken to be cancelled at the end of the period of 14 days beginning with the day on which the change occurred, unless during that period, or within such further time as may be allowed by the local authority, a fresh notice is given under sub-paragraph (1) above in respect of the shop.

   (8)   Where a fresh notice is given under sub-paragraph (1) above by reason of a change of the kind mentioned in sub-paragraph (7) above, the local authority may dispense with the certificate required by sub-paragraph (3) above in the case of any person in respect of whom such a certificate has been provided in connection with a former notice in respect of that shop or any other shop in the area of the local authority.

   (9)   A notice given under sub-paragraph (1) above in respect of any shop shall be cancelled on application in that behalf being made to the local authority by the occupier of the shop.

   (10)   A person who, in a notice or certificate given for the purposes of this paragraph, makes a statement which is false in a material respect and which he knows to be false or does not believe to be true shall be liable on summary conviction to a fine not exceeding level 5 on the standard scale.

   (11)   Where a person is convicted of an offence under sub-paragraph (10) above, the local authority may cancel any notice under sub-paragraph (1) above to which the offence relates.

   (12)   In this paragraph—
   "authorised person", in relation to a notice under sub-paragraph (1) above, means—
- (a)   the Minister of the synagogue of which the person giving the notice is a member,
- (b)   the secretary of that synagogue, or
- (c)   any other person nominated for the purposes of this paragraph by the President of the London Committee of Deputies of the British Jews (otherwise known as the Board of Deputies of British Jews),

   "large shop" and "shop" have the same meaning as in Schedule 1 to this Act, and
   "secretary of a synagogue" has the same meaning as in Part IV of the Marriage Act 1949.

Members of other religious bodies observing the Jewish Sabbath

9. Paragraph 8 above shall apply to persons who are members of any religious body regularly observing the Jewish Sabbath as it applies to persons of the Jewish religion, and accordingly—

    (a) references to persons of the Jewish religion shall be construed as including any person who is a member of such a body, and

    (b) in the application of that paragraph to such persons "authorised person" means a Minister of the religious body concerned.

Transitional provisions

10.—(1) Any shop which is registered under section 53 of the Shops Act 1950 at the commencement of this Schedule and is at that time a large shop within the meaning of Schedule 1 to this Act shall be taken to be a shop in respect of which a notice has been given under sub-paragraph (1) of paragraph 8 above by the person who was then registered as the occupier of the shop; and the provisions of that paragraph in relation to the cancellation of such a notice shall have effect accordingly.

(2) In paragraph 8(8) above, the reference to a certificate provided in connection with a former notice includes a reference to a statutory declaration provided under subsection (2) of section 53 of the Shops Act 1950 in connection with the registration of a shop under that section before the commencement of this Schedule.

[1542K]

SCHEDULE 3
LOADING AND UNLOADING AT LARGE SHOPS ON SUNDAY MORNING
Section 2

Shops to which Schedule applies

1. This Schedule applies to any shop—

    (a) which is a large shop, within the meaning of Schedule 1 to this Act, [that is permitted to be open on a Sunday by virtue of paragraph 2(3) of that Schedule and which the occupier opens on Sunday for the serving of retail customers], and

    (b) which is situated in an area designated as a loading control area under section 2 of this Act.

Consent required for early Sunday loading and unloading

2. The occupier of a shop to which this Schedule applies shall not load or unload, or permit any other person to load or unload, goods from a vehicle at the shop before 9 am on Sunday in connection with the trade or business carried on in the shop, unless the loading or unloading is carried on—

    (a) with the consent of the local authority for the area in which the shop is situated granted under this Schedule, and

    (b) in accordance with any conditions subject to which that consent is granted.

3.—(1) A consent under this Schedule may be granted subject to such conditions as the local authority consider appropriate.

(2) The local authority may at any time vary the conditions subject to which a consent is granted, and shall give notice of the variation to the person to whom the consent was granted.

Application for consent

4. An application for a consent under this Schedule shall be made in writing and shall contain such information as the local authority may reasonably require.

5. An applicant for a consent under this Schedule shall pay such reasonable fee in respect of his application as the local authority may determine.

6.—(1) Where an application is duly made to the local authority for a consent under this Schedule, the authority shall grant the consent unless they are satisfied that the loading or unloading of goods from vehicles before 9 am on Sunday at the shop to which the application relates, in connection with the trade or business carried on at the shop, has caused, or would be likely to cause, undue annoyance to local residents.

(2) The authority shall determine the application and notify the applicant in writing of their decision within the period of 21 days beginning with the day on which the application is received by the authority.

(3) In a case where a consent is granted, the notification under sub-paragraph (2) above shall specify the conditions, if any, subject to which the consent is granted.

Revocation of consent

7. Where—
   (a) the occupier of a shop in respect of which a consent under this Schedule is in force is convicted of an offence under paragraph 9 below by reason of his failure to comply with the conditions subject to which the consent was granted, or
   (b) the local authority are satisfied that the loading or unloading authorised by virtue of a consent under this Schedule has caused undue annoyance to local residents,

the local authority may revoke the consent.

Publication of consent

8. Where a local authority grant a consent under this Schedule, the authority may cause a notice giving details of that consent to be published in a local newspaper circulating in their area.

Offence

9. A person who contravenes paragraph 2 above shall be liable on summary conviction to a fine not exceeding level 3 on the standard scale.

[Christmas Day

10. Paragraph 2 does not apply where the Sunday is Christmas Day (loading and unloading at large shops on Christmas Day being regulated by section 2 of the Christmas Day (Trading) Act 2004).]

[1542L]

NOTES
Para 1: in sub-para (a) words in square brackets substituted by the Regulatory Reform (Sunday Trading) Order 2004, SI 2004/470, art 2(1), (3).
Para 10: inserted by the Christmas Day (Trading) Act 2004, s 4(1), (3).
See further, in relation to the application of paras 3–8 above, with modifications, for the purposes of the Christmas Day (Trading) Act 2004, s 2(1): the Christmas Day (Trading) Act 2004, s 2(2) at **[2037]**.

(Schs 4, 5 outside the scope of this work.)

ARBITRATION ACT 1996

(1996 c 23)

ARRANGEMENT OF SECTIONS

PART I
ARBITRATION PURSUANT TO AN ARBITRATION AGREEMENT

PART II
OTHER PROVISIONS RELATING TO ARBITRATION

Domestic arbitration agreements

Consumer arbitration agreements

Small claims arbitration in the county court

Appointment of judges as arbitrators

Statutory arbitrations

PART III
RECOGNITION AND ENFORCEMENT OF CERTAIN FOREIGN AWARDS

Enforcement of Geneva Convention awards

Recognition and enforcement of New York Convention awards

PART IV
GENERAL PROVISIONS

PART 1
STATUTES

An Act to restate and improve the law relating to arbitration pursuant to an arbitration agreement; to make other provision relating to arbitration and arbitration awards; and for connected purposes

[17 June 1996]

PART I
ARBITRATION PURSUANT TO AN ARBITRATION AGREEMENT

Introductory

1 General principles

The provisions of this Part are founded on the following principles, and shall be construed accordingly—

    (a)   the object of arbitration is to obtain the fair resolution of disputes by an impartial tribunal without unnecessary delay or expense;

    (b)   the parties should be free to agree how their disputes are resolved, subject only to such safeguards as are necessary in the public interest;

    (c)   in matters governed by this Part the court should not intervene except as provided by this Part.

[1543]

2 Scope of application of provisions

(1) The provisions of this Part apply where the seat of the arbitration is in England and Wales or Northern Ireland.

(2) The following sections apply even if the seat of the arbitration is outside England and Wales or Northern Ireland or no seat has been designated or determined—

    (a)   sections 9 to 11 (stay of legal proceedings, &c), and

    (b)   section 66 (enforcement of arbitral awards).

(3) The powers conferred by the following sections apply even if the seat of the arbitration is outside England and Wales or Northern Ireland or no seat has been designated or determined—

    (a)   section 43 (securing the attendance of witnesses), and

    (b)   section 44 (court powers exercisable in support of arbitral proceedings);

but the court may refuse to exercise any such power if, in the opinion of the court, the fact that the seat of the arbitration is outside England and Wales or Northern Ireland, or that when designated or determined the seat is likely to be outside England and Wales or Northern Ireland, makes it inappropriate to do so.

(4) The court may exercise a power conferred by any provision of this Part not mentioned in subsection (2) or (3) for the purpose of supporting the arbitral process where—

    (a)   no seat of the arbitration has been designated or determined, and

    (b)   by reason of a connection with England and Wales or Northern Ireland the court is satisfied that it is appropriate to do so.

(5) Section 7 (separability of arbitration agreement) and section 8 (death of a party) apply where the law applicable to the arbitration agreement is the law of England and Wales or Northern Ireland even if the seat of the arbitration is outside England and Wales or Northern Ireland or has not been designated or determined.

[1544]

3 The seat of the arbitration

In this Part "the seat of the arbitration" means the juridical seat of the arbitration designated—

    (a)   by the parties to the arbitration agreement, or

    (b)   by any arbitral or other institution or person vested by the parties with powers in that regard, or

    (c)   by the arbitral tribunal if so authorised by the parties,

or determined, in the absence of any such designation, having regard to the parties' agreement and all the relevant circumstances.

[1545]

4 Mandatory and non-mandatory provisions

(1) The mandatory provisions of this Part are listed in Schedule 1 and have effect notwithstanding any agreement to the contrary.

(2)   The other provisions of this Part (the "non-mandatory provisions") allow the parties to make their own arrangements by agreement but provide rules which apply in the absence of such agreement.

(3)   The parties may make such arrangements by agreeing to the application of institutional rules or providing any other means by which a matter may be decided.

(4)   It is immaterial whether or not the law applicable to the parties' agreement is the law of England and Wales or, as the case may be, Northern Ireland.

(5)   The choice of a law other than the law of England and Wales or Northern Ireland as the applicable law in respect of a matter provided for by a non-mandatory provision of this Part is equivalent to an agreement making provision about that matter.

For this purpose an applicable law determined in accordance with the parties' agreement, or which is objectively determined in the absence of any express or implied choice, shall be treated as chosen by the parties.

[1546]

5   Agreements to be in writing

(1)   The provisions of this Part apply only where the arbitration agreement is in writing, and any other agreement between the parties as to any matter is effective for the purposes of this Part only if in writing.

The expressions "agreement", "agree" and "agreed" shall be construed accordingly.

(2)   There is an agreement in writing—
   (a)   if the agreement is made in writing (whether or not it is signed by the parties),
   (b)   if the agreement is made by exchange of communications in writing, or
   (c)   if the agreement is evidenced in writing.

(3)   Where parties agree otherwise than in writing by reference to terms which are in writing, they make an agreement in writing.

(4)   An agreement is evidenced in writing if an agreement made otherwise than in writing is recorded by one of the parties, or by a third party, with the authority of the parties to the agreement.

(5)   An exchange of written submissions in arbitral or legal proceedings in which the existence of an agreement otherwise than in writing is alleged by one party against another party and not denied by the other party in his response constitutes as between those parties an agreement in writing to the effect alleged.

(6)   References in this Part to anything being written or in writing include its being recorded by any means.

[1547]

The arbitration agreement

6   Definition of arbitration agreement

(1)   In this Part an "arbitration agreement" means an agreement to submit to arbitration present or future disputes (whether they are contractual or not).

(2)   The reference in an agreement to a written form of arbitration clause or to a document containing an arbitration clause constitutes an arbitration agreement if the reference is such as to make that clause part of the agreement.

[1548]

7   Separability of arbitration agreement

Unless otherwise agreed by the parties, an arbitration agreement which forms or was intended to form part of another agreement (whether or not in writing) shall not be regarded as invalid, non-existent or ineffective because that other agreement is invalid, or did not come into existence or has become ineffective, and it shall for that purpose be treated as a distinct agreement.

[1549]

8   Whether agreement discharged by death of a party

(1)   Unless otherwise agreed by the parties, an arbitration agreement is not discharged by the death of a party and may be enforced by or against the personal representatives of that party.

(2)   Subsection (1) does not affect the operation of any enactment or rule of law by virtue of which a substantive right or obligation is extinguished by death.

[1550]

Stay of legal proceedings

9 Stay of legal proceedings

(1)   A party to an arbitration agreement against whom legal proceedings are brought (whether by way of claim or counterclaim) in respect of a matter which under the agreement is to be referred to arbitration may (upon notice to the other parties to the proceedings) apply to the court in which the proceedings have been brought to stay the proceedings so far as they concern that matter.

(2)   An application may be made notwithstanding that the matter is to be referred to arbitration only after the exhaustion of other dispute resolution procedures.

(3)   An application may not be made by a person before taking the appropriate procedural step (if any) to acknowledge the legal proceedings against him or after he has taken any step in those proceedings to answer the substantive claim.

(4)   On an application under this section the court shall grant a stay unless satisfied that the arbitration agreement is null and void, inoperative, or incapable of being performed.

(5)   If the court refuses to stay the legal proceedings, any provision that an award is a condition precedent to the bringing of legal proceedings in respect of any matter is of no effect in relation to those proceedings.

[1551]

10 Reference of interpleader issue to arbitration

(1)   Where in legal proceedings relief by way of interpleader is granted and any issue between the claimants is one in respect of which there is an arbitration agreement between them, the court granting the relief shall direct that the issue be determined in accordance with the agreement unless the circumstances are such that proceedings brought by a claimant in respect of the matter would not be stayed.

(2)   Where subsection (1) applies but the court does not direct that the issue be determined in accordance with the arbitration agreement, any provision that an award is a condition precedent to the bringing of legal proceedings in respect of any matter shall not affect the determination of that issue by the court.

[1552]

11 Retention of security where Admiralty proceedings stayed

(1)   Where Admiralty proceedings are stayed on the ground that the dispute in question should be submitted to arbitration, the court granting the stay may, if in those proceedings property has been arrested or bail or other security has been given to prevent or obtain release from arrest—
   (a)   order that the property arrested be retained as security for the satisfaction of any award given in the arbitration in respect of that dispute, or
   (b)   order that the stay of those proceedings be conditional on the provision of equivalent security for the satisfaction of any such award.

(2)   Subject to any provision made by rules of court and to any necessary modifications, the same law and practice shall apply in relation to property retained in pursuance of an order as would apply if it were held for the purposes of proceedings in the court making the order.

[1553]

Commencement of arbitral proceedings

12 Power of court to extend time for beginning arbitral proceedings, &c

(1)   Where an arbitration agreement to refer future disputes to arbitration provides that a claim shall be barred, or the claimant's right extinguished, unless the claimant takes within a time fixed by the agreement some step—
   (a)   to begin arbitral proceedings, or
   (b)   to begin other dispute resolution procedures which must be exhausted before arbitral proceedings can be begun,
the court may by order extend the time for taking that step.

(2)   Any party to the arbitration agreement may apply for such an order (upon notice to the other parties), but only after a claim has arisen and after exhausting any available arbitral process for obtaining an extension of time.

(3)   The court shall make an order only if satisfied—
   (a)   that the circumstances are such as were outside the reasonable contemplation of the parties when they agreed the provision in question, and that it would be just to extend the time, or
   (b)   that the conduct of one party makes it unjust to hold the other party to the strict terms of the provision in question.

(4)   The court may extend the time for such period and on such terms as it thinks fit, and may do so whether or not the time previously fixed (by agreement or by a previous order) has expired.

(5)   An order under this section does not affect the operation of the Limitation Acts (see section 13).

(6)   The leave of the court is required for any appeal from a decision of the court under this section.

[1554]

13   Application of Limitation Acts

(1)   The Limitation Acts apply to arbitral proceedings as they apply to legal proceedings.

(2)   The court may order that in computing the time prescribed by the Limitation Acts for the commencement of proceedings (including arbitral proceedings) in respect of a dispute which was the subject matter—

    (a)   of an award which the court orders to be set aside or declares to be of no effect, or

    (b)   of the affected part of an award which the court orders to be set aside in part, or declares to be in part of no effect,

the period between the commencement of the arbitration and the date of the order referred to in paragraph (a) or (b) shall be excluded.

(3)   In determining for the purposes of the Limitation Acts when a cause of action accrued, any provision that an award is a condition precedent to the bringing of legal proceedings in respect of a matter to which an arbitration agreement applies shall be disregarded.

(4)   In this Part "the Limitation Acts" means—

    (a)   in England and Wales, the Limitation Act 1980, the Foreign Limitation Periods Act 1984 and any other enactment (whenever passed) relating to the limitation of actions;

    (b)   in Northern Ireland, the Limitation (Northern Ireland) Order 1989, the Foreign Limitation Periods (Northern Ireland) Order 1985 and any other enactment (whenever passed) relating to the limitation of actions.

[1555]

14   Commencement of arbitral proceedings

(1)   The parties are free to agree when arbitral proceedings are to be regarded as commenced for the purposes of this Part and for the purposes of the Limitation Acts.

(2)   If there is no such agreement the following provisions apply.

(3)   Where the arbitrator is named or designated in the arbitration agreement, arbitral proceedings are commenced in respect of a matter when one party serves on the other party or parties a notice in writing requiring him or them to submit that matter to the person so named or designated.

(4)   Where the arbitrator or arbitrators are to be appointed by the parties, arbitral proceedings are commenced in respect of a matter when one party serves on the other party or parties notice in writing requiring him or them to appoint an arbitrator or to agree to the appointment of an arbitrator in respect of that matter.

(5)   Where the arbitrator or arbitrators are to be appointed by a person other than a party to the proceedings, arbitral proceedings are commenced in respect of a matter when one party gives notice in writing to that person requesting him to make the appointment in respect of that matter.

[1556]

The arbitral tribunal

15   The arbitral tribunal

(1)   The parties are free to agree on the number of arbitrators to form the tribunal and whether there is to be a chairman or umpire.

(2)   Unless otherwise agreed by the parties, an agreement that the number of arbitrators shall be two or any other even number shall be understood as requiring the appointment of an additional arbitrator as chairman of the tribunal.

(3)   If there is no agreement as to the number of arbitrators, the tribunal shall consist of a sole arbitrator.

[1557]

16   Procedure for appointment of arbitrators

(1)   The parties are free to agree on the procedure for appointing the arbitrator or arbitrators, including the procedure for appointing any chairman or umpire.

(2)   If or to the extent that there is no such agreement, the following provisions apply.

(3)   If the tribunal is to consist of a sole arbitrator, the parties shall jointly appoint the arbitrator not later than 28 days after service of a request in writing by either party to do so.

(4)   If the tribunal is to consist of two arbitrators, each party shall appoint one arbitrator not later than 14 days after service of a request in writing by either party to do so.

(5)   If the tribunal is to consist of three arbitrators—
   (a)   each party shall appoint one arbitrator not later than 14 days after service of a request in writing by either party to do so, and
   (b)   the two so appointed shall forthwith appoint a third arbitrator as the chairman of the tribunal.

(6)   If the tribunal is to consist of two arbitrators and an umpire—
   (a)   each party shall appoint one arbitrator not later than 14 days after service of a request in writing by either party to do so, and
   (b)   the two so appointed may appoint an umpire at any time after they themselves are appointed and shall do so before any substantive hearing or forthwith if they cannot agree on a matter relating to the arbitration.

(7)   In any other case (in particular, if there are more than two parties) section 18 applies as in the case of a failure of the agreed appointment procedure.

[1558]

17   Power in case of default to appoint sole arbitrator

(1)   Unless the parties otherwise agree, where each of two parties to an arbitration agreement is to appoint an arbitrator and one party ("the party in default") refuses to do so, or fails to do so within the time specified, the other party, having duly appointed his arbitrator, may give notice in writing to the party in default that he proposes to appoint his arbitrator to act as sole arbitrator.

(2)   If the party in default does not within 7 clear days of that notice being given—
   (a)   make the required appointment, and
   (b)   notify the other party that he has done so,
the other party may appoint his arbitrator as sole arbitrator whose award shall be binding on both parties as if he had been so appointed by agreement.

(3)   Where a sole arbitrator has been appointed under subsection (2), the party in default may (upon notice to the appointing party) apply to the court which may set aside the appointment.

(4)   The leave of the court is required for any appeal from a decision of the court under this section.

[1559]

18   Failure of appointment procedure

(1)   The parties are free to agree what is to happen in the event of a failure of the procedure for the appointment of the arbitral tribunal.

There is no failure if an appointment is duly made under section 17 (power in case of default to appoint sole arbitrator), unless that appointment is set aside.

(2)   If or to the extent that there is no such agreement any party to the arbitration agreement may (upon notice to the other parties) apply to the court to exercise its powers under this section.

(3)   Those powers are—
   (a)   to give directions as to the making of any necessary appointments;
   (b)   to direct that the tribunal shall be constituted by such appointments (or any one or more of them) as have been made;
   (c)   to revoke any appointments already made;
   (d)   to make any necessary appointments itself.

(4)   An appointment made by the court under this section has effect as if made with the agreement of the parties.

(5)   The leave of the court is required for any appeal from a decision of the court under this section.

[1560]

19   Court to have regard to agreed qualifications

In deciding whether to exercise, and in considering how to exercise, any of its powers under section 16 (procedure for appointment of arbitrators) or section 18 (failure of appointment procedure), the court shall have due regard to any agreement of the parties as to the qualifications required of the arbitrators.

[1561]

20   Chairman

(1)   Where the parties have agreed that there is to be a chairman, they are free to agree what the functions of the chairman are to be in relation to the making of decisions, orders and awards.

(2)   If or to the extent that there is no such agreement, the following provisions apply.

(3)   Decisions, orders and awards shall be made by all or a majority of the arbitrators (including the chairman).

(4)   The view of the chairman shall prevail in relation to a decision, order or award in respect of which there is neither unanimity nor a majority under subsection (3).

[1562]

21   Umpire

(1)   Where the parties have agreed that there is to be an umpire, they are free to agree what the functions of the umpire are to be, and in particular—

   (a)   whether he is to attend the proceedings, and
   (b)   when he is to replace the other arbitrators as the tribunal with power to make decisions, orders and awards.

(2)   If or to the extent that there is no such agreement, the following provisions apply.

(3)   The umpire shall attend the proceedings and be supplied with the same documents and other materials as are supplied to the other arbitrators.

(4)   Decisions, orders and awards shall be made by the other arbitrators unless and until they cannot agree on a matter relating to the arbitration.

In that event they shall forthwith give notice in writing to the parties and the umpire, whereupon the umpire shall replace them as the tribunal with power to make decisions, orders and awards as if he were sole arbitrator.

(5)   If the arbitrators cannot agree but fail to give notice of that fact, or if any of them fails to join in the giving of notice, any party to the arbitral proceedings may (upon notice to the other parties and to the tribunal) apply to the court which may order that the umpire shall replace the other arbitrators as the tribunal with power to make decisions, orders and awards as if he were sole arbitrator.

(6)   The leave of the court is required for any appeal from a decision of the court under this section.

[1563]

22   Decision-making where no chairman or umpire

(1)   Where the parties agree that there shall be two or more arbitrators with no chairman or umpire, the parties are free to agree how the tribunal is to make decisions, orders and awards.

(2)   If there is no such agreement, decisions, orders and awards shall be made by all or a majority of the arbitrators.

[1564]

23   Revocation of arbitrator's authority

(1)   The parties are free to agree in what circumstances the authority of an arbitrator may be revoked.

(2)   If or to the extent that there is no such agreement the following provisions apply.

(3)   The authority of an arbitrator may not be revoked except—

   (a)   by the parties acting jointly, or
   (b)   by an arbitral or other institution or person vested by the parties with powers in that regard.

(4)   Revocation of the authority of an arbitrator by the parties acting jointly must be agreed in writing unless the parties also agree (whether or not in writing) to terminate the arbitration agreement.

(5)   Nothing in this section affects the power of the court—

   (a)   to revoke an appointment under section 18 (powers exercisable in case of failure of appointment procedure), or
   (b)   to remove an arbitrator on the grounds specified in section 24.

[1565]

24   Power of court to remove arbitrator

(1)   A party to arbitral proceedings may (upon notice to the other parties, to the arbitrator concerned and to any other arbitrator) apply to the court to remove an arbitrator on any of the following grounds—

   (a)   that circumstances exist that give rise to justifiable doubts as to his impartiality;
   (b)   that he does not possess the qualifications required by the arbitration agreement;
   (c)   that he is physically or mentally incapable of conducting the proceedings or there are justifiable doubts as to his capacity to do so;
   (d)   that he has refused or failed—
      (i)   properly to conduct the proceedings, or
      (ii)   to use all reasonable despatch in conducting the proceedings or making an award,

and that substantial injustice has been or will be caused to the applicant.

(2)   If there is an arbitral or other institution or person vested by the parties with power to remove an arbitrator, the court shall not exercise its power of removal unless satisfied that the applicant has first exhausted any available recourse to that institution or person.

(3)   The arbitral tribunal may continue the arbitral proceedings and make an award while an application to the court under this section is pending.

(4)   Where the court removes an arbitrator, it may make such order as it thinks fit with respect to his entitlement (if any) to fees or expenses, or the repayment of any fees or expenses already paid.

(5)   The arbitrator concerned is entitled to appear and be heard by the court before it makes any order under this section.

(6)   The leave of the court is required for any appeal from a decision of the court under this section.

[1566]

25   Resignation of arbitrator

(1)   The parties are free to agree with an arbitrator as to the consequences of his resignation as regards—
   (a)   his entitlement (if any) to fees or expenses, and
   (b)   any liability thereby incurred by him.

(2)   If or to the extent that there is no such agreement the following provisions apply.

(3)   An arbitrator who resigns his appointment may (upon notice to the parties) apply to the court—
   (a)   to grant him relief from any liability thereby incurred by him, and
   (b)   to make such order as it thinks fit with respect to his entitlement (if any) to fees or expenses or the repayment of any fees or expenses already paid.

(4)   If the court is satisfied that in all the circumstances it was reasonable for the arbitrator to resign, it may grant such relief as is mentioned in subsection (3)(a) on such terms as it thinks fit.

(5)   The leave of the court is required for any appeal from a decision of the court under this section.

[1567]

26   Death of arbitrator or person appointing him

(1)   The authority of an arbitrator is personal and ceases on his death.

(2)   Unless otherwise agreed by the parties, the death of the person by whom an arbitrator was appointed does not revoke the arbitrator's authority.

[1568]

27   Filling of vacancy, &c

(1)   Where an arbitrator ceases to hold office, the parties are free to agree—
   (a)   whether and if so how the vacancy is to be filled,
   (b)   whether and if so to what extent the previous proceedings should stand, and
   (c)   what effect (if any) his ceasing to hold office has on any appointment made by him (alone or jointly).

(2)   If or to the extent that there is no such agreement, the following provisions apply.

(3)   The provisions of sections 16 (procedure for appointment of arbitrators) and 18 (failure of appointment procedure) apply in relation to the filling of the vacancy as in relation to an original appointment.

(4)   The tribunal (when reconstituted) shall determine whether and if so to what extent the previous proceedings should stand.

This does not affect any right of a party to challenge those proceedings on any ground which had arisen before the arbitrator ceased to hold office.

(5)   His ceasing to hold office does not affect any appointment by him (alone or jointly) of another arbitrator, in particular any appointment of a chairman or umpire.

[1569]

28   Joint and several liability of parties to arbitrators for fees and expenses

(1)   The parties are jointly and severally liable to pay to the arbitrators such reasonable fees and expenses (if any) as are appropriate in the circumstances.

(2)   Any party may apply to the court (upon notice to the other parties and to the arbitrators) which may order that the amount of the arbitrators' fees and expenses shall be considered and adjusted by such means and upon such terms as it may direct.

(3)   If the application is made after any amount has been paid to the arbitrators by way of fees or expenses, the court may order the repayment of such amount (if any) as is shown to be excessive, but shall not do so unless it is shown that it is reasonable in the circumstances to order repayment.

(4)   The above provisions have effect subject to any order of the court under section 24(4) or 25(3)(b) (order as to entitlement to fees or expenses in case of removal or resignation of arbitrator).

(5)   Nothing in this section affects any liability of a party to any other party to pay all or any of the costs of the arbitration (see sections 59 to 65) or any contractual right of an arbitrator to payment of his fees and expenses.

(6)   In this section references to arbitrators include an arbitrator who has ceased to act and an umpire who has not replaced the other arbitrators.

[1570]

29   Immunity of arbitrator

(1)   An arbitrator is not liable for anything done or omitted in the discharge or purported discharge of his functions as arbitrator unless the act or omission is shown to have been in bad faith.

(2)   Subsection (1) applies to an employee or agent of an arbitrator as it applies to the arbitrator himself.

(3)   This section does not affect any liability incurred by an arbitrator by reason of his resigning (but see section 25).

[1571]

Jurisdiction of the arbitral tribunal

30   Competence of tribunal to rule on its own jurisdiction

(1)   Unless otherwise agreed by the parties, the arbitral tribunal may rule on its own substantive jurisdiction, that is, as to—
   (a)   whether there is a valid arbitration agreement,
   (b)   whether the tribunal is properly constituted, and
   (c)   what matters have been submitted to arbitration in accordance with the arbitration agreement.

(2)   Any such ruling may be challenged by any available arbitral process of appeal or review or in accordance with the provisions of this Part.

[1572]

31   Objection to substantive jurisdiction of tribunal

(1)   An objection that the arbitral tribunal lacks substantive jurisdiction at the outset of the proceedings must be raised by a party not later than the time he takes the first step in the proceedings to contest the merits of any matter in relation to which he challenges the tribunal's jurisdiction.

A party is not precluded from raising such an objection by the fact that he has appointed or participated in the appointment of an arbitrator.

(2)   Any objection during the course of the arbitral proceedings that the arbitral tribunal is exceeding its substantive jurisdiction must be made as soon as possible after the matter alleged to be beyond its jurisdiction is raised.

(3)   The arbitral tribunal may admit an objection later than the time specified in subsection (1) or (2) if it considers the delay justified.

(4)   Where an objection is duly taken to the tribunal's substantive jurisdiction and the tribunal has power to rule on its own jurisdiction, it may—
   (a)   rule on the matter in an award as to jurisdiction, or
   (b)   deal with the objection in its award on the merits.

If the parties agree which of these courses the tribunal should take, the tribunal shall proceed accordingly.

(5)   The tribunal may in any case, and shall if the parties so agree, stay proceedings whilst an application is made to the court under section 32 (determination of preliminary point of jurisdiction).

[1573]

32   Determination of preliminary point of jurisdiction

(1)   The court may, on the application of a party to arbitral proceedings (upon notice to the other parties), determine any question as to the substantive jurisdiction of the tribunal.

A party may lose the right to object (see section 73).

(2)   An application under this section shall not be considered unless—
   (a)   it is made with the agreement in writing of all the other parties to the proceedings, or

  (b) it is made with the permission of the tribunal and the court is satisfied—
    (i) that the determination of the question is likely to produce substantial savings in costs,
    (ii) that the application was made without delay, and
    (iii) that there is good reason why the matter should be decided by the court.

(3) An application under this section, unless made with the agreement of all the other parties to the proceedings, shall state the grounds on which it is said that the matter should be decided by the court.

(4) Unless otherwise agreed by the parties, the arbitral tribunal may continue the arbitral proceedings and make an award while an application to the court under this section is pending.

(5) Unless the court gives leave, no appeal lies from a decision of the court whether the conditions specified in subsection (2) are met.

(6) The decision of the court on the question of jurisdiction shall be treated as a judgment of the court for the purposes of an appeal.

But no appeal lies without the leave of the court which shall not be given unless the court considers that the question involves a point of law which is one of general importance or is one which for some other special reason should be considered by the Court of Appeal.

                            [1574]

The arbitral proceedings

33 General duty of the tribunal

(1) The tribunal shall—
  (a) act fairly and impartially as between the parties, giving each party a reasonable opportunity of putting his case and dealing with that of his opponent, and
  (b) adopt procedures suitable to the circumstances of the particular case, avoiding unnecessary delay or expense, so as to provide a fair means for the resolution of the matters falling to be determined.

(2) The tribunal shall comply with that general duty in conducting the arbitral proceedings, in its decisions on matters of procedure and evidence and in the exercise of all other powers conferred on it.

                            [1575]

34 Procedural and evidential matters

(1) It shall be for the tribunal to decide all procedural and evidential matters, subject to the right of the parties to agree any matter.

(2) Procedural and evidential matters include—
  (a) when and where any part of the proceedings is to be held;
  (b) the language or languages to be used in the proceedings and whether translations of any relevant documents are to be supplied;
  (c) whether any and if so what form of written statements of claim and defence are to be used, when these should be supplied and the extent to which such statements can be later amended;
  (d) whether any and if so which documents or classes of documents should be disclosed between and produced by the parties and at what stage;
  (e) whether any and if so what questions should be put to and answered by the respective parties and when and in what form this should be done;
  (f) whether to apply strict rules of evidence (or any other rules) as to the admissibility, relevance or weight of any material (oral, written or other) sought to be tendered on any matters of fact or opinion, and the time, manner and form in which such material should be exchanged and presented;
  (g) whether and to what extent the tribunal should itself take the initiative in ascertaining the facts and the law;
  (h) whether and to what extent there should be oral or written evidence or submissions.

(3) The tribunal may fix the time within which any directions given by it are to be complied with, and may if it thinks fit extend the time so fixed (whether or not it has expired).

                            [1576]

35 Consolidation of proceedings and concurrent hearings

(1) The parties are free to agree—
  (a) that the arbitral proceedings shall be consolidated with other arbitral proceedings, or
  (b) that concurrent hearings shall be held,
on such terms as may be agreed.

(2)   Unless the parties agree to confer such power on the tribunal, the tribunal has no power to order consolidation of proceedings or concurrent hearings.

[1577]

36   Legal or other representation

Unless otherwise agreed by the parties, a party to arbitral proceedings may be represented in the proceedings by a lawyer or other person chosen by him.

[1578]

37   Power to appoint experts, legal advisers or assessors

(1)   Unless otherwise agreed by the parties—
   (a)   the tribunal may—
      (i)   appoint experts or legal advisers to report to it and the parties, or
      (ii)   appoint assessors to assist it on technical matters,
      and may allow any such expert, legal adviser or assessor to attend the proceedings; and
   (b)   the parties shall be given a reasonable opportunity to comment on any information, opinion or advice offered by any such person.

(2)   The fees and expenses of an expert, legal adviser or assessor appointed by the tribunal for which the arbitrators are liable are expenses of the arbitrators for the purposes of this Part.

[1579]

38   General powers exercisable by the tribunal

(1)   The parties are free to agree on the powers exercisable by the arbitral tribunal for the purposes of and in relation to the proceedings.

(2)   Unless otherwise agreed by the parties the tribunal has the following powers.

(3)   The tribunal may order a claimant to provide security for the costs of the arbitration.

This power shall not be exercised on the ground that the claimant is—
   (a)   an individual ordinarily resident outside the United Kingdom, or
   (b)   a corporation or association incorporated or formed under the law of a country outside the United Kingdom, or whose central management and control is exercised outside the United Kingdom.

(4)   The tribunal may give directions in relation to any property which is the subject of the proceedings or as to which any question arises in the proceedings, and which is owned by or is in the possession of a party to the proceedings—
   (a)   for the inspection, photographing, preservation, custody or detention of the property by the tribunal, an expert or a party, or
   (b)   ordering that samples be taken from, or any observation be made of or experiment conducted upon, the property.

(5)   The tribunal may direct that a party or witness shall be examined on oath or affirmation, and may for that purpose administer any necessary oath or take any necessary affirmation.

(6)   The tribunal may give directions to a party for the preservation for the purposes of the proceedings of any evidence in his custody or control.

[1580]

39   Power to make provisional awards

(1)   The parties are free to agree that the tribunal shall have power to order on a provisional basis any relief which it would have power to grant in a final award.

(2)   This includes, for instance, making—
   (a)   a provisional order for the payment of money or the disposition of property as between the parties, or
   (b)   an order to make an interim payment on account of the costs of the arbitration.

(3)   Any such order shall be subject to the tribunal's final adjudication; and the tribunal's final award, on the merits or as to costs, shall take account of any such order.

(4)   Unless the parties agree to confer such power on the tribunal, the tribunal has no such power.

This does not affect its powers under section 47 (awards on different issues, &c).

[1581]

40   General duty of parties

(1)   The parties shall do all things necessary for the proper and expeditious conduct of the arbitral proceedings.

(2)   This includes—
   (a)   complying without delay with any determination of the tribunal as to procedural or evidential matters, or with any order or directions of the tribunal, and

(b)   where appropriate, taking without delay any necessary steps to obtain a decision of the court on a preliminary question of jurisdiction or law (see sections 32 and 45).

[1582]

41   Powers of tribunal in case of party's default

(1)   The parties are free to agree on the powers of the tribunal in case of a party's failure to do something necessary for the proper and expeditious conduct of the arbitration.

(2)   Unless otherwise agreed by the parties, the following provisions apply.

(3)   If the tribunal is satisfied that there has been inordinate and inexcusable delay on the part of the claimant in pursuing his claim and that the delay—
  (a)   gives rise, or is likely to give rise, to a substantial risk that it is not possible to have a fair resolution of the issues in that claim, or
  (b)   has caused, or is likely to cause, serious prejudice to the respondent,
the tribunal may make an award dismissing the claim.

(4)   If without showing sufficient cause a party—
  (a)   fails to attend or be represented at an oral hearing of which due notice was given, or
  (b)   where matters are to be dealt with in writing, fails after due notice to submit written evidence or make written submissions,
the tribunal may continue the proceedings in the absence of that party or, as the case may be, without any written evidence or submissions on his behalf, and may make an award on the basis of the evidence before it.

(5)   If without showing sufficient cause a party fails to comply with any order or directions of the tribunal, the tribunal may make a peremptory order to the same effect, prescribing such time for compliance with it as the tribunal considers appropriate.

(6)   If a claimant fails to comply with a peremptory order of the tribunal to provide security for costs, the tribunal may make an award dismissing his claim.

(7)   If a party fails to comply with any other kind of peremptory order, then, without prejudice to section 42 (enforcement by court of tribunal's peremptory orders), the tribunal may do any of the following—
  (a)   direct that the party in default shall not be entitled to rely upon any allegation or material which was the subject matter of the order;
  (b)   draw such adverse inferences from the act of non-compliance as the circumstances justify;
  (c)   proceed to an award on the basis of such materials as have been properly provided to it;
  (d)   make such order as it thinks fit as to the payment of costs of the arbitration incurred in consequence of the non-compliance.

[1583]

Powers of court in relation to arbitral proceedings

42   Enforcement of peremptory orders of tribunal

(1)   Unless otherwise agreed by the parties, the court may make an order requiring a party to comply with a peremptory order made by the tribunal.

(2)   An application for an order under this section may be made—
  (a)   by the tribunal (upon notice to the parties),
  (b)   by a party to the arbitral proceedings with the permission of the tribunal (and upon notice to the other parties), or
  (c)   where the parties have agreed that the powers of the court under this section shall be available.

(3)   The court shall not act unless it is satisfied that the applicant has exhausted any available arbitral process in respect of failure to comply with the tribunal's order.

(4)   No order shall be made under this section unless the court is satisfied that the person to whom the tribunal's order was directed has failed to comply with it within the time prescribed in the order or, if no time was prescribed, within a reasonable time.

(5)   The leave of the court is required for any appeal from a decision of the court under this section.

[1584]

43   Securing the attendance of witnesses

(1)   A party to arbitral proceedings may use the same court procedures as are available in relation to legal proceedings to secure the attendance before the tribunal of a witness in order to give oral testimony or to produce documents or other material evidence.

(2)   This may only be done with the permission of the tribunal or the agreement of the other parties.

(3) The court procedures may only be used if—
    (a) the witness is in the United Kingdom, and
    (b) the arbitral proceedings are being conducted in England and Wales or, as the case may be, Northern Ireland.

(4) A person shall not be compelled by virtue of this section to produce any document or other material evidence which he could not be compelled to produce in legal proceedings.

[1585]

44 Court powers exercisable in support of arbitral proceedings

(1) Unless otherwise agreed by the parties, the court has for the purposes of and in relation to arbitral proceedings the same power of making orders about the matters listed below as it has for the purposes of and in relation to legal proceedings.

(2) Those matters are—
    (a) the taking of the evidence of witnesses;
    (b) the preservation of evidence;
    (c) making orders relating to property which is the subject of the proceedings or as to which any question arises in the proceedings—
        (i) for the inspection, photographing, preservation, custody or detention of the property, or
        (ii) ordering that samples be taken from, or any observation be made of or experiment conducted upon, the property;
    and for that purpose authorising any person to enter any premises in the possession or control of a party to the arbitration;
    (d) the sale of any goods the subject of the proceedings;
    (e) the granting of an interim injunction or the appointment of a receiver.

(3) If the case is one of urgency, the court may, on the application of a party or proposed party to the arbitral proceedings, make such orders as it thinks necessary for the purpose of preserving evidence or assets.

(4) If the case is not one of urgency, the court shall act only on the application of a party to the arbitral proceedings (upon notice to the other parties and to the tribunal) made with the permission of the tribunal or the agreement in writing of the other parties.

(5) In any case the court shall act only if or to the extent that the arbitral tribunal, and any arbitral or other institution or person vested by the parties with power in that regard, has no power or is unable for the time being to act effectively.

(6) If the court so orders, an order made by it under this section shall cease to have effect in whole or in part on the order of the tribunal or of any such arbitral or other institution or person having power to act in relation to the subject-matter of the order.

(7) The leave of the court is required for any appeal from a decision of the court under this section.

[1586]

45 Determination of preliminary point of law

(1) Unless otherwise agreed by the parties, the court may on the application of a party to arbitral proceedings (upon notice to the other parties) determine any question of law arising in the course of the proceedings which the court is satisfied substantially affects the rights of one or more of the parties.

An agreement to dispense with reasons for the tribunal's award shall be considered an agreement to exclude the court's jurisdiction under this section.

(2) An application under this section shall not be considered unless—
    (a) it is made with the agreement of all the other parties to the proceedings, or
    (b) it is made with the permission of the tribunal and the court is satisfied—
        (i) that the determination of the question is likely to produce substantial savings in costs, and
        (ii) that the application was made without delay.

(3) The application shall identify the question of law to be determined and, unless made with the agreement of all the other parties to the proceedings, shall state the grounds on which it is said that the question should be decided by the court.

(4) Unless otherwise agreed by the parties, the arbitral tribunal may continue the arbitral proceedings and make an award while an application to the court under this section is pending.

(5) Unless the court gives leave, no appeal lies from a decision of the court whether the conditions specified in subsection (2) are met.

(6) The decision of the court on the question of law shall be treated as a judgment of the court for the purposes of an appeal.

But no appeal lies without the leave of the court which shall not be given unless the court considers that the question is one of general importance, or is one which for some other special reason should be considered by the Court of Appeal.

[1587]

The award

46 Rules applicable to substance of dispute

(1) The arbitral tribunal shall decide the dispute—

    (a) in accordance with the law chosen by the parties as applicable to the substance of the dispute, or

    (b) if the parties so agree, in accordance with such other considerations as are agreed by them or determined by the tribunal.

(2) For this purpose the choice of the laws of a country shall be understood to refer to the substantive laws of that country and not its conflict of laws rules.

(3) If or to the extent that there is no such choice or agreement, the tribunal shall apply the law determined by the conflict of laws rules which it considers applicable.

[1588]

47 Awards on different issues, &c

(1) Unless otherwise agreed by the parties, the tribunal may make more than one award at different times on different aspects of the matters to be determined.

(2) The tribunal may, in particular, make an award relating—

    (a) to an issue affecting the whole claim, or

    (b) to a part only of the claims or cross-claims submitted to it for decision.

(3) If the tribunal does so, it shall specify in its award the issue, or the claim or part of a claim, which is the subject matter of the award.

[1589]

48 Remedies

(1) The parties are free to agree on the powers exercisable by the arbitral tribunal as regards remedies.

(2) Unless otherwise agreed by the parties, the tribunal has the following powers.

(3) The tribunal may make a declaration as to any matter to be determined in the proceedings.

(4) The tribunal may order the payment of a sum of money, in any currency.

(5) The tribunal has the same powers as the court—

    (a) to order a party to do or refrain from doing anything;

    (b) to order specific performance of a contract (other than a contract relating to land);

    (c) to order the rectification, setting aside or cancellation of a deed or other document.

[1590]

49 Interest

(1) The parties are free to agree on the powers of the tribunal as regards the award of interest.

(2) Unless otherwise agreed by the parties the following provisions apply.

(3) The tribunal may award simple or compound interest from such dates, at such rates and with such rests as it considers meets the justice of the case—

    (a) on the whole or part of any amount awarded by the tribunal, in respect of any period up to the date of the award;

    (b) on the whole or part of any amount claimed in the arbitration and outstanding at the commencement of the arbitral proceedings but paid before the award was made, in respect of any period up to the date of payment.

(4) The tribunal may award simple or compound interest from the date of the award (or any later date) until payment, at such rates and with such rests as it considers meets the justice of the case, on the outstanding amount of any award (including any award of interest under subsection (3) and any award as to costs).

(5) References in this section to an amount awarded by the tribunal include an amount payable in consequence of a declaratory award by the tribunal.

(6) The above provisions do not affect any other power of the tribunal to award interest.

[1591]

50 Extension of time for making award

(1) Where the time for making an award is limited by or in pursuance of the arbitration agreement, then, unless otherwise agreed by the parties, the court may in accordance with the following provisions by order extend that time.

(2)   An application for an order under this section may be made—
(a)   by the tribunal (upon notice to the parties), or
(b)   by any party to the proceedings (upon notice to the tribunal and the other parties),
but only after exhausting any available arbitral process for obtaining an extension of time.

(3)   The court shall only make an order if satisfied that a substantial injustice would otherwise be done.

(4)   The court may extend the time for such period and on such terms as it thinks fit, and may do so whether or not the time previously fixed (by or under the agreement or by a previous order) has expired.

(5)   The leave of the court is required for any appeal from a decision of the court under this section.

[1592]

51   Settlement

(1)   If during arbitral proceedings the parties settle the dispute, the following provisions apply unless otherwise agreed by the parties.

(2)   The tribunal shall terminate the substantive proceedings and, if so requested by the parties and not objected to by the tribunal, shall record the settlement in the form of an agreed award.

(3)   An agreed award shall state that it is an award of the tribunal and shall have the same status and effect as any other award on the merits of the case.

(4)   The following provisions of this Part relating to awards (sections 52 to 58) apply to an agreed award.

(5)   Unless the parties have also settled the matter of the payment of the costs of the arbitration, the provisions of this Part relating to costs (sections 59 to 65) continue to apply.

[1593]

52   Form of award

(1)   The parties are free to agree on the form of an award.

(2)   If or to the extent that there is no such agreement, the following provisions apply.

(3)   The award shall be in writing signed by all the arbitrators or all those assenting to the award.

(4)   The award shall contain the reasons for the award unless it is an agreed award or the parties have agreed to dispense with reasons.

(5)   The award shall state the seat of the arbitration and the date when the award is made.

[1594]

53   Place where award treated as made

Unless otherwise agreed by the parties, where the seat of the arbitration is in England and Wales or Northern Ireland, any award in the proceedings shall be treated as made there, regardless of where it was signed, despatched or delivered to any of the parties.

[1595]

54   Date of award

(1)   Unless otherwise agreed by the parties, the tribunal may decide what is to be taken to be the date on which the award was made.

(2)   In the absence of any such decision, the date of the award shall be taken to be the date on which it is signed by the arbitrator or, where more than one arbitrator signs the award, by the last of them.

[1596]

55   Notification of award

(1)   The parties are free to agree on the requirements as to notification of the award to the parties.

(2)   If there is no such agreement, the award shall be notified to the parties by service on them of copies of the award, which shall be done without delay after the award is made.

(3)   Nothing in this section affects section 56 (power to withhold award in case of non-payment).

[1597]

56   Power to withhold award in case of non-payment

(1)   The tribunal may refuse to deliver an award to the parties except upon full payment of the fees and expenses of the arbitrators.

(2)   If the tribunal refuses on that ground to deliver an award, a party to the arbitral proceedings may (upon notice to the other parties and the tribunal) apply to the court, which may order that—

(a)   the tribunal shall deliver the award on the payment into court by the applicant of the fees and expenses demanded, or such lesser amount as the court may specify,

(b)   the amount of the fees and expenses properly payable shall be determined by such means and upon such terms as the court may direct, and

(c)   out of the money paid into court there shall be paid out such fees and expenses as may be found to be properly payable and the balance of the money (if any) shall be paid out to the applicant.

(3)   For this purpose the amount of fees and expenses properly payable is the amount the applicant is liable to pay under section 28 or any agreement relating to the payment of the arbitrators.

(4)   No application to the court may be made where there is any available arbitral process for appeal or review of the amount of the fees or expenses demanded.

(5)   References in this section to arbitrators include an arbitrator who has ceased to act and an umpire who has not replaced the other arbitrators.

(6)   The above provisions of this section also apply in relation to any arbitral or other institution or person vested by the parties with powers in relation to the delivery of the tribunal's award.

As they so apply, the references to the fees and expenses of the arbitrators shall be construed as including the fees and expenses of that institution or person.

(7)   The leave of the court is required for any appeal from a decision of the court under this section.

(8)   Nothing in this section shall be construed as excluding an application under section 28 where payment has been made to the arbitrators in order to obtain the award.

[1598]

57   Correction of award or additional award

(1)   The parties are free to agree on the powers of the tribunal to correct an award or make an additional award.

(2)   If or to the extent there is no such agreement, the following provisions apply.

(3)   The tribunal may on its own initiative or on the application of a party—

(a)   correct an award so as to remove any clerical mistake or error arising from an accidental slip or omission or clarify or remove any ambiguity in the award, or

(b)   make an additional award in respect of any claim (including a claim for interest or costs) which was presented to the tribunal but was not dealt with in the award.

These powers shall not be exercised without first affording the other parties a reasonable opportunity to make representations to the tribunal.

(4)   Any application for the exercise of those powers must be made within 28 days of the date of the award or such longer period as the parties may agree.

(5)   Any correction of an award shall be made within 28 days of the date the application was received by the tribunal or, where the correction is made by the tribunal on its own initiative, within 28 days of the date of the award or, in either case, such longer period as the parties may agree.

(6)   Any additional award shall be made within 56 days of the date of the original award or such longer period as the parties may agree.

(7)   Any correction of an award shall form part of the award.

[1599]

58   Effect of award

(1)   Unless otherwise agreed by the parties, an award made by the tribunal pursuant to an arbitration agreement is final and binding both on the parties and on any persons claiming through or under them.

(2)   This does not affect the right of a person to challenge the award by any available arbitral process of appeal or review or in accordance with the provisions of this Part.

[1600]

Costs of the arbitration

59   Costs of the arbitration

(1)   References in this Part to the costs of the arbitration are to—

(a)   the arbitrators' fees and expenses,

(b)   the fees and expenses of any arbitral institution concerned, and

(c)   the legal or other costs of the parties.

(2)   Any such reference includes the costs of or incidental to any proceedings to determine the amount of the recoverable costs of the arbitration (see section 63).

[1601]

60   Agreement to pay costs in any event

An agreement which has the effect that a party is to pay the whole or part of the costs of the arbitration in any event is only valid if made after the dispute in question has arisen.

[1602]

61   Award of costs

(1)   The tribunal may make an award allocating the costs of the arbitration as between the parties, subject to any agreement of the parties.

(2)   Unless the parties otherwise agree, the tribunal shall award costs on the general principle that costs should follow the event except where it appears to the tribunal that in the circumstances this is not appropriate in relation to the whole or part of the costs.

[1603]

62   Effect of agreement or award about costs

Unless the parties otherwise agree, any obligation under an agreement between them as to how the costs of the arbitration are to be borne, or under an award allocating the costs of the arbitration, extends only to such costs as are recoverable.

[1604]

63   The recoverable costs of the arbitration

(1)   The parties are free to agree what costs of the arbitration are recoverable.

(2)   If or to the extent there is no such agreement, the following provisions apply.

(3)   The tribunal may determine by award the recoverable costs of the arbitration on such basis as it thinks fit.

If it does so, it shall specify—
  (a)   the basis on which it has acted, and
  (b)   the items of recoverable costs and the amount referable to each.

(4)   If the tribunal does not determine the recoverable costs of the arbitration, any party to the arbitral proceedings may apply to the court (upon notice to the other parties) which may—
  (a)   determine the recoverable costs of the arbitration on such basis as it thinks fit, or
  (b)   order that they shall be determined by such means and upon such terms as it may specify.

(5)   Unless the tribunal or the court determines otherwise—
  (a)   the recoverable costs of the arbitration shall be determined on the basis that there shall be allowed a reasonable amount in respect of all costs reasonably incurred, and
  (b)   any doubt as to whether costs were reasonably incurred or were reasonable in amount shall be resolved in favour of the paying party.

(6)   The above provisions have effect subject to section 64 (recoverable fees and expenses of arbitrators).

(7)   Nothing in this section affects any right of the arbitrators, any expert, legal adviser or assessor appointed by the tribunal, or any arbitral institution, to payment of their fees and expenses.

[1605]

64   Recoverable fees and expenses of arbitrators

(1)   Unless otherwise agreed by the parties, the recoverable costs of the arbitration shall include in respect of the fees and expenses of the arbitrators only such reasonable fees and expenses as are appropriate in the circumstances.

(2)   If there is any question as to what reasonable fees and expenses are appropriate in the circumstances, and the matter is not already before the court on an application under section 63(4), the court may on the application of any party (upon notice to the other parties)—
  (a)   determine the matter, or
  (b)   order that it be determined by such means and upon such terms as the court may specify.

(3)   Subsection (1) has effect subject to any order of the court under section 24(4) or 25(3)(b) (order as to entitlement to fees or expenses in case of removal or resignation of arbitrator).

(4)   Nothing in this section affects any right of the arbitrator to payment of his fees and expenses.

[1606]

65   Power to limit recoverable costs

(1)   Unless otherwise agreed by the parties, the tribunal may direct that the recoverable costs of the arbitration, or of any part of the arbitral proceedings, shall be limited to a specified amount.

(2)   Any direction may be made or varied at any stage, but this must be done sufficiently in advance of the incurring of costs to which it relates, or the taking of any steps in the proceedings which may be affected by it, for the limit to be taken into account.

[1607]

Powers of the court in relation to award

66   Enforcement of the award

(1)   An award made by the tribunal pursuant to an arbitration agreement may, by leave of the court, be enforced in the same manner as a judgment or order of the court to the same effect.

(2)   Where leave is so given, judgment may be entered in terms of the award.

(3)   Leave to enforce an award shall not be given where, or to the extent that, the person against whom it is sought to be enforced shows that the tribunal lacked substantive jurisdiction to make the award.

The right to raise such an objection may have been lost (see section 73).

(4)   Nothing in this section affects the recognition or enforcement of an award under any other enactment or rule of law, in particular under Part II of the Arbitration Act 1950 (enforcement of awards under Geneva Convention) or the provisions of Part III of this Act relating to the recognition and enforcement of awards under the New York Convention or by an action on the award.

[1608]

67   Challenging the award: substantive jurisdiction

(1)   A party to arbitral proceedings may (upon notice to the other parties and to the tribunal) apply to the court—
  (a)   challenging any award of the arbitral tribunal as to its substantive jurisdiction; or
  (b)   for an order declaring an award made by the tribunal on the merits to be of no effect, in whole or in part, because the tribunal did not have substantive jurisdiction.

A party may lose the right to object (see section 73) and the right to apply is subject to the restrictions in section 70(2) and (3).

(2)   The arbitral tribunal may continue the arbitral proceedings and make a further award while an application to the court under this section is pending in relation to an award as to jurisdiction.

(3)   On an application under this section challenging an award of the arbitral tribunal as to its substantive jurisdiction, the court may by order—
  (a)   confirm the award,
  (b)   vary the award, or
  (c)   set aside the award in whole or in part.

(4)   The leave of the court is required for any appeal from a decision of the court under this section.

[1609]

68   Challenging the award: serious irregularity

(1)   A party to arbitral proceedings may (upon notice to the other parties and to the tribunal) apply to the court challenging an award in the proceedings on the ground of serious irregularity affecting the tribunal, the proceedings or the award.

A party may lose the right to object (see section 73) and the right to apply is subject to the restrictions in section 70(2) and (3).

(2)   Serious irregularity means an irregularity of one or more of the following kinds which the court considers has caused or will cause substantial injustice to the applicant—
  (a)   failure by the tribunal to comply with section 33 (general duty of tribunal);
  (b)   the tribunal exceeding its powers (otherwise than by exceeding its substantive jurisdiction: see section 67);
  (c)   failure by the tribunal to conduct the proceedings in accordance with the procedure agreed by the parties;
  (d)   failure by the tribunal to deal with all the issues that were put to it;
  (e)   any arbitral or other institution or person vested by the parties with powers in relation to the proceedings or the award exceeding its powers;
  (f)   uncertainty or ambiguity as to the effect of the award;
  (g)   the award being obtained by fraud or the award or the way in which it was procured being contrary to public policy;
  (h)   failure to comply with the requirements as to the form of the award; or
  (i)   any irregularity in the conduct of the proceedings or in the award which is admitted by the tribunal or by any arbitral or other institution or person vested by the parties with powers in relation to the proceedings or the award.

(3)   If there is shown to be serious irregularity affecting the tribunal, the proceedings or the award, the court may—

(a)   remit the award to the tribunal, in whole or in part, for reconsideration,

(b)   set the award aside in whole or in part, or

(c)   declare the award to be of no effect, in whole or in part.

The court shall not exercise its power to set aside or to declare an award to be of no effect, in whole or in part, unless it is satisfied that it would be inappropriate to remit the matters in question to the tribunal for reconsideration.

(4)   The leave of the court is required for any appeal from a decision of the court under this section.

[1610]

69   Appeal on point of law

(1)   Unless otherwise agreed by the parties, a party to arbitral proceedings may (upon notice to the other parties and to the tribunal) appeal to the court on a question of law arising out of an award made in the proceedings.

An agreement to dispense with reasons for the tribunal's award shall be considered an agreement to exclude the court's jurisdiction under this section.

(2)   An appeal shall not be brought under this section except—

(a)   with the agreement of all the other parties to the proceedings, or

(b)   with the leave of the court.

The right to appeal is also subject to the restrictions in section 70(2) and (3).

(3)   Leave to appeal shall be given only if the court is satisfied—

(a)   that the determination of the question will substantially affect the rights of one or more of the parties,

(b)   that the question is one which the tribunal was asked to determine,

(c)   that, on the basis of the findings of fact in the award—

(i)   the decision of the tribunal on the question is obviously wrong, or

(ii)   the question is one of general public importance and the decision of the tribunal is at least open to serious doubt, and

(d)   that, despite the agreement of the parties to resolve the matter by arbitration, it is just and proper in all the circumstances for the court to determine the question.

(4)   An application for leave to appeal under this section shall identify the question of law to be determined and state the grounds on which it is alleged that leave to appeal should be granted.

(5)   The court shall determine an application for leave to appeal under this section without a hearing unless it appears to the court that a hearing is required.

(6)   The leave of the court is required for any appeal from a decision of the court under this section to grant or refuse leave to appeal.

(7)   On an appeal under this section the court may by order—

(a)   confirm the award,

(b)   vary the award,

(c)   remit the award to the tribunal, in whole or in part, for reconsideration in the light of the court's determination, or

(d)   set aside the award in whole or in part.

The court shall not exercise its power to set aside an award, in whole or in part, unless it is satisfied that it would be inappropriate to remit the matters in question to the tribunal for reconsideration.

(8)   The decision of the court on an appeal under this section shall be treated as a judgment of the court for the purposes of a further appeal.

But no such appeal lies without the leave of the court which shall not be given unless the court considers that the question is one of general importance or is one which for some other special reason should be considered by the Court of Appeal.

[1611]

70   Challenge or appeal: supplementary provisions

(1)   The following provisions apply to an application or appeal under section 67, 68 or 69.

(2)   An application or appeal may not be brought if the applicant or appellant has not first exhausted—

(a)   any available arbitral process of appeal or review, and

(b)   any available recourse under section 57 (correction of award or additional award).

(3)   Any application or appeal must be brought within 28 days of the date of the award or, if there has been any arbitral process of appeal or review, of the date when the applicant or appellant was notified of the result of that process.

(4) If on an application or appeal it appears to the court that the award—

    (a) does not contain the tribunal's reasons, or

    (b) does not set out the tribunal's reasons in sufficient detail to enable the court properly to consider the application or appeal,

the court may order the tribunal to state the reasons for its award in sufficient detail for that purpose.

(5) Where the court makes an order under subsection (4), it may make such further order as it thinks fit with respect to any additional costs of the arbitration resulting from its order.

(6) The court may order the applicant or appellant to provide security for the costs of the application or appeal, and may direct that the application or appeal be dismissed if the order is not complied with.

The power to order security for costs shall not be exercised on the ground that the applicant or appellant is—

    (a) an individual ordinarily resident outside the United Kingdom, or

    (b) a corporation or association incorporated or formed under the law of a country outside the United Kingdom, or whose central management and control is exercised outside the United Kingdom.

(7) The court may order that any money payable under the award shall be brought into court or otherwise secured pending the determination of the application or appeal, and may direct that the application or appeal be dismissed if the order is not complied with.

(8) The court may grant leave to appeal subject to conditions to the same or similar effect as an order under subsection (6) or (7).

This does not affect the general discretion of the court to grant leave subject to conditions.

[1612]

71 Challenge or appeal: effect of order of court

(1) The following provisions have effect where the court makes an order under section 67, 68 or 69 with respect to an award.

(2) Where the award is varied, the variation has effect as part of the tribunal's award.

(3) Where the award is remitted to the tribunal, in whole or in part, for reconsideration, the tribunal shall make a fresh award in respect of the matters remitted within three months of the date of the order for remission or such longer or shorter period as the court may direct.

(4) Where the award is set aside or declared to be of no effect, in whole or in part, the court may also order that any provision that an award is a condition precedent to the bringing of legal proceedings in respect of a matter to which the arbitration agreement applies, is of no effect as regards the subject matter of the award or, as the case may be, the relevant part of the award.

[1613]

Miscellaneous

72 Saving for rights of person who takes no part in proceedings

(1) A person alleged to be a party to arbitral proceedings but who takes no part in the proceedings may question—

    (a) whether there is a valid arbitration agreement,

    (b) whether the tribunal is properly constituted, or

    (c) what matters have been submitted to arbitration in accordance with the arbitration agreement,

by proceedings in the court for a declaration or injunction or other appropriate relief.

(2) He also has the same right as a party to the arbitral proceedings to challenge an award—

    (a) by an application under section 67 on the ground of lack of substantive jurisdiction in relation to him, or

    (b) by an application under section 68 on the ground of serious irregularity (within the meaning of that section) affecting him;

and section 70(2) (duty to exhaust arbitral procedures) does not apply in his case.

[1614]

73 Loss of right to object

(1) If a party to arbitral proceedings takes part, or continues to take part, in the proceedings without making, either forthwith or within such time as is allowed by the arbitration agreement or the tribunal or by any provision of this Part, any objection—

    (a) that the tribunal lacks substantive jurisdiction,

    (b) that the proceedings have been improperly conducted,

    (c) that there has been a failure to comply with the arbitration agreement or with any provision of this Part, or

    (d) that there has been any other irregularity affecting the tribunal or the proceedings,

PART 1
STATUTES

he may not raise that objection later, before the tribunal or the court, unless he shows that, at the time he took part or continued to take part in the proceedings, he did not know and could not with reasonable diligence have discovered the grounds for the objection.

(2)   Where the arbitral tribunal rules that it has substantive jurisdiction and a party to arbitral proceedings who could have questioned that ruling—
  (a)   by any available arbitral process of appeal or review, or
  (b)   by challenging the award,
does not do so, or does not do so within the time allowed by the arbitration agreement or any provision of this Part, he may not object later to the tribunal's substantive jurisdiction on any ground which was the subject of that ruling.

[1615]

74   Immunity of arbitral institutions, &c

(1)   An arbitral or other institution or person designated or requested by the parties to appoint or nominate an arbitrator is not liable for anything done or omitted in the discharge or purported discharge of that function unless the act or omission is shown to have been in bad faith.

(2)   An arbitral or other institution or person by whom an arbitrator is appointed or nominated is not liable, by reason of having appointed or nominated him, for anything done or omitted by the arbitrator (or his employees or agents) in the discharge or purported discharge of his functions as arbitrator.

(3)   The above provisions apply to an employee or agent of an arbitral or other institution or person as they apply to the institution or person himself.

[1616]

75   Charge to secure payment of solicitors' costs

The powers of the court to make declarations and orders under section 73 of the Solicitors Act 1974 or Article 71H of the Solicitors (Northern Ireland) Order 1976 (power to charge property recovered in the proceedings with the payment of solicitors' costs) may be exercised in relation to arbitral proceedings as if those proceedings were proceedings in the court.

[1617]

Supplementary

76   Service of notices, &c

(1)   The parties are free to agree on the manner of service of any notice or other document required or authorised to be given or served in pursuance of the arbitration agreement or for the purposes of the arbitral proceedings.

(2)   If or to the extent that there is no such agreement the following provisions apply.

(3)   A notice or other document may be served on a person by any effective means.

(4)   If a notice or other document is addressed, pre-paid and delivered by post—
  (a)   to the addressee's last known principal residence or, if he is or has been carrying on a trade, profession or business, his last known principal business address, or
  (b)   where the addressee is a body corporate, to the body's registered or principal office,
it shall be treated as effectively served.

(5)   This section does not apply to the service of documents for the purposes of legal proceedings, for which provision is made by rules of court.

(6)   References in this Part to a notice or other document include any form of communication in writing and references to giving or serving a notice or other document shall be construed accordingly.

[1618]

77   Powers of court in relation to service of documents

(1)   This section applies where service of a document on a person in the manner agreed by the parties, or in accordance with provisions of section 76 having effect in default of agreement, is not reasonably practicable.

(2)   Unless otherwise agreed by the parties, the court may make such order as it thinks fit—
  (a)   for service in such manner as the court may direct, or
  (b)   dispensing with service of the document.

(3)   Any party to the arbitration agreement may apply for an order, but only after exhausting any available arbitral process for resolving the matter.

(4)   The leave of the court is required for any appeal from a decision of the court under this section.

[1619]

78 Reckoning periods of time

(1) The parties are free to agree on the method of reckoning periods of time for the purposes of any provision agreed by them or any provision of this Part having effect in default of such agreement.

(2) If or to the extent there is no such agreement, periods of time shall be reckoned in accordance with the following provisions.

(3) Where the act is required to be done within a specified period after or from a specified date, the period begins immediately after that date.

(4) Where the act is required to be done a specified number of clear days after a specified date, at least that number of days must intervene between the day on which the act is done and that date.

(5) Where the period is a period of seven days or less which would include a Saturday, Sunday or a public holiday in the place where anything which has to be done within the period falls to be done, that day shall be excluded.

In relation to England and Wales or Northern Ireland, a "public holiday" means Christmas Day, Good Friday or a day which under the Banking and Financial Dealings Act 1971 is a bank holiday.

[1620]

79 Power of court to extend time limits relating to arbitral proceedings

(1) Unless the parties otherwise agree, the court may by order extend any time limit agreed by them in relation to any matter relating to the arbitral proceedings or specified in any provision of this Part having effect in default of such agreement.

This section does not apply to a time limit to which section 12 applies (power of court to extend time for beginning arbitral proceedings, &c).

(2) An application for an order may be made—
    (a) by any party to the arbitral proceedings (upon notice to the other parties and to the tribunal), or
    (b) by the arbitral tribunal (upon notice to the parties).

(3) The court shall not exercise its power to extend a time limit unless it is satisfied—
    (a) that any available recourse to the tribunal, or to any arbitral or other institution or person vested by the parties with power in that regard, has first been exhausted, and
    (b) that a substantial injustice would otherwise be done.

(4) The court's power under this section may be exercised whether or not the time has already expired.

(5) An order under this section may be made on such terms as the court thinks fit.

(6) The leave of the court is required for any appeal from a decision of the court under this section.

[1621]

80 Notice and other requirements in connection with legal proceedings

(1) References in this Part to an application, appeal or other step in relation to legal proceedings being taken "upon notice" to the other parties to the arbitral proceedings, or to the tribunal, are to such notice of the originating process as is required by rules of court and do not impose any separate requirement.

(2) Rules of court shall be made—
    (a) requiring such notice to be given as indicated by any provision of this Part, and
    (b) as to the manner, form and content of any such notice.

(3) Subject to any provision made by rules of court, a requirement to give notice to the tribunal of legal proceedings shall be construed—
    (a) if there is more than one arbitrator, as a requirement to give notice to each of them; and
    (b) if the tribunal is not fully constituted, as a requirement to give notice to any arbitrator who has been appointed.

(4) References in this Part to making an application or appeal to the court within a specified period are to the issue within that period of the appropriate originating process in accordance with rules of court.

(5) Where any provision of this Part requires an application or appeal to be made to the court within a specified time, the rules of court relating to the reckoning of periods, the extending or abridging of periods, and the consequences of not taking a step within the period prescribed by the rules, apply in relation to that requirement.

(6) Provision may be made by rules of court amending the provisions of this Part—
    (a) with respect to the time within which any application or appeal to the court must be made,

    (b)   so as to keep any provision made by this Part in relation to arbitral proceedings in step with the corresponding provision of rules of court applying in relation to proceedings in the court, or

    (c)   so as to keep any provision made by this Part in relation to legal proceedings in step with the corresponding provision of rules of court applying generally in relation to proceedings in the court.

(7)   Nothing in this section affects the generality of the power to make rules of court.

[1622]

81 Saving for certain matters governed by common law

(1)   Nothing in this Part shall be construed as excluding the operation of any rule of law consistent with the provisions of this Part, in particular, any rule of law as to—

    (a)   matters which are not capable of settlement by arbitration;

    (b)   the effect of an oral arbitration agreement; or

    (c)   the refusal of recognition or enforcement of an arbitral award on grounds of public policy.

(2)   Nothing in this Act shall be construed as reviving any jurisdiction of the court to set aside or remit an award on the ground of errors of fact or law on the face of the award.

[1623]

82 Minor definitions

(1)   In this Part—

    "arbitrator", unless the context otherwise requires, includes an umpire;

    "available arbitral process", in relation to any matter, includes any process of appeal to or review by an arbitral or other institution or person vested by the parties with powers in relation to that matter;

    "claimant", unless the context otherwise requires, includes a counterclaimant, and related expressions shall be construed accordingly;

    "dispute" includes any difference;

    "enactment" includes an enactment contained in Northern Ireland legislation;

    "legal proceedings" means civil proceedings in the High Court or a county court;

    "peremptory order" means an order made under section 41(5) or made in exercise of any corresponding power conferred by the parties;

    "premises" includes land, buildings, moveable structures, vehicles, vessels, aircraft and hovercraft;

    "question of law" means—

        (a)   for a court in England and Wales, a question of the law of England and Wales, and

        (b)   for a court in Northern Ireland, a question of the law of Northern Ireland;

    "substantive jurisdiction", in relation to an arbitral tribunal, refers to the matters specified in section 30(1)(a) to (c), and references to the tribunal exceeding its substantive jurisdiction shall be construed accordingly.

(2)   References in this Part to a party to an arbitration agreement include any person claiming under or through a party to the agreement.

[1624]

83 Index of defined expressions: Part I

In this Part the expressions listed below are defined or otherwise explained by the provisions indicated—

agreement, agree and agreed	section 5(1)
agreement in writing	section 5(2) to (5)
arbitration agreement	sections 6 and 5(1)
arbitrator	section 82(1)
available arbitral process	section 82(1)
claimant	section 82(1)
commencement (in relation to arbitral proceedings)	section 14
costs of the arbitration	section 59
the court	section 105
dispute	section 82(1)
enactment	section 82(1)

legal proceedings	section 82(1)
Limitation Acts	section 13(4)
notice (or other document)	section 76(6)
party—	
— in relation to an arbitration agreement	section 82(2)
— where section 106(2) or (3) applies	section 106(4)
peremptory order	section 82(1) (and see section 41(5))
premises	section 82(1)
question of law	section 82(1)
recoverable costs	sections 63 and 64
seat of the arbitration	section 3
serve and service (of notice or other document)	section 76(6)
substantive jurisdiction (in relation to an arbitral tribunal)	section 82(1) (and see section 30(1)(a) to (c))
upon notice (to the parties or the tribunal)	section 80
written and in writing	section 5(6)

[1625]

84 Transitional provisions

(1) The provisions of this Part do not apply to arbitral proceedings commenced before the date on which this Part comes into force.

(2) They apply to arbitral proceedings commenced on or after that date under an arbitration agreement whenever made.

(3) The above provisions have effect subject to any transitional provision made by an order under section 109(2) (power to include transitional provisions in commencement order).

[1626]

PART II
OTHER PROVISIONS RELATING TO ARBITRATION

Domestic arbitration agreements

85 Modification of Part I in relation to domestic arbitration agreement

(1) In the case of a domestic arbitration agreement the provisions of Part I are modified in accordance with the following sections.

(2) For this purpose a "domestic arbitration agreement" means an arbitration agreement to which none of the parties is—
   (a) an individual who is a national of, or habitually resident in, a state other than the United Kingdom, or
   (b) a body corporate which is incorporated in, or whose central control and management is exercised in, a state other than the United Kingdom,

and under which the seat of the arbitration (if the seat has been designated or determined) is in the United Kingdom.

(3) In subsection (2) "arbitration agreement" and "seat of the arbitration" have the same meaning as in Part I (see sections 3, 5(1) and 6).

[1627]

NOTES
  Commencement: to be appointed.

---

86 Staying of legal proceedings

(1) In section 9 (stay of legal proceedings), subsection (4) (stay unless the arbitration agreement is null and void, inoperative, or incapable of being performed) does not apply to a domestic arbitration agreement.

(2) On an application under that section in relation to a domestic arbitration agreement the court shall grant a stay unless satisfied—
   (a) that the arbitration agreement is null and void, inoperative, or incapable of being performed, or

(b)   that there are other sufficient grounds for not requiring the parties to abide by the arbitration agreement.

(3)   The court may treat as a sufficient ground under subsection (2)(b) the fact that the applicant is or was at any material time not ready and willing to do all things necessary for the proper conduct of the arbitration or of any other dispute resolution procedures required to be exhausted before resorting to arbitration.

(4)   For the purposes of this section the question whether an arbitration agreement is a domestic arbitration agreement shall be determined by reference to the facts at the time the legal proceedings are commenced.

[1628]

NOTES
Commencement: to be appointed.

87 Effectiveness of agreement to exclude court's jurisdiction

(1)   In the case of a domestic arbitration agreement any agreement to exclude the jurisdiction of the court under—

(a)   section 45 (determination of preliminary point of law), or
(b)   section 69 (challenging the award: appeal on point of law),

is not effective unless entered into after the commencement of the arbitral proceedings in which the question arises or the award is made.

(2)   For this purpose the commencement of the arbitral proceedings has the same meaning as in Part I (see section 14).

(3)   For the purposes of this section the question whether an arbitration agreement is a domestic arbitration agreement shall be determined by reference to the facts at the time the agreement is entered into.

[1629]

NOTES
Commencement: to be appointed.

88 Power to repeal or amend sections 85 to 87

(1)   The Secretary of State may by order repeal or amend the provisions of sections 85 to 87.

(2)   An order under this section may contain such supplementary, incidental and transitional provisions as appear to the Secretary of State to be appropriate.

(3)   An order under this section shall be made by statutory instrument and no such order shall be made unless a draft of it has been laid before and approved by a resolution of each House of Parliament.

[1630]

Consumer arbitration agreements

89 Application of unfair terms regulations to consumer arbitration agreements

(1)   The following sections extend the application of the Unfair Terms in Consumer Contracts Regulations 1994 in relation to a term which constitutes an arbitration agreement.

For this purpose "arbitration agreement" means an agreement to submit to arbitration present or future disputes or differences (whether or not contractual).

(2)   In those sections "the Regulations" means those regulations and includes any regulations amending or replacing those regulations.

(3)   Those sections apply whatever the law applicable to the arbitration agreement.

[1631]

NOTES
Unfair Terms in Consumer Contracts Regulations 1994, SI 1994/3159: revoked and replaced by the Unfair Terms in Consumer Contracts Regulations 1999, SI 1999/2083 at **[3228]**.

90 Regulations apply where consumer is a legal person

The Regulations apply where the consumer is a legal person as they apply where the consumer is a natural person.

[1632]

91 Arbitration agreement unfair where modest amount sought

(1)   A term which constitutes an arbitration agreement is unfair for the purposes of the Regulations so far as it relates to a claim for a pecuniary remedy which does not exceed the amount specified by order for the purposes of this section.

(2)   Orders under this section may make different provision for different cases and for different purposes.

(3)   The power to make orders under this section is exercisable—
   (a)   for England and Wales, by the Secretary of State with the concurrence of the Lord Chancellor,
   (b)   for Scotland, by the Secretary of State ... , and
   (c)   for Northern Ireland, by the Department of Economic Development for Northern Ireland with the concurrence of the Lord Chancellor.

(4)   Any such order for England and Wales or Scotland shall be made by statutory instrument which shall be subject to annulment in pursuance of a resolution of either House of Parliament.

(5)   Any such order for Northern Ireland shall be a statutory rule for the purposes of the Statutory Rules (Northern Ireland) Order 1979 and shall be subject to negative resolution, within the meaning of section 41(6) of the Interpretation Act (Northern Ireland) 1954.

[1633]

NOTES
Sub-s (3): words omitted from para (b) repealed by the Transfer of Functions (Lord Advocate and Secretary of State) Order 1999, SI 1999/678, art 6.
Order: the Unfair Arbitration Agreements (Specified Amount) Order 1999, SI 1999/2167.

Small claims arbitration in the county court

92 Exclusion of Part I in relation to small claims arbitration in the county court

Nothing in Part I of this Act applies to arbitration under section 64 of the County Courts Act 1984.

[1634]

Appointment of judges as arbitrators

93 Appointment of judges as arbitrators

(1)   A judge of the Commercial Court or an official referee may, if in all the circumstances he thinks fit, accept appointment as a sole arbitrator or as umpire by or by virtue of an arbitration agreement.

(2)   A judge of the Commercial Court shall not do so unless the Lord Chief Justice has informed him that, having regard to the state of business in the High Court and the Crown Court, he can be made available.

(3)   An official referee shall not do so unless the Lord Chief Justice has informed him that, having regard to the state of official referees' business, he can be made available.

(4)   The fees payable for the services of a judge of the Commercial Court or official referee as arbitrator or umpire shall be taken in the High Court.

(5)   In this section—
   "arbitration agreement" has the same meaning as in Part I; and
   "official referee" means a person nominated under section 68(1)(a) of the [Senior Courts Act 1981] to deal with official referees' business.

(6)   The provisions of Part I of this Act apply to arbitration before a person appointed under this section with the modifications specified in Schedule 2.

[1635]

NOTES
Sub-s (5): words in square brackets in definition "official referee" substituted by the Constitutional Reform Act 2005, s 59(5), Sch 11, Pt 1, para 1(2).

Statutory arbitrations

94 Application of Part I to statutory arbitrations

(1)   The provisions of Part I apply to every arbitration under an enactment (a "statutory arbitration"), whether the enactment was passed or made before or after the commencement of this Act, subject to the adaptations and exclusions specified in sections 95 to 98.

(2)   The provisions of Part I do not apply to a statutory arbitration if or to the extent that their application—
   (a)   is inconsistent with the provisions of the enactment concerned, with any rules or procedure authorised or recognised by it, or

(b)   is excluded by any other enactment.

(3)   In this section and the following provisions of this Part "enactment"—
    (a)   in England and Wales, includes an enactment contained in subordinate legislation within the meaning of the Interpretation Act 1978;
    (b)   in Northern Ireland, means a statutory provision within the meaning of section 1(f) of the Interpretation Act (Northern Ireland) 1954.

[1636]

95   General adaptation of provisions in relation to statutory arbitrations

(1)   The provisions of Part I apply to a statutory arbitration—
    (a)   as if the arbitration were pursuant to an arbitration agreement and as if the enactment were that agreement, and
    (b)   as if the persons by and against whom a claim subject to arbitration in pursuance of the enactment may be or has been made were parties to that agreement.

(2)   Every statutory arbitration shall be taken to have its seat in England and Wales or, as the case may be, in Northern Ireland.

[1637]

96   Specific adaptations of provisions in relation to statutory arbitrations

(1)   The following provisions of Part I apply to a statutory arbitration with the following adaptations.

(2)   In section 30(1) (competence of tribunal to rule on its own jurisdiction), the reference in paragraph (a) to whether there is a valid arbitration agreement shall be construed as a reference to whether the enactment applies to the dispute or difference in question.

(3)   Section 35 (consolidation of proceedings and concurrent hearings) applies only so as to authorise the consolidation of proceedings, or concurrent hearings in proceedings, under the same enactment.

(4)   Section 46 (rules applicable to substance of dispute) applies with the omission of subsection (1)(b) (determination in accordance with considerations agreed by parties).

[1638]

97   Provisions excluded from applying to statutory arbitrations

The following provisions of Part I do not apply in relation to a statutory arbitration—
    (a)   section 8 (whether agreement discharged by death of a party);
    (b)   section 12 (power of court to extend agreed time limits);
    (c)   sections 9(5), 10(2) and 71(4) (restrictions on effect of provision that award condition precedent to right to bring legal proceedings).

[1639]

98   Power to make further provision by regulations

(1)   The Secretary of State may make provision by regulations for adapting or excluding any provision of Part I in relation to statutory arbitrations in general or statutory arbitrations of any particular description.

(2)   The power is exercisable whether the enactment concerned is passed or made before or after the commencement of this Act.

(3)   Regulations under this section shall be made by statutory instrument which shall be subject to annulment in pursuance of a resolution of either House of Parliament.

[1640]

PART III
RECOGNITION AND ENFORCEMENT OF CERTAIN FOREIGN AWARDS

Enforcement of Geneva Convention awards

99   Continuation of Part II of the Arbitration Act 1950

Part II of the Arbitration Act 1950 (enforcement of certain foreign awards) continues to apply in relation to foreign awards within the meaning of that Part which are not also New York Convention awards.

[1641]

Recognition and enforcement of New York Convention awards

100   New York Convention awards

(1)   In this Part a "New York Convention award" means an award made, in pursuance of an arbitration agreement, in the territory of a state (other than the United Kingdom) which is a party to the New York Convention.

(2)   For the purposes of subsection (1) and of the provisions of this Part relating to such awards—

(a)   "arbitration agreement" means an arbitration agreement in writing, and

(b)   an award shall be treated as made at the seat of the arbitration, regardless of where it was signed, despatched or delivered to any of the parties.

In this subsection "agreement in writing" and "seat of the arbitration" have the same meaning as in Part I.

(3)   If Her Majesty by Order in Council declares that a state specified in the Order is a party to the New York Convention, or is a party in respect of any territory so specified, the Order shall, while in force, be conclusive evidence of that fact.

(4)   In this section "the New York Convention" means the Convention on the Recognition and Enforcement of Foreign Arbitral Awards adopted by the United Nations Conference on International Commercial Arbitration on 10th June 1958.

[1642]

NOTES

Orders: by virtue of the Interpretation Act 1978, s 17(2)(b), the following Orders in Council have effect as if made under this section: the Arbitration (Foreign Awards) Order 1984, SI 1984/1168; the Arbitration (Foreign Awards) Order 1989, SI 1989/1348; the Arbitration (Foreign Awards) Order 1993, SI 1993/1256.

101   Recognition and enforcement of awards

(1)   A New York Convention award shall be recognised as binding on the persons as between whom it was made, and may accordingly be relied on by those persons by way of defence, set-off or otherwise in any legal proceedings in England and Wales or Northern Ireland.

(2)   A New York Convention award may, by leave of the court, be enforced in the same manner as a judgment or order of the court to the same effect.

As to the meaning of "the court" see section 105.

(3)   Where leave is so given, judgment may be entered in terms of the award.

[1643]

102   Evidence to be produced by party seeking recognition or enforcement

(1)   A party seeking the recognition or enforcement of a New York Convention award must produce—

(a)   the duly authenticated original award or a duly certified copy of it, and

(b)   the original arbitration agreement or a duly certified copy of it.

(2)   If the award or agreement is in a foreign language, the party must also produce a translation of it certified by an official or sworn translator or by a diplomatic or consular agent.

[1644]

103   Refusal of recognition or enforcement

(1)   Recognition or enforcement of a New York Convention award shall not be refused except in the following cases.

(2)   Recognition or enforcement of the award may be refused if the person against whom it is invoked proves—

(a)   that a party to the arbitration agreement was (under the law applicable to him) under some incapacity;

(b)   that the arbitration agreement was not valid under the law to which the parties subjected it or, failing any indication thereon, under the law of the country where the award was made;

(c)   that he was not given proper notice of the appointment of the arbitrator or of the arbitration proceedings or was otherwise unable to present his case;

(d)   that the award deals with a difference not contemplated by or not falling within the terms of the submission to arbitration or contains decisions on matters beyond the scope of the submission to arbitration (but see subsection (4));

(e)   that the composition of the arbitral tribunal or the arbitral procedure was not in accordance with the agreement of the parties or, failing such agreement, with the law of the country in which the arbitration took place;

(f)   that the award has not yet become binding on the parties, or has been set aside or suspended by a competent authority of the country in which, or under the law of which, it was made.

(3)   Recognition or enforcement of the award may also be refused if the award is in respect of a matter which is not capable of settlement by arbitration, or if it would be contrary to public policy to recognise or enforce the award.

(4) An award which contains decisions on matters not submitted to arbitration may be recognised or enforced to the extent that it contains decisions on matters submitted to arbitration which can be separated from those on matters not so submitted.

(5) Where an application for the setting aside or suspension of the award has been made to such a competent authority as is mentioned in subsection (2)(f), the court before which the award is sought to be relied upon may, if it considers it proper, adjourn the decision on the recognition or enforcement of the award.

It may also on the application of the party claiming recognition or enforcement of the award order the other party to give suitable security.

[1645]

104 Saving for other bases of recognition or enforcement

Nothing in the preceding provisions of this Part affects any right to rely upon or enforce a New York Convention award at common law or under section 66.

[1646]

PART IV
GENERAL PROVISIONS

105 Meaning of "the court": jurisdiction of High Court and county court

(1) In this Act "the court" means the High Court or a county court, subject to the following provisions.

(2) The Lord Chancellor may by order make provision—
    (a) allocating proceedings under this Act to the High Court or to county courts; or
    (b) specifying proceedings under this Act which may be commenced or taken only in the High Court or in a county court.

(3) The Lord Chancellor may by order make provision requiring proceedings of any specified description under this Act in relation to which a county court has jurisdiction to be commenced or taken in one or more specified county courts.

Any jurisdiction so exercisable by a specified county court is exercisable throughout England and Wales or, as the case may be, Northern Ireland.

[(3A) The Lord Chancellor must consult the Lord Chief Justice of England and Wales or the Lord Chief Justice of Northern Ireland (as the case may be) before making an order under this section.

(3B) The Lord Chief Justice of England and Wales may nominate a judicial office holder (as defined in section 109(4) of the Constitutional Reform Act 2005) to exercise his functions under this section.

(3C) The Lord Chief Justice of Northern Ireland may nominate any of the following to exercise his functions under this section—
    (a) the holder of one of the offices listed in Schedule 1 to the Justice (Northern Ireland) Act 2002;
    (b) a Lord Justice of Appeal (as defined in section 88 of that Act).]

(4) An order under this section—
    (a) may differentiate between categories of proceedings by reference to such criteria as the Lord Chancellor sees fit to specify, and
    (b) may make such incidental or transitional provision as the Lord Chancellor considers necessary or expedient.

(5) An order under this section for England and Wales shall be made by statutory instrument which shall be subject to annulment in pursuance of a resolution of either House of Parliament.

(6) An order under this section for Northern Ireland shall be a statutory rule for the purposes of the Statutory Rules (Northern Ireland) Order 1979 which shall be subject to [negative resolution (within the meaning of section 41(6) of the Interpretation Act (Northern Ireland) 1954)].

[1647]

NOTES
Sub-ss (3A)–(3C): inserted by the Constitutional Reform Act 2005, s 15(1), Sch 4, Pt 1, para 250.
Sub-s (6): words in square brackets substituted by the Northern Ireland Act 1998 (Devolution of Policing and Justice Functions) Order 2010, SI 2010/976, art 15(5), Sch 18, Pt 1, para 50, subject to transitional provisions in arts 28–31 thereof.
Order: the High Court and County Courts (Allocation of Arbitration Proceedings) Order 1996, SI 1996/3215.

---

106 Crown application

(1) Part I of this Act applies to any arbitration agreement to which Her Majesty, either in right of the Crown or of the Duchy of Lancaster or otherwise, or the Duke of Cornwall, is a party.

(2)   Where Her Majesty is party to an arbitration agreement otherwise than in right of the Crown, Her Majesty shall be represented for the purposes of any arbitral proceedings—

  (a)   where the agreement was entered into by Her Majesty in right of the Duchy of Lancaster, by the Chancellor of the Duchy or such person as he may appoint, and

  (b)   in any other case, by such person as Her Majesty may appoint in writing under the Royal Sign Manual.

(3)   Where the Duke of Cornwall is party to an arbitration agreement, he shall be represented for the purposes of any arbitral proceedings by such person as he may appoint.

(4)   References in Part I to a party or the parties to the arbitration agreement or to arbitral proceedings shall be construed, where subsection (2) or (3) applies, as references to the person representing Her Majesty or the Duke of Cornwall.

[1648]

107   Consequential amendments and repeals

(1)   The enactments specified in Schedule 3 are amended in accordance with that Schedule, the amendments being consequential on the provisions of this Act.

(2)   The enactments specified in Schedule 4 are repealed to the extent specified.

[1649]

108   Extent

(1)   The provisions of this Act extend to England and Wales and, except as mentioned below, to Northern Ireland.

(2)   The following provisions of Part II do not extend to Northern Ireland—

  section 92 (exclusion of Part I in relation to small claims arbitration in the county court), and

  section 93 and Schedule 2 (appointment of judges as arbitrators).

(3)   Sections 89, 90 and 91 (consumer arbitration agreements) extend to Scotland and the provisions of Schedules 3 and 4 (consequential amendments and repeals) extend to Scotland so far as they relate to enactments which so extend, subject as follows.

(4)   The repeal of the Arbitration Act 1975 extends only to England and Wales and Northern Ireland.

[1650]

109   Commencement

(1)   The provisions of this Act come into force on such day as the Secretary of State may appoint by order made by statutory instrument, and different days may be appointed for different purposes.

(2)   An order under subsection (1) may contain such transitional provisions as appear to the Secretary of State to be appropriate.

[1651]

NOTES

  Order: the Arbitration Act 1996 (Commencement No 1) Order 1996, SI 1996/3146.

110   Short title

This Act may be cited as the Arbitration Act 1996.

[1652]

SCHEDULES

SCHEDULE 1
MANDATORY PROVISIONS OF PART I

Section 4(1)

  sections 9 to 11 (stay of legal proceedings);
  section 12 (power of court to extend agreed time limits);
  section 13 (application of Limitation Acts);
  section 24 (power of court to remove arbitrator);
  section 26(1) (effect of death of arbitrator);
  section 28 (liability of parties for fees and expenses of arbitrators);
  section 29 (immunity of arbitrator);
  section 31 (objection to substantive jurisdiction of tribunal);
  section 32 (determination of preliminary point of jurisdiction);
  section 33 (general duty of tribunal);
  section 37(2) (items to be treated as expenses of arbitrators);
  section 40 (general duty of parties);
  section 43 (securing the attendance of witnesses);

section 56 (power to withhold award in case of non-payment);

section 60 (effectiveness of agreement for payment of costs in any event);

section 66 (enforcement of award);

sections 67 and 68 (challenging the award: substantive jurisdiction and serious irregularity), and sections 70 and 71 (supplementary provisions; effect of order of court) so far as relating to those sections;

section 72 (saving for rights of person who takes no part in proceedings);

section 73 (loss of right to object);

section 74 (immunity of arbitral institutions, &c);

section 75 (charge to secure payment of solicitors' costs).

[1653]

SCHEDULE 2
MODIFICATIONS OF PART I IN RELATION TO JUDGE-ARBITRATORS
Section 93(6)

Introductory

1. In this Schedule "judge-arbitrator" means a judge of the Commercial Court or official referee appointed as arbitrator or umpire under section 93.

General

2.—(1) Subject to the following provisions of this Schedule, references in Part I to the court shall be construed in relation to a judge-arbitrator, or in relation to the appointment of a judge-arbitrator, as references to the Court of Appeal.

(2) The references in sections 32(6), 45(6) and 69(8) to the Court of Appeal shall in such a case be construed as references to the [Supreme Court].

Arbitrator's fees

3.—(1) The power of the court in section 28(2) to order consideration and adjustment of the liability of a party for the fees of an arbitrator may be exercised by a judge-arbitrator.

(2) Any such exercise of the power is subject to the powers of the Court of Appeal under sections 24(4) and 25(3)(b) (directions as to entitlement to fees or expenses in case of removal or resignation).

Exercise of court powers in support of arbitration

4.—(1) Where the arbitral tribunal consists of or includes a judge-arbitrator the powers of the court under sections 42 to 44 (enforcement of peremptory orders, summoning witnesses, and other court powers) are exercisable by the High Court and also by the judge-arbitrator himself.

(2) Anything done by a judge-arbitrator in the exercise of those powers shall be regarded as done by him in his capacity as judge of the High Court and have effect as if done by that court.

Nothing in this sub-paragraph prejudices any power vested in him as arbitrator or umpire.

Extension of time for making award

5.—(1) The power conferred by section 50 (extension of time for making award) is exercisable by the judge-arbitrator himself.

(2) Any appeal from a decision of a judge-arbitrator under that section lies to the Court of Appeal with the leave of that court.

Withholding award in case of non-payment

6.—(1) The provisions of paragraph 7 apply in place of the provisions of section 56 (power to withhold award in the case of non-payment) in relation to the withholding of an award for non-payment of the fees and expenses of a judge-arbitrator.

(2) This does not affect the application of section 56 in relation to the delivery of such an award by an arbitral or other institution or person vested by the parties with powers in relation to the delivery of the award.

7.—(1) A judge-arbitrator may refuse to deliver an award except upon payment of the fees and expenses mentioned in section 56(1).

(2) The judge-arbitrator may, on an application by a party to the arbitral proceedings, order that if he pays into the High Court the fees and expenses demanded, or such lesser amount as the judge-arbitrator may specify—

(a) the award shall be delivered,

(b) the amount of the fees and expenses properly payable shall be determined by such means and upon such terms as he may direct, and

(c) out of the money paid into court there shall be paid out such fees and expenses as may be found to be properly payable and the balance of the money (if any) shall be paid out to the applicant.

(3) For this purpose the amount of fees and expenses properly payable is the amount the applicant is liable to pay under section 28 or any agreement relating to the payment of the arbitrator.

(4) No application to the judge-arbitrator under this paragraph may be made where there is any available arbitral process for appeal or review of the amount of the fees or expenses demanded.

(5) Any appeal from a decision of a judge-arbitrator under this paragraph lies to the Court of Appeal with the leave of that court.

(6) Where a party to arbitral proceedings appeals under sub-paragraph (5), an arbitrator is entitled to appear and be heard.

Correction of award or additional award

8. Subsections (4) to (6) of section 57 (correction of award or additional award: time limit for application or exercise of power) do not apply to a judge-arbitrator.

Costs

9. Where the arbitral tribunal consists of or includes a judge-arbitrator the powers of the court under section 63(4) (determination of recoverable costs) shall be exercised by the High Court.

10.—(1) The power of the court under section 64 to determine an arbitrator's reasonable fees and expenses may be exercised by a judge-arbitrator.

(2) Any such exercise of the power is subject to the powers of the Court of Appeal under sections 24(4) and 25(3)(b) (directions as to entitlement to fees or expenses in case of removal or resignation).

Enforcement of award

11. The leave of the court required by section 66 (enforcement of award) may in the case of an award of a judge-arbitrator be given by the judge-arbitrator himself.

Solicitors' costs

12. The powers of the court to make declarations and orders under the provisions applied by section 75 (power to charge property recovered in arbitral proceedings with the payment of solicitors' costs) may be exercised by the judge-arbitrator.

Powers of court in relation to service of documents

13.—(1) The power of the court under section 77(2) (powers of court in relation to service of documents) is exercisable by the judge-arbitrator.

(2) Any appeal from a decision of a judge-arbitrator under that section lies to the Court of Appeal with the leave of that court.

Powers of court to extend time limits relating to arbitral proceedings

14.—(1) The power conferred by section 79 (power of court to extend time limits relating to arbitral proceedings) is exercisable by the judge-arbitrator himself.

(2) Any appeal from a decision of a judge-arbitrator under that section lies to the Court of Appeal with the leave of that court.

[1654]

NOTES
Para 2: words in square brackets in sub-para (2) substituted by the Constitutional Reform Act 2005, s 40(4), Sch 9, Pt 1, para 60.

(*Sch 3 (Consequential Amendments) and Sch 4 (Repeals) outside the scope of this work.*)

LATE PAYMENT OF COMMERCIAL DEBTS (INTEREST) ACT 1998

(1998 c 20)

ARRANGEMENT OF SECTIONS

PART I
STATUTORY INTEREST ON QUALIFYING DEBTS

An Act to make provision with respect to interest on the late payment of certain debts arising under commercial contracts for the supply of goods or services; and for connected purposes

[11 June 1998]

PART I
STATUTORY INTEREST ON QUALIFYING DEBTS

1   Statutory interest

(1)   It is an implied term in a contract to which this Act applies that any qualifying debt created by the contract carries simple interest subject to and in accordance with this Part.

(2)   Interest carried under that implied term (in this Act referred to as "statutory interest") shall be treated, for the purposes of any rule of law or enactment (other than this Act) relating to interest on debts, in the same way as interest carried under an express contract term.

(3)   This Part has effect subject to Part II (which in certain circumstances permits contract terms to oust or vary the right to statutory interest that would otherwise be conferred by virtue of the term implied by subsection (1)).

[1655]

2   Contracts to which Act applies

(1)   This Act applies to a contract for the supply of goods or services where the purchaser and the supplier are each acting in the course of a business, other than an excepted contract.

(2)   In this Act "contract for the supply of goods or services" means—
    (a)   a contract of sale of goods; or
    (b)   a contract (other than a contract of sale of goods) by which a person does any, or any combination, of the things mentioned in subsection (3) for a consideration that is (or includes) a money consideration.

(3)   Those things are—
    (a)   transferring or agreeing to transfer to another the property in goods;
    (b)   bailing or agreeing to bail goods to another by way of hire or, in Scotland, hiring or agreeing to hire goods to another; and
    (c)   agreeing to carry out a service.

(4)   For the avoidance of doubt a contract of service or apprenticeship is not a contract for the supply of goods or services.

(5)   The following are excepted contracts—
    (a)   a consumer credit agreement;
    (b)   a contract intended to operate by way of mortgage, pledge, charge or other security; and
    (c)   ...

(6)   ...

(7)   In this section—
    "business" includes a profession and the activities of any government department or local or public authority;
    "consumer credit agreement" has the same meaning as in the Consumer Credit Act 1974;

"contract of sale of goods" and "goods" have the same meaning as in the Sale of Goods Act 1979;

["government department" means any part of the Scottish Administration;]

"property in goods" means the general property in them and not merely a special property.

[1656]

NOTES

Sub-s (5): para (c) repealed by the Late Payment of Commercial Debts Regulations 2002, SI 2002/1674, reg 2(1), (2), in relation to contracts made on or after 7 August 2002.

Sub-s (6): repealed by SI 2002/1674, reg 2(1), (2), in relation to contracts made on or after 7 August 2002.

Sub-s (7): definition "government department" inserted by the Scotland Act 1998 (Consequential Modifications) (No 2) Order 1999, SI 1999/1820, art 4, Sch 2, Pt I, para 132.

Note: the repeals made by SI 2002/1674 as noted above apply to England, Wales and Northern Ireland. The same repeals are made in relation to Scotland by the Late Payment of Commercial Debts (Scotland) Regulations 2002, SSI 2002/335.

2A (*Inserted in relation to Scotland by the Late Payment of Commercial Debts (Scotland) Regulations 2002, SSI 2002/335.*)

3 Qualifying debts

(1) A debt created by virtue of an obligation under a contract to which this Act applies to pay the whole or any part of the contract price is a "qualifying debt" for the purposes of this Act, unless (when created) the whole of the debt is prevented from carrying statutory interest by this section.

(2) A debt does not carry statutory interest if or to the extent that it consists of a sum to which a right to interest or to charge interest applies by virtue of any enactment (other than section 1 of this Act).

This subsection does not prevent a sum from carrying statutory interest by reason of the fact that a court, arbitrator or arbiter would, apart from this Act, have power to award interest on it.

(3) A debt does not carry (and shall be treated as never having carried) statutory interest if or to the extent that a right to demand interest on it, which exists by virtue of any rule of law, is exercised.

(4), (5) ...

[1657]

NOTES

Sub-ss (4), (5): repealed by the Late Payment of Commercial Debts Regulations 2002, SI 2002/1674, reg 2(1), (3), in relation to contracts made on or after 7 August 2002.

Note: the repeals made by SI 2002/1674 as noted above apply to England, Wales and Northern Ireland. The same repeals are made in relation to Scotland by the Late Payment of Commercial Debts (Scotland) Regulations 2002, SSI 2002/335.

4 Period for which statutory interest runs

(1) Statutory interest runs in relation to a qualifying debt in accordance with this section (unless section 5 applies).

(2) Statutory interest starts to run on the day after the relevant day for the debt, at the rate prevailing under section 6 at the end of the relevant day.

(3) Where the supplier and the purchaser agree a date for payment of the debt (that is, the day on which the debt is to be created by the contract), that is the relevant day unless the debt relates to an obligation to make an advance payment.

A date so agreed may be a fixed one or may depend on the happening of an event or the failure of an event to happen.

(4) Where the debt relates to an obligation to make an advance payment, the relevant day is the day on which the debt is treated by section 11 as having been created.

(5) In any other case, the relevant day is the last day of the period of 30 days beginning with—

(a) the day on which the obligation of the supplier to which the debt relates is performed; or

(b) the day on which the purchaser has notice of the amount of the debt or (where that amount is unascertained) the sum which the supplier claims is the amount of the debt,

whichever is the later.

(6) Where the debt is created by virtue of an obligation to pay a sum due in respect of a period of hire of goods, subsection (5)(a) has effect as if it referred to the last day of that period.

(7) Statutory interest ceases to run when the interest would cease to run if it were carried under an express contract term.

(8) In this section "advance payment" has the same meaning as in section 11.

[1658]

5   Remission of statutory interest

(1)   This section applies where, by reason of any conduct of the supplier, the interests of justice require that statutory interest should be remitted in whole or part in respect of a period for which it would otherwise run in relation to a qualifying debt.

(2)   If the interests of justice require that the supplier should receive no statutory interest for a period, statutory interest shall not run for that period.

(3)   If the interests of justice require that the supplier should receive statutory interest at a reduced rate for a period, statutory interest shall run at such rate as meets the justice of the case for that period.

(4)   Remission of statutory interest under this section may be required—

(a)   by reason of conduct at any time (whether before or after the time at which the debt is created); and

(b)   for the whole period for which statutory interest would otherwise run or for one or more parts of that period.

(5)   In this section "conduct" includes any act or omission.

[1659]

[5A   Compensation arising out of late payment

(1)   Once statutory interest begins to run in relation to a qualifying debt, the supplier shall be entitled to a fixed sum (in addition to the statutory interest on the debt).

(2)   That sum shall be—

(a)   for a debt less than £1,000, the sum of £40;

(b)   for a debt of £1,000 or more, but less than £10,000, the sum of £70;

(c)   for a debt of £10,000 or more, the sum of £100.

(3)   The obligation to pay an additional fixed sum under this section in respect of a qualifying debt shall be treated as part of the term implied by section 1(1) in the contract creating the debt.]

[1660]

NOTES

Inserted by the Late Payment of Commercial Debts Regulations 2002, SI 2002/1674, reg 2(1), (4), in relation to contracts made on or after 7 August 2002.

Note: this section as inserted by SI 2002/1674 as noted above applies to England, Wales and Northern Ireland. The same insertion is made in relation to Scotland by the Late Payment of Commercial Debts (Scotland) Regulations 2002, SSI 2002/335.

6   Rate of statutory interest

(1)   The Secretary of State shall by order made with the consent of the Treasury set the rate of statutory interest by prescribing—

(a)   a formula for calculating the rate of statutory interest; or

(b)   the rate of statutory interest.

(2)   Before making such an order the Secretary of State shall, among other things, consider the extent to which it may be desirable to set the rate so as to—

(a)   protect suppliers whose financial position makes them particularly vulnerable if their qualifying debts are paid late; and

(b)   deter generally the late payment of qualifying debts.

[1661]

NOTES

Order: the Late Payment of Commercial Debts (Rate of Interest) (No 3) Order 2002, SI 2002/1675, which provides that the rate of interest for the purposes of this Act shall be 8 per cent per annum over the official dealing rate (ie, the rate announced from time to time by the Monetary Policy Committee of the Bank of England and for the time being in force as the official dealing rate, being the rate at which the Bank is willing to enter into transactions for providing short term liquidity in the money markets) in force on the 30 June (in respect of interest which starts to run between 1 July and 31 December) or the 31 December (in respect of interest which starts to run between 1 January and 30 June) immediately before the day on which statutory interest starts to run.

PART II

CONTRACT TERMS RELATING TO LATE PAYMENT OF QUALIFYING DEBTS

7   Purpose of Part II

(1)   This Part deals with the extent to which the parties to a contract to which this Act applies may by reference to contract terms oust or vary the right to statutory interest that would otherwise apply when a qualifying debt created by the contract (in this Part referred to as "the debt") is not paid.

(2) This Part applies to contract terms agreed before the debt is created; after that time the parties are free to agree terms dealing with the debt.

(3) This Part has effect without prejudice to any other ground which may affect the validity of a contract term.

[1662]

8 Circumstances where statutory interest may be ousted or varied

(1) Any contract terms are void to the extent that they purport to exclude the right to statutory interest in relation to the debt, unless there is a substantial contractual remedy for late payment of the debt.

(2) Where the parties agree a contractual remedy for late payment of the debt that is a substantial remedy, statutory interest is not carried by the debt (unless they agree otherwise).

(3) The parties may not agree to vary the right to statutory interest in relation to the debt unless either the right to statutory interest as varied or the overall remedy for late payment of the debt is a substantial remedy.

(4) Any contract terms are void to the extent that they purport to—
    (a)   confer a contractual right to interest that is not a substantial remedy for late payment of the debt, or
    (b)   vary the right to statutory interest so as to provide for a right to statutory interest that is not a substantial remedy for late payment of the debt,
unless the overall remedy for late payment of the debt is a substantial remedy.

(5) Subject to this section, the parties are free to agree contract terms which deal with the consequences of late payment of the debt.

[1663]

9 Meaning of "substantial remedy"

(1) A remedy for the late payment of the debt shall be regarded as a substantial remedy unless—
    (a)   the remedy is insufficient either for the purpose of compensating the supplier for late payment or for deterring late payment; and
    (b)   it would not be fair or reasonable to allow the remedy to be relied on to oust or (as the case may be) to vary the right to statutory interest that would otherwise apply in relation to the debt.

(2) In determining whether a remedy is not a substantial remedy, regard shall be had to all the relevant circumstances at the time the terms in question are agreed.

(3) In determining whether subsection (1)(b) applies, regard shall be had (without prejudice to the generality of subsection (2)) to the following matters—
    (a)   the benefits of commercial certainty;
    (b)   the strength of the bargaining positions of the parties relative to each other;
    (c)   whether the term was imposed by one party to the detriment of the other (whether by the use of standard terms or otherwise); and
    (d)   whether the supplier received an inducement to agree to the term.

[1664]

10 Interpretation of Part II

(1) In this Part—
    "contract term" means a term of the contract creating the debt or any other contract term binding the parties (or either of them);
    "contractual remedy" means a contractual right to interest or any contractual remedy other than interest;
    "contractual right to interest" includes a reference to a contractual right to charge interest;
    "overall remedy", in relation to the late payment of the debt, means any combination of a contractual right to interest, a varied right to statutory interest or a contractual remedy other than interest;
    "substantial remedy" shall be construed in accordance with section 9.

(2) In this Part a reference (however worded) to contract terms which vary the right to statutory interest is a reference to terms altering in any way the effect of Part I in relation to the debt (for example by postponing the time at which interest starts to run or by imposing conditions on the right to interest).

(3) In this Part a reference to late payment of the debt is a reference to late payment of the sum due when the debt is created (excluding any part of that sum which is prevented from carrying statutory interest by section 3).

[1665]

PART III
GENERAL AND SUPPLEMENTARY

11 Treatment of advance payments of the contract price

(1)   A qualifying debt created by virtue of an obligation to make an advance payment shall be treated for the purposes of this Act as if it was created on the day mentioned in subsection (3), (4) or (5) (as the case may be).

(2)   In this section "advance payment" means a payment falling due before the obligation of the supplier to which the whole contract price relates ("the supplier's obligation") is performed, other than a payment of a part of the contract price that is due in respect of any part performance of that obligation and payable on or after the day on which that part performance is completed.

(3)   Where the advance payment is the whole contract price, the debt shall be treated as created on the day on which the supplier's obligation is performed.

(4)   Where the advance payment is a part of the contract price, but the sum is not due in respect of any part performance of the supplier's obligation, the debt shall be treated as created on the day on which the supplier's obligation is performed.

(5)   Where the advance payment is a part of the contract price due in respect of any part performance of the supplier's obligation, but is payable before that part performance is completed, the debt shall be treated as created on the day on which the relevant part performance is completed.

(6)   Where the debt is created by virtue of an obligation to pay a sum due in respect of a period of hire of goods, this section has effect as if—

   (a)   references to the day on which the supplier's obligation is performed were references to the last day of that period; and

   (b)   references to part performance of that obligation were references to part of that period.

(7)   For the purposes of this section an obligation to pay the whole outstanding balance of the contract price shall be regarded as an obligation to pay the whole contract price and not as an obligation to pay a part of the contract price.

[1666]

12 Conflict of laws

(1)   This Act does not have effect in relation to a contract governed by the law of a part of the United Kingdom by choice of the parties if—

   (a)   there is no significant connection between the contract and that part of the United Kingdom; and

   (b)   but for that choice, the applicable law would be a foreign law.

(2)   This Act has effect in relation to a contract governed by a foreign law by choice of the parties if—

   (a)   but for that choice, the applicable law would be the law of a part of the United Kingdom; and

   (b)   there is no significant connection between the contract and any country other than that part of the United Kingdom.

(3)   In this section—

"contract" means a contract falling within section 2(1); and

"foreign law" means the law of a country outside the United Kingdom.

[1667]

13 Assignments, etc

(1)   The operation of this Act in relation to a qualifying debt is not affected by—

   (a)   any change in the identity of the parties to the contract creating the debt; or

   (b)   the passing of the right to be paid the debt, or the duty to pay it (in whole or in part) to a person other than the person who is the original creditor or the original debtor when the debt is created.

(2)   Any reference in this Act to the supplier or the purchaser is a reference to the person who is for the time being the supplier or the purchaser or, in relation to a time after the debt in question has been created, the person who is for the time being the creditor or the debtor, as the case may be.

(3)   Where the right to be paid part of a debt passes to a person other than the person who is the original creditor when the debt is created, any reference in this Act to a debt shall be construed as (or, if the context so requires, as including) a reference to part of a debt.

(4)   A reference in this section to the identity of the parties to a contract changing, or to a right or duty passing, is a reference to it changing or passing by assignment or assignation, by operation of law or otherwise.

[1668]

14 Contract terms relating to the date for payment of the contract price

(1) This section applies to any contract term which purports to have the effect of postponing the time at which a qualifying debt would otherwise be created by a contract to which this Act applies.

(2) Sections 3(2)(b) and 17(1)(b) of the Unfair Contract Terms Act 1977 (no reliance to be placed on certain contract terms) shall apply in cases where such a contract term is not contained in written standard terms of the purchaser as well as in cases where the term is contained in such standard terms.

(3) In this section "contract term" has the same meaning as in section 10(1).

[1669]

15 Orders and regulations

(1) Any power to make an order or regulations under this Act is exercisable by statutory instrument.

(2) Any statutory instrument containing an order or regulations under this Act, other than an order under section 17(2), shall be subject to annulment in pursuance of a resolution of either House of Parliament.

[1670]

16 Interpretation

(1) In this Act—
"contract for the supply of goods or services" has the meaning given in section 2(2);
"contract price" means the price in a contract of sale of goods or the money consideration referred to in section 2(2)(b) in any other contract for the supply of goods or services;
"purchaser" means (subject to section 13(2)) the buyer in a contract of sale or the person who contracts with the supplier in any other contract for the supply of goods or services;
"qualifying debt" means a debt falling within section 3(1);
"statutory interest" means interest carried by virtue of the term implied by section 1(1); and
"supplier" means (subject to section 13(2)) the seller in a contract of sale of goods or the person who does one or more of the things mentioned in section 2(3) in any other contract for the supply of goods or services.

(2) In this Act any reference (however worded) to an agreement or to contract terms includes a reference to both express and implied terms (including terms established by a course of dealing or by such usage as binds the parties).

[1671]

17 Short title, commencement and extent

(1) This Act may be cited as the Late Payment of Commercial Debts (Interest) Act 1998.

(2) This Act (apart from this section) shall come into force on such day as the Secretary of State may by order appoint; and different days may be appointed for different descriptions of contract or for other different purposes.

An order under this subsection may specify a description of contract by reference to any feature of the contract (including the parties).

(3) The Secretary of State may by regulations make such transitional, supplemental or incidental provision (including provision modifying any provision of this Act) as the Secretary of State may consider necessary or expedient in connection with the operation of this Act while it is not fully in force.

(4) This Act does not affect contracts of any description made before this Act comes into force for contracts of that description.

(5) This Act extends to Northern Ireland.

[1672]

NOTES

Orders: the Late Payment of Commercial Debts (Interest) Act 1998 (Commencement No 1) Order 1998, SI 1998/2479; the Late Payment of Commercial Debts (Interest) Act 1998 (Commencement No 2) Order 1999, SI 1999/1816; the Late Payment of Commercial Debts (Interest) Act 1998 (Commencement No 3) Order 2000, SI 2000/2225; the Late Payment of Commercial Debts (Interest) Act 1998 (Commencement No 4) Order 2000, SI 2000/2740; the Late Payment of Commercial Debts (Interest) Act 1998 (Commencement No 5) Order 2002, SI 2002/1673.

DATA PROTECTION ACT 1998

(1998 c 29)

ARRANGEMENT OF SECTIONS

PART I
PRELIMINARY

PART II
RIGHTS OF DATA SUBJECTS AND OTHERS

PART VI
MISCELLANEOUS AND GENERAL

General

An Act to make new provision for the regulation of the processing of information relating to individuals, including the obtaining, holding, use or disclosure of such information

[16 July 1998]

PART I
PRELIMINARY

1   Basic interpretative provisions

(1)   In this Act, unless the context otherwise requires—
    "data" means information which—
        (a)   is being processed by means of equipment operating automatically in response to instructions given for that purpose,
        (b)   is recorded with the intention that it should be processed by means of such equipment,
        (c)   is recorded as part of a relevant filing system or with the intention that it should form part of a relevant filing system, ...
        (d)   does not fall within paragraph (a), (b) or (c) but forms part of an accessible record as defined by section 68, [or
        (e)   is recorded information held by a public authority and does not fall within any of paragraphs (a) to (d);]
    "data controller" means, subject to subsection (4), a person who (either alone or jointly or in common with other persons) determines the purposes for which and the manner in which any personal data are, or are to be, processed;
    "data processor", in relation to personal data, means any person (other than an employee of the data controller) who processes the data on behalf of the data controller;

"data subject" means an individual who is the subject of personal data;

"personal data" means data which relate to a living individual who can be identified—

(a)   from those data, or

(b)   from those data and other information which is in the possession of, or is likely to come into the possession of, the data controller,

and includes any expression of opinion about the individual and any indication of the intentions of the data controller or any other person in respect of the individual;

"processing", in relation to information or data, means obtaining, recording or holding the information or data or carrying out any operation or set of operations on the information or data, including—

(a)   organisation, adaptation or alteration of the information or data,

(b)   retrieval, consultation or use of the information or data,

(c)   disclosure of the information or data by transmission, dissemination or otherwise making available, or

(d)   alignment, combination, blocking, erasure or destruction of the information or data;

["public authority" means a public authority as defined by the Freedom of Information Act 2000 or a Scottish public authority as defined by the Freedom of Information (Scotland) Act 2002;]

"relevant filing system" means any set of information relating to individuals to the extent that, although the information is not processed by means of equipment operating automatically in response to instructions given for that purpose, the set is structured, either by reference to individuals or by reference to criteria relating to individuals, in such a way that specific information relating to a particular individual is readily accessible.

(2)   In this Act, unless the context otherwise requires—

(a)   "obtaining" or "recording", in relation to personal data, includes obtaining or recording the information to be contained in the data, and

(b)   "using" or "disclosing", in relation to personal data, includes using or disclosing the information contained in the data.

(3)   In determining for the purposes of this Act whether any information is recorded with the intention—

(a)   that it should be processed by means of equipment operating automatically in response to instructions given for that purpose, or

(b)   that it should form part of a relevant filing system,

it is immaterial that it is intended to be so processed or to form part of such a system only after being transferred to a country or territory outside the European Economic Area.

(4)   Where personal data are processed only for purposes for which they are required by or under any enactment to be processed, the person on whom the obligation to process the data is imposed by or under that enactment is for the purposes of this Act the data controller.

[(5)   In paragraph (e) of the definition of "data" in subsection (1), the reference to information "held" by a public authority shall be construed in accordance with section 3(2) of the Freedom of Information Act 2000 [or section 3(2), (4) and (5) of the Freedom of Information (Scotland) Act 2002].

(6)   Where—

[(a)]   section 7 of the Freedom of Information Act 2000 prevents Parts I to V of that Act [or

(b)   section 7(1) of the Freedom of Information (Scotland) Act 2002 prevents that Act,]

from applying to certain information held by a public authority, that information is not to be treated for the purposes of paragraph (e) of the definition of "data" in subsection (1) as held by a public authority.]

[1673]

NOTES

Sub-s (1): in definition "data" word omitted from para (c) repealed, and para (e) and word immediately preceding it inserted by the Freedom of Information Act 2000, ss 68(1), (2)(a), 86, Sch 8, Pt III; definition "public authority" inserted by the Freedom of Information Act 2000, s 68(1), (2)(b), substituted by the Freedom of Information (Scotland) Act 2002 (Consequential Modifications) Order 2004, SI 2004/3089, art 2(1), (2)(a).

Sub-s (5): added, together with sub-s (6), by the Freedom of Information Act 2000, s 68(1), (3); words in square brackets inserted by SI 2004/3089, art 2(1), (2)(b).

Sub-s (6): added as noted to sub-s (5); para (a) numbered as such and para (b) and the word immediately preceding it inserted by SI 2004/3089, art 2(1), (2)(c).

---

2   Sensitive personal data

In this Act "sensitive personal data" means personal data consisting of information as to—

(a)   the racial or ethnic origin of the data subject,

(b)   his political opinions,

(c)   his religious beliefs or other beliefs of a similar nature,

(d) whether he is a member of a trade union (within the meaning of the Trade Union and Labour Relations (Consolidation) Act 1992,

(e) his physical or mental health or condition,

(f) his sexual life,

(g) the commission or alleged commission by him of any offence, or

(h) any proceedings for any offence committed or alleged to have been committed by him, the disposal of such proceedings or the sentence of any court in such proceedings.

[1674]

3 The special purposes

In this Act "the special purposes" means any one or more of the following—

(a) the purposes of journalism,

(b) artistic purposes, and

(c) literary purposes.

[1675]

4 The data protection principles

(1) References in this Act to the data protection principles are to the principles set out in Part I of Schedule 1.

(2) Those principles are to be interpreted in accordance with Part II of Schedule 1.

(3) Schedule 2 (which applies to all personal data) and Schedule 3 (which applies only to sensitive personal data) set out conditions applying for the purposes of the first principle; and Schedule 4 sets out cases in which the eighth principle does not apply.

(4) Subject to section 27(1), it shall be the duty of a data controller to comply with the data protection principles in relation to all personal data with respect to which he is the data controller.

[1676]

5 Application of Act

(1) Except as otherwise provided by or under section 54, this Act applies to a data controller in respect of any data only if—

(a) the data controller is established in the United Kingdom and the data are processed in the context of that establishment, or

(b) the data controller is established neither in the United Kingdom nor in any other EEA State but uses equipment in the United Kingdom for processing the data otherwise than for the purposes of transit through the United Kingdom.

(2) A data controller falling within subsection (1)(b) must nominate for the purposes of this Act a representative established in the United Kingdom.

(3) For the purposes of subsections (1) and (2), each of the following is to be treated as established in the United Kingdom—

(a) an individual who is ordinarily resident in the United Kingdom,

(b) a body incorporated under the law of, or of any part of, the United Kingdom,

(c) a partnership or other unincorporated association formed under the law of any part of the United Kingdom, and

(d) any person who does not fall within paragraph (a), (b) or (c) but maintains in the United Kingdom—

(i) an office, branch or agency through which he carries on any activity, or

(ii) a regular practice;

and the reference to establishment in any other EEA State has a corresponding meaning.

[1677]

6 The Commissioner …

[(1) For the purposes of this Act and of the Freedom of Information Act 2000 there shall be an officer known as the Information Commissioner (in this Act referred to as "the Commissioner").]

(2) The Commissioner shall be appointed by Her Majesty by Letters Patent.

(3)–(6) …

(7) Schedule 5 has effect in relation to the Commissioner …

[1678]

NOTES

Section heading: words omitted repealed by the Transfer of Tribunal Functions Order 2010, SI 2010/22, art 5(1), Sch 2, paras 24, 25(a), subject to transitional provisions in Sch 5 thereto.

Sub-s (1): substituted by the Freedom of Information Act 2000, s 18(4), Sch 2, Pt I, para 13(1), (2).

Sub-ss (3)–(6): repealed by SI 2010/22, art 5(1), Sch 2, paras 24, 25(b), subject to transitional provisions in Sch 5 thereto.

Sub-s (7): words omitted repealed by SI 2010/22, art 5(1), Sch 2, paras 24, 25(c), subject to transitional provisions in Sch 5 thereto.

PART II

RIGHTS OF DATA SUBJECTS AND OTHERS

7 Right of access to personal data

(1) Subject to the following provisions of this section and to [sections 8, 9 and 9A], an individual is entitled—

    (a) to be informed by any data controller whether personal data of which that individual is the data subject are being processed by or on behalf of that data controller,

    (b) if that is the case, to be given by the data controller a description of—

        (i) the personal data of which that individual is the data subject,

        (ii) the purposes for which they are being or are to be processed, and

        (iii) the recipients or classes of recipients to whom they are or may be disclosed,

    (c) to have communicated to him in an intelligible form—

        (i) the information constituting any personal data of which that individual is the data subject, and

        (ii) any information available to the data controller as to the source of those data, and

    (d) where the processing by automatic means of personal data of which that individual is the data subject for the purpose of evaluating matters relating to him such as, for example, his performance at work, his creditworthiness, his reliability or his conduct, has constituted or is likely to constitute the sole basis for any decision significantly affecting him, to be informed by the data controller of the logic involved in that decision-taking.

(2) A data controller is not obliged to supply any information under subsection (1) unless he has received—

    (a) a request in writing, and

    (b) except in prescribed cases, such fee (not exceeding the prescribed maximum) as he may require.

[(3) Where a data controller—

    (a) reasonably requires further information in order to satisfy himself as to the identity of the person making a request under this section and to locate the information which that person seeks, and

    (b) has informed him of that requirement,

the data controller is not obliged to comply with the request unless he is supplied with that further information.]

(4) Where a data controller cannot comply with the request without disclosing information relating to another individual who can be identified from that information, he is not obliged to comply with the request unless—

    (a) the other individual has consented to the disclosure of the information to the person making the request, or

    (b) it is reasonable in all the circumstances to comply with the request without the consent of the other individual.

(5) In subsection (4) the reference to information relating to another individual includes a reference to information identifying that individual as the source of the information sought by the request; and that subsection is not to be construed as excusing a data controller from communicating so much of the information sought by the request as can be communicated without disclosing the identity of the other individual concerned, whether by the omission of names or other identifying particulars or otherwise.

(6) In determining for the purposes of subsection (4)(b) whether it is reasonable in all the circumstances to comply with the request without the consent of the other individual concerned, regard shall be had, in particular, to—

    (a) any duty of confidentiality owed to the other individual,

    (b) any steps taken by the data controller with a view to seeking the consent of the other individual,

    (c) whether the other individual is capable of giving consent, and

    (d) any express refusal of consent by the other individual.

(7) An individual making a request under this section may, in such cases as may be prescribed, specify that his request is limited to personal data of any prescribed description.

(8) Subject to subsection (4), a data controller shall comply with a request under this section promptly and in any event before the end of the prescribed period beginning with the relevant day.

(9) If a court is satisfied on the application of any person who has made a request under the foregoing provisions of this section that the data controller in question has failed to comply with the request in contravention of those provisions, the court may order him to comply with the request.

(10) In this section—

"prescribed" means prescribed by the [Secretary of State] by regulations;

"the prescribed maximum" means such amount as may be prescribed;

"the prescribed period" means forty days or such other period as may be prescribed;

"the relevant day", in relation to a request under this section, means the day on which the data controller receives the request or, if later, the first day on which the data controller has both the required fee and the information referred to in subsection (3).

(11)   Different amounts or periods may be prescribed under this section in relation to different cases.

[1679]

NOTES

Sub-s (1): words in square brackets substituted by the Freedom of Information Act 2000, s 69(1).

Sub-s (3): substituted by the Freedom of Information Act 2000, s 73, Sch 6, para 1.

Sub-s (10): in definition "prescribed" words in square brackets substituted by the Secretary of State for Constitutional Affairs Order 2003, SI 2003/1887, art 9, Sch 2, para 9(1)(a).

Regulations: the Data Protection (Subject Access) (Fees and Miscellaneous Provisions) Regulations 2000, SI 2000/191.

8   Provisions supplementary to section 7

(1)   The [Secretary of State] may by regulations provide that, in such cases as may be prescribed, a request for information under any provision of subsection (1) of section 7 is to be treated as extending also to information under other provisions of that subsection.

(2)   The obligation imposed by section 7(1)(c)(i) must be complied with by supplying the data subject with a copy of the information in permanent form unless—

(a)   the supply of such a copy is not possible or would involve disproportionate effort, or

(b)   the data subject agrees otherwise;

and where any of the information referred to in section 7(1)(c)(i) is expressed in terms which are not intelligible without explanation the copy must be accompanied by an explanation of those terms.

(3)   Where a data controller has previously complied with a request made under section 7 by an individual, the data controller is not obliged to comply with a subsequent identical or similar request under that section by that individual unless a reasonable interval has elapsed between compliance with the previous request and the making of the current request.

(4)   In determining for the purposes of subsection (3) whether requests under section 7 are made at reasonable intervals, regard shall be had to the nature of the data, the purpose for which the data are processed and the frequency with which the data are altered.

(5)   Section 7(1)(d) is not to be regarded as requiring the provision of information as to the logic involved in any decision-taking if, and to the extent that, the information constitutes a trade secret.

(6)   The information to be supplied pursuant to a request under section 7 must be supplied by reference to the data in question at the time when the request is received, except that it may take account of any amendment or deletion made between that time and the time when the information is supplied, being an amendment or deletion that would have been made regardless of the receipt of the request.

(7)   For the purposes of section 7(4) and (5) another individual can be identified from the information being disclosed if he can be identified from that information, or from that and any other information which, in the reasonable belief of the data controller, is likely to be in, or to come into, the possession of the data subject making the request.

[1680]

NOTES

Sub-s (1): words in square brackets substituted by the Secretary of State for Constitutional Affairs Order 2003, SI 2003/1887, art 9, Sch 2, para 9(1)(a).

Regulations: the Data Protection (Subject Access) (Fees and Miscellaneous Provisions) Regulations 2000, SI 2000/191.

9   Application of section 7 where data controller is credit reference agency

(1)   Where the data controller is a credit reference agency, section 7 has effect subject to the provisions of this section.

(2)   An individual making a request under section 7 may limit his request to personal data relevant to his financial standing, and shall be taken to have so limited his request unless the request shows a contrary intention.

(3)   Where the data controller receives a request under section 7 in a case where personal data of which the individual making the request is the data subject are being processed by or on behalf of the data controller, the obligation to supply information under that section includes an obligation to give the individual making the request a statement, in such form as may be prescribed by the [Secretary of State] by regulations, of the individual's rights—

(a)   under section 159 of the Consumer Credit Act 1974, and

(b)   to the extent required by the prescribed form, under this Act.

[1681]

NOTES
Sub-s (3): words in square brackets substituted by the Secretary of State for Constitutional Affairs Order 2003, SI 2003/1887, art 9, Sch 2, para 9(1)(a).

[9A Unstructured personal data held by public authorities

(1) In this section "unstructured personal data" means any personal data falling within paragraph (e) of the definition of "data" in section 1(1), other than information which is recorded as part of, or with the intention that it should form part of, any set of information relating to individuals to the extent that the set is structured by reference to individuals or by reference to criteria relating to individuals.

(2) A public authority is not obliged to comply with subsection (1) of section 7 in relation to any unstructured personal data unless the request under that section contains a description of the data.

(3) Even if the data are described by the data subject in his request, a public authority is not obliged to comply with subsection (1) of section 7 in relation to unstructured personal data if the authority estimates that the cost of complying with the request so far as relating to those data would exceed the appropriate limit.

(4) Subsection (3) does not exempt the public authority from its obligation to comply with paragraph (a) of section 7(1) in relation to the unstructured personal data unless the estimated cost of complying with that paragraph alone in relation to those data would exceed the appropriate limit.

(5) In subsections (3) and (4) "the appropriate limit" means such amount as may be prescribed by the [Secretary of State] by regulations, and different amounts may be prescribed in relation to different cases.

(6) Any estimate for the purposes of this section must be made in accordance with regulations under section 12(5) of the Freedom of Information Act 2000.]

[1682]

NOTES
Inserted by the Freedom of Information Act 2000, s 69(2).
Sub-s (5): words in square brackets substituted by the Secretary of State for Constitutional Affairs Order 2003, SI 2003/1887, art 9, Sch 2, paras 9(1)(a), 12(1)(b).
Regulations: the Freedom of Information and Data Protection (Appropriate Limit and Fees) Regulations 2004, SI 2004/3244.

10 Right to prevent processing likely to cause damage or distress

(1) Subject to subsection (2), an individual is entitled at any time by notice in writing to a data controller to require the data controller at the end of such period as is reasonable in the circumstances to cease, or not to begin, processing, or processing for a specified purpose or in a specified manner, any personal data in respect of which he is the data subject, on the ground that, for specified reasons—

    (a) the processing of those data or their processing for that purpose or in that manner is causing or is likely to cause substantial damage or substantial distress to him or to another, and

    (b) that damage or distress is or would be unwarranted.

(2) Subsection (1) does not apply—

    (a) in a case where any of the conditions in paragraphs 1 to 4 of Schedule 2 is met, or

    (b) in such other cases as may be prescribed by the [Secretary of State] by order.

(3) The data controller must within twenty-one days of receiving a notice under subsection (1) ("the data subject notice") give the individual who gave it a written notice—

    (a) stating that he has complied or intends to comply with the data subject notice, or

    (b) stating his reasons for regarding the data subject notice as to any extent unjustified and the extent (if any) to which he has complied or intends to comply with it.

(4) If a court is satisfied, on the application of any person who has given a notice under subsection (1) which appears to the court to be justified (or to be justified to any extent), that the data controller in question has failed to comply with the notice, the court may order him to take such steps for complying with the notice (or for complying with it to that extent) as the court thinks fit.

(5) The failure by a data subject to exercise the right conferred by subsection (1) or section 11(1) does not affect any other right conferred on him by this Part.

[1683]

NOTES
Sub-s (2): words in square brackets in para (b) substituted by the Secretary of State for Constitutional Affairs Order 2003, SI 2003/1887, art 9, Sch 2, para 9(1)(a).

11 Right to prevent processing for purposes of direct marketing

(1) An individual is entitled at any time by notice in writing to a data controller to require the data controller at the end of such period as is reasonable in the circumstances to cease, or not to begin, processing for the purposes of direct marketing personal data in respect of which he is the data subject.

(2) If the court is satisfied, on the application of any person who has given a notice under subsection (1), that the data controller has failed to comply with the notice, the court may order him to take such steps for complying with the notice as the court thinks fit.

[(2A) This section shall not apply in relation to the processing of such data as are mentioned in paragraph (1) of regulation 8 of the Telecommunications (Data Protection and Privacy) Regulations 1999 (processing of telecommunications billing data for certain marketing purposes) for the purposes mentioned in paragraph (2) of that regulation.]

(3) In this section "direct marketing" means the communication (by whatever means) of any advertising or marketing material which is directed to particular individuals.

[1684]

NOTES

Sub-s (2A): inserted by the Telecommunications (Data Protection and Privacy) Regulations 1999, SI 1999/2093, reg 3(3), Sch 1, Pt II, para 3.

12 Rights in relation to automated decision-taking

(1) An individual is entitled at any time, by notice in writing to any data controller, to require the data controller to ensure that no decision taken by or on behalf of the data controller which significantly affects that individual is based solely on the processing by automatic means of personal data in respect of which that individual is the data subject for the purpose of evaluating matters relating to him such as, for example, his performance at work, his creditworthiness, his reliability or his conduct.

(2) Where, in a case where no notice under subsection (1) has effect, a decision which significantly affects an individual is based solely on such processing as is mentioned in subsection (1)—

(a) the data controller must as soon as reasonably practicable notify the individual that the decision was taken on that basis, and

(b) the individual is entitled, within twenty-one days of receiving that notification from the data controller, by notice in writing to require the data controller to reconsider the decision or to take a new decision otherwise than on that basis.

(3) The data controller must, within twenty-one days of receiving a notice under subsection (2)(b) ("the data subject notice") give the individual a written notice specifying the steps that he intends to take to comply with the data subject notice.

(4) A notice under subsection (1) does not have effect in relation to an exempt decision; and nothing in subsection (2) applies to an exempt decision.

(5) In subsection (4) "exempt decision" means any decision—

(a) in respect of which the condition in subsection (6) and the condition in subsection (7) are met, or

(b) which is made in such other circumstances as may be prescribed by the [Secretary of State] by order.

(6) The condition in this subsection is that the decision—

(a) is taken in the course of steps taken—

(i) for the purpose of considering whether to enter into a contract with the data subject,

(ii) with a view to entering into such a contract, or

(iii) in the course of performing such a contract, or

(b) is authorised or required by or under any enactment.

(7) The condition in this subsection is that either—

(a) the effect of the decision is to grant a request of the data subject, or

(b) steps have been taken to safeguard the legitimate interests of the data subject (for example, by allowing him to make representations).

(8) If a court is satisfied on the application of a data subject that a person taking a decision in respect of him ("the responsible person") has failed to comply with subsection (1) or (2)(b), the court may order the responsible person to reconsider the decision, or to take a new decision which is not based solely on such processing as is mentioned in subsection (1).

(9) An order under subsection (8) shall not affect the rights of any person other than the data subject and the responsible person.

[1685]–[1686]

NOTES

Sub-s (5): words in square brackets in para (b) substituted by the Secretary of State for Constitutional Affairs Order 2003, SI 2003/1887, art 9, Sch 2, para 9(1)(a).

13 Compensation for failure to comply with certain requirements

(1) An individual who suffers damage by reason of any contravention by a data controller of any of the requirements of this Act is entitled to compensation from the data controller for that damage.

(2) An individual who suffers distress by reason of any contravention by a data controller of any of the requirements of this Act is entitled to compensation from the data controller for that distress if—

(a) the individual also suffers damage by reason of the contravention, or

(b) the contravention relates to the processing of personal data for the special purposes.

(3) In proceedings brought against a person by virtue of this section it is a defence to prove that he had taken such care as in all the circumstances was reasonably required to comply with the requirement concerned.

[1687]

14 Rectification, blocking, erasure and destruction

(1) If a court is satisfied on the application of a data subject that personal data of which the applicant is the subject are inaccurate, the court may order the data controller to rectify, block, erase or destroy those data and any other personal data in respect of which he is the data controller and which contain an expression of opinion which appears to the court to be based on the inaccurate data.

(2) Subsection (1) applies whether or not the data accurately record information received or obtained by the data controller from the data subject or a third party but where the data accurately record such information, then—

(a) if the requirements mentioned in paragraph 7 of Part II of Schedule 1 have been complied with, the court may, instead of making an order under subsection (1), make an order requiring the data to be supplemented by such statement of the true facts relating to the matters dealt with by the data as the court may approve, and

(b) if all or any of those requirements have not been complied with, the court may, instead of making an order under that subsection, make such order as it thinks fit for securing compliance with those requirements with or without a further order requiring the data to be supplemented by such a statement as is mentioned in paragraph (a).

(3) Where the court—

(a) makes an order under subsection (1), or

(b) is satisfied on the application of a data subject that personal data of which he was the data subject and which have been rectified, blocked, erased or destroyed were inaccurate,

it may, where it considers it reasonably practicable, order the data controller to notify third parties to whom the data have been disclosed of the rectification, blocking, erasure or destruction.

(4) If a court is satisfied on the application of a data subject—

(a) that he has suffered damage by reason of any contravention by a data controller of any of the requirements of this Act in respect of any personal data, in circumstances entitling him to compensation under section 13, and

(b) that there is a substantial risk of further contravention in respect of those data in such circumstances,

the court may order the rectification, blocking, erasure or destruction of any of those data.

(5) Where the court makes an order under subsection (4) it may, where it considers it reasonably practicable, order the data controller to notify third parties to whom the data have been disclosed of the rectification, blocking, erasure or destruction.

(6) In determining whether it is reasonably practicable to require such notification as is mentioned in subsection (3) or (5) the court shall have regard, in particular, to the number of persons who would have to be notified.

[1688]

15 Jurisdiction and procedure

(1) The jurisdiction conferred by sections 7 to 14 is exercisable by the High Court or a county court or, in Scotland, by the Court of Session or the sheriff.

(2) For the purpose of determining any question whether an applicant under subsection (9) of section 7 is entitled to the information which he seeks (including any question whether any relevant data are exempt from that section by virtue of Part IV) a court may require the information

constituting any data processed by or on behalf of the data controller and any information as to the logic involved in any decision-taking as mentioned in section 7(1)(d) to be made available for its own inspection but shall not, pending the determination of that question in the applicant's favour, require the information sought by the applicant to be disclosed to him or his representatives whether by discovery (or, in Scotland, recovery) or otherwise.

[1689]

16–50   ((*Pts III–V*) *outside the scope of this work.*)

PART I
STATUTES

PART VI
MISCELLANEOUS AND GENERAL

51–62   (*Outside the scope of this work.*)

General

63–74   (*Outside the scope of this work.*)

75   Short title, commencement and extent

(1)   This Act may be cited as the Data Protection Act 1998.

(2)   The following provisions of this Act—
   (a)   sections 1 to 3,
   (b)–(d)   (*outside the scope of this work.*)
   (e)   this section,
   (f)–(h)   (*outside the scope of this work.*)
   (i)   so much of any other provision of this Act as confers any power to make subordinate legislation,
shall come into force on the day on which this Act is passed.

(3)   The remaining provisions of this Act shall come into force on such day as the [Secretary of State] may by order appoint; and different days may be appointed for different purposes.

(4)   The day appointed under subsection (3) for the coming into force of section 56 must not be earlier than the first day on which sections 112, 113 and 115 of the Police Act 1997 (which provide for the issue by the Secretary of State of criminal conviction certificates, criminal record certificates and enhanced criminal record certificates) are all in force.

[(4A)   Subsection (4) does not apply to section 56 so far as that section relates to a record containing information relating to—
   (a)   the Secretary of State's functions under the Safeguarding Vulnerable Groups Act 2006 [or the Safeguarding Vulnerable Groups (Northern Ireland) Order 2007], or
   (b)   the [Independent Safeguarding Authority's] functions under that Act [or that Order].]

(5)   Subject to subsection (6), this Act extends to Northern Ireland.

(6)   Any amendment, repeal or revocation made by Schedule 15 or 16 has the same extent as that of the enactment or instrument to which it relates.

[1690]

NOTES

Sub-s (3): words in square brackets substituted by the Secretary of State for Constitutional Affairs Order 2003, SI 2003/1887, art 9, Sch 2, para 9(1)(a).

Sub-s (4A): inserted by the Safeguarding Vulnerable Groups Act 2006, s 63(1), Sch 9, Pt 2, para 15(1), (3); words in square brackets in para (a) and words in second pair of square brackets in para (b) inserted by the Safeguarding Vulnerable Groups (Northern Ireland) Order 2007, SI 2007/1351, art 60(1), Sch 7, para 4(2), as from a day to be appointed; words in first pair of square brackets in para (b) substituted by the Policing and Crime Act 2009, s 81(2), (3)(i).

Orders: the Data Protection Act 1998 (Commencement) Order 2000, SI 2000/183; the Data Protection Act 1998 (Commencement No 2) Order 2008, SI 2008/1592.

SCHEDULES

SCHEDULE 1
THE DATA PROTECTION PRINCIPLES

Section 4(1) and (2)

PART I
THE PRINCIPLES

1.   Personal data shall be processed fairly and lawfully and, in particular, shall not be processed unless—

    (a)   at least one of the conditions in Schedule 2 is met, and

    (b)   in the case of sensitive personal data, at least one of the conditions in Schedule 3 is also met.

2.   Personal data shall be obtained only for one or more specified and lawful purposes, and shall not be further processed in any manner incompatible with that purpose or those purposes.

3.   Personal data shall be adequate, relevant and not excessive in relation to the purpose or purposes for which they are processed.

4.   Personal data shall be accurate and, where necessary, kept up to date.

5.   Personal data processed for any purpose or purposes shall not be kept for longer than is necessary for that purpose or those purposes.

6.   Personal data shall be processed in accordance with the rights of data subjects under this Act.

7.   Appropriate technical and organisational measures shall be taken against unauthorised or unlawful processing of personal data and against accidental loss or destruction of, or damage to, personal data.

8.   Personal data shall not be transferred to a country or territory outside the European Economic Area unless that country or territory ensures an adequate level of protection for the rights and freedoms of data subjects in relation to the processing of personal data.

[1691]

PART II
INTERPRETATION OF THE PRINCIPLES IN PART I

The first principle

1.—(1)   In determining for the purposes of the first principle whether personal data are processed fairly, regard is to be had to the method by which they are obtained, including in particular whether any person from whom they are obtained is deceived or misled as to the purpose or purposes for which they are to be processed.

    (2)   Subject to paragraph 2, for the purposes of the first principle data are to be treated as obtained fairly if they consist of information obtained from a person who—

    (a)   is authorised by or under any enactment to supply it, or

    (b)   is required to supply it by or under any enactment or by any convention or other instrument imposing an international obligation on the United Kingdom.

2.—(1)   Subject to paragraph 3, for the purposes of the first principle personal data are not to be treated as processed fairly unless—

    (a)   in the case of data obtained from the data subject, the data controller ensures so far as practicable that the data subject has, is provided with, or has made readily available to him, the information specified in sub-paragraph (3), and

    (b)   in any other case, the data controller ensures so far as practicable that, before the relevant time or as soon as practicable after that time, the data subject has, is provided with, or has made readily available to him, the information specified in sub-paragraph (3).

    (2)   In sub-paragraph (1)(b) "the relevant time" means—

    (a)   the time when the data controller first processes the data, or

    (b)   in a case where at that time disclosure to a third party within a reasonable period is envisaged—

        (i)   if the data are in fact disclosed to such a person within that period, the time when the data are first disclosed,

        (ii)   if within that period the data controller becomes, or ought to become, aware that the data are unlikely to be disclosed to such a person within that period, the time when the data controller does become, or ought to become, so aware, or

        (iii)   in any other case, the end of that period.

    (3)   The information referred to in sub-paragraph (1) is as follows, namely—

    (a)   the identity of the data controller,

    (b)   if he has nominated a representative for the purposes of this Act, the identity of that representative,

    (c)   the purpose or purposes for which the data are intended to be processed, and

    (d)   any further information which is necessary, having regard to the specific circumstances in which the data are or are to be processed, to enable processing in respect of the data subject to be fair.

3.—(1)   Paragraph 2(1)(b) does not apply where either of the primary conditions in subparagraph (2), together with such further conditions as may be prescribed by the [Secretary of State] by order, are met.

    (2)   The primary conditions referred to in sub-paragraph (1) are—

    (a)   that the provision of that information would involve a disproportionate effort, or

(b)   that the recording of the information to be contained in the data by, or the disclosure of the data by, the data controller is necessary for compliance with any legal obligation to which the data controller is subject, other than an obligation imposed by contract.

4.—(1)   Personal data which contain a general identifier falling within a description prescribed by the [Secretary of State] by order are not to be treated as processed fairly and lawfully unless they are processed in compliance with any conditions so prescribed in relation to general identifiers of that description.

(2)   In sub-paragraph (1) "a general identifier" means any identifier (such as, for example, a number or code used for identification purposes) which—

(a)   relates to an individual, and

(b)   forms part of a set of similar identifiers which is of general application.

The second principle

5.   The purpose or purposes for which personal data are obtained may in particular be specified—

(a)   in a notice given for the purposes of paragraph 2 by the data controller to the data subject, or

(b)   in a notification given to the Commissioner under Part III of this Act.

6.   In determining whether any disclosure of personal data is compatible with the purpose or purposes for which the data were obtained, regard is to be had to the purpose or purposes for which the personal data are intended to be processed by any person to whom they are disclosed.

The fourth principle

7.   The fourth principle is not to be regarded as being contravened by reason of any inaccuracy in personal data which accurately record information obtained by the data controller from the data subject or a third party in a case where—

(a)   having regard to the purpose or purposes for which the data were obtained and further processed, the data controller has taken reasonable steps to ensure the accuracy of the data, and

(b)   if the data subject has notified the data controller of the data subject's view that the data are inaccurate, the data indicate that fact.

The sixth principle

8.   A person is to be regarded as contravening the sixth principle if, but only if—

(a)   he contravenes section 7 by failing to supply information in accordance with that section,

(b)   he contravenes section 10 by failing to comply with a notice given under subsection (1) of that section to the extent that the notice is justified or by failing to give a notice under subsection (3) of that section,

(c)   he contravenes section 11 by failing to comply with a notice given under subsection (1) of that section, or

(d)   he contravenes section 12 by failing to comply with a notice given under subsection (1) or (2)(b) of that section or by failing to give a notification under subsection (2)(a) of that section or a notice under subsection (3) of that section.

The seventh principle

9.   Having regard to the state of technological development and the cost of implementing any measures, the measures must ensure a level of security appropriate to—

(a)   the harm that might result from such unauthorised or unlawful processing or accidental loss, destruction or damage as are mentioned in the seventh principle, and

(b)   the nature of the data to be protected.

10.   The data controller must take reasonable steps to ensure the reliability of any employees of his who have access to the personal data.

11.   Where processing of personal data is carried out by a data processor on behalf of a data controller, the data controller must in order to comply with the seventh principle—

(a)   choose a data processor providing sufficient guarantees in respect of the technical and organisational security measures governing the processing to be carried out, and

(b)   take reasonable steps to ensure compliance with those measures.

12.   Where processing of personal data is carried out by a data processor on behalf of a data controller, the data controller is not to be regarded as complying with the seventh principle unless—

(a)   the processing is carried out under a contract—

(i)   which is made or evidenced in writing, and

(ii)   under which the data processor is to act only on instructions from the data controller, and

(b)   the contract requires the data processor to comply with obligations equivalent to those imposed on a data controller by the seventh principle.

The eighth principle

13.   An adequate level of protection is one which is adequate in all the circumstances of the case, having regard in particular to—
  (a)   the nature of the personal data,
  (b)   the country or territory of origin of the information contained in the data,
  (c)   the country or territory of final destination of that information,
  (d)   the purposes for which and period during which the data are intended to be processed,
  (e)   the law in force in the country or territory in question,
  (f)   the international obligations of that country or territory,
  (g)   any relevant codes of conduct or other rules which are enforceable in that country or territory (whether generally or by arrangement in particular cases), and
  (h)   any security measures taken in respect of the data in that country or territory.

14.   The eighth principle does not apply to a transfer falling within any paragraph of Schedule 4, except in such circumstances and to such extent as the [Secretary of State] may by order provide.

15.—(1)   Where—
  (a)   in any proceedings under this Act any question arises as to whether the requirement of the eighth principle as to an adequate level of protection is met in relation to the transfer of any personal data to a country or territory outside the European Economic Area, and
  (b)   a Community finding has been made in relation to transfers of the kind in question,
that question is to be determined in accordance with that finding.

  (2)   In sub-paragraph (1) "Community finding" means a finding of the European Commission, under the procedure provided for in Article 31(2) of the Data Protection Directive, that a country or territory outside the European Economic Area does, or does not, ensure an adequate level of protection within the meaning of Article 25(2) of the Directive.

[1692]

NOTES
  Paras 3, 4, 14: words in square brackets substituted by the Secretary of State for Constitutional Affairs Order 2003, SI 2003/1887, art 9, Sch 2, para 9(1)(b).
  Order: the Data Protection (Conditions under Paragraph 3 of Part II of Schedule 1) Order 2000, SI 2000/185.

SCHEDULE 2
CONDITIONS RELEVANT FOR PURPOSES OF THE FIRST PRINCIPLE: PROCESSING OF ANY PERSONAL DATA

Section 4(3)

1.   The data subject has given his consent to the processing.

2.   The processing is necessary—
  (a)   for the performance of a contract to which the data subject is a party, or
  (b)   for the taking of steps at the request of the data subject with a view to entering into a contract.

3.   The processing is necessary for compliance with any legal obligation to which the data controller is subject, other than an obligation imposed by contract.

4.   The processing is necessary in order to protect the vital interests of the data subject.

5.   The processing is necessary—
  (a)   for the administration of justice,
  [(aa) for the exercise of any functions of either House of Parliament,]
  (b)   for the exercise of any functions conferred on any person by or under any enactment,
  (c)   for the exercise of any functions of the Crown, a Minister of the Crown or a government department, or
  (d)   for the exercise of any other functions of a public nature exercised in the public interest by any person.

6.—(1)   The processing is necessary for the purposes of legitimate interests pursued by the data controller or by the third party or parties to whom the data are disclosed, except where the processing is unwarranted in any particular case by reason of prejudice to the rights and freedoms or legitimate interests of the data subject.

  (2)   The [Secretary of State] may by order specify particular circumstances in which this condition is, or is not, to be taken to be satisfied.

[1693]

NOTES
  Para 5: sub-para (aa) inserted by the Freedom of Information Act 2000, s 73, Sch 6, para 4.
  Para 6: words in square brackets in sub-para (2) substituted by the Secretary of State for Constitutional Affairs Order 2003, SI 2003/1887, art 9, Sch 2, para 9(1)(b).

See further: the National Assembly for Wales Commission is treated as a government department for the purposes of para 5 above; see the National Assembly for Wales Commission (Crown Status) Order 2007, SI 2007/1118, art 5(1), (2)(b).

SCHEDULE 3
CONDITIONS RELEVANT FOR PURPOSES OF THE FIRST PRINCIPLE: PROCESSING OF SENSITIVE PERSONAL DATA

Section 4(3)

1. The data subject has given his explicit consent to the processing of the personal data.

2.—(1) The processing is necessary for the purposes of exercising or performing any right or obligation which is conferred or imposed by law on the data controller in connection with employment.

    (2) The [Secretary of State] may by order—
       (a) exclude the application of sub-paragraph (1) in such cases as may be specified, or
       (b) provide that, in such cases as may be specified, the condition in subparagraph (1) is not to be regarded as satisfied unless such further conditions as may be specified in the order are also satisfied.

3. The processing is necessary—
       (a) in order to protect the vital interests of the data subject or another person, in a case where—
          (i) consent cannot be given by or on behalf of the data subject, or
          (ii) the data controller cannot reasonably be expected to obtain the consent of the data subject, or
       (b) in order to protect the vital interests of another person, in a case where consent by or on behalf of the data subject has been unreasonably withheld.

4. The processing—
       (a) is carried out in the course of its legitimate activities by any body or association which—
          (i) is not established or conducted for profit, and
          (ii) exists for political, philosophical religious or trade-union purposes,
       (b) is carried out with appropriate safeguards for the rights and freedoms of data subjects,
       (c) relates only to individuals who either are members of the body or association or have regular contact with it in connection with its purposes, and
       (d) does not involve disclosure of the personal data to a third party without the consent of the data subject.

5. The information contained in the personal data has been made public as a result of steps deliberately taken by the data subject.

6. The processing—
       (a) is necessary for the purpose of, or in connection with, any legal proceedings (including prospective legal proceedings),
       (b) is necessary for the purpose of obtaining legal advice, or
       (c) is otherwise necessary for the purposes of establishing, exercising or defending legal rights.

7.—(1) The processing is necessary—
       (a) for the administration of justice,
       [(aa) for the exercise of any functions of either House of Parliament,]
       (b) for the exercise of any functions conferred on any person by or under an enactment, or
       (c) for the exercise of any functions of the Crown, a Minister of the Crown or a government department.

    (2) The [Secretary of State] may by order—
       (a) exclude the application of sub-paragraph (1) in such cases as may be specified, or
       (b) provide that, in such cases as may be specified, the condition in subparagraph (1) is not to be regarded as satisfied unless such further conditions as may be specified in the order are also satisfied.

[7A.—(1) The processing—
       (a) is either—
          (i) the disclosure of sensitive personal data by a person as a member of an anti-fraud organisation or otherwise in accordance with any arrangements made by such an organisation; or
          (ii) any other processing by that person or another person of sensitive personal data so disclosed; and
       (b) is necessary for the purposes of preventing fraud or a particular kind of fraud.

    (2) In this paragraph "an anti-fraud organisation" means any unincorporated association, body corporate or other person which enables or facilitates any sharing of information to prevent fraud or a particular kind of fraud or which has any of these functions as its purpose or one of its purposes.]

8.—(1) The processing is necessary for medical purposes and is undertaken by—
    (a)   a health professional, or
    (b)   a person who in the circumstances owes a duty of confidentiality which is equivalent to that which would arise if that person were a health professional.

(2) In this paragraph "medical purposes" includes the purposes of preventative medicine, medical diagnosis, medical research, the provision of care and treatment and the management of healthcare services.

9.—(1) The processing—
    (a)   is of sensitive personal data consisting of information as to racial or ethnic origin,
    (b)   is necessary for the purpose of identifying or keeping under review the existence or absence of equality of opportunity or treatment between persons of different racial or ethnic origins, with a view to enabling such equality to be promoted or maintained, and
    (c)   is carried out with appropriate safeguards for the rights and freedoms of data subjects.

(2) The [Secretary of State] may by order specify circumstances in which processing falling within sub-paragraph (1)(a) and (b) is, or is not, to be taken for the purposes of subparagraph (1)(c) to be carried out with appropriate safeguards for the rights and freedoms of data subjects.

10. The personal data are processed in circumstances specified in an order made by the [Secretary of State] for the purposes of this paragraph.

[1694]

NOTES
    Paras 2, 9, 10: words in square brackets substituted by the Secretary of State for Constitutional Affairs Order 2003, SI 2003/1887, art 9, Sch 2, para 9(1)(b).
    Para 7: sub-para (1)(aa) inserted by the Freedom of Information Act 2000, s 73, Sch 6, para 5; words in square brackets in sub-para (2) substituted by SI 2003/1887, art 9, Sch 2, para 9(1)(b).
    Para 7A: inserted by the Serious Crime Act 2007, s 72.
    Orders: the Data Protection (Processing of Sensitive Personal Data) Order 2000, SI 2000/417; the Data Protection (Processing of Sensitive Personal Data) (Elected Representatives) Order 2002, SI 2002/2905; the Data Protection (Processing of Sensitive Personal Data) Order 2006, SI 2006/2068; Data Protection (Processing of Sensitive Personal Data) Order 2009, SI 2009/1811.
    See further: the National Assembly for Wales Commission is treated as a government department for the purposes of para 7 above; see the National Assembly for Wales Commission (Crown Status) Order 2007, SI 2007/1118, art 5(1), (2)(c).

SCHEDULE 4
CASES WHERE THE EIGHTH PRINCIPLE DOES NOT APPLY

Section 4(3)

1. The data subject has given his consent to the transfer.

2. The transfer is necessary—
    (a)   for the performance of a contract between the data subject and the data controller, or
    (b)   for the taking of steps at the request of the data subject with a view to his entering into a contract with the data controller.

3. The transfer is necessary—
    (a)   for the conclusion of a contract between the data controller and a person other than the data subject which—
        (i)   is entered into at the request of the data subject, or
        (ii)   is in the interests of the data subject, or
    (b)   for the performance of such a contract.

4.—(1) The transfer is necessary for reasons of substantial public interest.

(2) The [Secretary of State] may by order specify—
    (a)   circumstances in which a transfer is to be taken for the purposes of sub-paragraph (1) to be necessary for reasons of substantial public interest, and
    (b)   circumstances in which a transfer which is not required by or under an enactment is not to be taken for the purpose of sub-paragraph (1) to be necessary for reasons of substantial public interest.

5. The transfer—
    (a)   is necessary for the purpose of, or in connection with, any legal proceedings (including prospective legal proceedings),
    (b)   is necessary for the purpose of obtaining legal advice, or
    (c)   is otherwise necessary for the purposes of establishing, exercising or defending legal rights.

6. The transfer is necessary in order to protect the vital interests of the data subject.

7. The transfer is of part of the personal data on a public register and any conditions subject to which the register is open to inspection are complied with by any person to whom the data are or may be disclosed after the transfer.

8.   The transfer is made on terms which are of a kind approved by the Commissioner as ensuring adequate safeguards for the rights and freedoms of data subjects.

9.   The transfer has been authorised by the Commissioner as being made in such a manner as to ensure adequate safeguards for the rights and freedoms of data subjects.

[1695]

NOTES
  Para 4: words in square brackets in sub-para (2) substituted by the Secretary of State for Constitutional Affairs Order 2003, SI 2003/1887, art 9, Sch 2, para 9(1)(b).

(Schs 5–16 outside the scope of this work.)

COMPETITION ACT 1998

(1998 c 41)

ARRANGEMENT OF SECTIONS

PART I
COMPETITION

CHAPTER I
AGREEMENTS

Introduction

CHAPTER II
ABUSE OF DOMINANT POSITION

The prohibition

CHAPTER III
INVESTIGATION AND ENFORCEMENT

Investigations

An Act to make provision about competition and the abuse of a dominant position in the market; to confer powers in relation to investigations conducted in connection with [Article 81 or 82] of the treaty establishing the European Community; to amend the Fair Trading Act 1973 in relation to information which may be required in connection with investigations under that Act; to make provision with respect to the meaning of "supply of services" in the Fair Trading Act 1973; and for connected purposes

[9 November 1998]

NOTES

Long title: words in square brackets substituted by the Competition Act 1998 and Other Enactments (Amendment) Regulations 2004, SI 2004/1261, reg 4, Sch 1, para 1.

Substitution of references to the Director General of Fair Trading: the Enterprise Act 2002, s 2(1), at **[1860]**, provides that, as from the coming into force of that section (on 1 April 2003, see the Enterprise Act 2002 (Commencement No 2, Transitional and Transitory Provisions) Order 2003, SI 2003/766), the functions of the

Director General of Fair Trading, his property, rights and liabilities are transferred to the Office of Fair Trading. Accordingly, (by virtue of s 2(2), (3) of the 2002 Act) the office of the Director is abolished, and amendments are made to this Act by the 2002 Act to take account of this (see Sch 25, para 38). Consequently, throughout this Act, unless noted otherwise, the words "OFT", "OFT's", "it", "it" and "its" are substituted for the original words "Director", "Director's", "he", "him" and "his" respectively. For transitional provisions in connection with the transfer, see s 276(1) of, and Sch 24, para 6 to, the 2002 Act.

PART I
COMPETITION

CHAPTER I
AGREEMENTS

Introduction

1 Enactments replaced

The following shall cease to have effect—
- (a) the Restrictive Practices Court Act 1976 (c 33),
- (b) the Restrictive Trade Practices Act 1976 (c 34),
- (c) the Resale Prices Act 1976 (c 53), and
- (d) the Restrictive Trade Practices Act 1977 (c 19).

[1696]

NOTES
  Commencement: 1 March 2000 (paras (b)–(d)); to be appointed (para (a)).

The prohibition

2 Agreements etc preventing, restricting or distorting competition

(1) Subject to section 3, agreements between undertakings, decisions by associations of undertakings or concerted practices which—
- (a) may affect trade within the United Kingdom, and
- (b) have as their object or effect the prevention, restriction or distortion of competition within the United Kingdom,

are prohibited unless they are exempt in accordance with the provisions of this Part.

(2) Subsection (1) applies, in particular, to agreements, decisions or practices which—
- (a) directly or indirectly fix purchase or selling prices or any other trading conditions;
- (b) limit or control production, markets, technical development or investment;
- (c) share markets or sources of supply;
- (d) apply dissimilar conditions to equivalent transactions with other trading parties, thereby placing them at a competitive disadvantage;
- (e) make the conclusion of contracts subject to acceptance by the other parties of supplementary obligations which, by their nature or according to commercial usage, have no connection with the subject of such contracts.

(3) Subsection (1) applies only if the agreement, decision or practice is, or is intended to be, implemented in the United Kingdom.

(4) Any agreement or decision which is prohibited by subsection (1) is void.

(5) A provision of this Part which is expressed to apply to, or in relation to, an agreement is to be read as applying equally to, or in relation to, a decision by an association of undertakings or a concerted practice (but with any necessary modifications).

(6) Subsection (5) does not apply where the context otherwise requires.

(7) In this section "the United Kingdom" means, in relation to an agreement which operates or is intended to operate only in a part of the United Kingdom, that part.

(8) The prohibition imposed by subsection (1) is referred to in this Act as "the Chapter I prohibition".

[1697]

Excluded agreements

3 Excluded agreements

(1) The Chapter I prohibition does not apply in any of the cases in which it is excluded by or as a result of—
- (a) Schedule 1 (mergers and concentrations);
- (b) Schedule 2 (competition scrutiny under other enactments);
- (c) Schedule 3 (planning obligations and other general exclusions); …

(d) ...

(2)   The Secretary of State may at any time by order amend Schedule 1, with respect to the Chapter I prohibition, by—
   (a)   providing for one or more additional exclusions; or
   (b)   amending or removing any provision (whether or not it has been added by an order under this subsection).

(3)   The Secretary of State may at any time by order amend Schedule 3, with respect to the Chapter I prohibition, by—
   (a)   providing for one or more additional exclusions; or
   (b)   amending or removing any provision—
      (i)   added by an order under this subsection; or
      (ii)   included in paragraph 1, 2, 8 or 9 of Schedule 3.

(4)   The power under subsection (3) to provide for an additional exclusion may be exercised only if it appears to the Secretary of State that agreements which fall within the additional exclusion—
   (a)   do not in general have an adverse effect on competition, or
   (b)   are, in general, best considered under Chapter II or [the Enterprise Act 2002].

(5)   An order under subsection (2)(a) or (3)(a) may include provision (similar to that made with respect to any other exclusion provided by the relevant Schedule) for the exclusion concerned to cease to apply to a particular agreement.

(6)   Schedule 3 also gives the Secretary of State power to exclude agreements from the Chapter I prohibition in certain circumstances.

[1698]–[1700]

NOTES
Sub-s (1): para (d) and the word immediately preceding it repealed by the Enterprise Act 2002, ss 207, 278(2), Sch 26.
Sub-s (4): words in square brackets in para (b) substituted by the Enterprise Act 2002, s 278(1), Sch 25, para 38(1), (2).

Exemptions

4, 5   (*Repealed by the Competition Act 1998 and Other Enactments (Amendment) Regulations 2004, SI 2004/1261, reg 4, Sch 1, paras 2, 3.*)

6   Block exemptions

(1)   If agreements which fall within a particular category of agreement are, in the opinion of the [OFT], likely to be [exempt agreements], the [OFT] may recommend that the Secretary of State make an order specifying that category for the purposes of this section.

(2)   The Secretary of State may make an order ("a block exemption order") giving effect to such a recommendation—
   (a)   in the form in which the recommendation is made; or
   (b)   subject to such modifications as he considers appropriate.

(3)   An agreement which falls within a category specified in a block exemption order is exempt from the Chapter I prohibition.

(4)   An exemption under this section is referred to in this Part as a block exemption.

(5)   A block exemption order may impose conditions or obligations subject to which a block exemption is to have effect.

(6)   A block exemption order may provide—
   (a)   that breach of a condition imposed by the order has the effect of cancelling the block exemption in respect of an agreement;
   (b)   that if there is a failure to comply with an obligation imposed by the order, the [OFT] may, by notice in writing, cancel the block exemption in respect of the agreement;
   (c)   that if the [OFT] considers that a particular agreement is not [an exempt agreement], [it] may cancel the block exemption in respect of that agreement.

(7)   A block exemption order may provide that the order is to cease to have effect at the end of a specified period.

[(8)   In this section—
   "exempt agreement" means an agreement which is exempt from the Chapter I prohibition as a result of section 9; and
   "specified" means specified in a block exemption order.]

[1701]–[1702]

NOTES

Sub-s (1): words in second pair of square brackets substituted by the Competition Act 1998 and Other Enactments (Amendment) Regulations 2004, SI 2004/1261, reg 4, Sch 1, para 4(1), (2).

Sub-s (6): words in second pair of square brackets substituted by SI 2004/1261, reg 4, Sch 1, para 4(1), (3).

Sub-s (8): substituted by SI 2004/1261, reg 4, Sch 1, para 4(1), (4).

References to the OFT, etc: as to the abolition of the office of the Director General of Fair Trading and the substitution of the original references to the Director (and related expressions), see the note preceding s 1 at **[1696]**.

Orders: the Competition Act 1998 (Public Transport Ticketing Schemes Block Exemption) Order 2001, SI 2001/319.

7 *(Repealed by the Competition Act 1998 and Other Enactments (Amendment) Regulations 2004, SI 2004/1261, reg 4, Sch 1, para 5.)*

8 Block exemptions: procedure

(1) Before making a recommendation under section 6(1), the [OFT] must—
- (a) publish details of [its] proposed recommendation in such a way as [it] thinks most suitable for bringing it to the attention of those likely to be affected; and
- (b) consider any representations about it which are made to [it].

(2) If the Secretary of State proposes to give effect to such a recommendation subject to modifications, he must inform the [OFT] of the proposed modifications and take into account any comments made by the [OFT].

(3) If, in the opinion of the [OFT], it is appropriate to vary or revoke a block exemption order [it] may make a recommendation to that effect to the Secretary of State.

(4) Subsection (1) also applies to any proposed recommendation under subsection (3).

(5) Before exercising his power to vary or revoke a block exemption order (in a case where there has been no recommendation under subsection (3)), the Secretary of State must—
- (a) inform the [OFT] of the proposed variation or revocation; and
- (b) take into account any comments made by the [OFT].

(6) A block exemption order may provide for a block exemption to have effect from a date earlier than that on which the order is made.

[1703]

NOTES

References to the OFT, etc: as to the abolition of the office of the Director General of Fair Trading and the substitution of the original references to the Director (and related expressions), see the note preceding s 1 at **[1696]**.

Order: the Competition Act 1998 (Public Transport Ticketing Schemes Block Exemption) Order 2001, SI 2001/319.

9 [Exempt agreements]

[(1)] [An agreement is exempt from the Chapter I prohibition if it]—
- (a) contributes to—
  - (i) improving production or distribution, or
  - (ii) promoting technical or economic progress,

  while allowing consumers a fair share of the resulting benefit; [and]
- (b) does not—
  - (i) impose on the undertakings concerned restrictions which are not indispensable to the attainment of those objectives; or
  - (ii) afford the undertakings concerned the possibility of eliminating competition in respect of a substantial part of the products in question.

[(2) In any proceedings in which it is alleged that the Chapter I prohibition is being or has been infringed by an agreement, any undertaking or association of undertakings claiming the benefit of subsection (1) shall bear the burden of proving that the conditions of that subsection are satisfied.]

[1704]

NOTES

Section heading: substituted by the Competition Act 1998 and Other Enactments (Amendment) Regulations 2004, SI 2004/1261, reg 4, Sch 1, para 6(5).

Sub-s (1): numbered as such and words in square brackets substituted by SI 2004/1261, reg 4, Sch 1, para 6(1)–(3).

Sub-s (2): added by SI 2004/1261, reg 4, Sch 1, para 6(4).

10 Parallel exemptions

(1) An agreement is exempt from the Chapter I prohibition if it is exempt from the Community prohibition—

(a)   by virtue of a Regulation, [or
(b)   because of a decision of the Commission under Article 10 of the EC Competition Regulation].

(2)   An agreement is exempt from the Chapter I prohibition if it does not affect trade between Member States but otherwise falls within a category of agreement which is exempt from the Community prohibition by virtue of a Regulation.

(3)   An exemption from the Chapter I prohibition under this section is referred to in this Part as a parallel exemption.

(4)   A parallel exemption—
    (a)   takes effect on the date on which the relevant exemption from the Community prohibition takes effect or, in the case of a parallel exemption under subsection (2), would take effect if the agreement in question affected trade between Member States; and
    (b)   ceases to have effect—
        (i)   if the relevant exemption from the Community prohibition ceases to have effect; or
        (ii)   on being cancelled by virtue of subsection (5) or (7).

(5)   In such circumstances and manner as may be specified in rules made under section 51, the [OFT] may—
    (a)   impose conditions or obligations subject to which a parallel exemption is to have effect;
    (b)   vary or remove any such condition or obligation;
    (c)   impose one or more additional conditions or obligations;
    (d)   cancel the exemption.

(6)   In such circumstances as may be specified in rules made under section 51, the date from which cancellation of an exemption is to take effect may be earlier than the date on which notice of cancellation is given.

(7)   Breach of a condition imposed by the [OFT] has the effect of cancelling the exemption.

(8)   In exercising [its] powers under this section, the [OFT] may require any person who is a party to the agreement in question to give [it] such information as [it] may require.

(9)   For the purpose of this section references to an agreement being exempt from the Community prohibition are to be read as including references to the prohibition being inapplicable to the agreement by virtue of a Regulation [other than the EC Competition Regulation] or a decision by the Commission.

(10)   In this section—
    "the Community prohibition" means the prohibition contained in—
        [(a)   Article 81(1);]
        (b)   any corresponding provision replacing, or otherwise derived from, that provision;
        (c)   such other Regulation as the Secretary of State may by order specify; and
    "Regulation" means a Regulation adopted by the Commission or by the Council.

(11)   This section has effect in relation to the prohibition contained in paragraph 1 of Article 53 of the EEA Agreement (and the EFTA Surveillance Authority) as it has effect in relation to the Community prohibition (and the Commission) subject to any modifications which the Secretary of State may by order prescribe.

                                                                          [1705]

NOTES
    Sub-s (1): para (b) and word "or" immediately preceding it substituted, for original paras (b), (c), by the Competition Act 1998 and Other Enactments (Amendment) Regulations 2004, SI 2004/1261, reg 4, Sch 1, para 7(1), (2), subject to savings and transitional provision in reg 7 of those Regulations.
    Sub-s (9): words in square brackets substituted by SI 2004/1261, reg 4, Sch 1, para 7(1), (3).
    Sub-s (10): in definition "the community prohibition" para (a) substituted by SI 2004/1261, reg 4, Sch 1, para 7(1), (4).
    References to the OFT, etc: as to the abolition of the office of the Director General of Fair Trading and the substitution of the original references to the Director (and related expressions), see the note preceding s 1 at **[1696]**.

11   Exemption for certain other agreements

(1)   The fact that a ruling may be given by virtue of [Article 84] of the Treaty on the question whether or not agreements of a particular kind are prohibited by [Article 81(1)] does not prevent such agreements from being subject to the Chapter I prohibition.

(2)   But the Secretary of State may by regulations make such provision as he considers appropriate for the purpose of granting an exemption from the Chapter I prohibition, in prescribed circumstances, in respect of such agreements.

(3) An exemption from the Chapter I prohibition by virtue of regulations under this section is referred to in this Part as a section 11 exemption.

[1706]–[1711]

NOTES
  Sub-s (1): words in square brackets substituted by the Competition Act 1998 and Other Enactments (Amendment) Regulations 2004, SI 2004/1261, reg 4, Sch 1, para 8.
  Regulations: the Competition Act 1998 (Section 11 Exemption) Regulations 2001, SI 2001/2993.

12–16 (*Repealed by the Competition Act 1998 and Other Enactments (Amendment) Regulations 2004, SI 2004/1261, reg 4, Sch 1, para 9.*)

CHAPTER II
ABUSE OF DOMINANT POSITION

17 (*Repeals the Competition Act 1980, ss 2–10.*)

The prohibition

18 Abuse of dominant position

(1) Subject to section 19, any conduct on the part of one or more undertakings which amounts to the abuse of a dominant position in a market is prohibited if it may affect trade within the United Kingdom.

(2) Conduct may, in particular, constitute such an abuse if it consists in—
  (a) directly or indirectly imposing unfair purchase or selling prices or other unfair trading conditions;
  (b) limiting production, markets or technical development to the prejudice of consumers;
  (c) applying dissimilar conditions to equivalent transactions with other trading parties, thereby placing them at a competitive disadvantage;
  (d) making the conclusion of contracts subject to acceptance by the other parties of supplementary obligations which, by their nature or according to commercial usage, have no connection with the subject of the contracts.

(3) In this section—
  "dominant position" means a dominant position within the United Kingdom; and
  "the United Kingdom" means the United Kingdom or any part of it.

(4) The prohibition imposed by subsection (1) is referred to in this Act as "the Chapter II prohibition".

[1712]

Excluded cases

19 Excluded cases

(1) The Chapter II prohibition does not apply in any of the cases in which it is excluded by or as a result of—
  (a) Schedule 1 (mergers and concentrations); or
  (b) Schedule 3 (general exclusions).

(2) The Secretary of State may at any time by order amend Schedule 1, with respect to the Chapter II prohibition, by—
  (a) providing for one or more additional exclusions; or
  (b) amending or removing any provision (whether or not it has been added by an order under this subsection).

(3) The Secretary of State may at any time by order amend paragraph 8 of Schedule 3 with respect to the Chapter II prohibition.

(4) Schedule 3 also gives the Secretary of State power to provide that the Chapter II prohibition is not to apply in certain circumstances.

[1713]–[1718]

20–24 (*Repealed by the Competition Act 1998 and Other Enactments (Amendment) Regulations 2004, SI 2004/1261, reg 4, Sch 1, para 9.*)

CHAPTER III
INVESTIGATION AND ENFORCEMENT

Investigations

[25   Power of OFT to investigate

(1)   In any of the following cases, the OFT may conduct an investigation.

(2)   The first case is where there are reasonable grounds for suspecting that there is an agreement which—
  (a)   may affect trade within the United Kingdom; and
  (b)   has as its object or effect the prevention, restriction or distortion of competition within the United Kingdom.

(3)   The second case is where there are reasonable grounds for suspecting that there is an agreement which—
  (a)   may affect trade between Member States; and
  (b)   has as its object or effect the prevention, restriction or distortion of competition within the Community.

(4)   The third case is where there are reasonable grounds for suspecting that the Chapter II prohibition has been infringed.

(5)   The fourth case is where there are reasonable grounds for suspecting that the prohibition in Article 82 has been infringed.

(6)   The fifth case is where there are reasonable grounds for suspecting that, at some time in the past, there was an agreement which at that time—
  (a)   may have affected trade within the United Kingdom; and
  (b)   had as its object or effect the prevention, restriction or distortion of competition within the United Kingdom.

(7)   The sixth case is where there are reasonable grounds for suspecting that, at some time in the past, there was an agreement which at that time—
  (a)   may have affected trade between Member States; and
  (b)   had as its object or effect the prevention, restriction or distortion of competition within the Community.

(8)   Subsection (2) does not permit an investigation to be conducted in relation to an agreement if the OFT—
  (a)   considers that the agreement is exempt from the Chapter I prohibition as a result of a block exemption or a parallel exemption; and
  (b)   does not have reasonable grounds for suspecting that the circumstances may be such that it could exercise its power to cancel the exemption.

(9)   Subsection (3) does not permit an investigation to be conducted if the OFT—
  (a)   considers that the agreement is an agreement to which the prohibition in Article 81(1) is inapplicable by virtue of a regulation of the Commission ("the relevant regulation"); and
  (b)   does not have reasonable grounds for suspecting that the conditions set out in Article 29(2) of the EC Competition Regulation for the withdrawal of the benefit of the relevant regulation may be satisfied in respect of that agreement.

(10)   Subsection (6) does not permit an investigation to be conducted in relation to any agreement if the OFT considers that, at the time in question, the agreement was exempt from the Chapter I prohibition as a result of a block exemption or a parallel exemption.

(11)   Subsection (7) does not permit an investigation to be conducted in relation to any agreement if the OFT considers that, at the time in question, the agreement was an agreement to which the prohibition in Article 81(1) was inapplicable by virtue of a regulation of the Commission.

(12)   It is immaterial for the purposes of subsection (6) or (7) whether the agreement in question remains in existence.]

[1719]

NOTES
  Substituted by the Competition Act 1998 and Other Enactments (Amendment) Regulations 2004, SI 2004/1261, reg 4, Sch 1, para 10.

26   Powers when conducting investigations

(1)   For the purposes of an investigation ... , the [OFT] may require any person to produce to [it] a specified document, or to provide [it] with specified information, which [it] considers relates to any matter relevant to the investigation.

(2)   The power conferred by subsection (1) is to be exercised by a notice in writing.

(3)   A notice under subsection (2) must indicate—

    (a)   the subject matter and purpose of the investigation; and

    (b)   the nature of the offences created by sections 42 to 44.

(4)   In subsection (1) "specified" means—

    (a)   specified, or described, in the notice; or

    (b)   falling within a category which is specified, or described, in the notice.

(5)   The [OFT] may also specify in the notice—

    (a)   the time and place at which any document is to be produced or any information is to be provided;

    (b)   the manner and form in which it is to be produced or provided.

(6)   The power under this section to require a person to produce a document includes power—

    (a)   if the document is produced—

        (i)   to take copies of it or extracts from it;

        (ii) to require him, or any person who is a present or past officer of his, or is or was at any time employed by him, to provide an explanation of the document;

    (b)   if the document is not produced, to require him to state, to the best of his knowledge and belief, where it is.

[1720]

NOTES

Sub-s (1): words omitted repealed by the Competition Act 1998 and Other Enactments (Amendment) Regulations 2004, SI 2004/1261, reg 4, Sch 1, para 11, subject to savings and transitional provision in reg 6(1), (2), (4) of those Regulations.

References to the OFT, etc: as to the abolition of the office of the Director General of Fair Trading and the substitution of the original references to the Director (and related expressions), see the note preceding s 1 at **[1696]**.

27 [Power to enter business premises without a warrant]

(1)   Any officer of the [OFT] who is authorised in writing by the [OFT] to do so ("an investigating officer") may enter [any business premises] in connection with an investigation ...

(2)   No investigating officer is to enter any premises in the exercise of his powers under this section unless he has given to the occupier of the premises a written notice which—

    (a)   gives at least two working days' notice of the intended entry;

    (b)   indicates the subject matter and purpose of the investigation; and

    (c)   indicates the nature of the offences created by sections 42 to 44.

(3)   Subsection (2) does not apply—

    (a)   if the [OFT] has a reasonable suspicion that the premises are, or have been, occupied by—

        (i)   a party to an agreement which [it] is investigating under [section 25]; or

        (ii) an undertaking the conduct of which [it] is investigating under [section 25]; or

    (b)   if the investigating officer has taken all such steps as are reasonably practicable to give notice but has not been able to do so.

(4)   In a case falling within subsection (3), the power of entry conferred by subsection (1) is to be exercised by the investigating officer on production of—

    (a)   evidence of his authorisation; and

    (b)   a document containing the information referred to in subsection (2)(b) and (c).

(5)   An investigating officer entering any premises under this section may—

    (a)   take with him such equipment as appears to him to be necessary;

    (b)   require any person on the premises—

        (i)   to produce any document which he considers relates to any matter relevant to the investigation; and

        (ii) if the document is produced, to provide an explanation of it;

    (c)   require any person to state, to the best of his knowledge and belief, where any such document is to be found;

    (d)   take copies of, or extracts from, any document which is produced;

    (e)   require any information which is [stored in any electronic form] and is accessible from the premises and which the investigating officer considers relates to any matter relevant to the investigation, to be produced in a form—

        (i)   in which it can be taken away, and

        (ii) in which it is visible and legible [or from which it can readily be produced in a visible and legible form].

    [(f)   take any steps which appear to be necessary for the purpose of preserving or preventing interference with any document which he considers relates to any matter relevant to the investigation.]

[(6)   In this section "business premises" means premises (or any part of premises) not used as a dwelling.]

[1721]

PART 1
STATUTES

NOTES

Section heading: substituted by the Competition Act 1998 and Other Enactments (Amendment) Regulations 2004, SI 2004/1261, reg 4, Sch 1, para 12(1), (6).

Sub-s (1): words in third pair of square brackets substituted and words omitted repealed by SI 2004/1261, reg 4, Sch 1, para 12(1), (2).

Sub-s (3): in para (a)(i), (a)(ii) words in second pair of square brackets substituted by SI 2004/1261, reg 4, Sch 1, para 12(1), (3).

Sub-s (5): in para (e) words in first pair of square brackets substituted, and words in second pair of square brackets added, by the Criminal Justice and Police Act 2001, s 70, Sch 2, Pt 2, para 21; para (f) added by SI 2004/1261, reg 4, Sch 1, para 12(1), (4).

Sub-s (6): added by SI 2004/1261, reg 4, Sch 1, para 12(1), (5).

References to the OFT, etc: as to the abolition of the office of the Director General of Fair Trading and the substitution of the original references to the Director (and related expressions), see the note preceding s 1 at **[1696]**.

28   [Power to enter business premises under a warrant]

(1)   On an application made by the [OFT] to the court in accordance with rules of court, a judge may issue a warrant if he is satisfied that—

(a)   there are reasonable grounds for suspecting that there are on [any business premises] documents—
   (i)   the production of which has been required under section 26 or 27; and
   (ii)   which have not been produced as required;

(b)   there are reasonable grounds for suspecting that—
   (i)   there are on [any business premises] documents which the [OFT] has power under section 26 to require to be produced; and
   (ii)   if the documents were required to be produced, they would not be produced but would be concealed, removed, tampered with or destroyed; or

(c)   an investigating officer has attempted to enter premises in the exercise of his powers under section 27 but has been unable to do so and that there are reasonable grounds for suspecting that there are on the premises documents the production of which could have been required under that section.

(2)   A warrant under this section shall authorise a named officer of the [OFT], and any other of [the OFT's officers whom the OFT] has authorised in writing to accompany the named officer—

(a)   to enter the premises specified in the warrant, using such force as is reasonably necessary for the purpose;

(b)   to search the premises and take copies of, or extracts from, any document appearing to be of a kind in respect of which the application under subsection (1) was granted ("the relevant kind");

(c)   to take possession of any documents appearing to be of the relevant kind if—
   (i)   such action appears to be necessary for preserving the documents or preventing interference with them; or
   (ii)   it is not reasonably practicable to take copies of the documents on the premises;

(d)   to take any other steps which appear to be necessary for the purpose mentioned in paragraph (c)(i);

(e)   to require any person to provide an explanation of any document appearing to be of the relevant kind or to state, to the best of his knowledge and belief, where it may be found;

(f)   to require any information which is [stored in any electronic form] and is accessible from the premises and which the named officer considers relates to any matter relevant to the investigation, to be produced in a form—
   (i)   in which it can be taken away, and
   (ii)   in which it is visible and legible [or from which it can readily be produced in a visible and legible form].

(3)   If, in the case of a warrant under subsection (1)(b), the judge is satisfied that it is reasonable to suspect that there are also on the premises other documents relating to the investigation concerned, the warrant shall also authorise action mentioned in subsection (2) to be taken in relation to any such document.

[(3A)   A warrant under this section may authorise persons specified in the warrant to accompany the named officer who is executing it.]

(4)   Any person entering premises by virtue of a warrant under this section may take with him such equipment as appears to him to be necessary.

(5)   On leaving any premises which he has entered by virtue of a warrant under this section, the named officer must, if the premises are unoccupied or the occupier is temporarily absent, leave them as effectively secured as he found them.

(6) A warrant under this section continues in force until the end of the period of one month beginning with the day on which it is issued.

(7) Any document of which possession is taken under subsection (2)(c) may be retained for a period of three months.

[(8) In this section "business premises" has the same meaning as in section 27.]

[1722]

NOTES
Section heading: substituted by the Competition Act 1998 and Other Enactments (Amendment) Regulations 2004, SI 2004/1261, reg 4, Sch 1, para 13(1), (4).
Sub-s (1): in paras (a), (b)(i) words in first pair of square brackets substituted by SI 2004/1261, reg 4, Sch 1, para 13(1), (2).
Sub-s (2): words in second pair of square brackets substituted by the Enterprise Act 2002, s 278(1), Sch 25, para 38(1), (22)(b)(ii); in para (f) words in first pair of square brackets substituted, and words in second pair of square brackets added, by the Criminal Justice and Police Act 2001, s 70, Sch 2, Pt 2, para 21.
Sub-s (3A): inserted by the Enterprise Act 2002, s 203(1), (2).
Sub-s (8): added by SI 2004/1261, reg 4, Sch 1, para 13(1), (3).
References to the OFT, etc: as to the abolition of the office of the Director General of Fair Trading and the substitution of the original references to the Director (and related expressions), see the note preceding s 1 at **[1696]**.
The power of seizure conferred by sub-s (2) is a power to which the Criminal Justice and Police Act 2001, s 50 applies (additional powers of seizure from premises); see s 50 of, and Sch 1, Pt 1, para 67 to, that Act.

[28A Power to enter domestic premises under a warrant

(1) On an application made by the OFT to the court in accordance with rules of court, a judge may issue a warrant if he is satisfied that—
    (a) there are reasonable grounds for suspecting that there are on any domestic premises documents—
        (i) the production of which has been required under section 26; and
        (ii) which have not been produced as required; or
    (b) there are reasonable grounds for suspecting that—
        (i) there are on any domestic premises documents which the OFT has power under section 26 to require to be produced; and
        (ii) if the documents were required to be produced, they would not be produced but would be concealed, removed, tampered with or destroyed.

(2) A warrant under this section shall authorise a named officer of the OFT, and any other of its officers whom the OFT has authorised in writing to accompany the named officer—
    (a) to enter the premises specified in the warrant, using such force as is reasonably necessary for the purpose;
    (b) to search the premises and take copies of, or extracts from, any document appearing to be of a kind in respect of which the application under subsection (1) was granted ("the relevant kind");
    (c) to take possession of any documents appearing to be of the relevant kind if—
        (i) such action appears to be necessary for preserving the documents or preventing interference with them; or
        (ii) it is not reasonably practicable to take copies of the documents on the premises;
    (d) to take any other steps which appear to be necessary for the purpose mentioned in paragraph (c)(i);
    (e) to require any person to provide an explanation of any document appearing to be of the relevant kind or to state, to the best of his knowledge and belief, where it may be found;
    (f) to require any information which is stored in any electronic form and is accessible from the premises and which the named officer considers relates to any matter relevant to the investigation, to be produced in a form—
        (i) in which it can be taken away, and
        (ii) in which it is visible and legible or from which it can readily be produced in a visible and legible form.

(3) If, in the case of a warrant under subsection (1)(b), the judge is satisfied that it is reasonable to suspect that there are also on the premises other documents relating to the investigation concerned, the warrant shall also authorise action mentioned in subsection (2) to be taken in relation to any such document.

(4) A warrant under this section may authorise persons specified in the warrant to accompany the named officer who is executing it.

(5) Any person entering premises by virtue of a warrant under this section may take with him such equipment as appears to him to be necessary.

(6)   On leaving any premises which he has entered by virtue of a warrant under this section, the named officer must, if the premises are unoccupied or the occupier is temporarily absent, leave them as effectively secured as he found them.

(7)   A warrant under this section continues in force until the end of the period of one month beginning with the day on which it is issued.

(8)   Any document of which possession is taken under subsection (2)(c) may be retained for a period of three months.

(9)   In this section, "domestic premises" means premises (or any part of premises) that are used as a dwelling and are—

    (a)   premises also used in connection with the affairs of an undertaking or association of undertakings; or

    (b)   premises where documents relating to the affairs of an undertaking or association of undertakings are kept.]

[1722A]

NOTES
Inserted by the Competition Act 1998 and Other Enactments (Amendment) Regulations 2004, SI 2004/1261, reg 4, Sch 1, para 14.

29   Entry of premises under warrant: supplementary

(1)   A warrant issued under section 28 [or 28A] must indicate—

    (a)   the subject matter and purpose of the investigation;

    (b)   the nature of the offences created by sections 42 to 44.

(2)   The powers conferred by section 28 [or 28A] are to be exercised on production of a warrant issued under that section.

(3)   If there is no one at the premises when the named officer proposes to execute such a warrant he must, before executing it—

    (a)   take such steps as are reasonable in all the circumstances to inform the occupier of the intended entry; and

    (b)   if the occupier is informed, afford him or his legal or other representative a reasonable opportunity to be present when the warrant is executed.

(4)   If the named officer is unable to inform the occupier of the intended entry he must, when executing the warrant, leave a copy of it in a prominent place on the premises.

(5)   In this section—

"named officer" means the officer named in the warrant; and

"occupier", in relation to any premises, means a person whom the named officer reasonably believes is the occupier of those premises.

[1723]

NOTES
Sub-ss (1), (2): words in square brackets inserted by the Competition Act 1998 and Other Enactments (Amendment) Regulations 2004, SI 2004/1261, reg 4, Sch 1, para 15.

30   Privileged communications

(1)   A person shall not be required, under any provision of this Part, to produce or disclose a privileged communication.

(2)   "Privileged communication" means a communication—

    (a)   between a professional legal adviser and his client, or

    (b)   made in connection with, or in contemplation of, legal proceedings and for the purposes of those proceedings,

which in proceedings in the High Court would be protected from disclosure on grounds of legal professional privilege.

(3)   In the application of this section to Scotland—

    (a)   references to the High Court are to be read as references to the Court of Session; and

    (b)   the reference to legal professional privilege is to be read as a reference to confidentiality of communications.

[1724]

[30A   Use of statements in prosecution

A statement made by a person in response to a requirement imposed by virtue of any of sections 26 [to 28A] may not be used in evidence against him on a prosecution for an offence under section 188 of the Enterprise Act 2002 unless, in the proceedings—

    (a)   in giving evidence, he makes a statement inconsistent with it, and

(b)   evidence relating to it is adduced, or a question relating to it is asked, by him or on his behalf.]

[1725]

NOTES
Inserted by the Enterprise Act 2002, s 198.
Words in square brackets substituted by the Competition Act 1998 and Other Enactments (Amendment) Regulations 2004, SI 2004/1261, reg 4, Sch 1, para 16.

[31 Decisions following an investigation

(1)   If as a result of an investigation the OFT proposes to make a decision, the OFT must—
  (a)   give written notice to the person (or persons) likely to be affected by the proposed decision; and
  (b)   give that person (or those persons) an opportunity to make representations.

(2)   For the purposes of this section and sections 31A and 31B "decision" means a decision of the OFT—
  (a)   that the Chapter I prohibition has been infringed;
  (b)   that the Chapter II prohibition has been infringed;
  (c)   that the prohibition in Article 81(1) has been infringed; or
  (d)   that the prohibition in Article 82 has been infringed.]

[1726]

NOTES
Substituted by the Competition Act 1998 and Other Enactments (Amendment) Regulations 2004, SI 2004/1261, reg 4, Sch 1, para 17.

[31A Commitments

(1)   Subsection (2) applies in a case where the OFT has begun an investigation under section 25 but has not made a decision (within the meaning given by section 31(2)).

(2)   For the purposes of addressing the competition concerns it has identified, the OFT may accept from such person (or persons) concerned as it considers appropriate commitments to take such action (or refrain from taking such action) as it considers appropriate.

(3)   At any time when commitments are in force the OFT may accept from the person (or persons) who gave the commitments—
  (a)   a variation of them if it is satisfied that the commitments as varied will address its current competition concerns;
  (b)   commitments in substitution for them if it is satisfied that the new commitments will address its current competition concerns.

(4)   Commitments under this section—
  (a)   shall come into force when accepted; and
  (b)   may be released by the OFT where—
    (i)   it is requested to do so by the person (or persons) who gave the commitments; or
    (ii)   it has reasonable grounds for believing that the competition concerns referred to in subsection (2) or (3) no longer arise.

(5)   The provisions of Schedule 6A to this Act shall have effect with respect to procedural requirements for the acceptance, variation and release of commitments under this section.]

[1726A]

NOTES
Inserted, together with ss 31B–31E, by the Competition Act 1998 and Other Enactments (Amendment) Regulations 2004, SI 2004/1261, reg 4, Sch 1, para 18.

[31B Effect of commitments under section 31A

(1)   Subsection (2) applies if the OFT has accepted commitments under section 31A (and has not released them).

(2)   In such a case, the OFT shall not—
  (a)   continue the investigation,
  (b)   make a decision (within the meaning of section 31(2)), or
  (c)   give a direction under section 35,
in relation to the agreement or conduct which was the subject of the investigation (but this subsection is subject to subsections (3) and (4)).

(3)   Nothing in subsection (2) prevents the OFT from taking any action in relation to competition concerns which are not addressed by commitments accepted by it.

(4)   Subsection (2) also does not prevent the OFT from continuing the investigation, making a decision, or giving a direction where—
  (a)   it has reasonable grounds for believing that there has been a material change of circumstances since the commitments were accepted;
  (b)   it has reasonable grounds for suspecting that a person has failed to adhere to one or more of the terms of the commitments; or
  (c)   it has reasonable grounds for suspecting that information which led it to accept the commitments was incomplete, false or misleading in a material particular.

(5)   If, pursuant to subsection (4), the OFT makes a decision or gives a direction the commitments are to be treated as released from the date of that decision or direction.]

[1726B]

NOTES
Inserted as noted to s 31A at **[1726A]**.

[31C   Review of commitments

(1)   Where the OFT is reviewing or has reviewed the effectiveness of commitments accepted under section 31A it must, if requested to do so by the Secretary of State, prepare a report of its findings.

(2)   The OFT must—
  (a)   give any report prepared by it under subsection (1) to the Secretary of State; and
  (b)   publish the report.]

[1726C]

NOTES
Inserted as noted to s 31A at **[1726A]**.

[31D   Guidance

(1)   The OFT must prepare and publish guidance as to the circumstances in which it may be appropriate to accept commitments under section 31A.

(2)   The OFT may at any time alter the guidance.

(3)   If the guidance is altered, the OFT must publish it as altered.

(4)   No guidance is to be published under this section without the approval of the Secretary of State.

(5)   The OFT may, after consulting the Secretary of State, choose how it publishes its guidance.

(6)   If the OFT is preparing or altering guidance under this section it must consult such persons as it considers appropriate.

(7)   If the proposed guidance or alteration relates to a matter in respect of which a regulator exercises concurrent jurisdiction, those consulted must include that regulator.

(8)   When exercising its discretion to accept commitments under section 31A, the OFT must have regard to the guidance for the time being in force under this section.]

[1726D]

NOTES
Inserted as noted to s 31A at **[1726A]**.

[31E   Enforcement of commitments

(1)   If a person from whom the OFT has accepted commitments fails without reasonable excuse to adhere to the commitments (and has not been released from them), the OFT may apply to the court for an order—
  (a)   requiring the defaulter to make good his default within a time specified in the order; or
  (b)   if the commitments relate to anything to be done in the management or administration of an undertaking, requiring the undertaking or any of its officers to do it.

(2)   An order of the court under subsection (1) may provide for all the costs of, or incidental to, the application for the order to be borne by—
  (a)   the person in default; or
  (b)   any officer of an undertaking who is responsible for the default.

(3)   In the application of subsection (2) to Scotland, the reference to "costs" is to be read as a reference to "expenses".]

[1726E]

Enforcement

32 Directions in relation to agreements

(1)   If the [OFT] has made a decision that an agreement infringes the Chapter I prohibition [or that it infringes the prohibition in Article 81(1)], [it] may give to such person or persons as [it] considers appropriate such directions as [it] considers appropriate to bring the infringement to an end.

(2)   ...

(3)   A direction under this section may, in particular, include provision—
   (a)   requiring the parties to the agreement to modify the agreement; or
   (b)   requiring them to terminate the agreement.

(4)   A direction under this section must be given in writing.

[**1727**]

NOTES
Sub-s (1): words in second pair of square brackets inserted by the Competition Act 1998 and Other Enactments (Amendment) Regulations 2004, SI 2004/1261, reg 4, Sch 1, para 19(1), (2).
Sub-s (2): repealed by SI 2004/1261, reg 4, Sch 1, para 19(1), (3).
References to the OFT, etc: as to the abolition of the office of the Director General of Fair Trading and the substitution of the original references to the Director (and related expressions), see the note preceding s 1 at [**1696**].

33 Directions in relation to conduct

(1)   If the [OFT] has made a decision that conduct infringes the Chapter II prohibition [or that it infringes the prohibition in Article 82], [it] may give to such person or persons as [it] considers appropriate such directions as [it] considers appropriate to bring the infringement to an end.

(2)   ...

(3)   A direction under this section may, in particular, include provision—
   (a)   requiring the person concerned to modify the conduct in question; or
   (b)   requiring him to cease that conduct.

(4)   A direction under this section must be given in writing.

[**1728**]

NOTES
Sub-s (1): words in second pair of square brackets inserted by the Competition Act 1998 and Other Enactments (Amendment) Regulations 2004, SI 2004/1261, reg 4, Sch 1, para 20(1), (2).
Sub-s (2): repealed by SI 2004/1261, reg 4, Sch 1, para 20(1), (3).
References to the OFT, etc: as to the abolition of the office of the Director General of Fair Trading and the substitution of the original references to the Director (and related expressions), see the note preceding s 1 at [**1696**].

34 Enforcement of directions

(1)   If a person fails, without reasonable excuse, to comply with a direction under section 32 or 33, the [OFT] may apply to the court for an order—
   (a)   requiring the defaulter to make good his default within a time specified in the order; or
   (b)   if the direction related to anything to be done in the management or administration of an undertaking, requiring the undertaking or any of its officers to do it.

(2)   An order of the court under subsection (1) may provide for all of the costs of, or incidental to, the application for the order to be borne by—
   (a)   the person in default; or
   (b)   any officer of an undertaking who is responsible for the default.

(3)   In the application of subsection (2) to Scotland, the reference to "costs" is to be read as a reference to "expenses".

[**1729**]

NOTES
References to the OFT, etc: as to the abolition of the office of the Director General of Fair Trading and the substitution of the original references to the Director (and related expressions), see the note preceding s 1 at [**1696**].

35 Interim measures

[(1) Subject to subsections (8) and (9), this section applies if the OFT has begun an investigation under section 25 and not completed it (but only applies so long as the OFT has power under section 25 to conduct that investigation).]

(2) If the [OFT] considers that it is necessary for [it] to act under this section as a matter of urgency for the purpose—

    (a)   of preventing serious, irreparable damage to a particular person or category of person, or

    (b)   of protecting the public interest,

[it] may give such directions as [it] considers appropriate for that purpose.

(3) Before giving a direction under this section, the [OFT] must—

    (a)   give written notice to the person (or persons) to whom [it] proposes to give the direction; and

    (b)   give that person (or each of them) an opportunity to make representations.

(4) A notice under subsection (3) must indicate the nature of the direction which the [OFT] is proposing to give and [its] reasons for wishing to give it.

[(5) A direction given under this section may if the circumstances permit be replaced by—

    (a)   a direction under section 32 or (as appropriate) section 33, or

    (b)   commitments accepted under section 31A,

but, subject to that, has effect while this section applies.]

(6) In the [cases mentioned in section 25(2), (3), (6) and (7)], sections 32(3) and 34 also apply to directions given under this section.

(7) In the [cases mentioned in section 25(4) and (5)], sections 33(3) and 34 also apply to directions given under this section.

[(8) In the case of an investigation conducted by virtue of section 25(2) or (6), this section does not apply if a person has produced evidence to the OFT in connection with the investigation that satisfies it on the balance of probabilities that, in the event of it reaching the basic infringement conclusion, it would also reach the conclusion that the suspected agreement is exempt from the Chapter I prohibition as a result of section 9(1); and in this subsection "the basic infringement conclusion" is the conclusion that there is an agreement which—

    (a)   may affect trade within the United Kingdom, and

    (b)   has as its object or effect the prevention, restriction or distortion of competition within the United Kingdom

(9) In the case of an investigation conducted by virtue of section 25(3) or (7), this section does not apply if a person has produced evidence to the OFT in connection with the investigation that satisfies it on the balance of probabilities that, in the event of it reaching the basic infringement conclusion, it would also reach the conclusion that the suspected agreement is an agreement to which the prohibition in Article 81(1) is inapplicable because the agreement satisfies the conditions in Article 81(3); and in this subsection "the basic infringement conclusion" is the conclusion that there is an agreement which—

    (a)   may affect trade between Member States, and

    (b)   has as its object or effect the prevention, restriction or distortion of competition within the Community.]

[1730]

NOTES

Sub-ss (1), (5): substituted by the Competition Act 1998 and Other Enactments (Amendment) Regulations 2004, SI 2004/1261, reg 4, Sch 1, para 21(1)–(3).

Sub-ss (6), (7): words in square brackets substituted by SI 2004/1261, reg 4, Sch 1, para 21(1), (4), (5).

Sub-ss (8), (9): added by SI 2004/1261, reg 4, Sch 1, para 21(1), (6).

References to the OFT, etc: as to the abolition of the office of the Director General of Fair Trading and the substitution of the original references to the Director (and related expressions), see the note preceding s 1 at **[1696]**.

36 [Penalties]

(1) On making a decision that an agreement has infringed the Chapter I prohibition [or that it has infringed the prohibition in Article 81(1)], the [OFT] may require an undertaking which is a party to the agreement to pay [the OFT] a penalty in respect of the infringement.

(2) On making a decision that conduct has infringed the Chapter II prohibition [or that it has infringed the prohibition in Article 82], the [OFT] may require the undertaking concerned to pay [the OFT] a penalty in respect of the infringement.

(3) The [OFT] may impose a penalty on an undertaking under subsection (1) or (2) only if [the OFT] is satisfied that the infringement has been committed intentionally or negligently by the undertaking.

(4)   Subsection (1) is subject to section 39 and does not apply [in relation to a decision that an agreement has infringed the Chapter I prohibition] if the [OFT] is satisfied that the undertaking acted on the reasonable assumption that that section gave it immunity in respect of the agreement.

(5)   Subsection (2) is subject to section 40 and does not apply [in relation to a decision that conduct has infringed the Chapter II prohibition] if the [OFT] is satisfied that the undertaking acted on the reasonable assumption that that section gave it immunity in respect of the conduct.

(6)   Notice of a penalty under this section must—
  (a)   be in writing; and
  (b)   specify the date before which the penalty is required to be paid.

(7)   The date specified must not be earlier than the end of the period within which an appeal against the notice may be brought under section 46.

(8)   No penalty fixed by the [OFT] under this section may exceed 10% of the turnover of the undertaking (determined in accordance with such provisions as may be specified in an order made by the Secretary of State).

(9)   Any sums received by the [OFT] under this section are to be paid into the Consolidated Fund.

[1731]

NOTES
Section heading: substituted by the Competition Act 1998 and Other Enactments (Amendment) Regulations 2004, SI 2004/1261, reg 4, Sch 1, para 22(1), (6).
Sub-ss (1), (2): words in second pairs of square brackets inserted by SI 2004/1261, reg 4, Sch 1, para 22(1)–(3); words in third pairs of square brackets substituted by the Enterprise Act 2002, s 278(1), Sch 25, para 38(1), (28)(b).
Sub-s (3): words in second pair of square brackets substituted by the Enterprise Act 2002, s 278(1), Sch 25, para 38(1), (28)(b).
Sub-ss (4), (5): words in first pair of square brackets inserted by SI 2004/1261, reg 4, Sch 1, para 22(1), (4), (5).
References to the OFT, etc: as to the abolition of the office of the Director General of Fair Trading and the substitution of the original references to the Director (and related expressions), see the note preceding s 1 at **[1696]**.
Order: the Competition Act 1998 (Determination of Turnover for Penalties) Order 2000, SI 2000/309.

37   Recovery of penalties

(1)   If the specified date in a penalty notice has passed and—
  (a)   the period during which an appeal against the imposition, or amount, of the penalty may be made has expired without an appeal having been made, or
  (b)   such an appeal has been made and determined,
the [OFT] may recover from the undertaking, as a civil debt due to [the OFT], any amount payable under the penalty notice which remains outstanding.

(2)   In this section—
  "penalty notice" means a notice given under section 36; and
  "specified date" means the date specified in the penalty notice.

[1732]

NOTES
Sub-s (1): words in second pair of square brackets substituted by the Enterprise Act 2002, s 278(1), Sch 25, para 38(1), (29).
References to the OFT, etc: as to the abolition of the office of the Director General of Fair Trading and the substitution of the original references to the Director (and related expressions), see the note preceding s 1 at **[1696]**.

38   The appropriate level of a penalty

(1)   The [OFT] must prepare and publish guidance as to the appropriate amount of any penalty under this Part.

[(1A)   The guidance must include provision about the circumstances in which, in determining a penalty under this Part, the OFT may take into account effects in another Member State of the agreement or conduct concerned.]

(2)   The [OFT] may at any time alter the guidance.

(3)   If the guidance is altered, the [OFT] must publish it as altered.

(4)   No guidance is to be published under this section without the approval of the Secretary of State.

(5)   The [OFT] may, after consulting the Secretary of State, choose how [it] publishes [its] guidance.

(6)   If the [OFT] is preparing or altering guidance under this section [it] must consult such persons as [it] considers appropriate.

(7)   If the proposed guidance or alteration relates to a matter in respect of which a regulator exercises concurrent jurisdiction, those consulted must include that regulator.

(8)   When setting the amount of a penalty under this Part, the [OFT] must have regard to the guidance for the time being in force under this section.

(9)   If a penalty or a fine has been imposed by the Commission, or by a court or other body in another Member State, in respect of an agreement or conduct, the [OFT], an appeal tribunal or the appropriate court must take that penalty or fine into account when setting the amount of a penalty under this Part in relation to that agreement or conduct.

(10)   In subsection (9) "the appropriate court" means—
- (a)   in relation to England and Wales, the Court of Appeal;
- (b)   in relation to Scotland, the Court of Session;
- (c)   in relation to Northern Ireland, the Court of Appeal in Northern Ireland;
- [(d) the Supreme Court.]

[1733]

NOTES

Sub-s (1A): inserted by the Competition Act 1998 and Other Enactments (Amendment) Regulations 2004, SI 2004/1261, reg 4, Sch 1, para 23.

Sub-s (10): para (d) substituted by the Constitutional Reform Act 2005, s 40(4), Sch 9, Pt 1, para 65(1), (2).

References to the OFT, etc: as to the abolition of the office of the Director General of Fair Trading and the substitution of the original references to the Director (and related expressions), see the note preceding s 1 at **[1696]**.

---

39 [Limited immunity in relation to the Chapter I prohibition]

(1)   In this section "small agreement" means an agreement—
- (a)   which falls within a category prescribed for the purposes of this section; but
- (b)   is not a price fixing agreement.

(2)   The criteria by reference to which a category of agreement is prescribed may, in particular, include—
- (a)   the combined turnover of the parties to the agreement (determined in accordance with prescribed provisions);
- (b)   the share of the market affected by the agreement (determined in that way).

(3)   A party to a small agreement is immune from the effect of section 36(1) [so far as that provision relates to decisions about infringement of the Chapter I prohibition]; but the [OFT] may withdraw that immunity under subsection (4).

(4)   If the [OFT] has investigated a small agreement, [it] may make a decision withdrawing the immunity given by subsection (3) if, as a result of [its] investigation, [it] considers that the agreement is likely to infringe the Chapter I prohibition.

(5)   The [OFT] must give each of the parties in respect of which immunity is withdrawn written notice of [its] decision to withdraw the immunity.

(6)   A decision under subsection (4) takes effect on such date ("the withdrawal date") as may be specified in the decision.

(7)   The withdrawal date must be a date after the date on which the decision is made.

(8)   In determining the withdrawal date, the [OFT] must have regard to the amount of time which the parties are likely to require in order to secure that there is no further infringement of the Chapter I prohibition with respect to the agreement.

(9)   In subsection (1) "price fixing agreement" means an agreement which has as its object or effect, or one of its objects or effects, restricting the freedom of a party to the agreement to determine the price to be charged (otherwise than as between that party and another party to the agreement) for the product, service or other matter to which the agreement relates.

[1734]

NOTES

Section heading: substituted by the Competition Act 1998 and Other Enactments (Amendment) Regulations 2004, SI 2004/1261, reg 4, Sch 1, para 24(1), (3).

Sub-s (3): words in first pair of square brackets inserted by SI 2004/1261, reg 4, Sch 1, para 24(1), (2).

References to the OFT, etc: as to the abolition of the office of the Director General of Fair Trading and the substitution of the original references to the Director (and related expressions), see the note preceding s 1 at **[1696]**.

Regulations: the Competition Act 1998 (Small Agreements and Conduct of Minor Significance) Regulations 2000, SI 2000/262.

40 Limited immunity in relation to the Chapter II prohibition

(1) In this section "conduct of minor significance" means conduct which falls within a category prescribed for the purposes of this section.

(2) The criteria by reference to which a category is prescribed may, in particular, include—
    (a) the turnover of the person whose conduct it is (determined in accordance with prescribed provisions);
    (b) the share of the market affected by the conduct (determined in that way).

(3) A person is immune from the effect of section 36(2)[, so far as that provision relates to decisions about infringement of the Chapter II prohibition,] if his conduct is conduct of minor significance; but the [OFT] may withdraw that immunity under subsection (4).

(4) If the [OFT] has investigated conduct of minor significance, [it] may make a decision withdrawing the immunity given by subsection (3) if, as a result of [its] investigation, [it] considers that the conduct is likely to infringe the Chapter II prohibition.

(5) The [OFT] must give the person, or persons, whose immunity has been withdrawn written notice of [its] decision to withdraw the immunity.

(6) A decision under subsection (4) takes effect on such date ("the withdrawal date") as may be specified in the decision.

(7) The withdrawal date must be a date after the date on which the decision is made.

(8) In determining the withdrawal date, the [OFT] must have regard to the amount of time which the person or persons affected are likely to require in order to secure that there is no further infringement of the Chapter II prohibition.

[1735]–[1736]

NOTES
Sub-s (3): words in first pair of square brackets inserted by the Competition Act 1998 and Other Enactments (Amendment) Regulations 2004, SI 2004/1261, reg 4, Sch 1, para 25.

References to the OFT, etc: as to the abolition of the office of the Director General of Fair Trading and the substitution of the original references to the Director (and related expressions), see the note preceding s 1 at [1696].

Regulations: the Competition Act 1998 (Small Agreements and Conduct of Minor Significance) Regulations 2000, SI 2000/262.

41 *(Repealed by the Competition Act 1998 and Other Enactments (Amendment) Regulations 2004, SI 2004/1261, reg 4, Sch 1, para 26.)*

Offences

42 Offences

(1) A person is guilty of an offence if he fails to comply with a requirement imposed on him under section 26, 27[, 28 or 28A].

(2) If a person is charged with an offence under subsection (1) in respect of a requirement to produce a document, it is a defence for him to prove—
    (a) that the document was not in his possession or under his control; and
    (b) that it was not reasonably practicable for him to comply with the requirement.

(3) If a person is charged with an offence under subsection (1) in respect of a requirement—
    (a) to provide information,
    (b) to provide an explanation of a document, or
    (c) to state where a document is to be found,
it is a defence for him to prove that he had a reasonable excuse for failing to comply with the requirement.

(4) Failure to comply with a requirement imposed under section 26 or 27 is not an offence if the person imposing the requirement has failed to act in accordance with that section.

(5) A person is guilty of an offence if he intentionally obstructs an officer acting in the exercise of his powers under section 27.

(6) A person guilty of an offence under subsection (1) or (5) is liable—
    (a) on summary conviction, to a fine not exceeding the statutory maximum;
    (b) on conviction on indictment, to a fine.

(7) A person who intentionally obstructs an officer in the exercise of his powers under a warrant issued under [section 28 or 28A] is guilty of an offence and liable—
    (a) on summary conviction, to a fine not exceeding the statutory maximum;
    (b) on conviction on indictment, to imprisonment for a term not exceeding two years or to a fine or to both.

[1737]

NOTES

Sub-ss (1), (7): words in square brackets substituted by the Competition Act 1998 and Other Enactments (Amendment) Regulations 2004, SI 2004/1261, reg 4, Sch 1, para 27.

43 Destroying or falsifying documents

(1)   A person is guilty of an offence if, having been required to produce a document under section 26, 27[, 28 or 28A]—

    (a)   he intentionally or recklessly destroys or otherwise disposes of it, falsifies it or conceals it, or

    (b)   he causes or permits its destruction, disposal, falsification or concealment.

(2)   A person guilty of an offence under subsection (1) is liable—

    (a)   on summary conviction, to a fine not exceeding the statutory maximum;

    (b)   on conviction on indictment, to imprisonment for a term not exceeding two years or to a fine or to both.

[1738]

NOTES

Sub-s (1): words in square brackets substituted by the Competition Act 1998 and Other Enactments (Amendment) Regulations 2004, SI 2004/1261, reg 4, Sch 1, para 28.

44 False or misleading information

(1)   If information is provided by a person to the [OFT] in connection with any function of the [OFT] under this Part, that person is guilty of an offence if—

    (a)   the information is false or misleading in a material particular, and

    (b)   he knows that it is or is reckless as to whether it is.

(2)   A person who—

    (a)   provides any information to another person, knowing the information to be false or misleading in a material particular, or

    (b)   recklessly provides any information to another person which is false or misleading in a material particular,

knowing that the information is to be used for the purpose of providing information to the [OFT] in connection with any of [its] functions under this Part, is guilty of an offence.

(3)   A person guilty of an offence under this section is liable—

    (a)   on summary conviction, to a fine not exceeding the statutory maximum;

    (b)   on conviction on indictment, to imprisonment for a term not exceeding two years or to a fine or to both.

[1739]

NOTES

References to the OFT, etc: as to the abolition of the office of the Director General of Fair Trading and the substitution of the original references to the Director (and related expressions), see the note preceding s 1 at **[1696]**.

CHAPTER IV
THE COMPETITION COMMISSION AND APPEALS

The Commission

45 The Competition Commission

(1)   There is to be a body corporate known as the Competition Commission.

(2)   The Commission is to have such functions as are conferred on it by or as a result of this Act.

(3)   The Monopolies and Mergers Commission is dissolved and its functions are transferred to the Competition Commission.

(4)   In any enactment, instrument or other document, any reference to the Monopolies and Mergers Commission which has continuing effect is to be read as a reference to the Competition Commission.

(5)   The Secretary of State may by order make such consequential, supplemental and incidental provision as he considers appropriate in connection with—

    (a)   the dissolution of the Monopolies and Mergers Commission; and

    (b)   the transfer of functions effected by subsection (3).

(6)   An order made under subsection (5) may, in particular, include provision—

    (a)   for the transfer of property, rights, obligations and liabilities and the continuation of proceedings, investigations and other matters; or

    (b)   amending any enactment which makes provision with respect to the Monopolies and Mergers Commission or any of its functions.

    (7)   [Schedules 7 and 7A make] further provision about the Competition Commission.

    [(8)   The Secretary of State may by order make such modifications in Part 2 of Schedule 7 and in Schedule 7A (performance of the Competition Commission's general functions) as he considers appropriate for improving the performance by the Competition Commission of its functions.]

                                                                                         [1740]

NOTES

Sub-s (7): words in square brackets substituted by the Enterprise Act 2002, s 187(1).
Sub-s (8): added by the Enterprise Act 2002, s 278(1), Sch 25, para 38(1), (35).
Orders: the Competition Act 1998 (Competition Commission) Transitional, Consequential and Supplemental Provisions Order 1999, SI 1999/506; the Competition Act 1998 (Transitional, Consequential and Supplemental Provisions) Order 2000, SI 2000/311; the Competition Act 1998 (Consequential and Supplemental Provisions) Order 2000, SI 2000/2031.

Appeals

46 Appealable decisions

    (1)   Any party to an agreement in respect of which the [OFT] has made a decision may appeal to [the Tribunal] against, or with respect to, the decision.

    (2)   Any person in respect of whose conduct the [OFT] has made a decision may appeal to [the Tribunal] against, or with respect to, the decision.

    [(3)   In this section "decision" means a decision of the OFT—
    (a)   as to whether the Chapter I prohibition has been infringed,
    (b)   as to whether the prohibition in Article 81(1) has been infringed,
    (c)   as to whether the Chapter II prohibition has been infringed,
    (d)   as to whether the prohibition in Article 82 has been infringed,
    (e)   cancelling a block or parallel exemption,
    (f)   withdrawing the benefit of a regulation of the Commission pursuant to Article 29(2) of the EC Competition Regulation,
    (g)   not releasing commitments pursuant to a request made under section 31A(4)(b)(i),
    (h)   releasing commitments under section 31A(4)(b)(ii),
    (i)   as to the imposition of any penalty under section 36 or as to the amount of any such penalty,
and includes a direction under section 32, 33 or 35 and such other decisions under this Part as may be prescribed.]

    (4)   Except in the case of an appeal against the imposition, or the amount, of a penalty, the making of an appeal under this section does not suspend the effect of the decision to which the appeal relates.

    (5)   Part I of Schedule 8 makes further provision about appeals.

                                                                                          [1741]

NOTES

Sub-ss (1), (2): words in second pairs of square brackets substituted by the Enterprise Act 2002, s 21, Sch 5, paras 1, 2(a).
Sub-s (3): substituted by the Competition Act 1998 and Other Enactments (Amendment) Regulations 2004, SI 2004/1261, reg 4, Sch 1, para 29, subject to savings and transitional provisions in regs 6, 8 of those Regulations.
References to the OFT, etc: as to the abolition of the office of the Director General of Fair Trading and the substitution of the original references to the Director (and related expressions), see the note preceding s 1 at **[1696]**.
Regulations: the Competition Act 1998 (Appealable Decisions and Revocation of Notification of Excluded Agreements) Regulations 2004, SI 2004/1078.

[47 Third party appeals

    [(1)   A person who does not fall within section 46(1) or (2) may appeal to the Tribunal with respect to—
    (a)   a decision falling within paragraphs (a) to (f) of section 46(3);
    (b)   a decision falling within paragraph (g) of section 46(3);
    (c)   a decision of the OFT to accept or release commitments under section 31A, or to accept a variation of such commitments other than a variation which is not material in any respect;
    (d)   a decision of the OFT to make directions under section 35;
    (e)   a decision of the OFT not to make directions under section 35; or
    (f)   such other decision of the OFT under this Part as may be prescribed.]

(2)　A person may make an appeal under subsection (1) only if the Tribunal considers that he has a sufficient interest in the decision with respect to which the appeal is made, or that he represents persons who have such an interest.

(3)　The making of an appeal under this section does not suspend the effect of the decision to which the appeal relates.]

[1742]

NOTES

Substituted by the Enterprise Act 2002, s 17.

Sub-s (1): substituted by the Competition Act 1998 and Other Enactments (Amendment) Regulations 2004, SI 2004/1261, reg 4, Sch 1, para 30, subject to savings and transitional provisions in regs 6, 8 of those Regulations.

Regulations: the Competition Act 1998 (Appealable Decisions and Revocation of Notification of Excluded Agreements) Regulations 2004, SI 2004/1078.

[47A　Monetary claims before Tribunal

(1)　This section applies to—
- (a)　any claim for damages, or
- (b)　any other claim for a sum of money,

which a person who has suffered loss or damage as a result of the infringement of a relevant prohibition may make in civil proceedings brought in any part of the United Kingdom.

(2)　In this section "relevant prohibition" means any of the following—
- (a)　the Chapter I prohibition;
- (b)　the Chapter II prohibition;
- (c)　the prohibition in Article 81(1) of the Treaty;
- (d)　the prohibition in Article 82 of the Treaty;
- (e)　the prohibition in Article 65(1) of the Treaty establishing the European Coal and Steel Community;
- (f)　the prohibition in Article 66(7) of that Treaty.

(3)　For the purpose of identifying claims which may be made in civil proceedings, any limitation rules that would apply in such proceedings are to be disregarded.

(4)　A claim to which this section applies may (subject to the provisions of this Act and Tribunal rules) be made in proceedings brought before the Tribunal.

(5)　But no claim may be made in such proceedings—
- (a)　until a decision mentioned in subsection (6) has established that the relevant prohibition in question has been infringed; and
- (b)　otherwise than with the permission of the Tribunal, during any period specified in subsection (7) or (8) which relates to that decision.

(6)　The decisions which may be relied on for the purposes of proceedings under this section are—
- (a)　a decision of the OFT that the Chapter I prohibition or the Chapter II prohibition has been infringed;
- (b)　a decision of the OFT that the prohibition in Article 81(1) or Article 82 of the Treaty has been infringed;
- (c)　a decision of the Tribunal (on an appeal from a decision of the OFT) that the Chapter I prohibition, the Chapter II prohibition or the prohibition in Article 81(1) or Article 82 of the Treaty has been infringed;
- (d)　a decision of the European Commission that the prohibition in Article 81(1) or Article 82 of the Treaty has been infringed; or
- (e)　a decision of the European Commission that the prohibition in Article 65(1) of the Treaty establishing the European Coal and Steel Community has been infringed, or a finding made by the European Commission under Article 66(7) of that Treaty.

(7)　The periods during which proceedings in respect of a claim made in reliance on a decision mentioned in subsection (6)(a), (b) or (c) may not be brought without permission are—
- (a)　in the case of a decision of the OFT, the period during which an appeal may be made to the Tribunal under [section 46 or section 47];
- (b)　in the case of a decision of the OFT which is the subject of an appeal mentioned in paragraph (a), the period following the decision of the Tribunal on the appeal during which a further appeal may be made under section 49 … ;
- (c)　in the case of a decision of the Tribunal mentioned in subsection (6)(c), the period during which a further appeal may be made under section 49 … ;
- (d)　in the case of any decision which is the subject of a further appeal, the period during which an appeal may be made to the [Supreme Court] from a decision on the further appeal;

and, where any appeal mentioned in paragraph (a), (b), (c) or (d) is made, the period specified in that paragraph includes the period before the appeal is determined.

(8) The periods during which proceedings in respect of a claim made in reliance on a decision or finding of the European Commission may not be brought without permission are—

(a) the period during which proceedings against the decision or finding may be instituted in the European Court; and

(b) if any such proceedings are instituted, the period before those proceedings are determined.

(9) In determining a claim to which this section applies the Tribunal is bound by any decision mentioned in subsection (6) which establishes that the prohibition in question has been infringed.

(10) The right to make a claim to which this section applies in proceedings before the Tribunal does not affect the right to bring any other proceedings in respect of the claim.]

[1743]

NOTES

Inserted by the Enterprise Act 2002, s 18(1), as from 20 June 2003, with effect in relation to claims arising before and after that date (see s 18(2) of the 2002 Act).

Sub-s (7): words in square brackets in para (a) substituted and words omitted from paras (b), (c) repealed by the EC Competition Law (Articles 84 and 85) Enforcement (Revocation) Regulations 2007, SI 2007/1846, reg 3, Schedule; words in square brackets in para (d) substituted by the Constitutional Reform Act 2005, s 40(4), Sch 9, Pt 1, para 65(1), (3).

[47B Claims brought on behalf of consumers

(1) A specified body may (subject to the provisions of this Act and Tribunal rules) bring proceedings before the Tribunal which comprise consumer claims made or continued on behalf of at least two individuals.

(2) In this section "consumer claim" means a claim to which section 47A applies which an individual has in respect of an infringement affecting (directly or indirectly) goods or services to which subsection (7) applies.

(3) A consumer claim may be included in proceedings under this section if it is—

(a) a claim made in the proceedings on behalf of the individual concerned by the specified body; or

(b) a claim made by the individual concerned under section 47A which is continued in the proceedings on his behalf by the specified body;

and such a claim may only be made or continued in the proceedings with the consent of the individual concerned.

(4) The consumer claims included in proceedings under this section must all relate to the same infringement.

(5) The provisions of section 47A(5) to (10) apply to a consumer claim included in proceedings under this section as they apply to a claim made in proceedings under that section.

(6) Any damages or other sum (not being costs or expenses) awarded in respect of a consumer claim included in proceedings under this section must be awarded to the individual concerned; but the Tribunal may, with the consent of the specified body and the individual, order that the sum awarded must be paid to the specified body (acting on behalf of the individual).

(7) This subsection applies to goods or services which—

(a) the individual received, or sought to receive, otherwise than in the course of a business carried on by him (notwithstanding that he received or sought to receive them with a view to carrying on a business); and

(b) were, or would have been, supplied to the individual (in the case of goods whether by way of sale or otherwise) in the course of a business carried on by the person who supplied or would have supplied them.

(8) A business includes—

(a) a professional practice;

(b) any other undertaking carried on for gain or reward;

(c) any undertaking in the course of which goods or services are supplied otherwise than free of charge.

(9) "Specified" means specified in an order made by the Secretary of State, in accordance with criteria to be published by the Secretary of State for the purposes of this section.

(10) An application by a body to be specified in an order under this section is to be made in a form approved by the Secretary of State for the purpose.]

[1744]

PART 1
STATUTES

NOTES
Inserted by the Enterprise Act 2002, s 19.
Order: the Specified Body (Consumer Claims) Order 2005, SI 2005/2365.

48 (*Repealed by the Enterprise Act 2002, ss 21, 278(2), Sch 5, paras 1, 3, Sch 26; for a saving in relation to rules made under this section, see s 276(1) of, and Sch 24, para 12 to, the 2002 Act.*)

[49 Further appeals

(1) An appeal lies to the appropriate court—
 (a) from a decision of the Tribunal as to the amount of a penalty under section 36;
 (b) from a decision of the Tribunal as to the award of damages or other sum in respect of a claim made in proceedings under section 47A or included in proceedings under section 47B (other than a decision on costs or expenses) or as to the amount of any such damages or other sum; and
 (c) on a point of law arising from any other decision of the Tribunal on an appeal under section 46 or 47.

(2) An appeal under this section—
 (a) may be brought by a party to the proceedings before the Tribunal or by a person who has a sufficient interest in the matter; and
 (b) requires the permission of the Tribunal or the appropriate court.

(3) In this section "the appropriate court" means the Court of Appeal or, in the case of an appeal from Tribunal proceedings in Scotland, the Court of Session.]

[1745]

NOTES
Substituted by the Enterprise Act 2002, s 21, Sch 5, paras 1, 4.

CHAPTER V
MISCELLANEOUS

Vertical agreements and land agreements

50 Vertical agreements and land agreements

(1) The Secretary of State may by order provide for any provision of this Part to apply in relation to—
 (a) vertical agreements, or
 (b) land agreements,
with such modifications as may be prescribed.

(2) An order may, in particular, provide for exclusions or exemptions, or otherwise provide for prescribed provisions not to apply, in relation to—
 (a) vertical agreements, or land agreements, in general; or
 (b) vertical agreements, or land agreements, of any prescribed description.

(3) An order may empower the [OFT] to give directions to the effect that in prescribed circumstances an exclusion, exemption or modification is not to apply (or is to apply in a particular way) in relation to an individual agreement.

(4) Subsections (2) and (3) are not to be read as limiting the powers conferred by section 71.

(5) In this section—
"land agreement" and "vertical agreement" have such meaning as may be prescribed; and
"prescribed" means prescribed by an order.

[1746]

NOTES
References to the OFT, etc: as to the abolition of the office of the Director General of Fair Trading and the substitution of the original references to the Director (and related expressions), see the note preceding s 1 at **[1696]**.
Order: the Competition Act 1998 (Land Agreements Exclusion and Revocation) Order 2004, SI 2004/1260.

[OFT's] rules, guidance and fees

51 Rules

(1) The [OFT] may make such rules about procedural and other matters in connection with the carrying into effect of the provisions of this Part as [it] considers appropriate.

(2) Schedule 9 makes further provision about rules made under this section but is not to be taken as restricting the [OFT's] powers under this section.

(3)   If the [OFT] is preparing rules under this section [it] must consult such persons as [it] considers appropriate.

(4)   If the proposed rules relate to a matter in respect of which a regulator exercises concurrent jurisdiction, those consulted must include that regulator.

(5)   No rule made by the [OFT] is to come into operation until it has been approved by an order made by the Secretary of State.

(6)   The Secretary of State may approve any rule made by the [OFT]—
   (a)   in the form in which it is submitted; or
   (b)   subject to such modifications as he considers appropriate.

(7)   If the Secretary of State proposes to approve a rule subject to modifications he must inform the [OFT] of the proposed modifications and take into account any comments made by the [OFT].

(8)   Subsections (5) to (7) apply also to any alteration of the rules made by the [OFT].

(9)   The Secretary of State may, after consulting the [OFT], by order vary or revoke any rules made under this section.

(10)   If the Secretary of State considers that rules should be made under this section with respect to a particular matter he may direct the [OFT] to exercise [its] powers under this section and make rules about that matter.

[1747]

NOTES
   References to the OFT, etc: as to the abolition of the office of the Director General of Fair Trading and the substitution of the original references to the Director (and related expressions), see the note preceding s 1 at [1696].
   Order: the Competition Act 1998 (Office of Fair Trading's Rules) Order 2004, SI 2004/2751.

52   Advice and information

(1)   As soon as is reasonably practicable after the passing of this Act, the Director must prepare and publish general advice and information about—
   (a)   the application of the Chapter I prohibition and the Chapter II prohibition, and
   (b)   the enforcement of those prohibitions.

[(1A)   As soon as is reasonably practicable after 1st May 2004, the OFT must prepare and publish general advice and information about—
   (a)   the application of the prohibitions in Article 81(1) and Article 82; and
   (b)   the enforcement by it of those prohibitions.]

(2)   The [OFT] may at any time publish revised, or new, advice or information.

(3)   Advice and information published under this section must be prepared with a view to—
   (a)   explaining provisions of this Part to persons who are likely to be affected by them; and
   (b)   indicating how the [OFT] expects such provisions to operate.

(4)   Advice (or information) published by virtue of subsection (3)(b) may include advice (or information) about the factors which the [OFT] may take into account in considering whether, and if so how, to exercise a power conferred on [it] by Chapter I, II or III.

(5)   Any advice or information published by the [OFT] under this section is to be published in such form and in such manner as [it] considers appropriate.

(6)   If the [OFT] is preparing any advice or information under this section [it] must consult such persons as [it] considers appropriate.

(7)   If the proposed advice or information relates to a matter in respect of which a regulator exercises concurrent jurisdiction, those consulted must include that regulator.

(8)   In preparing any advice or information under this section about a matter in respect of which he may exercise functions under this Part, a regulator must consult—
   (a)   the [OFT];
   (b)   the other regulators; and
   (c)   such other persons as he considers appropriate.

[1748]–[1749]

NOTES
   Sub-s (1A): inserted by the Competition Act 1998 and Other Enactments (Amendment) Regulations 2004, SI 2004/1261, reg 4, Sch 1, para 31.
   References to the OFT, etc: as to the abolition of the office of the Director General of Fair Trading and the substitution of the original references to the Director (and related expressions), see the note preceding s 1 at [1696].

53 _(Repealed by the Competition Act 1998 and Other Enactments (Amendment) Regulations 2004, SI 2004/1261, reg 4, Sch 1, para 32.)_

Regulators

54 Regulators

(1)   In this Part "regulator" means[—
[(a)   the Office of Communications;]
   (b)   the Gas and Electricity Markets Authority;
   (c)   the Director General of Electricity Supply for Northern Ireland;
[(d)   the Water Services Regulation Authority;]
   (e)   [the Office of Rail Regulation];
   (f)   the Director General of Gas for Northern Ireland; and
   (g)   the Civil Aviation Authority.]

(2)   Parts II and III of Schedule 10 provide for functions of the [OFT] under this Part to be exercisable concurrently by regulators.

(3)   Parts IV and V of Schedule 10 make minor and consequential amendments in connection with the regulators' competition functions.

(4)   The Secretary of State may make regulations for the purpose of co-ordinating the performance of functions under this Part ("Part I functions") which are exercisable concurrently by two or more competent persons as a result of [any enactment (including any subordinate legislation) whenever passed or made].

(5)   The regulations may, in particular, make provision—
   (a)   as to the procedure to be followed by competent persons when determining who is to exercise Part I functions in a particular case;
   (b)   as to the steps which must be taken before a competent person exercises, in a particular case, such Part I functions as may be prescribed;
   (c)   as to the procedure for determining, in a particular case, questions arising as to which competent person is to exercise Part I functions in respect of the case;
   (d)   for Part I functions in a particular case to be exercised jointly—
      (i)   by the [OFT] and one or more regulators, or
      (ii)   by two or more regulators,
      and as to the procedure to be followed in such cases;
   (e)   as to the circumstances in which the exercise by a competent person of such Part I functions as may be prescribed is to preclude the exercise of such functions by another such person;
   (f)   for cases in respect of which Part I functions are being, or have been, exercised by a competent person to be transferred to another such person;
   (g)   for the person ("A") exercising Part I functions in a particular case—
      (i)   to appoint another competent person ("B") to exercise Part I functions on A's behalf in relation to the case; or
      (ii)   to appoint officers of B (with B's consent) to act as officers of A in relation to the case;
   (h)   for notification as to who is exercising Part I functions in respect of a particular case.

(6)   Provision made by virtue of subsection (5)(c) may provide for questions to be referred to and determined by the Secretary of State or by such other person as may be prescribed.

(7)   "Competent person" means the [OFT] or any of the regulators.

[(8)   In this section, "subordinate legislation" has the same meaning as in section 21(1) of the Interpretation Act 1978 (c 30) and includes an instrument made under—
   (a)   an Act of the Scottish Parliament;
   (b)   Northern Ireland legislation.]

[1750]–[1752]

NOTES

Sub-s (1): words in first (outer) pair of square brackets substituted by the Enterprise Act 2002, s 278(1), Sch 25, para 38(1), (41)(a); para (a) substituted by the Communications Act 2003, s 371(5)(a); para (d) substituted by the Water Act 2003, s 101(1), Sch 7, Pt 2, para 32(1), (2); words in square brackets in para (e) substituted by the Railways and Transport Safety Act 2003, s 16(5), Sch 2, Pt 2, para 19(p).

Sub-s (4): words in square brackets substituted by the Competition Act 1998 and Other Enactments (Amendment) Regulations 2004, SI 2004/1261, reg 4, Sch 1, para 33(1), (2).

Sub-s (8): added by SI 2004/1261, reg 4, Sch 1, para 33(1), (3).

References to the OFT, etc: as to the abolition of the office of the Director General of Fair Trading and the substitution of the original references to the Director (and related expressions), see the note preceding s 1 at **[1696]**.

Regulations: the Competition Act 1998 (Concurrency) Regulations 2004, SI 2004/1077.

Confidentiality and immunity from defamation

55, 56   *(Repealed by the Enterprise Act 2002, ss 247(j), 278(2), Sch 26.)*

57 Defamation

For the purposes of the law relating to defamation, absolute privilege attaches to any advice, guidance, notice or direction given, or decision made, by the [OFT] in the exercise of any of [its] functions under this Part.

[1753]

NOTES
  References to the OFT, etc: as to the abolition of the office of the Director General of Fair Trading and the substitution of the original references to the Director (and related expressions), see the note preceding s 1 at **[1696]**.

Findings of fact by [OFT]

58 Findings of fact by [OFT]

  (1)   Unless the court directs otherwise ... , [an OFT's] finding which is relevant to an issue arising in Part I proceedings is binding on the parties if—

  (a)   the time for bringing an appeal [under section 46 or 47] in respect of the finding has expired and the relevant party has not brought such an appeal; or
  (b)   the decision of [the Tribunal] on such an appeal has confirmed the finding.

  (2)   In this section—
  ["an OFT's finding" means a finding of fact made by the OFT in the course of conducting an investigation;]
  ["Part 1 proceedings" means proceedings brought otherwise than by the OFT—
  (a)   in respect of an alleged infringement of the Chapter I prohibition or of the Chapter II prohibition; or
  (b)   in respect of an alleged infringement of the prohibitions in Article 81(1) or Article 82;]
  "relevant party" means—
  (a)   in relation to the Chapter I prohibition [or the prohibition in Article 81(1)], a party to the agreement which is alleged to have infringed the prohibition; and
  (b)   in relation to the Chapter II prohibition [or the prohibition in Article 82], the undertaking whose conduct is alleged to have infringed the prohibition.

  (3)   Rules of court may make provision in respect of assistance to be given by the [OFT] to the court in Part I proceedings.

[1754]

NOTES
  Sub-s (1): words omitted repealed by the Competition Act 1998 and Other Enactments (Amendment) Regulations 2004, SI 2004/1261, reg 4, Sch 1, para 34(1), (2); words in first and third pairs of square brackets substituted, and words in second pair of square brackets inserted, by the Enterprise Act 2002, ss 21, 278(1), Sch 5, paras 1, 5, Sch 25, para 38(1), (43)(b).
  Sub-s (2): definitions "an OFT's finding" and "Part 1 Proceedings" substituted and in definition "relevant party" words in square brackets inserted by SI 2004/1261, reg 4, Sch 1, para 34(1), (3).
  References to the OFT, etc: as to the abolition of the office of the Director General of Fair Trading and the substitution of the original references to the Director (and related expressions), see the note preceding s 1 at **[1696]**.

[Findings of infringements

58A Findings of infringements

  (1)   This section applies to proceedings before the court in which damages or any other sum of money is claimed in respect of an infringement of—
  (a)   the Chapter I prohibition;
  (b)   the Chapter II prohibition;
  (c)   the prohibition in Article 81(1) of the Treaty;
  (d)   the prohibition in Article 82 of the Treaty.

  (2)   In such proceedings, the court is bound by a decision mentioned in subsection (3) once any period specified in subsection (4) which relates to the decision has elapsed.

  (3)   The decisions are—
  (a)   a decision of the OFT that the Chapter I prohibition or the Chapter II prohibition has been infringed;
  (b)   a decision of the OFT that the prohibition in Article 81(1) or Article 82 of the Treaty has been infringed;
  (c)   a decision of the Tribunal (on an appeal from a decision of the OFT) that the Chapter I

prohibition or the Chapter II prohibition has been infringed, or that the prohibition in Article 81(1) or Article 82 of the Treaty has been infringed.

(4)   The periods mentioned in subsection (2) are—

(a)   in the case of a decision of the OFT, the period during which an appeal may be made to the Tribunal under section 46 or 47 ... ;

(b)   in the case of a decision of the Tribunal mentioned in subsection (3)(c), the period during which a further appeal may be made under section 49 ... ;

(c)   in the case of any decision which is the subject of a further appeal, the period during which an appeal may be made to the [Supreme Court] from a decision on the further appeal;

and, where any appeal mentioned in paragraph (a), (b) or (c) is made, the period specified in that paragraph includes the period before the appeal is determined.]

[1755]

NOTES

Inserted, together with the preceding cross-heading, by the Enterprise Act 2002, s 20(1).

Sub-s (4): words omitted from paras (a), (b) repealed by the EC Competition Law (Articles 84 and 85) Enforcement (Revocation) Regulations 2007, SI 2007/1846, reg 3(1), Schedule; words in square brackets in para (c) substituted by the Constitutional Reform Act 2005, s 40(4), Sch 9, Pt 1, para 65(1), (4).

Interpretation and governing principles

59   [Interpretation of Part 1]

(1)   In this Part—

["agreement" is to be read with section 2(5) and (6);]

.....

["Article 81(1)" means Article 81(1) of the Treaty;

"Article 81(3)" means Article 81(3) of the Treaty;]

["Article 82" means Article 82 of the Treaty;]

"block exemption" has the meaning given in section 6(4);

"block exemption order" has the meaning given in section 6(2);

"the Chapter I prohibition" has the meaning given in section 2(8);

"the Chapter II prohibition" has the meaning given in section 18(4);

"the Commission" (except in relation to the Competition Commission) means the European Commission;

"the Council" means the Council of the European Union;

"the court", except in sections 58[, 58A] and 60 and the expression "European Court", means—

(a)   in England and Wales, the High Court;

(b)   in Scotland, the Court of Session; and

(c)   in Northern Ireland, the High Court;

.....

"document" includes information recorded in any form;

"the EEA Agreement" means the Agreement on the European Economic Area signed at Oporto on 2nd May 1992 as it has effect for the time being;

"the European Court" means the Court of Justice of the European Communities and includes the Court of First Instance;

["the EC Competition Regulation" means Council Regulation (EC) No 1/2003 of 16th December 2002 on the implementation of the rules on competition laid down in Articles 81 and 82 of the Treaty;]

.....

"information" includes estimates and forecasts;

"investigating officer" has the meaning given in section 27(1);

["investigation" means an investigation under section 25;]

"Minister of the Crown" has the same meaning as in the Ministers of the Crown Act 1975;

["OFCOM" means the Office of Communications;]

"officer", in relation to a body corporate, includes a director, manager or secretary and, in relation to a partnership in Scotland, includes a partner;

["the OFT" means the Office of Fair Trading;]

"parallel exemption" has the meaning given in section 10(3);

"person", in addition to the meaning given by the Interpretation Act 1978, includes any undertaking;

["premises" includes any land or means of transport;]

"prescribed" means prescribed by regulations made by the Secretary of State;

"regulator" has the meaning given by section 54;

"section 11 exemption" has the meaning given in section 11(3); and

"the Treaty" means the treaty establishing the European Community.

["the Tribunal" means the Competition Appeal Tribunal;
"Tribunal rules" means rules under section 15 of the Enterprise Act 2002.]
["working day" means a day which is not—
    (a)   Saturday,
    (b)   Sunday,
    (c)   Christmas Day,
    (d)   Good Friday, or
    (e)   a day which is a bank holiday under the Banking and Financial Dealings Act 1971
        (c 80) in any part of the United Kingdom.]

(2)   The fact that to a limited extent the Chapter I prohibition does not apply to an agreement, because of an exclusion provided by or under this Part or any other enactment, does not require those provisions of the agreement to which the exclusion relates to be disregarded when considering whether the agreement infringes the prohibition for other reasons.

(3)   For the purposes of this Part, the power to require information, in relation to information recorded otherwise than in a legible form, includes power to require a copy of it in a legible form.

(4)   Any power conferred on the [OFT] by this Part to require information includes power to require any document which [it] believes may contain that information.

[1756]

NOTES

Section heading: substituted by the Competition Act 1998 and Other Enactments (Amendment) Regulations 2004, SI 2004/1261, reg 4, Sch 1, para 35(1), (3).

Sub-s (1): definitions "agreement", "the EC Competition Regulation", "investigation", "working day" inserted, definitions "Article 81(1)", "Article 81(3)" substituted for original definition "Article 85", definition "Article 82" substituted for original definition "Article 86", definition "premises" substituted, and definition "individual exemption" (omitted) repealed by SI 2004/1261, reg 4, Sch 1, para 35(1), (2); definitions "appeal tribunal" and "the Director" (both omitted) repealed, and definitions "the OFT", "the Tribunal" and "Tribunal rules" inserted, by the Enterprise Act 2002, ss 21, 278, Sch 5, paras 1, 6, Sch 25, para 38(1), (44)(a), Sch 26; figure in square brackets in definition "the court" inserted by s 20(3) of the 2002 Act; definition "OFCOM" inserted by the Communications Act 2003, s 371(7).

Regulations: the Competition Act 1998 (Small Agreements and Conduct of Minor Significance) Regulations 2000, SI 2000/262; the Competition Act 1998 (Appealable Decisions and Revocation of Notification of Excluded Agreements) Regulations 2004, SI 2004/1078.

References to the OFT, etc: as to the abolition of the office of the Director General of Fair Trading and the substitution of the original references to the Director (and related expressions), see the note preceding s 1 at **[1696]**.

---

60 Principles to be applied in determining questions

(1)   The purpose of this section is to ensure that so far as is possible (having regard to any relevant differences between the provisions concerned), questions arising under this Part in relation to competition within the United Kingdom are dealt with in a manner which is consistent with the treatment of corresponding questions arising in Community law in relation to competition within the Community.

(2)   At any time when the court determines a question arising under this Part, it must act (so far as is compatible with the provisions of this Part and whether or not it would otherwise be required to do so) with a view to securing that there is no inconsistency between—
    (a)   the principles applied, and decision reached, by the court in determining that question; and
    (b)   the principles laid down by the Treaty and the European Court, and any relevant decision of that Court, as applicable at that time in determining any corresponding question arising in Community law.

(3)   The court must, in addition, have regard to any relevant decision or statement of the Commission.

(4)   Subsections (2) and (3) also apply to—
    (a)   the [OFT]; and
    (b)   any person acting on behalf of the [OFT], in connection with any matter arising under this Part.

(5)   In subsections (2) and (3), "court" means any court or tribunal.

(6)   In subsections (2)(b) and (3), "decision" includes a decision as to—
    (a)   the interpretation of any provision of Community law;
    (b)   the civil liability of an undertaking for harm caused by its infringement of Community law.

[1757]

NOTES

References to the OFT, etc: as to the abolition of the office of the Director General of Fair Trading and the substitution of the original references to the Director (and related expressions), see the note preceding s 1 at **[1696]**.

[PART 2
INSPECTIONS UNDER ARTICLES 20, 21 AND 22(2)

61 Interpretation of Part 2

In this Part—

"Article 20 inspection" means an inspection ordered by a decision of the Commission under Article 20(4) of the EC Competition Regulation which is not an Article 22(2) inspection;

"Article 21 inspection" means an inspection ordered by a decision of the Commission under Article 21 of the EC Competition Regulation;

"Article 22(2) inspection" means an inspection requested by the Commission under Article 22(2) of the EC Competition Regulation;

"books and records" includes books and records stored on any medium;

"the Commission" means the European Commission;

"the EC Competition Regulation" means Council Regulation (EC) No 1/2003 of 16th December 2002 on the implementation of the rules on competition laid down in Articles 81 and 82 of the Treaty;

"the OFT" means the Office of Fair Trading;

"premises" includes any land or means of transport;

"the Treaty" means the treaty establishing the European Community.]

[1758]

NOTES

Substituted, together with preceding Part heading, by the Competition Act 1998 and Other Enactments (Amendment) Regulations 2004, SI 2004/1261, reg 4, Sch 1, para 36.

62 [Power to enter business premises under a warrant: Article 20 inspections]

(1)   A judge of the High Court [shall] issue a warrant if satisfied, on an application made to the High Court in accordance with rules of court by the [OFT], that—

[(a)   the Commission has ordered an Article 20 inspection;

(b)   the Article 20 inspection is being, or is likely to be, obstructed; and

(c)   the measures that would be authorised by the warrant are neither arbitrary nor excessive having regard to the subject matter of the Article 20 inspection].

(2)   [An Article 20 inspection] is being obstructed if—

(a)   [a Commission official], exercising his power in accordance with [Article 20(3) of the EC Competition Regulation], has attempted to enter [any business premises] but has been unable to do so; and

(b)   there are reasonable grounds for suspecting that there are [on any business premises] books or records … which the Commission official has power to examine.

(3)   [An Article 20 inspection] is also being obstructed if there are reasonable grounds for suspecting that there are [on any business premises] books or records … —

(a)   the production of which has been required by [a Commission official] exercising his power in accordance with [Article 20(3) of the EC Competition Regulation]; and

(b)   which have not been produced as required.

(4)   [An Article 20 inspection] is likely to be obstructed if—

(a)   …

(b)   there are reasonable grounds for suspecting that there are [on any business premises] books or records … which [a Commission official] has power to examine; and

(c)   there are also reasonable grounds for suspecting that, if the Commission official attempted to exercise his power to examine any of the books or records, they would not be produced but would be concealed, removed, tampered with or destroyed.

[(5)   A warrant under this section shall authorise a named officer of the OFT and any other OFT officer, or Commission official, accompanying the named officer—

(a)   to enter any business premises specified in the warrant using such force as is reasonably necessary for the purpose;

(b)   to search for books and records which a Commission official has power to examine, using such force as is reasonably necessary for the purpose;

(c)   to take or obtain copies of or extracts from such books and records;

(d)   to seal the premises, any part of the premises or any books or records which a Commission official has power to seal, for the period and to the extent necessary for the inspection.]

[(5A)   A warrant under this section may authorise persons specified in the warrant to accompany the named officer who is executing it.]

(6)   Any person entering any premises by virtue of a warrant under this section may take with him such equipment as appears to him to be necessary.

(7)   On leaving any premises entered by virtue of the warrant the named officer must, if the premises are unoccupied or the occupier is temporarily absent, leave them as effectively secured as he found them.

(8)   A warrant under this section continues in force until the end of the period of one month beginning with the day on which it is issued.

(9)   In the application of this section to Scotland, references to the High Court are to be read as references to the Court of Session.

[(10)   In this section—
   "business premises" means any premises of an undertaking or association of undertakings which a Commission official has under Article 20 of the EC Competition Regulation power to enter in the course of the Article 20 inspection;
   "Commission official" means any of the persons authorised by the Commission to conduct the Article 20 inspection; and
   "OFT officer" means any officer of the OFT whom the OFT has authorised in writing to accompany the named officer.

(11)   In subsection (10), the reference in the definition of "business premises" to Article 20 of the EC Competition Regulation does not include a reference to that Article as applied by Article 21 of that Regulation.]

[1759]

NOTES
   Section heading: substituted by the Competition Act 1998 and Other Enactments (Amendment) Regulations 2004, SI 2004/1261, reg 4, Sch 1, para 37(1), (8).
   Sub-s (1): words in first and third pairs of square brackets substituted by SI 2004/1261, reg 4, Sch 1, para 37(1), (2).
   Sub-s (2): words in first pair of square brackets and words in square brackets in para (a) substituted, words omitted from para (a) repealed and words in square brackets in para (b) inserted by SI 2004/1261, reg 4, Sch 1, para 37(1), (3).
   Sub-s (3): words in first pair of square brackets and words in square brackets in para (a) substituted, words in second pair of square brackets inserted and words omitted repealed by SI 2004/1261, reg 4, Sch 1, para 37(1), (4).
   Sub-s (4): words in first pair of square brackets and words in second pair of square brackets in para (b) substituted, para (a) and words omitted from para (b) repealed, and words in first pair of square brackets in para (b) inserted, by SI 2004/1261, reg 4, Sch 1, para 37(1), (5).
   Sub-s (5): substituted by SI 2004/1261, reg 4, Sch 1, para 37(1), (6).
   Sub-s (5A): inserted by the Enterprise Act 2002, s 203(1), (3).
   Sub-ss (10), (11): added by SI 2004/1261, reg 4, Sch 1, para 37(1), (7).
   References to the OFT, etc: as to the abolition of the office of the Director General of Fair Trading and the substitution of the original references to the Director (and related expressions), see the note preceding s 1 at **[1696]**.

[62A   Power to enter non-business premises under a warrant: Article 21 inspections

(1)   A judge of the High Court shall issue a warrant if satisfied, on an application made to the High Court in accordance with the rules of court by the OFT, that—
   (a)   the Commission has ordered an Article 21 inspection; and
   (b)   the measures that would be authorised by the warrant are neither arbitrary nor excessive having regard in particular to the matters mentioned in subsection (2).

(2)   Those matters are—
   (a)   the seriousness of the suspected infringement of Article 81(1) or 82 of the Treaty;
   (b)   the importance of the evidence sought;
   (c)   the involvement of the undertaking or association of undertakings concerned; and
   (d)   whether it is reasonably likely that business books and records relating to the subject matter of the Article 21 inspection are kept on the non-business premises that would be specified in the warrant.

(3)   A warrant under this section shall authorise a named officer of the OFT and any other OFT officer, or Commission official, accompanying the named officer to enter any non-business premises specified in the warrant.

(4)   A warrant under this section may authorise a named officer of the OFT and any other OFT officer, or Commission official, accompanying the named officer to search for books or records which a Commission official has power to examine.

(5)   A warrant under this section may authorise a named officer of the OFT and any other OFT officer, or Commission official, accompanying the named officer to take or obtain copies of books or records of which a Commission official has power to take or obtain copies.

(6)   A warrant granted under this section may authorise the use, for either or both of the purposes mentioned in subsections (3) and (4), of such force as is reasonably necessary.

(7)   A warrant under this section may authorise persons specified in the warrant to accompany the named officer who is executing it.

(8)   Any person entering any premises by virtue of a warrant under this section may take with him such equipment as appears to him to be necessary.

(9)   On leaving any premises entered by virtue of a warrant the named officer must, if the premises are unoccupied or the occupier is temporarily absent, leave them as effectively secured as he found them.

(10)   A warrant under this section continues in force until the end of the period of one month beginning with the day on which it is issued.

(11)   In the application of this section to Scotland, references to the High Court are to be read as references to the Court of Session.

(12)   In this section—
"non-business premises" means any premises to which a decision of the Commission ordering the Article 21 inspection relates;
"Commission official" means any of the persons authorised by the Commission to conduct the Article 21 inspection; and
"OFT officer" means any officer of the OFT whom the OFT has authorised in writing to accompany the named officer.]

[1759A]

NOTES
Inserted by the Competition Act 1998 and Other Enactments (Amendment) Regulations 2004, SI 2004/1261, reg 4, Sch 1, para 38.

[62B   Powers when conducting an Article 22(2) inspection

(1)   For the purposes of an Article 22(2) inspection, an authorised officer of the OFT has the powers specified in Article 20(2) of the EC Competition Regulation.

(2)   For the purposes of this section and section 63—
"authorised officer of the OFT" means any officer of the OFT to whom an authorisation has been given; and
"authorisation" means an authorisation given in writing by the OFT for the purposes of the Article 22(2) inspection which—
    (i)   identifies the officer;
    (ii)   indicates the subject matter and purpose of the inspection; and
    (iii)   draws attention to any penalties which a person may incur under the EC Competition Regulation in connection with the inspection.]

[1759B]

NOTES
Inserted by the Competition Act 1998 and Other Enactments (Amendment) Regulations 2004, SI 2004/1261, reg 4, Sch 1, para 39.

63   [Power to enter business premises under a warrant: Article 22(2) inspections]

(1)   A judge of the High Court [shall] issue a warrant if satisfied, on an application made to the High Court in accordance with rules of court by the [OFT, that]—
[(a)   the Commission has requested the OFT to conduct an Article 22(2) inspection which the Commission has ordered by a decision under Article 20(4) of the EC Competition Regulation;
(b)   the Article 22(2) inspection is being, or is likely to be, obstructed; and
(c)   the measures that would be authorised by the warrant are neither arbitrary nor excessive having regard to the subject matter of the Article 22(2) inspection.]

(2)   [An Article 22(2) inspection] is being obstructed if—
(a)   an authorised officer of the [OFT] has attempted to enter [any business] premises but has been unable to do so;
(b)   the officer has produced his authorisation to the undertaking, or association of undertakings, concerned; and
(c)   there are reasonable grounds for suspecting that there are [on any business premises] books or records … which the officer has power to examine.

(3)   [An Article 22(2) inspection] is also being obstructed if—

(a)   there are reasonable grounds for suspecting that there are [on any business premises] books or records ... which an authorised officer of the [OFT] has power to examine;

(b)   the officer has produced his authorisation to the undertaking, or association of undertakings, and has required production of the books or records; and

(c)   the books and records have not been produced as required.

(4) [An Article 22(2) inspection] is likely to be obstructed if—

(a)   there are reasonable grounds for suspecting that there are [on any business premises] books or records ... which an authorised officer of the [OFT] has power to examine; and

(b)   there are also reasonable grounds for suspecting that, if the officer attempted to exercise his power to examine any of the books or records, they would not be produced but would be concealed, removed, tampered with or destroyed.

[(5) A warrant under this section shall authorise a named authorised officer of the OFT and any other authorised officer of the OFT, or Commission official, accompanying the named authorised officer—

(a)   to enter any business premises specified in the warrant using such force as is reasonably necessary for the purpose;

(b)   to search for books and records which an authorised officer of the OFT has power to examine, using such force as is reasonably necessary for the purpose;

(c)   to take or obtain copies of or extracts from such books and records; and

(d)   to seal the premises, any part of the premises or any books or records which an authorised officer of the OFT has power to seal, for the period and to the extent necessary for the inspection.]

[(5A) A warrant under this section may authorise persons specified in the warrant to accompany the named authorised officer who is executing it.]

(6) Any person entering any premises by virtue of a warrant under this section may take with him such equipment as appears to him to be necessary.

(7) On leaving any premises which he has entered by virtue of the warrant the [named authorised officer] must, if the premises are unoccupied or the occupier is temporarily absent, leave them as effectively secured as he found them.

(8) A warrant under this section continues in force until the end of the period of one month beginning with the day on which it is issued.

(9) In the application of this section to Scotland, references to the High Court are to be read as references to the Court of Session.

[(10) In this section—

"business premises" means any premises of an undertaking or association of undertakings which an authorised officer of the OFT has power to enter in the course of the Article 22(2) inspection;

"Commission official" means any person authorised by the Commission to assist with the Article 22(2) inspection.]

[1760]

NOTES

Section heading: substituted by the Competition Act 1998 and Other Enactments (Amendment) Regulations 2004, SI 2004/1261, reg 4, Sch 1, para 40(1), (9).

Sub-s (1): words in first and third pairs of square brackets substituted by SI 2004/1261, reg 4, Sch 1, para 40(1), (2); words in second pair of square brackets substituted by the Enterprise Act 2002, s 278(1), Sch 25, para 38(1), (48)(a).

Sub-s (2): words in first pair of square brackets substituted, words in second pair of square brackets in para (a) and words in square brackets in para (c) inserted, and words omitted from para (c) repealed by SI 2004/1261, reg 4, Sch 1, para 40(1), (3).

Sub-s (3): words in first pair of square brackets and words in first pair of square brackets in para (a) substituted, and words omitted from para (a) repealed by SI 2004/1261, reg 4, Sch 1, para 40(1), (4).

Sub-s (4): words in first pair of square brackets substituted, words in first pair of square brackets in para (a) inserted and words omitted from para (b) repealed by SI 2004/1261, reg 4, Sch 1, para 37(1), (5).

Sub-s (5): substituted by SI 2004/1261, reg 4, Sch 1, para 40(1), (6).

Sub-s (5A): inserted by the Enterprise Act 2002, s 203(1), (4).

Sub-s (7): words in square brackets substituted by SI 2004/1261, reg 4, Sch 1, para 40(1), (6).

Sub-s (10): added by SI 2004/1261, reg 4, Sch 1, para 40(1), (7).

References to the OFT, etc: as to the abolition of the office of the Director General of Fair Trading and the substitution of the original references to the Director (and related expressions), see the note preceding s 1 at [1696].

---

64 Entry of premises under sections 62[, 62A] and 63: supplementary

(1) A warrant issued under section 62[, 62A] or 63 must indicate—

(a)   the subject matter and purpose of the [inspection];

(b)   the nature of the offence created by section 65.

(2)   The powers conferred by section 62[, 62A] or 63 are to be exercised on production of a warrant issued under that section.

(3)   If there is no one at the premises when the named officer proposes to execute such a warrant he must, before executing it—

    (a)   take such steps as are reasonable in all the circumstances to inform the occupier of the intended entry; and

    (b)   if the occupier is informed, afford him or his legal or other representative a reasonable opportunity to be present when the warrant is executed.

(4)   If the named officer is unable to inform the occupier of the intended entry he must, when executing the warrant, leave a copy of it in a prominent place on the premises.

(5)   In this section—

    ["named officer" means—

      (a)   for the purposes of a warrant issued under section 62 or 62A, the officer named in the warrant; and

      (b)   for the purposes of a warrant issued under section 63, the authorised officer named in the warrant;]

    "occupier", in relation to any premises, means a person whom the named officer reasonably believes is the occupier of those premises.

[1761]

NOTES

    Section heading: number in square brackets inserted by the Competition Act 1998 and Other Enactments (Amendment) Regulations 2004, SI 2004/1261, reg 4, Sch 1, para 41(1), (4).

    Sub-s (1): number in first pair of square brackets inserted and word in square brackets in para (a) substituted by SI 2004/1261, reg 4, Sch 1, para 41(1), (2), (4).

    Sub-s (2): number in square brackets inserted by SI 2004/1261, reg 4, Sch 1, para 41(1), (4).

    Sub-s (5): definition "named officer" substituted by SI 2004/1261, reg 4, Sch 1, para 41(1), (3).

65   Offences

(1)   A person is guilty of an offence if he intentionally obstructs any person in the exercise of his powers under a warrant issued under section 62[, 62A] or 63.

(2)   A person guilty of an offence under subsection (1) is liable—

    (a)   on summary conviction, to a fine not exceeding the statutory maximum;

    (b)   on conviction on indictment, to imprisonment for a term not exceeding two years or to a fine or to both.

[1762]

NOTES

    Sub-s (1): number in square brackets inserted by the Competition Act 1998 and Other Enactments (Amendment) Regulations 2004, SI 2004/1261, reg 4, Sch 1, para 42.

[65A   Privileged communications: Article 22(2) inspections

(1)   A person shall not be required, by virtue of any provision of section 62B or 63, to produce or disclose a privileged communication.

(2)   "Privileged communication" means a communication—

    (a)   between a professional legal adviser and his client, or

    (b)   made in connection with, or in contemplation of, legal proceedings and for the purposes of those proceedings,

which in proceedings in the High Court would be protected from disclosure on grounds of legal professional privilege.

(3)   In the application of this section to Scotland—

    (a)   the reference to the High Court is to be read as a reference to the Court of Session; and

    (b)   the reference to legal professional privilege is to be read as a reference to confidentiality of communications.]

[1762A]

NOTES

    Inserted, together with s 65B, by the Competition Act 1998 and Other Enactments (Amendment) Regulations 2004, SI 2004/1261, reg 4, Sch 1, para 43.

[65B   Use of statements in prosecution: Article 22(2) inspections

A statement made by a person in response to a requirement imposed by virtue of section 62B or 63 may not be used in evidence against him on a prosecution for an offence under section 188 of the Enterprise Act 2002 unless, in the proceedings—

    (a)   in giving evidence, he makes a statement inconsistent with it, and

(b)   evidence relating to it is adduced, or a question relating to it is asked, by him or on his behalf.]

[1762B]

NOTES

Inserted as noted to s 65A at **[1762A]**.

[PART 2A
ARTICLE 22(1) INVESTIGATIONS

65C   Interpretation of Part 2A

(1)   In this Part—

"Article 22(1) investigation" means an investigation conducted by the OFT on behalf and for the account of a competition authority of another Member State pursuant to Article 22(1) of the EC Competition Regulation;

"the Commission" means the European Commission;

"competition authority of another Member State" means a competition authority designated as such under Article 35 of the EC Competition Regulation by a Member State other than the United Kingdom;

"the EC Competition Regulation" means Council Regulation (EC) No 1/2003 of 16th December 2002 on the implementation of the rules on competition laid down in Articles 81 and 82 of the Treaty; and

"investigating officer" has the meaning given in section 65F(1).

(2)   In this Part, the following expressions have the same meanings as in Part 1—

"Article 81(1)";
"Article 82";
"the court";
"document";
"information";
"officer";
"the OFT";
"person";
"premises"
"the Treaty"; and
"working day".

(3)   For the purposes of this Part, the power to require information, in relation to information recorded otherwise than in a legible form, includes power to require a copy of it in a legible form.

(4)   Any power conferred on the OFT by this Part to require information includes power to require any document which it believes may contain that information.]

[1762C]

NOTES

Part 2A (ss 65C–65N) inserted by the Competition Act 1998 and Other Enactments (Amendment) Regulations 2004, SI 2004/1261, reg 4, Sch 1, para 44.

[65D   Power to conduct an Article 22(1) investigation

(1)   In any of the following cases, the OFT may conduct an Article 22(1) investigation.

(2)   The first case is where there are reasonable grounds for suspecting that there is an agreement which—

(a)   may affect trade between Member States; and

(b)   has as its object or effect the prevention, restriction or distortion of competition within the Community.

(3)   The second case is where there are reasonable grounds for suspecting that the prohibition in Article 82 has been infringed.

(4)   The third case is where there are reasonable grounds for suspecting that, at some time in the past, there was an agreement which at that time—

(a)   may have affected trade between Member States; and

(b)   had as its object or effect the prevention, restriction or distortion of competition within the Community.

(5)   It is immaterial for the purposes of subsection (4) whether the agreement in question remains in existence.

(6)   A provision of this Part which is expressed to apply to, or in relation to, an agreement is to be read as applying equally to, or in relation to, a decision by an association of undertakings or a concerted practice.]

[1762D]

NOTES
Inserted as noted to s 65C at **[1762C]**.

[65E   Powers when conducting Article 22(1) investigations

(1)   For the purposes of an Article 22(1) investigation, the OFT may require any person to produce to it a specified document, or to provide it with specified information, which it considers relates to any matter relevant to the investigation.

(2)   The power conferred by subsection (1) is to be exercised by a notice in writing.

(3)   A notice under subsection (2) must indicate—
  (a)   the subject matter and purpose of the Article 22(1) investigation; and
  (b)   the nature of the offences created by sections 65L to 65N.

(4)   In subsection (1) "specified" means—
  (a)   specified, or described, in the notice; or
  (b)   falling within a category which is specified, or described, in the notice.

(5)   The OFT may also specify in the notice—
  (a)   the time and place at which any document is to be produced or any information is to be provided;
  (b)   the manner and form in which it is to be produced or provided.

(6)   The power under this section to require a person to produce a document includes power—
  (a)   if the document is produced—
    (i)   to take copies of it or extracts from it;
    (ii)   to require him, or any person who is a present or past officer of his, or is or was at any time employed by him, to provide an explanation of the document;
  (b)   if the document is not produced, to require him to state, to the best of his knowledge and belief, where it is.]

[1762E]

NOTES
Inserted as noted to s 65C at **[1762C]**.

[65F   Power to enter business premises without a warrant

(1)   Any officer of the OFT who is authorised in writing by the OFT to do so ("an investigating officer") may enter any business premises in connection with an Article 22(1) investigation.

(2)   No investigating officer is to enter any premises in the exercise of his powers under this section unless he has given to the occupier of the premises a written notice which—
  (a)   gives at least two working days' notice of the intended entry;
  (b)   indicates the subject matter and purpose of the Article 22(1) investigation; and
  (c)   indicates the nature of the offences created by sections 65L to 65N.

(3)   Subsection (2) does not apply—
  (a)   if the OFT has a reasonable suspicion that the premises are, or have been, occupied by—
    (i)   a party to an agreement which it is investigating under section 65D; or
    (ii)   an undertaking the conduct of which it is investigating under section 65D; or
  (b)   if the investigating officer has taken all such steps as are reasonably practicable to give notice but has not been able to do so.

(4)   In a case falling within subsection (3), the power of entry conferred by subsection (1) is to be exercised by the investigating officer on production of—
  (a)   evidence of his authorisation; and
  (b)   a document containing the information referred to in subsection (2)(b) and (c).

(5)   An investigating officer entering any premises under this section may—
  (a)   take with him such equipment as appears to him to be necessary;
  (b)   require any person on the premises—
    (i)   to produce any document which he considers relates to any matter relevant to the investigation; and
    (ii)   if the document is produced, to provide an explanation of it;
  (c)   require any person to state, to the best of his knowledge and belief, where any such document is to be found;
  (d)   take copies of, or extracts from, any document which is produced;
  (e)   require any information which is stored in any electronic form and is accessible from the

premises and which the investigating officer considers relates to any matter relevant to the investigation, to be produced in a form—
  (i) in which it can be taken away, and
  (ii) in which it is visible and legible or from which it can readily be produced in a visible and legible form;

(f) take any steps which appear to be necessary for the purpose of preserving or preventing interference with any document which he consider relates to any matter relevant to the investigation.

(6) In this section "business premises" means premises (or any part of premises) not used as a dwelling.]

[1762F]

NOTES
Inserted as noted to s 65C at **[1762C]**.

[65G Power to enter business premises under a warrant

(1) On an application made by the OFT to the court in accordance with rules of court, a judge may issue a warrant if he is satisfied that—

(a) there are reasonable grounds for suspecting that there are on any business premises documents—
  (i) the production of which has been required under section 65E or 65F; and
  (ii) which have not been produced as required;

(b) there are reasonable grounds for suspecting that—
  (i) there are on any business premises documents which the OFT has power under section 65E to require to be produced; and
  (ii) if the documents were required to be produced, they would not be produced but would be concealed, removed, tampered with or destroyed; or

(c) an investigating officer has attempted to enter premises in the exercise of his powers under section 65F but has been unable to do so and that there are reasonable grounds for suspecting that there are on the premises documents the production of which could have been required under that section.

(2) A warrant under this section shall authorise a named officer of the OFT and any other of its officers whom the OFT has authorised in writing to accompany the named officer—

(a) to enter the premises specified in the warrant, using such force as is reasonably necessary for the purpose;

(b) to search the premises and take copies of, or extracts from, any document appearing to be of a kind in respect of which the application under subsection (1) was granted ("the relevant kind");

(c) to take possession of any documents appearing to be of the relevant kind if—
  (i) such action appears to be necessary for preserving the documents or preventing interference with them; or
  (ii) it is not reasonably practicable to take copies of the documents on the premises;

(d) to take any other steps which appear to be necessary for the purpose mentioned in paragraph (c)(i);

(e) to require any person to provide an explanation of any document appearing to be of the relevant kind or to state, to the best of his knowledge and belief, where it may be found;

(f) to require any information which is stored in any electronic form and is accessible from the premises and which the named officer considers relates to any matter relevant to the Article 22(1) investigation, to be produced in a form—
  (i) in which it can be taken away, and
  (ii) in which it is visible and legible or from which it can readily be produced in a visible and legible form.

(3) If, in the case of a warrant under subsection (1)(b), the judge is satisfied that it is reasonable to suspect that there are also on the premises other documents relating to the Article 22(1) investigation concerned, the warrant shall also authorise action mentioned in subsection (2) to be taken in relation to any such document.

(4) A warrant under this section may authorise persons specified in the warrant to accompany the named officer who is executing it.

(5) Any person entering premises by virtue of a warrant under this section may take with him such equipment as appears to him to be necessary.

(6) On leaving any premises which he has entered by virtue of a warrant under this section, the named officer must, if the premises are unoccupied or the occupier is temporarily absent, leave them as effectively secured as he found them.

(7) A warrant under this section continues in force until the end of the period of one month beginning with the day on which it is issued.

(8)   Any document of which possession is taken under subsection (2)(c) may be retained for a period of three months.

(9)   In this section "business premises" has the same meaning as in section 65F.]

NOTES
  Inserted as noted to s 65C at **[1762C]**.

[65H   Power to enter domestic premises under a warrant

(1)   On an application made by the OFT to the court in accordance with rules of court, a judge may issue a warrant if he is satisfied that—
  (a)   there are reasonable grounds for suspecting that there are on any domestic premises documents—
    (i)   the production of which has been required under section 65E; and
    (ii)   which have not been produced as required; or
  (b)   there are reasonable grounds for suspecting that—
    (i)   there are on any domestic premises documents which the OFT has power under section 65E to require to be produced; and
    (ii)   if the documents were required to be produced, they would not be produced but would be concealed, removed, tampered with or destroyed.

(2)   A warrant under this section shall authorise a named officer of the OFT, and any other of its officers whom the OFT has authorised in writing to accompany the named officer—
  (a)   to enter the premises specified in the warrant, using such force as is reasonably necessary for the purpose;
  (b)   to search the premises and take copies of, or extracts from, any document appearing to be of a kind in respect of which the application under subsection (1) was granted ("the relevant kind");
  (c)   to take possession of any documents appearing to be of the relevant kind if—
    (i)   such action appears to be necessary for preserving the documents or preventing interference with them; or
    (ii)   it is not reasonably practicable to take copies of the documents on the premises;
  (d)   to take any other steps which appear to be necessary for the purpose mentioned in paragraph (c)(i);
  (e)   to require any person to provide an explanation of any document appearing to be of the relevant kind or to state, to the best of his knowledge or belief, where it may be found;
  (f)   to require any information which is stored in any electronic form and is accessible from the premises and which the named officer considers relates to any matter relevant to the investigation, to be produced in a form—
    (i)   in which it can be taken away; and
    (ii)   in which it is visible and legible or from which it can readily be produced in a visible and legible form.

(3)   If, in the case of a warrant under subsection (1)(b), the judge is satisfied that it is reasonable to suspect that there are also on the premises other documents relating to the investigation concerned, the warrant shall also authorise action mentioned in subsection (2) to be taken in relation to any such document.

(4)   A warrant under this section may authorise persons specified in the warrant to accompany the named officer who is executing it.

(5)   Any person entering premises by virtue of a warrant under this section may take with him such equipment as appears to him to be necessary.

(6)   On leaving any premises which he has entered by virtue of a warrant under this section, the named officer must, if the premises are unoccupied or the occupier is temporarily absent, leave them as effectively secured as he found them.

(7)   A warrant under this section continues in force until the end of the period of one month beginning with the day on which it is issued.

(8)   Any document of which possession is taken under subsection (2)(c) may be retained for a period of three months.

(9)   In this section, "domestic premises" means premises (or any part of premises) that are used as a dwelling and are—
  (a)   premises also used in connection with the affairs of an undertaking or association of undertakings; or
  (b)   premises where documents relating to the affairs of an undertaking or association of undertakings are kept.]

NOTES
Inserted as noted to s 65C at **[1762C]**.

[65I Entry of premises under a warrant: supplementary

(1)   A warrant issued under section 65G or 65H must indicate—
   (a)   the subject matter of the Article 22(1) investigation;
   (b)   the nature of the offences created by sections 65L to 65N.

(2)   The powers conferred by section 65G or 65H are to be exercised on production of a warrant issued under that section.

(3)   If there is no one at the premises when the named officer proposes to execute such a warrant he must, before executing it—
   (a)   take such steps as are reasonable in all the circumstances to inform the occupier of the intended entry; and
   (b)   if the occupier is informed, afford him or his legal or other representative a reasonable opportunity to be present when the warrant is executed.

(4)   If the named officer is unable to inform the occupier of the intended entry he must, when executing the warrant, leave a copy of it in a prominent place on the premises.

(5)   In this section—
"named officer" means the officer named in the warrant; and
"occupier", in relation to any premises, means a person whom the named officer reasonably believes is the occupier of those premises.]

[1762I]

NOTES
Inserted as noted to s 65C at **[1762C]**.

[65J Privileged communications

(1)   A person shall not be required, under any provision of this Part, to produce or disclose a privileged communication.

(2)   "Privileged communication" means a communication—
   (a)   between a professional legal adviser and his client, or
   (b)   made in connection with, or in contemplation of, legal proceedings and for the purposes of those proceedings,
which in proceedings in the High Court would be protected from disclosure on grounds of legal professional privilege.

(3)   (*Applies to Scotland only.*)]

[1762J]

NOTES
Inserted as noted to s 65C at **[1762C]**.

[65K Use of statements in prosecution

A statement made by a person in response to a requirement imposed by virtue of any of sections 65E to 65H may not be used in evidence against him on a prosecution for an offence under section 188 of the Enterprise Act 2002 unless, in the proceedings—
   (a)   in giving evidence, he makes a statement inconsistent with it, and
   (b)   evidence relating to it is adduced, or a question relating to it is asked, by him or on his behalf.]

[1762K]

NOTES
Inserted as noted to s 65C at **[1762C]**.

[65L Offences

(1)   A person is guilty of an offence if he fails to comply with a requirement imposed on him under section 65E, 65F, 65G or 65H.

(2)   If a person is charged with an offence under subsection (1) in respect of a requirement to produce a document, it is a defence for him to prove—
   (a)   that the document was not in his possession or under his control; and
   (b)   that it was not reasonably practicable for him to comply with the requirement.

(3)   If a person is charged with an offence under subsection (1) in respect of a requirement—
   (a)   to provide information,

(b) to provide an explanation of a document, or

(c) to state where a document is to be found,

it is a defence for him to prove that he had a reasonable excuse for failing to comply with the requirement.

(4) Failure to comply with a requirement imposed under section 65E or 65F is not an offence if the person imposing the requirement has failed to act in accordance with that section.

(5) A person is guilty of an offence if he intentionally obstructs an officer acting in the exercise of his powers under section 65F.

(6) A person guilty of an offence under subsection (1) or (5) is liable—

(a) on summary conviction, to a fine not exceeding the statutory maximum;

(b) on conviction on indictment, to a fine.

(7) A person who intentionally obstructs an officer in the exercise of his powers under a warrant issued under section 65G or 65H is guilty of an offence and liable—

(a) on summary conviction, to a fine not exceeding the statutory maximum;

(b) on conviction on indictment, to imprisonment for a term not exceeding two years or to a fine or to both.]

[1762L]

NOTES

Inserted as noted to s 65C at **[1762C]**.

[65M Destroying or falsifying documents

(1) A person is guilty of an offence if, having been required to produce a document under section 65E, 65F, 65G or 65H—

(a) he intentionally or recklessly destroys or otherwise disposes of it, falsifies it or conceals it, or

(b) he causes or permits its destruction, disposal, falsification or concealment.

(2) A person guilty of an offence under subsection (1) is liable—

(a) on summary conviction, to a fine not exceeding the statutory maximum;

(b) on conviction on indictment, to imprisonment for a term not exceeding two years or to a fine or to both.]

[1762M]

NOTES

Inserted as noted to s 65C at **[1762C]**.

[65N False or misleading information

(1) If information is provided by a person to the OFT in connection with any function of the OFT under this Part, that person is guilty of an offence if—

(a) the information is false or misleading in a material particular; and

(b) he knows that it is or is reckless as to whether it is.

(2) A person who—

(a) provides any information to another person, knowing the information to be false or misleading in a material particular, or

(b) recklessly provides any information to another person which is false or misleading in a material particular,

knowing that the information is to be used for the purpose of providing information to the OFT in connection with any of its functions under this Part, is guilty of an offence.

(3) A person guilty of an offence under this section is liable—

(a) on summary conviction, to a fine not exceeding the statutory maximum;

(b) on conviction on indictment, to imprisonment for a term not exceeding two years or to a fine or to both.]

[1762N]

NOTES

Inserted as noted to s 65C at **[1762C]**.

66–69 ((Pt III) ss 66, 67 repealed by the Enterprise Act 2002, s 278(2), Sch 26; s 68 inserts s 137(3A)–(3C) of the Fair Trading Act 1973 at **[631]**; s 69 amends s 83 of the 1973 Act (repealed).)

PART IV
SUPPLEMENTAL AND TRANSITIONAL

70   (*Repeals the Patents Act 1977, ss 44, 45.*)

71   Regulations, orders and rules

(1)   Any power to make regulations or orders which is conferred by this Act is exercisable by statutory instrument.

(2)   The power to make rules which is conferred by section 48 is exercisable by statutory instrument.

(3)   Any statutory instrument made under this Act may—
  (a)   contain such incidental, supplemental, consequential and transitional provision as the Secretary of State considers appropriate; and
  (b)   make different provision for different cases.

(4)   No order is to be made under—
  (a)   section 3,
  (b)   section 19,
  (c)   section 36(8),
  [(ca)   section 45(8),]
  (d)   section 50, or
  (e)   paragraph 6(3) of Schedule 4,

unless a draft of the order has been laid before Parliament and approved by a resolution of each House.

(5)   Any statutory instrument made under this Act, apart from one made—
  (a)   under any of the provisions mentioned in subsection (4), or
  (b)   under section 76(3),

shall be subject to annulment by a resolution of either House of Parliament.

[1763]

NOTES
Sub-s (4): para (ca) inserted by the Enterprise Act 2002, s 278(1), Sch 25, para 38(1), (49).

72   Offences by bodies corporate etc

(1)   This section applies to an offence under any of sections 42 to 44, [65 or 65L to 65N].

(2)   If an offence committed by a body corporate is proved—
  (a)   to have been committed with the consent or connivance of an officer, or
  (b)   to be attributable to any neglect on his part,

the officer as well as the body corporate is guilty of the offence and liable to be proceeded against and punished accordingly.

(3)   In subsection (2) "officer", in relation to a body corporate, means a director, manager, secretary or other similar officer of the body, or a person purporting to act in any such capacity.

(4)   If the affairs of a body corporate are managed by its members, subsection (2) applies in relation to the acts and defaults of a member in connection with his functions of management as if he were a director of the body corporate.

(5)   If an offence committed by a partnership in Scotland is proved—
  (a)   to have been committed with the consent or connivance of a partner, or
  (b)   to be attributable to any neglect on his part,

the partner as well as the partnership is guilty of the offence and liable to be proceeded against and punished accordingly.

(6)   In subsection (5) "partner" includes a person purporting to act as a partner.

[1764]

NOTES
Sub-s (1): words in square brackets substituted by the Competition Act 1998 and Other Enactments (Amendment) Regulations 2004, SI 2004/1261, reg 4, Sch 1, para 45.

73   Crown application

(1)   Any provision made by or under this Act binds the Crown except that—
  (a)   the Crown is not criminally liable as a result of any such provision;
  (b)   the Crown is not liable for any penalty under any such provision; and
  (c)   nothing in this Act affects Her Majesty in her private capacity.

(2)   Subsection (1)(a) does not affect the application of any provision of this Act in relation to persons in the public service of the Crown.

(3)   Subsection (1)(c) is to be interpreted as if section 38(3) of the Crown Proceedings Act 1947 (interpretation of references in that Act to Her Majesty in her private capacity) were contained in this Act.

[(4)   If an investigation is conducted under section 25 or 65D in respect of an agreement where none of the parties is the Crown or a person in the public service of the Crown, or in respect of conduct otherwise than by the Crown or such a person—

    (a)   the power conferred by section 27 or (as the case may be) section 65F may not be exercised in relation to land which is occupied by a government department, or otherwise for purposes of the Crown, without the written consent of the appropriate person; and

    (b)   none of sections 28, 28A, 65G and 65H applies in relation to land so occupied.]

(5)   In any case in which consent is required under subsection (4), the person who is the appropriate person in relation to that case is to be determined in accordance with regulations made by the Secretary of State.

(6)   Sections 62[, 62A] and 63 do not apply in relation to land which is occupied by a government department, or otherwise for purposes of the Crown, unless the matter being investigated is [an agreement to which the Crown or a person in the service of the Crown is a party, or conduct by the Crown or such a person].

[(6A)   In subsections (4) and (6) "agreement" includes a suspected agreement and is to be read as applying equally to, or in relation to, a decision by an association of undertakings or a concerted practice; and "conduct" includes suspected conduct.]

(7)   …

(8)   If the Secretary of State certifies that it appears to him to be in the interests of national security that the powers of entry—

    (a)   conferred by section 27 [or 65F], or

    (b)   that may be conferred by a warrant under [section 28, 28A, 62, 62A, 63, 65G or 65H],

should not be exercisable in relation to premises held or used by or on behalf of the Crown and which are specified in the certificate, those powers are not exercisable in relation to those premises.

(9)   Any amendment, repeal or revocation made by this Act binds the Crown to the extent that the enactment amended, repealed or revoked binds the Crown.

[1765]

NOTES
Sub-s (4): substituted by the Competition Act 1998 and Other Enactments (Amendment) Regulations 2004, SI 2004/1261, reg 4, Sch 1, para 46(1), (2).
Sub-s (6): words in first pair of square brackets inserted and words in second pair of square brackets substituted by SI 2004/1261, reg 4, Sch 1, para 46(1), (3).
Sub-s (6A): inserted by SI 2004/1261, reg 4, Sch 1, para 46(1), (4).
Sub-s (7): repealed by SI 2004/1261, reg 4, Sch 1, para 46(1), (5), subject to savings and transitional provision in reg 6(1), (2), (4) of those Regulations.
Sub-s (8): words in square brackets in para (a) inserted and words in square brackets in para (b) substituted by SI 2004/1261, reg 4, Sch 1, para 46(1), (6).
Regulations: the Competition Act 1998 (Definition of Appropriate Person) Regulations 1999, SI 1999/2282.

74   Amendments, transitional provisions, savings and repeals

(1)   The minor and consequential amendments set out in Schedule 12 are to have effect.

(2)   The transitional provisions and savings set out in Schedule 13 are to have effect.

(3)   The enactments set out in Schedule 14 are repealed.

[1766]

NOTES
9 November 1998 (certain purposes); 11 January 1999 (certain purposes); 10 November 1999 (certain purposes); 1 March 2000 (certain purposes); to be appointed (otherwise).

75   Consequential and supplementary provision

(1)   The Secretary of State may by order make such incidental, consequential, transitional or supplemental provision as he thinks necessary or expedient for the general purposes, or any particular purpose, of this Act or in consequence of any of its provisions or for giving full effect to it.

(2)   An order under subsection (1) may, in particular, make provision—

    (a)   for enabling any person by whom any powers will become exercisable, on a date specified by or under this Act, by virtue of any provision made by or under this Act to take before that date any steps which are necessary as a preliminary to the exercise of those powers;

(b)   for making savings, or additional savings, from the effect of any repeal made by or under this Act.

(3)   Amendments made under this section shall be in addition, and without prejudice, to those made by or under any other provision of this Act.

(4)   No other provision of this Act restricts the powers conferred by this section.

[1767]

NOTES
Orders: the Competition Act 1998 (Competition Commission) Transitional, Consequential and Supplemental Provisions Order 1999, SI 1999/506; the Judicial Pensions (Qualifying Judicial Offices) (President of the Competition Commission Appeal Tribunals) Order 1999, SI 1999/2283; the Competition Act 1998 (Transitional, Consequential and Supplemental Provisions) Order 2000, SI 2000/311; the Competition Act 1998 (Consequential and Supplemental Provisions) Order 2000, SI 2000/2031; the Competition Act 1998 (Public Transport Ticketing Schemes Block Exemption) Order 2001, SI 2001/319.

[75A   Rules in relation to Part 2 and Part 2A

(1)   The OFT may make such rules about procedural and other matters in connection with the carrying into effect of the provisions of Parts 2 and 2A as it considers appropriate.

(2)   If the OFT is preparing rules under this section it must consult such persons as it considers appropriate.

(3)   No rule made by the OFT is to come into operation until it has been approved by an order made by the Secretary of State.

(4)   The Secretary of State may approve any rule made by the OFT—
(a)   in the form in which it is submitted; or
(b)   subject to such modifications as he considers appropriate.

(5)   If the Secretary of State proposes to approve a rule subject to modifications he must inform the OFT of the proposed modifications and take into account any comments made by the OFT.

(6)   Subsections (3) to (5) apply also to any alteration of the rules made by the OFT.

(7)   The Secretary of State may, after consulting the OFT, by order vary or revoke any rules made under this section.

(8)   If the Secretary of State considers that rules should be made under this section with respect to a particular matter he may direct the OFT to exercise its powers under this section and make rules about that matter.]

[1767A]

NOTES
Inserted by the Competition Act 1998 and Other Enactments (Amendment) Regulations 2004, SI 2004/1261, reg 4, Sch 1, para 47.
Order: the Competition Act 1998 (Office of Fair Trading's Rules) Order 2004, SI 2004/2751.

76   Short title, commencement and extent

(1)   This Act may be cited as the Competition Act 1998.

(2)   Sections 71 and 75 and this section and paragraphs 1 to 7 and 35 of Schedule 13 come into force on the passing of this Act.

(3)   The other provisions of this Act come into force on such day as the Secretary of State may by order appoint; and different days may be appointed for different purposes.

(4)   This Act extends to Northern Ireland.

[1768]

NOTES
Orders: the Competition Act 1998 (Commencement No 1) Order 1998, SI 1998/2750; the Competition Act 1998 (Commencement No 2) Order 1998, SI 1998/3166; the Competition Act 1998 (Commencement No 3) Order 1999, SI 1999/505; the Competition Act 1998 (Commencement No 4) Order 1999, SI 1999/2859; the Competition Act 1998 (Commencement No 5) Order 2000, SI 2000/344.

SCHEDULES

SCHEDULE 1
EXCLUSIONS: MERGERS AND CONCENTRATIONS
Sections 3(1)(a) and 19(1)(a)

PART I
MERGERS

Enterprises ceasing to be distinct: the Chapter I prohibition

1.—(1)   To the extent to which an agreement (either on its own or when taken together with another agreement) results, or if carried out would result, in any two enterprises ceasing to be distinct enterprises for the purposes of [Part 3 of the Enterprise Act 2002 ("the 2002 Act")], the Chapter I prohibition does not apply to the agreement.

(2)   The exclusion provided by sub-paragraph (1) extends to any provision directly related and necessary to the implementation of the merger provisions.

(3)   In sub-paragraph (2) "merger provisions" means the provisions of the agreement which cause, or if carried out would cause, the agreement to have the result mentioned in sub-paragraph (1).

(4)   [Section 26 of the 2002 Act] applies for the purposes of this paragraph as if—
   (a)   in subsection (3) (circumstances in which a person or group of persons may be treated as having control of an enterprise), and
   (b)   in subsection (4) (circumstances in which a person or group of persons may be treated as bringing an enterprise under their control),
for "may" there were substituted "must".

Enterprises ceasing to be distinct: the Chapter II prohibition

2.—(1)   To the extent to which conduct (either on its own or when taken together with other conduct)—
   (a)   results in any two enterprises ceasing to be distinct enterprises for the purposes of [Part 3 of the 2002 Act], or
   (b)   is directly related and necessary to the attainment of the result mentioned in paragraph (a),
the Chapter II prohibition does not apply to that conduct.

(2)   [Section 26 of the 2002 Act] applies for the purposes of this paragraph as it applies for the purposes of paragraph 1.

3.   ...

Withdrawal of the paragraph 1 exclusion

4.—(1)   The exclusion provided by paragraph 1 does not apply to a particular agreement if the [OFT] gives a direction under this paragraph to that effect.

(2)   If the [OFT] is considering whether to give a direction under this paragraph, [it] may by notice in writing require any party to the agreement in question to give [the OFT] such information in connection with the agreement as [it] may require.

(3)   The [OFT] may give a direction under this paragraph only as provided in sub-paragraph (4) or (5).

(4)   If at the end of such period as may be specified in rules under section 51 a person has failed, without reasonable excuse, to comply with a requirement imposed under sub-paragraph (2), the [OFT] may give a direction under this paragraph.

(5)   The [OFT] may also give a direction under this paragraph if—
   [(a)   it considers that the agreement will, if not excluded, infringe the Chapter I prohibition; and]
   (b)   the agreement is not a protected agreement.

(6)   ...

(7)   A direction under this paragraph—
   (a)   must be in writing;
   (b)   may be made so as to have effect from a date specified in the direction (which may not be earlier than the date on which it is given).

Protected agreements

5.   An agreement is a protected agreement for the purposes of paragraph 4 if—
   [(a)   the OFT or (as the case may be) the Secretary of State has published its or his decision

not to make a reference to the Competition Commission under section 22, 33, 45 or 62 of the 2002 Act in connection with the agreement;

(b)   the OFT or (as the case may be) the Secretary of State has made a reference to the Competition Commission under section 22, 33, 45 or 62 of the 2002 Act in connection with the agreement and the Commission has found that the agreement has given rise to, or would if carried out give rise to, a relevant merger situation or (as the case may be) a special merger situation;

(c)   the agreement does not fall within paragraph (a) or (b) but has given rise to, or would if carried out give rise to, enterprises to which it relates being regarded under section 26 of the 2002 Act as ceasing to be distinct enterprises (otherwise than as the result of subsection (3) or (4)(b) of that section); or

(d)   the OFT has made a reference to the Competition Commission under section 32 of the Water Industry Act 1991 in connection with the agreement and the Commission has found that the agreement has given rise to, or would if carried out give rise to, a merger of any two or more water enterprises of the kind to which that section applies.]

[1769]

NOTES

References to the OFT, etc: as to the abolition of the office of the Director General of Fair Trading and the substitution of the original references to the Director (and related expressions), see the note preceding s 1 at **[1696]**.

Para 1: words in square brackets in sub-paras (1), (4) substituted by the Enterprise Act 2002, s 278(1), Sch 25, para 38(1), (50)(a).

Para 2: words in square brackets in sub-paras (1)(a), (2) substituted by the Enterprise Act 2002, s 278(1), Sch 25, para 38(1), (50)(b).

Para 3: repealed by the Communications Act 2003, s 406(7), Sch 19(1).

Para 4: words in square brackets in sub-para (2) substituted by the Enterprise Act 2002, s 278(1), Sch 25, para 38(1), (50)(c)(ii); sub-para (5)(a) substituted and sub-para (6) repealed by the Competition Act 1998 and Other Enactments (Amendment) Regulations 2004, SI 2004/1261, reg 4, Sch 1, para 48.

Para 5: sub-paras (a)–(d) substituted by the Enterprise Act 2002, s 278(1), Sch 25, para 38(1), (50)(d).

PART II
CONCENTRATIONS SUBJECT TO EC CONTROLS

6.—(1)   To the extent to which an agreement (either on its own or when taken together with another agreement) gives rise to, or would if carried out give rise to, a concentration, the Chapter I prohibition does not apply to the agreement if the Merger Regulation gives the Commission exclusive jurisdiction in the matter.

(2)   To the extent to which conduct (either on its own or when taken together with other conduct) gives rise to, or would if pursued give rise to, a concentration, the Chapter II prohibition does not apply to the conduct if the Merger Regulation gives the Commission exclusive jurisdiction in the matter.

(3)   In this paragraph—
"concentration" means a concentration with a Community dimension within the meaning of Articles 1 and 3 of the Merger Regulation; and
["Merger Regulation" means Council Regulation (EC) No 139/2004 of 20th January 2004 on the control of concentrations between undertakings].

[1770]

NOTES

Para (3): definition "Merger Regulation" substituted by the EC Merger Control (Consequential Amendments) Regulations 2004, SI 2004/1079, reg 2, Schedule, para 1.

(Sch 2 outside the scope of this work.)

SCHEDULE 3
GENERAL EXCLUSIONS

Sections 3(1)(c) and 19(1)(b)

Planning obligations

1.—(1)   The Chapter I prohibition does not apply to an agreement—
(a)   to the extent to which it is a planning obligation;
(b)   which is made under section 75 (agreements regulating development or use of land) or 246 (agreements relating to Crown land) of the Town and Country Planning (Scotland) Act 1997; or
(c)   which is made under Article 40 of the Planning (Northern Ireland) Order 1991.

(2)   In sub-paragraph (1)(a), "planning obligation" means—
(a)   a planning obligation for the purposes of section 106 of the Town and Country Planning Act 1990; or

(b)   a planning obligation for the purposes of section 299A of that Act.

2.   ...

EEA Regulated Markets

3.—(1)   The Chapter I prohibition does not apply to an agreement for the constitution of an EEA regulated market to the extent to which the agreement relates to any of the rules made, or guidance issued, by that market.

(2)   The Chapter I prohibition does not apply to a decision made by an EEA regulated market, to the extent to which the decision relates to any of the market's regulating provisions.

(3)   The Chapter I prohibition does not apply to—
   (a)   any practices of an EEA regulated market; or
   (b)   any practices which are trading practices in relation to an EEA regulated market.

(4)   The Chapter I prohibition does not apply to an agreement the parties to which are or include—
   (a)   an EEA regulated market, or
   (b)   a person who is subject to the rules of that market,
to the extent to which the agreement consists of provisions the inclusion of which is required or contemplated by the regulating provisions of that market.

(5)   In this paragraph—
   "EEA regulated market" is a market which—
      (a)   is listed by an EEA State other than the United Kingdom pursuant to [Article 47 of Directive 2004/39/EC of the European Parliament and of the Council of 21 April 2004 on markets in financial instruments]; and
      (b)   operates without any requirement that a person dealing on the market should have a physical presence in the EEA State from which any trading facilities are provided or on any trading floor that the market may have;
   "EEA State" means a State which is a contracting party to the EEA Agreement;
   "regulating provisions", in relation to an EEA regulated market, means—
      (a)   rules made, or guidance issued, by that market,
      (b)   practices of that market, or
      (c)   practices which, in relation to that market, are trading practices;
   "trading practices", in relation to an EEA regulated market, means practices of persons who are subject to the rules made by that market, and—
      (a)   which relate to business in respect of which those persons are subject to the rules of that market, and which are required or contemplated by those rules or by guidance issued by that market; or
      (b)   which are otherwise attributable to the conduct of that market as such.

Services of general economic interest etc

4.   Neither the Chapter I prohibition nor the Chapter II prohibition applies to an undertaking entrusted with the operation of services of general economic interest or having the character of a revenue-producing monopoly in so far as the prohibition would obstruct the performance, in law or in fact, of the particular tasks assigned to that undertaking.

Compliance with legal requirements

5.—(1)   The Chapter I prohibition does not apply to an agreement to the extent to which it is made in order to comply with a legal requirement.

(2)   The Chapter II prohibition does not apply to conduct to the extent to which it is engaged in an order to comply with a legal requirement.

(3)   In this paragraph "legal requirement" means a requirement—
   (a)   imposed by or under any enactment in force in the United Kingdom;
   (b)   imposed by or under the Treaty or the EEA Agreement and having legal effect in the United Kingdom without further enactment; or
   (c)   imposed by or under the law in force in another Member State and having legal effect in the United Kingdom.

Avoidance of conflict with international obligations

6.—(1)   If the Secretary of State is satisfied that, in order to avoid a conflict between provisions of this Part and an international obligation of the United Kingdom, it would be appropriate for the Chapter I prohibition not to apply to—
   (a)   a particular agreement, or
   (b)   any agreement of a particular description,
he may by order exclude the agreement, or agreements of that description, from the Chapter I prohibition.

(2)　An order under sub-paragraph (1) may make provision for the exclusion of the agreement or agreements to which the order applies, or of such of them as may be specified, only in specified circumstances.

(3)　An order under sub-paragraph (1) may also provide that the Chapter I prohibition is to be deemed never to have applied in relation to the agreement or agreements, or in relation to such of them as may be specified.

(4)　If the Secretary of State is satisfied that, in order to avoid a conflict between provisions of this Part and an international obligation of the United Kingdom, it would be appropriate for the Chapter II prohibition not to apply in particular circumstances, he may by order provide for it not to apply in such circumstances as may be specified.

(5)　An order under sub-paragraph (4) may provide that the Chapter II prohibition is to be deemed never to have applied in relation to specified conduct.

(6)　An international arrangement relating to civil aviation and designated by an order made by the Secretary of State is to be treated as an international obligation for the purposes of this paragraph.

(7)　In this paragraph and paragraph 7 "specified" means specified in the order.

Public policy

7.—(1)　If the Secretary of State is satisfied that there are exceptional and compelling reasons of public policy why the Chapter I prohibition ought not to apply to—
(a)　a particular agreement, or
(b)　any agreement of a particular description,
he may by order exclude the agreement, or agreements of that description, from the Chapter I prohibition.

(2)　An order under sub-paragraph (1) may make provision for the exclusion of the agreement or agreements to which the order applies, or of such of them as may be specified, only in specified circumstances.

(3)　An order under sub-paragraph (1) may also provide that the Chapter I prohibition is to be deemed never to have applied in relation to the agreement or agreements, or in relation to such of them as may be specified.

(4)　If the Secretary of State is satisfied that there are exceptional and compelling reasons of public policy why the Chapter II prohibition ought not to apply in particular circumstances, he may by order provide for it not to apply in such circumstances as may be specified.

(5)　An order under sub-paragraph (4) may provide that the Chapter II prohibition is to be deemed never to have applied in relation to specified conduct.

Coal and steel

8.—(1)　The Chapter I prohibition does not apply to an agreement which relates to a coal or steel product to the extent to which the ECSC Treaty gives the Commission exclusive jurisdiction in the matter.

(2)　Sub-paragraph (1) ceases to have effect on the date on which the ECSC Treaty expires ("the expiry date").

(3)　The Chapter II prohibition does not apply to conduct which relates to a coal or steel product to the extent to which the ECSC Treaty gives the Commission exclusive jurisdiction in the matter.

(4)　Sub-paragraph (3) ceases to have effect on the expiry date.

(5)　In this paragraph—
"coal or steel product" means any product of a kind listed in Annex I to the ECSC Treaty; and
"ECSC Treaty" means the Treaty establishing the European Coal and Steel Community.

Agricultural products

9.—(1)　The Chapter I prohibition does not apply to an agreement to the extent to which it relates to production of or trade in an agricultural product and—
(a)　forms an integral part of a national market organisation;
(b)　is necessary for the attainment of the objectives set out in [Article 33] of the Treaty; or
(c)　is an agreement of farmers or farmers' associations (or associations of such associations) belonging to a single member State which concerns—
(i)　the production or sale of agricultural products, or
(ii)　the use of joint facilities for the storage, treatment or processing of agricultural products,
and under which there is no obligation to charge identical prices.

(2)   If the Commission determines that an agreement does not fulfil the conditions specified by the provision for agricultural products for exclusion from [Article 81(1)], the exclusion provided by this paragraph ("the agriculture exclusion") is to be treated as ceasing to apply to the agreement on the date of the decision.

(3)   The agriculture exclusion does not apply to a particular agreement if the [OFT] gives a direction under this paragraph to that effect.

(4)   If the [OFT] is considering whether to give a direction under this paragraph, [it] may by notice in writing require any party to the agreement in question to give [the OFT] such information in connection with the agreement as [it] may require.

(5)   The [OFT] may give a direction under this paragraph only as provided in sub-paragraph (6) or (7).

(6)   If at the end of such period as may be specified in rules under section 51 a person has failed, without reasonable excuse, to comply with a requirement imposed under sub-paragraph (4), the [OFT] may give a direction under this paragraph.

(7)   The [OFT] may also give a direction under this paragraph if [it] considers that an agreement (whether or not [it] considers that it infringes the Chapter I prohibition) is likely, or is intended, substantially and unjustifiably to prevent, restrict or distort competition in relation to an agricultural product.

(8)   A direction under this paragraph—
    (a)   must be in writing;
    (b)   may be made so as to have effect from a date specified in the direction (which may not be earlier than the date on which it is given).

(9)   In this paragraph—
    "agricultural product" means any product of a kind listed in [Annex I] to the Treaty; and
    "provision for agricultural products" means Council Regulation (EEC) No 26/62 of 4th April 1962 applying certain rules of competition to production of and trade in agricultural products.

[1771]

NOTES
    Para 2: repealed by the Competition Act 1998 and Other Enactments (Amendment) Regulations 2004, SI 2004/1261, reg 4, Sch 1, para 50(a).
    Para 3: in sub-para (5) in definition "EEA regulated market" words in square brackets in para (a) substituted by the Financial Services and Markets Act 2000 (Markets in Financial Instruments) Regulations 2007, SI 2007/126, reg 3(6), Sch 6, Pt 1, para 13.
    Para 9: words in square brackets in sub-paras (1)(b), (2), (9) substituted by SI 2004/1261, reg 4, Sch 1, para 50(b); words in third pair of square brackets in sub-para (4) substituted by the Enterprise Act 2002, s 278(1), Sch 25, para 38(1), (51)(b)(ii).
    Orders: the Competition Act 1998 (Public Policy Exclusion) Order 2006, SI 2006/605; the Competition Act 1998 (Public Policy Exclusion) Order 2007, SI 2007/1896; the Competition Act 1998 (Public Policy Exclusion) Order 2008, SI 2008/1820.
    References to the OFT, etc: as to the abolition of the office of the Director General of Fair Trading and the substitution of the original references to the Director (and related expressions), see the note preceding s 1 at **[1696]**.
    Restrictive Trade Practices Act 1976: repealed by ss 1, 74(3) of, and Sch 14, Pt I to, this Act, subject to transitional provisions in Sch 13 at **[1783]**.

(*Sch 4 repealed by the Enterprise Act 2002, ss 207, 278(2), Sch 26; Schs 5, 6 repealed by the Competition Act 1998 and Other Enactments (Amendment) Regulations 2004, SI 2004/1261, reg 4, Sch 1, para 51.*)

[SCHEDULE 6A
COMMITMENTS

Section 31A

PART 1
PROCEDURAL REQUIREMENTS FOR THE ACCEPTANCE AND VARIATION
OF COMMITMENTS

1.   Paragraph 2 applies where the OFT proposes to—
    (a)   accept any commitments under section 31A; or
    (b)   accept any variation of such commitments other than a variation which is not material in any respect.

2.—(1)   Before accepting the commitments or variation, the OFT must—
    (a)   give notice under this paragraph; and
    (b)   consider any representations made in accordance with the notice and not withdrawn.

(2)   A notice under this paragraph must state—
    (a)   that the OFT proposes to accept the commitments or variation;

(b)   the purpose of the commitments or variation and the way in which the commitments or variation would meet the OFT's competition concerns;

(c)   any other facts which the OFT considers are relevant to the acceptance or variation of the commitments; and

(d)   the period within which representations may be made in relation to the proposed commitments or variation.

(3)   The period stated for the purposes of sub-paragraph (2)(d) must be at least 11 working days starting with the date the notice is given or, if that date is not a working day, with the date of the first working day after that date.

3.—(1)   The OFT must not accept the commitments or variation of which notice has been given under paragraph 2(1) with modifications unless it—

(a)   gives notice under this paragraph of the proposed modifications; and

(b)   considers any representations made in accordance with the notice and not withdrawn.

(2)   A notice under this paragraph must state—

(a)   the proposed modifications;

(b)   the reasons for them; and

(c)   the period within which representations may be made in relation to the proposed modifications.

(3)   The period stated for the purposes of sub-paragraph (2)(c) must be at least 6 working days starting with the date the notice is given or, if that date is not a working day, with the date of the first working day after that date.

4.   If, after giving notice under paragraph 2 or 3 the OFT decides—

(a)   not to accept the commitments or variation concerned, and

(b)   not to proceed by virtue of paragraph 5 or 6,

the OFT must give notice that it has so decided.

5.   The requirements of paragraph 3 shall not apply if the OFT—

(a)   has already given notice under paragraph 2 but not under paragraph 3; and

(b)   considers that the modifications which are now being proposed are not material in any respect.

6.   The requirements of paragraph 3 shall not apply if the OFT—

(a)   has already given notices under paragraphs 2 and 3; and

(b)   considers that the further modifications which are now being proposed are not material in any respect or do not differ in any material respect from the modifications in relation to which notice was last given under paragraph 3.

7.   As soon as practicable after accepting commitments or a variation under section 31A the OFT must publish the commitments or the variation in such manner as the OFT considers appropriate.

8.   A notice under paragraph 2 or 3 shall be given by—

(a)   sending a copy of the notice to such person or persons as the OFT considers appropriate for the purpose of bringing the matter to which it relates to the attention of those likely to be affected by it; or

(b)   publishing the notice in such manner as the OFT considers appropriate for the purpose of bringing the matter to which it relates to the attention of those likely to be affected by it.]

[1772]

NOTES

Schedule inserted by the Competition Act 1998 and Other Enactments (Amendment) Regulations 2004, SI 2004/1261, reg 4, Sch 1, para 52.

[PART 2
PROCEDURAL REQUIREMENTS FOR THE RELEASE OF COMMITMENTS

10.   Paragraph 11 applies where the OFT proposes to release any commitments under section 31A.

11.—(1)   Before releasing the commitments, the OFT must—

(a)   give notice under this paragraph;

(b)   send a copy of the notice to the person (or persons) who gave the commitments; and

(c)   consider any representations made in accordance with the notice and not withdrawn.

(2)   A notice under this paragraph must state—

(a)   the fact that a release is proposed;

(b)   the reasons for it; and

(c)   the period within which representations may be made in relation to the proposed release.

(3)   The period stated for the purposes of sub-paragraph (2)(c) must be at least 11 working days starting with the date the notice is given or, if that date is not a working day, with the date of the first working day after that date.

12. If after giving notice under paragraph 11 the OFT decides not to proceed with the release, it must—
- (a) give notice that it has so decided; and
- (b) send a copy of the notice to the person (or persons) who gave the commitments.

13. As soon as practicable after releasing the commitments, the OFT must—
- (a) publish the release in such manner as it considers appropriate; and
- (b) send a copy of the release to the person (or persons) who gave the commitments.

14. A notice under paragraph 11 or 12 shall be given by—
- (a) sending a copy of the notice to such other person or persons as the OFT considers appropriate for the purpose of bringing the matter to which it relates to the attention of those likely to be affected by it; or
- (b) publishing the notice in such manner as the OFT considers appropriate for the purpose of bringing the matter to which it relates to the attention of those likely to be affected by it.]

[1773]

NOTES

Inserted as noted to Pt 1 at **[1772]**.

SCHEDULE 7
THE COMPETITION COMMISSION

Section 45(7)

PART I
GENERAL

Interpretation

1. In this Schedule—
    "the 1973 Act" means the Fair Trading Act 1973;
    .....
    "Chairman" means the chairman of the Commission;
    "the Commission" means the Competition Commission;
    "Council" has the meaning given in paragraph 5;
    "general functions" means any functions of the Commission other than functions—
        (a) ...
        (b) which are to be discharged by the Council;
    "member" means a member of the Commission;
    "newspaper merger reference" means a [reference under section 45 of the Enterprise Act 2002 which specifies a newspaper public interest consideration (within the meaning of paragraph 20A of Schedule 8 to that Act) or a reference under section 62 of that Act which specifies a consideration specified in section 58(2A) or (2B) of that Act];
    ["newspaper panel member" means a member of the panel maintained under paragraph 22;]
    .....
    "reporting panel member" means a member appointed under paragraph 2(1)(b);
    "secretary" means the secretary of the Commission appointed under paragraph 9; and
    "specialist panel member" means a member appointed under any of the provisions mentioned in paragraph 2(1)(d).

Membership of the Commission

2.—(1) The Commission is to consist of—
- (a) ...
- (b) members appointed by the Secretary of State to form a panel for the purposes of the Commission's general functions;
- (c) [the members of] the panel maintained under paragraph 22;
- (d) members appointed by the Secretary of State under or by virtue of—
    - (i) ...
    - [(ii) section 104 of the Utilities Act 2000;]
    - [(iii) section 194(1) of the Communications Act 2003;]
    - (iv) Article 15(9) of the Electricity (Northern Ireland) Order 1992;
- [(e) one or members appointed by the Secretary of State to serve on the Council].

[(1A) A person may not be, at the same time, a member of the Commission and a member of the Tribunal.]

(2) A person who is appointed as a member of a kind mentioned in one of paragraphs [(aa)] to (c) of sub-paragraph (3) may also be appointed as a member of either or both of the other kinds mentioned in those paragraphs.

(3) The kinds of member are—

(a) ...
[(aa) a newspaper panel member;]
(b) a reporting panel member;
(c) a specialist panel member.

(4) ...

(5) The validity of the Commission's proceedings is not affected by a defect in the appointment of a member.

Chairman and deputy chairmen

3.—(1) The Commission is to have a chairman appointed by the Secretary of State from among the reporting panel members.

(2) The Secretary of State may appoint one or more of the reporting panel members to act as deputy chairman.

(3) The Chairman, and any deputy chairman, may resign that office at any time by notice in writing addressed to the Secretary of State.

(4) If the Chairman (or a deputy chairman) ceases to be a member he also ceases to be Chairman (or a deputy chairman).

(5) If the Chairman is absent or otherwise unable to act, or there is no chairman, any of his functions may be performed—
    (a) if there is one deputy chairman, by him;
    (b) if there is more than one—
        (i) by the deputy chairman designated by the Secretary of State; or
        (ii) if no such designation has been made, by the deputy chairman designated by the deputy chairmen;
    (c) if there is no deputy chairman able to act—
        (i) by the member designated by the Secretary of State; or
        (ii) if no such designation has been made, by the member designated by the Commission.

4. ...

The Council

5.—(1) The Commission is to have a ... board to be known as the Competition Commission Council (but referred to in this Schedule as "the Council").

(2) The Council is to consist of—
    (a) the Chairman [and any deputy chairmen of the Commission];
    (b) ...
    [(bb) the member or members appointed under paragraph 2(1)(e);]
    (c) such other members as the Secretary of State may appoint; and
    (d) the secretary.

(3) In exercising its functions under paragraphs 3 and 7 to 12 ... the Commission is to act through the Council.

[(3A) Without prejudice to the question whether any other functions of the Commission are to be so discharged, the functions of the Commission under sections 106, 116, and 171 of the Enterprise Act 2002 (and under section 116 as applied for the purposes of references under Part 4 of that Act by section 176 of that Act) are to be discharged by the Council.]

(4) The Council may determine its own procedure including, in particular, its quorum.

(5) The Chairman (and any person acting as Chairman) is to have a casting vote on any question being decided by the Council.

Term of office

6.—(1) Subject to the provisions of this Schedule, each member is to hold and vacate office in accordance with the terms of his appointment.

(2) A person is not to be appointed as a member for more than *five years at a time* [eight years (but this does not prevent a re-appointment for the purpose only of continuing to act as a member of a group selected under paragraph 15 before the end of his term of office)].

(3) Any member may at any time resign by notice in writing addressed to the Secretary of State.

(4) The Secretary of State may remove a member on the ground of incapacity or misbehaviour.

(5) *No person is to be prevented from being appointed as a member merely because he has previously been a member.*

Expenses, remuneration and pensions

7.—(1)   The Secretary of State shall pay to the Commission such sums as he considers appropriate to enable it to perform its functions.

(2)   The Commission may pay, or make provision for paying, to or in respect of each member such salaries or other remuneration and such pensions, allowances, fees, expenses or gratuities as the Secretary of State may determine.

(3)   If a person ceases to be a member otherwise than on the expiry of his term of office and it appears to the Secretary of State that there are special circumstances which make it right for him to receive compensation, the Commission may make a payment to him of such amount as the Secretary of State may determine.

(4)   ...

[7A.   The Commission may publish advice and information in relation to any matter connected with the exercise of its functions.]

The Commission's powers

8.   Subject to the provisions of this Schedule, the Commission has power to do anything (except borrow money)—
  (a)   calculated to facilitate the discharge of its functions; or
  (b)   incidental or conducive to the discharge of its functions.

Staff

9.—(1)   The Commission is to have a secretary, appointed by the Secretary of State on such terms and conditions of service as he considers appropriate.

(2)   ...

(3)   Before appointing a person to be secretary, the Secretary of State must consult the Chairman ...

(4)   Subject to obtaining the approval of [the Secretary of State as to numbers and terms and conditions of service] the Commission may appoint such staff as it thinks appropriate.

10.   ...

Application of seal and proof of instruments

11.—(1)   The application of the seal of the Commission must be authenticated by the signature of the secretary or of some other person authorised for the purpose.

(2)   Sub-paragraph (1) does not apply in relation to any document which is or is to be signed in accordance with the law of Scotland.

(3)   A document purporting to be duly executed under the seal of the Commission—
  (a)   is to be received in evidence; and
  (b)   is to be taken to have been so executed unless the contrary is proved.

Accounts

12.—(1)   The Commission must—
  (a)   keep proper accounts and proper records in relation to its accounts;
  (b)   prepare a statement of accounts in respect of each of its financial years; and
  (c)   send copies of the statement to the Secretary of State and to the Comptroller and Auditor General before the end of the month of August next following the financial year to which the statement relates.

(2)   The statement of accounts must comply with any directions given by the Secretary of State with the approval of the Treasury as to—
  (a)   the information to be contained in it,
  (b)   the manner in which the information contained in it is to be presented, or
  (c)   the methods and principles according to which the statement is to be prepared,
and must contain such additional information as the Secretary of State may with the approval of the Treasury require to be provided for informing Parliament.

(3)   The Comptroller and Auditor General must—
  (a)   examine, certify and report on each statement received by him as a result of this paragraph; and
  (b)   lay copies of each statement and of his report before each House of Parliament.

(4)   In this paragraph "financial year" means the period beginning with the date on which the Commission is established and ending with March 31st next, and each successive period of twelve months.

[Annual reports

12A.—(1)   The Commission shall make to the Secretary of State a report for each financial year on its activities during the year.

(2)   The annual report must be made before the end of August next following the financial year to which it relates.

(3)   The Secretary of State shall lay a copy of the annual report before Parliament and arrange for the report to be published.]

Status

13.—(1)   The Commission is not to be regarded as the servant or agent of the Crown or as enjoying any status, privilege or immunity of the Crown.

(2)   The Commission's property is not to be regarded as property of, or held on behalf of, the Crown.

[1774]

NOTES

Para 1: definitions "appeal panel member" and "President" (both omitted) and words omitted from definition "general functions" repealed, and definition "newspaper panel member" inserted, by the Enterprise Act 2002, ss 21, 185, 278(2), Sch 5, paras 1, 7(1), (2), Sch 11, paras 1, 2, Sch 26; in definition "newspaper merger reference" words in square brackets substituted by the Communications Act 2003, s 388.

Para 2: sub-paras (1)(a), (3)(a), (4) repealed, words in square brackets in sub-paras (1)(c), (2) substituted, and sub-paras (1)(e), (3)(aa) inserted, by the Enterprise Act 2002, ss 21, 185, 278(2), Sch 5, paras 1, 7(1), (3), Sch 11, paras 1, 3(a), (b), (d), (e); sub-para (1)(d)(i) repealed by the Water Act 2003, s 101, Sch 7, Pt 2, para 32(1), (3), Sch 9, Pt 3; sub-para (1)(d)(ii) substituted by the Utilities Act 2000, s 104(3); sub-para (1)(d)(iii) substituted by the Communications Act 2003, s 406(1), Sch 17, para 153(1), (2); sub-para (1A) inserted by s 185 of, and Sch 11, paras 1, 3(c) to, the 2002 Act.

Para 4: repealed by the Enterprise Act 2002, ss 21, 278(2), Sch 5, paras 1, 7(1), (4), Sch 26.

Para 5: words omitted from sub-paras (1), (3), and the whole of sub-para (2)(b), repealed, and words in square brackets in sub-para (2)(a), and sub-paras (2)(bb) inserted, by the Enterprise Act 2002, ss 21, 185, 278(2), Sch 5, paras 1, 7(1), (5), Sch 11, paras 1, 4(a)–(c), Sch 26; sub-para (3A) inserted by s 185 of, and Sch 11, paras 1, 4(d) to, the 2002 Act.

Para 6: words in italics in sub-para (2) substituted by subsequent words in square brackets, and sub-para (5) repealed, by the Enterprise Act 2002, ss 185, 278(2), Sch 11, paras 1, 5, Sch 26, as from 1 April 2003 (except in relation to the re-appointment as a member of any person who is a member on that date), and as from a day to be appointed (otherwise).

Para 7: sub-para (4) repealed by the Enterprise Act 2002, ss 185, 278(2), Sch 11, paras 1, 6, Sch 26.

Para 7A: inserted by the Enterprise Act 2002, s 185, Sch 11, paras 1, 7.

Para 9: sub-para (2), and words omitted from sub-para (3) repealed, and words in square brackets in sub-para (4) substituted, by the Enterprise Act 2002, ss 185, 278(2), Sch 11, paras 1, 8, Sch 26.

Para 10: repealed by the Enterprise Act 2002, ss 185, 278(2), Sch 11, paras 1, 9, Sch 26.

Para 12A: inserted by the Enterprise Act 2002, s 186.

PART II

PERFORMANCE OF THE COMMISSION'S GENERAL FUNCTIONS

Interpretation

14.   In this Part of this Schedule "group" means a group selected under paragraph 15.

Discharge of certain functions by groups

15.—(1)   Except where sub-paragraph (7) [or (8)] gives the Chairman power to act on his own, any general function of the Commission must be performed through a group selected for the purpose by the Chairman.

(2)   The group must consist of at least three persons one of whom may be the Chairman.

(3)   In selecting the members of the group, the Chairman must comply with any requirement as to its constitution imposed by any enactment applying to specialist panel members.

(4)   If the functions to be performed through the group relate to a newspaper merger reference, the group must, subject to sub-paragraph (5), consist of such reporting panel members as the Chairman may select.

[(5)   The Chairman must select one or more newspaper panel members to be members of the group dealing with functions relating to a newspaper merger reference and, if he selects at least three such members, the group may consist entirely of those members.]

(6)   Subject to sub-paragraphs (2) to (5), a group must consist of reporting panel members or specialist panel members selected by the Chairman.

(7)   While a group is being constituted to perform a particular general function of the Commission, the Chairman may—

(a)   take such steps (falling within that general function) as he considers appropriate to facilitate the work of the group when it has been constituted; ...
(b)   ...

[(8)   The Chairman may exercise the power conferred by section 37(1), 48(1) or 64(1) of the Enterprise Act 2002 while a group is being constituted to perform a relevant general function of the Commission or, when it has been so constituted, before it has held its first meeting.]

Chairmen of groups

16.   The Chairman must appoint one of the members of a group to act as the chairman of the group.

Replacement of member of group

17.—(1)   If, during the proceedings of a group—
(a)   a member of the group ceases to be a member of the Commission,
(b)   the Chairman is satisfied that a member of the group will be unable for a substantial period to perform his duties as a member of the group, or
(c)   it appears to the Chairman that because of a particular interest of a member of the group it is inappropriate for him to remain in the group,
the Chairman may appoint a replacement.

(2)   The Chairman may also at any time appoint any reporting panel member to be an additional member of a group.

Attendance of other members

18.—(1)   At the invitation of the chairman of a group, any reporting panel member who is not a member of the group may attend meetings or otherwise take part in the proceedings of the group.

(2)   But any person attending in response to such an invitation may not—
(a)   vote in any proceedings of the group; or
(b)   have a statement of his dissent from a conclusion of the group included in a report made by them.

(3)   Nothing in sub-paragraph (1) is to be taken to prevent a group, or a member of a group, from consulting any member of the Commission with respect to any matter or question with which the group is concerned.

Procedure

19.—(1)   Subject to any special or general directions given by the Secretary of State, each group may determine its own procedure.

(2)   Each group may, in particular, determine its quorum and determine—
(a)   the extent, if any, to which persons interested or claiming to be interested in the subject-matter of the reference are allowed—
(i)   to be present or to be heard, either by themselves or by their representatives;
(ii)   to cross-examine witnesses; or
(iii)   otherwise to take part; and
(b)   the extent, if any, to which sittings of the group are to be held in public.

(3)   In determining its procedure a group must have regard to any guidance issued by the Chairman.

(4)   Before issuing any guidance for the purposes of this paragraph the Chairman must consult the members of the Commission.

[(5)   This paragraph does not apply to groups for which rules must be made under paragraph 19A.]

[19A.—(1)   The Chairman must make rules of procedure in relation to merger reference groups, market reference groups and special reference groups.

(2)   Schedule 7A makes further provision about rules made under this paragraph but is not to be taken as restricting the Chairman's powers under this paragraph.

(3)   The Chairman must publish rules made under this paragraph in such manner as he considers appropriate for the purpose of bringing them to the attention of those likely to be affected by them.

(4)   The Chairman must consult the members of the Commission and such other persons as he considers appropriate before making rules under this paragraph.

(5)   Rules under this paragraph may—
(a)   make different provision for different cases or different purposes;
(b)   be varied or revoked by subsequent rules made under this paragraph.

(6)   Subject to rules made under this paragraph, each merger reference group, market reference group and special reference group may determine its own procedure.

(7)   In determining how to proceed in accordance with rules made under this paragraph and in determining its procedure under sub-paragraph (6), a group must have regard to any guidance issued by the Chairman.

(8)   Before issuing any guidance for the purposes of this paragraph the Chairman shall consult the members of the Commission and such other persons as he considers appropriate.

(9)   In this paragraph and in Schedule 7A—
    "market reference group" means any group constituted in connection with a reference under section 131 or 132 of the Enterprise Act 2002 (including that section as it has effect by virtue of another enactment);
    "merger reference group" means any group constituted in connection with a reference under section 59 of the Fair Trading Act 1973 (c 41), section 32 of the Water Industry Act 1991 (c 56) or section 22, 33, 45 or 62 of the Enterprise Act 2002; and
    "special reference group" means any group constituted in connection with a reference or (in the case of the Financial Services and Markets Act 2000 (c 8)) an investigation under—

(a)	section 11 of the Competition Act 1980 (c 21);
(b)	...
(c)	section 43 of the Airports Act 1986 (c 31);
(d)	section 24 or 41E of the Gas Act 1986 (c 44);
(e)	section 12 or 56C of the Electricity Act 1989 (c 29);
(f)	...
(g)	section 12[, 14 or 17K] of the Water Industry Act 1991 (c 56);
(h)	article 15 of the Electricity (Northern Ireland) Order 1992 (SI 1992/231 (NI 1));
(i)	section 13 of, or Schedule 4A to, the Railways Act 1993 (c 43);
(j)	article 34 of the Airports (Northern Ireland) Order 1994 (SI 1994/426 (NI 1));
(k)	article 15 of the Gas (Northern Ireland) Order 1996 (SI 1996/275 (NI 2));
(l)	section 15 of the Postal Services Act 2000 (c 26);
(m)	section 162 or 306 of the Financial Services and Markets Act 2000 (c 8); ...
(n)	section 12 of the Transport Act 2000 (c 38); [...
(o)	section 193 of the Communications Act 2003][; or
(p)	article 3 of the Water Services etc (Scotland) Act 2005 (Consequential Provisions and Modifications) Order 2005].]

Effect of exercise of functions by group

20.—(1)   Subject to [sub-paragraphs (2) to (9)], anything done by or in relation to a group in, or in connection with, the performance of functions to be performed by the group is to have the same effect as if done by or in relation to the Commission.

[(2)   For the purposes of Part 3 of the Enterprise Act 2002 (mergers) any decision of a group under section 35(1) or 36(1) of that Act (questions to be decided on non-public interest merger references) that there is an anti-competitive outcome is to be treated as a decision under that section that there is not an anti-competitive outcome if the decision is not that of at least two-thirds of the members of the group.

(3)   For the purposes of Part 3 of the Act of 2002, if the decision is not that of at least two-thirds of the members of the group—
    (a)   any decision of a group under section 47 of that Act (questions to be decided on public interest merger references) that a relevant merger situation has been created is to be treated as a decision under that section that no such situation has been created;
    (b)   any decision of a group under section 47 of that Act that the creation of a relevant merger situation has resulted, or may be expected to result, in a substantial lessening of competition within any market or markets in the United Kingdom for goods or services is to be treated as a decision under that section that the creation of that situation has not resulted, or may be expected not to result, in such a substantial lessening of competition;
    (c)   any decision of a group under section 47 of that Act that arrangements are in progress or in contemplation which, if carried into effect, will result in the creation of a relevant merger situation is to be treated as a decision under that section that no such arrangements are in progress or in contemplation; and
    (d)   any decision of a group under section 47 of that Act that the creation of such a situation as is mentioned in paragraph (c) may be expected to result in a substantial lessening of competition within any market or markets in the United Kingdom for goods or services is to be treated as a decision under that section that the creation of that situation may be expected not to result in such a substantial lessening of competition.

(4)   For the purposes of Part 3 of the Act of 2002, if the decision is not that of at least two-thirds of the members of the group—
    (a)   any decision of a group under section 63 of that Act (questions to be decided on special public interest merger references) that a special merger situation has been created is to be treated as a decision under that section that no such situation has been created; and
    (b)   any decision of a group under section 63 of that Act that arrangements are in progress or

in contemplation which, if carried into effect, will result in the creation of a special merger situation is to be treated as a decision under that section that no such arrangements are in progress or in contemplation.

(5)   For the purposes of Part 4 of the Act of 2002 (market investigations), if the decision is not that of at least two-thirds of the members of the group, any decision of a group under section 134 or 141 (questions to be decided on market investigation references) that a feature, or combination of features, of a relevant market prevents, restricts or distorts competition in connection with the supply or acquisition of any goods or services in the United Kingdom or a part of the United Kingdom is to be treated as a decision that the feature or (as the case may be) combination of features does not prevent, restrict or distort such competition.

(6)   Accordingly, for the purposes of Part 4 of the Act of 2002, a group is to be treated as having decided under section 134 or 141 that there is no adverse effect on competition if—

    (a)   one or more than one decision of the group is to be treated as mentioned in sub-paragraph (5); and

    (b)   there is no other relevant decision of the group.

(7)   In sub-paragraph (6) "relevant decision" means a decision which is not to be treated as mentioned in sub-paragraph (5) and which is that a feature, or combination of features, of a relevant market prevents, restricts or distorts competition in connection with the supply or acquisition of any goods or services in the United Kingdom or a part of the United Kingdom.

(8)   Expressions used in sub-paragraphs (2) to (7) shall be construed in accordance with Part 3 or (as the case may be) 4 of the Act of 2002.

(9)   Sub-paragraph (1) is also subject to specific provision made by or under other enactments about decisions which are not decisions of at least two-thirds of the members of a group.]

Casting votes

21.   The chairman of a group is to have a casting vote on any question to be decided by the group.

Newspaper merger references

22.   [There are to be members of the Commission appointed by the Secretary of State to form a panel of persons available] for selection as members of a group constituted in connection with a newspaper merger reference.

NOTES

Para 15: words in square brackets in sub-para (1), and sub-para (8) inserted, and sub-para (7)(b) and the word preceding it repealed, by the Enterprise Act 2002, ss 185, 278(2), Sch 11, paras 1, 10(1), (2), (4), (5), Sch 26; sub-para (5) substituted by s 185 of, and Sch 11, para 10(3) to, the 2002 Act.

Para 19: sub-para (5) inserted by the Enterprise Act 2002, s 187(2).

Para 19A: inserted by the Enterprise Act 2002, s 187(3); in sub-para (9) in definition "merger reference group" words omitted repealed, in definition "special reference group" paras (b), (f) repealed, word omitted from para (m) repealed and para (o) and word omitted immediately preceding it inserted by the Communications Act 2003, s 406(1), (7), Sch 17, para 153(1), (3), Sch 19(1); in definition "special reference group" words in square brackets in para (g) substituted by the Water Act 2003, s 101(1), Sch 8, para 54, word omitted from para (n) repealed and para (p) and word "; or" immediately preceding it inserted by the Water Services etc (Scotland) Act 2005 (Consequential Provisions and Modifications) Order 2005, SI 2005/3172, art 11, Schedule, Pt 1, para 3(a).

Para 20: words in square brackets in sub-para (1) substituted and sub-paras (2)–(9) substituted for original sub-s (2), by the Enterprise Act 2002, ss 185, Sch 11, paras 1, 11.

Para 22: words in square brackets substituted by the Enterprise Act 2002, ss 185, Sch 11, paras 1, 12.

(Pt III repealed by the Enterprise Act 2002, ss 21, 278(2), Sch 5, paras 1, 7(1), (6), Sch 26; Pt IV amends the House of Commons Disqualification Act 1975, Sch 1, Pt II, and the Northern Ireland Assembly Disqualification Act 1975, Sch 1, Pt II.)

PART V
TRANSITIONAL PROVISIONS

Interpretation

30.   In this Part of this Schedule—

"commencement date" means the date on which section 45 comes into force; and

"MMC" means the Monopolies and Mergers Commission.

Chairman

31.—(1)   The person who is Chairman of the MMC immediately before the commencement date is on that date to become both a member of the Commission and its chairman as if he had been duly appointed under paragraphs 2(1)(b) and 3.

(2) He is to hold office as Chairman of the Commission for the remainder of the period for which he was appointed as Chairman of the MMC and on the terms on which he was so appointed.

Deputy chairmen

32. The persons who are deputy chairmen of the MMC immediately before the commencement date are on that date to become deputy chairmen of the Commission as if they had been duly appointed under paragraph 3(2).

Reporting panel members

33.—(1) The persons who are members of the MMC immediately before the commencement date are on that date to become members of the Commission as if they had been duly appointed under paragraph 2(1)(b).

(2) Each of them is to hold office as a member for the remainder of the period for which he was appointed as a member of the MMC and on the terms on which he was so appointed.

Specialist panel members

34.—(1) The persons who are members of the MMC immediately before the commencement date by virtue of appointments made under any of the enactments mentioned in paragraph 2(1)(d) are on that date to become members of the Commission as if they had been duly appointed to the Commission under the enactment in question.

(2) Each of them is to hold office as a member for such period and on such terms as the Secretary of State may determine.

Secretary

35. The person who is the secretary of the MMC immediately before the commencement date is on that date to become the secretary of the Commission as if duly appointed under paragraph 9, on the same terms and conditions.

Council

36.—(1) The members who become deputy chairmen of the Commission under paragraph 32 are also to become members of the Council as if they had been duly appointed under paragraph 5(2)(c).

(2) Each of them is to hold office as a member of the Council for such period as the Secretary of State determines.

[1776]

[SCHEDULE 7A
THE COMPETITION COMMISSION: PROCEDURAL RULES FOR MERGERS AND MARKET REFERENCES ETC

1. In this Schedule—
   "market investigation" means an investigation carried out by a market reference group in connection with a reference under section 131 or 132 of the Enterprise Act 2002 (including that section as it has effect by virtue of another enactment);
   "market reference group" has the meaning given by paragraph 19A(9) of Schedule 7 to this Act;
   "merger investigation" means an investigation carried out by a merger reference group in connection with a reference under … section 32 of the Water Industry Act 1991 (c 56) or section 22, 33, 45 or 62 of the Act of 2002;
   "merger reference group" has the meaning given by paragraph 19A(9) of Schedule 7 to this Act;
   "relevant group" means a market reference group, merger reference group or special reference group;
   "special investigation" means an investigation carried out by a special reference group—
       (a)   in connection with a reference under a provision mentioned in any of paragraphs (a) to (l) [and (n) to (p)] of the definition of "special reference group" in paragraph 19A(9) of Schedule 7 to this Act; or
       (b)   under a provision mentioned in paragraph (m) of that definition; and
   "special reference group" has the meaning given by paragraph 19A(9) of Schedule 7 to this Act.

2. Rules may make provision—
       (a)   for particular stages of a merger investigation, a market investigation or a special investigation to be dealt with in accordance with a timetable and for the revision of that timetable;
       (b)   as to the documents and information which must be given to a relevant group in connection with a merger investigation, a market investigation or a special investigation;

(c) as to the documents or information which a relevant group must give to other persons in connection with such an investigation.

3. Rules made by virtue of paragraph 2(a) and (b) may, in particular, enable or require a relevant group to disregard documents or information given after a particular date.

4. Rules made by virtue of paragraph 2(c) may, in particular, make provision for the notification or publication of, and for consultation about, provisional findings of a relevant group.

5. Rules may make provision as to the quorum of relevant groups.

6. Rules may make provision—
   (a) as to the extent (if any) to which persons interested or claiming to be interested in a matter under consideration which is specified or described in the rules are allowed—
       (i) to be (either by themselves or by their representatives) present before a relevant group or heard by that group;
       (ii) to cross-examine witnesses; or
       (iii) otherwise to take part;
   (b) as to the extent (if any) to which sittings of a relevant group are to be held in public; and
   (c) generally in connection with any matters permitted by rules made under paragraph (a) or (b) (including, in particular, provision for a record of any hearings).

7. Rules may make provision for—
   (a) the notification or publication of information in relation to merger investigations, market investigations or special investigations;
   (b) consultation about such investigations.]

[1777]

NOTES

Inserted by the Enterprise Act 2002, s 187(4), Sch 12.

Para 1: in definition "merger investigation" words omitted repealed by the Communications Act 2003, s 406(7), Sch 19(1); in definition "special investigation" words in square brackets in para (a) substituted by the Water Services etc (Scotland) Act 2005 (Consequential Provisions and Modifications) Order 2005, SI 2005/3172, art 11, Schedule, Pt 1, para 3(b).

SCHEDULE 8
APPEALS

Sections 46(5) and 48(4)

PART I
GENERAL

1. …

General procedure

2.—(1) An appeal to the [Tribunal under section 46 or 47 must be made by sending a notice of appeal to it] within the specified period.

(2) The notice of appeal must set out the grounds of appeal in sufficient detail to indicate—
   (a) under which provision of this Act the appeal is brought;
   (b) to what extent (if any) the appellant contends that the decision against, or with respect to which, the appeal is brought was based on an error of fact or was wrong in law; and
   (c) to what extent (if any) the appellant is appealing against the [OFT's exercise of its] discretion in making the disputed decision.

(3) The [Tribunal] may give an appellant leave to amend the grounds of appeal identified in the notice of appeal.

[(4) In this paragraph references to the Tribunal are to the Tribunal as constituted (in accordance with section 14 of the Enterprise Act 2002) for the purposes of the proceedings in question.

(5) Nothing in this paragraph restricts the power under section 15 of the Enterprise Act 2002 (Tribunal rules) to make provision as to the manner of instituting proceedings before the Tribunal.]

Decisions of the [Tribunal]

3.—[(A1) This paragraph applies to any appeal under section 46 or 47 other than—
   (a) an appeal under section 46 against, or with respect to, a decision of the kind specified in subsection (3)(g) or (h) of that section, and
   (b) an appeal under section 47(1)(b) or (c).]

(1) The [Tribunal] must determine the appeal on the merits by reference to the grounds of appeal set out in the notice of appeal.

(2) The [Tribunal] may confirm or set aside the decision which is the subject of the appeal, or any part of it, and may—

(a)   remit the matter to the [OFT],
(b)   impose or revoke, or vary the amount of, a penalty,
(c)   …
(d)   give such directions, or take such other steps, as the [OFT] could [itself] have given or taken, or
(e)   make any other decision which the [OFT] could [itself] have made.

((3)   Any decision of the [Tribunal] on an appeal has the same effect, and may be enforced in the same manner, as a decision of the [OFT].

(4)   If the [Tribunal] confirms the decision which is the subject of the appeal it may nevertheless set aside any finding of fact on which the decision was based.

[3A.—(1)   This paragraph applies to—
(a)   any appeal under section 46 against, or with respect to, a decision of the kind specified in subsection (3)(g) or (h) of that section, and
(b)   any appeal under section 47(1)(b) or (c).

(2)   The Tribunal must, by reference to the grounds of appeal set out in the notice of appeal, determine the appeal by applying the same principles as would be applied by a court on an application for judicial review.

(3)   The Tribunal may—
(a)   dismiss the appeal or quash the whole or part of the decision to which it relates; and
(b)   where it quashes the whole or part of that decision, remit the matter back to the OFT with a direction to reconsider and make a new decision in accordance with the ruling of the Tribunal.]

4.   …

                                                                                    [1778]

NOTES
Paras 1, 4: repealed by the Enterprise Act 2002, ss 21, 278(2), Sch 5, paras 1, 8(1), (2), (5), Sch 26.
Para 2: words in square brackets in sub-paras (1), (2)(c), (3) substituted, and sub-paras (4), (5) added, by the Enterprise Act 2002, ss 21, 278(1), Sch 5, paras 1, 8(1), (3), Sch 25, para 38(1), (54)(b).
Para 3: sub-para (A1) inserted and sub-para (2)(c) repealed by the Competition Act 1998 and Other Enactments (Amendment) Regulations 2004, SI 2004/1261, reg 4, Sch 1, para 53(1)–(3); words in first pairs of square brackets in sub-paras (1)–(4) and words in second pairs of square brackets in sub-paras (2)(d), (e) substituted by the Enterprise Act 2002, ss 21, 278(1), Sch 5, paras 1, 8(1), (4), Sch 25, para 38(1), (54)(c).
Para 3A: inserted by SI 2004/1261, reg 4, Sch 1, para 53(1), (4).
References to the OFT, etc: as to the abolition of the office of the Director General of Fair Trading and the substitution of the original references to the Director (and related expressions), see the note preceding s 1 at **[1696]**.

(*Pt II repealed by the Enterprise Act 2002, ss 21, 278(2), Sch 5, paras 1, 8(1), (5), Sch 26.*)

SCHEDULE 9
[OFT'S] RULES
Section 51(2)

General
[1.   In this Schedule "rules" means rules made by the OFT under section 51.]
2–4.   …

Decisions
5.—(1)   Rules may make provision as to—
(a)   the form and manner in which notice of any decision is to be given;
(b)   the person or persons to whom the notice is to be given;
(c)   the manner in which the [OFT] is to publish a decision;
[(d)   the procedure to be followed if—
(i)   the OFT takes further action with respect to an agreement after having decided that it does not infringe the Chapter I prohibition;
(ii)   the OFT takes further action with respect to an agreement after having decided that it does not infringe the prohibition in Article 81(1);
(iii)   the OFT takes further action with respect to conduct after having decided that it does not infringe the Chapter II prohibition; or
(iv)   the OFT takes further action with respect to conduct after having decided that it does not infringe the prohibition in Article 82.]

[(2)   In this paragraph "decision" means a decision of the OFT—
(a)   as to whether or not an agreement has infringed the Chapter I prohibition;
(b)   as to whether or not an agreement has infringed the prohibition in Article 81(1);
(c)   as to whether or not conduct has infringed the Chapter II prohibition; or
(d)   as to whether or not conduct has infringed the prohibition in Article 82.]

6, 7. ...

Block exemptions

[8.   Rules may make provision as to—
     (a)   the procedure to be followed by the OFT if it cancels a block exemption;
     (b)   the procedure to be followed by the OFT if it withdraws the benefit of a regulation of the Commission pursuant to Article 29(2) of the EC Competition Regulation.]

Parallel exemptions

9.   Rules may make provision as to—
     (a)   the circumstances in which the [OFT] may—
         (i)   impose conditions or obligations in relation to a parallel exemption,
         (ii)   vary or remove any such conditions or obligations,
         (iii)   impose additional conditions or obligations, or
         (iv)   cancel the exemption;
     (b)   as to the procedure to be followed by the [OFT] if [it] is acting under section 10(5);
     (c)   the form and manner in which notice of a decision to take any of the steps in sub-paragraph (a) is to be given;
     (d)   the circumstances in which an exemption may be cancelled with retrospective effect.

Section 11 exemptions

10.   Rules may, with respect to any exemption provided by regulations made under section 11, make provision similar to that made with respect to parallel exemptions by section 10 or by rules under paragraph 9.

Directions withdrawing exclusions

11.   Rules may make provision as to the factors which the [OFT] may take into account when [it] is determining the date on which a direction given under paragraph 4(1) of Schedule 1 or paragraph ... 9(3) of Schedule 3 is to have effect.

Disclosure of information

12.—(1)   Rules may make provision as to the circumstances in which the [OFT] is to be required, before disclosing information given to [it] by a third party in connection with the exercise of any of the [OFT's] functions under Part I, to give notice, and an opportunity to make representations, to the third party.

     (2)   In relation to the agreement (or conduct) concerned, "third party" means a person who is not a party to the agreement (or who has not engaged in the conduct).

Applications under section 47

13.   Rules may make provision as to—
     (a)   the period within which an application under section 47(1) must be made;
     (b)   the procedure to be followed by the [OFT] in dealing with the application;
     (c)   the person or persons to whom notice of the [OFT's] response to the application is to be given.

Enforcement

14.   Rules may make provision as to the procedure to be followed when the [OFT] takes action under any of sections [32 to 40] with respect to the enforcement of the provisions of this Part.

                                                 [1779]–[1780]

NOTES

    Paras 1, 8: substituted by the Competition Act 1998 and Other Enactments (Amendment) Regulations 2004, SI 2004/1261, reg 4, Sch 1, para 54(1), (2), (7).

    Paras 2–4, 6, 7: repealed by SI 2004/1261, reg 4, Sch 1, para 54(1), (3), (6), subject to savings and transitional provisions in reg 6(1), (2), (4) in those Regulations.

    Para 5: sub-paras (1)(d), (2) substituted by SI 2004/1261, reg 4, Sch 1, para 54(1), (4), (5).

    Para 11: words omitted repealed by SI 2004/1261, reg 4, Sch 1, para 54(1), (8).

    Para 14: words in second pair of square brackets substituted by SI 2004/1261, reg 4, Sch 1, para 54(1), (9).

    References to the OFT, etc: as to the abolition of the office of the Director General of Fair Trading and the substitution of the original references to the Director (and related expressions), see the note preceding s 1 at **[1696]**.

PART 1
STATUTES

SCHEDULE 10
REGULATORS

Sections 54 and 66(5)

(Pt I repealed by the Enterprise Act 2002, s 278(2), Sch 26.)

PART II
THE PROHIBITIONS

2. ...

Gas

3.—(1) In consequence of the repeal by this Act of provisions of the Competition Act 1980, the functions transferred by subsection (3) of section 36A of the Gas Act 1986 (functions with respect to competition) are no longer exercisable by the Director General of Gas Supply.

(2)–(11) ...

Electricity

4.—(1) In consequence of the repeal by this Act of provisions of the Competition Act 1980, the functions transferred by subsection (3) of section 43 of the Electricity Act 1989 (functions with respect to competition) are no longer exercisable by the Director General of Electricity Supply.

(2)–(9) ...

Water

5.—(1) In consequence of the repeal by this Act of provisions of the Competition Act 1980, the functions exercisable by virtue of subsection (3) of section 31 of the Water Industry Act 1991 (functions of Director with respect to competition) are no longer exercisable by the Director General of Water Services.

(2)–(13) ...

Railways

6.—(1) In consequence of the repeal by this Act of provisions of the Competition Act 1980, the functions transferred by subsection (3) of section 67 of the Railways Act 1993 (respective functions of the Regulator and the Director etc) are no longer exercisable by [the Office of Rail Regulation].

(2)–(9) ...

[1781]–[1782]

NOTES

Para 2: repealed by the Communications Act 2003, s 406(7), Sch 19(1) and the Enterprise Act 2002, s 278(2), Sch 26.

Para 3: sub-paras (2)–(11) amend the Gas Act 1986, ss 4, 36A; repealed in part by the Utilities Act 2000, s 108, Sch 8, and the Enterprise Act 2002, s 278(2), Sch 26.

Para 4: sub-paras (2)–(9) amend the Electricity Act 1989, ss 3, 43; repealed in part by the Utilities Act 2000, s 108, Sch 8, and the Enterprise Act 2002, s 278(2), Sch 26.

Para 5: sub-paras (2)–(13) amend the Water Industry Act 1991, ss 2, 31; repealed in part by the Water Act 2003, s 101, Sch 7, Pt 2, para 32(1), (4)(a), Sch 9, Pt 3 and the Enterprise Act 2002, s 278(2), Sch 26.

Para 6: words in square brackets in sub-para (1) substituted by virtue of the Railways and Transport Safety Act 2003, s 16(4), (5), Sch 3, para 4; sub-paras (2)–(9) amend the Railways Act 1993, ss 4, 67; repealed in part by the Enterprise Act 2002, s 278(2), Sch 26.

Director General of Gas Supply and the Director General of Electricity Supply: the functions of the Director General of Gas Supply and the Director General of Electricity Supply are transferred to the Gas and Electricity Markets Authority by virtue of the Utilities Act 2000, s 3(2). References in paras 3 and 4 above to either of those Directors should be construed accordingly.

(Pt III applies to Northern Ireland only; Pt IV (minor and consequential amendments), Pt V (minor and consequential amendments in relation to Northern Ireland) outside the scope of this work; Sch 11 repealed by the Enterprise Act 2002, ss 247(j), 278(2), Sch 26; Sch 12 (minor and consequential amendments) outside the scope of this work.)

SCHEDULE 13
TRANSITIONAL PROVISIONS AND SAVINGS
Section 74(2)

PART I
STATUTES

PART I
GENERAL
Interpretation

1.—(1) In this Schedule—

"RPA" means the Resale Prices Act 1976;

"RTPA" means the Restrictive Trade Practices Act 1976;

"continuing proceedings" has the meaning given by paragraph 15;

"the Court" means the Restrictive Practices Court;

"Director" means the Director General of Fair Trading;

"document" includes information recorded in any form;

"enactment date" means the date on which this Act is passed;

"information" includes estimates and forecasts;

"interim period" means the period beginning on the enactment date and ending immediately before the starting date;

"prescribed" means prescribed by an order made by the Secretary of State;

"regulator" means any person mentioned in paragraphs (a) to (g) of paragraph 1 of Schedule 10 [and the Civil Aviation Authority];

"starting date" means the date on which section 2 comes into force;

"transitional period" means the transitional period provided for in Chapters III and IV of Part IV of this Schedule.

(2) Sections 30, 44, 51, 53, 55, 56, 57 and 59(3) and (4) and paragraph 12 of Schedule 9 ("the applied provisions") apply for the purposes of this Schedule as they apply for the purposes of Part I of this Act.

(3) Section 2(5) applies for the purposes of any provisions of this Schedule which are concerned with the operation of the Chapter I prohibition as it applies for the purposes of Part I of this Act.

(4) In relation to any of the matters in respect of which a regulator may exercise powers as a result of paragraph 35(1), the applied provisions are to have effect as if references to the Director included references to the regulator.

(5) The fact that to a limited extent the Chapter I prohibition does not apply to an agreement, because a transitional period is provided by virtue of this Schedule, does not require those provisions of the agreement in respect of which there is a transitional period to be disregarded when considering whether the agreement infringes the prohibition for other reasons.

General power to make transitional provision and savings

2.—(1) Nothing in this Schedule affects the power of the Secretary of State under section 75 to make transitional provisions or savings.

(2) An order under that section may modify any provision made by this Schedule.

Advice and information

3.—(1) The Director may publish advice and information explaining provisions of this Schedule to persons who are likely to be affected by them.

(2) Any advice or information published by the Director under this paragraph is to be published in such form and manner as he considers appropriate.

[1783]

NOTES

Para 1: in sub-para (1) words in square brackets in definition "regulator" inserted by the Transport Act 2000, s 97, Sch 8, Pt IV, para 16(1), (2).

The Director: the Enterprise Act 2002, s 2(1), at **[1860]**, provides that, as from the coming into force of that section (on 1 April 2003, see the Enterprise Act 2002 (Commencement No 2, Transitional and Transitory Provisions) Order 2003, SI 2003/766), the functions of the Director General of Fair Trading, his property, rights and liabilities are transferred to the Office of Fair Trading. Accordingly, (by virtue of s 2(2), (3) of the 2002 Act) the office of the Director is abolished, and any reference to the Director in any enactment, instrument or other document passed or made before the commencement of s 2(1) has effect as if it were a reference to the Office of Fair Trading. For transitional provisions in connection with the transfer, see s 276(1) of, and Sch 24, para 6 to, the 2002 Act.

PART II
DURING THE INTERIM PERIOD

Block exemptions

4.—(1)   The Secretary of State may, at any time during the interim period, make one or more orders for the purpose of providing block exemptions which are effective on the starting date.

(2)   An order under this paragraph has effect as if properly made under section 6.

Certain agreements to be non-notifiable agreements

5.   An agreement which—
  (a)   is made during the interim period, and
  (b)   satisfies the conditions set out in paragraphs (a), (c) and (d) of section 27A(1) of the RTPA,
is to be treated as a non-notifiable agreement for the purposes of RTPA.

Application of RTPA during the interim period

6.   In relation to agreements made during the interim period—
  (a)   the Director is no longer under the duty to take proceedings imposed by section 1(2)(c) of the RTPA but may continue to do so;
  (b)   section 21 of that Act has effect as if subsections (1) and (2) were omitted; and
  (c)   section 35(1) of that Act has effect as if the words "or within such further time as the Director may, upon application made within that time, allow" were omitted.

Guidance

7.—(1)   Sub-paragraphs (2) to (4) apply in relation to agreements made during the interim period.

(2)   An application may be made to the Director in anticipation of the coming into force of section 13 in accordance with directions given by the Director and such an application is to have effect on and after the starting date as if properly made under section 13.

(3)   The Director may, in response to such an application—
  (a)   give guidance in anticipation of the coming into force of section 2; or
  (b)   on and after the starting date, give guidance under section 15 as if the application had been properly made under section 13.

(4)   Any guidance so given is to have effect on and after the starting date as if properly given under section 15.

[1784]

NOTES
  The Director: the Enterprise Act 2002, s 2(1), at **[1860]**, provides that, as from the coming into force of that section (on 1 April 2003, see the Enterprise Act 2002 (Commencement No 2, Transitional and Transitory Provisions) Order 2003, SI 2003/766), the functions of the Director General of Fair Trading, his property, rights and liabilities are transferred to the Office of Fair Trading. Accordingly, (by virtue of s 2(2), (3) of the 2002 Act) the office of the Director is abolished, and any reference to the Director in any enactment, instrument or other document passed or made before the commencement of s 2(1) has effect as if it were a reference to the Office of Fair Trading. For transitional provisions in connection with the transfer, see s 276(1) of, and Sch 24, para 6 to, the 2002 Act.
  Note: references to the Director should be construed in accordance with the note preceding s 1 at **[1696]**.

PART III
ON THE STARTING DATE

Applications which fall

8.—(1)   Proceedings in respect of an application which is made to the Court under any of the provisions mentioned in sub-paragraph (2), but which is not determined before the starting date, cease on that date.

(2)   The provisions are—
  (a)   sections 2(2), 35(3), 37(1) and 40(1) of the RTPA and paragraph 5 of Schedule 4 to that Act;
  (b)   section 4(1) of the RTPA so far as the application relates to an order under section 2(2) of that Act; and
  (c)   section 25(2) of the RPA.

(3)   The power of the Court to make an order for costs in relation to any proceedings is not affected by anything in this paragraph or by the repeals made by section 1.

Orders and approvals which fall

9.—(1)   An order in force immediately before the starting date under—

(a)　section 2(2), 29(1), 30(1), 33(4), 35(3) or 37(1) of the RTPA; or
(b)　section 25(2) of the RPA,
ceases to have effect on that date.

(2)　An approval in force immediately before the starting date under section 32 of the RTPA ceases to have effect on that date.

[1785]

PART IV
ON AND AFTER THE STARTING DATE

CHAPTER I
GENERAL

Duty of Director to maintain register etc

10.—(1)　This paragraph applies even though the relevant provisions of the RTPA are repealed by this Act.

(2)　The Director is to continue on and after the starting date to be under the duty imposed by section 1(2)(a) of the RTPA to maintain a register in respect of agreements—
(a)　particulars of which are, on the starting date, entered or filed on the register;
(b)　which fall within sub-paragraph (4);
(c)　which immediately before the starting date are the subject of proceedings under the RTPA which do not cease on that date by virtue of this Schedule; or
(d)　in relation to which a court gives directions to the Director after the starting date in the course of proceedings in which a question arises as to whether an agreement was, before that date—
　(i)　one to which the RTPA applied;
　(ii)　subject to registration under that Act;
　(iii)　a non-notifiable agreement for the purposes of that Act.

(3)　The Director is to continue on and after the starting date to be under the duties imposed by section 1(2)(a) and (b) of the RTPA of compiling a register of agreements and entering or filing certain particulars in the register, but only in respect of agreements of a kind referred to in paragraph (b), (c) or (d) of sub-paragraph (2).

(4)　An agreement falls within this sub-paragraph if—
(a)　it is subject to registration under the RTPA but—
　(i)　is not a non-notifiable agreement within the meaning of section 27A of the RTPA, or
　(ii)　is not one to which paragraph 5 applies;
(b)　particulars of the agreement have been provided to the Director before the starting date; and
(c)　as at the starting date no entry or filing has been made in the register in respect of the agreement.

(5)　Sections 23 and 27 of the RTPA are to apply after the starting date in respect of the register subject to such modifications, if any, as may be prescribed.

(6)　In sub-paragraph (2)(d) "court" means—
(a)　the High Court;
(b)　the Court of Appeal;
(c)　the Court of Session;
(d)　the High Court or Court of Appeal in Northern Ireland; or
[(e)　the Supreme Court].

RTPA section 3 applications

11.—(1)　Even though section 3 of the RTPA is repealed by this Act, its provisions (and so far as necessary that Act) are to continue to apply, with such modifications (if any) as may be prescribed—
(a)　in relation to a continuing application under that section; or
(b)　so as to allow an application to be made under that section on or after the starting date in respect of a continuing application under section 1(3) of the RTPA.

(2)　"Continuing application" means an application made, but not determined, before the starting date.

RTPA section 26 applications

12.—(1)　Even though section 26 of the RTPA is repealed by this Act, its provisions (and so far as necessary that Act) are to continue to apply, with such modifications (if any) as may be prescribed, in relation to an application which is made under that section, but not determined, before the starting date.

(2)   If an application under section 26 is determined on or after the starting date, this Schedule has effect in relation to the agreement concerned as if the application had been determined immediately before that date.

Right to bring civil proceedings

13.—(1)   Even though section 35 of the RTPA is repealed by this Act, its provisions (and so far as necessary that Act) are to continue to apply in respect of a person who, immediately before the starting date, has a right by virtue of section 27ZA or 35(2) of that Act to bring civil proceedings in respect of an agreement (but only so far as that right relates to any period before the starting date or, where there are continuing proceedings, the determination of the proceedings).

(2)   Even though section 25 of the RPA is repealed by this Act, the provisions of that section (and so far as necessary that Act) are to continue to apply in respect of a person who, immediately before the starting date, has a right by virtue of subsection (3) of that section to bring civil proceedings (but only so far as that right relates to any period before the starting date or, where there are continuing proceedings, the determination of the proceedings).

CHAPTER II
CONTINUING PROCEEDINGS

The general rule

14.—(1)   The Chapter I prohibition does not apply to an agreement at any time when the agreement is the subject of continuing proceedings under the RTPA.

(2)   The Chapter I prohibition does not apply to an agreement relating to goods which are the subject of continuing proceedings under section 16 or 17 of the RPA to the extent to which the agreement consists of exempt provisions.

(3)   In sub-paragraph (2) "exempt provisions" means those provisions of the agreement which would, disregarding section 14 of the RPA, be—
(a)   void as a result of section 9(1) of the RPA; or
(b)   unlawful as a result of section 9(2) or II of the RPA.

(4)   If the Chapter I prohibition does not apply to an agreement because of this paragraph, the provisions of, or made under, the RTPA or the RPA are to continue to have effect in relation to the agreement.

(5)   The repeals made by section 1 do not affect—
(a)   continuing proceedings; or
(b)   proceedings of the kind referred to in paragraph 11 or 12 of this Schedule which are continuing after the starting date.

Meaning of "continuing proceedings"

15.—(1)   For the purposes of this Schedule "continuing proceedings" means proceedings in respect of an application made to the Court under the RTPA or the RPA, but not determined, before the starting date.

(2)   But proceedings under section 3 or 26 of the RTPA to which paragraph 11 or 12 applies are not continuing proceedings.

(3)   The question whether (for the purposes of Part III, or this Part, of this Schedule) an application has been determined is to be decided in accordance with sub-paragraphs (4) and (5).

(4)   If an appeal against the decision on the application is brought, the application is not determined until—
(a)   the appeal is disposed of or withdrawn; or
(b)   if as a result of the appeal the case is referred back to the Court—
     (i)   the expiry of the period within which an appeal ("the further appeal") in respect of the Court's decision on that reference could have been brought had this Act not been passed; or
     (ii)   if later, the date on which the further appeal is disposed of or withdrawn.

(5)   Otherwise, the application is not determined until the expiry of the period within which any party to the application would have been able to bring an appeal against the decision on the application had this Act not been passed.

RTPA section 4 proceedings

16.   Proceedings on an application for an order under section 4 of the RTPA are also continuing proceedings if—
(a)   leave to make the application is applied for before the starting date but the proceedings in respect of that application for leave are not determined before that date; or

(b)   leave to make an application for an order under that section is granted before the starting date but the application itself is not made before that date.

RPA section 16 or 17 proceedings

17.   Proceedings on an application for an order under section 16 or 17 of the RPA are also continuing proceedings if—
    (a)   leave to make the application is applied for before the starting date but the proceedings in respect of that application for leave are not determined before that date; or
    (b)   leave to make an application for an order under section 16 or 17 of the RPA is granted before the starting date, but the application itself is not made before that date.

Continuing proceedings which are discontinued

18.—(1)   On an application made jointly to the Court by all the parties to any continuing proceedings, the Court must, if it is satisfied that the parties wish it to do so, discontinue the proceedings.

(2)   If, on an application under sub-paragraph (1) or for any other reason, the Court orders the proceedings to be discontinued, this Schedule has effect (subject to paragraphs 21 and 22) from the date on which the proceedings are discontinued as if they had never been instituted.

CHAPTER III
THE TRANSITIONAL PERIOD

The general rule

19.—(1)   Except where this Chapter or Chapter IV provides otherwise, there is a transitional period, beginning on the starting date and lasting for one year, for any agreement made before the starting date.

(2)   The Chapter I prohibition does not apply to an agreement to the extent to which there is a transitional period for the agreement.

(3)   The Secretary of State may by regulations provide for sections 13 to 16 and Schedule 5 to apply with such modifications (if any) as may be specified in the regulations, in respect of applications to the Director about agreements for which there is a transitional period.

Cases for which there is no transitional period

20.—(1)   There is no transitional period for an agreement to the extent to which, immediately before the starting date, it is—
    (a)   void under section 2(1) or 35(1)(a) of the RTPA;
    (b)   the subject of an order under section 2(2) or 35(3) of the RTPA; or
    (c)   unlawful under section 1, 2 or 11 of the RPA or void under section 9 of that Act.

(2)   There is no transitional period for an agreement to the extent to which, before the starting date, a person has acted unlawfully for the purposes of section 27ZA(2) or (3) of the RTPA in respect of the agreement.

(3)   There is no transitional period for an agreement to which paragraph 25(4) applies.

(4)   There is no transitional period for—
    (a)   an agreement in respect of which there are continuing proceedings, or
    (b)   an agreement relating to goods in respect of which there are continuing proceedings,
to the extent to which the agreement is, when the proceedings are determined, void or unlawful.

Continuing proceedings under the RTPA

21.   In the case of an agreement which is the subject of continuing proceedings under the RTPA, the transitional period begins—
    (a)   if the proceedings are discontinued, on the date of discontinuance;
    (b)   otherwise, when the proceedings are determined.

Continuing proceedings under the RPA

22.—(1)   In the case of an agreement relating to goods which are the subject of continuing proceedings under the RPA, the transitional period for the exempt provisions of the agreement begins—
    (a)   if the proceedings are discontinued, on the date of discontinuance;
    (b)   otherwise, when the proceedings are determined.

(2)   In sub-paragraph (1) "exempt provisions" has the meaning given by paragraph 14(3).

Provisions not contrary to public interest

23.—(1) To the extent to which an agreement contains provisions which, immediately before the starting date, are provisions which the Court has found not to be contrary to the public interest, the transitional period lasts for five years.

(2) Sub-paragraph (1) is subject to paragraph 20(4).

(3) To the extent to which an agreement which on the starting date is the subject of continuing proceedings is, when the proceedings are determined, found by the Court not to be contrary to the public interest, the transitional period lasts for five years.

Goods

24.—(1) In the case of an agreement relating to goods which, immediately before the starting date, are exempt under section 14 of the RPA, there is a transitional period for the agreement to the extent to which it consists of exempt provisions.

(2) Sub-paragraph (1) is subject to paragraph 20(4).

(3) In the case of an agreement relating to goods—
    (a) which on the starting date are the subject of continuing proceedings, and
    (b) which, when the proceedings are determined, are found to be exempt under section 14 of the RPA,
there is a transitional period for the agreement, to the extent to which it consists of exempt provisions.

(4) In each case, the transitional period lasts for five years.

(5) In sub-paragraphs (1) and (3) "exempt provisions" means those provisions of the agreement which would, disregarding section 14 of the RPA, be—
    (a) void as a result of section 9(1) of the RPA; or
    (b) unlawful as a result of section 9(2) or 11 of the RPA.

Transitional period for certain agreements

25.—(1) This paragraph applies to agreements—
    (a) which are subject to registration under the RTPA but which—
        (i) are not non-notifiable agreements within the meaning of section 27A of the RTPA, or
        (ii) are not agreements to which paragraph 5 applies; and
    (b) in respect of which the time for furnishing relevant particulars as required by or under the RTPA expires on or after the starting date.

(2) "Relevant particulars" means—
    (a) particulars which are required to be furnished by virtue of section 24 of the RTPA; or
    (b) particulars of any variation of an agreement which are required to be furnished by virtue of sections 24 and 27 of the RTPA.

(3) There is a transitional period of one year for an agreement to which this paragraph applies if—
    (a) relevant particulars are furnished before the starting date; and
    (b) no person has acted unlawfully (for the purposes of section 27ZA(2) or (3) of the RTPA) in respect of the agreement.

(4) If relevant particulars are not furnished by the starting date, section 35(1)(a) of the RTPA does not apply in relation to the agreement (unless sub-paragraph (5) applies).

(5) This sub-paragraph applies if a person falling within section 27ZA(2) or (3) of the RTPA has acted unlawfully for the purposes of those subsections in respect of the agreement.

Special cases

26.—(1) In the case of an agreement in respect of which—
    (a) a direction under section 127(2) of the Financial Services Act 1986 ("the 1986 Act") is in force immediately before the starting date, or
    (b) a direction under section 194A(3) of the Broadcasting Act 1990 ("the 1990 Act") is in force immediately before the starting date,
the transitional period lasts for five years.

(2) To the extent to which an agreement is the subject of a declaration—
    (a) made by the Treasury under section 127(3) of the 1986 Act, and
    (b) in force immediately before the starting date,
the transitional period lasts for five years.

(3) Sub-paragraphs (1) and (2) do not affect the power of—
    (a) the Treasury to make a declaration under section 127(2) of the 1986 Act (as amended by Schedule 2 to this Act),

(b)   the Secretary of State to make a declaration under section 194A of the 1990 Act (as amended by Schedule 2 to this Act),

in respect of an agreement for which there is a transitional period.

CHAPTER IV
THE UTILITIES

General

27.   In this Chapter "the relevant period" means the period beginning with the starting date and ending immediately before the fifth anniversary of that date.

Electricity

28.—(1)   For an agreement to which, immediately before the starting date, the RTPA does not apply by virtue of a section 100 order, there is a transitional period—

(a)   beginning on the starting date; and

(b)   ending at the end of the relevant period.

(2)   For an agreement which is made at any time after the starting date and to which, had the RTPA not been repealed, that Act would not at the time at which the agreement is made have applied by virtue of a section 100 order, there is a transitional period—

(a)   beginning on the date on which the agreement is made; and

(b)   ending at the end of the relevant period.

(3)   For an agreement (whether made before or after the starting date) which, during the relevant period, is varied at any time in such a way that it becomes an agreement which, had the RTPA not been repealed, would at that time have been one to which that Act did not apply by virtue of a section 100 order, there is a transitional period—

(a)   beginning on the date on which the variation is made; and

(b)   ending at the end of the relevant period.

(4)   If an agreement for which there is a transitional period as a result of sub-paragraph (1), (2) or (3) is varied during the relevant period, the transitional period for the agreement continues if, had the RTPA not been repealed, the agreement would have continued to be one to which that Act did not apply by virtue of a section 100 order.

(5)   But if an agreement for which there is a transitional period as a result of sub-paragraph (1), (2) or (3) ceases to be one to which, had it not been repealed, the RTPA would not have applied by virtue of a section 100 order, the transitional period ends on the date on which the agreement so ceases.

(6)   Sub-paragraph (3) is subject to paragraph 20.

(7)   In this paragraph and paragraph 29—

"section 100 order" means an order made under section 100 of the Electricity Act 1989; and expressions which are also used in Part I of the Electricity Act 1989 have the same meaning as in that Part.

Electricity: power to make transitional orders

29.—(1)   There is a transitional period for an agreement (whether made before or after the starting date) relating to the generation, transmission or supply of electricity which—

(a)   is specified, or is of a description specified, in an order ("a transitional order") made by the Secretary of State (whether before or after the making of the agreement but before the end of the relevant period); and

(b)   satisfies such conditions as may be specified in the order.

(2)   A transitional order may make provision as to when the transitional period in respect of such an agreement is to start or to be deemed to have started.

(3)   The transitional period for such an agreement ends at the end of the relevant period.

(4)   But if the agreement—

(a)   ceases to be one to which a transitional order applies, or

(b)   ceases to satisfy one or more of the conditions specified in the transitional order,

the transitional period ends on the date on which the agreement so ceases.

(5)   Before making a transitional order, the Secretary of State must consult [the Gas and Electricity Markets Authority].

(6)   The conditions specified in a transitional order may include conditions which refer any matter to the Secretary of State for determination after such consultation as may be so specified.

(7)   In the application of this paragraph to Northern Ireland, the reference in sub-paragraph (5) to [the Gas and Electricity Markets Authority] is to be read as a reference to the Director General of Electricity Supply for Northern Ireland.

Gas

30.—(1) For an agreement to which, immediately before the starting date, the RTPA does not apply by virtue of section 62 or a section 62 order, there is a transitional period—

(a) beginning on the starting date; and

(b) ending at the end of the relevant period.

(2) For an agreement which is made at any time after the starting date and to which, had the RTPA not been repealed, that Act would not at the time at which the agreement is made have applied by virtue of section 62 or a section 62 order, there is a transitional period—

(a) beginning on the date on which the agreement is made; and

(b) ending at the end of the relevant period.

(3) For an agreement (whether made before or after the starting date) which, during the relevant period, is varied at any time in such a way that it becomes an agreement which, had the RTPA not been repealed, would at that time have been one to which that Act did not apply by virtue of section 62 or a section 62 order, there is a transitional period—

(a) beginning on the date on which the variation is made; and

(b) ending at the end of the relevant period.

(4) If an agreement for which there is a transitional period as a result of sub-paragraph (1), (2) or (3) is varied during the relevant period, the transitional period for the agreement continues if, had the RTPA not been repealed, the agreement would have continued to be one to which that Act did not apply by virtue of section 62 or a section 62 order.

(5) But if an agreement for which there is a transitional period as a result of sub-paragraph (1), (2) or (3) ceases to be one to which, had it not been repealed, the RTPA would not have applied by virtue of section 62 or a section 62 order, the transitional period ends on the date on which the agreement so ceases.

(6) Sub-paragraph (3) also applies in relation to a modification which is treated as an agreement made on or after 28th November 1985 by virtue of section 62(4).

(7) Sub-paragraph (3) is subject to paragraph 20.

(8) In this paragraph and paragraph 31—

"section 62" means section 62 of the Gas Act 1986;

"section 62 order" means an order made under section 62.

Gas: power to make transitional orders

31.—(1) There is a transitional period for an agreement of a description falling within section 62(2)(a) and (b) or section 62(2A)(a) and (b) which—

(a) is specified, or is of a description specified, in an order ("a transitional order") made by the Secretary of State (whether before or after the making of the agreement but before the end of the relevant period); and

(b) satisfies such conditions as may be specified in the order.

(2) A transitional order may make provision as to when the transitional period in respect of such an agreement is to start or to be deemed to have started.

(3) The transitional period for such an agreement ends at the end of the relevant period.

(4) But if the agreement—

(a) ceases to be one to which a transitional order applies, or

(b) ceases to satisfy one or more of the conditions specified in the transitional order,

the transitional period ends on the date when the agreement so ceases.

(5) Before making a transitional order, the Secretary of State must consult [the Gas and Electricity Markets Authority] and the Director.

(6) The conditions specified in a transitional order may include—

(a) conditions which are to be satisfied in relation to a time before the coming into force of this paragraph;

(b) conditions which refer any matter (which may be the general question whether the Chapter I prohibition should apply to a particular agreement) to the Secretary of State, the Director or [the Gas and Electricity Markets Authority] for determination after such consultation as may be so specified.

Gas: Northern Ireland

32.—(1) For an agreement to which, immediately before the starting date, the RTPA does not apply by virtue of an Article 41 order, there is a transitional period—

(a) beginning on the starting date; and

(b) ending at the end of the relevant period.

(2)   For an agreement which is made at any time after the starting date and to which, had the RTPA not been repealed, that Act would not at the time at which the agreement is made have applied by virtue of an Article 41 order, there is a transitional period—
(a)   beginning on the date on which the agreement is made; and
(b)   ending at the end of the relevant period.

(3)   For an agreement (whether made before or after the starting date) which, during the relevant period, is varied at any time in such a way that it becomes an agreement which, had the RTPA not been repealed, would at that time have been one to which that Act did not apply by virtue of an Article 41 order, there is a transitional period—
(a)   beginning on the date on which the variation is made; and
(b)   ending at the end of the relevant period.

(4)   If an agreement for which there is a transitional period as a result of sub-paragraph (1), (2) or (3) is varied during the relevant period, the transitional period for the agreement continues if, had the RTPA not been repealed, the agreement would have continued to be one to which that Act did not apply by virtue of an Article 41 order.

(5)   But if an agreement for which there is a transitional period as a result of sub-paragraph (1), (2) or (3) ceases to be one to which, had it not been repealed, the RTPA would not have applied by virtue of an Article 41 order, the transitional period ends on the date on which the agreement so ceases.

(6)   Sub-paragraph (3) is subject to paragraph 20.

(7)   In this paragraph and paragraph 33—
"Article 41 order" means an order under Article 41 of the Gas (Northern Ireland) Order 1996;
"Department" means the Department of Economic Development.

Gas: Northern Ireland—power to make transitional orders

33.—(1)   There is a transitional period for an agreement of a description falling within Article 41(1) which—
(a)   is specified, or is of a description specified, in an order ("a transitional order") made by the Department (whether before or after the making of the agreement but before the end of the relevant period); and
(b)   satisfies such conditions as may be specified in the order.

(2)   A transitional order may make provision as to when the transitional period in respect of such an agreement is to start or to be deemed to have started.

(3)   The transitional period for such an agreement ends at the end of the relevant period.

(4)   But if the agreement—
(a)   ceases to be one to which a transitional order applies, or
(b)   ceases to satisfy one or more of the conditions specified in the transitional order,
the transitional period ends on the date when the agreement so ceases.

(5)   Before making a transitional order, the Department must consult the Director General of Gas for Northern Ireland and the Director.

(6)   The conditions specified in a transitional order may include conditions which refer any matter (which may be the general question whether the Chapter I prohibition should apply to a particular agreement) to the Department for determination after such consultation as may be so specified.

Railways

34.—(1)   In this paragraph—
"section 131" means section 131 of the Railways Act 1993 ("the 1993 Act");
"section 131 agreement" means an agreement—
(a)   to which the RTPA does not apply immediately before the starting date by virtue of section 131(1); or
(b)   in respect of which a direction under section 131(3) is in force immediately before that date;
"non-exempt agreement" means an agreement relating to the provision of railway services (whether made before or after the starting date) which is not a section 131 agreement; and
"railway services" has the meaning given by section 82 of the 1993 Act.

(2)   For a section 131 agreement there is a transitional period of five years.

(3)   There is a transitional period for a non-exempt agreement to the extent to which the agreement is at any time before the end of the relevant period required or approved—
(a)   by the Secretary of State or [the Office of Rail Regulation] in pursuance of any function assigned or transferred to him under or by virtue of any provision of the 1993 Act;
(b)   by or under any agreement the making of which is required or approved by the Secretary of State or [the Office of Rail Regulation] in the exercise of any such function; or

PART I
STATUTES

(c)   by or under a licence granted under Part I of the 1993 Act.

(4)   The transitional period conferred by sub-paragraph (3)—
    (a)   is to be taken to have begun on the starting date; and
    (b)   ends at the end of the relevant period.

(5)   Sub-paragraph (3) is subject to paragraph 20.

(6)   Any variation of a section 131 agreement on or after the starting date is to be treated, for the purposes of this paragraph, as a separate non-exempt agreement.

The regulators

35.—(1)   Subject to sub-paragraph (3), each of the regulators may exercise, in respect of sectoral matters and concurrently with the Director, the functions of the Director under paragraph 3, 7, 19(3), 36, 37, 38 or 39.

(2)   In sub-paragraph (1) "sectoral matters" means—
    (a)   ...
    (b)   in the case of [the Gas and Electricity Markets Authority], the matters referred to in section 36A(3) and (4) of the Gas Act 1986;
    (c)   in the case of [the Gas and Electricity Markets Authority], the matters referred to in section 43(3) of the Electricity Act 1989;
    (d)   in the case of the Director General of Electricity Supply for Northern Ireland, the matters referred to in Article 46(3) of the Electricity (Northern Ireland) Order 1992;
    (e)   in the case of the [Water Services Regulation Authority], the matters referred to in section 31(3) of the Water Industry Act 1991;
    (f)   in the case of [the Office of Rail Regulation], the matters referred to in section 67(3) of the Railways Act 1993;
    (g)   in the case of the Director General of Gas for Northern Ireland, the matters referred to in Article 23(3) of the Gas (Northern Ireland) Order 1996;
    [(h)   in the case of the Civil Aviation Authority, the supply of air traffic services within the meaning given by section 98 of the Transport Act 2000.]

(3)   The power to give directions in paragraph 7(2) is exercisable by the Director only but if the Director is preparing directions which relate to a matter in respect of which a regulator exercises concurrent jurisdiction, he must consult that regulator.

(4)   Consultations conducted by the Director before the enactment date, with a view to preparing directions which have effect on or after that date, are to be taken to satisfy sub-paragraph (3).

(5)   References to enactments in sub-paragraph (2) are to the enactments as amended by or under this Act.

CHAPTER V
EXTENDING THE TRANSITIONAL PERIOD

36.—(1)   A party to an agreement for which there is a transitional period may apply to the Director, not less than three months before the end of the period, for the period to be extended.

(2)   The Director may (on his own initiative or on an application under sub-paragraph (1))—
    (a)   extend a one-year transitional period by not more than twelve months;
    (b)   extend a transitional period of any period other than one year by not more than six months.

(3)   An application under sub-paragraph (1) must—
    (a)   be in such form as may be specified; and
    (b)   include such documents and information as may be specified.

(4)   If the Director extends the transitional period under this paragraph, he must give notice in such form, and to such persons, as may be specified.

(5)   The Director may not extend a transitional period more than once.

(6)   In this paragraph—
    "person" has the same meaning as in Part I; and
    "specified" means specified in rules made by the Director under section 51.

CHAPTER VI
TERMINATING THE TRANSITIONAL PERIOD

General

37.—(1)   Subject to sub-paragraph (2), the Director may by a direction in writing terminate the transitional period for an agreement, but only in accordance with paragraph 38.

(2)   The Director may not terminate the transitional period, nor exercise any of the powers in paragraph 38, in respect of an agreement which is excluded from the Chapter I prohibition by virtue

of any of the provisions of Part I of this Act other than paragraph 1 of Schedule 1 or paragraph 2 or 9 of Schedule 3 [or the Competition Act 1998 (Land and Vertical Agreements Exclusion) Order 2000].

Circumstances in which the Director may terminate the transitional period

38.—(1)   If the Director is considering whether to give a direction under paragraph 37 ("a direction"), he may in writing require any party to the agreement concerned to give him such information in connection with that agreement as he may require.

(2)   If at the end of such period as may be specified in rules made under section 51, a person has failed, without reasonable excuse, to comply with a requirement imposed under sub-paragraph (1), the Director may give a direction.

(3)   The Director may also give a direction if he considers—
(a)   that the agreement would, but for the transitional period or a relevant exclusion, infringe the Chapter I prohibition; and
(b)   that he would not be likely to grant the agreement an unconditional individual exemption.

(4)   For the purposes of sub-paragraph (3) an individual exemption is unconditional if no conditions or obligations are imposed in respect of it under section 4(3)(a).

(5)   In this paragraph—
"person" has the same meaning as in Part I;
"relevant exclusion" means an exclusion under paragraph 1 of Schedule 1 or paragraph 2 or 9 of Schedule 3 [or the Competition Act 1998 (Land and Vertical Agreements Exclusion) Order 2000].

Procedural requirements on giving a paragraph 37 direction

39.—(1)   The Director must specify in a direction under paragraph 37 ("a direction") the date on which it is to have effect (which must not be less than 28 days after the direction is given).

(2)   Copies of the direction must be given to—
(a)   each of the parties concerned, and
(b)   the Secretary of State,
not less than 28 days before the date on which the direction is to have effect.

(3)   In relation to an agreement to which a direction applies, the transitional period (if it has not already ended) ends on the date specified in the direction unless, before that date, the direction is revoked by the Director or the Secretary of State.

(4)   If a direction is revoked, the Director may give a further direction in respect of the same agreement only if he is satisfied that there has been a material change of circumstance since the revocation.

(5)   If, as a result of paragraph 24(1) or (3), there is a transitional period in respect of provisions of an agreement relating to goods—
(a)   which immediately before the starting date are exempt under section 14 of the RPA, or
(b)   which, when continuing proceedings are determined, are found to be exempt under section 14 of the RPA,
the period is not affected by paragraph 37 or 38.

[1786]

NOTES

Commencement: 9 November 1998 (para 35); 11 January 1999 (paras 10(5), 19(3), paras 11, 12(1) certain purposes); 1 March 2000 (paras 10(1)–(4), (6), 12(2), 13–18, 19(1), (2), 20–34, 36–39, para 12(1) remaining purposes); to be appointed (otherwise).

Para 10: sub-para (6)(e) substituted by the Constitutional Reform Act 2005, s 40(4), Sch 9, Pt 1, para 65(1), (5).

Para 29: words in square brackets in sub-paras (5), (7) substituted by virtue of the Utilities Act 2000, s 3(2).

Para 31: words in square brackets in sub-paras (5), (6)(b) substituted by virtue of the Utilities Act 2000, s 3(2).

Para 34: in sub-para (3) words in square brackets substituted by virtue of the Railways and Transport Safety Act 2003, s 16(4), (5), Sch 3, para 4.

Para 35: sub-para (a) repealed by the Communications Act 2003, s 406(7), Sch 19(1); words in square brackets in sub-para (2)(b), (c) substituted by virtue of the Utilities Act 2000, s 3(2)(2); words in square brackets in sub-para (2)(e) substituted by the Water Act 2003, s 101(1), Sch 7, Pt 2, para 32(1), (5); words in square brackets in sub-para (2)(f) substituted by virtue of the Railways and Transport Safety Act 2003, s 16(4), (5), Sch 3, para 4; sub-para (2)(h) added by the Transport Act 2000, s 97, Sch 8, Pt IV, para 16(1), (3).

Para 37: words in square brackets in sub-para (2) added by the Competition Act 1998 (Transitional, Consequential and Supplemental Provisions) Order 2000, SI 2000/311, art 2.

Para 38: words in square brackets in sub-para (5) inserted by the Competition Act 1998 (Consequential and Supplemental Provisions) Order 2000, SI 2000/2031, art 2.

The Director: the Enterprise Act 2002, s 2(1), at **[1860]**, provides that, as from the coming into force of that section (on 1 April 2003, see the Enterprise Act 2002 (Commencement No 2, Transitional and Transitory Provisions) Order 2003, SI 2003/766), the functions of the Director General of Fair Trading, his property, rights and liabilities are transferred to the Office of Fair Trading. Accordingly, (by virtue of s 2(2), (3) of the 2002 Act) the office of the Director is abolished, and any reference to the Director in any enactment, instrument or other document passed or made before the commencement of s 2(1) has effect as if it were a reference to the Office of Fair Trading. For transitional provisions in connection with the transfer, see s 276(1) of, and Sch 24, para 6 to, the 2002 Act.

Financial Services Act 1986, s 127: repealed.

Regulations: the Competition Act 1998 (Appealable Decisions and Revocation of Notification of Excluded Agreements) Regulations 2004, SI 2004/1078.

PART V
THE FAIR TRADING ACT 1973

References to the Monopolies and Mergers Commission

40.—(1) If, on the date on which the repeal by this Act of a provision mentioned in sub-paragraph (2) comes into force, the Monopolies and Mergers Commission has not completed a reference which was made to it before that date, continued consideration of the reference may include consideration of a question which could not have been considered if the provision had not been repealed.

(2) The provisions are—

    (a)   sections 10(2), 54(5) and 78(3) and paragraph 3(1) and (2) of Schedule 8 to the Fair Trading Act 1973 (c 41);

    (b)   section 11(8)(b) of the Competition Act 1980 (c 21);

    (c)   section 14(2) of the Telecommunications Act 1984 (c 12);

    (d)   section 45(3) of the Airports Act 1986 (c 31);

    (e)   section 25(2) of the Gas Act 1986 (c 44);

    (f)   section 13(2) of the Electricity Act 1989 (c 29);

    (g)   section 15(2) of the Water Industry Act 1991 (c 56);

    (h)   article 16(2) of the Electricity (Northern Ireland) Order 1992;

    (i)   section 14(2) of the Railways Act 1993 (c 43);

    (j)   article 36(3) of the Airports (Northern Ireland) Order 1994;

    (k)   article 16(2) of the Gas (Northern Ireland) Order 1996.

Orders under Schedule 8

41.—(1) In this paragraph—

"the 1973 Act" means the Fair Trading Act 1973;

"agreement" means an agreement entered into before the date on which the repeal of the limiting provisions comes into force;

"the order" means an order under section 56 or 73 of the 1973 Act;

"the limiting provisions" means sub-paragraph (1) or (2) of paragraph 3 of Schedule 8 to the 1973 Act (limit on power to make orders under paragraph 1 or 2 of that Schedule) and includes any provision of the order included because of either of those sub-paragraphs; and

"transitional period" means the period which—

    (a)   begins on the day on which the repeal of the limiting provisions comes into force; and

    (b)   ends on the first anniversary of the starting date.

(2) Sub-paragraph (3) applies to any agreement to the extent to which it would have been unlawful (in accordance with the provisions of the order) but for the limiting provisions.

(3) As from the end of the transitional period, the order is to have effect in relation to the agreement as if the limiting provisions had never had effect.

Part III of the Act

42.—(1) The repeals made by section 1 do not affect any proceedings in respect of an application which is made to the Court under Part III of the Fair Trading Act 1973, but is not determined, before the starting date.

(2) The question whether (for the purposes of sub-paragraph (1)) an application has been determined is to be decided in accordance with sub-paragraphs (3) and (4).

(3) If an appeal against the decision on the application is brought, the application is not determined until—

    (a)   the appeal is disposed of or withdrawn; or

    (b)   if as a result of the appeal the case is referred back to the Court—

        (i)   the expiry of the period within which an appeal ("the further appeal") in respect of the Court's decision on that reference could have been brought had this Act not been passed; or

        (ii)   if later, the date on which the further appeal is disposed of or withdrawn.

(4) Otherwise, the application is not determined until the expiry of the period within which any party to the application would have been able to bring an appeal against the decision on the application had this Act not been passed.

(5) Any amendment made by Schedule 12 to this Act which substitutes references to a relevant Court for references to the Court is not to affect proceedings of the kind referred to in sub-paragraph (1).

[1787]

PART VI
THE COMPETITION ACT 1980

Undertakings

43.—(1) Subject to sub-paragraph (2), an undertaking accepted by the Director under section 4 or 9 of the Competition Act 1980 ceases to have effect on the coming into force of the repeal by this Act of that section.

(2) If the undertaking relates to an agreement which on the starting date is the subject of continuing proceedings, the undertaking continues to have effect for the purposes of section 29 of the Competition Act 1980 until the proceedings are determined.

Application of sections 25 and 26

44. The repeals made by section 1 do not affect—
    (a) the operation of section 25 of the Competition Act 1980 in relation to an application under section 1(3) of the RTPA which is made before the starting date;
    (b) an application under section 26 of the Competition Act 1980 which is made before the starting date.

[1788]

NOTES
    The Director: the Enterprise Act 2002, s 2(1), at **[1860]**, provides that, as from the coming into force of that section (on 1 April 2003, see the Enterprise Act 2002 (Commencement No 2, Transitional and Transitory Provisions) Order 2003, SI 2003/766), the functions of the Director General of Fair Trading, his property, rights and liabilities are transferred to the Office of Fair Trading. Accordingly, (by virtue of s 2(2), (3) of the 2002 Act) the office of the Director is abolished, and any reference to the Director in any enactment, instrument or other document passed or made before the commencement of s 2(1) has effect as if it were a reference to the Office of Fair Trading. For transitional provisions in connection with the transfer, see s 276(1) of, and Sch 24, para 6 to, the 2002 Act.

PART VII
MISCELLANEOUS

Disclosure of information

45.—(1) Section 55 of this Act applies in relation to information which, immediately before the starting date, is subject to section 41 of the RTPA as it applies in relation to information obtained under or as a result of Part I.

(2) But section 55 does not apply to any disclosure of information of the kind referred to in sub-paragraph (1) if the disclosure is made—
    (a) for the purpose of facilitating the performance of functions of a designated person under the Control of Misleading Advertisements Regulations 1988; or
    (b) for the purposes of any proceedings before the Court or of any other legal proceedings under the RTPA or the Fair Trading Act 1973 or the Control of Misleading Advertisements Regulations 1988.

(3) Section 56 applies in relation to information of the kind referred to in sub-paragraph (1) if particulars containing the information have been entered or filed on the special section of the register maintained by the Director under, or as a result of, section 27 of the RTPA or paragraph 10 of this Schedule.

(4) Section 55 has effect, in relation to the matters as to which section 41(2) of the RTPA had effect, as if it contained a provision similar to section 41(2).

The Court

46. If it appears to the Lord Chancellor that a person who ceases to be a non-judicial member of the Court as a result of this Act should receive compensation for loss of office, he may pay to him out of moneys provided by Parliament such sum as he may with the approval of the Treasury determine.

[1789]

NOTES
The Director: the Enterprise Act 2002, s 2(1), at **[1860]**, provides that, as from the coming into force of that section (on 1 April 2003, see the Enterprise Act 2002 (Commencement No 2, Transitional and Transitory Provisions) Order 2003, SI 2003/766), the functions of the Director General of Fair Trading, his property, rights and liabilities are transferred to the Office of Fair Trading. Accordingly, (by virtue of s 2(2), (3) of the 2002 Act) the office of the Director is abolished, and any reference to the Director in any enactment, instrument or other document passed or made before the commencement of s 2(1) has effect as if it were a reference to the Office of Fair Trading. For transitional provisions in connection with the transfer, see s 276(1) of, and Sch 24, para 6 to, the 2002 Act.

(Sch 14 contains repeals and revocations.)

CONTRACTS (RIGHTS OF THIRD PARTIES) ACT 1999

(1999 c 31)

ARRANGEMENT OF SECTIONS

An Act to make provision for the enforcement of contractual terms by third parties

[11 November 1999]

1   Right of third party to enforce contractual term

(1)   Subject to the provisions of this Act, a person who is not a party to a contract (a "third party") may in his own right enforce a term of the contract if—
    (a)   the contract expressly provides that he may, or
    (b)   subject to subsection (2), the term purports to confer a benefit on him.

(2)   Subsection (1)(b) does not apply if on a proper construction of the contract it appears that the parties did not intend the term to be enforceable by the third party.

(3)   The third party must be expressly identified in the contract by name, as a member of a class or as answering a particular description but need not be in existence when the contract is entered into.

(4)   This section does not confer a right on a third party to enforce a term of a contract otherwise than subject to and in accordance with any other relevant terms of the contract.

(5)   For the purpose of exercising his right to enforce a term of the contract, there shall be available to the third party any remedy that would have been available to him in an action for breach of contract if he had been a party to the contract (and the rules relating to damages, injunctions, specific performance and other relief shall apply accordingly).

(6)   Where a term of a contract excludes or limits liability in relation to any matter references in this Act to the third party enforcing the term shall be construed as references to his availing himself of the exclusion or limitation.

(7)   In this Act, in relation to a term of a contract which is enforceable by a third party—
    "the promisor" means the party to the contract against whom the term is enforceable by the third party, and
    "the promisee" means the party to the contract by whom the term is enforceable against the promisor.

[1790]

2   Variation and rescission of contract

(1)   Subject to the provisions of this section, where a third party has a right under section 1 to enforce a term of the contract, the parties to the contract may not, by agreement, rescind the contract, or vary it in such a way as to extinguish or alter his entitlement under that right, without his consent if—

(a)   the third party has communicated his assent to the term to the promisor,

(b)   the promisor is aware that the third party has relied on the term, or

(c)   the promisor can reasonably be expected to have foreseen that the third party would rely on the term and the third party has in fact relied on it.

(2)   The assent referred to in subsection (1)(a)—

(a)   may be by words or conduct, and

(b)   if sent to the promisor by post or other means, shall not be regarded as communicated to the promisor until received by him.

(3)   Subsection (1) is subject to any express term of the contract under which—

(a)   the parties to the contract may by agreement rescind or vary the contract without the consent of the third party, or

(b)   the consent of the third party is required in circumstances specified in the contract instead of those set out in subsection (1)(a) to (c).

(4)   Where the consent of a third party is required under subsection (1) or (3), the court or arbitral tribunal may, on the application of the parties to the contract, dispense with his consent if satisfied—

(a)   that his consent cannot be obtained because his whereabouts cannot reasonably be ascertained, or

(b)   that he is mentally incapable of giving his consent.

(5)   The court or arbitral tribunal may, on the application of the parties to a contract, dispense with any consent that may be required under subsection (1)(c) if satisfied that it cannot reasonably be ascertained whether or not the third party has in fact relied on the term.

(6)   If the court or arbitral tribunal dispenses with a third party's consent, it may impose such conditions as it thinks fit, including a condition requiring the payment of compensation to the third party.

(7)   The jurisdiction conferred on the court by subsections (4) to (6) is exercisable by both the High Court and a county court.

[1791]

3   Defences etc available to promisor

(1)   Subsections (2) to (5) apply where, in reliance on section 1, proceedings for the enforcement of a term of a contract are brought by a third party.

(2)   The promisor shall have available to him by way of defence or setoff any matter that—

(a)   arises from or in connection with the contract and is relevant to the term, and

(b)   would have been available to him by way of defence or setoff if the proceedings had been brought by the promisee.

(3)   The promisor shall also have available to him by way of defence or setoff any matter if—

(a)   an express term of the contract provides for it to be available to him in proceedings brought by the third party, and

(b)   it would have been available to him by way of defence or setoff if the proceedings had been brought by the promisee.

(4)   The promisor shall also have available to him—

(a)   by way of defence or setoff any matter, and

(b)   by way of counterclaim any matter not arising from the contract,

that would have been available to him by way of defence or setoff or, as the case may be, by way of counterclaim against the third party if the third party had been a party to the contract.

(5)   Subsections (2) and (4) are subject to any express term of the contract as to the matters that are not to be available to the promisor by way of defence, setoff or counterclaim.

(6)   Where in any proceedings brought against him a third party seeks in reliance on section 1 to enforce a term of a contract (including, in particular, a term purporting to exclude or limit liability), he may not do so if he could not have done so (whether by reason of any particular circumstances relating to him or otherwise) had he been a party to the contract.

[1792]

4   Enforcement of contract by promisee

Section 1 does not affect any right of the promisee to enforce any term of the contract.

[1793]

5   Protection of party promisor from double liability

Where under section 1 a term of a contract is enforceable by a third party, and the promisee has recovered from the promisor a sum in respect of—

(a)   the third party's loss in respect of the term, or

(b)   the expense to the promisee of making good to the third party the default of the promisor, then, in any proceedings brought in reliance on that section by the third party, the court or arbitral tribunal shall reduce any award to the third party to such extent as it thinks appropriate to take account of the sum recovered by the promisee.

[1794]

6 Exceptions

(1) Section 1 confers no rights on a third party in the case of a contract on a bill of exchange, promissory note or other negotiable instrument.

(2) Section 1 confers no rights on a third party in the case of any contract binding on a company and its members under [section 33 of the Companies Act 2006 (effect of company's constitution)].

[(2A) Section 1 confers no rights on a third party in the case of any incorporation document of a limited liability partnership [or any agreement (express or implied) between the members of a limited liability partnership, or between a limited liability partnership and its members, that determines the mutual rights and duties of the members and their rights and duties in relation to the limited liability partnership].]

(3) Section 1 confers no right on a third party to enforce—
   (a) any term of a contract of employment against an employee,
   (b) any term of a worker's contract against a worker (including a home worker), or
   (c) any term of a relevant contract against an agency worker.

(4) In subsection (3)—
   (a) "contract of employment", "employee", "worker's contract", and "worker" have the meaning given by section 54 of the National Minimum Wage Act 1998,
   (b) "home worker" has the meaning given by section 35(2) of that Act,
   (c) "agency worker" has the same meaning as in section 34(1) of that Act, and
   (d) "relevant contract" means a contract entered into, in a case where section 34 of that Act applies, by the agency worker as respects work falling within subsection (1)(a) of that section.

(5) Section 1 confers no rights on a third party in the case of—
   (a) a contract for the carriage of goods by sea, or
   (b) a contract for the carriage of goods by rail or road, or for the carriage of cargo by air, which is subject to the rules of the appropriate international transport convention,

except that a third party may in reliance on that section avail himself of an exclusion or limitation of liability in such a contract.

(6) In subsection (5) "contract for the carriage of goods by sea" means a contract of carriage—
   (a) contained in or evidenced by a bill of lading, sea waybill or a corresponding electronic transaction, or
   (b) under or for the purposes of which there is given an undertaking which is contained in a ship's delivery order or a corresponding electronic transaction.

(7) For the purposes of subsection (6)—
   (a) "bill of lading", "sea waybill" and "ship's delivery order" have the same meaning as in the Carriage of Goods by Sea Act 1992, and
   (b) a corresponding electronic transaction is a transaction within section 1(5) of that Act which corresponds to the issue, indorsement, delivery or transfer of a bill of lading, sea waybill or ship's delivery order.

(8) In subsection (5) "the appropriate international transport convention" means—
   (a) in relation to a contract for the carriage of goods by rail, the Convention which has the force of law in the United Kingdom under [regulation 3 of the Railways (Convention on International Carriage by Rail) Regulations 2005],
   (b) in relation to a contract for the carriage of goods by road, the Convention which has the force of law in the United Kingdom under section 1 of the Carriage of Goods by Road Act 1965, and
   (c) in relation to a contract for the carriage of cargo by air—
      (i) the Convention which has the force of law in the United Kingdom under section 1 of the Carriage by Air Act 1961, or
      (ii) the Convention which has the force of law under section 1 of the Carriage by Air (Supplementary Provisions) Act 1962, or
      (iii) either of the amended Conventions set out in Part B of Schedule 2 or 3 to the Carriage by Air Acts (Application of Provisions) Order 1967.

[1795]

NOTES

Sub-s (2): words in square brackets substituted by the Companies Act 2006 (Consequential Amendments, Transitional Provisions and Savings) Order 2009, SI 2009/1941, art 2(1), Sch 1, para 179(1), (2)(a).

Sub-s (2A): inserted by the Limited Liability Partnerships Regulations 2001, SI 2001/1090, reg 9(1), Sch 5, para 20; words in square brackets substituted by SI 2009/1941, art 2(1), Sch 1, para 179(1), (2)(b).

Sub-s (8): words in square brackets in para (a) substituted by the Railways (Convention on International Carriage by Rail) Regulations 2005, SI 2005/2092, reg 9(2), Sch 3, para 3.

7   Supplementary provisions relating to third party

(1)   Section 1 does not affect any right or remedy of a third party that exists or is available apart from this Act.

(2)   Section 2(2) of the Unfair Contract Terms Act 1977 (restriction on exclusion etc of liability for negligence) shall not apply where the negligence consists of the breach of an obligation arising from a term of a contract and the person seeking to enforce it is a third party acting in reliance on section 1.

(3)   In sections 5 and 8 of the Limitation Act 1980 the references to an action founded on a simple contract and an action upon a specialty shall respectively include references to an action brought in reliance on section 1 relating to a simple contract and an action brought in reliance on that section relating to a specialty.

(4)   A third party shall not, by virtue of section 1(5) or 3(4) or (6), be treated as a party to the contract for the purposes of any other Act (or any instrument made under any other Act).

                                                      [1796]

8   Arbitration provisions

(1)   Where—

    (a)   a right under section 1 to enforce a term ("the substantive term") is subject to a term providing for the submission of disputes to arbitration ("the arbitration agreement"), and

    (b)   the arbitration agreement is an agreement in writing for the purposes of Part I of the Arbitration Act 1996,

the third party shall be treated for the purposes of that Act as a party to the arbitration agreement as regards disputes between himself and the promisor relating to the enforcement of the substantive term by the third party.

(2)   Where—

    (a)   a third party has a right under section 1 to enforce a term providing for one or more descriptions of dispute between the third party and the promisor to be submitted to arbitration ("the arbitration agreement"),

    (b)   the arbitration agreement is an agreement in writing for the purposes of Part I of the Arbitration Act 1996, and

    (c)   the third party does not fall to be treated under subsection (1) as a party to the arbitration agreement,

the third party shall, if he exercises the right, be treated for the purposes of that Act as a party to the arbitration agreement in relation to the matter with respect to which the right is exercised, and be treated as having been so immediately before the exercise of the right.

                                                      [1797]

9   Northern Ireland

(1)   In its application to Northern Ireland, this Act has effect with the modifications specified in subsections (2) and (3).

(2)   ...

(3)   In section 7, for subsection (3) there is substituted—

"(3)   In Articles 4(a) and 15 of the Limitation (Northern Ireland) Order 1989, the references to an action founded on a simple contract and an action upon an instrument under seal shall respectively include references to an action brought in reliance on section 1 relating to a simple contract and an action brought in reliance on that section relating to a contract under seal.".

(4)   ...

                                                      [1798]

NOTES

Sub-s (2): repealed by the Companies Act 2006 (Consequential Amendments, Transitional Provisions and Savings) Order 2009, SI 2009/1941, art 2(1), Sch 1, para 179(1), (3).

Sub-s (4): amends the Law Reform (Husband and Wife) (Northern Ireland) Act 1964.

10   Short title, commencement and extent

(1)   This Act may be cited as the Contracts (Rights of Third Parties) Act 1999.

(2)   This Act comes into force on the day on which it is passed but, subject to subsection (3), does not apply in relation to a contract entered into before the end of the period of six months beginning with that day.

(3)   The restriction in subsection (2) does not apply in relation to a contract which—
    (a)   is entered into on or after the day on which this Act is passed, and
    (b)   expressly provides for the application of this Act.

(4)   This Act extends as follows—
    (a)   section 9 extends to Northern Ireland only;
    (b)   the remaining provisions extend to England and Wales and Northern Ireland only.

[1799]–[1805]

ELECTRONIC COMMUNICATIONS ACT 2000

(2000 c 7)

ARRANGEMENT OF SECTIONS

PART II

FACILITATION OF ELECTRONIC COMMERCE, DATA STORAGE, ETC

PART III

MISCELLANEOUS AND SUPPLEMENTAL

Supplemental

An Act to make provision to facilitate the use of electronic communications and electronic data storage; to make provision about the modification of licences granted under section 7 of the Telecommunications Act 1984; and for connected purposes

[25 May 2000]

1–6   ((*Pt I) repealed by virtue of s 16(4) of this Act at* **[1813]**.)

PART II

FACILITATION OF ELECTRONIC COMMERCE, DATA STORAGE, ETC

7   Electronic signatures and related certificates

(1)   In any legal proceedings—
    (a)   an electronic signature incorporated into or logically associated with a particular electronic communication or particular electronic data, and
    (b)   the certification by any person of such a signature,
shall each be admissible in evidence in relation to any question as to the authenticity of the communication or data or as to the integrity of the communication or data.

(2)   For the purposes of this section an electronic signature is so much of anything in electronic form as—
    (a)   is incorporated into or otherwise logically associated with any electronic communication or electronic data; and
    (b)   purports to be so incorporated or associated for the purpose of being used in establishing the authenticity of the communication or data, the integrity of the communication or data, or both.

(3)   For the purposes of this section an electronic signature incorporated into or associated with a particular electronic communication or particular electronic data is certified by any person if that person (whether before or after the making of the communication) has made a statement confirming that—
    (a)   the signature,
    (b)   a means of producing, communicating or verifying the signature, or
    (c)   a procedure applied to the signature,

is (either alone or in combination with other factors) a valid means of establishing the authenticity of the communication or data, the integrity of the communication or data, or both.

[1806]

8 Power to modify legislation

(1) Subject to subsection (3), the appropriate Minister may by order made by statutory instrument modify the provisions of—

(a) any enactment or subordinate legislation, or

(b) any scheme, licence, authorisation or approval issued, granted or given by or under any enactment or subordinate legislation,

in such manner as he may think fit for the purpose of authorising or facilitating the use of electronic communications or electronic storage (instead of other forms of communication or storage) for any purpose mentioned in subsection (2).

(2) Those purposes are—

(a) the doing of anything which under any such provisions is required to be or may be done or evidenced in writing or otherwise using a document, notice or instrument;

(b) the doing of anything which under any such provisions is required to be or may be done by post or other specified means of delivery;

(c) the doing of anything which under any such provisions is required to be or may be authorised by a person's signature or seal, or is required to be delivered as a deed or witnessed;

(d) the making of any statement or declaration which under any such provisions is required to be made under oath or to be contained in a statutory declaration;

(e) the keeping, maintenance or preservation, for the purposes or in pursuance of any such provisions, of any account, record, notice, instrument or other document;

(f) the provision, production or publication under any such provisions of any information or other matter;

(g) the making of any payment that is required to be or may be made under any such provisions.

(3) The appropriate Minister shall not make an order under this section authorising the use of electronic communications or electronic storage for any purpose, unless he considers that the authorisation is such that the extent (if any) to which records of things done for that purpose will be available will be no less satisfactory in cases where use is made of electronic communications or electronic storage than in other cases.

(4) Without prejudice to the generality of subsection (1), the power to make an order under this section shall include power to make an order containing any of the following provisions—

(a) provision as to the electronic form to be taken by any electronic communications or electronic storage the use of which is authorised by an order under this section;

(b) provision imposing conditions subject to which the use of electronic communications or electronic storage is so authorised;

(c) provision, in relation to cases in which any such conditions are not satisfied, for treating anything for the purposes of which the use of such communications or storage is so authorised as not having been done;

(d) provision, in connection with anything so authorised, for a person to be able to refuse to accept receipt of something in electronic form except in such circumstances as may be specified in or determined under the order;

(e) provision, in connection with any use of electronic communications so authorised, for intermediaries to be used, or to be capable of being used, for the transmission of any data or for establishing the authenticity or integrity of any data;

(f) provision, in connection with any use of electronic storage so authorised, for persons satisfying such conditions as may be specified in or determined under the regulations to carry out functions in relation to the storage;

(g) provision, in relation to cases in which the use of electronic communications or electronic storage is so authorised, for the determination of any of the matters mentioned in subsection (5), or as to the manner in which they may be proved in legal proceedings;

(h) provision, in relation to cases in which fees or charges are or may be imposed in connection with anything for the purposes of which the use of electronic communications or electronic storage is so authorised, for different fees or charges to apply where use is made of such communications or storage;

(i) provision, in relation to any criminal or other liabilities that may arise (in respect of the making of false or misleading statements or otherwise) in connection with anything for the purposes of which the use of electronic communications or electronic storage is so authorised, for corresponding liabilities to arise in corresponding circumstances where use is made of such communications or storage;

(j) provision requiring persons to prepare and keep records in connection with any use of electronic communications or electronic storage which is so authorised;

    (k)   provision requiring the production of the contents of any records kept in accordance with an order under this section;

    (l)   provision for a requirement imposed by virtue of paragraph (j) or (k) to be enforceable at the suit or instance of such person as may be specified in or determined in accordance with the order;

    (m)   any such provision, in relation to electronic communications or electronic storage the use of which is authorised otherwise than by an order under this section, as corresponds to any provision falling within any of the preceding paragraphs that may be made where it is such an order that authorises the use of the communications or storage.

(5)   The matters referred to in subsection (4)(g) are—

    (a)   whether a thing has been done using an electronic communication or electronic storage;

    (b)   the time at which, or date on which, a thing done using any such communication or storage was done;

    (c)   the place where a thing done using such communication or storage was done;

    (d)   the person by whom such a thing was done; and

    (e)   the contents, authenticity or integrity of any electronic data.

(6)   An order under this section—

    (a)   shall not (subject to paragraph (b)) require the use of electronic communications or electronic storage for any purpose; but

    (b)   may make provision that a period of notice specified in the order must expire before effect is given to a variation or withdrawal of an election or other decision which—

        (i)   has been made for the purposes of such an order; and

        (ii)   is an election or decision to make use of electronic communications or electronic storage.

(7)   The matters in relation to which provision may be made by an order under this section do not include any matter under the care and management of the Commissioners of Inland Revenue or any matter under the care and management of the Commissioners of Customs and Excise.

(8)   In this section references to doing anything under the provisions of any enactment include references to doing it under the provisions of any subordinate legislation the power to make which is conferred by that enactment.

[1807]

NOTES

Orders: the Local Government and Housing Act 1989 (Electronic Communications) (England) Order 2000, SI 2000/3056; the Companies Act 1985 (Electronic Communications) Order 2000, SI 2000/3373; the Local Government and Housing Act 1989 (Electronic Communications) (Wales) Order 2001, SI 2001/605; the Unsolicited Goods and Services Act 1971 (Electronic Communications) Order 2001, SI 2001/2778; the National Health Service (Charges for Drugs and Appliances) (Electronic Communications) Order 2001, SI 2001/2887; the National Health Service (Pharmaceutical Services) and (Misuse of Drugs) (Electronic Communications) Order 2001, SI 2001/2888; the Public Records Act 1958 (Admissibility of Electronic Copies of Public Records) Order 2001, SI 2001/4058; the Building Societies Act 1986 (Electronic Communications) Order 2003, SI 2003/404; the Patents Act 1977 (Electronic Communications) Order 2003, SI 2003/512; the Town and Country Planning (Electronic Communications) (England) Order 2003, SI 2003/956; the Council Tax and Non-Domestic Rating (Electronic Communications) (England) Order 2003, SI 2003/2604; the Social Security (Electronic Communications) (Carer's Allowance) Order 2003, SI 2003/2800; the Council Tax and Non-Domestic Rating (Electronic Communications) (England) (No 2) Order 2003, SI 2003/3052; the Education Act 1996 (Electronic Communications) Order 2004, SI 2004/2521; the Town and Country Planning (Electronic Communications) (Wales) (No 1) Order 2004, SI 2004/3156; the Town and Country Planning (Electronic Communications) (Wales) (No 2) Order 2004, SI 2004/3157; the Town and Country Planning (Electronic Communications) (Wales) (No 3) Order 2004, SI 2004/3172; the Consumer Credit Act 1974 (Electronic Communications) Order 2004, SI 2004/3236; the Social Security (Electronic Communications) (Miscellaneous Benefits) Order 2005, SI 2005/3321; the Non-Domestic Rating and Council Tax (Electronic Communications) (England) Order 2006, SI 2006/237; the Registered Designs Act 1949 and Patents Act 1977 (Electronic Communications) Order 2006, SI 2006/1229; the Transport Security (Electronic Communications) Order 2006, SI 2006/2190; the Registration of Births and Deaths (Electronic Communications and Electronic Storage) Order 2006, SI 2006/2809; the Housing Benefit and Council Tax Benefit (Electronic Communications) Order 2006, SI 2006/2968; the Income-related Benefits (Subsidy to Authorities) (Miscellaneous Amendments and Electronic Communications) Order 2007, SI 2007/26; the Council Tax (Electronic Communications) (England) Order 2008, SI 2008/316; the Building (Electronic Communications) Order 2008, SI 2008/2334; the Police Act 1997 (Criminal Records) (Electronic Communications) Order 2009, SI 2009/203; the Unit Trusts (Electronic Communications) Order 2009, SI 2009/555; the Council Tax and Non-Domestic Rating (Electronic Communications) (Wales) Order 2009, SI 2009/2706; the Registration of Marriages etc (Electronic Communications and Electronic Storage) Order 2009, SI 2009/2821; the Health and Social Care Act 2008 (Commencement No 13, Transitory and Transitional Provisions and Electronic Communications) Order 2009, SI 2009/3023; the Council Tax (Electronic Communications) (Wales) Order 2010, SI 2010/613; the Motor Vehicles (Electronic Communication of Certificates of Insurance) Order 2010, SI 2010/1117.

9 Section 8 orders

(1)   In this Part "the appropriate Minister" means (subject to subsections (2) and (7) and section 10(1))—

(a) in relation to any matter with which a department of the Secretary of State is concerned, the Secretary of State;

(b) in relation to any matter with which the Treasury is concerned, the Treasury; and

(c) in relation to any matter with which any Government department other than a department of the Secretary of State or the Treasury is concerned, the Minister in charge of the other department.

(2) Where in the case of any matter—

(a) that matter falls within more than one paragraph of subsection (1),

(b) there is more than one such department as is mentioned in paragraph (c) of that subsection that is concerned with that matter, or

(c) both paragraphs (a) and (b) of this subsection apply,

references, in relation to that matter, to the appropriate Minister are references to any one or more of the appropriate Ministers acting (in the case of more than one) jointly.

(3) Subject to subsection (4) and section 10(6), a statutory instrument containing an order under section 8 shall be subject to annulment in pursuance of a resolution of either House of Parliament.

(4) Subsection (3) does not apply in the case of an order a draft of which has been laid before Parliament and approved by a resolution of each House.

(5) An order under section 8 may—

(a) provide for any conditions or requirements imposed by such an order to be framed by reference to the directions of such persons as may be specified in or determined in accordance with the order;

(b) provide that any such condition or requirement is to be satisfied only where a person so specified or determined is satisfied as to specified matters.

(6) The provision made by such an order may include—

(a) different provision for different cases;

(b) such exceptions and exclusions as the person making the order may think fit; and

(c) any such incidental, supplemental, consequential and transitional provision as he may think fit;

and the provision that may be made by virtue of paragraph (c) includes provision modifying any enactment or subordinate legislation or any scheme, licence, authorisation or approval issued, granted or given by or under any enactment or subordinate legislation.

(7) In the case of any matter which is not one of the reserved matters within the meaning of the Scotland Act 1998 or in respect of which functions are, by virtue of section 63 of that Act, exercisable by the Scottish Ministers instead of by or concurrently with a Minister of the Crown, this section and section 8 shall apply to Scotland subject to the following modifications—

(a) subsections (1) and (2) of this section are omitted;

(b) any reference to the appropriate Minister is to be read as a reference to the Secretary of State;

(c) any power of the Secretary of State, by virtue of paragraph (b), to make an order under section 8 may also be exercised by the Scottish Ministers with the consent of the Secretary of State; and

(d) where the Scottish Ministers make an order under section 8—

(i) any reference to the Secretary of State (other than a reference in this subsection) shall be construed as a reference to the Scottish Ministers; and

(ii) any reference to Parliament or to a House of Parliament shall be construed as a reference to the Scottish Parliament.

[1808]

NOTES

Orders: the Health and Social Care Act 2008 (Commencement No 13, Transitory and Transitional Provisions and Electronic Communications) Order 2009, SI 2009/3023; the Motor Vehicles (Electronic Communication of Certificates of Insurance) Order 2010, SI 2010/1117.

10 Modifications in relation to Welsh matters

(1) For the purposes of the exercise of the powers conferred by section 8 in relation to any matter the functions in respect of which are exercisable by the National Assembly for Wales, the appropriate Minister is the Secretary of State.

(2) Subject to the following provisions of this section, the powers conferred by section 8, so far as they fall within subsection (3), shall be exercisable by the National Assembly for Wales, as well as by the appropriate Minister.

(3) The powers conferred by section 8 fall within this subsection to the extent that they are exercisable in relation to—

(a) the provisions of any subordinate legislation made by the National Assembly for Wales;

(b) so much of any other subordinate legislation as makes provision the power to make which is exercisable by that Assembly;

(c) any power under any enactment to make provision the power to make which is so exercisable;

(d) the giving, sending or production of any notice, account, record or other document or of any information to or by a body mentioned in subsection (4); or

(e) the publication of anything by a body mentioned in subsection (4).

(4) Those bodies are—

(a) the National Assembly for Wales;

(b) any body specified in Schedule 4 to the Government of Wales Act 1998 (Welsh public bodies subject to reform by that Assembly);

(c) any other such body as may be specified for the purposes of this section by an order made by the Secretary of State with the consent of that Assembly.

(5) The National Assembly for Wales shall not make an order under section 8 except with the consent of the Secretary of State.

(6) Section 9(3) shall not apply to any order made under section 8 by the National Assembly for Wales.

(7) Nothing in this section shall confer any power on the National Assembly for Wales to modify any provision of the Government of Wales Act 1998.

(8) The power of the Secretary of State to make an order under subsection (4)(c)—

(a) shall include power to make any such incidental, supplemental, consequential and transitional provision as he may think fit; and

(b) shall be exercisable by statutory instrument subject to annulment in pursuance of a resolution of either House of Parliament.

[1809]

NOTES

Orders: the Council Tax and Non-Domestic Rating (Electronic Communications) (Wales) Order 2009, SI 2009/2706; the Council Tax (Electronic Communications) (Wales) Order 2010, SI 2010/613.

PART III
MISCELLANEOUS AND SUPPLEMENTAL

11, 12   *(Repealed by the Communications Act 2003, s 406(7), Sch 19(1).)*

Supplemental

13   Ministerial expenditure etc

There shall be paid out of money provided by Parliament—

(a) any expenditure incurred by the Secretary of State for or in connection with the carrying out of his functions under this Act; and

(b) any increase attributable to this Act in the sums which are payable out of money so provided under any other Act.

[1810]

14   Prohibition on key escrow requirements

(1) Subject to subsection (2), nothing in this Act shall confer any power on any Minister of the Crown, on the Scottish Ministers, on the National Assembly for Wales or on any person appointed under section 3—

(a) by conditions of an approval under Part I, or

(b) by any regulations or order under this Act,

to impose a requirement on any person to deposit a key for electronic data with another person.

(2) Subsection (1) shall not prohibit the imposition by an order under section 8 of—

(a) a requirement to deposit a key for electronic data with the intended recipient of electronic communications comprising the data; or

(b) a requirement for arrangements to be made, in cases where a key for data is not deposited with another person, which otherwise secure that the loss of a key, or its becoming unusable, does not have the effect that the information contained in a record kept in pursuance of any provision made by or under any enactment or subordinate legislation becomes inaccessible or incapable of being put into an intelligible form.

(3) In this section "key", in relation to electronic data, means any code, password, algorithm, key or other data the use of which (with or without other keys)—

(a) allows access to the electronic data, or

(b) facilitates the putting of the electronic data into an intelligible form;

and references in this section to depositing a key for electronic data with a person include references to doing anything that has the effect of making the key available to that person.

[1811]

15   General interpretation

(1)   In this Act, except in so far as the context otherwise requires—

"document" includes a map, plan, design, drawing, picture or other image;

"communication" includes a communication comprising sounds or images or both and a communication effecting a payment;

"electronic communication" means a communication transmitted (whether from one person to another, from one device to another or from a person to a device or vice versa)—

(a)   by means of [an electronic communications network]; or

(b)   by other means but while in an electronic form;

"enactment" includes—

(a)   an enactment passed after the passing of this Act,

(b)   an enactment comprised in an Act of the Scottish Parliament, and

(c)   an enactment contained in Northern Ireland legislation,

but does not include an enactment contained in Part I or II of this Act;

"modification" includes any alteration, addition or omission, and cognate expressions shall be construed accordingly;

"record" includes an electronic record; and

"subordinate legislation" means—

(a)   any subordinate legislation (within the meaning of the Interpretation Act 1978);

(b)   any instrument made under an Act of the Scottish Parliament; or

(c)   any statutory rules (within the meaning of the Statutory Rules (Northern Ireland) Order 1979).

(2)   In this Act—

(a)   references to the authenticity of any communication or data are references to any one or more of the following—

(i)   whether the communication or data comes from a particular person or other source;

(ii)   whether it is accurately timed and dated;

(iii)   whether it is intended to have legal effect; and

(b)   references to the integrity of any communication or data are references to whether there has been any tampering with or other modification of the communication or data.

(3)   References in this Act to something's being put into an intelligible form include references to its being restored to the condition in which it was before any encryption or similar process was applied to it.

[1812]

NOTES

Sub-s (1): in definition "electronic communication" words in square brackets substituted by the Communications Act 2003, s 406(1), Sch 17, para 158.

16   Short title, commencement, extent

(1)   This Act may be cited as the Electronic Communications Act 2000.

(2)   Part I of this Act and sections 7, 11 and 12 shall come into force on such day as the Secretary of State may by order made by statutory instrument appoint; and different days may be appointed under this subsection for different purposes.

(3)   An order shall not be made for bringing any of Part I of this Act into force for any purpose unless a draft of the order has been laid before Parliament and approved by a resolution of each House.

(4)   If no order for bringing Part I of this Act into force has been made under subsection (2) by the end of the period of five years beginning with the day on which this Act is passed, that Part shall, by virtue of this subsection, be repealed at the end of that period.

(5)   This Act extends to Northern Ireland.

[1813]

NOTES

Orders: the Electronic Communications Act 2000 (Commencement No 1) Order 2000, SI 2000/1798.

FINANCIAL SERVICES AND MARKETS ACT 2000

(2000 c 8)

ARRANGEMENT OF SECTIONS

PART XVI
THE OMBUDSMAN SCHEME

An Act to make provision about the regulation of financial services and markets; to provide for the transfer of certain statutory functions relating to building societies, friendly societies, industrial and provident societies and certain other mutual societies; and for connected purposes.

[14 June 2000]

1–224   ((*Pts I–XV*) outside the scope of this work.)

PART XVI
THE OMBUDSMAN SCHEME

The scheme

225 The scheme and the scheme operator

(1)   This Part provides for a scheme under which certain disputes may be resolved quickly and with minimum formality by an independent person.

(2)   The scheme is to be administered by a body corporate ("the scheme operator").

(3)   The scheme is to be operated under a name chosen by the scheme operator but is referred to in this Act as "the ombudsman scheme".

(4)   Schedule 17 makes provision in connection with the ombudsman scheme and the scheme operator.

[1813A]

226 Compulsory jurisdiction

(1)   A complaint which relates to an act or omission of a person ("the respondent") in carrying on an activity to which compulsory jurisdiction rules apply is to be dealt with under the ombudsman scheme if the conditions mentioned in subsection (2) are satisfied.

(2)   The conditions are that—
- (a)   the complainant is eligible and wishes to have the complaint dealt with under the scheme;
- (b)   the respondent was an authorised person[, or a payment service provider within the meaning of the Payment Services Regulations 2009,] at the time of the act or omission to which the complaint relates; and
- (c)   the act or omission to which the complaint relates occurred at a time when compulsory jurisdiction rules were in force in relation to the activity in question.

(3)   "Compulsory jurisdiction rules" means rules—
- (a)   made by the Authority for the purposes of this section; and
- (b)   specifying the activities to which they apply.

(4)   Only activities which are regulated activities, or which could be made regulated activities by an order under section 22, may be specified.

(5)   Activities may be specified by reference to specified categories (however described).

(6)   A complainant is eligible, in relation to the compulsory jurisdiction of the ombudsman scheme, if he falls within a class of person specified in the rules as eligible.

(7)   The rules—
- (a)   may include provision for persons other than individuals to be eligible; but
- (b)   may not provide for authorised persons to be eligible except in specified circumstances or in relation to complaints of a specified kind.

(8)   The jurisdiction of the scheme which results from this section is referred to in this Act as the "compulsory jurisdiction".

[1813B]

NOTES

Sub-s (2): words in square brackets inserted by the Payment Services Regulations 2009, SI 2009/209, reg 126, Sch 6, Pt 1, para 1(1)(a).

[226A Consumer credit jurisdiction

(1)   A complaint which relates to an act or omission of a person ("the respondent") is to be dealt with under the ombudsman scheme if the conditions mentioned in subsection (2) are satisfied.

(2)   The conditions are that—
- (a)   the complainant is eligible and wishes to have the complaint dealt with under the scheme;
- (b)   the complaint falls within a description specified in consumer credit rules;
- (c)   at the time of the act or omission the respondent was the licensee under a standard licence or was authorised to carry on an activity by virtue of section 34A of the Consumer Credit Act 1974;
- (d)   the act or omission occurred in the course of a business being carried on by the respondent which was of a type mentioned in subsection (3);
- (e)   at the time of the act or omission that type of business was specified in an order made by the Secretary of State; and
- (f)   the complaint cannot be dealt with under the compulsory jurisdiction.

(3)   The types of business referred to in subsection (2)(d) are—
- (a)   a consumer credit business;
- (b)   a consumer hire business;
- (c)   a business so far as it comprises or relates to credit brokerage;
- (d)   a business so far as it comprises or relates to debt-adjusting;
- (e)   a business so far as it comprises or relates to debt-counselling;
- (f)   a business so far as it comprises or relates to debt-collecting;
- (g)   a business so far as it comprises or relates to debt administration;
- (h)   a business so far as it comprises or relates to the provision of credit information services;
- (i)   a business so far as it comprises or relates to the operation of a credit reference agency.

(4)   A complainant is eligible if—
   (a)   he is—
      (i)   an individual; or
      (ii)   a surety in relation to a security provided to the respondent in connection with the business mentioned in subsection (2)(d); and
   (b)   he falls within a class of person specified in consumer credit rules.

(5)   The approval of the Treasury is required for an order under subsection (2)(e).

(6)   The jurisdiction of the scheme which results from this section is referred to in this Act as the "consumer credit jurisdiction".

(7)   In this Act "consumer credit rules" means rules made by the scheme operator with the approval of the Authority for the purposes of the consumer credit jurisdiction.

(8)   Consumer credit rules under this section may make different provision for different cases.

(9)   Expressions used in the Consumer Credit Act 1974 have the same meaning in this section as they have in that Act.]

[1813C]

NOTES
  Commencement: 16 June 2006.
  Inserted by the Consumer Credit Act 2006, s 59(1), subject to transitional provisions in s 69(1) of, and Sch 3, paras 1, 29 to, that Act at **[2077]**, **[2079]**.
  Order: the Financial Services and Markets Act 2000 (Ombudsman Scheme) (Consumer Credit Jurisdiction) Order 2007, SI 2007/383 at **[3486]**.

227   Voluntary jurisdiction

(1)   A complaint which relates to an act or omission of a person ("the respondent") in carrying on an activity to which voluntary jurisdiction rules apply is to be dealt with under the ombudsman scheme if the conditions mentioned in subsection (2) are satisfied.

(2)   The conditions are that—
   (a)   the complainant is eligible and wishes to have the complaint dealt with under the scheme;
   (b)   at the time of the act or omission to which the complaint relates, the respondent was participating in the scheme;
   (c)   at the time when the complaint is referred under the scheme, the respondent has not withdrawn from the scheme in accordance with its provisions;
   (d)   the act or omission to which the complaint relates occurred at a time when voluntary jurisdiction rules were in force in relation to the activity in question; and
   (e)   the complaint cannot be dealt with under the compulsory jurisdiction [or the consumer credit jurisdiction].

(3)   "Voluntary jurisdiction rules" means rules—
   (a)   made by the scheme operator for the purposes of this section; and
   (b)   specifying the activities to which they apply.

(4)   The only activities which may be specified in the rules are activities which are, or could be, specified in compulsory jurisdiction rules.

(5)   Activities may be specified by reference to specified categories (however described).

(6)   The rules require the Authority's approval.

(7)   A complainant is eligible, in relation to the voluntary jurisdiction of the ombudsman scheme, if he falls within a class of person specified in the rules as eligible.

(8)   The rules may include provision for persons other than individuals to be eligible.

(9)   A person qualifies for participation in the ombudsman scheme if he falls within a class of person specified in the rules in relation to the activity in question.

(10)   Provision may be made in the rules for persons other than authorised persons to participate in the ombudsman scheme.

(11)   The rules may make different provision in relation to complaints arising from different activities.

(12)   The jurisdiction of the scheme which results from this section is referred to in this Act as the "voluntary jurisdiction".

(13)   In such circumstances as may be specified in voluntary jurisdiction rules, a complaint—
   (a)   which relates to an act or omission occurring at a time before the rules came into force, and
   (b)   which could have been dealt with under a scheme which has to any extent been replaced by the voluntary jurisdiction,

is to be dealt with under the ombudsman scheme even though paragraph (b) or (d) of subsection (2) would otherwise prevent that.

(14)   In such circumstances as may be specified in voluntary jurisdiction rules, a complaint is to be dealt with under the ombudsman scheme even though—

(a)   paragraph (b) or (d) of subsection (2) would otherwise prevent that, and

(b)   the complaint is not brought within the scheme as a result of subsection (13),

but only if the respondent has agreed that complaints of that kind were to be dealt with under the scheme.

[1813D]

NOTES

Sub-s (2): words in square brackets in para (e) inserted by the Consumer Credit Act 2006, s 61(2).

Determination of complaints

228   Determination under the compulsory jurisdiction

(1)   This section applies only in relation to the compulsory jurisdiction [and to the consumer credit jurisdiction].

(2)   A complaint is to be determined by reference to what is, in the opinion of the ombudsman, fair and reasonable in all the circumstances of the case.

(3)   When the ombudsman has determined a complaint he must give a written statement of his determination to the respondent and to the complainant.

(4)   The statement must—

(a)   give the ombudsman's reasons for his determination;

(b)   be signed by him; and

(c)   require the complainant to notify him in writing, before a date specified in the statement, whether he accepts or rejects the determination.

(5)   If the complainant notifies the ombudsman that he accepts the determination, it is binding on the respondent and the complainant and final.

(6)   If, by the specified date, the complainant has not notified the ombudsman of his acceptance or rejection of the determination he is to be treated as having rejected it.

(7)   The ombudsman must notify the respondent of the outcome.

(8)   A copy of the determination on which appears a certificate signed by an ombudsman is evidence (or in Scotland sufficient evidence) that the determination was made under the scheme.

(9)   Such a certificate purporting to be signed by an ombudsman is to be taken to have been duly signed unless the contrary is shown.

[1813E]

NOTES

Sub-s (1): words in square brackets inserted by the Consumer Credit Act 2006, s 61(3).

229   Awards

(1)   This section applies only in relation to the compulsory jurisdiction [and to the consumer credit jurisdiction].

(2)   If a complaint which has been dealt with under the scheme is determined in favour of the complainant, the determination may include—

(a)   an award against the respondent of such amount as the ombudsman considers fair compensation for loss or damage (of a kind falling within subsection (3)) suffered by the complainant ("a money award");

(b)   a direction that the respondent take such steps in relation to the complainant as the ombudsman considers just and appropriate (whether or not a court could order those steps to be taken).

(3)   A money award may compensate for—

(a)   financial loss; or

(b)   any other loss, or any damage, of a specified kind.

(4)   The Authority may specify [for the purposes of the compulsory jurisdiction] the maximum amount which may be regarded as fair compensation for a particular kind of loss or damage specified under subsection (3)(b).

[(4A)   The scheme operator may specify for the purposes of the consumer credit jurisdiction the maximum amount which may be regarded as fair compensation for a particular kind of loss or damage specified under subsection (3)(b).]

(5)   A money award may not exceed the monetary limit; but the ombudsman may, if he considers that fair compensation requires payment of a larger amount, recommend that the respondent pay the complainant the balance.

(6)   The monetary limit is such amount as may be specified.

(7)   Different amounts may be specified in relation to different kinds of complaint.

(8)   A money award—
  (a)   may provide for the amount payable under the award to bear interest at a rate and as from a date specified in the award; and
  (b)   is enforceable by the complainant in accordance with Part III of Schedule 17 [or (as the case may be) Part 3A of that Schedule].

(9)   Compliance with a direction under subsection (2)(b)—
  (a)   is enforceable by an injunction; or
  (b)   in Scotland, is enforceable by an order under section 45 of the Court of Session Act 1988.

(10)   Only the complainant may bring proceedings for an injunction or proceedings for an order.

[(11)   "Specified" means—
  (a)   for the purposes of the compulsory jurisdiction, specified in compulsory jurisdiction rules;
  (b)   for the purposes of the consumer credit jurisdiction, specified in consumer credit rules.

(12)   Consumer credit rules under this section may make different provision for different cases.]

[1813F]

NOTES
Sub-ss (1), (4): words in square brackets inserted by the Consumer Credit Act 2006, s 61(3), (4).
Sub-s (4A): inserted by the Consumer Credit Act 2006, s 61(5).
Sub-s (8): words in square brackets in para (b) inserted by the Consumer Credit Act 2006, s 61(6).
Sub-ss (11), (12): substituted, for original sub-s (11), by the Consumer Credit Act 2006, s 61(7).

230   Costs

(1)   The scheme operator may by rules ("costs rules") provide for an ombudsman to have power, on determining a complaint under the compulsory jurisdiction [or the consumer credit jurisdiction]; to award costs in accordance with the provisions of the rules.

(2)   Costs rules require the approval of the Authority.

(3)   Costs rules may not provide for the making of an award against the complainant in respect of the respondent's costs.

(4)   But they may provide for the making of an award against the complainant in favour of the scheme operator, for the purpose of providing a contribution to resources deployed in dealing with the complaint, if in the opinion of the ombudsman—
  (a)   the complainant's conduct was improper or unreasonable; or
  (b)   the complainant was responsible for an unreasonable delay.

(5)   Costs rules may authorise an ombudsman making an award in accordance with the rules to order that the amount payable under the award bears interest at a rate and as from a date specified in the order.

(6)   An amount due under an award made in favour of the scheme operator is recoverable as a debt due to the scheme operator.

(7)   Any other award made against the respondent is to be treated as a money award for the purposes of paragraph 16 of Schedule 17 [or (as the case may be) paragraph 16D of that Schedule].

[1813G]

NOTES
Sub-ss (1), (7): words in square brackets inserted by the Consumer Credit Act 2006, s 61(8).

Information

231   Ombudsman's power to require information

(1)   An ombudsman may, by notice in writing given to a party to a complaint, require that party—
  (a)   to provide specified information or information of a specified description; or
  (b)   to produce specified documents or documents of a specified description.

(2)   The information or documents must be provided or produced—
  (a)   before the end of such reasonable period as may be specified; and
  (b)   in the case of information, in such manner or form as may be specified.

(3)   This section applies only to information and documents the production of which the ombudsman considers necessary for the determination of the complaint.

(4)   If a document is produced in response to a requirement imposed under this section, the ombudsman may—

    (a)   take copies or extracts from the document; or

    (b)   require the person producing the document to provide an explanation of the document.

(5)   If a person who is required under this section to produce a document fails to do so, the ombudsman may require him to state, to the best of his knowledge and belief, where the document is.

(6)   If a person claims a lien on a document, its production under this Part does not affect the lien.

(7)   "Specified" means specified in the notice given under subsection (1).

[1813H]

232   Powers of court where information required

(1)   If a person ("the defaulter") fails to comply with a requirement imposed under section 231, the ombudsman may certify that fact in writing to the court and the court may enquire into the case.

(2)   If the court is satisfied that the defaulter failed without reasonable excuse to comply with the requirement, it may deal with the defaulter (and, in the case of a body corporate, any director or officer) as if he were in contempt[; and "officer", in relation to a limited liability partnership, means a member of the limited liability partnership].

(3)   "Court" means—

    (a)   the High Court;

    (b)   in Scotland, the Court of Session.

[1813I]

NOTES

Sub-s (2): words in square brackets inserted by the Limited Liability Partnerships Regulations 2001, SI 2001/1090, reg 9(1), Sch 5, para 21.

Modification: the Limited Liability Partnerships Act 2000 provides for the creation of Limited Liability Partnerships (LLPs). The Limited Liability Partnerships Regulations 2001, SI 2001/1090, regulate LLPs by applying to them, with appropriate modifications, the appropriate provisions of this Act: see SI 2001/1090, regs 6, 10.

---

233   (*Amends the Data Protection Act 1998, s 31.*)

Funding

234   Industry funding

(1)   For the purpose of funding—

    (a)   the establishment of the ombudsman scheme (whenever any relevant expense is incurred), and

    (b)   its operation in relation to the compulsory jurisdiction,

the Authority may make rules requiring the payment to it or to the scheme operator, by authorised persons or any class of authorised person [or any payment service provider within the meaning of the Payment Services Regulations 2009] of specified amounts (or amounts calculated in a specified way).

(2)   "Specified" means specified in the rules.

[1813J]

NOTES

Sub-s (1): words in square brackets inserted by the Payment Services Regulations 2009, SI 2009/209, reg 126, Sch 6, Pt 1, para 1(1)(b).

[234A   Funding by consumer credit licensees etc

(1)   For the purpose of funding—

    (a)   the establishment of the ombudsman scheme so far as it relates to the consumer credit jurisdiction (whenever any relevant expense is incurred), and

    (b)   its operation in relation to the consumer credit jurisdiction,

the scheme operator may from time to time with the approval of the Authority determine a sum which is to be raised by way of contributions under this section.

(2)   A sum determined under subsection (1) may include a component to cover the costs of the collection of contributions to that sum ("collection costs") under this section.

(3)   The scheme operator must notify the OFT of every determination under subsection (1).

(4)   The OFT must give general notice of every determination so notified.

(5)   The OFT may by general notice impose requirements on—
  (a)   licensees to whom this section applies, or
  (b)   persons who make applications to which this section applies,
to pay contributions to the OFT for the purpose of raising sums determined under subsection (1).

(6)   The amount of the contribution payable by a person under such a requirement—
  (a)   shall be the amount specified in or determined under the general notice; and
  (b)   shall be paid before the end of the period or at the time so specified or determined.

(7)   A general notice under subsection (5) may—
  (a)   impose requirements only on descriptions of licensees or applicants specified in the notice;
  (b)   provide for exceptions from any requirement imposed on a description of licensees or applicants;
  (c)   impose different requirements on different descriptions of licensees or applicants;
  (d)   make provision for refunds in specified circumstances.

(8)   Contributions received by the OFT must be paid to the scheme operator.

(9)   As soon as practicable after the end of—
  (a)   each financial year of the scheme operator, or
  (b)   if the OFT and the scheme operator agree that this paragraph is to apply instead of paragraph (a) for the time being, each period agreed by them,
the scheme operator must pay to the OFT an amount representing the extent to which collection costs are covered in accordance with subsection (2) by the total amount of the contributions paid by the OFT to it during the year or (as the case may be) the agreed period.

(10)   Amounts received by the OFT from the scheme operator are to be retained by it for the purpose of meeting its costs.

(11)   The Secretary of State may by order provide that the functions of the OFT under this section are for the time being to be carried out by the scheme operator.

(12)   An order under subsection (11) may provide that while the order is in force this section shall have effect subject to such modifications as may be set out in the order.

(13)   The licensees to whom this section applies are licensees under standard licences which cover to any extent the carrying on of a type of business specified in an order under section 226A(2)(e).

(14)   The applications to which this section applies are applications for—
  (a)   standard licences covering to any extent the carrying on of a business of such a type;
  (b)   the renewal of standard licences on terms covering to any extent the carrying on of a business of such a type.

(15)   Expressions used in the Consumer Credit Act 1974 have the same meaning in this section as they have in that Act.]

[1813K]

NOTES
  Commencement: 16 June 2006.
  Inserted by the Consumer Credit Act 2006, s 60.

235–284   ((*Pt XVII*) *outside the scope of this work.*)

PART XVIII
RECOGNISED INVESTMENT EXCHANGES AND CLEARING HOUSES

CHAPTER I
EXEMPTION

285, 286   (*Outside the scope of this work.*)

Applications for recognition

287–290   (*Outside the scope of this work.*)

[290A   Refusal of recognition on ground of excessive regulatory provision

(1)   The Authority must not make a recognition order if it appears to the Authority that an existing or proposed regulatory provision of the applicant in connection with—
  (a)   the applicant's business as an investment exchange, or
  (b)   the provision by the applicant of clearing services,

imposes or will impose an excessive requirement on the persons affected (directly or indirectly) by it.

(2) The reference in section 290(1) (making of recognition order) to satisfying the applicable recognition requirements shall be read accordingly.

(3) Expressions used in subsection (1) above that are defined for the purposes of section 300A (power of Authority to disallow excessive regulatory provision) have the same meaning as in that section.

(4) The provisions of section 300A(3) and (4) (determination whether regulatory provision excessive) apply for the purposes of this section as for the purposes of section 300A.

(5) Section 298 has effect in relation to a decision under this section to refuse a recognition order—

    (a)   as it has effect in relation to a decision to revoke such an order, and

    (b)   as if references to a recognised body were references to the applicant.

(6) This section does not apply to an application for recognition as an overseas investment exchange or overseas clearing house.]

[1813L]

NOTES

Commencement: 20 December 2006.

Inserted by the Investment Exchanges and Clearing Houses Act 2006, s 4.

291–300 (*Outside the scope of this work.*)

[Power to disallow excessive regulatory provision

300A Power of Authority to disallow excessive regulatory provision

(1) This section applies where a recognised body proposes to make any regulatory provision in connection with its business as an investment exchange or the provision by it of clearing services.

(2) If it appears to the Authority—

    (a)   that the proposed provision will impose a requirement on persons affected (directly or indirectly) by it, and

    (b)   that the requirement is excessive,

the Authority may direct that the proposed provision must not be made.

(3) A requirement is excessive if—

    (a)   it is not required under Community law or any enactment or rule of law in the United Kingdom, and

    (b)   either—

        (i)   it is not justified as pursuing a reasonable regulatory objective, or

        (ii)   it is disproportionate to the end to be achieved.

(4) In considering whether a requirement is excessive the Authority must have regard to all the relevant circumstances, including—

    (a)   the effect of existing legal and other requirements,

    (b)   the global character of financial services and markets and the international mobility of activity,

    (c)   the desirability of facilitating innovation, and

    (d)   the impact of the proposed provision on market confidence.

(5) In this section "requirement" includes any obligation or burden.

(6) Any provision made in contravention of a direction under this section is of no effect.]

[1813M]

NOTES

Commencement: 20 December 2006.

Inserted, together with preceding cross-heading, by the Investment Exchanges and Clearing Houses Act 2006, s 1; for further effect see s 5(3) of the 2006 Act at **[2101]**.

[300B Duty to notify proposal to make regulatory provision

(1) A recognised body that proposes to make any regulatory provision must give written notice of the proposal to the Authority without delay.

(2) The Authority may by rules under section 293 (notification requirements)—

    (a)   specify descriptions of regulatory provision in relation to which, or circumstances in which, the duty in subsection (1) above does not apply, or

    (b)   provide that the duty applies only to specified descriptions of regulatory provision or in specified circumstances.

(3) The Authority may also by rules under that section—
    (a) make provision as to the form and contents of the notice required, and
    (b) require the body to provide such information relating to the proposal as may be specified in the rules or as the Authority may reasonably require.]

[1813N]

NOTES
Commencement: 20 December 2006.
Inserted, together with ss 300C–300E, by the Investment Exchanges and Clearing Houses Act 2006, s 2; for further effect see s 5(3) of the 2006 Act at **[2101]**.

[300C Restriction on making provision before Authority decides whether to act

(1) Where notice of a proposal to make regulatory provision is required to be given to the Authority under section 300B, the provision must not be made—
    (a) before that notice is given, or
    (b) subject to the following provisions of this section, before the end of the initial period.

(2) The initial period is—
    (a) the period of 30 days beginning with the day on which the Authority receives notice of the proposal, or
    (b) if any consultation period announced by the body in relation to the proposal ends after that 30-day period, the end of the consultation period.

(3) If before the end of the initial period the Authority notifies the body that it is calling in the proposal, the provisions of section 300D (consideration by Authority whether to disallow proposed provision) apply as to when the provision may be made.

(4) If—
    (a) before the end of the initial period the Authority notifies the body that it is not calling in the proposal, or
    (b) the initial period ends without the Authority having notified the body that it is calling in the proposal,
the body may then make the proposed provision.

(5) Any provision made in contravention of this section is of no effect.]

[1813O]

NOTES
Commencement: 20 December 2006.
Inserted as noted to s 300B at **[1813N]**.

[300D Consideration by Authority whether to disallow proposed provision

(1) This section applies where the Authority notifies a recognised body that it is calling in a proposal to make regulatory provision.

(2) The Authority must publish a notice—
    (a) giving details of the proposed provision,
    (b) stating that it has called in the proposal in order to consider whether to disallow it, and
    (c) specifying a period during which representations with respect to that question may be made to it.

(3) The Authority may extend the period for making representations.

(4) The Authority must notify the body of its decision whether to disallow the provision not later than 30 days after the end of the period for making representations, and must publish the decision and the reasons for it.

(5) The body must not make the provision unless and until—
    (a) the Authority notifies it of its decision not to disallow it, or
    (b) the 30-day period specified in subsection (4) ends without the Authority having notified any decision.

(6) If the Authority notifies the body of its decision to disallow the provision and that decision is questioned in legal proceedings—
    (a) the body must not make the provision until those proceedings, and any proceedings on appeal, are finally determined,
    (b) if the Authority's decision is quashed and the matter is remitted to it for reconsideration, the court may give directions as to the period within which the Authority is to complete its reconsideration, and
    (c) the body must not make the provision until—
        (i) the Authority notifies it of its decision on reconsideration not to disallow the provision, or

        (ii)   the period specified by the court ends without the Authority having notified any decision.

(7)   Any provision made in contravention of subsection (5) or (6) is of no effect.]

[1813P]

NOTES
Commencement: 20 December 2006.
Inserted as noted to s 300B at **[1813N]**.

[300E   Power to disallow excessive regulatory provision: supplementary

(1)   In sections 300A to 300D—
   (a)   "regulatory provision" means any rule, guidance, arrangements, policy or practice, and
   (b)   references to making provision shall be read accordingly as including, as the case may require, issuing guidance, entering into arrangements or adopting a policy or practice.

(2)   For the purposes of those sections a variation of a proposal is treated as a new proposal.

(3)   Those sections do not apply to an overseas investment exchange or overseas clearing house.]

[1813Q]

NOTES
Commencement: 20 December 2006.
Inserted as noted to s 300B at **[1813N]**.

301–425   (*Outside the scope of this work.*)

PART XXX
SUPPLEMENTAL

426–432   (*Outside the scope of this work.*)

433   Short title

This Act may be cited as the Financial Services and Markets Act 2000.

[1813R]

(*Schs 1–16 outside the scope of this work.*)

SCHEDULE 17
THE OMBUDSMAN SCHEME

Section 225(4)

PART I
GENERAL

Interpretation

1.   In this Schedule—
   "ombudsman" means a person who is a member of the panel; and
   "the panel" means the panel established under paragraph 4.

[1813S]

PART II
THE SCHEME OPERATOR

Establishment by the Authority

2.—(1)   The Authority must establish a body corporate to exercise the functions conferred on the scheme operator by or under this Act.

(2)   The Authority must take such steps as are necessary to ensure that the scheme operator is, at all times, capable of exercising those functions.

Constitution

3.—(1)   The constitution of the scheme operator must provide for it to have—
   (a)   a chairman; and
   (b)   a board (which must include the chairman) whose members are the scheme operator's directors.

(2)   The chairman and other members of the board must be persons appointed, and liable to removal from office, by the Authority (acting, in the case of the chairman, with the approval of the Treasury).

(3)   But the terms of their appointment (and in particular those governing removal from office) must be such as to secure their independence from the Authority in the operation of the scheme.

(4)   The function of making voluntary jurisdiction rules under section 227[, the function of making consumer credit rules, the function of making determinations under section 234A(1)] and the functions conferred by paragraphs 4, 5, 7, 9 or 14 may be exercised only by the board.

(5)   The validity of any act of the scheme operator is unaffected by—
    (a)   a vacancy in the office of chairman; or
    (b)   a defect in the appointment of a person as chairman or as a member of the board.

The panel of ombudsmen

4.—(1)   The scheme operator must appoint and maintain a panel of persons, appearing to it to have appropriate qualifications and experience, to act as ombudsmen for the purposes of the scheme.

(2)   A person's appointment to the panel is to be on such terms (including terms as to the duration and termination of his appointment and as to remuneration) as the scheme operator considers—
    (a)   consistent with the independence of the person appointed; and
    (b)   otherwise appropriate.

The Chief Ombudsman

5.—(1)   The scheme operator must appoint one member of the panel to act as Chief Ombudsman.

(2)   The Chief Ombudsman is to be appointed on such terms (including terms as to the duration and termination of his appointment) as the scheme operator considers appropriate.

Status

6.—(1)   The scheme operator is not to be regarded as exercising functions on behalf of the Crown.

(2)   The scheme operator's board members, officers and staff are not to be regarded as Crown servants.

(3)   Appointment as Chief Ombudsman or to the panel or as a deputy ombudsman does not confer the status of Crown servant.

Annual reports

7.—(1)   At least once a year—
    (a)   the scheme operator must make a report to the Authority on the discharge of its functions; and
    (b)   the Chief Ombudsman must make a report to the Authority on the discharge of his functions.

(2)   Each report must distinguish between functions in relation to the scheme's compulsory jurisdiction[, functions in relation to its consumer credit jurisdiction] and functions in relation to its voluntary jurisdiction.

(3)   Each report must also comply with any requirements specified in rules made by the Authority.

(4)   The scheme operator must publish each report in the way it considers appropriate.

Guidance

8.   The scheme operator may publish guidance consisting of such information and advice as it considers appropriate and may charge for it or distribute it free of charge.

Budget

9.—(1)   The scheme operator must, before the start of each of its financial years, adopt an annual budget which has been approved by the Authority.

(2)   The scheme operator may, with the approval of the Authority, vary the budget for a financial year at any time after its adoption.

(3)   The annual budget must include an indication of—
    (a)   the distribution of resources deployed in the operation of the scheme, and
    (b)   the amounts of income of the scheme operator arising or expected to arise from the operation of the scheme,
distinguishing between the scheme's compulsory[, consumer credit] and voluntary jurisdiction.

Exemption from liability in damages

10.—(1)   No person is to be liable in damages for anything done or omitted in the discharge, or purported discharge, of any functions under this Act in relation to the compulsory jurisdiction [or to the consumer credit jurisdiction].

(2)   Sub-paragraph (1) does not apply—
   (a)   if the act or omission is shown to have been in bad faith; or
   (b)   so as to prevent an award of damages made in respect of an act or omission on the ground that the act or omission was unlawful as a result of section 6(1) of the Human Rights Act 1998.

Privilege

11.   For the purposes of the law relating to defamation, proceedings in relation to a complaint which is subject to the compulsory jurisdiction [or to the consumer credit jurisdiction] are to be treated as if they were proceedings before a court.

[1813T]

NOTES

Paras 3, 7, 9, 10, 11: words in square brackets inserted by the Consumer Credit Act 2006, s 61(10).

PART III
THE COMPULSORY JURISDICTION

Introduction

12.   This Part of this Schedule applies only in relation to the compulsory jurisdiction.

Authority's procedural rules

13.—(1)   The Authority must make rules providing that a complaint is not to be entertained unless the complainant has referred it under the ombudsman scheme before the applicable time limit (determined in accordance with the rules) has expired.

(2)   The rules may provide that an ombudsman may extend that time limit in specified circumstances.

(3)   The Authority may make rules providing that a complaint is not to be entertained (except in specified circumstances) if the complainant has not previously communicated its substance to the respondent and given him a reasonable opportunity to deal with it.

(4)   The Authority may make rules requiring an authorised person[, or a payment service provider within the meaning of the Payment Services Regulations 2009,] who may become subject to the compulsory jurisdiction as a respondent to establish such procedures as the Authority considers appropriate for the resolution of complaints which—
   (a)   may be referred to the scheme; and
   (b)   arise out of activity to which the Authority's powers under Part X do not apply.

The scheme operator's rules

14.—(1)   The scheme operator must make rules, to be known as "scheme rules", which are to set out the procedure for reference of complaints and for their investigation, consideration and determination by an ombudsman.

(2)   Scheme rules may, among other things—
   (a)   specify matters which are to be taken into account in determining whether an act or omission was fair and reasonable;
   (b)   provide that a complaint may, in specified circumstances, be dismissed without consideration of its merits;
   (c)   provide for the reference of a complaint, in specified circumstances and with the consent of the complainant, to another body with a view to its being determined by that body instead of by an ombudsman;
   (d)   make provision as to the evidence which may be required or admitted, the extent to which it should be oral or written and the consequences of a person's failure to produce any information or document which he has been required (under section 231 or otherwise) to produce;
   (e)   allow an ombudsman to fix time limits for any aspect of the proceedings and to extend a time limit;
   (f)   provide for certain things in relation to the reference, investigation or consideration (but not determination) of a complaint to be done by a member of the scheme operator's staff instead of by an ombudsman;
   (g)   make different provision in relation to different kinds of complaint.

(3)   The circumstances specified under sub-paragraph (2)(b) may include the following—

    (a)   the ombudsman considers the complaint frivolous or vexatious;

    (b)   legal proceedings have been brought concerning the subject-matter of the complaint and the ombudsman considers that the complaint is best dealt with in those proceedings; or

    (c)   the ombudsman is satisfied that there are other compelling reasons why it is inappropriate for the complaint to be dealt with under the ombudsman scheme.

(4)   If the scheme operator proposes to make any scheme rules it must publish a draft of the proposed rules in the way appearing to it to be best calculated to bring them to the attention of persons appearing to it to be likely to be affected.

(5)   The draft must be accompanied by a statement that representations about the proposals may be made to the scheme operator within a time specified in the statement.

(6)   Before making the proposed scheme rules, the scheme operator must have regard to any representations made to it under sub-paragraph (5).

(7)   The consent of the Authority is required before any scheme rules may be made.

Fees

15.—(1)   Scheme rules may require a respondent to pay to the scheme operator such fees as may be specified in the rules.

(2)   The rules may, among other things—

    (a)   provide for the scheme operator to reduce or waive a fee in a particular case;

    (b)   set different fees for different stages of the proceedings on a complaint;

    (c)   provide for fees to be refunded in specified circumstances;

    (d)   make different provision for different kinds of complaint.

Enforcement of money awards

16.   A money award, including interest, which has been registered in accordance with scheme rules may—

    (a)   if a county court so orders in England and Wales, be recovered *by execution issued from the county court* [under section 85 of the County Courts Act 1984] (or otherwise) as if it were payable under an order of that court;

    (b)   be enforced in Northern Ireland as a money judgment under the Judgments Enforcement (Northern Ireland) Order 1981;

    (c)   be enforced in Scotland by the sheriff, as if it were a judgment or order of the sheriff and whether or not the sheriff could himself have granted such judgment or order.

[1813U]

NOTES

Para 13: words in square brackets in sub-para (4) inserted by the Payment Services Regulations 2009, SI 2009/209, reg 126, Sch 6, Pt 1, para 1(2).

Para 16: in sub-para (a) words in italics substituted by subsequent words in square brackets by the Tribunals, Courts and Enforcement Act 2007, s 62(3), Sch 13, para 134, as from a day to be appointed.

[PART 3A
THE CONSUMER CREDIT JURISDICTION

Introduction

16A.   This Part of this Schedule applies only in relation to the consumer credit jurisdiction.

Procedure for complaints etc

16B.—(1)   Consumer credit rules—

    (a)   must provide that a complaint is not to be entertained unless the complainant has referred it under the ombudsman scheme before the applicable time limit (determined in accordance with the rules) has expired;

    (b)   may provide that an ombudsman may extend that time limit in specified circumstances;

    (c)   may provide that a complaint is not to be entertained (except in specified circumstances) if the complainant has not previously communicated its substance to the respondent and given him a reasonable opportunity to deal with it;

    (d)   may make provision about the procedure for the reference of complaints and for their investigation, consideration and determination by an ombudsman.

(2)   Sub-paragraphs (2) and (3) of paragraph 14 apply in relation to consumer credit rules under sub-paragraph (1) of this paragraph as they apply in relation to scheme rules under that paragraph.

(3)   Consumer credit rules may require persons falling within sub-paragraph (6) to establish such procedures as the scheme operator considers appropriate for the resolution of complaints which may be referred to the scheme.

(4)   Consumer credit rules under sub-paragraph (3) may make different provision in relation to persons of different descriptions or to complaints of different descriptions.

(5)   Consumer credit rules under sub-paragraph (3) may authorise the scheme operator to dispense with or modify the application of such rules in particular cases where the scheme operator—

(a)   considers it appropriate to do so; and
(b)   is satisfied that the specified conditions (if any) are met.

(6)   A person falls within this sub-paragraph if he is licensed by a standard licence (within the meaning of the Consumer Credit Act 1974) to carry on to any extent a business of a type specified in an order under section 226A(2)(e) of this Act.

Fees

16C.—(1)   Consumer credit rules may require a respondent to pay to the scheme operator such fees as may be specified in the rules.

(2)   Sub-paragraph (2) of paragraph 15 applies in relation to consumer credit rules under this paragraph as it applies in relation to scheme rules under that paragraph.

Enforcement of money awards

16D.   A money award, including interest, which has been registered in accordance with consumer credit rules may—

(a)   if a county court so orders in England and Wales, be recovered by execution issued from the county court (or otherwise) as if it were payable under an order of that court;
(b)   be enforced in Northern Ireland as a money judgment under the Judgments Enforcement (Northern Ireland) Order 1981;
(c)   be enforced in Scotland as if it were a decree of the sheriff and whether or not the sheriff could himself have granted such a decree.

Procedure for consumer credit rules

16E.—(1)   If the scheme operator makes any consumer credit rules, it must give a copy of them to the Authority without delay.

(2)   If the scheme operator revokes any such rules, it must give written notice to the Authority without delay.

(3)   The power to make such rules is exercisable in writing.

(4)   Immediately after the making of such rules, the scheme operator must arrange for them to be printed and made available to the public.

(5)   The scheme operator may charge a reasonable fee for providing a person with a copy of any such rules.

Verification of consumer credit rules

16F.—(1)   The production of a printed copy of consumer credit rules purporting to be made by the scheme operator—

(a)   on which there is endorsed a certificate signed by a member of the scheme operator's staff authorised by the scheme operator for that purpose, and
(b)   which contains the required statements,

is evidence (or in Scotland sufficient evidence) of the facts stated in the certificate.

(2)   The required statements are—

(a)   that the rules were made by the scheme operator;
(b)   that the copy is a true copy of the rules; and
(c)   that on a specified date the rules were made available to the public in accordance with paragraph 16E(4).

(3)   A certificate purporting to be signed as mentioned in sub-paragraph (1) is to be taken to have been duly signed unless the contrary is shown.

Consultation

16G.—(1)   If the scheme operator proposes to make consumer credit rules, it must publish a draft of the proposed rules in the way appearing to it to be best calculated to bring the draft to the attention of the public.

(2)   The draft must be accompanied by—

(a)   an explanation of the proposed rules; and
(b)   a statement that representations about the proposals may be made to the scheme operator within a specified time.

PART 1
STATUTES

(3) Before making any consumer credit rules, the scheme operator must have regard to any representations made to it in accordance with sub-paragraph (2)(b).

(4) If consumer credit rules made by the scheme operator differ from the draft published under sub-paragraph (1) in a way which the scheme operator considers significant, the scheme operator must publish a statement of the difference.]

[1813V]

NOTES

Commencement: 16 June 2006.
Inserted by the Consumer Credit Act 2006, s 59(2), Sch 2.

PART IV
THE VOLUNTARY JURISDICTION

Introduction

17. This Part of this Schedule applies only in relation to the voluntary jurisdiction.

Terms of reference to the scheme

18.—(1) Complaints are to be dealt with and determined under the voluntary jurisdiction on standard terms fixed by the scheme operator with the approval of the Authority.

(2) Different standard terms may be fixed with respect to different matters or in relation to different cases.

(3) The standard terms may, in particular—
    (a) require the making of payments to the scheme operator by participants in the scheme of such amounts, and at such times, as may be determined by the scheme operator;
    (b) make provision as to the award of costs on the determination of a complaint.

(4) The scheme operator may not vary any of the standard terms or add or remove terms without the approval of the Authority.

(5) The standard terms may include provision to the effect that (unless acting in bad faith) none of the following is to be liable in damages for anything done or omitted in the discharge or purported discharge of functions in connection with the voluntary jurisdiction—
    (a) the scheme operator;
    (b) any member of its governing body;
    (c) any member of its staff;
    (d) any person acting as an ombudsman for the purposes of the scheme.

Delegation by and to other schemes

19.—(1) The scheme operator may make arrangements with a relevant body—
    (a) for the exercise by that body of any part of the voluntary jurisdiction of the ombudsman scheme on behalf of the scheme; or
    (b) for the exercise by the scheme of any function of that body as if it were part of the voluntary jurisdiction of the scheme.

(2) A "relevant body" is one which the scheme operator is satisfied—
    (a) is responsible for the operation of a broadly comparable scheme (whether or not established by statute) for the resolution of disputes; and
    (b) in the case of arrangements under sub-paragraph (1)(a), will exercise the jurisdiction in question in a way compatible with the requirements imposed by or under this Act in relation to complaints of the kind concerned.

(3) Such arrangements require the approval of the Authority.

Voluntary jurisdiction rules: procedure

20.—(1) If the scheme operator makes voluntary jurisdiction rules, it must give a copy to the Authority without delay.

(2) If the scheme operator revokes any such rules, it must give written notice to the Authority without delay.

(3) The power to make voluntary jurisdiction rules is exercisable in writing.

(4) Immediately after making voluntary jurisdiction rules, the scheme operator must arrange for them to be printed and made available to the public.

(5) The scheme operator may charge a reasonable fee for providing a person with a copy of any voluntary jurisdiction rules.

Verification of the rules

21.—(1)   The production of a printed copy of voluntary jurisdiction rules purporting to be made by the scheme operator—

    (a)   on which is endorsed a certificate signed by a member of the scheme operator's staff authorised by the scheme operator for that purpose, and

    (b)   which contains the required statements,

is evidence (or in Scotland sufficient evidence) of the facts stated in the certificate.

    (2)   The required statements are—

    (a)   that the rules were made by the scheme operator;

    (b)   that the copy is a true copy of the rules; and

    (c)   that on a specified date the rules were made available to the public in accordance with paragraph 20(4).

    (3)   A certificate purporting to be signed as mentioned in sub-paragraph (1) is to be taken to have been duly signed unless the contrary is shown.

Consultation

22.—(1)   If the scheme operator proposes to make voluntary jurisdiction rules, it must publish a draft of the proposed rules in the way appearing to it to be best calculated to bring them to the attention of the public.

    (2)   The draft must be accompanied by—

    (a)   an explanation of the proposed rules; and

    (b)   a statement that representations about the proposals may be made to the scheme operator within a specified time.

    (3)   Before making any voluntary jurisdiction rules, the scheme operator must have regard to any representations made to it in accordance with sub-paragraph (2)(b).

    (4)   If voluntary jurisdiction rules made by the scheme operator differ from the draft published under sub-paragraph (1) in a way which the scheme operator considers significant, the scheme operator must publish a statement of the difference.

[1813W]

(Schs 18–22 outside the scope of this work.)

LIMITED LIABILITY PARTNERSHIPS ACT 2000

(2000 c 12)

ARRANGEMENT OF SECTIONS

An Act to make provision for limited liability partnerships

[20 July 2000]

Introductory

1   Limited liability partnerships

   (1)   There shall be a new form of legal entity to be known as a limited liability partnership.

   (2)   A limited liability partnership is a body corporate (with legal personality separate from that of its members) which is formed by being incorporated under this Act; and—

   (a)   in the following provisions of this Act (except in the phrase "oversea limited liability partnership"), and

   (b)   in any other enactment (except where provision is made to the contrary or the context otherwise requires),

references to a limited liability partnership are to such a body corporate.

   (3)   A limited liability partnership has unlimited capacity.

   (4)   The members of a limited liability partnership have such liability to contribute to its assets in the event of its being wound up as is provided for by virtue of this Act.

   (5)   Accordingly, except as far as otherwise provided by this Act or any other enactment, the law relating to partnerships does not apply to a limited liability partnership.

   (6)   The Schedule (which makes provision about the names and registered offices of limited liability partnerships) has effect.

[1814]

Incorporation

2   Incorporation document etc

   (1)   For a limited liability partnership to be incorporated—

   (a)   two or more persons associated for carrying on a lawful business with a view to profit must have subscribed their names to an incorporation document,

   [(b)   the incorporation document or a copy of it must have been delivered to the registrar, and]

   (c)   there must have been so delivered a statement ... made by either a solicitor engaged in the formation of the limited liability partnership or anyone who subscribed his name to the incorporation document, that the requirement imposed by paragraph (a) has been complied with.

   (2)   The incorporation document must—

   (a)   ...

   (b)   state the name of the limited liability partnership,

   (c)   state whether the registered office of the limited liability partnership is to be situated in England and Wales, in Wales[, in Scotland or in Northern Ireland],

   (d)   state the address of that registered office,

   [(e)   give the required particulars of each of the persons who are to be members of the limited liability partnership on incorporation, and]

   (f)   either specify which of those persons are to be designated members or state that every person who from time to time is a member of the limited liability partnership is a designated member.

   [(2ZA)   The required particulars mentioned in subsection (2)(e) are the particulars required to be stated in the LLP's register of members and register of members' residential addresses.]

   [(2A), (2B)   ...]

   (3)   If a person makes a false statement under subsection (1)(c) which he—

   (a)   knows to be false, or

   (b)   does not believe to be true,

he commits an offence.

   (4)   A person guilty of an offence under subsection (3) is liable—

   (a)   on summary conviction, to imprisonment for a period not exceeding six months or a fine not exceeding the statutory maximum, or to both, or

(b)   on conviction on indictment, to imprisonment for a period not exceeding two years or a fine, or to both.

[1815]

NOTES

    Sub-s (1): para (b) substituted and words omitted from para (c) repealed by the Limited Liability Partnerships (Application of Companies Act 2006) Regulations 2009, SI 2009/1804, reg 85, Sch 3, Pt 1, para 1(1)–(3), except in relation to an obligation arising before 1 October 2009 to deliver a document to the registrar.

    Sub-s (2): para (a) repealed, words in square brackets in para (c), and para (e) substituted by SI 2009/1804, reg 85, Sch 3, Pt 1, para 1(1), (4), except in relation to an obligation arising before 1 October 2009 to deliver a document to the registrar.

    Sub-s (2ZA): inserted by SI 2009/1804, reg 85, Sch 3, Pt 1, para 1(1), (5), except in relation to an obligation arising before 1 October 2009 to deliver a document to the registrar.

    Sub-ss (2A), (2B): inserted by the Limited Liability Partnerships (Particulars of Usual Residential Address) (Confidentiality Orders) Regulations 2002, SI 2002/915, reg 16, Sch 2, para 1; repealed by SI 2009/1804, reg 85, Sch 3, Pt 1, para 1(1), (6), except in relation to an obligation arising before 1 October 2009 to deliver a document to the registrar.

3 Incorporation by registration

    [(1)   The registrar, if satisfied that the requirements of section 2 are complied with, shall—

    (a)   register the documents delivered under that section, and

    (b)   give a certificate that the limited liability partnership is incorporated.

    (1A)   The certificate must state—

    (a)   the name and registered number of the limited liability partnership,

    (b)   the date of its incorporation, and

    (c)   whether the limited liability partnership's registered office is situated in England and Wales (or in Wales), in Scotland or in Northern Ireland.]

    (2)   The registrar may accept the statement delivered under paragraph (c) of subsection (1) of section 2 as sufficient evidence that the requirement imposed by paragraph (a) of that subsection has been complied with.

    (3)   The certificate shall either be signed by the registrar or be authenticated by his official seal.

    (4)   The certificate is conclusive evidence that the requirements of section 2 are complied with and that the limited liability partnership is incorporated by the name specified in the incorporation document.

[1816]

NOTES

    Sub-ss (1), (1A): substituted for original sub-s (1) by the Limited Liability Partnerships (Application of Companies Act 2006) Regulations 2009, SI 2009/1804, reg 85, Sch 3, Pt 1, para 2, except in relation to an obligation arising before 1 October 2009 to deliver a document to the registrar.

Membership

4 Members

    (1)   On the incorporation of a limited liability partnership its members are the persons who subscribed their names to the incorporation document (other than any who have died or been dissolved).

    (2)   Any other person may become a member of a limited liability partnership by and in accordance with an agreement with the existing members.

    (3)   A person may cease to be a member of a limited liability partnership (as well as by death or dissolution) in accordance with an agreement with the other members or, in the absence of agreement with the other members as to cessation of membership, by giving reasonable notice to the other members.

    (4)   A member of a limited liability partnership shall not be regarded for any purpose as employed by the limited liability partnership unless, if he and the other members were partners in a partnership, he would be regarded for that purpose as employed by the partnership.

[1817]

[4A Minimum membership for carrying on business

    (1)   This section applies where a limited liability partnership carries on business without having at least two members, and does so for more than 6 months.

    (2)   A person who, for the whole or any part of the period that it so carries on business after those 6 months—

    (a)   is a member of the limited liability partnership, and

    (b)   knows that it is carrying on business with only one member, is liable (jointly and severally with the limited liability partnership) for the payment of the limited liability partnership's debts contracted during the period or, as the case may be, that part of it.]

[1817A]

NOTES
Commencement: 1 October 2009.
Inserted by the Limited Liability Partnerships (Application of Companies Act 2006) Regulations 2009, SI 2009/1804, reg 85, Sch 3, Pt 1, para 3, except in relation to an obligation arising before 1 October 2009 to deliver a document to the registrar.

5 Relationship of members etc

(1)   Except as far as otherwise provided by this Act or any other enactment, the mutual rights and duties of the members of a limited liability partnership, and the mutual rights and duties of a limited liability partnership and its members, shall be governed—
  (a)   by agreement between the members, or between the limited liability partnership and its members, or
  (b)   in the absence of agreement as to any matter, by any provision made in relation to that matter by regulations under section 15(c).

(2)   An agreement made before the incorporation of a limited liability partnership between the persons who subscribe their names to the incorporation document may impose obligations on the limited liability partnership (to take effect at any time after its incorporation).

[1818]

6 Members as agents

(1)   Every member of a limited liability partnership is the agent of the limited liability partnership.

(2)   But a limited liability partnership is not bound by anything done by a member in dealing with a person if—
  (a)   the member in fact has no authority to act for the limited liability partnership by doing that thing, and
  (b)   the person knows that he has no authority or does not know or believe him to be a member of the limited liability partnership.

(3)   Where a person has ceased to be a member of a limited liability partnership, the former member is to be regarded (in relation to any person dealing with the limited liability partnership) as still being a member of the limited liability partnership unless—
  (a)   the person has notice that the former member has ceased to be a member of the limited liability partnership, or
  (b)   notice that the former member has ceased to be a member of the limited liability partnership has been delivered to the registrar.

(4)   Where a member of a limited liability partnership is liable to any person (other than another member of the limited liability partnership) as a result of a wrongful act or omission of his in the course of the business of the limited liability partnership or with its authority, the limited liability partnership is liable to the same extent as the member.

[1819]

7 Ex-members

(1)   This section applies where a member of a limited liability partnership has either ceased to be a member or—
  (a)   has died,
  (b)   has become bankrupt or had his estate sequestrated or has been wound up,
  (c)   has granted a trust deed for the benefit of his creditors, or
  (d)   has assigned the whole or any part of his share in the limited liability partnership (absolutely or by way of charge or security).

(2)   In such an event the former member or—
  (a)   his personal representative,
  (b)   his trustee in bankruptcy or permanent or interim trustee (within the meaning of the Bankruptcy (Scotland) Act 1985) or liquidator,
  (c)   his trustee under the trust deed for the benefit of his creditors, or
  (d)   his assignee,
may not interfere in the management or administration of any business or affairs of the limited liability partnership.

(3)   But subsection (2) does not affect any right to receive an amount from the limited liability partnership in that event.

[1820]

8   Designated members

  (1)   If the incorporation document specifies who are to be designated members—

    (a)   they are designated members on incorporation, and

    (b)   any member may become a designated member by and in accordance with an agreement with the other members,

and a member may cease to be a designated member in accordance with an agreement with the other members.

  (2)   But if there would otherwise be no designated members, or only one, every member is a designated member.

  (3)   If the incorporation document states that every person who from time to time is a member of the limited liability partnership is a designated member, every member is a designated member.

  (4)   A limited liability partnership may at any time deliver to the registrar—

    (a)   notice that specified members are to be designated members, or

    (b)   notice that every person who from time to time is a member of the limited liability partnership is a designated member,

and, once it is delivered, subsection (1) (apart from paragraph (a)) and subsection (2), or subsection (3), shall have effect as if that were stated in the incorporation document.

  (5)   ...

  (6)   A person ceases to be a designated member if he ceases to be a member.

[1821]

NOTES

Sub-s (5): repealed by the Limited Liability Partnerships (Application of Companies Act 2006) Regulations 2009, SI 2009/1804, reg 85, Sch 3, Pt 1, para 4, except in relation to an obligation arising before 1 October 2009 to deliver a document to the registrar.

9   Registration of membership changes

  (1)   A limited liability partnership must ensure that—

    (a)   where a person becomes or ceases to be a member or designated member, notice is delivered to the registrar within fourteen days, and

    (b)   where there is any change in the [particulars contained in its register of members or its register of members' residential addresses], notice is delivered to the registrar within [14 days].

  (2)   Where all the members from time to time of a limited liability partnership are designated members, subsection (1)(a) does not require notice that a person has become or ceased to be a designated member as well as a member.

  [(3)   A notice delivered under subsection (1) that relates to a person becoming a member or designated member must contain—

    (a)   a statement that the member or designated member consents to acting in that capacity, and

    (b)   in the case of a person becoming a member, a statement of the particulars of the new member that are required to be included in the limited liability partnership's register of members and its register of residential addresses.]

  [(3ZA)   Where—

    (a)   a limited liability partnership gives notice of a change of a member's service address as stated in its register of members, and

    (b)   the notice is not accompanied by notice of any resulting change in the particulars contained in its register of members' residential addresses,

the notice must be accompanied by a statement that no such change is required.]

  [(3A), (3B)   ...]

  (4)   If a limited liability partnership fails to comply with [this section], the partnership and every designated member commits an offence.

  (5)   But it is a defence for a designated member charged with an offence under subsection (4) to prove that he took all reasonable steps for securing that [this section] was complied with.

  (6)   A person guilty of an offence under subsection (4) is liable on summary conviction to a fine not exceeding level 5 on the standard scale.

[1822]

NOTES

Sub-s (1): words in square brackets substituted by the Limited Liability Partnerships (Application of Companies Act 2006) Regulations 2009, SI 2009/1804, reg 85, Sch 3, Pt 1, para 5(1), (2), except in relation to an obligation arising before 1 October 2009 to deliver a document to the registrar.

Sub-s (3): substituted by SI 2009/1804, reg 85, Sch 3, Pt 1, para 5(1), (3), except in relation to an obligation arising before 1 October 2009 to deliver a document to the registrar.

Sub-s (3ZA): inserted by SI 2009/1804, reg 85, Sch 3, Pt 1, para 5(1), (4), except in relation to an obligation arising before 1 October 2009 to deliver a document to the registrar.

Sub-ss (3A), (3B): inserted by the Limited Liability Partnerships (Particulars of Usual Residential Address) (Confidentiality Orders) Regulations 2002, SI 2002/915, reg 16, Sch 2, para 1; repealed by SI 2009/1804, reg 85, Sch 3, Pt 1, para 5(1), (5), except in relation to an obligation arising before 1 October 2009 to deliver a document to the registrar.

Sub-ss (4), (5): words in square brackets substituted by SI 2009/1804, reg 85, Sch 3, Pt 1, para 5(1), (6), except in relation to an obligation arising before 1 October 2009 to deliver a document to the registrar.

Taxation

10, 11 *(S 10 repealed in part by the Income Tax Act 2007, s 1031, Sch 3, Pt 1 and the Corporation Tax Act 2010, s 1181(1), Sch 3, Pt 1; remainder inserts the Taxation of Chargeable Gains Act 1992, ss 59A, 156A; s 11 inserts the Inheritance Tax Act 1984, s 267A.)*

12 Stamp duty

(1)　Stamp duty shall not be chargeable on an instrument by which property is conveyed or transferred by a person to a limited liability partnership in connection with its incorporation within the period of one year beginning with the date of incorporation if the following two conditions are satisfied.

(2)　The first condition is that at the relevant time the person—
  (a)　is a partner in a partnership comprised of all the persons who are or are to be members of the limited liability partnership (and no-one else), or
  (b)　holds the property conveyed or transferred as nominee or bare trustee for one or more of the partners in such a partnership.

(3)　The second condition is that—
  (a)　the proportions of the property conveyed or transferred to which the persons mentioned in subsection (2)(a) are entitled immediately after the conveyance or transfer are the same as those to which they were entitled at the relevant time, or
  (b)　none of the differences in those proportions has arisen as part of a scheme or arrangement of which the main purpose, or one of the main purposes, is avoidance of liability to any duty or tax.

(4)　For the purposes of subsection (2) a person holds property as bare trustee for a partner if the partner has the exclusive right (subject only to satisfying any outstanding charge, lien or other right of the trustee to resort to the property for payment of duty, taxes, costs or other outgoings) to direct how the property shall be dealt with.

(5)　In this section "the relevant time" means—
  (a)　if the person who conveyed or transferred the property to the limited liability partnership acquired the property after its incorporation, immediately after he acquired the property, and
  (b)　in any other case, immediately before its incorporation.

(6)　An instrument in respect of which stamp duty is not chargeable by virtue of subsection (1) shall not be taken to be duly stamped unless—
  (a)　it has, in accordance with section 12 of the Stamp Act 1891, been stamped with a particular stamp denoting that it is not chargeable with any duty or that it is duly stamped, or
  (b)　it is stamped with the duty to which it would be liable apart from that subsection.

[1823]

13　*(Amends the Social Security Contributions and Benefits Act 1992, s 15, and the Social Security Contributions and Benefits (Northern Ireland) Act 1992, s 15.)*

Regulations

14 Insolvency and winding up

(1)　Regulations shall make provision about the insolvency and winding up of limited liability partnerships by applying or incorporating, with such modifications as appear appropriate[—
  (a)　in relation to a limited liability partnership registered in Great Britain, Parts 1 to 4, 6 and 7 of the Insolvency Act 1986;
  (b)　in relation to a limited liability partnership registered in Northern Ireland, Parts 2 to 5 and 7 of the Insolvency (Northern Ireland) Order 1989, and so much of Part 1 of that Order as applies for the purposes of those Parts].

(2) Regulations may make other provision about the insolvency and winding up of limited liability partnerships, and provision about the insolvency and winding up of oversea limited liability partnerships, by—

(a) applying or incorporating, with such modifications as appear appropriate, any law relating to the insolvency or winding up of companies or other corporations which would not otherwise have effect in relation to them, or

(b) providing for any law relating to the insolvency or winding up of companies or other corporations which would otherwise have effect in relation to them not to apply to them or to apply to them with such modifications as appear appropriate.

(3) In this Act "oversea limited liability partnership" means a body incorporated or otherwise established outside [the United Kingdom] and having such connection with [the United Kingdom], and such other features, as regulations may prescribe.

[1824]

NOTES

Sub-s (1): words in square brackets substituted by the Limited Liability Partnerships (Application of Companies Act 2006) Regulations 2009, SI 2009/1804, reg 85, Sch 3, Pt 1, para 6(1), (2), except in relation to an obligation arising before 1 October 2009 to deliver a document to the registrar.

Sub-s (3): words in square brackets substituted by SI 2009/1804, reg 85, Sch 3, Pt 1, para 6(1), (3), except in relation to an obligation arising before 1 October 2009 to deliver a document to the registrar.

Regulations: the Limited Liability Partnerships Regulations 2001, SI 2001/1090.

15 Application of company law etc

Regulations may make provision about limited liability partnerships and oversea limited liability partnerships (not being provision about insolvency or winding up) by—

(a) applying or incorporating, with such modifications as appear appropriate, any law relating to companies or other corporations which would not otherwise have effect in relation to them,

(b) providing for any law relating to companies or other corporations which would otherwise have effect in relation to them not to apply to them or to apply to them with such modifications as appear appropriate, or

(c) applying or incorporating, with such modifications as appear appropriate, any law relating to partnerships.

[1825]

NOTES

Regulations: the Limited Liability Partnerships Regulations 2001, SI 2001/1090; the Companies (Registrar, Languages and Trading Disclosures) Regulations 2006, SI 2006/3429; the Companies (Late Filing Penalties) and Limited Liability Partnerships (Filing Periods and Late Filing Penalties) Regulations 2008, SI 2008/497; the Limited Liability Partnerships (Accounts and Audit) (Application of Companies Act 2006) Regulations 2008, SI 2008/1911; the Small Limited Liability Partnerships (Accounts) Regulations 2008, SI 2008/1912; the Large and Medium-sized Limited Liability Partnerships (Accounts) Regulations 2008, SI 2008/1913; the Limited Liability Partnerships (Application of Companies Act 2006) Regulations 2009, SI 2009/1804.

16 Consequential amendments

(1) Regulations may make in any enactment such amendments or repeals as appear appropriate in consequence of this Act or regulations made under it.

(2) The regulations may, in particular, make amendments and repeals affecting companies or other corporations or partnerships.

[1826]

NOTES

Regulations: the Limited Liability Partnerships Regulations 2001, SI 2001/1090.

17 General

(1) In this Act "regulations" means regulations made by the Secretary of State by statutory instrument.

(2) Regulations under this Act may in particular—

(a) make provisions for dealing with non-compliance with any of the regulations (including the creation of criminal offences),

(b) impose fees (which shall be paid into the Consolidated Fund), and

(c) provide for the exercise of functions by persons prescribed by the regulations.

(3) Regulations under this Act may—

(a) contain any appropriate consequential, incidental, supplementary or transitional provisions or savings, and

(b) make different provision for different purposes.

PART 1
STATUTES

(4)   No regulations to which this subsection applies shall be made unless a draft of the statutory instrument containing the regulations (whether or not together with other provisions) has been laid before, and approved by a resolution of, each House of Parliament.

(5)   Subsection (4) applies to—

(a)   regulations under section 14(2) not consisting entirely of the application or incorporation (with or without modifications) of provisions contained in or made under the Insolvency Act 1986 [or the Insolvency (Northern Ireland) Order 1989],

[(b)   regulations under section 15 not consisting entirely of the application or incorporation (with or without modifications) of provisions contained in or made under the following provisions of the Companies Act 2006 (c 46)—

Part 4 (a company's capacity and related matters);
Part 5 (a company's name);
Part 6 (a company's registered office);
Chapters 1 and 8 of Part 10 (register of directors);
Part 15 (accounts and reports);
Part 16 (audit);
Part 19 (debentures);
Part 21 (certification and transfer of securities);
Part 24 (a company's annual return);
Part 25 (company charges);
Part 26 (arrangements and reconstructions);
Part 29 (fraudulent trading);
Part 30 (protection of members against unfair prejudice);
Part 31 (dissolution and restoration to the register);
Part 35 (the registrar of companies);
Part 36 (offences under the Companies Acts);
Part 37 (supplementary provisions);
Part 38 (interpretation),]

(c)   regulations under section 14 or 15 making provision about oversea limited liability partnerships, and

(d)   regulations under section 16.

(6)   A statutory instrument containing regulations under this Act shall (unless a draft of it has been approved by a resolution of each House of Parliament) be subject to annulment in pursuance of a resolution of either House of Parliament.

[1827]

NOTES

Sub-s (5): words in square brackets in para (a) inserted and para (b) substituted by the Limited Liability Partnerships (Application of Companies Act 2006) Regulations 2009, SI 2009/1804, reg 85, Sch 3, Pt 1, para 7, except in relation to an obligation arising before 1 October 2009 to deliver a document to the registrar.

Regulations: the Companies (Registrar, Languages and Trading Disclosures) Regulations 2006, SI 2006/3429; the Limited Liability Partnerships (Accounts and Audit) (Application of Companies Act 2006) Regulations 2008, SI 2008/1911; the Small Limited Liability Partnerships (Accounts) Regulations 2008, SI 2008/1912; the Limited Liability Partnerships (Application of Companies Act 2006) Regulations 2009, SI 2009/1804.

Supplementary

18 Interpretation

In this Act—

...

"business" includes every trade, profession and occupation,

"designated member" shall be construed in accordance with section 8,

"enactment" includes subordinate legislation (within the meaning of the Interpretation Act 1978),

"incorporation document" shall be construed in accordance with section 2,

"limited liability partnership" has the meaning given by section 1(2),

"member" shall be construed in accordance with section 4,

"modifications" includes additions and omissions,

"name", in relation to a member of a limited liability partnership, means—

(a)   if an individual, his forename and surname (or, in the case of a peer or other person usually known by a title, his title instead of or in addition to either or both his forename and surname), and

(b)   if a corporation or Scottish firm, its corporate or firm name,

"oversea limited liability partnership" has the meaning given by section 14(3),

["the registrar" means—

(a)   if the registered office of the limited liability partnership is, or is to be, in England and Wales (or Wales), the registrar of companies for England and Wales,

(b)   if the registered office of the limited liability partnership is, or is to be, in Scotland, the registrar of companies for Scotland, and

(c)   if the registered office of the limited liability partnership is, or is to be, in Northern Ireland, the registrar of companies for Northern Ireland;] and

"regulations" has the meaning given by section 17(1).

[1828]

NOTES

Definition "address" (omitted) repealed and definition "the registrar" substituted by the Limited Liability Partnerships (Application of Companies Act 2006) Regulations 2009, SI 2009/1804, reg 85, Sch 3, Pt 1, para 8, except in relation to an obligation arising before 1 October 2009 to deliver a document to the registrar.

19   Commencement, extent and short title

(1)   The preceding provisions of this Act shall come into force on such day as the Secretary of State may by order made by statutory instrument appoint; and different days may be appointed for different purposes.

(2)   The Secretary of State may by order made by statutory instrument make any transitional provisions and savings which appear appropriate in connection with the coming into force of any provision of this Act.

(3)   For the purposes of the Scotland Act 1998 this Act shall be taken to be a pre-commencement enactment within the meaning of that Act.

[(4)   This Act extends to the whole of the United Kingdom.]

(5)   This Act may be cited as the Limited Liability Partnerships Act 2000.

[1829]

NOTES

Sub-s (4): substituted by the Limited Liability Partnerships (Application of Companies Act 2006) Regulations 2009, SI 2009/1804, reg 85, Sch 3, Pt 1, para 9, except in relation to an obligation arising before 1 October 2009 to deliver a document to the registrar.

Order: the Limited Liability Partnerships Act 2000 (Commencement) Order 2000, SI 2000/3316.

SCHEDULE
NAMES AND REGISTERED OFFICES

Section 1

PART I
NAMES

1.   ...

Name to indicate status

2.—(1)   The name of a limited liability partnership must end with—

(a)   the expression "limited liability partnership", or

(b)   the abbreviation "llp" or "LLP".

(2)   But if the incorporation document for a limited liability partnership states that the registered office is to be situated in Wales, its name must end with—

(a)   one of the expressions "limited liability partnership" and "partneriaeth atebolrwydd cyfyngedig", or

(b)   one of the abbreviations "llp", "LLP", "pac" and "PAC".

3.   ...

Change of name

4.—(1)   A limited liability partnership may change its name at any time.

[(2)   The name of a limited liability partnership may also be changed—

(a)   on the determination of a new name by a company names adjudicator under section 73 of the Companies Act 2006 (C 46) as applied to limited liability partnerships (powers of adjudicator on upholding objection to name);

(b)   on the determination of a new name by the court under section 74 of the Companies Act 2006 as so applied (appeal against decision of company names adjudicator);

(c)   under section 1033 as so applied (name on restoration to the register).]

Notification of change of name

5.—(1)   Where a limited liability partnership changes its name it shall deliver notice of the change to the registrar.

(2)   ...

(3)   Where the registrar receives [notice of a change of name] he shall (unless the new name is one by which a limited liability partnership may not be registered)—

[(a)   enter the new name on the register in place of the former name, and]

(b)   issue a certificate of the change of name.

(4)   The change of name has effect from the date on which the certificate is issued.

Effect of change of name

6.   A change of name by a limited liability partnership does not—

(a)   affect any of its rights or duties,

(b)   render defective any legal proceedings by or against it,

and any legal proceedings that might have been commenced or continued against it by its former name may be commenced or continued against it by its new name.

Improper use of "limited liability partnership" etc

7.—(1)   If any person carries on a business under a name or title which includes as the last words—

(a)   the expression "limited liability partnership" or "partneriaeth atebolrwydd cyfyngedig", or

(b)   any contraction or imitation of either of those expressions,

that person, unless a limited liability partnership or oversea limited liability partnership, commits an offence.

(2)   A person guilty of an offence under sub-paragraph (1) is liable on summary conviction to a fine not exceeding level 3 on the standard scale.

8.   ...

[1830]–[1831]

NOTES

Para 1: repealed by the Companies Act 2006, s 1295, Sch 16.

Para 3: repealed by the Limited Liability Partnerships (Application of Companies Act 2006) Regulations 2009, SI 2009/1804, reg 85, Sch 3, Pt 1, para 10(1), (2), except in relation to an obligation arising before 1 October 2009 to deliver a document to the registrar.

Para 4: sub-para (2) substituted for original sub-paras (2)–(9) by SI 2009/1804, reg 85, Sch 3, Pt 1, para 10(1), (3), except in relation to an obligation arising before 1 October 2009 to deliver a document to the registrar.

Para 5: sub-para (2) repealed and words in square brackets in sub-para (3) substituted by SI 2009/1804, Sch 3, Pt 1, para 10(1), (4), except in relation to an obligation arising before 1 October 2009 to deliver a document to the registrar.

Para 8: repealed by SI 2009/1804, reg 85, Sch 3, Pt 1, para 10(1), (5), except in relation to an obligation arising before 1 October 2009 to deliver a document to the registrar.

(*Pt II repealed by the Limited Liability Partnerships (Application of Companies Act 2006) Regulations 2009, SI 2009/1804, reg 85, Sch 3, Pt 1, para 10(1), (6), except in relation to an obligation arising before 1 October 2009 to deliver a document to the registrar.*)

REGULATION OF INVESTIGATORY POWERS ACT 2000

(2000 c 23)

ARRANGEMENT OF SECTIONS

PART I
COMMUNICATIONS

CHAPTER I
INTERCEPTION

Unlawful and authorised interception

PART IV
SCRUTINY ETC OF INVESTIGATORY POWERS AND OF THE
FUNCTIONS OF THE INTELLIGENCE SERVICES

Codes of practice

PART V
MISCELLANEOUS AND SUPPLEMENTAL

Supplemental

An Act to make provision for and about the interception of communications, the acquisition and disclosure of data relating to communications, the carrying out of surveillance, the use of covert human intelligence sources and the acquisition of the means by which electronic data protected by encryption or passwords may be decrypted or accessed; to provide for Commissioners and a tribunal with functions and jurisdiction in relation to those matters, to entries on and interferences with property or with wireless telegraphy and to the carrying out of their functions by the Security Service, the Secret Intelligence Service and the Government Communications Headquarters; and for connected purposes

[28 July 2000]

PART I
COMMUNICATIONS

CHAPTER I
INTERCEPTION

Unlawful and authorised interception

1   Unlawful interception

(1)   It shall be an offence for a person intentionally and without lawful authority to intercept, at any place in the United Kingdom, any communication in the course of its transmission by means of—
    (a)   a public postal service; or
    (b)   a public telecommunication system.

(2)   It shall be an offence for a person—
    (a)   intentionally and without lawful authority, and
    (b)   otherwise than in circumstances in which his conduct is excluded by subsection (6) from criminal liability under this subsection,
to intercept, at any place in the United Kingdom, any communication in the course of its transmission by means of a private telecommunication system.

(3)   Any interception of a communication which is carried out at any place in the United Kingdom by, or with the express or implied consent of, a person having the right to control the operation or the use of a private telecommunication system shall be actionable at the suit or instance of the sender or recipient, or intended recipient, of the communication if it is without lawful authority and is either—
    (a)   an interception of that communication in the course of its transmission by means of that private system; or
    (b)   an interception of that communication in the course of its transmission, by means of a public telecommunication system, to or from apparatus comprised in that private telecommunication system.

(4)   Where the United Kingdom is a party to an international agreement which—
    (a)   relates to the provision of mutual assistance in connection with, or in the form of, the interception of communications,
    (b)   requires the issue of a warrant, order or equivalent instrument in cases in which assistance is given, and
    (c)   is designated for the purposes of this subsection by an order made by the Secretary of State,
it shall be the duty of the Secretary of State to secure that no request for assistance in accordance with the agreement is made on behalf of a person in the United Kingdom to the competent authorities of a country or territory outside the United Kingdom except with lawful authority.

(5)   Conduct has lawful authority for the purposes of this section if, and only if—
    (a)   it is authorised by or under section 3 or 4;
    (b)   it takes place in accordance with a warrant under section 5 ("an interception warrant"); or
    (c)   it is in exercise, in relation to any stored communication, of any statutory power that is exercised (apart from this section) for the purpose of obtaining information or of taking possession of any document or other property;
and conduct (whether or not prohibited by this section) which has lawful authority for the purposes of this section by virtue of paragraph (a) or (b) shall also be taken to be lawful for all other purposes.

PART I
STATUTES

(6)   The circumstances in which a person makes an interception of a communication in the course of its transmission by means of a private telecommunication system are such that his conduct is excluded from criminal liability under subsection (2) if—

(a)   he is a person with a right to control the operation or the use of the system; or

(b)   he has the express or implied consent of such a person to make the interception.

(7)   A person who is guilty of an offence under subsection (1) or (2) shall be liable—

(a)   on conviction on indictment, to imprisonment for a term not exceeding two years or to a fine, or to both;

(b)   on summary conviction, to a fine not exceeding the statutory maximum.

(8)   No proceedings for any offence which is an offence by virtue of this section shall be instituted—

(a)   in England and Wales, except by or with the consent of the Director of Public Prosecutions;

(b)   in Northern Ireland, except by or with the consent of the Director of Public Prosecutions for Northern Ireland.

[1832]

NOTES

Order: the Regulation of Investigatory Powers (Designation of an International Agreement) Order 2004, SI 2004/158.

---

2   Meaning and location of "interception" etc

(1)   In this Act—

"postal service" means any service which—

(a)   consists in the following, or in any one or more of them, namely, the collection, sorting, conveyance, distribution and delivery (whether in the United Kingdom or elsewhere) of postal items; and

(b)   is offered or provided as a service the main purpose of which, or one of the main purposes of which, is to make available, or to facilitate, a means of transmission from place to place of postal items containing communications;

"private telecommunication system" means any telecommunication system which, without itself being a public telecommunication system, is a system in relation to which the following conditions are satisfied—

(a)   it is attached, directly or indirectly and whether or not for the purposes of the communication in question, to a public telecommunication system; and

(b)   there is apparatus comprised in the system which is both located in the United Kingdom and used (with or without other apparatus) for making the attachment to the public telecommunication system;

"public postal service" means any postal service which is offered or provided to, or to a substantial section of, the public in any one or more parts of the United Kingdom;

"public telecommunications service" means any telecommunications service which is offered or provided to, or to a substantial section of, the public in any one or more parts of the United Kingdom;

"public telecommunication system" means any such parts of a telecommunication system by means of which any public telecommunications service is provided as are located in the United Kingdom;

"telecommunications service" means any service that consists in the provision of access to, and of facilities for making use of, any telecommunication system (whether or not one provided by the person providing the service); and

"telecommunication system" means any system (including the apparatus comprised in it) which exists (whether wholly or partly in the United Kingdom or elsewhere) for the purpose of facilitating the transmission of communications by any means involving the use of electrical or electro-magnetic energy.

(2)   For the purposes of this Act, but subject to the following provisions of this section, a person intercepts a communication in the course of its transmission by means of a telecommunication system if, and only if, he—

(a)   so modifies or interferes with the system, or its operation,

(b)   so monitors transmissions made by means of the system, or

(c)   so monitors transmissions made by wireless telegraphy to or from apparatus comprised in the system,

as to make some or all of the contents of the communication available, while being transmitted, to a person other than the sender or intended recipient of the communication.

(3)   References in this Act to the interception of a communication do not include references to the interception of any communication broadcast for general reception.

(4)   For the purposes of this Act the interception of a communication takes place in the United Kingdom if, and only if, the modification, interference or monitoring or, in the case of a postal item, the interception is effected by conduct within the United Kingdom and the communication is either—

    (a)   intercepted in the course of its transmission by means of a public postal service or public telecommunication system; or

    (b)   intercepted in the course of its transmission by means of a private telecommunication system in a case in which the sender or intended recipient of the communication is in the United Kingdom.

(5)   References in this Act to the interception of a communication in the course of its transmission by means of a postal service or telecommunication system do not include references to—

    (a)   any conduct that takes place in relation only to so much of the communication as consists in any traffic data comprised in or attached to a communication (whether by the sender or otherwise) for the purposes of any postal service or telecommunication system by means of which it is being or may be transmitted; or

    (b)   any such conduct, in connection with conduct falling within paragraph (a), as gives a person who is neither the sender nor the intended recipient only so much access to a communication as is necessary for the purpose of identifying traffic data so comprised or attached.

(6)   For the purposes of this section references to the modification of a telecommunication system include references to the attachment of any apparatus to, or other modification of or interference with—

    (a)   any part of the system; or

    (b)   any wireless telegraphy apparatus used for making transmissions to or from apparatus comprised in the system.

(7)   For the purposes of this section the times while a communication is being transmitted by means of a telecommunication system shall be taken to include any time when the system by means of which the communication is being, or has been, transmitted is used for storing it in a manner that enables the intended recipient to collect it or otherwise to have access to it.

(8)   For the purposes of this section the cases in which any contents of a communication are to be taken to be made available to a person while being transmitted shall include any case in which any of the contents of the communication, while being transmitted, are diverted or recorded so as to be available to a person subsequently.

(9)   In this section "traffic data", in relation to any communication, means—

    (a)   any data identifying, or purporting to identify, any person, apparatus or location to or from which the communication is or may be transmitted,

    (b)   any data identifying or selecting, or purporting to identify or select, apparatus through which, or by means of which, the communication is or may be transmitted,

    (c)   any data comprising signals for the actuation of apparatus used for the purposes of a telecommunication system for effecting (in whole or in part) the transmission of any communication, and

    (d)   any data identifying the data or other data as data comprised in or attached to a particular communication,

but that expression includes data identifying a computer file or computer program access to which is obtained, or which is run, by means of the communication to the extent only that the file or program is identified by reference to the apparatus in which it is stored.

(10)   In this section—

    (a)   references, in relation to traffic data comprising signals for the actuation of apparatus, to a telecommunication system by means of which a communication is being or may be transmitted include references to any telecommunication system in which that apparatus is comprised; and

    (b)   references to traffic data being attached to a communication include references to the data and the communication being logically associated with each other;

and in this section "data", in relation to a postal item, means anything written on the outside of the item.

(11)   In this section "postal item" means any letter, postcard or other such thing in writing as may be used by the sender for imparting information to the recipient, or any packet or parcel.

3 Lawful interception without an interception warrant

(1)   Conduct by any person consisting in the interception of a communication is authorised by this section if the communication is one which, or which that person has reasonable grounds for believing, is both—

    (a)   a communication sent by a person who has consented to the interception; and

    (b)   a communication the intended recipient of which has so consented.

    (2)   Conduct by any person consisting in the interception of a communication is authorised by this section if—

        (a)   the communication is one sent by, or intended for, a person who has consented to the interception; and

        (b)   surveillance by means of that interception has been authorised under Part II.

    (3)   Conduct consisting in the interception of a communication is authorised by this section if—

        (a)   it is conduct by or on behalf of a person who provides a postal service or a telecommunications service; and

        (b)   it takes place for purposes connected with the provision or operation of that service or with the enforcement, in relation to that service, of any enactment relating to the use of postal services or telecommunications services.

    [(3A)   Conduct consisting in the interception of a communication in the course of its transmission by means of a public postal service is authorised by this section if it is conduct—

        (a)   under section 159 of the Customs and Excise Management Act 1979 as applied by virtue of—

            (i)   section 105 of the Postal Services Act 2000 (power to open postal items etc); or

            (ii)   that section 105 and another enactment; and

        (b)   by an officer of Revenue and Customs.]

    (4)   Conduct by any person consisting in the interception of a communication in the course of its transmission by means of wireless telegraphy is authorised by this section if it takes place—

        (a)   with the authority of a designated person under [section 48 of the Wireless Telegraphy Act 2006 (interception and disclosure of wireless telegraphy messages)]; and

        (b)   for purposes connected with anything falling within subsection (5).

    (5)   Each of the following falls within this subsection—

        [(a)   the grant of wireless telegraphy licences under the Wireless Telegraphy Act 2006;]

        (b)   the prevention or detection of anything which constitutes interference with wireless telegraphy; and

        (c)   the enforcement of[—

            (i)   any provision of Part 2 (other than Chapter 2 and sections 27 to 31) or Part 3 of that Act, or

            (ii)   any enactment not falling within sub-paragraph (i),]

        that relates to such interference.

[1834]

NOTES

    Sub-s (3A): inserted by the Policing and Crime Act 2009, s 100(1).

    Sub-s (4): words in square brackets in para (a) substituted by the Wireless Telegraphy Act 2006, s 123, Sch 7, paras 21, 22(1), (2).

    Sub-s (5): paras (a), (c)(i), (ii) substituted by the Wireless Telegraphy Act 2006, s 123, Sch 7, paras 21, 22(1), (3).

4 Power to provide for lawful interception

    (1)   Conduct by any person ("the interceptor") consisting in the interception of a communication in the course of its transmission by means of a telecommunication system is authorised by this section if—

        (a)   the interception is carried out for the purpose of obtaining information about the communications of a person who, or who the interceptor has reasonable grounds for believing, is in a country or territory outside the United Kingdom;

        (b)   the interception relates to the use of a telecommunications service provided to persons in that country or territory which is either—

            (i)   a public telecommunications service; or

            (ii)   a telecommunications service that would be a public telecommunications service if the persons to whom it is offered or provided were members of the public in a part of the United Kingdom;

        (c)   the person who provides that service (whether the interceptor or another person) is required by the law of that country or territory to carry out, secure or facilitate the interception in question;

        (d)   the situation is one in relation to which such further conditions as may be prescribed by regulations made by the Secretary of State are required to be satisfied before conduct may be treated as authorised by virtue of this subsection; and

        (e)   the conditions so prescribed are satisfied in relation to that situation.

    (2)   Subject to subsection (3), the Secretary of State may by regulations authorise any such conduct described in the regulations as appears to him to constitute a legitimate practice reasonably required for the purpose, in connection with the carrying on of any business, of monitoring or keeping a record of—

(a) communications by means of which transactions are entered into in the course of that business; or

(b) other communications relating to that business or taking place in the course of its being carried on.

(3) Nothing in any regulations under subsection (2) shall authorise the interception of any communication except in the course of its transmission using apparatus or services provided by or to the person carrying on the business for use wholly or partly in connection with that business.

(4) Conduct taking place in a prison is authorised by this section if it is conduct in exercise of any power conferred by or under any rules made under section 47 of the Prison Act 1952, section 39 of the Prisons (Scotland) Act 1989 or section 13 of the Prison Act (Northern Ireland) 1953 (prison rules).

(5) Conduct taking place in any hospital premises where high security psychiatric services are provided is authorised by this section if it is conduct in pursuance of, and in accordance with, any direction given under [section 8 of the National Health Service Act 2006, or section 19 or 23 of the National Health Service (Wales) Act 2006] (directions as to the carrying out of their functions by health bodies) to the body providing those services at those premises.

(6) Conduct taking place in a state hospital is authorised by this section if it is conduct in pursuance of, and in accordance with, any direction given to the State Hospitals Board for Scotland under section 2(5) of the National Health Service (Scotland) Act 1978 (regulations and directions as to the exercise of their functions by health boards) as applied by Article 5(1) of and the Schedule to The State Hospitals Board for Scotland Order 1995 (which applies certain provisions of that Act of 1978 to the State Hospitals Board).

(7) In this section references to a business include references to any activities of a government department, of any public authority or of any person or office holder on whom functions are conferred by or under any enactment.

(8) In this section—

"government department" includes any part of the Scottish Administration, a Northern Ireland department and [the Welsh Assembly Government];

"high security psychiatric services" has the same meaning as in [section 4 of the National Health Service Act 2006];

"hospital premises" has the same meaning as in section 4(3) of that Act; and

"state hospital" has the same meaning as in the National Health Service (Scotland) Act 1978.

(9) In this section "prison" means—

(a) any prison, young offender institution, young offenders centre or remand centre which is under the general superintendence of, or is provided by, the Secretary of State under the Prison Act 1952 or the Prison Act (Northern Ireland) 1953, or

(b) any prison, young offenders institution or remand centre which is under the general superintendence of the Scottish Ministers under the Prisons (Scotland) Act 1989,

and includes any contracted out prison, within the meaning of Part IV of the Criminal Justice Act 1991 or section 106(4) of the Criminal Justice and Public Order Act 1994, and any legalised police cells within the meaning of section 14 of the Prisons (Scotland) Act 1989.

[1835]

NOTES

Sub-s (5): words in square brackets substituted by the National Health Service (Consequential Provisions) Act 2006, s 2, Sch 1, paras 207, 208(a).

Sub-s (8): in definition "government department" words in square brackets substituted by the Government of Wales Act 2006 (Consequential Modifications and Transitional Provisions) Order 2007, SI 2007/1388, art 3, Sch 1, paras 76(1), (2); in definition "high security psychiatric services" words in square brackets substituted by the National Health Service (Consequential Provisions) Act 2006, s 2, Sch 1, paras 207, 208(b).

Regulations: the Telecommunications (Lawful Business Practice) (Interception of Communications) Regulations 2000, SI 2000/2699 at **[3328]**; the Regulation of Investigatory Powers (Conditions for the Lawful Interception of Persons outside the United Kingdom) Regulations 2004, SI 2004/157.

5–56 (*Ss 5–25, ss 26–56 (Pts II, III) outside the scope of this work.*)

PART IV
SCRUTINY ETC OF INVESTIGATORY POWERS AND OF THE FUNCTIONS OF THE INTELLIGENCE SERVICES

57–70 (*Outside the scope of this work.*)

Codes of practice

71 Issue and revision of codes of practice

(1)   The Secretary of State shall issue one or more codes of practice relating to the exercise and performance of the powers and duties mentioned in subsection (2).

(2)   Those powers and duties are those (excluding any power to make subordinate legislation) that are conferred or imposed otherwise than on the Surveillance Commissioners by or under—
  (a)   Parts I to III of this Act;
  (b)   section 5 of the Intelligence Services Act 1994 (warrants for interference with property or wireless telegraphy for the purposes of the intelligence services); and
  (c)   Part III of the Police Act 1997 (authorisation by the police or [Her Majesty's Revenue and Customs] of interference with property or wireless telegraphy).

(3)   Before issuing a code of practice under subsection (1), the Secretary of State shall—
  (a)   prepare and publish a draft of that code; and
  (b)   consider any representations made to him about the draft;
and the Secretary of State may incorporate in the code finally issued any modifications made by him to the draft after its publication.

(4)   The Secretary of State shall lay before both Houses of Parliament every draft code of practice prepared and published by him under this section.

(5)   A code of practice issued by the Secretary of State under this section shall not be brought into force except in accordance with an order made by the Secretary of State.

(6)   An order under subsection (5) may contain such transitional provisions and savings as appear to the Secretary of State to be necessary or expedient in connection with the bringing into force of the code brought into force by that order.

(7)   The Secretary of State may from time to time—
  (a)   revise the whole or any part of a code issued under this section; and
  (b)   issue the revised code.

(8)   Subsections (3) to (6) shall apply (with appropriate modifications) in relation to the issue of any revised code under this section as they apply in relation to the first issue of such a code.

(9)   The Secretary of State shall not make an order containing provision for any of the purposes of this section unless a draft of the order has been laid before Parliament and approved by a resolution of each House.

[1836]

NOTES
Commencement: 25 September 2000 (in so far as relating to Pt II of this Act (ss 26–48), the Intelligence Services Act 1994, s 5 or the Police Act 1997, Pt III); 2 October 2000 (in so far as relating to ss 1–20 of this Act); 13 August 2001 (in so far as relating to ss 21–25 of this Act); 1 October 2007 (otherwise).
Sub-s (2): words in square brackets in para (c) substituted by the Serious Crime Act 2007, s 88, Sch 12, paras 5, 25.
Orders: the Regulation of Investigatory Powers (Interception of Communications: Code of Practice) Order 2002, SI 2002/1693; the Regulation of Investigatory Powers (Covert Human Intelligence Sources: Code of Practice) Order 2002, SI 2002/1932; the Regulation of Investigatory Powers (Covert Surveillance: Code of Practice) Order 2002, SI 2002/1933; the Regulation of Investigatory Powers (Acquisition and Disclosure of Communications Data: Code of Practice) Order 2007, SI 2007/2197; the Regulation of Investigatory Powers (Investigation of Protected Electronic Information: Code of Practice) Order 2007, SI 2007/2200; the Regulation of Investigatory Powers (Covert Human Intelligence Sources: Code of Practice) Order 2010, SI 2010/462; the Regulation of Investigatory Powers (Covert Surveillance and Property Interference: Code of Practice) Order 2010, SI 2010/463.

72 Effect of codes of practice

(1)   A person exercising or performing any power or duty in relation to which provision may be made by a code of practice under section 71 shall, in doing so, have regard to the provisions (so far as they are applicable) of every code of practice for the time being in force under that section.

(2)   A failure on the part of any person to comply with any provision of a code of practice for the time being in force under section 71 shall not of itself render him liable to any criminal or civil proceedings.

(3)   A code of practice in force at any time under section 71 shall be admissible in evidence in any criminal or civil proceedings.

(4)   If any provision of a code of practice issued or revised under section 71 appears to—
  (a)   the court or tribunal conducting any civil or criminal proceedings,
  (b)   the Tribunal,
  (c)   a relevant Commissioner carrying out any of his functions under this Act,
  (d)   a Surveillance Commissioner carrying out his functions under this Act or the Police Act 1997, or

(e)   any Assistant Surveillance Commissioner carrying out any functions of his under section 63 of this Act,

to be relevant to any question arising in the proceedings, or in connection with the exercise of that jurisdiction or the carrying out of those functions, in relation to a time when it was in force, that provision of the code shall be taken into account in determining that question.

(5)   In this section "relevant Commissioner" means the Interception of Communications Commissioner, the Intelligence Services Commissioner or the Investigatory Powers Commissioner for Northern Ireland.

[1837]

NOTES
Commencement: 25 September 2000 (in so far as relating to Pt II of this Act (ss 26–48), the Intelligence Services Act 1994, s 5 or the Police Act 1997, Pt III); 2 October 2000 (in so far as relating to ss 1–20 of this Act); 13 August 2001 (in so far as relating to ss 21–25 of this Act); 1 October 2007 (otherwise).

PART V
MISCELLANEOUS AND SUPPLEMENTAL

73–76A   (*Outside the scope of this work.*)

Supplemental

77–82   (*Outside the scope of this work.*)

83   Short title, commencement and extent

(1)   This Act may be cited as the Regulation of Investigatory Powers Act 2000.

(2)   The provisions of this Act, other than this section, shall come into force on such day as the Secretary of State may by order appoint; and different days may be appointed under this subsection for different purposes.

(3)   This Act extends to Northern Ireland.

[1838]

NOTES
Orders: the Regulation of Investigatory Powers (Commencement No 1 and Transitional Provisions) Order 2000, SI 2000/2543; the Regulation of Investigatory Powers Act 2000 (Commencement No 2) Order 2001, SI 2001/2727; the Regulation of Investigatory Powers Act 2000 (Commencement No 3) Order 2003, SI 2003/3140; the Regulation of Investigatory Powers Act 2000 (Commencement No 4) Order 2007, SI 2007/2196.

(*Schs 1–5 outside the scope of this work.*)

PROCEEDS OF CRIME ACT 2002

(2002 c 29)

ARRANGEMENT OF SECTIONS

PART 7
MONEY LAUNDERING

Offences

CHAPTER 4
INTERPRETATION

PART 12
MISCELLANEOUS AND GENERAL

General

An Act to establish the Assets Recovery Agency and make provision about the appointment of its Director and his functions (including Revenue functions), to provide for confiscation orders in relation to persons who benefit from criminal conduct and for restraint orders to prohibit dealing with property, to allow the recovery of property which is or represents property obtained through unlawful conduct or which is intended to be used in unlawful conduct, to make provision about money laundering, to make provision about investigations relating to benefit from criminal conduct or to property which is or represents property obtained through unlawful conduct or to money laundering, to make provision to give effect to overseas requests and orders made where property is found or believed to be obtained through criminal conduct, and for connected purposes

[24 July 2002]

1–326　((Pts 1–6) *outside the scope of this work.*)

PART 7
MONEY LAUNDERING

Offences

327　Concealing etc

(1)　A person commits an offence if he—
　　(a)　conceals criminal property;
　　(b)　disguises criminal property;
　　(c)　converts criminal property;
　　(d)　transfers criminal property;
　　(e)　removes criminal property from England and Wales or from Scotland or from Northern Ireland.

(2)　But a person does not commit such an offence if—
　　(a)　he makes an authorised disclosure under section 338 and (if the disclosure is made before he does the act mentioned in subsection (1)) he has the appropriate consent;
　　(b)　he intended to make such a disclosure but had a reasonable excuse for not doing so;
　　(c)　the act he does is done in carrying out a function he has relating to the enforcement of any provision of this Act or of any other enactment relating to criminal conduct or benefit from criminal conduct.

[(2A)   Nor does a person commit an offence under subsection (1) if—
(a)   he knows, or believes on reasonable grounds, that the relevant criminal conduct occurred in a particular country or territory outside the United Kingdom, and
(b)   the relevant criminal conduct—
(i)   was not, at the time it occurred, unlawful under the criminal law then applying in that country or territory, and
(ii)   is not of a description prescribed by an order made by the Secretary of State.

(2B)   In subsection (2A) "the relevant criminal conduct" is the criminal conduct by reference to which the property concerned is criminal property.]

[(2C)   A deposit-taking body that does an act mentioned in paragraph (c) or (d) of subsection (1) does not commit an offence under that subsection if—
(a)   it does the act in operating an account maintained with it, and
(b)   the value of the criminal property concerned is less than the threshold amount determined under section 339A for the act.]

(3)   Concealing or disguising criminal property includes concealing or disguising its nature, source, location, disposition, movement or ownership or any rights with respect to it.

[1839]

NOTES
Sub-ss (2A), (2B): inserted by the Serious Organised Crime and Police Act 2005, s 102(1), (2).
Sub-s (2C): inserted by the Serious Organised Crime and Police Act 2005, s 103(1), (2).
Transitional provisions: by virtue of the Proceeds of Crime Act 2002 (Commencement No 4, Transitional Provisions and Savings) Order 2003, SI 2003/120, the new principal money laundering offences (ie, those contained in ss 327, 328 and 329 of this Act) do not have effect where the conduct constituting an offence under those provisions began before 24 February 2003 and ended on or after that date. In such a case, the old principal money laundering offences (ie, those contained in (i) the Criminal Justice Act 1988, ss 93A, 93B, 93C, (ii) the Criminal Justice (International Co-operation) Act 1990, s 14, (iii) the Drug Trafficking Act 1994, ss 49, 50, 51, (iv) the Criminal Law (Consolidation) (Scotland) Act 1995, ss 37, 38, and (v) the Proceeds of Crime (Northern Ireland) Order 1996, arts 45, 46, 47, continue to have effect.
Order: the Proceeds of Crime Act 2002 (Money Laundering: Exceptions to Overseas Conduct Defence) Order 2006, SI 2006/1070.

328   Arrangements

(1)   A person commits an offence if he enters into or becomes concerned in an arrangement which he knows or suspects facilitates (by whatever means) the acquisition, retention, use or control of criminal property by or on behalf of another person.

(2)   But a person does not commit such an offence if—
(a)   he makes an authorised disclosure under section 338 and (if the disclosure is made before he does the act mentioned in subsection (1)) he has the appropriate consent;
(b)   he intended to make such a disclosure but had a reasonable excuse for not doing so;
(c)   the act he does is done in carrying out a function he has relating to the enforcement of any provision of this Act or of any other enactment relating to criminal conduct or benefit from criminal conduct.

[(3)   Nor does a person commit an offence under subsection (1) if—
(a)   he knows, or believes on reasonable grounds, that the relevant criminal conduct occurred in a particular country or territory outside the United Kingdom, and
(b)   the relevant criminal conduct—
(i)   was not, at the time it occurred, unlawful under the criminal law then applying in that country or territory, and
(ii)   is not of a description prescribed by an order made by the Secretary of State.

(4)   In subsection (3) "the relevant criminal conduct" is the criminal conduct by reference to which the property concerned is criminal property.]

[(5)   A deposit-taking body that does an act mentioned in subsection (1) does not commit an offence under that subsection if—
(a)   it does the act in operating an account maintained with it, and
(b)   the arrangement facilitates the acquisition, retention, use or control of criminal property of a value that is less than the threshold amount determined under section 339A for the act.]

[1840]

NOTES
Sub-ss (3), (4): added by the Serious Organised Crime and Police Act 2005, s 102(1), (3).
Sub-s (5): added by the Serious Organised Crime and Police Act 2005, s 103(1), (3).
Order: the Proceeds of Crime Act 2002 (Money Laundering: Exceptions to Overseas Conduct Defence) Order 2006, SI 2006/1070.
Transitional provisions: see the note to s 327 at **[1839]**.

329   Acquisition, use and possession

(1)   A person commits an offence if he—
    (a)   acquires criminal property;
    (b)   uses criminal property;
    (c)   has possession of criminal property.

(2)   But a person does not commit such an offence if—
    (a)   he makes an authorised disclosure under section 338 and (if the disclosure is made before he does the act mentioned in subsection (1)) he has the appropriate consent;
    (b)   he intended to make such a disclosure but had a reasonable excuse for not doing so;
    (c)   he acquired or used or had possession of the property for adequate consideration;
    (d)   the act he does is done in carrying out a function he has relating to the enforcement of any provision of this Act or of any other enactment relating to criminal conduct or benefit from criminal conduct.

[(2A)   Nor does a person commit an offence under subsection (1) if—
    (a)   he knows, or believes on reasonable grounds, that the relevant criminal conduct occurred in a particular country or territory outside the United Kingdom, and
    (b)   the relevant criminal conduct—
        (i)   was not, at the time it occurred, unlawful under the criminal law then applying in that country or territory, and
        (ii)   is not of a description prescribed by an order made by the Secretary of State.

(2B)   In subsection (2A) "the relevant criminal conduct" is the criminal conduct by reference to which the property concerned is criminal property.]

[(2C)   A deposit-taking body that does an act mentioned in subsection (1) does not commit an offence under that subsection if—
    (a)   it does the act in operating an account maintained with it, and
    (b)   the value of the criminal property concerned is less than the threshold amount determined under section 339A for the act.]

(3)   For the purposes of this section—
    (a)   a person acquires property for inadequate consideration if the value of the consideration is significantly less than the value of the property;
    (b)   a person uses or has possession of property for inadequate consideration if the value of the consideration is significantly less than the value of the use or possession;
    (c)   the provision by a person of goods or services which he knows or suspects may help another to carry out criminal conduct is not consideration.

[1841]

NOTES
Sub-ss (2A), (2B): inserted by the Serious Organised Crime and Police Act 2005, s 102(1), (4).
Sub-s (2C): inserted by the Serious Organised Crime and Police Act 2005, s 103(1), (4).
Order: the Proceeds of Crime Act 2002 (Money Laundering: Exceptions to Overseas Conduct Defence) Order 2006, SI 2006/1070.
Transitional provisions: see the note to s 327 at **[1839]**.

330   Failure to disclose: regulated sector

(1)   A person commits an offence if [the conditions in subsections (2) to (4) are satisfied].

(2)   The first condition is that he—
    (a)   knows or suspects, or
    (b)   has reasonable grounds for knowing or suspecting,
that another person is engaged in money laundering.

(3)   The second condition is that the information or other matter—
    (a)   on which his knowledge or suspicion is based, or
    (b)   which gives reasonable grounds for such knowledge or suspicion,
came to him in the course of a business in the regulated sector.

[(3A)   The third condition is—
    (a)   that he can identify the other person mentioned in subsection (2) or the whereabouts of any of the laundered property, or
    (b)   that he believes, or it is reasonable to expect him to believe, that the information or other matter mentioned in subsection (3) will or may assist in identifying that other person or the whereabouts of any of the laundered property.

(4)   The fourth condition is that he does not make the required disclosure to—
    (a)   a nominated officer, or
    (b)   a person authorised for the purposes of this Part by the Director General of [SOCA],
as soon as is practicable after the information or other matter mentioned in subsection (3) comes to him.

PART 1
STATUTES

(5)   The required disclosure is a disclosure of—
   (a)   the identity of the other person mentioned in subsection (2), if he knows it,
   (b)   the whereabouts of the laundered property, so far as he knows it, and
   (c)   the information or other matter mentioned in subsection (3).

(5A)   The laundered property is the property forming the subject-matter of the money laundering that he knows or suspects, or has reasonable grounds for knowing or suspecting, that other person to be engaged in.

(6)   But he does not commit an offence under this section if—
   (a)   he has a reasonable excuse for not making the required disclosure,
   (b)   he is a professional legal adviser [or … relevant professional adviser] and—
        (i)   if he knows either of the things mentioned in subsection (5)(a) and (b), he knows the thing because of information or other matter that came to him in privileged circumstances, or
        (ii)   the information or other matter mentioned in subsection (3) came to him in privileged circumstances, or
   (c)   subsection (7) [or (7B)] applies to him.]

(7)   This subsection applies to a person if—
   (a)   he does not know or suspect that another person is engaged in money laundering, and
   (b)   he has not been provided by his employer with such training as is specified by the Secretary of State by order for the purposes of this section.

[(7A)   Nor does a person commit an offence under this section if—
   (a)   he knows, or believes on reasonable grounds, that the money laundering is occurring in a particular country or territory outside the United Kingdom, and
   (b)   the money laundering—
        (i)   is not unlawful under the criminal law applying in that country or territory, and
        (ii)   is not of a description prescribed in an order made by the Secretary of State.]

[(7B)   This subsection applies to a person if—
   (a)   he is employed by, or is in partnership with, a professional legal adviser or a relevant professional adviser to provide the adviser with assistance or support,
   (b)   the information or other matter mentioned in subsection (3) comes to the person in connection with the provision of such assistance or support, and
   (c)   the information or other matter came to the adviser in privileged circumstances.]

(8)   In deciding whether a person committed an offence under this section the court must consider whether he followed any relevant guidance which was at the time concerned—
   (a)   issued by a supervisory authority or any other appropriate body,
   (b)   approved by the Treasury, and
   (c)   published in a manner it approved as appropriate in its opinion to bring the guidance to the attention of persons likely to be affected by it.

(9)   A disclosure to a nominated officer is a disclosure which—
   (a)   is made to a person nominated by the alleged offender's employer to receive disclosures under this section, and
   (b)   is made in the course of the alleged offender's employment …

[(9A)   But a disclosure which satisfies paragraphs (a) and (b) of subsection (9) is not to be taken as a disclosure to a nominated officer if the person making the disclosure—
   (a)   is a professional legal adviser [or … relevant professional adviser],
   (b)   makes it for the purpose of obtaining advice about making a disclosure under this section, and
   (c)   does not intend it to be a disclosure under this section.]

(10)   Information or other matter comes to a professional legal adviser [or … relevant professional adviser] in privileged circumstances if it is communicated or given to him—
   (a)   by (or by a representative of) a client of his in connection with the giving by the adviser of legal advice to the client,
   (b)   by (or by a representative of) a person seeking legal advice from the adviser, or
   (c)   by a person in connection with legal proceedings or contemplated legal proceedings.

(11)   But subsection (10) does not apply to information or other matter which is communicated or given with the intention of furthering a criminal purpose.

(12)   Schedule 9 has effect for the purpose of determining what is—
   (a)   a business in the regulated sector;
   (b)   a supervisory authority.

(13)   An appropriate body is any body which regulates or is representative of any trade, profession, business or employment carried on by the alleged offender.

[(14)   A relevant professional adviser is an accountant, auditor or tax adviser who is a member of a professional body which is established for accountants, auditors or tax advisers (as the case may be) and which makes provision for—

    (a)   testing the competence of those seeking admission to membership of such a body as a condition for such admission; and

    (b)   imposing and maintaining professional and ethical standards for its members, as well as imposing sanctions for non-compliance with those standards.]

[1842]

NOTES

Sub-s (1): words in square brackets substituted by the Serious Organised Crime and Police Act 2005, s 104(1), (2).

Sub-ss (3A), (5), (5A): substituted, together with sub-ss (4), (6), for original sub-ss (4)–(6), by the Serious Organised Crime and Police Act 2005, s 104(1), (3), subject to transitional provisions in the Serious Organised Crime and Police Act 2005 (Commencement No 1, Transitional and Transitory Provisions) Order 2005, SI 2005/1521, art 3(4).

Sub-s (4): substituted as noted above; word in square brackets in para (b) substituted by the Serious Crime Act 2007, s 74(2)(f), Sch 8, Pt 6, paras 121, 126.

Sub-s (6): substituted as noted above; words in square brackets in paras (b), (c) inserted by the Proceeds of Crime Act 2002 and Money Laundering Regulations 2003 (Amendment) Order 2006, SI 2006/308, art 2(1)–(3); word omitted from para (b) repealed by the Terrorism Act 2000 and Proceeds of Crime Act 2002 (Amendment) Regulations 2007, SI 2007/3398, reg 3, Sch 2, paras 1, 2.

Sub-s (7A): inserted by the Serious Organised Crime and Police Act 2005, s 102(1), (5).

Sub-s (7B): inserted by SI 2006/308, art 2(1), (4).

Sub-s (9): words omitted from para (b) repealed by the Serious Organised Crime and Police Act 2005, ss 105(1), (2), 174(2), Sch 17, Pt 2.

Sub-s (9A): inserted by the Serious Organised Crime and Police Act 2005, s 106(1), (2); in para (a) words in square brackets inserted by SI 2006/308, art 2(1), (2); word omitted from para (a) repealed by SI 2007/3398, reg 3, Sch 2, paras 1, 2.

Sub-s (10): words in square brackets inserted by SI 2006/308, art 2(1), (2); word omitted repealed by SI 2007/3398, reg 3, Sch 2, paras 1, 2.

Sub-s (14): added by SI 2006/308, art 2(1), (5).

Transitional provisions: by virtue of the Proceeds of Crime Act 2002 (Commencement No 4, Transitional Provisions and Savings) Order 2003, SI 2003/120, the new failure to disclose offences (ie, those contained in ss 330, 331 and 332 of this Act) do not have effect where the information or other matter on which knowledge or suspicion that another person is engaged in money laundering is based, or which gives reasonable grounds for such knowledge or suspicion, came to a person before 24 February 2003. In such a case, the old failure to disclose offences (ie, those contained in (i) the Drug Trafficking Act 1994, s 53, (ii) the Criminal Law (Consolidation) (Scotland) Act 1995, s 39, and (iii) the Proceeds of Crime (Northern Ireland) Order 1996, art 44, continue to have effect.

Transitional provisions: the Serious Crime Act 2007 (Commencement No 2 and Transitional and Transitory Provisions and Savings) Order 2008, SI 2008/755, arts 3–14 ensure that, notwithstanding the abolition of the Assets Recovery Agency ("the Agency") and its Director, the cases of the Agency or its Director in relation to Part 5 (civil recovery), Part 6 (revenue), Part 8 (investigations) and section 3 (accreditation and training of civilian financial investigators) will be continued by specified successors. The successors are the National Policing Improvement Agency in relation to accreditation and training of civilian financial investigators and the Serious Organised Crime Agency for all other cases. Cases being dealt with by the Agency and its Director concerning the confiscation of the proceeds of crime will be continued by the Serious Organised Crime Agency. The 2008 Order makes further transitional and transitory provision and savings in relation to the abolition of the Agency and its Director.

Order: the Proceeds of Crime Act 2002 (Failure to Disclose Money Laundering: Specified Training) Order 2003, SI 2003/171.

331   Failure to disclose: nominated officers in the regulated sector

(1)   A person nominated to receive disclosures under section 330 commits an offence if the conditions in subsections (2) to (4) are satisfied.

(2)   The first condition is that he—

    (a)   knows or suspects, or

    (b)   has reasonable grounds for knowing or suspecting,

that another person is engaged in money laundering.

(3)   The second condition is that the information or other matter—

    (a)   on which his knowledge or suspicion is based, or

    (b)   which gives reasonable grounds for such knowledge or suspicion,

came to him in consequence of a disclosure made under section 330.

[(3A)   The third condition is—

    (a)   that he knows the identity of the other person mentioned in subsection (2), or the whereabouts of any of the laundered property, in consequence of a disclosure made under section 330,

    (b)   that that other person, or the whereabouts of any of the laundered property, can be identified from the information or other matter mentioned in subsection (3), or

    (c)   that he believes, or it is reasonable to expect him to believe, that the information or other matter will or may assist in identifying that other person or the whereabouts of any of the laundered property.

(4)   The fourth condition is that he does not make the required disclosure to a person authorised for the purposes of this Part by the Director General of [SOCA] as soon as is practicable after the information or other matter mentioned in subsection (3) comes to him.

(5)   The required disclosure is a disclosure of—
    (a)   the identity of the other person mentioned in subsection (2), if disclosed to him under section 330,
    (b)   the whereabouts of the laundered property, so far as disclosed to him under section 330, and
    (c)   the information or other matter mentioned in subsection (3).

(5A)   The laundered property is the property forming the subject-matter of the money laundering that he knows or suspects, or has reasonable grounds for knowing or suspecting, that other person to be engaged in.

(6)   But he does not commit an offence under this section if he has a reasonable excuse for not making the required disclosure.]

[(6A)   Nor does a person commit an offence under this section if—
    (a)   he knows, or believes on reasonable grounds, that the money laundering is occurring in a particular country or territory outside the United Kingdom, and
    (b)   the money laundering—
        (i)   is not unlawful under the criminal law applying in that country or territory, and
        (ii)   is not of a description prescribed in an order made by the Secretary of State.]

(7)   In deciding whether a person committed an offence under this section the court must consider whether he followed any relevant guidance which was at the time concerned—
    (a)   issued by a supervisory authority or any other appropriate body,
    (b)   approved by the Treasury, and
    (c)   published in a manner it approved as appropriate in its opinion to bring the guidance to the attention of persons likely to be affected by it.

(8)   Schedule 9 has effect for the purpose of determining what is a supervisory authority.

(9)   An appropriate body is a body which regulates or is representative of a trade, profession, business or employment.

[1843]

NOTES

Sub-ss (3A), (5), (5A), (6): substituted, together with sub-s (4), for original sub-ss (4)–(6), by the Serious Organised Crime and Police Act 2005, s 104(1), (4), subject to transitional provisions in the Serious Organised Crime and Police Act 2005 (Commencement No 1, Transitional and Transitory Provisions) Order 2005, SI 2005/1521, art 3(4).

Sub-s (4): substituted as noted above; word in square brackets substituted by the Serious Crime Act 2007, s 74(2)(f), Sch 8, Pt 6, paras 121, 127, except in relation to anything done (or having effect as if done) by or in relation to the transferor before 1 April 2008.

Sub-s (6A): inserted by the Serious Organised Crime and Police Act 2005, s 102(1), (6).

Transitional provisions: see the notes to s 330 at **[1842]**.

---

332 Failure to disclose: other nominated officers

(1)   A person nominated to receive disclosures under section 337 or 338 commits an offence if the conditions in subsections (2) to (4) are satisfied.

(2)   The first condition is that he knows or suspects that another person is engaged in money laundering.

(3)   The second condition is that the information or other matter on which his knowledge or suspicion is based came to him in consequence of a disclosure made under [the applicable section].

[(3A)   The third condition is—
    (a)   that he knows the identity of the other person mentioned in subsection (2), or the whereabouts of any of the laundered property, in consequence of a disclosure made under the applicable section,
    (b)   that that other person, or the whereabouts of any of the laundered property, can be identified from the information or other matter mentioned in subsection (3), or
    (c)   that he believes, or it is reasonable to expect him to believe, that the information or other matter will or may assist in identifying that other person or the whereabouts of any of the laundered property.

(4)   The fourth condition is that he does not make the required disclosure to a person authorised for the purposes of this Part by the Director General of [SOCA] as soon as is practicable after the information or other matter mentioned in subsection (3) comes to him.

(5)   The required disclosure is a disclosure of—
    (a)   the identity of the other person mentioned in subsection (2), if disclosed to him under the applicable section,
    (b)   the whereabouts of the laundered property, so far as disclosed to him under the applicable section, and
    (c)   the information or other matter mentioned in subsection (3).

(5A)   The laundered property is the property forming the subject-matter of the money laundering that he knows or suspects that other person to be engaged in.

(5B)   The applicable section is section 337 or, as the case may be, section 338.

(6)   But he does not commit an offence under this section if he has a reasonable excuse for not making the required disclosure.]

[(7)   Nor does a person commit an offence under this section if—
    (a)   he knows, or believes on reasonable grounds, that the money laundering is occurring in a particular country or territory outside the United Kingdom, and
    (b)   the money laundering—
        (i)   is not unlawful under the criminal law applying in that country or territory, and
        (ii)   is not of a description prescribed in an order made by the Secretary of State.]
[1844]

PART I
STATUTES

NOTES
Sub-s (3): words in square brackets substituted by the Serious Organised Crime and Police Act 2005, s 104(1), (5).
Sub-ss (3A), (4), (5), (5A), (5B), (6): substituted, for original sub-ss (4)–(6), by the Serious Organised Crime and Police Act 2005, s 104(1), (6).
Sub-s (4): word in square brackets substituted by the Serious Crime Act 2007, s 74(2)(f), Sch 8, Pt 6, paras 121, 128, except in relation to anything done (or having effect as if done) by or in relation to the transferor before 1 April 2008.
Sub-s (7): added by the Serious Organised Crime and Police Act 2005, s 102(1), (7).
Transitional provisions: see the notes to s 330 at **[1842]**.

333   (*Repealed by the Terrorism Act 2000 and Proceeds of Crime Act 2002* (*Amendment*) *Regulations 2007, SI 2007/3398, reg 3, Sch 2, paras 1, 3.*)

[333A   Tipping off: regulated sector
(1)   A person commits an offence if—
    (a)   the person discloses any matter within subsection (2);
    (b)   the disclosure is likely to prejudice any investigation that might be conducted following the disclosure referred to in that subsection; and
    (c)   the information on which the disclosure is based came to the person in the course of a business in the regulated sector.

(2)   The matters are that the person or another person has made a disclosure under this Part—
    (a)   to a constable,
    (b)   to an officer of Revenue and Customs,
    (c)   to a nominated officer, or
    (d)   to a member of staff of the Serious Organised Crime Agency authorised for the purposes of this Part by the Director General of that Agency,
of information that came to that person in the course of a business in the regulated sector.

(3)   A person commits an offence if—
    (a)   the person discloses that an investigation into allegations that an offence under this Part has been committed is being contemplated or is being carried out;
    (b)   the disclosure is likely to prejudice that investigation; and
    (c)   the information on which the disclosure is based came to the person in the course of a business in the regulated sector.

(4)   A person guilty of an offence under this section is liable—
    (a)   on summary conviction to imprisonment for a term not exceeding three months, or to a fine not exceeding level 5 on the standard scale, or to both;
    (b)   on conviction on indictment to imprisonment for a term not exceeding two years, or to a fine, or to both.

(5)   This section is subject to—
    (a)   section 333B (disclosures within an undertaking or group etc),
    (b)   section 333C (other permitted disclosures between institutions etc), and
    (c)   section 333D (other permitted disclosures etc).]

[1845]

NOTES
Commencement: 26 December 2007.
Inserted, together with ss 333B–333E, by the Terrorism Act 2000 and Proceeds of Crime Act 2002 (Amendment) Regulations 2007, SI 2007/3398, reg 3, Sch 2, paras 1, 4.

[333B Disclosures within an undertaking or group etc

(1) An employee, officer or partner of an undertaking does not commit an offence under section 333A if the disclosure is to an employee, officer or partner of the same undertaking.

(2) A person does not commit an offence under section 333A in respect of a disclosure by a credit institution or a financial institution if—

(a) the disclosure is to a credit institution or a financial institution,

(b) the institution to whom the disclosure is made is situated in an EEA State or in a country or territory imposing equivalent money laundering requirements, and

(c) both the institution making the disclosure and the institution to whom it is made belong to the same group.

(3) In subsection (2) "group" has the same meaning as in Directive 2002/87/EC of the European Parliament and of the Council of 16th December 2002 on the supplementary supervision of credit institutions, insurance undertakings and investment firms in a financial conglomerate.

(4) A professional legal adviser or a relevant professional adviser does not commit an offence under section 333A if—

(a) the disclosure is to professional legal adviser or a relevant professional adviser,

(b) both the person making the disclosure and the person to whom it is made carry on business in an EEA State or in a country or territory imposing equivalent money laundering requirements, and

(c) those persons perform their professional activities within different undertakings that share common ownership, management or control.]

[1845A]

NOTES
Commencement: 26 December 2007.
Inserted as noted to s 333A at [1845].

[333C Other permitted disclosures between institutions etc

(1) This section applies to a disclosure—

(a) by a credit institution to another credit institution,

(b) by a financial institution to another financial institution,

(c) by a professional legal adviser to another professional legal adviser, or

(d) by a relevant professional adviser of a particular kind to another relevant professional adviser of the same kind.

(2) A person does not commit an offence under section 333A in respect of a disclosure to which this section applies if—

(a) the disclosure relates to—

(i) a client or former client of the institution or adviser making the disclosure and the institution or adviser to whom it is made,

(ii) a transaction involving them both, or

(iii) the provision of a service involving them both;

(b) the disclosure is for the purpose only of preventing an offence under this Part of this Act;

(c) the institution or adviser to whom the disclosure is made is situated in an EEA State or in a country or territory imposing equivalent money laundering requirements; and

(d) the institution or adviser making the disclosure and the institution or adviser to whom it is made are subject to equivalent duties of professional confidentiality and the protection of personal data (within the meaning of section 1 of the Data Protection Act 1998).]

[1845B]

NOTES
Commencement: 26 December 2007.
Inserted as noted to s 333A at [1845].

[333D Other permitted disclosures etc

(1) A person does not commit an offence under section 333A if the disclosure is—

(a) to the authority that is the supervisory authority for that person by virtue of the Money Laundering Regulations 2007 (SI 2007/2157); or

(b) for the purpose of—

(i) the detection, investigation or prosecution of a criminal offence (whether in the United Kingdom or elsewhere),

    (ii)   an investigation under this Act, or

    (iii)   the enforcement of any order of a court under this Act.

(2)   A professional legal adviser or a relevant professional adviser does not commit an offence under section 333A if the disclosure—

    (a)   is to the adviser's client, and

    (b)   is made for the purpose of dissuading the client from engaging in conduct amounting to an offence.

(3)   A person does not commit an offence under section 333A(1) if the person does not know or suspect that the disclosure is likely to have the effect mentioned in section 333A(1)(b).

(4)   A person does not commit an offence under section 333A(3) if the person does not know or suspect that the disclosure is likely to have the effect mentioned in section 333A(3)(b).]

[1845C]

NOTES

Commencement: 26 December 2007.

Inserted as noted to s 333A at **[1845]**.

[333E   Interpretation of sections 333A to 333D

(1)   For the purposes of sections 333A to 333D, Schedule 9 has effect for determining—

    (a)   what is a business in the regulated sector, and

    (b)   what is a supervisory authority.

(2)   In those sections—

    "credit institution" has the same meaning as in Schedule 9;

    "financial institution" means an undertaking that carries on a business in the regulated sector by virtue of any of paragraphs (b) to (i) of paragraph 1(1) of that Schedule.

(3)   References in those sections to a disclosure by or to a credit institution or a financial institution include disclosure by or to an employee, officer or partner of the institution acting on its behalf.

(4)   For the purposes of those sections a country or territory imposes "equivalent money laundering requirements" if it imposes requirements equivalent to those laid down in Directive 2005/60/EC of the European Parliament and of the Council of 26th October 2005 on the prevention of the use of the financial system for the purpose of money laundering and terrorist financing.

(5)   In those sections "relevant professional adviser" means an accountant, auditor or tax adviser who is a member of a professional body which is established for accountants, auditors or tax advisers (as the case may be) and which makes provision for—

    (a)   testing the competence of those seeking admission to membership of such a body as a condition for such admission; and

    (b)   imposing and maintaining professional and ethical standards for its members, as well as imposing sanctions for non-compliance with those standards.]

[1845D]

NOTES

Commencement: 26 December 2007.

Inserted as noted to s 333A at **[1845]**.

334   Penalties

(1)   A person guilty of an offence under section 327, 328 or 329 is liable—

    (a)   on summary conviction, to imprisonment for a term not exceeding six months or to a fine not exceeding the statutory maximum or to both, or

    (b)   on conviction on indictment, to imprisonment for a term not exceeding 14 years or to a fine or to both.

(2)   A person guilty of an offence under section 330, 331 [or 332] is liable—

    (a)   on summary conviction, to imprisonment for a term not exceeding six months or to a fine not exceeding the statutory maximum or to both, or

    (b)   on conviction on indictment, to imprisonment for a term not exceeding five years or to a fine or to both.

[(3)   A person guilty of an offence under section 339(1A) is liable on summary conviction to a fine not exceeding level 5 on the standard scale.]

[1846]

NOTES

Sub-s (2): words in square brackets substituted by the Terrorism Act 2000 and Proceeds of Crime Act 2002 (Amendment) Regulations 2007, SI 2007/3398, reg 3, Sch 2, paras 1, 5.

Sub-s (3): added by the Serious Organised Crime and Police Act 2005, s 105(1), (3).

Consent

335 Appropriate consent

(1) The appropriate consent is—

    (a) the consent of a nominated officer to do a prohibited act if an authorised disclosure is made to the nominated officer;

    (b) the consent of a constable to do a prohibited act if an authorised disclosure is made to a constable;

    (c) the consent of a customs officer to do a prohibited act if an authorised disclosure is made to a customs officer.

(2) A person must be treated as having the appropriate consent if—

    (a) he makes an authorised disclosure to a constable or a customs officer, and

    (b) the condition in subsection (3) or the condition in subsection (4) is satisfied.

(3) The condition is that before the end of the notice period he does not receive notice from a constable or customs officer that consent to the doing of the act is refused.

(4) The condition is that—

    (a) before the end of the notice period he receives notice from a constable or customs officer that consent to the doing of the act is refused, and

    (b) the moratorium period has expired.

(5) The notice period is the period of seven working days starting with the first working day after the person makes the disclosure.

(6) The moratorium period is the period of 31 days starting with the day on which the person receives notice that consent to the doing of the act is refused.

(7) A working day is a day other than a Saturday, a Sunday, Christmas Day, Good Friday or a day which is a bank holiday under the Banking and Financial Dealings Act 1971 (c 80) in the part of the United Kingdom in which the person is when he makes the disclosure.

(8) References to a prohibited act are to an act mentioned in section 327(1), 328(1) or 329(1) (as the case may be).

(9) A nominated officer is a person nominated to receive disclosures under section 338.

(10) Subsections (1) to (4) apply for the purposes of this Part.

[1847]

336 Nominated officer: consent

(1) A nominated officer must not give the appropriate consent to the doing of a prohibited act unless the condition in subsection (2), the condition in subsection (3) or the condition in subsection (4) is satisfied.

(2) The condition is that—

    (a) he makes a disclosure that property is criminal property to a person authorised for the purposes of this Part by [the Director General of [SOCA]], and

    (b) such a person gives consent to the doing of the act.

(3) The condition is that—

    (a) he makes a disclosure that property is criminal property to a person authorised for the purposes of this Part by [the Director General of [SOCA]], and

    (b) before the end of the notice period he does not receive notice from such a person that consent to the doing of the act is refused.

(4) The condition is that—

    (a) he makes a disclosure that property is criminal property to a person authorised for the purposes of this Part by [the Director General of [SOCA]],

    (b) before the end of the notice period he receives notice from such a person that consent to the doing of the act is refused, and

    (c) the moratorium period has expired.

(5) A person who is a nominated officer commits an offence if—

    (a) he gives consent to a prohibited act in circumstances where none of the conditions in subsections (2), (3) and (4) is satisfied, and

    (b) he knows or suspects that the act is a prohibited act.

(6) A person guilty of such an offence is liable—

    (a) on summary conviction, to imprisonment for a term not exceeding six months or to a fine not exceeding the statutory maximum or to both, or

    (b) on conviction on indictment, to imprisonment for a term not exceeding five years or to a fine or to both.

(7) The notice period is the period of seven working days starting with the first working day after the nominated officer makes the disclosure.

(8) The moratorium period is the period of 31 days starting with the day on which the nominated officer is given notice that consent to the doing of the act is refused.

(9) A working day is a day other than a Saturday, a Sunday, Christmas Day, Good Friday or a day which is a bank holiday under the Banking and Financial Dealings Act 1971 (c 80) in the part of the United Kingdom in which the nominated officer is when he gives the appropriate consent.

(10) References to a prohibited act are to an act mentioned in section 327(1), 328(1) or 329(1) (as the case may be).

(11) A nominated officer is a person nominated to receive disclosures under section 338.

[1848]

NOTES
Sub-ss (2)–(4): in para (a) words in first (outer) pair of square brackets substituted by the Serious Organised Crime and Police Act 2005, s 59, Sch 4, paras 168, 173, word in second (inner) pair of square brackets substituted by the Serious Crime Act 2007, s 74(2)(f), Sch 8, Pt 6, paras 121, 129, except in relation to anything done (or having effect as if done) by or in relation to the transferor before 1 April 2008.

Disclosures

337 Protected disclosures

(1) A disclosure which satisfies the following three conditions is not to be taken to breach any restriction on the disclosure of information (however imposed).

(2) The first condition is that the information or other matter disclosed came to the person making the disclosure (the discloser) in the course of his trade, profession, business or employment.

(3) The second condition is that the information or other matter—
    (a)   causes the discloser to know or suspect, or
    (b)   gives him reasonable grounds for knowing or suspecting,
that another person is engaged in money laundering.

(4) The third condition is that the disclosure is made to a constable, a customs officer or a nominated officer as soon as is practicable after the information or other matter comes to the discloser.

[(4A) Where a disclosure consists of a disclosure protected under subsection (1) and a disclosure of either or both of—
    (a)   the identity of the other person mentioned in subsection (3), and
    (b)   the whereabouts of property forming the subject-matter of the money laundering that the discloser knows or suspects, or has reasonable grounds for knowing or suspecting, that other person to be engaged in,
the disclosure of the thing mentioned in paragraph (a) or (b) (as well as the disclosure protected under subsection (1)) is not to be taken to breach any restriction on the disclosure of information (however imposed).]

(5) A disclosure to a nominated officer is a disclosure which—
    (a)   is made to a person nominated by the discloser's employer to receive disclosures under [section 330 or] this section, and
    (b)   is made in the course of the discloser's employment ...

[1849]

NOTES
Sub-s (4A): inserted by the Serious Organised Crime and Police Act 2005, s 104(1), (7).
Sub-s (5): in para (a) words in square brackets inserted and words omitted repealed by the Serious Organised Crime and Police Act 2005, ss 105(1), (2), 106(1), (3), 174(2), Sch 17, Pt 2.

338 Authorised disclosures

(1) For the purposes of this Part a disclosure is authorised if—
    (a)   it is a disclosure to a constable, a customs officer or a nominated officer by the alleged offender that property is criminal property,
    (b)   ... and
    (c)   the first[, second or third] condition set out below is satisfied.

(2) The first condition is that the disclosure is made before the alleged offender does the prohibited act.

[(2A) The second condition is that—
    (a)   the disclosure is made while the alleged offender is doing the prohibited act,
    (b)   he began to do the act at a time when, because he did not then know or suspect that the property constituted or represented a person's benefit from criminal conduct, the act was not a prohibited act, and

(c) the disclosure is made on his own initiative and as soon as is practicable after he first knows or suspects that the property constitutes or represents a person's benefit from criminal conduct.]

(3) The [third] condition is that—

(a) the disclosure is made after the alleged offender does the prohibited act,

(b) [he has a reasonable excuse] for his failure to make the disclosure before he did the act, and

(c) the disclosure is made on his own initiative and as soon as it is practicable for him to make it.

(4) An authorised disclosure is not to be taken to breach any restriction on the disclosure of information (however imposed).

(5) A disclosure to a nominated officer is a disclosure which—

(a) is made to a person nominated by the alleged offender's employer to receive authorised disclosures, and

(b) is made in the course of the alleged offender's employment …

(6) References to the prohibited act are to an act mentioned in section 327(1), 328(1) or 329(1) (as the case may be).

[1850]

NOTES

Sub-s (1): para (b) repealed and words in square brackets in para (c) substituted by the Serious Organised Crime and Police Act 2005, ss 105(1), (4), 106(1), (4), 174(2), Sch 17, Pt 2.

Sub-s (2A): inserted by the Serious Organised Crime and Police Act 2005, s 106(1), (5).

Sub-s (3): word in first pair of square brackets substituted by the Serious Organised Crime and Police Act 2005, s 106(1), (6); words in square brackets in para (b) substituted by the Terrorism Act 2000 and Proceeds of Crime Act 2002 (Amendment) Regulations 2007, SI 2007/3398, reg 3, Sch 2, paras 1, 6.

Sub-s (5): words omitted from para (b) repealed by the Serious Organised Crime and Police Act 2005, ss 105(1), (2), 174(2), Sch 17, Pt 2.

339 Form and manner of disclosures

(1) The Secretary of State may by order prescribe the form and manner in which a disclosure under section 330, 331, 332 or 338 must be made.

[(1A) A person commits an offence if he makes a disclosure under section 330, 331, 332 or 338 otherwise than in the form prescribed under subsection (1) or otherwise than in the manner so prescribed.

(1B) But a person does not commit an offence under subsection (1A) if he has a reasonable excuse for making the disclosure otherwise than in the form prescribed under subsection (1) or (as the case may be) otherwise than in the manner so prescribed.

(2) The power under subsection (1) to prescribe the form in which a disclosure must be made includes power to provide for the form to include a request to a person making a disclosure that the person provide information specified or described in the form if he has not provided it in making the disclosure.

(3) Where under subsection (2) a request is included in a form prescribed under subsection (1), the form must—

(a) state that there is no obligation to comply with the request, and

(b) explain the protection conferred by subsection (4) on a person who complies with the request.]

(4) A disclosure made in pursuance of a request under subsection (2) is not to be taken to breach any restriction on the disclosure of information (however imposed).

(5), (6) …

(7) Subsection (2) does not apply to a disclosure made to a nominated officer.

[1851]

NOTES

Sub-ss (1A), (1B), (2), (3): substituted, for original sub-ss (2), (3), by the Serious Organised Crime and Police Act 2005, s 105(1), (5).

Sub-ss (5), (6): repealed by the Serious Organised Crime and Police Act 2005, s 174(2), Sch 17, Pt 2.

[339ZA Disclosures to SOCA

Where a disclosure is made under this Part to a constable or an officer of Revenue and Customs, the constable or officer of Revenue and Customs must disclose it in full to a person authorised for the purposes of this Part by the Director General of the Serious Organised Crime Agency as soon as practicable after it has been made.]

[1851A]

NOTES
  Commencement: 26 December 2007.
  Inserted by the Terrorism Act 2000 and Proceeds of Crime Act 2002 (Amendment) Regulations 2007, SI 2007/3398, reg 3, Sch 2, paras 1, 7.

[Threshold amounts

339A   Threshold amounts
  (1)   This section applies for the purposes of sections 327(2C), 328(5) and 329(2C).

  (2)   The threshold amount for acts done by a deposit-taking body in operating an account is £250 unless a higher amount is specified under the following provisions of this section (in which event it is that higher amount).

  (3)   An officer of Revenue and Customs, or a constable, may specify the threshold amount for acts done by a deposit-taking body in operating an account—
  (a)   when he gives consent, or gives notice refusing consent, to the deposit-taking body's doing of an act mentioned in section 327(1), 328(1) or 329(1) in opening, or operating, the account or a related account, or
  (b)   on a request from the deposit-taking body.

  (4)   Where the threshold amount for acts done in operating an account is specified under subsection (3) or this subsection, an officer of Revenue and Customs, or a constable, may vary the amount (whether on a request from the deposit-taking body or otherwise) by specifying a different amount.

  (5)   Different threshold amounts may be specified under subsections (3) and (4) for different acts done in operating the same account.

  (6)   The amount specified under subsection (3) or (4) as the threshold amount for acts done in operating an account must, when specified, not be less than the amount specified in subsection (2).

  (7)   The Secretary of State may by order vary the amount for the time being specified in subsection (2).

  (8)   For the purposes of this section, an account is related to another if each is maintained with the same deposit-taking body and there is a person who, in relation to each account, is the person or one of the persons entitled to instruct the body as respects the operation of the account.]
[1851B]

NOTES
  Inserted, together with preceding cross-heading, by the Serious Organised Crime and Police Act 2005, s 103(1), (5).

Interpretation

340   Interpretation
  (1)   This section applies for the purposes of this Part.

  (2)   Criminal conduct is conduct which—
  (a)   constitutes an offence in any part of the United Kingdom, or
  (b)   would constitute an offence in any part of the United Kingdom if it occurred there.

  (3)   Property is criminal property if—
  (a)   it constitutes a person's benefit from criminal conduct or it represents such a benefit (in whole or part and whether directly or indirectly), and
  (b)   the alleged offender knows or suspects that it constitutes or represents such a benefit.

  (4)   It is immaterial—
  (a)   who carried out the conduct;
  (b)   who benefited from it;
  (c)   whether the conduct occurred before or after the passing of this Act.

  (5)   A person benefits from conduct if he obtains property as a result of or in connection with the conduct.

  (6)   If a person obtains a pecuniary advantage as a result of or in connection with conduct, he is to be taken to obtain as a result of or in connection with the conduct a sum of money equal to the value of the pecuniary advantage.

  (7)   References to property or a pecuniary advantage obtained in connection with conduct include references to property or a pecuniary advantage obtained in both that connection and some other.

  (8)   If a person benefits from conduct his benefit is the property obtained as a result of or in connection with the conduct.

(9)   Property is all property wherever situated and includes—
   (a)   money;
   (b)   all forms of property, real or personal, heritable or moveable;
   (c)   things in action and other intangible or incorporeal property.

(10)   The following rules apply in relation to property—
   (a)   property is obtained by a person if he obtains an interest in it;
   (b)   references to an interest, in relation to land in England and Wales or Northern Ireland, are to any legal estate or equitable interest or power;
   (c)   references to an interest, in relation to land in Scotland, are to any estate, interest, servitude or other heritable right in or over land, including a heritable security;
   (d)   references to an interest, in relation to property other than land, include references to a right (including a right to possession).

(11)   Money laundering is an act which—
   (a)   constitutes an offence under section 327, 328 or 329,
   (b)   constitutes an attempt, conspiracy or incitement to commit an offence specified in paragraph (a),
   (c)   constitutes aiding, abetting, counselling or procuring the commission of an offence specified in paragraph (a), or
   (d)   would constitute an offence specified in paragraph (a), (b) or (c) if done in the United Kingdom.

(12)   For the purposes of a disclosure to a nominated officer—
   (a)   references to a person's employer include any body, association or organisation (including a voluntary organisation) in connection with whose activities the person exercises a function (whether or not for gain or reward), and
   (b)   references to employment must be construed accordingly.

(13)   References to a constable include references to a person authorised for the purposes of this Part by [the Director General of [SOCA]].

[(14)   "Deposit-taking body" means—
   (a)   a business which engages in the activity of accepting deposits, or
   (b)   the National Savings Bank.]

                                                                                    [1852]

NOTES
   Sub-s (13): words in first (outer) pair of square brackets substituted by the Serious Organised Crime and Police Act 2005, s 59, Sch 4, paras 168, 174; word in second (inner) pair of square brackets substituted by the Serious Crime Act 2007, s 74(2)(f), Sch 8, Pt 6, paras 121, 130, except in relation to anything done (or having effect as if done) by or in relation to the transferor before 1 April 2008.
   Sub-s (14): added by the Serious Organised Crime and Police Act 2005, s 103(1), (6).
   See further, in relation to England, Wales and Northern Ireland, the Serious Crime Act 2007, s 63(1), Sch 6, Pt 1, para 44(a), which provides that the reference in sub-s (11)(b) above to (or to conduct amounting to) the common law offence of inciting the commission of another offence, has effect (as from the day that offence is abolished) as a reference to (or to conduct amounting to) offences under the Serious Crime Act 2007, Pt 2.

PART 8
INVESTIGATIONS

CHAPTER 1
INTRODUCTION

341   Investigations
   (1)   For the purposes of this Part a confiscation investigation is an investigation into—
   (a)   whether a person has benefited from his criminal conduct, or
   (b)   the extent or whereabouts of his benefit from his criminal conduct.

   (2)   For the purposes of this Part a civil recovery investigation is an investigation into—
   (a)   whether property is recoverable property or associated property,
   (b)   who holds the property, or
   (c)   its extent or whereabouts.

   (3)   But an investigation is not a civil recovery investigation if—
   (a)   proceedings for a recovery order have been started in respect of the property in question,
   (b)   an interim receiving order applies to the property in question,
   (c)   an interim administration order applies to the property in question, or
   (d)   the property in question is detained under section 295.

   [(3A)   For the purposes of this Part a detained cash investigation is—
   (a)   an investigation for the purposes of Chapter 3 of Part 5 into the derivation of cash detained under *section 295* [that Chapter] or a part of such cash, or

(b)   an investigation for the purposes of Chapter 3 of Part 5 into whether cash detained under *section 295* [that Chapter], or a part of such cash, is intended by any person to be used in unlawful conduct.]

(4)   For the purposes of this Part a money laundering investigation is an investigation into whether a person has committed a money laundering offence.

[(5)   For the purposes of this Part an exploitation proceeds investigation is an investigation for the purposes of Part 7 of the Coroners and Justice Act 2009 (criminal memoirs etc) into—
(a)   whether a person is a qualifying offender,
(b)   whether a person has obtained exploitation proceeds from a relevant offence,
(c)   the value of any benefits derived by a person from a relevant offence, or
(d)   the available amount in respect of a person.
Paragraphs (a) to (d) are to be construed in accordance with that Part of that Act.]

[1852A]

_____

NOTES
Sub-s (3A): inserted by the Serious Crime Act 2007, s 75(1); words in italics in both places they appear substituted by subsequent words in square brackets by the Policing and Crime Act 2009, s 112(1), Sch 7, Pt 7, paras 99, 110, as from a day to be appointed.
Sub-s (5): inserted, in relation to England and Wales, by the Coroners and Justice Act 2009, s 169, Sch 19, paras 1, 2.
Modification: this section is applied, with modifications, in so far as it relates to bank insolvency or administration under the Banking Act 2009, Pts 2, 3, by the Banking Act 2009 (Parts 2 and 3 Consequential Amendments) Order 2009, SI 2009/317, art 3, Schedule.

_____

342 Offences of prejudicing investigation

(1)   This section applies if a person knows or suspects that an appropriate officer or (in Scotland) a proper person is acting (or proposing to act) in connection with a confiscation investigation, a civil recovery investigation[, a detained cash investigation][, an exploitation proceeds investigation] or a money laundering investigation which is being or is about to be conducted.

(2)   The person commits an offence if—
(a)   he makes a disclosure which is likely to prejudice the investigation, or
(b)   he falsifies, conceals, destroys or otherwise disposes of, or causes or permits the falsification, concealment, destruction or disposal of, documents which are relevant to the investigation.

(3)   A person does not commit an offence under subsection (2)(a) if—
(a)   he does not know or suspect that the disclosure is likely to prejudice the investigation,
(b)   the disclosure is made in the exercise of a function under this Act or any other enactment relating to criminal conduct or benefit from criminal conduct or in compliance with a requirement imposed under or by virtue of this Act,
[(ba)   the disclosure is of a matter within section 333A(2) or (3)(a) (money laundering: tipping off) and the information on which the disclosure is based came to the person in the course of a business in the regulated sector,]
[(bb)   the disclosure is made in the exercise of a function under Part 7 of the Coroners and Justice Act 2009 (criminal memoirs etc) or in compliance with a requirement imposed under or by virtue of that Act,] or
(c)   he is a professional legal adviser and the disclosure falls within subsection (4).

(4)   A disclosure falls within this subsection if it is a disclosure—
(a)   to (or to a representative of) a client of the professional legal adviser in connection with the giving by the adviser of legal advice to the client, or
(b)   to any person in connection with legal proceedings or contemplated legal proceedings.

(5)   But a disclosure does not fall within subsection (4) if it is made with the intention of furthering a criminal purpose.

(6)   A person does not commit an offence under subsection (2)(b) if—
(a)   he does not know or suspect that the documents are relevant to the investigation, or
(b)   he does not intend to conceal any facts disclosed by the documents from any appropriate officer or (in Scotland) proper person carrying out the investigation.

(7)   A person guilty of an offence under subsection (2) is liable—
(a)   on summary conviction, to imprisonment for a term not exceeding six months or to a fine not exceeding the statutory maximum or to both, or
(b)   on conviction on indictment, to imprisonment for a term not exceeding five years or to a fine or to both.

(8)   For the purposes of this section—
(a)   "appropriate officer" must be construed in accordance with section 378;

(b) "proper person" must be construed in accordance with section 412;

[(c) Schedule 9 has effect for determining what is a business in the regulated sector].

[1852B]

NOTES

Sub-s (1): words in first pair of square brackets inserted by the Serious Crime Act 2007, s 77, Sch 10, paras 1, 2; words in second pair of square brackets inserted by the Coroners and Justice Act 2009, s 169, Sch 19, paras 1, 3(a).

Sub-s (3): para (ba) inserted by the Terrorism Act 2000 and Proceeds of Crime Act 2002 (Amendment) Regulations 2007, SI 2007/3398, reg 3, Sch 2, paras 1, 8(1), (2); para (bb) inserted by the Coroners and Justice Act 2009, s 169, Sch 19, paras 1, 3(b).

Sub-s (8): para (c) added by SI 2007/3398, reg 3, Sch 2, paras 1, 8(1), (3).

CHAPTER 2
ENGLAND AND WALES AND NORTHERN IRELAND

Judges and courts

343 Judges

(1) In this Chapter references to a judge in relation to an application must be construed in accordance with this section.

(2) In relation to an application for the purposes of a confiscation investigation *or a money laundering investigation*[, a money laundering investigation or a detained cash investigation] a judge is—

    (a)   in England and Wales, a judge entitled to exercise the jurisdiction of the Crown Court;

    (b)   in Northern Ireland, a Crown Court judge.

(3) In relation to an application for the purposes of a civil recovery investigation [or an exploitation proceeds investigation] [*or a detained cash investigation*] a judge is a judge of the High Court.

[1852C]

NOTES

Sub-s (2): words in italics substituted by subsequent words in square brackets by the Policing and Crime Act 2009, s 66(1), (2)(a), as from a day to be appointed.

Sub-s (3): words in first pair of square brackets inserted by the Coroners and Justice Act 2009, s 169, Sch 19, paras 1, 4; words (in italics) in second pair of square brackets inserted by the Serious Crime Act 2007, s 77, Sch 10, paras 1, 3 and repealed by the Policing and Crime Act 2009, ss 66(1), (2)(b), 112(2), Sch 8, Pt 5, as from a day to be appointed.

344 Courts

In this Chapter references to the court are to—

    (a)   the Crown Court, in relation to an order for the purposes of a confiscation investigation *or a money laundering investigation* [, a money laundering investigation or a detained cash investigation];

    (b)   the High Court, in relation to an order for the purposes of a civil recovery investigation [or an exploitation proceeds investigation] [*or a detained cash investigation*].

[1852D]

NOTES

Para (a): words in italics substituted by subsequent words in square brackets by the Policing and Crime Act 2009, s 66(1), (3)(a), as from a day to be appointed.

Para (b): words in first pair of square brackets inserted by the Coroners and Justice Act 2009, s 169, Sch 19, paras 1, 5; words (in italics) in second pair of square brackets inserted by the Serious Crime Act 2007, s 77, Sch 10, paras 1, 4 and repealed by the Policing and Crime Act 2009, ss 66(1), (3)(b), 112(2), Sch 8, Pt 5, as from a day to be appointed.

Production orders

345 Production orders

(1) A judge may, on an application made to him by an appropriate officer, make a production order if he is satisfied that each of the requirements for the making of the order is fulfilled.

(2) The application for a production order must state that—

    (a)   a person specified in the application is subject to a confiscation investigation[, an exploitation proceeds investigation] or a money laundering investigation, or

    (b)   property specified in the application is subject to a civil recovery investigation [or a detained cash investigation].

(3) The application must also state that—

    (a)   the order is sought for the purposes of the investigation;

PART 1
STATUTES

    (b)   the order is sought in relation to material, or material of a description, specified in the application;

    (c)   a person specified in the application appears to be in possession or control of the material.

(4)   A production order is an order either—

    (a)   requiring the person the application for the order specifies as appearing to be in possession or control of material to produce it to an appropriate officer for him to take away, or

    (b)   requiring that person to give an appropriate officer access to the material,

within the period stated in the order.

(5)   The period stated in a production order must be a period of seven days beginning with the day on which the order is made, unless it appears to the judge by whom the order is made that a longer or shorter period would be appropriate in the particular circumstances.

[1852E]

NOTES

Sub-s (2): words in square brackets in para (a) inserted by the Coroners and Justice Act 2009, s 169, Sch 19, paras 1, 6; words in square brackets in para (b) added by the Serious Crime Act 2007, s 75(2).

See further, in relation to the enforcement in England and Wales of production orders made in Northern Ireland for the purposes of a confiscation investigation or money laundering investigation: the Proceeds of Crime Act 2002 (Investigations in different parts of the United Kingdom) Order 2003, SI 2003/425, art 3.

346   Requirements for making of production order

(1)   These are the requirements for the making of a production order.

(2)   There must be reasonable grounds for suspecting that—

    (a)   in the case of a confiscation investigation, the person the application for the order specifies as being subject to the investigation has benefited from his criminal conduct;

    (b)   in the case of a civil recovery investigation, the property the application for the order specifies as being subject to the investigation is recoverable property or associated property;

    [(ba) in the case of a detained cash investigation into the derivation of cash, the property the application for the order specifies as being subject to the investigation, or a part of it, is recoverable property;

    (bb) in the case of a detained cash investigation into the intended use of cash, the property the application for the order specifies as being subject to the investigation, or a part of it, is intended by any person to be used in unlawful conduct;]

    (c)   in the case of a money laundering investigation, the person the application for the order specifies as being subject to the investigation has committed a money laundering offence.

    [(d)   in the case of an exploitation proceeds investigation, the person the application for the order specifies as being subject to the investigation is within subsection (2A)].

[(2A)   A person is within this subsection if, for the purposes of Part 7 of the Coroners and Justice Act 2009 (criminal memoirs etc), exploitation proceeds have been obtained by the person from a relevant offence by reason of any benefit derived by the person.

This subsection is to be construed in accordance with that Part.]

(3)   There must be reasonable grounds for believing that the person the application specifies as appearing to be in possession or control of the material so specified is in possession or control of it.

(4)   There must be reasonable grounds for believing that the material is likely to be of substantial value (whether or not by itself) to the investigation for the purposes of which the order is sought.

(5)   There must be reasonable grounds for believing that it is in the public interest for the material to be produced or for access to it to be given, having regard to—

    (a)   the benefit likely to accrue to the investigation if the material is obtained;

    (b)   the circumstances under which the person the application specifies as appearing to be in possession or control of the material holds it.

[1852F]

NOTES

Sub-s (2): paras (ba), (bb) inserted by the Serious Crime Act 2007, s 75(3); para (d) inserted by the Coroners and Justice Act 2009, s 169, Sch 19, paras 1, 7(a).

Sub-s (2A): inserted by the Coroners and Justice Act 2009, s 169, Sch 19, paras 1, 7(b).

347   Order to grant entry

(1)   This section applies if a judge makes a production order requiring a person to give an appropriate officer access to material on any premises.

(2) The judge may, on an application made to him by an appropriate officer and specifying the premises, make an order to grant entry in relation to the premises.

(3) An order to grant entry is an order requiring any person who appears to an appropriate officer to be entitled to grant entry to the premises to allow him to enter the premises to obtain access to the material.

[1852G]

NOTES
See further, in relation to the enforcement in England and Wales of production orders made in Northern Ireland for the purposes of a confiscation investigation or money laundering investigation: the Proceeds of Crime Act 2002 (Investigations in different parts of the United Kingdom) Order 2003, SI 2003/425, art 3.

348 Further provisions

(1) A production order does not require a person to produce, or give access to, privileged material.

(2) Privileged material is any material which the person would be entitled to refuse to produce on grounds of legal professional privilege in proceedings in the High Court.

(3) A production order does not require a person to produce, or give access to, excluded material.

(4) A production order has effect in spite of any restriction on the disclosure of information (however imposed).

(5) An appropriate officer may take copies of any material which is produced, or to which access is given, in compliance with a production order.

(6) Material produced in compliance with a production order may be retained for so long as it is necessary to retain it (as opposed to copies of it) in connection with the investigation for the purposes of which the order was made.

(7) But if an appropriate officer has reasonable grounds for believing that—
    (a) the material may need to be produced for the purposes of any legal proceedings, and
    (b) it might otherwise be unavailable for those purposes,
it may be retained until the proceedings are concluded.

[1852H]

NOTES
See further, in relation to the enforcement in England and Wales of production orders made in Northern Ireland for the purposes of a confiscation investigation or money laundering investigation: the Proceeds of Crime Act 2002 (Investigations in different parts of the United Kingdom) Order 2003, SI 2003/425, art 3.

349 Computer information

(1) This section applies if any of the material specified in an application for a production order consists of information contained in a computer.

(2) If the order is an order requiring a person to produce the material to an appropriate officer for him to take away, it has effect as an order to produce the material in a form in which it can be taken away by him and in which it is visible and legible.

(3) If the order is an order requiring a person to give an appropriate officer access to the material, it has effect as an order to give him access to the material in a form in which it is visible and legible.

[1852I]

NOTES
See further, in relation to the enforcement in England and Wales of production orders made in Northern Ireland for the purposes of a confiscation investigation or money laundering investigation: the Proceeds of Crime Act 2002 (Investigations in different parts of the United Kingdom) Order 2003, SI 2003/425, art 3.

350 Government departments

(1) A production order may be made in relation to material in the possession or control of an authorised government department.

(2) An order so made may require any officer of the department (whether named in the order or not) who may for the time being be in possession or control of the material to comply with it.

(3) An order containing such a requirement must be served as if the proceedings were civil proceedings against the department.

(4) If an order contains such a requirement—
    (a) the person on whom it is served must take all reasonable steps to bring it to the attention of the officer concerned;

(b)   any other officer of the department who is in receipt of the order must also take all reasonable steps to bring it to the attention of the officer concerned.

(5)   If the order is not brought to the attention of the officer concerned within the period stated in the order (in pursuance of section 345(4)) the person on whom it is served must report the reasons for the failure to—

(a)   a judge entitled to exercise the jurisdiction of the Crown Court or (in Northern Ireland) a Crown Court judge, in the case of an order made for the purposes of a confiscation investigation *or a money laundering investigation*[, a money laundering investigation or a detained cash investigation];

(b)   a High Court judge, in the case of an order made for the purposes of a civil recovery investigation [or an exploitation proceeds investigation] [*or a detained cash investigation*].

(6)   An authorised government department is a government department, or a Northern Ireland department, which is an authorised department for the purposes of the Crown Proceedings Act 1947 (c 44).

[1852J]

NOTES

Sub-s (5): words in italics in para (a) substituted by subsequent words in square brackets by the Policing and Crime Act 2009, s 66(1), (4)(a), as from a day to be appointed; in para (b), words in first pair of square brackets inserted by the Coroners and Justice Act 2009, s 169, Sch 19, paras 1, 8, and words (in italics) in second pair of square brackets inserted by the Serious Crime Act 2007, s 77, Sch 10, paras 1, 5 and repealed by the Policing and Crime Act 2009, ss 66(1), (4)(b), 112(2), Sch 8, Pt 5, as from a day to be appointed.

See further, in relation to the enforcement in England and Wales of production orders made in Northern Ireland for the purposes of a confiscation investigation or money laundering investigation: the Proceeds of Crime Act 2002 (Investigations in different parts of the United Kingdom) Order 2003, SI 2003/425, art 3.

351 Supplementary

(1)   An application for a production order or an order to grant entry may be made ex parte to a judge in chambers.

(2)   Rules of court may make provision as to the practice and procedure to be followed in connection with proceedings relating to production orders and orders to grant entry.

(3)   An application to discharge or vary a production order or an order to grant entry may be made to the court by—

(a)   the person who applied for the order;

(b)   any person affected by the order.

(4)   The court—

(a)   may discharge the order;

(b)   may vary the order.

(5)   If an accredited financial investigator, [a member of SOCA's staff,] a constable or a customs officer applies for a production order or an order to grant entry, an application to discharge or vary the order need not be by the same accredited financial investigator, [member of SOCA's staff,] constable or customs officer.

(6)   References to a person who applied for a production order or an order to grant entry must be construed accordingly.

(7)   Production orders and orders to grant entry have effect as if they were orders of the court.

(8)   Subsections (2) to (7) do not apply to orders made in England and Wales for the purposes of a civil recovery investigation [or an exploitation proceeds investigation] [*or a detained cash investigation*].

[1852K]

NOTES

Sub-s (5): words in square brackets inserted by the Serious Crime Act 2007, s 74(2)(d), Sch 8, Pt 4, paras 103, 104.

Sub-s (8): words in first pair of square brackets inserted by the Coroners and Justice Act 2009, s 169, Sch 19, paras 1, 9; words (in italics) in second pair of square brackets inserted by the Serious Crime Act 2007, s 77, Sch 10, paras 1, 6 and repealed by the Policing and Crime Act 2009, ss 66(1), (5), 112(2), Sch 8, Pt 5, as from a day to be appointed.

Transitional provisions: see the second note to s 330 at **[1842]**.

Rules: the Criminal Procedure Rules 2010, SI 2010/60.

Search and seizure warrants

352 Search and seizure warrants

(1)   A judge may, on an application made to him by an appropriate officer, issue a search and seizure warrant if he is satisfied that either of the requirements for the issuing of the warrant is fulfilled.

(2)   The application for a search and seizure warrant must state that—
  (a)   a person specified in the application is subject to a confiscation investigation [, an exploitation proceeds investigation] or a money laundering investigation, or
  (b)   property specified in the application is subject to a civil recovery investigation [or a detained cash investigation].

(3)   The application must also state—
  (a)   that the warrant is sought for the purposes of the investigation;
  (b)   that the warrant is sought in relation to the premises specified in the application;
  (c)   that the warrant is sought in relation to material specified in the application, or that there are reasonable grounds for believing that there is material falling within section 353(6), (7)[, (7A), (7B)] or (8) on the premises.

(4)   A search and seizure warrant is a warrant authorising an appropriate person—
  (a)   to enter and search the premises specified in the application for the warrant, and
  (b)   to seize and retain any material found there which is likely to be of substantial value (whether or not by itself) to the investigation for the purposes of which the application is made.

(5)   An appropriate person is—
  (a)   a constable[, an accredited financial investigator] or a customs officer, if the warrant is sought for the purposes of a confiscation investigation or a money laundering investigation;
  (b)   a [member of SOCA's staff or of the staff of the relevant Director], if the warrant is sought for the purposes of a civil recovery investigation;
  [(c)   a constable[, an accredited financial investigator] or an officer of Revenue and Customs, if the warrant is sought for the purposes of a detained cash investigation];
  [(d)   a member of SOCA's staff, if the warrant is sought for the purposes of an exploitation proceeds investigation].

[(5A)   In this Part "relevant Director"—
  (a)   in relation to England and Wales, means the Director of Public Prosecutions, the Director of Revenue and Customs Prosecutions or the Director of the Serious Fraud Office; and
  (b)   in relation to Northern Ireland, means the Director of the Serious Fraud Office or the Director of Public Prosecutions for Northern Ireland.]

(6)   The requirements for the issue of a search and seizure warrant are—
  (a)   that a production order made in relation to material has not been complied with and there are reasonable grounds for believing that the material is on the premises specified in the application for the warrant, or
  (b)   that section 353 is satisfied in relation to the warrant.

[(7)   The reference in paragraph (a) or (c) of subsection (5) to an accredited financial investigator is a reference to an accredited financial investigator who falls within a description specified in an order made for the purposes of that paragraph by the Secretary of State under section 453.]

[1852L]

NOTES

Sub-s (2): words in square brackets in para (a) inserted by the Coroners and Justice Act 2009, s 169, Sch 19, paras 1, 10(a); words in square brackets in para (b) inserted by the Serious Crime Act 2007, s 76(1).

Sub-s (3): reference in square brackets in para (c) inserted by the Serious Crime Act 2007, s 77, Sch 10, paras 1, 7(1), (2).

Sub-s (5): words in square brackets in para (a) inserted and words in square brackets in para (b) substituted by the Serious Crime Act 2007, ss 74(2)(d), 80(1)(a), Sch 8, Pt 4, paras 103, 105; para (c) inserted by s 77 of, and Sch 10, paras 1, 7(1), (3) to, the 2007 Act, words in square brackets therein inserted by s 80(1)(b) of the 2007 Act; para (d) inserted by the Coroners and Justice Act 2009, s 169, Sch 19, paras 1, 10(b).

Sub-s (5A): inserted by the Serious Crime Act 2007, s 74(2)(d), Sch 8, Pt 4, paras 103, 105(1), (3).

Sub-s (7): added by the Serious Crime Act 2007, s 80(2).

See further, in relation to the enforcement in England and Wales of search and seizure warrants issued in Northern Ireland for the purposes of a confiscation investigation or money laundering investigation: the Proceeds of Crime Act 2002 (Investigations in different parts of the United Kingdom) Order 2003, SI 2003/425, art 5.

Transitional provisions: see the second note to s 330 at [**1842**].

353 Requirements where production order not available

(1)   This section is satisfied in relation to a search and seizure warrant if—

(a)   subsection (2) applies, and

(b)   either the first or the second set of conditions is complied with.

(2)   This subsection applies if there are reasonable grounds for suspecting that—

    (a)   in the case of a confiscation investigation, the person specified in the application for the warrant has benefited from his criminal conduct;

    (b)   in the case of a civil recovery investigation, the property specified in the application for the warrant is recoverable property or associated property;

    [(ba)   in the case of a detained cash investigation into the derivation of cash, the property specified in the application for the warrant, or a part of it, is recoverable property;

    (bb)   in the case of a detained cash investigation into the intended use of cash, the property specified in the application for the warrant, or a part of it, is intended by any person to be used in unlawful conduct;]

    (c)   in the case of a money laundering investigation, the person specified in the application for the warrant has committed a money laundering offence;

    [(d)   in the case of an exploitation proceeds investigation, the person specified in the application for the warrant is within section 346(2A).]

(3)   The first set of conditions is that there are reasonable grounds for believing that—

    (a)   any material on the premises specified in the application for the warrant is likely to be of substantial value (whether or not by itself) to the investigation for the purposes of which the warrant is sought,

    (b)   it is in the public interest for the material to be obtained, having regard to the benefit likely to accrue to the investigation if the material is obtained, and

    (c)   it would not be appropriate to make a production order for any one or more of the reasons in subsection (4).

(4)   The reasons are—

    (a)   that it is not practicable to communicate with any person against whom the production order could be made;

    (b)   that it is not practicable to communicate with any person who would be required to comply with an order to grant entry to the premises;

    (c)   that the investigation might be seriously prejudiced unless an appropriate person is able to secure immediate access to the material.

(5)   The second set of conditions is that—

    (a)   there are reasonable grounds for believing that there is material on the premises specified in the application for the warrant and that the material falls within subsection (6), (7)[, (7A), (7B)][, (8) or (8A)],

    (b)   there are reasonable grounds for believing that it is in the public interest for the material to be obtained, having regard to the benefit likely to accrue to the investigation if the material is obtained, and

    (c)   any one or more of the requirements in subsection (9) is met.

(6)   In the case of a confiscation investigation, material falls within this subsection if it cannot be identified at the time of the application but it—

    (a)   relates to the person specified in the application, the question whether he has benefited from his criminal conduct or any question as to the extent or whereabouts of his benefit from his criminal conduct, and

    (b)   is likely to be of substantial value (whether or not by itself) to the investigation for the purposes of which the warrant is sought.

(7)   In the case of a civil recovery investigation, material falls within this subsection if it cannot be identified at the time of the application but it—

    (a)   relates to the property specified in the application, the question whether it is recoverable property or associated property, the question as to who holds any such property, any question as to whether the person who appears to hold any such property holds other property which is recoverable property, or any question as to the extent or whereabouts of any property mentioned in this paragraph, and

    (b)   is likely to be of substantial value (whether or not by itself) to the investigation for the purposes of which the warrant is sought.

[(7A)   In the case of a detained cash investigation into the derivation of cash, material falls within this subsection if it cannot be identified at the time of the application but it—

    (a)   relates to the property specified in the application, the question whether the property, or a part of it, is recoverable property or any other question as to its derivation, and

    (b)   is likely to be of substantial value (whether or not by itself) to the investigation for the purposes of which the warrant is sought.

(7B)   In the case of a detained cash investigation into the intended use of cash, material falls within this subsection if it cannot be identified at the time of the application but it—

    (a)   relates to the property specified in the application or the question whether the property, or a part of it, is intended by any person to be used in unlawful conduct, and

(b)   is likely to be of substantial value (whether or not by itself) to the investigation for the purposes of which the warrant is sought.]

(8)   In the case of a money laundering investigation, material falls within this subsection if it cannot be identified at the time of the application but it—

    (a)   relates to the person specified in the application or the question whether he has committed a money laundering offence, and

    (b)   is likely to be of substantial value (whether or not by itself) to the investigation for the purposes of which the warrant is sought.

[(8A)   In the case of an exploitation proceeds investigation, material falls within this subsection if it cannot be identified at the time of the application but it—

    (a)   relates to the person specified in the application, the question whether exploitation proceeds have been obtained from a relevant offence in relation to that person, any question as to the extent or whereabouts of any benefit as a result of which exploitation proceeds are obtained or any question about the person's available amount, and

    (b)   is likely to be of substantial value (whether or not by itself) to the investigation for the purposes of which the warrant is sought.

This subsection is to be construed in accordance with Part 7 of the Coroners and Justice Act 2009 (criminal memoirs etc).]

(9)   The requirements are—

    (a)   that it is not practicable to communicate with any person entitled to grant entry to the premises;

    (b)   that entry to the premises will not be granted unless a warrant is produced;

    (c)   that the investigation might be seriously prejudiced unless an appropriate person arriving at the premises is able to secure immediate entry to them.

(10)   An appropriate person is—

    (a)   a constable[, an accredited financial investigator] or a customs officer, if the warrant is sought for the purposes of a confiscation investigation or a money laundering investigation;

    (b)   a member of [SOCA's staff or of the staff of the relevant Director], if the warrant is sought for the purposes of a civil recovery investigation;

    [(c)   a constable[, an accredited financial investigator] or an officer of Revenue and Customs, if the warrant is sought for the purposes of a detained cash investigation];

    [(d)   a member of SOCA's staff, if the warrant is sought for the purposes of an exploitation proceeds investigation].

[(11)   The reference in paragraph (a) or (c) of subsection (10) to an accredited financial investigator is a reference to an accredited financial investigator who falls within a description specified in an order made for the purposes of that paragraph by the Secretary of State under section 453.]

[1852M]

NOTES

Sub-s (2): paras (ba), (bb) inserted by the Serious Crime Act 2007, s 76(2); para (d) inserted by the Coroners and Justice Act 2009, s 169, Sch 19, paras 1, 11(a).

Sub-s (5): reference in first pair of square brackets in para (a) inserted by the Serious Crime Act 2007, s 77, Sch 10, paras 1, 8(1), (2); reference in second pair of square brackets in para (a) substituted by the Coroners and Justice Act 2009, s 169, Sch 19, paras 1, 11(b).

Sub-ss (7A), (7B): inserted by the Serious Crime Act 2007, s 76(3).

Sub-s (8A): inserted by the Coroners and Justice Act 2009, s 169, Sch 19, paras 1, 11(c).

Sub-s (10): words in square brackets in paras (a), (b) inserted by the Serious Crime Act 2007, ss 74(2)(d), 80(3)(a), Sch 8, Pt 4, paras 103, 106; para (c) added by s 77 of, and Sch 10, paras 1, 8(1), (3) to, the 2007 Act and words in square brackets inserted by s 80(3)(b) of the 2007 Act; para (d) inserted by the Coroners and Justice Act 2009, s 169, Sch 19, paras 1, 11(d).

Sub-s (11): added by the Serious Crime Act 2007, s 80(4).

Transitional provisions: see the second note to s 330 at **[1842]**.

354   Further provisions: general

(1)   A search and seizure warrant does not confer the right to seize privileged material.

(2)   Privileged material is any material which a person would be entitled to refuse to produce on grounds of legal professional privilege in proceedings in the High Court.

(3)   A search and seizure warrant does not confer the right to seize excluded material.

[1852N]

NOTES

See further, in relation to the enforcement in England and Wales of search and seizure warrants issued in Northern Ireland for the purposes of a confiscation investigation or money laundering investigation: the Proceeds of Crime Act 2002 (Investigations in different parts of the United Kingdom) Order 2003, SI 2003/425, art 5.

355   Further provisions: confiscation and money laundering

(1)   This section applies to—
   (a)   search and seizure warrants sought for the purposes of a confiscation investigation *or a money laundering investigation*[, a money laundering investigation or a detained cash investigation], and
   (b)   powers of seizure under them.

(2)   In relation to such warrants and powers, the Secretary of State may make an order which applies[, in relation to England and Wales,] the provisions to which [subsection (3) applies] subject to any specified modifications.

(3)   This subsection applies to the following provisions of the Police and Criminal Evidence Act 1984 (c 60)—
   (a)   section 15 (search warrants – safeguards);
   (b)   section 16 (execution of warrants);
   (c)   section 21 (access and copying);
   (d)   section 22 (retention).

[(3A)   In relation to such warrants and powers, the Department of Justice in Northern Ireland may make an order which applies, in relation to Northern Ireland, the provisions to which subsection (4) applies subject to any specified modifications.]

(4)   This subsection applies to the following provisions of the Police and Criminal Evidence (Northern Ireland) Order 1989 (SI 1989/1341 (NI 12))—
   (a)   Article 17 (search warrants -safeguards);
   (b)   Article 18 (execution of warrants);
   (c)   Article 23 (access and copying);
   (d)   Article 24 (retention).

[1852O]

NOTES
   Sub-s (1): words in italics substituted by subsequent words in square brackets by the Policing and Crime Act 2009, s 66(1), (6), as from a day to be appointed.
   Sub-s (2): words in first pair of square brackets inserted and words in second pair of square brackets substituted by the Northern Ireland Act 1998 (Devolution of Policing and Justice Functions) Order 2010, SI 2010/976, art 12, Sch 14, paras 47, 66(1), (2), subject to transitional provisions in arts 28–31 thereof.
   Sub-s (3A): inserted by SI 2010/976, art 12, Sch 14, paras 47, 66(1), (3), subject to transitional provisions in arts 28–31 thereof.
   Order: the Proceeds of Crime Act 2002 (Application of Police and Criminal Evidence Act 1984 and Police and Criminal Evidence (Northern Ireland) Order 1989) Order 2003, SI 2003/174.

356   Further provisions: civil recovery [and detained cash]

(1)   This section applies to search and seizure warrants sought for the purposes of civil recovery investigations [or exploitation proceeds investigations] [*or detained cash investigations*].

(2)   An application for a warrant may be made ex parte to a judge in chambers.

(3)   A warrant may be issued subject to conditions.

(4)   A warrant continues in force until the end of the period of one month starting with the day on which it is issued.

(5)   A warrant authorises the person it names to require any information which is held in a computer and is accessible from the premises specified in the application for the warrant, and which the named person believes relates to any matter relevant to the investigation, to be produced in a form—
   (a)   in which it can be taken away, and
   (b)   in which it is visible and legible.

(6)   …

(7)   A warrant may include provision authorising a person who is exercising powers under it to do other things which—
   (a)   are specified in the warrant, and
   (b)   need to be done in order to give effect to it.

(8)   Copies may be taken of any material seized under a warrant.

(9)   Material seized under a warrant may be retained for so long as it is necessary to retain it (as opposed to copies of it) in connection with the investigation for the purposes of which the warrant was issued.

(10)   But *[if the appropriate person has reasonable]* [if an appropriate officer has reasonable] grounds for believing that—
   (a)   the material may need to be produced for the purposes of any legal proceedings, and
   (b)   it might otherwise be unavailable for those purposes,

it may be retained until the proceedings are concluded.

[*(11)*   *The appropriate person is—*
  (*a*)   *[an appropriate officer], if the warrant was issued for the purposes of a civil recovery investigation;*
  (*b*)   *a constable[, an accredited financial investigator] or an officer of Revenue and Customs, if the warrant was issued for the purposes of a detained cash investigation.]*

[*(12)*   *The reference in paragraph (b) of subsection (11) to an accredited financial investigator is a reference to an accredited financial investigator who falls within a description specified in an order made for the purposes of that paragraph by the Secretary of State under section 453.]*

[1852P]

NOTES
Section heading: words in italics in square brackets inserted by the Serious Crime Act 2007, s 77, Sch 10, paras 1, 9(1), (2) and repealed by the Policing and Crime Act 2009, ss 66(1), (7)(a), 112(2), Sch 8, Pt 5, as from a day to be appointed.
Sub-s (1): words in first pair of square brackets inserted by the Coroners and Justice Act 2009, s 169, Sch 19, paras 1, 12; words in italics in second pair of square brackets inserted by the Serious Crime Act 2007, s 77, Sch 10, paras 1, 9(1), (3) and repealed by the Policing and Crime Act 2009, ss 66(1), (7)(b), 112(2), Sch 8, Pt 5, as from a day to be appointed.
Sub-s (6): repealed by the Serious Crime Act 2007, ss 74(2)(d), 92, Sch 8, Pt 4, paras 103, 107(1), (2), Sch 14.
Sub-s (10): words in italics in square brackets substituted by the Serious Crime Act 2007, s 77, Sch 10, paras 1, 9(1), (5); those words in italics substituted by subsequent words in square brackets by the Policing and Crime Act 2009, s 66(1), (7)(c), as from a day to be appointed.
Sub-s (11): added by the Serious Crime Act 2007, s 77, Sch 10, paras 1, 9(1), (6); words in square brackets in para (a) substituted and words in square brackets in para (b) inserted by ss 74(2)(d), 80(5) of, and Sch 8, Pt 4, paras 103, 107(1), (3) to, the 2007 Act; repealed by the Policing and Crime Act 2009, ss 66(1), (7)(d), 112(2), Sch 8, Pt 5, as from a day to be appointed.
Sub-s (12): added by the Serious Crime Act 2007, s 80(6); repealed by the Policing and Crime Act 2009, ss 66(1), (7)(d), 112(2), Sch 8, Pt 5, as from a day to be appointed.
Transitional provisions: see the second note to s 330 at **[1842]**.

Disclosure orders

357   Disclosure orders

(1)   A judge may, on an application made to him by [the relevant authority], make a disclosure order if he is satisfied that each of the requirements for the making of the order is fulfilled.

(2)   No application for a disclosure order may be made in relation to a [detained cash investigation or a] money laundering investigation.

[(2A)   The relevant authority may only make an application for a disclosure order in relation to a confiscation investigation if the relevant authority is in receipt of a request to do so from an appropriate officer.]

(3)   The application for a disclosure order must state that—
  (*a*)   a person specified in the application is subject to a confiscation investigation which is being carried out by [an appropriate officer] and the order is sought for the purposes of the investigation, or
  (*b*)   property specified in the application is subject to a civil recovery investigation and the order is sought for the purposes of the investigation[, or
  (*c*)   a person specified in the application is subject to an exploitation proceeds investigation and the order is sought for the purposes of the investigation].

(4)   A disclosure order is an order authorising [an appropriate officer] to give to any person [the appropriate officer] considers has relevant information notice in writing requiring him to do, with respect to any matter relevant to the investigation for the purposes of which the order is sought, any or all of the following—
  (*a*)   answer questions, either at a time specified in the notice or at once, at a place so specified;
  (*b*)   provide information specified in the notice, by a time and in a manner so specified;
  (*c*)   produce documents, or documents of a description, specified in the notice, either at or by a time so specified or at once, and in a manner so specified.

(5)   Relevant information is information (whether or not contained in a document) which [the appropriate officer concerned] considers to be relevant to the investigation.

(6)   A person is not bound to comply with a requirement imposed by a notice given under a disclosure order unless evidence of authority to give the notice is produced to him.

[(7)   In this Part "relevant authority" means—
  (*a*)   in relation to a confiscation investigation, a prosecutor; and
  (*b*)   in relation to a civil recovery investigation, a member of SOCA's staff or the relevant Director[; and
  (*c*)   in relation to an exploitation proceeds investigation, a member of SOCA's staff].

(8)   For the purposes of subsection (7)(a) a prosecutor is—
 (a)   in relation to a confiscation investigation carried out by a member of SOCA's staff, the relevant Director or any specified person;
 (b)   in relation to a confiscation investigation carried out by an accredited financial investigator, the Director of Public Prosecutions, the Director of Public Prosecutions for Northern Ireland or any specified person;
 (c)   in relation to a confiscation investigation carried out by a constable, the Director of Public Prosecutions, the Director of Public Prosecutions for Northern Ireland, the Director of the Serious Fraud Office or any specified person; and
 (d)   in relation to a confiscation investigation carried out by an officer of Revenue and Customs, the Director of Revenue and Customs Prosecutions, the Director of Public Prosecutions for Northern Ireland or any specified person.

(9)   In subsection (8) "specified person" means any person specified, or falling within a description specified, by an order of the Secretary of State.]

[1852Q]

NOTES

Sub-s (1): words in square brackets substituted by the Serious Crime Act 2007, s 74(2)(d), Sch 8, Pt 4, paras 103, 108(1), (2).
Sub-s (2): words in square brackets inserted by the Serious Crime Act 2007, s 77, Sch 10, paras 1, 10.
Sub-s (2A): inserted by the Serious Crime Act 2007, s 74(2)(d), Sch 8, Pt 4, paras 103, 108(1), (3).
Sub-s (3): words in square brackets in para (a) substituted by the Serious Crime Act 2007, s 74(2)(d), Sch 8, Pt 4, paras 103, 108(1), (4); para (c) inserted together with word immediately preceding it by the Coroners and Justice Act 2009, s 169, Sch 19, paras 1, 13(a).
Sub-ss (4), (5): words in square brackets substituted by the Serious Crime Act 2007, s 74(2)(d), Sch 8, Pt 4, paras 103, 108(1), (5), 6.
Sub-s (7): added together with sub-ss (8), (9) by the Serious Crime Act 2007, s 74(2)(d), Sch 8, Pt 4, paras 103, 108(7); para (c) inserted together with word immediately preceding it by the Coroners and Justice Act 2009, s 169, Sch 19, paras 1, 13(b).
Sub-ss (8), (9): added as noted above.
Transitional provisions: see the second note to s 330 at **[1842]**.

358   Requirements for making of disclosure order

(1)   These are the requirements for the making of a disclosure order.
(2)   There must be reasonable grounds for suspecting that—
 (a)   in the case of a confiscation investigation, the person specified in the application for the order has benefited from his criminal conduct;
 (b)   in the case of a civil recovery investigation, the property specified in the application for the order is recoverable property or associated property;
 [(c)   in the case of an exploitation proceeds investigation, the person specified in the application for the order is a person within section 346(2A)].

(3)   There must be reasonable grounds for believing that information which may be provided in compliance with a requirement imposed under the order is likely to be of substantial value (whether or not by itself) to the investigation for the purposes of which the order is sought.

(4)   There must be reasonable grounds for believing that it is in the public interest for the information to be provided, having regard to the benefit likely to accrue to the investigation if the information is obtained.

[1852R]

NOTES

Sub-s (2): para (c) inserted by the Coroners and Justice Act 2009, s 169, Sch 19, paras 1, 14.

359   Offences

(1)   A person commits an offence if without reasonable excuse he fails to comply with a requirement imposed on him under a disclosure order.

(2)   A person guilty of an offence under subsection (1) is liable on summary conviction to—
 (a)   imprisonment for a term not exceeding six months,
 (b)   a fine not exceeding level 5 on the standard scale, or
 (c)   both.

(3)   A person commits an offence if, in purported compliance with a requirement imposed on him under a disclosure order, he—
 (a)   makes a statement which he knows to be false or misleading in a material particular, or
 (b)   recklessly makes a statement which is false or misleading in a material particular.

(4)   A person guilty of an offence under subsection (3) is liable—
 (a)   on summary conviction, to imprisonment for a term not exceeding six months or to a fine not exceeding the statutory maximum or to both, or

(b)   on conviction on indictment, to imprisonment for a term not exceeding two years or to a fine or to both.

[1852S]

NOTES

See further, in relation to the enforcement in England and Wales of disclosure orders made in Northern Ireland for the purposes of a confiscation investigation: the Proceeds of Crime Act 2002 (Investigations in different parts of the United Kingdom) Order 2003, SI 2003/425, art 7.

360 Statements

(1)   A statement made by a person in response to a requirement imposed on him under a disclosure order may not be used in evidence against him in criminal proceedings.

(2)   But subsection (1) does not apply—

(a)   in the case of proceedings under Part 2 or 4,

(b)   on a prosecution for an offence under section 359(1) or (3),

(c)   on a prosecution for an offence under section 5 of the Perjury Act 1911 (c 6) or Article 10 of the Perjury (Northern Ireland) Order 1979 (SI 1979/1714 (NI 19)) (false statements), or

(d)   on a prosecution for some other offence where, in giving evidence, the person makes a statement inconsistent with the statement mentioned in subsection (1).

(3)   A statement may not be used by virtue of subsection (2)(d) against a person unless—

(a)   evidence relating to it is adduced, or

(b)   a question relating to it is asked,

by him or on his behalf in the proceedings arising out of the prosecution.

[1852T]

NOTES

See further, in relation to the enforcement in England and Wales of disclosure orders made in Northern Ireland for the purposes of a confiscation investigation: the Proceeds of Crime Act 2002 (Investigations in different parts of the United Kingdom) Order 2003, SI 2003/425, art 7.

361 Further provisions

(1)   A disclosure order does not confer the right to require a person to answer any privileged question, provide any privileged information or produce any privileged document, except that a lawyer may be required to provide the name and address of a client of his.

(2)   A privileged question is a question which the person would be entitled to refuse to answer on grounds of legal professional privilege in proceedings in the High Court.

(3)   Privileged information is any information which the person would be entitled to refuse to provide on grounds of legal professional privilege in proceedings in the High Court.

(4)   Privileged material is any material which the person would be entitled to refuse to produce on grounds of legal professional privilege in proceedings in the High Court.

(5)   A disclosure order does not confer the right to require a person to produce excluded material.

(6)   A disclosure order has effect in spite of any restriction on the disclosure of information (however imposed).

(7)   [An appropriate officer] may take copies of any documents produced in compliance with a requirement to produce them which is imposed under a disclosure order.

(8)   Documents so produced may be retained for so long as it is necessary to retain them (as opposed to a copy of them) in connection with the investigation for the purposes of which the order was made.

(9)   But if [an appropriate officer] has reasonable grounds for believing that—

(a)   the documents may need to be produced for the purposes of any legal proceedings, and

(b)   they might otherwise be unavailable for those purposes,

they may be retained until the proceedings are concluded.

[1852U]

NOTES

Sub-ss (7), (9): words in square brackets substituted by the Serious Crime Act 2007, s 74(2)(d), Sch 8, Pt 4, paras 103, 109.

See further, in relation to the enforcement in England and Wales of disclosure orders made in Northern Ireland for the purposes of a confiscation investigation: the Proceeds of Crime Act 2002 (Investigations in different parts of the United Kingdom) Order 2003, SI 2003/425, art 7.

Transitional provisions: see the second note to s 330 at **[1842]**.

362 Supplementary

(1)   An application for a disclosure order may be made ex parte to a judge in chambers.

(2)   Rules of court may make provision as to the practice and procedure to be followed in connection with proceedings relating to disclosure orders.

(3)   An application to discharge or vary a disclosure order may be made to the court by—
  (a)   the [person who applied for the order];
  (b)   any person affected by the order.

(4)   The court—
  (a)   may discharge the order;
  (b)   may vary the order.

[(4A)   If a member of SOCA's staff or a person falling within a description of persons specified by virtue of section 357(9) applies for a disclosure order, an application to discharge or vary the order need not be by the same member of SOCA's staff or (as the case may be) the same person falling within that description.

(4B)   References to a person who applied for a disclosure order must be construed accordingly.]

(5)   Subsections (2) to [(4B)] do not apply to orders made in England and Wales for the purposes of a civil recovery investigation [or an exploitation proceeds investigation].

[1852V]

NOTES

Sub-s (3): words in square brackets in para (a) substituted by the Serious Crime Act 2007, s 74(2)(d), Sch 8, Pt 4, paras 103, 110(1), (2).

Sub-ss (4A), (4B): inserted by the Serious Crime Act 2007, s 74(2)(d), Sch 8, Pt 4, paras 103, 110(1), (3).

Sub-s (5): reference in first pair of square brackets substituted by the Serious Crime Act 2007, s 74(2)(d), Sch 8, Pt 4, paras 103, 110(1), (4); words in second pair of square brackets added by the Coroners and Justice Act 2009, s 169, Sch 19, paras 1, 15.

Transitional provisions: see the second note to s 330 at **[1842]**.

Rules: the Criminal Procedure Rules 2010, SI 2010/60.

Customer information orders

363 Customer information orders

(1)   A judge may, on an application made to him by an appropriate officer, make a customer information order if he is satisfied that each of the requirements for the making of the order is fulfilled.

[(1A)   No application for a customer information order may be made in relation to a detained cash investigation.]

(2)   The application for a customer information order must state that—
  (a)   a person specified in the application is subject to a confiscation investigation[, an exploitation proceeds investigation] or a money laundering investigation, or
  (b)   property specified in the application is subject to a civil recovery investigation and a person specified in the application appears to hold the property.

(3)   The application must also state that—
  (a)   the order is sought for the purposes of the investigation;
  (b)   the order is sought against the financial institution or financial institutions specified in the application.

(4)   An application for a customer information order may specify—
  (a)   all financial institutions,
  (b)   a particular description, or particular descriptions, of financial institutions, or
  (c)   a particular financial institution or particular financial institutions.

(5)   A customer information order is an order that a financial institution covered by the application for the order must, on being required to do so by notice in writing given by an appropriate officer, provide any such customer information as it has relating to the person specified in the application.

(6)   A financial institution which is required to provide information under a customer information order must provide the information to an appropriate officer in such manner, and at or by such time, as an appropriate officer requires.

(7)   If a financial institution on which a requirement is imposed by a notice given under a customer information order requires the production of evidence of authority to give the notice, it is not bound to comply with the requirement unless evidence of the authority has been produced to it.

[1852W]

NOTES
Sub-s (1A): inserted by the Serious Crime Act 2007, s 77, Sch 10, paras 1, 11.
Sub-s (2): words in square brackets inserted by the Coroners and Justice Act 2009, s 169, Sch 19, paras 1, 16.

364 Meaning of customer information

(1)   "Customer information", in relation to a person and a financial institution, is information whether the person holds, or has held, an account or accounts [or any safe deposit box] at the financial institution (whether solely or jointly with another) and (if so) information as to—
- (a)   the matters specified in subsection (2) if the person is an individual;
- (b)   the matters specified in subsection (3) if the person is a company or limited liability partnership or a similar body incorporated or otherwise established outside the United Kingdom.

(2)   The matters referred to in subsection (1)(a) are—
- (a)   the account number or numbers [or the number of any safe deposit box];
- (b)   the person's full name;
- (c)   his date of birth;
- (d)   his most recent address and any previous addresses;
- (e)   [in the case of an account or accounts,] the date or dates on which he began to hold the account or accounts and, if he has ceased to hold the account or any of the accounts, the date or dates on which he did so;
- [(ee) in the case of any safe deposit box, the date on which the box was made available to him and if the box has ceased to be available to him the date on which it so ceased;]
- (f)   such evidence of his identity as was obtained by the financial institution under or for the purposes of any legislation relating to money laundering;
- (g)   the full name, date of birth and most recent address, and any previous addresses, of any person who holds, or has held, an account at the financial institution jointly with him;
- (h)   the account number or numbers of any other account or accounts held at the financial institution to which he is a signatory and details of the person holding the other account or accounts.

(3)   The matters referred to in subsection (1)(b) are—
- (a)   the account number or numbers [or the number of any safe deposit box];
- (b)   the person's full name;
- (c)   a description of any business which the person carries on;
- (d)   the country or territory in which it is incorporated or otherwise established and any number allocated to it under [the Companies Act 2006] or corresponding legislation of any country or territory outside the United Kingdom;
- (e)   any number assigned to it for the purposes of value added tax in the United Kingdom;
- (f)   its registered office, and any previous registered offices, under [the Companies Act 2006 (or corresponding earlier legislation)] or anything similar under corresponding legislation of any country or territory outside the United Kingdom;
- (g)   its registered office, and any previous registered offices, under the Limited Liability Partnerships Act 2000 (c 12) or anything similar under corresponding legislation of any country or territory outside Great Britain;
- (h)   [in the case of an account or accounts,] the date or dates on which it began to hold the account or accounts and, if it has ceased to hold the account or any of the accounts, the date or dates on which it did so;
- [(hh) in the case of any safe deposit box, the date on which the box was made available to it and if the box has ceased to be available to it the date on which it so ceased;]
- (i)   such evidence of its identity as was obtained by the financial institution under or for the purposes of any legislation relating to money laundering;
- (j)   the full name, date of birth and most recent address and any previous addresses of any person who is a signatory to the account or any of the accounts.

(4)   The Secretary of State may by order provide for information of a description specified in the order—
- (a)   to be customer information, or
- (b)   no longer to be customer information.

(5)   Money laundering is an act which—
- (a)   constitutes an offence under section 327, 328 or 329 of this Act or section 18 of the Terrorism Act 2000 (c 11),
- [(aa) constitutes an offence specified in section 415(1A) of this Act,] or
- (b)   would constitute an offence specified in paragraph (a) [or (aa)] if done in the United Kingdom.

[(6) A "safe deposit box" includes any procedure under which a financial institution provides a facility to hold items for safe keeping on behalf of another person.]

[1852X]

NOTES

Sub-s (1): words in square brackets inserted, in relation to Northern Ireland, by the Criminal Justice (Northern Ireland) Order 2005, SI 2005/1965, art 14(1), (2).

Sub-s (2): in paras (a), (e) words in square brackets inserted, and para (ee) inserted, in relation to Northern Ireland, by the Criminal Justice (Northern Ireland) Order 2005, SI 2005/1965, art 14(1), (3).

Sub-s (3): in paras (a), (h) words in square brackets inserted, and para (hh) inserted, in relation to Northern Ireland, by the Criminal Justice (Northern Ireland) Order 2005, SI 2005/1965, art 14(1), (4); words in square brackets in paras (d), (f) substituted by the Companies Act 2006 (Consequential Amendments, Transitional Provisions and Savings) Order 2009, SI 2009/1941, art 2(1), Sch 1, para 196(1), (2).

Sub-s (5): para (aa) inserted and words in square brackets in para (b) inserted by the Serious Organised Crime and Police Act 2005, s 107(1), (2).

Sub-s (6): inserted, in relation to Northern Ireland, by the Criminal Justice (Northern Ireland) Order 2005, SI 2005/1965, art 14(1), (5).

365 Requirements for making of customer information order

(1) These are the requirements for the making of a customer information order.

(2) In the case of a confiscation investigation, there must be reasonable grounds for suspecting that the person specified in the application for the order has benefited from his criminal conduct.

(3) In the case of a civil recovery investigation, there must be reasonable grounds for suspecting that—

(a) the property specified in the application for the order is recoverable property or associated property;

(b) the person specified in the application holds all or some of the property.

(4) In the case of a money laundering investigation, there must be reasonable grounds for suspecting that the person specified in the application for the order has committed a money laundering offence.

(5) In the case of any investigation, there must be reasonable grounds for believing that customer information which may be provided in compliance with the order is likely to be of substantial value (whether or not by itself) to the investigation for the purposes of which the order is sought.

(6) In the case of any investigation, there must be reasonable grounds for believing that it is in the public interest for the customer information to be provided, having regard to the benefit likely to accrue to the investigation if the information is obtained.

[1852Y]

366 Offences

(1) A financial institution commits an offence if without reasonable excuse it fails to comply with a requirement imposed on it under a customer information order.

(2) A financial institution guilty of an offence under subsection (1) is liable on summary conviction to a fine not exceeding level 5 on the standard scale.

(3) A financial institution commits an offence if, in purported compliance with a customer information order, it—

(a) makes a statement which it knows to be false or misleading in a material particular, or

(b) recklessly makes a statement which is false or misleading in a material particular.

(4) A financial institution guilty of an offence under subsection (3) is liable—

(a) on summary conviction, to a fine not exceeding the statutory maximum, or

(b) on conviction on indictment, to a fine.

[1852Z]

NOTES

See further, in relation to the provision for the enforcement in England and Wales of customer information orders made in Northern Ireland for the purposes of a confiscation investigation or money laundering investigation: the Proceeds of Crime Act 2002 (Investigations in different parts of the United Kingdom) Order 2003, SI 2003/425, art 9.

367 Statements

(1) A statement made by a financial institution in response to a customer information order may not be used in evidence against it in criminal proceedings.

(2) But subsection (1) does not apply—

(a) in the case of proceedings under Part 2 or 4,

(b) on a prosecution for an offence under section 366(1) or (3), or

(c) on a prosecution for some other offence where, in giving evidence, the financial institution makes a statement inconsistent with the statement mentioned in subsection (1).

(3) A statement may not be used by virtue of subsection (2)(c) against a financial institution unless—

(a) evidence relating to it is adduced, or
(b) a question relating to it is asked,

by or on behalf of the financial institution in the proceedings arising out of the prosecution.

[1852AA]

NOTES

See further, in relation to the provision for the enforcement in England and Wales of customer information orders made in Northern Ireland for the purposes of a confiscation investigation or money laundering investigation: the Proceeds of Crime Act 2002 (Investigations in different parts of the United Kingdom) Order 2003, SI 2003/425, art 9.

368 Disclosure of information

A customer information order has effect in spite of any restriction on the disclosure of information (however imposed).

[1852AB]

NOTES

See further, in relation to the provision for the enforcement in England and Wales of customer information orders made in Northern Ireland for the purposes of a confiscation investigation or money laundering investigation: the Proceeds of Crime Act 2002 (Investigations in different parts of the United Kingdom) Order 2003, SI 2003/425, art 9.

369 Supplementary

(1) An application for a customer information order may be made ex parte to a judge in chambers.

(2) Rules of court may make provision as to the practice and procedure to be followed in connection with proceedings relating to customer information orders.

(3) An application to discharge or vary a customer information order may be made to the court by—

(a) the person who applied for the order;
(b) any person affected by the order.

(4) The court—

(a) may discharge the order;
(b) may vary the order.

(5) If an accredited financial investigator, [a member of SOCA's staff,] a constable or a customs officer applies for a customer information order, an application to discharge or vary the order need not be by the same accredited financial investigator, [member of SOCA's staff,] constable or customs officer.

(6) References to a person who applied for a customer information order must be construed accordingly.

(7) An accredited financial investigator, [a member of SOCA's staff,] a constable or a customs officer may not make an application for a customer information order or an application to vary such an order unless he is a senior appropriate officer or he is authorised to do so by a senior appropriate officer.

(8) Subsections (2) to (6) do not apply to orders made in England and Wales for the purposes of a civil recovery investigation.

[1852AC]

NOTES

Sub-ss (5), (7): words in square brackets inserted by the Serious Crime Act 2007, s 74(2)(d), Sch 8, Pt 4, paras 103, 111(1).

Transitional provisions: see the second note to s 330 at **[1842]**.

Rules: the Criminal Procedure Rules 2010, SI 2010/60.

Account monitoring orders

370 Account monitoring orders

(1) A judge may, on an application made to him by an appropriate officer, make an account monitoring order if he is satisfied that each of the requirements for the making of the order is fulfilled.

[(1A)   No application for an account monitoring order may be made in relation to a detained cash investigation.]

(2)   The application for an account monitoring order must state that—
   (a)   a person specified in the application is subject to a confiscation investigation[, an exploitation proceeds investigation] or a money laundering investigation, or
   (b)   property specified in the application is subject to a civil recovery investigation and a person specified in the application appears to hold the property.

(3)   The application must also state that—
   (a)   the order is sought for the purposes of the investigation;
   (b)   the order is sought against the financial institution specified in the application in relation to account information of the description so specified.

(4)   Account information is information relating to an account or accounts held at the financial institution specified in the application by the person so specified (whether solely or jointly with another).

(5)   The application for an account monitoring order may specify information relating to—
   (a)   all accounts held by the person specified in the application for the order at the financial institution so specified,
   (b)   a particular description, or particular descriptions, of accounts so held, or
   (c)   a particular account, or particular accounts, so held.

(6)   An account monitoring order is an order that the financial institution specified in the application for the order must, for the period stated in the order, provide account information of the description specified in the order to an appropriate officer in the manner, and at or by the time or times, stated in the order.

(7)   The period stated in an account monitoring order must not exceed the period of 90 days beginning with the day on which the order is made.

[1852AD]

NOTES
Sub-s (1A): inserted by the Serious Crime Act 2007, s 77, Sch 10, paras 1, 12.
Sub-s (2): words in square brackets inserted by the Coroners and Justice Act 2009, s 169, Sch 19, paras 1, 17.
See further, in relation to the enforcement in England and Wales of account monitoring orders made in Northern Ireland for the purpose of a confiscation investigation or money laundering investigation: the Proceeds of Crime Act 2002 (Investigations in different parts of the United Kingdom) Order 2003, SI 2003/425, art 11.

371   Requirements for making of account monitoring order

(1)   These are the requirements for the making of an account monitoring order.

(2)   In the case of a confiscation investigation, there must be reasonable grounds for suspecting that the person specified in the application for the order has benefited from his criminal conduct.

(3)   In the case of a civil recovery investigation, there must be reasonable grounds for suspecting that—
   (a)   the property specified in the application for the order is recoverable property or associated property;
   (b)   the person specified in the application holds all or some of the property.

(4)   In the case of a money laundering investigation, there must be reasonable grounds for suspecting that the person specified in the application for the order has committed a money laundering offence.

(5)   In the case of any investigation, there must be reasonable grounds for believing that account information which may be provided in compliance with the order is likely to be of substantial value (whether or not by itself) to the investigation for the purposes of which the order is sought.

(6)   In the case of any investigation, there must be reasonable grounds for believing that it is in the public interest for the account information to be provided, having regard to the benefit likely to accrue to the investigation if the information is obtained.

[1852AE]

372   Statements

(1)   A statement made by a financial institution in response to an account monitoring order may not be used in evidence against it in criminal proceedings.

(2)   But subsection (1) does not apply—
   (a)   in the case of proceedings under Part 2 or 4,
   (b)   in the case of proceedings for contempt of court, or
   (c)   on a prosecution for an offence where, in giving evidence, the financial institution makes a statement inconsistent with the statement mentioned in subsection (1).

(3)   A statement may not be used by virtue of subsection (2)(c) against a financial institution unless—

    (a)   evidence relating to it is adduced, or

    (b)   a question relating to it is asked,

by or on behalf of the financial institution in the proceedings arising out of the prosecution.

[1852AF]

NOTES

See further, in relation to the enforcement in England and Wales of account monitoring orders made in Northern Ireland for the purpose of a confiscation investigation or money laundering investigation: the Proceeds of Crime Act 2002 (Investigations in different parts of the United Kingdom) Order 2003, SI 2003/425, art 11.

373   Applications

An application for an account monitoring order may be made ex parte to a judge in chambers.

[1852AG]

374   Disclosure of information

An account monitoring order has effect in spite of any restriction on the disclosure of information (however imposed).

[1852AH]

NOTES

See further, in relation to the enforcement in England and Wales of account monitoring orders made in Northern Ireland for the purpose of a confiscation investigation or money laundering investigation: the Proceeds of Crime Act 2002 (Investigations in different parts of the United Kingdom) Order 2003, SI 2003/425, art 11.

375   Supplementary

(1)   Rules of court may make provision as to the practice and procedure to be followed in connection with proceedings relating to account monitoring orders.

(2)   An application to discharge or vary an account monitoring order may be made to the court by—

    (a)   the person who applied for the order;

    (b)   any person affected by the order.

(3)   The court—

    (a)   may discharge the order;

    (b)   may vary the order.

(4)   If an accredited financial investigator, [a member of SOCA's staff,] a constable or a customs officer applies for an account monitoring order, an application to discharge or vary the order need not be by the same accredited financial investigator, [member of SOCA's staff,] constable or customs officer.

(5)   References to a person who applied for an account monitoring order must be construed accordingly.

(6)   Account monitoring orders have effect as if they were orders of the court.

(7)   This section does not apply to orders made in England and Wales for the purposes of a civil recovery investigation.

[1852AI]–[1852AJ]

NOTES

Sub-s (4): words in square brackets inserted by the Serious Crime Act 2007, s 74(2)(d), Sch 8, Pt 4, paras 103, 112.

Transitional provisions: see the second note to s 330 at **[1842]**.

Rules: the Criminal Procedure Rules 2010, SI 2010/60.

376   *(Repealed by the Serious Crime Act 2007, ss 74(2)(d), 92, Sch 8, Pt 4, paras 103, 113, Sch 14, except in relation to anything done (or having effect as if done) by or in relation to the transferor before 1 April 2008.)*

Code of practice

377   Code of practice [of Secretary of State etc]

(1)   The Secretary of State must prepare a code of practice as to the exercise by all of the following of functions they have under this Chapter—

    (a)   [the Director General of SOCA];

    (b)   [other members of SOCA's staff];

    (c)   [in relation to England and Wales,] accredited financial investigators;

(d)　[in relation to England and Wales,] constables;
(e)　customs officers.

(2)　After preparing a draft of the code the Secretary of State—
(a)　must publish the draft;
(b)　must consider any representations made to him about the draft;
(c)　may amend the draft accordingly.

(3)　After the Secretary of State has proceeded under subsection (2) he must lay the code before Parliament.

(4)　When he has done so the Secretary of State may bring the code into operation on such day as he may appoint by order.

(5)　A person specified in subsection (1)(a) to (e) must comply with a code of practice which is in operation under this section in the exercise of any function he has under this Chapter.

(6)　If such a person fails to comply with any provision of such a code of practice he is not by reason only of that failure liable in any criminal or civil proceedings.

(7)　But the code of practice is admissible in evidence in such proceedings and a court may take account of any failure to comply with its provisions in determining any question in the proceedings.

(8)　The Secretary of State may from time to time revise a code previously brought into operation under this section; and the preceding provisions of this section apply to a revised code as they apply to the code as first prepared.

(9)　......

[1852AK]

NOTES

Section heading: words in square brackets inserted by the Serious Crime Act 2007, s 74(2)(d), Sch 8, Pt 4, paras 103, 114(1), (2).

Sub-s (1): words in square brackets in paras (a), (b) substituted by the Serious Crime Act 2007, s 74(2)(d), Sch 8, Pt 4, paras 103, 114(1), (3); words in square brackets in paras (c), (d) inserted by the Northern Ireland Act 1998 (Devolution of Policing and Justice Functions) Order 2010, SI 2010/976, art 12, Sch 14, paras 47, 67(1), (2), subject to transitional provisions in arts 28–31 thereof.

Sub-s (9): repealed by SI 2010/976, art 12, Sch 14, paras 47, 67(1), (3), subject to transitional provisions in arts 28–31 thereof.

Transitional provisions: see the second note to s 330 at **[1842]**.

Order: the Proceeds of Crime Act 2002 (Investigations in England, Wales and Northern Ireland: Code of Practice) Order 2008, SI 2008/946.

[377ZA　Code of practice (Northern Ireland)

(1)　The Department of Justice in Northern Ireland must prepare a code of practice as to the exercise, in relation to Northern Ireland, by constables and accredited financial investigators of functions they have under this Chapter.

(2)　After preparing a draft of the code the Department of Justice—
(a)　must publish the draft;
(b)　must consider any representations made to the Department of Justice about the draft;
(c)　may amend the draft accordingly.

(3)　After the Department of Justice has proceeded under subsection (2) it must lay the code before the Northern Ireland Assembly.

(4)　When the Department of Justice has done so it may bring the code into operation on such day as the Department of Justice may appoint by order.

(5)　Section 41(3) of the Interpretation Act (Northern Ireland) 1954 applies for the purposes of subsection (3) in relation to the laying of a code as it applies in relation to the laying of a statutory document under an enactment.

(6)　A constable or accredited financial investigator must comply with a code of practice which is in operation under this section in the exercise of any function he has under this Chapter.

(7)　If a constable or accredited financial investigator fails to comply with any provision of such a code of practice he is not by reason only of that failure liable in any criminal or civil proceedings.

(8)　But the code of practice is admissible in evidence in such proceedings and a court may take account of any failure to comply with its provisions in determining any question in the proceedings.

(9)　The Department of Justice may from time to time revise a code previously brought into operation under this section; and the preceding provisions of this section apply to a revised code as they apply to the code as first prepared.]

[1852AKA]

NOTES

Commencement: 12 April 2010.

Inserted, together with s 377ZB, by the Northern Ireland Act 1998 (Devolution of Policing and Justice Functions) Order 2010, SI 2010/976, art 12, Sch 14, paras 47, 68, subject to transitional provisions in arts 28–31 thereof.

[377ZB Disapplication of PACE codes

The following provisions do not apply to an appropriate officer or the relevant authority in the exercise of any function either has under this Chapter—
(a) section 67(9) of the Police and Criminal Evidence Act 1984 (application of codes of practice under that Act to persons other than police officers);
(b) Article 66(8) of the Police and Criminal Evidence (Northern Ireland) Order 1989 (which makes similar provision for Northern Ireland).]

[1852AKB]

NOTES
Commencement: 12 April 2010.
Inserted as noted to s 377ZA at **[1852AKA]**.

[377A Code of practice of Attorney General or Advocate General for Northern Ireland

(1) The Attorney General must prepare a code of practice as to—
(a) the exercise by the Director of Public Prosecutions, the Director of Revenue and Customs Prosecutions and the Director of the Serious Fraud Office of functions they have under this Chapter; and
(b) the exercise by any other person, who is the relevant authority by virtue of section 357(9) in relation to a confiscation investigation, of functions he has under this Chapter in relation to England and Wales as the relevant authority.

(2) The Advocate General for Northern Ireland must prepare a code of practice as to—
(a) the exercise by the Director of Public Prosecutions for Northern Ireland of functions he has under this Chapter; and
(b) the exercise by any other person, who is the relevant authority by virtue of section 357(9) in relation to a confiscation investigation, of functions he has under this Chapter in relation to Northern Ireland as the relevant authority.

(3) After preparing a draft of the code the Attorney General or (as the case may be) the Advocate General for Northern Ireland—
(a) must publish the draft;
(b) must consider any representations made to him about the draft;
(c) may amend the draft accordingly.

(4) After the Attorney General or the Advocate General for Northern Ireland has proceeded under subsection (3) he must lay the code before Parliament.

(5) When the code has been so laid the Attorney General or (as the case may be) the Advocate General for Northern Ireland may bring the code into operation on such day as he may appoint by order.

(6) A person specified in subsection (1)(a) or (b) or (2)(a) or (b) must comply with a code of practice which is in operation under this section in the exercise of any function he has under this Chapter to which the code relates.

(7) If such a person fails to comply with any provision of such a code of practice the person is not by reason only of that failure liable in any criminal or civil proceedings.

(8) But the code of practice is admissible in evidence in such proceedings and a court may take account of any failure to comply with its provisions in determining any question in the proceedings.

(9) The Attorney General or (as the case may be) the Advocate General for Northern Ireland may from time to time revise a code previously brought into operation under this section; and the preceding provisions of this section apply to a revised code as they apply to the code as first prepared.

(10) In this section references to the Advocate General for Northern Ireland are to be read, before the coming into force of section 27(1) of the Justice (Northern Ireland) Act 2002 (c 26), as references to the Attorney General for Northern Ireland.]

[1852AL]

NOTES
Commencement: 1 March 2008 (sub-ss (1)–(5), (10)); 1 April 2008 (otherwise).
Inserted by the Serious Crime Act 2007, s 74(2)(d), Sch 8, Pt 4, paras 103, 115.
Transitional provisions: see the second note to s 330 at **[1842]**.
Order: the Proceeds of Crime Act 2002 (Investigative Powers of Prosecutors in England, Wales and Northern Ireland: Code of Practice) Order 2008, SI 2008/1978.

Interpretation

378 Officers

(1)   In relation to a confiscation investigation these are appropriate officers—
   (a)   [a member of SOCA's staff];
   (b)   an accredited financial investigator;
   (c)   a constable;
   (d)   a customs officer.

(2)   In relation to a confiscation investigation these are senior appropriate officers—
   (a)   [a senior member of SOCA's staff];
   (b)   a police officer who is not below the rank of superintendent;
   (c)   a customs officer who is not below such grade as is designated by the Commissioners of Customs and Excise as equivalent to that rank;
   (d)   an accredited financial investigator who falls within a description specified in an order made for the purposes of this paragraph by the Secretary of State under section 453.

(3)   In relation to a civil recovery investigation—
   (a)   a member of SOCA's staff or the relevant Director is an appropriate officer;
   (b)   a senior member of SOCA's staff is a senior appropriate officer].

[(3A)   In relation to a detained cash investigation these are appropriate officers—
   (a)   a constable;
   [(ab)   an accredited financial investigator;]
   (b)   an officer of Revenue and Customs.]

[(3B)   The reference in paragraph (ab) of subsection (3A) to an accredited financial investigator is a reference to an accredited financial investigator who falls within a description specified in an order made for the purposes of that paragraph by the Secretary of State under section 453.]

(4)   In relation to a money laundering investigation these are appropriate officers—
   (a)   an accredited financial investigator;
   (b)   a constable;
   (c)   a customs officer.

(5)   For the purposes of section 342, in relation to a money laundering investigation a person authorised for the purposes of money laundering investigations by [the Director General of [SOCA]] is also an appropriate officer.

(6)   In relation to a money laundering investigation these are senior appropriate officers—
   (a)   a police officer who is not below the rank of superintendent;
   (b)   a customs officer who is not below such grade as is designated by the Commissioners of Customs and Excise as equivalent to that rank;
   (c)   an accredited financial investigator who falls within a description specified in an order made for the purposes of this paragraph by the Secretary of State under section 453.

[(6A)   In relation to an exploitation proceeds investigation, a member of SOCA's staff is an appropriate officer.]

(7)   …

[(8)   For the purposes of this Part a senior member of SOCA's staff is—
   (a)   the Director General of SOCA; or
   (b)   any member of SOCA's staff authorised by the Director General (whether generally or specifically) for this purpose.]

[1852AM]

NOTES

Sub-ss (1)–(3): words in square brackets substituted by the Serious Crime Act 2007, s 74(2)(d), Sch 8, Pt 4, paras 103, 116(1)–(4).

Sub-s (3A): inserted by the Serious Crime Act 2007, s 77, Sch 10, paras 1, 13; para (ab) inserted by s 80(7) of the 2007 Act.

Sub-s (3B): inserted by the Serious Crime Act 2007, s 80(8).

Sub-s (5): words in first (outer) pair of square brackets substituted by the Serious Organised Crime and Police Act 2005, s 59, Sch 4, paras 168, 175; word in second (inner) pair of square brackets substituted by the Serious Crime Act 2007, s 74(2)(d), Sch 8, Pt 4, paras 103, 116(1), (5).

Sub-s (6A): inserted by the Coroners and Justice Act 2009, s 169, Sch 19, paras 1, 18.

Sub-s (7): repealed by the Serious Crime Act 2007, ss 74(2)(d), 92, Sch 8, Pt 4, paras 103, 116(1), (6), Sch 14.

Sub-s (8): added by the Serious Crime Act 2007, s 74(2)(d), Sch 8, Pt 4, paras 103, 116(1), (7).

Transitional provisions: see the second note to s 330 at **[1842]**.

379 Miscellaneous

"Document", "excluded material" and "premises" have the same meanings as in the Police and Criminal Evidence Act 1984 (c 60) or (in relation to Northern Ireland) the Police and Criminal Evidence (Northern Ireland) Order 1989 (SI 1989/1341 (NI 12)).

[1852AN]

380–412   ((*Ch 3*) *outside the scope of this work.*)

CHAPTER 4
INTERPRETATION

413 Criminal conduct

(1)   Criminal conduct is conduct which—
  (a)   constitutes an offence in any part of the United Kingdom, or
  (b)   would constitute an offence in any part of the United Kingdom if it occurred there.

(2)   A person benefits from conduct if he obtains property or a pecuniary advantage as a result of or in connection with the conduct.

(3)   References to property or a pecuniary advantage obtained in connection with conduct include references to property or a pecuniary advantage obtained in both that connection and some other.

(4)   If a person benefits from conduct his benefit is the property or pecuniary advantage obtained as a result of or in connection with the conduct.

(5)   It is immaterial—
  (a)   whether conduct occurred before or after the passing of this Act, and
  (b)   whether property or a pecuniary advantage constituting a benefit from conduct was obtained before or after the passing of this Act.

[1852AO]

414 Property

(1)   Property is all property wherever situated and includes—
  (a)   money;
  (b)   all forms of property, real or personal, heritable or moveable;
  (c)   things in action and other intangible or incorporeal property.

(2)   "Recoverable property" and "associated property" have the same meanings as in Part 5.

(3)   The following rules apply in relation to property—
  (a)   property is obtained by a person if he obtains an interest in it;
  (b)   references to an interest, in relation to land in England and Wales or Northern Ireland, are to any legal estate or equitable interest or power;
  (c)   references to an interest, in relation to land in Scotland, are to any estate, interest, servitude or other heritable right in or over land, including a heritable security;
  (d)   references to an interest, in relation to property other than land, include references to a right (including a right to possession).

[1852AP]

415 Money laundering offences

(1)   An offence under section 327, 328 or 329 is a money laundering offence.

[(1A)   Each of the following is a money laundering offence—
  (a)   an offence under section 93A, 93B or 93C of the Criminal Justice Act 1988;
  (b)   an offence under section 49, 50 or 51 of the Drug Trafficking Act 1994;
  (c)   an offence under section 37 or 38 of the Criminal Law (Consolidation) (Scotland) Act 1995;
  (d)   an offence under article 45, 46 or 47 of the Proceeds of Crime (Northern Ireland) Order 1996.]

(2)   Each of the following is a money laundering offence—
  (a)   an attempt, conspiracy or incitement to commit an offence specified in subsection (1);
  (b)   aiding, abetting, counselling or procuring the commission of an offence specified in subsection (1).

[1852AQ]

NOTES

Sub-s (1A): inserted by the Serious Organised Crime and Police Act 2005, s 107(1), (4).

See further, in relation to England, Wales and Northern Ireland, the Serious Crime Act 2007, s 63(1), Sch 6, Pt 1, para 44(b), which provides that the reference in sub-s (2)(a) above to (or to conduct amounting to) the common law offence of inciting the commission of another offence, has effect (as from the day that offence is abolished) as a reference to (or to conduct amounting to) offences under the Serious Crime Act 2007, Pt 2.

416 Other interpretative provisions

(1)   These expressions are to be construed in accordance with these provisions of this Part—
civil recovery investigation: section 341(2) and (3)
confiscation investigation: section 341(1)
[detained cash investigation: section 341(3A)]
money laundering investigation: section 341(4).

(2)   In the application of this Part to England and Wales and Northern Ireland, these expressions are to be construed in accordance with these provisions of this Part—
account information: section 370(4)
account monitoring order: section 370(6)
appropriate officer: section 378
customer information: section 364
customer information order: section 363(5)
disclosure order: section 357(4)
document: section 379
order to grant entry: section 347(3)
production order: section 345(4)
[relevant authority: section 357(7) to (9)
relevant Director: section 352(5A)]
search and seizure warrant: section 352(4)
senior appropriate officer: section 378
[senior member of SOCA's staff: section 378(8)].

(3)   In the application of this Part to Scotland, these expressions are to be construed in accordance with these provisions of this Part—
account information: section 404(5)
account monitoring order: section 404(7)
customer information: section 398
customer information order: section 397(6)
disclosure order: section 391(4)
production order: section 380(5)
proper person: section 412
search warrant: section 387(4).

(4)   "Financial institution" means a person carrying on a business in the regulated sector.

(5)   But a person who ceases to carry on a business in the regulated sector (whether by virtue of paragraph 5 of Schedule 9 or otherwise) is to continue to be treated as a financial institution for the purposes of any requirement under—

(a)   a customer information order, or

(b)   an account monitoring order,

to provide information which relates to a time when the person was a financial institution.

(6)   References to a business in the regulated sector must be construed in accordance with Schedule 9.

(7)   "Recovery order", "interim receiving order" and "interim administration order" have the same meanings as in Part 5.

[(7A)   "Unlawful conduct" has the meaning given by section 241.]

(8)   References to notice in writing include references to notice given by electronic means.

(9)   This section and sections 413 to 415 apply for the purposes of this Part.

[1852AR]

NOTES

Sub-s (1): words in square brackets inserted by the Serious Crime Act 2007, s 77, Sch 10, paras 1, 24(1), (2).
Sub-s (2): entries relating to "relevant authority" and "relevant Director" and "senior member of SOCA's staff" inserted by the Serious Crime Act 2007, s 74(2)(d), Sch 8, Pt 4, paras 103, 117.
Sub-s (7A): inserted by the Serious Crime Act 2007, s 77, Sch 10, paras 1, 24(1), (3).
Transitional provisions: see the second note to s 330 at **[1842]**.

417–447   ((*Pts 9–11*) *outside the scope of this work.*)

PART 12
MISCELLANEOUS AND GENERAL

448–455   (*Outside the scope of this work.*)

General

456, 457   (*Outside the scope of this work.*)

458   Commencement

(1)   The preceding provisions of this Act (except the provisions specified in subsection (3) [or (4)]) come into force in accordance with provision made by the Secretary of State by order.

(2)   But no order may be made [by the Secretary of State] which includes provision for the commencement of Part 5, 8 or 10 unless the Secretary of State has consulted the Scottish Ministers.

(3)   The following provisions come into force in accordance with provision made by the Scottish Ministers by order after consultation with the Secretary of State—
  (a)   Part 3;
  (b)   this Part, to the extent that it relates to Part 3.

[(4)   Any provision of this Act which provides for the repeal of any provision of the Proceeds of Crime (Northern Ireland) Order 1996 comes into force in accordance with provision made by the Department of Justice in Northern Ireland by order.]

[1853]

NOTES

Sub-ss (1), (2): words in square brackets inserted by the Northern Ireland Act 1998 (Devolution of Policing and Justice Functions) Order 2010, SI 2010/976, art 12, Sch 14, paras 47, 73(a), (b), subject to transitional provisions in arts 28–31 thereof.
Sub-s (4): added by SI 2010/976, art 12, Sch 14, paras 47, 73(c), subject to transitional provisions in arts 28–31 thereof.
Orders: the commencement order relevant to the provisions of this Act reproduced in this work is the Proceeds of Crime Act 2002 (Commencement No 4, Transitional Provisions and Savings) Order 2003, SI 2003/120 (as amended by SI 2003/333).

459, 460   (*Outside the scope of this work.*)

461   Extent

(1)   Part 2 extends to England and Wales only.

(2)   In Part 8, Chapter 2 extends to England and Wales and Northern Ireland only.

(3)   These provisions extend to Scotland only—
  (a)   Part 3;
  (b)   in Part 8, Chapter 3.

(4)   Part 4 extends to Northern Ireland only.

(5)   The amendments in Schedule 11 have the same extent as the provisions amended.

(6)   The repeals and revocations in Schedule 12 have the same extent as the provisions repealed or revoked.

[1854]

462   Short title

This Act may be cited as the Proceeds of Crime Act 2002.

[1855]

SCHEDULES

(*Schs 1–8 outside the scope of this work.*)

SCHEDULE 9
REGULATED SECTOR AND SUPERVISORY AUTHORITIES
Section 330

[PART 1
REGULATED SECTOR

Business in the Regulated Sector

1.—(1)   A business is in the regulated sector to the extent that it consists of—
  (a)   the acceptance by a credit institution of deposits or other repayable funds from the public, or the granting by a credit institution of credits for its own account;
  (b)   the carrying on of one or more of the activities listed in points 2 to 12 and 14 of Annex 1 to the Banking Consolidation Directive by an undertaking other than—
    (i)   a credit institution; or
    (ii)   an undertaking whose only listed activity is trading for own account in one or

more of the products listed in point 7 of Annex 1 to the Banking Consolidation Directive and which does not act on behalf of a customer (that is, a third party which is not a member of the same group as the undertaking);

(c)   the carrying on of activities covered by the Life Assurance Consolidation Directive by an insurance company authorised in accordance with that Directive;

(d)   the provision of investment services or the performance of investment activities by a person (other than a person falling within Article 2 of the Markets in Financial Instruments Directive) whose regular occupation or business is the provision to other persons of an investment service or the performance of an investment activity on a professional basis;

(e)   the marketing or other offering of units or shares by a collective investment undertaking;

(f)   the activities of an insurance intermediary as defined in Article 2(5) of the Insurance Mediation Directive, other than a tied insurance intermediary as mentioned in Article 2(7) of that Directive, in respect of contracts of long-term insurance within the meaning given by article 3(1) of, and Part II of Schedule 1 to, the Financial Services and Markets Act 2000 (Regulated Activities) Order 2001;

(g)   the carrying on of any of the activities mentioned in paragraphs (b) to (f) by a branch located in an EEA State of a person referred to in those paragraphs (or of an equivalent person in any other State), wherever its head office is located;

(h)   the activities of the National Savings Bank;

(i)   any activity carried on for the purpose of raising money authorised to be raised under the National Loans Act 1968 under the auspices of the Director of Savings;

(j)   the carrying on of statutory audit work within the meaning of section 1210 of the Companies Act 2006 (meaning of "statutory auditor" etc) by any firm or individual who is a statutory auditor within the meaning of Part 42 of that Act (statutory auditors);

(k)   the activities of a person appointed to act as an insolvency practitioner within the meaning of section 388 of the Insolvency Act 1986 (meaning of "act as insolvency practitioner") or article 3 of the Insolvency (Northern Ireland) Order 1989;

(l)   the provision to other persons of accountancy services by a firm or sole practitioner who by way of business provides such services to other persons;

(m)   the provision of advice about the tax affairs of other persons by a firm or sole practitioner who by way of business provides advice about the tax affairs of other persons;

(n)   the participation in financial or real property transactions concerning—

    (i)   the buying and selling of real property (or, in Scotland, heritable property) or business entities;

    (ii)   the managing of client money, securities or other assets;

    (iii)   the opening or management of bank, savings or securities accounts;

    (iv)   the organisation of contributions necessary for the creation, operation or management of companies; or

    (v)   the creation, operation or management of trusts, companies or similar structures,

by a firm or sole practitioner who by way of business provides legal or notarial services to other persons;

(o)   the provision to other persons by way of business by a firm or sole practitioner of any of the services mentioned in sub-paragraph (4);

(p)   the carrying on of estate agency work (within the meaning given by section 1 of the Estate Agents Act 1979 (estate agency work)) by a firm or a sole practitioner who carries on, or whose employees carry on, such work;

(q)   the trading in goods (including dealing as an auctioneer) whenever a transaction involves the receipt of a payment or payments in cash of at least 15,000 euros in total, whether the transaction is executed in a single operation or in several operations which appear to be linked, by a firm or sole trader who by way of business trades in goods;

(r)   operating a casino under a casino operating licence (within the meaning given by section 65(2) of the Gambling Act 2005 (nature of licence)).

(2)   For the purposes of sub-paragraph (1)(a) and (b) "credit institution" means—

(a)   a credit institution as defined in Article 4(1)(a) of the Banking Consolidation Directive; or

(b)   a branch (within the meaning of Article 4(3) of that Directive) located in an EEA state of an institution falling within paragraph (a) (or of an equivalent institution in any other State) wherever its head office is located.

(3)   For the purposes of sub-paragraph (1)(n) a person participates in a transaction by assisting in the planning or execution of the transaction or otherwise acting for or on behalf of a client in the transaction.

(4)   The services referred to in sub-paragraph (1)(o) are—

(a)   forming companies or other legal persons;

(b)   acting, or arranging for another person to act—

    (i)   as a director or secretary of a company;

    (ii)   as a partner of a partnership; or

(iii)   in a similar position in relation to other legal persons;

(c)   providing a registered office, business address, correspondence or administrative address or other related services for a company, partnership or any other legal person or arrangement;

(d)   acting, or arranging for another person to act, as—
   (i)   a trustee of an express trust or similar legal arrangement; or
   (ii)   a nominee shareholder for a person other than a company whose securities are listed on a regulated market.

(5)   For the purposes of sub-paragraph (4)(d) "regulated market"—
   (a)   in relation to any EEA State, has the meaning given by point 14 of Article 4(1) of the Markets in Financial Instruments Directive; and
   (b)   in relation to any other State, means a regulated financial market which subjects companies whose securities are admitted to trading to disclosure obligations which are contained in international standards and are equivalent to the specified disclosure obligations.

(6)   For the purposes of sub-paragraph (5) "the specified disclosure obligations" means disclosure requirements consistent with—
   (a)   Article 6(1) to (4) of Directive 2003/6/EC of the European Parliament and of the Council of 28th January 2003 on insider dealing and market manipulation;
   (b)   Articles 3, 5, 7, 8, 10, 14 and 16 of Directive 2003/71/EC of the European Parliament and of the Council of 4th November 2003 on the prospectuses to be published when securities are offered to the public or admitted to trading;
   (c)   Articles 4 to 6, 14, 16 to 19 and 30 of Directive 2004/109/EC of the European Parliament and of the Council of 15th December 2004 relating to the harmonisation of transparency requirements in relation to information about issuers whose securities are admitted to trading on a regulated market; or
   (d)   Community legislation made under the provisions mentioned in paragraphs (a) to (c).

(7)   For the purposes of sub-paragraph (1)(j) and (l) to (q) "firm" means any entity, whether or not a legal person, that is not an individual and includes a body corporate and a partnership or other unincorporated association.

(8)   For the purposes of sub-paragraph (1)(q) "cash" means notes, coins or travellers' cheques in any currency.

Excluded Activities

2.—(1)   A business is not in the regulated sector to the extent that it consists of—
   (a)   the issuing of withdrawable share capital within the limit set by section 6 of the Industrial and Provident Societies Act 1965 (maximum shareholding in society), or the acceptance of deposits from the public within the limit set by section 7(3) of that Act (carrying on of banking by societies), by a society registered under that Act;
   (b)   the issuing of withdrawable share capital within the limit set by section 6 of the Industrial and Provident Societies Act (Northern Ireland) 1969 (maximum shareholding in society), or the acceptance of deposits from the public within the limit set by section 7(3) of that Act (carrying on of banking by societies), by a society registered under that Act;
   (c)   the carrying on of any activity in respect of which a person who is (or falls within a class of persons) specified in any of paragraphs 2 to 23, 25 to 38 or 40 to 49 of the Schedule to the Financial Services and Markets Act 2000 (Exemption) Order 2001 is exempt;
   (d)   the exercise of the functions specified in section 45 of the Financial Services Act 1986 (miscellaneous exemptions) by a person who was an exempted person for the purposes of that section immediately before its repeal;
   (e)   the engaging in financial activity which fulfils all of the conditions set out in paragraphs (a) to (g) of sub-paragraph (3) of this paragraph by a person whose main activity is that of a high value dealer; or
   (f)   the preparation of a home information pack (within the meaning of Part 5 of the Housing Act 2004 (home information packs)) or a document or information for inclusion in a home information pack.

(2)   For the purposes of sub-paragraph (1)(e) a "high value dealer" means a person mentioned in paragraph 1(1)(q) when carrying on the activities mentioned in that paragraph.

(3)   A business is not in the regulated sector to the extent that it consists of financial activity if—
   (a)   the person's total annual turnover in respect of the financial activity does not exceed £64,000;
   (b)   the financial activity is limited in relation to any customer to no more than one transaction exceeding 1,000 euros, whether the transaction is carried out in a single operation, or a series of operations which appear to be linked;
   (c)   the financial activity does not exceed 5% of the person's total annual turnover;

(d)   the financial activity is ancillary to the person's main activity and directly related to that activity;

(e)   the financial activity is not the transmission or remittance of money (or any representation of monetary value) by any means;

(f)   the main activity of the person carrying on the financial activity is not an activity mentioned in paragraph 1(1)(a) to (p) or (r); and

(g)   the financial activity is provided only to customers of the person's main activity and is not offered to the public.

(4)   A business is not in the regulated sector if it is carried on by—

(a)   the Auditor General for Scotland;
(b)   the Auditor General for Wales;
(c)   the Bank of England;
(d)   the Comptroller and Auditor General;
(e)   the Comptroller and Auditor General for Northern Ireland;
(f)   the Official Solicitor to the Supreme Court, when acting as trustee in his official capacity; or
(g)   the Treasury Solicitor.

Interpretation

3.—(1)   In this Part—

"the Banking Consolidation Directive" means directive 2006/48/EC of the European Parliament and of the Council of 14th June 2006 relating to the taking up and pursuit of the business of credit institutions;

"the Insurance Mediation Directive" means directive 2002/92/EC of the European Parliament and of the Council of 9th December 2002 on insurance mediation;

"the Life Assurance Consolidation Directive" means directive 2002/83/EC of the European Parliament and of the Council of 5th November 2002 concerning life assurance; and

"the Markets in Financial Instruments Directive" means directive 2004/39/EC of the European Parliament and of the Council of 12th April 2004 on markets in financial instruments.

(2)   In this Part references to amounts in euros include references to equivalent amounts in another currency.

(3)   Terms used in this Part and in the Banking Consolidation Directive or the Markets in Financial Instruments Directive have the same meaning in this Part as in those Directives.]

[1856]

NOTES

Commencement: 15 December 2007.

Substituted, together with Pt 2, by the Proceeds of Crime Act 2002 (Business in the Regulated Sector and Supervisory Authorities) Order 2007, SI 2007/3287, art 2.

[PART 2
SUPERVISORY AUTHORITIES

4.—(1)   The following bodies are supervisory authorities—

(a)   the Commissioners for Her Majesty's Revenue and Customs;
(b)   the Department of Enterprise, Trade and Investment in Northern Ireland;
(c)   the Financial Services Authority;
(d)   the Gambling Commission;
(e)   the Office of Fair Trading;
(f)   the Secretary of State; and
(g)   the professional bodies listed in sub-paragraph (2).

(2)   The professional bodies referred to in sub-paragraph (1)(g) are—

(a)   the Association of Accounting Technicians;
(b)   the Association of Chartered Certified Accountants;
(c)   the Association of International Accountants;
(d)   the Association of Taxation Technicians;
(e)   the Chartered Institute of Management Accountants;
(f)   the Chartered Institute of Public Finance and Accountancy;
(g)   the Chartered Institute of Taxation;
(h)   the Council for Licensed Conveyancers;
(i)   the Faculty of Advocates;
(j)   the Faculty Office of the Archbishop of Canterbury;
(k)   the General Council of the Bar;
(l)   the General Council of the Bar of Northern Ireland;
(m)   the Insolvency Practitioners Association;
(n)   the Institute of Certified Bookkeepers;
(o)   the Institute of Chartered Accountants in England and Wales;

(p)   the Institute of Chartered Accountants in Ireland;
(q)   the Institute of Chartered Accountants of Scotland;
(r)   the Institute of Financial Accountants;
(s)   the International Association of Book-keepers;
(t)   the Law Society;
(u)   the Law Society for Northern Ireland; and
(v)   the Law Society of Scotland.]

[1857]

NOTES
Commencement: 15 December 2007.
Substituted as noted to Pt 1 at **[1856]**.

PART 3
POWER TO AMEND

5.   The Treasury may by order amend Part 1 or 2 of this Schedule.

[1858]

NOTES
Order: the Proceeds of Crime Act 2002 (Business in the Regulated Sector and Supervisory Authorities) Order 2007, SI 2007/3287.

(Schs 10–12 outside the scope of this work.)

ENTERPRISE ACT 2002

(2002 c 40)

ARRANGEMENT OF SECTIONS

PART 1
THE OFFICE OF FAIR TRADING

Establishment of OFT

General functions of OFT

Miscellaneous

PART 2
THE COMPETITION APPEAL TRIBUNAL

The Competition Appeal Tribunal

PART 4
MARKET INVESTIGATIONS

CHAPTER 1
MARKET INVESTIGATION REFERENCES

Making of references

CHAPTER 2
PUBLIC INTEREST CASES

Intervention notices

Intervention notices under section 139(1)

Intervention notices under section 139(2)

Other

CHAPTER 3
ENFORCEMENT

Undertakings and orders

Enforcement functions of OFT

Supplementary

CHAPTER 4
SUPPLEMENTARY

Regulated markets

Consultation, information and publicity

PART 1
STATUTES

PART 6
CARTEL OFFENCE

Cartel offence

Criminal investigations by OFT

PART 7
MISCELLANEOUS COMPETITION PROVISIONS

Miscellaneous

PART 8
ENFORCEMENT OF CERTAIN CONSUMER LEGISLATION

Introduction

Enforcement procedure

Establish and provide for the functions of the Office of Fair Trading, the Competition Appeal Tribunal and the Competition Service; to make provision about mergers and market structures and conduct; to amend the constitution and functions of the Competition Commission; to create an offence for those entering into certain anticompetitive agreements; to provide for the disqualification of directors of companies engaging in certain anticompetitive practices; to make other provision about competition law; to amend the law relating to the protection of the collective interests of consumers; to make further provision about the disclosure of information obtained under competition and consumer legislation; to amend the Insolvency Act 1986 and make other provision about insolvency; and for connected purposes

[7 November 2002]

PART 1
THE OFFICE OF FAIR TRADING

Establishment of OFT

1   The Office of Fair Trading

(1)   There shall be a body corporate to be known as the Office of Fair Trading (in this Act referred to as "the OFT").

(2)   The functions of the OFT are carried out on behalf of the Crown.

(3)   Schedule 1 (which makes further provision about the OFT) has effect.

(4)   In managing its affairs the OFT shall have regard, in addition to any relevant general guidance as to the governance of public bodies, to such generally accepted principles of good corporate governance as it is reasonable to regard as applicable to the OFT.

[1859]

2   The Director General of Fair Trading

(1)   The functions of the Director General of Fair Trading (in this Act referred to as "the Director"), and his property, rights and liabilities, are transferred to the OFT.

(2)   The office of the Director is abolished.

(3)   Any enactment, instrument or other document passed or made before the commencement of subsection (1) which refers to the Director shall have effect, so far as necessary for the purposes of or in consequence of anything being transferred, as if any reference to the Director were a reference to the OFT.

[1860]

3   Annual plan

(1)   The OFT shall, before each financial year, publish a document (the "annual plan") containing a statement of its main objectives and priorities for the year.

(2)   The OFT shall for the purposes of public consultation publish a document containing proposals for its annual plan at least two months before publishing the annual plan for any year.

(3)   The OFT shall lay before Parliament a copy of each document published under subsection (2) and each annual plan.

[1861]

4   Annual and other reports

(1)   The OFT shall, as soon as practicable after the end of each financial year, make to the Secretary of State a report (the "annual report") on its activities and performance during that year.

(2)   The annual report for each year shall include—
  (a)   a general survey of developments in respect of matters relating to the OFT's functions;
  (b)   an assessment of the extent to which the OFT's main objectives and priorities for the year (as set out in the annual plan) have been met;
  (c)   a summary of the significant decisions, investigations or other activities made or carried out by the OFT during the year;
  (d)   a summary of the allocation of the OFT's financial resources to its various activities during the year; and
  (e)   an assessment of the OFT's performance and practices in relation to its enforcement functions.

(3)   The OFT shall lay a copy of each annual report before Parliament and arrange for the report to be published.

(4)   The OFT may—
  (a)   prepare other reports in respect of matters relating to any of its functions; and
  (b)   arrange for any such report to be published.

[1862]

General functions of OFT

5   Acquisition of information etc

(1)   The OFT has the function of obtaining, compiling and keeping under review information about matters relating to the carrying out of its functions.

(2)   That function is to be carried out with a view to (among other things) ensuring that the OFT has sufficient information to take informed decisions and to carry out its other functions effectively.

(3)   In carrying out that function the OFT may carry out, commission or support (financially or otherwise) research.

[1863]

6   Provision of information etc to the public

(1)   The OFT has the function of—
  (a)   making the public aware of the ways in which competition may benefit consumers in, and the economy of, the United Kingdom; and
  (b)   giving information or advice in respect of matters relating to any of its functions to the public.

(2)   In carrying out those functions the OFT may—
  (a)   publish educational materials or carry out other educational activities; or

(b)   support (financially or otherwise) the carrying out by others of such activities or the provision by others of information or advice.

[1864]

7   Provision of information and advice to Ministers etc

(1)   The OFT has the function of—
   (a)   making proposals, or
   (b)   giving other information or advice,
on matters relating to any of its functions to any Minister of the Crown or other public authority (including proposals, information or advice as to any aspect of the law or a proposed change in the law).

(2)   A Minister of the Crown may request the OFT to make proposals or give other information or advice on any matter relating to any of its functions; and the OFT shall, so far as is reasonably practicable and consistent with its other functions, comply with the request.

[1865]

8   Promoting good consumer practice

(1)   The OFT has the function of promoting good practice in the carrying out of activities which may affect the economic interests of consumers in the United Kingdom.

(2)   In carrying out that function the OFT may (without prejudice to the generality of subsection (1)) make arrangements for approving consumer codes and may, in accordance with the arrangements, give its approval to or withdraw its approval from any consumer code.

(3)   Any such arrangements must specify the criteria to be applied by the OFT in determining whether to give approval to or withdraw approval from a consumer code.

(4)   Any such arrangements may in particular—
   (a)   specify descriptions of consumer code which may be the subject of an application to the OFT for approval (and any such description may be framed by reference to any feature of a consumer code, including the persons who are, or are to be, subject to the code, the manner in which it is, or is to be, operated and the persons responsible for its operation); and
   (b)   provide for the use in accordance with the arrangements of an official symbol intended to signify that a consumer code is approved by the OFT.

(5)   The OFT shall publish any arrangements under subsection (2) in such manner it considers appropriate.

(6)   In this section "consumer code" means a code of practice or other document (however described) intended, with a view to safeguarding or promoting the interests of consumers, to regulate by any means the conduct of persons engaged in the supply of goods or services to consumers (or the conduct of their employees or representatives).

[1866]

Miscellaneous

9   *(Repeals the Fair Trading Act 1973, s 12, and the Competition Act 1980, s 13.)*

10   Part 2 of the 1973 Act

(1)   The following provisions of the 1973 Act shall cease to have effect—
   (a)   section 3 and Schedule 2 (which establish, and make provision with respect to, the Consumer Protection Advisory Committee);
   (b)   sections 13 to 21 (which relate to references made to, and reports of, that Committee); and
   (c)   section 22 (power of Secretary of State to make orders in pursuance of a report of that Committee).

(2)–(4)   ...

[1867]

NOTES

Sub-ss (2)–(4): repealed by the Consumer Protection from Unfair Trading Regulations 2008, SI 2008/1277, reg 30(1), (3), Sch 2, Pt 1, paras 68, 69, Sch 4, subject to savings in reg 30(2) of, and Sch 3 to, those Regulations at **[3702]**, **[3704]**.

---

11   Super-complaints to OFT

(1)   This section applies where a designated consumer body makes a complaint to the OFT that any feature, or combination of features, of a market in the United Kingdom for goods or services is or appears to be significantly harming the interests of consumers.

(2)   The OFT must, within 90 days after the day on which it receives the complaint, publish a response stating how it proposes to deal with the complaint, and in particular—
- (a)   whether it has decided to take any action, or to take no action, in response to the complaint, and
- (b)   if it has decided to take action, what action it proposes to take.

(3)   The response must state the OFT's reasons for its proposals.

(4)   The Secretary of State may by order amend subsection (2) by substituting any period for the period for the time being specified there.

(5)   "Designated consumer body" means a body designated by the Secretary of State by order.

(6)   The Secretary of State—
- (a)   may designate a body only if it appears to him to represent the interests of consumers of any description, and
- (b)   must publish (and may from time to time vary) other criteria to be applied by him in determining whether to make or revoke a designation.

(7)   The OFT—
- (a)   must issue guidance as to the presentation by the complainant of a reasoned case for the complaint, and
- (b)   may issue such other guidance as appears to it to be appropriate for the purposes of this section.

(8)   An order under this section—
- (a)   shall be made by statutory instrument, and
- (b)   shall be subject to annulment in pursuance of a resolution of either House of Parliament.

(9)   In this section—
- (a)   references to a feature of a market in the United Kingdom for goods or services have the same meaning as if contained in Part 4, and
- (b)   "consumer" means an individual who is a consumer within the meaning of that Part.

[1868]

NOTES

Order: the Enterprise Act 2002 (Bodies Designated to make Super-complaints) Order 2004, SI 2004/1517.

PART 2
THE COMPETITION APPEAL TRIBUNAL

The Competition Appeal Tribunal

12   The Competition Appeal Tribunal

(1)   There shall be a tribunal, to be called the Competition Appeal Tribunal (in this Part referred to as "the Tribunal").

(2)   The Tribunal shall consist of—
- (a)   a person appointed by the Lord Chancellor to preside over the Tribunal (in this Part referred to as "the President");
- (b)   members appointed by the Lord Chancellor to form a panel of chairmen; and
- (c)   members appointed by the Secretary of State to form a panel of ordinary members.

(3)   The Tribunal shall have a Registrar appointed by the Secretary of State.

(4)   The expenses of the Tribunal shall be paid by the Competition Service.

(5)   Schedule 2 (which makes further provision about the Tribunal) has effect.

[1869]

NOTES

Transitional provisions: see the Enterprise Act 2002 (Commencement No 2, Transitional and Transitory Provisions) Order 2003, SI 2003/766, art 3 for transitional and transitory provisions in relation to any appeal made to the Competition Commission under the Competition Act 1998, ss 46, 47, or the EC Competition Law (Articles 84 and 85) Enforcement Regulations 2001, SI 2001/2916, regs 24, 25 which has not been finally determined before 1 April 2003.

13   The Competition Service

(1)   There shall be a body corporate called the Competition Service (in this Part referred to as "the Service").

(2)   The purpose of the Service is to fund, and provide support services to, the Competition Appeal Tribunal.

(3)   In subsection (2) "support services" includes the provision of staff, accommodation and equipment and any other services which facilitate the carrying out by the Tribunal of its functions.

(4)   The activities of the Service are not carried out on behalf of the Crown (and its property is not to be regarded as held on behalf of the Crown).

(5)   The Secretary of State shall pay to the Service such sums as he considers appropriate to enable it to fund the activities of the Tribunal and to carry out its other activities.

(6)   Schedule 3 (which makes further provision about the Service) has effect.

[1870]

NOTES
Transitional provisions: see the note to s 12 at **[1869]**.

14   Constitution of Tribunal for particular proceedings and its decisions

(1)   For the purposes of any proceedings before it the Tribunal shall consist of a chairman and two other members.

(2)   The chairman must be the President or a member of the panel of chairmen.

(3)   The other members may be chosen from either the panel of chairmen or the panel of ordinary members.

(4)   If the members of the Tribunal as constituted in accordance with this section are unable to agree on any decision, the decision is to be taken by majority vote.

(5)   This section has effect subject to paragraph 18 of Schedule 4 (consequences of a member of the Tribunal being unable to continue after the proceedings have begun to be heard).

(6)   Part 1 of Schedule 4 (which makes further provision about the decisions of the Tribunal and their enforcement) has effect.

[1871]

NOTES
Transitional provisions: see the note to s 12 at **[1869]**.

15   Tribunal rules

(1)   The Secretary of State may, after consulting the President and such other persons as he considers appropriate, make rules (in this Part referred to as "Tribunal rules") with respect to proceedings before the Tribunal.

(2)   Tribunal rules may make provision with respect to matters incidental to or consequential upon appeals provided for by or under any Act to the Court of Appeal or the Court of Session in relation to a decision of the Tribunal.

(3)   Tribunal rules may—
 (a)   specify qualifications for appointment as Registrar;
 (b)   confer functions on the President or the Registrar in relation to proceedings before the Tribunal; and
 (c)   contain incidental, supplemental, consequential or transitional provision.

(4)   The power to make Tribunal rules is exercisable by statutory instrument subject to annulment in pursuance of a resolution of either House of Parliament.

(5)   Part 2 of Schedule 4 (which makes further provision about the rules) has effect, but without prejudice to the generality of subsection (1).

[1872]

NOTES
Transitional provisions: see the note to s 12 at **[1869]**.
Rules: the Competition Appeal Tribunal Rules 2003, SI 2003/1372.

16   Transfers of certain proceedings to and from Tribunal

(1)   The Lord Chancellor may by regulations—
 (a)   make provision enabling the court—
  (i)   to transfer to the Tribunal for its determination so much of any proceedings before the court as relates to an infringement issue; and
  (ii)   to give effect to the determination of that issue by the Tribunal; and
 (b)   make such incidental, supplementary, consequential, transitional or saving provision as the Lord Chancellor may consider appropriate.

(2)   The power to make regulations under subsection (1) is exercisable by statutory instrument subject to annulment in pursuance of a resolution of either House of Parliament.

(3)   Rules of court may prescribe the procedure to be followed in connection with a transfer mentioned in subsection (1).

(4)   The court may transfer to the Tribunal, in accordance with rules of court, so much of any proceedings before it as relates to a claim to which section 47A of the 1998 Act applies.

(5)   Rules of court may make provision in connection with the transfer from the Tribunal to the High Court or the Court of Session of a claim made in proceedings under section 47A of the 1998 Act.

(6)   In this section—
"the court" means—
    (a)   the High Court or a county court; or
    (b)   the Court of Session or a sheriff court; and
"infringement issue" means any question relating to whether or not an infringement of—
    (a)   the Chapter I prohibition or the Chapter II prohibition; or
    (b)   Article 81 or 82 of the Treaty,
    has been or is being committed;
but otherwise any terms used in this section and Part 1 of the 1998 Act have the same meaning as they have in that Part.

[1873]

17–130   (*S 17 substitutes the Competition Act 1998, s 47 at* **[1742]**; *s 18 inserts s 47A of the 1998 Act at* **[1743]**, *in relation to claims arising both before and after the commencement of s 18; s 19 inserts s 47B of the 1998 Act at* **[1744]**; *s 20 inserts s 58A of the 1998 Act at* **[1755]**, *except in relation to decisions made before 20 June 2003, and amends 59(1) of that Act at* **[1756]**; *s 21 introduces Sch 5 to this Act (further amendments of the 1998 Act); ss 22–130 (Pt 3: Mergers) outside the scope of this work.*)

PART 4
MARKET INVESTIGATIONS

CHAPTER 1
MARKET INVESTIGATION REFERENCES
Making of references

131   Power of OFT to make references

(1)   The OFT may, subject to subsection (4), make a reference to the Commission if the OFT has reasonable grounds for suspecting that any feature, or combination of features, of a market in the United Kingdom for goods or services prevents, restricts or distorts competition in connection with the supply or acquisition of any goods or services in the United Kingdom or a part of the United Kingdom.

(2)   For the purposes of this Part any reference to a feature of a market in the United Kingdom for goods or services shall be construed as a reference to—
    (a)   the structure of the market concerned or any aspect of that structure;
    (b)   any conduct (whether or not in the market concerned) of one or more than one person who supplies or acquires goods or services in the market concerned; or
    (c)   any conduct relating to the market concerned of customers of any person who supplies or acquires goods or services.

(3)   In subsection (2) "conduct" includes any failure to act (whether or not intentional) and any other unintentional conduct.

(4)   No reference shall be made under this section if—
    (a)   the making of the reference is prevented by section 156(1); or
    (b)   a reference has been made under section 132 in relation to the same matter but has not been finally determined.

(5)   References in this Part to a market investigation reference being finally determined shall be construed in accordance with section 183(3) to (6).

(6)   In this Part—
"market in the United Kingdom" includes—
    (a)   so far as it operates in the United Kingdom or a part of the United Kingdom, any market which operates there and in another country or territory or in a part of another country or territory; and
    (b)   any market which operates only in a part of the United Kingdom;
"market investigation reference" means a reference under this section or section 132;
and references to a market for goods or services include references to a market for goods and services.

[1874]

132 Ministerial power to make references

(1)   Subsection (3) applies where, in relation to any goods or services, the appropriate Minister is not satisfied with a decision of the OFT not to make a reference under section 131.

(2)   Subsection (3) also applies where, in relation to any goods or services, the appropriate Minister—

(a)   has brought to the attention of the OFT information which the appropriate Minister considers to be relevant to the question of whether the OFT should make a reference under section 131; but

(b)   is not satisfied that the OFT will decide, within such period as the appropriate Minister considers to be reasonable, whether to make such a reference.

(3)   The appropriate Minister may, subject to subsection (4), make a reference to the Commission if he has reasonable grounds for suspecting that any feature, or combination of features, of a market in the United Kingdom for goods or services prevents, restricts or distorts competition in connection with the supply or acquisition of any goods or services in the United Kingdom or a part of the United Kingdom.

(4)   No reference shall be made under this section if the making of the reference is prevented by section 156(1).

(5)   In this Part "the appropriate Minister" means—

(a)   the Secretary of State; or

(b)   the Secretary of State and one or more than one other Minister of the Crown acting jointly.

[1875]

133 Contents of references

(1)   A market investigation reference shall, in particular, specify—

(a)   the enactment under which it is made;

(b)   the date on which it is made; and

(c)   the description of goods or services to which the feature or combination of features concerned relates.

(2)   A market investigation reference may be framed so as to require the Commission to confine its investigation into the effects of features of markets in the United Kingdom for goods or services of a description specified in the reference to the effects of features of such of those markets as exist in connection with—

(a)   a supply, of a description specified in the reference, of the goods or services concerned; or

(b)   an acquisition, of a description specified in the reference, of the goods or services concerned.

(3)   A description of the kind mentioned in subsection (2)(a) or (b) may, in particular, be by reference to—

(a)   the place where the goods or services are supplied or acquired; or

(b)   the persons by or to whom they are supplied or by or from whom they are acquired.

[1876]

Determination of references

134 Questions to be decided on market investigation references

(1)   The Commission shall, on a market investigation reference, decide whether any feature, or combination of features, of each relevant market prevents, restricts or distorts competition in connection with the supply or acquisition of any goods or services in the United Kingdom or a part of the United Kingdom.

(2)   For the purposes of this Part, in relation to a market investigation reference, there is an adverse effect on competition if any feature, or combination of features, of a relevant market prevents, restricts or distorts competition in connection with the supply or acquisition of any goods or services in the United Kingdom or a part of the United Kingdom.

(3)   In subsections (1) and (2) "relevant market" means—

(a)   in the case of subsection (2) so far as it applies in connection with a possible reference, a market in the United Kingdom—

(i)   for goods or services of a description to be specified in the reference; and

(ii)   which would not be excluded from investigation by virtue of section 133(2); and

(b)   in any other case, a market in the United Kingdom—

(i)   for goods or services of a description specified in the reference concerned; and

(ii)   which is not excluded from investigation by virtue of section 133(2).

(4)   The Commission shall, if it has decided on a market investigation reference that there is an adverse effect on competition, decide the following additional questions—

    (a)   whether action should be taken by it under section 138 for the purpose of remedying, mitigating or preventing the adverse effect on competition concerned or any detrimental effect on customers so far as it has resulted from, or may be expected to result from, the adverse effect on competition;

    (b)   whether it should recommend the taking of action by others for the purpose of remedying, mitigating or preventing the adverse effect on competition concerned or any detrimental effect on customers so far as it has resulted from, or may be expected to result from, the adverse effect on competition; and

    (c)   in either case, if action should be taken, what action should be taken and what is to be remedied, mitigated or prevented.

(5)   For the purposes of this Part, in relation to a market investigation reference, there is a detrimental effect on customers if there is a detrimental effect on customers or future customers in the form of—

    (a)   higher prices, lower quality or less choice of goods or services in any market in the United Kingdom (whether or not the market to which the feature or features concerned relate); or

    (b)   less innovation in relation to such goods or services.

(6)   In deciding the questions mentioned in subsection (4), the Commission shall, in particular, have regard to the need to achieve as comprehensive a solution as is reasonable and practicable to the adverse effect on competition and any detrimental effects on customers so far as resulting from the adverse effect on competition.

(7)   In deciding the questions mentioned in subsection (4), the Commission may, in particular, have regard to the effect of any action on any relevant customer benefits of the feature or features of the market concerned.

(8)   For the purposes of this Part a benefit is a relevant customer benefit of a feature or features of a market if—

    (a)   it is a benefit to customers or future customers in the form of—

        (i)   lower prices, higher quality or greater choice of goods or services in any market in the United Kingdom (whether or not the market to which the feature or features concerned relate); or

        (ii)   greater innovation in relation to such goods or services; and

    (b)   the Commission, the Secretary of State or (as the case may be) the OFT believes that—

        (i)   the benefit has accrued as a result (whether wholly or partly) of the feature or features concerned or may be expected to accrue within a reasonable period as a result (whether wholly or partly) of that feature or those features; and

        (ii)   the benefit was, or is, unlikely to accrue without the feature or features concerned.

[1877]

135 Variation of market investigation references

(1)   The OFT or (as the case may be) the appropriate Minister may at any time vary a market investigation reference made by it or (as the case may be) him.

(2)   The OFT or (as the case may be) the appropriate Minister shall consult the Commission before varying any such reference.

(3)   Subsection (2) shall not apply if the Commission has requested the variation concerned.

(4)   No variation under this section shall be capable of altering the period permitted by section 137 within which the report of the Commission under section 136 is to be prepared and published or (as the case may be) the period permitted by section 144 within which the report of the Commission under section 142 is to be prepared and published or given.

[1878]

136 Investigations and reports on market investigation references

(1)   The Commission shall prepare and publish a report on a market investigation reference within the period permitted by section 137.

(2)   The report shall, in particular, contain—

    (a)   the decisions of the Commission on the questions which it is required to answer by virtue of section 134;

    (b)   its reasons for its decisions; and

    (c)   such information as the Commission considers appropriate for facilitating a proper understanding of those questions and of its reasons for its decisions.

(3)   The Commission shall carry out such investigations as it considers appropriate for the purposes of preparing a report under this section.

(4)   The Commission shall, at the same time as a report under this section is published—

    (a)   in the case of a reference under section 131, give it to the OFT; and

(b)   in the case of a reference under section 132, give it to the appropriate Minister and give a copy of it to the OFT.

(5)   Where a reference has been made by the OFT under section 131 or by the appropriate Minister under section 132 in circumstances in which a reference could have been made by a relevant sectoral regulator under section 131 as it has effect by virtue of a relevant sectoral enactment, the Commission shall, at the same time as the report under this section is published, give a copy of it to the relevant sectoral regulator concerned.

(6)   Where a reference has been made by a relevant sectoral regulator under section 131 as it has effect by virtue of a relevant sectoral enactment, the Commission shall, at the same time as the report under this section is published, give a copy of it to the OFT.

(7)   In this Part "relevant sectoral enactment" means—
(a)   ...
(b)   in relation to the Gas and Electricity Markets Authority, section 36A of the Gas Act 1986 (c 44) or (as the case may be) section 43 of the Electricity Act 1989 (c 29);
(c)   in relation to [the Water Services Regulation Authority], section 31 of the Water Industry Act 1991 (c 56);
(d)   ...
(e)   in relation to [the Office of Rail Regulation], section 67 of the Railways Act 1993 (c 43);
(f)   ...
(g)   in relation to the Civil Aviation Authority, section 86 of the Transport Act 2000 (c 38);
[(h)   in relation to the Office of Communications, sections 370 and 371 of the Communications Act 2003];
[(h)   in relation to the Northern Ireland Authority for Utility Regulation, Article 46 of the Electricity (Northern Ireland) Order 1992, Article 23 of the Gas (Northern Ireland) Order 1996 or Article 29 of the Water and Sewerage Services (Northern Ireland) Order 2006].

(8)   In this Part "relevant sectoral regulator" means ... the Gas and Electricity Markets Authority, [the Water Services Regulation Authority], ... , [the Office of Rail Regulation], ... [, the Civil Aviation Authority or the Office of Communications] [or the Northern Ireland Authority for Utility Regulation].

(9)   The Secretary of State may by order modify subsection (7) or (8).

[1879]

NOTES

Sub-s (7): para (a) repealed and first para (h) added by the Communications Act 2003, s 406(1), (7), Sch 17, para 174(1), (4)(a), Sch 19(1); words in square brackets in para (c) substituted by the Water Act 2003, s 101(1), Sch 7, Pt 2, para 36(1), (2); paras (d), (f) repealed and second para (h) added by the Water and Sewerage Services (Northern Ireland) Order 2006, SI 2006/3336, art 308(1), (2), Sch 12, para 46(1), Sch 13; words in square brackets in para (e) substituted by the Railways and Transport Safety Act 2003, s 16(5), Sch 2, Pt 2, para 19(u).

Sub-s (8): words omitted in the first place repealed and words in third pair of square brackets substituted by the Communications Act 2003, s 406(1), (7), Sch 17, para 174(1), (4)(b), Sch 19(1); words in first pair of square brackets substituted by the Water Act 2003, s 101(1), Sch 7, Pt 2, para 36(1), (2); words omitted in the second and third places repealed and words in fourth pair of square brackets inserted by SI 2006/3336, art 308(1), (2), Sch 12, para 46(2), Sch 13; words in second pair of square brackets substituted by the Railways and Transport Safety Act 2003, s 16(5), Sch 2, Pt 2, para 19(u).

---

137   Time-limits for market investigations and reports

(1)   The Commission shall prepare and publish its report under section 136 within the period of two years beginning with the date of the market investigation reference concerned.

(2)   Subsection (1) is subject to section 151(3) and (5).

(3)   The Secretary of State may by order amend subsection (1) so as to alter the period of two years mentioned in that subsection or any period for the time being mentioned in that subsection in substitution for that period.

(4)   No alteration shall be made by virtue of subsection (3) which results in the period for the time being mentioned in subsection (1) exceeding two years.

(5)   An order under subsection (3) shall not affect any period of time within which the Commission is under a duty to prepare and publish its report under section 136 in relation to a market investigation reference if the Commission is already under that duty in relation to that reference when the order is made.

(6)   Before making an order under subsection (3) the Secretary of State shall consult the Commission and such other persons as he considers appropriate.

(7)   References in this Part to the date of a market investigation reference shall be construed as references to the date specified in the reference as the date on which it is made.

[1880]

138 Duty to remedy adverse effects

(1)   Subsection (2) applies where a report of the Commission has been prepared and published under section 136 within the period permitted by section 137 and contains the decision that there is one or more than one adverse effect on competition.

(2)   The Commission shall, in relation to each adverse effect on competition, take such action under section 159 or 161 as it considers to be reasonable and practicable—
  (a)   to remedy, mitigate or prevent the adverse effect on competition concerned; and
  (b)   to remedy, mitigate or prevent any detrimental effects on customers so far as they have resulted from, or may be expected to result from, the adverse effect on competition.

(3)   The decisions of the Commission under subsection (2) shall be consistent with its decisions as included in its report by virtue of section 134(4) unless there has been a material change of circumstances since the preparation of the report or the Commission otherwise has a special reason for deciding differently.

(4)   In making a decision under subsection (2), the Commission shall, in particular, have regard to the need to achieve as comprehensive a solution as is reasonable and practicable to the adverse effect on competition concerned and any detrimental effects on customers so far as resulting from the adverse effect on competition.

(5)   In making a decision under subsection (2), the Commission may, in particular, have regard to the effect of any action on any relevant customer benefits of the feature or features of the market concerned.

(6)   The Commission shall take no action under subsection (2) to remedy, mitigate or prevent any detrimental effect on customers so far as it may be expected to result from the adverse effect on competition concerned if—
  (a)   no detrimental effect on customers has resulted from the adverse effect on competition; and
  (b)   the adverse effect on competition is not being remedied, mitigated or prevented.

                                                                                [1881]

CHAPTER 2
PUBLIC INTEREST CASES

Intervention notices

139 Public interest intervention by Secretary of State

(1)   The Secretary of State may give a notice to the Commission if—
  (a)   a market investigation reference has been made to the Commission;
  (b)   no more than four months has passed since the date of the reference;
  (c)   the reference is not finally determined; and
  (d)   the Secretary of State believes that it is or may be the case that one or more than one public interest consideration is relevant to the case.

(2)   The Secretary of State may give a notice to the OFT if—
  (a)   the OFT is considering whether to accept—
      (i)   an undertaking under section 154 instead of making a reference under section 131; or
      (ii)   an undertaking varying or superseding any such undertaking;
  (b)   the OFT has published a notice under section 155(1) or (4); and
  (c)   the Secretary of State believes that it is or may be the case that one or more than one public interest consideration is relevant to the case.

(3)   In this Part "intervention notice" means a notice under subsection (1) or (2).

(4)   No more than one intervention notice shall be given under subsection (1) in relation to the same market investigation reference and no more than one intervention notice shall be given under subsection (2) in relation to the same proposed undertaking or in relation to proposed undertakings which do not differ from each other in any material respect.

(5)   For the purposes of this Part a public interest consideration is a consideration which, at the time of the giving of the intervention notice concerned, is specified in section 153 or is not so specified but, in the opinion of the Secretary of State, ought to be so specified.

(6)   Where the Secretary of State has given an intervention notice mentioning a public interest consideration which, at that time, is not finalised, he shall, as soon as practicable, take such action as is within his power to ensure that it is finalised.

(7)   For the purposes of this Part a public interest consideration is finalised if—
  (a)   it is specified in section 153 otherwise than by virtue of an order under subsection (3) of that section; or
  (b)   it is specified in that section by virtue of an order under subsection (3) of that section

and the order providing for it to be so specified has been laid before, and approved by, Parliament in accordance with subsection (6) of section 181 and within the period mentioned in that subsection.

Intervention notices under section 139(1)

140   Intervention notices under section 139(1)

(1)   An intervention notice under section 139(1) shall state—
  (a)   the market investigation reference concerned;
  (b)   the date of the market investigation reference concerned;
  (c)   the public interest consideration or considerations which are, or may be, relevant to the case; and
  (d)   where any public interest consideration concerned is not finalised, the proposed timetable for finalising it.

(2)   Where the Secretary of State believes that it is or may be the case that two or more public interest considerations are relevant to the case, he may decide not to mention in the intervention notice such of those considerations as he considers appropriate.

(3)   The Secretary of State may at any time revoke an intervention notice which has been given under section 139(1) and which is in force.

(4)   An intervention notice under section 139(1) shall come into force when it is given and shall cease to be in force when the matter to which it relates is finally determined under this Chapter.

(5)   For the purposes of subsection (4) a matter to which an intervention notice under section 139(1) relates is finally determined under this Chapter if—
  (a)   the period permitted by section 144 for the preparation of the report of the Commission under section 142 and for action to be taken in relation to it under section 143(1) or (3) has expired and no such report has been so prepared or no such action has been taken;
  (b)   the Commission decides under section 145(1) to terminate its investigation;
  (c)   the report of the Commission has been prepared under section 142 and published under section 143(1) within the period permitted by section 144;
  (d)   the Secretary of State fails to make and publish a decision under subsection (2) of section 146 within the period required by subsection (3) of that section;
  (e)   the Secretary of State decides under section 146(2) that no eligible public interest consideration is relevant;
  (f)   the Secretary of State decides under section 147(2) neither to accept an undertaking under section 159 nor to make an order under section 161;
  (g)   the Secretary of State accepts an undertaking under section 159 or makes an order under section 161; or
  (h)   the Secretary of State decides to revoke the intervention notice concerned.

(6)   For the purposes of subsections (4) and (5) the time when a matter to which an intervention notice under section 139(1) relates is finally determined under this Chapter is—
  (a)   in a case falling within subsection (5)(a) or (d), the expiry of the period concerned;
  (b)   in a case falling within subsection (5)(b), (e), (f) or (h), the making of the decision concerned;
  (c)   in a case falling within subsection (5)(c), the publication of the report concerned; and
  (d)   in a case falling within subsection (5)(g), the acceptance of the undertaking concerned or (as the case may be) the making of the order concerned.

(7)   In subsection (6)(d) the reference to the acceptance of the undertaking concerned or the making of the order concerned shall, in a case where the enforcement action under section 147(2) involves the acceptance of a group of undertakings, the making of a group of orders or the acceptance and making of a group of undertakings and orders, be treated as a reference to the acceptance or making of the last undertaking or order in the group; but undertakings or orders which vary, supersede or revoke earlier undertakings or orders shall be disregarded for the purposes of subsections (5)(g) and (6)(d).

141   Questions to be decided by Commission

(1)   This section applies where an intervention notice under section 139(1) is in force in relation to a market investigation reference.

(2)   The Commission shall decide whether any feature, or combination of features, of each relevant market (within the meaning given by section 134(3)) prevents, restricts or distorts competition in connection with the supply or acquisition of any goods or services in the United Kingdom or a part of the United Kingdom.

(3)   The Commission shall, if it has decided that there is an adverse effect on competition, decide the following additional questions—

    (a)   whether action should be taken by the Secretary of State under section 147 for the purpose of remedying, mitigating or preventing the adverse effect on competition concerned or any detrimental effect on customers so far as it has resulted from, or may be expected to result from, the adverse effect on competition;

    (b)   whether the Commission should recommend the taking of other action by the Secretary of State or action by persons other than itself and the Secretary of State for the purpose of remedying, mitigating or preventing the adverse effect on competition concerned or any detrimental effect on customers so far as it has resulted from, or may be expected to result from, the adverse effect on competition; and

    (c)   in either case, if action should be taken, what action should be taken and what is to be remedied, mitigated or prevented.

(4)   The Commission shall, if it has decided that there is an adverse effect on competition, also decide separately the following questions (on the assumption that it is proceeding as mentioned in section 148(1))—

    (a)   whether action should be taken by it under section 138 for the purpose of remedying, mitigating or preventing the adverse effect on competition concerned or any detrimental effect on customers so far as it has resulted from, or may be expected to result from, the adverse effect on competition;

    (b)   whether the Commission should recommend the taking of action by other persons for the purpose of remedying, mitigating or preventing the adverse effect on competition concerned or any detrimental effect on customers so far as it has resulted from, or may be expected to result from, the adverse effect on competition; and

    (c)   in either case, if action should be taken, what action should be taken and what is to be remedied, mitigated or prevented.

(5)   In deciding the questions mentioned in subsections (3) and (4), the Commission shall, in particular, have regard to the need to achieve as comprehensive a solution as is reasonable and practicable to the adverse effect on competition concerned and any detrimental effects on customers so far as resulting from the adverse effect on competition.

(6)   In deciding the questions mentioned in subsections (3) and (4), the Commission may, in particular, have regard to the effect of any action on any relevant customer benefits of the feature or features of the market concerned.

[1884]

142 Investigations and reports by Commission

(1)   Where an intervention notice under section 139(1) is in force in relation to a market investigation reference, the Commission shall prepare a report on the reference and take action in relation to it under section 143(1) or (3) within the period permitted by section 144.

(2)   The report shall, in particular, contain—

    (a)   the decisions of the Commission on the questions which it is required to answer by virtue of section 141;

    (b)   its reasons for its decisions; and

    (c)   such information as the Commission considers appropriate for facilitating a proper understanding of those questions and of its reasons for its decisions.

(3)   The Commission shall carry out such investigations as it considers appropriate for the purposes of preparing a report under this section.

[1885]

143 Publication etc of reports of Commission

(1)   The Commission shall publish a report under section 142 if it contains—

    (a)   the decision of the Commission that there is no adverse effect on competition; or

    (b)   the decisions of the Commission that there is one or more than one adverse effect on competition but, on the question mentioned in section 141(4)(a) and in relation to each adverse effect on competition, that no action should be taken by it.

(2)   The Commission shall, at the same time as the report is published under subsection (1)—

    (a)   in the case of a reference under section 131, give it to the OFT; and

    (b)   in the case of a reference under section 132, give it to the appropriate Minister and give a copy of it to the OFT.

(3)   Where a report under section 142 contains the decisions of the Commission that there is one or more than one adverse effect on competition and, on the question mentioned in section 141(4)(a) and in relation to at least one such adverse effect, that action should be taken by it, the Commission shall give the report to the Secretary of State.

(4)   The Secretary of State shall publish, no later than publication of his decision under section 146(2) in relation to the case, a report of the Commission given to him under subsection (3) and not required to be published by virtue of section 148(2).

(5) The Secretary of State shall, at the same time as a report of the Commission given to him under subsection (3) is published under subsection (4), give a copy of it—
  (a) in the case of a reference under section 131, to the OFT; and
  (b) in the case of a reference under section 132, to any other Minister of the Crown who made the reference and to the OFT.

(6) Where a reference has been made by the OFT under section 131 or by the appropriate Minister under section 132 in circumstances in which a reference could have been made by a relevant sectoral regulator under section 131 as it has effect by virtue of a relevant sectoral enactment, the relevant authority shall, at the same time as the report under section 142 is published under subsection (1) or (4), give a copy of it to the relevant sectoral regulator concerned.

(7) Where a reference has been made by a relevant sectoral regulator under section 131 as it has effect by virtue of a relevant sectoral enactment, the relevant authority shall, at the same time as the report under section 142 is published under subsection (1) or (4), give a copy of it to the OFT.

(8) In subsections (6) and (7) "the relevant authority" means—
  (a) in the case of a report published under subsection (1), the Commission; and
  (b) in the case of a report published under subsection (4), the Secretary of State.

[1886]

144 Time-limits for investigations and reports: Part 4

(1) The Commission shall, within the period of two years beginning with the date of the reference, prepare its report under section 142 and publish it under subsection (1) of section 143 or (as the case may be) give it to the Secretary of State under subsection (3) of that section.

(2) The Secretary of State may by order amend subsection (1) so as to alter the period of two years mentioned in that subsection or any period for the time being mentioned in that subsection in substitution for that period.

(3) No alteration shall be made by virtue of subsection (2) which results in the period for the time being mentioned in subsection (1) exceeding two years.

(4) An order under subsection (2) shall not affect any period of time within which, in relation to a market investigation reference, the Commission is under a duty to prepare its report under section 142 and take action in relation to it under section 143(1) or (3) if the Commission is already under that duty in relation to that reference when the order is made.

(5) Before making an order under subsection (2) the Secretary of State shall consult the Commission and such other persons as he considers appropriate.

[1887]

145 Restrictions where public interest considerations not finalised: Part 4

(1) The Commission shall terminate its investigation under section 142 if—
  (a) the intervention notice concerned mentions a public interest consideration which was not finalised on the giving of that notice or public interest considerations which, at that time, were not finalised;
  (b) no other public interest consideration is mentioned in the notice;
  (c) at least 24 weeks has elapsed since the giving of the notice; and
  (d) the public interest consideration mentioned in the notice has not been finalised within that period of 24 weeks or (as the case may be) none of the public interest considerations mentioned in the notice has been finalised within that period of 24 weeks.

(2) Where the intervention notice concerned mentions a public interest consideration which is not finalised on the giving of the notice, the Commission shall not give its report under section 142 to the Secretary of State in accordance with section 143(3) unless the period of 24 weeks beginning with the giving of the intervention notice concerned has expired or the public interest consideration concerned has been finalised.

(3) The Commission shall, in reporting on any of the questions mentioned in section 141(3), disregard any public interest consideration which has not been finalised before the giving of the report.

(4) The Commission shall, in reporting on any of the questions mentioned in section 141(3), disregard any public interest consideration which was not finalised on the giving of the intervention notice concerned and has not been finalised within the period of 24 weeks beginning with the giving of the notice concerned.

(5) Subsections (1) to (4) are without prejudice to the power of the Commission to carry out investigations in relation to any public interest consideration to which it might be able to have regard in its report.

[1888]

146   Decision of Secretary of State

(1)   Subsection (2) applies where the Secretary of State has received a report of the Commission which—
    (a)   has been prepared under section 142;
    (b)   contains the decisions that there is one or more than one adverse effect on competition and, on the question mentioned in section 141(4)(a) and in relation to at least one such adverse effect, that action should be taken by it; and
    (c)   has been given to the Secretary of State as required by section 143(3).

(2)   The Secretary of State shall decide whether—
    (a)   any eligible public interest consideration is relevant; or
    (b)   any eligible public interest considerations are relevant;

to any action which is mentioned in the report by virtue of section 141(4)(a) and (c) and which the Commission should take for the purpose of remedying, mitigating or preventing any adverse effect on competition concerned or any detrimental effect on customers so far as it has resulted or may be expected to result from any adverse effect on competition.

(3)   The Secretary of State shall make and publish his decision under subsection (2) within the period of 90 days beginning with the receipt of the report of the Commission under section 142.

(4)   In this section "eligible public interest consideration" means a public interest consideration which—
    (a)   was mentioned in the intervention notice concerned; and
    (b)   was not disregarded by the Commission for the purposes of its report under section 142.
[1889]

147   Remedial action by Secretary of State

(1)   Subsection (2) applies where the Secretary of State—
    (a)   has decided under subsection (2) of section 146 within the period required by subsection (3) of that section that an eligible public interest consideration is relevant as mentioned in subsection (2) of that section or eligible public interest considerations are so relevant; and
    (b)   has published his decision within the period required by subsection (3) of that section.

(2)   The Secretary of State may, in relation to any adverse effect on competition identified in the report concerned, take such action under section 159 or 161 as he considers to be—
    (a)   reasonable and practicable—
        (i)   to remedy, mitigate or prevent the adverse effect on competition concerned; or
        (ii)   to remedy, mitigate or prevent any detrimental effect on customers so far as it has resulted from, or may be expected to result from, the adverse effect on competition; and
    (b)   appropriate in the light of the eligible public interest consideration concerned or (as the case may be) the eligible public interest considerations concerned.

(3)   In making a decision under subsection (2), the Secretary of State shall, in particular, have regard to—
    (a)   the need to achieve as comprehensive a solution as is reasonable and practicable to the adverse effect on competition concerned and any detrimental effects on customers so far as resulting from the adverse effect on competition; and
    (b)   the report of the Commission under section 142.

(4)   In having regard by virtue of subsection (3) to the report of the Commission under section 142, the Secretary of State shall not challenge the decision of the Commission contained in the report that there is one or more than one adverse effect on competition.

(5)   In making a decision under subsection (2), the Secretary of State may, in particular, have regard to the effect of any action on any relevant customer benefits of the feature or features of the market concerned.

(6)   The Secretary of State shall take no action under subsection (2) to remedy, mitigate or prevent any detrimental effect on customers so far as it may be expected to result from the adverse effect on competition concerned if—
    (a)   no detrimental effect on customers has resulted from the adverse effect on competition; and
    (b)   the adverse effect on competition is not being remedied, mitigated or prevented.

(7)   In this section "eligible public interest consideration" has the same meaning as in section 146.
[1890]

148   Reversion of the matter to the Commission

(1)   If—

(a)   the Secretary of State fails to make and publish his decision under subsection (2) of section 146 within the period required by subsection (3) of that section; or

(b)   the Secretary of State decides that no eligible public interest consideration is relevant as mentioned in subsection (2) of that section;

the Commission shall proceed under section 138 as if the report had been prepared and published under section 136 within the period permitted by section 137.

(2)   The Commission shall publish the report which has been prepared by it under section 142 (if still unpublished) as soon as it becomes able to proceed by virtue of subsection (1).

(3)   The Commission shall, at the same time as its report is published under subsection (2), give a copy of it—

(a)   in the case of a reference under section 131, to the OFT; and

(b)   in the case of a reference under section 132, to any Minister of the Crown who made the reference (other than the Secretary of State) and to the OFT.

(4)   Where a reference has been made by the OFT under section 131 or by the appropriate Minister under section 132 in circumstances in which a reference could have been made by a relevant sectoral regulator under section 131 as it has effect by virtue of a relevant sectoral enactment, the Commission shall, at the same time as its report is published under subsection (2), give a copy of it to the relevant sectoral regulator concerned.

(5)   Where a reference has been made by a relevant sectoral regulator under section 131 as it has effect by virtue of a relevant sectoral enactment, the Commission shall, at the same time as its report is published under subsection (2), give a copy of it to the OFT.

(6)   In relation to proceedings by virtue of subsection (1), the reference in section 138(3) to decisions of the Commission included in its report by virtue of section 134(4) shall be construed as a reference to decisions which were included in the report of the Commission by virtue of section 141(4).

(7)   Where the Commission, in proceeding by virtue of subsection (1), intends to proceed in a way which is not consistent with its decisions as included in its report by virtue of section 141(4), it shall not so proceed without the consent of the Secretary of State.

(8)   The Secretary of State shall not withhold his consent under subsection (7) unless he believes that the proposed alternative way of proceeding will operate against the public interest.

(9)   For the purposes of subsection (8) a proposed alternative way of proceeding will operate against the public interest only if any eligible public interest consideration or considerations outweigh the considerations which have led the Commission to propose proceeding in that way.

(10)   In deciding whether to withhold his consent under subsection (7), the Secretary of State shall accept the Commission's view of what, if the only relevant consideration were how to remedy, mitigate or prevent the adverse effect on competition concerned or any detrimental effect on customers so far as resulting from the adverse effect on competition, would be the most appropriate way to proceed.

(11)   In this section "eligible public interest consideration" has the same meaning as in section 146.

[1891]

Intervention notices under section 139(2)

149   Intervention notices under section 139(2)

(1)   An intervention notice under section 139(2) shall state—

(a)   the proposed undertaking which may be accepted by the OFT;

(b)   the notice under section 155(1) or (4);

(c)   the public interest consideration or considerations which are, or may be, relevant to the case; and

(d)   where any public interest consideration concerned is not finalised, the proposed timetable for finalising it.

(2)   Where the Secretary of State believes that it is or may be the case that two or more public interest considerations are relevant to the case, he may decide not to mention in the intervention notice such of those considerations as he considers appropriate.

(3)   The Secretary of State may at any time revoke an intervention notice which has been given under section 139(2) and which is in force.

(4)   An intervention notice under section 139(2) shall come into force when it is given and shall cease to be in force on the occurrence of any of the events mentioned in subsection (5).

(5)   The events are—

(a)   the acceptance by the OFT with the consent of the Secretary of State of an undertaking which is the same as the proposed undertaking mentioned in the intervention notice by virtue of subsection (1)(a) or which does not differ from it in any material respect;

(b) the decision of the OFT to proceed neither with the proposed undertaking mentioned in the intervention notice by virtue of subsection (1)(a) nor a proposed undertaking which does not differ from it in any material respect; or

(c) the decision of the Secretary of State to revoke the intervention notice concerned.

[1892]

150 Power of veto of Secretary of State

(1) Where an intervention notice under section 139(2) is in force, the OFT shall not, without the consent of the Secretary of State, accept the proposed undertaking concerned or a proposed undertaking which does not differ from it in any material respect.

(2) The Secretary of State shall withhold his consent if he believes that it is or may be the case that the proposed undertaking will, if accepted, operate against the public interest.

(3) For the purposes of subsection (2) a proposed undertaking will, if accepted, operate against the public interest only if any public interest consideration which is mentioned in the intervention notice concerned and has been finalised, or any public interest considerations which are so mentioned and have been finalised, outweigh the considerations which have led the OFT to propose accepting the undertaking.

(4) In making his decision under subsection (2) the Secretary of State shall accept the OFT's view of what undertakings, if the only relevant consideration were how to remedy, mitigate or prevent the adverse effect on competition concerned or any detrimental effect on customers so far as resulting from the adverse effect on competition, would be most appropriate.

(5) Where a public interest consideration which is mentioned in the intervention notice concerned is not finalised on the giving of the notice, the Secretary of State shall not make his decision as to whether to give his consent under this section before—

(a) the end of the period of 24 weeks beginning with the giving of the intervention notice; or

(b) if earlier, the date on which the public interest consideration concerned has been finalised.

(6) Subject to subsections (2) to (5), the Secretary of State shall not withhold his consent under this section.

[1893]

Other

151 Further interaction of intervention notices with general procedure

(1) Where an intervention notice under section 139(1) comes into force in relation to a market investigation reference, sections 134(1), (4), (6) and (7), 136(1) to (6), 137(1) to (6) and 138 shall cease to apply in relation to that reference.

(2) Where the Secretary of State revokes an intervention notice which has been given under section 139(1), the Commission shall instead proceed under sections 134 and 136 to 138.

(3) Where the Commission is proceeding by virtue of subsection (2), the period within which the Commission shall prepare and publish its report under section 136 shall be extended by an additional period of 20 days.

(4) Where the Commission terminates its investigation under section 145(1), the Commission shall proceed under sections 134 and 136 to 138.

(5) Where the Commission is proceeding by virtue of subsection (4), the period within which the Commission shall prepare and publish its report under section 136 shall be extended by an additional period of 20 days.

(6) In determining the period of 20 days mentioned in subsection (3) or (5) no account shall be taken of—

(a) Saturday, Sunday, Good Friday and Christmas Day; and

(b) any day which is a bank holiday in England and Wales.

[1894]

152 Certain duties of OFT and Commission

(1) The OFT shall, in considering whether to make a reference under section 131, bring to the attention of the Secretary of State any case which it believes raises any consideration specified in section 153 unless it believes that the Secretary of State would consider any such consideration immaterial in the context of the particular case.

(2) The Commission shall, in investigating any reference made to it under section 131 or 132 within the previous four months, bring to the attention of the Secretary of State any case which it believes raises any consideration specified in section 153 unless it believes that the Secretary of State would consider any such consideration immaterial in the context of the particular case.

(3)   The OFT and the Commission shall bring to the attention of the Secretary of State any representations about exercising his power under section 153(3) which have been made to the OFT or (as the case may be) the Commission.

[1895]

153   Specified considerations: Part 4

(1)   The interests of national security are specified in this section.

(2)   In subsection (1) "national security" includes public security; and in this subsection "public security" has the same meaning as in article [21(4) of Council Regulation (EC) No 139/2004 of 20th January 2004 on the control of concentrations between undertakings].

(3)   The Secretary of State may by order modify this section for the purpose of specifying in this section a new consideration or removing or amending any consideration which is for the time being specified in this section.

(4)   An order under this section may apply in relation to cases under consideration by the OFT, by the Secretary of State, by the appropriate Minister (other than the Secretary of State acting alone) or by the Commission before the making of the order as well as cases under consideration on or after the making of the order.

[1896]

NOTES
Sub-s (2): words in square brackets substituted by the EC Merger Control (Consequential Amendments) Regulations 2004, SI 2004/1079, reg 2, Schedule, para 2(1), (27).

CHAPTER 3
ENFORCEMENT

Undertakings and orders

154   Undertakings in lieu of market investigation references

(1)   Subsection (2) applies if the OFT considers that it has the power to make a reference under section 131 and otherwise intends to make such a reference.

(2)   The OFT may, instead of making such a reference and for the purpose of remedying, mitigating or preventing—
  (a)   any adverse effect on competition concerned; or
  (b)   any detrimental effect on customers so far as it has resulted from, or may be expected to result from, the adverse effect on competition;
accept, from such persons as it considers appropriate, undertakings to take such action as it considers appropriate.

(3)   In proceeding under subsection (2), the OFT shall, in particular, have regard to the need to achieve as comprehensive a solution as is reasonable and practicable to the adverse effect on competition concerned and any detrimental effects on customers so far as resulting from the adverse effect on competition.

(4)   In proceeding under subsection (2), the OFT may, in particular, have regard to the effect of any action on any relevant customer benefits of the feature or features of the market concerned.

(5)   The OFT shall take no action under subsection (2) to remedy, mitigate or prevent any detrimental effect on customers so far as it may be expected to result from the adverse effect on competition concerned if—
  (a)   no detrimental effect on customers has resulted from the adverse effect on competition; and
  (b)   the adverse effect on competition is not being remedied, mitigated or prevented.

(6)   An undertaking under this section—
  (a)   shall come into force when accepted;
  (b)   may be varied or superseded by another undertaking; and
  (c)   may be released by the OFT.

(7)   The OFT shall, as soon as reasonably practicable, consider any representations received by it in relation to varying or releasing an undertaking under this section.

(8)   This section is subject to sections 150 and 155.

[1897]

155   Undertakings in lieu: procedural requirements

(1)   Before accepting an undertaking under section 154 (other than an undertaking under that section which varies an undertaking under that section but not in any material respect), the OFT shall—
  (a)   publish notice of the proposed undertaking; and

(b)   consider any representations made in accordance with the notice and not withdrawn.

(2)   A notice under subsection (1) shall state—
    (a)   that the OFT proposes to accept the undertaking;
    (b)   the purpose and effect of the undertaking;
    (c)   the situation that the undertaking is seeking to deal with;
    (d)   any other facts which the OFT considers justify the acceptance of the undertaking;
    (e)   a means of gaining access to an accurate version of the proposed undertaking at all reasonable times; and
    (f)   the period (not less than 15 days starting with the date of publication of the notice) within which representations may be made in relation to the proposed undertaking.

(3)   The matters to be included in a notice under subsection (1) by virtue of subsection (2) shall, in particular, include—
    (a)   the terms of the reference under section 131 which the OFT considers that it has power to make and which it otherwise intends to make; and
    (b)   the adverse effect on competition, and any detrimental effect on customers so far as resulting from the adverse effect on competition, which the OFT has identified.

(4)   The OFT shall not accept the undertaking with modifications unless it—
    (a)   publishes notice of the proposed modifications; and
    (b)   considers any representations made in accordance with the notice and not withdrawn.

(5)   A notice under subsection (4) shall state—
    (a)   the proposed modifications;
    (b)   the reasons for them; and
    (c)   the period (not less than 7 days starting with the date of the publication of the notice under subsection (4)) within which representations may be made in relation to the proposed modifications.

(6)   If, after publishing notice under subsection (1) or (4), the OFT decides—
    (a)   not to accept the undertaking concerned; and
    (b)   not to proceed by virtue of subsection (8) or (9);
it shall publish notice of that decision.

(7)   As soon as practicable after accepting an undertaking to which this section applies, the OFT shall—
    (a)   serve a copy of the undertaking on any person by whom it is given; and
    (b)   publish the undertaking.

(8)   The requirements of subsection (4) (and those of subsection (1)) shall not apply if the OFT—
    (a)   has already published notice under subsection (1) but not subsection (4) in relation to the proposed undertaking; and
    (b)   considers that the modifications which are now being proposed are not material in any respect.

(9)   The requirements of subsection (4) (and those of subsection (1)) shall not apply if the OFT—
    (a)   has already published notice under subsections (1) and (4) in relation to the matter concerned; and
    (b)   considers that the further modifications which are now being proposed do not differ in any material respect from the modifications in relation to which notice was last given under subsection (4).

(10)   Paragraphs 6 to 8 (but not paragraph 9) of Schedule 10 (procedural requirements before terminating undertakings) shall apply in relation to the proposed release of undertakings under section 154 (other than in connection with accepting an undertaking under that section which varies or supersedes an undertaking under that section) as they apply in relation to the proposed release of undertakings under section 73.

[1898]

156   Effect of undertakings under section 154

(1)   No market investigation reference shall be made by the OFT or the appropriate Minister in relation to any feature, or combination of features, of a market in the United Kingdom for goods or services if—
    (a)   the OFT has accepted an undertaking or group of undertakings under section 154 within the previous 12 months; and
    (b)   the goods or services to which the undertaking or group of undertakings relates are of the same description as the goods or services to which the feature, or combination of features, relates.

(2)   Subsection (1) does not prevent the making of a market investigation reference if—

(a) the OFT considers that any undertaking concerned has been breached and has given notice of that fact to the person responsible for giving the undertaking; or

(b) the person responsible for giving any undertaking concerned supplied, in connection with the matter, information to the OFT which was false or misleading in a material respect.

[1899]

157 Interim undertakings: Part 4

(1) Subsection (2) applies where—
(a) a market investigation reference has been made;
(b) a report has been published under section 136 within the period permitted by section 137 or (as the case may be) a report prepared under section 142 and given to the Secretary of State under section 143(3) within the period permitted by section 144 has been published; and
(c) the market investigation reference concerned is not finally determined.

(2) The relevant authority may, for the purpose of preventing pre-emptive action, accept, from such persons as the relevant authority considers appropriate, undertakings to take such action as the relevant authority considers appropriate.

(3) An undertaking under this section—
(a) shall come into force when accepted;
(b) may be varied or superseded by another undertaking; and
(c) may be released by the relevant authority.

(4) An undertaking under this section shall, if it has not previously ceased to be in force, cease to be in force when the market investigation reference is finally determined.

(5) The relevant authority shall, as soon as reasonably practicable, consider any representations received by the relevant authority in relation to varying or releasing an undertaking under this section.

(6) In this section and section 158—
"pre-emptive action" means action which might impede the taking of any action under section 138(2) or (as the case may be) 147(2) in relation to the market investigation reference concerned; and
"the relevant authority" means—
(a) where an intervention notice is in force in relation to the market investigation reference, the Secretary of State;
(b) in any other case, the Commission.

[1900]

158 Interim orders: Part 4

(1) Subsection (2) applies where—
(a) a market investigation reference has been made;
(b) a report has been published under section 136 within the period permitted by section 137 or (as the case may be) a report prepared under section 142 and given to the Secretary of State under section 143(3) within the period permitted by section 144 has been published; and
(c) the market investigation reference concerned is not finally determined.

(2) The relevant authority may by order, for the purpose of preventing pre-emptive action—
(a) prohibit or restrict the doing of things which the relevant authority considers would constitute pre-emptive action;
(b) impose on any person concerned obligations as to the carrying on of any activities or the safeguarding of any assets;
(c) provide for the carrying on of any activities or the safeguarding of any assets either by the appointment of a person to conduct or supervise the conduct of any activities (on such terms and with such powers as may be specified or described in the order) or in any other manner;
(d) do anything which may be done by virtue of paragraph 19 of Schedule 8.

(3) An order under this section—
(a) shall come into force at such time as is determined by or under the order; and
(b) may be varied or revoked by another order.

(4) An order under this section shall, if it has not previously ceased to be in force, cease to be in force when the market investigation reference is finally determined.

(5) The relevant authority shall, as soon as reasonably practicable, consider any representations received by the relevant authority in relation to varying or revoking an order under this section.

[1901]

159 Final undertakings: Part 4

(1)   The Commission may, in accordance with section 138, accept, from such persons as it considers appropriate, undertakings to take action specified or described in the undertakings.

(2)   The Secretary of State may, in accordance with section 147, accept, from such persons as he considers appropriate, undertakings to take action specified or described in the undertakings.

(3)   An undertaking under this section shall come into force when accepted.

(4)   An undertaking under subsection (1) or (2) may be varied or superseded by another undertaking under that subsection.

(5)   An undertaking under subsection (1) may be released by the Commission and an undertaking under subsection (2) may be released by the Secretary of State.

(6)   The Commission or (as the case may be) the Secretary of State shall, as soon as reasonably practicable, consider any representations received by it or (as the case may be) him in relation to varying or releasing an undertaking under this section.

[1902]

160 Order-making power where final undertakings not fulfilled: Part 4

(1)   Subsection (2) applies where the relevant authority considers that—
   (a)   an undertaking accepted by the relevant authority under section 159 has not been, is not being or will not be fulfilled; or
   (b)   in relation to an undertaking accepted by the relevant authority under that section, information which was false or misleading in a material respect was given to the relevant authority or the OFT by the person giving the undertaking before the relevant authority decided to accept the undertaking.

(2)   The relevant authority may, for any of the purposes mentioned in section 138(2) or (as the case may be) 147(2), make an order under this section.

(3)   Subsections (3) to (6) of section 138 or (as the case may be) 147 shall apply for the purposes of subsection (2) above as they apply for the purposes of that section.

(4)   An order under this section may contain—
   (a)   anything permitted by Schedule 8; and
   (b)   such supplementary, consequential or incidental provision as the relevant authority considers appropriate.

(5)   An order under this section—
   (a)   shall come into force at such time as is determined by or under the order;
   (b)   may contain provision which is different from the provision contained in the undertaking concerned; and
   (c)   may be varied or revoked by another order.

(6)   No order shall be varied or revoked under this section unless the OFT advises that such a variation or revocation is appropriate by reason of a change of circumstances.

(7)   In this section "the relevant authority" means—
   (a)   in the case of an undertaking accepted under section 159 by the Commission, the Commission; and
   (b)   in the case of an undertaking accepted under that section by the Secretary of State, the Secretary of State.

[1903]

161 Final orders: Part 4

(1)   The Commission may, in accordance with section 138, make an order under this section.

(2)   The Secretary of State may, in accordance with section 147, make an order under this section.

(3)   An order under this section may contain—
   (a)   anything permitted by Schedule 8; and
   (b)   such supplementary, consequential or incidental provision as the person making it considers appropriate.

(4)   An order under this section—
   (a)   shall come into force at such time as is determined by or under the order; and
   (b)   may be varied or revoked by another order.

(5)   No order shall be varied or revoked under this section unless the OFT advises that such a variation or revocation is appropriate by reason of a change of circumstances.

[1904]

Enforcement functions of OFT

162   Duty of OFT to monitor undertakings and orders: Part 4

(1)   The OFT shall keep under review the carrying out of any enforcement undertaking or any enforcement order.

(2)   The OFT shall, in particular, from time to time consider—

    (a)   whether an enforcement undertaking or enforcement order has been or is being complied with;

    (b)   whether, by reason of any change of circumstances, an enforcement undertaking is no longer appropriate and—

        (i)   one or more of the parties to it can be released from it; or

        (ii)   it needs to be varied or to be superseded by a new enforcement undertaking; and

    (c)   whether, by reason of any change of circumstances, an enforcement order is no longer appropriate and needs to be varied or revoked.

(3)   The OFT shall give the Commission or (as the case may be) the Secretary of State such advice as it considers appropriate in relation to—

    (a)   any possible variation or release by the Commission or (as the case may be) the Secretary of State of an enforcement undertaking accepted by it or (as the case may be) him;

    (b)   any possible new enforcement undertaking to be accepted by the Commission or (as the case may be) the Secretary of State so as to supersede another enforcement undertaking given to the Commission or (as the case may be) the Secretary of State;

    (c)   any possible variation or revocation by the Commission or (as the case may be) the Secretary of State of an enforcement order made by the Commission or (as the case may be) the Secretary of State;

    (d)   any possible enforcement undertaking to be accepted by the Commission or (as the case may be) the Secretary of State instead of an enforcement order or any possible enforcement order to be made by the Commission or (as the case may be) the Secretary of State instead of an enforcement undertaking; or

    (e)   the enforcement by virtue of section 167(6) to (8) of any enforcement undertaking or enforcement order.

(4)   The OFT shall take such action as it considers appropriate in relation to—

    (a)   any possible variation or release by it of an undertaking accepted by it under section 154;

    (b)   any possible new undertaking to be accepted by it under section 154 so as to supersede another undertaking given to it under that section; or

    (c)   the enforcement by it by virtue of section 167(6) of any enforcement undertaking or enforcement order.

(5)   The OFT shall keep under review the effectiveness of enforcement undertakings accepted under this Part and enforcement orders made under this Part.

(6)   The OFT shall, whenever requested to do so by the Secretary of State and otherwise from time to time, prepare a report of its findings under subsection (5).

(7)   The OFT shall—

    (a)   give any report prepared by it under subsection (6) to the Commission;

    (b)   give a copy of the report to the Secretary of State; and

    (c)   publish the report.

(8)   In this Part—

"enforcement order" means an order made under section 158, 160 or 161; and

"enforcement undertaking" means an undertaking accepted under section 154, 157 or 159.

[1905]

163   Further role of OFT in relation to undertakings and orders: Part 4

(1)   Subsections (2) and (3) apply where the Commission or the Secretary of State (in this section "the relevant authority") is considering whether to accept undertakings under section 157 or 159.

(2)   The relevant authority may require the OFT to consult with such persons as the relevant authority considers appropriate with a view to discovering whether they will offer undertakings which the relevant authority would be prepared to accept under section 157 or (as the case may be) 159.

(3)   The relevant authority may require the OFT to report to the relevant authority on the outcome of the OFT's consultations within such period as the relevant authority may require.

(4)   A report under subsection (3) shall, in particular, contain advice from the OFT as to whether any undertakings offered should be accepted by the relevant authority under section 157 or (as the case may be) 159.

(5)   The powers conferred on the relevant authority by subsections (1) to (4) are without prejudice to the power of the relevant authority to consult the persons concerned itself.

(6)   If asked by the relevant authority for advice in relation to the taking of enforcement action (whether or not by way of undertakings) in a particular case, the OFT shall give such advice as it considers appropriate.

[1906]

Supplementary

164   Enforcement undertakings and orders under this Part: general provisions

(1)   The provision which may be contained in an enforcement undertaking is not limited to the provision which is permitted by Schedule 8.

(2)   The following enactments in Part 3 shall apply in relation to enforcement orders under this Part as they apply in relation to enforcement orders under that Part—
   (a)   section 86(1) to (5) (enforcement orders: general provisions); and
   (b)   section 87 (power of directions conferred by enforcement order).

(3)   An enforcement order under section 160 or 161 or any explanatory material accompanying the order shall state—
   (a)   the actions that the persons or description of persons to whom the order is addressed must do or (as the case may be) refrain from doing;
   (b)   the date on which the order comes into force;
   (c)   the possible consequences of not complying with the order; and
   (d)   the section of this Part under which a review can be sought in relation to the order.

[1907]

165   Procedural requirements for certain undertakings and orders: Part 4

Schedule 10 (procedural requirements for certain undertakings and orders), other than paragraph 9 of that Schedule, shall apply in relation to undertakings under section 159 and orders under section 160 or 161 as it applies in relation to undertakings under section 82 and orders under section 83 or 84.

[1908]

166   Register of undertakings and orders: Part 4

(1)   The OFT shall compile and maintain a register for the purposes of this Part.

(2)   The register shall be kept in such form as the OFT considers appropriate.

(3)   The OFT shall ensure that the following matters are entered in the register—
   (a)   the provisions of any enforcement undertaking accepted by virtue of this Part (whether by the OFT, the Commission, the Secretary of State or a relevant sectoral regulator);
   (b)   the provisions of any enforcement order made by virtue of this Part (whether by the Commission, the Secretary of State or a relevant sectoral regulator); and
   (c)   the details of any variation, release or revocation of such an undertaking or order.

(4)   The duty in subsection (3) does not extend to anything of which the OFT is unaware.

(5)   The Commission, the Secretary of State and any relevant sectoral regulator shall inform the OFT of any matters which are to be included in the register by virtue of subsection (3) and which relate to enforcement undertakings accepted by them or enforcement orders made by them.

(6)   The OFT shall ensure that the contents of the register are available to the public—
   (a)   during (as a minimum) such hours as may be specified in an order made by the Secretary of State; and
   (b)   subject to such reasonable fees (if any) as the OFT may determine.

(7)   If requested by any person to do so and subject to such reasonable fees (if any) as the OFT may determine, the OFT shall supply the person concerned with a copy (certified to be true) of the register or of an extract from it.

[1909]

NOTES

Order: the OFT Registers of Undertakings and Orders (Available Hours) Order 2003, SI 2003/1373.

167   Rights to enforce undertakings and orders under this Part

(1)   This section applies to any enforcement undertaking or enforcement order.

(2)   Any person to whom such an undertaking or order relates shall have a duty to comply with it.

(3)   The duty shall be owed to any person who may be affected by a contravention of the undertaking or (as the case may be) order.

(4)   Any breach of the duty which causes such a person to sustain loss or damage shall be actionable by him.

(5)   In any proceedings brought under subsection (4) against a person to whom an enforcement undertaking or enforcement order relates it shall be a defence for that person to show that he took all reasonable steps and exercised all due diligence to avoid contravening the undertaking or (as the case may be) order.

(6)   Compliance with an enforcement undertaking or an enforcement order shall also be enforceable by civil proceedings brought by the OFT for an injunction or for interdict or for any other appropriate relief or remedy.

(7)   Compliance with an undertaking accepted under section 157 or 159, or an order under section 158, 160 or 161, shall also be enforceable by civil proceedings brought by the relevant authority for an injunction or for interdict or for any other appropriate relief or remedy.

(8)   In subsection (7) "the relevant authority" means—
   (a)   in the case of an undertaking accepted by the Commission or an order made by the Commission, the Commission; and
   (b)   in the case of an undertaking accepted by the Secretary of State or an order made by the Secretary of State, the Secretary of State.

(9)   Subsections (6) to (8) shall not prejudice any right that a person may have by virtue of subsection (4) to bring civil proceedings for contravention or apprehended contravention of an enforcement undertaking or an enforcement order.

[1910]

CHAPTER 4
SUPPLEMENTARY
Regulated markets

168   Regulated markets

(1)   Subsection (2) applies where the Commission or the Secretary of State is considering for the purposes of this Part whether relevant action would be reasonable and practicable for the purpose of remedying, mitigating or preventing an adverse effect on competition or any detrimental effect on customers so far as resulting from such an effect.

(2)   The Commission or (as the case may be) the Secretary of State shall, in deciding whether such action would be reasonable and practicable, have regard to the relevant statutory functions of the sectoral regulator concerned.

(3)   In this section "relevant action" means—
   (a)   …
   (b)   modifying conditions in force under Part 4 of the Airports Act 1986 (c 31) other than any conditions imposed or modified in pursuance of section 40(3) or (4) of that Act;
   (c)   modifying the conditions of a licence granted under section 7 or 7A of the Gas Act 1986 (c 44);
   (d)   modifying the conditions of a licence granted under section 6 of the Electricity Act 1989 (c 29);
   (e)   modifying networking arrangements (within the meaning given by [section 290 of the Communications Act 2003]);
   (f)   modifying the conditions of a company's appointment under Chapter 1 of Part 2 of the Water Industry Act 1991 (c 56);
   [(ff)   modifying the conditions of a licence granted under Chapter 1A of Part 2 of the Act of 1991 or modifying the terms and conditions of an agreement under section 66D of that Act;]
   (g)   modifying the conditions of a licence granted under article 10 of the Electricity (Northern Ireland) Order 1992 (SI 1992/231 (NI 1));
   (h)   modifying the conditions of a licence granted under section 8 of the Railways Act 1993 (c 43);
   [(hh)   modifying the conditions of a SNRP issued pursuant to the Railways Infrastructure (Access, Management and Licensing of Railway Undertakings) Regulations (Northern Ireland) 2005;]
   (i)   modifying an access agreement (within the meaning given by section 83(1) of the Act of 1993) or a franchise agreement (within the meaning given by section 23(3) of that Act);
   (j)   modifying conditions in force under Part 4 of the Airports (Northern Ireland) Order 1994 (SI 1994/426 (NI 1)) other than any conditions imposed or modified in pursuance of article 40(3) or (4) of that Order;
   (k)   modifying the conditions of a licence granted under article 8 of the Gas (Northern Ireland) Order 1996 (SI 1996/275 (NI 2));
   (l)   modifying the conditions of a licence granted under section 11 of the Postal Services Act 2000 (c 26); or

(m) modifying the conditions of a licence granted under section 5 of the Transport Act 2000 (c 38);

[(n) modifying the conditions of a company's appointment under Chapter I of Part III of the Water and Sewerage Services (Northern Ireland) Order 2006].

(4) In this section "relevant statutory functions" means—

(a) ...

(b) in relation to conditions in force under Part 4 of the Airports Act 1986 (c 31) other than any conditions imposed or modified in pursuance of section 40(3) or (4) of that Act, the duties of the Civil Aviation Authority under section 39(2) and (3) of that Act;

(c) in relation to any licence granted under section 7 or 7A of the Gas Act 1986 (c 44), the objectives and duties of the Gas and Electricity Markets Authority under section 4AA and 4AB(2) of that Act;

(d) in relation to any licence granted under section 6 of the Electricity Act 1989 (c 29), the objectives and duties of the Gas and Electricity Markets Authority under section 3A and 3B(2) of that Act;

[(e) in relation to any networking arrangements (within the meaning given by section 290 of the Communications Act 2003), the duty of the Office of Communications under subsection (1) of section 3 of that Act to secure the matters mentioned in subsection (2)(c) of that section;]

(f) in relation to a company's appointment under Chapter 1 of Part 2 of the Water Industry Act 1991 (c 56), the duties of [the Water Services Regulation Authority] under section 2 of that Act;

[(ff) in relation to a licence granted under Chapter 1A of Part 2 of the Act of 1991 or an agreement under section 66D of that Act, the duties of the Authority under section 2 of that Act or under that section and section 66D of that Act (as the case may be);]

(g) in relation to any licence granted under article 10 of the Electricity (Northern Ireland) Order 1992 (SI 1992/231 (NI 1)), the duty of the Director General of Electricity Supply for Northern Ireland under article 6 of that Order;

(h) in relation to any licence granted under section 8 of the Railways Act 1993 (c 43) ... , the duties of [the Office of Rail Regulation] under section 4 of that Act;

[(hh) in relation to a SNRP issued pursuant to the Railways Infrastructure (Access, Management and Licensing of Railway Undertakings) Regulations (Northern Ireland) 2005 where none of the conditions of the SNRP relate to consumer protection, the duties of the Department for Regional Development under regulation 36 of those Regulations;]

(i) ...

(j) in relation to any access agreement (within the meaning given by section 83(1) of the Act of 1993), the duties of [the Office of Rail Regulation] under section 4 of the Act of 1993;

(k) in relation to any franchise agreement (within the meaning given by section 23(3) of the Act of 1993), the duties of the [Secretary of State, the Scottish Ministers and the National Assembly for Wales under section 4 of the Act of 1993];

(l) in relation to conditions in force under Part 4 of the Airports (Northern Ireland) Order 1994 (SI 1994/426 (NI 1)) other than any conditions imposed or modified in pursuance of article 40(3) or (4) of that Order, the duties of the Civil Aviation Authority under article 30(2) and (3) of that Order;

(m) in relation to any licence granted under article 8 of the Gas (Northern Ireland) Order 1996 (SI 1996/275 (NI 2)), the duties of the Director General of Gas for Northern Ireland under article 5 of that Order;

(n) in relation to any licence granted under section 11 of the Postal Services Act 2000 (c 26), the duties of the Postal Services Commission under sections 3 and 5 of that Act; and

(o) in relation to any licence granted under section 5 of the Transport Act 2000, the duties of the Civil Aviation Authority under section 87 of that Act;

[(p) in relation to a company's appointment under Chapter I of Part III of the Water and Sewerage Services (Northern Ireland) Order 2006, the duties of the Northern Ireland Authority for Utility Regulation under Article 6 of that Order].

(5) In this section "sectoral regulator" means—

(a) the Civil Aviation Authority;

[(b) the Northern Ireland Authority for Utility Regulation;]

(d) ...

[(e) the Water Services Regulation Authority;]

(f) the Gas and Electricity Markets Authority;

[(g) the Office of Communications;]

(h) the Postal Services Commission;

(i) [the Office of Rail Regulation]; ...

[(j) the Secretary of State;

(k) the Scottish Ministers; or

(l) the National Assembly for Wales].

(6) Subsection (7) applies where the Commission or the Secretary of State is considering for the purposes of this Part whether modifying the conditions of a licence granted under section 7 or 7A of the Gas Act 1986 (c 44) or section 6 of the Electricity Act 1989 (c 29) would be reasonable and practicable for the purpose of remedying, mitigating or preventing an adverse effect on competition or any detrimental effect on customers so far as resulting from such an effect.

(7) The Commission or (as the case may be) the Secretary of State may, in deciding whether modifying the conditions of such a licence would be reasonable and practicable, have regard to those matters to which the Gas and Electricity Markets Authority may have regard by virtue of section 4AA(4) of the Act of 1986 or (as the case may be) section 3A(4) of the Act of 1989.

(8) The Secretary of State may by order modify subsection (3), (4), (5), (6) or (7).

(9) Part 2 of Schedule 9 (which makes provision for functions under this Part to be exercisable by various sectoral regulators) shall have effect.

NOTES

Sub-s (3): para (a) repealed and words in square brackets in para (e) substituted by the Communications Act 2003, s 406(1), (7), Sch 17, para 174(1), (5)(a), Sch 19(1); para (ff) inserted by the Water Act 2003, s 101(1), Sch 8, para 55(1), (2)(a); para (hh) inserted by the Railways Infrastructure (Access, Management and Licensing of Railway Undertakings) Regulations (Northern Ireland) 2005, SR 2005/537, reg 45, Sch 5, para 4(a); para (n) inserted by the Water and Sewerage Services (Northern Ireland) Order 2006, SI 2006/3336, art 308(1), Sch 12, para 46(3).

Sub-s (4): para (a) repealed and para (e) substituted by the Communications Act 2003, s 406(1), (7), Sch 17, para 174(1), (5)(b), Sch 19(1); in para (f) words in square brackets substituted and para (ff) inserted by the Water Act 2003, s 101(1), Sch 7, Pt 2, para 36(1), (3)(a), Sch 8, para 55(1), (2)(b); in para (h) words omitted repealed by the Railways Act 2005, s 59(1), (6), Sch 12, para 18(1), (2)(a), Sch 13, Pt 1, words in square brackets substituted by the Railways and Transport Safety Act 2003, s 16(5), Sch 2, Pt 2, para 19(u); para (hh) inserted by the Railways Infrastructure (Access, Management and Licensing of Railway Undertakings) Regulations (Northern Ireland) 2005, SR 2005/537, reg 45, Sch 5, para 4(b); para (i) repealed and words in square brackets in para (k) substituted by the Railways Act 2005, s 59(1), (6), Sch 12, para 18(1), (2)(b), (c), Sch 13, Pt 1; words in square brackets in para (j) substituted by the Railways and Transport Safety Act 2003, s 16(5), Sch 2, Pt 2, para 19(u); para (p) inserted by SI 2006/3336, art 308(1), Sch 12, para 46(4).

Sub-s (5): para (b) substituted, for original paras (b), (c), by SI 2006/3336, art 308(1), Sch 12, para 46(5); para (d) repealed and para (g) substituted by the Communications Act 2003, s 406(1), (7), Sch 17, para 174(1), (5)(c), Sch 19(1); para (e) substituted by the Water Act 2003, s 101(1), Sch 7, Pt 2, para 36(1), (3)(b); in para (i) words in square brackets substituted by the Railways and Transport Safety Act 2003, s 16(5), Sch 2, Pt 2, para 19(u), word omitted repealed in relation to England, Scotland and Wales by the Railways Act 2005, s 59(6), Sch 13, Pt 1 and in relation to Northern Ireland by the Railways Infrastructure (Access, Management and Licensing of Railway Undertakings) Regulations (Northern Ireland) 2005, SR 2005/537, reg 45, Sch 5, para 4(c)(i); paras (j)–(l) substituted, for original para (j), by the Railways Act 2005, s 59(1), Sch 12, paras 18(1), (3), and a corresponding amendment, substituting para (k) in relation to Northern Ireland, has been made by the Railways Infrastructure (Access, Management and Licensing of Railway Undertakings) Regulations (Northern Ireland) 2005, SR 2005/537, reg 45, Sch 5, para 4(c)(ii).

Consultation, information and publicity

169 Certain duties of relevant authorities to consult: Part 4

(1) Subsection (2) applies where the relevant authority is proposing to make a relevant decision in a way which the relevant authority considers is likely to have a substantial impact on the interests of any person.

(2) The relevant authority shall, so far as practicable, consult that person about what is proposed before making that decision.

(3) In consulting the person concerned, the relevant authority shall, so far as practicable, give the reasons of the relevant authority for the proposed decision.

(4) In considering what is practicable for the purposes of this section the relevant authority shall, in particular, have regard to—
 (a) any restrictions imposed by any timetable for making the decision; and
 (b) any need to keep what is proposed, or the reasons for it, confidential.

(5) The duty under this section shall not apply in relation to the making of any decision so far as particular provision is made elsewhere by virtue of this Part for consultation before the making of that decision.

(6) In this section—
 "the relevant authority" means the OFT, the appropriate Minister or the Commission; and
 "relevant decision" means—
  (a) in the case of the OFT, any decision by the OFT—
   (i) as to whether to make a reference under section 131 or accept undertakings under section 154 instead of making such a reference; or
   (ii) to vary under section 135 such a reference;
  (b) in the case of the appropriate Minister, any decision by the appropriate Minister—

    (i)   as to whether to make a reference under section 132; or

    (ii)   to vary under section 135 such a reference; and

  (c)   in the case of the Commission, any decision on the questions mentioned in section 134 or 141.

[1912]

170 General information duties

(1)   The OFT shall give the Commission—

  (a)   such information in its possession as the Commission may reasonably require to enable the Commission to carry out its functions under this Part; and

  (b)   any other assistance which the Commission may reasonably require for the purpose of assisting it in carrying out its functions under this Part and which it is within the power of the OFT to give.

(2)   The OFT shall give the Commission any information in its possession which has not been requested by the Commission but which, in the opinion of the OFT, would be appropriate to give to the Commission for the purpose of assisting it in carrying out its functions under this Part.

(3)   The OFT and the Commission shall give the Secretary of State or the appropriate Minister so far as he is not the Secretary of State acting alone—

  (a)   such information in their possession as the Secretary of State or (as the case may be) the appropriate Minister concerned may by direction reasonably require to enable him to carry out his functions under this Part; and

  (b)   any other assistance which the Secretary of State or (as the case may be) the appropriate Minister concerned may by direction reasonably require for the purpose of assisting him in carrying out his functions under this Part and which it is within the power of the OFT or (as the case may be) the Commission to give.

(4)   The OFT shall give the Secretary of State or the appropriate Minister so far as he is not the Secretary of State acting alone any information in its possession which has not been requested by the Secretary of State or (as the case may be) the appropriate Minister concerned but which, in the opinion of the OFT, would be appropriate to give to the Secretary of State or (as the case may be) the appropriate Minister concerned for the purpose of assisting him in carrying out his functions under this Part.

(5)   The Commission shall have regard to any information given to it under subsection (1) or (2); and the Secretary of State or (as the case may be) the appropriate Minister concerned shall have regard to any information given to him under subsection (3) or (4).

(6)   Any direction given under subsection (3)—

  (a)   shall be in writing; and

  (b)   may be varied or revoked by a subsequent direction.

[1913]

171 Advice and information: Part 4

(1)   As soon as reasonably practicable after the passing of this Act, the OFT shall prepare and publish general advice and information about the making of references by it under section 131.

(2)   The OFT may at any time publish revised, or new, advice or information.

(3)   As soon as reasonably practicable after the passing of this Act, the Commission shall prepare and publish general advice and information about the consideration by it of market investigation references and the way in which relevant customer benefits may affect the taking of enforcement action in relation to such references.

(4)   The Commission may at any time publish revised, or new, advice or information.

(5)   Advice and information published under this section shall be prepared with a view to—

  (a)   explaining relevant provisions of this Part to persons who are likely to be affected by them; and

  (b)   indicating how the OFT or (as the case may be) the Commission expects such provisions to operate.

(6)   Advice and information published by virtue of subsection (1) or (3) shall include such advice and information about the effect of Community law, and anything done under or in accordance with it, on the provisions of this Part as the OFT or (as the case may be) the Commission considers appropriate.

(7)   Advice (or information) published by virtue of subsection (1) or (3) may include advice (or information) about the factors which the OFT or (as the case may be) the Commission may take into account in considering whether, and if so how, to exercise a function conferred by this Part.

(8)   Any advice or information published by the OFT or the Commission under this section shall be published in such manner as the OFT or (as the case may be) the Commission considers appropriate.

(9)　　In preparing any advice or information under this section, the OFT shall consult the Commission and such other persons as it considers appropriate.

(10)　　In preparing any advice or information under this section, the Commission shall consult the OFT and such other persons as it considers appropriate.

(11)　　In this section "Community law" means—
- (a)　all the rights, powers, liabilities, obligations and restrictions from time to time created or arising by or under the Community Treaties; and
- (b)　all the remedies and procedures from time to time provided for by or under the Community Treaties.

[1914]

172　Further publicity requirements: Part 4

(1)　　The OFT shall publish—
- (a)　any reference made by it under section 131;
- (b)　any variation made by it under section 135 of a reference under section 131;
- (c)　any decision of a kind mentioned in section 149(5)(b); and
- (d)　such information as it considers appropriate about any decision made by it under section 152(1) to bring a case to the attention of the Secretary of State.

(2)　　The Commission shall publish—
- (a)　any decision made by it under section 138(2) neither to accept an undertaking under section 159 nor to make an order under section 161;
- (b)　any decision made by it that there has been a material change of circumstances as mentioned in section 138(3) or there is another special reason as mentioned in that section;
- (c)　any termination under section 145(1) of an investigation by it;
- (d)　such information as it considers appropriate about any decision made by it under section 152(2) to bring a case to the attention of the Secretary of State;
- (e)　any enforcement undertaking accepted by it under section 157;
- (f)　any enforcement order made by it under section 158; and
- (g)　any variation, release or revocation of such an undertaking or order.

(3)　　The Secretary of State shall publish—
- (a)　any reference made by him under section 132;
- (b)　any variation made by him under section 135 of a reference under section 132;
- (c)　any intervention notice given by him;
- (d)　any decision made by him to revoke such a notice;
- (e)　any decision made by him under section 147(2) neither to accept an undertaking under section 159 nor to make an order under section 161;
- (f)　any enforcement undertaking accepted by him under section 157;
- (g)　any variation or release of such an undertaking; and
- (h)　any direction given by him under section 170(3) in connection with the exercise by him of his functions under section 132(3).

(4)　　The appropriate Minister (other than the Secretary of State acting alone) shall publish—
- (a)　any reference made by him under section 132;
- (b)　any variation made by him under section 135 of a reference under section 132; and
- (c)　any direction given by him under section 170(3) in connection with the exercise by him of his functions under section 132(3).

(5)　　Where any person is under an obligation by virtue of subsection (1), (2), (3) or (4) to publish the result of any action taken by that person or any decision made by that person, the person concerned shall, subject to subsections (6) and (7), also publish that person's reasons for the action concerned or (as the case may be) the decision concerned.

(6)　　Such reasons need not, if it is not reasonably practicable to do so, be published at the same time as the result of the action concerned or (as the case may be) as the decision concerned.

(7)　　Subsections (5) and (6) shall not apply in relation to any case falling within subsection (1)(d) or (2)(d).

(8)　　The Secretary of State shall publish his reasons for—
- (a)　any decision made by him under section 146(2); or
- (b)　any decision to make an order under section 153(3) or vary or revoke such an order.

(9)　　Such reasons may be published after—
- (a)　in the case of subsection (8)(a), the publication of the decision concerned; and
- (b)　in the case of subsection (8)(b), the making of the order or of the variation or revocation;

if it is not reasonably practicable to publish them at the same time as the publication of the decision or (as the case may be) the making of the order or variation or revocation.

(10)　　Where the Secretary of State has decided under section 147(2) to accept an undertaking under section 159 or to make an order under section 161, he shall (after the acceptance of the

PART 1
STATUTES

undertaking or (as the case may be) the making of the order) lay details of his decision and his reasons for it, and the Commission's report under section 142, before each House of Parliament.

[1915]

173 Defamation: Part 4

For the purposes of the law relating to defamation, absolute privilege attaches to any advice, guidance, notice or direction given, or decision or report made, by the OFT, by the Secretary of State, by the appropriate Minister (other than the Secretary of State acting alone) or by the Commission in the exercise of any of their functions under this Part.

[1916]

Investigation powers

174 Investigation powers of OFT

(1)   The OFT may exercise any of the powers in subsections (3) to (5) for the purpose of assisting it in deciding whether to make a reference under section 131 or to accept undertakings under section 154 instead of making such a reference.

(2)   The OFT shall not exercise any of the powers in subsections (3) to (5) for the purpose of assisting it as mentioned in subsection (1) unless it already believes that it has power to make such a reference.

(3)   The OFT may give notice to any person requiring him—
(a)   to attend at a time and place specified in the notice; and
(b)   to give evidence to the OFT or a person nominated by the OFT for the purpose.

(4)   The OFT may give notice to any person requiring him—
(a)   to produce any documents which—
(i)   are specified or described in the notice, or fall within a category of document which is specified or described in the notice; and
(ii)   are in that person's custody or under his control; and
(b)   to produce them at a time and place so specified and to a person so specified.

(5)   The OFT may give notice to any person who carries on any business requiring him—
(a)   to supply to the OFT such estimates, forecasts, returns or other information as may be specified or described in the notice; and
(b)   to supply it at a time and place, and in a form and manner, so specified and to a person so specified.

(6)   A notice under this section shall include information about the possible consequences of not complying with the notice.

(7)   The person to whom any document is produced in accordance with a notice under this section may, for the purpose mentioned in subsection (1), copy the document so produced.

(8)   No person shall be required under this section—
(a)   to give any evidence or produce any documents which he could not be compelled to give or produce in civil proceedings before the court; or
(b)   to supply any information which he could not be compelled to supply in evidence in such proceedings.

(9)   No person shall be required, in compliance with a notice under this section, to go more than 10 miles from his place of residence unless his necessary travelling expenses are paid or offered to him.

(10)   Any reference in this section to the production of a document includes a reference to the production of a legible and intelligible copy of information recorded otherwise than in legible form.

(11)   In this section "the court" means—
(a)   in relation to England and Wales or Northern Ireland, the High Court; and
(b)   in relation to Scotland, the Court of Session.

[1917]

175 Enforcement of powers under section 174: offences

(1)   A person commits an offence if he, intentionally and without reasonable excuse, fails to comply with any requirement of a notice under section 174.

(2)   A person commits an offence if he intentionally and without reasonable excuse alters, suppresses or destroys any document which he has been required to produce by a notice under section 174.

(3)   A person who commits an offence under subsection (1) or (2) shall be liable—
(a)   on summary conviction, to a fine not exceeding the statutory maximum;
(b)   on conviction on indictment, to imprisonment for a term not exceeding two years or to a fine or to both.

(4) A person commits an offence if he intentionally obstructs or delays—
  (a) the OFT in the exercise of its powers under section 174; or
  (b) any person in the exercise of his powers under subsection (7) of that section.

(5) A person who commits an offence under subsection (4) shall be liable—
  (a) on summary conviction, to a fine not exceeding the statutory maximum;
  (b) on conviction on indictment, to a fine.

[1918]

176 Investigation powers of the Commission

(1) The following sections in Part 3 shall apply, with the modifications mentioned in subsections (2) and (3) below, for the purposes of references under this Part as they apply for the purposes of references under that Part—
  (a) section 109 (attendance of witnesses and production of documents etc);
  (b) section 110 (enforcement of powers under section 109: general);
  (c) section 111 (penalties);
  (d) section 112 (penalties: main procedural requirements);
  (e) section 113 (payments and interest by instalments);
  (f) section 114 (appeals in relation to penalties);
  (g) section 115 (recovery of penalties); and
  (h) section 116 (statement of policy).

(2) Section 110 shall, in its application by virtue of subsection (1) above, have effect as if—
  (a) subsection (2) were omitted; and
  (b) in subsection (9) the words from "or section" to "section 65(3))" were omitted.

(3) Section 111(5)(b)(ii) shall, in its application by virtue of subsection (1) above, have effect as if—
  (a) for the words "section 50 or 65, given" there were substituted "section 142, published or given under section 143(1) or (3)"; and
  (b) for the words "(or given)", in both places where they appear, there were substituted "(or published or given)".

[1919]

Reports

177 Excisions from reports: Part 4

(1) Subsection (2) applies where the Secretary of State is under a duty to publish a report of the Commission under section 142.

(2) The Secretary of State may exclude a matter from the report if he considers that publication of the matter would be inappropriate.

(3) In deciding what is inappropriate for the purposes of subsection (2) the Secretary of State shall have regard to the considerations mentioned in section 244.

(4) The Commission shall advise the Secretary of State as to the matters (if any) which it considers should be excluded by him under subsection (2).

(5) References in sections 136(4) to (6), 143(2) and (5) to (7), 148(3) to (5) and 172(10) to the giving or laying of a report of the Commission shall be construed as references to the giving or laying of the report as published.

[1920]

178 Minority reports of Commission: Part 4

(1) Subsection (2) applies where, on a market investigation reference, a member of a group constituted in connection with the reference in pursuance of paragraph 15 of Schedule 7 to the Competition Act 1998 (c 41), disagrees with any decisions contained in the report of the Commission under this Part as the decisions of the Commission.

(2) The report shall, if the member so wishes, include a statement of his disagreement and of his reasons for disagreeing.

[1921]

Other

179 Review of decisions under Part 4

(1) Any person aggrieved by a decision of the OFT, the appropriate Minister, the Secretary of State or the Commission in connection with a reference or possible reference under this Part may apply to the Competition Appeal Tribunal for a review of that decision.

(2) For this purpose "decision"—
  (a) does not include a decision to impose a penalty under section 110(1) or (3) as applied by section 176; but

    (b)   includes a failure to take a decision permitted or required by this Part in connection with a reference or possible reference.

(3)   Except in so far as a direction to the contrary is given by the Competition Appeal Tribunal, the effect of the decision is not suspended by reason of the making of the application.

(4)   In determining such an application the Competition Appeal Tribunal shall apply the same principles as would be applied by a court on an application for judicial review.

(5)   The Competition Appeal Tribunal may—
    (a)   dismiss the application or quash the whole or part of the decision to which it relates; and
    (b)   where it quashes the whole or part of that decision, refer the matter back to the original decision maker with a direction to reconsider and make a new decision in accordance with the ruling of the Competition Appeal Tribunal.

(6)   An appeal lies on any point of law arising from a decision of the Competition Appeal Tribunal under this section to the appropriate court.

(7)   An appeal under subsection (6) requires the permission of the Tribunal or the appropriate court.

(8)   In this section—
"the appropriate court" means the Court of Appeal or, in the case of Tribunal proceedings in Scotland, the Court of Session; and
"Tribunal rules" has the meaning given by section 15(1).

[1922]

180 Offences

(1)   Sections 117 (false or misleading information) and 125 (offences by bodies corporate) shall apply, with the modifications mentioned in subsection (2) below, for the purposes of this Part as they apply for the purposes of Part 3.

(2)   Section 117 shall, in its application by virtue of subsection (1) above, have effect as if references to the Secretary of State included references to the appropriate Minister so far as he is not the Secretary of State acting alone [and as if the references to OFCOM were omitted].

[1923]

NOTES
Sub-s (2): words in square brackets added by the Communications Act 2003, s 389, Sch 16, para 26.

---

181 Orders under Part 4

(1)   Any power of the Secretary of State to make an order under this Part shall be exercisable by statutory instrument.

(2)   Any power of the Secretary of State to make an order under this Part—
    (a)   may be exercised so as to make different provision for different cases or different purposes;
    (b)   includes power to make such incidental, supplementary, consequential, transitory, transitional or saving provision as the Secretary of State considers appropriate.

(3)   The power of the Secretary of State under section 136(9), 137(3), 144(2), 153(3) or 168(8) as extended by subsection (2) above may be exercised by modifying any enactment comprised in or made under this Act, or any other enactment.

(4)   An order made by the Secretary of State under section 137(3), 144(2), 158, 160 or 161, or under section 111(4) or (6) or 114(3)(b) or (4)(b) as applied by section 176, shall be subject to annulment in pursuance of a resolution of either House of Parliament.

(5)   No order shall be made by the Secretary of State under section 136(9) or 168(8), or section 128(6) as applied by section 183(2), unless a draft of it has been laid before, and approved by a resolution of, each House of Parliament.

(6)   An order made by the Secretary of State under section 153(3) shall be laid before Parliament after being made and shall cease to have effect unless approved, within the period of 28 days beginning with the day on which it is made, by a resolution of each House of Parliament.

(7)   In calculating the period of 28 days mentioned in subsection (6), no account shall be taken of any time during which Parliament is dissolved or prorogued or during which both Houses are adjourned for more than four days.

(8)   If an order made by the Secretary of State ceases to have effect by virtue of subsection (6), any modification made by it of an enactment is repealed (and the previous enactment revived) but without prejudice to the validity of anything done in connection with that modification before the order ceased to have effect and without prejudice to the making of a new order.

(9)   If, apart from this subsection, an order made by the Secretary of State under section 153(3) would be treated for the purposes of the standing orders of either House of Parliament as a hybrid instrument, it shall proceed in that House as if it were not such an instrument.

(10)   References in this section to an order made under this Part include references to an order made under section 111(4) or (6) or 114(3)(b) or (4)(b) as applied by section 176 and an order made under section 128(6) as applied by section 183(2).

[1924]

182   Service of documents: Part 4

Section 126 shall apply for the purposes of this Part as it applies for the purposes of Part 3.

[1925]

183   Interpretation: Part 4

(1)   In this Part, unless the context otherwise requires—
  "action" includes omission; and references to the taking of action include references to refraining from action;
  "business" includes a professional practice and includes any other undertaking which is carried on for gain or reward or which is an undertaking in the course of which goods or services are supplied otherwise than free of charge;
  "change of circumstances" includes any discovery that information has been supplied which is false or misleading in a material respect;
  "consumer" means any person who is—
    (a)   a person to whom goods are or are sought to be supplied (whether by way of sale or otherwise) in the course of a business carried on by the person supplying or seeking to supply them; or
    (b)   a person for whom services are or are sought to be supplied in the course of a business carried on by the person supplying or seeking to supply them;
    and who does not receive or seek to receive the goods or services in the course of a business carried on by him;
  "customer" includes a customer who is not a consumer;
  "enactment" includes an Act of the Scottish Parliament, Northern Ireland legislation and an enactment comprised in subordinate legislation, and includes an enactment whenever passed or made;
  "goods" includes buildings and other structures, and also includes ships, aircraft and hovercraft;
  "Minister of the Crown" means the holder of an office in Her Majesty's Government in the United Kingdom and includes the Treasury;
  "modify" includes amend or repeal;
  "notice" means notice in writing;
  "subordinate legislation" has the same meaning as in the Interpretation Act 1978 (c 30) and also includes an instrument made under an Act of the Scottish Parliament and an instrument made under Northern Ireland legislation; and
  "supply", in relation to the supply of goods, includes supply by way of sale, lease, hire or hire-purchase, and, in relation to buildings or other structures, includes the construction of them by a person for another person.

(2)   Sections 127(1)(b) and (4) to (6) and 128 shall apply for the purposes of this Part as they apply for the purposes of Part 3.

(3)   For the purposes of this Part a market investigation reference is finally determined if—
  (a)   where no intervention notice under section 139(1) has been given in relation to it—
    (i)   the period permitted by section 137 for preparing and publishing a report under section 136 has expired and no such report has been prepared and published;
    (ii)   such a report has been prepared and published within the period permitted by section 137 and contains the decision that there is no adverse effect on competition;
    (iii)   the Commission has decided under section 138(2) neither to accept undertakings under section 159 nor to make an order under section 161; or
    (iv)   the Commission has accepted an undertaking under section 159 or made an order under section 161;
  (b)   where an intervention notice under section 139(1) has been given in relation to it—
    (i)   the period permitted by section 144 for the preparation of the report of the Commission under section 142 and for action to be taken in relation to it under section 143(1) or (3) has expired while the intervention notice is still in force and no such report has been so prepared or no such action has been taken;
    (ii)   the Commission has terminated under section 145(1) its investigation and the reference is finally determined under paragraph (a) above (disregarding the fact that the notice was given);

(iii) the report of the Commission has been prepared under section 142 and published under section 143(1) within the period permitted by section 144;

(iv) the intervention notice was revoked and the reference is finally determined under paragraph (a) above (disregarding the fact that the notice was given);

(v) the Secretary of State has failed to make and publish a decision under subsection (2) of section 146 within the period permitted by subsection (3) of that section and the reference is finally determined under paragraph (a) above (disregarding the fact that the notice was given);

(vi) the Secretary of State has decided under section 146(2) that no eligible public interest consideration is relevant and the reference is finally determined under paragraph (a) above (disregarding the fact that the notice was given);

(vii) the Secretary of State has decided under 146(2) that a public interest consideration is relevant but has decided under section 147(2) neither to accept an undertaking under section 159 nor to make an order under section 161; or

(viii) the Secretary of State has decided under section 146(2) that a public interest consideration is relevant and has accepted an undertaking under section 159 or made an order under section 161.

(4) For the purposes of this Part the time when a market investigation reference is finally determined is—

(a) in a case falling within subsection (3)(a)(i) or (b)(i), the expiry of the time concerned;

(b) in a case falling within subsection (3)(a)(ii) or (b)(iii), the publication of the report;

(c) in a case falling within subsection (3)(a)(iv) or (b)(viii), the acceptance of the undertaking concerned or (as the case may be) the making of the order concerned; and

(d) in any other case, the making of the decision or last decision concerned or the taking of the action concerned.

(5) The references in subsection (4) to subsections (3)(a)(i), (ii) and (iv) include those enactments as applied by subsection (3)(b)(ii), (iv), (v) or (vi).

(6) In subsection (4)(c) the reference to the acceptance of the undertaking concerned or the making of the order concerned shall, in a case where the enforcement action concerned involves the acceptance of a group of undertakings, the making of a group of orders or the acceptance and making of a group of undertakings and orders, be treated as a reference to the acceptance or making of the last undertaking or order in the group; but undertakings or orders which vary, supersede or revoke earlier undertakings or orders shall be disregarded for the purposes of subsections (3)(a)(iv) and (b)(viii) and (4)(c).

(7) Any duty to publish which is imposed on a person by this Part shall, unless the context otherwise requires, be construed as a duty on that person to publish in such manner as that person considers appropriate for the purpose of bringing the matter concerned to the attention of those likely to be affected by it.

[1926]

184 Index of defined expressions: Part 4

In this Part, the expressions listed in the left-hand column have the meaning given by, or are to be interpreted in accordance with, the provisions listed in the right-hand column.

Expression	Provision of this Act
Action (and the taking of action)	Section 183(1)
Adverse effect on competition	Section 134(2)
Appropriate Minister	Section 132(5)
Business	Section 183(1)
Change of circumstances	Section 183(1)
The Commission	Section 273
Consumer	Section 183(1)
Customer	Section 183(1)
Date of market investigation reference	Section 137(7)
Detrimental effect on customers	Section 134(5)
Enactment	Section 183(1)
Enforcement order	Section 162(8)
Enforcement undertaking	Section 162(8)

Expression	Provision of this Act
Feature of a market	Section 131(2)
Final determination of market investigation reference	Section 183(3) to (6)
Goods	Section 183(1)
Intervention notice	Section 139(3)
Market for goods or services	Section 131(6)
Market in the United Kingdom	Section 131(6)
Market investigation reference	Section 131(6)
Minister of the Crown	Section 183(1)
Modify	Section 183(1)
Notice	Section 183(1)
The OFT	Section 273
Public interest consideration	Section 139(5)
Public interest consideration being finalised	Section 139(7)
Publish	Section 183(7)
Relevant customer benefit	Section 134(8)
Relevant sectoral enactment	Section 136(7)
Relevant sectoral regulator	Section 136(8)
Reports of the Commission	Section 177(5)
Subordinate legislation	Section 183(1)
Supply (in relation to the supply of goods)	Section 183(1)
The supply of services (and a market for services etc)	Section 183(2)

[1927]

185–187   ((*Pt 5*) *s 185 introduces Sch 11 to this Act (amendments to the Competition Act 1998 relating to the constitution and powers of the Competition Commission); s 186 inserts the Competition Act 1998, Sch 7, para 12A at* **[1774]**; *s 187 amends s 45 of the 1998 Act at* **[1740]**, *inserts Sch 7, paras 19(5), 19A to that Act at* **[1775]**, *and introduces Sch 12 to this Act (insertion of the Competition Act 1998, Sch 7A at* **[1777]**).)

PART 6
CARTEL OFFENCE
Cartel offence

188   Cartel offence

(1)   An individual is guilty of an offence if he dishonestly agrees with one or more other persons to make or implement, or to cause to be made or implemented, arrangements of the following kind relating to at least two undertakings (A and B).

(2)   The arrangements must be ones which, if operating as the parties to the agreement intend, would—

(a)   directly or indirectly fix a price for the supply by A in the United Kingdom (otherwise than to B) of a product or service,

(b)   limit or prevent supply by A in the United Kingdom of a product or service,

(c)   limit or prevent production by A in the United Kingdom of a product,

(d)   divide between A and B the supply in the United Kingdom of a product or service to a customer or customers,

(e)   divide between A and B customers for the supply in the United Kingdom of a product or service, or

(f)   be bid-rigging arrangements.

(3)   Unless subsection (2)(d), (e) or (f) applies, the arrangements must also be ones which, if operating as the parties to the agreement intend, would—
-   (a)   directly or indirectly fix a price for the supply by B in the United Kingdom (otherwise than to A) of a product or service,
-   (b)   limit or prevent supply by B in the United Kingdom of a product or service, or
-   (c)   limit or prevent production by B in the United Kingdom of a product.

(4)   In subsections (2)(a) to (d) and (3), references to supply or production are to supply or production in the appropriate circumstances (for which see section 189).

(5)   "Bid-rigging arrangements" are arrangements under which, in response to a request for bids for the supply of a product or service in the United Kingdom, or for the production of a product in the United Kingdom—
-   (a)   A but not B may make a bid, or
-   (b)   A and B may each make a bid but, in one case or both, only a bid arrived at in accordance with the arrangements.

(6)   But arrangements are not bid-rigging arrangements if, under them, the person requesting bids would be informed of them at or before the time when a bid is made.

(7)   "Undertaking" has the same meaning as in Part 1 of the 1998 Act.

[1928]

189   Cartel offence: supplementary

(1)   For section 188(2)(a), the appropriate circumstances are that A's supply of the product or service would be at a level in the supply chain at which the product or service would at the same time be supplied by B in the United Kingdom.

(2)   For section 188(2)(b), the appropriate circumstances are that A's supply of the product or service would be at a level in the supply chain—
-   (a)   at which the product or service would at the same time be supplied by B in the United Kingdom, or
-   (b)   at which supply by B in the United Kingdom of the product or service would be limited or prevented by the arrangements.

(3)   For section 188(2)(c), the appropriate circumstances are that A's production of the product would be at a level in the production chain—
-   (a)   at which the product would at the same time be produced by B in the United Kingdom, or
-   (b)   at which production by B in the United Kingdom of the product would be limited or prevented by the arrangements.

(4)   For section 188(2)(d), the appropriate circumstances are that A's supply of the product or service would be at the same level in the supply chain as B's.

(5)   For section 188(3)(a), the appropriate circumstances are that B's supply of the product or service would be at a level in the supply chain at which the product or service would at the same time be supplied by A in the United Kingdom.

(6)   For section 188(3)(b), the appropriate circumstances are that B's supply of the product or service would be at a level in the supply chain—
-   (a)   at which the product or service would at the same time be supplied by A in the United Kingdom, or
-   (b)   at which supply by A in the United Kingdom of the product or service would be limited or prevented by the arrangements.

(7)   For section 188(3)(c), the appropriate circumstances are that B's production of the product would be at a level in the production chain—
-   (a)   at which the product would at the same time be produced by A in the United Kingdom, or
-   (b)   at which production by A in the United Kingdom of the product would be limited or prevented by the arrangements.

[1929]

190   Cartel offence: penalty and prosecution

(1)   A person guilty of an offence under section 188 is liable—
-   (a)   on conviction on indictment, to imprisonment for a term not exceeding five years or to a fine, or to both;
-   (b)   on summary conviction, to imprisonment for a term not exceeding six months or to a fine not exceeding the statutory maximum, or to both.

(2)   In England and Wales and Northern Ireland, proceedings for an offence under section 188 may be instituted only—
-   (a)   by the Director of the Serious Fraud Office, or
-   (b)   by or with the consent of the OFT.

(3)   No proceedings may be brought for an offence under section 188 in respect of an agreement outside the United Kingdom, unless it has been implemented in whole or in part in the United Kingdom.

(4)   Where, for the purpose of the investigation or prosecution of offences under section 188, the OFT gives a person written notice under this subsection, no proceedings for an offence under section 188 that falls within a description specified in the notice may be brought against that person in England and Wales or Northern Ireland except in circumstances specified in the notice.

[1930]–[1931]

191   (*Repealed by the Extradition Act 2003, ss 219(1), 220, Sch 3, paras 1, 14, Sch 4, except in relation to any request for extradition, whether made under the Extradition Act 1989 or the Backing of Warrants (Republic of Ireland) Act 1965 or otherwise, which is received by the relevant authority in the United Kingdom and an extradition made from or to the United Kingdom on or before 31 December 2003.*)

Criminal investigations by OFT

192   Investigation of offences under section 188

(1)   The OFT may conduct an investigation if there are reasonable grounds for suspecting that an offence under section 188 has been committed.

(2)   The powers of the OFT under sections 193 and 194 are exercisable, but only for the purposes of an investigation under subsection (1), in any case where it appears to the OFT that there is good reason to exercise them for the purpose of investigating the affairs, or any aspect of the affairs, of any person ("the person under investigation").

[1932]

193   Powers when conducting an investigation

(1)   The OFT may by notice in writing require the person under investigation, or any other person who it has reason to believe has relevant information, to answer questions, or otherwise provide information, with respect to any matter relevant to the investigation at a specified place and either at a specified time or forthwith.

(2)   The OFT may by notice in writing require the person under investigation, or any other person, to produce, at a specified place and either at a specified time or forthwith, specified documents, or documents of a specified description, which appear to the OFT to relate to any matter relevant to the investigation.

(3)   If any such documents are produced, the OFT may—
   (a)   take copies or extracts from them;
   (b)   require the person producing them to provide an explanation of any of them.

(4)   If any such documents are not produced, the OFT may require the person who was required to produce them to state, to the best of his knowledge and belief, where they are.

(5)   A notice under subsection (1) or (2) must indicate—
   (a)   the subject matter and purpose of the investigation; and
   (b)   the nature of the offences created by section 201.

[1933]

194   Power to enter premises under a warrant

(1)   On an application made by the OFT to the High Court, or, in Scotland, by the procurator fiscal to the sheriff, in accordance with rules of court, a judge or the sheriff may issue a warrant if he is satisfied that there are reasonable grounds for believing—
   (a)   that there are on any premises documents which the OFT has power under section 193 to require to be produced for the purposes of an investigation; and
   (b)   that—
      (i)   a person has failed to comply with a requirement under that section to produce the documents;
      (ii)   it is not practicable to serve a notice under that section in relation to them; or
      (iii)   the service of such a notice in relation to them might seriously prejudice the investigation.

(2)   A warrant under this section shall authorise a named officer of the OFT, and any other officers of the OFT whom the OFT has authorised in writing to accompany the named officer—
   (a)   to enter the premises, using such force as is reasonably necessary for the purpose;
   (b)   to search the premises and—
      (i)   take possession of any documents appearing to be of the relevant kind, or
      (ii)   take, in relation to any documents appearing to be of the relevant kind, any other steps which may appear to be necessary for preserving them or preventing interference with them;

    (c)   to require any person to provide an explanation of any document appearing to be of the relevant kind or to state, to the best of his knowledge and belief, where it may be found;

    (d)   to require any information which is stored in any electronic form and is accessible from the premises and which the named officer considers relates to any matter relevant to the investigation, to be produced in a form—

        (i)   in which it can be taken away, and

        (ii)   in which it is visible and legible or from which it can readily be produced in a visible and legible form.

(3)   Documents are of the relevant kind if they are of a kind in respect of which the application under subsection (1) was granted.

(4)   A warrant under this section may authorise persons specified in the warrant to accompany the named officer who is executing it.

(5)   …

[1934]

NOTES

Sub-s (5): inserts the Criminal Justice and Police Act 2001, Sch 1, Pt 1, para 73A.

---

195 Exercise of powers by authorised person

(1)   The OFT may authorise any competent person who is not an officer of the OFT to exercise on its behalf all or any of the powers conferred by section 193 or 194.

(2)   No such authority may be granted except for the purpose of investigating the affairs, or any aspect of the affairs, of a person specified in the authority.

(3)   No person is bound to comply with any requirement imposed by a person exercising powers by virtue of any authority granted under this section unless he has, if required to do so, produced evidence of his authority.

[1935]

196 Privileged information etc

(1)   A person may not under section 193 or 194 be required to disclose any information or produce any document which he would be entitled to refuse to disclose or produce on grounds of legal professional privilege in proceedings in the High Court, except that a lawyer may be required to provide the name and address of his client.

(2)   A person may not under section 193 or 194 be required to disclose any information or produce any document in respect of which he owes an obligation of confidence by virtue of carrying on any banking business unless—

    (a)   the person to whom the obligation of confidence is owed consents to the disclosure or production; or

    (b)   the OFT has authorised the making of the requirement.

(3)   In the application of this section to Scotland, the reference in subsection (1)—

    (a)   to proceedings in the High Court is to be read as a reference to legal proceedings generally; and

    (b)   to an entitlement on grounds of legal professional privilege is to be read as a reference to an entitlement by virtue of any rule of law whereby—

        (i)   communications between a professional legal adviser and his client, or

        (ii)   communications made in connection with or in contemplation of legal proceedings and for the purposes of those proceedings,

    are in such proceedings protected from disclosure on the ground of confidentiality.

[1936]

197 Restriction on use of statements in court

(1)   A statement by a person in response to a requirement imposed by virtue of section 193 or 194 may only be used in evidence against him—

    (a)   on a prosecution for an offence under section 201(2); or

    (b)   on a prosecution for some other offence where in giving evidence he makes a statement inconsistent with it.

(2)   However, the statement may not be used against that person by virtue of paragraph (b) of subsection (1) unless evidence relating to it is adduced, or a question relating to it is asked, by or on behalf of that person in the proceedings arising out of the prosecution.

[1937]

198–200   (*S 198 inserts the Competition Act 1998, s 30A at* **[1725]***; s 199 amends the Regulation of Investigatory Powers Act 2000, ss 32–37, 40, 46, 48; s 200 amends the Police Act 1997, ss 93, 94.*)

201 Offences

(1)   Any person who without reasonable excuse fails to comply with a requirement imposed on him under section 193 or 194 is guilty of an offence and liable on summary conviction to imprisonment for a term not exceeding six months or to a fine not exceeding level 5 on the standard scale or to both.

(2)   A person who, in purported compliance with a requirement under section 193 or 194—
  (a)   makes a statement which he knows to be false or misleading in a material particular; or
  (b)   recklessly makes a statement which is false or misleading in a material particular,
is guilty of an offence.

(3)   A person guilty of an offence under subsection (2) is liable—
  (a)   on conviction on indictment, to imprisonment for a term not exceeding two years or to a fine or to both; and
  (b)   on summary conviction, to imprisonment for a term not exceeding six months or to a fine not exceeding the statutory maximum, or to both.

(4)   Where any person—
  (a)   knows or suspects that an investigation by the Serious Fraud Office or the OFT into an offence under section 188 is being or is likely to be carried out; and
  (b)   falsifies, conceals, destroys or otherwise disposes of, or causes or permits the falsification, concealment, destruction or disposal of documents which he knows or suspects are or would be relevant to such an investigation,
he is guilty of an offence unless he proves that he had no intention of concealing the facts disclosed by the documents from the persons carrying out such an investigation.

(5)   A person guilty of an offence under subsection (4) is liable—
  (a)   on conviction on indictment, to imprisonment for a term not exceeding 5 years or to a fine or to both; and
  (b)   on summary conviction, to imprisonment for a term not exceeding six months or to a fine not exceeding the statutory maximum, or to both.

(6)   A person who intentionally obstructs a person in the exercise of his powers under a warrant issued under section 194 is guilty of an offence and liable—
  (a)   on conviction on indictment, to imprisonment for a term not exceeding 2 years or to a fine or to both; and
  (b)   on summary conviction, to a fine not exceeding the statutory maximum.

[1938]

202   Interpretation of sections 192 to 201

In sections 192 to 201—
  "documents" includes information recorded in any form and, in relation to information recorded otherwise than in a form in which it is visible and legible, references to its production include references to producing it in a form in which it is visible and legible or from which it can readily be produced in a visible and legible form;
  "person under investigation" has the meaning given in section 192(2).

[1939]

PART 7
MISCELLANEOUS COMPETITION PROVISIONS

203, 204   (*S 203 inserts the Competition Act 1998, ss 28(3A), 62(5A), 63(5A) at* **[1722]**, **[1759]**, **[1760]**; *s 204 outside the scope of this work.*)

Miscellaneous

205   Super-complaints to regulators other than OFT

(1)   The Secretary of State may by order provide that section 11 is to apply to complaints made to a specified regulator in relation to a market of a specified description as it applies to complaints made to the OFT, with such modifications as may be specified.

(2)   An order under this section—
  (a)   shall be made by statutory instrument, and
  (b)   shall be subject to annulment in pursuance of a resolution of either House of Parliament.

(3)   In this section—
  "regulator" has the meaning given in section 54(1) of the 1998 Act; and
  "specified" means specified in the order.

[1940]

NOTES

Orders: the Enterprise Act 2002 (Super-complaints to Regulators) Order 2003, SI 2003/1368; the Enterprise Act 2002 (Water Services Regulation Authority) Order 2006, SI 2006/522.

206 Power to modify Schedule 8

(1)   The Secretary of State may by order made by statutory instrument modify Schedule 8.

(2)   An order under this section may make—
    (a)   different provision for different cases or different purposes;
    (b)   such incidental, supplementary, consequential, transitory, transitional or saving provision as the Secretary of State considers appropriate.

(3)   An order under this section may, in particular, modify that Schedule in its application by virtue of Part 3 of this Act, in its application by virtue of Part 4 of this Act, in its application by virtue of any other enactment (whether by virtue of Part 4 of this Act as applied by that enactment or otherwise) or in its application by virtue of every enactment that applies it.

(4)   An order under this section as extended by subsection (2) may modify any enactment comprised in or made under this Act, or any other enactment.

(5)   No order shall be made under this section unless a draft of it has been laid before, and approved by a resolution of, each House of Parliament.

(6)   No modification of Schedule 8 in its application by virtue of Part 3 of this Act shall be made by an order under this section if the modification relates to a relevant merger situation or (as the case may be) a special merger situation which has been created before the coming into force of the order.

(7)   No modification shall be made by an order under this section of Schedule 8 in its application in relation to references made under section 22, 33, 45 or 62 before the coming into force of the order.

(8)   No modification shall be made by an order under this section of Schedule 8 in its application in relation to references made under section 131 or 132 before the coming into force of the order (including references made under section 131 as applied by another enactment).

(9)   Before making an order under this section, the Secretary of State shall consult the OFT and the Commission.

(10)   Expressions used in this section which are also used in Part 3 of this Act have the same meaning in this section as in that Part.

[1941]

207, 208   (*S 207 repeals the Competition Act 1998, s 3(1)(d), Sch 4; s 208 repeals the Fair Trading Act 1973, ss 78–80.*)

209   Reform of Community competition law

(1)   The Secretary of State may by regulations make such modifications of the 1998 Act as he considers appropriate for the purpose of eliminating or reducing any differences between—
    (a)   the domestic provisions of the 1998 Act, and
    (b)   European Community competition law,
which result (or would otherwise result) from a relevant Community instrument made after the passing of this Act.

(2)   In subsection (1)—
"the domestic provisions of the 1998 Act" means the provisions of the 1998 Act so far as they do not implement or give effect to a relevant Community instrument;
"European Community competition law" includes any Act or subordinate legislation so far as it implements or gives effect to a relevant Community instrument;
"relevant Community instrument" means a regulation or directive under Article 83 of the Treaty establishing the European Community.

(3)   The Secretary of State may by regulations repeal or otherwise modify any provision of an Act (other than the 1998 Act) which excludes any matter from the Chapter I prohibition or the Chapter II prohibition (within the meaning of Part 1 of the 1998 Act).

(4)   The power under subsection (3) may not be exercised—
    (a)   before the power under subsection (1) has been exercised; or
    (b)   so as to extend the scope of any exclusion that is not being removed by the regulations.

(5)   Regulations under this section may—
    (a)   confer power to make subordinate legislation;
    (b)   make such consequential, supplementary, incidental, transitory, transitional or saving provision as the Secretary of State considers appropriate (including provision modifying any Act or subordinate legislation); and
    (c)   make different provision for different cases or circumstances.

(6) The power to make regulations under this section is exercisable by statutory instrument.

(7) No regulations may be made under this section unless a draft of them has been laid before and approved by a resolution of each House of Parliament.

(8) Paragraph 1(1)(c) of Schedule 2 to the European Communities Act 1972 (c 68) (restriction on powers to legislate) shall not apply to regulations which implement or give effect to a relevant Community instrument made after the passing of this Act.

[1942]

PART 8
ENFORCEMENT OF CERTAIN CONSUMER LEGISLATION
Introduction

210 Consumers

(1) In this Part references to consumers must be construed in accordance with this section.

(2) In relation to a domestic infringement a consumer is an individual in respect of whom the first and second conditions are satisfied.

(3) The first condition is that—
  (a) goods are or are sought to be supplied to the individual (whether by way of sale or otherwise) in the course of a business carried on by the person supplying or seeking to supply them, or
  (b) services are or are sought to be supplied to the individual in the course of a business carried on by the person supplying or seeking to supply them.

(4) The second condition is that—
  (a) the individual receives or seeks to receive the goods or services otherwise than in the course of a business carried on by him, or
  (b) the individual receives or seeks to receive the goods or services with a view to carrying on a business but not in the course of a business carried on by him.

(5) For the purposes of a domestic infringement it is immaterial whether a person supplying goods or services has a place of business in the United Kingdom.

(6) In relation to a Community infringement a consumer is a person who is a consumer for the purposes of—
  (a) the Injunctions Directive, and
  (b) the listed Directive [or the listed Regulation] concerned.

(7) A Directive is a listed Directive—
  (a) if it is a Directive of the Council of the European Communities or of the European Parliament and of the Council, and
  (b) if it is specified in Schedule 13 or to the extent that any of its provisions is so specified.

[(7A) A Regulation is a listed Regulation—
  (a) if it is a Regulation of the Council of the European Communities or of the European Parliament and of the Council, and
  (b) if it is specified in Schedule 13 or to the extent that any of its provisions is so specified.]

(8) A business includes—
  (a) a professional practice;
  (b) any other undertaking carried on for gain or reward;
  (c) any undertaking in the course of which goods or services are supplied otherwise than free of charge.

(9) The Secretary of State may by order modify Schedule 13.

(10) An order under this section must be made by statutory instrument subject to annulment in pursuance of a resolution of either House of Parliament.

[1943]

NOTES

Sub-s (6): words in square brackets in para (b) inserted by the Enterprise Act 2002 (Amendment) Regulations 2006, SI 2006/3363, regs 3, 4.

Sub-s (7A): inserted by SI 2006/3363, regs 3, 5.

Order: the Enterprise Act 2002 (Part 8 Community Infringements Specified UK Laws) Order 2003, SI 2003/1374.

---

211 Domestic infringements

(1) In this Part a domestic infringement is an act or omission which—
  (a) is done or made by a person in the course of a business,
  (b) falls within subsection (2), and
  (c) harms the collective interests of consumers in the United Kingdom.

(2)   An act or omission falls within this subsection if it is of a description specified by the Secretary of State by order and consists of any of the following—

(a)   a contravention of an enactment which imposes a duty, prohibition or restriction enforceable by criminal proceedings;

(b)   an act done or omission made in breach of contract;

(c)   an act done or omission made in breach of a non-contractual duty owed to a person by virtue of an enactment or rule of law and enforceable by civil proceedings;

(d)   an act or omission in respect of which an enactment provides for a remedy or sanction enforceable by civil proceedings;

(e)   an act done or omission made by a person supplying or seeking to supply goods or services as a result of which an agreement or security relating to the supply is void or unenforceable to any extent;

(f)   an act or omission by which a person supplying or seeking to supply goods or services purports or attempts to exercise a right or remedy relating to the supply in circumstances where the exercise of the right or remedy is restricted or excluded under or by virtue of an enactment;

(g)   an act or omission by which a person supplying or seeking to supply goods or services purports or attempts to avoid (to any extent) liability relating to the supply in circumstances where such avoidance is restricted or prevented under an enactment.

(3)   But an order under this section may provide that any description of act or omission falling within subsection (2) is not a domestic infringement.

(4)   For the purposes of subsection (2) it is immaterial—

(a)   whether or not any duty, prohibition or restriction exists in relation to consumers as such;

(b)   whether or not any remedy or sanction is provided for the benefit of consumers as such;

(c)   whether or not any proceedings have been brought in relation to the act or omission;

(d)   whether or not any person has been convicted of an offence in respect of the contravention mentioned in subsection (2)(a);

(e)   whether or not there is a waiver in respect of the breach of contract mentioned in subsection (2)(b).

(5)   References to an enactment include references to subordinate legislation (within the meaning of the Interpretation Act 1978 (c 30)).

(6)   The power to make an order under this section must be exercised by statutory instrument.

(7)   But no such order may be made unless a draft of it has been laid before Parliament and approved by a resolution of each House.

[1944]

NOTES

Order: the Enterprise Act 2002 (Part 8 Domestic Infringements) Order 2003, SI 2003/1593.

212   Community infringements

(1)   In this Part a Community infringement is an act or omission which harms the collective interests of consumers and which—

(a)   contravenes a listed Directive as given effect by the laws, regulations or administrative provisions of an EEA State, ...

(b)   contravenes such laws, regulations or administrative provisions which provide additional permitted protections,

[(c)   contravenes a listed Regulation, or

(d)   contravenes any laws, regulations or administrative provisions of an EEA State which give effect to a listed Regulation.]

(2)   The laws, regulations or administrative provisions of an EEA State which give effect to a listed Directive provide additional permitted protections if—

(a)   they provide protection for consumers which is in addition to the minimum protection required by the Directive concerned, and

(b)   such additional protection is permitted by that Directive.

(3)   The Secretary of State may by order specify for the purposes of this section the law in the United Kingdom which—

(a)   gives effect to the listed Directives;

(b)   provides additional permitted protections[; or]

[(c)   gives effect to a listed Regulation].

(4)   References to a listed Directive [or to a listed Regulation] must be construed in accordance with section 210.

[(5)   EEA State has the meaning given by Schedule 1 to the Interpretation Act 1978.]

(6) An order under this section must be made by statutory instrument subject to annulment in pursuance of a resolution of either House of Parliament.

[1945]

NOTES
Sub-s (1): word omitted repealed and paras (c), (d) added by the Enterprise Act 2002 (Amendment) Regulations 2006, SI 2006/3363, regs 3, 6, 7.
Sub-s (3): para (c) and word "or" immediately preceding it added by SI 2006/3363, regs 3, 8.
Sub-s (4): words in square brackets inserted by SI 2006/3363, regs 3, 9.
Sub-s (5): substituted by the Enterprise Act 2002 (EEA State) (Amendment) Regulations 2007, SI 2007/528, reg 2.
Orders: the Enterprise Act 2002 (Part 8 Community Infringements Specified UK Laws) Order 2003, SI 2003/1374; the Enterprise Act 2002 (Part 8 Community Infringements Specified UK Laws) Order 2006, SI 2006/3372.

---

213 Enforcers

(1) Each of the following is a general enforcer—
   (a) the OFT;
   (b) every local weights and measures authority in Great Britain;
   (c) the Department of Enterprise, Trade and Investment in Northern Ireland.

(2) A designated enforcer is any person or body (whether or not incorporated) which the Secretary of State—
   (a) thinks has as one of its purposes the protection of the collective interests of consumers, and
   (b) designates by order.

(3) The Secretary of State may designate a public body only if he is satisfied that it is independent.

(4) The Secretary of State may designate a person or body which is not a public body only if the person or body (as the case may be) satisfies such criteria as the Secretary of State specifies by order.

(5) A Community enforcer is a qualified entity for the purposes of the Injunctions Directive—
   (a) which is for the time being specified in the list published in the Official Journal of the European Communities in pursuance of Article 4.3 of that Directive, but
   [(b) which is not a general enforcer, a designated enforcer or a CPC enforcer.]

[(5A) Each of the following (being bodies or persons designated by the Secretary of State under Article 4(1) or 4(2) of the CPC Regulation) is a CPC enforcer—
   (a) the OFT;
   (b) the Civil Aviation Authority;
   (c) the Financial Services Authority;
   (d) the Secretary of State for Health;
   (e) the Department of Health, Social Services and Public Safety in Northern Ireland;
   (f) the Office of Communications;
   (g) the Department of Enterprise, Trade and Investment in Northern Ireland;
   (h) every local weights and measures authority in Great Britain;
   (i) the Independent Committee for the Supervision of Standards of the Telephone Information Services.]

(6) An order under this section may designate an enforcer in respect of—
   (a) all infringements;
   (b) infringements of such descriptions as are specified in the order.

(7) An order under this section may make different provision for different purposes.

(8) The designation of a body by virtue of subsection (3) is conclusive evidence for the purposes of any question arising under this Part that the body is a public body.

(9) An order under this section must be made by statutory instrument subject to annulment in pursuance of a resolution of either House of Parliament.

(10) If requested to do so by a designated enforcer which is designated in respect of one or more Community infringements the Secretary of State must notify the Commission of the European Communities—
   (a) of its name and purpose;
   (b) of the Community infringements in respect of which it is designated.

(11) The Secretary of State must also notify the Commission—
   (a) of the fact that a person or body in respect of which he has given notice under subsection (10) ceases to be a designated enforcer;
   (b) of any change in the name or purpose of a designated enforcer in respect of which he has given such notice;

(c)   of any change to the Community infringements in respect of which a designated enforcer is designated.

[1946]

NOTES

Sub-s (5): para (b) substituted by the Enterprise Act 2002 (Amendment) Regulations 2006, SI 2006/3363, regs 3, 10.

Sub-s (5A): inserted by SI 2006/3363, regs 3, 11.

Orders: the Enterprise Act 2002 (Part 8 Designated Enforcers: Criteria for Designation, Designation of Public Bodies as Designated Enforcers and Transitional Provisions) Order 2003, SI 2003/1399; the Enterprise Act 2002 (Part 8) (Designation of the Financial Services Authority as a Designated Enforcer) Order 2004, SI 2004/935; the Enterprise Act 2002 (Part 8) (Designation of the Consumers' Association) Order 2005, SI 2005/917; the Enterprise Act 2002 (Water Services Regulation Authority) Order 2006, SI 2006/522.

Enforcement procedure

214 Consultation

(1)   An enforcer must not make an application for an enforcement order unless he has engaged in appropriate consultation with—

(a)   the person against whom the enforcement order would be made, and

(b)   the OFT (if it is not the enforcer).

(2)   Appropriate consultation is consultation for the purpose of—

(a)   achieving the cessation of the infringement in a case where an infringement is occurring;

(b)   ensuring that there will be no repetition of the infringement in a case where the infringement has occurred;

(c)   ensuring that there will be no repetition of the infringement in a case where the cessation of the infringement is achieved under paragraph (a);

(d)   ensuring that the infringement does not take place in the case of a Community infringement which the enforcer believes is likely to take place.

(3)   Subsection (1) does not apply if the OFT thinks that an application for an enforcement order should be made without delay.

(4)   Subsection (1) ceases to apply—

(a)   for the purposes of an application for an enforcement order at the end of the period of 14 days beginning with the day after the person against whom the enforcement order would be made receives a request for consultation from the enforcer;

(b)   for the purposes of an application for an interim enforcement order at the end of the period of seven days beginning with the day after the person against whom the interim enforcement order would be made receives a request for consultation from the enforcer.

(5)   The Secretary of State may by order make rules in relation to consultation under this section.

(6)   Such an order must be made by statutory instrument subject to annulment in pursuance of a resolution of either House of Parliament.

(7)   In this section (except subsection (4)) and in sections 215 and 216 references to an enforcement order include references to an interim enforcement order.

[1947]

NOTES

Order: the Enterprise Act 2002 (Part 8 Request for Consultation) Order 2003, SI 2003/1375.

215 Applications

(1)   An application for an enforcement order must name the person the enforcer thinks—

(a)   has engaged or is engaging in conduct which constitutes a domestic or a Community infringement, or

(b)   is likely to engage in conduct which constitutes a Community infringement.

(2)   A general enforcer may make an application for an enforcement order in respect of any infringement.

(3)   A designated enforcer may make an application for an enforcement order in respect of an infringement to which his designation relates.

(4)   A Community enforcer may make an application for an enforcement order in respect of a Community infringement.

[(4A)   A CPC enforcer may make an application for an enforcement order in respect of a Community infringement.]

(5)   The following courts have jurisdiction to make an enforcement order—

(a)   the High Court or a county court if the person against whom the order is sought carries on business or has a place of business in England and Wales or Northern Ireland;

   (b)   the Court of Session or the sheriff if the person against whom the order is sought carries
          on business or has a place of business in Scotland.

   (6)   If an application for an enforcement order is made by a Community enforcer the court may
examine whether the purpose of the enforcer justifies its making the application.

   (7)   If the court thinks that the purpose of the Community enforcer does not justify its making
the application the court may refuse the application on that ground alone.

   (8)   The purpose of a Community enforcer must be construed by reference to the Injunctions
Directive.

   (9)   An enforcer which is not the OFT must notify the OFT of the result of an application under
this section.

                                                                                    [1948]

NOTES

   Sub-s (4A): inserted by the Enterprise Act 2002 (Amendment) Regulations 2006, SI 2006/3363, regs 3, 12.

---

216   Applications: directions by OFT

   (1)   This section applies if the OFT believes that an enforcer other than the OFT intends to
apply for an enforcement order.

   (2)   In such a case the OFT may direct that if an application in respect of a particular
infringement is to be made it must be made—
   (a)   only by the OFT, or
   (b)   only by such other enforcer as the OFT directs.

   (3)   If the OFT directs that only it may make an application that does not prevent—
   (a)   the OFT or any enforcer from accepting an undertaking under section 219, or
   (b)   the OFT from taking such other steps it thinks appropriate (apart from making an
          application) for the purpose of securing that the infringement is not committed,
          continued or repeated.

   (4)   The OFT may vary or withdraw a direction given under this section.

   (5)   The OFT must take such steps as it thinks appropriate to bring a direction (or a variation or
withdrawal of a direction) to the attention of enforcers it thinks may be affected by it.

   (6)   But this section does not prevent an application for an enforcement order being made by a
Community enforcer.

                                                                                    [1949]

217   Enforcement orders

   (1)   This section applies if an application for an enforcement order is made under section 215
and the court finds that the person named in the application has engaged in conduct which
constitutes the infringement.

   (2)   This section also applies if such an application is made in relation to a Community
infringement and the court finds that the person named in the application is likely to engage in
conduct which constitutes the infringement.

   (3)   If this section applies the court may make an enforcement order against the person.

   (4)   In considering whether to make an enforcement order the court must have regard to whether
the person named in the application—
   (a)   has given an undertaking under section 219 in respect of conduct such as is mentioned in
          subsection (3) of that section;
   (b)   has failed to comply with the undertaking.

   (5)   An enforcement order must—
   (a)   indicate the nature of the conduct to which the finding under subsection (1) or (2)
          relates, and
   (b)   direct the person to comply with subsection (6).

   (6)   A person complies with this subsection if he—
   (a)   does not continue or repeat the conduct;
   (b)   does not engage in such conduct in the course of his business or another business;
   (c)   does not consent to or connive in the carrying out of such conduct by a body corporate
          with which he has a special relationship (within the meaning of section 222(3)).

   (7)   But subsection (6)(a) does not apply in the case of a finding under subsection (2).

   (8)   An enforcement order may require a person against whom the order is made to publish in
such form and manner and to such extent as the court thinks appropriate for the purpose of
eliminating any continuing effects of the infringement—
   (a)   the order;
   (b)   a corrective statement.

(9)   If the court makes a finding under subsection (1) or (2) it may accept an undertaking by the person—

    (a)   to comply with subsection (6), or

    (b)   to take steps which the court believes will secure that he complies with subsection (6).

(10)   An undertaking under subsection (9) may include a further undertaking by the person to publish in such form and manner and to such extent as the court thinks appropriate for the purpose of eliminating any continuing effects of the infringement—

    (a)   the terms of the undertaking;

    (b)   a corrective statement.

(11)   If the court—

    (a)   makes a finding under subsection (1) or (2), and

    (b)   accepts an undertaking under subsection (9),

it must not make an enforcement order in respect of the infringement to which the undertaking relates.

(12)   An enforcement order made by a court in one part of the United Kingdom has effect in any other part of the United Kingdom as if made by a court in that part.

[1950]

218   Interim enforcement order

(1)   The court may make an interim enforcement order against a person named in the application for the order if it appears to the court—

    (a)   that it is alleged that the person is engaged in conduct which constitutes a domestic or Community infringement or is likely to engage in conduct which constitutes a Community infringement,

    (b)   that if the application had been an application for an enforcement order it would be likely to be granted,

    (c)   that it is expedient that the conduct is prohibited or prevented (as the case may be) immediately, and

    (d)   if no notice of the application has been given to the person named in the application that it is appropriate to make an interim enforcement order without notice.

(2)   An interim enforcement order must—

    (a)   indicate the nature of the alleged conduct, and

    (b)   direct the person to comply with subsection (3).

(3)   A person complies with this subsection if he—

    (a)   does not continue or repeat the conduct;

    (b)   does not engage in such conduct in the course of his business or another business;

    (c)   does not consent to or connive in the carrying out of such conduct by a body corporate with which he has a special relationship (within the meaning of section 222(3)).

(4)   But subsection (3)(a) does not apply in so far as the application is made in respect of an allegation that the person is likely to engage in conduct which constitutes a Community infringement.

(5)   An application for an interim enforcement order against a person may be made at any time before an application for an enforcement order against the person in respect of the same conduct is determined.

(6)   An application for an interim enforcement order must refer to all matters—

    (a)   which are known to the applicant, and

    (b)   which are material to the question whether or not the application is granted.

(7)   If an application for an interim enforcement order is made without notice the application must state why no notice has been given.

(8)   The court may vary or discharge an interim enforcement order on the application of—

    (a)   the enforcer who applied for the order;

    (b)   the person against whom it is made.

(9)   An interim enforcement order against a person is discharged on the determination of an application for an enforcement order made against the person in respect of the same conduct.

(10)   If it appears to the court as mentioned in subsection (1)(a) to (c) the court may instead of making an interim enforcement order accept an undertaking from the person named in the application—

    (a)   to comply with subsection (3), or

    (b)   to take steps which the court believes will secure that he complies with subsection (3).

(11)   An interim enforcement order made by a court in one part of the United Kingdom has effect in any other part of the United Kingdom as if made by a court in that part.

[1951]

[218A Unfair commercial practices: substantiation of claims

(1) This section applies where an application for an enforcement order or for an interim enforcement order is made in respect of a Community infringement involving a contravention of Directive 2005/29/EC of the European Parliament and of the Council of 11 May 2005 concerning unfair business-to-consumer commercial practices in the internal market.

(2) For the purposes of considering the application the court may require the person named in the application to provide evidence as to the accuracy of any factual claim made as part of a commercial practice of that person if, taking into account the legitimate interests of that person and any other party to the proceedings, it appears appropriate in the circumstances.

(3) If, having been required under subsection (2) to provide evidence as to the accuracy of a factual claim, a person—

    (a)   fails to provide such evidence, or

    (b)   provides evidence as to the accuracy of the factual claim that the court considers inadequate,

the court may consider that the factual claim is inaccurate.

(4) In this section "commercial practice" has the meaning given by regulation 2 of the Consumer Protection from Unfair Trading Regulations 2008.]

[1951A]

NOTES

Commencement: 26 May 2008.

Inserted by the Consumer Protection from Unfair Trading Regulations 2008, SI 2008/1277, reg 27.

219 Undertakings

(1) This section applies if an enforcer has power to make an application under section 215.

(2) In such a case the enforcer may accept from a person to whom subsection (3) applies an undertaking that the person will comply with subsection (4).

(3) This subsection applies to a person who the enforcer believes—

    (a)   has engaged in conduct which constitutes an infringement;

    (b)   is engaging in such conduct;

    (c)   is likely to engage in conduct which constitutes a Community infringement.

(4) A person complies with this subsection if he—

    (a)   does not continue or repeat the conduct;

    (b)   does not engage in such conduct in the course of his business or another business;

    (c)   does not consent to or connive in the carrying out of such conduct by a body corporate with which he has a special relationship (within the meaning of section 222(3)).

(5) But subsection (4)(a) does not apply in the case of an undertaking given by a person in so far as subsection (3) applies to him by virtue of paragraph (c).

[(5A) A CPC enforcer who has accepted an undertaking under this section may—

    (a)   accept a further undertaking from the person concerned to publish the terms of the undertaking; or

    (b)   take steps itself to publish the undertaking.

(5B) In each case the undertaking shall be published in such form and manner and to such extent as the CPC enforcer thinks appropriate for the purpose of eliminating any continuing effects of the Community infringement.]

(6) If an enforcer accepts an undertaking under this section it must notify the OFT—

    (a)   of the terms of the undertaking;

    (b)   of the identity of the person who gave it.

[1952]

NOTES

Sub-ss (5A), (5B): inserted by the Enterprise Act 2002 (Amendment) Regulations 2006, SI 2006/3363, regs 3, 13.

220 Further proceedings

(1) This section applies if the court—

    (a)   makes an enforcement order under section 217,

    (b)   makes an interim enforcement order under section 218, or

    (c)   accepts an undertaking under either of those sections.

(2) In such a case the OFT has the same right to apply to the court in respect of a failure to comply with the order or undertaking as the enforcer who made the application for the order.

(3) An application to the court in respect of a failure to comply with an undertaking may include an application for an enforcement order or for an interim enforcement order.

(4)   If the court finds that an undertaking is not being complied with it may make an enforcement order or an interim enforcement order (instead of making any other order it has power to make).

(5)   In the case of an application for an enforcement order or for an interim enforcement order as mentioned in subsection (3) sections 214 and 216 must be ignored and sections 215 and 217 or 218 (as the case may be) apply subject to the following modifications—

    (a)   section 215(1)(b) must be ignored;

    (b)   section 215(5) must be ignored and the application must be made to the court which accepted the undertaking;

    (c)   section 217(9) to (11) must be ignored;

    (d)   section 218(10) must be ignored.

(6)   If an enforcer which is not the OFT makes an application in respect of the failure of a person to comply with an enforcement order, an interim enforcement order or an undertaking given under section 217 or 218 the enforcer must notify the OFT—

    (a)   of the application;

    (b)   of any order made by the court on the application.

[1953]

221   Community infringements: proceedings

(1)   Subsection (2) applies to—

    (a)   every general enforcer;

    (b)   every designated enforcer which is a public body.

(2)   An enforcer to which this subsection applies has power to take proceedings in EEA States other than the United Kingdom for the cessation or prohibition of a Community infringement.

(3)   Subsection (4) applies to—

    (a)   every general enforcer;

    (b)   every designated enforcer;

    [(c)   every CPC enforcer.]

(4)   An enforcer to which this subsection applies may co-operate with a Community enforcer—

    (a)   for the purpose of bringing proceedings mentioned in subsection (2);

    (b)   in connection with the exercise by the Community enforcer of its functions under this Part.

(5)   An EEA State is a State which is a contracting party to the Agreement on the European Economic Area signed at Oporto on 2nd May 1992 as adjusted by the Protocol signed at Brussels on 17th March 1993.

[1954]

NOTES

Sub-s (3): para (c) added by the Enterprise Act 2002 (Amendment) Regulations 2006, SI 2006/3363, regs 3, 14.

222   Bodies corporate: accessories

(1)   This section applies if the person whose conduct constitutes a domestic infringement or a Community infringement is a body corporate.

(2)   If the conduct takes place with the consent or connivance of a person (an accessory) who has a special relationship with the body corporate, the consent or connivance is also conduct which constitutes the infringement.

(3)   A person has a special relationship with a body corporate if he is—

    (a)   a controller of the body corporate, or

    (b)   a director, manager, secretary or other similar officer of the body corporate or a person purporting to act in such a capacity.

(4)   A person is a controller of a body corporate if—

    (a)   the directors of the body corporate or of another body corporate which is its controller are accustomed to act in accordance with the person's directions or instructions, or

    (b)   either alone or with an associate or associates he is entitled to exercise or control the exercise of one third or more of the voting power at any general meeting of the body corporate or of another body corporate which is its controller.

(5)   An enforcement order or an interim enforcement order may be made against an accessory in respect of an infringement whether or not such an order is made against the body corporate.

(6)   The court may accept an undertaking under section 217(9) or 218(10) from an accessory in respect of an infringement whether or not it accepts such an undertaking from the body corporate.

(7)   An enforcer may accept an undertaking under section 219 from an accessory in respect of an infringement whether or not it accepts such an undertaking from the body corporate.

(8)   Subsection (9) applies if—
  (a)   an order is made as mentioned in subsection (5), or
  (b)   an undertaking is accepted as mentioned in subsection (6) or (7).

(9)   In such a case for subsection (6) of section 217, subsection (3) of section 218 or subsection (4) of section 219 (as the case may be) there is substituted the following subsection—

"( )   A person complies with this subsection if he—
  (a)   does not continue or repeat the conduct;
  (b)   does not in the course of any business carried on by him engage in conduct such as that which constitutes the infringement committed by the body corporate mentioned in section 222(1);
  (c)   does not consent to or connive in the carrying out of such conduct by another body corporate with which he has a special relationship (within the meaning of section 222(3))."

(10)   A person is an associate of an individual if—
  (a)   he is the spouse [or civil partner] of the individual;
  (b)   he is a relative of the individual;
  (c)   he is a relative of the individual's spouse [or civil partner];
  (d)   he is the spouse [or civil partner] of a relative of the individual;
  (e)   he is the spouse [or civil partner] of a relative of the individual's spouse [or civil partner];
  (f)   he lives in the same household as the individual otherwise than merely because he or the individual is the other's employer, tenant, lodger or boarder;
  (g)   he is a relative of a person who is an associate of the individual by virtue of paragraph (f);
  (h)   he has at some time in the past fallen within any of paragraphs (a) to (g).

(11)   A person is also an associate of—
  (a)   an individual with whom he is in partnership;
  (b)   an individual who is an associate of the individual mentioned in paragraph (a);
  (c)   a body corporate if he is a controller of it or he is an associate of a person who is a controller of the body corporate.

(12)   A body corporate is an associate of another body corporate if—
  (a)   the same person is a controller of both;
  (b)   a person is a controller of one and persons who are his associates are controllers of the other;
  (c)   a person is a controller of one and he and persons who are his associates are controllers of the other;
  (d)   a group of two or more persons is a controller of each company and the groups consist of the same persons;
  (e)   a group of two or more persons is a controller of each company and the groups may be regarded as consisting of the same persons by treating (in one or more cases) a member of either group as replaced by a person of whom he is an associate.

(13)   A relative is a brother, sister, uncle, aunt, nephew, niece, lineal ancestor or lineal descendant.

[1955]

NOTES
  Sub-s (10): words in square brackets inserted by the Civil Partnership Act 2004, s 261(1), Sch 27, para 169.

223   Bodies corporate: orders

(1)   This section applies if a court makes an enforcement order or an interim enforcement order against a body corporate and—
  (a)   at the time the order is made the body corporate is a member of a group of interconnected bodies corporate,
  (b)   at any time when the order is in force the body corporate becomes a member of a group of interconnected bodies corporate, or
  (c)   at any time when the order is in force a group of interconnected bodies corporate of which the body corporate is a member is increased by the addition of one or more further members.

(2)   The court may direct that the order is binding upon all of the members of the group as if each of them were the body corporate against which the order is made.

(3)   A group of interconnected bodies corporate is a group consisting of two or more bodies corporate all of whom are interconnected with each other.

(4)   Any two bodies corporate are interconnected—
  (a)   if one of them is a subsidiary of the other, or

(b)   if both of them are subsidiaries of the same body corporate.

[(5)   In this section "subsidiary" has the meaning given by section 1159 of the Companies Act 2006.]

[1956]

NOTES
Sub-s (5): substituted by the Companies Act 2006 (Consequential Amendments, Transitional Provisions and Savings) Order 2009, SI 2009/1941, art 2(1), Sch 1, para 199(1), (4).

Information

224   OFT

(1)   The OFT may for any of the purposes mentioned in subsection (2) give notice to any person requiring the person to provide it with the information specified in the notice.

(2)   The purposes are—
    (a)   to enable the OFT to exercise or to consider whether to exercise any function it has under this Part;
    (b)   to enable a designated enforcer to which section 225 does not apply to consider whether to exercise any function it has under this Part;
    (c)   to enable a Community enforcer to consider whether to exercise any function it has under this Part;
    (d)   to ascertain whether a person has complied with or is complying with an enforcement order, an interim enforcement order or an undertaking given under section 217(9), 218(10) or 219.

[1957]

225   Other enforcers

(1)   This section applies to—
    (a)   every general enforcer (other than the OFT);
    (b)   every designated enforcer which is a public body;
    [(c)   every CPC enforcer (other than the OFT).]

(2)   An enforcer to which this section applies may for any of the purposes mentioned in subsection (3) give notice to any person requiring the person to provide the enforcer with the information specified in the notice.

(3)   The purposes are—
    (a)   to enable the enforcer to exercise or to consider whether to exercise any function it has under this Part;
    (b)   to ascertain whether a person has complied with or is complying with an enforcement order or an interim enforcement order made on the application of the enforcer or an undertaking given under section 217(9) or 218(10) (as the case may be) following such an application or an undertaking given to the enforcer under section 219.

[1958]

NOTES
Sub-s (1): para (c) added by the Enterprise Act 2002 (Amendment) Regulations 2006, SI 2006/3363, regs 3, 15.

226   Notices: procedure

(1)   This section applies to a notice given under section 224 or 225.

(2)   The notice must—
    (a)   be in writing;
    (b)   specify the purpose for which the information is required.

(3)   If the purpose is as mentioned in section 224(2)(a), (b) or (c) or 225(3)(a) the notice must specify the function concerned.

(4)   A notice may specify the time within which and manner in which it is to be complied with.

(5)   A notice may require the production of documents or any description of documents.

(6)   An enforcer may take copies of any documents produced in compliance with such a requirement.

[(6A)   A notice may specify the form in which information is to be provided.]

(7)   A notice may be varied or revoked by a subsequent notice.

(8)   But a notice must not require a person to provide any information or produce any document which he would be entitled to refuse to provide or produce—
    (a)   in proceedings in the High Court on the grounds of legal professional privilege;

(b)   in proceedings in the Court of Session on the grounds of confidentiality of communications.

[1959]

NOTES

Sub-s (6A): inserted by the Enterprise Act 2002 (Amendment) Regulations 2006, SI 2006/3363, regs 3, 16.

227   Notices: enforcement

(1)   If a person fails to comply with a notice given under section 224 or 225 the enforcer who gave the notice may make an application under this section.

(2)   If it appears to the court that the person to whom the notice was given has failed to comply with the notice the court may make an order under this section.

(3)   An order under this section may require the person to whom the notice was given to do anything the court thinks it is reasonable for him to do for any of the purposes mentioned in section 224 or 225 (as the case may be) to ensure that the notice is complied with.

(4)   An order under this section may require the person to meet all the costs or expenses of the application.

(5)   If the person is a company or association the court in proceeding under subsection (4) may require any officer of the company or association who is responsible for the failure to meet the costs or expenses.

(6)   The court is a court which may make an enforcement order.

(7)   In subsection (5) an officer of a company is a person who is a director, manager, secretary or other similar officer of the company.

[1960]

[227A   Power to enter premises without warrant

(1)   An officer of a CPC enforcer who reasonably suspects that there has been, or is likely to be, a Community infringement may for any purpose relating to the functions of the CPC enforcer under this Part enter any premises to investigate whether there has been, or is likely to be, such an infringement.

(2)   An officer of a CPC enforcer who reasonably suspects that there is, or has been, a failure to comply with a relevant enforcement measure may for any purpose relating to the functions of the CPC enforcer under this Part enter any premises to investigate whether a person is complying with, or has complied with, the relevant enforcement measure.

(3)   An appropriate notice must be given to the occupier of the premises before an officer of a CPC enforcer enters them under subsection (1) and (2).

(4)   An appropriate notice is a notice in writing given by an officer of a CPC enforcer which—
  (a)   gives at least two working days' notice of entry on the premises;
  (b)   sets out why the entry is necessary; and
  (c)   indicates the nature of the offence created by section 227E.

(5)   Subsection (3) does not apply if such a notice cannot be given despite all reasonably practicable steps having been taken to do so.

(6)   In that case, the officer entering the premises must produce to any occupier that he finds on the premises a document setting out why the entry is necessary and indicating the nature of the offence created by section 227E.

(7)   In all cases, the officer entering the premises must produce to any occupier evidence of—
  (a)   his identity; and
  (b)   in the case of an authorised officer of a CPC enforcer, his authorisation;
if asked to do so.

(8)   In this section—
  "give", in relation to the giving of a notice to the occupier of premises, includes delivering or leaving it at the premises or sending it there by post; and
  "working day" means a day which is not—
    (a)   Saturday or Sunday; or
    (b)   Christmas Day, Good Friday or a day which is a bank holiday under the Banking and Financial Dealings Act 1971 in the part of the United Kingdom in which the premises are situated.

(9)   In this section and sections 227B to 227F—
  "authorised officer of a CPC enforcer" means an officer of a CPC enforcer who is authorised by that enforcer for the purposes of this Part;
  "occupier" means any person whom the officer concerned reasonably suspects to be the occupier;

"officer of a CPC enforcer" means—
    (a)   an officer of a local weights and measures authority in Great Britain; or
    (b)   an authorised officer of a CPC enforcer which is not a local weights and measures authority in Great Britain;
"premises" includes vehicles but does not include any premises which are used only as a dwelling; and
"relevant enforcement measure" means—
    (a)   an enforcement order made under section 217 on the application of the CPC enforcer;
    (b)   an interim enforcement order made under section 218 on the application of the CPC enforcer;
    (c)   an undertaking under section 217(9) in connection with an application made by the CPC enforcer for an enforcement order under section 217;
    (d)   an undertaking under section 218(10) in connection with an application made by the CPC enforcer for an interim enforcement order under section 218; or
    (e)   an undertaking under section 219 to the CPC enforcer.]

[1960A]

NOTES
Commencement: 8 January 2007.
Inserted, together with ss 227B–227F, by the Enterprise Act 2002 (Amendment) Regulations 2006, SI 2006/3363, regs 3, 17.

[227B   Powers exercisable on the premises

    (1)   An officer of a CPC enforcer may, in the exercise of his powers under section 227A—
    (a)   observe the carrying on of a business on the premises;
    (b)   inspect goods or documents on the premises;
    (c)   require any person on the premises to produce goods or documents within such period as the officer considers to be reasonable;
    (d)   seize goods or documents to carry out tests on them on the premises or seize, remove and retain them to carry out tests on them elsewhere; or
    (e)   seize, remove and retain goods or documents which he reasonably suspects may be required as evidence of a Community infringement or a breach of a relevant enforcement measure.

    (2)   The power in subsection (1)(c) to require a person to produce goods or documents includes the power to require him—
    (a)   to state, to the best of his knowledge and belief, where the goods or documents are;
    (b)   to give an explanation of the goods or documents; and
    (c)   to secure that any goods or documents produced are authenticated or verified in such manner as the officer considers appropriate.

    (3)   An officer of a CPC enforcer may take copies of, or extracts from, any documents to which he has access by virtue of subsection (1).

    (4)   But nothing in this section authorises action to be taken in relation to anything which, in proceedings in the High Court, a person would be entitled to refuse to produce on the grounds of legal professional privilege.

    (5)   In this section document includes information recorded in any form.

    (6)   The reference in subsection (1)(c) to the production of documents is, in the case of a document which contains information recorded otherwise than in legible form, a reference to the production of a copy of the information in legible form.

    (7)   *(Applies to Scotland only.)*]

[1960B]

NOTES
Commencement: 8 January 2007.
Inserted as noted to s 227A at **[1960A]**.

[227C   Power to enter premises with warrant

    (1)   A justice of the peace may issue a warrant authorising an officer of a CPC enforcer to enter premises for purposes falling within section 227A(1) or (2) if the justice of the peace considers that there are reasonable grounds for believing that—
    (a)   condition A is met; and
    (b)   either condition B, C or D is met.

    (2)   Condition A is that there are, on the premises, goods or documents to which an officer of a CPC enforcer would be entitled to have access under sections 227A and 227B.

(3)   Condition B is that an officer of a CPC enforcer acting under sections 227A and 227B has been, or would be likely to be, refused admission to the premises or access to the goods or documents.

(4)   Condition C is that the goods or documents would be likely to be concealed or interfered with if an appropriate notice were given under section 227A.

(5)   Condition D is that there is likely to be nobody at the premises capable of granting admission.

(6)   A warrant under this section authorises the officer of the CPC enforcer—
- (a)   to enter the premises specified in the warrant (using reasonable force if necessary);
- (b)   to do anything on the premises that an officer of the CPC enforcer would be able to do if he had entered the premises under section 227A;
- (c)   to search for goods or documents which he has required a person on the premises to produce where that person has failed to comply with such a requirement;
- (d)   to the extent that it is reasonably necessary to do so, to require any person to whom subsection (7) applies to break open a container and, if that person does not comply with the requirement, or if such a person cannot be identified after all reasonably practicable steps have been taken to identify such a person, to do so himself;
- (e)   to take any other steps which he considers to be reasonably necessary to preserve, or prevent interference with, goods or documents to which he would be entitled to have access under sections 227A and 227B.

(7)   This subsection applies to a person who is responsible for discharging any of the functions of the business being carried on at the premises under inspection.

(8)   A warrant under this section—
- (a)   is issued on information on oath given by an officer of a CPC enforcer;
- (b)   ceases to have effect at the end of the period of one month beginning with the day of issue; and
- (c)   must, on request, be produced to the occupier of the premises for inspection.

(9)   Any reference in this section to goods or documents being interfered with includes a reference to them being destroyed.

(10)   (*Applies to Scotland only.*)

(11)   In its application to Northern Ireland, this section has effect as if the references in subsection (1) to a justice of the peace were references to a lay magistrate.]

[1960C]

NOTES
Commencement: 8 January 2007.
Inserted as noted to s 227A at **[1960A]**.

[227D   Ancillary provisions about powers of entry

(1)   An officer of a CPC enforcer who enters premises by virtue of section 227A may only do so at a reasonable time.

(2)   An officer of a CPC enforcer who enters premises by virtue of section 227A or 227C may take with him such persons and equipment as he considers appropriate.

(3)   An officer of a CPC enforcer who enters premises by virtue of section 227A or 227C must, if the premises are unoccupied or the occupier is temporarily absent, take reasonable steps to ensure that when he leaves the premises they are as secure as they were before he entered.]

[1960D]

NOTES
Commencement: 8 January 2007.
Inserted as noted to s 227A at **[1960A]**.

[227E   Obstructing, or failing to co-operate with, powers of entry

(1)   A person commits an offence if, without reasonable excuse, he intentionally obstructs, or fails to co-operate with, an officer of a CPC enforcer who is exercising or seeking to exercise a power under sections 227A to 227D.

(2)   A person guilty of an offence under subsection (1) is liable, on summary conviction, to a fine not exceeding level 5 on the standard scale.]

[1960E]

NOTES
Commencement: 8 January 2007.
Inserted as noted to s 227A at **[1960A]**.

[227F Retention of documents and goods

(1)   No documents seized under sections 227A to 227D may be retained for a period of more than three months.

(2)   No goods seized under sections 227A to 227D may be retained for a period of more than three months unless they are reasonably required in connection with the exercise of any function of a CPC enforcer under this Part.

(3)   Where goods are so required they may be retained for as long as they are so required.]

[1960F]

NOTES
Commencement: 8 January 2007.
Inserted as noted to s 227A at **[1960A]**.

Miscellaneous

228 Evidence

(1)   Proceedings under this Part are civil proceedings for the purposes of—
(a)   section 11 of the Civil Evidence Act 1968 (c 64) (convictions admissible as evidence in civil proceedings);
(b)   section 10 of the Law Reform (Miscellaneous Provisions) (Scotland) Act 1968 (c 70) (corresponding provision in Scotland);
(c)   section 7 of the Civil Evidence Act (Northern Ireland) 1971 (c 36 (NI)) (corresponding provision in Northern Ireland).

(2)   In proceedings under this Part any finding by a court in civil proceedings that an act or omission mentioned in section 211(2)(b), (c) or (d) or 212(1) has occurred—
(a)   is admissible as evidence that the act or omission occurred;
(b)   unless the contrary is proved, is sufficient evidence that the act or omission occurred.

(3)   But subsection (2) does not apply to any finding—
(a)   which has been reversed on appeal;
(b)   which has been varied on appeal so as to negative it.

[(4)   This section does not apply to proceedings for an offence under section 227E.]

[1961]

NOTES
Sub-s (4): added by the Enterprise Act 2002 (Amendment) Regulations 2006, SI 2006/3363, regs 3, 18.

229 Advice and information

(1)   As soon as is reasonably practicable after the passing of this Act the OFT must prepare and publish advice and information with a view to—
(a)   explaining the provisions of this Part to persons who are likely to be affected by them, and
(b)   indicating how the OFT expects such provisions to operate.

(2)   The OFT may at any time publish revised or new advice or information.

(3)   Advice or information published in pursuance of subsection (1)(b) may include advice or information about the factors which the OFT may take into account in considering how to exercise the functions conferred on it by this Part.

(4)   Advice or information published by the OFT under this section is to be published in such form and in such manner as it considers appropriate.

(5)   In preparing advice or information under this section the OFT must consult such persons as it thinks are representative of persons affected by this Part.

(6)   If any proposed advice or information relates to a matter in respect of which another general [or CPC] enforcer or a designated enforcer may act the persons to be consulted must include that enforcer.

[1962]

NOTES
Sub-s (6): words in square brackets inserted by the Enterprise Act 2002 (Amendment) Regulations 2006, SI 2006/3363, regs 3, 19.

230 Notice to OFT of intended prosecution

(1)   This section applies if a local weights and measures authority in England and Wales intends to start proceedings for an offence under an enactment or subordinate legislation specified by the Secretary of State by order for the purposes of this section.

(2) The authority must give the OFT—
  (a) notice of its intention to start the proceedings;
  (b) a summary of the evidence it intends to lead in respect of the charges.

(3) The authority must not start the proceedings until whichever is the earlier of the following—
  (a) the end of the period of 14 days starting with the day on which the authority gives the notice;
  (b) the day on which it is notified by the OFT that the OFT has received the notice and summary given under subsection (2).

(4) The authority must also notify the OFT of the outcome of the proceedings after they are finally determined.

(5) But such proceedings are not invalid by reason only of the failure of the authority to comply with this section.

(6) Subordinate legislation has the same meaning as in section 21(1) of the Interpretation Act 1978 (c 30).

(7) An order under this section must be made by statutory instrument subject to annulment in pursuance of a resolution of either House of Parliament.

[1963]

NOTES

Orders: the Enterprise Act 2002 (Part 8 Notice to OFT of Intended Prosecution Specified Enactments, Revocation and Transitional Provision) Order 2003, SI 2003/1376; the Enterprise Act 2002 (Part 8 Notice to OFT of Intended Prosecution Specified Enactments) Order 2006, SI 2006/3371.

231 Notice of convictions and judgments to OFT

(1) This section applies if—
  (a) a person is convicted of an offence by or before a court in the United Kingdom, or
  (b) a judgment is given against a person by a court in civil proceedings in the United Kingdom.

(2) The court may make arrangements to bring the conviction or judgment to the attention of the OFT if it appears to the court—
  (a) having regard to the functions of the OFT under this Part or under the Estate Agents Act 1979 (c 38) that it is expedient for the conviction or judgment to be brought to the attention of the OFT, and
  (b) without such arrangements the conviction or judgment may not be brought to the attention of the OFT.

(3) For the purposes of subsection (2) it is immaterial that the proceedings have been finally disposed of by the court.

(4) Judgment includes an order or decree and references to the giving of the judgment must be construed accordingly.

[1964]

Interpretation

232 Goods and services

(1) References in this Part to goods and services must be construed in accordance with this section.

(2) Goods include—
  (a) buildings and other structures;
  (b) ships, aircraft and hovercraft.

(3) The supply of goods includes—
  (a) supply by way of sale, lease, hire or hire purchase;
  (b) in relation to buildings and other structures, construction of them by one person for another.

(4) Goods or services which are supplied wholly or partly outside the United Kingdom must be taken to be supplied to or for a person in the United Kingdom if they are supplied in accordance with arrangements falling within subsection (5).

(5) Arrangements fall within this subsection if they are made by any means and—
  (a) at the time the arrangements are made the person seeking the supply is in the United Kingdom, or
  (b) at the time the goods or services are supplied (or ought to be supplied in accordance with the arrangements) the person responsible under the arrangements for effecting the supply is in or has a place of business in the United Kingdom.

[1965]

233 Person supplying goods

(1) This section has effect for the purpose of references in this Part to a person supplying or seeking to supply goods under—

    (a)   a hire-purchase agreement;

    (b)   a credit-sale agreement;

    (c)   a conditional sale agreement.

(2) The references include references to a person who conducts any antecedent negotiations relating to the agreement.

(3) The following expressions must be construed in accordance with section 189 of the Consumer Credit Act 1974 (c 39)—

    (a)   hire-purchase agreement;

    (b)   credit-sale agreement;

    (c)   conditional sale agreement;

    (d)   antecedent negotiations.

[1966]

234 Supply of services

(1) References in this Part to the supply of services must be construed in accordance with this section.

(2) The supply of services does not include the provision of services under a contract of service or of apprenticeship whether it is express or implied and (if it is express) whether it is oral or in writing.

(3) The supply of services includes—

    (a)   performing for gain or reward any activity other than the supply of goods;

    (b)   rendering services to order;

    (c)   the provision of services by making them available to potential users.

(4) The supply of services includes making arrangements for the use of computer software or for granting access to data stored in any form which is not readily accessible.

(5) The supply of services includes making arrangements by means of a relevant agreement (within the meaning of [paragraph 29 of Schedule 2 to the Telecommunications Act 1984]) for sharing the use of telecommunications apparatus.

(6) The supply of services includes permitting or making arrangements to permit the use of land in such circumstances as the Secretary of State specifies by order.

(7) The power to make an order under subsection (6) must be exercised by statutory instrument.

(8) But no such order may be made unless a draft of it has been laid before Parliament and approved by a resolution of each House.

[1967]

NOTES

Sub-s (5): words in square brackets substituted by the Communications Act 2003, s 406(1), Sch 17, para 174(1), (6).

Order: the Enterprise Act 2002 (Supply of Services) Order 2003, SI 2003/1594.

235 Injunctions Directive

In this Part the Injunctions Directive is Directive 98/27/EC of the European Parliament and of the Council on injunctions for the protection of consumers' interests.

[1968]

[235A CPC Regulation

In this Part—

    (a)   the CPC Regulation is Regulation (EC) No 2006/2004 of the European Parliament and of the Council of 27 October 2004 on cooperation between national authorities responsible for the enforcement of consumer protection laws as amended by the Unfair Commercial Practices Directive;

    (b)   the Unfair Commercial Practices Directive is Directive 2005/29/EC of the European Parliament and of the Council of 11 May 2005 concerning unfair business-to-consumer commercial practices in the internal market.]

[1968A]

NOTES

Commencement: 8 January 2007.

Inserted, together with s 235B, by the Enterprise Act 2002 (Amendment) Regulations 2006, SI 2006/3363, regs 3, 20.

[235B   Dual enforcers

References in this Part to a general enforcer, a designated enforcer or a CPC enforcer are to be read, in the case of a person or body which is more than one kind of enforcer, as references to that person or body acting in its capacity as a general enforcer, designated enforcer or (as the case may be) CPC enforcer.]

[1968B]

NOTES
Commencement: 8 January 2007.
Inserted as noted to s 235A at **[1968A]**.

Crown

[236   Crown

(1)   This Part binds the Crown.

(2)   But the powers conferred by sections 227A to 227D are not exercisable in relation to premises occupied by the Crown.]

[1969]

NOTES
Commencement: 8 January 2007.
Substituted by the Enterprise Act 2002 (Amendment) Regulations 2006, SI 2006/3363, regs 3, 21.

237–272   (*Ss 237–247 (Pt 9: Information); ss 248–272 (Pt 10: Insolvency) outside the scope of this work.*)

PART 11
SUPPLEMENTARY

273   Interpretation

In this Act—
"the 1973 Act" means the Fair Trading Act 1973 (c 41);
"the 1998 Act" means the Competition Act 1998 (c 41);
"the Commission" means the Competition Commission;
"the Director" means the Director General of Fair Trading; and
"the OFT" means the Office of Fair Trading.

[1970]

274   Provision of financial assistance for consumer purposes

The Secretary of State may give financial assistance to any person for the purpose of assisting—
(a)   activities which the Secretary of State considers are of benefit to consumers; or
(b)   the provision of—
(i)   advice or information about consumer matters;
(ii)   educational materials relating to consumer matters; or
(iii)   advice or information to the Secretary of State in connection with the formulation of policy in respect of consumer matters.

[1971]

275   Financial provision

There shall be paid out of money provided by Parliament—
(a)   any expenditure incurred by the OFT, the Secretary of State, any other Minister of the Crown or a government department by virtue of this Act; and
(b)   any increase attributable to this Act in the sums payable out of money so provided by virtue of any other Act.

[1972]

276   Transitional or transitory provision and savings

(1)   Schedule 24 (which makes transitional and transitory provisions and savings) has effect.

(2)   The Secretary of State may by order made by statutory instrument make such transitional or transitory provisions and savings as he considers appropriate in connection with the coming into force of any provision of this Act.

(3)   An order under subsection (2) may modify any Act or subordinate legislation.

(4)   Schedule 24 does not restrict the power under subsection (2) to make other transitional or transitory provisions and savings.

[1973]

NOTES

Orders: the Enterprise Act 2002 (Commencement No 2, Transitional and Transitory Provisions) Order 2003, SI 2003/766; the Enterprise Act 2002 (Commencement No 3, Transitional and Transitory Provisions and Savings) Order 2003, SI 2003/1397; the Enterprise Act 2002 (Part 8 Designated Enforcers: Criteria for Designation, Designation of Public Bodies as Designated Enforcers and Transitional Provisions) Order 2003, SI 2003/1399; the Enterprise Act 2002 (Commencement No 4 and Transitional Provisions and Savings) Order 2003, SI 2003/2093; the Enterprise Act 2002 (Transitional Provisions) (Insolvency) Order 2003, SI 2003/2332; the Enterprise Act 2002 (Commencement No 7 and Transitional Provisions and Savings) Order 2004, SI 2004/3233.

277   Power to make consequential amendments etc

(1)   The Secretary of State may by order make such supplementary, incidental or consequential provision as he thinks appropriate—
    (a)   for the general purposes, or any particular purpose, of this Act; or
    (b)   in consequence of any provision made by or under this Act or for giving full effect to it.

(2)   An order under this section may—
    (a)   modify any Act or subordinate legislation (including this Act);
    (b)   make incidental, supplementary, consequential, transitional, transitory or saving provision.

(3)   The power to make an order under this section is exercisable by statutory instrument subject to annulment in pursuance of a resolution of either House of Parliament.

(4)   The power conferred by this section is not restricted by any other provision of this Act.

[1974]–[1975]

NOTES

Orders: the Enterprise Act 2002 (Consequential and Supplemental Provisions) Order 2003, SI 2003/1398; the Enterprise Act 2002 (Insolvency) Order 2003, SI 2003/2096; the Enterprise Act 2002 (Part 9 Restrictions on Disclosure of Information) (Specification) Order 2004, SI 2004/693; the Enterprise Act 2002 (Part 8) (Designation of the Financial Services Authority as a Designated Enforcer) Order 2004, SI 2004/935; the Enterprise Act 2002 (Insolvency) Order 2004, SI 2004/2312; the Enterprise Act 2002 (Enforcement Undertakings) Order 2006, SI 2006/354; the Enterprise Act 2002 (Enforcement Undertakings and Orders) Order 2006, SI 2006/355; the Enterprise Act 2002 (Enforcement Undertakings) (No 2) Order 2006, SI 2006/3095.

278   (*Introduces Sch 25* (*minor and consequential amendments*) *and Sch 26* (*repeals and revocations*).)

279   Commencement

The preceding provisions of this Act shall come into force on such day as the Secretary of State may by order made by statutory instrument appoint; and different days may be appointed for different purposes.

[1976]

NOTES

Orders: the Enterprise Act 2002 (Commencement No 1) Order 2003, SI 2003/765; the Enterprise Act 2002 (Commencement No 2, Transitional and Transitory Provisions) Order 2003, SI 2003/766; the Enterprise Act 2002 (Commencement No 3, Transitional and Transitory Provisions and Savings) Order 2003, SI 2003/1397; the Enterprise Act 2002 (Commencement No 4 and Transitional Provisions and Savings) Order 2003, SI 2003/2093; the Enterprise Act 2002 (Commencement No 5 and Amendment) Order 2003, SI 2003/3340; the Enterprise Act 2002 (Commencement No 6) Order 2004, SI 2004/1866; the Enterprise Act 2002 (Commencement No 7 and Transitional Provisions and Savings) Order 2004, SI 2004/3233.

280   Extent

(1)   Sections 256 to 265, 267, 269 and 272 extend only to England and Wales.

(2)   Sections 204, 248 to 255 and 270 extend only to England and Wales and Scotland (but subsection (3) of section 415A as inserted by section 270 extends only to England and Wales).

(3)   Any other modifications by this Act of an enactment have the same extent as the enactment being modified.

(4)   Otherwise, this Act extends to England and Wales, Scotland and Northern Ireland.

[1977]

281   Short title

This Act may be cited as the Enterprise Act 2002.

[1978]

SCHEDULES

SCHEDULE 1
THE OFFICE OF FAIR TRADING

Section 1

Membership

1.—(1)   The OFT shall consist of a chairman and no fewer than four other members, appointed by the Secretary of State.

(2)   The Secretary of State shall consult the chairman before appointing any other member.

Terms of appointment, remuneration, pensions etc

2.—(1)   Subject to this Schedule, the chairman and other members shall hold and vacate office in accordance with the terms of their respective appointments.

(2)   The terms of appointment of the chairman and other members shall be determined by the Secretary of State.

3.—(1)   An appointment of a person to hold office as chairman or other member shall be for a term not exceeding five years.

(2)   A person holding office as chairman or other member—
  (a)   may resign that office by giving notice in writing to the Secretary of State; and
  (b)   may be removed from office by the Secretary of State on the ground of incapacity or misbehaviour.

(3)   A previous appointment as chairman or other member does not affect a person's eligibility for appointment to either office.

4.—(1)   The OFT shall pay to the chairman and other members such remuneration, and such travelling and other allowances, as may be determined by the Secretary of State.

(2)   The OFT shall, if required to do so by the Secretary of State—
  (a)   pay such pension, allowances or gratuities as may be determined by the Secretary of State to or in respect of a person who holds or has held office as chairman or other member; or
  (b)   make such payments as may be so determined towards provision for the payment of a pension, allowances or gratuities to or in respect of such a person.

(3)   If, where any person ceases to hold office as chairman or other member, the Secretary of State determines that there are special circumstances which make it right that he should receive compensation, the OFT shall pay to him such amount by way of compensation as the Secretary of State may determine.

Staff

5.—(1)   The Secretary of State shall, after consulting the chairman, appoint a person (who may, subject to sub-paragraph (2), also be a member of the OFT) to act as chief executive of the OFT on such terms and conditions as the Secretary of State may think appropriate.

(2)   A person appointed as chief executive after the end of the transitional period may not at the same time be chairman.

(3)   In sub-paragraph (2) "the transitional period" means the period of two years beginning with the day on which this paragraph comes into force.

6.   The OFT may, with the approval of the Minister for the Civil Service as to numbers and terms and conditions of service, appoint such other staff as it may determine.

Membership of committees or sub-committees of OFT

7.   The members of a committee or sub-committee of the OFT may include persons who are not members of the OFT (and a sub-committee may include persons who are not members of the committee which established it).

Proceedings etc

8.—(1)   The OFT may regulate its own procedure (including quorum).

(2)   The OFT shall consult the Secretary of State before making or revising its rules and procedures for dealing with conflicts of interest.

(3)   The OFT shall from time to time publish a summary of its rules and procedures for dealing with conflicts of interest.

9.   The validity of anything done by the OFT is not affected by a vacancy among its members or by a defect in the appointment of a member.

10.—(1)   The application of the seal of the OFT shall be authenticated by the signature of—

(a)   any member; or

(b)   some other person who has been authorised for that purpose by the OFT, whether generally or specially.

(2)   Sub-paragraph (1) does not apply in relation to any document which is, or is to be, signed in accordance with the law of Scotland.

11.   A document purporting to be duly executed under the seal of the OFT, or signed on its behalf, shall be received in evidence and, unless the contrary is proved, be taken to be so executed or signed.

Performance of functions

12.—(1)   Anything authorised or required to be done by the OFT (including exercising the power under this paragraph) may be done by—

(a)   any member or employee of the OFT who is authorised for that purpose by the OFT, whether generally or specially;

(b)   any committee of the OFT which has been so authorised.

(2)   Sub-paragraph (1)(b) does not apply to a committee whose members include any person who is not a member or employee of the OFT.

Supplementary powers

13.   The OFT has power to do anything which is calculated to facilitate, or is conducive or incidental to, the performance of its functions.

14–16.   ...

[1979]

NOTES

Paras 14–16: amend the Parliamentary Commissioner Act 1967, Sch 2, the House of Commons Disqualification Act 1975, Sch 1, Pt II, and the Northern Ireland Assembly Disqualification Act 1975, Sch 1, Pt II.

SCHEDULE 2
THE COMPETITION APPEAL TRIBUNAL

Section 12

Appointment, etc of President and chairmen

1.—(1)   A person is not eligible for appointment as President unless—

[(a)   he satisfies the judicial-appointment eligibility condition on a 7-year basis;]

(b)   he is an advocate or solicitor in Scotland of at least [7] years' standing; or

(c)   he is a member of the Bar of Northern Ireland or [solicitor of the Court of Judicature of Northern Ireland] of at least [7] years' standing;

and he appears to the Lord Chancellor to have appropriate experience and knowledge of competition law and practice.

(2)   A person is not eligible for appointment as a chairman unless—

[(a)   he satisfies the judicial-appointment eligibility condition on a 5-year basis,]

(b)   he is an advocate or solicitor in Scotland of at least [5] years' standing; or

(c)   he is a member of the Bar of Northern Ireland or [solicitor of the Court of Judicature of Northern Ireland] of at least [5] years' standing;

and he appears to the Lord Chancellor to have appropriate experience and knowledge (either of competition law and practice or any other relevant law and practice).

(3)   Before appointing an advocate or solicitor in Scotland under this paragraph, the Lord Chancellor must consult the Lord President of the Court of Session.

(4)   ...

[(5)   The Lord Chancellor may remove a person from office as President under sub-paragraph (4) only with the concurrence of all of the following—

(a)   the Lord Chief Justice of England and Wales;

(b)   the Lord President of the Court of Session;

(c)   the Lord Chief Justice of Northern Ireland.

(6)   The Lord Chancellor may remove a person from office as chairman under sub-paragraph (4) only with the concurrence of the appropriate senior judge.

(7)   The appropriate senior judge is the Lord Chief Justice of England and Wales, unless—

(a)   the person to be removed exercises functions wholly or mainly in Scotland, in which case it is the Lord President of the Court of Session, or

(b)   the person to be removed exercises functions wholly or mainly in Northern Ireland, in which case it is the Lord Chief Justice of Northern Ireland.]

2.—(1) The members appointed as President or as chairmen shall hold and vacate office in accordance with their terms of appointment, subject to the following provisions.

(2) A person may not be a chairman for more than 8 years (but this does not prevent a temporary reappointment for the purpose of continuing to act as a member of the Tribunal as constituted for the purposes of any proceedings instituted before the end of his term of office).

(3) The President and the chairmen may resign their offices by notice in writing to the Lord Chancellor.

(4) The Lord Chancellor may remove a person from office as President or chairman on the ground of incapacity or misbehaviour.

3. If the President is absent or otherwise unable to act the Lord Chancellor may appoint as acting President any person qualified for appointment as a chairman.

Appointment, etc of ordinary members

4.—(1) Ordinary members shall hold and vacate office in accordance with their terms of appointment, subject to the following provisions.

(2) A person may not be an ordinary member for more than 8 years (but this does not prevent a temporary reappointment for the purpose of continuing to act as a member of the Tribunal as constituted for the purposes of any proceedings instituted before the end of his term of office).

(3) An ordinary member may resign his office by notice in writing to the Secretary of State.

(4) The Secretary of State may remove a person from office as an ordinary member on the ground of incapacity or misbehaviour.

Remuneration etc for members

5.—(1) The Competition Service shall pay to the President, the chairmen and the ordinary members such remuneration (whether by way of salaries or fees), and such allowances, as the Secretary of State may determine.

(2) The Competition Service shall, if required to do so by the Secretary of State—
   (a) pay such pension, allowances or gratuities as may be determined by the Secretary of State to or in respect of a person who holds or has held office as President, a chairman or an ordinary member; or
   (b) make such payments as may be so determined towards provision for the payment of a pension, allowance or gratuities to or in respect of such a person.

Compensation for loss of office

6. If, where any person ceases to hold office as President, a chairman or ordinary member, the Secretary of State determines that there are special circumstances which make it right that he should receive compensation, the Competition Service shall pay to him such amount by way of compensation as the Secretary of State may determine.

Staff, accommodation and property

7. Any staff, office accommodation or equipment required for the Tribunal shall be provided by the Competition Service.

Miscellaneous

8. The President must arrange such training for members of the Tribunal as he considers appropriate.

9. In this Schedule "chairman" and "ordinary member" mean respectively a member of the panel of chairmen, or a member of the panel of ordinary members, appointed under section 12.

10, 11. ...

[1980]

NOTES
   Para 1: sub-paras (1)(a), (2)(a) and numbers in square brackets in sub-paras (1)(b), (c), (2)(b), (c)substituted and sub-para (4) repealed by the Tribunals, Courts and Enforcement Act 2007, ss 50, 146, Sch 10, Pt 1, para 36, Sch 23, Pt 2; words in square brackets in sub-paras (1)(c), (2)(c) substituted by the Constitutional Reform Act 2005, s 59(5), Sch 11, Pt 3, para 5.
   Para 2: sub-paras (5)–(7) added by the Constitutional Reform Act 2005, s 15(1), Sch 4, Pt 1, paras 304, 306.
   Paras 10, 11: amend the House of Commons Disqualification Act 1975, Sch 1, Pt II, and the Northern Ireland Assembly Disqualification Act 1975, Sch 1, Pt II.
   Transitional provisions: see the note to s 12 at **[1869]**.

(Schs 3–26 outside the scope of this work.)

FIREWORKS ACT 2003

(2003 c 22)

ARRANGEMENT OF SECTIONS

Introductory

An Act to make provision about fireworks and other explosives

[18 September 2003]

Introductory

1 Introduction

(1)   In this Act "fireworks" means devices which—
    (a)   are fireworks for the purposes of the British Standard Specification relating to fireworks published on 30th November 1988 (BS 7114) or any British Standard Specification replacing it, or
    (b)   would be fireworks for those purposes if they were intended as a form of entertainment.

(2)   The Secretary of State may by regulations substitute a new definition of "fireworks" for the definition in subsection (1).

(3)   References in this Act to supplying fireworks include—
    (a)   selling them,
    (b)   exchanging them for any consideration other than money, and
    (c)   giving them as a prize or otherwise making a gift of them,
but do not include supplying them otherwise than in the course of a business.

[1981]

Fireworks regulations

2 Power to make regulations about fireworks

(1)   The Secretary of State may by regulations ("fireworks regulations") make any provision which the Secretary of State considers appropriate—
    (a)   for securing that there is no risk that use of fireworks will have the consequences specified in subsection (2), or
    (b)   for securing that the risk that the use of fireworks will have those consequences is the minimum that is compatible with their being used.

(2)   The consequences are—
    (a)   death of persons or injury, alarm, distress or anxiety to persons,
    (b)   death of animals or injury or distress to animals, and
    (c)   destruction of, or damage to, property.

(3)   Before making fireworks regulations the Secretary of State must consult—
    (a)   [the Health and Safety Executive],

(b)   organisations which appear to the Secretary of State to be representative of interests substantially affected by the proposal, and

(c)   other persons whom the Secretary of State considers it appropriate to consult.

(4)   Before making fireworks regulations the Secretary of State must issue a full regulatory impact assessment setting out details of the costs and benefits and the wider economic, social and environmental impact of the proposed regulations.

(5)   But subsection (3) does not apply if the regulations are to—

(a)   cease to have effect at the end of the period of not more than twelve months beginning with the day on which they come into force, and

(b)   contain a statement that it appears to the Secretary of State that the need to protect the public requires that the regulations should be made without delay.

(6)   The power to make fireworks regulations includes power—

(a)   to make different provision for different cases, and

(b)   to make any incidental, supplementary, consequential and transitional provision which the Secretary of State considers appropriate.

(7)   Section 18 of the Consumer Protection Act 1987 (c 43) (power to require information for deciding whether to make, vary or revoke regulations under section 11 of that Act) applies in relation to fireworks regulations as in relation to regulations under section 11 of that Act.

(8)   Nothing in this Act shall be construed as in any way limiting the provision that may be made in regulations under section 11 of the Consumer Protection Act 1987.

[1982]

NOTES

Sub-s (3): words in square brackets substituted by the Legislative Reform (Health and Safety Executive) Order 2008, SI 2008/960, art 22, Sch 3, subject to transitional provisions in art 21 of, and Sch 2 to, that Order. Regulations: the Fireworks Regulations 2004, SI 2004/1836.

---

3   Prohibition of supply etc to young persons

(1)   Fireworks regulations may include provision prohibiting persons from—

(a)   supplying, or

(b)   offering or agreeing to supply,

fireworks, or fireworks of a description specified in the regulations, to persons who are below an age so specified.

(2)   Fireworks regulations may include provision prohibiting the purchase or possession of fireworks, or fireworks of a description specified in the regulations, by persons who are below an age so specified.

(3)   If fireworks regulations impose any prohibition by virtue of this section, they may contain—

(a)   exceptions from the prohibition, or

(b)   provision for the granting of dispensations from the prohibition.

[1983]

NOTES

Regulations: the Fireworks Regulations 2004, SI 2004/1836.

---

4   Prohibition of supply etc in certain circumstances

(1)   Fireworks regulations may include provision prohibiting persons from supplying, purchasing, possessing or using fireworks, or fireworks of a description specified in the regulations, during hours of the day so specified.

(2)   Fireworks regulations may include provision prohibiting persons from supplying, exposing for supply, purchasing, possessing or using fireworks, or fireworks of a description specified in the regulations—

(a)   in places or places of a description, or

(b)   in circumstances,

specified in the regulations.

(3)   If fireworks regulations impose any prohibition by virtue of this section, they may contain—

(a)   exceptions from the prohibition, or

(b)   provision for the granting of dispensations from the prohibition.

[1984]

NOTES

Regulations: the Fireworks Regulations 2004, SI 2004/1836.

---

5 Prohibition of supply etc of certain fireworks

(1)   Fireworks regulations may include provision—
    (a)   prohibiting persons from supplying, or offering or agreeing to supply, fireworks of a description specified in the regulations, or
    (b)   prohibiting persons from supplying, or offering or agreeing to supply, fireworks of a description specified in the regulations to persons of a description so specified.

(2)   Fireworks regulations may include provision—
    (a)   prohibiting the purchase or possession of fireworks of a description specified in the regulations, or
    (b)   prohibiting the purchase or possession of fireworks of a description specified in the regulations by persons of a description so specified.

(3)   Subsections (1) and (2) shall not apply to class I and class II fireworks.

(4)   The descriptions of persons which may be specified in fireworks regulations by virtue of subsection (1) or (2) include in particular persons who do not satisfy any conditions which are specified in the regulations and relate to any of the matters mentioned in subsection (5).

(5)   Those matters are—
    (a)   the satisfactory completion of a course, or courses, of training relating to fireworks and the means of proving the satisfactory completion of such a course or courses,
    (b)   proficiency or experience in the use of fireworks and the means of proving such proficiency or experience, and
    (c)   the possession of insurance cover against liability arising from the use of fireworks and the means of proving possession of such cover.

(6)   If fireworks regulations impose any prohibition by virtue of this section, they may contain—
    (a)   exceptions from the prohibition, or
    (b)   provision for the granting of dispensations from the prohibition.

[1985]

NOTES
Regulations: the Fireworks Regulations 2004, SI 2004/1836.

6 Public fireworks displays

(1)   Fireworks regulations may include provision prohibiting persons from operating a public fireworks display unless—
    (a)   notice of the display has been given in accordance with the regulations to any local or other authority to which the regulations require it to be given,
    (b)   any other information relating to the display which is required by the regulations to be given to any local or other authority has been so given,
    (c)   any fee imposed by any local or other authority in accordance with the regulations has been paid, and
    (d)   such other conditions relating to the holding of public fireworks displays as are specified in the regulations have been complied with.

(2)   Fireworks regulations may include provision prohibiting persons from operating public fireworks displays unless they satisfy—
    (a)   any conditions which are specified in the regulations and relate to the satisfactory completion of a course, or courses, of training relating to fireworks and to the means of proving the satisfactory completion of such a course or courses, or
    (b)   any other conditions which are so specified.

(3)   Fireworks regulations may include provision prohibiting persons from operating, or assisting in the operation of, public fireworks displays if they are below an age specified in the regulations.

(4)   If fireworks regulations impose any prohibition by virtue of this section, they may contain—
    (a)   exceptions from the prohibition, or
    (b)   provision for the granting of dispensations from the prohibition.

(5)   In this section "public fireworks display" means a fireworks display at which the public, or any section of the public, are present (whether or not they have paid to be).

[1986]

7 Licensing of suppliers

(1)   Fireworks regulations may include provision prohibiting persons, or persons of a description specified in the regulations, from supplying, exposing for supply or possessing for supply fireworks, or fireworks of a description so specified, unless—
    (a)   they are licensed in accordance with the regulations, and

(b)   the fireworks are supplied, exposed for supply or kept at premises which are so licensed.

(2)   If fireworks regulations impose any prohibition by virtue of subsection (1), they may contain provision—

(a)   specifying the local or other authority by which a licence relating to any person or premises may be granted, varied and revoked,

(b)   relating to the grant, variation and revocation of licences,

(c)   about conditions which may be attached to licences (including, in particular, conditions as to the time of year for which persons or premises are licensed),

(d)   for the charging of fees for the grant or variation of licences, and

(e)   about appeals against refusals to grant or vary, or variations of, licences.

(3)   The provision that may be contained in fireworks regulations by virtue of subsection (1) includes, in particular, provision that a person may not be licensed unless any conditions which are specified in the regulations are satisfied by the person or his employees (or both).

(4)   Those conditions may include conditions relating to the satisfactory completion of a course, or courses, of training about fireworks and the means of proving the satisfactory completion of such course or courses.

(5)   If fireworks regulations impose any prohibition by virtue of this section, they may contain—

(a)   exceptions from the prohibition, or

(b)   provision for the granting of dispensations from the prohibition.

[1987]

NOTES

Regulations: the Fireworks Regulations 2004, SI 2004/1836.

---

8   Information about fireworks

(1)   Fireworks regulations may include provision for securing that—

(a)   appropriate information is, and

(b)   inappropriate information is not,

given in relation to fireworks, or fireworks of a description specified in the regulations.

(2)   The provision that may be contained in fireworks regulations by virtue of subsection (1) includes, in particular, provision—

(a)   requiring that a mark, warning or instruction relating to the fireworks be put on or accompany the fireworks, or

(b)   requiring that information specified in the regulations be given to any person so specified.

(3)   If fireworks regulations impose any requirement by virtue of this section, they may contain—

(a)   exceptions from the requirement, or

(b)   provision for the granting of dispensations from the requirement.

(4)   If fireworks regulations impose any requirement by virtue of this section, they may contain provision requiring the keeping of records by any person to whom information is given under the regulations.

[1988]

NOTES

Regulations: the Fireworks Regulations 2004, SI 2004/1836.

---

9   Prohibition of importation etc of fireworks

(1)   Fireworks regulations may include provision prohibiting persons from—

(a)   importing,

(b)   completing the manufacture of, or

(c)   placing on the market,

fireworks, or fireworks of a description specified in the regulations, unless they have complied with any requirement imposed by the regulations for the giving of information.

(2)   If fireworks regulations impose any prohibition by virtue of subsection (1)(b) or (c), they shall specify the circumstances in which—

(a)   (if the prohibition is imposed by virtue of subsection (1)(b)) a person completes the manufacture of fireworks, or

(b)   (if the prohibition is imposed by virtue of subsection (1)(c)) a person places fireworks on the market.

(3)   If fireworks regulations impose any prohibition by virtue of this section, they may contain—

(a)   exceptions from the prohibition, or

(b) provision for the granting of dispensations from the prohibition.

(4) If fireworks regulations impose any prohibition by virtue of this section, they may contain provision requiring the keeping of records by any person to whom information is given under the regulations.

[1989]

NOTES
  Regulations: the Fireworks Regulations 2004, SI 2004/1836.

10 Training courses

(1) If fireworks regulations specify conditions relating to the satisfactory completion of a course, or courses, of training about fireworks, they may make provision for courses to be provided by—

(a) the Secretary of State,

(b) a body or bodies established or recognised by the Secretary of State, or

(c) licensed persons.

(2) If fireworks regulations make provision for courses to be provided by licensed persons, they may—

(a) make provision for the licensing of persons by the Secretary of State or by any body or bodies established or recognised by the Secretary of State,

(b) authorise the making by the Secretary of State of provision about the charging of fees for the grant or variation of licences, and

(c) authorise the making by the Secretary of State, or by any such body or bodies, of provision about any of the matters mentioned in subsection (3).

(3) Those matters are—

(a) the grant, variation and revocation of licences,

(b) conditions which may be attached to licences, and

(c) appeals against refusals to grant or vary, or variations of, licences.

(4) Fireworks regulations may authorise—

(a) the making by the Secretary of State of provision about the charging of fees for attendance at courses of training about fireworks, and

(b) the making by the Secretary of State, or by any body or bodies established or recognised by the Secretary of State under this section, of provision about any of the matters mentioned in subsection (5).

(5) Those matters are—

(a) the descriptions of persons who are to be eligible to attend courses of training about fireworks,

(b) the subject matter to be covered by courses and the conduct of courses,

(c) the criteria to be applied in determining whether persons have satisfactorily completed courses,

(d) the form and content of certificates to be awarded to persons who have satisfactorily completed courses,

(e) appeals against refusals to award certificates to persons who have attended courses, and

(f) the keeping of records about persons who have attended courses.

[1990]

NOTES
  Commencement: to be appointed.

Supplementary

11 Offences

(1) Any person who contravenes a prohibition imposed by fireworks regulations is guilty of an offence.

(2) Any person who fails to comply with a requirement imposed by or under fireworks regulations to give or not to give information is guilty of an offence.

(3) Where a requirement to give information is imposed by or under fireworks regulations, a person is guilty of an offence if, in giving the information, he—

(a) makes a statement which he knows is false in a material particular, or

(b) recklessly makes a statement which is false in a material particular.

(4) A person guilty of an offence under this section is liable on summary conviction to—

(a) imprisonment for a term not exceeding six months, or

(b) a fine not exceeding level 5 on the standard scale,

or to both.

(5) Fireworks regulations may not provide for any contravention of the regulations to be an offence.

(6) Paragraphs (c), (e) and (f) of section 11(3) of the Consumer Protection Act 1987 (c 43) (provision about offences which may be included in regulations) apply in relation to fireworks regulations as to regulations under section 11 of that Act, but as if references to an offence under section 12 of that Act were references to an offence under this section.

(7) Section 39 of that Act (defence of due diligence) applies to offences under subsections (1) and (2) of this section; and section 40(1) of that Act (liability of persons other than the principal offender) has effect accordingly.

(8) In proceedings against any person for an offence of contravening a prohibition imposed by fireworks regulations made by virtue of section 3(1) it is a defence for that person to show that he had no reason to suspect that the person to whom he supplied, offered to supply or agreed to supply the fireworks was below the age specified in the regulations.

(9) Section 40(2) and (3) of the Consumer Protection Act 1987 (c 43) (offences by bodies corporate) applies to an offence under this section as to an offence under that Act.

[1991]

NOTES
Commencement: 28 November 2003 (for the purposes of fireworks regulations made in exercise of powers conferred by the provisions of the Act brought into force on that date); 15 July 2004 (for the purposes of fireworks regulations made in exercise of powers conferred by the provisions of the Act brought into force on that date); to be appointed (otherwise).

11A, 11B *(Inserted by the Police, Public Order and Criminal Justice (Scotland) Act 2006, s 76; apply to Scotland only.)*

12 Enforcement

(1) Section 27 of the Consumer Protection Act 1987 (enforcement authorities), apart from subsection (1)(b), applies in relation to fireworks regulations as to regulations under section 11 of that Act.

(2) The following provisions of that Act—
  (a) section 28(1)(a) and (2) to (4) (test purchases), apart from the references to forfeiture and suspension notices,
  (b) section 29(1) to (5), (6)(a) and (7) and section 30(1) to (9) (powers of search etc), apart from the references to forfeiture and suspension notices,
  (c) section 32 (obstruction of officer),
  (d) section 33 (appeals against detention), apart from subsections (2)(a)(ii) and (3)(a)(ii),
  (e) section 34 (compensation for seizure and detention),
  (f) section 35 (recovery of enforcement expenses), apart from subsections (1)(b) and (2)(b),
  (g) section 37 (disclosure of information by Customs and Excise),
  (h) section 41 (civil proceedings), and
  (i) section 44 (service of documents),
apply in relation to fireworks regulations as to regulations under section 11 of that Act.

(3) ...

[1992]

NOTES
Commencement: 28 November 2003 (for the purposes of fireworks regulations made in exercise of powers conferred by the provisions of the Act brought into force on that date); 15 July 2004 (for the purposes of fireworks regulations made in exercise of powers conferred by the provisions of the Act brought into force on that date); to be appointed (otherwise).
Sub-s (3): amends the Enterprise Act 2002, Schs 14, 15.

13 Savings for certain privileges

Section 47 of the Consumer Protection Act 1987 (savings for privileges) applies in relation to this Act.

[1993]

NOTES
Commencement: 28 November 2003 (for the purposes of fireworks regulations made in exercise of powers conferred by the provisions of the Act brought into force on that date); 15 July 2004 (for the purposes of fireworks regulations made in exercise of powers conferred by the provisions of the Act brought into force on that date); to be appointed (otherwise).

14 Prohibition of supply etc of other explosives

(1) The power to make regulations under section 3 or 4(2) applies to explosives other than fireworks as to fireworks; and regulations made by virtue of this subsection are fireworks regulations for all the purposes of this Act.

(2) In subsection (1) "explosives" has the same meaning as in the Explosives Act 1875 (c 17).

(3) The Secretary of State may by regulations substitute a new definition of "explosives" for the definition in subsection (2).

[1994]

NOTES
Commencement: to be appointed.

15 (*Introduces the Schedule to this Act* (*outside the scope of this work*).)

16 Parliamentary procedure for regulations

(1) Any power to make regulations under this Act is exercisable by statutory instrument.

(2) Regulations under section 1(2) or 14(3) must not be made unless a draft of the statutory instrument containing them has been laid before Parliament and approved by a resolution of each House.

(3) A statutory instrument containing fireworks regulations is subject to annulment in pursuance of a resolution of either House of Parliament.

[1995]

NOTES
Commencement: 28 November 2003 (for the purposes of fireworks regulations made in exercise of powers conferred by the provisions of the Act brought into force on that date); 15 July 2004 (for the purposes of fireworks regulations made in exercise of powers conferred by the provisions of the Act brought into force on that date); to be appointed (otherwise).

17 Financial provisions

(1) There is to be paid out of money provided by Parliament—
   (a) any expenses incurred by the Secretary of State in consequence of any provision of this Act, and
   (b) any increase attributable to this Act in the sums payable out of money so provided under any other Act.

(2) Any sums received by the Secretary of State by virtue of this Act are to be paid into the Consolidated Fund.

[1996]

18 Commencement

(1) Sections 1 to 16 (and the Schedule) do not come into force until a day appointed by order made by the Secretary of State by statutory instrument; and different days may be appointed for different purposes.

(2) The Secretary of State may by order made by statutory instrument make such transitional provision in connection with the coming into force of any provision of this Act as the Secretary of State considers appropriate.

[1997]

NOTES
Orders: the Fireworks Act 2003 (Commencement No 1) Order 2003, SI 2003/3084; the Fireworks Act 2003 (Commencement No 2) Order 2004, SI 2004/1831.

19 Short title and extent

(1) This Act may be cited as the Fireworks Act 2003.

(2) This Act does not extend to Northern Ireland.

[1998]

(*Schedule* (*Repeals and Revocation*) *outside the scope of this work.*)

DEALING IN CULTURAL OBJECTS (OFFENCES) ACT 2003

(2003 c 27)

An Act to provide for an offence of acquiring, disposing of, importing or exporting tainted cultural objects, or agreeing or arranging to do so; and for connected purposes

[30 October 2003]

PART 1
STATUTES

1   Offence of dealing in tainted cultural objects

(1)   A person is guilty of an offence if he dishonestly deals in a cultural object that is tainted, knowing or believing that the object is tainted.

(2)   It is immaterial whether he knows or believes that the object is a cultural object.

(3)   A person guilty of the offence is liable—
   (a)   on conviction on indictment, to imprisonment for a term not exceeding seven years or a fine (or both),
   (b)   on summary conviction, to imprisonment for a term not exceeding six months or a fine not exceeding the statutory maximum (or both).

[1999]

2   Meaning of "tainted cultural object"

(1)   "Cultural object" means an object of historical, architectural or archaeological interest.

(2)   A cultural object is tainted if, after the commencement of this Act—
   (a)   a person removes the object in a case falling within subsection (4) or he excavates the object, and
   (b)   the removal or excavation constitutes an offence.

(3)   It is immaterial whether—
   (a)   the removal or excavation was done in the United Kingdom or elsewhere,
   (b)   the offence is committed under the law of a part of the United Kingdom or under the law of any other country or territory.

(4)   An object is removed in a case falling within this subsection if—
   (a)   it is removed from a building or structure of historical, architectural or archaeological interest where the object has at any time formed part of the building or structure, or
   (b)   it is removed from a monument of such interest.

(5)   "Monument" means—
   (a)   any work, cave or excavation,
   (b)   any site comprising the remains of any building or structure or of any work, cave or excavation,
   (c)   any site comprising, or comprising the remains of, any vehicle, vessel, aircraft or other movable structure, or part of any such thing.

(6)   "Remains" includes any trace or sign of the previous existence of the thing in question.

(7)   It is immaterial whether—
   (a)   a building, structure or work is above or below the surface of the land,
   (b)   a site is above or below water.

(8)   This section has effect for the purposes of section 1.

[2000]

3   Meaning of "deals in"

(1)   A person deals in an object if (and only if) he—
   (a)   acquires, disposes of, imports or exports it,
   (b)   agrees with another to do an act mentioned in paragraph (a), or
   (c)   makes arrangements under which another person does such an act or under which another person agrees with a third person to do such an act.

(2)   "Acquires" means buys, hires, borrows or accepts.

(3)   "Disposes of" means sells, lets on hire, lends or gives.

(4)   In relation to agreeing or arranging to do an act, it is immaterial whether the act is agreed or arranged to take place in the United Kingdom or elsewhere.

(5)   This section has effect for the purposes of section 1.

[2001]

[4   Revenue and Customs prosecutions]

(1)   Proceedings for an offence relating to the dealing in a tainted cultural object may be instituted [by the Director of Revenue and Customs Prosecutions or by order of the Commissioners

for Her Majesty's Revenue and Customs] [if it appears to the Director or to the Commissioners] that the offence has involved the importation or exportation of such an object.

(2)   An offence relates to the dealing in a tainted cultural object if it is—

  (a)   an offence under section 1, or

  (b)   an offence of inciting the commission of, or attempting or conspiring to commit, such an offence.

(3)   Proceedings for an offence which are instituted [by order of the Commissioners] under subsection (1) are to be commenced in the name of an officer [of Revenue and Customs], but may be continued by another officer.

(4)   Where the Commissioners ... investigate, or propose to investigate, any matter with a view to determining—

  (a)   whether there are grounds for believing that a person has committed an offence which relates to the dealing in a tainted cultural object and which involves the importation or exportation of such an object, or

  (b)   whether a person should be prosecuted for such an offence,

the matter is to be treated as an assigned matter within the meaning of the Customs and Excise Management Act 1979 (c 2).

(5)   Nothing in this section affects any powers of any person (including any officer) apart from this section.

(6)   ...

[2002]

NOTES

Section heading: substituted by the Commissioners for Revenue and Customs Act 2005, s 50(6), Sch 4, para 128(e).

Sub-s (1): words in square brackets substituted by the Commissioners for Revenue and Customs Act 2005, s 50(6), Sch 4, para 128(a).

Sub-s (3): words in square brackets inserted by the Commissioners for Revenue and Customs Act 2005, s 50(6), Sch 4, para 128(b).

Sub-s (4): words omitted repealed by the Commissioners for Revenue and Customs Act 2005, s 50(6), Sch 4, para 128(c).

Sub-s (6): repealed by the Commissioners for Revenue and Customs Act 2005, ss 50(6), 52(2), Sch 4, para 128(d), Sch 5.

See further, the Serious Crime Act 2007, s 63(1), Sch 6, Pt 1, para 45, which provides that the reference above to (or to conduct amounting to) the common law offence of inciting the commission of another offence, has effect (as from the day that offence is abolished) as a reference to (or to conduct amounting to) offences under the Serious Crime Act 2007, Pt 2.

5   Offences by bodies corporate

(1)   If an offence under section 1 committed by a body corporate is proved—

  (a)   to have been committed with the consent or connivance of an officer, or

  (b)   to be attributable to any neglect on his part,

he (as well as the body corporate) is guilty of the offence and liable to be proceeded against and punished accordingly.

(2)   "Officer", in relation to a body corporate, means—

  (a)   a director, manager, secretary or other similar officer of the body,

  (b)   a person purporting to act in any such capacity.

(3)   If the affairs of a body corporate are managed by its members, subsection (1) applies in relation to the acts and defaults of a member in connection with his functions of management as if he were a director of the body.

[2003]

6   Short title, commencement and extent

(1)   This Act may be cited as the Dealing in Cultural Objects (Offences) Act 2003.

(2)   This Act comes into force at the end of the period of two months beginning with the day on which it is passed.

(3)   This Act does not extend to Scotland.

[2004]

GANGMASTERS (LICENSING) ACT 2004

(2004 c 11)

ARRANGEMENT OF SECTIONS

An Act to make provision for the licensing of activities involving the supply or use of workers in connection with agricultural work, the gathering of wild creatures and wild plants, the harvesting of fish from fish farms, and certain processing and packaging; and for connected purposes

[8 July 2004]

The Gangmasters Licensing Authority

1   The Gangmasters Licensing Authority

(1)   There shall be a body known as the Gangmasters Licensing Authority (in this Act referred to as "the Authority").

(2)   The functions of the Authority shall be—

    (a)   to carry out the functions relating to licensing that are conferred on it by this Act,

    (b)   to ensure the carrying out of such inspections as it considers necessary of persons holding licences under this Act,

    (c)   to keep under review generally the activities of persons acting as gangmasters,

    (d)   to supply information held by it to specified persons in accordance with the provisions of this Act,

    (e)   to keep under review the operation of this Act, and

    (f)   such other functions as may be prescribed in regulations made by the Secretary of State.

(3)   The Authority may do anything that it considers is calculated to facilitate, or is incidental or conducive to, the carrying out of any of its functions.

(4)   The Authority shall not be regarded—

    (a)   as the servant or agent of the Crown, or

    (b)   as enjoying any status, immunity or privilege of the Crown,

and the property of the Authority shall not be regarded as property of, or property held on behalf of, the Crown.

(5)   The Secretary of State may by regulations make provision as to—

    (a)   the status and constitution of the Authority,

    (b)   the appointment of its members,

    (c)   the payment of remuneration and allowances to its members, and

    (d)   such other matters in connection with its establishment and operation as he thinks fit.

(6)   Schedule 1 amends certain enactments in consequence of the establishment of the Authority.

[2005]

NOTES

Regulations: the Gangmasters (Licensing Authority) Regulations 2005, SI 2005/448.

---

2 Directions etc by the Secretary of State

(1)   In carrying out its functions the Authority shall comply with any general or specific directions given to it in writing by the Secretary of State.

(2)   Before giving any such directions the Secretary of State shall consult the Authority.

(3)   The Authority shall provide the Secretary of State with such information about its activities as he may request.

[2006]

Scope of Act

3 Work to which this Act applies

(1)   The work to which this Act applies is—

    (a)   agricultural work,

    (b)   gathering shellfish, and

    (c)   processing or packaging—

        (i)   any produce derived from agricultural work, or

        (ii)   shellfish, fish or products derived from shellfish or fish.

This is subject to any provision made by regulations under subsection (5) below and to section 5 (territorial scope of application).

(2)   In subsection (1)(a) "agricultural work" means work in agriculture.

(3)   In this Act "agriculture" includes—

    (a)   dairy-farming,

    (b)   the production for the purposes of any trade, business or other undertaking (whether carried on for profit or not) of consumable produce,

    (c)   the use of land as grazing, meadow or pasture land,

    (d)   the use of land as an orchard or as osier land or woodland, and

    (e)   the use of land for market gardens or nursery grounds.

In paragraph (b) "consumable produce" means produce grown for sale, consumption or other use after severance from the land on which it is grown.

(4)   In this Act "shellfish" means crustaceans and molluscs of any kind, and includes any part of a shellfish and any (or any part of any) brood, ware, halfware or spat of shellfish, and any spawn of shellfish, and the shell, or any part of the shell, of a shellfish.

(5)   The Secretary of State may by regulations make provision—

    (a)   excluding work of a prescribed description from being work to which this Act applies;

    (b)   including work of the following nature as being work to which this Act applies—

        (i)   the gathering (by any manner) of wild creatures, or wild plants, of a prescribed description and the processing and packaging of anything so gathered, and

        (ii)   the harvesting of fish from a fish farm (within the meaning of [the Salmon and Freshwater Fisheries Act 1975]).

[2007]

NOTES

Sub-s (5): words in square brackets substituted by the Aquatic Animal Health (England and Wales) Regulations 2009, SI 2009/463, reg 45, Sch 2, para 10.

4 Acting as a gangmaster

(1) This section defines what is meant in this Act by a person acting as a gangmaster.

(2) A person ("A") acts as a gangmaster if he supplies a worker to do work to which this Act applies for another person ("B").

(3) For the purposes of subsection (2) it does not matter—

(a) whether the worker works under a contract with A or is supplied to him by another person,

(b) whether the worker is supplied directly under arrangements between A and B or indirectly under arrangements involving one or more intermediaries,

(c) whether A supplies the worker himself or procures that the worker is supplied,

(d) whether the work is done under the control of A, B or an intermediary,

(e) whether the work done for B is for the purposes of a business carried on by him or in connection with services provided by him to another person.

(4) A person ("A") acts as a gangmaster if he uses a worker to do work to which this Act applies in connection with services provided by him to another person.

(5) A person ("A") acts as a gangmaster if he uses a worker to do any of the following work to which this Act applies for the purposes of a business carried on by him—

(a) harvesting or otherwise gathering agricultural produce following—

(i) a sale, assignment or lease of produce to A, or

(ii) the making of any other agreement with A,

where the sale, assignment, lease or other agreement was entered into for the purpose of enabling the harvesting or gathering to take place;

(b) gathering shellfish;

(c) processing or packaging agricultural produce harvested or gathered as mentioned in paragraph (a).

In this subsection "agricultural produce" means any produce derived from agriculture.

(6) For the purposes of subsection (4) or (5) A shall be treated as using a worker to do work to which this Act applies if he makes arrangements under which the worker does the work—

(a) whether the worker works for A (or for another) or on his own account, and

(b) whether or not he works under a contract (with A or another).

(7) Regulations under section 3(5)(b) may provide for the application of subsections (5) and (6) above in relation to work that is work to which this Act applies by virtue of the regulations.

[2008]

5 Territorial scope of application

(1) The work to which this Act applies is work—

(a) in the United Kingdom,

(b) on any portion of the shore or bed of the sea, or of an estuary or tidal river, adjacent to the United Kingdom, whether above or below (or partly above and partly below) the low water mark, or

(c) in UK coastal waters.

(2) In subsection (1)(c) "UK coastal waters" means waters adjacent to the United Kingdom to a distance of six miles measured from the baselines from which the breadth of the territorial sea is measured.

In this subsection "miles" means international nautical miles of 1,852 metres.

(3) The provisions of this Act apply where a person acts as a gangmaster, whether in the United Kingdom or elsewhere, in relation to work to which this Act applies.

[2009]

Licensing

6 Prohibition of unlicensed activities

(1) A person shall not act as a gangmaster except under the authority of a licence.

(2) Regulations made by the Secretary of State may specify circumstances in which a licence is not required.

[2010]

NOTES

Commencement: 1 December 2004 (sub-s (2)); 1 October 2006 (sub-s (1), for purposes related to work falling within s 3(1)(a) and (c)); 6 April 2007 (sub-s (1), otherwise).

Regulations: the Gangmasters Licensing (Exclusions) Regulations 2010, SI 2010/649.

7 Grant of licence

(1) The Authority may grant a licence if it thinks fit.

(2) A licence shall describe the activities authorised by it and shall be granted for such period as the Authority thinks fit.

(3) A licence authorises activities—
  (a) by the holder of the licence, and
  (b) by persons employed or engaged by the holder of the licence who are named or otherwise specified in the licence.

(4) In the case of a licence held otherwise than by an individual, the reference in subsection (3)(a) to activities by the holder of the licence shall be read as a reference only to such activities as are mentioned in whichever of the following provisions applies—
  section 20(2) (body corporate);
  section 21(2) (unincorporated association);
  section 22(4) (partnership that is regarded as a legal person under the law of the country or territory under which it is formed).

(5) A licence shall be granted subject to such conditions as the Authority considers appropriate.

[2011]

8 General power of Authority to make rules

(1) The Authority may make such rules as it thinks fit in connection with the licensing of persons acting as gangmasters.

(2) The rules may, in particular—
  (a) prescribe the form and contents of applications for licences and other documents to be filed in connection with applications;
  (b) regulate the procedure to be followed in connection with applications and authorise the rectification of procedural irregularities;
  (c) prescribe time limits for doing anything required to be done in connection with an application and provide for the extension of any period so prescribed;
  (d) prescribe the requirements which must be met before a licence is granted;
  (e) provide for the manner in which the meeting of those requirements is to be verified;
  (f) allow for the grant of licences on a provisional basis before it is determined whether the requirements for the grant of a licence are met and for the withdrawal of such licences (if appropriate) if it appears that those requirements are not met;
  (g) prescribe the form of licences and the information to be contained in them;
  (h) require the payment of such fees as may be prescribed or determined in accordance with the rules;
  (i) provide that licences are to be granted subject to conditions requiring the licence holder—
    (i) to produce, in prescribed circumstances, evidence in a prescribed form of his being licensed, and
    (ii) to comply with any prescribed requirements relating to the recruitment, use and supply of workers.

(3) The Authority must consult the Secretary of State before making any rules about fees.

(4) In subsection (2) "prescribed" means prescribed by the rules.

[2012]

NOTES

Rules: the Gangmasters (Licensing Conditions) Rules 2009, SI 2009/307.

---

9 Modification, revocation or transfer of licence

(1) The Authority may by notice in writing to the licensee modify or revoke any licence granted to him (including any of the conditions of that licence)—
  (a) with the consent of the licensee, or
  (b) where it appears to him that a condition of the licence or any requirement of this Act has not been complied with.

(2) The modifications that may be made include one suspending the effect of the licence for such period as the Authority may determine.

(3) A licence may be transferred with the written consent of the Authority and in such other cases as may be determined by the Authority.

[2013]

10 Appeals

(1) The Secretary of State shall by regulations make provision for an appeal against any decision of the Authority—

(a)   to refuse an application for a licence,
(b)   as to the conditions to which the grant of the licence is subject,
(c)   to refuse consent to the transfer of a licence, or
(d)   to modify or revoke a licence.

(2)   The regulations shall make provision—
(a)   for and in connection with the appointment of a person to hear and determine such appeals (including provision for the payment of remuneration and allowances to such a person), and
(b)   as to the procedure to be followed in connection with an appeal.

[2014]

NOTES
Regulations: the Gangmasters (Appeals) Regulations 2006, SI 2006/662.

11   Register of licences

(1)   The Authority shall establish and maintain a register of persons licensed under this Act.

(2)   The register shall contain such particulars as the Authority may determine of every person who for the time being holds a licence or whose activities are authorised by a licence (whether or not they are named in the licence).

(3)   The Authority shall ensure that appropriate arrangements are in force for allowing members of the public to inspect the contents of the register.

[2015]

NOTES
Commencement: 1 October 2006.

Offences

12   Offences: acting as a gangmaster, being in possession of false documents etc

(1)   A person commits an offence if he acts as a gangmaster in contravention of section 6 (prohibition of unlicensed activities).

For this purpose a person acting as a gangmaster does not contravene section 6 by reason only of the fact that he breaches a condition of the licence which authorises him to so act.

(2)   A person commits an offence if he has in his possession or under his control—
(a)   a relevant document that is false and that he knows or believes to be false,
(b)   a relevant document that was improperly obtained and that he knows or believes to have been improperly obtained, or
(c)   a relevant document that relates to someone else,

with the intention of inducing another person to believe that he or another person acting as a gangmaster in contravention of section 6 is acting under the authority of a licence.

(3)   A person guilty of an offence under subsection (1) or (2) is liable on summary conviction—
(a)   in England and Wales, to imprisonment for a term not exceeding twelve months, or to a fine not exceeding the statutory maximum, or to both;
(b)   in Scotland or Northern Ireland, to imprisonment for a term not exceeding six months, or to a fine not exceeding the statutory maximum, or to both.

In relation to an offence committed before the commencement of section 154(1) of the Criminal Justice Act 2003 (c 44), for "twelve months" in paragraph (a) substitute "six months".

(4)   A person guilty of an offence under subsection (1) or (2) is liable on conviction on indictment to imprisonment for a term not exceeding ten years, or to a fine, or to both.

(5)   For the purposes of this section—
(a)   except in Scotland, a document is false only if it is false within the meaning of Part 1 of the Forgery and Counterfeiting Act 1981 (c 45) (see section 9(1) of that Act), and
(b)   a document was improperly obtained if false information was provided, in or in connection with the application for its issue or an application for its modification, to the person who issued it or (as the case may be) to a person entitled to modify it,

and references to the making of a false document include references to the modification of a document so that it becomes false.

(6)   In this section "relevant document" means—
(a)   a licence, or
(b)   any document issued by the Authority in connection with a licence.

[2016]

NOTES
Commencement: 1 October 2006 (for purposes related to work falling within s 3(1)(a) and (c)); 6 April 2007 (otherwise).

13 Offences: entering into arrangements with gangmasters

(1)　A person commits an offence if—

- (a)　he enters into arrangements under which a person ("the gangmaster") supplies him with workers or services, and
- (b)　the gangmaster in supplying the workers or services contravenes section 6 (prohibition of unlicensed activities).

(2)　In proceedings against a person for an offence under subsection (1) it is a defence for him to prove that he—

- (a)　took all reasonable steps to satisfy himself that the gangmaster was acting under the authority of a valid licence, and
- (b)　did not know, and had no reasonable grounds for suspecting that the gangmaster was not the holder of a valid licence.

(3)　The Secretary of State may by regulations make provision as to what constitutes "reasonable steps" for the purposes of subsection (2)(a).

(4)　A person guilty of an offence under subsection (1) is liable—

- (a)　on summary conviction in England and Wales, to imprisonment for a term not exceeding 51 weeks, or to a fine not exceeding the statutory maximum, or to both,
- (b)　on summary conviction in Scotland or Northern Ireland, to imprisonment for a term not exceeding six months, or to a fine not exceeding the statutory maximum, or to both.

In relation to an offence committed before the commencement of section 281(5) of the Criminal Justice Act 2003 (c 44), for "51 weeks" in paragraph (a) substitute "six months".

[2017]

NOTES
Commencement: 1 October 2006 (sub-s (3)); 1 December 2006 (sub-ss (1), (2), (4), for purposes related to work falling within s 3(1)(a) and (c)); 6 April 2007 (otherwise).

14 Offences: supplementary provisions

(1)　An enforcement officer (see section 15) has the powers of arrest mentioned in subsection (2) (in addition to powers under [section 24A] of the Police and Criminal Evidence Act 1984 (c 60)) in relation to any of the following offences—

- (a)　an offence under section 12(1) or (2),
- (b)　conspiring to commit any such offence,
- (c)　attempting to commit any such offence,
- (d)　inciting, aiding, abetting, counselling or procuring the commission of any such offence.

(2)　Those powers are as follows—

- (a)　if he has reasonable grounds for suspecting that such an offence has been committed, he may arrest without warrant anyone whom he has reasonable grounds for suspecting to be guilty of the offence;
- (b)　he may arrest without warrant—
  - (i)　anyone who is about to commit such an offence;
  - (ii)　anyone whom he has reasonable grounds for suspecting to be about to commit such an offence.

(3)　Subsections (1) and (2) do not apply in Scotland.

(4)　...

[2018]

NOTES
Commencement: 1 October 2006.
Sub-s (1): words in square brackets substituted by the Serious Organised Crime and Police Act 2005, s 111, Sch 7, Pt 4, para 62(a).
Sub-s (4): amends the Proceeds of Crime Act 2002, Schs 2, 4, 5.
See further, in relation to England, Wales and Northern Ireland, the Serious Crime Act 2007, s 63(1), Sch 6, Pt 1, para 50, which provides that the reference above to (or to conduct amounting to) the common law offence *of inciting the commission of another offence*, has effect (as from the day that offence is abolished) as a reference to (or to conduct amounting to) offences under the Serious Crime Act 2007, Pt 2.

Enforcement

15 Enforcement and compliance officers

(1)   The Secretary of State may appoint officers ("enforcement officers") to act for the purposes of this Act—
-   (a)   in enforcing the provisions of section 6 (prohibition of unlicensed activities), and
-   (b)   in taking action in circumstances in which it appears that an offence under section 13 (persons entering into arrangements with gangmasters) has been, is being, or may be committed.

(2)   The Secretary of State may, instead of or in addition to appointing enforcement officers under subsection (1), make arrangements with a relevant authority for officers of that authority to be enforcement officers.

(3)   The following are relevant authorities for this purpose—
-   (a)   the Authority,
-   (b)   any Minister of the Crown or government department,
-   (c)   the National Assembly for Wales,
-   (d)   the Scottish Ministers,
-   (e)   any body performing functions on behalf of the Crown.

(4)   The Authority may appoint officers ("compliance officers") to act for the purposes of this Act in verifying, from time to time or in such circumstances as the Authority may determine, compliance by a licence holder with the conditions of the licence.

(5)   When acting for the purposes of this Act, an enforcement officer or a compliance officer shall, if so required, produce some duly authenticated document showing his authority to act.

(6)   If it appears to an enforcement officer or a compliance officer that any person with whom he is dealing while acting for the purposes of this Act does not know that he is an officer so acting, the officer shall identify himself as such to that person.

[2019]

16 Powers of officers

(1)   An enforcement officer or a compliance officer acting for the purposes of this Act shall have power for the performance of his duties—
-   (a)   to require the production by a relevant person of any records required to be kept by virtue of this Act, to inspect and examine those records, to remove those records from the premises where they are kept and to copy any material part of them,
-   (b)   to require a relevant person to furnish to him (either alone or in the presence of any other person, as the officer thinks fit) an explanation of any such records,
-   (c)   to require a relevant person to furnish to him (either alone or in the presence of any other person, as the officer thinks fit) any additional information known to the relevant person which might reasonably be needed in order to establish whether—
    -   (i)   any provision of this Act, or
    -   (ii)   any condition of any licence granted under it,
    is being complied with,
-   (d)   at all reasonable times to enter any relevant premises in order to exercise any power conferred on the officer by virtue of paragraphs (a) to (c).

(2)   The powers conferred by subsection (1) include power, on reasonable written notice, to require a relevant person—
-   (a)   to produce any such records as are mentioned in paragraph (a) of that subsection to an officer at such time and place as may be specified in the notice, or
-   (b)   to attend before an officer at such time and place as may be specified in the notice to furnish any such explanation or additional information as is mentioned in paragraph (b) or (c) of that subsection.

(3)   The power conferred by subsection (1)(a) includes, in relation to records which are kept by means of a computer, power to require the records to be produced in a form in which they are legible and can be taken away.

(4)   A person authorised by virtue of subsection (1)(a) to inspect any records is entitled to have access to, and to check the operation of, any computer and any associated apparatus or material which is or has been in use in connection with the records in question.

(5)   In this section "relevant person" means any person whom an officer acting for the purposes of this Act has reasonable cause to believe to be—
-   (a)   a person acting as a gangmaster,
-   (b)   a person supplied with workers or services by a person acting as a gangmaster,
-   (c)   any employee or agent of a person falling within paragraph (a) or (b).

(6)   In this section and section 17—

"relevant premises" means any premises which an officer acting for the purposes of this Act has reasonable cause to believe to be—

    (a)   premises at which a person mentioned in subsection (5)(a) or (b) carries on business, and

    (b)   premises which such a person uses in connection with his business,

"premises" includes any place and, in particular, includes—

    (a)   any vehicle, vessel, aircraft or hovercraft, and

    (b)   any tent or movable structure.

[2020]

17 Entry by warrant

(1)   If a justice of the peace is satisfied by written information on oath that there are reasonable grounds for an enforcement officer to enter relevant premises for the purpose of ascertaining whether there has been any contravention of section 6 (prohibition of unlicensed activities), and is also satisfied—

    (a)   that admission to the premises has been refused, or that a refusal is expected, and (in either case) that notice of the intention to apply for a warrant has been given to the occupier,

    (b)   that an application for admission, or the giving of such a notice, would defeat the object of the entry,

    (c)   that the case is one of extreme urgency, or

    (d)   that the premises are unoccupied or the occupier is temporarily absent,

the justice may issue a warrant authorising the enforcement officer to enter the premises, if necessary using reasonable force.

(2)   An enforcement officer entering any premises by virtue of a warrant under this section may—

    (a)   take with him when he enters those premises such other persons and such other equipment as he considers necessary,

    (b)   carry out on those premises such inspections and examinations as he considers necessary for the purpose of ascertaining whether there has been any contravention of section 6, and

    (c)   take possession of any book, document, data, record (in whatever form it is held) or product which is on the premises and retain it for as long as he considers necessary for that purpose.

(3)   On leaving any premises which an enforcement officer is authorised to enter by a warrant under this section, that officer shall, if the premises are unoccupied or the occupier is temporarily absent, leave the premises as effectively secured against trespassers as he found them.

(4)   Where by virtue of subsection (2)(c) an enforcement officer takes possession of any item, he shall leave on the premises from which the item was removed a statement giving particulars of what he has taken and stating that he has taken possession of it.

(5)   In the application of this section to Scotland—

    (a)   the reference to a justice of the peace being satisfied by written information on oath, shall be read as a reference to a sheriff or a justice of the peace being satisfied; and

    (b)   "the justice" shall be read as a reference to the sheriff, or as the case may be, to the justice.

[2021]

18 Obstruction of officers

(1)   A person commits an offence who—

    (a)   intentionally obstructs an enforcement officer or compliance officer who is acting in the exercise of his functions under this Act, or

    (b)   without reasonable cause, fails to comply with any requirement made of him by such an officer who is so acting.

(2)   A person who, in giving any information which is required of him by an enforcement officer or compliance officer, makes a statement which is false in a material particular commits an offence.

(3)   A person guilty of an offence under this section is liable—

    (a)   on summary conviction in England and Wales, to imprisonment for a term not exceeding 51 weeks, or to a fine not exceeding the statutory maximum, or to both,

    (b)   on summary conviction in Scotland or Northern Ireland, to imprisonment for a term not exceeding six months, or to a fine not exceeding the statutory maximum, or to both.

In relation to an offence committed before the commencement of section 281(5) of the Criminal Justice Act 2003 (c 44), for "51 weeks" in paragraph (a) substitute "six months".

[2022]

19 Information relating to gangmasters

(1)   Information held by any person for the purposes of, or for any purpose connected with, the exercise of functions under this Act—
  (a)   may be supplied to any other person for use for any such purpose, and
  (b)   may be supplied to any person having functions in relation to—
    (i)   the enforcement of any other enactment applying to the operations of a person acting as a gangmaster,
    (ii)   the enforcement of any other enactment in connection with accommodation, meals or facilities provided to workers, or the conditions in which they work, or
    (iii)   offences committed by workers in connection with or by reason of their doing work to which this Act applies,
  for use for the purposes of, or for any purpose connected with, those functions.

(2)   Information relating to the operations of a person acting as a gangmaster which is held by any person for the purposes of, or for any purpose connected with, such functions as are mentioned in subsection (1)(b) may be supplied to any person having functions under this Act for the purposes of, or for any purpose connected with, the exercise of those functions.

(3)   Information supplied under subsection (2) by or on behalf of the Commissioners of Inland Revenue or the Commissioners of Customs and Excise must not be supplied by the recipient to any other person without the consent of the Commissioners concerned.

(4)   This section—
  (a)   has effect notwithstanding any restriction on the disclosure of information imposed by any enactment or rule of law, and
  (b)   does not limit the circumstances in which information may be used or supplied apart from this section.

(5)   In this section "enactment" means an Act of Parliament, an Act of the Scottish Parliament or any Northern Ireland legislation or any instrument made under or having effect by virtue of an Act of Parliament, an Act of the Scottish Parliament or any Northern Ireland legislation.

(6)   References in this section to a person having functions of any description include references to any person providing, or employed in the provision of, services for that person in connection with those functions.

[2023]

Supplementary

20 Application of Act to bodies corporate

(1)   A licence under this Act may be granted to a body corporate.

(2)   A licence granted to a body corporate authorises activities carried on by the body through such persons representing, or acting on behalf of, the body as are named or otherwise specified in the licence.

(3)   If an offence under this Act committed by a body corporate is shown—
  (a)   to have been committed with the consent or connivance of an officer of the body corporate, or
  (b)   to be attributable to any neglect on his part,
the officer, as well as the body corporate, is guilty of the offence and liable to be proceeded against and punished accordingly.

(4)   In subsection (3) "officer" means—
  (a)   any director, manager, secretary or other similar officer of the body corporate, or
  (b)   any person purporting to act in any such capacity.

(5)   If the affairs of a body corporate are managed by its members, subsection (3) applies in relation to the acts and defaults of a member in connection with his functions of management as if he were a director of the body corporate.

[2024]

21 Application of Act to unincorporated associations

(1)   A licence under this Act may be granted to an unincorporated association (other than a partnership).

(2)   A licence granted to an unincorporated association authorises activities carried on by the association through such persons representing, or acting on behalf of, the association as are named or otherwise specified in the licence.

(3)   Proceedings for an offence under this Act alleged to have been committed by an unincorporated association may be brought against the association in the name of the association.

(4)   For the purposes of such proceedings—

(a) rules of court relating to the service of documents have effect as if the association were a body corporate, and

(b) the following provisions apply as they apply in relation to a body corporate—
section 33 of the Criminal Justice Act 1925 (c 86) and Schedule 3 to the Magistrates' Courts Act 1980 (c 43),
sections 70 and 143 of the Criminal Procedure (Scotland) Act 1995,
section 18 of the Criminal Justice Act (Northern Ireland) 1945 (c 15 (NI)) and Schedule 4 to the Magistrates' Courts (Northern Ireland) Order 1981 (SI 1981/1675 (NI 26)).

(5) A fine imposed on the association on its conviction of an offence shall be paid out of the funds of the association.

(6) If an offence under this Act committed by an unincorporated association is shown—
(a) to have been committed with the consent or connivance of an officer of the association, or
(b) to be attributable to any neglect on his part,
the officer, as well as the association, is guilty of the offence and liable to be proceeded against and punished accordingly.

(7) In subsection (6) "officer", in relation to any association, means—
(a) any officer of the association or any member of its governing body, or
(b) any person purporting to act in such a capacity.

[2025]

22 Application of Act to partnerships

(1) A licence under this Act may be granted to a partnership in the firm name.

(2) Where the partnership is not regarded as a legal person under the law of the country or territory under which it is formed, the grant of a licence to the partnership in the firm name—
(a) continues to have effect notwithstanding a change of partners, so long as at least one of the persons who was a partner before the change remains a partner after it; and
(b) has effect as the grant of a licence to those partners named in the licence.

(3) If in the case of such a partnership an offence under this Act committed by a partner is shown—
(a) to have been committed with the consent or connivance of another partner, or
(b) to be attributable to any neglect on the part of another partner,
that other partner, as well as the first-mentioned partner, is guilty of the offence and liable to be proceeded against and punished accordingly.

(4) A licence granted to a partnership that is regarded as a legal person under the law of the country or territory under which it is formed authorises activities carried on by the partnership through those partners named in the licence.

(5) Proceedings for an offence under this Act alleged to have been committed by such a partnership may be brought against the partnership in the firm name.

(6) For the purposes of such proceedings—
(a) rules of court relating to the service of documents have effect as if the partnership were a body corporate, and
(b) the following provisions apply as they apply in relation to a body corporate—
section 33 of the Criminal Justice Act 1925 (c 86) and Schedule 3 to the Magistrates' Courts Act 1980 (c 43),
sections 70 and 143 of the Criminal Procedure (Scotland) Act 1995,
section 18 of the Criminal Justice Act (Northern Ireland) 1945 (c 15 (NI)) and Schedule 4 to the Magistrates' Courts (Northern Ireland) Order 1981 (SI 1981/1675 (NI 26)).

(7) A fine imposed on a partnership on its conviction of an offence shall be paid out of the funds of the partnership.

(8) If an offence under this Act committed by a partnership is shown—
(a) to have been committed with the consent or connivance of a partner, or
(b) to be attributable to any neglect on the part of a partner,
the partner, as well as the partnership, is guilty of the offence and liable to be proceeded against and punished accordingly.

(9) In subsections (3) and (8) "partner" includes a person purporting to act as a partner.

[2026]

Miscellaneous and general

23   Annual report

The Secretary of State shall each year lay a report before each House of Parliament on the operation of this Act.

[2027]

24   Financial provision

(1)   The Secretary of State may make payments to the Authority of such amounts, at such times and on such conditions (if any) as he considers appropriate.

(2)   The Authority shall (unless the Secretary of State directs otherwise) pay to the Secretary of State all sums received by it in the course of, or in connection with, the carrying out of its functions.

(3)   Any sums received by the Secretary of State under subsection (2) shall be paid into the Consolidated Fund.

[2028]

25   Regulations, rules and orders

(1)   In this Act, unless otherwise indicated, "prescribed" means prescribed by regulations made by the Secretary of State.

(2)   Any power to make regulations or rules under this Act includes power to make different provision for different cases.

(3)   Any power of the Secretary of State to make regulations or orders under this Act is exercisable by statutory instrument.

(4)   Any power of the Authority to make rules under this Act is exercisable by statutory instrument.

(5)   A statutory instrument containing regulations made by the Secretary of State under—
    (a)   section 1(5) (regulations as to status, constitution, etc of the Authority), or
    (b)   section 3(5)(b) (regulations extending work to which this Act applies),

must not be made unless a draft of the instrument has been laid before, and approved by a resolution of, each House of Parliament.

(6)   A statutory instrument containing—
    (a)   regulations made by the Secretary of State under any other provision of this Act, or
    (b)   rules made by the Authority under section 8 (general power of Authority to make rules),

is subject to annulment in pursuance of a resolution of either House of Parliament.

[2029]

26   Meaning of "worker"

(1)   In this Act "worker" means an individual who does work to which this Act applies.

(2)   A person is not prevented from being a worker for the purposes of this Act by reason of the fact that he has no right to be, or to work, in the United Kingdom.

[2030]

27   Exclusion of provisions relating to employment agencies and businesses

(1)   The Employment Agencies Act 1973 (c 35) does not apply to an employment agency or an employment business in so far as it consists of activities for which a licence is required under this Act.

(2)   In subsection (1) "employment agency" and "employment business" have the same meaning as in that Act.

[2031]

NOTES

Commencement: 1 October 2006 (for purposes related to work falling within s 3(1)(a) and (c)); 6 April 2007 (otherwise).

---

28   Application of Act to Northern Ireland

The provisions of Schedule 2 to this Act have effect with respect to the application of this Act to Northern Ireland.

[2032]

NOTES

Commencement: 1 December 2004 (certain purposes); 1 April 2005 (certain purposes); 1 October 2006 (certain purposes); 6 April 2007 (otherwise).

29 Commencement and transitional provision

(1)   The provisions of this Act come into force on such day as the Secretary of State may by order appoint.

(2)   Different days may be appointed for different purposes and for different areas.

(3)   The Secretary of State may by order make such transitional provision as he considers appropriate in connection with the coming into force of any provision of this Act.

[2033]

NOTES

Orders: the Gangmasters (Licensing) Act 2004 (Commencement No 1) Order 2004, SI 2004/2857; the Gangmasters (Licensing) Act 2004 (Commencement No 2) Order 2005, SI 2005/447; the Gangmasters (Licensing) Act 2004 (Commencement No 3) Order 2006, SI 2006/2406; the Gangmasters (Licensing) Act 2004 (Commencement No 4) Order 2006, SI 2006/2906; the Gangmasters (Licensing) Act 2004 (Commencement No 5) Order 2007, SI 2007/695.

30 Short title and extent

(1)   This Act may be cited as the Gangmasters (Licensing) Act 2004.

(2)   This Act extends to England and Wales, Scotland and Northern Ireland.

[2034]

(Sch 1 (Consequential Amendments) outside the scope of this work.)

SCHEDULE 2
APPLICATION OF ACT TO NORTHERN IRELAND
Section 28

Introduction

1.—(1)   The following provisions have effect in relation to the application of this Act to Northern Ireland.

(2)   For the purposes of this Schedule the relevant Northern Ireland department is the Department of Agriculture and Rural Development in Northern Ireland.

General

2.—(1)   References in this Schedule to "work in Northern Ireland" are to work—
   (a)   in Northern Ireland,
   (b)   on any portion of the shore or bed of the sea, or of an estuary or tidal river, adjacent to Northern Ireland, whether above or below (or partly above and partly below) the low water mark, or
   (c)   in Northern Ireland coastal waters.

(2)   In sub-paragraph (1)(c) "Northern Ireland coastal waters" means waters adjacent to Northern Ireland to a distance of six miles measured from the baselines from which the breadth of the territorial sea is measured.

In this sub-paragraph "miles" means international nautical miles of 1,852 metres.

(3)   The provisions of this Act relating to work in Northern Ireland apply where a person acts as a gangmaster, whether in Northern Ireland or elsewhere, in relation to work in Northern Ireland to which this Act applies.

(4)   References in this Schedule to "Northern Ireland licences" are to licences under this Act in respect of activities as a gangmaster in relation to work in Northern Ireland.

Section 1: The Gangmasters Licensing Authority

3.   In relation to persons acting as gangmasters in Northern Ireland or persons acting as gangmasters in relation to work in Northern Ireland, the reference to the Secretary of State in section 1(2)(f) (power to prescribe additional functions of Authority) shall be read as a reference to the relevant Northern Ireland department.

4.   Before making any regulations under that provision, the relevant Northern Ireland department shall consult the Secretary of State.

5.   Before making any regulations under section 1(5) (regulations as to status, constitution etc of the Authority), the Secretary of State shall consult the relevant Northern Ireland department.

Section 2: Directions etc by the Secretary of State

6.   In relation to the Authority's functions in connection with persons acting as gangmasters in Northern Ireland or persons acting as gangmasters in relation to work in Northern Ireland, the references in section 2 to the Secretary of State shall be read as references to the relevant Northern Ireland department.

Section 3: Work to which this Act applies

7.   In section 3(5) (power to make regulations excluding or including work) as it applies in relation to work in Northern Ireland—

    (a)   the reference to the Secretary of State shall be read as a reference to the relevant Northern Ireland department, and

    (b)   for the reference to the Diseases of Fish Act 1937 (c 33) substitute a reference to the Fisheries Act (NI) 1966 (c 17 (NI)).

Section 6: Prohibition of unlicensed activities

8.   In section 6(2) (power to specify circumstances in which licence not required) as it applies in relation to work in Northern Ireland, the reference to the Secretary of State shall be read as a reference to the relevant Northern Ireland department.

Section 7: Grant of licences

9.   The Authority shall grant separate licences in respect of activities as a gangmaster in relation to work in Northern Ireland.

Section 8: General power of Authority to make rules

10.—(1)   Rules under section 8 (general power of Authority to make rules) may make different provision for Northern Ireland licences.

    (2)   In section 8(3) as it applies in relation to rules requiring the payment of fees in connection with Northern Ireland licences, the reference to the Secretary of State shall be read as a reference to the relevant Northern Ireland department.

Section 10: Appeals

11.   In section 10 as it applies in relation to decisions made in connection with Northern Ireland licences, the reference to the Secretary of State shall be read as a reference to the relevant Northern Ireland department.

Section 11: Register of licences

12.   The Authority shall establish and maintain a separate register of Northern Ireland licences.

Section 13: Offences: entering into arrangements with gangmasters

13.   In section 13(3) (power to make regulations as to what constitutes "reasonable steps") as it applies in relation to persons entering into arrangements with gangmasters in relation to work in Northern Ireland, the reference to the Secretary of State shall be read as a reference to the relevant Northern Ireland department.

Section 14: Offences: supplementary provisions

14.   In section 14(1) (additional powers of arrest) the reference to [section 24A] of the Police and Criminal Evidence Act 1984 (c 60) shall be read as a reference to Article 26(4) and (5) of the Police and Criminal Evidence (Northern Ireland) Order 1989 (SI 1989/ 1341 (NI 12)).

Section 15: Enforcement and compliance officers

15.—(1)   The relevant Northern Ireland department may appoint officers ("enforcement officers") to act for the purposes of this Act in Northern Ireland—

    (a)   in enforcing the provisions of section 6 (prohibition of unlicensed activities), and

    (b)   in taking action in circumstances in which it appears that an offence under section 13 (persons entering into arrangements with gangmasters) has been, is being, or may be committed.

    (2)   The relevant Northern Ireland department may, instead of or in addition to appointing enforcement officers under sub-paragraph (1), make arrangements with a relevant authority for officers of that authority to be enforcement officers in Northern Ireland.

    (3)   The following are relevant authorities for this purpose—

    (a)   the Authority,

    (b)   any Minister of the Crown or government department,

(c) any Minister within the meaning of the Northern Ireland Act 1998 (c 47) or Northern Ireland department,

(d) any body performing functions on behalf of the Crown.

Section 17: Entry by warrant

16. In section 17 the reference in subsection (1) to information on oath shall be read as a reference to a complaint on oath.

Section 23: Annual report

17.—(1) The Secretary of State shall send to the relevant Northern Ireland department a copy of every report laid by him before Parliament under section 23.

(2) The relevant Northern Ireland department shall lay a copy of the report before the Northern Ireland Assembly.

Section 24: Financial provision

18. In relation to payments to the Authority with respect to its functions in connection with persons acting as gangmasters in Northern Ireland or persons acting as gangmasters in relation to work in Northern Ireland, the reference in section 24(1) to the Secretary of State shall be read as a reference to the relevant Northern Ireland department.

Section 25: Regulations, rules and orders

19.—(1) In section 25(1) (meaning of "prescribed") as it applies in relation to matters in relation to which the relevant Northern Ireland department has power to make regulations the reference to the Secretary of State shall be read as a reference to the relevant Northern Ireland department.

(2) Regulations under this Act made by the relevant Northern Ireland department shall be made by statutory rule (for the purposes of the Statutory Rules (Northern Ireland) Order 1979 (SI 1979/1573 (NI 12)).

(3) A statutory rule containing regulations under section 3(5)(b) (regulations extending work to which this Act applies) must not be made unless a draft of the rule has been laid before and approved by the Northern Ireland Assembly.

(4) Any other power under this Act to make a statutory rule is subject to negative resolution.

In this sub-paragraph "negative resolution" shall be construed in accordance with section 41 of the Interpretation Act (Northern Ireland) 1954 (c 33 (NI)).

Section 27: Exclusion of provisions relating to employment agencies and businesses

20. In section 27 as it applies in relation to activities in relation to work in Northern Ireland, the references to the Employment Agencies Act 1973 (c 35) shall be read as references to Part 2 of the Employment (Miscellaneous Provisions) (Northern Ireland) Order 1981 (SI 1981/839 (NI 20)).

Section 29: Commencement and transitional provision

21. Before exercising the power under section 29(1) or (3) in relation to the coming into force of any provision of this Act in relation to persons acting as gangmasters in relation to work in Northern Ireland, the Secretary of State shall consult the relevant Northern Ireland department.

[2035]

NOTES

Commencement: 1 December 2004 (paras 1–8, 11, 19, 21); 1 April 2005 (paras 9, 10, 15–18); 1 October 2006 (paras 12–14, para 20 for purposes related to work falling within s 3(1)(a) and (c)); 6 April 2007 (otherwise).

Para 14: words in square brackets substituted by the Serious Organised Crime and Police Act 2005, s 111, Sch 7, Pt 4, para 62(b).

CHRISTMAS DAY (TRADING) ACT 2004

(2004 c 26)

An Act to prohibit the opening of large shops on Christmas Day and to restrict the loading or unloading of goods at such shops on Christmas Day

[28 October 2004]

1 Prohibition of opening of large shops on Christmas Day

(1) A large shop must not be open on Christmas Day for the serving of retail customers.

(2)   Subsection (1) does not apply to any of the shops mentioned in paragraph 3(1) of Schedule 1 to the 1994 Act (shops exempt from restrictions on Sunday trading).

(3)   If subsection (1) is contravened in relation to a shop, the occupier of the shop is liable on summary conviction to a fine not exceeding £50,000.

(4)   In its application for the purposes of subsection (2), paragraph 3(2) of Schedule 1 to the 1994 Act (which relates to the interpretation of paragraph 3(1) of that Schedule) has effect as if—
   (a)   the reference to weekdays were a reference to days of the year other than Christmas Day, and
   (b)   the reference to Sunday were a reference to Christmas Day.

(5)   In this section—
   "large shop" has the same meaning as in Schedule 1 to the 1994 Act, except that for the purposes of this section the definition of "relevant floor area" in paragraph 1 of that Schedule is to be read as if the reference to the week ending with the Sunday in question were a reference to the period of seven days ending with the Christmas Day in question;
   "retail customer" and "shop" have the same meaning as in that Schedule.

[2036]

2   Loading and unloading early on Christmas Day

(1)   Where a shop which is prohibited by section 1 from opening on Christmas Day is located in a loading control area, the occupier of the shop must not load or unload, or permit any other person to load or unload, goods from a vehicle at the shop before 9am on Christmas Day in connection with the trade or business carried on in the shop, unless the loading or unloading is carried on—
   (a)   with the consent of the local authority for the area in which the shop is situated, granted in accordance with this section, and
   (b)   in accordance with any conditions subject to which that consent is granted.

(2)   The provisions of paragraphs 3 to 8 of Schedule 3 to the 1994 Act shall apply in relation to consent under subsection (1) as they apply in relation to consent under that Schedule, but as if—
   (a)   the reference in paragraph 6(1) to Sunday were a reference to Christmas Day, and
   (b)   the reference in paragraph 7(a) to an offence under paragraph 9 of that Schedule were a reference to an offence under subsection (3).

(3)   A person who contravenes subsection (1) is liable on summary conviction to a fine not exceeding level 3 on the standard scale.

(4)   In this section, "loading control area" means any area designated by a local authority as a loading control area in accordance with section 2 of the 1994 Act.

[2037]

3   Enforcement

(1)   It is the duty of every local authority to enforce within their area the provisions of sections 1 and 2.

(2)   For the purposes of their duties under subsection (1), it is the duty of every local authority to appoint inspectors, who may be the same persons as those appointed as inspectors by the local authority under paragraph 2 of Schedule 2 to the 1994 Act.

(3)   Paragraphs 3 and 4 of Schedule 2 to the 1994 Act (powers of entry and obstruction of inspectors) apply in respect of inspectors appointed under subsection (2) as they apply to inspectors appointed under paragraph 2 of that Schedule and, for the purposes of paragraph 3 of that Schedule as so applied, the reference in that paragraph to the provisions of Schedules 1 and 3 to the 1994 Act is to be taken to be a reference to the provisions of sections 1 and 2 of this Act.

(4)   Paragraphs 5, 6 and 7 of Schedule 2 to the 1994 Act (offences due to fault of other person, offences by body corporate and defence of due diligence) apply in respect of the offences under sections 1 and 2 as they apply in respect of offences under the 1994 Act.

(5)   In this section "local authority" has the meaning given by section 8 of the 1994 Act.

[2038]

4   (*Amends the Sunday Trading Act 1994, Schs 1, 3 at* **[1542I]**, **[1542L]**.)

5   Expenses

There is to be paid out of money provided by Parliament any increase attributable to this Act in the sums which under any other Act are payable out of money so provided.

[2039]

6   Short title, interpretation, commencement and extent

(1)   This Act may be cited as the Christmas Day (Trading) Act 2004.

(2)   In this Act "the 1994 Act" means the Sunday Trading Act 1994 (c 20).

(3)   This Act comes into force on such day as the Secretary of State may by order made by statutory instrument appoint.

(4)   This Act extends to England and Wales only.

[2040]

NOTES

Orders: the Christmas Day (Trading) Act 2004 (Commencement) Order 2004, SI 2004/3235.

MENTAL CAPACITY ACT 2005

(2005 c 9)

ARRANGEMENT OF SECTIONS

PART 1
PERSONS WHO LACK CAPACITY

PART 3
MISCELLANEOUS AND GENERAL

An Act to make new provision relating to persons who lack capacity; to establish a superior court of record called the Court of Protection in place of the office of the Supreme Court called by that name; to make provision in connection with the Convention on the International Protection of Adults signed at the Hague on 13th January 2000; and for connected purposes

[7 April 2005]

PART 1
PERSONS WHO LACK CAPACITY

The principles

1 The principles

(1)   The following principles apply for the purposes of this Act.

(2)   A person must be assumed to have capacity unless it is established that he lacks capacity.

(3)   A person is not to be treated as unable to make a decision unless all practicable steps to help him to do so have been taken without success.

(4)   A person is not to be treated as unable to make a decision merely because he makes an unwise decision.

(5)   An act done, or decision made, under this Act for or on behalf of a person who lacks capacity must be done, or made, in his best interests.

(6)   Before the act is done, or the decision is made, regard must be had to whether the purpose for which it is needed can be as effectively achieved in a way that is less restrictive of the person's rights and freedom of action.

[2041]

NOTES

Commencement: 1 April 2007 (for the purposes of s 44 of this Act and in England for purposes relating to the independent mental capacity advocate service); 1 October 2007 (otherwise).

Preliminary

2 People who lack capacity

(1)   For the purposes of this Act, a person lacks capacity in relation to a matter if at the material time he is unable to make a decision for himself in relation to the matter because of an impairment of, or a disturbance in the functioning of, the mind or brain.

(2)   It does not matter whether the impairment or disturbance is permanent or temporary.

(3)   A lack of capacity cannot be established merely by reference to—
   (a)   a person's age or appearance, or
   (b)   a condition of his, or an aspect of his behaviour, which might lead others to make unjustified assumptions about his capacity.

(4)   In proceedings under this Act or any other enactment, any question whether a person lacks capacity within the meaning of this Act must be decided on the balance of probabilities.

(5)   No power which a person ("D") may exercise under this Act—
   (a)   in relation to a person who lacks capacity, or
   (b)   where D reasonably thinks that a person lacks capacity,
is exercisable in relation to a person under 16.

(6)   Subsection (5) is subject to section 18(3).

[2042]

NOTES

Commencement: 1 April 2007 (for the purposes of s 44 of this Act and in England for purposes relating to the independent mental capacity advocate service); 1 October 2007 (otherwise).

3 Inability to make decisions

(1)   For the purposes of section 2, a person is unable to make a decision for himself if he is unable—
   (a)   to understand the information relevant to the decision,
   (b)   to retain that information,
   (c)   to use or weigh that information as part of the process of making the decision, or
   (d)   to communicate his decision (whether by talking, using sign language or any other means).

(2)   A person is not to be regarded as unable to understand the information relevant to a decision if he is able to understand an explanation of it given to him in a way that is appropriate to his circumstances (using simple language, visual aids or any other means).

(3)   The fact that a person is able to retain the information relevant to a decision for a short period only does not prevent him from being regarded as able to make the decision.

(4)   The information relevant to a decision includes information about the reasonably foreseeable consequences of—
    (a)   deciding one way or another, or
    (b)   failing to make the decision.

[2043]

NOTES
  Commencement: 1 April 2007 (for the purposes of s 44 of this Act and in England for purposes relating to the independent mental capacity advocate service); 1 October 2007 (otherwise).

---

4   Best interests

(1)   In determining for the purposes of this Act what is in a person's best interests, the person making the determination must not make it merely on the basis of—
    (a)   the person's age or appearance, or
    (b)   a condition of his, or an aspect of his behaviour, which might lead others to make unjustified assumptions about what might be in his best interests.

(2)   The person making the determination must consider all the relevant circumstances and, in particular, take the following steps.

(3)   He must consider—
    (a)   whether it is likely that the person will at some time have capacity in relation to the matter in question, and
    (b)   if it appears likely that he will, when that is likely to be.

(4)   He must, so far as reasonably practicable, permit and encourage the person to participate, or to improve his ability to participate, as fully as possible in any act done for him and any decision affecting him.

(5)   Where the determination relates to life-sustaining treatment he must not, in considering whether the treatment is in the best interests of the person concerned, be motivated by a desire to bring about his death.

(6)   He must consider, so far as is reasonably ascertainable—
    (a)   the person's past and present wishes and feelings (and, in particular, any relevant written statement made by him when he had capacity),
    (b)   the beliefs and values that would be likely to influence his decision if he had capacity, and
    (c)   the other factors that he would be likely to consider if he were able to do so.

(7)   He must take into account, if it is practicable and appropriate to consult them, the views of—
    (a)   anyone named by the person as someone to be consulted on the matter in question or on matters of that kind,
    (b)   anyone engaged in caring for the person or interested in his welfare,
    (c)   any donee of a lasting power of attorney granted by the person, and
    (d)   any deputy appointed for the person by the court,
as to what would be in the person's best interests and, in particular, as to the matters mentioned in subsection (6).

(8)   The duties imposed by subsections (1) to (7) also apply in relation to the exercise of any powers which—
    (a)   are exercisable under a lasting power of attorney, or
    (b)   are exercisable by a person under this Act where he reasonably believes that another person lacks capacity.

(9)   In the case of an act done, or a decision made, by a person other than the court, there is sufficient compliance with this section if (having complied with the requirements of subsections (1) to (7)) he reasonably believes that what he does or decides is in the best interests of the person concerned.

(10)   "Life-sustaining treatment" means treatment which in the view of a person providing health care for the person concerned is necessary to sustain life.

(11)   "Relevant circumstances" are those—
    (a)   of which the person making the determination is aware, and
    (b)   which it would be reasonable to regard as relevant.

[2044]

NOTES

Commencement: 1 April 2007 (for the purposes of s 44 of this Act and in England for purposes relating to the independent mental capacity advocate service); 1 October 2007 (otherwise).

[4A Restriction on deprivation of liberty

(1) This Act does not authorise any person ("D") to deprive any other person ("P") of his liberty.

(2) But that is subject to—
  (a) the following provisions of this section, and
  (b) section 4B.

(3) D may deprive P of his liberty if, by doing so, D is giving effect to a relevant decision of the court.

(4) A relevant decision of the court is a decision made by an order under section 16(2)(a) in relation to a matter concerning P's personal welfare.

(5) D may deprive P of his liberty if the deprivation is authorised by Schedule A1 (hospital and care home residents: deprivation of liberty).]

[2045]

NOTES

Commencement: 1 April 2009.
Inserted, together with s 4B, by the Mental Health Act 2007, s 50(1), (2).

[4B Deprivation of liberty necessary for life-sustaining treatment etc

(1) If the following conditions are met, D is authorised to deprive P of his liberty while a decision as respects any relevant issue is sought from the court.

(2) The first condition is that there is a question about whether D is authorised to deprive P of his liberty under section 4A.

(3) The second condition is that the deprivation of liberty—
  (a) is wholly or partly for the purpose of—
    (i) giving P life-sustaining treatment, or
    (ii) doing any vital act, or
  (b) consists wholly or partly of—
    (i) giving P life-sustaining treatment, or
    (ii) doing any vital act.

(4) The third condition is that the deprivation of liberty is necessary in order to—
  (a) give the life-sustaining treatment, or
  (b) do the vital act.

(5) A vital act is any act which the person doing it reasonably believes to be necessary to prevent a serious deterioration in P's condition.]

[2046]

NOTES

Commencement: 1 April 2009.
Inserted as noted to s 4A at **[2045]**.

5 Acts in connection with care or treatment

(1) If a person ("D") does an act in connection with the care or treatment of another person ("P"), the act is one to which this section applies if—
  (a) before doing the act, D takes reasonable steps to establish whether P lacks capacity in relation to the matter in question, and
  (b) when doing the act, D reasonably believes—
    (i) that P lacks capacity in relation to the matter, and
    (ii) that it will be in P's best interests for the act to be done.

(2) D does not incur any liability in relation to the act that he would not have incurred if P—
  (a) had had capacity to consent in relation to the matter, and
  (b) had consented to D's doing the act.

(3) Nothing in this section excludes a person's civil liability for loss or damage, or his criminal liability, resulting from his negligence in doing the act.

(4) Nothing in this section affects the operation of sections 24 to 26 (advance decisions to refuse treatment).

[2047]

6 Section 5 acts: limitations

(1) If D does an act that is intended to restrain P, it is not an act to which section 5 applies unless two further conditions are satisfied.

(2) The first condition is that D reasonably believes that it is necessary to do the act in order to prevent harm to P.

(3) The second is that the act is a proportionate response to—
    (a) the likelihood of P's suffering harm, and
    (b) the seriousness of that harm.

(4) For the purposes of this section D restrains P if he—
    (a) uses, or threatens to use, force to secure the doing of an act which P resists, or
    (b) restricts P's liberty of movement, whether or not P resists.

(5) …

(6) Section 5 does not authorise a person to do an act which conflicts with a decision made, within the scope of his authority and in accordance with this Part, by—
    (a) a donee of a lasting power of attorney granted by P, or
    (b) a deputy appointed for P by the court.

(7) But nothing in subsection (6) stops a person—
    (a) providing life-sustaining treatment, or
    (b) doing any act which he reasonably believes to be necessary to prevent a serious deterioration in P's condition,
while a decision as respects any relevant issue is sought from the court.

[2048]

7 Payment for necessary goods and services

(1) If necessary goods or services are supplied to a person who lacks capacity to contract for the supply, he must pay a reasonable price for them.

(2) "Necessary" means suitable to a person's condition in life and to his actual requirements at the time when the goods or services are supplied.

[2049]

8 Expenditure

(1) If an act to which section 5 applies involves expenditure, it is lawful for D—
    (a) to pledge P's credit for the purpose of the expenditure, and
    (b) to apply money in P's possession for meeting the expenditure.

(2) If the expenditure is borne for P by D, it is lawful for D—
    (a) to reimburse himself out of money in P's possession, or
    (b) to be otherwise indemnified by P.

(3) Subsections (1) and (2) do not affect any power under which (apart from those subsections) a person—
    (a) has lawful control of P's money or other property, and
    (b) has power to spend money for P's benefit.

[2050]

Lasting powers of attorney

9 Lasting powers of attorney

(1) A lasting power of attorney is a power of attorney under which the donor ("P") confers on the donee (or donees) authority to make decisions about all or any of the following—
    (a) P's personal welfare or specified matters concerning P's personal welfare, and

(b)   P's property and affairs or specified matters concerning P's property and affairs,

and which includes authority to make such decisions in circumstances where P no longer has capacity.

(2)   A lasting power of attorney is not created unless—
- (a)   section 10 is complied with,
- (b)   an instrument conferring authority of the kind mentioned in subsection (1) is made and registered in accordance with Schedule 1, and
- (c)   at the time when P executes the instrument, P has reached 18 and has capacity to execute it.

(3)   An instrument which—
- (a)   purports to create a lasting power of attorney, but
- (b)   does not comply with this section, section 10 or Schedule 1,

confers no authority.

(4)   The authority conferred by a lasting power of attorney is subject to—
- (a)   the provisions of this Act and, in particular, sections 1 (the principles) and 4 (best interests), and
- (b)   any conditions or restrictions specified in the instrument.

[2051]

NOTES

Commencement: 1 October 2007.

---

10 Appointment of donees

(1)   A donee of a lasting power of attorney must be—
- (a)   an individual who has reached 18, or
- (b)   if the power relates only to P's property and affairs, either such an individual or a trust corporation.

(2)   An individual who is bankrupt may not be appointed as donee of a lasting power of attorney in relation to P's property and affairs.

(3)   Subsections (4) to (7) apply in relation to an instrument under which two or more persons are to act as donees of a lasting power of attorney.

(4)   The instrument may appoint them to act—
- (a)   jointly,
- (b)   jointly and severally, or
- (c)   jointly in respect of some matters and jointly and severally in respect of others.

(5)   To the extent to which it does not specify whether they are to act jointly or jointly and severally, the instrument is to be assumed to appoint them to act jointly.

(6)   If they are to act jointly, a failure, as respects one of them, to comply with the requirements of subsection (1) or (2) or Part 1 or 2 of Schedule 1 prevents a lasting power of attorney from being created.

(7)   If they are to act jointly and severally, a failure, as respects one of them, to comply with the requirements of subsection (1) or (2) or Part 1 or 2 of Schedule 1—
- (a)   prevents the appointment taking effect in his case, but
- (b)   does not prevent a lasting power of attorney from being created in the case of the other or others.

(8)   An instrument used to create a lasting power of attorney—
- (a)   cannot give the donee (or, if more than one, any of them) power to appoint a substitute or successor, but
- (b)   may itself appoint a person to replace the donee (or, if more than one, any of them) on the occurrence of an event mentioned in section 13(6)(a) to (d) which has the effect of terminating the donee's appointment.

[2052]

NOTES

Commencement: 1 October 2007.

---

11 Lasting powers of attorney: restrictions

(1)   A lasting power of attorney does not authorise the donee (or, if more than one, any of them) to do an act that is intended to restrain P, unless three conditions are satisfied.

(2)   The first condition is that P lacks, or the donee reasonably believes that P lacks, capacity in relation to the matter in question.

(3)   The second is that the donee reasonably believes that it is necessary to do the act in order to prevent harm to P.

(4)   The third is that the act is a proportionate response to—
   (a)   the likelihood of P's suffering harm, and
   (b)   the seriousness of that harm.

(5)   For the purposes of this section, the donee restrains P if he—
   (a)   uses, or threatens to use, force to secure the doing of an act which P resists, or
   (b)   restricts P's liberty of movement, whether or not P resists,
or if he authorises another person to do any of those things.

(6)   ...

(7)   Where a lasting power of attorney authorises the donee (or, if more than one, any of them) to make decisions about P's personal welfare, the authority—
   (a)   does not extend to making such decisions in circumstances other than those where P lacks, or the donee reasonably believes that P lacks, capacity,
   (b)   is subject to sections 24 to 26 (advance decisions to refuse treatment), and
   (c)   extends to giving or refusing consent to the carrying out or continuation of a treatment by a person providing health care for P.

(8)   But subsection (7)(c)—
   (a)   does not authorise the giving or refusing of consent to the carrying out or continuation of life-sustaining treatment, unless the instrument contains express provision to that effect, and
   (b)   is subject to any conditions or restrictions in the instrument.

[2053]

NOTES
Commencement: 1 October 2007.
Sub-s (6): repealed by the Mental Health Act 2007, ss 50(1), (4)(b), 55, Sch 11, Pt 10.

12   Scope of lasting powers of attorney: gifts

(1)   Where a lasting power of attorney confers authority to make decisions about P's property and affairs, it does not authorise a donee (or, if more than one, any of them) to dispose of the donor's property by making gifts except to the extent permitted by subsection (2).

(2)   The donee may make gifts—
   (a)   on customary occasions to persons (including himself) who are related to or connected with the donor, or
   (b)   to any charity to whom the donor made or might have been expected to make gifts,
if the value of each such gift is not unreasonable having regard to all the circumstances and, in particular, the size of the donor's estate.

(3)   "Customary occasion" means—
   (a)   the occasion or anniversary of a birth, a marriage or the formation of a civil partnership, or
   (b)   any other occasion on which presents are customarily given within families or among friends or associates.

(4)   Subsection (2) is subject to any conditions or restrictions in the instrument.

[2054]

NOTES
Commencement: 1 October 2007.

13   Revocation of lasting powers of attorney etc

(1)   This section applies if—
   (a)   P has executed an instrument with a view to creating a lasting power of attorney, or
   (b)   a lasting power of attorney is registered as having been conferred by P,
and in this section references to revoking the power include revoking the instrument.

(2)   P may, at any time when he has capacity to do so, revoke the power.

(3)   P's bankruptcy revokes the power so far as it relates to P's property and affairs.

(4)   But where P is bankrupt merely because an interim bankruptcy restrictions order has effect in respect of him, the power is suspended, so far as it relates to P's property and affairs, for so long as the order has effect.

(5)   The occurrence in relation to a donee of an event mentioned in subsection (6)—
   (a)   terminates his appointment, and
   (b)   except in the cases given in subsection (7), revokes the power.

(6)   The events are—
(a)   the disclaimer of the appointment by the donee in accordance with such requirements as may be prescribed for the purposes of this section in regulations made by the Lord Chancellor,
(b)   subject to subsections (8) and (9), the death or bankruptcy of the donee or, if the donee is a trust corporation, its winding-up or dissolution,
(c)   subject to subsection (11), the dissolution or annulment of a marriage or civil partnership between the donor and the donee,
(d)   the lack of capacity of the donee.

(7)   The cases are—
(a)   the donee is replaced under the terms of the instrument,
(b)   he is one of two or more persons appointed to act as donees jointly and severally in respect of any matter and, after the event, there is at least one remaining donee.

(8)   The bankruptcy of a donee does not terminate his appointment, or revoke the power, in so far as his authority relates to P's personal welfare.

(9)   Where the donee is bankrupt merely because an interim bankruptcy restrictions order has effect in respect of him, his appointment and the power are suspended, so far as they relate to P's property and affairs, for so long as the order has effect.

(10)   Where the donee is one of two or more appointed to act jointly and severally under the power in respect of any matter, the reference in subsection (9) to the suspension of the power is to its suspension in so far as it relates to that donee.

(11)   The dissolution or annulment of a marriage or civil partnership does not terminate the appointment of a donee, or revoke the power, if the instrument provided that it was not to do so.
[2055]

NOTES
Commencement: 1 October 2007.
Regulations: the Lasting Powers of Attorney, Enduring Powers of Attorney and Public Guardian Regulations 2007, SI 2007/1253.

14   Protection of donee and others if no power created or power revoked

(1)   Subsections (2) and (3) apply if—
(a)   an instrument has been registered under Schedule 1 as a lasting power of attorney, but
(b)   a lasting power of attorney was not created,
whether or not the registration has been cancelled at the time of the act or transaction in question.

(2)   A donee who acts in purported exercise of the power does not incur any liability (to P or any other person) because of the non-existence of the power unless at the time of acting he—
(a)   knows that a lasting power of attorney was not created, or
(b)   is aware of circumstances which, if a lasting power of attorney had been created, would have terminated his authority to act as a donee.

(3)   Any transaction between the donee and another person is, in favour of that person, as valid as if the power had been in existence, unless at the time of the transaction that person has knowledge of a matter referred to in subsection (2).

(4)   If the interest of a purchaser depends on whether a transaction between the donee and the other person was valid by virtue of subsection (3), it is conclusively presumed in favour of the purchaser that the transaction was valid if—
(a)   the transaction was completed within 12 months of the date on which the instrument was registered, or
(b)   the other person makes a statutory declaration, before or within 3 months after the completion of the purchase, that he had no reason at the time of the transaction to doubt that the donee had authority to dispose of the property which was the subject of the transaction.

(5)   In its application to a lasting power of attorney which relates to matters in addition to P's property and affairs, section 5 of the Powers of Attorney Act 1971 (c 27) (protection where power is revoked) has effect as if references to revocation included the cessation of the power in relation to P's property and affairs.

(6)   Where two or more donees are appointed under a lasting power of attorney, this section applies as if references to the donee were to all or any of them.
[2056]

NOTES
Commencement: 1 October 2007.

General powers of the court and appointment of deputies

15   Power to make declarations

(1)   The court may make declarations as to—
    (a)   whether a person has or lacks capacity to make a decision specified in the declaration;
    (b)   whether a person has or lacks capacity to make decisions on such matters as are described in the declaration;
    (c)   the lawfulness or otherwise of any act done, or yet to be done, in relation to that person.

(2)   "Act" includes an omission and a course of conduct.

[2057]

NOTES
    Commencement: 1 October 2007.

16   Powers to make decisions and appoint deputies: general

(1)   This section applies if a person ("P") lacks capacity in relation to a matter or matters concerning—
    (a)   P's personal welfare, or
    (b)   P's property and affairs.

(2)   The court may—
    (a)   by making an order, make the decision or decisions on P's behalf in relation to the matter or matters, or
    (b)   appoint a person (a "deputy") to make decisions on P's behalf in relation to the matter or matters.

(3)   The powers of the court under this section are subject to the provisions of this Act and, in particular, to sections 1 (the principles) and 4 (best interests).

(4)   When deciding whether it is in P's best interests to appoint a deputy, the court must have regard (in addition to the matters mentioned in section 4) to the principles that—
    (a)   a decision by the court is to be preferred to the appointment of a deputy to make a decision, and
    (b)   the powers conferred on a deputy should be as limited in scope and duration as is reasonably practicable in the circumstances.

(5)   The court may make such further orders or give such directions, and confer on a deputy such powers or impose on him such duties, as it thinks necessary or expedient for giving effect to, or otherwise in connection with, an order or appointment made by it under subsection (2).

(6)   Without prejudice to section 4, the court may make the order, give the directions or make the appointment on such terms as it considers are in P's best interests, even though no application is before the court for an order, directions or an appointment on those terms.

(7)   An order of the court may be varied or discharged by a subsequent order.

(8)   The court may, in particular, revoke the appointment of a deputy or vary the powers conferred on him if it is satisfied that the deputy—
    (a)   has behaved, or is behaving, in a way that contravenes the authority conferred on him by the court or is not in P's best interests, or
    (b)   proposes to behave in a way that would contravene that authority or would not be in P's best interests.

[2058]

NOTES
    Commencement: 1 October 2007.

[16A   Section 16 powers: Mental Health Act patients etc

(1)   If a person is ineligible to be deprived of liberty by this Act, the court may not include in a welfare order provision which authorises the person to be deprived of his liberty.

(2)   If—
    (a)   a welfare order includes provision which authorises a person to be deprived of his liberty, and
    (b)   that person becomes ineligible to be deprived of liberty by this Act,
the provision ceases to have effect for as long as the person remains ineligible.

(3)   Nothing in subsection (2) affects the power of the court under section 16(7) to vary or discharge the welfare order.

(4)   For the purposes of this section—

(a) Schedule 1A applies for determining whether or not P is ineligible to be deprived of liberty by this Act;

(b) "welfare order" means an order under section 16(2)(a),]

[2059]

NOTES
Commencement: 1 April 2009.
Inserted by the Mental Health Act 2007, s 50(1), (3).

17 Section 16 powers: personal welfare

(1) The powers under section 16 as respects P's personal welfare extend in particular to—

(a) deciding where P is to live;

(b) deciding what contact, if any, P is to have with any specified persons;

(c) making an order prohibiting a named person from having contact with P;

(d) giving or refusing consent to the carrying out or continuation of a treatment by a person providing health care for P;

(e) giving a direction that a person responsible for P's health care allow a different person to take over that responsibility.

(2) Subsection (1) is subject to section 20 (restrictions on deputies).

[2060]

NOTES
Commencement: 1 October 2007.

18 Section 16 powers: property and affairs

(1) The powers under section 16 as respects P's property and affairs extend in particular to—

(a) the control and management of P's property;

(b) the sale, exchange, charging, gift or other disposition of P's property;

(c) the acquisition of property in P's name or on P's behalf;

(d) the carrying on, on P's behalf, of any profession, trade or business;

(e) the taking of a decision which will have the effect of dissolving a partnership of which P is a member;

(f) the carrying out of any contract entered into by P;

(g) the discharge of P's debts and of any of P's obligations, whether legally enforceable or not;

(h) the settlement of any of P's property, whether for P's benefit or for the benefit of others;

(i) the execution for P of a will;

(j) the exercise of any power (including a power to consent) vested in P whether beneficially or as trustee or otherwise;

(k) the conduct of legal proceedings in P's name or on P's behalf.

(2) No will may be made under subsection (1)(i) at a time when P has not reached 18.

(3) The powers under section 16 as respects any other matter relating to P's property and affairs may be exercised even though P has not reached 16, if the court considers it likely that P will still lack capacity to make decisions in respect of that matter when he reaches 18.

(4) Schedule 2 supplements the provisions of this section.

(5) Section 16(7) (variation and discharge of court orders) is subject to paragraph 6 of Schedule 2.

(6) Subsection (1) is subject to section 20 (restrictions on deputies).

[2061]

NOTES
Commencement: 1 October 2007.

19 Appointment of deputies

(1) A deputy appointed by the court must be—

(a) an individual who has reached 18, or

(b) as respects powers in relation to property and affairs, an individual who has reached 18 or a trust corporation.

(2) The court may appoint an individual by appointing the holder for the time being of a specified office or position.

(3) A person may not be appointed as a deputy without his consent.

(4) The court may appoint two or more deputies to act—

(a) jointly,

(b)   jointly and severally, or

(c)   jointly in respect of some matters and jointly and severally in respect of others.

(5)   When appointing a deputy or deputies, the court may at the same time appoint one or more other persons to succeed the existing deputy or those deputies—

(a)   in such circumstances, or on the happening of such events, as may be specified by the court;

(b)   for such period as may be so specified.

(6)   A deputy is to be treated as P's agent in relation to anything done or decided by him within the scope of his appointment and in accordance with this Part.

(7)   The deputy is entitled—

(a)   to be reimbursed out of P's property for his reasonable expenses in discharging his functions, and

(b)   if the court so directs when appointing him, to remuneration out of P's property for discharging them.

(8)   The court may confer on a deputy powers to—

(a)   take possession or control of all or any specified part of P's property;

(b)   exercise all or any specified powers in respect of it, including such powers of investment as the court may determine.

(9)   The court may require a deputy—

(a)   to give to the Public Guardian such security as the court thinks fit for the due discharge of his functions, and

(b)   to submit to the Public Guardian such reports at such times or at such intervals as the court may direct.

[2062]

NOTES

Commencement: 1 October 2007.

20   Restrictions on deputies

(1)   A deputy does not have power to make a decision on behalf of P in relation to a matter if he knows or has reasonable grounds for believing that P has capacity in relation to the matter.

(2)   Nothing in section 16(5) or 17 permits a deputy to be given power—

(a)   to prohibit a named person from having contact with P;

(b)   to direct a person responsible for P's health care to allow a different person to take over that responsibility.

(3)   A deputy may not be given powers with respect to—

(a)   the settlement of any of P's property, whether for P's benefit or for the benefit of others,

(b)   the execution for P of a will, or

(c)   the exercise of any power (including a power to consent) vested in P whether beneficially or as trustee or otherwise.

(4)   A deputy may not be given power to make a decision on behalf of P which is inconsistent with a decision made, within the scope of his authority and in accordance with this Act, by the donee of a lasting power of attorney granted by P (or, if there is more than one donee, by any of them).

(5)   A deputy may not refuse consent to the carrying out or continuation of life-sustaining treatment in relation to P.

(6)   The authority conferred on a deputy is subject to the provisions of this Act and, in particular, sections 1 (the principles) and 4 (best interests).

(7)   A deputy may not do an act that is intended to restrain P unless four conditions are satisfied.

(8)   The first condition is that, in doing the act, the deputy is acting within the scope of an authority expressly conferred on him by the court.

(9)   The second is that P lacks, or the deputy reasonably believes that P lacks, capacity in relation to the matter in question.

(10)   The third is that the deputy reasonably believes that it is necessary to do the act in order to prevent harm to P.

(11)   The fourth is that the act is a proportionate response to—

(a)   the likelihood of P's suffering harm, [and]

(b)   the seriousness of that harm.

(12)   For the purposes of this section, a deputy restrains P if he—

(a)   uses, or threatens to use, force to secure the doing of an act which P resists, or

(b)   restricts P's liberty of movement, whether or not P resists,

or if he authorises another person to do any of those things.

(13)   ...

[2063]

PART 1
STATUTES

NOTES
Commencement: 1 October 2007.
Sub-s (11): word in square brackets in para (a) substituted by the Mental Health Act 2007, s 51.
Sub-s (13): repealed by the Mental Health Act 2007, ss 50(1), (4)(c), 55, Sch 11, Pt 10.

21 Transfer of proceedings relating to people under 18

[(1)] The [Lord Chief Justice, with the concurrence of the Lord Chancellor,] may by order make provision as to the transfer of proceedings relating to a person under 18, in such circumstances as are specified in the order—

(a) from the Court of Protection to a court having jurisdiction under the Children Act 1989 (c 41), or

(b) from a court having jurisdiction under that Act to the Court of Protection.

[(2) The Lord Chief Justice may nominate any of the following to exercise his functions under this section—

(a) the President of the Court of Protection;

(b) a judicial office holder (as defined in section 109(4) of the Constitutional Reform Act 2005).]

[2064]

NOTES
Commencement: 1 October 2007.
Sub-s (1): numbered as such and words in square brackets substituted by the Lord Chancellor (Transfer of Functions and Supplementary Provisions) (No 2) Order 2006, SI 2006/1016, art 2, Sch 1, paras 30, 31(1)–(3).
Sub-s (2): added by SI 2006/1016, art 2, Sch 1, paras 30, 31(1), (4).
Order: the Mental Capacity Act 2005 (Transfer of Proceedings) Order 2007, SI 2007/1899.

[Powers of the court in relation to Schedule A1

21A Powers of court in relation to Schedule A1

(1) This section applies if either of the following has been given under Schedule A1—

(a) a standard authorisation;

(b) an urgent authorisation.

(2) Where a standard authorisation has been given, the court may determine any question relating to any of the following matters—

(a) whether the relevant person meets one or more of the qualifying requirements;

(b) the period during which the standard authorisation is to be in force;

(c) the purpose for which the standard authorisation is given;

(d) the conditions subject to which the standard authorisation is given.

(3) If the court determines any question under subsection (2), the court may make an order—

(a) varying or terminating the standard authorisation, or

(b) directing the supervisory body to vary or terminate the standard authorisation.

(4) Where an urgent authorisation has been given, the court may determine any question relating to any of the following matters—

(a) whether the urgent authorisation should have been given;

(b) the period during which the urgent authorisation is to be in force;

(c) the purpose for which the urgent authorisation is given.

(5) Where the court determines any question under subsection (4), the court may make an order—

(a) varying or terminating the urgent authorisation, or

(b) directing the managing authority of the relevant hospital or care home to vary or terminate the urgent authorisation.

(6) Where the court makes an order under subsection (3) or (5), the court may make an order about a person's liability for any act done in connection with the standard or urgent authorisation before its variation or termination.

(7) An order under subsection (6) may, in particular, exclude a person from liability.]

[2065]

NOTES
Commencement: 1 April 2009.
Inserted, together with preceding cross-heading, by the Mental Health Act 2007, s 50(7), Sch 9, Pt 1, paras 1, 2.

Powers of the court in relation to lasting powers of attorney

22   Powers of court in relation to validity of lasting powers of attorney

  (1)   This section and section 23 apply if—

  (a)   a person ("P") has executed or purported to execute an instrument with a view to creating a lasting power of attorney, or

  (b)   an instrument has been registered as a lasting power of attorney conferred by P.

  (2)   The court may determine any question relating to—

  (a)   whether one or more of the requirements for the creation of a lasting power of attorney have been met;

  (b)   whether the power has been revoked or has otherwise come to an end.

  (3)   Subsection (4) applies if the court is satisfied—

  (a)   that fraud or undue pressure was used to induce P—

  (i)   to execute an instrument for the purpose of creating a lasting power of attorney, or

  (ii)   to create a lasting power of attorney, or

  (b)   that the donee (or, if more than one, any of them) of a lasting power of attorney—

  (i)   has behaved, or is behaving, in a way that contravenes his authority or is not in P's best interests, or

  (ii)   proposes to behave in a way that would contravene his authority or would not be in P's best interests.

  (4)   The court may—

  (a)   direct that an instrument purporting to create the lasting power of attorney is not to be registered, or

  (b)   if P lacks capacity to do so, revoke the instrument or the lasting power of attorney.

  (5)   If there is more than one donee, the court may under subsection (4)(b) revoke the instrument or the lasting power of attorney so far as it relates to any of them.

  (6)   "Donee" includes an intended donee.

                                                                                 [2066]

NOTES

Commencement: 1 October 2007.

23   Powers of court in relation to operation of lasting powers of attorney

  (1)   The court may determine any question as to the meaning or effect of a lasting power of attorney or an instrument purporting to create one.

  (2)   The court may—

  (a)   give directions with respect to decisions—

  (i)   which the donee of a lasting power of attorney has authority to make, and

  (ii)   which P lacks capacity to make;

  (b)   give any consent or authorisation to act which the donee would have to obtain from P if P had capacity to give it.

  (3)   The court may, if P lacks capacity to do so—

  (a)   give directions to the donee with respect to the rendering by him of reports or accounts and the production of records kept by him for that purpose;

  (b)   require the donee to supply information or produce documents or things in his possession as donee;

  (c)   give directions with respect to the remuneration or expenses of the donee;

  (d)   relieve the donee wholly or partly from any liability which he has or may have incurred on account of a breach of his duties as donee.

  (4)   The court may authorise the making of gifts which are not within section 12(2) (permitted gifts).

  (5)   Where two or more donees are appointed under a lasting power of attorney, this section applies as if references to the donee were to all or any of them.

                                                                                 [2067]

NOTES

Commencement: 1 October 2007.

24–61   (*Ss 24–44, ss 45–61 (Pt 2) outside the scope of this work.*)

PART 3
MISCELLANEOUS AND GENERAL

62, 63   (*Outside the scope of this work.*)

General

64, 65   (*Outside the scope of this work.*)

66   Existing receivers and enduring powers of attorney etc

(1)   The following provisions cease to have effect—
    (a)   Part 7 of the Mental Health Act,
    (b)   the Enduring Powers of Attorney Act 1985 (c 29).

(2)   No enduring power of attorney within the meaning of the 1985 Act is to be created after the commencement of subsection (1)(b).

(3)   Schedule 4 has effect in place of the 1985 Act in relation to any enduring power of attorney created before the commencement of subsection (1)(b).

(4)   Schedule 5 contains transitional provisions and savings in relation to Part 7 of the Mental Health Act and the 1985 Act.

[2068]

NOTES
    Commencement: 1 October 2007.

67, 68   (*Outside the scope of this work.*)

69   Short title

This Act may be cited as the Mental Capacity Act 2005.

[2069]

(*Sch A1 outside the scope of this work.*)

SCHEDULE 1
LASTING POWERS OF ATTORNEY: FORMALITIES
Section 9

PART 1
MAKING INSTRUMENTS

General requirements as to making instruments

1.—(1)   An instrument is not made in accordance with this Schedule unless—
    (a)   it is in the prescribed form,
    (b)   it complies with paragraph 2, and
    (c)   any prescribed requirements in connection with its execution are satisfied.

(2)   Regulations may make different provision according to whether—
    (a)   the instrument relates to personal welfare or to property and affairs (or to both);
    (b)   only one or more than one donee is to be appointed (and if more than one, whether jointly or jointly and severally).

(3)   In this Schedule—
    (a)   "prescribed" means prescribed by regulations, and
    (b)   "regulations" means regulations made for the purposes of this Schedule by the Lord Chancellor.

Requirements as to content of instruments

2.—(1)   The instrument must include—
    (a)   the prescribed information about the purpose of the instrument and the effect of a lasting power of attorney,
    (b)   a statement by the donor to the effect that he—
        (i)   has read the prescribed information or a prescribed part of it (or has had it read to him), and
        (ii)   intends the authority conferred under the instrument to include authority to make decisions on his behalf in circumstances where he no longer has capacity,
    (c)   a statement by the donor—
        (i)   naming a person or persons whom the donor wishes to be notified of any application for the registration of the instrument, or

(ii) stating that there are no persons whom he wishes to be notified of any such application,

(d) a statement by the donee (or, if more than one, each of them) to the effect that he—

(i) has read the prescribed information or a prescribed part of it (or has had it read to him), and

(ii) understands the duties imposed on a donee of a lasting power of attorney under sections 1 (the principles) and 4 (best interests), and

(e) a certificate by a person of a prescribed description that, in his opinion, at the time when the donor executes the instrument—

(i) the donor understands the purpose of the instrument and the scope of the authority conferred under it,

(ii) no fraud or undue pressure is being used to induce the donor to create a lasting power of attorney, and

(iii) there is nothing else which would prevent a lasting power of attorney from being created by the instrument.

(2) Regulations may—

(a) prescribe a maximum number of named persons;

(b) provide that, where the instrument includes a statement under sub-paragraph (1)(c)(ii), two persons of a prescribed description must each give a certificate under sub-paragraph (1)(e).

(3) The persons who may be named persons do not include a person who is appointed as donee under the instrument.

(4) In this Schedule, "named person" means a person named under sub-paragraph (1)(c).

(5) A certificate under sub-paragraph (1)(e)—

(a) must be made in the prescribed form, and

(b) must include any prescribed information.

(6) The certificate may not be given by a person appointed as donee under the instrument.

Failure to comply with prescribed form

3.—(1) If an instrument differs in an immaterial respect in form or mode of expression from the prescribed form, it is to be treated by the Public Guardian as sufficient in point of form and expression.

(2) The court may declare that an instrument which is not in the prescribed form is to be treated as if it were, if it is satisfied that the persons executing the instrument intended it to create a lasting power of attorney.

[2070]

NOTES

Commencement: 1 October 2007.

PART 2
REGISTRATION

Applications and procedure for registration

4.—(1) An application to the Public Guardian for the registration of an instrument intended to create a lasting power of attorney—

(a) must be made in the prescribed form, and

(b) must include any prescribed information.

(2) The application may be made—

(a) by the donor,

(b) by the donee or donees, or

(c) if the instrument appoints two or more donees to act jointly and severally in respect of any matter, by any of the donees.

(3) The application must be accompanied by—

(a) the instrument, and

(b) any fee provided for under section 58(4)(b).

(4) A person who, in an application for registration, makes a statement which he knows to be false in a material particular is guilty of an offence and is liable—

(a) on summary conviction, to imprisonment for a term not exceeding 12 months or a fine not exceeding the statutory maximum or both;

(b) on conviction on indictment, to imprisonment for a term not exceeding 2 years or a fine or both.

5.   Subject to paragraphs 11 to 14, the Public Guardian must register the instrument as a lasting power of attorney at the end of the prescribed period.

Notification requirements

6.—(1)   A donor about to make an application under paragraph 4(2)(a) must notify any named persons that he is about to do so.

(2)   The donee (or donees) about to make an application under paragraph 4(2)(b) or (c) must notify any named persons that he is (or they are) about to do so.

7.   As soon as is practicable after receiving an application by the donor under paragraph 4(2)(a), the Public Guardian must notify the donee (or donees) that the application has been received.

8.—(1)   As soon as is practicable after receiving an application by a donee (or donees) under paragraph 4(2)(b), the Public Guardian must notify the donor that the application has been received.

(2)   As soon as is practicable after receiving an application by a donee under paragraph 4(2)(c), the Public Guardian must notify—
- (a)   the donor, and
- (b)   the donee or donees who did not join in making the application,

that the application has been received.

9.—(1)   A notice under paragraph 6 must be made in the prescribed form.

(2)   A notice under paragraph 6, 7 or 8 must include such information, if any, as may be prescribed.

Power to dispense with notification requirements

10.   The court may—
- (a)   on the application of the donor, dispense with the requirement to notify under paragraph 6(1), or
- (b)   on the application of the donee or donees concerned, dispense with the requirement to notify under paragraph 6(2),

if satisfied that no useful purpose would be served by giving the notice.

Instrument not made properly or containing ineffective provision

11.—(1)   If it appears to the Public Guardian that an instrument accompanying an application under paragraph 4 is not made in accordance with this Schedule, he must not register the instrument unless the court directs him to do so.

(2)   Sub-paragraph (3) applies if it appears to the Public Guardian that the instrument contains a provision which—
- (a)   would be ineffective as part of a lasting power of attorney, or
- (b)   would prevent the instrument from operating as a valid lasting power of attorney.

(3)   The Public Guardian—
- (a)   must apply to the court for it to determine the matter under section 23(1), and
- (b)   pending the determination by the court, must not register the instrument.

(4)   Sub-paragraph (5) applies if the court determines under section 23(1) (whether or not on an application by the Public Guardian) that the instrument contains a provision which—
- (a)   would be ineffective as part of a lasting power of attorney, or
- (b)   would prevent the instrument from operating as a valid lasting power of attorney.

(5)   The court must—
- (a)   notify the Public Guardian that it has severed the provision, or
- (b)   direct him not to register the instrument.

(6)   Where the court notifies the Public Guardian that it has severed a provision, he must register the instrument with a note to that effect attached to it.

Deputy already appointed

12.—(1)   Sub-paragraph (2) applies if it appears to the Public Guardian that—
- (a)   there is a deputy appointed by the court for the donor, and
- (b)   the powers conferred on the deputy would, if the instrument were registered, to any extent conflict with the powers conferred on the attorney.

(2)   The Public Guardian must not register the instrument unless the court directs him to do so.

Objection by donee or named person

13.—(1)   Sub-paragraph (2) applies if a donee or a named person—
- (a)   receives a notice under paragraph 6, 7 or 8 of an application for the registration of an instrument, and
- (b)   before the end of the prescribed period, gives notice to the Public Guardian of an

objection to the registration on the ground that an event mentioned in section 13(3) or (6)(a) to (d) has occurred which has revoked the instrument.

(2)   If the Public Guardian is satisfied that the ground for making the objection is established, he must not register the instrument unless the court, on the application of the person applying for the registration—

(a)   is satisfied that the ground is not established, and
(b)   directs the Public Guardian to register the instrument.

(3)   Sub-paragraph (4) applies if a donee or a named person—

(a)   receives a notice under paragraph 6, 7 or 8 of an application for the registration of an instrument, and
(b)   before the end of the prescribed period—
    (i)   makes an application to the court objecting to the registration on a prescribed ground, and
    (ii)   notifies the Public Guardian of the application.

(4)   The Public Guardian must not register the instrument unless the court directs him to do so.

Objection by donor

14.—(1)   This paragraph applies if the donor—

(a)   receives a notice under paragraph 8 of an application for the registration of an instrument, and
(b)   before the end of the prescribed period, gives notice to the Public Guardian of an objection to the registration.

(2)   The Public Guardian must not register the instrument unless the court, on the application of the donee or, if more than one, any of them—

(a)   is satisfied that the donor lacks capacity to object to the registration, and
(b)   directs the Public Guardian to register the instrument.

Notification of registration

15.   Where an instrument is registered under this Schedule, the Public Guardian must give notice of the fact in the prescribed form to—

(a)   the donor, and
(b)   the donee or, if more than one, each of them.

Evidence of registration

16.—(1)   A document purporting to be an office copy of an instrument registered under this Schedule is, in any part of the United Kingdom, evidence of—

(a)   the contents of the instrument, and
(b)   the fact that it has been registered.

(2)   Sub-paragraph (1) is without prejudice to—

(a)   section 3 of the Powers of Attorney Act 1971 (c 27) (proof by certified copy), and
(b)   any other method of proof authorised by law.

[2071]

NOTES

Commencement: 1 October 2007.

PART 3
CANCELLATION OF REGISTRATION AND NOTIFICATION OF SEVERANCE

17.—(1)   The Public Guardian must cancel the registration of an instrument as a lasting power of attorney on being satisfied that the power has been revoked—

(a)   as a result of the donor's bankruptcy, or
(b)   on the occurrence of an event mentioned in section 13(6)(a) to (d).

(2)   If the Public Guardian cancels the registration of an instrument he must notify—

(a)   the donor, and
(b)   the donee or, if more than one, each of them.

18.   The court must direct the Public Guardian to cancel the registration of an instrument as a lasting power of attorney if it—

(a)   determines under section 22(2)(a) that a requirement for creating the power was not met,
(b)   determines under section 22(2)(b) that the power has been revoked or has otherwise come to an end, or
(c)   revokes the power under section 22(4)(b) (fraud etc).

19.—(1)   Sub-paragraph (2) applies if the court determines under section 23(1) that a lasting power of attorney contains a provision which—

(a)   is ineffective as part of a lasting power of attorney, or

(b)   prevents the instrument from operating as a valid lasting power of attorney.

(2)   The court must—
    (a)   notify the Public Guardian that it has severed the provision, or
    (b)   direct him to cancel the registration of the instrument as a lasting power of attorney.

20.   On the cancellation of the registration of an instrument, the instrument and any office copies of it must be delivered up to the Public Guardian to be cancelled.

[2072]

NOTES
Commencement: 1 October 2007.

PART 4
RECORDS OF ALTERATIONS IN REGISTERED POWERS

Partial revocation or suspension of power as a result of bankruptcy

21.   If in the case of a registered instrument it appears to the Public Guardian that under section 13 a lasting power of attorney is revoked, or suspended, in relation to the donor's property and affairs (but not in relation to other matters), the Public Guardian must attach to the instrument a note to that effect.

Termination of appointment of donee which does not revoke power

22.   If in the case of a registered instrument it appears to the Public Guardian that an event has occurred—
    (a)   which has terminated the appointment of the donee, but
    (b)   which has not revoked the instrument,
the Public Guardian must attach to the instrument a note to that effect.

Replacement of donee

23.   If in the case of a registered instrument it appears to the Public Guardian that the donee has been replaced under the terms of the instrument the Public Guardian must attach to the instrument a note to that effect.

Severance of ineffective provisions

24.   If in the case of a registered instrument the court notifies the Public Guardian under paragraph 19(2)(a) that it has severed a provision of the instrument, the Public Guardian must attach to it a note to that effect.

Notification of alterations

25.   If the Public Guardian attaches a note to an instrument under paragraph 21, 22, 23 or 24 he must give notice of the note to the donee or donees of the power (or, as the case may be, to the other donee or donees of the power).

[2073]

NOTES
Commencement: 1 October 2007.

(Schs 1A–7 outside the scope of this work.)

CONSUMER CREDIT ACT 2006

(2006 c 14)

An Act to amend the Consumer Credit Act 1974; to extend the ombudsman scheme under the Financial Services and Markets Act 2000 to cover licensees under the Consumer Credit Act 1974; and for connected purposes

[30 March 2006]

1–65   (Ss 1–54, 56(1), (3), 62–65 amend the Consumer Credit Act 1974 at **[651]** et seq and amend other provisions outside the scope of this work; ss 55, 56(2), 57, 58 repealed by the Transfer of Functions of the Consumer Credit Appeals Tribunal Order 2009, SI 2009/1835, art 4(3), Sch 3, subject to transitional provisions in Sch 4 thereto at **[3908]**; s 59 inserts the Financial Services and Markets Act 2000, s 226A at **[1813C]**, and amends Sch 17 to that Act at **[1813V]**; s 60 inserts

PART 1
STATUTES

s 234A of the 2000 Act at **[1813K]**; s 61 amends s 4 of the 1974 Act at **[653]** and amends ss 227–230, 353 of and Sch 17 to the 2000 Act at **[1813D]**–**[1813G]**, **[1813T]**.)

Final provisions

66 Financial provision

There shall be payable out of money provided by Parliament—
  (a) any expenditure incurred by a Minister of the Crown or the Office of Fair Trading by virtue of this Act; and
  (b) any increase attributable to this Act in the sums payable out of money so provided by virtue of any other Act.

[2074]

NOTES
Commencement: 16 June 2006.

67 Interpretation

In this Act—
  "the 1974 Act" means the Consumer Credit Act 1974 (c 39);
  "the 2000 Act" means the Financial Services and Markets Act 2000 (c 8).

[2075]

NOTES
Commencement: 16 June 2006.

68 Consequential amendments

  (1) The Secretary of State may by order made by statutory instrument make such modifications of—
  (a) any Act or subordinate legislation (within the meaning of the Interpretation Act 1978 (c 30)), or
  (b) any Northern Ireland legislation or instrument made under such legislation,
as he thinks fit in consequence of any provision of this Act.

  (2) An order under this section may include transitional or transitory provisions and savings.

  (3) A statutory instrument containing an order under this section may not be made by the Secretary of State unless a draft has been laid before and approved by a resolution of each House of Parliament.

[2076]

NOTES
Commencement: 16 June 2006.

69 Transitional provision and savings

  (1) Schedule 3 (which sets out transitional provision and savings) has effect.

  (2) The Secretary of State may by order made by statutory instrument make such transitional or transitory provisions and savings as he thinks fit in connection with the coming into force of any provision of this Act.

  (3) An order under this section may (amongst other things)—
  (a) where a provision of this Act is brought into force for limited purposes only, make provision about how references in Schedule 3 to the commencement of that provision of this Act are to apply;
  (b) make provision for or in connection with the application of any provision of this Act in relation to—
      (i) things existing or done, or
      (ii) persons who have done something or in relation to whom something has been done,
    before the coming into force of that provision of this Act.

  (4) An order under this section may—
  (a) modify any Act or any subordinate legislation (within the meaning of the Interpretation Act 1978);
  (b) modify any Northern Ireland legislation or any instrument made under such legislation;
  (c) make different provision for different cases.

  (5) Schedule 3 does not restrict the power under this section to make transitional or transitory provisions or savings.

[2077]

PART 1
STATUTES

NOTES

Commencement: 16 June 2006 (sub-s (1) certain purposes, sub-ss (2)–(5)); 1 October 2006 (sub-s (1) certain purposes); 31 January 2007 (sub-s (1) certain purposes); 6 April 2007 (sub-s (1) certain purposes); 1 December 2007 (sub-s (1) certain purposes); 6 April 2008 (sub-s (1) certain purposes); 1 October 2008 (sub-s (1) certain purposes).

Orders: the Consumer Credit Act 2006 (Commencement No 2 and Transitional Provisions and Savings) Order 2007, SI 2007/123; the Consumer Credit Act 2006 (Commencement No 3) Order 2007, SI 2007/3300; the Consumer Credit Act 2006 (Commencement No 4 and Transitional Provisions) Order 2008, SI 2008/831.

70   (*Introduces Sch 4 (outside the scope of this work).*)

71   Short title, commencement and extent

(1)   This Act may be cited as the Consumer Credit Act 2006.

(2)   This Act (apart from this section) shall come into force on such day as the Secretary of State may by order made by statutory instrument appoint; and different days may be appointed for different purposes.

(3)   This Act extends to Northern Ireland.

[2078]

NOTES

Commencement: 30 March 2006.

Orders: the Consumer Credit Act 2006 (Commencement No 1) Order 2006, SI 2006/1508; the Consumer Credit Act 2006 (Commencement No 2 and Transitional Provisions and Savings) Order 2007, SI 2007/123; the Consumer Credit Act 2006 (Commencement No 2 and Transitional Provisions and Savings) (Amendment) Order 2007, SI 2007/387; the Consumer Credit Act 2006 (Commencement No 3) Order 2007, SI 2007/3300; the Consumer Credit Act 2006 (Commencement No 4 and Transitional Provisions) Order 2008, SI 2008/831; the Consumer Credit Act 2006 (Commencement No 4 and Transitional Provisions) (Amendment) Order 2008, SI 2008/2444.

(*Sch 1 repealed by the Transfer of Functions of the Consumer Credit Appeals Tribunal Order 2009, SI 2009/1835, art 4(3), Sch 3, subject to transitional provisions in Sch 4 thereto at* **[3908]***; Sch 2 inserts the Financial Services and Markets Act 2000, Sch 2, Pt 3A.*)

SCHEDULE 3
TRANSITIONAL PROVISION AND SAVINGS
Section 69

Interpretation

1.—(1)   Expressions used in the 1974 Act have the same meaning in this Schedule (apart from paragraphs 14 to 16 and 26) as they have in that Act.

(2)   For the purposes of this Schedule an agreement becomes a completed agreement once—
    (a)   there is no sum payable under the agreement; and
    (b)   there is no sum which will or may become so payable.

Statements to be provided in relation to regulated agreements

2.   ...

3.   Regulations made under section 78(4A) of the 1974 Act may apply in relation to agreements regardless of when they were made.

4.—(1)   Section 7(3) of this Act shall have effect in relation to agreements whenever made.

(2)   A dispensing notice given under section 185(2) of the 1974 Act which is operative immediately before the commencement of section 7(3)—
    (a)   shall, on the commencement of section 7(3), be treated as having been given under section 185(2) as substituted by section 7(3); and
    (b)   shall continue to be operative accordingly.

Default under regulated agreements

5.   The OFT shall prepare, and give general notice of, the arrears information sheet and the default information sheet required under section 86A of the 1974 Act as soon as practicable after the commencement of section 8 of this Act.

6.—(1)   Section 86B of the 1974 Act applies in relation to agreements whenever made.

(2)   In the application of section 86B in relation to an agreement made before the commencement of section 9 of this Act, the conditions under subsection (1) can be satisfied only if the two payments mentioned in paragraph (c) were not required to have been made before the commencement of section 9.

(3)   In the case of an agreement within subsection (9) of section 86B, sub-paragraph (2) has effect as if for "two" there were substituted "four".

7.—(1)   Section 86C of the 1974 Act applies in relation to agreements whenever made.

(2)   In the application of section 86C in relation to an agreement made before the commencement of section 10 of this Act, the conditions mentioned in subsection (1) can be satisfied only if the two payments mentioned in paragraph (b) were not required to have been made before the commencement of section 10.

8.   Section 86E of the 1974 Act applies in relation to agreements whenever made but only as regards default sums which become payable after the commencement of section 12 of this Act.

9.—(1)   Section 86F of the 1974 Act applies in relation to agreements whenever made but only as regards default sums which become payable after the commencement of section 13 of this Act.

(2)   Where section 86F applies in relation to an agreement made before the commencement of section 13, the agreement shall have effect as if any right of the creditor or owner to recover compound interest in connection with the default sum in question at a particular rate were a right to recover simple interest in that connection at that rate.

10.   Section 14 of this Act shall have effect in relation to any default notice served after the commencement of that section, regardless of—
(a)   when the breach of the agreement in question occurred; or
(b)   when that agreement was made.

11.   The repeal by this Act of—
(a)   the words "(subject to subsections (3) and (4))" in subsection (1) of section 127 of the 1974 Act,
(b)   subsections (3) to (5) of that section, and
(c)   the words "or 127(3)" in subsection (3) of section 185 of that Act,
has no effect in relation to improperly-executed agreements made before the commencement of section 15 of this Act.

12.   A debtor or hirer under an agreement may make an application under section 129(1)(ba) of the 1974 Act regardless of when that agreement was made.

13.   Section 130A of the 1974 Act applies in relation to agreements whenever made but only as regards sums that are required to be paid under judgments given after the commencement of section 17 of this Act.

Unfair relationships

14.—(1)   The court may make an order under section 140B of the 1974 Act in connection with a credit agreement made before the commencement of section 20 of this Act but only—
(a)   on an application of the kind mentioned in paragraph (a) of subsection (2) of section 140B made at a time after the end of the transitional period; or
(b)   at the instance of the debtor or a surety in any proceedings of the kind mentioned in paragraph (b) or (c) of that subsection which were commenced at such a time.

(2)   But the court shall not make such an order in connection with such an agreement so made if the agreement—
(a)   became a completed agreement before the commencement of section 20; or
(b)   becomes a completed agreement during the transitional period.

(3)   Expressions used in sections 140A to 140C of the 1974 Act have the same meaning in this paragraph as they have in those sections.

(4)   In this paragraph "the transitional period" means the period of one year beginning with the day of the commencement of section 20.

(5)   An order under section 69 of this Act may extend, or further extend, the transitional period.

15.—(1)   The repeal by this Act of sections 137 to 140 of the 1974 Act shall not affect the court's power to reopen an existing agreement under those sections as set out in this paragraph.

(2)   The court's power to reopen an existing agreement which—
(a)   became a completed agreement before the commencement of section 22(3) of this Act, or
(b)   becomes a completed agreement during the transitional period,
is not affected at all.

(3)   The court may also reopen an existing agreement—
(a)   on an application of the kind mentioned in paragraph (a) of subsection (1) of section 139 made at a time before the end of the transitional period; or
(b)   at the instance of the debtor or a surety in any proceedings of the kind mentioned in paragraph (b) or (c) of that subsection which were commenced at such a time.

(4)   Nothing in section 16A or 16B of the 1974 Act shall affect the application of sections 137 to 140 (whether by virtue of this paragraph or otherwise).

(5)   The repeal or revocation by this Act of the following provisions has no effect in relation to existing agreements so far as they may be reopened as set out in this paragraph—

 (a) section 16(7) of the 1974 Act;

 (b) in section 143(b) of that Act, the words ", 139(1)(a)";

 (c) section 171(7) of that Act;

 (d) in subsection (1) of section 181 of that Act, the words "139(5) and (7),";

 (e) in subsection (2) of that section, the words "or 139(5) or (7)";

 (f) in section 61(6) of the Bankruptcy (Scotland) Act 1985 (c 66), the words from the beginning to "but";

 (g) in section 343(6) of the Insolvency Act 1986 (c 45), the words from the beginning to "But";

 (h) Article 316(6) of the Insolvency (Northern Ireland) Order 1989 (SI 1989/2405 (NI 19)).

(6)   Expressions used in sections 137 to 140 of the 1974 Act have the same meaning in this paragraph as they have in those sections.

(7)   In this paragraph—

 "existing agreement" means a credit agreement made before the commencement of section 22(3) of this Act;

 "the transitional period" means the period of one year beginning with the day of the commencement of section 22(3).

(8)   An order under section 69 of this Act may extend, or further extend, the transitional period.

16.—(1)   It is immaterial for the purposes of section 140C(4)(a) to (c) of the 1974 Act when (as the case may be) a credit agreement or a linked transaction was made or a security was provided.

(2)   In relation to an order made under section 140B of the 1974 Act during the transitional period in connection with a credit agreement—

 (a) references in subsection (1) of that section to any related agreement shall not include references to a related agreement to which this sub-paragraph applies;

 (b) the reference to a security in paragraph (d) of that subsection shall not include a reference to a security to which this sub-paragraph applies;

and the order shall not under paragraph (g) of that subsection direct accounts to be taken, or (in Scotland) an accounting to be made, between any persons in relation to a related agreement to which this sub-paragraph applies.

(3)   Sub-paragraph (2) applies to a related agreement or a security if—

 (a) it was made or provided before the commencement of section 21 of this Act; and

 (b) it ceased to have any operation before the order under section 140B is made.

(4)   In relation to an order made under section 140B after the end of the transitional period in connection with a credit agreement—

 (a) references in subsection (1) of that section to any related agreement shall not include references to a related agreement to which this sub-paragraph applies;

 (b) the reference to a security in paragraph (d) of that subsection shall not include a reference to a security to which this sub-paragraph applies;

and the order shall not under paragraph (g) of that subsection direct accounts to be taken, or (in Scotland) an accounting to be made, between any persons in relation to a related agreement to which this sub-paragraph applies.

(5)   Sub-paragraph (4) applies to a related agreement or a security if—

 (a) it was made or provided before the commencement of section 21; and

 (b) it ceased to have any operation before the end of the transitional period.

(6)   Expressions used in sections 140A to 140C of the 1974 Act have the same meanings in this paragraph as they have in those sections.

(7)   In this paragraph "the transitional period" means the period of one year beginning with the day of the commencement of section 21.

(8)   An order under section 69 of this Act may extend, or further extend, the transitional period.

17.   Section 1 of this Act shall have no effect for the purposes of section 140C(1) of the 1974 Act in relation to agreements made before the commencement of section 1.

Applications for licences and fitness to hold a licence etc

18.—(1)   Section 6A of the 1974 Act shall not apply in relation to applications made before the commencement of section 27 of this Act.

(2)   Section 6(2A) of the 1974 Act shall not apply in relation to applications so made.

(3)   The repeal by this Act of the words "and must be accompanied by the specified fee" in section 6(2) of the 1974 Act has no effect in relation to applications so made.

19.—(1)   The OFT shall prepare and publish the guidance required by section 25A of the 1974 Act as soon as practicable after the commencement of section 30 of this Act.

(2)   The requirements of subsection (4) of section 25A may be satisfied in relation to the preparation of that guidance by steps taken wholly or partly before the commencement of section 30.

Further powers of OFT to regulate conduct of licensees etc

20.   The cases in which the OFT may impose requirements under section 33A of the 1974 Act include cases where the matter with which the OFT is dissatisfied arose before the commencement of section 38 of this Act.

21.   The cases in which the OFT may impose requirements under section 33B of the 1974 Act include cases where the matters giving rise to the OFT's dissatisfaction arose before the commencement of section 39 of this Act.

22.—(1)   The OFT shall prepare and publish the guidance required by section 33E of the 1974 Act as soon as practicable after the commencement of section 42 of this Act.

(2)   The requirements of subsection (4) of section 33E may be satisfied in relation to the preparation of that guidance by steps taken wholly or partly before the commencement of section 42.

Powers and duties in relation to information

23.—(1)   Section 44 of this Act has no effect in relation to applications made before the commencement of that section.

(2)   Paragraph 12(6) of Schedule A1 to the 1974 Act does not apply in relation to applications so made.

24.   A person is not required by section 36A of the 1974 Act to do anything in relation to an application made by him before the commencement of section 45 of this Act.

Civil penalties

25.—(1)   The OFT shall prepare and publish the statement of policy required by section 39C of the 1974 Act as soon as practicable after the commencement of section 54 of this Act.

(2)   The requirements of subsection (5) of section 39C may be satisfied in relation to the preparation of that statement of policy by steps taken wholly or partly before the commencement of section 54.

Appeals

26.—(1)   A person who—
  (a)   immediately before the commencement of section 55 of this Act is a member of a panel established under regulation 24 of the appeals regulations, and
  (b)   at the time of his appointment to that panel fell within paragraph (2)(a) of that regulation,
shall be treated as having been appointed to the panel of chairmen on the day of the commencement of section 55.

(2)   A person who—
  (a)   immediately before the commencement of section 55 is a member of a panel established under regulation 24 of the appeals regulations, and
  (b)   is not to be treated as having been appointed to the panel of chairmen in accordance with sub-paragraph (1),
shall be treated as having been appointed to the lay panel on the day of the commencement of section 55.

(3)   A person who is to be treated as having been appointed to the panel of chairmen or to the lay panel in accordance with this paragraph shall, subject to paragraph 4(2) and (3) of Schedule A1 to the 1974 Act, hold office as a member of the panel in question—
  (a)   for the remainder of the period for which he was appointed under regulation 24 of the appeals regulations; and
  (b)   on the terms on which he was so appointed (except as to the renewal of his appointment).

(4)   In this paragraph—
  "appeals regulations" means the Consumer Credit Licensing (Appeals) Regulations 1998 (SI 1998/1203);
  "lay panel" and "panel of chairmen" have the same meanings as in Schedule A1 to the 1974 Act.

27.—(1)   Neither—
  (a)   subsections (1) and (2) of section 56 of this Act, nor
  (b)   the repeal by this Act of subsections (2) to (5) of section 41 of the 1974 Act,
has effect in relation to determinations of the OFT made before the commencement of section 56.

(2)   This Act, so far as it repeals section 11 of the Tribunals and Inquiries Act 1992 (c 53), has no effect in relation to such determinations so made.

(3)   The repeal by this Act of paragraph 27(2) of Schedule 25 to the Enterprise Act 2002 (c 40) has no effect in relation to such determinations so made.

28.   Neither subsection (1) nor (4)(a) of section 58 of this Act has effect in relation to determinations of the OFT made before the commencement of that section.

Ombudsman scheme

29.   Section 1 of this Act shall have no effect for the purposes of section 226A(4)(a) of the 2000 Act in relation to a complaint which relates to an act or omission occurring before the commencement of section 1.

[2079]

NOTES

Commencement: 16 June 2006 (para 1(1)); 1 October 2006 (para 10): 31 January 2007 (para 5); 6 April 2007 (paras 1(2), 11, 14–16, 29); 1 December 2007 (paras 19, 22–25); 6 April 2008 (paras 18, 20, 21, 26–28); 1 October 2008 (paras 2–4, 6–9 12, 13).

Para 2: repealed by the Legislative Reform (Consumer Credit) Order 2008, SI 2008/2826, art 6.

(*Sch 4 (Repeals) outside the scope of this work.*)

COMPENSATION ACT 2006

(2006 c 29)

An Act to specify certain factors that may be taken into account by a court determining a claim in negligence or breach of statutory duty; to make provision about damages for mesothelioma; and to make provision for the regulation of claims management services

[25 July 2006]

PART 1
STANDARD OF CARE

1   Deterrent effect of potential liability

A court considering a claim in negligence or breach of statutory duty may, in determining whether the defendant should have taken particular steps to meet a standard of care (whether by taking precautions against a risk or otherwise), have regard to whether a requirement to take those steps might—

(a)   prevent a desirable activity from being undertaken at all, to a particular extent or in a particular way, or

(b)   discourage persons from undertaking functions in connection with a desirable activity.

[2080]

NOTES

Commencement: 25 July 2006.

---

2   Apologies, offers of treatment or other redress

An apology, an offer of treatment or other redress, shall not of itself amount to an admission of negligence or breach of statutory duty.

[2081]

NOTES

Commencement: 25 July 2006.

---

3   Mesothelioma: damages

(1)   This section applies where—

(a)   a person ("the responsible person") has negligently or in breach of statutory duty caused or permitted another person ("the victim") to be exposed to asbestos,

(b)   the victim has contracted mesothelioma as a result of exposure to asbestos,

(c)   because of the nature of mesothelioma and the state of medical science, it is not possible to determine with certainty whether it was the exposure mentioned in paragraph (a) or another exposure which caused the victim to become ill, and

(d)   the responsible person is liable in tort, by virtue of the exposure mentioned in paragraph (a), in connection with damage caused to the victim by the disease (whether by reason of having materially increased a risk or for any other reason).

(2) The responsible person shall be liable—
- (a) in respect of the whole of the damage caused to the victim by the disease (irrespective of whether the victim was also exposed to asbestos—
  - (i) other than by the responsible person, whether or not in circumstances in which another person has liability in tort, or
  - (ii) by the responsible person in circumstances in which he has no liability in tort), and
- (b) jointly and severally with any other responsible person.

(3) Subsection (2) does not prevent—
- (a) one responsible person from claiming a contribution from another, or
- (b) a finding of contributory negligence.

(4) In determining the extent of contributions of different responsible persons in accordance with subsection (3)(a), a court shall have regard to the relative lengths of the periods of exposure for which each was responsible; but this subsection shall not apply—
- (a) if or to the extent that responsible persons agree to apportion responsibility amongst themselves on some other basis, or
- (b) if or to the extent that the court thinks that another basis for determining contributions is more appropriate in the circumstances of a particular case.

(5) In subsection (1) the reference to causing or permitting a person to be exposed to asbestos includes a reference to failing to protect a person from exposure to asbestos.

(6) In the application of this section to Scotland—
- (a) a reference to tort shall be taken as a reference to delict, and
- (b) a reference to a court shall be taken to include a reference to a jury.

(7) The Treasury may make regulations about the provision of compensation to a responsible person where—
- (a) he claims, or would claim, a contribution from another responsible person in accordance with subsection (3)(a), but
- (b) he is unable or likely to be unable to obtain the contribution, because an insurer of the other responsible person is unable or likely to be unable to satisfy the claim for a contribution.

(8) The regulations may, in particular—
- (a) replicate or apply (with or without modification) a provision of the Financial Services Compensation Scheme;
- (b) replicate or apply (with or without modification) a transitional compensation provision;
- (c) provide for a specified person to assess and pay compensation;
- (d) provide for expenses incurred (including the payment of compensation) to be met out of levies collected in accordance with section 213(3)(b) of the Financial Services and Markets Act 2000 (c 8) (the Financial Services Compensation Scheme);
- (e) modify the effect of a transitional compensation provision;
- (f) enable the Financial Services Authority to amend the Financial Services Compensation Scheme;
- (g) modify the Financial Services and Markets Act 2000 in its application to an amendment pursuant to paragraph (f);
- (h) make, or require the making of, provision for the making of a claim by a responsible person for compensation whether or not he has already satisfied claims in tort against him;
- (i) make, or require the making of, provision which has effect in relation to claims for contributions made on or after the date on which this Act is passed.

(9) Provision made by virtue of subsection (8)(a) shall cease to have effect when the Financial Services Compensation Scheme is amended by the Financial Services Authority by virtue of subsection (8)(f).

(10) In subsections (7) and (8)—
- (a) a reference to a responsible person includes a reference to an insurer of a responsible person, and
- (b) "transitional compensation provision" means a provision of an enactment which is made under the Financial Services and Markets Act 2000 and—
  - (i) preserves the effect of the Policyholders Protection Act 1975 (c 75), or
  - (ii) applies the Financial Services Compensation Scheme in relation to matters arising before its establishment.

(11) Regulations under subsection (7)—
- (a) may include consequential or incidental provision,

    (b)   may make provision which has effect generally or only in relation to specified cases or circumstances,

    (c)   may make different provision for different cases or circumstances,

    (d)   shall be made by statutory instrument, and

    (e)   may not be made unless a draft has been laid before and approved by resolution of each House of Parliament.

[2082]

NOTES

    Commencement: 25 July 2006. By virtue of s 16(3) of this Act, this section is treated as having always had effect.

    Regulations: the Compensation Act 2006 (Contribution for Mesothelioma Claims) Regulations 2006, SI 2006/3259.

4–15   ((*Pt 2*) *Outside the scope of this work.*)

PART 3

GENERAL

16, 17   (*Outside the scope of this work.*)

18 Short title

This Act may be cited as the Compensation Act 2006.

[2083]

NOTES

    Commencement: 25 July 2006.

(*Schedule outside the scope of this work.*)

FRAUD ACT 2006

(2006 c 35)

ARRANGEMENT OF SECTIONS

Fraud

An Act to make provision for, and in connection with, criminal liability for fraud and obtaining services dishonestly

[8 November 2006]

Fraud

1 Fraud

    (1)   A person is guilty of fraud if he is in breach of any of the sections listed in subsection (2) (which provide for different ways of committing the offence).

(2)   The sections are—
- (a)   section 2 (fraud by false representation),
- (b)   section 3 (fraud by failing to disclose information), and
- (c)   section 4 (fraud by abuse of position).

(3)   A person who is guilty of fraud is liable—
- (a)   on summary conviction, to imprisonment for a term not exceeding 12 months or to a fine not exceeding the statutory maximum (or to both);
- (b)   on conviction on indictment, to imprisonment for a term not exceeding 10 years or to a fine (or to both).

(4)   Subsection (3)(a) applies in relation to Northern Ireland as if the reference to 12 months were a reference to 6 months.

[2084]

NOTES
Commencement: 15 January 2007.

2   Fraud by false representation

(1)   A person is in breach of this section if he—
- (a)   dishonestly makes a false representation, and
- (b)   intends, by making the representation—
    - (i)   to make a gain for himself or another, or
    - (ii)   to cause loss to another or to expose another to a risk of loss.

(2)   A representation is false if—
- (a)   it is untrue or misleading, and
- (b)   the person making it knows that it is, or might be, untrue or misleading.

(3)   "Representation" means any representation as to fact or law, including a representation as to the state of mind of—
- (a)   the person making the representation, or
- (b)   any other person.

(4)   A representation may be express or implied.

(5)   For the purposes of this section a representation may be regarded as made if it (or anything implying it) is submitted in any form to any system or device designed to receive, convey or respond to communications (with or without human intervention).

[2085]

NOTES
Commencement: 15 January 2007.

3   Fraud by failing to disclose information

A person is in breach of this section if he—
- (a)   dishonestly fails to disclose to another person information which he is under a legal duty to disclose, and
- (b)   intends, by failing to disclose the information—
    - (i)   to make a gain for himself or another, or
    - (ii)   to cause loss to another or to expose another to a risk of loss.

[2086]

NOTES
Commencement: 15 January 2007.

4   Fraud by abuse of position

(1)   A person is in breach of this section if he—
- (a)   occupies a position in which he is expected to safeguard, or not to act against, the financial interests of another person,
- (b)   dishonestly abuses that position, and
- (c)   intends, by means of the abuse of that position—
    - (i)   to make a gain for himself or another, or
    - (ii)   to cause loss to another or to expose another to a risk of loss.

(2)   A person may be regarded as having abused his position even though his conduct consisted of an omission rather than an act.

[2087]

NOTES
Commencement: 15 January 2007.

5 "Gain" and "loss"

(1)   The references to gain and loss in sections 2 to 4 are to be read in accordance with this section.

(2)   "Gain" and "loss"—
  (a)   extend only to gain or loss in money or other property;
  (b)   include any such gain or loss whether temporary or permanent;
and "property" means any property whether real or personal (including things in action and other intangible property).

(3)   "Gain" includes a gain by keeping what one has, as well as a gain by getting what one does not have.

(4)   "Loss" includes a loss by not getting what one might get, as well as a loss by parting with what one has.

[2088]

NOTES
Commencement: 15 January 2007.

6 Possession etc of articles for use in frauds

(1)   A person is guilty of an offence if he has in his possession or under his control any article for use in the course of or in connection with any fraud.

(2)   A person guilty of an offence under this section is liable—
  (a)   on summary conviction, to imprisonment for a term not exceeding 12 months or to a fine not exceeding the statutory maximum (or to both);
  (b)   on conviction on indictment, to imprisonment for a term not exceeding 5 years or to a fine (or to both).

(3)   Subsection (2)(a) applies in relation to Northern Ireland as if the reference to 12 months were a reference to 6 months.

[2089]

NOTES
Commencement: 15 January 2007.

7 Making or supplying articles for use in frauds

(1)   A person is guilty of an offence if he makes, adapts, supplies or offers to supply any article—
  (a)   knowing that it is designed or adapted for use in the course of or in connection with fraud, or
  (b)   intending it to be used to commit, or assist in the commission of, fraud.

(2)   A person guilty of an offence under this section is liable—
  (a)   on summary conviction, to imprisonment for a term not exceeding 12 months or to a fine not exceeding the statutory maximum (or to both);
  (b)   on conviction on indictment, to imprisonment for a term not exceeding 10 years or to a fine (or to both).

(3)   Subsection (2)(a) applies in relation to Northern Ireland as if the reference to 12 months were a reference to 6 months.

[2090]

NOTES
Commencement: 15 January 2007.

8 "Article"

(1)   For the purposes of—
  (a)   sections 6 and 7, and
  (b)   the provisions listed in subsection (2), so far as they relate to articles for use in the course of or in connection with fraud,
"article" includes any program or data held in electronic form.

(2)   The provisions are—
  (a)   section 1(7)(b) of the Police and Criminal Evidence Act 1984 (c 60),
  (b)   section 2(8)(b) of the Armed Forces Act 2001 (c 19), and
  (c)   Article 3(7)(b) of the Police and Criminal Evidence (Northern Ireland) Order 1989 (SI 1989/1341 (NI 12));
(meaning of "prohibited articles" for the purposes of stop and search powers).

[2091]

9 Participating in fraudulent business carried on by sole trader etc

(1)   A person is guilty of an offence if he is knowingly a party to the carrying on of a business to which this section applies.

(2)   This section applies to a business which is carried on—
  (a)   by a person who is outside the reach of [section 993 of the Companies Act 2006] (offence of fraudulent trading), and
  (b)   with intent to defraud creditors of any person or for any other fraudulent purpose.

(3)   The following are within the reach of [that section]—
  (a)   a company [(as defined in section 1(1) of the Companies Act 2006)];
  (b)   a person to whom that section applies (with or without adaptations or modifications) as if the person were a company;
  (c)   a person exempted from the application of that section.

(4)   ...

(5)   "Fraudulent purpose" has the same meaning as in [that section].

(6)   A person guilty of an offence under this section is liable—
  (a)   on summary conviction, to imprisonment for a term not exceeding 12 months or to a fine not exceeding the statutory maximum (or to both);
  (b)   on conviction on indictment, to imprisonment for a term not exceeding 10 years or to a fine (or to both).

(7)   Subsection (6)(a) applies in relation to Northern Ireland as if the reference to 12 months were a reference to 6 months.

[2092]–[2093]

10   *(Repealed by the Companies Act 2006 (Consequential Amendments, Transitional Provisions and Savings) Order 2009, SI 2009/1941, art 2(2), Sch 2.)*

Obtaining services dishonestly

11 Obtaining services dishonestly

(1)   A person is guilty of an offence under this section if he obtains services for himself or another—
  (a)   by a dishonest act, and
  (b)   in breach of subsection (2).

(2)   A person obtains services in breach of this subsection if—
  (a)   they are made available on the basis that payment has been, is being or will be made for or in respect of them,
  (b)   he obtains them without any payment having been made for or in respect of them or without payment having been made in full, and
  (c)   when he obtains them, he knows—
    (i)   that they are being made available on the basis described in paragraph (a), or
    (ii)   that they might be,
    but intends that payment will not be made, or will not be made in full.

(3)   A person guilty of an offence under this section is liable—

(a) on summary conviction, to imprisonment for a term not exceeding 12 months or to a fine not exceeding the statutory maximum (or to both);

(b) on conviction on indictment, to imprisonment for a term not exceeding 5 years or to a fine (or to both).

(4) Subsection (3)(a) applies in relation to Northern Ireland as if the reference to 12 months were a reference to 6 months.

[2094]

NOTES
Commencement: 15 January 2007.

Supplementary

12 Liability of company officers for offences by company

(1) Subsection (2) applies if an offence under this Act is committed by a body corporate.

(2) If the offence is proved to have been committed with the consent or connivance of—
   (a) a director, manager, secretary or other similar officer of the body corporate, or
   (b) a person who was purporting to act in any such capacity,

he (as well as the body corporate) is guilty of the offence and liable to be proceeded against and punished accordingly.

(3) If the affairs of a body corporate are managed by its members, subsection (2) applies in relation to the acts and defaults of a member in connection with his functions of management as if he were a director of the body corporate.

[2095]

NOTES
Commencement: 15 January 2007.

13 Evidence

(1) A person is not to be excused from—
   (a) answering any question put to him in proceedings relating to property, or
   (b) complying with any order made in proceedings relating to property,

on the ground that doing so may incriminate him or his spouse or civil partner of an offence under this Act or a related offence.

(2) But, in proceedings for an offence under this Act or a related offence, a statement or admission made by the person in—
   (a) answering such a question, or
   (b) complying with such an order,

is not admissible in evidence against him or (unless they married or became civil partners after the making of the statement or admission) his spouse or civil partner.

(3) "Proceedings relating to property" means any proceedings for—
   (a) the recovery or administration of any property,
   (b) the execution of a trust, or
   (c) an account of any property or dealings with property,

and "property" means money or other property whether real or personal (including things in action and other intangible property).

(4) "Related offence" means—
   (a) conspiracy to defraud;
   (b) any other offence involving any form of fraudulent conduct or purpose.

[2096]

NOTES
Commencement: 15 January 2007.

14 Minor and consequential amendments etc

(1) Schedule 1 contains minor and consequential amendments.

(2) Schedule 2 contains transitional provisions and savings.

(3) Schedule 3 contains repeals and revocations.

[2097]

NOTES
Commencement: 15 January 2007.

15 Commencement and extent

(1)   This Act (except this section and section 16) comes into force on such day as the Secretary of State may appoint by an order made by statutory instrument; and different days may be appointed for different purposes.

(2)   Subject to subsection (3), sections 1 to 9 and 11 to 13 extend to England and Wales and Northern Ireland only.

(3)   Section 8, so far as it relates to the Armed Forces Act 2001 (c 19), extends to any place to which that Act extends.

(4)   Any amendment in section 10 or Schedule 1, and any related provision in section 14 or Schedule 2 or 3, extends to any place to which the provision which is the subject of the amendment extends.

[2098]

NOTES

Commencement: 8 November 2006.
Order: the Fraud Act 2006 (Commencement) Order 2006, SI 2006/3200.

16 Short title

This Act may be cited as the Fraud Act 2006.

[2099]

NOTES

Commencement: 8 November 2006.

(*Sch 1* (*Minor and Consequential Amendments*) *outside the scope of this work.*)

SCHEDULE 2
TRANSITIONAL PROVISIONS AND SAVINGS

Section 14(2)

Maximum term of imprisonment for offences under this Act

1.   In relation to an offence committed before the commencement of section 154(1) of the Criminal Justice Act 2003 (c 44), the references to 12 months in sections 1(3)(a), 6(2)(a), 7(2)(a), 9(6)(a) and 11(3)(a) are to be read as references to 6 months.

Increase in penalty for fraudulent trading

2.   Section 10 does not affect the penalty for any offence committed before that section comes into force.

Abolition of deception offences

3.—(1)   Paragraph 1 of Schedule 1 does not affect any liability, investigation, legal proceeding or penalty for or in respect of any offence partly committed before the commencement of that paragraph.

(2)   An offence is partly committed before the commencement of paragraph 1 of Schedule 1 if—

(a)   a relevant event occurs before its commencement, and
(b)   another relevant event occurs on or after its commencement.

(3)   "Relevant event", in relation to an offence, means any act, omission or other event (including any result of one or more acts or omissions) proof of which is required for conviction of the offence.

Scope of offences relating to stolen goods under the Theft Act 1968 (c 60)

4.   Nothing in paragraph 6 of Schedule 1 affects the operation of section 24 of the Theft Act 1968 in relation to goods obtained in the circumstances described in section 15(1) of that Act where the obtaining is the result of a deception made before the commencement of that paragraph.

Dishonestly retaining a wrongful credit under the Theft Act 1968

5.   Nothing in paragraph 7 of Schedule 1 affects the operation of section 24A(7) and (8) of the Theft Act 1968 in relation to credits falling within section 24A(3) or (4) of that Act and made before the commencement of that paragraph.

Scope of offences relating to stolen goods under the Theft Act (Northern Ireland) 1969 (c 16 (NI))

6.   Nothing in paragraph 11 of Schedule 1 affects the operation of section 23 of the Theft Act (Northern Ireland) 1969 in relation to goods obtained in the circumstances described in section 15(1) of that Act where the obtaining is the result of a deception made before the commencement of that paragraph.

Dishonestly retaining a wrongful credit under the Theft Act (Northern Ireland) 1969

7.   Nothing in paragraph 12 of Schedule 1 affects the operation of section 23A(7) and (8) of the Theft Act (Northern Ireland) 1969 in relation to credits falling within section 23A(3) or (4) of that Act and made before the commencement of that paragraph.

Limitation periods under the Limitation Act 1980 (c 58)

8.   Nothing in paragraph 18 of Schedule 1 affects the operation of section 4 of the Limitation Act 1980 in relation to chattels obtained in the circumstances described in section 15(1) of the Theft Act 1968 where the obtaining is a result of a deception made before the commencement of that paragraph.

Limitation periods under the Limitation (Northern Ireland) Order 1989 (SI 1989/1339 (NI 11))

9.   Nothing in paragraph 22 of Schedule 1 affects the operation of Article 18 of the Limitation (Northern Ireland) Order 1989 in relation to chattels obtained in the circumstances described in section 15(1) of the Theft Act (Northern Ireland) 1969 where the obtaining is a result of a deception made before the commencement of that paragraph.

Scheduled offences under the Terrorism Act 2000 (c 11)

10.   Nothing in paragraph 30 of Schedule 1 affects the operation of Part 7 of the Terrorism Act 2000 in relation to an offence under section 15(1) of the Theft Act (Northern Ireland) 1969 where the obtaining is a result of a deception made before the commencement of that paragraph.

Powers of arrest under Asylum and Immigration (Treatment of Claimants, etc) Act 2004 (c 19)

11.—(1)   Nothing in paragraph 35 of Schedule 1 affects the power of arrest conferred by section 14 of the Asylum and Immigration (Treatment of Claimants, etc) Act 2004 in relation to an offence partly committed before the commencement of that paragraph.

(2)   An offence is partly committed before the commencement of paragraph 35 of Schedule 1 if—

    (a)   a relevant event occurs before its commencement, and
    (b)   another relevant event occurs on or after its commencement.

(3)   "Relevant event", in relation to an offence, means any act, omission or other event (including any result of one or more acts or omissions) proof of which is required for conviction of the offence.

[2100]

NOTES
Commencement: 15 January 2007.

(Sch 3 (Repeals and Revocations) outside the scope of this work.)

COMPANIES ACT 2006

(2006 c 46)

ARRANGEMENT OF SECTIONS

PART 41
BUSINESS NAMES

CHAPTER 1
RESTRICTED OR PROHIBITED NAMES

Introductory

Sensitive words or expressions

An Act to reform company law and restate the greater part of the enactments relating to companies; to make other provision relating to companies and other forms of business organisation; to make provision about directors' disqualification, business names, auditors and actuaries; to amend Part 9 of the Enterprise Act 2002; and for connected purposes

[8 November 2006]

1–1191   ((Pts 1–40) Outside the scope of this work.)

PART 41
BUSINESS NAMES

CHAPTER 1
RESTRICTED OR PROHIBITED NAMES

Introductory

1192 Application of this Chapter

(1)   This Chapter applies to any person carrying on business in the United Kingdom.

(2)   The provisions of this Chapter do not prevent—

   (a)   an individual carrying on business under a name consisting of his surname without any addition other than a permitted addition, or

   (b)   individuals carrying on business in partnership under a name consisting of the surnames of all the partners without any addition other than a permitted addition.

(3)   The following are the permitted additions—

   (a)   in the case of an individual, his forename or initial;

   (b)   in the case of a partnership—

      (i)   the forenames of individual partners or the initials of those forenames, or

(ii)   where two or more individual partners have the same surname, the addition of "s" at the end of that surname;

(c)   in either case, an addition merely indicating that the business is carried on in succession to a former owner of the business.

[2100A]

NOTES

Commencement: 1 October 2009 (subject to transitional provisions and savings in SI 2008/2860, art 5, Sch 2, para 1).

Sensitive words or expressions

1193   Name suggesting connection with government or public authority

(1)   A person must not, without the approval of the Secretary of State, carry on business in the United Kingdom under a name that would be likely to give the impression that the business is connected with—

(a)   Her Majesty's Government, any part of the Scottish administration[, the Welsh Assembly Government] or Her Majesty's Government in Northern Ireland,

(b)   any local authority, or

(c)   any public authority specified for the purposes of this section by regulations made by the Secretary of State.

(2)   For the purposes of this section—

"local authority" means—

(a)   a local authority within the meaning of the Local Government Act 1972 (c 70), the Common Council of the City of London or the Council of the Isles of Scilly,

(b)   a council constituted under section 2 of the Local Government etc (Scotland) Act 1994 (c 39), or

(c)   a district council in Northern Ireland;

"public authority" includes any person or body having functions of a public nature.

(3)   Regulations under this section are subject to affirmative resolution procedure.

(4)   A person who contravenes this section commits an offence.

(5)   Where an offence under this section is committed by a body corporate, an offence is also committed by every officer of the body who is in default.

(6)   A person guilty of an offence under this section is liable on summary conviction to a fine not exceeding level 3 on the standard scale and, for continued contravention, a daily default fine not exceeding one-tenth of level 3 on the standard scale.

[2100B]

NOTES

Commencement: 20 January 2007 (for the purpose of enabling the exercise of powers to make regulations); 1 October 2009 (otherwise, subject to transitional provisions and savings in SI 2008/2860, art 5, Sch 2, para 1).

Sub-s (1): words in square brackets inserted by the Government of Wales Act 2006 (Consequential Modifications, Transitional Provisions and Saving) Order 2009, SI 2009/2958, arts 8, 11.

1194   Other sensitive words or expressions

(1)   A person must not, without the approval of the Secretary of State, carry on business in the United Kingdom under a name that includes a word or expression for the time being specified in regulations made by the Secretary of State under this section.

(2)   Regulations under this section are subject to approval after being made.

(3)   A person who contravenes this section commits an offence.

(4)   Where an offence under this section is committed by a body corporate, an offence is also committed by every officer of the body who is in default.

(5)   A person guilty of an offence under this section is liable on summary conviction to a fine not exceeding level 3 on the standard scale and, for continued contravention, a daily default fine not exceeding one-tenth of level 3 on the standard scale.

[2100C]

NOTES

Commencement: 20 January 2007 (for the purpose of enabling the exercise of powers to make regulations); 1 October 2009 (otherwise, subject to transitional provisions and savings in SI 2008/2860, art 5, Sch 2, para 1).

Regulations: the Company, Limited Liability Partnership and Business Names (Sensitive Words and Expressions) Regulations 2009, SI 2009/2615.

1195   Requirement to seek comments of government department or other relevant body

(1)   The Secretary of State may by regulations under—

(a) section 1193 (name suggesting connection with government or public authority), or

(b) section 1194 (other sensitive words or expressions),

require that, in connection with an application for the approval of the Secretary of State under that section, the applicant must seek the view of a specified Government department or other body.

(2) Where such a requirement applies, the applicant must request the specified department or other body (in writing) to indicate whether (and if so why) it has any objections to the proposed name.

(3) He must submit to the Secretary of State a statement that such a request has been made and a copy of any response received from the specified body.

(4) If these requirements are not complied with, the Secretary of State may refuse to consider the application for approval.

(5) In this section "specified" means specified in the regulations.

[2100D]

NOTES

Commencement: 20 January 2007 (for the purpose of enabling the exercise of powers to make regulations); 1 October 2009 (otherwise, subject to transitional provisions and savings in SI 2008/2860, art 5, Sch 2, para 1).

Regulations: the Company, Limited Liability Partnership and Business Names (Sensitive Words and Expressions) Regulations 2009, SI 2009/2615; the Company, Limited Liability Partnership and Business Names (Public Authorities) Regulations 2009, SI 2009/2982.

1196 Withdrawal of Secretary of State's approval

(1) This section applies to approval given for the purposes of—

section 1193 (name suggesting connection with government or public authority), or

section 1194 (other sensitive words or expressions).

(2) If it appears to the Secretary of State that there are overriding considerations of public policy that require such approval to be withdrawn, the approval may be withdrawn by notice in writing given to the person concerned.

(3) The notice must state the date as from which approval is withdrawn.

[2100E]

NOTES

Commencement: 1 October 2009 (subject to transitional provisions and savings in SI 2008/2860, art 5, Sch 2, para 1).

Misleading names

1197 Name containing inappropriate indication of company type or legal form

(1) The Secretary of State may make provision by regulations prohibiting a person from carrying on business in the United Kingdom under a name consisting of or containing specified words, expressions or other indications—

(a) that are associated with a particular type of company or form of organisation, or

(b) that are similar to words, expressions or other indications associated with a particular type of company or form of organisation.

(2) The regulations may prohibit the use of words, expressions or other indications—

(a) in a specified part, or otherwise than in a specified part, of a name;

(b) in conjunction with, or otherwise than in conjunction with, such other words, expressions or indications as may be specified.

(3) In this section "specified" means specified in the regulations.

(4) Regulations under this section are subject to negative resolution procedure.

(5) A person who uses a name in contravention of regulations under this section commits an offence.

(6) Where an offence under this section is committed by a body corporate, an offence is also committed by every officer of the body who is in default.

(7) A person guilty of an offence under this section is liable on summary conviction to a fine not exceeding level 3 on the standard scale and, for continued contravention, a daily default fine not exceeding one-tenth of level 3 on the standard scale.

[2100F]

NOTES

Commencement: 20 January 2007 (for the purpose of enabling the exercise of powers to make regulations); 1 October 2009 (otherwise, subject to transitional provisions and savings in SI 2008/2860, art 5, Sch 2, para 1).

Regulations: the Company and Business Names (Miscellaneous Provisions) Regulations 2009, SI 2009/1085 at **[3886]**.

1198   Name giving misleading indication of activities

(1)   A person must not carry on business in the United Kingdom under a name that gives so misleading an indication of the nature of the activities of the business as to be likely to cause harm to the public.

(2)   A person who uses a name in contravention of this section commits an offence.

(3)   Where an offence under this section is committed by a body corporate, an offence is also committed by every officer of the body who is in default.

(4)   A person guilty of an offence under this section is liable on summary conviction to a fine not exceeding level 3 on the standard scale and, for continued contravention, a daily default fine not exceeding one-tenth of level 3 on the standard scale.

[2100G]

NOTES
Commencement: 1 October 2009 (subject to transitional provisions and savings in SI 2008/2860, art 5, Sch 2, para 1).

Supplementary

1199   Savings for existing lawful business names

(1)   This section has effect in relation to—
sections 1192 to 1196 (sensitive words or expressions), and
section 1197 (inappropriate indication of company type or legal form).

(2)   Those sections do not apply to the carrying on of a business by a person who—
  (a)   carried on the business immediately before the date on which this Chapter came into force, and
  (b)   continues to carry it on under the name that immediately before that date was its lawful business name.

(3)   Where—
  (a)   a business is transferred to a person on or after the date on which this Chapter came into force, and
  (b)   that person carries on the business under the name that was its lawful business name immediately before the transfer,
those sections do not apply in relation to the carrying on of the business under that name during the period of twelve months beginning with the date of the transfer.

(4)   In this section "lawful business name", in relation to a business, means a name under which the business was carried on without contravening—
  (a)   section 2(1) of the Business Names Act 1985 (c 7) or Article 4(1) of the Business Names (Northern Ireland) Order 1986 (SI 1986/1033 NI 7)), or
  (b)   after this Chapter has come into force, the provisions of this Chapter.

[2100H]

NOTES
Commencement: 1 October 2009 (subject to transitional provisions and savings in SI 2008/2860, art 5, Sch 2, para 1).

CHAPTER 2
DISCLOSURE REQUIRED IN CASE OF INDIVIDUAL OR PARTNERSHIP
Introductory

1200   Application of this Chapter

(1)   This Chapter applies to an individual or partnership carrying on business in the United Kingdom under a business name.

References in this Chapter to "a person to whom this Chapter applies" are to such an individual or partnership.

(2)   For the purposes of this Chapter a "business name" means a name other than—
  (a)   in the case of an individual, his surname without any addition other than a permitted addition;
  (b)   in the case of a partnership—
    (i)   the surnames of all partners who are individuals, and
    (ii)   the corporate names of all partners who are bodies corporate,
    without any addition other than a permitted addition.

(3)   The following are the permitted additions—
  (a)   in the case of an individual, his forename or initial;

(b)   in the case of a partnership—
    (i)   the forenames of individual partners or the initials of those forenames, or
    (ii)   where two or more individual partners have the same surname, the addition of "s" at the end of that surname;
(c)   in either case, an addition merely indicating that the business is carried on in succession to a former owner of the business.

[2100I]

NOTES
Commencement: 1 October 2009 (subject to transitional provisions and savings in SI 2008/2860, art 5, Sch 2, para 1).

[1201   Information required to be disclosed

(1)   The "information required by this Chapter" is—
    (a)   in the case of an individual, the individual's name;
    (b)   in the case of a partnership, the name of each member of the partnership;
and, in relation to each person so named, an address at which service of any document relating in any way to the business will be effective.

(2)   If the individual or partnership has a place of business in the United Kingdom, the address must be in the United Kingdom.

(3)   If the individual or partnership does not have a place of business in the United Kingdom, the address must be an address at which service of documents can be effected by physical delivery and the delivery of documents is capable of being recorded by the obtaining of an acknowledgement of delivery.]

[2100J]

NOTES
Commencement: 28 December 2009.
Substituted by the Companies Act 2006 (Substitution of Section 1201) Regulations 2009, SI 2009/3182, reg 2.

Disclosure requirements

1202   Disclosure required: business documents etc

(1)   A person to whom this Chapter applies must state the information required by this Chapter, in legible characters, on all—
    (a)   business letters,
    (b)   written orders for goods or services to be supplied to the business,
    (c)   invoices and receipts issued in the course of the business, and
    (d)   written demands for payment of debts arising in the course of the business.

This subsection has effect subject to section 1203 (exemption for large partnerships if certain conditions met).

(2)   A person to whom this Chapter applies must secure that the information required by this Chapter is immediately given, by written notice, to any person with whom anything is done or discussed in the course of the business and who asks for that information.

(3)   The Secretary of State may by regulations require that such notices be given in a specified form.

(4)   Regulations under this section are subject to negative resolution procedure.

[2100K]

NOTES
Commencement: 20 January 2007 (for the purpose of enabling the exercise of powers to make regulations); 1 October 2009 (otherwise, subject to transitional provisions and savings in SI 2008/2860, art 5, Sch 2, para 1).

1203   Exemption for large partnerships if certain conditions met

(1)   Section 1202(1) (disclosure required in business documents) does not apply in relation to a document issued by a partnership of more than 20 persons if the following conditions are met.

(2)   The conditions are that—
    (a)   the partnership maintains at its principal place of business a list of the names of all the partners,
    (b)   no partner's name appears in the document, except in the text or as a signatory, and
    (c)   the document states in legible characters the address of the partnership's principal place of business and that the list of the partners' names is open to inspection there.

(3)   Where a partnership maintains a list of the partners' names for the purposes of this section, any person may inspect the list during office hours.

(4)   Where an inspection required by a person in accordance with this section is refused, an offence is committed by any member of the partnership concerned who without reasonable excuse refused the inspection or permitted it to be refused.

(5)   A person guilty of an offence under subsection (4) is liable on summary conviction to a fine not exceeding level 3 on the standard scale and, for continued contravention, a daily default fine not exceeding one-tenth of level 3 on the standard scale.

[2100L]

NOTES
Commencement: 1 October 2009 (subject to transitional provisions and savings in SI 2008/2860, art 5, Sch 2, para 1).

1204   Disclosure required: business premises

(1)   A person to whom this Chapter applies must, in any premises—
(a)   where the business is carried on, and
(b)   to which customers of the business or suppliers of goods or services to the business have access,

display in a prominent position, so that it may easily be read by such customers or suppliers, a notice containing the information required by this Chapter.

(2)   The Secretary of State may by regulations require that such notices be displayed in a specified form.

(3)   Regulations under this section are subject to negative resolution procedure.

[2100M]

NOTES
Commencement: 20 January 2007 (for the purpose of enabling the exercise of powers to make regulations); 1 October 2009 (otherwise, subject to transitional provisions and savings in SI 2008/2860, art 5, Sch 2, para 1).

Consequences of failure to make required disclosure

1205   Criminal consequences of failure to make required disclosure

(1)   A person who without reasonable excuse fails to comply with the requirements of—
section 1202 (disclosure required: business documents etc), or
section 1204 (disclosure required: business premises),
commits an offence.

(2)   Where an offence under this section is committed by a body corporate, an offence is also committed by every officer of the body who is in default.

(3)   A person guilty of an offence under this section is liable on summary conviction to a fine not exceeding level 3 on the standard scale and, for continued contravention, a daily default fine not exceeding one-tenth of level 3 on the standard scale.

(4)   References in this section to the requirements of section 1202 or 1204 include the requirements of regulations under that section.

[2100N]

NOTES
Commencement: 1 October 2009 (subject to transitional provisions and savings in SI 2008/2860, art 5, Sch 2, para 1).

1206   Civil consequences of failure to make required disclosure

(1)   This section applies to any legal proceedings brought by a person to whom this Chapter applies to enforce a right arising out of a contract made in the course of a business in respect of which he was, at the time the contract was made, in breach of section 1202(1) or (2) (disclosure in business documents etc) or section 1204(1) (disclosure at business premises).

(2)   The proceedings shall be dismissed if the defendant (in Scotland, the defender) to the proceedings shows—
(a)   that he has a claim against the claimant (pursuer) arising out of the contract that he has been unable to pursue by reason of the latter's breach of the requirements of this Chapter, or
(b)   that he has suffered some financial loss in connection with the contract by reason of the claimant's (pursuer's) breach of those requirements,

unless the court before which the proceedings are brought is satisfied that it is just and equitable to permit the proceedings to continue.

(3)   References in this section to the requirements of this Chapter include the requirements of regulations under this Chapter.

(4) This section does not affect the right of any person to enforce such rights as he may have against another person in any proceedings brought by that person.

[2100O]

CHAPTER 3
SUPPLEMENTARY

1207 Application of general provisions about offences

The provisions of sections 1121 to 1123 (liability of officer in default) and 1125 to 1131 (general provisions about offences) apply in relation to offences under this Part as in relation to offences under the Companies Acts.

[2100P]

1208 Interpretation

In this Part—
    "business" includes a profession;
    "initial" includes any recognised abbreviation of a name;
    "partnership" means—
        (a)   a partnership within the Partnership Act 1890 (c 39), or
        (b)   a limited partnership registered under the Limited Partnerships Act 1907 (c 24),
        or a firm or entity of a similar character formed under the law of a country or territory outside the United Kingdom;
    "surname", in relation to a peer or person usually known by a British title different from his surname, means the title by which he is known.

[2100Q]

1209–1297   ((*Pts 42–46*) *Outside the scope of this work.*)

PART 47
FINAL PROVISIONS

1298 Short title

The short title of this Act is the Companies Act 2006.

[2100R]

1299 Extent

Except as otherwise provided (or the context otherwise requires), the provisions of this Act extend to the whole of the United Kingdom.

[2100S]

1300 Commencement

(1)   The following provisions come into force on the day this Act is passed—
    (a)   Part 43 (transparency obligations and related matters), except the amendment in paragraph 11(2) of Schedule 15 of the definition of "regulated market" in Part 6 of the Financial Services and Markets Act 2000 (c 8),
    (b)   in Part 44 (miscellaneous provisions)—
        section 1274 (grants to bodies concerned with actuarial standards etc), and

section 1276 (application of provisions to Scotland and Northern Ireland),

(c) Part 46 (general supplementary provisions), except section 1295 and Schedule 16 (repeals), and

(d) this Part.

(2) The other provisions of this Act come into force on such day as may be appointed by order of the Secretary of State or the Treasury.

[2100T]

NOTES

Commencement: 8 November 2006.

Orders: the Companies Act 2006 (Commencement No 1, Transitional Provisions and Savings) Order 2006, SI 2006/3428; the Companies Act 2006 (Commencement No 2, Consequential Amendments, Transitional Provisions and Savings) Order 2007, SI 2007/1093; the Companies Act 2006 (Commencement No 3, Consequential Amendments, Transitional Provisions and Savings) Order 2007, SI 2007/2194; the Companies Act 2006 (Commencement No 4 and Commencement No 3 (Amendment)) Order 2007, SI 2007/2607; the Companies Act 2006 (Commencement No 5, Transitional Provisions and Savings) Order 2007, SI 2007/3495; the Companies Act 2006 (Commencement No 6, Saving and Commencement Nos 3 and 5 (Amendment)) Order 2008, SI 2008/674; the Companies Act 2006 (Commencement No 7, Transitional Provisions and Savings) Order 2008, SI 2008/1886; the Companies Act 2006 (Commencement No 8, Transitional Provisions and Savings) Order 2008, SI 2008/2860.

(Schs 1–16 outside the scope of this work.)

INVESTMENT EXCHANGES AND CLEARING HOUSES ACT 2006

(2006 c 55)

An Act to confer power on the Financial Services Authority to disallow excessive regulatory provision by recognised investment exchanges and clearing houses; and for connected purposes

[19 December 2006]

1–4 (*S 1 inserts the Financial Services and Markets Act 2000, s 300A at* **[1813M]**; *s 2 inserts ss 300B–300E of the 2000 Act at* **[1813N]–[1813Q]**; *s 3 repealed by s 3(8) of this Act; s 4 inserts s 290A of the 2000 Act at* **[1813L]**.)

5 Short title and commencement

(1) The short title of this Act is the Investment Exchanges and Clearing Houses Act 2006.

(2) This Act comes into force on the day after that on which it is passed.

(3) Sections 300A to 300E of the Financial Services and Markets Act 2000 (c 8) (as inserted by this Act)—

(a) do not apply to regulatory provision made before that day, and

(b) apply to regulatory provision proposed on or after that day, whenever originally proposed.

Expressions used in this subsection that are defined for the purposes of those sections have the same meaning as in those sections.

[2101]

NOTES

Commencement: 20 December 2006.

CONSUMERS, ESTATE AGENTS AND REDRESS ACT 2007

(2007 c 17)

ARRANGEMENT OF SECTIONS

PART 1
THE NATIONAL CONSUMER COUNCIL

The National Consumer Council and territorial committees

PART 2
COMPLAINTS HANDLING AND REDRESS SCHEMES

Introductory

An Act to make provision for the establishment of the National Consumer Council and its functions; to make provision for the abolition of other consumer bodies; to make provision about the handling of consumer complaints by certain providers; to make provision requiring certain providers to be members of redress schemes in respect of consumer complaints; to amend the Estate Agents Act 1979; to make provision about the cancellation of certain contracts concluded away from business premises; and for connected purposes

[19 July 2007]

PART 1
THE NATIONAL CONSUMER COUNCIL

The National Consumer Council and territorial committees

1   Establishment of the National Consumer Council and its territorial committees

(1)   There is to be a body corporate called the National Consumer Council or, in Welsh, Cyngor Defnyddwyr Cenedlaethol ("the Council").

(2)   The Council must establish and maintain—
    (a)   a committee for Scotland to be known as the Scottish Consumer Council;
    (b)   a committee for Wales to be known as the Welsh Consumer Council or, in Welsh, Cyngor Defnyddwyr Cymru;
    (c)   a committee for Northern Ireland to be known as the Northern Ireland Postal Services Committee.

(3)   In this Part references to a "territorial committee" are to a committee established under subsection (2).

(4)   Schedule 1 is about the Council and its territorial committees.

[2102]

NOTES
Commencement: 21 December 2007 (sub-ss (1), (2)(a), (b), (3), sub-s (4) certain purposes); 1 April 2008 (sub-s (4) certain purposes); 1 October 2008 (otherwise).

2   The territorial committees

(1)   The territorial committees may exercise, on behalf of the Council, the following functions—

    (a)   in the case of the Scottish Consumer Council, the Council's functions under sections [7A,] 8 to 17, 19[, 20A] and 21 to 26, so far as they are exercisable in relation to Scotland;

    (b)   in the case of the Welsh Consumer Council, the Council's functions under those sections, so far as they are exercisable in relation to Wales;

    (c)   in the case of the Northern Ireland Postal Services Committee—

        (i)   the Council's functions under sections 8 to 12, 15 to 17, 19, 21 and 23 to 26 so far as they are exercisable in relation to Northern Ireland, and

        (ii)   the Council's functions under section 22 so far as they are exercisable in relation to consumer matters which relate to relevant postal services in relation to Northern Ireland.

(2)   For the purpose of facilitating or improving co-ordination in relation to the carrying out of its functions, the Council may from time to time—

    (a)   impose restrictions or conditions on the exercise by a territorial committee of a function by virtue of subsection (1);

    (b)   give a territorial committee general or specific directions relating to the exercise of a function by virtue of that subsection.

(3)   Nothing in subsection (1) prevents the Council from exercising any of its functions referred to in that subsection.

(4)   A territorial committee also has the following purposes—

    (a)   the provision of advice and information to the Council about consumer matters affecting the area for which the committee is established,

    (b)   the provision of advice to the Council about the exercise of the Council's functions in so far as they affect that area, and

    (c)   such other purposes as the Council may determine (including the exercise of any functions delegated to the committee under paragraph 23 of Schedule 1).

[2103]

NOTES
Commencement: 21 December 2007 (sub-s (1)(a), (b) in so far as they relate to ss 9, 10(1)(a) and (2), sub-ss (2)–(4)); 1 October 2008 (otherwise).
Sub-s (1): figures in square brackets inserted in relation to Scotland only by the Public Services Reform (Scotland) Act 2010, s 3(6), Sch 2, Pt 1, paras 15, 16, as from a day to be appointed.

"Consumer", "consumer matters" and "designated consumers"

3   "Consumer" and "consumer matters"

(1)   In this Part "consumer" and "consumer matters" have the meaning given by this section.

(2)   "Consumer" means—

    (a)   a person who purchases, uses or receives, in Great Britain, goods or services which are supplied in the course of a business carried on by the person supplying or seeking to supply them, or

    (b)   a person who purchases, uses or receives relevant postal services in Northern Ireland.

(3)   "Consumer" includes both an existing consumer and a future consumer.

(4)   For the purposes of subsection (2)—

    (a)   a person who uses services includes, in relation to relevant postal services, an addressee;

    (b)   "goods" includes land or an interest in land;

    (c)   "business" includes a profession and the activities of any government department, local or public authority or other public body.

(5)   "Consumer matters" means—

    (a)   the interests of consumers, and

    (b)   any matter connected with those interests.

[2104]

PART 1
STATUTES

4   "Designated consumers"

(1)   In this Part "designated consumers" means—
- (a)   consumers in relation to gas conveyed through pipes or electricity conveyed by distribution systems or transmission systems, and
- (b)   consumers in relation to relevant postal services.

(2)   The Secretary of State may, by order, amend subsection (1) so as—
- (a)   to make any description of consumers within subsection (3) "designated consumers" for the purposes of this Part;
- (b)   to provide for any description of consumers to cease to be "designated consumers" for those purposes.

(3)   The consumers within this subsection are consumers in England and Wales in relation to services provided by a water undertaker, a sewerage undertaker or a licensed water supplier, in its capacity as such.

(4)   Before making an order under subsection (2), the Secretary of State must consult—
- (a)   the Council,
- (b)   in the case of a relevant order, the Scottish Ministers,
- (c)   the Welsh Ministers, and
- (d)   such other persons as the Secretary of State considers appropriate.

(5)   For this purpose a "relevant order" is an order which relates to any description of—
- (a)   consumers in relation to gas conveyed through pipes or electricity conveyed by distribution systems or transmission systems, or
- (b)   consumers in relation to relevant postal services.

[2105]

NOTES
Commencement: 21 December 2007.

Determining priorities

5   Forward work programmes

(1)   The Council must before each financial year publish a document (the "forward work programme") containing—
- (a)   a statement of any priorities of the Council for the year in relation to designated consumers generally or any description of designated consumers;
- (b)   a general description of the main activities (including any projects) which it plans to undertake during the year in relation to designated consumers generally or any description of designated consumers;
- (c)   a statement of any other priorities of the Council for the year;
- (d)   a general description of any other projects which it plans to undertake during the year (other than those comprising routine activities in the exercise of its functions).

(2)   The description of a project under subsection (1)(b) or (d) must include the objectives of the project.

(3)   The forward work programme for any year must also include—
- (a)   an estimate of the overall expenditure which the Council expects to incur during the year in the exercise of its functions, and
- (b)   an estimate of the expenditure (if any) which the Council expects to incur during the year in the exercise of its functions in relation to designated consumers.

(4)   An estimate under subsection (3)(b) must identify the expenditure (if any) which the Council expects to incur in the exercise of its functions in relation to each of the following—
- (a)   consumers in relation to gas conveyed through pipes or electricity conveyed by distribution systems or transmission systems;
- (b)   consumers in relation to relevant postal services;
- (c)   consumers who are designated consumers by virtue of an order under section 4(2)(a).

(5)   Before publishing the forward work programme for any year, the Council must publish a notice—
- (a)   containing a draft of the forward work programme, and
- (b)   specifying the period within which representations about the proposals contained in it may be made,

and must consider any representations which are duly made and not withdrawn.

(6)   The notice under subsection (5) must be published by the Council in such manner as it considers appropriate for the purpose of bringing the matters contained in the notice to the attention of persons likely to have an interest in them.

(7)   The Council must send a copy of any notice given by it under subsection (5) to—
    (a)   the Secretary of State,
    (b)   the Scottish Ministers,
    (c)   the Welsh Ministers,
    (d)   the Office of Fair Trading, and
    (e)   any regulatory body which the Council considers might have an interest in the content of the notice.

[2106]

NOTES
Commencement: 7 May 2008.

6   General provision about functions

(1)   In exercising its functions the Council must comply with the requirements of this section.

(2)   The Council must have regard to the forward work programme published under section 5.

(3)   The Council must have regard to the interests of consumers in different areas.

(4)   The Council must have regard to the interests of consumers that are one or more of the following—
    (a)   disabled or chronically sick individuals;
    (b)   individuals of pensionable age;
    (c)   individuals with low incomes;
    (d)   individuals residing in rural areas.

(5)   But nothing in subsection (4) is to be taken as implying that regard may not be had to the interests of other descriptions of consumers.

(6)   The Council must have regard to the need to use its resources in the most efficient and economic way.

(7)   In discharging the duty imposed by subsection (6), the Council must take account of the existence of any other public bodies with the same functions as, or similar functions to, those of the Council and the activities carried on by such bodies.

(8)   The Council must exercise its functions in the manner which it considers is best calculated to contribute to the achievement of sustainable development.

(9)   Subject to section 13 (investigation of complaints relating to disconnection of gas or electricity), nothing in this Part imposes on the Council a duty to exercise any of its functions on behalf of or at the request of a particular consumer.

(10)   A person is of pensionable age for the purposes of this section if—
    (a)   the person has attained pensionable age (within the meaning given by the rules in paragraph 1 of Schedule 4 to the Pensions Act 1995 (c 26)), or
    (b)   in the case of a man born before 6 April 1955, he is the same age as a woman who has attained pensionable age (within the meaning so given).

[2107]

NOTES
Commencement: 21 December 2007 (sub-ss (1), (3)–(10)); 1 October 2008 (sub-s (2)).

Annual report

7   Annual report

(1)   The Council must prepare a report for each financial year on its activities during the year ("the annual report").

(2)   The annual report must—
    (a)   contain a report on the progress of the projects described in the Council's forward work programme for that year published under section 5,
    (b)   contain details of any activities undertaken in that year under section 22 (voluntary activities), and
    (c)   deal with such other matters as the Secretary of State may from time to time direct.

(3)   As soon as reasonably practicable after the end of each financial year, the Council must send a copy of the annual report prepared for that year to—
    (a)   the Secretary of State,
    (b)   the Scottish Ministers, and
    (c)   the Welsh Ministers.

(4)   The Secretary of State must lay a copy of the annual report before Parliament.

(5)   The Council must arrange for the annual report to be published.

[2108]

NOTES
Commencement: 1 October 2008.

7A   (*Inserted in relation to Scotland only by the Public Services Reform (Scotland) Act 2010, s 3(6), Sch 2, Pt 1, paras 15, 17, as from a day to be appointed.*)

The core functions

8   The representative function

(1)   The Council may—
   (a)   provide advice and information to persons within subsection (2) about consumer matters,
   (b)   make proposals to such persons about consumer matters, and
   (c)   represent the views of consumers on consumer matters to such persons.

(2)   Those persons are—
   (a)   any Minister of the Crown or government department;
   (b)   the Scottish Ministers;
   (c)   the Welsh Ministers;
   (d)   any regulatory body established by or under an enactment;
   (e)   the European Commission or any other international organisation;
   (f)   any other person whom the Council considers might have an interest in the matter in question.

(3)   In this section "enactment" means—
   (a)   an Act of Parliament,
   (b)   an Act of the Scottish Parliament,
   (c)   a Measure or Act of the National Assembly for Wales, or
   (d)   Northern Ireland legislation,
whenever passed or made.

[2109]

NOTES
Commencement: 1 October 2008.

9   The research function

The Council may obtain and keep under review—
   (a)   information about consumer matters,
   (b)   information about the views of consumers on consumer matters, and
   (c)   information of such other description as may be prescribed by the Secretary of State by order.

[2110]

NOTES
Commencement: 21 December 2007.

10   The information function

(1)   The Council may facilitate the dissemination to consumers of advice and information—
   (a)   about the Council and its functions,
   (b)   about consumer matters, and
   (c)   about such other matters as may be prescribed by the Secretary of State by order.

(2)   In exercising the power conferred by subsection (1) the Council may (among other things)—
   (a)   publish or otherwise make available information in any manner the Council thinks appropriate for the purpose of bringing it to the attention of those likely to be interested;
   (b)   support (financially or otherwise), facilitate or co-ordinate the activities of other persons.

[2111]

NOTES
Commencement: 21 December 2007 (sub-ss (1)(a), (2)); 1 October 2008 (sub-s (1)(b), (c)).

Powers of investigation

11 General powers of investigation

(1) The Council may investigate—

(a) a complaint made by or on behalf of a consumer which appears to the Council to raise one or more issues of general relevance;

(b) any matter which appears to the Council to be, or to be related to, a problem which affects or may affect consumers generally or consumers of a particular description.

(2) For this purpose, a complaint raises an issue of general relevance if it raises—

(a) a novel issue which affects or may affect consumers generally or consumers of a particular description, or

(b) any other issue which has or may have an important effect on consumers generally or consumers of a particular description.

[2112]

NOTES
Commencement: 1 October 2008.

12 Investigation of complaints made by vulnerable designated consumers

(1) Subsection (3) applies to a complaint which is made—

(a) by or on behalf of a vulnerable person in that person's capacity as a designated consumer ("the designated consumer"),

(b) against a person ("the supplier") who in the course of a business carried on by the supplier supplies or seeks to supply, or refuses to supply, goods or services to the designated consumer, and

(c) in respect of a matter connected with the supply of goods or services by the supplier to the designated consumer or a refusal by the supplier to supply goods or services to the designated consumer.

(2) For this purpose a person is "vulnerable" if the Council is satisfied that it is not reasonable to expect that person to pursue the complaint on that person's own behalf.

(3) Where a complaint to which this subsection applies is referred to the Council by or on behalf of the designated consumer, the Council may investigate the complaint for the purpose of determining whether it is appropriate to take any action under subsection (4).

(4) Where it appears to the Council to be appropriate to do so with a view to assisting in reaching a satisfactory resolution of a complaint referred to it under this section, the Council may—

(a) provide advice to the designated consumer or, if the complaint was made by another person on the designated consumer's behalf, that person;

(b) make representations on behalf of the designated consumer to the supplier about anything to which the complaint relates.

[2113]

NOTES
Commencement: 1 October 2008.

13 Investigation of complaints relating to disconnection of gas or electricity

(1) This section applies to—

(a) a complaint by a gas consumer against a gas transporter, in respect of the disconnection of, or a threat to disconnect, the consumer's premises by the gas transporter;

(b) a complaint by a gas consumer against a gas transporter, following such a disconnection, in respect of a refusal by the gas transporter to reconnect the premises;

(c) a complaint by a gas consumer against a gas supplier, in respect of the cutting off of, or a threat to cut off, a supply of gas to the consumer's premises by the gas supplier;

(d) a complaint by a gas consumer against a gas supplier, following such a cutting off, in respect of a refusal by the gas supplier to restore the supply to the premises;

(e) a complaint by a gas consumer against a gas supplier, in respect of the failure of a prepayment system;

(f) a complaint by an electricity consumer against an electricity supplier, an electricity distributor or a transmission licence holder, in respect of the disconnection of, or a threat to disconnect, the consumer's premises by the electricity supplier, electricity distributor or licence holder;

(g) a complaint by an electricity consumer against an electricity supplier, electricity distributor or transmission licence holder, following such a disconnection by the supplier, distributor or licence holder, in respect of a refusal by the supplier, distributor or licence holder to reconnect the premises;

(h) a complaint by an electricity consumer against an electricity supplier, in respect of the failure of a prepayment system.

(2)   Where a complaint to which this section applies is referred to the Council by or on behalf of the complainant, the Council must investigate the complaint for the purpose of determining whether it is appropriate to take any action under subsection (3).

(3)   Where it appears to the Council to be appropriate to do so with a view to assisting in reaching a satisfactory resolution of a complaint referred to it under this section, the Council must—

    (a)   provide advice to the complainant, or

    (b)   make representations on behalf of the complainant to the person against whom the complaint is made about anything to which the complaint relates.

(4)   The Council may refuse to investigate a complaint, or part of a complaint, if—

    (a)   the complaint or part appears to the Council to be frivolous or vexatious;

    (b)   the complaint or part falls within a class of matter which a regulatory body is under a duty (whether imposed by or under an enactment or otherwise) to investigate;

    (c)   the complaint or part is being dealt with, or the Council is satisfied that it would be better dealt with, under an ombudsman scheme or any other redress scheme or in legal proceedings;

    (d)   the Council considers that there has been undue delay in the making of the complaint or part, or the provision of evidence to support it;

    (e)   the Council considers that there are other compelling reasons why it is inappropriate for the complaint or part to be investigated by the Council.

(5)   The Council may refuse to investigate a complaint until the complainant has taken such steps as appear to the Council to be reasonable for the purpose of giving the person against whom the complaint is made a reasonable opportunity to deal with it.

(6)   In subsection (1)—

    (a)   in paragraphs (a) and (b) "disconnection" in relation to any premises, means disconnection from a main of a gas transporter or the discontinuation of the conveyance of gas to the premises;

    (b)   in paragraphs (b), (d) and (g), the references to a gas consumer or electricity consumer are references to a person who was such a consumer at the time the disconnection of, or cutting off of the supply to, the premises occurred;

    (c)   in paragraphs (e) and (h), references to the failure of a prepayment system are references to—

        (i)   a failure in the facilities for payment for the supply of gas or electricity which results in a consumer with a prepayment meter being unable to make a payment for the supply of gas or electricity, or

        (ii)   where a payment has been made for the supply of gas or electricity through a prepayment meter, a case where the supply is not given through the prepayment meter because of a defect in the meter or in the facilities for payment.

(7)   In this section—

    "electricity consumer" means an individual who is a consumer in relation to electricity supplied by an authorised supplier;

    "enactment" means—

        (a)   an Act of Parliament,

        (b)   an Act of the Scottish Parliament, or

        (c)   a Measure or Act of the National Assembly for Wales,

    whenever passed or made;

    "gas consumer" means an individual who is a consumer in relation to gas supplied by an authorised supplier;

    "the consumer's premises"—

        (a)   in relation to an electricity consumer, means the premises to which the electricity supplied to the consumer by the authorised supplier is supplied;

        (b)   in relation to a gas consumer, means the premises to which the gas supplied to the consumer is conveyed by the gas transporter;

    "redress scheme" means a scheme under which complaints may be made to, and investigated and determined by, an independent person.

[2114]

NOTES

Commencement: 1 October 2008.

---

14 Reference of matters to the Gas and Electricity Markets Authority

(1)   In this section references to a complaint are to a complaint within section 11(1)(a) or to which section 12(3) or 13 applies.

(2)   Where it appears to the Council that a complaint relates to a matter in respect of which any of the Authority's enforcement functions may be exercisable, the Council must refer the complaint to the Authority unless it is satisfied that the Authority is already aware of the matter.

(3)   Where a complaint to which section 13 applies is referred to the Authority under subsection (2), the Council is not required to investigate the complaint under subsection (2) of that section until the Authority has had a reasonable opportunity to exercise its enforcement functions in relation to the matter to which the complaint relates.

(4)   On investigating a complaint, the Council must inform the complainant if it considers that the complaint relates to a matter of a kind which can be referred by the complainant to the Authority under any provision of the Gas Act 1986 (c 44) or the Electricity Act 1989 (c 29).

(5)   In this section—

"the Authority" means the Gas and Electricity Markets Authority;

"enforcement function", in relation to the Authority, means any of its functions under section 28 or 30A of the Gas Act 1986 or section 25 or 27A of the Electricity Act 1989.

[2115]

NOTES
Commencement: 1 October 2008.

15   Reference of matters to the Postal Services Commission

(1)   The Council must refer any complaint within section 11(1)(a), or to which section 12(3) applies, to the Postal Services Commission ("the Commission") if the Council considers that—

(a)   the subject matter of the complaint indicates that a condition of a licence under Part 2 of the Postal Services Act 2000 (c 26) has been contravened,

(b)   the subject matter of the complaint is a referable matter, or

(c)   it is appropriate to do so.

(2)   The Council and the Commission must, from time to time, agree the descriptions of matters which are to be referred to the Commission and, for the purposes of subsection (1)(b), a matter is a "referable matter" if it is of a description for the time being so agreed.

[2116]

NOTES
Commencement: 1 October 2008.

16   Investigations relating to public post offices

(1)   Without prejudice to the generality of section 11, the Council may investigate any matter relating to—

(a)   the number and location of public post offices in England and Wales and Scotland;

(b)   the number and location of public post offices in Northern Ireland.

(2)   In this section "public post office" has the same meaning as in the Postal Services Act 2000 (c 26) (see section 42(3) of that Act).

[2117]

NOTES
Commencement: 1 October 2008.

Other functions of the Council

17   Reports by the Council

(1)   The Council may prepare a report in relation to any matter falling within the scope of its functions.

(2)   The Council may publish any report prepared under this section.

[2118]

NOTES
Commencement: 1 October 2008.

18   Secretary of State's power to require reports

(1)   The Secretary of State may direct the Council to prepare, and submit to the Secretary of State within a specified period, a report in respect of any matter specified in the direction which relates to consumer matters.

(2)   The Secretary of State may publish any report submitted under this section.

[2119]

NOTES
Commencement: 1 October 2008.

19   Advice, information and guidance

(1)   The Council may issue advice or guidance to any person with a view to improving standards of service and promoting best practice in connection with the handling of complaints made by consumers or any other matter affecting the interests of consumers.

(2)   The Council may publish advice or information about consumer matters if it appears to the Council that its publication would promote the interests of consumers.

(3)   For this purpose "information about consumer matters" includes information about the views of consumers on consumer matters.

[2120]

NOTES

Commencement: 1 October 2008.

20   Duty to enter into co-operation arrangements

(1)   It is the duty of the Council and each designated body to enter into co-operation arrangements under this section.

(2)   In this section—

"co-operation arrangements" means arrangements made by the Council and a designated body with a view to securing co-operation between them, including—

(a)   the exchange of information between them,

(b)   the co-ordination of any activities they carry on in connection with their functions relating to the provision of advice or information to consumers, and

(c)   consistent treatment of matters which affect both of them;

"designated body" means—

(a)   the Office of Fair Trading;

(b)   the Consumer Panel established by the Financial Services Authority under the Financial Services and Markets Act 2000 (c 8) ("the Financial Services Consumer Panel");

(c)   the Consumer Panel established by the Office of Communications under the Communications Act 2003 (c 21) ("the OFCOM Consumer Panel");

(d)   a person designated by the Secretary of State by order for the purposes of this section.

(3)   The co-operation arrangements must set out—

(a)   in the case of the Financial Services Consumer Panel, the procedure for consulting and making nominations for the purposes of paragraph 1(4)(a) of Schedule 1 to this Act and section 10(5A) of the Financial Services and Markets Act 2000 (c 8);

(b)   in the case of the OFCOM Consumer Panel, the procedure for consulting and making nominations for the purposes of paragraph 1(4)(b) of Schedule 1 to this Act and section 17(4A) of the Communications Act 2003.

(4)   As soon as practicable after agreement is reached between the Council and a designated body on co-operation arrangements, the Council and the body must prepare a memorandum setting them out and send a copy of it to the Secretary of State.

(5)   The Council and a designated body must keep under review any co-operation arrangements entered into by them under this section.

(6)   As soon as practicable after agreement is reached on any changes to co-operation arrangements, the Council and the designated body to which they relate must revise their memorandum and send a copy of the revised memorandum to the Secretary of State.

(7)   The Secretary of State must lay a copy of any document received under this section before each House of Parliament.

[2121]

NOTES

Commencement: 21 December 2007.

20A   (*Inserted in relation to Scotland only by the Public Services Reform (Scotland) Act 2010, s 3(6), Sch 2, Pt 1, paras 15, 18, as from a day to be appointed.*)

21   Power to co-operate and give assistance

The Council may make arrangements to co-operate with and give assistance to any person if it considers that to do so would facilitate or be conducive to the exercise of its own functions.

[2122]

NOTES
Commencement: 1 October 2008.

22   Voluntary activities

(1)   The Council may provide for any person advice or assistance, including research or other services, as respects any matter in which the Council has skill, experience or expertise.

(2)   The Council may make such charges as it thinks fit in respect of anything done in exercise of its powers under this section.

(3)   The Council may spend such sums as it considers reasonable in the exploitation of commercial opportunities arising from the activities it carries on in the exercise of its functions.

(4)   The Council may—
    (a)   establish one or more bodies corporate to exercise on behalf of the Council such of its functions under this section, in such circumstances, as the Council may determine;
    (b)   acquire an interest in an existing body corporate with a view to it exercising on behalf of the Council such of its functions under this section, in such circumstances, as the Council may determine.

(5)   The Council may acquire an interest in a body corporate under subsection (4)(b) only with the consent of the Secretary of State.

(6)   If the Secretary of State gives such consent, the Secretary of State must publish a notice stating that consent has been given and specifying the reasons for giving consent.

[2123]

NOTES
Commencement: 21 December 2007.

23   Supplementary powers etc

(1)   The Council may do anything (other than borrow money) which is calculated to facilitate, or is incidental or conducive to, the exercise of any of its functions.

(2)   The Council must not acquire or dispose of any interest in land, except with the approval of the Secretary of State.

(3)   Subsection (2) does not apply to an acquisition of an interest in land under a transfer scheme (within the meaning of section 35).

[2124]

NOTES
Commencement: 21 December 2007.

Information

24   Provision of information to the Council

(1)   The Council may, by notice, require a person within subsection (3) to supply it with such information as is specified or described in the notice within such reasonable period as is so specified.

(2)   The information specified or described in a notice under subsection (1) must be information the Council requires for the purpose of exercising its functions.

(3)   The persons referred to in subsection (1) are—
    (a)   the Office of Fair Trading;
    (b)   a designated regulator;
    (c)   any person who supplies goods or services in the course of a business carried on by that person;
    (d)   any other person specified or of a description specified by the Secretary of State by order for the purposes of this subsection.

(4)   A notice under subsection (1) may specify the manner and form in which any information is to be provided.

(5)   Before giving a notice under subsection (1), or specifying the manner or form in which any information is to be provided, the Council must have regard to the desirability of minimising the costs, or any other detriment, to the person to whom the notice is to be given.

(6)   If a person within subsection (3)(a) or (b) fails to comply with a notice under subsection (1), the person must, if so required by the Council, give notice to the Council of the reasons for the failure.

(7)   An order under subsection (3)(d) may provide either—

    (a)   that subsection (6) is to apply in relation to a person specified or of a description specified by the order as it applies to a person within subsection (3)(a) or (b), or

    (b)   that section 26 is to apply in relation to such a person.

(8)   The Council may publish any notice received under subsection (6).

(9)   In this section—

"designated regulator" means—

    (a)   the Gas and Electricity Markets Authority;

    (b)   the Postal Services Commission;

    (c)   the Water Services Regulation Authority;

    [(ca) the Water Industry Commission for Scotland;]

    (d)   any other person prescribed by the Secretary of State by order for the purposes of this subsection;

"goods" includes land or an interest in land.

[2125]

NOTES

Commencement: 1 October 2008.

Sub-s (9): para (ca) inserted in relation to Scotland only by the Public Services Reform (Scotland) Act 2010, s 3(6), Sch 2, Pt 1, paras 15, 19, as from a day to be appointed.

---

25 Enforcement by regulator of section 24 notice

(1)   Where a regulated provider fails to comply with a notice under section 24(1), the Council may refer the failure to—

    (a)   a person prescribed by the Secretary of State by order for the purposes of this section, or

    (b)   if no person has been so prescribed, the relevant regulator.

(2)   Subsection (1) applies only to the extent that the notice relates to information which is held or may be obtained by the regulated provider in its capacity as a regulated provider.

(3)   For the purposes of this section—

"designated investigator", in relation to a failure to comply with a notice under section 24(1), means the person to whom the failure is referred under subsection (1);

"regulated provider" means a person listed in the first column of the following table;

"relevant regulator", in relation to a regulated provider, means the body listed in relation to the regulated provider in the second column of that table.

TABLE

Regulated provider	*Relevant regulator*
A person holding a licence under section 7, 7ZA or 7A of the Gas Act 1986 (c 44).	The Gas and Electricity Markets Authority.
A person holding a licence under section 6 of the Electricity Act 1989 (c 29).	The Gas and Electricity Markets Authority.
A person holding a licence under Part 2 of the Postal Services Act 2000 (c 26).	The Postal Services Commission.
A water undertaker, sewerage undertaker or licensed water supplier.	The Water Services Regulation Authority.
[Scottish Water	The Water Industry Commission for Scotland.]

(4)   Where a failure is referred under subsection (1), the designated investigator must—

    (a)   consider any representations made by the Council or the regulated provider, and

    (b)   determine whether the regulated provider is entitled to refuse to comply with the notice by virtue of provision made under section 28 (exemptions from requirements to provide information).

(5)   If the designated investigator determines that the regulated provider is not entitled to refuse to comply with the notice, the designated investigator must direct the regulated provider to comply with it.

(6)   The designated investigator must give the Council and the regulated provider notice of—

    (a)   a determination under subsection (4)(b) and the reasons for it, and

    (b)   any direction under subsection (5).

(7)   An obligation imposed by virtue of subsection (5) on a water undertaker, sewerage undertaker or licensed water supplier is enforceable by the Water Services Regulation Authority under section 18 of the Water Industry Act 1991 (c 56) (orders for securing compliance).

(8)   Schedule 2 makes provision about the enforcement of obligations imposed by virtue of subsection (5) on other regulated providers.

[2126]

NOTES
Commencement: 1 October 2008.
Sub-s (3): words in square brackets in the Table inserted in relation to Scotland only by the Public Services Reform (Scotland) Act 2010, s 3(6), Sch 2, Pt 1, paras 15, 20, as from a day to be appointed.

26   Enforcement by court of section 24 notice

(1)   This section applies where a person ("the defaulter") refuses, or otherwise fails, to comply with a notice given to the defaulter under section 24(1) and the defaulter is—
   (a)   within section 24(3)(c), or
   (b)   a person in relation to whom this section applies by virtue of provision made under section 24(7)(b).

(2)   But this section does not apply in relation to a notice if, or to the extent that, section 25(1) applies in relation to the notice.

(3)   The Council may apply to the court for an order requiring the defaulter to comply with the notice or with such directions for the like purpose as may be contained in the order.

(4)   An order under this section may, in particular, provide that all the costs or expenses of and incidental to the application are to be borne—
   (a)   by the defaulter, or
   (b)   if officers of a company or other association are responsible for the failure to comply with the notice, by those officers.

(5)   In this section "the court"—
   (a)   in relation to England and Wales or Northern Ireland, means the High Court, and
   (b)   in relation to Scotland, means the Court of Session.

[2127]

NOTES
Commencement: 1 October 2008.

27   Provision of information by the Council

(1)   An authorised person may, by notice, require the Council to supply it with such information as is specified or described in the notice within such reasonable period as is so specified.

(2)   The information specified or described in a notice under subsection (1) must be information the authorised person requires for the purpose of exercising its functions.

(3)   "Authorised person" means—
   (a)   the Office of Fair Trading;
   (b)   a designated regulator (within the meaning of section 24(9);
   (c)   any person specified or of a description specified by the Secretary of State by order.

(4)   A notice under subsection (1) may specify the manner and form in which any information is to be provided.

(5)   Before giving a notice under subsection (1) or specifying the manner or form in which any information is to be provided, an authorised person must have regard to the desirability of minimising the costs, or any other detriment, to the Council.

(6)   If the Council fails to comply with a notice under subsection (1), it must, if so required by the authorised person which gave that notice, give notice to the authorised person of the reasons for the failure.

(7)   An authorised person may publish any notice received by it under subsection (6).

[2128]

NOTES
Commencement: 1 October 2008.

28   Exemptions from requirements to provide information

(1)   The Secretary of State may make regulations prescribing—
   (a)   descriptions of persons to whom the Council may not give a notice under section 24(1);
   (b)   descriptions of information which a person may refuse to supply in accordance with a notice under section 24(1) or 27(1);

    (c)   circumstances in which a person may refuse to comply with such a notice.

    (2)   No person may be required by a notice under section 24(1) or 27(1) or a court order under section 26—

    (a)   to provide any information which that person could not be compelled to supply in evidence in civil proceedings before the High Court or the Court of Session, or

    (b)   to produce any document which that person could not be compelled to produce in such proceedings.

[2129]

NOTES
Commencement: 1 October 2008.

29   Disclosure of information

    (1), (2)   ...

    (3)   For the purposes of Part 9 of the Enterprise Act 2002 (c 40) (information) the following information is to be regarded as "specified information" within the meaning of that Part—

    (a)   information obtained by the Council under or by virtue of Part 1 of the Gas Act 1986 (c 44), Part 1 of the Electricity Act 1989 (c 29) or the Utilities Act 2000 (c 27);

    (b)   information obtained by the Council under or by virtue of the Postal Services Act 2000 (c 26).

    (4)   Part 9 of the Enterprise Act 2002 (which among other things restricts the disclosure of certain information) does not limit the information which may be—

    (a)   made available by the Council under section 8 or 10,

    (b)   included in, or made public as part of, a report of the Council under any provision of this Part,

    (c)   published by the Council under section 19(2) or 24(8),

    (d)   published by an authorised person under section 27(7),

    (e)   published by the Council under section 45, or

    (f)   published by the Council under section 33DA of the Gas Act 1986 or section 42AA of the Electricity Act 1989.

    (5)   Before disclosing any specified information by virtue of subsection (4) (other than by publishing it as mentioned in subsection (4)(e) or (f)), the Council or authorised person must consult—

    (a)   if the information relates to the affairs of an individual, that individual, and

    (b)   if the information relates to the business of an undertaking, the person for the time being carrying on the business.

    (6)   Before disclosing any specified information by virtue of subsection (4) (other than by publishing it as mentioned in subsection (4)(e) or (f)), the Council or authorised person must also have regard to the considerations set out in subsections (2) to (4) of section 244 of the Enterprise Act 2002.

For this purpose, references to "the authority" in those subsections are to be read as references to the Council or the authorised person, as appropriate.

    (7)   In this section—

"authorised person" has the same meaning as in section 27;

"specified information" has the meaning given by section 238(1) of the Enterprise Act 2002.

[2130]

NOTES
Commencement: 1 October 2008.
Sub-ss (1), (2): amend the Enterprise Act 2002, Schs 14, 15.

Abolition of consumer bodies

30   Abolition of "Energywatch" and "Postwatch"

    (1)   The Gas and Electricity Consumer Council is abolished.

    (2)   The Consumer Council for Postal Services is abolished.

    (3)   Subject to any modifications made by this Act—

    (a)   the functions of the Gas and Electricity Consumer Council under the Gas Act 1986 (c 44), the Electricity Act 1989 (c 29) and the Utilities Act 2000 (c 27), and

    (b)   the functions of the Consumer Council for Postal Services under the Postal Services Act 2000 (c 26),

are transferred by this section to the Council.

(4)   ...

(5)   Schedule 3 contains transitional provisions.

[2131]

NOTES
Commencement: 21 December 2007 (sub-s (4), for the purposes of the Postal Services Act 2000, s 39A and the Utilities Act 2000, s 8); 1 October 2008 (otherwise).
Sub-s (4): amends the Gas Act 1986, s 66, the Electricity Act 1989, s 111(1), the Postal Services Act 2000, s 125(1), the Utilities Act 2000, s 106(1).

31   Designation of the Consumer Council for Water for abolition

(1)   The Secretary of State may by order designate the Consumer Council for Water for abolition.

(2)   An order under this section must specify the earliest date on which a transfer order or an abolition order under section 32 may take effect in respect of the Consumer Council for Water.

(3)   Before making an order under this section the Secretary of State must consult—
  (a)   the Consumer Council for Water,
  (b)   the Council, and
  (c)   such other persons as the Secretary of State considers appropriate.

(4)   An order under this section may only be made with the consent of the Welsh Ministers.

[2132]

NOTES
Commencement: 1 October 2008.

32   Transfer orders and abolition orders

(1)   Where the Consumer Council for Water is designated for abolition under section 31, the Secretary of State may make in respect of it—
  (a)   one or more transfer orders;
  (b)   an abolition order.

(2)   A transfer order is an order which provides for the transfer to the Council of any function of the Consumer Council for Water.

(3)   An abolition order is an order which provides for the abolition of the Consumer Council for Water.

(4)   No provision of an order under this section may take effect before the date specified under section 31(2).

(5)   A transfer order or abolition order may be made only with the consent of the Welsh Ministers.

[2133]

NOTES
Commencement: 1 October 2008.

33   Supplementary provision about transfer and abolition orders

(1)   This section applies where the Consumer Council for Water has been designated for abolition under section 31.

(2)   In this section "payment conditions" means—
  (a)   in the case of an appointment under Chapter 1 of Part 2 of the Water Industry Act 1991 (c 56), conditions included in the appointment by virtue of section 11(1)(c) of that Act, and
  (b)   in the case of a water supply licence under Chapter 1A of that Part, conditions included in the licence by virtue of section 17G(1)(b) of that Act.

(3)   The payment conditions of such an appointment or licence may (without prejudice to the generality of sections 11(1)(c) and 17G(1)(b) of that Act) require the payment by the company holding the appointment or licence of sums relating to any of the expenses mentioned in subsection (4).

(4)   Those expenses are—
  (a)   the appropriate proportion of the expenses of the Council (other than those expenses within paragraph (b) and any expenses relating to the establishment of the Council);
  (b)   any expenses of the Council, the Secretary of State or the Consumer Council for Water which relate to a transfer scheme made in respect of the Consumer Council for Water under section 35(2)(a) or (7);

(c)   the expenses of the Secretary of State which relate to the abolition of the Consumer Council for Water;

(d)   the expenses of expanding an OFT scheme to enable it to cater for water consumers;

(e)   the appropriate proportion of the expenses of the Office of Fair Trading on, or in connection with, the support of any OFT scheme.

(5)   The "appropriate proportion" of any relevant expenses means such proportion of the expenses as the Secretary of State considers is reasonable having regard to—

(a)   in the case of expenses within subsection (4)(a), the functions exercisable by the Council in relation to water consumers;

(b)   in the case of expenses within subsection (4)(e), the functions under the OFT scheme which are exercisable in relation to water consumers.

(6)   The Authority may, in accordance with this section, modify any payment conditions where it considers it necessary or expedient to do so in consequence of, or of preparations for—

(a)   the abolition of the Consumer Council for Water, or

(b)   a transfer order or abolition order under section 32.

(7)   The Authority may, in accordance with this section, make such incidental or consequential modifications of the other conditions which are included in—

(a)   an appointment under Chapter 1 of Part 2 of the Water Industry Act 1991 (c 56), or

(b)   a water supply licence under Chapter 1A of that Part,

as it considers necessary or expedient in consequence of, or of preparations for, an event mentioned in subsection (6)(a) or (b).

(8)   Before modifying under subsection (6) or (7) the conditions included in an appointment or licence, the Authority must consult the company holding the appointment or licence.

(9)   The Secretary of State may, after consulting the Welsh Ministers, give directions to the Authority for the purpose of securing that sums relating to any of the expenses mentioned in subsection (4) are included in the sums payable by virtue of payment conditions; and the Authority must comply with any such direction.

(10)   In this section—

"the Authority" means the Water Services Regulation Authority;

"OFT scheme" means any public consumer advice scheme supported by the Office of Fair Trading;

"water consumers" means consumers in relation to services provided by a water undertaker, a sewerage undertaker or a licensed water supplier, in its capacity as such.

[2134]

NOTES

Commencement: 1 October 2008.

Abolition: supplementary provision

34 Compensation for loss of office

(1)   The Secretary of State may pay such sums as the Secretary of State may, with the approval of the Treasury, determine by way of compensation to any person who—

(a)   ceases to be a member of the Consumer Council for Postal Services, the Gas and Electricity Consumer Council, or the Consumer Council for Water by virtue of the abolition of the body in question by or under this Part, or

(b)   ceases to be a member of the company called the National Consumer Council (a company limited by guarantee and registered under the Companies Acts) by virtue of its dissolution.

(2)   The compensation is payable in respect of loss of office, or loss or diminution of pension rights.

[2135]

NOTES

Commencement: 1 October 2008.

35 Transfer of property etc

(1)   This section applies to—

(a)   the Consumer Council for Postal Services;

(b)   the Gas and Electricity Consumer Council;

(c)   if a transfer order has been made under section 32 (whether or not it has taken effect), the Consumer Council for Water;

(d)   the company called the National Consumer Council (a company limited by guarantee and registered under the Companies Acts).

(2) The Secretary of State may direct a body to which this section applies—

    (a) to make a scheme or schemes for the transfer of its property, rights and liabilities to the Council;

    (b) to transfer such property, rights or obligations as are specified in the direction to a person (other than the Council) so specified ("the specified transferee").

(3) Before giving, varying or revoking a direction under subsection (2), the Secretary of State must consult—

    (a) the body to which the direction is to be or has been given,

    (b) the Council, and

    (c) in the case of a direction under subsection (2)(b), the specified transferee.

(4) A body given a direction under subsection (2)(a) must consult the Council before making a transfer scheme.

(5) A transfer scheme made pursuant to a direction under subsection (2)(a) has effect—

    (a) only if approved by the Secretary of State, and

    (b) subject to any modifications made by the Secretary of State.

(6) Before making any modifications the Secretary of State must consult the body to which the direction was given.

(7) The Secretary of State may make a scheme or schemes for the transfer to the Council of the property, rights and liabilities of a body to which this section applies.

(8) Schedule 4 makes further provision about transfer schemes.

(9) In this section "transfer scheme" means a scheme made under or by virtue of subsection (2)(a) or (7).

[2136]

NOTES

Commencement: 21 December 2007.

36 Directions

(1) The Secretary of State may direct a body to which section 35 applies to supply to the Secretary of State such information specified or described in the direction as the Secretary of State may require in relation to—

    (a) the body's property, rights or liabilities, or

    (b) the exercise by the body of its functions.

(2) A direction under subsection (1)—

    (a) must specify the period within which the information is to be provided, and

    (b) may require the information to be supplied in a specified form.

(3) A body given a direction under subsection (1) must comply with it within the specified period.

(4) The Secretary of State may direct a body to which section 35 applies not to take any action of a specified kind, or in specified circumstances.

(5) Before giving, varying or revoking a direction under this section, the Secretary of State must consult—

    (a) the body to which the direction is to be or has been given, and

    (b) the Council.

(6) In this section "specified" means specified in the direction given by the Secretary of State.

[2137]

NOTES

Commencement: 21 December 2007.

Alteration of the Council's functions

37 Extension of the Council's functions: Great Britain

(1) The Secretary of State may, by order, confer on the Council any other function or functions if the Secretary of State considers that it is in the interests of consumers generally, or consumers of a particular description, to do so.

(2) The Secretary of State may only confer a function on the Council under this section if the function appears to the Secretary of State to be connected (directly or indirectly) to an existing or former function of the Council.

(3) Before making an order under subsection (1), the Secretary of State must consult—

    (a) the Council,

    (b) if it appears to the Secretary of State that the exercise of any function conferred by the order might affect Wales in relation to any matter as respects which functions are exercisable by the Welsh Ministers, those Ministers, and

(c)   such other persons as the Secretary of State considers appropriate.

(4)   An order under this section may not make provision which would be within the legislative competence of the Scottish Parliament if it were contained in an Act of that Parliament.

(5)   An order under this section which makes provision which would be within the legislative competence of the National Assembly for Wales if it were contained in a Measure of the Assembly (or, if the order is made after the Assembly Act provisions come into force, an Act of the Assembly) may only be made with the consent of the Assembly.

(6)   In subsection (5) "the Assembly Act provisions" has the meaning given by section 103(8) of the Government of Wales Act 2006 (c 32).

[2138]

NOTES

Commencement: 1 October 2008.

38   Removal of the Council's functions in relation to Northern Ireland

(1)   This section applies where the Secretary of State is satisfied that satisfactory arrangements are in place for a body (other than the Council) to exercise functions corresponding to the functions exercisable by the Council in relation to Northern Ireland.

(2)   The Secretary of State may by order repeal—
(a)   section 1(2)(c) (requirement to establish and maintain the Northern Ireland Postal Services Committee);
(b)   section 2(1)(c) (functions which the Northern Ireland Postal Services Committee is authorised to exercise);
(c)   section 3(2)(b) (Northern Ireland consumers of relevant postal services);
(d)   section 16(1)(b)(investigations relating to public post offices in Northern Ireland);
(e)   any other provision of this Part, so far as it extends to Northern Ireland.

(3)   Before making an order under this section, the Secretary of State must consult—
(a)   the Council, and
(b)   such other persons as the Secretary of State considers appropriate.

[2139]

NOTES

Commencement: 1 October 2008.

39, 40   (*Outside the scope of this work.*)

Interpretation

41   Interpretation of Part 1

(1)   In this Part—

"distribution system" has the meaning given by section 4(4) of the Electricity Act 1989 (c 29);

"financial year" (except in Schedule 3) means—
(a)   the period beginning with the day on which the Council is established and ending with the next following 31 March, and
(b)   each successive period of 12 months;

"functions" includes powers and duties;

"gas" has the meaning given by section 48(1) of the Gas Act 1986 (c 44);

"licensed water supplier" means a company holding a water supply licence under Chapter 1A of Part 2 of the Water Industry Act 1991 (c 56);

"modify" includes amend, add to, revoke or repeal (and references to "modification" are to be read accordingly);

"postal services" has the same meaning as in the Postal Services Act 2000 (c 26) (see section 125(1) of that Act);

"regulatory body" means a person who exercises regulatory functions in relation to a particular description of persons with a view to ensuring compliance with particular standards of conduct (whether statutory or non-statutory) by those persons;

"relevant postal services" means any postal services provided in connection with the provision of a universal postal service (within the meaning of the Postal Services Act 2000) and any other postal services which are provided, or authorised or required to be provided, by a licence holder under Part 2 of that Act in accordance with a licence under that Part.

(2)   In this Part—
(a)   expressions used, as regards matters relating to gas, which are defined in section 48 of the Gas Act 1986 have the same meaning as in Part 1 of that Act, and

(b) expressions used, as regards matters relating to electricity, which are defined in section 64 of the Electricity Act 1989, have the same meaning as in Part 1 of that Act.

[2140]

NOTES
Commencement: 21 December 2007.
Modification: for the purposes of s 5 of this Act, para (a) of the definition "financial year" has effect as if it referred to the period beginning with 1 October 2008 and ending with 31 March 2010: see the Consumers, Estate Agents and Redress Act 2007 (Commencement No 3 and Supplementary Provision) Order 2008, SI 2008/1262, art 4.

PART 2
COMPLAINTS HANDLING AND REDRESS SCHEMES

Introductory

42 Interpretation of Part 2

(1) In this Part—
"regulated provider" means a person within an entry in column 1 of the table;
"relevant consumer", in relation to a regulated provider, means a person within the corresponding entry in column 2 of the table;
"relevant regulator", in relation to a regulated provider, means the body specified in the corresponding entry in column 3 of the table.

TABLE

Regulated provider	*Relevant consumer*	*Relevant regulator*
A person holding a licence under section 7A(1) of the Gas Act 1986 (c 44) (supply licences).	A person who is a consumer in relation to gas supplied by a gas supplier (within the meaning of Part 1 of that Act).	The Gas and Electricity Markets Authority.
A person holding a licence under section 7(2) of the Gas Act 1986 (transportation licences).	A person (other than a gas licensee) who is a consumer in relation to services provided by a gas transporter (within the meaning of Part 1 of that Act).	The Gas and Electricity Markets Authority.
A person holding a licence under section 6(1)(d) of the Electricity Act 1989 (c 29) (supply licences).	A person who is a consumer in relation to electricity supplied by an electricity supplier (within the meaning of Part 1 of that Act).	The Gas and Electricity Markets Authority.
A person holding a licence under section 6(1)(c) of the Electricity Act 1989 (distribution licences).	A person (other than an electricity licensee) who is a consumer in relation to services provided by an electricity distributor (within the meaning of Part 1 of that Act).	The Gas and Electricity Markets Authority.
A person holding a licence under Part 2 of the Postal Services Act 2000 (c 26).	A person who is a consumer in relation to relevant postal services (within the meaning of section 41).	The Postal Services Commission.
A water undertaker, sewerage undertaker or licensed water supplier.	A person who is a consumer in relation to services provided by a water undertaker, sewerage undertaker or licensed water supplier in its capacity as such.	The Water Services Regulation Authority.

(2)   In this Part—

"consumer" has the same meaning as in Part 1;

"consumer complaint" means a complaint which is made against a regulated provider by or on behalf of a person in that person's capacity as a relevant consumer in relation to the regulated provider;

"licensed water supplier" has the same meaning as in Part 1;

"regulator" means a body listed in column 3 of the table.

(3)   In this Part references to a regulator's regulated providers are to the regulated providers in relation to which the regulator is the relevant regulator.

(4)   In this section—

"electricity licensee" means—

     (a)   an electricity supplier (within the meaning of Part 1 of the Electricity Act 1989);

     (b)   an electricity distributor (within the meaning of that Part);

     (c)   the holder of a licence under section 6(1)(a), (b) or (e) of that Act (generation licences, transmission licences and interconnector licences), except where the holder is acting otherwise than for purposes connected with the carrying on of activities authorised by the licence;

"gas licensee" means—

     (a)   a gas supplier (within the meaning of Part 1 of the Gas Act 1986 (c 44));

     (b)   a gas transporter (within the meaning of that Part);

     (c)   a gas shipper (within the meaning of that Part);

     (d)   the holder of a licence under section 7ZA of that Act (licences for operation of gas interconnectors), except where the holder is acting otherwise than for purposes connected with the carrying on of activities authorised by the licence.

[2141]

NOTES

Commencement: 21 December 2007.

Standards for handling complaints

43   Standards for handling complaints

(1)   A regulator must by regulations prescribe standards for the handling by its regulated providers of consumer complaints made to them.

(2)   The regulations may prescribe standards in relation to all consumer complaints, or consumer complaints of a kind specified in the regulations.

(3)   In particular, the regulations may specify a kind of consumer complaint by reference to the subject-matter of a complaint, or the description of person making a complaint.

(4)   Regulations under this section may be made only with the consent of the Secretary of State.

(5)   A regulator must make arrangements for securing that regulations made by it under this section are available to the public, by whatever means it considers appropriate.

(6)   If a date is prescribed in relation to a regulator for the purposes of this subsection, from that date subsection (1) has effect in relation to that regulator as if, in that subsection, for "must" there were substituted "may".

(7)   In subsection (6) "prescribed" means prescribed by order made by the Secretary of State under this section.

(8)   Before prescribing a date in relation to a regulator for the purposes of subsection (6), the Secretary of State must consult—

     (a)   the regulator,

     (b)   the Council, and

     (c)   such other persons as the Secretary of State considers appropriate.

(9)   This section does not apply to the Water Services Regulation Authority.

[2142]

NOTES

Commencement: 21 December 2007.

Regulations: the Gas and Electricity (Consumer Complaints Handling Standards) Regulations 2008, SI 2008/1898; the Postal Services (Consumer Complaints Handling Standards) Regulations 2008, SI 2008/2355.

44   Requirements for making regulations under section 43

(1)   Before making regulations under section 43 a regulator must—

     (a)   arrange for such research as it considers appropriate with a view to discovering the views of a representative sample of persons likely to be affected, and consider the results,

    (b)   publish a notice of its proposals (a "proposals notice") in such manner as the regulator considers appropriate for bringing it to the attention of those likely to be affected by the proposals,

    (c)   consider any representations duly made, and

    (d)   consult persons or bodies appearing to it to be representative of persons likely to be affected by the proposals.

  (2)   The proposals notice must—

    (a)   set out the standards the regulator proposes to prescribe,

    (b)   give the reasons why the regulator proposes to prescribe those standards,

    (c)   explain how the standards will be enforced, and

    (d)   specify a time (not being earlier than the end of the period of 30 days beginning with the day on which the notice is published) before which representations may be made.

  (3)   The requirements of subsection (1) may be satisfied by action taken before the commencement of this section or the passing of this Act.

[2143]

NOTES

  Commencement: 21 December 2007.

  Regulations: the Gas and Electricity (Consumer Complaints Handling Standards) Regulations 2008, SI 2008/1898; the Postal Services (Consumer Complaints Handling Standards) Regulations 2008, SI 2008/2355.

45 Information with respect to compliance with complaints handling standards

  (1)   This section applies in relation to standards prescribed by a regulator by regulations under section 43 in relation to its regulated providers (or some of them).

  (2)   The Council must publish such statistical information as it considers appropriate relating to the levels of compliance with the standards which those regulated providers have achieved.

  (3)   That information must be published in such form and manner, and with such frequency, as the Council thinks appropriate.

  (4)   Schedule 5 makes further provision with respect to information about compliance with complaints handling standards.

[2144]

NOTES

  Commencement: 1 October 2008.

46 Supply of information to consumers

  (1)   A regulator may make regulations requiring each of its regulated providers in relation to which standards are prescribed under section 43 to give to the provider's relevant consumers such information as may be specified or described in the regulations about—

    (a)   the standards, and

    (b)   the levels of compliance with those standards achieved by the provider.

  (2)   Regulations under this section may include provision specifying the form and manner in which, and the frequency with which, information is to be given.

[2145]

NOTES

  Commencement: 21 December 2007.

  Regulations: the Gas and Electricity (Consumer Complaints Handling Standards) Regulations 2008, SI 2008/1898; the Postal Services (Consumer Complaints Handling Standards) Regulations 2008, SI 2008/2355.

Requirements relating to redress schemes

47 Membership of redress scheme

  (1)   The Secretary of State may by order require regulated providers to be members of a redress scheme which is—

    (a)   approved by their relevant regulator in accordance with section 49, or

    (b)   administered by the Secretary of State (or a person appointed by the Secretary of State) and designated by the Secretary of State as an appropriate redress scheme in relation to them.

  (2)   The order may provide that the requirement applies only in relation to consumer complaints of a kind specified in the order.

  (3)   In particular, the order may specify a kind of consumer complaint by reference to the subject-matter of a complaint, or the description of person making a complaint.

  (4)   Before making an order under this section the Secretary of State must consult—

(a)　each relevant regulator (in relation to regulated providers to which the order will apply), and

(b)　other persons appearing to the Secretary of State to be representative of persons who have an interest in the matter.

(5)　The requirements of subsection (4) may be satisfied by consultation undertaken before the commencement of this section or the passing of this Act.

(6)　An order under this section which applies to a water undertaker or sewerage undertaker for an area which is wholly or mainly in Wales may be made only with the consent of the Welsh Ministers.

(7)　The Secretary of State may not make an order under this section unless satisfied, in relation to each regulated provider to which the order will apply, that—

(a)　there is at least one qualifying redress scheme which the provider is eligible to join and membership of which will satisfy the requirement imposed by the order, or

(b)　there will be such a scheme when the order comes into force.

(8)　The Secretary of State may not designate a scheme in relation to regulated providers under subsection (1)(b) unless the Secretary of State is satisfied that the scheme is one which could be approved by their relevant regulator in accordance with section 49.

(9)　The Secretary of State may establish or administer a scheme for the purposes of subsection (1)(b), or provide financial assistance to a person who establishes or administers such a scheme; and such a scheme may provide for fees to be payable by members of the scheme.

[2146]

NOTES

Commencement: 21 December 2007.

Orders: the Postal Services Regulated Providers (Redress Scheme) Order 2008, SI 2008/2267; the Gas and Electricity Regulated Providers (Redress Scheme) Order 2008, SI 2008/2268.

48　Membership of redress schemes: supplementary

(1)　In this Part—

"qualifying redress scheme" means a redress scheme within paragraph (a) or (b) of section 47(1);

"redress scheme" means a scheme under which consumer complaints may be made to, and investigated and determined by, an independent person ("the independent person");

"scheme administrator", in relation to a redress scheme, means the person who administers the scheme,

and references to approval of a redress scheme are to approval of the scheme for the purposes of section 47(1)(a).

(2)　In the definition of "redress scheme", "independent", in relation to a consumer complaint, means independent of—

(a)　the regulated provider against whom the complaint is made, and

(b)　the regulator who is the relevant regulator in relation to the regulated provider.

(3)　Nothing in this Part prevents a qualifying redress scheme providing—

(a)　for membership to be open to persons who are not subject to any duty to belong to a qualifying redress scheme;

(b)　for the investigation and determination of complaints other than those in relation to which such a duty applies, made against members who have voluntarily accepted the jurisdiction of the scheme over such complaints.

(4)　For the purposes of the law relating to defamation, proceedings under a qualifying redress scheme (in relation to a consumer complaint and a regulated provider to which an order under section 47 applies) are to be treated in the same way as proceedings before a court.

[2147]

NOTES

Commencement: 21 December 2007.

49　Approval of redress schemes

(1)　In deciding whether to approve a redress scheme, a regulator must have regard to—

(a)　the provisions of the scheme;

(b)　the manner in which the scheme will be operated (so far as that can be judged from the facts known to the regulator);

(c)　the interests of relevant consumers (in relation to the regulator's regulated providers);

(d)　such principles as—

(i)　in the opinion of the regulator constitute generally accepted principles of best practice in relation to schemes for providing redress to consumers, and

(ii)   it is reasonable to regard as applicable to the scheme.

(2)   In considering the interests of relevant consumers under subsection (1)(c), the regulator must in particular have regard to the number of other redress schemes applying to its regulated providers which are (or are likely to become) qualifying redress schemes.

(3)   A regulator must not approve a redress scheme unless—

    (a)   membership of the scheme is open to all the regulator's regulated providers, and those regulated providers may not be expelled from membership of the scheme,

    (b)   if, at the time the approval is given, any of the regulator's regulated providers are required under section 47 to be a member of a redress scheme (or would be so required but for the fact that an order which has been made under that section is not yet in force), the scheme covers all the consumer complaints to which the requirement applies,

    (c)   the independent person may require regulated providers to provide complainants with the types of redress listed in subsection (6) (whether or not other types of redress are available), and

    (d)   the regulator considers that the scheme makes satisfactory provision about the matters listed in subsection (7).

(4)   Subsection (3)(a) does not prevent the Gas and Electricity Markets Authority approving—

    (a)   a scheme which is open to all regulated gas providers, but not regulated electricity providers,

    (b)   a scheme which is open to all regulated electricity providers, but not regulated gas providers,

and, in the case of such a scheme, subsection (3)(b) applies as if the reference to the regulator's regulated providers were to the regulated gas providers or, as the case may be, regulated electricity providers.

(5)   For this purpose—
"regulated electricity provider" means a person holding a licence under section 6(1)(c) or (d) of the Electricity Act 1989 (c 29);
"regulated gas provider" means a person holding a licence under section 7(2) or 7A(1) of the Gas Act 1986 (c 44).

(6)   The types of redress mentioned in subsection (3)(c) are—

    (a)   providing an apology or explanation,

    (b)   paying compensation, and

    (c)   taking such other action in the interests of the complainant as the independent person may specify.

(7)   The matters mentioned in subsection (3)(d) are—

    (a)   the matters about which complaints may be made (which may include non-compliance with a code of practice or other document);

    (b)   the independent person's duties and powers in relation to the investigation and determination of complaints (which may include power to decide not to investigate or determine a complaint);

    (c)   the enforcement of any requirement to provide redress imposed on a regulated provider in accordance with the scheme;

    (d)   the provision of information by the independent person to the regulator and to persons within subsection (8);

    (e)   the provision of information by the independent person—

        (i)   to the Office of Fair Trading, for the purposes of any public consumer advice scheme supported by it, and

        (ii)   to persons who operate a public consumer advice scheme supported by the Office of Fair Trading, for the purposes of that scheme;

    (f)   the acceptance and handling of complaints transferred from redress schemes which have their approval withdrawn under section 51.

(8)   The persons within this subsection are—

    (a)   any other body having regulatory functions in relation to the regulated providers to which the scheme applies;

    (b)   persons exercising functions under other redress schemes which apply to the regulator's regulated providers;

    (c)   the Council;

    (d)   the Secretary of State.

[2148]

NOTES

Commencement: 21 December 2007.

50   Approval of redress schemes: supplementary

(1)   An application for approval of a redress scheme must be made in such manner, and accompanied by such information, as the regulator to which the application is made may determine.

(2)   Section 51 applies if the regulator is minded to refuse an application for approval.

(3)   The scheme administrator of a redress scheme approved by a regulator must notify the regulator of any change to the scheme before the end of the period of 14 days beginning with the day on which the change is made.

(4)   A regulator may, in accordance with section 51, withdraw its approval of a redress scheme, and may do so generally or in relation to consumer complaints of a description specified by the regulator.

(5)   In particular, a regulator may withdraw its approval in relation to consumer complaints made on or after a date specified by the regulator.

[2149]

NOTES
    Commencement: 21 December 2007.

51   Procedure for refusing or withdrawing approval

(1)   Before refusing or withdrawing its approval of a redress scheme, the regulator must give the scheme administrator a notice—
   (a)   stating that the regulator proposes to refuse or withdraw its approval,
   (b)   giving the reasons for the proposed refusal or withdrawal, and
   (c)   specifying a time (not being earlier than the end of the period of 30 days beginning with the day on which the notice is given to the scheme administrator) before which representations about the proposed refusal or withdrawal may be made.

(2)   The regulator must give notice to the scheme administrator of—
   (a)   the regulator's decision on a proposal to refuse or withdraw approval, and
   (b)   the reasons for its decision.

(3)   In the case of a decision to withdraw approval, the regulator must also give notice of its decision and the reasons for it to the Secretary of State.

(4)   The scheme administrator must give a copy of the notice under subsection (2) to each member of the scheme.

(5)   If the regulator decides to withdraw approval, the withdrawal has effect in accordance with, and from the date specified in, the notice under subsection (2).

(6)   Where a redress scheme designated under section 47(1)(b) is administered by a person appointed by the Secretary of State, this section (other than subsection (3)) applies in relation to a revocation by the Secretary of State of that person's appointment as it applies in relation to a withdrawal by a regulator of the approval of a redress scheme.

[2150]

NOTES
    Commencement: 21 December 2007.

Enforcement

52   Enforcement of requirements imposed under Part 2

(1), (2)   ...

(3)   A requirement imposed under section 47 on a water undertaker, sewerage undertaker or licensed water supplier is enforceable by the Water Services Regulation Authority under section 18 of the Water Industry Act 1991 (c 56) (orders for securing compliance).

(4)   ...

[2151]

NOTES
    Commencement: 1 October 2008.
    Sub-s (1): amends the Gas Act 1986, s 28.
    Sub-s (2): amends the Electricity Act 1989, s 25.
    Sub-s (4): amends the Postal Services Act 2000, s 22.

53–58   *(S 53(1) introduces Sch 6; s 53(2) amends the Estate Agents Act 1979, s 3 at* **[915]***; s 53(3) repeals the Housing Act 2004, ss 172–174; s 54 inserts s 21A of the 1979 Act at* **[932A]** *and amends s 3 of that Act at* **[915]***; s 55 amends ss 3, 5 of, and Sch 1 to, the 1979 Act at* **[915]**, **[917]**, **[947]***; s 56*

PART 1 STATUTES

amends s 4 of the 1979 Act at **[916]**; *s 57 amends s 11 of the 1979 Act at* **[923]**; *s 58 inserts s 11A of the 1979 Act at* **[923A]** *and amends ss 3, 9, 27 of the 1979 Act at* **[915]**, **[921]**, **[938]**.)

PART 4
MISCELLANEOUS AND GENERAL

Contracts concluded away from business premises

59   Contracts concluded away from business premises

(1)   The Secretary of State may make regulations entitling a consumer who is a party to a protected contract to cancel the contract.

(2)   A protected contract is a contract between a consumer and a trader which is for the supply of goods or services to the consumer by a trader and is made—
  (a)   during a solicited visit by a trader to the consumer's home or place of work, or to the home of another individual, or
  (b)   after an offer made by the consumer during such a visit.

(3)   A visit is solicited if it is made at the express request of the consumer.

(4)   Regulations made under this section may make any provision which may be made by regulations under section 2(2) of the European Communities Act 1972 (c 68) (by virtue of section 2(4) of that Act).

(5)   The regulations may in particular make provision—
  (a)   as to the circumstances in which the consumer may cancel the contract and the effect of such a cancellation;
  (b)   requiring the trader to inform the consumer of the matters within paragraph (a);
  (c)   for the enforcement of any requirement imposed by virtue of paragraph (b).

(6)   For the purposes of this section, "consumer" and "trader" in relation to a contract have the same meaning as they have for the purposes of the relevant Directive in relation to transactions within that Directive.

(7)   "The relevant Directive" means—
  (a)   Council Directive 85/577/EEC to protect the consumer in respect of contracts negotiated away from business premises, as it has effect from time to time, or
  (b)   if that Directive is repealed and re-enacted (with or without modification), that Directive as re-enacted.

[2152]

NOTES
Commencement: 21 December 2007.
Regulations: the Cancellation of Contracts made in a Consumer's Home or Place of Work etc Regulations 2008, SI 2008/1816 at **[3705]**.

Subordinate legislation

60   Orders and regulations

(1)   An order or regulations under this Act must be made by statutory instrument.

(2)   The Statutory Instruments Act 1946 (c 36) is to apply in relation to any power of a regulator to make regulations under section 43 or 46 as if the regulator were a Minister of the Crown.

(3)   Any order or regulations under this Act may—
  (a)   make provision generally or subject to exceptions or in relation to specified cases or descriptions of case;
  (b)   make different provision for different cases or circumstances or for different purposes;
  (c)   provide for a person to exercise a discretion in dealing with any matter;
  (d)   make incidental, supplementary, consequential, transitory and transitional provision and savings.

(4)   A provision of this Act which permits regulations or orders to make provision of a specified kind is without prejudice to the generality of subsection (3).

(5)   In the case of an order or regulations made by the Secretary of State, the provision which may be made by virtue of subsection (3)(d) includes provision modifying any provision made by or under any enactment.

(6)   For this purpose—
"enactment" means—
  (a)   an Act of Parliament (including, in the case of an order under section 32, this Act),
  (b)   an Act of the Scottish Parliament,
  (c)   a Measure or Act of the National Assembly for Wales, or
  (d)   Northern Ireland legislation,

whenever passed or made;
"modify" has the same meaning as in Part 1.

(7)   Nothing in this section authorises an order or regulations under this Act to make provision which would be within the legislative competence of the Scottish Parliament if it were contained in an Act of that Parliament.

(8)   The Documentary Evidence Act 1868 (c 37) (proof of order and regulations etc) has effect as if—

(a)   the regulators were included in column 1 of the Schedule to that Act, and
(b)   the entry in column 2 of that Schedule corresponding to each regulator mentioned the regulator and persons authorised to act on the regulator's behalf.

(9)   Nothing in this section applies in relation to a court order under section 26.

(10)   In this section "regulator" means—
(a)   the Gas and Electricity Markets Authority, or
(b)   the Postal Services Commission.

[2153]

NOTES
Commencement: 19 July 2007.

61   Directions

(1)   A requirement or power under this Act to give a notice (or to notify) is a requirement or power to give notice in writing.

(2)   A requirement or power under this Act to give a direction (or to direct) is a requirement or power to give a direction in writing.

(3)   Any power conferred by this Act to give a direction includes power to vary or revoke the direction.

[2154]

NOTES
Commencement: 19 July 2007.

62   Parliamentary control of orders and regulations

(1)   Any instrument to which this subsection applies is subject to annulment in pursuance of a resolution of either House of Parliament.

(2)   Subsection (1) applies to any order or regulations made by the Secretary of State under any provision of this Act except—
(a)   an order or regulations to which subsection (3) applies, or
(b)   an order under section 66 (commencement).

(3)   An order or regulations containing (whether alone or with other provision) provision made under or by virtue of any of the following provisions may not be made unless a draft of the order or regulations has been laid before, and approved by a resolution of, each House of Parliament—
(a)   section 4 ("designated consumers");
(b)   section 24(3)(d) (power to specify persons from whom Council may require information);
(c)   section 31 (designation of the Consumer Council for Water for abolition);
(d)   section 37(1) (conferral of additional functions on the Council);
(e)   section 38 (removal of Council's functions in relation to Northern Ireland);
(f)   section 59 (contracts concluded away from business premises), so far as it enables provision to be made modifying an Act of Parliament;
(g)   section 60(5) (consequential provision etc), so far as it enables such provision to be made;
(h)   section 63(2) (consequential provision etc), so far as it enables such provision to be made.

(4)   In subsection (3), "modify" has the same meaning as in Part 1.

[2155]

NOTES
Commencement: 19 July 2007.

Amendments, transitional provision and repeals

63   Minor, consequential and transitional provision

(1)   Schedule 7 contains minor and consequential amendments.

(2)   The Secretary of State may by order make such consequential, supplementary, incidental, transitory or transitional provision or savings (including provision modifying any provision made by or under an enactment) as the Secretary of State considers necessary or expedient in connection with the coming into force of any provision made by or under this Act.

(3)   An order under this section may make such adaptations of provisions of this Act brought into force as appear to be necessary or expedient in consequence of other provisions of this Act not yet having come into force.

(4)   In this section—
   "enactment" means—
      (a)   an Act of Parliament,
      (b)   an Act of the Scottish Parliament,
      (c)   a Measure or Act of the National Assembly for Wales, or
      (d)   Northern Ireland legislation,
    whenever passed or made;
   "modify" has the same meaning as in Part 1.

(5)   An order under this section may not make provision which would be within the legislative competence of the Scottish Parliament if it were contained in an Act of that Parliament.

[2156]

NOTES
Commencement: 21 December 2007 (sub-s (1) certain purposes; sub-ss (2)–(5)); 1 October 2008 (sub-s (1), certain purposes); to be appointed (otherwise).
Order: the Consumers, Estate Agents and Redress Act 2007 (Commencement No 3 and Supplementary Provision) Order 2008, SI 2008/1262.

64   (*Introduces Sch 8 (outside the scope of this work).*)

General

65   Extent

(1)   Subject to subsections (2) to (6), this Act extends to England and Wales, Scotland and Northern Ireland.

(2)   The following provisions extend to England and Wales and Scotland only—
    (a)   section 13 (investigation of complaints relating to disconnection of gas or electricity);
    (b)   section 14 (reference of matters to Gas and Electricity Markets Authority);
    (c)   section 37 (extension of the Council's functions: Great Britain).

(3)   Sections 31 to 33 (abolition of Consumer Council for Water) extend to England and Wales only.

(4)   Section 43 (standards for handling complaints) extends to Northern Ireland, but only to the extent that it applies to the Postal Services Commission.

(5)   Section 47 (membership of redress scheme) extends to Northern Ireland, but only to the extent that it applies in relation to regulated providers (within the meaning of Part 2) holding a licence under Part 2 of the Postal Services Act 2000 (c 26).

(6)   Any amendment or repeal made by this Act has the same extent as the enactment to which it relates.

(7)   This section is subject to any provision made under section 38 (removal of the Council's functions in relation to Northern Ireland).

[2157]

NOTES
Commencement: 19 July 2007.

66   Commencement

(1)   This section and sections 60 to 62, 65 and 67 come into force on the day this Act is passed.

(2)   Subject to that, the provisions of this Act come into force on such day as may be appointed by order of the Secretary of State.

[2158]

NOTES
Commencement: 19 July 2007.
Orders: the Consumers, Estate Agents and Redress Act 2007 (Commencement No 1) Order 2007, SI 2007/2934; the Consumers, Estate Agents and Redress Act 2007 (Commencement No 2) Order 2007, SI 2007/3546; the Consumers, Estate Agents and Redress Act 2007 (Commencement No 4) Order 2008, SI 2008/905; the Consumers, Estate Agents and Redress Act 2007 (Commencement No 3 and Supplementary

Provision) Order 2008, SI 2008/1262; the Consumers, Estate Agents and Redress Act 2007 (Commencement No 5 and Savings and Transitional Provisions) Order 2008, SI 2008/2550.

67   Short title

This Act may be cited as the Consumers, Estate Agents and Redress Act 2007.

[2159]

NOTES
Commencement: 19 July 2007.

SCHEDULE 1
THE NATIONAL CONSUMER COUNCIL

Section 1

PART 1
MEMBERS OF THE COUNCIL

Membership

1.—(1)   The Council is to consist of the following members—
- (a)   a chairman ("the Council Chairman") appointed by the Secretary of State,
- (b)   the chairman of each territorial committee, and
- (c)   such other members as may be appointed by the Secretary of State.

(2)   In this Schedule—
- (a)   references to executive members of the Council are to the members of the Council appointed from the staff of the Council, and
- (b)   references to non-executive members of the Council are to the members of the Council who are not executive members.

(3)   The Council Chairman must be a non-executive member of the Council.

(4)   The persons appointed under sub-paragraph (1)(c) may include one or both of the following—
- (a)   a member of the Consumer Panel established by the Financial Services Authority under the Financial Services and Markets Act 2000 (c 8) nominated for the appointment by that Panel after consultation with the Council Chairman and the Financial Services Authority;
- (b)   a member of the Consumer Panel established by the Office of Communications under the Communications Act 2003 (c 21) nominated for the appointment by that Panel after consultation with the Council Chairman and the Office of Communications.

(5)   Nothing in sub-paragraph (4) prevents the Secretary of State from appointing under sub-paragraph (1)(c) a person who is a member of either Panel but is not the subject of a nomination for the purposes of sub-paragraph (4).

(6)   A person may be appointed under sub-paragraph (1)(c) only if—
- (a)   in the case of an appointment of a non-executive member, the Secretary of State has consulted the Council Chairman about the appointment;
- (b)   in the case of an appointment of an executive member, the person has been nominated by the Council Chairman for appointment to the Council.

(7)   In making appointments to the Council under sub-paragraph (1)(c) the Secretary of State must secure that a majority of the members of the Council are non-executive members.

(8)   In making appointments to the Council, the Secretary of State must have regard to the desirability of including among the members of the Council one or more persons with experience of work among, and the special needs of, disabled persons.

Terms of appointment and tenure of members

2.   Subject to this Schedule, a member of the Council—
- (a)   is to hold and vacate office in accordance with the terms and conditions of the member's appointment, and
- (b)   may resign or be removed from office in accordance with those terms and conditions.

3.—(1)   The Council may pay, or make provision for paying—
- (a)   its non-executive members such remuneration as the Secretary of State may determine, and
- (b)   any of its members such travelling and other allowances as the Secretary of State may determine.

(2)   The Council may—
- (a)   pay to or in respect of any person who is or has been a non-executive member such pension, allowances or gratuities as the Secretary of State may determine, or

    (b)   make such payments as the Secretary of State may determine towards provision for the payment of a pension, allowance or gratuity to or in respect of such a person.

4.—(1)   A non-executive member must be appointed for a fixed period.

    (2)   The period for which a non-executive member is appointed must not exceed 5 years.

    (3)   A person who has held office as a non-executive member may be re-appointed as a non-executive member, once only, for a further period (whether consecutive or not) not exceeding 5 years.

5.—(1)   A person ceases to be a member of the Council if—
    (a)   in the case of the Council Chairman, the person ceases to hold that office or becomes a member of the staff of the Council;
    (b)   in the case of a member within paragraph 1(1)(b), the person ceases to be the chairman of a territorial committee;
    (c)   in the case of any other non-executive member, the person becomes a member of the staff of the Council;
    (d)   in the case of an executive member, the person ceases to be a member of the staff of the Council;
    (e)   in the case of a non-executive member appointed by virtue of a nomination within paragraph 1(4), the person ceases to be a member of the Panel which made the nomination.

    (2)   The Secretary of State may remove any person from office as chairman or another member of the Council on the grounds that the person is unable, unfit or unwilling to discharge the functions of the office.

6.   Where—
    (a)   a non-executive member ceases to be a member otherwise than on the expiry of the member's term of office, and
    (b)   it appears to the Secretary of State that there are circumstances which make it right for that person to receive compensation,

the Council may make a payment to that person of such amount as the Secretary of State may determine.

[2160]

NOTES
    Commencement: 21 December 2007.

PART 2
STAFF OF THE COUNCIL

The Chief Executive

7.—(1)   The Council is to employ a person as its Chief Executive.

    (2)   The first appointment of a Chief Executive—
    (a)   is to be made by the Secretary of State, and
    (b)   is to be on such terms and conditions as are determined by the Secretary of State.

    (3)   Subsequent appointments of a Chief Executive—
    (a)   are to be made by the Council with the approval of the Secretary of State, and
    (b)   are to be on such terms and conditions as are determined by the Council with the approval of the Secretary of State.

Other staff

8.—(1)   The Council may appoint such other staff, on such terms and conditions, as it considers appropriate.

    (2)   The approval of the Secretary of State as to numbers and as to terms and conditions of staff is required for the exercise by the Council of its powers under sub-paragraph (1).

The Superannuation Act 1972

9.—(1)   The persons to whom section 1 of the Superannuation Act 1972 (c 11) (persons to or in respect of whom benefits may be provided by schemes under that section) applies are to include the Chief Executive and the other employees of the Council.

    (2)   ...

    (3)   The Council must pay to the Minister for the Civil Service, at such times as that Minister may direct, such sums as that Minister may determine in respect of the increase attributable to sub-paragraph (1) in the sums payable out of money provided by Parliament under that Act.

Arrangements for assistance

10.—(1)   The Council may make arrangements with such persons as it considers appropriate for assistance to be provided to it.

(2)   Arrangements may include the paying of fees to such persons.

[2161]

NOTES
Commencement: 21 December 2007.
Para 9: sub-para (2) amends the Superannuation Act 1972, Sch 1.

PART 3
TERRITORIAL, REGIONAL AND OTHER COMMITTEES

Constitution of territorial committees

11.—(1)   A territorial committee is to consist of a chairman, and such other members, as the Secretary of State may appoint.

(2)   In this Schedule—
  (a)   references to executive members of a territorial committee are to the members of the committee appointed from the staff of the Council, and
  (b)   references to non-executive members of a territorial committee are to the members who are not executive members of the committee.

(3)   The chairman of a territorial committee must be a non-executive member of the committee.

(4)   In appointing persons to a territorial committee the Secretary of State must secure that a majority of the members of the committee are non-executive members.

(5)   Before appointing a person as a non-executive member of a territorial committee the Secretary of State must consult—
  (a)   the Council Chairman,
  (b)   except where the appointment is as chairman, the chairman of the territorial committee,
  (c)   in the case of the Scottish Consumer Council, the Scottish Ministers, and
  (d)   in the case of the Welsh Consumer Council, the Welsh Ministers,
about the appointment.

(6)   A person may be appointed as an executive member of a territorial committee only if the person has been nominated for the appointment by the Council Chairman, after consultation with the chairman of the territorial committee.

(7)   In making appointments to a territorial committee, the Secretary of State must have regard to the desirability of including among the members of the committee one or more persons with experience of work among, and the special needs of, disabled persons.

Regional committees

12.—(1)   The Council may, with the approval of the Secretary of State, establish one or more committees for areas within the United Kingdom.

(2)   In this Schedule references to a "regional committee" are to a committee established under sub-paragraph (1).

(3)   The purposes of a regional committee are—
  (a)   the provision of advice and information to the Council about such consumer matters affecting the area for which the committee is established as may be specified by the Council, and
  (b)   such other purposes as the Council may determine.

(4)   The Council may not abolish a regional committee, or alter the area for which a regional committee is established, except with the approval of the Secretary of State.

(5)   If the Council proposes to do anything mentioned in sub-paragraph (1) or (4), it must, after consulting the Secretary of State, give notice—
  (a)   describing its proposals, and
  (b)   specifying the period (not being less than 2 months) starting with the date of the notice within which representations may be made with respect to the proposals,
and consider any representations that are duly made and not withdrawn.

(6)   A notice under sub-paragraph (5) must be given by publishing it in such manner as the Council considers appropriate for bringing the proposals to the attention of those likely to be affected by them.

(7)   The Secretary of State may not give his approval under sub-paragraph (4) until after the period specified in the notice under sub-paragraph (5).

Constitution of regional committees

13.—(1)   A regional committee is to consist of a chairman, and such other members, as the Council may appoint.

(2)   In this Schedule—
   (a)   references to executive members of a regional committee are to the members of the committee appointed from the staff of the Council, and
   (b)   references to non-executive members of a regional committee are to the members who are not executive members of the committee.

(3)   The chairman of a regional committee must be a non-executive member of the committee.

(4)   In appointing persons to a regional committee the Council must secure that a majority of the members of the committee are non-executive members.

(5)   In making appointments to a regional committee, the Council must have regard to the desirability of including among the members of the committee one or more persons with experience of work among, and the special needs of, disabled persons.

Other committees

14.   The Council may establish such other committees as it considers appropriate.

General provision about committees

15.—(1)   In this paragraph and paragraphs 16 and 17 "committee" means—
   (a)   a territorial committee,
   (b)   a regional committee, or
   (c)   a committee established under paragraph 14.

(2)   A committee may establish sub-committees.

(3)   The members of a committee or sub-committee may include persons who are not members of the Council.

(4)   The members of a sub-committee established by a committee may include persons who are not members of the committee.

Terms of appointment etc

16.   Subject to this Schedule, a member of a committee—
   (a)   is to hold and vacate office in accordance with the terms and conditions of the member's appointment, and
   (b)   may resign or be removed from office in accordance with those terms and conditions.

17.—(1)   The Council may—
   (a)   pay to any non-executive member of a committee or sub-committee, such remuneration as the Secretary of State may determine;
   (b)   pay to any member of a committee or sub-committee, such travelling and other allowances as the Secretary of State may determine.

(2)   For the purposes of sub-paragraph (1), the non-executive members of a committee established under paragraph 14 or a sub-committee are such of its members as are not also members of the staff of the Council.

(3)   The Council may—
   (a)   pay to or in respect of any person who is or has been a non-executive member of a territorial committee such pension, allowances or gratuities as the Secretary of State may determine, or
   (b)   make such payments as the Secretary of State may determine towards provision for the payment of a pension, allowance or gratuity to or in respect of such a person.

18.—(1)   A non-executive member of a territorial or regional committee must be appointed for a fixed period.

(2)   The period for which a non-executive member of a territorial or regional committee is appointed must not exceed 5 years.

(3)   A person who has held office as a non-executive member of a territorial or regional committee may be re-appointed as a non-executive member of that committee, once only, for a further period (whether consecutive or not) not exceeding 5 years.

19.—(1)   A person ceases to be a member of a territorial or regional committee where—
   (a)   in the case of the chairman of the committee, the person ceases to hold that office or becomes a member of the staff of the Council;
   (b)   in the case of any other non-executive member, the person becomes a member of the staff of the Council;
   (c)   in the case of an executive member, the person ceases to be a member of the staff of the Council.

(2)   The Secretary of State may remove any person from office as chairman or another member of a territorial committee on the grounds that the person is unable, unfit or unwilling to discharge the functions of the office.

20.   Where—
- (a)   a non-executive member of a territorial committee ceases to be a member of the committee otherwise than on the expiry of the member's term of office, and
- (b)   it appears to the Secretary of State that there are circumstances which make it right for that person to receive compensation,

the Council may make a payment to that person of such amount as the Secretary of State may determine.

[2162]

NOTES

Commencement: 21 December 2007.

PART 4
PROCEDURE ETC

Procedure

21.   The Council may regulate—
- (a)   its own procedure (including quorum), and
- (b)   the procedure (including quorum) of its committees and sub-committees.

22.   The validity of any act of the Council is not affected by—
- (a)   any vacancy among the members of the Council or of any of its committees or sub-committees, or
- (b)   any defect in the appointment of any member of the Council or of any of its committees or sub-committees, or any disqualification of a person as chairman or another member of the Council.

Delegation

23.—(1)   The Council may authorise—
- (a)   the Council Chairman or any other member of the Council,
- (b)   any of its committees or sub-committees, or
- (c)   the Chief Executive or any other member of staff,

to exercise, on behalf of the Council, such of its functions, in such circumstances, as the Council may determine.

(2)   Any committee established by the Council may delegate functions (including functions delegated to the committee) to—
- (a)   the Council Chairman or any other member of the Council,
- (b)   any member of the committee,
- (c)   a sub-committee of the committee, or
- (d)   the Chief Executive or any other member of staff.

Application of seal and proof of instruments

24.   The application of the seal of the Council is to be authenticated by the signature of—
- (a)   any member of the Council,
- (b)   the Chief Executive of the Council, or
- (c)   any person who has been authorised (whether generally or specifically) by the Council for the purpose.

25.   Any contract or instrument which, if entered into or executed by an individual, would not need to be under seal may be entered into or executed on behalf of the Council by any person who has been authorised (whether generally or specifically) by the Council for the purpose.

26.   A document purporting to be duly executed under the seal of the Council, or signed on its behalf—
- (a)   is to be received in evidence, and
- (b)   is to be taken to be executed or signed in that way, unless the contrary is proved.

Offices

27.—(1)   The Council must maintain an office in each of England, Northern Ireland, Scotland and Wales.

(2)   The Council may, with the approval of the Secretary of State, establish additional offices in the United Kingdom.

[2163]

NOTES

Commencement: 21 December 2007 (paras 21–26); 1 October 2008 (para 27).

PART 5
FUNDING AND ACCOUNTS

Funding

28. The Secretary of State may pay the Council out of money provided by Parliament such sums as the Secretary of State may determine towards the Council's expenses.

29–31. ...

Accounts

32.—(1) The Council must—
  (a) keep proper accounts and proper records in relation to the accounts, and
  (b) prepare in respect of each financial year a statement of accounts.

(2) Each statement of accounts must comply with any directions given by the Secretary of State, with the approval of the Treasury, as to—
  (a) the information to be contained in it and the manner in which it is to be presented;
  (b) the methods and principles according to which the statement is to be prepared;
  (c) the additional information (if any) which is to be provided for the information of Parliament.

(3) The Council must give a copy of each statement of accounts—
  (a) to the Secretary of State, and
  (b) to the Comptroller and Auditor General,
before the end of the month of August next following the financial year to which the statement relates.

(4) The Comptroller and Auditor General must—
  (a) examine, certify and report on each statement of accounts which is received under sub-paragraph (3), and
  (b) send a copy of the certified statement and the Comptroller and Auditor General's report to the Secretary of State, who shall lay them before Parliament.

[2164]

NOTES

Commencement: 21 December 2007 (paras 28–31); 1 April 2008 (para 32).
Paras 29–31: outside the scope of this work.

PART 6
STATUS ETC

Status

33.—(1) The Council is not to be regarded—
  (a) as the servant or agent of the Crown, or
  (b) as enjoying any status, immunity or privilege of the Crown.

(2) Accordingly, the Council's property is not to be regarded as property of or held on behalf of the Crown.

34, 35. ...

Public records

36.—(1) ...

(2) The records of the Council are to include—
  (a) on and after commencement of section 30(1), the records of the Gas and Electricity Consumer Council, and
  (b) on and after commencement of section 30(2), the records of the Consumer Council for Postal Services,
and those records are to be dealt with accordingly under the Public Records Act 1958.

37. ...

Exemption from liability in damages

38.—(1) This paragraph applies to—
  (a) the Council;

(b)   a member of the Council;
(c)   a member of any territorial committee, regional committee or other committee or sub-committee of the Council;
(d)   the Chief Executive or any other member of the Council's staff,

(2)   A person to whom this paragraph applies is not liable in damages for anything done or omitted in the exercise or purported exercise of the functions of the Council conferred by or by virtue of this or any other enactment.

(3)   But sub-paragraph (2) does not apply—
(a)   if it is shown that the act or omission was in bad faith, or
(b)   so as to prevent an award of damages made in respect of an act or omission on the ground that the act or omission was unlawful as a result of section 6(1) of the Human Rights Act 1998 (c 42).

(4)   In this paragraph "enactment" means—
(a)   an Act of Parliament,
(b)   an Act of the Scottish Parliament,
(c)   a Measure or Act of the National Assembly for Wales, or
(d)   Northern Ireland legislation,

whenever passed or made.

[2165]

NOTES

Commencement: 21 December 2007.
Paras 34, 35, 37: outside the scope of this work.
Para 36: sub-para (1) amends the Public Records Act 1958, Sch 1.

(Sch 2 outside the scope of this work.)

SCHEDULE 3
ABOLITION OF CONSUMER BODIES: TRANSITIONAL PROVISION

Section 30

Complaints and investigations functions of Gas and Electricity Consumer Council

1.—(1)   This paragraph applies to—
(a)   any complaint to which section 32(1) of the Gas Act 1986 (c 44) applies which is referred to the Gas and Electricity Consumer Council before the appointed day;
(b)   any matter under investigation by the Gas and Electricity Consumer Council under section 33 of that Act immediately before the appointed day.

(2)   The functions of the Gas and Electricity Consumer Council under section 32 or 33 of the Gas Act 1986 are exercisable by the Council in relation to the complaint or matter, but as if in section 32(8) of that Act the reference to the Utilities Act 2000 (c 27) or the Gas Act 1986 included a reference to this Act and to Part 9 of the Enterprise Act 2002 (c 40).

(3)   Sub-paragraph (2) applies—
(a)   notwithstanding the repeal of sections 32 and 33 of the Gas Act 1986 by this Act, and
(b)   whether or not the complaint is within section 11, 12 or 13, or the matter is within section 11.

(4)   "The appointed day" is the day on which section 30(1) comes into force.

2.—(1)   This paragraph applies to—
(a)   any complaint to which section 46(1) of the Electricity Act 1989 (c 29) applies which is referred to the Gas and Electricity Consumer Council before the appointed day;
(b)   any matter under investigation by the Gas and Electricity Consumer Council under section 46A of that Act immediately before the appointed day.

(2)   The functions of the Gas and Electricity Consumer Council under section 46 or 46A of the Electricity Act 1989 are exercisable by the Council in relation to the complaint or matter, but as if in section 46(8) of that Act the reference to the Utilities Act 2000 or the Electricity Act 1989 included a reference to this Act and Part 9 of the Enterprise Act 2002.

(3)   Sub-paragraph (2) applies—
(a)   notwithstanding the repeal of sections 46 and 46A of the Electricity Act 1989 by this Act, and
(b)   whether or not the complaint is within section 11, 12 or 13, or the matter is within section 11.

(4)   "The appointed day" is the day on which section 30(1) comes into force.

Annual reports of the Gas and Electricity Consumer Council

3.—(1)   After the abolition of the Gas and Electricity Consumer Council under section 30(1), any duty of the Gas and Electricity Consumer Council to make an annual report, in relation to any financial year for which such a report has not been made, is to be discharged by the Council.

(2)   The period between the abolition of the Gas and Electricity Consumer Council and the end of the preceding financial year (if less than 12 months) is to be treated as its financial year for which the last annual report is required.

(3)   If that period is 9 months or longer the Council must make the last annual report as soon as practicable after the end of that period.

(4)   If that period is shorter than 9 months the last annual report must be made no later than the first report of the Council under section 7.

(5)   In this paragraph—
"annual report" means a report required by paragraph 6 of Schedule 2 to the Utilities Act 2000 (c 27);
"financial year" means a year ending with 31 March.

Complaints and investigations functions of Consumer Council for Postal Services

4.—(1)   This paragraph applies to any matter which, immediately before the appointed day, is under investigation by the Consumer Council for Postal Services under—
(a)   section 56(1) of the Postal Services Act 2000 (c 26) (complaints referred to the Consumer Council for Postal Services), or
(b)   section 57 of that Act (power of that Council to investigate other matters).

(2)   The functions of the Consumer Council for Postal Services under section 56 or 57 of the Postal Services Act 2000 are exercisable by the Council in relation to the matter, and any agreement between the Consumer Council for Postal Services and the Commission under section 56(3) of that Act has effect as if agreed between the Council and the Commission.

(3)   Sub-paragraph (2) applies—
(a)   notwithstanding the repeal of sections 56 and 57 of the Postal Services Act 2000 by this Act;
(b)   whether or not the matter is within section 11 or 16.

(4)   "The appointed day" is the day on which section 30(2) comes into force.

Annual reports of the Consumer Council for Postal Services

5.—(1)   After the abolition of the Consumer Council for Postal Services under section 30(2), any duty of the Consumer Council for Postal Services to make an annual report, in relation to any financial year for which such a report has not been made, is to be discharged by the Council.

(2)   The period between the abolition of the Consumer Council for Postal Services and the end of the preceding financial year (if less than 12 months) is to be treated as the financial year for which the last annual report is required.

(3)   If that period is 9 months or longer the Council must make the last annual report as soon as practicable after the end of that period.

(4)   If that period is shorter than 9 months the last annual report must be made no later than the first report of the Council under section 7.

(5)   In this paragraph—
"annual report" means a report required by section 55(1) of the Postal Services Act 2000 (c 26);
"financial year" means a year ending with 31 March.

[2166]

NOTES
Commencement: 1 October 2008.

SCHEDULE 4
TRANSFER OF PROPERTY ETC TO COUNCIL
Section 35

Preliminary

1.   In this Schedule—
"transfer scheme" has the meaning given by section 35;
"transferor" means the body to which section 35 applies and to which the transfer scheme relates.

Contents of transfer schemes

2.—(1)   The property, rights and liabilities that may be transferred by a transfer scheme include property, rights and liabilities that would not otherwise be capable of being transferred or assigned.

(2)   The transfers authorised by sub-paragraph (1) include transfers of interests and rights that are to take effect in accordance with the scheme as if there were—

    (a)   no such requirement to obtain a person's consent or concurrence,

    (b)   no such liability in respect of a contravention of any other requirement, and

    (c)   no such interference with any interest or right,

as there would otherwise be by reason of a provision within sub-paragraph (3).

(3)   A provision is within this sub-paragraph to the extent that it has effect (whether under an enactment or agreement or otherwise) in relation to the terms on which the transferor is entitled or subject to anything to which the transfer relates.

3.   A transfer scheme may define the property, rights and liabilities to be transferred by specifying them or describing them.

4.   A transfer scheme may contain supplementary, incidental, transitional and consequential provision.

Effect of transfers

5.—(1)   On the day appointed by a transfer scheme the property, rights and liabilities which are the subject of the scheme are transferred to the Council in accordance with the provisions of the scheme.

(2)   Sub-paragraph (1) has effect in relation to property, rights or liabilities to which it applies in spite of any provision (of whatever nature) which would prevent or restrict the transfer of the property, rights or liabilities otherwise than by virtue of that sub-paragraph.

6.—(1)   So far as is appropriate in consequence of the transfer, anything done by the transferor for the purposes of or in connection with anything transferred which is in effect immediately before it is transferred is to be treated as if done by the Council.

(2)   A transfer does not affect the validity of anything done by or in relation to the transferor before the transfer takes effect.

(3)   There may be continued by or in relation to the Council anything (including legal proceedings) relating to anything transferred which is in the process of being done by or in relation to the transferor immediately before it is transferred.

(4)   So far as is appropriate in consequence of the transfer, the Council is substituted for the transferor in any agreement, instrument or other document relating to anything transferred.

Staff

7.   The Transfer of Undertakings (Protection of Employment) Regulations 2006 (SI 2006/246) apply to a transfer which relates to rights or liabilities under a contract of employment whether or not the transfer would, apart from this paragraph, be a relevant transfer for the purposes of those regulations.

8.   Where an employee of the transferor becomes an employee of the Council by virtue of a transfer scheme—

    (a)   a period of employment with the transferor is to be treated as a period of employment with the Council, and

    (b)   the transfer to the Council is not to be treated as a break in service.

Chargeable gains: asset to be treated as disposed of without a gain or loss

9.   For the purposes of the Taxation of Chargeable Gains Act 1992 (c 12), a transfer of an asset by a transfer scheme is to be treated as a disposal of that asset to the Council for a consideration of such amount as would secure that, on the disposal, neither a gain nor a loss accrues to the transferor.

Continuity in relation to transfer of intangible assets

10.—(1)   For the purposes of Schedule 29 to the Finance Act 2002 (c 23)—

    (a)   a transfer by a transfer scheme of a chargeable intangible asset of the transferor is to be treated as a tax-neutral transfer, and

    (b)   an intangible fixed asset which is an existing asset of the transferor at the time of the transfer is to be treated, on and after the transfer, as an existing asset in the hands of the Council.

(2)   Expressions used in this paragraph and in that Schedule have the same meanings in this paragraph as in that Schedule.

Corporation Tax Acts

11.   So far as it relates to corporation tax, this Schedule is to be construed as one with the Corporation Tax Acts.

Modification of transfer schemes after appointed day

12.—(1)   If, after the day appointed by a transfer scheme, the transferor and the Council so agree in writing, the scheme shall for all purposes be deemed to have come into force on that day with such modifications as may be agreed.

(2)   An agreement under this paragraph may, in connection with giving effect to modifications to the scheme, include supplementary, incidental, transitional and consequential provision.

[2167]

NOTES
Commencement: 21 December 2007.

(Schs 5, 7, 8 outside the scope of this work; Sch 6 inserts the Estate Agents Act 1979, ss 23A–23C at **[934A]**–**[935]** *and inserts Schs 3, 4 to that Act at* **[949A]**, **[949B]**.*)*

CORPORATE MANSLAUGHTER AND CORPORATE HOMICIDE ACT 2007

(2007 c 19)

ARRANGEMENT OF SECTIONS

An Act to create a new offence that, in England and Wales or Northern Ireland, is to be called corporate manslaughter and, in Scotland, is to be called corporate homicide; and to make provision in connection with that offence

[26 July 2007]

Corporate manslaughter and corporate homicide

1   The offence

(1)   An organisation to which this section applies is guilty of an offence if the way in which its activities are managed or organised—

(a)   causes a person's death, and

(b)　　amounts to a gross breach of a relevant duty of care owed by the organisation to the deceased.

(2)　The organisations to which this section applies are—
(a)　a corporation;
(b)　a department or other body listed in Schedule 1;
(c)　a police force;
(d)　a partnership, or a trade union or employers' association, that is an employer.

(3)　An organisation is guilty of an offence under this section only if the way in which its activities are managed or organised by its senior management is a substantial element in the breach referred to in subsection (1).

(4)　For the purposes of this Act—
(a)　"relevant duty of care" has the meaning given by section 2, read with sections 3 to 7;
(b)　a breach of a duty of care by an organisation is a "gross" breach if the conduct alleged to amount to a breach of that duty falls far below what can reasonably be expected of the organisation in the circumstances;
(c)　"senior management", in relation to an organisation, means the persons who play significant roles in—
(i)　the making of decisions about how the whole or a substantial part of its activities are to be managed or organised, or
(ii)　the actual managing or organising of the whole or a substantial part of those activities.

(5)　The offence under this section is called—
(a)　corporate manslaughter, in so far as it is an offence under the law of England and Wales or Northern Ireland;
(b)　corporate homicide, in so far as it is an offence under the law of Scotland.

(6)　An organisation that is guilty of corporate manslaughter or corporate homicide is liable on conviction on indictment to a fine.

(7)　The offence of corporate homicide is indictable only in the High Court of Justiciary.

[2168]

NOTES
Commencement: 6 April 2008 (except in relation to anything done or omitted before that date).

Relevant duty of care

2　Meaning of "relevant duty of care"

(1)　A "relevant duty of care", in relation to an organisation, means any of the following duties owed by it under the law of negligence—
(a)　a duty owed to its employees or to other persons working for the organisation or performing services for it;
(b)　a duty owed as occupier of premises;
(c)　a duty owed in connection with—
(i)　the supply by the organisation of goods or services (whether for consideration or not),
(ii)　the carrying on by the organisation of any construction or maintenance operations,
(iii)　the carrying on by the organisation of any other activity on a commercial basis, or
(iv)　the use or keeping by the organisation of any plant, vehicle or other thing;
(d)　a duty owed to a person who, by reason of being a person within subsection (2), is someone for whose safety the organisation is responsible.

(2)　A person is within this subsection if—
(a)　he is detained at a custodial institution or in a custody area at a court or police station;
(b)　he is detained at a removal centre or short-term holding facility;
(c)　he is being transported in a vehicle, or being held in any premises, in pursuance of prison escort arrangements or immigration escort arrangements;
(d)　he is living in secure accommodation in which he has been placed;
(e)　he is a detained patient.

(3)　Subsection (1) is subject to sections 3 to 7.

(4)　A reference in subsection (1) to a duty owed under the law of negligence includes a reference to a duty that would be owed under the law of negligence but for any statutory provision under which liability is imposed in place of liability under that law.

(5)　For the purposes of this Act, whether a particular organisation owes a duty of care to a particular individual is a question of law.

The judge must make any findings of fact necessary to decide that question.

(6)   For the purposes of this Act there is to be disregarded—
  (a)   any rule of the common law that has the effect of preventing a duty of care from being owed by one person to another by reason of the fact that they are jointly engaged in unlawful conduct;
  (b)   any such rule that has the effect of preventing a duty of care from being owed to a person by reason of his acceptance of a risk of harm.

(7)   In this section—
"construction or maintenance operations" means operations of any of the following descriptions—
  (a)   construction, installation, alteration, extension, improvement, repair, maintenance, decoration, cleaning, demolition or dismantling of—
      (i)   any building or structure,
      (ii)   anything else that forms, or is to form, part of the land, or
      (iii)   any plant, vehicle or other thing;
  (b)   operations that form an integral part of, or are preparatory to, or are for rendering complete, any operations within paragraph (a);
"custodial institution" means a prison, a young offender institution, a secure training centre, a young offenders institution, a young offenders centre, a juvenile justice centre or a remand centre;
"detained patient" means—
  (a)   a person who is detained in any premises under—
      (i)   Part 2 or 3 of the Mental Health Act 1983 (c 20) ("the 1983 Act"), or
      (ii)   Part 2 or 3 of the Mental Health (Northern Ireland) Order 1986 (SI 1986/595 (NI 4)) ("the 1986 Order");
  (b)   a person who (otherwise than by reason of being detained as mentioned in paragraph (a)) is deemed to be in legal custody by—
      (i)   section 137 of the 1983 Act,
      (ii)   Article 131 of the 1986 Order, or
      (iii)   article 11 of the Mental Health (Care and Treatment) (Scotland) Act 2003 (Consequential Provisions) Order 2005 (SI 2005/2078);
  (c)   a person who is detained in any premises, or is otherwise in custody, under the Mental Health (Care and Treatment) (Scotland) Act 2003 (asp 13) or Part 6 of the Criminal Procedure (Scotland) Act 1995 (c 46) or who is detained in a hospital under section 200 of that Act of 1995;
"immigration escort arrangements" means arrangements made under section 156 of the Immigration and Asylum Act 1999 (c 33);
"the law of negligence" includes—
  (a)   in relation to England and Wales, the Occupiers' Liability Act 1957 (c 31), the Defective Premises Act 1972 (c 35) and the Occupiers' Liability Act 1984 (c 3);
  (b)   in relation to Scotland, the Occupiers' Liability (Scotland) Act 1960 (c 30);
  (c)   in relation to Northern Ireland, the Occupiers' Liability Act (Northern Ireland) 1957 (c 25), the Defective Premises (Northern Ireland) Order 1975 (SI 1975/1039 (NI 9)), the Occupiers' Liability (Northern Ireland) Order 1987 (SI 1987/1280 (NI 15)) and the Defective Premises (Landlord's Liability) Act (Northern Ireland) 2001 (c 10);
"prison escort arrangements" means arrangements made under section 80 of the Criminal Justice Act 1991 (c 53) or under section 102 or 118 of the Criminal Justice and Public Order Act 1994 (c 33);
"removal centre" and "short-term holding facility" have the meaning given by section 147 of the Immigration and Asylum Act 1999;
"secure accommodation" means accommodation, not consisting of or forming part of a custodial institution, provided for the purpose of restricting the liberty of persons under the age of 18.

[2169]

NOTES
Commencement: 6 April 2008 (sub-ss (1)(a)–(c), (2)–(7)); to be appointed (otherwise).

3 Public policy decisions, exclusively public functions and statutory inspections

(1)   Any duty of care owed by a public authority in respect of a decision as to matters of public policy (including in particular the allocation of public resources or the weighing of competing public interests) is not a "relevant duty of care".

(2)   Any duty of care owed in respect of things done in the exercise of an exclusively public function is not a "relevant duty of care" unless it falls within section 2(1)(a), (b) or (d).

(3)   Any duty of care owed by a public authority in respect of inspections carried out in the exercise of a statutory function is not a "relevant duty of care" unless it falls within section 2(1)(a) or (b).

(4)   In this section—

"exclusively public function" means a function that falls within the prerogative of the Crown or is, by its nature, exercisable only with authority conferred—

(a)   by the exercise of that prerogative, or

(b)   by or under a statutory provision;

"statutory function" means a function conferred by or under a statutory provision.

[2170]

NOTES

Commencement: 6 April 2008.

---

4   Military activities

(1)   Any duty of care owed by the Ministry of Defence in respect of—

(a)   operations within subsection (2),

(b)   activities carried on in preparation for, or directly in support of, such operations, or

(c)   training of a hazardous nature, or training carried out in a hazardous way, which it is considered needs to be carried out, or carried out in that way, in order to improve or maintain the effectiveness of the armed forces with respect to such operations,

is not a "relevant duty of care".

(2)   The operations within this subsection are operations, including peacekeeping operations and operations for dealing with terrorism, civil unrest or serious public disorder, in the course of which members of the armed forces come under attack or face the threat of attack or violent resistance.

(3)   Any duty of care owed by the Ministry of Defence in respect of activities carried on by members of the special forces is not a "relevant duty of care".

(4)   In this section "the special forces" means those units of the armed forces the maintenance of whose capabilities is the responsibility of the Director of Special Forces or which are for the time being subject to the operational command of that Director.

[2171]

NOTES

Commencement: 6 April 2008.

---

5   Policing and law enforcement

(1)   Any duty of care owed by a public authority in respect of—

(a)   operations within subsection (2),

(b)   activities carried on in preparation for, or directly in support of, such operations, or

(c)   training of a hazardous nature, or training carried out in a hazardous way, which it is considered needs to be carried out, or carried out in that way, in order to improve or maintain the effectiveness of officers or employees of the public authority with respect to such operations,

is not a "relevant duty of care".

(2)   Operations are within this subsection if—

(a)   they are operations for dealing with terrorism, civil unrest or serious disorder,

(b)   they involve the carrying on of policing or law-enforcement activities, and

(c)   officers or employees of the public authority in question come under attack, or face the threat of attack or violent resistance, in the course of the operations.

(3)   Any duty of care owed by a public authority in respect of other policing or law-enforcement activities is not a "relevant duty of care" unless it falls within section 2(1)(a), (b) or (d).

(4)   In this section "policing or law-enforcement activities" includes—

(a)   activities carried on in the exercise of functions that are—

(i)   functions of police forces, or

(ii)   functions of the same or a similar nature exercisable by public authorities other than police forces;

(b)   activities carried on in the exercise of functions of constables employed by a public authority;

(c)   activities carried on in the exercise of functions exercisable under Chapter 4 of Part 2 of the Serious Organised Crime and Police Act 2005 (c 15) (protection of witnesses and other persons);

    (d)   activities carried on to enforce any provision contained in or made under the Immigration Acts.

[2172]

NOTES

Commencement: 6 April 2008 (except in relation to anything done or omitted before that date).

6 Emergencies

(1)   Any duty of care owed by an organisation within subsection (2) in respect of the way in which it responds to emergency circumstances is not a "relevant duty of care" unless it falls within section 2(1)(a) or (b).

(2)   The organisations within this subsection are—
    (a)   a fire and rescue authority in England and Wales;
    (b)   a fire and rescue authority or joint fire and rescue board in Scotland;
    (c)   the Northern Ireland Fire and Rescue Service Board;
    (d)   any other organisation providing a service of responding to emergency circumstances either—
        (i)   in pursuance of arrangements made with an organisation within paragraph (a), (b) or (c), or
        (ii) (if not in pursuance of such arrangements) otherwise than on a commercial basis;
    (e)   a relevant NHS body;
    (f)   an organisation providing ambulance services in pursuance of arrangements—
        (i)   made by, or at the request of, a relevant NHS body, or
        (ii) made with the Secretary of State or with the Welsh Ministers;
    (g)   an organisation providing services for the transport of organs, blood, equipment or personnel in pursuance of arrangements of the kind mentioned in paragraph (f);
    (h)   an organisation providing a rescue service;
    (i)   the armed forces.

(3)   For the purposes of subsection (1), the way in which an organisation responds to emergency circumstances does not include the way in which—
    (a)   medical treatment is carried out, or
    (b)   decisions within subsection (4) are made.

(4)   The decisions within this subsection are decisions as to the carrying out of medical treatment, other than decisions as to the order in which persons are to be given such treatment.

(5)   Any duty of care owed in respect of the carrying out, or attempted carrying out, of a rescue operation at sea in emergency circumstances is not a "relevant duty of care" unless it falls within section 2(1)(a) or (b).

(6)   Any duty of care owed in respect of action taken—
    (a)   in order to comply with a direction under Schedule 3A to the Merchant Shipping Act 1995 (c 21) (safety directions), or
    (b)   by virtue of paragraph 4 of that Schedule (action in lieu of direction),
is not a "relevant duty of care" unless it falls within section 2(1)(a) or (b).

(7)   In this section—
"emergency circumstances" means circumstances that are present or imminent and—
    (a)   are causing, or are likely to cause, serious harm or a worsening of such harm, or
    (b)   are likely to cause the death of a person;
"medical treatment" includes any treatment or procedure of a medical or similar nature;
"relevant NHS body" means—
    (a)   a Strategic Health Authority, Primary Care Trust, NHS trust, Special Health Authority or NHS foundation trust in England;
    (b)   a Local Health Board, NHS trust or Special Health Authority in Wales;
    (c)   a Health Board or Special Health Board in Scotland, or the Common Services Agency for the Scottish Health Service;
    (d)   a Health and Social Services trust or Health and Social Services Board in Northern Ireland;
"serious harm" means—
    (a)   serious injury to or the serious illness (including mental illness) of a person;
    (b)   serious harm to the environment (including the life and health of plants and animals);
    (c)   serious harm to any building or other property.

(8)   A reference in this section to emergency circumstances includes a reference to circumstances that are believed to be emergency circumstances.

[2173]

NOTES

Commencement: 6 April 2008.

7   Child-protection and probation functions

(1)   A duty of care to which this section applies is not a "relevant duty of care" unless it falls within section 2(1)(a), (b) or (d).

(2)   This section applies to any duty of care that a local authority or other public authority owes in respect of the exercise by it of functions conferred by or under—

(a)   Parts 4 and 5 of the Children Act 1989 (c 41),
(b)   Part 2 of the Children (Scotland) Act 1995 (c 36), or
(c)   Parts 5 and 6 of the Children (Northern Ireland) Order 1995 (SI 1995/755 (NI 2)).

(3)   This section also applies to any duty of care that a local probation board[, a provider of probation services] or other public authority owes in respect of the exercise by it of functions conferred by or under—

(a)   Chapter 1 of Part 1 of the Criminal Justice and Court Services Act 2000 (c 43),
[(aa)   section 13 of the Offender Management Act 2007 (c 21)]
(b)   section 27 of the Social Work (Scotland) Act 1968 (c 49), or
(c)   Article 4 of the Probation Board (Northern Ireland) Order 1982 (SI 1982/713 (NI 10)).

[(4)   This section also applies to any duty of care that a provider of probation services owes in respect of the carrying out by it of activities in pursuance of arrangements under section 3 of the Offender Management Act 2007.]

[2174]

NOTES

Commencement: 6 April 2008 (except in relation to anything done or omitted before that date).

Sub-s (3): words in first pair of square brackets and para (aa) inserted by the Offender Management Act 2007 (Consequential Amendments) Order 2008, SI 2008/912, art 3, Sch 1, para 25(1), (2).

Sub-s (4): added by SI 2008/912, art 3, Sch 1, para 25(1), (3).

Gross breach

8   Factors for jury

(1)   This section applies where—

(a)   it is established that an organisation owed a relevant duty of care to a person, and
(b)   it falls to the jury to decide whether there was a gross breach of that duty.

(2)   The jury must consider whether the evidence shows that the organisation failed to comply with any health and safety legislation that relates to the alleged breach, and if so—

(a)   how serious that failure was;
(b)   how much of a risk of death it posed.

(3)   The jury may also—

(a)   consider the extent to which the evidence shows that there were attitudes, policies, systems or accepted practices within the organisation that were likely to have encouraged any such failure as is mentioned in subsection (2), or to have produced tolerance of it;
(b)   have regard to any health and safety guidance that relates to the alleged breach.

(4)   This section does not prevent the jury from having regard to any other matters they consider relevant.

(5)   In this section "health and safety guidance" means any code, guidance, manual or similar publication that is concerned with health and safety matters and is made or issued (under a statutory provision or otherwise) by an authority responsible for the enforcement of any health and safety legislation.

[2175]

NOTES

Commencement: 6 April 2008.

Remedial orders and publicity orders

9   Power to order breach etc to be remedied

(1)   A court before which an organisation is convicted of corporate manslaughter or corporate homicide may make an order (a "remedial order") requiring the organisation to take specified steps to remedy—

(a)   the breach mentioned in section 1(1) ("the relevant breach");

(b)   any matter that appears to the court to have resulted from the relevant breach and to have been a cause of the death;

(c)   any deficiency, as regards health and safety matters, in the organisation's policies, systems or practices of which the relevant breach appears to the court to be an indication.

(2)   A remedial order may be made only on an application by the prosecution specifying the terms of the proposed order.

Any such order must be on such terms (whether those proposed or others) as the court considers appropriate having regard to any representations made, and any evidence adduced, in relation to that matter by the prosecution or on behalf of the organisation.

(3)   Before making an application for a remedial order the prosecution must consult such enforcement authority or authorities as it considers appropriate having regard to the nature of the relevant breach.

(4)   A remedial order—

(a)   must specify a period within which the steps referred to in subsection (1) are to be taken;

(b)   may require the organisation to supply to an enforcement authority consulted under subsection (3), within a specified period, evidence that those steps have been taken.

A period specified under this subsection may be extended or further extended by order of the court on an application made before the end of that period or extended period.

(5)   An organisation that fails to comply with a remedial order is guilty of an offence, and liable on conviction on indictment to a fine.

[2176]

NOTES

Commencement: 6 April 2008.

10   Power to order conviction etc to be publicised

(1)   A court before which an organisation is convicted of corporate manslaughter or corporate homicide may make an order (a "publicity order") requiring the organisation to publicise in a specified manner—

(a)   the fact that it has been convicted of the offence;

(b)   specified particulars of the offence;

(c)   the amount of any fine imposed;

(d)   the terms of any remedial order made.

(2)   In deciding on the terms of a publicity order that it is proposing to make, the court must—

(a)   ascertain the views of such enforcement authority or authorities (if any) as it considers appropriate, and

(b)   have regard to any representations made by the prosecution or on behalf of the organisation.

(3)   A publicity order—

(a)   must specify a period within which the requirements referred to in subsection (1) are to be complied with;

(b)   may require the organisation to supply to any enforcement authority whose views have been ascertained under subsection (2), within a specified period, evidence that those requirements have been complied with.

(4)   An organisation that fails to comply with a publicity order is guilty of an offence, and liable on conviction on indictment to a fine.

[2177]

NOTES

Commencement: 15 February 2010 (except in relation to an offence committed before that date).

11–14   (*Outside the scope of this work.*)

Miscellaneous

15, 16   (*Outside the scope of this work.*)

17   DPP's consent required for proceedings

Proceedings for an offence of corporate manslaughter—

(a)   may not be instituted in England and Wales without the consent of the Director of Public Prosecutions;

(b)   may not be instituted in Northern Ireland without the consent of the Director of Public Prosecutions for Northern Ireland.

[2178]

PART 1
STATUTES

NOTES
Commencement: 6 April 2008.

18   No individual liability

(1)   An individual cannot be guilty of aiding, abetting, counselling or procuring the commission of an offence of corporate manslaughter.

[(1A)   An individual cannot be guilty of an offence under Part 2 of the Serious Crime Act 2007 (encouraging or assisting crime) by reference to an offence of corporate manslaughter.]

(2)   An individual cannot be guilty of aiding, abetting, counselling or procuring, or being art and part in, the commission of an offence of corporate homicide.

[2179]

NOTES
Commencement: 6 April 2008.
Sub-s (1A): inserted, in relation to England, Wales and Northern Ireland, by the Serious Crime Act 2007, s 62.

19   Convictions under this Act and under health and safety legislation

(1)   Where in the same proceedings there is—
  (a)   a charge of corporate manslaughter or corporate homicide arising out of a particular set of circumstances, and
  (b)   a charge against the same defendant of a health and safety offence arising out of some or all of those circumstances,
the jury may, if the interests of justice so require, be invited to return a verdict on each charge.

(2)   An organisation that has been convicted of corporate manslaughter or corporate homicide arising out of a particular set of circumstances may, if the interests of justice so require, be charged with a health and safety offence arising out of some or all of those circumstances.

(3)   In this section "health and safety offence" means an offence under any health and safety legislation.

[2180]

NOTES
Commencement: 6 April 2008.

20   Abolition of liability of corporations for manslaughter at common law

The common law offence of manslaughter by gross negligence is abolished in its application to corporations, and in any application it has to other organisations to which section 1 applies.

[2181]

NOTES
Commencement: 6 April 2008 (except in relation to any liability, investigation, legal proceeding or penalty for or in respect of an offence committed wholly or partly before that date).

General and supplemental

21–28   (*Outside the scope of this work.*)

29   Short title

This Act may be cited as the Corporate Manslaughter and Corporate Homicide Act 2007.

[2182]

NOTES
Commencement: 26 July 2007.

(*Schs 1, 2 outside the scope of this work.*)

THIRD PARTIES (RIGHTS AGAINST INSURERS) ACT 2010

(2010 c 10)

ARRANGEMENT OF SECTIONS

An Act to make provision about the rights of third parties against insurers of liabilities to third parties in the case where the insured is insolvent, and in certain other cases.

[25 March 2010]

Transfer of rights to third parties

1   Rights against insurer of insolvent person etc

(1)   This section applies if—

    (a)   a relevant person incurs a liability against which that person is insured under a contract of insurance, or

    (b)   a person who is subject to such a liability becomes a relevant person.

(2)   The rights of the relevant person under the contract against the insurer in respect of the liability are transferred to and vest in the person to whom the liability is or was incurred (the "third party").

(3)   The third party may bring proceedings to enforce the rights against the insurer without having established the relevant person's liability; but the third party may not enforce those rights without having established that liability.

(4)   For the purposes of this Act, a liability is established only if its existence and amount are established; and, for that purpose, "establish" means establish—

(a)   by virtue of a declaration under section 2 or a declarator under section 3,
(b)   by a judgment or decree,
(c)   by an award in arbitral proceedings or by an arbitration, or
(d)   by an enforceable agreement.

(5)   In this Act—
(a)   references to an "insured" are to a person who incurs or who is subject to a liability to a third party against which that person is insured under a contract of insurance;
(b)   references to a "relevant person" are to a person within sections 4 to 7;
(c)   references to a "third party" are to be construed in accordance with subsection (2);
(d)   references to "transferred rights" are to rights under a contract of insurance which are transferred under this section.

[2183]

NOTES
Commencement: to be appointed.

---

2   Establishing liability in England and Wales and Northern Ireland

(1)   This section applies where a person (P)—
(a)   claims to have rights under a contract of insurance by virtue of a transfer under section 1, but
(b)   has not yet established the insured's liability which is insured under that contract.

(2)   P may bring proceedings against the insurer for either or both of the following—
(a)   a declaration as to the insured's liability to P;
(b)   a declaration as to the insurer's potential liability to P.

(3)   In such proceedings P is entitled, subject to any defence on which the insurer may rely, to a declaration under subsection (2)(a) or (b) on proof of the insured's liability to P or (as the case may be) the insurer's potential liability to P.

(4)   Where proceedings are brought under subsection (2)(a) the insurer may rely on any defence on which the insured could rely if those proceedings were proceedings brought against the insured in respect of the insured's liability to P.

(5)   Subsection (4) is subject to section 12(1).

(6)   Where the court makes a declaration under this section, the effect of which is that the insurer is liable to P, the court may give the appropriate judgment against the insurer.

(7)   Where a person applying for a declaration under subsection (2)(b) is entitled or required, by virtue of the contract of insurance, to do so in arbitral proceedings, that person may also apply in the same proceedings for a declaration under subsection (2)(a).

(8)   In the application of this section to arbitral proceedings, subsection (6) is to be read as if "tribunal" were substituted for "court" and "make the appropriate award" for "give the appropriate judgment".

(9)   When bringing proceedings under subsection (2)(a), P may also make the insured a defendant to those proceedings.

(10)   If (but only if) the insured is a defendant to proceedings under this section (whether by virtue of subsection (9) or otherwise), a declaration under subsection (2) binds the insured as well as the insurer.

(11)   In this section, references to the insurer's potential liability to P are references to the insurer's liability in respect of the insured's liability to P, if established.

[2184]

NOTES
Commencement: to be appointed.

---

3   (*Applies to Scotland only.*)

Relevant persons

4   Individuals

(1)   An individual is a relevant person if any of the following is in force in respect of that individual in England and Wales—
(a)   a deed of arrangement registered in accordance with the Deeds of Arrangement Act 1914,
(b)   an administration order made under Part 6 of the County Courts Act 1984,
(c)   an enforcement restriction order made under Part 6A of that Act,

    (d)   subject to subsection (4), a debt relief order made under Part 7A of the Insolvency Act 1986,

    (e)   a voluntary arrangement approved in accordance with Part 8 of that Act, or

    (f)   a bankruptcy order made under Part 9 of that Act.

(2)   An individual is a relevant person if any of the following is in force in respect of that individual (or, in the case of paragraph (a) or (b), that individual's estate) in Scotland—

    (a)   an award of sequestration made under section 5 of the Bankruptcy (Scotland) Act 1985,

    (b)   a protected trust deed within the meaning of that Act, or

    (c)   a composition approved in accordance with Schedule 4 to that Act.

(3)   An individual is a relevant person if any of the following is in force in respect of that individual in Northern Ireland—

    (a)   an administration order made under Part 6 of the Judgments Enforcement (Northern Ireland) Order 1981 (SI 1981/226 (NI 6)),

    (b)   a deed of arrangement registered in accordance with Chapter 1 of Part 8 of the Insolvency (Northern Ireland) Order 1989 (SI 1989/2405 (NI 19)),

    (c)   a voluntary arrangement approved under Chapter 2 of Part 8 of that Order, or

    (d)   a bankruptcy order made under Part 9 of that Order.

(4)   If an individual is a relevant person by virtue of subsection (1)(d), that person is a relevant person for the purposes of section 1(1)(b) only.

(5)   Where an award of sequestration made under section 5 of the Bankruptcy (Scotland) Act 1985 is recalled or reduced, any rights which were transferred under section 1 as a result of that award are re-transferred to and vest in the person who became a relevant person as a result of the award.

(6)   Where an order discharging an individual from an award of sequestration made under section 5 of the Bankruptcy (Scotland) Act 1985 is recalled or reduced under paragraph 17 or 18 of Schedule 4 to that Act, the order is to be treated for the purposes of this section as never having been made.

[2185]

NOTES
Commencement: to be appointed.

5   Individuals who die insolvent

(1)   An individual who dies insolvent is a relevant person for the purposes of section 1(1)(b) only.

(2)   For the purposes of this section an individual (D) is to be regarded as having died insolvent if, following D's death—

    (a)   D's estate falls to be administered in accordance with an order under section 421 of the Insolvency Act 1986 or Article 365 of the Insolvency (Northern Ireland) Order 1989 (SI 1989/2405 (NI 19)),

    (b)   an award of sequestration is made under section 5 of the Bankruptcy (Scotland) Act 1985 in respect of D's estate and the award is not recalled or reduced, or

    (c)   a judicial factor is appointed under section 11A of the Judicial Factors (Scotland) Act 1889 in respect of D's estate and the judicial factor certifies that the estate is absolutely insolvent within the meaning of the Bankruptcy (Scotland) Act 1985.

(3)   Where a transfer of rights under section 1 takes place as a result of an insured person being a relevant person by virtue of this section, references in this Act to an insured are, where the context so requires, to be read as references to the insured's estate.

[2186]

NOTES
Commencement: to be appointed.

6   Corporate bodies etc

(1)   A body corporate or an unincorporated body is a relevant person if—

    (a)   a compromise or arrangement between the body and its creditors (or a class of them) is in force, having been sanctioned in accordance with section 899 of the Companies Act 2006, or

    (b)   the body has been dissolved under section 1000, 1001 or 1003 of that Act, and the body has not been—

        (i)   restored to the register by virtue of section 1025 of that Act, or

        (ii)   ordered to be restored to the register by virtue of section 1031 of that Act.

(2)   A body corporate or an unincorporated body is a relevant person if, in England and Wales or Scotland—

(a) a voluntary arrangement approved in accordance with Part 1 of the Insolvency Act 1986 is in force in respect of it,

(b) an administration order made under Part 2 of that Act is in force in respect of it,

(c) there is a person appointed in accordance with Part 3 of that Act who is acting as receiver or manager of the body's property (or there would be such a person so acting but for a temporary vacancy),

(d) the body is, or is being, wound up voluntarily in accordance with Chapter 2 of Part 4 of that Act,

(e) there is a person appointed under section 135 of that Act who is acting as provisional liquidator in respect of the body (or there would be such a person so acting but for a temporary vacancy), or

(f) the body is, or is being, wound up by the court following the making of a winding-up order under Chapter 6 of Part 4 of that Act or Part 5 of that Act.

(3) A body corporate or an unincorporated body is a relevant person if, in Scotland—

(a) an award of sequestration has been made under section 6 of the Bankruptcy (Scotland) Act 1985 in respect of the body's estate, and the body has not been discharged under that Act,

(b) the body has been dissolved and an award of sequestration has been made under that section in respect of its estate,

(c) a protected trust deed within the meaning of the Bankruptcy (Scotland) Act 1985 is in force in respect of the body's estate, or

(d) a composition approved in accordance with Schedule 4 to that Act is in force in respect of the body.

(4) A body corporate or an unincorporated body is a relevant person if, in Northern Ireland—

(a) a voluntary arrangement approved in accordance with Part 2 of the Insolvency (Northern Ireland) Order 1989 (SI 1989/2405 (NI 19)) is in force in respect of the body,

(b) an administration order made under Part 3 of that Order is in force in respect of the body,

(c) there is a person appointed in accordance with Part 4 of that Order who is acting as receiver or manager of the body's property (or there would be such a person so acting but for a temporary vacancy),

(d) the body is, or is being, wound up voluntarily in accordance with Chapter 2 of Part 5 of that Order,

(e) there is a person appointed under Article 115 of that Order who is acting as provisional liquidator in respect of the body (or there would be such a person so acting but for a temporary vacancy), or

(f) the body is, or is being, wound up by the court following the making of a winding-up order under Chapter 6 of Part 5 of that Order or Part 6 of that Order.

(5) A body within subsection (1)(a) is not a relevant person in relation to a liability that is transferred to another body by the order sanctioning the compromise or arrangement.

(6) Where a body is a relevant person by virtue of subsection (1)(a), section 1 has effect to transfer rights only to a person on whom the compromise or arrangement is binding.

(7) Where an award of sequestration made under section 6 of the Bankruptcy (Scotland) Act 1985 is recalled or reduced, any rights which were transferred under section 1 as a result of that award are re-transferred to and vest in the person who became a relevant person as a result of the award.

(8) Where an order discharging a body from an award of sequestration made under section 6 of the Bankruptcy (Scotland) Act 1985 is recalled or reduced under paragraph 17 or 18 of Schedule 4 to that Act, the order is to be treated for the purposes of this section as never having been made.

(9) In this section—

(a) a reference to a person appointed in accordance with Part 3 of the Insolvency Act 1986 includes a reference to a person appointed under section 101 of the Law of Property Act 1925;

(b) a reference to a receiver or manager of a body's property includes a reference to a receiver or manager of part only of the property and to a receiver only of the income arising from the property or from part of it;

(c) for the purposes of subsection (3) "body corporate or unincorporated body" includes any entity, other than a trust, the estate of which may be sequestrated under section 6 of the Bankruptcy (Scotland) Act 1985;

(d) a reference to a person appointed in accordance with Part 4 of the Insolvency (Northern Ireland) Order 1989 (SI 1989/2405 (NI 19)) includes a reference to a person appointed under section 19 of the Conveyancing Act 1881.

[2187]

NOTES
Commencement: to be appointed.

7 Scottish trusts

(1) A trustee of a Scottish trust is, in respect of a liability of that trustee that falls to be met out of the trust estate, a relevant person if—

(a) an award of sequestration has been made under section 6 of the Bankruptcy (Scotland) Act 1985 in respect of the trust estate, and the trust has not been discharged under that Act,

(b) a protected trust deed within the meaning of that Act is in force in respect of the trust estate, or

(c) a composition approved in accordance with Schedule 4 to that Act is in force in respect of the trust estate.

(2) Where an award of sequestration made under section 6 of the Bankruptcy (Scotland) Act 1985 is recalled or reduced any rights which were transferred under section 1 as a result of that award are re-transferred to and vest in the person who became a relevant person as a result of the award.

(3) Where an order discharging an individual, body or trust from an award of sequestration made under section 6 of the Bankruptcy (Scotland) Act 1985 is recalled or reduced under paragraph 17 or 18 of Schedule 4 to that Act, the order is to be treated for the purposes of this section as never having been made.

(4) In this section "Scottish trust" means a trust the estate of which may be sequestrated under section 6 of the Bankruptcy (Scotland) Act 1985.

[2188]

NOTES
Commencement: to be appointed.

Transferred rights: supplemental

8 Limit on rights transferred

Where the liability of an insured to a third party is less than the liability of the insurer to the insured (ignoring the effect of section 1), no rights are transferred under that section in respect of the difference.

[2189]

NOTES
Commencement: to be appointed.

9 Conditions affecting transferred rights

(1) This section applies where transferred rights are subject to a condition (whether under the contract of insurance from which the transferred rights are derived or otherwise) that the insured has to fulfil.

(2) Anything done by the third party which, if done by the insured, would have amounted to or contributed to fulfilment of the condition is to be treated as if done by the insured.

(3) The transferred rights are not subject to a condition requiring the insured to provide information or assistance to the insurer if that condition cannot be fulfilled because the insured is—

(a) an individual who has died, or

(b) a body corporate that has been dissolved.

(4) A condition requiring the insured to provide information or assistance to the insurer does not include a condition requiring the insured to notify the insurer of the existence of a claim under the contract of insurance.

(5) The transferred rights are not subject to a condition requiring the prior discharge by the insured of the insured's liability to the third party.

(6) In the case of a contract of marine insurance, subsection (5) applies only to the extent that the liability of the insured is a liability in respect of death or personal injury.

(7) In this section—

"contract of marine insurance" has the meaning given by section 1 of the Marine Insurance Act 1906;

"dissolved" means dissolved under—

(a) Chapter 9 of Part 4 of the Insolvency Act 1986,

(b) section 1000, 1001 or 1003 of the Companies Act 2006, or

(c) Chapter 9 of Part 5 of the Insolvency (Northern Ireland) Order 1989 (SI 1989/2405 (NI 19));

"personal injury" includes any disease and any impairment of a person's physical or mental condition.

[2190]

10   Insurer's right of set off

(1)   This section applies if—

    (a)   rights of an insured under a contract of insurance have been transferred to a third party under section 1,

    (b)   the insured is under a liability to the insurer under the contract ("the insured's liability"), and

    (c)   if there had been no transfer, the insurer would have been entitled to set off the amount of the insured's liability against the amount of the insurer's own liability to the insured.

(2)   The insurer is entitled to set off the amount of the insured's liability against the amount of the insurer's own liability to the third party in relation to the transferred rights.

[2191]

Provision of information etc

11   Information and disclosure for third parties

Schedule 1 (information and disclosure for third parties) has effect.

[2192]

Enforcement of transferred rights

12   Limitation and prescription

(1)   Subsection (2) applies where a person brings proceedings for a declaration under section 2(2)(a), or for a declarator under section 3(2)(a), and the proceedings are started or, in Scotland, commenced—

    (a)   after the expiry of a period of limitation applicable to an action against the insured to enforce the insured's liability, or of a period of prescription applicable to that liability, but

    (b)   while such an action is in progress.

(2)   The insurer may not rely on the expiry of that period as a defence unless the insured is able to rely on it in the action against the insured.

(3)   For the purposes of subsection (1), an action is to be treated as no longer in progress if it has been concluded by a judgment or decree, or by an award, even if there is an appeal or a right of appeal.

(4)   Where a person who has already established an insured's liability to that person brings proceedings under this Act against the insurer, nothing in this Act is to be read as meaning—

    (a)   that, for the purposes of the law of limitation in England and Wales, that person's cause of action against the insurer arose otherwise than at the time when that person established the liability of the insured,

    (b)   that, for the purposes of the law of prescription in Scotland, the obligation in respect of which the proceedings are brought became enforceable against the insurer otherwise than at that time, or

    (c)   that, for the purposes of the law of limitation in Northern Ireland, that person's cause of action against the insurer arose otherwise than at the time when that person established the liability of the insured.

[2193]

13   Jurisdiction within the United Kingdom

(1)   Where a person (P) domiciled in a part of the United Kingdom is entitled to bring proceedings under this Act against an insurer domiciled in another part, P may do so in the part where P is domiciled or in the part where the insurer is domiciled (whatever the contract of insurance may stipulate as to where proceedings are to be brought).

(2)   The following provisions of the Civil Jurisdiction and Judgments Act 1982 (relating to determination of domicile) apply for the purposes of subsection (1)—

    (a)   section 41(2), (3), (5) and (6) (individuals);
    (b)   section 42(1), (3), (4) and (8) (corporations and associations);
    (c)   section 45(2) and (3) (trusts);
    (d)   section 46(1), (3) and (7) (the Crown).

(3)   ...

[2194]

NOTES
Commencement: to be appointed.
Sub-s (3): amends the Civil Jurisdiction and Judgments Act 1982, Sch 5.

Enforcement of insured's liability

14   Effect of transfer on insured's liability

(1)   Where rights in respect of an insured's liability to a third party are transferred under section 1, the third party may enforce that liability against the insured only to the extent (if any) that it exceeds the amount recoverable from the insurer by virtue of the transfer.

(2)   Subsection (3) applies if a transfer of rights under section 1 occurs because the insured person is a relevant person by virtue of—

    (a)   section 4(1)(a) or (e), (2)(b) or (3)(b) or (c),
    (b)   section 6(1)(a), (2)(a), (3)(c) or (4)(a), or
    (c)   section 7(1)(b).

(3)   If the liability is subject to the arrangement, trust deed or compromise by virtue of which the insured is a relevant person, the liability is to be treated as subject to that arrangement, trust deed or compromise only to the extent that the liability exceeds the amount recoverable from the insurer by virtue of the transfer.

(4)   Subsection (5) applies if a transfer of rights under section 1 occurs in respect of a liability which, after the transfer, becomes one that is subject to a composition approved in accordance with Schedule 4 to the Bankruptcy (Scotland) Act 1985.

(5)   The liability is to be treated as subject to the composition only to the extent that the liability exceeds the amount recoverable from the insurer by virtue of the transfer.

(6)   For the purposes of this section the amount recoverable from the insurer does not include any amount that the third party is unable to recover as a result of—

    (a)   a shortage of assets on the insurer's part, in a case where the insurer is a relevant person, or
    (b)   a limit set by the contract of insurance on the fund available to meet claims in respect of a particular description of liability of the insured.

(7)   Where a third party is eligible to make a claim in respect of the insurer's liability under or by virtue of rules made under Part 15 of the Financial Services and Markets Act 2000 (the Financial Services Compensation Scheme)—

    (a)   subsection (6)(a) applies only if the third party has made such a claim, and
    (b)   the third party is to be treated as being able to recover from the insurer any amount paid to, or due to, the third party as a result of the claim.

[2195]

NOTES
Commencement: to be appointed.

Application of Act

15   Reinsurance

This Act does not apply to a case where the liability referred to in section 1(1) is itself a liability incurred by an insurer under a contract of insurance.

[2196]

NOTES
Commencement: to be appointed.

16   Voluntarily-incurred liabilities

It is irrelevant for the purposes of section 1 whether or not the liability of the insured is or was incurred voluntarily.

[2197]

PART 1
STATUTES

NOTES
Commencement: to be appointed.

17   Avoidance

(1)   A contract of insurance to which this section applies is of no effect in so far as it purports, whether directly or indirectly, to avoid or terminate the contract or alter the rights of the parties under it in the event of the insured—

    (a)   becoming a relevant person, or

    (b)   dying insolvent (within the meaning given by section 5(2)).

(2)   A contract of insurance is one to which this section applies if the insured's rights under it are capable of being transferred under section 1.

[2198]

NOTES
Commencement: to be appointed.

18   Cases with a foreign element

Except as expressly provided, the application of this Act does not depend on whether there is a connection with a part of the United Kingdom; and in particular it does not depend on—

    (a)   whether or not the liability (or the alleged liability) of the insured to the third party was incurred in, or under the law of, England and Wales, Scotland or Northern Ireland;

    (b)   the place of residence or domicile of any of the parties;

    (c)   whether or not the contract of insurance (or a part of it) is governed by the law of England and Wales, Scotland or Northern Ireland;

    (d)   the place where sums due under the contract of insurance are payable.

[2199]

NOTES
Commencement: to be appointed.

Supplemental

19   Power to amend Act

(1)   The Secretary of State may by order made by statutory instrument amend section 4, 5 or 6 so as to—

    (a)   substitute a reference to a provision of Northern Ireland legislation with a reference to a different provision of Northern Ireland legislation, or

    (b)   add a reference to a provision of a description within subsection (2).

(2)   A provision is within this subsection if—

    (a)   it is made by or under Northern Ireland legislation, and

    (b)   in the opinion of the Secretary of State, it corresponds with a provision under the law of England and Wales or the law of Scotland that is referred to in the section being amended.

(3)   An order under this section may include consequential, incidental, supplementary, transitional, transitory or saving provision.

(4)   An order under this section may not be made unless a draft of the statutory instrument containing the order has been laid before, and approved by a resolution of, each House of Parliament.

[2200]

NOTES
Commencement: to be appointed.

20   Amendments, transitionals, repeals, etc

(1)   Schedule 2 (amendments) has effect.

(2)   Schedule 3 (transitory, transitional and saving provisions) has effect.

(3)   Schedule 4 (repeals and revocations) has effect.

[2201]

NOTES
Commencement: to be appointed.

21 Short title, commencement and extent

(1)   This Act may be cited as the Third Parties (Rights against Insurers) Act 2010.

(2)   This Act comes into force on such day as the Secretary of State may by order made by statutory instrument appoint.

(3)   This Act extends to England and Wales, Scotland and Northern Ireland, subject as follows.

(4)   Section 2 and paragraphs 3 and 4 of Schedule 1 do not extend to Scotland.

(5)   Section 3 extends to Scotland only.

(6)   Any amendment, repeal or revocation made by this Act has the same extent as the provision to which it relates.

[2202]

NOTES

Commencement: to be appointed.

SCHEDULE 1
INFORMATION AND DISCLOSURE FOR THIRD PARTIES

Section 11

Notices requesting information

1.—(1)   If a person (A) reasonably believes that—
   (a)   another person (B) has incurred a liability to A, and
   (b)   B is a relevant person,

A may, by notice in writing, request from B such information falling within sub-paragraph (3) as the notice specifies.

(2)   If a person (A) reasonably believes that—
   (a)   a liability has been incurred to A,
   (b)   the person who incurred the liability is insured against it under a contract of insurance,
   (c)   rights of that person under the contract have been transferred to A under section 1, and
   (d)   there is a person (C) who is able to provide information falling within sub-paragraph (3),

A may, by notice in writing, request from C such information falling within that sub-paragraph as the notice specifies.

(3)   The following is the information that falls within this sub-paragraph—
   (a)   whether there is a contract of insurance that covers the supposed liability or might reasonably be regarded as covering it;
   (b)   if there is such a contract—
      (i)   who the insurer is;
      (ii)   what the terms of the contract are;
      (iii) whether the insured has been informed that the insurer has claimed not to be liable under the contract in respect of the supposed liability;
      (iv)   whether there are or have been any proceedings between the insurer and the insured in respect of the supposed liability and, if so, relevant details of those proceedings;
      (v)   in a case where the contract sets a limit on the fund available to meet claims in respect of the supposed liability and other liabilities, how much of it (if any) has been paid out in respect of other liabilities;
      (vi)   whether there is a fixed charge to which any sums paid out under the contract in respect of the supposed liability would be subject.

(4)   For the purpose of sub-paragraph (3)(b)(iv), relevant details of proceedings are—
   (a)   in the case of court proceedings—
      (i)   the name of the court;
      (ii)   the case number;
      (iii) the contents of all documents served in the proceedings in accordance with rules of court or orders made in the proceedings, and the contents of any such orders;
   (b)   in the case of arbitral proceedings or, in Scotland, an arbitration—
      (i)   the name of the arbitrator;
      (ii)   information corresponding with that mentioned in paragraph (a)(iii).

(5)   In sub-paragraph (3)(b)(vi), in its application to Scotland, "fixed charge" means a fixed security within the meaning given by section 47(1) of the Bankruptcy and Diligence etc (Scotland) Act 2007 (asp 3).

(6)   A notice given by a person under this paragraph must include particulars of the facts on which that person relies as entitlement to give the notice.

Provision of information where notice given under paragraph 1

2.—(1)   A person (R) who receives a notice under paragraph 1 must, within the period of 28 days beginning with the day of receipt of the notice—

    (a)   provide to the person who gave the notice any information specified in it that R is able to provide;

    (b)   in relation to any such information that R is not able to provide, notify that person why R is not able to provide it.

  (2)   Where—

    (a)   a person (R) receives a notice under paragraph 1,

    (b)   there is information specified in the notice that R is not able to provide because it is contained in a document that is not in R's control,

    (c)   the document was at one time in R's control, and

    (d)   R knows or believes that it is now in another person's control,

R must, within the period of 28 days beginning with the day of receipt of the notice, provide the person who gave the notice with whatever particulars R can as to the nature of the information and the identity of that other person.

  (3)   If R fails to comply with a duty imposed on R by this paragraph, the person who gave R the notice may apply to court for an order requiring R to comply with the duty.

  (4)   No duty arises by virtue of this paragraph in respect of information as to which a claim to legal professional privilege or, in Scotland, to confidentiality as between client and professional legal adviser could be maintained in legal proceedings.

Notices requiring disclosure: defunct bodies

3.—(1)   If—

    (a)   a person (P) has started proceedings under this Act against an insurer in respect of a liability that P claims has been incurred to P by a body corporate, and

    (b)   the body is defunct,

P may by notice in writing require a person to whom sub-paragraph (2) applies to disclose to P any documents that are relevant to that liability.

  (2)   This sub-paragraph applies to a person if—

    (a)   immediately before the time of the alleged transfer under section 1, that person was an officer or employee of the body, or

    (b)   immediately before the body became defunct, that person was—

      (i)   acting as an insolvency practitioner in relation to the body (within the meaning given by section 388(1) of the Insolvency Act 1986 or Article 3 of the Insolvency (Northern Ireland) Order 1989 (SI 1989/2405 NI 19)), or

      (ii)   acting as the official receiver in relation to the winding up of the body.

  (3)   A notice under this paragraph must be accompanied by—

    (a)   a copy of the particulars of claim required to be served in connection with the proceedings mentioned in sub-paragraph (1), or

    (b)   where those proceedings are arbitral proceedings, the particulars of claim that would be required to be so served if they were court proceedings.

  (4)   For the purposes of this paragraph a body corporate is defunct if, subject to sub-paragraph (5), it has been dissolved under—

    (a)   Chapter 9 of Part 4 of the Insolvency Act 1986,

    (b)   Chapter 9 of Part 5 of the Insolvency (Northern Ireland) Order 1989 (SI 1989/2405 NI 19)), or

    (c)   section 1000, 1001 or 1003 of the Companies Act 2006.

  (5)   But a body corporate is not defunct for the purposes of this paragraph if the body has been—

    (a)   restored to the register by virtue of section 1025 of the Companies Act 2006, or

    (b)   ordered to be restored to the register by virtue of section 1031 of that Act.

Disclosure and inspection where notice given under paragraph 3

4.—(1)   Subject to the provisions of this paragraph and to any necessary modifications—

    (a)   the duties of disclosure of a person who receives a notice under paragraph 3, and

    (b)   the rights of inspection of the person giving the notice,

are the same as the corresponding duties and rights under Civil Procedure Rules of parties to court proceedings in which an order for standard disclosure has been made.

  (2)   In sub-paragraph (1), in its application to Northern Ireland—

    (a)   the reference to Civil Procedure Rules is—

      (i)   in the case of proceedings in the High Court, to be read as a reference to the Rules of the Court of Judicature (Northern Ireland) 1980 (SR 1980 No 346), and

(ii) in the case of proceedings in the county court, to be read as a reference to the County Court Rules (Northern Ireland) 1981 (SR 1981 No 225), and

(b) the reference to an order for standard disclosure is to be read as a reference to an order for discovery.

(3) A person who by virtue of sub-paragraph (1) or (2) has to serve a list of documents must do so within the period of 28 days beginning with the day of receipt of the notice.

(4) A person who has received a notice under paragraph 3 and has served a list of documents in response to it is not under a duty of disclosure by reason of that notice in relation to documents that the person did not have when the list was served.

Avoidance

5. A contract of insurance is of no effect in so far as it purports, whether directly or indirectly—
(a) to avoid or terminate the contract or alter the rights of the parties under it in the event of a person providing information, or giving disclosure, that the person is required to provide or give by virtue of a notice under paragraph 1 or 3, or
(b) otherwise to prohibit, prevent or restrict a person from providing such information or giving such disclosure.

Other rights to information etc

6. Rights to information, or to inspection of documents, that a person has by virtue of paragraph 1 or 3 are in addition to any such rights as the person has apart from that paragraph.

Interpretation

7. For the purposes of this Schedule—
(a) a person is able to provide information only if—
(i) that person can obtain it without undue difficulty from a document that is in that person's control, or
(ii) where that person is an individual, the information is within that person's knowledge;
(b) a document is in a person's control if it is in that person's possession or if that person has a right to possession of it or to inspect or take copies of it.

[2203]

NOTES

Commencement: to be appointed.

(Sch 2 contains amendments outside the scope of this work.)

SCHEDULE 3
TRANSITORY, TRANSITIONAL AND SAVING PROVISIONS

Section 20

1.—(1) Section 1(1)(a) applies where the insured became a relevant person before, as well as when the insured becomes such a person on or after, commencement day.

(2) Section 1(1)(b) applies where the liability was incurred before, as well as where it is incurred on or after, commencement day.

2. Until the coming into force of section 47(1) of the Bankruptcy and Diligence etc (Scotland) Act 2007 (asp 3), the reference to that provision in paragraph 1(5) of Schedule 1 is to be read as a reference to section 486(1) of the Companies Act 1985.

3. Despite its repeal by this Act, the Third Parties (Rights against Insurers) Act 1930 continues to apply in relation to—
(a) cases where the event referred to in subsection (1) of section 1 of that Act and the incurring of the liability referred to in that subsection both happened before commencement day;
(b) cases where the death of the deceased person referred to in subsection (2) of that section happened before that day.

4. Despite its repeal by this Act, the Third Parties (Rights against Insurers) Act (Northern Ireland) 1930 continues to apply in relation to—
(a) cases where the event referred to in subsection (1) of section 1 of that Act and the incurring of the liability referred to in that subsection both happened before commencement day;
(b) cases where the death of the deceased person referred to in subsection (2) of that section happened before that day.

5. In this Schedule "commencement day" means the day on which this Act comes into force.

[2204]

NOTES

Commencement: to be appointed.

(Sch 4 contains repeals and revocations outside the scope of this work.)

BRIBERY ACT 2010

(2010 c 23)

ARRANGEMENT OF SECTIONS

General bribery offences

An Act to make provision about offences relating to bribery; and for connected purposes.

[8 April 2010]

General bribery offences

1 Offences of bribing another person

(1)   A person ("P") is guilty of an offence if either of the following cases applies.

(2)   Case 1 is where—

    (a)   P offers, promises or gives a financial or other advantage to another person, and

    (b)   P intends the advantage—

        (i)   to induce a person to perform improperly a relevant function or activity, or

        (ii)   to reward a person for the improper performance of such a function or activity.

(3)   Case 2 is where—

    (a)   P offers, promises or gives a financial or other advantage to another person, and

    (b)   P knows or believes that the acceptance of the advantage would itself constitute the improper performance of a relevant function or activity.

(4)   In case 1 it does not matter whether the person to whom the advantage is offered, promised or given is the same person as the person who is to perform, or has performed, the function or activity concerned.

(5)   In cases 1 and 2 it does not matter whether the advantage is offered, promised or given by P directly or through a third party.

[2205]

NOTES
Commencement: to be appointed.

2   Offences relating to being bribed

(1)   A person ("R") is guilty of an offence if any of the following cases applies.

(2)   Case 3 is where R requests, agrees to receive or accepts a financial or other advantage intending that, in consequence, a relevant function or activity should be performed improperly (whether by R or another person).

(3)   Case 4 is where—
  (a)   R requests, agrees to receive or accepts a financial or other advantage, and
  (b)   the request, agreement or acceptance itself constitutes the improper performance by R of a relevant function or activity.

(4)   Case 5 is where R requests, agrees to receive or accepts a financial or other advantage as a reward for the improper performance (whether by R or another person) of a relevant function or activity.

(5)   Case 6 is where, in anticipation of or in consequence of R requesting, agreeing to receive or accepting a financial or other advantage, a relevant function or activity is performed improperly—
  (a)   by R, or
  (b)   by another person at R's request or with R's assent or acquiescence.

(6)   In cases 3 to 6 it does not matter—
  (a)   whether R requests, agrees to receive or accepts (or is to request, agree to receive or accept) the advantage directly or through a third party,
  (b)   whether the advantage is (or is to be) for the benefit of R or another person.

(7)   In cases 4 to 6 it does not matter whether R knows or believes that the performance of the function or activity is improper.

(8)   In case 6, where a person other than R is performing the function or activity, it also does not matter whether that person knows or believes that the performance of the function or activity is improper.

[2206]

NOTES
Commencement: to be appointed.

3   Function or activity to which bribe relates

(1)   For the purposes of this Act a function or activity is a relevant function or activity if—
  (a)   it falls within subsection (2), and
  (b)   meets one or more of conditions A to C.

(2)   The following functions and activities fall within this subsection—
  (a)   any function of a public nature,
  (b)   any activity connected with a business,
  (c)   any activity performed in the course of a person's employment,
  (d)   any activity performed by or on behalf of a body of persons (whether corporate or unincorporate).

(3)   Condition A is that a person performing the function or activity is expected to perform it in good faith.

(4)   Condition B is that a person performing the function or activity is expected to perform it impartially.

(5)   Condition C is that a person performing the function or activity is in a position of trust by virtue of performing it.

(6)   A function or activity is a relevant function or activity even if it—
  (a)   has no connection with the United Kingdom, and
  (b)   is performed in a country or territory outside the United Kingdom.

(7)   In this section "business" includes trade or profession.

[2207]

NOTES
Commencement: to be appointed.

4 Improper performance to which bribe relates

(1) For the purposes of this Act a relevant function or activity—
    (a) is performed improperly if it is performed in breach of a relevant expectation, and
    (b) is to be treated as being performed improperly if there is a failure to perform the function or activity and that failure is itself a breach of a relevant expectation.

(2) In subsection (1) "relevant expectation"—
    (a) in relation to a function or activity which meets condition A or B, means the expectation mentioned in the condition concerned, and
    (b) in relation to a function or activity which meets condition C, means any expectation as to the manner in which, or the reasons for which, the function or activity will be performed that arises from the position of trust mentioned in that condition.

(3) Anything that a person does (or omits to do) arising from or in connection with that person's past performance of a relevant function or activity is to be treated for the purposes of this Act as being done (or omitted) by that person in the performance of that function or activity.

[2208]

NOTES
Commencement: to be appointed.

5 Expectation test

(1) For the purposes of sections 3 and 4, the test of what is expected is a test of what a reasonable person in the United Kingdom would expect in relation to the performance of the type of function or activity concerned.

(2) In deciding what such a person would expect in relation to the performance of a function or activity where the performance is not subject to the law of any part of the United Kingdom, any local custom or practice is to be disregarded unless it is permitted or required by the written law applicable to the country or territory concerned.

(3) In subsection (2) "written law" means law contained in—
    (a) any written constitution, or provision made by or under legislation, applicable to the country or territory concerned, or
    (b) any judicial decision which is so applicable and is evidenced in published written sources.

[2209]

NOTES
Commencement: to be appointed.

Bribery of foreign public officials

6 Bribery of foreign public officials

(1) A person ("P") who bribes a foreign public official ("F") is guilty of an offence if P's intention is to influence F in F's capacity as a foreign public official.

(2) P must also intend to obtain or retain—
    (a) business, or
    (b) an advantage in the conduct of business.

(3) P bribes F if, and only if—
    (a) directly or through a third party, P offers, promises or gives any financial or other advantage—
        (i) to F, or
        (ii) to another person at F's request or with F's assent or acquiescence, and
    (b) F is neither permitted nor required by the written law applicable to F to be influenced in F's capacity as a foreign public official by the offer, promise or gift.

(4) References in this section to influencing F in F's capacity as a foreign public official mean influencing F in the performance of F's functions as such an official, which includes—
    (a) any omission to exercise those functions, and
    (b) any use of F's position as such an official, even if not within F's authority.

(5) "Foreign public official" means an individual who—
    (a) holds a legislative, administrative or judicial position of any kind, whether appointed or elected, of a country or territory outside the United Kingdom (or any subdivision of such a country or territory),
    (b) exercises a public function—
        (i) for or on behalf of a country or territory outside the United Kingdom (or any subdivision of such a country or territory), or

      (ii)   for any public agency or public enterprise of that country or territory (or subdivision), or

(c)   is an official or agent of a public international organisation.

(6) "Public international organisation" means an organisation whose members are any of the following—

    (a)   countries or territories,
    (b)   governments of countries or territories,
    (c)   other public international organisations,
    (d)   a mixture of any of the above.

(7) For the purposes of subsection (3)(b), the written law applicable to F is—

    (a)   where the performance of the functions of F which P intends to influence would be subject to the law of any part of the United Kingdom, the law of that part of the United Kingdom,
    (b)   where paragraph (a) does not apply and F is an official or agent of a public international organisation, the applicable written rules of that organisation,
    (c)   where paragraphs (a) and (b) do not apply, the law of the country or territory in relation to which F is a foreign public official so far as that law is contained in—
        (i)   any written constitution, or provision made by or under legislation, applicable to the country or territory concerned, or
        (ii)   any judicial decision which is so applicable and is evidenced in published written sources.

(8) For the purposes of this section, a trade or profession is a business.

                                                        [2210]

NOTES
Commencement: to be appointed.

Failure of commercial organisations to prevent bribery

7   Failure of commercial organisations to prevent bribery

(1) A relevant commercial organisation ("C") is guilty of an offence under this section if a person ("A") associated with C bribes another person intending—

    (a)   to obtain or retain business for C, or
    (b)   to obtain or retain an advantage in the conduct of business for C.

(2) But it is a defence for C to prove that C had in place adequate procedures designed to prevent persons associated with C from undertaking such conduct.

(3) For the purposes of this section, A bribes another person if, and only if, A—

    (a)   is, or would be, guilty of an offence under section 1 or 6 (whether or not A has been prosecuted for such an offence), or
    (b)   would be guilty of such an offence if section 12(2)(c) and (4) were omitted.

(4) See section 8 for the meaning of a person associated with C and see section 9 for a duty on the Secretary of State to publish guidance.

(5) In this section—

"partnership" means—

    (a)   a partnership within the Partnership Act 1890, or
    (b)   a limited partnership registered under the Limited Partnerships Act 1907,
    or a firm or entity of a similar character formed under the law of a country or territory outside the United Kingdom,

"relevant commercial organisation" means—

    (a)   a body which is incorporated under the law of any part of the United Kingdom and which carries on a business (whether there or elsewhere),
    (b)   any other body corporate (wherever incorporated) which carries on a business, or part of a business, in any part of the United Kingdom,
    (c)   a partnership which is formed under the law of any part of the United Kingdom and which carries on a business (whether there or elsewhere), or
    (d)   any other partnership (wherever formed) which carries on a business, or part of a business, in any part of the United Kingdom,

and, for the purposes of this section, a trade or profession is a business.

                                                         [2211]

NOTES
Commencement: to be appointed.

8 Meaning of associated person

(1) For the purposes of section 7, a person ("A") is associated with C if (disregarding any bribe under consideration) A is a person who performs services for or on behalf of C.

(2) The capacity in which A performs services for or on behalf of C does not matter.

(3) Accordingly A may (for example) be C's employee, agent or subsidiary.

(4) Whether or not A is a person who performs services for or on behalf of C is to be determined by reference to all the relevant circumstances and not merely by reference to the nature of the relationship between A and C.

(5) But if A is an employee of C, it is to be presumed unless the contrary is shown that A is a person who performs services for or on behalf of C.

[2212]

NOTES
Commencement: to be appointed.

9 Guidance about commercial organisations preventing bribery

(1) The Secretary of State must publish guidance about procedures that relevant commercial organisations can put in place to prevent persons associated with them from bribing as mentioned in section 7(1).

(2) The Secretary of State may, from time to time, publish revisions to guidance under this section or revised guidance.

(3) The Secretary of State must consult the Scottish Ministers before publishing anything under this section.

(4) Publication under this section is to be in such manner as the Secretary of State considers appropriate.

(5) Expressions used in this section have the same meaning as in section 7.

[2213]

NOTES
Commencement: to be appointed.

Prosecution and penalties

10 Consent to prosecution

(1) No proceedings for an offence under this Act may be instituted in England and Wales except by or with the consent of—
    (a) the Director of Public Prosecutions,
    (b) the Director of the Serious Fraud Office, or
    (c) the Director of Revenue and Customs Prosecutions.

(2) No proceedings for an offence under this Act may be instituted in Northern Ireland except by or with the consent of—
    (a) the Director of Public Prosecutions for Northern Ireland, or
    (b) the Director of the Serious Fraud Office.

(3) No proceedings for an offence under this Act may be instituted in England and Wales or Northern Ireland by a person—
    (a) who is acting—
        (i) under the direction or instruction of the Director of Public Prosecutions, the Director of the Serious Fraud Office or the Director of Revenue and Customs Prosecutions, or
        (ii) on behalf of such a Director, or
    (b) to whom such a function has been assigned by such a Director,
except with the consent of the Director concerned to the institution of the proceedings.

(4) The Director of Public Prosecutions, the Director of the Serious Fraud Office and the Director of Revenue and Customs Prosecutions must exercise personally any function under subsection (1), (2) or (3) of giving consent.

(5) The only exception is if—
    (a) the Director concerned is unavailable, and
    (b) there is another person who is designated in writing by the Director acting personally as the person who is authorised to exercise any such function when the Director is unavailable.

(6) In that case, the other person may exercise the function but must do so personally.

(7)   Subsections (4) to (6) apply instead of any other provisions which would otherwise have enabled any function of the Director of Public Prosecutions, the Director of the Serious Fraud Office or the Director of Revenue and Customs Prosecutions under subsection (1), (2) or (3) of giving consent to be exercised by a person other than the Director concerned.

(8)   No proceedings for an offence under this Act may be instituted in Northern Ireland by virtue of section 36 of the Justice (Northern Ireland) Act 2002 (delegation of the functions of the Director of Public Prosecutions for Northern Ireland to persons other than the Deputy Director) except with the consent of the Director of Public Prosecutions for Northern Ireland to the institution of the proceedings.

(9)   The Director of Public Prosecutions for Northern Ireland must exercise personally any function under subsection (2) or (8) of giving consent unless the function is exercised personally by the Deputy Director of Public Prosecutions for Northern Ireland by virtue of section 30(4) or (7) of the Act of 2002 (powers of Deputy Director to exercise functions of Director).

(10)   Subsection (9) applies instead of section 36 of the Act of 2002 in relation to the functions of the Director of Public Prosecutions for Northern Ireland and the Deputy Director of Public Prosecutions for Northern Ireland under, or (as the case may be) by virtue of, subsections (2) and (8) above of giving consent.

[2214]

NOTES
Commencement: to be appointed.

11   Penalties

(1)   An individual guilty of an offence under section 1, 2 or 6 is liable—
    (a)   on summary conviction, to imprisonment for a term not exceeding 12 months, or to a fine not exceeding the statutory maximum, or to both,
    (b)   on conviction on indictment, to imprisonment for a term not exceeding 10 years, or to a fine, or to both.

(2)   Any other person guilty of an offence under section 1, 2 or 6 is liable—
    (a)   on summary conviction, to a fine not exceeding the statutory maximum,
    (b)   on conviction on indictment, to a fine.

(3)   A person guilty of an offence under section 7 is liable on conviction on indictment to a fine.

(4)   The reference in subsection (1)(a) to 12 months is to be read—
    (a)   in its application to England and Wales in relation to an offence committed before the commencement of section 154(1) of the Criminal Justice Act 2003, and
    (b)   in its application to Northern Ireland,
as a reference to 6 months.

[2215]

NOTES
Commencement: to be appointed.

Other provisions about offences

12   Offences under this Act: territorial application

(1)   An offence is committed under section 1, 2 or 6 in England and Wales, Scotland or Northern Ireland if any act or omission which forms part of the offence takes place in that part of the United Kingdom.

(2)   Subsection (3) applies if—
    (a)   no act or omission which forms part of an offence under section 1, 2 or 6 takes place in the United Kingdom,
    (b)   a person's acts or omissions done or made outside the United Kingdom would form part of such an offence if done or made in the United Kingdom, and
    (c)   that person has a close connection with the United Kingdom.

(3)   In such a case—
    (a)   the acts or omissions form part of the offence referred to in subsection (2)(a), and
    (b)   proceedings for the offence may be taken at any place in the United Kingdom.

(4)   For the purposes of subsection (2)(c) a person has a close connection with the United Kingdom if, and only if, the person was one of the following at the time the acts or omissions concerned were done or made—
    (a)   a British citizen,
    (b)   a British overseas territories citizen,
    (c)   a British National (Overseas),
    (d)   a British Overseas citizen,

(e)   a person who under the British Nationality Act 1981 was a British subject,

(f)   a British protected person within the meaning of that Act,

(g)   an individual ordinarily resident in the United Kingdom,

(h)   a body incorporated under the law of any part of the United Kingdom,

(i)   a Scottish partnership.

(5)   An offence is committed under section 7 irrespective of whether the acts or omissions which form part of the offence take place in the United Kingdom or elsewhere.

(6)   Where no act or omission which forms part of an offence under section 7 takes place in the United Kingdom, proceedings for the offence may be taken at any place in the United Kingdom.

(7)   Subsection (8) applies if, by virtue of this section, proceedings for an offence are to be taken in Scotland against a person.

(8)   Such proceedings may be taken—

(a)   in any sheriff court district in which the person is apprehended or in custody, or

(b)   in such sheriff court district as the Lord Advocate may determine.

(9)   In subsection (8) "sheriff court district" is to be read in accordance with section 307(1) of the Criminal Procedure (Scotland) Act 1995.

[2216]

NOTES

Commencement: to be appointed.

13   Defence for certain bribery offences etc

(1)   It is a defence for a person charged with a relevant bribery offence to prove that the person's conduct was necessary for—

(a)   the proper exercise of any function of an intelligence service, or

(b)   the proper exercise of any function of the armed forces when engaged on active service.

(2)   The head of each intelligence service must ensure that the service has in place arrangements designed to ensure that any conduct of a member of the service which would otherwise be a relevant bribery offence is necessary for a purpose falling within subsection (1)(a).

(3)   The Defence Council must ensure that the armed forces have in place arrangements designed to ensure that any conduct of—

(a)   a member of the armed forces who is engaged on active service, or

(b)   a civilian subject to service discipline when working in support of any person falling within paragraph (a),

which would otherwise be a relevant bribery offence is necessary for a purpose falling within subsection (1)(b).

(4)   The arrangements which are in place by virtue of subsection (2) or (3) must be arrangements which the Secretary of State considers to be satisfactory.

(5)   For the purposes of this section, the circumstances in which a person's conduct is necessary for a purpose falling within subsection (1)(a) or (b) are to be treated as including any circumstances in which the person's conduct—

(a)   would otherwise be an offence under section 2, and

(b)   involves conduct by another person which, but for subsection (1)(a) or (b), would be an offence under section 1.

(6)   In this section—

"active service" means service in—

(a)   an action or operation against an enemy,

(b)   an operation outside the British Islands for the protection of life or property, or

(c)   the military occupation of a foreign country or territory,

"armed forces" means Her Majesty's forces (within the meaning of the Armed Forces Act 2006),

"civilian subject to service discipline" and "enemy" have the same meaning as in the Act of 2006,

"GCHQ" has the meaning given by section 3(3) of the Intelligence Services Act 1994,

"head" means—

(a)   in relation to the Security Service, the Director General of the Security Service,

(b)   in relation to the Secret Intelligence Service, the Chief of the Secret Intelligence Service, and

(c)   in relation to GCHQ, the Director of GCHQ,

"intelligence service" means the Security Service, the Secret Intelligence Service or GCHQ,

"relevant bribery offence" means—

(a)   an offence under section 1 which would not also be an offence under section 6,

(b)   an offence under section 2,

(c)   an offence committed by aiding, abetting, counselling or procuring the commission of an offence falling within paragraph (a) or (b),

(d)   an offence of attempting or conspiring to commit, or of inciting the commission of, an offence falling within paragraph (a) or (b), or

(e)   an offence under Part 2 of the Serious Crime Act 2007 (encouraging or assisting crime) in relation to an offence falling within paragraph (a) or (b).

[2217]

NOTES
Commencement: to be appointed.

14   Offences under sections 1, 2 and 6 by bodies corporate etc

(1)   This section applies if an offence under section 1, 2 or 6 is committed by a body corporate or a Scottish partnership.

(2)   If the offence is proved to have been committed with the consent or connivance of—
   (a)   a senior officer of the body corporate or Scottish partnership, or
   (b)   a person purporting to act in such a capacity,

the senior officer or person (as well as the body corporate or partnership) is guilty of the offence and liable to be proceeded against and punished accordingly.

(3)   But subsection (2) does not apply, in the case of an offence which is committed under section 1, 2 or 6 by virtue of section 12(2) to (4), to a senior officer or person purporting to act in such a capacity unless the senior officer or person has a close connection with the United Kingdom (within the meaning given by section 12(4)).

(4)   In this section—
   "director", in relation to a body corporate whose affairs are managed by its members, means a member of the body corporate,
   "senior officer" means—
      (a)   in relation to a body corporate, a director, manager, secretary or other similar officer of the body corporate, and
      (b)   in relation to a Scottish partnership, a partner in the partnership.

[2218]

NOTES
Commencement: to be appointed.

15   Offences under section 7 by partnerships

(1)   Proceedings for an offence under section 7 alleged to have been committed by a partnership must be brought in the name of the partnership (and not in that of any of the partners).

(2)   For the purposes of such proceedings—
   (a)   rules of court relating to the service of documents have effect as if the partnership were a body corporate, and
   (b)   the following provisions apply as they apply in relation to a body corporate—
      (i)   section 33 of the Criminal Justice Act 1925 and Schedule 3 to the Magistrates' Courts Act 1980,
      (ii)   section 18 of the Criminal Justice Act (Northern Ireland) 1945 (c 15 (NI)) and Schedule 4 to the Magistrates' Courts (Northern Ireland) Order 1981 (SI 1981/1675 (NI 26)),
      (iii)   section 70 of the Criminal Procedure (Scotland) Act 1995.

(3)   A fine imposed on the partnership on its conviction for an offence under section 7 is to be paid out of the partnership assets.

(4)   In this section "partnership" has the same meaning as in section 7.

[2219]

NOTES
Commencement: to be appointed.

Supplementary and final provisions

16   Application to Crown

This Act applies to individuals in the public service of the Crown as it applies to other individuals.

[2220]

NOTES
Commencement: 8 April 2010.

17 Consequential provision

(1) The following common law offences are abolished—
  (a) the offences under the law of England and Wales and Northern Ireland of bribery and embracery,
  (b) the offences under the law of Scotland of bribery and accepting a bribe.

(2) Schedule 1 (which contains consequential amendments) has effect.

(3) Schedule 2 (which contains repeals and revocations) has effect.

(4) The relevant national authority may by order make such supplementary, incidental or consequential provision as the relevant national authority considers appropriate for the purposes of this Act or in consequence of this Act.

(5) The power to make an order under this section—
  (a) is exercisable by statutory instrument,
  (b) includes power to make transitional, transitory or saving provision,
  (c) may, in particular, be exercised by amending, repealing, revoking or otherwise modifying any provision made by or under an enactment (including any Act passed in the same Session as this Act).

(6) Subject to subsection (7), a statutory instrument containing an order of the Secretary of State under this section may not be made unless a draft of the instrument has been laid before, and approved by a resolution of, each House of Parliament.

(7) A statutory instrument containing an order of the Secretary of State under this section which does not amend or repeal a provision of a public general Act or of devolved legislation is subject to annulment in pursuance of a resolution of either House of Parliament.

(8) Subject to subsection (9), a statutory instrument containing an order of the Scottish Ministers under this section may not be made unless a draft of the instrument has been laid before, and approved by a resolution of, the Scottish Parliament.

(9) A statutory instrument containing an order of the Scottish Ministers under this section which does not amend or repeal a provision of an Act of the Scottish Parliament or of a public general Act is subject to annulment in pursuance of a resolution of the Scottish Parliament.

(10) In this section—
  "devolved legislation" means an Act of the Scottish Parliament, a Measure of the National Assembly for Wales or an Act of the Northern Ireland Assembly,
  "enactment" includes an Act of the Scottish Parliament and Northern Ireland legislation,
  "relevant national authority" means—
  (a) in the case of provision which would be within the legislative competence of the Scottish Parliament if it were contained in an Act of that Parliament, the Scottish Ministers, and
  (b) in any other case, the Secretary of State.

[2221]

NOTES
Commencement: 8 April 2010 (sub-ss (4)–(10)); to be appointed (sub-ss (1)–(3)).

18 Extent

(1) Subject as follows, this Act extends to England and Wales, Scotland and Northern Ireland.

(2) Subject to subsections (3) to (5), any amendment, repeal or revocation made by Schedule 1 or 2 has the same extent as the provision amended, repealed or revoked.

(3) The amendment of, and repeals in, the Armed Forces Act 2006 do not extend to the Channel Islands.

(4) The amendments of the International Criminal Court Act 2001 extend to England and Wales and Northern Ireland only.

(5) Subsection (2) does not apply to the repeal in the Civil Aviation Act 1982.

[2222]

NOTES
Commencement: 8 April 2010.

19 Commencement and transitional provision etc

(1) Subject to subsection (2), this Act comes into force on such day as the Secretary of State may by order made by statutory instrument appoint.

(2) Sections 16, 17(4) to (10) and 18, this section (other than subsections (5) to (7)) and section 20 come into force on the day on which this Act is passed.

(3)   An order under subsection (1) may—
  (a)   appoint different days for different purposes,
  (b)   make such transitional, transitory or saving provision as the Secretary of State considers appropriate in connection with the coming into force of any provision of this Act.

(4)   The Secretary of State must consult the Scottish Ministers before making an order under this section in connection with any provision of this Act which would be within the legislative competence of the Scottish Parliament if it were contained in an Act of that Parliament.

(5)   This Act does not affect any liability, investigation, legal proceeding or penalty for or in respect of—
  (a)   a common law offence mentioned in subsection (1) of section 17 which is committed wholly or partly before the coming into force of that subsection in relation to such an offence, or
  (b)   an offence under the Public Bodies Corrupt Practices Act 1889 or the Prevention of Corruption Act 1906 committed wholly or partly before the coming into force of the repeal of the Act by Schedule 2 to this Act.

(6)   For the purposes of subsection (5) an offence is partly committed before a particular time if any act or omission which forms part of the offence takes place before that time.

(7)   Subsections (5) and (6) are without prejudice to section 16 of the Interpretation Act 1978 (general savings on repeal).

[2223]

NOTES
Commencement: 8 April 2010 (sub-ss (1)–(4)); to be appointed (sub-ss (5)–(7)).

20   Short title
This Act may be cited as the Bribery Act 2010.

[2224]–[3009]

NOTES
Commencement: 8 April 2010.

(Schs 1, 2 contain amendments, repeals and revocations outside the scope of this work.)

PART 2
STATUTORY INSTRUMENTS

CONSUMER CREDIT (TOTAL CHARGE FOR CREDIT) REGULATIONS 1980

(SI 1980/51)

NOTES
Made: 17 January 1980.
Authority: Consumer Credit Act 1974, ss 20, 182(2).
Commencement: 28 April 1980.

ARRANGEMENT OF REGULATIONS

PART I
GENERAL

PART II
TOTAL CHARGE FOR CREDIT

PART III
RATE OF TOTAL CHARGE FOR CREDIT

PART IV
ASSUMPTIONS FOR CALCULATIONS

PART I
GENERAL

1   Citation, commencement, interpretation and revocation

(1)   These Regulations may be cited as the Consumer Credit (Total Charge for Credit) Regulations 1980 and shall come into operation on 28th April 1980.

(2)   In these Regulations—

"the Act" means the Consumer Credit Act 1974;

"agreement" means a consumer credit agreement;

["land-related agreement" means an agreement which is—
 (a)   intended primarily to finance the acquisition or retention of land, or
 (b)   intended to finance the renovation or improvement of a building,
 or any other agreement secured by a mortgage on land or, in Scotland, by a standard security within the meaning of the Conveyancing and Feudal Reform (Scotland) Act 1970;]

["period rate of charge" means a percentage rate of charge for a period, comprising all charges included in the total charge for credit determined in accordance with Part II of these Regulations;]

"the relevant date" means, in a case where a date is specified in or determinable under an agreement at the date of its making as that on which the debtor is entitled to require provision of anything the subject of the agreement, the earliest such date and, in any other case, the date of the making of the agreement; and

"transaction", except in regulation 5(1)(c) below, means an agreement, any transaction which is a linked transaction by virtue of section 19(1)(a) of the Act, any contract for the provision

PART 2
STATUTORY INSTRUMENTS

of security relating to the agreement[, any credit brokerage contract relating to the agreement] and any other contract to which the debtor or a relative of his is a party and which the creditor requires to be made or maintained as a condition of the making of the agreement,

and, except where the contrary intention appears, other expressions used in these Regulations have the same respective meanings as in the Act.

(3)　For the purposes of these Regulations, references to the period for which credit is provided,—

(a)　in the case of an agreement under which the period for which credit is to be provided is ascertainable at the date of the making of the agreement, are references to the period beginning with the relevant date and ending with the end of the period for which credit is to be provided;

(b)　in the case of an agreement under which the period for which credit is to be provided can be ascertained at the relevant date if the assumption set out in regulation 13 below is applied, are references to the period beginning with the relevant date and ending with the end of the period for which credit would be provided under the agreement if the amount given by that assumption were the amount of the credit so provided; and

(c)　in any other case, are references to the period of one year referred to in regulation 14 below.

(4)　References in these Regulations to repayment of the credit under an agreement and of the total charge for credit include references to any repayment or payment, as the case may require, of any part of the credit and of the total charge for credit.

(5)　...

[3010]

NOTES

Para (2): definition "land-related agreement" inserted, and definition "period rate of charge" substituted, by the Consumer Credit (Total Charge for Credit, Agreements and Advertisements) (Amendment) Regulations 1999, SI 1999/3177, reg 3(a); in definition "transaction" words in square brackets inserted by the Consumer Credit (Total Charge for Credit and Rebate on Early Settlement) (Amendment) Regulations 1989, SI 1989/596, reg 2(a).

Para (5): revokes the Consumer Credit (Total Charge for Credit) Regulations 1977, SI 1977/327.

[1A　Application

These Regulations apply to regulated consumer credit agreements which are secured on land or to prospective regulated consumer credit agreements which are to be secured on land except to the extent that the Consumer Credit (Disclosure of Information) Regulations 2010 apply to such agreements.]

[3010A]

NOTES

Commencement: 1 February 2011.

Inserted by the Consumer Credit (EU Directive) Regulations 2010, SI 2010/1010, reg 50, as from 1 February 2011, with effect in relation to certain agreements before that date, as provided for in regs 101, 101A of the 2010 Regulations at **[3942]**, **[3942A]**.

2　General provisions about calculation

(1)　Any calculation under these Regulations shall be made on the following assumptions—

(a)　the assumption that the debtor will not be entitled to any income tax relief relating to the transaction other than relief under section 19 of the Income and Corporation Taxes Act 1970 and Schedule 4 to the Finance Act 1976 (which afford relief in respect of premiums under certain policies of insurance) without any deduction under section 21 of the said Act of 1970;

(b)　the assumption that no assistance is given under the Home Purchase Assistance and Housing Corporation Guarantee Act 1978;

(c)

(i)　in the case of a transaction which provides for repayment of the credit or of the total charge for credit at or not later than a specified time or times, the assumption that the creditor will not exercise any right under the transaction to require repayment at any other time or times; and

(ii)　in any other case, the assumption that the creditor will not exercise any right under the transaction to require repayment;

the debtor, in any case, performing all his obligations under the transaction; ...

(d)　[subject to sub-paragraph (e) below,] in the case of a transaction which provides for variation of the rate or amount of any item included in the total charge for credit in consequence of the occurrence after the relevant date of any event, the assumption that the event will not occur; and, in this sub-paragraph, "event" means an act or omission of the debtor or of the creditor or any other event (including where the transaction makes provision for variation upon the continuation of any circumstance, the continuation of that circumstance) but does not include an event which is certain to occur and of which the date of occurrence, or the earliest date of occurrence, can be ascertained at the date of the making of the agreement[; and]

[(e)   in the case of a land-related agreement which provides for the possibility of any variation of the rate of interest in consequence of the occurrence after the relevant date of any event (being an event which is certain to occur and of which the date of occurrence, or the earliest date of occurrence, can be ascertained at the date of the making of the agreement), the assumption that such a variation will, when the event occurs, take place.]

(2)   For the purposes of these Regulations—

(a)   subject to sub-paragraph (b) below and regulation 18 below, in the case of any agreement each provision of credit and each repayment of the credit and of the total charge for credit shall be taken to be made:—

(i)   at the earliest time provided under the transaction, and

(ii)   in a case where any such provision or repayment is to be made at or not later than a specified time, at that time

and, where any such repayment is to be made before the relevant date, it shall be taken to be made on the relevant date;

(b)   where under an agreement for running-account credit or an agreement for fixed-sum credit where the credit is not repayable at specified intervals or in specified amounts a constant period rate of charge in respect of periods of equal or of nearly equal length is charged, it shall be assumed for the purposes of calculations under these Regulations, notwithstanding regulation 17 below, that—

(i)   the amount of credit outstanding at the beginning of a period is to remain outstanding throughout the period;

(ii)   the amount of any credit provided during a period is provided immediately after the end of the period; and

(iii)   any repayment of credit or of the total charge for credit made during a period is made immediately after the end of the period; and

(c)   the assumption that the amount of any repayment of credit or of the total charge for credit will, at the time when the repayment is made, be the smallest for which the agreement provides.

(3)   In determining the amount of the total of the interest on the credit which may be provided under the agreement, any subsidy receivable by any person under Part II of the Housing Subsidies Act 1967 shall be deducted.

[3011]

NOTES

Para (1): word omitted from sub-para (c) revoked, in sub-para (d) words in first pair of square brackets inserted, and word in second pair of square brackets substituted, and sub-para (e) added, by the Consumer Credit (Total Charge for Credit, Agreements and Advertisements) (Amendment) Regulations 1999, SI 1999/3177, reg 3(b)–(d).

PART II
TOTAL CHARGE FOR CREDIT

3 Total charge for credit

For the purposes of the Act, the total charge for the credit which may be provided under an actual or prospective agreement shall be the total of the amounts determined as at the date of the making of the agreement of such of the charges specified in regulation 4 below as apply in relation to the agreement but excluding the amount of the charges specified in regulation 5 below.

[3012]

4 Items included in total charge for credit

Except as provided in regulation 5 below, the amounts of the following charges are included in the total charge for credit in relation to an agreement:—

(a)   the total of the interest on the credit which may be provided under the agreement; ...

(b)   other charges at any time payable under the transaction by or on behalf of the debtor or a relative of his whether to the creditor or any other person[; and]

[(c)   a premium under a contract of insurance, payable under the transaction by the debtor or a relative of his, where the making or maintenance of the contract of insurance is required by the creditor—

(i)   as a condition of making the agreement, and

(ii)   for the sole purpose of ensuring complete or partial repayment of the credit, and complete or partial payment to the creditor of such of those charges included in the total charge for credit as are payable to him under the transaction, in the event of the death, invalidity, illness or unemployment of the debtor,]

notwithstanding that the whole or part of the charge may be repayable at any time or that the consideration therefor may include matters not within the transaction or subsisting at a time not within the duration of the agreement.

[3013]

NOTES
Word omitted from para (a) revoked, in para (b) word in square brackets substituted, and para (c) inserted, by the Consumer Credit (Total Charge for Credit, Agreements and Advertisements) (Amendment) Regulations 1999, SI 1999/3177, reg 3(e), (f).

5 Items excluded from total charge for credit

(1)   The amounts of the following items are not included in the total charge for credit in relation to an agreement:—

(a)   any charge payable under the transaction to the creditor upon failure by the debtor or a relative of his to do or to refrain from doing anything which he is required to do or to refrain from doing, as the case may be;

(b)   any charge—
   (i)   which is payable by the creditor to any person upon failure by the debtor or a relative of his to do or to refrain from doing anything which he is required under the transaction to do or to refrain from doing, as the case may be, and
   (ii)   which the creditor may under the transaction require the debtor or a relative of his to pay to him or to another person on his behalf;

(c)   any charge relating to an agreement which is an agreement to finance a transaction of a description referred to in paragraph (a) or (b) of section 11(1) of the Act, being a charge which would be payable if the transaction were for cash;

(d)   any charge [(other than a fee or commission charged by a credit-broker)] not within sub-paragraph (c) above—
   (i)   of a description which relates to services or benefits incidental to the agreement and also to other services or benefits which may be supplied to the debtor, and
   (ii)   which is payable pursuant to an obligation incurred by the debtor under arrangements effected before he applies to enter into the agreement, not being arrangements under which the debtor is bound to enter into any personal credit agreement;

(e)   subject to paragraph (2) below, any charge under arrangements for the care, maintenance or protection of any land or goods;

(f)   charges for money transmission services relating to an arrangement for a current account whereby the debtor may, by cheques or similar orders payable to himself or to any other person, obtain or have the use of money held or made available by the creditor and which records alterations in the financial relationship between the creditor and debtor, being charges which vary with the use made by the debtor of the arrangement.

[(g)   any charge for a guarantee other than a guarantee—
   (i)   which is required by the creditor as a condition of making the agreement, and
   (ii)   the purpose of which is to ensure complete or partial repayment of the credit, and complete or partial payment to the creditor of such of those charges included in the total charge for credit as are payable to him under the transaction, in the event of the death, invalidity, illness or unemployment of the debtor;

(h)   charges for the transfer of funds (other than charges within sub-paragraph (f) above) and charges for keeping an account intended to receive payments towards the repayment of the credit and the payment of interest and other charges, except where the debtor does not have reasonable freedom of choice in the matter and where such charges are abnormally high; but this sub-paragraph does not exclude from the total charge for credit charges for collection of the payments to which it refers, whether such payments are made in cash or otherwise;

(i)   a premium under a contract of insurance other than a contract of insurance referred to in regulation 4(c) above.]

(2)   Paragraph (1) above has effect only—

(a)   in the case of a charge within sub-paragraph (e), where, in pursuance of the arrangements—
   (i)   the services are to be performed if, after the date of the making of the agreement, the condition of the land or goods becomes or is in immediate danger of becoming such that the land or goods cannot reasonably be enjoyed or used, and
   (ii)   the charge will not accrue unless the services are performed; and

(b)   in the case of any other charge within sub-paragraph (e) … —
   (i)   where provision of substantially the same description as that to which the

arrangements ... relate is available under comparable arrangements from a person who is not the creditor or a supplier or a credit-broker who introduced the debtor and the creditor, and

(ii)   where the arrangements ... are made with a person chosen by the debtor, and

(iii)   if, in accordance with the transaction, the consent of the creditor or of a supplier or of the credit-broker who introduced the debtor and the creditor is required to the making of the arrangements ... , where the transaction provides that such consent may not be unreasonably withheld whether because no incidental benefit will or may accrue to the creditor or to the supplier or to the credit-broker or on any other ground;

and references in this paragraph to the creditor, a supplier and a credit-broker include references to his near relative, his partner and a member of a group of which he is a member, to any person nominated by him or any such person in relation to the arrangements ... , and to a near relative of his partner; and "near relative" means, in relation to any person, the husband, wife, father, mother, brother, sister, son or daughter of that person and "group" means the person (including a company) having control of a company together with all the companies directly or indirectly controlled by him.

[3014]

NOTES
Para (1): in sub-para (d) words in square brackets inserted by the Consumer Credit (Total Charge for Credit and Rebate on Early Settlement) (Amendment) Regulations 1989, SI 1989/596, reg 2(b); sub-paras (g)–(i) substituted, for original sub-paras (g)–(l), by the Consumer Credit (Total Charge for Credit, Agreements and Advertisements) (Amendment) Regulations 1999, SI 1999/3177, reg 3(g).
Para (2): words omitted revoked by SI 1999/3177, reg 3(h).

PART III
RATE OF TOTAL CHARGE FOR CREDIT

6   Rate of total charge for credit
The rate of the total charge for credit in the case of an actual or prospective agreement shall be the annual percentage rate of charge determined in accordance with the following provisions of this Part of these Regulations and [(where it has more than one decimal place) rounded to one decimal place in accordance with regulation 6A below].

[3015]

NOTES
Words in square brackets substituted by the Consumer Credit (Total Charge for Credit, Agreements and Advertisements) (Amendment) Regulations 1999, SI 1999/3177, reg 3(i).

[6A   The annual percentage rate of charge referred to in regulation 6 above shall be rounded to one decimal place as follows—

(a)   where the figure at the second decimal place is greater than or equal to 5, the figure at the first decimal place shall be increased by one and the decimal place (or places) following the first decimal place shall be disregarded; and

(b)   where the figure at the second decimal place is less than 5, that decimal place and any decimal places following it shall be disregarded.]

[3016]

NOTES
Inserted by the Consumer Credit (Total Charge for Credit, Agreements and Advertisements) (Amendment) Regulations 1999, SI 1999/3177, reg 3(j).

[7   Calculation where a period rate is charged

(1)   Subject to paragraph (4) below, the annual percentage rate of charge is the rate for i which satisfies the equation set out in paragraph (2) below, expressed as a percentage.

(2)   The equation referred to in paragraph (1) above is—

$$\sum_{K=1}^{K=m} \frac{A_K}{(1+i)^{tK}} = \sum_{K'=1}^{K'=m'} \frac{A'_{K'}}{(1+i)^{tK'}}$$

where

K is the number identifying a particular advance of credit;
K' is the number identifying a particular instalment;
A_K is the amount of advance K;
$A'_{K'}$ is the amount of instalment K';
$\sum$ represents the sum of all the terms indicated;

PART 2
STATUTORY INSTRUMENTS

m is the number of advances of credit;

m' is the total number of instalments;

'K is the interval, expressed in years, between the relevant date and the date of the second advance and those of any subsequent advances numbered three to m; and

'K'   is the interval, expressed in years, between the relevant date and the dates of instalments numbered one to m'.

(3)   In paragraph (2) above, references to instalments are references to any payment made by or on behalf of the debtor or a relative of his which comprises—

    (a)   a repayment of all or part of the credit under the agreement;

    (b)   a payment of all or part of the total charge for credit; or

    (c)   both a repayment of all or part of the credit and a payment of all or part of the total charge for credit.

(4)   Where more than one rate is given under paragraph (1) above, the annual percentage rate of charge is the positive rate nearest to zero or, if no positive rate is so given, the negative rate nearest to zero.]

[3017]

NOTES

Substituted, for original regs 7–9, by the Consumer Credit (Total Charge for Credit, Agreements and Advertisements) (Amendment) Regulations 1999, SI 1999/3177, reg 3(k).

---

10   (*Revoked by the Consumer Credit (Total Charge for Credit, Agreements and Advertisements) (Amendment) Regulations 1999, SI 1999/3177, reg 3(l).*)

11   Computation of time

(1)   This regulation has effect for determining the length of any period for the purposes of calculations under this Part of these Regulations.

(2)   A period which is not a whole number of calendar months or a whole number of weeks shall be counted in years and days.

(3)   Subject to paragraph (4) below, a period which is a whole number of calendar months or a whole number of weeks shall be counted in calendar months or in weeks, as the case may be.

(4)   Where a period is both a whole number of calendar months and a whole number of weeks and—

    (a)   one repayment only is to be made, the period shall be counted in calendar months, or

    (b)   more than one repayment is to be made,—

        (i)   if all such repayments are to be made at intervals from the relevant date of one or more weeks, the period shall be counted in weeks, and

        (ii)   in any other case, the period shall be counted in calendar months.

(5)   A period which is to be counted—

    (a)   in calendar months shall be taken to be of a length equal to the relevant number of twelfth parts of a year, and

    (b)   in weeks, shall be taken to be of a length equal to the relevant number of fifty-second parts of a year.

[(6)   A day may be taken to be either—

    (a)   one three hundred and sixty-fifth part of a year or, if it is a leap year, one three hundred and sixty-sixth part of a year; or

    (b)   1/365.25 of a year.]

(7)   Every day shall be taken to be a working day.

[3018]

NOTES

Para (6): substituted by the Consumer Credit (Total Charge for Credit, Agreements and Advertisements) (Amendment) Regulations 1999, SI 1999/3177, reg 3(m).

PART IV

ASSUMPTIONS FOR CALCULATIONS

12   Effect of Part IV

(1)   The provisions of this Part of these Regulations shall have effect as the case may require for the purpose of the calculation of the total charge for credit under Part II above and of the rate of such charge under Part III above in relation to any actual or prospective agreement in respect of matters necessary for the calculation which cannot be ascertained by the creditor at the date of the making of the agreement.

(2)   In a case where apart from this paragraph regulation 13 below and one or more other provisions of this Part would fall to be applied the said regulation 13 shall be applied first.

[3019]

13   Assumption about the amount of credit

Where the amount of the credit to be provided under the agreement cannot be ascertained at the date of the making of the agreement,—

(a)   in the case of an agreement for running-account credit under which there is a credit limit, that amount shall be taken to be such credit limit; and

(b)   in any other case, that amount shall be taken to be £100.

[3020]

14   Assumption about period for which credit is provided

Where the period for which credit is to be provided is not ascertainable at the date of the making of the agreement, it shall be assumed that credit is provided for one year beginning with the relevant date.

[3021]

15   Assumption about index-linked rates and amounts

[Subject to regulation 15A below,] where the rate or amount of any item included in the total charge for credit or the amount of any repayment of credit under a transaction falls to be ascertained thereunder by reference to the level of any index or other factor in accordance with any formula specified therein, the rate or amount, as the case may be, shall be taken to be the rate or amount so ascertained, the formula being applied as if the level of such index or other factor subsisting at the date of the making of the agreement were that subsisting at the date by reference to which the formula is to be applied.

[3022]

NOTES

Words in square brackets inserted by the Consumer Credit (Total Charge for Credit, Agreements and Advertisements) (Amendment) Regulations 1999, SI 1999/3177, reg 3(n).

[15A   Assumptions about variations of interest rates in land-related agreements

(1)   This regulation applies to any land-related agreement which provides for the possibility of any variation of the rate of interest if it is to be assumed, by virtue of regulation 2(1)(e) above, that the variation will take place but the amount of the variation cannot be ascertained at the date of the making of the agreement.

(2)   In this regulation—

"initial standard variable rate" means—

(a)   the standard variable rate of interest which would be applied by the creditor to the agreement on the date of the making of the agreement if the agreement provided for interest to be paid at the creditor's standard variable rate with effect from that date, or

(b)   if there is no such rate, the standard variable rate of interest applied by the creditor on the date of the making of the agreement in question to other land-related agreements or, where there is more than one such rate, the highest such rate,

taking no account (for the avoidance of doubt) of any discount or other reduction to which the debtor would or might be entitled; and

"varied rate" means any rate of interest charged when a variation of the rate of interest is to be assumed to take place by virtue of regulation 2(1)(e) above.

(3)   Where a land-related agreement provides a formula for calculating a varied rate by reference to a standard variable rate of interest applied by the creditor, or any other fluctuating rate of interest, but does not enable the varied rate to be ascertained at the date of the making of the agreement because it is not known on that date what the standard variable rate will be or (as the case may be) at what level the fluctuating rate will be fixed when the varied rate falls to be calculated, it shall be assumed that that rate or level will be the same as the initial standard variable rate.

(4)   Where a land-related agreement provides for the possibility of any variation in the rate of interest (other than a variation referred to in paragraph (3) above) which it is to be assumed, by virtue of regulation 2(1)(e) above, will take place but does not enable the amount of that variation to be ascertained at the date of the making of the agreement, it shall be assumed that the varied rate will be the same as the initial standard variable rate.]

[3023]

PART 2
STATUTORY INSTRUMENTS

NOTES
Inserted by the Consumer Credit (Total Charge for Credit, Agreements and Advertisements) (Amendment) Regulations 1999, SI 1999/3177, reg 3(n).

16 Assumption about changes in charges

Where—

(a) the period for which the credit or any part thereof is to be or may be provided cannot be ascertained at the date of the making of the agreement; and

(b) the rate or amount of any item included in the total charge for credit will change at a time provided in the transaction within one year beginning with the relevant date,

the rate or amount shall be taken to be the highest rate or amount at any time obtaining under the transaction in that year.

[3024]

17 Assumption about time of provision of credit

Where the earliest date on which credit is to be provided cannot be ascertained at the date of the making of the agreement, it shall be assumed that credit is provided on that date.

[3025]

18 Assumptions about time of payment of charges

In the case of any transaction it shall be assumed—

(a) that a charge payable at a time which cannot be ascertained at the date of the making of the agreement shall be payable on the relevant date or, where it may reasonably be expected that a debtor will not make payment on that date, on the earliest date at which it may reasonably be expected that he will make payment; or

(b) where more than one payment of a charge of the same description falls to be made at times which cannot be ascertained at the date of the making of the agreement, that the first such payment will be payable on the relevant date (or, where it may reasonably be expected that a debtor will not make payment on that date, at the earliest date on which it may reasonably be expected that he will make payment), that the last such payment will be payable at the end of the period for which credit is provided and that all other such payments (if any) will be payable at equal intervals between such times,

as the case may require.

[3026]

SUPPLY OF SERVICES (EXCLUSION OF IMPLIED TERMS) ORDER 1982

(SI 1982/1771)

NOTES
Made: 8 December 1982.
Authority: Supply of Goods and Services Act 1982, s 12(4).
Commencement: 4 July 1983.

1 This Order may be cited as the Supply of Services (Exclusion of Implied Terms) Order 1982 and shall come into operation on 4th July 1983.

[3027]

2 Section 13 of the Supply of Goods and Services Act 1982 (which provides that, in a contract for the supply of a service where the supplier is acting in the course of a business, there is an implied term that the supplier will carry out the service with reasonable care and skill) shall not apply to the following services:—

(1) the services of an advocate in court or before any tribunal, inquiry or arbitrator and in carrying out preliminary work directly affecting the conduct of the hearing;

(2) the services rendered to a company by a director of the company in his capacity as such.

[3028]

SUPPLY OF SERVICES (EXCLUSION OF IMPLIED TERMS) ORDER 1983

(SI 1983/902)

NOTES
Made: 24 June 1983.
Authority: Supply of Goods and Services Act 1982, s 12(4).
Commencement: 4 July 1983.

1 This Order may be cited as the Supply of Services (Exclusion of Implied Terms) Order 1983 and shall come into operation on 4th July 1983.

[3029]

2—(1) Section 13 of the Supply of Goods and Services Act 1982 (which provides that, in a contract for the supply of a service where the supplier is acting in the course of a business, there is an implied term that the supplier will carry out the service with reasonable care and skill) shall not apply to the following services:—

(a) the services rendered to a building society by a director of the society in his capacity as such;

(b) the services rendered to a society registered or deemed to be registered under the Industrial and Provident Societies Act 1965 or the Industrial and Provident Societies Act (Northern Ireland) 1969 by any member of the committee of management or other directing body of such a society in his capacity as such.

(2) In this Article, "building society" and "director" shall have the same meaning as in the Building Societies Act 1962 or the Building Societies Act (Northern Ireland) 1967.

[3030]

CONSUMER CREDIT (AGREEMENTS) REGULATIONS 1983

(SI 1983/1553)

NOTES
Made: 19 January 2004.
Authority: Consumer Credit Act 1974, ss 60, 61(1)(a), 105(9), 114(1), 127(3), 182(2), 189(1).
Commencement: 19 May 1985; see reg 1(1).

ARRANGEMENT OF REGULATIONS

1 Citation, commencement and interpretation

(1)   These Regulations may be cited as the Consumer Credit (Agreements) Regulations 1983 and shall come into operation on 19th May 1985.

(2)   In these Regulations, unless the context otherwise requires—

"the Act" means the Consumer Credit Act 1974;

"advance payment" includes any deposit and in relation to a regulated consumer credit agreement includes also any part-exchange allowance in respect of any goods agreed in antecedent negotiations to be taken by the creditor in part-exchange but does not include a repayment of credit or any insurance premium or any amount entering into the total charge for credit;

"the APR" means the annual percentage rate of charge for credit determined in accordance with the Total Charge for Credit Regulations and Schedule 7 to, these Regulations and, in the case of modifying agreements, Regulation 7 of, and Part I of Schedule 8 to, these Regulations;

"cancellable agreement" includes an agreement which is a modifying agreement treated under section 82(5) of the Act as a cancellable agreement;

"cash price" in relation to any goods, services, land or other things means the price or charge at which the goods, services, land or other things may be purchased by, or supplied to, the debtor for cash;

[...]

["contract of shortfall insurance" means anything in writing which contains or purports to contain some promise or assurance (however worded or presented) that if a sum payable under a contract of insurance against loss of or damage to goods is less than the amount necessary to defray—

    (a)   any amount of credit provided to finance the purchase of those goods; and

    (b)   any other amount included in the total charge for that credit,

    to the extent that these remain unpaid at the date of the loss or damage, a sum up to but not exceeding that shortfall will be paid;]

"earlier credit agreement" means an earlier agreement for the provision of credit;

"earlier hire agreement" means an earlier agreement for the bailment or the hiring of goods;

["guarantee of goods" means anything in writing which contains or purports to contain some promise or assurance (however worded or presented) that defects in goods will be made good by complete or partial replacement, or by repair, monetary compensation or otherwise;]

"hire payment" means any payment to be made by the hirer in relation to any period in consideration of the bailment or hiring to him of goods under a regulated consumer hire agreement;

"lettering" includes figures and symbols;

"modified agreement" means an earlier agreement as varied or supplemented by a modifying agreement, which is treated as—

    (a)   revoking the earlier agreement, and

    (b)   containing provisions reproducing the combined effect of the two agreements;

"the relevant date" shall be determined in accordance with the Total Charge for Credit Regulations and, in the case of modifying agreements, Regulation 7(7) below;

["the relevant date" means—

    (a)   where a date is specified in or determinable under an agreement at the date of its making as that on which the debtor is entitled to require the provision of anything under the agreement, the earliest such date, or

    (b)   where no such date is specified or determinable, the date of the making of the agreement;]

"total charge for credit" shall be determined in accordance with the Total Charge for Credit Regulations [and Schedule 7 to these Regulations] and, in the case of modifying agreements, Regulation 7 of, and Part I of Schedule 8 to, these Regulations; and

"the Total Charge for Credit Regulations" means the Consumer Credit (Total Charge for Credit) Regulations 1980.

["the Total Charge for Credit Regulations" means, unless the context otherwise requires—

    (a)   in relation to a regulated consumer credit agreement that is secured on land, the Consumer Credit (Total Charge for Credit) Regulations 1980,

    (b)   in relation to any other regulated consumer credit agreement, the Consumer Credit (Total Charge for Credit) Regulations 2010, and references in these regulations to regulation 6 of and the Schedule to the Total Charge for Credit Regulations are to be read, in the case of regulated consumer credit agreements that are secured on land, as references to Part 4 and regulation 7 respectively of the Total Charge for Credit Regulations 1980.]

[(2A) References in these Regulations to contracts of insurance must be read with—
    (a) section 22 of the Financial Services and Markets Act 2000;
    (b) any relevant order under that section; and
    (c) Schedule 2 to that Act.]

(3) In these Regulations, any reference to a repayment is a reference to—
    (a) a repayment of the whole or any part of the credit;
    (b) a payment of the whole or any part of the total charge for credit; or
    (c) a combination of such repayments and payments.

[3030A]

NOTES

Para (2): definition "contract of insurance" (omitted) inserted by the Consumer Credit (Agreements) (Amendment) Regulations 1984, SI 1984/1600, reg 2(a) and revoked by the Financial Services and Markets Act 2000 (Consequential Amendments and Repeals) Order 2001, SI 2001/3649, art 375(1); definition "contract of shortfall insurance" and words in square brackets in definition "total charge for credit" inserted by the Consumer Credit (Agreements) (Amendment) Regulations 2004, SI 2004/1482, regs 2, 3; definition "guarantee of goods" inserted by SI 1984/1600, reg 2(a); definitions "the relevant date" and "the Total Charge for Credit Regulations" in italics substituted by subsequent definitions in square brackets, by the Consumer Credit (EU Directive) Regulations 2010, SI 2010/1010, regs 51, 52 (as substituted by the Consumer Credit (Amendment) Regulations 2010, SI 2010/1969, regs 4, 12), as from 1 February 2011, with effect in relation to certain agreements before that date, as provided for in regs 101, 101A of SI 2010/1010 at **[3942]**, **[3942A]**.

Para (2A): inserted by SI 2001/3649, art 375(2).

[2 Form and content of regulated consumer credit agreements

(1) Subject to paragraphs (2) and (9) below, documents embodying regulated consumer credit agreements (other than modifying agreements) shall contain the information set out in Column 2 of Schedule 1 to these Regulations in so far as it relates to the type of agreement referred to in Column 1.

(2) Where any information about financial and related particulars set out in paragraphs 9 to 11 of Schedule 1 to these Regulations cannot be exactly ascertained by the creditor, estimated information based on the assumptions referred to in paragraph 10 of that Schedule, where applicable, and otherwise such assumptions as the creditor may reasonably make in all the circumstances of the case and a statement of the assumptions made shall be included in documents embodying regulated consumer credit agreements.

(3) Subject to paragraph (9) below, documents embodying regulated consumer credit agreements, other than agreements of the description specified in the Schedule to the Consumer Credit (Notices of Cancellation Rights) (Exemptions) Regulations 1983 in relation to which there are no charges forming part of the total charge for credit (in this regulation referred to as "exempted agreements"), shall contain statements of the protection and remedies available to debtors under the Act, in the Form numbered in Column 1 of Part 1 of Schedule 2 to these Regulations and set out in Column 3, in so far as they relate to the type of agreement referred to in Column 2.

(4) Subject to paragraphs (5) and (9) below, the information, statements of the protection and remedies, signature and separate boxes which this regulation requires documents embodying regulated consumer credit agreements to contain, shall be set out in the order given by paragraphs (a) to (f) below under, where applicable, the headings specified below—
    (a) the nature of the agreement as set out in paragraph 1 of Schedule 1 to these Regulations;
    (b) the parties to the agreement as set out in paragraph 2 of Schedule 1 to these Regulations;
    [(c) under the heading "Key Financial Information", the financial and related particulars set out in paragraphs 6 to 8B, 11 to 14 and 15 to 17 of Schedule 1 to these Regulations;]
    (d) under the heading "Other Financial Information", the financial and related particulars set out in paragraphs 3 to 5, 9, 10, 14A and 18 to 19A of Schedule 1 to these regulations;
    (e) under the heading "Key Information"—
        (i) the information set out in paragraphs 20 to 24 of Schedule 1 to these Regulations; and
        (ii) the statements of protection and remedies set out in Schedule 2 to these Regulations; and
    (f) the signature box and, where applicable, the separate box required by paragraph (7)(b) below;

and such information, statements of protection and remedies, signature and separate boxes shall be shown together as a whole and shall not be preceded by any information apart from trade names, logos or the reference number of the agreement or interspersed with any other information or wording apart from subtotals of total amounts and cross references to the terms of the agreement.

(5)   In the case of documents embodying restricted-use debtor-creditor-supplier agreements for fixed-sum credit to finance a transaction comprising the acquisition of goods, services, land or other things specified in the agreement or identified and agreed on at the time the agreement is made and relating to more than one description of goods, services, land or other things, the cash prices, and the total cash price, referred to in paragraph 4 of Schedule 1 to these Regulations may be shown in a schedule to such document together with each description of the goods, services, land or other things, provided that the total cash price and a reference to the schedule to such document are shown together with the information required by paragraph (4)(d) above.

(6)   The APR referred to in paragraphs 15 to 17 of Schedule 1 to these Regulations shall in documents embodying regulated consumer credit agreements, other than exempted agreements—

    (a)   be denoted as "APR" or "annual percentage rate" or "annual percentage rate of the total charge for credit; and

    (b)   where it is subject to change, be accompanied by the word "variable".

(7)   Documents embodying regulated consumer credit agreements other than exempted agreements shall, subject to paragraph (9) below, contain a signature box in the Form numbered in Column 1 of Part 1 of Schedule 5 to these Regulations and set out in Column 3 in so far as it relates to the type of agreement referred to in Column 2 and shall—

    (a)   if—

        (i)   the documents embody a principal agreement and subsidiary agreement to which paragraph (9) below applies; or

        (ii)   at the time of entering into the agreement the debtor is also purchasing an optional contract of insurance which will be financed by credit advanced under that agreement,

    contain a form of consent in the Form set out in Part III of Schedule 5 immediately below the signature box required by this paragraph; and

    (b)   if the agreement is one to which section 58(1) of the Act applies, is a cancellable agreement or is an agreement under which a person takes any article in pawn and under which the pawn-receipt is not separate from the document embodying the agreement, contain a separate box immediately above, below or adjacent to the signature box in which shall be included the appropriate statements specified in Forms 1 and 4 to 6 of Part 1, and in Part II, of Schedule 2.

(8)   Paragraph (9) applies to documents embodying a debtor-creditor-supplier agreement falling within section 12(a) of the Act or a debtor-creditor agreement (in this paragraph and paragraph (9) in either case referred to as "the principal agreement") and also embodying, or containing the option of, a debtor-creditor-supplier agreement falling within section 12(b) of the Act (in this paragraph and paragraph (9) referred to as "the subsidiary agreement") where the subsidiary agreement is to finance a premium under one or more of—

    (a)   a contract of insurance to provide a sum payable in the event of the death of a debtor or a debtor suffering one or more of the following:—

        (i)   accident;

        (ii)   sickness; and

        (iii)   unemployment,

    at any time before the credit under the principal agreement and the subsidiary agreement has been repaid, where the sum payable does not exceed the amount sufficient to defray the sums payable to the creditor in respect of that credit and of the total charge for credit and where the policy monies payable under the contract of insurance are to be used for a repayment under the principal agreement and the subsidiary agreement;

    (b)   a contract of shortfall insurance; and

    (c)   a contract of insurance in so far as it relates to the guarantee of goods.

(9)   Documents to which this paragraph applies may contain instead of the headings specified in paragraph 1 of Schedules 1 or 8 to these Regulations, statements of protection and remedies available to debtors under the Act and signature boxes that would otherwise apply—

    (a)   a heading and signature box in so far as they relate to the principal agreement;

    (b)   a statement in Form 14 of Part I of Schedule 2 to these Regulations; and

    (c)   other statements (other than in Form 16 of Part I of Schedule 2) of the protection and remedies available to debtors under the Act in so far as they relate to the principal agreement.

(10)   Documents embodying regulated consumer credit agreements shall embody any security provided in relation to the regulated agreement by the debtor.]

[3030B]

NOTES

Substituted by the Consumer Credit (Agreements) (Amendment) Regulations 2004, SI 2004/1482, regs 2, 4 (as amended by SI 2004/2619, reg 2(1), (2)).

3   Form and content of regulated consumer hire agreements

(1)   Subject to paragraph (2) below, documents embodying regulated consumer hire agreements (other than modifying agreements) shall contain the information set out in Column 2 of Schedule 3 to these Regulations in so far as it relates to the type of agreement referred to in Column 1.

(2)   Where any information about financial and related particulars set out in paragraphs 5 and 6 of Schedule 3 to these Regulations cannot be exactly ascertained by the owner, estimated information based on such assumptions as the owner may reasonably make in all the circumstances of the case and an indication of the assumptions made shall be included in documents embodying regulated consumer hire agreements.

(3)   Documents embodying regulated consumer hire agreements shall contain statements of the protection and remedies available to hirers under the Act, in the Form numbered in Column 1 of Schedule 4 to these Regulations and set out in Column 3, in so far as they relate to the type of agreement referred to in Column 2.

[(4)   Subject to paragraph (5) below the information, statements of the protection and remedies, signature and separate boxes which this regulation requires documents embodying regulated consumer hire agreements to contain, shall be set out in the order given by paragraphs (a) to (e) below under, where applicable, the headings specified below:—

    (a)   the nature of the agreement as set out in paragraph 1 of Schedule 3 to these Regulations;
    (b)   the parties to the agreement as set out in paragraph 2 of Schedule 3 to these Regulations;
    (c)   under the heading "Key Financial Information", the financial and related particulars set out in paragraphs 3 to 8 of Schedule 3 to these Regulations;
    (d)   under the heading "Key Information"—
        (i)   the information set out in paragraphs 9 to 11 of Schedule 3 to these Regulations; and
        (ii)   the statements of protection and remedies set out in Schedule 4 to these Regulations; and
    (e)   the signature box and, where applicable, the separate box required by paragraph (6) below,

and such information, statements of protection and remedies, signature and separate boxes shall be shown together as a whole and shall not be preceded by any information apart from trade names, logos or the reference number of the agreement or interspersed with any other information or wording apart from subtotals of total amounts and cross references to the terms of the agreement.]

(5)   In the case of documents embodying consumer hire agreements relating to more than one description of goods to be bailed or hired under the agreement, the list or other description of the goods referred to in paragraph 3 of Schedule 3 to these Regulations may be shown in a schedule to such document, provided that a reference to the schedule to such document is shown together with the remaining financial and related particulars specified in [paragraph (4)(c) above].

(6)   Documents embodying regulated consumer hire agreements shall contain a signature box in the Form numbered in Column 1 of Part II of Schedule 5 to these Regulations and set out in Column 3, so far as it relates to the type of agreement referred to in Column 2 and shall, if the agreement is one to which section 58(1) of the Act applies or is a cancellable agreement, contain a separate box immediately above, below or adjacent to the signature box in which shall be included the appropriate statements specified in [Forms 1, 4 and 5] of Schedule 4.

(7)   Documents embodying regulated consumer hire agreements shall embody any security provided in relation to the regulated agreement by the hirer.

[3030C]

NOTES
    Para (4): substituted by the Consumer Credit (Agreements) (Amendment) Regulations 2004, SI 2004/1482, regs 2, 5(1), (2).
    Para (5): in square brackets substituted by SI 2004/1482, regs 2, 5(1), (3).
    Para (6): in square brackets substituted by SI 2004/1482, regs 2, 5(1), (4) (as amended by SI 2004/2619, reg 2(1), (3)).

4   Pawn-receipts

Where a pawn-receipt is given under section 114(1) of the Act, by a person who takes any article in pawn under a regulated consumer credit agreement or a modifying agreement varying or supplementing an earlier credit agreement which is, or is treated under section 82(3) of the Act as, a regulated agreement, and where the pawn-receipt is not separate from any document embodying such an agreement, it shall—

    (a)   contain the information set out in paragraphs 1, 2 and 20 of Schedule 1 to these Regulations, or, in the case of a modifying agreement varying or supplementing an earlier credit agreement, in paragraphs 1, 2 and 20 of Part I of Schedule 8; and

(b)   contain a notice in the Form [numbered 18] in Column 1 of Part II of Schedule 2 to these
Regulations and set out in Column 3.

[3030D]

NOTES
Para (b): words in square brackets substituted by the Consumer Credit (Agreements) (Amendment)
Regulations 2004, SI 2004/1482, regs 2, 6.

5   Statutory Forms

(1)   The wording of any Form specified in Schedules 2, 4 and 5 to these Regulations shall be
reproduced in documents embodying regulated agreements without any alteration or addition,
except that—

(a)   the words "the creditor" or "the owner" may be replaced by the name of the creditor or
owner, by the expression by which the creditor or owner is referred to in the agreement
or by an appropriate pronoun, and any consequential changes to pronouns and verbs or
other consequential grammatical changes may be made;

(b)   the word "DEBTOR" may be replaced by "BORROWER" or "CUSTOMER" and the
word "Debtor(s)" may be replaced by "Borrower(s)" or "Customer(s)"; and

(c)   every Form shall be completed in accordance with any footnote.

(2)   Any such footnote shall not be treated as part of any Form specified in the said Schedules
and may be reproduced in addition to any such Form.

(3)   Where any such footnote requires any words to be omitted, those words shall be omitted or
deleted.

(4)   Where words are shown in capital letters in any Form specified in Schedule 2, 4 or 5 to
these Regulations, and are reproduced in documents embodying regulated agreements, they shall be
afforded more prominence (whether by capital letters, underlining, larger or bold print or otherwise)
than any other lettering in that Form except lettering inserted in accordance with paragraph (1)(c)
above and no less prominence than that given to any other information in the document apart from
the heading to the document, ... trade names, names of parties to the agreement or lettering in the
document inserted in handwriting.

[3030E]

NOTES
Para (4): words omitted revoked by the Consumer Credit (Agreements) (Amendment) Regulations 2004,
SI 2004/1482, regs 2, 7.

6   Signing of agreement

(1)   The terms specified in Column 2 of Schedule 6 to these Regulations in relation to the type
of regulated agreement referred to in Column 1 (and no other terms) are hereby prescribed for the
purposes of section 61(1)(a) of the Act (the terms which must be contained in a document if a
regulated agreement is not to be improperly executed) and of section 127(3) (the terms which must
be contained in a document before any enforcement order can be made under section 65(1), if
section 61(1)(a) was not complied with).

[(2)   The lettering of the terms of the agreement included in the document referred to in
section 61(1)(a) of the Act, containing all the prescribed terms of the regulated agreement, and of
the information contained in that document for the purpose of conforming to these Regulations
shall—

(a)   apart from any signature, be easily legible and, where applicable, be of a colour which is
readily distinguishable from the background medium upon which the information is
displayed; and

(b)   apart from that inserted in handwriting, be of equal prominence, except that headings,
trade names and names of parties to the agreement may be afforded more prominence
whether by capital letters, underlining, larger or bold print or otherwise.]

(3)   The signature of the said document shall be made in the following manner—

(a)   by the debtor or hirer, or by or on behalf of the debtor or hirer in the case of a
partnership or an unincorporated body of persons, in the space in the document indicated
for the purpose, and, subject to sub-paragraph (c) below, the date of the signature shall
be inserted in the space in the document indicated for the purpose;

(b)   by the creditor or owner, or by a person on his behalf, outside any signature box in
which the debtor or hirer may sign and, subject to sub-paragraph (c) below, the date of
the signature shall be inserted outside any such signature box;

(c)   in the case of a regulated agreement which is not a cancellable agreement, the date on
which the unexecuted agreement becomes an executed agreement may be inserted in the
document and in such a case any other date specified in paragraphs (a) and (b) above
need not be inserted; and

(d)   nothing in this Regulation shall prohibit the inclusion in the said document, near to any such signature, of the signature by any witness outside any signature box in which the debtor or hirer may sign.

(4)   In Scotland any provision in paragraph (3) above requiring the said document to be signed shall be complied with by a body corporate if the document is properly executed in accordance with the law of Scotland.

[(5)   Where an agreement is intended to be concluded by the use of an electronic communication nothing in this Regulation shall prohibit the inclusion in the signature box of information about the process or means of providing, communicating or verifying the signature to be made by the debtor or hirer.]

[3030F]

NOTES

Para (2): substituted by the Consumer Credit (Agreements) (Amendment) Regulations 2004, SI 2004/1482, regs 2, 8.

Para (5): inserted by the Consumer Credit Act 1974 (Electronic Communications) Order 2004, SI 2004/3236, art 4(1), (2)(b).

S 127(3): Repealed, subject to transitional provisions and savings, by the Consumer Credit Act 2006, ss 15, 69(1), 70, Sch 3, paras 1, 11(b), Sch 4.

7   Modifying agreements which are, or are treated as, regulated agreements

(1)   The provisions of these Regulations shall apply to modifying agreements which vary or supplement earlier credit agreements or earlier hire agreements and which are, or are treated under section 82(3) of the Act as, regulated agreements, subject as hereinafter mentioned.

(2)   Subject to paragraphs (3) and (12) below, documents embodying modifying agreements varying or supplementing earlier credit agreements shall contain the information set out in Column 2 of Part I of Schedule 8 to these Regulations in so far as it relates to the type of modifying agreement referred to in Column 1.

[(3)   Where any information about financial and related particulars set out in paragraphs 8 to 10 of Part 1 of Schedule 8 to these Regulations cannot be exactly ascertained by the creditor, estimated information based on the assumptions referred to in paragraph 9 of that Schedule, where applicable, and otherwise such assumptions as the creditor may reasonably make in all the circumstances of the case and a statement of the assumptions made shall be included in documents embodying modifying agreements varying or supplementing earlier credit agreements.]

[(4)   Subject to paragraph (5) below and regulation 2(9), the information, statements of the protection and remedies, signature and separate boxes which under these Regulations must be contained in documents embodying modifying agreements varying or supplementing earlier credit agreements in relation to the credit being provided under the modifying agreement, shall be set out in the order given by paragraphs (a) to (f) below under, where applicable, the headings specified below—

(a)   the nature of the agreement as set out in paragraph 1 of Part 1 of Schedule 8 to these Regulations;

(b)   parties to the agreement as set out in paragraph 2 of Part 1 of Schedule 8 to these Regulations;

(c)   under the heading "Key Financial Information", the financial and related particulars set out in paragraphs 5 to 7B, 10 to 13 and 14 to 17 of Part 1 of Schedule 8 to these Regulations;

(d)   under the heading "Other Financial Information", the financial and related particulars set out in paragraphs 3, 4, 8, 9, 13A and 18 to 19A of Part 1 of Schedule 8 to these Regulations;

(e)   under the heading "Key Information"—

     (i)   the information set out in paragraphs 20 to 24 of Part 1 of Schedule 8 to these Regulations; and

     (ii)   the statements of protection and remedies set out in Schedule 2 to these Regulations; and

(f)   the signature box and, where applicable, separate box required by regulation 2(7)(b),

and such information, statements of protection and remedies, signature and separate boxes shall be shown together as a whole and shall not be preceded by any information apart from trade names, logos or the reference number of the agreement or interspersed with any other information or wording apart from subtotals of total amounts and cross references to the terms of the agreement.]

(5)   In the case of documents embodying modifying agreements varying or supplementing earlier restricted-use debtor-creditor-supplier agreements for fixed-sum credit which were to finance a transaction comprising the acquisition of goods, services, land or other things specified in the earlier agreement or identified and agreed on at the time the earlier agreement was made and relating to more than one description of goods, services, land or other things, the cash prices, and the

total cash price, referred to in paragraph 3 of Part I of Schedule 8 to these Regulations may be shown in a schedule to such document together with each description of the goods, services, land or other things, provided that the total cash price and a reference to the schedule to such document are shown together with the [the information required by paragraph (4)(d) above].

(6)   The APR referred to in paragraphs 14 to 17 of Part I of Schedule 8 to these Regulations shall in documents embodying agreements varying or supplementing earlier credit agreements—

    (a)   be denoted as "APR" or "annual percentage rate" or "annual percentage rate of the total charge for credit"; and

    [(b) where it is subject to change, be accompanied by the word "variable"].

(7)   For the purposes of Part I of Schedule 8 to these Regulations, in calculating—

    (a)   the amount of repayments or of any capital outstanding under an earlier agreement;

    (b)   the total charge for credit (or any items included in it) in relation to the credit to be provided under the modified agreement; or

    (c)   the APR in relation to the modified agreement,

the relevant date shall be determined by reference to the date of the modifying agreement.

(8)   For the purposes of Part I of Schedule 8 to these Regulations, the total cash price under the modified agreement shall be taken to be the total of—

    (a)   the total amount of the capital outstanding under the earlier agreement on the relevant date within the meaning of paragraph 5 of Part I of Schedule 8; and

    (b)   the cash price in relation to each list or other description of any additional goods, services, land or other things the acquisition of which is to be financed by credit under the modifying agreement.

(9)   Subject to paragraphs (10), (12) and (15) below, documents embodying modifying agreements varying or supplementing earlier hire agreements shall contain the information set out in Column 2 of Part II of Schedule 8 to these Regulations in so far as it relates to the type of modifying agreement referred to in Column 1.

(10)   Where any information about financial and related particulars set out in paragraphs 5 and 6 of Part II of Schedule 8 to these Regulations cannot be exactly ascertained by the owner, estimated information based on such assumptions as the owner may reasonably make in all the circumstances of the case and an indication of the assumptions made shall be included in documents embodying modifying agreements varying or supplementing earlier hire agreements.

[(11)   The information, statements of the protection and remedies, signature and separate boxes which under these Regulations must be contained in documents embodying modifying agreements varying or supplementing earlier hire agreements in relation to the goods to be bailed or hired under the modifying agreement, shall be set out in the order given by paragraphs (a) to (e) below under, where applicable, the headings specified below—

    (a)   the nature of the agreement as set out in paragraph 1 of Part II of Schedule 8 to these Regulations;

    (b)   the parties to the agreement as set out in paragraph 2 of Part II of Schedule 8 to these Regulations;

    (c)   under the heading "Key Financial Information", the financial and related particulars set out in paragraphs 3 to 8 of Part II of Schedule 8 to these Regulations;

    (d)   under the heading "Key Information"—

        (i)   the information set out in paragraphs 9 to 11 of Part II of Schedule 8 to these Regulations; and

        (ii) the information set out in Schedule 4 to these Regulations; and

    (e)   the signature box and, where applicable, separate box required by regulation 3(6)

and such information, statements of protection and remedies, signature and separate boxes shall be shown together as a whole and shall not be preceded by any information apart from trade names, logos or the reference number of the agreement or interspersed with any other information or wording apart from subtotals of total amounts and cross references to the terms of the agreement.]

(12)   Where any information about financial and related particulars set out in paragraphs 3 to 19 of Schedule 1 to these Regulations and paragraphs 3 to 8 of Schedule 3 is contained in any document embodying an earlier agreement, nothing in the preceding provisions of this Regulation shall require the information to be contained in any document embodying a modifying agreement varying or supplementing an earlier agreement except as mentioned in Schedule 8 if the information is not varied or supplemented by the modifying agreement and the document contains a statement to this effect.

(13)   Documents embodying modifying agreements shall identify clearly the terms and financial and related particulars of earlier agreements varied or supplemented by modifying agreements.

(14)   In the application of Regulation 6(1) above and Schedule 6 to these Regulations to modifying agreements, which are, or are treated under section 82(3) of the Act as, regulated agreements—

(a) for any reference to the type of agreement referred to in Column 1 of Schedule 6 there shall be substituted a reference to modifying agreements which vary or supplement the type of agreement referred to in Column 1 of Schedule 6;

(b) any reference in Column 2 of Schedule 6 to an agreement, or a term, shall be a reference to a modified agreement, or a term of a modified agreement, as the case may be; and

(c) any term referred to in Column 2 of Schedule 6 in relation to the type of modifying agreement referred to in sub-paragraph (a) above shall not be a prescribed term for the purposes of sections 61(1)(a) and 127(3) of the Act, if the term was a term of the earlier agreement and has not been varied or supplemented by the modifying agreement.

(15) Where a modifying agreement varies or supplements an earlier hire agreement and the modified agreement is, or is treated as, a restricted-use debtor-creditor-supplier agreement, the provisions of this Regulation shall apply to any document embodying the modifying agreement as though it varied or supplemented an earlier restricted-use debtor-creditor-supplier agreement, except that its heading shall be "Agreement modifying a Hire Agreement and regulated by the Consumer Credit Act 1974".

[3030G]

NOTES

Para (3): substituted by the Consumer Credit (Agreements) (Amendment) Regulations 2004, SI 2004/1482, regs 2, 9(1), (2).

Para (4): substituted by SI 2004/1482, regs 2, 9(1), (3) (as amended by SI 2004/2619, reg 2(1), (4)).

Paras (5), (6): words in square brackets substituted by SI 2004/1482, regs 2, 9(1), (4), (5).

Para (11): substituted by SI 2004/1482, regs 2, 9(1), (6).

S 127(3) of the Act: Repealed, subject to transitional provisions and savings, by the Consumer Credit Act 2006, ss 15, 69(1), 70, Sch 3, paras 1, 11(b), Sch 4.

---

8   Application of Regulations

(1) Subject to *[paragraphs (2) and (4)]* [paragraphs (1A) to (2) and (4)] below, Regulations 1 to 3 and 5 to 7 shall apply to regulated agreements, and modifying agreements treated under section 82(3) of the Act as regulated agreements, made on or after 19th May 1985.

[(1A) Where an agreement is a regulated consumer credit agreement these Regulations apply where that agreement is—

(a) an agreement secured on land;

(b) an agreement under which the creditor provides the debtor with credit exceeding £60,260; or

(c) an agreement entered into by the debtor wholly or predominantly for the purposes of a business carried on, or intended to be carried on, by him.

except to the extent that the Consumer Credit (Agreements) Regulations 2010 apply to such agreements.

(1B) Subsections (2) to (5) of section 16B of the Act (declaration by the debtor as to the purposes of the agreement) apply for the purposes of paragraph (1A)(c)).]

(2) In the case of a modifying agreement of a type specified in paragraphs 3 to 19 of Part I and 3 to 8 of Part II of Schedule 8 to these Regulations made on or after 19th May 1985 which varies or supplements an earlier credit agreement or an earlier hire agreement made before that date, nothing in these Regulations shall require the information about financial and related particulars specified in those paragraphs to be contained in any document embodying the modifying agreement if no term of the earlier agreement relating to such financial and related particulars has been varied or supplemented by the modifying agreement.

(3) Nothing in these Regulations applies to a regulated agreement which purports to bind a person to enter as debtor or hirer into a prospective regulated agreement and which is excluded from the operation of section 59(1) of the Act by the Consumer Credit (Agreements to enter Prospective Agreements) (Exemptions) Regulations 1983.

[(4) These Regulations do not apply to an agreement entered into on or after 26th August 2010 and before 1st February 2011 where—

(a) that agreement is an agreement secured on land to which section 58 of the Act applies, and

(b) the Consumer Credit (Agreements) Regulations 2010 apply to that agreement.]

[3030H]

NOTES

Para (1): words in square brackets and italics substituted for original words "paragraph (2)" by the Consumer Credit (Amendment) Regulations 2010, SI 2010/1969, reg 2(1), (2)(a), as from 26 August 2010, and those words are further substituted by subsequent words in square brackets by the Consumer Credit (EU Directive) Regulations 2010, SI 2010/1010, regs 51, 53(a) (as substituted by SI 2010/1969, regs 4, 13) as from 1 February 2011, with effect in relation to certain agreements before that date, as provided for in regs 101, 101A of SI 2010/1010 at **[3942]**, **[3942A]**.

Paras (1A), (1B): inserted by SI 2010/1010, regs 51, 53(b) (as substituted by SI 2010/1969, regs 4, 13), as from 1 February 2011, with effect in relation to certain agreements before that date, as provided for in regs 101, 101A of SI 2010/1010 at **[3942]**, **[3942A]**.

Para (4): added by SI 2010/1969, reg 2(1), (2)(b), as from 26 August 2010.

SCHEDULE 1
INFORMATION TO BE CONTAINED IN DOCUMENTS EMBODYING REGULATED CONSUMER CREDIT AGREEMENTS OTHER THAN MODIFYING AGREEMENTS
Regulation 2(1)

TYPE OF AGREEMENT (1)	INFORMATION (2)
Nature of agreement	
[1 All types.	(1) Subject to paragraph (2) below, a heading in one of the following forms of words—
	(a) "Hire-Purchase Agreement regulated by the Consumer Credit Act 1974";
	(b) "Conditional Sale Agreement regulated by the Consumer Credit Act 1974";
	(c) "Fixed-Sum Loan Agreement regulated by the Consumer Credit Act 1974"; or
	(d) "Credit Card Agreement regulated by the Consumer Credit Act 1974",
	as the case may require.
	(2) If none of the headings in 1(a) to (d) above are applicable a heading in the following form of words—"Credit Agreement regulated by the Consumer Credit Act 1974".
	(3) Where the document and a pawn-receipt are combined, the words ", and Pawn-Receipt," shall be inserted in the heading after the word "Agreement".
	(4) Where the document embodies an agreement of which at least one part is a credit agreement not regulated by the Act, the word "partly" shall be inserted before "regulated" unless the regulated and unregulated parts of the agreement are clearly separate.
	(5) Where the credit is being secured on land the words "secured on" followed by the address of the land shall be inserted at the end of the heading.]
Parties to agreement	
2 All types.	(1) The name[, postal address and, where appropriate, any other address] of the creditor.
	(2) The name[, postal address and, where appropriate, any other address] of the debtor.
FINANCIAL AND RELATED PARTICULARS	
Description of goods, services, land etc	
3 Restricted-use debtor-creditor-supplier agreements for fixed-sum credit to finance a transaction comprising the acquisition of goods, services, land or other things specified in the agreement or identified and agreed on at the time the agreement is made.	A list or other description of the goods, services or other things and, in the case of land, a general description of the land, the acquisition of which is to be financed by credit under the agreement.

TYPE OF AGREEMENT (1)	INFORMATION (2)
Cash price	
4 Agreements falling within paragraph 3.	The cash price in relation to each list or other description of goods, services, land or other things, to be shown under paragraph 3 above, and the total cash price.
Advance payments	
5 All types in relation to which any advance payment is to be made by the debtor (whether under the agreement or as a condition precedent to the making of the agreement) before he is provided with credit under the agreement or, as the case may be, before he enters into the agreement.	The amount of the advance payments to be made by the debtor and, in the case of a cancellable agreement, the nature of such payments.
Amount of credit	
6 Agreements falling within paragraph 3 except agreements under which both— (a) the total amount payable by the debtor is not greater than the total cash price referred to in paragraph 4; and (b) there is no advance payment falling within paragraph 5.	The amount of the credit to be provided under the agreement, namely the difference between the total cash price to be shown under paragraph 4 above and the total of any advance payments to be shown under paragraph 5 above.
7 Agreements for fixed-sum credit not falling within paragraph 3.	The amount of the credit to be provided under the agreement.
Credit limit	
8 Agreements for running-account credit.	The credit limit expressed as:— (a) a sum of money; (b) a statement that the credit limit will be determined by the creditor from time to time under the agreement and that notice of it will be given by him to the debtor; (c) a sum of money together with a statement that the creditor may vary the credit limit to such sum as he may from time to time determine under the agreement and that notice of it will be given by him to the debtor; or (d) in a case not falling within head (a), (b) or (c) above, either a statement indicating the manner in which the credit limit will be determined and that notice of it will be given by the creditor to the debtor or a statement indicating that there is no credit limit.
[Term of the agreement	
8A Agreements of fixed duration for running-account credit.	The duration of the agreement.
8B Agreements for fixed-sum credit.	The duration or minimum duration of the agreement.]
Total charge for credit, rate of interest, etc	
[9 Agreements for fixed-sum credit except agreements— (a) which do not specify either the intervals between repayments or the amounts of repayments or both the intervals and the amounts;	(1) The total charge for credit, with a list of its constituent parts. (2) The rate of interest on the credit to be provided under the agreement or, where more than one such rate applies, all the rates in all cases quoted on a per annum basis with details of when each rate applies.

TYPE OF AGREEMENT (1)	INFORMATION (2)
(b) under which the total amount payable by the debtor to discharge his indebtedness in respect of the amount of credit provided may vary according to any formula specified in the agreement having effect by reference to movements in the level of any index or to any other factor; (c) which provide for a variation of, or permit the creditor to vary, (whether or not by reference to any index) the amount or rate of any item included in the total charge for credit after the relevant date; or (d) under which the total amount payable by the debtor is not greater than the total cash price referred to in paragraph 4.	(3) A statement explaining how and when interest charges are calculated and applied under the agreement.]
[10 Agreements for— (a) running-account credit; and (b) fixed-sum credit falling within the exceptions in paragraph 9(a) to (c).	(1) The total charge for credit with a list of its constituent parts and in the case of running-account credit, the total charge for credit shall be calculated on the same assumptions as are set out in paragraph 1 of Schedule 7 for the purpose of calculating the APR in place of the assumptions in *Part 4* [regulation 6] of the Total Charge for Credit Regulations that might otherwise apply. (2) The rate of interest on the credit to be provided under the agreement or, where more than one such rate applies, all the rates in all cases quoted on a per annum basis with details of when each rate applies. (3) A statement whether any interest rate to be shown under (2) above is fixed or variable. (4) A statement explaining how and when interest charges are calculated and applied under the agreement.]
Total amount payable	
11 Agreements falling within paragraph 9.	The total amount payable, being the total of any amounts to be shown under paragraphs 5, 6 or 7, and 9 above.
Timing of repayments	
12 All types	The timing of repayments to be made under the agreement expressed by reference to one or more of the following— (a) the dates on which each repayment is to be made; (b) the frequency and number of the repayments and the date of the first repayment or a statement indicating the manner in which that date will be determined; (c) a statement indicating the manner in which the dates of the repayments will be determined.
Amounts of repayments	
13 All types except those falling within paragraph 14.	The amount of each repayment to be made under the agreement expressed as— (a) a sum of money; (b) a specified proportion of a specified amount (including the amount outstanding from time to time);

TYPE OF AGREEMENT (1)	INFORMATION (2)
	(c) a combination of heads (a) and (b) above; or
	(d) in a case where the amount of any repayment cannot be expressed in accordance with head (a), (b) or (c) above, a statement indicating the manner in which the amount will be determined.
14 Agreements where— (i) the credit to be provided is repayable by two or more instalments; and (ii) the interest on the credit is of a type to which section 26 of, and Schedule 7 to, the Finance Act 1982 apply.	The amount of each repayment to be made under the agreement (with or without the equivalent repayment after deduction of tax in accordance with section 26 of, and Schedule 7 to, the Finance Act 1982), expressed as—
	(a) a sum of money;
	(b) a specified proportion of a specified amount (including the amount outstanding from time to time);
	(c) a combination of heads (a) and (b) above; or
	(d) in a case where the amount of any repayment cannot be expressed in accordance with head (a), (b) or (c) above, a statement indicating the manner in which the amount will be determined:
	Provided that, where the amounts to be paid by the debtor after deduction of tax in accordance with section 26 of, and Schedule 7 to, the Finance Act 1982 are the same, the requirements of this paragraph may be satisfied by a statement indicating the lowest and highest amounts of the repayments to be made under the agreement before deduction of tax.
[14A All types where different interest rates or different charges or both are or will be at any time during the term of the agreement payable in respect of— (a) credit provided under the agreement for different purposes; or (b) under each of the different parts of the agreement, whether or not the agreement is a multiple agreement.	A statement of the order or proportions in which any amount paid by the debtor which is not sufficient to discharge the total debt then due under the agreement will be applied or appropriated by the creditor towards the discharge of the sums due— (a) in respect of the amounts of credit provided for different purposes, or (b) different parts of the agreement, as the case may be.]
	APR
15 All types except those referred to in paragraph 16.	The APR in relation to the agreement or a statement indicating that the total amount payable under the agreement is not greater than the total cash price of the goods, services, land or other things the acquisition of which is to be financed by credit under the agreement.
16 Debtor-creditor-supplier agreements for running-account credit under which—	(1) The APR in relation to the agreement calculated on the assumptions specified in sub-paragraphs (2) and (3) below.
(a) the debtor agrees to pay the creditor an amount specified in the agreement on specified occasions;	(2) The first assumption referred to in sub-paragraph (1) above is the assumption that—
(b) there is a credit limit; and (c) charges for credit are either—	(a) the debtor is provided with an amount of credit at the date of the making of the agreement which, taken with the amount of the charge for that credit ascertained at that date, is equal to the credit limit; and

TYPE OF AGREEMENT (1)	INFORMATION (2)
(i) a fixed amount in respect of each transaction, or (ii) calculated as a proportion of the price payable under a transaction financed by the credit.	(b) the debtor repays the sum of the amounts referred to in head (a) above by payments of the amounts specified in the agreement on the occasions specified in the agreement and makes no other payment and obtains no further credit in relation to the account. (3) The second assumption referred to in sub-paragraph (1) above is the like assumption as in sub-paragraph (2) above save that the sum of the amounts referred to in head (a) thereof shall be taken to be one third of the credit limit. A statement indicating that it has been assumed in the calculation of the APR in relation to the agreement that relief may be available under section 19 of the Income and Corporation Taxes Act 1970 and Schedule 4 to the Finance Act 1976 in respect of premiums under certain policies of insurance without any deduction under section 21 of the said Act of 1970.
17 Agreements where the APR is based on a total charge for credit which is calculated to take account of relief available under section 19 of the Income and Corporation Taxes Act 1970 and Schedule 4 to the Finance Act 1976.	A statement indicating that it has been assumed in the calculation of the APR in relation to the agreement that relief may be available under section 19 of the Income and Corporation Taxes Act 1970 and Schedule 4 to the Finance Act 1976 in respect of premiums under certain policies of insurance without any deduction under section 21 of the said Act of 1970.

Variable rates or items

18 Agreements under which the rate or amount of any item included in the total charge for credit will or may be varied (other than a variation in consequence of an event which is certain to occur).	A statement indicating that in calculating the APR no account has been taken of any variation which may occur under the agreement of the rate or amount of any item entering into that calculation.
19 Agreements falling within paragraph 18.	A statement indicating the circumstances in which any variation referred to in paragraph 18 above may occur and where that information is ascertainable at the time at which the document referred to in section 61(1) of the Act is presented or sent to the debtor for signature, the time at which any such variation may occur.
[19A Agreements to which regulation 15A of the Total Charge for Credit Regulations [1980] applies.	The initial standard variable rate within the meaning of regulation 15A(2) of the Total Charge for Credit Regulations [1980] together with a statement explaining— (a) what that rate is; and (b) that it has been taken into account in calculating the APR.]

OTHER INFORMATION

Security provided by the debtor

20 Agreements, to which section 114 of the Act applies, under which a person takes any article in pawn and where no separate pawn-receipt is given.	A statement indicating that an article has been taken in pawn under the agreement and a description of the article sufficient to identify it.

TYPE OF AGREEMENT (1)	INFORMATION (2)
21 All types except those referred to in paragraph 20 in relation to which any security is to be provided by the debtor to secure the carrying out of the obligations of the debtor under the agreement.	A description of the security to be provided by the debtor in relation to the agreement sufficient to identify it and— (a) a general description of any stocks and shares (including any right to become a stockholder or shareholder) to which it relates; and (b) in any other case a description of the subject matter to which it relates.
[Charges	
22 All types.	(1) A list of any charges payable under the agreement to the creditor upon failure by the debtor or a relative of his to do or refrain from doing anything which he is required to do or refrain from doing, as the case may be. (2) A statement indicating any term of the agreement which provides for charges— (a) not required to be shown under (1) above; or (b) not included in the total charge for credit.]
[Cancellation rights	
23 Agreements that cannot be cancelled by the debtor under the Act, the Timeshare Act 1992 or the Financial Services (Distance Marketing) Regulations 2004.	A statement that the debtor has no right to cancel the agreement under the Consumer Credit Act 1974, the Timeshare Act 1992 or the Financial Services (Distance Marketing) Regulations 2004.]
[Right of withdrawal	
23A Agreements falling within regulation 8(1A)(c)	A statement providing details of the debtor's right under section 66A of the Act to withdraw from the consumer credit agreement including— (1) the right to withdraw within 14 days without the debtor having to give any reason; (2) when that period of withdrawal begins and ends; (3) the requirement of the debtor to notify the creditor of his intention to withdraw, in writing or orally; (4) contact details of the person/creditor whom he must notify of this intention to withdraw from the agreement; (5) the requirement to repay the credit without delay and no later than 30 calendar days of giving notice of withdrawal; (6) the requirement to pay, without delay and no later than 30 calendar days of giving notice of withdrawal, the interest accrued from the date of drawing down the credit to the date of repaying it; and (7) the amount of interest payable per day expressed as a sum of money; Paragraph (7) does not apply [in respect of agreements for running account credit] where it is not practicable for the creditor to state the amount of interest payable per day. In such cases, the agreement shall state that where credit is drawn down during the withdrawal period, the creditor shall inform the debtor, on request, without delay, of the amount of interest payable per day.]

PART 2 STATUTORY INSTRUMENTS

TYPE OF AGREEMENT (1)	INFORMATION (2)

[Amount payable on early settlement

TYPE OF AGREEMENT (1)	INFORMATION (2)
24 Agreements for fixed-sum credit [secured on land] for a term of more than one month.	(1) Examples based on the amount of credit to be provided under the agreement or the nominal amount of either £1000 or £100, showing the amount that would be payable if the debtor exercised the right under section 94 of the Act to discharge his indebtedness on the date when— (a) a quarter of the term of the agreement elapses; (b) half of the term elapses; and (c) three quarters of the term elapses. or on the first repayment date after each of those dates. (2) A statement explaining that, in calculating the amounts shown, no account has been taken of any variation which might occur under the agreement, and that the amounts are accordingly only illustrative.]
[24A Agreements falling within regulation 8(1A)(b) and (c)	A statement providing details of the debtor's right of early repayment under section 94 of the Act including— (1) the fact that the debtor has a right to repay early in full or part, (2) the procedure for early repayment, and (3) where applicable details of the creditor's right to compensation under section 95A of the Act and the manner in which that compensation shall be determined.]

[3030I]

NOTES

Paras 1, 9, 22: substituted by the Consumer Credit (Agreements) (Amendment) Regulations 2004, SI 2004/1482, regs 2, 10(1), (2), (4), (7).

Para 2: words in square brackets substituted by the Consumer Credit Act 1974 (Electronic Communications) Order 2004, SI 2004/3236, art 4(1), (3).

Paras 8A, 8B, 14A: inserted by SI 2004/1482, regs 2, 10(1), (3), (6).

Para 10: substituted by SI 2004/1482, regs 2, 10(1), (5); words in italics in column 2 substituted by subsequent words in square brackets by the Consumer Credit (EU Directive) Regulations 2010, SI 2010/1010, regs 51, 54(za) (as inserted by the Consumer Credit (Amendment) Regulations 2010, SI 2010/1969, regs 4, 14), as from 1 February 2011, with effect in relation to certain agreements before that date, as provided for in regs 101, 101A of SI 2010/1010 at **[3942]**, **[3942A]**.

Para 19A: inserted by the Consumer Credit (Total Charge for Credit, Agreements and Advertisements) (Amendment) Regulations 1999, SI 1999/3177, reg 4(a); year in square brackets in both places inserted by SI 2010/1010, regs 51, 54(zb) (as inserted by SI 2010/1969, regs 4, 14), as from 1 February 2011, with effect in relation to certain agreements before that date, as provided for in regs 101, 101A of SI 2010/1010 at **[3942]**, **[3942A]**.

Para 23: inserted by SI 2004/1482, regs 2, 10(1), (8) (as amended by SI 2004/2619, reg 2(1), (5)).

Paras 23A, 24A: inserted by SI 2010/1010, regs 51, 54(a), (c), as from 1 February 2011, with effect in relation to certain agreements before that date, as provided for in regs 101, 101A of the 2010 Regulations at **[3942]**, **[3942A]**.

Para 24: inserted by SI 2004/1482, regs 2, 10(1), (8) (as amended by SI 2004/2619, reg 2(1), (5)); words in square brackets inserted by SI 2010/1010, regs 51, 54(b), as from 1 February 2011, with effect in relation to certain agreements before that date, as provided for in regs 101, 101A of the 2010 Regulations at **[3942]**, **[3942A]**.

[SCHEDULE 2

PART I
FORMS OF STATEMENT OF PROTECTION AND REMEDIES AVAILABLE UNDER THE
CONSUMER CREDIT ACT 1974 TO DEBTORS UNDER REGULATED CONSUMER
CREDIT AGREEMENTS
Regulation 2(3)

[FORM NO (1)	TYPE OF AGREEMENT (2)	FORM OF STATEMENT (3)
1	Agreement to which section 58(1) of the Act applies.	**YOUR RIGHTS** Under the Consumer Credit Act 1974, you should have been given a copy of this agreement at least seven days ago so you could consider whether you wanted to go ahead. If the creditor did not give you a copy of this agreement he can only enforce it with a court order.
2	All types.	**MISSING PAYMENTS** Missing payments could have severe consequences and make obtaining credit more difficult.
3	All agreements which are secured on land.	**YOUR HOME MAY BE REPOSSESSED** Your home may be repossessed if you do not keep up repayments on a mortgage or other debt secured on it.
4	Cancellable agreements to which section 68(b) of the Act applies.	**YOUR RIGHT TO CANCEL** You can cancel this agreement within FOURTEEN days (starting the day after you signed it) by giving WRITTEN notice to*. If you intend to cancel, you should not use any goods you have under the agreement and you should keep them safe. You can wait for them to be collected and you do not need to hand them over until you receive a written request for them. … Notes: *Creditor or agent to insert the name and address of person to whom the notice may be given or an indication of the person to whom a notice may be given with clear reference to the place in the document embodying the agreement where his name and address appear. …
5	Cancellable agreements not included in paragraphs [4 or 6].	**YOUR RIGHT TO CANCEL**

[FORM NO (1)	TYPE OF AGREEMENT (2)	FORM OF STATEMENT (3)
		Once you have signed this agreement, you will have a short time in which you can cancel [it]*[that part of this agreement which is regulated by the Consumer Credit Act 1974]*. The creditor will send you exact details of how and when you can do this.
		Notes:
		*Creditor to omit passage in square brackets which does not apply to the agreement.
6	Modifying agreements treated under section 82(5) of the Act as cancellable agreements.	YOUR RIGHT TO CANCEL
		This agreement modifies an earlier agreement. Once you have signed this agreement your right to cancel [that part of]* the earlier agreement [which was regulated by the Consumer Credit Act 1974]* will be widened to cover the [regulated]* agreement as modified. The cancellation period itself will be unchanged. Details of how to cancel are given in your copy of this agreement.
		Notes:
		*Creditor to omit passages in square brackets except in the case of an agreement of which at least one part is a credit agreement not regulated by the Act.
7	Hire purchase and conditional sale agreements relating to goods, not included in paragraph 8.	TERMINATION: YOUR RIGHTS
		You have a right to end this agreement. To do so, you should write to the person you make your payments to. They will then be entitled to the return of the goods and to [the cost of installing the goods plus half the rest of the total amount payable under this agreement, that is] [half the total amount payable under this agreement, that is] *£x**. If you have already paid at least this amount plus any overdue instalments and have taken reasonable care of the goods, you will not have to pay any more.
		Notes:
		*Creditor to insert the appropriate passage in square brackets where the amount calculated in accordance with the provisions of section 100 of the Act applies. If the agreement provides for a sum below the minimum prescribed in the Act, both passages in square brackets are to be omitted.
		**Creditor to insert the amount calculated in accordance with the provisions of section 100 of the Act or such lesser sum as the agreement may provide.

[FORM NO (1)	TYPE OF AGREEMENT (2)	FORM OF STATEMENT (3)
8	Agreements modifying hire-purchase and conditional sale agreements relating to goods.	TERMINATION: YOUR RIGHTS You have a right to end this agreement. To do so, write to the person you make your payments to. They will then be entitled to the return of the goods and to [the cost of installing the goods plus half the total amount yet to be paid under the earlier agreement as modified by this agreement, that is] [half the total amount payable under the earlier agreement as modified by this agreement, that is]* £x**. If you have already paid at least this amount, plus any overdue instalments and have taken reasonable care of the goods, you will not have to pay any more. Notes: *Creditor to insert the appropriate passage in square brackets where the amount calculated in accordance with the provisions of section 100 of the Act applies. If the modified agreement provides for a sum below the minimum prescribed in the Act, both passages in square brackets are to be omitted. **Creditor to insert the amount calculated in accordance with the provisions of section 100 of the Act or such lesser sum as the agreement may provide.
9	Conditional sale agreements relating to land, not included in paragraph 10.	TERMINATION: YOUR RIGHTS Until the title to the land has passed to you, you have a right to end this agreement. To do so write to the person you make your payments to. They will then be entitled to the return of the land and to [half the total amount payable under this agreement, that is]* £x.** If, at the time you end this agreement, you have already paid at least this amount plus any overdue instalments and you have taken reasonable care of the land, you will not have to pay any more. Notes: *Creditor to insert the passage in square brackets where the amount calculated in accordance with the provisions of section 100 of the Act applies. If the agreement provides for a sum below the minimum prescribed in the Act, the passage in square brackets is to be omitted. **Creditor to insert the amount calculated in accordance with the provisions of section 100 of the Act or such lesser sum as the agreement may provide.
10	Agreements modifying conditional sale agreements relating to land.	TERMINATION: YOUR RIGHTS

PART 2
STATUTORY INSTRUMENTS

[FORM NO (1)	TYPE OF AGREEMENT (2)	FORM OF STATEMENT (3)
		Until the title to the land has passed to you, you have a right to end this agreement. To do so write to the person you make your payments to. They will then be entitled to the return of the land and to [half the total amount payable under your earlier agreement as modified by this agreement, that is]* £x**. If you have already paid at least this amount plus any overdue instalments and taken reasonable care of the land, you will not have to pay any more. Notes: *Creditor to insert the passage in square brackets where the amount calculated in accordance with the provisions of section 100 of the Act applies. If the modified agreement provides for a sum below the minimum prescribed in the Act, the passage in square brackets is to be omitted. **Creditor to insert the amount calculated in accordance with the provisions of section 100 of the Act or such lesser sum as the modified agreement may provide.
11	Hire-purchase and conditional sale agreements relating to goods, not included in paragraph 12.	REPOSSESSION: YOUR RIGHTS If you do not keep your side of this agreement but you have paid at least [the cost of installing the goods plus one third of the rest of the total amount payable under this agreement, that is] [one third of the total amount payable under this agreement, that is]*£x** the creditor may not take back the goods against your wishes unless he gets a court order. (In Scotland he may need to get a court order at any time.) If he does take the goods without your consent or a court order, you have the right to get back any money that you have paid under this agreement. Notes: *Creditor to insert the appropriate passage in square brackets. **Creditor to insert the amount calculated in accordance with the provisions of section 90 of the Act.
12	Agreements modifying hire-purchase and conditional sale agreements relating to goods.	REPOSSESSION: YOUR RIGHTS

[FORM NO (1)	TYPE OF AGREEMENT (2)	FORM OF STATEMENT (3)
		If you do not keep to your side of this agreement [but you have paid at least £x*]** the creditor may not take back the goods against your wishes unless he gets a court order. (In Scotland he may need to get a court order at any time.) If he does take the goods without your consent or a court order, you have the right to get back all the money you have paid under this agreement.
		Notes:
		*Creditor to insert the amount calculated in accordance with the provisions of section 90 of the Act.
		**Creditor to omit both passages in square brackets in the case of a modifying agreement where the goods are protected at the time the modifying agreement is made.
13	Agreements, to which section 114 of the Act applies, under which a person takes any article in pawn.	IMPORTANT—READ THIS CAREFULLY TO FIND OUT ABOUT YOUR RIGHTS
		The Consumer Credit Act 1974 lays down certain requirements for your protection which should have been complied with when this agreement was made. If they were not, the creditor cannot enforce this agreement without getting a court order.
		The Act also gives you a number of rights. In particular you should read the NOTICE TO DEBTOR [in this agreement]* [in your pawn receipt].**
		If you would like to know more about your rights under the Act, contact either your local Trading Standards Department or your nearest Citizens' Advice Bureau.
		Notes:
		*Phrase in square brackets to be included by creditor in agreements where any document embodying the agreement is not separate from the pawn-receipt. Creditor to omit "in your pawn receipt".
		** Phrase in square brackets to be included by creditor in agreements where a separate pawn-receipt is given to the debtor. Creditor to omit "in this agreement".
14	Debtor-creditor-supplier agreements falling within section 12(b) and (c) of the Act, and multiple agreements not falling within paragraph 15 of which at least one part is a debtor-creditor-supplier agreement falling within section 12(b) or (c) of the Act.	IMPORTANT—READ THIS CAREFULLY TO FIND OUT ABOUT YOUR RIGHTS

[FORM NO (1)	TYPE OF AGREEMENT (2)	FORM OF STATEMENT (3)
		The Consumer Credit Act 1974 lays down certain requirements for your protection which should have been complied with when this agreement was made. If they were not, the creditor cannot enforce this agreement without getting a court order.
		The Act also gives you a number of rights:
		1) You can settle this agreement at any time by giving notice in writing and paying off the amount you owe under the agreement [which may be reduced by a rebate]* [Examples indicating the amount you have to pay appear in the agreement.]**
		2) If you received unsatisfactory goods or services paid for under this agreement[, apart from any bought with a cash loan,]*** you may have a right to sue the supplier, the creditor or both.
		3) If the contract is not fulfilled, perhaps because the supplier has gone out of business, you may still be able to sue the creditor.
		If you would like to know more about your rights under the Act, contact either your local Trading Standards Department or your nearest Citizens' Advice Bureau.
		Notes:
		*Creditor to insert phrase in square brackets in any agreement where rebate would be payable on early settlement under the agreement or the Consumer Credit (Early Settlement) Regulations 2004.
		** Creditor to insert phrase in second pair of square brackets in any agreement for fixed-sum credit for a term of more than one month.
		***Creditor to insert phrase in square brackets in any multiple agreement, of which, at least one part is a debtor-creditor-supplier agreement falling within section 12(b) or (c) of the Act and at least one part is a debtor-creditor agreement falling within section 13(c) of the Act.
		[1] You can settle this agreement at any time by giving notice in writing and paying off the amount you owe under the agreement [which may be reduced by a rebate]* [Examples indicating the amount you have to pay appear in the agreement.]**
		[2] You can settle this agreement in part at any time by giving notice and paying off some of the amount you owe.]***
		[3] If you received unsatisfactory goods or services paid for under this agreement [, apart from any bought with a cash loan,]**** you may have a right to sue the supplier, the creditor or both.

[FORM NO (1)	TYPE OF AGREEMENT (2)	FORM OF STATEMENT (3)
		4) If the contract is not fulfilled, perhaps because the supplier has gone out of business, you may still be able to sue the creditor.]*****
		If you would like to know more about your rights under the Act, contact either your local Trading Standards Department or your nearest Citizens' Advice Bureau.
		Notes:
		*Creditor to insert phrase in square brackets in any agreement where rebate would be payable on early settlement under the agreement or the Consumer Credit (Early Settlement) Regulations 2004.
		** Creditor to insert phrase in second pair of square brackets in any agreement for fixed-sum credit for a term of more than one month that is an agreement secured on land.
		*** Creditor to delete where agreement is secured on land.
		**** Creditor to insert phrase in square brackets in any multiple agreement, of which at least one part is a debtor-creditor-supplier agreement falling within section 12(b) or (c) of the Act and at least one part is a debtor-creditor agreement falling within section 13(c) of the Act.
		***** Creditor may delete text in 3) and 4) where agreement is a debtor-creditor-supplier agreement for running-account credit— (i) which provides for the making of payments by the debtor in relation to specified periods which, in the case of an agreement which is not secured on land, do not exceed three months, and (ii) which requires that the number of payments to be made by the debtor in repayments of the whole amount of credit provided in such period shall not exceed one.]
15	Multiple agreements of which at least one part is a credit agreement not regulated by the Act.	IMPORTANT—READ THIS CAREFULLY TO FIND OUT ABOUT YOUR RIGHTS
		That part of this agreement which deals with [..........]* is a regulated agreement under the Consumer Credit Act 1974. As a result certain requirements for your protection should have been complied with when it was made. If they were not, the creditor cannot enforce this agreement without a court order.
		The Act also gives you a number of rights. You can settle the regulated agreement at any time by giving notice in writing and paying off the amount you owe under this agreement [which may be reduced by a rebate]** [Examples indicating the amount you have to pay appear in the agreement.]***

[FORM NO (1)	TYPE OF AGREEMENT (2)	FORM OF STATEMENT (3)
		[[You can settle this agreement in part at any time by giving notice and paying off some of the amount you owe.]****] If you would like to know more about your rights under the Act, contact either your local Trading Standards Department or your nearest Citizens' Advice Bureau. Notes: * Creditor to insert description of regulated agreement example, "the cash advance facility". ** Creditor to insert phrase in square brackets in any agreement where rebate would be payable on early settlement under the agreement or the Consumer Credit (Early Settlement) Regulations 2004. *** *Creditor to insert phrase in second pair of square brackets in any agreement for fixed-sum credit for a term of more than one month.* [*** Creditor to insert phrase in second pair of square brackets in any agreement for fixed-sum credit for a term of more than one month that is an agreement secured on land.] [**** Creditor to delete where agreement is secured on land.]
16	All types not included in paragraphs 13,14 and 15.	IMPORTANT—READ THIS CAREFULLY TO FIND OUT ABOUT YOUR RIGHTS The Consumer Credit Act 1974 lays down certain requirements for your protection which should have been complied with when this agreement was made. If they were not, the creditor cannot enforce this agreement without getting a court order. The Act also gives you a number of rights. You can settle this agreement at any time by giving notice in writing and paying off the amount you owe under the agreement [which may be reduced by a rebate]*. [Examples indicating the amount you might have to pay appear in the agreement.]** [[You can settle this agreement in part at any time by giving notice and paying off some of the amount you owe.]****] If you would like to know more about your rights under the Act, contact either your local Trading Standards Department or your nearest Citizens' Advice Bureau. Notes: * Creditor to insert phrase in square brackets in any agreement where rebate would be payable on early settlement under the agreement or the Consumer Credit (Early Settlement) Regulations 2004.

[FORM NO (1)	TYPE OF AGREEMENT (2)	FORM OF STATEMENT (3)
		*** Creditor to insert phrase in second pair of square brackets in any agreement for fixed-sum credit for a term of more than one month.* [** Creditor to insert phrase in second pair of square brackets in any agreement for fixed sum credit for a term of more than one month that is an agreement secured on land.]
		[*** Creditor to delete where agreement is secured on land.]
17	Credit-token agreements which make debtors liable for loss to the creditor resulting from the misuse of credit-tokens by other persons.	THEFT, LOSS OR MISUSE OF CREDIT-TOKEN*
		If your credit-token* is lost, stolen or misused by someone without your permission, you may have to pay up to £x** of any loss to the creditor. If it is misused with your permission you will probably be liable for ALL losses. You will not be liable to the creditor for losses which take place after you have told the creditor about the theft, etc [as long as you confirm this in writing within seven days]. ***[However, the credit-token* can also be used under an agreement to which this protection does not apply. As a result, there may be circumstances under which you may have to pay for all the losses to the creditor.]****
		Notes:
		*Creditor may insert specific designation or trade name of credit-token for example, credit card instead of "credit-token".
		**Creditor to insert the extent of the liability laid down in section 84(1) of the Act or the credit limit if lower or such lower figure as he may decide.
		***Creditor to omit phrase in square brackets if written confirmation is not required under the credit-token agreement.
		****Creditor to omit passage in square brackets if inapplicable.]

[3030J]

NOTES

Substituted by the Consumer Credit (Agreements) (Amendment) Regulations 2004, SI 2004/1482, regs 2, 11 (as amended by SI 2004/2619).

Form 14: in column 3, words in italics substituted by subsequent words underlined in square brackets by the Consumer Credit (EU Directive) Regulations 2010, SI 2010/1010, regs 51, 55(a) (as substituted by the Consumer Credit (Amendment) Regulations 2010, SI 2010/1969, regs 4, 15), as from 1 February 2011, with effect in relation to certain agreements before that date, as provided for in regs 101, 101A of SI 2010/1010 at **[3942]**, **[3942A]**.

Form 15: in column 3, first and third words underlined in square brackets inserted and words in italics substituted by subsequent words underlined in square brackets by SI 2010/1010, regs 51, 55(b) (as substituted by SI 2010/1969, regs 4, 15), as from 1 February 2011, with effect in relation to certain agreements before that date, as provided for regs 101, 101A of SI 2010/1010 at **[3942]**, **[3942A]**.

Form 16: in column 3, first and third words underlined in square brackets inserted and words in italics substituted by subsequent words underlined in square brackets by SI 2010/1010, regs 51, 55(c) (as substituted by

SI 2010/1969, regs 4, 15), as from 1 February 2011, with effect in relation to certain agreements before that date, as provided for in regs 101, 101A of SI 2010/1010 at **[3942]**, **[3942A]**.

[PART II
NOTICE TO BE CONTAINED IN DOCUMENTS EMBODYING A COMBINED CONSUMER CREDIT AGREEMENT AND PAWN-RECEIPT]
Regulation 4

FORM NO (1)	TYPE OF AGREEMENT (2)	FORM OF STATEMENT (3)
18	Agreements, to which section 114 of the Act applies, under which a person takes any article in pawn and where any document embodying the agreement is not separate from the pawn-receipt.	**NOTICE TO THE DEBTOR IMPORTANT— YOU SHOULD READ THIS CAREFULLY** Right to Redeem Articles If you hand in this agreement (which is also your pawn-receipt) and pay the amount you owe, you may redeem the article(s) in pawn at any time within 6 months of the date of this agreement or any longer time agreed with the creditor ("the redemption period"). IF YOU DO NOT REDEEM THE ARTICLE(S) ON OR BEFORE * YOU MAY LOSE YOUR RIGHT TO REDEEM IT (THEM). Loss of Receipt If you lose your receipt you may provide either a statutory declaration or, if the credit (or credit limit) is not more than £x** and the creditor agrees, a signed statement instead. The creditor may provide the form to be used and may charge for doing so. Unredeemed Articles An article not redeemed within the redemption period becomes the creditor's property if the credit (or credit limit) is not more than £x**** and the redemption period is 6 months. In any other case it may be sold by the creditor, but it continues to be redeemable until it is sold. Interest is payable until the actual date of redemption. Where the credit (or credit limit) is more than £x**** the creditor must give you 14 days notice of his intention to sell. When an article has been sold you will receive information about the sale. If the proceeds (less expenses) are more that the amount that would have been payable to redeem the article on the date of the sale you will be entitled to receive the extra amount. If the proceeds are less than the amount you will owe the creditor the shortfall. Your goods will not be insured by the creditor while they are in pawn. ***** Notes:

FORM NO (1)	TYPE OF AGREEMENT (2)	FORM OF STATEMENT (3)
		*Creditor to insert the date at the end of the redemption period. **Creditor to insert the amount specified in section 118(1)(b) of the Act. ***Creditor to insert the amount specified in section 120(1)(a) of the Act. ****Creditor to insert the amount specified in the Consumer Credit (Realisation of Pawn) Regulations 1983 *****Creditor to omit this paragraph if inapplicable.]

[3030K]

NOTES

Substituted by the Consumer Credit (Agreements) (Amendment) Regulations 2004, SI 2004/1482, regs 2, 11.

SCHEDULE 3
INFORMATION TO BE CONTAINED IN DOCUMENTS EMBODYING REGULATED CONSUMER HIRE AGREEMENTS OTHER THAN MODIFYING AGREEMENTS
Regulation 3(1)

TYPE OF AGREEMENT (1)	INFORMATION (2)
[Nature of agreement	
1 All types.	(1) A heading in the following form of words— "Hire Agreement regulated by the Consumer Credit Act 1974". (2) Where the agreement to hire is being secured on land the words "secured on" and the address of the land shall be inserted at the end of the heading.]
Parties to agreement	
2 All types.	(1) The name[, postal address and, where appropriate, any other address] of the owner. (2) The name[, postal address and, where appropriate, any other address] of the hirer.
FINANCIAL AND RELATED PARTICULARS	
Description of goods	
3 All types.	A list or other description of the goods to be bailed or hired under the agreement.
Advance payments	
4 All types in relation to which any advance payment is to be made by the hirer (whether under the agreement or as a condition precedent to the making of the agreement) before he is to take possession of the goods to be bailed or hired under the agreement or, as the case may be, before he enters into the agreement.	The amount of the advance payments to be made by the hirer and, in the case of a cancellable agreement, the nature of such payments.

TYPE OF AGREEMENT (1)	INFORMATION (2)
Hire payments	
5 All types.	(1) The amount of each hire payment, other than an advance payment to be shown under paragraph 4 above
	(2) The timing of such payments to be made under the agreement expressed by reference to one or more of the following—
	(a) the dates on which each payment is to be made;
	(b) the frequency and number of the payments and the date of the first payment or a statement indicating the manner in which that date will be determined.
	(c) a statement indicating the manner in which the dates of the payments will be determined.
Other payments	
6 All types including provisions for payments other than advance payments and hire payments.	(1) The amount (or a statement indicating the manner in which the amount will be determined) of each of the following descriptions of payments (not being an advance payment to be shown under paragraph 4 above or a hire payment to be shown under paragraph 5) to be made under the agreement by, or on behalf of,' the hirer, or a relative of his, to the owner, that is to say,—
	(a) any payment under arrangements for the installation, care, maintenance or protection of any goods;
	(b) any premium under a contract of insurance; or
	(c) any payment payable on termination of the agreement (other than a payment on default to be shown under paragraph 10 below).
	(2) The timing of such payments expressed by reference to one or more of the following—
	(a) the dates on which each payment is to be made;
	(b) the frequency and number of the payments and the date of the first payment or a statement indicating the manner in which that date will be determined;
	(c) a statement indicating the manner in which the dates of the payments will be determined.
	(3) References in this paragraph to the owner include references to his near relative, his partner and a member of a group of which he is a member to any person nominated by him or by any such person in relation to the arrangements, the contract of insurance or the termination of the agreement, and to a near relative of his partner; and "near relative" means, in relation to any person, the husband, wife, father, mother, brother, sister, son or daughter of that person and "group" means the person (including a company) having control of a company together with all the companies directly or indirectly controlled by him.

TYPE OF AGREEMENT (1)	INFORMATION (2)

Variable payments

7 All types including provisions for variation of hire or other payments, where the amount of any such payment following any variation cannot be ascertained at the time of the making of the agreement.	(1) Subject to sub-paragraph (2) below, a statement indicating the circumstances in which any hire payment to be shown under paragraph 5 above or any other payment to be shown under paragraph 6 may be varied under the agreement and, where that information is ascertainable at the time at which the document referred to in section 61(1) of the Act is presented or sent to the hirer for signature, the time at which any such variation may occur.
	(2) Sub-paragraph (1) above does not apply to a variation under the agreement which takes account only of a change in value added tax.
	(3) References in sub-paragraph (2) above to a change in value added tax include references to a change to or from no tax being charged.

Duration of hire

8 All types including a provision that goods are to be bailed or hired for a fixed period or a minimum period.	A statement indicating that goods are to be bailed or hired under the agreement for a fixed period or a minimum period, as the case may be, and the duration of that period.

OTHER INFORMATION

Security provided by the hirer

9 All types in relation to which any security is to be provided by the hirer to secure the carrying out of the obligations of the hirer under the agreement.	A description of the security to be provided by the hirer in relation to the agreement sufficient to identify it and a description of the subject matter to which it relates.

[Charges

10 All types.	(1) A list of any charges payable under the agreement to the owner upon failure by the hirer or a relative of his to do or refrain from doing anything which he is required to do or refrain from doing, as the case may be.
	(2) A statement indicating any term of the agreement which provides for charges not required to be shown under (1) above.]

[Cancellation rights

11. Agreements that are not cancellable agreements.	A statement that the agreement is not cancellable.]

[3030L]

NOTES

    Paras 1, 10: substituted by the Consumer Credit (Agreements) (Amendment) Regulations 2004, SI 2004/1482, regs 2, 12(1)–(3).

    Para 2: words in square brackets substituted by the Consumer Credit Act 1974 (Electronic Communications) Order 2004, SI 2004/3236, art 4(1), (5).

    Para 11: inserted by SI 2004/1482, regs 2, 12(1), (4).

PART 2
STATUTORY INSTRUMENTS

[SCHEDULE 4
FORMS OF STATEMENT OF PROTECTION AND REMEDIES AVAILABLE UNDER THE
CONSUMER CREDIT ACT 1974 TO HIRERS UNDER REGULATED CONSUMER
HIRE AGREEMENTS

Regulation 3(3)

FORM (1)	TYPE OF AGREEMENT (2)	FORM OF STATEMENT (3)
1	Agreement to which section 58(1) of the Act applies.	YOUR RIGHTS Under the Consumer Credit Act 1974, you should have been given a copy of this agreement at least seven days ago so you could consider whether to go ahead. If the owner did not give you a copy this agreement can only be enforced with a court order.
2	All types.	MISSING PAYMENTS Missing payments could have severe consequences and may make obtaining credit more difficult.
3	All agreements which are secured on property.	YOUR HOME MAY BE REPOSSESSED Your home may be repossessed if you do not keep up repayments on a hire agreement secured by a mortgage or other security on your home.
4	All cancellable agreements not included in paragraph 5.	YOUR RIGHT TO CANCEL Once you have signed this agreement you have a short time in which you can cancel it. Details of how to cancel it will be sent to you by the owner.
5	Modifying agreements treated under section 82(5) of the Act as cancellable agreements.	YOUR RIGHT TO CANCEL This agreement modifies an earlier agreement. Once you have signed it, your right to cancel the earlier agreement will cover this modified agreement. The cancellation period itself is unchanged. Details of how you can cancel can be found in the copy of this agreement.
6	Agreements to which the hirer is entitled to terminate by notice under section 101(1) of the Act and which provides for the bailment or hiring of goods for at least 18 months after the making of the agreement.	IMPORTANT—READ THIS CAREFULLY TO FIND OUT ABOUT YOUR RIGHTS] The Consumer Credit Act 1974 lays down certain requirements for your protection which should have been complied with when this agreement was made. If they were not, the owner cannot enforce this agreement without getting a court order.

FORM (1)	TYPE OF AGREEMENT (2)	FORM OF STATEMENT (3)
7	Agreements not included in paragraph 6.	The Act also gives you a number of rights. You can end this agreement by writing to the person you make your payments to and giving at least * notice. In order to do this the agreement must have been allowed to run for at least 18 months [from the date of the original agreement]** though this may include the period of notice. You will have to make all payments and pay any amounts you owe until the date the agreement comes to an end. If you would like to know more about your rights under the Act, contact either your local Trading Standards Department or your nearest Citizens' Advice Bureau. Notes: *Owner to insert minimum period of notice as determined by section 101. **Owner to omit passage in square brackets except where this notice appears in a modifying agreement. IMPORTANT—READ THIS CAREFULLY TO FIND OUT ABOUT YOUR RIGHTS The Consumer Credit Act 1974 covers this agreement and lays down certain requirements for your protection which should have been complied with when this agreement was made. If they were not, the owner cannot enforce this agreement against you without getting a court order. If you would like to know more about your rights under the Act, contact either your local Trading Standards Department or your nearest Citizens' Advice Bureau.]

[3030M]

NOTES

Substituted by the Consumer Credit (Agreements) (Amendment) Regulations 2004, SI 2004/1482, regs 2, 13.

SCHEDULE 5
FORMS OF SIGNATURE BOX

PART I
REGULATED CONSUMER CREDIT AGREEMENTS

Regulation 2(7)

FORM NO (1)	TYPE OF AGREEMENT (2)	FORM OF SIGNATURE BOX (3)
1	Hire-purchase agreements.	This is a Hire-Purchase Agreement regulated by the Consumer Credit Act 1974. Sign it only if you want to be legally bound by its terms. Signature(s) of Debtor(s) Date(s) of signature(s)*

FORM NO (1)	TYPE OF AGREEMENT (2)	FORM OF SIGNATURE BOX (3)
		The goods will not become your property until you have made all the payments. You must not sell them before then.
		Note:
		* Creditor may omit "Date(s) of signature(s)" where, by virtue of Regulation 6(3)(c), the date is not required.
2	Conditional sale agreements relating to land.	This is a Conditional Sale Agreement regulated by the Consumer Credit Act 1974. Sign it only if you want to be legally bound by its terms.
		Signature(s)
		of Debtor(s)
		Date(s) of signature(s)*
		The land will not become your property until you have made** payments. You must not sell it before then.
		Notes:
		* Creditor may omit "Date(s) of signature(s)" where, by virtue of Regulation 6(3)(c) the date is not required.
		** Creditor to insert "all the" or the number of payments as appropriate.
3	Conditional sale agreements relating to goods.	This is a Conditional Sale Agreement regulated by the Consumer Credit Act 1974. Sign it only if you want to be legally bound by its terms.
		Signature(s)
		of Debtor(s)
		Date(s) of signature(s)*
		The goods will not become your property until you have made** payments. You must not sell them before then.
		Notes:
		* Creditor may omit "Date(s) of signature(s)" where, by virtue of Regulation 6(3)(c), the date is not required.
		** Creditor to insert "all the" or the number of payments as appropriate.
4	Agreements under which a person takes any article in pawn and where the agreement is not separate from the pawn-receipt.	This is a Credit Agreement regulated by the Consumer Credit Act 1974. Sign it only if you want to be legally bound by its terms.
		Signature(s)*
		of Debtor(s)
		Date(s) of signature(s)*
		This document is also your PAWN-RECEIPT. Keep it safely.
		Note:

FORM NO (1)	TYPE OF AGREEMENT (2)	FORM OF SIGNATURE BOX (3)
		* Creditor may omit "Date(s) of signature(s)" where, by virtue of Regulation 6(3)(c), the date is not required.
5	Multiple agreements of which at least one part is a credit agreement not regulated by the Act.	This is a Credit Agreement partly regulated by the Consumer Credit Act 1974. Sign it only if you want to be legally bound by its terms.
		Signature(s)
		of Debtor(s)
		Date(s) of signature(s)*
		Note:
		* Creditor may omit "Date(s) of signature(s)" where, by virtue of Regulation 6(3)(c), the date is not required.
6	Agreements not included in paragraphs 1–5 or 7–8.	This is a Credit Agreement regulated by the Consumer Credit Act 1974. Sign it only if you want to be legally bound by its terms.
		Signature(s)
		of Debtor(s)
		Date(s) of signature(s)*
		Note:
		* Creditor may omit "Date(s) of signature(s)" where, by virtue of Regulation 6(3)(c), the date is not required.
7	Modifying agreements varying or supplementing earlier multiple agreements of which at least one part was a credit agreement not regulated by the Act and where at least one part of the modified agreement is not regulated.	This Agreement varies and/or supplements a Credit Agreement and is partly regulated by the Consumer Credit Act 1974. Sign it only if you want to be legally bound by the new terms.
		Signature(s)
		Debtor(s)
		Date(s) of signature(s)*
		Note:
		* Creditor may omit "Date(s) of signature(s)" where, by virtue of Regulation 6(3)(c), the date is not required.
8	Modifying agreements other than those included in paragraph 7.	This Agreement varies and/or supplements a* Agreement regulated by the Consumer Credit Act 1974. Sign it only if you want to be legally bound by the new terms.
		Signature(s)
		of Debtor(s)
		Date(s) of signature(s)**
		Notes:
		* Creditor to insert "Hire-Purchase" or "Conditional Sale" or "Credit" as appropriate

PART 2
STATUTORY INSTRUMENTS

FORM NO	TYPE OF AGREEMENT	FORM OF SIGNATURE BOX
(1)	(2)	(3)
		** Creditor may omit "Date(s) of signature(s)" where, by virtue of Regulation 6(3)(c), the date is not required.

[3030N]

PART II
REGULATED CONSUMER HIRE AGREEMENTS

Regulation 3(6)

FORM NO (1)	TYPE OF AGREEMENT (2)	FORM OF SIGNATURE BOX (3)
9	All types not included in paragraph 10.	This is a Hire Agreement regulated by the Consumer Credit Act 1974. Sign it only if you want to be legally bound by its terms. (Signature(s) of Hirer(s) Date(s) of signature(s)* Under this agreement the goods do not become your property and you must not sell them. Note: * Owner may omit "Date(s) of signature(s)" where, by virtue of Regulation 6(3)(c), the date is not required.
10	Modifying agreements.	This Agreement varies and/or supplements a Hire Agreement regulated by the Consumer Credit Act 1974. Sign it only if you want to be legally bound by the new terms. (Signature(s) of Hirer(s) Date(s) of signature(s)* Note: * Owner may omit "Date(s) of signature(s)" where, by virtue of Regulation 6(3)(c), the date is not required.

[3030O]

[PART III
AGREEMENTS UNDER WHICH A SEPARATE FORM OF CONSENT IS REQUIRED]
[Regulation 2(7)]

[1 (1)	TYPE OF AGREEMENT (2)	FORM OF CONSENT (3)
	Agreements under which a separate form of consent is required.	I wish to purchase [.....................] * / **

[1	TYPE OF AGREEMENT	FORM OF CONSENT
(1)	(2)	(3)
		I understand that I am purchasing the product(s) ticked above on credit provided by you and that the terms relating to the credit for the products can be found [......................]*** in this agreement.
		Your signature(s):
		Notes:
		* Creditor to list the products being offered to the debtor for purchase.
		** Debtor to indicate which products they wish to purchase by putting a tick next to the name(s) of the product(s).
		*** Creditor to insert the cross-references to the terms of the agreement containing the terms relating to the credit for the products being purchased.]

[3030P]

NOTES
 Inserted by the Consumer Credit (Agreements) (Amendment) Regulations 2004, SI 2004/1482, regs 2, 14.

SCHEDULE 6
PRESCRIBED TERMS FOR THE PURPOSES OF SECTIONS 61(1)(A) AND 127(3) OF THE CONSUMER CREDIT ACT 1974

Regulation 6(1)

TYPE OF AGREEMENT (1)	PRESCRIBED TERMS (2)
Amount of credit	
1 Restricted-use debtor-creditor-supplier agreements for fixed-sum credit—	A term stating the amount of the credit, which may be expressed as the total cash price of the goods, services, land or other things, the acquisition of which is to be financed by credit under the agreement.
(a) to finance a transaction comprising the acquisition of goods, services, land or other things specified in the agreement or identified and agreed on at the time the agreement is made;	
(b) under which the total amount payable by the debtor is not greater than the total cash price; and	
(c) under which there is no advance payment.	
2 Agreements for fixed-sum credit not falling within paragraph 1.	A term stating the amount of the credit.
Credit limit	
3 Agreements for running-account credit.	A term stating the credit limit or the manner in which it will be
Rate of interest	
4 Agreements for—	A term stating the rate of any interest on the credit to be provided under the agreement.
(a) running-account credit; and	

TYPE OF AGREEMENT (1)	PRESCRIBED TERMS (2)
(b) fixed-sum credit falling within the exceptions in paragraph 9(a) to (c) of Schedule 1 to these Regulations.	
Repayments	
5 Consumer credit agreements.	A term stating how the debtor is to discharge his obligations under the agreement to make the repayments, which may be expressed by reference to a combination of any of the following— (a) number of repayments; (b) amount of repayments; (c) frequency and timing of repayments; (d) dates of repayments; (e) the manner in which any of the above may be determined; or in any other way, and any power of the creditor to vary what is payable.
6 Consumer hire agreements.	A term stating how the hirer is to discharge his obligations under the agreement to pay the hire payments, which may be expressed by reference to a combination of any of the following— (a) number of payments; (b) amount of payments; (c) frequency and timing of payments; (d) dates of payments; (e) the manner in which any of the above may be determined; or in any other way, and any power of the owner to vary what is payable.

[3030Q]

NOTES

Consumer Credit Act 1974, s 127(3): Repealed, subject to transitional provisions and savings, by the Consumer Credit Act 2006, ss 15, 69(1), 70, Sch 3, paras 1, 11(b), Sch 4.

SCHEDULE 7
PROVISIONS RELATING TO DISCLOSURE OF THE APR
Regulation 1(2)

[1 Assumptions about running-account credit

In the case of an agreement for running-account credit, the following assumptions shall have effect for the purpose of calculating the APR in place of the assumptions in *Part 4* [regulation 6] of the Total Charge for Credit Regulations that might otherwise apply—

(1) in any case where there will be a credit limit but that limit is not known at the date of making the agreement the amount of the credit to be provided shall be taken to be £1,500 or, in a case where the credit limit will be less than £1,500, an amount equal to that limit;

(2) it shall be assumed that the credit is provided for a period of one year beginning with the relevant date;

(3) it shall be assumed that the credit is provided in full on the relevant date;

(4) where the rate of interest will change at a time provided in the agreement within a period of three years beginning with the date of the making of the agreement, the rate shall be taken to be the highest rate at any time obtaining under the agreement in that period;

(5)　where the agreement provides credit to finance the purchase of goods, services, land or other things and also provides one or more of—

    (a)　cash loans;

    (b)　credit to refinance existing indebtedness of the debtor's, whether to the creditor or another person; and

    (c)　credit for any other purpose,

and either or both different rates of interest and different charges are payable in relation to the credit provided for all or some of these purposes, it shall be assumed that the rate of interest and charges payable in relation to the whole of the credit are those applicable to the provision of credit for the purchase of goods, services, land or other things;

(6)　it shall be assumed that the credit is repaid—

    (a)　in twelve equal instalments, and

    (b)　at monthly intervals, beginning one month after the relevant date.

1A　Permissible tolerances in disclosure of the APR

For the purposes of these Regulations, it shall be sufficient compliance with the requirement to show the APR if there is included in the document—

(1)　a rate which exceed the APR by not more than one; or

(2)　a rate which falls short of the APR by not more than 0.1; or

(3)　in a case to which either of paragraphs 2 or 3 below applies, a rate determined in accordance with the paragraph or such of them as apply to that case.]

2　Tolerance where repayments are nearly equal

In the case of an agreement under which all repayments but one are equal and that one repayment does not differ from any other repayment by more whole pence than there are repayments, there may be included in the document a rate found under *[regulation 7] of* [the Schedule to] the Total Charge for Credit Regulations as if that one repayment were equal to the other repayments.

3　Tolerance where interval between relevant date and first repayment is greater than interval between repayments

In the case of an agreement under which:—

    (a)　three or more repayments are to be made at equal intervals; and

    (b)　the interval between the relevant date and the first repayment is greater than the interval between the repayments,

there may be included in the document a rate found under any of *[regulation 7] of* [the Schedule to] the Total Charge for Credit Regulations as if the interval between the relevant date and the first repayment were shortened so as to be equal to the interval between the repayments.

4, 5　...

[3030R]

NOTES

    Para 1: substituted together with para 1A, for original para 1, by the Consumer Credit (Agreements) (Amendment) Regulations 2004, SI 2004/1482, regs 2, 15; words in italics substituted by subsequent words in square brackets by the Consumer Credit (EU Directive) Regulations 2010, SI 2010/1010, regs 51, 55A(a) (as inserted by the Consumer Credit (Amendment) Regulations 2010, SI 2010/1969, regs 4, 16), as from 1 February 2011, with effect in relation to certain agreements before that date, as provided for in regs 101, 101A of SI 2010/1010 at **[3942]**, **[3942A]**.

    Para 1A: substituted as noted to para 1 above.

    Paras 2, 3: words in square brackets substituted by the Consumer Credit (Total Charge for Credit, Agreements and Advertisements) (Amendment) Regulations 1999, SI 1999/3177, reg 4(b), (c); words in italics substituted by subsequent words in square brackets by SI 2010/1010, regs 51, 55A(b) (as inserted by SI 2010/1969, regs 4, 16), as from 1 February 2011, with effect in relation to certain agreements before that date, as provided for in regs 101, 101A of SI 2010/1010 at **[3942]**, **[3942A]**.

    Paras 4, 5: revoked by SI 1999/3177, reg 4(d).

SCHEDULE 8
REGULATED MODIFYING AGREEMENTS

Regulation 7(2)

PART I
INFORMATION TO BE CONTAINED IN DOCUMENTS EMBODYING REGULATED MODIFYING AGREEMENTS VARYING OR SUPPLANTING EARLIER CREDIT AGREEMENTS

TYPE OF MODIFYING AGREEMENT (1)	INFORMATION (2)
Nature of modifying agreement	
[1 All types.	(1) A heading in one of the following forms of words—
	(a) "Agreement modifying a Hire-Purchase Agreement and regulated by the Consumer Credit Act 1974";
	(b) "Agreement modifying a Conditional Sale Agreement and regulated by the Consumer Credit Act 1974"; or
	(c) "Agreement modifying a Fixed-Sum Loan Agreement and regulated by the Consumer Credit Act 1974";
	(d) "Agreement modifying a Credit Card Agreement and regulated by the Consumer Credit Act 1974"; or
	(e) "Agreement modifying a Credit Agreement and regulated by the Consumer Credit Act 1974";
	as the case may require.
	(2) Where the document and a pawn-receipt are combined, the words ", and Pawn-Receipt," shall be inserted in the heading after the word "Agreement" in the second place that it occurs.
	(3) Where the document embodies an agreement of which at least one part is a credit agreement not regulated by the Act, the word "partly" shall be inserted before "regulated" unless the regulated and unregulated parts of the agreement are clearly separate.
	(4) Where the loan is being secured on land the words "secured on" and the address of the land shall be inserted at the end of the heading.]
Parties to modifying agreement	
2 All types	(1) The name[, postal address and, where appropriate, any other address] of the creditor.
	(2) The name[, postal address and, where appropriate, any other address] of the debtor.

TYPE OF MODIFYING AGREEMENT (1)	INFORMATION (2)

FINANCIAL AND RELATED PARTICULARS

Description of goods, services, land etc and cash price

3 Modifying agreements under which— (a) goods, services, land or other things, the acquisition of which was to be comprised in a transaction to be financed by an earlier restricted-use debtor-creditor-supplier agreement for fixed-sum credit and which were specified in the earlier agreement or identified and agreed on at the time the earlier agreement was made, are varied or supplemented; or	(1) A list or other description of the goods, services or other things and, in the case of land, a general description of the land (whether or not varied or supplemented under the modifying agreement) the acquisition of which is to be financed by credit under the modified agreement and the cash price (whether or not so varied or supplemented) in relation to each such list or other description:
(b) the cash price of goods, services, land or other things, the acquisition of which was to be comprised in a transaction to be financed by an earlier restricted-use debtor-creditor-supplier agreement for fixed-sum credit and which were specified in the earlier agreement or identified and agreed on at the time the earlier agreement was made, is varied but the goods, services, land or other things are not varied or supplemented.	Provided that, where both the description and the cash price of all the goods, services, land or other things the acquisition of which was to be comprised in a transaction to be financed by the earlier agreement are unchanged, the requirements of this paragraph may be satisfied in relation to such goods, services, land or other things by a statement clearly indicating that the descriptions and cash prices in the earlier agreement are unchanged.
	(2) The total cash price under the modified agreement.

Advance payments

4 Modifying agreements in relation to which any advance payment is to be made by the debtor additional to any made in relation to an earlier agreement (whether under the modifying agreement or as a condition precedent to the making of that agreement) before he is provided with additional credit under that agreement, or, as the case may be, before he enters into that agreement.	The amount of the additional advance payments to be made by the debtor in relation to the modifying agreement, and, where the modifying agreement is a cancellable agreement, the nature of such payments.

Amount of credit

5 Modifying agreements under which any charge included in the total charge for credit in relation to an earlier agreement for fixed-sum credit is varied or supplemented or under which the amount of the credit to be provided under such an earlier agreement is varied or supplemented, except—	(1) The total amount of the credit to be provided under the modified agreement calculated as follows, namely the total amount of the capital outstanding under the earlier agreement on the relevant date calculated in accordance with sub-paragraph (2) below, increased or reduced, as the case may require, by—
(a) modifying agreements falling within paragraph 3 under which both—	(a) the amount of any additional credit to be provided under the modifying agreement.
(i) the total amount payable by the debtor under the modified agreement is not greater than the total cash price under the agreement; and	(b) the amount of any reduction of credit to be effected under the modifying agreement.
(ii) there is no advance payment under the modifying agreement;	(2) The total amount of the capital outstanding referred to in sub-paragraph (1) above shall be the difference between—
[(b) modifying agreements where the earlier agreement is an agreement excluded from the scope of the Consumer Credit (Early Settlement) Regulations 2004 by regulation 2(2) of these Regulations.]	(a) the total amount of the repayments outstanding under the earlier agreement at the relevant date (whether or not due at that date); and

PART 2
STATUTORY INSTRUMENTS

TYPE OF MODIFYING AGREEMENT (1)	INFORMATION (2)
	(b) the total amount of the charges on the credit not yet accrued under the earlier agreement calculated in accordance with sub-paragraph (3) below.
	[(3) The total amount of the charges on the credit not yet accrued referred to in sub-paragraph (2) above shall be the amount of a notional rebate calculated in accordance with the Consumer Credit (Early Settlement) Regulations 2004 as if early settlement had taken place and as if the settlement date were the relevant date disregarding any deferment of the settlement date under regulation 6 of those Regulations.]
[6 Modifying agreements both under which the amount of credit to be provided under an earlier agreement for fixed-sum credit is varied or supplemented and where the earlier agreement is an agreement excluded from the scope of the Consumer Credit (Early Settlement) Regulations 2004 by regulation 2(2) of those Regulations.	The total amount of the credit to be provided under the modified agreement calculated as follows, namely the total of— (a) the balance of the credit outstanding under the earlier agreement at the relevant date; (b) any charges thereon (included in the total charge for credit in relation to the credit to be provided under the earlier agreement) due and unpaid at the relevant date; (c) the amount of any additional credit to be provided under the modifying agreement, with a list of its constituent parts.]
Credit limit	
7 Modifying agreements under which the provisions relating to any credit limit under an earlier agreement for running-account credit are varied, including a change to or from there being no credit limit.	The varied credit limit under the modified agreement expressed as— (a) a sum of money; (b) a statement that the credit limit will be determined by the creditor from time to time under that agreement and that notice of it will be given by him to the debtor; (c) a sum of money together with a statement that the creditor may vary the credit limit to such sum as he may from time to time determine under that agreement and that notice of it will be given by him to the debtor; or (d) in a case not falling within head (a), (b) or (c) above, either a statement indicating the manner in which the credit limit will be determined and that notice of it will be given by the creditor to the debtor or a statement indicating that there is no credit limit.
[Term of the agreement	
7A. Modifying agreements under which the duration of an earlier agreement for running account credit of fixed duration is varied.	The duration of the modified agreement.
7B. Modifying agreements under which the duration of an earlier agreement for fixed-sum credit is varied.	The duration or minimum duration of the modified agreement.]

TYPE OF MODIFYING AGREEMENT (1)	INFORMATION (2)
Total charge for credit, rate of interest, etc	
[8 Modifying agreements under which any charge included in the total charge for credit in relation to an earlier agreement for fixed-sum credit is varied or supplemented, except modifying agreements—	(1) The total charge for credit in relation to the credit to be provided under the modified agreement, with a list of its constituent parts.
(a) which do not specify either the intervals between repayments under the modified agreement or the amounts of repayments or both the intervals and the amounts;	(2) The varied or supplemented rates of any interest on the credit to be provided under the modified agreement quoted on a per annum basis, or a statement that the rates of interest under the earlier agreement are unchanged.
(b) under which the total amount payable by the debtor under the modified agreement to discharge his indebtedness in respect of the amount of credit provided may vary according to any formula specified in such agreement having effect by reference to movements in the level of any index or to any other factor;	(3) A statement explaining how and when interest charges are calculated and applied under the modified agreement.]
(c) which provide for a variation of, or permit the creditor to vary, (whether or not by reference to any index) the amount or rate of any item included in the total charge for credit in relation to the modified agreement after the relevant date; or	
(d) under which the total amount payable by the debtor under the modified agreement is not greater than the total cash price under that agreement.	
[9 Modifying agreements under which— (a) any charge included in the total charge for credit in relation to an earlier agreement for fixed-sum credit is varied or supplemented and which fall within the exceptions in paragraph 8(a) to (c); or (b) the rate of any other charge included in the total charge for credit in relation to an earlier agreement for running-account credit is varied or supplemented.	(1) The total charge for credit in relation to the credit to be provided under the modified agreement with a list of its constituent parts and in the case of running-account credit, the total charge for credit shall be calculated on the same assumptions as are set out in paragraph 1 of Schedule 7 for the purpose of calculating the APR in place of the assumptions in *Part 4* [regulation 6] of the Total Charge for Credit Regulations that might otherwise apply.
	(2) The varied or supplemented rates of any interest on the credit to be provided under the modified agreement quoted on a per annum basis, or a statement that the rates of interest under the earlier agreement are unchanged.
	(3) A statement whether the interest rates to be shown under (2) above are fixed or variable.
	(4) A statement explaining how and when interest charges are calculated and applied under the modified agreement.]
Total amount payable	
10 Modifying agreements falling within paragraph 8.	The total amount payable under the modified agreement, being the total of any amounts to be shown under paragraphs 4, 5 or 6, and 8 above.
Timing of repayments	
11 Modifying agreements under which—	The timing of repayments to be made under the modified agreement expressed by reference to one or more of the following—

PART 2
STATUTORY INSTRUMENTS

TYPE OF MODIFYING AGREEMENT (1)	INFORMATION (2)
(i) the amount of the credit to be provided under an earlier agreement for fixed-sum credit is varied or supplemented;	(a) the dates on which each repayment is to be made;
(ii) the repayment provisions of an earlier agreement for fixed-sum or for running-account credit are varied or supplemented; or	(b) the frequency and number of the repayments and the date of the first repayment or a statement indicating the manner in which that date will be determined;
(iii) any charge included in the total charge for credit in relation to an earlier agreement for fixed-sum or for running-account credit is varied or supplemented.	(c) a statement indicating the manner in which the dates of the repayments will be determined.

Amount of repayments

12 Modifying agreements falling within paragraph 11 but not falling within paragraph 13.	The amount of each repayment to be made under the modified agreement expressed as—
	(a) a sum of money;
	(b) a specified proportion of a specified amount (including the amount outstanding from time to time);
	(c) a combination of heads (a) and (b) above; or
	(d) in a case where the amount of any repayment cannot be expressed in accordance with head (a), (b) or (c) above, a statement indicating the manner in which the amount will be determined.
13 Modifying agreements falling within paragraph 11 where—	The amount of each repayment to be made under the modified agreement (with or without the equivalent repayment after deduction of tax in accordance with section 26 of, and Schedule 7 to, the Finance Act 1982) expressed as—
(i) the credit to be provided under the modified agreement is repayable by two or more instalments; and	(a) a sum of money;
(ii) the interest on such credit is of a type to which section 26 of, and Schedule 7 to, the Finance Act 1982 apply.	(b) a specified proportion of a specified amount (including the amount outstanding from time to time);
	(c) a combination of heads (a) and (b) above; or
	(d) in a case where the amount of any repayment cannot be expressed in accordance with head (a), (b) or (c) above, a statement indicating the manner in which the amount will be determined:
	Provided that, where the amounts to be paid by the debtor after deduction of tax in accordance with section 26 of, and Schedule 7 to, the Finance Act 1982 are the same, the requirements of this paragraph may be satisfied by a statement indicating the lowest and highest amounts of the repayments to be made under the modified agreement before deduction of tax.

TYPE OF MODIFYING AGREEMENT (1)	INFORMATION (2)
[13A Modifying agreements under which— (a) an earlier agreement is varied or supplemented so that different interest rates or different charges forming part of the total charge for credit or both are payable in respect of—	A statement of the order or proportions in which any amount paid by the debtor which is not sufficient to discharge the total debt then due under the agreement will be applied or appropriated by the creditor towards the discharge of the sums due—
(i) credit provided under the agreement for different purposes; or	(a) in respect of the amounts of credit provided for different purposes, or
(ii) different parts of the agreement,	(b) under each of the different parts of the agreement,
whether or not the agreement is a multiple agreement; or	as the case may be.]
(b) an earlier agreement is varied by varying the order or proportions in which any amount paid by the debtor which is not sufficient to discharge the total debt then due under the agreement will be applied or appropriated by the creditor towards the discharge of the sums due—	
(i) in respect of the amounts of credit provided for different purposes, or	
(ii) under each of the different parts of the agreement, as the case may require.	

APR

14 Modifying agreements under which— (a) the amount of the credit to be provided under an earlier agreement for fixed-sum credit is varied or supplemented; (b) the repayment provisions of such an agreement are varied or supplemented; or (c) any charge included in the total charge for credit in relation to such an agreement is varied or supplemented.	The APR in relation to the modified agreement or a statement indicating that the total amount payable under the modified agreement is not greater than the total cash price of the goods, services, land or other things, the acquisition of which is to be financed by credit under that agreement.
15 Modifying agreements not falling within paragraph 16 under which—	The APR in relation to the modified agreement.
(a) the provisions relating to any credit limit under an earlier agreement for running-account credit are varied, including a change to or from there being no credit limit;	
(b) the repayment provisions of such an agreement are varied or supplemented; or	
(c) any charge included in the total charge for credit in relation to such an agreement is varied or supplemented.	
16 (a) Modifying agreements under which—	(1) The APR in relation to the modified agreement calculated on the assumptions specified in sub-paragraphs (2) and (3) below.
(i) the provisions relating to the credit limit under an earlier debtor-creditor-supplier agreement for running-account credit which fulfils all the criteria in sub-paragraph (b) below are varied;	(2) The first assumption referred to in sub-paragraph (1) above is the assumption that—

TYPE OF MODIFYING AGREEMENT (1)	INFORMATION (2)
(ii) the repayment provisions of such an agreement are varied or supplemented; or (iii) any charge included in the total charge for credit in relation to such an agreement is varied or supplemented.	(a) the debtor is provided with an amount of credit at the date of the making of the modifying agreement which, taken with the amount of the charge for that credit ascertained at that date under the provisions of the modified agreement, is equal to the credit limit under the modified agreement; and
(b) The criteria referred to in sub-paragraph (a) above are that— (i) the debtor agrees to pay the creditor an amount specified in the agreement on specified occasions; (ii) there is a credit limit; and (iii) charges for credit are either—	(b) the debtor repays the sum of the amounts referred to in head (a) above by payments of the amounts specified in the modified agreement on the occasions specified in that agreement and makes no other payment and obtains no further credit in relation to the account.
(aa) a fixed amount in respect of each transaction; or (bb) calculated as a proportion of the price payable under a transaction financed by the credit.	(3) The second assumption referred to in sub-paragraph (1) above is the like assumption as in sub-paragraph (2) above save that the sum of the amounts referred to in head (a) thereof shall be taken to be one third of the credit limit under the modified agreement.
17 Modifying agreements which are required under paragraph 14, 15 or 16 to disclose an APR in relation to the modified agreement and where the APR is based on a total charge for credit which is calculated to take account of relief available under section 19 of the Income and Corporation Taxes Act 1970 and Schedule 4 to the Finance Act 1976.	A statement indicating that it has been assumed in the calculation of the APR in relation to the modified agreement that relief may be available under section 19 of the Income and Corporation Taxes Act 1970 and Schedule 4 to the Finance Act 1976 in respect of premiums under certain policies of insurance without any deduction under section 21 of the said Act of 1970.

Variable rates or items

18 Modifying agreements which are required under paragraph 14, 15 or 16 to disclose an APR in relation to the modified agreement and under which the rate or amount of any item included in the total charge for credit in relation to the modified agreement will or may be varied (other than a variation in consequence of an event which is certain to occur).	A statement indicating that in calculating the APR in relation to the credit to be provided under the modified agreement no account has been taken of any variation which may occur under that agreement of the rate or amount of any item entering into that calculation.
19 Modifying agreements falling within paragraph 18.	A statement indicating the circumstances in which any variation referred to in paragraph 18 above may occur and, where that information is ascertainable at the time at which the document referred to in section 61(1) of the Act is presented or sent to the debtor for signature, the time at which any such variation may occur.
[19A Modifying agreements which are required under paragraph 14, 15 or 16 to disclose an APR in relation to the modified agreement and under which the provisions of an earlier agreement are varied or supplemented with the result that the modified agreement is an agreement to which regulation 15A of the Total Charge for Credit Regulations [1980] applies.	The initial standard variable rate (within the meaning of regulation 15A(2) of the Total Charge for Credit Regulations [1980]) in relation to the modified agreement, together with a statement explaining— (a) what that rate is; and (b) that it has been taken into account in calculating the APR in relation to the modified agreement.]

TYPE OF MODIFYING AGREEMENT (1)	INFORMATION (2)

OTHER INFORMATION

Security provided by the debtor

20 Modifying agreements (to which section 114 of the Act applies) under which an article taken in pawn by any person under an earlier agreement is varied or supplemented and where no separate pawn-receipt is given.	A statement indicating that an article has been taken in pawn under the modified agreement and a description of the article, unless unchanged from that in the earlier agreement, sufficient to identify it.
21 Modifying agreements (except those referred to in paragraph 20) under which— (a) any provisions for security provided by the debtor in relation to an earlier agreement to secure the carrying out of the obligations of the debtor under the earlier agreement are varied (including a variation to or from there being no security provided by the debtor); or (b) new or additional security is to be provided by the debtor.	A description of the new, additional or varied security to be provided by the debtor in relation to the modified agreement and of the subject matter to which it relates, sufficient to identify the new, additional or varied security, or a statement indicating that the debtor is no longer providing any security in relation to that agreement.

[Charges

22 Modifying agreements under which any provision for charges under an earlier agreement are varied, including a variation to or from there being no such charges.	(1) A list of any charges payable under the modified agreement to the creditor upon failure by the debtor or a relative of his to do or refrain from doing anything which he is required to do or refrain from doing, as the case may be, or a statement indicating that no such charges are payable as the case may be.
	(2) A statement indicating any term of the modified agreement which provides for charges
	(a) not required to be shown under (1) above; or
	(b) included in the total charge for credit.]

[Cancellation rights

23 Modifying agreements that are not treated as cancellable agreements under section 82(5) of the Act.	A statement that the modifying agreement is not cancellable.

Amount payable on early settlement

24 Agreements for fixed sum credit [secured on land] for a term of more than one month.	(1) Examples based on the amount of credit to be provided under the agreement or the nominal amount of either £1000 or £100, showing the amount that would be payable if the debtor exercised the right under section 94 of the Act to discharge his indebtedness on the date when—
	(a) a quarter of the term of the agreement elapses;
	(b) half of the term elapses; and
	(c) three quarters of the term elapses,
	or on the first repayment date after each of those dates.
	(2) A statement explaining that, in calculating the amounts shown, no account has been taken of any variation which might occur under the agreement, and that the amounts are accordingly only illustrative.]

PART 2
STATUTORY INSTRUMENTS

TYPE OF MODIFYING AGREEMENT (1)	INFORMATION (2)
[24A Modifying agreements falling within regulation 8(1A)(b) or (c)	A statement providing details of the debtor's right of early repayment under section 94 of the Act including— (1) the fact that the debtor has a right to repay early in full or part; (2) the procedure for early repayment, and (3) where applicable details of the creditor's right to compensation under section 95A of the Act and the manner in which that compensation shall be determined.]

[3030S]

NOTES

Paras 1, 6, 8, 22: substituted by the Consumer Credit (Agreements) (Amendment) Regulations 2004, SI 2004/1482, regs 2, 16(1), (2), (4), (6), (9).

Para 2: words in brackets substituted by the Consumer Credit Act 1974 (Electronic Communications) Order 2004, SI 2004/3236, art 4(1), (7).

Para 5: words in square brackets substituted by SI 2004/1482, regs 2, 16(1), (3).

Paras 7A, 7B, 13A: inserted by SI 2004/1482, regs 2, 16(1), (5), (8).

Para 9: substituted by SI 2004/1482, regs 2, 16(1), (7); in column 2, words in italics substituted by subsequent words in square brackets by the Consumer Credit (EU Directive) Regulations 2010, SI 2010/1010, regs 51, 56(za) (as inserted by the Consumer Credit (Amendment) Regulations 2010, SI 2010/1969, regs 4, 17), as from 1 February 2011, with effect in relation to certain agreements before that date, as provided for in regs 101, 101A of SI 2010/1010 at **[3942]**, **[3942A]**.

Para 19A: inserted by the Consumer Credit (Total Charge for Credit, Agreements and Advertisements) (Amendment) Regulations 1999, SI 1999/3177, reg 4(e); words in square brackets inserted by SI 2010/1010, regs 51, 56(zb) (as inserted by SI 2010/1969, regs 4, 17), as from 1 February 2011, with effect in relation to certain agreements before that date, as provided for in regs 101, 101A of SI 2010/1010 at **[3942]**, **[3942A]**.

Para 23: inserted by SI 2004/1482, regs 2, 16(1), (10).

Para 24: inserted by SI 2004/1482, regs 2, 16(1), (10); words in square brackets inserted by SI 2010/1010, regs 51, 56(a), as from 1 February 2011, with effect in relation to certain agreements before that date, as provided for in regs 101, 101A of the 2010 Regulations at **[3942]**, **[3942A]**.

Para 24A: inserted by SI 2010/1010, regs 51, 56(b), as from 1 February 2011, with effect in relation to certain agreements before that date, as provided for in regs 101, 101A of the 2010 Regulations at **[3942]**, **[3942A]**.

PART II

INFORMATION TO BE CONTAINED IN DOCUMENTS EMBODYING REGULATED MODIFYING AGREEMENTS VARYING OR SUPPLEMENTING EARLIER HIRE AGREEMENTS

Regulation 7(9)

TYPE OF MODIFYING AGREEMENT (1)	INFORMATION (2)
Nature of modifying agreement	
[1 All types.	(1) A heading in the following form of words— "Agreement modifying a Hire Agreement and regulated by the Consumer Credit Act 1974". (2) Where the credit is being secured on land the words "secured on" followed by the address of the land shall be inserted at the end of the heading.]
Parties to modifying agreement	
2 All types.	(1) The name[, postal address and, where appropriate, any other address] of the owner. (2) The name[, postal address and, where appropriate, any other address] of the hirer.

TYPE OF MODIFYING AGREEMENT (1)	INFORMATION (2)

FINANCIAL AND RELATED PARTICULARS

Description of goods

3 Modifying agreements under which— (a) goods to be bailed or hired under an earlier agreement are varied or supplemented; or	A list or other description of the goods to be bailed or hired under the modified agreement (whether or not varied or supplemented under the modifying agreement);
(b) any provision of an earlier agreement relating to advance, hire or other payments is varied but the goods to be bailed or hired under the earlier agreement are not varied or supplemented.	Provided that, where the description of all goods to be bailed or hired under the earlier agreement is unchanged, the requirements of this paragraph may be satisfied in relation to such goods by a statement clearly indicating that the descriptions in the earlier agreement are unchanged.

Advance payments

4 Modifying agreements in relation to which any advance payment is to be made by the hirer additional to any made in relation to an earlier agreement (whether under the modifying agreement or as a condition precedent to the making of that agreement) before he is to take possession of any additional goods to be bailed or hired under that agreement or, as the case may be, before he enters into that agreement.	The amount of the additional advance payments to be made by the hirer in relation to the modifying agreement, and, where the modifying agreement is a cancellable agreement, the nature of such payments.

Hire payments

5 Modifying agreements under which any provisions of an earlier agreement relating to hire payments, other than advance payments, are varied or supplemented.	(1) The amount of each hire payment (other than an advance payment) to be made by the hirer under the modified agreement in relation to any period on or after the date of the modifying agreement. (2) The timing of such payments expressed by reference to one or more of the following— (a) the dates on which each payment is to be made; (b) the frequency and number of payments and the date of the first payment or a statement indicating the manner in which that date will be determined (c) a statement indicating the manner in which the dates of the payments will be determined.

Other payments

6 Modifying agreements under which any provisions of an earlier agreement relating to payments other than advance payments and hire payments are varied or supplemented, including a change to or from there being no such other payments.	(1) The amount (or a statement indicating the manner in which the amount will be determined) of each of the following descriptions of payments (not being an advance payment or a hire payment) to be made under the modified agreement by, or on behalf of, the hirer, or a relative of his, to the owner in relation to any period on or after the date of the modifying agreement, that is to say,— (a) any payment under arrangements for the installation, care, maintenance or protection of any goods; (b) any premium under a contract of insurance; or (c) any payment payable on termination of the modified agreement (other than a payment on default to be shown under paragraph 10 below).

PART 2
STATUTORY INSTRUMENTS

TYPE OF MODIFYING AGREEMENT (1)	INFORMATION (2)
	(2) The timing of such payments to be made under the modified agreement expressed by reference to one or more of the following—
	(a) the dates on which each payment is to be made;
	(b) the frequency and number of the payments and the date of the first payment or a statement indicating the manner in which that date will be determined; or
	(c) a statement indicating the manner in which the dates of the payments will be determined.
	(3) References in this paragraph to the owner include references to his near relative, his partner and a member of a group of which he is a member, to any person nominated by him or by any such person in relation to the arrangements, the contract of insurance or the termination of the modified agreement, and to a near relative of his partner; and "near relative" means, in relation to any person, the husband, wife, father, mother, brother, sister, son or daughter of that person and "group" means the person (including a company) having control of a company together with all the companies directly or indirectly controlled by him.

Variable payments

7 Modifying agreements including provisions for variation of hire or other payments, where the amount of any such payment following any variation cannot be ascertained at the time of the making of the modifying agreement.	(1) Subject to sub-paragraph (2) below, a statement indicating the circumstances in which any hire payment to be shown under paragraph 5 above or any other payment to be shown under paragraph 6 may be varied under the modified agreement and, where that information is ascertainable at the time at which the document referred to in section 61(1) of the Act is presented or sent to the hirer for signature, the time at which any such variation may occur.
	(2) Sub-paragraph (1) above does not apply to a variation under the modified agreement which takes account only of a change in value added tax.
	(3) References in sub-paragraph (2) above to a change in value added tax include references to a change to or from no tax being charged.

Duration of hire

8 Modifying agreements under which— (a) additional goods are to be bailed or hired for a fixed period or a minimum period; or	A statement indicating that goods are to be bailed or hired under the modified agreement for a fixed-period or a minimum period, as the case may be, and the duration of that period.
(b) any provisions of any earlier agreement that goods are to be bailed or hired for a fixed period or a minimum period are varied, including a variation to or from there being no such fixed or minimum period.	

TYPE OF MODIFYING AGREEMENT (1)	INFORMATION (2)
OTHER INFORMATION *Security provided by the hirer*	
9 Modifying agreements under which— (a) any provisions for security provided by the hirer in relation to an earlier agreement to secure the carrying out of the obligations of the hirer under the earlier agreement are varied (including a variation to or from there being no security provided by the hirer); or (b) new or additional security is to be provided by the hirer.	A description of the new, additional or varied security to be provided by the hirer in relation to the modified agreement and of the subject matter to which it relates, sufficient to identify the new, additional or varied security, or a statement indicating that the hirer is no longer providing any security in relation to that agreement.
Charges on default	
10 Modifying agreements under which any provisions for charges on default under an earlier agreement are varied, including a variation to or from there being no such charges.	[A list of all] charges payable under the modified agreement to the owner upon failure by the hirer or a relative of his to do or refrain from doing, as the case may be, or a statement indicating that no such charges are payable under that agreement.
[Cancellation rights	
11. Modifying agreements that are not treated as cancellable agreements under section 82(5) of the Act.	A statement that the modifying agreement is not cancellable.]

[3030T]

NOTES
    Para 1: substituted by the Consumer Credit (Agreements) (Amendment) Regulations 2004, SI 2004/1482, regs 2, 17(1), (2).
    Para 2: words in brackets substituted by the Consumer Credit Act 1974 (Electronic Communications) Order 2004, SI 2004/3236, art 4(1), (8).
    Para 10: in column (2) words in square brackets substituted by SI 2004/1482, regs 2, 17(1), (3).
    Para 11: inserted by SI 2004/1482, regs 2, 17(1), (4).

CONSUMER CREDIT (LINKED TRANSACTIONS) (EXEMPTIONS) REGULATIONS 1983

(SI 1983/1560)

NOTES
    Made: 24 October 1983.
    Authority: Consumer Credit Act 1974, ss 19(4), 69(5), 96(3), 189(1).
    Commencement: 19 May 1985.

1 Citation, commencement and interpretation

    (1) These Regulations may be cited as the Consumer Credit (Linked Transactions) (Exemptions) Regulations 1983 and shall come into operation on 19th May 1985.

    (2) In these Regulations—
       "the Act" means the Consumer Credit Act 1974;

            .....

       ... and
       "guarantee of goods" means anything in writing which contains or purports to contain some promise of assurance (however worded or presented) that defects in goods will be made good by complete or partial replacement, or by repair, monetary compensation or otherwise.

    [(2A) References in these Regulations to contracts of insurance and to deposits must be read with—
       (a)   section 22 of the Financial Services and Markets Act 2000;
       (b)   any relevant order under that section; and

PART 2 STATUTORY INSTRUMENTS

(c)   Schedule 2 to that Act.]

[3031]

NOTES
Para (2): definitions omitted revoked by the Financial Services and Markets Act 2000 (Consequential Amendments and Repeals) Order 2001, SI 2001/3649, art 376(1).
Para (2A): added by SI 2001/3649, art 376(2).

2   Exempted linked transactions

(1)   The linked transactions of the descriptions specified in paragraph (2) below shall be excluded from—

(a)   the operation of section 19(3) of the Act (which provides that a linked transaction entered into before the making of the regulated consumer credit agreement or regulated consumer hire agreement to which it relates has no effect until such time (if any) as that agreement is made);

(b)   section 69(1)(i) and (ii) (which provides that a notice of cancellation served by the debtor or hirer under a cancellable agreement shall operate to cancel any linked transaction and to withdraw any offer by the debtor or hirer, or his relative, to enter into a linked transaction); and

(c)   the operation of section 96(1) (which provides that where the indebtedness of the debtor under a regulated consumer credit agreement is discharged before the time fixed by the agreement, he, and any relative of his, shall be discharged from any liability under a linked transaction, other than a debt which has already become payable).

(2)   The linked transactions referred to in paragraph (1) above are as follows—

(a)   contracts of insurance;

(b)   other contracts in so far as they contain a guarantee of goods; or

(c)   transactions comprising or effected under—

(i)   any agreement for the operation of any account (including any savings account) for the deposit of money; or

(ii)   any agreement for the operation of a current account, under which the customer may, by means of cheques or similar orders payable to himself or to any other person, obtain or have the use of money held or made available by the person with whom the account is kept and which records alterations in the financial relationship between the said person and the customer.

[3032]

CONSUMER CREDIT (REBATE ON EARLY SETTLEMENT) REGULATIONS 1983

(SI 1983/1562)

NOTES
Made: 4 October 1983.
Authority: Consumer Credit Act 1974, ss 95, 182(2), 189(1).
Commencement: 19 May 1985.

ARRANGEMENT OF REGULATIONS

1   Citation, commencement and interpretation

*(1)   These Regulations may be cited as the Consumer Credit (Rebate on Early Settlement)
Regulations 1983 and shall come into operation on 19th May 1985.*

(2)   In these Regulations—
    "the Act" means the Consumer Credit Act 1974;
    "early settlement" shall be construed in accordance with Regulation 2(1) below;
    "rebate" means a rebate of charges for credit included in the total charge for credit;
    *"the relevant date" shall be determined in accordance with the Total Charge for Credit
        Regulations;*
    "settlement date" has the meaning given by Regulation 6 below;
    *"total charge for credit" shall be determined in accordance with the Total Charge for Credit
        Regulations, subject to Regulations 3(2) and 7 below; and*
    *"the Total Charge for Credit Regulations" means the Consumer Credit (Total Charge for
        Credit) Regulations 1980.*

*(3)   The length of any period for the purposes of calculations under these Regulations shall be
determined in accordance with Regulation 11 of the Total Charge for Credit Regulations, other than
paragraph (5)(a) of that Regulation.*

*(4)   In these Regulations, references to repayment of credit are references to repayment of credit
with any amount included in the total charge for credit payable at the same time.*

[3033]

NOTES
    These Regulations are revoked by the Consumer Credit (Early Settlement) Regulations 2004, SI 2004/1483,
reg 8, as from 31 May 2005, subject to SI 2004/1483, reg 10 at **[3398]**, which provides for the continuing effect
of these Regulations in specified circumstances.

2   Entitlement to rebate

*(1)   Subject to the following provisions of this Regulation, the creditor shall allow to the debtor
under a regulated consumer credit agreement a rebate at least equal to that calculated in
accordance with the following provisions of these Regulations whenever early settlement takes
place, that is to say whenever, under section 94 of the Act, on refinancing, on breach of the
agreement, or for any other reason, the indebtedness of the debtor is discharged or becomes payable
before the time fixed by the agreement, or any sum becomes payable by him before the time so fixed.*

*(2)   Paragraph (1) above does not apply in the case of agreements of the following
descriptions—*
    *(a)   agreements under which no payments of items included in the total charge for credit are
        required to be made in respect of the period of time commencing on the settlement date;
        or*
    (b)   agreements for running-account credit.

*(3)   Paragraph (1) above does not apply where a hire-purchase or conditional sale agreement is
terminated by the debtor under section 99 of the Act.*

*(4)   Where a sum less than the total remaining indebtedness of the debtor is required to be paid
before the time fixed by the agreement, no consequential payment of any subsequent instalment
required to be paid under the agreement, or under a modifying agreement not relating to the
provision of additional credit or an increase in the total charge for credit, shall entitle the debtor to
a rebate.*

[3034]

NOTES
    Revoked as noted to reg 1 at **[3033]**.

3   Items included in the calculation of rebate

*(1)   Subject to paragraph (2) below, the rebate shall be calculated by reference to all sums paid
or payable by the debtor or a relative of his under or in connection with the agreement (whether to
the creditor or any other person) and included in the total charge for credit.*

(2)   There may be excluded from the calculation of the rebate—
    (a)   taxes, duties, fees and charges payable under or by virtue of any statute or payable to

PART 2
STATUTORY INSTRUMENTS

the Secretary of State or any other Minister or government department (including for
this purpose the Civil Aviation Authority and a Minister or department of the
Government of Northern Ireland or of any country outside the United Kingdom) or to a
local authority or similar body outside the United Kingdom;

(b)   sums paid or payable under linked transactions, except sums paid before the settlement
       date in respect of cash, goods or services to be supplied under the transaction wholly or
       partly after that date;

(c)   sums payable under linked transactions excluded under Regulations made under
       section 96(3) of the Act from the operation of section 96(1);

[(d)   any fee or commission paid by the debtor or a relative of his under a credit brokerage
       contract relating to the agreement.]

[3035]

NOTES
Revoked as noted to reg 1 at **[3033]**.
Para (2): sub-para (d) inserted by the Consumer Credit (Total Charge for Credit and Rebate on Early
Settlement) (Amendment) Regulations 1989, SI 1989/596, reg 3.

4   Formulae for calculating rebate

(1)   In the case of an agreement for fixed-sum credit provided, and to be repayable, in a single
lump sum at the end of a specified period, the amount of the rebate shall be given by the formula set
out in Schedule 1 to these Regulations.

(2)   Subject as hereinafter mentioned, in the case of agreements under which credit is repayable
by instalments, the amount of the rebate shall be as follows—

(i)   where credit is repayable in equal instalments at equal intervals, the amount of the
       rebate shall be given by the formula set out in Part I of Schedule 2 to these Regulations;

(ii)   where credit is repayable in unequal instalments or in instalments at unequal intervals,
       the amount of the rebate shall be given by the formula set out in Part II of Schedule 2 to
       these Regulations.

(3)   In the case of agreements under which credit is repayable by instalments to be made at
other than monthly or shorter intervals and where early settlement takes place between two
instalment dates for the repayment of credit under the agreement, the amount of the rebate shall be
given by the formula set out in Schedule 3 to these Regulations.

(4)   Where a sum less than the total remaining indebtedness of the debtor is required to be paid
before the time fixed by the agreement, the amount of the rebate shall be given by the formula set out
in Schedule 4 to these Regulations.

(5)   The provisions of Schedule 5 to these Regulations shall have effect for the purpose of
determining whether repayments of credit under the agreement may be regarded as being in equal
instalments or at equal intervals for the purpose of any formula set out in Schedules 2 to 4 to these
Regulations.

(6)   The examples set out in Schedules 1 to 4 to these Regulations shall have effect only for
illustrating the use of the formulae in those Schedules, and in the case of conflict between any
example and any other provision of these Regulations, that other provision shall prevail.

[3036]

NOTES
Revoked as noted to reg 1 at **[3033]**.

5   Deferment of settlement date

The settlement date for calculation of the rebate in Schedules 1 to 4 to these Regulations may be
deferred as follows—

(a)   where the agreement provides for the credit to be repaid over, or at the end of, a period
       of 5 years or less, by 2 months;

(b)   where the agreement provides for the credit to be repaid over, or at the end of, a period
       of more than 5 years, by 1 month.

[3037]

NOTES
Revoked as noted to reg 1 at **[3033]**.

6   Settlement date

(1)   Subject to paragraph (3) below, where the agreement provides for the credit to be repaid by
instalments to be made only at monthly or shorter intervals and early settlement takes place
between two instalment dates for repayment of credit under the agreement, the settlement date shall
be taken to be the date of the instalment due under the agreement immediately following—

(a)   the date of service of a notice on the creditor under section 94 of the Act, if accompanied by payment of the amount due on early settlement (less any rebate allowable under these Regulations), or any later date specified as the date for early settlement in the notice, if the debtor pays the amount in question not later than that date;

(b)   the date specified as the date for payment of any sum by the debtor involving early settlement in any notice served under section 76(1) of the Act, any default notice or any notice served under section 98(1), if the debtor pays the amount in question (less any rebate allowable under these Regulations) not later than that date;

(c)   in any other case, the date on which the debtor pays any sum involving early settlement.

(2)   Subject to paragraph (3) below, where the agreement provides for the credit to be repaid by instalments to be made at other than monthly or shorter intervals and early settlement takes place between two instalment dates for repayment of credit under the agreement, the settlement date shall be taken to be 14 days after the date referred to in paragraph (1)(a), (b) or (c) above, as the case may be.

(3)   Where the creditor has given the debtor a statement under section 97 of the Act indicating the amount of the payment required to discharge the debtor's indebtedness under the agreement, the settlement date shall be taken to be the date specified in Regulation 3 of the Consumer Credit (Settlement Information) Regulations 1983, if the debtor pays the amount (less any rebate allowable under these Regulations) not later than that date.

(4)   In any other case, the settlement date shall be the date on which the debtor pays any sum involving early settlement.

[3038]

NOTES
Revoked as noted to reg 1 at **[3033]**.

---

7   Variation of rates and amounts

Where, under a power contained in the agreement, the rate or amount of any item included in the total charge for credit, the amount of any instalment of repayment of credit or the time fixed by the agreement for the debtor's indebtedness to be discharged is or can be varied, the rate or amount, as the case may be, of any item to be included in the total charge for credit or the amount of any instalment of repayment of credit or the time fixed by the agreement for the debtor's indebtedness to be discharged for the purpose of calculation of the rebate shall be taken to be, in respect of any period of time commencing on or after the settlement date, the rate or amount or time subsisting at that date.

[3039]

NOTES
Revoked as noted to reg 1 at **[3033]**.

---

8   Old agreements

Any sums paid or payable by the debtor or a relative of his under or in connection with an agreement made before 1st April 1977 to a person other than the creditor may be excluded from the calculation of the rebate under these Regulations, and in this paragraph "creditor" has the same meaning as in Regulation 5(2) of the Total Charge for Credit Regulations.

[3040]

NOTES
Revoked as noted to reg 1 at **[3033]**.

SCHEDULES

SCHEDULE 1
PRO RATA RULE: FORMULA FOR CALCULATION OF REBATE WHERE FIXED-SUM CREDIT IS PROVIDED AND REPAYABLE IN A SINGLE LUMP SUM AT THE END OF A SPECIFIED PERIOD

Regulation 4(1)

The rebate of charges is given by the following formula, whereby it is calculated pro rata to the period of the agreement outstanding at the settlement date—

$$\frac{d}{e} \times K$$

where

d = period beginning with the settlement date and ending with the date for the repayment of credit under the agreement (the settlement date being deferable in accordance with Regulation 5)

e = period beginning with the relevant date, as defined in the Total Charge for Credit Regulations, and ending with the date for the repayment of credit under the agreement

K = total charge for credit on which rebate is to be allowed

EXAMPLE
Facts

A loan of £160 is agreed to be repaid by 1 repayment of £185 after 273 days. The consumer settles the loan on 131st day (ie on 1st May when 142 days are outstanding)

Calculation of Rebate

$d = (142 - 61) = 81$ where the settlement date is deferred by 2 months (in this case by a month of 31 days followed by a month of 30 days) in accordance with Regulation 5(a)

$e = 273$

$K = £25$ (ie £185 – £160)

$$\text{Rebate} = \frac{81}{273} \times £25$$

$$= £7.42$$

[3041]

NOTES

Revoked as noted to reg 1 at [3033].

SCHEDULE 2
RULE OF 78

Regulation 4(2)

PART I
SIMPLE FORMULA FOR CALCULATION OF REBATE WHERE CREDIT IS REPAYABLE IN EQUAL INSTALMENTS AT EQUAL INTERVALS

Where credit is repayable in equal instalments at equal intervals, the rebate of charges is given by the following formula—

$$\frac{m(m+1)}{n(n+1)} \times K$$

Where

m = total number of instalments not yet due at the settlement date (deferable in accordance with Regulation 5)

n = total number of instalments payable under the agreement after the relevant date, as defined in the Total Charge for Credit Regulations

K = total charge for credit on which rebate is to be allowed

EXAMPLE
Facts

A loan of £1000 is agreed to be repaid by 36 monthly instalments of £48 starting one month after the date of the loan and the consumer settles the loan at the end of the 30th month (ie when 6 monthly instalments are outstanding)

Calculation of Rebate

$K = £728$ (ie 36 x £48 – £1000)

$m = (6 - 2) = 4$ where the number of outstanding instalments is reduced by 2 because the settlement date is deferred by 2 months in accordance with Regulation 5(a)

$n = 36$

$$\text{Rebate} = \frac{4(4+1)}{36(36+1)} \times £728$$

$$= \frac{20}{1332} \times £728$$

$$= £10.93$$

[3042]

NOTES

Revoked as noted to reg 1 at [3033].

PART II
GENERAL FORMULA FOR CALCULATION OF REBATE WHERE CREDIT IS REPAYABLE IN UNEQUAL INSTALMENTS AT UNEQUAL INTERVALS

Where credit is repayable in unequal instalments or in instalments at unequal intervals, the rebate of charges is given by the following formula—

$$\frac{B_1b_1+B_2b_2 \ldots +B_mb_m}{A_1a_1+A_2a_2 \ldots +A_na_n} \times K$$

Where
m = *total number of instalments not yet due at the settlement date (deferable in accordance with Regulation 5)*
n = *total number of instalments payable under the agreement after the relevant date, as defined in the Total Charge for Credit Regulations*
K = *total charge for credit on which rebate is to be allowed*
A = *amount of instalment*
B = *amount of instalment not yet due at the settlement date (deferable in accordance with Regulation 5)*
a = *period of instalment from the relevant date*
b = *period of instalment from the settlement date counted on the same basis*

EXAMPLE I
Facts
    A loan of £1000 is agreed to be repaid by 1 monthly instalment after the date of the loan of £100, 22 monthly instalments thereafter of £50 and 1 monthly instalment thereafter of £40 and the consumer settles the loan at the end of the 18th month (i e when 6 monthly instalments are outstanding)
Calculation of Rebate
$K = £240$ *(i e £100 + (£50 x 22) + £40 – £1000)*
$A_1 = £100, A_2$ *to* $A_{23} = £50, A_{24} = £40$
B_1 *to* $B_3* = £50, B_4* = £40$
$a_1 = 1, a_2 = 2, etc, a_{24} = 24$
$b_1 = 1, b_2 = 2, etc, b_4 = 4$
$m = 4*, n = 24$
* *(Where the number of outstanding instalments is reduced by 2 because the settlement date is deferred by 2 months in accordance with Regulation 5(a))*

$$\text{Rebate} = \frac{£50\,(1+2+3)+£40\,(4)}{£100\,(1)+£50\,(2+3+4+\ldots\ 21+22+23)+£40\,(24)} \times £240$$

$$= \frac{(£50 \times 6)+£160}{£100+(£50 \times 275)+£960} \times £240$$

$$= \frac{£460}{£14810} \times £240$$

$$= £7.45$$

EXAMPLE II
Facts
A loan of £1000 is agreed to be repaid by 4 three-monthly instalments of £110, 4 two-monthly instalments of £110 and 4 monthly instalments of £110. The consumer settles the loan at the end of the 16th month (i e when 6 instalments are outstanding consisting of 2 two-monthly instalments and 4 monthly instalments)
Calculation of Rebate
$K = £320$ *(i e (12 x £110) – £1000)*
A_1 *to* $A_{12} = £110$
B_1 *to* $B_5* = £110$
$a_1 = 3, a_2 = 6, a_3 = 9, a_4 = 12, a_5 = 14, a_6 = 16, a_7 = 18, a_8 = 20, a_9 = 21, a_{10} = 22, a_{11} = 23, a_{12} = 24$
$b_1 = 2, b_2 = 3, b_3 = 4, b_4 = 5, b_5 = 6$
$m = 5*, n = 12$
* *(Where the number of outstanding instalments is reduced by 1 because the settlement date is deferred by 2 months in accordance with Regulation 5(a))*

$$\text{Rebate} = \frac{£110\,(2+3+4+5+6)}{£110\,(3+6+9+12+14+16+18+20+21+22+23+24)} \times £320$$

$$= \frac{£110 \times 20}{£110 \times 188} \times £320$$

$$= £34.04$$

[3043]

NOTES

Revoked as noted to reg 1 at **[3033]**.

SCHEDULE 3
FORMULA FOR CALCULATION OF REBATE WHERE SETTLEMENT TAKES PLACE
BETWEEN TWO INSTALMENT DATES AND CREDIT IS REPAYABLE BY INSTALMENTS
AT OTHER THAN MONTHLY OR SHORTER INTERVALS

Regulation 4(3)

$$R_1 - \frac{f}{g}(R_1 + R_2)$$

*where R_1 = rebate if early settlement had taken place at the instalment date immediately
before the settlement date*
*R_2 = rebate if early settlement had taken place at the instalment date immediately following
the settlement date*
*f = inclusive period between the settlement date (determined by Regulation 6 and deferable in
accordance with Regulation 5) and the instalment date immediately before it (in days)*
*g = period commencing on the instalment date immediately before the settlement date and
ending on the day before the next instalment date (in days)*

EXAMPLE

Facts
*A loan of £1000 is agreed to be repaid by 36 quarterly instalments of £48, with repayment
being made on the 1st day of each quarter. The consumer settles the loan on 1st April
between the 30th payment made on 1st March and the 31st payment due on 1st June. Under
Regulation 6(2) the settlement date is 15th April and under Regulation 5(b) it is deferred by
1 month (ie to 15th May when 6 quarterly instalments are outstanding)*
Calculation of Rebate
R_1 = £22.95 (using in this case the formula in Part I of Schedule 2 on the basis that m = 6)
R_2 = £16.40 (using in this case the formula in Part I of Schedule 2 on the basis that m = 5)
f = 76 (31 days in March + 30 days in April + 15 days in May)
g = 92 (31 days in March + 30 days in April + 31 days in May)

$$\text{Rebate} = £22.95 - \frac{76}{92}\,(£22.95 - £16.40)$$

$$= £22.95 - 0.826\,(£6.55)$$

$$= £22.95 - £5.41$$

$$= £17.54$$

[3044]

NOTES

Revoked as noted to reg 1 at **[3033]**.

SCHEDULE 4
FORMULA FOR CALCULATION OF REBATE WHERE A SUM LESS THAN THE TOTAL
REMAINING INDEBTEDNESS OF THE DEBTOR IS REQUIRED TO BE PAID EARLY

Regulation 4(4)

$$R_2 = R_1 \times \frac{A_1}{A_2}$$

where R_1 = rebate if total early settlement had taken place

R_2 = rebate on the sum required to be paid early
A_1 = amount of the sum required to be paid early
A_2 = amount of the repayments of credit not yet due under the agreement at the date when A_1 is paid

EXAMPLE

Facts

     A loan of £1000 is agreed to be repaid by 36 monthly instalments of £48 and the consumer is required partly to settle the loan at the end of the 30th month (ie when 6 monthly instalments totalling £288 are outstanding) by a payment of £150

Calculation of Rebate

R_1 = £10.93 (see Example in Part I of Schedule 2)
A_1 = £150
A_2 = £288

$$\text{Rebate} = £10.93 \times \frac{£150}{£228}$$

$$= £5.69$$

[3045]

NOTES
Revoked as noted to reg 1 at **[3033]**.

SCHEDULE 5
PROVISIONS RELATING TO DETERMINING WHETHER PAYMENTS OF CREDIT ARE IN EQUAL INSTALMENTS OR AT EQUAL INTERVALS FOR THE PURPOSE OF CALCULATION OF REBATE

Regulation 4(5)

1   Where credit is repayable in nearly equal instalments

In the case of an agreement under which all repayments of credit but one are equal and that one repayment does not differ from any other repayment by more whole pence than there are repayments of credit, that one repayment may be regarded as equal to the other repayments.

2   Where interval between relevant date and first repayment of credit is greater than interval between repayments

In the case of an agreement under which—

     (a)   *the credit is repayable by three or more repayments at equal intervals; and*
     (b)   *the interval between the relevant date and the first repayment of credit is greater than the interval between the repayments,*

the interval between the relevant date, as defined in the Total Charge for Credit Regulations, and the first repayment of credit may be regarded as equal to the interval between the repayments.

[3046]

NOTES
Revoked as noted to reg 1 at **[3033]**.

SUPPLY OF SERVICES (EXCLUSION OF IMPLIED TERMS) ORDER 1985

(SI 1985/1)

NOTES
Made: 4 January 1985.
Authority: Supply of Goods and Services Act 1982, s 12(4).
Commencement: 1 March 1985.

1   This Order may be cited as the Supply of Services (Exclusion of Implied Terms) Order 1985 and shall come into operation on 1st March 1985.

[3047]

2   Section 13 of the Supply of Goods and Services Act 1982 (which provides that, in a contract for the supply of a service where the supplier is acting in the course of a business, there is an implied term that the supplier will carry out the service with reasonable care and skill) shall not apply to the services rendered by an arbitrator (including an umpire) in his capacity as such.

[3048]

CONSUMER PROTECTION (CANCELLATION OF CONTRACTS CONCLUDED AWAY FROM BUSINESS PREMISES) REGULATIONS 1987

(SI 1987/2117)

NOTES
Made: 7 December 1987.
Authority: European Communities Act 1972, s 2(2).
Commencement: 1 July 1988.
These Regulations are revoked by the Cancellation of Contracts made in a Consumer's Home or Place of Work etc Regulations 2008, SI 2008/1816, reg 4(1), Sch 2, as from 1 October 2008, except in relation to contracts to which the 1987 Regulations applied before that date (see SI 2008/1816, reg 4(2) at **[3708]**).

ARRANGEMENT OF REGULATIONS

1 Citation and commencement

These Regulations may be cited as the Consumer Protection (Cancellation of Contracts Concluded away from Business Premises) Regulations 1987 and shall come into force on 1st July 1988.

[3049]

NOTES
Revoked as noted at the beginning of these Regulations.

2 Interpretation

(1)   In these Regulations—
  "business" includes a trade or profession;
  "consumer" means a person, other than a body corporate, who, in making a contract to which these Regulations apply, is acting for purposes which can be regarded as outside his business;
  ["enforcement authority" means, in Great Britain, a weights and measures authority and, in Northern Ireland, the Department of Economic Development;]
  "goods" has the meaning given by section 61(1) of the Sale of Goods Act 1979;
  "land mortgage" includes any security charged on land and in relation to Scotland includes any heritable security;
  "notice of cancellation" has the meaning given by regulation 4(5) below;
  "security" in relation to a contract means a mortgage, charge, pledge, bond, debenture, indemnity, guarantee, bill, note or other right provided by the consumer, or at his request (express or implied), to secure the carrying out of his obligations under the contract;

"*signed*" *has the same meaning as in the Consumer Credit Act 1974; and*
"*trader*" *means a person who, in making a contract to which these Regulations apply, is acting for the purposes of his business, and anyone acting in the name or on behalf of such a person.*

(2)   (*Applies to Scotland only.*)

[3050]

NOTES
Revoked as noted at the beginning of these Regulations.
Para (1): definition "enforcement authority" inserted by the Consumer Protection (Cancellation of Contracts Concluded away from Business Premises) (Amendment) Regulations 1998, SI 1998/3050, reg 2(a).

3 Contracts to which the Regulations apply

(*1*)   *These Regulations apply to a contract, other than an excepted contract, for the supply by a trader of goods or services to a consumer which is made—*
    (*a*)   *during an unsolicited visit by a trader—*
        (*i*)   *to the consumer's home or to the home of another person; or*
        (*ii*)   *to the consumer's place of work;*
    (*b*)   *during a visit by a trader as mentioned in paragraph (a)(i) or (ii) above at the express request of the consumer where the goods or services to which the contract relates are other than those concerning which the consumer requested the visit of the trader, provided that when the visit was requested the consumer did not know, or could not reasonably have known, that the supply of those other goods or services formed part of the trader's business activities;*
    (*c*)   *after an offer was made by the consumer in respect of the supply by a trader of the goods or services in the circumstances mentioned in paragraph (a) or (b) above or (d) below; or*
    (*d*)   *during an excursion organised by the trader away from premises on which he is carrying on any business (whether on a permanent or temporary basis).*

(*2*)   *For the purposes of this regulation an excepted contract means*
    (*a*)   *any contract—*
        (*i*)   *for the sale or other disposition of land, or for a lease or land mortgage;*
        (*ii*)   *to finance the purchase of land;*
        (*iii*) *for a bridging loan in connection with the purchase of land; or*
        (*iv*)   *for the construction or extension of a building or other erection on land:*
            Provided that these Regulations shall apply to a contract for the supply of goods and their incorporation in any land or a contract for the repair or improvement of a building or other erection on land, where the contract is not financed by a loan secured by a land mortgage;
    (*b*)   *any contract for the supply of food, drink or other goods intended for current consumption by use in the household and supplied by regular roundsmen;*
    (*c*)   *any contract for the supply of goods or services which satisfies all the following conditions, namely—*
        (*i*)   *terms of the contract are contained in a trader's catalogue which is readily available to the consumer to read in the absence of the trader or his representative before the conclusion of the contract;*
        (*ii*)   *the parties to the contract intend that there shall be maintained continuity of contact between the trader or his representative and the consumer in relation to the transaction in question or any subsequent transaction; and*
        (*iii*) *both the catalogue and the contract contain or are accompanied by a prominent notice indicating that the consumer has a right to return to the trader or his representative goods supplied to him within the period of not less than 7 days from the day on which the goods are received by the consumer and otherwise to cancel the contract within that period without the consumer incurring any liability, other than any liability which may arise from the failure of the consumer to take reasonable care of the goods while they are in his possession;*
    [(*d*)   *contracts of insurance;*]
    [(*e*)   *any agreement the making or performance of which by either party constitutes a relevant regulated activity;*]
    (*f*)   *any contract not falling within sub-paragraph (g) below under which the total payments to be made by the consumer do not exceed £35; and*
    (*g*)   *any contract under which credit within the meaning of the Consumer Credit Act 1974 is provided not exceeding £35 other than a hire-purchase or conditional sale agreement.*

[(*3*)   *In this regulation "unsolicited visit" means a visit by a trader, whether or not he is the trader who supplies the goods or services, which does not take place at the express request of the consumer and includes—*

(a) *a visit by a trader which takes place after he, or a person acting in his name or on his behalf, telephones the consumer (otherwise than at the consumer's express request) and indicates during the course of the telephone call (either expressly or by implication) that he, or the trader in whose name or on whose behalf he is acting, is willing to visit the consumer; and*

(b) *a visit by a trader which takes place after he, or a person acting in his name or on his behalf, visits the consumer (otherwise than at the consumer's express request) and indicates during the course of that visit (either expressly or by implication) that he, or the trader in whose name or on whose behalf he is acting, is willing to make a subsequent visit to the consumer.]*

[(4) *For the purposes of paragraph (2)(e)—*
(a) *"a relevant regulated activity" means an activity of the following kind, namely—*
    (i)   *dealing in investments, as principal or as agent,*
    (ii) *arranging deals in investments,*
    [(iia) *operating a multilateral trading facility,]*
    (iii) *managing investments,*
    (iv) *safeguarding and administering investments,*
    (v)   *establishing etc a collective investment scheme; and*
(b) *"investment" means—*
    (i)   *shares,*
    (ii)   *instruments creating or acknowledging indebtedness,*
    (iii) *government and public securities,*
    (iv)   *instruments giving entitlement to investments,*
    (v)   *certificates representing securities,*
    (vi)   *units in a collective investment scheme,*
    (vii) *options,*
    (viii) *futures,*
    (ix)   *contracts for differences, and*
    (x)   *rights to or interests in investments.*

(5) *Paragraphs (2)(d) and (4) must be read with—*
(a) *section 22 of the Financial Services and Markets Act 2000;*
(b) *any relevant order under that section; and*
(c) *Schedule 22 to that Act,*

but any restriction on or exclusion from the meaning of a regulated activity (which is a relevant regulated activity for the purposes of paragraph (2)(e)) which arises from the identity of the person carrying it on is to be disregarded.]

[3051]

NOTES
Revoked as noted at the beginning of these Regulations.
Para (2): sub-paras (d), (e) substituted by the Financial Services and Markets Act 2000 (Consequential Amendments and Repeals) Order 2001, SI 2001/3649, art 386(1)–(3).
Para (3): substituted by the Consumer Protection (Cancellation of Contracts Concluded away from Business Premises) (Amendment) Regulations 1998, SI 1998/3050, reg 2(b).
Para (4): added, together with para (5), by SI 2001/3649, art 386(1), (4); sub-para (a)(iia) inserted by the Financial Services and Markets Act 2000 (Regulated Activities) (Amendment No 3) Order 2006, SI 2006/3384, art 34.
Para (5): added, together with para (4), by SI 2001/3649, art 386(1), (4).

4 Cancellation of Contract

(*1*) *No contract to which these Regulations apply shall be enforceable against the consumer unless the trader has delivered to the consumer notice in writing in accordance with paragraphs (3) and (4) below indicating the right of the consumer to cancel the contract within the period of 7 days mentioned in paragraph (5) below containing both the information set out in Part I of the Schedule to these Regulations and a Cancellation Form in the form set out in Part II of the Schedule and completed in accordance with the footnotes.*

(*2*) *Paragraph (1) above does not apply to a cancellable agreement within the meaning of the Consumer Credit Act 1974 or to an agreement which may be cancelled by the consumer in accordance with terms of the agreement conferring upon him similar rights as if the agreement were such a cancellation agreement.*

(*3*) *The information to be contained in the notice under paragraph (1) above shall be easily legible and if incorporated in the contract or other document shall be afforded no less prominence than that given to any other information in the document apart from the heading to the document and the names of the parties to the contract and any information inserted in handwriting.*

(*4*) *The notice shall be dated and delivered to the consumer—*

(a)   *in the cases mentioned in regulation 3(1)(a), (b) and (d) above, at the time of the making of the contract; and*

(b)   *in the case mentioned in regulation 3(1)(c) above, at the time of the making of the offer by the consumer.*

(5)   *If within the period of 7 days following the making of the contract the consumer serves a notice in writing (a "notice of cancellation") on the trader or any other person specified in a notice referred to in paragraph (1) above as a person to whom notice of cancellation may be given which, however expressed and whether or not conforming to the cancellation form set out in Part II of the Schedule to these Regulations, indicates the intention of the consumer to cancel the contract, the notice of cancellation shall operate to cancel the contract.*

(6)   *Except as otherwise provided under these Regulations, a contract cancelled under paragraph (5) above shall be treated as if it had never been entered into by the consumer.*

(7)   *Notwithstanding anything in section 7 of the Interpretation Act 1978, a notice of cancellation sent by post by a consumer shall be deemed to have been served at the time of posting, whether or not it is actually received.*

[3052]

NOTES
Revoked as noted at the beginning of these Regulations.

[4A   Offence relating to the failure to provide notice of cancellation rights

(1)   *A trader is guilty of an offence if he enters into a contract to which these Regulations apply (other than an agreement referred to in regulation 4(2) above) with a consumer but fails (or, in the case mentioned in regulation 3(1)(c) above, has failed) to deliver to the consumer the notice in writing referred to in regulation 4(1) above in accordance with paragraph (2) below.*

(2)   *A notice is delivered in accordance with this paragraph if it—*
(a)   *contains what is required by regulation 4(1) above;*
(b)   *complies with the requirements of regulation 4(3) above; and*
(c)   *is dated and delivered to the consumer at the time specified in regulation 4(4) above.*

(3)   *A person who is guilty of an offence under paragraph (1) above shall be liable on summary conviction to a fine not exceeding level 4 on the standard scale.]*

[3053]

NOTES
Revoked as noted at the beginning of these Regulations.
Inserted, together with regs 4B–4H, by the Consumer Protection (Cancellation of Contracts Concluded away from Business Premises) (Amendment) Regulations 1998, SI 1998/3050, reg 2(c).

[4B   Defence of due diligence

(1)   *In proceedings against any person for an offence under regulation 4A above it shall be a defence for that person to show that he took all reasonable steps and exercised all due diligence to avoid committing the offence.*

(2)   *Where in proceedings against a person for such an offence the defence provided for by paragraph (1) above involves an allegation that the commission of the offence was due—*
(a)   *to the act or default of another, or*
(b)   *to reliance on information given by another,*
that person shall not, without the leave of the court, be entitled to rely on the defence unless he has served a notice under paragraph (3) below on the person bringing the proceedings not less than seven clear days before the hearing of the proceedings or, in Scotland, the diet of the trial.

(3)   *A notice under this paragraph shall give such information identifying or assisting in the identification of the person who committed the act or default or gave the information as is in the possession of the person serving the notice at the time when he serves it.]*

[3054]

NOTES
Revoked as noted at the beginning of these Regulations.
Inserted as noted to reg 4A at **[3053]**.

[4C   Liability of persons other than the principal offender

(1)   *Where the commission by a person of an offence under regulation 4A above is due to the act or default of some other person, that other person is guilty of the offence and may be proceeded against and punished by virtue of this regulation whether or not proceedings are taken against the first-mentioned person.*

(2)   Where a body corporate is guilty of an offence under regulation 4A above in respect of any act or default which is shown to have been committed with the consent or connivance of, or to be attributable to any neglect on the part of, any director, manager, secretary or other similar officer of the body corporate or any person who was purporting to act in any such capacity he, as well as the body corporate, shall be guilty of that offence and shall be liable to be proceeded against and punished accordingly.

(3)   Where the affairs of a body corporate are managed by its members, paragraph (2) above shall apply in relation to the acts and defaults of a member in connection with his functions of management as if he were a director of the body corporate.

(4)   Where an offence under regulation 4A above committed in Scotland by a Scottish partnership is proved to have been committed with the consent or connivance of, or to be attributable to neglect on the part of, a partner, he (as well as the partnership) is guilty of the offence and liable to be proceeded against and punished accordingly.]

[3055]

NOTES
Revoked as noted at the beginning of these Regulations.
Inserted as noted to reg 4A at **[3053]**.

[4D   Duty to enforce regulation 4A

(1)   Subject to paragraph (2) below—
    (a)   it shall be the duty of every weights and measures authority in Great Britain to enforce regulation 4A above within its area; and
    (b)   it shall be the duty of the Department of Economic Development to enforce regulation 4A above in Northern Ireland.

(2)   Nothing in paragraph (1) above shall authorise any weights and measures authority to bring proceedings in Scotland for an offence.]

[3056]

NOTES
Revoked as noted at the beginning of these Regulations.
Inserted as noted to reg 4A at **[3053]**.

[4E   Enforcement powers, obstruction of authorised officers and restrictions on disclosure of information

(1)   If a duly authorised officer of an enforcement authority has reasonable grounds for suspecting that an offence has been committed under regulation 4A above, he may—
    (a)   require a person carrying on or employed in a business to produce any book, document or record in non-documentary form relating to the business, and take copies of it or any entry in it, or
    (b)   require such a person to produce in a visible and legible documentary form any information so relating which is contained in a computer, and take copies of it,
for the purposes of ascertaining whether such an offence has been committed.

(2)   If such an officer has reasonable grounds for believing that any books, documents or records may be required as evidence in proceedings for such an offence, he may seize and detain them and shall, if he does so, inform the person from whom they are seized.

(3)   The powers of an officer under this regulation may be exercised by him only at a reasonable hour and on production (if required) of his credentials.

(4)   Nothing in this regulation requires a person to produce, or authorises the taking from a person of, a book, document or record which he could not be compelled to produce in civil proceedings before the High Court or (in Scotland) the Court of Session.]

[3057]

NOTES
Revoked as noted at the beginning of these Regulations.
Inserted as noted to reg 4A at **[3053]**.

[4F—(1)   A person who—
    (a)   intentionally obstructs an officer of an enforcement authority acting in pursuance of his functions under these Regulations,
    (b)   without reasonable cause fails to comply with the requirement made of him by regulation 4E(1) above, or
    (c)   without reasonable excuse fails to give an officer of an enforcement authority acting in pursuance of his functions under these Regulations any other assistance or information

which the officer has reasonably required of him for the purpose of the performance of the officer's functions under these Regulations,

is guilty of an offence.

(2)   If a person, in giving information to an officer of an enforcement authority who is acting in pursuance of his functions under these Regulations—

(a)   makes a statement which he knows is false in a material particular, or

(b)   recklessly makes a statement which is false in a material particular,

he is guilty of an offence.

(3)   A person guilty of an offence under paragraph (1) or (2) above shall be liable on summary conviction to a fine not exceeding level 3 on the standard scale.]

[3058]–[3059]

NOTES
Revoked as noted at the beginning of these Regulations.
Inserted as noted to reg 4A at **[3053]**.

4G   (Inserted as noted to reg 4A at **[3053]**; revoked by the Enterprise Act 2002 (Part 9 Restrictions on Disclosure of Information) (Amendment and Specification) Order 2003, SI 2003/1400, art 7, Sch 5.)

[4H   Nothing in regulations 4E or 4F above requires a person to answer any question or give any information if to do so might incriminate him.]

[3060]

NOTES
Revoked as noted at the beginning of these Regulations.
Inserted as noted to reg 4A at **[3053]**.

5   Recovery of money paid by consumer

(1)   Subject to regulation 7(2) below, on the cancellation of a contract under regulation 4 above, any sum paid by or on behalf of the consumer under or in contemplation of the contract shall become repayable.

(2)   If under the terms of the cancelled contract the consumer or any person on his behalf is in possession of any goods, he shall have a lien on them for any sum repayable to him under paragraph (1) above.

(3)   Where any security has been provided in relation to the cancelled contract, the security, so far as it is so provided, shall be treated as never having had effect and any property lodged with the trader solely for the purposes of the security as so provided shall be returned by him forthwith.

[3061]

NOTES
Revoked as noted at the beginning of these Regulations.

6   Repayment of credit

(1)   Notwithstanding the cancellation of a contract under regulation 4 above under which credit is provided, the contract shall continue in force so far as it relates to repayment of credit and payment of interest.

(2)   If, following the cancellation of the contract, the consumer repays the whole or a portion of the credit—

(a)   before the expiry of one month following service of the notice of cancellation, or

(b)   in the case of a credit repayable by instalments, before the date on which the first instalment is due,

no interest shall be payable on the amount repaid.

(3)   If the whole of a credit repayable by instalments is not repaid on or before the date specified in paragraph (2)(b) above, the consumer shall not be liable to repay any of the credit except on receipt of a request in writing signed by the trader stating the amounts of the remaining instalments (recalculated by the trader as nearly as may be in accordance with the contract and without extending the repayment period), but excluding any sum other than principal and interest.

(4)   Repayment of a credit, or payment of interest, under a cancelled contract shall be treated as duly made if it is made to any person on whom, under regulation 4(5) above, a notice of cancellation could have been served.

(5)   Where any security has been provided in relation to the contract, the duty imposed on the consumer by this regulation shall not be enforceable before the trader has discharged any duty imposed on him by regulation 5(3) above.

[(6)   In this regulation, the following expressions have the meanings hereby assigned to them:—
  "cash" includes money in any form;
  "credit" means a cash loan and any facility enabling the consumer to overdraw on a current account;
  "current account" means an account under which the customer may, by means of cheques or similar orders payable to himself or to any other person, obtain or have the use of money held or made available by the person with whom the account is kept and which records alterations in the financial relationship between the said person and the customer; and
  "repayment", in relation to credit, means the repayment of money—
    (a)   paid to a consumer before the cancellation of the contract; or
    (b)   to the extent that he has overdrawn on his current account before the cancellation.]

[3062]

NOTES
Revoked as noted at the beginning of these Regulations.
Para (6): substituted by the Consumer Protection (Cancellation of Contracts Concluded away from Business Premises) (Amendment) Regulations 1988, SI 1988/958, reg 2.

7   Return of goods by consumer after cancellation

(1)   Subject to paragraph (2) below, a consumer who has before cancelling a contract under regulation 4 above acquired possession of any goods by virtue of the contract shall be under a duty, subject to any lien, on the cancellation to restore the goods to the trader in accordance with this regulation, and meanwhile to retain possession of the goods and take reasonable care of them.

(2)   The consumer shall not be under a duty to restore—
  (i)   perishable goods;
  (ii)   goods which by their nature are consumed by use and which, before the cancellation, were so consumed;
  (iii)   goods supplied to meet an emergency; or
  (iv)   goods which, before the cancellation, had become incorporated in any land or thing not comprised in the cancelled contract,

but he shall be under a duty to pay in accordance with the cancelled contract for the supply of the goods and for the provision of any services in connection with the supply of the goods before the cancellation.

(3)   The consumer shall not be under any duty to deliver the goods except at his own premises and in pursuance of a request in writing signed by the trader and served on the consumer either before, or at the time when, the goods are collected from those premises.

(4)   If the consumer—
  (i)   delivers the goods (whether at his own premises or elsewhere) to any person on whom, under regulation 4(5) above, a notice of cancellation could have been served; or
  (ii)   sends the goods at his own expense to such a person,

he shall be discharged from any duty to retain possession of the goods or restore them to the trader.

(5)   Where the consumer delivers the goods as mentioned in paragraph (4)(i) above, his obligation to take care of the goods shall cease; and if he sends the goods as mentioned in paragraph (4)(ii) above, he shall be under a duty to take reasonable care to see that they are received by the trader and not damaged in transit, but in other respects his duty to take care of the goods shall cease.

(6)   Where, at any time during the period of 21 days following the cancellation, the consumer receives such a request as is mentioned in paragraph (3) above and unreasonably refuses or unreasonably fails to comply with it, his duty to retain possession and take reasonable care of the goods shall continue until he delivers or sends the goods as mentioned in paragraph (4) above, but if within that period he does not receive such a request his duty to take reasonable care of the goods shall cease at the end of that period.

(7)   Where any security has been provided in relation to the cancelled contract, the duty imposed on the consumer to restore goods by this regulation shall not be enforceable before the trader has discharged any duty imposed on him by regulation 5(3) above.

(8)   Breach of a duty imposed by this regulation on a consumer is actionable as a breach of statutory duty.

[3063]

PART 2
STATUTORY INSTRUMENTS

NOTES

Revoked as noted at the beginning of these Regulations.

8   Goods given in part-exchange

(1)   *This regulation applies on the cancellation of a contract under regulation 4 above where the trader agreed to take goods in part-exchange (the "part-exchange goods") and those goods have been delivered to him.*

(2)   *Unless, before the end of the period of ten days beginning with the date of cancellation, the part-exchange goods are returned to the consumer in a condition substantially as good as when they were delivered to the trader, the consumer shall be entitled to recover from the trader a sum equal to the part-exchange allowance.*

(3)   *During the period of ten days beginning with the date of cancellation, the consumer, if he is in possession of goods to which the cancelled contract relates, shall have a lien on them for—*
  (a)   *delivery of the part-exchange goods in a condition substantially as good as when they were delivered to the trader; or*
  (b)   *a sum equal to the part-exchange allowance;*

and if the lien continues to the end of that period it shall thereafter subsist only as a lien for a sum equal to the part-exchange allowance.

(4)   *In this regulation the part-exchange allowance means the sum agreed as such in the cancelled contract, or if no such sum was agreed, such sum as it would have been reasonable to allow in respect of the part-exchange goods if no notice of cancellation had been served.*

[3064]

NOTES

Revoked as noted at the beginning of these Regulations.

9   *(Adds the Consumer Credit Act 1974, s 74(2A) at* **[720]***; revoked as noted at the beginning of these Regulations.)*

10   No contracting-out

(1)   *A term contained in a contract to which these Regulations apply is void if, and to the extent that, it is inconsistent with a provision for the protection of the consumer contained in these Regulations.*

(2)   *Where a provision of these Regulations specifies the duty or liability of the consumer in certain circumstances a term contained in a contract to which these Regulations apply is inconsistent with that provision if it purports to impose, directly or indirectly, an additional duty or liability on him in those circumstances.*

[3065]

NOTES

Revoked as noted at the beginning of these Regulations.

11   Service of documents

(1)   *A document to be served under these Regulations on a person may be so served—*
  (a)   *by delivering it to him, or by sending it by post to him, or by leaving it with him, at his proper address addressed to him by name;*
  (b)   *if the person is a body corporate, by serving it in accordance with paragraph (a) above on the secretary or clerk of that body; or*
  (c)   *if the person is a partnership, by serving it in accordance with paragraph (a) above on a partner or on a person having the control or management of the partnership business.*

(2)   *For the purposes of these Regulations, a document sent by post to, or left at, the address last known to the server of the document as the address of a person shall be treated as sent by post to, or left at, his proper address.*

[3066]

NOTES

Revoked as noted at the beginning of these Regulations.

SCHEDULE

Regulation 4(i)

PART I
INFORMATION TO BE CONTAINED IN NOTICE OF CANCELLATION RIGHTS

1.   *The name of the trader.*

2.   *The trader's reference number, code or other details to enable the contract or offer to be identified.*

3.   *A statement that the consumer has a right to cancel the contract if he wishes and that this right can be exercised by sending or taking a written notice of cancellation to the person mentioned in paragraph 4 within the period of 7 days following the making of the contract.*

4.   *The name and address of a person to whom notice of cancellation may be given.*

5.   *A statement that the consumer can use the cancellation form provided if he wishes.*

[3067]

NOTES
  Revoked as noted at the beginning of these Regulations.

PART II
CANCELLATION FORM TO BE INCLUDED IN NOTICE OF CANCELLATION RIGHTS
(*Complete, detach and return this form ONLY IF YOU WISH TO CANCEL THE CONTRACT.*)

To: **1**
I/We* hereby give notice that I/we* wish to cancel my/our* contract   **2**
Signed
Date
* Delete as appropriate

Notes:

  1.   *Trader to insert name and address of person to whom notice may be given.*

  2.   *Trader to insert reference number, code or other details to enable the contract or offer to be identified. He may also insert the name and address of the consumer.*

[3068]–[3079]

NOTES
  Revoked as noted at the beginning of these Regulations.

CONSUMER CREDIT (EXEMPT AGREEMENTS) ORDER 1989

(SI 1989/869)

NOTES
  Made: 19 May 1989.
  Authority: Consumer Credit Act 1974, ss 16(1), (4)–(6), 182(2), (4).
  Commencement: 19 June 1989.

ARRANGEMENT OF ARTICLES

1   Citation, commencement, interpretation and revocation

(1)   This Order may be cited as the Consumer Credit (Exempt Agreements) Order 1989 and shall come into force on 19th June 1989.

(2)   In this Order—
  "the Act" means the Consumer Credit Act 1974;

"business premises" means premises for occupation for the purposes of a business (including any activity carried on by a body of persons, whether corporate or unincorporate) or for those and other purposes;

and references to the total charge for credit and the rate thereof are respectively references to the total charge for credit and the rate thereof calculated in accordance with the *Consumer Credit (Total Charge for Credit) Regulations 1980* [Consumer Credit (Total Charge for Credit) Regulations 2010].

[(2A) In relation to a consumer credit agreement secured on land, paragraph (2) shall apply as if for the words "Consumer Credit (Total Charge for Credit) Regulations 2010" there were substituted "Consumer Credit (Total Charge for Credit) Regulations 1980.]

(3) The Orders specified in Schedule 2 to this Order are hereby revoked.

[3080]

NOTES

Para (2): words in italics substituted by subsequent words in square brackets by the Consumer Credit (EU Directive) Regulations 2010, SI 2010/1010, regs 64, 65(a), as from 1 February 2011, with effect in relation to certain agreements before that date, as provided for in regs 101, 101A of the 2010 Regulations at **[3942]**, **[3942A]**.

Para (2A): inserted by SI 2010/1010, regs 64, 65(b) (as amended by the Consumer Credit (Amendment) Regulations 2010, SI 2010/1969, regs 4, 20), as from 1 February 2011, with effect in relation to certain agreements before that date, as provided for in regs 101, 101A of SI 2010/1010 at **[3942]**, **[3942A]**.

2 Exemption of certain consumer credit agreements secured on land

(1) The Act shall not regulate a consumer credit agreement which falls within section 16(2) of the Act, being an agreement to which this paragraph applies.

(2) Where the creditor is a body specified in Part I of Schedule 1 to this Order, [or a deposit taker (within the meaning given by section 16(10) of the Act),] paragraph (1) above applies only to—

    (a) a debtor-creditor-supplier agreement falling within section 16(2)(a) or (c) of the Act;

    (b) a debtor-creditor agreement secured by any land mortgage to finance—

        (i) the purchase of land; or

        (ii) the provision of dwellings or business premises on any land; or

        (iii) subject to paragraph (3) below, the alteration, enlarging, repair or improvement of a dwelling or business premises on any land;

    (c) a debtor-creditor agreement secured by any land mortgage to refinance any existing indebtedness of the debtor, whether to the creditor or another person, under any agreement by which the debtor was provided with credit for any of the purposes specified in heads (i) to (iii) of sub-paragraph (b) above.

(3) Head (iii) of sub-paragraph (b) of paragraph (2) above applies only—

    (i) where the creditor is the creditor under—

        (a) an agreement (whenever made) by which the debtor is provided with credit for any of the purposes specified in head (i) and head (ii) of that sub-paragraph; or

        (b) an agreement (whenever made) refinancing an agreement under which the debtor is provided with credit for any of the said purposes,

        being, in either case, an agreement relating to the land referred to in the said head (iii) and secured by a land mortgage on that land; or

    (ii) where a debtor-creditor agreement to finance the alteration, enlarging, repair or improvement of a dwelling, secured by a land mortgage on that dwelling, is made as a result of any such services as are described in [section 4(3)(e) of the Housing Associations Act 1985] which are certified as having been provided by—

        (a) a local authority;

        (b) a housing association within the meaning of section 1 of the Housing Associations Act 1985 or [Article 3 of the Housing (Northern Ireland) Order 1992];

        (c) a body established by such a housing association for the purpose of providing such services as are described in the said [section 4(3)(e) of the Housing Associations Act 1985];

        (d) a charity;

        (e) the National Home Improvement Council; ...

        (f) the Northern Ireland Housing Executive[; or

        (g) a body, or a body of any description, that has been approved by the Secretary of State under section 169(4)(c) of the Local Government and Housing Act 1989 [or the Department of the Environment for Northern Ireland under article 103(4)(c) of the Housing (Northern Ireland) Order 1992.]]

(4) Where the creditor is a body specified in Part II of Schedule 1 to this Order, paragraph (1) above applies only to an agreement of a description specified in that Part in relation to that body and made pursuant to an enactment or for a purpose so specified.

PART 2
STATUTORY INSTRUMENTS

(5)   Where the creditor is a body specified in Part III of Schedule 1 to this Order, paragraph (1) above applies only to an agreement of a description falling within Article 2(2)(a) to (c) above, being an agreement advancing money on the security of a dwelling-house.

[3081]

NOTES

Para (2): words in square brackets substituted by the Financial Services and Markets Act 2000 (Consequential Amendments and Repeals) Order 2001, SI 2001/3649, art 396.

Para (3): words in first, second and third pairs of square brackets substituted by the Consumer Credit (Exempt Agreements) (Amendment) (No 2) Order 1993, SI 1993/2922, art 2(a); word omitted revoked and words in fourth pair of square brackets added, by the Consumer Credit (Exempt Agreements) (Amendment) (No 3) Order 1991, SI 1991/2844, art 2(a); words in square brackets therein added by SI 1993/2922, art 2(a).

3   Exemption of certain consumer credit agreements by reference to the number of payments to be made by the debtor

(1)   The Act shall not regulate a consumer credit agreement which is an agreement of one of the following descriptions, that is to say—

(a)   a debtor-creditor-supplier agreement being either—

   (i)   *an agreement for fixed-sum credit under which the total number of payments to be made by the debtor does not exceed four, and those payments are required to be made within a period not exceeding 12 months beginning with the date of the agreement; or*

   (ii)   *an agreement for running-account credit which provides for the making of payments by the debtor in relation to specified periods and requires that the number of payments to be made by the debtor in repayment of the whole amount of the credit provided in each such period shall not exceed one;*

   [(i)   an agreement for fixed-sum credit under which—

      (aa)   the total number of payments to be made by the debtor does not exceed four;

      (bb)   those payments are required to be made within a period not exceeding 12 months beginning with the date of the agreement; and

      (cc)   the credit is provided without interest and without any other charges; or

   (ii)   an agreement for running-account credit—

      (aa)   which provides for the making of payments by the debtor in relation to specified periods not exceeding 3 months;

      (bb)   which requires that the number of payments to be made by the debtor in repayment of the whole amount of the credit provided in each such period shall not exceed one; and

      (cc)   in relation to which no or insignificant charges are payable for the credit;]

   not being, in either case, an agreement of a description specified in paragraph (2) below; and in this sub-paragraph, "payment" means a payment comprising an amount in respect of credit with or without any other amount;

(b)   *a debtor-creditor-supplier agreement financing the purchase of land being an agreement under which the number of payments to be made by the debtor does not exceed four; and in this sub-paragraph, "payment" means a payment comprising or including an amount in respect of credit or the total charge for credit (if any);*

   [(b)   a debtor-creditor-supplier agreement financing the purchase of land under which—

      (i)   number of payments to be made by the debtor does not exceed four; and

      (ii)   the credit is provided without interest and without any other charges;

   and in this sub-paragraph, "payment" means a payment comprising or including an amount in respect of credit.]

(c)   a debtor-creditor-supplier agreement for fixed-sum credit to finance a premium under a contract of insurance relating to any land or to anything thereon where—

   (i)   the creditor is the creditor under an agreement secured by a land mortgage on that land which either is an exempt agreement by virtue of section 16(1) of the Act or of article 2 above, or is a personal credit agreement which would be an exempt agreement by virtue of either of those provisions if the credit provided were not to exceed £15,000;

   (ii)   the amount of the credit is to be repaid within the period to which the premium relates, not being a period exceeding 12 months; and

   (iii)   *there is no charge forming part of the total charge for credit under the agreement other than interest at a rate not exceeding the rate of interest from time to time payable under the agreement mentioned in head (i) above,*

   [(iii)   the credit is provided without interest and without any other charges;]

   and the number of payments to be made by the debtor does not exceed twelve; and in this sub-paragraph "payment" has the same meaning as it has in paragraph (1)(b) above; and

(d)   a debtor-creditor-supplier agreement for fixed-sum credit where—

    (i)   the creditor is the creditor under an agreement secured by a land mortgage on any land which either is an exempt agreement by virtue of section 16(1) of the Act or of article 2 above, or is a personal credit agreement which would be an exempt agreement by virtue of either of those provisions if the credit provided were not to exceed £15,000;

    (ii)   the agreement is to finance a premium under a contract of life insurance which provides, in the event of the death before the credit under the agreement referred to in head (i) above has been repaid of the person on whose life the contract is effected, for payment of a sum not exceeding the amount sufficient to defray the sums which, immediately after that credit has been advanced, would be payable to the creditor in respect of that credit and of the total charge for that credit; and

    (iii)   there is no charge forming part of the total charge for credit under the agreement other than interest at a rate not exceeding the rate of interest from time to time payable under the agreement referred to in head (i) above,

    [(iii)   the credit is provided without interest and without any other charges;]

and the number of payments to be made by the debtor does not exceed twelve; and in this sub-paragraph, "payment" has the same meaning as it has in sub-paragraph (1)(b) above.

[(1A)   In relation to a consumer credit agreement secured on land—

    (a)   <u>paragraph (1)(a)(i) shall apply as if sub-paragraph (cc) were omitted</u>

    (b)   <u>paragraph (1) (a)(ii) shall apply as if—</u>

        (i)   <u>in sub-paragraph (aa) the words "not exceeding 3 months" were omitted; and</u>

        (ii)   <u>sub-paragraph (cc) were omitted;</u>

    (c)   <u>paragraph (1)(b) shall apply as if sub-paragraph (ii) were omitted;</u>

    (d)   <u>paragraph (1)(c)(iii) shall apply as if for the words "the credit is" to the end there were substituted—</u>

        <u>"there is no charge forming part of the total charge for credit under the agreement other than interest at a rate not exceeding the rate of interest from time to time payable under the agreement mentioned in subparagraph (i);";</u>

    (e)   <u>paragraph (1)(d)(iii) shall apply as if for the words "the credit is" to the end there were substituted—</u>

        <u>there is no charge forming part of the total charge for credit under the agreement other than interest at a rate not exceeding the rate of interest from time to time payable under the agreement referred to in sub-paragraph (i);]</u>

(2)   The descriptions of agreement referred to in sub-paragraph (a) of paragraph (1) above and to which accordingly that sub-paragraph does not apply are—

    (a)   agreements financing the purchase of land;

    (b)   agreements which are conditional sale agreements or hire-purchase agreements; and

    (c)   agreements secured by a pledge (other than a pledge of documents of title or of bearer bonds).

[3082]

NOTES

Para (1): sub-paras (a)(i), (ii), (b), (c)(iii), (d)(iii) in italics substituted by subsequent sub-paras (a)(i), (ii), (b), (c)(iii), (d)(iii) in square brackets by the Consumer Credit (EU Directive) Regulations 2010, SI 2010/1010, regs 64, 66(a)–(e), as from 1 February 2011, with effect in relation to certain agreements before that date, as provided for in regs 101, 101A of the 2010 Regulations at **[3942]**, **[3942A]**.

Para (1A): inserted by SI 2010/1010, regs 64, 66(f), as from 1 February 2011, with effect in relation to certain agreements before that date, as provided for in regs 101, 101A of the 2010 Regulations at **[3942]**, **[3942A]**.

[4 Exemption of certain consumer credit agreements by reference to the rate of the total charge for credit

(1)   The Act shall not regulate—

    (a)   a debtor-creditor agreement where the creditor is a credit union and the rate of the total charge for credit does not exceed [26.9 per cent];

    (b)   (*subject to paragraph (2)* [subject to paragraphs (2) and (2A)] below) a debtor-creditor agreement—

        (i)   which is an agreement of a type offered to a particular class, or particular classes, of individuals and not offered to the public generally; and

        (ii)   under the terms of which the only charge included in the total charge for credit is interest which cannot at any time exceed the sum of one per cent and the highest of the base rates published by the banks named in paragraph (3) below, being the latest rates in operation on the date 28 days before any such time; or

    (c)   (*subject to paragraph (2)* [subject to paragraphs (2) and (2A)] below) a debtor-creditor agreement—

        (i)   which is an agreement of a type offered to a particular class, or particular classes, of individuals and not offered to the public generally;

(ii)   under which there can be no increase after the relevant date in the rate or amount of any item which is included in the total charge for credit or which would be included but for regulation 14 of the Total Charge for Credit Regulations; and

(iii)   in respect of which the rate of the total charge for credit does not exceed the sum of one per cent and the highest of the base rates published by the banks named in paragraph (3) below, being the latest rates in operation on the date 28 days before the date on which the agreement is made.

(2)   Paragraph (1)(b) and (c) above does not apply to an agreement under which the total amount to be repaid by the debtor to discharge his indebtedness in respect of the amount of credit provided may vary according to a formula which is specified in the agreement and which has effect by reference to movements in the level of any index or to any other factor.

[(2A)   Where the agreement referred to in paragraph (1)(b) or (c)—
   (a)   is not an agreement offered by a creditor who is an employer to a debtor as an incident of employment with the creditor, or
   (b)   is not an agreement secured on land,
those paragraphs do not apply to the agreement unless the conditions in paragraph (2B) are satisfied.

(2B)   The conditions referred to in paragraph (2A) are—
   (a)   the agreement is offered under an enactment with a general interest purpose, and
   (b)   the rate of interest (if any) on the credit which may be provided under the agreement is—
      (i)   at a rate which is lower than that prevailing on the market, or
      (ii)   at a rate which is not higher than that prevailing on the market where the other terms on which credit may be provided are more favourable for the debtor than those prevailing on the market.]

(3)   The banks referred to in paragraph (1)(b) and (c) above are—
Bank of England
Bank of Scotland
Barclays Bank PLC
Clydesdale Bank PLC
Co-operative Bank Public Limited Company
Coutts & Co
Lloyds TSB Bank plc
Midland Bank Public Limited Company
National Westminster Bank Public Limited Company
The Royal Bank of Scotland plc

(4)   In this article—
"credit union" means—
   (a)   a society registered under the Industrial and Provident Societies Act 1965 by virtue of section 1 of the Credit Unions Act 1979; or
   (b)   a society registered under the Credit Unions (Northern Ireland) Order 1985 or a society registered under the Industrial and Provident Societies Act (Northern Ireland) 1969 as a credit union;
"interest" means interest at a rate determined in accordance with the formula set out in regulation 7(1) of the Total Charge for Credit Regulations, and in that formula as applied by paragraph (1)(b) above;
"period rate of charge" has the meaning given in regulation 7(2) of those Regulations;
"the relevant date" has the meaning given in regulation 1(2) of the Total Charge for Credit Regulations; and
"the Total Charge for Credit Regulations" means the Consumer Credit (Total Charge for Credit) Regulations 1980.]

[3083]

NOTES
Substituted by the Consumer Credit (Exempt Agreements) (Amendment) Order 1999, SI 1999/1956, art 3.
Para (1): words in square brackets in sub-para (a) substituted by the Consumer Credit (Exempt Agreements) (Amendment) Order 2006, SI 2006/1273, arts 2, 3; words in italics in sub-paras (b), (c) substituted by subsequent words in square brackets by the Consumer Credit (EU Directive) Regulations 2010, SI 2010/1010, regs 64, 67(a), (b), as from 1 February 2011, with effect in relation to certain agreements before that date, as provided for in regs 101, 101A of the 2010 Regulations at **[3942]**, **[3942A]**.
Paras (2A), (2B): inserted by SI 2010/1010, regs 64, 67(c), as from 1 February 2011, with effect in relation to certain agreements before that date, as provided for in regs 101, 101A of the 2010 Regulations at **[3942]**, **[3942A]**.

5   Exemption of certain consumer credit agreements having a connection with a country outside the United Kingdom
The Act shall not regulate a consumer credit agreement made—

    (a)   in connection with trade in goods or services between the United Kingdom and a country outside the United Kingdom or within a country or between countries outside the United Kingdom, being an agreement under which credit is provided to the debtor in the course of a business carried on by him; or

    (b)   between a creditor listed in Part IV of Schedule 1 to this Order and a debtor who is—

        (i)   a member of any of the armed forces of the United States of America;

        (ii)   an employee not habitually resident in the United Kingdom of any of those forces; or

        (iii)   any such member's or employee's wife or husband or any other person (whether or not a child of his) whom he wholly or partly maintains and treats as a child of the family.

[3084]

[5A—(1)   The Act shall not regulate a consumer credit agreement concluded with—

    (a)   an investment firm, or

    (b)   a credit institution,

for the purposes of allowing a debtor to carry out a transaction relating to one or more of the instruments listed in Section C of Annex 1 to MIFID, where the investment firm or credit institution providing the credit is involved in that transaction.

    (2)   In this article—

    "credit institution" means an undertaking the business of which is to receive deposits or other repayable funds from the public and to grant credits on its own account;

    "investment firm" has the meaning given in article 4.1.1 of MIFID;

    "MIFID" means Directive 2004/39/EC of the European Parliament and of the Council of 21 April 2004 on markets in financial instruments.]

[3084A]

NOTES

Commencement: 1 February 2011

Inserted by the Consumer Credit (EU Directive) Regulations 2010, SI 2010/1010, regs 64, 67A (as inserted by the Consumer Credit (Amendment) Regulations 2010, SI 2010/1969, regs 4, 21), as from 1 February 2011, with effect in relation to certain agreements before that date, as provided for in regs 101, 101A of SI 2010/1010 at **[3942]**, **[3942A]**.

6   Exemption of certain consumer hire agreements

The Act shall not regulate a consumer hire agreement where the owner is a body corporate authorised by or under any enactment to supply [gas,] electricity or water and the subject of the agreement is a meter or metering equipment used or to be used in connection with the supply of [gas,] electricity or water, as the case may be.

[3085]–[3098]

NOTES

Words in square brackets inserted by the Consumer Credit (Exempt Agreements) (Amendment) Order 1991, SI 1991/1393, art 2(b).

(Sch 1 (Bodies Whose Agreements of the Specified Description are Exempt Agreements), Sch 2 (Revocations) outside the scope of this work.)

CREDIT CARDS (PRICE DISCRIMINATION) ORDER 1990

(SI 1990/2159)

NOTES

Made: 31 October 1990.

Authority: Fair Trading Act 1973, ss 56(2), 90(2), (3), (4), Sch 8, paras 1, 2. The enabling powers of this order have been repealed, subject to transitional and transitory provisions and savings, by the Enterprise Act 2002, ss 276, 278(2), Schs 24, 26, as from 20 June 2003 and 29 December 2004. However, pursuant to the saving provisions in paras 14, 19 of Sch 24 to the 2002 Act and SI 2003/1397, the relevant provisions of the 1973 Act continue to apply in respect of monopoly references made before 20 June 2003 under s 50 of the 1973 Act.

Commencement: 28 February 1991.

1   Citation and Commencement

This Order may be cited as the Credit Cards (Price Discrimination) Order 1990 and shall come into force on 28th February 1991.

[3099]

PART 2
STATUTORY INSTRUMENTS

NOTES

Application: see note "Authority" at the beginning of this order.

2 Interpretation

(1)   In this Order—

"credit card" means a payment card the holder of which is permitted under his contract with the issuer of the card to discharge less than the whole of any outstanding balance on his payment card account on or before the expiry of a specified period (subject to any contractual requirements with respect to minimum or fixed amounts of payment), other than—

(a)   a payment card issued with respect to the purchase of the goods, services, accommodation or facilities of only one supplier or of suppliers who are members of a single group of interconnected bodies corporate or who trade under a common name,

(b)   a payment card with respect to which the payment card account is a current account, or

(c)   a trading check;

"credit card transaction" means a transaction under which goods, services, accommodation or facilities are supplied on the production in the United Kingdom of—

(a)   a credit card, or

(b)   any other type of payment card which—

(i)   bears a trade mark or service mark which is also borne by a credit card,

(ii)   does not bear a trade mark or service mark registered in a Member State of the European Economic Community and borne by (and only by) a type of payment card which is not a credit card, and

(iii)   is not readily distinguishable from a credit card;

"payment card" means a card, the production of which (whether or not any other action is required) enables the person to whom it is issued ("the holder") to discharge his obligation to a supplier in respect of payment for the acquisition of goods, services, accommodation or facilities, the supplier being reimbursed by a third party (whether or not the third party is the issuer of the card and whether or not a fee or charge is imposed for such reimbursement);

"price" means the aggregate of the sums required to be paid by a purchaser for or otherwise in respect of the supply of the goods, services, accommodation or facilities in question.

(2)   For the purposes of the definition of "credit card transaction"—

(a)   "production in the United Kingdom" includes the identification of a payment card described in paragraph (a) or (b) of the definition in a telephone order or mail order received at a place of business in the United Kingdom, and

(b)   without prejudice to it otherwise being readily distinguishable, a payment card shall be deemed to be readily distinguishable from a credit card when—

(i)   either it bears a trade mark, service mark or other distinguishing feature which is borne only by the payment card or it does not bear such a feature which is borne only by the credit card,

(ii)   the supplier in question has received in writing a clear description of the distinguishing feature and notice that such a payment card is not a credit card, and

(iii)   with the facilities and equipment which he possesses, the supplier is able quickly and easily to ascertain by reference to the distinguishing feature or its absence (if shown to the supplier or identified to him in a telephone order or mail order) whether or not the payment card is a credit card.

(3)   For the purposes of this Order, a person shall not be treated as carrying out an agreement by reason only that he refrains from doing something the doing of which is the subject of a prohibition or restriction imposed by the agreement.

(4)   In the case of a person falling within paragraph (a), (b) or (c) of section 90(3) of the Fair Trading Act 1973, this Order shall extend to his acts and omissions outside the United Kingdom.

(5)   This Order shall extend so as to prohibit the carrying out of agreements already in existence on the making of this Order as it prohibits the carrying out of agreements made subsequently.

[3100]

NOTES

Application: see note "Authority" at the beginning of this order.

Modification: references to trade marks or registered trade marks within the meaning of the Trade Marks Act 1938 shall, unless the context otherwise requires, be construed as references to trade marks or registered trade marks within the meaning of the Trade Marks Act 1994; see the Trade Marks Act 1994, Sch 4, para 1.

3 Prohibition

(*1*)   Subject to article 4 below, the parties to any agreement relating to payment cards which—

(*a*)   imposes or has the effect of imposing any prohibition or restriction on the charging by any party to the agreement of prices for credit card transactions which differ from prices charged by him for other transactions with respect to goods, services, accommodation or facilities of the same description;

(*b*)   requires or has the effect of requiring any party to the agreement to charge prices for credit card transactions which are the same as prices charged by him for other transactions with respect to goods, services, accommodation or facilities of the same description; or

(*c*)   requires or has the effect of requiring any party to the agreement to include in any other agreement made by him a prohibition or restriction falling within sub-paragraph (*a*) above or a requirement falling within sub-paragraph (*b*) above,

shall terminate it before 7th March 1991 to the extent of that prohibition, restriction or requirement.

(*2*)   On and after 7th March 1991, it shall be unlawful for any person to make or carry out an agreement relating to payment cards to the extent that it imposes or has the effect of imposing any prohibition, restriction or requirement falling within the preceding provisions of this article.

[3101]

NOTES

Application: see note "Authority" at the beginning of this order.

4   *Article 3 does not apply to a requirement—*

(*a*)   to comply with any provision of the law of the United Kingdom; or

(*b*)   to limit the maximum amount of a difference in price to the amount of the fee or charge imposed under the agreement with respect to the reimbursement for supplies made on the production of a credit card.

[3102]–[3111]

NOTES

Application: see note "Authority" at the beginning of this order.

5   (*Revoked by the Competition Act 1988 (Consequential and Supplemental Provisions) Order 2000, SI 2000/2031, art 13.*)

TIMESHARE (CANCELLATION NOTICES) ORDER 1992

(SI 1992/1942)

NOTES

Made: 6 August 1992.
Authority: Timeshare Act 1992, ss 4(2), 12(6)–(8).
Commencement: 12 October 1992.

1   This Order may be cited as the Timeshare (Cancellation Notices) Order 1992 and shall come into force on 12th October 1992.

[3112]

2   In this Order, "the Act" means the Timeshare Act 1992.

[3113]

3   Subject to the following provisions of this Order—

(*a*)   a notice of the right to cancel a timeshare agreement given under section 2 of the Act shall be in the form set out in schedule 1 to this Order;

(*b*)   a blank notice of cancellation which is required by section 4(2) of the Act to accompany a notice as described in (a) above shall be attached to that notice and shall be in the form set out in schedule 2 to this Order;

(*c*)   a notice of the right to cancel a timeshare credit agreement given under section 3 of the Act shall be in the form set out in schedule 3 to this Order;

(*d*)   a blank notice of cancellation which is required by section 4(2) of the Act to accompany a notice as described in (c) above shall be attached to that notice and shall be in the form set out in schedule 4 to this Order.

[3114]

4 A notice referred to in article 3(a) or (c) shall be printed on a single sheet of paper with the part which sets out section 7 of the Act appearing on the back of the sheet.

[3115]

5 The lettering of the notices referred to in article 3 shall be easily legible and of a colour which is easily distinguishable from the colour of the paper; and capital letters shall be used in all the places in which they are shown in each schedule and phrases shall be in bold lettering and underlined in accordance with the schedules.

[3116]

6 No capital letter in any of the notices referred to in article 3 shall be less than 2 millimetres high with lower case letters in proportion.

[3117]

7 The lettering of the words "YOUR RIGHT TO CANCEL" and "PLEASE READ CAREFULLY" in the notices referred to in article 3(a) and (c) shall be larger than any other lettering on those notices.

[3118]

8 In the notices referred to in article 3 there shall be inserted in the blank spaces beside the numbers shown in the form set out in the appropriate schedule the following wording or information and the numbers shall not appear in the notices—

in schedule 1—
1. the offeror's reference number, code or other details to enable the contract or offer to be identified;
2. the name of the offeror;
3. the last date on which notice of cancellation may be given;
4. the name and address of a person to whom notice of cancellation may be given;

in schedule 2—
1. the name and address of a person to whom notice of cancellation may be given;
2. the offeror's reference number, code or other details to enable the contract or offer to be identified;

in schedule 3—
1. the creditor's reference number, code or other details to enable the timeshare credit agreement to be identified;
2. the name of the creditor;
3. the last date on which notice of cancellation may be given;
4. the name and address of a person to whom notice of cancellation may be given;

in schedule 4—
1. the name and address of a person to whom notice of cancellation may be given;
2. the creditor's reference number, code or other details to enable the timeshare credit agreement to be identified.

[3119]

SCHEDULES

SCHEDULE 1
TIMESHARE FORM 1

Article 3(a)

Your Right To Cancel
Please Read Carefully

Notice of Right to Cancel Timeshare Agreement Given under Section 2 of the Timeshare Act 1992

1   This notice refers to timeshare agreement   (1) with   (2) that you propose to enter into.

2   **YOU HAVE UNTIL**   (3) **IN WHICH TO CHANGE YOUR MIND**

At any time before or on the above date you may cancel the agreement. If you do so (unless the agreement also includes provisions for credit to help you pay for the timeshare—see paragraph 4 below) you will be able to claim back any money that you have paid under or in contemplation of the agreement. You will then have no other rights or obligations under the agreement.

3   If you wish to cancel the agreement you must send or take written notice of cancellation to   (4)
before or on   (3). You may use the cancellation form provided if you wish to but you do not need to.

4   **If your timeshare agreement includes a credit agreement**

If your timeshare agreement includes provision for credit with which to pay for the timeshare, then if you cancel the agreement as set out above, the part of it that relates to the repayment of the credit and the payment of interest will still be enforceable subject to section 7 of the Timeshare Act 1992 (see over page). This section sets out the procedure to be followed if you wish to withdraw from the credit arrangements.

5   If you are paying for your timeshare purchase by means of credit provided or to be provided under a separate timeshare credit agreement, and not under your timeshare agreement itself, you may also have a right to cancel the timeshare credit agreement. If you have, you should receive or have received a separate notice setting out what these rights are and you will have to give notice separately if cancelling that agreement.

Section 7 of the Timeshare Act 1992 provides as follows:—

"(1)   This section applies following—
    (a)   the giving of notice of cancellation of a timeshare agreement in accordance with section 5 of this Act in a case where subsection (9) of that section applies, or
    (b)   the giving of notice of cancellation of a timeshare credit agreement in accordance with section 6 of this Act.

(2)   If the offeree repays the whole or a portion of the credit—
    (a)   before the expiry of one month following the giving of the notice, or
    (b)   in the case of a credit repayable by instalments, before the date on which the first instalment is due,
no interest shall be payable on the amount repaid.

(3)   If the whole of a credit repayable by instalments is not repaid on or before the date specified in subsection (2)(b) above, the offeree shall not be liable to repay any of the credit except on receipt of a request in writing in such form as may be prescribed, signed by or on behalf of the offeror or (as the case may be) creditor, stating the amounts of the remaining instalments (recalculated by the offeror or creditor as nearly as may be in accordance with the agreement and without extending the repayment period), but excluding any sum other than principal and interest."

[3120]

SCHEDULE 2
TIMESHARE FORM 2

Article 3(b)

Notice of Cancellation of Timeshare Agreement Given under Section 5 of the Timeshare Act 1992

Complete and return this notice **ONLY** if you wish to cancel the timeshare agreement or to withdraw your offer to enter into the agreement.
To

(1)

I/we* hereby give notice that I/we* wish to cancel my/our* timeshare agreement.
Contract or Reference No   (2)
Signed ....
Dated ....
* Delete as appropriate
If this notice is sent by post in a properly addressed and pre-paid letter the notice is treated as given at the time of posting.

[3121]

SCHEDULE 3
TIMESHARE FORM 3

Article 3(c)

Your Right to Cancel
Please Read Carefully

Notice of Right to Cancel Timeshare Credit Agreement Given Under Section 3 of the Timeshare Act 1992

1   Before you entered into your timeshare agreement you should have received notice of your right to cancel that agreement within a specified period of not less than fourteen days after the date when you entered into that agreement.

2   This notice refers to timeshare credit agreement   (1) with   (2) that you propose to enter into.

3   **YOU HAVE UNTIL**   **(3) IN WHICH TO CHANGE YOUR MIND**

At any time before or on the above date you may cancel the agreement and, if you do so, then

(i)   repayment of any credit you may have received, and payment of interest on it, will become subject to section 7 of the Timeshare Act 1992 (see over page); and

(ii)   subject to (i) above you will have no other rights or obligations under the timeshare credit agreement.

4   If you wish to cancel the agreement you must send or take written notice of cancellation to:

         (4)

before or on   (3). You may use the cancellation form provided if you wish to but you do not need to.

5   Cancelling your timeshare credit agreement does not cancel your timeshare agreement. If you also wish to cancel your timeshare agreement you must do that separately.

Section 7 of the Timeshare Act 1992 provides as follows:—

"(1)   This section applies following—

(a)   the giving of notice of cancellation of a timeshare agreement in accordance with section 5 of this Act in a case where subsection (9) of that section applies, or

(b)   the giving of notice of cancellation of a timeshare credit agreement in accordance with section 6 of this Act.

(2)   If the offeree repays the whole or a portion of the credit—

(a)   before the expiry of one month following the giving of the notice, or

(b)   in the case of a credit repayable by instalments, before the date on which the first instalment is due,

no interest shall be payable on the amount repaid.

(3)   If the whole of a credit repayable by instalments is not repaid on or before the date specified in subsection (2)(b) above, the offeree shall not be liable to repay any of the credit except on receipt of a request in writing in such form as may be prescribed, signed by or on behalf of the offeror or (as the case may be) creditor, stating the amounts of the remaining instalments (recalculated by the offeror or creditor as nearly as may be in accordance with the agreement and without extending the repayment period), but excluding any sum other than principal and interest."

[3122]

SCHEDULE 4
TIMESHARE FORM 4

Article 3(d)

Notice of Cancellation of Timeshare Credit Agreement Given under Section 6 of the Timeshare Act 1992

Complete and return this notice **ONLY** if you wish to cancel the timeshare credit agreement.
To:

         (1)

I/we* hereby give notice that I/we* wish to cancel my/our* timeshare credit agreement.

Contract or Reference No   (2)
Signed ....
Dated ....
* Delete as appropriate
If this notice is sent by post in a properly addressed and pre-paid letter the notice is treated as given at the time of posting.

[3123]

TIMESHARE (REPAYMENT OF CREDIT ON CANCELLATION) ORDER 1992

(SI 1992/1943)

NOTES
  Made: 6 August 1992.
  Authority: Timeshare Act 1992, ss 7(3), 12(6)–(8).
  Commencement: 12 October 1992.

1   This Order may be cited as the Timeshare (Repayment of Credit on Cancellation) Order 1992 and shall come into force on 12th October 1992.

[3124]

2   In this Order "the Act" means the Timeshare Act 1992.

[3125]

3—(1)   Any request in writing, to be made to an offeree under section 7(3) of the Act, following the giving of notice of cancellation of a timeshare agreement in accordance with section 5 of the Act in a case where subsection (9) of that section applies shall contain the information set out in schedule 1 to this Order.

(2)   Any request in writing, to be given to an offeree under section 7(3) of the Act, following the giving of notice of cancellation of a timeshare credit agreement in accordance with section 6 of the Act shall contain the information set out in schedule 2 to this Order.

[3126]

SCHEDULES

SCHEDULE 1
FORM OF REQUEST FOR REPAYMENT OF CREDIT REPAYABLE BY INSTALMENTS UNDER A TIMESHARE AGREEMENT IN RESPECT OF WHICH NOTICE OF CANCELLATION HAS BEEN GIVEN IN ACCORDANCE WITH SECTION 5 OF THE ACT IN A CASE WHERE SUBSECTION (9) OF THAT SECTION APPLIES
Article 3(1)

1.   A description of the cancelled agreement sufficient to identify it.

2.   The name and a postal address of the offeror.

3.   The name and a postal address of the offeree.

4.   The amount of credit received by the offeree under the agreement.

5.   The date when the first instalment was due under the agreement.

6.   The amount of credit repaid by the offeree before that date or a statement that none of the credit was repaid before that date.

7.   The amounts of the remaining instalments (recalculated in accordance with section 7(3) of the Act) which the offeree is required to pay, i.e. excluding any sum other than principal and interest.

8.   A precise indication of the dates on which the instalments are due or a statement indicating clearly the manner in which those dates will be determined.

9.   A clear and unambiguous statement by the offeror that payment of the amounts of the remaining instalments is demanded on the dates indicated.

[3127]

SCHEDULE 2
FORM OF REQUEST FOR REPAYMENT OF CREDIT REPAYABLE BY INSTALMENTS UNDER A TIMESHARE CREDIT AGREEMENT IN RESPECT OF WHICH NOTICE OF CANCELLATION HAS BEEN GIVEN IN ACCORDANCE WITH SECTION 6 OF THE ACT
Article 3(2)

1.   A description of the cancelled agreement sufficient to identify it.

2. The name and a postal address of the creditor.

3. The name and a postal address of the offeree.

4. The amount of credit received by the offeree under the agreement.

5. The date when the first instalment was due under the agreement.

6. The amount of credit repaid by the offeree before that date or a statement that none of the credit was repaid before that date.

7. The amounts of the remaining instalments (recalculated in accordance with section 7(3) of the Act) which the offeree is required to pay, ie excluding any sum other than principal and interest.

8. A precise indication of the dates on which the instalments are due or a statement indicating clearly the manner in which those dates will be determined.

9. A clear and unambiguous statement by the creditor that payment of the amounts of the remaining instalments is demanded on the dates indicated.

[3128]

PROPERTY MISDESCRIPTIONS (SPECIFIED MATTERS) ORDER 1992

(SI 1992/2834)

NOTES

Made: 11 November 1992.
Authority: Property Misdescriptions Act 1991, s 1.
Commencement: 4 April 1993.

1 This Order may be cited as the Property Misdescriptions (Specified Matters) Order 1992 and shall come into force on 4th April 1993.

[3129]

2 The matters contained in the Schedule to this Order are hereby specified to the extent described in that Schedule for the purposes of section 1(1) of the Property Misdescriptions Act 1991.

[3130]

SCHEDULE
SPECIFIED MATTERS

Article 2

1. Location or address.

2. Aspect, view, outlook or environment.

3. Availability and nature of services, facilities or amenities.

4. Proximity to any services, places, facilities or amenities.

5. Accommodation, measurements or sizes.

6. Fixtures and fittings.

7. Physical or structural characteristics, form of construction or condition.

8. Fitness for any purpose or strength of any buildings or other structures on land or of land itself.

9. Treatments, processes, repairs or improvements or the effects thereof.

10. Conformity or compliance with any scheme, standard, test or regulations or the existence of any guarantee.

11. Survey, inspection, investigation, valuation or appraisal by any person or the results thereof.

12. The grant or giving of any award or prize for design or construction.

13. History, including the age, ownership or use of land or any building or fixture and the date of any alterations thereto.

14. Person by whom any building, (or part of any building), fixture or component was designed, constructed, built, produced, treated, processed, repaired, reconditioned or tested.

15. The length of time during which land has been available for sale either generally or by or through a particular person.

16. Price (other than the price at which accommodation or facilities are available and are to be provided by means of the creation or disposal of an interest in land in the circumstances specified in

section 23(1)(a) and (b) of the Consumer Protection Act 1987 or Article 16(1)(a) and (b) of the Consumer Protection (NI) Order 1987 (which relate to the creation or disposal of certain interests in new dwellings)) and previous price.

17.   Tenure or estate.

18.   Length of any lease or of the unexpired term of any lease and the terms and conditions of a lease (and, in relation to land in Northern Ireland, any fee farm grant creating the relation of landlord and tenant shall be treated as a lease).

19.   Amount of any ground-rent, rent or premium and frequency of any review.

20.   Amount of any rent-charge.

21.   Where all or any part of any land is let to a tenant or is subject to a licence, particulars of the tenancy or licence, including any rent, premium or other payment due and frequency of any review.

22.   Amount of any service or maintenance charge or liability for common repairs.

23.   Council tax payable in respect of a dwelling within the meaning of section 3, or in Scotland section 72, of the Local Government Finance Act 1992 or the basis or any part of the basis on which that tax is calculated.

24.   Rates payable in respect of a non-domestic hereditament within the meaning of section 64 of the Local Government Finance Act 1988 or, in Scotland, in respect of lands and heritages shown on a valuation roll or the basis or any part of the basis on which those rates are calculated.

25.   Rates payable in respect of a hereditament within the meaning of the Rates (Northern Ireland) Order 1977 or the basis or any part of the basis on which those rates are calculated.

26.   Existence or nature of any planning permission or proposals for development, construction or change of use.

27.   In relation to land in England and Wales, the passing or rejection of any plans of proposed building work in accordance with section 16 of the Building Act 1984 and the giving of any completion certificate in accordance with regulation 15 of the Building Regulations 1991.

28.   In relation to land in Scotland, the granting of a warrant under section 6 of the Building (Scotland) Act 1959 or the granting of a certificate of completion under section 9 of that Act.

29.   In relation to land in Northern Ireland, the passing or rejection of any plans of proposed building work in accordance with Article 13 of the Building Regulations (Northern Ireland) Order 1979 and the giving of any completion certificate in accordance with building regulations made under that Order.

30.   Application of any statutory provision which restricts the use of land or which requires it to be preserved or maintained in a specified manner.

31.   Existence or nature of any restrictive covenants, or of any restrictions on resale, restrictions on use, or pre-emption rights and, in relation to land in Scotland, (in addition to the matters mentioned previously in this paragraph) the existence or nature of any reservations or real conditions.

32.   Easements, servitudes or wayleaves.

33.   Existence and extent of any public or private right of way.

[3131]

PACKAGE TRAVEL, PACKAGE HOLIDAYS AND PACKAGE TOURS REGULATIONS 1992

(SI 1992/3288)

NOTES
   Made: 22 December 1992.
   Authority: European Communities Act 1972, s 2(2).
   Commencement: 23 December 1992.

ARRANGEMENT OF REGULATIONS

1 Citation and commencement

These Regulations may be cited as the Package Travel, Package Holidays and Package Tours Regulations 1992 and shall come into force on the day after the day on which they are made.

[3132]

2 Interpretation

(1) In these Regulations—

"brochure" means any brochure in which packages are offered for sale;

"contract" means the agreement linking the consumer to the organiser or to the retailer, or to both, as the case may be;

"the Directive" means Council Directive 90/314/EEC on package travel, package holidays and package tours;

["member State" means a member State of the European Community or another State in the European Economic Area;]

"offer" includes an invitation to treat whether by means of advertising or otherwise, and cognate expressions shall be construed accordingly;

"organiser" means the person who, otherwise than occasionally, organises packages and sells or offers them for sale, whether directly or through a retailer;

"the other party to the contract" means the party, other than the consumer, to the contract, that is, the organiser or the retailer, or both, as the case may be;

"package" means the pre-arranged combination of at least two of the following components when sold or offered for sale at an inclusive price and when the service covers a period of more than twenty-four hours or includes overnight accommodation:—

 (a) transport;

 (b) accommodation;

 (c) other tourist services not ancillary to transport or accommodation and accounting for a significant proportion of the package,

  and

   (i) the submission of separate accounts for different components shall not cause the arrangements to be other than a package;

   (ii) the fact that a combination is arranged at the request of the consumer and in accordance with his specific instructions (whether modified or not) shall not of itself cause it to be treated as other than pre-arranged;

  and

"retailer" means the person who sells or offers for sale the package put together by the organiser.

(2) In the definition of "contract" in paragraph (1) above, "consumer" means the person who takes or agrees to take the package ("the principal contractor") and elsewhere in these Regulations "consumer" means, as the context requires, the principal contractor, any person on whose behalf the

principal contractor agrees to purchase the package ("the other beneficiaries") or any person to whom the principal contractor or any of the other beneficiaries transfers the package ("the transferee").

[3133]

NOTES

Para (1): definition "member State" inserted by the Package Travel, Package Holidays and Package Tours (Amendment) Regulations 1995, SI 1995/1648, reg 2(a).

3 Application of Regulations

(1)   These Regulations apply to packages sold or offered for sale in the territory of the United Kingdom.

(2)   Regulations 4 to 15 apply to packages so sold or offered for sale on or after 31st December 1992.

(3)   Regulations 16 to 22 apply to contracts which, in whole or part, remain to be performed on 31st December 1992.

[3134]

4 Descriptive matter relating to packages must not be misleading

(1)   No organiser or retailer shall supply to a consumer any descriptive matter concerning a package, the price of a package or any other conditions applying to the contract which contains any misleading information.

(2)   If an organiser or retailer is in breach of paragraph (1) he shall be liable to compensate the consumer for any loss which the consumer suffers in consequence.

[3135]

5 Requirements as to brochures

(1)   Subject to paragraph (4) below, no organiser shall make available a brochure to a possible consumer unless it indicates in a legible, comprehensible and accurate manner the price and adequate information about the matters specified in Schedule 1 to these Regulations in respect of the packages offered for sale in the brochure to the extent that those matters are relevant to the packages so offered.

(2)   Subject to paragraph (4) below, no retailer shall make available to a possible consumer a brochure which he knows or has reasonable cause to believe does not comply with the requirements of paragraph (1).

(3)   An organiser who contravenes paragraph (1) of this regulation and a retailer who contravenes paragraph (2) thereof shall be guilty of an offence and liable:—

    (a)   on summary conviction, to a fine not exceeding level 5 on the standard scale; and

    (b)   on conviction on indictment, to a fine.

(4)   Where a brochure was first made available to consumers generally before 31st December 1992 no liability shall arise under this regulation in respect of an identical brochure being made available to a consumer at any time.

[3136]

6 Circumstances in which particulars in brochure are to be binding

(1)   Subject to paragraphs (2) and (3) of this regulation, the particulars in the brochure (whether or not they are required by regulation 5(1) above to be included in the brochure) shall constitute implied warranties (or, as regards Scotland, implied terms) for the purposes of any contract to which the particulars relate.

(2)   Paragraph (1) of this regulation does not apply—

    (a)   in relation to information required to be included by virtue of paragraph 9 of Schedule 1 to these Regulations; or

    (b)   where the brochure contains an express statement that changes may be made in the particulars contained in it before a contract is concluded and changes in the particulars so contained are clearly communicated to the consumer before a contract is concluded.

(3)   Paragraph (1) of this regulation does not apply when the consumer and the other party to the contract agree after the contract has been made that the particulars in the brochure, or some of those particulars, should not form part of the contract.

[3137]

7 Information to be provided before contract is concluded

(1)   Before a contract is concluded, the other party to the contract shall provide the intending consumer with the information specified in paragraph (2) below in writing or in some other appropriate form.

PART 2
STATUTORY INSTRUMENTS

(2)   The information referred to in paragraph (1) is:—
 (a)   general information about passport and visa requirements which apply to [nationals of the member State or States concerned] who purchase the package in question, including information about the length of time it is likely to take to obtain the appropriate passports and visas;
 (b)   information about health formalities required for the journey and the stay; and
 (c)   the arrangements for security for the money paid over and (where applicable) for the repatriation of the consumer in the event of insolvency.

(3)   If the intending consumer is not provided with the information required by paragraph (1) in accordance with that paragraph the other party to the contract shall be guilty of an offence and liable:—
 (a)   on summary conviction, to a fine not exceeding level 5 on the standard scale; and
 (b)   on conviction on indictment, to a fine.

[3138]

NOTES
Para (2): words in square brackets substituted by the Package Travel, Package Holidays and Package Tours (Amendment) Regulations 1998, SI 1998/1208, reg 5.

8   Information to be provided in good time

(1)   The other party to the contract shall in good time before the start of the journey provide the consumer with the information specified in paragraph (2) below in writing or in some other appropriate form.

(2)   The information referred to in paragraph (1) is the following:—
 (a)   the times and places of intermediate stops and transport connections and particulars of the place to be occupied by the traveller (for example, cabin or berth on ship, sleeper compartment on train);
 (b)   the name, address and telephone number—
  (i)   of the representative of the other party to the contract in the locality where the consumer is to stay,
   or, if there is no such representative,
  (ii)   of an agency in that locality on whose assistance a consumer in difficulty would be able to call,
   or, if there is no such representative or agency, a telephone number or other information which will enable the consumer to contact the other party to the contract during the stay; and
 (c)   in the case of a journey or stay abroad by a child under the age of 16 on the day when the journey or stay is due to start, information enabling direct contact to be made with the child or the person responsible at the place where he is to stay; and
 (d)   except where the consumer is required as a term of the contract to take out an insurance policy in order to cover the cost of cancellation by the consumer or the cost of assistance, including repatriation, in the event of accident or illness, information about an insurance policy which the consumer may, if he wishes, take out in respect of the risk of those costs being incurred.

(3)   If the consumer is not provided with the information required by paragraph (1) in accordance with that paragraph the other party to the contract shall be guilty of an offence and liable:—
 (a)   on summary conviction, to a fine not exceeding level 5 on the standard scale; and
 (b)   on conviction on indictment, to a fine.

[3139]

9   Contents and form of contract

(1)   The other party to the contract shall ensure that—
 (a)   depending on the nature of the package being purchased, the contract contains at least the elements specified in Schedule 2 to these Regulations;
 (b)   subject to paragraph (2) below, all the terms of the contract are set out in writing or such other form as is comprehensible and accessible to the consumer and are communicated to the consumer before the contract is made; and
 (c)   a written copy of these terms is supplied to the consumer.

(2)   Paragraph (1)(b) above does not apply when the interval between the time when the consumer approaches the other party to the contract with a view to entering into a contract and the time of departure under the proposed contract is so short that it is impracticable to comply with the sub-paragraph.

(3)   It is an implied condition (or, as regards Scotland, an implied term) of the contract that the other party to the contract complies with the provisions of paragraph (1).

(4) *(Applies to Scotland only.)*

[3140]

10 Transfer of bookings

(1) In every contract there is an implied term that where the consumer is prevented from proceeding with the package the consumer may transfer his booking to a person who satisfies all the conditions applicable to the package, provided that the consumer gives reasonable notice to the other party to the contract of his intention to transfer before the date when departure is due to take place.

(2) Where a transfer is made in accordance with the implied term set out in paragraph (1) above, the transferor and the transferee shall be jointly and severally liable to the other party to the contract for payment of the price of the package (or, if part of the price has been paid, for payment of the balance) and for any additional costs arising from such transfer.

[3141]

11 Price revision

(1) Any term in a contract to the effect that the prices laid down in the contract may be revised shall be void and of no effect unless the contract provides for the possibility of upward or downward revision and satisfies the conditions laid down in paragraph (2) below.

(2) The conditions mentioned in paragraph (1) are that—
    (a) the contract states precisely how the revised price is to be calculated;
    (b) the contract provides that price revisions are to be made solely to allow for variations in:—
        (i) transportation costs, including the cost of fuel,
        (ii) dues, taxes or fees chargeable for services such as landing taxes or embarkation or disembarkation fees at ports and airports, or
        (iii) the exchange rates applied to the particular package; and

(3) Notwithstanding any terms of a contract,
    (i) no price increase may be made in a specified period which may not be less than 30 days before the departure date stipulated; and
    (ii) as against an individual consumer liable under the contract, no price increase may be made in respect of variations which would produce an increase of less than 2 per cent, or such greater percentage as the contract may specify, ("non-eligible variations") and that the non-eligible variations shall be left out of account in the calculation.

[3142]

12 Significant alterations to essential terms

In every contract there are implied terms to the effect that—
    (a) where the organiser is constrained before the departure to alter significantly an essential term of the contract, such as the price (so far as regulation 11 permits him to do so), he will notify the consumer as quickly as possible in order to enable him to take appropriate decisions and in particular to withdraw from the contract without penalty or to accept a rider to the contract specifying the alterations made and their impact on the price; and
    (b) the consumer will inform the organiser or the retailer of his decision as soon as possible.

[3143]

13 Withdrawal by consumer pursuant to regulation 12 and cancellation by organiser

(1) The terms set out in paragraphs (2) and (3) below are implied in every contract and apply where the consumer withdraws from the contract pursuant to the term in it implied by virtue of regulation 12(a), or where the organiser, for any reason other than the fault of the consumer, cancels the package before the agreed date of departure.

(2) The consumer is entitled—
    (a) to take a substitute package of equivalent or superior quality if the other party to the contract is able to offer him such a substitute; or
    (b) to take a substitute package of lower quality if the other party to the contract is able to offer him one and to recover from the organiser the difference in price between the price of the package purchased and that of the substitute package; or
    (c) to have repaid to him as soon as possible all the monies paid by him under the contract.

(3) The consumer is entitled, if appropriate, to be compensated by the organiser for non-performance of the contract except where—
    (a) the package is cancelled because the number of persons who agree to take it is less than the minimum number required and the consumer is informed of the cancellation, in writing, within the period indicated in the description of the package; or
    (b) the package is cancelled by reason of unusual and unforeseeable circumstances beyond the control of the party by whom this exception is pleaded, the consequences of which could not have been avoided even if all due care had been exercised.

(4)   Overbooking shall not be regarded as a circumstance falling within the provisions of sub-paragraph (b) of paragraph (3) above.

[3144]

14 Significant proportion of services not provided

(1)   The terms set out in paragraphs (2) and (3) below are implied in every contract and apply where, after departure, a significant proportion of the services contracted for is not provided or the organiser becomes aware that he will be unable to procure a significant proportion of the services to be provided.

(2)   The organiser will make suitable alternative arrangements, at no extra cost to the consumer, for the continuation of the package and will, where appropriate, compensate the consumer for the difference between the services to be supplied under the contract and those supplied.

(3)   If it is impossible to make arrangements as described in paragraph (2), or these are not accepted by the consumer for good reasons, the organiser will, where appropriate, provide the consumer with equivalent transport back to the place of departure or to another place to which the consumer has agreed and will, where appropriate, compensate the consumer.

[3145]

15 Liability of other party to the contract for proper performance of obligations under contract

(1)   The other party to the contract is liable to the consumer for the proper performance of the obligations under the contract, irrespective of whether such obligations are to be performed by that other party or by other suppliers of services but this shall not affect any remedy or right of action which that other party may have against those other suppliers of services.

(2)   The other party to the contract is liable to the consumer for any damage caused to him by the failure to perform the contract or the improper performance of the contract unless the failure or the improper performance is due neither to any fault of that other party nor to that of another supplier of services, because—

    (a)   the failures which occur in the performance of the contract are attributable to the consumer;

    (b)   such failures are attributable to a third party unconnected with the provision of the services contracted for, and are unforeseeable or unavoidable; or

    (c)   such failures are due to—

        (i)   unusual and unforeseeable circumstances beyond the control of the party by whom this exception is pleaded, the consequences of which could not have been avoided even if all due care had been exercised; or

        (ii)   an event which the other party to the contract or the supplier of services, even with all due care, could not foresee or forestall.

(3)   In the case of damage arising from the non-performance or improper performance of the services involved in the package, the contract may provide for compensation to be limited in accordance with the international conventions which govern such services.

(4)   In the case of damage other than personal injury resulting from the non-performance or improper performance of the services involved in the package, the contract may include a term limiting the amount of compensation which will be paid to the consumer, provided that the limitation is not unreasonable.

(5)   Without prejudice to paragraph (3) and paragraph (4) above, liability under paragraphs (1) and (2) above cannot be excluded by any contractual term.

(6)   The terms set out in paragraphs (7) and (8) below are implied in every contract.

(7)   In the circumstances described in paragraph (2)(b) and (c) of this regulation, the other party to the contract will give prompt assistance to a consumer in difficulty.

(8)   If the consumer complains about a defect in the performance of the contract, the other party to the contract, or his local representative, if there is one, will make prompt efforts to find appropriate solutions.

(9)   The contract must clearly and explicitly oblige the consumer to communicate at the earliest opportunity, in writing or any other appropriate form, to the supplier of the services concerned and to the other party to the contract any failure which he perceives at the place where the services concerned are supplied.

[3146]

16 Security in event of insolvency—requirements and offences

(1)   The other party to the contract shall at all times be able to provide sufficient evidence of security for the refund of money paid over and for the repatriation of the consumer in the event of insolvency.

(2)   Without prejudice to paragraph (1) above, and subject to paragraph (4) below, save to the extent that—

(a)   the package is covered by measures adopted or retained by the member State where he is established for the purpose of implementing Article 7 of the Directive; or

(b)   the package is one in respect of which he is required to hold a licence under the Civil Aviation (Air Travel Organisers' Licensing) Regulations 1972 or the package is one that is covered by the arrangements he has entered into for the purposes of those Regulations,

the other party to the contract shall at least ensure that there are in force arrangements as described in regulations 17,18, 19 or 20 or, if that party is acting otherwise than in the course of business, as described in any of those regulations or in regulation 21.

(3)   Any person who contravenes paragraph (1) or (2) of this regulation shall be guilty of an offence and liable:—

(a)   on summary conviction to a fine not exceeding level 5 on the standard scale; and

(b)   on conviction on indictment, to a fine.

(4)   A person shall not be guilty of an offence under paragraph (3) above by reason only of the fact that arrangements such as are mentioned in paragraph (2) above are not in force in respect of any period before 1 April 1993 unless money paid over is not refunded when it is due or the consumer is not repatriated in the event of insolvency.

(5)   For the purposes of regulations 17 to 21 below a contract shall be treated as having been fully performed if the package or, as the case may be, the part of the package has been completed irrespective of whether the obligations under the contract have been properly performed for the purposes of regulation 15.

[3147]

17   Bonding

(1)   The other party to the contract shall ensure that a bond is entered into by an authorised institution under which the institution binds itself to pay to an approved body of which that other party is a member a sum calculated in accordance with paragraph (3) below in the event of the insolvency of that other party.

(2)   Any bond entered into pursuant to paragraph (1) above shall not be expressed to be in force for a period exceeding eighteen months.

(3)   The sum referred to in paragraph (1) above shall be such sum as may reasonably be expected to enable all monies paid over by consumers under or in contemplation of contracts for relevant packages which have not been fully performed to be repaid and shall not in any event be a sum which is less than the minimum sum calculated in accordance with paragraph (4) below.

(4)   The minimum sum for the purposes of paragraph (3) above shall be a sum which represents:—

(a)   not less than 25 per cent of all the payments which the other party to the contract estimates that he will receive under or in contemplation of contracts for relevant packages in the twelve month period from the date of entry into force of the bond referred to in paragraph (1) above; or

(b)   the maximum amount of all the payments which the other party to the contract expects to hold at any one time, in respect of contracts which have not been fully performed,

whichever sum is the smaller.

(5)   Before a bond is entered into pursuant to paragraph (1) above, the other party to the contract shall inform the approved body of which he is a member of the minimum sum which he proposes for the purposes of paragraphs (3) and (4) above and it shall be the duty of the approved body to consider whether such sum is sufficient for the purpose mentioned in paragraph (3) and, if it does not consider that this is the case, it shall be the duty of the approved body so to inform the other party to the contract and to inform him of the sum which, in the opinion of the approved body, is sufficient for that purpose.

(6)   Where an approved body has informed the other party to the contract of a sum pursuant to paragraph (5) above, the minimum sum for the purposes of paragraphs (3) and (4) above shall be that sum.

(7)   In this regulation—

"approved body" means a body which is for the time being approved by the Secretary of State for the purposes of this regulation;

"authorised institution" means a person authorised under the law of a member State[, of the Channel Islands or of the Isle of Man] to carry on the business of entering into bonds of the kind required by this regulation.

[3148]

NOTES
Para (7): words in square brackets in definition "authorised institution" inserted by the Package Travel, Package Holidays and Package Tours (Amendment) Regulations 1995, SI 1995/1648, reg 2(b).

18 Bonding where approved body has reserve fund or insurance

(1)   The other party to the contract shall ensure that a bond is entered into by an authorised institution, under which the institution agrees to pay to an approved body of which that other party is a member a sum calculated in accordance with paragraph (3) below in the event of the insolvency of that other party.

(2)   Any bond entered into pursuant to paragraph (1) above shall not be expressed to be in force for a period exceeding eighteen months.

(3)   The sum referred to in paragraph (1) above shall be such sum as may be specified by the approved body as representing the lesser of—

    (a)   the maximum amount of all the payments which the other party to the contract expects to hold at any one time in respect of contracts which have not been fully performed; or

    (b)   the minimum sum calculated in accordance with paragraph (4) below.

(4)   The minimum sum for the purposes of paragraph (3) above shall be a sum which represents not less than 10 per cent of all the payments which the other party to the contract estimates that he will receive under or in contemplation of contracts for relevant packages in the twelve month period from the date of entry referred to in paragraph (1) above.

(5)   In this regulation "approved body" means a body which is for the time being approved by the Secretary of State for the purposes of this regulation and no such approval shall be given unless the conditions mentioned in paragraph (6) below are satisfied in relation to it.

(6)   A body may not be approved for the purposes of this regulation unless—

    (a)   it has a reserve fund or insurance cover with an insurer authorised in respect of such business in a member State[, the Channel Islands or the Isle of Man] of an amount in each case which is designed to enable all monies paid over to a member of the body of consumers under or in contemplation of contracts for relevant packages which have not been fully performed to be repaid to those consumers in the event of the insolvency of the member; and

    (b)   where it has a reserve fund, it agrees that the fund will be held by persons and in a manner approved by the Secretary of State.

(7)   In this regulation, authorised institution has the meaning given to that expression by paragraph (7) of regulation 17.

[3149]

NOTES
Para (6): words in square brackets in sub-para (a) inserted by the Package Travel, Package Holidays and Package Tours (Amendment) Regulations 1995, SI 1995/1648, reg 2(c).

19 Insurance

(1)   The other party to the contract shall have insurance under one or more appropriate policies with an insurer authorised in respect of such business in a member State under which the insurer agrees to indemnify consumers, who shall be insured persons under the policy, against the loss of money paid over by them under or in contemplation of contracts for packages in the event of the insolvency of the contractor.

(2)   The other party to the contract shall ensure that it is a term of every contract with a consumer that the consumer acquires the benefit of a policy of a kind mentioned in paragraph (1) above in the event of the insolvency of the other party to the contract.

(3)   In this regulation:

   "appropriate policy" means one which does not contain a condition which provides (in whatever terms) that no liability shall arise under the policy, or that any liability so arising shall cease:—

    (i)   in the event of some specified thing being done or omitted to be done after the happening of the event giving rise to a claim under the policy;

    (ii)   in the event of the policy holder not making payments under or in connection with other policies; or

    (iii)   unless the policy holder keeps specified records or provides the insurer with or makes available to him information therefrom.

[3150]

20 Monies in trust

(1)   The other party to the contract shall ensure that all monies paid over by a consumer under or in contemplation of a contract for a relevant package are held in the United Kingdom by a person

as trustee for the consumer until the contract has been fully performed or any sum of money paid by the consumer in respect of the contract has been repaid to him or has been forfeited on cancellation by the consumer.

(2)   The costs of administering the trust mentioned in paragraph (1) above shall be paid for by the other party to the contract.

(3)   Any interest which is earned on the monies held by the trustee pursuant to paragraph (1) shall be held for the other party to the contract and shall be payable to him on demand.

(4)   Where there is produced to the trustee a statement signed by the other party to the contract to the effect that—

(a)   a contract for a package the price of which is specified in that statement has been fully performed;

(b)   the other party to the contract has repaid to the consumer a sum of money specified in that statement which the consumer had paid in respect of a contract for a package; or

(c)   the consumer has on cancellation forfeited a sum of money specified in that statement which he had paid in respect of a contract for a relevant package,

the trustee shall (subject to paragraph (5) below) release to the other party to the contract the sum specified in the statement.

(5)   Where the trustee considers it appropriate to do so, he may require the other party to the contract to provide further information or evidence of the matters mentioned in sub-paragraph (a), (b) or (c) of paragraph (4) above before he releases any sum to that other party pursuant to that paragraph.

(6)   Subject to paragraph (7) below, in the event of the insolvency of the other party to the contract the monies held in trust by the trustee pursuant to paragraph (1) of this regulation shall be applied to meet the claims of consumers who are creditors of that other party in respect of contracts for packages in respect of which the arrangements were established and which have not been fully performed and, if there is a surplus after those claims have been met, it shall form part of the estate of that insolvent other party for the purposes of insolvency law.

(7)   If the monies held in trust by the trustee pursuant to paragraph (1) of this regulation are insufficient to meet the claims of consumers as described in paragraph (6), payments to those consumers shall be made by the trustee on a pari passu basis.

[3151]

21   Monies in trust where other party to contract is acting otherwise than in the course of business

(1)   The other party to the contract shall ensure that all monies paid over by a consumer under or in contemplation of a contract for a relevant package are held in the United Kingdom by a person as trustee for the consumer for the purpose of paying for the consumer's package.

(2)   The costs of administering the trust mentioned in paragraph (1) shall be paid for out of the monies held in trust and the interest earned on those monies.

(3)   Where there is produced to the trustee a statement signed by the other party to the contract to the effect that—

(a)   the consumer has previously paid over a sum of money specified in that statement in respect of a contract for a package and that sum is required for the purpose of paying for a component (or part of a component) of the package;

(b)   the consumer has previously paid over a sum of money specified in that statement in respect of a contract for a package and the other party to the contract has paid that sum in respect of a component (or part of a component) of the package;

(c)   the consumer requires the repayment to him of a sum of money specified in that statement which was previously paid over by the consumer in respect of a contract for a package; or

(d)   the consumer has on cancellation forfeited a sum of money specified in that statement which he had paid in respect of a contract for a package,

the trustee shall (subject to paragraph (4) below) release to the other party to the contract the sum specified in the statement.

(4)   Where the trustee considers it appropriate to do so, he may require the other party to the contract to provide further information or evidence of the matters mentioned in sub-paragraph (a), (b), (c) or (d) of paragraph (3) above before he releases to that other party any sum from the monies held in trust for the consumer.

(5)   Subject to paragraph (6) below, in the event of the insolvency of the other party to the contract and of contracts for packages not being fully performed (whether before or after the insolvency) the monies held in trust by the trustee pursuant to paragraph (1) of this regulation shall be applied to meet the claims of consumers who are creditors of that other party in respect of amounts paid over by them and remaining in the trust fund after deductions have been made in

respect of amounts released to that other party pursuant to paragraph (3) and, if there is a surplus after those claims have been met, it shall be divided amongst those consumers pro rata.

(6)   If the monies held in trust by the trustee pursuant to paragraph (1) of this regulation are insufficient to meet the claims of consumers as described in paragraph (5) above, payments to those consumers shall be made by the trustee on a pari passu basis.

(7)   Any sums remaining after all the packages in respect of which the arrangements were established have been fully performed shall be dealt with as provided in the arrangements or, in default of such provision, may be paid to the other party to the contract.

[3152]

22   Offences arising from breach of regulations 20 and 21

(1)   If the other party to the contract makes a false statement under paragraph (4) of regulation 20 or paragraph (3) of regulation 21 he shall be guilty of an offence.

(2)   If the other party to the contract applies monies released to him on the basis of a statement made by him under regulation 21(3)(a) or (c) for a purpose other than that mentioned in the statement he shall be guilty of an offence.

(3)   If the other party to the contract is guilty of an offence under paragraph (1) or (2) of this regulation shall be liable—
   (a)   on summary conviction to a fine not exceeding level 5 on the standard scale; and
   (b)   on conviction on indictment, to a fine.

[3153]

23   Enforcement

Schedule 3 to these Regulations (which makes provision about the enforcement of regulations 5, 7, 8, 16 and 22 of these Regulations) shall have effect.

[3154]

24   Due diligence defence

(1)   Subject to the following provisions of this regulation, in proceedings against any person for an offence under regulation 5, 7, 8, 16 or 22 of these Regulations, it shall be a defence for that person to show that he took all reasonable steps and exercised all due diligence to avoid committing the offence.

(2)   Where in any proceedings against any person for such an offence the defence provided by paragraph (1) above involves an allegation that the commission of the offence was due—
   (a)   to the act or default of another; or
   (b)   to reliance on information given by another,
that person shall not, without the leave of the court, be entitled to rely on the defence unless, not less than seven clear days before the hearing of the proceedings, or, in Scotland, the trial diet, he has served a notice under paragraph (3) below on the person bringing the proceedings.

(3)   A notice under this paragraph shall give such information identifying or assisting in the identification of the person who committed the act or default or gave the information as is in the possession of the person serving the notice at the time he serves it.

(4)   It is hereby declared that a person shall not be entitled to rely on the defence provided by paragraph (1) above by reason of his reliance on information supplied by another, unless he shows that it was reasonable in all the circumstances for him to have relied on the information, having regard in particular—
   (a)   to the steps which he took, and those which might reasonably have been taken, for the purpose of verifying the information; and
   (b)   to whether he had any reason to disbelieve the information.

[3155]

25   Liability of persons other than principal offender

(1)   Where the commission by any person of an offence under regulation 5, 7, 8, 16 or 22 of these Regulations is due to an act or default committed by some other person in the course of any business of his, the other person shall be guilty of the offence and may be proceeded against and punished by virtue of this paragraph whether or not proceedings are taken against the first-mentioned person.

(2)   Where a body corporate is guilty of an offence under any of the provisions mentioned in paragraph (1) above (including where it is so guilty by virtue of the said paragraph (1)) in respect of any act or default which is shown to have been committed with the consent or connivance of, or to be attributable to any neglect on the part of, any director, manager, secretary or other similar officer of the body corporate or any person who was purporting to act in any such capacity he, as well as the body corporate, shall be guilty of that offence and shall be liable to be proceeded against and punished accordingly.

(3)   Where the affairs of a body corporate are managed by its members, paragraph (2) above shall apply in relation to the acts and defaults of a member in connection with his functions of management as if he were a director of the body corporate.

(4)   (*Applies to Scotland only.*)

(5)   On proceedings for an offence under regulation 5 by virtue of paragraph (1) above committed by the making available of a brochure it shall be a defence for the person charged to prove that he is a person whose business it is to publish or arrange for the publication of brochures and that he received the brochure for publication in the ordinary course of business and did not know and had no reason to suspect that its publication would amount to an offence under these Regulations.

[3156]

26   Prosecution time limit

(1)   No proceedings for an offence under regulation 5, 7, 8, 16 or 22 of these Regulations or under paragraphs 5(3), 6 or 7 of Schedule 3 thereto shall be commenced after—
- (a)   the end of the period of three years beginning with the date of the commission of the offence; or
- (b)   the end of the period of one year beginning with the date of the discovery of the offence by the prosecutor,

whichever is the earlier.

(2)   For the purposes of this regulation a certificate signed by or on behalf of the prosecutor and stating the date on which the offence was discovered by him shall be conclusive evidence of that fact; and a certificate stating that matter and purporting to be so signed shall be treated as so signed unless the contrary is proved.

(3)   (*Applies to Scotland only.*)

[3157]

27   Saving for civil consequences

No contract shall be void or unenforceable, and no right of action in civil proceedings in respect of any loss shall arise, by reason only of the commission of an offence under regulations 5, 7, 8, 16 or 22 of these Regulations.

[3158]

28   Terms implied in contract

Where it is provided in these Regulations that a term (whether so described or whether described as a condition or warranty) is implied in the contract it is so implied irrespective of the law which governs the contract.

[3159]

SCHEDULES

SCHEDULE 1
INFORMATION TO BE INCLUDED (IN ADDITION TO THE PRICE) IN BROCHURES WHERE RELEVANT TO PACKAGES OFFERED

Regulation 5

1.   The destination and the means, characteristics and categories of transport used.

2.   The type of accommodation, its location, category or degree of comfort and its main features and, where the accommodation is to be provided in a member State, its approval or tourist classification under the rules of that member State.

3.   The meals which are included in the package.

4.   The itinerary.

5.   General information about passport and visa requirements which apply for [nationals of the member State or States in which the brochure is made available] and health formalities required for the journey and the stay.

6.   Either the monetary amount or the percentage of the price which is to be paid on account and the timetable for payment of the balance.

7.   Whether a minimum number of persons is required for the package to take place and, if so, the deadline for informing the consumer in the event of cancellation.

8.   The arrangements (if any) which apply if consumers are delayed at the outward or homeward points of departure.

9.   The arrangements for security for money paid over and for the repatriation of the consumer in the event of insolvency.

[3160]

NOTES

Para 5: words in square brackets substituted by SI 1998/1208, reg 4.

SCHEDULE 2

ELEMENTS TO BE INCLUDED IN THE CONTRACT IF RELEVANT TO THE
PARTICULAR PACKAGE

Regulation 9

1.   The travel destination(s) and, where periods of stay are involved, the relevant periods, with dates.

2.   The means, characteristics and categories of transport to be used and the dates, times and points of departure and return.

3.   Where the package includes accommodation, its location, its tourist category or degree of comfort, its main features and, where the accommodation is to be provided in a member State, its compliance with the rules of that member State.

4.   The meals which are included in the package.

5.   Whether a minimum number of persons is required for the package to take place and, if so, the deadline for informing the consumer in the event of cancellation.

6.   The itinerary.

7.   Visits, excursions or other services which are included in the total price agreed for the package.

8.   The name and address of the organiser, the retailer and, where appropriate, the insurer.

9.   The price of the package, if the price may be revised in accordance with the term which may be included in the contract under regulation 11, an indication of the possibility of such price revisions, and an indication of any dues, taxes or fees chargeable for certain services (landing, embarkation or disembarkation fees at ports and airports and tourist taxes) where such costs are not included in the package.

10.   The payment schedule and method of payment.

11.   Special requirements which the consumer has communicated to the organiser or retailer when making the booking and which both have accepted.

12.   The periods within which the consumer must make any complaint about the failure to perform or the inadequate performance of the contract.

[3161]

SCHEDULE 3
ENFORCEMENT

Regulation 23

Enforcement authority

1.—(1)   Every local weights and measures authority in Great Britain shall be an enforcement authority for the purposes of regulations 5, 7, 8, 16 and 22 of these Regulations ("the relevant regulations"), and it shall be the duty of each such authority to enforce those provisions within their area.

(2)   The Department of Economic Development in Northern Ireland shall be an enforcement authority for the purposes of the relevant regulations, and it shall be the duty of the Department to enforce those provisions within Northern Ireland.

2.—....

Powers of officers of enforcement authority

3.—(1)   If a duly authorised officer of an enforcement authority has reasonable grounds for suspecting that an offence has been committed under any of the relevant regulations, he may—

(a)   require a person whom he believes on reasonable grounds to be engaged in the organisation or retailing of packages to produce any book or document relating to the activity and take copies of it or any entry in it, or

(b)   require such a person to produce in a visible and legible documentary form any information so relating which is contained in a computer, and take copies of it,

for the purpose of ascertaining whether such an offence has been committed.

(2)   Such an officer may inspect any goods for the purpose of ascertaining whether such an offence has been committed.

(3)   If such an officer has reasonable grounds for believing that any documents or goods may be required as evidence in proceedings for such an offence, he may seize and detain them.

(4)   An officer seizing any documents or goods in the exercise of his power under sub-paragraph (3) above shall inform the person from whom they are seized.

(5) The powers of an officer under this paragraph may be exercised by him only at a reasonable hour and on production (if required) of his credentials.

(6) Nothing in this paragraph—
- (a) requires a person to produce a document if he would be entitled to refuse to produce it in proceedings in a court on the ground that it is the subject of legal professional privilege or, in Scotland, that it contains a confidential communication made by or to an advocate or a solicitor in that capacity; or
- (b) authorises the taking possession of a document which is in the possession of a person who would be so entitled.

4.—(1) A duly authorised officer of an enforcement authority may, at a reasonable hour and on production (if required) of his credentials, enter any premises for the purpose of ascertaining whether an offence under any of the relevant regulations has been committed.

(2) If a justice of the peace, or in Scotland a justice of the peace or a sheriff, is satisfied—
- (a) that any relevant books, documents or goods are on, or that any relevant information contained in a computer is available from, any premises, and that production or inspection is likely to disclose the commission of an offence under the relevant regulations; or
- (b) that any such an offence has been, is being or is about to be committed on any premises,

and that any of the conditions specified in sub-paragraph (3) below is met, he may by warrant under his hand authorise an officer of an enforcement authority to enter the premises, if need be by force.

(3) The conditions referred to in sub-paragraph (2) above are—
- (a) that admission to the premises has been or is likely to be refused and that notice of intention to apply for a warrant under that sub-paragraph has been given to the occupier;
- (b) that an application for admission, or the giving of such a notice, would defeat the object of the entry;
- (c) that the premises are unoccupied; and
- (d) that the occupier is temporarily absent and it might defeat the object of the entry to await his return.

(4) In sub-paragraph (2) above "relevant", in relation to books, documents, goods or information, means books, documents, goods or information which, under paragraph 3 above, a duly authorised officer may require to be produced or may inspect.

(5) A warrant under sub-paragraph (2) above may be issued only if—
- (a) in England and Wales, the justice of the peace is satisfied as required by that sub-paragraph by written information on oath;
- (b) in Scotland, the justice of the peace or sheriff is so satisfied by evidence on oath; or
- (c) in Northern Ireland, the justice of the peace is so satisfied by complaint on oath.

(6) A warrant under sub-paragraph (2) above shall continue in force for a period of one month.

(7) An officer entering any premises by virtue of this paragraph may take with him such other persons as may appear to him necessary.

(8) On leaving premises which he has entered by virtue of a warrant under sub-paragraph (2) above, an officer shall, if the premises are unoccupied or the occupier is temporarily absent, leave the premises as effectively secured against trespassers as he found them.

(9) In this paragraph "premises" includes any place (including any vehicle, ship or aircraft) except premises used only as a dwelling.

Obstruction of officers

5.—(1) A person who—
- (a) intentionally obstructs an officer of an enforcement authority acting in pursuance of this Schedule;
- (b) without reasonable excuse fails to comply with a requirement made of him by such an officer under paragraph 3(1) above; or
- (c) without reasonable excuse fails to give an officer of an enforcement authority acting in pursuance of this Schedule any other assistance or information which the officer may reasonably require of him for the purpose of the performance of the officer's functions under this Schedule,

shall be guilty of an offence.

(2) A person guilty of an offence under sub-paragraph (1) above shall be liable on summary conviction to a fine not exceeding level 5 on the standard scale.

(3) If a person, in giving any such information as is mentioned in sub-paragraph (1)(c) above,—
- (a) makes a statement which he knows is false in a material particular; or
- (b) recklessly makes a statement which is false in a material particular,

he shall be guilty of an offence.

(4)   A person guilty of an offence under sub-paragraph (3) above shall be liable—
  (a)   on summary conviction, to a fine not exceeding level 5 on the standard scale; and
  (b)   on conviction on indictment, to a fine.

Impersonation of officers

6.—(1)   If a person who is not a duly authorised officer of an enforcement authority purports to act as such under this Schedule he shall be guilty of an offence.

(2)   A person guilty of an offence under sub-paragraph (1) above shall be liable—
  (a)   on summary conviction, to a fine not exceeding level 5 on the standard scale; and
  (b)   on conviction on indictment, to a fine.

7.   …

Privilege against self-incrimination

8.   Nothing in this Schedule requires a person to answer any question or give any information if to do so might incriminate him.

[3162]

NOTES
    Para 2: revoked by the Enterprise Act 2002 (Part 8 Notice to OFT of Intended Prosecution Specified Enactments, Revocation and Transitional Provision) Order 2003, SI 2003/1376, art 3.
    Para 7: revoked by the Enterprise Act 2002 (Part 9 Restrictions on Disclosure of Information) (Amendment and Specification) Order 2003, SI 2003/1400, art 7, Sch 5.

COMMERCIAL AGENTS (COUNCIL DIRECTIVE) REGULATIONS 1993

(SI 1993/3053)

NOTES
    Made: 7 December 1993.
    Authority: European Communities Act 1972, s 2(2).
    Commencement: 1 January 1994.

ARRANGEMENT OF REGULATIONS

PART I
GENERAL

PART II
RIGHTS AND OBLIGATIONS

PART III
REMUNERATION

PART IV
CONCLUSION AND TERMINATION OF THE AGENCY CONTRACT

PART I
GENERAL

1　Citation, commencement and applicable law

(1)　These Regulations may be cited as the Commercial Agents (Council Directive) Regulations 1993 and shall come into force on 1st January 1994.

(2)　These Regulations govern the relations between commercial agents and their principals and, subject to paragraph (3), apply in relation to the activities of commercial agents in Great Britain.

[(3)　A court or tribunal shall—
　(a)　apply the law of the other member State concerned in place of regulations 3 to 22 where the parties have agreed that the agency contract is to be governed by the law of that member State;
　(b)　(whether or not it would otherwise be required to do so) apply these regulations where the law of another member State corresponding to these regulations enables the parties to agree that the agency contract is to be governed by the law of a different member State and the parties have agreed that it is to be governed by the law of England and Wales or Scotland.]

[3163]

NOTES
　Para (3): substituted by the Commercial Agents (Council Directive) (Amendment) Regulations 1998, SI 1998/2868, reg 2(a).

2　Interpretation, application and extent

(1)　In these Regulations—
　"commercial agent" means a self-employed intermediary who has continuing authority to negotiate the sale or purchase of goods on behalf of another person (the "principal"), or to negotiate and conclude the sale or purchase of goods on behalf of and in the name of that principal; but shall be understood as not including in particular:
　　(i)　a person who, in his capacity as an officer of a company or association, is empowered to enter into commitments binding on that company or association;
　　(ii)　a partner who is lawfully authorised to enter into commitments binding on his partners;
　　(iii)　a person who acts as an insolvency practitioner (as that expression is defined in section 388 of the Insolvency Act 1986) or the equivalent in any other jurisdiction;
　"commission" means any part of the remuneration of a commercial agent which varies with the number or value of business transactions;
　["EEA Agreement" means the Agreement on the European Economic Area signed at Oporto on 2nd May 1992 as adjusted by the Protocol signed at Brussels on 17th March 1993;
　"member State" includes a State which is a contracting party to the EEA Agreement;]
　"restraint of trade clause" means an agreement restricting the business activities of a commercial agent following termination of the agency contract.

(2)　These Regulations do not apply to—
　(a)　commercial agents whose activities are unpaid;
　(b)　commercial agents when they operate on commodity exchanges or in the commodity market;
　(c)　the Crown Agents for Overseas Governments and Administrations, as set up under the Crown Agents Act 1979, or its subsidiaries.

(3)　The provisions of the Schedule to these Regulations have effect for the purpose of determining the persons whose activities as commercial agents are to be considered secondary.

(4)　These Regulations shall not apply to the persons referred to in paragraph (3) above.

(5)   These Regulations do not extend to Northern Ireland.

[3164]

NOTES
Para (1): definitions "EEA Agreement" and "member State" inserted by the Commercial Agents (Council Directive) (Amendment) Regulations 1998, SI 1998/2868, reg 2(b).

PART II
RIGHTS AND OBLIGATIONS

3 Duties of a commercial agent to his principal

(1)   In performing his activities a commercial agent must look after the interests of his principal and act dutifully and in good faith.

(2)   In particular, a commercial agent must—
(a)   make proper efforts to negotiate and where appropriate conclude the transactions he is instructed to take care of;
(b)   communicate to his principal all the necessary information available to him;
(c)   comply with reasonable instructions given by his principal.

[3165]

4 Duties of a principal to his commercial agent

(1)   In his relations with his commercial agent a principal must act dutifully and in good faith.

(2)   In particular, a principal must—
(a)   provide his commercial agent with the necessary documentation relating to the goods concerned;
(b)   obtain for his commercial agent the information necessary for the performance of the agency contract, and in particular notify his commercial agent within a reasonable period once he anticipates that the volume of commercial transactions will be significantly lower than that which the commercial agent could normally have expected.

(3)   A principal shall, in addition, inform his commercial agent within a reasonable period of his acceptance or refusal of, and of any non-execution by him of, a commercial transaction which the commercial agent has procured for him.

[3166]

5 Prohibition on derogation from regulations 3 and 4 and consequence of breach

(1)   The parties may not derogate from regulations 3 and 4 above.

(2)   The law applicable to the contract shall govern the consequence of breach of the rights and obligations under regulations 3 and 4 above.

[3167]

PART III
REMUNERATION

6 Form and amount of remuneration in absence of agreement

(1)   In the absence of any agreement as to remuneration between the parties, a commercial agent shall be entitled to the remuneration that commercial agents appointed for the goods forming the subject of his agency contract are customarily allowed in the place where he carries on his activities and, if there is no such customary practice, a commercial agent shall be entitled to reasonable remuneration taking into account all the aspects of the transaction.

(2)   This regulation is without prejudice to the application of any enactment or rule of law concerning the level of remuneration.

(3)   Where a commercial agent is not remunerated (wholly or in part) by commission, regulations 7 to 12 below shall not apply.

[3168]

7 Entitlement to commission on transactions concluded during agency contract

(1)   A commercial agent shall be entitled to commission on commercial transactions concluded during the period covered by the agency contract—
(a)   where the transaction has been concluded as a result of his action; or
(b)   where the transaction is concluded with a third party whom he has previously acquired as a customer for transactions of the same kind.

(2)   A commercial agent shall also be entitled to commission on transactions concluded during the period covered by the agency contract where he has an exclusive right to a specific geographical area or to a specific group of customers and where the transaction has been entered into with a customer belonging to that area or group.

[3169]

8   Entitlement to commission on transactions concluded after agency contract has terminated

Subject to regulation 9 below, a commercial agent shall be entitled to commission on commercial transactions concluded after the agency contract has terminated if—

(a)   the transaction is mainly attributable to his efforts during the period covered by the agency contract and if the transaction was entered into within a reasonable period after that contract terminated; or

(b)   in accordance with the conditions mentioned in regulation 7 above, the order of the third party reached the principal or the commercial agent before the agency contract terminated.

[3170]

9   Apportionment of commission between new and previous commercial agents

(1)   A commercial agent shall not be entitled to the commission referred to in regulation 7 above if that commission is payable, by virtue of regulation 8 above, to the previous commercial agent, unless it is equitable because of the circumstances for the commission to be shared between the commercial agents.

(2)   The principal shall be liable for any sum due under paragraph (1) above to the person entitled to it in accordance with that paragraph, and any sum which the other commercial agent receives to which he is not entitled shall be refunded to the principal.

[3171]

10   When commission due and date for payment

(1)   Commission shall become due as soon as, and to the extent that, one of the following circumstances occurs:

(a)   the principal has executed the transaction; or

(b)   the principal should, according to his agreement with the third party, have executed the transaction; or

(c)   the third party has executed the transaction.

(2)   Commission shall become due at the latest when the third party has executed his part of the transaction or should have done so if the principal had executed his part of the transaction, as he should have.

(3)   The commission shall be paid not later than on the last day of the month following the quarter in which it became due, and, for the purposes of these Regulations, unless otherwise agreed between the parties, the first quarter period shall run from the date the agency contract takes effect, and subsequent periods shall run from that date in the third month thereafter or the beginning of the fourth month, whichever is the sooner.

(4)   Any agreement to derogate from paragraphs (2) and (3) above to the detriment of the commercial agent shall be void.

[3172]

11   Extinction of right to commission

(1)   The right to commission can be extinguished only if and to the extent that—

(a)   it is established that the contract between the third party and the principal will not be executed; and

(b)   that fact is due to a reason for which the principal is not to blame.

(2)   Any commission which the commercial agent has already received shall be refunded if the right to it is extinguished.

(3)   Any agreement to derogate from paragraph (1) above to the detriment of the commercial agent shall be void.

[3173]

12 Periodic supply of information as to commission due and right of inspection of principal's books

(1)   The principal shall supply his commercial agent with a statement of the commission due, not later than the last day of the month following the quarter in which the commission has become due, and such statement shall set out the main components used in calculating the amount of the commission.

(2)   A commercial agent shall be entitled to demand that he be provided with all the information (and in particular an extract from the books) which is available to his principal and which he needs in order to check the amount of the commission due to him.

(3)   Any agreement to derogate from paragraphs (1) and (2) above shall be void.

(4)   Nothing in this regulation shall remove or restrict the effect of, or prevent reliance upon, any enactment or rule of law which recognises the right of an agent to inspect the books of a principal.

[3174]

PART IV
CONCLUSION AND TERMINATION OF THE AGENCY CONTRACT

13   Right to signed written statement of terms of agency contract

(1)   The commercial agent and principal shall each be entitled to receive from the other on request, a signed written document setting out the terms of the agency contract including any terms subsequently agreed.

(2)   Any purported waiver of the right referred to in paragraph (1) above shall be void.

[3175]

14   Conversion of agency contract after expiry of fixed period

An agency contract for a fixed period which continues to be performed by both parties after that period has expired shall be deemed to be converted into an agency contract for an indefinite period.

[3176]

15   Minimum periods of notice for termination of agency contract

(1)   Where an agency contract is concluded for an indefinite period either party may terminate it by notice.

(2)   The period of notice shall be—
  (a)   1 month for the first year of the contract;
  (b)   2 months for the second year commenced;
  (c)   3 months for the third year commenced and for the subsequent years;
and the parties may not agree on any shorter periods of notice.

(3)   If the parties agree on longer periods than those laid down in paragraph (2) above, the period of notice to be observed by the principal must not be shorter than that to be observed by the commercial agent.

(4)   Unless otherwise agreed by the parties, the end of the period of notice must coincide with the end of a calendar month.

(5)   The provisions of this regulation shall also apply to an agency contract for a fixed period where it is converted under regulation 14 above into an agency contract for an indefinite period subject to the proviso that the earlier fixed period must be taken into account in the calculation of the period of notice.

[3177]

16   Savings with regard to immediate termination

These Regulations shall not affect the application of any enactment or rule of law which provides for the immediate termination of the agency contract—
  (a)   because of the failure of one party to carry out all or part of his obligations under that contract; or
  (b)   where exceptional circumstances arise.

[3178]

17   Entitlement of commercial agent to indemnity or compensation on termination of agency contract

(1)   This regulation has effect for the purpose of ensuring that the commercial agent is, after termination of the agency contract, indemnified in accordance with paragraphs (3) to (5) below or compensated for damage in accordance with paragraphs (6) and (7) below.

(2)   Except where the agency [contract] otherwise provides, the commercial agent shall be entitled to be compensated rather than indemnified.

(3)   Subject to paragraph (9) and to regulation 18 below, the commercial agent shall be entitled to an indemnity if and to the extent that—
  (a)   he has brought the principal new customers or has significantly increased the volume of business with existing customers and the principal continues to derive substantial benefits from the business with such customers; and
  (b)   the payment of this indemnity is equitable having regard to all the circumstances and, in particular, the commission lost by the commercial agent on the business transacted with such customers.

(4)   The amount of the indemnity shall not exceed a figure equivalent to an indemnity for one year calculated from the commercial agent's average annual remuneration over the preceding five years and if the contract goes back less than five years the indemnity shall be calculated on the average for the period in question.

(5)   The grant of an indemnity as mentioned above shall not prevent the commercial agent from seeking damages.

(6)   Subject to paragraph (9) and to regulation 18 below, the commercial agent shall be entitled to compensation for the damage he suffers as a result of the termination of his relations with his principal.

(7)   For the purpose of these Regulations such damage shall be deemed to occur particularly when the termination takes place in either or both of the following circumstances, namely circumstances which—

   (a)   deprive the commercial agent of the commission which proper performance of the agency contract would have procured for him whilst providing his principal with substantial benefits linked to the activities of the commercial agent; or

   (b)   have not enabled the commercial agent to amortize the costs and expenses that he had incurred in the performance of the agency contract on the advice of his principal.

(8)   Entitlement to the indemnity or compensation for damage as provided for under paragraphs (2) to (7) above shall also arise where the agency contract is terminated as a result of the death of the commercial agent.

(9)   The commercial agent shall lose his entitlement to the indemnity or compensation for damage in the instances provided for in paragraphs (2) to (8) above if within one year following termination of his agency contract he has not notified his principal that he intends pursuing his entitlement.

[3179]

NOTES

Para (2): word in square brackets substituted by the Commercial Agents (Council Directive) (Amendment) Regulations 1998, SI 1998/2868, reg 2(c).

18   Grounds for excluding payment of indemnity or compensation under regulation 17

The [indemnity or] compensation referred to in regulation 17 above shall not be payable to the commercial agent where—

   (a)   the principal has terminated the agency contract because of default attributable to the commercial agent which would justify immediate termination of the agency contract pursuant to regulation 16 above; or

   (b)   the commercial agent has himself terminated the agency contract, unless such termination is justified—

      (i)   by circumstances attributable to the principal, or

      (ii)   on grounds of the age, infirmity or illness of the commercial agent in consequence of which he cannot reasonably be required to continue his activities; or

   (c)   the commercial agent, with the agreement of his principal, assigns his rights and duties under the agency contract to another person.

[3180]

NOTES

Words in square brackets inserted by the Commercial Agents (Council Directive) (Amendment) Regulations 1993, SI 1993/3173, reg 2.

19   Prohibition on derogation from regulations 17 and 18

The parties may not derogate from regulations 17 and 18 to the detriment of the commercial agent before the agency contract expires.

[3181]

20   Restraint of trade clauses

(1)   A restraint of trade clause shall be valid only if and to the extent that—

   (a)   it is concluded in writing; and

   (b)   it relates to the geographical area or the group of customers and the geographical area entrusted to the commercial agent and to the kind of goods covered by his agency under the contract.

(2)   A restraint of trade clause shall be valid for not more than two years after termination of the agency contract.

(3) Nothing in this regulation shall affect any enactment or rule of law which imposes other restrictions on the validity or enforceability of restraint of trade clauses or which enables a court to reduce the obligations on the parties resulting from such clauses.

[3182]

PART V
MISCELLANEOUS AND SUPPLEMENTAL

21 Disclosure of information

Nothing in these Regulations shall require information to be given where such disclosure would be contrary to public policy.

[3183]

22 Service of notice etc

(1) Any notice, statement or other document to be given or supplied to a commercial agent or to be given or supplied to the principal under these Regulations may be so given or supplied:
- (a) by delivering it to him;
- (b) by leaving it at his proper address addressed to him by name;
- (c) by sending it by post to him addressed either to his registered address or to the address of his registered or principal office;

or by any other means provided for in the agency contract.

(2) Any such notice, statement or document may—
- (a) in the case of a body corporate, be given or served on the secretary or clerk of that body;
- (b) in the case of a partnership, be given to or served on any partner or on any person having the control or management of the partnership business.

[3184]

23 Transitional provisions

(1) Notwithstanding any provision in an agency contract made before 1st January 1994, these Regulations shall apply to that contract after that date and, accordingly any provision which is inconsistent with these Regulations shall have effect subject to them.

(2) Nothing in these Regulations shall affect the rights and liabilities of a commercial agent or a principal which have accrued before 1st January 1994.

[3185]

SCHEDULE

Regulation 2(3)

1. The activities of a person as a commercial agent are to be considered secondary where it may reasonably be taken that the primary purpose of the arrangement with his principal is other than as set out in paragraph 2 below.

2. An arrangement falls within this paragraph if—
- (a) the business of the principal is the sale, or as the case may be purchase, of goods of a particular kind; and
- (b) the goods concerned are such that—
  - (i) transactions are normally individually negotiated and concluded on a commercial basis, and
  - (ii) procuring a transaction on one occasion is likely to lead to further transactions in those goods with that customer on future occasions, or to transactions in those goods with other customers in the same geographical area or among the same group of customers, and

  that accordingly it is in the commercial interests of the principal in developing the market in those goods to appoint a representative to such customers with a view to the representative devoting effort, skill and expenditure from his own resources to that end.

3. The following are indications that an arrangement falls within paragraph 2 above, and the absence of any of them is an indication to the contrary—
- (a) the principal is the manufacturer, importer or distributor of the goods;
- (b) the goods are specifically identified with the principal in the market in question rather than, or to a greater extent than, with any other person;
- (c) the agent devotes substantially the whole of his time to representative activities (whether for one principal or for a number of principals whose interests are not conflicting);
- (d) the goods are not normally available in the market in question other than by means of the agent;
- (e) the arrangement is described as one of commercial agency.

4. The following are indications that an arrangement does not fall within paragraph 2 above—
- (a) promotional material is supplied direct to potential customers;

(b)   persons are granted agencies without reference to existing agents in a particular area or in relation to a particular group;

(c)   customers normally select the goods for themselves and merely place their orders through the agent.

5.   The activities of the following categories of persons are presumed, unless the contrary is established, not to fall within paragraph 2 above—

Mail order catalogue agents for consumer goods.

Consumer credit agents.

[3186]–[3211]

TRADING SCHEMES REGULATIONS 1997

(SI 1997/30)

NOTES
Made: 13 January 1997.
Authority: Fair Trading Act 1973, s 119.
Commencement: 6 February 1997.

ARRANGEMENT OF REGULATIONS

1   Citation, commencement and application

(1)   These Regulations may be cited as the Trading Schemes Regulations 1997 and shall come into force on 6th February 1997.

(2)   Subject to paragraph (3) below, these Regulations shall apply—

(a)   from the date of their coming into force to any trading scheme to which Part XI of the Fair Trading Act 1973 applies and which came into existence on or after the date of coming into force of these Regulations, and to any agreement made under such a trading scheme;

(b)   after a period of six months from the date of their coming into force to any trading scheme in existence prior to the coming into force of the Act and to which Part XI of the Fair Trading Act 1973 did not apply prior to that date.

(3)   Where an agreement is made after the date of coming into force of these Regulations but prior to the expiry of a six months period after that date under a trading scheme to which Part XI of the Fair Trading Act 1973 applied prior to the coming into force of the Act such agreement shall comply either with the 1989 Regulations or these Regulations.

(4)   Subject to paragraph (3) above the 1989 Regulations shall not apply to any trading scheme coming into operation after the date of the coming into force of these Regulations or to any agreement made after that date under any trading scheme to which Part XI of the Fair Trading Act 1973 applies.

[3212]

2   Interpretation

In these Regulations—

"the Act" means the Trading Schemes Act 1996;

"advertisement" means any advertisement, document, prospectus, circular or notice, whether transmitted in electronic or any other form, which promotes a trading scheme;

"the 1989 Regulations" means the Pyramid Selling Schemes Regulations 1989;

"the 1990 Regulations" means the Pyramid Selling Schemes (Amendment) Regulations 1990;

"participant" has the same meaning as in Part XI of the Fair Trading Act 1973;

"security" means a mortgage, charge, pledge, bond, debenture, indemnity, guarantee, bill, note or other right provided by the participant, or at his request (expressed or implied), to secure the carrying out of the obligations of the participant under an agreement referred to in regulation 4.

"trading scheme" has the same meaning as in Part XI of the Fair Trading Act 1973.

[3213]

3 Contents of advertisements

(1) Subject to paragraph (2) of this regulation, a promoter of, or a participant in, a trading scheme shall not issue, circulate or distribute any advertisement which contains information likely to lead directly or indirectly to persons becoming participants in a trading scheme by any means unless such advertisement

  (a) states the name and address of the promoter, or in the case of a scheme promoted by more than one person, the names and addresses of all of the promoters;

  (b) describes the goods or services acquired or supplied under the trading scheme; and

  (c) contains the words set out in Schedule 1 to these Regulations which must

    (i) not appear at the beginning or the end of the advertisement;

    (ii) insofar as the advertisement contains any information as to the sources of income for participants from participation in the trading scheme, appear together with such information and be given no less prominence than such information;

    (iii) be easily legible or audible; and

    (iv) be afforded no less prominence than that given to any other information in the advertisement apart from the heading of the advertisement.

(2) This regulation does not apply to any advertisement which—

  (a) forms part of a newspaper or magazine; or

  (b) is transmitted by way of a radio or television broadcast.

[3214]

4 Pre-performance requirements

(1) Save where the requirements set out in paragraph (2) below are satisfied, no promoter of, nor participant in, a trading scheme shall—

  (a) supply goods or services to a participant in the trading scheme;

  (b) provide any goods or services under a transaction effected by such a participant;

  (c) be a party to any arrangement under which goods or services are supplied or provided as aforesaid; or

  (d) accept from any such participant any payment or undertaking to make a payment in respect of any goods or services supplied or provided as mentioned in any of the preceding paragraphs (a) to (c) above or in respect of any goods or services to be so supplied or provided.

(2) The requirements referred to in paragraph (1) above are that—

  (a) the arrangements with a participant do not include a statement or promise that the participant will receive a payment or benefit in respect of the continued participation of another person in the trading scheme to which such arrangements relate or in any other trading scheme;

  (b) the promoter or a participant and the participant joining the trading scheme shall have signed a written agreement which contains all the terms under which the participant joining the trading scheme is participating in the trading scheme and which complies with regulation 5;

  (c) a copy of that agreement shall have been furnished to the participant joining the trading scheme.

[3215]

5 Contents of contracts

The agreement referred to in regulation 4 shall include:—

  (a) the name and address of the promoter or, in the case of a scheme promoted by more than one person, the names and addresses of all the promoters;

  (b) a description of the goods or services to be acquired by or supplied to the participant by the promoter or promoters, other participants or suppliers nominated by the promoter or promoters or any other person under the trading scheme;

  (c) a statement describing the capacity in which the participant shall act for the purposes of any transaction which he may effect under the trading scheme;

  (d) a statement describing the financial obligation of the participant during the period of twelve months from the commencement date of the agreement. The promoter shall give to the participant at least 60 days advance written notice of any subsequent changes in such financial obligation;

  (e) a statement describing the right of the participant to cancel the agreement:—

    (i) within 14 days of entering into the agreement without penalty and with the right to recover any monies which he had paid to or for the benefit of the promoter or any of the promoters or any other participant in connection with his participation in the trading scheme or paid to any other participant in accordance with the provisions of the trading scheme and the manner in which that cancellation and recovery shall be effected;

 (ii) within 14 days of entering into the agreement the right to return to an address specified in the agreement which must be an address in the United Kingdom, any goods the participant has purchased within that period under the trading scheme and which remain unsold provided that such unsold goods remain in the condition in which they were in at the time of purchase, whether or not their external wrappings have been broken and to recover any monies paid in respect of such goods;

 (iii) within 14 days of entering into the agreement the right to cancel any services ordered within that period under the trading scheme and to recover any monies paid in respect of such services not yet supplied to the participant;

and that the promoter or any other person who has supplied goods to the participant under the trading scheme shall not be entitled to make a handling charge in respect of goods returned under sub-paragraph (ii) above or services cancelled under sub-paragraph (iii) above;

(f) a statement describing the rights of the participant to terminate the agreement at any time without penalty by giving 14 days written notice to the promoter or any of the promoters at an address which is specified in the agreement;

(g) a statement describing the rights of the participant following termination of the agreement by the promoter or the participant as set out in these Regulations;

(h) the written warnings in the form set out in Part I and Part II of Schedule 2 hereto which comply with the following:—
  (i) the words are easily legible; and
  (ii) the words in Part II are printed immediately above the space for the participant's signature;

(i) a statement setting out the conditions under which the participant shall be entitled to return goods to the promoter or any promoters or any other participant which shall include at least the rights conferred on the participant by regulation 6 below and which must include an address in the United Kingdom to which such goods can be returned;

(j) a statement setting out the conditions when commission already paid by the promoter or another participant will be recoverable from the participant which shall include at least the rights conferred on the participant by regulation 9;

(k) where the agreement comprises more than one document, a statement setting out all documents which form part of the contract between the parties and that those documents form the entire agreement between the parties.

[3216]

6　Right to return goods to promoter on termination

(1) The rights referred to in regulation 5(i) are, that if a participant or the promoter or any of the promoters terminates an agreement referred to in regulation 4 or any agreement entered into in consequence of such an agreement with a participant, the participant shall, subject to subsection (2) below, have the right to be released from all future contractual obligations and to return to the promoter or any of the promoters or any other participant any goods the participant has purchased within a period of 90 days prior to such termination under the scheme and which remain unsold and to recover from the promoter or such other participant who supplied the goods—

(a) where the participant has terminated the agreement, the price (inclusive of Value Added Tax) which the participant paid for them less—
  (i) in the case of any goods the condition of which has deteriorated due to an act or default on the part of the participant, an amount equal to the diminution in their value resulting from such deterioration; and
  (ii) a reasonable handling charge;

(b) where the promoter or any of the promoters or any other participant has terminated the agreement the price (inclusive of Value Added Tax) which the participant paid for them together with any costs incurred by the participant for returning the goods to the promoter or any other participant;

(c) on terms whereby the purchase price is payable upon delivery of the goods or, if the goods are already held by the promoter or any of the promoters, forthwith, and

(d) on terms whereby the goods not already held by the promoter or any of the promoters will be delivered within 21 days of such termination at the promoter's expense to the address stated in the agreement.

(2)   Where an agreement referred to in regulation 4 contains an obligation on the participant not to compete with the business of the promoter after termination of such agreement, such non-competition provision shall continue in force after the date of termination.

[3217]

7   Securities and guarantees

A promoter of, or a participant in, a trading scheme shall not accept from a participant any guarantee or security in whatever form in respect of goods or services supplied or to be supplied or in respect of the payment of the price for goods or services supplied or to be supplied or an undertaking to provide such a guarantee or such security unless the creditor or a promoter or other supplier who is not a creditor has agreed in writing to refund the amount of that payment to the debtor upon his returning the relevant goods in an undamaged condition to the creditor or to any promoter or supplier.

[3218]

8   Supply of goods and services

A promoter of, or a participant in, a trading scheme shall not make a supply of goods or services to the participant unless, in respect of every supply of goods or services under a trading scheme, such promoter or participant has provided the participant to whom the goods are supplied or to be supplied with an adequate record of the transaction in respect of which payment is due from that participant. For the purposes of this regulation an itemised order form, invoice or receipt shall constitute an adequate record.

[3219]

9   Recovery of commission

The rights referred to in regulation 5(j) are the right to retain, after termination of an agreement referred to in regulation 4 or any agreement made thereunder, any commission paid to the participant under a trading scheme unless—

(a)   the commission was paid in respect of goods returned to the promoter or another participant who paid the commission;

(b)   the promoter has refunded all monies due to the participant under the agreement referred to in regulation 4 in respect of goods returned to him by the participant;

(c)   the commission payment is claimed within 120 days of the date of having been made; and

(d)   the promoter has entered into an agreement with the participant that complies with the requirements in regulation 5 and that agreement and any subsequent agreement contains a statement describing when commission becomes repayable to the promoter and the terms upon which recovery of that payment may be made; and

(e)   the promoter recovers the commission payment in accordance with the terms referred to in paragraph (d) above.

[3220]

10   £200 liability limit

A promoter of, or a participant in, a trading scheme shall not accept from a participant joining the trading scheme any payment or an undertaking to make a payment of any sum exceeding £200 unless 7 days have expired from the making of the agreement relating to goods or services supplied or to be supplied under that agreement to the participant by the promoter or any other participant under the trading scheme.

[3221]

11   Civil consequences of contraventions

(1)   Where a participant makes a payment to or for the benefit of a promoter of, or to a participant in, a trading scheme and the acceptance of that payment involves a contravention of these Regulations, that contravention shall be actionable at the suit of the participant who suffers loss as a result of the contravention subject to the defences and other incidents applying to actions for breach of statutory duty.

(2)   No undertaking to make any payment given by a participant in a trading scheme involving a contravention of sub-paragraph (d) of paragraph (1) of regulation 4 or regulation 10 shall be enforceable against him in any civil proceedings or recoverable in any other way.

(3)   A participant in a trading scheme shall be under no liability to pay for any goods or services as the case may be—

(a)   supplied to him in circumstances involving a contravention of regulations 4 to 10; or

(b)   unless it was clearly explained to him by a promoter or a participant supplying or seeking to supply goods or services under the trading scheme, before he purchased the goods or services, that he had a free choice whether or not to purchase those goods or services and the purchase price for those goods or services and his annual financial obligation under the agreement was clearly stated.

[3222]

SCHEDULES

SCHEDULE 1

Regulation 3(1)(c)

Warning for use in advertisements—

1. It is illegal for a promoter or a participant in a trading scheme to persuade anyone to make a payment by promising benefits from getting others to join a scheme.

2. Do not be misled by claims that high earnings are easily achieved.

[3223]

SCHEDULE 2

Regulation 5

Warning for use in contracts—

PART I

1. It is illegal for a promoter or a participant in a trading scheme to persuade anyone to make a payment by promising benefits from getting others to join a scheme.

2. Do not be misled by claims that high earnings are easily achieved.

PART II

3. If you sign this contract, you have 14 days in which to cancel and get your money back.

[3224]

TRADING SCHEMES (EXCLUSION) REGULATIONS 1997

(SI 1997/31)

NOTES
Made: 13 January 1997.
Authority: Fair Trading Act 1973, s 118(6)(b).
Commencement: 6 February 1997.

1 Citation and Commencement

These Regulations may be cited as the Trading Schemes (Exclusion) Regulations 1997 and shall come into force on 6th February 1997.

[3225]

2 Interpretation

In these Regulations—

"the Act" means the Fair Trading Act 1973.

"annual profit of the trading scheme" means for each financial year the net profit of the promoter or promoters of the trading scheme as shown in the accounts of the trading scheme.

"chain letter" means any trading scheme under which a letter is sent to participants or prospective participants directly or indirectly instructing or requesting them to—

    (a)   send monies or other benefits to at least one of the individuals on a list of individuals, shown with their mailing addresses, which is contained in or accompanying that letter; and

    (b)   carry on the chain by sending copies of the letter to other individuals not on the list and removing from the list any one name and address and adding their own to it.

"participant" has the same meaning as in section 118(8) of the Act.

"single tier trading scheme" means a trading scheme the only members of which are the promoter or promoters and one or more participants and under which, in the United Kingdom, either a single promoter or a single participant operates at one level and any other participant or participants of the trading scheme operate at the same level below such promoter or participant aforesaid.

"trading scheme" has the same meaning as in section 118(8) of the Act.

[3226]

3 Disapplication of Part XI of the Act

For the purpose of section 118(6)(b) of the Act the Secretary of State hereby prescribes trading schemes of the following description, that is to say—

(a) [any trading scheme which is a single tier trading scheme under which a participant operating at a level immediately below that of the promoter or single participant in the UK, who introduces another participant to the scheme at that level,] does not receive any payment or benefit, or can only receive a single benefit or payment, in respect of the introduction of that participant, such payment or benefit not exceeding £50 and can receive no other benefit or payment in respect of or flowing directly or indirectly from the membership or activities of that participant in that or any other trading scheme, unless such other benefit or payment results from—

    (i) a sharing of expenses of the operation of the trading scheme;

    (ii) a share in the annual profit of the trading scheme; or

    (iii) the sale of the participant's business, being a business in respect of which a registration under the Value Added Taxes Act 1994 was in force at the date of sale.

[(b) any trading scheme all of the participants in which are making or have the intention of making taxable supplies in the UK and are registered for Value Added Tax; or]

(c) any trading scheme which is a chain letter provided there is no requirement on the participant to send monies or other benefits

    (i) to a central address or the promoter of the trading scheme for onward distribution; or

    (ii) to any person or organisation other than or additional to the person whose name and address is to be deleted from the list when the participant sends the letter to others; or

    (iii) to an organisation or person for onward transmission to a participant (whether or not that participant is identified on the list); and

where the promoter does not benefit from the provision of any other service or facilities offered or provided either by him or any other person or organisation to participants.

[3227]

NOTES
Words in square brackets substituted by the Trading Schemes (Exclusion) (Amendment) Regulations 1997, SI 1997/1887, reg 2.

UNFAIR TERMS IN CONSUMER CONTRACTS REGULATIONS 1999

(SI 1999/2083)

NOTES
Made: 22 July 1999.
Authority: European Communities Act 1972, s 2(2).
Commencement: 1 October 1999.

ARRANGEMENT OF REGULATIONS

1   Citation and commencement

These Regulations may be cited as the Unfair Terms in Consumer Contracts Regulations 1999 and shall come into force on 1st October 1999.

[3228]

2   (*Revokes the Unfair Terms in Consumer Contracts Regulations 1994, SI 1994/3159.*)

3   Interpretation

In these Regulations—

"the Community" means the European Community;

"consumer" means any natural person who, in contracts covered by these Regulations, is acting for purposes which are outside his trade, business or profession;

"court" in relation to England and Wales and Northern Ireland means a county court or the High Court, and in relation to Scotland, the Sheriff or the Court of Session;

"[OFT]" means the [Office of Fair Trading];

"EEA Agreement" means the Agreement on the European Economic Area signed at Oporto on 2nd May 1992 as adjusted by the protocol signed at Brussels on 17th March 1993;

"Member State" means a State which is a contracting party to the EEA Agreement;

"notified" means notified in writing;

"qualifying body" means a person specified in Schedule 1;

"seller or supplier" means any natural or legal person who, in contracts covered by these Regulations, is acting for purposes relating to his trade, business or profession, whether publicly owned or privately owned;

"unfair terms" means the contractual terms referred to in regulation 5.

[(1A)   The references—

(a)   in regulation 4(1) to a seller or a supplier, and

(b)   in regulation 8(1) to a seller or supplier,

include references to a distance supplier and to an intermediary.

(1B)   In paragraph (1A) and regulation 5(6)—

"distance supplier" means—

(a)   a supplier under a distance contract within the meaning of the Financial Services (Distance Marketing) Regulations 2004, or

(b)   a supplier of unsolicited financial services within regulation 15 of those Regulations; and

"intermediary" has the same meaning as in those Regulations.]

(2)   (*Applies to Scotland only.*)

[3229]

NOTES

Paras (1A), (1B): inserted by the Financial Services (Distance Marketing) Regulations 2004, SI 2004/2095, reg 24(1), (2).

Director General of Fair Trading: the Enterprise Act 2002, s 2(1), at **[1860]**, provides that, as from the coming into force of that section (on 1 April 2003, see the Enterprise Act 2002 (Commencement No 2, Transitional and Transitory Provisions) Order 2003, SI 2003/766), the functions of the Director General of Fair Trading, his property, rights and liabilities are transferred to the Office of Fair Trading. Accordingly, (by virtue of s 2(2), (3) of the 2002 Act) the office of the Director is abolished, and any reference to the Director in any enactment, instrument or other document passed or made before the commencement of s 2(1) shall have effect as if it were a reference to the Office of Fair Trading. Consequently, throughout these Regulations, unless noted otherwise, the words "Office of Fair Trading", "OFT", "OFT's", "it", "it" and "its" are substituted for the original words "Director General of Fair Trading", "Director", "Director's", "he", "him" and "his" respectively. For transitional provisions in connection with the transfer, see s 276(1) of, and Sch 24, para 6 to, the 2002 Act.

---

4   Terms to which these Regulations apply

(1)   These Regulations apply in relation to unfair terms in contracts concluded between a seller or a supplier and a consumer.

(2)   These Regulations do not apply to contractual terms which reflect—

(a)   mandatory statutory or regulatory provisions (including such provisions under the law of any Member State or in Community legislation having effect in the United Kingdom without further enactment);

(b)   the provisions or principles of international conventions to which the Member States or the Community are party.

[3230]

5   Unfair Terms

(1)   A contractual term which has not been individually negotiated shall be regarded as unfair if, contrary to the requirement of good faith, it causes a significant imbalance in the parties' rights and obligations arising under the contract, to the detriment of the consumer.

(2)   A term shall always be regarded as not having been individually negotiated where it has been drafted in advance and the consumer has therefore not been able to influence the substance of the term.

(3)   Notwithstanding that a specific term or certain aspects of it in a contract has been individually negotiated, these Regulations shall apply to the rest of a contract if an overall assessment of it indicates that it is a pre-formulated standard contract.

(4)   It shall be for any seller or supplier who claims that a term was individually negotiated to show that it was.

(5)   Schedule 2 to these Regulations contains an indicative and non-exhaustive list of the terms which may be regarded as unfair.

[(6)   Any contractual term providing that a consumer bears the burden of proof in respect of showing whether a distance supplier or an intermediary complied with any or all of the obligations placed upon him resulting from the Directive and any rule or enactment implementing it shall always be regarded as unfair.

(7)   In paragraph (6)—
"the Directive" means Directive 2002/65/EC of the European Parliament and of the Council of 23 September 2002 concerning the distance marketing of consumer financial services and amending Council Directive 90/619/EEC and Directives 97/7/EC and 98/27/EC; and
"rule" means a rule made by the Financial Services Authority under the Financial Services and Markets Act 2000 or by a designated professional body within the meaning of section 326(2) of that Act.]

[3231]

NOTES

Paras (6), (7): added by the Financial Services (Distance Marketing) Regulations 2004, SI 2004/2095, reg 24(1), (3).

---

6 Assessment of unfair terms

(1)   Without prejudice to regulation 12, the unfairness of a contractual term shall be assessed, taking into account the nature of the goods or services for which the contract was concluded and by referring, at the time of conclusion of the contract, to all the circumstances attending the conclusion of the contract and to all the other terms of the contract or of another contract on which it is dependent.

(2)   In so far as it is in plain intelligible language, the assessment of fairness of a term shall not relate—
    (a)   to the definition of the main subject matter of the contract, or
    (b)   to the adequacy of the price or remuneration, as against the goods or services supplied in exchange.

[3232]

7 Written contracts

(1)   A seller or supplier shall ensure that any written term of a contract is expressed in plain, intelligible language.

(2)   If there is doubt about the meaning of a written term, the interpretation which is most favourable to the consumer shall prevail but this rule shall not apply in proceedings brought under regulation 12.

[3233]

8 Effect of unfair term

(1)   An unfair term in a contract concluded with a consumer by a seller or supplier shall not be binding on the consumer.

(2)   The contract shall continue to bind the parties if it is capable of continuing in existence without the unfair term.

[3234]

9 Choice of law clauses

These Regulations shall apply notwithstanding any contract term which applies or purports to apply the law of a non-Member State, if the contract has a close connection with the territory of the Member States.

[3235]

10 Complaints—consideration by [OFT]

(1)   It shall be the duty of the [OFT] to consider any complaint made to [it] that any contract term drawn up for general use is unfair, unless—
    (a)   the complaint appears to the [OFT] to be frivolous or vexatious; or

(b)   a qualifying body has notified the [OFT] that it agrees to consider the complaint.

(2)   The [OFT] shall give reasons for [its] decision to apply or not to apply, as the case may be, for an injunction under regulation 12 in relation to any complaint which these Regulations require [it] to consider.

(3)   In deciding whether or not to apply for an injunction in respect of a term which the [OFT] considers to be unfair, [it] may, if [it] considers it appropriate to do so, have regard to any undertakings given to [it] by or on behalf of any person as to the continued use of such a term in contracts concluded with consumers.

[3236]

NOTES
   References to the OFT, etc: as to the abolition of the office of the Director General of Fair Trading and the substitution of the original references to the Director (and related expressions), see the note to reg 3 at **[3229]**.

11   Complaints—consideration by qualifying bodies

(1)   If a qualifying body specified in Part One of Schedule 1 notifies the [OFT] that it agrees to consider a complaint that any contract term drawn up for general use is unfair, it shall be under a duty to consider that complaint.

(2)   Regulation 10(2) and (3) shall apply to a qualifying body which is under a duty to consider a complaint as they apply to the [OFT].

[3237]

NOTES
   References to the OFT, etc: as to the abolition of the office of the Director General of Fair Trading and the substitution of the original references to the Director (and related expressions), see the note to reg 3 at **[3229]**.

12   Injunctions to prevent continued use of unfair terms

(1)   The [OFT] or, subject to paragraph (2), any qualifying body may apply for an injunction (including an interim injunction) against any person appearing to the [OFT] or that body to be using, or recommending use of, an unfair term drawn up for general use in contracts concluded with consumers.

(2)   A qualifying body may apply for an injunction only where—
   (a)   it has notified the [OFT] of its intention to apply at least fourteen days before the date on which the application is made, beginning with the date on which the notification was given; or
   (b)   the [OFT] consents to the application being made within a shorter period.

(3)   The court on an application under this regulation may grant an injunction on such terms as it thinks fit.

(4)   An injunction may relate not only to use of a particular contract term drawn up for general use but to any similar term, or a term having like effect, used or recommended for use by any person.

[3238]

NOTES
   References to the OFT, etc: as to the abolition of the office of the Director General of Fair Trading and the substitution of the original references to the Director (and related expressions), see the note to reg 3 at **[3229]**.

13   Powers of the [OFT] and qualifying bodies to obtain documents and information

(1)   The [OFT] may exercise the power conferred by this regulation for the purpose of—
   (a)   facilitating [its] consideration of a complaint that a contract term drawn up for general use is unfair; or
   (b)   ascertaining whether a person has complied with an undertaking or court order as to the continued use, or recommendation for use, of a term in contracts concluded with consumers.

(2)   A qualifying body specified in Part One of Schedule 1 may exercise the power conferred by this regulation for the purpose of—
   (a)   facilitating its consideration of a complaint that a contract term drawn up for general use is unfair; or
   (b)   ascertaining whether a person has complied with—
      (i)   an undertaking given to it or to the court following an application by that body, or
      (ii)   a court order made on an application by that body,
      as to the continued use, or recommendation for use, of a term in contracts concluded with consumers.

(3)   The [OFT] may require any person to supply to [it], and a qualifying body specified in Part One of Schedule 1 may require any person to supply to it—

   (a)   a copy of any document which that person has used or recommended for use, at the time the notice referred to in paragraph (4) below is given, as a pre-formulated standard contract in dealings with consumers;

   (b)   information about the use, or recommendation for use, by that person of that document or any other such document in dealings with consumers.

(4)   The power conferred by this regulation is to be exercised by a notice in writing which may—

   (a)   specify the way in which and the time within which it is to be complied with; and

   (b)   be varied or revoked by a subsequent notice.

(5)   Nothing in this regulation compels a person to supply any document or information which he would be entitled to refuse to produce or give in civil proceedings before the court.

(6)   If a person makes default in complying with a notice under this regulation, the court may, on the application of the [OFT] or of the qualifying body, make such order as the court thinks fit for requiring the default to be made good, and any such order may provide that all the costs or expenses of and incidental to the application shall be borne by the person in default or by any officers of a company or other association who are responsible for its default.

[3239]

NOTES

References to the OFT, etc: as to the abolition of the office of the Director General of Fair Trading and the substitution of the original references to the Director (and related expressions), see the note to reg 3 at **[3229]**.

14   Notification of undertakings and orders to [OFT]

A qualifying body shall notify the [OFT]—

   (a)   of any undertaking given to it by or on behalf of any person as to the continued use of a term which that body considers to be unfair in contracts concluded with consumers;

   (b)   of the outcome of any application made by it under regulation 12, and of the terms of any undertaking given to, or order made by, the court;

   (c)   of the outcome of any application made by it to enforce a previous order of the court.

[3240]

NOTES

References to the OFT, etc: as to the abolition of the office of the Director General of Fair Trading and the substitution of the original references to the Director (and related expressions), see the note to reg 3 at **[3229]**.

15   Publication, information and advice

(1)   The [OFT] shall arrange for the publication in such form and manner as [it] considers appropriate, of—

   (a)   details of any undertaking or order notified to [it] under regulation 14;

   (b)   details of any undertaking given to [it] by or on behalf of any person as to the continued use of a term which the [OFT] considers to be unfair in contracts concluded with consumers;

   (c)   details of any application made by [it] under regulation 12, and of the terms of any undertaking given to, or order made by, the court;

   (d)   details of any application made by the [OFT] to enforce a previous order of the court.

(2)   The [OFT] shall inform any person on request whether a particular term to which these Regulations apply has been—

   (a)   the subject of an undertaking given to the [OFT] or notified to [it] by a qualifying body; or

   (b)   the subject of an order of the court made upon application by [it] or notified to [it] by a qualifying body;

and shall give that person details of the undertaking or a copy of the order, as the case may be, together with a copy of any amendments which the person giving the undertaking has agreed to make to the term in question.

(3)   The [OFT] may arrange for the dissemination in such form and manner as [it] considers appropriate of such information and advice concerning the operation of these Regulations as may appear to [it] to be expedient to give to the public and to all persons likely to be affected by these Regulations.

[3241]

NOTES

References to the OFT, etc: as to the abolition of the office of the Director General of Fair Trading and the substitution of the original references to the Director (and related expressions), see the note to reg 3 at **[3229]**.

[16   The functions of the Financial Services Authority

The functions of the Financial Services Authority under these Regulations shall be treated as functions of the Financial Services Authority under the [Financial Services and Markets Act 2000].]

[3242]

NOTES

Inserted by the Unfair Terms in Consumer Contracts (Amendment) Regulations 2001, SI 2001/1186, reg 2(a); words in square brackets substituted by the Financial Services and Markets Act 2000 (Consequential Amendments and Repeals) Order 2001, SI 2001/3649, art 583.

SCHEDULES

SCHEDULE 1
QUALIFYING BODIES
Regulation 3

PART ONE

[1.   The Information Commissioner.

2.   The Gas and Electricity Markets Authority.

3.   The Director General of Electricity Supply for Northern Ireland.

4.   The Director General of Gas for Northern Ireland.

5.   [The Office of Communications].

6.   [The Water Services Regulation Authority].

7.   [The Office of Rail Regulation].

8.   Every weights and measures authority in Great Britain.

9.   The Department of Enterprise, Trade and Investment in Northern Ireland.

10.   The Financial Services Authority.]

[3243]

NOTES

Substituted by the Unfair Terms in Consumer Contracts (Amendment) Regulations 2001, SI 2001/1186, reg 2(b).

Entry 5 relating to "The Office of Communications" substituted by the Communications Act 2003 (Consequential Amendments No 2) Order 2003, SI 2003/3182, art 2; entry 6 relating to "The Water Services Regulation Authority" substituted by the Unfair Terms in Consumer Contracts (Amendment) and Water Act 2003 (Transitional Provision) Regulations 2006, SI 2006/523, reg 2, subject to transitional provisions in reg 3 of those Regulations; entry 7 relating to "The Office of Rail Regulation" in square brackets substituted by virtue of the Railways and Transport Safety Act 2003, s 16(4), (5), Sch 3, para 4.

PART TWO
11.   Consumers' Association.

[3244]

SCHEDULE 2
INDICATIVE AND NON-EXHAUSTIVE LIST OF TERMS WHICH MAY BE REGARDED AS UNFAIR
Regulation 5(5)

1.   Terms which have the object or effect of—

(a)   excluding or limiting the legal liability of a seller or supplier in the event of the death of a consumer or personal injury to the latter resulting from an act or omission of that seller or supplier;

(b)   inappropriately excluding or limiting the legal rights of the consumer vis-à-vis the seller or supplier or another party in the event of total or partial non-performance or inadequate performance by the seller or supplier of any of the contractual obligations, including the option of offsetting a debt owed to the seller or supplier against any claim which the consumer may have against him;

(c)   making an agreement binding on the consumer whereas provision of services by the seller or supplier is subject to a condition whose realisation depends on his own will alone;

(d)   permitting the seller or supplier to retain sums paid by the consumer where the latter decides not to conclude or perform the contract, without providing for the consumer to receive compensation of an equivalent amount from the seller or supplier where the latter is the party cancelling the contract;

(e) requiring any consumer who fails to fulfil his obligation to pay a disproportionately high sum in compensation;

(f) authorising the seller or supplier to dissolve the contract on a discretionary basis where the same facility is not granted to the consumer, or permitting the seller or supplier to retain the sums paid for services not yet supplied by him where it is the seller or supplier himself who dissolves the contract;

(g) enabling the seller or supplier to terminate a contract of indeterminate duration without reasonable notice except where there are serious grounds for doing so;

(h) automatically extending a contract of fixed duration where the consumer does not indicate otherwise, when the deadline fixed for the consumer to express his desire not to extend the contract is unreasonably early;

(i) irrevocably binding the consumer to terms with which he had no real opportunity of becoming acquainted before the conclusion of the contract;

(j) enabling the seller or supplier to alter the terms of the contract unilaterally without a valid reason which is specified in the contract;

(k) enabling the seller or supplier to alter unilaterally without a valid reason any characteristics of the product or service to be provided;

(l) providing for the price of goods to be determined at the time of delivery or allowing a seller of goods or supplier of services to increase their price without in both cases giving the consumer the corresponding right to cancel the contract if the final price is too high in relation to the price agreed when the contract was concluded;

(m) giving the seller or supplier the right to determine whether the goods or services supplied are in conformity with the contract, or giving him the exclusive right to interpret any term of the contract;

(n) limiting the seller's or supplier's obligation to respect commitments undertaken by his agents or making his commitments subject to compliance with a particular formality;

(o) obliging the consumer to fulfil all his obligations where the seller or supplier does not perform his;

(p) giving the seller or supplier the possibility of transferring his rights and obligations under the contract, where this may serve to reduce the guarantees for the consumer, without the latter's agreement;

(q) excluding or hindering the consumer's right to take legal action or exercise any other legal remedy, particularly by requiring the consumer to take disputes exclusively to arbitration not covered by legal provisions, unduly restricting the evidence available to him or imposing on him a burden of proof which, according to the applicable law, should lie with another party to the contract.

2. Scope of paragraphs 1(g), (j) and (l)

(a) Paragraph 1(g) is without hindrance to terms by which a supplier of financial services reserves the right to terminate unilaterally a contract of indeterminate duration without notice where there is a valid reason, provided that the supplier is required to inform the other contracting party or parties thereof immediately.

(b) Paragraph 1(j) is without hindrance to terms under which a supplier of financial services reserves the right to alter the rate of interest payable by the consumer or due to the latter, or the amount of other charges for financial services without notice where there is a valid reason, provided that the supplier is required to inform the other contracting party or parties thereof at the earliest opportunity and that the latter are free to dissolve the contract immediately.

Paragraph 1(j) is also without hindrance to terms under which a seller or supplier reserves the right to alter unilaterally the conditions of a contract of indeterminate duration, provided that he is required to inform the consumer with reasonable notice and that the consumer is free to dissolve the contract.

(c) Paragraphs 1(g), (j) and (l) do not apply to:

— transactions in transferable securities, financial instruments and other products or services where the price is linked to fluctuations in a stock exchange quotation or index or a financial market rate that the seller or supplier does not control;

— contracts for the purchase or sale of foreign currency, traveller's cheques or international money orders denominated in foreign currency.

(d) Paragraph 1(1) is without hindrance to price indexation clauses, where lawful, provided that the method by which prices vary is explicitly described.

[3245]–[3299]

CONSUMER PROTECTION (DISTANCE SELLING) REGULATIONS 2000

(SI 2000/2334)

NOTES
Made: 31 August 2000.
Authority: European Communities Act 1972, s 2(2).
Commencement: 31 October 2000.

ARRANGEMENT OF REGULATIONS

1 Title, commencement and extent

(1) These Regulations may be cited as the Consumer Protection (Distance Selling) Regulations 2000 and shall come into force on 31st October 2000.

(2) These Regulations extend to Northern Ireland.

[3300]

2 *(Revokes the Mail Order Transactions (Information) Order 1976, SI 1976/1812.)*

3 Interpretation

(1) In these Regulations—
["the 2000 Act" means the Financial Services and Markets Act 2000;
"appointed representative" has the same meaning as in section 39(2) of the 2000 Act;
"authorised person" has the same meaning as in section 31(2) of the 2000 Act;]
"breach" means contravention by a supplier of a prohibition in, or failure to comply with a requirement of, these Regulations;
"business" includes a trade or profession;
"consumer" means any natural person who, in contracts to which these Regulations apply, is acting for purposes which are outside his business;
"court" in relation to England and Wales and Northern Ireland means a county court or the High Court, and in relation to Scotland means the Sheriff Court or the Court of Session;
"credit" includes a cash loan and any other form of financial accommodation, and for this purpose "cash" includes money in any form;
"[OFT]" means the [Office of Fair Trading];
"distance contract" means any contract concerning goods or services concluded between a supplier and a consumer under an organised distance sales or service provision scheme run

by the supplier who, for the purpose of the contract, makes exclusive use of one or more means of distance communication up to and including the moment at which the contract is concluded;

"EEA Agreement" means the Agreement on the European Economic Area signed at Oporto on 2 May 1992 as adjusted by the Protocol signed at Brussels on 17 March 1993;

"enactment" includes an enactment comprised in, or in an instrument made under, an Act of the Scottish Parliament;

"enforcement authority" means the [OFT], every weights and measures authority in Great Britain, and the Department of Enterprise, Trade and Investment in Northern Ireland;

"excepted contract" means a contract such as is mentioned in regulation 5(1);

["financial service" means any service of a banking, credit, insurance, personal pension, investment or payment nature;]

"means of distance communication" means any means which, without the simultaneous physical presence of the supplier and the consumer, may be used for the conclusion of a contract between those parties; and an indicative list of such means is contained in Schedule 1;

"Member State" means a State which is a contracting party to the EEA Agreement;

"operator of a means of communication" means any public or private person whose business involves making one or more means of distance communication available to suppliers;

"period for performance" has the meaning given by regulation 19(2);

"personal credit agreement" has the meaning given by regulation 14(8);

["regulated activity" has the same meaning as in section 22 of the 2000 Act;]

"related credit agreement" has the meaning given by regulation 15(5);

"supplier" means any person who, in contracts to which these Regulations apply, is acting in his commercial or professional capacity; and

"working days" means all days other than Saturdays, Sundays and public holidays.

(2) (*Applies to Scotland only.*)

[3301]

NOTES

Para (1): definitions "the 2000 Act", "appointed representative", "authorised person", "financial service" and "regulated activity" inserted by the Financial Services (Distance Marketing) Regulations 2004, SI 2004/2095, reg 25(1), (2).

Director General of Fair Trading: the Enterprise Act 2002, s 2(1), at **[1860]**, provides that, as from the coming into force of that section (1 April 2003, see the Enterprise Act 2002 (Commencement No 2, Transitional and Transitory Provisions) Order 2003, SI 2003/766), the functions of the Director General of Fair Trading, his property, rights and liabilities are transferred to the Office of Fair Trading. Accordingly, (by virtue of s 2(2), (3) of the 2002 Act) the office of the Director is abolished, and any reference to the Director in any enactment, instrument or other document passed or made before the commencement of s 2(1) shall have effect as if it were a reference to the Office of Fair Trading. Consequently, throughout these Regulations, unless noted otherwise, the words "Office of Fair Trading", "OFT", "it" and "it" are substituted for the original words "Director General of Fair Trading", "Director", "he" and "him" respectively. For transitional provisions in connection with the transfer, see s 276(1) of, and Sch 24, para 6 to, the 2002 Act.

4 Contracts to which these Regulations apply

These Regulations apply, subject to regulation 6, to distance contracts other than excepted contracts.

[3302]

5 Excepted contracts

(1) The following are excepted contracts, namely any contract—

    (a) for the sale or other disposition of an interest in land except for a rental agreement;

    (b) for the construction of a building where the contract also provides for a sale or other disposition of an interest in land on which the building is constructed, except for a rental agreement;

    (c) relating to financial services … ;

    (d) concluded by means of an automated vending machine or automated commercial premises;

    (e) concluded with a telecommunications operator through the use of a public pay-phone;

    (f) concluded at an auction.

(2) References in paragraph (1) to a rental agreement—

    (a) if the land is situated in England and Wales, are references to any agreement which does not have to be made in writing (whether or not in fact made in writing) because of section 2(5)(a) of the Law of Property (Miscellaneous Provisions) Act 1989;

    (b) (*applies to Scotland only*); and

    (c) if the land is situated in Northern Ireland, are references to any agreement which is not one to which section II of the Statute of Frauds, (Ireland) 1695 applies.

(3)   Paragraph (2) shall not be taken to mean that a rental agreement in respect of land situated outside the United Kingdom is not capable of being a distance contract to which these Regulations apply.

[3303]

NOTES
    Para (1): words omitted from sub-para (c) revoked by the Financial Services (Distance Marketing) Regulations 2004, SI 2004/2095, reg 25(1), (3).

6   Contracts to which only part of these Regulations apply

(1)   Regulations 7 to 20 shall not apply to a contract which is a "timeshare agreement" within the meaning of the Timeshare Act 1992 and to which that Act applies.

(2)   Regulations 7 to 19(1) shall not apply to—
    (a)   contracts for the supply of food, beverages or other goods intended for everyday consumption supplied to the consumer's residence or to his workplace by regular roundsmen; or
    (b)   contracts for the provision of accommodation, transport, catering or leisure services, where the supplier undertakes, when the contract is concluded, to provide these services on a specific date or within a specific period.

(3)   Regulations 19(2) to (8) and 20 do not apply to a contract for a "package" within the meaning of the Package Travel, Package Holidays and Package Tours Regulations 1992 which is sold or offered for sale in the territory of the Member States.

[(4)   Regulations 7 to 14, 17 to 20 and 25 do not apply to any contract which is made, and regulation 24 does not apply to any unsolicited services which are supplied, by an authorised person where the making or performance of that contract or the supply of those services, as the case may be, constitutes or is part of a regulated activity carried on by him.

(5)   Regulations 7 to 9, 17 to 20 and 25 do not apply to any contract which is made, and regulation 24 does not apply to any unsolicited services which are supplied, by an appointed representative where the making or performance of that contract or the supply of those services, as the case may be, constitutes or is part of a regulated activity carried on by him.]

[3304]

NOTES
    Paras (4), (5): added by the Financial Services (Distance Marketing) Regulations 2004, SI 2004/2095, reg 25(1), (4).

7   Information required prior to the conclusion of the contract

(1)   Subject to paragraph (4), in good time prior to the conclusion of the contract the supplier shall—
    (a)   provide to the consumer the following information—
       (i)   the identity of the supplier and, where the contract requires payment in advance, the supplier's address;
       (ii)   a description of the main characteristics of the goods or services;
       (iii)   the price of the goods or services including all taxes;
       (iv)   delivery costs where appropriate;
       (v)   the arrangements for payment, delivery or performance;
       (vi)   the existence of a right of cancellation except in the cases referred to in regulation 13;
       (vii)   the cost of using the means of distance communication where it is calculated other than at the basic rate;
       (viii)   the period for which the offer or the price remains valid; and
       (ix)   where appropriate, the minimum duration of the contract, in the case of contracts for the supply of goods or services to be performed permanently or recurrently;
    (b)   inform the consumer if he proposes, in the event of the goods or services ordered by the consumer being unavailable, to provide substitute goods or services (as the case may be) of equivalent quality and price; and
    (c)   inform the consumer that the cost of returning any such substitute goods to the supplier in the event of cancellation by the consumer would be met by the supplier.

(2)   The supplier shall ensure that the information required by paragraph (1) is provided in a clear and comprehensible manner appropriate to the means of distance communication used, with due regard in particular to the principles of good faith in commercial transactions and the principles governing the protection of those who are unable to give their consent such as minors.

(3)   Subject to paragraph (4), the supplier shall ensure that his commercial purpose is made clear when providing the information required by paragraph (1).

(4)   In the case of a telephone communication, the identity of the supplier and the commercial purpose of the call shall be made clear at the beginning of the conversation with the consumer.

[3305]

8   Written and additional information

(1)   Subject to regulation 9, the supplier shall provide to the consumer in writing, or in another durable medium which is available and accessible to the consumer, the information referred to in paragraph (2), either—

    (a)   prior to the conclusion of the contract, or

    (b)   thereafter, in good time and in any event—

        (i)   during the performance of the contract, in the case of services; and

        (ii)   at the latest at the time of delivery where goods not for delivery to third parties are concerned.

(2)   The information required to be provided by paragraph (1) is—

    (a)   the information set out in paragraphs (i) to (vi) of Regulation 7(1)(a);

    (b)   information about the conditions and procedures for exercising the right to cancel under regulation 10, including—

        (i)   where a term of the contract requires (or the supplier intends that it will require) that the consumer shall return the goods to the supplier in the event of cancellation, notification of that requirement; ...

        (ii)   information as to whether the consumer or the supplier would be responsible under these Regulations for the cost of returning any goods to the supplier, or the cost of his recovering them, if the consumer cancels the contract under regulation 10;

        [(iii)   in the case of a contract for the supply of services, information as to how the right to cancel may be affected by the consumer agreeing to performance of the services beginning before the end of the seven working day period referred to in regulation 12;]

    (c)   the geographical address of the place of business of the supplier to which the consumer may address any complaints;

    (d)   information about any after-sales services and guarantees; and

    (e)   the conditions for exercising any contractual right to cancel the contract, where the contract is of an unspecified duration or a duration exceeding one year.

(3)   Subject to regulation 9, prior to the conclusion of a contract for the supply of services, the supplier shall inform the consumer in writing or in another durable medium which is available and accessible to the consumer that, unless the parties agree otherwise, he will not be able to cancel the contract under regulation 10 once the performance of the services has begun with his agreement.

[3306]

NOTES

Para (2): word omitted and sub-para (b)(iii) added by the Consumer Protection (Distance Selling) (Amendment) Regulations 2005, SI 2005/689, reg 2, Schedule, para 1(1), (2).

Para (3): revoked by SI 2005/689, reg 2, Schedule, para 1(1), (3).

---

9   Services performed through the use of a means of distance communication

(1)   Regulation 8 shall not apply to a contract for the supply of services which are performed through the use of a means of distance communication, where those services are supplied on only one occasion and are invoiced by the operator of the means of distance communication.

(2)   But the supplier shall take all necessary steps to ensure that a consumer who is a party to a contract to which paragraph (1) applies is able to obtain the supplier's geographical address and the place of business to which the consumer may address any complaints.

[3307]

10   Right to cancel

(1)   Subject to regulation 13, if within the cancellation period set out in regulations 11 and 12, the consumer gives a notice of cancellation to the supplier, or any other person previously notified by the supplier to the consumer as a person to whom notice of cancellation may be given, the notice of cancellation shall operate to cancel the contract.

(2)   Except as otherwise provided by these Regulations, the effect of a notice of cancellation is that the contract shall be treated as if it had not been made.

(3)   For the purposes of these Regulations, a notice of cancellation is a notice in writing or in another durable medium available and accessible to the supplier (or to the other person to whom it is given) which, however expressed, indicates the intention of the consumer to cancel the contract.

(4)   A notice of cancellation given under this regulation by a consumer to a supplier or other person is to be treated as having been properly given if the consumer—

(a)   leaves it at the address last known to the consumer and addressed to the supplier or other person by name (in which case it is to be taken to have been given on the day on which it was left);

(b)   sends it by post to the address last known to the consumer and addressed to the supplier or other person by name (in which case, it is to be taken to have been given on the day on which it was posted);

(c)   sends it by facsimile to the business facsimile number last known to the consumer (in which case it is to be taken to have been given on the day on which it is sent); or

(d)   sends it by electronic mail, to the business electronic mail address last known to the consumer (in which case it is to be taken to have been given on the day on which it is sent).

(5)   Where a consumer gives a notice in accordance with paragraph (4)(a) or (b) to a supplier who is a body corporate or a partnership, the notice is to be treated as having been properly given if—

(a)   in the case of a body corporate, it is left at the address of, or sent to, the secretary or clerk of that body; or

(b)   in the case of a partnership, it is left with or sent to a partner or a person having control or management of the partnership business.

[3308]

11   Cancellation period in the case of contracts for the supply of goods

(1)   For the purposes of regulation 10, the cancellation period in the case of contracts for the supply of goods begins with the day on which the contract is concluded and ends as provided in paragraphs (2) to (5).

(2)   Where the supplier complies with regulation 8, the cancellation period ends on the expiry of the period of seven working days beginning with the day after the day on which the consumer receives the goods.

(3)   Where a supplier who has not complied with regulation 8 provides to the consumer the information referred to in regulation 8(2), and does so in writing or in another durable medium available and accessible to the consumer, within the period of three months beginning with the day after the day on which the consumer receives the goods, the cancellation period ends on the expiry of the period of seven working days beginning with the day after the day on which the consumer receives the information.

(4)   Where neither paragraph (2) nor (3) applies, the cancellation period ends on the expiry of the period of three months and seven working days beginning with the day after the day on which the consumer receives the goods.

(5)   In the case of contracts for goods for delivery to third parties, paragraphs (2) to (4) shall apply as if the consumer had received the goods on the day on which they were received by the third party.

[3309]

12   Cancellation period in the case of contracts for the supply of services

(1)   For the purposes of regulation 10, the cancellation period in the case of contracts for the supply of services begins with the day on which the contract is concluded and ends as provided in paragraphs (2) to (4).

(2)   Where the supplier complies with regulation 8 on or before the day on which the contract is concluded, the cancellation period ends on the expiry of the period of seven working days beginning with the day after the day on which the contract is concluded.

(3)   [Subject to paragraph (3A)] where a supplier who has not complied with regulation 8 on or before the day on which the contract is concluded provides to the consumer the information referred to in regulation 8(2) … , and does so in writing or in another durable medium available and accessible to the consumer, within the period of three months beginning with the day after the day on which the contract is concluded, the cancellation period ends on the expiry of the period of seven working days beginning with the day after the day on which the consumer receives the information.

[(3A)   Where the performance of the contract has begun with the consumer's agreement before the expiry of the period of seven working days beginning with the day after the day on which the contract was concluded and the supplier has not complied with regulation 8 on or before the day on which performance began, but provides to the consumer the information referred to in regulation 8(2) in good time during the performance of the contract, the cancellation period ends—

(a)   on the expiry of the period of seven working days beginning with the day after the day on which the consumer receives the information; or

(b)   if the performance of the contract is completed before the expiry of the period referred to in sub-paragraph (a), on the day when the performance of the contract is completed.]

(4)   Where [none of paragraphs (2) to (3A) applies], the cancellation period ends on the expiry of the period of three months and seven working days beginning with the day after the day on which the contract is concluded.

[3310]

NOTES
Para (3): words in square brackets inserted and words omitted revoked by the Consumer Protection (Distance Selling) (Amendment) Regulations 2005, SI 2005/689, reg 2, Schedule, para 2(1), (2).
Para (3A): inserted by SI 2005/689, reg 2, Schedule, para 2(1), (3).
Para (4): words in square brackets substituted by SI 2005/689, reg 2, Schedule, para 2(1), (4).

13 Exceptions to the right to cancel

(1)   Unless the parties have agreed otherwise, the consumer will not have the right to cancel the contract by giving notice of cancellation pursuant to regulation 10 in respect of contracts—

    [(a)   for the supply of services if the performance of the contract has begun with the consumer's agreement—
        (i)   before the end of the cancellation period applicable under regulation 12(2); and
        (ii)   after the supplier has provided the information referred to in regulation 8(2).]
    (b)   for the supply of goods or services the price of which is dependent on fluctuations in the financial market which cannot be controlled by the supplier;
    (c)   for the supply of goods made to the consumer's specifications or clearly personalised or which by reason of their nature cannot be returned or are liable to deteriorate or expire rapidly;
    (d)   for the supply of audio or video recordings or computer software if they are unsealed by the consumer;
    (e)   for the supply of newspapers, periodicals or magazines; or
    (f)   for gaming, betting or lottery services.

[3311]

NOTES
Para (a) substituted by the Consumer Protection (Distance Selling) (Amendment) Regulations 2005, SI 2005/689, reg 2, Schedule, para 3.

14 Recovery of sums paid by or on behalf of the consumer on cancellation, and return of security

(1)   On the cancellation of a contract under regulation 10, the supplier shall reimburse any sum paid by or on behalf of the consumer under or in relation to the contract to the person by whom it was made free of any charge, less any charge made in accordance with paragraph (5).

(2)   The reference in paragraph (1) to any sum paid on behalf of the consumer includes any sum paid by a creditor who is not the same person as the supplier under a personal credit agreement with the consumer.

(3)   The supplier shall make the reimbursement referred to in paragraph (1) as soon as possible and in any case within a period not exceeding 30 days beginning with the day on which the notice of cancellation was given.

(4)   Where any security has been provided in relation to the contract, the security (so far as it is so provided) shall, on cancellation under regulation 10, be treated as never having had effect and any property lodged with the supplier solely for the purposes of the security as so provided shall be returned by him forthwith.

(5)   Subject to paragraphs (6) and (7), the supplier may make a charge, not exceeding the direct costs of recovering any goods supplied under the contract, where a term of the contract provides that the consumer must return any goods supplied if he cancels the contract under regulation 10 but the consumer does not comply with this provision or returns the goods at the expense of the supplier.

(6)   Paragraph (5) shall not apply where—
    (a)   the consumer cancels in circumstances where he has the right to reject the goods under a term of the contract, including a term implied by virtue of any enactment, or
    (b)   the term requiring the consumer to return any goods supplied if he cancels the contract is an "unfair term" within the meaning of the Unfair Terms in Consumer Contracts Regulations 1999.

(7)   Paragraph (5) shall not apply to the cost of recovering any goods which were supplied as substitutes for the goods ordered by the consumer.

(8)   For the purposes of these Regulations, a personal credit agreement is an agreement between the consumer and any other person ("the creditor") by which the creditor provides the consumer with credit of any amount.

[3312]

15   Automatic cancellation of a related credit agreement

(1)   Where a notice of cancellation is given under regulation 10 which has the effect of cancelling the contract, the giving of the notice shall also have the effect of cancelling any related credit agreement.

(2)   Where a related credit agreement is cancelled by virtue of paragraph (1), the supplier shall, if he is not the same person as the creditor under that agreement, forthwith on receipt of the notice of cancellation inform the creditor that the notice has been given.

(3)   Where a related credit agreement is cancelled by virtue of paragraph (1)—
- (a)   any sum paid by or on behalf of the consumer under, or in relation to, the credit agreement which the supplier is not obliged to reimburse under regulation 14(1) shall be reimbursed, except for any sum which, if it had not already been paid, would have to be paid under sub-paragraph (b);
- (b)   the agreement shall continue in force so far as it relates to repayment of the credit and payment of interest, subject to regulation 16; and
- (c)   subject to sub-paragraph (b), the agreement shall cease to be enforceable.

(4)   Where any security has been provided under a related credit agreement, the security, so far as it is so provided, shall be treated as never having had effect and any property lodged with the creditor solely for the purposes of the security as so provided shall be returned by him forthwith.

(5)   For the purposes of this regulation and regulation 16, a "related credit agreement" means an agreement under which fixed sum credit which fully or partly covers the price under a contract cancelled under regulation 10 is granted—
- (a)   by the supplier, or
- (b)   by another person, under an arrangement between that person and the supplier.

(6)   For the purposes of this regulation and regulation 16—
- (a)   "creditor" is a person who grants credit under a related credit agreement;
- (b)   "fixed sum credit" has the same meaning as in section 10 of the Consumer Credit Act 1974;
- (c)   "repayment" in relation to credit means repayment of money received by the consumer, and cognate expressions shall be construed accordingly; and
- (d)   "interest" means interest on money so received.

[3313]

16   Repayment of credit and interest after cancellation of a related credit agreement

(1)   This regulation applies following the cancellation of a related credit agreement by virtue of regulation 15(1).

(2)   If the consumer repays the whole or a portion of the credit—
- (a)   before the expiry of one month following the cancellation of the credit agreement, or
- (b)   in the case of a credit repayable by instalments, before the date on which the first instalment is due,

no interest shall be payable on the amount repaid.

(3)   If the whole of a credit repayable by instalments is not repaid on or before the date referred to in paragraph (2)(b), the consumer shall not be liable to repay any of the credit except on receipt of a request in writing, signed by the creditor, stating the amounts of the remaining instalments (recalculated by the creditor as nearly as may be in accordance with the agreement and without extending the repayment period), but excluding any sum other than principal and interest.

(4)   Where any security has been provided under a related credit agreement the duty imposed on the consumer to repay credit and to pay interest shall not be enforceable before the creditor has discharged any duty imposed on him by regulation 15(4) to return any property lodged with him as security on cancellation.

[3314]

17   Restoration of goods by consumer after cancellation

(1)   This regulation applies where a contract is cancelled under regulation 10 after the consumer has acquired possession of any goods under the contract other than any goods mentioned in regulation 13(1)(b) to (e).

(2)   The consumer shall be treated as having been under a duty throughout the period prior to cancellation—
- (a)   to retain possession of the goods, and
- (b)   to take reasonable care of them.

(3)   On cancellation, the consumer shall be under a duty to restore the goods to the supplier in accordance with this regulation, and in the meanwhile to retain possession of the goods and take reasonable care of them.

(4)   The consumer shall not be under any duty to deliver the goods except at his own premises and in pursuance of a request in writing, or in another durable medium available and accessible to the consumer, from the supplier and given to the consumer either before, or at the time when, the goods are collected from those premises.

(5)   If the consumer—

(a)   delivers the goods (whether at his own premises or elsewhere) to any person to whom, under regulation 10(1), a notice of cancellation could have been given; or

(b)   sends the goods at his own expense to such a person,

he shall be discharged from any duty to retain possession of the goods or restore them to the supplier.

(6)   Where the consumer delivers the goods in accordance with paragraph (5)(a), his obligation to take care of the goods shall cease; and if he sends the goods in accordance with paragraph (5)(b), he shall be under a duty to take reasonable care to see that they are received by the supplier and not damaged in transit, but in other respects his duty to take care of the goods shall cease when he sends them.

(7)   Where, at any time during the period of 21 days beginning with the day notice of cancellation was given, the consumer receives such a request as is mentioned in paragraph (4), and unreasonably refuses or unreasonably fails to comply with it, his duty to retain possession and take reasonable care of the goods shall continue until he delivers or sends the goods as mentioned in paragraph (5), but if within that period he does not receive such a request his duty to take reasonable care of the goods shall cease at the end of that period.

(8)   Where—

(a)   a term of the contract provides that if the consumer cancels the contract, he must return the goods to the supplier, and

(b)   the consumer is not otherwise entitled to reject the goods under the terms of the contract or by virtue of any enactment,

paragraph (7) shall apply as if for the period of 21 days there were substituted the period of 6 months.

(9)   Where any security has been provided in relation to the cancelled contract, the duty to restore goods imposed on the consumer by this regulation shall not be enforceable before the supplier has discharged any duty imposed on him by regulation 14(4) to return any property lodged with him as security on cancellation.

(10)   Breach of a duty imposed by this regulation on a consumer is actionable as a breach of statutory duty.

[3315]

18   Goods given in part-exchange

(1)   This regulation applies on the cancellation of a contract under regulation 10 where the supplier agreed to take goods in part-exchange (the "part-exchange goods") and those goods have been delivered to him.

(2)   Unless, before the end of the period of 10 days beginning with the date of cancellation, the part-exchange goods are returned to the consumer in a condition substantially as good as when they were delivered to the supplier, the consumer shall be entitled to recover from the supplier a sum equal to the part-exchange allowance.

(3)   In this regulation the part-exchange allowance means the sum agreed as such in the cancelled contract, or if no such sum was agreed, such sum as it would have been reasonable to allow in respect of the part-exchange goods if no notice of cancellation had been served.

(4)   Where the consumer recovers from the supplier a sum equal to the part-exchange allowance, the title of the consumer to the part-exchange goods shall vest in the supplier (if it has not already done so) on recovery of that sum.

[3316]

19   Performance

(1)   Unless the parties agree otherwise, the supplier shall perform the contract within a maximum of 30 days beginning with the day after the day the consumer sent his order to the supplier.

(2)   Subject to paragraphs (7) and (8), where the supplier is unable to perform the contract because the goods or services ordered are not available, within the period for performance referred to in paragraph (1) or such other period as the parties agree ("the period for performance"), he shall—

(a)   inform the consumer; and

(b)   reimburse any sum paid by or on behalf of the consumer under or in relation to the contract to the person by whom it was made.

(3)   The reference in paragraph (2)(b) to any sum paid on behalf of the consumer includes any sum paid by a creditor who is not the same person as the supplier under a personal credit agreement with the consumer.

(4)   The supplier shall make the reimbursement referred to in paragraph (2)(b) as soon as possible and in any event within a period of 30 days beginning with the day after the day on which the period for performance expired.

(5)   A contract which has not been performed within the period for performance shall be treated as if it had not been made, save for any rights or remedies which the consumer has under it as a result of the non-performance.

(6)   Where any security has been provided in relation to the contract, the security (so far as it is so provided) shall, where the supplier is unable to perform the contract within the period for performance, be treated as never having had any effect and any property lodged with the supplier solely for the purposes of the security as so provided shall be returned by him forthwith.

(7)   Where the supplier is unable to supply the goods or services ordered by the consumer, the supplier may perform the contract for the purposes of these Regulations by providing substitute goods or services (as the case may be) of equivalent quality and price provided that—
   (a)   this possibility was provided for in the contract;
   (b)   prior to the conclusion of the contract the supplier gave the consumer the information required by regulation 7(1)(b) and (c) in the manner required by regulation 7(2).

(8)   In the case of outdoor leisure events which by their nature cannot be rescheduled, paragraph 2(b) shall not apply where the consumer and the supplier so agree.

[3317]

20   Effect of non-performance on related credit agreement

Where a supplier is unable to perform the contract within the period for performance—
   (a)   regulations 15 and 16 shall apply to any related credit agreement as if the consumer had given a valid notice of cancellation under regulation 10 on the expiry of the period for performance; and
   (b)   the reference in regulation 15(3)(a) to regulation 14(1) shall be read, for the purposes of this regulation, as a reference to regulation 19(2).

[3318]–[3319]

21–23   (*Reg 21 revoked by the Payment Services Regulations 2009, SI 2009/209, reg 126, Sch 6, Pt 2, para 3; reg 22 repeals the Unsolicited Goods and Services Act 1971, s 1 and amends s 2 to that Act at* **[501]**; *reg 23 repeals the Unsolicited Goods and Services (Northern Ireland) Order 1976, art 3 and amends art 4 of that Order.*)

24   Inertia Selling

(1)   Paragraphs (2) and (3) apply if—
   (a)   unsolicited goods are sent to a person ("the recipient") with a view to his acquiring them;
   (b)   the recipient has no reasonable cause to believe that they were sent with a view to their being acquired for the purposes of a business; and
   (c)   the recipient has neither agreed to acquire nor agreed to return them.

(2)   The recipient may, as between himself and the sender, use, deal with or dispose of the goods as if they were an unconditional gift to him.

(3)   The rights of the sender to the goods are extinguished.

(4), (5)   …

(6)   In this regulation—
   "acquire" includes hire;
   "send" includes deliver;
   "sender", in relation to any goods, includes—
      (a)   any person on whose behalf or with whose consent the goods are sent;
      (b)   any other person claiming through or under the sender or any person mentioned in paragraph (a); and
      (c)   any person who delivers the goods; and
   "unsolicited" means, in relation to goods sent or services supplied to any person, that they are sent or supplied without any prior request made by or on behalf of the recipient.

(7)–(9)   …

(10)   This regulation applies only to goods sent and services supplied after the date on which it comes into force.

[3320]

NOTES
Paras (4), (5), (7)–(9): revoked by the Consumer Protection from Unfair Trading Regulations 2008, SI 2008/1277, reg 30(1), (3), Sch 2, Pt 2, para 96, Sch 4.

25 No contracting-out

(1) A term contained in any contract to which these Regulations apply is void if, and to the extent that, it is inconsistent with a provision for the protection of the consumer contained in these Regulations.

(2) Where a provision of these Regulations specifies a duty or liability of the consumer in certain circumstances, a term contained in a contract to which these Regulations apply, other than a term to which paragraph (3) applies, is inconsistent with that provision if it purports to impose, directly or indirectly, an additional duty or liability on him in those circumstances.

(3) This paragraph applies to a term which requires the consumer to return any goods supplied to him under the contract if he cancels it under regulation 10.

(4) A term to which paragraph (3) applies shall, in the event of cancellation by the consumer under regulation 10, have effect only for the purposes of regulation 14(5) and 17(8).

(5) These Regulations shall apply notwithstanding any contract term which applies or purports to apply the law of a non-Member State if the contract has a close connection with the territory of a Member State.

[3321]

26 Consideration of complaints

(1) It shall be the duty of an enforcement authority to consider any complaint made to it about a breach unless—

  (a) the complaint appears to the authority to be frivolous or vexatious; or
  (b) another enforcement authority has notified the [OFT] that it agrees to consider the complaint.

(2) If an enforcement authority notifies the [OFT] that it agrees to consider a complaint made to another enforcement authority, the first mentioned authority shall be under a duty to consider the complaint.

(3) An enforcement authority which is under a duty to consider a complaint shall give reasons for its decision to apply or not to apply, as the case may be, for an injunction under regulation 27.

(4) In deciding whether or not to apply for an injunction in respect of a breach an enforcement authority may, if it considers it appropriate to do so, have regard to any undertaking given to it or another enforcement authority by or on behalf of any person as to compliance with these Regulations.

[3322]

NOTES
References to the OFT, etc: as to the abolition of the office of the Director General of Fair Trading and the substitution of the original references to the Director (and related expressions), see the note to reg 3 at [3301].

27 Injunctions to secure compliance with these Regulations

(1) The [OFT] or, subject to paragraph (2), any other enforcement authority may apply for an injunction (including an interim injunction) against any person who appears to the [OFT] or that authority to be responsible for a breach.

(2) An enforcement authority other than the [OFT] may apply for an injunction only where—

  (a) it has notified the [OFT] of its intention to apply at least fourteen days before the date on which the application is to be made, beginning with the date on which the notification was given; or
  (b) the [OFT] consents to the application being made within a shorter period.

(3) The court on an application under this regulation may grant an injunction on such terms as it thinks fit to secure compliance with these Regulations.

[3323]

NOTES
References to the OFT, etc: as to the abolition of the office of the Director General of Fair Trading and the substitution of the original references to the Director (and related expressions), see the note to reg 3 at [3301].

28 Notification of undertakings and orders to the [OFT]

An enforcement authority other than the [OFT] shall notify the [OFT]—

  (a) of any undertaking given to it by or on behalf of any person who appears to it to be responsible for a breach;

(b)   of the outcome of any application made by it under regulation 27 and of the terms of any undertaking given to or order made by the court;

(c)   of the outcome of any application made by it to enforce a previous order of the court.

[3324]

NOTES
References to the OFT, etc: as to the abolition of the office of the Director General of Fair Trading and the substitution of the original references to the Director (and related expressions), see the note to reg 3 at **[3301]**.

29   Publication, information and advice

(1)   The [OFT] shall arrange for the publication in such form and manner as [it] considers appropriate of—
(a)   details of any undertaking or order notified to [it] under regulation 28;
(b)   details of any undertaking given to [it] by or on behalf of any person as to compliance with these Regulations;
(c)   details of any application made by [it] under regulation 27, and of the terms of any undertaking given to, or order made by, the court;
(d)   details of any application made by the [OFT] to enforce a previous order of the court.

(2)   The [OFT] may arrange for the dissemination in such form and manner as [it] considers appropriate of such information and advice concerning the operation of these Regulations as it may appear to [it] to be expedient to give to the public and to all persons likely to be affected by these Regulations.

[3325]

NOTES
References to the OFT, etc: as to the abolition of the office of the Director General of Fair Trading and the substitution of the original references to the Director (and related expressions), see the note to reg 3 at **[3301]**.

SCHEDULES

SCHEDULE 1
INDICATIVE LIST OF MEANS OF DISTANCE COMMUNICATION
Regulation 3
1.   Unaddressed printed matter.
2.   Addressed printed matter.
3.   Letter.
4.   Press advertising with order form.
5.   Catalogue.
6.   Telephone with human intervention.
7.   Telephone without human intervention (automatic calling machine, audiotext).
8.   Radio.
9.   Videophone (telephone with screen).
10.   Videotext (microcomputer and television screen) with keyboard or touch screen.
11.   Electronic mail.
12.   Facsimile machine (fax).
13.   Television (teleshopping).

[3326]–[3327]

(Sch 2 revoked by the Financial Services (Distance Marketing) Regulations 2004, SI 2004/2095, reg 25(1), (5).)

TELECOMMUNICATIONS (LAWFUL BUSINESS PRACTICE) (INTERCEPTION OF COMMUNICATIONS) REGULATIONS 2000

(SI 2000/2699)

NOTES
Made: 2 October 2000.
Authority: Regulation of Investigatory Powers Act 2000, ss 4(2), 78(5).
Commencement: 24 October 2000.

1 Citation and commencement

These Regulations may be cited as the Telecommunications (Lawful Business Practice) (Interception of Communications) Regulations 2000 and shall come into force on 24th October 2000.

[3328]

2 Interpretation

In these Regulations—

(a) references to a business include references to activities of a government department, of any public authority or of any person or office holder on whom functions are conferred by or under any enactment;

(b) a reference to a communication as relevant to a business is a reference to—

    (i) a communication—

        (aa) by means of which a transaction is entered into in the course of that business, or

        (bb) which otherwise relates to that business, or

    (ii) a communication which otherwise takes place in the course of the carrying on of that business;

(c) "regulatory or self-regulatory practices or procedures" means practices or procedures—

    (i) compliance with which is required or recommended by, under or by virtue of—

        (aa) any provision of the law of a member state or other state within the European Economic Area, or

        (bb) any standard or code of practice published by or on behalf of a body established in a member state or other state within the European Economic Area which includes amongst its objectives the publication of standards or codes of practice for the conduct of business, or

    (ii) which are otherwise applied for the purpose of ensuring compliance with anything so required or recommended;

(d) "system controller" means, in relation to a particular telecommunication system, a person with a right to control its operation or use.

[3329]

3 Lawful interception of a communication

(1) For the purpose of section 1(5)(a) of the Act, conduct is authorised, subject to paragraphs (2) and (3) below, if it consists of interception of a communication, in the course of its transmission by means of a telecommunication system, which is effected by or with the express or implied consent of the system controller for the purpose of—

(a) monitoring or keeping a record of communications—

    (i) in order to—

        (aa) establish the existence of facts, or

        (bb) ascertain compliance with regulatory or self-regulatory practices or procedures which are—

            applicable to the system controller in the carrying on of his business or applicable to another person in the carrying on of his business where that person is supervised by the system controller in respect of those practices or procedures, or

        (cc) ascertain or demonstrate the standards which are achieved or ought to be achieved by persons using the system in the course of their duties, or

    (ii) in the interests of national security, or

    (iii) for the purpose of preventing or detecting crime, or

    (iv) for the purpose of investigating or detecting the unauthorised use of that or any other telecommunication system, or

    (v) where that is undertaken—

        (aa) in order to secure, or

        (bb) as an inherent part of,

        the effective operation of the system (including any monitoring or keeping of a record which would be authorised by section 3(3) of the Act if the conditions in paragraphs (a) and (b) thereof were satisfied); or

(b) monitoring communications for the purpose of determining whether they are communications relevant to the system controller's business which fall within regulation 2(b)(i) above; or

(c) monitoring communications made to a confidential voice-telephony counselling or support service which is free of charge (other than the cost, if any, of making a telephone call) and operated in such a way that users may remain anonymous if they so choose.

(2) Conduct is authorised by paragraph (1) of this regulation only if—

(a) the interception in question is effected solely for the purpose of monitoring or (where appropriate) keeping a record of communications relevant to the system controller's business;

(b) the telecommunication system in question is provided for use wholly or partly in connection with that business;

(c) the system controller has made all reasonable efforts to inform every person who may use the telecommunication system in question that communications transmitted by means thereof may be intercepted; and

(d) in a case falling within—

    (i) paragraph (1)(a)(ii) above, the person by or on whose behalf the interception is effected is a person specified in section 6(2)(a) to (i) of the Act;

    (ii) paragraph (1)(b) above, the communication is one which is intended to be received (whether or not it has been actually received) by a person using the telecommunication system in question.

[(3) Conduct falling within paragraph (1)(a)(i) above is authorised only to the extent that Article 5 of Directive 2002/58/EC of the European Parliament and of the Council of 12 July 2002 concerning the processing of personal data and the protection of privacy in the electronic communications sector so permits.]

NOTES

Para (3): substituted by the Privacy and Electronic Communications (EC Directive) Regulations 2003, SI 2003/2426, reg 34.

[3330]–[3340]

LATE PAYMENT OF COMMERCIAL DEBTS REGULATIONS 2002

(SI 2002/1674)

NOTES

Made: 22 June 2002.
Authority: European Communities Act 1972, s 2(2).
Commencement: 7 August 2002.

1 Citation, commencement and extent

(1) These Regulations may be cited as the Late Payment of Commercial Debts Regulations 2002 and shall come into force on 7th August 2002.

(2) These Regulations extend to England and Wales and Northern Ireland.

[3341]

2 (*Amends the Late Payment of Commercial Debts (Interest) Act 1998, ss 2, 3 at* **[1656]**, **[1657]**, *and inserts s 5A at* **[1660]**.)

3 Proceedings restraining use of grossly unfair terms

(1) In this regulation:

(a) "small and medium-sized enterprises" means those enterprises defined in Annex 1 to Commission Regulation (EC) No 70/2001 of 12th January 2001 on the application of Articles 87 and 88 of the EC Treaty to State aid to small and medium-sized enterprises;

(b) "representative body" means an organisation established to represent the collective interests of small and medium-sized enterprises in general or in a particular sector or area.

(2) This regulation applies where a person acting in the course of a business has written standard terms on which he enters (or intends to enter) as purchaser into contracts to which the Late Payment of Commercial Debts (Interest) Act 1998 applies which include a term purporting to oust or vary the right to statutory interest in relation to qualifying debts created by those contracts.

(3) If it appears to the High Court that in all or any circumstances the purported use of such a term in a relevant contract would be void under the Late Payment of Commercial Debts (Interest) Act 1998, the court on the application of a representative body may grant an injunction against that person restraining him in those circumstances from using the offending term, on such terms as the court may think fit.

(4) Only a representative body may apply to the High Court under this regulation.

[3342]

PART 2
STATUTORY INSTRUMENTS

4 (*Revokes the Late Payment of Commercial Debts* (*Interest*) (*Legal Aid Exceptions*) *Order 1998, SI 1998/2482.*)

5 Saving for existing contracts

These Regulations do not affect contracts made before 7th August 2002.

[3343]

ELECTRONIC COMMERCE (EC DIRECTIVE) REGULATIONS 2002

(SI 2002/2013)

NOTES
Made: 30 July 2002.
Authority: European Communities Act 1972, s 2(2).
Commencement: 21 August 2002 (regs 1–15, 17–22, Schedule); 23 October 2002 (reg 16).

ARRANGEMENT OF REGULATIONS

1 Citation and commencement

(1) These Regulations may be cited as the Electronic Commerce (EC Directive) Regulations 2002 and except for regulation 16 shall come into force on 21st August 2002.

(2) Regulation 16 shall come into force on 23rd October 2002.

[3344]

2 Interpretation

(1) In these Regulations and in the Schedule—
    "commercial communication" means a communication, in any form, designed to promote, directly or indirectly, the goods, services or image of any person pursuing a commercial, industrial or craft activity or exercising a regulated profession, other than a communication—
        (a)   consisting only of information allowing direct access to the activity of that person including a geographic address, a domain name or an electronic mail address; or
        (b)   relating to the goods, services or image of that person provided that the communication has been prepared independently of the person making it (and for this purpose, a communication prepared without financial consideration is to be taken to have been prepared independently unless the contrary is shown);
    "the Commission" means the Commission of the European Communities;
    "consumer" means any natural person who is acting for purposes other than those of his trade, business or profession;
    "coordinated field" means requirements applicable to information society service providers or information society services, regardless of whether they are of a general nature or specifically designed for them, and covers requirements with which the service provider has to comply in respect of—

    (a)   the taking up of the activity of an information society service, such as requirements concerning qualifications, authorisation or notification, and

    (b)   the pursuit of the activity of an information society service, such as requirements concerning the behaviour of the service provider, requirements regarding the quality or content of the service including those applicable to advertising and contracts, or requirements concerning the liability of the service provider,

but does not cover requirements such as those applicable to goods as such, to the delivery of goods or to services not provided by electronic means;

"the Directive" means Directive 2000/31/EC of the European Parliament and of the Council of 8 June 2000 on certain legal aspects of information society services, in particular electronic commerce, in the Internal Market (Directive on electronic commerce);

"EEA Agreement" means the Agreement on the European Economic Area signed at Oporto on 2 May 1992 as adjusted by the Protocol signed at Brussels on 17 March 1993;

"enactment" includes an enactment comprised in Northern Ireland legislation and comprised in, or an instrument made under, an Act of the Scottish Parliament;

"enforcement action" means any form of enforcement action including, in particular—

    (a)   in relation to any legal requirement imposed by or under any enactment, any action taken with a view to or in connection with imposing any sanction (whether criminal or otherwise) for failure to observe or comply with it; and

    (b)   in relation to a permission or authorisation, anything done with a view to removing or restricting that permission or authorisation;

"enforcement authority" does not include courts but, subject to that, means any person who is authorised, whether by or under an enactment or otherwise, to take enforcement action;

"established service provider" means a service provider who is a national of a member State or a company or firm as mentioned in Article 48 of the Treaty and who effectively pursues an economic activity by virtue of which he is a service provider using a fixed establishment in a member State for an indefinite period, but the presence and use of the technical means and technologies required to provide the information society service do not, in themselves, constitute an establishment of the provider; in cases where it cannot be determined from which of a number of places of establishment a given service is provided, that service is to be regarded as provided from the place of establishment where the provider has the centre of his activities relating to that service; references to a service provider being established or to the establishment of a service provider shall be construed accordingly;

"information society services" (which is summarised in recital 17 of the Directive as covering "any service normally provided for remuneration, at a distance, by means of electronic equipment for the processing (including digital compression) and storage of data, and at the individual request of a recipient of a service") has the meaning set out in Article 2(a) of the Directive, (which refers to Article 1(2) of Directive 98/34/EC of the European Parliament and of the Council of 22 June 1998 laying down a procedure for the provision of information in the field of technical standards and regulations, as amended by Directive 98/48/EC of 20 July 1998);

"member State" includes a State which is a contracting party to the EEA Agreement;

"recipient of the service" means any person who, for professional ends or otherwise, uses an information society service, in particular for the purposes of seeking information or making it accessible;

"regulated profession" means any profession within the meaning of either Article 1(d) of Council Directive 89/48/EEC of 21 December 1988 on a general system for the recognition of higher-education diplomas awarded on completion of professional education and training of at least three years' duration or of Article 1(f) of Council Directive 92/51/EEC of 18 June 1992 on a second general system for the recognition of professional education and training to supplement Directive 89/48/EEC;

"service provider" means any person providing an information society service;

"the Treaty" means the treaty establishing the European Community.

(2)   In regulation 4 and 5, "requirement" means any legal requirement under the law of the United Kingdom, or any part of it, imposed by or under any enactment or otherwise.

(3)   Terms used in the Directive other than those in paragraph (1) above shall have the same meaning as in the Directive.

[3345]

3   Exclusions

(1)   Nothing in these Regulations shall apply in respect of—

    (a)   the field of taxation;

    (b)   questions relating to information society services covered by the Data Protection Directive and the Telecommunications Data Protection Directive and Directive 2002/58/EC of the European Parliament and of the Council of 12th July 2002 concerning the processing of personal data and the protection of privacy in the electronic communications sector (Directive on privacy and electronic communications);

    (c)   questions relating to agreements or practices governed by cartel law; and

    (d)   the following activities of information society services—

        (i)   the activities of a public notary or equivalent professions to the extent that they involve a direct and specific connection with the exercise of public authority,

        (ii)   the representation of a client and defence of his interests before the courts, and

        (iii)   betting, gaming or lotteries which involve wagering a stake with monetary value.

[(2)   These Regulations shall not apply in relation to any Act passed on or after the date these Regulations are made or in relation to the exercise of a power to legislate after that date.]

    (3)   In this regulation—

"cartel law" means so much of the law relating to agreements between undertakings, decisions by associations of undertakings or concerted practices as relates to agreements to divide the market or fix prices;

"Data Protection Directive" means Directive 95/46/EC of the European Parliament and of the Council of 24 October 1995 on the protection of individuals with regard to the processing of personal data and on the free movement of such data; and

"Telecommunications Data Protection Directive" means Directive 97/66/EC of the European Parliament and of the Council of 15 December 1997 concerning the processing of personal data and the protection of privacy in the telecommunications sector.

[3346]

NOTES

Para (2): substituted by the Electronic Commerce (EC Directive) (Extension) Regulations 2004, SI 2004/1178, reg 3.

4 Internal market

    (1)   Subject to paragraph (4) below, any requirement which falls within the coordinated field shall apply to the provision of an information society service by a service provider established in the United Kingdom irrespective of whether that information society service is provided in the United Kingdom or another member State.

    (2)   Subject to paragraph (4) below, an enforcement authority with responsibility in relation to any requirement in paragraph (1) shall ensure that the provision of an information society service by a service provider established in the United Kingdom complies with that requirement irrespective of whether that service is provided in the United Kingdom or another member State and any power, remedy or procedure for taking enforcement action shall be available to secure compliance.

    (3)   Subject to paragraphs (4), (5) and (6) below, any requirement shall not be applied to the provision of an information society service by a service provider established in a member State other than the United Kingdom for reasons which fall within the coordinated field where its application would restrict the freedom to provide information society services to a person in the United Kingdom from that member State.

    (4)   Paragraphs (1), (2) and (3) shall not apply to those fields in the annex to the Directive set out in the Schedule.

    (5)   The reference to any requirements the application of which would restrict the freedom to provide information society services from another member State in paragraph (3) above does not include any requirement maintaining the level of protection for public health and consumer interests established by Community acts.

    (6)   To the extent that anything in these Regulations creates any new criminal offence, it shall not be punishable with imprisonment for more than two years or punishable on summary conviction with imprisonment for more than three months or with a fine of more than level 5 on the standard scale (if not calculated on a daily basis) or with a fine of more than £100 a day.

[3347]

5 Derogations from Regulation 4

    (1)   Notwithstanding regulation 4(3), an enforcement authority may take measures, including applying any requirement which would otherwise not apply by virtue of regulation 4(3) in respect of a given information society service, where those measures are necessary for reasons of—

    (a)   public policy, in particular the prevention, investigation, detection and prosecution of criminal offences, including the protection of minors and the fight against any incitement to hatred on grounds of race, sex, religion or nationality, and violations of human dignity concerning individual persons;

    (b)   the protection of public health;

    (c)   public security, including the safeguarding of national security and defence, or

    (d)   the protection of consumers, including investors,

and proportionate to those objectives.

(2)　Notwithstanding regulation 4(3), in any case where an enforcement authority with responsibility in relation to the requirement in question is not party to the proceedings, a court may, on the application of any person or of its own motion, apply any requirement which would otherwise not apply by virtue of regulation 4(3) in respect of a given information society service, if the application of that enactment or requirement is necessary for and proportionate to any of the objectives set out in paragraph (1) above.

(3)　Paragraphs (1) and (2) shall only apply where the information society service prejudices or presents a serious and grave risk of prejudice to an objective in paragraph (1)(a) to (d).

(4)　Subject to paragraphs (5) and (6), an enforcement authority shall not take the measures in paragraph (1) above, unless it—
- (a)　asks the member State in which the service provider is established to take measures and the member State does not take such measures or they are inadequate; and
- (b)　notifies the Commission and the member State in which the service provider is established of its intention to take such measures.

(5)　Paragraph (4) shall not apply to court proceedings, including preliminary proceedings and acts carried out in the course of a criminal investigation.

(6)　If it appears to the enforcement authority that the matter is one of urgency, it may take the measures under paragraph (1) without first asking the member State in which the service provider is established to take measures and notifying the Commission and the member State in derogation from paragraph (4).

(7)　In a case where a measure is taken pursuant to paragraph (6) above, the enforcement authority shall notify the measures taken to the Commission and to the member State concerned in the shortest possible time thereafter and indicate the reasons for urgency.

(8)　In paragraph (2), "court" means any court or tribunal.

[3348]

6　General information to be provided by a person providing an information society service

(1)　A person providing an information society service shall make available to the recipient of the service and any relevant enforcement authority, in a form and manner which is easily, directly and permanently accessible, the following information—
- (a)　the name of the service provider;
- (b)　the geographic address at which the service provider is established;
- (c)　the details of the service provider, including his electronic mail address, which make it possible to contact him rapidly and communicate with him in a direct and effective manner;
- (d)　where the service provider is registered in a trade or similar register available to the public, details of the register in which the service provider is entered and his registration number, or equivalent means of identification in that register;
- (e)　where the provision of the service is subject to an authorisation scheme, the particulars of the relevant supervisory authority;
- (f)　where the service provider exercises a regulated profession—
  - (i)　the details of any professional body or similar institution with which the service provider is registered;
  - (ii)　his professional title and the member State where that title has been granted;
  - (iii)　a reference to the professional rules applicable to the service provider in the member State of establishment and the means to access them; and
- (g)　where the service provider undertakes an activity that is subject to value added tax, the identification number referred to in Article 22(1) of the sixth Council Directive 77/388/EEC of 17 May 1977 on the harmonisation of the laws of the member States relating to turnover taxes—Common system of value added tax: uniform basis of assessment.

(2)　Where a person providing an information society service refers to prices, these shall be indicated clearly and unambiguously and, in particular, shall indicate whether they are inclusive of tax and delivery costs.

[3349]

7　Commercial communications

A service provider shall ensure that any commercial communication provided by him and which constitutes or forms part of an information society service shall—
- (a)　be clearly identifiable as a commercial communication;
- (b)　clearly identify the person on whose behalf the commercial communication is made;
- (c)　clearly identify as such any promotional offer (including any discount, premium or gift) and ensure that any conditions which must be met to qualify for it are easily accessible, and presented clearly and unambiguously; and

(d)   clearly identify as such any promotional competition or game and ensure that any conditions for participation are easily accessible and presented clearly and unambiguously.

[3350]

8 Unsolicited commercial communications

A service provider shall ensure that any unsolicited commercial communication sent by him by electronic mail is clearly and unambiguously identifiable as such as soon as it is received.

[3351]

9 Information to be provided where contracts are concluded by electronic means

(1)   Unless parties who are not consumers have agreed otherwise, where a contract is to be concluded by electronic means a service provider shall, prior to an order being placed by the recipient of a service, provide to that recipient in a clear, comprehensible and unambiguous manner the information set out in (a) to (d) below—

(a)   the different technical steps to follow to conclude the contract;
(b)   whether or not the concluded contract will be filed by the service provider and whether it will be accessible;
(c)   the technical means for identifying and correcting input errors prior to the placing of the order; and
(d)   the languages offered for the conclusion of the contract.

(2)   Unless parties who are not consumers have agreed otherwise, a service provider shall indicate which relevant codes of conduct he subscribes to and give information on how those codes can be consulted electronically.

(3)   Where the service provider provides terms and conditions applicable to the contract to the recipient, the service provider shall make them available to him in a way that allows him to store and reproduce them.

(4)   The requirements of paragraphs (1) and (2) above shall not apply to contracts concluded exclusively by exchange of electronic mail or by equivalent individual communications.

[3352]

10 Other information requirements

Regulations 6, 7, 8 and 9(1) have effect in addition to any other information requirements in legislation giving effect to Community law.

[3353]

11 Placing of the order

(1)   Unless parties who are not consumers have agreed otherwise, where the recipient of the service places his order through technological means, a service provider shall–

(a)   acknowledge receipt of the order to the recipient of the service without undue delay and by electronic means; and
(b)   make available to the recipient of the service appropriate, effective and accessible technical means allowing him to identify and correct input errors prior to the placing of the order.

(2)   For the purposes of paragraph (1)(a) above—

(a)   the order and the acknowledgement of receipt will be deemed to be received when the parties to whom they are addressed are able to access them; and
(b)   the acknowledgement of receipt may take the form of the provision of the service paid for where that service is an information society service.

(3)   The requirements of paragraph (1) above shall not apply to contracts concluded exclusively by exchange of electronic mail or by equivalent individual communications.

[3354]

12 Meaning of the term "order"

Except in relation to regulation 9(1)(c) and regulation 11(1)(b) where "order" shall be the contractual offer, "order" may be but need not be the contractual offer for the purposes of regulations 9 and 11.

[3355]

13 Liability of the service provider

The duties imposed by regulations 6, 7, 8, 9(1) and 11(1)(a) shall be enforceable, at the suit of any recipient of a service, by an action against the service provider for damages for breach of statutory duty.

[3356]

14   Compliance with Regulation 9(3)

Where on request a service provider has failed to comply with the requirement in regulation 9(3), the recipient may seek an order from any court having jurisdiction in relation to the contract requiring that service provider to comply with that requirement.

[3357]

15   Right to rescind contract

Where a person—
- (a)   has entered into a contract to which these Regulations apply, and
- (b)   the service provider has not made available means of allowing him to identify and correct input errors in compliance with regulation 11(1)(b),

he shall be entitled to rescind the contract unless any court having jurisdiction in relation to the contract in question orders otherwise on the application of the service provider.

[3358]

16   (*Amends the Stop Now Orders* (*EC Directive*) *Regulations 2001, SI 2001/1422, reg 2, Sch 1.*)

17   Mere conduit

(1)   Where an information society service is provided which consists of the transmission in a communication network of information provided by a recipient of the service or the provision of access to a communication network, the service provider (if he otherwise would) shall not be liable for damages or for any other pecuniary remedy or for any criminal sanction as a result of that transmission where the service provider—
- (a)   did not initiate the transmission;
- (b)   did not select the receiver of the transmission; and
- (c)   did not select or modify the information contained in the transmission.

(2)   The acts of transmission and of provision of access referred to in paragraph (1) include the automatic, intermediate and transient storage of the information transmitted where—
- (a)   this takes place for the sole purpose of carrying out the transmission in the communication network, and
- (b)   the information is not stored for any period longer than is reasonably necessary for the transmission.

[3359]

18   Caching

Where an information society service is provided which consists of the transmission in a communication network of information provided by a recipient of the service, the service provider (if he otherwise would) shall not be liable for damages or for any other pecuniary remedy or for any criminal sanction as a result of that transmission where—
- (a)   the information is the subject of automatic, intermediate and temporary storage where that storage is for the sole purpose of making more efficient onward transmission of the information to other recipients of the service upon their request, and
- (b)   the service provider—
  - (i)   does not modify the information;
  - (ii)   complies with conditions on access to the information;
  - (iii) complies with any rules regarding the updating of the information, specified in a manner widely recognised and used by industry;
  - (iv)   does not interfere with the lawful use of technology, widely recognised and used by industry, to obtain data on the use of the information; and
  - (v)   acts expeditiously to remove or to disable access to the information he has stored upon obtaining actual knowledge of the fact that the information at the initial source of the transmission has been removed from the network, or access to it has been disabled, or that a court or an administrative authority has ordered such removal or disablement.

[3360]

19   Hosting

Where an information society service is provided which consists of the storage of information provided by a recipient of the service, the service provider (if he otherwise would) shall not be liable for damages or for any other pecuniary remedy or for any criminal sanction as a result of that storage where—
- (a)   the service provider—
  - (i)   does not have actual knowledge of unlawful activity or information and, where a claim for damages is made, is not aware of facts or circumstances from which it would have been apparent to the service provider that the activity or information was unlawful; or

PART 2
STATUTORY INSTRUMENTS

(ii)   upon obtaining such knowledge or awareness, acts expeditiously to remove or to disable access to the information, and

(b)   the recipient of the service was not acting under the authority or the control of the service provider.

[3361]

20 Protection of rights

(1)   Nothing in regulations 17, 18 and 19 shall—

(a)   prevent a person agreeing different contractual terms; or

(b)   affect the rights of any party to apply to a court for relief to prevent or stop infringement of any rights.

(2)   Any power of an administrative authority to prevent or stop infringement of any rights shall continue to apply notwithstanding regulations 17, 18 and 19.

[3362]

21 Defence in Criminal Proceedings: burden of proof

(1)   This regulation applies where a service provider charged with an offence in criminal proceedings arising out of any transmission, provision of access or storage falling within regulation 17, 18 or 19 relies on a defence under any of regulations 17, 18 and 19.

(2)   Where evidence is adduced which is sufficient to raise an issue with respect to that defence, the court or jury shall assume that the defence is satisfied unless the prosecution proves beyond reasonable doubt that it is not.

[3363]

22 Notice for the purposes of actual knowledge

In determining whether a service provider has actual knowledge for the purposes of regulations 18(b)(v) and 19(a)(i), a court shall take into account all matters which appear to it in the particular circumstances to be relevant and, among other things, shall have regard to—

(a)   whether a service provider has received a notice through a means of contact made available in accordance with regulation 6(1)(c), and

(b)   the extent to which any notice includes—

(i)   the full name and address of the sender of the notice;

(ii)   details of the location of the information in question; and

(iii)   details of the unlawful nature of the activity or information in question.

[3364]

SCHEDULE

Regulation 4(4)

1.   Copyright, neighbouring rights, rights referred to in Directive 87/54/EEC and Directive 96/9/EC and industrial property rights.

2.   The freedom of the parties to a contract to choose the applicable law.

3.   Contractual obligations concerning consumer contracts.

4.   Formal validity of contracts creating or transferring rights in real estate where such contracts are subject to mandatory formal requirements of the law of the member State where the real estate is situated.

5.   The permissibility of unsolicited commercial communications by electronic mail.

[3365]

SALE AND SUPPLY OF GOODS TO CONSUMERS REGULATIONS 2002

(SI 2002/3045)

NOTES

Made: 10 December 2002.

Authority: European Communities Act 1972, s 2(2).

Commencement: 31 March 2003.

1 Title, commencement and extent

(1)   These Regulations may be cited as the Sale and Supply of Goods to Consumers Regulations 2002 and shall come into force on 31st March 2003.

(2)   These Regulations extend to Northern Ireland.

[3366]

2 Interpretation

In these Regulations—

"consumer" means any natural person who, in the contracts covered by these Regulations, is acting for purposes which are outside his trade, business or profession;

"consumer guarantee" means any undertaking to a consumer by a person acting in the course of his business, given without extra charge, to reimburse the price paid or to replace, repair or handle consumer goods in any way if they do not meet the specifications set out in the guarantee statement or in the relevant advertising;

"court" in relation to England and Wales and Northern Ireland means a county court or the High Court, and in relation to Scotland, the sheriff or the Court of Session;

"enforcement authority" means [the Office of Fair Trading], every local weights and measures authority in Great Britain and the Department of Enterprise, Trade and Investment for Northern Ireland;

"goods" has the same meaning as in section 61 of the Sale of Goods Act 1979;

"guarantor" means a person who offers a consumer guarantee to a consumer; and

"supply" includes supply by way of sale, lease, hire or hire-purchase.

[3367]

NOTES

In definition "enforcement authority" words in square brackets substituted by virtue of the Enterprise Act 2002, s 2.

3–14 (*Reg 3 amends the Sale of Goods Act 1979, s 14 at* **[963]***; reg 4 amends s 20 of the 1979 Act, at* **[970]***; reg 5 inserts Pt 5A of the 1979 Act at* **[1001]***; reg 6 amends s 61(1) of the 1979 Act at* **[1018]***; reg 7 inserts s 4 of the Supply of Goods and Services Act 1982 at* **[1050]***; reg 8 amends s 11D of the 1982 Act; reg 9 inserts Pt 1B of the 1982 Act; reg 10 amends s 9 of the 1982 Act at* **[1056]***; reg 11 amends s 11J of the 1982 Act; reg 12 amends s 18(1) of the 1982 Act at* **[1065]***; reg 13 amends s 10 of the Supply of Goods* (*Implied Terms*) *Act 1973 at* **[510]***; reg 14 amends ss 12, 25 of the Unfair Contract Terms Act 1977 at* **[891]**).

15 Consumer guarantees

(1) Where goods are sold or otherwise supplied to a consumer which are offered with a consumer guarantee, the consumer guarantee takes effect at the time the goods are delivered as a contractual obligation owed by the guarantor under the conditions set out in the guarantee statement and the associated advertising.

(2) The guarantor shall ensure that the guarantee sets out in plain intelligible language the contents of the guarantee and the essential particulars necessary for making claims under the guarantee, notably the duration and territorial scope of the guarantee as well as the name and address of the guarantor.

[(2A) The guarantor shall also ensure that the guarantee contains a statement that the consumer has statutory rights in relation to the goods which are sold or supplied and that those rights are not affected by the guarantee.]

(3) On request by the consumer to a person to whom paragraph (4) applies, the guarantee shall within a reasonable time be made available in writing or in another durable medium available and accessible to him.

(4) This paragraph applies to the guarantor and any other person who offers to consumers the goods which are the subject of the guarantee for sale or supply.

(5) Where consumer goods are offered with a consumer guarantee, and where those goods are offered within the territory of the United Kingdom, then the guarantor shall ensure that the consumer guarantee is written in English.

(6) If the guarantor fails to comply with the provisions of paragraphs (2) or (5) above, or a person to whom paragraph (4) applies fails to comply with paragraph (3) then the enforcement authority may apply for an injunction or (in Scotland) an order of specific implement against that person requiring him to comply.

(7) The court on application under this Regulation may grant an injunction or (in Scotland) an order of specific implement on such terms as it thinks fit.

[3368]

NOTES

Para (2A): inserted by the Consumer Protection from Unfair Trading Regulations 2008, SI 2008/1277, reg 30(1), Sch 2, Pt 2, para 97.

PRIVACY AND ELECTRONIC COMMUNICATIONS (EC DIRECTIVE) REGULATIONS 2003

(SI 2003/2426)

NOTES

Made: 18 September 2003.
Authority: European Communities Act 1972, s 2(2).
Commencement: 11 December 2003.

ARRANGEMENT OF ARTICLES

1   Citation and commencement

These Regulations may be cited as the Privacy and Electronic Communications (EC Directive) Regulations 2003 and shall come into force on 11th December 2003.

[3368A]

2   Interpretation

(1)   In these Regulations—
   "bill" includes an invoice, account, statement or other document of similar character and "billing" shall be construed accordingly;
   "call" means a connection established by means of a telephone service available to the public allowing two-way communication in real time;
   "communication" means any information exchanged or conveyed between a finite number of parties by means of a public electronic communications service, but does not include information conveyed as part of a programme service, except to the extent that such information can be related to the identifiable subscriber or user receiving the information;

"communications provider" has the meaning given by section 405 of the Communications Act 2003;

"corporate subscriber" means a subscriber who is—

(a)   a company within the meaning of section 735(1) of the Companies Act 1985;

(b)   a company incorporated in pursuance of a royal charter or letters patent;

(c)   a partnership in Scotland;

(d)   a corporation sole; or

(e)   any other body corporate or entity which is a legal person distinct from its members;

"the Directive" means Directive 2002/58/EC of the European Parliament and of the Council of 12 July 2002 concerning the processing of personal data and the protection of privacy in the electronic communications sector (Directive on privacy and electronic communications);

"electronic communications network" has the meaning given by section 32 of the Communications Act 2003;

"electronic communications service" has the meaning given by section 32 of the Communications Act 2003;

"electronic mail" means any text, voice, sound or image message sent over a public electronic communications network which can be stored in the network or in the recipient's terminal equipment until it is collected by the recipient and includes messages sent using a short message service;

"enactment" includes an enactment comprised in, or in an instrument made under, an Act of the Scottish Parliament;

"individual" means a living individual and includes an unincorporated body of such individuals;

"the Information Commissioner" and "the Commissioner" both mean the Commissioner appointed under section 6 of the Data Protection Act 1998;

"information society service" has the meaning given in regulation 2(1) of the Electronic Commerce (EC Directive) Regulations 2002;

"location data" means any data processed in an electronic communications network indicating the geographical position of the terminal equipment of a user of a public electronic communications service, including data relating to—

(f)   the latitude, longitude or altitude of the terminal equipment;

(g)   the direction of travel of the user; or

(h)   the time the location information was recorded;

"OFCOM" means the Office of Communications as established by section 1 of the Office of Communications Act 2002;

"programme service" has the meaning given in section 201 of the Broadcasting Act 1990;

"public communications provider" means a provider of a public electronic communications network or a public electronic communications service;

"public electronic communications network" has the meaning given in section 151 of the Communications Act 2003;

"public electronic communications service" has the meaning given in section 151 of the Communications Act 2003;

"subscriber" means a person who is a party to a contract with a provider of public electronic communications services for the supply of such services;

"traffic data" means any data processed for the purpose of the conveyance of a communication on an electronic communications network or for the billing in respect of that communication and includes data relating to the routing, duration or time of a communication;

"user" means any individual using a public electronic communications service; and

"value added service" means any service which requires the processing of traffic data or location data beyond that which is necessary for the transmission of a communication or the billing in respect of that communication.

(2)   Expressions used in these Regulations that are not defined in paragraph (1) and are defined in the Data Protection Act 1998 shall have the same meaning as in that Act.

(3)   Expressions used in these Regulations that are not defined in paragraph (1) or the Data Protection Act 1998 and are defined in the Directive shall have the same meaning as in the Directive.

(4)   Any reference in these Regulations to a line shall, without prejudice to paragraph (3), be construed as including a reference to anything that performs the function of a line, and "connected", in relation to a line, is to be construed accordingly.

[3368B]

3   *(Revokes the Telecommunications (Data Protection and Privacy) Regulations 1999, SI 1999/2093, and the amending SI 2000/157.)*

4 Relationship between these Regulations and the Data Protection Act 1998

Nothing in these Regulations shall relieve a person of his obligations under the Data Protection Act 1998 in relation to the processing of personal data.

[3368C]

5 Security of public electronic communications services

(1) Subject to paragraph (2), a provider of a public electronic communications service ("the service provider") shall take appropriate technical and organisational measures to safeguard the security of that service.

(2) If necessary, the measures required by paragraph (1) may be taken by the service provider in conjunction with the provider of the electronic communications network by means of which the service is provided, and that network provider shall comply with any reasonable requests made by the service provider for these purposes.

(3) Where, notwithstanding the taking of measures as required by paragraph (1), there remains a significant risk to the security of the public electronic communications service, the service provider shall inform the subscribers concerned of—

    (a)   the nature of that risk;

    (b)   any appropriate measures that the subscriber may take to safeguard against that risk; and

    (c)   the likely costs to the subscriber involved in the taking of such measures.

(4) For the purposes of paragraph (1), a measure shall only be taken to be appropriate if, having regard to—

    (a)   the state of technological developments, and

    (b)   the cost of implementing it,

it is proportionate to the risks against which it would safeguard.

(5) Information provided for the purposes of paragraph (3) shall be provided to the subscriber free of any charge other than the cost to the subscriber of receiving or collecting the information.

[3368D]

6 Confidentiality of communications

(1) Subject to paragraph (4), a person shall not use an electronic communications network to store information, or to gain access to information stored, in the terminal equipment of a subscriber or user unless the requirements of paragraph (2) are met.

(2) The requirements are that the subscriber or user of that terminal equipment—

    (a)   is provided with clear and comprehensive information about the purposes of the storage of, or access to, that information; and

    (b)   is given the opportunity to refuse the storage of or access to that information.

(3) Where an electronic communications network is used by the same person to store or access information in the terminal equipment of a subscriber or user on more than one occasion, it is sufficient for the purposes of this regulation that the requirements of paragraph (2) are met in respect of the initial use.

(4) Paragraph (1) shall not apply to the technical storage of, or access to, information—

    (a)   for the sole purpose of carrying out or facilitating the transmission of a communication over an electronic communications network; or

    (b)   where such storage or access is strictly necessary for the provision of an information society service requested by the subscriber or user.

[3368E]

7 Restrictions on the processing of certain traffic data

(1) Subject to paragraphs (2) and (3), traffic data relating to subscribers or users which are processed and stored by a public communications provider shall, when no longer required for the purpose of the transmission of a communication, be—

    (a)   erased;

    (b)   in the case of an individual, modified so that they cease to constitute personal data of that subscriber or user; or

    (c)   in the case of a corporate subscriber, modified so that they cease to be data that would be personal data if that subscriber was an individual.

(2) Traffic data held by a public communications provider for purposes connected with the payment of charges by a subscriber or in respect of interconnection payments may be processed and stored by that provider until the time specified in paragraph (5).

(3) Traffic data relating to a subscriber or user may be processed and stored by a provider of a public electronic communications service if—

    (a)   such processing and storage are for the purpose of marketing electronic communications services, or for the provision of value added services to that subscriber or user; and

(b)   the subscriber or user to whom the traffic data relate has given his consent to such processing or storage; and

(c)   such processing and storage are undertaken only for the duration necessary for the purposes specified in subparagraph (a).

(4)   Where a user or subscriber has given his consent in accordance with paragraph (3), he shall be able to withdraw it at any time.

(5)   The time referred to in paragraph (2) is the end of the period during which legal proceedings may be brought in respect of payments due or alleged to be due or, where such proceedings are brought within that period, the time when those proceedings are finally determined.

(6)   Legal proceedings shall not be taken to be finally determined—

(a)   until the conclusion of the ordinary period during which an appeal may be brought by either party (excluding any possibility of an extension of that period, whether by order of a court or otherwise), if no appeal is brought within that period; or

(b)   if an appeal is brought, until the conclusion of that appeal.

(7)   References in paragraph (6) to an appeal include references to an application for permission to appeal.

[3368F]

8   Further provisions relating to the processing of traffic data under regulation 7

(1)   Processing of traffic data in accordance with regulation 7(2) or (3) shall not be undertaken by a public communications provider unless the subscriber or user to whom the data relate has been provided with information regarding the types of traffic data which are to be processed and the duration of such processing and, in the case of processing in accordance with regulation 7(3), he has been provided with that information before his consent has been obtained.

(2)   Processing of traffic data in accordance with regulation 7 shall be restricted to what is required for the purposes of one or more of the activities listed in paragraph (3) and shall be carried out only by the public communications provider or by a person acting under his authority.

(3)   The activities referred to in paragraph (2) are activities relating to—

(a)   the management of billing or traffic;

(b)   customer enquiries;

(c)   the prevention or detection of fraud;

(d)   the marketing of electronic communications services; or

(e)   the provision of a value added service.

(4)   Nothing in these Regulations shall prevent the furnishing of traffic data to a person who is a competent authority for the purposes of any provision relating to the settling of disputes (by way of legal proceedings or otherwise) which is contained in, or made by virtue of, any enactment.

[3368G]

9   Itemised billing and privacy

(1)   At the request of a subscriber, a provider of a public electronic communications service shall provide that subscriber with bills that are not itemised.

(2)   OFCOM shall have a duty, when exercising their functions under Chapter 1 of Part 2 of the Communications Act 2003, to have regard to the need to reconcile the rights of subscribers receiving itemised bills with the rights to privacy of calling users and called subscribers, including the need for sufficient alternative privacy-enhancing methods of communications or payments to be available to such users and subscribers.

[3368H]

10   Prevention of calling line identification—outgoing calls

(1)   This regulation applies, subject to regulations 15 and 16, to outgoing calls where a facility enabling the presentation of calling line identification is available.

(2)   The provider of a public electronic communications service shall provide users originating a call by means of that service with a simple means to prevent presentation of the identity of the calling line on the connected line as respects that call.

(3)   The provider of a public electronic communications service shall provide subscribers to the service, as respects their line and all calls originating from that line, with a simple means of preventing presentation of the identity of that subscriber's line on any connected line.

(4)   The measures to be provided under paragraphs (2) and (3) shall be provided free of charge.

[3368I]

11   Prevention of calling or connected line identification—incoming calls

(1)   This regulation applies to incoming calls.

PART 2
STATUTORY INSTRUMENTS

(2)   Where a facility enabling the presentation of calling line identification is available, the provider of a public electronic communications service shall provide the called subscriber with a simple means to prevent, free of charge for reasonable use of the facility, presentation of the identity of the calling line on the connected line.

(3)   Where a facility enabling the presentation of calling line identification prior to the call being established is available, the provider of a public electronic communications service shall provide the called subscriber with a simple means of rejecting incoming calls where the presentation of the calling line identification has been prevented by the calling user or subscriber.

(4)   Where a facility enabling the presentation of connected line identification is available, the provider of a public electronic communications service shall provide the called subscriber with a simple means to prevent, without charge, presentation of the identity of the connected line on any calling line.

(5)   In this regulation "called subscriber" means the subscriber receiving a call by means of the service in question whose line is the called line (whether or not it is also the connected line).

[3368J]

12   Publication of information for the purposes of regulations 10 and 11

Where a provider of a public electronic communications service provides facilities for calling or connected line identification, he shall provide information to the public regarding the availability of such facilities, including information regarding the options to be made available for the purposes of regulations 10 and 11.

[3368K]

13   Co-operation of communications providers for the purposes of regulations 10 and 11

For the purposes of regulations 10 and 11, a communications provider shall comply with any reasonable requests made by the provider of the public electronic communications service by means of which facilities for calling or connected line identification are provided.

[3368L]

14   Restrictions on the processing of location data

(1)   This regulation shall not apply to the processing of traffic data.

(2)   Location data relating to a user or subscriber of a public electronic communications network or a public electronic communications service may only be processed—

(a)   where that user or subscriber cannot be identified from such data; or

(b)   where necessary for the provision of a value added service, with the consent of that user or subscriber.

(3)   Prior to obtaining the consent of the user or subscriber under paragraph (2)(b), the public communications provider in question must provide the following information to the user or subscriber to whom the data relate—

(a)   the types of location data that will be processed;

(b)   the purposes and duration of the processing of those data; and

(c)   whether the data will be transmitted to a third party for the purpose of providing the value added service.

(4)   A user or subscriber who has given his consent to the processing of data under paragraph (2)(b) shall—

(a)   be able to withdraw such consent at any time, and

(b)   in respect of each connection to the public electronic communications network in question or each transmission of a communication, be given the opportunity to withdraw such consent, using a simple means and free of charge.

(5)   Processing of location data in accordance with this regulation shall—

(a)   only be carried out by—

   (i)   the public communications provider in question;

   (ii)   the third party providing the value added service in question; or

   (iii) a person acting under the authority of a person falling within (i) or (ii); and

(b)   where the processing is carried out for the purposes of the provision of a value added service, be restricted to what is necessary for those purposes.

[3368M]

15   Tracing of malicious or nuisance calls

(1)   A communications provider may override anything done to prevent the presentation of the identity of a calling line where—

(a)   a subscriber has requested the tracing of malicious or nuisance calls received on his line; and

(b)   the provider is satisfied that such action is necessary and expedient for the purposes of tracing such calls.

(2)   Any term of a contract for the provision of public electronic communications services which relates to such prevention shall have effect subject to the provisions of paragraph (1).

(3)   Nothing in these Regulations shall prevent a communications provider, for the purposes of any action relating to the tracing of malicious or nuisance calls, from storing and making available to a person with a legitimate interest data containing the identity of a calling subscriber which were obtained while paragraph (1) applied.

[3368N]

16   Emergency calls

(1)   For the purposes of this regulation, "emergency calls" means calls to either the national emergency call number 999 or the single European emergency call number 112.

(2)   In order to facilitate responses to emergency calls—
-   (a)   all such calls shall be excluded from the requirements of regulation 10;
-   (b)   no person shall be entitled to prevent the presentation on the connected line of the identity of the calling line; and
-   (c)   the restriction on the processing of location data under regulation 14(2) shall be disregarded.

[3368O]

17   Termination of automatic call forwarding

(1)   Where—
-   (a)   calls originally directed to another line are being automatically forwarded to a subscriber's line as a result of action taken by a third party, and
-   (b)   the subscriber requests his provider of electronic communications services ("the subscriber's provider") to stop the forwarding of those calls,

the subscriber's provider shall ensure, free of charge, that the forwarding is stopped without any avoidable delay.

(2)   For the purposes of paragraph (1), every other communications provider shall comply with any reasonable requests made by the subscriber's provider to assist in the prevention of that forwarding.

[3368P]

18   Directories of subscribers

(1)   This regulation applies in relation to a directory of subscribers, whether in printed or electronic form, which is made available to members of the public or a section of the public, including by means of a directory enquiry service.

(2)   The personal data of an individual subscriber shall not be included in a directory unless that subscriber has, free of charge, been—
-   (a)   informed by the collector of the personal data of the purposes of the directory in which his personal data are to be included, and
-   (b)   given the opportunity to determine whether such of his personal data as are considered relevant by the producer of the directory should be included in the directory.

(3)   Where personal data of an individual subscriber are to be included in a directory with facilities which enable users of that directory to obtain access to that data solely on the basis of a telephone number—
-   (a)   the information to be provided under paragraph (2)(a) shall include information about those facilities; and
-   (b)   for the purposes of paragraph (2)(b), the express consent of the subscriber to the inclusion of his data in a directory with such facilities must be obtained.

(4)   Data relating to a corporate subscriber shall not be included in a directory where that subscriber has advised the producer of the directory that it does not want its data to be included in that directory.

(5)   Where the data of an individual subscriber have been included in a directory, that subscriber shall, without charge, be able to verify, correct or withdraw those data at any time.

(6)   Where a request has been made under paragraph (5) for data to be withdrawn from or corrected in a directory, that request shall be treated as having no application in relation to an edition of a directory that was produced before the producer of the directory received the request.

(7)   For the purposes of paragraph (6), an edition of a directory which is revised after it was first produced shall be treated as a new edition.

(8)   In this regulation, "telephone number" has the same meaning as in section 56(5) of the Communications Act 2003 but does not include any number which is used as an internet domain name, an internet address or an address or identifier incorporating either an internet domain name or an internet address, including an electronic mail address.

[3368Q]

PART 2
STATUTORY INSTRUMENTS

19 Use of automated calling systems

(1)   A person shall neither transmit, nor instigate the transmission of, communications comprising recorded matter for direct marketing purposes by means of an automated calling system except in the circumstances referred to in paragraph (2).

(2)   Those circumstances are where the called line is that of a subscriber who has previously notified the caller that for the time being he consents to such communications being sent by, or at the instigation of, the caller on that line.

(3)   A subscriber shall not permit his line to be used in contravention of paragraph (1).

(4)   For the purposes of this regulation, an automated calling system is a system which is capable of—
- (a)   automatically initiating a sequence of calls to more than one destination in accordance with instructions stored in that system; and
- (b)   transmitting sounds which are not live speech for reception by persons at some or all of the destinations so called.

[3368R]

20 Use of facsimile machines for direct marketing purposes

(1)   A person shall neither transmit, nor instigate the transmission of, unsolicited communications for direct marketing purposes by means of a facsimile machine where the called line is that of—
- (a)   an individual subscriber, except in the circumstances referred to in paragraph (2);
- (b)   a corporate subscriber who has previously notified the caller that such communications should not be sent on that line; or
- (c)   a subscriber and the number allocated to that line is listed in the register kept under regulation 25.

(2)   The circumstances referred to in paragraph (1)(a) are that the individual subscriber has previously notified the caller that he consents for the time being to such communications being sent by, or at the instigation of, the caller.

(3)   A subscriber shall not permit his line to be used in contravention of paragraph (1).

(4)   A person shall not be held to have contravened paragraph (1)(c) where the number allocated to the called line has been listed on the register for less than 28 days preceding that on which the communication is made.

(5)   Where a subscriber who has caused a number allocated to a line of his to be listed in the register kept under regulation 25 has notified a caller that he does not, for the time being, object to such communications being sent on that line by that caller, such communications may be sent by that caller on that line, notwithstanding that the number allocated to that line is listed in the said register.

(6)   Where a subscriber has given a caller notification pursuant to paragraph (5) in relation to a line of his—
- (a)   the subscriber shall be free to withdraw that notification at any time, and
- (b)   where such notification is withdrawn, the caller shall not send such communications on that line.

(7)   The provisions of this regulation are without prejudice to the provisions of regulation 19.

[3368S]

21 Unsolicited calls for direct marketing purposes

(1)   A person shall neither use, nor instigate the use of, a public electronic communications service for the purposes of making unsolicited calls for direct marketing purposes where—
- (a)   the called line is that of a subscriber who has previously notified the caller that such calls should not for the time being be made on that line; or
- (b)   the number allocated to a subscriber in respect of the called line is one listed in the register kept under regulation 26.

(2)   A subscriber shall not permit his line to be used in contravention of paragraph (1).

(3)   A person shall not be held to have contravened paragraph (1)(b) where the number allocated to the called line has been listed on the register for less than 28 days preceding that on which the call is made.

(4)   Where a subscriber who has caused a number allocated to a line of his to be listed in the register kept under regulation 26 has notified a caller that he does not, for the time being, object to such calls being made on that line by that caller, such calls may be made by that caller on that line, notwithstanding that the number allocated to that line is listed in the said register.

(5)   Where a subscriber has given a caller notification pursuant to paragraph (4) in relation to a line of his—
- (a)   the subscriber shall be free to withdraw that notification at any time, and

(b)   where such notification is withdrawn, the caller shall not make such calls on that line.

[3368T]

22   Use of electronic mail for direct marketing purposes

(1)   This regulation applies to the transmission of unsolicited communications by means of electronic mail to individual subscribers.

(2)   Except in the circumstances referred to in paragraph (3), a person shall neither transmit, nor instigate the transmission of, unsolicited communications for the purposes of direct marketing by means of electronic mail unless the recipient of the electronic mail has previously notified the sender that he consents for the time being to such communications being sent by, or at the instigation of, the sender.

(3)   A person may send or instigate the sending of electronic mail for the purposes of direct marketing where—

(a)   that person has obtained the contact details of the recipient of that electronic mail in the course of the sale or negotiations for the sale of a product or service to that recipient;

(b)   the direct marketing is in respect of that person's similar products and services only; and

(c)   the recipient has been given a simple means of refusing (free of charge except for the costs of the transmission of the refusal) the use of his contact details for the purposes of such direct marketing, at the time that the details were initially collected, and, where he did not initially refuse the use of the details, at the time of each subsequent communication.

(4)   A subscriber shall not permit his line to be used in contravention of paragraph (2).

[3368U]

23   Use of electronic mail for direct marketing purposes where the identity or address of the sender is concealed

A person shall neither transmit, nor instigate the transmission of, a communication for the purposes of direct marketing by means of electronic mail—

(a)   where the identity of the person on whose behalf the communication has been sent has been disguised or concealed; or

(b)   where a valid address to which the recipient of the communication may send a request that such communications cease has not been provided.

[3368V]

24   Information to be provided for the purposes of regulations 19, 20 and 21

(1)   Where a public electronic communications service is used for the transmission of a communication for direct marketing purposes the person using, or instigating the use of, the service shall ensure that the following information is provided with that communication—

(a)   in relation to a communication to which regulations 19 (automated calling systems) and 20 (facsimile machines) apply, the particulars mentioned in paragraph (2)(a) and (b);

(b)   in relation to a communication to which regulation 21 (telephone calls) applies, the particulars mentioned in paragraph (2)(a) and, if the recipient of the call so requests, those mentioned in paragraph (2)(b).

(2)   The particulars referred to in paragraph (1) are—

(a)   the name of the person;

(b)   either the address of the person or a telephone number on which he can be reached free of charge.

[3368W]

25   Register to be kept for the purposes of regulation 20

(1)   For the purposes of regulation 20 OFCOM shall maintain and keep up-to-date, in printed or electronic form, a register of the numbers allocated to subscribers, in respect of particular lines, who have notified them (notwithstanding, in the case of individual subscribers, that they enjoy the benefit of regulation 20(1)(a) and (2)) that they do not for the time being wish to receive unsolicited communications for direct marketing purposes by means of facsimile machine on the lines in question.

(2)   OFCOM shall remove a number from the register maintained under paragraph (1) where they have reason to believe that it has ceased to be allocated to the subscriber by whom they were notified pursuant to paragraph (1).

(3)   On the request of—

(a)   a person wishing to send, or instigate the sending of, such communications as are mentioned in paragraph (1), or

(b)   a subscriber wishing to permit the use of his line for the sending of such communications,

PART 2
STATUTORY INSTRUMENTS

for information derived from the register kept under paragraph (1), OFCOM shall, unless it is not reasonably practicable so to do, on the payment to them of such fee as is, subject to paragraph (4), required by them, make the information requested available to that person or that subscriber.

(4) For the purposes of paragraph (3) OFCOM may require different fees—
  (a) for making available information derived from the register in different forms or manners, or
  (b) for making available information derived from the whole or from different parts of the register,

but the fees required by them shall be ones in relation to which the Secretary of State has notified OFCOM that he is satisfied that they are designed to secure, as nearly as may be and taking one year with another, that the aggregate fees received, or reasonably expected to be received, equal the costs incurred, or reasonably expected to be incurred, by OFCOM in discharging their duties under paragraphs (1), (2) and (3).

(5) The functions of OFCOM under paragraphs (1), (2) and (3), other than the function of determining the fees to be required for the purposes of paragraph (3), may be discharged on their behalf by some other person in pursuance of arrangements made by OFCOM with that other person.

[3368X]

26 Register to be kept for the purposes of regulation 21

(1) For the purposes of regulation 21 OFCOM shall maintain and keep up-to-date, in printed or electronic form, a register of the numbers allocated to ... subscribers, in respect of particular lines, who have notified them that they do not for the time being wish to receive unsolicited calls for direct marketing purposes on the lines in question.

[(1A) Notifications to OFCOM made for the purposes of paragraph (1) by corporate subscribers shall be in writing.]

(2) OFCOM shall remove a number from the register maintained under paragraph (1) where they have reason to believe that it has ceased to be allocated to the subscriber by whom they were notified pursuant to paragraph (1).

[(2A) Where a number allocated to a corporate subscriber is listed in the register maintained under paragraph (1), OFCOM shall, within the period of 28 days following each anniversary of the date of that number being first listed in the register, send to the subscriber a written reminder that the number is listed in the register.]

(3) On the request of—
  (a) a person wishing to make, or instigate the making of, such calls as are mentioned in paragraph (1), or
  (b) a subscriber wishing to permit the use of his line for the making of such calls,

for information derived from the register kept under paragraph (1), OFCOM shall, unless it is not reasonably practicable so to do, on the payment to them of such fee as is, subject to paragraph (4), required by them, make the information requested available to that person or that subscriber.

(4) For the purposes of paragraph (3) OFCOM may require different fees—
  (a) for making available information derived from the register in different forms or manners, or
  (b) for making available information derived from the whole or from different parts of the register,

but the fees required by them shall be ones in relation to which the Secretary of State has notified OFCOM that he is satisfied that they are designed to secure, as nearly as may be and taking one year with another, that the aggregate fees received, or reasonably expected to be received, equal the costs incurred, or reasonably expected to be incurred, by OFCOM in discharging their duties under paragraphs (1), (2) and (3).

(5) The functions of OFCOM under paragraphs (1), (2)[, (2A)] and (3), other than the function of determining the fees to be required for the purposes of paragraph (3), may be discharged on their behalf by some other person in pursuance of arrangements made by OFCOM with that other person.

[3368Y]

NOTES
Para (1): word omitted revoked by the Privacy and Electronic Communications (EC Directive) (Amendment) Regulations 2004, SI 2004/1039, reg 2(1), (2).
Para (1A): inserted by SI 2004/1039, reg 2(1), (3).
Para (2A): inserted by SI 2004/1039, reg 2(1), (4).
Para (5): reference in square brackets inserted by SI 2004/1039, reg 2(1), (5).

27   Modification of contracts

To the extent that any term in a contract between a subscriber to and the provider of a public electronic communications service or such a provider and the provider of an electronic communications network would be inconsistent with a requirement of these Regulations, that term shall be void.

[3368Z]

28   National security

(1)   Nothing in these Regulations shall require a communications provider to do, or refrain from doing, anything (including the processing of data) if exemption from the requirement in question is required for the purpose of safeguarding national security.

(2)   Subject to paragraph (4), a certificate signed by a Minister of the Crown certifying that exemption from any requirement of these Regulations is or at any time was required for the purpose of safeguarding national security shall be conclusive evidence of that fact.

(3)   A certificate under paragraph (2) may identify the circumstances in which it applies by means of a general description and may be expressed to have prospective effect.

(4)   Any person directly affected by the issuing of a certificate under paragraph (2) may appeal to the Tribunal against the issuing of the certificate.

(5)   If, on an appeal under paragraph (4), the Tribunal finds that, applying the principles applied by a court on an application for judicial review, the Minister did not have reasonable grounds for issuing the certificate, the Tribunal may allow the appeal and quash the certificate.

(6)   Where, in any proceedings under or by virtue of these Regulations, it is claimed by a communications provider that a certificate under paragraph (2) which identifies the circumstances in which it applies by means of a general description applies in the circumstances in question, any other party to the proceedings may appeal to the Tribunal on the ground that the certificate does not apply in those circumstances and, subject to any determination under paragraph (7), the certificate shall be conclusively presumed so to apply.

(7)   On any appeal under paragraph (6), the Tribunal may determine that the certificate does not so apply.

(8)   In this regulation—
  [(a)   "the Tribunal", in relation to any appeal under this regulation, means—
    (i)   the Upper Tribunal, in any case where it is determined by or under Tribunal Procedure Rules that the Upper Tribunal is to hear the appeal; or
    (ii)   the First-tier Tribunal, in any other case;]
  (b)   Subsections (8), (9), (10) and (12) of section 28 of and Schedule 6 to that Act apply for the purposes of this regulation as they apply for the purposes of section 28;
  (c)   section 58 of that Act shall apply for the purposes of this regulation as if the reference in that section to the functions of the Tribunal under that Act included a reference to the functions of the Tribunal under paragraphs (4) to (7) of this regulation; and
  (d)   subsections (1), (2) and (5)(f) of section 67 of that Act shall apply in respect of the making of rules relating to the functions of the Tribunal under this regulation.

[3368ZA]

NOTES

Para (8): sub-para (a) substituted by the Transfer of Tribunal Functions Order 2010, SI 2010/22, art 5(2), Sch 3, para 40, subject to transitional provisions and savings in Sch 5 thereto.

29   Legal requirements, law enforcement etc

(1)   Nothing in these Regulations shall require a communications provider to do, or refrain from doing, anything (including the processing of data)—
  (a)   if compliance with the requirement in question—
    (i)   would be inconsistent with any requirement imposed by or under an enactment or by a court order; or
    (ii)   would be likely to prejudice the prevention or detection of crime or the apprehension or prosecution of offenders; or
  (b)   if exemption from the requirement in question—
    (i)   is required for the purposes of, or in connection with, any legal proceedings (including prospective legal proceedings);
    (ii)   is necessary for the purposes of obtaining legal advice; or
    (iii)   is otherwise necessary for the purposes of establishing, exercising or defending legal rights.

[3368ZB]

30   Proceedings for compensation for failure to comply with requirements of the Regulations

(1)   A person who suffers damage by reason of any contravention of any of the requirements of these Regulations by any other person shall be entitled to bring proceedings for compensation from that other person for that damage.

(2)   In proceedings brought against a person by virtue of this regulation it shall be a defence to prove that he had taken such care as in all the circumstances was reasonably required to comply with the relevant requirement.

(3)   The provisions of this regulation are without prejudice to those of regulation 31.

[3368ZC]

31   Enforcement—extension of Part V of the Data Protection Act 1998

(1)   The provisions of Part V of the Data Protection Act 1998 and of Schedules 6 and 9 to that Act are extended for the purposes of these Regulations and, for those purposes, shall have effect subject to the modifications set out in Schedule 1.

(2)   In regulations 32 and 33, "enforcement functions" means the functions of the Information Commissioner under the provisions referred to in paragraph (1) as extended by that paragraph.

(3)   The provisions of this regulation are without prejudice to those of regulation 30.

[3368ZD]

32   Request that the Commissioner exercise his enforcement functions

Where it is alleged that there has been a contravention of any of the requirements of these Regulations either OFCOM or a person aggrieved by the alleged contravention may request the Commissioner to exercise his enforcement functions in respect of that contravention, but those functions shall be exercisable by the Commissioner whether or not he has been so requested.

[3368ZE]

33   Technical advice to the Commissioner

OFCOM shall comply with any reasonable request made by the Commissioner, in connection with his enforcement functions, for advice on technical and similar matters relating to electronic communications.

[3368ZF]

34, 35   (*Reg 34 substitutes reg 3(3) of the Telecommunications* (*Lawful Business Practice*) (*Interception of Communications*) *Regulations 2000, SI 2000/2699, at* **[3328]**; *reg 35 amends the Schedule to the Electronic Communications* (*Universal Service*) *Order 2003, SI 2003/1904*).

36   Transitional provisions

The provisions in Schedule 2 shall have effect.

[3368ZG]

SCHEDULE 1
MODIFICATIONS FOR THE PURPOSES OF THESE REGULATIONS TO PART V OF THE
DATA PROTECTION ACT 1998 AND SCHEDULES 6 AND 9 TO THAT ACT AS EXTENDED
BY REGULATION 31

Regulation 31

1.   In section 40—
    (a)   in subsection (1), for the words "data controller" there shall be substituted the word "person", for the words "data protection principles" there shall be substituted the words "requirements of the Privacy and Electronic Communications (EC Directive) Regulations 2003 (in this Part referred to as "the relevant requirements")" and for the words "principle or principles" there shall be substituted the words "requirement or requirements";
    (b)   in subsection (2), the words "or distress" shall be omitted;
    (c)   subsections (3), (4), (5), (9) and (10) shall be omitted; and
    (d)   in subsection (6)(a), for the words "data protection principle or principles" there shall be substituted the words "relevant requirement or requirements."

2.   In section 41(1) and (2), for the words "data protection principle or principles", in both places where they occur, there shall be substituted the words "relevant requirement or requirements".

3.   Section 42 shall be omitted.

4.   In section 43—
    (a)   for subsections (1) and (2) there shall be substituted the following provisions—

        "(1)   If the Commissioner reasonably requires any information for the purpose of determining whether a person has complied or is complying with the relevant requirements, he may serve that person with a notice (in this Act referred to as "an information notice") requiring him, within such time as is specified in the notice, to furnish the Commissioner, in such form as may be so specified, with such information relating to compliance with the relevant requirements as is so specified.

(2)   An information notice must contain a statement that the Commissioner regards the specified information as relevant for the purpose of determining whether the person has complied or is complying with the relevant requirements and his reason for regarding it as relevant for that purpose."

   (b)   in subsection (6)(a), after the word "under" there shall be inserted the words "the Privacy and Electronic Communications (EC Directive) Regulations 2003 or";

   (c)   in subsection (6)(b), after the words "arising out of" there shall be inserted the words "the said Regulations or"; and

   (d)   subsection (10) shall be omitted.

5.   Sections 44, 45 and 46 shall be omitted.

6.   In section 47—

   (a)   in subsection (1), for the words "an information notice or special information notice" there shall be substituted the words "or an information notice"; and

   (b)   in subsection (2) the words "or a special information notice" shall be omitted.

7.   In section 48—

   (a)   in subsections (1) and (3), for the words "an information notice or a special information notice", in both places where they occur, there shall be substituted the words "or an information notice";

   (b)   in subsection (3) for the words "43(5) or 44(6)" there shall be substituted the words "or 43(5)"; and

   (c)   subsection (4) shall be omitted.

8.   In section 49 subsection (5) shall be omitted.

9.   In paragraph 4(1) of Schedule (6), for the words " (2) or (4)" there shall be substituted the words "or (2)".

10.   In paragraph 1 of Schedule 9—

   (a)   for subparagraph (1)(a) there shall be substituted the following provision—

      "(a)   that a person has contravened or is contravening any of the requirements of the Privacy and Electronic Communications (EC Directive) Regulations 2003 (in this Schedule referred to as "the 2003 Regulations") or";

      and

   (b)   subparagraph (2) shall be omitted.

11.   In paragraph 9 of Schedule 9—

   (a)   in subparagraph (1)(a) after the words "rights under" there shall be inserted the words "the 2003 Regulations or"; and

   (b)   in subparagraph (1)(b) after the words "arising out of" there shall be inserted the words "the 2003 Regulations or".

[3368ZH]

PART 2
STATUTORY INSTRUMENTS

SCHEDULE 2
TRANSITIONAL PROVISIONS

Regulation 36

Interpretation

1.   In this Schedule "the 1999 Regulations" means the Telecommunications (Data Protection and Privacy) Regulations 1999 and "caller" has the same meaning as in regulation 21 of the 1999 Regulations.

Directories

2.—(1)   Regulation 18 of these Regulations shall not apply in relation to editions of directories first published before 11th December 2003.

(2)   Where the personal data of a subscriber have been included in a directory in accordance with Part IV of the 1999 Regulations, the personal data of that subscriber may remain included in that directory provided that the subscriber—

   (a)   has been provided with information in accordance with regulation 18 of these Regulations; and

   (b)   has not requested that his data be withdrawn from that directory.

(3)   Where a request has been made under subparagraph (2) for data to be withdrawn from a directory, that request shall be treated as having no application in relation to an edition of a directory that was produced before the producer of the directory received the request.

(4)   For the purposes of subparagraph (3), an edition of a directory, which is revised after it was first produced, shall be treated as a new edition.

Notifications

3.—(1) A notification of consent given to a caller by a subscriber for the purposes of regulation 22(2) of the 1999 Regulations is to have effect on and after 11th December 2003 as a notification given by that subscriber for the purposes of regulation 19(2) of these Regulations.

(2) A notification given to a caller by a corporate subscriber for the purposes of regulation 23(2)(a) of the 1999 Regulations is to have effect on and after 11th December 2003 as a notification given by that subscriber for the purposes of regulation 20(1)(b) of these Regulations.

(3) A notification of consent given to a caller by an individual subscriber for the purposes of regulation 24(2) of the 1999 Regulations is to have effect on and after 11th December 2003 as a notification given by that subscriber for the purposes of regulation 20(2) of these Regulations.

(4) A notification given to a caller by an individual subscriber for the purposes of regulation 25(2)(a) of the 1999 Regulations is to have effect on and after the 11th December 2003 as a notification given by that subscriber for the purposes of regulation 21(1) of these Regulations.

Registers Kept Under Regulations 25 and 26

4.—(1) A notification given by a subscriber pursuant to regulation 23(4)(a) of the 1999 Regulations to the Director General of Telecommunications (or to such other person as is discharging his functions under regulation 23(4) of the 1999 Regulations on his behalf by virtue of an arrangement made under regulation 23(6) of those Regulations) is to have effect on or after 11th December 2003 as a notification given pursuant to regulation 25(1) of these Regulations.

(2) A notification given by a subscriber who is an individual pursuant to regulation 25(4)(a) of the 1999 Regulations to the Director General of Telecommunications (or to such other person as is discharging his functions under regulation 25(4) of the 1999 Regulations on his behalf by virtue of an arrangement made under regulation 25(6) of those Regulations) is to have effect on or after 11th December 2003 as a notification given pursuant to regulation 26(1) of these Regulations.

References in these Regulations to OFCOM

5. In relation to times before an order made under section 411 of the Communications Act 2003 brings any of the provisions of Part 2 of Chapter 1 of that Act into force for the purpose of conferring on OFCOM the functions contained in those provisions, references to OFCOM in these Regulations are to be treated as references to the Director General of Telecommunications.

[3368ZI]

PRICE MARKING ORDER 2004

(SI 2004/102)

NOTES
Made: 19 January 2004.
Authority: Prices Act 1974, s 4.
Commencement: 22 July 2004.

ARRANGEMENT OF ARTICLES

1   Citation, commencement and interpretation

(1)   This Order may be cited as the Price Marking Order 2004 and shall come into force on 22nd July 2004.

(2)   In this Order—

"advertisement" means any form of advertisement which is made in order to promote the sale of a product but does not include any advertisement by means of which the trader intends to encourage a consumer to enter into a distance contract, a catalogue, a price list, a container or a label;

"consumer" means any individual who buys a product for purposes that do not fall within the sphere of his commercial or professional activity;

"cosmetic products" means any substance or preparation intended to be placed in contact with an external part of the human body, or with the teeth, inside of the mouth or throat with a view exclusively or mainly to one or more of the following purposes: cleaning, perfuming, changing the appearance of, protecting, and keeping in good condition it or them or correcting body odour;

"distance contract" means any contract concerning products concluded between a trader and a consumer, by any means, without the simultaneous physical presence of the trader and the consumer;

"itinerant trader" means any trader who, as a pedestrian, or from a train, aircraft, vessel, vehicle, stall, barrow, or other mobile sales unit, offers products to consumers other than by means of pre-printed material;

"liquid medium" has the meaning given for the purposes of paragraph 4 of Article 8 of Directive 2000/13/EC of the European Parliament and of the Council on the approximation of the laws of the Member States relating to the labelling, presentation and advertising of foodstuffs;

"make-up products" means cosmetic products solely intended temporarily to change the appearance of the face or nails, including (but not limited to) lipsticks, mascaras, eye shadows, blushers and concealers;

"net drained weight" means the weight of a solid food product when it is presented in a liquid medium;

"precious metal" means gold, silver or platinum, or any other metal to which by an order under section 17 of the Hallmarking Act 1973 the provisions of that Act are applied;

"products sold from bulk" means products which are not pre-packaged and are weighed or measured at the request of the consumer;

"relevant floor area" in relation to a shop means the internal floor area of the shop excluding any area not used for the retail sale of products or for the display of such products for retail sale;

"selling price" means the final price for a unit of a product, or a given quantity of a product, including VAT and all other taxes;

"shop" includes a store, kiosk and a franchise or concession within a shop;

"small shop" means any shop which has a "relevant floor area" not exceeding 280 square metres;

"standard of fineness" means any one of the standards of fineness specified in column (2) of paragraph 2 of Schedule 2 to the Hallmarking Act 1973;

"trader" means any person who sells or offers or exposes for sale products which fall within his commercial or professional activity;

"unit price" means the final price, including VAT and all other taxes, for one kilogram, one litre, one metre, one square metre or one cubic metre of a product, except (i) in respect of the products specified in Schedule 1, where unit price means the final price including VAT and all other taxes for the corresponding units of quantity set out in that Schedule; and (ii) in respect of products sold by number, where unit price means the final price including VAT and all other taxes for an individual item of the product.

[3369]

2   *(Revokes the Price Marking Order 1999, SI 1999/3042.)*

3   Scope of application of the Order

(1)   This Order shall not apply:

    (a)   to products which are supplied in the course of the provision of a service; or

    (b)   to sales by auction or sales of works of art or antiques.

(2)   The Electronic Commerce (EC Directive) Regulations 2002 shall apply to this Order notwithstanding Regulation 3(2) of those Regulations.

[3370]

PART 2
STATUTORY INSTRUMENTS

4 Obligation to indicate selling price

(1) Subject to paragraph (2) and articles 9 and 10, where a trader indicates that any product is or may be for sale to a consumer, he shall indicate the selling price of that product in accordance with the provisions of this Order.

(2) The requirement in paragraph (1) above shall not apply in respect of:
(a) products sold from bulk; or
(b) an advertisement for a product.

[3371]

5 Obligation to indicate unit price

(1) Subject to paragraph (2), (3) and (4) and article 9, where a trader indicates that any product is or may be for sale to a consumer, he shall indicate the unit price of that product in accordance with the provisions of this Order.

(2) The requirement in paragraph (1) only applies in respect of products sold from bulk or required by or under Parts IV or V of the Weights and Measures Act 1985 to be:
(a) marked with an indication of quantity; or
(b) made up in a quantity prescribed by or under that Act.

(3) The requirement in paragraph (1) shall not apply in relation to:
(a) any product which falls within Schedule 2;
(b) any product the unit price of which is identical to its selling price;
(c) bread made up in a prescribed quantity which is or may be for sale in a small shop, by an itinerant trader or from a vending machine; or
(d) any product which is pre-packaged in a constant quantity which is or may be for sale in a small shop, by an itinerant trader or from a vending machine.

(4) The requirement in paragraph (1) applies in relation to an advertisement for a product only where the selling price of the product is indicated in the advertisement.

[3372]

6 Manner of indication of selling price and unit price

(1) The indication of selling price and unit price shall be in sterling.

(2) If a trader indicates his willingness to accept foreign currency in payment for a product, he shall, in addition to the required price indications in sterling:
(a) give an indication of the selling price and any unit price required for the product in the foreign currency in question together with any commission to be charged; or
(b) clearly identify the conversion rate on the basis of which the foreign currency price will be calculated together with any commission to be charged; and

indicate that such selling price, unit price or conversion rate as the case may be does not apply to transactions via a payment card to be applied to accounts denominated in currencies other than sterling, the conversion rate for which will be that applied by the relevant payment scheme which processes the transaction.

[3373]

7—(1) An indication of selling price, unit price, commission, conversion rate or a change in the rate or coverage of value added tax given in accordance with article 11 shall be—
(a) unambiguous, easily identifiable and clearly legible;
(b) subject to paragraph 2, given in proximity to:
(i) the product; or
(ii) in the case of distance contracts and advertisements, a visual or written description of the product; and
(c) so placed as to be available to consumers without the need for them to seek assistance from the trader or someone on his behalf in order to ascertain it.

(2) Paragraph (1)(b)(i) does not apply to an indication given in relation to any item of jewellery, item of precious metal, or watch displayed in a window of the premises where it is or may be for sale and the selling price of which is in excess of £3,000.

(3) The indication of any charges for postage, package or delivery of a product shall be unambiguous, easily identifiable and clearly legible.

(4) Where, in addition to a unit price, a price per quantity is indicated in relation to a supplementary indication of quantity the unit price shall predominate and the price per supplementary indication of quantity shall be expressed in characters no larger than the unit price.

(5) In paragraph (4) "supplementary indication of quantity" refers to an indication of quantity expressed in a unit of measurement other than a metric unit as authorised by section 8(5A) of the Weights and Measures Act 1985.

[3374]

8   In the case of a pre-packaged solid food product presented in a liquid medium, the unit price shall refer to the net drained weight of the product. Where a unit price is also given with reference to the net weight of the product, it shall be clearly indicated which unit price relates to net drained weight and which to net weight.

[3375]

9   Special provisions relating to general reductions

Where a trader proposes to sell products to which this Order applies at less than the selling price or the unit price previously applicable and indicated in accordance with article 7(1), he may comply with the obligations specified in articles 4(1) (to indicate the selling price) and 5(1) (to indicate the unit price) by indicating by a general notice or any other visible means that the products are or may be for sale at a reduction, provided that the details of the reduction are prominently displayed, unambiguous, easily identifiable and clearly legible.

[3376]

10   Special provisions relating to precious metals

In the case of products the selling price of which varies from day to day according to the price of the precious metals contained in them the obligation to indicate the selling price referred to in article 4(1) may be complied with by indicating in a manner which is unambiguous, easily identifiable and clearly legible:

    (a)   the weight, type and standard of fineness of each precious metal contained in the product; and

    (b)   any element of the selling price which is not referable to weight,

accompanied by a clearly legible and prominent notice stating the price per unit of weight for the type and standard of fineness of each precious metal contained in the product.

[3377]

11   Change in Value Added Tax etc

Where there is a change in the rate or coverage of VAT or any other tax, a trader who adjusts his prices in consequence may comply with the provisions of this Order—

    (a)   by means of a general notice or notices for a period of [28] days from the date any such change takes effect, indicating that any products subject to that change are not for sale at the price indicated and that such price will be adjusted to take account of the change; and

    (b)   if he continues to distribute any catalogue or sales literature printed or ordered to be printed before a change is announced and there is firmly attached to it a label which prominently states that some or all of the prices printed in it are to be adjusted to reflect the change, and:

        (i)   the label includes sufficient information to enable consumers to establish the adjusted price of any product listed, or

        (ii)   the label refers to and is accompanied by a supplement which enables them to do so.

[3378]

NOTES

Number in square brackets substituted by the Price Marking (Amendment) Order 2009, SI 2009/3231, art 2.

---

12   Decimal places and rounding of unit prices

Where the unit price of a product falls below £1 it shall be expressed to the nearest 0.1p. Where the figure denoting one hundredths of one penny in the unit price is 5 or higher, it shall be rounded up and where it is 4 or lower it shall be rounded down.

[3379]

13   Where the unit price of a product falls above £1 it may be expressed to the nearest:

    (a)   1p, in which case where the figure denoting tenths of one penny in the unit price is 5 or higher, it shall be rounded up and where it is 4 or lower it shall be rounded down; or

    (b)   0.1p, in which case where the figure denoting one hundredths of one penny in the unit price is 5 or higher it shall be rounded up and where it is 4 or lower it shall be rounded down.

[3380]

14   Units of Quantity

For the purposes of Schedule 1, the figure denoting the relevant units of quantity in the second column of the table for the corresponding product in the first column of the table refers, as indicated by or under the Weights and Measures Act 1985, and unless specified otherwise to:

    (a)   grams where the product is sold by weight;

    (b)   millilitres where the product is sold by volume; and

(c) either grams or millilitres, as indicated by the manufacturer of the product, where the product is permitted to be sold by either weight or volume.

[3381]

15 Enforcement

For the purpose of ascertaining whether any trader enjoys exemption from unit pricing under article 5(3)(c) or (d) in respect of a small shop, a local weights and measures authority may require that trader to produce such documentary evidence relating to the shop in question as it considers necessary.

[3382]

SCHEDULE 1
RELEVANT UNITS OF QUANTITY FOR SPECIFIED PRODUCTS FOR THE PURPOSE OF THE DEFINITION OF "UNIT PRICE"
Articles 1(2) and 14

Product	Units of Quantity
Flavouring essences	10
Food colourings	10
Herbs	10
Make-up Products	10 (except where sold by number)
Seeds other than pea, bean, grass and wild bird seeds	10
Spices	10
Biscuits and shortbread	100 (except where sold by number)
Bread	100 (except where sold by number)
Breakfast cereal products	100 (except where required to be quantity marked by number)
Chocolate confectionery and sugar confectionery	100
Coffee	100
Cooked or ready-to-eat fish, seafoods and crustacea	100
Cooked or ready-to-eat meat including game and poultry	100
Cosmetic products other than make-up products	100
Cream and non-dairy alternatives to cream	100
Dips and spreads excluding edible fats	100
Dry sauce mixes	100
Fresh processed salad	100
Fruit juices, soft drinks	100
Handrolling and pipe tobacco	100
Ice cream and frozen desserts	100
Lubricating oils other than oils for internal combustion engines	100
Pickles	100
Pies, pasties, sausage rolls, puddings and flans indicating net quantity	100 (except where sold by number)
Potato crisps and similar products commonly known as snack foods	100
Preserves including honey	100
Ready to eat desserts	100
Sauces, edible oils	100

Product	Units of Quantity
Soups	100
Tea and other beverages prepared with liquid	100
Waters, including spa waters and aerated waters	100
Wines, sparkling wine, liqueur wine, fortified wine	75 cl
Coal, where sold by the kilogram	50 kg
Ballast, where sold by the kilogram	1,000 kg

[3383]

SCHEDULE 2
PRODUCTS IN RESPECT OF WHICH A TRADER IS EXEMPT FROM THE REQUIREMENT
TO UNIT PRICE

Article 5(3)

1.   Any product which is offered by traders to consumers by means of an advertisement which is:
    (a)   purely aural;
    (b)   broadcast on television;
    (c)   shown at a cinema; or
    (d)   inside a small shop.

2.   Any product the price of which has been reduced from the usual price at which it is sold, on account of:
    (a)   its damaged condition; or
    (b)   the danger of its deterioration.

3.   Any product which comprises an assortment of different items sold in a single package.

4.   Any product the unit price of which is 0.0p as a result of article 12 (Decimal places and rounding of unit prices) of this Order.

[3384]

CONSUMER CREDIT (DISCLOSURE OF INFORMATION) REGULATIONS 2004

(SI 2004/1481)

NOTES
Made: 5 June 2004.
Authority: Consumer Credit Act 1974, ss 55(1), 182(2), 189(1).
Commencement: 31 May 2005.

1   Citation, commencement and interpretation

(1)   These Regulations may be cited as the Consumer Credit (Disclosure of Information) Regulations 2004 and shall come into force on 31st May 2005.

(2)   In these Regulations—
    ["the Act" means the Consumer Credit Act 1974;]
    "the Agreements Regulations" mean the Consumer Credit (Agreements) Regulations 1983;
    "distance contract" means any regulated agreement made under an organised distance sales or service-provision scheme run by the creditor or owner or by an intermediary of the creditor or owner who, in any such case, for the purpose of that agreement makes exclusive use of one or more means of distance communication up to and including the time at which the agreement is made and for this purpose any means of communication is a means of distance communication if, without the simultaneous physical presence of the creditor or owner or any intermediary of the creditor or owner and of the debtor or hirer, it may be used for the distance marketing of a regulated agreement between the parties to that agreement;
    "durable medium" means any instrument which enables the debtor or hirer to store information addressed personally to him in a way accessible for future reference for a period of time adequate for the purposes of the information and which allows the unchanged reproduction of the information stored.

[3385]

NOTES
Definition "the Act" inserted by the Consumer Credit (EU Directive) Regulations 2010, SI 2010/1010, regs 73, 74, as from 1 February 2011, with effect in relation to certain agreements before that date, as provided for in regs 101, 101A of the 2010 Regulations at **[3942]**, **[3942A]**.

2 Agreements to which these Regulations apply

These Regulations apply in respect of all regulated agreements except—

(a) *agreements to which section 58 of the Consumer Credit Act 1974 (opportunity for withdrawal from prospective land mortgage) applies; and*

(b) *distance contracts.*

[(1) Subject to paragraph (3) these Regulations apply in respect of the following regulated agreements—

(a) consumer credit agreements secured on land except those to which section 58 of the Act (opportunity for withdrawal from prospective land mortgage) applies,

(b) consumer hire agreements,

(c) consumer credit agreements under which the creditor provides the debtor with credit which exceeds £60,260,

(d) consumer credit agreements entered into by the debtor wholly or predominantly for the purposes of a business carried on, or intended to be carried on, by him, and

(e) small debtor-creditor-supplier agreements for restricted-use credit,

except to the extent the Consumer Credit (Disclosure of Information) Regulations 2010 apply to such agreements.

(2) Subsections (2) to (5) of section 16B of the Act (declaration by the debtor as to the purposes of the agreement) apply for the purposes of paragraph (1)(d).

(3) These Regulations do not apply to—

(a) a distance contract;

(b) an authorised non-business overdraft agreement;

(c) an agreement which would be an authorised non-business overdraft agreement but for the fact that the credit is not repayable on demand or within three months.]

[3386]

NOTES
Text in italics substituted for subsequent text in square brackets, by the Consumer Credit (EU Directive) Regulations 2010, SI 2010/1010, regs 73, 75 (as amended by the Consumer Credit (Amendment) Regulations 2010, SI 2010/1969, regs 4, 24), as from 1 February 2011, with effect in relation to certain agreements before that date, as provided for in regs 101, 101A of SI 2010/1010 at **[3942]**, **[3942A]**.

3 Information to be disclosed to a debtor or hirer before a regulated agreement is made

(1) Before a regulated agreement ("the relevant agreement") is made, the creditor or owner must disclose to the debtor or hirer in the manner set out in regulation 4 the information and statements of protection and remedies that are required to be given—

(a) in the case of a regulated consumer credit agreement, under regulation 2 of the Agreements Regulations;

(b) in the case of a regulated consumer hire agreement, under regulation 3 of the Agreements Regulations;

(c) in the case of a modifying agreement which is, or is treated as, a regulated consumer credit agreement, under regulations 2(3) and 7(2) of the Agreements Regulations;

(d) in the case of a modifying agreement which is or is treated as a regulated consumer hirer agreement, under regulations 3(3) and 7(9) of the Agreements Regulations.

[(1A) In the case of an agreement falling within regulation 2(1)(c), (d) or (e), the creditor shall provide, in addition to the information specified in paragraph (1), a statement that if he decided not to proceed with a prospective regulated consumer credit agreement on the basis of information from a credit reference agency, he will, when informing the debtor of that decision, inform the debtor that the decision has been reached on the basis of information from a credit reference agency and of the particulars of that agency (in compliance with section 157(A1) of the Act.]

(2) The information and statements of protection required to be disclosed under paragraph (1) shall be the information and statements that will be included in the document embodying the relevant agreement save that, where any of the information is not known at the time of disclosure, the creditor or owner shall disclose estimated information based on such assumptions as he may reasonably make in all the circumstances of the case.

[3387]

NOTES
Para (1A): inserted by the Consumer Credit (EU Directive) Regulations 2010, SI 2010/1010, regs 73, 76 (as amended by the Consumer Credit (Amendment) Regulations 2010, SI 2010/1969, regs 4, 25), as from 1 February 2011, with effect in relation to certain agreements before that date, as provided for in regs 101, 101A of SI 2010/1010 at **[3942]**, **[3942A]**.

4 Manner of disclosure

The information and statements of protection and remedies required to be disclosed under regulation 3 must be—

- (a) easily legible and, where applicable, of a colour which is readily distinguishable from the background medium upon which they are displayed;
- (b) not interspersed with any other information or wording apart from subtotals of total amounts and cross references to the terms of the agreement;
- (c) of equal prominence except that headings may be afforded more prominence whether by capital letters, underlining, larger or bold print or otherwise; and
- (d) contained in a document which:
  - (i) is separate from the document embodying the relevant agreement (within the meaning of regulation 3) and any other document referred to in the document embodying that agreement;
  - (ii) is headed with the words "Pre-contract Information";
  - (iii) does not contain any other information or wording apart from the heading referred to in sub-paragraph (ii);
  - (iv) is on paper or on another durable medium which is available and accessible to the debtor or hirer; and
  - (v) is of a nature that enables the debtor or hirer to remove it from the place where it is disclosed to him.

[3388]

CONSUMER CREDIT (EARLY SETTLEMENT) REGULATIONS 2004

(SI 2004/1483)

NOTES
Made: 5 June 2004.
Authority: Consumer Credit Act 1974, ss 95, 97(1), 182(2), 189(1).
Commencement: 31 May 2005.

ARRANGEMENT OF REGULATIONS

1 Citation, commencement and interpretation

(1) These Regulations may be cited as the Consumer Credit (Early Settlement) Regulations 2004, and shall come into force on 31st May 2005.

(2) In these Regulations—

"the Act" means the Consumer Credit Act 1974;

"the APR" means the annual percentage rate of charge for credit determined in accordance with the Total Charge for Credit Regulations, subject to regulation 3(2) below;

"early settlement" shall be construed in accordance with *regulation 2(1)* [regulation 2(1A)] below;

"rebate" means a rebate of charges for credit included in the total charge for credit;

"the relevant date" *shall be determined in accordance with the Total Charge for Credit Regulations;* [means—

- (a) where a date is specified in or determinable under an agreement at the date of its making as that on which the debtor is entitled to require the provision of anything under the agreement, the earliest such date, or

(b) where no such date is specified or determinable, the date of making of the agreement;]

"the settlement date", means the settlement date provided for in regulation 5 and, where applicable, regulation 6;

"the total charge for credit" shall be determined in accordance with the Total Charge for Credit Regulations, subject to regulations 3(2) and 7 below; and

"the Total Charge for Credit Regulations" means the Consumer Credit (Total Charge for Credit) Regulations 1980.

["the Total Charge for Credit Regulations" means—

(a) in relation to a regulated consumer credit agreement that is secured on land and to which the Consumer Credit (Disclosure of Information) Regulations 2010 do not apply, the Consumer Credit (Total Charge for Credit) Regulations 1980,

(b) in relation to any other regulated consumer credit agreement, the Consumer Credit (Total Charge for Credit) Regulations 2010.]

(3)   The length of any period for the purposes of calculations under these Regulations shall be determined in accordance with regulation 11 of the Total Charge for Credit Regulations, other than paragraph (5)(a) of that regulation.

[(4)   In relation to a regulated consumer credit agreement secured on land and to which the Consumer Credit (Disclosure of Information) Regulations 2010 do not apply, the definition of the Total Charge for Credit Regulations in paragraph (2) shall apply as if for the words "Consumer Credit (Total Charge for Credit Regulations 2010" there were substituted "Consumer Credit (Total Charge for Credit) Regulations 1980.]

(4)   In these Regulations, references to repayment of credit are references to repayment of credit with any amount included in the total charge for credit payable at the same time.

[3389]

NOTES

Para (2): in definitions "early settlement" and "the relevant date", words in italics substituted by subsequent words in square brackets, and definition "the Total Charge for Credit Regulations" substituted by subsequent definition in square brackets, by the Consumer Credit (EU Directive) Regulations 2010, SI 2010/1010, regs 77, 78(a) (as amended by the Consumer Credit (Amendment) Regulations 2010, SI 2010/1969, regs 4, 26), as from 1 February 2011, with effect in relation to certain agreements before that date, as provided for in regs 100–101A of SI 2010/1010 at **[3941]**–**[3942A]**.

Para (3): revoked by SI 2010/1010, regs 77, 78(b), as from 1 February 2011, with effect in relation to certain agreements before that date, as provided for in regs 100–101A of the 2010 Regulations at **[3941]**–**[3942A]**.

First para (4): inserted by SI 2010/1010, regs 77, 78(c), as from 1 February 2011, with effect in relation to certain agreements before that date, as provided for in regs 100–101A of the 2010 Regulations at **[3941]**–**[3942A]**.

2   Entitlement to rebate

(1)   Subject to the following provisions of this regulation, the creditor shall allow to the debtor under a regulated consumer credit agreement a rebate at least equal to that calculated in accordance with the following provisions of these Regulations whenever early settlement takes place, that is to say whenever, under section 94 of the Act, on refinancing, on breach of the agreement or for any other reason, the indebtedness of the debtor is discharged or becomes payable before the time fixed by the agreement, or any sum becomes payable by him before the time so fixed.

[(1)   Where early settlement takes place the creditor shall, subject to the following provisions of this regulation, allow to the debtor under a regulated consumer credit agreement a rebate at least equal to that calculated in accordance with the following provisions of these Regulations.]

[(1A)   Early settlement takes place under paragraph (1) where—

(a) the indebtedness of the debtor is discharged or becomes payable before the time fixed by the agreement—
  (i) under section 94(1) of the Act,
  (ii) on refinancing,
  (iii) on breach of the agreement, or
  (iv) for any other reason,

(b) the indebtedness of the debtor is discharged in part under section 94(3) of the Act, or

(c) any sum becomes payable by the debtor before the time fixed by the agreement.]

(2)   Paragraph (1) does not apply in the case of agreements of the following descriptions—

(a) agreements under which no payments of items included in the total charge for credit are required to be made in respect of the period of time commencing on the settlement date;

(b) agreements for running-account credit;

(c) land mortgages under which no instalment repayments secured by the mortgage on the debtor's home, and no payment of interest on the credit (other than interest charged when all or part of the credit is repaid voluntarily by the debtor), are due or capable of becoming due while the debtor continues to occupy the mortgaged land as his main residence.

(3)   Paragraph (1) does not apply where a hire-purchase or conditional sale agreement is terminated by the debtor under section 99 of the Act.

(4)   Where a sum less than the total remaining indebtedness of the debtor is required to be paid before the time fixed by the agreement, no consequential payment of any subsequent instalment required to be paid under the agreement, or under a modifying agreement not relating to the provision of additional credit or an increase in the total charge for credit, shall entitle the debtor to a rebate.

[3390]

NOTES

Para (1): para (1) in italics substituted by subsequent para (1) in square brackets, by the Consumer Credit (EU Directive) Regulations 2010, SI 2010/1010, regs 77, 79(a), as from 1 February 2011, with effect in relation to certain agreements before that date, as provided for in regs 100–101A of the 2010 Regulations at **[3941]**–**[3942A]**.

Para (1A): inserted by SI 2010/1010, regs 77, 79(b), as from 1 February 2011, with effect in relation to certain agreements before that date, as provided for in regs 100–101A of the 2010 Regulations at **[3941]**–**[3942A]**.

3   Items included in the calculation of rebate

(1)   Subject to paragraph (2), the rebate shall be calculated by reference to all sums paid or payable by the debtor or a relative of his under or in connection with the agreement (whether to the creditor or any other person) and included in the total charge for credit.

(2)   There may be excluded from the calculation of the rebate—

    (a)   [so much of the amount of] taxes, duties, fees and charges payable under or by virtue of any statute or payable to the Secretary of State or any other Minister or government department (including for this purpose a Northern Ireland department or a government department in any country outside the United Kingdom) or to a local authority or similar body outside the United Kingdom [as is attributable to the period before the settlement date];

    (b)   sums paid or payable under linked transactions, except sums paid before the settlement date in respect of cash, goods or services to be supplied under the transaction wholly or partly after that date;

    (c)   sums payable under linked transactions excluded under regulations made under section 96(3) of the Act from the operation of section 96(1);

    (d)   [so much of] any fee or commission paid by the debtor or a relative of his under a credit brokerage contract relating to the agreement [as is attributable to the period before the settlement date] ...

[(3)   In relation to a regulated consumer credit agreement secured on land—

    (a)   paragraph (2)(a) shall apply as if the words "so much of the amount of" and "as is attributable to the period before the settlement date" were omitted; and

    (b)   paragraph (2)(d) shall apply as if the words "so much of" and "as is attributable to the period before the settlement date" were omitted.]

[3391]

NOTES

Para (2): words in square brackets in sub-paras (a), (d) inserted by the Consumer Credit (EU Directive) Regulations 2010, SI 2010/1010, regs 77, 80(a), as from 1 February 2011, with effect in relation to certain agreements before that date, as provided for in regs 100–101A of the 2010 Regulations at **[3941]**–**[3942A]**; words omitted from sub-para (d) revoked by the Consumer Credit (Miscellaneous Amendments) Regulations 2004, SI 2004/2619, reg 4.

Para (3): added by SI 2010/1010, regs 77, 80(b), as from 1 February 2011, with effect in relation to certain agreements before that date, as provided for in regs 100–101A of the 2010 Regulations at **[3941]**–**[3942A]**.

4   Calculation of the amount of rebate

[(A1)   This regulation provides for the calculation of the amount of the rebate where early settlement takes place as provided in regulation 2(1A)(a) or (c) and the debtor pays the amount or sum by the time specified in regulation 5(1).]

(1)   The amount of the rebate is the difference between the total amount of the repayments of credit that would fall due for payment after the settlement date if early settlement did not take place and the amount given by the following formula—

$$\sum_{i=1}^{m} A_i (1+r)^{a_i} \text{ minus } \sum_{j=1}^{n} B_j (1+r)^{b_j}$$

where:

A_i = the amount of the *ith* advance of credit,

B_j = the amount of the *jth* repayment of credit,

r = the periodic rate equivalent of the APR/100,

m = the number of advances of credit made before the settlement date,

n = the number of repayments of credit made before the settlement date,

a_i = the time between the *ith* advance of credit and the settlement date, expressed in periods,

b_j = the time between the *jth* repayment of credit and the settlement date, expressed in periods, and

Σ represents the sum of all the terms indicated.

(2) In calculating the rebate, where the creditor so elects, any repayment of credit [not] made at a time or a rate *other than that* provided for in the agreement [(other than one made under section 94(3) of the Act)] shall be taken to have been made at the time or rate provided for.

(3) *The examples set out in the Schedule to these Regulations have effect for the purpose of illustrating the calculation provided for in paragraph (1); in the case of conflict between any example and any other provision of these Regulations, that other provision shall prevail.*

[3392]

NOTES

Para (A1): inserted by the Consumer Credit (EU Directive) Regulations 2010, SI 2010/1010, regs 77, 81(a), as from 1 February 2011, with effect in relation to certain agreements before that date, as provided for in regs 100–101A of the 2010 Regulations at **[3941]–[3942A]**.

Para (2): words in square brackets inserted and words in italics revoked by SI 2010/1010, regs 77, 81(b), as from 1 February 2011, with effect in relation to certain agreements before that date, as provided for in regs 100–101A of the 2010 Regulations at **[3941]–[3942A]**.

Para (3): revoked by SI 2010/1010, regs 77, 81(c), as from 1 February 2011, with effect in relation to certain agreements before that date, as provided for in regs 100–101A of the 2010 Regulations at **[3941]–[3942A]**.

[4A   Calculation of the amount of rebate (indebtedness discharged in part)

(1) This regulation provides for the calculation of the amount of the rebate where early settlement takes place as provided in regulation 2(1A)(b) and the debtor pays the amount by the time specified in regulation 5(2).

(2) The amount of the rebate is the amount given by the following formula—

$$F - K - P$$

where:

F = the total amount of repayments of credit that would fall due for payment after the settlement date if early settlement did not take place,

K = the total amount of repayments of credit that will fall due for payment after the settlement date if early settlement takes place; in calculating K—

(i)   the amount of the credit outstanding from the debtor and the amount of the accrued charges remaining unpaid by the debtor under the agreement on the settlement date if early settlement takes place are to be determined in accordance with the formula given in regulation 4(1), and

(ii)   the amount paid by the debtor to the creditor where early settlement takes place shall be treated as though it were reduced by the amount (if any) which the creditor may claim under section 95A(2) of the Act,

and

P = the amount paid by the debtor to the creditor where early settlement takes place.

(3) In calculating the rebate, where the creditor so elects, any repayment of credit not made at a time or a rate provided for in the agreement (other than one made under section 94(3) of the Act) shall be taken to have been made at the time or rate provided for.]

[3392A]

NOTES

Commencement: 1 February 2011.

Inserted by the Consumer Credit (EU Directive) Regulations 2010, SI 2010/1010, regs 77, 82, as from 1 February 2011, with effect in relation to certain agreements before that date, as provided for in regs 100–101A of the 2010 Regulations at **[3941]–[3942A]**.

5 Settlement date

[(1)] The settlement date for calculation of the rebate [in regulation 4] shall be taken to be—

(a)   where the debtor has given notice under *section 94* [section 94(1)] of the Act with a view to discharging his indebtedness under the agreement, the date falling 28 days after the date on which the notice was received by the creditor, or any later date specified as the date of early settlement in the notice, if the debtor pays the amount in question (less any rebate allowable under these Regulations) not later than that date;

(b)   the date specified as the date for payment of any sum by the debtor involving early settlement in any notice served under section 76(1) of the Act, any default notice or any notice served under section 98(1), if the debtor pays the amount in question (less any rebate allowable under these Regulations) not later than that date;

(c)   in any other case, the date on which the debtor pays any sum involving early settlement.

[(2)   The settlement date for the calculation of the rebate in regulation 4A shall be taken to be the date falling 28 days after the date on which the notice under section 94(4)(a) of the Act was received by the creditor, or any later date specified as the date of early settlement in the notice, if the debtor pays the amount in question not later than that date.]

[3393]

NOTES

Para (1): original provision renumbered as such, words in first pair of square brackets inserted and words in italics in sub-para (a) substituted by subsequent words in square brackets, by the Consumer Credit (EU Directive) Regulations 2010, SI 2010/1010, regs 77, 83(a), (b), as from 1 February 2011, with effect in relation to certain agreements before that date, as provided for in regs 100–101A of the 2010 Regulations at **[3941]–[3942A]**.

Para (2): added by SI 2010/1010, regs 77, 83(c), as from 1 February 2011, with effect in relation to certain agreements before that date, as provided for in regs 100–101A of the 2010 Regulations at **[3941]–[3942A]**.

6 Deferment of settlement date

Where the agreement provides for the credit to be repaid over, or at the end of, a period which is more than a year after the relevant date, the settlement date for calculation of the rebate may be deferred by—

(a)   one month, or

(b)   where the length of a month's deferment would be more or less than 30 days and the creditor so elects, 30 days.

[3394]

7 Variation of rates and amounts

Where, under a power contained in the agreement, the rate or amount of any item included in the total charge for credit, the amount of any instalment of repayment of credit or the time fixed by the agreement for the debtor's indebtedness to be discharged is or can be varied, the rate or amount, as the case may be, of any item to be included in the total charge for credit or the amount of any instalment of repayment of credit or the time fixed by the agreement for the debtor's indebtedness to be discharged for the purpose of calculation of the rebate shall be taken to be, in respect of any period of time commencing on or after the settlement date, the rate or amount or time subsisting at that date.

[3395]

8 Revocation of Regulations

Subject to regulation 10, the Consumer Credit (Rebate on Early Settlement) Regulations 1983 are revoked.

[3396]

9 Amendment of Regulations

(1)   Subject to regulation 10, the Consumer Credit (Settlement Information) Regulations 1983 are amended as follows.

(2)   In regulation 3 (which determines the settlement date to be taken for the purposes of the Regulations)—

(a)   paragraph (1) (which applies in the case of an agreement for credit to be repaid in instalments) is omitted, and

(b)   in paragraph (2) (which applies in all other cases), the words "Where paragraph (1) does not apply" are omitted.

(3)   In regulation 4 (which prescribes the number of working days within which a creditor is required to respond to a request for a statement indicating the amount required to discharge a debt), for "12" there is substituted "7".

(4)   In paragraph 7(a) of the Schedule (which provides for the statement to indicate, where any rebate is due, that the rebate has been calculated having regard to Regulations), for "the Consumer Credit (Rebate on Early Settlement) Regulations 1983" there is substituted "the Consumer Credit (Early Settlement) Regulations 2004".

[3397]

10 Savings

(1)   The Regulations referred to in regulation 8 continue to apply, in place of regulations 1–7 of these Regulations, and the amendments in regulation 9 do not apply, in the case of a regulated consumer credit agreement entered into before the date on which these Regulations come into force—

(a)   until 31st May 2007, if the agreement is for a term of 10 years or less;

(b)   until 31st May 2010, if the agreement is for a term of more than 10 years.

(2)   For the purposes of paragraph (1), the term of an agreement is the term originally provided for, or, in the case where the term was varied before the date on which these Regulations are made, the term provided for on that date.

[3398]

SCHEDULE
EXAMPLES ILLUSTRATING USE OF FORMULA FOR CALCULATING REBATE
Regulation 4(3)

Example 1—medium term, medium value loan

A loan of £5,000 is repayable by 48 monthly instalments of £134.57, starting one month after the relevant date. The monthly repayments include interest and all other charges included in the total charge for credit. Thus the total amount repayable = £134.57 x 48 = £6,459.36. The total charge for credit = £6,459.36 – £5,000 = £1,459.36.

The creditor receives notice from the debtor requesting early settlement immediately after payment of the 12th instalment (ie after one year).

Assuming that no charges are excluded from the calculation of the rebate under regulation 3(2), the APR on the loan required for the calculation of the rebate is 14% per annum.

The creditor opts to calculate the rebate using periods of one month, giving a period rate equivalent of the APR = $(1.14^{(1/12)} – 1)$ x 100 = 1.0979% per month. Hence, for the purposes of the formula in regulation 4(1)—

$A_1 = 5,000$

$B_1 = 134.57 = B_2 = \ldots . = B_{48}$

$r = 1.0979/100 = 0.010979$

$m = 1$

$n = 12$

$a_1 = 12$ (working in periods of 1 month)

$b_1 = 11$

$b_2 = 10$

$b_3 = 9$

$\vdots$

$b_{11} = 1$

$b_{12} = 0$

Then the loan outstanding immediately after payment of the12th instalment as calculated by the formula in regulation 4(1) is—

$5,000 \times (1.010979)^{12} – (134.57 \times 1.010979^{11} + 134.57 \times 1.010979^{10} + \ldots . + 134.57 \times 1.010979^1 + 134.57 \times 1.010979^0;)$

$= 5,700.01 – (151.74 + 150.10 + 148.47 + 146.85 + 145.26 + 143.68 + 142.12 + 140.58 + 139.05 + 137.54 + 136.05 + 134.57)$

$= 5,700.01 – 1,716.01 = £3,984.00.$

If regulation 5(a) applies (making the settlement date 28 days after the debtor's notice is received) no further payments will be due; thus the amount outstanding at the settlement date is—

$£3,984.00 \times 1.010979^{(28/30)} = £4,024.81.$

(this assumes that there are 30 days between the date for the 12th instalment and the 13th instalment; for months of 31 days, the amount outstanding would be

$£3,984.00 \times 1.010979^{(28/31)} = £4,023.49.)$

If the creditor elects to defer the settlement date by a further month under regulation 6, this makes the date for calculating the rebate the 28th day after the payment date for the 13th instalment.

For the calculation using the formula in regulation 4(1)—

$n = 13$

$a_1 = 13$ (working in periods of 1 month)

$b_1 = 12$

$b_2 = 11$

$b_3 = 10$

$b_{12} = 1$

$b_{13} = 0$

Then the loan outstanding to be repaid immediately after payment of the 13th instalment as calculated by the formula in regulation 4(1) is—

$5,000 \times (1.010979)^{13} - (134.57 \times 1.010979^{12} + 134.57 \times 1.010979^{11} + \ldots + 134.57 \times 1.0109791 + 134.57 \times 1.010979^0)$

$= 5,762.59 - (153.41 + 151.74 + 150.10 + 148.47 + 146.85 + 145.26 + 143.68 + 142.12 + 140.58$
$= 139.05 + 137.54 + 136.05 + 134.57)$

$= 5,762.59 - 1,869.42 = £3,893.17.$

The formula gives an amount outstanding after payment of the 13th instalment of £3,893.17. The amount outstanding at the settlement date is £3,893.17 $\times$ 1.010979$^{(28/30)}$ = £3,933.05 (assuming that the period between the 13th and 14th instalment dates is 30 days).

The debtor will also have to pay the instalment due between the date of request for early settlement and the settlement date assumed for calculating the rebate (i e the 13th repayment of £134.57).

Hence the total amount to be paid at the settlement date (which is 58 days after the date of request for early settlement) is £4,067.62.

For this example, the rebate would be £776.90; this is calculated by deducting the early settlement figure of £3,933.05 from the total payments outstanding after the date assumed for calculating the rebate, which is £4,709.95 (= 35 x £134.57).

NB If the period between the 13th and 14th instalments were 31 days, the amount outstanding would be £3,893.17 $\times$ 1.010979$^{(28/31)}$ = £3,931.76 and the total amount still to be repaid would be £4,066.33. Other adjustments may be appropriate where the lender opted to choose the period of deferment as 30 days. In this case the settlement date for calculating the rebate would be 58 days after the date on which notice was received).

Example 2—longer term, high value loan

A loan of £10,000 is repayable by 180 monthly instalments of £139.51 starting one month after the relevant date. The monthly repayments include interest and all other charges included in the total charge for credit.

Thus total amount repayable = £139.51 x 180 = £25,111.80. The total charge for credit = £25,111.80 – £10,000 = £15,111.80.

The creditor receives notice from the borrower requesting early settlement immediately after payment of the 72nd instalment (i e after six years).

Assuming that no charges are excluded from the calculation of the rebate under regulation 3(2), the APR on the loan required for the calculation of the rebate is 16% per annum.

The creditor opts to calculate the rebate using periods of one month, giving a period rate equivalent of the APR = (1.16$^{(1/12)}$ – 1) x 100 = 1.2445% per month. The creditor also opts to defer the settlement date for 30 days under regulation 6, so that the settlement date for the purposes of calculating the rebate is the 28th day after the payment date of the 73rd instalment. Hence, for the purposes of the formula in regulation 4(1)—

$A_1 = 10,000$

$B_1 = 139.51 = B_2 = \ldots . = B_{180}$

$r = 1.2445/100 = 0.012445$

$m = 1$

$n = 73$

$a_1 = 73$ *(working in periods of 1 month)*

$b_1 = 72$

$b_2 = 71$

$b_3 = 70$

$:$

$b_{71} = 1$

$b_{72} = 0$

Then the loan outstanding to be repaid immediately after payment of the 73rd instalment as calculated by the formula in regulation 4(1) is—

$10,000 \times (1.012445)^{73} - (139.51 \times 1.012445^{72} + 139.51 \times 1.012445^{71} + \ldots . + 139.51 \times 1.012445^1 + 139.51 \times 1.012445^0)$

$= 24,363.72 - (339.90 + 335.72 + \ldots . + 141.25 + 139.51)$

$= 24,666.93 - 16,441.81 = £8,225.12$

The amount outstanding at the settlement date is then—

$£8,225.12 \times 1.012445^{(28/30)}) = £8,320.62$

(assuming that the period between the 72nd and 73rd instalments is 30 days or the creditor has opted for an additional deferment period of 30 days). The debtor will also have to pay the instalment due between the date of request for early repayment and the settlement date assumed for calculating the rebate (i e the 73rd repayment of £139.51).

Hence the total amount to be paid at the settlement date (which is 28 days after the date of request for early repayment) is £8,460.13.

NB If the period between the 72nd and 73rd instalments were not 30 days, the amount outstanding would be slightly different.)

For this example, the rebate is £6,606.95; this is calculated by deducting the early settlement figure of £8,320.62 from the total payments outstanding after the date assumed for calculating the rebate which is £14,927.57 (= 107 x £139.51).

[3399]

NOTES

Schedule revoked by the Consumer Credit (EU Directive) Regulations 2010, SI 2010/1010, regs 77, 84, as from 1 February 2011, with effect in relation to certain agreements before that date, as provided for in regs 100–101A of the 2010 Regulations at **[3941]**–**[3942A]**.

CONSUMER CREDIT (ADVERTISEMENTS) REGULATIONS 2004

(SI 2004/1484)

NOTES

Made: 5 June 2004.
Authority: Consumer Credit Act 1974, ss 44, 151(1), 182(2), 189(1).
Commencement: 31 October 2004.

ARRANGEMENT OF REGULATIONS

1 Citation, commencement and interpretation

(1) These Regulations may be cited as the Consumer Credit (Advertisements) Regulations 2004, and shall come into force on 31st October 2004.

(2) In these Regulations—

"the Act" means the Consumer Credit Act 1974;

"advance payment" does not include a repayment of credit or any insurance premium or any amount entering into the total charge for credit;

"APR" means the annual percentage rate of charge for credit determined in accordance with the Total Charge for Credit Regulations and Schedule 1 to these Regulations;

"authorised deposit taker" means—

    (a)   a person who has permission under Part 4 of the Financial Services and Markets Act 2000 to accept deposits, or

    (b)   an EEA firm of the kind mentioned in paragraph 5(b) of Schedule 3 to that Act which has permission under paragraph 15 of that Schedule (as a result of qualifying for authorisation under paragraph 12(1)) to accept deposits, but sub-paragraph (a) does not include a person who is a credit union within the meaning of the Credit Unions Act 1979 or the Credit Unions (Northern Ireland) Order 1985, or a specially authorised friendly society within the meaning of section 7(1)(f) of the Friendly Societies Act 1974;

"cash price" in relation to any goods, services, land or other things means the price or charge at which the goods, services, land or other things may be purchased by, or supplied to, persons for cash, account being taken of any discount generally available from the dealer or supplier in question;

"cash purchaser" means, in relation to any advertisement, a person who, for a money consideration—

    (a)   acquires goods, land or other things, or

    (b)   is provided with services,

    under a transaction which is not financed by credit;

"credit advertisement" means an advertisement to which Part 4 of the Act applies by virtue of it falling within section 43(1)(a), or which falls within section 151(1) of the Act in so far as section 44 is applied to such an advertisement;

"current account" means an account under which the customer may, by means of cheques or similar orders payable to himself or to any other person or by any other means, obtain or have the use of money held or made available by the person with whom the account is kept and which records alterations in the financial relationship between the said person and the customer;

"dealer" means, in relation to a hire-purchase, credit sale or conditional sale agreement under which he is not the creditor, a person who sells or proposes to sell goods, land or other things to the creditor before they form the subject matter of any such agreement and, in relation to any other agreement, means a supplier or his agent;

.....

"identified dealer" means, in relation to an advertisement—

    (a)   a dealer who is named in the advertisement or is identified in it by reference to a business connection he has with the advertiser, or

    (b)   a dealer upon whose premises the advertisement is published;

"premises" includes any place, stall, vehicle, aircraft or hovercraft at which a person is carrying on any business (whether on a permanent or temporary basis);

"relevant date", in relation to an advertisement relating to credit to be provided under a consumer credit agreement, means—

    (a)   in a case where a date is specified in or determinable under the agreement at the date of its making as that on which the debtor is entitled to require provision of anything the subject of the agreement, the earliest such date, and

    (b)   in any other case, the date of the making of the agreement;

"supplier" has the meaning assigned to it by section 189(1) of the Act, except that it does not include, in relation to a hire-purchase, credit sale or conditional sale agreement, a creditor to whom goods, land or other things are sold or proposed to be sold by a dealer before becoming the subject matter of such an agreement;

"the total charge for credit" means the total charge for credit determined in accordance with the Total Charge for Credit Regulations and Schedule 1 to these Regulations;

"the Total Charge for Credit Regulations" means the Consumer Credit (Total Charge for Credit) Regulations 1980, and

["the typical APR" is an APR at or below which the advertiser reasonably expects, at the date on which the advertisement is published, that credit would be provided under at least 66% of the agreements which will be entered into as a result of the advertisement. In the case of an advertisement which falls within section 151(1) of the Act, "advertiser" means the person carrying on the business of credit brokerage].

(3)   The definition of "authorised deposit taker" in paragraph (2) must be read with—

    (a)   section 22 of the Financial Services and Markets Act 2000;

    (b)   any relevant order under that section; and

    (c)   Schedule 2 to that Act.

(4)   In these Regulations as they apply to Scotland—

    (a)   any reference to bailment is a reference to hiring;

    (b)   any reference to a mortgage or charge on land, or any other security on land, is a reference to a standard security over land within the meaning of the Conveyancing and Feudal Reform (Scotland) Act 1970.

(5)   In these Regulations, references to repayment of credit are references to repayment of credit with or without any other amount.

(6)   In these Regulations, any reference to the name of any person is—

    (a)   in the case of any person covered by a standard licence, a reference to any name of his specified in the licence; and

(b)   in the case of any other person, a reference to any name under which he carries on business.

(7)   Where any expression is used in these Regulations and in the Act, for the purposes of these Regulations that expression shall be construed as if, in the Act (except section 8), references to consumer credit agreements and to regulated agreements (being consumer credit agreements) included references to personal credit agreements.

[3400]

NOTES
Para (2): definitions "hire advertisement" and "hire payment" (omitted) revoked by the Consumer Protection from Unfair Trading Regulations 2008, SI 2008/1277, reg 30(1), (3), Sch 2, Pt 2, para 108(1), (2), Sch 4; definition "the typical APR" substituted by the Consumer Credit (Advertisements) (Amendment) Regulations 2007, SI 2007/827, reg 2(1), (2).

[1A Application

These Regulations apply to a credit advertisement in so far as it relates to a regulated consumer credit agreement secured on land.]

[3400A]

NOTES
Commencement: 1 February 2011.
Inserted by the Consumer Credit (EU Directive) Regulations 2010, SI 2010/1010, regs 70, 72 (as amended by the Consumer Credit (Amendment) Regulations 2010, SI 2010/1969, regs 4, 23), as from 1 February 2011, with effect in relation to certain agreements before that date, as provided for in regs 101, 101A of SI 2010/1010 at **[3942]**, **[3942A]**.

2 Duty to comply

A person who causes a credit advertisement ... to be published shall ensure that the advertisement complies with all applicable requirements of these Regulations.

[3401]

NOTES
Words omitted revoked by the Consumer Protection from Unfair Trading Regulations 2008, SI 2008/1277, reg 30(1), (3), Sch 2, Pt 2, para 108(1), (3), Sch 4.

3 General requirements

Every credit advertisement ... shall—
  (a)   use plain and intelligible language;
  (b)   be easily legible (or, in the case of any information given orally, clearly audible), and
  (c)   specify the name of the advertiser.

[3402]

NOTES
Words omitted revoked by the Consumer Protection from Unfair Trading Regulations 2008, SI 2008/1277, reg 30(1), (3), Sch 2, Pt 2, para 108(1), (4), Sch 4.

4 Content of advertisements

(1)   Where a credit advertisement includes any of the amounts referred to in paragraphs 5 to 7 of Schedule 2 to these Regulations ... the advertisement shall also—
  (a)   include all the other items of information (other than any item inapplicable to the particular case) listed in the relevant Schedule, and
  (b)   specify a postal address at which the advertiser may be contacted, except—
      (i)   in the case of advertisements published by means of television or radio broadcast;
      (ii)   in the case of advertisements in any form on the premises of a dealer or creditor (not being advertisements in writing which customers are intended to take away);
      (iii)   in the case of advertisements which include the name and address of a dealer, and
      (iv)   in the case of advertisements which include the name and a postal address of a credit-broker.

(2)   The items of information listed in Schedule 2 ... shall be given equal prominence and shall be shown together as a whole.

(3)   Any information in any book, catalogue, leaflet or other document which is likely to vary from time to time shall be taken for the purpose of paragraph (2) to be shown together as a whole if—
  (a)   it is set out together as a whole in a separate document issued with the book, catalogue, leaflet or other document;

(b)   the other information in the credit advertisement … is shown together as a whole in the book, catalogue, leaflet or other document, and

(c)   the book, catalogue, leaflet or other document identifies the separate document in which the information likely to vary is set out.

[3403]

NOTES

Words omitted revoked by the Consumer Protection from Unfair Trading Regulations 2008, SI 2008/1277, reg 30(1), (3), Sch 2, Pt 2, para 108(1), (5), Sch 4.

5   Credit advertisements in dealers' publications covering a calendar or seasonal period

(1)   Regulation 4 shall not apply to a credit advertisement contained in, or in a separate document issued with, a publication published by or on behalf of a dealer which relates to goods or services which may be sold or supplied by him in a calendar or seasonal period specified in the publication if the advertisement contains the information specified in paragraph (2) and no other indication that a person is willing to provide credit.

(2)   The information referred to in paragraph (1) is—

(a)   the name of the creditor, credit-broker or dealer and a postal address of his with or without his occupation or a statement of the general nature of his occupation, and

(b)   an indication that individuals may obtain on request details of the terms on which the advertiser is prepared to do business.

[3404]

6   Advertisements in dealers' publications relating to credit under a debtor-creditor-supplier agreement

Information contained in a credit advertisement relating to credit to be provided under a debtor-creditor-supplier agreement, being an advertisement contained in a publication published by or on behalf of a dealer which relates to goods or services which may be sold or supplied by him, shall be taken for the purpose of regulation 4(2) to be shown together as a whole if—

(a)   the advertisement clearly indicates—

    (i)   the cash price alone, or

    (ii)   the cash price, any advance payment and the information specified in paragraphs 5 to 7 of Schedule 2, and (except in the case of agreements for credit under which the total amount payable by the debtor is not greater than the cash price of the goods or services the acquisition of which is to be financed by the credit under the agreement) the APR,

in close proximity to every description of, or specific reference to, goods or services to which the information in the publication relates, and

(b)   the remaining information in the advertisement is so presented as to be readily comprehensible as a whole by a prospective debtor and an indication is given in close proximity to any of that information that it relates to all or specified descriptions of goods or services, and

(c)   except as mentioned in paragraph (a), no information relating to the provision of credit is shown together with the cash price.

[3405]

7   Security

(1)   Where the subject-matter of a credit advertisement … is a facility for which security is or may be required, the advertisement shall—

(a)   state that security is or may be required, and

(b)   specify the nature of the security.

(2)   Where, in the case of a credit advertisement, the security comprises or may comprise a mortgage or charge on the debtor's home—

(a)   except where sub-paragraph (c) applies, the advertisement shall contain a warning in the form—

"YOUR HOME MAY BE REPOSSESSED IF YOU DO NOT KEEP UP REPAYMENTS ON A MORTGAGE OR ANY OTHER DEBT SECURED ON IT";

(b)   where the advertisement indicates that credit is available for the payment of debts due to other creditors, the warning in sub-paragraph (a) shall be preceded by the words—

"THINK CAREFULLY BEFORE SECURING OTHER DEBTS AGAINST YOUR HOME."

(c)   where the credit agreement is or would be an agreement of a kind described in paragraph (3), the advertisement shall contain a warning in the form—

"CHECK THAT THIS MORTGAGE WILL MEET YOUR NEEDS IF YOU WANT TO MOVE OR SELL YOUR HOME OR YOU WANT YOUR FAMILY TO INHERIT IT. IF YOU ARE IN ANY DOUBT, SEEK INDEPENDENT ADVICE".

(3)   The kinds of agreement referred to in paragraph (2)(c) are—

(a)   any credit agreement under which no instalment repayments secured by the mortgage on the debtor's home, and no payment of interest on the credit (other than interest charged when all or part of the credit is repaid voluntarily by the debtor), are due or capable of becoming due while the debtor continues to occupy the mortgaged land as his main residence; and

(b)   any credit agreement—

(i)   which is secured by a mortgage which the creditor cannot enforce by taking possession of or selling (or concurring with any other person in selling) the mortgaged land or any part of it while the debtor continues to occupy it as his main residence, and

(ii)   under which, although interest payments may become due, no full or partial repayment of the credit secured by the mortgage is due or capable of becoming due while the debtor continues to occupy the mortgaged land as his main residence.

(4)   Where a credit advertisement is for a mortgage or other loan secured on property and repayments are to be made in a currency other than sterling, the advertisement shall contain a warning in the form—

"CHANGES IN THE EXCHANGE RATE MAY INCREASE THE STERLING EQUIVALENT OF YOUR DEBT".

(5)   ...

(6)   The warnings provided for in paragraphs (2) and (4)—

(a)   shall be given greater prominence in a credit advertisement than is given to—

(i)   any rate of charge other than the typical APR, or

(ii)   any indication or incentive of a kind referred to in regulation 8(1)(c) or (d), and

(b)   shall be given no less prominence in a credit advertisement than is given to any of the items listed in Schedule 2 to these Regulations that appear in the advertisement.

(7)   ...

(8)   [Paragraphs (2), (3), (4) and (6)] do not apply in the case of an advertisement which—

(a)   is published by means of television or radio broadcast in the course of programming the primary purpose of which is not advertising;

(b)   is published by exhibition of a film (other than exhibition by television broadcast), or

(c)   contains only the name of the advertiser.

[3406]

NOTES

Para (1): words omitted revoked by the Consumer Protection from Unfair Trading Regulations 2008, SI 2008/1277, reg 30(1), (3), Sch 2, Pt 2, para 108(1), (6)(a), Sch 4.

Paras (5), (7): revoked by SI 2008/1277, reg 30(1), (3), Sch 2, Pt 2, para 108(1), (6)(b), (c), Sch 4.

Para (8): words in square brackets substituted by SI 2008/1277, reg 30(1), (3), Sch 2, Pt 2, para 108(1), (6)(d).

---

8   APR

(1)   A credit advertisement shall specify the typical APR if the advertisement—

(a)   specifies any other rate of charge;

(b)   includes any of the items of information listed in paragraphs 5 to 7 of Schedule 2 to these Regulations;

(c)   indicates in any way, including by means of the name given to a business or of an address used by a business for the purposes of electronic communication, that—

(i)   credit is available to persons who might otherwise consider their access to credit restricted, or

(ii)   any of the terms on which credit is available is more favourable (either in relation to a limited period or generally) than corresponding terms applied in any other case or by any other creditors, or

(d)   includes any incentive to apply for credit or to enter into an agreement under which credit is provided.

(2)   A credit advertisement may not indicate the range of APRs charged where credit is provided otherwise than by specifying, with equal prominence, both—

(a)   the APR which the advertiser reasonably expects, at the date on which the advertisement is published, would be the lowest APR at which credit would be provided under not less than 10% of the agreements [which will be entered] into as a result of that advertisement, and

(b)   the APR which the advertiser reasonably expects, at that date, would be the highest APR at which credit would be provided under any of the agreements [which will be entered] into as a result of that advertisement.

(3)   An APR shall be denoted in an advertisement as "%APR".

(4)　Where an APR is subject to change, it shall be accompanied by the word "variable".

(5)　The typical APR shall be—
- (a)　accompanied by the word "typical";
- (b)　presented together with any of the items listed in Schedule 2 that are included in the advertisement;
- (c)　given greater prominence in the advertisement than—
  - (i)　any other rate of charge;
  - (ii)　any of the items listed in Schedule 2, and
  - (iii)　any indication or incentive of a kind referred to in paragraph (1)(c) or (d), and
- (d)　in the case of an advertisement in printed or electronic form which includes any of the items listed in Schedule 2, shown in characters at least one and a half times the size of the characters in which those items appear.

(6)　In the case of an advertisement relating to a debtor-creditor agreement enabling the debtor to overdraw on a current account under which the creditor is the Bank of England or an authorised deposit taker, there may be substituted for the typical APR a reference to the statement of—
- (a)　a rate, expressed to be a rate of interest, being a rate determined as the rate of the total charge for credit calculated on the assumption that only interest is included in the total charge for credit, and
- (b)　the nature and amount of any other charge included in the total charge for credit.

[3407]

NOTES

Para (2): words in square brackets substituted by the Consumer Credit (Advertisements) (Amendment) Regulations 2007, SI 2007/827, reg 2(1), (3).

9　Restrictions on certain expressions in credit advertisements

(1)　A credit advertisement shall not include—
- (a)　the word "overdraft" or any similar expression as describing any agreement for running-account credit except an agreement enabling the debtor to overdraw on a current account;
- (b)　the expression "interest free" or any similar expression indicating that a customer is liable to pay no greater amount in respect of a transaction financed by credit than he would be liable to pay as a cash purchaser in relation to the like transaction, except where the total amount payable by the debtor does not exceed the cash price;
- (c)　the expression "no deposit" or any similar expression, except where no advance payments are to be made;
- (d)　the expression "loan guaranteed" or "pre-approved" or any similar expression, except where the agreement is free of any conditions regarding the credit status of the debtor, or
- (e)　the expression "gift", "present" or any similar expression except where there are no conditions which would require the debtor to return the credit or items that are the subject of the claim.

(2)　A credit advertisement shall not include in relation to any repayment of credit … the expression "weekly equivalent" or any expression to the like effect or any expression of any other periodical equivalent, unless weekly payments or the other periodical payments are provided for under the agreement.

[3408]

NOTES

Para (2): words omitted revoked by the Consumer Protection from Unfair Trading Regulations 2008, SI 2008/1277, reg 30(1), (3), Sch 2, Pt 2, para 108(1), (6), Sch 4.

10　Exclusions

(1)　These Regulations do not apply to any advertisement which—
- (a)　whether expressly or by implication indicates clearly that a person is willing—
  - (i)　to provide credit, or
  - (ii)　to enter into an agreement for the bailment of goods,
  for the purposes of another person's business, and
- (b)　does not indicate (whether expressly or by implication) that a person is willing to do either of those things otherwise than for the purposes of such a business.

(2)　References in paragraph (1) to a business do not include references to a business carried on by the advertiser or any person acting as a credit-broker in relation to the credit or hire facility to which the advertisement relates.

(3)　These Regulations do not apply to any advertisement in so far as it is a communication of an invitation or inducement to engage in investment activity within the meaning of section 21 of the Financial Services and Markets Act 2000, other than an exempt generic communication.

(4) An "exempt generic communication" is a communication to which subsection (1) of section 21 of the Financial Services and Markets Act does not apply, as a result of an order under subsection (5) of that section, because it does not identify a person as providing an investment or as carrying on an activity to which the communication relates.

[(5) These regulations do not apply to any advertisement in so far as it is a communication of an invitation or inducement to enter into—
- (a) a regulated mortgage contract within the meaning of article 61 of the Financial Services and Markets Act (Regulated Activities) Order 2001; or
- (b) a regulated home purchase plan within the meaning of article 63F of that Order.]

[3409]

NOTES

Para (5): substituted by the Financial Services and Markets Act 2000 (Regulated Activities) (Amendment) (No 2) Order 2006, SI 2006/2383, art 34, subject to transitional provisions in arts 37–39 of that Order.

11 (*Revokes the Consumer Credit (Advertisements) Regulations 1989, SI 1989/1125, the Consumer Credit (Content of Quotations) and Consumer Credit (Advertisements) (Amendment) Regulations 1999, SI 1999/2725, Pt III and the Consumer Credit (Advertisements and Content of Quotations) (Amendment) Regulations 2000, SI 2000/1797, reg 2.*)

12 Transitional provisions

(1) Subject to paragraph (2), a person shall not be guilty of an offence under section 47(1) or 167 of the Act for contravention of these Regulations in the case of an advertisement that would have complied with the requirements of the Consumer Credit (Advertisements) Regulations 1989 if those Regulations had not been revoked by these Regulations.

(2) Paragraph (1) only applies to advertisements published in a catalogue, diary or work of reference comprising at least 50 printed pages—
- (a) copies of which are first published, or made available for publication in the ordinary course of business, before 31st May 2005, and
- (b) which, in a reasonably prominent position either contains the date of its first publication or specifies a period, being a calendar or seasonal period, throughout which it is intended to have effect.

[3410]

SCHEDULE 1
PROVISIONS RELATING TO CALCULATION AND DISCLOSURE OF THE TOTAL CHARGE FOR CREDIT AND ANY APR
Regulation 1(2)

1 Assumptions about running-account credit

In the case of an advertisement relating to running-account credit, the following assumptions shall have effect for the purpose of calculating the total charge for credit and any APR, notwithstanding the terms of the transaction advertised and in place of any assumptions in Part 4 of the Total Charge for Credit Regulations that might otherwise apply—
- (a) the amount of the credit to be provided shall be taken to be £1,500, or, in a case where credit is to be provided subject to a credit limit of less than £1,500, an amount equal to that limit;
- (b) it shall be assumed that the credit is provided for a period of one year beginning with the relevant date;
- (c) it shall be assumed that the credit is provided in full on the relevant date;
- (d) where the rate of interest will change at a time provided in the transaction within a period of three years beginning with the relevant date, the rate shall be taken to be the highest rate at any time obtaining under the transaction in that period;
- (e) where the agreement provides credit to finance the purchase of goods, services, land or other things and also provides one or more of—
  - (i) cash loans
  - (ii) credit to refinance existing indebtedness of the debtor's, whether to the creditor or another person; and
  - (iii) credit for any other purpose,
  and either or both different rates of interest and different charges are payable in relation to the credit provided for all or some of these purposes, it shall be assumed that the rate of interest and charges payable in relation to the whole of the credit are those applicable to the provision of credit for the purchase of goods, services land or other things;
- (f) it shall be assumed that the credit is repaid—
  - (i) in twelve equal instalments, and
  - (ii) at monthly intervals, beginning one month after the relevant date.

2   Permissible tolerances in disclosure of an APR

For the purposes of these Regulations, it shall be sufficient compliance with the requirement to show an APR if there is included in the advertisement—

    (a)   a rate which exceeds the APR by not more than one, or

    (b)   a rate which falls short of the APR by not more than 0.1,

or in a case to which paragraph 3 or 4 of this Schedule applies, a rate determined in accordance with those paragraphs or whichever of them applies to that case.

3   Tolerance where repayments are nearly equal

In the case of an agreement under which all repayments but one are equal and that one repayment does not differ from any other repayment by more whole pence than there are repayments of credit, there may be included in an advertisement relating to the agreement a rate found under regulation 7 of the Total Charge for Credit Regulations as if that one repayment were equal to the other repayments to be made under the agreement.

4   Tolerance where interval between relevant date and first repayment is greater than interval between repayments

In the case of an agreement under which—

    (a)   three or more repayments are to be made at equal intervals, and

    (b)   the interval between the relevant date and the first repayment is greater than the interval between the repayments,

there may be included in the advertisement relating to the agreement a rate found under regulation 7 of the Total Charge for Credit Regulations as if the interval between the relevant date and the first repayment were shortened so as to be equal to the interval between repayments.

[3411]

SCHEDULE 2
INFORMATION TO BE CONTAINED IN A CREDIT ADVERTISEMENT
Regulations 4(1), 7(6), 8(1) [and (5)]

1   Amount of credit

The amount of credit which may be provided under a consumer credit agreement or an indication of one or both of the maximum amount and the minimum amount of credit which may be provided.

2   Deposit of money in an account

A statement of any requirement to place on deposit any sum of money in any account with any person.

3   Cash price

In the case of an advertisement relating to credit to be provided under a debtor-creditor-supplier agreement, where the advertisement specifies goods, services, land or other things having a particular cash price, the acquisition of which from an identified dealer may be financed by the credit, the cash price of such goods, services, land or other things.

4   Advance payment

A statement as to whether an advance payment is required and if so the amount or minimum amount of the payment expressed as a sum of money or a percentage.

5   Frequency, number and amount of repayments of credit

    (1)   In the case of an advertisement relating to running-account credit, a statement of the frequency of the repayments of credit under the advertised transaction and of the amount of each repayment stating whether it is a fixed or minimum amount, or a statement indicating the manner in which the amount will be determined.

    (2)   In the case of other credit advertisements, a statement of the frequency, number and amounts of repayments of credit.

    (3)   The amount of any repayment under this paragraph may be expressed as a sum of money or as a specified proportion of a specified amount (including the amount outstanding from time to time).

6   Other payments and charges

    (1)   Subject to sub-paragraphs (2) and (3) below, a statement indicating the description and amount of any other payments and charges which may be payable under the transaction advertised.

    (2)   Where the liability of the debtor to make any payment cannot be ascertained at the date the advertisement is published, a statement indicating the description of the payment in question and the circumstances in which the liability to make it will arise.

(3)   Sub-paragraphs (1) and (2) above do not apply to any charge payable under the transaction to the creditor or any other person on his behalf upon failure by the debtor or a relative of his to do or refrain from doing anything which he is required to do or refrain from doing, as the case may be.

[7   Total amount payable by the debtor

In the case of an advertisement relating to fixed-sum credit to be provided under a consumer credit agreement which is repayable at specified intervals or in specified amounts and other than cases under which the sum of the payments within sub-paragraphs (a) to (c) below is not greater than the cash price referred to in paragraph 3, the total amount payable by the debtor, being the total of—
  (a)   advance payments;
  (b)   the amount of credit repayable by the debtor, and
  (c)   the amount of the total charge for credit.]

[3412]

NOTES
  Enabling provision: words in square brackets substituted by the Consumer Credit (Miscellaneous Amendments) Regulations 2004, SI 2004/2619, reg 3(1), (2).
  Para 7: substituted by SI 2004/2619, reg 3(1), (3).

(Sch 3 revoked by the Consumer Protection from Unfair Trading Regulations 2008, SI 2008/1277, reg 30(1), (3), Sch 2, Pt 2, para 108(1), (8), Sch 4.)

FINANCIAL SERVICES (DISTANCE MARKETING) REGULATIONS 2004

(SI 2004/2095)

NOTES
  Made: 4 August 2004.
  Authority: European Communities Act 1972, s 2(2).
  Commencement: 31 October 2004.

ARRANGEMENT OF REGULATIONS

1   Citation, commencement and extent

These Regulations may be cited as the Financial Services (Distance Marketing) Regulations 2004 and come into force on 31st October 2004.

[3413]

2   Interpretation

  (1)   In these Regulations—
    "the 1974 Act" means the Consumer Credit Act 1974;

"the 2000 Act" means the Financial Services and Markets Act 2000;

"the Authority" means the Financial Services Authority;

"appointed representative" has the same meaning as in section 39(2) of the 2000 Act (exemption of appointed representatives);

["authorised non-business overdraft agreement" has the same meaning as in section 189 of the 1974 Act;]

"authorised person" has the same meaning as in section 31(2) of the 2000 Act (authorised persons);

"breach" means a contravention by a supplier of a prohibition in, or a failure by a supplier to comply with a requirement of, these Regulations;

"business" includes a trade or profession;

"consumer" means any individual who, in contracts to which these Regulations apply, is acting for purposes which are outside any business he may carry on;

["consumer credit agreement" has the same meaning as in section 189 of the 1974 Act;]

"court" in relation to England and Wales and Northern Ireland means a county court or the High Court, and in relation to Scotland means the Sheriff Court or the Court of Session;

"credit" includes a cash loan and any other form of financial accommodation, and for this purpose "cash" includes money in any form;

"designated professional body" has the same meaning as in section 326(2) of the 2000 Act (designation of professional bodies);

"the Directive" means Directive 2002/65/EC of the European Parliament and of the Council of 23 September 2002 concerning the distance marketing of consumer financial services and amending Council Directive 90/619/EEC and Directives 97/7/EC and 98/27/EC;

["the Disclosure of Information Regulations" means the Consumer Credit (Disclosure of Information) Regulations 2010;]

"distance contract" means any contract concerning one or more financial services concluded between a supplier and a consumer under an organised distance sales or service-provision scheme run by the supplier or by an intermediary, who, for the purpose of that contract, makes exclusive use of one or more means of distance communication up to and including the time at which the contract is concluded;

"durable medium" means any instrument which enables a consumer to store information addressed personally to him in a way accessible for future reference for a period of time adequate for the purposes of the information and which allows the unchanged reproduction of the information stored;

["the European Consumer Credit Information form" means the form set out in schedule 3 to the Disclosure of Information Regulations;]

"EEA supplier" means a supplier who is a national of an EEA State, or a company or firm (within the meaning of Article 48 of the Treaty establishing the European Community) formed in accordance with the law of an EEA State;

["EEA State" has the meaning given by Schedule 1 to the Interpretation Act 1978;]

"exempt regulated activity" has the same meaning as in section 325(2) of the 2000 Act;

"financial service" means any service of a banking, credit, insurance, personal pension, investment or payment nature;

"means of distance communication" means any means which, without the simultaneous physical presence of the supplier and the consumer, may be used for the marketing of a service between those parties;

"the OFT" means the Office of Fair Trading;

"regulated activity" has the same meaning as in section 22 of the 2000 Act (the classes of activity and categories of investment);

"Regulated Activities Order" means the Financial Services and Markets Act 2000 (Regulated Activities) Order 2001;

["regulated consumer credit agreement" means a consumer credit agreement regulated by the 1974 Act;]

"rule" means a rule—

    (a)   made by the Authority under the 2000 Act, or

    (b)   made by a designated professional body, and approved by the Authority, under section 332 of the 2000 Act,

    as the context requires;

"supplier" means any person who, acting in his commercial or professional capacity, is the contractual provider of services.

(2)   In these Regulations, subject to paragraph (1), any expression used in these Regulations which is also used in the Directive has the same meaning as in the Directive.

[3414]

NOTES

Para (1): definitions "authorised non-business overdraft agreement", "consumer credit agreement", "the Disclosure of Information Regulations", "the European Consumer Credit Information form" and "regulated consumer credit agreement" inserted by the Consumer Credit (EU Directive) Regulations 2010, SI 2010/1010, regs 85, 86, as from 1 February 2011, with effect in relation to certain agreements before that date, as provided for in regs 101, 101A of the 2010 Regulations at **[3942]**, **[3942A]**; definition "EEA State" substituted by the Financial Services (EEA State) Regulations 2007, SI 2007/108, reg 10.

3   Scope of these Regulations

(1)   Regulations 7 to 14 apply, subject to regulations 4 and 5, in relation to distance contracts made on or after 31st October 2004.

(2)   Regulation 15 applies in relation to financial services supplied on or after 31st October 2004 under an organised distance sales or service-provision scheme run by the supplier or by an intermediary, who, for the purpose of that supply, makes exclusive use of one or more means of distance communication up to and including the time at which the financial services are supplied.

[3415]

4—(1)   Where an EEA State, other than the United Kingdom, has transposed the Directive or has obligations in its domestic law corresponding to those provided for in the Directive—

(a)   regulations 7 to 14 do not apply in relation to any contract made between an EEA supplier contracting from an establishment in that EEA State and a consumer in the United Kingdom, and

(b)   regulation 15 does not apply to any supply of financial services by an EEA supplier from an establishment in that EEA State to a consumer in the United Kingdom,

if the provisions by which that State has transposed the Directive, or the obligations in the domestic law of that State corresponding to those provided for in the Directive, as the case may be, apply to that contract or that supply.

(2)   Subject to paragraph (5) and regulation 6(3) and (4)—

(a)   regulations 7 to 11 do not apply in relation to any contract made by a supplier who is an authorised person, the making or performance of which constitutes or is part of a regulated activity carried on by him;

(b)   regulation 15 does not apply to any supply of financial services by a supplier who is an authorised person, where that supply constitutes or is part of a regulated activity carried on by him.

(3)   Subject to regulation 6(3) and (4)—

(a)   regulations 7 and 8 do not apply in relation to any contract made by a supplier who is an appointed representative, the making or performance of which constitutes or is part of a regulated activity (other than an exempt regulated activity) carried on by him;

(b)   regulation 15 does not apply to any supply of financial services by a supplier who is an appointed representative, where that supply constitutes or is part of a regulated activity (other than an exempt regulated activity) carried on by him.

(4)   Subject to regulation 6(3) and (4)—

(a)   regulations 7 and 8 do not apply in relation to any contract where—

(i)   the supplier is bound, or is controlled or managed by one or more persons who are bound, by rules of a designated professional body which are equivalent to those regulations, and

(ii)   the making or performance of that contract constitutes or is part of an exempt regulated activity carried on by the supplier;

(b)   regulation 15 does not apply to any supply of financial services where—

(i)   the supplier is bound, or is controlled or managed by one or more persons who are bound, by rules of a designated professional body which are equivalent to that regulation, and

(ii)   that supply constitutes or is part of an exempt regulated activity carried on by the supplier.

(5)   Paragraph (2) does not apply in relation to any contract or supply of financial services made by a supplier who is the operator, trustee or depositary of a scheme which is a recognised scheme by virtue of section 264 of the 2000 Act (schemes constituted in other EEA States), where the making or performance of the contract or the supply of the financial services constitutes or is part of a regulated activity for which he has permission in that capacity.

(6)   In paragraph (5)—

"the operator", "trustee" and "depositary" each has the same meaning as in section 237(2) of the 2000 Act (other definitions); and

"permission" has the same meaning as in section 266 of that Act (disapplication of rules).

[3416]

5—(1)   Where a consumer and a supplier enter an initial service agreement and—

(a)   successive operations of the same nature, or

(b)   a series of separate operations of the same nature,

are subsequently performed between them over time and within the framework of that agreement, then, if any of regulations 7 to 14 apply, they apply only to the initial service agreement.

(2)   Where a consumer and a supplier do not enter an initial service agreement and—
   (a)   successive operations of the same nature, or
   (b)   a series of separate operations of the same nature,

are performed between them over time, then, if regulations 7 and 8 apply, they apply only—
      (i)   when the first operation is performed, and
     (ii)   to any operation which is performed more than one year after the previous operation.

(3)   For the purposes of this regulation, "initial service agreement" includes, for example, an agreement for the provision of—
   (a)   a bank account;
   (b)   a credit card; or
   (c)   portfolio management services.

(4)   For the purposes of this regulation, "operations" includes, for example—
   (a)   deposits to or withdrawals from a bank account;
   (b)   payments by a credit card;
   (c)   transactions carried out within the framework of an initial service agreement for portfolio management services; and
   (d)   subscriptions to new units of the same collective investment fund,

but does not include adding new elements to an existing initial service agreement, for example adding the possibility of using an electronic payment instrument together with an existing bank account.

[3417]

6   Financial services marketed by an intermediary

(1)   This regulation applies where a financial service is marketed by an intermediary.

(2)   These Regulations have effect as if—
   (a)   each reference to a supplier in the definition of "breach" in regulation 2(1) were a reference to a supplier or an intermediary;
   (b)   the reference to the supplier in the definition of "means of distance communication" in regulation 2(1), each reference to the supplier in regulations 7, 8(1) and (2), 10 and 11(3)(b), and the first reference to the supplier in regulation 8(4), were a reference to the intermediary;
   (c)   the reference to the supplier in regulation 8(3) were a reference to the supplier or the intermediary;
   (d)   for regulation 11(2) there were substituted—

"(2)   Paragraph (1) does not apply to a distance contract if the intermediary has not complied with regulation 8(1) (and the supplier has not done what the intermediary was required to do by regulation 8(1)), unless—
   (a)   the circumstances fall within regulation 8(1)(b); and
   (b)   either—
      (i)   the intermediary has complied with regulation 7(1) and (2) or, if applicable, regulation 7(4)(b), and with regulation 7(5), or
     (ii)   the supplier has done what the intermediary was required to do by regulation 7(1) and (2) or, if applicable, regulation 7(4)(b), and by regulation 7(5).";

   (e)   the reference to a supplier in regulation 22(1) were a reference to an intermediary; and
   (f)   each reference to the supplier in paragraphs 2, 4, 5 and 19 of Schedule 1 were a reference to the supplier and the intermediary.

(3)   Notwithstanding paragraphs (2) to (4) of regulation 4, regulations 7 and 8 apply in relation to the intermediary unless—
   (a)   the intermediary is an authorised person and the marketing of the financial service constitutes or is part of a regulated activity carried on by him;
   (b)   the intermediary is an appointed representative and the marketing of the financial service constitutes or is part of a regulated activity (other than an exempt regulated activity) carried on by him; or
   (c)   the intermediary is not an authorised person, but—
      (i)   he is bound, or is controlled or managed by one or more persons who are bound, by rules of a designated professional body which are equivalent to regulations 7 and 8, and
     (ii)   the marketing of the financial service constitutes or is part of an exempt regulated activity carried on by him.

(4) Notwithstanding paragraphs (2) to (4) of regulation 4, regulation 15 applies to the intermediary unless—

  (a) the intermediary is an authorised person and is acting in the course of a regulated activity carried on by him;

  (b) the intermediary is an appointed representative and is acting in the course of a regulated activity (other than an exempt regulated activity) carried on by him; or

  (c) the intermediary is not an authorised person, but—

  (i) he is bound, or is controlled or managed by one or more persons who are bound, by rules of a designated professional body which are equivalent to regulation 15, and

  (ii) he is acting in the course an exempt regulated activity carried on by him.

[3418]

7 Information required prior to the conclusion of the contract

(1) Subject to *[paragraphs (1A) and (4)]* [paragraphs (1A), (4), (6) and (7)], in good time prior to the consumer being bound by any distance contract, the supplier shall provide to the consumer the information specified in Schedule 1.

[(1A) Where a distance contract to which paragraph (1) applies is also a contract for payment services to which the Payment Services Regulations 2009 apply, the supplier is required to provide to the consumer only the information specified in paragraphs 8 to 13, 16, 17 and 21 of Schedule 1.]

(2) The supplier shall provide the information specified in Schedule 1 in a clear and comprehensible manner appropriate to the means of distance communication used, with due regard in particular to the principles of good faith in commercial transactions and the principles governing the protection of those who are unable to give their consent such as minors.

(3) Subject to paragraph (4), the supplier shall make clear his commercial purpose when providing the information specified in Schedule 1.

(4) In the case of a voice telephone communication—

  (a) the supplier shall make clear his identity and the commercial purpose of any call initiated by him at the beginning of any conversation with the consumer; and

  (b) if the consumer explicitly consents, only the information specified in Schedule 2 need be given.

(5) The supplier shall ensure that the information he provides to the consumer pursuant to this regulation, regarding the contractual obligations which would arise if the distance contract were concluded, accurately reflects the contractual obligations which would arise under the law presumed to be applicable to that contract.

[(6) This regulation shall not apply to a distance contract which is also a consumer credit agreement (other than an authorised non-business overdraft agreement) in respect of which the supplier has disclosed the pre-contract credit information required by regulations 3, 4 or 5, as the case may be, and 7, of the Disclosure of Information Regulations (information to be disclosed to a debtor before a regulated consumer credit agreement is made) in accordance with those Regulations.

(7) This regulation shall not apply to a distance contract which is also an authorised non-business overdraft agreement in respect of which—

  (a) the supplier has disclosed the information required by regulation 10(2) of the Disclosure of Information Regulations (authorised non-business overdraft agreements) by means of the European Consumer Credit Information form in accordance with those Regulations; or

  (b) in the case of a voice telephone communication, the supplier has—

  (i) disclosed the information required by regulation 10(5) of the Disclosure of Information Regulations in accordance with those Regulations; and

  (ii) provided a copy of the written agreement in accordance with section 61B(2)(b) of the Consumer Credit Act 1974; or

  (c) in the case of an agreement made using a means of distance communication, other than voice telephone communication, such that the supplier is unable to provide the information required by regulation 10(2) of the Disclosure of Information Regulations, the supplier has—

  (i) provided a copy of the written agreement in accordance with section 61B(2)(c) of the Consumer Credit Act 1974, and

  (ii) in relation to the contractual obligations which would arise if the distance contract were concluded, provided information which accurately reflects the contractual obligations which would arise under the law presumed to be applicable to that contract.]

[3419]

NOTES

Para (1): words in italics (as substituted by the Payment Services Regulations 2009, SI 2009/209, reg 126, Sch 6, Pt 2, para 5(a)(i)) further substituted by subsequent words in square brackets, by the Consumer Credit (EU

Directive) Regulations 2010, SI 2010/1010, regs 85, 87(a), as from 1 February 2011, with effect in relation to certain agreements before that date, as provided for in regs 101, 101A of the 2010 Regulations at **[3942]**, **[3942A]**.

Para (1A): inserted by SI 2009/209, reg 126, Sch 6, Pt 2, para 5(a)(ii).

Paras (6), (7): added by SI 2010/1010, regs 85, 87(b), as from 1 February 2011, with effect in relation to certain agreements before that date, as provided for in regs 101, 101A of the 2010 Regulations at **[3942]**, **[3942A]**.

8   Written and additional information

(1)   [Subject to *paragraph (1A)* [paragraphs (1A) to (1C)],] the supplier under a distance contract shall communicate to the consumer on paper, or in another durable medium which is available and accessible to the consumer, all the contractual terms and conditions and the information specified in Schedule 1, either—

   (a)   in good time prior to the consumer being bound by that distance contract; or
   (b)   immediately after the conclusion of the contract, where the contract has been concluded at the consumer's request using a means of distance communication which does not enable provision in accordance with sub-paragraph (a) of the contractual terms and conditions and the information specified in Schedule 1.

[(1A)   Where a distance contract to which paragraph (1) applies is also a contract for payment services to which the Payment Services Regulations 2009 apply, the supplier is required to communicate to the consumer all the contractual terms and conditions and the information specified in paragraphs 8 to 13, 16, 17 and 21 of Schedule 1.]

[(1B)   Paragraph (1) shall not apply to a distance contract which is also a consumer credit agreement (other than an authorised non-business overdraft agreement) in respect of which the supplier has disclosed the pre-contract credit information required by regulations 3, 4 or 5, as the case may be, and 7 of the Disclosure of Information Regulations in accordance with those Regulations.

(1C)   Paragraph (1) shall not apply to a distance contract which is also an authorised non-business overdraft agreement in respect of which—

   (a)   the supplier has—
       (i)   disclosed the information required by regulation 10(2) of the Disclosure of Information Regulations (authorised non-business overdraft agreements) by means of the European Consumer Credit Information form in accordance with those Regulations; and
       (ii)   provided a copy of the contractual terms and conditions, or
   (b)   in the case of a voice telephone communication the supplier has—
       (i)   disclosed the information required by regulation 10(5) of the Disclosure of Information Regulations in accordance with those Regulations; and
       (ii)   provided a copy of the written agreement in accordance with section 61B(2)(b) of the Consumer Credit Act 1974; or
   (c)   in the case of an agreement made using a means of distance communication, other than voice telephone communication, such that the supplier is unable to provide the information required by regulation 10(2) of the Disclosure of Information Regulations, the supplier has provided a copy of the written agreement in accordance with section 61B(2)(c) of the Consumer Credit Act 1974.]

(2)   The supplier shall communicate the contractual terms and conditions to the consumer on paper, if the consumer so requests at any time during their contractual relationship.

(3)   Paragraph (2) does not apply if the supplier has already communicated the contractual terms and conditions to the consumer on paper during that contractual relationship, and those terms and conditions have not changed since they were so communicated.

(4)   The supplier shall change the means of distance communication with the consumer if the consumer so requests at any time during his contractual relationship with the supplier, unless that is incompatible with the distance contract or the nature of the financial service provided to the consumer.

[3420]

NOTES

Para (1): words in first (outer) pair of square brackets inserted by the Payment Services Regulations 2009, SI 2009/209, reg 126, Sch 6, Pt 2, para 5(b)(i); words in italics substituted by subsequent words in square brackets, by the Consumer Credit (EU Directive) Regulations 2010, SI 2010/1010, regs 85, 88(a), as from 1 February 2011, with effect in relation to certain agreements before that date, as provided for in regs 101, 101A of the 2010 Regulations at **[3942]**, **[3942A]**.

Para (1A): inserted by SI 2009/209, reg 126, Sch 6, Pt 2, para 5(b)(ii).

Paras (1B), (1C): inserted by SI 2010/1010, regs 85, 88(b), as from 1 February 2011, with effect in relation to certain agreements before that date, as provided for in regs 101, 101A of the 2010 Regulations at **[3942]**, **[3942A]**.

9 Right to cancel

(1) Subject to regulation 11, if within the cancellation period set out in regulation 10 notice of cancellation is properly given by the consumer to the supplier, the notice of cancellation shall operate to cancel the distance contract.

(2) Cancelling the contract has the effect of terminating the contract at the time at which the notice of cancellation is given.

(3) For the purposes of these Regulations, a notice of cancellation is a notification given—
- (a) orally (where the supplier has informed the consumer that notice of cancellation may be given orally),
- (b) in writing, or
- (c) in another durable medium available and accessible to the supplier,

which, however expressed, indicates the intention of the consumer to cancel the contract by that notification.

(4) Notice of cancellation given under this regulation by a consumer to a supplier is to be treated as having been properly given if the consumer—
- (a) gives it orally to the supplier (where the supplier has informed the consumer that notice of cancellation may be given orally);
- (b) leaves it at the address of the supplier last known to the consumer and addressed to the supplier by name (in which case it is to be taken to have been given on the day on which it was left);
- (c) sends it by post to the address of the supplier last known to the consumer and addressed to the supplier by name (in which case it is to be taken to have been given on the day on which it was posted);
- (d) sends it by facsimile to the business facsimile number of the supplier last known to the consumer (in which case it is to be taken to have been given on the day on which it was sent);
- (e) sends it by electronic mail to the business electronic mail address of the supplier last known to the consumer (in which case it is to be taken to have been given on the day on which it is sent); or
- (f) by other electronic means—
  - (i) sends it to an internet address or web-site which the supplier has notified the consumer may be used for the purpose, or
  - (ii) indicates it on such a web-site in accordance with instructions which are on the web-site or which the supplier has provided to the consumer,
  - (in which case it is to be taken to have been given on the day on which it is sent to that address or web-site or indicated on that web-site).

(5) The references in paragraph (4)(b) and (c) to the address of the supplier shall, in the case of a supplier which is a body corporate, be treated as including a reference to the address of the secretary or clerk of that body.

(6) The references in paragraph (4)(b) and (c) to the address of the supplier shall, in the case of a supplier which is a partnership, be treated as including a reference to the address of a partner or a person having control or management of the partnership business.

(7) In this regulation—
- (a) every reference to the supplier includes a reference to any other person previously notified by or on behalf of the supplier to the consumer as a person to whom notice of cancellation may be given;
- (b) the references to giving notice of cancellation orally include giving such notice by voice telephone communication, where the supplier has informed the consumer that notice of cancellation may be given in that way; and
- (c) "electronic mail" has the same meaning as in regulation 2(1) of the Privacy and Electronic Communications (EC Directive) Regulations 2003 (interpretation).

[3421]

10 Cancellation period

(1) For the purposes of regulation 9, the cancellation period begins on the day on which the distance contract is concluded ("conclusion day") and ends as provided for in paragraphs (2) to (5).

(2) Where the supplier complies with regulation 8(1) on or before conclusion day, the cancellation period ends on the expiry of fourteen calendar days beginning with the day after conclusion day.

(3) Where the supplier does not comply with regulation 8(1) on or before conclusion day, but subsequently communicates to the consumer on paper, or in another durable medium which is available and accessible to the consumer, all the contractual terms and conditions and the

information required under regulation 8(1), the cancellation period ends on the expiry of fourteen calendar days beginning with the day after the day on which the consumer receives the last of those terms and conditions and that information.

(4)   In the case of a distance contract relating to life insurance, for the references to conclusion day in paragraphs (2) and (3) there are substituted references to the day on which the consumer is informed that the distance contract has been concluded.

(5)   In the case of a distance contract relating to life insurance or a personal pension, for the references to fourteen calendar days in paragraphs (2) and (3) there are substituted references to thirty calendar days.

[3422]

11   Exceptions to the right to cancel

(1)   Subject to paragraphs (2) and (3), regulation 9 does not confer on a consumer a right to cancel a distance contract which is—

    (a)   a contract for a financial service where the price of that service depends on fluctuations in the financial market outside the supplier's control, which may occur during the cancellation period, such as services related to—

        (i)   foreign exchange,

        (ii)   money market instruments,

        (iii)   transferable securities,

        (iv)   units in collective investment undertakings,

        (v)   financial-futures contracts, including equivalent cash-settled instruments,

        (vi)   forward interest-rate agreements,

        (vii)   interest-rate, currency and equity swaps,

        (viii)   options to acquire or dispose of any instruments referred to in sub-paragraphs (i) to (vii), including cash-settled instruments and options on currency and on interest rates;

    (b)   a contract whose performance has been fully completed by both parties at the consumer's express request before the consumer gives notice of cancellation;

    (c)   a contract which—

        (i)   is a connected contract of insurance within the meaning of article 72B(1) of the Regulated Activities Order (activities carried on by a provider of relevant goods or services),

        (ii)   covers travel risks within the meaning of article 72B(1)(d)(ii) of that Order, and

        (iii)   has a total duration of less than one month;

    (d)   a contract under which a supplier provides credit to a consumer and the consumer's obligation to repay is secured by a legal mortgage on land;

    (e)   a credit agreement cancelled under regulation 15(1) of the Consumer Protection (Distance Selling) Regulations 2000 (automatic cancellation of a related credit agreement);

    (f)   a credit agreement cancelled under section 6A of the Timeshare Act 1992 (automatic cancellation of timeshare credit agreement); or

    (g)   a restricted-use credit agreement (within the meaning of the 1974 Act) to finance the purchase of land or an existing building, or an agreement for a bridging loan in connection with the purchase of land or an existing building;

    [(h)   a regulated consumer credit agreement within the meaning of the 1974 Act to which the right of withdrawal applies under section 66A of that Act.]

(2)   Paragraph (1) does not apply to a distance contract if the supplier has not complied with regulation 8(1), unless—

    (a)   the circumstances fall within regulation 8(1)(b); and

    (b)   the supplier has complied with regulation 7(1) and (2) or, if applicable, regulation 7(4)(b), and with regulation 7(5).

(3)   Where—

    (a)   the conditions in sub-paragraphs (a) and (b) of paragraph (2) are satisfied in relation to a distance contract falling within paragraph (1),

    (b)   the supplier has not complied with regulation 8(1), and

    (c)   the consumer has not, by the end of the sixth day after the day on which the distance contract is concluded, received all the contractual terms and conditions and the information required under regulation 8(1),

the consumer may cancel the contract under regulation 9 during the period beginning on the seventh day after the day on which the distance contract is concluded and ending when he receives the last of the contractual terms and conditions and the information required under regulation 8(1).

[3423]

NOTES

Para (1): sub-para (h) added by the Consumer Credit (EU Directive) Regulations 2010, SI 2010/1010, regs 85, 89, as from 1 February 2011, with effect in relation to certain agreements before that date, as provided for in regs 101, 101A of the 2010 Regulations at **[3942]**, **[3942A]**.

12   Automatic cancellation of an attached distance contract

(1)   For the purposes of this regulation, where there is a distance contract for the provision of a financial service by a supplier to a consumer ("the main contract") and there is a further distance contract ("the secondary contract") for the provision to that consumer of a further financial service by—

    (a)   the same supplier, or

    (b)   a third party, the further financial service being provided pursuant to an agreement between the third party and the supplier under the main contract,

then the secondary contract (referred to in these Regulations as an "attached contract") is attached to the main contract if any of the conditions in paragraph (2) are satisfied.

(2)   The conditions referred to in paragraph (1) are—

    (a)   the secondary contract is entered into in compliance with a term of the main contract;

    (b)   the main contract is, or is to be, financed by the secondary contract;

    (c)   the main contract is a debtor-creditor-supplier agreement within the meaning of the 1974 Act, and the secondary contract is, or is to be, financed by the main contract;

    (d)   the secondary contract is entered into by the consumer to induce the supplier to enter into the main contract;

    (e)   performance of the secondary contract requires performance of the main contract.

(3)   Where a main contract is cancelled by a notice of cancellation given under regulation 9—

    (a)   the cancellation of the main contract also operates to cancel, at the time at which the main contract is cancelled, any attached contract which is not a contract or agreement of a type listed in regulation 11(1); and

    (b)   the supplier under the main contract shall, if he is not the supplier under the attached contract, forthwith on receipt of the notice of cancellation inform the supplier under the attached contract.

(4)   Paragraph (3)(a) does not apply to an attached contract if, at or before the time at which the notice of cancellation in respect of the main contract is given, the consumer has given and not withdrawn a notice to the supplier under the main contract that cancellation of the main contract is not to operate to cancel that attached contract.

(5)   Where a main contract made by an authorised person, the making or performance of which constitutes or is part of a regulated activity carried on by him, is cancelled under rules made by the Authority corresponding to regulation 9—

    (a)   the cancellation of the main contract also operates to cancel, at the time at which the main contract is cancelled, any attached contract which is not a contract or agreement of a type listed in regulation 11(1); and

    (b)   the supplier under the main contract shall, if he is not the supplier under the attached contract, inform the supplier under the attached contract forthwith on receiving notification of the consumer's intention to cancel the main contract by that notification.

(6)   Paragraph (5)(a) does not apply to an attached contract if, at or before the time at which the consumer gives notification of his intention to cancel the main contract by that notification, the consumer has given and not withdrawn a notice to the supplier under the main contract that cancellation of the main contract is not to operate to cancel that attached contract.

                                                                                   [3424]

13   Payment for services provided before cancellation

(1)   This regulation applies where a cancellation event occurs in relation to a distance contract.

(2)   In this regulation, "cancellation event" means the cancellation of a distance contract under regulation 9 or 12.

(3)   The supplier shall refund any sum paid by or on behalf of the consumer under or in relation to the contract to the person by whom it was paid, less any charge made in accordance with paragraph (6), as soon as possible and in any event within a period not exceeding 30 calendar days beginning with—

    (a)   the day on which the cancellation event occurred; or

    (b)   if the supplier proves that this is later—

        (i)   in the case of a contract cancelled under regulation 9, the day on which the supplier in fact received the notice of cancellation, or

        (ii)   in the case of an attached contract under which the supplier is not the supplier under the main contract, the day on which, pursuant to regulation 12(3)(b) or (5)(b), he was in fact informed by the supplier under the main contract of the cancellation of the main contract.

(4)   The reference in paragraph (3) to any sum paid on behalf of the consumer includes any sum paid by any other person ("the creditor"), who is not the supplier, under an agreement between the consumer and the creditor by which the creditor provides the consumer with credit of any amount.

(5)   Where any security has been provided in relation to the contract, the security (so far as it has been provided) shall, on cancellation under regulation 9 or 12, be treated as never having had effect; and any property lodged solely for the purposes of the security as so provided shall be returned forthwith by the person with whom it is lodged.

(6)   Subject to paragraphs (7), (8) and (9), the supplier may make a charge for any service actually provided by the supplier in accordance with the contract.

(7)   The charge shall not exceed an amount which is in proportion to the extent of the service provided to the consumer prior to the time at which the cancellation event occurred (including the service of arranging to provide the financial service) in comparison with the full coverage of the contract, and in any event shall not be such that it could be construed as a penalty.

(8)   The supplier may not make any charge unless he can prove on the balance of probabilities that the consumer was informed about the amount payable in accordance with—
(a)   regulation 7(1) and paragraph 13 of Schedule 1,
(b)   regulation 7(4) and paragraph 5 of Schedule 2, or
(c)   rules corresponding to those provisions,
as the case may be.

(9)   The supplier may not make any charge if, without the consumer's prior request, he commenced performance of the contract prior to the expiry of the relevant cancellation period.

(10)   In paragraph (9), the relevant cancellation period is the cancellation period which—
(a)   in the case of a main contract, is applicable to that contract, or
(b)   in the case of an attached contract, would be applicable to that contract if that contract were a main contract,
under regulation 10, or under rules corresponding to that regulation, as the case may be.

(11)   The consumer shall, as soon as possible and in any event within a period not exceeding 30 calendar days beginning with the day on which the cancellation event occurred—
(a)   refund any sum paid by or on behalf of the supplier under or in relation to that contract to the person by whom it was paid; and
(b)   either restore to the supplier any property of which he has acquired possession under that contract, or deliver or send that property to any person to whom, under regulation 9, a notice of cancellation could have been given in respect of that contract.

(12)   Breach of a duty imposed by paragraph (11) on a consumer is actionable as a breach of statutory duty.

[3425]–[3426]

14   (*Revoked by the Payment Services Regulations 2009, SI 2009/209, reg 126, Sch 6, Pt 2, para 5(c).*)

15   Unsolicited services

(1)   A person ("the recipient") who receives unsolicited financial services for purposes other than those of his business from another person who supplies those services in the course of his business, shall not thereby become subject to any obligation (to make payment, or otherwise).

(2), (3)   …

(4)   In this regulation, "unsolicited" means, in relation to financial services supplied to any person, that they are supplied without any prior request made by or on behalf of that person.

(5)–(7)   …

(8)   This regulation is without prejudice to any right a supplier may have at any time, by contract or otherwise, to renew a distance contract with a consumer without any request made by or on behalf of that consumer prior to the renewal of that contract.

[3427]

NOTES
Paras (2), (3), (5)–(7): revoked by the Consumer Protection from Unfair Trading Regulations 2008, SI 2008/1277, reg 30(1), (3), Sch 2, Pt 2, para 110(1), (2), Sch 4.

PART 2
STATUTORY INSTRUMENTS

16 Prevention of contracting-out

(1)   A term contained in any contract is void if, and to the extent that, it is inconsistent with the application of a provision of these Regulations to a distance contract or the application of regulation 15 to a supply of unsolicited financial services.

(2)   Where a provision of these Regulations specifies a duty or liability of the consumer in certain circumstances, a term contained in a contract is inconsistent with that provision if it purports to impose, directly or indirectly, an additional or greater duty or liability on him in those circumstances.

(3)   These Regulations apply notwithstanding any contract term which applies or purports to apply the law of a State which is not an EEA State if the contract or supply has a close connection with the territory of an EEA State.

[3428]

17 Enforcement authorities

(1)   For the purposes of regulations 18 to 21—
  (a)   in relation to any alleged breach concerning a specified contract, the Authority is the enforcement authority;
  (b)   in relation to any alleged breach concerning a contract under which the supplier is a local authority, but which is not a specified contract, the OFT is the enforcement authority;
  (c)   in relation to any other alleged breach—
    (i)   the OFT, and
    (ii)   in Great Britain every local weights and measures authority, and in Northern Ireland the Department of Enterprise, Trade and Investment,
  is an enforcement authority.

(2)   For the purposes of paragraph (1) and regulation 22(6), each of the following is a specified contract—
  (a)   a contract the making or performance of which constitutes or is part of a regulated activity carried on by the supplier;
  (b)   a contract for the provision of a debit card;
  (c)   a contract relating to the issuing of electronic money by a supplier to whom the Authority has given a certificate under article 9C of the Regulated Activities Order (persons certified as small issuers etc);
  (d)   a contract the effecting or carrying out of which is excluded from article 10(1) or (2) of the Regulated Activities Order (effecting and carrying out contracts of insurance) by article 12 of that order (breakdown insurance), where the supplier is a person who does not otherwise carry on an activity of the kind specified by article 10 of that order;
  (e)   a contract under which a supplier provides credit to a consumer and the obligation of the consumer to repay is secured by a first legal mortgage on land;
  (f)   a contract, made before 14th January 2005, for insurance mediation activity other than in respect of a contract of long-term care insurance.

(3)   For the purposes of the application of this regulation and regulations 18 to 22 in relation to breaches of, and offences under, regulation 15, "contract"—
  (a)   wherever it appears in this regulation other than in the expression "contract of long-term care insurance", and
  (b)   in regulation 22(6),
is to be taken to mean "supply of financial services".

(4)   For the purposes of this regulation—
  "contract of long-term care insurance" has the same meaning as in the Financial Services and Markets Act 2000 (Regulated Activities) (Amendment) (No 2) Order 2003;
  "insurance mediation activity" means any activity which is not a regulated activity at the time the contract is made but will be a regulated activity of the kind specified by article 21, 25(1) or (2), 39A or 53 of the Regulated Activities Order when the amendments to that order made by the Financial Services and Markets Act 2000 (Regulated Activities) (Amendment) (No 2) Order 2003 come into force;
  "local authority" means—
    (a)   in England and Wales, a local authority within the meaning of the Local Government Act 1972, the Greater London Authority, the Common Council of the City of London or the Council of the Isles of Scilly,
    (b)   in Scotland, a council constituted under section 2 of the Local Government etc (Scotland) Act 1994, and
    (c)   in Northern Ireland, a district council within the meaning of the Local Government Act (Northern Ireland) 1972.

[3429]

18   Consideration of complaints

(1)   An enforcement authority shall consider any complaint made to it about a breach unless—

    (a)   the complaint appears to that authority to be frivolous or vexatious; or

    (b)   that authority is aware that another enforcement authority has notified the OFT that it agrees to consider the complaint.

(2)   If an enforcement authority notifies the OFT that it agrees to consider a complaint made to another enforcement authority, the first mentioned authority shall be under a duty to consider the complaint.

[3430]

19   Injunctions to secure compliance with these Regulations

(1)   Subject to paragraph (2), an enforcement authority may apply for an injunction (including an interim injunction) against any person who appears to that authority to be responsible for a breach.

(2)   An enforcement authority, other than the OFT or the Authority, may apply for an injunction only where—

    (a)   that authority has notified the OFT, at least fourteen days before the date on which the application is to be made, of its intention to apply; or

    (b)   the OFT consents to the application being made within a shorter period.

(3)   On an application made under this regulation, the court may grant an injunction on such terms as it thinks fit to secure compliance with these Regulations.

(4)   An enforcement authority which has a duty under regulation 18 to consider a complaint shall give reasons for its decision to apply or not to apply, as the case may be, for an injunction.

(5)   In deciding whether or not to apply for an injunction in respect of a breach, an enforcement authority may, if it considers it appropriate to do so, have regard to any undertaking as to compliance with these Regulations given to it or to another enforcement authority by or on behalf of any person.

(6)   In the application of this regulation to Scotland, for references to an "injunction" or an "interim injunction" there are substituted references to an "interdict" or an "interim interdict" respectively.

[3431]

20   Notification of undertakings and orders to the OFT

An enforcement authority, other than the OFT and the Authority, shall notify the OFT of—

    (a)   any undertaking given to it by or on behalf of any person who appears to it to be responsible for a breach;

    (b)   the outcome of any application made by it under regulation 19 and the terms of any undertaking given to, or order made by, the court; and

    (c)   the outcome of any application made by it to enforce a previous order of the court.

[3432]

21   Publication, information and advice

(1)   The OFT shall arrange for the publication, in such form and manner as it considers appropriate, of details of any undertaking or order notified to it under regulation 20.

(2)   Each of the OFT and the Authority shall arrange for the publication in such form and manner as it considers appropriate of—

    (a)   details of any undertaking as to compliance with these Regulations given to it by or on behalf of any person;

    (b)   details of any application made by it under regulation 19, and of the terms of any undertaking given to, or order made by, the court; and

    (c)   details of any application made by it to enforce a previous order of the court.

(3)   Each of the OFT and the Authority may arrange for the dissemination, in such form and manner as it considers appropriate, of such information and advice concerning the operation of these Regulations as may appear to it to be expedient to give to the public and to all persons likely to be affected by these Regulations.

[3433]

22   Offences

(1)   A supplier under a distance contract who fails to comply with regulation 7(3) or (4)(a) or regulation 8(2) or (4) is guilty of an offence and liable, on summary conviction, to a fine not exceeding level 3 on the standard scale.

(2)   If an offence under paragraph (1) … committed by a body corporate is shown—

    (a)   to have been committed with the consent or connivance of any director, manager, secretary or other similar officer of the body corporate, or any person who was purporting to act in any such capacity, or

PART 2
STATUTORY INSTRUMENTS

(b)   to be attributable to any neglect on his part,

he as well as the body corporate is guilty of the offence and liable to be proceeded against and punished accordingly.

(3)   If the affairs of a body corporate are managed by its members, paragraph (2) applies in relation to the acts and defaults of a member in connection with his functions of management as if he were a director of the body.

(4)   If an offence under paragraph (1) … committed by a partnership is shown—

    (a)   to have been committed with the consent or connivance of any partner, or any person who was purporting to act as a partner, or

    (b)   to be attributable to any neglect on his part,

he as well as the partnership is guilty of an offence and liable to be proceeded against and punished accordingly.

(5)   If an offence under paragraph (1) … committed by an unincorporated association (other than a partnership) is shown—

    (a)   to have been committed with the consent or connivance of an officer of the association or a member of its governing body, or any person who was purporting to act in any such capacity, or

    (b)   to be attributable to any neglect on his part,

he as well as the association is guilty of an offence and liable to be proceeded against and punished accordingly.

(6)   Except in Scotland—

    (a)   the Authority may institute proceedings for an offence under these Regulations which relates to a specified contract;

    (b)   the OFT, and—

        (i)   in Great Britain, every local weights and measures authority,

        (ii)   in Northern Ireland, the Department of Enterprise, Trade and Investment,

may institute proceedings for any other offence under these Regulations.

[3434]

NOTES

Paras (2), (4), (5): words omitted revoked by the Consumer Protection from Unfair Trading Regulations 2008, SI 2008/1277, reg 30(1), (3), Sch 2, Pt 2, para 110(1), (3), Sch 4.

23   Functions of the Authority

The functions conferred on the Authority by these Regulations shall be treated as if they were conferred by the 2000 Act.

[3435]

24–28   (*Reg 24 amends the Unfair Terms in Consumer Contracts Regulations 1999, SI 1999/2083, regs 3, 5 at* **[3229]**, **[3231]**; *reg 25 amends the Consumer Protection (Distance Selling) Regulations 2000, SI 2000/2334, regs 3, 5, 6 at* **[3301]**, **[3303]**, **[3304]** *and repeals Sch 2 to those Regulations; regs 26–28 amend provisions outside the scope of this work.*)

29   Transitional provisions

(1)   In relation to any contract made before 31st May 2005 which is a consumer credit agreement within the meaning of the 1974 Act and a regulated agreement within the meaning of that Act—

    (a)   regulations 7, 8, 10 and 11 apply subject to the modifications in paragraphs (2) to (5); and

    (b)   references in these Regulations to regulations 7, 8, 10 and 11 or to provisions contained in them shall be construed accordingly.

(2)   In regulation 7—

    (a)   in paragraphs (1) to (3), before "Schedule 1" at each place where it occurs insert "paragraph 13 of"; and

    (b)   in paragraph (4)(b), before "Schedule 2" insert "paragraph 5 of".

(3)   In regulation 8(1), for "contractual terms and conditions and the information specified in" at each place where it occurs substitute "information specified in paragraph 13 of".

(4)   In regulation 10(3), omit—

    (a)   "the contractual terms and conditions and"; and

    (b)   "those terms and conditions and".

(5)   In regulation 11(3), omit "the contractual terms and conditions and" at each place where it occurs.

[3436]

SCHEDULE 1
INFORMATION REQUIRED PRIOR TO THE CONCLUSION OF THE CONTRACT

Regulations 7(1) and 8(1)

1.   The identity and the main business of the supplier, the geographical address at which the supplier is established and any other geographical address relevant to the consumer's relations with the supplier.

2.   Where the supplier has a representative established in the consumer's State of residence, the identity of that representative and the geographical address relevant to the consumer's relations with him.

3.   Where the consumer's dealings are with any professional other than the supplier, the identity of that professional, the capacity in which he is acting with respect to the consumer, and the geographical address relevant to the consumer's relations with that professional.

4.   Where the supplier is registered in a trade or similar public register, the particulars of the register in which the supplier is entered and his registration number or an equivalent means of identification in that register.

5.   Where the supplier's activity is subject to an authorisation scheme, the particulars of the relevant supervisory authority.

6.   A description of the main characteristics of the financial service.

7.   The total price to be paid by the consumer to the supplier for the financial service, including all related fees, charges and expenses, and all taxes paid via the supplier or, where an exact price cannot be indicated, the basis for the calculation of the price enabling the consumer to verify it.

8.   Where relevant, notice indicating that: (i) the financial service is related to instruments involving special risks related to their specific features or the operations to be executed or whose price depends on fluctuations in the financial markets outside the supplier's control; and (ii) historical performances are no indicators for future performances.

9.   Notice of the possibility that other taxes or costs may exist that are not paid via the supplier or imposed by him.

10.   Any limitations of the period for which the information provided is valid.

11.   The arrangements for payment and for performance.

12.   Any specific additional cost for the consumer of using the means of distance communication, if such additional cost is charged.

13.   Whether or not there is a right of cancellation and, where there is a right of cancellation, its duration and the conditions for exercising it, including information on the amount which the consumer may be required to pay in accordance with regulation 13, as well as the consequences of not exercising that right.

14.   The minimum duration of the distance contract in the case of financial services to be performed indefinitely or recurrently.

15.   Information on any rights the parties may have to terminate the distance contract early or unilaterally by virtue of the terms of the contract, including any penalties imposed by the contract in such cases.

16.   Practical instructions for exercising the right to cancel in accordance with regulation 9 indicating, among other things, the address at which the notice of cancellation should be left or to which it should be sent by post, and any facsimile number or electronic mail address to which it should be sent.

17.   The EEA State or States whose laws are taken by the supplier as a basis for the establishment of relations with the consumer prior to the conclusion of the distance contract.

18.   Any contractual clause on the law applicable to the distance contract or on the competent court.

19.   In which language, or languages: (i) the contractual terms and conditions, and the prior information specified in this Schedule, are supplied; and (ii) the supplier, with the agreement of the consumer, undertakes to communicate during the duration of the distance contract.

20.   Whether or not there is an out-of-court complaint and redress mechanism for the consumer and, if so, the methods for having access to it.

21.   The existence of guarantee funds or other compensation arrangements, except to the extent that they are required by Directive 94/19/EC of the European Parliament and of the Council of 30 May 1994 on deposit guarantee schemes or Directive 97/9/EC of the European Parliament and of the Council of 3 March 1997 on investor compensation schemes.

[3437]

PART 2
STATUTORY INSTRUMENTS

SCHEDULE 2
INFORMATION REQUIRED IN THE CASE OF VOICE TELEPHONE COMMUNICATIONS
Regulation 7(4)(b)

1.   The identity of the person in contact with the consumer and his link with the supplier.

2.   A description of the main characteristics of the financial service.

3.   The total price to be paid by the consumer to the supplier for the financial service including all taxes paid via the supplier or, if an exact price cannot be indicated, the basis for the calculation of the price enabling the consumer to verify it.

4.   Notice of the possibility that other taxes or costs may exist that are not paid via the supplier or imposed by him.

5.   Whether or not there is a right to cancel and, where there is such a right, its duration and the conditions for exercising it, including information on the amount which the consumer may be required to pay in accordance with regulation 13, as well as the consequences of not exercising that right.

6.   That other information is available on request and the nature of that information.

[3438]

GENERAL PRODUCT SAFETY REGULATIONS 2005

(SI 2005/1803)

NOTES
Made: 30 June 2005.
Authority: European Communities Act 1972, s 2(2).
Commencement: see reg 1(1) at **[3439]**.

ARRANGEMENT OF REGULATIONS
PART 1
GENERAL

PART 2
OBLIGATIONS OF PRODUCERS AND DISTRIBUTORS

PART 3
ENFORCEMENT

PART 1
GENERAL

1 Citation, commencement and revocation

(1) These Regulations may be cited as the General Product Safety Regulations 2005 and shall come into force on 1st October 2005 with the exception of the reference to a civil partner in regulation 43(2) which shall come into force on 5th December 2005.

(2) The General Product Safety Regulations 1994 are hereby revoked.

[3439]

NOTES

Commencement: 1 October 2005.

---

2 Interpretation

In these Regulations:-

"the 1987 Act" means the Consumer Protection Act 1987;

"Community law" includes a law in any part of the United Kingdom which implements a Community obligation;

"contravention" includes a failure to comply and cognate expressions shall be construed accordingly;

"dangerous product" means a product other than a safe product;

"distributor" means a professional in the supply chain whose activity does not affect the safety properties of a product;

"enforcement authority" means the Secretary of State, any other Minister of the Crown in charge of a government department, any such department and any authority or council mentioned in regulation 10;

"general safety requirement" means the requirement that only safe products should be placed on the market;

"the GPS Directive" means Directive 2001/95/EC of the European Parliament and of the Council of 3 December 2001 on general product safety;

"magistrates' court" in relation to Northern Ireland, means a court of summary jurisdiction;

"Member State" means a member State, Norway, Iceland or Liechtenstein;

"notice" means a notice in writing;

"officer", in relation to an enforcement authority, means a person authorised in writing to assist the authority in carrying out its functions under or for the purposes of the enforcement of these Regulations and safety notices, except in relation to an enforcement authority which is a government department where it means an officer of that department;

"producer" means—

    (a)   the manufacturer of a product, when he is established in a Member State and any other person presenting himself as the manufacturer by affixing to the product his name, trade mark or other distinctive mark, or the person who reconditions the product;

    (b)   when the manufacturer is not established in a Member State—

       (i)   if he has a representative established in a Member State, the representative,

       (ii)   in any other case, the importer of the product from a state that is not a Member State into a Member State;

(c)   other professionals in the supply chain, insofar as their activities may affect the safety properties of a product;

"product" means a product which is intended for consumers or likely, under reasonably foreseeable conditions, to be used by consumers even if not intended for them and which is supplied or made available, whether for consideration or not, in the course of a commercial activity and whether it is new, used or reconditioned and includes a product that is supplied or made available to consumers for their own use in the context of providing a service. "product" does not include equipment used by service providers themselves to supply a service to consumers, in particular equipment on which consumers ride or travel which is operated by a service provider;

"recall" means any measure aimed at achieving the return of a dangerous product that has already been supplied or made available to consumers;

"recall notice" means a notice under regulation 15;

"record" includes any book or document and any record in any form;

"requirement to mark" means a notice under regulation 12;

"requirement to warn" means a notice under regulation 13;

"safe product" means a product which, under normal or reasonably foreseeable conditions of use including duration and, where applicable, putting into service, installation and maintenance requirements, does not present any risk or only the minimum risks compatible with the product's use, considered to be acceptable and consistent with a high level of protection for the safety and health of persons. In determining the foregoing, the following shall be taken into account in particular—

(a)   the characteristics of the product, including its composition, packaging, instructions for assembly and, where applicable, instructions for installation and maintenance,

(b)   the effect of the product on other products, where it is reasonably foreseeable that it will be used with other products,

(c)   the presentation of the product, the labelling, any warnings and instructions for its use and disposal and any other indication or information regarding the product, and

(d)   the categories of consumers at risk when using the product, in particular children and the elderly.

The feasibility of obtaining higher levels of safety or the availability of other products presenting a lesser degree of risk shall not constitute grounds for considering a product to be a dangerous product;

"safety notice" means a suspension notice, a requirement to mark, a requirement to warn, a withdrawal notice or a recall notice;

"serious risk" means a serious risk, including one the effects of which are not immediate, requiring rapid intervention;

"supply" in relation to a product includes making it available, in the context of providing a service, for use by consumers;

"suspension notice" means a notice under regulation 11;

"withdrawal" means any measure aimed at preventing the distribution, display or offer of a dangerous product to a consumer;

"withdrawal notice" means a notice under regulation 14.

[3440]

NOTES
Commencement: 1 October 2005.

3   Application

(1)   Each provision of these Regulations applies to a product in so far as there are no specific provisions with the same objective in rules of Community law governing the safety of the product other than the GPS Directive.

(2)   Where a product is subject to specific safety requirements imposed by rules of Community law other than the GPS Directive, these Regulations shall apply only to the aspects and risks or category of risks not covered by those requirements. This means that:

(a)   the definition of "safe product" and "dangerous product" in regulation 2 and regulations 5 and 6 shall not apply to such a product in so far as concerns the risks or category of risks covered by the specific rules, and

(b)   the remainder of these Regulations shall apply except where there are specific provisions governing the aspects covered by those regulations with the same objective.

[3441]

NOTES
Commencement: 1 October 2005.

4   These Regulations do not apply to a second-hand product supplied as a product to be repaired or reconditioned prior to being used, provided the supplier clearly informs the person to whom he supplies the product to that effect.

[3442]

PART 2
OBLIGATIONS OF PRODUCERS AND DISTRIBUTORS

5 General safety requirement

(1)   No producer shall place a product on the market unless the product is a safe product.

(2)   No producer shall offer or agree to place a product on the market or expose or possess a product for placing on the market unless the product is a safe product.

(3)   No producer shall offer or agree to supply a product or expose or possess a product for supply unless the product is a safe product.

(4)   No producer shall supply a product unless the product is a safe product.

[3443]

6 Presumption of conformity

(1)   Where, in the absence of specific provisions in rules of Community law governing the safety of a product, the product conforms to the specific rules of the law of part of the United Kingdom laying down the health and safety requirements which the product must satisfy in order to be marketed in the United Kingdom, the product shall be deemed safe so far as concerns the aspects covered by such rules.

(2)   Where a product conforms to a voluntary national standard of the United Kingdom giving effect to a European standard the reference of which has been published in the Official Journal of the European Union in accordance with Article 4 of the GPS Directive, the product shall be presumed to be a safe product so far as concerns the risks and categories of risk covered by that national standard. The Secretary of State shall publish the reference number of such national standards in such manner as he considers appropriate.

(3)   In circumstances other than those referred to in paragraphs (1) and (2), the conformity of a product to the general safety requirement shall be assessed taking into account—

    (a)   any voluntary national standard of the United Kingdom giving effect to a European standard, other than one referred to in paragraph (2),

    (b)   other national standards drawn up in the United Kingdom,

    (c)   recommendations of the European Commission setting guidelines on product safety assessment,

    (d)   product safety codes of good practice in the sector concerned,

    (e)   the state of the art and technology, and

    (f)   reasonable consumer expectations concerning safety.

(4)   Conformity of a product with the criteria designed to ensure the general safety requirement is complied with, in particular the provisions mentioned in paragraphs (1) to (3), shall not bar an enforcement authority from exercising its powers under these Regulations in relation to that product where there is evidence that, despite such conformity, it is dangerous.

[3444]

7 Other obligations of producers

(1)   Within the limits of his activities, a producer shall provide consumers with the relevant information to enable them—

    (a)   to assess the risks inherent in a product throughout the normal or reasonably foreseeable period of its use, where such risks are not immediately obvious without adequate warnings, and

    (b)   to take precautions against those risks.

(2)   The presence of warnings does not exempt any person from compliance with the other requirements of these Regulations.

(3)   Within the limits of his activities, a producer shall adopt measures commensurate with the characteristics of the products which he supplies to enable him to—
- (a)   be informed of the risks which the products might pose, and
- (b)   take appropriate action including, where necessary to avoid such risks, withdrawal, adequately and effectively warning consumers as to the risks or, as a last resort, recall.

(4)   The measures referred to in paragraph (3) include—
- (a)   except where it is not reasonable to do so, an indication by means of the product or its packaging of—
  - (i)   the name and address of the producer, and
  - (ii)   the product reference or where applicable the batch of products to which it belongs; and
- (b)   where and to the extent that it is reasonable to do so—
  - (i)   sample testing of marketed products,
  - (ii)   investigating and if necessary keeping a register of complaints concerning the safety of the product, and
  - (iii)   keeping distributors informed of the results of such monitoring where a product presents a risk or may present a risk.

[3445]

NOTES

Commencement: 1 October 2005.

---

8   Obligations of distributors

(1)   A distributor shall act with due care in order to help ensure compliance with the applicable safety requirements and in particular he—
- (a)   shall not expose or possess for supply or offer or agree to supply, or supply, a product to any person which he knows or should have presumed, on the basis of the information in his possession and as a professional, is a dangerous product; and
- (b)   shall, within the limits of his activities, participate in monitoring the safety of a product placed on the market, in particular by—
  - (i)   passing on information on the risks posed by the product,
  - (ii)   keeping the documentation necessary for tracing the origin of the product,
  - (iii)   producing the documentation necessary for tracing the origin of the product, and cooperating in action taken by a producer or an enforcement authority to avoid the risks.

(2)   Within the limits of his activities, a distributor shall take measures enabling him to cooperate efficiently in the action referred to in paragraph (1)(b)(iii).

[3446]

NOTES

Commencement: 1 October 2005.

---

9   Obligations of producers and distributors

(1)   Subject to paragraph (2), where a producer or a distributor knows that a product he has placed on the market or supplied poses risks to the consumer that are incompatible with the general safety requirement, he shall forthwith notify an enforcement authority in writing of that information and—
- (a)   the action taken to prevent risk to the consumer; and
- (b)   where the product is being or has been marketed or otherwise supplied to consumers outside the United Kingdom, of the identity of each Member State in which, to the best of his knowledge, it is being or has been so marketed or supplied.

(2)   Paragraph (1) shall not apply—
- (a)   in the case of a second-hand product supplied as an antique or as a product to be repaired or reconditioned prior to being used, provided the supplier clearly informed the person to whom he supplied the product to that effect,
- (b)   in conditions concerning isolated circumstances or products.

(3)   In the event of a serious risk the notification under paragraph (1) shall include the following—
- (a)   information enabling a precise identification of the product or batch of products in question,
- (b)   a full description of the risks that the product presents,
- (c)   all available information relevant for tracing the product, and
- (d)   a description of the action undertaken to prevent risks to the consumer.

(4)   Within the limits of his activities, a person who is a producer or a distributor shall co-operate with an enforcement authority (at the enforcement authority's request) in action taken to

avoid the risks posed by a product which he supplies or has supplied. Every enforcement authority shall maintain procedures for such co-operation, including procedures for dialogue with the producers and distributors concerned on issues related to product safety.

[3447]

NOTES
    Commencement: 1 October 2005.

PART 3
ENFORCEMENT

10 Enforcement

(1)   It shall be the duty of every authority to which paragraph (4) applies to enforce within its area these Regulations and safety notices.

(2)   An authority in England or Wales to which paragraph (4) applies shall have the power to investigate and prosecute for an alleged contravention of any provision imposed by or under these Regulations which was committed outside its area in any part of England and Wales.

(3)   A district council in Northern Ireland shall have the power to investigate and prosecute for an alleged contravention of any provision imposed by or under these Regulations which was committed outside its area in any part of Northern Ireland.

(4)   The authorities to which this paragraph applies are:
- (a)   in England, a county council, district council, London Borough Council, the Common Council of the City of London in its capacity as a local authority and the Council of the Isles of Scilly,
- (b)   in Wales, a county council or a county borough council,
- (c)   in Scotland, a council constituted under section 2 of the Local Government etc (Scotland) Act 1994,
- (d)   in Northern Ireland any district council.

(5)   An enforcement authority shall in enforcing these Regulations act in a manner proportionate to the seriousness of the risk and shall take due account of the precautionary principle. In this context, it shall encourage and promote voluntary action by producers and distributors. Notwithstanding the foregoing, an enforcement authority may take any action under these Regulations urgently and without first encouraging and promoting voluntary action if a product poses a serious risk.

[3448]

NOTES
    Commencement: 1 October 2005.

11 Suspension notices

(1)   Where an enforcement authority has reasonable grounds for suspecting that a requirement of these Regulations has been contravened in relation to a product, the authority may, for the period needed to organise appropriate safety evaluations, checks and controls, serve a notice ("a suspension notice") prohibiting the person on whom it is served from doing any of the following things without the consent of the authority, that is to say—
- (a)   placing the product on the market, offering to place it on the market, agreeing to place it on the market or exposing it for placing on the market, or
- (b)   supplying the product, offering to supply it, agreeing to supply it or exposing it for supply.

(2)   A suspension notice served by an enforcement authority in relation to a product may require the person on whom it is served to keep the authority informed of the whereabouts of any such product in which he has an interest.

(3)   A consent given by the enforcement authority for the purposes of paragraph (1) may impose such conditions on the doing of anything for which the consent is required as the authority considers appropriate.

[3449]

NOTES
    Commencement: 1 October 2005.

12 Requirements to mark

(1)   Where an enforcement authority has reasonable grounds for believing that a product is a dangerous product in that it could pose risks in certain conditions, the authority may serve a notice

("a requirement to mark") requiring the person on whom the notice is served at his own expense to undertake either or both of the following, as specified in the notice—

(a)   to ensure that the product is marked in accordance with requirements specified in the notice with warnings as to the risks it may present,

(b)   to make the marketing of the product subject to prior conditions as specified in the notice so as to ensure the product is a safe product.

(2)   The requirements referred to in paragraph (1)(a) shall be such as to ensure that the product is marked with a warning which is suitable, clearly worded and easily comprehensible.

[3450]

NOTES
Commencement: 1 October 2005.

13   Requirements to warn

Where an enforcement authority has reasonable grounds for believing that a product is a dangerous product in that it could pose risks for certain persons, the authority may serve a notice ("a requirement to warn") requiring the person on whom the notice is served at his own expense to undertake one or more of the following, as specified in the notice—

(a)   where and to the extent it is practicable to do so, to ensure that any person who could be subject to such risks and who has been supplied with the product be given warning of the risks in good time and in a form specified in the notice,

(b)   to publish a warning of the risks in such form and manner as is likely to bring those risks to the attention of any such person,

(c)   to ensure that the product carries a warning of the risks in a form specified in the notice.

[3451]

NOTES
Commencement: 1 October 2005.

14   Withdrawal notices

(1)   Where an enforcement authority has reasonable grounds for believing that a product is a dangerous product, the authority may serve a notice ("a withdrawal notice") prohibiting the person on whom it is served from doing any of the following things without the consent of the authority, that is to say—

(a)   placing the product on the market, offering to place it on the market, agreeing to place it on the market or exposing it for placing on the market, or

(b)   supplying the product, offering to supply it, agreeing to supply it or exposing it for supply.

(2)   A withdrawal notice may require the person on whom it is served to take action to alert consumers to the risks that the product presents.

(3)   In relation to a product that is already on the market, a withdrawal notice may only be served by an enforcement authority where the action being undertaken by the producer or the distributor concerned in fulfilment of his obligations under these Regulations is unsatisfactory or insufficient to prevent the risks concerned to the health and safety of persons.

(4)   Paragraph (3) shall not apply in the case of a product posing a serious risk requiring, in the view of the enforcement authority, urgent action.

(5)   A withdrawal notice served by an enforcement authority in relation to a product may require the person on whom it is served to keep the authority informed of the whereabouts of any such product in which he has an interest.

(6)   A consent given by the enforcement authority for the purposes of paragraph (1) may impose such conditions on the doing of anything for which the consent is required as the authority considers appropriate.

[3452]

NOTES
Commencement: 1 October 2005.

15   Recall notices

(1)   Subject to paragraph (4), where an enforcement authority has reasonable grounds for believing that a product is a dangerous product and that it has already been supplied or made available to consumers, the authority may serve a notice ("a recall notice") requiring the person on whom it is served to use his reasonable endeavours to organise the return of the product from consumers to that person or to such other person as is specified in the notice.

(2)   A recall notice may require—

(a) the recall to be effected in accordance with a code of practice applicable to the product concerned, or

(b) the recipient of the recall notice to—

   (i) contact consumers who have purchased the product in order to inform them of the recall, where and to the extent it is practicable to do so,

   (ii) publish a notice in such form and such manner as is likely to bring to the attention of purchasers of the product the risk the product poses and the fact of the recall, or

   (iii) make arrangements for the collection or return of the product from consumers who have purchased it or for its disposal,

and may impose such additional requirements on the recipient of the notice as are reasonable and practicable with a view to achieving the return of the product from consumers to the person specified in the notice or its disposal.

(3) In determining what requirements to include in a recall notice, the enforcement authority shall take into consideration the need to encourage distributors, users and consumers to contribute to its implementation.

(4) A recall notice may only be issued by an enforcement authority where—

(a) other action which it may require under these Regulations would not suffice to prevent the risks concerned to the health and safety of persons,

(b) the action being undertaken by the producer or the distributor concerned in fulfilment of his obligations under these Regulations is unsatisfactory or insufficient to prevent the risks concerned to the health and safety of persons, and

(c) the authority has given not less than seven days notice to the person on whom the recall notice is to be served of its intention to serve such a notice and where that person has before the expiry of that period by notice required the authority to seek the advice of such person as the Institute determines on the questions of—

   (i) whether the product is a dangerous product,

   (ii) whether the issue of a recall notice is proportionate to the seriousness of the risk, and

the authority has taken account of such advice.

(5) Paragraphs (4)(b) and (c) shall not apply in the case of a product posing a serious risk requiring, in the view of the enforcement authority, urgent action.

(6) Where a person requires an enforcement authority to seek advice as referred to in paragraph (4)(c), that person shall be responsible for the fees, costs and expenses of the Institute and of the person appointed by the Institute to advise the authority.

(7) In paragraphs 4(c) and (6) "the Institute" means the charitable organisation with registered number 803725 and known as the Chartered Institute of Arbitrators.

(8) A recall notice served by an enforcement authority in relation to a product may require the person on whom it is served to keep the authority informed of the whereabouts of any such product to which the recall notice relates, so far as he is able to do so.

(9) Where the conditions in paragraph (1) for serving a recall notice are satisfied and either the enforcement authority has been unable to identify any person on whom to serve a recall notice, or the person on whom such a notice has been served has failed to comply with it, then the authority may itself take such action as could have been required by a recall notice.

(10) Where—

(a) an authority has complied with the requirements of paragraph (4); and

(b) the authority has exercised its powers under paragraph (9) to take action following the failure of the person on whom the recall notice has been served to comply with that notice,

then the authority may recover from the person on whom the notice was served summarily as a civil debt, any costs or expenses reasonably incurred by it in undertaking the action referred to in sub-paragraph (b).

(11) A civil debt recoverable under the preceding paragraph may be recovered—

(a) in England and Wales by way of complaint (as mentioned in section 58 of the Magistrates' Courts Act 1980,

(b) in Northern Ireland in proceedings under Article 62 of the Magistrate's Court (Northern Ireland) Order 1981.

[3453]

NOTES

Commencement: 1 October 2005.

16 Supplementary provisions relating to safety notices

(1) Whenever feasible, prior to serving a safety notice the authority shall give an opportunity to the person on whom the notice is to be served to submit his views to the authority. Where, due to the urgency of the situation, this is not feasible the person shall be given an opportunity to submit his views to the authority after service of the notice.

(2) A safety notice served by an enforcement authority in respect of a product shall—
  (a) describe the product in a manner sufficient to identify it;
  (b) state the reasons on which the notice is based;
  (c) indicate the rights available to the recipient of the notice under these Regulations and (where applicable) the time limits applying to their exercise; and
  (d) in the case of a suspension notice, state the period of time for which it applies.

(3) A safety notice shall have effect throughout the United Kingdom.

(4) Where an enforcement authority serves a suspension notice in respect of a product, the authority shall be liable to pay compensation to a person having an interest in the product in respect of any loss or damage suffered by reason of the notice if—
  (a) there has been no contravention of any requirement of these Regulations in relation to the product; and
  (b) the exercise by the authority of the power to serve the suspension notice was not attributable to any neglect or default by that person.

(5) Where an enforcement authority serves a withdrawal notice in respect of a product, the authority shall be liable to pay compensation to a person having an interest in the product in respect of any loss or damage suffered by reason of the notice if—
  (a) the product was not a dangerous product; and
  (b) the exercise by the authority of the power to serve the withdrawal notice was not attributable to any neglect or default by that person.

(6) Where an enforcement authority serves a recall notice in respect of a product, the authority shall be liable to pay compensation to the person on whom the notice was served in respect of any loss or damage suffered by reason of the notice if—
  (a) the product was not a dangerous product; and
  (b) the exercise by the authority of the power to serve the recall notice was not attributable to any neglect or default by that person.

(7) An enforcement authority may vary or revoke a safety notice which it has served provided that the notice is not made more restrictive for the person on whom it is served or more onerous for that person to comply with.

(8) Wherever feasible prior to varying a safety notice the authority shall give an opportunity to the person on whom the original notice was served to submit his views to the authority.

[3454]

NOTES
  Commencement: 1 October 2005.

17 Appeals against safety notices

(1) A person on whom a safety notice has been served and a person having an interest in a product in respect of which a safety notice (other than a recall notice) has been served may, before the end of the period of 21 days beginning with the day on which the notice was served, apply for an order to vary or set aside the terms of the notice.

(2) On an application under paragraph (1) the court or the sheriff, as the case may be, shall make an order setting aside the notice only if satisfied that—
  (a) in the case of a suspension notice, there has been no contravention in relation to the product of any requirement of these Regulations,
  (b) in the case of a requirement to mark or a requirement to warn, the product is not a dangerous product,
  (c) in the case of a withdrawal notice—
    (i) the product is not a dangerous product, or
    (ii) where applicable, regulation 14(3) has not been complied with by the enforcement authority concerned,
  (d) in the case of a recall notice—
    (i) the product is not a dangerous product, or
    (ii) regulation 15(4) has not been complied with,
  (e) in any case, the serving of the safety notice concerned was not proportionate to the seriousness of the risk.

(3)   On an application concerning the period of time specified in a suspension notice as the period for which it applies, the court or the sheriff, as the case may be, may reduce the period to such period as it considers sufficient for organising appropriate safety evaluations, checks and controls.

(4)   On an application to vary the terms of a notice, the court or the sheriff, as the case may be, may vary the requirements specified in the notice as it considers appropriate.

(5)   A person on whom a recall notice has been served and who proposes to make an application under paragraph (1) in relation to the notice may, before the end of the period of seven days beginning with the day on which the notice was served, apply to the court or the sheriff for an order suspending the effect of the notice and the court or the sheriff may, in any case where it considers it appropriate to do so, make an order suspending the effect of the notice.

(6)   If the court or the sheriff makes an order suspending the effect of a recall notice under paragraph (5) in the absence of the enforcement authority, the enforcement authority may apply for the revocation of such order.

(7)   An order under paragraph (5) shall take effect from the time it is made until—

   (a)   it is revoked under paragraph (6),

   (b)   where no application is made under paragraph (1) in respect of the recall notice within the time specified in that paragraph, the expiration of that time,

   (c)   where such an application is made but is withdrawn or dismissed for want of prosecution, the date of dismissal or withdrawal of the application, or

   (d)   where such an application is made and is not withdrawn or dismissed for want of prosecution, the determination of the application.

(8)   Subject to paragraph (6), in Scotland the sheriff's decision under paragraph (5) shall be final.

(9)   An application under this regulation may be made—

   (a)   by way of complaint to any magistrates' court in which proceedings have been brought in England and Wales or Northern Ireland—

      (i)   in respect of a contravention in relation to the product of a requirement imposed by or under these Regulations; or

      (ii)   for the forfeiture of the product under regulation 18;

   (b)   where no such proceedings have been brought, by way of complaint to any magistrates' court; or

   (c)   in Scotland, by summary application to the sheriff.

(10)   A person aggrieved by an order made pursuant to an application under paragraph (1) by a magistrates' court in England, Wales or Northern Ireland, or by a decision of such a court not to make such an order, may appeal against that order or decision—

   (a)   in England and Wales, to the Crown Court;

   (b)   in Northern Ireland, to the county court.

[3455]

NOTES

Commencement: 1 October 2005.

18   Forfeiture: England and Wales and Northern Ireland

(1)   An enforcement authority in England and Wales or Northern Ireland may apply for an order for the forfeiture of a product on the grounds that the product is a dangerous product.

(2)   An application under paragraph (1) may be made—

   (a)   where proceedings have been brought in a magistrates' court for an offence in respect of a contravention in relation to the product of a requirement imposed by or under these Regulations, to that court,

   (b)   where an application with respect to the product has been made to a magistrates' court under regulation 17 (appeals against safety notices) or 25 (appeals against detention of products and records) to that court, and

   (c)   otherwise, by way of complaint to a magistrates' court.

(3)   An enforcement authority making an application under paragraph (1) shall serve a copy of the application on any person appearing to it to be the owner of, or otherwise to have an interest in, the product to which the application relates, together with a notice giving him the opportunity to appear at the hearing of the application to show cause why the product should not be forfeited.

(4)   A person on whom notice is served under paragraph (3) and any other person claiming to be the owner of, or otherwise to have an interest in, the product to which the application relates shall be entitled to appear at the hearing of the application and show cause why the product should not be forfeited.

(5)   The court shall not make an order for the forfeiture of a product—

(a)   if any person on whom notice is served under paragraph (3) does not appear, unless service of the notice on that person is proved, or

(b)   if no notice under paragraph (3) has been served, unless the court is satisfied that in the circumstances it was reasonable not to serve notice on any person.

(6)   The court may make an order for the forfeiture of a product only if it is satisfied that the product is a dangerous product.

(7)   Any person aggrieved by an order made by a magistrates' court for the forfeiture of a product, or by a decision of such a court not to make such an order, may appeal against that order or decision—

(a)   in England and Wales, to the Crown Court;

(b)   in Northern Ireland, to the county court.

(8)   An order for the forfeiture of a product shall not take effect until the later of—

(i)   the end of the period within which an appeal under paragraph (7) may be brought or within which an application under section 111 of the Magistrates' Courts Act 1980 or article 146 of the Magistrates' Courts (Northern Ireland) Order 1981 (statement of case) may be made, or

(ii)   if an appeal or an application is so made, when the appeal or application is determined or abandoned.

(9)   Subject to the following paragraph, where a product is forfeited it shall be destroyed in accordance with such directions as the court may give.

(10)   On making an order for forfeiture of a product a magistrates' court may, if it considers it appropriate to do so, direct that the product shall (instead of being destroyed) be delivered up to such person as the court may specify, on condition that the person—

(a)   does not supply the product to any person otherwise than as mentioned in paragraph (11), and

(b)   on condition, if the court considers it appropriate, that he complies with any order to pay costs or expenses (including any order under regulation 28) which has been made against him in the proceedings for the order for forfeiture.

(11)   The supplies which may be permitted under the preceding paragraph are—

(a)   a supply to a person who carries on a business of buying products of the same description as the product concerned and repairing or reconditioning them,

(b)   a supply to a person as scrap (that is to say, for the value of materials included in the product rather than for the value of the product itself),

(c)   a supply to any person, provided that being so supplied the product is repaired by or on behalf of the person to whom the product was delivered up by direction of the court and that following such repair it is not a dangerous product.

[3456]

NOTES
Commencement: 1 October 2005.

---

19   (*Applies to Scotland only.*)

20   Offences

(1)   A person who contravenes regulations 5 or 8(1)(a) shall be guilty of an offence and liable on conviction on indictment to imprisonment for a term not exceeding 12 months or to a fine not exceeding £20,000 or to both, or on summary conviction to imprisonment for a term not exceeding three months or to a fine not exceeding the statutory maximum or to both.

(2)   A person who contravenes regulation 7(1), 7(3) (by failing to take any of the measures specified in regulation 7(4)), 8(1)(b)(i), (ii) or (iii) or 9(1) shall be guilty of an offence and liable on summary conviction to imprisonment for a term not exceeding three months or to a fine not exceeding level 5 on the standard scale or to both.

(3)   A producer or distributor who does not give notice to an enforcement authority under regulation 9(1) in respect of a product he has placed on the market or supplied commits an offence where it is proved that he ought to have known that the product poses risks to consumers that are incompatible with the general safety requirement and he shall be liable on summary conviction to imprisonment for a term not exceeding three months or to a fine not exceeding level 5 on the standard scale or to both.

(4)   A person who contravenes a safety notice shall be guilty of an offence and liable on conviction on indictment to imprisonment for a term not exceeding 12 months or to a fine not exceeding £20,000 or to both, or on summary conviction to imprisonment for a term not exceeding three months or to a fine not exceeding the statutory maximum or to both.

[3457]

NOTES
  Commencement: 1 October 2005.

21   Test purchases

(1)   An enforcement authority shall have power to organise appropriate checks on the safety properties of a product, on an adequate scale, up to the final stage of use or consumption and for that purpose may make a purchase of a product or authorise an officer of the authority to make a purchase of a product.

(2)   Where a product purchased under paragraph (1) is submitted to a test and the test leads to—

   (a)   the bringing of proceedings for an offence in respect of a contravention in relation to the product of any requirement imposed by or under these Regulations or for the forfeiture of the product under regulation 18 or 19, or

   (b)   the serving of a safety notice in respect of the product, and

   (c)   the authority is requested to do so and it is practicable for the authority to comply with the request,

then the authority shall allow the person from whom the product was purchased, a person who is a party to the proceedings, on whom the notice was served or who has an interest in the product to which the notice relates, to have the product tested.

[3458]

NOTES
  Commencement: 1 October 2005.

22   Powers of entry and search etc

(1)   An officer of an enforcement authority may at any reasonable hour and on production, if required, of his credentials exercise any of the powers conferred by the following provisions of this regulation.

(2)   The officer may, for the purposes of ascertaining whether there has been a contravention of a requirement imposed by or under these Regulations, enter any premises other than premises occupied only as a person's residence and inspect any record or product.

(3)   The officer may, for the purpose of ascertaining whether there has been a contravention of a requirement imposed by or under these Regulations, examine any procedure (including any arrangements for carrying out a test) connected with the production of a product.

(4)   If the officer has reasonable grounds for suspecting that the product has not been placed on the market or supplied in the United Kingdom since it was manufactured or imported he may for the purpose of ascertaining whether there has been a contravention in relation to the product of a requirement imposed by or under these Regulations—

   (a)   require a person carrying on a commercial activity, or employed in connection with a commercial activity, to supply all necessary information relating to the activity, including by the production of records,

   (b)   require any record which is stored in an electronic form and is accessible from the premises to be produced in a form—

      (i)   in which it can be taken away, and

      (ii)   in which it is visible and legible.

   (c)   for the purpose of ascertaining (by testing or otherwise) whether there has been any such contravention, seize and detain samples of the product,

   (d)   take copies of, or of an entry in, any records produced by virtue of sub-paragraph (a).

(5)   If the officer has reasonable grounds for suspecting that there has been a contravention in relation to a product of a requirement imposed by or under these Regulations, he may—

   (a)   for the purpose of ascertaining whether there has been any such contravention, require a person carrying on a commercial activity, or employed in connection with a commercial activity, to supply all necessary information relating to the activity, including by the production of records,

   (b)   for the purpose of ascertaining whether there has been any such contravention, require any record which is stored in an electronic form and is accessible from the premises to be produced in a form—

      (i)   in which it can be taken away, and

      (ii)   in which it is visible and legible,

   (c)   for the purpose of ascertaining (by testing or otherwise) whether there has been any such contravention, seize and detain samples of the product,

   (d)   take copies of, or of an entry in, any records produced by virtue of sub-paragraph (a).

(6)   The officer may seize and detain any products or records which he has reasonable grounds for believing may be required as evidence in proceedings for an offence in respect of a contravention of any requirement imposed by or under these Regulations.

(7)   If and to the extent that it is reasonably necessary to do so to prevent a contravention of any requirement imposed by or under these Regulations, the officer may, for the purpose of exercising his power under paragraphs (4) to (6) to seize products or records—

    (a)   require any person having authority to do so to open any container or to open any vending machine; and

    (b)   himself open or break open any such container or machine where a requirement made under sub-paragraph (a) in relation to the container or machine has not been complied with.

[3459]

NOTES

Commencement: 1 October 2005.

23   Provisions supplemental to regulation 22 and search warrants etc

(1)   An officer seizing any products or records shall, before he leaves the premises, provide to the person from whom they were seized a written notice—

    (a)   specifying the products (including the quantity thereof) and records seized,

    (b)   stating the reasons for their seizure, and

    (c)   explaining the right of appeal under regulation 25.

(2)   References in paragraph (1) and regulation 25 to the person from whom something has been seized, in relation to a case in which the power of seizure was exercisable by reason of the product having been found on any premises, are references to the occupier of the premises at the time of the seizure.

(3)   If a justice of the peace—

    (a)   is satisfied by written information on oath that there are reasonable grounds for believing either—

        (i)   that any products or records which an officer has power to inspect under regulation 22 are on any premises and that their inspection is likely to disclose evidence that there has been a contravention of any requirement imposed by or under these Regulations, or

        (ii)   that such a contravention has taken place, is taking place or is about to take place on any premises, and

    (b)   is also satisfied by such information either—

        (i)   that admission to the premises has been or is likely to be refused and that notice of the intention to apply for a warrant under this paragraph has been given to the occupier, or

        (ii)   that an application for admission, or the giving of such a notice, would defeat the object of the entry or that the premises are unoccupied or that the occupier is temporarily absent and it might defeat the object of the entry to await his return.

the justice may by warrant under his hand, which shall continue in force for a period of one month, authorise any officer of an enforcement authority to enter the premises, if need be by force.

(4)   An officer entering premises by virtue of regulation 22 or a warrant under paragraph (3) may take him such other persons and equipment as may appear to him necessary.

(5)   On leaving any premises which a person is authorised to enter by a warrant under paragraph (3), that person shall, if the premises are unoccupied or the occupier is temporarily absent—

    (a)   leave the premises as effectively secured against trespassers as he found them,

    (b)   attach a notice such as is mentioned in paragraph (1) in a prominent place at the premises.

(6)   Where a product seized by an officer of an enforcement authority under regulation 22 or 23 is submitted to a test, the authority shall inform the person mentioned in paragraph (1) of the result of the test and, if—

    (a)   proceedings are brought for an offence in respect of a contravention in relation to the product of any requirement imposed by or under these Regulations or for the forfeiture of the product under regulation 18 or 19; or

    (b)   a safety notice is served in respect of the product; and

    (c)   the authority is requested to do so and it is practicable for him to comply with the request,

then the authority shall allow a person who is a party to the proceedings or, on whom the notice was served or who has an interest in the product to which the notice relates to have the product tested.

(7)   If a person who is not an officer of an enforcement authority purports to act as such under regulation 22 or under this regulation he shall be guilty of an offence and liable on summary conviction to a fine not exceeding level 5 on the standard scale.

(8)   *(Applies to Scotland only.)*

(9)   In the application of this section to Northern Ireland, the reference in paragraph (3) to a justice of the peace shall include a reference to a lay magistrate and the references to an information on oath shall be construed as a reference to a complaint on oath.

[3460]

NOTES
Commencement: 1 October 2005.

24   Obstruction of officers

(1)   A person who—
- (a)   intentionally obstructs an officer of an enforcement authority who is acting in pursuance of any provision of regulations 22 or 23; or
- (b)   intentionally fails to comply with a requirement made of him by an officer of an enforcement authority under any provision of those regulations; or
- (c)   without reasonable cause fails to give an officer of an enforcement authority who is so acting any other assistance or information which the officer may reasonably require of him for the purposes of the exercise of the officer's functions under any provision of those regulations,

shall be guilty of an offence and liable on summary conviction to a fine not exceeding level 5 on the standard scale.

(2)   A person shall be guilty of an offence if, in giving any information which is required by him by virtue of paragraph (1)(c)—
- (a)   he makes a statement which he knows is false in a material particular; or
- (b)   he recklessly makes a statement which is false in a material particular.

(3)   A person guilty of an offence under paragraph (2) shall be liable—
- (a)   on conviction on indictment, to a fine;
- (b)   on summary conviction, to a fine not exceeding the statutory maximum.

[3461]

NOTES
Commencement: 1 October 2005.

25   Appeals against detention of products and records

(1)   A person referred to in regulation 23(1) may apply for an order requiring any product or record which is for the time being detained under regulation 22 or 23 by an enforcement authority or by an officer of such an authority to be released to him or to another person.

(2)   An application under the preceding paragraph may be made—
- (a)   to any magistrates' court in which proceedings have been brought in England and Wales or Northern Ireland—
  - (i)   for an offence in respect of a contravention in relation to the product of a requirement imposed by or under these Regulation, or
  - (ii)   for the forfeiture of the product under regulation 18,
- (b)   where no such proceedings have been brought, by way of complaint to a magistrates' court;
- (c)   in Scotland, by summary application to the sheriff.

(3)   On an application under paragraph (1) to a magistrates' court or to the sheriff, the court or the sheriff may make an order requiring a product or record to be released only if the court or sheriff is satisfied—
- (a)   that proceedings
  - (i)   for an offence in respect of any contravention in relation to the product or, in the case of a record, the product to which the record relates, of any requirement imposed by or under these Regulations; or
  - (ii)   for the forfeiture of the product or, in the case of a record, the product to which the record relate, under regulation 18 or 19,

have not been brought or, having been brought, have been concluded without the product being forfeited; and
- (b)   where no such proceedings have been brought, that more than six months have elapsed since the product or records was seized.

(4)   In determining whether to make an order under this regulation requiring the release of a product or record the court or sheriff shall take all the circumstances into account including the results of any tests on the product which have been carried out by or on behalf of the enforcement authority and any statement made by the enforcement authority to the court or sheriff as to its intention to bring proceedings for an offence in respect of a contravention in relation to the product of any requirement imposed by or under these Regulations.

(5)　Where—

(a)　more than 12 months have elapsed since a product or records were seized and the enforcement authority has not commenced proceedings for an offence in respect of a contravention in relation to the product (or, in the case of records, the product to which the records relate) of any requirement imposed by or under these Regulations or for the forfeiture of the product under regulation 18 or 19, or

(b)　an enforcement authority has brought proceedings for an offence as mentioned in sub-paragraph (a) and the proceedings were dismissed and all rights of appeal have been exercised or the time for appealing has expired,

the authority shall be under a duty to return the product or records detained under regulation 22 or 23 to the person from whom they were seized.

(6)　Where the authority is satisfied that some other person has a better right to a product or record than the person from whom they were seized, the authority shall, instead of the duty in paragraph (5), be under a duty to return it to that other person or, as the case may be, to the person appearing to the authority to have the best right to the product or record in question.

(7)　Where different persons claim to be entitled to the return of a product or record that is required to be returned under paragraph (5), then it may be retained for as long as it reasonably necessary for the determination in accordance with paragraph (6) of the person to whom it must be returned.

(8)　A person aggrieved by an order made under this regulation by a magistrates' court in England and Wales or Northern Ireland, or by a decision of such a court not to make such an order, may appeal against that order or decision—

(a)　in England and Wales, to the Crown Court;

(b)　in Northern Ireland, to the county court;

and an order so made may contain such provision as appears to the court to be appropriate for delaying the coming into force of the order pending the making and determination of any appeal (including any application under section 111 of the Magistrates' Courts Act 1980 or article 146 of the Magistrates' Courts (Northern Ireland) Order 1981 (statement of case)).

[3462]

NOTES
Commencement: 1 October 2005.

26　Compensation for seizure and detention

Where an officer of an enforcement authority exercises any power under regulation 22 or 23 to seize and detain a product, the enforcement authority shall be liable to pay compensation to any person having an interest in the product in respect of any loss or damage caused by reason of the exercise of the power if—

(a)　there has been no contravention in relation to the product of any requirement imposed by or under these Regulations, and

(b)　the exercise of the power is not attributable to any neglect or default by that person.

[3463]

NOTES
Commencement: 1 October 2005.

27　Recovery of expenses of enforcement

(1)　This regulation shall apply where a court—

(a)　convicts a person of an offence in respect of a contravention in relation to a product of any requirement imposed by or under these Regulations, or

(b)　makes an order under regulation 18 or 19 for the forfeiture of a product.

(2)　The court may (in addition to any other order it may make as to costs or expenses) order the person convicted or, as the case may be, any person having an interest in the product to reimburse an enforcement authority for any expenditure which has been or may be incurred by that authority—

(a)　in connection with any seizure or detention of the product by or on behalf of the authority, or

(b)　in connection with any compliance by the authority with directions given by the court for the purposes of any order for the forfeiture of the product.

[3464]

NOTES
Commencement: 1 October 2005.

28 Power of Secretary of State to obtain information

(1) If the Secretary of State considers that, for the purposes of deciding whether to serve a safety notice, or to vary or revoke a safety notice which he has already served, he requires information or a sample of a product he may serve on a person a notice requiring him:

    (a) to furnish to the Secretary of State, within a period specified in the notice, such information as is specified;

    (b) to produce such records as are specified in the notice at a time and place so specified (and to produce any such records which are stored in any electronic form in a form in which they are visible and legible) and to permit a person appointed by the Secretary of State for that purpose to take copies of the records at that time and place;

    (c) to produce such samples of a product as are specified in the notice at a time and place so specified.

(2) A person shall be guilty of an offence if he—

    (a) fails, without reasonable cause, to comply with a notice served on him under paragraph (1); or

    (b) in purporting to comply with a requirement which by virtue of paragraph (1)(a) or (b) is contained in such a notice—

        (i) furnishes information or records which he knows are false in a material particular, or

        (ii) recklessly furnishes information or records which are false in a material particular.

(3) A person guilty of an offence under paragraph (2) shall—

    (a) in the case of an offence under sub-paragraph (a) of that paragraph, be liable on summary conviction to a fine not exceeding level 5 on the standard scale; and

    (b) in the case of an offence under sub-paragraph (b) of that paragraph, be liable—

        (i) on conviction on indictment, to a fine;

        (ii) on summary conviction, to a fine not exceeding the statutory maximum.

[3465]

NOTES

Commencement: 1 October 2005.

29 Defence of due diligence

(1) Subject to the following provisions of this regulation, in proceedings against a person for an offence under these Regulations it shall be a defence for that person to show that he took all reasonable steps and exercised all due diligence to avoid committing the offence.

(2) Where in any proceedings against any person for such an offence the defence provided by paragraph (1) involves an allegation that the commission of the offence was due—

    (a) to the act or default of another, or

    (b) to reliance on information given by another,

that person shall not, without the leave of the court, be entitled to rely on the defence unless, not less than seven clear days before, in England, Wales and Northern Ireland, the hearing of the proceedings or, in Scotland, the trial diet, he has served a notice under paragraph (3) on the person bringing the proceedings.

(3) A notice under this paragraph shall give such information identifying or assisting in the identification of the person who—

    (a) committed the act or default, or

    (b) gave the information,

as is in the possession of the person serving the notice at the time he serves it.

(4) A person may not rely on the defence provided by paragraph (1) by reason of his reliance on information supplied by another, unless he shows that it was reasonable in all the circumstances to have relied on the information, having regard in particular—

    (a) to the steps which he took, and those which might reasonably have been taken, for the purpose of verifying the information; and

    (b) to whether he had any reason to disbelieve the information.

[3466]

NOTES

Commencement: 1 October 2005.

30 Defence in relation to antiques

(1) This regulation shall apply in proceedings against any person for an offence under regulation 20(1) in respect of the supply, offer or agreement to supply or exposure or possession for supply of second hand products supplied as antiques.

PART 2
STATUTORY INSTRUMENTS

(2)   It shall be a defence for that person to show that the terms on which he supplied the product or agreed or offered to supply the product or, in the case of a product which he exposed or possessed for supply, the terms on which he intended to supply the product, contemplated the acquisition of an interest in the product by the person supplied or to be supplied.

(3)   Paragraph (2) applies only if the producer or distributor clearly informed the person to whom he supplied the product, or offered or agreed to supply the product or, in the case of a product which he exposed or possessed for supply, he intended to so inform that person, that the product is an antique.

[3467]

NOTES
Commencement: 1 October 2005.

31   Liability of person other than principal offender

(1)   Where the commission by a person of an offence under these Regulations is due to an act or default committed by some other person in the course of a commercial activity of his, the other person shall be guilty of the offence and may be proceeded against and punished by virtue of this paragraph whether or not proceedings are taken against the first-mentioned person.

(2)   Where a body corporate is guilty of an offence under these Regulations (including where it is so guilty by virtue of paragraph (1)) in respect of any act or default which is shown to have been committed with the consent or connivance of, or to be attributable to any neglect on the part of, any director, manager, secretary or other similar officer of the body corporate or any person who was purporting to act in any such capacity he, as well as the body corporate, shall be guilty of that offence and shall be liable to be proceeded against and punished accordingly.

(3)   Where the affairs of a body corporate are managed by its members, paragraph (2) shall apply in relation to the acts and defaults of a member in connection with his functions of management as if he were a director of the body corporate.

(4)   Where a Scottish partnership is guilty of an offence under these Regulations (including where it is so guilty by virtue of paragraph (1)) in respect of any act or default which is shown to have been committed with the consent or connivance of, or to be attributable to any neglect on the part of, a partner in the partnership, he, as well as the partnership, shall be guilty of that offence and shall be liable to be proceeded against and punished accordingly.

[3468]

NOTES
Commencement: 1 October 2005.

PART 4
MISCELLANEOUS

32   Reports

(1)   It shall be the duty of the Secretary of State to lay before each House of Parliament a report on the exercise during the period to which the report relates of the functions which are exercisable by enforcement authorities under these Regulations.

(2)   The first such report shall relate to the period beginning on the day on which these Regulations come into force and ending on 31 March 2008 and subsequent reports shall relate to a period of not more than five years beginning on the day after the day on which the period to which the previous report relates ends.

(3)   The Secretary of State may from time to time prepare and lay before each House of Parliament such other reports on the exercise of those functions as he considers appropriate.

(4)   The Secretary of State may direct an enforcement authority to report at such intervals as he may specify in the direction on the discharge by that authority of the functions exercisable by it under these Regulations.

(5)   A report under paragraph (4) shall be in such form and shall contain such particulars as are specified in the direction of the Secretary of State.

[3469]

NOTES
Commencement: 1 October 2005.

33   Duty to notify Secretary of State and Commission

(1)   An enforcement authority which has received a notification under regulation 9(1) shall immediately pass the same on to the Secretary of State, who shall immediately pass it on to the

competent authorities appointed for the purpose in the Member States where the product in question is or has been marketed or otherwise supplied to consumers.

(2)   Where an enforcement authority takes a measure which restricts the placing on the market of a product, or requires its withdrawal or recall, it shall immediately notify the Secretary of State, specifying its reasons for taking the action. It shall also immediately notify the Secretary of State of any modification or lifting of such a measure.

(3)   On receiving a notification under paragraph (2), or if he takes a measure which restricts the placing on the market of a product, or requires its withdrawal or recall, the Secretary of State shall (to the extent that such notification is not required under article 12 of the GPS Directive or any other Community legislation) immediately notify the European Commission of the measure taken, specifying the reasons for taking it. The Secretary of State shall also immediately notify the European Commission of any modification or lifting of such a measure. If the Secretary of State considers that the effects of the risk do not or cannot go beyond the territory of the United Kingdom, he shall notify the European Commission of the measure concerned insofar as it involves information likely to be of interest to Member States from the product safety standpoint, and in particular if it is in response to a new risk which has not yet been reported in other notifications.

(4)   Where an enforcement authority adopts or decides to adopt, recommend or agree with producers and distributors, whether on a compulsory or voluntary basis, a measure or action to prevent, restrict or impose specific conditions on the possible marketing or use of a product (other than a pharmaceutical product) by reason of a serious risk, it shall immediately notify the Secretary of State. It shall also immediately notify the Secretary of State of any modification or withdrawal of any such measure or action.

(5)   On receiving a notification under paragraph (4), or if he adopts or decides to adopt, recommend or agree with producers and distributors, whether on a compulsory or voluntary basis, a measure or action to prevent, restrict or impose specific conditions on the possible marketing or use of a product (other than a pharmaceutical product) by reason of a serious risk, the Secretary of State shall immediately notify the European Commission of it through the Community Rapid Information System, known as RAPEX. The Secretary of State shall also inform the European Commission without delay of any modification or withdrawal of any such measure or action.

(6)   If the Secretary of State considers that the effects of the risk do not or cannot go beyond the territory of the United Kingdom, he shall notify the European Commission of the measures or action concerned insofar as they involve information likely to be of interest to Member States of the European Union from the product safety standpoint, and in particular if they are in response to a new risk which has not been reported in other notifications.

(7)   Before deciding to adopt such a measure or take such an action as is referred to in paragraph (5), the Secretary of State may pass on to the European Commission any information in his possession regarding the existence of a serious risk. Where he does so, he must inform the European Commission, within 45 days of the day of passing the information to it, whether he confirms or modifies that information.

(8)   Upon receipt of a notification from the European Commission under article 12(2) of the GPS Directive, the Secretary of State shall notify the Commission of the following—
(a)   whether the product the subject of the notification has been marketed in the United Kingdom;
(b)   what measure concerning the product the enforcement authorities in the United Kingdom may be adopting, stating the reasons, including any differing assessment of risk or any other special circumstance justifying the decision as to the measure, in particular lack of action or follow-up; and
(c)   any relevant supplementary information he has obtained on the risk involved, including the results of any test or analysis carried out.

(9)   The Secretary of State shall notify the European Commission without delay of any modification or withdrawal of any measures notified to it under paragraph (8)(b).

(10)   In this regulation—
(a)   references to a product excludes a second hand product supplied as an antique or as a product to be repaired or reconditioned prior to being used, provided the supplier clearly informs the person to whom he supplies the product to that effect;
(b)   "pharmaceutical product" means a product falling within Council Directive 2001/83/EC of the European Parliament and of the Council on the Community code relating to medicinal products for human use [as amended by Directive 2002/98/EC of the European Parliament and of the Council setting standards of quality and safety for the collection, testing, processing, storage and distribution of human blood and blood components, Commission Directive 2003/63/EC amending Directive 2001/83/EC on the Community code relating to medicinal products for human use, Directive 2004/24/EC of the European Parliament and of the Council amending, as regards traditional herbal medicinal products, Directive 2001/83/EC on the Community code relating to medicinal

products for human use and Directive 2004/27/EC of the European Parliament and of the Council amending Directive 2001/83/EC on the Community code relating to medicinal products for human use].

[3470]

NOTES
Commencement: 1 October 2005.
Para (10): words in square brackets in sub-para (b) inserted by the Medicines (Marketing Authorisations Etc) Amendment Regulations 2005, SI 2005/2759, reg 4, Schedule, para 18.

34 Provisions supplemental to regulation 33

(1) A notification under regulation 33(2) to (6), (8) or (9) to the Secretary of State or the Commission shall be in writing and shall provide all available details and at least the following information—

    (a) information enabling the product to be identified,

    (b) a description of the risk involved, including a summary of the results of any test or analysis and of their conclusions which are relevant to assessing the level of risk,

    (c) the nature and the duration of the measures or action taken or decided on, if applicable,

    (d) information on supply chains and distribution of the product, in particular on destination countries.

(2) Where a measure notified to the Commission under regulation 33 seeks to limit the marketing or use of a chemical substance or preparation, the Secretary of State shall provide to the Commission as soon as possible either a summary or the references of the relevant data relating to the substance or preparation considered and to known and available substitutes, where such information is available. The Secretary of State shall also notify the Commission of the anticipated effects of the measure on consumer health and safety together with the assessment of the risk carried out in accordance with the general principles for the risk evaluation of chemical substances as referred to in article 10(4) of Council Regulation (EEC) No 793/93 of 23 March 1993 on the evaluation and control of the risks of existing substances, in the case of an existing substance, or in article 3(2) of Council Directive 67/548/EEC on the approximation of laws, regulations and administrative provisions relating to the classification, packaging and labelling of dangerous substances in the case of a new substance.

(3) Where the Commission carries out an investigation under paragraph 5 of Annex II to the GPS Directive, the Secretary of State shall supply the Commission with such information as it requests, to the best of his ability.

[3471]

NOTES
Commencement: 1 October 2005.

35 Implementation of Commission decisions

(1) This regulation applies where the Commission adopts a decision pursuant to article 13 of the GPS Directive.

(2) The Secretary of State shall—

    (a) take such action under these Regulations, or

    (b) direct another enforcement authority to take such action under these Regulations

as is necessary to comply with the decision.

(3) Where an enforcement authority serves a safety notice pursuant to paragraph (2), the following provisions of these Regulations shall not apply in relation to that notice, namely regulations 14(3), 15(4) to (6) and 16(1), 16(2)(c) and (d), 16(5) to (7) and 17.

(4) Unless the Commission's decision provides otherwise, export from the Community of a dangerous product which is the subject of such a decision is prohibited with effect from the date the decision comes into force.

(5) The enforcement of the prohibition in paragraph (4) shall be treated as an assigned matter within the meaning of section 1(1) of the Customs and Excise Management Act 1979.

(6) The measures necessary to implement the decision shall be taken within 20 days, unless the decision specifies a different period.

(7) The Secretary of State or, where the Secretary of State has directed another enforcement authority to take action under paragraph (2)(b), that enforcement authority shall, within one month, give the parties concerned an opportunity to submit their views and shall inform the Commission accordingly.

[3472]

PART 2
STATUTORY INSTRUMENTS

NOTES
Commencement: 1 October 2005.

36 Market surveillance

In order to ensure a high level of consumer health and safety protection, enforcement authorities shall within the limits of their responsibility and to the extent of their ability undertake market surveillance of products employing appropriate means and procedures and co-operating with other enforcement authorities and competent authorities of other Member States which may include:

  (a) establishment, periodical updating and implementation of sectoral surveillance programmes by categories of products or risks and the monitoring of surveillance activities, findings and results,

  (b) follow-up and updating of scientific and technical knowledge concerning the safety of products,

  (c) the periodical review and assessment of the functioning of the control activities and their effectiveness and, if necessary revision of the surveillance approach and organisation put in place.

[3473]

NOTES
Commencement: 1 October 2005.

37 Complaints procedures

An enforcement authority shall maintain and publish a procedure by which complaints may be submitted by any person on product safety and on surveillance and control activities, which complaints shall be followed up as appropriate.

[3474]

NOTES
Commencement: 1 October 2005.

38 Co-operation between enforcement authorities

  (1) It shall be the duty of an enforcement authority to co-operate with other enforcement authorities in carrying out the functions conferred on them by these Regulations. In particular—

  (a) enforcement authorities shall share their expertise and best practices with each other;

  (b) enforcement authorities shall undertake collaborative working where they have a shared interest.

  (2) The Secretary of State shall inform the European Commission as to the arrangements for the enforcement of these Regulations, including which bodies are enforcement authorities.

[3475]

NOTES
Commencement: 1 October 2005.

39 Information

  (1) An enforcement authority shall in general make available to the public such information as is available to it on the following matters relating to the risks to consumer health and safety posed by a product—

  (a) the nature of the risk,

  (b) the product identification,

and the measures taken in respect of the risk, without prejudice to the need not to disclose information for effective monitoring and investigation activities.

  (2) Paragraph (1) shall not apply to any information obtained by an enforcement authority for the purposes of these Regulations which, by its nature, is covered by professional secrecy, unless the circumstances require such information to be made public in order to protect the health and safety of consumers.

  (3) ...

[3476]

NOTES
Commencement: 1 October 2005.
Para (3): amends the Enterprise Act 2002 (Part 9 Restrictions on Disclosure of Information) (Amendment and Specification) Order 2003, SI 2003/1400.

40 Service of documents

(1)   A document required or authorised by virtue of these Regulations to be served on a person may be so served—

(a)   on an individual by delivering it to him or by leaving it at his proper address or by sending it by post to him at that address;

(b)   on a body corporate other than a limited liability partnership, by serving it in accordance with sub-paragraph (a) on the secretary of the body;

(c)   on a limited liability partnership, by serving it in accordance with sub-paragraph (a) on a member of the partnership; or

(d)   on a partnership, by serving it in accordance with sub-paragraph (a) on a partner or a person having the control or management of the partnership business;

(e)   on any other person by leaving it at his proper address or by sending it by post to him at that address.

(2)   For the purposes of paragraph (1), and for the purposes of section 7 of the Interpretation Act 1978 (which relates to the service of documents by post) in its application to that paragraph, the proper address of a person on whom a document is to be served by virtue of these Regulations shall be his last known address except that—

(a)   in the case of a body corporate (other than a limited liability partnership) or its secretary, it shall be the address of the registered or principal office of the body;

(b)   in the case of a limited liability partnership or a member of the partnership, it shall be the address of the registered or principal office of the partnership;

(c)   in the case of a partnership or a partner or a person having the control or management of a partnership business, it shall be the address of the principal office of the partnership,

and for the purposes of this paragraph the principal officer of a company constituted under the law of a country or territory outside the United Kingdom or of a partnership carrying on business outside the United Kingdom is its principal office within the United Kingdom.

(3)   A document required or authorised by virtue of these Regulations to be served on a person may also be served by transmitting the request by any means of electronic communication to an electronic address (which includes a fax number and an e-mail address) being an address which the person has held out as an address at which he or it can be contacted for the purposes of receiving such documents.

(4)   A document transmitted by any means of electronic communication in accordance with the preceding paragraph is, unless the contrary is proved, deemed to be received on the business day after the notice was transmitted over a public electronic communications network.

[3477]

NOTES

Commencement: 1 October 2005.

41 Extension of time for bringing summary proceedings

(1)   Notwithstanding section 127 of the Magistrates' Courts Act 1980 or article 19 of the Magistrates' Courts (Northern Ireland) Order 1981, in England, Wales and Northern Ireland a magistrates' court may try an information (in the case of England and Wales) or a complaint (in the case of Northern Ireland) in respect of an offence under these Regulations if (in the case of England and Wales) the information is laid or (in the case of Northern Ireland) the complaint is made within three years from the date of the offence or within one year from the discovery of the offence by the prosecutor whichever is the earlier.

(2)   Notwithstanding section 136 of the Criminal Procedure (Scotland) Act 1995, in Scotland summary proceedings for an offence under these Regulations may be commenced within three years from the date of the offence or within one year from the discovery of the offence by the prosecutor whichever is the earlier.

(3)   For the purposes of paragraph (2), section 136(3) of the Criminal Procedure (Scotland) Act 1995 shall apply as it applies for the purposes of that section.

[3478]

NOTES

Commencement: 1 October 2005.

42 Civil proceedings

These Regulations shall not be construed as conferring any right of action in civil proceedings in respect of any loss or damage suffered in consequence of a contravention of these Regulations.

[3479]

NOTES
Commencement: 1 October 2005.

43 Privileged information

(1) Nothing in these Regulations shall be taken as requiring a person to produce any records if he would be entitled to refuse to produce those records in any proceedings in any court on the grounds that they are the subject of legal professional privilege or, in Scotland, that they contain a confidential communication made by or to an advocate or solicitor in that capacity, or as authorising a person to take possession of any records which are in the possession of a person who would be so entitled.

(2) Nothing in these Regulations shall be construed as requiring a person to answer any question or give any information if to do so would incriminate that person or that person's spouse or civil partner.

[3480]

NOTES
Commencement: 1 October 2005 (para (1), para (2) certain purposes); 5 December 2005 (para (2), otherwise).

44 Evidence in proceedings for offence relating to regulation 9(1)

(1) This regulation applies where a person has given a notification to an enforcement authority pursuant to regulation 9(1).

(2) No evidence relating to that statement may be adduced and no question relating to it may be asked by the prosecution in any criminal proceedings (other than proceedings in which that person is charged with an offence under regulation 20 for a contravention of regulation 9(1)), unless evidence relating to it is adduced, or a question relating to it is asked, in the proceedings by or on behalf of that person.

[3481]

NOTES
Commencement: 1 October 2005.

45 Transitional provisions

Where, in relation to a product, a suspension notice (within the meaning of the 1987 Act) has (by virtue of regulation 11(b) of the General Product Safety Regulations 1994) been served under section 14 of the 1987 Act and is in force immediately prior to the coming into force of these Regulations, it shall continue in force notwithstanding the revocation of the General Product Safety Regulations 1994 by these Regulations, and those Regulations shall continue to apply accordingly.

[3482]–[3485]

NOTES
Commencement: 1 October 2005.

46, 47   (*Reg 46 repeals the Consumer Protection Act 1987, s 10 and amends ss 11, 13, 19, 39, 45 of that Act at* **[1397]**, **[1399]**, **[1404]**, **[1423]**, **[1429]**; *reg 47 amends the Gas Act 1995, Sch 4, the Criminal Justice and Police Act 2001, s 66, Schs 1, 2.*)

FINANCIAL SERVICES AND MARKETS ACT 2000 (OMBUDSMAN SCHEME) (CONSUMER CREDIT JURISDICTION) ORDER 2007

(SI 2007/383)

NOTES
Made: 7 February 2007.
Authority: Financial Services and Markets Act 2000, s 226A(2)(e).
Commencement: see art 1.

1 Citation and commencement

This Order may be cited as the Financial Services and Markets Act 2000 (Ombudsman Scheme) (Consumer Credit Jurisdiction) Order 2007 and shall come into force—
    (a)   for the purposes of article 2(a) to (f) and (i) on 8th March 2007; and

(b)   for all other purposes on the day sections 24 and 25 of the Consumer Credit Act 2006 come fully into force.

[3486]

NOTES
Commencement: 8 March 2007.

2 Types of Business

The Secretary of State specifies the following types of business for the purposes of section 226A(2)(e) of the Financial Services and Markets Act 2000—

(a)   a consumer credit business;
(b)   a consumer hire business;
(c)   a business so far as it comprises or relates to credit brokerage;
(d)   a business so far as it comprises or relates to debt-adjusting;
(e)   a business so far as it comprises or relates to debt-counselling;
(f)   a business so far as it comprises or relates to debt-collecting;
(g)   a business so far as it comprises or relates to debt administration;
(h)   a business so far as it comprises or relates to the provision of credit information services;
(i)   a business so far as it comprises or relates to the operation of a credit reference agency.

[3487]

NOTES
Commencement: 8 March 2007 (paras (a)–(f), (i)); 1 October 2008 (otherwise).

CONSUMER CREDIT (INFORMATION REQUIREMENTS AND DURATION OF LICENCES AND CHARGES) REGULATIONS 2007

(SI 2007/1167)

NOTES
Made: 31 March 2007.
Authority: Consumer Credit Act 1974, ss 22(1B), (1E), 28A(3)(b), (6), 77A(2), 78(4A), 86B(8), 86C(6), 86E(2), (7)(b), 88(1), (4), 130A(6), 182(2), 189(1).
Commencement: in accordance with reg 1(2), (3).

ARRANGEMENT OF REGULATIONS

1 Citation and commencement

(1)　These Regulations may be cited as the Consumer Credit (Information Requirements and Duration of Licences and Charges) Regulations 2007.

(2)　This regulation and regulations 2 and 42 to 44 shall come into force on 6th April 2008.

(3)　The remaining regulations shall come into force on 1st October 2008.

[3488]

NOTES
　Commencement: 6 April 2008.

2　Interpretation

In these Regulations—

　"the 1974 Act" means the Consumer Credit Act 1974;

　"agreement to aggregate" means an agreement (whether arising by conduct or otherwise) made between the creditor and the debtor—

　　　(a)　concerning two or more agreements for fixed-sum credit between the creditor and the debtor where at least one such agreement is a regulated credit agreement; and

　　　(b)　which permits or requires the debtor to aggregate all individual payments under the agreements mentioned in paragraph (a) and pay them at the same time; and

　"home credit loan agreement" means a debtor-creditor agreement which satisfies either or both of the following conditions—

　　　(a)　the agreement provides that all or most of the sums payable by the debtor are to be collected by or on behalf of the creditor at the debtor's home or at the home of a natural person who makes payments to the creditor on the debtor's behalf (or, in either case, to be so collected if the debtor so wishes);

　　　(b)　at the time the agreement is entered into, the debtor could reasonably expect, from representations made by or on behalf of the creditor at or before that time, that all or most of the sums payable would be collected as specified in paragraph (a) (or, in either case would be so collected if the debtor wished).

[3489]

NOTES
　Commencement: 6 April 2008.

3　Content of statements provided in relation to fixed-sum credit agreements

Regulations 4 to 11 shall apply to a statement given under section 77A of the 1974 Act (statements to be provided in relation to fixed-sum credit agreements).

[3490]

NOTES
　Commencement: 1 October 2008.

4　Subject to regulations 5 to 9, the statement shall contain—

　　(a)　the information set out in Part 1 of Schedule 1;

　　(b)　each of the forms of wording set out in Part 2 of Schedule 1;

　　(c)　subject to paragraph (d),

　　　　(i)　where the statement relates to a hire-purchase or conditional sale agreement, the first form of wording in paragraph 5 of Schedule 1; and

　　　　(ii)　where the statement relates to a hire-purchase or conditional sale agreement and the debtor purchased a contract of insurance as referred to in regulation 2(8) of the Consumer Credit (Agreement) Regulations 1983 (information requirements in relation to credit and insurance finance agreements), each form of wording set out in paragraph 5 of Schedule 1;

(d) where the statement referred to in paragraph (c) is required to be given after the final payment under the agreement has fallen due, the statement need not include either of the forms of wording set out in paragraph 5 of Schedule 1.

[3491]

NOTES
Commencement: 1 October 2008.

5 The creditor shall indicate in the statement which of the two pieces of information referred to in each of paragraphs 3(d) and 3(e) of Schedule 1 it has included in the statement.

[3492]

NOTES
Commencement: 1 October 2008.

6 Where the rate or rates of interest provided for under the agreement are not applicable on a per annum basis, paragraph 3(h) of Schedule 1 shall not require amounts [and dates] of interest which become due during the period to which the statement relates to be set out separately in the statement.

[3493]

NOTES
Commencement: 1 October 2008.
Words in square brackets inserted by the Consumer Credit (Information Requirements and Duration of Licences and Charges) (Amendment) Regulations 2008, SI 2008/1751, reg 2(a).

7 Subject to regulations 8 and 9, where the creditor and the debtor have entered into an agreement to aggregate—

[(za) the reference to opening balance in paragraph 3(f) of Schedule 1 may be construed as a reference to the aggregated opening balance;]

(a) the reference to payments made in paragraph 3(g) of Schedule 1 may be construed as a reference to the aggregated payments which the debtor is permitted or required to make;

(b) the reference to interest and charges which became due in paragraph 3(h) of Schedule 1 may be construed as the aggregated interest and charges which became due;

(c) the reference to movements in paragraph 3(i) of Schedule 1 may be construed as a reference to the aggregated movements in all the accounts maintained by the creditor in relation to the agreements to which the agreement to aggregate relates;

[(cc) the reference to balance in paragraph 3(j) of Schedule 1 may be construed as a reference to the aggregated balance;]

(d) where any of the forms of wording set out in Parts 2 and 3 of Schedule 1 do not apply to all the agreements to which the agreement to aggregate relates the creditor shall identify for each form of wording which does not so apply the regulated agreement or agreements to which it relates;

(e) the information required under paragraphs 1, 2, 3(c), 3(d) and 3(e) of Schedule 1 need only be shown once where the information which would otherwise have to be included for the agreements to which the agreement to aggregate relates is the same for each agreement.

[3494]

NOTES
Commencement: 1 October 2008.
Paras (za), (cc) inserted by the Consumer Credit (Information Requirements and Duration of Licences and Charges) (Amendment) Regulations 2008, SI 2008/1751, reg 2(b).

8 Subject to regulation 9, where not all the sums permitted to be shown in the statement as an aggregated figure under regulation 7 are so shown the creditor shall indicate where each figure for payment made or interest or charges which became due or the movement which occurred is an aggregated figure.

[3495]

NOTES
Commencement: 1 October 2008.

9—(1)   Paragraphs (2) to (4) shall apply where the agreement to aggregate concerns agreements to which regulation 2(8) of the Consumer Credit (Agreements) Regulations 1983 applies.

[(2)   Where the statement is not the first statement given under section 77A of the 1974 Act in relation to the agreements to which the agreement to aggregate relates, the reference to the amount of credit in paragraph 3(b) of Schedule 1 may be construed as a reference to the aggregated amount of credit provided, and where applicable, to be provided under those agreements.]

(3)   …

(4)   The creditor shall not be required to comply with regulation 8.

[3496]

NOTES
Commencement: 1 October 2008.
Para (2): substituted by the Consumer Credit (Information Requirements and Duration of Licences and Charges) (Amendment) Regulations 2008, SI 2008/1751, reg 2(c)(i).
Para (3): revoked by SI 2008/1751, reg 2(c)(ii).

10   Where the creditor and the debtor have entered into an arrangement under which interest or charges payable under a fixed-sum credit agreement are applied to an account which is separate from the account to which payments referred to in paragraph 3(g) of Schedule 1 are applied, the statement shall include a form of wording referring to that arrangement [and the information referred to in paragraph 3(h) of Schedule 1 may be omitted from the statement].

[3497]–[3498]

NOTES
Commencement: 1 October 2008.
Words in square brackets added by the Consumer Credit (Information Requirements and Duration of Licences and Charges) (Amendment) Regulations 2008, SI 2008/1751, reg 2(d).

11   (*Revoked by the Legislative Reform (Consumer Credit) Order 2008, SI 2008/2826, art 7.*)

12 Additional information in statements provided in relation to certain fixed-sum credit agreements

(1)   A statement given under section 77A of the 1974 Act in relation to a home credit loan agreement shall include—
   (a)   the total charge for credit provided under the agreement; and
   (b)   a statement in the following form:

"You are entitled to request one free statement per quarter or one per loan (whichever allows for more requests). We are required to provide you with a statement free of charge within seven days of receiving your request.".

(2)   Such a statement, if given during a period when any relevant website is being [operated], shall also contain the statement—"You can compare our loans with other home credit loans available in your area by accessing the website", followed by the location of the website in question.

[(3)   For the purposes of paragraph (2), "relevant website" has the same meaning as in article 14 of the Home Credit Market Investigation Order 2007.]

[3499]

NOTES
Commencement: 1 October 2008.
Para (2): word in square brackets substituted by the Consumer Credit (Information Requirements and Duration of Licences and Charges) (Amendment) Regulations 2008, SI 2008/1751, reg 2(e)(i).
Para (3): substituted by SI 2008/1751, reg 2(e)(ii).

13 Additional information in statements provided in relation to running-account credit agreements

Regulations 14 to 18 shall apply to a statement given under section 78(4) of the 1974 Act (duty to give information to debtor under running-account credit agreement).

[3500]

NOTES
Commencement: 1 October 2008.

[**14**   Subject to regulations 17 and 18, where the agreement to which the statement relates requires the payment each month of a minimum sum, the statement shall include the forms of wording set

PART 2
STATUTORY INSTRUMENTS

out in paragraphs 1 and 4 of Schedule 2, and in paragraph 2 of that Schedule if applicable, and the information set out in paragraph 3 of that Schedule.]

[3501]–[3502]

NOTES
Commencement: 1 October 2008.
Substituted by the Consumer Credit (Information Requirements and Duration of Licences and Charges) (Amendment) Regulations 2008, SI 2008/1751, reg 2(f).

15 (*Revoked by the Consumer Credit* (*Information Requirements and Duration of Licences and Charges*) (*Amendment*) *Regulations 2008, SI 2008/1751, reg 2(g).*)

[**16** Where the agreement to which the statement relates does not require the payment each month of a minimum sum, and the creditor has at any time during the period to which the statement relates required the debtor to repay sums which are due under the agreement, only the second form of wording set out in paragraph 4 of Schedule 2 shall be given.]

[3503]

NOTES
Commencement: 1 October 2008.
Substituted by the Consumer Credit (Information Requirements and Duration of Licences and Charges) (Amendment) Regulations 2008, SI 2008/1751, reg 2(h).

17 For the purposes of regulations [14] and 16, "minimum sum" means a sum which is less than the total sum due under the agreement at the time the duty to give the notice arises.

[3504]

NOTES
Commencement: 1 October 2008.
Number in square brackets substituted by the Consumer Credit (Information Requirements and Duration of Licences and Charges) (Amendment) Regulations 2008, SI 2008/1751, reg 2(i).

18—(1) Subject to paragraph (2), the form of wording in paragraph 2 of Schedule 2 need not be included in a statement where the total amount which the debtor has failed to pay in relation to all the payments due under the running-account credit agreement during the period to which the statement relates does not exceed £1.

(2) Paragraph (1) shall not apply where, at the date on which the duty to give the statement arose, a default sum or other charge has become payable as a result of the debtors failure to pay sums not exceeding £1 as set out in paragraph (1).

[3505]

NOTES
Commencement: 1 October 2008.

19 Content of notices of sums in arrears under fixed-sum credit agreements etc

(1) Subject to regulations 20 to 23, a notice given under section 86B of the 1974 Act (notice of sums in arrears under fixed-sum credit agreements etc) shall contain—
  (a) a form of wording to the effect that the notice is given in compliance with the 1974 Act because the debtor or hirer is behind with [the sums payable] under the agreement;
  (b) a form of wording encouraging the debtor or the hirer to discuss the state of his account with the creditor or owner;
  (c) the information required by paragraphs 1 to 3 of Schedule 3;
  (d) statements in the form specified in paragraphs 4 and 5 of Schedule 3 as applicable; and
  (e) a statement in the form specified in Part 5 of Schedule 3.

(2) In addition, where the notice is required to be given under section 86B(2)(a) of the 1974 Act—
  (a) it shall include the information set out in Part 2 of Schedule 3;
  (b) the creditor or owner shall within fifteen working days of receiving the debtor's or hirer's request for further information about the shortfall which gave rise to the duty to give the notice, give the debtor or hirer in relation to each of the sums which comprise the shortfall, notice of—
    (i) the amount of the sums due which comprise the shortfall;
    (ii) the date on which the sums became due; and
    (iii) the amounts the debtor or hirer paid in respect of the sums due and the dates of those payments;

(c)   it shall, except where it contains all the information specified in regulation [19(2)(b)], include a statement in the following form:

"If you want more information about which payments you failed to make please get in touch with us. We are required to give you this information within fifteen working days of receiving your request for it.";

(d)   where the creditor or owner and the debtor or hirer have entered into an agreement to aggregate, the references to sums due and the reference to amounts paid in sub-paragraph (b) may be construed as a reference to the aggregated sums due to the creditor or owner and the aggregated amounts paid by the debtor or hirer in accordance with the terms of that agreement.

(3)   [Subject to paragraph (3A),] where the notice is required to be given under section 86B(2)(b) of the 1974 Act it shall also include the information set out in Part 3 of Schedule 3 and the statement in paragraph 4(1) of that Schedule shall be amended as specified in paragraph 13 of that Schedule.

[(3A)   Where the rate or rates of interest provided for under the agreement are not applicable on a per annum basis, paragraph 9 of Schedule 3 shall not require amounts and dates of interest which became due during the period to which the notice relates to be set out separately in the notice.]

(4)   Where the notice includes a form of wording to the effect that it is not a demand for immediate payment, the creditor or owner shall include wording explaining why it is not such a demand.

(5)   Subject to regulation 20(3)(c), the reference to the account in paragraphs 8 and 10 of Schedule 3 shall be construed as a reference to all accounts maintained by the creditor or owner which relate to the agreement with the debtor or hirer.

[3506]

NOTES

Commencement: 1 October 2008.

Para (1): words in square brackets substituted by the Consumer Credit (Information Requirements and Duration of Licences and Charges) (Amendment) Regulations 2008, SI 2008/1751, reg 2(j)(i).

Para (2): figure in square brackets substituted by SI 2008/1751, reg 2(j)(ii).

Para (3): words in square brackets inserted by SI 2008/1751, reg 2(j)(iii).

Para (3A): inserted by SI 2008/1751, reg 2(j)(iv).

20—(1)   Where the creditor and the debtor have entered into an agreement to aggregate and an arrears notice is required to be given in relation to two or more of the agreements to which the agreement to aggregate relates—

(a)   the information required under paragraphs 1 and 2 of Schedule 3 need only be shown once where the information which would otherwise have to be included for the agreements to which the agreement to aggregate relates is the same for each agreement;

(b)   where any of the forms of wording set out in paragraphs 4, 5 and 13 of that Schedule do not apply to all the agreements to which the agreement to aggregate relates the creditor shall identify for each such form of wording which does not so apply the regulated agreement or agreements to which it relates.

(2)   Where the creditor and the debtor have entered into an agreement to aggregate and the notice is required to be given under section 86B(2)(a) of the 1974 Act, the reference to the amount which comprises the shortfall in Part 2 of Schedule 3 may be construed as a reference to the aggregated shortfall due under the agreements to which the agreement to aggregate relates.

(3)   Subject to regulation 22, where the creditor and the debtor have entered into an agreement to aggregate and the notice is required to be given under section 86B(2)(b) of the 1974 Act—

[(a)   the reference to sums paid in paragraph 8 of Schedule 3 may be construed as a reference to the aggregated sums which the debtor is permitted or required to pay;]

(b)   the reference to interest or other charges in paragraph 9 of that Schedule may be construed as a reference to the aggregated interest or other charges which became due during the period to which the notice relates; and

(c)   the reference to movements in paragraph 10 of that Schedule may be construed as a reference to the aggregated movements in all the accounts maintained by the creditor in relation to the agreements to which the agreement to aggregate relates.

[3507]

NOTES

Commencement: 1 October 2008.

Para (3): sub-para (a) substituted by the Consumer Credit (Information Requirements and Duration of Licences and Charges) (Amendment) Regulations 2008, SI 2008/1751, reg 2(k).

21   Subject to regulation 22(c), where not all the sums permitted to be shown in the notice as an aggregated figure under regulation 20(3) are so shown, the creditor shall indicate where each figure for [a sum paid] or interest or charges which became due or the movement in the account which occurred is an aggregated figure.

[3508]

NOTES
Commencement: 1 October 2008.
Words in square brackets substituted by the Consumer Credit (Information Requirements and Duration of Licences and Charges) (Amendment) Regulations 2008, SI 2008/1751, reg 2(l).

22   Where the agreement to aggregate concerns agreements to which regulation 2(8) of the Consumer Credit (Agreements) Regulations 1983 applies and the notice is required to be given under [section 86B(2)] of the 1974 Act—
  (a)   the references to—
        (i)   the opening balance in paragraph 3(b) of Schedule 3; ...
        [(ia)   the amount of the shortfall in paragraph 6 of that Schedule; and]
        (ii)   the opening balance in paragraph 7 of that Schedule,
        may be construed as references to, respectively, the aggregated opening balance[, the aggregated amount of the shortfall] and the aggregated opening balance of those sums to which paragraph 7 refers, under the agreements to which the agreement to aggregate relates;
  (b)   the reference to the balance under the agreement at the end of the period to which the notice relates may be construed as a reference to the aggregated balance under the agreements to which the agreement to aggregate relates at the end of that period; and
  (c)   the creditor shall not be required to comply with regulation 21.

[3509]

NOTES
Commencement: 1 October 2008.
Words in first pair of square brackets substituted, word omitted revoked and words in second and third pairs of square brackets inserted by the Consumer Credit (Information Requirements and Duration of Licences and Charges) (Amendment) Regulations 2008, SI 2008/1751, reg 2(m).

23   Where all the sums payable under two or more agreements made between the creditor and the debtor at least one of which is a regulated fixed-sum credit agreement have become due and the creditor aggregates the sums due under those agreements for the purpose of recovering those sums—
  (a)   the reference to the opening balance in paragraph 3(b) of Schedule 3 may be construed as a reference to the aggregated opening balance under those agreements;
  (b)   the reference to opening balance in paragraph 7 of that Schedule may be construed as a reference to a sum equal to the aggregated parts of the opening balance under those agreements which the debtor has failed to pay in full when they became due;
  [(c)   the reference to sums paid in paragraph 8 of that Schedule may be construed as a reference to the aggregated sums which the debtor is permitted or required to pay;]
  (d)   the reference to interest and other charges becoming due to the creditor in paragraph 9 of that Schedule may be construed as a reference to the aggregated interest and other charges becoming due;
  (e)   the reference to movements in paragraph 10 of that Schedule may be construed as a reference to the aggregated movements in all the accounts maintained by the creditor in relation to those agreements;
  (f)   the reference to the balance in paragraph 11 of that Schedule may be construed as a reference to the aggregated balance under those agreements;
  (g)   the reference to the balance in paragraph 12 of that Schedule may be construed as a reference to a sum equal to the aggregated balance under those agreements which the debtor has failed to pay in full when it became due and which remains unpaid at the end of the period to which the notice relates;
  (h)   the information required under paragraphs 1 and 2 of Schedule 3 need only to be shown once where the information which would otherwise have to be included for those agreements is the same for each agreement; and
  (i)   where any of the forms of wording set out in paragraphs 4, 5 and 13 of that Schedule do not apply to all those agreements the creditor shall identify for each form of wording which does not so apply the regulated agreement or agreements to which it relates.

[3510]

NOTES
Commencement: 1 October 2008.

Para (c): substituted by the Consumer Credit (Information Requirements and Duration of Licences and Charges) (Amendment) Regulations 2008, SI 2008/1751, reg 2(n).

24   Content of notices of sums in arrears under running-account credit agreements

(1)   Subject to regulations 25 and 26, a notice given under section 86C of the 1974 Act (notice of sums in arrears under running-account credit agreements) ("the regulation 24 notice") shall contain—

   (a)   a form of wording to the effect that it is given in compliance with the 1974 Act because the debtor is behind with his payments under the agreement;

   (b)   a form of wording encouraging the debtor to discuss the state of his account with the creditor;

   (c)   the information required by paragraphs 14 to 17 of Schedule 3;

   (d)   a statement in the form set out in paragraph 18 of Schedule 3 and the appropriate statement specified in paragraph 19 of that Schedule; and

   (e)   a statement in the form specified in Part 5 of Schedule 3.

(2)   Where a regulation 24 notice includes wording to the effect that it is not a demand for immediate payment the creditor shall include wording explaining why it is not such a demand.

[3511]

NOTES

Commencement: 1 October 2008.

25   Where a regulation 24 notice is incorporated into another notice or statement which the creditor gives the debtor in relation to the agreement by virtue of another provision of the 1974 Act ("the other notice"), the regulation 24 notice need not contain so much of the information required under paragraphs 14 to 17 of Schedule 3 as is required to be included in the other notice by or under the provision of the 1974 Act under which the other notice is given.

[3512]

NOTES

Commencement: 1 October 2008.

26—(1)   Subject to paragraphs (2) and (3), where the total amount which the debtor has failed to pay in relation to the last two payments due under the agreement prior to the date on which the creditor came under a duty to give the debtor a regulation 24 notice is not more than £2, the notice—

   (a)   need not include any of the information or statements referred to in regulation 24;

   (b)   but in that event shall contain a statement in the following form—

"You have failed to make two minimum payments

Failing to make minimum payments can mean that you have broken the terms of this credit agreement. This could result in your having to pay additional costs. A copy of the Office of Fair Trading Arrears information sheet is enclosed, which contains more information about what to do when you get behind with your payments.".

(2)   Paragraph (1) shall not apply where at the date on which the duty to give notice arose a default sum or other charge has become payable as a result of the debtor's failure to pay sums as set out in paragraph (1).

(3)   Where a regulation 24 notice is incorporated into a statement which the creditor is required to give the debtor under section 78(4) of the 1974 Act, the statement shall not contain the wording specified in paragraph 2 of Schedule 2.

[3513]

NOTES

Commencement: 1 October 2008.

27   Giving of notices of default sums

Regulations 28 to 32 shall apply to a notice of default sums given under section 86E of the 1974 Act (notice of default sums) ("the regulation 27 notice").

[3514]

NOTES

Commencement: 1 October 2008.

28 A regulation 27 notice shall be given to the debtor or hirer by the creditor or owner within 35 days of a default sum becoming payable by the debtor or hirer.

[3515]

NOTES
    Commencement: 1 October 2008.

29 Content of notices of default sums

A regulation 27 notice shall contain a form of wording to the effect that it relates to default sums and is given in compliance with the 1974 Act.

[3516]

NOTES
    Commencement: 1 October 2008.

30 A regulation 27 notice shall contain the information and the form of wording set out in Part 1 of Schedule 4.

[3517]

NOTES
    Commencement: 1 October 2008.

31 If a regulation 27 notice is given in relation to an agreement which provides that interest is payable in connection with default sums it shall contain the appropriate form of wording set out in Part 2 of Schedule 4.

[3518]

NOTES
    Commencement: 1 October 2008.

32 Where a regulation 27 notice is incorporated into another notice or statement which the creditor gives the debtor in relation to the agreement by virtue of another provision of the 1974 Act ("the other notice"), the regulation 27 notice need not contain such of the information required under paragraphs 1 to 3 of Schedule 4 as is required to be included in the other notice by the provision of the 1974 Act under which the other notice is given.

[3519]

NOTES
    Commencement: 1 October 2008.

33 (*Amends the Consumer Credit (Enforcement, Default and Termination Notices) Regulations 1983, SI 1983/1561, reg 2, Sch 2.*)

34 Content of notices of intention to recover post-judgment interest

Subject to regulation 35, a notice given under section 130A(1) of the 1974 Act (notice of intention to recover post-judgment interest in connection with a judgment sum) shall contain:
    (a)   if the notice is the first required notice—
        (i)   the information listed and forms of wording set out in Part 1 of Schedule 5; and
        (ii)   the form of wording set out in Part 3 of Schedule 5;
    (b)   if the notice is not the first required notice, the information and forms of wording set out in Part 1 of and the information set out in Part 2 of Schedule 5.

[3520]

NOTES
    Commencement: 1 October 2008.

35 The creditor may, instead of including in the notice the form of wording set out in paragraph 6 of Schedule 5, include the wording which concerns advice and information available to consumers which is contained in the default information sheet referred to in section 86A of the 1974 Act and which is in effect in accordance with subsection (5) of that section at the time the duty to give the notice arose.

[3521]

NOTES
Commencement: 1 October 2008.

36 Form of notices and statements required under these Regulations

The wording required by regulations 10, 19(1)(a) and (b) and (4), 24(1)(a) and (b) and (2), 29 and 48(c) to be included in a notice or statement to be given under the 1974 Act shall be expressed in plain, intelligible language.

[3522]

NOTES
Commencement: 1 October 2008.

37—(1) Subject to paragraph (2), the first form of wording set out in paragraph 4 of Schedule 1 and the first form of wording set out in paragraph 5 of that Schedule shall appear together as a whole and shall not be interspersed with any other information or wording.

(2) The first form of wording set out in paragraph 4 of Schedule 1 and the first form of wording set out in paragraph 5 of that Schedule may be interspersed with the second form of wording set out in paragraph 5 of that Schedule.

[3523]

NOTES
Commencement: 1 October 2008.

38—(1) The first form of wording set out in paragraph 4 of Schedule 2 and the closing balance shall be shown together as a whole and not interspersed with any other information or wording.

(2) For the purposes of this regulation—
    (a)   ...
    (b)   closing balance means, in relation to a statement required to be given under section 78(4) of the 1974 Act, the balance at the end of the period to which the statement relates which is required to be included in the statement under paragraph 1 of the Schedule to the Consumer Credit (Running-Account) Credit Information Regulations 1983.

[3524]

NOTES
Commencement: 1 October 2008.
Para (2): sub-para (a) revoked by the Consumer Credit (Information Requirements and Duration of Licences and Charges) (Amendment) Regulations 2008, SI 2008/1751, reg 2(o).

39 The lettering of the information and wording required by these Regulations to be included in a statement or notice and any figures and symbols forming part of that information or wording shall be easily legible and of a colour which is readily distinguishable from the background medium upon which it is or they are displayed.

[3525]

NOTES
Commencement: 1 October 2008.

40—(1) Subject to paragraph (2), the information and wording required by these Regulations[, other than regulation 33,] to be included in a statement or notice to be given under the 1974 Act shall be no less prominent than any other information and wording included in the document in which that notice or statement is embodied.

(2) But—
    (a)   the date of the notice or statement, trade names and names of parties to the agreement, logos, headings or the reference number of the agreement may be more prominent; and
    (b)   the form of wording set out in paragraph 2 of Schedule 2 shall be more prominent,

than any such other information and wording, whether prominence is achieved by capital letters, underlining, larger or bold print or otherwise.

[3526]

NOTES
Commencement: 1 October 2008.

Para (1): words in square brackets inserted by the Consumer Credit (Information Requirements and Duration of Licences and Charges) (Amendment) Regulations 2008, SI 2008/1751, reg 2(p).

41 Errors and omissions

Where a notice or statement contains an error or omission which does not affect the substance of the information or forms of wording which it is required by these Regulations to contain, that notice or statement shall not breach these Regulations on this ground alone.

[3527]

NOTES
Commencement: 1 October 2008.

42 Duration of licences and charges

For the purposes of sections 22(1B) and (1E) of the 1974 Act, the prescribed period shall be a period of five years.

[3528]

NOTES
Commencement: 6 April 2008.

43—(1) For the purposes of section 28A(3)(b) of the 1974 Act, the day shall be the date three months before the end of the person's payment period.

(2) The payment period for the purposes of section 28A of the Act shall be five years beginning—
(a) in the case of a person's first payment period, on the day that his standard licence or, where a person is the original applicant for a group licence, that group licence takes effect; and
(b) in the case of all subsequent payment periods, on the day after the day on which the immediately preceding payment period expires.

[3529]

NOTES
Commencement: 6 April 2008.

44 (*Revokes the Consumer Credit (Period of Standard Licence) Regulations 1975, SI 1975/2124.*)

45 Transitional provisions

Regulations 46 to 50 shall apply where a statement is given under section 77A of the 1974 Act in relation to a fixed-sum credit agreement made before 1 October 2008.

[3530]

NOTES
Commencement: 1 October 2008.

46 A statement to which this regulation applies need not include the information under paragraphs 3(b), 3(c)(ii), 3(d) and 3(e) of Schedule 1.

[3531]

NOTES
Commencement: 1 October 2008.

47—(1) Where the conditions set out in paragraph (2) are met and the statement includes the information under paragraph 3(b) of Schedule 1, regulation 9(2) shall apply to that statement as if the words "Where the statement is not the first statement given under section 77A of the 1974 Act in relation to the agreements to which the agreement to aggregate relates" were omitted.

(2) Those conditions are—
(a) a statement to which this regulation applies is the first given on or after 1 October 2008;
(b) the creditor and the debtor have entered into an agreement to aggregate;
(c) the agreement to aggregate was entered into prior to 1 October 2008; and
(d) regulation 9 applies to that agreement to aggregate.

[3532]

NOTES
Commencement: 1 October 2008.

48   Where a statement to which this regulation applies does not include some or all of the information referred to in regulation 46—

    (a)   the creditor shall give the debtor in writing such of the information referred to in regulation 46 as was omitted from the statement within fifteen working days of receipt of the debtor's request for that information;

    (b)   the statement shall contain the following wording:

"**More information**

This statement does not contain all the information which you are entitled to receive from us about your agreement. If you would like to receive this extra information please get in touch with us to obtain it. We are required to provide you with this information within fifteen working days of receiving your request for it.";

    (c)   the creditor shall include a form of words that identifies which pieces of the information referred to in regulation 46 it has not included in the statement;

    (d)   where the debtor requests some but not all of the information which the creditor has omitted from the statement in accordance with regulation 46 (whether or not the information requested amounts to all the information which the creditor has so omitted) paragraph (a) shall only require the creditor to give the debtor the information requested; and

    (e)   where it is not clear from the debtor's request which pieces of the information so omitted the debtor has requested, the creditor shall give the debtor all the information so omitted.

        [3533]

NOTES

Commencement: 1 October 2008.

49   Regulations 45 to 48 shall apply until 30 September 2018.

        [3534]

NOTES

Commencement: 1 October 2008.

50—(1)   Subject to paragraph (2), where a notice of sums in arrears is given pursuant to section 86B of the 1974 Act in relation to a regulated agreement for fixed-sum credit or a regulated consumer hire agreement made before 1 October 2008 the notice may contain pre-commencement information.

   [(2)   Where pre-commencement information is included in a notice to which section 86(B)(2) applies it may be aggregated with—

    (a)   the amount of the shortfall in paragraph 6 of Schedule 3;

    (b)   the sum required to be included in the notice under paragraph 7 of that Schedule; or

    (c)   the sum required to be included in the notice under paragraph 12 of that Schedule.]

   (3)   For the purposes of this regulation, "pre-commencement information" means any sum which—

    (a)   became due before 1 October 2008;

    (b)   the debtor or hirer failed to pay in full when it became due under the agreement; and

    (c)   remains unpaid at the date the duty to give the notice arose.

        [3535]

NOTES

Commencement: 1 October 2008.

Para (2): substituted by the Consumer Credit (Information Requirements and Duration of Licences and Charges) (Amendment) Regulations 2008, SI 2008/1751, reg 2(q).

SCHEDULE 1

PART 1

INFORMATION TO BE INCLUDED IN STATEMENTS RELATING TO FIXED-SUM
CREDIT AGREEMENTS

Regulation 4(a)

1.   The period to which the statement relates.

2.—(1)   The name, telephone number or numbers, postal address and, where appropriate, any other address of the creditor.

   (2)   Where the creditor and the debtor have entered into an arrangement under which the creditor has given the debtor details of a particular employee or category of employee of the creditor

whom the debtor is entitled to contact in relation to all his dealings with the creditor, the creditor may, instead of including the telephone number or numbers referred to in sub-paragraph (1), refer to that arrangement.

3. Information specific to the agreement—
    (a)   a description of the agreement sufficient to identify it;
    (b)   the amount of credit provided and, where applicable, to be provided under the agreement (shown as one figure);
    (c)
        (i)   any rate or rates of interest applicable on a per annum basis which applied during the period to which the statement relates and—
            (aa)   the periods during which each rate applied; and
            (bb)   if applicable, the element of the credit to which each rate applied; or
        (ii)   where the rate or rates of interest are not applicable on a per annum basis, the rate or rates of interest on the credit provided under the agreement, in each case quoted on a per annum basis and a statement explaining how and when interest charges are calculated and applied under the agreement;
    (d)
        (i)   the date on which the agreement became an executed agreement; or
        (ii)   the date of first movement on the account;
    (e)
        (i)   the duration; or
        (ii)   the minimum duration,
    of the agreement as provided in the agreement;
    (f)   any opening balance under the agreement at the beginning of the period to which the statement relates;
    (g)   the amount and date of any payment made into the account by, or to the credit of, the debtor during the period to which the statement relates;
    (h)   the amount and date of any interest or other charges payable by the debtor which became due during the period to which the statement relates, whether or not the interest or other charges relate only to that period;
    (i)   the amount and date of any movement in the account during the period to which the statement relates which is not required to be included in the statement under sub-paragraphs (g) and (h); and
    (j)   the balance under the agreement at the end of the period to which the statement relates.

[3536]

NOTES
    Commencement: 1 October 2008.

PART 2
FORMS OF WORDING TO BE INCLUDED IN STATEMENTS RELATING TO FIXED-SUM CREDIT AGREEMENTS

Regulation 4(b)

4. Each of the following forms of wording shall be contained in a statement under this Part:

    "Settling your credit agreement early

    You can settle this agreement at any time by giving us notice in writing and paying off the amount you owe. If you wish to settle early you should contact us for a final settlement figure.";

    "Dispute resolution

    If you have a problem with your agreement, please try to resolve it with us in the first instance. If you are not happy with the way in which we handled your complaint or the result, you may be able to complain to the Financial Ombudsman Service. If you do not take up your problem with us first you will not be entitled to complain to the Ombudsman. We can provide details of how to contact the Ombudsman.";

    "Paying less than the agreed sum:

    If you pay less than your agreed payment in most cases it is likely to take you longer and may cost you more to pay off the debt under the agreement.

    If you have difficulties making payments under your credit agreement please contact us if you have not already done so to discuss terms for the rest of the agreement. You may also want to seek advice on what to do from an independent free advice agency such as the Citizens Advice Bureau.".

[3537]

NOTES
Commencement: 1 October 2008.

PART 3
FORMS OF WORDING TO BE INCLUDED IN FIXED-SUM CREDIT STATEMENTS RELATING TO HIRE-PURCHASE OR CONDITIONAL SALE AGREEMENTS

Regulation 4(c)

5.   The following forms of wording shall be included, as appropriate, in a statement under this Part:

"Termination: Your rights

You also have the right to end this agreement early in accordance with section 99 of the Consumer Credit Act 1974. You will not have to pay all the sums due under the agreement but you will not be entitled to retain the goods if you do this. Details were set out in your credit agreement. If you wish to terminate the agreement you should contact us for further information including any amount payable on termination.".

"If you wish we can provide you with separate settlement figures for your [hire purchase] [conditional sale] [NOTE 1] agreement and for your insurance finance agreement. Please contact us in writing to obtain this.".

NOTE 1: Delete as applicable.

[3538]

NOTES
Commencement: 1 October 2008.

SCHEDULE 2
FORMS OF WORDING AND INFORMATION TO BE INCLUDED IN STATEMENTS RELATING TO RUNNING-ACCOUNT CREDIT AGREEMENTS

Regulation 14

1.   The following form of wording shall be contained in a statement under this Part—

"Minimum payments

If you make only the minimum payment each month, it will take you longer and cost you more to clear your balance.".

2.   If at the end of the period to which the statement relates, the debtor has paid less than the minimum payment required to be paid by him in accordance with the agreement, the statement shall contain the following form of wording—

"You have failed to make a minimum payment

Failing to make your minimum payment can mean that you have broken the terms of this credit agreement and could result in us taking legal action against you. It could lead to your having to pay additional costs and make it more difficult for you to obtain credit in future.".

3.   The following information shall be contained in the statement—

A statement of the order or proportions in which any amount paid by the debtor which is not sufficient to discharge the total debt then due under the agreement will be applied or appropriated by the creditor towards the discharge of the sums due in respect of:

(a)   the amounts of credit provided for different purposes; or
(b)   different parts of the agreement.

4.   The following forms of wording shall be contained in the statement—

"If you do not pay off the full amount outstanding, we will allocate your payment to the outstanding balance in a specific order, which is set out [NOTE 1]. The way in which payments are allocated can make a significant difference to the amount of interest you will pay until the balance is cleared completely.";

NOTE 1: state where in relation to this form of wording this information is located on the statement;

"Dispute resolution

If you have a problem with your agreement, please try to resolve it with us in the first instance. If you are not happy with the way in which we handled your complaint or the result, you may be able to complain to the Financial Ombudsman Service. If you do not take up your problem with us first you will not be entitled to complain to the Ombudsman. We can provide details of how to contact the Ombudsman.".

[3539]

NOTES
Commencement: 1 October 2008.

SCHEDULE 3

PART 1
INFORMATION AND STATEMENTS TO BE INCLUDED IN NOTICES OF SUMS IN ARREARS UNDER FIXED-SUM CREDIT AGREEMENTS ETC

Regulation 19(1)(c), (d)

1.   The date of the notice.

2.—(1)   The name, telephone number or numbers, the postal address, and, where appropriate, any other address of the creditor or owner.

(2)   Where the creditor and the debtor or the owner and the hirer have entered into an arrangement under which the debtor or the hirer has been given details of a particular employee or category of employee of the creditor or owner whom the debtor or hirer is entitled to contact in relation to all his dealings with the creditor or owner, the creditor or owner may, instead of including the telephone number or numbers referred to in sub-paragraph (1), refer to that arrangement.

3.   Information specific to the agreement:
    (a)   a description of the agreement sufficient to identify it; and
    (b)   the opening balance under the agreement at the date on which the duty to give the notice arose.

4.—(1)   Where default sums or interest (other than any set out in the notice) may be payable in connection with the amounts set out in the notice, a statement in the following form—

> **"Default sums and interest**
>
> You may have to pay default sums and interest in relation to the missed or partly made payments referred to in this notice. Please contact us if you would like further details. This notice does not take account of any payments received after the date of the notice.".

(2)   In any other case, a statement in the following form—

> **"Default sums and interest**
>
> You will not incur any default sums or extra interest in relation to the missed or partly made payments referred to in this notice. This notice does not take account of any payments received after the date of the notice.".

5.   A statement in the following form:

> **"Notices**
>
> For so long as you continue to be behind with your payments by any amount, you will be sent notices about this at least every six months. We are not required to send you notices more frequently than this, even if you get further behind with your payments in between notices.".

[3540]

NOTES
Commencement: 1 October 2008.

PART 2
INFORMATION TO BE INCLUDED IN FIRST REQUIRED NOTICES OF SUMS IN ARREARS UNDER FIXED-SUM CREDIT AGREEMENTS ETC

Regulation 19(2)(a)

6.   The amount of the shortfall under the agreement which gave rise to the duty to give the notice.

[3541]

NOTES
Commencement: 1 October 2008.

PART 3
INFORMATION AND STATEMENT TO BE INCLUDED IN ALL NOTICES OF SUMS IN ARREARS UNDER FIXED-SUM CREDIT AGREEMENTS ETC EXCEPT FIRST REQUIRED NOTICES

Regulation 19(3)

7.   That part of the opening balance referred to in paragraph 3(b) of this Schedule which comprises any sum which the debtor or hirer has failed to pay in full when it became due under the agreement, whether or not such sums have been included in a previous notice.

8.   The amount and date of any [sums paid] into the account by, or to the credit of, the debtor or hirer during the period to which the notice relates.

9.   The amount and date of any interest or other charges payable by the debtor or hirer which became due during the period to which the notice relates, whether or not the interest or other charges relate only to that period.

10.   The amount and date of any movement in the account during the period to which the notice relates which is not required to be included in the notice under paragraphs 8 [and 9].

11.   The balance under the agreement at the end of the period to which the notice relates.

12.   That part of the balance referred to in paragraph 11 which comprises any sum which the debtor or hirer has failed to pay in full when it became due under the agreement and which remains unpaid at the end of the period to which the notice relates, whether or not such a sum has been included in a previous notice.

13.   Add the following words to the end of the first sentence of the statement in paragraph 4(1): "(in addition to any default sums and interest included in this notice).".

[3542]

NOTES

Commencement: 1 October 2008.

Para 8: words in square brackets substituted by the Consumer Credit (Information Requirements and Duration of Licences and Charges) (Amendment) Regulations 2008, SI 2008/1751, reg 2(r)(i).

Para 10: words in square brackets added by SI 2008/1751, reg 2(r)(ii).

PART 4
INFORMATION AND STATEMENTS TO BE INCLUDED IN NOTICES OF SUMS IN ARREARS UNDER RUNNING-ACCOUNT CREDIT AGREEMENTS

Regulation 24(1)(c) and (d)

14.   The date of the notice.

15.   A description of the agreement sufficient to identify it.

16.—(1)   The name, telephone number, postal address and, where appropriate, any other address of the creditor.

(2)   Where the creditor and the debtor have entered into an arrangement under which the creditor has given the debtor details of a particular employee or category of employee of the creditor whom the debtor is entitled to contact in relation to all his dealings with the creditor, the creditor may, instead of including the telephone number or numbers referred to in sub-paragraph (1), refer to that arrangement.

17.   In relation to each of the last two payments which the debtor is required under the agreement to have made and which have not been paid or not fully paid:

    (a)   the amount payable;
    (b)   the date on which that amount became due;
    (c)   in the event that the debtor has paid part of that amount, the amount he has paid and the date on which that payment was made; and
    (d)   the nature of the amount due,

together with the aggregate of the amounts payable as shown under sub-paragraph (a) less the aggregate of the amounts paid as shown under sub-paragraph (c).

18.   A statement in the following form—

"Missed and partly made payments

This notice does not give details of missed or partly made payments previously notified whether or not they remain unpaid.".

19.—(1)   Where default sums or interest (other than any set out in the notice) may be payable in connection with the amounts set out in the notice, a statement in the following form—

"Default sums and Interest

You may have to pay default sums and interest in relation to the missed or partly made payments indicated above in addition to any default sums and interest already included in this notice. Please contact us if you would like further details. This notice does not take account of any payments received after the date of the notice.".

(2)   In any other case, a statement in the following form—

"Default sums and Interest

You will not incur any default sums or extra interest in relation to the missed or partly made payments indicated above. This notice does not take account of any payments received after the date of the notice.".

[3543]

NOTES
Commencement: 1 October 2008.

PART 5
STATEMENT TO BE INCLUDED IN NOTICES OF SUMS IN ARREARS UNDER FIXED-SUM
CREDIT AGREEMENTS ETC AND RUNNING-ACCOUNT CREDIT AGREEMENTS
Regulation 19(1)(e) and 24(1)(e)

A statement in the following form shall be contained in a notice under this Part—

"Office of Fair Trading Information Sheet

This notice should include a copy of the current information sheet on arrears prepared by the Office of Fair Trading. This contains important information about your rights and where to go for support and advice, for example on applying for a Time Order as well as our right to charge you interest. If it is not included you should contact us to get one. Please refer to the Office of Fair Trading information sheet for more information about how to get advice on dealing with your debt.".

[3544]

NOTES
Commencement: 1 October 2008.

SCHEDULE 4

PART 1
INFORMATION AND FORM OF WORDING TO BE INCLUDED IN NOTICES OF
DEFAULT SUMS
Regulation 30

1.   The date of the notice.

2.   A description of the agreement sufficient to identify it.

3.—(1)   The name, telephone number, postal address and, where appropriate, any other address of the creditor or owner.

(2)   Where the creditor and the debtor or the owner and the hirer have entered into an arrangement under which the debtor or the hirer has been given details of a particular employee or category of employee of the creditor or owner whom the debtor or hirer is entitled to contact in relation to all his dealings with the creditor or owner, the creditor or owner may, instead of including the telephone number or numbers referred to in sub-paragraph (1), refer to that arrangement.

4.   The amount and nature of each default sum payable under the agreement which has not been the subject of a previous notice of default sums.

5.   The date upon which each default sum referred to in the notice became payable under the agreement.

6.   The following statement:

"This Notice does not take account of default sums which we have already told you about in another default sum notice, whether or not those sums remain unpaid.".

7.   The total amount of all the default sums included in the notice.

[3545]

NOTES
Commencement: 1 October 2008.

PART 2
FORMS OF WORDING TO BE INCLUDED IN NOTICES OF DEFAULT SUMS WHERE
INTEREST IS PAYABLE ON DEFAULT SUMS
Regulation 31

8.   Where the interest rate which applies to the default sum in the event that it is not paid or not paid in full when it falls due is a variable rate the following form of wording shall be contained in a notice under this Part—

"Interest

We are not entitled to charge you interest on the default sums for the first 28 days after we have given you this notice. However if the sums are not paid in full by that date interest will be charged at the rate of ......[NOTE 1]. Since this interest rate is a variable rate, the rate which we will apply to the default sum once the 28 days have passed may be different.".

NOTE 1: Insert the interest rate applicable at the date of the notice.

9. Where the interest rate which applies to the default sum in the event that it is not paid or not paid in full when it falls due is a fixed rate the following form of wording shall be contained in the notice—

"**Interest**

We are not entitled to charge you interest on the default sums for the first 28 days after we have given you this notice. However if the sum is not paid in full by that date interest will be charged at the rate of ......[NOTE 1].".

NOTE 1: Insert applicable interest rate.

[3546]

NOTES
Commencement: 1 October 2008.

SCHEDULE 5

PART 1
INFORMATION AND STATEMENT TO BE INCLUDED IN ALL NOTICES UNDER SECTION 130A OF THE 1974 ACT

Regulation 34(a)(i) and (b)

1. The date of the notice.

2. A description of the agreement sufficient to identify it and the claim number of the judgment given in relation to the agreement.

3.—(1) The name, telephone number, postal address and, where appropriate, any other address of the creditor or owner.

(2) Where the creditor and the debtor or the owner and the hirer have entered into an arrangement under which the debtor or the hirer has been given details of a particular employee or category of employee of the creditor or owner whom the debtor or hirer is entitled to contact in relation to all his dealings with the creditor or owner, the creditor or owner may, instead of including the telephone number or numbers referred to in sub-paragraph (1), refer to that arrangement.

4. The amount on which post-judgment interest is or will be charged at the date of the notice.

5. A statement in the following form—

"If you are having problems making repayments you should contact us in the first instance. If we cannot help you resolve the problem and if you are making payments under an instalment order you may be able to apply to the court to have the terms of the instalment order varied. If you do so you may also ask the court to reduce the amount of interest payable on the judgment debt.".

[6. A statement in the following form—

'**Advice and information**

You can also obtain advice and information about dealing with your debt issues from Citizens Advice, Consumer Credit Counselling Service, National Debtline, Consumer Direct, Consumerline and Community Legal Advice. [NOTE 1].'.

NOTE 1: Insert the contact details for the organisations referred to which are contained in the current Office of Fair Trading Default information sheet.]

[3547]

NOTES
Commencement: 1 October 2008.
Para 6: substituted by the Consumer Credit (Information Requirements and Duration of Licences and Charges) (Amendment) Regulations 2008, SI 2008/1751, reg 2(s).

PART 2
INFORMATION AND STATEMENT TO BE INCLUDED IN ALL EXCEPT FIRST REQUIRED NOTICE UNDER SECTION 130A OF THE 1974 ACT

Regulation 34(b)

7. The total amount of post-judgment interest charged since the date of the last notice given under section130A in relation to the agreement.

8. The date or dates on which post-judgment interest has been charged since that date.

9. The rate or rates at which post-judgment interest was charged. Where the rate is a variable rate it shall be stated to be variable.

[3548]

NOTES
    Commencement: 1 October 2008.

PART 3
FORM OF WORDING TO BE INCLUDED IN FIRST REQUIRED NOTICE
Regulation 34(a)(ii)

"Interest payable after a judgment

This notice is being given to you because a court judgment has been obtained against you in relation to the agreement. Under the agreement we are allowed to continue to charge you interest on all the sums which the judgment states you owe us.

This notice is to advise you that we intend to charge interest. The rate of interest payable will be .... [NOTE 1] (variable) [NOTE 2].

Interest will be charged from the day you were given this notice (i.e. when the notice is deemed to have been delivered to you in the ordinary course of post) onwards.

This means that even if you pay off the whole amount of the judgment, you may still have a further sum to pay.

For so long as we intend to charge interest on the monies which the judgment states you owe us, you will be given a notice about this at least every six months. This will also include information about the amount of interest that has been charged since the previous notice was given.

If you are not given such a notice within 6 months starting with the day after the previous notice was given to you then we will not be able to charge further interest until you are given such a notice."

NOTE 1: Insert interest rate or rates. Where the rate is variable insert the rate applicable at the date of the notice.

NOTE 2: Delete where the rate or rates are fixed.

[3549]

NOTES
    Commencement: 1 October 2008.

CONSUMER CREDIT (EXEMPT AGREEMENTS) ORDER 2007

(SI 2007/1168)

NOTES
    Made: 31 March 2007.
    Authority: Consumer Credit Act 1974, ss 16A, 16B(4), 182(2).
    Commencement: 6 April 2008.

ARRANGEMENT OF ARTICLES

1   Citation and Commencement

This Order may be cited as the Consumer Credit (Exempt Agreements) Order 2007 and shall come into force on 6th April 2008.

[3550]

NOTES
    Commencement: 6 April 2008.

2   Exemption for high net worth debtors and hirers

The Consumer Credit Act 1974 shall not regulate a consumer credit agreement or a consumer hire agreement where—

    (a)   the debtor or hirer is a natural person;

[(aa)   in the case of a consumer credit agreement other than an agreement secured on land, the agreement is for credit which exceeds £60,260;]

    (b)   the agreement includes a declaration made by him complying with article 3 and Schedule 1;

    (c)   a statement of high net worth complying with articles 4 and 5 and Schedule 2 has been made in relation to him;

    (d)   that statement was made during the period of one year ending with the day on which the agreement was made; and

    (e)   before the agreement was made a copy of that statement was provided to the debtor or hirer and, if the statement was not made by the creditor or owner, to the creditor or owner.

[3551]

NOTES

Commencement: 6 April 2008.

Para (aa): inserted by the Consumer Credit (EU Directive) Regulations 2010, SI 2010/1010, reg 92, as from 1 February 2011, with effect in relation to certain agreements before that date, as provided for in regs 101, 101A of the 2010 Regulations at **[3942]**, **[3942A]**.

3   A declaration for the purposes of article 2(b) shall—

    (a)   be set out in the consumer credit agreement or consumer hire agreement no less prominently than other information in the agreement and be readily distinguishable from the background medium; and

    (b)   be signed by the debtor or hirer, unless the agreement is so signed.

[3552]

NOTES

Commencement: 6 April 2008.

4—(1)   Subject to article 5, a statement of high net worth shall be signed by—

    (a)   the creditor or owner; or

    (b)   an accountant who is a member of any of the bodies listed in paragraph (2).

    (2)   The bodies referred to in paragraph (1)(b) are:

    (a)   the Institute of Chartered Accountants in England and Wales;

    (b)   the Institute of Chartered Accountants of Scotland;

    (c)   the Institute of Chartered Accounts in Ireland;

    (d)   the Association of Chartered Certified Accountants;

    (e)   the Chartered Institute of Management Accountants;

    (f)   the Chartered Institute of Public Finance and Accountancy;

    (g)   a professional body for accountants established in a jurisdiction outside the United Kingdom.

[3553]

NOTES

Commencement: 6 April 2008.

5   A person who is—

    (a)   the creditor or owner;

    (b)   an employee or agent of the creditor or owner or a person who otherwise acts on behalf of the creditor or owner in relation to the consumer credit agreement or consumer hire agreement; or

    (c)   an associate of the creditor or owner,

may only make a statement of high net worth if the creditor or owner is a person who has permission under Part 4 of the Financial Services and Markets Act 2000 to accept deposits.

[3554]

NOTES

Commencement: 6 April 2008.

6 **Declaration for exemption relating to businesses**

A declaration for the purposes of section 16B(2) of the Consumer Credit Act 1974 shall—

    (a)   comply with Schedule 3;

(b)   be set out in the consumer credit agreement or consumer hire agreement no less prominently than other information in the agreement and be readily distinguishable from the background medium; and

(c)   be signed by the debtor or hirer or where the debtor or hirer is a partnership or unincorporated body of persons be signed by or on behalf of the debtor or hirer, unless the agreement is so signed.

[3555]

NOTES

Commencement: 6 April 2008.

SCHEDULE 1
DECLARATION BY HIGH NET WORTH DEBTOR OR HIRER

Article 2

The declaration for the purposes of article 2(b) must have the following form and content—

"Declaration by high net worth debtor or hirer

(section 16A(1)(b) Consumer Credit Act 1974)

I confirm that I have received a copy of the statement of high net worth made in relation to me for the purposes of section 16A(1)(c) of the Consumer Credit Act 1974.

I understand that by making this declaration I will not have the benefit of the protection and remedies that would be available to me under the Consumer Credit Act 1974 if this agreement were a regulated agreement under that Act.

I understand that this declaration does not affect the powers of the court to make an order under section 140B of the Consumer Credit Act 1974 in relation to a credit agreement where it determines that the relationship between the creditor and the debtor is unfair to the debtor.*

I am aware that if I am in any doubt as to the consequences of making this declaration I should seek independent legal advice.".

This sentence should be omitted in the case of a consumer hire agreement.

[3556]

NOTES

Commencement: 6 April 2008.

SCHEDULE 2
STATEMENT OF HIGH NET WORTH

Article 2

A statement of high net worth for the purposes of article 2(c) must have the following form and content—

"Statement of High Net Worth

(section 16A(1)(c) Consumer Credit Act 1974)

I/We* (insert full name) .... of

(insert address and postcode) ....

confirm that I am/we are* a person qualified to make a statement of high net worth under article 4 of the Consumer Credit (Exempt Agreements) Order 2007, by virtue of the fact that ....

In my/our* opinion (insert full name of debtor or hirer) ....

of (insert address and post code of debtor or hirer) ....

is an individual of high net worth because he/she*—

(a)   received during the previous financial year net income totalling an amount of not less than £150,000*; and/or*

(b)   had throughout that year net assets with a total value of not less than £500,000*.

(insert one of the following declarations as appropriate)

I/We* declare that I am/we are* not connected to [insert name of the creditor(s)/owner(s)] [any person who is a creditor/owner offering consumer credit agreements/consumer hire agreements*].

I/We* declare that I am/we are* [connected to] [insert name of creditor(s)/owner(s)] as I am/we are* [the creditor(s)/owner(s)/an employee of/an agent of the creditor(s)/owner(s)/a person who otherwise acts on behalf of the creditor(s)/owner(s) in relation to the consumer credit agreement/ consumer hire agreement/an associate of the creditor(s)/owner(s)].*

I/We* declare that I am/we are*/[a/an] creditor(s)/owner(s) offering consumer credit agreements/ consumer hire agreements/an employee of/an agent of/a person who otherwise acts on behalf of/an associate of creditor(s)/owner(s) offering consumer credit agreements/consumer hire agreements.*

In this statement—

(a) "associate" shall be construed in accordance with section 184 of the Consumer Credit Act 1974;

(b) "financial year" means a period of one year ending with 31st March;

(c) "net assets" shall not include—

  (i) the value of the debtor's or hirer's primary residence or any loan secured on that residence;

  (ii) any rights of the debtor or hirer under a qualifying contract of insurance within the meaning of the Financial Services and Markets Act 2000 (Regulated Activities) Order 2001 (SI 2001/544); and

  (iii) any benefits (in the form of pensions or otherwise) which are payable on the termination of the service of the debtor or hirer or on his death or retirement and to which he is (or his dependents are), or may be, entitled;

(d) "net income" means the total income of the debtor or hirer from all sources reduced by the amount of income tax and national insurance contributions payable in respect of it; and

(e) "previous financial year" means the financial year immediately preceding the financial year during which the statement is made.".

*Delete as appropriate.

[3557]

NOTES

Commencement: 6 April 2008.

SCHEDULE 3
DECLARATION FOR EXEMPTION RELATING TO BUSINESSES
Article 6

A declaration for the purposes of article 6 must have the following form and content—

"Declaration for Exemption Relating to Businesses

(sections 16B and 189(1) and (2) Consumer Credit Act 1974)

I am/We are* entering this agreement wholly or predominantly for the purposes of a business carried on by me/us* or intended to be carried by me/us.*

I/We* understand that I/we* will not have the benefit of the protection and remedies that would be available to me/us* under the Consumer Credit Act 1974 if this agreement were a regulated agreement under that Act.

I/We* understand that this declaration does not affect the powers of the court to make an order under section 140B of the Consumer Credit Act 1974 in relation to a credit agreement where it determines that the relationship between the creditor and the debtor is unfair to the debtor.**

I am/We are* aware that, if I am/we are* in any doubt as to the consequences of the agreement not being regulated by the Consumer Credit Act 1974 I/we should seek independent legal advice.".

*Delete as appropriate.

**This section should be omitted in the case of a consumer hire agreement.

[3558]

NOTES

Commencement: 6 April 2008.

MONEY LAUNDERING REGULATIONS 2007

(SI 2007/2157)

NOTES

Made: 24 July 2007.

Authority: European Communities Act 1972, s 2(2); Financial Services and Markets Act 2000, ss 168(4)(b), 402(1)(b), 417(1), 428(3).

Commencement: 15 December 2007.

ARRANGEMENT OF REGULATIONS

PART 1
GENERAL

PART 1
GENERAL

1 Citation, commencement etc

(1) These Regulations may be cited as the Money Laundering Regulations 2007 and come into force on 15th December 2007.

(2) These Regulations are prescribed for the purposes of sections 168(4)(b) (appointment of persons to carry out investigations in particular cases) and 402(1)(b) (power of the Authority to institute proceedings for certain other offences) of the 2000 Act.

(3) …

[3559]

NOTES
Commencement: 15 December 2007.
Para (3): revokes the Money Laundering Regulations 2003, SI 2003/3075.

2 Interpretation

(1) In these Regulations—
"the 2000 Act" means the Financial Services and Markets Act 2000;
"Annex I financial institution" has the meaning given by regulation 22(1);
"auditor", except in regulation 17(2)(c) and (d), has the meaning given by regulation 3(4) and (5);
"authorised person" means a person who is authorised for the purposes of the 2000 Act;
"the Authority" means the Financial Services Authority;
"the banking consolidation directive" means Directive 2006/48/EC of the European Parliament and of the Council of 14th June 2006 relating to the taking up and pursuit of the business of credit institutions;
"beneficial owner" has the meaning given by regulation 6;
["bill payment service provider" means an undertaking which provides a payment service enabling the payment of utility and other household bills;]

"business relationship" means a business, professional or commercial relationship between a relevant person and a customer, which is expected by the relevant person, at the time when contact is established, to have an element of duration;

"cash" means notes, coins or travellers' cheques in any currency;

"casino" has the meaning given by regulation 3(13);

"the Commissioners" means the Commissioners for Her Majesty's Revenue and Customs;

"consumer credit financial institution" has the meaning given by regulation 22(1);

"credit institution" has the meaning given by regulation 3(2);

"customer due diligence measures" has the meaning given by regulation 5;

"DETI" means the Department of Enterprise, Trade and Investment in Northern Ireland;

"the electronic money directive" means Directive 2000/46/EC of the European Parliament and of the Council of 18th September 2000 on the taking up, pursuit and prudential supervision of the business of electronic money institutions;

"estate agent" has the meaning given by regulation 3(11);

"external accountant" has the meaning given by regulation 3(7);

"financial institution" has the meaning given by regulation 3(3);

"firm" means any entity, whether or not a legal person, that is not an individual and includes a body corporate and a partnership or other unincorporated association;

"high value dealer" has the meaning given by regulation 3(12);

"the implementing measures directive" means Commission Directive 2006/70/EC of 1st August 2006 laying down implementing measures for the money laundering directive;

"independent legal professional" has the meaning given by regulation 3(9);

"insolvency practitioner", except in regulation 17(2)(c) and (d), has the meaning given by regulation 3(6);

"the life assurance consolidation directive" means Directive 2002/83/EC of the European Parliament and of the Council of 5th November 2002 concerning life assurance;

"local weights and measures authority" has the meaning given by section 69 of the Weights and Measures Act 1985 (local weights and measures authorities);

"the markets in financial instruments directive" means Directive 2004/39/EC of the European Parliament and of the Council of 12th April 2004 on markets in financial instruments;

"money laundering" means an act which falls within section 340(11) of the Proceeds of Crime Act 2002;

"the money laundering directive" means Directive 2005/60/EC of the European Parliament and of the Council of 26th October 2005 on the prevention of the use of the financial system for the purpose of money laundering and terrorist financing;

"money service business" means an undertaking which by way of business operates a currency exchange office, transmits money (or any representations of monetary value) by any means or cashes cheques which are made payable to customers;

"nominated officer" means a person who is nominated to receive disclosures under Part 7 of the Proceeds of Crime Act 2002 (money laundering) or Part 3 of the Terrorism Act 2000 (terrorist property);

"non-EEA state" means a state that is not an EEA state;

"notice" means a notice in writing;

"occasional transaction" means a transaction (carried out other than as part of a business relationship) amounting to 15,000 euro or more, whether the transaction is carried out in a single operation or several operations which appear to be linked;

"the OFT" means the Office of Fair Trading;

"ongoing monitoring" has the meaning given by regulation 8(2);

["payment services" has the meaning given by regulation 2(1) of the Payment Services Regulations 2009;]

"regulated market"—

    (a)   within the EEA, has the meaning given by point 14 of Article 4(1) of the markets in financial instruments directive; and

    (b)   outside the EEA, means a regulated financial market which subjects companies whose securities are admitted to trading to disclosure obligations which are contained in international standards and are equivalent to the specified disclosure obligations;

"relevant person" means a person to whom, in accordance with regulations 3 and 4, these Regulations apply;

"the specified disclosure obligations" means disclosure requirements consistent with—

    (a)   Article 6(1) to (4) of Directive 2003/6/EC of the European Parliament and of the Council of 28th January 2003 on insider dealing and market manipulation;

    (b)   Articles 3, 5, 7, 8, 10, 14 and 16 of Directive 2003/71/EC of the European Parliament and of the Council of 4th November 2003 on the prospectuses to be published when securities are offered to the public or admitted to trading;

    (c)   Articles 4 to 6, 14, 16 to 19 and 30 of Directive 2004/109/EC of the European Parliament and of the Council of 15th December 2004 relating to the harmonisation of transparency requirements in relation to information about issuers whose securities are admitted to trading on a regulated market; or

(d) Community legislation made under the provisions mentioned in sub-paragraphs (a) to (c);

"supervisory authority" in relation to any relevant person means the supervisory authority specified for such a person by regulation 23;

"tax adviser" (except in regulation 11(3)) has the meaning given by regulation 3(8);

["telecommunication, digital and IT payment service provider" means an undertaking which provides payment services falling within paragraph 1(g) of Schedule 1 to the Payment Services Regulations 2009;]

"terrorist financing" means an offence under—

(a) section 15 (fund-raising), 16 (use and possession), 17 (funding arrangements), 18 (money laundering) or 63 (terrorist finance: jurisdiction) of the Terrorism Act 2000;

(b) paragraph 7(2) or (3) of Schedule 3 to the Anti-Terrorism, Crime and Security Act 2001 (freezing orders);

(c) article 7, 8 or 10 of the Terrorism (United Nations Measures) Order 2006; ...

(d) article 7, 8 or 10 of the Al-Qaida and Taliban (United Nations Measures) Order 2006; [or

(e) article 10, 11, 12, 13, 14 or 16 of the Terrorism (United Nations Measures) Order 2009;]

"trust or company service provider" has the meaning given by regulation 3(10).

(2) In these Regulations, references to amounts in euro include references to equivalent amounts in another currency.

(3) Unless otherwise defined, expressions used in these Regulations and the money laundering directive have the same meaning as in the money laundering directive and expressions used in these Regulations and in the implementing measures directive have the same meaning as in the implementing measures directive.

[3560]

NOTES
Commencement: 15 December 2007.

Para (1): definitions "bill payment service provider", "payment services" and "telecommunication, digital and IT payment service provider" inserted by the Payment Services Regulations 2009, SI 2009/209, reg 126, Sch 6, Pt 2, para 6(a); in definition "terrorist financing", word omitted from para (c) revoked and para (e) inserted together with word immediately preceding it, by the Terrorism (United Nations Measures) Order (Consequential Amendments) Regulations 2009, SI 2009/1912, reg 2.

3 Application of the Regulations

(1) Subject to regulation 4, these Regulations apply to the following persons acting in the course of business carried on by them in the United Kingdom ("relevant persons")—

(a) credit institutions;
(b) financial institutions;
(c) auditors, insolvency practitioners, external accountants and tax advisers;
(d) independent legal professionals;
(e) trust or company service providers;
(f) estate agents;
(g) high value dealers;
(h) casinos.

(2) "Credit institution" means—

(a) a credit institution as defined in Article 4(1)(a) of the banking consolidation directive; or
(b) a branch (within the meaning of Article 4(3) of that directive) located in an EEA state of an institution falling within sub-paragraph (a) (or an equivalent institution whose head office is located in a non-EEA state) wherever its head office is located,

when it accepts deposits or other repayable funds from the public or grants credits for its own account (within the meaning of the banking consolidation directive).

(3) "Financial institution" means—

(a) an undertaking, including a money service business, when it carries out one or more of the activities listed in points 2 to 12 and 14 of Annex 1 to the banking consolidation directive (the relevant text of which is set out in Schedule 1 to these Regulations), other than—

(i) a credit institution;
(ii) an undertaking whose only listed activity is trading for own account in one or more of the products listed in point 7 of Annex 1 to the banking consolidation directive where the undertaking does not have a customer,

and, for this purpose, "customer" means a third party which is not a member of the same group as the undertaking;

(b) an insurance company duly authorised in accordance with the life assurance consolidation directive, when it carries out activities covered by that directive;

(c) a person whose regular occupation or business is the provision to other persons of an investment service or the performance of an investment activity on a professional basis, when providing or performing investment services or activities (within the meaning of the markets in financial instruments directive), other than a person falling within Article 2 of that directive;

(d) a collective investment undertaking, when marketing or otherwise offering its units or shares;

(e) an insurance intermediary as defined in Article 2(5) of Directive 2002/92/EC of the European Parliament and of the Council of 9th December 2002 on insurance mediation, with the exception of a tied insurance intermediary as mentioned in Article 2(7) of that Directive, when it acts in respect of contracts of long-term insurance within the meaning given by article 3(1) of, and Part II of Schedule 1 to, the Financial Services and Markets Act 2000 (Regulated Activities) Order 2001;

(f) a branch located in an EEA state of a person referred to in sub-paragraphs (a) to (e) (or an equivalent person whose head office is located in a non-EEA state), wherever its head office is located, when carrying out any activity mentioned in sub-paragraphs (a) to (e);

(g) the National Savings Bank;

(h) the Director of Savings, when money is raised under the auspices of the Director under the National Loans Act 1968.

(4) "Auditor" means any firm or individual who is a statutory auditor within the meaning of Part 42 of the Companies Act 2006 (statutory auditors), when carrying out statutory audit work within the meaning of section 1210 of that Act.

(5) Before the entry into force of Part 42 of the Companies Act 2006 the reference in paragraph (4) to—

(a) a person who is a statutory auditor shall be treated as a reference to a person who is eligible for appointment as a company auditor under section 25 of the Companies Act 1989 (eligibility for appointment) or article 28 of the Companies (Northern Ireland) Order 1990; and

(b) the carrying out of statutory audit work shall be treated as a reference to the provision of audit services.

(6) "Insolvency practitioner" means any person who acts as an insolvency practitioner within the meaning of section 388 of the Insolvency Act 1986 (meaning of "act as insolvency practitioner") or article 3 of the Insolvency (Northern Ireland) Order 1989.

(7) "External accountant" means a firm or sole practitioner who by way of business provides accountancy services to other persons, when providing such services.

(8) "Tax adviser" means a firm or sole practitioner who by way of business provides advice about the tax affairs of other persons, when providing such services.

(9) "Independent legal professional" means a firm or sole practitioner who by way of business provides legal or notarial services to other persons, when participating in financial or real property transactions concerning—

(a) the buying and selling of real property or business entities;

(b) the managing of client money, securities or other assets;

(c) the opening or management of bank, savings or securities accounts;

(d) the organisation of contributions necessary for the creation, operation or management of companies; or

(e) the creation, operation or management of trusts, companies or similar structures,

and, for this purpose, a person participates in a transaction by assisting in the planning or execution of the transaction or otherwise acting for or on behalf of a client in the transaction.

(10) "Trust or company service provider" means a firm or sole practitioner who by way of business provides any of the following services to other persons—

(a) forming companies or other legal persons;

(b) acting, or arranging for another person to act—

(i) as a director or secretary of a company;

(ii) as a partner of a partnership; or

(iii) in a similar position in relation to other legal persons;

(c) providing a registered office, business address, correspondence or administrative address or other related services for a company, partnership or any other legal person or arrangement;

(d) acting, or arranging for another person to act, as—

(i) a trustee of an express trust or similar legal arrangement; or

      (ii)   a nominee shareholder for a person other than a company whose securities are listed on a regulated market,

    when providing such services.

    (11)   "Estate agent" means—

  (a)   a firm; or

  (b)   sole practitioner,

who, or whose employees, carry out estate agency work (within the meaning given by section 1 of the Estate Agents Act 1979 (estate agency work)), when in the course of carrying out such work.

    (12)   "High value dealer" means a firm or sole trader who by way of business trades in goods (including an auctioneer dealing in goods), when he receives, in respect of any transaction, a payment or payments in cash of at least 15,000 euros in total, whether the transaction is executed in a single operation or in several operations which appear to be linked.

    (13)   "Casino" means the holder of a casino operating licence and, for this purpose, a "casino operating licence" has the meaning given by section 65(2) of the Gambling Act 2005 (nature of licence).

    (14)   In the application of this regulation to Scotland, for "real property" in paragraph (9) substitute "heritable property".

[3561]

NOTES

Commencement: 15 December 2007.

---

4 Exclusions

    (1)   These Regulations do not apply to the following persons when carrying out any of the following activities—

  (a)   a society registered under the Industrial and Provident Societies Act 1965, when it—

      (i)   issues withdrawable share capital within the limit set by section 6 of that Act (maximum shareholding in society); or

      (ii)   accepts deposits from the public within the limit set by section 7(3) of that Act (carrying on of banking by societies);

  (b)   a society registered under the Industrial and Provident Societies Act (Northern Ireland) 1969, when it—

      (i)   issues withdrawable share capital within the limit set by section 6 of that Act (maximum shareholding in society); or

      (ii)   accepts deposits from the public within the limit set by section 7(3) of that Act (carrying on of banking by societies);

  (c)   a person who is (or falls within a class of persons) specified in any of paragraphs 2 to 23, 25 to 38 or 40 to 49 of the Schedule to the Financial Services and Markets Act 2000 (Exemption) Order 2001, when carrying out any activity in respect of which he is exempt;

  (d)   a person who was an exempted person for the purposes of section 45 of the Financial Services Act 1986 (miscellaneous exemptions) immediately before its repeal, when exercising the functions specified in that section;

  (e)   a person whose main activity is that of a high value dealer, when he engages in financial activity on an occasional or very limited basis as set out in paragraph 1 of Schedule 2 to these Regulations; or

  (f)   a person, when he prepares a home information pack or a document or information for inclusion in a home information pack.

    (2)   These Regulations do not apply to a person who falls within regulation 3 solely as a result of his engaging in financial activity on an occasional or very limited basis as set out in paragraph 1 of Schedule 2 to these Regulations.

    (3)   Parts 2 to 5 of these Regulations do not apply to—

  (a)   the Auditor General for Scotland;

  (b)   the Auditor General for Wales;

  (c)   the Bank of England;

  (d)   the Comptroller and Auditor General;

  (e)   the Comptroller and Auditor General for Northern Ireland;

  (f)   the Official Solicitor to the Supreme Court, when acting as trustee in his official capacity;

  (g)   the Treasury Solicitor.

    (4)   In paragraph (1)(f), "home information pack" has the same meaning as in Part 5 of the Housing Act 2004 (home information packs).

[3562]

NOTES
Commencement: 15 December 2007.

PART 2
CUSTOMER DUE DILIGENCE

5 Meaning of customer due diligence measures

"Customer due diligence measures" means—

    (a)   identifying the customer and verifying the customer's identity on the basis of documents, data or information obtained from a reliable and independent source;

    (b)   identifying, where there is a beneficial owner who is not the customer, the beneficial owner and taking adequate measures, on a risk-sensitive basis, to verify his identity so that the relevant person is satisfied that he knows who the beneficial owner is, including, in the case of a legal person, trust or similar legal arrangement, measures to understand the ownership and control structure of the person, trust or arrangement; and

    (c)   obtaining information on the purpose and intended nature of the business relationship.

[3563]

NOTES
Commencement: 15 December 2007.

6 Meaning of beneficial owner

(1)   In the case of a body corporate, "beneficial owner" means any individual who—

    (a)   as respects any body other than a company whose securities are listed on a regulated market, ultimately owns or controls (whether through direct or indirect ownership or control, including through bearer share holdings) more than 25% of the shares or voting rights in the body; or

    (b)   as respects any body corporate, otherwise exercises control over the management of the body.

(2)   In the case of a partnership (other than a limited liability partnership), "beneficial owner" means any individual who—

    (a)   ultimately is entitled to or controls (whether the entitlement or control is direct or indirect) more than a 25% share of the capital or profits of the partnership or more than 25% of the voting rights in the partnership; or

    (b)   otherwise exercises control over the management of the partnership.

(3)   In the case of a trust, "beneficial owner" means—

    (a)   any individual who is entitled to a specified interest in at least 25% of the capital of the trust property;

    (b)   as respects any trust other than one which is set up or operates entirely for the benefit of individuals falling within sub-paragraph (a), the class of persons in whose main interest the trust is set up or operates;

    (c)   any individual who has control over the trust.

(4)   In paragraph (3)—

"specified interest" means a vested interest which is—

        (a)   in possession or in remainder or reversion (or, in Scotland, in fee); and

        (b)   defeasible or indefeasible;

"control" means a power (whether exercisable alone, jointly with another person or with the consent of another person) under the trust instrument or by law to—

        (a)   dispose of, advance, lend, invest, pay or apply trust property;

        (b)   vary the trust;

        (c)   add or remove a person as a beneficiary or to or from a class of beneficiaries;

        (d)   appoint or remove trustees;

        (e)   direct, withhold consent to or veto the exercise of a power such as is mentioned in sub-paragraph (a), (b), (c) or (d).

(5)   For the purposes of paragraph (3)—

    (a)   where an individual is the beneficial owner of a body corporate which is entitled to a specified interest in the capital of the trust property or which has control over the trust, the individual is to be regarded as entitled to the interest or having control over the trust; and

    (b)   an individual does not have control solely as a result of—

        (i)   his consent being required in accordance with section 32(1)(c) of the Trustee Act 1925 (power of advancement);

        (ii)   any discretion delegated to him under section 34 of the Pensions Act 1995 (power of investment and delegation);

(iii) the power to give a direction conferred on him by section 19(2) of the Trusts of Land and Appointment of Trustees Act 1996 (appointment and retirement of trustee at instance of beneficiaries); or

(iv) the power exercisable collectively at common law to vary or extinguish a trust where the beneficiaries under the trust are of full age and capacity and (taken together) absolutely entitled to the property subject to the trust (or, in Scotland, have a full and unqualified right to the fee).

(6) In the case of a legal entity or legal arrangement which does not fall within paragraph (1), (2) or (3), "beneficial owner" means—

(a) where the individuals who benefit from the entity or arrangement have been determined, any individual who benefits from at least 25% of the property of the entity or arrangement;

(b) where the individuals who benefit from the entity or arrangement have yet to be determined, the class of persons in whose main interest the entity or arrangement is set up or operates;

(c) any individual who exercises control over at least 25% of the property of the entity or arrangement.

(7) For the purposes of paragraph (6), where an individual is the beneficial owner of a body corporate which benefits from or exercises control over the property of the entity or arrangement, the individual is to be regarded as benefiting from or exercising control over the property of the entity or arrangement.

(8) In the case of an estate of a deceased person in the course of administration, "beneficial owner" means—

(a) in England and Wales and Northern Ireland, the executor, original or by representation, or administrator for the time being of a deceased person;

(b) in Scotland, the executor for the purposes of the Executors (Scotland) Act 1900.

(9) In any other case, "beneficial owner" means the individual who ultimately owns or controls the customer or on whose behalf a transaction is being conducted.

(10) In this regulation—

"arrangement", "entity" and "trust" means an arrangement, entity or trust which administers and distributes funds;

"limited liability partnership" has the meaning given by the Limited Liability Partnerships Act 2000.

[3564]

NOTES

Commencement: 15 December 2007.

7 Application of customer due diligence measures

(1) Subject to regulations 9, 10, 12, 13, 14, 16(4) and 17, a relevant person must apply customer due diligence measures when he—

(a) establishes a business relationship;

(b) carries out an occasional transaction;

(c) suspects money laundering or terrorist financing;

(d) doubts the veracity or adequacy of documents, data or information previously obtained for the purposes of identification or verification.

(2) Subject to regulation 16(4), a relevant person must also apply customer due diligence measures at other appropriate times to existing customers on a risk-sensitive basis.

(3) A relevant person must—

(a) determine the extent of customer due diligence measures on a risk-sensitive basis depending on the type of customer, business relationship, product or transaction; and

(b) be able to demonstrate to his supervisory authority that the extent of the measures is appropriate in view of the risks of money laundering and terrorist financing.

(4) Where—

(a) a relevant person is required to apply customer due diligence measures in the case of a trust, legal entity (other than a body corporate) or a legal arrangement (other than a trust); and

(b) the class of persons in whose main interest the trust, entity or arrangement is set up or operates is identified as a beneficial owner,

the relevant person is not required to identify all the members of the class.

(5) Paragraph (3)(b) does not apply to the National Savings Bank or the Director of Savings.

[3565]

8 Ongoing monitoring

(1)   A relevant person must conduct ongoing monitoring of a business relationship.

(2)   "Ongoing monitoring" of a business relationship means—
  (a)   scrutiny of transactions undertaken throughout the course of the relationship (including, where necessary, the source of funds) to ensure that the transactions are consistent with the relevant person's knowledge of the customer, his business and risk profile; and
  (b)   keeping the documents, data or information obtained for the purpose of applying customer due diligence measures up-to-date.

(3)   Regulation 7(3) applies to the duty to conduct ongoing monitoring under paragraph (1) as it applies to customer due diligence measures.

[3566]

9 Timing of verification

(1)   This regulation applies in respect of the duty under regulation 7(1)(a) and (b) to apply the customer due diligence measures referred to in regulation 5(a) and (b).

(2)   Subject to paragraphs (3) to (5) and regulation 10, a relevant person must verify the identity of the customer (and any beneficial owner) before the establishment of a business relationship or the carrying out of an occasional transaction.

(3)   Such verification may be completed during the establishment of a business relationship if—
  (a)   this is necessary not to interrupt the normal conduct of business; and
  (b)   there is little risk of money laundering or terrorist financing occurring,
provided that the verification is completed as soon as practicable after contact is first established.

(4)   The verification of the identity of the beneficiary under a life insurance policy may take place after the business relationship has been established provided that it takes place at or before the time of payout or at or before the time the beneficiary exercises a right vested under the policy.

(5)   The verification of the identity of a bank account holder may take place after the bank account has been opened provided that there are adequate safeguards in place to ensure that—
  (a)   the account is not closed; and
  (b)   transactions are not carried out by or on behalf of the account holder (including any payment from the account to the account holder),
before verification has been completed.

[3567]

10   Casinos

(1)   A casino must establish and verify the identity of—
  (a)   all customers to whom the casino makes facilities for gaming available—
    (i)   before entry to any premises where such facilities are provided; or
    (ii)   where the facilities are for remote gaming, before access is given to such facilities; or
  (b)   if the specified conditions are met, all customers who, in the course of any period of 24 hours—
    (i)   purchase from, or exchange with, the casino chips with a total value of 2,000 euro or more;
    (ii)   pay the casino 2,000 [euro] or more for the use of gaming machines; or
    (iii) pay to, or stake with, the casino 2,000 euro or more in connection with facilities for remote gaming.

(2)   The specified conditions are—
  (a)   the casino verifies the identity of each customer before or immediately after such purchase, exchange, payment or stake takes place, and
  (b)   the Gambling Commission is satisfied that the casino has appropriate procedures in place to monitor and record—
    (i)   the total value of chips purchased from or exchanged with the casino;
    (ii)   the total money paid for the use of gaming machines; or

      (iii)   the total money paid or staked in connection with facilities for remote gaming, by each customer.

  (3)   In this regulation—

"gaming", "gaming machine", "remote operating licence" and "stake" have the meanings given by, respectively, sections 6(1) (gaming & game of chance), 235 (gaming machine), 67 (remote gambling) and 353(1) (interpretation) of the Gambling Act 2005;

"premises" means premises subject to—

    (a)   a casino premises licence within the meaning of section 150(1)(a) of the Gambling Act 2005 (nature of licence); or

    (b)   a converted casino premises licence within the meaning of paragraph 65 of Part 7 of Schedule 4 to the Gambling Act 2005 (Commencement No 6 and Transitional Provisions) Order 2006;

"remote gaming" means gaming provided pursuant to a remote operating licence.

[3568]

NOTES

Commencement: 15 December 2007.

Para (1): word in square brackets in sub-para (b)(ii) inserted by the Money Laundering (Amendment) Regulations 2007, SI 2007/3299, reg 2(a).

---

11   Requirement to cease transactions etc

  (1)   Where, in relation to any customer, a relevant person is unable to apply customer due diligence measures in accordance with the provisions of this Part, he—

    (a)   must not carry out a transaction with or for the customer through a bank account;

    (b)   must not establish a business relationship or carry out an occasional transaction with the customer;

    (c)   must terminate any existing business relationship with the customer;

    (d)   must consider whether he is required to make a disclosure by Part 7 of the Proceeds of Crime Act 2002 or Part 3 of the Terrorism Act 2000.

  (2)   Paragraph (1) does not apply where a lawyer or other professional adviser is in the course of ascertaining the legal position for his client or performing his task of defending or representing that client in, or concerning, legal proceedings, including advice on the institution or avoidance of proceedings.

  (3)   In paragraph (2), "other professional adviser" means an auditor, accountant or tax adviser who is a member of a professional body which is established for any such persons and which makes provision for—

    (a)   testing the competence of those seeking admission to membership of such a body as a condition for such admission; and

    (b)   imposing and maintaining professional and ethical standards for its members, as well as imposing sanctions for non-compliance with those standards.

[3569]

NOTES

Commencement: 15 December 2007.

---

12   Exception for trustees of debt issues

  (1)   A relevant person—

    (a)   who is appointed by the issuer of instruments or securities specified in paragraph (2) as trustee of an issue of such instruments or securities; or

    (b)   whose customer is a trustee of an issue of such instruments or securities,

is not required to apply the customer due diligence measure referred to in regulation 5(b) in respect of the holders of such instruments or securities.

  (2)   The specified instruments and securities are—

    (a)   instruments which fall within article 77 [or 77A] of the Financial Services and Markets Act 2000 (Regulated Activities) Order 2001; and

    (b)   securities which fall within article 78 of that Order.

[3570]

NOTES

Commencement: 15 December 2007.

Para (2): words in square brackets in sub-para (a) inserted by the Financial Services and Markets Act 2000 (Regulated Activities) (Amendment) Order 2010, SI 2010/86, art 4, Schedule, para 10.

13 Simplified due diligence

(1)   A relevant person is not required to apply customer due diligence measures in the circumstances mentioned in regulation 7(1)(a), (b) or (d) where he has reasonable grounds for believing that the customer, transaction or product related to such transaction, falls within any of the following paragraphs.

(2)   The customer is—

    (a)   a credit or financial institution which is subject to the requirements of the money laundering directive; or

    (b)   a credit or financial institution (or equivalent institution) which—

        (i)   is situated in a non-EEA state which imposes requirements equivalent to those laid down in the money laundering directive; and

        (ii)   is supervised for compliance with those requirements.

(3)   The customer is a company whose securities are listed on a regulated market subject to specified disclosure obligations.

(4)   The customer is an independent legal professional and the product is an account into which monies are pooled, provided that—

    (a)   where the pooled account is held in a non-EEA state—

        (i)   that state imposes requirements to combat money laundering and terrorist financing which are consistent with international standards; and

        (ii)   the independent legal professional is supervised in that state for compliance with those requirements; and

    (b)   information on the identity of the persons on whose behalf monies are held in the pooled account is available, on request, to the institution which acts as a depository institution for the account.

(5)   The customer is a public authority in the United Kingdom.

(6)   The customer is a public authority which fulfils all the conditions set out in paragraph 2 of Schedule 2 to these Regulations.

(7)   The product is—

    (a)   a life insurance contract where the annual premium is no more than 1,000 euro or where a single premium of no more than 2,500 euro is paid;

    (b)   an insurance contract for the purposes of a pension scheme where the contract contains no surrender clause and cannot be used as collateral;

    (c)   a pension, superannuation or similar scheme which provides retirement benefits to employees, where contributions are made by an employer or by way of deduction from an employee's wages and the scheme rules do not permit the assignment of a member's interest under the scheme (other than an assignment permitted by section 44 of the Welfare Reform and Pensions Act 1999 (disapplication of restrictions on alienation) or section 91(5)(a) of the Pensions Act 1995 (inalienability of occupational pension)); or

    (d)   electronic money, within the meaning of Article 1(3)(b) of the electronic money directive, where—

        (i)   if the device cannot be recharged, the maximum amount stored in the device is no more than 150 euro; or

        (ii)   if the device can be recharged, a limit of 2,500 euro is imposed on the total amount transacted in a calendar year, except when an amount of 1,000 euro or more is redeemed in the same calendar year by the bearer (within the meaning of Article 3 of the electronic money directive).

(8)   The product and any transaction related to such product fulfils all the conditions set out in paragraph 3 of Schedule 2 to these Regulations.

(9)   The product is a child trust fund within the meaning given by section 1(2) of the Child Trust Funds Act 2004.

[3571]

NOTES
Commencement: 15 December 2007.

---

14 Enhanced customer due diligence and ongoing monitoring

(1)   A relevant person must apply on a risk-sensitive basis enhanced customer due diligence measures and enhanced ongoing monitoring—

    (a)   in accordance with paragraphs (2) to (4);

    (b)   in any other situation which by its nature can present a higher risk of money laundering or terrorist financing.

(2)   Where the customer has not been physically present for identification purposes, a relevant person must take specific and adequate measures to compensate for the higher risk, for example, by applying one or more of the following measures—

(a) ensuring that the customer's identity is established by additional documents, data or information;
(b) supplementary measures to verify or certify the documents supplied, or requiring confirmatory certification by a credit or financial institution which is subject to the money laundering directive;
(c) ensuring that the first payment is carried out through an account opened in the customer's name with a credit institution.

(3) A credit institution ("the correspondent") which has or proposes to have a correspondent banking relationship with a respondent institution ("the respondent") from a non-EEA state must—
(a) gather sufficient information about the respondent to understand fully the nature of its business;
(b) determine from publicly-available information the reputation of the respondent and the quality of its supervision;
(c) assess the respondent's anti-money laundering and anti-terrorist financing controls;
(d) obtain approval from senior management before establishing a new correspondent banking relationship;
(e) document the respective responsibilities of the respondent and correspondent; and
(f) be satisfied that, in respect of those of the respondent's customers who have direct access to accounts of the correspondent, the respondent—
  (i) has verified the identity of, and conducts ongoing monitoring in respect of, such customers; and
  (ii) is able to provide to the correspondent, upon request, the documents, data or information obtained when applying customer due diligence measures and ongoing monitoring.

(4) A relevant person who proposes to have a business relationship or carry out an occasional transaction with a politically exposed person must—
(a) have approval from senior management for establishing the business relationship with that person;
(b) take adequate measures to establish the source of wealth and source of funds which are involved in the proposed business relationship or occasional transaction; and
(c) where the business relationship is entered into, conduct enhanced ongoing monitoring of the relationship.

(5) In paragraph (4), "a politically exposed person" means a person who is—
(a) an individual who is or has, at any time in the preceding year, been entrusted with a prominent public function by—
  (i) a state other than the United Kingdom;
  (ii) a Community institution; or
  (iii) an international body,
  including a person who falls in any of the categories listed in paragraph 4(1)(a) of Schedule 2;
(b) an immediate family member of a person referred to in sub-paragraph (a), including a person who falls in any of the categories listed in paragraph 4(1)(c) of Schedule 2; or
(c) a known close associate of a person referred to in sub-paragraph (a), including a person who falls in either of the categories listed in paragraph 4(1)(d) of Schedule 2.

(6) For the purpose of deciding whether a person is a known close associate of a person referred to in paragraph (5)(a), a relevant person need only have regard to information which is in his possession or is publicly known.

[3572]

NOTES
Commencement: 15 December 2007.

15 Branches and subsidiaries

(1) A credit or financial institution must require its branches and subsidiary undertakings which are located in a non-EEA state to apply, to the extent permitted by the law of that state, measures at least equivalent to those set out in these Regulations with regard to customer due diligence measures, ongoing monitoring and record-keeping.

(2) Where the law of a non-EEA state does not permit the application of such equivalent measures by the branch or subsidiary undertaking located in that state, the credit or financial institution must—
(a) inform its supervisory authority accordingly; and
(b) take additional measures to handle effectively the risk of money laundering and terrorist financing.

(3) In this regulation "subsidiary undertaking"—
(a) except in relation to an incorporated friendly society, has the meaning given by

section 1162 of the Companies Act 2006 (parent and subsidiary undertakings) and, in relation to a body corporate in or formed under the law of an EEA state other than the United Kingdom, includes an undertaking which is a subsidiary undertaking within the meaning of any rule of law in force in that state for purposes connected with implementation of the European Council Seventh Company Law Directive 83/349/EEC of 13th June 1983 on consolidated accounts;

    (b)   in relation to an incorporated friendly society, means a body corporate of which the society has control within the meaning of section 13(9)(a) or (aa) of the Friendly Societies Act 1992 (control of subsidiaries and other bodies corporate).

(4)   Before the entry into force of section 1162 of the Companies Act 2006 the reference to that section in paragraph (3)(a) shall be treated as a reference to section 258 of the Companies Act 1985 (parent and subsidiary undertakings).

[3573]

NOTES

Commencement: 15 December 2007.

16 Shell banks, anonymous accounts etc

(1)   A credit institution must not enter into, or continue, a correspondent banking relationship with a shell bank.

(2)   A credit institution must take appropriate measures to ensure that it does not enter into, or continue, a corresponding banking relationship with a bank which is known to permit its accounts to be used by a shell bank.

(3)   A credit or financial institution carrying on business in the United Kingdom must not set up an anonymous account or an anonymous passbook for any new or existing customer.

(4)   As soon as reasonably practicable on or after 15th December 2007 all credit and financial institutions carrying on business in the United Kingdom must apply customer due diligence measures to, and conduct ongoing monitoring of, all anonymous accounts and passbooks in existence on that date and in any event before such accounts or passbooks are used.

(5)   A "shell bank" means a credit institution, or an institution engaged in equivalent activities, incorporated in a jurisdiction in which it has no physical presence involving meaningful decision-making and management, and which is not part of a financial conglomerate or third-country financial conglomerate.

(6)   In this regulation, "financial conglomerate" and "third-country financial conglomerate" have the meanings given by regulations 1(2) and 7(1) respectively of the Financial Conglomerates and Other Financial Groups Regulations 2004.

[3574]

NOTES

Commencement: 15 December 2007.

17 Reliance

(1)   A relevant person may rely on a person who falls within paragraph (2) (or who the relevant person has reasonable grounds to believe falls within paragraph (2)) to apply any customer due diligence measures provided that—

    (a)   the other person consents to being relied on; and

    (b)   notwithstanding the relevant person's reliance on the other person, the relevant person remains liable for any failure to apply such measures.

(2)   The persons are—

    (a)   a credit or financial institution which is an authorised person;

    (b)   a relevant person who is—

        (i)   an auditor, insolvency practitioner, external accountant, tax adviser or independent legal professional; and

        (ii)   supervised for the purposes of these Regulations by one of the bodies listed in Part 1 of Schedule 3;

    (c)   a person who carries on business in another EEA state who is—

        (i)   a credit or financial institution, auditor, insolvency practitioner, external accountant, tax adviser or independent legal professional;

        (ii)   subject to mandatory professional registration recognised by law; and

        (iii)   supervised for compliance with the requirements laid down in the money laundering directive in accordance with section 2 of Chapter V of that directive; or

    (d)   a person who carries on business in a non-EEA state who is—

(i) a credit or financial institution (or equivalent institution), auditor, insolvency practitioner, external accountant, tax adviser or independent legal professional;
(ii) subject to mandatory professional registration recognised by law;
(iii) subject to requirements equivalent to those laid down in the money laundering directive; and
(iv) supervised for compliance with those requirements in a manner equivalent to section 2 of Chapter V of the money laundering directive.

(3) In paragraph (2)(c)(i) and (d)(i), "auditor" and "insolvency practitioner" includes a person situated in another EEA state or a non-EEA state who provides services equivalent to the services provided by an auditor or insolvency practitioner.

(4) Nothing in this regulation prevents a relevant person applying customer due diligence measures by means of an outsourcing service provider or agent provided that the relevant person remains liable for any failure to apply such measures.

[(5) In this regulation, "financial institution" excludes—
(a) any money service business;
(b) any authorised payment institution, EEA authorised payment institution or small payment institution (within the meaning of the Payment Services Regulations 2009) which provides payment services mainly falling within paragraph 1(f) of Schedule 1 to those Regulations.]

[3575]

NOTES
Commencement: 15 December 2007.
Para (5): substituted by the Payment Services Regulations 2009, SI 2009/209, reg 126, Sch 6, Pt 2, para 6(b).

18 Directions where Financial Action Task Force applies counter-measures

The Treasury may direct any relevant person—
(a) not to enter into a business relationship;
(b) not to carry out an occasional transaction; or
(c) not to proceed any further with a business relationship or occasional transaction,

with a person who is situated or incorporated in a non-EEA state to which the Financial Action Task Force has decided to apply counter-measures.

[3576]

NOTES
Commencement: 15 December 2007.

PART 3
RECORD-KEEPING, PROCEDURES AND TRAINING

19 Record-keeping

(1) Subject to paragraph (4), a relevant person must keep the records specified in paragraph (2) for at least the period specified in paragraph (3).

(2) The records are—
(a) a copy of, or the references to, the evidence of the customer's identity obtained pursuant to regulation 7, 8, 10, 14 or 16(4);
(b) the supporting records (consisting of the original documents or copies) in respect of a business relationship or occasional transaction which is the subject of customer due diligence measures or ongoing monitoring.

(3) The period is five years beginning on—
(a) in the case of the records specified in paragraph (2)(a), the date on which—
(i) the occasional transaction is completed; or
(ii) the business relationship ends; or
(b) in the case of the records specified in paragraph (2)(b)—
(i) where the records relate to a particular transaction, the date on which the transaction is completed;
(ii) for all other records, the date on which the business relationship ends.

(4) A relevant person who is relied on by another person must keep the records specified in paragraph (2)(a) for five years beginning on the date on which he is relied on for the purposes of regulation 7, 10, 14 or 16(4) in relation to any business relationship or occasional transaction.

(5) A person referred to in regulation 17(2)(a) or (b) who is relied on by a relevant person must, if requested by the person relying on him within the period referred to in paragraph (4)—
(a) as soon as reasonably practicable make available to the person who is relying on him any

information about the customer (and any beneficial owner) which he obtained when applying customer due diligence measures; and

(b) as soon as reasonably practicable forward to the person who is relying on him copies of any identification and verification data and other relevant documents on the identity of the customer (and any beneficial owner) which he obtained when applying those measures.

(6) A relevant person who relies on a person referred to in regulation 17(2)(c) or (d) (a "third party") to apply customer due diligence measures must take steps to ensure that the third party will, if requested by the relevant person within the period referred to in paragraph (4)—

(a) as soon as reasonably practicable make available to him any information about the customer (and any beneficial owner) which the third party obtained when applying customer due diligence measures; and

(b) as soon as reasonably practicable forward to him copies of any identification and verification data and other relevant documents on the identity of the customer (and any beneficial owner) which the third party obtained when applying those measures.

(7) Paragraphs (5) and (6) do not apply where a relevant person applies customer due diligence measures by means of an outsourcing service provider or agent.

(8) For the purposes of this regulation, a person relies on another person where he does so in accordance with regulation 17(1).

[3577]

NOTES

Commencement: 15 December 2007.

20 Policies and procedures

(1) A relevant person must establish and maintain appropriate and risk-sensitive policies and procedures relating to—

(a) customer due diligence measures and ongoing monitoring;

(b) reporting;

(c) record-keeping;

(d) internal control;

(e) risk assessment and management;

(f) the monitoring and management of compliance with, and the internal communication of, such policies and procedures,

in order to prevent activities related to money laundering and terrorist financing.

(2) The policies and procedures referred to in paragraph (1) include policies and procedures—

(a) which provide for the identification and scrutiny of—

 (i) complex or unusually large transactions;

 (ii) unusual patterns of transactions which have no apparent economic or visible lawful purpose; and

 (iii) any other activity which the relevant person regards as particularly likely by its nature to be related to money laundering or terrorist financing;

(b) which specify the taking of additional measures, where appropriate, to prevent the use for money laundering or terrorist financing of products and transactions which might favour anonymity;

(c) to determine whether a customer is a politically exposed person;

(d) under which—

 (i) an individual in the relevant person's organisation is a nominated officer under Part 7 of the Proceeds of Crime Act 2002 and Part 3 of the Terrorism Act 2000;

 (ii) anyone in the organisation to whom information or other matter comes in the course of the business as a result of which he knows or suspects or has reasonable grounds for knowing or suspecting that a person is engaged in money laundering or terrorist financing is required to comply with Part 7 of the Proceeds of Crime Act 2002 or, as the case may be, Part 3 of the Terrorism Act 2000; and

 (iii) where a disclosure is made to the nominated officer, he must consider it in the light of any relevant information which is available to the relevant person and determine whether it gives rise to knowledge or suspicion or reasonable grounds for knowledge or suspicion that a person is engaged in money laundering or terrorist financing.

(3) Paragraph (2)(d) does not apply where the relevant person is an individual who neither employs nor acts in association with any other person.

(4) A credit or financial institution must establish and maintain systems which enable it to respond fully and rapidly to enquiries from financial investigators accredited under section 3 of the

Proceeds of Crime Act 2002 (accreditation and training), persons acting on behalf of the Scottish Ministers in their capacity as an enforcement authority under that Act, officers of Revenue and Customs or constables as to—

    (a)   whether it maintains, or has maintained during the previous five years, a business relationship with any person; and

    (b)   the nature of that relationship.

(5)   A credit or financial institution must communicate where relevant the policies and procedures which it establishes and maintains in accordance with this regulation to its branches and subsidiary undertakings which are located outside the United Kingdom.

(6)   In this regulation—

"politically exposed person" has the same meaning as in regulation 14(4);

"subsidiary undertaking" has the same meaning as in regulation 15.

[3578]

NOTES

Commencement: 15 December 2007.

---

21 Training

A relevant person must take appropriate measures so that all relevant employees of his are—

    (a)   made aware of the law relating to money laundering and terrorist financing; and

    (b)   regularly given training in how to recognise and deal with transactions and other activities which may be related to money laundering or terrorist financing.

[3579]

NOTES

Commencement: 15 December 2007.

PART 4
SUPERVISION AND REGISTRATION

Interpretation

22 Interpretation

(1)   In this Part—

"Annex I financial institution" means any undertaking which falls within regulation 3(3)(a) other than—

    (a)   a consumer credit financial institution;

    (b)   a money service business; ...

    (c)   an authorised person;

    [(d)   a bill payment service provider; or

    (e)   a telecommunication, digital and IT payment service provider;]

"consumer credit financial institution" means any undertaking which falls within regulation 3(3)(a) and which requires, under section 21 of the Consumer Credit Act 1974 (businesses needing a licence), a licence to carry on a consumer credit business, other than—

    (a)   a person covered by a group licence issued by the OFT under section 22 of that Act (standard and group licences);

    (b)   a money service business; ...

    (c)   an authorised person.

    [(d)   a bill payment service provider; or

    (e)   a telecommunication, digital and IT payment service provider.]

(2)   In paragraph (1), "consumer credit business" has the meaning given by section 189(1) of the Consumer Credit Act 1974 (definitions) and, on the entry into force of section 23(a) of the Consumer Credit Act 2006 (definitions of "consumer credit business" and "consumer hire business"), has the meaning given by section 189(1) of the Consumer Credit Act 1974 as amended by section 23(a) of the Consumer Credit Act 2006.

[3580]

NOTES

Commencement: 15 December 2007.

Para (1): in definitions "Annex I financial institution" and "consumer credit financial institution" words omitted revoked and words in square brackets inserted by the Payment Services Regulations 2009, SI 2009/209, reg 126, Sch 6, Pt 2, para 6(c).

Supervision

23 Supervisory authorities

(1) Subject to paragraph (2), the following bodies are supervisory authorities—
  (a) the Authority is the supervisory authority for—
    (i) credit and financial institutions which are authorised persons;
    (ii) trust or company service providers which are authorised persons;
    (iii) Annex I financial institutions;
  (b) the OFT is the supervisory authority for—
    (i) consumer credit financial institutions;
    (ii) estate agents;
  (c) each of the professional bodies listed in Schedule 3 is the supervisory authority for relevant persons who are regulated by it;
  (d) the Commissioners are the supervisory authority for—
    (i) high value dealers;
    (ii) money service businesses which are not supervised by the Authority;
    (iii) trust or company service providers which are not supervised by the Authority or one of the bodies listed in Schedule 3;
    (iv) auditors, external accountants and tax advisers who are not supervised by one of the bodies listed in Schedule 3;
    [(v) bill payment service providers which are not supervised by the Authority;
    (vi) telecommunication, digital and IT payment service providers which are not supervised by the Authority.]
  (e) the Gambling Commission is the supervisory authority for casinos;
  (f) DETI is the supervisory authority for—
    (i) credit unions in Northern Ireland;
    (ii) insolvency practitioners authorised by it under article 351 of the Insolvency (Northern Ireland) Order 1989;
  (g) the Secretary of State is the supervisory authority for insolvency practitioners authorised by him under section 393 of the Insolvency Act 1986 (grant, refusal and withdrawal of authorisation).

(2) Where under paragraph (1) there is more than one supervisory authority for a relevant person, the supervisory authorities may agree that one of them will act as the supervisory authority for that person.

(3) Where an agreement has been made under paragraph (2), the authority which has agreed to act as the supervisory authority must notify the relevant person or publish the agreement in such manner as it considers appropriate.

(4) Where no agreement has been made under paragraph (2), the supervisory authorities for a relevant person must cooperate in the performance of their functions under these Regulations.

[3581]

NOTES
Commencement: 15 December 2007.
Para (1): sub-para (d)(v), (vi) inserted by the Payment Services Regulations 2009, SI 2009/209, reg 126, Sch 6, Pt 2, para 6(d).

24 Duties of supervisory authorities

(1) A supervisory authority must effectively monitor the relevant persons for whom it is the supervisory authority and take necessary measures for the purpose of securing compliance by such persons with the requirements of these Regulations.

(2) A supervisory authority which, in the course of carrying out any of its functions under these Regulations, knows or suspects that a person is or has engaged in money laundering or terrorist financing must promptly inform the Serious Organised Crime Agency.

(3) A disclosure made under paragraph (2) is not to be taken to breach any restriction, however imposed, on the disclosure of information.

(4) The functions of the Authority under these Regulations shall be treated for the purposes of Parts 1, 2 and 4 of Schedule 1 to the 2000 Act (the Financial Services Authority) as functions conferred on the Authority under that Act.

[3582]

NOTES
Commencement: 15 December 2007.

*Registration of high value dealers, money service businesses
and trust or company service providers*

25 Duty to maintain registers

(1)   The Commissioners must maintain registers of—
- (a)   high value dealers;
- (b)   money service businesses for which they are the supervisory authority; ...
- (c)   trust or company service providers for which they are the supervisory authority.
- [(d)   bill payment service providers for which they are the supervisory authority; and
- (e)   telecommunication, digital and IT payment service providers for which they are the supervisory authority.]

(2)   The Commissioners may keep the registers in any form they think fit.

(3)   The Commissioners may publish or make available for public inspection all or part of a register maintained under this regulation.

[3583]

NOTES

Commencement: 15 December 2007.

Para (1): word omitted from sub-para (b) revoked and sub-paras (d), (e) inserted by the Payment Services Regulations 2009, SI 2009/209, reg 126, Sch 6, Pt 2, para 6(e).

26 Requirement to be registered

(1)   A person in respect of whom the Commissioners are required to maintain a register under regulation 25 must not act as a—
- (a)   high value dealer;
- (b)   money service business; ...
- (c)   trust or company service provider,
- [(d)   bill payment service provider; or
- (e)   telecommunication, digital and IT payment service provider,]

unless he is included in the register.

(2)   Paragraph (1) and regulation 29 are subject to the transitional provisions set out in regulation 50.

[3584]

NOTES

Commencement: 15 December 2007.

Para (1): word omitted from sub-para (b) revoked and sub-paras (d), (e) inserted by the Payment Services Regulations 2009, SI 2009/209, reg 126, Sch 6, Pt 2, para 6(f).

27 Applications for registration in a register maintained under regulation 25

(1)   An applicant for registration in a register maintained under regulation 25 must make an application in such manner and provide such information as the Commissioners may specify.

(2)   The information which the Commissioners may specify includes—
- (a)   the applicant's name and (if different) the name of the business;
- (b)   the nature of the business;
- (c)   the name of the nominated officer (if any);
- (d)   in relation to a money service business or trust or company service provider—
  - (i)   the name of any person who effectively directs or will direct the business and any beneficial owner of the business; and
  - (ii)   information needed by the Commissioners to decide whether they must refuse the application pursuant to regulation 28.

(3)   At any time after receiving an application and before determining it, the Commissioners may require the applicant to provide, within 21 days beginning with the date of being requested to do so, such further information as they reasonably consider necessary to enable them to determine the application.

(4)   If at any time after the applicant has provided the Commissioners with any information under paragraph (1) or (3)—
- (a)   there is a material change affecting any matter contained in that information; or
- (b)   it becomes apparent to that person that the information contains a significant inaccuracy,

he must provide the Commissioners with details of the change or, as the case may be, a correction of the inaccuracy within 30 days beginning with the date of the occurrence of the change (or the discovery of the inaccuracy) or within such later time as may be agreed with the Commissioners.

(5)   The obligation in paragraph (4) applies also to material changes or significant inaccuracies affecting any matter contained in any supplementary information provided pursuant to that paragraph.

(6)   Any information to be provided to the Commissioners under this regulation must be in such form or verified in such manner as they may specify.

[3585]

NOTES
Commencement: 15 December 2007.

28 Fit and proper test

(1)   The Commissioners must refuse to register an applicant as a money service business or trust or company service provider if they are satisfied that—
  (a)   the applicant;
  (b)   a person who effectively directs, or will effectively direct, the business or service provider;
  (c)   a beneficial owner of the business or service provider; or
  (d)   the nominated officer of the business or service provider,
is not a fit and proper person.

(2)   For the purposes of paragraph (1), a person is not a fit and proper person if he—
  (a)   has been convicted of—
      (i)   an offence under the Terrorism Act 2000;
      (ii)   an offence under paragraph 7(2) or (3) of Schedule 3 to the Anti-Terrorism, Crime and Security Act 2001 (offences);
      (iii)   an offence under the Terrorism Act 2006;
      (iv)   an offence under Part 7 (money laundering) of, or listed in Schedule 2 (lifestyle offences: England and Wales), 4 (lifestyle offences: Scotland) or 5 (lifestyle offences: Northern Ireland) to, the Proceeds of Crime Act 2002;
      (v)   an offence under the Fraud Act 2006 or, in Scotland, the common law offence of fraud;
      (vi)   an offence under section 72(1), (3) or (8) of the Value Added Tax Act 1994 (offences); or
      (vii)   the common law offence of cheating the public revenue;
  (b)   has been adjudged bankrupt or sequestration of his estate has been awarded and (in either case) he has not been discharged;
  (c)   is subject to a disqualification order under the Company Directors Disqualification Act 1986;
  (d)   is or has been subject to a confiscation order under the Proceeds of Crime Act 2002;
  (e)   has consistently failed to comply with the requirements of these Regulations, the Money Laundering Regulations 2003 or the Money Laundering Regulations 2001;
  (f)   has consistently failed to comply with the requirements of regulation 2006/1781/EC of the European Parliament and of the Council of 15th November 2006 on information on the payer accompanying the transfer of funds;
  (g)   has effectively directed a business which falls within sub-paragraph (e) or (f);
  (h)   is otherwise not a fit and proper person with regard to the risk of money laundering or terrorist financing.

(3)   For the purposes of this regulation, a conviction for an offence listed in paragraph (2)(a) is to be disregarded if it is spent for the purposes of the Rehabilitation of Offenders Act 1974.

[3586]

NOTES
Commencement: 15 December 2007.

29 Determination of applications under regulation 27

(1)   Subject to regulation 28, the Commissioners may refuse to register an applicant for registration in a register maintained under regulation 25 only if—
  (a)   any requirement of, or imposed under, regulation 27 has not been complied with;
  (b)   it appears to the Commissioners that any information provided pursuant to regulation 27 is false or misleading in a material particular; or
  (c)   the applicant has failed to pay a charge imposed by them under regulation 35(1).

(2)   The Commissioners must within 45 days beginning either with the date on which they receive the application or, where applicable, with the date on which they receive any further information required under regulation 27(3), give the applicant notice of—
  (a)   their decision to register the applicant; or
  (b)   the following matters—
      (i)   their decision not to register the applicant;
      (ii)   the reasons for their decision;
      [(iii)   the right to a review under regulation 43A; and]

      (iv)   the right to appeal under regulation [43].

(3)   The Commissioners must, as soon as practicable after deciding to register a person, include him in the relevant register.

[3587]

NOTES
Commencement: 15 December 2007.
Para (2): sub-para (b)(iii) and number in square brackets in sub-para (b)(iv) substituted by the Transfer of Tribunal Functions and Revenue and Customs Appeals Order 2009, SI 2009/56, art 3, Sch 2, paras 168, 169, subject to transitional provisions and savings in Sch 3 to the 2009 Order.

30   Cancellation of registration in a register maintained under regulation 25

(1)   The Commissioners must cancel the registration of a money service business or trust or company service provider in a register maintained under regulation 25(1) if, at any time after registration, they are satisfied that he or any person mentioned in regulation 28(1)(b), (c) or (d) is not a fit and proper person within the meaning of regulation 28(2).

(2)   The Commissioners may cancel a person's registration in a register maintained by them under regulation 25 if, at any time after registration, it appears to them that they would have had grounds to refuse registration under regulation 29(1).

(3)   Where the Commissioners decide to cancel a person's registration they must give him notice of—
      (a)   their decision and, subject to paragraph (4), the date from which the cancellation takes effect;
      (b)   the reasons for their decision;
      [(c)   the right to a review under regulation 43A; and]
      (d)   the right to appeal under regulation [43].

(4)   If the Commissioners—
      (a)   consider that the interests of the public require the cancellation of a person's registration to have immediate effect; and
      (b)   include a statement to that effect and the reasons for it in the notice given under paragraph (3),
the cancellation takes effect when the notice is given to the person.

[3588]

NOTES
Commencement: 15 December 2007.
Para (3): sub-para (c) and number in square brackets in sub-para (d) substituted by the Transfer of Tribunal Functions and Revenue and Customs Appeals Order 2009, SI 2009/56, art 3, Sch 2, paras 168, 170, subject to transitional provisions and savings in Sch 3 to the 2009 Order.

Requirement to inform the authority

31   Requirement on authorised person to inform the Authority

(1)   An authorised person whose supervisory authority is the Authority must, before acting as a money service business or a trust or company service provider or within 28 days of so doing, inform the Authority that he intends, or has begun, to act as such.

(2)   Paragraph (1) does not apply to an authorised person who—
      (a)   immediately before 15th December 2007 was acting as a money service business or a trust or company service provider and continues to act as such after that date; and
      (b)   before 15th January 2008 informs the Authority that he is or was acting as such.

(3)   Where an authorised person whose supervisory authority is the Authority ceases to act as a money service business or a trust or company service provider, he must immediately inform the Authority.

(4)   Any requirement imposed by this regulation is to be treated as if it were a requirement imposed by or under the 2000 Act.

(5)   Any information to be provided to the Authority under this regulation must be in such form or verified in such manner as it may specify.

[3589]

NOTES
Commencement: 15 December 2007.

PART 2
STATUTORY INSTRUMENTS

Registration of Annex I financial institutions, estate agents etc

32 Power to maintain registers

(1)   The supervisory authorities mentioned in paragraph (2), (3) or (4) may, in order to fulfil their duties under regulation 24, maintain a register under this regulation.

(2)   The Authority may maintain a register of Annex I financial institutions.

(3)   The OFT may maintain registers of—
    (a)   consumer credit financial institutions; and
    (b)   estate agents.

(4)   The Commissioners may maintain registers of—
    (a)   auditors;
    (b)   external accountants; and
    (c)   tax advisers,

who are not supervised by the Secretary of State, DETI or any of the professional bodies listed in Schedule 3.

(5)   Where a supervisory authority decides to maintain a register under this regulation, it must take reasonable steps to bring its decision to the attention of those relevant persons in respect of whom the register is to be established.

(6)   A supervisory authority may keep a register under this regulation in any form it thinks fit.

(7)   A supervisory authority may publish or make available to public inspection all or part of a register maintained by it under this regulation.

[3590]

NOTES
Commencement: 15 December 2007.

33 Requirement to be registered

Where a supervisory authority decides to maintain a register under regulation 32 in respect of any description of relevant persons and establishes a register for that purpose, a relevant person of that description may not carry on the business or profession in question for a period of more than six months beginning on the date on which the supervisory authority establishes the register unless he is included in the register.

[3591]

NOTES
Commencement: 15 December 2007.

34 Applications for and cancellation of registration in a register maintained under regulation 32

(1)   Regulations 27, 29 (with the omission of the words "Subject to regulation 28" in regulation 29(1)) and 30(2), (3) and (4) apply to registration in a register maintained by the Commissioners under regulation 32 as they apply to registration in a register maintained under regulation 25.

(2)   Regulation 27 applies to registration in a register maintained by the Authority or the OFT under regulation 32 as it applies to registration in a register maintained under regulation 25 and, for this purpose, references to the Commissioners are to be treated as references to the Authority or the OFT, as the case may be.

(3)   The Authority and the OFT may refuse to register an applicant for registration in a register maintained under regulation 32 only if—
    (a)   any requirement of, or imposed under, regulation 27 has not been complied with;
    (b)   it appears to the Authority or the OFT, as the case may be, that any information provided pursuant to regulation 27 is false or misleading in a material particular; or
    (c)   the applicant has failed to pay a charge imposed by the Authority or the OFT, as the case may be, under regulation 35(1).

(4)   The Authority or the OFT, as the case may be, must, within 45 days beginning either with the date on which it receives an application or, where applicable, with the date on which it receives any further information required under regulation 27(3), give the applicant notice of—
    (a)   its decision to register the applicant; or
    (b)   the following matters—
        (i)   that it is minded not to register the applicant;
        (ii)   the reasons for being minded not to register him; and
        (iii) the right to make representations to it within a specified period (which may not be less than 28 days).

(5)   The Authority or the OFT, as the case may be, must then decide, within a reasonable period, whether to register the applicant and it must give the applicant notice of—

     (a)   its decision to register the applicant; or

     (b)   the following matters—

         (i)   its decision not to register the applicant;

         (ii)   the reasons for its decision; and

         (iii)   the right to appeal under regulation 44(1)(b).

(6)   The Authority or the OFT, as the case may be, must, as soon as reasonably practicable after deciding to register a person, include him in the relevant register.

(7)   The Authority or the OFT may cancel a person's registration in a register maintained by them under regulation 32 if, at any time after registration, it appears to them that they would have had grounds to refuse registration under paragraph (3).

(8)   Where the Authority or the OFT proposes to cancel a person's registration, it must give him notice of—

     (a)   its proposal to cancel his registration;

     (b)   the reasons for the proposed cancellation; and

     (c)   the right to make representations to it within a specified period (which may not be less than 28 days).

(9)   The Authority or the OFT, as the case may be, must then decide, within a reasonable period, whether to cancel the person's registration and it must give him notice of—

     (a)   its decision not to cancel his registration; or

     (b)   the following matters—

         (i)   its decision to cancel his registration and, subject to paragraph (10), the date from which cancellation takes effect;

         (ii)   the reasons for its decision; and

         (iii)   the right to appeal under regulation 44(1)(b).

(10)   If the Authority or the OFT, as the case may be—

     (a)   considers that the interests of the public require the cancellation of a person's registration to have immediate effect; and

     (b)   includes a statement to that effect and the reasons for it in the notice given under paragraph (9)(b),

the cancellation takes effect when the notice is given to the person.

(11)   In paragraphs (3) and (4), references to regulation 27 are to be treated as references to that paragraph as applied by paragraph (2) of this regulation.

[3592]

NOTES

Commencement: 15 December 2007.

Financial provisions

35   Costs of supervision

(1)   The Authority, the OFT and the Commissioners may impose charges—

     (a)   on applicants for registration;

     (b)   on relevant persons supervised by them.

(2)   Charges levied under paragraph (1) must not exceed such amount as the Authority, the OFT or the Commissioners (as the case may be) consider will enable them to meet any expenses reasonably incurred by them in carrying out their functions under these Regulations or for any incidental purpose.

(3)   Without prejudice to the generality of paragraph (2), a charge may be levied in respect of each of the premises at which a person carries on (or proposes to carry on) business.

(4)   The Authority must apply amounts paid to it by way of penalties imposed under regulation 42 towards expenses incurred in carrying out its functions under these Regulations or for any incidental purpose.

(5)   In paragraph (2), "expenses" in relation to the OFT includes expenses incurred by a local weights and measures authority or DETI pursuant to arrangements made for the purposes of these Regulations with the OFT—

     (a)   by or on behalf of the authority; or

     (b)   by DETI.

[3593]

NOTES

Commencement: 15 December 2007.

PART 5
ENFORCEMENT

Powers of designated authorities

36 Interpretation

In this Part—
"designated authority" means—
  (a)   the Authority;
  (b)   the Commissioners;
  (c)   the OFT; and
  (d)   in relation to credit unions in Northern Ireland, DETI;
"officer", except in regulations 40(3), 41 and 47 means—
  (a)   an officer of the Authority, including a member of the Authority's staff or an agent of the Authority;
  (b)   an officer of Revenue and Customs;
  (c)   an officer of the OFT;
  (d)   a relevant officer; or
  (e)   an officer of DETI acting for the purposes of its functions under these Regulations in relation to credit unions in Northern Ireland;
"recorded information" includes information recorded in any form and any document of any nature;
"relevant officer" means—
  (a)   in Great Britain, an officer of a local weights and measures authority;
  (b)   in Northern Ireland, an officer of DETI acting pursuant to arrangements made with the OFT for the purposes of these Regulations.

[3594]

NOTES

Commencement: 15 December 2007.

37 Power to require information from, and attendance of, relevant and connected persons

(1)   An officer may, by notice to a relevant person or to a person connected with a relevant person, require the relevant person or the connected person, as the case may be—
  (a)   to provide such information as may be specified in the notice;
  (b)   to produce such recorded information as may be so specified; or
  (c)   to attend before an officer at a time and place specified in the notice and answer questions.

(2)   For the purposes of paragraph (1), a person is connected with a relevant person if he is, or has at any time been, in relation to the relevant person, a person listed in Schedule 4 to these Regulations.

(3)   An officer may exercise powers under this regulation only if the information sought to be obtained as a result is reasonably required in connection with the exercise by the designated authority for whom he acts of its functions under these Regulations.

(4)   Where an officer requires information to be provided or produced pursuant to paragraph (1)(a) or (b)—
  (a)   the notice must set out the reasons why the officer requires the information to be provided or produced; and
  (b)   such information must be provided or produced—
    (i)   before the end of such reasonable period as may be specified in the notice; and
    (ii)   at such place as may be so specified.

(5)   In relation to information recorded otherwise than in legible form, the power to require production of it includes a power to require the production of a copy of it in legible form or in a form from which it can readily be produced in visible and legible form.

(6)   The production of a document does not affect any lien which a person has on the document.

(7)   A person may not be required under this regulation to provide or produce information or to answer questions which he would be entitled to refuse to provide, produce or answer on grounds of legal professional privilege in proceedings in the High Court, except that a lawyer may be required to provide the name and address of his client.

(8)   Subject to paragraphs (9) and (10), a statement made by a person in compliance with a requirement imposed on him under paragraph (1)(c) is admissible in evidence in any proceedings, so long as it also complies with any requirements governing the admissibility of evidence in the circumstances in question.

(9)   In criminal proceedings in which a person is charged with an offence to which this paragraph applies—

(a) no evidence relating to the statement may be adduced; and
(b) no question relating to it may be asked,

by or on behalf of the prosecution unless evidence relating to it is adduced, or a question relating to it is asked, in the proceedings by or on behalf of that person.

(10) Paragraph (9) applies to any offence other than one under—
(a) section 5 of the Perjury Act 1911 (false statements without oath);
(b) section 44(2) of the Criminal Law (Consolidation) (Scotland) Act 1995 (false statements and declarations); or
(c) Article 10 of the Perjury (Northern Ireland) Order 1979 (false unsworn statements).

(11) In the application of this regulation to Scotland, the reference in paragraph (7) to—
(a) proceedings in the High Court is to be read as a reference to legal proceedings generally; and
(b) an entitlement on grounds of legal professional privilege is to be read as a reference to an entitlement on the grounds of confidentiality of communications[—
  (i) between a professional legal adviser and his client; or
  (ii) made in connection with or in contemplation of legal proceedings and for the purposes of those proceedings].

[3595]

NOTES
Commencement: 15 December 2007.
Para (11): sub-paras (b)(i), (ii) inserted by the Money Laundering (Amendment) Regulations 2007, SI 2007/3299, reg 2(b).

38 Entry, inspection without a warrant etc

(1) Where an officer has reasonable cause to believe that any premises are being used by a relevant person in connection with his business or professional activities, he may on producing evidence of his authority at any reasonable time—
(a) enter the premises;
(b) inspect the premises;
(c) observe the carrying on of business or professional activities by the relevant person;
(d) inspect any recorded information found on the premises;
(e) require any person on the premises to provide an explanation of any recorded information or to state where it may be found;
(f) in the case of a money service business or a high value dealer, inspect any cash found on the premises.

(2) An officer may take copies of, or make extracts from, any recorded information found under paragraph (1).

(3) Paragraphs (1)(d) and (e) and (2) do not apply to recorded information which the relevant person would be entitled to refuse to disclose on grounds of legal professional privilege in proceedings in the High Court, except that a lawyer may be required to provide the name and address of his client and, for this purpose, regulation 37(11) applies to this paragraph as it applies to regulation 37(7).

(4) An officer may exercise powers under this regulation only if the information sought to be obtained as a result is reasonably required in connection with the exercise by the designated authority for whom he acts of its functions under these Regulations.

(5) In this regulation, "premises" means any premises other than premises used only as a dwelling.

[3596]

NOTES
Commencement: 15 December 2007.

39 Entry to premises under warrant

(1) A justice may issue a warrant under this paragraph if satisfied on information on oath given by an officer that there are reasonable grounds for believing that the first, second or third set of conditions is satisfied.

(2) The first set of conditions is—
(a) that there is on the premises specified in the warrant recorded information in relation to which a requirement could be imposed under regulation 37(1)(b); and
(b) that if such a requirement were to be imposed—
  (i) it would not be complied with; or
  (ii) the recorded information to which it relates would be removed, tampered with or destroyed.

(3) The second set of conditions is—

    (a)   that a person on whom a requirement has been imposed under regulation 37(1)(b) has failed (wholly or in part) to comply with it; and

    (b)   that there is on the premises specified in the warrant recorded information which has been required to be produced.

(4) The third set of conditions is—

    (a)   that an officer has been obstructed in the exercise of a power under regulation 38; and

    (b)   that there is on the premises specified in the warrant recorded information or cash which could be inspected under regulation 38(1)(d) or (f).

(5) A justice may issue a warrant under this paragraph if satisfied on information on oath given by an officer that there are reasonable grounds for suspecting that—

    (a)   an offence under these Regulations has been, is being or is about to be committed by a relevant person; and

    (b)   there is on the premises specified in the warrant recorded information relevant to whether that offence has been, or is being or is about to be committed.

(6) A warrant issued under this regulation shall authorise an officer—

    (a)   to enter the premises specified in the warrant;

    (b)   to search the premises and take possession of any recorded information or anything appearing to be recorded information specified in the warrant or to take, in relation to any such recorded information, any other steps which may appear to be necessary for preserving it or preventing interference with it;

    (c)   to take copies of, or extracts from, any recorded information specified in the warrant;

    (d)   to require any person on the premises to provide an explanation of any recorded information appearing to be of the kind specified in the warrant or to state where it may be found;

    (e)   to use such force as may reasonably be necessary.

(7) Where a warrant is issued by a justice under paragraph (1) or (5) on the basis of information [on oath] given by an officer of the Authority, for "an officer" in paragraph (6) substitute "a constable".

(8) In paragraphs (1), (5) and (7), "justice" means—

    (a)   in relation to England and Wales, a justice of the peace;

    (b)   in relation to Scotland, a justice within the meaning of section 307 of the Criminal Procedure (Scotland) Act 1995 (interpretation);

    (c)   in relation to Northern Ireland, a lay magistrate.

(9) In the application of this regulation to Scotland, the references in paragraphs [(1), (5) and (7)] to information on oath are to be read as references to evidence on oath.

[3597]

NOTES

Commencement: 15 December 2007.

Para (7): words in square brackets inserted by the Money Laundering (Amendment) Regulations 2007, SI 2007/3299, reg 2(c)(i).

Para (9): words in square brackets substituted by SI 2007/3299, reg 2(c)(ii).

40 Failure to comply with information requirement

(1) If, on an application made by—

    (a)   a designated authority; or

    (b)   a local weights and measures authority or DETI pursuant to arrangements made with the OFT—

        (i)   by or on behalf of the authority; or

        (ii)   by DETI,

it appears to the court that a person (the "information defaulter") has failed to do something that he was required to do under regulation 37(1), the court may make an order under this regulation.

(2) An order under this regulation may require the information defaulter—

    (a)   to do the thing that he failed to do within such period as may be specified in the order;

    (b)   otherwise to take such steps to remedy the consequences of the failure as may be so specified.

(3) If the information defaulter is a body corporate, a partnership or an unincorporated body of persons which is not a partnership, the order may require any officer of the body corporate, partnership or body, who is (wholly or partly) responsible for the failure to meet such costs of the application as are specified in the order.

(4) In this regulation, "court" means—

(a) in England and Wales and Northern Ireland, the High Court or the county court;

(b) in Scotland, the Court of Session or the sheriff [court].

[3598]

NOTES

Commencement: 15 December 2007.

Para (4): word in square brackets in sub-para (b) inserted by the Money Laundering (Amendment) Regulations 2007, SI 2007/3299, reg 2(d).

41 Powers of relevant officers

(1) A relevant officer may only exercise powers under regulations 37 to 39 pursuant to arrangements made with the OFT—

(a) by or on behalf of the local weights and measures authority of which he is an officer ("his authority"); or

(b) by DETI.

(2) Anything done or omitted to be done by, or in relation to, a relevant officer in the exercise or purported exercise of a power in this Part shall be treated for all purposes as having been done or omitted to be done by, or in relation to, an officer of the OFT.

(3) Paragraph (2) does not apply for the purposes of any criminal proceedings brought against the relevant officer, his authority, DETI or the OFT, in respect of anything done or omitted to be done by the officer.

(4) A relevant officer shall not disclose to any person other than the OFT and his authority or, as the case may be, DETI information obtained by him in the exercise of such powers unless—

(a) he has the approval of the OFT to do so; or

(b) he is under a duty to make the disclosure.

[3599]

NOTES

Commencement: 15 December 2007.

Civil penalties, review and appeals

42 Power to impose civil penalties

(1) A designated authority may impose a penalty of such amount as it considers appropriate on a relevant person who fails to comply with any requirement in regulation 7(1), (2) or (3), 8(1) or (3), 9(2), 10(1), 11(1), 14(1), 15(1) or (2), 16(1), (2), (3) or (4), 19(1), (4), (5) or (6), 20(1), (4) or (5), 21, 26, 27(4) or 33 or a direction made under regulation 18 and, for this purpose, "appropriate" means effective, proportionate and dissuasive.

(2) The designated authority must not impose a penalty on a person under paragraph (1) where there are reasonable grounds for it to be satisfied that the person took all reasonable steps and exercised all due diligence to ensure that the requirement would be complied with.

(3) In deciding whether a person has failed to comply with a requirement of these Regulations, the designated authority must consider whether he followed any relevant guidance which was at the time—

(a) issued by a supervisory authority or any other appropriate body;

(b) approved by the Treasury; and

(c) published in a manner approved by the Treasury as suitable in their opinion to bring the guidance to the attention of persons likely to be affected by it.

(4) In paragraph (3), an "appropriate body" means any body which regulates or is representative of any trade, profession, business or employment carried on by the [person].

(5) Where the Commissioners decide to impose a penalty under this regulation, they must give the person notice of—

(a) their decision to impose the penalty and its amount;

(b) the reasons for imposing the penalty;

(c) the right to a review under regulation [43A]; and

(d) the right to appeal under regulation [43].

(6) Where the Authority, the OFT or DETI proposes to impose a penalty under this regulation, it must give the person notice of—

(a) its proposal to impose the penalty and the proposed amount;

(b) the reasons for imposing the penalty; and

(c) the right to make representations to it within a specified period (which may not be less than 28 days).

(7) The Authority, the OFT or DETI, as the case may be, must then decide, within a reasonable period, whether to impose a penalty under this regulation and it must give the person notice of—

(a)   its decision not to impose a penalty; or
(b)   the following matters—
    (i)   its decision to impose a penalty and the amount;
    (ii)   the reasons for its decision; and
    (iii)   the right to appeal under regulation 44(1)(b).

(8)   A penalty imposed under this regulation is payable to the designated authority which imposes it.

[3600]

NOTES
Commencement: 15 December 2007.
Para (4): word in square brackets substituted by the Money Laundering (Amendment) Regulations 2007, SI 2007/3299, reg 2(e).
Para (5): numbers in square brackets in sub-paras (c), (d) substituted by the Transfer of Tribunal Functions and Revenue and Customs Appeals Order 2009, SI 2009/56, art 3, Sch 2, paras 168, 171, subject to transitional provisions and savings in Sch 3 to the 2009 Order.

43 [Appeals against decisions of the Commissioners]

(1)   This regulation applies to decisions of the Commissioners made under—
(a)   regulation 29, to refuse to register an applicant;
(b)   regulation 30, to cancel the registration of a registered person; and
(c)   regulation 42, to impose a penalty.

(2)   Any person who is the subject of a decision to which this regulation applies may [appeal to the tribunal in accordance with regulation 43F].

[(3)   The provisions of Part 5 of the Value Added Tax Act 1994 (appeals), subject to the modifications set out in paragraph 1 of Schedule 5 to these Regulations, apply in respect of appeals to a tribunal made under this regulation as they apply in respect of appeals made to the tribunal under section 83 (appeals) of that Act.

(4)   A tribunal hearing an appeal under paragraph (2) has the power to—
(a)   quash or vary any decision of the supervisory authority, including the power to reduce any penalty to such amount (including nil) as it thinks proper, and
(b)   substitute its own decision for any decision quashed on appeal.

(5)   The modifications in Schedule 5 have effect for the purposes of appeals made under this regulation.

(6)   For the purposes of appeals under this regulation, the meaning of "tribunal" is as defined in section 82 of the Value Added Tax Act 1994.]

[3601]

NOTES
Commencement: 15 December 2007.
Regulation heading: words in square brackets substituted by the Transfer of Tribunal Functions and Revenue and Customs Appeals Order 2009, SI 2009/56, art 3, Sch 2, paras 168, 172(1), (2), subject to transitional provisions and savings in Sch 3 to the 2009 Order.
Para (2): words in square brackets substituted by SI 2009/56, art 3, Sch 2, paras 168, 172(1), (3), subject to transitional provisions and savings in Sch 3 to the 2009 Order.
Paras (3)–(6): substituted for original paras (3)–(5) by SI 2009/56, art 3, Sch 2, paras 168, 172(1), (4), subject to transitional provisions and savings in Sch 3 to the 2009 Order.

[43A   Offer of review

(1)   The Commissioners must offer a person (P) a review of a decision that has been notified to P if an appeal lies under regulation 43 in respect of the decision.

(2)   The offer of the review must be made by notice given to P at the same time as the decision is notified to P.

(3)   This regulation does not apply to the notification of the conclusions of a review.]

[3601A]

NOTES
Commencement: 1 April 2009.
Inserted, together with regs 43B–43F, by the Transfer of Tribunal Functions and Revenue and Customs Appeals Order 2009, SI 2009/56, art 3, Sch 2, paras 168, 173, subject to transitional provisions and savings in Sch 3 to the 2009 Order.

[43B   Review by the Commissioners

(1)   The Commissioners must review a decision if—
(a)   they have offered a review of the decision under regulation 43A, and

(b)　P notifies the Commissioners accepting the offer within 30 days from the date of the document containing the notification of the offer.

(2)　But P may not notify acceptance of the offer if P has already appealed to the tribunal under regulation 43F.

(3)　The Commissioners shall not review a decision if P has appealed to the tribunal under regulation 43F in respect of the decision.]

[3601B]

NOTES

Commencement: 1 April 2009.
Inserted as noted to reg 43A at **[3601A]**.

[43C　Extensions of time

(1)　If under regulation 43A, the Commissioners have offered P a review of a decision, the Commissioners may within the relevant period notify P that the relevant period is extended.

(2)　If notice is given the relevant period is extended to the end of 30 days from—
(a)　the date of the notice, or
(b)　any other date set out in the notice or a further notice.

(3)　In this regulation "relevant period" means—
(a)　the period of 30 days referred to in regulation 43B(1)(b), or
(b)　if notice has been given under paragraph (1) that period as extended (or as most recently extended) in accordance with paragraph (2).]

[3601C]

NOTES

Commencement: 1 April 2009.
Inserted as noted to reg 43A at **[3601A]**.

[43D　Review out of time

(1)　This regulation applies if—
(a)　the Commissioners have offered a review of a decision under regulation 43A, and
(b)　P does not accept the offer within the time allowed under regulation 43B(1)(b) or 43C(2).

(2)　The Commissioners must review the decision under regulation 43B if—
(a)　after the time allowed, P notifies the Commissioners in writing requesting a review out of time,
(b)　the Commissioners are satisfied that P had a reasonable excuse for not accepting the offer or requiring review within the time allowed, and
(c)　the Commissioners are satisfied that P made the request without unreasonable delay after the excuse had ceased to apply.

(3)　The Commissioners shall not review a decision if P has appealed to the tribunal under regulation 43F in respect of the decision.]

[3601D]

NOTES

Commencement: 1 April 2009.
Inserted as noted to reg 43A at **[3601A]**.

[43E　Nature of review etc

(1)　This regulation applies if the Commissioners are required to undertake a review under regulation 43B or 43D.

(2)　The nature and extent of the review are to be such as appear appropriate to the Commissioners in the circumstances.

(3)　For the purpose of paragraph (2), the Commissioners must, in particular, have regard to steps taken before the beginning of the review—
(a)　by the Commissioners in reaching the decision, and
(b)　by any person in seeking to resolve disagreement about the decision.

(4)　The review must take account of any representations made by P at a stage which gives the Commissioners a reasonable opportunity to consider them.

(5)　The review may conclude that the decision is to be—
(a)　upheld,
(b)　varied, or
(c)　cancelled.

(6)   The Commissioners must give P notice of the conclusions of the review and their reasoning within—
  (a)   a period of 45 days beginning with the relevant date, or
  (b)   such other period as the Commissioners and P may agree.

(7)   In paragraph (6) "relevant date" means—
  (a)   the date the Commissioners received P's notification accepting the offer of a review (in a case falling within regulation 43A), or
  (b)   the date on which the Commissioners decided to undertake the review (in a case falling within regulation 43D).

(8)   Where the Commissioners are required to undertake a review but do not give notice of the conclusions within the time period specified in paragraph (6), the review is to be treated as having concluded that the decision is upheld.

(9)   If paragraph (8) applies, the Commissioners must notify P of the conclusion which the review is treated as having reached.]

[3601E]

NOTES
Commencement: 1 April 2009.
Inserted as noted to reg 43A at **[3601A]**.

[43F   Bringing of appeals against decisions of the Commissioners
  (1)   An appeal under regulation 43 is to be made to the tribunal before—
  (a)   the end of the period of 30 days beginning with the date of the document notifying the decision to which the appeal relates, or
  (b)   if later, the end of the relevant period (within the meaning of regulation 43C).

(2)   But that is subject to paragraphs (3) to (5).

(3)   In a case where the Commissioners are required to undertake a review under regulation 43B—
  (a)   an appeal may not be made until the conclusion date, and
  (b)   any appeal is to be made within the period of 30 days beginning with the conclusion date.

(4)   In a case where the Commissioners are requested to undertake a review in accordance with regulation 43D—
  (a)   an appeal may not be made—
    (i)   unless the Commissioners have decided whether or not to undertake a review, and
    (ii)   if the Commissioners decide to undertake a review, until the conclusion date; and
  (b)   any appeal is to be made within the period of 30 days beginning with—
    (i)   the conclusion date (if the Commissioners decide to undertake a review), or
    (ii)   the date on which the Commissioners decide not to undertake a review.

(5)   In a case where regulation 43E(8) applies, an appeal may be made at any time from the end of the period specified in regulation 43E(6) to the date 30 days after the conclusion date.

(6)   An appeal may be made after the end of the period specified in paragraph (1), (3)(b), (4)(b) or (5) if the tribunal gives permission to do so.

(7)   In this regulation "conclusion date" means the date of the document notifying the conclusions of the review.]

[3601F]

NOTES
Commencement: 1 April 2009.
Inserted as noted to reg 43A at **[3601A]**.

44   Appeals
  (1)   A person may appeal from a decision by—
  (a)   ...
  (b)   the Authority, the OFT or DETI under regulation 34 or 42.

(2)   An appeal from a decision by—
  (a)   ...
  (b)   the Authority is to the [Upper Tribunal];
  (c)   the OFT is to the [First-tier Tribunal]; and
  (d)   DETI is to the High Court.

(3)   ...

(4)   The provisions of Part 9 of the 2000 Act (hearings and appeals), subject to the modifications set out in paragraph 2 of Schedule 5, apply in respect of appeals to the [Upper Tribunal] made under this regulation as they apply in respect of references made to that Tribunal under that Act.

(5)   *Sections 40A (the Consumer Credit Appeals Tribunal), 41 (appeals to the Secretary of State under Part 3) and 41A (appeals from the Consumer Credit Appeals Tribunal) of the Consumer Credit Act 1974 apply in respect of appeals to the Consumer Credit Appeal Tribunal made under this regulation as they apply in respect of appeals made to that Tribunal under section 41 of that Act.*

(6)   …

(7)   Notwithstanding paragraph (2)(c), until the coming into force of section 55 of the Consumer Credit Act 2006 (the Consumer Credit Appeals Tribunal), an appeal from a decision by the OFT is to the Financial Services and Markets Tribunal and, for these purposes, the coming into force of that section shall not affect—

     (a)   the hearing and determination by the Financial Service and Markets Tribunal of an appeal commenced before the coming into force of that section ("the original appeal"); or

     (b)   any appeal against the decision of the Financial Services and Markets Tribunal with respect to the original appeal.

(8)   The modifications in Schedule 5 have effect for the purposes of appeals made under this regulation.

[3602]

NOTES

Commencement: 15 December 2007.

Para (1): sub-para (a) revoked by the Transfer of Tribunal Functions and Revenue and Customs Appeals Order 2009, SI 2009/56, art 3, Sch 2, paras 168, 174(1), (2), subject to transitional provisions and savings in Sch 3 thereto.

Para (2): sub-para (a) revoked by SI 2009/56, art 3, Sch 2, paras 168, 174(1), (2), subject to transitional provisions and savings in Sch 3 thereto; words in square brackets in sub-para (b) substituted by the Transfer of Tribunal Functions Order 2010, SI 2010/22, art 5(2), Sch 3, paras 140, 141, subject to transitional provisions in Sch 5 thereto; words in square brackets in sub-para (c) substituted for original words "Consumer Credit Appeals Tribunal" by the Transfer of Functions of the Consumer Credit Appeals Tribunal Order 2009, SI 2009/1835, art 4(2), Sch 2, para 1(a), subject to transitional provisions and savings in Sch 4 thereto at **[3908]**.

Paras (3), (6): revoked by SI 2009/56, art 3, Sch 2, paras 168, 174(1), (3), (4), subject to transitional provisions and savings in Sch 3 to the 2009 Order.

Para (4): words in square brackets substituted by SI 2010/22, art 5(2), Sch 3, paras 140, 141, subject to transitional provisions in Sch 5 thereto.

Para (5): revoked by SI 2009/1835, art 4(2), Sch 2, para 1(b), subject to transitional provisions and savings in Sch 4 thereto at **[3908]**.

Criminal offences

45   Offences

(1)   A person who fails to comply with any requirement in regulation 7(1), (2) or (3), 8(1) or (3), 9(2), 10(1), 11(1)(a), (b) or (c), 14(1), 15(1) or (2), 16(1), (2), (3) or (4), 19(1), (4), (5) or (6), 20(1), (4) or (5), 21, 26, 27(4) or 33, or a direction made under regulation 18, is guilty of an offence and liable—

     (a)   on summary conviction, to a fine not exceeding the statutory maximum;

     (b)   on conviction on indictment, to imprisonment for a term not exceeding two years, to a fine or to both.

(2)   In deciding whether a person has committed an offence under paragraph (1), the court must consider whether he followed any relevant guidance which was at the time—

     (a)   issued by a supervisory authority or any other appropriate body;

     (b)   approved by the Treasury; and

     (c)   published in a manner approved by the Treasury as suitable in their opinion to bring the guidance to the attention of persons likely to be affected by it.

(3)   In paragraph (2), an "appropriate body" means any body which regulates or is representative of any trade, profession, business or employment carried on by the alleged offender.

(4)   A person is not guilty of an offence under this regulation if he took all reasonable steps and exercised all due diligence to avoid committing the offence.

(5)   Where a person is convicted of an offence under this regulation, he shall not also be liable to a penalty under regulation 42.

[3603]

NOTES

Commencement: 15 December 2007.

46 Prosecution of offences

(1) Proceedings for an offence under regulation 45 may be instituted by—
(a) the Director of Revenue and Customs Prosecutions or by order of the Commissioners;
(b) the OFT;
(c) a local weights and measures authority;
(d) DETI;
(e) the Director of Public Prosecutions; or
(f) the Director of Public Prosecutions for Northern Ireland.

(2) Proceedings for an offence under regulation 45 may be instituted only against a relevant person or, where such a person is a body corporate, a partnership or an unincorporated association, against any person who is liable to be proceeded against under regulation 47.

(3) Where proceedings under paragraph (1) are instituted by order of the Commissioners, the proceedings must be brought in the name of an officer of Revenue and Customs.

(4) Where a local weights and measures authority in England or Wales proposes to institute proceedings for an offence under regulation 45 it must give the OFT notice of the intended proceedings, together with a summary of the facts on which the charges are to be founded.

(5) A local weights and measures authority must also notify the OFT of the outcome of the proceedings after they are finally determined.

(6) A local weights and measures authority must, whenever the OFT requires, report in such form and with such particulars as the OFT requires on the exercise of its functions under these Regulations.

(7) Where the Commissioners investigate, or propose to investigate, any matter with a view to determining—
(a) whether there are grounds for believing that an offence under regulation 45 has been committed by any person; or
(b) whether such a person should be prosecuted for such an offence,
that matter is to be treated as an assigned matter within the meaning of section 1(1) of the Customs and Excise Management Act 1979.

(8) Paragraphs (1) and (3) to (6) do not extend to Scotland.

[(9) In its application to the Commissioners acting in Scotland, paragraph (7)(b) shall be read as referring to the Commissioners determining whether to refer the matter to the Crown Office and Procurator Fiscal Service with a view to the Procurator Fiscal determining whether a person should be prosecuted for such an offence.]

[3604]

NOTES
Commencement: 15 December 2007.
Para (9): added by the Money Laundering (Amendment) Regulations 2007, SI 2007/3299, reg 2(f).

47 Offences by bodies corporate etc

(1) If an offence under regulation 45 committed by a body corporate is shown—
(a) to have been committed with the consent or the connivance of an officer of the body corporate; or
(b) to be attributable to any neglect on his part,
the officer as well as the body corporate is guilty of an offence and liable to be proceeded against and punished accordingly.

(2) If an offence under regulation 45 committed by a partnership is shown—
(a) to have been committed with the consent or the connivance of a partner; or
(b) to be attributable to any neglect on his part,
the partner as well as the partnership is guilty of an offence and liable to be proceeded against and punished accordingly.

(3) If an offence under regulation 45 committed by an unincorporated association (other than a partnership) is shown—
(a) to have been committed with the consent or the connivance of an officer of the association; or
(b) to be attributable to any neglect on his part,
that officer as well as the association is guilty of an offence and liable to be proceeded against and punished accordingly.

(4) If the affairs of a body corporate are managed by its members, paragraph (1) applies in relation to the acts and defaults of a member in connection with his functions of management as if he were a director of the body.

(5) Proceedings for an offence alleged to have been committed by a partnership or an unincorporated association must be brought in the name of the partnership or association (and not in that of its members).

(6) A fine imposed on the partnership or association on its conviction of an offence is to be paid out of the funds of the partnership or association.

(7) Rules of court relating to the service of documents are to have effect as if the partnership or association were a body corporate.

(8) In proceedings for an offence brought against the partnership or association—
- (a) section 33 of the Criminal Justice Act 1925 (procedure on charge of offence against corporation) and Schedule 3 to the Magistrates' Courts Act 1980 (corporations) apply as they do in relation to a body corporate;
- (b) section 70 (proceedings against bodies corporate) of the Criminal Procedure (Scotland) Act 1995 applies as it does in relation to a body corporate;
- (c) section 18 of the Criminal Justice (Northern Ireland) Act 1945 (procedure on charge) and Schedule 4 to the Magistrates' Courts (Northern Ireland) Order 1981 (corporations) apply as they do in relation to a body corporate.

(9) In this regulation—
"officer"—
- (a) in relation to a body corporate, means a director, manager, secretary, chief executive, member of the committee of management, or a person purporting to act in such a capacity; and
- (b) in relation to an unincorporated association, means any officer of the association or any member of its governing body, or a person purporting to act in such capacity; and

"partner" includes a person purporting to act as a partner.

[3605]

NOTES
 Commencement: 15 December 2007.

PART 6
MISCELLANEOUS

48 Recovery of charges and penalties through the court
Any charge or penalty imposed on a person by a supervisory authority under regulation 35(1) or 42(1) is a debt due from that person to the authority, and is recoverable accordingly.

[3606]

NOTES
 Commencement: 15 December 2007.

---

49 Obligations on public authorities
(1) The following bodies and persons must, if they know or suspect or have reasonable grounds for knowing or suspecting that a person is or has engaged in money laundering or terrorist financing, as soon as reasonably practicable inform the Serious Organised Crime Agency—
- (a) the Auditor General for Scotland;
- (b) the Auditor General for Wales;
- (c) the Authority;
- (d) the Bank of England;
- (e) the Comptroller and Auditor General;
- (f) the Comptroller and Auditor General for Northern Ireland;
- (g) the Gambling Commission;
- (h) the OFT;
- (i) the Official Solicitor to the Supreme Court;
- (j) the Pensions Regulator;
- (k) the Public Trustee;
- (l) the Secretary of State, in the exercise of his functions under enactments relating to companies and insolvency;
- (m) the Treasury, in the exercise of their functions under the 2000 Act;
- (n) the Treasury Solicitor;
- (o) a designated professional body for the purposes of Part 20 of the 2000 Act (provision of financial services by members of the professions);
- (p) a person or inspector appointed under section 65 (investigations on behalf of Authority) or 66 (inspections and special meetings) of the Friendly Societies Act 1992;

PART 2
STATUTORY INSTRUMENTS

(q) an inspector appointed under section 49 of the Industrial and Provident Societies Act 1965 (appointment of inspectors) or section 18 of the Credit Unions Act 1979 (power to appoint inspector);

(r) an inspector appointed under section 431 (investigation of a company on its own application), 432 (other company investigations), 442 (power to investigate company ownership) or 446 (investigation of share dealing) of the Companies Act 1985 or under Article 424, 425, 435 or 439 of the Companies (Northern Ireland) Order 1986;

(s) a person or inspector appointed under section 55 (investigations on behalf of Authority) or 56 (inspections and special meetings) of the Building Societies Act 1986;

(t) a person appointed under section 167 (appointment of persons to carry out investigations), 168(3) or (5) (appointment of persons to carry out investigations in particular cases), 169(1)(b) (investigations to support overseas regulator) or 284 (power to investigate affairs of a scheme) of the 2000 Act, or under regulations made under section 262(2)(k) (open-ended investment companies) of that Act, to conduct an investigation; and

(u) a person authorised to require the production of documents under section 447 of the Companies Act 1985 (Secretary of State's power to require production of documents), Article 440 of the Companies (Northern Ireland) Order 1986 or section 84 of the Companies Act 1989 (exercise of powers by officer).

(2) A disclosure made under paragraph (1) is not to be taken to breach any restriction on the disclosure of information however imposed.

[3607]

NOTES
Commencement: 15 December 2007.

[49A Disclosure by the Commissioners

(1) The Commissioners may disclose to the Authority information held in connection with their functions under these Regulations if the disclosure is made for the purpose of enabling or assisting the Authority to discharge any of its functions under the Payment Services Regulations 2009.

(2) Information disclosed to the Authority under subsection (1) may not be disclosed by the Authority or any person who receives the information directly or indirectly from the Authority except—

(a) to, or in accordance with authority given by, the Commissioners;

(b) with a view to the institution of, or otherwise for the purposes of, any criminal proceedings;

(c) with a view to the institution of any other proceedings by the Authority, for the purposes of any such proceedings instituted by the Authority, or for the purposes of any reference to the Tribunal under the Payment Services Regulations 2009; or

(d) in the form of a summary or collection of information so framed as not to enable information relating to any particular person to be ascertained from it.

(3) Any person who discloses information in contravention of subsection (2) is guilty of an offence and liable—

(a) on summary conviction, to imprisonment for a term not exceeding three months, to a fine not exceeding the statutory maximum, or to both;

(b) on conviction on indictment, to imprisonment for a term not exceeding two years to a fine, or to both.

(4) It is a defence for a person charged with an offence under this regulation of disclosing information to prove that they reasonably believed

(a) that the disclosure was lawful; or

(b) that the information had already and lawfully been made available to the public.]

[3607A]

NOTES
Commencement: 2 March 2009.
Inserted by the Payment Services Regulations 2009, SI 2009/209, reg 126, Sch 6, Pt 2, para 6(g).

50 Transitional provisions: requirement to be registered

(1) Regulation 26 does not apply to an existing money service business, an existing trust or company service provider[, an existing high value dealer, an existing bill payment service provider or an existing telecommunication, digital and IT payment service provider] until—

(a) where it has applied in accordance with regulation 27 before the specified date for registration in a register maintained under regulation 25(1) (a "new register")—

(i) the date it is included in a new register following the determination of its application by the Commissioners; or

(ii) where the Commissioners give it notice under regulation 29(2)(b) of their decision not to register it, the date on which the Commissioners state that the decision takes effect or, where a statement is included in accordance with paragraph (3)(b), the time at which the Commissioners give it such notice;

    (b)   in any other case, the specified date.

(2)   The specified date is—

    (a)   in the case of an existing money service business, 1st February 2008;

    (b)   in the case of an existing trust or company service provider, 1st April 2008;

    (c)   in the case of an existing high value dealer, the first anniversary which falls on or after 1st January 2008 of the date of its registration in a register maintained under regulation 10 of the Money Laundering Regulations 2003;

    [(d)   in the case of an existing bill payment service provider or an existing telecommunication, digital and IT payment service provider, 1st March 2010.]

(3)   In the case of an application for registration in a new register made before the specified date by an existing money service business, an existing trust or company service provider[, an existing high value dealer, an existing bill payment service provider or an existing telecommunication, digital and IT payment service provider], the Commissioners must include in a notice given to it under regulation 29(2)(b)—

    (a)   the date on which their decision is to take effect; or

    (b)   if the Commissioners consider that the interests of the public require their decision to have immediate effect, a statement to that effect and the reasons for it.

(4)   In the case of an application for registration in a new register made before the specified date by an existing money services business or an existing trust or company service provider, the Commissioners must give it a notice under regulation 29(2) by—

    (a)   in the case of an existing money service business, 1st June 2008;

    (b)   in the case of an existing trust or company service provider, 1st July 2008; or

    (c)   where applicable, 45 days beginning with the date on which they receive any further information required under regulation 27(3).

(5)   In this regulation—

["existing bill payment service provider" and "existing telecommunication, digital and IT payment service provider" mean a bill payment service provider or a telecommunication, digital and IT payment service provider carrying on business in the United Kingdom immediately before 1st November 2009;]

"existing money service business" and an "existing high value dealer" mean a money service business or a high value dealer which, immediately before 15th December 2007, was included in a register maintained under regulation 10 of the Money Laundering Regulations 2003;

"existing trust or company service provider" means a trust or company service provider carrying on business in the United Kingdom immediately before 15th December 2007.

[3608]

NOTES
Commencement: 15 December 2007.
Para (1): words in square brackets substituted by the Payment Services Regulations 2009, SI 2009/209, reg 126, Sch 6, Pt 2, para 6(h)(i).
Para (2): sub-para (d) inserted by SI 2009/209, reg 126, Sch 6, Pt 2, para 6(h)(ii).
Para (3): words in square brackets substituted by SI 2009/209, reg 126, Sch 6, Pt 2, para 6(h)(iii).
Para (5): definition "existing bill payment service provider" and "existing telecommunication, digital and IT payment service provider" inserted by SI 2009/209, reg 126, Sch 6, Pt 2, para 6(h)(iv).

51   (*Introduces Sch 6* (*outside the scope of this work*).)

SCHEDULES

SCHEDULE 1
ACTIVITIES LISTED IN POINTS 2 TO 12 AND 14 OF ANNEX I
TO THE BANKING CONSOLIDATION DIRECTIVE

Regulation 3(3)(a)

2.   Lending including, inter alia: consumer credit, mortgage credit, factoring, with or without recourse, financing of commercial transactions (including forfeiting).

3.   Financial leasing.

[4.   Payment services as defined in Article 4(3) of Directive 2007/64/EC of the European Parliament and of the Council of 13 November 2007 on payment services in the internal market.

5.   Issuing and administering other means of payment (including travellers' cheques and bankers' drafts) insofar as this activity is not covered by point 4.]

6.   Guarantees and commitments.

7. Trading for own account or for account of customers in:
   (a) money market instruments (cheques, bills, certificates of deposit, etc);
   (b) foreign exchange;
   (c) financial futures and options;
   (d) exchange and interest-rate instruments; or
   (e) transferable securities.

8. Participation in securities issues and the provision of services related to such issues.

9. Advice to undertakings on capital structure, industrial strategy and related questions and advice as well as services relating to mergers and the purchase of undertakings.

10. Money broking.

11. Portfolio management and advice.

12. Safekeeping and administration of securities.

14. Safe custody services.

[3609]

NOTES

Commencement: 15 December 2007.

Paras 4, 5: substituted by the Payment Services Regulations 2009, SI 2009/209, reg 126, Sch 6, Pt 2, para 6(i).

SCHEDULE 2
FINANCIAL ACTIVITY, SIMPLIFIED DUE DILIGENCE AND POLITICALLY
EXPOSED PERSONS

Regulations 4(1)(e) and (2),
13(6) and (8) and 14(5)

1 Financial activity on an occasional or very limited basis

For the purposes of regulation 4(1)(e) and (2), a person is to be considered as engaging in financial activity on an occasional or very limited basis if all the following conditions are fulfilled—
   (a) the person's total annual turnover in respect of the financial activity does not exceed £64,000;
   (b) the financial activity is limited in relation to any customer to no more than one transaction exceeding 1,000 euro, whether the transaction is carried out in a single operation, or a series of operations which appear to be linked;
   (c) the financial activity does not exceed 5% of the person's total annual turnover;
   (d) the financial activity is ancillary and directly related to the person's main activity;
   (e) the financial activity is not the transmission or remittance of money (or any representation of monetary value) by any means;
   (f) the person's main activity is not that of a person falling within regulation 3(1)(a) to (f) or (h);
   (g) the financial activity is provided only to customers of the person's main activity and is not offered to the public.

2 Simplified due diligence

For the purposes of regulation 13(6), the conditions are—
   (a) the authority has been entrusted with public functions pursuant to the Treaty on the European Union, the Treaties on the European Communities or Community secondary legislation;
   (b) the authority's identity is publicly available, transparent and certain;
   (c) the activities of the authority and its accounting practices are transparent;
   (d) either the authority is accountable to a Community institution or to the authorities of an EEA state, or otherwise appropriate check and balance procedures exist ensuring control of the authority's activity.

3 For the purposes of regulation 13(8), the conditions are—
   (a) the product has a written contractual base;
   (b) any related transaction is carried out through an account of the customer with a credit institution which is subject to the money laundering directive or with a credit institution situated in a non-EEA state which imposes requirements equivalent to those laid down in that directive;
   (c) the product or related transaction is not anonymous and its nature is such that it allows for the timely application of customer due diligence measures where there is a suspicion of money laundering or terrorist financing;
   (d) the product is within the following maximum threshold—
      (i) in the case of insurance policies or savings products of a similar nature, the annual premium is no more than 1,000 euro or there is a single premium of no more than 2,500 euro;
      (ii) in the case of products which are related to the financing of physical assets where

the legal and beneficial title of the assets is not transferred to the customer until the termination of the contractual relationship (whether the transaction is carried out in a single operation or in several operations which appear to be linked), the annual payments do not exceed 15,000 euro;

 (iii) in all other cases, the maximum threshold is 15,000 euro;

(e) the benefits of the product or related transaction cannot be realised for the benefit of third parties, except in the case of death, disablement, survival to a predetermined advanced age, or similar events;

(f) in the case of products or related transactions allowing for the investment of funds in financial assets or claims, including insurance or other kinds of contingent claims—

 (i) the benefits of the product or related transaction are only realisable in the long term;

 (ii) the product or related transaction cannot be used as collateral; and

 (iii) during the contractual relationship, no accelerated payments are made, surrender clauses used or early termination takes place.

4 Politically exposed persons

(1) For the purposes of regulation 14(5)—

(a) individuals who are or have been entrusted with prominent public functions include the following—

 (i) heads of state, heads of government, ministers and deputy or assistant ministers;

 (ii) members of parliaments;

 (iii) members of supreme courts, of constitutional courts or of other high-level judicial bodies whose decisions are not generally subject to further appeal, other than in exceptional circumstances;

 (iv) members of courts of auditors or of the boards of central banks;

 (v) ambassadors, chargés d'affaires and high-ranking officers in the armed forces; and

 (vi) members of the administrative, management or supervisory bodies of state-owned enterprises;

(b) the categories set out in paragraphs (i) to (vi) of sub-paragraph (a) do not include middle-ranking or more junior officials;

(c) immediate family members include the following—

 (i) a spouse;

 (ii) a partner;

 (iii) children and their spouses or partners; and

 (iv) parents;

(d) persons known to be close associates include the following—

 (i) any individual who is known to have joint beneficial ownership of a legal entity or legal arrangement, or any other close business relations, with a person referred to in regulation 14(5)(a); and

 (ii) any individual who has sole beneficial ownership of a legal entity or legal arrangement which is known to have been set up for the benefit of a person referred to in regulation 14(5)(a).

(2) In paragraph (1)(c), "partner" means a person who is considered by his national law as equivalent to a spouse.

[3610]

NOTES
Commencement: 15 December 2007.

SCHEDULE 3
PROFESSIONAL BODIES

Regulations 17(2)(b), 23(1)(c) and 32(4)

PART 1

1. Association of Chartered Certified Accountants

2. Council for Licensed Conveyancers

3. Faculty of Advocates

4. General Council of the Bar

5. General Council of the Bar of Northern Ireland

6. Institute of Chartered Accountants in England and Wales

7. Institute of Chartered Accountants in Ireland

8. Institute of Chartered Accountants of Scotland

9. Law Society

10. Law Society of Scotland
11. Law Society of Northern Ireland

[3611]

NOTES
Commencement: 15 December 2007.

PART 2

12. Association of Accounting Technicians
13. Association of International Accountants
14. Association of Taxation Technicians
15. Chartered Institute of Management Accountants
16. Chartered Institute of Public Finance and Accountancy
17. Chartered Institute of Taxation
18. Faculty Office of the Archbishop of Canterbury
19. Insolvency Practitioners Association
20. Institute of Certified Bookkeepers
21. Institute of Financial Accountants
[22. International Association of Book-keepers]

[3612]

NOTES
Commencement: 15 December 2007.
Para 22: added by the Money Laundering (Amendment) Regulations 2007, SI 2007/3299, reg 2(g).

SCHEDULE 4
CONNECTED PERSONS

Regulation 37(2)

Corporate bodies

1. If the relevant person is a body corporate ("BC"), a person who is or has been—
    (a) an officer or manager of BC or of a parent undertaking of BC;
    (b) an employee of BC;
    (c) an agent of BC or of a parent undertaking of BC

Partnerships

2. If the relevant person is a partnership, a person who is or has been a member, manager, employee or agent of the partnership.

Unincorporated associations

3. If the relevant person is an unincorporated association of persons which is not a partnership, a person who is or has been an officer, manager, employee or agent of the association.

Individuals

4. If the relevant person is an individual, a person who is or has been an employee or agent of that individual.

[3613]

NOTES
Commencement: 15 December 2007.

SCHEDULE 5
MODIFICATIONS IN RELATION TO APPEALS

Regulation 44(8)

PART 1
PRIMARY LEGISLATION

1 The Value Added Tax Act 1994 (c 23)

[Part 5 of the Value Added Tax Act 1994 (appeals) is modified by omitting sections 83A to 84, 85A and 85B.]

2 The Financial Services and Markets Act 2000 (c 8)

Part 9 of the 2000 Act (hearings and appeals) is modified as follows—
> (a)   in the application of [sections 133 to 133B] to any appeal commenced before the coming into force of section 55 of the Consumer Credit Act 2006, for all the references to "the Authority", substitute "the Authority or the OFT (as the case may be)";
> (b)   ...
> [(c)   in section 133A omit subsections (1), (2), (3) and (5);] and
> (d)   in [section 133A(4)] for "decision notice" in both places where it occurs substitute "notice under regulation 34(5) or (9) or 42(7) of the Money Laundering Regulations 2007".

[3614]–[3615]

NOTES
Commencement: 15 December 2007.
Para 1: substituted by the Transfer of Tribunal Functions and Revenue and Customs Appeals Order 2009, SI 2009/56, art 3, Sch 2, paras 168, 175, subject to transitional provisions and savings in Sch 3 to the 2009 Order.
Para 2: words in square brackets in sub-paras (a), (d) and sub-para (c) substituted, and sub-para (b) revoked, by the Transfer of Tribunal Functions Order 2010, SI 2010/22, art 5(2), Sch 3, paras 140, 142(a), subject to transitional provisions and savings in Sch 5 thereto.

(Sch 5, Pt 2 revoked by the Transfer of Tribunal Functions Order 2010, SI 2010/22, art 5(2), Sch 3, paras 140, 142(b), subject to transitional provisions and savings in Sch 5 thereto; Sch 6 (Minor and Consequential Amendments) outside the scope of this work.)

CONSUMER CREDIT APPEALS TRIBUNAL RULES 2008

(SI 2008/668)

NOTES
Made: 10 March 2008.
Authority: Consumer Credit Act 1974, ss 40A(3), 41A(6), Sch A1, para 10. These enabling sections were repealed by the Transfer of Functions of the Consumer Credit Appeals Tribunal Order 2009, SI 2009/1835, art 4(1), Sch 1, paras 1, 3, 6, 9, as from 1 September 2009, subject to transitional provisions and savings in Sch 4 to the 2009 Order at **[3908]**.
Commencement: 6 April 2008.
These Rules were revoked by the Transfer of Functions of the Consumer Credit Appeals Tribunal Order 2009, SI 2009/1835, art 4(3), Sch 3, as from 1 September 2009, subject to transitional provisions and savings in Sch 4 to the 2009 Order at **[3908]**.

ARRANGEMENT OF RULES

PART 1
INTRODUCTION

PART 2
GENERAL MATTERS IN APPEALS

PART 3
INITIATING AN APPEAL

PART 4
HEARINGS OF APPEALS

PART 5
APPEALS FROM THE TRIBUNAL

PART 1
INTRODUCTION

1   Citation and commencement

These Rules may be cited as the Consumer Credit Appeals Tribunal Rules 2008 and come into force on 6th April 2008.

[3616]

NOTES

Commencement: 6 April 2008.
Revoked as noted at the beginning of these Rules.

2   Interpretation

(1)   A reference in these Rules to a rule by number alone means the rule so numbered in these Rules.

(2)   In these Rules—
    "the 1974 Act" means the Consumer Credit Act 1974;
    "the 2006 Act" means the Consumer Credit Act 2006;
    "the 2007 Regulations" means the Money Laundering Regulations 2007;
    "appeal" means an appeal to the Tribunal under section 41(1) of the 1974 Act or under regulation 44(2)(c) of the 2007 Regulations or, where the context requires, an appeal from the Tribunal to the Court of Appeal or the Court of Session;
    "appellant" means a person who makes an appeal to the Tribunal;
    "applicant" means a party who seeks permission to bring an appeal to the Court of Appeal or the Court of Session against a decision of the Tribunal;
    "document" means anything in which information is recorded in any form, and an obligation under these Rules to provide or allow access to a document or a copy of a document for any purpose means, unless the Tribunal directs otherwise, an obligation to provide or allow access to such a document or copy in a legible form or in a form which can be readily made into a legible form;
    "file" means send a document to the Tribunal so that the document is received by the Tribunal within any time limit specified by a direction or under these Rules;
    "legal representative" means an authorised advocate or authorised litigator as defined by section 119(1) of the Courts and Legal Services Act 1990 or any person who according to the law applicable to Scotland or to Northern Ireland has rights to conduct litigation on behalf of members of the public or has rights of audience;
    "notice of appeal" means a notice filed under rule 15(1) (notice of appeal);
    "panel of chairmen" has the meaning set out in paragraph 1 of Schedule A1 to the 1974 Act;
    "party" means the appellant or the Regulator and "other party" shall be construed accordingly;
    "register" means the register maintained in accordance with rule 14 (the register);
    "Regulator" means the Office of Fair Trading established under section 1 of the Enterprise Act 2002;
    "Regulator's decision" means the determination referred to in section 41(1) of the 1974 Act or a decision of the Regulator under regulations 34 or 42 of the 2007 Regulations;
    "serve" means send a document to a party so that the document is received by that party within any time limit specified by a direction or under these Rules;

"*statement of case*" *means a statement filed by the Regulator under rule 16(1)* (*Regulator's statement of case*);

"*Tribunal*" *means the Consumer Credit Appeals Tribunal established by section 40A(1) of the 1974 Act;*

"*working day*" *means any day except for Saturday, Sunday, Christmas Day, Good Friday or a bank holiday under the Banking and Financial Dealings Act 1971.*

(3)　*Unless the context requires otherwise, anything permitted or required by these Rules to be done by a party may be done by the representative of that party.*

[3617]

NOTES

Commencement: 6 April 2008.

Revoked as noted at the beginning of these Rules.

PART 2
GENERAL MATTERS IN APPEALS

3　Directions

(1)　*The Tribunal may at any time give a direction to—*
- (a)　*deal with any request or application made under these Rules;*
- (b)　*enable the parties to prepare for any hearing;*
- (c)　*assist the Tribunal to determine the issues; and*
- (d)　*ensure the just, expeditious and economical determination of the appeal.*

(2)　*The Tribunal may give a direction—*
- (a)　*at the request of any party; or*
- (b)　*of its own initiative.*

(3)　*Where the Tribunal gives a direction of its own initiative under paragraph (2)(b), it may (but need not) give prior notice to the parties of its intention to do so.*

(4)　*Any request for a direction must include the reasons for making that request.*

(5)　*Unless the Tribunal directs otherwise or the request is made during the course of a hearing, a request for a direction must be in writing and filed.*

(6)　*The party making the request must at the same time serve a copy of that request on the other party except where—*
- (a)　*the request is accompanied by the written consent of the other party;*
- (b)　*the request is made during a hearing; or*
- (c)　*the request is made under rule 5(4)* (*disclosure*).

(7)　*Where the Tribunal directs that an oral hearing is to be held to consider a request under this rule, the Tribunal must give the parties not less than 14 days notice of the hearing unless the parties consent to shorter notice.*

(8)　*A direction may be given in writing or orally at a hearing.*

(9)　*When the Tribunal gives a direction under these Rules containing a requirement, the Tribunal—*
- (a)　*must include a statement of the possible consequences, as set out in rule 7* (*failure to comply*), *of a party's failure to comply with the requirement; and*
- (b)　*may specify a time limit for complying with the requirement.*

(10)　*The Tribunal may, of the Tribunal's own initiative or at the request of a party or a witness, vary or set aside any direction given under these Rules.*

(11)　*The Tribunal must not vary or set aside a direction without first giving any party who requested the direction an opportunity to oppose that decision.*

[3618]

NOTES

Commencement: 6 April 2008.

Revoked as noted at the beginning of these Rules.

4　Consolidation of appeals

The Tribunal may direct that two or more appeals or any particular issue raised in the appeals, be consolidated or heard together.

[3619]

NOTES

Commencement: 6 April 2008.

Revoked as noted at the beginning of these Rules.

5 Disclosure and inspection of documents

(1)   In this rule "relevant document" means a document which is or has been in a party's possession or control and—
(a)   is to be relied upon by that party in the proceedings;
(b)   adversely affects that party's own case;
(c)   adversely affects another party's case; or
(d)   supports another party's case.

(2)   The Tribunal may give a direction that one or more parties must file and serve on any party a list of—
(a)   all relevant documents; or
(b)   relevant documents which relate to specified issues.

(3)   A list required under these Rules must indicate—
(a)   the documents in respect of which a right or duty to withhold inspection is claimed; and
(b)   the documents that are no longer in the party's possession or control, and their current location.

(4)   A party may make a request under rule 3 (directions), without notice to the other party, to exclude a document from a list required under these Rules.

(5)   The Tribunal may make such directions as are necessary to determine any matters that arise under this rule including a direction—
(a)   for documents to be produced;
(b)   for a hearing to be held; and
(c)   inviting representations.

(6)   Any party to whom a direction under paragraph (2) applies must, if a document to which the direction applies comes to the party's attention at any time during the proceedings immediately notify the Tribunal of that document.

(7)   Except where the matters in paragraph (8) apply, a party on whom a list has been served may inspect or take a copy of any document on that list on reasonable notice and at a reasonable time and place.

(8)   The matters referred to in paragraph (7) are that the—
(a)   document is no longer in the possession or control of the party who served the list; or
(b)   party who served the list has a right or duty to withhold inspection of the document.

(9)   Unless otherwise permitted by a direction, any document provided to the Tribunal or to a party under these Rules may only be used for the purpose of the proceedings in which it was disclosed.

(10)   No person may be compelled to produce any document that they could not be compelled to produce on a trial of an action in a court of law in the part of the United Kingdom where the proceedings are due to be determined.

[3620]

NOTES
Commencement: 6 April 2008.
Revoked as noted at the beginning of these Rules.

6 Powers of Tribunal to strike out

(1)   The Tribunal may, if it thinks fit order any appeal notice, statement of case or written representation to be struck out at any stage of the proceedings on the ground that it—
(a)   discloses no reasonable grounds;
(b)   is an abuse of the Tribunal's process;
(c)   is likely to obstruct the just disposal of proceedings; or
(d)   is inordinately delayed.

(2)   Before making any order under paragraph (1), the Tribunal must provide an opportunity for the party against whom it is proposed that the order should be made to make representations.

[3621]

NOTES
Commencement: 6 April 2008.
Revoked as noted at the beginning of these Rules.

7 Failure to comply

(1)   In addition to any direction that the Tribunal thinks it is reasonable to make, the Tribunal may take one of the steps in paragraph (2) in respect of a party, where that party has, without reasonable excuse, failed to comply—
(a)   with a direction given under these Rules; or

    (*b*)   with a provision of these Rules.

  (2)   The steps referred to in paragraph (1) are—
    (*a*)   where the party is the appellant, dismiss the whole or part of the appeal (or, if there is more than one appellant, that appellant's appeal); and
    (*b*)   where the party is the Regulator, strike out the whole or part of the statement of case and, where appropriate, direct that the Regulator is to be barred from contesting the appeal.

  (3)   The Tribunal must not take any of the steps under this rule in respect of a party unless it has given that party an opportunity to make representations against the taking of any such steps.

                                                [3622]

NOTES
Commencement: 6 April 2008.
Revoked as noted at the beginning of these Rules.

8   Notification of witnesses

  (1)   Unless the Tribunal directs otherwise, if a party intends to call any witness, that party must file a written notice stating the names of the witnesses that party intends to call not less than 14 days before the day fixed for the hearing of the appeal.

  (2)   A party calling an expert witness under rule 23(2)(c) must provide full details about that witness when making the request under that rule, including the nature of the expertise that witness is intended to provide.

                                                [3623]

NOTES
Commencement: 6 April 2008.
Revoked as noted at the beginning of these Rules.

9   Signature of documents

Any requirement in these Rules or in a direction of the Tribunal for a document to be signed by a person is satisfied, in the case of a document which is sent electronically in accordance with these Rules or in accordance with a direction of the Tribunal, by the individual who is required to sign the document producing their name by means of a computer or by other electronic means.

                                                [3624]

NOTES
Commencement: 6 April 2008.
Revoked as noted at the beginning of these Rules.

10   Calculation of time

Where the time prescribed for doing any act under these Rules expires on a day that is not a working day, the act is done in time if done on the next working day.

                                                [3625]

NOTES
Commencement: 6 April 2008.
Revoked as noted at the beginning of these Rules.

11   Sending of notices

  (1)   Any documents to be served by a party under these Rules must be served—
    (*a*)   by first class post or by personal delivery to the postal address given to that party as the address for service;
    (*b*)   where no address for service has been provided, by first class post or by personal delivery to the party's registered office, principal place of business, head or main office or last known address;
    (*c*)   subject to paragraph (2), by an alternative method.

  (2)   Documents may only be served on a party by an alternative method if the intended recipient has informed the Tribunal and each other party in writing—
    (*a*)   that they are willing to accept service by an alternative method; and
    (*b*)   of the relevant information to allow documents to be served in that way.

  (3)   Any documents to be filed with the Tribunal must be filed—
    (*a*)   by first class post or by personal delivery to an address specified by the Tribunal; or
    (*b*)   by such alternative method as the Tribunal may permit.

  (4)   Where the Tribunal gives permission for documents to be filed using an alternative method under paragraph (3)(b), the Tribunal may—

(a)   specify that the alternative method may be used generally or only in relation to certain documents;

(b)   direct that the alternative method is no longer available or substitute an alternative method with another alternative method; and

(c)   make such directions in relation to the use of an alternative method as the Tribunal considers appropriate.

(5)   Any document which is filed or served in accordance with this paragraph must, unless the contrary is proved, be regarded as having been received—

(a)   where it is sent by first class post, the second working day after it was posted;

(b)   where it is delivered to the specified address for service, if it is delivered on a working day before 5pm, on that day; or in any other case the working day after the day it is delivered;

(c)   where it is sent by email or by fax, if it is transmitted on a working day before 5pm, on that day; or in any other case, on the working day after the day that it is transmitted;

(d)   where it is sent by document exchange, the second working day after it is left at the document exchange.

(6)   The Tribunal may direct that filing or service of any documents under these Rules be dispensed with and, in those circumstances, may make such consequential directions as the Tribunal considers appropriate.

(7)   Any document that is served or filed under the Rules must specify the date on which it is being served or filed.

[3626]

NOTES
Commencement: 6 April 2008.
Revoked as noted at the beginning of these Rules.

12   Absence of a tribunal member

(1)   This rule applies when a member who is selected to hear an appeal becomes unable to act.

(2)   In the absence of any selected member, the remaining members may continue to hear the appeal if—

(a)   the parties consent in writing; and

(b)   the absent member was not selected from the panel of chairmen.

(3)   Except where paragraph (4) applies, where a member selected from the panel of chairmen to hear an appeal becomes unable to act the Tribunal must adjourn the hearing.

(4)   The Tribunal need not adjourn the hearing under paragraph (3) if—

(a)   one of the remaining members selected to hear the appeal is a member selected from the panel of chairmen; and

(b)   it is in the interests of justice to continue to hear the appeal.

[3627]

NOTES
Commencement: 6 April 2008.
Revoked as noted at the beginning of these Rules.

13   Member of the panel of chairmen acting alone

Any request, application or hearing under these Rules, except for the substantive hearing of the appeal, may be decided or heard by a member of the panel of chairmen acting alone.

[3628]

NOTES
Commencement: 6 April 2008.
Revoked as noted at the beginning of these Rules.

14   The register

(1)   Subject to rule 20 and 25 the Tribunal must maintain a register containing details of—

(a)   appeals to the Tribunal; and

(b)   decisions of the Tribunal that dispose of appeals.

(2)   The register must be reasonably accessible to any person without charge.

[3629]

NOTES
Commencement: 6 April 2008.
Revoked as noted at the beginning of these Rules.

PART 3
INITIATING AN APPEAL

15 Notice of appeal

(*1*)　An appeal must be made by way of a notice of appeal signed, dated and filed by the appellant.

(*2*)　Subject to paragraph (*3*) a notice of appeal must be filed not later than 28 days after the date on which the appellant receives notification of the Regulator's decision.

(*3*)　An appellant may request a direction under rule 3 (*directions*) to allow the appeal to be made later than the time limit under paragraph (*2*).

(*4*)　The notice of appeal must state—
    (*a*)　the name and address of the appellant;
    (*b*)　the name and address of the appellant's representative (*if any*);
    (*c*)　an address for service;
    (*d*)　whether the notice of appeal concerns the bringing of an appeal under—
        (i)　the 1974 Act; or
        (ii)　the 2007 Regulations;
    (*e*)　the grounds upon which the appeal should be granted in the appellant's favour; and
    (*f*)　the remedy sought by the appellant.

(*5*)　The appeal notice must be accompanied by a list of all of the documents the appellant relies on in support of the appeal.

(*6*)　In paragraph (*4*)(*a*), "address" in respect of—
    (*a*)　a company means the address of the registered or principal office;
    (*b*)　a partnership means the address of the principal or last known place of business of the firm.

(*7*)　Where a representative, other than a legal representative, is named under paragraph (*4*)(*b*) and the appeal notice is signed by that representative on behalf of the appellant, a statement that the representative is authorised to act on the appellant's behalf must be—
    (*a*)　filed with the appeal notice; and
    (*b*)　signed by the appellant or where the appellant is not an individual, by an individual authorised by the appellant (*not being the representative under paragraph (4)(b)*).

(*8*)　Unless it is not possible, a copy of the decision being appealed must be filed with the notice of appeal.

(*9*)　The appellant may include a request for directions under rule 3 (*directions*) with the notice of appeal.

(*10*)　At the same time as filing the notice of appeal, the appellant must serve a copy of that notice and any accompanying documents, including any request for directions (*unless rule 5(4) applies*), on the Regulator.

(*11*)　The Tribunal must—
    (*a*)　in accordance with rule 14 enter the particulars of the appeal in the register;
    (*b*)　inform the parties in writing that a notice of appeal has been received; and
    (*c*)　inform the parties in writing of any determination made in relation to a request for a direction.

[3630]

NOTES
Commencement: 6 April 2008.
Revoked as noted at the beginning of these Rules.

16 Regulator's statement of case

(*1*)　The Regulator must file a statement of case in accordance with this rule.

(*2*)　The Regulator must file a statement of case no later than 28 days after the date on which the Regulator receives the information from the Tribunal in accordance with rule 15(11)(b).

(*3*)　The Regulator may request a direction under rule 3 (*directions*) to allow the statement of case to be filed later than the time limit under paragraph (*2*).

(*4*)　The statement of case must—
    (*a*)　indicate whether the Regulator considers that the appeal should be allowed or refused and provide reasons;
    (*b*)　indicate whether the Regulator intends to take an active part in the proceedings;
    (*c*)　specify the name and address of the Regulator's representative (*if any*);
    (*d*)　identify an address for service and an individual contact at that address;
    (*e*)　be signed by a person authorised by the Regulator.

(*5*)　The statement of case must be accompanied by—

(*a*)   a list of the documents relied on by the Regulator; and
(*b*)   a copy of the Regulator's decision if not filed by the appellant under rule 15(8) (notice of appeal).

(6)   The Regulator may include a request for directions with the statement of case.

(7)   At the same time as the Regulator files the statement of case, the Regulator must serve on an appellant a copy of the statement of case and any document accompanying the statement of case, including any request for directions (unless rule 5(4) applies).

(8)   The Tribunal must inform the parties in writing of any determination made in relation to a request for a direction.

[3631]

NOTES
Commencement: 6 April 2008.
Revoked as noted at the beginning of these Rules.

PART 4
HEARINGS OF APPEALS

17   Fixing the time and place of the hearing of the appeal
(1)   Unless the Tribunal otherwise directs, the Tribunal must give the parties not less than 28 days notice of the time and place of the hearing of the appeal.

(2)   Before fixing the time and place of a hearing under paragraph (1), the Tribunal must consider—
(*a*)   whether the appeal should be dealt with as a matter of urgency; and
(*b*)   the ability of the appellant, and any witness, to prepare for and attend a hearing which is to take place at short notice.

[3632]

NOTES
Commencement: 6 April 2008.
Revoked as noted at the beginning of these Rules.

18   Determination without oral hearing
The Tribunal may determine an appeal or any particular issue without an oral hearing if—
(*a*)   the parties agree in writing; or
(*b*)   the issue concerns a request for directions.

[3633]

NOTES
Commencement: 6 April 2008.
Revoked as noted at the beginning of these Rules.

19   Withdrawal of appeal
(1)   The appellant may withdraw the appeal—
(*a*)   without the Tribunal's permission at any time before the hearing of the appeal, by filing a notice in writing to that effect; or
(*b*)   with the Tribunal's permission at the hearing of the appeal.

(2)   The Tribunal must dismiss any appeal that is withdrawn under paragraph (1)(a) or that is withdrawn with the Tribunal's permission under paragraph (1)(b).

(3)   The Regulator may state that it does not oppose the appeal or that it is withdrawing its opposition to it—
(*a*)   without the Tribunal's permission at any time before the hearing of the appeal, by filing a notice to that effect; or
(*b*)   with the Tribunal's permission at the hearing of the appeal.

(4)   The Tribunal must allow the appeal where the Regulator states that it does not oppose it or that the Regulator is withdrawing its opposition to it under paragraph (3)(a) or that the Regulator is, with the Tribunal's permission under paragraph (3)(b), not opposing it or is withdrawing its opposition to it.

(5)   An appellant who withdraws an appeal must obtain the permission of the Tribunal to make another appeal against the same decision of the Regulator.

[3634]

**PART 2
STATUTORY INSTRUMENTS**

NOTES
Commencement: 6 April 2008.
Revoked as noted at the beginning of these Rules.

20   Public hearings and directions for private hearings

(*1*)   *In this rule, "hearing" means any oral hearing under these Rules except for a directions hearing that takes place without notice to the other party under rule 5(4) (disclosure).*

(*2*)   *Subject to the following paragraphs of this rule, all hearings must be in public.*

(*3*)   *The Tribunal may upon the request of a party or of the Tribunal's own initiative direct that all or part of a hearing is to be in private if—*
   (*a*)   *the Tribunal is satisfied that a hearing in private is necessary in the circumstances; and*
   (*b*)   *it is in the interests of justice.*

(*4*)   *Before making a direction under paragraph (3), the Tribunal must give a party or the parties as the case may be, an opportunity to make representations.*

(*5*)   *Before giving a direction under paragraph (3) that all of a hearing should be in private, the Tribunal must consider whether it is only necessary that part of the hearing should be in private.*

(*6*)   *Where a hearing is in private, the Tribunal may direct that any particular individual be—*
   (*a*)   *excluded from that hearing; or*
   (*b*)   *permitted to attend that hearing.*

(*7*)   *Subject to any direction under paragraph (8), the Tribunal must allow for the public inspection of—*
   (*a*)   *a daily list of all hearings; and*
   (*b*)   *information about the time and place fixed for hearings.*

(*8*)   *Where all or part of a hearing is held or is to be held in private, the Tribunal may direct that information about the whole or the relevant part of the proceedings (including information that might help to identify any person) must not be made public.*

(*9*)   *Where a direction is given under paragraph (8), the Tribunal must state what information is to be withheld or removed from the register.*

[3635]

NOTES
Commencement: 6 April 2008.
Revoked as noted at the beginning of these Rules.

21   Representation at hearings

(*1*)   *Subject to paragraph (2), the parties may appear at a hearing and may be assisted or represented by any person, whether or not that person is a legal representative.*

(*2*)   *If the Tribunal is satisfied that there are good and sufficient reasons for doing so, it may refuse to permit a person to assist or represent a party at a hearing.*

[3636]

NOTES
Commencement: 6 April 2008.
Revoked as noted at the beginning of these Rules.

22   Adjournment of hearing

Where a hearing of an appeal is adjourned, the Tribunal must fix a new hearing date as soon as is practicable to do so.

[3637]

NOTES
Commencement: 6 April 2008.
Revoked as noted at the beginning of these Rules.

23   Procedure at hearings

(*1*)   *Subject to these Rules, the Tribunal may regulate its own procedure.*

(*2*)   *Subject to any directions by the Tribunal, the parties may—*
   (*a*)   *give evidence;*
   (*b*)   *present witness evidence;*
   (*c*)   *make a request under rule 3 (directions) to present expert evidence;*
   (*d*)   *question any witness; and*
   (*e*)   *address the Tribunal on the evidence, and generally on the subject matter of the appeal.*

(3)   Evidence may be admitted by the Tribunal—

(a)   whether or not it would be admissible in a civil trial in the jurisdiction in which the appeal is being determined; or

(b)   whether or not it was available to either of the parties when the Regulator's decision was made.

(4)   If the Tribunal considers it is in the interests of justice, the Tribunal may allow a party to amend a notice of appeal or a statement of case.

(5)   The Tribunal may exclude from the whole or part of any hearing any person whose conduct, in the opinion of the Tribunal, is likely to disrupt the hearing.

[3638]

NOTES
Commencement: 6 April 2008.
Revoked as noted at the beginning of these Rules.

24   Failure to attend an appeal hearing

(1)   If a party fails to attend or be represented at any hearing the Tribunal must adjourn the hearing unless paragraph (2) applies.

(2)   The Tribunal may proceed with the hearing and reach a substantive decision if the Tribunal is satisfied that the party received notification of the hearing and no good reason has been given for the party's absence.

(3)   Where a party can subsequently show sufficient reason for not attending or being represented at a hearing which the Tribunal proceeded in the party's absence, that party may request the Tribunal's permission to have the hearing re-opened.

[3639]

NOTES
Commencement: 6 April 2008.
Revoked as noted at the beginning of these Rules.

25   Restrictions on publication of decisions of the Tribunal

(1)   The Tribunal must publish its decisions except where the Tribunal is satisfied, on the application of a party or of its own initiative, that it is necessary to impose restrictions on publication.

(2)   Before imposing restrictions on publication under paragraph (1) the Tribunal must invite the parties to make representations.

(3)   If the Tribunal decides that a restriction on publication is necessary the Tribunal may take any appropriate steps, including any one or more of the steps specified in paragraph (5).

(4)   Any step taken under paragraph (3) must be taken with a view to ensuring the minimum restriction on publication that is consistent with the need for the restriction.

(5)   The specified steps that may be taken by the Tribunal under paragraph (3) are—

(a)   anonymising the decision;

(b)   editing the text of the decision; and

(c)   declining to publish the whole or part of the decision.

[3640]

NOTES
Commencement: 6 April 2008.
Revoked as noted at the beginning of these Rules.

26   Notification of the Tribunal's decision

(1)   The Tribunal must as soon as practicable—

(a)   whether there has been an oral hearing or not, serve notification of a decision and the reasons for reaching it on each of the parties to the appeal; and

(b)   subject to any steps taken under rules 20 (public or private hearing) or 25 (restrictions on publication) to restrict publication of a decision, enter into the register the decision and the reasons for reaching the decision.

(2)   Every notification under paragraph (1)(a) must be accompanied by a notification of—

(a)   any relevant provision of the 1974 Act or the 2007 Regulations relating to appeals from the Tribunal; and

(b)   the time and the manner in which an application for permission to appeal may be made.

[3641]

27 Review of the Tribunal's decision

(*1*)   *If the Tribunal is satisfied that a decision disposing of the appeal was wrongly made because of an administrative error by Tribunal staff, the Tribunal may at the request of a party or of the Tribunal's own initiative, review the decision.*

(*2*)   *No review under paragraph (1) shall take place unless either—*
- (*a*)   *the application for review is made not later than 14 days after the date that notification of the decision that is subject to review is received; or*
- (*b*)   *the Tribunal notified the parties of its intention to review a decision not later than 14 days after the decision was made.*

(*3*)   *When the Tribunal reviews a decision under paragraph (1) it may set aside that decision if the Tribunal considers that it is necessary in the interests of justice.*

(*4*)   *The Tribunal must not set aside a decision under paragraph (3) without giving the parties an opportunity to make representations.*

(*5*)   *If after completion of any review the Tribunal sets aside the decision, the Tribunal must—*
- (*a*)   *substitute such decision as it thinks fit; or*
- (*b*)   *order a re-hearing before either the same or a differently constituted Tribunal;*
- (*c*)   *make such correction as may be necessary in the register; and*
- (*d*)   *serve a copy of an entry so corrected under paragraph (c) on each party.*

(*6*)   *The Tribunal must notify the parties in writing of the Tribunal's decision following a review under this rule.*

[3642]

PART 5
APPEALS FROM THE TRIBUNAL

28 Permission to appeal to the Court of Appeal or Court of Session

(*1*)   *A request to the Tribunal for permission to appeal to the Court of Appeal or to the Court of Session may be made by the applicant—*
- (*a*)   *orally at the hearing immediately following the announcement of the decision by the Tribunal; or*
- (*b*)   *by way of a request filed not later than 14 days after the date on which the notification of the decision is received by the person seeking permission; or*
- (*c*)   *by way of a request filed not later than 14 days after the date on which the notification under rule 27(6) (review) is received by the person making the application.*

(*2*)   *When a request for permission is made under paragraph (1)(b) or (c), it must be signed by the applicant and must—*
- (*a*)   *state the name and address of the applicant and any representative of the applicant;*
- (*b*)   *identify the decision of the Tribunal to which the request relates; and*
- (*c*)   *state the grounds on which the applicant intends to rely before the Court of Appeal or the Court of Session.*

[3643]

29 Decision as to permission to appeal to the Court of Appeal or the Court of Session

(*1*)   *A request for permission to appeal to the Court of Appeal or to the Court of Session under rule 28(1)(b) or (c) (permission to appeal) must be decided without an oral hearing unless the Tribunal considers that special circumstances make a hearing desirable.*

(*2*)   *The decision of the Tribunal following a request for permission to appeal to the Court of Appeal or to the Court of Session, together with the reasons for the decision, must be recorded in writing.*

(*3*)   *The Tribunal must serve the written record in paragraph (2) on the applicant and each of the other parties.*

(4) If the Tribunal refuses the request, the notification under paragraph (3) must include notification of the time within which a request may be made to the Court of Appeal or the Court of Session for permission to appeal to that court.

[3644]

NOTES
Commencement: 6 April 2008.
Revoked as noted at the beginning of these Rules.

30 Appeal remitted by the Court of Appeal or the Court of Session for rehearing

Where the Court of Appeal or the Court of Session remits an appeal to the Tribunal—
  (a) these Rules, so far as relevant and subject to any direction that the court may give when remitting the matter, apply to the remitted case as they did to the original hearing of the appeal; and
  (b) the Tribunal must, within 28 days of the remittal, give directions in relation to the case.

[3645]

NOTES
Commencement: 6 April 2008.
Revoked as noted at the beginning of these Rules.

ESTATE AGENTS (REDRESS SCHEME) ORDER 2008

(SI 2008/1712)

NOTES
Made: 28 June 2008.
Authority: Estate Agents Act 1979, s 23A.
Commencement: 1 October 2008.

1 Citation and Commencement

This Order may be cited as the Estate Agents (Redress Scheme) Order 2008 and shall come into force on 1st October 2008.

[3645A]

NOTES
Commencement: 1 October 2008.

2 Requirement to belong to an approved redress scheme

Every person who engages in relevant estate agency work shall be required to be a member of an approved redress scheme.

[3645B]

NOTES
Commencement: 1 October 2008.

ESTATE AGENTS (REDRESS SCHEME) (PENALTY CHARGE) REGULATIONS 2008

(SI 2008/1713)

NOTES
Made: 28 June 2008.
Authority: Estate Agents Act 1979, Sch 4, para 2.
Commencement: 1 October 2008.

1 Citation and Commencement

These Regulations may be cited as the Estate Agents (Redress Scheme) (Penalty Charge) Regulations 2008 and shall come into force on 1st October 2008.

[3645C]

NOTES
Commencement: 1 October 2008.

2   Level of the penalty charge

The amount of the penalty charge specified in a notice given to a person under section 23B(1) of the Estate Agents Act 1979 shall be £1000.

[3645D]

NOTES
Commencement: 1 October 2008.

BUSINESS PROTECTION FROM MISLEADING MARKETING REGULATIONS 2008

(SI 2008/1276)

NOTES
Made: 8 May 2008.
Authority: European Communities Act 1972, s 2(2).
Commencement: 26 May 2008.

PART 2
STATUTORY INSTRUMENTS

ARRANGEMENT OF REGULATIONS

PART 1
DEFINITIONS AND PROHIBITIONS

PART 2
OFFENCES

PART 3
ENFORCEMENT

PART 4
INVESTIGATION POWERS

PART 1
DEFINITIONS AND PROHIBITIONS

1 Citation and Commencement

These Regulations may be cited as the Business Protection from Misleading Marketing Regulations 2008 and shall come into force on 26th May 2008.

[3646]

NOTES

Commencement: 26 May 2008.

2 Interpretation

(1)   In these Regulations—

"advertising" means any form of representation which is made in connection with a trade, business, craft or profession in order to promote the supply or transfer of a product and "advertiser" shall be construed accordingly;

"code owner" means a trader or a body responsible for—

(a)   the formulation and revision of a code of conduct; or

(b)   monitoring compliance with the code by those who have undertaken to be bound by it;

"comparative advertising" means advertising which in any way, either explicitly or by implication, identifies a competitor or a product offered by a competitor;

"court", in relation to England and Wales and Northern Ireland, means a county court or the High Court, and, in relation to Scotland, the sheriff or the Court of Session;

"enforcement authority" means the OFT, every local weights and measures authority in Great Britain (within the meaning of section 69 of the Weights and Measure Act 1985) and the Department of Enterprise, Trade and Investment in Northern Ireland;

"goods" includes ships, aircraft, animals, things attached to land and growing crops;

"OFT" means the Office of Fair Trading;

"premises" includes any place and any stall, vehicle, ship or aircraft;

"product" means any goods or services and includes immovable property, rights and obligations;

"ship" includes any boat and any other description of vessel used in navigation; and

"trader" means any person who is acting for purposes relating to his trade, craft, business or profession and anyone acting in the name of or on behalf of a trader.

(2)   *(Applies to Scotland only.)*

[3647]

NOTES

Commencement: 26 May 2008.

3 Prohibition of advertising which misleads traders

(1)   Advertising which is misleading is prohibited.

(2)   Advertising is misleading which—

(a)   in any way, including its presentation, deceives or is likely to deceive the traders to whom it is addressed or whom it reaches; and by reason of its deceptive nature, is likely to affect their economic behaviour; or

(b)   for those reasons, injures or is likely to injure a competitor.

(3)   In determining whether advertising is misleading, account shall be taken of all its features, and in particular of any information it contains concerning—

(a)   the characteristics of the product (as defined in paragraph (4));

(b)   the price or manner in which the price is calculated;

(c)   the conditions on which the product is supplied or provided; and

(d)   the nature, attributes and rights of the advertiser (as defined in paragraph (5)).

(4)   In paragraph (3)(a) the "characteristics of the product" include—

(a)   availability of the product;

(b)   nature of the product;

(c)   execution of the product;

(d)   composition of the product;

(e)   method and date of manufacture of the product;

(f)   method and date of provision of the product;

(g)   fitness for purpose of the product;

(h)   uses of the product;

(i)   quantity of the product;

(j)   specification of the product;

    (k)   geographical or commercial origin of the product;

    (l)   results to be expected from use of the product; or

    (m)   results and material features of tests or checks carried out on the product.

    (5)   In paragraph (3)(d) the "nature, attributes and rights" of the advertiser include the advertiser's—

    (a)   identity;

    (b)   assets;

    (c)   qualifications;

    (d)   ownership of industrial, commercial or intellectual property rights; or

    (e)   awards and distinctions.

[3648]

NOTES
    Commencement: 26 May 2008.

4   Comparative advertising

Comparative advertising shall, as far as the comparison is concerned, be permitted only when the following conditions are met—

    (a)   it is not misleading under regulation 3;

    (b)   it is not a misleading action under regulation 5 of the Consumer Protection from Unfair Trading Regulations 2008 or a misleading omission under regulation 6 of those Regulations;

    (c)   it compares products meeting the same needs or intended for the same purpose;

    (d)   it objectively compares one or more material, relevant, verifiable and representative features of those products, which may include price;

    (e)   it does not create confusion among traders—

        (i)   between the advertiser and a competitor, or

        (ii)   between the trade marks, trade names, other distinguishing marks or products of the advertiser and those of a competitor;

    (f)   it does not discredit or denigrate the trade marks, trade names, other distinguishing marks, products, activities, or circumstances of a competitor;

    (g)   for products with designation of origin, it relates in each case to products with the same designation;

    (h)   it does not take unfair advantage of the reputation of a trade mark, trade name or other distinguishing marks of a competitor or of the designation of origin of competing products;

    (i)   it does not present products as imitations or replicas of products bearing a protected trade mark or trade name.

[3649]

NOTES
    Commencement: 26 May 2008.

5   Promotion of misleading advertising and comparative advertising which is not permitted

A code owner shall not promote in a code of conduct—

    (a)   advertising which is misleading under regulation 3; or

    (b)   comparative advertising which is not permitted under regulation 4.

[3650]

NOTES
    Commencement: 26 May 2008.

PART 2
OFFENCES

6   Misleading advertising

A trader is guilty of an offence if he engages in advertising which is misleading under regulation 3.

[3651]

NOTES
    Commencement: 26 May 2008.

7   Penalty for offence under regulation 6

A person guilty of an offence under regulation 6 shall be liable—

    (a)   on summary conviction, to a fine not exceeding the statutory maximum; or

    (b)   on conviction on indictment, to a fine or imprisonment for a term not exceeding two years or both.

[3652]

NOTES
    Commencement: 26 May 2008.

---

8 Offences committed by bodies of persons

    (1)   Where an offence under these Regulations committed by a body corporate is proved—
        (a)   to have been committed with the consent or connivance of an officer of the body, or
        (b)   to be attributable to any neglect on his part,
the officer as well as the body corporate is guilty of the offence and liable to be proceeded against and punished accordingly.

    (2)   In paragraph (1) a reference to an officer of a body corporate includes a reference to—
        (a)   a director, manager, secretary or other similar officer; and
        (b)   a person purporting to act as a director, manager, secretary or other similar officer.

    (3)   Where an offence under these Regulations committed by a Scottish partnership is proved—
        (a)   to have been committed with the consent or connivance of a partner, or
        (b)   to be attributable to any neglect on his part,
the partner as well as the partnership is guilty of the offence and liable to be proceeded against and punished accordingly.

    (4)   In paragraph (3) a reference to a partner includes a person purporting to act as a partner.

[3653]

NOTES
    Commencement: 26 May 2008.

---

9 Offence due to the default of another person

    (1)   This regulation applies where a person "X"—
        (a)   commits an offence under regulation 6, or
        (b)   would have committed an offence under regulation 6 but for a defence under regulation 11 or 12,
and the commission of the offence, or of what would have been an offence but for X being able to rely on a defence under regulations 11 or 12, is due to the act or default of some other person "Y".

    (2)   Where this regulation applies Y shall be guilty of the offence subject to regulations 11 and 12 whether or not Y is a trader and whether or not Y's act or default is advertising.

    (3)   Y may be charged with and convicted of the offence by virtue of paragraph (2) whether or not proceedings are taken against X.

[3654]

NOTES
    Commencement: 26 May 2008.

---

10 Time limit for prosecution

    (1)   No proceedings for an offence under these Regulations shall be commenced after—
        (a)   the end of the period of three years beginning with the date of the commission of the offence; or
        (b)   the end of the period of one year beginning with the date of discovery of the offence by the prosecutor,
whichever is earlier.

    (2)   For the purposes of paragraph (1)(b) a certificate signed by or on behalf of the prosecutor and stating the date on which the offence was discovered by him shall be conclusive evidence of that fact and a certificate stating that matter and purporting to be so signed shall be treated as so signed unless the contrary is proved.

    (3)   Notwithstanding anything in section 127(1) of the Magistrates' Courts Act 1980, an information relating to an offence under these Regulations which is triable by a magistrates' court in England and Wales may be so tried if it is laid at any time before the end of the period of twelve months beginning with the date of the commission of the offence.

    (4)   Notwithstanding anything in section 136 of the Criminal Procedure (Scotland) Act 1995 summary proceedings in Scotland for an offence under these Regulations may be commenced at any time before the end of the period of twelve months beginning with the date of the commission of the offence.

(5) For the purposes of paragraph (4), section 136(3) of the Criminal Procedure (Scotland) Act 1995 shall apply as it applies for the purposes of that section.

(6) Notwithstanding anything in Article 19(1) of the Magistrates' Courts (Northern Ireland) Order 1981 a complaint charging an offence under these Regulations which is triable by a magistrates' court in Northern Ireland may be so tried if it is made at any time before the end of the period of twelve months beginning with the date of the commission of the offence.

[3655]

NOTES
Commencement: 26 May 2008.

11 Due diligence defence

(1) In any proceedings against a person for an offence under regulation 6 it is a defence for that person to prove—
- (a) that the commission of the offence was due to—
  - (i) a mistake;
  - (ii) reliance on information supplied to him by another person;
  - (iii) the act or default of another person;
  - (iv) an accident; or
  - (v) another cause beyond his control;
  and
- (b) that he took all reasonable precautions and exercised all due diligence to avoid the commission of such an offence by himself or any person under his control.

(2) A person shall not be entitled to rely on the defence provided by paragraph (1) by reason of the matters referred to in paragraph (ii) or (iii) of paragraph (1)(a) without the leave of the court unless—
- (a) he has served on the prosecutor a notice in writing giving such information identifying or assisting in the identification of that other person as was in his possession; and
- (b) the notice is served on the prosecutor at least seven clear days before the date of the hearing.

[3656]

NOTES
Commencement: 26 May 2008.

12 Innocent publication defence

In any proceedings against a person for an offence under regulation 6 committed by the publication of advertising it is a defence for that person to prove that—
- (a) he is a person whose business it is to publish or to arrange for the publication of advertising;
- (b) he received the advertising for publication in the ordinary course of business; and
- (c) he did not know and had no reason to suspect that its publication would amount to an offence under regulation 6.

[3657]

NOTES
Commencement: 26 May 2008.

PART 3
ENFORCEMENT

13 Duty to enforce

(1) It shall be the duty of every enforcement authority to enforce these Regulations.

(2) Where an enforcement authority is a local weights and measures authority the duty referred to in paragraph (1) shall apply to the enforcement of these Regulations within the authority's area.

(3) Where the enforcement authority is the Department of Enterprise, Trade and Investment in Northern Ireland the duty referred to in paragraph (1) shall apply to the enforcement of these Regulations within Northern Ireland.

(4) In determining how to comply with its duty of enforcement every enforcement authority shall have regard to the desirability of encouraging control of advertising which is misleading under regulation 3 and comparative advertising which is not permitted under regulation 4 by such established means as it considers appropriate having regard to all the circumstances of the particular case.

(5) Nothing in this regulation shall authorise any enforcement authority to bring proceedings in Scotland for an offence.

[3658]

NOTES
Commencement: 26 May 2008.

14 Notice to OFT of intended prosecution

(1) Where an enforcement authority is a local weights and measures authority in England and Wales it may bring proceedings for an offence under regulation 6 only if—

  (a) it has notified the OFT of its intention to bring proceedings at least fourteen days before the date on which proceedings are brought; or

  (b) the OFT consents to proceedings being brought in a shorter period.

(2) The enforcement authority must also notify the OFT of the outcome of the proceedings after they are finally determined.

(3) Such proceedings are not invalid by reason only of the failure to comply with this regulation.

[3659]

NOTES
Commencement: 26 May 2008.

15 Injunctions to secure compliance with the Regulations

(1) This regulation applies where an enforcement authority considers that there has been or is likely to be a breach of regulation 3, 4 or 5.

(2) Where this regulation applies an enforcement authority may, subject to paragraph (3), if it thinks it appropriate to do so, bring proceedings for an injunction (in which proceedings it may also apply for an interim injunction) against any person appearing to it to be concerned or likely to be concerned with the breach.

(3) Where the enforcement authority is a local weights and measures authority in Great Britain it may apply for an injunction only if—

  (a) it has notified the OFT of its intention to apply for an injunction at least fourteen days before the date on which the application is made; or

  (b) the OFT consents to the application for an injunction being made within a shorter period.

(4) Proceedings referred to in paragraph (2) are not invalid by reason only of the failure to comply with paragraph (3).

[3660]

NOTES
Commencement: 26 May 2008.

16 Undertakings

Where an enforcement authority considers that there has been or is likely to be a breach of regulation 3, 4 or 5 it may accept from the person concerned or likely to be concerned with the breach an undertaking that he will comply with those regulations.

[3661]

NOTES
Commencement: 26 May 2008.

17 Co-ordination

(1) If more than one local weights and measures authority in Great Britain is contemplating bringing proceedings under regulation 15 in any particular case, the OFT may direct which enforcement authority is to bring the proceedings or decide that only it may do so.

(2) Where the OFT directs that only it may bring such proceedings it may take into account whether compliance with regulation 3, 4 or 5 could be achieved by other means in deciding whether to bring proceedings.

[3662]

NOTES
Commencement: 26 May 2008.

18   Powers of the court

(1)   The court on an application by an enforcement authority may grant an injunction on such terms as it may think fit to secure compliance with regulation 3, 4 or 5.

(2)   Before granting an injunction the court shall have regard to all the interests involved and in particular the public interest.

(3)   An injunction may relate not only to particular advertising but to any advertising in similar terms or likely to convey a similar impression.

(4)   The court may also require any person against whom an injunction (other than an interim injunction) is granted to publish in such form and manner and to such extent as the court thinks appropriate for the purpose of eliminating any continuing effects of the advertising—

   (a)   the injunction; and
   (b)   a corrective statement.

(5)   In considering an application for an injunction the court may require the person named in the application to provide evidence as to the accuracy of any factual claim made as part of the advertising of that person if, taking into account the legitimate interests of that person and any other party to the proceedings, it appears appropriate in the circumstances.

(6)   If, having been required under paragraph (5) to provide evidence as to the accuracy of a factual claim, a person—

   (a)   fails to provide such evidence, or
   (b)   provides evidence as to the accuracy of the factual claim that the court considers inadequate,

the court may consider that the factual claim is inaccurate.

(7)   The court may grant an injunction even where there is no evidence of proof of actual loss or damage or of intention or negligence on the part of the advertiser.

[3663]

NOTES
Commencement: 26 May 2008.

19   Notifications of undertakings and orders to the OFT

An enforcement authority, other than the OFT, shall notify the OFT—

   (a)   of any undertaking given to it under regulation 16;
   (b)   of the outcome of any application made by it under regulation 15 and the terms of any order made by the court; and
   (c)   of the outcome of any application made by it to enforce a previous order of the court.

[3664]

NOTES
Commencement: 26 May 2008.

20   Publication, information and advice

(1)   The OFT must arrange for the publication, in such form and manner as it considers appropriate, of—

   (a)   details of any undertaking or order notified to it under regulation 19;
   (b)   details of any undertaking given to it under regulation 16;
   (c)   details of any application made by it under regulation 15 and of the terms of any undertaking given to, or order made by, the court;
   (d)   details of any application made by it to enforce a previous order of the court.

(2)   The OFT may arrange for the dissemination, in such form and manner as it considers appropriate, of such information and advice concerning the operation of these Regulations as appear to it to be expedient to give to the public and to all persons likely to be affected by these Regulations.

[3665]

NOTES
Commencement: 26 May 2008.

PART 4
INVESTIGATION POWERS

21 Powers of Enforcement Authorities to obtain information

(1) For the purpose of determining whether to bring proceedings for an injunction under regulation 15, an enforcement authority may by notice in writing require a person to provide to it such information as may be specified or described in the notice or to produce to it any documents so specified or described.

(2) A notice under paragraph (1) may—
    (a)   specify the way in which and the time within which it is to be complied with; and
    (b)   be varied or revoked by a subsequent notice.

(3) Nothing in this regulation gives an enforcement authority any power to require another person to provide or produce any information or document which the other person would be entitled to refuse to provide or produce in proceedings in the High Court on the grounds of legal professional privilege or (in Scotland) in proceedings in the Court of Session on the grounds of confidentiality of communications.

(4) In paragraph (3) "communications" means—
    (a)   communications between a professional legal adviser and his client; or
    (b)   communications made in connection with or in contemplation of legal proceedings and for the purposes of those proceedings.

(5) Nothing in this regulation shall be construed as requiring a person to provide information if to do so might incriminate him.

(6) If a person does not comply with a notice under paragraph (1) the court may, on the application of an enforcement authority, make such order as the court thinks fit for requiring the default to be made good, and any such order may provide that all the costs or expenses of and incidental to the application shall be borne by the person in default or by any officers of a company or other association who are responsible for its default.

[3666]

NOTES
Commencement: 26 May 2008.

22 Power to make test purchases

An enforcement authority may or may authorise any of its officers on its behalf to—
    (a)   make a purchase of a product; or
    (b)   enter into an agreement to secure the provision of a product,
for the purposes of determining whether these Regulations are being complied with.

[3667]

NOTES
Commencement: 26 May 2008.

23 Power of entry and investigation, etc

(1) A duly authorised officer of an enforcement authority may at all reasonable hours exercise the following powers—
    (a)   he may, for the purpose of ascertaining whether a breach of these Regulations has been committed, inspect any goods and enter any premises other than premises used only as a dwelling;
    (b)   if he has reasonable cause to suspect that a breach of these Regulations has been committed, he may, for the purpose of ascertaining whether it has been committed, require any trader to produce any documents relating to his trade, business, craft or profession and may take copies of, or of any entry in, any such document;
    (c)   if he has reasonable cause to believe that a breach of these Regulations has been committed, he may seize and detain any goods for the purpose of ascertaining, by testing or otherwise, whether the breach has been committed; and
    (d)   he may seize and detain goods or documents which he has reason to believe may be required as evidence in proceedings for a breach of these Regulations.

(2) If and to the extent that it is reasonably necessary to do so to secure that the provisions of these Regulations are observed, the officer may for the purpose of exercising his powers under paragraphs (1) (c) and (d) to seize goods or documents—
    (a)   require any person having authority to do so to break open any container or open any vending machine; and
    (b)   himself open or break open any such container or open any vending machine where a requirement made under sub-paragraph (a) in relation to the container or vending machine has not been complied with.

(3)   An officer seizing any goods or documents in exercise of his powers under this regulation shall—

    (a)   inform the person from whom they are seized; and

    (b)   where goods are seized from a vending machine, inform—

        (i)   the person whose name and address are stated on the vending machine as being the proprietor's, or

        (ii)   if there is no such name or address stated on the vending machine, the occupier of the premises on which the machine stands or to which it is affixed,

that the goods or documents have been so seized.

(4)   In this regulation "document" includes information recorded in any form.

(5)   The reference in paragraph (1)(b) to the production of documents is, in the case of a document which contains information recorded otherwise than in legible form, a reference to the production of a copy of the information in legible form.

(6)   An officer seeking to exercise a power under this regulation must produce evidence of his identity and authority to a person (if there is one) who appears to the officer to be the occupier of the premises.

(7)   Where an officer seizes goods or documents in exercise of a power under this regulation they may not be detained—

    (a)   for a period of more than 3 months; or

    (b)   where the goods or documents are reasonably required by the enforcement authority in connection with the enforcement of these Regulations, for longer than they are so required.

(8)   An officer entering any premises under this regulation may take with him such other persons and such equipment as may appear to him to be necessary.

(9)   Nothing in this regulation or in regulation 24 gives any power to an officer of an enforcement authority—

    (a)   to require any person to produce, or

    (b)   to seize from another person,

any document which the other person would be entitled to refuse to produce in proceedings in the High Court on the grounds of legal professional privilege or (in Scotland) in proceedings in the Court of Session on the grounds of confidentiality of communications.

(10)   In paragraph (9) "communications" means—

    (a)   communications between a professional legal adviser and his client; or

    (b)   communications made in connection with or in contemplation of legal proceedings and for the purposes of those proceedings.

(11)   If any person who is not an officer of an enforcement authority purports to act as such under this regulation or regulation 24 he shall be guilty of an offence and liable on summary conviction to a fine not exceeding level 5 on the standard scale.

[3668]

NOTES

Commencement: 26 May 2008.

---

24   Power to enter premises with a warrant

(1)   If a justice of the peace by a written information on oath is satisfied—

    (a)   that there are reasonable grounds for believing that Condition A or B is met, and

    (b)   that Condition C, D or E is met,

the justice may by warrant under his hand authorise an officer of an enforcement authority to enter the premises at all reasonable times, if necessary by force.

(2)   Condition A is that there are on any premises goods or documents which a duly authorised officer of the enforcement authority has power under regulation 23(1) to inspect and that their inspection is likely to disclose evidence of a breach of these Regulations.

(3)   Condition B is that a breach of these Regulations has occurred, is occurring or is about to occur on any premises.

(4)   Condition C is that the admission to the premises has been or is likely to be refused and that notice of intention to apply for a warrant under this regulation has been given to the occupier.

(5)   Condition D is that an application for admission, or the giving of a notice of intention to apply for a warrant, would defeat the object of the entry.

(6)   Condition E is that the premises are unoccupied or that the occupier is absent and it might defeat the object of the entry to await his return.

(7)   A warrant under paragraph (1)—

(a) ceases to have effect at the end of the period of one month beginning with the day it is issued;

(b) must be produced for inspection to the person (if there is one) who appears to the officer to be the occupier of the premises.

(8) An officer entering any premises under this regulation may take with him such other persons and such equipment as may appear to him to be necessary.

(9) On leaving any premises which an officer is authorised to enter by warrant under this regulation the officer shall, if the premises are unoccupied or the occupier is temporarily absent, leave the premises as effectively secured against trespassers as he found them.

(10) In its application to Scotland, this regulation has effect as if—

(a) the references in paragraph (1) to a justice of the peace included references to a sheriff; and

(b) the reference in paragraph (1) to information on oath were a reference to evidence on oath.

(11) In its application to Northern Ireland, this regulation has effect as if the references in paragraph (1) to a justice of the peace were references to a lay magistrate.

[3669]

NOTES
Commencement: 26 May 2008.

25 Obstruction of authorised officers

(1) Any person who—

(a) intentionally obstructs an officer of an enforcement authority acting in pursuance of these Regulations;

(b) intentionally fails to comply with any requirement properly made of him by such an officer under regulation 23; or

(c) without reasonable cause fails to give such an officer any other assistance or information which he may reasonably require of him for the purpose of the performance of his functions under these Regulations,

is guilty of an offence and liable, on summary conviction, to a fine not exceeding level 5 on the standard scale.

(2) Any person who, in giving any information which is required of him under paragraph (1)(c), makes any statement which he knows to be false in a material particular is guilty of an offence and liable—

(a) on summary conviction, to a fine not exceeding the statutory maximum; or

(b) on conviction on indictment, to a fine or imprisonment for a term not exceeding two years or both.

(3) Nothing in this regulation shall be construed as requiring a person to answer any question or give any information if to do so might incriminate him.

(4) Paragraph (1)(a) does not apply in relation to the exercise by an enforcement authority of its power to require information under regulation 21.

[3670]

NOTES
Commencement: 26 May 2008.

26 Notice of test and intended proceedings

(1) Where goods purchased by an officer pursuant to regulation 22 are submitted to a test and the test leads to the institution of any proceedings for a breach of these Regulations the officer shall inform—

(a) the person from whom the goods were purchased; or

(b) where the goods were sold through a vending machine, the person mentioned in regulation 23(3)(b);

of the result of the test.

(2) Where goods seized by an officer pursuant to regulation 23 are submitted to a test then the officer shall inform the person mentioned in regulation 23(3) of the result of the test.

(3) Where, as a result of the test, proceedings for a breach of these Regulations are taken against any person, the officer shall allow him to have the goods tested on his behalf if it is reasonably practicable to do so.

[3671]

NOTES

Commencement: 26 May 2008.

27 Compensation

(1) Where an officer of an enforcement authority seizes and detains goods in exercise of the powers under regulation 23 the enforcement authority shall be liable to pay compensation to any person having an interest in the goods in respect of any loss or damage caused by reason of the exercise of the power if—

    (a)   there has been no breach of these Regulations in relation to the goods, and

    (b)   the exercise of that power is not attributable to any neglect or default by that person.

(2) Any disputed question as to the right to or the amount of any compensation payable under this provision shall be determined by arbitration or, in Scotland, by a single arbiter appointed, failing agreement between the parties, by the sheriff.

    [3672]

NOTES

Commencement: 26 May 2008.

28 Crown

(1) The powers conferred by regulations 23 and 24 are not exercisable in relation to premises occupied by the Crown.

(2) The Crown is not criminally liable as a result of any provision of these Regulations.

(3) Paragraph (2) does not affect the application of any provision of these Regulations in relation to a person in the public service of the Crown.

    [3673]

NOTES

Commencement: 26 May 2008.

29 Validity of agreements

An agreement shall not be void or unenforceable by reason only of a breach of these Regulations.

    [3674]

NOTES

Commencement: 26 May 2008.

CONSUMER PROTECTION FROM UNFAIR TRADING REGULATIONS 2008

(SI 2008/1277)

NOTES

Made: 8 May 2008.
Authority: European Communities Act 1972, s 2(2).
Commencement: 26 May 2008.

ARRANGEMENT OF REGULATIONS

PART 1
GENERAL

PART 2
PROHIBITIONS

PART 3
OFFENCES

PART 4
ENFORCEMENT

PART 5
SUPPLEMENTARY

PART 1
GENERAL

1   Citation and commencement

These Regulations may be cited as the Consumer Protection from Unfair Trading Regulations 2008 and shall come into force on 26th May 2008.

[3675]

NOTES

Commencement: 26 May 2008.

2   Interpretation

(1)   In these Regulations—

"average consumer" shall be construed in accordance with paragraphs (2) to (6);

"business" includes a trade, craft or profession;

"code of conduct" means an agreement or set of rules (which is not imposed by legal or administrative requirements), which defines the behaviour of traders who undertake to be bound by it in relation to one or more commercial practices or business sectors;

"code owner" means a trader or a body responsible for—

(a)   the formulation and revision of a code of conduct; or

(b)   monitoring compliance with the code by those who have undertaken to be bound by it;

"commercial practice" means any act, omission, course of conduct, representation or commercial communication (including advertising and marketing) by a trader, which is directly connected with the promotion, sale or supply of a product to or from consumers, whether occurring before, during or after a commercial transaction (if any) in relation to a product;

"consumer" means any individual who in relation to a commercial practice is acting for purposes which are outside his business;

"enforcement authority" means the OFT, every local weights and measures authority in Great Britain (within the meaning of section 69 of the Weights and Measures Act 1985) and the Department of Enterprise, Trade and Investment in Northern Ireland;

"goods" includes ships, aircraft, animals, things attached to land and growing crops;

"invitation to purchase" means a commercial communication which indicates characteristics of the product and the price in a way appropriate to the means of that commercial communication and thereby enables the consumer to make a purchase;

"materially distort the economic behaviour" means in relation to an average consumer, appreciably to impair the average consumer's ability to make an informed decision thereby causing him to take a transactional decision that he would not have taken otherwise;

"OFT" means the Office of Fair Trading;

"premises" includes any place and any stall, vehicle, ship or aircraft;

"product" means any goods or service and includes immovable property, rights and obligations;

"professional diligence" means the standard of special skill and care which a trader may reasonably be expected to exercise towards consumers which is commensurate with either—

    (a)   honest market practice in the trader's field of activity, or

    (b)   the general principle of good faith in the trader's field of activity;

"ship" includes any boat and any other description of vessel used in navigation;

"trader" means any person who in relation to a commercial practice is acting for purposes relating to his business, and anyone acting in the name of or on behalf of a trader;

"transactional decision" means any decision taken by a consumer, whether it is to act or to refrain from acting, concerning—

    (a)   whether, how and on what terms to purchase, make payment in whole or in part for, retain or dispose of a product; or

    (b)   whether, how and on what terms to exercise a contractual right in relation to a product.

(2)   In determining the effect of a commercial practice on the average consumer where the practice reaches or is addressed to a consumer or consumers account shall be taken of the material characteristics of such an average consumer including his being reasonably well informed, reasonably observant and circumspect.

(3)   Paragraphs (4) and (5) set out the circumstances in which a reference to the average consumer shall be read as in addition referring to the average member of a particular group of consumers.

(4)   In determining the effect of a commercial practice on the average consumer where the practice is directed to a particular group of consumers, a reference to the average consumer shall be read as referring to the average member of that group.

(5)   In determining the effect of a commercial practice on the average consumer—

    (a)   where a clearly identifiable group of consumers is particularly vulnerable to the practice or the underlying product because of their mental or physical infirmity, age or credulity in a way which the trader could reasonably be expected to foresee, and

    (b)   where the practice is likely to materially distort the economic behaviour only of that group,

a reference to the average consumer shall be read as referring to the average member of that group.

(6)   Paragraph (5) is without prejudice to the common and legitimate advertising practice of making exaggerated statements which are not meant to be taken literally.

[3676]

NOTES

Commencement: 26 May 2008.

PART 2
PROHIBITIONS

3   Prohibition of unfair commercial practices

(1)   Unfair commercial practices are prohibited.

(2)   Paragraphs (3) and (4) set out the circumstances when a commercial practice is unfair.

(3)   A commercial practice is unfair if—

    (a)   it contravenes the requirements of professional diligence; and

    (b)   it materially distorts or is likely to materially distort the economic behaviour of the average consumer with regard to the product.

(4)   A commercial practice is unfair if—

    (a)   it is a misleading action under the provisions of regulation 5;

    (b)   it is a misleading omission under the provisions of regulation 6;

    (c)   it is aggressive under the provisions of regulation 7; or

    (d)   it is listed in Schedule 1.

[3677]

NOTES

Commencement: 26 May 2008.

4 Prohibition of the promotion of unfair commercial practices

The promotion of any unfair commercial practice by a code owner in a code of conduct is prohibited.

[3678]

NOTES

Commencement: 26 May 2008.

5 Misleading actions

(1) A commercial practice is a misleading action if it satisfies the conditions in either paragraph (2) or paragraph (3).

(2) A commercial practice satisfies the conditions of this paragraph—

    (a) if it contains false information and is therefore untruthful in relation to any of the matters in paragraph (4) or if it or its overall presentation in any way deceives or is likely to deceive the average consumer in relation to any of the matters in that paragraph, even if the information is factually correct; and

    (b) it causes or is likely to cause the average consumer to take a transactional decision he would not have taken otherwise.

(3) A commercial practice satisfies the conditions of this paragraph if—

    (a) it concerns any marketing of a product (including comparative advertising) which creates confusion with any products, trade marks, trade names or other distinguishing marks of a competitor; or

    (b) it concerns any failure by a trader to comply with a commitment contained in a code of conduct which the trader has undertaken to comply with, if—

        (i) the trader indicates in a commercial practice that he is bound by that code of conduct, and

        (ii) the commitment is firm and capable of being verified and is not aspirational,

and it causes or is likely to cause the average consumer to take a transactional decision he would not have taken otherwise, taking account of its factual context and of all its features and circumstances.

(4) The matters referred to in paragraph (2)(a) are—

    (a) the existence or nature of the product;

    (b) the main characteristics of the product (as defined in paragraph 5);

    (c) the extent of the trader's commitments;

    (d) the motives for the commercial practice;

    (e) the nature of the sales process;

    (f) any statement or symbol relating to direct or indirect sponsorship or approval of the trader or the product;

    (g) the price or the manner in which the price is calculated;

    (h) the existence of a specific price advantage;

    (i) the need for a service, part, replacement or repair;

    (j) the nature, attributes and rights of the trader (as defined in paragraph 6);

    (k) the consumer's rights or the risks he may face.

(5) In paragraph (4)(b), the "main characteristics of the product" include—

    (a) availability of the product;

    (b) benefits of the product;

    (c) risks of the product;

    (d) execution of the product;

    (e) composition of the product;

    (f) accessories of the product;

    (g) after-sale customer assistance concerning the product;

    (h) the handling of complaints about the product;

    (i) the method and date of manufacture of the product;

    (j) the method and date of provision of the product;

    (k) delivery of the product;

    (l) fitness for purpose of the product;

    (m) usage of the product;

    (n) quantity of the product;

    (o) specification of the product;

    (p) geographical or commercial origin of the product;

    (q) results to be expected from use of the product; and

    (r) results and material features of tests or checks carried out on the product.

(6) In paragraph (4)(j), the "nature, attributes and rights" as far as concern the trader include the trader's—

    (a) identity;

    (b) assets;

(c)   qualifications;
(d)   status;
(e)   approval;
(f)   affiliations or connections;
(g)   ownership of industrial, commercial or intellectual property rights; and
(h)   awards and distinctions.

(7)   In paragraph (4)(k) "consumer's rights" include rights the consumer may have under Part 5A of the Sale of Goods Act 1979 or Part 1B of the Supply of Goods and Services Act 1982.

[3679]

NOTES
Commencement: 26 May 2008.

6 Misleading omissions

(1)   A commercial practice is a misleading omission if, in its factual context, taking account of the matters in paragraph (2)—
(a)   the commercial practice omits material information,
(b)   the commercial practice hides material information,
(c)   the commercial practice provides material information in a manner which is unclear, unintelligible, ambiguous or untimely, or
(d)   the commercial practice fails to identify its commercial intent, unless this is already apparent from the context,

and as a result it causes or is likely to cause the average consumer to take a transactional decision he would not have taken otherwise.

(2)   The matters referred to in paragraph (1) are—
(a)   all the features and circumstances of the commercial practice;
(b)   the limitations of the medium used to communicate the commercial practice (including limitations of space or time); and
(c)   where the medium used to communicate the commercial practice imposes limitations of space or time, any measures taken by the trader to make the information available to consumers by other means.

(3)   In paragraph (1) "material information" means—
(a)   the information which the average consumer needs, according to the context, to take an informed transactional decision; and
(b)   any information requirement which applies in relation to a commercial communication as a result of a Community obligation.

(4)   Where a commercial practice is an invitation to purchase, the following information will be material if not already apparent from the context in addition to any other information which is material information under paragraph (3)—
(a)   the main characteristics of the product, to the extent appropriate to the medium by which the invitation to purchase is communicated and the product;
(b)   the identity of the trader, such as his trading name, and the identity of any other trader on whose behalf the trader is acting;
(c)   the geographical address of the trader and the geographical address of any other trader on whose behalf the trader is acting;
(d)   either—
  (i)   the price, including any taxes; or
  (ii)   where the nature of the product is such that the price cannot reasonably be calculated in advance, the manner in which the price is calculated;
(e)   where appropriate, either—
  (i)   all additional freight, delivery or postal charges; or
  (ii)   where such charges cannot reasonably be calculated in advance, the fact that such charges may be payable;
(f)   the following matters where they depart from the requirements of professional diligence—
  (i)   arrangements for payment,
  (ii)   arrangements for delivery,
  (iii) arrangements for performance,
  (iv)   complaint handling policy;
(g)   for products and transactions involving a right of withdrawal or cancellation, the existence of such a right.

[3680]

NOTES
Commencement: 26 May 2008.

7 Aggressive commercial practices

(1) A commercial practice is aggressive if, in its factual context, taking account of all of its features and circumstances—

    (a) it significantly impairs or is likely significantly to impair the average consumer's freedom of choice or conduct in relation to the product concerned through the use of harassment, coercion or undue influence; and

    (b) it thereby causes or is likely to cause him to take a transactional decision he would not have taken otherwise.

(2) In determining whether a commercial practice uses harassment, coercion or undue influence account shall be taken of—

    (a) its timing, location, nature or persistence;

    (b) the use of threatening or abusive language or behaviour;

    (c) the exploitation by the trader of any specific misfortune or circumstance of such gravity as to impair the consumer's judgment, of which the trader is aware, to influence the consumer's decision with regard to the product;

    (d) any onerous or disproportionate non-contractual barrier imposed by the trader where a consumer wishes to exercise rights under the contract, including rights to terminate a contract or to switch to another product or another trader; and

    (e) any threat to take any action which cannot legally be taken.

(3) In this regulation—

    (a) "coercion" includes the use of physical force; and

    (b) "undue influence" means exploiting a position of power in relation to the consumer so as to apply pressure, even without using or threatening to use physical force, in a way which significantly limits the consumer's ability to make an informed decision.

[3681]

NOTES

Commencement: 26 May 2008.

PART 3
OFFENCES

8 Offences relating to unfair commercial practices

(1) A trader is guilty of an offence if—

    (a) he knowingly or recklessly engages in a commercial practice which contravenes the requirements of professional diligence under regulation 3(3)(a); and

    (b) the practice materially distorts or is likely to materially distort the economic behaviour of the average consumer with regard to the product under regulation 3(3)(b).

(2) For the purposes of paragraph (1)(a) a trader who engages in a commercial practice without regard to whether the practice contravenes the requirements of professional diligence shall be deemed recklessly to engage in the practice, whether or not the trader has reason for believing that the practice might contravene those requirements.

[3682]

NOTES

Commencement: 26 May 2008.

9 A trader is guilty of an offence if he engages in a commercial practice which is a misleading action under regulation 5 otherwise than by reason of the commercial practice satisfying the condition in regulation 5(3)(b).

[3683]

NOTES

Commencement: 26 May 2008.

10 A trader is guilty of an offence if he engages in a commercial practice which is a misleading omission under regulation 6.

[3684]

NOTES

Commencement: 26 May 2008.

11 A trader is guilty of an offence if he engages in a commercial practice which is aggressive under regulation 7.

[3685]

NOTES

Commencement: 26 May 2008.

12 A trader is guilty of an offence if he engages in a commercial practice set out in any of paragraphs 1 to 10, 12 to 27 and 29 to 31 of Schedule 1.

[3686]

NOTES

Commencement: 26 May 2008.

13 Penalty for offences

A person guilty of an offence under regulation 8, 9, 10, 11 or 12 shall be liable—
- (a)   on summary conviction, to a fine not exceeding the statutory maximum; or
- (b)   on conviction on indictment, to a fine or imprisonment for a term not exceeding two years or both.

[3687]

NOTES

Commencement: 26 May 2008.

14 Time limit for prosecution

(1)   No proceedings for an offence under these Regulations shall be commenced after—
- (a)   the end of the period of three years beginning with the date of the commission of the offence, or
- (b)   the end of the period of one year beginning with the date of discovery of the offence by the prosecutor,

whichever is earlier.

(2)   For the purposes of paragraph (1)(b) a certificate signed by or on behalf of the prosecutor and stating the date on which the offence was discovered by him shall be conclusive evidence of that fact and a certificate stating that matter and purporting to be so signed shall be treated as so signed unless the contrary is proved.

(3)   Notwithstanding anything in section 127(1) of the Magistrates' Courts Act 1980, an information relating to an offence under these Regulations which is triable by a magistrates' court in England and Wales may be so tried if it is laid at any time before the end of the period of twelve months beginning with the date of the commission of the offence.

(4)   Notwithstanding anything in section 136 of the Criminal Procedure (Scotland) Act 1995 summary proceedings in Scotland for an offence under these Regulations may be commenced at any time before the end of the period of twelve months beginning with the date of the commission of the offence.

(5)   For the purposes of paragraph (4), section 136(3) of the Criminal Procedure (Scotland) Act 1995 shall apply as it applies for the purposes of that subsection.

(6)   Notwithstanding anything in Article 19(1) of the Magistrates' Courts (Northern Ireland) Order 1981 a complaint charging an offence under these Regulations which is triable by a magistrates' court in Northern Ireland may be so tried if it is made at any time before the end of the period of twelve months beginning with the date of the commission of the offence.

[3688]

NOTES

Commencement: 26 May 2008.

15 Offences committed by bodies of persons

(1)   Where an offence under these Regulations committed by a body corporate is proved—
- (a)   to have been committed with the consent or connivance of an officer of the body, or
- (b)   to be attributable to any neglect on his part,

the officer as well as the body corporate is guilty of the offence and liable to be proceeded against and punished accordingly.

(2)   In paragraph (1) a reference to an officer of a body corporate includes a reference to—
- (a)   a director, manager, secretary or other similar officer; and
- (b)   a person purporting to act as a director, manager, secretary or other similar officer.

(3) Where an offence under these Regulations committed by a Scottish partnership is proved—

    (a) to have been committed with the consent or connivance of a partner, or

    (b) to be attributable to any neglect on his part,

the partner as well as the partnership is guilty of the offence and liable to be proceeded against and punished accordingly.

(4) In paragraph (3) a reference to a partner includes a person purporting to act as a partner.

[3689]

NOTES

    Commencement: 26 May 2008.

16 Offence due to the default of another person

(1) This regulation applies where a person "X"—

    (a) commits an offence under regulation 9, 10, 11 or 12, or

    (b) would have committed an offence under those regulations but for a defence under regulation 17 or 18,

and the commission of the offence, or of what would have been an offence but for X being able to rely on a defence under regulation 17 or 18, is due to the act or default of some other person "Y".

(2) Where this regulation applies Y is guilty of the offence, subject to regulations 17 and 18, whether or not Y is a trader and whether or not Y's act or default is a commercial practice.

(3) Y may be charged with and convicted of the offence by virtue of paragraph (2) whether or not proceedings are taken against X.

[3690]

NOTES

    Commencement: 26 May 2008.

17 Due diligence defence

(1) In any proceedings against a person for an offence under regulation 9, 10, 11 or 12 it is a defence for that person to prove—

    (a) that the commission of the offence was due to—

        (i) a mistake;

        (ii) reliance on information supplied to him by another person;

        (iii) the act or default of another person;

        (iv) an accident; or

        (v) another cause beyond his control; and

    (b) that he took all reasonable precautions and exercised all due diligence to avoid the commission of such an offence by himself or any person under his control.

(2) A person shall not be entitled to rely on the defence provided by paragraph (1) by reason of the matters referred to in paragraph (ii) or (iii) of paragraph (1)(a) without leave of the court unless—

    (a) he has served on the prosecutor a notice in writing giving such information identifying or assisting in the identification of that other person as was in his possession; and

    (b) the notice is served on the prosecutor at least seven clear days before the date of the hearing.

[3691]

NOTES

    Commencement: 26 May 2008.

18 Innocent publication of advertisement defence

(1) In any proceedings against a person for an offence under regulation 9, 10, 11 or 12 committed by the publication of an advertisement it shall be a defence for a person to prove that—

    (a) he is a person whose business it is to publish or to arrange for the publication of advertisements;

    (b) he received the advertisement for publication in the ordinary course of business; and

    (c) he did not know and had no reason to suspect that its publication would amount to an offence under the regulation to which the proceedings relate.

(2) In paragraph (1) "advertisement" includes a catalogue, a circular and a price list.

[3692]

NOTES

    Commencement: 26 May 2008.

PART 4
ENFORCEMENT

19 Duty to enforce

(1)   It shall be the duty of every enforcement authority to enforce these Regulations.

(2)   Where the enforcement authority is a local weights and measures authority the duty referred to in paragraph (1) shall apply to the enforcement of these Regulations within the authority's area.

(3)   Where the enforcement authority is the Department of Enterprise, Trade and Investment in Northern Ireland the duty referred to in paragraph (1) shall apply to the enforcement of these Regulations within Northern Ireland.

(4)   In determining how to comply with its duty of enforcement every enforcement authority shall have regard to the desirability of encouraging control of unfair commercial practices by such established means as it considers appropriate having regard to all the circumstances of the particular case.

(5)   Nothing in this regulation shall authorise any enforcement authority to bring proceedings in Scotland for an offence.

[3693]

NOTES

Commencement: 26 May 2008.

20 Power to make test purchases

An enforcement authority may or may authorise any of its officers on its behalf to—

   (a)   make a purchase of a product, or

   (b)   enter into an agreement to secure the provision of a product,

for the purposes of determining whether these Regulations are being complied with.

[3694]

NOTES

Commencement: 26 May 2008.

21 Power of entry and investigation, etc

(1)   A duly authorised officer of an enforcement authority may at all reasonable hours exercise the following powers—

   (a)   he may, for the purposes of ascertaining whether a breach of these Regulations has been committed, inspect any goods and enter any premises other than premises used only as a dwelling;

   (b)   if he has reasonable cause to suspect that a breach of these Regulations has been committed, he may, for the purpose of ascertaining whether it has been committed, require any trader to produce any documents relating to his business and may take copies of, or of any entry in, any such document;

   (c)   if he has reasonable cause to believe that a breach of these Regulations has been committed, he may seize and detain any goods for the purpose of ascertaining, by testing or otherwise, whether the breach has been committed; and

   (d)   he may seize and detain goods or documents which he has reason to believe may be required as evidence in proceedings for a breach of these Regulations.

(2)   If and to the extent that it is reasonably necessary to secure that the provisions of these Regulations are observed, the officer may for the purpose of exercising his powers under paragraphs (1)(c) and (d) to seize goods or documents—

   (a)   require any person having authority to do so to break open any container or open any vending machine; and

   (b)   himself open or break open any such container or open any vending machine where a requirement made under sub-paragraph (a) in relation to the container or vending machine has not been complied with.

(3)   An officer seizing any goods or documents in exercise of his powers under this regulation shall—

   (a)   inform the person from whom they are seized, and,

   (b)   where goods are seized from a vending machine, inform—

      (i)   the person whose name and address are stated on the machine as being the proprietor's; or

      (ii)   if there is no such name or address stated on the machine the occupier of the premises on which the machine stands or to which it is affixed,

     that the goods or documents have been so seized.

(4)   In this regulation "document" includes information recorded in any form.

(5)   The reference in paragraph (1)(b) to the production of documents is, in the case of a document which contains information recorded otherwise than in legible form, a reference to the production of a copy of the information in legible form.

(6)   An officer seeking to exercise a power under this regulation must produce evidence of his identity and authority to a person (if there is one) who appears to the officer to be the occupier of the premises.

(7)   Where an officer seizes goods or documents in exercise of a power under this regulation they may not be detained—
    (a)   for a period of more than 3 months; or
    (b)   where the goods or documents are reasonably required by the enforcement authority in connection with the enforcement of these Regulations, for longer than they are so required.

(8)   An officer entering any premises under this regulation may take with him such other persons and such equipment as may appear to him to be necessary.

(9)   Nothing in this regulation or in regulation 22 gives any power to an officer of an enforcement authority—
    (a)   to require any person to produce, or
    (b)   to seize from another person,
any document which the other person would be entitled to refuse to produce in proceedings in the High Court on the grounds of legal professional privilege or (in Scotland) in proceedings in the Court of Session on the grounds of confidentiality of communications.

(10)   In paragraph (9) "communications" means—
    (a)   communications between a professional legal adviser and his client; or
    (b)   communications made in connection with or in contemplation of legal proceedings and for the purposes of those proceedings.

(11)   If any person who is not an officer of an enforcement authority purports to act as such under this regulation or under regulation 22 he shall be guilty of an offence and liable on summary conviction to a fine not exceeding level 5 on the standard scale.

[3695]

NOTES
Commencement: 26 May 2008.

22 Power to enter premises with a warrant

(1)   If a justice of the peace by any written information on oath is satisfied—
    (a)   that there are reasonable grounds for believing that Condition A or B is met, and
    (b)   that Condition C, D or E is met,
the justice may by warrant under his hand authorise an officer of an enforcement authority to enter the premises at all reasonable times, if necessary by force.

(2)   Condition A is that there are on any premises goods or documents which a duly authorised officer of the enforcement authority has power under regulation 21(1) to inspect and that their inspection is likely to disclose evidence of a breach of these Regulations.

(3)   Condition B is that a breach of these Regulations has been, is being or is about to be committed on any premises.

(4)   Condition C is that the admission to the premises has been or is likely to be refused and that notice of intention to apply for a warrant under this regulation has been given to the occupier.

(5)   Condition D is that an application for admission, or the giving of a notice of intention to apply for a warrant, would defeat the object of the entry.

(6)   Condition E is that the premises are unoccupied or that the occupier is absent and it might defeat the object of the entry to await his return.

(7)   A warrant under paragraph (1)—
    (a)   ceases to have effect at the end of the period of one month beginning with the day it is issued;
    (b)   must be produced for inspection to the person (if there is one) who appears to the officer to be the occupier of the premises.

(8)   An officer entering any premises under this regulation may take with him such other persons and such equipment as may appear to him to be necessary.

(9)   On leaving any premises which an officer is authorised to enter by warrant under this regulation the officer shall, if the premises are unoccupied or the occupier is temporarily absent, leave the premises as effectively secured against trespassers as he found them.

(10)   (*Applies to Scotland only.*)

(11) In its application to Northern Ireland, this regulation has effect as if the references in paragraph (1) to a justice of the peace were references to a lay magistrate.

[3696]

NOTES
Commencement: 26 May 2008.

23 Obstruction of authorised officers

(1) Any person who—
    (a)   intentionally obstructs an officer of an enforcement authority acting in pursuance of these Regulations,
    (b)   intentionally fails to comply with any requirement properly made of him by such an officer under regulation 21, or
    (c)   without reasonable cause fails to give such an officer any other assistance or information which he may reasonably require of him for the purpose of the performance of his functions under these Regulations,

is guilty of an offence and liable, on summary conviction, to a fine not exceeding level 5 on the standard scale.

(2) Any person who, in giving any information which is required of him under paragraph (1)(c), makes any statement which he knows to be false in a material particular is guilty of an offence and liable—
    (a)   on summary conviction, to a fine not exceeding the statutory maximum; or
    (b)   on conviction on indictment, to a fine or imprisonment for a term not exceeding two years or both.

(3) Nothing in this regulation shall be construed as requiring a person to answer any question or give any information if to do so might incriminate him.

[3697]

NOTES
Commencement: 26 May 2008.

24 Notice of test and intended proceedings

(1) Where goods purchased by an officer pursuant to regulation 20 are submitted to a test and the test leads to the institution of any proceedings for a breach of these Regulations the officer shall inform—
    (a)   the person from whom the goods were purchased, or
    (b)   where the goods were sold through a vending machine, the person mentioned in regulation 21(3)(b),
of the result of the test.

(2) Where goods seized by an officer pursuant to regulation 21 are submitted to a test then the officer shall inform the person mentioned in regulation 21(3) of the result of the test.

(3) Where, as a result of the test, any proceedings in respect of a breach of these Regulations are taken against any person, the officer shall allow him to have the goods tested on his behalf if it is reasonably practicable to do so.

[3698]

NOTES
Commencement: 26 May 2008.

25 Compensation

(1) Where an officer of an enforcement authority seizes and detains goods in exercise of the powers under regulation 21 the enforcement authority shall be liable to pay compensation to any person having an interest in the goods in respect of any loss or damage caused by reason of the exercise of the power if—
    (a)   there has been no breach of these Regulations in relation to the goods, and
    (b)   the exercise of that power is not attributable to any neglect or default by that person.

(2) Any disputed question as to the right to or the amount of any compensation payable under this provision shall be determined by arbitration or, in Scotland, by a single arbiter appointed, failing agreement between the parties, by the sheriff.

[3699]

NOTES
Commencement: 26 May 2008.

PART 2
STATUTORY INSTRUMENTS

26, 27 (*Reg 26 amends the Enterprise Act 2002, Sch 13; reg 27 inserts s 218A of the 2002 Act at* **[1951A]**.)

PART 5
SUPPLEMENTARY

28 Crown

(1) The powers conferred by regulations 21 and 22 are not exercisable in relation to premises occupied by the Crown.

(2) The Crown is not criminally liable as a result of any provision of these Regulations.

(3) Paragraph (2) does not affect the application of any provision of these Regulations in relation to a person in the public service of the Crown.

[3700]

NOTES
Commencement: 26 May 2008.

29 Validity of agreements

An agreement shall not be void or unenforceable by reason only of a breach of these Regulations.

[3701]

NOTES
Commencement: 26 May 2008.

30 Amendments, repeals and transitional and saving provisions

(1) Schedule 2 (which contains amendments) shall have effect.

(2) Schedule 3 (which contains transitional and saving provisions) shall have effect.

(3) Schedule 4 (which contains repeals and revocations) shall have effect.

[3702]

NOTES
Commencement: 26 May 2008.

SCHEDULE 1
COMMERCIAL PRACTICES WHICH ARE IN ALL CIRCUMSTANCES CONSIDERED UNFAIR

Regulation 3(4)(d)

1. Claiming to be a signatory to a code of conduct when the trader is not.

2. Displaying a trust mark, quality mark or equivalent without having obtained the necessary authorisation.

3. Claiming that a code of conduct has an endorsement from a public or other body which it does not have.

4. Claiming that a trader (including his commercial practices) or a product has been approved, endorsed or authorised by a public or private body when the trader, the commercial practices or the product have not or making such a claim without complying with the terms of the approval, endorsement or authorisation.

5. Making an invitation to purchase products at a specified price without disclosing the existence of any reasonable grounds the trader may have for believing that he will not be able to offer for supply, or to procure another trader to supply, those products or equivalent products at that price for a period that is, and in quantities that are, reasonable having regard to the product, the scale of advertising of the product and the price offered (bait advertising).

6. Making an invitation to purchase products at a specified price and then—
    (a) refusing to show the advertised item to consumers,
    (b) refusing to take orders for it or deliver it within a reasonable time, or
    (c) demonstrating a defective sample of it,
with the intention of promoting a different product (bait and switch).

7. Falsely stating that a product will only be available for a very limited time, or that it will only be available on particular terms for a very limited time, in order to elicit an immediate decision and deprive consumers of sufficient opportunity or time to make an informed choice.

8. Undertaking to provide after-sales service to consumers with whom the trader has communicated prior to a transaction in a language which is not an official language of the EEA State where the trader is located and then making such service available only in another language without clearly disclosing this to the consumer before the consumer is committed to the transaction.

9. Stating or otherwise creating the impression that a product can legally be sold when it cannot.

10. Presenting rights given to consumers in law as a distinctive feature of the trader's offer.

11. Using editorial content in the media to promote a product where a trader has paid for the promotion without making that clear in the content or by images or sounds clearly identifiable by the consumer (advertorial).

12. Making a materially inaccurate claim concerning the nature and extent of the risk to the personal security of the consumer or his family if the consumer does not purchase the product.

13. Promoting a product similar to a product made by a particular manufacturer in such a manner as deliberately to mislead the consumer into believing that the product is made by that same manufacturer when it is not.

14. Establishing, operating or promoting a pyramid promotional scheme where a consumer gives consideration for the opportunity to receive compensation that is derived primarily from the introduction of other consumers into the scheme rather than from the sale or consumption of products.

15. Claiming that the trader is about to cease trading or move premises when he is not.

16. Claiming that products are able to facilitate winning in games of chance.

17. Falsely claiming that a product is able to cure illnesses, dysfunction or malformations.

18. Passing on materially inaccurate information on market conditions or on the possibility of finding the product with the intention of inducing the consumer to acquire the product at conditions less favourable than normal market conditions.

19. Claiming in a commercial practice to offer a competition or prize promotion without awarding the prizes described or a reasonable equivalent.

20. Describing a product as 'gratis', 'free', 'without charge' or similar if the consumer has to pay anything other than the unavoidable cost of responding to the commercial practice and collecting or paying for delivery of the item.

21. Including in marketing material an invoice or similar document seeking payment which gives the consumer the impression that he has already ordered the marketed product when he has not.

22. Falsely claiming or creating the impression that the trader is not acting for purposes relating to his trade, business, craft or profession, or falsely representing oneself as a consumer.

23. Creating the false impression that after-sales service in relation to a product is available in an EEA State other than the one in which the product is sold.

24. Creating the impression that the consumer cannot leave the premises until a contract is formed.

25. Conducting personal visits to the consumer's home ignoring the consumer's request to leave or not to return, except in circumstances and to the extent justified to enforce a contractual obligation.

26. Making persistent and unwanted solicitations by telephone, fax, e-mail or other remote media except in circumstances and to the extent justified to enforce a contractual obligation.

27. Requiring a consumer who wishes to claim on an insurance policy to produce documents which could not reasonably be considered relevant as to whether the claim was valid, or failing systematically to respond to pertinent correspondence, in order to dissuade a consumer from exercising his contractual rights.

28. Including in an advertisement a direct exhortation to children to buy advertised products or persuade their parents or other adults to buy advertised products for them.

29. Demanding immediate or deferred payment for or the return or safekeeping of products supplied by the trader, but not solicited by the consumer, except where the product is a substitute supplied in accordance with regulation 19(7) of the Consumer Protection (Distance Selling) Regulations 2000 (inertia selling).

30. Explicitly informing a consumer that if he does not buy the product or service, the trader's job or livelihood will be in jeopardy.

31. Creating the false impression that the consumer has already won, will win, or will on doing a particular act win, a prize or other equivalent benefit, when in fact either—
    (a)   there is no prize or other equivalent benefit, or
    (b)   taking any action in relation to claiming the prize or other equivalent benefit is subject to the consumer paying money or incurring a cost.

[3703]

NOTES
   Commencement: 26 May 2008.

(Sch 2 (Amendments) outside the scope of this work.)

SCHEDULE 3
TRANSITIONAL AND SAVING PROVISIONS
Regulation 30(2)

Trade Descriptions Act 1968

1. Notwithstanding the repeal by these Regulations of section 5 of the Trade Descriptions Act 1968—

(a)   section 5(3) shall continue to apply for the purposes of section 1(8) of the Hallmarking Act 1973 as it applied before that repeal, and

(b)   section 5 shall continue to apply for the purposes of regulation 8(1) of the Crystal Glass (Descriptions) Regulations 1973 as it applied before that repeal.

2. The repeal of section 19(4)(b) and (c) of the Trade Descriptions Act 1968 shall not have effect in relation to the references to section 19 in—

(a)   regulation 8(2) of the Crystal Glass (Descriptions) Regulations 1973;

(b)   regulation 11(1) of the Textile Products (Indications of Fibre Content) Regulations 1986;

(c)   regulation 4(1) of the Electro-medical Equipment (EEC Requirements) Regulations 1988; and

(d)   regulation 10(1) of the Footwear (Indication of Composition) Labelling Regulations 1995.

3. The repeal of section 24(3) of the Trade Descriptions Act 1968 shall not have effect in relation to the references to section 24 in—

(a)   regulation 8(2) of the Crystal Glass (Descriptions) Regulations 1973;

(b)   regulation 11(1) of the Textile Products (Indications of Fibre Content) Regulations 1986;

(c)   regulation 4(1) of the Electro-medical Equipment (EEC Requirements) Regulations 1988; and

(d)   regulation 10(1) of the Footwear (Indication of Composition) Labelling Regulations 1995.

4. Notwithstanding the repeal by these Regulations of section 39(2) of the Trade Descriptions Act 1968, that subsection shall continue to apply for the purposes of section 1 of the Hallmarking Act 1973 as it applied before that repeal.

Application of the Consumer Protection Act 1987 to the Price Indications (Bureaux de Change) (No 2) Regulations 1992

5.—(1) Despite the repeal by these Regulations of section 26 of the Consumer Protection Act 1987, the Price Indications (Bureaux de Change) (No 2) Regulations 1992 shall continue in force, and that section shall continue to have effect as it had effect immediately before the coming into force of these Regulations for the purposes of amending or revoking those Regulations.

(2)   Where these Regulations repeal a provision of the Consumer Protection Act 1987 that, immediately before the coming into force of these Regulations, was applied by the Price Indications (Bureaux de Change) (No 2) Regulations 1992 to an offence under those Regulations, that provision shall continue to apply to that offence as it applied immediately before the coming into force of these Regulations, notwithstanding that repeal.

6. Notwithstanding the repeals and amendments made by these Regulations to the provisions of Parts 4 and 5 of the Consumer Protection Act 1987 those provisions shall continue to apply in relation to the Price Indications (Bureaux de Change) (No 2) Regulations 1992 as they applied before the coming into force of these Regulations.

Application of the Consumer Protection (Northern Ireland) Order 1987 to the Price Indications (Bureaux de Change) Regulations (Northern Ireland) 1992

7.—(1) Despite the repeal by these Regulations of Article 19 of the Consumer Protection (Northern Ireland) Order 1987, the Price Indications (Bureaux de Change) Regulations (Northern Ireland) 1992 shall continue in force, and that Article shall continue to have effect as it had effect immediately before the coming into force of these Regulations for the purpose of amending or revoking those Regulations.

(2)   Where these Regulations repeal a provision of the Consumer Protection (Northern Ireland) Order 1987 that, immediately before the coming into force of these Regulations, was applied by the Price Indications (Bureaux de Change) Regulations (Northern Ireland) 1992 to an offence under that Order, that provision shall continue to apply to that offence as it applied immediately before the coming into force of these Regulations, notwithstanding that repeal.

8. Notwithstanding the repeals and amendments made by these Regulations to the provisions of Parts IV and V of the Consumer Protection (Northern Ireland) Order 1987 those provisions shall continue to apply in relation to the Price Indications (Bureaux de Change) Regulations (Northern Ireland) 1992 as they applied before the coming into force of these Regulations.

Enterprise Act 2002 (Part 8 Notice to OFT of Intended Prosecution, Specified Enactments, Revocation and Transitional Provision) Order 2003

9.—(1) This paragraph applies to offences under the following provisions—

- (a) Part 3 of the Consumer Protection Act 1987;
- (b) section 23 of the Fair Trading Act 1973;
- (c) the Mock Auctions Act 1961;
- (d) section 29 of the Weights and Measures Act 1985.

(2) Notwithstanding the omission of the references to these provisions in the Enterprise Act 2002 (Part 8 Notice to OFT of Intended Prosecution, Specified Enactments, Revocation and Transitional Provision) Order 2003 by these Regulations section 230 of the Enterprise Act 2002 shall continue to apply in relation to an intention by a local weights and measures authority in England and Wales to start proceedings for an offence to which paragraph (1) applies.

10. Notwithstanding the amendments made by these Regulations to the Enterprise Act 2002 (Part 8 Notice to OFT of Intended Prosecution, Specified Enactments, Revocation and Transitional Provision) Order 2003 that Order shall continue to apply in relation to the Price Indications (Bureaux de Change) (No 2) Regulations 1992 as it applied before the coming into force of these Regulations.

Enterprise Act 2002 (Part 8 Domestic Infringements) Order 2003

11.—(1) This paragraph applies to an act or omission which immediately before the date on which these Regulations come into force is a domestic infringement under section 211 of the Enterprise Act 2002 in respect of the provisions of—
- (a) the Business Advertisements (Disclosure) Order 1977;
- (b) Part 3 of the Consumer Protection Act 1987;
- (c) Part III of the Consumer Protection (Northern Ireland) Order 1987;
- (d) the Consumer Transactions (Restrictions on Statements) Order 1976;
- (e) the Control of Misleading Advertisements Regulations 1988;
- (f) the Mock Auctions Act 1961;
- (g) section 29 of the Weights and Measures Act 1985;
- (h) Article 22(2) of the Weights and Measures (Northern Ireland) Order 1981.

(2) Notwithstanding the omission of the references to these provisions in the Enterprise Act 2002 (Part 8 Domestic Infringements) Order 2003 by these Regulations an act or omission to which paragraph (1) applies shall continue to be a domestic infringement.

12. Notwithstanding the amendments made by these Regulations to the Enterprise Act 2002 (Part 8 Domestic Infringements) Order 2003 that Order shall continue to apply in relation to the Price Indications (Bureaux de Change) (No 2) Regulations 1992 as it applied before the coming into force of these Regulations.

Enterprise Act 2002 (Part 8 Community Infringements Specified UK Laws) Order 2003

13.—(1) This paragraph applies to an act or omission which immediately before the date on which these Regulations come into force is a Community infringement under section 212 of the Enterprise Act 2002 by contravening the provisions of—
- (a) Council Directive 84/450/EEC of 10 September 1984 relating to the approximation of the laws, regulations and administrative provisions of the Member States concerning misleading advertising;
- (b) the Control of Misleading Advertisements Regulations 1988 except regulation 4A (comparative advertisements); or
- (c) regulation 4 or 5 of the Consumer Transactions (Restrictions on Statements) Order 1976.

(2) Notwithstanding the omission of the references to these provisions in the Enterprise Act 2002 (Part 8 Community Infringements Specified UK Laws) Order 2003 by these Regulations an act or omission to which paragraph (1) applies shall continue to be a Community infringement.

Enterprise Act 2002 (Part 8 Community Infringements Specified UK Laws) Order 2006

14.—(1) This paragraph applies to an act or omission which immediately before the date on which these Regulations come into force is a Community infringement under section 212 of the Enterprise Act 2002 by contravening the provisions of—
- (a) Directive 97/55/EC of the European Parliament and of the Council of 6 October 1997 amending Directive 84/450/EEC concerning misleading advertising so as to include comparative advertising; or
- (b) regulation 4A of the Control of Misleading Advertisements Regulations 1988.

(2) Notwithstanding the omission of the reference to these provisions in the Enterprise Act 2002 (Part 8 Community Infringements Specified UK Laws) Order 2006 by these Regulations an act or omission to which paragraph (1) applies shall continue to be a Community infringement.

Disclosure of information

15.—(1) This paragraph applies in relation to information which immediately before the date on which these Regulations come into force was subject to the provisions of any enactment which permitted the disclosure of information for the purposes of any function under, or proceedings brought under or by virtue of—
- (a) the Control of Misleading Advertisements Regulations 1988; or

(b)   Part 2 of the Fair Trading Act 1973.

(2)   Notwithstanding the repeal of such provisions by these Regulations such disclosure shall continue to be permitted.

[3704]

NOTES
Commencement: 26 May 2008.

(*Sch 4* (*Repeals and Revocations*) *outside the scope of this work.*)

CANCELLATION OF CONTRACTS MADE IN A CONSUMER'S HOME OR PLACE OF WORK ETC REGULATIONS 2008

(SI 2008/1816)

NOTES
Made: 8 July 2008.
Authority: European Communities Act 1972, s 2(2); Consumers, Estate Agents and Redress Act 2007, s 59.
Commencement: 1 October 2008.
These Regulations re-implement Council Directive 85/577/EEC at **[4198]** (originally implemented in the UK by the Consumer Protection (Cancellation of Contracts Concluded away from Business Premises) Regulations 1987, SI 1987/2117 at **[3049]**).

ARRANGEMENT OF REGULATIONS

1   Citation and commencement

These Regulations may be cited as the Cancellation of Contracts made in a Consumer's Home or Place of Work etc Regulations 2008 and shall come into force on 1st October 2008.

[3705]

NOTES
Commencement: 1 October 2008.

2   Interpretation

(1)   In these Regulations:
"the 1974 Act" means the Consumer Credit Act 1974;

33

"cancellable agreement" has the same meaning as in section 189(1) of the 1974 Act;

"cancellation notice" means a notice in writing given by the consumer which indicates that he wishes to cancel the contract;

"cancellation period" means the period of 7 days starting with the date of receipt by the consumer of a notice of the right to cancel;

"consumer" means a natural person who in making a contract to which these Regulations apply is acting for purposes which can be regarded as outside his trade or profession;

"consumer credit agreement" means an agreement between the consumer and any other person by which the other person provides the consumer with credit of any amount;

"credit" includes a cash loan and any other form of financial accommodation, and for this purpose "cash" includes money in any form;

"enforcement authority" means any person mentioned in regulation 21;

"fixed sum credit" has the same meaning as in section 10(1) of the 1974 Act;

"notice of the right to cancel" means a notice given in accordance with regulation 7;

"related credit agreement" means a consumer credit agreement under which fixed sum credit which fully or partly covers the price under a contract which may be cancelled under regulation 7 is granted—

    (i)   by the trader; or

    (ii) by another person, under an arrangement made between that person and the trader;

"solicited visit" has the meaning given in regulation 6(3);

"specified contract" has the meaning given in regulation 9; and

"trader" means a person who, in making a contract to which these Regulations apply, is acting in his commercial or professional capacity and anyone acting in the name or on behalf of a trader.

(2)   Paragraph 8(2) of Schedule 3 has effect for the purposes of paragraphs 7 and 8(1).

[3706]

NOTES

   Commencement: 1 October 2008.

3 Consequential amendments, revocations and saving

Schedule 1 (Consequential Amendments) shall have effect.

[3707]

NOTES

   Commencement: 1 October 2008.

4—(1)   Schedule 2 (Revocations) shall have effect.

(2)   The Consumer Protection (Cancellation of Contracts Concluded away from Business Premises) Regulations 1987 ("the 1987 Regulations") shall continue to have effect in relation to a contract to which they applied before their revocation by these Regulations.

(3)   These Regulations shall not apply to a contract to which the 1987 Regulations applied before their revocation.

[3708]

NOTES

   Commencement: 1 October 2008.

5 Scope of application

These Regulations apply to a contract, including a consumer credit agreement, between a consumer and a trader which is for the supply of goods or services to the consumer by a trader and which is made—

    (a)   during a visit by the trader to the consumer's home or place of work, or to the home of another individual;

    (b)   during an excursion organised by the trader away from his business premises; or

    (c)   after an offer made by the consumer during such a visit or excursion.

[3709]

NOTES

   Commencement: 1 October 2008.

6—(1)   These Regulations do not apply to—

    (a)   any contracts listed in Schedule 3 (Excepted Contracts);

    (b)   a cancellable agreement;

(c)   a consumer credit agreement which may be cancelled by the consumer in accordance with the terms of the agreement conferring upon him similar rights as if the agreement were a cancellable agreement;

[(ca) a consumer credit agreement regulated under the 1974 Act to which the right of withdrawal applies under section 66A of that Act;] or

(d)   a contract made during a solicited visit or a contract made after an offer made by a consumer during a solicited visit where the contract is—

    (i)   a regulated mortgage, home purchase plan or home reversion plan if the making or performance of such a contract constitutes a regulated activity for the purposes of the Financial Services and Markets Act 2000;

    (ii)   a consumer credit agreement secured on land which is—

        (aa)   regulated under the 1974 Act; or

        (bb)   to the extent that it is not regulated under the 1974 Act, exempt under that Act; or

    (iii) any other consumer credit agreement regulated under the 1974 Act.

(2)   Where any agreement referred to in paragraph (1)(b), *(c) or (d)(iii)* [(c), (ca) or (d)(iii)] is a related credit agreement the provisions of regulations 11 and 12 shall apply to the cancellation of that agreement.

(3)   A solicited visit means a visit by a trader, whether or not he is the trader who supplies the goods or services, to a consumer's home or place of work or to the home of another individual, which is made at the express request of the consumer but does not include—

(a)   a visit by a trader which is made after he, or a person acting in his name or on his behalf—

    (i)   telephones the consumer (otherwise than at the consumer's express request) and indicates during the course of the telephone call (either expressly or by implication) that he, or the trader in whose name or on whose behalf he is acting, is willing to visit the consumer; or

    (ii)   visits the consumer (otherwise than at the consumer's express request) and indicates during the course of that visit (either expressly or by implication) that he, or the trader in whose name or on whose behalf he is acting, is willing to make a subsequent visit to the consumer; or

(b)   a visit during which the contract which is made relates to goods and services other than those concerning which the consumer requested the visit of the trader, provided that when the visit was requested the consumer did not know, or could not reasonably have known, that the supply of such goods or services formed part of the trader's commercial or professional activities.

[3710]

NOTES

Commencement: 1 October 2008.

Para (1): sub-para (ca) inserted by the Consumer Credit (EU Directive) Regulations 2010, SI 2010/1010, regs 94, 95(a), as from 1 February 2011, with effect in relation to certain agreements before that date, as provided for in regs 101, 101A of the 2010 Regulations at **[3942]**, **[3942A]**.

Para (2): words in italics substituted by subsequent words in square brackets by SI 2010/1010, regs 94, 95(b), as from 1 February 2011, with effect in relation to certain agreements before that date, as provided for in regs 101, 101A of the 2010 Regulations at **[3942]**, **[3942A]**.

---

7   Right to cancel a contract to which these Regulations apply

(1)   A consumer has the right to cancel a contract to which these Regulations apply within the cancellation period.

(2)   The trader must give the consumer a written notice of his right to cancel the contract and such notice must be given at the time the contract is made except in the case of a contract to which regulation 5(c) applies in which case the notice must be given at the time the offer is made by the consumer.

(3)   The notice must—

    (a)   be dated;

    (b)   indicate the right of the consumer to cancel the contract within the cancellation period;

    (c)   be easily legible;

    (d)   contain—

        (i)   the information set out in Part I of Schedule 4; and

        (ii)   a cancellation form in the form set out in Part II of that Schedule provided as a detachable slip and completed by or on behalf of the trader in accordance with the notes; and

    (e)   indicate if applicable—

       (i)   that the consumer may be required to pay for the goods or services supplied if the performance of the contract has begun with his written agreement before the end of the cancellation period;

      (ii)   that a related credit agreement will be automatically cancelled if the contract for goods or services is cancelled.

(4)   Where the contract is wholly or partly in writing the notice must be incorporated in the same document.

(5)   If incorporated in the contract or another document the notice of the right to cancel must—

    (a)   be set out in a separate box with the heading "Notice of the Right to Cancel"; and

    (b)   have as much prominence as any other information in the contract or document apart from the heading and the names of the parties to the contract and any information inserted in handwriting.

(6)   A contract to which these Regulations apply shall not be enforceable against the consumer unless the trader has given the consumer a notice of the right to cancel and the information required in accordance with this regulation.

[3711]

NOTES
Commencement: 1 October 2008.

8   Exercise of the right to cancel a contract

(1)   If the consumer serves a cancellation notice within the cancellation period then the contract is cancelled.

(2)   A contract which is cancelled shall be treated as if it had never been entered into by the consumer except where these Regulations provide otherwise.

(3)   The cancellation notice must indicate the intention of the consumer to cancel the contract and does not need to follow the form of cancellation notice set out in Part II of Schedule 4.

(4)   The cancellation notice must be served on the trader or another person specified in the notice of the right to cancel as a person to whom the cancellation notice may be given.

(5)   A cancellation notice sent by post is taken to have been served at the time of posting, whether or not it is actually received.

(6)   Where a cancellation notice is sent by electronic mail it is taken to have been served on the day on which it is sent.

[3712]

NOTES
Commencement: 1 October 2008.

9   Cancellation of specified contracts commenced before expiry of the right to cancel

(1)   Where the consumer enters into a specified contract and he wishes the performance of the contract to begin before the end of the cancellation period, he must request this in writing.

(2)   Where the consumer cancels a specified contract in accordance with regulation 8 he shall be under a duty to pay in accordance with the reasonable requirements of the cancelled contract for goods or services that were supplied before the cancellation.

(3)   If the consumer fails to provide the request in writing referred to in paragraph (1) then—

    (a)   the trader is not obliged to begin performance of the specified contract before the end of the cancellation period; and

    (b)   the consumer is not bound by the duty referred to in paragraph (2) if he cancels the contract in accordance with regulation 8.

(4)   For the purposes of this regulation and regulation 13, a "specified contact" means a contract for any of the following—

    (a)   the supply of newspapers, periodicals or magazines;

    (b)   advertising in any medium;

    (c)   the supply of goods the price of which is dependent on fluctuations in the financial markets which cannot be controlled by the trader;

    (d)   the supply of goods to meet an emergency;

    (e)   the supply of goods made to a customer's specifications or clearly personalised and any services in connection with the provision of such goods;

    (f)   the supply of perishable goods;

    (g)   the supply of goods which by their nature are consumed by use and which, before the cancellation, were so consumed;

    (h)   the supply of goods which, before the cancellation, had become incorporated in any land or thing not comprised in the cancelled contract;

PART 2
STATUTORY INSTRUMENTS

(i)   the supply of goods or services relating to a funeral; or
(j)   the supply of services of any other kind.

[3713]

NOTES
Commencement: 1 October 2008.

10   Recovery of money paid by consumer

(1)   On the cancellation of a contract under regulation 8 any sum paid by or on behalf of the consumer in respect of the contract shall become repayable except where these Regulations provide otherwise.

(2)   If the consumer or any person on his behalf is in possession of any goods under the terms of the cancelled contract then he shall have a lien on them for any sum repayable to him under paragraph (1).

(3)   Where any security has been provided in relation to the cancelled contract, the security shall be treated as never having had effect for that purpose and the trader must immediately return any property lodged with him solely as security for the purposes of the cancelled contract.

[3714]

NOTES
Commencement: 1 October 2008.

11   Automatic cancellation of related credit agreement

(1)   A cancellation notice which cancels a contract for goods or services shall have the effect of cancelling any related credit agreement.

(2)   Subject to paragraphs (3) and (4), where a related credit agreement has been cancelled under paragraph (1)—
(a)   the trader must, if he is not the same person as the creditor under that agreement, immediately on receipt of the cancellation notice inform the creditor that the notice has been given;
(b)   any sum paid by or on behalf of the consumer in relation to the credit agreement must be reimbursed, except for any sum which would have to be paid under sub-paragraph (c);
(c)   the agreement shall continue in force so far as it relates to repayment of the credit and payment of interest in accordance with regulation 12, but shall otherwise cease to be enforceable; and
(d)   any security provided under the related credit agreement shall be treated as never having had effect for that purpose and the creditor must immediately return any property lodged with him solely as security for the purposes of the related credit agreement.

(3)   Where a related credit agreement is a cancellable agreement—
(a)   its cancellation under paragraph (1) shall take effect as if a notice of cancellation within the meaning of the 1974 Act had been served;
(b)   that Act shall apply in respect of the consequences of such cancellation;
(c)   paragraph (2)(b) to (d) and regulation 12 shall not apply in respect of its cancellation; and
(d)   regulations 13 and 14 shall not apply in respect of the cancellation of the related contract for goods or services.

(4)   Where a related credit agreement of a kind referred to in regulation 6(1)(c) is cancelled under paragraph (1)—
(a)   paragraph (2)(b) to (d) and regulation 12 shall not apply in respect of its cancellation; and
(b)   regulations 13 and 14 shall not apply in respect of the cancellation of the related contract for goods or services.

(5)   Where a related credit agreement of a kind referred to in *regulation 6(1)(d)(iii)* [regulation 6(1)(ca) or 6(1)(d)(iii)] is cancelled under paragraph (1)—
(a)   the provisions of this regulation and regulation 12 shall apply in respect of its cancellation; and
(b)   the provisions of regulations 13 and 14 shall apply in respect of the cancellation of the related contract for goods or services.

(6)   For the purposes of this regulation and regulation 12 "creditor" is the person who grants credit under a related credit agreement.

[3715]

NOTES
Commencement: 1 October 2008.

Para (5): words in italics substituted by subsequent words in square brackets by the Consumer Credit (EU Directive) Regulations 2010, SI 2010/1010, regs 94, 96, as from 1 February 2011, with effect in relation to certain agreements before that date, as provided for in regs 101, 101A of the 2010 Regulations at **[3942]**, **[3942A]**.

12 Repayment of credit and interest

(1)   Where—

(a)   a contract under which credit is provided to the consumer is cancelled under regulation 8; or

(b)   a related credit agreement (other than a cancellable agreement or an agreement of a kind referred to in regulation 6(1)(c)) is cancelled as a result of the cancellation of a contract for goods or services,

the contract or agreement shall continue in force so far as it relates to repayment of the credit and payment of interest.

(2)   If, following the cancellation of a contract or related credit agreement to which paragraph (1) applies, the consumer repays the whole or a portion of the credit—

(a)   before the expiry of one month following service of the cancellation notice; or

(b)   in the case of a credit repayable by instalments, before the date on which the first instalment is due,

no interest shall be payable on the amount repaid.

(3)   If the whole of a credit repayable by instalments is not repaid on or before the date specified in paragraph (2)(b), the consumer shall not be liable to repay any of the credit except on receipt of a request in writing signed by the trader stating the amounts of the remaining instalments (recalculated by the trader as nearly as may be in accordance with the contract and without extending the repayment period), but excluding any sum other than principal and interest.

(4)   Repayment of a credit, or payment of interest, under a cancelled contract or related credit agreement shall be treated as duly made if it is made to any person on whom, under regulation 8(4), a cancellation notice could have been served.

(5)   Where any security has been provided in relation to the contract or consumer credit agreement, the duty imposed on the consumer by this regulation shall not be enforceable before the trader or creditor has discharged any duty imposed on him by regulation 10(3) or 11(2)(d) respectively.

[3716]

NOTES

Commencement: 1 October 2008.

13 Return of goods by consumer after cancellation

(1)   A consumer who has acquired possession of any goods by virtue of the contract shall on the cancellation of that contract be under a duty, subject to any lien, to restore the goods to the trader and meanwhile to retain possession of the goods and take reasonable care of them.

(2)   The consumer shall not be under a duty to restore goods supplied under a specified contract in circumstances where—

(a)   he is required to pay, in accordance with the reasonable requirements of the cancelled contract, for the supply of such goods before cancellation; or

(b)   the trader has begun performance of the contract before the end of the cancellation period without a prior request in writing by the consumer.

(3)   The consumer shall not be under any duty to deliver the goods except at his own premises and following a request in writing signed by the trader and served on the consumer either before, or at the time when, the goods are collected from those premises.

(4)   If the consumer—

(a)   delivers the goods (whether at his own premises or elsewhere) to any person on whom, under regulation 8(4), a cancellation notice could have been served; or

(b)   sends the goods at his own expense to such a person,

he shall be discharged from any duty to retain possession of the goods or restore them to the trader.

(5)   Where the consumer delivers the goods as mentioned in paragraph (4)(a), his obligation to take care of the goods shall cease; and if he send the goods as mentioned in paragraph (4)(b), he shall be under a duty to take reasonable care to see that they are received by the trader and not damaged in transit, but in other respects his duty to take care of the goods shall cease.

(6)   Where, at any time during the period of 21 days following the cancellation, the consumer receives such a request as is mentioned in paragraph (3) and unreasonably refuses or unreasonably fails to comply with it, his duty to retain possession and take reasonable care of the goods shall

continue until he delivers or sends the goods as mentioned in paragraph (4); but if within that period he does not receive such a request his duty to take reasonable care of the goods shall cease at the end of that period.

(7) Where any security has been provided in relation to the cancelled contract, the duty imposed on the consumer to restore goods shall not be enforceable before the trader has discharged any duty imposed on him by regulation 10(3).

(8) Breach of a duty imposed on a consumer by this regulation is actionable as a breach of statutory duty.

[3717]

NOTES

Commencement: 1 October 2008.

14 Goods given in part-exchange

(1) This regulation applies on the cancellation of a contract where the trader agreed to take goods in part-exchange (the "part-exchange goods") and those goods have been delivered to him.

(2) Unless, before the end of the period of ten days beginning with the date of cancellation, the part-exchange goods are returned to the consumer in a condition substantially as good as when they were delivered to the trader, the consumer shall be entitled to recover from the trader a sum equal to the part-exchange allowance.

(3) During the period of ten days beginning with the date of cancellation, the consumer, if he is in possession of goods to which the cancelled contract relates, shall have a lien on them for—

   (a) delivery of the part-exchange goods in a condition substantially as good as when they were delivered to the trader; or

   (b) a sum equal to the part-exchange allowance,

and if the lien continues to the end of that period it shall thereafter subsist only as a lien for a sum equal to the part-exchange allowance.

(4) In this regulation the part-exchange allowance means the sum agreed as such in the cancelled contract, or if no such sum was agreed, such sum as it would have been reasonable to allow in respect of the part-exchange goods if no notice of cancellation had been served.

[3718]

NOTES

Commencement: 1 October 2008.

15 No contracting-out of contracts to which these Regulations apply

(1) A term contained in a contract is void if, and to the extent that, it is inconsistent with a provision for the protection of the consumer contained in these Regulations.

(2) Where a provision of these Regulations specifies the duty or liability of the consumer in certain circumstances, a term contained in a contract is inconsistent with that provision if it purports to impose, directly or indirectly, an additional or different duty or liability on the consumer in those circumstances.

[3719]

NOTES

Commencement: 1 October 2008.

16 Service of documents

(1) A document to be served under these Regulations on a person may be so served—

   (a) by delivering it to him, or by leaving it at his proper address or by sending it to him at that address;

   (b) if the person is a body corporate, by serving it in accordance with sub-paragraph (a) on the secretary or clerk of that body;

   (c) if the person is a partnership, by serving it in accordance with sub-paragraph (a) on a partner or on a person having the control or management of the partnership business; and

   (d) if the person is an unincorporated body, by serving it in accordance with sub-paragraph (a) on a person having control or management of that body.

(2) For the purposes of paragraph (1), the proper address of any person on whom a document is to be served under these Regulations is his last known address except that—

   (a) in the case of service on a body corporate or its secretary or clerk, it is the address of the registered or principal office of the body corporate in the United Kingdom; and

(b) in the case of service on a partnership or partner or person having the control or management of a partnership business, it is the partnership's principal place of business in the United Kingdom.

(3) A person's electronic mail address may also be his proper address for the purposes of paragraph (1).

[3720]

Enforcement

17 Offence relating to the failure to give notice of the right to cancel

(1) A trader is guilty of an offence if he enters into a contract to which these Regulations apply but fails to give the consumer a notice of the right to cancel in accordance with regulation 7.

(2) A person who is guilty of an offence under paragraph (1) shall be liable on summary conviction to a fine not exceeding level 5 on the standard scale.

[3721]

18 Defence of due diligence

(1) In any proceedings against a person for an offence under regulation 17 it is a defence for that person to prove—
    (a) that the commission of the offence was due to—
        (i) the act or default of another, or
        (ii) reliance on information given by another, and
    (b) that he took all reasonable precautions and exercised all due diligence to avoid the commission of such an offence by himself or any person under his control.

(2) A person shall not be entitled to rely on the defence provided by paragraph (1) without leave of the court unless—
    (a) he has served on the prosecutor a notice in writing giving such information identifying or assisting in the identification of that other person as was in his possession; and
    (b) the notice is served on the prosecutor not less than seven clear days before the hearing of the proceedings or, in Scotland, the diet of trial.

[3722]

19 Liability of persons other than the principal offender

Where the commission by a person of an offence under regulation 17 is due to the act or default of another person, that other person is guilty of the offence and may be proceeded against and punished whether or not proceedings are taken against the first person.

[3723]

20 Offences committed by bodies of persons

(1) Where an offence under regulation 17 committed by a body corporate is proved—
    (a) to have been committed with the consent or connivance of an officer of the body corporate or
    (b) to be attributable to any neglect on his part,
the officer, as well as the body corporate shall be guilty of the offence and liable to be proceeded against and punished accordingly.

(2) In paragraph (1) a reference to an officer of a body corporate includes a reference to—
    (a) a director, manager, secretary or other similar officer; and
    (b) a person purporting to act as a director, manager, secretary or other similar officer.

(3) Where an offence under regulation 17 committed in Scotland by a Scottish partnership is proved—
    (a) to have been committed with the consent or connivance of a partner; or
    (b) to be attributable to any neglect on his part,

that partner, as well as the partnership shall be guilty of the offence and liable to be proceeded against and punished accordingly.

(4)   In paragraph (3) a reference to a partner includes a person purporting to act as a partner.

[3724]

NOTES
Commencement: 1 October 2008.

21 Duty to enforce

(1)   Subject to paragraphs (2) and (3)—
    (a)   it shall be the duty of every weights and measures authority in Great Britain to enforce regulation 17 within its area; and
    (b)   it shall be the duty of the Department of Enterprise Trade and Investment in Northern Ireland to enforce regulation 17 within Northern Ireland.

(2)   No proceedings for an offence under these Regulations may be instituted in England and Wales except by or on behalf of an enforcement authority.

(3)   Nothing in paragraph (1) shall authorise any weights and measures authority to bring proceedings in Scotland for an offence.

[3725]

NOTES
Commencement: 1 October 2008.

22 Powers of investigation

(1)   If a duly authorised officer of an enforcement authority has reasonable grounds for suspecting that an offence has been committed under regulation 17, he may require a person carrying on or employed in a business to produce any document relating to the business, and take copies of it or any entry in it for the purposes of ascertaining whether such an offence has been committed.

(2)   If the officer has reasonable grounds for believing that any documents may be required as evidence in proceedings for such an offence, he may seize and detain them and shall, if he does so, inform the person from whom they are seized.

(3)   In this regulation "document" includes information recorded in any form.

(4)   The reference in paragraph (1) to production of documents is, in the case of a document which contains information recorded otherwise than in a legible form, a reference to the production of a copy of the information in a legible form.

(5)   An officer seeking to exercise a power under this regulation must do so only at a reasonable hour and on production (if required) of his identification and authority.

(6)   Nothing in this regulation requires a person to produce, or authorises the taking from a person of, a document which the other person would be entitled to refuse to produce in proceedings in the High Court on the grounds of legal professional privilege or (in Scotland) in the Court of Session on the grounds of confidentiality of communications.

(7)   In paragraph (6) "communications" means—
    (a)   communications between a professional legal adviser and his client; or
    (b)   communications made in connection with, or in contemplation of legal proceedings and for the purpose of those proceedings.

[3726]

NOTES
Commencement: 1 October 2008.

23 Obstruction of authorised officers

(1)   A person is guilty of an offence if he—
    (a)   intentionally obstructs an officer of an enforcement authority acting in pursuance of his functions under these Regulations;
    (b)   without reasonable cause fails to comply with any requirement properly made of him by such an officer under regulation 22; or
    (c)   without reasonable cause fails to give such an officer any other assistance or information which he may reasonably require of him for the purpose of the performance of his functions under these Regulations.

(2)   A person is guilty of an offence if, in giving any information which is required of him under paragraph (1)(c), he makes any statement which he knows to be false in a material particular.

(3)   A person guilty of an offence under paragraph (1) or (2) shall be liable on summary conviction to a fine not exceeding level 3 on the standard scale.

[3727]

NOTES
Commencement: 1 October 2008.

24   Nothing in regulation 22 or 23 shall be construed as requiring a person to answer any question or give any information if to do so might incriminate him.

[3728]

NOTES
Commencement: 1 October 2008.

(Sch 1 amends the Consumer Credit Act 1974, s 74 at **[720]** *and amends other provisions outside the scope of this work; Sch 2 revokes the Consumer Protection (Cancellation of Contracts Concluded away from Business Premises) Regulations 1987, SI 1987/2117 at* **[3049]** *and revokes other provisions outside the scope of this work.)*

SCHEDULE 3
EXCEPTED CONTRACTS

Regulations 2(2) and 6(1)(a)

1.   A contract for the construction, sale or rental of immovable property or a contract concerning other rights relating to immovable property other than—
    (a)   a contract for the construction of extensions, patios, conservatories or driveways;
    (b)   a contract for the supply of goods and their incorporation in immovable property; and
    (c)   a contract for the repair, refurbishment or improvement of immovable property.

2.   A contract for the supply of foodstuffs or beverages or other goods intended for current consumption in the household and supplied by a regular roundsman.

3.   A contract for the supply of goods or services provided that each of the following conditions is met:
    (a)   the contract is concluded on the basis of a trader's catalogue which the consumer has a proper opportunity of reading in the absence of the trader's representative;
    (b)   there is intended to be continuity of contact between the trader's representative and the consumer in relation to that or any subsequent transaction; and
    (c)   both the catalogue and the contract contain a prominent notice informing the consumer of his rights to return goods to the supplier within a period of not less than seven days of receipt or otherwise to cancel the contract within that period without obligation of any kind other than to take reasonable care of the goods.

4.   A contract of insurance.

5.   Any contract under which credit within the meaning of the 1974 Act is provided not exceeding £35 other than a hire purchase or conditional sale agreement.

6.   Any contract not falling within paragraph 5 under which the total payments to be made by the consumer do not exceed £35.

7.   Any agreement the making or performance of which by either party constitutes a relevant regulated activity.

8.—(1)   For the purposes of paragraph 7—
    (a)   "a relevant regulated activity" means an activity of the following kind—
        (i)   dealing in investments, as principal or as agent;
        (ii)   arranging deals in investments;
        (iii)   operating a multilateral trading facility;
        (iv)   managing investments;
        (v)   safeguarding and administering investments;
        (vi)   establishing, operating or winding up a collective investment scheme; and
    (b)   for these purposes "investment" means—
        (i)   shares;
        (ii)   instruments creating or acknowledging indebtedness;
        (iii)   instruments giving entitlement to investments
        (iv)   certificates representing securities;
        (v)   units in a collective investment scheme;
        (vi)   options;
        (vii)   futures;
        (viii)   contracts for differences; and
        (ix)   rights to or interests in investments.

(2)   Paragraph 7 and this paragraph must be read with—

(a) section 22 of the Financial Services and Markets Act 2000;

(b) any relevant order under that section; and

(c) Schedule 2 to that Act,

but any restriction on or exclusion from the meaning of a regulated activity for the purposes of paragraph 7 which arises from the identity of the person carrying on such activity is to be disregarded.

[3729]

NOTES

Commencement: 1 October 2008.

SCHEDULE 4
NOTICE OF THE RIGHT TO CANCEL

Regulation 7(3)

PART I
INFORMATION TO BE CONTAINED IN NOTICE OF THE RIGHT TO CANCEL

1. The identity of the trader including trading name if any.

2. The trader's reference number, code or other details to enable the contract or offer to be identified.

3. A statement that the consumer has a right to cancel the contract if he wishes and that this right can be exercised by delivering, or sending (including by electronic mail) a cancellation notice to the person mentioned in the next paragraph at any time within the period of 7 days starting with the day of receipt of a notice in writing of the right to cancel the contract.

4. The name and address, (including any electronic mail address as well as the postal address), of a person to whom a cancellation notice may be given.

5. A statement that notice of cancellation is deemed to be served as soon as it is posted or sent to a trader or in the case of an electronic communication from the day it is sent to the trader.

6. A statement that the consumer can use the cancellation form provided if he wishes.

[3730]

NOTES

Commencement: 1 October 2008.

PART II
CANCELLATION NOTICE TO BE INCLUDED IN NOTICE OF THE RIGHT TO CANCEL

If you wish to cancel the contract you MUST DO SO IN WRITING and deliver personally or send (which may be by electronic mail) this to the person named below. You may use this form if you want to but you do not have to.

(Complete, detach and return this form ONLY IF YOU WISH TO CANCEL THE CONTRACT).

To:................[trader to insert name and address of person to whom notice may be given.]

I/We (delete as appropriate) hereby give notice that I/we (delete as appropriate) wish to cancel my/our (delete as appropriate) contract ....[trader to insert reference number, code and other details to enable the contract or offer to be identified. He may also insert the name and address of the consumer.]

Signed

Name and Address

Date

[3731]

NOTES

Commencement: 1 October 2008.

PAYMENT SERVICES REGULATIONS 2009

(SI 2009/209)

NOTES
Made: 9 February 2009.
Authority: European Communities Act 1972, s 2(2).
Commencement: see reg 1(2) at **[3732]**.

ARRANGEMENT OF REGULATIONS

PART 1
INTRODUCTORY PROVISIONS

PART 2
REGISTRATION

The register

Authorisation as a payment institution

Registration as a small payment institution

Common provisions

PART 3
AUTHORISED PAYMENT INSTITUTIONS

Exercise of passport rights

PART 4
PROVISIONS APPLICABLE TO AUTHORISED PAYMENT INSTITUTIONS
AND SMALL PAYMENT INSTITUTIONS

PART 2
STATUTORY INSTRUMENTS

PART 1
INTRODUCTORY PROVISIONS

1   Citation and commencement

(1)   These Regulations may be cited as the Payment Services Regulations 2009.

(2)   These Regulations come into force—
   (a)   on 2nd March 2009 for the purposes of regulations 25, 80, 92 to 94, 95 in respect of paragraphs 5 and 10 of Schedule 5, 119 and 126 in respect of paragraphs 1 and 6(g) of Schedule 6;
   (b)   on 1st May 2009 for the purposes of—
      (i)   enabling applications for authorisation as a payment institution and the variation of an authorisation to be made under regulation 5 and the Authority to determine such applications in accordance with regulations 6 to 9;
      (ii)   enabling applications for registration as a small payment institution and the variation of a registration to be made under regulation 12 and the Authority to determine such applications in accordance with regulation 13 and regulations 7 to 9 (as applied by regulation 14);
      (iii)   enabling applications for an agent to be included on the register under regulation 29 and the Authority to determine such applications in accordance with that regulation;
      (iv)   enabling the Authority to give directions as to the manner in which an application under regulation 5(1) or (2), 12(1) or (2) or 29(3) is to be made and enabling the Authority to require the applicant to provide further information in accordance with regulation 5(4), 12(4) or 29(3)(a)(iv), as the case may be;
      (v)   enabling the Authority to cancel an authorisation or registration or vary an authorisation or registration on its own initiative in accordance with regulation 10 or 11 (as applied, in the case of a registration, by regulation 14);
      (vi)   requiring a person who has made an application under regulation 5(1) or (2) or 12(1) or (2) to provide information to the Authority in accordance with regulation 16 and enabling the Authority to give directions under that regulation;
      (vii)   enabling a person to make a reference to the [Upper Tribunal] under regulation 9(9), 10(4), 11(5), 24(4) or 29(11);
      (viii)   enabling an applicant for authorisation as a payment institution to give the Authority a notice of intention under regulation 23(1) and the Authority to give

              directions as to the manner in which such a notice is to be given and to inform the host state competent authority in accordance with regulation 23(2);

  (ix) enabling the Authority to decide whether to register an EEA branch, or to cancel such a registration, under regulation 24(1);

  (x) enabling the Authority to give directions under regulation 82 to a person whose application under regulation 5(1) or 12(1) has been granted before 1st November 2009 in respect of—

    (aa) its provision as from that date of payment services; and

    (bb) its compliance as from that date with requirements imposed by or under Parts 2 to 6 of these Regulations;

  (xi) enabling the Authority to give directions under paragraph 7, 11, 12 or 16(3) of Schedule 3 to a person whose application under regulation 5(1) has been granted before 1st November 2009;

  (xii) requiring a person whose application under regulation 5(1), 12(1) or 29(3) has been granted before 1st November 2009 to provide information to the Authority in accordance with regulation 32 and enabling the Authority to give directions under that regulation;

  (xiii) regulations 95 in respect of paragraphs 2 and 7 to 9 of Schedule 5, 114 to 118, and 121, 124 and 125; and

  (c) for all other purposes on 1st November 2009.

                                                                  [3732]

NOTES

Commencement: 2 March 2009 (for the purposes specified in reg 1(2)(a)), 1 May 2009 (for the purposes specified in reg 1(2)(b)), and 1 November 2009 (otherwise). See above.

Para (2): words in square brackets in sub-para (b)(vii) substituted by the Transfer of Tribunal Functions Order 2010, SI 2010/22, art 5(2), Sch 3, paras 177, 178, subject to transitional provisions and savings in Sch 5 thereto.

2   Interpretation

  (1) In these Regulations—

"the 2000 Act" means the Financial Services and Markets Act 2000;

"agent" means a person who acts on behalf of an authorised payment institution or a small payment institution in the provision of payment services;

"authorised payment institution" means—

  (a) a person included by the Authority in the register as an authorised payment institution pursuant to regulation 4(1)(a); or

  (b) a person deemed to have been granted authorisation by the Authority by virtue of regulation 121;

"the Authority" means the Financial Services Authority;

"the banking consolidation directive" means Directive 2006/48/EC of the European Parliament and of the Council of 14th June 2006 relating to the taking up and pursuit of the business of credit institutions;

"branch" means a place of business of an authorised payment institution, a small payment institution, or an EEA authorised payment institution, other than its head office, which forms a legally dependent part of the institution and which carries out directly all or some of the transactions inherent in its business; and, for the purposes of these Regulations, all places of business set up in the same EEA State other than the United Kingdom by an authorised payment institution are to be regarded as a single branch;

"business day" means any day on which the relevant payment service provider is open for business as required for the execution of a payment transaction;

"charity" means a body whose annual income is less than £1 million and is—

  (c) in England and Wales, a charity as defined by section 1(1) of the Charities Act 2006;

  (d) in Scotland, a charity as defined by section 106 of the Charities and Trustee Investment (Scotland) Act 2005;

  (e) in Northern Ireland, a charity as defined by section 1(1) of the Charities Act (Northern Ireland) 2008 or, until that section comes into force, a body which is recognised as a charity for tax purposes by Her Majesty's Revenue and Customs;

"the Commissioners" means the Commissioners for Her Majesty's Revenue and Customs;

"consumer" means an individual who, in contracts for payment services to which these Regulations apply, is acting for purposes other than a trade, business or profession;

"credit institution" has the meaning given in Article 4(1)(a) of the banking consolidation directive;

"direct debit" means a payment service for debiting the payer's payment account where a payment transaction is initiated by the payee on the basis of consent given by the payer to the payee, to the payee's payment service provider or to the payer's own payment service provider;

"durable medium" means any instrument which enables the payment service user to store information addressed personally to them in a way accessible for future reference for a period of time adequate for the purposes of the information and which allows the unchanged reproduction of the information stored;

"the EEA" means the European Economic Area;

"EEA agent" means an agent through which an authorised payment institution, in the exercise of its passport rights, provides payment services in an EEA State other than the United Kingdom;

"EEA authorised payment institution" means a person authorised in an EEA State other than the United Kingdom to provide payment services in accordance with the payment services directive;

"EEA branch" means a branch established by an authorised payment institution, in the exercise of its passport rights, to carry out payment services in an EEA State other than the United Kingdom;

"the electronic money directive" means Directive 2000/46/EC of the European Parliament and of the Council of 18th September 2000 on the taking up, pursuit and prudential supervision of the business of electronic money institutions;

"electronic money institution" has the meaning given in Article 1(3)(a) of the electronic money directive;

"framework contract" means a contract for payment services which governs the future execution of individual and successive payment transactions and which may contain the obligation and conditions for setting up a payment account;

"funds" means banknotes and coins, scriptural money, and electronic money as defined in Article 1(3)(b) of the electronic money directive;

"group" means a group of undertakings which consists of a parent undertaking, its subsidiary undertakings and the entities in which the parent undertaking or its subsidiary undertakings have a holding, as well as undertakings linked to each other by a relationship referred to in Article 12(1) of the Seventh Council Directive 83/349/EEC of 13th June 1983 based on Article 54(3)(g) of the Treaty on consolidated accounts;

"home state competent authority" means the competent authority designated in accordance with Article 20 of the payment services directive as being responsible for the authorisation and prudential supervision of an EEA authorised payment institution which is exercising (or intends to exercise) its passport rights in the United Kingdom;

"host state competent authority" means the competent authority designated in accordance with Article 20 of the payment services directive in an EEA State in which an authorised payment institution exercises (or intends to exercise) its passport rights;

"means of distance communication" means any means which, without the simultaneous physical presence of the payment service provider and the payment service user, may be used for the conclusion of a contract for payment services between those parties;

"micro-enterprise" means an enterprise which, at the time at which the contract for payment services is entered into, is an enterprise as defined in Article 1 and Article 2(1) and (3) of the Annex to Recommendation 2003/361/EC;

"the money laundering directive" means Directive 2005/60/EC of the European Parliament and of the Council of 26th October 2005 on the prevention of the use of the financial system for the purpose of money laundering and terrorist financing;

"money remittance" means a service for the transmission of money (or any representation of monetary value), without any payment accounts being created in the name of the payer or the payee, where—

    (a)   funds are received from a payer for the sole purpose of transferring a corresponding amount to a payee or to another payment service provider acting on behalf of the payee; or

    (b)   funds are received on behalf of, and made available to, the payee;

"notice" means a notice in writing;

"the OFT" means the Office of Fair Trading;

"parent undertaking" has the same meaning as in the Companies Acts (see section 1162 of, and Schedule 7 to, the Companies Act 2006);

"passport right" (except for the purposes of regulation 26(1)) means the entitlement of a person to establish a branch or provide services in an EEA State other than that in which they are authorised to provide payment services—

    (a)   in accordance with the Treaty establishing the European Community as applied in the EEA; and

    (b)   subject to the conditions of the payment services directive;

"payee" means a person who is the intended recipient of funds which have been the subject of a payment transaction;

"payer" means—

    (a)   a person who holds a payment account and initiates, or consents to the initiation of, a payment order from that payment account; or

    (b)   where there is no payment account, a person who gives a payment order;

"payment account" means an account held in the name of one or more payment service users which is used for the execution of payment transactions;

"payment instrument" means any—

    (a)   personalised device; or

    (b)   personalised set of procedures agreed between the payment service user and the payment service provider,

used by the payment service user in order to initiate a payment order;

"payment order" means any instruction by—

    (a)   a payer; or

    (b)   a payee,

to their respective payment service provider requesting the execution of a payment transaction;

"payment services" means any of the activities specified in Part 1 of Schedule 1 when carried out as a regular occupation or business activity, other than any of the activities specified in Part 2 of that Schedule;

"payment services directive" means Directive 2007/64/EC of the European Parliament and of the Council of 13th November 2007 on payment services in the internal market;

"payment service provider" means any of the following persons when they carry out payment services—

    (a)   authorised payment institutions;

    (b)   small payment institutions;

    (c)   EEA authorised payment institutions;

    (d)   credit institutions;

    (e)   electronic money institutions;

    (f)   the Post Office Limited;

    (g)   the Bank of England, the European Central Bank and the national central banks of EEA States other than the United Kingdom, other than when acting in their capacity as a monetary authority or carrying out other functions of a public nature; and

    (h)   government departments and local authorities, other than when carrying out functions of a public nature;

"payment service user" means a person when making use of a payment service in the capacity of either payer or payee, or both;

"payment system" means a funds transfer system with formal and standardised arrangements and common rules for the processing, clearing and settlement of payment transactions;

"payment transaction" means an act, initiated by the payer or payee, of placing, transferring or withdrawing funds, irrespective of any underlying obligations between the payer and payee;

"qualifying holding" has the meaning given in article 4(11) of the banking consolidation directive;

"reference exchange rate" means the exchange rate which is used as the basis to calculate any currency exchange and which is made available by the payment service provider or comes from a publicly available source;

"reference interest rate" means the interest rate which is used as the basis for calculating any interest to be applied and which comes from a publicly available source which can be verified by both parties to a contract for payment services;

"the register" means the register maintained by the Authority under regulation 4;

"regulated agreement" has the meaning given by section 189(1) of the Consumer Credit Act 1974 (definitions);

"single payment service contract" means a contract for a single payment transaction not covered by a framework contract;

"small payment institution" means a person included by the Authority in the register pursuant to regulation 4(1)(b);

"subsidiary undertaking" has the same meaning as in the Companies Acts (see section 1162 of, and Schedule 7 to, the Companies Act 2006);

...

"unique identifier" means a combination of letters, numbers or symbols specified to the payment service user by the payment service provider and to be provided by the payment service user in relation to a payment transaction in order to identify unambiguously one or both of—

    (a)   the other payment service user who is a party to the payment transaction;

    (b)   the other payment service user's payment account;

"value date" means a reference time used by a payment service provider for the calculation of interest on the funds debited from or credited to a payment account.

(2)   In these Regulations references to amounts in euro include references to equivalent amounts in another currency.

(3)   Unless otherwise defined, expressions used in these Regulations which are also used in the payment services directive have the same meaning as in that directive.

(4)   Expressions used in these Regulations and in a modification to a provision in primary or secondary legislation applied by these Regulations have the same meaning as in these Regulations.

[3733]

NOTES

Commencement: see reg 1 at **[3732]**.

Para (1): definition "the Tribunal" (omitted) revoked by the Transfer of Tribunal Functions Order 2010, SI 2010/22, art 5(2), Sch 3, paras 177, 179, subject to transitional provisions and savings in Sch 5 thereto.

3 Exemption for certain bodies

(1)   Subject to paragraph (2) and regulation 4(1)(d), these Regulations do not apply to the following persons—

    (a)   credit unions;

    (b)   municipal banks; and

    (c)   the National Savings Bank.

(2)   Where municipal banks provide or propose to provide payment services they must give notice to the Authority.

(3)   In this regulation—

"credit union" means a credit union within the meaning of—

    (a)   the Credit Unions Act 1979;

    (b)   the Credit Unions (Northern Ireland) Order 1985;

"municipal bank" means a company which, immediately before 1st December 2001, fell within the definition in section 103 of the Banking Act 1987.

[3734]

NOTES

Commencement: see reg 1 at **[3732]**.

PART 2

REGISTRATION

The register

4 The register of certain payment service providers

(1)   The Authority must maintain a register of—

    (a)   authorised payment institutions and their EEA branches;

    (b)   small payment institutions;

    (c)   agents of authorised payment institutions and small payment institutions required to be registered under regulation 29; and

    (d)   the persons specified in regulation 3(1) where they provide payment services.

(2)   The Authority may include on the register any of the persons mentioned in paragraphs (c) to (h) of the definition of a payment service provider in regulation 2(1) where such persons provide payment services.

(3)   Where a person mentioned in paragraph (f), (g) or (h) of the definition of a payment service provider in regulation 2(1)—

    (a)   is not included on the register; and

    (b)   provides, or proposes to provide, payment services,

the person must give notice to the Authority.

(4)   The Authority may—

    (a)   keep the register in any form it thinks fit;

    (b)   include on it such information as the Authority considers appropriate, provided that the register identifies the payment services for which an institution is authorised or registered under this Part; and

    (c)   exploit commercially the information contained in the register, or any part of that information.

(5)   The Authority must—

    (a)   publish the register online and make it available for public inspection;

    (b)   update the register on a regular basis; and

(c)   provide a certified copy of the register, or any part of it, to any person who asks for it—

        (i)   on payment of the fee (if any) fixed by the Authority; and

        (ii)   in a form (either written or electronic) in which it is legible to the person asking for it.

[3735]

NOTES

Commencement: see reg 1 at **[3732]**.

Authorisation as a payment institution

5 Application for authorisation as a payment institution or variation of an existing authorisation

(1)   An application for authorisation as a payment institution must contain or be accompanied by the information specified in Schedule 2.

(2)   An application for the variation of an authorisation as a payment institution must—

     (a)   contain a statement of the proposed variation;

     (b)   contain a statement of the payment services which the applicant proposes to carry on if the authorisation is varied; and

     (c)   contain, or be accompanied by, such other information as the Authority may reasonably require.

(3)   An application under paragraph (1) or (2) must be made in such manner as the Authority may direct.

(4)   At any time after receiving an application and before determining it, the Authority may require the applicant to provide it with such further information as it reasonably considers necessary to enable it to determine the application.

(5)   Different directions may be given, and different requirements imposed, in relation to different applications or categories of application.

[3736]

NOTES

Commencement: see reg 1 at **[3732]**.

6 Conditions for authorisation as a payment institution

(1)   The Authority may refuse to grant all or part of an application for authorisation as a payment institution only if any of the conditions set out in paragraphs (2) to (8) is not met.

(2)   The application must comply with the requirements of, and any requirements imposed under, regulation 5.

(3)   The applicant must immediately before the time of authorisation hold the amount of initial capital required in accordance with Part 1 of Schedule 3.

(4)   The applicant must be a body corporate constituted under the law of a part of the United Kingdom having—

     (a)   its head office, and

     (b)   if it has a registered office, that office,

in the United Kingdom.

(5)   The applicant must satisfy the Authority that, taking into account the need to ensure the sound and prudent conduct of the affairs of the institution, it has—

     (a)   robust governance arrangements for its payment service business, including a clear organisational structure with well-defined, transparent and consistent lines of responsibility;

     (b)   effective procedures to identify, manage, monitor and report any risks to which it might be exposed;

     (c)   adequate internal control mechanisms, including sound administrative, risk management and accounting procedures,

which are comprehensive and proportionate to the nature, scale and complexity of the payment services to be provided by the institution.

(6)   The applicant must satisfy the Authority that—

     (a)   any persons having a qualifying holding in it are fit and proper persons having regard to the need to ensure the sound and prudent conduct of the affairs of an authorised payment institution;

     (b)   the directors and persons responsible for the management of the institution and, where relevant, the persons responsible for the management of payment services, are of good repute and possess appropriate knowledge and experience to provide payment services;

     (c)   it has a business plan (including, for the first three years, a forecast budget calculation) under which appropriate and proportionate systems, resources and procedures will be employed by the institution to operate soundly; and

   (d)   it has taken adequate measures for the purpose of safeguarding payment service users' funds in accordance with regulation 19.

(7)   The applicant must comply with a requirement of the Money Laundering Regulations 2007 to be included in a register maintained under those Regulations where such a requirement applies to the applicant.

(8)   If the applicant has close links with another person ("CL") the applicant must satisfy the Authority—

   (a)   that those links are not likely to prevent the Authority's effective supervision of the applicant; and

   (b)   if it appears to the Authority that CL is subject to the laws, regulations or administrative provisions of a territory which is not an EEA State ("the foreign provisions"), that neither the foreign provisions, nor any deficiency in their enforcement, would prevent the Authority's effective supervision of the applicant.

(9)   For the purposes of paragraph (8), an applicant has close links with CL if—

   (a)   CL is a parent undertaking of the applicant;

   (b)   CL is a subsidiary undertaking of the applicant;

   (c)   CL is a parent undertaking of a subsidiary undertaking of the applicant;

   (d)   CL is a subsidiary undertaking of a parent undertaking of the applicant;

   (e)   CL owns or controls 20% or more of the voting rights or capital of the applicant; or

   (f)   the applicant owns or controls 20% or more of the voting rights or capital of CL.

[3737]

NOTES

Commencement: see reg 1 at **[3732]**.

7 Imposition of requirements

(1)   The Authority may include in an authorisation such requirements as it considers appropriate.

(2)   A requirement may, in particular, be imposed so as to require the person concerned to—

   (a)   take a specified action;

   (b)   refrain from taking a specified action.

(3)   A requirement may be imposed by reference to the person's relationship with its group or other members of its group.

(4)   Where—

   (a)   an applicant for authorisation as a payment institution intends to carry on business activities other than the provision of payment services; and

   (b)   the Authority considers that the carrying on of such other business activities will impair, or is likely to impair—

      (i)   the financial soundness of the applicant, or

      (ii)   the Authority's effective supervision of the applicant,

the Authority may require the applicant to establish a separate body corporate to carry on the payment service business.

(5)   A requirement expires at the end of such period as the Authority may specify in the authorisation.

(6)   Paragraph (5) does not affect the Authority's powers under regulation 8 or 11.

[3738]

NOTES

Commencement: see reg 1 at **[3732]**.

8 Variation etc at request of authorised payment institution

The Authority may, on the application of an authorised payment institution, vary that person's authorisation by—

   (a)   adding a payment service to those for which it has granted authorisation;

   (b)   removing a payment service from those for which it has granted authorisation;

   (c)   imposing a requirement such as may, under regulation 7, be included in an authorisation;

   (d)   cancelling a requirement included in the authorisation or previously imposed under paragraph (c); or

   (e)   varying such a requirement,

provided that the conditions set out in regulation 6(4) to (8) and, if applicable, the requirement in regulation 18(1) to maintain own funds, will continue to be met.

[3739]

NOTES
    Commencement: see reg 1 at **[3732]**.

9 Determination of application for authorisation or variation of authorisation

(1) The Authority must determine an application for authorisation or the variation of an authorisation before the end of the period of three months beginning with the date on which it received the completed application.

(2) The Authority may determine an incomplete application if it considers it appropriate to do so, and it must in any event determine any such application within 12 months beginning with the date on which it received the application.

(3) The applicant may withdraw its application, by giving the Authority notice, at any time before the Authority determines it.

(4) The Authority may grant authorisation to carry out the payment services to which the application relates or such of them as may be specified in the grant of the authorisation.

(5) If the Authority decides to grant an application for authorisation, or for the variation of an authorisation, it must give the applicant notice of its decision specifying—
    (a)   the payment services for which authorisation has been granted; or
    (b)   the variation granted,
described in such manner as the Authority considers appropriate.

(6) The notice must state the date on which the authorisation or variation takes effect.

(7) If the Authority proposes to refuse an application or to impose a requirement it must give the applicant a warning notice.

(8) The Authority must, having considered any representations made in response to the warning notice—
    (a)   if it decides to refuse the application or to impose a requirement, give the applicant a decision notice; or
    (b)   if it grants the application without imposing a requirement, give the applicant notice of its decision, stating the date on which the authorisation or variation takes effect.

(9) If the Authority decides to refuse the application or to impose a requirement the applicant may refer the matter to the [Upper Tribunal].

(10) If the Authority decides to authorise the applicant, or vary its authorisation, it must update the register as soon as practicable.

[3740]

NOTES
    Commencement: see reg 1 at **[3732]**.
    Para (9): words in square brackets substituted by the Transfer of Tribunal Functions Order 2010, SI 2010/22, art 5(2), Sch 3, paras 177, 180, subject to transitional provisions and savings in Sch 5 thereto.

10 Cancellation of authorisation

(1) The Authority may cancel a person's authorisation and remove the person from the register where—
    (a)   the person does not provide payment services within 12 months beginning with the date on which the authorisation took effect;
    (b)   the person requests, or consents to, the cancellation of the authorisation;
    (c)   the person ceases to engage in business activity for more than six months;
    (d)   the person has obtained authorisation through false statements or any other irregular means;
    (e)   the person no longer meets, or is unlikely to continue to meet, any of the conditions set out in regulation 6(4) to (8) or, if applicable, the requirement in regulation 18(1) to maintain own funds;
    (f)   the person has provided payment services other than in accordance with the authorisation granted to it;
    (g)   the person would constitute a threat to the stability of a payment system by continuing its payment services business;
    (h)   the cancellation is desirable in order to protect the interests of consumers; or
    (i)   the person's provision of payment services is otherwise unlawful.

(2) Where the Authority proposes to cancel a person's authorisation, other than at the person's request, it must give the person a warning notice.

(3) The Authority must, having considered any representations made in response to the warning notice—
    (a)   if it decides to cancel the authorisation, give the person a decision notice; or

(b)   if it decides not to cancel the authorisation, give the person notice of its decision.

(4)   If the Authority decides to cancel the authorisation, other than at the person's request, the person may refer the matter to the [Upper Tribunal].

(5)   Where the period for a reference to the [Upper Tribunal] has expired without a reference being made, the Authority must as soon as practicable update the register accordingly.

[3741]

NOTES
Commencement: see reg 1 at **[3732]**.
Paras (4), (5): words in square brackets substituted by the Transfer of Tribunal Functions Order 2010, SI 2010/22, art 5(2), Sch 3, paras 177, 181, subject to transitional provisions and savings in Sch 5 thereto.

[10A   Request for cancellation of authorisation

(1)   A request for cancellation of a person's authorisation under regulation 10(1)(b) must be made in such manner as the Authority may direct.

(2)   At any time after receiving a request and before determining it, the Authority may require the person making the request to provide it with such further information as it reasonably considers necessary to enable it to determine the request.

(3)   Different directions may be given and different requirements imposed, in relation to different requests or categories of request.]

[3742]

NOTES
Commencement: 1 October 2009 (certain purposes); 1 November 2009 (otherwise).
Inserted by the Payment Services (Amendment) Regulations 2009, SI 2009/2475, regs 2, 3, as from the dates noted above. Note: the Payment Services (Amendment) Regulations 2009, SI 2009/2475, reg 1(2), (3) provides as follows—

"(2)   Subject to paragraph (3), these Regulations come into force on 1st November 2009.

(3)   These Regulations come into force on 1st October 2009 for the purposes—
    (a)   referred to in regulation 1(2)(b)(v), (vii), (viii) and (ix) of the Payment Services Regulations 2009; and
    (b)   of enabling the Authority to give directions as to the manner in which an application or request under regulation 5(1) or (2), 10(1)(b), 12(1) or (2) or 29(3) of the Payment Services Regulations 2009 is to be made and enabling the Authority to require the applicant or the person making the request to provide further information in accordance with regulation 5(4), 10A(2), 12(4) or 29(3)(a)(iv) of those Regulations, as the case may be.".

11   Variation of authorisation on Authority's own initiative

(1)   The Authority may vary a person's authorisation in any of the ways mentioned in regulation 8 if it appears to the Authority that—
    (a)   the person no longer meets, or is unlikely to continue to meet, any of the conditions set out in regulation 6(4) to (8) or, if applicable, the requirement in regulation 18(1) to maintain own funds;
    (b)   the person has provided a particular payment service or payment services other than in accordance with the authorisation granted to it;
    (c)   the person would constitute a threat to the stability of a payment system by continuing to provide a particular payment service or payment services;
    (d)   the variation is desirable in order to protect the interests of consumers; or
    (e)   the person's provision of a particular payment service or payment services is otherwise unlawful.

(2)   A variation under this regulation takes effect—
    (a)   immediately, if the notice given under paragraph (6) states that that is the case;
    (b)   on such date as may be specified in the notice; or
    (c)   if no date is specified in the notice, when the matter to which the notice relates is no longer open to review.

(3)   A variation may be expressed to take effect immediately or on a specified date only if the Authority, having regard to the ground on which it is exercising the power under paragraph (1), reasonably considers that it is necessary for the variation to take effect immediately or, as the case may be, on that date.

(4)   The Authority must as soon as practicable after the variation takes effect update the register accordingly.

(5)   A person who is aggrieved by the variation of their authorisation under this regulation may refer the matter to the [Upper Tribunal].

(6)   Where the Authority proposes to vary a person's authorisation under this regulation, it must give the person notice.

(7)   The notice must—
- (a)   give details of the variation;
- (b)   state the Authority's reasons for the variation and for its determination as to when the variation takes effect;
- (c)   inform the person that they may make representations to the Authority within such period as may be specified in the notice (whether or not the person has referred the matter to the [Upper Tribunal]);
- (d)   inform the person of the date on which the variation takes effect; and
- (e)   inform the person of their right to refer the matter to the [Upper Tribunal] and the procedure for such a reference.

(8)   The Authority may extend the period allowed under the notice for making representations.

(9)   If, having considered any representations made by the person, the Authority decides—
- (a)   to vary the authorisation in the way proposed, or
- (b)   if the authorisation has been varied, not to rescind the variation,

it must give the person notice.

(10)   If, having considered any representations made by the person, the Authority decides—
- (a)   not to vary the authorisation in the way proposed,
- (b)   to vary the authorisation in a different way, or
- (c)   to rescind a variation which has taken effect,

it must give the person notice.

(11)   A notice given under paragraph (9) must inform the person of their right to refer the matter to the [Upper Tribunal] and the procedure for such a reference.

(12)   A notice under paragraph (10)(b) must comply with paragraph (7).

(13)   For the purposes of paragraph (2)(c), paragraphs (a) to (d) of section 391(8) of the 2000 Act (publication) apply to determine whether a matter is open to review.

[3743]

NOTES

Commencement: see reg 1 at **[3732]**.
Paras (5), (7), (11): words in square brackets substituted by the Transfer of Tribunal Functions Order 2010, SI 2010/22, art 5(2), Sch 3, paras 177, 182, subject to transitional provisions and savings in Sch 5 thereto.

Registration as a small payment institution

12   Application for registration as a small payment institution or variation of an existing registration

(1)   An application for registration as a small payment institution must contain, or be accompanied by, such information as the Authority may reasonably require.

(2)   An application for the variation of a registration as a small payment institution must—
- (a)   contain a statement of the proposed variation;
- (b)   contain a statement of the payment services which the applicant proposes to carry on if the registration is varied; and
- (c)   contain, or be accompanied by, such other information as the Authority may reasonably require.

(3)   An application under paragraph (1) or (2) must be made in such manner as the Authority may direct.

(4)   At any time after receiving an application and before determining it, the Authority may require the applicant to provide it with such further information as it reasonably considers necessary to enable it to determine the application.

(5)   Different directions may be given, and different requirements imposed, in relation to different applications or categories of application.

[3744]

NOTES

Commencement: see reg 1 at **[3732]**.

13   Conditions for registration as a small payment institution

(1)   The Authority may refuse to register an applicant as a small payment institution only if any of the conditions set out in paragraphs (2) to (6) is not met.

(2)   The application must comply with the requirements of, and any requirements imposed under, regulation 12.

(3)   The monthly average over the period of 12 months preceding the application of the total amount of payment transactions executed by the applicant, including any of its agents in the United Kingdom, must not exceed 3 million euros.

(4)   None of the individuals responsible for the management or operation of the business has been convicted of—

(a)   an offence under Part 7 of the Proceeds of Crime Act 2002 (money laundering) or under the Money Laundering Regulations 2007;

(b)   an offence under section 15 (fund-raising), 16 (use and possession), 17 (funding arrangements), 18 (money laundering) or 63 (terrorist finance: jurisdiction) of the Terrorism Act 2000;

(c)   an offence under the 2000 Act;

(d)   an offence under article 7, 8 or 10 of the Terrorism (United Nations Measures) Order 2006 or article 7, 8 or 10 of the Al-Qaida and Taliban (United Nations Measures) Order 2006;

[(da) an offence under article 10, 11, 12, 13, 14 or 16 of the Terrorism (United Nations Measures) Order 2009;]

(e)   an offence under these Regulations; or

(f)   any other financial crimes.

(5)   The applicant's head office, registered office or place of residence, as the case may be, must be in the United Kingdom.

(6)   The applicant must comply with a requirement of the Money Laundering Regulations 2007 to be included in a register maintained under those Regulations where such a requirement applies to the applicant.

(7)   For the purposes of paragraph (3), where the applicant has yet to commence the provision of payment services, or has been providing payment services for less than 12 months, the monthly average may be based on the projected total amount of payment transactions over a 12 month period.

(8)   In paragraph (4) "financial crime" includes any offence involving fraud or dishonesty and, for this purpose, "offence" includes any act or omission which would be an offence if it had taken place in the United Kingdom.

[3745]

NOTES

Commencement: see reg 1 at [3732].

Para (4): sub-para (da) inserted by the Terrorism (United Nations Measures) Order (Consequential Amendments) Regulations 2009, SI 2009/1912, art 4.

14 Supplementary provisions

Regulations 7 to 11 apply to registration as a small payment institution as they apply to authorisation as a payment institution with the following modifications—

(a)   references to authorisation are to be treated as references to registration;

(b)   omit regulation 7(4);

(c)   in regulation 8 for "an authorised payment institution" substitute "small payment institution" and for "provided that" to the end substitute—

"provided that the conditions set out in regulation 13(4) to (6) will continue to be met and that the monthly average over any period of 12 months of the total amount of payment transactions executed by the institution, including any of its agents in the United Kingdom, continues not to exceed 3 million euro ("the financial limit").";

(d)   in regulation 10 for paragraph (1)(e) substitute—

"(e)   the person no longer meets, or is unlikely to continue to meet, any of the conditions set out in regulation 13(4) to (6) or the financial limit referred to in regulation 8;"; and

(e)   in regulation 11 for paragraph (1)(a) substitute—

"(a)   the person no longer meets, or is unlikely to continue to meet, any of the conditions set out in regulation 13(4) to (6) or the financial limit referred to in regulation 8;".

[3746]

NOTES

Commencement: see reg 1 at [3732].

15 Application for authorisation as a payment institution where the financial limit is exceeded

Where the financial limit referred to in regulation 8 (as applied by regulation 14(c)) is exceeded, the institution concerned must, within 30 days of becoming aware of the change in circumstances, apply for authorisation as a payment institution under regulation 5 if it intends to continue providing payment services in the United Kingdom.

[3747]

NOTES
Commencement: see reg 1 at **[3732]**.

Common provisions

16 Duty to notify changes

(1) If at any time after an applicant has provided the Authority with any information under regulation 5(1), (2), or (4), or 12(1), (2) or (4) and before the Authority has determined the application—

(a) there is, or is likely to be, a material change affecting any matter contained in that information; or

(b) it becomes apparent to the applicant that the information is incomplete or contains a material inaccuracy,

the applicant must provide the Authority with details of the change, the complete information or a correction of the inaccuracy (as the case may be) without undue delay, or, in the case of a material change which has not yet taken place, the applicant must provide details of the likely change as soon as the applicant is aware of such change.

(2) The obligation in paragraph (1) also applies to material changes or significant inaccuracies affecting any matter contained in any supplementary information provided pursuant to that paragraph.

(3) Any information to be provided to the Authority under this regulation must be in such form or verified in such manner as it may direct.

[3748]

NOTES
Commencement: see reg 1 at **[3732]**.

17 Authorised payment institutions and small payment institutions acting without permission

If an authorised payment institution or a small payment institution carries on a payment service in the United Kingdom, or purports to do so, other than in accordance with an authorisation or registration granted, or deemed to be granted under regulation 121, to it by the Authority under these Regulations, it is to be taken to have contravened a requirement imposed on it under these Regulations.

[3749]

NOTES
Commencement: see reg 1 at **[3732]**.

PART 3
AUTHORISED PAYMENT INSTITUTIONS

18 Capital requirements

(1) Subject to paragraph (2), an authorised payment institution must maintain at all times own funds as defined for the purposes of Part 2 of Schedule 3 equal to or in excess of—

(a) the amount of initial capital specified in Part 1 of Schedule 3, or

(b) the amount of the own funds requirement calculated in accordance with paragraph 11 of Schedule 3 subject to any adjustment directed by the Authority under paragraph 12 of that Schedule,

whichever is greater.

(2) Paragraph (1) does not apply to an authorised payment institution—

(a) which is included in the consolidated supervision of a parent credit institution pursuant to the banking consolidation directive; and

(b) in respect of which all of the conditions specified in Article 69(1) of the banking consolidation directive are met.

[3750]

NOTES

Commencement: see reg 1 at **[3732]**.

19 Safeguarding requirements

(1)　For the purposes of this regulation "relevant funds" comprise the following—

    (a)　sums received from, or for the benefit of, a payment service user for the execution of a payment transaction; and

    (b)　sums received from a payment service provider for the execution of a payment transaction on behalf of a payment service user.

(2)　Where—

    (a)　only a portion of the sums referred to in paragraph (1)(a) or (b) is to be used for the execution of a payment transaction (with the remainder being used for non-payment services); and

    (b)　the precise portion attributable to the execution of the payment transaction is variable or unknown in advance,

the relevant funds are such amount as may be reasonably estimated, on the basis of historical data and to the satisfaction of the Authority, to be representative of the portion attributable to the execution of the payment transaction.

(3)　Where the relevant funds in respect of a payment transaction exceed £50, an authorised payment institution must safeguard such funds in accordance with either—

    (a)　paragraphs (4) to (8); or

    (b)　paragraphs (9) and (10).

(4)　An authorised payment institution must keep relevant funds segregated from any other funds that it holds.

(5)　Where the authorised payment institution continues to hold the relevant funds at the end of the business day following the day on which they were received it must—

    (a)　place them in a separate account that it holds with an authorised credit institution; or

    (b)　invest the relevant funds in such secure, liquid assets as the Authority may approve ("relevant assets") and place those assets in a separate account with an authorised custodian.

(6)　An account in which relevant funds or relevant assets are placed under paragraph (5) must—

    (a)　be designated in such a way as to show that it is an account which is held for the purpose of safeguarding relevant funds or relevant assets in accordance with this regulation; and

    (b)　be used only for holding those funds or assets.

(7)　No person other than the authorised payment institution may have any interest in or right over the relevant funds or relevant assets placed in an account in accordance with paragraph (5)(a) or (b) except as provided by this regulation.

(8)　The authorised payment institution must keep a record of—

    (a)　any relevant funds segregated in accordance with paragraph (4);

    (b)　any relevant funds placed in an account in accordance with paragraph (5)(a); and

    (c)　any relevant assets placed in an account in accordance with paragraph (5)(b).

(9)　The authorised payment institution must ensure that—

    (a)　any relevant funds are covered by—

        (i)　an insurance policy with an authorised insurer;

        (ii)　a guarantee from an authorised insurer; or

        (iii)　a guarantee from an authorised credit institution; and

    (b)　the proceeds of any such insurance policy or guarantee are payable upon an insolvency event into a separate account held by the authorised payment institution which must—

        (i)　be designated in such a way as to show that it is an account which is held for the purpose of safeguarding relevant funds in accordance with this regulation; and

        (ii)　be used only for holding such proceeds.

(10)　No person other than the authorised payment institution may have any interest in or right over the proceeds placed in an account in accordance with paragraph (9)(b) except as provided by this regulation.

(11)　Subject to paragraph (12), where there is an insolvency event—

    (a)　the claims of payment service users are to be paid from the asset pool in priority to all other creditors; and

    (b)　until all the claims of payment service users have been paid, no right of set-off or security right may be exercised in respect of the asset pool except to the extent that the right of set-off relates to fees and expenses in relation to operating an account held in accordance with paragraph (5)(a) or (b) or (9)(b).

(12) The claims referred to in paragraph (11)(a) shall not be subject to the priority of expenses of an insolvency proceeding except in respect of the costs of distributing the asset pool.

(13) Paragraphs (11) and (12) shall apply to any relevant funds which a small payment institution (or an authorised payment institution in relation to relevant funds of £50 or less) voluntarily safeguards in accordance with either paragraphs (4) to (8) or paragraphs (9) and (10).

(14) An authorised payment institution (and any small payment institution which voluntarily safeguards relevant funds) must maintain organisational arrangements sufficient to minimise the risk of the loss or diminution of relevant funds or relevant assets through fraud, misuse, negligence or poor administration.

(15) In this regulation—
"asset pool" means—
    (a)   any relevant funds segregated in accordance with paragraph (4);
    (b)   any relevant funds held in an account in accordance with paragraph (5)(a);
    (c)   any relevant assets held in an account in accordance with paragraph (5)(b); and
    (d)   any proceeds of an insurance policy or guarantee held in an account in accordance with paragraph (9)(b);
"authorised insurer" means a person authorised for the purposes of the 2000 Act to effect and carry out a contract of general insurance as principal or otherwise authorised in accordance with Article 6 of the First Council Directive 73/239/EEC of 24th July 1973 on the business of direct insurance other than life insurance, other than a person in the same group as the authorised payment institution;
"authorised credit institution" means a person authorised for the purposes of the 2000 Act to accept deposits or otherwise authorised as a credit institution in accordance with Article 6 of the banking consolidation directive other than a person in the same group as the authorised payment institution;
"authorised custodian" means a person authorised for the purposes of the 2000 Act to safeguard and administer investments or authorised as an investment firm under Article 5 of Directive 2004/39/EC of 12th April 2004 on markets in financial instruments which holds those investments under regulatory standards at least equivalent to those set out under Article 13 of that directive;
"insolvency event" means any of the following procedures in relation to an authorised payment institution or small payment institution—
    (e)   the making of a winding-up order;
    (f)   the passing of a resolution for voluntary winding-up;
    (g)   the entry of the institution into administration;
    (h)   the appointment of a receiver or manager of the institution's property;
    (i)   the approval of a proposed voluntary arrangement (being a composition in satisfaction of debts or a scheme of arrangement);
    (j)   the making of a bankruptcy order;
    (k)   in Scotland, the award of sequestration;
    (l)   the making of any deed of arrangement for the benefit of creditors or, in Scotland, the execution of a trust deed for creditors;
    (m)   the conclusion of any composition contract with creditors; or
    (n)   the making of an insolvency administration order or, in Scotland, sequestration, in respect of the estate of a deceased person;
"insolvency proceeding" means—
    (o)   winding-up, administration, receivership, bankruptcy or, in Scotland, sequestration;
    (p)   a voluntary arrangement, deed of arrangement or trust deed for the benefit of creditors; or
    (q)   the administration of the insolvent estate of a deceased person;
"security right" means—
    (r)   security for a debt owed by an authorised payment institution or a small payment institution and includes any charge, lien, mortgage or other security over the asset pool or any part of the asset pool; and
    (s)   any charge arising in respect of the expenses of a voluntary arrangement.

[3751]

NOTES
Commencement: see reg 1 at **[3732]**.

20 Accounting and statutory audit

(1) Where an authorised payment institution carries on activities other than the provision of payment services, it must provide to the Authority separate accounting information in respect of its provision of payment services.

(2)   Such accounting information must be subject, where relevant, to an auditor's report prepared by the institution's statutory auditors or an audit firm (within the meaning of Directive 2006/43/EC of the European Parliament and of the Council of 17th May 2006 on statutory audits of annual accounts and consolidated accounts).

(3)   A statutory auditor or audit firm ("the auditor") must, in any of the circumstances referred to in paragraph (4), communicate to the Authority information on, or its opinion on, matters—

(a)   of which it has become aware in its capacity as auditor of an authorised payment institution or of a person with close links to an authorised payment institution; and

(b)   which relate to payment services provided by that institution.

(4)   The circumstances are that—

(a)   the auditor reasonably believes that—

(i)   there is or has been, or may be or may have been, a contravention of any requirement imposed on the authorised payment institution by or under these Regulations; and

(ii)   the contravention may be of material significance to the Authority in determining whether to exercise, in relation to that institution, any functions conferred on the Authority by these Regulations;

(b)   the auditor reasonably believes that the information on, or his opinion on, those matters may be of material significance to the Authority in determining whether the institution meets or will continue to meet the conditions set out in regulation 6(4) to (8) and, if applicable, the requirement in regulation 18(1) to maintain own funds;

(c)   the auditor reasonably believes that the institution is not, may not be or may cease to be, a going concern;

(d)   the auditor is precluded from stating in his report that the annual accounts have been properly prepared in accordance with the Companies Act 2006;

(e)   the auditor is precluded from stating in his report, where applicable, that the annual accounts give a true and fair view of the matters referred to in section 495 of the Companies Act 2006 (auditor's report on company's annual accounts) including as it is applied and modified by regulation 39 of the Limited Liability Partnerships (Accounts and Audit) (Application of Companies Act 2006) Regulations 2008 ("the LLP Regulations"); or

(f)   the auditor is required to state in his report in relation to the person concerned any of the facts referred to in subsection (2), (3) or (5) of section 498 of the Companies Act 2006 (duties of auditor) or, in the case of limited liability partnerships, subsection (2), (3) or (4) of section 498 as applied and modified by regulation 40 of the LLP Regulations.

(5)   In this regulation a person has close links with an authorised payment institution ("A") if that person is—

(a)   a parent undertaking of A;

(b)   a subsidiary undertaking of A;

(c)   a parent undertaking of a subsidiary undertaking of A; or

(d)   a subsidiary undertaking of a parent undertaking of A.

[3752]

NOTES

Commencement: see reg 1 at **[3732]**.

21 Outsourcing

(1)   An authorised payment institution must notify the Authority of its intention to enter into a contract with another person under which that other person will carry out any operational function relating to its provision of payment services ("outsourcing").

(2)   Where an authorised payment institution intends to outsource any important operational function, all of the following conditions must be met—

(a)   the outsourcing is not undertaken in such a way as to impair—

(i)   the quality of the authorised payment institution's internal control; or

(ii)   the ability of the Authority to monitor the authorised payment institution's compliance with these Regulations;

(b)   the outsourcing does not result in any delegation by the senior management of the authorised payment institution of responsibility for complying with the requirements imposed by or under these Regulations;

(c)   the relationship and obligations of the authorised payment institution towards its payment service users under these Regulations is not substantially altered;

(d)   compliance with the conditions which the authorised payment institution must observe in order to be authorised and remain so is not adversely affected; and

(e)   none of the conditions of the payment institution's authorisation requires removal or variation.

(3)   For the purposes of paragraph (2), an operational function is important if a defect or failure in its performance would materially impair—

    (a)   compliance by the authorised payment institution with these Regulations and any requirements of its authorisation;

    (b)   the financial performance of the authorised payment institution; or

    (c)   the soundness or continuity of the authorised payment institution's payment services.

[3753]

NOTES

Commencement: see reg 1 at **[3732]**.

22 Record keeping

(1)   An authorised payment institution must maintain relevant records and keep them for at least five years from the date on which the record was created.

(2)   For the purposes of paragraph (1), records are relevant where they relate to the authorised payment institution's compliance with this Part and, in particular, would enable the Authority to supervise effectively such compliance.

[3754]

NOTES

Commencement: see reg 1 at **[3732]**.

Exercise of passport rights

23 Notice of intention

(1)   Where an authorised payment institution intends to exercise its passport rights for the first time in a particular EEA State it must give the Authority, in such manner as the Authority may direct, notice of its intention to do so ("a notice of intention") which—

    (a)   identifies the payment services which it seeks to carry on in exercise of those rights in that State;

    (b)   gives the names of those responsible for the management of a proposed EEA branch, if any; and

    (c)   provides details of the organisational structure of a proposed EEA branch, if any.

(2)   The Authority must, within one month beginning with the date on which it receives the notice of intention, inform the host state competent authority of—

    (a)   the name and address of the authorised payment institution; and

    (b)   the information contained in the notice of intention.

(3)   Where an authorised payment institution intends to exercise its passport rights through an EEA agent, the provisions of regulation 29 apply.

[3755]

NOTES

Commencement: see reg 1 at **[3732]**.

24 Registration of EEA branch

(1)   If the Authority, taking into account any information received from the host state competent authority, has reasonable grounds to suspect that, in connection with the establishment of an EEA branch by an authorised payment institution—

    (a)   money laundering or terrorist financing within the meaning of the money laundering directive is taking place, has taken place, or has been attempted; or

    (b)   the risk of such activities taking place would be increased,

the Authority may refuse to register the EEA branch or cancel any such registration already made and remove the branch from the register.

(2)   If the Authority proposes to refuse to register, or cancel the registration of, an EEA branch, it must give the relevant authorised payment institution a warning notice.

(3)   The Authority must, having considered any representations made in response to the warning notice—

    (a)   if it decides not to register the branch, or to cancel its registration, give the authorised payment institution a decision notice; or

    (b)   if it decides to register the branch, or not to cancel the registration, give the authorised payment institution notice of its decision.

(4)   If the Authority decides not to register the branch, or to cancel its registration, the authorised payment institution may refer the matter to the [Upper Tribunal].

PART 2

STATUTORY INSTRUMENTS

(5)   If the Authority decides to register an EEA branch, it must update the register as soon as practicable.

(6)   If the Authority decides to cancel the registration, the Authority must, where the period for a reference to the [Upper Tribunal] has expired without a reference being made, as soon as practicable update the register accordingly.

[3756]

NOTES
Commencement: see reg 1 at **[3732]**.
Paras (4), (6): words in square brackets substituted by the Transfer of Tribunal Functions Order 2010, SI 2010/22, art 5(2), Sch 3, paras 177, 183, subject to transitional provisions and savings in Sch 5 thereto.

25   Supervision of firms exercising passport rights

(1)   Without prejudice to the generality of regulation 119, the Authority must co-operate with the relevant host state competent authority or home state competent authority, as the case may be, in relation to the exercise of passport rights by any authorised payment institution or EEA authorised payment institution.

(2)   The Authority must, in particular—
  (a)   notify the host state competent authority whenever it intends to carry out an on-site inspection in the host state competent authority's territory; and
  (b)   provide the host state competent authority or home state competent authority, as the case may be—
     (i)   on request, with all relevant information; and
     (ii) on its own initiative, with all essential information,
relating to the exercise of passport rights by an authorised payment institution or EEA authorised payment institution, including where there is an infringement or suspected infringement of these Regulations or of the provisions of the payment services directive by an agent, branch or entity carrying out activities on behalf of such an institution.

(3)   Where the Authority and the home state competent authority agree, the Authority may carry out on-site inspections on behalf of the home state competent authority in respect of payment services provided by an EEA authorised payment institution exercising its passport rights.

(4)   If the Authority has reasonable grounds to suspect that, in connection with the proposed establishment of a branch or the proposed provision of services by an EEA authorised payment institution—
  (a)   money laundering or terrorist financing within the meaning of the Money Laundering Regulations 2007 is taking place, has taken place, or has been attempted; or
  (b)   the risk of such activities taking place would be increased,
it must inform the relevant home state competent authority of its grounds for suspicion.

[3757]

NOTES
Commencement: see reg 1 at **[3732]**.

26   Carrying on of Consumer Credit Act business by EEA authorised payment institutions

(1)   Sections 203 (power to prohibit the carrying on of Consumer Credit Act business) and 204 (power to restrict the carrying on of Consumer Credit Act business) of, and Schedule 16 (prohibitions and restrictions imposed by OFT) to, the 2000 Act apply in relation to EEA authorised payment institutions exercising passport rights in the United Kingdom under these Regulations as they apply in relation to EEA firms exercising passport rights under Part 2 of Schedule 3 to the 2000 Act (EEA passport rights) with the following modifications—
  (a)   in section 203(10)—
     (i)   for the definition of "a consumer credit EEA firm" substitute—
       ""a consumer credit EEA firm" means an EEA authorised payment institution (as defined by regulation 2(1) of the Payment Services Regulations 2009) which is exercising passport rights in the United Kingdom and is carrying on any Consumer Credit Act business;" and
     (ii) for the definition of "listed activity" substitute—
       ""listed activity" means an activity listed in the Annex to the payment services directive and any activity carried on in accordance with Article 16 of that directive;";
  (b)   in paragraph 2(5)(b) of Schedule 16, for "the firm's home state regulator" substitute "the home state competent authority (as defined by regulation 2(1) of the Payment Services Regulations 2009)".

(2)   Sections 21 (businesses needing a licence) and 39(1) (offences against Part 3) of the Consumer Credit Act 1974 do not apply in relation to the carrying on by an EEA authorised

payment institution of a payment service which is Consumer Credit Act business, unless the OFT has exercised the power conferred on it by section 203 of the 2000 Act, as applied with modifications by paragraph (1), in relation to that institution.

(3)   In this regulation "Consumer Credit Act business" has the same meaning as in section 203 of the 2000 Act.

[3758]

NOTES
Commencement: see reg 1 at **[3732]**.

PART 4
PROVISIONS APPLICABLE TO AUTHORISED PAYMENT INSTITUTIONS AND SMALL PAYMENT INSTITUTIONS

27   Additional activities

(1)   Authorised payment institutions and small payment institutions may, in addition to providing payment services, engage in the following activities—
   (a)   the provision of operational and closely related ancillary services, including—
       (i)   ensuring the execution of payment transactions;
      (ii)   foreign exchange services;
     (iii)   safe-keeping activities; and
     (iv)   the storage and processing of data;
   (b)   the operation of payment systems; and
   (c)   business activities other than the provision of payment services, subject to any relevant Community or national law.

(2)   Authorised payment institutions and small payment institutions may grant credit in relation to the provision of the payment services specified in paragraph 1(d), (e) and (g) of Schedule 1 only if—
   (a)   such credit is ancillary and granted exclusively in connection with the execution of a payment transaction;
   (b)   such credit is not granted from the funds received or held for the purposes of executing payment transactions;
   (c)   in cases where such credit is granted by an authorised payment institution exercising its passport rights, there is an obligation upon the payment service user to repay the credit within a period not exceeding 12 months; and
   (d)   in relation to an authorised payment institution, in the opinion of the Authority the institution's own funds (comprising the items specified in paragraph 3(a) to (j) of Schedule 3) are, and continue to be, adequate in the light of the overall amount of credit granted.

[3759]

NOTES
Commencement: see reg 1 at **[3732]**.

28   Payment accounts and sums received for the execution of payment transactions

Any payment account held by an authorised payment institution or a small payment institution must be used only in relation to payment transactions.

[3760]

NOTES
Commencement: see reg 1 at **[3732]**.

29   Use of agents

(1)   Authorised payment institutions and small payment institutions may not provide payment services in the United Kingdom through an agent unless the agent is included on the register.

(2)   Authorised payment institutions may not provide payment services in the exercise of their passport rights through an EEA agent unless the agent is included on the register.

(3)   An application for an agent to be included on the register must—
   (a)   contain, or be accompanied by, the following information—
      (i)   the name and address of the agent;
     (ii)   where relevant, a description of the internal control mechanisms that will be used by the agent—
         (aa)   in the case of an agent in the United Kingdom, to comply with the Money Laundering Regulations 2007; and

(bb) in the case of an EEA agent, to comply with provisions of the money laundering directive; and

(iii) in the case of an agent of an authorised payment institution, the identity of the directors and persons responsible for the management of the agent and evidence that they are fit and proper persons; and

(iv) such other information as the Authority may reasonably require; and

(b) be made in such manner as the Authority may direct.

(4) Different directions may be given, and different requirements imposed, in relation to different applications or categories of application.

(5) At any time after receiving an application and before determining it, the Authority may require the applicant to provide it with such further information as it reasonably considers necessary to enable it to determine the application.

(6) The Authority may refuse to include the agent on the register only if—

(a) it has not received the information referred to in paragraph (3)(a), or is not satisfied that such information is correct;

(b) it is not satisfied that the directors and persons responsible for the management of the agent are fit and proper persons;

(c) it has reasonable grounds to suspect that, in connection with the provision of services through the agent—

(i) money laundering or terrorist financing within the meaning of the money laundering directive (or, in the United Kingdom, the Money Laundering Regulations 2007) is taking place, has taken place, or has been attempted; or

(ii) the risk of such activities taking place would be increased.

(7) Where—

(a) an authorised payment institution intends to provide payment services through an EEA agent; and

(b) the Authority proposes to include the EEA agent on the register,

the Authority must inform the host state competent authority and take account of its opinion (if provided within such reasonable period as the Authority specifies) on any of the matters referred to in paragraph (6)(b) or (c).

(8) The Authority must decide whether to include the agent on the register within a reasonable period of it having received a completed application.

(9) If the Authority proposes to refuse to include the agent on the register, it must give the authorised payment institution or the small payment institution, as the case may be, a warning notice.

(10) The Authority must, having considered any representations made in response to the warning notice—

(a) if it decides not to include the agent on the register, give the applicant a decision notice; or

(b) if it decides to include the agent on the register, give the applicant notice of its decision, stating the date on which the registration takes effect.

(11) If the Authority decides not to include the agent on the register the applicant may refer the matter to the [Upper Tribunal].

(12) If the Authority decides to include the agent on the register, it must update the register as soon as practicable.

(13) An application under paragraph (3) may be combined with an application under regulation 5 or 12, in which case the application must be determined in the manner set out in regulation 9 (if relevant, as applied by regulation 14).

(14) An authorised payment institution or a small payment institution must ensure that agents acting on its behalf inform payment service users of the agency arrangement.

[3761]

NOTES

Commencement: see reg 1 at **[3732]**.

Para (11): words in square brackets substituted by the Transfer of Tribunal Functions Order 2010, SI 2010/22, art 5(2), Sch 3, paras 177, 184, subject to transitional provisions and savings in Sch 5 thereto.

30 Removal of agent from register

(1) The Authority may remove an agent of an authorised payment institution or small payment institution from the register where—

(a) the authorised payment institution or small payment institution requests, or consents to, the agent's removal from the register;

(b)   the authorised payment institution or small payment institution has obtained registration through false statements or any other irregular means;

(c)   regulation 29(6)(b) or (c) applies;

(d)   the removal is desirable in order to protect the interests of consumers; or

(e)   the agent's provision of payment services is otherwise unlawful.

(2)   Where the Authority proposes to remove an agent from the register, other than at the request of the authorised payment institution or small payment institution, it must give the authorised payment institution or small payment institution a warning notice.

(3)   The Authority must, having considered any representations made in response to the warning notice—

(a)   if it decides to remove the agent, give the authorised payment institution or small payment institution a decision notice; or

(b)   if it decides not to remove the agent, give the authorised payment institution or small payment institution notice of its decision.

(4)   If the Authority decides to remove the agent, other than at the request of the authorised payment institution or small payment institution, the institution concerned may refer the matter to the [Upper Tribunal].

(5)   Where the period for a reference to the [Upper Tribunal] has expired without a reference being made, the Authority must as soon as practicable update the register accordingly.

[3762]

NOTES

Commencement: see reg 1 at **[3732]**.

Paras (4), (5): words in square brackets substituted by the Transfer of Tribunal Functions Order 2010, SI 2010/22, art 5(2), Sch 3, paras 177, 185, subject to transitional provisions and savings in Sch 5 thereto.

31 Reliance

(1)   Where an authorised payment institution or a small payment institution relies on a third party for the performance of operational functions it must take all reasonable steps to ensure that these Regulations are complied with.

(2)   Without prejudice to paragraph (1), an authorised payment institution or a small payment institution is responsible, to the same extent as if it had expressly permitted it, for anything done or omitted by any of its employees, any agent or branch providing payment services on its behalf, or any entity to which activities are outsourced.

[3763]

NOTES

Commencement: see reg 1 at **[3732]**.

32 Duty to notify change in circumstance

(1)   Where it becomes apparent to an authorised payment institution or a small payment institution that there is, or is likely to be, a significant change in circumstances which is relevant to—

(a)   in the case of an authorised payment institution—

(i)   its fulfilment of any of the conditions set out in regulation 6(4) to (8) and, if applicable, the requirement in regulation 18(1) to maintain own funds;

(ii)   the payment services which it seeks to carry on in exercise of its passport rights;

(b)   in the case of a small payment institution, its fulfilment of any of the conditions set out in regulation 13(4) to (6) and compliance with the financial limit referred to in regulation 8 (as applied by regulation 14(c)); and

(c)   in the case of the use of an agent to provide payment services, the matters referred to in regulation 29(6)(b) and (c),

it must provide the Authority with details of the change without undue delay, or, in the case of a substantial change in circumstances which has not yet taken place, details of the likely change a reasonable period before it takes place.

(2)   Any information to be provided to the Authority under this regulation must be in such form or verified in such manner as it may direct.

[3764]

NOTES

Commencement: see reg 1 at **[3732]**.

PART 5
INFORMATION REQUIREMENTS FOR PAYMENT SERVICES
Application

33 Application of Part 5

(1)   This Part applies to a contract for payment services where—
   (a)   the services are provided from an establishment maintained by a payment service provider or its agent in the United Kingdom;
   (b)   the payment service providers of both the payer and the payee are located within the EEA; and
   (c)   the payment services are carried out either in euro or in the currency of an EEA State that has not adopted the euro as its currency.

(2)   Regulations 36 to 39 apply to payment services provided under a single payment service contract.

(3)   Regulations 40 to 46 apply to payment services provided under a framework contract.

(4)   Except where the payment service user is—
   (a)   a consumer,
   (b)   a micro-enterprise, or
   (c)   a charity,
the parties may agree that any or all of the provisions of this Part do not apply to a contract for payment services.

[3765]

NOTES
Commencement: see reg 1 at **[3732]**.

34 Disapplication of certain regulations in the case of consumer credit agreements

Where the contract under which a payment service is provided is, or would be, when entered into, a regulated agreement—
   (a)   regulations 41, 42 and 43 do not apply;
   (b)   the payment service provider is only required under regulation 40(1) to provide the information specified in paragraph 3(b) of Schedule 4; and
   (c)   the payment service provider is only required under regulation 45(1) to provide the information specified in paragraph (2)(d) of regulation 45.

[3766]

NOTES
Commencement: see reg 1 at **[3732]**.

35 Disapplication of certain regulations in the case of low-value payment instruments

(1)   This regulation applies in respect of payment instruments which, under the framework contract governing their use—
   (a)   can be used only to execute individual payment transactions of 30 euro or less, or in relation to payment transactions executed wholly within the United Kingdom, 60 euro or less;
   (b)   have a spending limit of 150 euro, or where payment transactions must be executed wholly within the United Kingdom, 300 euro; or
   (c)   store funds that do not exceed 500 euro at any time.

(2)   Where this regulation applies—
   (a)   regulations 40 and 44 do not apply and the payment service provider is only required to provide the payer with information about the main characteristics of the payment service, including—
      (i)   the way in which the payment instrument can be used;
      (ii)   the liability of the payer, as set out in regulation 62;
      (iii)   charges levied;
      (iv)   any other material information the payer might need to take an informed decision; and
      (v)   an indication of where the information specified in Schedule 4 is made available in an easily accessible manner;
   (b)   the parties may agree that regulations 45 and 46 do not apply and instead—
      (i)   the payment service provider must provide or make available a reference enabling the payment service user to identify—
         (aa)   the payment transaction;
         (bb)   the amount of the payment transaction;
         (cc)   any charges payable in respect of the payment transaction;

(ii)   in the case of several payment transactions of the same kind made to the same payee, the payment service provider must provide or make available to the payment service user information about the total amount of the payment transactions and any charges for those payment transactions; or

(iii)   where the payment instrument is used anonymously or the payment service provider is not otherwise technically able to provide or make available the information specified in paragraph (i) or (ii), the payment service provider must enable the payer to verify the amount of funds stored; and

(c)   the parties may agree that regulation 47(1) does not apply to information provided or made available in accordance with regulation 42.

[3767]

NOTES
Commencement: see reg 1 at **[3732]**.

Single payment service contracts

36 Information required prior to the conclusion of a single payment service contract

(1)   A payment service provider must provide or make available to the payment service user the information specified in paragraph (2), whether by supplying a copy of the draft single payment service contract or supplying a copy of the draft payment order or otherwise, either—

(a)   before the payment service user is bound by the single payment service contract; or

(b)   immediately after the execution of the payment transaction, where the contract is concluded at the payment service user's request using a means of distance communication which does not enable provision of such information in accordance with sub-paragraph (a).

(2)   The information referred to in paragraph (1) is—

(a)   the information or unique identifier that has to be provided by the payment service user in order for a payment order to be properly executed;

(b)   the maximum time in which the payment service will be executed;

(c)   the charges payable by the payment service user to the user's payment service provider and, where applicable, a breakdown of the amounts of such charges;

(d)   where applicable, the actual or reference exchange rate to be applied to the payment transaction; and

(e)   such of the information specified in Schedule 4 as is relevant to the single payment service contract in question.

[3768]

NOTES
Commencement: see reg 1 at **[3732]**.

37 Information required after receipt of the payment order

(1)   The payer's payment service provider must, immediately after receipt of the payment order, provide or make available to the payer the information specified in paragraph (2).

(2)   The information referred to in paragraph (1) is—

(a)   a reference enabling the payer to identify the payment transaction and, where appropriate, information relating to the payee;

(b)   the amount of the payment transaction in the currency used in the payment order;

(c)   the amount of any charges for the payment transaction payable by the payer and, where applicable, a breakdown of the amounts of such charges;

(d)   where an exchange rate is used in the payment transaction and the actual rate used in the payment transaction differs from the rate provided in accordance with regulation 36(2)(d), the actual rate used or a reference to it, and the amount of the payment transaction after that currency conversion; and

(e)   the date on which the payment service provider received the payment order.

[3769]

NOTES
Commencement: see reg 1 at **[3732]**.

38 Information for the payee after execution

(1)   The payee's payment service provider must, immediately after the execution of the payment transaction, provide or make available to the payee the information specified in paragraph (2).

(2)   The information referred to in paragraph (1) is—

(a)   a reference enabling the payee to identify the payment transaction and, where appropriate, the payer and any information transferred with the payment transaction;

(b) the amount of the payment transaction in the currency in which the funds are at the payee's disposal;

(c) the amount of any charges for the payment transaction payable by the payee and, where applicable, a breakdown of the amount of such charges;

(d) where applicable, the exchange rate used in the payment transaction by the payee's payment service provider, and the amount of the payment transaction before that currency conversion; and

(e) the credit value date.

[3770]

NOTES

Commencement: see reg 1 at **[3732]**.

39 Avoidance of duplication of information

Where a payment order for a single payment transaction is transmitted by way of a payment instrument issued under a framework contract, the payment service provider in respect of that single payment transaction need not provide or make available under regulations 36 to 38 information which has been provided or made available, or will be provided or made available, under regulations 40 to 45 by another payment service provider in respect of the framework contract.

[3771]

NOTES

Commencement: see reg 1 at **[3732]**.

Framework contracts

40 Prior general information for framework contracts

(1) A payment service provider must provide to the payment service user the information specified in Schedule 4, either—

(a) in good time before the payment service user is bound by the framework contract; or

(b) where the contract is concluded at the payment service user's request using a means of distance communication which does not enable provision of such information in accordance with sub-paragraph (a), immediately after the conclusion of the contract.

(2) The payment service provider may discharge the duty under paragraph (1) by supplying a copy of the draft framework contract provided that such contract includes the information specified in Schedule 4.

[3772]

NOTES

Commencement: see reg 1 at **[3732]**.

41 Information during period of contract

If the payment service user so requests at any time during the contractual relationship, the payment service provider must provide the information specified in Schedule 4 and the terms of the framework contract.

[3773]

NOTES

Commencement: see reg 1 at **[3732]**.

42 Changes in contractual information

(1) Subject to paragraph (4), any proposed changes to—

(a) the existing terms of the framework contract; or

(b) the information specified in Schedule 4,

must be [provided] by the payment service provider to the payment service user no later than two months before the date on which they are to take effect.

(2) The framework contract may provide for any such proposed changes to be made unilaterally by the payment service provider where the payment service user does not, before the proposed date of entry into force of the changes, notify the payment service provider to the contrary.

(3) Where paragraph (2) applies, the payment service provider must inform the payment service user that—

(a) the payment service user will be deemed to have accepted the changes in the circumstances referred to in that paragraph; and

(b) the payment service user has the right to terminate the framework contract immediately and without charge before the proposed date of their entry into force.

(4)   Changes in the interest or exchange rates may be applied immediately and without notice where—
    (a)   such a right is agreed under the framework contract and the changes are based on the reference interest or exchange rates information on which has been provided to the payment service user in accordance with this Part; or
    (b)   the changes are more favourable to the payment service user.

(5)   The payment service provider must inform the payment service user of any change to the interest rate as soon as possible unless the parties have agreed on a specific frequency or manner in which the information is to be provided or made available.

(6)   Any change in the interest or exchange rate used in payment transactions must be implemented and calculated in a neutral manner that does not discriminate against payment service users.

[3774]

NOTES
Commencement: see reg 1 at **[3732]**.
Para (1): word in square brackets substituted by the Payment Services (Amendment) Regulations 2009, SI 2009/2475, regs 2, 4; see further the note to reg 10A at **[3742]**.

43   Termination of framework contract

(1)   The payment service user may terminate the framework contract at any time unless the parties have agreed on a period of notice not exceeding one month.

(2)   Subject to paragraph (3), any charges for the termination of the contract must reasonably correspond to the actual costs to the payment service provider of termination.

(3)   The payment service provider may not charge the payment service user for the termination, after the expiry of 12 months, of a framework contract concluded for a fixed period of more than 12 months or for an indefinite period.

(4)   The payment service provider may terminate a framework contract concluded for an indefinite period by giving at least two months' notice, if the contract so provides.

(5)   Notice of termination given in accordance with paragraph (4) must be provided in the same way as information is required by regulation 47(1) to be provided or made available.

(6)   Where charges for the payment service are levied on a regular basis, such charges must be apportioned up until the time of the termination of the contract and any charges paid in advance must be reimbursed proportionally.

(7)   This regulation does not affect any right of a party to the framework contract to treat it[, in accordance with the general law of contract, as unenforceable, void or discharged].

[3775]

NOTES
Commencement: see reg 1 at **[3732]**.
Para (7): words in square brackets substituted by the Payment Services (Amendment) Regulations 2009, SI 2009/2475, regs 2, 5; see further the note to reg 10A at **[3742]**.

44   Information prior to execution of individual payment transaction

Where an individual payment transaction under a framework contract is initiated by the payer, at the payer's request the payer's payment service provider must inform the payer of—
    (a)   the maximum execution time;
    (b)   the charges payable by the payer in respect of the payment transaction; and
    (c)   where applicable, a breakdown of the amounts of such charges.

[3776]

NOTES
Commencement: see reg 1 at **[3732]**.

45   Information for the payer on individual payment transactions

(1)   The payer's payment service provider under a framework contract must provide to the payer the information specified in paragraph (2) as soon as reasonably practicable either—
    (a)   after the amount of an individual payment transaction is debited from the payer's payment account; or
    (b)   where the payer does not use a payment account, after receipt of the payment order.

(2)   The information referred to in paragraph (1) is—
    (a)   a reference enabling the payer to identify each payment transaction and, where appropriate, information relating to the payee;

PART 2 STATUTORY INSTRUMENTS

    (b)   the amount of the payment transaction in the currency in which the payer's payment account is debited or in the currency used for the payment order;

    (c)   the amount of any charges for the payment transaction and, where applicable, a breakdown of the amounts of such charges, or the interest payable by the payer;

    (d)   where applicable, the exchange rate used in the payment transaction by the payer's payment service provider and the amount of the payment transaction after that currency conversion; and

    (e)   the debit value date or the date of receipt of the payment order.

(3)   A framework contract may include a condition that the information specified in paragraph (2) be provided or made available periodically at least once a month and in an agreed manner which enables the payer to store and reproduce the information unchanged.

[3777]

NOTES

Commencement: see reg 1 at **[3732]**.

46 Information for the payee on individual payment transactions

(1)   As soon as reasonably practicable after the execution of an individual payment transaction under a framework contract, the payee's payment service provider must provide to the payee the information specified in paragraph (2).

(2)   The information referred to in paragraph (1) is—

    (a)   a reference enabling the payee to identify the payment transaction and, where appropriate, the payer, and any information transferred with the payment transaction;

    (b)   the amount of the payment transaction in the currency in which the payee's payment account is credited;

    (c)   the amount of any charges for the payment transaction and, where applicable, a breakdown of the amounts of such charges, or the interest payable by the payee;

    (d)   where applicable, the exchange rate used in the payment transaction by the payee's payment service provider, and the amount of the payment transaction before that currency conversion; and

    (e)   the credit value date.

(3)   A framework contract may include a condition that the information specified in paragraph (2) is to be provided or made available periodically at least once a month and in an agreed manner which enables the payee to store and reproduce the information unchanged.

[3778]

NOTES

Commencement: see reg 1 at **[3732]**.

Common provisions

47 Communication of information

(1)   Subject to regulation 35(2)(c), any information provided or made available in accordance with this Part must be provided or made available—

    (a)   [in the case of single payment service contracts,] in an easily accessible manner;

    (b)   [subject to paragraph (2)], on paper or on another durable medium;

    (c)   in easily understandable language and in a clear and comprehensible form; and

    (d)   in English or in the language agreed by the parties.

[(2)   Paragraph (1)(b)—

    (a)   in the case of single payment service contracts, only applies where the payment service user so requests; and

    (b)   in the case of framework contracts, is subject to any agreement in accordance with regulation 45(3) or 46(3) as to the manner in which information is to be provided or made available.]

[3779]

NOTES

Commencement: see reg 1 at **[3732]**.
Para (1): words in square brackets in sub-para (a) inserted, and words in square brackets in sub-para (b) substituted by the Payment Services (Amendment) Regulations 2009, SI 2009/2475, regs 2, 6(a), (b); see further the note to reg 10A at **[3742]**.
Para (2): substituted by SI 2009/2475, regs 2, 6(c); see further the note to reg 10A at **[3742]**.

48 Charges for information

(1)   A payment service provider may not charge for providing or making available information which is required to be provided or made available by this Part.

(2)   The payment service provider and the payment service user may agree on charges for any information which is provided at the request of the payment service user where such information is—

(a)   additional to the information required to be provided or made available by this Part;

(b)   provided more frequently than is specified in this Part; or

(c)   transmitted by means of communication other than those specified in the framework contract.

(3)   Any charges imposed under paragraph (2) must reasonably correspond to the payment service provider's actual costs.

[3780]

NOTES

Commencement: see reg 1 at **[3732]**.

49   Currency and currency conversion

(1)   Payment transactions must be executed in the currency agreed between the parties.

(2)   Where a currency conversion service is offered before the initiation of the payment transaction—

(a)   at the point of sale; or

(b)   by the payee,

the party offering the currency conversion service to the payer must disclose to the payer all charges as well as the exchange rate to be used for converting the payment transaction.

[3781]

NOTES

Commencement: see reg 1 at **[3732]**.

50   Information on additional charges or reductions

(1)   The payee must inform the payer of any charge requested or reduction offered by the payee for the use of a particular payment instrument before the initiation of the payment transaction.

(2)   The payment service provider, or any relevant third party, must inform the payment service user of any charge requested by the payment service provider or third party, as the case may be, for the use of a particular payment instrument before the initiation of the payment transaction.

[3782]

NOTES

Commencement: see reg 1 at **[3732]**.

PART 6
RIGHTS AND OBLIGATIONS IN RELATION TO THE PROVISION OF PAYMENT SERVICES

Application

51   Application of Part 6

(1)   This Part applies to a contract for payment services where—

(a)   the services are provided from an establishment maintained by a payment service provider or its agent in the United Kingdom;

(b)   subject to paragraph (2), the payment service providers of both the payer and the payee are located within the EEA; and

(c)   where the payment services are carried out in euro or in the currency of an EEA State that has not adopted the euro as its currency.

(2)   Regulation 73 applies whether or not the payment service providers of both the payer and the payee are located within the EEA.

(3)   Except where the payment service user is a consumer, a micro-enterprise or a charity, the parties may agree that—

(a)   any or all of regulations 54(1), [55(3) or (4)], 60, 62, 63, 64, 67, 75, 76 and 77 do not apply;

(b)   a different time period applies for the purposes of regulation 59(1).

[3783]

NOTES

Commencement: see reg 1 at **[3732]**.

Para (3): figure in square brackets substituted by the Payment Services (Amendment) Regulations 2009, SI 2009/2475, regs 2, 7; see further the note to reg 10A at **[3742]**.

52   Disapplication of certain regulations in the case of consumer credit agreements

The following provisions of the Consumer Credit Act 1974 shall apply in relation to contracts for
the provision of payment services which are regulated agreements for the purposes of that Act in
place of the following provisions of these Regulations—

(a)   section 51 (prohibition of unsolicited credit tokens) in place of regulation 58(1)(b);
(b)   sections 66 (acceptance of credit tokens) and 84 (misuse of credit tokens) in place of
      regulations 59, 61 and 62;
(c)   section 83 (liability for misuse of credit facilities) in place of regulations 59, 61 and 62;
(d)   sections 76 (duty to give notice before taking certain action) and 87 (need for default
      notice) in relation to the grounds mentioned in regulation 56(2) in place of
      regulation 56(3) to (6)[; and
(e)   section 98A(4) to (6) (termination of open-end consumer credit agreement) in place of
      regulation 56(2) to (6).]

                                                                                          [3784]

NOTES
   Commencement: see reg 1 at **[3732]**.
   Para (e): inserted, together with word immediately preceding it, by the Consumer Credit (EU Directive)
Regulations 2010, SI 2010/1010, reg 97, as from 1 February 2011, with effect in relation to certain agreements
before that date, as provided in regs 100–101A thereof at **[3941]**–**[3942A]**.

53   Disapplication of certain regulations in the case of low value payment instruments

(1)   This regulation applies in respect of payment instruments which, under the framework
contract governing their use—

(a)   can be used only to execute individual payment transactions of 30 euro or less, or in
      relation to payment transactions executed wholly within the United Kingdom, 60 euro or
      less;
(b)   have a spending limit of 150 euro, or where payment transactions must be executed
      wholly within the United Kingdom, 300 euro; or
(c)   store funds that do not exceed 500 euro at any time.

(2)   Where this regulation applies the parties may agree that—

(a)   regulations 57(1)(b), 58(1)(c), (d) and (e) and 62(3) do not apply where the payment
      instrument does not allow for the stopping or prevention of its use;
(b)   regulations 60, 61 and 62(1) and (2) do not apply where the payment instrument is used
      anonymously or the payment service provider is not in a position, for other reasons
      concerning the payment instrument, to prove that a payment transaction was authorised;
(c)   the payment service provider is not required under regulation 66(1) to notify the
      payment service user of the refusal of a payment order if the non-execution is apparent
      from the context;
(d)   the payer may not revoke the payment order under regulation 67 after transmitting the
      payment order or giving their consent to execute the payment transaction to the payee;
(e)   execution periods other than those provided by regulations 70 and 71 apply.

(3)   Subject to paragraph (2)(b), regulations 61 and 62(1) and (2) apply to electronic money as
defined in Article 1(3)(b) of the electronic money directive unless the payer's payment service
provider does not have the ability under the contract to—

(a)   freeze the payment account; or
(b)   stop the use of the payment instrument.

                                                                                          [3785]

NOTES
   Commencement: see reg 1 at **[3732]**.

Charges

54   Charges

(1)   The payment service provider may only charge the payment service user for the fulfilment
of any of its obligations under this Part—

(a)   in accordance with regulation 66(3), 67(6) or 74(2)(b);
(b)   where agreed between the parties; and
(c)   where such charges reasonably correspond to the payment service provider's actual
      costs.

(2)   Where a payment transaction does not involve any currency conversion, the respective
payment service providers must ensure that—

(a)   the payee pays any charges levied by the payee's payment service provider; and
(b)   the payer pays any charges levied by the payer's payment service provider.

(3)   The payee's payment service provider may not prevent the payee from—

(a)　requiring payment of a charge by; or

(b)　offering a reduction to,

the payer for the use of a particular payment instrument.

[3786]

NOTES

Commencement: see reg 1 at **[3732]**.

Authorisation of payment transactions

55　Consent and withdrawal of consent

(1)　A payment transaction is to be regarded as having been authorised by the payer for the purposes of this Part only if the payer has given its consent to—

(a)　the execution of the payment transaction; or

(b)　the execution of a series of payment transactions of which that payment transaction forms part.

(2)　Such consent—

(a)　may be given before or, if agreed between the payer and its payment service provider, after the execution of the payment transaction; and

(b)　must be given in the form, and in accordance with the procedure, agreed between the payer and its payment service provider.

(3)　The payer may withdraw its consent to a payment transaction at any time before the point at which the payment order can no longer be revoked under regulation 67.

(4)　Subject to regulation 67(3) to (5), the payer may withdraw its consent to the execution of a series of payment transactions at any time with the effect that any future payment transactions are not regarded as authorised for the purposes of this Part.

[3787]

NOTES

Commencement: see reg 1 at **[3732]**.

56　Limits on the use of payment instruments

(1)　Where a specific payment instrument is used for the purpose of giving consent to the execution of a payment transaction, the payer and its payment service provider may agree on spending limits for any payment transactions executed through that payment instrument.

(2)　A framework contract may provide for the payment service provider to have the right to stop the use of a payment instrument on reasonable grounds relating to—

(a)　the security of the payment instrument;

(b)　the suspected unauthorised or fraudulent use of the payment instrument; or

(c)　in the case of a payment instrument with a credit line, a significantly increased risk that the payer may be unable to fulfil its liability to pay.

(3)　The payment service provider must, in the manner agreed between the payment service provider and the payer and before carrying out any measures to stop the use of the payment instrument—

(a)　inform the payer that it intends to stop the use of the payment instrument; and

(b)　give its reasons for doing so.

(4)　Where the payment service provider is unable to inform the payer in accordance with paragraph (3) before carrying out any measures to stop the use of the payment instrument, it must do so immediately after.

(5)　Paragraphs (3) and (4) do not apply where provision of the information in accordance with paragraph (3) would compromise reasonable security measures or is otherwise unlawful.

(6)　The payment service provider must allow the use of the payment instrument or replace it with a new payment instrument as soon as practicable after the reasons for stopping its use cease to exist.

[3788]

NOTES

Commencement: see reg 1 at **[3732]**.

57　Obligations of the payment service user in relation to payment instruments

(1)　A payment service user to whom a payment instrument has been issued must—

(a)　use the payment instrument in accordance with the terms and conditions governing its issue and use; and

PART 2
STATUTORY INSTRUMENTS

(b)   notify the payment service provider in the agreed manner and without undue delay on becoming aware of the loss, theft, misappropriation or unauthorised use of the payment instrument.

(2)   The payment service user must on receiving a payment instrument take all reasonable steps to keep its personalised security features safe.

[3789]

NOTES
Commencement: see reg 1 at [3732].

58 Obligations of the payment service provider in relation to payment instruments

(1)   A payment service provider issuing a payment instrument must—
(a)   subject to regulation 57, ensure that the personalised security features of the payment instrument are not accessible to persons other than the payment service user to whom the payment instrument has been issued;
(b)   not send an unsolicited payment instrument, except where a payment instrument already issued to a payment service user is to be replaced;
(c)   ensure that appropriate means are available at all times to enable the payment service user to notify the payment service provider in accordance with regulation 57(1)(b) or to request that the use of the payment instrument is no longer stopped in accordance with regulation 56(6);
(d)   on request, provide the payment service user at any time during a period of 18 months after the alleged date of notification under regulation 57(1)(b) with the means to prove that such notification to the payment service provider was made;
(e)   prevent any use of the payment instrument once notification has been made under regulation 57(1)(b).

(2)   The payment service provider bears the risk of sending a payment instrument or any of its personalised security features to the payment service user.

[3790]

NOTES
Commencement: see reg 1 at [3732].

59 Notification of unauthorised or incorrectly executed payment transactions

(1)   A payment service user is entitled to redress under regulation 61, 75, 76 or 77 only if it notifies the payment service provider without undue delay, and in any event no later than 13 months after the debit date, on becoming aware of any unauthorised or incorrectly executed payment transaction.

(2)   Where the payment service provider has failed to provide or make available information concerning the payment transaction in accordance with Part 5 of these Regulations, the payment service user is entitled to redress under the regulations referred to in paragraph (1) notwithstanding that the payment service user has failed to notify the payment service provider as mentioned in that paragraph.

[3791]

NOTES
Commencement: see reg 1 at [3732].

60 Evidence on authentication and execution of payment transactions

(1)   Where a payment service user—
(a)   denies having authorised an executed payment transaction; or
(b)   claims that a payment transaction has not been correctly executed,
it is for the payment service provider to prove that the payment transaction was authenticated, accurately recorded, entered in the payment service provider's accounts and not affected by a technical breakdown or some other deficiency.

(2)   In paragraph (1) "authenticated" means the use of any procedure by which a payment service provider is able to verify the use of a specific payment instrument, including its personalised security features.

(3)   Where a payment service user denies having authorised an executed payment transaction, the use of a payment instrument recorded by the payment service provider is not in itself necessarily sufficient to prove either that—
(a)   the payment transaction was authorised by the payer; or
(b)   the payer acted fraudulently or failed with intent or gross negligence to comply with regulation 57.

[3792]

NOTES
Commencement: see reg 1 at **[3732]**.

61 Payment service provider's liability for unauthorised payment transactions

Subject to regulations 59 and 60, where an executed payment transaction was not authorised in accordance with regulation 55, the payment service provider must immediately—

    (a)   refund the amount of the unauthorised payment transaction to the payer; and

    (b)   where applicable, restore the debited payment account to the state it would have been in had the unauthorised payment transaction not taken place.

[3793]

NOTES
Commencement: see reg 1 at **[3732]**.

62 Payer's liability for unauthorised payment transaction

(1)   Subject to paragraphs (2) and (3), the payer is liable up to a maximum of £50 for any losses incurred in respect of unauthorised payment transactions arising—

    (a)   from the use of a lost or stolen payment instrument; or

    (b)   where the payer has failed to keep the personalised security features of the payment instrument safe, from the misappropriation of the payment instrument.

(2)   The payer is liable for all losses incurred in respect of an unauthorised payment transaction where the payer—

    (a)   has acted fraudulently; or

    (b)   has with intent or gross negligence failed to comply with regulation 57.

(3)   Except where the payer has acted fraudulently, the payer is not liable for any losses incurred in respect of an unauthorised payment transaction—

    (a)   arising after notification under regulation 57(1)(b);

    (b)   where the payment service provider has failed at any time to provide, in accordance with regulation 58(1)(c), appropriate means for notification; or

    (c)   where the payment instrument has been used in connection with a distance contract (other than an excepted contract).

(4)   In paragraph (3)(c) "distance contract" and "excepted contract" have the meanings given in the Consumer Protection (Distance Selling) Regulations 2000.

[3794]

NOTES
Commencement: see reg 1 at **[3732]**.

63 Refunds for payment transactions initiated by or through a payee

(1)   Where the conditions in paragraph (2) and the requirement in regulation 64(1) are satisfied, the payer is entitled to a refund from its payment service provider of the full amount of any authorised payment transaction initiated by or through the payee.

(2)   The conditions are that—

    (a)   the authorisation did not specify the exact amount of the payment transaction when the authorisation was given in accordance with regulation 55; and

    (b)   the amount of the payment transaction exceeded the amount that the payer could reasonably have expected taking into account the payer's previous spending pattern, the conditions of the framework contract and the circumstances of the case.

(3)   The payer and payment service provider may agree in the framework contract, in respect of direct debits, that the conditions in paragraph (2) need not be satisfied in order for the payer to be entitled to a refund.

(4)   For the purposes of paragraph (2)(b), the payer cannot rely on currency exchange fluctuations where the reference exchange rate provided under regulation 36(2)(d) or paragraph 3(b) of Schedule 4 was applied.

(5)   The payer and payment service provider may agree in the framework contract that the right to a refund does not apply where—

    (a)   the payer has given consent directly to the payment service provider for the payment transaction to be executed; and

    (b)   if applicable, information on the payment transaction was provided or made available in an agreed manner to the payer for at least four weeks before the due date by the payment service provider or by the payee.

[3795]

PART 2
STATUTORY INSTRUMENTS

NOTES
Commencement: see reg 1 at **[3732]**.

64 Requests for refunds for payment transactions initiated by or through a payee

(1) The payer must request a refund under regulation 63 from its payment service provider within 8 weeks from the date on which the funds were debited.

(2) The payment service provider may require the payer to provide such information as is reasonably necessary to ascertain whether the conditions in regulation 63(2) are satisfied.

(3) Subject to paragraph (4), the payment service provider must either—
  (a) refund the full amount of the payment transaction; or
  (b) provide justification for refusing to refund the payment transaction, indicating the bodies to which the payer may refer the matter if the payer does not accept the justification provided.

(4) Where an agreement in accordance with regulation 63(3) applies, the payment service provider must, notwithstanding that a condition in regulation 63(2) is not satisfied, refund the full amount of the payment transaction.

(5) Any refund or justification for refusing a refund must be provided within 10 business days of receiving a request for a refund or, where applicable, within 10 business days of receiving any further information requested under paragraph (2).

[3796]

NOTES
Commencement: see reg 1 at **[3732]**.

Execution of payment transactions

65 Receipt of payment orders

(1) Subject to paragraphs (2) to (5), for the purposes of these Regulations the time of receipt of a payment order is the time at which the payment order, given directly by the payer or indirectly by or through a payee, is received by the payer's payment service provider.

(2) If the time of receipt of a payment order does not fall on a business day for the payer's payment service provider, the payment order is deemed to have been received on the first business day thereafter.

(3) The payment service provider may set a time towards the end of a business day after which any payment order received will be deemed to have been received on the following business day.

(4) Where the payment service user initiating a payment order agrees with its payment service provider that execution of the payment order is to take place—
  (a) on a specific day;
  (b) on the last day of a certain period; or
  (c) on the day on which the payer has put funds at the disposal of its payment service provider,
the time of receipt is deemed to be the day so agreed.

(5) If the day agreed under paragraph (4) is not a business day for the payer's payment service provider, the payment order is deemed to have been received on the first business day thereafter.

[3797]

NOTES
Commencement: see reg 1 at **[3732]**.

66 Refusal of payment orders

(1) Subject to paragraph (4), where a payment service provider refuses to execute a payment order, it must notify the payment service user of—
  (a) the refusal;
  (b) if possible, the reasons for such refusal; and
  (c) [where it is possible to provide reasons for the refusal and those reasons relate to factual matters,] the procedure for rectifying any factual errors that led to the refusal.

(2) Any notification under paragraph (1) must be given or made available in an agreed manner and at the earliest opportunity, and in any event within the periods specified in regulation 70.

(3) The framework contract may provide for the payment service provider to charge the payment service user for such notification where the refusal is reasonably justified.

(4) The payment service provider is not required to notify the payment service user under paragraph (1) where such notification would be otherwise unlawful.

(5)   Where all the conditions set out in the payer's framework contract have been satisfied, the payment service provider may not refuse to execute an authorised payment order irrespective of whether the payment order is initiated by the payer or by or through a payee, unless such execution is otherwise unlawful.

(6)   For the purposes of regulations 70, 75 and 76 a payment order of which execution has been refused is deemed not to have been received.

[3798]

NOTES
Commencement: see reg 1 at **[3732]**.
Para (1): words in square brackets inserted by the Payment Services (Amendment) Regulations 2009, SI 2009/2475, regs 2, 8; see further the note to reg 10A at **[3742]**.

67   Revocation of a payment order

(1)   Subject to paragraphs (2) to (5), a payment service user may not revoke a payment order after it has been received by the payer's payment service provider.

(2)   In the case of a payment transaction initiated by or through the payee, the payer may not revoke the payment order after transmitting the payment order or giving consent to execute the payment transaction to the payee.

(3)   In the case of a direct debit, the payer may not revoke the payment order after the end of the business day preceding the day agreed for debiting the funds.

(4)   Where a day is agreed under regulation 65(4), the payment service user may not revoke a payment order after the end of the business day preceding the agreed day.

(5)   At any time after the time limits for revocation set out in paragraphs (1) to (4), the payment order may only be revoked if the revocation is—

    (a)   agreed between the payment service user and its payment service provider; and

    (b)   in the case of a payment transaction initiated by or through the payee, including in the case of a direct debit, also agreed with the payee.

(6)   A framework contract may provide for the payment service provider to charge for revocation under this regulation.

[3799]

NOTES
Commencement: see reg 1 at **[3732]**.

68   Amounts transferred and amounts received

(1)   Subject to paragraph (2), the payment service providers of the payer and payee must ensure that the full amount of the payment transaction is transferred and that no charges are deducted from the amount transferred.

(2)   The payee and its payment service provider may agree for the payment service provider to deduct its charges from the amount transferred before crediting it to the payee provided that the full amount of the payment transaction and the amount of the charges are clearly stated in the information provided to the payee.

(3)   If charges other than those provided for by paragraph (2) are deducted from the amount transferred—

    (a)   in the case of a payment transaction initiated by the payer, the payer's payment service provider must ensure that the payee receives the full amount of the payment transaction;

    (b)   in the case of a payment transaction initiated by the payee, the payee's payment service provider must ensure that the payee receives the full amount of the payment transaction.

[3800]

NOTES
Commencement: see reg 1 at **[3732]**.

Execution time and value date

69   Application of regulations 70 to 72

(1)   Regulations 70 to 72 apply to any [payment] transaction—

    (a)   in euro;

    [(b)   executed wholly within the United Kingdom in sterling; or]

    (c)   involving only one currency conversion between the euro and sterling, provided that—

        (i)   the currency conversion is carried out in the United Kingdom; and

        (ii)   in the case of cross-border payment transactions, the cross-border transfer takes place in euro.

(2)   In respect of any other [payment] transaction, the payment service user may agree with the payment service provider that regulations 70 (other than regulation 70(4)) to 72 do not apply.

[3801]

NOTES
Commencement: see reg 1 at **[3732]**.
Para (1): word in first pair of square brackets inserted, and sub-para (b) substituted by the Payment Services (Amendment) Regulations 2009, SI 2009/2475, regs 2, 9(a), (b); see further the note to reg 10A at **[3742]**.
Para (2): word in square brackets inserted by SI 2009/2475, regs 2, 9(a); see further the note to reg 10A at **[3742]**.

70   Payment transactions to a payment account

(1)   Subject to paragraphs (2), (3) and (4), the payer's payment service provider must ensure that the amount of the payment transaction is credited to the payee's payment service provider's account by the end of the business day following the time of receipt of the payment order.

(2)   Until 1st January 2012, the payer and their payment service provider may agree that the amount of the payment transaction is to be credited to the payee's payment service provider's account by the end of the third business day following the time of receipt of the payment order.

(3)   Where a payment transaction is initiated by way of a paper payment order—
    (a)   the reference in paragraph (1) to the end of the business day following the time of receipt of the payment order is to be treated as a reference to the end of the second business day following the time of receipt of the payment order; and
    (b)   the reference in paragraph (2) to the end of the third business day following the time of receipt of the payment order is to be treated as a reference to the end of the fourth business day following the time of receipt of the payment order.

(4)   Where a payment transaction—
    (a)   does not fall within paragraphs (a) to (c) of regulation 69(1); but
    (b)   is to be executed wholly within the EEA,
the payer's payment service provider must ensure that the amount of the payment transaction is credited to the payee's payment service provider's account by the end of the fourth business day following the time of receipt of the payment order.

(5)   The payee's payment service provider must value date and credit the amount of the payment transaction to the payee's payment account following its receipt of the funds.

(6)   The payee's payment service provider must transmit a payment order initiated by or through the payee to the payer's payment service provider within the time limits agreed between the payee and its payment service provider, enabling settlement in respect of a direct debit to occur on the agreed due date.

[3802]

NOTES
Commencement: see reg 1 at **[3732]**.

71   Absence of payee's payment account with the payment service provider

(1)   Paragraph (2) applies where a payment service provider accepts funds on behalf of a payee who does not have a payment account with that payment service provider.

(2)   The payment service provider must make the funds available to the payee immediately after the funds have been credited to that payment service provider's account.

[3803]

NOTES
Commencement: see reg 1 at **[3732]**.

72   Cash placed on a payment account

Where a payment service user places cash on its payment account with a payment service provider in the same currency as that payment account, the payment service provider must—
    (a)   if the user is a consumer, micro-enterprise or charity, ensure that the amount is made available and value dated immediately after the receipt of the funds;
    (b)   in any other case, ensure that the amount is made available and value dated no later than the end of the [next] business day after the receipt of the funds.

[3804]

NOTES
Commencement: see reg 1 at **[3732]**.
Para (b): word in square brackets inserted by the Payment Services (Amendment) Regulations 2009, SI 2009/2475, regs 2, 10; see further the note to reg 10A at **[3742]**.

73 Value date and availability of funds

(1) The credit value date for the payee's payment account must be no later than the business day on which the amount of the payment transaction is credited to the account of the payee's payment service provider.

(2) The payee's payment service provider must ensure that the amount of the payment transaction is at the payee's disposal immediately after that amount has been credited to that payment service provider's account.

(3) The debit value date for the payer's payment account must be no earlier than the time at which the amount of the payment transaction is debited to that payment account.

[3805]

NOTES

Commencement: see reg 1 at **[3732]**.

Liability

74 Incorrect unique identifiers

(1) Where a payment order is executed in accordance with the unique identifier, the payment order is deemed to have been correctly executed by each payment service provider involved in executing the payment order with respect to the payee specified by the unique identifier.

(2) Where the unique identifier provided by the payment service user is incorrect, the payment service provider is not liable under regulation 75 or 76 for non-execution or defective execution of the payment transaction, but the payment service provider—

    (a) must make reasonable efforts to recover the funds involved in the payment transaction; and

    (b) may, if agreed in the framework contract, charge the payment service user for any such recovery.

(3) Where the payment service user provides information additional to that specified in regulation 36(2)(a) or paragraph 2(b) of Schedule 4, the payment service provider is liable only for the execution of payment transactions in accordance with the unique identifier provided by the payment service user.

[3806]

NOTES

Commencement: see reg 1 at **[3732]**.

75 Non-execution or defective execution of payment transactions initiated by the payer

(1) This regulation applies where a payment order is initiated by the payer.

(2) The payer's payment service provider is liable to the payer for the correct execution of the payment transaction unless it can prove to the payer and, where relevant, to the payee's payment service provider, that the payee's payment service provider received the amount of the payment transaction in accordance with regulation 70.

(3) The payer's payment service provider must, on request, make immediate efforts to trace the payment transaction and notify the payer of the outcome.

(4) Where the payer's payment service provider is liable under paragraph (2), it must without undue delay refund to the payer the amount of the non-executed or defective payment transaction and, where applicable, restore the debited payment account to the state in which it would have been had the defective payment transaction not taken place.

(5) Where the payer's payment service provider can prove (as set out in paragraph (2)) that the payee's payment service provider received the amount of the payment transaction in accordance with regulation 70, the payee's payment service provider is liable to the payee for the correct execution of the payment transaction and must—

    (a) immediately make available the amount of the payment transaction to the payee; and

    (b) where applicable, credit the corresponding amount to the payee's payment account.

[3807]

NOTES

Commencement: see reg 1 at **[3732]**.

76 Non-execution or defective execution of payment transactions initiated by the payee

(1) This regulation applies where a payment order is initiated by the payee.

(2) The payee's payment service provider is liable to the payee for the correct transmission of the payment order to the payer's payment service provider in accordance with regulation 70(6).

(3) Where the payee's payment service provider is liable under paragraph (2), it must immediately re-transmit the payment order in question to the payer's payment service provider.

(4) The payee's payment service provider must, on request, make immediate efforts to trace the payment transaction and notify the payee of the outcome.

(5) Where the payee's payment service provider can prove to the payee and, where relevant, to the payer's payment service provider, that it is not liable under paragraph (2) in respect of a non-executed or defectively executed payment transaction, the payer's payment service provider is liable to the payer and must, as appropriate and without undue delay—
   (a) refund to the payer the amount of the payment transaction; and
   (b) restore the debited payment account to the state in which it would have been had the defective payment transaction not taken place.

[3808]

NOTES
   Commencement: see reg 1 at **[3732]**.

77 Liability of payment service provider for charges and interest

A payment service provider is liable to its payment service user for—
   (a) any charges for which the payment service user is responsible; and
   (b) any interest which the payment service user must pay,
as a consequence of the non-execution or defective execution of the payment transaction.

[3809]

NOTES
   Commencement: see reg 1 at **[3732]**.

78 Right of recourse

Where the liability of a payment service provider ("the first provider") under regulation 75 or 76 is attributable to another payment service provider or an intermediary, the other payment service provider or intermediary must compensate the first provider for any losses incurred or sums paid pursuant to those regulations.

[3810]

NOTES
   Commencement: see reg 1 at **[3732]**.

79 Force majeure

(1) A person is not liable for any contravention of a requirement imposed on it by or under this Part where the contravention is due to abnormal and unforeseeable circumstances beyond the person's control, the consequences of which would have been unavoidable despite all efforts to the contrary.

(2) A payment service provider is not liable for any contravention of a requirement imposed on it by or under this Part where the contravention is due to the obligations of the payment service provider under other provisions of Community or national law.

[3811]

NOTES
   Commencement: see reg 1 at **[3732]**.

PART 7
THE AUTHORITY

The functions of the Authority

80 Functions of the Authority

(1) The Authority is to have the functions conferred on it by these Regulations.

(2) In discharging its function of determining the general policy and principles by reference to which it performs particular functions under these Regulations, the Authority must have regard to—
   (a) the need to use its resources in the most efficient and economic way;
   (b) the responsibilities of those who manage the affairs of payment service providers;
   (c) the principle that a burden or restriction which is imposed on a person, or on the carrying on of an activity, should be proportionate to the benefits, considered in general terms, which are expected to result from the imposition of that burden or restriction;
   (d) the desirability of facilitating innovation in connection with payment services;

    (e)   the international character of financial services and markets and the desirability of maintaining the competitive position of the United Kingdom;

    (f)   the need to minimise the adverse effects on competition that may arise from anything done in the discharge of those functions; and

    (g)   the desirability of facilitating competition in relation to payment services.

[3812]

NOTES
Commencement: see reg 1 at **[3732]**.

Supervision and enforcement

81 Monitoring and enforcement

(1)   The Authority must maintain arrangements designed to enable it to determine whether—

    (a)   persons on whom requirements are imposed by or under Part 2, 3 or 4 of these Regulations are complying with them;

    (b)   there has been any contravention of regulation 110(1), 111(1) or 114(1)(a) or (2).

(2)   The Authority may maintain arrangements designed to enable it to determine whether persons on whom requirements are imposed by or under Part 5 or 6 of these Regulations are complying with them.

(3)   The arrangements referred to in paragraphs (1) and (2) may provide for functions to be performed on behalf of the Authority by any body or person who is, in its opinion, competent to perform them.

(4)   The Authority must also maintain arrangements for enforcing the provisions of these Regulations.

(5)   Paragraph (3) does not affect the Authority's duty under paragraph (1).

[3813]

NOTES
Commencement: see reg 1 at **[3732]**.

82 Reporting requirements

(1)   A payment service provider must give the Authority such information in respect of its provision of payment services and its compliance with requirements imposed by or under Parts 2 to 6 of these Regulations as the Authority may direct.

(2)   Information required under this regulation must be given at such times and in such form, and verified in such manner, as the Authority may direct.

[3814]

NOTES
Commencement: see reg 1 at **[3732]**.

83 Entry, inspection without a warrant etc

(1)   Paragraph (2) applies where an officer has reasonable cause to believe that any premises are being used by—

    (i)   an authorised payment institution, an EEA authorised payment institution or a small payment institution (including any of its branches) in connection with its business activities;

    (ii)   an agent providing payment services on behalf of an authorised payment institution, an EEA authorised payment institution or a small payment institution; or

    (iii)   an entity to which an authorised payment institution or an EEA authorised payment institution has outsourced any of its business activities.

(2)   The officer may on producing evidence of authority at any reasonable time—

    (a)   enter the premises;

    (b)   inspect the premises;

    (c)   observe the carrying on of business activities by the authorised payment institution, the EEA authorised payment institution or the small payment institution, as the case may be;

    (d)   inspect any document found on the premises;

    (e)   require any person on the premises to provide an explanation of any document or to state where it may be found.

(3)   An officer may take copies of, or make extracts from, any document found under paragraph (2).

PART 2
STATUTORY INSTRUMENTS

(4)   An officer may exercise powers under this regulation only if the information or document sought to be obtained as a result is reasonably required in connection with the exercise by the Authority of its functions under these Regulations.

(5)   An officer may not exercise powers under this regulation in relation to information or documents in respect of which a claim to legal professional privilege (in Scotland, to confidentiality of communications) could be maintained in legal proceedings.

(6)   In this regulation—
   "document" includes information recorded in any form;
   "officer" means an officer of the Authority and includes a member of the Authority's staff or an agent of the Authority;
   "premises" means any premises other than premises used only as a dwelling.

[3815]

NOTES
Commencement: see reg 1 at **[3732]**.

84   Public censure

If the Authority considers that a payment service provider has contravened a requirement imposed on them by or under these Regulations the Authority may publish a statement to that effect.

[3816]

NOTES
Commencement: see reg 1 at **[3732]**.

85   Financial penalties

(1)   The Authority may impose a penalty of such amount as it considers appropriate on—
   (a)   a payment service provider who has contravened a requirement imposed on them by or under these Regulations; or
   (b)   a person who has contravened regulation 110(1),111(1) or 114(1)(a) or (2).

(2)   The Authority may not in respect of any contravention both require a person to pay a penalty under this regulation and cancel their authorisation as a payment institution or their registration as a small payment institution (as the case may be).

(3)   A penalty under this regulation is a debt due from that person to the Authority, and is recoverable accordingly.

[3817]

NOTES
Commencement: see reg 1 at **[3732]**.

86   Proposal to take disciplinary measures

(1)   Where the Authority proposes to publish a statement under regulation 84 or to impose a penalty under regulation 85, it must give the person concerned a warning notice.

(2)   The warning notice must set out the terms of the proposed statement or state the amount of the proposed penalty.

(3)   If, having considered any representations made in response to the warning notice, the Authority decides to publish a statement under regulation 84 or to impose a penalty under regulation 85, it must without delay give the person concerned a decision notice.

(4)   The decision notice must set out the terms of the statement or state the amount of the penalty.

(5)   If the Authority decides to publish a statement under regulation 84 or impose a penalty on a person under regulation 85, the person concerned may refer the matter to the [Upper Tribunal].

(6)   Sections 210 (statements of policy) and 211 (statements of policy: procedure) of the 2000 Act apply in respect of the imposition of penalties under regulation 85 and the amount of such penalties as they apply in respect of the imposition of penalties under Part 14 of the 2000 Act (disciplinary measures) and the amount of penalties under that Part of that Act.

(7)   After a statement under regulation 84 is published, the Authority must send a copy of it to the person concerned and to any person to whom a copy of the decision notice was given under section 393(4) of the 2000 Act (third party rights) (as applied by paragraph 7 of Schedule 5 to these Regulations).

[3818]

NOTES
Commencement: see reg 1 at **[3732]**.

Para (5): words in square brackets substituted by the Transfer of Tribunal Functions Order 2010, SI 2010/22, art 5(2), Sch 3, paras 177, 186, subject to transitional provisions and savings in Sch 5 thereto.

87 Injunctions

(1) If, on the application of the Authority, the court is satisfied—

    (a) that there is a reasonable likelihood that any person will contravene a requirement imposed by or under these Regulations; or

    (b) that any person has contravened such a requirement and that there is a reasonable likelihood that the contravention will continue or be repeated,

the court may make an order restraining (or in Scotland an interdict prohibiting) the contravention.

(2) If, on the application of the Authority, the court is satisfied—

    (a) that any person has contravened a requirement imposed by or under these Regulations, and

    (b) that there are steps which could be taken for remedying the contravention,

the court may make an order requiring that person, and any other person who appears to have been knowingly concerned in the contravention, to take such steps as the court may direct to remedy it.

(3) If, on the application of the Authority, the court is satisfied that any person may have—

    (a) contravened a requirement imposed by or under these Regulations, or

    (b) been knowingly concerned in the contravention of such a requirement,

it may make an order restraining (or in Scotland an interdict prohibiting) them from disposing of, or otherwise dealing with, any assets of theirs which it is satisfied they are reasonably likely to dispose of or otherwise deal with.

(4) The jurisdiction conferred by this regulation is exercisable by the High Court and the Court of Session.

(5) In paragraph (2), references to remedying a contravention include references to mitigating its effect.

[3819]

NOTES

Commencement: see reg 1 at **[3732]**.

---

88 Power of Authority to require restitution

(1) The Authority may exercise the power in paragraph (2) if it is satisfied that a payment service provider (referred to in this regulation and regulation 89 as "the person concerned") has contravened a requirement imposed by or under these Regulations, or been knowingly concerned in the contravention of such a requirement, and that—

    (a) profits have accrued to the person concerned as a result of the contravention; or

    (b) one or more persons have suffered loss or been otherwise adversely affected as a result of the contravention.

(2) The power referred to in paragraph (1) is a power to require the person concerned, in accordance with such arrangements as the Authority considers appropriate, to pay to the appropriate person or distribute among the appropriate persons such amount as appears to the Authority to be just having regard—

    (a) in a case within sub-paragraph (a) of paragraph (1), to the profits appearing to the Authority to have accrued;

    (b) in a case within sub-paragraph (b) of that paragraph, to the extent of the loss or other adverse effect;

    (c) in a case within both of those paragraphs, to the profits appearing to the Authority to have accrued and to the extent of the loss or other adverse effect.

(3) In paragraph (2) "appropriate person" means a person appearing to the Authority to be someone—

    (a) to whom the profits mentioned in paragraph (1)(a) are attributable; or

    (b) who has suffered the loss or adverse effect mentioned in paragraph (1)(b).

[3820]

NOTES

Commencement: see reg 1 at **[3732]**.

---

89 Proposal to require restitution

(1) If the Authority proposes to exercise the power under regulation 88(2), it must give the person concerned a warning notice.

(2) The warning notice must state the amount which the Authority propose to require the person concerned to pay or distribute as mentioned in regulation 88(2).

(3) If, having considered any representations made in response to the warning notice, the Authority decides to exercise the power under regulation 88(2), it must without delay give the person concerned a decision notice.

(4) The decision notice must—

(a) state the amount that the person concerned is to pay or distribute;

(b) identify the person or persons to whom that amount is to be paid or among whom that amount is to be distributed; and

(c) state the arrangements in accordance with which the payment or distribution is to be made.

(5) If the Authority decides to exercise the power under regulation 88(2), the person concerned may refer the matter to the [Upper Tribunal].

[3821]

NOTES

Commencement: see reg 1 at [**3732**].

Para (5): words in square brackets substituted by the Transfer of Tribunal Functions Order 2010, SI 2010/22, art 5(2), Sch 3, paras 177, 187, subject to transitional provisions and savings in Sch 5 thereto.

90 Restitution orders

(1) The court may, on the application of the Authority, make an order under paragraph (2) if it is satisfied that a payment service provider has contravened a requirement imposed by or under these Regulations, or been knowingly concerned in the contravention of such a requirement, and that—

(a) profits have accrued to them as a result of the contravention; or

(b) one or more persons have suffered loss or been otherwise adversely affected as a result of the contravention.

(2) The court may order the person concerned to pay to the Authority such sum as appears to the court to be just having regard—

(a) in a case within sub-paragraph (a) of paragraph (1), to the profits appearing to the court to have accrued;

(b) in a case within sub-paragraph (b) of that paragraph, to the extent of the loss or other adverse effect;

(c) in a case within both of those sub-paragraphs, to the profits appearing to the court to have accrued and to the extent of the loss or other adverse effect.

(3) Any amount paid to the Authority in pursuance of an order under paragraph (2) must be paid by it to such qualifying person or distributed by it among such qualifying persons as the court may direct.

(4) In paragraph (3), "qualifying person" means a person appearing to the court to be someone—

(a) to whom the profits mentioned in paragraph (1)(a) are attributable; or

(b) who has suffered the loss or adverse effect mentioned in paragraph (1)(b).

(5) On an application under paragraph (1) the court may require the person concerned to supply it with such accounts or other information as it may require for any one or more of the following purposes—

(a) establishing whether any and, if so, what profits have accrued to them as mentioned in sub-paragraph (a) of that paragraph;

(b) establishing whether any person or persons have suffered any loss or adverse effect as mentioned in sub-paragraph (b) of that paragraph; and

(c) determining how any amounts are to be paid or distributed under paragraph (3).

(6) The court may require any accounts or other information supplied under paragraph (5) to be verified in such manner as it may direct.

(7) The jurisdiction conferred by this regulation is exercisable by the High Court and the Court of Session.

(8) Nothing in this regulation affects the right of any person other than the Authority to bring proceedings in respect of the matters to which this regulation applies.

[3822]

NOTES

Commencement: see reg 1 at [**3732**].

91 Complaints

(1) The Authority must maintain arrangements designed to enable payment service users and other interested parties to submit complaints to it that a requirement imposed by or under Parts 2 to 6 of these Regulations has been breached by a payment service provider.

(2)   Where it considers it appropriate, the Authority must include in any reply to a complaint under paragraph (1) details of the ombudsman scheme established under Part 16 of the 2000 Act (the ombudsman scheme).

[3823]

Miscellaneous

92   Costs of supervision

(1)   The functions of the Authority under these Regulations are to be treated for the purposes of paragraph 17 (fees) of Part 3 of Schedule 1 to the 2000 Act as functions conferred on the Authority under that Act with the following modifications—

    (a)   section 2(3) of the 2000 Act (the Authority's general duties) does not apply to the making of rules under paragraph 17 by virtue of this regulation;

    (b)   rules made under paragraph 17 by virtue of this regulation are not to be treated as regulating provisions for the purposes of section 159(1) of the 2000 Act (competition scrutiny);

    (c)   paragraph 17(2) and (3) are omitted.

(2)   The Authority must apply amounts paid to it by way of penalties imposed under regulation 85 towards expenses incurred in carrying out its functions under these Regulations or for any incidental purpose.

[3824]

93   Guidance

(1)   The Authority may give guidance consisting of such information and advice as it considers appropriate with respect to—

    (a)   the operation of these Regulations;

    (b)   any matters relating to the functions of the Authority under these Regulations;

    (c)   any other matters about which it appears to the Authority to be desirable to give information or advice in connection with these Regulations.

(2)   The Authority may—

    (a)   publish its guidance;

    (b)   offer copies of its published guidance for sale at a reasonable price;

    (c)   if it gives guidance in response to a request made by any person, make a reasonable charge for that guidance.

[3825]

94   Authority's exemption from liability in damages

The functions of the Authority under these Regulations are to be treated for the purposes of paragraph 19 (exemption from liability in damages) of Part 4 of Schedule 1 to the 2000 Act as functions conferred on the Authority under that Act.

[3826]

95   (*Introduces Sch 5 to the Regulations (outside the scope of this work).*)

PART 8
ACCESS TO PAYMENT SYSTEMS
General

96   Application of Part 8

(1)   This Part does not apply to the following kinds of payment systems—

    (a)   a designated system;

(b)   a payment system consisting solely of payment service providers belonging to the same group where one of the payment service providers enjoys effective control over the others;

(c)   a payment system where the sole payment service provider (whether as a single entity or a group)—
  (i)   acts or is able to act as the payment service provider for both the payer and the payee and is solely responsible for the management of the system; and
  (ii) licenses other payment service providers to participate in the system subject to their having no right to negotiate fees in respect of the system between or amongst themselves (although they may establish their own pricing in relation to payers and payees).

(2)   In paragraph (1)(a), "designated system" means a system which is declared by a designation order for the time being in force under regulation 4 of the Financial Markets and Insolvency (Settlement Finality) Regulations 1999 to be a designated system for the purposes of those Regulations.

[3827]

NOTES
Commencement: see reg 1 at **[3732]**.

97 Prohibition on restrictive rules on access to payment systems

(1)   Rules or conditions governing access to, or participation in, a payment system by authorised payment institutions, EEA authorised payment institutions and small payment institutions must—
  (a)   be objective, proportionate and non-discriminatory; and
  (b)   not prevent, restrict or inhibit access or participation more than is necessary to—
    (i)   safeguard against specific risks such as settlement risk, operational risk or business risk; or
    (ii) protect the financial and operational stability of the payment system.

(2)   Paragraph (1) applies only to such small payment institutions as are legal persons.

(3)   Rules or conditions governing access to, or participation in, a payment system which, in respect of payment service providers, payment service users or other payment systems—
  (a)   restrict effective participation in other payment systems;
  (b)   discriminate (whether directly or indirectly) between—
    (i)   different authorised payment institutions, or
    (ii) different small payment institutions,
    in relation to the rights, obligations or entitlements of participants in the payment system; or
  (c)   impose any restrictions on the basis that a person is not of a particular institutional status,
are prohibited.

[3828]

NOTES
Commencement: see reg 1 at **[3732]**.

Supervision and enforcement

98 Power of OFT to investigate

(1)   The OFT may conduct an investigation where there are reasonable grounds for suspecting that any rule or condition governing access to, or participation in, a payment system contravenes regulation 97(1) or (3).

(2)   Where the investigation relates to a possible breach of regulation 97(1)(b)(ii), the OFT must consult the Bank of England and the Authority.

[3829]

NOTES
Commencement: see reg 1 at **[3732]**.

99 OFT power to require information

(1)   For the purposes of an investigation under regulation 98 the OFT may require any person—
  (a)   to produce to it or to a person appointed by it, at a specified time and place, any specified document, or
  (b)   to provide to it or to a person appointed by it, at a specified time and place, any specified information,

which the OFT considers relates to any matter relevant to the investigation.

(2)   The power conferred by paragraph (1) is to be exercised by a notice indicating the subject matter and purpose of the investigation.

(3)   Information required to be provided under paragraph (1) must be provided in the specified manner and form, or, if that is not possible, in the nearest equivalent manner and form.

(4)   The power conferred by paragraph (1) to require a person to produce a document includes power—
    (a)   to require them to provide an explanation of the document, or
    (b)   if the document is not produced, to require them to state, to the best of their knowledge and belief, where it is.

(5)   In this regulation—
    "document" includes information recorded in any form;
    "information" includes estimates and forecasts;
    "specified" means—
        (a)   specified, or described, in the notice referred to in paragraph (2), or
        (b)   falling within a category which is specified, or described, in such notice.

[3830]

NOTES
Commencement: see reg 1 at **[3732]**.

100   Failure to comply with information requirement

(1)   If, on an application made by the OFT, it appears to the court that a person (the "information defaulter") has failed to do something that they were required to do under regulation 99, the court may make an order under this regulation.

(2)   An order under this regulation may require the information defaulter—
    (a)   to do the thing that they failed to do within such period as may be specified in the order;
    (b)   otherwise to take such steps to remedy the consequence of the failure as may be so specified.

(3)   In this regulation, "the court" means—
    (a)   in England and Wales and Northern Ireland, the High Court or the county court;
    (b)   in Scotland, the Court of Session or the sheriff court.

[3831]

NOTES
Commencement: see reg 1 at **[3732]**.

101   Privileged communications

(1)   A person is not required under regulation 99 to produce or disclose a privileged communication.

(2)   In paragraph (1) "privileged communication" means a communication—
    (a)   between a professional legal adviser and their client, or
    (b)   made in connection with, or in contemplation of, legal proceedings and for the purposes of those proceedings,
which in proceedings in the High Court would be protected from disclosure on grounds of legal professional privilege.

(3)   In the application of this regulation to Scotland the reference in paragraph (2) to—
    (a)   proceedings in the High Court is to be read as a reference to legal proceedings generally; and
    (b)   an entitlement on grounds of legal professional privilege is to be read as a reference to an entitlement on the grounds of confidentiality of communications.

[3832]

NOTES
Commencement: see reg 1 at **[3732]**.

102   Notice of OFT decision

Before the OFT, as the result of an investigation under regulation 98, makes a decision that any rules or conditions governing access to, or participation in, a payment system contravene regulation 97(1) or (3), the OFT must—
    (a)   give notice to the person (or persons) who the OFT considers are responsible for the contravention, and
    (b)   give that person (or those persons) an opportunity to make representations.

[3833]

PART 2
STATUTORY INSTRUMENTS

103 Publication of OFT decision

Where the OFT makes a decision after an investigation under regulation 98, the OFT must publish its decision, together with its reasons for making it.

[3834]

NOTES
Commencement: see reg 1 at **[3732]**.

104 Enforcement of decisions

(1) If the OFT makes a decision that any rules or conditions governing access to, or participation in, a payment system contravene regulation 97(1) or (3), the OFT may give such directions as the OFT considers appropriate to such person or persons as it considers appropriate.

(2) A direction under paragraph (1) may (in particular)—
  (a) require the person concerned to change any rule or condition so that it no longer contravenes regulation 97(1) or (3); and
  (b) relate to the conduct of the person in implementing any rule or condition.

(3) A direction under paragraph (1) must be given in writing.

(4) If a person fails, without reasonable excuse, to comply with a direction under paragraph (1), the OFT may apply to the High Court (or, in Scotland, the Court of Session) for an order requiring that person to comply with the direction within a time specified in the order.

(5) An order under paragraph (4) may provide for all of the costs of, or incidental to, the application for the order to be borne by the person in default.

[3835]

NOTES
Commencement: see reg 1 at **[3732]**.

105 Power of OFT to impose financial penalties

(1) Where the OFT is satisfied that any rules or conditions governing access to, or participation in, a payment system contravene regulation 97(1) or (3), the OFT may impose a penalty of such amount as it considers appropriate on such persons as it considers appropriate.

(2) The OFT may impose a penalty on a person under paragraph (1) only if the OFT is satisfied that the infringement has been committed intentionally or negligently by that person.

(3) Notice of a penalty under this regulation must—
  (a) be in writing; and
  (b) specify the date before which the penalty is required to be paid.

(4) The date specified must not be earlier than the end of the period within which an appeal against the notice may be brought under regulation 106.

(5) Any sums received by the OFT under this regulation are to be paid into the Consolidated Fund.

[3836]

NOTES
Commencement: see reg 1 at **[3732]**.

Miscellaneous

106 Appeal to the Competition Appeal Tribunal

(1) A person may appeal to the Competition Appeal Tribunal from a decision by the OFT to give a direction under regulation 104(1) to that person or to impose a penalty under regulation 105 on that person.

(2) In determining an appeal under paragraph (1) the Competition Appeal Tribunal shall apply the same principles as would be applied by a court on an application for judicial review.

(3) Sections 14 (constitution of tribunal) and 15 (tribunal rules) of the Enterprise Act 2002 apply in respect of appeals to the Competition Appeal Tribunal under paragraph (1) as they apply in respect of appeals to the Competition Appeal Tribunal under that Act.

[3837]

PART 2
STATUTORY INSTRUMENTS

NOTES
Commencement: see reg 1 at **[3732]**.

107 Disclosure of information by OFT

Subject to regulation 119(2) and (3), Part 9 of the Enterprise Act 2002 (information) applies in respect of information which comes to the OFT by virtue of these Regulations as it applies in respect of information which is specified information for the purposes of Part 9.

[3838]

NOTES
Commencement: see reg 1 at **[3732]**.

108 Defamation

For the purposes of the law relating to defamation, absolute privilege attaches to any decision made or notice given by the OFT in the exercise of any of its functions under this Part.

[3839]

NOTES
Commencement: see reg 1 at **[3732]**.

109 Guidance

(1) The OFT may give guidance consisting of such information and advice as it considers appropriate with respect to the exercise of its functions under this Part.

(2) The OFT may—
    (a) publish its guidance;
    (b) if it gives guidance in response to a request made by any person, make a reasonable charge for that guidance.

[3840]

NOTES
Commencement: see reg 1 at **[3732]**.

PART 9
GENERAL

Criminal Offences

110 Prohibition on provision of payment services by persons other than payment service providers

(1) A person may not provide a payment service in the United Kingdom, or purport to do so, unless the person is—
    (a) an authorised payment institution;
    (b) a small payment institution;
    (c) an EEA authorised payment institution exercising its passport rights;
    [(d) a credit institution authorised in the UK or exercising an EEA right in accordance with Part 2 of Schedule 3 to the 2000 Act (exercise of passport rights by EEA firms);
    (e) an electronic money institution authorised in the UK or exercising an EEA right in accordance with Part 2 of Schedule 3 to the 2000 Act;
    (f) the Post Office Limited;
    (g) the Bank of England, the European Central Bank or a national central bank of an EEA State other than the United Kingdom,
    (h) a government department or a local authority; or
    (i) exempt under regulation 3.]

(2) A person who contravenes paragraph (1) is guilty of an offence and is liable—
    (a) on summary conviction, to imprisonment for a term not exceeding three months or to a fine not exceeding the statutory maximum, or both;
    (b) on conviction on indictment, to imprisonment for a term not exceeding two years or to a fine, or both.

[3841]

NOTES
Commencement: see reg 1 at **[3732]**.
Para (1): sub-paras (d)–(i) substituted for original sub-paras (d), (e) by the Payment Services (Amendment) Regulations 2009, SI 2009/2475, regs 2, 11; see further the note to reg 10A at **[3742]**.

111 False claims to be a payment service provider or exempt

(1)   A person who does not fall within any of sub-paragraphs (a) to (e) of regulation 110(1) may not—

  (a)   describe themselves (in whatever terms) as a person falling within any of those sub-paragraphs; or

  (b)   behave, or otherwise hold themselves out, in a manner which indicates (or which is reasonably likely to be understood as indicating) that they are such a person.

(2)   A person who contravenes paragraph (1) is guilty of an offence and is liable on summary conviction to imprisonment for a term not exceeding three months or to a fine not exceeding level 5 on the standard scale, or both.

[3842]

NOTES
Commencement: see reg 1 at **[3732]**.

112 Defences

In proceedings for an offence under regulation 110 or 111 it is a defence for the accused to show that they took all reasonable precautions and exercised all due diligence to avoid committing the offence.

[3843]

NOTES
Commencement: see reg 1 at **[3732]**.

113 Contravention of regulations 49 and 50

(1)   A person (not being a payment service provider) who contravenes regulation 49(2) or 50(2) is guilty of an offence and liable on summary conviction to a fine not exceeding level 5 on the standard scale.

(2)   No offence is committed if the person took all reasonable steps and exercised all due diligence to ensure that the requirement imposed on the person by regulation 49(2) or 50(2), as the case may be, would be complied with.

[3844]

NOTES
Commencement: see reg 1 at **[3732]**.

114 Misleading the Authority or the OFT

(1)   A person may not, in purported compliance with any requirement imposed by or under these Regulations, knowingly or recklessly give—

  (a)   the Authority; or

  (b)   the OFT,

information which is false or misleading in a material particular.

(2)   A person may not—

  (a)   provide any information to another person, knowing the information to be false or misleading in a material particular, or

  (b)   recklessly provide to another person any information which is false or misleading in a material particular,

knowing that the information is to be used for the purpose of providing information to the Authority in connection with its functions under these Regulations.

(3)   A person may not—

  (a)   provide any information to another person, knowing the information to be false or misleading in a material particular, or

  (b)   recklessly provide to another person any information which is false or misleading in a material particular,

knowing that the information is to be used for the purpose of providing information to the OFT in connection with their functions under these Regulations.

(4)   A person who knows or suspects that an investigation by the OFT under regulation 98 is being or is likely to be conducted may not—

  (a)   intentionally or recklessly destroy or otherwise dispose of, falsify or conceal a document (as defined by regulation 99(5)) which may be relevant to such an investigation; or

  (b)   cause or permit its destruction, disposal, falsification or concealment.

(5)   A person who contravenes paragraph (1), (2), (3) or (4) is guilty of an offence and is liable—

(a)   on summary conviction, to a fine not exceeding the statutory maximum;

(b)   on conviction on indictment, to a fine.

[3845]

NOTES
Commencement: see reg 1 at **[3732]**.

115   Restriction on penalties

A person who is convicted of an offence under these Regulations is not liable to a penalty under regulation 85 or 105 in respect of the same contravention of a requirement imposed by or under these Regulations.

[3846]

NOTES
Commencement: see reg 1 at **[3732]**.

116   Liability of officers of bodies corporate etc

(1)   If an offence under these Regulations committed by a body corporate is shown—

(a)   to have been committed with the consent or connivance of an officer, or

(b)   to be attributable to any neglect on their part,

the officer as well as the body corporate is guilty of the offence and liable to be proceeded against and punished accordingly.

(2)   If the affairs of a body corporate are managed by its members, paragraph (1) applies in relation to the acts and defaults of a member in connection with such member's functions of management as if the member were a director of the body.

(3)   If an offence under these Regulations committed by a partnership is shown—

(a)   to have been committed with the consent or connivance of a partner, or

(b)   to be attributable to any neglect on their part,

the partner as well as the partnership is guilty of the offence and liable to be proceeded against and punished accordingly.

(4)   If an offence under these Regulations committed by an unincorporated association (other than a partnership) is shown—

(a)   to have been committed with the consent or connivance of an officer, or

(b)   to be attributable to any neglect of such officer,

the officer as well as the association is guilty of the offence and liable to be proceeded against and punished accordingly.

(5)   In this regulation—
"officer"—

(a)   in relation to a body corporate, means a director, manager, secretary, chief executive, member of the committee of management, or a person purporting to act in such a capacity; and

(b)   in relation to an unincorporated association, means any officer of the association or any member of its governing body, or a person purporting to act in such capacity; and

"partner" includes a person purporting to act as a partner.

[3847]

NOTES
Commencement: see reg 1 at **[3732]**.

117   Prosecution of offences

(1)   Proceedings for an offence under these Regulations may be instituted only—

(a)   in respect of an offence under regulation 110, 111, 113, or 114(1)(a) or (2), by the Authority;

(b)   in respect of an offence under regulation 114(1)(b), (3) or (4), by the OFT; or

(c)   by or with the consent of the Director of Public Prosecutions.

(2)   Paragraph (1) does not apply to proceedings in Scotland.

[3848]

NOTES
Commencement: see reg 1 at **[3732]**.

118 Proceedings against unincorporated bodies

(1) Proceedings for an offence alleged to have been committed by a partnership or an unincorporated association must be brought in the name of the partnership or association (and not in that of its members).

(2) A fine imposed on the partnership or association on its conviction of an offence is to be paid out of the funds of the partnership or association.

(3) Rules of court relating to the service of documents are to have effect as if the partnership or association were a body corporate.

(4) In proceedings for an offence brought against the partnership or association—
- (a) section 33 of the Criminal Justice Act 1925 (procedure on charge of offence against corporation) and section 46 of and Schedule 3 to the Magistrates' Courts Act 1980 (corporations) apply as they do in relation to a body corporate;
- (b) section 70 of the Criminal Procedure (Scotland) Act 1995 (proceedings against bodies corporate) applies as it does in relation to a body corporate;
- (c) section 18 of the Criminal Justice (Northern Ireland) Act 1945 (procedure on charge) and Schedule 4 to the Magistrates' Courts (Northern Ireland) Order 1981 (corporations) apply as they do in relation to a body corporate.

(5) Summary proceedings for an offence under these Regulations may be taken—
- (a) against a body corporate or unincorporated association at any place at which it has a place of business;
- (b) against an individual at any place where they are for the time being.

(6) Paragraph (5) does not affect any jurisdiction exercisable apart from this regulation.

[3849]

NOTES
Commencement: see reg 1 at **[3732]**.

Duties of the Authority, the Commissioners and the OFT to cooperate

119 Duty to co-operate and exchange of information

(1) The Authority, the Commissioners and the OFT must take such steps as they consider appropriate to co-operate with each other and—
- (a) the competent authorities designated under Article 20(1), or referred to in Article 82(1), of the payment services directive, of EEA States other than the United Kingdom;
- (b) the European Central Bank, the Bank of England and the national central banks of EEA States other than the United Kingdom; and
- (c) any other relevant competent authorities designated under Community law or the law of the United Kingdom or any other EEA State which is applicable to payment service providers,

for the purposes of the exercise by those bodies of their functions under the payment services directive and other relevant Community or national legislation.

(2) Subject to the requirements of the Data Protection Act 1998, sections 348 and 349 of the 2000 Act (as applied with modifications by paragraph 5 of Schedule 5 to these Regulations), regulation 49A of the Money Laundering Regulations 2007 (as inserted by paragraph 6(g) of Schedule 6 to these Regulations) and any other applicable restrictions on the disclosure of information, the Authority, the Commissioners and the OFT may provide information to each other and—
- (a) the bodies mentioned in paragraph (1)(a) and (c);
- (b) the European Central Bank, the Bank of England and the national central banks of EEA States other than the United Kingdom when acting in their capacity as monetary and oversight authorities;
- (c) where relevant, other public authorities responsible for the oversight of payment and settlement systems;

for the purposes of the exercise by those bodies of their functions under the payment services directive and other relevant Community or national legislation.

(3) Part 9 of the Enterprise Act 2002 does not prohibit disclosure by the OFT under paragraph (2) but the OFT must have regard to the considerations mentioned in section 244 of that Act (specified information: considerations relevant to disclosure) before making any such disclosure.

[3850]

NOTES
Commencement: see reg 1 at **[3732]**.

Actions for breach of requirements

120   Right to bring actions

(1)   A contravention—
     (a)   which is to be taken to have occurred by virtue of regulation 17;
     (b)   of a requirement imposed by regulation 19; or
     (c)   of a requirement imposed by or under Part 5 or 6,

is actionable at the suit of a private person who suffers loss as a result of the contravention, subject to the defences and other incidents applying to actions for breach of statutory duty.

(2)   A person acting in a fiduciary or representative capacity may bring an action under paragraph (1) on behalf of a private person if any remedy—
     (a)   will be exclusively for the benefit of the private person; and
     (b)   cannot be obtained by way of an action brought otherwise than at the suit of the fiduciary or representative.

(3)   In this regulation "private person" means—
     (a)   any individual, except where the individual suffers the loss in question in the course of providing payment services; and
     (b)   any person who is not an individual, except where that person suffers the loss in question in the course of carrying on business of any kind;

but does not include a government, a local authority (in the United Kingdom or elsewhere) or an international organisation.

[3851]

NOTES

Commencement: see reg 1 at **[3732]**.

Transitional provisions

121   Transitional provisions: deemed authorisation

(1)   Any financial institution (within the meaning of the banking consolidation directive) which—
     (a)   is constituted under the law of a part of the United Kingdom and has its head office and, if it has a registered office, that office, in the United Kingdom; and
     (b)   before 25th December 2007 had—
         (i)   lawfully provided payment services in the United Kingdom; and
         (ii)   met the condition in Article 24(1)(e) of the banking consolidation directive;

shall be deemed to have been granted authorisation by the Authority under regulation 9.

(2)   An institution which is deemed to have been granted authorisation by virtue of paragraph (1) shall continue on or after 25th December 2009 to be deemed to have been granted authorisation only if it has by that date—
     (a)   notified the Authority of the payment services referred to in sub-paragraph (b)(i); and
     (b)   provided the Authority with the information specified in paragraph 1, 4, 7 to 9 and 12 of Schedule 2 ("the required information").

(3)   Authorisation which continues on or after 25th December 2009 to be deemed to have been granted by virtue of paragraph (2) shall continue to be so deemed until such time as the Authority decides whether to include the institution in the register as an authorised payment institution.

(4)   If the Authority decides to include the institution in the register as an authorised payment institution—
     (a)   it must as soon as practicable update the register accordingly; and
     (b)   the institution shall cease to be deemed to have been granted authorisation by virtue of paragraph (1) or (2).

(5)   The Authority may decide that an institution is not to be included in the register as an authorised payment institution only if—
     (a)   it has not received the required information; or
     (b)   any of the conditions in regulation 6(4) to (6) (other than the condition that a person must be a body corporate) ("the required conditions") are not met in respect of that institution.

(6)   If the Authority is satisfied that—
     (a)   it has received the required information; and
     (b)   the required conditions are met,

it must give the institution notice of its decision.

(7)   If the Authority proposes to decide that—
     (a)   it has not received the required information; or
     (b)   any of the required conditions is not met,

it must give the institution a warning notice.

(8)   The Authority must, having considered any representations in response to the warning notice—

(a)   if it decides that it has not received the required information or that any of the required conditions is not met, give the institution a decision notice; or

(b)   if it decides that it has received the required information and that the required conditions have been met, give the institution notice of its decision.

(9)   If the Authority gives the institution a decision notice, the institution may refer the matter to the [Upper Tribunal].

(10)   Where the period for a reference to the [Upper Tribunal] has expired without a reference being made, the institution shall cease to be deemed to have been granted authorisation by virtue of paragraph (1) or (2).

(11)   Where an institution is deemed to have been granted authorisation by virtue of paragraph (1) or (2)—

(a)   the duty to which the Authority is subject under regulation 4(1)(a) to maintain a register shall not apply in respect of it; and

(b)   Parts 3 and 4 shall not apply to it.

[3852]

NOTES

Commencement: see reg 1 at [3732].

Paras (9), (10): words in square brackets substituted by the Transfer of Tribunal Functions Order 2010, SI 2010/22, art 5(2), Sch 3, paras 177, 188, subject to transitional provisions and savings in Sch 5 thereto.

122   Transitional provisions: requirement to be authorised as a payment institution

(1)   Any person which—

(a)   is a body corporate constituted under the law of a part of the United Kingdom and has its head office and, if it has a registered office, that office, in the United Kingdom;

(b)   is not a body—

(i)   mentioned in any of paragraphs (d) to (h) of the definition in regulation 2(1) of a payment service provider; or

(ii)   which is deemed to have been granted authorisation by virtue of regulation 121(1) or (2); and

(c)   immediately before 25th December 2007, was lawfully providing payment services in the United Kingdom,

may continue until 1st May 2011 to provide payment services in the United Kingdom notwithstanding that the person has not been granted authorisation by the Authority under regulation 9.

(2)   Parts 5 to 8 and regulation 110(1) apply to a person falling within paragraph (1) as if the person were an authorised payment institution.

[3853]

NOTES

Commencement: see reg 1 at [3732].

123   Transitional provisions: requirement to be registered as a small payment institution

(1)   Any person who—

(a)   immediately before 25th December 2007, was lawfully providing payment services in the United Kingdom;

(b)   is not a body—

(i)   mentioned in any of paragraphs (d) to (h) of the definition in regulation 2(1) of a payment service provider; or

(ii)   which is deemed to have been granted authorisation by virtue of regulation 121(1) or (2) or which falls within regulation 122(1); and

(c)   meets the conditions set out in regulation 13(4) to (6) and complies with the financial limit referred to in regulation 8 (as applied by regulation 14(c)),

may continue until 25th December 2010 to provide payment services in the United Kingdom notwithstanding that the person has not been granted registration by the Authority under regulation 9 (as applied by regulation 14).

(2)   Parts 5 to 8 and regulation 110(1) apply to a person falling within paragraph (1) as if the person were a small payment institution.

[3854]

PART 2
STATUTORY INSTRUMENTS

NOTES
  Commencement: see reg 1 at **[3732]**.

124　Transitional provisions: early applications

(1)　Where an application is made under regulation 5(1) or (2) or 12(1) or (2) before 1st August 2009 and is a completed application, the Authority must determine it before 1st November 2009.

(2)　The requirement under regulation 23(2) for information to be given to the host state competent authority within one month of receipt by the Authority of a notice of intention does not apply where the notice of intention is received by the Authority before 1st November 2009.

(3)　Any requirement under these Regulations to update the register does not apply until 1st November 2009.

[3855]

NOTES
  Commencement: see reg 1 at **[3732]**.

125　Transitional provisions: the ombudsman scheme

Part 16 of, and Schedule 17 to, the 2000 Act (the ombudsman scheme) shall apply as if persons who fall within regulation 122(1) or 123(1) were payment service providers within the meaning of these Regulations.

[3856]

NOTES
  Commencement: see reg 1 at **[3732]**.

Amendments to primary and secondary legislation

126　Amendments to primary and secondary legislation

Schedule 6, which contains amendments to primary and secondary legislation, has effect.

[3857]

NOTES
  Commencement: see reg 1 at **[3732]**.

[127　Application to Gibraltar

Schedule 7, which contains provisions concerning the application of these Regulations to Gibraltar, has effect.]

[3858]

NOTES
  Commencement: 1 October 2009 (certain purposes); 1 November 2009 (otherwise); see further the note to reg 10A at **[3742]**.
  Inserted by the Payment Services (Amendment) Regulations 2009, SI 2009/2475, regs 2, 12.

SCHEDULES

SCHEDULE 1
PAYMENT SERVICES

Regulation 2(1)

PART 1
PAYMENT SERVICES

1.　Subject to Part 2, the following activities, when carried out as a regular occupation or business activity, are payment services—
  (a)　services enabling cash to be placed on a payment account and all of the operations required for operating a payment account;
  (b)　services enabling cash withdrawals from a payment account and all of the operations required for operating a payment account;
  (c)　the execution of the following types of payment transaction—
    (i)　direct debits, including one-off direct debits;
    (ii)　payment transactions executed through a payment card or a similar device;
    (iii)　credit transfers, including standing orders;
  (d)　the execution of the following types of payment transaction where the funds are covered by a credit line for the payment service user—

        (i)   direct debits, including one-off direct debits;

        (ii)   payment transactions executed through a payment card or a similar device;

        (iii) credit transfers, including standing orders;

(e)   issuing payment instruments or acquiring payment transactions;

(f)   money remittance;

(g)   the execution of payment transactions where the consent of the payer to execute the payment transaction is given by means of any telecommunication, digital or IT device and the payment is made to the telecommunication, IT system or network operator acting only as an intermediary between the payment service user and the supplier of the goods or services.

[3859]

NOTES

Commencement: see reg 1 at **[3732]**.

PART 2
ACTIVITIES WHICH DO NOT CONSTITUTE PAYMENT SERVICES

2.   The following activities do not constitute payment services—

    (a)   payment transactions executed wholly in cash and directly between the payer and the payee, without any intermediary intervention;

    (b)   payment transactions between the payer and the payee through a commercial agent authorised to negotiate or conclude the sale or purchase of goods or services on behalf of the payer or the payee;

    (c)   the professional physical transport of banknotes and coins, including their collection, processing and delivery;

    (d)   payment transactions consisting of non-professional cash collection and delivery as part of a not-for-profit or charitable activity;

    (e)   services where cash is provided by the payee to the payer as part of a payment transaction for the purchase of goods or services following an explicit request by the payer immediately before the execution of the payment transaction;

    (f)   money exchange business consisting of cash-to-cash operations where the funds are not held on a payment account;

    (g)   payment transactions based on any of the following documents drawn on the payment service provider with a view to placing funds at the disposal of the payee—

        (i)   paper cheques of any kind, including traveller's cheques;

        (ii)   bankers' drafts;

        (iii) paper-based vouchers;

        (iv) paper postal orders;

    (h)   payment transactions carried out within a payment or securities settlement system between payment service providers and settlement agents, central counterparties, clearing houses, central banks or other participants in the system;

    (i)   payment transactions related to securities asset servicing, including dividends, income or other distributions, or redemption or sale, carried out by persons referred to in sub-paragraph (h) or by investment firms, credit institutions, collective investment undertakings or asset management companies providing investment services or by any other entities allowed to have the custody of financial instruments;

    (j)   services provided by technical service providers, which support the provision of payment services, without the provider entering at any time into possession of the funds to be transferred, including—

        (i)   the processing and storage of data;

        (ii)   trust and privacy protection services;

        (iii) data and entity authentication;

        (iv) information technology;

        (v)   communication network provision; and

        (vi) the provision and maintenance of terminals and devices used for payment services;

    (k)   services based on instruments that can be used to acquire goods or services only—

        (i)   in or on the issuer's premises; or

        (ii)   under a commercial agreement with the issuer, either within a limited network of service providers or for a limited range of goods or services,

    and for these purposes the "issuer" is the person who issues the instrument in question;

    (l)   payment transactions executed by means of any telecommunication, digital or IT device, where the goods or services purchased are delivered to and are to be used through a telecommunication, digital or IT device, provided that the telecommunication, digital or IT operator does not act only as an intermediary between the payment service user and the supplier of the goods and services;

    (m) payment transactions carried out between payment service providers, or their agents or branches, for their own account;

(n)   payment transactions between a parent undertaking and its subsidiary or between subsidiaries of the same parent undertaking, without any intermediary intervention by a payment service provider other than an undertaking belonging to the same group;

(o)   services by providers to withdraw cash by means of automated teller machines acting on behalf of one or more card issuers, which are not party to the framework contract with the customer withdrawing money from a payment account, where no other payment service is conducted by the provider.

[3860]

NOTES

Commencement: see reg 1 at **[3732]**.

SCHEDULE 2
INFORMATION TO BE INCLUDED IN OR WITH AN APPLICATION
FOR AUTHORISATION

Regulation 5(1)

1.   A programme of operations setting out, in particular, the type of payment services envisaged.

2.   A business plan including a forecast budget calculation for the first three financial years which demonstrates that the applicant is able to employ appropriate and proportionate systems, resources and procedures to operate soundly.

3.   Evidence that the applicant holds initial capital for the purposes of regulation 6(3).

4.   Where regulation 19 applies, a description of the measures taken for safeguarding payment service users' funds in accordance with that regulation.

5.   A description of the applicant's governance arrangements and internal control mechanisms, including administrative risk management and accounting procedures, which demonstrates that such arrangements, mechanisms and procedures are proportionate, appropriate, sound and adequate.

6.   A description of the internal control mechanisms which the applicant has established in order to comply with the Money Laundering Regulations 2007 and Regulation (EC) No 1781/2006 of the European Parliament and of the Council of 15 November 2006 on information on the payer accompanying transfers of funds.

7.   A description of the applicant's structural organisation, including, where applicable, a description of the intended use of agents and branches and a description of outsourcing arrangements, and of its participation in a national or international payment system.

8.—(1)   In relation to each person holding, directly or indirectly, a qualifying holding in the applicant—

(a)   the size and nature of their qualifying holding; and

(b)   evidence of their suitability taking into account the need to ensure the sound and prudent management of a payment institution.

9.—(1)   The identity of directors and persons who are or will be responsible for the management of the applicant and, where relevant, persons who are or will be responsible for the management of the payment services activities of the applicant.

(2)   Evidence that the persons described in sub-paragraph (1) are of good repute and that they possess appropriate knowledge and experience to perform payment services.

10.   The identity of the auditors of the applicant, if any.

11.—(1)   The legal status of the applicant and, where the applicant is a limited company, its articles.

(2)   In this paragraph "articles" has the meaning given in section 7 of the Companies Act 1985 (articles prescribing regulations for companies) until the coming into force of section 18 of the Companies Act 2006 (articles of association) when it will have the meaning given by that section.

12.   The address of the head office of the applicant.

13.   For the purposes of paragraphs 4, 5 and 7, a description of the audit arrangements of the applicant and of the organisational arrangements the applicant has set up with a view to taking all reasonable steps to protect the interests of its payment service users and to ensure continuity and reliability in the performance of payment services.

[3861]

NOTES

Commencement: see reg 1 at **[3732]**.

Note: para 8 above is reproduced as it appears in the Queen's Printer's copy of these Regulations, ie, there is no sub-paragraph (2).

PART 2
STATUTORY INSTRUMENTS

SCHEDULE 3
CAPITAL REQUIREMENTS

Regulations 6(3), 18

PART 1
INITIAL CAPITAL

1. For the purposes of this Part, "initial capital" comprises the items specified in paragraph 3(a), (b) and (c) of this Schedule.

2.—(1) An applicant for authorisation as a payment institution must hold the amount of initial capital specified in the second column of the table, corresponding to the payment services provided or to be provided (as specified in the first column).

(2) Where more than one initial capital requirement applies, the applicant must hold initial capital of whichever is the greater amount.

Payment services	Initial capital requirement (euro)
Payment services specified in paragraph 127(f) of Schedule 1	20,000
Payment services specified in paragraph 127(g) of Schedule 1	50,000
Any of the payment services specified in paragraph 127(a) to (e) of Schedule 1	125,000

[3862]

NOTES

Commencement: see reg 1 at [3732].

PART 2
OWN FUNDS

Qualifying items

3. For the purposes of this Part, "own funds" means the following items, subject to the deductions specified in paragraph 147 and to the limits specified in paragraph 149—

    (a)   paid up capital, including share premium accounts but excluding amounts arising in respect of cumulative preference shares;

    (b)   reserves other than—

        (i)   revaluation reserves;

        (ii)   fair value reserves related to gains or losses on cash flow hedges of financial instruments measured at amortised cost; and

        (iii)   that part of profit and loss reserves that arises from any gains on liabilities valued at fair value that are due to changes in the authorised payment institution's credit standing;

    (c)   profit or loss brought forward as a result of the application of the final profit or loss, provided that—

        (i)   interim profits may only be included if they are—

            (aa)   verified by persons responsible for the auditing of the authorised payment institution's accounts;

            (bb)   shown to the satisfaction of the Authority that the amount has been evaluated in accordance with the principles set out in directive 86/635/EEC of the Council of the 8th December 1986 on the annual accounts and consolidated accounts of banks and other financial institutions; and

            (cc)   net of any foreseeable charge or dividend;

        (ii)   in the case of an authorised payment institution which is the originator of a securitisation, net gains arising from the capitalisation of future income from the securitised assets and providing credit enhancement to positions in the securitisation are excluded;

    (d)   revaluation reserves;

    (e)   general or collective provisions if—

        (i)   they are freely available to the authorised payment institution to cover normal payment services risks where revenue or capital losses have not yet been identified;

        (ii)   their existence is disclosed in internal accounting records; and

        (iii)   their amount is determined by the management of the authorised payment institution, verified by a statutory auditor or audit firm (as defined by regulation 20(2)) and notified to the Authority;

(f) securities of indeterminate duration and other instruments that fulfil the following conditions—

   (i) they may not be reimbursed on the bearer's initiative or without the prior agreement of the Authority;

   (ii) the debt agreement provides for the authorised payment institution to have the option of deferring the payment of interest on the debt;

   (iii) the lender's claim on the authorised payment institution is wholly subordinated to those of all non-subordinated creditors;

   (iv) the documents governing the issue of the securities provide for debt and unpaid interest to be such as to absorb losses, whilst leaving the authorised payment institution in a position to continue trading;

provided that only fully paid-up amounts are to be taken into account;

(g) cumulative preferential shares, other than fixed-term cumulative preference shares referred to in paragraph (j);

(h) the commitments of the members of an authorised payment institution set up as a cooperative, comprising—

   (i) that institution's uncalled capital; and

   (ii) the legal commitments of the members of that institution to make additional non-refundable payments should the institution incur a loss provided that such payments can be demanded without delay;

(i) the joint and several commitments of the borrower in the case of an authorised payment institution organised as a fund, comprising—

   (i) that institution's uncalled capital; and

   (ii) the legal commitments of the borrowers of that institution to make additional non-refundable payments should the institution incur a loss provided that such payments can be demanded without delay;

(j) fixed-term cumulative preferential shares and subordinated loan capital if—

   (i) binding agreements exist under which, in the event of the winding-up of the authorised payment institution, they rank after the claims of all other creditors and are not to be repaid until all other debts outstanding at the time have been settled; and

   (ii) in the case of subordinated loan capital—

      (aa) only fully paid-up funds are taken into account;

      (bb) the loans involved have an original maturity of at least five years, after which they may be repaid;

      (cc) the extent to which they may rank as own funds is gradually reduced during at least the last five years before the repayment date; and

      (dd) the loan agreement does not include any clause providing that in specified circumstances, other than the winding-up of the authorised payment institution, the debt will become repayable before the agreed repayment date.

4. The items specified in paragraph 144(a) to (d) must be—

(a) available to the authorised payment institution for unrestricted and immediate use to cover risks or losses as soon as these occur; and

(b) net of any foreseeable tax charge at the moment of their calculation or be suitably adjusted in so far as such tax charges reduce the amount up to which these items may be applied to cover risks or losses.

5. Own funds are not to include guarantees provided by the Crown or a local authority to a payment institution which is a public sector entity for the purposes of the banking consolidation directive.

Deductions from own funds

6. The deductions from own funds are—

(a) own shares at book value held by the authorised payment institution;

(b) intangible assets;

(c) material losses of the current financial year;

(d) holdings of shares in credit institutions and financial institutions exceeding 10% of their capital;

(e) if sub-paragraph (d) applies, the items specified in paragraph 144(f), (g) and (j) held in the relevant credit institution or financial institution;

(f) holdings of shares or of the items specified in paragraph 3(f), (g) and (j) held in other credit institutions or financial institutions where—

   (i) the holding has not been deducted in accordance with sub-paragraph (d) or (e) of this paragraph; and

   (ii) the total amount of such holdings exceeds 10% of the authorised payment institution's own funds calculated before deduction of the items specified in this sub-paragraph and sub-paragraphs (d), (e), (g) and (h);

   (g)   participations which the authorised payment institution holds in an insurance undertaking, reinsurance undertaking or insurance holding company; and

   (h)   the following instruments held in an insurance undertaking, reinsurance undertaking or insurance holding company in which the authorised payment institution holds a participation—

      (i)   instruments referred to in article 16(3) of directive 73/239/EEC of the Council on the coordination of laws, regulations and administrative provisions relating to the taking-up and pursuit of the business of direct insurance other than life assurance;

      (ii)   instruments referred to in article 27(3) of directive 2002/83/EC of the European Parliament and of the Council of 5th November 2002 concerning life assurance.

7.   Where shares in another credit institution, financial institution, insurance undertaking, reinsurance undertaking or insurance holding company are held temporarily for the purposes of a financial assistance operation designed to reorganise and save that entity, the Authority may direct that any or all of the items specified in paragraph 147(d) to (h) are not to be deducted from own funds.

Limits on qualifying items

8.—(1)   The limits referred to in paragraph 144 are—

   (a)   that A must not exceed B; and

   (b)   that C must not exceed 50% of B.

  (2)   After applying such limits—

   (a)   50% of the total of the items specified in paragraph 6(d) to (h) must be deducted from A and the remaining 50% must be deducted from B; and

   (b)   the amount, if any, by which the amount to be deducted from A exceeds A must be deducted from B.

  (3)   In this paragraph—

   (a)   "A" means the total of the items specified in paragraph 144(d) to (j);

   (b)   "B" means the total of the items specified in paragraph 144(a) to (c) less the total of the items specified in paragraph 147(a) to (c); and

   (c)   "C" means the total of the items specified in paragraph 144(h) to (j).

9.   The Authority may in temporary and exceptional circumstances direct that an authorised payment institution may exceed one or more of the limits described in paragraph 8(1).

10.   An authorised payment institution must not include in its own funds calculation any item—

   (a)   used in an equivalent calculation by an authorised payment institution, credit institution, investment firm, asset management company or insurance undertaking in the same group; or

   (b)   in the case of an authorised payment institution which carries out activities other than providing payment services, is used in carrying out those activities.

Own funds requirement

11.   An authorised payment institution must hold own funds calculated in accordance with such of Method A, Method B or Method C as the Authority may direct.

Adjustment by the Authority

12.   The Authority may direct that an authorised payment institution must hold own funds up to 20% higher, or up to 20% lower, than the amount which would result from paragraph 152.

13.   A direction made under paragraph 153 must be on the basis of an evaluation of the relevant authorised payment institution including, if available and where the Authority considers it appropriate, any risk-management processes, risk loss database or internal control mechanisms of the authorised payment institution.

14.   The Authority may make a reasonable charge for making an evaluation required under paragraph 154.

Provision for start-up payment institutions

15.   If an authorised payment institution has not completed a full financial year's business, references to a figure for the preceding financial year are to be read as the equivalent figure projected in the business plan provided in the payment institution's application for authorisation, subject to any adjustment to that plan required by the Authority.

Method A

16.—(1)   "Method A" means the calculation method set out in this paragraph.

(2)   The own funds requirement is 10% of the authorised payment institution's fixed overheads for the preceding financial year.

(3)   If a material change has occurred in an authorised payment institution's business since the preceding financial year, the Authority may direct that the own funds requirement is to be a higher or lower amount than that calculated in accordance with sub-paragraph (2).

Method B

17.—(1)   "Method B" means the calculation method set out in this paragraph.

(2)   The own funds requirement is the sum of the following elements multiplied by the scaling factor—

    (a)   4% of the first 5,000,000 euro of payment volume;

    (b)   2.5% of the next 5,000,000 euro of payment volume;

    (c)   1% of the next 90,000,000 euro of payment volume;

    (d)   0.5% of the next 150,000,000 euro of payment volume; and

    (e)   0.25% of any remaining payment volume.

(3)   "Payment volume" means the total amount of payment transactions executed by the authorised payment institution in the preceding financial year divided by the number of months in that year.

(4)   The "scaling factor" is—

    (a)   0.5 for a payment institution that is authorised to provide the payment service specified in paragraph 127(f) of Schedule 1;

    (b)   0.8 for a payment institution that is authorised to provide the payment service specified in paragraph 127(g) of Schedule 1; and

    (c)   1 for a payment institution that is authorised to provide any other payment service.

Method C

18.—(1)   "Method C" means the calculation method set out in this paragraph.

(2)   The own funds requirement is the relevant indicator multiplied by—

    (a)   the multiplication factor; and

    (b)   the scaling factor;

subject to the proviso in sub-paragraph (7).

(3)   The "relevant indicator" is the sum of the following elements—

    (a)   interest income;

    (b)   interest expenses;

    (c)   gross commissions and fees received; and

    (d)   gross other operating income.

(4)   For the purpose of calculating the relevant indicator—

    (a)   each element must be included in the sum with its positive or negative sign;

    (b)   income from extraordinary or irregular items may not be used;

    (c)   expenditure on the outsourcing of services rendered by third parties may reduce the relevant indicator if the expenditure is incurred from a payment service provider;

    (d)   the relevant indicator is calculated on the basis of the twelve-monthly observation at the end of the previous financial year;

    (e)   the relevant indicator must be calculated over the previous financial year; and

    (f)   audited figures must be used unless they are not available in which case business estimates may be used.

(5)   The "multiplication factor" is the sum of—

    (a)   10% of the first 2,500,000 euro of the relevant indicator;

    (b)   8% of the next 2,500,000 euro of the relevant indicator;

    (c)   6% of the next 20,000,000 euro of the relevant indicator;

    (d)   3% of the next 25,000,000 euro of the relevant indicator; and

    (e)   1.5% of any remaining amount of the relevant indicator.

(6)   "Scaling factor" has the meaning given in paragraph 158(4).

(7)   The proviso is that the own funds requirement must not be less than 80 % of the average of the previous three financial years for the relevant indicator.

Application of accounting standards

19.   Except where this Schedule provides for a different method of recognition, measurement or valuation, whenever a provision in this Schedule refers to an asset, liability, equity or income statement item, an authorised payment institution must, for the purpose of that provision, recognise the asset, liability, equity or income statement item and measure its value in accordance with whichever of the following are applicable for the purpose of the institution's external financial reporting—

PART 2
STATUTORY INSTRUMENTS

(a)   Financial Reporting Standards and Statements of Standard Accounting Practice issued or adopted by the Accounting Standards Board;

(b)   Statements of Recommended Practice, issued by industry or sectoral bodies recognised for this purpose by the Accounting Standards Board;

(c)   International Financial Reporting Standards and International Accounting Standards issued or adopted by the International Accounting Standards Board;

(d)   International Standards on Auditing (United Kingdom and Ireland) issued by the Auditing Practices Board; and

(e)   the Companies Act 2006.

[3863]

NOTES

Commencement: see reg 1 at **[3732]**.

SCHEDULE 4
PRIOR GENERAL INFORMATION FOR FRAMEWORK CONTRACTS
Regulations 36(2), 40(1)

1.   The following information about the payment service provider—
(a)   the name of the payment service provider;
(b)   the address and contact details of the payment service provider's head office;
(c)   if different from the information under sub-paragraph (b), the address and contact details of the branch or agent from which the payment service is being provided;
(d)   details of the payment service provider's regulators, including any reference or registration number of the payment service provider.

2.   The following information about the payment service—
(a)   a description of the main characteristics of the payment service to be provided;
(b)   the information or unique identifier that must be provided by the payment service user in order for a payment order to be properly executed;
(c)   the form and procedure for giving consent to the execution of a payment transaction and for the withdrawal of consent in accordance with regulation 55;
(d)   a reference to the time of receipt of a payment order, as defined in regulation 65, and the cut-off time, if any, established by the payment service provider;
(e)   the maximum execution time for the payment services to be provided;
(f)   whether spending limits for the use of a payment instrument may be agreed in accordance with regulation 56(1).

3.   The following information about charges, interest and exchange rates—
(a)   details of all charges payable by the payment service user to the payment service provider and, where applicable, a breakdown of the amounts of any charges;
(b)   where relevant, details of the interest and exchange rates to be applied or, if reference interest and exchange rates are to be used, the method of calculating the actual interest and the relevant date and index or base for determining such reference interest or exchange rates;
(c)   if agreed, the immediate application of changes in reference interest or exchange rates and information requirements relating to the changes in accordance with regulation 42(4).

4.   The following information about communication—
(a)   the means of communication agreed between the parties for the transmission of information or notifications under these Regulations including, where relevant, any technical requirements for the payment service user's equipment for receipt of the information or notifications;
(b)   the manner in which and frequency with which information under these Regulations is to be provided or made available;
(c)   the language or languages in which the framework contract will be concluded and in which any information or notifications under these Regulations will be communicated;
(d)   the payment service user's right to receive the terms of the framework contract and information in accordance with regulation 41.

5.   The following information about safeguards and corrective measures—
(a)   where relevant, a description of the steps that the payment service user is to take in order to keep safe a payment instrument and how to notify the payment service provider for the purposes of regulation 57(1)(b);
(b)   where relevant, the conditions under which the payment service provider proposes to reserve the right to stop or prevent the use of a payment instrument in accordance with regulation 56;
(c)   the payer's liability under regulation 62, including details of any limits on such liability;
(d)   how and within what period of time the payment service user is to notify the payment

service provider of any unauthorised or incorrectly executed payment transaction under regulation 59, and the payment service provider's liability for unauthorised payment transactions under regulation 61;

(e) the payment service provider's liability for the execution of payment transactions under regulation 75 or 76;

(f) the conditions for the payment of any refund under regulation 63.

6. The following information about changes to and termination of the framework contract—

(a) where relevant, the proposed terms under which the payment service user will be deemed to have accepted changes to the framework contract in accordance with regulation 42(2), unless they notify the payment service provider that they do not accept such changes before the proposed date of their entry into force;

(b) the duration of the framework contract;

(c) the right of the payment service user to terminate the framework contract and any agreements relating to termination in accordance with regulation 43.

7. The following information about redress—

(a) any contractual clause on—
   (i) the law applicable to the framework contract;
   (ii) the competent courts;

(b) the availability of out-of-court complaint and redress procedures for the payment service user and the methods for having access to them.

[3864]

NOTES

Commencement: see reg 1 at **[3732]**.

(*Sch 5 makes modifications to legislation outside the scope of this work; Sch 6 amends the Financial Services and Markets Act 2000, ss 226, 234, Sch 17, Pt III at* **[1813B]**, **[1813J]**, **[1813U]**, *the Financial Services (Distance Marketing) Regulations 2004, SI 2004/2095 at* **[3413]**, *the Money Laundering Regulations 2007, SI 2007/2157 at* **[3559]**, *revokes the Consumer Protection (Distance Selling) Regulations 2000, SI 2000/2334, reg 21, and amends other legislation outside the scope of this work.*)

[SCHEDULE 7]

Regulation 127

1 Exercise of deemed passport rights by Gibraltar-based firms

(1) These Regulations apply in relation to a firm which—

(a) has its head office in Gibraltar; and

(b) is authorised in Gibraltar to provide payment services;

as follows.

(2) The firm is to be treated as having an entitlement, corresponding to its passport right deriving from the payment services directive, to establish a branch or provide services in the United Kingdom.

(3) References in these Regulations to—

(a) "an EEA authorised payment institution" are to be treated as references to the firm;

(b) "home state competent authority" are to be treated as references to the competent authority (within the meaning of the payment services directive) in Gibraltar in relation to the firm; and

(c) "passport rights" are to be treated as references to the entitlement mentioned in sub-paragraph (2).

2 Exercise by authorised payment institutions of deemed passport rights in Gibraltar

(1) For the purposes of these Regulations, an authorised payment institution is to be treated as having an entitlement, corresponding to its passport right, to establish a branch or provide services in Gibraltar.

(2) In relation to an authorised payment institution which establishes a branch, or provides services, in Gibraltar, references in these Regulations to—

(a) "EEA branch" are to be treated as including a reference to such a branch;

(b) "host state competent authority" are to be treated as including a reference to the competent authority (within the meaning of the payment services directive) in Gibraltar in relation to the institution;

(c) "passport rights" are to be treated as including references to the entitlement mentioned in sub-paragraph (1); and

(d) "EEA State" are to be treated as including references to Gibraltar.

3 Modification of legislation

(1) Section 155(7) of the 2000 Act (consultation) has effect for the purposes of these Regulations as if modified by adding at the end "or if it is making rules for the purpose of extending rules that apply to EEA authorised payment institutions to Gibraltar-based firms".

(2) Paragraph 14 of Schedule 17 to the 2000 Act (the ombudsman scheme) has effect for the purposes of these Regulations as if modified by adding at the end—

"(8) Sub-paragraphs (4), (5) and (6) above do not apply if the scheme operator is making rules for the purpose of extending rules that apply to EEA authorised payment institutions to Gibraltar-based firms".]

[3865]

NOTES
Commencement: 1 October 2009 (certain purposes); 1 November 2009 (otherwise); see further the note to reg 10A at **[3742]**.
Inserted by the Payment Services (Amendment) Regulations 2009, SI 2009/2475, regs 2, 13.

COMPANIES (DISCLOSURE OF ADDRESS) REGULATIONS 2009

(SI 2009/214)

NOTES
Made: 1 February 2009.
Authority: Companies Act 2006, ss 243(2)–(6), 1088(1)–(3), (5), 1292(1), (4).
Commencement: 1 October 2009.
Application: these Regulations are applied, with modifications, in so far as they relates to LLPs, by the Limited Liability Partnerships (Application of Companies Act 2006) Regulations 2009, SI 2009/1804, reg 83, Sch 1, Pt 4, para 11.

ARRANGEMENT OF REGULATIONS

PART 1

PART 1

1   Citation, commencement and interpretation

(1)   These Regulations may be cited as the Companies (Disclosure of Address) Regulations 2009 and come into force on 1st October 2009.

(2)   In these Regulations—

"the Act" means the Companies Act 2006 and, unless the context otherwise requires, any reference to a numbered section is to a section so numbered in that Act;

"the 1985 Act" means the Companies Act 1985;

"the 1986 Order" means the Companies (Northern Ireland) Order 1986;

"confidentiality order" means an order under section 723B of the 1985 Act (confidentiality orders);

"former name" means a name by which an individual was formerly known and which has been notified to the registrar under section 10 (documents to be sent to the registrar) or section 288 (register of directors and secretaries) of the 1985 Act, or Article 21 or 296 of the 1986 Order, [or regulation 80C of the SEs Regulations, or regulation 79 of the old SEs Regulations, or regulation 77 of the Northern Ireland SEs Regulations,] or section 12 (statement of proposed officers) or section 167 (duty to notify registrar of changes) of the Act;

"limited liability partnership" means a limited liability partnership incorporated under the Limited Liability Partnerships Act 2000 or Limited Liability Partnerships Act (Northern Ireland) 2002;

"name" means a person's Christian name (or other forename) and surname, except that in the case of—

    (a)   a peer; or

    (b)   an individual usually known by a title,

the title may be stated instead of his Christian name (or other forename) and surname or in addition to either or both of them;

["the Northern Ireland SEs Regulations" means the European Public Limited-Liability Company Regulations (Northern Ireland) 2004;]

["the old SEs Regulations" means the SEs Regulations, disregarding the amendments made by the European Public Limited-Liability Company (Amendment) Regulations 2009;]

"permanent representative" means an individual who was a permanent representative for the purposes of sections 723B and 723C (effect of confidentiality orders) of the 1985 Act;

"police force" means a police force within the meaning of section 101(1) of the Police Act 1996 (interpretation), section 50 of the Police (Scotland) Act 1967 (meaning of police area, etc) or section 1 of the Police (Northern Ireland) Act 2000 (name of the police in Northern Ireland);

"relevant body" means any police force and any other person whom the registrar considers may be able to assist in answering a question referred to that person by the registrar under these Regulations;

"relevant organisation" means the Government Communications Headquarters, the Secret Intelligence Service, the Security Service or a police force;

"section 243 applicant" means an individual by whom or in respect of whom a section 243 application has been made but in respect of which application the registrar either has not made a determination, or has made a determination, not being a section 243 decision, and any appeal to the court in respect of that application under regulation 14 has not been determined by the court;

"section 243 application" means an application under section 243(4) (permitted use or disclosure by the registrar) for the purpose of requiring the registrar to refrain from disclosing protected information relating to a director to a credit reference agency;

"section 243 beneficiary" means—

    (a)   an individual who has made a section 243 application in respect of which a section 243 decision has been made; or

    (b)   an individual on whose behalf a company or a subscriber to a memorandum of association has made a section 243 application in respect of which a section 243 decision has been made; or

    (c)   an individual in relation to whom a confidentiality order was in force immediately before 1st October 2009 and who, by paragraph 37 of Schedule 2 to the Companies Act 2006 (Commencement No 8, Transitional Provisions and Savings) Order 2008 is treated as having made a section 243 application in respect of which a section 243 decision has been made;

"section 243 decision" means a determination by the registrar on a section 243 application in favour of the applicant;

PART 2
STATUTORY INSTRUMENTS

"section 1088 application" means an application under section 1088 (application to registrar to make address unavailable for public inspection) for the purpose of requiring the registrar to make an address on the register unavailable for public inspection;

"section 1088 beneficiary" means a person who has made a section 1088 application in respect of which a section 1088 decision has been made;

"section 1088 decision" means a determination by the registrar on a section 1088 application in favour of the applicant;

["the SEs Regulations" means the European Public Limited-Liability Company Regulations 2004;]

"specified public authority" means any public authority specified in Schedule 1 to these Regulations; and

"working day" means a day that is not a Saturday or Sunday, Christmas Day, Good Friday or any day that is a bank holiday under the Banking and Financial Dealings Act 1971 in England and Wales.

[3866]

NOTES
Commencement: 1 October 2009.
Para (2): words in square brackets in definition "former name" inserted, and definitions "the Northern Ireland SEs Regulations", "the old SEs Regulations", "the SEs Regulations" inserted by the European Public Limited-Liability Company (Amendment) Regulations 2009, SI 2009/2400, reg 42(1), (2), subject to transitional provisions in reg 2 thereof.

PART 2
DISCLOSURE OF PROTECTED INFORMATION

2   Permitted disclosure by the registrar to specified public authorities

(1)   The registrar may disclose protected information to a specified public authority where the conditions specified in paragraphs 2 and 3 of Schedule 2 are satisfied.

(2)   A specified public authority shall deliver to the registrar such information or evidence as he may direct for the purpose of enabling him to determine in accordance with these Regulations whether to disclose protected information.

(3)   The registrar may require such information or evidence to be verified in such manner as he may direct.

(4)   The specified public authority must inform the registrar immediately of any change in respect of any statement delivered to the registrar pursuant to Schedule 2 or information or evidence provided for the purpose of enabling the registrar to determine whether to disclose protected information.

(5)   The public authorities specified for the purposes of section 243(2) are set out in Schedule 1 to these Regulations.

[3867]

NOTES
Commencement: 1 October 2009.

3   Permitted disclosure by the registrar to credit reference agencies

(1)   Subject to regulation 4, the registrar may disclose protected information to a credit reference agency where the conditions specified in paragraphs 6 to 10 of Schedule 2 are satisfied.

(2)   The registrar may rely on a statement delivered to him by a credit reference agency under paragraph 10 of Schedule 2 as sufficient evidence of the matters stated in it.

(3)   Notwithstanding paragraph (2), a credit reference agency shall deliver to the registrar such information or evidence in addition to the statement required by paragraph 10 of Schedule 2 as he may direct for the purpose of enabling him to determine in accordance with these Regulations whether to disclose protected information.

(4)   The registrar may require such information or evidence to be verified in such manner as he may direct.

(5)   The credit reference agency must inform the registrar immediately of any change in respect of any statement delivered to the registrar pursuant to Schedule 2 or information or evidence provided for the purpose of enabling the registrar to determine whether to disclose protected information.

[3868]

NOTES
Commencement: 1 October 2009.

4 Registrar to refrain from disclosure of protected information

The registrar shall refrain from disclosing protected information to a credit reference agency if such information relates to a section 243 beneficiary or a section 243 applicant.

[3869]

NOTES
Commencement: 1 October 2009.

5 Application under section 243 by an individual

(1) A section 243 application may be made to the registrar by an individual who is, or proposes to become, a director.

(2) The grounds on which an application under paragraph (1) may be made are that the individual making the application—
- (a) considers that there is a serious risk that he, or a person who lives with him, will be subjected to violence or intimidation as a result of the activities of at least one of—
  - (i) the companies of which he is, or proposes to become, a director;
  - (ii) the companies of which he was a director;
  - (iii) the overseas companies of which he is or has been a director, secretary or permanent representative; or,
  - (iv) the limited liability partnerships of which he is or has been a member; or
- (b) is or has been employed by a relevant organisation.

(3) The application shall—
- (a) contain—
  - (i) a statement of the grounds on which the application is made;
  - (ii) the name and any former name of the applicant;
  - (iii) the date of birth of the applicant;
  - (iv) the usual residential address of the applicant;
  - (v) where the registrar has allocated a unique identifier to the applicant, that unique identifier;
  - (vi) the name and registered number of each company of which the applicant is, or proposes to become, a director;
  - (vii) where the grounds of the application are those described in paragraph (2)(a)(ii), (iii) or (iv), the name and registered number of the company, overseas company or limited liability partnership; and
- (b) be accompanied by evidence which—
  - (i) where the grounds of the application are those described in paragraph (2)(a) supports the applicant's statement of the grounds of the application; or,
  - (ii) where the grounds of the application are those described in paragraph (2)(b), establishes that the applicant is or has been employed by a relevant organisation.

(4) The registrar may refer to a relevant body any question relating to an assessment of—
- (a) where the grounds of the application are those described in paragraph (2)(a), the nature and extent of any risk of violence or intimidation considered by the applicant to arise in relation to himself, or to a person who lives with him; or
- (b) where the grounds of the application are those described in paragraph (2)(b), whether the applicant is or has been employed by a relevant organisation.

(5) The registrar shall determine the application and send the applicant to his usual residential address, as stated in his application, notice of his determination on the section 243 application within five working days of that determination being made.

[3870]

NOTES
Commencement: 1 October 2009.

6 Application under section 243 by a company

(1) A section 243 application may be made to the registrar by a company on behalf of any of its directors who are individuals.

(2) The grounds on which an application under paragraph (1) may be made are that the company making the application considers that there is a serious risk that the director on behalf of whom the application is made, or a person who lives with that director, will be subjected to violence or intimidation as a result of the activities of the company making the application.

(3) The application shall—
- (a) contain—
  - (i) a statement of the grounds on which the application is made;
  - (ii) the name and registered number of the applicant;

    (iii) the name and any former name of each director on behalf of whom the application is made;

    (iv) the date of birth of each such director;

    (v) the usual residential address of each such director;

    (vi) where the registrar has allocated a unique identifier to any such director, that unique identifier;

    (vii) the name and registered number of each company of which each such director is a director; and

  (b) be accompanied by evidence which supports the applicant's statement of the grounds of the application.

(4) The registrar may refer to a relevant body any question relating to an assessment of the nature and extent of any risk of violence or intimidation considered by the applicant to arise in relation to its directors on behalf of whom the application is made or to persons who live with those directors as a result of any of its activities.

(5) The registrar shall determine the application and send—

  (a) the applicant, to its registered office; and

  (b) each director on behalf of whom the application was made, to his usual residential address as stated in the application,

notice of his determination on the section 243 application within five working days of that determination being made.

[3871]

NOTES

Commencement: 1 October 2009.

7 Application under section 243 by a subscriber to a memorandum of association

(1) A section 243 application may be made to the registrar by a subscriber to a memorandum of association on behalf of any of the proposed directors of a proposed company who are individuals.

(2) The grounds on which an application under paragraph (1) may be made are that the subscriber making the application considers that there is a serious risk that the proposed directors of the proposed company on behalf of whom the application is made, or persons who live with them, will be subjected to violence or intimidation as a result of the proposed activities of that proposed company.

(3) The application shall—

  (a) contain—

    (i) a statement of the grounds on which the application is made;

    (ii) the name of the applicant;

    (iii) the address of the applicant;

    (iv) the name of the proposed company;

    (v) the name and any former name of each of the proposed directors on behalf of whom the application is made;

    (vi) the date of birth of each such proposed director;

    (vii) the usual residential address of each such proposed director;

    (viii) the name and registered number of each company of which each such proposed director is a director; and

  (b) be accompanied by evidence which supports the applicant's statement of the grounds of the application.

(4) The registrar may refer to a relevant body any question relating to an assessment of the nature and extent of any risk of violence or intimidation considered by the applicant to arise in relation to its proposed directors on behalf of whom the application is made or to persons who live with those proposed directors as a result of any of the proposed activities of the proposed company.

(5) The registrar shall determine the application and send—

  (a) the applicant, to the address stated in the application, and

  (b) each of the proposed directors on behalf of whom the application was made, to their usual residential address as stated in the application,

notice of his determination on the section 243 application within five working days of that determination being made.

[3872]

NOTES

Commencement: 1 October 2009.

8   Matters relating to a section 243 application

(1)   For the purpose of regulations 5, 6 and 7 the registrar may direct that additional information or evidence should be delivered to him, what such information or evidence should be and how it should be verified.

(2)   The registrar shall not make available for public inspection—
    (a)   any section 243 application; or
    (b)   any documents provided in support of that application.

(3)   For the purpose of determining any section 243 application the registrar may accept any answer to a question referred in accordance with regulation 5(4), 6(4) or 7(4) as providing sufficient evidence of—
    (a)   the nature and extent of any risk relevant to—
       (i)   where the grounds of the application are those described in regulation 5(2)(a), the applicant;
       (ii)   where the grounds of the application are those described in regulation 6(2), the directors on behalf of whom the application is made;
       (iii)   where the grounds of the application are those described in regulation 7(2), the proposed directors on behalf of whom the application is made,
       or to persons who live with any of the above individuals, or
    (b)   whether an applicant is or has been employed by a relevant organisation.

[3873]

NOTES
Commencement: 1 October 2009.

PART 3

APPLICATION TO MAKE AN ADDRESS UNAVAILABLE FOR PUBLIC INSPECTION
UNDER SECTION 1088

9   Application under section 1088 to make an address unavailable for public inspection by an individual

(1)   A section 1088 application may be made to the registrar by an individual whose usual residential address was placed on the register under either—
    (a)   under section 10 (documents to be sent to registrar), 288 (register of directors and secretaries), 363 (duty to deliver annual returns), 691 (documents to be delivered to registrar) or 692 (registration of altered particulars) of or paragraph 2 of Schedule 21A to the 1985 Act;
    (b)   under Article 21, 296, 371, 641 or 642 of the 1986 Order; …
    [(ba)   as a service address under regulation 80C of the SEs Regulations (duty to notify registrar of changes of particulars of members of an SE's supervisory organ),
    (bb)   under regulation 79 of the old SEs Regulations or regulation 77 of the Northern Ireland SEs Regulations, or]
    (c)   as a service address under section 12 (statement of proposed officers), 167 (duty to notify registrar of changes of director's particulars) or 855 (contents of annual return) of the Act,

in respect of that usual residential address where it was placed on the register on or after 1st January 2003.

(2)   The grounds on which an application under paragraph (1) may be made are that the individual making the application—
    (a)   considers that there is a serious risk that he, or a person who lives with him, will be subjected to violence or intimidation as a result of the activities of at least one of the companies of which—
       (i)   he is, or proposes to become, a director; or
       (ii)   he is not a director but of which he has been at any time a director, secretary or permanent representative;
    (b)   he is or has been employed by a relevant organisation;
    (c)   is a section 243 beneficiary.

(3)   The application shall—
    (a)   contain—
       (i)   a statement of the grounds on which the application is made;
       (ii)   the name and any former name of the applicant;
       (iii)   the usual residential address of the applicant that is to be made unavailable for public inspection;
       (iv)   an address for correspondence in respect of the application;

(v) the name and registered number of each company of which the applicant is or has been at any time since 1st January 2003 a director, secretary or permanent representative;

(vi) the service address which is to replace that usual residential address on the register;

(vii) subject to paragraph (4)—

   (aa) the date of birth of the applicant;

   (bb) the name of each company of which the applicant proposes to become a director; and

   (cc) where the registrar has allotted a unique identifier to the applicant, that unique identifier; and

(b) be accompanied by evidence which—

   (i) where the grounds of the application are those described in paragraph (2)(a), supports the applicant's assertion that his application falls within the grounds stated in his application;

   (ii) where the grounds of the application are those described in paragraph (2)(b), establishes that the applicant is or has been employed by a relevant organisation;

   (iii) where the grounds of the application are those described in paragraph (2)(c), establishes that he is a section 243 beneficiary.

(4) The application need not contain the information described at paragraph (3)(a)(vii) where the application is delivered to the registrar on the same day as the applicant delivers a section 243 application.

(5) The registrar may refer to a relevant body any question relating to an assessment of—

(a) the nature and extent of any risk of violence or intimidation considered by the applicant to arise in relation to himself, or a person who lives with him, as a result of the activities of any company of which he is or proposes to become a director or has been at any time a director, secretary or permanent representative; or

(b) whether the applicant is or has been employed by a relevant organisation.

(6) The registrar shall determine the application and send the applicant to the address for correspondence stated in his application, notice of his determination on the section 1088 application within five working days of that determination being made.

[3874]

NOTES

Commencement: 1 October 2009.

Para (1): word omitted from sub-para (b) revoked and sub-paras (ba), (bb) inserted by the European Public Limited-Liability Company (Amendment) Regulations 2009, SI 2009/2400, reg 42(1), (3), subject to transitional provisions in reg 2 thereof.

10 Application under section 1088 to make an address unavailable for public inspection by a company

(1) A section 1088 application may be made to the registrar by a company in respect of the addresses of—

(a) all of its members and former members whose addresses were contained in—

   (i) an annual return; or

   (ii) a return of allotment of shares,

   delivered to the registrar on or after 1st January 2003; or

(b) the subscribers to its memorandum of association where that memorandum was delivered to the registrar on or after 1st January 2003.

(2) The grounds on which an application under paragraph (1) may be made are that the company making the application considers that, as a result of its activities, the availability to members of the public of the addresses described in paragraph (1) creates a serious risk that its members or former members or subscribers, or persons who live at those addresses, will be subjected to violence or intimidation.

(3) The application shall—

(a) contain—

   (i) the name of the applicant and its registered number; and

   (ii) a statement of the grounds on which the application is made; and

(b) be accompanied by evidence—

   (i) which supports the applicant's assertion that its application falls within the grounds stated in its application; or

   (ii) where the court has made an order under section 117(3) (register of members: response to request for inspection or copy) directing the applicant not to comply with a request under section 116 (rights to inspect and require copies), a copy of that order.

(4)   The registrar may refer to a relevant body any question relating to the assessment of the nature and extent of any risk of violence or intimidation considered by the applicant to arise in relation to any of its members or former members or subscribers, or persons who live at the addresses described in paragraph (1), as a result of its activities by virtue of the availability to members of the public of particulars of the addresses of such members or former members or subscribers.

(5)   The registrar shall determine the application and send the applicant to its registered office notice of his determination on the section 1088 application within five working days of that determination being made.

[3875]

NOTES

Commencement: 1 October 2009.

---

11   Application under section 1088 to make an address unavailable for public inspection by a person who registers a charge

(1)   A section 1088 application may be made to the registrar by a person who—
   (a)   (i)   on or after 1st January 2003, registered a charge under Part 12 of the 1985 Act (registration of charges) or Part 13 of the 1986 Order; or
          (ii)   has registered a charge under Part 25 of the Act (company charges); and
   (b)   is not the company which created the charge or acquired the property subject to a charge,
in respect of his address delivered to the registrar for the purposes of that registration.

(2)   The grounds on which an application under paragraph (1) may be made are that the person making the application considers that there is a serious risk that he, or if applicable his employees, or persons who live with him or his employees, will be subjected to violence or intimidation as a result of the activities of the company which is, or was, subject to the charge.

(3)   The application shall—
   (a)   contain—
          (i)   a statement of the grounds on which the application is made;
          (ii)   the name of the applicant, and where the applicant is a company, its registered number;
          (iii)   the address of the applicant that is to be made unavailable for public inspection;
          (iv)   the name and registered number of the company which is or was subject to the charge;
          (v)   an address for correspondence with the registrar in respect of the application;
          (vi)   where the applicant is the chargee, the service address which is to replace the address of the applicant on the register; and
   (b)   be accompanied by evidence which supports the applicant's assertion that there is a serious risk that he or, if applicable, his employees, or persons who live with him or his employees, will be subjected to violence or intimidation as a result of the activities of the company which is or was subject to the charge.

(4)   The registrar may refer to a relevant body any question relating to the assessment of the nature and extent of any risk of violence or intimidation considered by the applicant to arise in relation to himself or, if applicable, his employees, or persons who live with him or his employees, as a result of the activities of the company which is or was subject to the charge.

(5)   The registrar shall determine the application and send the applicant to the address stated in the application in accordance with paragraph (3)(a)(v) notice of his determination on the section 1088 application within five working days of that determination being made.

[3876]

NOTES

Commencement: 1 October 2009.

---

12   Matters relevant to section 1088 applications

(1)   For the purpose of regulations 9, 10 and 11 the registrar may direct that additional information or evidence should be delivered to him, what such information or evidence should be and how it should be verified.

(2)   For the purpose of determining any section 1088 application the registrar may accept any answer to a question referred in accordance with regulation 9(5), 10(4) or 11(4) as providing sufficient evidence of—
   (a)   the nature and extent of any risk relevant to—
          (i)   where the grounds of the application are those described in regulation 9(2)(a), the applicant;
          (ii)   where the grounds of the application are those described in regulation 10(2), the subscribers or members or former members of an applicant; or

(iii) where the grounds of the application are those described in regulation 11(2), where the applicant is an individual, the applicant, or any employees of an applicant,

or to persons who live with any of the above individuals or, in the case of members, former members or subscribers, to persons who live at their addresses, or

(b) whether an applicant is or has been employed by a relevant organisation.

[3877]

NOTES
Commencement: 1 October 2009.

13 Effect of a successful section 1088 application

(1) Where a section 1088 application has been determined in favour of the applicant the registrar shall—

(a) in the case of an application made under regulation 9(1) or 11(1) make the specified address unavailable for public inspection;

(b) in the case of an application under regulation 10(1) make all of the members', former members' or subscribers' addresses unavailable for public inspection;

(c) in the case of a person to whom paragraph 36 of Schedule 2 to the Companies Act 2006 (Commencement No 8, Transitional Provisions and Savings) Order 2008 applies, make unavailable for public inspection the address referred to in sub-paragraph (1)(a) of that paragraph.

(2) In this regulation "specified address" means the address specified in the application as being the one to be made unavailable for public inspection.

[3878]

NOTES
Commencement: 1 October 2009.

PART 4
MATTERS RELATING TO APPLICATIONS UNDER SECTION 243 AND UNDER SECTION 1088

14 Appeals

(1) An applicant who has received notice under regulation 5(5), 6(5), 7(5), 9(6), 10(5) or 11(5) that his application has been unsuccessful may appeal to the High Court or, in Scotland, the Court of Session on the grounds that the decision—

(a) is unlawful;

(b) is irrational or unreasonable;

(c) has been made on the basis of a procedural impropriety or otherwise contravenes the rules of natural justice.

(2) No appeal under this regulation may be brought unless the leave of the court has been obtained.

(3) An applicant must bring an appeal within 21 days of the date of the notice or, with the court's permission, after the end of such period, but only if the court is satisfied—

(a) where permission is sought before the end of that period, that there is good reason for the applicant being unable to bring the appeal in time; or

(b) where permission is sought after that time, that there was a good reason for the applicant's failure to bring the appeal in time and for any delay in applying for permission.

(4) The court determining an appeal may—

(a) dismiss the appeal; or

(b) quash the decision,

and where the court quashes a decision it may refer the matter to the registrar with a direction to reconsider it and make a determination in accordance with the findings of the court.

[3879]

NOTES
Commencement: 1 October 2009.

15 Duration of a section 243 decision or a section 1088 decision

(1) A section 243 decision shall continue to have effect until—

(a) either—

(i) the section 243 beneficiary, or

(ii) his personal representative,

has notified the registrar in writing that he wishes the section 243 decision to cease to apply; or

(b)   the registrar has made a revocation decision in relation to that beneficiary,

whichever first occurs.

(2)   A section 1088 decision shall continue to have effect until the registrar has made a revocation decision in relation to the section 1088 beneficiary.

(3)   In this regulation—

"personal representative" means the executor, original or by representation, or administrator for the time being of a deceased person; and

"revocation decision" in relation to a section 243 decision or a section 1088 decision means a determination by the registrar to revoke that decision in accordance with regulation 16.

[3880]

NOTES

Commencement: 1 October 2009.

16   Revocation of a section 243 decision or a section 1088 decision

(1)   The registrar may revoke a section 243 decision or a section 1088 decision at any time if he is satisfied that the section 243 beneficiary or section 1088 beneficiary, as the case may be, or any other person, in purported compliance with any provision of these Regulations, is found guilty of an offence under section 1112 (general false statement offence) ("a revocation decision").

(2)   If the registrar proposes to make a revocation decision he shall send the beneficiary notice of his intention.

(3)   The notice must—

(a)   inform the beneficiary that he may, within the period of 28 days beginning with the date of the notice, deliver representations in writing to the registrar; and

(b)   state that if representations are not received by the registrar within that period, the revocation decision will be made at the expiry of that period.

(4)   If within the period specified in paragraph (3) the beneficiary delivers representations as to why the revocation decision should not be made, the registrar shall have regard to the representations in determining whether to make the revocation decision, and shall, within five working days of making his decision, send notice of it to the beneficiary.

(5)   Any communication by the registrar in respect of a revocation decision or proposed revocation decision shall be sent to the beneficiary—

(a)   in the case of an individual, to his usual residential address;

(b)   in the case of a company, to its registered office; or

(c)   in the case of a partnership, to the address specified in its section 1088 application.

(6)   In this regulation—

"partnership" includes a limited liability partnership;

"section 243 beneficiary" includes where the section 243 decision was made following an application under regulation 6 or 7, the applicant.

[3881]

NOTES

Commencement: 1 October 2009.

SCHEDULE 1
SPECIFIED PUBLIC AUTHORITIES

Regulation 2

The Secretary of State;
any Northern Ireland Department;
the Scottish Ministers;
the Welsh Ministers;
the Treasury;
the Commissioners for Her Majesty's Revenue and Customs;
the Bank of England;
the Director of Public Prosecutions;
the Director of Public Prosecutions for Northern Ireland;
the Serious Fraud Office;
the Secret Intelligence Service;
the Security Service;
the Government Communications Headquarters;
the Financial Services Authority;
the Competition Commission;
the Pensions Regulator;

the Panel on Takeovers and Mergers;

the Regulator of Community Interest Companies;

the Registrar of Credit Unions for Northern Ireland;

the Office of Fair Trading;

the Office of the Information Commissioner;

the Charity Commission;

the Charity Commission for Northern Ireland;

the Office of the Scottish Charity Regulator;

the Postal Services Commission;

the Gas and Electricity Markets Authority;

the Northern Ireland Authority for Utility Regulation;

the Gambling Commission;

the Serious Organised Crime Agency;

the Health and Safety Executive;

the Health and Safety Executive for Northern Ireland;

the Food Standards Agency;

the Gangmasters Licensing Authority;

the Security Industry Authority;

a local authority within the meaning of section 54(2) of the Act;

an official receiver appointed under section 399 of the Insolvency Act 1986 (appointment, etc, of official receivers);

the Official Receiver for Northern Ireland;

the Crown Office and Procurator Fiscal Services;

a person acting as an insolvency practitioner within the meaning of section 388 of the Insolvency Act 1986 (meaning of "act as an insolvency practitioner") or Article 3 of the Insolvency (Northern Ireland) Order 1989 ("act as an insolvency practitioner");

an inspector appointed under Part 14 of the 1985 Act (investigation of companies and their affairs: requisition of documents) or Part 15 of the 1986 Order or a person appointed under regulation 30 of the Open-Ended Investment Companies Regulations 2001 (power to investigate) or regulation 22 of the Open-Ended Investment Companies Regulations (Northern Ireland) 2004;

any person authorised to exercise powers under section 447 of the 1985 Act (power to require documents and information), or section 84 of the Companies Act 1989 (exercise of powers by officers, etc) or Article 440 of the 1986 Order;

any person exercising functions conferred by Part 6 of the Financial Services and Markets Act 2000 (official listing) or the competent authority under that Part;

a person appointed to make a report under section 166 (reports by skilled persons) of the Financial Services and Markets Act 2000;

a person appointed to conduct an investigation under section 167 (appointment of persons to carry out general investigations) or 168(3) or (5) (appointment of persons to carry out investigations in particular cases) of the Financial Services and Markets Act 2000;

an inspector appointed under section 284 (power to investigate) of the Financial Services and Markets Act 2000;

an overseas regulatory authority within the meaning of section 82 of the Companies Act 1989 (request for assistance by overseas regulatory authority);

a police force.

[3882]

NOTES

Commencement: 1 October 2009.

SCHEDULE 2
CONDITIONS FOR PERMITTED DISCLOSURE
Regulations 2 and 3

PART 1
DISCLOSURE TO SPECIFIED PUBLIC AUTHORITIES

1.   Paragraphs 2 and 3 set out the conditions specified for the disclosure of protected information by the registrar to a specified public authority.

2.   The specified public authority has delivered to the registrar a statement that it intends to use the protected information only for the purpose of facilitating the carrying out by that specified public authority of a public function ("the permitted purpose").

3.   Subject to paragraph 4, the specified public authority ("the authority") has delivered to the registrar a statement that it will, where it supplies a copy of the protected information to a processor for the purpose of processing the information for use in respect of the permitted purpose—

(a)   ensure that the processor is one who carries on business in the European Economic Area;

   (b)   require that the information is not transmitted outside the European Economic Area by the processor; and

   (c)   require that the processor does not disclose the information except to the authority or an employee of the authority.

4.   Paragraph 3 does not apply where the specified public authority is the Secret Intelligence Service, Security Service or Government Communications Headquarters.

[3883]

NOTES

Commencement: 1 October 2009.

PART 2
DISCLOSURE TO A CREDIT REFERENCE AGENCY

5.   Paragraphs 6 to 10 set out the conditions specified for the disclosure of protected information by the registrar to a credit reference agency.

6.   The credit reference agency—

   (a)   is carrying on in the United Kingdom or in another EEA State a business comprising the furnishing of information relevant to the financial standing of individuals, being information collected by the agency for that purpose;

   (b)   maintains appropriate procedures—

      (i)   to ensure that an independent person can investigate and audit the measures maintained by the agency for the purposes of ensuring the security of any protected information disclosed to that agency; and

      (ii)   for the purposes of ensuring that it complies with its obligations under the Data Protection Act 1998, or, where the agency carries on business in a EEA State other than the United Kingdom, with its obligations under legislation implementing Directive 95/46/EC of the European Parliament and of the Council of 24 October 1995 on the protection of individuals with regard to the processing of personal data and on the free movement of such data;

   (c)   has not been found guilty of an offence under—

      (i)   section 1112 (general false statement offence) of the Act or section 2 of the Fraud Act 2006 (fraud by false representation); or

      (ii)   section 47 (failure to comply with enforcement notice) of the Data Protection Act 1998 in circumstances where it has used the protected information for purposes other than those described in sub-paragraphs (a) to (e) of paragraph 7 below.

7.   The credit reference agency has delivered to the registrar a statement that it intends to use the protected information only for the purposes of—

   (a)   providing an assessment of the financial standing of a person;

   (b)   meeting any obligations contained in the Money Laundering Regulations 2007 or any rules made pursuant to section 146 of the Financial Services and Markets Act 2000 (money laundering rules), or in any legislation of another EEA State implementing Directive 2005/60/EC of the European Parliament and of the Council of 26 October 2005 on the prevention of the use of the financial system for the purpose of money laundering and terrorist financing;

   (c)   conducting conflict of interest checks required or made necessary by any enactment;

   (d)   the provision of protected information to—

      (i)   a public authority specified in Schedule 1 which has satisfied the requirements of paragraphs 2 and 3 of this Schedule; or

      (ii)   a credit reference agency which has satisfied the requirements of this Part of this Schedule; or

   (e)   conducting checks for the prevention and detection of crime and fraud.

8.   The credit reference agency has delivered to the registrar a statement that it intends to take delivery of and to use the protected information only in the United Kingdom or in another EEA State.

9.   The credit reference agency has delivered to the registrar a statement that it will, where it supplies a copy of the protected information to a processor for the purpose of processing the information for use in respect of the purposes referred to in paragraph 7—

   (a)   ensure that the processor is one who carries on business in the European Economic Area;

   (b)   require that the information is not transmitted outside the European Economic Area by the processor; and

   (c)   require that the processor does not disclose the information except to the credit reference agency or an employee of the credit reference agency.

10.   The credit reference agency has delivered to the registrar a statement that it meets the conditions in paragraph 6 above.

[3884]

NOTES
Commencement: 1 October 2009.

PART 3
INTERPRETATION OF THIS SCHEDULE

11.—(1) In this Schedule—

"processor" means any person who provides a service which consists of putting information into data form or processing information in data form and any reference to a processor includes a reference to his employees; and

"public function" includes—

(a) any function conferred by or in accordance with any provision contained in any enactment;

(b) any function conferred by or in accordance with any provision contained in the Community Treaties or any Community instrument;

(c) any similar function conferred on persons by or under provisions having effect as part of the law of a country or territory outside the United Kingdom; and

(d) any function exercisable in relation to the investigation of any criminal offence or for the purpose of any criminal proceedings.

(2) In this Schedule any reference to—

(a) an employee of any person who has access to protected information shall be deemed to include any person working or providing services for the purposes of that person or employed by or on behalf of, or working for, any person who is so working or who is supplying such a service; and

(b) the disclosure for the purpose of facilitating the carrying out of a public function includes disclosure in relation to, and for the purpose of, any proceedings whether civil, criminal or disciplinary in which the specified public authority engages while carrying out its public functions.

[3885]

NOTES
Commencement: 1 October 2009.

COMPANY AND BUSINESS NAMES (MISCELLANEOUS PROVISIONS) REGULATIONS 2009

(SI 2009/1085)

NOTES
Made: 24 April 2009.
Authority: Companies Act 2006, ss 57(1)(a), (2), (5), 60(1), 65, 66, 1197, 1292(1).
Commencement: 1 October 2009.

ARRANGEMENT OF REGULATIONS
PART 1
INTRODUCTORY

PART 4
BUSINESS NAMES

PART 1
INTRODUCTORY

1   Citation, commencement and interpretation

(1)   These Regulations may be cited as the Company and Business Names (Miscellaneous Provisions) Regulations 2009 and come into force on 1st October 2009.

(2)   In these Regulations—
   "the Act" means the Companies Act 2006;
   "expression or abbreviation specified as similar" has the meaning given in paragraph 4 of Schedule 2 and "abbreviation specified as similar" has the meaning that would be given to it in that paragraph if that paragraph made no reference to "expressions";
   "permitted characters" has the meaning given in regulation 2(1);
   "word or abbreviation specified as similar" has the meaning given in paragraph 2 of Schedule 2; and
   "word specified as similar" has the meaning given in paragraph 2 of Schedule 2.

(3)   For the purposes of computing the number of permitted characters in regulation 2(4) and paragraph 7 of Schedule 3 (but not in regulation 2(3)), any blank space between one permitted character and another in the name shall be counted as though it was a permitted character.

[3886]

NOTES

Commencement: 1 October 2009.

PART 2
COMPANY NAMES

2   Permitted characters

(1)   This regulation sets out the characters, signs, symbols and punctuation that may be used in the name of a company registered under the Act ("the permitted characters").

(2)   The following permitted characters may be used in any part of the name—
   (a)   any character, sign or symbol set out in table 1 in Schedule 1;
   (b)   0, 1, 2, 3, 4, 5, 6, 7, 8 or 9;
   (c)   full stop, comma, colon, semi-colon or hyphen; and
   (d)   any other punctuation referred to in column 1 of table 2 in Schedule 1 but only in one of the forms set out opposite that punctuation in column 2 of that table.

(3)   The signs and symbols set out in table 3 in Schedule 1 are permitted characters that may be used but not as one of the first three permitted characters of the name.

(4)   The name must not consist of more than 160 permitted characters.

[3887]

NOTES

Commencement: 1 October 2009.

3   Exemption from requirement as to use of "limited"

(1)   A private company limited by guarantee is exempt from the requirement of section 59 of the Act (requirement to have name ending with "limited" or permitted alternative) so long as it meets the following two conditions.

(2)   The first condition is that the objects of that company are the promotion or regulation of commerce, art, science, education, religion, charity or any profession, and anything incidental or conducive to any of those objects.

PART 2
STATUTORY INSTRUMENTS

(3)   The second condition is that the company's articles—
(a)   require its income to be applied in promoting its objects;
(b)   prohibit the payment of dividends, or any return of capital, to its members; and
(c)   require all the assets that would otherwise be available to its members generally to be transferred on its winding up either—
    (i)   to another body with objects similar to its own; or
    (ii)   to another body the objects of which are the promotion of charity and anything incidental or conducive thereto,
(whether or not the body is a member of the company).

[3888]

NOTES
Commencement: 1 October 2009.

4   Inappropriate indication of company type or legal form: generally applicable provisions

(1)   A company must not be registered under the Act by a name that includes, otherwise than at the end of the name, an expression or abbreviation specified in inverted commas in paragraph 3(a) to (f) of Schedule 2 (or any expression or abbreviation specified as similar).

(2)   A company must not be registered under the Act by a name that includes in any part of the name an expression or abbreviation specified in inverted commas in paragraph 3(g) or (h) of Schedule 2 (or any expression or abbreviation specified as similar) unless that company is a RTE company within the meaning of section 4A of the Leasehold Reform, Housing and Urban Development Act 1993.

(3)   A company must not be registered under the Act by a name that includes in any part of the name an expression or abbreviation specified in inverted commas in paragraph 3(i) or (j) of Schedule 2 (or any expression or abbreviation specified as similar) unless that company is a RTM company within the meaning of section 73 of the Commonhold and Leasehold Reform Act 2002.

(4)   A company must not be registered under the Act by a name that includes in any part of the name an expression or abbreviation specified in inverted commas in paragraph 3(k) to (u) of Schedule 2 (or any expression or abbreviation specified as similar).

(5)   A company must not be registered under the Act by a name that includes immediately before an expression or abbreviation specified in inverted commas in paragraph 3(a) to (j) of Schedule 2 an abbreviation specified in inverted commas in paragraph 3(v) of that Schedule (or any abbreviation specified as similar).

(6)   Paragraph (1) is subject to regulations 5(b) and 6(b).

[3889]

NOTES
Commencement: 1 October 2009.

5   Inappropriate indication of company type or legal form: company exempt from requirement to have name ending in "limited"

A company which is exempt from the requirement of section 59 of the Act (requirement to have name ending with "limited" or permitted alternative) under section 60 of the Act must not be registered under the Act by a name that concludes with—
(a)   a word specified in inverted commas in paragraph 1(c) or (d) of Schedule 2 (or any word specified as similar); or
(b)   an expression or abbreviation specified in inverted commas in paragraph 3(a) to (f) or (v) of Schedule 2 (or any expression or abbreviation specified as similar).

[3890]

NOTES
Commencement: 1 October 2009.

6   Inappropriate indication of company type or legal form: unlimited company

An unlimited company must not be registered under the Act by a name that concludes with—
(a)   a word or abbreviation specified in inverted commas in paragraph 1(a) or (b) of Schedule 2 (or any word or abbreviation specified as similar); or
(b)   an expression or abbreviation specified in inverted commas in paragraph 3(a) to (f) or (v) of Schedule 2 (or any expression or abbreviation specified as similar).

[3891]

NOTES
Commencement: 1 October 2009.

7   Name not to be the same as another in the registrar's index of company names

For the purposes of section 66 of the Act (determining whether a name to be registered under the Act is the same as another name appearing in the registrar's index of company names) Schedule 3 has effect for setting out—

    (a)   the matters that are to be disregarded; and

    (b)   the words, expressions, signs and symbols that are to be regarded as the same.

[3892]

NOTES

Commencement: 1 October 2009.

8   Consent to registration of a name which is the same as another in the registrar's index of company names

    (1)   A company may be registered under the Act by a proposed same name if the conditions in paragraph (2) are met.

    (2)   The conditions are—

    (a)   the company or other body whose name already appears in the registrar's index of company names ("Body X") consents to the proposed same name being the name of a company ("Company Y");

    (b)   Company Y forms, or is to form, part of the same group as Body X; and

    (c)   Company Y provides to the registrar a copy of a statement made by Body X indicating—

        (i)   the consent of Body X as referred to in sub-paragraph (a); and

        (ii)   that Company Y forms, or is to form, part of the same group as Body X.

    (3)   If the proposed same name is to be taken by a company which has not yet been incorporated, the copy of such statement must be provided to the registrar instead by the person who delivers to the registrar the application for registration of the company (and the reference in paragraph (1) to the conditions in paragraph (2) shall be read accordingly).

    (4)   The registrar may accept the statement referred to in paragraph (2)(c) as sufficient evidence that the conditions referred to in paragraph (2)(a) and (b) have been met.

    (5)   If the consent referred to in paragraph (2)(a) is given by Body X, a subsequent withdrawal of that consent does not affect the registration of Company Y by that proposed same name.

    (6)   In this regulation—

    (a)   "group" has the meaning given in section 474(1) of the Act; and

    (b)   "proposed same name" means a name which is, due to the application of regulation 7 and Schedule 3, considered the same as a name appearing in the registrar's index of company names and differs from that name appearing in the index only by one of the matters set out in inverted commas in paragraph 4 of Schedule 3.

[3893]

NOTES

Commencement: 1 October 2009.

PART 3
OVERSEAS COMPANY NAMES

9   Interpretation and permitted characters

Regulations 1(2) and (3) and 2 apply to the name of an overseas company which is registered by that company under Part 34 of the Act (overseas companies) as they apply to the name of a company formed and registered under the Act.

[3894]

NOTES

Commencement: 1 October 2009.

10   Inappropriate indication of company type or legal form

    (1)   An overseas company must not be registered under the Act by a name that concludes with a word or abbreviation specified in inverted commas in paragraph 1(a) or (b) of Schedule 2 (or any word or abbreviation specified as similar) unless the liability of the members of the company is limited by its constitution.

    (2)   An overseas company must not be registered under the Act by a name that concludes with a word specified in inverted commas in paragraph 1(c) or (d) of Schedule 2 (or any word specified as similar) unless the liability of the members of the company is not limited by its constitution.

PART 2
STATUTORY INSTRUMENTS

(3)   An overseas company must not be registered under the Act by a name that includes in any part of the name an expression or abbreviation specified in inverted commas in paragraph 3 of Schedule 2 (or any expression or abbreviation specified as similar).

[3895]

NOTES
Commencement: 1 October 2009.

11   Name not to be the same as another in the registrar's index of company names

Regulation 7 applies to the name of an overseas company which is registered by that company under Part 34 of the Act as it applies to the name of a company formed and registered under the Act.

[3896]

NOTES
Commencement: 1 October 2009.

12   Consent to registration of a name which is the same as another in the registrar's index of company names

(1)   Regulation 8 applies to the proposed same name of an overseas company as it applies to the proposed same name of a company formed and registered under the Act.

(2)   In this regulation "proposed same name" has the same meaning as in regulation 8.

[3897]

NOTES
Commencement: 1 October 2009.

PART 4
BUSINESS NAMES

13   "Limited" and permitted alternatives

(1)   A person must not carry on business in the United Kingdom under a name that concludes with any word or abbreviation set out in inverted commas in paragraph 1(a) or (b) of Schedule 2 unless that person is—

    (a)   a company or an overseas company registered in the United Kingdom by that name;

    (b)   an overseas company incorporated with that name; ...

    (c)   a society registered under the Industrial and Provident Societies Act 1965 or the Industrial and Provident Societies Act (Northern Ireland) 1969 by that name;

    [(d)   an incorporated friendly society (as defined in section 116 of the Friendly Societies Act 1992) which has that name; or

    (e)   a company to which section 1040 of the Companies Act 2006 (companies authorised to register under the Companies Act 2006) applies which has that name].

(2)   A person must not carry on business in the United Kingdom under a name that concludes with any word or abbreviation specified as similar to any word or abbreviation set out in inverted commas in paragraph 1(a) or (b) of Schedule 2.

[3898]

NOTES
Commencement: 1 October 2009.
Para (1): word omitted from sub-para (b) revoked and sub-paras (d), (e) inserted by the Company, Limited Liability Partnership and Business Names (Miscellaneous Provisions) (Amendment) Regulations 2009, SI 2009/2404, reg 2(1), (2).

14   Other indications of legal form

(1)   A person must not carry on business in the United Kingdom under a name that includes any expression or abbreviation set out in inverted commas in paragraph 3 of Schedule 2 unless that person is such a company, partnership, grouping or organisation as is indicated in that expression or abbreviation.

(2)   A person must not carry on business in the United Kingdom under a name that includes any expression or abbreviation specified as similar to any expression or abbreviation set out in inverted commas in paragraph 3 of Schedule 2.

[3899]

NOTES
Commencement: 1 October 2009.

15 Transitional provisions

(1) Regulation 14 does not apply to the carrying on of a business under a name by a person who—

    (a) carried on that business under that name immediately before these Regulations came into force; and

    (b) continues to carry it on under that name,

if it was lawful for the business to be carried on under that name immediately before these Regulations came into force.

(2) Regulation 14 does not apply to the carrying on of a business under a name by a person to whom the business is transferred on or after the date on which these Regulations came into force—

    (a) where that person continues to carry on the business under that name; and

    (b) where it was lawful for the business to be carried on under that name immediately before the transfer,

during the period of 12 months beginning with the date of the transfer.

[3900]

NOTES

Commencement: 1 October 2009.

SCHEDULE 1

CHARACTERS, SIGNS, SYMBOLS AND PUNCTUATION

Regulation 2

Table 1				
Characters, signs and symbols				
A	B	C	D	E
F	G	H	I	J
K	L	M	N	O
P	Q	R	S	T
U	V	W	X	Y
Z	&	@	£	$
€	¥			

Table 2	
Type of punctuation	*Punctuation mark*
Apostrophe	,
	'
Bracket	(
	)
	[
	]
	{
	}
	<
	>
Exclamation mark	!
Guillemet	«
	»
Inverted comma	"
	"

Table 2

	‖	
Question mark	?	
Solidus	\	
	/	

Table 3

Signs and symbols

*
=
#
%
+

[3901]

NOTES

Commencement: 1 October 2009.

SCHEDULE 2
SPECIFIED WORDS, EXPRESSIONS AND ABBREVIATIONS
Regulations 1, 4 to 6, 10, 13 and 14

1.   The words and abbreviations specified are—
- (a) "LIMITED" or (with or without full stops) the abbreviation "LTD";
- (b) "CYFYNGEDIG" or (with or without full stops) the abbreviation "CYF";
- (c) "UNLIMITED"; and
- (d) "ANGHYFYNGEDIG".

2.   The words and abbreviations specified as similar to the words and abbreviations set out in inverted commas in paragraph 1(a) and (b) and the words specified as similar to the words set out in inverted commas in paragraph 1(c) and (d) are any in which—
- (a) one or more characters has been omitted;
- (b) one or more characters, signs, symbols or punctuation has been added; or
- (c) each of one or more characters has been substituted by one or more other characters, signs, symbols or punctuation,

in such a way as to be likely to mislead the public as to the legal form of a company or business if included in the registered name of the company or in a business name.

3.   The expressions and abbreviations specified are—
- (a) "PUBLIC LIMITED COMPANY" or (with or without full stops) the abbreviation "PLC";
- (b) "CWMNI CYFYNGEDIG CYHOEDDUS" or (with or without full stops) the abbreviation "CCC";
- (c) "COMMUNITY INTEREST COMPANY" or (with or without full stops) the abbreviation "CIC";
- (d) "CWMNI BUDDIANT CYMUNEDOL" or (with or without full stops) the abbreviation "CBC";
- (e) "COMMUNITY INTEREST PUBLIC LIMITED COMPANY" or (with or without full stops) the abbreviation "COMMUNITY INTEREST PLC";
- (f) "CWMNI BUDDIANT CYMUNEDOL CYHOEDDUS CYFYNGEDIG" or (with or without full stops) the abbreviation ["CWMNI BUDDIANT CYMUNEDOL CCC"];
- (g) "RIGHT TO ENFRANCHISEMENT" or (with or without full stops) the abbreviation "RTE";
- (h) "HAWL I RYDDFREINIAD";
- (i) "RIGHT TO MANAGE" or (with or without full stops) the abbreviation "RTM";
- (j) "CWMNI RTM CYFYNGEDIG";
- (k) "EUROPEAN ECONOMIC INTEREST GROUPING" or (with or without full stops) the abbreviation "EEIG";
- (l) "INVESTMENT COMPANY WITH VARIABLE CAPITAL";
- (m) "CWMNI BUDDSODDI A CHYFALAF NEWIDIOL";
- (n) "LIMITED PARTNERSHIP";

  (o) "PARTNERIAETH CYFYNGEDIG";

  (p) "LIMITED LIABILITY PARTNERSHIP";

  (q) "PARTNERIAETH ATEBOLRWYDD CYFYNGEDIG";

  (r) "OPEN-ENDED INVESTMENT COMPANY";

  (s) "CWMNI BUDDSODDIANT PENAGORED";

  (t) "CHARITABLE INCORPORATED ORGANISATION";

  (u) "SEFDYDLIAD ELUSENNOL CORFFOREDIG"; ...

 [(ua) "INDUSTRIAL AND PROVIDENT SOCIETY"; and]

  (v) the following abbreviations (with or without full stops) of the expressions specified in sub-paragraphs (n), (o), (p), (q), (t) and (u) respectively, namely "LP", "PC", "LLP", "PAC", "CIO" and "SEC".

4. The expressions and abbreviations specified as similar to the expressions and abbreviations set out in inverted commas in paragraph 3 are any in which—

  (a) one or more characters has been omitted;

  (b) one or more characters, signs, symbols or punctuation has been added; or

  (c) each of one or more characters has been substituted by one or more other characters, signs, symbols or punctuation,

in such a way as to be likely to mislead the public as to the legal form of a company or business if included in the registered name of the company or in a business name.

                                [3902]

NOTES

 Commencement: 1 October 2009.

 Para 3: words in square brackets in sub-para (f) substituted, word omitted from sub-para (u) revoked and sub-para (ua) inserted by the Company, Limited Liability Partnership and Business Names (Miscellaneous Provisions) (Amendment) Regulations 2009, SI 2009/2404, reg 2(1), (3).

SCHEDULE 3
NAME SAME AS ANOTHER IN THE REGISTRAR'S INDEX OF COMPANY NAMES
Regulations 7 and 8

1. In determining whether a name is the same as another name appearing in the registrar's index of company names the provisions in this Schedule are to be applied in the order set out in the Schedule.

2. Disregard any word, expression or abbreviation set out in inverted commas in Schedule 2 where it appears at the end of the name.

3.—(1) Taking the name remaining after the application of paragraph 2, regard each of the words, expressions, signs and symbols set out in inverted commas in any of the paragraphs of sub-paragraph (2) ("relevant matters") as the same as the other relevant matters set out in that paragraph where each relevant matter—

  (a) is preceded by and followed by a blank space; or

  (b) where the relevant matter is at the beginning of the name, where it is followed by a blank space.

 (2) The words, expressions, signs and symbols are—

  (a) "AND" and "&";

  (b) "PLUS" and "+";

  (c) "0", "ZERO" and "O";

  (d) "1" and "ONE";

  (e) "2", "TWO", "TO" and "TOO";

  (f) "3" and "THREE";

  (g) "4", "FOUR" and "FOR";

  (h) "5" and "FIVE";

  (i) "6" and "SIX";

  (j) "7" and "SEVEN";

  (k) "8" and "EIGHT";

  (l) "9" and "NINE";

  (m) "£" and "POUND";

  (n) "€" and "EURO";

  (o) "$" and "DOLLAR";

  (p) "¥" and "YEN";

  (q) "%", "PER CENT", "PERCENT", "PER CENTUM" and "PERCENTUM"; and

  (r) "@" and "AT".

4.—(1) Taking the name remaining after the application of paragraphs 2 and 3, disregard at the end of the name the matters set out in inverted commas in sub-paragraph (2) (or any combination of such matters) where the matter (or combination) is preceded by the following punctuation or symbol in inverted commas—

  (a) a blank space;

  (b) a full stop; or

 (c) "@".

 (2) The matters are—

  (a) "BIZ";
  (b) "CO";
  (c) "CO UK";
  (d) "CO.UK";
  (e) "COM";
  (f) "COMPANY";
  (g) "EU";
  (h) "EXPORTS";
  (i) "GB";
  (j) "GREAT BRITAIN";
  (k) "GROUP";
  (l) "HOLDINGS";
  (m) "IMPORTS";
  (n) "INTERNATIONAL";
  (o) "NET";
  (p) "NI";
  (q) "NORTHERN IRELAND";
  (r) "ORG";
  (s) "ORG UK";
  (t) "ORG.UK";
  (u) "SERVICES";
  (v) "UK";
  (w) "UNITED KINGDOM";
  (x) "WALES";
  (y) "ALLFORION";
  (z) "CWMNI";
  (aa) "CYM";
  (bb) "CYMRU";
  (cc) "CYNHEILIAID";
  (dd) "CYRDDAU";
  (ee) "DALIADAU";
  (ff) "DU";
  (gg) "GRWP";
  (hh) "GWASANAETHAU";
  (ii) "MEWNFORION";
  (jj) "PF";
  (kk) "PRYDAIN FAWR";
  (ll) "RHYNGWLADOL";
  (mm) "RYNGWLADOL"; and
  (nn) "Y DEYRNAS UNEDIG".

5. Taking the name remaining after the application of paragraphs 2 to 4, disregard the following matters in any part of the name—

  (a) any punctuation set out in regulation 2(2)(c) or in column 2 of table 2 in Schedule 1; and
  (b) the following symbols set out in inverted commas—

   (i) "*";
   (ii) "="; and
   (iii) "#".

6. Taking the name remaining after the application of paragraphs 2 to 5, disregard the letter "S" at the end of the name.

7. Taking the name remaining after the application of paragraphs 2 to 6, disregard any permitted character after the first 60 permitted characters of the name.

8. Taking the name remaining after the application of paragraphs 2 to 7, disregard the following matters or any combination of the following matters set out in inverted commas where they appear at the beginning of the name—

  (a) "@";
  (b) "THE" (but only where followed by a blank space); and
  (c) "WWW".

9. Taking the name remaining after the application of paragraphs 2 to 8, disregard blank spaces between permitted characters.

[3903]

NOTES
 Commencement: 1 October 2009.

TRANSFER OF FUNCTIONS OF THE CONSUMER CREDIT APPEALS TRIBUNAL ORDER 2009

(SI 2009/1835)

NOTES
Made: 7 July 2009.
Authority: Tribunals, Courts and Enforcement Act 2007, ss 30(1), (4), 31(1), (2), (9), 38, Sch 5, para 30.
Commencement: 1 September 2009.

1   Citation and commencement

This Order may be cited as the Transfer of Functions of the Consumer Credit Appeals Tribunal Order 2009 and comes into force on 1st September 2009.

[3904]

NOTES
Commencement: 1 September 2009.

2   Transfer of functions and abolition of tribunal

(1)   The functions of the Consumer Credit Appeals Tribunal are transferred to the First-tier Tribunal.

(2)   The Consumer Credit Appeals Tribunal is abolished.

[3905]

NOTES
Commencement: 1 September 2009.

3   Transfer of persons into the First-tier Tribunal and the Upper Tribunal

A person who, immediately before this Order comes into force, holds an office listed in column (1) of the following table is to hold the office or offices listed in the corresponding entry in column (2) of the table.

(*1*) *Office held*	(*2*) *Office to be held*
President of the Consumer Credit Appeals Tribunal appointed under paragraph 2(1) of Schedule A1 to the Consumer Credit Act 1974	Transferred-in judge of the First-tier Tribunal and deputy judge of the Upper Tribunal
Deputy President of the Consumer Credit Appeals Tribunal appointed under paragraph 2(3) of Schedule A1 to the Consumer Credit Act 1974	Transferred-in judge of the First-tier Tribunal
Member of the panel of chairmen of the Consumer Credit Appeals Tribunal appointed under paragraph 3(1) of Schedule A1 to the Consumer Credit Tribunal 1974	Transferred-in judge of the First-tier Tribunal
Other member of the Consumer Credit Appeals Tribunal appointed under paragraph 3(3) of Schedule A1 to the Consumer Credit Act 1974	Transferred-in other member of the First-tier Tribunal

[3906]

NOTES
Commencement: 1 September 2009.

4   Consequential and transitional provisions

(1)   Schedule 1 contains amendments to primary legislation as a consequence of the transfer effected by this Order.

(2)   Schedule 2 contains amendments to secondary legislation as a consequence of the transfer effected by this Order.

(3)   Schedule 3 contains repeals and revocations as a consequence of the amendments in Schedules 1 and 2.

(4)   Schedule 4 contains transitional and saving provisions.

[3907]

NOTES

Commencement: 1 September 2009.

(Sch 1: paras 1–9 amend the Consumer Credit Act 1974, ss 2, 41, 182, 189 at **[652]**, **[688]**, **[824]**, **[831]**, *insert ss 41ZA, 41ZB at* **[688ZA]**, **[688ZB]**, *and repeal ss 40A, 41A, Sch A1 at* **[687A]**, **[688A]**, **[835A]**; *paras 10, 11 amend provisions outside the scope of this work. Sch 2: para 1 amends the Money Laundering Regulations 2007, SI 2007/2157, reg 44 at* **[3602]**; *para 2 amends provisions outside the scope of this work. Sch 3 repeals the Consumer Credit Act 2006, ss 55, 56(2), 57, 58, Sch 1 and the Tribunals, Courts and Enforcement Act 2007, Sch 10, para 11 and revokes the Consumer Credit Appeals Tribunal Rules 2008, SI 2008/668 at* **[3616]**.*)*

SCHEDULE 4
TRANSITIONAL AND SAVING PROVISIONS

Article 4(4)

Transitional and saving provisions

1.   Any proceedings before the Consumer Credit Appeals Tribunal which are pending immediately before 1st September 2009 shall continue on and after 1st September 2009 as proceedings before the First-tier Tribunal.

2.—(1)   The following sub-paragraphs apply where proceedings are continued in the First-tier Tribunal by virtue of paragraph 1.

(2)   Where a hearing began before 1st September 2009 but was not completed by that date, the First-tier Tribunal must be comprised for the continuation of that hearing of the person or persons who began it.

(3)   The First-tier Tribunal may give any direction to ensure that proceedings are dealt with fairly and, in particular, may—

    (a)   apply any provision in procedural rules which applied to the proceedings before 1st September 2009; or

    (b)   disapply provisions of Tribunal Procedure Rules.

(4)   In sub-paragraph (3) "procedural rules" means provision (whether called rules or not) regulating practice or procedure before a tribunal.

(5)   Any direction or order given or made in proceedings which is in force immediately before 1st September 2009 remains in force on and after that date as if it were a direction or order of the First-tier Tribunal.

(6)   A time period which has started to run before 1st September 2009 and which has not expired shall continue to apply.

(7)   An order for costs may only be made if, and to the extent that, an order could have been made before 1st September 2009.

3.   Where an appeal lies to a court from any decision made by the Consumer Credit Appeals Tribunal before 1st September 2009, that right of appeal has not been exercised, and the time to exercise that right of appeal has not expired prior to 1st September 2009, section 11 of the Tribunals, Courts and Enforcement Act 2007 (right to appeal to Upper Tribunal) shall apply as if the decision were a decision made on or after 1st September 2009 by the First-tier Tribunal, and any reference to the Consumer Credit Appeals Tribunal in an enactment relating to such an appeal, express or otherwise, is to be taken as a reference to the First-tier Tribunal.

4.   Any case to be remitted by a court on or after 1st September 2009 and which, if it had been remitted before 1st September 2009, would have been remitted to the Consumer Credit Appeals Tribunal, shall be remitted to the First-tier Tribunal.

5.   Staff appointed to the Consumer Credit Appeals Tribunal before 1st September 2009 are to be treated on and after that date, for the purpose of any enactment, as if they had been appointed by the Lord Chancellor under section 40(1) of the Tribunals, Courts and Enforcement Act 2007 (tribunal staff and services).

6.   A decision made by the Consumer Credit Appeals Tribunal before 1st September 2009 is to be treated as a decision of the First-tier Tribunal on or after 1st September 2009.

[3908]

NOTES

Commencement: 1 September 2009.

CREDIT RATING AGENCIES REGULATIONS 2010

(SI 2010/906)

NOTES

Made: 22 March 2010.

Authority: European Communities Act 1972, s 2(2); Financial Services and Markets Act 2000, s 349(1)(b).

Commencement: 7 June 2010.

PART 1
GENERAL

1 Citation and commencement

These Regulations may be cited as the Credit Rating Agencies Regulations 2010 and shall come into force on 7th June 2010.

[3909]

NOTES
Commencement: 7 June 2010.

2 Interpretation

(1) In these Regulations—
"the Act" means the Financial Services and Markets Act 2000;
"the Authority" means the Financial Services Authority;
"the EC Regulation" means Regulation (EC) No 1060/2009 of the European Parliament and of the Council of 16 September 2009 on credit rating agencies;
"overseas competent authority" means an authority designated by a Member State other than the United Kingdom in accordance with Article 22(1) of the EC Regulation (competent authorities);
"protected item" has the same meaning as in section 413 of the Act (protected items).

(2) Expressions used in these Regulations which are listed in Article 3 of the EC Regulation (definitions) have the meaning given in that Article.

[3910]

NOTES
Commencement: 7 June 2010.

PART 2
THE AUTHORITY

3 Designation of competent authority

The Authority is the competent authority for the purposes of the EC Regulation.

[3911]

NOTES
Commencement: 7 June 2010.

4 Fees

A registration or supervisory fee charged by the Authority under Article 19 of the EC Regulation (registration and supervisory fees) may be recovered as a debt owed to the Authority.

[3912]

NOTES
Commencement: 7 June 2010.

5 Disclosure of confidential information

Section 348(1) of the Act (restrictions on disclosure of confidential information by Authority etc) does not prevent the Authority from disclosing confidential information where the disclosure is permitted by the EC Regulation.

[3913]

NOTES
Commencement: 7 June 2010.

6 Guidance

(1) The Authority may give guidance consisting of such information and advice as it considers appropriate with respect to—
    (a) the operation of the EC Regulation or these Regulations;
    (b) any matter relating to the functions of the Authority under the EC Regulation;
    (c) any other matter about which it appears to the Authority to be desirable to give information or advice in connection with the EC Regulation or these Regulations.

(2) The Authority may—
    (a) publish its guidance;
    (b) offer copies of its published guidance for sale at a reasonable price;

(c)   if it gives guidance in response to a request made by any person, make a reasonable charge for that guidance.

[3914]

NOTES

Commencement: 7 June 2010.

7   Miscellaneous

The functions of the Authority under the EC Regulation are to be treated for the purposes of Part 1 (general) and paragraphs 13 (status) and 19 (exemption from liability in damages) of Schedule 1 to the Act as functions conferred on the Authority under the Act.

[3915]

NOTES

Commencement: 7 June 2010.

PART 3

APPLICATIONS FOR CERTIFICATION AND REGISTRATION

8   Language for applications

Where a credit rating agency submits an application for registration under Article 15 of the EC Regulation (application for registration), the application must be in English if the United Kingdom is the home Member State of that agency.

[3916]

NOTES

Commencement: 7 June 2010.

9   Approval decisions

Where the Authority adopts—

    (a)   a certification decision in respect of an application for certification submitted by a credit rating agency under Article 5(2) of the EC Regulation (equivalence and certification based on equivalence); or

    (b)   a registration decision in respect of an application for registration submitted by a credit rating agency under Article 15 of the EC Regulation,

the decision takes effect when it is adopted.

[3917]

NOTES

Commencement: 7 June 2010.

10   Refusal decisions

Where the Authority adopts a refusal decision in respect of an application for certification submitted by a credit rating agency under Article 5(2) of the EC Regulation, or an application for registration submitted by a credit rating agency under Article 15 of the EC Regulation, the decision takes effect—

    (a)   on the expiry of the time period within which the credit rating agency may refer the matter to the Upper Tribunal under sub-paragraph (a) or (c) of regulation 29(1); or

    (b)   if the credit rating agency refers the matter to the Upper Tribunal within that period, on the determination of that reference, unless the Upper Tribunal directs otherwise.

[3918]

NOTES

Commencement: 7 June 2010.

PART 4

INVESTIGATORY POWERS

11   Application of this Part

The powers conferred on the Authority by this Part—

    (a)   may only be used to obtain information, documents or a report which is necessary for the exercise of the Authority's functions under the EC Regulation; and

    (b)   may not be used to require the production, disclosure or inspection of a protected item.

[3919]

NOTES
Commencement: 7 June 2010.

12   Interpretation of this Part

In this Part—

"document" includes information recorded in any form;

"information requirement" means a requirement imposed by the Authority under regulation 13(1), or by an investigator under sub-paragraph (a) or (b) of regulation 16(1);

"investigator" means a person appointed to conduct an investigation under regulation 15(1);

"person under investigation" means a person who is the subject of an investigation under regulation 15(1);

"premises" includes a vehicle;

"relevant person" means any of the persons referred to in the last sub-paragraph of Article 23(3) of the EC Regulation.

[3920]

NOTES
Commencement: 7 June 2010.

13   Information and documents

(1)   A relevant person must give the Authority such information or documents as the Authority may direct.

(2)   Information or documents required under this regulation must be given at such times, in such form and at such place, and verified in such manner, as the Authority may reasonably direct.

[3921]

NOTES
Commencement: 7 June 2010.

14   Reports by skilled persons

(1)   The Authority may, by written notice, require a credit rating agency which is registered in accordance with the EC Regulation to provide the Authority with a report on any relevant matter.

(2)   The Authority may require the report to be in such form, and to be provided by such date, as may be specified in the notice.

(3)   The person appointed to make a report required under paragraph (1) (the "skilled person") must be a person—

    (a)   nominated or approved by the Authority; and

    (b)   appearing to the Authority to have the skills necessary to make a report on the matter concerned.

(4)   The agency must—

    (a)   require the skilled person to prepare a report in accordance with the notice;

    (b)   permit the skilled person to disclose information to the Authority in accordance with paragraph (5)(b); and

    (c)   give the skilled person such assistance as the skilled person may reasonably require.

(5)   The skilled person must—

    (a)   give the Authority such assistance in connection with the report as the Authority may reasonably require; and

    (b)   disclose to the Authority any information which—

        (i)   the skilled person receives in their capacity as a skilled person; and

        (ii)   might reasonably suggest that the agency has not complied with a requirement imposed on the agency by the EC Regulation.

(6)   A relevant person who is providing, or who has provided, services to the reporting agency in relation to a matter on which a report is required under paragraph (1) must give the skilled person such assistance as the skilled person may reasonably require.

(7)   The obligations imposed by paragraphs (4) to (6) are enforceable, on the application of the Authority, by an injunction or, in Scotland, by an order for specific performance under section 45 of the Court of Session Act 1988.

[3922]

NOTES
Commencement: 7 June 2010.

15 Investigations

(1) If it appears to the Authority that there is good reason for doing so, the Authority may appoint a competent person to conduct an investigation on its behalf.

(2) Only a relevant person who is, or has been, a credit rating agency or a member of the senior management of such an agency may be the subject of an investigation under paragraph (1).

(3) The Authority must give written notice of the appointment of an investigator to the person under investigation.

(4) The notice under paragraph (3) must state the reason for the investigator's appointment.

(5) Nothing prevents the Authority from appointing a person who is a member of its staff as an investigator.

(6) An investigator must make a report of the investigation to the Authority.

(7) The Authority may, by a direction to an investigator, control—
    (a) the scope of the investigation;
    (b) the period during which the investigation is to be conducted;
    (c) the conduct of the investigation; and
    (d) the reporting of the investigation.

(8) A direction may, in particular—
    (a) confine the investigation to particular matters;
    (b) extend the investigation to additional matters;
    (c) require the investigator to discontinue the investigation or to take only such steps as are specified in the direction;
    (d) require the investigator to make such interim reports as are so specified.

(9) If there is a change in the scope or conduct of the investigation and, in the opinion of the Authority, the person under investigation is likely to be significantly prejudiced by not being made aware of it, that person must be given written notice of the change.

(10) Paragraphs (3) and (9) do not apply if the notice required by paragraph (3) or (9) would be likely to result in the investigation being frustrated.

[3923]

NOTES

Commencement: 7 June 2010.

---

16 Investigators: powers and evidence

(1) An investigator may require a relevant person to—
    (a) attend before the investigator at a specified time and place and answer questions;
    (b) give the investigator such information or documents as the investigator may require; or
    (c) give the investigator all assistance in connection with the investigation as the person is reasonably able to give.

(2) A requirement under paragraph (1)—
    (a) may be imposed only so far as the investigator reasonably considers the question, the provision of the information or production of the document, or the assistance to be relevant to the purposes of the investigation; and
    (b) may not be imposed so as to require the production, disclosure or inspection of a protected item.

(3) Information or documents required under paragraph (1)(b) must be given at such times, in such form and at such place, and verified in such manner, as the investigator may reasonably direct.

(4) Section 174 of the Act (admissibility of statements made to investigators) applies for the purposes of these Regulations as it applies for the purposes of the Act with the following modifications—
    (a) in subsection (2), omit "or in proceedings in relation to action to be taken against that person under section 123";
    (b) at the end of subsection (3)(a) insert "as applied by regulations 24 and 25 respectively of the Credit Rating Agencies Regulations 2010"; and
    (c) for subsections (4) and (5), substitute—

"(4) "Investigator" and "information requirement" have the meaning given in regulation 12 of the Credit Rating Agencies Regulations 2010.".

[3924]

NOTES

Commencement: 7 June 2010.

PART 2
STATUTORY INSTRUMENTS

17   Information and documents: supplemental provisions

Section 175 of the Act (information and documents: supplemental provisions) applies for the purposes of these Regulations as it applies for the purposes of Part 11 of the Act (information gathering and investigations) with the following modifications—

    (a)   omit subsection (1);

    (b)   in subsection (2)(b), omit ", or any relevant person,";

    (c)   omit subsection (7); and

    (d)   for subsection (8) substitute—

    "(8)   "Investigator" means a person appointed to conduct an investigation under regulation 15(1) of the Credit Rating Agencies Regulations 2010.".

[3925]

NOTES

Commencement: 7 June 2010.

---

18   Entry of premises under warrant

    (1)   A justice of the peace may, on an application by the Authority, issue a warrant under this regulation if satisfied on information on oath given on behalf of the Authority, an overseas competent authority or an investigator that there are reasonable grounds for believing that the first or second set of conditions is satisfied.

    (2)   The first set of conditions is—

    (a)   that a person on whom an information requirement has been imposed has failed (wholly or in part) to comply with it; and

    (b)   that on the premises specified in the warrant—

        (i)   there are documents which have been required; or

        (ii)   there is information which has been required.

    (3)   The second set of conditions is—

    (a)   that the premises specified in the warrant are premises used by a relevant person;

    (b)   that there are on the premises documents or information in relation to which an information requirement could be imposed; and

    (c)   that if such a requirement were imposed—

        (i)   it would not be complied with; or

        (ii)   the documents or information to which it related would be removed, tampered with or destroyed.

    (4)   A warrant under this regulation shall authorise a constable—

    (a)   to enter the premises specified in the warrant;

    (b)   to search the premises and take possession of any documents or information appearing to be documents or information of a kind in respect of which a warrant under this regulation was issued ("the relevant kind") or to take, in relation to any such documents or information, any other steps which may appear to be necessary for preserving them or preventing interference with them;

    (c)   to take copies of, or extracts from, any documents or information appearing to be of the relevant kind;

    (d)   to require any person on the premises to provide an explanation of any document or information appearing to be of the relevant kind or to state where it may be found; and

    (e)   to use such force as may be reasonably necessary.

    (5)   In England and Wales, sections 15(5) to (8) and 16 of the Police and Criminal Evidence Act 1984 (execution of search warrants and safeguards) apply to warrants issued under this regulation.

    (6)   In Northern Ireland, Articles 17(5) to (8) and 18 of the Police and Criminal Evidence (Northern Ireland) Order 1989 apply to warrants issued under this regulation.

    (7)   Any document of which possession is taken under this regulation may be retained—

    (a)   for a period of three months; or

    (b)   if within that period proceedings to which the document is relevant are commenced against any person for any criminal offence, until the conclusion of those proceedings.

    (8)   (*Applies to Scotland only.*)

    (9)   In the application of this regulation to Northern Ireland, for the reference in paragraph (1) to a justice of the peace substitute a reference to a lay magistrate appointed under section 9(1) of the Justice (Northern Ireland) Act 2002.

[3926]

NOTES

Commencement: 7 June 2010.

PART 5
SUPERVISORY MEASURES

19 Appropriate measures

(1) The Authority may for the purposes of Article 24(1)(d) (supervisory measures by the competent authorities of the home Member State) or Article 25(1)(b) (supervisory measures by competent authorities other than the competent authority of the home Member State) of the EC Regulation—

 (a) direct a credit rating agency to take such specified steps as are necessary for the purpose of securing its compliance with the EC Regulation; or

 (b) apply for an injunction under regulation 20.

(2) Where the Authority proposes to give a credit rating agency a direction under paragraph (1)(a), the Authority must give the agency a warning notice.

(3) A credit rating agency must comply with any directions given to it by the Authority under paragraph (1)(a).

(4) Paragraph (1) does not prevent the Authority from taking any other measures under Article 24(1) or 25(1) of the EC Regulation.

[3927]

NOTES
 Commencement: 7 June 2010.

20 Injunctions

(1) If, on the application of the Authority, the court is satisfied that—

 (a) there is a reasonable likelihood that a person will contravene a relevant requirement, or

 (b) a person has contravened a relevant requirement and there is a reasonable likelihood that the contravention will continue or be repeated,

the court may make an order restraining (or in Scotland an interdict prohibiting) the contravention.

(2) If, on the application of the Authority, the court is satisfied that—

 (a) a person has contravened a relevant requirement, and

 (b) there are steps which could be taken for remedying the contravention,

 the court may make an order requiring that person, and any person who has been knowingly concerned in the contravention, to take such steps as the court may direct to remedy it.

(3) The jurisdiction conferred by this regulation is exercisable by the High Court and the Court of Session.

(4) In paragraph (2), references to remedying a contravention include references to mitigating its effect.

(5) "Relevant requirement" means a requirement which is imposed by virtue of the EC Regulation or by a direction given under regulation 19(1)(a).

[3928]

NOTES
 Commencement: 7 June 2010.

PART 6
PENALTIES AND OFFENCES

21 Financial penalties

(1) The Authority may impose a penalty of such amount as it considers appropriate on a person—

 (a) which is, or has been, a credit rating agency and which has contravened a requirement imposed on that person by the EC Regulation; or

 (b) who has contravened a requirement imposed on that person by or under these Regulations.

(2) Where a credit rating agency has contravened a requirement imposed on the agency by the EC Regulation, or by or under these Regulations, the Authority may impose a penalty of such amount as it considers appropriate on any member of the senior management of the agency who has been knowingly concerned in the contravention.

(3) Where the Authority proposes to impose a penalty under this regulation, it must give the person concerned a warning notice.

(4) A penalty imposed under this regulation is payable to the Authority.

(5)   The Authority may not take action against a person under paragraph (2) after the end of the period of three years beginning with the first day on which it knew of the contravention unless proceedings against that person, in respect of the contravention, were begun before the end of that period.

(6)   For the purposes of paragraph (5)—

(a)   the Authority is to be treated as knowing of a contravention if it has information from which the contravention can reasonably be inferred; and

(b)   proceedings against a person in respect of a contravention are to be treated as begun when a warning notice is given to that person under paragraph (3).

[3929]

NOTES
Commencement: 7 June 2010.

22   Statements of policy

(1)   Sections 69 (statement of policy) and 70 (statements of policy: procedure) of the Act apply in respect of the imposition and amount of penalties under regulation 21(2) as they apply in respect of the imposition and amount of penalties under section 66 of the Act (disciplinary powers), but with the following subsection inserted at the end of section 69—

"(9)   Until such time as a statement of policy has been issued in respect of the imposition and amount of penalties under regulation 21(2) of the Credit Rating Agencies Regulations 2010, any statement issued under this section in relation to penalties under section 66 shall also apply for the purposes of this section as applied by regulation 22(1) of the Credit Rating Agencies Regulations 2010.".

(2)   Sections 210 (statements of policy) and 211 (statements of policy: procedure) of the Act apply in respect of the imposition and amount of penalties under regulation 21(1) as they apply in respect of the imposition and amount of penalties under Part 14 of the Act (disciplinary measures), but with the following subsection inserted at the end of section 210—

"(9)   Until such time as a statement of policy has been issued in respect of the imposition and amount of penalties under regulation 21(1) of the Credit Rating Agencies Regulations 2010, any statement issued under this section in relation to penalties under this Part shall also apply for the purposes of this section as applied by regulation 22(2) of the Credit Rating Agencies Regulations 2010."

(3)   In determining its policy with respect to the amount of penalties to be imposed by it under regulation 21, the Authority must take no account of the expenses which it incurs, or expects to incur, in discharging its functions under the EC Regulation.

(4)   The Authority must apply amounts paid to it by way of penalties imposed under regulation 21 towards expenses incurred in carrying out its functions under the EC Regulation or for any incidental purposes.

[3930]

NOTES
Commencement: 7 June 2010.

23   Publication of penalties

(1)   Where the Authority has—

(a)   imposed a penalty on a person under regulation 21; and

(b)   given that person a final notice about the penalty under section 390(5) of the Act (final notices) as applied by regulation 30,

it must publish a statement that it has imposed the penalty on that person.

(2)   Where the Authority publishes a statement under paragraph (1), it may publish such details of the penalty as it considers appropriate.

(3)   Paragraph (1) does not apply where publication would seriously jeopardise the financial markets or cause disproportionate damage to any party involved.

[3931]

NOTES
Commencement: 7 June 2010.

24   Offences relating to investigatory powers

Section 177 of the Act (offences) applies for the purposes of Part 4 of these Regulations as it applies for the purposes of Part 11 of the Act (information gathering and investigations) with the following modifications—

(a) in subsection (5)(a)—
    (i) for "six months" substitute "three months"; and
    (ii) for "the statutory maximum" substitute "level 5 on the standard scale";
(b) in subsection (6), for "section 176" substitute "regulation 18 of the Credit Rating Agencies Regulations 2010"; and
(c) after subsection (7) insert—

"(8) "Investigator" means a person appointed to make a report required under regulation 14(1) of the Credit Rating Agencies Regulations 2010, or a person appointed to conduct an investigation under regulation 15(1) of those Regulations.".

[3932]

NOTES
Commencement: 7 June 2010.

25 Offence of misleading the Authority

Section 398 of the Act (misleading the Authority: residual cases) applies in respect of requirements imposed by the EC Regulation, or by or under these Regulations, as it applies in respect of requirements imposed by or under the Act, but for the reference to "the statutory maximum" in section 398(3)(a) substitute a reference to "level 5 on the standard scale".

[3933]

NOTES
Commencement: 7 June 2010.

26 Offences by bodies corporate etc

Section 400 of the Act (offences by bodies corporate etc) applies for the purposes of these Regulations as it applies for the purposes of the Act, but with subsection (7) omitted.

[3934]

NOTES
Commencement: 7 June 2010.

27 Proceedings for offences

Section 401 of the Act (proceedings for offences) applies for the purposes of these Regulations as it applies for the purposes of the Act with the following modifications—
(a) in subsection (1), omit "or subordinate legislation made under this Act";
(b) in subsections (2)(a) and (3)(a), omit "or the Secretary of State"; and
(c) omit subsection (4).

[3935]

NOTES
Commencement: 7 June 2010.

28 Unincorporated associations

Section 403 of the Act (jurisdiction and procedure in respect of offences) applies for the purposes of these Regulations as it applies for the purposes of the Act.

[3936]

NOTES
Commencement: 7 June 2010.

PART 7
APPEALS

29 Appeals

(1) If the Authority—
(a) adopts a refusal decision in respect of an application for certification submitted by a credit rating agency under Article 5(2) of the EC Regulation;
(b) adopts a refusal decision in respect of an application for an exemption under Article 5(4) or Article 6(3) (independence and avoidance of conflicts of interest) of the EC Regulation;
(c) adopts a refusal decision in respect of an application for registration submitted by a credit rating agency under Article 15 of the EC Regulation;
(d) withdraws the certification or registration of a credit rating agency under Article 20(1) of the EC Regulation (withdrawal of registration);

PART 2
STATUTORY INSTRUMENTS

(e)   takes action against a person under paragraphs (a) to (e) of Article 24(1), or paragraphs (a) to (c) of Article 25(1), of the EC Regulation;

(f)   gives a credit rating agency a direction under regulation 19(1)(a); or

(g)   imposes a penalty on a person under regulation 21,

the credit rating agency or the person concerned may refer the matter to the Upper Tribunal.

(2)   Where a reference is made to the Upper Tribunal by a credit rating agency under paragraph (1)(a) or (c), and an overseas competent authority does not agree to the certification or registration of the agency, the Upper Tribunal is not required to determine for the purposes of section 133(5) of the Act that the Authority must adopt a refusal decision.

[3937]

NOTES
Commencement: 7 June 2010.

PART 8
NOTICES

30   Application of Part 26 of the Act

Part 26 of the Act (notices) applies for the purposes of these Regulations as it applies for the purposes of the Act with the following modifications—

(a)   in section 388 (decision notices), omit subsection (2);

(b)   in section 390 (final notices)—
    (i)   omit subsections (6) and (10); and
    (ii)   in subsection (8), omit "or (6)(c)";

(c)   in section 391 (publication)—
    (i)   after subsection (1) insert—

"(1A)   Subsection (1) does not—
    (a)   prevent the Authority from taking any action under Article 24(1) or 25(1) of the EC Regulation; or
    (b)   apply to any information which is available to the public as a result of any action taken by the Authority or an overseas competent authority under Article 24(1) or 25(1) of the EC Regulation.

(1B)   "EC Regulation" means Regulation (EC) No 1060/2009 of the European Parliament and of the Council of 16 September 2009 on credit rating agencies.

(1C)   "Overseas competent authority" has the meaning given by regulation 2 of the Credit Rating Agencies Regulations 2010."; and
    (ii)   omit subsections (2) to (11);

(d)   omit section 392 (application of sections 393 and 394);

(e)   in section 394(7)(c) (access to Authority material), for "section 413" substitute "regulation 2 of the Credit Rating Agencies Regulations 2010"; and

(f)   in section 395 (the Authority's procedures)—
    (i)   omit subsections (1)(a), (3), (4) and (13);
    (ii)   in subsection (9), omit the words "supervisory notice, or a"; and
    (iii)   at the end, insert—

"(14)   Until such time as a statement of procedure has been issued under this section as applied by regulation 30 of the Credit Rating Agencies Regulations 2010, the statement issued under this section for the purposes of the Act shall apply for the purposes of this section as applied by that regulation.".

[3938]

NOTES
Commencement: 7 June 2010.

31   (*Amends the Capital Requirements Regulations 2006, SI 2006/3221 (outside the scope of this work*).)

CONSUMER CREDIT (EU DIRECTIVE) REGULATIONS 2010

(SI 2010/1010)

NOTES
Made: 28 March 2010.
Authority: European Communities Act 1972, s 2(2).

Commencement: see regs 99, 101, 101A at **[3940]**, **[3942]**, **[3942A]**.
These Regulations implement European Parliament and Council Directive 2008/48/EC at **[4529]**.

PART 1
GENERAL

1 Citation and commencement

These Regulations may be cited as the Consumer Credit (EU Directive) Regulations 2010 and shall
come into force in accordance with *regulations 99 and 101* [regulations 99, 101 and 101A].

[3939]

NOTES
Commencement: 1 February 2011 (see further regs 99, 101, 101A at **[3940]**, **[3942]**, **[3942A]**).
Words in italics substituted by subsequent words in square brackets by the Consumer Credit (Amendment)
Regulations 2010, SI 2010/1969, regs 4, 5, as from 26 August 2010.

2–98   ((*Pts 2, 3*) *Reg 2 introduces amendments to the Consumer Credit Act 1974 specified in
regs 3–45; reg 3 inserts s 55A at* **[701A]***; reg 4 amends s 185 at* **[827]***; reg 5 inserts s 55B at* **[701B]***;
reg 6 inserts s 55C at* **[701C]***; reg 7 amends s 60 at* **[706]***; reg 8 inserts s 61A at* **[707A]***; reg 9
inserts s 61B at* **[707B]***; reg 10 amends s 62 at* **[708]***; reg 11 amends s 63 at* **[709]***; regs 12, 18
amend s 127 at* **[771]***; reg 13 inserts s 66A at* **[712A]***; reg 14 amends s 67 at* **[713]***; reg 15 amends
s 82 at* **[728]***; reg 16 amends s 55 at* **[701]***; reg 17 amends s 74 at* **[720]***; regs 19, 39, 42 amend s 189
at* **[831]***; reg 20 amends Sch 2 at* **[838]***; reg 21 inserts s 74A at* **[720A]***; reg 22 inserts s 74B at*
[720B]*; reg 23 amends s 77A at* **[723A]***; reg 24 amends s 75 at* **[721]***; reg 25 inserts s 75A at*
[721A]*; reg 26 inserts s 77B at* **[723B]***; reg 27 inserts s 78A at* **[724A]***; regs 28, 29 amend s 82 at*
[728]*; reg 30 amends s 94 at* **[740]***; reg 31 amends s 95 at* **[741]***; reg 32 inserts s 95A at* **[741A]***;
reg 33 amends s 97 at* **[743]***; reg 34 inserts s 97A at* **[743A]***; reg 35 amends s 120 at* **[765]***; reg 36
inserts s 82A at* **[728A]***; reg 37 amends s 87 at* **[733]***; reg 38 inserts s 98A at* **[744A]***; reg 40 amends
s 157 at* **[799]***; reg 41 inserts s 160A at* **[802A]***; reg 43 amends Sch 1 at* **[836]***; reg 44 amends s 10
at* **[658]***; reg 45 amends s 17 at* **[665]***; regs 46–49, 57–63, 68, 69, 90, 91, 93, 98 amend provisions
outside the scope of this work; reg 50 inserts the Consumer Credit (Total Charge for Credit)
Regulations 1980, SI 1980/51 at* **[3010A]***; regs 51–56 amend the Consumer Credit (Agreements)
Regulations 1983, SI 1983/1553, regs 1, 8 and Schs 1, 2, 8 at* **[3030A]**, **[3030H]**–**[3030J]**, **[3030S]***;
regs 64–67 amend the Consumer Credit (Exempt Agreements) Order 1989, SI 1989/869, arts 1, 3, 4
at* **[3080]**, **[3082]**, **[3083]***; regs 70–72 amend the Consumer Credit (Advertisements)
Regulations 2004, SI 2004/1484, reg 1 at* **[3400]** *and insert reg 1A thereof at* **[3400A]***; regs 73–76
amend the Consumer Credit (Disclosure of Information) Regulations 2004, SI 2004/1481, regs 1, 3
at* **[3385]**, **[3387]** *and substitute reg 2 thereof at* **[3386]***; regs 77–84 amend the Consumer Credit
(Early Settlement) Regulations 2004, SI 2004/1483, regs 1–5 at* **[3389]**–**[3393]***, insert reg 4A thereof
at* **[3392A]** *and revoke the Schedule thereto at* **[3399]***; regs 85–89 amend the Financial Services
(Distance Marketing) Regulations 2004, SI 2004/2095, regs 2, 7, 8, 11 at* **[3414]**, **[3419]**, **[3420]**,
[3423]*; reg 92 amends the Consumer Credit (Exempt Agreements) Order 2007, SI 2007/1168, art 2
at* **[3551]***; regs 94–96 amend the Cancellation of Contracts made in a Consumer's Home or Place of
Work etc Regulations 2008, SI 2008/1816, regs 6, 11 at* **[3710]**, **[3715]***; reg 97 amends the Payment
Services Regulations 2009, SI 2009/209, reg 52 at* **[3784]**.)

PART 4
COMMENCEMENT, TRANSITIONAL AND SAVING PROVISION

99   Commencement

(1)   Subject to paragraph (2) and *regulation 101* [regulations 101 and 101A], these Regulations
come into force on 1st February 2011.

(2)   The following provisions come into force on 30th April 2010—
    (a)   regulation 19 (definition of certain overdraft agreements);
    (b)   regulation 39 (definition of open-end);
    (c)   regulation 41 (credit intermediaries) for the purposes of the definition of credit
          intermediary;
    (d)   regulation 42 (definition of credit intermediary);
    (e)   the regulations in this Part.

[3940]

NOTES
Commencement: 30 April 2010 (see further regs 101, 101A at **[3942]**, **[3942A]**).
Para (1): words in italics substituted by subsequent words in square brackets by the Consumer Credit
(Amendment) Regulations 2010, SI 2010/1969, regs 4, 28, as from 26 August 2010.

100 Application of regulations to agreements entered into before 1st February 2011

(1)   Subject to paragraphs (2) to (5) and *regulation 101* [regulations 101 and 101A] these Regulations apply only to a regulated consumer credit agreement entered into on or after 1st February 2011.

(2)   The following regulations apply (from 1st February 2011) to a regulated consumer credit agreement which is an open-end agreement and is entered into before 11th June 2010—

[(za)   regulation 22 (information to be provided on significant overdrawing without prior arrangement);]
(a)   regulations 27 and 28 (information on change of interest rate etc);
(b)   regulation 36 (assignment);
(c)   regulations 37 to 39 (open-end agreements);
(d)   regulation 46(b) (amendments to Enterprise Act 2002);
(e)   regulation 63 (amendments to Consumer Credit (Running-Account Credit Information) Regulations 1983);
(f)   regulation 69(b) (amendments to Enterprise Act 2002 (Part 8 Community Infringements Specified UK Laws) Order 2003);
(g)   regulation 97 (amendments to Payment Services Regulations 2009).

(3)   The following regulations apply (from 1st February 2011) to a regulated consumer credit agreement which is an open-end agreement and is entered into on or after 11th June 2010 and before 1st February 2011—

[(za)   regulation 22 (information to be provided on significant overdrawing without prior arrangement);]
(a)   regulation 25 (linked credit agreements);
(b)   regulations 27 and 28 (information on change of interest rate etc);
(c)   regulations 29 to 35 (early repayment);
(d)   regulation 36 (assignment);
(e)   regulations 37 to 39 (open-end agreements);
(f)   regulation 46 (amendments to Enterprise Act 2002);
(g)   regulations 59 to 62 (amendments to Consumer Credit (Settlement Information) Regulations 1983);
(h)   regulation 63 (amendments to Consumer Credit (Running-Account Credit Information) Regulations 1983);
(i)   regulation 69 (amendments to Enterprise Act 2002 (Part 8 Community Infringements Specified UK Laws) Order 2003);
(j)   regulations 77 to 84 (amendments to Consumer Credit (Early Settlement) Regulations 2004);
(k)   regulation 97 (amendments to Payment Services Regulations 2009).

(4)   The following regulations apply (from 1st February 2011) to a regulated consumer credit agreement which not an open-end agreement and is entered into on or after 11th June 2010 and before 1st February 2011—

(a)   regulation 25 (linked credit agreements);
(b)   regulation 26 (statement of account);
(c)   regulations 29 to 35 (early repayment);
(d)   regulation 36 (assignment);
(e)   regulation 46 (amendments to Enterprise Act 2002);
(f)   regulations 59 to 62 (amendments to Consumer Credit (Settlement Information) Regulations 1983);
(g)   regulation 69 (amendments to Enterprise Act 2002 (Part 8 Community Infringements Specified UK Laws) Order 2003);
(h)   regulations 77 to 84 (amendments to Consumer Credit (Early Settlement) Regulations 2004).

(5)   Section 95A of the Consumer Credit Act 1974 (compensation for early repayment) applies in relation to an agreement by virtue of sub-paragraph (3)(c) or (4)(c) only where the debtor's entitlement to discharge his indebtedness arises by virtue of a notice made on or after 1st February 2011.

[3941]

NOTES

Commencement: 30 April 2010 (see further regs 99, 101, 101A at **[3940]**, **[3942]**, **[3942A]**).

Para (1): words in italics substituted by subsequent words in square brackets by the Consumer Credit (Amendment) Regulations 2010, SI 2010/1969, regs 4, 29(a), as from 26 August 2010.

Para (2): sub-para (za) inserted by SI 2010/1969, regs 4, 29(b), as from 26 August 2010.

Para (3): sub-para (za) inserted by SI 2010/1969, regs 4, 29(c), as from 26 August 2010.

101   Early application of regulations to certain agreements before 1st February 2011

(1)   Where one of the conditions A to E is satisfied in relation to a prospective regulated consumer credit agreement on a date on or after 30th April 2010 and before 1st February 2011, Parts 1 to 3 of these Regulations apply to that agreement (and to any subsequent regulated consumer credit agreement entered into before 1st February 2011), from the date and time that the condition is satisfied.

(2)   Condition A is that information relating to the agreement is disclosed by a creditor or a credit intermediary before the agreement is made in compliance or in purported compliance with the Information Regulations 2010.

(3)   Condition B is that—
- (a)   the agreement would, if made, be an agreement entered into at the debtor's request using a means of distance communication (other than voice telephony) which does not enable the provision before the agreement is made of the information referred to in regulation 3(4) of the Information Regulations 2010, and
- (b)   the debtor is informed by the creditor before the agreement is made that the information referred to in regulation 3(4) of the Information Regulations 2010 will be disclosed immediately after the agreement is made in accordance with regulation 5 of those Regulations.

(4)   Condition C is that—
- (a)   the agreement would, if made, be a distance agreement entered into by the debtor wholly or predominantly for the purposes of a business carried on, or intended to be carried on, by him, and
- (b)   the debtor is informed by the creditor before the agreement is made that information referred to in regulation 3(4) of the Information Regulations 2010 will be disclosed immediately after the agreement is made in accordance with regulation 6 of those Regulations.

(5)   Condition D is that—
- (a)   the agreement would, if made, be an authorised non-business overdraft agreement (other than a qualifying overdraft agreement referred to in paragraph (7)(b)),
- (b)   the agreement would, if made, be one made at the debtor's request using a means of distance communication which does not enable the provision before the agreement is made of the information referred to in regulation 10(2) of the Information Regulations 2010, and
- (c)   the creditor has informed the debtor before the agreement is made that a document containing the terms of the agreement will be provided immediately after the agreement is made as though the amendment made by regulation 9 of these Regulations (insertion of section 61B in the Consumer Credit Act 1974) applied.

(6)   Condition E is that the agreement would, if made, be a qualifying overdraft agreement and—
- (a)   the creditor has provided a document containing the terms of the agreement before the agreement is made as though the amendment made by regulation 9 (insertion of section 61B in the Consumer Credit Act 1974) applied, or
- (b)   the creditor has informed the debtor before the agreement is made that a document containing the terms of the agreement will be provided at, or immediately after, the time the agreement is made as though the amendment made by regulation 9 applied.

(7)   In paragraph (6) "qualifying overdraft agreement" means—
- (a)   an authorised business overdraft agreement, or
- (b)   an authorised non-business overdraft agreement under which the creditor provides the debtor with credit exceeding £60,260 or which is secured on land.

[3942]

PART 2
STATUTORY INSTRUMENTS

NOTES

Commencement: 30 April 2010 (see further regs 99, 101A at **[3940]**, **[3942A]**).

[101A—(1)   Where condition F is satisfied on a date on or after 26th August 2010 and before 1st February 2011 in relation to a prospective regulated consumer credit agreement falling within paragraph (2), Parts 1 to 3 of these Regulations apply to that agreement (and to any subsequent regulated consumer credit agreement entered into before 1st February 2011), from the date and time that the condition is satisfied.

(2)   An agreement falls within this paragraph if it is an agreement which would, if made, be—
- (a)   an agreement under which the creditor provides the debtor with credit exceeding £60,260 and is not an authorised non-business overdraft agreement, or
- (b)   an agreement entered into by the debtor wholly or predominantly for the purposes of a business carried on, or intended to be carried on, by him.

(3)   Condition F is that the Consumer Credit (Disclosure of Information) Regulations 2004 apply to the agreement, but the creditor—

(a)   does what would be required by regulations 3(1)(a) and (c) of those Regulations (pre-contractual information requirement to disclose information and statements required by the Consumer Credit (Agreements) Regulations 1983) if the amendments to the Consumer Credit (Agreements) Regulations 1983 made by regulations 52 to 56 were in force; and

(b)   also provides the debtor with a statement before the agreement is made that, if the creditor decides not to proceed with the agreement on the basis of information obtained from a credit reference agency, the creditor will, when informing the debtor of the decision—

(i)   inform the debtor that this decision has been reached on the basis of information from a credit reference agency, and

(ii)   provide the debtor with the particulars of the agency including its name, address and telephone number.]

[3942A]

NOTES
Commencement: 26 August 2010.
Inserted by the Consumer Credit (Amendment) Regulations 2010, SI 2010/1969, regs 4, 30, as from 26 August 2010.

102   Interpretation

In this Part—

(a)   "authorised business overdraft agreement", "authorised non-business overdraft agreement", "consumer credit agreement", "creditor", "debtor", "open-end" and "regulated" have the meanings given by section 189(1) of the Consumer Credit Act 1974;

(b)   "distance agreement" means any regulated consumer credit agreement made under an organised distance sales or service-provision scheme run by the creditor or on behalf of the creditor who, in any such case, for the purpose of that agreement makes exclusive use of one or more means of distance communication up to and including the time at which the agreement is made;

(c)   "Information Regulations 2010" means the Consumer Credit (Disclosure of Information) Regulations 2010;

(d)   "means of distance communication" means any means which, without the simultaneous physical presence of the creditor or a person acting on behalf of the creditor and of the debtor, may be used for the making of a regulated consumer credit agreement between the parties to that agreement.

[3943]

NOTES
Commencement: 30 April 2010 (see further regs 99, 101, 101A at **[3940]**, **[3942]**, **[3942A]**).

CONSUMER CREDIT (TOTAL CHARGE FOR CREDIT) REGULATIONS 2010

(SI 2010/1011)

NOTES
Made: 28 March 2010.
Authority: Consumer Credit Act 1974, ss 20, 182(2).
Commencement: see reg 1(2) at **[3944]**.
These Regulations implement European Parliament and Council Directive 2008/48/EC, Art 19, Annex 1 at **[4547]**, **[4561]**.

ARRANGEMENT OF REGULATIONS

1 Citation and commencement

(1) These Regulations may be cited as the Consumer Credit (Total Charge for Credit) Regulations 2010.

(2) These Regulations shall come into force—

    (a) on 1st February 2011, or

    (b) in relation to a prospective or actual regulated consumer credit agreement, on the date and at the time Parts 1 to 3 of the Consumer Credit (EU Directive) Regulations 2010 apply to such an agreement, being a date before 1st February 2011.

[3944]

NOTES

Commencement: 1 February 2011 (see further para (2)(b) above).

2 Interpretation

(1) In these Regulations—

"annual percentage rate of charge" means the rate of the total charge for credit (calculated in accordance with regulation 4), expressed as an annual percentage of the total amount of credit;

"current account" means an account under which the customer may, by means of cheques or similar orders payable to the customer or to any other person or by any other means, obtain or have the use of money held or made available by the person with whom the account is kept and which records alterations in the financial relationship between the said person and the customer;

"overdraft facility" means an explicit agreement whereby a creditor makes available to a debtor funds which exceed the current balance in the debtor's current account;

"total amount of credit" means the credit limit or the total sums made available under a consumer credit agreement;

"total cost of credit to the debtor" means all costs, including interest, commissions, taxes and any other kind of fees which are required to be paid by or on behalf of the debtor or a relative of the debtor in connection with the consumer credit agreement, whether payable to the creditor or to any other person, and which are known to the creditor, except for notarial costs.

(2) In these Regulations—

    (a) a reference to a rate of interest is a reference to the interest rate expressed as a fixed or variable percentage applied on an annual basis to the amount of credit drawn down;

    (b) a reference to a consumer credit agreement is to a consumer credit agreement regulated by the Act.

[3945]

NOTES

Commencement: 1 February 2011 (see further reg 1(2)(b) at **[3944]**).

3 Application

These Regulations shall not apply to consumer credit agreements which are secured on land or to prospective consumer credit agreements which are to be secured on land except to the extent that the Consumer Credit (Disclosure of Information) Regulations 2010 apply to such agreements.

[3946]

NOTES

Commencement: 1 February 2011 (see further reg 1(2)(b) at **[3944]**).

4 Total charge for credit

(1) The total charge for credit which may be provided under an actual or prospective consumer credit agreement shall be the total cost of credit to the debtor determined in accordance with the requirements in paragraphs (2) to (5) below.

(2) Subject to paragraph (3), the following costs shall be included in the total cost of credit to the debtor—

    (a) the costs of maintaining an account recording both payment transactions and drawdowns;

    (b) the costs of using a means of payment for both payment transactions and drawdowns;

    (c) other costs relating to payment transactions.

(3) The costs at paragraph (2) shall not be included in the total cost of credit to the debtor where—

(a) the opening of the account is optional and the costs of the account have been clearly and separately shown in the consumer credit agreement or in any other agreement made with the debtor;

(b) in the case of an overdraft facility the costs do not relate to that facility.

(4) Costs in respect of an ancillary service shall be included in the total cost of credit to the debtor if the conclusion of a service contract is compulsory in order to obtain the credit or to obtain it on the terms and conditions marketed.

(5) The total cost of credit to the debtor shall not include—

(a) any charges payable by or on behalf of the debtor or a relative of his for non-compliance with his commitments contained in the consumer credit agreement;

(b) charges which, for purchases of goods or services, he or a relative of his is obliged to pay whether the transaction is effected in cash or on credit.

(6) In paragraph (4), the reference to an ancillary service means a service that relates to the provision of credit under the consumer credit agreement and includes in particular an insurance or payment protection policy.

[3947]

NOTES

Commencement: 1 February 2011 (see further reg 1(2)(b) at **[3944]**).

5 Calculation of the annual percentage rate of charge

The annual percentage rate of charge shall be calculated in accordance with the mathematical formula set out in the Schedule to these Regulations.

[3948]

NOTES

Commencement: 1 February 2011 (see further reg 1(2)(b) at **[3944]**).

6 Assumptions for calculation

For the purposes of calculating the total charge for credit and the annual percentage rate of charge——

(a) it shall be assumed that the consumer credit agreement is to remain valid for the period agreed and that the creditor and the debtor will fulfil their obligations under the terms and by the dates specified in that agreement;

(b) in the case of a consumer credit agreement allowing variations in—

(i) the rate of interest, or

(ii) where applicable, charges contained in the annual percentage rate of charge,

where these cannot be quantified at the time of calculation, it shall be assumed that they will remain at the initial level and will be applicable for the duration of the agreement;

(c) where not all rates of interest are determined in the consumer credit agreement, a rate of interest shall be assumed to be fixed only for the partial periods for which the rate of interest is determined exclusively by a fixed specific percentage agreed when the agreement is made;

(d) where the duration of the consumer credit agreement cannot be determined at the date of calculation and where different rates of interest and charges are to be offered for limited periods during that agreement, the rate of interest and the charge shall be assumed to be at the highest level for the duration of the agreement;

(e) where there is a fixed rate of interest agreed in relation to an initial period under a consumer credit agreement, at the end of which a new rate of interest is determined and subsequently periodically adjusted according to an agreed indicator, it shall be assumed that, at the end of the period of the fixed rate of interest, the rate of interest is the same as at the time of making the calculation, based on the value of the agreed indicator at that time;

(f) where the consumer credit agreement gives the debtor freedom of drawdown, the total amount of credit shall be assumed to be drawn down immediately and in full;

(g) where the consumer credit agreement provides different ways of drawdown with different charges or rates of interest, the total amount of credit shall be assumed to be drawn down at the highest charge and rate of interest applied to the most common drawdown mechanism for the credit product to which the agreement relates;

(h) for the purposes of paragraph (g), the most common drawdown mechanism for a particular credit product shall be assessed on the basis of the volume of transactions for that product in the preceding 12 months, or expected volumes in the case of a new credit product;

(i) where the consumer credit agreement imposes, amongst the different ways of drawdown, a limitation with regard to the amount and period of time, the amount of credit shall be assumed to be the maximum amount provided for in the agreement and to be drawn down on the earliest date provided for in the agreement;

(j)   subject to paragraphs (p) and (q), where there is no fixed timetable for repayment under a consumer credit agreement, it shall be assumed—

    (i)   that the credit is provided for a period of one year;

    (ii)   that the credit will be repaid in 12 equal instalments and at monthly intervals;

(k)   repayment of credit in paragraph (j)(ii) includes repayment of interest and other charges;

(l)   there is no fixed timetable for repayment under a consumer credit agreement where the agreement does not set a specific date by which the entire credit must be repaid;

(m)   where there is a fixed timetable for repayment under a consumer credit agreement but the amount of repayment instalments is flexible, the amount of each instalment (other than the last instalment) shall be assumed to be the lowest for which the agreement provides;

(n)   unless otherwise provided, where the consumer credit agreement provides for more than one repayment date, it shall be assumed that the credit is to be made available and repayment made on the earliest date provided for in the agreement;

(o)   in the case of an agreement for running-account credit, where the credit limit applicable to the credit is not yet known, that credit limit shall be assumed to be £1,200;

(p)   in the case of an overdraft facility, the total amount of credit shall be assumed to be drawn down in full and for the entire duration of the consumer credit agreement;

(q)   for the purposes of paragraph (p) if the duration of the consumer credit agreement is not known it shall be assumed that the duration of the agreement is three months.

[3949]

NOTES

Commencement: 1 February 2011 (see further reg 1(2)(b) at **[3944]**).

SCHEDULE
CALCULATION OF THE ANNUAL PERCENTAGE RATE OF CHARGE

Regulation 5

1.   The annual percentage rate of charge ("APR") is calculated by means of the equation in paragraph 2 which equates, on an annual basis, the total present value of drawdowns with the total present value of repayments and payments of charges.

2.   The equation referred to in paragraph 1 is—

$$\sum_{k=1}^{m} C_k(1+X)^{-t_k} = \sum_{l=1}^{m'} D_l(1+X)^{-S_l}$$

where

    X is the APR;

    m is the number of the last drawdown;

    k is the number of a drawdown, thus $1 \leq k = m$;

    C_k is the amount of drawdown k;

    t_k is the interval, expressed in years and fractions of a year, between the date of the first drawdown and the date of each subsequent drawdown, thus $t_1 = 0$;

    m' is the number of the last repayment or payment of charges;

    l is the number of a repayment or payment of charges;

    D_l is the amount of a repayment or payment of charges;

    S_l is the interval, expressed in years and fractions of a year, between the date of the first drawdown and the date of each repayment or payment of charges.

3.   For the purposes of paragraph 2—

(a)   the amounts paid by both parties at different times shall not necessarily be equal and shall not necessarily be paid at equal intervals;

(b)   the starting date shall be that of the first drawdown;

(c)   intervals between dates used in the calculations shall be expressed in years or in fractions of a year;

(d)   a year is assumed to have 365 days (366 days for leap years), 52 weeks or 12 equal months;

(e)   an equal month is assumed to have 30.41666 days (365/12) regardless of whether or not it is a leap year;

(f)   the result of the calculation shall be expressed with an accuracy of at least one decimal place; if the figure at the following decimal place is greater than or equal to 5, the figure at that particular decimal place shall be increased by one;

(g)   the equation can be rewritten as set out in sub-paragraph (h) using a single sum and the concept of flows (A_k), which will be positive or negative, either paid or received during periods 1 to n, expressed in years;

(h)   the equation referred to in sub-paragraph (g) is—

PART 2
STATUTORY INSTRUMENTS

$$S = \sum_{k=1}^{n} A_k (1+X)^{-t_k}$$

S being the present balance of flows; if the aim is to maintain the equivalence of flows, the value will be zero.

[3950]–[3963]

NOTES
Commencement: 1 February 2011 (see further reg 1(2)(b) at **[3944]**).

CONSUMER CREDIT (DISCLOSURE OF INFORMATION) REGULATIONS 2010

(SI 2010/1013)

NOTES
Made: 28 March 2010.
Authority: European Communities Act 1972, s 2(2); Consumer Credit Act 1974, ss 55(1), 182(2), 189(1).
Commencement: 30 April 2010.
These Regulations implement European Parliament and Council Directive 2002/65/EC, Arts 3, 5 at **[4428]**, **[4430]** and European Parliament and Council Directive 2008/48/EC, Arts 5, 6 at **[4533]**, **[4534]**.

ARRANGEMENT OF REGULATIONS

1 Citation, commencement and interpretation

(1) These Regulations may be cited as the Consumer Credit (Disclosure of Information) Regulations 2010 and shall come into force on 30th April 2010.

(2) In these Regulations—
   "the Act" means the Consumer Credit Act 1974;
   "advance payment" includes any deposit and in relation to a regulated consumer credit agreement includes also any part-exchange allowance in respect of any goods agreed in antecedent negotiations *not* to be taken by the creditor in part exchange but does not include a repayment of credit or any insurance premium or any amount entering into the total charge for credit;
   "ancillary service" means a service that relates to the provision of credit under the agreement and includes in particular an insurance or payment protection policy;
   "the APR" means the annual percentage rate of charge for credit determined in accordance with Schedule 2 to these Regulations and the Total Charge for Credit Regulations;
   "cash price" in relation to any goods, services, land or other things means the price or charge at which the goods, services, land or other things may be purchased by, or supplied to, the debtor for cash account being taken of any discount generally available from the dealer or supplier in question;
   "credit intermediary" has the same meaning as in section 160A of the Act;
   "distance contract" means any regulated agreement made under an organised distance sales or service-provision scheme run by or on behalf of the creditor who, in any such case, for the purpose of that agreement makes exclusive use of one or more means of distance communication up to and including the time at which the agreement is made. For this

purpose, "means of distance communication" means any means which, without the simultaneous physical presence of the creditor or a person acting on behalf of the creditor and of the debtor, may be used for the making of a regulated agreement between the parties to that agreement;

"excluded pawn agreement" means a pawn agreement—

    (a)   where the debtor is not a new customer of the creditor (see *paragraph (5)* [paragraph (6)]), and

    (b)   where, before the agreement is made, the creditor has not received a request from the debtor for the pre-contract credit information (see regulation 9);

"linked credit agreement" means a regulated consumer credit agreement which—

    (a)   serves exclusively to finance an agreement for the supply of specific goods or the provision of a specific service or land, and

        (i)   where the supplier or service provider himself finances the credit for the debtor, or if it is financed by a third party, where the creditor uses the services of the supplier or service provider in connection with the preparation or making of the credit agreement, or

        (ii)   where the specific goods or land or the provision of a specific service are explicitly specified in the credit agreement;

"pawn agreement" means a consumer credit agreement under which the creditor takes an article in pawn;

"pre-contract credit information" means the information specified in regulation 3(4);

"total amount of credit" means the credit limit or the total sums made available under a consumer credit agreement;

"total amount payable" means the sum of the total charge for credit and the total amount of credit payable under the agreement as well as any advance payment;

"total charge for credit" means the total charge for credit determined in accordance with the Total Charge for Credit Regulations and the Schedule to these Regulations;

"the Total Charge for Credit Regulations" means the Consumer Credit (Total Charge for Credit) Regulations 2010.

(3)   In these Regulations, a reference to a repayment is a reference to—

    (a)   a repayment of the whole or any part of the credit,

    (b)   a payment of the whole or any part of the total charge for credit, or

    (c)   a combination of such repayments and payments.

(4)   In these Regulations, a reference to rate of interest is a reference to the interest rate expressed as a fixed or variable percentage applied on an annual basis to the amount of credit drawn down.

(5)   In these Regulations, a reference to an agreement includes a reference to a prospective agreement.

(6)   For the purposes of the definition of "excluded pawn agreement" and regulation 8 the debtor is a new customer if the debtor has not entered into a pawn agreement with the creditor in the three years preceding the start of the negotiations antecedent to the agreement.

(7)   In relation to a regulated consumer credit agreement secured on land and to which these Regulations do not apply, the definition of Total Charge for Credit Regulations shall apply as if for the words "Consumer Credit (Total Charge for Credit) Regulations 2010" there were substituted "Consumer Credit (Total Charge for Credit) Regulations 1980".

[3964]

NOTES

Commencement: 30 April 2010.

Para (2): word in italics in definition "advance payment" revoked and words in italics in definition "excluded pawn agreement" substituted by subsequent words in square brackets by the Consumer Credit (Amendment) Regulations 2010, SI 2010/1969, regs 31, 32, as from 26 August 2010.

2 Agreements to which these Regulations apply

(1)   These Regulations apply in respect of a regulated consumer credit agreement, except as provided for in paragraphs (2) to (4).

(2)   These regulations do not apply to an agreement to which section 58 of the Act (opportunity for withdrawal from prospective land mortgage) applies.

(3)   These Regulations do not apply to an authorised non-business overdraft agreement which is—

    (a)   for credit which exceeds £60,260, or

    (b)   secured on land.

(4)   Except as provided for in paragraph (5) these Regulations do not apply to an agreement—

    (a)   under which the creditor provides the debtor with credit exceeding £60,260,

    (b)   secured on land,

     (c)   entered into by the debtor wholly or predominantly for the purposes of a business also carried on, or intended to be carried on, by him, or

     (d)   made before 1st February 2011.

(5) These Regulations apply to an agreement mentioned in paragraph (4) (which is not also an agreement mentioned in paragraph (2) or (3)) where a creditor or, where applicable a credit intermediary, discloses or purports to disclose the pre-contract credit information in accordance with these Regulations rather than in accordance with the Consumer Credit (Disclosure of Information) Regulations 2004 or the Financial Services (Distance Marketing) Regulations 2004 (as the case may be).

(6) Subsections (2) to (5) of section 16B of the Act (declaration by the debtor as to the purposes of the agreement) apply for the purposes of *paragraph (3)(c)* [paragraph (4)(c)].

[3965]

NOTES

Commencement: 30 April 2010.

Para (6): words in italics substituted by subsequent words in square brackets by the Consumer Credit (Amendment) Regulations 2010, SI 2010/1969, regs 31, 33, as from 26 August 2010.

---

3 Information to be disclosed: agreements other than telephone contracts, non-telephone distance contracts, excluded pawn agreements and overdraft agreements

(1) This regulation applies to an agreement other than—

     (a)   *an agreement made by way of a voice telephone communication (whether or not it is a distance contract) (see regulation 4);*

     [(a)   an agreement made by voice telephone communication where it is a distance contract and the debtor consents to the disclosure of the information referred to in regulation 4(2);

     (aa)   an agreement made by voice telephone communication where it is not a distance contract (see regulation 4(3));]

     (b)   an agreement made using a means of distance communication other than a voice telephone communication, which does not enable the provision of the pre-contract credit information before the agreement is made (see regulation 5);

     (c)   an excluded pawn agreement;

     (d)   an authorised non-business overdraft agreement (see regulations 10 and 11).

(2) In good time before the agreement is made, the creditor must disclose to the debtor, in the manner set out in regulation 8, the pre-contract credit information.

(3) Paragraph (2) does not require a creditor to disclose the pre-contract credit information where it has already been disclosed to the debtor by a credit intermediary in a manner which complies with paragraph (2).

(4) For the purposes of these Regulations, the pre-contract credit information comprises—

     (a)   the type of credit,

     (b)   the identity and geographical address of the creditor and, where applicable, of the credit intermediary,

     (c)   the total amount of credit to be provided under the agreement and the conditions governing the draw down of credit. In the case of an agreement for running-account credit, the total amount of credit may be expressed as a statement indicating the manner in which the credit limit will be determined where it is not practicable to express the limit as a sum of money,

     (d)   the duration or minimum duration of the agreement or a statement that the agreement has no fixed or minimum duration,

     (e)   in the case of—

         (i)   credit in the form of deferred payment for specific goods, services or land, or

         (ii)   a linked credit agreement,

         a description of the goods, services or land and the cash price of each and the total cash price,

     (f)   the rate of interest charged, any conditions applicable to that rate, where available, any reference rate on which that rate is based and any information on any changes to the rate of interest (including the periods that the rate applies, and any conditions or procedure applicable to changing the rate),

     (g)   where different rates of interest are charged in different circumstances the creditor must provide the information in paragraph (f) in respect of each rate,

     (h)   the APR and the total amount payable under the agreement illustrated (if not known) by way of a representative example mentioning all the assumptions used in order to calculate that rate and amount,

     (i)   the amount (expressed as a sum of money), number (if applicable) and frequency of repayments to be made by the debtor and, where appropriate, the order in which repayments will be allocated to different outstanding balances charged at different rates of interest,

(j)   in the case of an agreement for running-account credit, the amount of each repayment is to be expressed as (a) a sum of money; (b) a specified proportion of a specified amount; (c) a combination of (a) or (b); or (d) in a case where the amount of any repayment cannot be expressed in accordance with (a), (b) or (c), a statement indicating the manner in which the amount will be determined,

(k)   if applicable, any charges for maintaining an account recording both payment transactions and draw downs, unless the opening of an account is optional, and any charge payable for using a method of payment in respect of payment transactions or draw downs,

(l)   any other charges payable deriving from the credit agreement and the conditions under which those charges may be changed,

(m)   if applicable, a statement that fees will be payable by the debtor to a notary on conclusion of the credit agreement,

(n)   the obligation, if any, to enter into a contract for ancillary services relating to the consumer credit agreement, in particular insurance services, where the conclusion of such a contract is compulsory in order to obtain the credit or to obtain it on the terms and conditions marketed,

(o)   the rate of interest applicable in the case of late payments and the arrangements for its adjustment, and, where applicable, any charges payable for default,

(p)   a warning regarding the consequences of missing payments (for example, the possibility of legal proceedings and the possibility that the debtor's home may be repossessed),

(q)   where applicable, any security to be provided by the debtor or on behalf of the debtor,

(r)   the existence or absence of a right of withdrawal,

(s)   the debtor's right of early repayment under section 94 of the Act, and where applicable, information concerning the creditor's right to compensation and the way in which that compensation will be determined,

(t)   the requirement for a creditor to inform a debtor in accordance with section 157(A1) of the Act that a decision not to proceed with a prospective regulated consumer credit agreement has been reached on the basis of information from a credit reference agency and of the particulars of that agency,

(u)   the debtor's right to be supplied under section 55C of the Act on request and free of charge, with a copy of the draft agreement except where—

     (i)   the creditor is at the time of the request unwilling to proceed to the making of the agreement, or

     (ii)   the agreement is an agreement referred to in regulation 2(4)(a) to (c) or a pawn agreement, and

(v)   if applicable, the period of time during which the creditor is bound by the pre-contract credit information.

(5)   For the purpose of the representative example referred to in paragraph (4)(h)—

     (i)   where the debtor has informed the creditor or credit intermediary of one or more components of his preferred credit, such as the duration of the consumer credit agreement or the total amount of credit, and

     (ii)   where the creditor would in principle agree to offer credit on such terms,

the creditor or credit intermediary must take those components into account when calculating the representative APR and the total amount payable;

(b)   where the creditor uses the assumption set out in regulation 6(g) of the Consumer Credit (Total Charge for Credit) Regulations 2010 the creditor must indicate that other draw down mechanisms for this type of consumer credit agreement may result in a higher APR;

(c)   subject to paragraph (a), in the case of an agreement for running-account credit, where the credit limit is not known at the date on which the pre-contract credit information is disclosed, the total amount of credit is to be assumed to be £1,200 or in a case where credit is to be provided subject to a maximum credit limit of less than £1,200, an amount equal to that maximum limit.

(6)   In the case of a consumer credit agreement under which repayments do not give rise to an immediate reduction in the total amount of credit advanced but are used to constitute capital as provided for under the agreement or under an ancillary agreement, the creditor or credit intermediary must provide a clear and concise statement that such agreements do not provide for a guarantee of repayment of the total amount of credit drawn down under the credit agreement unless such a guarantee is given.

[3966]

NOTES
Commencement: 30 April 2010.

Para (1): original sub-para (a) in italics substituted by subsequent sub-paras (a), (aa) in square brackets by the Consumer Credit (Amendment) Regulations 2010, SI 2010/1969, regs 31, 34, as from 26 August 2010.

4 Information to be disclosed: telephone contracts

(1)   This regulation applies to an agreement (other than an authorised non-business overdraft agreement) made by way of a voice telephone communication (whether or not it is a distance contract).

(2)   Where the agreement is a distance contract and where the debtor explicitly consents, the creditor must disclose the following information before the agreement is made—

    (a)   the identity of the person in contact with the debtor and that person's link with the creditor,

    (b)   a description of the main characteristics of the credit agreement which includes the information set out in regulation 3(4)(c), (d), (e), (f), (g), (h), (i) and (j),

    (c)   the total price to be paid by the debtor to the creditor for the credit including all taxes paid via the creditor or, if an exact price cannot be indicated, the basis for the calculation of the price enabling the debtor to verify it,

    (d)   notice of the possibility that other taxes or costs may exist that are not paid via the creditor or imposed by the creditor,

    (e)   whether or not there is—

        (i)   a right to withdraw under section 66A of the Act, or

        (ii)   a right to cancel under regulation 9 of the Financial Services (Distance Marketing) Regulations 2004 and, where there is such a right, its duration and the conditions for exercising it, including information on the amount which the consumer may be required to pay in accordance with regulation 13 of those Regulations, as well as the consequences of not exercising that right,

    (f)   that other information is available on request and the nature of that information.

(3)   Where the agreement is not a distance contract the creditor must disclose the information in paragraph (2)(b) before the agreement is made.

(4)   The creditor must disclose the pre-contract credit information in the manner set out in regulation 8 immediately after the agreement is made.

[3967]

NOTES
    Commencement: 30 April 2010.

5 Information to be disclosed: non-telephone distance contracts

(1)   This regulation applies to an agreement (other than an authorised non-business overdraft agreement) made—

    (a)   at the debtor's request, and

    (b)   using a means of distance communication other than a voice telephone communication which does not enable the provision before the agreement is made of the pre-contract credit information.

(2)   The creditor must disclose the pre-contract credit information in the manner set out in regulation 8 immediately after the agreement is made.

[3968]

NOTES
    Commencement: 30 April 2010.

6 Information to be disclosed: distance contracts for the purpose of a business

(1)   This regulation applies to an agreement that is a distance contract entered into by the debtor wholly or predominantly for the purposes of a business carried on, or intended to be carried on by him.

(2)   Where the agreement is an agreement to which *regulations 3 or 4* [regulations 3, 4 or 5] would otherwise apply the creditor may comply with those regulations by disclosing the pre-contract credit information immediately after the agreement is entered into.

(3)   Subsections (2) to (5) of section 16B of the Act (declaration by the debtor as to the purposes of the agreement) apply for the purposes of paragraph (1).

[3969]

NOTES
    Commencement: 30 April 2010.
    Para (2): words in italics substituted by subsequent words in square brackets by the Consumer Credit (Amendment) Regulations 2010, SI 2010/1969, regs 31, 35, as from 26 August 2010.

7   Information about contractual terms and conditions: regulations 3 and 4 [regulations 3, 4 and 5]

(1)   This regulation applies to an agreement which is—
  (a)   a distance contract to which *regulation 3 or 4* [regulation 3, 4 or 5] applies, and
  (b)   which is not entered into by the debtor wholly or predominantly for the purposes of a business carried on, or intended to be carried on, by him.

(2)   The creditor must ensure that—
  (a)   the information provided to the debtor pursuant to *regulation 3 or 4* [regulation 3, 4 or 5] includes the contractual terms and conditions, and
  (b)   the information provided to the debtor in relation to the contractual obligations which would arise if the distance contract were made accurately reflects the contractual obligations which would arise under the law presumed to be applicable to that contract.

(3)   Subsections (2) to (5) of section 16B of the Act (declaration by the debtor as to the purposes of the agreement) apply for the purposes of paragraph (1).

[3970]

NOTES
Commencement: 30 April 2010.
Heading: words in italics substituted by subsequent words in square brackets by the Consumer Credit (Amendment) Regulations 2010, SI 2010/1969, regs 31, 36(a), as from 26 August 2010.
Paras (1), (2): words in italics substituted by subsequent words in square brackets by SI 2010/1969, regs 31, 36(b), (c), as from 26 August 2010.

8   Manner of disclosure

(1)   The pre-contract credit information must be disclosed by means of the form contained in Schedule 1.

(2)   The form must be—
  (a)   in writing, and
  (b)   of a nature that enables the debtor to remove it from the place where it is disclosed to him.

(3)   The form must be completed as specified in this paragraph—
  (a)   the relevant pre-contract credit information is to be provided in the appropriate row,
  (b)   the form is to be completed in accordance with the notes to that form,
  (c)   the asterisks and notes may be deleted,
  (d)   gridlines and boxes may be omitted, and
  (e)   any information contained in the form must be clear and easily legible.

(4)   Any additional information relating to the credit which is provided in writing by the creditor to the debtor must be provided in a separate document to the form.

(5)   Where a consumer credit agreement is a multiple agreement containing more than one part for the purposes of section 18 of the Act, the pre-contract credit information in respect of each part may be provided in the same form provided that—
  (a)   information that is not common to each part of the agreement is disclosed separately within the relevant section of the form, and
  (b)   it is clear which information relates to which part.

[3971]

NOTES
Commencement: 30 April 2010.

9   Information to be disclosed: pawn agreements

(1)   This Regulation applies to a pawn agreement.

(2)   In good time before a pawn agreement is made (unless the debtor is a new customer), the creditor must inform the debtor of his right to receive the pre-contract credit information in the form contained in Schedule 1, free of charge, on request.

[3972]

NOTES
Commencement: 30 April 2010.

10   Information to be disclosed: overdraft agreements

(1)   This regulation applies to an agreement which is an authorised non-business overdraft agreement.

(2)   In good time before an authorised non-business overdraft agreement is made, the creditor must disclose to the debtor, the information in paragraph (3) in the manner set out in regulation 11.

(3)   The information referred to in paragraph (2) is as follows—

(a)   the type of credit,

(b)   the identity and geographical address of the creditor and, where applicable, of the credit intermediary,

(c)   the total amount of credit,

(d)   the duration of the agreement,

(e)   the rate of interest charged, any conditions applicable to that rate, any reference rate on which that rate is based and any information on any changes to the rate of interest (including the periods that the rate applies, and any conditions or procedure applicable to changing the rate),

(f)   where different rates of interest are charged in different circumstances the creditor must provide the information in paragraph (e) in respect of each rate,

(g)   the conditions and procedure for terminating the agreement,

(h)   where applicable, an indication that the debtor may be requested to repay the amount of credit in full on demand at any time,

(i)   the rate of interest applicable in the case of late payments and the arrangements for its adjustment, and, where applicable, any charges payable for default,

(j)   the requirement for a creditor to inform a debtor in accordance with section 157(A1) of the Act that a decision not to proceed with a prospective regulated consumer credit agreement has been reached on the basis of information from a credit reference agency and of the particulars of that agency,

(k)   the charges, other than the rates of interest, payable by the debtor under the agreement (and the conditions under which those charges may be varied),

(l)   if applicable, the period of time during which the creditor is bound by the information set out in this paragraph.

(4)   Paragraph (2) does not apply to—

(a)   an agreement made by a voice telephone communication (whether or not it is a distance contract),

(b)   an agreement made at the debtor's request using a means of distance communication, other than a voice telephone communication, which does not enable the provision of the information required by paragraph (2) before the agreement is made, or

(c)   an agreement that does not come within sub-paragraph (a) or (b) but where the debtor requests the overdraft be made available with immediate effect.

(5)   In the case of an agreement that falls within paragraph (4)(a) that is also a distance contract, where the debtor explicitly consents the creditor must disclose the following information before the agreement is made—

(a)   the identity of the person in contact with the debtor and that person's link with the creditor,

(b)   a description of the main characteristics of the financial service including at least the information in paragraph (3)(c), (e), (f), (h) and (k),

(c)   the total price to be paid by the debtor to the creditor for the credit including all taxes paid via the creditor or, if an exact price cannot be indicated, the basis for the calculation of the price enabling the debtor to verify it,

(d)   notice of the possibility that other taxes or costs may exist that are not paid via the creditor or imposed by the creditor,

(e)   whether or not there is a right to cancel under regulation 9 of the Financial Services (Distance Marketing) Regulations 2004 and where there is such a right, its duration and the conditions for exercising it including information on the amount which the consumer may be required to pay in accordance with regulation 13 of those regulations, as well as the consequences of not exercising that right, and

(f)   that other information is available on request and the nature of that information.

[(5A)   In the case of an agreement that falls within paragraph (4)(a) that is also a distance contract, where the debtor does not explicitly consent to the disclosure of the information in paragraph (5), the creditor must disclose the information in paragraph (3) to the debtor before the regulation is made.]

(6)   In the case of an agreement that falls within paragraph (4)(a) that is not a distance contract the creditor must disclose the information in paragraph (5)(b) before the agreement is made.

(7)   In the case of an agreement that is a distance contract to which this regulation applies the creditor must ensure that the information he provides to the debtor pursuant to this regulation regarding the contractual obligations which would arise if the distance contract were concluded, accurately reflects the contractual obligations which would arise under the law presumed to be applicable to that contract.

(8)   In the case of an agreement that falls within paragraph (4)(c), the creditor must disclose the information in paragraph (3)(c), (e), (f), (h), and (k) to the debtor before the agreement is made in the manner set out in regulation 11.

(9)   Where a current account is an agreement for two or more debtors jointly the creditor may comply with paragraphs (5), [(5A),] (6) or (8) by disclosing the information to one debtor provided that each of the debtors have given the creditor their consent that the creditor may not comply in each debtor's case with the relevant paragraph.

[3973]

NOTES
Commencement: 30 April 2010.
Para (5A): inserted by the Consumer Credit (Amendment) Regulations 2010, SI 2010/1969, regs 31, 37(a), as from 26 August 2010.
Para (9): figure in square brackets inserted by SI 2010/1969, regs 31, 37(b), as from 26 August 2010.

11—(1)   Where regulation 10(2) applies, the creditor must comply with that regulation by—
     (a)   disclosing the information by means of the European Consumer Credit Information form set out in Schedule 3 to these Regulations and as specified in paragraph (2), or
     (b)   disclosing the information in writing so that all information is equally prominent.

(2)   The specifications referred to in paragraph (1)(a) are that—
     (a)   the relevant information must be provided in the appropriate row,
     (b)   the form must be completed in accordance with the notes to that form,
     (c)   the asterisks and notes may be deleted,
     (d)   gridlines and boxes may be omitted, and
     (e)   any information contained in the form must be clear and easily legible.

(3)   Where regulation 10(8) applies, the creditor may provide the information orally.

[3974]

NOTES
Commencement: 30 April 2010.

12   Modifying agreements

(1)   Subject to paragraphs (2) to (4), these Regulations apply to a modifying agreement which varies or supplements an earlier agreement and which is, or is treated under section 82(3) of the Act as, a regulated agreement.

(2)   *Where a modifying agreement modifies an earlier consumer credit agreement, the requirements of regulations 3, 4 and 10 will be deemed to be satisfied if, in good time before the modifying agreement is made—*
     (a)   the information specified by regulations 3(4) and 10(3) is disclosed to the debtor in respect of any provision of the earlier agreement which is varied or supplemented,
     (b)   the creditor informs the debtor in writing that the other information in the earlier agreement remains unchanged, and
     (c)   where the Financial Services (Distance Marketing) Regulations 2004 apply, the creditor complies with regulation 7 and 8 of those Regulations.

[(2)   Where a modifying agreement modifies an earlier consumer credit agreement, the requirements of regulations 3, 4 and 10 will be deemed to be satisfied if—
     (a)   in good time before the modifying agreement is made—
         (i)   the information specified by regulations 3(4) and 10(3) is disclosed to the debtor in respect of any provision of the earlier agreement which is varied or supplemented, and
         (ii)   the creditor informs the debtor in writing that the other information in the earlier agreement remains unchanged, and
     (b)   where the Financial Services (Distance Marketing) Regulations 2004 apply, the creditor complies with regulations 7 and 8 of those Regulations.]

(3)   Where a modifying agreement is made in a manner that does not allow the creditor to comply with the requirement in *paragraph (2)(b)* [paragraph (2)(a)(ii)], the creditor is deemed to have complied with that requirement if—
     (a)   before the agreement is made the creditor informs the debtor orally that the other information in the earlier agreement remains unchanged, and
     (b)   this is confirmed to the debtor in writing immediately after the agreement is made.

(4)   This regulation does not apply to an excluded pawn agreement.

[3975]

NOTES
Commencement: 30 April 2010.
Para (2): text in italics substituted by subsequent text in square brackets by the Consumer Credit (Amendment) Regulations 2010, SI 2010/1969, regs 31, 38(a), as from 26 August 2010.

Para (3): words in italics substituted by subsequent words in square brackets by SI 2010/1969, regs 31, 38(b), as from 26 August 2010.

SCHEDULE 1
PRE-CONTRACT CREDIT INFORMATION
Regulation 8(1)

(Standard European Consumer Credit Information)

1 Contact details	
Creditor.	[Identity.]
Address.	[Geographical address of the creditor
Telephone number(s).*	to be used by the debtor.]
E-mail address.*	
Fax number.*	
Web address.*	
If applicable	
Credit intermediary.	[Identity.]
Address.	[Geographical address of the credit
Telephone number(s).*	intermediary to be used by the debtor.]
E-mail address.*	
Fax number.*	
Web address.*	

* This information is optional for the creditor. The row may be deleted if the information is not provided.

Wherever "if applicable" is indicated, the creditor must give the information relevant to the credit product or, if the information is not relevant for the type of credit considered, delete the respective information or the entire row, or indicate that the information is not applicable.

Indications between square brackets provide explanations for the creditor and must be replaced with the corresponding information.

2 Key features of the credit product	
The type of credit [The type of credit].	
The total amount of credit. This means the amount of credit to be provided under the proposed credit agreement or the credit limit.	[The amount is to be expressed as a sum of money. In the case of running-account credit, the total amount may be expressed as a statement indicating the manner in which the credit limit will be determined where it is not practicable to express the limit as a sum of money.]
How and when credit would be provided.	[Details of how and when any credit being advanced is to be drawn down.]
The duration of the credit agreement.	[The duration or minimum duration of the agreement or a statement that the agreement has no fixed or minimum duration.]

Repayments. If applicable: Your repayments will pay off what you owe in the following order.	[The amount (expressed as a sum of money), number (if applicable) and frequency of repayments to be made by the debtor. In the case of an agreement for running-account credit, the amount may be expressed as a sum of money or a specified proportion of a specified amount or both, or in a case where the amount of any repayment cannot be expressed as a sum of money or a specified proportion, a statement indicating the manner in which the amount will be determined. [The order in which repayments will be allocated to different outstanding balances charged at different rates of interest.]
The total amount you will have to pay. This means the amount you have borrowed plus interest and other costs.	[The amount payable by the debtor under the agreement (where necessary, illustrated by means of a representative example). The total amount payable will be the sum of the total amount of credit and the total charge for credit payable under the agreement as well as any advance payment where required. In the case of running account credit, where it is not practicable to express the limit as a sum of money, a credit limit of £1200 should be assumed. In a case where credit is to be provided subject to a maximum credit limit of less than £1200, an amount equal to that maximum limit. The total charge for credit is to be calculated using the relevant APR assumptions set out in Schedule 2 to the Consumer Credit (Disclosure of Information) Regulations 2010 and the Total Charge for Credit Regulations, and where appropriate the relevant components of the debtor's preferred credit.]
If applicable [The proposed credit will be granted in the form of a deferred payment for goods or service.] or [The proposed credit will be linked to the supply of specific goods or the provision of a service.] Description of goods/services/land (as applicable). Cash price.	[A list or other description] [Cash price of goods or service.] [Total cash price.]
If applicable Security required. This is a description of the security to be provided by you in relation to the credit agreement.	[Description of any security to be provided by or on behalf of the debtor.]

PART 2
STATUTORY INSTRUMENTS

If applicable Repayments will not immediately reduce the amount you owe.	[In the case of a credit agreement under which repayments do not give rise to an immediate reduction in the total amount of credit advanced but are used to constitute capital as provided by the agreement (or an ancillary agreement a clear and concise statement) where applicable, that the agreement does not provide for a guarantee of the repayment of the total amount of credit drawn down under the credit agreement.]

3 Costs of the credit	
The rates of interest which apply to the credit agreement	[Details of the rate of interest charged, any conditions applicable to that rate, where available, any reference rate on which that rate is based and any information on changes to the rate of interest (including the periods that the rate applies, and any conditions or procedure applicable to changing the rate). Where different rates of interest are charged in different circumstances, the creditor must provide the above information in respect of each rate.]
Annual Percentage Rate of Charge (APR). This is the total cost expressed as an annual percentage of the total amount of credit. The APR is there to help you compare different offers.	[% if known. If the APR is not known a representative example (expressed as a %) mentioning all the necessary assumptions used for calculating the rate (as set out in Schedule 2 to the Consumer Credit (Disclosure of Information) Regulations 2010, the Total Charge for Credit Regulations and, where appropriate, the relevant components of the debtor's preferred credit). Where the creditor uses the assumption set out in regulation 6(g) of the Total Charge for Credit Regulations, the creditor shall indicate that other draw down mechanisms for this type of agreement may result in a higher APR.]
If applicable In order to obtain the credit or to obtain it on the terms and conditions marketed, you must take out: —an insurance policy securing the credit, or —another ancillary service contract. If we do not know the costs of these services they are not included in the APR.	[Nature and description of any insurance or other ancillary service contract required.]
Related costs	
If applicable You must have a separate account for recording both payment transactions and drawdowns.	[Details of any account or accounts that the creditor requires to be set up in order to obtain the credit together with the amount of any charge for this.]
If applicable Charge for using a specific payment method.	[Specify means of payment and the amount of charge.]

If applicable Any other costs deriving from the credit agreement.	[Description and amount of any other charges not otherwise referred to in this form.]
If applicable Conditions under which the above charges can be changed.	[Details of the conditions under which any of the charges mentioned above can be changed.]
If applicable You will be required to pay notarial fees.	[Description and amount of any fee.]
Costs in the case of late payments.	Either [A statement that there are no charges for late or missed payments.] Or [Applicable rate of interest in the case of late payments and arrangements for its adjustment and, where applicable any charges payable for default.]
Consequences of missing payments.	[A statement warning about the consequences of missing payments, including: —a reference to possible legal proceedings and repossession of the debtor's home where this is a possibility, and —the possibility of missing payments making it more difficult to obtain credit in the future.]

4 Other important legal aspects	
Right of withdrawal.	Either: [A statement that the debtor has the right to withdraw from the credit agreement before the end of 14 days beginning with the day after the day on which the agreement is made, or if information is provided after the agreement is made, the day on which the debtor receives a copy of the executed agreement under sections 61A or 63 of the Consumer Credit Act 1974, the day on which the debtor receives the information required in section 61A(3) of that Act or the day on which the creditor notifies the debtor of the credit limit, the first time it is provided, whichever is the latest.] Or [There is no right to withdraw from this agreement—if there is a right to cancel the agreement this should be stated.] [If the right to cancel is under the Financial Services (Distance Marketing) Regulations 2004 refer to section 5 of the form.]
Early repayment. If applicable	[A statement that the debtor has the right to repay the credit early at any time in full or partially.].

Compensation payable in the case of early repayment.	[Determination of the compensation (calculation method) in accordance with section 95A of the Consumer Credit Act 1974.]
Consultation with a Credit Reference Agency.	[A statement that if the creditor decides not to proceed with a prospective regulated consumer credit agreement on the basis of information from a credit reference agency the creditor must, when informing the debtor of the decision, inform the debtor that it has been reached on the basis of information from a credit reference agency and of the particulars of that agency.]
Right to a draft credit agreement.	[A statement that the debtor has the right, upon request, to obtain a copy of the draft credit agreement free of charge, unless the creditor is unwilling at the time of the request to proceed to the conclusion of the credit agreement.]
If applicable The period of time during which the creditor is bound by the pre-contractual information.	[This information is valid from [—] until [—].] or [Period of time during which the information on this form is valid.]

If applicable

5 Additional information in the case of distance marketing of financial services	
(a) concerning the creditor	
If applicable The creditor's representative in your Member State of residence.	[ie where different from section 1.] [Identity.]
Address.	[Geographical address to be used by the debtor.]
Telephone number(s). E-mail address.* Fax number.* Web address.*	
If applicable Registration number.	[Consumer credit licence number and any other relevant registration number of the creditor.]
If applicable The supervisory authority.	[The Office of Fair Trading or any other relevant supervisory authority or both.]
(b) concerning the credit agreement	
If applicable Right to cancel the credit agreement.	[Practical instructions for exercising the right to cancel indicating, amongst other things, the period for exercising the right, the address to which notification of exercise of the right to cancel should be sent and the consequences of non- exercise of that right.]

If applicable	
The law taken by the creditor as a basis for the establishment of relations with you before the conclusion of the credit agreement.	[English/other law]
If applicable	
The law applicable to the credit agreement and/or the competent court.	[A statement concerning the law which governs the contract and the courts to which disputes may be referred.]
If applicable	
Language to be used in connection with the credit agreement.	[Details of the language that the information and contractual terms will be supplied in and used, with your consent, for communication during the duration of the credit agreement.]
(c) concerning redress	
Access to out-of-court complaint and redress mechanism.	[Whether or not there is an out-of-court complaint and redress mechanism for the debtor and, if so, the methods of access to it.]

* This information is optional for the creditor. The row may be deleted if the information is not provided.

[3976]

NOTES
Commencement: 30 April 2010.
Para 2: words "The type of credit" in italics substituted by subsequent words in square brackets underlined, by the Consumer Credit (Amendment) Regulations 2010, SI 2010/1969, regs 31, 39, as from 26 August 2010.

SCHEDULE 2
PROVISIONS RELATING TO CALCULATION AND DISCLOSURE OF THE TOTAL
CHARGE FOR CREDIT AND APR

Regulation 1(2)

Assumptions about running-account credit

1.—(a)   In the case of an agreement for running-account credit, the assumption in paragraph (b) shall have effect for the purpose of calculating the total charge for credit and any APR in place of any assumptions in regulation 6(o) of the Consumer Credit (Total Charge for Credit) Regulations 2010 that might otherwise apply—

(b)   in a case where the credit limit applicable to the credit is not known at the time the pre-contract credit information is disclosed but it is known that it will be subject to a maximum limit of less than £1,200, the credit limit shall be assumed to be an amount equal to that maximum limit.

Permissible tolerances in disclosure of an APR

2.   For the purposes of these Regulations, it shall be sufficient compliance with the requirement to show an APR if there is included in the pre-contract credit information—

(a)   a rate which exceeds the APR by not more than one,

(b)   a rate which falls short of the APR by not more than 0.1, or

(c)   in a case to which paragraph 3 or 4 of this Schedule applies, a rate determined in accordance with those paragraphs or whichever of them applies to that case.

Tolerance where repayments are nearly equal

3.   In the case of an agreement under which all repayments but one are equal and that one repayment does not differ from any other repayment by more whole pence than there are repayments of credit, there may be included in the pre-contract credit information a rate found under regulation 5 of the Consumer Credit (Total Charge for Credit) Regulations 2010 as if that one repayment were equal to the other repayments to be made under the agreement.

Tolerance where interval between relevant date and first repayment is greater than interval between repayments

4.   In the case of an agreement under which—

(a)   three or more repayments are to be made at equal intervals, and

(b)   the interval between the relevant date and the first repayment is greater than the interval between the repayments,

there may be included in the pre-contract credit information a rate found under regulation 5 of the Consumer Credit (Total Charge for Credit) Regulations 2010 as if the interval between the relevant date and the first repayment were shortened so as to be equal to the interval between repayments.

[3977]

NOTES

Commencement: 30 April 2010.

SCHEDULE 3

EUROPEAN CONSUMER CREDIT INFORMATION

Regulation 11(1)

1 Contact details	
Creditor.	[Identity.]
Address.	[Geographical address of the creditor to be used by the debtor.]
Telephone number(s).*	
E-mail address.*	
Fax number.*	
Web address.*	
If applicable	
Credit intermediary.	[Identity.]
Address.	[Geographical address of the credit intermediary to be used by the debtor.]
Telephone number(s).*	
E-mail address.*	
Fax number.*	
Web address.*	
* This information is optional for the creditor. The row may be deleted if the information is not provided. Wherever "if applicable" is indicated, the creditor must give the information relevant to the credit product or, if the information is not relevant for the type of credit considered, delete the respective information or the entire row or indicate that the information is not applicable. Indications between square brackets provide explanations for the creditor and must be replaced with the corresponding information.	

2 Description of the main features of the credit product	
The type of credit [The type of credit].	
The total amount of credit. This means the amount of credit to be provided under the agreement or the credit limit.	[The amount is to be expressed as a sum of money. In the case of running account credit, the total amount may be expressed as a statement indicating the manner in which the credit limit will be determined where it is not practicable to express the limit as a sum of money.]
The duration of the credit agreement.	[The duration or minimum duration of the agreement or a statement that the agreement has no fixed or minimum duration.]

If applicable Repayment of the credit.	[A statement informing the debtor that the debtor may be required to repay the amount of credit in full on demand at any time.]

3 Costs of the credit	
The rates of interest which apply to the credit agreement.	[Details of the rates of interest charged, any conditions applicable to that rate, where available any reference rate on which that rate is based and any information on changes to the rate of interest (including the periods that the rate applies and any conditions or procedure applicable to changing the rate). Where different rates of interest are charged in different circumstances, the creditor must provide the above information in respect of each rate.]
If applicable Costs. If applicable The conditions under which those costs may be changed.	[The costs applicable from the time the credit agreement is concluded.]
Costs in the case of late payments.	Either [A statement that there are no charges for late or missed payments.] Or [Applicable rate of interest, in the case of late payments and arrangements for its adjustment and, where applicable, any charges payable for default.]

4 Other important legal aspects	
Termination of the credit agreement.	[The conditions and procedure for termination of the credit agreement.]
Consultation with a credit reference agency.	[A statement that if the creditor decides not to proceed with a prospective regulated consumer credit agreement on the basis of information from a credit reference agency the creditor must, when informing the debtor of that decision, inform the debtor that it has been reached on the basis of information from a credit reference agency and of the particulars of that agency.]
If applicable The period of time during which the creditor is bound by the pre-contractual information.	[This information is valid from [—] until [—] or [Period of time during which the information on this form is valid.]
If applicable	

PART 2
STATUTORY INSTRUMENTS

5 Additional information to be given in the case of distance marketing of financial services	
(a) concerning the creditor	
If applicable The creditor's representative in [the UK] [your Member State of residence.] Address. Telephone number.* E-mail address.* Fax number.* Web address.*	[ie where different from section 1.] [Identity.] [Geographical address to be used by the debtor.]
If applicable Registration number.	[Consumer credit licence number and any other relevant registration number of the creditor.]
If applicable The supervisory authority.	[The Office of Fair Trading or any other relevant supervisory authority or both.]
(b) concerning the credit agreement	
If applicable The law taken by the creditor as a basis for the establishment of relations with you before the conclusion of the credit contract.	[English/other law.]
If applicable The law applicable to the credit agreement and/or the competent court.	[A statement concerning the law which governs the contract and the courts to which disputes may be referred.]
If applicable Language to be used in connection your agreement.	[Details of the language that the information and contractual terms will be supplied in and used, with the debtor's consent, for communication during the duration of the credit agreement.]
(c) concerning redress	
Access to out-of-court complaint and redress mechanism.	[Whether or not there is an out-of-court complaint and redress mechanism for the debtor who is party to the distance contract and, if so, the methods of access to it.]
* This information is optional for the creditor. The row may be deleted if the information is not provided.	

[3978]

NOTES
Commencement: 30 April 2010.
Para 2: words "The type of credit" in italics substituted by subsequent words in square brackets underlined, by the Consumer Credit (Amendment) Regulations 2010, SI 2010/1969, regs 31, 40, as from 26 August 2010.

CONSUMER CREDIT (AGREEMENTS) REGULATIONS 2010

(SI 2010/1014)

NOTES
Made: 28 March 2010.
Authority: Consumer Credit Act 1974, ss 60, 61(1)(a), 105(9), 114(1), 182(2), 189(1).
Commencement: see reg 1(2) at **[3979]**.
These Regulations implement European Parliament and Council Directive 2008/48/EC, Art 10 at **[4538]**.

ARRANGEMENT OF REGULATIONS

1   Citation, commencement and interpretation

(1)   These Regulations may be cited as the Consumer Credit (Agreements) Regulations 2010.

(2)   [Except as provided for in paragraphs (2A) and (2B)] these Regulations shall come into force—

    (a)   on 1st February 2011, or

    (b)   in relation to a regulated consumer credit agreement, on the date and at the time Parts 1 to 3 of the Consumer Credit (EU Directive) Regulations 2010 apply to such an agreement, being a date before 1st February 2011.

[(2A)   Where the condition in paragraph (2B) is satisfied on a date on or after 26th August 2010 and before 1st February 2011 in relation to a prospective regulated consumer credit agreement to which section 58 of the Act applies, these Regulations apply to that agreement (and to any subsequent regulated consumer credit agreement entered into before 1st February 2011) from the date and time the condition is satisfied.

(2B)   The condition referred to in paragraph (2A) is that—

    (a)   before the creditor gives the debtor the unexecuted agreement for his signature the creditor gives the debtor a copy of the unexecuted agreement in compliance or purported compliance with regulations 3 and 7 of, and Schedules 1 and 2 to, these Regulations and

    (b)   the copy of the unexecuted agreement contains a heading and notice as set out in regulation 4(a)(ii) and (b)(ii) respectively of the Consumer Credit (Cancellation Notices and Copies of Documents) Regulations 1983.]

(3)   In these Regulations, unless the context otherwise requires—

"the Act" means the Consumer Credit Act 1974;

"advance payment" includes any deposit and in relation to a regulated consumer credit agreement includes also any part-exchange allowance in respect of any goods agreed in antecedent negotiations to be taken by the creditor in part-exchange but does not include a repayment of credit or any insurance premium or any amount entering into the total charge for credit;

"the APR" means the annual percentage rate of charge for credit determined in accordance with Schedule 4 and the Total Charge for Credit Regulations;

"cash price" in relation to any goods, services, land or other things means the price or charge at which the goods, services, land or other things may be purchased by, or supplied to, the debtor for cash;

"contract of shortfall insurance" means anything in writing which contains or purports to contain some promise or assurance (however worded or presented) that if a sum payable under a contract of insurance against loss of or damage to goods is less than the amount necessary to defray—

    (a)   any amount of credit provided to finance the purchase of those goods, and

    (b)   any other amount included in the total charge for that credit,
        to the extent that these remain unpaid at the date of the loss or damage, a sum up to but not exceeding that shortfall will be paid;

"credit intermediary" has the same meaning as in section 160A of the Act;

"distance contract" means any regulated agreement made under an organised distance sales or service provision scheme run by or on behalf of the creditor who, in any such case, for the purpose of the agreement makes exclusive use of one or more means of distance communication up to and including the time at which the agreement is made. For this purpose, "means of distance communication" means any means which, without the simultaneous physical presence of the creditor or a person acting on behalf of the creditor, and of the debtor, may be used for the making of a regulated agreement between the parties to that agreement;

"earlier agreement" means an earlier consumer credit agreement for the provision of credit;

"exempted agreement" means an agreement of the description specified in the Schedule to the Consumer Credit (Notices of Cancellation Rights) (Exemptions) Regulations 1983 in relation to which there are no charges forming part of the total charge for credit;

"the Information Regulations 2010" means the Consumer Credit (Disclosure of Information) Regulations 2010;

"lettering" includes figures and symbols;

"modified agreement" means an earlier agreement as varied or supplemented by a modifying agreement, which is treated as—
    (a)   revoking the earlier agreement, and
    (b)   containing provisions reproducing the combined effect of the two agreements;

"pawn agreement" means a regulated consumer credit agreement under which the creditor takes an article in pawn;

"pre-contract credit information" means the information required to be disclosed by regulation 3(4) of the Information Regulations 2010;

"total amount of credit" means the credit limit or the total sums made available under a consumer credit agreement;

"total amount payable" means the sum of the total charge for credit and the total amount of credit payable under the consumer credit agreement as well as any advance payment;

"total charge for credit" means the total charge for credit determined in accordance with Schedule 4 and the Total Charge for Credit Regulations;

"the Total Charge for Credit Regulations" means the Consumer Credit (Total Charge for Credit) Regulations 2010.

(4)   References in these Regulations to a contract of insurance shall be read with—
    (a)   section 22 of the Financial Services and Markets Act 2000,
    (b)   any relevant order under that section, and
    (c)   Schedule 2 to that Act.

(5)   In these Regulations—
    (a)   a reference to a repayment is a reference to—
        (i)   a repayment of the whole or any part of the credit,
        (ii)   a payment of the whole or any part of the total charge for credit, or
        (iii)   a combination of such repayments and payments.
    (b)   a reference to rate of interest is a reference to the interest rate expressed as a fixed or variable percentage applied on an annual basis to the amount of credit drawn down.

(6)   In relation to a regulated consumer credit agreement secured on land and to which the Information Regulations 2010 do not apply, the definition of Total Charge for Credit Regulations) shall apply as if for the words "Consumer Credit (Total Charge for Credit) Regulations 2010" there were substituted "Consumer Credit (Total Charge for Credit) Regulations 1980".

[3979]

NOTES

    Commencement: 1 February 2011, subject to reg 1(2)(b) above.
    Para (2): words in square brackets inserted by the Consumer Credit (Amendment) Regulations 2010, SI 2010/1969, regs 41, 42(a), as from 26 August 2010.
    Paras (2A), (2B): inserted by SI 2010/1969, regs 41, 42(b), as from 26 August 2010.

2   Agreements to which these regulations apply

(1)   These Regulations apply in respect of a regulated consumer credit agreement except as provided for in *paragraphs (2) to (5)* [paragraphs (1A) to (5)].

[(1A)   These Regulations apply to an agreement to which section 58 of the Act applies where—
    (a)   before the creditor gives the debtor the unexecuted agreement for his signature the creditor gives the debtor a copy of the unexecuted agreement in compliance or purported compliance with regulations 3 and 7 of, and Schedules 1 and 2 to, these Regulations, and
    (b)   the copy of the unexecuted agreement contains a heading and notice as set out in

regulation 4(a)(ii) and (b)(ii) respectively of the Consumer Credit (Cancellation Notices and Copies of Documents) Regulations 1983.]

(2)   These Regulations do not apply to an agreement mentioned in paragraph (3) unless pre-contract credit information has been disclosed in compliance (or in purported compliance) with the Information Regulations 2010.

(3)   The agreements referred to in paragraph (2) are—
- (a)   an agreement secured on land [other than an agreement to which section 58 applies];
- (b)   an agreement under which the creditor provides the debtor with credit which exceeds £60,260;
- (c)   an agreement entered into by the debtor wholly or predominantly for the purposes of a business carried on, or intended to be carried on, by him.

(4)   Paragraph (2) and regulations 3 to 4 and 6 to 7 do not apply to an authorised non-business overdraft agreement or an authorised business overdraft agreement.

(5)   Regulation 5 does not apply to a regulated consumer credit agreement which is also a distance contract unless the agreement is entered into by the debtor wholly or predominantly for the purposes of a business carried on, or intended to be carried on, by him.

(6)   Subsections (2) to (5) of section 16B of the Act (declaration by the debtor as to the purposes of the agreement) apply for the purposes of paragraphs (3)(c) and (5).

[3980]

NOTES
   Commencement: 1 February 2011, subject to reg 1(2)(b) at **[3979]**.
   Para (1): words in italics substituted by subsequent words in square brackets by the Consumer Credit (Amendment) Regulations 2010, SI 2010/1969, regs 41, 43(a), as from 26 August 2010.
   Para (1A): inserted by SI 2010/1969, regs 41, 43(b), as from 26 August 2010.
   Para (3): words in square brackets inserted by SI 2010/1969, regs 41, 43(c), as from 26 August 2010.

---

3   Form and content of regulated consumer credit agreements

(1)   Documents embodying a regulated consumer credit agreement shall contain the information set out in column 2 of Schedule 1 to these Regulations in so far as that information relates to the type of agreement referred to in column 1.

(2)   The information specified in Schedule 1 shall be presented in a clear and concise manner.

(3)   For the purposes of this regulation, the requirement for the information to be "clear" includes a requirement that the wording, apart from any signature, is to be easily legible and of a colour which is readily distinguishable from the background medium upon which the information is displayed.

(4)   Documents embodying a regulated consumer credit agreement, other than an exempted agreement, shall contain statements of the protection and remedies available to debtors under the Act, in the Form numbered in column 1 of Schedule 2 to these Regulations and set out in column 3, in so far as those statements relate to the type of agreement referred to in column 2.

(5)   Documents embodying a regulated consumer credit agreement shall contain details of any security provided in relation to the regulated agreement by the debtor.

(6)   Paragraph (7) applies to documents embodying a debtor-creditor-supplier agreement falling within section 12(a) of the Act or a debtor-creditor agreement (in this paragraph and paragraph (7) referred to as "the principal agreement") and also embodying, or containing the option of, a debtor-creditor-supplier agreement falling within section 12(b) of the Act (in this paragraph referred to as "the subsidiary agreement") where the subsidiary agreement is to finance a premium under one or more of—
- (a)   a contract of insurance to provide a sum payable in the event of the death of a debtor or a debtor suffering one or more of the following—
   - (i)   accident;
   - (ii)   sickness;
   - (iii)   unemployment,
   at any time before the credit under the principal agreement and the subsidiary agreement has been repaid, where
   - (i)   the sum payable does not exceed the amount sufficient to defray the sums payable to the creditor in respect of that credit and of the total charge for credit, and
   - (ii)   the policy monies payable under the contract of insurance are to be used for a repayment under the principal agreement and the subsidiary agreement;
- (b)   a contract of shortfall insurance;
- (c)   a contract of insurance in so far as it relates to the guarantee of goods.

(7)   Documents to which this regulation applies may contain instead of the headings specified in paragraph 1 of Schedule 1 to these Regulations and any applicable statements of protection and remedies available to debtors under the Act that would otherwise apply—

(a) a heading in so far as it relates to the principal agreement, and

(b) if applicable, statements of the protection and remedies available to debtors under the Act in so far as they relate to the principal agreement.

[3981]

NOTES

Commencement: 1 February 2011, subject to reg 1(2)(b) at **[3979]**.

4 Signing of agreement

(1) The information specified in paragraphs 5, 6, 7, 11 and 14 of Schedule 1 to these Regulations in relation to the type of regulated consumer credit agreement referred to in column 1 shall be "the prescribed terms" for the purposes of section 61(1)(a) of the Act (the terms which must be contained in a document if a regulated consumer credit agreement is not to be improperly executed).

(2) The document containing the prescribed terms of the regulated consumer credit agreement referred to in paragraph (1) shall contain a space indicated for the purpose of the debtor's signature.

(3) The signature of the document shall be made in the following manner—

(a) by the debtor, or by or on behalf of the debtor in the case of a partnership or an unincorporated body of persons, in the space in the document indicated for the purpose and, subject to sub-paragraph (c), the date of the signature shall be inserted in the space in the document indicated for the purpose,

(b) by the creditor, or by a person on behalf of the creditor, and subject to sub-paragraph (c), the date of the signature shall be inserted in the document,

(c) except where the agreement is cancellable, the date on which the unexecuted agreement becomes an executed agreement may be inserted in the document and in such a case any other date specified in paragraphs (a) and (b) need not be inserted, and

(d) nothing in this regulation shall prohibit the inclusion in the said document, near to any such signature, of the signature by any witness.

(4) *(Applies to Scotland only.)*

(5) Where an agreement is intended to be concluded by the use of electronic communication nothing in this regulation shall prohibit the inclusion in the document of information about the process or means of providing, communicating or verifying the signature to be made by the debtor.

[3982]

NOTES

Commencement: 1 February 2011, subject to reg 1(2)(b) at **[3979]**.

5 Modifying agreements

(1) These Regulations shall apply to a modifying agreement which varies or supplements an earlier agreement and which is, or is treated under section 82(3) of the Act as, a regulated agreement.

(2) Where an item of information required by regulation 3(1) or 8(1) is unchanged by the modifying agreement, the requirements of regulation 3(1) or 8(1) may be satisfied in relation to such item of information by a statement in the modifying agreement clearly indicating that the information in the earlier agreement remains unchanged.

(3) [Except as provided for in paragraph (3A)] a statement referred to in paragraph (2) shall be contained in the document which is signed by the debtor.

[(3A) Where a modifying agreement is an authorised business overdraft agreement or an authorised non-business overdraft agreement the document referred to in paragraph (3) does not have to be signed by the debtor.]

(4) The information referred to in regulation 4(1) as prescribed terms for the purposes of section 61(1)(a) of the Act shall not be prescribed for the purposes of a modifying agreement if the information contained in the earlier agreement has not been varied or supplemented by the modifying agreement.

(5) For the purposes of Schedule 1 to these Regulations, in calculating—

(a) the amount of repayments of credit or of any capital outstanding under an earlier agreement,

(b) the total charge for credit (or any items included in it) in relation to the credit to be provided under the modified agreement, or

(c) the APR in relation to the modified agreement,

the relevant date shall be determined by reference to the date of the modifying agreement.

[3983]

PART 2
STATUTORY INSTRUMENTS

NOTES
  Commencement: 1 February 2011, subject to reg 1(2)(b) at **[3979]**.
  Para (3): words in square brackets inserted by the Consumer Credit (Amendment) Regulations 2010, SI 2010/1969, regs 41, 44(a), as from 26 August 2010.
  Para (3A): inserted by SI 2010/1969, regs 41, 44(b), as from 26 August 2010.

6   Pawn agreements

Where a pawn-receipt is given under section 114(1) of the Act by a person who takes any article in pawn under a regulated consumer credit agreement (or a modifying agreement varying or supplementing an earlier credit agreement which is, or is treated under section 82(3) of the Act as, a regulated consumer credit agreement) and where the pawn-receipt is not separate from any document embodying such an agreement, it shall contain—

  (a)   the information set out in paragraphs 1, 2 and 22 of Schedule 1 to these Regulations, and
  (b)   a notice in the form contained in Schedule 3 to these Regulations.

                                                                        [3984]

NOTES
  Commencement: 1 February 2011, subject to reg 1(2)(b) at **[3979]**.

7   Statutory Forms

  (1)   The wording of any Form specified in Schedules 2 and 3 to these Regulations shall be reproduced in documents embodying regulated consumer credit agreements where applicable without any alteration, except that—

  (a)   the words "the creditor" may be replaced by the name of the creditor, by the expression by which the creditor is referred to in the agreement or by an appropriate pronoun, and any consequential changes to pronouns and verbs or other consequential grammatical changes may be made,
  (b)   the word "DEBTOR" may be replaced by "BORROWER" or "CUSTOMER" and the word "Debtor(s)" may be replaced by "Borrower(s)" or "Customer(s)", and
  (c)   every Form shall be completed in accordance with any note.

  (2)   Any such note shall not be treated as part of any Form specified in the said Schedules and may be reproduced in addition to any such Form.

  (3)   Where any such note requires any words to be omitted, those words shall be omitted or deleted.

  (4)   Where words are shown in capital letters in any Form specified in Schedule 2 or 3 to these Regulations, and are reproduced in documents embodying regulated consumer credit agreements, they shall be afforded more prominence (whether by capital letters, underlining, larger or bold print or otherwise) than any other lettering in that Form except lettering inserted in accordance with paragraph 1(c) and no less prominence than that given to any other information in the document apart from the heading to the document, trade names, names of parties to the agreement or lettering in the document inserted in handwriting.

                                                                        [3985]

NOTES
  Commencement: 1 February 2011, subject to reg 1(2)(b) at **[3979]**.

8   Form and content of an authorised overdraft agreement

  (1)   Subject to paragraph (3), in the case of an authorised non-business overdraft agreement or an authorised business overdraft agreement, the following information shall be specified in writing in a clear and concise manner—

  (a)   the type of credit,
  (b)   the identities and geographical addresses of the creditor, debtor and, where relevant, of any credit intermediary involved,
  (c)   the duration of the agreement,
  (d)   the credit limit and the conditions governing its drawdown,
  (e)   the rate of interest charged, any conditions applicable to that rate, any reference rate on which that rate is based and any information on changes to the rate of interest (including the periods that the rate applies, and any conditions or procedure applicable to changing the rate),
  (f)   where different rates of interest are charged in different circumstances the creditor must provide the information in paragraph (e) in respect of each rate,
  (g)   the total charge for credit, calculated at the time the agreement is made, mentioning all the assumptions used in order to calculate it,
  (h)   an indication that the debtor may be requested to repay the amount of credit in full on demand at any time, and

    (i)   the charges payable by the debtor under the agreement (and the conditions under which those charges may be varied).

(2)   For the purposes of paragraph (1), the requirement for the information to be "clear" includes a requirement that the wording is easily legible and of a colour which is readily distinguishable from the background medium upon which the information is displayed.

(3)   Paragraph (1)(g) shall not apply—
    (a)   in the case of an authorised business overdraft agreement, or
    (b)   in the case of an authorised non-business overdraft agreement that is also an agreement secured on land.

[3986]

NOTES

Commencement: 1 February 2011, subject to reg 1(2)(b) at **[3979]**.

SCHEDULE 1
INFORMATION TO BE INCLUDED IN REGULATED CONSUMER CREDIT AGREEMENTS
Regulation 3

Paragraph	Type of agreement (*1*)	Information (2)
	Nature of the agreement	
1	All types.	(1) Subject to paragraph (2) below, a heading in one of the following forms of words—
		a) "Hire Purchase Agreement regulated by the Consumer Credit Act 1974"
		b) "Conditional Sale Agreement regulated by the Consumer Credit Act 1974
		c) "Fixed Sum Loan Agreement regulated by the Consumer Credit Act 1974"
		d) "Credit Card Agreement regulated by the Consumer Credit Act 1974"
		e) "Agreement modifying a Credit Agreement regulated by the Consumer Credit Act 1974."
		as the case may require.
		(2) If none of the headings in (1)(a) to (e) above are applicable—
		a) a heading in the following form of words—"Credit Agreement regulated by the Consumer Credit Act 1974" and
		b) a description of the type of credit.
		(3) Where the document and a pawn-receipt are combined, the words "and Pawn-Receipt" shall be inserted in the heading after the word "Agreement".
		(4) Where the document embodies an agreement of which at least one part is a consumer credit agreement not regulated by the Act, the word "partly" shall be inserted before "regulated" unless the regulated and unregulated parts of the agreement are clearly separate.
		(5) Where the credit is secured on land the words "and secured on" followed by the address of the land shall be inserted at the end of the heading.

Paragraph	Type of agreement (1)	Information (2)
2	**Parties to the agreement** All types.	The identity and geographical address of the creditor, debtor and, where relevant, the identity and geographical address of any credit intermediary involved.
3	**Duration of the agreement** Agreement of fixed duration.	The duration of the agreement.
4	Open end agreements.	A statement indicating that the agreement has no fixed duration. The statement shall include details of the minimum duration of the agreement where such a period is provided for under the agreement.
5	**Amount of credit** Agreements falling within paragraph 9 except agreements under which both— a) the total amount payable by the debtor is not greater than the total cash price referred to in paragraph 10; and b) there is no advance payment.	The amount of the credit to be provided under the agreement, namely the difference between the total cash price to be referred to in paragraph 10 and the total of any advance payments.
6	Agreements for fixed-sum credit not falling within paragraph 9.	The amount of the credit to be provided under the agreement.
7	**Credit limit** Agreements for running-account credit.	The credit limit expressed as— a) a sum of money, b) a statement that the credit limit will be determined by the creditor from time to time under the agreement and that notice of it will be given by the creditor to the debtor, c) a sum of money together with a statement that the creditor may vary the credit limit to such sum as the creditor may from time to time determine under the agreement and that notice of it will be given by the creditor to the debtor, or d) in a case not falling within head (a), (b) or (c), either a statement indicating the manner in which the credit limit will be determined and that notice of it will be given by the creditor to the debtor, or a statement indicating that there is no credit limit.
8	How and when credit will be provided. All types.	A statement indicating how and when the credit to be advanced under the agreement is to be drawn down.

Paragraph	Type of agreement (1)	Information (2)
9	**Description of goods, services, land etc** Restricted use debtor-creditor-supplier agreements for fixed-sum credit to finance a transaction comprising the acquisition of goods, services, land or other things specified in the agreement or identified and agreed on at the time the agreement is made	A list or other description of the goods, services or other things and, in the case of land, a general description of the land, the acquisition of which is to be financed by credit under the agreement.
10	**Cash price** Agreements falling within paragraph 9.	The cash price in relation to each item referred to in paragraph 9 and, where applicable, the total cash price.
11	**Rate of interest** All types.	The rate(s) of interest and, where available, any reference rate on which that rate is based. The following additional information shall be given in relation to each rate that applies: (1) the conditions governing the application of the rate; (2) the period during which the rate will apply; (3) the conditions and procedure for changing the rate.
12	**Total amount payable** All types.	(1) The total amount payable by the debtor being the sum of the total amount of credit and the total charge for credit payable under the agreement as well as any advance payment. (2) In the case of running-account credit, where the credit limit is not known at the time the credit agreement is made, the total amount of credit referred to in paragraph (1) shall be assumed to be £1,200 or in a case where credit is to be provided subject to a maximum credit limit of less than £1,200, an amount equal to that maximum limit.
13	**APR** All Types.	The APR in relation to the agreement calculated at the time the credit agreement is made. All the assumptions used in order to calculate that rate shall be specified. Alternatively, where applicable, a statement indicating that the total amount payable under the agreement is not greater than the total cash price of the goods, services, land or other things the acquisition of which is to be financed by credit under the agreement.

Paragraph	Type of agreement (1)	Information (2)
14	*Timing of repayments [Repayments]* All types.	The timing of repayments to be made under the agreement expressed by reference to one or more of the following— a) the dates on which each repayment is to be made; b) the frequency and number of the repayments and the date of the first repayment or a statement indicating the manner in which that date will be determined; c) a statement indicating the number of repayments and the manner in which the dates of the repayments will be determined.
		[The number (if applicable) and frequency of repayments to be made by the debtor]
14A	*Allocation of payments* All types where different rates of interest are or will be at any time during the term of the agreement payable in respect of— a) credit provided under the agreement for different purposes, or b) credit provided under each of the different parts of the agreement, whether or not the agreement is a multiple agreement.	A statement of the order or proportions in which any amount paid by the debtor which is not sufficient to discharge the total debt then due under the agreement will be applied or appropriated by the creditor towards the discharge of the sums due— a) in respect of the amounts of credit provided for different purposes, or b) different parts of the agreement as the case may be.
15	*Amounts of repayments* All types.	The amount of each repayment to be made under the agreement expressed as— a) a sum of money; b) a specified proportion of a specified amount (including the amount outstanding from time to time); c) a combination of heads (a) and (b); or d) in a case where the amount of any repayment cannot be expressed in accordance with head (a), (b) or (c), a statement indicating the manner in which the amount will be determined.
16	*Statement of account* Agreements of fixed duration where the debtor's repayments under the agreement result in an immediate reduction in the total amount of credit owed, other than— a) agreements referred to in regulation 2(2), or	The right to receive, on request, and free of charge, at any time throughout the duration of the agreement pursuant to section 77B of the Act, a statement in the form of a table showing— a) the details of each instalment owing under the agreement;

Paragraph	Type of agreement *(1)*	Information *(2)*
	b) agreements where the total amount payable by the debtor does not exceed the total amount of credit.	b) the date on which each instalment is due, the amount and any conditions relating to the payment of the instalment; c) a breakdown of each instalment showing how much comprises— i) capital repayment, ii) interest payment, and iii) if applicable, any other charges. Where the interest rate is variable or the other charges may be varied the statement shall indicate clearly and concisely that the information contained in the statement is valid only until the rates of interest or charges are varied.
17	*Statement where no credit reduction* Agreements under which payments of interest and charges made by the debtor are not accompanied by a reduction in the total amount of credit owed under the agreement.	A statement indicating the periods and conditions for the payment of the interest and of any associated recurrent or non-recurrent charges.
17A	Agreements under which repayments made by the debtor do not give rise to an immediate corresponding reduction in the total amount of credit owed but are used to constitute capital during periods and under conditions laid down in the credit agreement or in an ancillary agreement.	A statement indicating that— a) the debtor's regular repayments will not repay the capital advanced, and b) at the termination of the agreement the debtor must repay the capital advanced unless the agreement provides a guarantee that any capital constituted by the debtor's repayments will repay the total amount of credit.
18	*Charges* All types where applicable.	(1) Where applicable, the charges for maintaining an account recording both payment transactions and draw downs, unless the opening of the account is optional. (2) Any charge payable as a result of using a method of payment in respect of repayment transactions or drawdown.

Paragraph	Type of agreement (1)	Information (2)
		(3) Any other charges deriving from the credit agreements (other than those referred to in paragraph 19(3)) and the conditions under which those charges may be changed.
19	*Interest for late payment* All types where applicable.	(1) The rate of interest which applies in the case of late payments applicable at the time of the making of the credit agreement, (2) the arrangements for its adjustment and, (3) where applicable, any charges payable for late payment.
20	*Missing payment warning* All types under which periodic repayments are to be made except pawn agreements.	A statement warning about the consequences of missing payments, including, for example, a reference to possible legal proceedings and the possibility that the debtor's home may be repossessed and the possibility of missing payments making it more difficult to obtain credit.
21	*Notarial fees* All types.	Where applicable, a statement that notarial fees will be payable.
22	*Security provided by the debtor* Pawn agreements, to which section 114 of the Act applies and where no separate pawn receipt is given.	A statement indicating that an article has been taken in pawn under the agreement and a description of the article sufficient to identify it.
23	All types except those referred to in paragraph 22 in relation to which any security or guarantee is to be provided by the debtor or on his behalf.	A description of the security or guarantee as applicable.
24	*Compulsory insurance* All types.	A description of any contract of insurance which the debtor is required to conclude under the terms of the agreement.
25	*Right of withdrawal* All types except where the agreement is—	A statement providing details of the debtor's right under section 66A of the Act to withdraw from the regulated consumer credit agreement including—
	a) an agreement secured on land,	(1) the right to withdraw within 14 days without the debtor having to give any reason,
	b) restricted-use credit agreements to finance the purchase of land,	(2) when that period of withdrawal begins and ends;
	c) an agreement for a bridging loan in connection with the purchase of land,	(3) the requirement of the debtor to notify the creditor of his intention to withdraw, in writing or orally,
	d) for credit which exceeds £60,260, or	(4) contact details of the person/creditor whom he must notify of his intention to withdraw from the agreement;

Paragraph	Type of agreement (1)	Information (2)
	e) a cancellable agreement.	(5) the requirement to repay the credit without delay and no later than 30 calendar days after giving notice of withdrawal,
		(6) the requirement to pay, without delay and no later than 30 calendar days after giving notice of withdrawal, the interest accrued from the date the credit was provided to the date of repaying it,
		(7) the amount of interest payable per day expressed as a sum of money, and
		(8) details of how and to whom he must pay the credit and interest.
		Paragraph (7) does not apply in respect of agreements for running-account credit where it is not practicable for the creditor to state the amount of interest payable per day. In such cases, the agreement shall state that where credit is drawn down during the withdrawal period, the creditor shall inform the debtor, on request, without delay, of the amount of interest payable per day.
25A	Agreements referred to in paragraph 25 (a) to (e).	(1) A statement that there is no right of withdrawal under section 66A of the Act.
		(2) An indication of any other right to cancel the credit agreement whether under the Act or otherwise, with details as appropriate.
	Linked credit agreements [Linked credit agreements to which section 75A of the Act applies]	
26	Linked credit agreements except those—	A statement explaining—
	a) falling within paragraph 27;	(1) that the credit agreement finances the supply of specific goods or services,
	b) under which the credit provided exceeds £60,260.	(2) that if the goods or services are not supplied, or are supplied only in part, or do not conform with the contract, the debtor has the right to seek redress from the creditor, if he is unable to obtain redress from the supplier of the goods or services.
27	Agreements falling within section 12(b) or (c) of the Act to which section 75 of the Act applies.	A statement explaining that the debtor may have a right to sue the supplier, the creditor or both if he has received unsatisfactory goods or services paid for under the agreement costing more than £100 and not more than £30,000.
	Early repayment	
28	All types.	A statement providing details of the debtor's right of early repayment under section 94 of the Act including—
		(1) the fact that the debtor has a right to repay early in full or (except where the agreement is secured on land) in part,
		(2) the procedure for early repayment, and

Paragraph	Type of agreement (1)	Information (2)
		(3) where applicable, details of the creditor's right to compensation under section 95A of the Act and the manner in which that compensation shall be determined.
29	*Termination by debtor* Open-end agreements.	A statement explaining how and when the debtor can terminate the agreement.
30.	Hire-purchase and conditional sale agreements.	A statement explaining— (1) how and when the debtor can terminate the agreement under section 99 of the Act, and (2) the debtor's maximum liability under section 100 of the Act.
31	*Ombudsman Scheme* All types.	A statement explaining that the debtor who is not a business debtor has the right to complain to the Financial Ombudsman Service. A debtor who is a business debtor may have a right to complain to the Financial Ombudsman Service.
32	*Contractual terms and conditions* All types.	Where applicable, the other contractual terms and conditions.
33	*Supervisory authority* All types.	A statement specifying that the Office of Fair Trading, [geographical address] is the supervisory authority under the Act.

[3987]

NOTES

Commencement: 1 February 2011, subject to reg 1(2)(b) at **[3979]**.

Para 14: words in italics in columns 2, 3 substituted by subsequent words in square brackets by the Consumer Credit (Amendment) Regulations 2010, SI 2010/1969, regs 41, 45(a), as from 26 August 2010.

Para 26: words in italics in column 2 substituted by subsequent words in square brackets by SI 2010/1969, regs 41, 45(b), as from 26 August 2010.

SCHEDULE 2
FORMS OF STATEMENT OF PROTECTION AND REMEDIES AVAILABLE UNDER THE CONSUMER CREDIT ACT 1974 TO DEBTORS UNDER REGULATED CONSUMER CREDIT AGREEMENTS

Regulations 3(4) and 7

FORM (1)	TYPE OF AGREEMENT (2)	FORM OF STATEMENT (3)
1	Agreement to which section 58(1) of the Act applies.	YOUR RIGHTS Under the Consumer Credit Act 1974, you should have been given a copy of this agreement at least seven days ago so you could consider whether you wanted to go ahead. If the creditor did not give you a copy of this agreement he can only enforce it with a court order.

FORM (1)	TYPE OF AGREEMENT (2)	FORM OF STATEMENT (3)
2	All agreements which are secured on land.	YOUR HOME MAY BE REPOSSESSED. Your home may be repossessed if you do not keep up repayments on a mortgage or other debt secured on it.
3	Cancellable agreements to which section 68(b) of the Act applies.	YOUR RIGHT TO CANCEL You can cancel this agreement within FOURTEEN days (starting the day after you signed it) by giving WRITTEN notice to*. If you intend to cancel you should not use any goods you have under the agreement and you should keep them safe. You can wait for them to be collected and you do not need to hand them over until you receive a written request for them. *Creditor or agent to insert the name and address of the person to whom the notice may be given or an indication of the person to whom a notice may be given with clear reference to the place in the document embodying the agreement where his name and address appear.
4	Cancellable agreements not included in paragraphs 3 or 5.	YOUR RIGHT TO CANCEL Once you have signed this agreement you will have a short time in which you can cancel [it]* [that part of this agreement which is regulated by the Consumer Credit Act 1974]*. The creditor will send you exact details of how and when you can do this. *Creditor to omit passage in square brackets which does not apply to the agreement.
5	Modifying agreement treated under section 82(5) of the Act as cancellable arrangements.	YOUR RIGHT TO CANCEL This agreement modifies an earlier agreement. Once you have signed this agreement your right to cancel [that part of]* the earlier agreement [which was regulated by the Consumer Credit Act 1974]* will be widened to cover the [regulated]* agreement as modified. The cancellation period itself will be unchanged. Details of how to cancel are given in your copy of this agreement. *Creditor to omit passages in square brackets except in the case of an agreement of which at least one part is credit agreement not regulated by the Act.

FORM (1)	TYPE OF AGREEMENT (2)	FORM OF STATEMENT (3)
6	Pawn agreements to which section 114 of the Act applies.	**IMPORTANT—READ THIS CAREFULLY TO FIND OUT ABOUT YOUR RIGHTS** The Consumer Credit Act 1974 ("the Act") lays down certain requirements for your protection which should have been complied with when this agreement was made. If they were not, the creditor cannot enforce this agreement without getting a court order. The Act also gives you a number of rights. In particular, you should read the NOTICE TO DEBTOR [in this agreement]* [in your pawn-receipt].** If you would like to know more about your rights under the Act, contact Consumer Direct, your local Trading Standards Department or your nearest Citizens' Advice Bureau. *Phrase in square brackets to be included by creditor in agreements where any document embodying the agreement is not separate from the pawn-receipt. Creditor to omit "in your pawn-receipt". **Phrase in square brackets to be included by creditor in agreements where a separate pawn-receipt is given to the debtor. Creditor to omit "in this agreement".
7	Conditional sale agreements secured on land.	**TERMINATION: YOUR RIGHTS** Until the title to the land has passed to you, you have a right to end this agreement. To do so write to the person you make your payments to. They will then be entitled to the return of the land and to [half the total amount payable under this agreement, that is]* £x. ** If, at the time you end this agreement, you have already paid at least this amount plus any overdue instalments and you have taken reasonable care of the land, you will not have to pay any more. *Creditor to insert the passage in square brackets where the amount calculated in accordance with the provisions of section 100 of the Act applies. If the agreement provides for a sum below the minimum prescribed in the Act, the passage in square brackets is to be omitted **Creditor to insert the amount calculated in accordance with the provisions of section 100 of the Act or such lesser sum as the agreement may provide.

FORM (1)	TYPE OF AGREEMENT (2)	FORM OF STATEMENT (3)
8	Agreements modifying conditional sale agreements relating to land.	**TERMINATION: YOUR RIGHTS** Until the title to the land has passed to you, you have a right to end this agreement. To do so write to the person you make your payments to. They will then be entitled to the return of the land and to [half the total amount payable under this agreement, that is]* [£[—**] If at the time you end this agreement, you have already paid at least this amount plus any overdue instalments and you have taken reasonable care of the land, you will not have to pay any more. *Creditor to insert the passage in square brackets where the amount calculated in accordance with the provisions of section 100 of the Act applies. If the agreement provides for a sum below the minimum prescribed in the Act, the passage in square brackets is to be omitted. ** Creditor to insert the amount calculated in accordance with the provisions of section 100 of the Act or such lesser sum as the agreement may provide.
9	Hire purchase and conditional sale agreements relating to goods, not included in paragraph 10.	**TERMINATION: YOUR RIGHTS** You have a right to end this agreement. To do so, you should write to the person you make your payments to. They will then be entitled to the return of the goods and to [the cost of installing the goods plus half the rest of the total amount payable under this agreement, that is][half the total amount payable under this agreement, that is]*£x**. If you have already paid at least this amount plus any overdue instalments and have taken reasonable care of the goods, you will not have to pay any more. *Creditor to insert the appropriate passage in square brackets where the amount calculated in accordance with the provisions of section 100 of the Act apply. If the agreement provides for a sum below the minimum prescribed in the Act, both passages in square brackets are to be omitted. **Creditor to insert the amount calculated in accordance with the provisions of section 100 of the Act or such lesser sum as the agreement may provide.

FORM (1)	TYPE OF AGREEMENT (2)	FORM OF STATEMENT (3)
10	Agreements modifying hire-purchase and conditional sale agreements relating to goods.	**TERMINATION: YOUR RIGHTS** You have the right to end this agreement. To do so, write to the person you make your payments to. They will then be entitled to the return of the goods and to [the cost of installing the goods plus half the total amount yet to be paid under the earlier agreement as modified by this agreement, that is][half the total amount payable under the earlier agreement as modified by this agreement, that is]*£x**. If you have already paid at least this amount, plus any overdue instalments and have taken reasonable care of the goods, you will not have to pay any more. *Creditor to insert the appropriate passage in square brackets where the amount calculated in accordance with the provisions of section 100 of the Act applies. If the modified agreement provides for a sum below the minimum prescribed in the Act, both passages in square brackets are to be omitted. **Creditor to insert the amount calculated in accordance with the provisions of section 100 of the Act or such lesser sum as the agreement may provide.
11	Hire-purchase and conditional sale agreements relating to goods, not included in paragraph 12.	**REPOSSESSION: YOUR RIGHTS** If you do not keep your side of the agreement but you have paid at least [the cost of installing the goods plus one third of the rest of the total amount payable under this agreement, that is][one third of the total amount payable under this agreement, that is] *£x **the creditor may not take back the goods against your wishes unless he gets a court order. (In Scotland he may need to get a court order at any time). If he does take the goods without your consent or a court order, you have the right to get back any money that you have paid under this agreement. *Creditor to insert the appropriate passage in square brackets. **Creditor to insert the amount calculated in accordance with the provision of section 90 of the Act.

FORM (1)	TYPE OF AGREEMENT (2)	FORM OF STATEMENT (3)
12	Agreements modifying hire-purchase and conditional sale agreements relating to goods.	REPOSSESSION: YOUR RIGHTS If you do not keep your side of this agreement [but you have paid at least £x*]** the creditor may not take back the goods against your wishes unless he gets a court order. (In Scotland he may need to get a court order at any time). If he does take the goods back without your consent or a court order, you have the right to get back all the money you have paid under this agreement. *Creditor to insert the amount calculated in accordance with the provisions of section 90 of the Act. ** Creditor to omit both passages in square brackets in the case of a modifying agreement where the goods are protected at the time the modifying agreement is made.

[3988]

NOTES

  Commencement: 1 February 2011, subject to reg 1(2)(b) at **[3979]**.

SCHEDULE 3
NOTICE TO BE CONTAINED IN DOCUMENTS EMBODYING A COMBINED CONSUMER CREDIT AGREEMENT AND PAWN-RECEIPT
Regulation 6

NOTICE TO DEBTOR

IMPORTANT—YOU SHOULD READ THIS CAREFULLY

Right to Redeem Articles

If you hand in this agreement (which is also your pawn receipt) and pay the amount you owe, you may redeem the article(s) in pawn at any time within 6 months of the date of this agreement or any longer time agreed with the creditor ("the redemption period").

IF YOU DO NOT REDEEM THE ARTICLE(S) ON OR BEFORE[1] **YOU MAY LOSE YOUR RIGHT TO REDEEM IT (THEM).**

Loss of Receipt

If you lose your receipt you may provide either a statutory declaration or, if the credit (or credit limit) is not more than £x [2] and the creditor agrees, a signed statement instead. The creditor may provide the form to be used and may charge for doing so.

Unredeemed Articles

An article not redeemed within the redemption period becomes the creditor's property if the credit (or credit limit) is not more than £x [3] and the redemption period is 6 months. In any other case it may be sold by the creditor, but it continues to be redeemable until it is sold. Interest is payable until the actual date of redemption. Where the credit (or credit limit) is more than £x [4] the creditor must give you 14 days notice of his intention to sell. When an article has been sold you will receive information about the sale. If the proceeds (less expenses) are more that the amount that would have been payable to redeem the article on the date of the sale you will be entitled to receive the extra amount. If the proceeds are less than the amount you will owe the creditor the shortfall.

Your goods will not be insured by the creditor while they are in pawn. [5]

[1] Creditor to insert the date at the end of the redemption period.

[2] Creditor to insert the amount specified in section 118(1)(b) of the Act.

(3) Creditor to insert the amount specified in section 120(1)(a) of the Act.

(4) Creditor to insert the amount specified in the Consumer Credit (Realisation of Pawn) Regulations 1983 (SI 1983/1568).

(5) Creditor to omit this paragraph if inapplicable.

[3989]

NOTES

Commencement: 1 February 2011, subject to reg 1(2)(b) at **[3979]**.

SCHEDULE 4
PROVISIONS RELATING TO CALCULATION AND DISCLOSURE OF THE TOTAL CHARGE FOR CREDIT AND APR

Regulation 1(2)

Assumptions about running-account credit

1.—(a) In the case of an agreement for running-account credit, the assumption in paragraph (b) below shall have effect for the purpose of calculating the total charge for credit and any APR in place of the assumption in regulation 6(o) of the Consumer Credit (Total Charge for Credit) Regulations 2010 that might otherwise apply.

  (b) In a case where credit is to be provided subject to a maximum credit limit of less than £1,200, the credit limit shall be assumed to be an amount equal to that maximum limit.

Permissible tolerances in disclosure of an APR

2. For the purposes of these Regulations, it shall be sufficient compliance with the requirement to show an APR if there is included in the consumer credit agreement—

  (a) a rate which exceeds the APR by not more than one, or
  (b) a rate which falls short of the APR by not more than 0.1, or
  (c) in a case to which either of paragraphs 3 or 4 of this Schedule applies, a rate determined in accordance with those paragraphs or whichever of them applies to that case.

Tolerance where repayments are nearly equal

3. In the case of an agreement under which all repayments of credit but one are equal and that one repayment does not differ from any other repayment by more whole pence than there are repayments of credit, there may be included in a consumer credit agreement a rate found under regulation 5 of the Consumer Credit (Total Charge for Credit) Regulations 2010 as if that one repayment were equal to the other repayments to be made under the agreement.

Tolerance where interval between relevant date and first repayment is greater than interval between repayments

4.—(a) In the case of a consumer credit agreement under which—
  (i) three or more repayments are to be made at equal intervals, and
  (ii) the interval between the relevant date and the first repayment is greater than the interval between the repayments,
  there may be included in the agreement a rate found under regulation 5 of the Consumer Credit (Total Charge for Credit) Regulations 2010 as if the interval between the relevant date and the first repayment were shortened so as to be equal to the interval between repayments.

  (b) In this paragraph "relevant date" means—
  (i) in a case where a date is specified in or determinable under the consumer credit agreement at the date of its making as that on which the debtor is entitled to require provision of anything the subject of the agreement, the earliest such date, and
  (ii) in any other case, the date of the making of the agreement.

[3990]

NOTES

Commencement: 1 February 2011, subject to reg 1(2)(b) at **[3979]**.

CONSUMER CREDIT (ADVERTISEMENTS) REGULATIONS 2010

(SI 2010/1970)

NOTES
Made: 3 August 2010.
Authority: Consumer Credit Act 1974, ss 44, 151(1), 182(2).
Commencement: 1 February 2011.
These Regulations implement European Parliament and Council Directive 2008/48/EC, Art 4 at [4532].

ARRANGEMENT OF REGULATIONS

1   Citation, commencement, revocation and interpretation

(1)   These Regulations may be cited as the Consumer Credit (Advertisements) Regulations 2010 and shall come into force on 1st February 2011.

(2)   …

(3)   In these Regulations, unless the context otherwise requires—

"the Act" means the Consumer Credit Act 1974;

"advance payment" includes any deposit but does not include a repayment of credit or any insurance premium or any amount entering into the total charge for credit;

"ancillary service" means a service that relates to the provision of credit under the consumer credit agreement and includes in particular an insurance or payment protection policy;

"APR" means the annual percentage rate of charge for credit determined in accordance with the Total Charge for Credit Regulations and the Schedule to these Regulations;

"cash price" in relation to any goods, services, land or other things means the price or charge at which the goods, services, land or other things may be purchased by, or supplied to, the debtor for cash, account being taken of any discount generally available from the dealer or supplier in question;

"cost of the credit" means any costs, including interest, commissions, taxes and any other kind of fees which are required to be paid by or on behalf of the debtor or a relative of the debtor in connection with the consumer credit agreement, whether payable to the creditor or to any other person, and which are known to the creditor, except for notarial costs;

"credit advertisement" means an advertisement to which Part 4 of the Act applies by virtue of it falling within section 43(1)(a), or which falls within section 151(1) of the Act in so far as section 44 is applied to such an advertisement;

"dealer" means, in relation to a hire-purchase, credit sale or conditional sale agreement under which he is not the creditor, a person who sells or proposes to sell goods, land or other things to the creditor before they form the subject matter of any such agreement and, in relation to any other agreement, means a supplier or his agent;

"the representative APR" is an APR at or below which the advertiser reasonably expects, at the date on which the credit advertisement is published, that credit would be provided under at least 51% of the consumer credit agreements which will be entered into as a result of the advertisement. For these purposes, in the case of a credit advertisement which falls within section 151(1) of the Act, "advertiser" means the person carrying on the business of credit brokerage;

"standard information" means the information listed in regulation 5(1);

"supplier" has the meaning assigned to it by section 189(1) of the Act, except that it does not include, in relation to a hire purchase, credit sale or conditional sale agreement, a creditor to whom goods, land or other things are sold or proposed to be sold by a dealer before becoming the subject matter of such an agreement;

"total amount of credit" means the credit limit or the total sums made available under a consumer credit agreement;

"total amount payable" means the sum of the total charge for credit and the total amount of credit payable under the consumer credit agreement as well as any advance payment;

"total charge for credit" means the total charge for credit determined in accordance with the Total Charge for Credit Regulations and the Schedule to these Regulations;

"the Total Charge for Credit Regulations" means the Consumer Credit (Total Charge for Credit) Regulations 2010;

"the 2004 Regulations" means the Consumer Credit (Advertisements) Regulations 2004.

(4)   In these Regulations—

    (a)   a reference to repayment of credit is a reference to repayment of credit with or without any other amount;

    (b)   a reference to the name of any person is—

        (i)   in the case of any person covered by a standard licence, a reference to any name of his specified in the licence;

        (ii)   in the case of any other person, a reference to any name under which he carries on business.

[3991]

NOTES

Commencement: 1 February 2011.

Para (2): revokes the Consumer Credit (Advertisements) Regulations 2010, SI 2010/1012.

2   Duty to comply

A person who causes a credit advertisement to be published shall ensure that the advertisement complies with all applicable requirements of these Regulations.

[3992]

NOTES

Commencement: 1 February 2011.

3   General requirements

Every credit advertisement shall—

    (a)   use plain and intelligible language,

    (b)   be easily legible (or, in the case of any information given orally, clearly audible), and

    (c)   specify the name of the advertiser.

[3993]

NOTES

Commencement: 1 February 2011.

4   Content of advertisements

(1)   Where a credit advertisement includes a rate of interest or an amount relating to the cost of the credit whether expressed as a sum of money or a proportion of a specified amount, the advertisement shall also—

    (a)   subject to paragraph (2), include standard information by means of a representative example in accordance with regulation 5, and

    (b)   specify a postal address at which the advertiser may be contacted, except in the case of credit advertisements—

        (i)   published by means of television or radio broadcast,

        (ii)   in any form on the premises of a dealer or creditor (not being advertisements in writing which customers are intended to take away),

        (iii)   which include the name and address of a dealer, or

        (iv)   which include the name and a postal address of a credit broker.

(2)   Paragraph (1)(a) shall not apply where regulation 6(1) applies and the credit advertisement does not indicate a rate of interest or other amount relating to the cost of the credit other than the representative APR.

[3994]

NOTES

Commencement: 1 February 2011.

5   Representative Example

(1)   Subject to paragraph (5), the representative example referred to in regulation 4(1)(a) shall comprise the following items of information—

    (a)   the rate of interest, whether fixed, variable or both,

    (b)   the nature and amount of any other charge included in the total charge for credit,

    (c)   the total amount of credit,

    (d)   the representative APR,

    (e)   in the case of credit in the form of a deferred payment for specific goods, services, land or other things, the cash price and the amount of any advance payment, and

    (f)   except where the consumer credit agreement is an open-end agreement—

        (i)   the duration of the agreement, and

        (ii)   the total amount payable by the debtor and the amount of each repayment of credit.

(2)   For the purposes of the representative example, the information referred to in sub-paragraphs (a) to (c), (e) and (f) of paragraph (1) shall be that which the advertiser reasonably expects at the date on which the credit advertisement is published to be representative of consumer credit agreements to which the representative APR applies and which are expected to be entered into as a result of the advertisement. For these purposes in the case of a credit advertisement which falls within section 151(1) of the Act, "advertiser" means the person carrying on the business of credit brokerage.

(3)   For the purposes of paragraph (2), "agreements to which the representative APR applies" in the case of paragraph (1)(e) means agreements providing credit for the purchase of specific goods, services, land or other things to which the representative APR applies.

(4)   For the purposes of paragraph (1)(a), where the consumer credit agreement provides different ways of draw down with different rates of interest, the rate of interest shall be assumed to be the highest rate applied to the most common draw down mechanism for the product to which the agreement relates.

(5)   Paragraphs (1)(d) and (2) shall not apply to a credit advertisement relating to an authorised non-business overdraft agreement.

(6)   The standard information contained in the representative example shall be—

    (a)   specified in a clear and concise way,

    (b)   accompanied by the words "representative example",

    (c)   presented together with each item of information being given equal prominence, and

    (d)   given greater prominence than—

        (i)   any other information relating to the cost of the credit in the credit advertisement except for any statement relating to an obligation to enter into a contract for an ancillary service referred to in regulation 8(1), and

        (ii)   any indication or incentive of a kind referred to in regulation 6(1).

(7)   In this regulation a reference to a rate of interest is a reference to the interest rate expressed as a fixed or variable percentage applied on an annual basis to the amount of credit drawn down.

[3995]

NOTES
Commencement: 1 February 2011.

6   Other advertisements requiring representative APR

(1)   A credit advertisement shall specify the representative APR if the advertisement—

    (a)   indicates in any way, including by means of the name given to a business or of an address used by a business for the purposes of electronic communication, that—

        (i)   credit is available to persons who might otherwise consider their access to credit restricted, or

        (ii)   any of the terms on which credit is available is more favourable (either in relation to a limited period or generally) than corresponding terms applied in any other case or by any other creditors, or

    (b)   includes any incentive to apply for credit or to enter into an agreement under which credit is provided.

(2)   For the purposes of this regulation, the representative APR shall be given greater prominence than any indication or incentive of a kind referred to in paragraph (1).

(3)   This regulation does not apply to a credit advertisement relating to an authorised non-business overdraft agreement.

[3996]

NOTES
Commencement: 1 February 2011.

7   APR

(1)   An APR shall be denoted in a credit advertisement as "%APR".

(2)   Where an APR is subject to change it shall be accompanied by the word "variable".

(3)   The representative APR shall be accompanied by the word "representative".

[3997]

NOTES
Commencement: 1 February 2011.

8   Ancillary services

(1)   Subject to paragraph (3), a credit advertisement shall include a clear and concise statement in respect of any obligation to enter into a contract for an ancillary service , where—

   (a)   the conclusion of that service contract is compulsory in order to obtain the credit or to obtain it on the terms and conditions advertised, and

   (b)   the cost of that ancillary service cannot be determined in advance.

(2)   The statement referred to in paragraph (1) shall—

   (a)   be no less prominent than any standard information included in the credit advertisement, and

   (b)   be presented together with any representative APR included in the advertisement.

(3)   This regulation does not apply to a credit advertisement relating to an authorised non-business overdraft agreement.

[3998]

NOTES
Commencement: 1 February 2011.

9   Security

Where the subject matter of a credit advertisement is a facility for which security is or may be required, the advertisement shall—

   (a)   state that security is or may be required, and

   (b)   specify the nature of the security.

[3999]

NOTES
Commencement: 1 February 2011.

10   Restrictions on certain expressions in credit advertisements

(1)   A credit advertisement shall not include—

   (a)   the word "overdraft" or any similar expression as describing any agreement for running-account credit except an agreement enabling the debtor to overdraw on a current account,

   (b)   the expression "interest free" or any similar expression indicating that a customer is liable to pay no greater amount in respect of a transaction financed by credit than he would be liable to pay as a cash purchaser in relation to the like transaction, except where the total amount payable by the debtor does not exceed the cash price,

   (c)   the expression "no deposit" or any similar expression, except where no advance payments are to be made,

   (d)   the expression "loan guaranteed" or "pre-approved" or any similar expression, except where the agreement is free of any conditions regarding the credit status of the debtor, or

   (e)   the expression "gift", "present" or any similar expression except where there are no conditions which would require the debtor to return the credit or items that are the subject of the claim.

(2)   A credit advertisement shall not include in relation to any repayment of credit the expression "weekly equivalent" or any expression to the like effect or any expression of any other periodical equivalent, unless weekly payments or the other periodical payments are provided for under the agreement.

(3)   In this regulation—

   (a)   "cash purchaser" means, in relation to any credit advertisement, a person who for a money consideration—

      (i)   acquires goods, land or other things, or

      (ii)   is provided with services,

   under a transaction which is not financed by credit;

   (b)   "current account" means an account under which the customer may, by means of cheques or similar orders payable to the customer or to any other person or by any other means, obtain or have the use of money held or made available by the person with whom the account is kept and which records alterations in the financial relationship between the said person and the customer.

[4000]

NOTES
Commencement: 1 February 2011.

11 Exclusions

(1) These Regulations do not apply to a credit advertisement which—

(a) whether expressly or by implication indicates clearly that a person is willing to provide credit for the purposes of another person's business, and

(b) does not indicate (whether expressly or by implication) that a person is willing to provide credit otherwise than for the purposes of such a business.

(2) References in paragraph (1) to a business do not include references to a business carried on by the advertiser or any person acting as a credit-broker in relation to the credit facility to which the credit advertisement relates.

(3) These Regulations do not apply to any credit advertisement in so far as it is a communication of an invitation or inducement to—

(a) engage in investment activity within the meaning of section 21 of the Financial Services and Markets Act 2000, other than an exempt generic communication;

(b) enter into a regulated home purchase plan within the meaning of article 63F of the Financial Services and Markets Act (Regulated Activities) Order 2001.

(4) An "exempt generic communication" is a communication to which subsection (1) of section 21 of the Financial Services and Markets Act 2000 does not apply, as a result of an order under subsection (5) of that section, because it does not identify a person as providing an investment or carrying on an activity to which the communication relates.

(5) These Regulations do not apply to a credit advertisement in so far as it relates to a consumer credit agreement secured on land.

[4000A]

NOTES
Commencement: 1 February 2011.

12 Transitional provisions

(1) Subject to paragraph (2), a person shall not be guilty of an offence under section 47(1) or 167 of the Act for contravention of these Regulations in respect of a credit advertisement that would have complied with the requirements of the 2004 Regulations had those Regulations not been disapplied in relation to a consumer credit agreement not secured on land by virtue of regulation 72 of the Consumer Credit (EU Directive) Regulations 2010.

(2) Paragraph (1) only applies to—

(a) credit advertisements published in a catalogue, diary or work of reference comprising at least 50 printed pages—

(i) copies of which are first published, or made available for publication in the ordinary course of business before 1st March 2011, and

(ii) which, in a reasonably prominent position either contains the date of its first publication or specifies a period, being a calendar or seasonal period, throughout which it is intended to have effect;

(b) other credit advertisements—

(i) which are first published before 1st February 2011, and

(ii) which cease to be published before 1st March 2011.

[4000B]

NOTES
Commencement: 1 February 2011.

SCHEDULE
PROVISIONS RELATING TO CALCULATION AND DISCLOSURE OF TOTAL CHARGE
FOR CREDIT AND APR

Regulation 1(3)

1 Assumptions about running-account credit

(a) In the case of a credit advertisement relating to running-account credit, the assumption in paragraph (b) below shall have effect for the purpose of calculating the total charge for credit and any APR in place of the assumption in regulation 6(o) of the Total Charge for Credit Regulations that might otherwise apply.

(b) In a case where the credit limit applicable to the credit is not yet known on the date the credit advertisement is published but it is known that it will be less than £1,200, the credit limit shall be assumed to be an amount equal to that maximum limit.

2   Permissible tolerances in disclosure of an APR

For the purposes of these Regulations, it shall be sufficient compliance with the requirement to show an APR if there is included in the credit advertisement—

    (a)   a rate which exceeds the APR by not more than one,

    (b)   a rate which falls short of the APR by not more than 0.1, or

    (c)   in a case to which paragraph 3 or 4 of this Schedule applies, a rate determined in accordance with those paragraphs or whichever of them applies to that case.

3   Tolerance where repayments are nearly equal

In the case of an agreement under which all repayments of credit but one are equal and that one repayment does not differ from any other repayment by more whole pence than there are repayments of credit, there may be included in a credit advertisement relating to the agreement a rate found under regulation 5 of the Total Charge for Credit Regulations as if that one repayment were equal to the other repayments to be made under the agreement.

4   Tolerance where interval between relevant date and first repayment is greater than interval between repayments

    (a)   In the case of a consumer credit agreement under which—

        (i)   three or more repayments of credit are to be made at equal intervals, and

        (ii)   the interval between the relevant date and the first repayment is greater than the interval between the repayments,

    there may be included in the credit advertisement relating to the agreement a rate found under regulation 5 of the Total Charge for Credit Regulations as if the interval between the relevant date and the first repayment were shortened so as to be equal to the interval between repayments.

    (b)

        (i)   In this paragraph "relevant date", in relation to a credit advertisement, means—

        (ii)   in a case where a date is specified in or determinable under a consumer credit agreement at the date of its making as that on which the debtor is entitled to require provision of anything the subject of the agreement, the earliest such date, and

        (iii)   in any other case, the date of the making of the agreement.

[4000C]

NOTES

Commencement: 1 February 2011.

PART 3
EU AND INTERNATIONAL MATERIALS

CONSOLIDATED VERSION OF THE TREATY ON THE FUNCTIONING OF THE EUROPEAN UNION

NOTES

Date of publication in OJ: OJ C83, 30.03.2010, p 47.

Formerly titled the "Treaty Establishing the European Community" (Treaty of Rome). This is the Treaty currently in force which is the successor to the Treaty of Rome, as consolidated following the amendments to and the renaming of the Treaty, by the Treaty of Lisbon which came into force on 1 December 2009.

Cross-references to the equivalent article in the pre-Lisbon Treaty version of the Treaty are given at the beginning of each of the Articles reproduced; these cross-references are part of the official text. The abbreviation "TEC" refers to the Treaty Establishing the European Community.

PART THREE
POLICIES AND INTERNAL ACTIONS OF THE UNION

TITLE VII
COMMON RULES ON COMPETITION, TAXATION AND APPROXIMATION OF LAWS

CHAPTER 1
RULES ON COMPETITION

SECTION 1
RULES APPLYING TO UNDERTAKINGS

Article 101 (ex Article 81 TEC)

1.   The following shall be prohibited as incompatible with the internal market: all agreements between undertakings, decisions by associations of undertakings and concerted practices which may affect trade between Member States and which have as their object or effect the prevention, restriction or distortion of competition within the internal market, and in particular those which:

(a)   directly or indirectly fix purchase or selling prices or any other trading conditions;
(b)   limit or control production, markets, technical development, or investment;
(c)   share markets or sources of supply;
(d)   apply dissimilar conditions to equivalent transactions with other trading parties, thereby placing them at a competitive disadvantage;
(e)   make the conclusion of contracts subject to acceptance by the other parties of supplementary obligations which, by their nature or according to commercial usage, have no connection with the subject of such contracts.

2.   Any agreements or decisions prohibited pursuant to this Article shall be automatically void.

3.   The provisions of paragraph 1 may, however, be declared inapplicable in the case of:
— any agreement or category of agreements between undertakings,
— any decision or category of decisions by associations of undertakings,
— any concerted practice or category of concerted practices,
which contributes to improving the production or distribution of goods or to promoting technical or economic progress, while allowing consumers a fair share of the resulting benefit, and which does not:

(a)   impose on the undertakings concerned restrictions which are not indispensable to the attainment of these objectives;
(b)   afford such undertakings the possibility of eliminating competition in respect of a substantial part of the products in question.

[4001]

Article 102 (ex Article 82 TEC)

Any abuse by one or more undertakings of a dominant position within the internal market or in a substantial part of it shall be prohibited as incompatible with the internal market in so far as it may affect trade between Member States.

Such abuse may, in particular, consist in:

(a)   directly or indirectly imposing unfair purchase or selling prices or other unfair trading conditions;
(b)   limiting production, markets or technical development to the prejudice of consumers;
(c)   applying dissimilar conditions to equivalent transactions with other trading parties, thereby placing them at a competitive disadvantage;
(d)   making the conclusion of contracts subject to acceptance by the other parties of supplementary obligations which, by their nature or according to commercial usage, have no connection with the subject of such contracts.

[4002]

Article 103 (ex Article 83 TEC)

1. The appropriate regulations or directives to give effect to the principles set out in Articles 101 and 102 shall be laid down by the Council, on a proposal from the Commission and after consulting the European Parliament.

2. The regulations or directives referred to in paragraph 1 shall be designed in particular:
    (a) to ensure compliance with the prohibitions laid down in Article 101(1) and in Article 102 by making provision for fines and periodic penalty payments;
    (b) to lay down detailed rules for the application of Article 101(3), taking into account the need to ensure effective supervision on the one hand, and to simplify administration to the greatest possible extent on the other;
    (c) to define, if need be, in the various branches of the economy, the scope of the provisions of Articles 101 and 102;
    (d) to define the respective functions of the Commission and of the Court of Justice of the European Union in applying the provisions laid down in this paragraph;
    (e) to determine the relationship between national laws and the provisions contained in this Section or adopted pursuant to this Article.

[4003]

Article 104 (ex Article 84 TEC)

Until the entry into force of the provisions adopted in pursuance of Article 103, the authorities in Member States shall rule on the admissibility of agreements, decisions and concerted practices and on abuse of a dominant position in the internal market in accordance with the law of their country and with the provisions of Article 101, in particular paragraph 3, and of Article 102.

[4004]

Article 105 (ex Article 85 TEC)

1. Without prejudice to Article 104, the Commission shall ensure the application of the principles laid down in Articles 101 and 102. On application by a Member State or on its own initiative, and in cooperation with the competent authorities in the Member States, which shall give it their assistance, the Commission shall investigate cases of suspected infringement of these principles. If it finds that there has been an infringement, it shall propose appropriate measures to bring it to an end.

2. If the infringement is not brought to an end, the Commission shall record such infringement of the principles in a reasoned decision. The Commission may publish its decision and authorise Member States to take the measures, the conditions and details of which it shall determine, needed to remedy the situation.

3. The Commission may adopt regulations relating to the categories of agreement in respect of which the Council has adopted a regulation or a directive pursuant to Article 103(2)(b).

[4005]

Article 106 (ex Article 86 TEC)

1. In the case of public undertakings and undertakings to which Member States grant special or exclusive rights, Member States shall neither enact nor maintain in force any measure contrary to the rules contained in the Treaties, in particular to those rules provided for in Article 18 and Articles 101 to 109.

2. Undertakings entrusted with the operation of services of general economic interest or having the character of a revenue-producing monopoly shall be subject to the rules contained in the Treaties, in particular to the rules on competition, in so far as the application of such rules does not obstruct the performance, in law or in fact, of the particular tasks assigned to them. The development of trade must not be affected to such an extent as would be contrary to the interests of the Union.

3. The Commission shall ensure the application of the provisions of this Article and shall, where necessary, address appropriate directives or decisions to Member States.

[4006]

SECTION 2
AIDS GRANTED BY STATES

Article 107 (ex Article 87 TEC)

1. Save as otherwise provided in the Treaties, any aid granted by a Member State or through State resources in any form whatsoever which distorts or threatens to distort competition by favouring certain undertakings or the production of certain goods shall, in so far as it affects trade between Member States, be incompatible with the internal market.

2. The following shall be compatible with the internal market:
    (a) aid having a social character, granted to individual consumers, provided that such aid is granted without discrimination related to the origin of the products concerned;

  (b)   aid to make good the damage caused by natural disasters or exceptional occurrences;

  (c)   aid granted to the economy of certain areas of the Federal Republic of Germany affected by the division of Germany, in so far as such aid is required in order to compensate for the economic disadvantages caused by that division. Five years after the entry into force of the Treaty of Lisbon, the Council, acting on a proposal from the Commission, may adopt a decision repealing this point.

3.   The following may be considered to be compatible with the internal market:

  (a)   aid to promote the economic development of areas where the standard of living is abnormally low or where there is serious underemployment, and of the regions referred to in Article 349, in view of their structural, economic and social situation;

  (b)   aid to promote the execution of an important project of common European interest or to remedy a serious disturbance in the economy of a Member State;

  (c)   aid to facilitate the development of certain economic activities or of certain economic areas, where such aid does not adversely affect trading conditions to an extent contrary to the common interest;

  (d)   aid to promote culture and heritage conservation where such aid does not affect trading conditions and competition in the Union to an extent that is contrary to the common interest;

  (e)   such other categories of aid as may be specified by decision of the Council on a proposal from the Commission.

[4007]

Article 108 (ex Article 88 TEC)

1.   The Commission shall, in cooperation with Member States, keep under constant review all systems of aid existing in those States. It shall propose to the latter any appropriate measures required by the progressive development or by the functioning of the internal market.

2.   If, after giving notice to the parties concerned to submit their comments, the Commission finds that aid granted by a State or through State resources is not compatible with the internal market having regard to Article 107, or that such aid is being misused, it shall decide that the State concerned shall abolish or alter such aid within a period of time to be determined by the Commission.

If the State concerned does not comply with this decision within the prescribed time, the Commission or any other interested State may, in derogation from the provisions of Articles 258 and 259, refer the matter to the Court of Justice of the European Union direct.

On application by a Member State, the Council may, acting unanimously, decide that aid which that State is granting or intends to grant shall be considered to be compatible with the internal market, in derogation from the provisions of Article 107 or from the regulations provided for in Article 109, if such a decision is justified by exceptional circumstances. If, as regards the aid in question, the Commission has already initiated the procedure provided for in the first subparagraph of this paragraph, the fact that the State concerned has made its application to the Council shall have the effect of suspending that procedure until the Council has made its attitude known.

If, however, the Council has not made its attitude known within three months of the said application being made, the Commission shall give its decision on the case.

3.   The Commission shall be informed, in sufficient time to enable it to submit its comments, of any plans to grant or alter aid. If it considers that any such plan is not compatible with the internal market having regard to Article 107, it shall without delay initiate the procedure provided for in paragraph 2. The Member State concerned shall not put its proposed measures into effect until this procedure has resulted in a final decision.

4.   The Commission may adopt regulations relating to the categories of State aid that the Council has, pursuant to Article 109, determined may be exempted from the procedure provided for by paragraph 3 of this Article.

[4008]

Article 109 (ex Article 89 TEC)

The Council, on a proposal from the Commission and after consulting the European Parliament, may make any appropriate regulations for the application of Articles 107 and 108 and may in particular determine the conditions in which Article 108(3) shall apply and the categories of aid exempted from this procedure.

[4009]

COUNCIL OF EUROPE: EUROPEAN CONVENTION ON PRODUCTS LIABILITY IN REGARD TO PERSONAL INJURY AND DEATH

[Done at Strasbourg, 27 January 1977]

NOTES
On the occasion of the 59th Session of the Committee of Ministers of the Council of Europe, the Convention was opened to signature on 27 January 1977. It was signed by the plenipotentiaries of Belgium, France, and Luxembourg.

The member States of the Council of Europe, signatory hereto,

Considering that the aim of the Council of Europe is to achieve a greater unity between its Members;

Considering the development of case law in the majority of member States extending liability of producers prompted by a desire to protect consumers taking into account the new production techniques and marketing and sales methods;

Desiring to ensure better protection of the public and, at the same time, to take producers' legitimate interests into account;

Considering that priority should be given to compensation for personal injury and death;

Aware of the importance of introducing special rules on the liability of producers at European level,

Have agreed as follows—

Article 1

1. Each Contracting State shall make its national law conform with the provisions of this Convention not later than the date of the entry into force of the Convention in respect of that State.

2. Each Contracting State shall communicate to the Secretary General of the Council of Europe, not later than the date of the entry into force of the Convention in respect of that State, any text adopted or a statement of the contents of the existing law which it relies on to implement the Convention.

[4010]

Article 2

For the purpose of this Convention—
    (a)   the term 'product' indicates all movables, natural or industrial, whether raw or manufactured, even though incorporated into another movable or into an immovable;
    (b)   the term 'producer' indicates the manufacturers of finished products or of component parts and the producers of natural products;
    (c)   a product has a 'defect' when it does not provide the safety which a person is entitled to expect, having regard to all the circumstances including the presentation of the product;
    (d)   a product has been 'put into circulation' when the producer has delivered it to another person.

[4011]

Article 3

1. The producer shall be liable to pay compensation for death or personal injuries caused by a defect in his product.

2. Any person who has imported a product for putting it into circulation in the course of a business and any person who has presented a product as his product by causing his name, trademark or other distinguishing feature to appear on the product, shall be deemed to be producers for the purpose of this Convention and shall be liable as such.

3. When the product does not indicate the identity of any of the persons liable under paragraphs 1 and 2 of this article, each supplier shall be deemed to be a producer for the purpose of this Convention and liable as such, unless he discloses, within a reasonable time, at the request of the claimant, the identity of the producer or of the person who supplied him with the product. The same shall apply, in the case of an imported product, if this product does not indicate the identity of the importer referred to in paragraph 2, even if the name of the producer is indicated.

4. In the case of damage caused by a defect in a product incorporated into another product, the producer of the incorporated product and the producer incorporating that product shall be liable.

5. Where several persons are liable under this Convention for the same damage, each shall be liable in full (*in solidum*).

[4012]

Article 4

1. If the injured person or the person entitled to claim compensation has by his own fault contributed to the damage, the compensation may be reduced or disallowed having regard to all the circumstances.

2. The same shall apply if a person, for whom the injured person or the person entitled to claim compensation is responsible under national law, has contributed to the damage by his fault.

[4013]

Article 5

1. A producer shall not be liable under this Convention if he proves—
   (a) that the product has not been put into circulation by him; or
   (b) that, having regard to the circumstances, it is probable that the defect which caused the damage did not exist at the time when the product was put into circulation by him or that this defect came into being afterwards; or
   (c) that the product was neither manufactured for sale, hire or any other form of distribution for the economic purposes of the producer nor manufactured or distributed in the course of his business.

2. The liability of a producer shall not be reduced when the damage is caused both by a defect in the product and by the act or by omission of a third party.

[4014]

Article 6

Proceedings for the recovery of the damages shall be subject to a limitation period of three years from the day the claimant became aware or should reasonably have been aware of the damage, the defect and the identity of the producer.

[4015]

Article 7

The right to compensation under this Convention against a producer shall be extinguished if an action is not brought within ten years from the date on which the producer put into circulation the individual product which caused the damage.

[4016]

Article 8

The liability of the producer under this Convention cannot be excluded or limited by any exemption or exoneration clause.

[4017]

Article 9

This Convention shall not apply to—
   (a) the liability of producers inter se and their rights of recourse against third parties;
   (b) nuclear damage.

[4018]

Article 10

Contracting States shall not adopt rules derogating from this Convention, even if these rules are more favourable to the victim.

[4019]

Article 11

States may replace the liability of the producer, in a principal or subsidiary way, wholly or in part, in a general way, or for certain risks only, by the liability of a guarantee fund or other form of collective guarantee, provided that the victim shall receive protection at least equivalent to the protection he would have had under the liability scheme provided for by this Convention.

[4020]

Article 12

This Convention shall not affect any rights which a person suffering damage may have according to the ordinary rules of the law of contractual and extra-contractual liability including any rules concerning the duties of a seller who sells goods in the course of his business.

[4021]

Article 13

1. This Convention shall be open to signature by the member States of the Council of Europe. It shall be subject to ratification, acceptance or approval. Instruments of ratification, acceptance or approval shall be deposited with the Secretary General of the Council of Europe.

2.   This Convention shall enter into force on the first day of the month following the expiration of a period of six months after the date of deposit of the third instrument of ratification, acceptance or approval.

3.   In respect of a signatory State ratifying, accepting or approving subsequently, the Convention shall come into force on the first day of the month following the expiration of a period of six months after the date of the deposit of its instrument of ratification, acceptance or approval.

[4022]

Article 14

1.   After the entry into force of this Convention, the Committee of Ministers of the Council of Europe may invite any non-member State to accede thereto.

2.   Such accession shall be effected by depositing with the Secretary General of the Council of Europe an instrument of accession which shall take effect on the first day of the month following the expiration of a period of six months after the date of its deposit.

[4023]

Article 15

1.   Any State may, at the time of signature or when depositing its instrument of ratification, acceptance, approval or accession, specify the territory or territories to which this Convention shall apply.

2.   Any State may, when depositing its instrument of ratification, acceptance, approval or accession or at any later date, by declaration addressed to the Secretary General of the Council of Europe, extend this Convention to any other territory or territories specified in the declaration and for whose international relations it is responsible or on whose behalf it is authorised to give undertakings.

3.   Any declaration made in pursuance of the preceding paragraph may, in respect of any territory mentioned in such declaration, be withdrawn by means of a notification addressed to the Secretary General of the Council of Europe. Such withdrawal shall take effect on the first day of the month following the expiration of a period of six months after the date of receipt by the Secretary General of the Council of Europe of the declaration of withdrawal.

[4024]

Article 16

1.   Any State may, at the time of signature or when depositing its instrument of ratification, acceptance, approval or accession, or at any later date, by notification addressed to the Secretary General of the Council of Europe, declare that, in pursuance of an international agreement to which it is a Party, it will not consider imports from one or more specified States also Parties to that agreement as imports for the purpose of paragraphs 2 and 3 of Article 3; in this case the person importing the product into any of these States from another State shall be deemed to be an importer for all the States Parties to this agreement.

2.   Any declaration made in pursuance of the preceding paragraph may be withdrawn by means of a notification addressed to the Secretary General of the Council of Europe. Such withdrawal shall take effect the first day of the month following the expiration of a period of one month after the date of receipt by the Secretary General of the Council of Europe of the declaration of withdrawal.

[4025]

Article 17

1.   No reservation shall be made to the provisions of this Convention except those mentioned in the Annex to this Convention.

2.   The Contracting State which has made one of the reservations mentioned in the Annex to this Convention may withdraw it by means of a declaration addressed to the Secretary General of the Council of Europe which shall become effective the first day of the month following the expiration of a period of one month after the date of its receipt by the Secretary General.

[4026]

Article 18

1.   Any Contracting State may, in so far as it is concerned, denounce this Convention by means of a notification addressed to the Secretary General of the Council of Europe.

2.   Such denunciation shall take effect on the first day of the month following the expiration of a period of six months after the date of receipt by the Secretary General of such notification.

[4027]

Article 19

The Secretary General of the Council of Europe shall notify the member States of the Council and any State which has acceded to this Convention of—

(a)   any signature;

(b)   any deposit of an instrument of ratification, acceptance, approval or accession;

(c)   any date of entry into force of this Convention in accordance with Article 13 thereof;

(d)   any reservation made in pursuance of the provisions of Article 17, paragraph 1;

(e)   withdrawal of any reservation carried out in pursuance of the provisions of Article 17, paragraph 2;

(f)   any communication or notification received in pursuance of the provisions of Article 1, paragraph 2, Article 15, paragraphs 2 and 3 and Article 16, paragraphs 1 and 2;

(g)   any notification received in pursuance of the provisions of Article 18 and the date on which denunciation takes effect.

[4028]

In witness whereof, the undersigned, being duly authorised thereto, have signed this Convention.

Done at Strasbourg, this 27th day of January 1977, in English and in French, both texts being equally authoritative, in a single copy which shall remain deposited in the archives of the Council of Europe. The Secretary General of the Council of Europe shall transmit certified copies to each of the signatory and acceding Parties.

ANNEX

Each State may declare, at the moment of signature or at the moment of the deposit of its instrument of ratification, acceptance, approval or accession, that it reserves the right—

1.   to apply its ordinary law, in place of the provisions of Article 4, in so far as such law provides that compensation may be reduced or disallowed only in case of gross negligence or intentional conduct by the injured person or the person entitled to claim compensation;

2.   to limit, by provisions of its national law, the amount of compensation to be paid by a producer under this national law in compliance with the present Convention. However, this limit shall not be less than—

    (a)   the sum in national currency corresponding to 70,000 Special Drawing Rights as defined by the International Monetary Fund at the time of the ratification, for each deceased person or person suffering personal injury;

    (b)   the sum in national currency corresponding to 10 million Special Drawing Rights as defined by the International Monetary Fund at the time of ratification, for all damage caused by identical products having the same defect;

3.   to exclude the retailer of primary agricultural products from liability under the terms of paragraph 3 of Article 3 providing he discloses to the claimant all information in his possession concerning the identity of the persons mentioned in Article 3.

[4029]

UNITED NATIONS CONVENTION ON THE CARRIAGE OF GOODS BY SEA, 1978

(Hamburg, 31 March 1978)

NOTES

This Convention was adopted by the United Nations Conference on the Carriage of Goods by Sea convened in Hamburg, at the invitation of the Government of the Federal Republic of Germany, from 6 to 31 March 1978.

PREAMBLE

THE STATES PARTIES TO THIS CONVENTION,

HAVING RECOGNISED the desirability of determining by agreement certain rules relating to the carriage of goods by sea,

HAVE DECIDED to conclude a Convention for this purpose and have thereto agreed as follows—

PART I
GENERAL PROVISIONS

Article 1
Definitions

In this Convention—

1.   'Carrier' means any person by whom or in whose name a contract of carriage of goods by sea has been concluded with a shipper.

2.   'Actual carrier' means any person to whom the performance of the carriage of the goods,

or of part of the carriage, has been entrusted by the carrier, and includes any other person to whom such performance has been entrusted.

3. 'Shipper' means any person by whom or in whose name or on whose behalf a contract of carriage of goods by sea has been concluded with a carrier, or any person by whom or in whose name or on whose behalf the goods are actually delivered to the carrier in relation to the contract of carriage by sea.

4. 'Consignee' means the person entitled to take delivery of the goods.

5. 'Goods' includes live animals; where the goods are consolidated in a container, pallet or similar article of transport or where they are packed, goods includes such article of transport or packaging if supplied by the shipper.

6. 'Contract of carriage by sea' means any contract whereby the carrier undertakes against payment of freight to carry goods by sea from one port to another; however, a contract which involves carriage by sea and also carriage by some other means is deemed to be a contract of carriage by sea for the purposes of this Convention only in so far as it relates to the carriage by sea.

7. 'Bill of lading' means a document which evidences a contract of carriage by sea and the taking over or loading of the goods by the carrier, and by which the carrier undertakes to deliver the goods against surrender of the document. A provision in the document that the goods are to be delivered to the order of a named person, or to order, or to bearer, constitutes such an undertaking.

8. 'Writing' includes, *inter alia*, telegram and telex.

[4030]

Article 2
Scope of application

1. The provisions of this Convention are applicable to all contracts of carriage by sea between two different States, if—

   (a) the port of loading as provided for in the contract of carriage by sea is located in a Contracting State, or

   (b) the port of discharge as provided for in the contract of carriage by sea is located in a Contracting State, or

   (c) one of the optional ports of discharge provided for in the contract of carriage by sea is the actual port of discharge and such port is located in a Contracting State, or

   (d) the bill of lading or other document evidencing the contract of carriage by sea is issued in a Contracting State, or

   (e) the bill of lading or other document evidencing the contract of carriage by sea provides that the provisions of this Convention or the legislation of any State giving effect to them are to govern the contract.

2. The provisions of this Convention are applicable without regard to the nationality of the ship, the carrier, the actual carrier, the shipper, the consignee or any other interested person.

3. The provisions of this Convention are not applicable to charter-parties. However, where a bill of lading is issued pursuant to a charter-party, the provisions of the Convention apply to such a bill of lading if it governs the relation between the carrier and the holder of the bill of lading, not being the charterer.

4. If a contract provides for future carriage of goods in a series of shipments during an agreed period, the provisions of this Convention apply to each shipment. However, where a shipment is made under a charter-party, the provisions of paragraph 3 of this article apply.

[4031]

Article 3
Interpretation of the Convention

In the interpretation and application of the provisions of this Convention regard shall be had to its international character and to the need to promote uniformity.

[4032]

PART II
LIABILITY OF THE CARRIER

Article 4
Period of responsibility

1. The responsibility of the carrier for the goods under this Convention covers the period during which the carrier is in charge of the goods at the port of loading, during the carriage and at the port of discharge.

2. For the purpose of paragraph 1 of this article, the carrier is deemed to be in charge of the goods—

   (a) from the time he has taken over the goods from—

       (i) the shipper, or a person acting on his behalf; or

      (ii) an authority or other third party to whom, pursuant to law or regulations applicable at the port of loading, the goods must be handed over for shipment;

   (b) until the time he has delivered the goods—

      (i) by handing over the goods to the consignee; or

      (ii) in cases where the consignee does not receive the goods from the carrier, by placing them at the disposal of the consignee in accordance with the contract or with the law or with the usage of the particular trade, applicable at the port of discharge; or

      (iii) by handing over the goods to an authority or other third party to whom, pursuant to law or regulations applicable at the port of discharge, the goods must be handed over.

3.   In paragraphs 1 and 2 of this article, reference to the carrier or to the consignee means, in addition to the carrier or the consignee, the servants or agents, respectively of the carrier or the consignee.

[4033]

Article 5
Basis of liability

1.   The carrier is liable for loss resulting from loss of or damage to the goods, as well as from delay in delivery, if the occurrence which caused the loss, damage or delay took place while the goods were in his charge as defined in article 4, unless the carrier proves that he, his servants or agents took all measures that could reasonably be required to avoid the occurrence and its consequences.

2.   Delay in delivery occurs when the goods have not been delivered at the port of discharge provided for in the contract of carriage by sea within the time expressly agreed upon or, in the absence of such agreement, within the time which it would be reasonable to require of a diligent carrier, having regard to the circumstances of the case.

3.   The person entitled to make a claim for the loss of goods may treat the goods as lost if they have not been delivered as required by article 4 within 60 consecutive days following the expiry of the time for delivery according to paragraph 2 of this article.

4.

   (a) The carrier is liable

      (i) for loss of or damage to the goods or delay in delivery caused by fire, if the claimant proves that the fire arose from fault or neglect on the part of the carrier, his servants or agents;

      (ii) for such loss, damage or delay in delivery which is proved by the claimant to have resulted from the fault or neglect of the carrier, his servants or agents in taking all measures that could reasonably be required to put out the fire and avoid or mitigate its consequences.

   (b) In case of fire on board the ship affecting the goods, if the claimant or the carrier so desires, a survey in accordance with shipping practices must be held into the cause and circumstances of the fire, and a copy of the surveyor's report shall be made available on demand to the carrier and the claimant.

5.   With respect to live animals, the carrier is not liable for loss, damage or delay in delivery resulting from any special risks inherent in that kind of carriage. If the carrier proves that he has complied with any special instructions given to him by the shipper respecting the animals and that, in the circumstances of the case, the loss, damage or delay in delivery could be attributed to such risks, it is presumed that the loss, damage or delay in delivery was so caused, unless there is proof that all or a part of the loss, damage or delay in delivery resulted from fault or neglect on the part of the carrier, his servants or agents.

6.   The carrier is not liable, except in general average, where loss, damage or delay in delivery resulted from measures to save life or from reasonable measures to save property at sea.

7.   Where fault or neglect on the part of the carrier, his servants or agents combines with another cause to produce loss, damage or delay in delivery, the carrier is liable only to the extent that the loss, damage or delay in delivery is attributable to such fault or neglect, provided that the carrier proves the amount of the loss, damage or delay in delivery not attributable thereto.

[4034]

Article 6
Limits of liability

1.

   (a) The liability of the carrier for loss resulting from loss of or damage to goods according to the provisions of article 5 is limited to an amount equivalent to 835 units of account per package or other shipping unit or 2.5 units of account per kilogram of gross weight of the goods lost or damaged, whichever is the higher.

   (b) The liability of the carrier for delay in delivery according to the provisions of article 5 is limited to an amount equivalent to two and a half times the freight payable for the goods delayed, but not exceeding the total freight payable under the contract of carriage of goods by sea.

(c)   In no case shall the aggregate liability of the carrier, under both subparagraphs (a) and (b) of this paragraph, exceed the limitation which would be established under subparagraph (a) of this paragraph for total loss of the goods with respect to which such liability was incurred.

2.   For the purpose of calculating which amount is the higher in accordance with paragraph 1(a) of this article, the following rules apply—

(a)   Where a container, pallet or similar article of transport is used to consolidate goods, the package or other shipping units enumerated in the bill of lading, if issued, or otherwise in any other document evidencing the contract of carriage by sea, as packed in such article of transport are deemed packages or shipping units. Except as aforesaid the goods in such article of transport are deemed one shipping unit.

(b)   In cases where the article of transport itself has been lost or damaged, that article of transport, if not owned or otherwise supplied by the carrier, is considered one separate shipping unit.

3.   Unit of account means the unit of account mentioned in article 26.

4.   By agreement between the carrier and the shipper, limits of liability exceeding those provided for in paragraph 1 may be fixed.

[4035]

Article 7
Application to non-contractual claims

1.   The defences and limits of liability provided for in this Convention apply in any action against the carrier in respect of loss or damage to the goods covered by the contract of carriage by sea, as well as of delay in delivery whether the action is founded in contract, in tort or otherwise.

2.   If such an action is brought against a servant or agent of the carrier, such servant or agent, if he proves that he acted within the scope of his employment, is entitled to avail himself of the defences and limits of liability which the carrier is entitled to invoke under this Convention.

3.   Except as provided in article 8, the aggregate of the amounts recoverable from the carrier and from any persons referred to in paragraph 2 of this article shall not exceed the limits of liability provided for in this Convention.

[4036]

Article 8
Loss of right to limit responsibility

1.   The carrier is not entitled to the benefit of the limitation of liability provided for in article 6 if it is proved that the loss, damage or delay in delivery resulted from an act or omission of the carrier done with the intent to cause such loss, damage or delay, or recklessly and with knowledge that such loss, damage or delay would probably result.

2.   Notwithstanding the provisions of paragraph 2 of article 7, a servant or agent of the carrier is not entitled to the benefit of the limitation of liability provided for in article 6 if it is proved that the loss, damage or delay in delivery resulted from an act or omission of such servant or agent, done with the intent to cause such loss, damage or delay, or recklessly and with knowledge that such loss, damage or delay would probably result.

[4037]

Article 9
Deck cargo

1.   The carrier is entitled to carry the goods on deck only if such carriage is in accordance with an agreement with the shipper or with the usage of the particular trade or is required by statutory rules or regulations.

2.   If the carrier and the shipper have agreed that the goods shall or may be carried on deck, the carrier must insert in the bill of lading or other document evidencing the contract of carriage by sea a statement to that effect. In the absence of such a statement the carrier has the burden of proving that an agreement for carriage on deck has been entered into; however, the carrier is not entitled to invoke such an agreement against a third party, including a consignee, who has acquired the bill of lading in good faith.

3.   Where the goods have been carried on deck contrary to the provisions of paragraph 1 of this article or where the carrier may not under paragraph 2 of this article invoke an agreement for carriage on deck, the carrier, notwithstanding the provisions of paragraph 1 of article 5, is liable for loss of or damage to the goods, as well as for delay in delivery, resulting solely from the carriage on deck, and the extent of his liability is to be determined in accordance with the provisions of article 6 or article 8 of this Convention, as the case may be.

4.   Carriage of goods on deck contrary to express agreement for carriage under deck is deemed to be an act or omission of the carrier within the meaning of article 8.

[4038]

Article 10
Liability of the carrier and actual carrier

1.   Where the performance of the carriage or part thereof has been entrusted to an actual carrier, whether or not in pursuance of a liberty under the contract of carriage by sea to do so, the carrier nevertheless remains responsible for the entire carriage according to the provisions of this Convention. The carrier is responsible, in relation to the carriage performed by the actual carrier, for the acts and omissions of the actual carrier and of his servants and agents acting within the scope of their employment.

2.   All the provisions of this Convention governing the responsibility of the carrier also apply to the responsibility of the actual carrier for the carriage performed by him. The provisions of paragraphs 2 and 3 of article 7 and of paragraph 2 of article 8 apply if an action is brought against a servant or agent of the actual carrier.

3.   Any special agreement under which the carrier assumes obligations not imposed by this Convention or waives rights conferred by this Convention affects the actual carrier only if agreed to by him expressly and in writing. Whether or not the actual carrier has so agreed, the carrier nevertheless remains bound by the obligations or waivers resulting from such special agreement.

4.   Where and to the extent that both the carrier and the actual carrier are liable, their liability is joint and several.

5.   The aggregate of the amounts recoverable from the carrier, the actual carrier and their servants and agents shall not exceed the limits of liability provided for in this Convention.

6.   Nothing in this article shall prejudice any right of recourse as between the carrier and the actual carrier.

[4039]

Article 11
Through carriage

1.   Notwithstanding the provisions of paragraph 1 of article 10, where a contract of carriage by sea provides explicitly that a specified part of the carriage covered by the said contract is to be performed by a named person other than the carrier, the contract may also provide that the carrier is not liable for loss, damage or delay in delivery caused by an occurrence which takes place while the goods are in the charge of the actual carrier during such part of the carriage. Nevertheless, any stipulation limiting or excluding such liability is without effect if no judicial proceedings can be instituted against the actual carrier in a court competent under paragraph 1 or 2 of article 21. The burden of proving that any loss, damage or delay in delivery has been caused by such an occurrence rests upon the carrier.

2.   The actual carrier is responsible in accordance with the provisions of paragraph 2 of article 10 for loss, damage or delay in delivery caused by an occurrence which takes place while the goods are in his charge.

[4040]

PART III
LIABILITY OF THE SHIPPER

Article 12
General rule

The shipper is not liable for loss sustained by the carrier or the actual carrier, or for damage sustained by the ship, unless such loss or damage was caused by the fault or neglect of the shipper, his servants or agents. Nor is any servant or agent of the shipper liable for such loss or damage unless the loss or damage was caused by fault or neglect on his part.

[4041]

Article 13
Special rules on dangerous goods

1.   The shipper must mark or label in a suitable manner dangerous goods as dangerous.

2.   Where the shipper hands over dangerous goods to the carrier or an actual carrier, as the case may be, the shipper must inform him of the dangerous character of the goods and, if necessary, of the precautions to be taken. If the shipper fails to do so and such carrier or actual carrier does not otherwise have knowledge of their dangerous character—

    (a)   the shipper is liable to the carrier and any actual carrier for the loss resulting from the shipment of such goods, and

    (b)   the goods may at any time be unloaded, destroyed or rendered innocuous, as the circumstances may require, without payment of compensation.

3.   The provisions of paragraph 2 of this article may not be invoked by any person if during the carriage he has taken the goods in his charge with knowledge of their dangerous character.

4.   If, in cases where the provisions of paragraph 2, subparagraph (b), of this article do not apply or may not be invoked, dangerous goods become an actual danger to life or property, they may be unloaded, destroyed or rendered innocuous, as the circumstances may require, without payment of compensation except where there is an obligation to contribute in general average or where the carrier is liable in accordance with the provisions of article 5.

[4042]

PART IV
TRANSPORT DOCUMENTS

Article 14
Issue of bill of lading

1.   When the carrier or the actual carrier takes the goods in his charge, the carrier must, on demand of the shipper, issue to the shipper a bill of lading.

2.   The bill of lading may be signed by a person having authority from the carrier. A bill of lading signed by the master of the ship carrying the goods is deemed to have been signed on behalf of the carrier.

3.   The signature on the bill of lading may be in handwriting, printed in facsimile, perforated, stamped, in symbols, or made by any other mechanical or electronic means, if not inconsistent with the law of the country where the bill of lading is issued.

[4043]

Article 15
Contents of bill of lading

1.   The bill of lading must include, *inter alia*, the following particulars—

   (a)   the general nature of the goods, the leading marks necessary for identification of the goods, an express statement, if applicable, as to the dangerous character of the goods, the number of packages or pieces, and the weight of the goods or their quantity otherwise expressed, all such particulars as furnished by the shipper;
   (b)   the apparent condition of the goods;
   (c)   the name and principal place of business of the carrier;
   (d)   the name of the shipper;
   (e)   the consignee if named by the shipper;
   (f)   the port of loading under the contract of carriage by sea and the date on which the goods were taken over by the carrier at the port of loading;
   (g)   the port of discharge under the contract of carriage by sea;
   (h)   the number of originals of the bill of lading, if more than one;
   (i)   the place of issuance of the bill of lading;
   (j)   the signature of the carrier or a person acting on his behalf;
   (k)   the freight to the extent payable by the consignee or other indication that freight is payable by him;
   (l)   the statement referred to in paragraph 3 of article 23;
   (m)   the statement, if applicable, that the goods shall or may be carried on deck;
   (n)   the date or the period of delivery of the goods at the port of discharge if expressly agreed upon between the parties; and
   (o)   any increased limit or limits of liability where agreed in accordance with paragraph 4 of article 6.

2.   After the goods have been loaded on board, if the shipper so demands, the carrier must issue to the shipper a "shipped" bill of lading which, in addition to the particulars required under paragraph 1 of this article, must state that the goods are on board a named ship or ships, and the date or dates of loading. If the carrier has previously issued to the shipper a bill of lading or other document of title with respect to any of such goods, on request of the carrier the shipper must surrender such document in exchange for a "shipped" bill of lading. The carrier may amend any previously issued document in order to meet the shipper's demand for a "shipped" bill of lading if, as amended, such document includes all the information required to be contained in a "shipped" bill of lading.

3.   The absence in the bill of lading of one or more particulars referred to in this article does not affect the legal character of the document as a bill of lading provided that it nevertheless meets the requirements set out in paragraph 7 of article 1.

[4044]

Article 16
Bills of lading: reservations and evidentiary effect

1.   If the bill of lading contains particulars concerning the general nature, leading marks, number of packages or pieces, weight or quantity of the goods which the carrier or other person

issuing the bill of lading on his behalf knows or has reasonable grounds to suspect do not accurately represent the goods actually taken over or, where a "shipped" bill of lading is issued, loaded, or if he had no reasonable means of checking such particulars, the carrier or such other person must insert in the bill of lading a reservation specifying these inaccuracies, grounds of suspicion or the absence of reasonable means of checking.

2.   If the carrier or other person issuing the bill of lading on his behalf fails to note on the bill of lading the apparent condition of the goods, he is deemed to have noted on the bill of lading that the goods were in apparent good condition.

3.   Except for particulars in respect of which and to the extent to which a reservation permitted under paragraph 1 of this article has been entered—

    (a)   the bill of lading is *prima facie* evidence of the taking over or, where a "shipped" bill of lading is issued, loading, by the carrier of the goods as described in the bill of lading; and

    (b)   proof to the contrary by the carrier is not admissible if the bill of lading has been transferred to a third party, including a consignee, who in good faith has acted in reliance on the description of the goods therein.

4.   A bill of lading which does not, as provided in paragraph 1, subparagraph (k), of article 15, set forth the freight or otherwise indicate that freight is payable by the consignee or does not set forth demurrage incurred at the port of loading payable by the consignee, is *prima facie* evidence that no freight or such demurrage is payable by him. However, proof to the contrary by the carrier is not admissible when the bill of lading has been transferred to a third party, including a consignee, who in good faith has acted in reliance on the absence in the bill of lading of any such indication.

[4045]

Article 17
Guarantees by the shipper

1.   The shipper is deemed to have guaranteed to the carrier the accuracy of particulars relating to the general nature of the goods, their marks, number, weight and quantity as furnished by him for insertion in the bill of lading. The shipper must indemnify the carrier against the loss resulting from inaccuracies in such particulars. The shipper remains liable even if the bill of lading has been transferred by him. The right of the carrier to such indemnity in no way limits his liability under the contract of carriage by sea to any person other than the shipper.

2.   Any letter of guarantee or agreement by which the shipper undertakes to indemnify the carrier against loss resulting from the issuance of the bill of lading by the carrier, or by a person acting on his behalf, without entering a reservation relating to particulars furnished by the shipper for insertion in the bill of lading, or to the apparent condition of the goods, is void and of no effect as against any third party, including a consignee, to whom the bill of lading has been transferred.

3.   Such a letter of guarantee or agreement is valid as against the shipper unless the carrier or the person acting on his behalf, by omitting the reservation referred to in paragraph 2 of this article, intends to defraud a third party, including a consignee, who acts in reliance on the description of the goods in the bill of lading. In the latter case, if the reservation omitted relates to particulars furnished by the shipper for insertion in the bill of lading, the carrier has no right of indemnity from the shipper pursuant to paragraph 1 of this article.

4.   In the case of intended fraud referred to in paragraph 3 of this article, the carrier is liable, without the benefit of the limitation of liability provided for in this Convention, for the loss incurred by a third party, including a consignee, because he has acted in reliance on the description of the goods in the bill of lading.

[4046]

Article 18
Documents other than bills of lading

Where a carrier issues a document other than a bill of lading to evidence the receipt of the goods to be carried, such a document is *prima facie* evidence of the conclusion of the contract of carriage by sea and the taking over by the carrier of the goods as therein described.

[4047]

PART V
CLAIMS AND ACTIONS

Article 19
Notice of loss, damage or delay

1.   Unless notice of loss or damage, specifying the general nature of such loss or damage, is given in writing by the consignee to the carrier not later than the working day after the day when the goods were handed over to the consignee, such handing over is *prima facie* evidence of the delivery by the carrier of the goods as described in the document of transport or, if no such document has been issued, in good condition.

2. Where the loss or damage is not apparent, the provisions of paragraph 1 of this article apply correspondingly if notice in writing is not given within 15 consecutive days after the day when the goods were handed over to the consignee.

3. If the state of the goods at the time they were handed over to the consignee has been the subject of a joint survey or inspection by the parties, notice in writing need not be given of loss or damage ascertained during such survey or inspection.

4. In the case of any actual or apprehended loss or damage, the carrier and the consignee must give all reasonable facilities to each other for inspecting and tallying the goods.

5. No compensation shall be payable for loss resulting from delay in delivery unless a notice has been given in writing to the carrier within 60 consecutive days after the day when the goods were handed over to the consignee.

6. If the goods have been delivered by an actual carrier, any notice given under this article to him shall have the same effect as if it had been given to the carrier; and any notice given to the carrier shall have effect as if given to such actual carrier.

7. Unless notice of loss or damage, specifying the general nature of the loss or damage, is given in writing by the carrier or actual carrier to the shipper not later than 90 consecutive days after the occurrence of such loss or damage or after the delivery of the goods in accordance with paragraph 2 of article 4, whichever is later, the failure to give such notice is *prima facie* evidence that the carrier or the actual carrier has sustained no loss or damage due to the fault or neglect of the shipper, his servants or agents.

8. For the purpose of this article, notice given to a person acting on the carrier's or the actual carrier's behalf, including the master or the officer in charge of the ship, or to a person acting on the shipper's behalf is deemed to have been given to the carrier, to the actual carrier or to the shipper, respectively.

[4048]

Article 20
Limitation of actions

1. Any action relating to carriage of goods under this Convention is time-barred if judicial or arbitral proceedings have not been instituted within a period of two years.

2. The limitation period commences on the day on which the carrier has delivered the goods or part thereof or, in cases where no goods have been delivered, on the last day on which the goods should have been delivered.

3. The day on which the limitation period commences is not included in the period.

4. The person against whom a claim is made may at any time during the running of the limitation period extend that period by a declaration in writing to the claimant. This period may be further extended by another declaration or declarations.

5. An action for indemnity by a person held liable may be instituted even after the expiration of the limitation period provided for in the preceding paragraphs if instituted within the time allowed by the law of the State where proceedings are instituted. However, the time allowed shall not be less than 90 days commencing from the day when the person instituting such action for indemnity has settled the claim or has been served with process in the action against himself.

[4049]

Article 21
Jurisdiction

1. In judicial proceedings relating to carriage of goods under this Convention the plaintiff, at his option, may institute an action in a court which according to the law of the State where the court is situated, is competent and within the jurisdiction of which is situated one of the following places—

   (a)   the principal place of business or, in the absence thereof, the habitual residence of the defendant; or
   (b)   the place where the contract was made, provided that the defendant has there a place of business, branch or agency through which the contract was made; or
   (c)   the port of loading or the port of discharge; or
   (d)   any additional place designated for that purpose in the contract of carriage by sea.

2.

   (a)   Notwithstanding the preceding provisions of this article, an action may be instituted in the courts of any port or place in a Contracting State at which the carrying vessel or any other vessel of the same ownership may have been arrested in accordance with applicable rules of the law of that State and of international law. However, in such a case, at the petition of the defendant, the claimant must remove the action, at his choice, to one of the jurisdictions referred to in paragraph 1 of this article for the determination of the claim, but before such removal the defendant must furnish security sufficient to ensure payment of any judgment that may subsequently be awarded to the claimant in the action.

  (b)   All questions relating to the sufficiency or otherwise of the security shall be determined by the court of the port or place of the arrest.

3.   No judicial proceedings relating to carriage of goods under this Convention may be instituted in a place not specified in paragraph 1 or 2 of this article. The provisions of this paragraph do not constitute an obstacle to the jurisdiction of the Contracting States for provisional or protective measures.

4.

  (a)   Where an action has been instituted in a court competent under paragraphs 1 and 2 of this article or where judgment has been delivered by such a court, no new action may be started between the same parties on the same grounds unless the judgment of the court before which the first action was instituted is not enforceable in the country in which the new proceedings are instituted;

  (b)   for the purpose of this article, the institution of measures with a view to obtaining enforcement of a judgment is not to be considered as the starting of a new action;

  (c)   for the purpose of this article, the removal of an action to a different court within the same country, or to a court in another country, in accordance with paragraph 2(a) of this article, is not to be considered as the starting of a new action.

5.   Notwithstanding the provisions of the preceding paragraphs, an agreement made by the parties, after a claim under the contract of carriage by sea has arisen, which designates the place where the claimant may institute an action, is effective.

[4050]

Article 22
Arbitration

1.   Subject to the provisions of this article, parties may provide by agreement evidenced in writing that any dispute that may arise relating to carriage of goods under this Convention shall be referred to arbitration.

2.   Where a charter-party contains a provision that disputes arising thereunder shall be referred to arbitration and a bill of lading issued pursuant to the charter-party does not contain a special annotation providing that such provision shall be binding upon the holder of the bill of lading, the carrier may not invoke such provision as against a holder having acquired the bill of lading in good faith.

3.   The arbitration proceedings shall, at the option of the claimant, be instituted at one of the following places—

  (a)   a place in a State within whose territory is situated—

     (i)   the principal place of business of the defendant or, in the absence thereof, the habitual residence of the defendant; or

    (ii)   the place where the contract was made, provided that the defendant has there a place of business, branch or agency through which the contract was made; or

    (iii)   the port of loading or the port of discharge; or

  (b)   any place designated for that purpose in the arbitration clause or agreement.

4.   The arbitrator or arbitration tribunal shall apply the rules of this Convention.

5.   The provisions of paragraphs 3 and 4 of this article are deemed to be part of every arbitration clause or agreement, and any term of such clause or agreement which is inconsistent therewith is null and void.

6.   Nothing in this article affects the validity of an agreement relating to arbitration made by the parties after the claim under the contract of carriage by sea has arisen.

[4051]

PART VI
SUPPLEMENTARY PROVISIONS

Article 23
Contractual stipulations

1.   Any stipulation in a contract of carriage by sea, in a bill of lading, or in any other document evidencing the contract of carriage by sea is null and void to the extent that it derogates, directly or indirectly, from the provisions of this Convention. The nullity of such a stipulation does not affect the validity of the other provisions of the contract or document of which it forms a part. A clause assigning benefit of insurance of goods in favour of the carrier, or any similar clause, is null and void.

2.   Notwithstanding the provisions of paragraph 1 of this article, a carrier may increase his responsibilities and obligations under this Convention.

3. Where a bill of lading or any other document evidencing the contract of carriage by sea is issued, it must contain a statement that the carriage is subject to the provisions of this Convention which nullify any stipulation derogating therefrom to the detriment of the shipper or the consignee.

4. Where the claimant in respect of the goods has incurred loss as a result of a stipulation which is null and void by virtue of the present article, or as a result of the omission of the statement referred to in paragraph 3 of this article, the carrier must pay compensation to the extent required in order to give the claimant compensation in accordance with the provisions of this Convention for any loss of or damage to the goods as well as for delay in delivery. The carrier must, in addition, pay compensation for costs incurred by the claimant for the purpose of exercising his right, provided that costs incurred in the action where the foregoing provision is invoked are to be determined in accordance with the law of the State where proceedings are instituted.

[4052]

Article 24
General average

1. Nothing in this Convention shall prevent the application of provisions in the contract of carriage by sea or national law regarding the adjustment of general average.

2. With the exception of article 20, the provisions of this Convention relating to the liability of the carrier for loss of or damage to the goods also determine whether the consignee may refuse contribution in general average and the liability of the carrier to indemnify the consignee in respect of any such contribution made or any salvage paid.

[4053]

Article 25
Other conventions

1. This Convention does not modify the rights or duties of the carrier, the actual carrier and their servants and agents, provided for in international conventions or national law relating to the limitation of liability of owners of seagoing ships.

2. The provisions of articles 21 and 22 of this Convention do not prevent the application of the mandatory provisions of any other multilateral convention already in force at the date of this Convention relating to matters dealt with in the said articles, provided that the dispute arises exclusively between parties having their principal place of business in States members of such other convention. However, this paragraph does not affect the application of paragraph 4 of article 22 of this Convention.

3. No liability shall arise under the provisions of this Convention for damage caused by a nuclear incident if the operator of a nuclear installation is liable for such damage—
   (a) under either the Paris Convention of 29 July 1960 on Third Party Liability in the Field of Nuclear Energy as amended by the Additional Protocol of 28 January 1964, or the Vienna Convention of 21 May 1963 on Civil Liability for Nuclear Damage, or
   (b) by virtue of national law governing the liability for such damage, provided that such law is in all respects as favourable to persons who may suffer damage as either the Paris Convention or the Vienna Convention.

4. No liability shall arise under the provisions of this Convention for any loss of or damage to or delay in delivery of luggage for which the carrier is responsible under any international convention or national law relating to the carriage of passengers and their luggage by sea.

5. Nothing contained in this Convention prevents a Contracting State from applying any other international convention which is already in force at the date of this Convention and which applies mandatorily to contracts of carriage of goods primarily by a mode of transport other than transport by sea. This provision also applies to any subsequent revision or amendment of such international convention.

[4054]

Article 26
Unit of account

1. The unit of account referred to in article 6 of this Convention is the special drawing right as defined by the International Monetary Fund. The amounts mentioned in article 6 are to be converted into the national currency of a State according to the value of such currency at the date of judgment or the date agreed upon by the parties. The value of a national currency, in terms of the special drawing right, of a Contracting State which is a member of the International Monetary Fund is to be calculated in accordance with the method of valuation applied by the International Monetary Fund in effect at the date in question for its operations and transactions. The value of a national currency, in terms of the special drawing right, of a Contracting State which is not a member of the International Monetary Fund is to be calculated in a manner determined by that State.

2. Nevertheless, those States which are not members of the International Monetary Fund and whose law does not permit the application of the provisions of paragraph 1 of this article may, at the

time of signature, or at the time of ratification, acceptance, approval or accession or at any time thereafter, declare that the limits of liability provided for in this Convention to be applied in their territories shall be fixed as 12,500 monetary units per package or other shipping unit or 37.5 monetary units per kilogram of gross weight of the goods.

3.   The monetary unit referred to in paragraph 2 of this article corresponds to sixty-five and a half milligrams of gold of millesimal fineness nine hundred. The conversion of the amounts referred to in paragraph 2 into the national currency is to be made according to the law of the State concerned.

4.   The calculation mentioned in the last sentence of paragraph 1 and the conversion mentioned in paragraph 3 of this article is to be made in such a manner as to express in the national currency of the Contracting State as far as possible the same real value for the amounts in article 6 as is expressed there in units of account. Contracting States must communicate to the depositary the manner of calculation pursuant to paragraph 1 of this article, or the result of the conversion mentioned in paragraph 3 of this article, as the case may be, at the time of signature or when depositing their instruments of ratification, acceptance, approval or accession, or when availing themselves of the option provided for in paragraph 2 of this article and whenever there is a change in the manner of such calculation or in the result of such conversion.

[4055]

PART VII
FINAL CLAUSES

Article 27
Depository
The Secretary-General of the United Nations is hereby designated as the depositary of this Convention.

[4056]

Article 28
Signature, Ratification, Acceptance, Approval, Accession
1.   This Convention is open for signature by all States until 30 April 1979 at the Headquarters of the United Nations, New York.

2.   This Convention is subject to ratification, acceptance or approval by the signatory States.

3.   After 30 April 1979, this Convention will be open for accession by all States which are not signatory States.

4.   Instruments of ratification, acceptance, approval and accession are to be deposited with the Secretary-General of the United Nations.

[4057]

Article 29
Reservations
No reservations may be made to this Convention.

[4058]

Article 30
Entry into force
1.   This Convention enters into force on the first day of the month following the expiration of one year from the date of deposit of the twentieth instrument of ratification, acceptance, approval or accession.

2.   For each State which becomes a Contracting State to this Convention after the date of the deposit of the twentieth instrument of ratification, acceptance, approval or accession, this Convention enters into force on the first day of the month following the expiration of one year after the deposit of the appropriate instrument on behalf of that State.

3.   Each Contracting State shall apply the provisions of this Convention to contracts of carriage by sea concluded on or after the date of the entry into force of this Convention in respect of that State.

[4059]

Article 31
Denunciation of other conventions
1.   Upon becoming a Contracting State to this Convention, any State party to the International Convention for the Unification of certain Rules relating to Bills of Lading signed at Brussels on 25 August 1924 (1924 Convention) must notify the Government of Belgium as the depositary of the 1924 Convention of its denunciation of the said Convention with a declaration that the denunciation is to take effect as from the date when this Convention enters into force in respect of that State.

2.   Upon the entry into force of this Convention under paragraph 1 of article 30, the depositary of this Convention must notify the Government of Belgium as the depositary of the 1924 Convention of the date of such entry into force, and of the names of the Contracting States in respect of which the Convention has entered into force.

3.   The provisions of paragraphs 1 and 2 of this article apply correspondingly in respect of States parties to the Protocol signed on 23 February 1968 to amend the International Convention for the Unification of certain Rules relating to Bills of Lading signed at Brussels on 25 August 1924.

4.   Notwithstanding article 2 of this Convention, for the purposes of paragraph 1 of this article, a Contracting State may, if it deems it desirable, defer the denunciation of the 1924 Convention and of the 1924 Convention as modified by the 1968 Protocol for a maximum period of five years from the entry into force of this Convention. It will then notify the Government of Belgium of its intention. During this transitory period, it must apply to the Contracting States this Convention to the exclusion of any other one.

[4060]

Article 32
Revision and amendment

1.   At the request of not less than one third of the Contracting States to this Convention, the depositary shall convene a conference of the Contracting States for revising or amending it.

2.   Any instrument of ratification, acceptance, approval or accession deposited after the entry into force of an amendment to this Convention is deemed to apply to the Convention as amended.

[4061]

Article 33
Revision of the limitation amounts and unit of account or monetary unit

1.   Notwithstanding the provisions of article 32, a conference only for the purpose of altering the amount specified in article 6 and paragraph 2 of article 26, or of substituting either or both of the units defined in paragraphs 1 and 3 of article 26 by other units is to be convened by the depositary in accordance with paragraph 2 of this article. An alteration of the amounts shall be made only because of a significant change in their real value.

2.   A revision conference is to be convened by the depositary when not less than one fourth of the Contracting States so request.

3.   Any decision by the conference must be taken by a two thirds majority of the participating States. The amendment is communicated by the depositary to all the Contracting States for acceptance and to all the States signatories of the Convention for information.

4.   Any amendment adopted enters into force on the first day of the month following one year after its acceptance by two thirds of the Contracting States. Acceptance is to be effected by the deposit of a formal instrument to that effect with the depositary.

5.   After entry into force of an amendment a Contracting State which has accepted the amendment is entitled to apply the Convention as amended in its relations with Contracting States which have not within six months after the adoption of the amendment notified the depositary that they are not bound by the amendment.

6.   Any instrument of ratification, acceptance, approval or accession deposited after the entry into force of an amendment to this Convention is deemed to apply to the Convention as amended.

[4062]

Article 34
Denunciation

1.   A Contracting State may denounce this Convention at any time by means of a notification in writing addressed to the depositary.

2.   The denunciation takes effect on the first day of the month following the expiration of one year after the notification is received by the depositary. Where a longer period is specified in the notification, the denunciation takes effect upon the expiration of such longer period after the notification is received by the depositary.

[4063]

DONE at Hamburg, this thirty-first day of March, one thousand nine hundred and seventy-eight, in a single original, of which the Arabic, Chinese, English, French, Russian and Spanish texts are equally authentic.

IN WITNESS WHEREOF the undersigned plenipotentiaries, being duly authorised by their respective Governments, have signed the present Convention.

COMMON UNDERSTANDING ADOPTED BY THE UNITED NATIONS CONFERENCE ON THE CARRIAGE OF GOODS BY SEA

It is the common understanding that the liability of the carrier under this Convention is based on the principle of presumed fault or neglect. This means that, as a rule, the burden of proof rests on the carrier but, with respect to certain cases, the provisions of the Convention modify this rule.

RESOLUTION ADOPTED BY THE UNITED NATIONS CONFERENCE ON THE CARRIAGE OF GOODS BY SEA

The United Nations Conference on the Carriage of Goods by Sea,

Noting with appreciation the kind invitation of the Federal Republic of Germany to hold the Conference in Hamburg,

Being aware that the facilities placed at the disposal of the Conference and the generous hospitality bestowed on the participants by the Government of the Federal Republic of Germany and by the Free and Hanseatic City of Hamburg, have in no small measure contributed to the success of the Conference,

Expresses its gratitude to the Government and people of the Federal Republic of Germany, and

Having adopted the Convention on the Carriage of Goods by Sea on the basis of a draft Convention prepared by the United Nations Commission on International Trade Law at the request of the United Nations Conference on Trade and Development,

Expresses its gratitude to the United Nations Commission on International Trade Law and to the United Nations Conference on Trade and Development for their outstanding contribution to the simplification and harmonisation of the law of the carriage of goods by sea, and

Decides to designate the Convention adopted by the Conference as the—

'UNITED NATIONS CONVENTION ON THE CARRIAGE OF GOODS BY SEA', 1978, and

Recommends that the rues embodied therein be known as the 'HAMBURG RULES'.

[4064]

NOTES

The text of this Convention was prepared by the United Nations Commission on International Trade Law.

UNITED NATIONS CONVENTION ON CONTRACTS FOR THE INTERNATIONAL SALE OF GOODS, 1980

The States Parties to this Convention,

Bearing in mind the broad objectives in the resolutions adopted by the sixth special session of the General Assembly of the United Nations on the establishment of a New International Economic Order,

Considering that the development of international trade on the basis of equality and mutual benefit is an important element in promoting friendly relations among States,

Being of the opinion that the adoption of uniform rules which govern contracts for the international sale of goods and take into account the different social, economic and legal systems would contribute to the removal of legal barriers in international trade and promote the development of international trade,

Have agreed as follows—

PART I
SPHERE OF APPLICATION AND GENERAL PROVISIONS

CHAPTER I
SPHERE OF APPLICATION

Article 1

(1)   This Convention applies to contracts of sale of goods between parties whose places of business are in different States—
  (a)   when the States are Contracting States; or
  (b)   when the rules of private international law lead to the application of the law of a Contracting State.

(2)   The fact that the parties have their places of business in different States is to be disregarded whenever this fact does not appear either from the contract or from any dealings between, or from information disclosed by, the parties at any time before or at the conclusion of the contract.

(3)   Neither the nationality of the parties nor the civil or commercial character of the parties or of the contract is to be taken into consideration in determining the application of this Convention.

[4065]

Article 2

This Convention does not apply to sales—

(a)   of goods bought for personal, family or household use, unless the seller, at any time before or at the conclusion of the contract, neither knew nor ought to have known that the goods were bought for any such use;

(b)   by auction;

(c)   on execution or otherwise by authority of law;

(d)   of stocks, shares, investment securities, negotiable instruments or money;

(e)   of ships, vessels, hovercraft or aircraft;

(f)   of electricity.

[4066]

Article 3

(1)   Contracts for the supply of goods to be manufactured or produced are to be considered sales unless the party who orders the goods undertakes to supply a substantial part of the materials necessary for such manufacture or production.

(2)   This Convention does not apply to contracts in which the preponderant part of the obligations of the party who furnishes the goods consists in the supply of labour or other services.

[4067]

Article 4

This Convention governs only the formation of the contract of sale and the rights and obligations of the seller and the buyer arising from such a contract. In particular, except as otherwise expressly provided in this Convention, it is not concerned with—

(a)   the validity of the contract or of any of its provisions or of any usage;

(b)   the effect which the contract may have on the property in the goods sold.

[4068]

Article 5

This Convention does not apply to the liability of the seller for death or personal injury caused by the goods to any person.

[4069]

Article 6

The parties may exclude the application of this Convention or, subject to article 12, derogate from or vary the effect of any of its provisions.

[4070]

CHAPTER II
GENERAL PROVISIONS

Article 7

(1)   In the interpretation of this Convention, regard is to be had to its international character and to the need to promote uniformity in its application and the observance of good faith in international trade.

(2)   Questions concerning matters governed by this Convention which are not expressly settled in it are to be settled in conformity with the general principles on which it is based or, in the absence of such principles, in conformity with the law applicable by virtue of the rules of private international law.

[4071]

Article 8

(1)   For the purposes of this Convention statements made by and other conduct of a party are to be interpreted according to his intent where the other party knew or could not have been unaware what that intent was.

(2)   If the preceding paragraph is not applicable, statements made by and other conduct of a party are to be interpreted according to the understanding that a reasonable person of the same kind as the other party would have had in the same circumstances.

(3)   In determining the intent of a party or the understanding a reasonable person would have had, due consideration is to be given to all relevant circumstances of the case including the negotiations, any practices which the parties have established between themselves, usages and any subsequent conduct of the parties.

[4072]

Article 9

(1)   The parties are bound by any usage to which they have agreed and by any practices which they have established between themselves.

(2)   The parties are considered, unless otherwise agreed, to have impliedly made applicable to their contract or its formation a usage of which the parties knew or ought to have known and which in international trade is widely known to, and regularly observed by, parties to contracts of the type involved in the particular trade concerned.

[4073]

Article 10

For the purposes of this Convention—
- (a)   if a party has more than one place of business, the place of business is that which has the closest relationship to the contract and its performance, having regard to the circumstances known to or contemplated by the parties at any time before or at the conclusion of the contract;
- (b)   if a party does not have a place of business, reference is to be made to his habitual residence.

[4074]

Article 11

A contract of sale need not be concluded in or evidenced by writing and is not subject to any other requirement as to form. It may be proved by any means, including witnesses.

[4075]

Article 12

Any provision of article 11, article 29 or Part II of this Convention that allows a contract of sale or its modification or termination by agreement or any offer, acceptance or other indication of intention to be made in any form other than in writing does not apply where any party has his place of business in a Contracting State which has made a declaration under article 96 of this Convention. The parties may not derogate from or vary the effect of this article.

[4076]

Article 13

For the purposes of this Convention "writing" includes telegram and telex.

[4077]

PART II
FORMATION OF THE CONTRACT

Article 14

(1)   A proposal for concluding a contract addressed to one or more specific persons constitutes an offer if it is sufficiently definite and indicates the intention of the offeror to be bound in case of acceptance. A proposal is sufficiently definite if it indicates the goods and expressly or implicitly fixes or makes provision for determining the quantity and the price.

(2)   A proposal other than one addressed to one or more specific persons is to be considered merely as an invitation to make offers, unless the contrary is clearly indicated by the person making the proposal.

[4078]

Article 15

(1)   An offer becomes effective when it reaches the offeree.

(2)   An offer, even if it is irrevocable, may be withdrawn if the withdrawal reaches the offeree before or at the same time as the offer.

[4079]

Article 16

(1)   Until a contract is concluded an offer may be revoked if the revocation reaches the offeree before he has dispatched an acceptance.

(2)   However, an offer cannot be revoked—
- (a)   if it indicates, whether by stating a fixed time for acceptance or otherwise, that it is irrevocable; or
- (b)   if it was reasonable for the offeree to rely on the offer as being irrevocable and the offeree has acted in reliance on the offer.

[4080]

Article 17

An offer, even if it is irrevocable, is terminated when a rejection reaches the offeror.

[4081]

Article 18

(1)   A statement made by or other conduct of the offeree indicating assent to an offer is an acceptance. Silence or inactivity does not in itself amount to acceptance.

(2)   An acceptance of an offer becomes effective at the moment the indication of assent reaches the offeror. An acceptance is not effective if the indication of assent does not reach the offeror within the time he has fixed or, if no time is fixed, within a reasonable time, due account being taken of the circumstances of the transaction, including the rapidity of the means of communication employed by the offeror. An oral offer must be accepted immediately unless the circumstances indicate otherwise.

(3)   However, if, by virtue of the offer or as a result of practices which the parties have established between themselves or of usage, the offeree may indicate assent by performing an act, such as one relating to the dispatch of the goods or payment of the price, without notice to the offeror, the acceptance is effective at the moment the act is performed, provided that the act is performed within the period of time laid down in the preceding paragraph.

[4082]

Article 19

(1)   A reply to an offer which purports to be an acceptance but contains additions, limitations or other modifications is a rejection of the offer and constitutes a counter-offer.

(2)   However, a reply to an offer which purports to be an acceptance but contains additional or different terms which do not materially alter the terms of the offer constitutes an acceptance, unless the offeror, without undue delay, objects orally to the discrepancy or dispatches a notice to that effect. If he does not so object, the terms of the contract are the terms of the offer with the modifications contained in the acceptance.

(3)   Additional or different terms relating, among other things, to the price, payment, quality and quantity of the goods, place and time of delivery, extent of one party's liability to the other or the settlement of disputes are considered to alter the terms of the offer materially.

[4083]

Article 20

(1)   A period of time for acceptance fixed by the offeror in a telegram or a letter begins to run from the moment the telegram is handed in for dispatch or from the date shown on the letter or, if no such date is shown, from the date shown on the envelope. A period of time for acceptance fixed by the offeror by telephone, telex or other means of instantaneous communication, begins to run from the moment that the offer reaches the offeree.

(2)   Official holidays or non-business days occurring during the period for acceptance are included in calculating the period. However, if a notice of acceptance cannot be delivered at the address of the offeror on the last day of the period because that day falls on an official holiday or a non-business day at the place of business of the offeror, the period is extended until the first business day which follows.

[4084]

Article 21

(1)   A late acceptance is nevertheless effective as an acceptance if without delay the offeror orally so informs the offeree or dispatches a notice to that effect.

(2)   If a letter or other writing containing a late acceptance shows that it has been sent in such circumstances that if its transmission had been normal it would have reached the offeror in due time, the late acceptance is effective as an acceptance unless, without delay, the offeror orally informs the offeree that he considers his offer as having lapsed or dispatches a notice to that effect.

[4085]

Article 22

An acceptance may be withdrawn if the withdrawal reaches the offeror before or at the same time as the acceptance would have become effective.

[4086]

Article 23

A contract is concluded at the moment when an acceptance of an offer becomes effective in accordance with the provisions of this Convention.

[4087]

Article 24

For the purposes of this Part of the Convention, an offer, declaration of acceptance or any other indication of intention "reaches" the addressee when it is made orally to him or delivered by any other means to him personally, to his place of business or mailing address or, if he does not have a place of business or mailing address, to his habitual residence.

[4088]

PART III
SALE OF GOODS

CHAPTER I
GENERAL PROVISIONS

Article 25

A breach of contract committed by one of the parties is fundamental if it results in such detriment to the other party as substantially to deprive him of what he is entitled to expect under the contract, unless the party in breach did not foresee and a reasonable person of the same kind in the same circumstances would not have foreseen such a result.

[4089]

Article 26

A declaration of avoidance of the contract is effective only if made by notice to the other party.

[4090]

Article 27

Unless otherwise expressly provided in this Part of the Convention, if any notice, request or other communication is given or made by a party in accordance with this Part and by means appropriate in the circumstances, a delay or error in the transmission of the communication or its failure to arrive does not deprive that party of the right to rely on the communication.

[4091]

Article 28

If, in accordance with the provisions of this Convention, one party is entitled to require performance of any obligation by the other party, a court is not bound to enter a judgment for specific performance unless the court would do so under its own law in respect of similar contracts of sale not governed by this Convention.

[4092]

Article 29

(1)   A contract may be modified or terminated by the mere agreement of the parties.

(2)   A contract in writing which contains a provision requiring any modification or termination by agreement to be in writing may not be otherwise modified or terminated by agreement. However, a party may be precluded by his conduct from asserting such a provision to the extent that the other party has relied on that conduct.

[4093]

CHAPTER II
OBLIGATIONS OF THE SELLER

Article 30

The seller must deliver the goods, hand over any documents relating to them and transfer the property in the goods, as required by the contract and this Convention.

[4094]

SECTION I
DELIVERY OF THE GOODS AND HANDING OVER OF DOCUMENTS

Article 31

If the seller is not bound to deliver the goods at any other particular place, his obligation to deliver consists—

    (a)   if the contract of sale involves carriage of the goods—in handing the goods over to the first carrier for transmission to the buyer;

    (b)   if, in cases not within the preceding subparagraph, the contract relates to specific goods, or unidentified goods to be drawn from a specific stock or to be manufactured or produced, and at the time of the conclusion of the contract the parties knew that the goods were at, or were to be manufactured or produced at, a particular place—in placing the goods at the buyer's disposal at that place;

    (c)   in other cases—in placing the goods at the buyer's disposal at the place where the seller had his place of business at the time of the conclusion of the contract.

[4095]

Article 32

(1)   If the seller, in accordance with the contract or this Convention, hands the goods over to a carrier and if the goods are not clearly identified to the contract by markings on the goods, by shipping documents or otherwise, the seller must give the buyer notice of the consignment specifying the goods.

(2)   If the seller is bound to arrange for carriage of the goods, he must make such contracts as are necessary for carriage to the place fixed by means of transportation appropriate in the circumstances and according to the usual terms for such transportation.

(3)   If the seller is not bound to effect insurance in respect of the carriage of the goods, he must, at the buyer's request, provide him with all available information necessary to enable him to effect such insurance.

[4096]

Article 33

The seller must deliver the goods—
    (a)   if a date is fixed by or determinable from the contract, on that date;
    (b)   if a period of time is fixed by or determinable from the contract, at any time within that period unless circumstances indicate that the buyer is to choose a date; or
    (c)   in any other case, within a reasonable time after the conclusion of the contract.

[4097]

Article 34

If the seller is bound to hand over documents relating to the goods, he must hand them over at the time and place and in the form required by the contract. If the seller has handed over documents before that time, he may, up to that time, cure any lack of conformity in the documents, if the exercise of this right does not cause the buyer unreasonable inconvenience or unreasonable expense. However, the buyer retains any right to claim damages as provided for in this Convention.

[4098]

SECTION II
CONFORMITY OF THE GOODS AND THIRD PARTY CLAIMS

Article 35

(1)   The seller must deliver goods which are of the quantity, quality and description required by the contract and which are contained or packaged in the manner required by the contract.

(2)   Except where the parties have agreed otherwise, the goods do not conform with the contract unless they—
    (a)   are fit for the purposes for which goods of the same description would ordinarily be used;
    (b)   are fit for any particular purpose expressly or impliedly made known to the seller at the time of the conclusion of the contract, except where the circumstances show that the buyer did not rely, or that it was unreasonable for him to rely, on the seller's skill and judgment;
    (c)   possess the qualities of goods which the seller has held out to the buyer as a sample or model;
    (d)   are contained or packaged in the manner usual for such goods or, where there is no such manner, in a manner adequate to preserve and protect the goods.

(3)   The seller is not liable under subparagraphs (a) to (d) of the preceding paragraph for any lack of conformity of the goods if at the time of the conclusion of the contract the buyer knew or could not have been unaware of such lack of conformity.

[4099]

Article 36

(1)   The seller is liable in accordance with the contract and this Convention for any lack of conformity which exists at the time when the risk passes to the buyer, even though the lack of conformity becomes apparent only after that time.

(2)   The seller is also liable for any lack of conformity which occurs after the time indicated in the preceding paragraph and which is due to a breach of any of his obligations, including a breach of any guarantee that for a period of time the goods will remain fit for their ordinary purpose or for some particular purpose or will retain specified qualities or characteristics.

[4100]

Article 37

If the seller has delivered goods before the date for delivery, he may, up to that date, deliver any missing part or make up any deficiency in the quantity of the goods delivered, or deliver goods in replacement of any non-conforming goods delivered or remedy any lack of conformity in the goods delivered, provided that the exercise of this right does not cause the buyer unreasonable inconvenience or unreasonable expense. However, the buyer retains any right to claim damages as provided for in this Convention.

[4101]

Article 38

(1)   The buyer must examine the goods, or cause them to be examined, within as short a period as is practicable in the circumstances.

(2)   If the contract involves carriage of the goods, examination may be deferred until after the goods have arrived at their destination.

(3)   If the goods are redirected in transit or redispatched by the buyer without a reasonable opportunity for examination by him and at the time of the conclusion of the contract the seller knew or ought to have known of the possibility of such redirection or redispatch, examination may be deferred until after the goods have arrived at the new destination.

[4102]

Article 39

(1)   The buyer loses the right to rely on a lack of conformity of the goods if he does not give notice to the seller specifying the nature of the lack of conformity within a reasonable time after he has discovered it or ought to have discovered it.

(2)   In any event, the buyer loses the right to rely on a lack of conformity of the goods if he does not give the seller notice thereof at the latest within a period of two years from the date on which the goods were actually handed over to the buyer, unless this time-limit is inconsistent with a contractual period of guarantee.

[4103]

Article 40

The seller is not entitled to rely on the provisions of articles 38 and 39 if the lack of conformity relates to facts of which he knew or could not have been unaware and which he did not disclose to the buyer.

[4104]

Article 41

The seller must deliver goods which are free from any right or claim of a third party, unless the buyer agreed to take the goods subject to that right or claim. However, if such right or claim is based on industrial property or other intellectual property, the seller's obligation is governed by article 42.

[4105]

Article 42

(1)   The seller must deliver goods which are free from any right or claim of a third party based on industrial property or other intellectual property, of which at the time of the conclusion of the contract the seller knew or could not have been unaware, provided that the right or claim is based on industrial property or other intellectual property—

    (a)   under the law of the State where the goods will be resold or otherwise used, if it was contemplated by the parties at the time of the conclusion of the contract that the goods would be resold or otherwise used in that State; or

    (b)   in any other case, under the law of the State where the buyer has his place of business.

(2)   The obligation of the seller under the preceding paragraph does not extend to cases where—

    (a)   at the time of the conclusion of the contract the buyer knew or could not have been unaware of the right or claim; or

    (b)   the right or claim results from the seller's compliance with technical drawings, designs, formulae or other such specifications furnished by the buyer.

[4106]

Article 43

(1)   The buyer loses the right to rely on the provisions of article 41 or article 42 if he does not give notice to the seller specifying the nature of the right or claim of the third party within a reasonable time after he has become aware or ought to have become aware of the right or claim.

(2)   The seller is not entitled to rely on the provisions of the preceding paragraph if he knew of the right or claim of the third party and the nature of it.

[4107]

PART 3   EU AND INTERNATIONAL MATERIALS

Article 44

Notwithstanding the provisions of paragraph (1) of article 39 and paragraph (1) of article 43, the buyer may reduce the price in accordance with article 50 or claim damages, except for loss of profit, if he has a reasonable excuse for his failure to give the required notice.

[4108]

SECTION III
REMEDIES FOR BREACH OF CONTRACT BY THE SELLER

Article 45

(1)   If the seller fails to perform any of his obligations under the contract or this Convention, the buyer may—
   (a)   exercise the rights provided in articles 46 to 52;
   (b)   claim damages as provided in articles 74 to 77.

(2)   The buyer is not deprived of any right he may have to claim damages by exercising his right to other remedies.

(3)   No period of grace may be granted to the seller by a court or arbitral tribunal when the buyer resorts to a remedy for breach of contract.

[4109]

Article 46

(1)   The buyer may require performance by the seller of his obligations unless the buyer has resorted to a remedy which is inconsistent with this requirement.

(2)   If the goods do not conform with the contract, the buyer may require delivery of substitute goods only if the lack of conformity constitutes a fundamental breach of contract and a request for substitute goods is made either in conjunction with notice given under article 39 or within a reasonable time thereafter.

(3)   If the goods do not conform with the contract, the buyer may require the seller to remedy the lack of conformity by repair, unless this is unreasonable having regard to all the circumstances. A request for repair must be made either in conjunction with notice given under article 39 or within a reasonable time thereafter.

[4110]

Article 47

(1)   The buyer may fix an additional period of time of reasonable length for performance by the seller of his obligations.

(2)   Unless the buyer has received notice from the seller that he will not perform within the period so fixed, the buyer may not, during that period, resort to any remedy for breach of contract. However, the buyer is not deprived thereby of any right he may have to claim damages for delay in performance.

[4111]

Article 48

(1)   Subject to article 49, the seller may, even after the date for delivery, remedy at his own expense any failure to perform his obligations, if he can do so without unreasonable delay and without causing the buyer unreasonable inconvenience or uncertainty of reimbursement by the seller of expenses advanced by the buyer. However, the buyer retains any right to claim damages as provided for in this Convention.

(2)   If the seller requests the buyer to make known whether he will accept performance and the buyer does not comply with the request within a reasonable time, the seller may perform within the time indicated in his request. The buyer may not, during that period of time, resort to any remedy which is inconsistent with performance by the seller.

(3)   A notice by the seller that he will perform within a specified period of time is assumed to include a request, under the preceding paragraph, that the buyer make known his decision.

(4)   A request or notice by the seller under paragraph (2) or (3) of this article is not effective unless received by the buyer.

[4112]

Article 49

(1)   The buyer may declare the contract avoided—
   (a)   if the failure by the seller to perform any of his obligations under the contract or this Convention amounts to a fundamental breach of contract; or
   (b)   in case of non-delivery, if the seller does not deliver the goods within the additional period of time fixed by the buyer in accordance with paragraph (1) of article 47 or declares that he will not deliver within the period so fixed.

(2)   However, in cases where the seller has delivered the goods, the buyer loses the right to declare the contract avoided unless he does so—

(a)   in respect of late delivery, within a reasonable time after he has become aware that delivery has been made;

(b)   in respect of any breach other than late delivery, within a reasonable time—

    (i)   after he knew or ought to have known of the breach;

    (ii)   after the expiration of any additional period of time fixed by the buyer in accordance with paragraph (1) of article 47, or after the seller has declared that he will not perform his obligations within such an additional period; or

    (iii)   after the expiration of any additional period of time indicated by the seller in accordance with paragraph (2) of article 48, or after the buyer has declared that he will not accept performance.

[4113]

Article 50

If the goods do not conform with the contract and whether or not the price has already been paid, the buyer may reduce the price in the same proportion as the value that the goods actually delivered had at the time of the delivery bears to the value that conforming goods would have had at that time. However, if the seller remedies any failure to perform his obligations in accordance with article 37 or article 48 or if the buyer refuses to accept performance by the seller in accordance with those articles, the buyer may not reduce the price.

[4114]

Article 51

(1)   If the seller delivers only a part of the goods or if only a part of the goods delivered is in conformity with the contract, articles 46 to 50 apply in respect of the part which is missing or which does not conform.

(2)   The buyer may declare the contract avoided in its entirety only if the failure to make delivery completely or in conformity with the contract amounts to a fundamental breach of the contract.

[4115]

Article 52

(1)   If the seller delivers the goods before the date fixed, the buyer may take delivery or refuse to take delivery.

(2)   If the seller delivers a quantity of goods greater than that provided for in the contract, the buyer may take delivery or refuse to take delivery of the excess quantity. If the buyer takes delivery of all or part of the excess quantity, he must pay for it at the contract rate.

[4116]

CHAPTER III
OBLIGATIONS OF THE BUYER

Article 53

The buyer must pay the price for the goods and take delivery of them as required by the contract and this Convention.

[4117]

SECTION I
PAYMENT OF THE PRICE

Article 54

The buyer's obligation to pay the price includes taking such steps and complying with such formalities as may be required under the contract or any laws and regulations to enable payment to be made.

[4118]

Article 55

Where a contract has been validly concluded but does not expressly or implicitly fix or make provision for determining the price, the parties are considered, in the absence of any indication to the contrary, to have impliedly made reference to the price generally charged at the time of the conclusion of the contract for such goods sold under comparable circumstances in the trade concerned.

[4119]

Article 56

If the price is fixed according to the weight of goods, in case of doubt it is to be determined by the net weight.

[4120]

Article 57

(1)   If the buyer is not bound to pay the price at any other particular place, he must pay it to the seller—
    (a)   at the seller's place of business; or
    (b)   if the payment is to be made against the handing over of the goods or of documents, at the place where the handing over takes place.

(2)   The seller must bear any increase in the expenses incidental to payment which is caused by a change in his place of business subsequent to the conclusion of the contract.

[4121]

Article 58

(1)   If the buyer is not bound to pay the price at any other specific time he must pay it when the seller places either the goods or documents controlling their disposition at the buyer's disposal in accordance with the contract and this Convention. The seller may make such payment a condition for handing over the goods or documents.

(2)   If the contract involves carriage of the goods, the seller may dispatch the goods on terms whereby the goods, or documents controlling their disposition, will not be handed over to the buyer except against payment of the price.

(3)   The buyer is not bound to pay the price until he has had an opportunity to examine the goods, unless the procedures for delivery or payment agreed upon by the parties are inconsistent with his having such an opportunity.

[4122]

Article 59

The buyer must pay the price on the date fixed by or determinable from the contract and this Convention without the need for any request or compliance with any formality on the part of the seller.

[4123]

SECTION II
TAKING DELIVERY

Article 60

The buyer's obligation to take delivery consists—
    (a)   in doing all the acts which could reasonably be expected of him in order to enable the seller to make delivery; and
    (b)   in taking over the goods.

[4124]

SECTION III
REMEDIES FOR BREACH OF CONTRACT BY THE BUYER

Article 61

(1)   If the buyer fails to perform any of his obligations under the contract or this Convention, the seller may—
    (a)   exercise the rights provided in articles 62 to 65;
    (b)   claim damages as provided in articles 74 to 77.

(2)   The seller is not deprived of any right he may have to claim damages by exercising his right to other remedies.

(3)   No period of grace may be granted to the buyer by a court or arbitral tribunal when the seller resorts to a remedy for breach of contract.

[4125]

Article 62

The seller may require the buyer to pay the price, take delivery or perform his other obligations, unless the seller has resorted to a remedy which is inconsistent with this requirement.

[4126]

Article 63

(1)   The seller may fix an additional period of time of reasonable length for performance by the buyer of his obligations.

(2) Unless the seller has received notice from the buyer that he will not perform within the period so fixed, the seller may not, during that period, resort to any remedy for breach of contract. However, the seller is not deprived thereby of any right he may have to claim damages for delay in performance.

[4127]

Article 64

(1) The seller may declare the contract avoided—

- (a) if the failure by the buyer to perform any of his obligations under the contract or this Convention amounts to a fundamental breach of contract; or
- (b) if the buyer does not, within the additional period of time fixed by the seller in accordance with paragraph (1) of article 63, perform his obligation to pay the price or take delivery of the goods, or if he declares that he will not do so within the period so fixed.

(2) However, in cases where the buyer has paid the price, the seller loses the right to declare the contract avoided unless he does so—

- (a) in respect of late performance by the buyer, before the seller has become aware that performance has been rendered; or
- (b) in respect of any breach other than late performance by the buyer, within a reasonable time—
  - (i) after the seller knew or ought to have known of the breach; or
  - (ii) after the expiration of any additional period of time fixed by the seller in accordance with paragraph (1) of article 63, or after the buyer has declared that he will not perform his obligations within such an additional period.

[4128]

Article 65

(1) If under the contract the buyer is to specify the form, measurement or other features of the goods and he fails to make such specification either on the date agreed upon or within a reasonable time after receipt of a request from the seller, the seller may, without prejudice to any other rights he may have, make the specification himself in accordance with the requirements of the buyer that may be known to him.

(2) If the seller makes the specification himself, he must inform the buyer of the details thereof and must fix a reasonable time within which the buyer may make a different specification. If, after receipt of such a communication, the buyer fails to do so within the time so fixed, the specification made by the seller is binding.

[4129]

CHAPTER IV
PASSING OF RISK

Article 66

Loss of or damage to the goods after the risk has passed to the buyer does not discharge him from his obligation to pay the price, unless the loss or damage is due to an act or omission of the seller.

[4130]

Article 67

(1) If the contract of sale involves carriage of the goods and the seller is not bound to hand them over at a particular place, the risk passes to the buyer when the goods are handed over to the first carrier for transmission to the buyer in accordance with the contract of sale. If the seller is bound to hand the goods over to a carrier at a particular place, the risk does not pass to the buyer until the goods are handed over to the carrier at that place. The fact that the seller is authorised to retain documents controlling the disposition of the goods does not affect the passage of the risk.

(2) Nevertheless, the risk does not pass to the buyer until the goods are clearly identified to the contract, whether by markings on the goods, by shipping documents, by notice given to the buyer or otherwise.

[4131]

Article 68

The risk in respect of goods sold in transit passes to the buyer from the time of the conclusion of the contract. However, if the circumstances so indicate, the risk is assumed by the buyer from the time the goods were handed over to the carrier who issued the documents embodying the contract of carriage. Nevertheless, if at the time of the conclusion of the contract of sale the seller knew or ought to have known that the goods had been lost or damaged and did not disclose this to the buyer, the loss or damage is at the risk of the seller.

[4132]

Article 69

(1)   In cases not within articles 67 and 68, the risk passes to the buyer when he takes over the goods or, if he does not do so in due time, from the time when the goods are placed at his disposal and he commits a breach of contract by failing to take delivery.

(2)   However, if the buyer is bound to take over the goods at a place other than a place of business of the seller, the risk passes when delivery is due and the buyer is aware of the fact that the goods are placed at his disposal at that place.

(3)   If the contract relates to goods not then identified, the goods are considered not to be placed at the disposal of the buyer until they are clearly identified to the contract.

[4133]

Article 70

If the seller has committed a fundamental breach of contract, articles 67, 68 and 69 do not impair the remedies available to the buyer on account of the breach.

[4134]

CHAPTER V
PROVISIONS COMMON TO THE OBLIGATIONS OF THE SELLER AND OF THE BUYER

SECTION I
ANTICIPATORY BREACH AND INSTALMENT CONTRACTS

Article 71

(1)   A party may suspend the performance of his obligations if, after the conclusion of the contract, it becomes apparent that the other party will not perform a substantial part of his obligations as a result of—
    (a)   a serious deficiency in his ability to perform or in his creditworthiness; or
    (b)   his conduct in preparing to perform or in performing the contract.

(2)   If the seller has already dispatched the goods before the grounds described in the preceding paragraph become evident, he may prevent the handing over of the goods to the buyer even though the buyer holds a document which entitles him to obtain them. The present paragraph relates only to the rights in the goods as between the buyer and the seller.

(3)   A party suspending performance, whether before or after dispatch of the goods, must immediately give notice of the suspension to the other party and must continue with performance if the other party provides adequate assurance of his performance.

[4135]

Article 72

(1)   If prior to the date for performance of the contract it is clear that one of the parties will commit a fundamental breach of contract, the other party may declare the contract avoided.

(2)   If time allows, the party intending to declare the contract avoided must give reasonable notice to the other party in order to permit him to provide adequate assurance of his performance.

(3)   The requirements of the preceding paragraph do not apply if the other party has declared that he will not perform his obligations.

[4136]

Article 73

(1)   In the case of a contract for delivery of goods by instalments, if the failure of one party to perform any of his obligations in respect of any instalment constitutes a fundamental breach of contract with respect to that instalment, the other party may declare the contract avoided with respect to that instalment.

(2)   If one party's failure to perform any of his obligations in respect of any instalment gives the other party good grounds to conclude that a fundamental breach of contract will occur with respect to future instalments, he may declare the contract avoided for the future, provided that he does so within a reasonable time.

(3)   A buyer who declares the contract avoided in respect of any delivery may, at the same time, declare it avoided in respect of deliveries already made or of future deliveries if, by reason of their interdependence, those deliveries could not be used for the purpose contemplated by the parties at the time of the conclusion of the contract.

[4137]

SECTION II
DAMAGES

Article 74

Damages for breach of contract by one party consist of a sum equal to the loss, including loss of profit, suffered by the other party as a consequence of the breach. Such damages may not exceed the loss which the party in breach foresaw or ought to have foreseen at the time of the conclusion of the contract, in the light of the facts and matters of which he then knew or ought to have known, as a possible consequence of the breach of contract.

[4138]

Article 75

If the contract is avoided and if, in a reasonable manner and within a reasonable time after avoidance, the buyer has bought goods in replacement or the seller has resold the goods, the party claiming damages may recover the difference between the contract price and the price in the substitute transaction as well as any further damages recoverable under article 74.

[4139]

Article 76

(1)   If the contract is avoided and there is a current price for the goods, the party claiming damages may, if he has not made a purchase or resale under article 75, recover the difference between the price fixed by the contract and the current price at the time of avoidance as well as any further damages recoverable under article 74. If, however, the party claiming damages has avoided the contract after taking over the goods, the current price at the time of such taking over shall be applied instead of the current price at the time of avoidance.

(2)   For the purposes of the preceding paragraph, the current price is the price prevailing at the place where delivery of the goods should have been made or, if there is no current price at that place, the price at such other place as serves as a reasonable substitute, making due allowance for differences in the cost of transporting the goods.

[4140]

Article 77

A party who relies on a breach of contract must take such measures as are reasonable in the circumstances to mitigate the loss, including loss of profit, resulting from the breach. If he fails to take such measures, the party in breach may claim a reduction in the damages in the amount by which the loss should have been mitigated.

[4141]

SECTION III
INTEREST

Article 78

If a party fails to pay the price or any other sum that is in arrears, the other party is entitled to interest on it, without prejudice to any claim for damages recoverable under article 74.

[4142]

SECTION IV
EXEMPTION

Article 79

(1)   A party is not liable for a failure to perform any of his obligations if he proves that the failure was due to an impediment beyond his control and that he could not reasonably be expected to have taken the impediment into account at the time of the conclusion of the contract or to have avoided or overcome it or its consequences.

(2)   If the party's failure is due to the failure by a third person whom he has engaged to perform the whole or a part of the contract, that party is exempt from liability only if—
    (a)   he is exempt under the preceding paragraph; and
    (b)   the person whom he has so engaged would be so exempt if the provisions of that paragraph were applied to him.

(3)   The exemption provided by this article has effect for the period during which the impediment exists.

(4)   The party who fails to perform must give notice to the other party of the impediment and its effect on his ability to perform. If the notice is not received by the other party within a reasonable time after the party who fails to perform knew or ought to have known of the impediment, he is liable for damages resulting from such non receipt.

(5)   Nothing in this article prevents either party from exercising any right other than to claim damages under this Convention.

[4143]

Article 80

A party may not rely on a failure of the other party to perform, to the extent that such failure was caused by the first party's act or omission.

[4144]

SECTION V
EFFECTS OF AVOIDANCE

Article 81

(1)   Avoidance of the contract releases both parties from their obligations under it, subject to any damages which may be due. Avoidance does not affect any provision of the contract for the settlement of disputes or any other provision of the contract governing the rights and obligations of the parties consequent upon the avoidance of the contract.

(2)   A party who has performed the contract either wholly or in part may claim restitution from the other party of whatever the first party has supplied or paid under the contract. If both parties are bound to make restitution, they must do so concurrently.

[4145]

Article 82

(1)   The buyer loses the right to declare the contract avoided or to require the seller to deliver substitute goods if it is impossible for him to make restitution of the goods substantially in the condition in which he received them.

(2)   The preceding paragraph does not apply—
  (a)   if the impossibility of making restitution of the goods or of making restitution of the goods substantially in the condition in which the buyer received them is not due to his act or omission;
  (b)   if the goods or part of the goods have perished or deteriorated as a result of the examination provided for in article 38; or
  (c)   if the goods or part of the goods have been sold in the normal course of business or have been consumed or transformed by the buyer in the course of normal use before he discovered or ought to have discovered the lack of conformity.

[4146]

Article 83

A buyer who has lost the right to declare the contract avoided or to require the seller to deliver substitute goods in accordance with article 82 retains all other remedies under the contract and this Convention.

[4147]

Article 84

(1)   If the seller is bound to refund the price, he must also pay interest on it, from the date on which the price was paid.

(2)   The buyer must account to the seller for all benefits which he has derived from the goods or part of them—
  (a)   if he must make restitution of the goods or part of them; or
  (b)   if it is impossible for him to make restitution of all or part of the goods or to make restitution of all or part of the goods substantially in the condition in which he received them, but he has nevertheless declared the contract avoided or required the seller to deliver substitute goods.

[4148]

SECTION VI
PRESERVATION OF THE GOODS

Article 85

If the buyer is in delay in taking delivery of the goods or, where payment of the price and delivery of the goods are to be made concurrently, if he fails to pay the price, and the seller is either in possession of the goods or otherwise able to control their disposition, the seller must take such steps as are reasonable in the circumstances to preserve them. He is entitled to retain them until he has been reimbursed his reasonable expenses by the buyer.

[4149]

Article 86

(1)   If the buyer has received the goods and intends to exercise any right under the contract or this Convention to reject them, he must take such steps to preserve them as are reasonable in the circumstances. He is entitled to retain them until he has been reimbursed his reasonable expenses by the seller.

(2)   If goods dispatched to the buyer have been placed at his disposal at their destination and he exercises the right to reject them, he must take possession of them on behalf of the seller, provided that this can be done without payment of the price and without unreasonable inconvenience or unreasonable expense. This provision does not apply if the seller or a person authorised to take charge of the goods on his behalf is present at the destination. If the buyer takes possession of the goods under this paragraph, his rights and obligations are governed by the preceding paragraph.

[4150]

Article 87

A party who is bound to take steps to preserve the goods may deposit them in a warehouse of a third person at the expense of the other party provided that the expense incurred is not unreasonable.

[4151]

Article 88

(1)   A party who is bound to preserve the goods in accordance with article 85 or 86 may sell them by any appropriate means if there has been an unreasonable delay by the other party in taking possession of the goods or in taking them back or in paying the price or the cost of preservation, provided that reasonable notice of the intention to sell has been given to the other party.

(2)   If the goods are subject to rapid deterioration or their preservation would involve unreasonable expense, a party who is bound to preserve the goods in accordance with article 85 or 86 must take reasonable measures to sell them. To the extent possible he must give notice to the other party of his intention to sell.

(3)   A party selling the goods has the right to retain out of the proceeds of sale an amount equal to the reasonable expenses of preserving the goods and of selling them. He must account to the other party for the balance.

[4152]

PART IV
FINAL PROVISIONS

Article 89

The Secretary-General of the United Nations is hereby designated as the depositary for this Convention.

[4153]

Article 90

This Convention does not prevail over any international agreement which has already been or may be entered into and which contains provisions concerning the matters governed by this Convention, provided that the parties have their places of business in States parties to such agreement.

[4154]

Article 91

(1)   This Convention is open for signature at the concluding meeting of the United Nations Conference on Contracts for the International Sale of Goods and will remain open for signature by all States at the Headquarters of the United Nations, New York until 30 September 1981.

(2)   This Convention is subject to ratification, acceptance or approval by the signatory States.

(3)   This Convention is open for accession by all States which are not signatory States as from the date it is open for signature.

(4)   Instruments of ratification, acceptance, approval and accession are to be deposited with the Secretary-General of the United Nations.

[4155]

Article 92

(1)   A Contracting State may declare at the time of signature, ratification, acceptance, approval or accession that it will not be bound by Part II of this Convention or that it will not be bound by Part III of this Convention.

(2)   A Contracting State which makes a declaration in accordance with the preceding paragraph in respect of Part II or Part III of this Convention is not to be considered a Contracting State within paragraph (1) of article 1 of this Convention in respect of matters governed by the Part to which the declaration applies.

[4156]

Article 93

(1) If a Contracting State has two or more territorial units in which, according to its constitution, different systems of law are applicable in relation to the matters dealt with in this Convention, it may, at the time of signature, ratification, acceptance, approval or accession, declare that this Convention is to extend to all its territorial units or only to one or more of them, and may amend its declaration by submitting another declaration at any time.

(2) These declarations are to be notified to the depositary and are to state expressly the territorial units to which the Convention extends.

(3) If, by virtue of a declaration under this article, this Convention extends to one or more but not all of the territorial units of a Contracting State, and if the place of business of a party is located in that State, this place of business, for the purposes of this Convention, is considered not to be in a Contracting State, unless it is in a territorial unit to which the Convention extends.

(4) If a Contracting State makes no declaration under paragraph (1) of this article, the Convention is to extend to all territorial units of that State.

[4157]

Article 94

(1) Two or more Contracting States which have the same or closely related legal rules on matters governed by this Convention may at any time declare that the Convention is not to apply to contracts of sale or to their formation where the parties have their places of business in those States. Such declarations may be made jointly or by reciprocal unilateral declarations.

(2) A Contracting State which has the same or closely related legal rules on matters governed by this Convention as one or more non-Contracting States may at any time declare that the Convention is not to apply to contracts of sale or to their formation where the parties have their places of business in those States.

(3) If a State which is the object of a declaration under the preceding paragraph subsequently becomes a Contracting State, the declaration made will, as from the date on which the Convention enters into force in respect of the new Contracting State, have the effect of a declaration made under paragraph (1), provided that the new Contracting State joins in such declaration or makes a reciprocal unilateral declaration.

[4158]

Article 95

Any State may declare at the time of the deposit of its instrument of ratification, acceptance, approval or accession that it will not be bound by subparagraph (1)(b) of article 1 of this Convention.

[4159]

Article 96

A Contracting State whose legislation requires contracts of sale to be concluded in or evidenced by writing may at any time make a declaration in accordance with article 12 that any provision of article 11, article 29, or Part II of this Convention, that allows a contract of sale or its modification or termination by agreement or any offer, acceptance, or other indication of intention to be made in any form other than in writing, does not apply where any party has his place of business in that State.

[4160]

Article 97

(1) Declarations made under this Convention at the time of signature are subject to confirmation upon ratification, acceptance or approval.

(2) Declarations and confirmations of declarations are to be in writing and be formally notified to the depositary.

(3) A declaration takes effect simultaneously with the entry into force of this Convention in respect of the State concerned. However, a declaration of which the depositary receives formal notification after such entry into force takes effect on the first day of the month following the expiration of six months after the date of its receipt by the depositary. Reciprocal unilateral declarations under article 94 take effect on the first day of the month following the expiration of six months after the receipt of the latest declaration by the depositary.

(4) Any State which makes a declaration under this Convention may withdraw it at any time by a formal notification in writing addressed to the depositary. Such withdrawal is to take effect on the first day of the month following the expiration of six months after the date of the receipt of the notification by the depositary.

(5)   A withdrawal of a declaration made under article 94 renders inoperative, as from the date on which the withdrawal takes effect, any reciprocal declaration made by another State under that article.

[4161]

Article 98

No reservations are permitted except those expressly authorised in this Convention.

[4162]

Article 99

(1)   This Convention enters into force, subject to the provisions of paragraph (6) of this article, on the first day of the month following the expiration of twelve months after the date of deposit of the tenth instrument of ratification, acceptance, approval or accession, including an instrument which contains a declaration made under article 92.

(2)   When a State ratifies, accepts, approves or accedes to this Convention after the deposit of the tenth instrument of ratification, acceptance, approval or accession, this Convention, with the exception of the Part excluded, enters into force in respect of that State, subject to the provisions of paragraph (6) of this article, on the first day of the month following the expiration of twelve months after the date of the deposit of its instrument of ratification, acceptance, approval or accession.

(3)   A State which ratifies, accepts, approves or accedes to this Convention and is a party to either or both the Convention relating to a Uniform Law on the Formation of Contracts for the International Sale of Goods done at The Hague on 1 July 1964 (1964 Hague Formation Convention) and the Convention relating to a Uniform Law on the International Sale of Goods done at The Hague on 1 July 1964 (1964 Hague Sales Convention) shall at the same time denounce, as the case may be, either or both the 1964 Hague Sales Convention and the 1964 Hague Formation Convention by notifying the Government of the Netherlands to that effect.

(4)   A State party to the 1964 Hague Sales Convention which ratifies, accepts, approves or accedes to the present Convention and declares or has declared under article 92 that it will not be bound by Part II of this Convention shall at the time of ratification, acceptance, approval or accession denounce the 1964 Hague Sales Convention by notifying the Government of the Netherlands to that effect.

(5)   A State party to the 1964 Hague Formation Convention which ratifies, accepts, approves or accedes to the present Convention and declares or has declared under article 92 that it will not be bound by Part III of this Convention shall at the time of ratification, acceptance, approval or accession denounce the 1964 Hague Formation Convention by notifying the Government of the Netherlands to that effect.

(6)   For the purpose of this article, ratifications, acceptances, approvals and accessions in respect of this Convention by States parties to the 1964 Hague Formation Convention or to the 1964 Hague Sales Convention shall not be effective until such denunciations as may be required on the part of those States in respect of the latter two Conventions have themselves become effective. The depositary of this Convention shall consult with the Government of the Netherlands, as the depositary of the 1964 Conventions, so as to ensure necessary co-ordination in this respect.

[4163]

Article 100

(1)   This Convention applies to the formation of a contract only when the proposal for concluding the contract is made on or after the date when the Convention enters into force in respect of the Contracting States referred to in subparagraph (1)(a) or the Contracting State referred to in subparagraph (1)(b) of article 1.

(2)   This Convention applies only to contracts concluded on or after the date when the Convention enters into force in respect of the Contracting States referred to in subparagraph (1)(a) or the Contracting State referred to in subparagraph (1)(b) of article 1.

[4164]

Article 101

(1)   A Contracting State may denounce this Convention, or Part II or Part III of the Convention, by a formal notification in writing addressed to the depositary.

(2)   The denunciation takes effect on the first day of the month following the expiration of twelve months after the notification is received by the depositary. Where a longer period for the denunciation to take effect is specified in the notification, the denunciation takes effect upon the expiration of such longer period after the notification is received by the depositary.

[4165]–[4175]

DONE at Vienna, this day of eleventh day of April, one thousand nine hundred and eighty, in a single original, of which the Arabic, Chinese, English, French, Russian and Spanish texts are equally authentic.

IN WITNESS WHEREOF the undersigned plenipotentiaries, being duly authorised by their respective Governments, have signed this Convention.

NOTES

The text of this Convention was prepared by the United Nations Commission on International Trade Law.

COUNCIL DIRECTIVE

of 25 July 1985

on the approximation of the laws, regulations and administrative provisions of the Member States concerning liability for defective products

(85/374/EEC)

NOTE

Date of publication in OJ: OJ L210, 7.8.85, p 29.
This Directive has been implemented in the UK by the Consumer Protection Act 1987 at **[1387]**.

THE COUNCIL OF THE EUROPEAN COMMUNITIES,

Having regard to the Treaty establishing the European Economic Community, and in particular Article 100 thereof,

Having regard to the proposal from the Commission,[1]

Having regard to the opinion of the European Parliament,[2]

Having regard to the opinion of the Economic and Social Committee,[3]

Whereas approximation of the laws of the Member States concerning the liability of the producer for damage caused by the defectiveness of his products is necessary because the existing divergences may distort competition and affect the movement of goods within the common market and entail a differing degree of protection of the consumer against damage caused by a defective product to his health or property;

Whereas liability without fault on the part of the producer is the sole means of adequately solving the problem, peculiar to our age of increasing technicality, of a fair apportionment of the risks inherent in modern technological production;

Whereas liability without fault should apply only to movables which have been industrially produced; whereas, as a result, it is appropriate to exclude liability for agricultural products and game, except where they have undergone a processing of an industrial nature which could cause a defect in these products; whereas the liability provided for in this Directive should also apply to movables which are used in the construction of immovables or are installed in immovables;

Whereas protection of the consumer requires that all producers involved in the production process should be made liable, in so far as their finished product, component part or any raw material supplied by them was defective; whereas, for the same reason, liability should extend to importers of products into the Community and to persons who present themselves as producers by affixing their name, trade mark or other distinguishing feature or who supply a product the producer of which cannot be identified;

Whereas, in situations where several persons are liable for the same damage, the protection of the consumer requires that the injured person should be able to claim full compensation for the damage from any one of them;

Whereas, to protect the physical well-being and property of the consumer, the defectiveness of the product should be determined by reference not to its fitness for use but to the lack of the safety which the public at large is entitled to expect; whereas the safety is assessed by excluding any misuse of the product not reasonable under the circumstances;

Whereas a fair apportionment of risk between the injured person and the producer implies that the producer should be able to free himself from liability if he furnishes proof as to the existence of certain exonerating circumstances;

Whereas the protection of the consumer requires that the liability of the producer remains unaffected by acts or omissions of other persons having contributed to cause the damage; whereas, however, the contributory negligence of the injured person may be taken into account to reduce or disallow such liability;

Whereas the protection of the consumer requires compensation for death and personal injury as well as compensation for damage to property; whereas the latter should nevertheless be limited to goods for private use or consumption and be subject to a deduction of a lower threshold of a fixed amount in order to avoid litigation in an excessive number of cases; whereas this Directive should not prejudice compensation for pain and suffering and other nonmaterial damages payable, where appropriate, under the law applicable to the case;

Whereas a uniform period of limitation for the bringing of action for compensation is in the interests both of the injured person and of the producer;

Whereas products age in the course of time, higher safety standards are developed and the state of science and technology progresses; whereas, therefore, it would not be reasonable to make the producer liable for an unlimited period for the defectiveness of his product; whereas, therefore, liability should expire after a reasonable length of time, without prejudice to claims pending at law;

Whereas, to achieve effective protection of consumers, no contractual derogation should be permitted as regards the liability of the producer in relation to the injured person;

Whereas under the legal systems of the Member States an injured party may have a claim for damages based on grounds of contractual liability or on grounds of non-contractual liability other than that provided for in this Directive; in so far as these provisions also serve to attain the objective of effective protection of consumers, they should remain unaffected by this Directive; whereas, in so far as effective protection of consumers in the sector of pharmaceutical products is already also attained in a Member State under a special liability system, claims based on this system should similarly remain possible;

Whereas, to the extent that liability for nuclear injury or damage is already covered in all Member States by adequate special rules, it has been possible to exclude damage of this type from the scope of this Directive;

Whereas, since the exclusion of primary agricultural products and game from the scope of this Directive may be felt, in certain Member States, in view of what is expected for the protection of consumers, to restrict unduly such protection, it should be possible for a Member State to extend liability to such products;

Whereas, for similar reasons, the possibility offered to a producer to free himself from liability if he proves that the state of scientific and technical knowledge at the time when he put the product into circulation was not such as to enable the existence of a defect to be discovered may be felt in certain Member States to restrict unduly the protection of the consumer; whereas it should therefore be possible for a Member State to maintain in its legislation or to provide by new legislation that this exonerating circumstance is not admitted; whereas, in the case of new legislation, making use of this derogation should, however, be subject to a Community stand-still procedure, in order to raise, if possible, the level of protection in a uniform manner throughout the Community;

Whereas, taking into account the legal traditions in most of the Member States, it is inappropriate to set any financial ceiling on the producer's liability without fault; whereas, in so far as there are, however, differing traditions, it seems possible to admit that a Member State may derogate from the principle of unlimited liability by providing a limit for the total liability of the producer for damage resulting from a death or personal injury and caused by identical items with the same defect, provided that this limit is established at a level sufficiently high to guarantee adequate protection of the consumer and the correct functioning of the common market;

Whereas the harmonisation resulting from this cannot be total at the present stage, but opens the way towards greater harmonisation; whereas it is therefore necessary that the Council receive at regular intervals, reports from the Commission on the application of this Directive, accompanied, as the case may be, by appropriate proposals;

Whereas it is particularly important in this respect that a re-examination be carried out of those parts of the Directive relating to the derogations open to the Member States, at the expiry of a period of sufficient length to gather practical experience on the effects of these derogations on the protection of consumers and on the functioning of the common market,

NOTES

1　　OJ C241, 14.10.76, p 9; OJ C271, 26.10.79, p 3.
2　　OJ C127, 21.5.79, p 61.
3　　OJ C114, 7.5.79, p 15.

HAS ADOPTED THIS DIRECTIVE:

Article 1

The producer shall be liable for damage caused by a defect in his product.

[4176]

[Article 2

For the purpose of this Directive, "product" means all movables even if incorporated into another movable or into an immovable. "Product" includes electricity.]

[4177]

NOTES

Substituted by European Parliament and Council Directive 1999/34/EC, Art 1(1).

Article 3

1.　"Producer" means the manufacturer of a finished product, the producer of any raw material or the manufacturer of a component part and any person who, by putting his name, trade mark or other distinguishing feature on the product presents himself as its producer.

2.   Without prejudice to the liability of the producer, any person who imports into the Community a product for sale, hire, leasing or any form of distribution in the course of his business shall be deemed to be a producer within the meaning of this Directive and shall be responsible as a producer.

3.   Where the producer of the product cannot be identified, each supplier of the product shall be treated as its producer unless he informs the injured person, within a reasonable time, of the identity of the producer or of the person who supplied him with the product. The same shall apply, in the case of an imported product, if this product does not indicate the identity of the importer referred to in paragraph 2, even if the name of the producer is indicated.

[4178]

Article 4

The injured person shall be required to prove the damage, the defect and the causal relationship between defect and damage.

[4179]

Article 5

Where, as a result of the provisions of this Directive, two or more persons are liable for the same damage, they shall be liable jointly and severally, without prejudice to the provisions of national law concerning the rights of contribution or recourse.

[4180]

Article 6

1.   A product is defective when it does not provide the safety which a person is entitled to expect, taking all circumstances into account, including—
   (a)   the presentation of the product;
   (b)   the use to which it could reasonably be expected that the product would be put;
   (c)   the time when the product was put into circulation.

2.   A product shall not be considered defective for the sole reason that a better product is subsequently put into circulation;

[4181]

Article 7

The producer shall not be liable as a result of this Directive if he proves—
   (a)   that he did not put the product into circulation; or
   (b)   that, having regard to the circumstances, it is probable that the defect which caused the damage did not exist at the time when the product was put into circulation by him or that this defect came into being afterwards; or
   (c)   that the product was neither manufactured by him for sale or any form of distribution for economic purpose nor manufactured or distributed by him in the course of his business; or
   (d)   that the defect is due to compliance of the product with mandatory regulations issued by the public authorities; or
   (e)   that the state of scientific and technical knowledge at the time when he put the product into circulation was not such as to enable the existence of the defect to be discovered; or
   (f)   in the case of a manufacturer of a component, that the defect is attributable to the design of the product in which the component has been fitted or to the instructions given by the manufacturer of the product.

[4182]

Article 8

1.   Without prejudice to the provisions of national law concerning the right of contribution or recourse, the liability of the producer shall not be reduced when the damage is caused both by a defect in product and by the act or omission of a third party.

2.   The liability of the producer may be reduced or disallowed when, having regard to all the circumstances, the damage is caused both by a defect in the product and by the fault of the injured person or any person for whom the injured person is responsible.

[4183]

Article 9

For the purpose of Article 1, "damage" means—
   (a)   damage caused by death or by personal injuries;
   (b)   damage to, or destruction of, any item of property other than the defective product itself, with a lower threshold of 500 ECU, provided that the item of property—
       (i)   is of a type ordinarily intended for private use or consumption, and
       (ii)   was used by the injured person mainly for his own private use or consumption.

This Article shall be without prejudice to national provisions relating to nonmaterial damage.

[4184]

Article 10

1.　Member States shall provide in their legislation that a limitation period of three years shall apply to proceedings for the recovery of damages as provided for in this Directive. The limitation period shall begin to run from the day on which the plaintiff became aware, or should reasonably have become aware, of the damage, the defect and the identity of the producer.

2.　The laws of Member States regulating suspension or interruption of the limitation period shall not be affected by this Directive.

[4185]

Article 11

Member States shall provide in their legislation that the rights conferred upon the injured person pursuant to this Directive shall be extinguished upon the expiry of a period of 10 years from the date on which the producer put into circulation the actual product which caused the damage, unless the injured person has in the meantime instituted proceedings against the producer.

[4186]

Article 12

The liability of the producer arising from this Directive may not, in relation to the injured person, be limited or excluded by a provision limiting his liability or exempting him from liability.

[4187]

Article 13

This Directive shall not affect any rights which an injured person may have according to the rules of the law of contractual or non-contractual liability or a special liability system existing at the moment when this Directive is notified.

[4188]

Article 14

This Directive shall not apply to injury or damage arising from nuclear accidents and covered by international conventions ratified by the Member States.

[4189]

Article 15

1.　Each Member State may—
    (a)　…
    (b)　by way of derogation from Article 7(e), maintain or, subject to the procedure set out in paragraph 2 of this Article, provide in this legislation that the producer shall be liable even if he proves that the state of scientific and technical knowledge at the time when he put the product into circulation was not such as to enable the existence of a defect to be discovered.

2.　A Member State wishing to introduce the measure specified in paragraph 1(b) shall communicate the text of the proposed measure to the Commission. The Commission shall inform the other Member States thereof.

The Member State concerned shall hold the proposed measure in abeyance for nine months after the Commission is informed and provided that in the meantime the Commission has not submitted to the Council a proposal amending this Directive on the relevant matter. However, if within three months of receiving the said information, the Commission does not advise the Member State concerned that it intends submitting such a proposal to the Council, the Member State may take the proposed measure immediately.

If the Commission does submit to the Council such a proposal amending this Directive within the aforementioned nine months, the Member State concerned shall hold the proposed measure in abeyance for a further period of 18 months from the date on which the proposal is submitted.

3.　Ten years after the date of notification of this Directive, the Commission shall submit to the Council a report on the effect that rulings by the courts as to the application of Article 7(e) and of paragraph 1(b) of this Article have on consumer protection and the functioning of the common market. In the light of this report the Council, acting on a proposal from the Commission and pursuant to the terms of Article 100 of the Treaty, shall decide whether to repeal Article 7(e).

[4190]

NOTES

Para 1: sub-para (a) revoked by European Parliament and Council Directive 1999/34/EC, Art 1(2).

Article 16

1.　Any Member State may provide that a producer's total liability for damage resulting from a death or personal injury and caused by identical items with the same defect shall be limited to an amount which may not be less than 70 million ECU.

2. Ten years after the date of notification of this Directive, the Commission shall submit to the Council a report on the effect on consumer protection and the functioning of the common market of the implementation of the financial limit on liability by those Member States which have used the option provided for in paragraph 1. In the light of this report the Council, acting on a proposal from the Commission and pursuant to the terms of Article 100 of the Treaty, shall decide whether to repeal paragraph 1.

[4191]

Article 17

This Directive shall not apply to products put into circulation before the date on which the provisions referred to in Article 19 enter into force.

[4192]

Article 18

1. For the purposes of this Directive, the ECU shall be that defined by Regulation (EEC) No 3180/78,[1] as amended by Regulation (EEC) No 2626/84.[2] The equivalent in national currency shall initially be calculated at the rate obtaining on the date of adoption of this Directive.

2. Every five years the Council, acting on a proposal from the Commission, shall examine and, if need be, revise the amounts in this Directive, in the light of economic and monetary trends in the Community.

[4193]

NOTES
[1]   OJ L379, 30.12.78, p 1.
[2]   OJ L247, 16.9.84, p 1.

Article 19

1. Member States shall bring into force, not later than three years from the date of notification of this Directive, the laws, regulations and administrative provisions necessary to comply with this Directive. They shall forthwith inform the Commission thereof.

2. The procedure set out in Article 15(2) shall apply from the date of notification of this Directive.

[4194]

NOTES
   This Directive was notified to the Member States on 30 July 1985.

Article 20

Member States shall communicate to the Commission the texts of the main provisions of national law which they subsequently adopt in the field governed by this Directive.

[4195]

Article 21

Every five years the Commission shall present a report to the Council on the application of this Directive and, if necessary, shall submit appropriate proposals to it.

[4196]

Article 22

This Directive is addressed to the Member States.

[4197]

Done at Brussels, 25 July 1985.

COUNCIL DIRECTIVE

of 20 December 1985

to protect the consumer in respect of contracts negotiated away from business premises

(85/577/EEC)

NOTES
Date of publication in OJ: OJ L372, 31,12,85, p 31.

This Directive has been implemented in the UK by the Consumer Protection (Cancellation of Contracts Concluded away from Business Premises) Regulations 1987, SI 1987/2117 at **[3049]** and the Cancellation of Contracts made in a Consumer's Home or Place of Work etc Regulations 2008, SI 2008/1816 at **[3705]**.

THE COUNCIL OF THE EUROPEAN COMMUNITIES,

Having regard to the Treaty establishing the European Economic Community, and in particular Article 100 thereof,

Having regard to the proposal from the Commission,[1]

Having regard to the opinion of the European Parliament,[2]

Having regard to the opinion of the Economic and Social Committee,[3]

Whereas it is a common form of commercial practice in the Member States for the conclusion of a contract or a unilateral engagement between a trader and consumer to be made away from the business premises of the trader, and whereas such contracts and engagements are the subject of legislation which differs from one Member State to another;

Whereas any disparity between such legislation may directly affect the functioning of the common market; whereas it is therefore necessary to approximate laws in this field;

Whereas the preliminary programme of the European Economic Community for a consumer protection and information policy[4] provides inter alia, under paragraphs 24 and 25, that appropriate measures be taken to protect consumers against unfair commercial practices in respect of doorstep selling; whereas the second programme of the European Economic Community for a consumer protection and information policy[5] confirmed that the action and priorities defined in the preliminary programme would be pursued;

Whereas the special feature of contracts concluded away from the business premises of the trader is that as a rule it is the trader who initiates the contract negotiations, for which the consumer is unprepared or which he does not except; whereas the consumer is often unable to compare the quality and price of the offer with other offers; whereas this surprise element generally exists not only in contracts made at the doorstep but also in other forms of contract concluded by the trader away from his business premises;

Whereas the consumer should be given a right of cancellation over a period of at least seven days in order to enable him to assess the obligations arising under the contract;

Whereas appropriate measures should be taken to ensure that the consumer is informed in writing of this period for reflection;

Whereas the freedom of Member States to maintain or introduce a total or partial prohibition on the conclusion of contracts away from business premises, inasmuch as they consider this to be in the interest of consumers, must not be affected;

NOTES
1   OJ C22, 29.1.77, p 6 and OJ C127, 1.6.78, p 6.
2   OJ C241, 10.10.77, p 26.
3   OJ C180, 18.7.77, p 39.
4   OJ C92, 25.4.75, p 2.
5   OJ C133, 3.6.81, p 1.

HAS ADOPTED THIS DIRECTIVE—

Article 1

1. This Directive shall apply to contracts under which a trader supplies goods or services to a consumer and which are concluded—
   — during an excursion organised by the trader away from his business premises, or
   — during a visit by a trader—
      (i) to the consumer's home or to that of another consumer;
      (ii) to the consumer's place of work;
   where the visit does not take place at the express request of the consumer.

2. This Directive shall also apply to contracts for the supply of goods or services other than those concerning which the consumer requested the visit of the trader, provided that when he requested the visit the consumer did not know, or could not reasonably have known, that the supply of those other goods or services formed part of the trader's commercial or professional activities.

3. This Directive shall also apply to contracts in respect of which an offer was made by the consumer under conditions similar to those described in paragraph 1 or paragraph 2 although the consumer was not bound by that offer before its acceptance by the trader.

4. This Directive shall also apply to offers made contractually by the consumer under conditions similar to those described in paragraph 1 or paragraph 2 where the consumer is bound by his offer.

[4198]

Article 2

For the purposes of this Directive—

"consumer" means a natural person who, in transactions covered by this Directive, is acting for purposes which can be regarded as outside his trade or profession;

"trader" means a natural or legal person who, for the transaction in question, acts in his commercial or professional capacity, and anyone acting in the name or on behalf of a trader.

[4199]

Article 3

1.   The Member States may decide that this Directive shall apply only to contracts for which the payment to be made by the consumer exceeds a specified amount. This amount may not exceed 60 ECU.

The Council, acting on a proposal from the Commission, shall examine and, if necessary, revise this amount for the first time no later than four years after notification of the Directive and thereafter every two years, taking into account economic and monetary developments in the Community.

2.   This Directive shall not apply to—
   (a)   contracts for the construction, sale and rental of immovable property or contracts concerning other rights relating to immovable property.
   Contracts for the supply of goods and for their incorporation in immovable property or contracts for repairing immovable property shall fall within the scope of this Directive;
   (b)   contracts for the supply of foodstuffs or beverages or other goods intended for current consumption in the household and supplied by regular roundsmen;
   (c)   contracts for the supply of goods or services, provided that all three of the following conditions are met—
      (i)   the contract is concluded on the basis of a trader's catalogue which the consumer has a proper opportunity of reading in the absence of the trader's representative,
      (ii)   there is intended to be continuity of contact between the trader's representative and the consumer in relation to that or any subsequent transaction,
      (iii) both the catalogue and the contract clearly inform the consumer of his right to return goods to the supplier within a period of not less than seven days of receipt or otherwise to cancel the contract within that period without obligation of any kind other than to take reasonable care of the goods;
   (d)   insurance contracts;
   (e)   contracts for securities.

3.   By way of derogation from Article 1(2), Member States may refrain from applying this Directive to contracts for the supply of goods or services having a direct connection with the goods or services concerning which the consumer requested the visit of the trader.

[4200]

Article 4

In the case of transactions within the scope of Article 1, traders shall be required to give consumers written notice of their right of cancellation within the period laid down in Article 5, together with the name and address of a person against whom that right may be exercised.

Such notice shall be dated and shall state particulars enabling the contract to be identified. It shall be given to the consumer—
   (a)   in the case of Article 1(1), at the time of conclusion of the contract;
   (b)   in the case of Article 1(2), not later than the time of conclusion of the contract;
   (c)   in the case of Article 1(3) and 1(4), when the offer is made by the consumer.

Member States shall ensure that their national legislation lays down appropriate consumer protection measures in cases where the information referred to in this Article is not supplied.

[4201]

Article 5

1.   The consumer shall have the right to renounce the effects of his undertaking by sending notice within a period of not less than seven days from receipt by the consumer of the notice referred to in Article 4, in accordance with the procedure laid down by national law. It shall be sufficient if the notice is dispatched before the end of such period.

2.   The giving of the notice shall have the effect of releasing the consumer from any obligations under the cancelled contract.

[4202]

Article 6

The consumer may not waive the rights conferred on him by this Directive.

[4203]

Article 7

If the consumer exercises his right of renunciation, the legal effects of such renunciation shall be governed by national laws, particularly regarding the reimbursement of payments for goods or services provided and the return of goods received.

[4204]

Article 8

This Directive shall not prevent Member States from adopting or maintaining more favourable provisions to protect consumers in the field which it covers.

[4205]

Article 9

1.   Member States shall take the measures necessary to comply with this Directive within 24 months of its notification.[1] They shall forthwith inform the Commission thereof.

2.   Member States shall ensure that the texts of the main provisions of national law which they adopt in the field covered by this Directive are communicated to the Commission.

[4206]

NOTES

[1]   This Directive was notified to the Member States on 23 December 1985.

Article 10

This Directive is addressed to the Member States.

[4207]

Done at Brussels, 20 December 1985.

COUNCIL DIRECTIVE

of 18 December 1986

on the coordination of the laws of the Member States relating to self-employed commercial agents

(86/653/EEC)

NOTES

Date of publication in OJ: OJ L382, 31.12.86, p 17.
This Directive has been implemented in the UK by the Commercial Agents (Council Directive) Regulations 1993, SI 1993/3053 at **[3163]**.

THE COUNCIL OF THE EUROPEAN COMMUNITIES,

Having regard to the Treaty establishing the European Economic Community, and in particular Articles 57(2) and 100 thereof,

Having regard to the proposal from the Commission,[1]

Having regard to the opinion of the European Parliament,[2]

Having regard to the opinion of the Economic and Social Committee,[3]

Whereas the restrictions on the freedom of establishment and the freedom to provide services in respect of activities of intermediaries in commerce, industry and small craft industries were abolished by Directive 64/224/EEC;[4]

Whereas the differences in national laws concerning commercial representation substantially affect the conditions of competition and the carrying-on of that activity within the Community and are detrimental both to the protection available to commercial agents *vis-à-vis* their principals and to the security of commercial transactions; whereas moreover those differences are such as to inhibit substantially the conclusion and operation of commercial representation contracts where principal and commercial agent are established in different Member States;

Whereas trade in goods between Member States should be carried on under conditions which are similar to those of a single market, and this necessitates approximation of the legal systems of the Member States to the extent required for the proper functioning of the common market; whereas in this regard the rules concerning conflict of laws do not, in the matter of commercial representation, remove the inconsistencies referred to above, nor would they even if they were made uniform, and accordingly the proposed harmonisation is necessary notwithstanding the existence of those rules;

Whereas in this regard the legal relationship between commercial agent and principal must be given priority;

Whereas it is appropriate to be guided by the principles of Article 117 of the Treaty and to maintain improvements already made, when harmonising the laws of the Member States relating to commercial agents;

Whereas additional transitional periods should be allowed for certain Member States which have to make a particular effort to adapt their regulations, especially those concerning indemnity for termination of contract between the principal and the commercial agent, to the requirements of this Directive,

NOTES

1	OJ C13, 18.1.77, p 2 and OJ C56, 2.3.79, p.5.
2	OJ C239, 9.10.78, p 17.
3	OJ C59, 8.3.78, p 31.
4	OJ C56, 4.4.19, p 869/64.

HAS ADOPTED THIS DIRECTIVE—

CHAPTER I
SCOPE

Article 1

1. The harmonisation measures prescribed by this Directive shall apply to the laws, regulations and administrative provisions of the Member States governing the relations between commercial agents and their principals.

2. For the purposes of this Directive, "commercial agent" shall mean a self-employed intermediary who has continuing authority to negotiate the sale or the purchase of goods on behalf of another person, hereinafter called the "principal", or to negotiate and conclude such transactions on behalf of and in the name of that principal.

3. A commercial agent shall be understood within the meaning of this Directive as not including in particular—
   — a person who, in his capacity as an officer, is empowered to enter into commitments binding on a company or association,
   — a partner who is lawfully authorised to enter into commitments binding on his partners,
   — a receiver, a receiver and manager, a liquidator or a trustee in bankruptcy.

[4208]

Article 2

1. This Directive shall not apply to—
   — commercial agents whose activities are unpaid,
   — commercial agents when they operate on commodity exchanges or in the commodity market, or
   — the body known as the Crown Agents for Overseas Governments and Administrations, as set up under the Crown Agents Act 1979 in the United Kingdom, or its subsidiaries.

2. Each of the Member States shall have the right to provide that the Directive shall not apply to those persons whose activities as commercial agents are considered secondary by the law of that Member State.

[4209]

CHAPTER II
RIGHTS AND OBLIGATIONS

Article 3

1. In performing his activities a commercial agent must look after his principal's interests and act dutifully and in good faith.

2. In particular, a commercial agent must—
   (a) make proper efforts to negotiate and, where appropriate, conclude the transactions he is instructed to take care of;
   (b) communicate to his principal all the necessary information available to him;
   (c) comply with reasonable instructions given by his principal.

[4210]

Article 4

1. In his relations with his commercial agent a principal must act dutifully and in good faith.

2. A principal must in particular—
   (a) provide his commercial agent with the necessary documentation relating to the goods concerned;
   (b) obtain for his commercial agent the information necessary for the performance of the

agency contract, and in particular notify the commercial agent within a reasonable period once he anticipates that the volume of commercial transactions will be significantly lower than that which the commercial agent could normally have expected.

3. A principal must, in addition, inform the commercial agent within a reasonable period of his acceptance, refusal, and of any non-execution of a commercial transaction which the commercial agent has procured for the principal.

[4211]

Article 5

The parties may not derogate from the provisions of Articles 3 and 4.

[4212]

CHAPTER III
REMUNERATION

Article 6

1. In the absence of any agreement on this matter between the parties, and without prejudice to the application of the compulsory provisions of the Member States concerning the level of remuneration, a commercial agent shall be entitled to the remuneration that commercial agents appointed for the goods forming the subject of his agency contract are customarily allowed in the place where he carries on his activities. If there is no such customary practice a commercial agent shall be entitled to reasonable remuneration taking into account all the aspects of the transaction.

2. Any part of the remuneration which varies with the number or value of business transactions shall be deemed to be commission within the meaning of this Directive.

3. Articles 7 to 12 shall not apply if the commercial agent is not remunerated wholly or in part by commission.

[4213]

Article 7

1. A commercial agent shall be entitled to commission on commercial transactions concluded during the period covered by the agency contract—
  (a) where the transaction has been concluded as a result of his action; or
  (b) where the transaction is concluded with a third party whom he has previously acquired as a customer for transactions of the same kind.

2. A commercial agent shall also be entitled to commission on transactions concluded during the period covered by the agency contract—
  — either where he is entrusted with a specific geographical area or group of customers,
  — or where he has an exclusive right to a specific geographical area or group of customers,
and where the transaction has been entered into with a customer belonging to that area or group.

Member States shall include in their legislation one of the possibilities referred to in the above two indents.

[4214]

Article 8

A commercial agent shall be entitled to commission on commercial transactions concluded after the agency contract has terminated—
  (a) if the transaction is mainly attributable to the commercial agent's efforts during the period covered by the agency contract and if the transaction was entered into within a reasonable period, after that contract terminated; or
  (b) if, in accordance with the conditions mentioned in Article 7, the order of the third party reached the principal or the commercial agent before the agency contract terminated.

[4215]

Article 9

A commercial agent shall not be entitled to the commission referred to in Article 7, if that commission is payable, pursuant to Article 8, to the previous commercial agent, unless it is equitable because of the circumstances for the commission to be shared between the commercial agents.

[4216]

Article 10

1. The commission shall become due as soon as and to the extent that one of the following circumstances obtains—
  (a) the principal has executed the transaction; or
  (b) the principal should, according to his agreement with the third party, have executed the transaction; or
  (c) the third party has executed the transaction.

2.　The commission shall become due at the latest when the third party has executed his part of the transaction or should have done so if the principal had executed his part of the transaction, as he should have.

3.　The commission shall be paid not later than on the last day of the month following the quarter in which it became due.

4.　Agreements to derogate from paragraphs 2 and 3 to the detriment of the commercial agent shall not be permitted.

[4217]

Article 11

1.　The right to commission can be extinguished only if and to the extent that—
   —　it is established that the contract between the third party and the principal will not be executed, and
   —　that face is due to a reason for which the principal is not to blame.

2.　Any commission which the commercial agent has already received shall be refunded if the right to it is extinguished.

3.　Agreements to derogate from paragraph 1 to the detriment of the commercial agent shall not be permitted.

[4218]

Article 12

1.　The principal shall supply his commercial agent with a statement of the commission due, not later than the last day of the month following the quarter in which the commission has become due. This statement shall set out the main components used in calculating the amount of commission.

2.　A commercial agent shall be entitled to demand that he be provided with all the information, and in particular an extract from the books, which is available to his principal and which he needs in order to check the amount of the commission due to him.

3.　Agreements to derogate from paragraphs 1 and 2 to the detriment of the commercial agent shall not be permitted.

4.　This Directive shall not conflict with the internal provisions of Member States which recognise the right of a commercial agent to inspect a principal's books.

[4219]

CHAPTER IV
CONCLUSION AND TERMINATION OF THE AGENCY CONTRACT

Article 13

1.　Each party shall be entitled to receive from the other on request a signed written document setting out the terms of the agency contract including any terms subsequently agreed. Waiver of this right shall not be permitted.

2.　Notwithstanding paragraph 1 a Member State may provide that an agency contract shall not be valid unless evidenced in writing.

[4220]

Article 14

An agency contract for a fixed period which continues to be performed by both parties after that period has expired shall be deemed to be converted into an agency contract for an indefinite period.

[4221]

Article 15

1.　Where an agency contract is concluded for an indefinite period either party may terminate it by notice.

2.　The period of notice shall be one month for the first year of the contract, two months for the second year commenced, and three months for the third year commenced and subsequent years. The parties may not agree on shorter periods of notice.

3.　Member States may fix the period of notice at four months for the fourth year of the contract, five months for the fifth year and six months for the sixth and subsequent years. They may decide that the parties may not agree to shorter periods.

4.　If the parties agree on longer periods than those laid down in paragraphs 2 and 3, the period of notice to be observed by the principal must not be shorter than that to be observed by the commercial agent.

5.　Unless otherwise agreed by the parties, the end of the period of notice must coincide with the end of a calendar month.

6. The provisions of this Article shall apply to an agency contract for a fixed period where it is converted under Article 14 into an agency contract for an indefinite period, subject to the proviso that the earlier fixed period must be taken into account in the calculation of the period of notice.

[4222]

Article 16

Nothing in this Directive shall affect the application of the law of the Member States where the latter provides for the immediate termination of the agency contract—
    (a)   because of the failure of one party to carry out all or part of his obligations;
    (b)   where exceptional circumstances arise.

[4223]

Article 17

1. Member States shall take the measures necessary to ensure that the commercial agent is, after termination of the agency contract, indemnified in accordance with paragraph 2 or compensated for damage in accordance with paragraph 3.

2.
    (a)   The commercial agent shall be entitled to an indemnity if and to the extent that—
        —   he has brought the principal new customers or has significantly increased the volume of business with existing customers and the principal continues to derive substantial benefits from the business with such customers, and
        —   the payment of this indemnity is equitable having regard to all the circumstances and, in particular, the commission lost by the commercial agent on the business transacted with such customers. Member States may provide for such circumstances also to include the application or otherwise of a restraint of trade clause, within the meaning of Article 20;
    (b)   The amount of the indemnity may not exceed a figure equivalent to an indemnity for one year calculated from the commercial agent's average annual remuneration over the preceding five years and if the contract goes back less than five years the indemnity shall be calculated on the average for the period in question;
    (c)   The grant of such an indemnity shall not prevent the commercial agent from seeking damages.

3. The commercial agent shall be entitled to compensation for the damage he suffers as a result of the termination, of his relations with the principal.

Such damage shall be deemed to occur particularly when the termination takes place in circumstances—
    —   depriving the commercial agent of the commission which proper performance of the agency contract would have procured him whilst providing the principal with substantial benefits linked to the commercial agent's activities,
    —   and/or which have not enabled the commercial agent to amortise the costs and expenses that he had incurred for the performance of the agency contract on the principal's advice.

4. Entitlement to the indemnity as provided for in paragraph 2 or to compensation for damage as provided for under paragraph 3, shall also arise where the agency contract is terminated as a result of the commercial agent's death.

5. The commercial agent shall lose his entitlement to the indemnity in the instances provided for in paragraph 2 or to compensation for damage in the instances provided for in paragraph 3, if within one year following termination of the contract he has not notified the principal that he intends pursuing his entitlement.

6. The Commission shall submit to the Council, within eight years following the date of notification of this Directive, a report on the implementation of this Article, and shall if necessary submit to it proposals for amendments.

[4224]

Article 18

The indemnity or compensation referred to in Article 17 shall not be payable—
    (a)   where the principal has terminated the agency contract because of default attributable to the commercial agent which would justify immediate termination of the agency contract under national law;
    (b)   where the commercial agent has terminated the agency contract, unless such termination is justified by circumstances attributable to the principal or on grounds of age, infirmity or illness of the commercial agent in consequence of which he cannot reasonably be required to continue his activities;
    (c)   where, with the agreement of the principal, the commercial agent assigns his rights and duties under the agency contract to another person.

[4225]

PART 3   EU AND INTERNATIONAL MATERIALS

Article 19

The parties may not derogate from Articles 17 and 18 to the detriment of the commercial agent before the agency contract expires.

[4226]

Article 20

1.   For the purposes of this Directive, an agreement restricting the business activities of a commercial agent following termination of the agency contract is hereinafter referred to as a restraint of trade clause.

2.   A restraint of trade clause shall be valid only if and to the extent that—
   (a)   it is concluded in writing; and
   (b)   it relates to the geographical area or the group of customers and the geographical area entrusted to the commercial agent and to the kind of goods covered by his agency under the contract.

3.   A restraint of trade clause shall be valid for not more than two years after termination of the agency contract.

4.   This Article shall not affect provisions of national law which impose other restrictions on the validity or enforceability of restraint of trade clauses or which enable the courts to reduce the obligations on the parties resulting from such an agreement.

[4227]

CHAPTER V
GENERAL AND FINAL PROVISIONS

Article 21

Nothing in this Directive shall require a Member State to provide for the disclosure of information where such disclosure would be contrary to public policy.

[4228]

Article 22

1.   Member States shall bring into force the provisions necessary to comply with this Directive before 1 January 1990. They shall forthwith inform the Commission thereof. Such provisions shall apply at least to contracts concluded after their entry into force. They shall apply to contracts in operation by 1 January 1994 at the latest.

2.   As from the notification of this Directive, Member States shall communicate to the Commission the main laws, regulations and administrative provisions which they adopt in the field governed by this Directive.

3.   However, with regard to Ireland and the United Kingdom, 1 January 1990 referred to in paragraph 1 shall be replaced by 1 January 1994.

With regard to Italy, 1 January 1990 shall be replaced by 1 January 1993 in the case of the obligations deriving from Article 17.

[4229]

Article 23

This Directive is addressed to the Member States.

[4230]–[4248]

Done at Brussels, 18 December 1986.

COUNCIL DIRECTIVE

of 13 June 1990

on package travel, package holidays and package tours

(90/314/EEC)

NOTES

Date of publication in OJ: OJ L158, 23.6.90, p 59.

This Directive has been implemented in the UK by the Package Travel, Package Holidays and Package Tours Regulations 1992, SI 1992/3288 at [3132].

THE COUNCIL OF THE EUROPEAN COMMUNITIES,

Having regard to the Treaty establishing the European Economic Community, and in particular Article 100a thereof,

Having regard to the proposal from the Commission,[1]

In cooperation with the European Parliament,[2]

Having regard to the opinion of the Economic and Social Committee,[3]

Whereas one of the main objectives of the Community is to complete the internal market, of which the tourist sector is an essential part;

Whereas the national laws of Member States concerning package travel, package holidays and package tours, hereinafter referred to as 'packages', show many disparities and national practices in this field are markedly different, which gives rise to obstacles to the freedom to provide services in respect of packages and distortions of competition amongst operators established in different Member States;

Whereas the establishment of common rules on packages will contribute to the elimination of these obstacles and thereby to the achievement of a common market in services, thus enabling operators established in one Member State to offer their services in other Member States and Community consumers to benefit from comparable conditions when buying a package in any Member State;

Whereas paragraph 36(b) of the Annex to the Council resolution of 19 May 1981 on a second programme of the European Economic Community for a consumer protection and information policy[4] invites the Commission to study, *inter alia*, tourism and, if appropriate, to put forward suitable proposals, with due regard for their significance for consumer protection and the effects of differences in Member States' legislation on the proper functioning of the common market;

Whereas in the resolution on a Community policy on tourism on 10 April 1984[5] the Council welcomed the Commission's initiative in drawing attention to the importance of tourism and took note of the Commission's initial guidelines for a Community policy on tourism;

Whereas the Commission communication to the Council entitled 'A New Impetus for Consumer Protection Policy', which was approved by resolution of the Council on 6 May 1986,[6] lists in paragraph 37, among the measures proposed by the Commission, the harmonization of legislation on packages;

Whereas tourism plays an increasingly important role in the economies of the Member States; whereas the package system is a fundamental part of tourism; whereas the package travel industry in Member States would be stimulated to greater growth and productivity if at least a minimum of common rules were adopted in order to give it a Community dimension; whereas this would not only produce benefits for Community citizens buying packages organized on the basis of those rules, but would attract tourists from outside the Community seeking the advantages of guaranteed standards in packages;

Whereas disparities in the rules protecting consumers in different Member States are a disincentive to consumers in one Member State from buying packages in another Member State;

Whereas this disincentive is particularly effective in deterring consumers from buying packages outside their own Member State, and more effective than it would be in relation to the acquisition of other services, having regard to the special nature of the services supplied in a package which generally involve the expenditure of substantial amounts of money in advance and the supply of the services in a State other than that in which the consumer is resident;

Whereas the consumer should have the benefit of the protection introduced by this Directive irrespective of whether he is a direct contracting party, a transferee or a member of a group on whose behalf another person has concluded a contract in respect of a package;

Whereas the organizer of the package and/or the retailer of it should be under obligation to ensure that in descriptive matter relating to packages which they respectively organize and sell, the information which is given is not misleading and brochures made available to consumers contain information which is comprehensible and accurate;

Whereas the consumer needs to have a record of the terms of contract applicable to the package; whereas this can conveniently be achieved by requiring that all the terms of the contract be stated in writing of such other documentary form as shall be comprehensible and accessible to him, and that he be given a copy thereof;

Whereas the consumer should be at liberty in certain circumstances to transfer to a willing third person a booking made by him for a package;

Whereas the price established under the contract should not in principle be subject to revision except where the possibility of upward or downward revision is expressly provided for in the contract; whereas that possibility should nonetheless be subject to certain conditions;

Whereas the consumer should in certain circumstances be free to withdraw before departure from a package travel contract;

Whereas there should be a clear definition of the rights available to the consumer in circumstances where the organizer of the package cancels it before the agreed date of departure;

Whereas if, after the consumer has departed, there occurs a significant failure of performance of the services for which he has contracted or the organizer perceives that he will be unable to procure a significant part of the services to be provided; the organizer should have certain obligations towards the consumer;

Whereas the organizer and/or retailer party to the contract should be liable to the consumer for the proper performance of the obligations arising from the contract; whereas, moreover, the organizer and/or retailer should be liable for the damage resulting for the consumer from failure to perform or improper performance of the contract unless the defects in the performance of the contract are attributable neither to any fault of theirs nor to that of another supplier of services;

Whereas in cases where the organizer and/or retailer is liable for failure to perform or improper performance of the services involved in the package, such liability should be limited in accordance with the international conventions governing such services, in particular the Warsaw Convention of 1929 in International Carriage by Air, the Berne Convention of 1961 on Carriage by Rail, the Athens Convention of 1974 on Carriage by Sea and the Paris Convention of 1962 on the Liability of Hotel-keepers; whereas, moreover, with regard to damage other than personal injury, it should be possible for liability also to be limited under the package contract provided, however, that such limits are not unreasonable;

Whereas certain arrangements should be made for the information of consumers and the handling of complaints;

Whereas both the consumer and the package travel industry would benefit if organizers and/or retailers were placed under an obligation to provide sufficient evidence of security in the event of insolvency;

Whereas Member States should be at liberty to adopt, or retain, more stringent provisions relating to package travel for the purpose of protecting the consumer,

NOTES

1 OJ C96, 12.4.88, p 5.
2 OJ C69, 20.3.89, p 102 and OJ C149, 18.6.90.
3 OJ C102, 24.4.89, p 27.
4 OJ C165, 23.6.81, p 24.
5 OJ C115, 30.4.84, p 1.
6 OJ C118, 7.3.86, p 28.

HAS ADOPTED THIS DIRECTIVE—

Article 1

The purpose of this Directive is to approximate the laws, regulations and administrative provisions of the Member States relating to packages sold or offered for sale in the territory of the Community.

[4249]

Article 2

For the purposes of this Directive—

1. 'package' means the pre-arranged combination of not fewer than two of the following when sold or offered for sale at an inclusive price and when the service covers a period of more than twenty-four hours or includes overnight accommodation—
   (a) transport;
   (b) accommodation;
   (c) other tourist services not ancillary to transport or accommodation and accounting for a significant proportion of the package.
   The separate billing of various components of the same package shall not absolve the organiser or retailer from the obligations under this Directive;
2. 'organiser' means the person who, other than occasionally, organises packages and sells or offers them for sale, whether directly or through a retailer;
3. 'retailer' means the person who sells or offers for sale the package put together by the organiser;
4. 'consumer' means the person who takes or agrees to take the package ('the principal contractor'), or any person on whose behalf the principal contractor agrees to purchase the package ('the other beneficiaries') or any person to whom the principal contractor or any of the other beneficiaries transfers the package ('the transferee');
5. 'contract' means the agreement linking the consumer to the organiser and/or the retailer.

[4250]

Article 3

1. Any descriptive matter concerning a package and supplied by the organiser or the retailer to the consumer, the price of the package and any other conditions applying to the contract must not contain any misleading information.

2. When a brochure is made available to the consumer, it shall indicate in a legible, comprehensible and accurate manner both the price and adequate information concerning—
   (a) the destination and the means, characteristics and categories of transport used;
   (b) the type of accommodation, its location, category or degree of comfort and its main features, its approval and tourist classification under the rules of the host Member State concerned;

(c)   the meal plan;

(d)   the itinerary;

(e)   general information on passport and visa requirements for nationals of the Member State or States concerned and health formalities required for the journey and the stay;

(f)   either the monetary amount or the percentage of the price which is to be paid on account, and the timetable for payment of the balance;

(g)   whether a minimum number of persons is required for the package to take place and, if so, the deadline for informing the consumer in the event of cancellation.

The particulars contained in the brochure are binding on the organiser or retailer, unless—

—   changes in such particulars have been clearly communicated to the consumer before conclusion of the contract, in which case the brochure shall expressly state so,

—   changes are made later following an agreement between the parties to the contract.

[4251]

Article 4

1.

(a)   The organiser and/or the retailer shall provide the consumer, in writing or any other appropriate form, before the contract is concluded, with general information on passport and visa requirements applicable to nationals of the Member State or States concerned and in particular on the periods for obtaining them, as well as with information on the health formalities required for the journey and the stay;

(b)   The organiser and/or retailer shall also provide the consumer, in writing or any other appropriate form, with the following information in good time before the start of the journey—

    (i)   the times and places of intermediate stops and transport connections as well as details of the place to be occupied by the traveller, e g cabin or berth on ship, sleeper compartment on train;

    (ii)   the name, address and telephone number of the organiser's and/or retailer's local representative or, failing that, of local agencies on whose assistance a consumer in difficulty could call.

    Where no such representatives or agencies exist, the consumer must in any case be provided with an emergency telephone number or any other information that will enable him to contract the organiser and/or the retailer;

    (iii)   in the case of journeys or stays abroad by minors, information enabling direct contact to be established with the child or the person responsible at the child's place of stay;

    (iv)   information on the optional conclusion of an insurance policy to cover the cost of cancellation by the consumer or the cost of assistance, including repatriation, in the event of accident or illness.

2.   Member States shall ensure that in relation to the contract the following principles apply—

(a)   depending on the particular package, the contract shall contain at least the elements listed in the Annex;

(b)   all the terms of the contract are set out in writing or such other form as is comprehensible and accessible to the consumer and must be communicated to him before the conclusion of the contract; the consumer is given a copy of these terms;

(c)   the provision under (b) shall not preclude the belated conclusion of last-minute reservations or contracts.

3.   Where the consumer is prevented from proceeding with the package, he may transfer his booking, having first given the organiser or the retailer reasonable notice of his intention before departure, to a person who satisfies all the conditions applicable to the package. The transferor of the package and the transferee shall be jointly and severally liable to the organiser or retailer party to the contract for payment of the balance due and for any additional costs arising from such transfer.

4.

(a)   The prices laid down in the contract shall not be subject to revision unless the contract expressly provides for the possibility of upward or downward revision and states precisely how the revised price is to be calculated, and solely to allow for variations in—

—   transportation costs, including the cost of fuel,

—   dues, taxes or fees chargeable for certain services, such as landing taxes or embarkation or disembarkation fees at ports and airports,

—   the exchange rates applied to the particular package.

(b)   During the twenty days prior to the departure date stipulated, the price stated in the contract shall not be increased.

5.   If the organiser finds that before the departure he is constrained to alter significantly any of the essential terms, such as the price, he shall notify the consumer as quickly as possible in order to enable him to take appropriate decisions and in particular—

—   either to withdraw from the contract without penalty,

PART 3
EU AND INTERNATIONAL MATERIALS

— or to accept a rider to the contract specifying the alterations made and their impact on the price.

The consumer shall inform the organiser or the retailer of his decision as soon as possible.

6. If the consumer withdraws from the contract pursuant to paragraph 5, or if, for whatever cause, other than the fault of the consumer, the organiser cancels the package before the agreed date of departure, the consumer shall be entitled—

    (a) either to take a substitute package of equivalent or higher quality where the organiser and/or retailer is able to offer him such a substitute. If the replacement package offered is of lower quality, the organiser shall refund the difference in price to the consumer;

    (b) or to be repaid as soon as possible all sums paid by him under the contract.

In such a case, he shall be entitled, if appropriate, to be compensated by either the organiser or the retailer, whichever the relevant Member State's law requires, for non-performance of the contract, except where—

    (i) cancellation is on the grounds that the number of persons enrolled for the package is less than the minimum number required and the consumer is informed of the cancellation, in writing, within the period indicated in the package description; or

    (ii) cancellation, excluding overbooking, is for reasons of *force majeure*, ie unusual and unforeseeable circumstances beyond the control of the party by whom it is pleaded, the consequences of which could not have been avoided even if all due care had been exercised.

7. Where, after departure, a significant proportion of the services contracted for is not provided or the organiser perceives that he will be unable to procure a significant proportion of the services to be provided, the organiser shall make suitable alternative arrangements, at no extra cost to the consumer, for the continuation of the package and where appropriate compensate the consumer for the difference between the services offered and those supplied.

If it is impossible to make such arrangements or these are not accepted by the consumer for good reasons, the organiser shall, where appropriate, provide the consumer, at no extra cost, with equivalent transport back to the place of departure, or to another return-point to which the consumer has agreed and shall, where appropriate, compensate the consumer.

                                                                      [4252]

Article 5

1. Member States shall take the necessary steps to ensure that the organiser and/or retailer party to the contract is liable to the consumer for the proper performance of the obligations arising from the contract, irrespective of whether such obligations are to be performed by that organiser and/or retailer or by other suppliers of services without prejudice to the right of the organiser and/or retailer to pursue those other suppliers of services.

2. With regard to the damage resulting for the consumer from the failure to perform or the improper performance of the contract, Member States shall take the necessary steps to ensure that the organiser and/or retailer is/are liable unless such failure to perform or improper performance is attributable neither to any fault of theirs nor to that of another supplier of services, because—

    — the failures which occur in the performance of the contract are attributable to the consumer,

    — such failures are attributable to a third party unconnected with the provision of the services contracted for, and are unforeseeable or unavoidable,

    — such failures are due to a case of *force majeure* such as that defined in Article 4(6), second subparagraph (ii), or to an event which the organiser and/or retailer or the supplier of services, even with all due care, could not foresee or forestall.

In the cases referred to in the second and third indents, the organiser and/or retailer party to the contract shall be required to give prompt assistance to a consumer in difficulty.

In the matter of damages arising from the non-performance or improper performance of the services involved in the package, the Member States may allow compensation to be limited in accordance with the international conventions governing such services.

In the matter of damage other than personal injury resulting from the non-performance or improper performance of the services involved in the package, the Member States may allow compensation to be limited under the contract. Such limitation shall not be unreasonable.

3. Without prejudice to the fourth subparagraph of paragraph 2, there may be no exclusion by means of a contractual clause from the provisions of paragraphs 1 and 2.

4. The consumer must communicate any failure in the performance of a contract which he perceives on the spot to the supplier of the services concerned and to the organiser and/or retailer in writing or any other appropriate form at the earliest opportunity.

This obligation must be stated clearly and explicitly in the contract.

                                                                      [4253]

Article 6

In cases of complaint, the organiser and/or retailer or his local representative, if there is one, must make prompt efforts to find appropriate solutions.

[4254]

Article 7

The organiser and/or retailer party to the contract shall provide sufficient evidence of security for the refund of money paid over and for the repatriation of the consumer in the event of insolvency.

[4255]

Article 8

Member States may adopt or return more stringent provisions in the field covered by this Directive to protect the consumer.

[4256]

Article 9

1. Member States shall bring into force the measures necessary to comply with this Directive before 31 December 1992. They shall forthwith inform the Commission thereof.

2. Member States shall communicate to the Commission the texts of the main provisions of national law which they adopt in the field governed by this Directive. The Commission shall inform the other Member States thereof.

[4257]

Article 10

This Directive is addressed to the Member States.

[4258]

Done at Luxembourg, 13 June 1990.

ANNEX

Elements to be included in the contract if relevant to the particular package;

(a)   the travel destination(s) and, where periods of stay are involved, the relevant periods, with dates;

(b)   the means, characteristics and categories of transport to be used, the dates, times and points of departure and return;

(c)   where the package includes accommodation, its location, its tourist category or degree of comfort, its main features, its compliance with the rules of the host Member State concerned and the meal plan;

(d)   whether a minimum number of persons is required for the package to take place and, if so, the deadline for informing the consumer in the event of cancellation;

(e)   the itinerary;

(f)   visits, excursions or other services which are included in the total price agreed for the package;

(g)   the name and address of the organiser, the retailer and, where appropriate, the insurer;

(h)   the price of the package, an indication of the possibility of price revisions under Article 4(4) and an indication of any dues, taxes or fees chargeable for certain services (landing, embarkation or disembarkation fees at ports and airports, tourist taxes) where such costs are not included in the package;

(i)   the payment schedule and method of payment;

(j)   special requirements which the consumer has communicated to the organiser or retailer when making the booking, and which both have accepted;

(k)   periods within which the consumer must make any complaint concerning failure to perform or improper performance of the contract.

[4259]–[4278]

COUNCIL DIRECTIVE

of 5 April 1993

on unfair terms in consumer contracts

(93/13/EEC)

NOTES
Date of publication in OJ: OJ L95, 21.4.93, p 29.

This Directive has been implemented in the UK by the Unfair Terms in Consumer Contracts Regulations 1999, SI 1999/2083 at **[3228]**.

THE COUNCIL OF THE EUROPEAN COMMUNITIES,

Having regard to the Treaty establishing the European Economic Community, and in particular Article 100A thereof,

Having regard to the proposal from the Commission,[1]

In co-operation with the European Parliament,[2]

Having regard to the opinion of the Economic and Social Committee,[3]

Whereas it is necessary to adopt measures with the aim of progressively establishing the internal market before 31 December 1992; whereas the internal market comprises an area without internal frontiers in which goods, persons, services and capital move freely;

Whereas the laws of Member States relating to the terms of contract between the seller of goods or supplier of services, on the one hand, and the consumer of them, on the other hand, show many disparities, with the result that the national markets for the sale of goods and services to consumers differ from each other and that distortions of competition may arise amongst the sellers and suppliers, notably when they sell and supply in other Member States;

Whereas, in particular, the laws of Member States relating to unfair terms in consumer contracts show marked divergences;

Whereas it is the responsibility of the Member States to ensure that contracts concluded with consumers do not contain unfair terms;

Whereas, generally speaking, consumers do not know the rules of law which, in Member States other than their own, govern contracts for the sale of goods or services; whereas this lack of awareness may deter them from direct transactions for the purchase of goods or services in another Member State;

Whereas, in order to facilitate the establishment of the internal market and to safeguard the citizen in his role as consumer when acquiring goods and services under contracts which are governed by the laws of Member States other than his own, it is essential to remove unfair terms from those contracts;

Whereas sellers of goods and suppliers of services will thereby be helped in their task of selling goods and supplying services, both at home and throughout the internal market; whereas competition will thus be stimulated, so contributing to increased choice for Community citizens as consumers;

Whereas the two Community programmes for a consumer protection and information policy[4] underlined the importance of safeguarding consumers in the matter of unfair terms of contract; whereas this protection ought to be provided by laws and regulations which are either harmonised at Community level or adopted directly at that level;

Whereas in accordance with the principle laid down under the heading "Protection of the economic interests of the consumers", as stated in those programmes: "acquirers of goods and services should be protected against the abuse of power by the seller or supplier, in particular against one-sided standard contracts and the unfair exclusion of essential rights in contracts";

Whereas more effective protection of the consumer can be achieved by adopting uniform rules of law in the matter of unfair terms; whereas those rules should apply to all contracts concluded between sellers or suppliers and consumers; whereas as a result inter alia contracts relating to employment, contracts relating to succession rights, contracts relating to rights under family law and contracts relating to the incorporation and organisation of companies or partnership agreements must be excluded from this Directive;

Whereas the consumer must receive equal protection under contracts concluded by word of mouth and written contracts regardless, in the latter case, of whether the terms of the contract are contained in one or more documents;

Whereas, however, as they now stand, national laws allow only partial harmonisation to be envisaged; whereas, in particular, only contractual terms which have not been individually negotiated are covered by this Directive; whereas Member States should have the option, with due regard for the Treaty, to afford consumers a higher level of protection through national provisions that are more stringent than those of this Directive;

Whereas the statutory or regulatory provisions of the Member States which directly or indirectly determine the terms of consumer contracts are presumed not to contain unfair terms; whereas, therefore, it does not appear to be necessary to subject the terms which reflect mandatory statutory or regulatory provisions and the principles or provisions of international conventions to which the Member States or the Community are party; whereas in that respect the wording "mandatory statutory or regulatory provisions" in Article 1(2) also covers rules which, according to the law, shall apply between the contracting parties provided that no other arrangements have been established;

Whereas Member States must however ensure that unfair terms are not included, particularly because this Directive also applies to trades, business or professions of a public nature;

Whereas it is necessary to fix in a general way the criteria for assessing the unfair character of contract terms;

Whereas the assessment, according to the general criteria chosen, of the unfair character of terms, in particular in sale or supply activities of a public nature providing collective services which take account of solidarity among users, must be supplemented by a means of making an overall evaluation of the different interests involved; whereas this constitutes the requirement of good faith; whereas, in making an assessment of good faith, particular regard shall be had to the strength of the bargaining positions of the parties, whether the consumer had an inducement to agree to the term and whether the goods or services were sold or supplied to the special order of the consumer; whereas the requirement of good faith may be satisfied by the seller or supplier where he deals fairly and equitably with the other party whose legitimate interests he has to take into account;

Whereas, for the purposes of this Directive, the annexed list of terms can be of indicative value only and, because of the cause of the minimal character of the Directive, the scope of these terms may be the subject of amplification or more restrictive editing by the Member States in their national laws;

Whereas the nature of goods or services should have an influence on assessing the unfairness of contractual terms;

Whereas, for the purposes of this Directive, assessment of unfair character shall not be made of terms which describe the main subject matter of the contract nor the quality/price ratio of the goods or services supplied; whereas the main subject matter of the contract and the price/quality ratio may nevertheless be taken into account in assessing the fairness of other terms; whereas it follows, inter alia, that in insurance contracts, the terms which clearly define or circumscribe the insured risk and the insurer's liability shall not be subject to such assessment since these restrictions are taken into account in calculating the premium paid by the consumer;

Whereas contracts should be drafted in plain, intelligible language, the consumer should actually be given an opportunity to examine all the terms and, if in doubt, the interpretation most favourable to the consumer should prevail;

Whereas Member States should ensure that unfair terms are not used in contracts concluded with consumers by a seller or supplier and that if, nevertheless, such terms are so used, they will not bind the consumer, and the contract will continue to bind the parties upon those terms if it is capable of continuing in existence without the unfair provisions;

Whereas there is a risk that, in certain cases, the consumer may be deprived of protection under this Directive by designating the law of a non-Member country as the law applicable to the contract; whereas provisions should therefore be included in this Directive designed to avert this risk;

Whereas persons or organisations, if regarded under the law of a Member State as having a legitimate interest in the matter, must have facilities for initiating proceedings concerning terms of contract drawn up for general use in contracts concluded with consumers, and in particular unfair terms, either before a court or before an administrative authority competent to decide upon complaints or to initiate appropriate legal proceedings; whereas this possibility does not, however, entail prior verification of the general conditions obtaining in individual economic sectors;

Whereas the courts or administrative authorities of the Member States must have at their disposal adequate and effective means of preventing the continued application of unfair terms in consumer contracts,

---

NOTES

1   OJ C73, 24.3.92, p 7.
2   OJ C326, 16.12.91, p 108 and OJ C21, 25.1.93.
3   OJ C159, 17.6.91, p 34.
4   OJ C92, 25.4.75 and OJ C133, 3.6.81, p 1.

HAS ADOPTED THIS DIRECTIVE:

Article 1

1. The purpose of this Directive is to approximate the laws, regulations and administrative provisions of the Member States relating to unfair terms in contracts concluded between a seller or supplier and a consumer.

2. The contractual terms which reflect mandatory statutory or regulatory provisions and the provisions or principles of international conventions to which the Member States or the Community are party, particularly in the transport area, shall not be subject to the provisions of this Directive.

[4279]

Article 2

For the purposes of this Directive—

    (a)   "unfair terms" means the contractual terms defined in Article 3;
    (b)   "consumer" means any natural person who, in contracts covered by this Directive, is acting for purposes which are outside his trade, business or profession;
    (c)   "seller or supplier" means any natural or legal person who, in contracts covered by this Directive, is acting for purposes relating to his trade, business or profession, whether publicly owned or privately owned.

[4280]

Article 3

1.   A contractual term which has not been individually negotiated shall be regarded as unfair if, contrary to the requirement of good faith, it causes a significant imbalance in the parties' rights and obligations arising under the contract, to the detriment of the consumer.

2.   A term shall always be regarded as not individually negotiated where it has been drafted in advance and the consumer has therefore not been able to influence the substance of the term, particularly in the context of a pre-formulated standard contract.

The fact that certain aspects of a term or one specific term have been individually negotiated shall not exclude the application of this Article to the rest of a contract if an overall assessment of the contract indicates that it is nevertheless a pre-formulated standard contract.

Where any seller or supplier claims that a standard term has been individually negotiated, the burden of proof in this respect shall be incumbent on him.

3.   The Annex shall contain an indicative and non-exhaustive list of the terms which may be regarded as unfair.

[4281]

Article 4

1.   Without prejudice to Article 7, the unfairness of a contractual term shall be assessed, taking into account the nature of the goods or services for which the contract was concluded and by referring, at the time of conclusion of the contract, to all the circumstances attending the conclusion of the contract and to all the other terms of the contract or of another contract on which it is dependent.

2.   Assessment of the unfair nature of the terms shall relate neither to the definition of the main subject matter of the contract nor to the adequacy of the price and remuneration, on the one hand, as against the services or goods supplies in exchange, on the other, in so far as these terms are in plain intelligible language.

[4282]

Article 5

In the case of contracts where all or certain terms offered to the consumer are in writing, these terms must always be drafted in plain, intelligible language. Where there is doubt about the meaning of a term, the interpretation most favourable to the consumer shall prevail. This rule on interpretation shall not apply in the context of the procedures laid down in Article 7(2).

[4283]

Article 6

1.   Member States shall lay down that unfair terms used in a contract concluded with a consumer by a seller or supplier shall, as provided for under their national law, not be binding on the consumer and that the contract shall continue to bind the parties upon those terms if it is capable of continuing in existence without the unfair terms.

2.   Member States shall take the necessary measures to ensure that the consumer does not lose the protection granted by this Directive by virtue of the choice of the law of a non-Member country as the law applicable to the contract if the latter has a close connection with the territory of the Member States.

[4284]

Article 7

1.   Member States shall ensure that, in the interests of consumers and of competitors, adequate and effective means exist to prevent the continued use of unfair terms in contracts concluded with consumers by sellers or suppliers.

2.   The means referred to in paragraph 1 shall include provisions whereby persons or organisations, having a legitimate interest under national law in protecting consumers, may take action according to the national law concerned before the courts or before competent administrative bodies for a decision as to whether contractual terms drawn up for general use are unfair, so that they can apply appropriate and effective means to prevent the continued use of such terms.

3.   With due regard for national laws, the legal remedies referred to in paragraph 2 may be directed separately or jointly against a number of sellers or suppliers from the same economic sector or their associations which use or recommend the use of the same general contractual terms or similar terms.

[4285]

Article 8

Member States may adopt or retain the most stringent provisions compatible with the Treaty in the area covered by this Directive, to ensure a maximum degree of protection for the consumer.

[4286]

Article 9

The Commission shall present a report to the European Parliament and to the Council concerning the application of this Directive five years at the latest after the date in Article 10(1).

[4287]

Article 10

1. Member States shall bring into force the laws, regulations and administrative provisions necessary to comply with this Directive no later than 31 December 1994. They shall forthwith inform the Commission thereof.

These provisions shall be applicable to all contracts concluded after 31 December 1994.

2. When Member States adopt these measures, they shall contain a reference to this Directive or shall be accompanied by such reference on the occasion of their official publication. The methods of making such a reference shall be laid down by the Member States.

3. Member States shall communicate the main provisions of national law which they adopt in the field covered by this Directive to the Commission.

[4288]

Article 11

This Directive is addressed to the Member States.

[4289]

Done at Luxembourg, 5 April 1993.

ANNEX

TERMS REFERRED TO IN ARTICLE 3(3)

1. Terms which have the object or effect of—

   (a)   excluding or limiting the legal liability of a seller or supplier in the event of the death of a consumer or personal injury to the latter resulting from an act or omission of that seller or supplier;

   (b)   inappropriately excluding or limiting the legal rights of the consumer *vis-à-vis* the seller or supplier or another party in the event of total or partial non-performance or inadequate performance by the seller or supplier of any of the contractual obligations, including the option of offsetting a debt owed to the seller or supplier against any claim which the consumer may have against him;

   (c)   making an agreement binding on the consumer whereas provision of services by the seller or supplier is subject to a condition whose realisation depends on his own will alone;

   (d)   permitting the seller or supplier to retain sums paid by the consumer where the latter decides not to conclude or perform the contract, without providing for the consumer to receive compensation of an equivalent amount from the seller or supplier where the latter is the party cancelling the contract;

   (e)   requiring any consumer who fails to fulfil his obligation to pay a disproportionately high sum in compensation;

   (f)   authorising the seller or supplier to dissolve the contract on a discretionary basis where the same facility is not granted to the consumer, or permitting the seller or supplier to retain the sums paid for services not yet supplied by him where it is the seller or supplier himself who dissolves the contract;

   (g)   enabling the seller or supplier to terminate a contract of indeterminate duration without reasonable notice except where there are serious grounds for doing so;

   (h)   automatically extending a contract of fixed duration where the consumer does not indicate otherwise, when the deadline fixed for the consumer to express this desire not to extend the contract is unreasonably early;

   (i)   irrevocably binding the consumer to terms with which he had no real opportunity of becoming acquainted before the conclusion of the contract;

   (j)   enabling the seller or supplier to alter the terms of the contract unilaterally without a valid reason which is specified in the contract;

   (k)   enabling the seller or supplier to alter unilaterally without a valid reason any characteristics of the product or service to be provided;

   (l)   providing for the price of goods to be determined at the time of delivery or allowing a seller of goods or supplier of services to increase their price without in both cases giving the consumer the corresponding right to cancel the contract if the final price is too high in relation to the price agreed when the contract was concluded;

   (m)   giving the seller or supplier the right to determine whether the goods or services supplied are in conformity with the contract, or giving him the exclusive right to interpret any term of the contract;

   (n)   limiting the seller's or supplier's obligation to respect commitments undertaken by his agents or making his commitments subject to compliance with a particular formality;

(o) obliging the consumer to fulfil all his obligations where the seller or supplier does not perform his;

(p) giving the seller or supplier the possibility of transferring his rights and obligations under the contract, where this may serve to reduce the guarantees for the consumer, without the latter's agreement;

(q) excluding or hindering the consumer's right to take legal action or exercise any other legal remedy, particularly by requiring the consumer to take disputes exclusively to arbitration not covered by legal provisions, unduly restricting the evidence available to him or imposing on him a burden of proof which, according to the applicable law, should lie with another party to the contract.

2. Scope of subparagraphs (g), (j) and (l)—

(a) Subparagraph (g) is without hindrance to terms by which a supplier of financial services reserves the right to terminate unilaterally a contract of indeterminate duration without notice where there is a valid reason, provided that the supplier is required to inform the other contracting party or parties thereof immediately.

(b) Subparagraph (j) is without hindrance to terms under which a supplier of financial services reserves the right to alter the rate of interest payable by the consumer or due to the latter, or the amount of other charges for financial services without notice where there is a valid reason, provided that the supplier is required to inform the other contracting party or parties thereof at the earliest opportunity and that the latter are free to dissolve the contract immediately.

Subparagraph (j) is also without hindrance to terms under which a seller or supplier reserves the right to alter unilaterally the conditions of a contract of indeterminate duration, provided that he is required to inform the consumer with reasonable notice and that the consumer is free to dissolve the contract.

(c) Subparagraphs (g), (j) and (l) do not apply to—

— transactions in transferable securities, financial instruments and other products or services where the price is linked to fluctuations in a stock exchange quotation or index or a financial market rate that the seller or supplier does not control;

— contracts for the purchase or sale of foreign currency, traveller's cheques or international money orders denominated in foreign currency;

(d) Subparagraph (l) is without hindrance to price-indexation clauses, where lawful, provided that the method by which prices vary is explicitly described.

[4290]–[4304]

DIRECTIVE OF THE EUROPEAN PARLIAMENT AND OF THE COUNCIL

of 20 May 1997

on the protection of consumers in respect of distance contracts

(97/7/EC)

NOTES
Date of publication in OJ: OJ L144, 4.6.97, p 19.
This Directive has been implemented in the UK by the Consumer Protection (Distance Selling) Regulations 2000, SI 2000/2334 at **[3300]**.

THE EUROPEAN PARLIAMENT AND THE COUNCIL OF THE EUROPEAN UNION,

Having regard to the Treaty establishing the European Community, and in particular Article 100a thereof,

Having regard to the proposal from the Commission,[1]

Having regard to the opinion of the Economic and Social Committee,[2]

Acting in accordance with the procedure laid down in Article 189b of the Treaty,[3] in the light of the joint text approved by the Conciliation Committee on 27 November 1996,

(1) Whereas, in connection with the attainment of the aims of the internal market, measures must be taken for the gradual consolidation of that market;

(2) Whereas the free movement of goods and services affects not only the business sector but also private individuals; whereas it means that consumers should be able to have access to the goods and services of another Member State on the same terms as the population of that State;

(3) Whereas, for consumers, cross-border distance selling could be one of the main tangible results of the completion of the internal market, as noted, *inter alia*, in the communication from the Commission to the Council entitled 'Towards a single market in distribution'; whereas it is essential to the smooth operation of the internal market for consumers to be able to have dealings with a business outside their country, even if it has a subsidiary in the consumer's country of residence;

(4)   Whereas the introduction of new technologies is increasing the number of ways for consumers to obtain information about offers anywhere in the Community and to place orders; whereas some Member States have already taken different or diverging measures to protect consumers in respect of distance selling, which has had a detrimental effect on competition between businesses in the internal market; whereas it is therefore necessary to introduce at Community level a minimum set of common rules in this area;

(5)   Whereas paragraphs 18 and 19 of the Annex to the Council resolution of 14 April 1975 on a preliminary programme of the European Economic Community for a consumer protection and information policy[4] point to the need to protect the purchasers of goods or services from demands for payment for unsolicited goods and from high-pressure selling methods;

(6)   Whereas paragraph 33 of the communication from the Commission to the Council entitled 'A new impetus for consumer protection policy', which was approved by the Council resolution of 23 June 1986,[5] states that the Commission will submit proposals regarding the use of new information technologies enabling consumers to place orders with suppliers from their homes;

(7)   Whereas the Council resolution of 9 November 1989 on future priorities for relaunching consumer protection policy[6] calls upon the Commission to give priority to the areas referred to in the Annex to that resolution; whereas that Annex refers to new technologies involving teleshopping; whereas the Commission has responded to that resolution by adopting a three-year action plan for consumer protection policy in the European Economic Community (1990–1992); whereas that plan provides for the adoption of a Directive;

(8)   Whereas the languages used for distance contracts are a matter for the Member States;

(9)   Whereas contracts negotiated at a distance involve the use of one or more means of distance communication; whereas the various means of communication are used as part of an organised distance sales or service-provision scheme not involving the simultaneous presence of the supplier and the consumer; whereas the constant development of those means of communication does not allow an exhaustive list to be compiled but does require principles to be defined which are valid even for those which are not as yet in widespread use;

(10)   Whereas the same transaction comprising successive operations or a series of separate operations over a period of time may give rise to different legal descriptions depending on the law of the Member States; whereas the provisions of this Directive cannot be applied differently according to the law of the Member States, subject to their recourse to Article 14; whereas, to that end, there is therefore reason to consider that there must at least be compliance with the provisions of this Directive at the time of the first of a series of successive operations or the first of a series of separate operations over a period of time which may be considered as forming a whole, whether that operation or series of operations are the subject of a single contract or successive, separate contracts;

(11)   Whereas the use of means of distance communication must not lead to a reduction in the information provided to the consumer; whereas the information that is required to be sent to the consumer should therefore be determined, whatever the means of communication used; whereas the information supplied must also comply with the other relevant Community rules, in particular those in Council Directive 84/450/EEC of 10 September 1984 relating to the approximation of the laws, regulations and administrative provisions of the Member States concerning misleading advertising;[7] whereas, if exceptions are made to the obligation to provide information, it is up to the consumer, on a discretionary basis, to request certain basic information such as the identity of the supplier, the main characteristics of the goods or services and their price;

(12)   Whereas in the case of communication by telephone it is appropriate that the consumer receive enough information at the beginning of the conversation to decide whether or not to continue;

(13)   Whereas information disseminated by certain electronic technologies is often ephemeral in nature insofar as it is not received on a permanent medium; whereas the consumer must therefore receive written notice in good time of the information necessary for proper performance of the contract;

(14)   Whereas the consumer is not able actually to see the product or ascertain the nature of the service provided before concluding the contract; whereas provision should be made, unless otherwise specified in this Directive, for a right of withdrawal from the contract; whereas, if this right is to be more than formal, the costs, if any, borne by the consumer when exercising the right of withdrawal must be limited to the direct costs for returning the goods; whereas this right of withdrawal shall be without prejudice to the consumer's rights under national laws, with particular regard to the receipt of damaged products and services or of products and services not corresponding to the description given in the offer of such products or services; whereas it is for the Member States to determine the other conditions and arrangements following exercise of the right of withdrawal;

(15)   Whereas it is also necessary to prescribe a time limit for performance of the contract if this is not specified at the time of ordering;

(16)   Whereas the promotional technique involving the dispatch of a product or the provision of a service to the consumer in return for payment without a prior request from, or the explicit agreement of, the consumer cannot be permitted, unless a substitute product or service is involved;

(17)   Whereas the principles set out in Articles 8 and 10 of the European Convention for the Protection of Human Rights and Fundamental Freedoms of 4 November 1950 apply; whereas the consumer's right to privacy, particularly as regards freedom from certain particularly intrusive

means of communication, should be recognised; whereas specific limits on the use of such means should therefore be stipulated; whereas Member States should take appropriate measures to protect effectively those consumers, who do not wish to be contacted through certain means of communication, against such contacts, without prejudice to the particular safeguards available to the consumer under Community legislation concerning the protection of personal data and privacy;

(18)　Whereas it is important for the minimum binding rules contained in this Directive to be supplemented where appropriate by voluntary arrangements among the traders concerned, in line with Commission recommendation 92/295/EEC of 7 April 1992 on codes of practice for the protection of consumers in respect of contracts negotiated at a distance;[8]

(19)　Whereas in the interest of optimum consumer protection it is important for consumers to be satisfactorily informed of the provisions of this Directive and of codes of practice that may exist in this field;

(20)　Whereas non-compliance with this Directive may harm not only consumers but also competitors; whereas provisions may therefore be laid down enabling public bodies or their representatives, or consumer organisations which, under national legislation, have a legitimate interest in consumer protection, or professional organisations which have a legitimate interest in taking action, to monitor the application thereof;

(21)　Whereas it is important, with a view to consumer protection, to address the question of cross-border complaints as soon as this is feasible; whereas the Commission published on 14 February 1996 a plan of action on consumer access to justice and the settlement of consumer disputes in the internal market; whereas that plan of action includes specific initiatives to promote out-of-court procedures; whereas objective criteria (Annex II) are suggested to ensure the reliability of those procedures and provision is made for the use of standardised claims forms (Annex III);

(22)　Whereas in the use of new technologies the consumer is not in control of the means of communication used; whereas it is therefore necessary to provide that the burden of proof may be on the supplier;

(23)　Whereas there is a risk that, in certain cases, the consumer may be deprived of protection under this Directive through the designation of the law of a non-member country as the law applicable to the contract; whereas provisions should therefore be included in this Directive to avert that risk;

(24)　Whereas a Member State may ban, in the general interest, the marketing on its territory of certain goods and services through distance contracts; whereas that ban must comply with Community rules; whereas there is already provision for such bans, notably with regard to medicinal products, under Council Directive 89/552/EEC of 3 October 1989 on the coordination of certain provisions laid down by law, regulation or administrative action in Member States concerning the pursuit of television broadcasting activities[9] and Council Directive 92/28/EEC of 31 March 1992 on the advertising of medicinal products for human use,[10]

NOTES

[1]	OJ C156, 23.6.92, p 14 and OJ C308, 15.11.93, p 18.
[2]	OJ C19, 25.1.93, p 111.
[3]	Opinion of the European Parliament of 26 May 1993 (OJ C176, 28.6.93, p 95), Council common position of 29 June 1995 (OJ C288, 30.10.95, p.1) and Decision of the European Parliament of 13 December 1995 (OJ C17, 22.1.96, p 51). Decision of the European Parliament of 16 January 1997 and Council Decision of 20 January 1997.
[4]	OJ C92, 25.4.75, p 1.
[5]	OJ C167, 5.7.86, p 1.
[6]	OJ C294, 22.11.89, p 1.
[7]	OJ L250, 19.9.84, p 17.
[8]	OJ L156, 10.6.92, p 21.
[9]	OJ L298, 17.10.89, p 23.
[10]	OJ L113, 30.4.92, p 13.

HAVE ADOPTED THIS DIRECTIVE—

Article 1
Object

The object of this Directive is to approximate the laws, regulations and administrative provisions of the Member States concerning distance contracts between consumers and suppliers.

[4305]

Article 2
Definitions

For the purposes of this Directive—

(1)　'distance contract' means any contract concerning goods or services concluded between a supplier and a consumer under an organised distance sales or service-provision scheme run by the supplier, who, for the purpose of the contract, makes exclusive use of one or more means of distance communication up to and including the moment at which the contract is concluded;

(2)   'consumer' means any natural person who, in contracts covered by this Directive, is acting for purposes which are outside his trade, business or profession;

(3)   'supplier' means any natural or legal person who, in contracts covered by this Directive, is acting in his commercial or professional capacity;

(4)   'means of distance communication' means any means which, without the simultaneous physical presence of the supplier and the consumer, may be used for the conclusion of a contract between those parties. An indicative list of the means covered by this Directive is contained in Annex I;

(5)   'operator of a means of communication' means any public or private natural or legal person whose trade, business or profession involves making one or more means of distance communication available to suppliers.

[4306]

Article 3
Exemptions

1.   This Directive shall not apply to contracts—

[—   relating to any financial service to which Directive 2002/65/EC of the European Parliament and of the Council of 23 September 2002 concerning the distance marketing of consumer financial services and amending Council Directive 90/619/EEC and Directives 97/7/EC and 98/27/EC[1] applies,]

—   concluded by means of automatic vending machines or automated commercial premises,

—   concluded with telecommunications operators through the use of public payphones,

—   concluded for the construction and sale of immovable property or relating to other immovable property rights, except for rental,

—   concluded at an auction.

2.   Articles 4, 5, 6 and 7(1) shall not apply—

—   to contracts for the supply of foodstuffs, beverages or other goods intended for everyday consumption supplied to the home of the consumer, to his residence or to his workplace by regular roundsmen,

—   to contracts for the provision of accommodation, transport, catering or leisure services, where the supplier undertakes, when the contract is concluded, to provide these services on a specific date or within a specific period; exceptionally, in the case of outdoor leisure events, the supplier can reserve the right not to apply Article 7(2) in specific circumstances.

[4307]

NOTES

Para 1: words in square brackets substituted by European Parliament and Council Directive 2002/65/EC, Art 18(1).

[1]   OJ L271, 9.10.2002, p 16.

Article 4
Prior information

1.   In good time prior to the conclusion of any distance contract, the consumer shall be provided with the following information—

(a)   the identity of the supplier and, in the case of contracts requiring payment in advance, his address;

(b)   the main characteristics of the goods or services;

(c)   the price of the goods or services including all taxes;

(d)   delivery costs, where appropriate;

(e)   the arrangements for payment, delivery or performance;

(f)   the existence of a right of withdrawal, except in the cases referred to in Article 6(3);

(g)   the cost of using the means of distance communication, where it is calculated other than at the basic rate;

(h)   the period for which the offer or the price remains valid;

(i)   where appropriate, the minimum duration of the contract in the case of contracts for the supply of products or services to be performed permanently or recurrently.

2.   The information referred to in paragraph 1, the commercial purpose of which must be made clear, shall be provided in a clear and comprehensible manner in any way appropriate to the means of distance communication used, with due regard, in particular, to the principles of good faith in commercial transactions, and the principles governing the protection of those who are unable, pursuant to the legislation of the Member States, to give their consent, such as minors.

3.   Moreover, in the case of telephone communications, the identity of the supplier and the commercial purpose of the call shall be made explicitly clear at the beginning of any conversation with the consumer.

[4308]

Article 5
Written confirmation of information

1.   The consumer must receive written confirmation or confirmation in another durable medium available and accessible to him of the information referred to in Article 4(1)(a) to (f), in good time during the performance of the contract, and at the latest at the time of delivery where goods not for delivery to third parties are concerned, unless the information has already been given to the consumer prior to conclusion of the contract in writing or on another durable medium available and accessible to him.

In any event the following must be provided—
— written information on the conditions and procedures for exercising the right of withdrawal, within the meaning of Article 6, including the cases referred to in the first indent of Article 6(3),
— the geographical address of the place of business of the supplier to which the consumer may address any complaints,
— information on after-sales services and guarantees which exist,
— the conclusion for cancelling the contract, where it is of unspecified duration or a duration exceeding one year.

2.   Paragraph 1 shall not apply to services which are performed through the use of a means of distance communication, where they are supplied on only one occasion and are invoiced by the operator of the means of distance communication. Nevertheless, the consumer must in all cases be able to obtain the geographical address of the place of business of the supplier to which he may address any complaints.

[4309]

Article 6
Right of withdrawal

1.   For any distance contract the consumer shall have a period of at least seven working days in which to withdraw from the contract without penalty and without giving any reason. The only charge that may be made to the consumer because of the exercise of his right of withdrawal is the direct cost of returning the goods.

The period for exercise of this right shall begin—
— in the case of goods, from the day of receipt by the consumer where the obligations laid down in Article 5 have been fulfilled,
— in the case of services, from the day of conclusion of the contract or from the day on which the obligations laid down in Article 5 were fulfilled if they are fulfilled after conclusion of the contract, provided that this period does not exceed the three-month period referred to in the following subparagraph.

If the supplier has failed to fulfil the obligations laid down in Article 5, the period shall be three months. The period shall begin   —
— in the case of goods, from the day of receipt by the consumer,
— in the case of services, from the day of conclusion of the contract.

If the information referred to in Article 5 is supplied within this three-month period, the seven working day period referred to in the first subparagraph shall begin as from that moment.

2.   Where the right of withdrawal has been exercised by the consumer pursuant to this Article, the supplier shall be obliged to reimburse the sums paid by the consumer free of charge. The only charge that may be made to the consumer because of the exercise of his right of withdrawal is the direct cost of returning the goods. Such reimbursement must be carried out as soon as possible and in any case within 30 days.

3.   Unless the parties have agreed otherwise, the consumer may not exercise the right of withdrawal provided for in paragraph 1 in respect of contracts—
— for the provision of services if performance has begun, with the consumer's agreement, before the end of the seven working day period referred to in paragraph 1,
— for the supply of goods or services the price of which is dependent on fluctuations in the financial market which cannot be controlled by the supplier,
— for the supply of goods made to the consumer's specifications or clearly personalised or which, by reason of their nature, cannot be returned or are liable to deteriorate or expire rapidly,
— for the supply of audio or video recordings or computer software which were unsealed by the consumer,
— for the supply of newspapers, periodicals and magazines,
— for gaming and lottery services.

4.   The Member States shall make provision in their legislation to ensure that—
— if the price of goods or services is fully or partly covered by credit granted by the supplier, or

— if that price is fully or partly covered by credit granted to the consumer by a third party on the basis of an agreement between the third party and the supplier,

the credit agreement shall be cancelled, without any penalty, if the consumer exercises his right to withdraw from the contract in accordance with paragraph 1.

Member States shall determine the detailed rules for cancellation of the credit agreement.

[4310]

Article 7
Performance

1. Unless the parties have agreed otherwise, the supplier must execute the order within a maximum of 30 days from the day following that on which the consumer forwarded his order to the supplier.

2. Where a supplier fails to perform his side of the contract on the grounds that the goods or services ordered are unavailable, the consumer must be informed of this situation and must be able to obtain a refund of any sums he has paid as soon as possible and in any case within 30 days.

3. Nevertheless, Member States may lay down that the supplier may provide the consumer with goods or services of equivalent quality and price provided that this possibility was provided for prior to the conclusion of the contract or in the contract. The consumer shall be informed of this possibility in a clear and comprehensible manner. The cost of returning the goods following exercise of the right of withdrawal shall, in this case, be borne by the supplier, and the consumer must be informed of this. In such cases the supply of goods or services may not be deemed to constitute inertia selling within the meaning of Article 9.

[4311]–[4312]

Article 8

(Repealed by European Parliament and Council Directive 2007/64/EC, Art 89.)

[Article 9
Inertia selling

Given the prohibition of inertia selling practices laid down in Directive 2005/29/EC of 11 May 2005 of the European Parliament and of the Council concerning unfair business-to-consumer commercial practices in the internal market,[1] Member States shall take the measures necessary to exempt the consumer from the provision of any consideration in cases of unsolicited supply, the absence of a response not constituting consent.]

[4313]

NOTES

Substituted by European Parliament and Council Directive 2005/29/EC, Art 15(1).

[1]   OJ L149, 11.6.2005, p 22.

Article 10
Restrictions on the use of certain means of distance communication

1. Use by a supplier of the following means requires the prior consent of the consumer—
   — automated calling system without human intervention (automatic calling machine),
   — facsimile machine (fax).

2. Member States shall ensure that means of distance communication, other than those referred to in paragraph 1, which allow individual communications may be used only where there is no clear objection from the consumer.

[4314]

Article 11
Judicial or administrative redress

1. Member States shall ensure that adequate and effective means exist to ensure compliance with this Directive in the interests of consumers.

2. The means referred to in paragraph 1 shall include provisions whereby one or more of the following bodies, as determined by national law, may take action under national law before the courts or before the competent administrative bodies to ensure that the national provisions for the implementation of this Directive are applied—
   (a) public bodies or their representatives;
   (b) consumer organisations having a legitimate interest in protecting consumers;
   (c) professional organisations having a legitimate interest in acting.

3.
   (a) Member States may stipulate that the burden of proof concerning the existence of prior information, written confirmation, compliance with time-limits or consumer consent can be placed on the supplier.

(b)   Member States shall take the measures needed to ensure that suppliers and operators of means of communication, where they are able to do so, cease practices which do not comply with measures adopted pursuant to this Directive.

4.   Member States may provide for voluntary supervision by self-regulatory bodies of compliance with the provisions of this Directive and recourse to such bodies for the settlement of disputes to be added to the means which Member States must provided to ensure compliance with the provisions of this Directive.

[4315]

Article 12
Binding nature

1.   The consumer may not waive the rights conferred on him by the transposition of this Directive into national law.

2.   Member States shall take the measures needed to ensure that the consumer does not lose the protection granted by this Directive by virtue of the choice of the law of a non-member country as the law applicable to the contract if the latter has close connection with the territory of one or more Member States.

[4316]

Article 13
Community rules

1.   The provisions of this Directive shall apply insofar as there are no particular provisions in rules of Community law governing certain types of distance contracts in their entirety.

2.   Where specific Community rules contain provisions governing only certain aspects of the supply of goods or provision of services, those provisions, rather than the provisions of this Directive, shall apply to these specific aspects of the distance contracts.

[4317]

Article 14
Minimal clause

Member States may introduce or maintain, in the area covered by this Directive, more stringent provisions compatible with the Treaty, to ensure a higher level of consumer protection. Such provisions shall, where appropriate, include a ban, in the general interest, on the marketing of certain goods or services, particularly medicinal products, within their territory by means of distance contracts, with due regard for the Treaty.

[4318]

Article 15
Implementation

1.   Member States shall bring into force the laws, regulations and administrative provisions necessary to comply with this Directive no later than three years after it enters into force. They shall forthwith inform the Commission thereof.

2.   When Member States adopt the measures referred to in paragraph 1, these shall contain a reference to this Directive or shall be accompanied by such reference on the occasion of their official publication. The procedure for such reference shall be laid down by Member States.

3.   Member States shall communicate to the Commission the text of the provisions of national law which they adopt in the field governed by this Directive.

4.   No later than four years after the entry into force of this Directive the Commission shall submit a report to the European Parliament and the Council on the implementation of this Directive, accompanied if appropriate by a proposal for the revision thereof.

[4319]

Article 16
Consumer information

Member States shall take appropriate measures to inform the consumer of the national law transposing this Directive and shall encourage, where appropriate, professional organisations to inform consumers of their codes of practice.

[4320]

Article 17
Complaints systems

The Commission shall study the feasibility of establishing effective means to deal with consumers' complaints in respect of distance selling. Within two years after the entry into force of this Directive the Commission shall submit a report to the European Parliament and the Council on the results of the studies, accompanied if appropriate by proposals.

[4321]

Article 18

This Directive shall enter into force on the day of its publication in the *Official Journal of the European Communities*.

[4322]

Article 19

This Directive is addressed to the Member States.

[4323]

Done at Brussels, 20 May 1997.

ANNEX I

MEANS OF COMMUNICATION COVERED BY ARTICLE 2(4)

— Unaddressed printed matter
— Addressed printed matter
— Standard letter
— Press advertising with order form
— Catalogue
— Telephone with human intervention
— Telephone without human intervention (automatic calling machine, audiotext)
— Radio
— Videophone (telephone with screen)
— Videotex (microcomputer and television screen) with keyboard or touch screen
— Electronic mail
— Facsimile machine (fax)
— Television (teleshopping).

[4324]

(Annex II repealed by European Parliament and Council Directive 2002/65/EC, Art 18(2).)

DIRECTIVE OF THE EUROPEAN PARLIAMENT AND OF THE COUNCIL

of 16 February 1998

on consumer protection in the indication of the prices of products offered to consumers

(98/6/EC)

NOTES
Date of publication in OJ: OJ L80, 18.3.98, p 27.
This Directive has been implemented in the UK by the Price Marking Order 2004, SI 2004/102 at **[3369]**.

THE EUROPEAN PARLIAMENT AND THE COUNCIL OF THE EUROPEAN UNION,

Having regard to the Treaty establishing the European Community, and in particular Article 129a(2) thereof,

Having regard to the proposal from the Commission,[1]

Having regard to the opinion of the Economic and Social Committee,[2]

Acting in accordance with the procedure laid down in Article 189b of the Treaty,[3] in the light of the joint text approved by the Conciliation Committee on 9 December 1997,

(1) Whereas transparent operation of the market and correct information is of benefit to consumer protection and healthy competition between enterprises and products;

(2) Whereas consumers must be guaranteed a high level of protection; whereas the Community should contribute thereto by specific action which supports and supplements the policy pursued by the Member States regarding precise, transparent and unambiguous information for consumers on the prices of products offered to them;

(3) Whereas the Council Resolution of 14 April 1975 on a preliminary programme of the European Economic Community for a consumer protection and information policy[4] and the Council Resolution of 19 May 1981 on a second programme of the European Economic Community for a consumer protection and information policy[5] provide for the establishment of common principles for indicating prices;

(4) Whereas these principles have been established by Directive 79/581/EEC concerning the indication of prices of certain foodstuffs[6] and Directive 88/314/EEC concerning the indication of prices of non-food products;[7]

(5)   Whereas the link between indication of the unit price of products and their pre-packaging in pre-established quantities or capacities corresponding to the values of the ranges adopted at Community level has proved overly complex to apply; whereas it is thus necessary to abandon this link in favour of a new simplified mechanism and in the interest of the consumer, without prejudice to the rules governing packaging standardisation;

(6)   Whereas the obligation to indicate the selling price and the unit price contributes substantially to improving consumer information, as this is the easiest way to enable consumers to evaluate and compare the price of products in an optimum manner and hence to make informed choices on the basis of simple comparisons;

(7)   Whereas, therefore, there should be a general obligation to indicate both the selling price and the unit price for all products except for products sold in bulk, where the selling price cannot be determined until the consumer indicates how much of the product is required;

(8)   Whereas it is necessary to take into account the fact that certain products are customarily sold in quantities different from one kilogramme, one litre, one metre, one square metre or one cubic metre; whereas it is thus appropriate to allow Member States to authorise that the unit price refer to a different single unit of quantity, taking into account the nature of the product and the quantities in which it is customarily sold in the Member State concerned;

(9)   Whereas the obligation to indicate the unit price may entail an excessive burden for certain small retail businesses under certain circumstances; whereas Member States should therefore be allowed to refrain from applying this obligation during an appropriate transitional period;

(10)   Whereas Member States should also remain free to waive the obligation to indicate the unit price in the case of products for which such price indication would not be useful or would be liable to cause confusion for instance when indication of the quantity is not relevant for price comparison purposes, or when different products are marketed in the same packaging;

(11)   Whereas in the case of non-food products, Member States, with a view to facilitating application of the mechanism implemented, are free to draw up a list of products or categories of products for which the obligation to indicate the unit price remains applicable;

(12)   Whereas Community-level rules can ensure homogenous and transparent information that will benefit all consumers in the context of the internal market; whereas the new, simplified approach is both necessary and sufficient to achieve this objective;

(13)   Whereas Member States must make sure that the system is effective; whereas the transparency of the system should also be maintained when the euro is introduced; whereas, to that end, the maximum number of prices to be indicated should be limited;

(14)   Whereas particular attention should be paid to small retail businesses; whereas, to this end, the Commission should, in its report on the application of this Directive to be presented no later than three years after the date referred to in Article 11(1), take particular account of the experience gleaned in the application of the Directive by small retail businesses, *inter alia*, regarding technological developments and the introduction of the single currency; whereas this report, having regard to the transitional period referred to in Article 6, should be accompanied by a proposal,

NOTES

1   OJ C260, 5.10.95, p 5 and OJ C249, 27.8.96, p 2.
2   OJ C82, 19.3.96, p 32.
3   Opinion of the European Parliament of 18 April 1996 (OJ C141, 13.5.96, p 191). Council Common Position of 27 September 1996 (OJ C333, 7.11.96, p 7) and Decision of the European Parliament of 18 February 1997 (OJ C85, 17.3.97, p 26). Decision of the European Parliament of 16 December 1997 and Decision of the Council of 18 December 1997.
4   OJ C92, 25.4.75, p 1.
5   OJ C133, 3.6.81, p 1.
6   OJ L158, 26.6.79, p 19. Directive as last amended by Directive 95/58/EC (OJ L299, 12.12.95, p 11).
7   OJ L142, 9.6.88, p 19. Directive as last amended by Directive 95/58/EC (OJ L299, 12.12.95, p 11).

HAVE ADOPTED THIS DIRECTIVE—

Article 1

The purpose of this Directive is to stipulate indication of the selling price and the price per unit of measurement of products offered by traders to consumers in order to improve consumer information and to facilitate comparison of prices.

[4325]

Article 2

For the purposes of this Directive—

(a)   *selling price* shall mean the final price for a unit of the product, or a given quantity of the product, including VAT and all other taxes;

(b)   *unit price* shall mean the final price, including VAT and all other taxes, for one kilogramme, one litre, one metre, one square metre or one cubic metre of the product or a different single unit of quantity which is widely and customarily used in the Member State concerned in the marketing of specific products;

(c) *products sold in bulk* shall mean products which are not pre-packaged and are measured in the presence of the consumer;

(d) *trader* shall mean any natural or legal person who sells or offers for sale products which fall within his commercial or professional activity;

(e) *consumer* shall mean any natural person who buys a product for purposes that do not fall within the sphere of his commercial or professional activity.

[4326]

Article 3

1. The selling price and the unit price shall be indicated for all products referred to in Article 1, the indication of the unit price being subject to the provisions of Article 5. The unit price need not be indicated if it is identical to the sales price.

2. Member States may decide not to apply paragraph 1 to—
— products supplied in the course of the provision of a service,
— sales by auction and sales of works of art and antiques.

3. For products sold in bulk, only the unit price must be indicated.

4. Any advertisement which mentions the selling price of products referred to in Article 1 shall also indicate the unit price subject to Article 5.

[4327]

Article 4

1. The selling price and the unit price must be unambiguous, easily identifiable and clearly legible. Member States may provide that the maximum number of prices to be indicated be limited.

2. The unit price shall refer to a quantity declared in accordance with national and Community provisions.

Where national or Community provisions require the indication of the net weight and the net drained weight for certain pre-packed products, it shall be sufficient to indicate the unit price of the net drained weight.

[4328]

Article 5

1. Member States may waive the obligation to indicate the unit price of products for which such indication would not be useful because of the products' nature or purpose or would be liable to create confusion.

2. With a view to implementing paragraph 1, Member States may, in the case of non-food products, establish a list of the products or product categories to which the obligation to indicate the unit price shall remain applicable.

[4329]

Article 6

If the obligation to indicate the unit price were to constitute an excessive burden for certain small retail businesses because of the number of products on sale, the sales area, the nature of the place of sale, specific conditions of sale where the product is not directly accessible for the consumer or certain forms of business, such as certain types of itinerant trade, Member States may, for a transitional period following the date referred to in Article 11(1), provide that the obligation to indicate the unit price of products other than those sold in bulk, which are sold in the said businesses, shall not apply, subject to Article 12.

[4330]

Article 7

Member States shall provide appropriate measures to inform all persons concerned of the national law transposing this Directive.

[4331]

Article 8

Member States shall lay down penalties for infringements of national provisions adopted in application of this Directive, and shall take all necessary measures to ensure that these are enforced. These penalties must be effective, proportionate and dissuasive.

[4332]

Article 9

1. The transition period of nine years referred to in Article 1 of Directive 95/58/EC of the European Parliament and of the Council of 29 November 1995 amending Directive 79/581/EEC on consumer protection in the indication of the prices of foodstuffs and Directive 88/314/EEC on consumer protection in the indication of the prices of non-food products[1] shall be extended until the date referred to in Article 11(1) of this Directive.

2.   Directives 79/581/EEC and 88/314/EEC shall be repealed with effect from the date referred to in Article 11(1) of this Directive.

[4333]

NOTES

¹   OJ L299, 12.12.95, p 11.

Article 10

This Directive shall not prevent Member States from adopting or maintaining provisions which are more favourable as regards consumer information and comparison of prices, without prejudice to their obligations under the Treaty.

[4334]

Article 11

1.   Member States shall bring into force the laws, regulations and administrative provisions necessary to comply with this Directive not later than 18 March 2000. They shall forthwith inform the Commission thereof. The provisions adopted shall be applicable as of that date.

When Member States adopt these measures, they shall contain a reference to this Directive or shall be accompanied by such reference at the time of their official publication. The methods of making such reference shall be laid down by Member States.

2.   Member States shall communicate to the Commission the text of the provisions of national law which they adopt in the field governed by this Directive.

3.   Member States shall communicate the provisions governing the penalties provided for in Article 8, and any later amendments thereto.

[4335]

Article 12

The Commission shall, not later than three years after the date referred to in Article 11(1), submit to the European Parliament and the Council a comprehensive report on the application of this Directive, in particular on the application of Article 6, accompanied by a proposal.

The European Parliament and the Council shall, on this basis, re-examine the provisions of Article 6 and shall act, in accordance with the Treaty, within three years of the presentation by the Commission of the proposal referred to in the first paragraph.

[4336]

Article 13

This Directive shall enter into force on the day of its publication in the *Official Journal of the European Communities*.

[4337]

Article 14

This Directive is addressed to the Member States.

[4338]

Done at Brussels, 16 February 1998.

Commission Declaration

Article 2(b)—

The Commission takes the view that the expression 'for one kilogramme, one litre, one metre, one square metre or cubic metre of the product or a different single unit of quantity' in Article 2(b) also applies to products sold by individual item or singly.

[4339]

Commission Declaration

Article 12, first paragraph—

The Commission considers that Article 12, first paragraph, of the Directive cannot be construed as calling into question its right of initiative.

[4340]–[4351]

DIRECTIVE OF THE EUROPEAN PARLIAMENT AND OF THE COUNCIL

of 25 May 1999

on certain aspects of the sale of consumer goods and associated guarantees

(99/44/EC)

NOTES

Date of publication in OJ: OJ L171, 7.7.99, p 12.

This Directive has been implemented in the UK by the Sale and Supply of Goods to Consumers Regulations 2002, SI 2002/3045 at **[3366]**.

THE EUROPEAN PARLIAMENT AND THE COUNCIL OF THE EUROPEAN UNION,

Having regard to the Treaty establishing the European Community, and in particular Article 95 thereof,

Having regard to the proposal from the Commission,[1]

Having regard to the opinion of the Economic and Social Committee,[2]

Acting in accordance with the procedure laid down in Article 251 of the Treaty in the light of the joint text approved by the Conciliation Committee on 18 May 1999,[3]

(1) Whereas Article 153(1) and (3) of the Treaty provides that the Community should contribute to the achievement of a high level of consumer protection by the measures it adopts pursuant to Article 95 thereof;

(2) Whereas the internal market comprises an area without internal frontiers in which the free movement of goods, persons, services and capital is guaranteed; whereas free movement of goods concerns not only transactions by persons acting in the course of a business but also transactions by private individuals; whereas it implies that consumers resident in one Member State should be free to purchase goods in the territory of another Member State on the basis of a uniform minimum set of fair rules governing the sale of consumer goods;

(3) Whereas the laws of the Member States concerning the sale of consumer goods are somewhat disparate, with the result that national consumer goods markets differ from one another and that competition between sellers may be distorted;

(4) Whereas consumers who are keen to benefit from the large market by purchasing goods in Member States other than their State of residence play a fundamental role in the completion of the internal market; whereas the artificial reconstruction of frontiers and the compartmentalisation of markets should be prevented; whereas the opportunities available to consumers have been greatly broadened by new communication technologies which allow ready access to distribution systems in other Member States or in third countries; whereas, in the absence of minimum harmonisation of the rules governing the sale of consumer goods, the development of the sale of goods through the medium of new distance communication technologies risks being impeded;

(5) Whereas the creation of a common set of minimum rules of consumer law, valid no matter where goods are purchased within the Community, will strengthen consumer confidence and enable consumers to make the most of the internal market;

(6) Whereas the main difficulties encountered by consumers and the main source of disputes with sellers concern the non-conformity of goods with the contract; whereas it is therefore appropriate to approximate national legislation governing the sale of consumer goods in this respect, without however impinging on provisions and principles of national law relating to contractual and non-contractual liability;

(7) Whereas the goods must, above all, conform with the contractual specifications; whereas the principle of conformity with the contract may be considered as common to the different national legal traditions; whereas in certain national legal traditions it may not be possible to rely solely on this principle to ensure a minimum level of protection for the consumer; whereas under such legal traditions, in particular, additional national provisions may be useful to ensure that the consumer is protected in cases where the parties have agreed no specific contractual terms or where the parties have concluded contractual terms or agreements which directly or indirectly waive or restrict the rights of the consumer and which, to the extent that these rights result from this Directive, are not binding on the consumer;

(8) Whereas, in order to facilitate the application of the principle of conformity with the contract, it is useful to introduce a rebuttable presumption of conformity with the contract covering the most common situations; whereas that presumption does not restrict the principle of freedom of contract; whereas, furthermore, in the absence of specific contractual terms, as well as where the minimum protection clause is applied, the elements mentioned in this presumption may be used to determine the lack of conformity of the goods with the contract; whereas the quality and performance which consumers can reasonably expect will depend *inter alia* on whether the goods are new or second-hand; whereas the elements mentioned in the presumption are cumulative;

whereas, if the circumstances of the case render any particular element manifestly inappropriate, the remaining elements of the presumption nevertheless still apply;

(9)   Whereas the seller should be directly liable to the consumer for the conformity of the goods with the contract; whereas this is the traditional solution enshrined in the legal orders of the Member States; whereas nevertheless the seller should be free, as provided for by national law, to pursue remedies against the producer, a previous seller in the same chain of contracts or any other intermediary, unless he has renounced that entitlement; whereas this Directive does not affect the principle of freedom of contract between the seller, the producer, a previous seller or any other intermediary; whereas the rules governing against whom and how the seller may pursue such remedies are to be determined by national law;

(10)   Whereas, in the case of non-conformity of the goods with the contract, consumers should be entitled to have the goods restored to conformity with the contract free of charge, choosing either repair or replacement, or, failing this, to have the price reduced or the contract rescinded;

(11)   Whereas the consumer in the first place may require the seller to repair the goods or to replace them unless those remedies are impossible or disproportionate; whereas whether a remedy is disproportionate should be determined objectively; whereas a remedy would be disproportionate if it imposed, in comparison with the other remedy, unreasonable costs; whereas, in order to determine whether the costs are unreasonable, the costs of one remedy should be significantly higher than the costs of the other remedy;

(12)   Whereas in cases of a lack of conformity, the seller may always offer the consumer, by way of settlement, any available remedy; whereas it is for the consumer to decide whether to accept or reject this proposal;

(13)   Whereas, in order to enable consumers to take advantage of the internal market and to buy consumer goods in another Member State, it should be recommended that, in the interests of consumers, the producers of consumer goods that are marketed in several Member States attach to the product a list with at least one contact address in every Member State where the product is marketed;

(14)   Whereas the references to the time of delivery do not imply that Member States have to change their rules on the passing of the risk;

(15)   Whereas Member States may provide that any reimbursement to the consumer may be reduced to take account of the use the consumer has had of the goods since they were delivered to him; whereas the detailed arrangements whereby rescission of the contract is effected may be laid down in national law;

(16)   Whereas the specific nature of second-hand goods makes it generally impossible to replace them; whereas therefore the consumer's right of replacement is generally not available for these goods; whereas for such goods, Member States may enable the parties to agree a shortened period of liability;

(17)   Whereas it is appropriate to limit in time the period during which the seller is liable for any lack of conformity which exists at the time of delivery of the goods; whereas Member States may also provide for a limitation on the period during which consumers can exercise their rights, provided such a period does not expire within two years from the time of delivery; whereas where, under national legislation, the time when a limitation period starts is not the time of delivery of the goods, the total duration of the limitation period provided for by national law may not be shorter than two years from the time of delivery;

(18)   Whereas Member States may provide for suspension or interruption of the period during which any lack of conformity must become apparent and of the limitation period, where applicable and in accordance with their national law, in the event of repair, replacement or negotiations between seller and consumer with a view to an amicable settlement;

(19)   Whereas Member States should be allowed to set a period within which the consumer must inform the seller of any lack of conformity; whereas Member States may ensure a higher level of protection for the consumer by not introducing such an obligation; whereas in any case consumers throughout the Community should have at least two months in which to inform the seller that a lack of conformity exists;

(20)   Whereas Member States should guard against such a period placing at a disadvantage consumers shopping across borders; whereas all Member States should inform the Commission of their use of this provision; whereas the Commission should monitor the effect of the varied application of this provision on consumers and on the internal market; whereas information on the use made of this provision by a Member State should be available to the other Member States and to consumers and consumer organisations throughout the Community; whereas a summary of the situation in all Member States should therefore be published in the *Official Journal of the European Communities*;

(21)   Whereas, for certain categories of goods, it is current practice for sellers and producers to offer guarantees on goods against any defect which becomes apparent within a certain period; whereas this practice can stimulate competition; whereas, while such guarantees are legitimate marketing tools, they should not mislead the consumer; whereas, to ensure that consumers are not misled, guarantees should contain certain information, including a statement that the guarantee does not affect the consumer's legal rights;

(22)   Whereas the parties may not, by common consent, restrict or waive the rights granted to consumers, since otherwise the legal protection afforded would be thwarted; whereas this principle

should apply also to clauses which imply that the consumer was aware of any lack of conformity of the consumer goods existing at the time the contract was concluded; whereas the protection granted to consumers under this Directive should not be reduced on the grounds that the law of a non-member State has been chosen as being applicable to the contract;

(23)   Whereas legislation and case-law in this area in the various Member States show that there is growing concern to ensure a high level of consumer protection; whereas, in the light of this trend and the experience acquired in implementing this Directive, it may be necessary to envisage more far-reaching harmonisation, notably by providing for the producer's direct liability for defects for which he is responsible;

(24)   Whereas Member States should be allowed to adopt or maintain in force more stringent provisions in the field covered by this Directive to ensure an even higher level of consumer protection;

(25)   Whereas, according to the Commission recommendation of 30 March 1998 on the principles applicable to the bodies responsible for out-of-court settlement of consumer disputes,[4] Member States can create bodies that ensure impartial and efficient handling of complaints in a national and cross-border context and which consumers can use as mediators;

(26)   Whereas it is appropriate, in order to protect the collective interests of consumers, to add this Directive to the list of Directives contained in the Annex to Directive 98/27/EC of the European Parliament and of the Council of 19 May 1998 on injunctions for the protection of consumers' interests,[5]

NOTES

[1]   OJ C307, 16.10.1996, p 8 and OJ C148, 14.5.1998, p 12.
[2]   OJ C66, 3.3.1997, p 5.
[3]   Opinion of the European Parliament of 10 March 1998 (OJ C104, 6.4.1998, p 30), Council Common Position of 24 September 1998 (OJ C333, 30.10.1998, p 46) and Decision of the European Parliament of 17 December 1998 (OJ C98, 9.4.1999, p 226). Decision of the European Parliament of 5 May 1999. Council Decision of 17 May 1999.
[4]   OJ L115, 17.4.1998, p 31.
[5]   OJ L166, 11.6.1998, p 51.

HAVE ADOPTED THIS DIRECTIVE—

Article 1
Scope and definitions

1.   The purpose of this Directive is the approximation of the laws, regulations and administrative provisions of the Member States on certain aspects of the sale of consumer goods and associated guarantees in order to ensure a uniform minimum level of consumer protection in the context of the internal market.

2.   For the purposes of this Directive—
  (a)   *consumer:* shall mean any natural person who, in the contracts covered by this Directive, is acting for purposes which are not related to his trade, business or profession;
  (b)   *consumer goods:* shall mean any tangible movable item, with the exception of—
    —   goods sold by way of execution or otherwise by authority of law,
    —   water and gas where they are not put up for sale in a limited volume or set quantity,
    —   electricity;
  (c)   *seller:* shall mean any natural or legal person who, under a contract, sells consumer goods in the course of his trade, business or profession;
  (d)   *producer:* shall mean the manufacturer of consumer goods, the importer of consumer goods into the territory of the Community or any person purporting to be a producer by placing his name, trade mark or other distinctive sign on the consumer goods;
  (e)   *guarantee:* shall mean any undertaking by a seller or producer to the consumer, given without extra charge, to reimburse the price paid or to replace, repair or handle consumer goods in any way if they do not meet the specifications set out in the guarantee statement or in the relevant advertising;
  (f)   *repair:* shall mean, in the event of lack of conformity, bringing consumer goods into conformity with the contract of sale.

3.   Member States may provide that the expression "consumer goods" does not cover second-hand goods sold at public auction where consumers have the opportunity of attending the sale in person.

4.   Contracts for the supply of consumer goods to be manufactured or produced shall also be deemed contracts of sale for the purpose of this Directive.

[4352]

Article 2
Conformity with the contract

1.   The seller must deliver goods to the consumer which are in conformity with the contract of sale.

2.   Consumer goods are presumed to be in conformity with the contract if they—
   (a)   comply with the description given by the seller and possess the qualities of the goods which the seller has held out to the consumer as a sample or model;
   (b)   are fit for any particular purpose for which the consumer requires them and which he made known to the seller at the time of conclusion of the contract and which the seller has accepted;
   (c)   are fit for the purposes for which goods of the same type are normally used;
   (d)   show the quality and performance which are normal in goods of the same type and which the consumer can reasonably expect, given the nature of the goods and taking into account any public statements on the specific characteristics of the goods made about them by the seller, the producer or his representative, particularly in advertising or on labelling.

3.   There shall be deemed not to be a lack of conformity for the purposes of this Article if, at the time the contract was concluded, the consumer was aware, or could not reasonably be unaware of, the lack of conformity, or if the lack of conformity has its origin in materials supplied by the consumer.

4.   The seller shall not be bound by public statements, as referred to in paragraph 2(d) if he—
   —   shows that he was not, and could not reasonably have been, aware of the statement in question,
   —   shows that by the time of conclusion of the contract the statement had been corrected, or
   —   shows that the decision to buy the consumer goods could not have been influenced by the statement.

5.   Any lack of conformity resulting from incorrect installation of the consumer goods shall be deemed to be equivalent to lack of conformity of the goods if installation forms part of the contract of sale of the goods and the goods were installed by the seller or under his responsibility. This shall apply equally if the product, intended to be installed by the consumer, is installed by the consumer and the incorrect installation is due to a shortcoming in the installation instructions.

[4353]

Article 3
Rights of the consumer

1.   The seller shall be liable to the consumer for any lack of conformity which exists at the time the goods were delivered.

2.   In the case of a lack of conformity, the consumer shall be entitled to have the goods brought into conformity free of charge by repair or replacement, in accordance with paragraph 3, or to have an appropriate reduction made in the price or the contract rescinded with regard to those goods, in accordance with paragraphs 5 and 6.

3.   In the first place, the consumer may require the seller to repair the goods or he may require the seller to replace them, in either case free of charge, unless this is impossible or disproportionate.

A remedy shall be deemed to be disproportionate if it imposes costs on the seller which, in comparison with the alternative remedy, are unreasonable, taking into account—
   —   the value the goods would have if there were no lack of conformity,
   —   the significance of the lack of conformity, and
   —   whether the alternative remedy could be completed without significant inconvenience to the consumer.

Any repair or replacement shall be completed within a reasonable time and without any significant inconvenience to the consumer, taking account of the nature of the goods and the purpose for which the consumer required the goods.

4.   The terms "free of charge" in paragraphs 2 and 3 refer to the necessary costs incurred to bring the goods into conformity, particularly the cost of postage, labour and materials.

5.   The consumer may require an appropriate reduction of the price or have the contract rescinded—
   —   if the consumer is entitled to neither repair nor replacement, or
   —   if the seller has not completed the remedy within a reasonable time, or
   —   if the seller has not completed the remedy without significant inconvenience to the consumer.

6.   The consumer is not entitled to have the contract rescinded if the lack of conformity is minor.

[4354]

Article 4
Right of redress

Where the final seller is liable to the consumer because of a lack of conformity resulting from an act or omission by the producer, a previous seller in the same chain of contracts or any other intermediary, the final seller shall be entitled to pursue remedies against the person or persons liable in the contractual chain. The person or persons liable against whom the final seller may pursue remedies, together with the relevant actions and conditions of exercise, shall be determined by national law.

[4355]

Article 5
Time limits

1. The seller shall be held liable under Article 3 where the lack of conformity becomes apparent within two years as from delivery of the goods. If, under national legislation, the rights laid down in Article 3(2) are subject to a limitation period, that period shall not expire within a period of two years from the time of delivery.

2. Member States may provide that, in order to benefit from his rights, the consumer must inform the seller of the lack of conformity within a period of two months from the date on which he detected such lack of conformity.

Member States shall inform the Commission of their use of this paragraph. The Commission shall monitor the effect of the existence of this option for the Member States on consumers and on the internal market.

Not later than 7 January 2003, the Commission shall prepare a report on the use made by Member States of this paragraph. This report shall be published in the *Official Journal of the European Communities*.

3. Unless proved otherwise, any lack of conformity which becomes apparent within six months of delivery of the goods shall be presumed to have existed at the time of delivery unless this presumption is incompatible with the nature of the goods or the nature of the lack of conformity.

[4356]

Article 6
Guarantees

1. A guarantee shall be legally binding on the offerer under the conditions laid down in the guarantee statement and the associated advertising.

2. The guarantee shall—
   — state that the consumer has legal rights under applicable national legislation governing the sale of consumer goods and make clear that those rights are not affected by the guarantee,
   — set out in plain intelligible language the contents of the guarantee and the essential particulars necessary for making claims under the guarantee, notably the duration and territorial scope of the guarantee as well as the name and address of the guarantor.

3. On request by the consumer, the guarantee shall be made available in writing or feature in another durable medium available and accessible to him.

4. Within its own territory, the Member State in which the consumer goods are marketed may, in accordance with the rules of the Treaty, provide that the guarantee be drafted in one or more languages which it shall determine from among the official languages of the Community.

5. Should a guarantee infringe the requirements of paragraphs 2, 3 or 4, the validity of this guarantee shall in no way be affected, and the consumer can still rely on the guarantee and require that it be honoured.

[4357]

Article 7
Binding nature

1. Any contractual terms or agreements concluded with the seller before the lack of conformity is brought to the seller's attention which directly or indirectly waive or restrict the rights resulting from this Directive shall, as provided for by national law, not be binding on the consumer.

Member States may provide that, in the case of second-hand goods, the seller and consumer may agree contractual terms or agreements which have a shorter time period for the liability of the seller than that set down in Article 5(1). Such period may not be less than one year.

2. Member States shall take the necessary measures to ensure that consumers are not deprived of the protection afforded by this Directive as a result of opting for the law of a non-member State as the law applicable to the contract where the contract has a close connection with the territory of the Member States.

[4358]

Article 8
National law and minimum protection

1.   The rights resulting from this Directive shall be exercised without prejudice to other rights which the consumer may invoke under the national rules governing contractual or non-contractual liability.

2.   Member States may adopt or maintain in force more stringent provisions, compatible with the Treaty in the field covered by this Directive, to ensure a higher level of consumer protection.

[4359]

Article 9

Member States shall take appropriate measures to inform the consumer of the national law transposing this Directive and shall encourage, where appropriate, professional organisations to inform consumers of their rights.

[4360]

Article 10

(Spent: amended Directive 98/27/EC, Annex (repealed).)

Article 11
Transposition

1.   Member States shall bring into force the laws, regulations and administrative provisions necessary to comply with this Directive not later than 1 January 2002. They shall forthwith inform the Commission thereof.

When Member States adopt these measures, they shall contain a reference to this Directive, or shall be accompanied by such reference at the time of their official publication. The procedure for such reference shall be adopted by Member States.

2.   Member States shall communicate to the Commission the provisions of national law which they adopt in the field covered by this Directive.

[4361]

Article 12
Review

The Commission shall, not later than 7 July 2006, review the application of this Directive and submit to the European Parliament and the Council a report. The report shall examine, *inter alia*, the case for introducing the producer's direct liability and, if appropriate, shall be accompanied by proposals.

[4362]

Article 13
Entry into force

This Directive shall enter into force on the day of its publication in the *Official Journal of the European Communities*.

[4363]

Article 14

This Directive is addressed to the Member States.

[4364]

Done at Brussels, 25 May 1999.

DIRECTIVE OF THE EUROPEAN PARLIAMENT AND OF THE COUNCIL

of 8 June 2000

on certain legal aspects of information society services, in particular electronic commerce, in the Internal Market (Directive on electronic commerce)

(2000/31/EC)

NOTES
Date of publication in OJ: OJ L178, 17.7.2000, p 1.

This Directive has been implemented in the UK by the Electronic Commerce (Financial Services and Markets) Regulations 2002, SI 2002/1775 (as amended) and by the Electronic Commerce (EC Directive) Regulations 2002, SI 2002/2013 at **[3344]**.

THE EUROPEAN PARLIAMENT AND THE COUNCIL OF THE EUROPEAN UNION,

Having regard to the Treaty establishing the European Community, and in particular Articles 47(2), 55 and 95 thereof,

Having regard to the proposal from the Commission,[1]

Having regard to the opinion of the Economic and Social Committee,[2]

Acting in accordance with the procedure laid down in Article 251 of the Treaty,[3]

Whereas—

(1)   The European Union is seeking to forge ever closer links between the States and peoples of Europe, to ensure economic and social progress; in accordance with Article 14(2) of the Treaty, the internal market comprises an area without internal frontiers in which the free movements of goods, services and the freedom of establishment are ensured; the development of information society services within the area without internal frontiers is vital to eliminating the barriers which divide the European peoples.

(2)   The development of electronic commerce within the information society offers significant employment opportunities in the Community, particularly in small and medium-sized enterprises, and will stimulate economic growth and investment in innovation by European companies, and can also enhance the competitiveness of European industry, provided that everyone has access to the Internet.

(3)   Community law and the characteristics of the Community legal order are a vital asset to enable European citizens and operators to take full advantage, without consideration of borders, of the opportunities afforded by electronic commerce; this Directive therefore has the purpose of ensuring a high level of Community legal integration in order to establish a real area without internal borders for information society services.

(4)   It is important to ensure that electronic commerce could fully benefit from the internal market and therefore that, as with Council Directive 89/552/EEC of 3 October 1989 on the coordination of certain provisions laid down by law, regulation or administrative action in Member States concerning the pursuit of television broadcasting activities,[4] a high level of Community integration is achieved.

(5)   The development of information society services within the Community is hampered by a number of legal obstacles to the proper functioning of the internal market which make less attractive the exercise of the freedom of establishment and the freedom to provide services; these obstacles arise from divergences in legislation and from the legal uncertainty as to which national rules apply to such services; in the absence of coordination and adjustment of legislation in the relevant areas, obstacles might be justified in the light of the case-law of the Court of Justice of the European Communities; legal uncertainty exists with regard to the extent to which Member States may control services originating from another Member State.

(6)   In the light of Community objectives, of Articles 43 and 49 of the Treaty and of secondary Community law, these obstacles should be eliminated by coordinating certain national laws and by clarifying certain legal concepts at Community level to the extent necessary for the proper functioning of the internal market; by dealing only with certain specific matters which give rise to problems for the internal market, this Directive is fully consistent with the need to respect the principle of subsidiarity as set out in Article 5 of the Treaty.

(7)   In order to ensure legal certainty and consumer confidence, this Directive must lay down a clear and general framework to cover certain legal aspects of electronic commerce in the internal market.

(8)   The objective of this Directive is to create a legal framework to ensure the free movement of information society services between Member States and not to harmonise the field of criminal law as such.

(9)   The free movement of information society services can in many cases be a specific reflection in Community law of a more general principle, namely freedom of expression as enshrined in Article 10(1) of the Convention for the Protection of Human Rights and Fundamental Freedoms, which has been ratified by all the Member States; for this reason, directives covering the supply of information society services must ensure that this activity may be engaged in freely in the light of that Article, subject only to the restrictions laid down in paragraph 2 of that Article and in Article 46(1) of the Treaty; this Directive is not intended to affect national fundamental rules and principles relating to freedom of expression.

(10)   In accordance with the principle of proportionality, the measures provided for in this Directive are strictly limited to the minimum needed to achieve the objective of the proper functioning of the internal market; where action at Community level is necessary, and in order to guarantee an area which is truly without internal frontiers as far as electronic commerce is concerned, the Directive must ensure a high level of protection of objectives of general interest, in particular the protection of minors and human dignity, consumer protection and the protection of public health; according to Article 152 of the Treaty, the protection of public health is an essential component of other Community policies.

(11)   This Directive is without prejudice to the level of protection for, in particular, public health and consumer interests, as established by Community acts; amongst others, Council Directive 93/13/EEC of 5 April 1993 on unfair terms in consumer contracts[5] and Directive 97/7/EC of the European Parliament and of the Council of 20 May 1997 on the protection of consumers in respect of distance contracts[6] form a vital element for protecting consumers in contractual matters; those Directives also apply in their entirety to information society services; that same Community acquis, which is fully applicable to information society services, also embraces in particular Council Directive 84/450/EEC of 10 September 1984 concerning misleading and comparative advertising,[7] Council Directive 87/102/EEC of 22 December 1986 for the approximation of the laws, regulations and administrative provisions of the Member States concerning consumer credit,[8] Council Directive 93/22/EEC of 10 May 1993 on investment services in the securities field,[9] Council Directive 90/314/EEC of 13 June 1990 on package travel, package holidays and package tours,[10] Directive 98/6/EC of the European Parliament and of the Council of 16 February 1998 on consumer production in the indication of prices of products offered to consumers,[11] Council Directive 92/59/EEC of 29 June 1992 on general product safety,[12] Directive 94/47/EC of the European Parliament and of the Council of 26 October 1994 on the protection of purchasers in respect of certain aspects on contracts relating to the purchase of the right to use immovable properties on a timeshare basis,[13] Directive 98/27/EC of the European Parliament and of the Council of 19 May 1998 on injunctions for the protection of consumers' interests,[14] Council Directive 85/374/EEC of 25 July 1985 on the approximation of the laws, regulations and administrative provisions concerning liability for defective products,[15] Directive 1999/44/EC of the European Parliament and of the Council of 25 May 1999 on certain aspects of the sale of consumer goods and associated guarantees,[16] the future Directive of the European Parliament and of the Council concerning the distance marketing of consumer financial services and Council Directive 92/28/EEC of 31 March 1992 on the advertising of medicinal products;[17] this Directive should be without prejudice to Directive 98/43/EC of the European Parliament and of the Council of 6 July 1998 on the approximation of the laws, regulations and administrative provisions of the Member States relating to the advertising and sponsorship of tobacco products[18] adopted within the framework of the internal market, or to directives on the protection of public health; this Directive complements information requirements established by the abovementioned Directives and in particular Directive 97/7/EC.

(12)   It is necessary to exclude certain activities from the scope of this Directive, on the grounds that the freedom to provide services in these fields cannot, at this stage, be guaranteed under the Treaty or existing secondary legislation; excluding these activities does not preclude any instruments which might prove necessary for the proper functioning of the internal market; taxation, particularly value added tax imposed on a large number of the services covered by this Directive, must be excluded from the scope of this Directive.

(13)   This Directive does not aim to establish rules on fiscal obligations nor does it pre-empt the drawing up of Community instruments concerning fiscal aspects of electronic commerce.

(14)   The protection of individuals with regard to the processing of personal data is solely governed by Directive 95/46/EC of the European Parliament and of the Council of 24 October 1995 on the protection of individuals with regard to the processing of personal data and on the free movement of such data[19] and Directive 97/66/EC of the European Parliament and of the Council of 15 December 1997 concerning the processing of personal data and the protection of privacy in the telecommunications sector[20] which are fully applicable to information society services; these Directives already establish a Community legal framework in the field of personal data and therefore it is not necessary to cover this issue in this Directive in order to ensure the smooth functioning of the internal market, in particular the free movement of personal data between Member States; the implementation and application of this Directive should be made in full compliance with the principles relating to the protection of personal data, in particular as regards unsolicited commercial communication and the liability of intermediaries; this Directive cannot prevent the anonymous use of open networks such as the Internet.

(15)   The confidentiality of communications is guaranteed by Article 5 Directive 97/66/EC; in accordance with that Directive, Member States must prohibit any kind of interception or surveillance of such communications by others than the senders and receivers, except when legally authorised.

(16)   The exclusion of gambling activities from the scope of application of this Directive covers only games of chance, lotteries and betting transactions, which involve wagering a stake with monetary value; this does not cover promotional competitions or games where the purpose is to encourage the sale of goods or services and where payments, if they arise, serve only to acquire the promoted goods or services.

(17)   The definition of information society services already exists in Community law in Directive 98/34/EC of the European Parliament and of the Council of 22 June 1998 laying down a procedure for the provision of information in the field of technical standards and regulations and of rules on information society services[21] and in Directive 98/84/EC of the European Parliament and of the Council of 20 November 1998 on the legal protection of services based on, or consisting of, conditional access;[22] this definition covers any service normally provided for remuneration, at a distance, by means of electronic equipment for the processing (including digital compression) and

storage of data, and at the individual request of a recipient of a service; those services referred to in the indicative list in Annex V to Directive 98/34/EC which do not imply data processing and storage are not covered by this definition.

(18) Information society services span a wide range of economic activities which take place on-line; these activities can, in particular, consist of selling goods on-line; activities such as the delivery of goods as such or the provision of services off-line are not covered; information society services are not solely restricted to services giving rise to on-line contracting but also, in so far as they represent an economic activity, extend to services which are not remunerated by those who receive them, such as those offering on-line information or commercial communications, or those providing tools allowing for search, access and retrieval of data; information society services also include services consisting of the transmission of information via a communication network, in providing access to a communication network or in hosting information provided by a recipient of the service; television broadcasting within the meaning of Directive EEC/89/552 and radio broadcasting are not information society services because they are not provided at individual request; by contrast, services which are transmitted point to point, such as video-on-demand or the provision of commercial communications by electronic mail are information society services; the use of electronic mail or equivalent individual communications for instance by natural persons acting outside their trade, business or profession including their use for the conclusion of contracts between such persons is not an information society service; the contractual relationship between an employee and his employer is not an information society service; activities which by their very nature cannot be carried out at a distance and by electronic means, such as the statutory auditing of company accounts or medical advice requiring the physical examination of a patient are not information society services.

(19) The place at which a service provider is established should be determined in conformity with the case-law of the Court of Justice according to which the concept of establishment involves the actual pursuit of an economic activity through a fixed establishment for an indefinite period; this requirement is also fulfilled where a company is constituted for a given period; the place of establishment of a company providing services via an Internet website is not the place at which the technology supporting its website is located or the place at which its website is accessible but the place where it pursues its economic activity; in cases where a provider has several places of establishment it is important to determine from which place of establishment the service concerned is provided; in cases where it is difficult to determine from which of several places of establishment a given service is provided, this is the place where the provider has the centre of his activities relating to this particular service.

(20) The definition of "recipient of a service" covers all types of usage of information society services, both by persons who provide information on open networks such as the Internet and by persons who seek information on the Internet for private or professional reasons.

(21) The scope of the coordinated field is without prejudice to future Community harmonisation relating to information society services and to future legislation adopted at national level in accordance with Community law; the coordinated field covers only requirements relating to on-line activities such as on-line information, on-line advertising, online shopping, on-line contracting and does not concern Member States' legal requirements relating to goods such as safety standards, labelling obligations, or liability for goods, or Member States' requirements relating to the delivery or the transport of goods, including the distribution of medicinal products; the coordinated field does not cover the exercise of rights of pre-emption by public authorities concerning certain goods such as works of art.

(22) Information society services should be supervised at the source of the activity, in order to ensure an effective protection of public interest objectives; to that end, it is necessary to ensure that the competent authority provides such protection not only for the citizens of its own country but for all Community citizens; in order to improve mutual trust between Member States, it is essential to state clearly this responsibility on the part of the Member State where the services originate; moreover, in order to effectively guarantee freedom to provide services and legal certainty for suppliers and recipients of services, such information society services should in principle be subject to the law of the Member State in which the service provider is established.

(23) This Directive neither aims to establish additional rules on private international law relating to conflicts of law nor does it deal with the jurisdiction of Courts; provisions of the applicable law designated by rules of private international law must not restrict the freedom to provide information society services as established in this Directive.

(24) In the context of this Directive, notwithstanding the rule on the control at source of information society services, it is legitimate under the conditions established in this Directive for Member States to take measures to restrict the free movement of information society services.

(25) National courts, including civil courts, dealing with private law disputes can take measures to derogate from the freedom to provide information society services in conformity with conditions established in this Directive.

(26) Member States, in conformity with conditions established in this Directive, may apply their national rules on criminal law and criminal proceedings with a view to taking all investigative and other measures necessary for the detection and prosecution of criminal offences, without there being a need to notify such measures to the Commission.

(27)   This Directive, together with the future Directive of the European Parliament and of the Council concerning the distance marketing of consumer financial services, contributes to the creating of a legal framework for the on-line provision of financial services; this Directive does not pre-empt future initiatives in the area of financial services in particular with regard to the harmonisation of rules of conduct in this field; the possibility for Member States, established in this Directive, under certain circumstances of restricting the freedom to provide information society services in order to protect consumers also covers measures in the area of financial services in particular measures aiming at protecting investors.

(28)   The Member States' obligation not to subject access to the activity of an information society service provider to prior authorisation does not concern postal services covered by Directive 97/67/EC of the European Parliament and of the Council of 15 December 1997 on common rules for the development of the internal market of Community postal services and the improvement of quality of service[23] consisting of the physical delivery of a printed electronic mail message and does not affect voluntary accreditation systems, in particular for providers of electronic signature certification service.

(29)   Commercial communications are essential for the financing of information society services and for developing a wide variety of new, charge-free services; in the interests of consumer protection and fair trading, commercial communications, including discounts, promotional offers and promotional competitions or games, must meet a number of transparency requirements; these requirements are without prejudice to Directive 97/7/EC; this Directive should not affect existing Directives on commercial communications, in particular Directive 98/43/EC.

(30)   The sending of unsolicited commercial communications by electronic mail may be undesirable for consumers and information society service providers and may disrupt the smooth functioning of interactive networks; the question of consent by recipient of certain forms of unsolicited commercial communications is not addressed by this Directive, but has already been addressed, in particular, by Directive 97/7/EC and by Directive 97/66/EC; in Member States which authorise unsolicited commercial communications by electronic mail, the setting up of appropriate industry filtering initiatives should be encouraged and facilitated; in addition it is necessary that in any event unsolicited commercial communities are clearly identifiable as such in order to improve transparency and to facilitate the functioning of such industry initiatives; unsolicited commercial communications by electronic mail should not result in additional communication costs for the recipient.

(31)   Member States which allow the sending of unsolicited commercial communications by electronic mail without prior consent of the recipient by service providers established in their territory have to ensure that the service providers consult regularly and respect the opt-out registers in which natural persons not wishing to receive such commercial communications can register themselves.

(32)   In order to remove barriers to the development of cross-border services within the Community which members of the regulated professions might offer on the Internet, it is necessary that compliance be guaranteed at Community level with professional rules aiming, in particular, to protect consumers or public health; codes of conduct at Community level would be the best means of determining the rules on professional ethics applicable to commercial communication; the drawing-up or, where appropriate, the adaptation of such rules should be encouraged without prejudice to the autonomy of professional bodies and associations.

(33)   This Directive complements Community law and national law relating to regulated professions maintaining a coherent set of applicable rules in this field.

(34)   Each Member State is to amend its legislation containing requirements, and in particular requirements as to form, which are likely to curb the use of contracts by electronic means; the examination of the legislation requiring such adjustment should be systematic and should cover all the necessary stages and acts of the contractual process, including the filing of the contract; the result of this amendment should be to make contracts concluded electronically workable; the legal effect of electronic signatures is dealt with by Directive 1999/93/EC of the European Parliament and of the Council of 13 December 1999 on a Community framework for electronic signatures;[24] the acknowledgement of receipt by a service provider may take the form of the on-line provision of the service paid for.

(35)   This Directive does not affect Member States' possibility of maintaining or establishing general or specific legal requirements for contracts which can be fulfilled by electronic means, in particular requirements concerning secure electronic signatures.

(36)   Member States may maintain restrictions for the use of electronic contracts with regard to contracts requiring by law the involvement of courts, public authorities, or professions exercising public authority; this possibility also covers contracts which require the involvement of courts, public authorities, or professions exercising public authority in order to have an effect with regard to third parties as well as contracts requiring by law certification or attestation by a notary.

(37)   Member States' obligation to remove obstacles to the use of electronic contracts concerns only obstacles resulting from legal requirements and not practical obstacles resulting from the impossibility of using electronic means in certain cases.

(38)   Member States' obligation to remove obstacles to the use of electronic contracts is to be implemented in conformity with legal requirements for contracts enshrined in Community law.

(39)   The exceptions to the provisions concerning the contracts concluded exclusively by electronic mail or by equivalent individual communications provided for by this Directive, in relation to information to be provided and the placing of orders, should not enable, as a result, the by-passing of those provisions by providers of information society services.

(40)   Both existing and emerging disparities in Member States' legislation and case-law concerning liability of service providers acting as intermediaries prevent the smooth functioning of the internal market, in particular by impairing the development of cross-border services and producing distortions of competition; service providers have a duty to act, under certain circumstances, with a view to preventing or stopping illegal activities; this Directive should constitute the appropriate basis for the development of rapid and reliable procedures for removing and disabling access to illegal information; such mechanisms could be developed on the basis of voluntary agreements between all parties concerned and should be encouraged by Member States; it is in the interest of all parties involved in the provision of information society services to adopt and implement such procedures; the provisions of this Directive relating to liability should not preclude the development and effective operation, by the different interested parties, of technical systems of protection and identification and of technical surveillance instruments made possible by digital technology within the limits laid down by Directives 95/46/EC and 97/66/EC.

(41)   This Directive strikes a balance between the different interests at stake and establishes principles upon which industry agreements and standards can be based.

(42)   The exemptions from liability established in this Directive cover only cases where the activity of the information society service provider is limited to the technical process of operating and giving access to a communication network over which information made available by third parties is transmitted or temporarily stored, for the sole purpose of making the transmission more efficient; this activity is of a mere technical, automatic and passive nature, which implies that the information society service provider has neither knowledge of nor control over the information which is transmitted or stored.

(43)   A service provider can benefit from the exemptions for "mere conduit" and for "caching" when he is in no way involved with the information transmitted; this requires among other things that he does not modify the information that he transmits; this requirement does not cover manipulations of a technical nature which take place in the course of the transmission as they do not alter the integrity of the information contained in the transmission.

(44)   A service provider who deliberately collaborates with one of the recipients of his service in order to undertake illegal acts goes beyond the activities of "mere conduit" or "caching" and as a result cannot benefit from the liability exemptions established for these activities.

(45)   The limitations of the liability of intermediary service providers established in this Directive do not affect the possibility of injunctions of different kinds; such injunctions can in particular consist of orders by courts or administrative authorities requiring the termination or prevention of any infringement, including the removal of illegal information or the disabling of access to it.

(46)   In order to benefit from a limitation of liability, the provider of an information society service, consisting of the storage of information, upon obtaining actual knowledge or awareness of illegal activities has to act expeditiously to remove or to disable access to the information concerned; the removal or disabling of access has to be undertaken in the observance of the principle of freedom of expression and of procedures established for this purpose at national level; this Directive does not affect Member States' possibility of establishing specific requirements which must be fulfilled expeditiously prior to the removal or disabling of information.

(47)   Member States are prevented from imposing a monitoring obligation on service providers only with respect to obligations of a general nature; this does not concern monitoring obligations in a specific case and, in particular, does not affect orders by national authorities in accordance with national legislation.

(48)   This Directive does not affect the possibility for Member States of requiring service providers, who host information provided by recipients of their service, to apply duties of care, which can reasonably be expected from them and which are specified by national law, in order to detect and prevent certain types of illegal activities.

(49)   Member States and the Commission are to encourage the drawing-up of codes of conduct; this is not to impair the voluntary nature of such codes and the possibility for interested parties of deciding freely whether to adhere to such codes.

(50)   It is important that the proposed directive on the harmonisation of certain aspects of copyright and related rights in the information society and this Directive come into force within a similar time scale with a view to establishing a clear framework of rules relevant to the issue of liability of intermediaries for copyright and relating rights infringements at Community level.

(51)   Each Member State should be required, where necessary, to amend any legislation which is liable to hamper the use of schemes for the out-of-court settlement of disputes through electronic channels; the result of this amendment must be to make the functioning of such schemes genuinely and effectively possible in law and in practice, even across borders.

(52)   The effective exercise of the freedoms of the internal market makes it necessary to guarantee victims effective access to means of settling disputes; damage which may arise in connection with information society services is characterised both by its rapidity and by its geographical extent; in view of this specific character and the need to ensure that national authorities

do not endanger the mutual confidence which they should have in one another, this Directive requests Member States to ensure that appropriate court actions are available; Member States should examine the need to provide access to judicial procedures by appropriate electronic means.

(53)   Directive 98/27/EC, which is applicable to information society services, provides a mechanism relating to actions for an injunction aimed at the protection of the collective interests of consumers; this mechanism will contribute to the free movement of information society services by ensuring a high level of consumer protection.

(54)   The sanctions provided for under this Directive are without prejudice to any other sanction or remedy provided under national law; Member States are not obliged to provide criminal sanctions for infringement of national provisions adopted pursuant to this Directive.

(55)   This Directive does not affect the law applicable to contractual obligations relating to consumer contracts; accordingly, this Directive cannot have the result of depriving the consumer of the protection afforded to him by the mandatory rules relating to contractual obligations of the law of the Member State in which he has his habitual residence.

(56)   As regards the derogation contained in this Directive regarding contractual obligations concerning contracts concluded by consumers, those obligations should be interpreted as including information on the essential elements of the content of the contract, including consumer rights, which have a determining influence on the decision to contract.

(57)   The Court of Justice has consistently held that a Member State retains the right to take measures against a service provider that is established in another Member State but directs all or most of his activity to the territory of the first Member State if the choice of establishment was made with a view to evading the legislation that would have applied to the provider had he been established on the territory of the first Member State.

(58)   This Directive should not apply to services supplied by service providers established in a third country; in view of the global dimension of electronic commerce, it is, however, appropriate to ensure that the Community rules are consistent with international rules; this Directive is without prejudice to the results of discussions within international organisations (amongst others WTO, OECD, Uncitral) on legal issues.

(59)   Despite the global nature of electronic communications, coordination of national regulatory measures at European Union level is necessary in order to avoid fragmentation of the internal market, and for the establishment of an appropriate European regulatory framework; such coordination should also contribute to the establishment of a common and strong negotiating position in international forums.

(60)   In order to allow the unhampered development of electronic commerce, the legal framework must be clear and simple, predictable and consistent with the rules applicable at international level so that it does not adversely affect the competitiveness of European industry or impede innovation in that sector.

(61)   If the market is actually to operate by electronic means in the context of globalisation, the European Union and the major non-European areas need to consult each other with a view to making laws and procedures compatible.

(62)   Cooperation with third countries should be strengthened in the area of electronic commerce, in particular with applicant countries, the developing countries and the European Union's other trading partners.

(63)   The adoption of this Directive will not prevent the Member States from taking into account the various social, societal and cultural implications which are inherent in the advent of the information society; in particular it should not hinder measures which Member States might adopt in conformity with Community law to achieve social, cultural and democratic goals taking into account their linguistic diversity, national and regional specificities as well as their cultural heritage, and to ensure and maintain public access to the widest possible range of information society services; in any case, the development of the information society is to ensure that Community citizens can have access to the cultural European heritage provided in the digital environment.

(64)   Electronic communication offers the Member States an excellent means of providing public services in the cultural, educational and linguistic fields.

(65)   The Council, in its resolution of 19 January 1999 on the consumer dimension of the information society,[25] stressed that the protection of consumers deserved special attention in this field; the Commission will examine the degree to which existing consumer protection rules provide insufficient protection in the context of the information society and will identify, where necessary, the deficiencies of this legislation and those issues which could require additional measures; if need be, the Commission should make specific additional proposals to resolve such deficiencies that will thereby have been identified,

NOTES

1.   OJ C30, 5.2.1999, p 4.
2.   OJ C169, 16.6.1999, p 36.
3.   Opinion of the European Parliament of 6 May 1999 (OJ C279, 1.10.1999, p 389), Council common position of 28 February 2000 (OJ C128, 8.5.2000, p 32) and Decision of the European Parliament of 4 May 2000 (not yet published in the Official Journal).
4.   OJ L298, 17.10.1989, p 23. Directive as amended by Directive 97/36/EC of the European Parliament and of the Council (OJ L202, 30.7.1997, p 60).

5   OJ L95, 21.4.1993, p 29.
6   OJ L144, 4.6.1999, p 19.
7   OJ L250, 19.9.1984, p 17. Directive as amended by Directive 97/55/EC of the European Parliament and of the Council (OJ L290, 23.10.1997, p 18).
8   OJ L42, 12.2.1987, p 48. Directive as last amended by Directive 98/7/EC of the European Parliament and of the Council (OJ L101, 1.4.1998, p 17).
9   OJ L141, 11.6.1993, p 27. Directive as last amended by Directive 97/9/EC of the European Parliament and of the Council (OJ L84, 26.3.1997, p 22).
10   OJ L158, 23.6.1990, p 59.
11   OJ L80, 18.3.1998, p 27.
12   OJ L228, 11.8.1992, p 24.
13   OJ L280, 29.10.1994, p 83.
14   OJ L166, 11.6.1998, p 51. Directive as amended by Directive 1999/44/EC (OJ L171, 7.7.1999, p 12).
15   OJ L210, 7.8.1985, p 29. Directive as amended by Directive 1999/34/EC (OJ L141, 4.6.1999, p 20).
16   OJ L171, 7.7.1999, p 12.
17   OJ L113, 30.4.1992, p 13.
18   OJ L213, 30.7.1998, p 9.
19   OJ L281, 23.11.1995, p 31.
20   OJ L24, 30.1.1998, p 1.
21   OJ L204, 21.7.1998, p 37. Directive as amended by Directive 98/48/EC (OJ L217, 5.8.1998, p 18).
22   OJ L320, 28.11.1998, p 54.
23   OJ L15, 21.1.1998, p 14.
24   OJ L13, 19.1.2000, p 12.
25   OJ C23, 28.1.1999, p 1.

HAVE ADOPTED THIS DIRECTIVE—

CHAPTER I
GENERAL PROVISIONS

Article 1
Objective and scope

1.   This Directive seeks to contribute to the proper functioning of the internal market by ensuring the free movement of information society services between the Member States.

2.   This Directive approximates, to the extent necessary for the achievement of the objective set out in paragraph 1, certain national provisions on information society services relating to the internal market, the establishment of service providers, commercial communications, electronic contracts, the liability of intermediaries, codes of conduct, out-of-court dispute settlements, court actions and cooperation between Member States.

3.   This Directive complements Community law applicable to information society services without prejudice to the level of protection for, in particular, public health and consumer interests, as established by Community acts and national legislation implementing them in so far as this does not restrict the freedom to provide information society services.

4.   This Directive does not establish additional rules on private international law nor does it deal with the jurisdiction of Courts.

5.   This Directive shall not apply to—
     (a)   the field of taxation;
     (b)   questions relating to information society services covered by Directives 95/46/EC and 97/66/EC;
     (c)   questions relating to agreements or practices governed by cartel law;
     (d)   the following activities of information society services—
         —   the activities of notaries or equivalent professions to the extent that they involve a direct and specific connection with the exercise of public authority,
         —   the representation of a client and defence of his interests before the courts,
         —   gambling activities which involve wagering a stake with monetary value in games of chance, including lotteries and betting transactions.

6.   This Directive does not affect measures taken at Community or national level, in the respect of Community law, in order to promote cultural and linguistic diversity and to ensure the defence of pluralism.

[4365]

Article 2
Definitions

For the purpose of this Directive, the following terms shall bear the following meanings—
     (a)   "information society services": services within the meaning of Article 1(2) of Directive 98/34/EC as amended by Directive 98/48/EC;
     (b)   "service provider": any natural or legal person providing an information society service;
     (c)   "established service provider": a service provider who effectively pursues an economic

activity using a fixed establishment for an indefinite period. The presence and use of the technical means and technologies required to provide the service do not, in themselves, constitute an establishment of the provider;

(d) "recipient of the service": any natural or legal person who, for professional ends or otherwise, uses an information society service, in particular for the purposes of seeking information or making it accessible;

(e) "consumer": any natural person who is acting for purposes which are outside his or her trade, business or profession;

(f) "commercial communication": any form of communication designed to promote, directly or indirectly, the goods, services or image of a company, organisation or person pursuing a commercial, industrial or craft activity or exercising a regulated profession. The following do not in themselves constitute commercial communications—

— information allowing direct access to the activity of the company, organisation or person, in particular a domain name or an electronic-mail address,

— communications relating to the goods, services or image of the company, organisation or person compiled in an independent manner, particularly when this is without financial consideration;

(g) "regulated profession": any profession within the meaning of either Article 1(d) of Council Directive 89/48/EEC of 21 December 1988 on a general system for the recognition of higher-education diplomas awarded on completion of professional education and training of at least three-years duration[1] or of Article 1(f) of Council Directive 92/51/EEC of 18 June 1992 on a second general system for the recognition of professional education and training to supplement Directive 89/48/EEC;[2]

(h) "coordinated field": requirements laid down in Member States' legal systems applicable to information society service providers or information society services, regardless of whether they are of a general nature or specifically designed for them.

(i) The coordinated field concerns requirements with which the service provider has to comply in respect of—

— the taking up of the activity of an information society service, such as requirements concerning qualifications, authorisation or notification,

— the pursuit of the activity of an information society service, such as requirements concerning the behaviour of the service provider, requirements regarding the quality or content of the service including those applicable to advertising and contracts, or requirements concerning the liability of the service provider;

(ii) The coordinated field does not cover requirements such as—

— requirements applicable to goods as such,

— requirements applicable to the delivery of goods,

— requirements applicable to services not provided by electronic means.

[4366]

NOTES

[1]   OJ L19, 24.1.1989, p 16.

[2]   OJ L209, 24.7.1992, p 25. Directive as last amended by Commission Directive 97/38/EC (OJ L184, 12.7.1997, p 31).

Article 3
Internal market

1.   Each Member State shall ensure that the information society services provided by a service provider established on its territory comply with the national provisions applicable in the Member State in question which fall within the coordinated field.

2.   Member States may not, for reasons falling within the coordinated field, restrict the freedom to provide information society services from another Member State.

3.   Paragraphs 1 and 2 shall not apply to the fields referred to in the Annex.

4.   Member States may take measures to derogate from paragraph 2 in respect of a given information society service if the following conditions are fulfilled—

(a) the measures shall be—

(i) necessary for one of the following reasons—

— public policy, in particular the prevention, investigation, detection and prosecution of criminal offences, including the protection of minors and the fight against any incitement to hatred on grounds of race, sex, religion or nationality, and violations of human dignity concerning individual persons,

— the protection of public health,

— public security, including the safeguarding of national security and defence,

— the protection of consumers, including investors;

      (ii)   taken against a given information society service which prejudices the objectives referred to in point (i) or which presents a serious and grave risk of prejudice to those objectives;

      (iii)   proportionate to those objectives;

  (b)   before taking the measures in question and without prejudice to court proceedings, including preliminary proceedings and acts carried out in the framework of a criminal investigation, the Member State has—

     —   asked the Member State referred to in paragraph 1 to take measures and the latter did not take such measures, or they were inadequate,

     —   notified the Commission and the Member State referred to in paragraph 1 of its intention to take such measures.

5.   Member States may, in the case of urgency, derogate from the conditions stipulated in paragraph 4(b). Where this is the case, the measures shall be notified in the shortest possible time to the Commission and to the Member State referred to in paragraph 1, indicating the reasons for which the Member State considers that there is urgency.

6.   Without prejudice to the Member State's possibility of proceeding with the measures in question, the Commission shall examine the compatibility of the notified measures with Community law in the shortest possible time; where it comes to the conclusion that the measure is incompatible with Community law, the Commission shall ask the Member State in question to refrain from taking any proposed measures or urgently to put an end to the measures in question.

[4367]

CHAPTER II

PRINCIPLES

Section 1: Establishment and information requirements

Article 4
Principle excluding prior authorisation

1.   Member States shall ensure that the taking up and pursuit of the activity of an information society service provider may not be made subject to prior authorisation or any other requirement having equivalent effect.

2.   Paragraph 1 shall be without prejudice to authorisation schemes which are not specifically and exclusively targeted at information society services, or which are covered by Directive 97/13/EC of the European Parliament and of the Council of 10 April 1997 on a common framework for general authorisations and individual licences in the field of telecommunications services.[1]

[4368]

NOTES

  [1]   OJ L117, 7.5.1997, p 15.

Article 5
General information to be provided

1.   In addition to other information requirements established by Community law, Member States shall ensure that the service provider shall render easily, directly and permanently accessible to the recipients of the service and competent authorities, at least the following information—

  (a)   the name of the service provider;

  (b)   the geographic address at which the service provider is established;

  (c)   the details of the service provider, including his electronic mail address, which allow him to be contacted rapidly and communicated with in a direct and effective manner;

  (d)   where the service provider is registered in a trade or similar public register, the trade register in which the service provider is entered and his registration number, or equivalent means of identification in that register;

  (e)   where the activity is subject to an authorisation scheme, the particulars of the relevant supervisory authority;

  (f)   as concerns the regulated professions—

     —   any professional body or similar institution with which the service provider is registered,

     —   the professional title and the Member State where it has been granted,

     —   a reference to the applicable professional rules in the Member State of establishment and the means to access them;

  (g)   where the service provider undertakes an activity that is subject to VAT, the identification number referred to in Article 22(1) of the sixth Council Directive 77/388/EEC of 17 May 1977 on the harmonisation of the laws of the Member States relating to turnover taxes—Common system of value added tax: uniform basis of assessment.[1]

PART 3

EU AND INTERNATIONAL MATERIALS

2. In addition to other information requirements established by Community law, Member States shall at least ensure that, where information society services refer to prices, these are to be indicated clearly and unambiguously and, in particular, must indicate whether they are inclusive of tax and delivery costs.

[4369]

NOTES

1   OJ L145, 13.6.1977, p 1. Directive as last amended by Directive 1999/85/EC (OJ L277, 28.10.1999, p 34).

Section 2: Commercial communications

Article 6
Information to be provided

In addition to other information requirements established by Community law, Member States shall ensure that commercial communications which are part of, or constitute, an information society service comply at least with the following conditions—

(a)   the commercial communication shall be clearly identifiable as such;

(b)   the natural or legal person on whose behalf the commercial communication is made shall be clearly identifiable;

(c)   promotional offers, such as discounts, premiums and gifts, where permitted in the Member State where the service provider is established, shall be clearly identifiable as such, and the conditions which are to be met to qualify for them shall be easily accessible and be presented clearly and unambiguously;

(d)   promotional competitions or games, where permitted in the Member State where the service provider is established, shall be clearly identifiable as such, and the conditions for participation shall be easily accessible and be presented clearly and unambiguously.

[4370]

Article 7
Unsolicited commercial communication

1.   In addition to other requirements established by Community law, Member States which permit unsolicited commercial communication by electronic mail shall ensure that such commercial communication by a service provider established in their territory shall be identifiable clearly and unambiguously as such as soon as it is received by the recipient.

2.   Without prejudice to Directive 97/7/EC and Directive 97/66/EC, Member States shall take measures to ensure that service providers undertaking unsolicited commercial communications by electronic mail consult regularly and respect the opt-out registers in which natural persons not wishing to receive such commercial communications can register themselves.

[4371]

Article 8
Regulated professions

1.   Member States shall ensure that the use of commercial communications which are part of, or constitute, an information society service provided by a member of a regulated profession is permitted subject to compliance with the professional rules regarding, in particular, the independence, dignity and honour of the profession, professional secrecy and fairness towards clients and other members of the profession.

2.   Without prejudice to the autonomy of professional bodies and associations, Member States and the Commission shall encourage professional associations and bodies to establish codes of conduct at Community level in order to determine the types of information that can be given for the purposes of commercial communication in conformity with the rules referred to in paragraph 1.

3.   When drawing up proposals for Community initiatives which may become necessary to ensure the proper functioning of the Internal Market with regard to the information referred to in paragraph 2, the Commission shall take due account of codes of conduct applicable at Community level and shall act in close cooperation with the relevant professional associations and bodies.

4.   This Directive shall apply in addition to Community Directives concerning access to, and the exercise of, activities of the regulated professions.

[4372]

Section 3: Contracts concluded by electronic means

Article 9
Treatment of contracts

1.   Member States shall ensure that their legal system allows contracts to be concluded by electronic means. Member States shall in particular ensure that the legal requirements applicable to

the contractual process neither create obstacles for the use of electronic contracts nor result in such contracts being deprived of legal effectiveness and validity on account of their having been made by electronic means.

2. Member States may lay down that paragraph 1 shall not apply to all or certain contracts falling into one of the following categories—
   (a) contracts that create or transfer rights in real estate, except for rental rights;
   (b) contracts requiring by law the involvement of courts, public authorities or professions exercising public authority;
   (c) contracts of suretyship granted and on collateral securities furnished by persons acting for purposes outside their trade, business or profession;
   (d) contracts governed by family law or by the law of succession.

3. Member States shall indicate to the Commission the categories referred to in paragraph 2 to which they do not apply paragraph 1. Member States shall submit to the Commission every five years a report on the application of paragraph 2 explaining the reasons why they consider it necessary to maintain the category referred to in paragraph 2(b) to which they do not apply paragraph 1.

[4373]

Article 10
Information to be provided

1. In addition to other information requirements established by Community law, Member States shall ensure, except when otherwise agreed by parties who are not consumers, that at least the following information is given by the service provider clearly, comprehensibly and unambiguously and prior to the order being placed by the recipient of the service—
   (a) the different technical steps to follow to conclude the contract;
   (b) whether or not the concluded contract will be filed by the service provider and whether it will be accessible;
   (c) the technical means for identifying and correcting input errors prior to the placing of the order;
   (d) the languages offered for the conclusion of the contract.

2. Member States shall ensure that, except when otherwise agreed by parties who are not consumers, the service provider indicates any relevant codes of conduct to which he subscribes and information on how those codes can be consulted electronically.

3. Contract terms and general conditions provided to the recipient must be made available in a way that allows him to store and reproduce them.

4. Paragraphs 1 and 2 shall not apply to contracts concluded exclusively by exchange of electronic mail or by equivalent individual communications.

[4374]

Article 11
Placing of the order

1. Member States shall ensure, except when otherwise agreed by parties who are not consumers, that in cases where the recipient of the service places his order through technological means, the following principles apply—
   — the service provider has to acknowledge the receipt of the recipient's order without undue delay and by electronic means,
   — the order and the acknowledgement of receipt are deemed to be received when the parties to whom they are addressed are able to access them.

2. Member States shall ensure that, except when otherwise agreed by parties who are not consumers, the service provider makes available to the recipient of the service appropriate, effective and accessible technical means allowing him to identify and correct input errors, prior to the placing of the order.

3. Paragraph 1, first indent, and paragraph 2 shall not apply to contracts concluded exclusively by exchange of electronic mail or by equivalent individual communications.

[4375]

Section 4: Liability of intermediary service providers

Article 12
"Mere conduit"

1. Where an information society service is provided that consists of the transmission in a communication network of information provided by a recipient of the service, or the provision of access to a communication network, Member States shall ensure that the service provider is not liable for the information transmitted, on condition that the provider—
   (a) does not initiate the transmission;

(b)   does not select the receiver of the transmission; and
(c)   does not select or modify the information contained in the transmission.

2.   The acts of transmission and of provision of access referred to in paragraph 1 include the automatic, intermediate and transient storage of the information transmitted in so far as this takes place for the sole purpose of carrying out the transmission in the communication network, and provided that the information is not stored for any period longer than is reasonably necessary for the transmission.

3.   This Article shall not affect the possibility for a court or administrative authority, in accordance with Member States' legal systems, of requiring the service provider to terminate or prevent an infringement.

[4376]

Article 13
"Caching"

1.   Where an information society service is provided that consists of the transmission in a communication network of information provided by a recipient of the service, Member States shall ensure that the service provider is not liable for the automatic, intermediate and temporary storage of that information, performed for the sole purpose of making more efficient the information's onward transmission to other recipients of the service upon their request, on condition that—
(a)   the provider does not modify the information;
(b)   the provider complies with conditions on access to the information;
(c)   the provider complies with rules regarding the updating of the information, specified in a manner widely recognised and used by industry;
(d)   the provider does not interfere with the lawful use of technology, widely recognised and used by industry, to obtain data on the use of the information; and
(e)   the provider acts expeditiously to remove or to disable access to the information it has stored upon obtaining actual knowledge of the fact that the information at the initial source of the transmission has been removed from the network, or access to it has been disabled, or that a court or an administrative authority has ordered such removal or disablement.

2.   This Article shall not affect the possibility for a court or administrative authority, in accordance with Member States' legal systems, of requiring the service provider to terminate or prevent an infringement.

[4377]

Article 14
Hosting

1.   Where an information society service is provided that consists of the storage of information provided by a recipient of the service, Member States shall ensure that the service provider is not liable for the information stored at the request of a recipient of the service, on condition that—
(a)   the provider does not have actual knowledge of illegal activity or information and, as regards claims for damages, is not aware of facts or circumstances from which the illegal activity or information is apparent; or
(b)   the provider, upon obtaining such knowledge or awareness, acts expeditiously to remove or to disable access to the information.

2.   Paragraph 1 shall not apply when the recipient of the service is acting under the authority or the control of the provider.

3.   This Article shall not affect the possibility for a court or administrative authority, in accordance with Member States' legal systems, of requiring the service provider to terminate or prevent an infringement, nor does it affect the possibility for Member States of establishing procedures governing the removal or disabling of access to information.

[4378]

Article 15
No general obligation to monitor

1.   Member States shall not impose a general obligation on providers, when providing the services covered by Articles 12, 13 and 14, to monitor the information which they transmit or store, nor a general obligation actively to seek facts or circumstances indicating illegal activity.

2.   Member States may establish obligations for information society service providers promptly to inform the competent public authorities of alleged illegal activities undertaken or information provided by recipients of their service or obligations to communicate to the competent authorities, at their request, information enabling the identification of recipients of their service with whom they have storage agreements.

[4379]

CHAPTER III

IMPLEMENTATION

Article 16

Codes of conduct

  1.   Member States and the Commission shall encourage—

    (a)   the drawing up of codes of conduct at Community level, by trade, professional and consumer associations or organisations, designed to contribute to the proper implementation of Articles 5 to 15;

    (b)   the voluntary transmission of draft codes of conduct at national or Community level to the Commission;

    (c)   the accessibility of these codes of conduct in the Community languages by electronic means;

    (d)   the communication to the Member States and the Commission, by trade, professional and consumer associations or organisations, of their assessment of the application of their codes of conduct and their impact upon practices, habits or customs relating to electronic commerce;

    (e)   the drawing up of codes of conduct regarding the protection of minors and human dignity.

  2.   Member States and the Commission shall encourage the involvement of associations or organisations representing consumers in the drafting and implementation of codes of conduct affecting their interests and drawn up in accordance with paragraph 1(a). Where appropriate, to take account of their specific needs, associations representing the visually impaired and disabled should be consulted.

[4380]

Article 17

Out-of-court dispute settlement

  1.   Member States shall ensure that, in the event of disagreement between an information society service provider and the recipient of the service, their legislation does not hamper the use of out-of-court schemes, available under national law, for dispute settlement, including appropriate electronic means.

  2.   Member States shall encourage bodies responsible for the out-of-court settlement of, in particular, consumer disputes to operate in a way which provides adequate procedural guarantees for the parties concerned.

  3.   Member States shall encourage bodies responsible for out-of-court dispute settlement to inform the Commission of the significant decisions they take regarding information society services and to transmit any other information on the practices, usages or customs relating to electronic commerce.

[4381]

Article 18

Court actions

  1.   Member States shall ensure that court actions available under national law concerning information society services' activities allow for the rapid adoption of measures, including interim measures, designed to terminate any alleged infringement and to prevent any further impairment of the interests involved.

  2.   ...

[4382]

NOTES

  Para 2: spent (amended Directive 98/27/EC, Annex (repealed)).

Article 19

Cooperation

  1.   Member States shall have adequate means of supervision and investigation necessary to implement this Directive effectively and shall ensure that service providers supply them with the requisite information.

  2.   Member States shall cooperate with other Member States; they shall, to that end, appoint one or several contact points, whose details they shall communicate to the other Member States and to the Commission.

  3.   Member States shall, as quickly as possible, and in conformity with national law, provide the assistance and information requested by other Member States or by the Commission, including by appropriate electronic means.

  4.   Member States shall establish contact points which shall be accessible at least by electronic means and from which recipients and service providers may—

(a)   obtain general information on contractual rights and obligations as well as on the complaint and redress mechanisms available in the event of disputes, including practical aspects involved in the use of such mechanisms;

(b)   obtain the details of authorities, associations or organisations from which they may obtain further information or practical assistance.

5.   Member States shall encourage the communication to the Commission of any significant administrative or judicial decisions taken in their territory regarding disputes relating to information society services and practices, usages and customs relating to electronic commerce. The Commission shall communicate these decisions to the other Member States.

[4383]

Article 20
Sanctions

Member States shall determine the sanctions applicable to infringements of national provisions adopted pursuant to this Directive and shall take all measures necessary to ensure that they are enforced. The sanctions they provide for shall be effective, proportionate and dissuasive.

[4384]

CHAPTER IV
FINAL PROVISIONS

Article 21
Re-examination

1.   Before 17 July 2003, and thereafter every two years, the Commission shall submit to the European Parliament, the Council and the Economic and Social Committee a report on the application of this Directive, accompanied, where necessary, by proposals for adapting it to legal, technical and economic developments in the field of information society services, in particular with respect to crime prevention, the protection of minors, consumer protection and to the proper functioning of the internal market.

2.   In examining the need for an adaptation of this Directive, the report shall in particular analyse the need for proposals concerning the liability of providers of hyperlinks and location tool services, "notice and take down" procedures and the attribution of liability following the taking down of content. The report shall also analyse the need for additional conditions for the exemption from liability, provided for in Articles 12 and 13, in the light of technical developments, and the possibility of applying the internal market principles to unsolicited commercial communications by electronic mail.

[4385]

Article 22
Transposition

1.   Member States shall bring into force the laws, regulations and administrative provisions necessary to comply with this Directive before 17 January 2002. They shall forthwith inform the Commission thereof.

2.   When Member States adopt the measures referred to in paragraph 1, these shall contain a reference to this Directive or shall be accompanied by such reference at the time of their official publication. The methods of making such reference shall be laid down by Member States.

[4386]

Article 23
Entry into force

This Directive shall enter into force on the day of its publication in the *Official Journal of the European Communities*.

[4387]

Article 24
Addressees

This Directive is addressed to the Member States.

[4388]

Done at Luxembourg, 8 June 2000.

ANNEX

DEROGATIONS FROM ARTICLE 3

As provided for in Article 3(3), Article 3(1) and (2) do not apply to—

—   copyright, neighbouring rights, rights referred to in Directive 87/54/EEC[1] and Directive 96/9/EC[2] as well as industrial property rights,

— the emission of electronic money by institutions in respect of which Member States have
applied one of the derogations provided for in Article 8(1) of Directive 2000/46/EC,[3]
— Article 44(2) of Directive 85/611/EEC,[4]
— Article 30 and Title IV of Directive 92/49/EEC,[5] Title IV of Directive 92/96/EEC,[6]
Articles 7 and 8 of Directive 88/357/EEC[7] and Article 4 of Directive 90/619/EEC,[8]
— the freedom of the parties to choose the law applicable to their contract,
— contractual obligations concerning consumer contacts,
— formal validity of contracts creating or transferring rights in real estate where such
contracts are subject to mandatory formal requirements of the law of the Member State
where the real estate is situated,
— the permissibility of unsolicited commercial communications by electronic mail.

[4389]

NOTES
1   OJ L24, 27.1.1987, p 36.
2   OJ L77, 27.3.1996, p 20.
3   Not yet published in the Official Journal.
4   OJ L375, 31.12.1985, p 3. Directive as last amended by Directive 95/26/EC (OJ L168, 18.7.1995, p 7).
5   OJ L228, 11.8.1992, p 1. Directive as last amended by Directive 95/26/EC.
6   OJ L360, 9.12.1992, p 2. Directive as last amended by Directive 95/26/EC.
7   OJ L172, 4.7.1988, p 1. Directive as last amended by Directive 92/49/EC.
8   OJ L330, 29.11.1990, p 50. Directive as last amended by Directive 92/96/EC.

DIRECTIVE OF THE EUROPEAN PARLIAMENT AND OF
THE COUNCIL

of 29 June 2000

on combating late payment in commercial transactions

(2000/35/EC)

NOTES
Date of publication in OJ: OJ L200, 8.8.2000, p 35.
This Directive has been mainly implemented in the UK by the Late Payment of Commercial Debts
Regulations 2002, SI 2002/1674 at **[3341]**.

THE EUROPEAN PARLIAMENT AND THE COUNCIL OF THE EUROPEAN UNION,
Having regard to the Treaty establishing the European Community, and in particular Article 95
thereof,
Having regard to the proposal from the Commission,[1]
Having regard to the opinion of the Economic and Social Committee,[2]
Acting in accordance with the procedure laid down in Article 251 of the Treaty,[3] in the light of
the joint text approved by the Conciliation Committee on 4 May 2000,
Whereas:
(1)   In its resolution on the integrated programme in favour of SMEs and the craft sector,[4] the
European Parliament urged the Commission to submit proposals to deal with the problem of late
payment.
(2)   On 12 May 1995 the Commission adopted a recommendation on payment periods in
commercial transactions.[5]
(3)   In its resolution on the Commission recommendation on payment periods in commercial
transactions,[6] the European Parliament called on the Commission to consider transforming its
recommendation into a proposal for a Council directive to be submitted as soon as possible.
(4)   On 29 May 1997 the Economic and Social Committee adopted an opinion on the
Commission's Green Paper on Public procurement in the European Union: Exploring the way
forward.[7]
(5)   On 4 June 1997 the Commission published an action plan for the single market, which
underlined that late payment represents an increasingly serious obstacle for the success of the single
market.
(6)   On 17 July 1997 the Commission published a report on late payments in commercial
transactions,[8] summarising the results of an evaluation of the effects of the Commission's
recommendation of 12 May 1995.
(7)   Heavy administrative and financial burdens are placed on businesses, particularly small and
medium-sized ones, as a result of excessive payment periods and late payment. Moreover, these
problems are a major cause of insolvencies threatening the survival of businesses and result in
numerous job losses.

(8)   In some Member States contractual payment periods differ significantly from the Community average.

(9)   The differences between payment rules and practices in the Member States constitute an obstacle to the proper functioning of the internal market.

(10)   This has the effect of considerably limiting commercial transactions between Member States. This is in contradiction with Article 14 of the Treaty as entrepreneurs should be able to trade throughout the internal market under conditions which ensure that transborder operations do not entail greater risks than domestic sales. Distortions of competition would ensue if substantially different rules applied to domestic and transborder operations.

(11)   The most recent statistics indicate that there has been, at best, no improvement in late payments in many Member States since the adoption of the recommendation of 12 May 1995.

(12)   The objective of combating late payments in the internal market cannot be sufficiently achieved by the Member States acting individually and can, therefore, be better achieved by the Community. This Directive does not go beyond what is necessary to achieve that objective. This Directive complies therefore, in its entirety, with the requirements of the principles of subsidiarity and proportionality as laid down in Article 5 of the Treaty.

(13)   This Directive should be limited to payments made as remuneration for commercial transactions and does not regulate transactions with consumers, interest in connection with other payments, e g payments under the laws on cheques and bills of exchange, payments made as compensation for damages including payments from insurance companies.

(14)   The fact that the liberal professions are covered by this Directive does not mean that Member States have to treat them as undertakings or merchants for purposes not covered by this Directive.

(15)   This Directive only defines the term 'enforceable title' but does not regulate the various procedures of forced execution of such a title and the conditions under which forced execution of such a title can be stopped or suspended.

(16)   Late payment constitutes a breach of contract which has been made financially attractive to debtors in most Member States by low interest rates on late payments and/or slow procedures for redress. A decisive shift, including compensation of creditors for the costs incurred, is necessary to reverse this trend and to ensure that the consequences of late payments are such as to discourage late payment.

(17)   The reasonable compensation for the recovery costs has to be considered without prejudice to national provisions according to which a national judge can award to the creditor any additional damage caused by the debtor's late payment, taking also into account that such incurred costs may be already compensated for by the interest for late payment.

(18)   This Directive takes into account the issue of long contractual payment periods and, in particular, the existence of certain categories of contracts where a longer payment period in combination with a restriction of freedom of contract or a higher interest rate can be justified.

(19)   This Directive should prohibit abuse of freedom of contract to the disadvantage of the creditor. Where an agreement mainly serves the purpose of procuring the debtor additional liquidity at the expense of the creditor, or where the main contractor imposes on his suppliers and subcontractors terms of payment which are not justified on the grounds of the terms granted to himself, these may be considered to be factors constituting such an abuse. This Directive does not affect national provisions relating to the way contracts are concluded or regulating the. validity of contractual terms which are unfair to the debtor.

(20)   The consequences of late payment can be dissuasive only if they are accompanied by procedures for redress which are rapid and effective for the creditor. In conformity with the principle of non-discrimination contained in Article 12 of the Treaty, those procedures should be available to all creditors who are established in the Community.

(21)   It is desirable to ensure that creditors are in a position to exercise a retention of title on a non-discriminatory basis throughout the Community, if the retention of title clause is valid under the applicable national provisions designated by private international law.

(22)   This Directive should regulate all commercial transactions irrespective of whether they are carried out between private or public undertakings or between undertakings and public authorities, having regard to the fact that the latter handle a considerable volume of payments to business. It should therefore also regulate all commercial transactions between main contractors and their suppliers and subcontractors.

(23)   Article 5 of this Directive requires that the recovery procedure for unchallenged claims be completed within a short period of time in conformity with national legislation, but does not require Member States to adopt a specific procedure or to amend their existing legal procedures in a specific way,

---

NOTES

1   OJ C168, 3.6.1998, p 13, and OJ C374, 3.12.1998, p 4.
2   OJ C407, 28.12.1998, p 50.
3   Opinion of the European Parliament of 17 September 1998 (OJ C313, 12.10.1998, p 142), Council Common Position of 29 July 1999 (OJ C284, 6.10.1999, p 1) and decision of the European Parliament of 16 December 1999. Decision of the European Parliament of 15 June 2000 and Decision of the Council of 18 May 2000.

4   OJ C323, 21.11.1994, p 19.
5   OJ L127, 10.6.1995, p 19.
6   OJ C211, 22.7.1996, p 43.
7   OJ C287, 22.9.1997, p 92.
8   OJ C216, 17.7.1997, p 10.

HAVE ADOPTED THIS DIRECTIVE:

Article 1
Scope

This Directive shall apply to all payments made as remuneration for commercial transactions.

[4390]

Article 2
Definitions

For the purposes of this Directive—

1.   'commercial transactions' means transactions between undertakings or between undertakings and public authorities which lead to the delivery of goods or the provision of services for remuneration,

   'public authority' means any contracting authority or entity, as defined by the Public Procurement Directives (92/50/EEC,[1] 93/36/EEC,[2] 93/37/EEC[3] and 93/38/EEC),[4]

   'undertaking' means any organisation acting in the course of its independent economic or professional activity, even where it is carried on by a single person;

2.   'late payment' means exceeding the contractual or statutory period of payment;

3.   'retention of title' means the contractual agreement according to which the seller retains title to the goods in question until the price has been paid in full;

4.   'interest rate applied by the European Central Bank to its main refinancing operations' means the interest rate applied to such operations in the rate of fixed-rate tenders. In the event that a main refinancing operation was conducted according to a variable-rate tender procedure, this interest rate refers to the marginal interest rate which resulted from that tender. This applies both in the case of single-rate and variable-rate auctions;

5.   'enforceable title' means any decision, judgment or order for payment issued by a court or other competent authority, whether for immediate payment or payment by instalments, which permits the creditor to have his claim against the debtor collected by means of forced execution; it shall include a decision, judgment or order for payment that is provisionally enforceable and remains so even if the debtor appeals against it.

[4391]

NOTES

1   OJ L209, 24.7.1992, p 1.
2   OJ L199, 9.8.1993, p 1.
3   OJ L199, 9.8.1993. p 54.
4   OJ L199, 9.8.1993, p 84.

Article 3
Interest in case of late payment

Member States shall ensure that—

(a)   interest in accordance with point (d) shall become payable from the day following the date or the end of the period for payment fixed in the contract;

(b)   if the date or period for payment is not fixed in the contract, interest shall become payable automatically without the necessity of a reminder—

     (i)   30 days following the date of receipt by the debtor of the invoice or an equivalent request for payment; or

     (ii)   if the date of the receipt of the invoice or the equivalent request for payment is uncertain, 30 days after the date of receipt of the goods or services; or

     (iii)   if the debtor receives the invoice or the equivalent request for payment earlier than the goods or the services, 30 days after the receipt of the goods or services; or

     (iv)   if a procedure of acceptance or verification, by which the conformity of the goods or services with the contract is to be ascertained, is provided for by statute or in the contract and if the debtor receives the invoice or the equivalent request for payment earlier or on the date on which such acceptance or verification takes place, 30 days after this latter date;

(c)   the creditor shall be entitled to interest for late payment to the extent that—

     (i)   he has fulfilled his contractual and legal obligations; and

     (ii)   he has not received the amount due on time, unless the debtor is not responsible for the delay;

(d) the level of interest for late payment ('the statutory rate'), which the debtor is obliged to pay, shall be the sum of the interest rate applied by the European Central Bank to its most recent main refinancing operation carried out before the first calendar day of the half-year in question ('the reference rate'), plus at least seven percentage points ('the margin'), unless otherwise specified in the contract. For a Member State which is not participating in the third stage of economic and monetary union, the reference rate referred to above shall be the equivalent rate set by its national central bank. In both cases, the reference rate in force on the first calendar day of the half-year in question shall apply for the following six months;

(e) unless the debtor is not responsible for the delay, the creditor shall be entitled to claim reasonable compensation from the debtor for all relevant recovery costs incurred through the latter's late payment. Such recovery costs shall respect the principles of transparency and proportionality as regards the debt in question. Member States may, while respecting the principles referred to above, fix maximum amounts as regards the recovery costs for different levels of debt.

2. For certain categories of contracts to be defined by national law, Member States may fix the period after which interest becomes payable to a maximum of 60 days provided that they either restrain the parties to the contract from exceeding this period or fix a mandatory interest rate that substantially exceeds the statutory rate.

3. Member States shall provide that an agreement on the date for payment or on the consequences of late payment which is not in line with the provisions of paragraphs 1(b) to (d) and 2 either shall not be enforceable or shall give rise to a claim for damages if, when all circumstances of the case, including good commercial practice and the nature of the product, are considered, it is grossly unfair to the creditor. In determining whether an agreement is grossly unfair to the creditor, it will be taken, inter alia, into account whether the debtor has any objective reason to deviate from the provisions of paragraphs 1(b) to (d) and 2. If such an agreement is determined to be grossly unfair, the statutory terms will apply, unless the national courts determine different conditions which are fair.

4. Member States shall ensure that, in the interests of creditors and of competitors, adequate and effective means exist to prevent the continued use of terms which are grossly unfair within the meaning of paragraph 3.

5. The means referred to in paragraph 4 shall include provisions whereby organisations officially recognised as, or having a legitimate interest in, representing small and medium-sized enterprises may take action according to the national law concerned before the courts or before competent administrative bodies on the grounds that contractual terms drawn up for general use are grossly unfair within the meaning of paragraph 3, so that they can apply appropriate and effective means to prevent the continued use of such terms.

[4392]

Article 4
Retention of title

1. Member States shall provide in conformity with the applicable national provisions designated by private international law that the seller retains title to goods until they are fully paid for if a retention of title clause has been expressly agreed between the buyer and the seller before the delivery of the goods.

2. Member States may adopt or retain provisions dealing with down payments already made by the debtor.

[4393]

Article 5
Recovery procedures for unchallenged claims

1. Member States shall ensure that an enforceable title can be obtained, irrespective of the amount of the debt, normally within 90 calendar days of the lodging of the creditor's action or application at the court or other competent authority, provided that the debt or aspects of the procedure are not disputed. This duty shall be carried out by Member States in conformity with their respective national legislation, regulations and administrative provisions.

2. The respective national legislation, regulations and administrative provisions shall apply the same conditions for all creditors who are established in the European Community.

3. The 90 calendar day period referred to in paragraph 1 shall not include the following:
(a) periods for service of documents;
(b) any delays caused by the creditor, such as periods devoted to correcting applications.

4. This Article shall be without prejudice to the provisions of the Brussels Convention on jurisdiction and enforcement of judgments in civil and commercial matters.

[4394]

Article 6
Transposition

1. Member States shall bring into force the laws, regulations and administrative provisions necessary to comply with this Directive before 8 August 2002. They shall forthwith inform the Commission thereof.

When Member States adopt these measures, they shall contain a reference to this Directive or shall be accompanied by such reference on the occasion of their official publication. The methods of making such reference shall be laid down by Member States.

2. Member States may maintain or bring into force provisions which are more favourable to the creditor than the provisions necessary to comply with this Directive.

3. In transposing this Directive, Member States may exclude:
    (a) debts that are subject to insolvency proceedings instituted against the debtor;
    (b) contracts that have been concluded prior to 8 August 2002; and
    (c) claims for interest of less than EUR 5.

4. Member States shall communicate to the Commission the text of the main provisions of national law which they adopt in the field covered by this Directive.

5. The Commission shall undertake two years after 8 August 2002 a review of, inter alia, the statutory rate, contractual payment periods and late payments, to assess the impact on commercial transactions and the operation of the legislation in practice. The results of this review and of other reviews will be made known to the European Parliament and the Council, accompanied where appropriate by proposals for improvement of this Directive.

[4395]

Article 7
Entry into force

This Directive shall enter into force on the day of its publication in the *Official Journal of the European Communities*.

[4396]

Article 8
Addressees

This Directive is addressed to the Member States.

[4397]

Done at Luxembourg, 29 June 2000.

DIRECTIVE OF THE EUROPEAN PARLIAMENT AND OF THE COUNCIL

of 3 December 2001

on general product safety

(2001/95/EC)

(Text with EEA relevance)

NOTES
Date of publication in OJ: OJ L11, 15.1.2002, p 4.
This Directive has been implemented in the UK by the General Product Safety Regulations 2005, SI 2005/1803 at **[3439]**.

THE EUROPEAN PARLIAMENT AND THE COUNCIL OF THE EUROPEAN UNION,
Having regard to the Treaty establishing the European Community, and in particular Article 95 thereof,
Having regard to the proposal from the Commission,[1]
Having regard to the opinion of the Economic and Social Committee,[2]
Acting in accordance with the procedure referred to in Article 251 of the Treaty,[3] in the light of the joint text approved by the Conciliation Committee on 2 August 2001,
Whereas—
(1) Under Article 16 of Council Directive 92/59/EEC of 29 June 1992 on general product safety,[4] the Council was to decide, four years after the date set for the implementation of the said Directive, on the basis of a report of the Commission on the experience acquired, together with

appropriate proposals, whether to adjust Directive 92/59/EEC. It is necessary to amend Directive 92/59/EEC in several respects, in order to complete, reinforce or clarify some of its provisions in the light of experience as well as new and relevant developments on consumer product safety, together with the changes made to the Treaty, especially in Articles 152 concerning public health and 153 concerning consumer protection, and in the light of the precautionary principle. Directive 92/59/EEC should therefore be recast in the interest of clarity. This recasting leaves the safety of services outside the scope of this Directive, since the Commission intends to identify the needs, possibilities and priorities for Community action on the safety of services and liability of service providers, with a view to presenting appropriate proposals.

(2) It is important to adopt measures with the aim of improving the functioning of the internal market, comprising an area without internal frontiers in which the free movement of goods, persons, services and capital is assured.

(3) In the absence of Community provisions, horizontal legislation of the Member States on product safety, imposing in particular a general obligation on economic operators to market only safe products, might differ in the level of protection afforded to consumers. Such disparities, and the absence of horizontal legislation in some Member States, would be liable to create barriers to trade and distortion of competition within the internal market.

(4) In order to ensure a high level of consumer protection, the Community must contribute to protecting the health and safety of consumers. Horizontal Community legislation introducing a general product safety requirement, and containing provisions on the general obligations of producers and distributors, on the enforcement of Community product safety requirements and on rapid exchange of information and action at Community level in certain cases, should contribute to that aim.

(5) It is very difficult to adopt Community legislation for every product which exists or which may be developed; there is a need for a broad-based, legislative framework of a horizontal nature to deal with such products, and also to cover lacunae, in particular pending revision of the existing specific legislation, and to complement provisions in existing or forthcoming specific legislation, in particular with a view to ensuring a high level of protection of safety and health of consumers, as required by Article 95 of the Treaty.

(6) It is therefore necessary to establish at Community level a general safety requirement for any product placed on the market, or otherwise supplied or made available to consumers, intended for consumers, or likely to be used by consumers under reasonably foreseeable conditions even if not intended for them. In all these cases the products under consideration can pose risks for the health and safety of consumers which must be prevented. Certain second-hand goods should nevertheless be excluded by their very nature.

(7) This Directive should apply to products irrespective of the selling techniques, including distance and electronic selling.

(8) The safety of products should be assessed taking into account all the relevant aspects, in particular the categories of consumers which can be particularly vulnerable to the risks posed by the products under consideration, in particular children and the elderly.

(9) This Directive does not cover services, but in order to secure the attainment of the protection objectives in question, its provisions should also apply to products that are supplied or made available to consumers in the context of service provision for use by them. The safety of the equipment used by service providers themselves to supply a service to consumers does not come within the scope of this Directive since it has to be dealt with in conjunction with the safety of the service provided. In particular, equipment on which consumers ride or travel which is operated by a service provider is excluded from the scope of this Directive.

(10) Products which are designed exclusively for professional use but have subsequently migrated to the consumer market should be subject to the requirements of this Directive because they can pose risks to consumer health and safety when used under reasonably foreseeable conditions.

(11) In the absence of more specific provisions, within the framework of Community legislation covering safety of the products concerned, all the provisions of this Directive should apply in order to ensure consumer health and safety.

(12) If specific Community legislation sets out safety requirements covering only certain risks or categories of risks, with regard to the products concerned the obligations of economic operators in respect of these risks are those determined by the provisions of the specific legislation, while the general safety requirement of this Directive should apply to the other risks.

(13) The provisions of this Directive relating to the other obligations of producers and distributors, the obligations and powers of the Member States, the exchanges of information and rapid intervention situations and dissemination of information and confidentiality apply in the case of products covered by specific rules of Community law, if those rules do not already contain such obligations.

(14) In order to facilitate the effective and consistent application of the general safety requirement of this Directive, it is important to establish European voluntary standards covering certain products and risks in such a way that a product which conforms to a national standard transposing a European standard is to be presumed to be in compliance with the said requirement.

(15) With regard to the aims of this Directive, European standards should be established by European standardisation bodies, under mandates set by the Commission assisted by appropriate

Committees. In order to ensure that products in compliance with the standards fulfil the general safety requirement, the Commission assisted by a committee composed of representatives of the Member States, should fix the requirements that the standards must meet. These requirements should be included in the mandates to the standardisation bodies.

(16) In the absence of specific regulations and when the European standards established under mandates set by the Commission are not available or recourse is not made to such standards, the safety of products should be assessed taking into account in particular national standards transposing any other relevant European or international standards, Commission recommendations or national standards, international standards, codes of good practice, the state of the art and the safety which consumers may reasonably expect. In this context, the Commission's recommendations may facilitate the consistent and effective application of this Directive pending the introduction of European standards or as regards the risks and/or products for which such standards are deemed not to be possible or appropriate.

(17) Appropriate independent certification recognised by the competent authorities may facilitate proof of compliance with the applicable product safety criteria.

(18) It is appropriate to supplement the duty to observe the general safety requirement by other obligations on economic operators because action by such operators is necessary to prevent risks to consumers under certain circumstances.

(19) The additional obligations on producers should include the duty to adopt measures commensurate with the characteristics of the products, enabling them to be informed of the risks that these products may present, to supply consumers with information enabling them to assess and prevent risks, to warn consumers of the risks posed by dangerous products already supplied to them, to withdraw those products from the market and, as a last resort, to recall them when necessary, which may involve, depending on the provisions applicable in the Member States, an appropriate form of compensation, for example exchange or reimbursement.

(20) Distributors should help in ensuring compliance with the applicable safety requirements. The obligations placed on distributors apply in proportion to their respective responsibilities. In particular, it may prove impossible, in the context of charitable activities, to provide the competent authorities with information and documentation on possible risks and origin of the product in the case of isolated used objects provided by private individuals.

(21) Both producers and distributors should cooperate with the competent authorities in action aimed at preventing risks and inform them when they conclude that certain products supplied are dangerous. The conditions regarding the provision of such information should be set in this Directive to facilitate its effective application, while avoiding an excessive burden for economic operators and the authorities.

(22) In order to ensure the effective enforcement of the obligations incumbent on producers and distributors, the Member States should establish or designate authorities which are responsible for monitoring product safety and have powers to take appropriate measures, including the power to impose effective, proportionate and dissuasive penalties, and ensure appropriate coordination between the various designated authorities.

(23) It is necessary in particular for the appropriate measures to include the power for Member States to order or organise, immediately and efficiently, the withdrawal of dangerous products already placed on the market and as a last resort to order, coordinate or organise the recall from consumers of dangerous products already supplied to them. Those powers should be applied when producers and distributors fail to prevent risks to consumers in accordance with their obligations. Where necessary, the appropriate powers and procedures should be available to the authorities to decide and apply any necessary measures rapidly.

(24) The safety of consumers depends to a great extent on the active enforcement of Community product safety requirements. The Member States should, therefore, establish systematic approaches to ensure the effectiveness of market surveillance and other enforcement activities and should ensure their openness to the public and interested parties.

(25) Collaboration between the enforcement authorities of the Member States is necessary in ensuring the attainment of the protection objectives of this Directive. It is, therefore, appropriate to promote the operation of a European network of the enforcement authorities of the Member States to facilitate, in a coordinated manner with other Community procedures, in particular the Community Rapid Information System (RAPEX), improved collaboration at operational level on market surveillance and other enforcement activities, in particular risk assessment, testing of products, exchange of expertise and scientific knowledge, execution of joint surveillance projects and tracing, withdrawing or recalling dangerous products.

(26) It is necessary, for the purpose of ensuring a consistent, high level of consumer health and safety protection and preserving the unity of the internal market, that the Commission be informed of any measure restricting the placing on the market of a product or requiring its withdrawal or recall from the market. Such measures should be taken in compliance with the provisions of the Treaty, and in particular Articles 28, 29 and 30 thereof.

(27) Effective supervision of product safety requires the setting-up at national and Community levels of a system of rapid exchange of information in situations of serious risk requiring rapid intervention in respect of the safety of a product. It is also appropriate in this Directive to set out detailed procedures for the operation of the system and to give the Commission, assisted by an advisory committee, power to adapt them.

(28) This Directive provides for the establishment of non-binding guidelines aimed at indicating simple and clear criteria and practical rules which may change, in particular for the purpose of allowing efficient notification of measures restricting the placing on the market of products in the cases referred to in this Directive, whilst taking into account the range of situations dealt with by Member States and economic operators. The guidelines should in particular include criteria for the application of the definition of serious risks in order to facilitate consistent implementation of the relevant provisions in case of such risks.

(29) It is primarily for Member States, in compliance with the Treaty and in particular with Articles 28, 29 and 30 thereof, to take appropriate measures with regard to dangerous products located within their territory.

(30) However, if the Member States differ as regards the approach to dealing with the risk posed by certain products, such differences could entail unacceptable disparities in consumer protection and constitute a barrier to intra-Community trade.

(31) It may be necessary to deal with serious product-safety problems requiring rapid intervention which affect or could affect, in the immediate future, all or a significant part of the Community and which, in view of the nature of the safety problem posed by the product, cannot be dealt with effectively in a manner commensurate with the degree of urgency, under the procedures laid down in the specific rules of Community law applicable to the products or category of products in question.

(32) It is therefore necessary to provide for an adequate mechanism allowing, as a last resort, for the adoption of measures applicable throughout the Community, in the form of a decision addressed to the Member States, to cope with situations created by products presenting a serious risk. Such a decision should entail a ban on the export of the product in question, unless in the case in point exceptional circumstances allow a partial ban or even no ban to be decided upon, particularly when a system of prior consent is established. In addition, the banning of exports should be examined with a view to preventing risks to the health and safety of consumers. Since such a decision is not directly applicable to economic operators, Member States should take all necessary measures for its implementation. Measures adopted under such a procedure are interim measures, save when they apply to individually identified products or batches of products. In order to ensure the appropriate assessment of the need for, and the best preparation of such measures, they should be taken by the Commission, assisted by a committee, in the light of consultations with the Member States, and, if scientific questions are involved falling within the competence of a Community scientific committee, with the scientific committee competent for the risk concerned.

(33) The measures necessary for the implementation of this Directive should be adopted in accordance with Council Decision 1999/468/EC of 28 June 1999 laying down the procedures for the exercise of implementing powers conferred on the Commission.[5]

(34) In order to facilitate effective and consistent application of this Directive, the various aspects of its application may need to be discussed within a committee.

(35) Public access to the information available to the authorities on product safety should be ensured. However, professional secrecy, as referred to in Article 287 of the Treaty, must be protected in a way which is compatible with the need to ensure the effectiveness of market surveillance activities and of protection measures.

(36) This Directive should not affect victims' rights within the meaning of Council Directive 85/374/EEC of 25 July 1985 on the approximation of the laws, regulations and administrative provisions of the Member States concerning liability for defective products.[6]

(37) It is necessary for Member States to provide for appropriate means of redress before the competent courts in respect of measures taken by the competent authorities which restrict the placing on the market of a product or require its withdrawal or recall.

(38) In addition, the adoption of measures concerning imported products, like those concerning the banning of exports, with a view to preventing risks to the safety and health of consumers must comply with the Community's international obligations.

(39) The Commission should periodically examine the manner in which this Directive is applied and the results obtained, in particular in relation to the functioning of market surveillance systems, the rapid exchange of information and measures adopted at Community level, together with other issues relevant for consumer product safety in the Community, and submit regular reports to the European Parliament and the Council on the subject.

(40) This Directive should not affect the obligations of Member States concerning the deadline for transposition and application of Directive 92/59/EEC;

NOTES

[1]   OJ C337E, 28.11.2000, p 109 and OJ C154E, 29.5.2000, p 265.
[2]   OJ C367, 20.12.2000, p 34.
[3]   Opinion of the European Parliament of 15.11.2000 (OJ C223, 8.8.2001, p 154), Council Common Position of 12.2.2001 (OJ C93, 23.3.2001, p 24) and Decision of the European Parliament of 16.5.2001 (not yet published in the Official Journal). Decision of the European Parliament of 4.10.2001 and Council Decision of 27.9.2001.
[4]   OJ L228, 11.8.1992, p 24.
[5]   OJ L184, 17.7.1999, p 23.

⁶   OJ L210, 7.8.1985, p 29. Directive as amended by Directive 1999/34/EC of the European Parliament and of the Council (OJ L141, 4.6.1999, p 20).

HAVE ADOPTED THIS DIRECTIVE—

CHAPTER I
OBJECTIVE—SCOPE—DEFINITIONS

Article 1

1.   The purpose of this Directive is to ensure that products placed on the market are safe.

2.   This Directive shall apply to all the products defined in Article 2(a). Each of its provisions shall apply in so far as there are no specific provisions with the same objective in rules of Community law governing the safety of the products concerned.

Where products are subject to specific safety requirements imposed by Community legislation, this Directive shall apply only to the aspects and risks or categories of risks not covered by those requirements. This means that—

    (a)   Articles 2(b) and (c), 3 and 4 shall not apply to those products insofar as concerns the risks or categories of risks covered by the specific legislation;

    (b)   Articles 5 to 18 shall apply except where there are specific provisions governing the aspects covered by the said Articles with the same objective.

[4398]

Article 2

For the purposes of this Directive—

    (a)   "product" shall mean any product—including in the context of providing a service—which is intended for consumers or likely, under reasonably foreseeable conditions, to be used by consumers even if not intended for them, and is supplied or made available, whether for consideration or not, in the course of a commercial activity, and whether new, used or reconditioned.

         This definition shall not apply to second-hand products supplied as antiques or as products to be repaired or reconditioned prior to being used, provided that the supplier clearly informs the person to whom he supplies the product to that effect;

    (b)   "safe product" shall mean any product which, under normal or reasonably foreseeable conditions of use including duration and, where applicable, putting into service, installation and maintenance requirements, does not present any risk or only the minimum risks compatible with the product's use, considered to be acceptable and consistent with a high level of protection for the safety and health of persons, taking into account the following points in particular—

        (i)   the characteristics of the product, including its composition, packaging, instructions for assembly and, where applicable, for installation and maintenance;

        (ii)   the effect on other products, where it is reasonably foreseeable that it will be used with other products;

        (iii)   the presentation of the product, the labelling, any warnings and instructions for its use and disposal and any other indication or information regarding the product;

        (iv)   the categories of consumers at risk when using the product, in particular children and the elderly.

         The feasibility of obtaining higher levels of safety or the availability of other products presenting a lesser degree of risk shall not constitute grounds for considering a product to be "dangerous";

    (c)   "dangerous product" shall mean any product which does not meet the definition of "safe product" in (b);

    (d)   "serious risk" shall mean any serious risk, including those the effects of which are not immediate, requiring rapid intervention by the public authorities;

    (e)   "producer" shall mean—

        (i)   the manufacturer of the product, when he is established in the Community, and any other person presenting himself as the manufacturer by affixing to the product his name, trade mark or other distinctive mark, or the person who reconditions the product;

        (ii)   the manufacturer's representative, when the manufacturer is not established in the Community or, if there is no representative established in the Community, the importer of the product;

        (iii)   other professionals in the supply chain, insofar as their activities may affect the safety properties of a product;

    (f)   "distributor" shall mean any professional in the supply chain whose activity does not affect the safety properties of a product;

(g)   "recall" shall mean any measure aimed at achieving the return of a dangerous product that has already been supplied or made available to consumers by the producer or distributor;

(h)   "withdrawal" shall mean any measure aimed at preventing the distribution, display and offer of a product dangerous to the consumer.

[4399]

CHAPTER II
GENERAL SAFETY REQUIREMENT, CONFORMITY ASSESSMENT CRITERIA AND EUROPEAN STANDARDS

Article 3

1.   Producers shall be obliged to place only safe products on the market.

2.   A product shall be deemed safe, as far as the aspects covered by the relevant national legislation are concerned, when, in the absence of specific Community provisions governing the safety of the product in question, it conforms to the specific rules of national law of the Member State in whose territory the product is marketed, such rules being drawn up in conformity with the Treaty, and in particular Articles 28 and 30 thereof, and laying down the health and safety requirements which the product must satisfy in order to be marketed.

A product shall be presumed safe as far as the risks and risk categories covered by relevant national standards are concerned when it conforms to voluntary national standards transposing European standards, the references of which have been published by the Commission in the *Official Journal of the European Communities* in accordance with Article 4. The Member States shall publish the references of such national standards.

3.   In circumstances other than those referred to in paragraph 2, the conformity of a product to the general safety requirement shall be assessed by taking into account the following elements in particular, where they exist—

(a)   voluntary national standards transposing relevant European standards other than those referred to in paragraph 2;

(b)   the standards drawn up in the Member State in which the product is marketed;

(c)   Commission recommendations setting guidelines on product safety assessment;

(d)   product safety codes of good practice in force in the sector concerned;

(e)   the state of the art and technology;

(f)   reasonable consumer expectations concerning safety.

4.   Conformity of a product with the criteria designed to ensure the general safety requirement, in particular the provisions mentioned in paragraphs 2 or 3, shall not bar the competent authorities of the Member States from taking appropriate measures to impose restrictions on its being placed on the market or to require its withdrawal from the market or recall where there is evidence that, despite such conformity, it is dangerous.

[4400]

Article 4

1.   For the purposes of this Directive, the European standards referred to in the second subparagraph of Article 3(2) shall be drawn up as follows—

[(a)   the requirements intended to ensure that products which conform to those standards satisfy the general safety requirement shall be determined by the Commission. Those measures, designed to amend non-essential elements of this Directive by supplementing it, shall be adopted in accordance with the regulatory procedure with scrutiny referred to in Article 15(4);]

(b)   on the basis of those requirements, the Commission shall, in accordance with Directive 98/34/EC of the European Parliament and of the Council of 22 June 1998 laying down a procedure for the provision of information in the field of technical standards and regulations and of rules on information society services[1] call on the European standardisation bodies to draw up standards which satisfy these requirements;

(c)   on the basis of those mandates, the European standardisation bodies shall adopt the standards in accordance with the principles contained in the general guidelines for cooperation between the Commission and those bodies;

(d)   the Commission shall report every three years to the European Parliament and the Council, within the framework of the report referred to in Article 19(2), on its programmes for setting the requirements and the mandates for standardisation provided for in subparagraphs (a) and (b) above. This report will, in particular, include an analysis of the decisions taken regarding requirements and mandates for standardisation referred to in subparagraphs (a) and (b) and regarding the standards referred to in subparagraph (c). It will also include information on the products for which the Commission intends to set the requirements and the mandates in question, the product risks to be considered and the results of any preparatory work launched in this area.

2. The Commission shall publish in the *Official Journal of the European Communities* the references of the European standards adopted in this way and drawn up in accordance with the requirements referred to in paragraph 1.

If a standard adopted by the European standardisation bodies before the entry into force of this Directive ensures compliance with the general safety requirement, the Commission shall decide to publish its references in the *Official Journal of the European Communities*.

If a standard does not ensure compliance with the general safety requirement, the Commission shall withdraw reference to the standard from publication in whole or in part.

In the cases referred to in the second and third subparagraphs, the Commission shall, on its own initiative or at the request of a Member State, decide in accordance with the procedure laid down in Article 15(2) whether the standard in question meets the general safety requirement. The Commission shall decide to publish or withdraw after consulting the Committee established by Article 5 of Directive 98/34/EC. The Commission shall notify the Member States of its decision.

[4401]

NOTES

Para 1: sub-para (a) substituted by European Parliament and Council Regulation 596/2009/EC, Art 2, Annex, para 5.8(1).

¹   OJ L204, 21.7.1998, p 37. Directive amended by Directive 98/48/EC (OJ L217, 5.8.1998, p 18).

CHAPTER III
OTHER OBLIGATIONS OF PRODUCERS AND OBLIGATIONS OF DISTRIBUTORS

Article 5

1. Within the limits of their respective activities, producers shall provide consumers with the relevant information to enable them to assess the risks inherent in a product throughout the normal or reasonably foreseeable period of its use, where such risks are not immediately obvious without adequate warnings, and to take precautions against those risks.

The presence of warnings does not exempt any person from compliance with the other requirements laid down in this Directive.

Within the limits of their respective activities, producers shall adopt measures commensurate with the characteristics of the products which they supply, enabling them to—
  (a) be informed of risks which these products might pose;
  (b) choose to take appropriate action including, if necessary to avoid these risks, withdrawal from the market, adequately and effectively warning consumers or recall from consumers.

The measures referred to in the third subparagraph shall include, for example—
  (a) an indication, by means of the product or its packaging, of the identity and details of the producer and the product reference or, where applicable, the batch of products to which it belongs, except where not to give such indication is justified and
  (b) in all cases where appropriate, the carrying out of sample testing of marketed products, investigating and, if necessary, keeping a register of complaints and keeping distributors informed of such monitoring.

Action such as that referred to in (b) of the third subparagraph shall be undertaken on a voluntary basis or at the request of the competent authorities in accordance with Article 8(1)(f). Recall shall take place as a last resort, where other measures would not suffice to prevent the risks involved, in instances where the producers consider it necessary or where they are obliged to do so further to a measure taken by the competent authority. It may be effected within the framework of codes of good practice on the matter in the Member State concerned, where such codes exist.

2. Distributors shall be required to act with due care to help to ensure compliance with the applicable safety requirements, in particular by not supplying products which they know or should have presumed, on the basis of the information in their possession and as professionals, do not comply with those requirements. Moreover, within the limits of their respective activities, they shall participate in monitoring the safety of products placed on the market, especially by passing on information on product risks, keeping and providing the documentation necessary for tracing the origin of products, and cooperating in the action taken by producers and competent authorities to avoid the risks. Within the limits of their respective activities they shall take measures enabling them to cooperate efficiently.

3. Where producers and distributors know or ought to know, on the basis of the information in their possession and as professionals, that a product that they have placed on the market poses risks to the consumer that are incompatible with the general safety requirement, they shall immediately inform the competent authorities of the Member States thereof under the conditions laid down in Annex I, giving details, in particular, of action taken to prevent risk to the consumer.

[The Commission shall adapt the specific requirements relating to the obligation to provide information laid down in Annex I. Those measures, designed to amend non-essential elements of this Directive by supplementing it, shall be adopted in accordance with the regulatory procedure with scrutiny referred to in Article 15(5).]

4. Producers and distributors shall, within the limits of their respective activities, cooperate with the competent authorities, at the request of the latter, on action taken to avoid the risks posed by products which they supply or have supplied. The procedures for such cooperation, including procedures for dialogue with the producers and distributors concerned on issues related to product safety, shall be established by the competent authorities.

[4402]

NOTES

Para 3: words in square brackets substituted by European Parliament and Council Regulation 596/2009/EC, Art 2, Annex, para 5.8(2).

CHAPTER IV
SPECIFIC OBLIGATIONS AND POWERS OF THE MEMBER STATES

Article 6

1. Member States shall ensure that producers and distributors comply with their obligations under this Directive in such a way that products placed on the market are safe.

2. Member States shall establish or nominate authorities competent to monitor the compliance of products with the general safety requirements and arrange for such authorities to have and use the necessary powers to take the appropriate measures incumbent upon them under this Directive.

3. Member States shall define the tasks, powers, organisation and cooperation arrangements of the competent authorities. They shall keep the Commission informed, and the Commission shall pass on such information to the other Member States.

[4403]

Article 7

Member States shall lay down the rules on penalties applicable to infringements of the national provisions adopted pursuant to this Directive and shall take all measures necessary to ensure that they are implemented. The penalties provided for shall be effective, proportionate and dissuasive. Member States shall notify those provisions to the Commission by 15 January 2004 and shall also notify it, without delay, of any amendment affecting them.

[4404]

Article 8

1. For the purposes of this Directive, and in particular of Article 6 thereof, the competent authorities of the Member States shall be entitled to take, *inter alia*, the measures in (a) and in (b) to (f) below, where appropriate—
  (a) for any product—
    (i) to organise, even after its being placed on the market as being safe, appropriate checks on its safety properties, on an adequate scale, up to the final stage of use or consumption;
    (ii) to require all necessary information from the parties concerned;
    (iii) to take samples of products and subject them to safety checks;
  (b) for any product that could pose risks in certain conditions—
    (i) to require that it be marked with suitable, clearly worded and easily comprehensible warnings, in the official languages of the Member State in which the product is marketed, on the risks it may present;
    (ii) to make its marketing subject to prior conditions so as to make it safe;
  (c) for any product that could pose risks for certain persons—
    to order that they be given warning of the risk in good time and in an appropriate form, including the publication of special warnings;
  (d) for any product that could be dangerous—
    for the period needed for the various safety evaluations, checks and controls, temporarily to ban its supply, the offer to supply it or its display;
  (e) for any dangerous product—
    to ban its marketing and introduce the accompanying measures required to ensure the ban is complied with;
  (f) for any dangerous product already on the market—
    (i) to order or organise its actual and immediate withdrawal, and alert consumers to the risks it presents;
    (ii) to order or coordinate or, if appropriate, to organise together with producers and distributors its recall from consumers and its destruction in suitable conditions.

2.   When the competent authorities of the Member States take measures such as those provided for in paragraph 1, in particular those referred to in (d) to (f), they shall act in accordance with the Treaty, and in particular Articles 28 and 30 thereof, in such a way as to implement the measures in a manner proportional to the seriousness of the risk, and taking due account of the precautionary principle.

In this context, they shall encourage and promote voluntary action by producers and distributors, in accordance with the obligations incumbent on them under this Directive, and in particular Chapter III thereof, including where applicable by the development of codes of good practice.

If necessary, they shall organise or order the measures provided for in paragraph 1(f) if the action undertaken by the producers and distributors in fulfilment of their obligations is unsatisfactory or insufficient. Recall shall take place as a last resort. It may be effected within the framework of codes of good practice on the matter in the Member State concerned, where such codes exist.

[3.   In the case of products posing a serious risk, the competent authorities shall with due dispatch take the appropriate measures referred to in paragraph 1(b) to (f). The existence of a serious risk shall be determined by the Member States, assessing each individual case on its merits and taking into account the guidelines referred to in point 8 of Annex II.]

4.   The measures to be taken by the competent authorities under this Article shall be addressed, as appropriate, to—
     (a)   the producer;
     (b)   within the limits of their respective activities, distributors and in particular the party responsible for the first stage of distribution on the national market;
     (c)   any other person, where necessary, with a view to cooperation in action taken to avoid risks arising from a product.

                                                     [4405]

NOTES
Para 3: substituted by European Parliament and Council Regulation 765/2008/EC, Art 42.

Article 9

1.   In order to ensure effective market surveillance, aimed at guaranteeing a high level of consumer health and safety protection, which entails cooperation between their competent authorities, Member States shall ensure that approaches employing appropriate means and procedures are put in place, which may include in particular—
     (a)   establishment, periodical updating and implementation of sectoral surveillance programmes by categories of products or risks and the monitoring of surveillance activities, findings and results;
     (b)   follow-up and updating of scientific and technical knowledge concerning the safety of products;
     (c)   periodical review and assessment of the functioning of the control activities and their effectiveness and, if necessary, revision of the surveillance approach and organisation put in place.

2.   Member States shall ensure that consumers and other interested parties are given an opportunity to submit complaints to the competent authorities on product safety and on surveillance and control activities and that these complaints are followed up as appropriate. Member States shall actively inform consumers and other interested parties of the procedures established to that end.

                                                     [4406]

Article 10

1.   The Commission shall promote and take part in the operation in a European network of the authorities of the Member States competent for product safety, in particular in the form of administrative cooperation.

2.   This network operation shall develop in a coordinated manner with the other existing Community procedures, particularly RAPEX. Its objective shall be, in particular, to facilitate—
     (a)   the exchange of information on risk assessment, dangerous products, test methods and results, recent scientific developments as well as other aspects relevant for control activities;
     (b)   the establishment and execution of joint surveillance and testing projects;
     (c)   the exchange of expertise and best practices and cooperation in training activities;
     (d)   improved cooperation at Community level with regard to the tracing, withdrawal and recall of dangerous products.

                                                     [4407]

CHAPTER V
EXCHANGES OF INFORMATION AND RAPID INTERVENTION SITUATIONS

Article 11

1. Where a Member State takes measures which restrict the placing on the market of products—or require their withdrawal or recall—such as those provided for in Article 8(1)(b) to (f), the Member State shall, to the extent that such notification is not required under Article 12 or any specific Community legislation, inform the Commission of the measures, specifying its reasons for adopting them. It shall also inform the Commission of any modification or lifting of such measures.

If the notifying Member State considers that the effects of the risk do not or cannot go beyond its territory, it shall notify the measures concerned insofar as they involve information likely to be of interest to Member States from the product safety standpoint, and in particular if they are in response to a new risk which has not yet been reported in other notifications.

In accordance with the procedure laid down in Article 15(3) of this Directive, the Commission shall, while ensuring the effectiveness and proper functioning of the system, adopt the guidelines referred to in point 8 of Annex II. These shall propose the content and standard form for the notifications provided for in this Article, and, in particular, shall provide precise criteria for determining the conditions for which notification is relevant for the purposes of the second subparagraph.

2. The Commission shall forward the notification to the other Member States, unless it concludes, after examination on the basis of the information contained in the notification, that the measure does not comply with Community law. In such a case, it shall immediately inform the Member State which initiated the action.

[4408]

Article 12

1. Where a Member State adopts or decides to adopt, recommend or agree with producers and distributors, whether on a compulsory or voluntary basis, measures or actions to prevent, restrict or impose specific conditions on the possible marketing or use, within its own territory, of products by reason of a serious risk, it shall immediately notify the Commission thereof through RAPEX. It shall also inform the Commission without delay of modification or withdrawal of any such measure or action.

If the notifying Member State considers that the effects of the risk do not or cannot go beyond its territory, it shall follow the procedure laid down in Article 11, taking into account the relevant criteria proposed in the guidelines referred to in point 8 of Annex II.

Without prejudice to the first subparagraph, before deciding to adopt such measures or to take such action, Member States may pass on to the Commission any information in their possession regarding the existence of a serious risk.

In the case of a serious risk, they shall notify the Commission of the voluntary measures laid down in Article 5 of this Directive taken by producers and distributors.

2. On receiving such notifications, the Commission shall check whether they comply with this Article and with the requirements applicable to the functioning of RAPEX, and shall forward them to the other Member States, which, in turn, shall immediately inform the Commission of any measures adopted.

[3. Detailed procedures for RAPEX are set out in Annex II. They shall be adapted by the Commission. Those measures, designed to amend non-essential elements of this Directive by supplementing it, shall be adopted in accordance with the regulatory procedure with scrutiny referred to in Article 15(5).]

4. Access to RAPEX shall be open to applicant countries, third countries or international organisations, within the framework of agreements between the Community and those countries or international organisations, according to arrangements defined in these agreements. Any such agreements shall be based on reciprocity and include provisions on confidentiality corresponding to those applicable in the Community.

[4409]

NOTES

Para 3: substituted by European Parliament and Council Regulation 596/2009/EC, Art 2, Annex, para 5.8(3).

Article 13

1. If the Commission becomes aware of a serious risk from certain products to the health and safety of consumers in various Member States, it may, after consulting the Member States, and, if scientific questions arise which fall within the competence of a Community Scientific Committee, the Scientific Committee competent to deal with the risk concerned, adopt a decision in the light of

the result of those consultations, in accordance with the procedure laid down in Article 15(2), requiring Member States to take measures from among those listed in Article 8(1)(b) to (f) if, at one and the same time—

    (a)   it emerges from prior consultations with the Member States that they differ significantly on the approach adopted or to be adopted to deal with the risk; and

    (b)   the risk cannot be dealt with, in view of the nature of the safety issue posed by the product, in a manner compatible with the degree of urgency of the case, under other procedures laid down by the specific Community legislation applicable to the products concerned; and

    (c)   the risk can be eliminated effectively only by adopting appropriate measures applicable at Community level, in order to ensure a consistent and high level of protection of the health and safety of consumers and the proper functioning of the internal market.

2.   The decisions referred to in paragraph 1 shall be valid for a period not exceeding one year and may be confirmed, under the same procedure, for additional periods none of which shall exceed one year.

However, decisions concerning specific, individually identified products or batches of products shall be valid without a time limit.

3.   Export from the Community of dangerous products which have been the subject of a decision referred to in paragraph 1 shall be prohibited unless the decision provides otherwise.

4.   Member States shall take all necessary measures to implement the decisions referred to in paragraph 1 within less than 20 days, unless a different period is specified in those decisions.

5.   The competent authorities responsible for carrying out the measures referred to in paragraph 1 shall, within one month, give the parties concerned an opportunity to submit their views and shall inform the Commission accordingly.

[4410]

CHAPTER VI
COMMITTEE PROCEDURES

Article 14

1.   The measures necessary for the implementation of this Directive relating to the matters referred to below shall be adopted in accordance with the regulatory procedure provided for in Article 15(2)—

    (a)   the measures referred to in Article 4 concerning standards adopted by the European standardisation bodies;

    (b)   the decisions referred to in Article 13 requiring Member States to take measures as listed in Article 8(1)(b) to (f).

2.   The measures necessary for the implementation of this Directive in respect of all other matters shall be adopted in accordance with the advisory procedure provided for in Article 15(3).

[4411]

[Article 15

1.   The Commission shall be assisted by a Committee.

2.   Where reference is made to this paragraph, Articles 5 and 7 of Decision 1999/468/EC shall apply, having regard to the provisions of Article 8 thereof.

The period laid down in Article 5(6) of Decision 1999/468/EC shall be set at 15 days.

3.   Where reference is made to this paragraph, Articles 3 and 7 of Decision 1999/468/EC shall apply, having regard to the provisions of Article 8 thereof.

4.   Where reference is made to this paragraph, Article 5a(1) to (4) and Article 7 of Decision 1999/468/EC shall apply, having regard to the provisions of Article 8 thereof.

5.   Where reference is made to this paragraph, Article 5a(1) to (4) and (5)(b) and Article 7 of Decision 1999/468/EC shall apply, having regard to the provisions of Article 8 thereof.

The time-limits laid down in Article 5a(3)(c) and (4)(b) and (e) of Decision 1999/468/EC shall be set at two months, one month and two months respectively.]

[4412]

NOTES

  Substituted by European Parliament and Council Regulation 596/2009/EC, Art 2, Annex, para 5.8(4).

CHAPTER VII
FINAL PROVISIONS

Article 16

1.   Information available to the authorities of the Member States or the Commission relating to risks to consumer health and safety posed by products shall in general be available to the public, in accordance with the requirements of transparency and without prejudice to the restrictions required for monitoring and investigation activities. In particular the public shall have access to information on product identification, the nature of the risk and the measures taken.

However, Member States and the Commission shall take the steps necessary to ensure that their officials and agents are required not to disclose information obtained for the purposes of this Directive which, by its nature, is covered by professional secrecy in duly justified cases, except for information relating to the safety properties of products which must be made public if circumstances so require, in order to protect the health and safety of consumers.

2.   Protection of professional secrecy shall not prevent the dissemination to the competent authorities of information relevant for ensuring the effectiveness of market monitoring and surveillance activities. The authorities receiving information covered by professional secrecy shall ensure its protection.

[4413]

Article 17

This Directive shall be without prejudice to the application of Directive 85/374/EEC.

[4414]

Article 18

1.   Any measure adopted under this Directive and involving restrictions on the placing of a product on the market or requiring its withdrawal or recall must state the appropriate reasons on which it is based. It shall be notified as soon as possible to the party concerned and shall indicate the remedies available under the provisions in force in the Member State in question and the time limits applying to such remedies.

The parties concerned shall, whenever feasible, be given an opportunity to submit their views before the adoption of the measure. If this has not been done in advance because of the urgency of the measures to be taken, they shall be given such opportunity in due course after the measure has been implemented.

Measures requiring the withdrawal of a product or its recall shall take into consideration the need to encourage distributors, users and consumers to contribute to the implementation of such measures.

2.   Member States shall ensure that any measure taken by the competent authorities involving restrictions on the placing of a product on the market or requiring its withdrawal or recall can be challenged before the competent courts.

3.   Any decision taken by virtue of this Directive and involving restrictions on the placing of a product on the market or requiring its withdrawal or its recall shall be without prejudice to assessment of the liability of the party concerned, in the light of the national criminal law applying in the case in question.

[4415]

Article 19

1.   The Commission may bring before the Committee referred to in Article 15 any matter concerning the application of this Directive and particularly those relating to market monitoring and surveillance activities.

2.   Every three years, following 15 January 2004, the Commission shall submit a report on the implementation of this Directive to the European Parliament and the Council.

The report shall in particular include information on the safety of consumer products, in particular on improved traceability of products, the functioning of market surveillance, standardisation work, the functioning of RAPEX and Community measures taken on the basis of Article 13. To this end the Commission shall conduct assessments of the relevant issues, in particular the approaches, systems and practices put in place in the Member States, in the light of the requirements of this Directive and the other Community legislation relating to product safety. The Member States shall provide the Commission with all the necessary assistance and information for carrying out the assessments and preparing the reports.

[4416]

Article 20

The Commission shall identify the needs, possibilities and priorities for Community action on the safety of services and submit to the European Parliament and the Council, before 1 January 2003, a report, accompanied by proposals on the subject as appropriate.

[4417]

Article 21

1.   Member States shall bring into force the laws, regulations and administrative provisions necessary in order to comply with this Directive with effect from 15 January 2004. They shall forthwith inform the Commission thereof.

When Member States adopt those measures, they shall contain a reference to this Directive or be accompanied by such reference on the occasion of their official publication. The methods of making such reference shall be laid down by Member States.

2.   Member States shall communicate to the Commission the provisions of national law which they adopt in the field covered by this Directive.

[4418]

Article 22

Directive 92/59/EEC is hereby repealed from 15 January 2004, without prejudice to the obligations of Member States concerning the deadlines for transposition and application of the said Directive as indicated in Annex III.

References to Directive 92/59/EEC shall be construed as references to this Directive and shall be read in accordance with the correlation table in Annex IV.

[4419]

Article 23

This Directive shall enter into force on the day of its publication in the *Official Journal of the European Communities*.

[4420]

Article 24

This Directive is addressed to the Member States.

[4421]

Done at Brussels, 3 December 2001.

ANNEX I

REQUIREMENTS CONCERNING INFORMATION ON PRODUCTS THAT DO NOT COMPLY WITH THE GENERAL SAFETY REQUIREMENT TO BE PROVIDED TO THE COMPETENT AUTHORITIES BY PRODUCERS AND DISTRIBUTORS

1.   The information specified in Article 5(3), or where applicable by specific requirements of Community rules on the product concerned, shall be passed to the competent authorities appointed for the purpose in the Member States where the products in question are or have been marketed or otherwise supplied to consumers.

2.   The Commission, assisted by the Committee referred to in Article 15, shall define the content and draw up the standard form of the notifications provided for in this Annex, while ensuring the effectiveness and proper functioning of the system. In particular, it shall put forward, possibly in the form of a guide, simple and clear criteria for determining the special conditions, particularly those concerning isolated circumstances or products, for which notification is not relevant in relation to this Annex.

3.   In the event of serious risks, this information shall include at least the following—
   (a)   information enabling a precise identification of the product or batch of products in question;
   (b)   a full description of the risk that the products in question present;
   (c)   all available information relevant for tracing the product;
   (d)   a description of the action undertaken to prevent risks to consumers.

[4422]

ANNEX II

PROCEDURES FOR THE APPLICATION OF RAPEX AND GUIDELINES FOR NOTIFICATIONS

1.   RAPEX covers products as defined in Article 2(a) that pose a serious risk to the health and safety of consumers.

Pharmaceuticals, which come under Directives 75/319/EEC[1] and 81/851/EEC,[2] are excluded from the scope of RAPEX.

2.   RAPEX is essentially aimed at a rapid exchange of information in the event of a serious risk. The guidelines referred to in point 8 define specific criteria for identifying serious risks.

3.   Member States notifying under Article 12 shall provide all available details. In particular, the notification shall contain the information stipulated in the guidelines referred to in point 8 and at least—

(a)   information enabling the product to be identified;
(b)   a description of the risk involved, including a summary of the results of any tests/analyses and of their conclusions which are relevant to assessing the level of risk;
(c)   the nature and the duration of the measures or action taken or decided on, if applicable;
(d)   information on supply chains and distribution of the product, in particular on destination countries.

Such information must be transmitted using the special standard notification form and by the means stipulated in the guidelines referred to in point 8.

When the measure notified pursuant to Article 11 or Article 12 seeks to limit the marketing or use of a chemical substance or preparation, the Member States shall provide as soon as possible either a summary or the references of the relevant data relating to the substance or preparation considered and to known and available substitutes, where such information is available. They will also communicate the anticipated effects of the measure on consumer health and safety together with the assessment of the risk carried out in accordance with the general principles for the risk evaluation of chemical substances as referred to in Article 10(4) of Regulation (EEC) No 793/93[3] in the case of an existing substance or in Article 3(2) of Directive 67/548/EEC[4] in the case of a new substance. The guidelines referred to in point 8 shall define the details and procedures for the information requested in that respect.

4.   When a Member State has informed the Commission, in accordance with Article 12(1), third subparagraph, of a serious risk before deciding to adopt measures, it must inform the Commission within 45 days whether it confirms or modifies this information.

5.   The Commission shall, in the shortest time possible, verify the conformity with the provisions of the Directive of the information received under RAPEX and, may, when it considers it to be necessary and in order to assess product safety, carry out an investigation on its own initiative. In the case of such an investigation, Member States shall supply the Commission with the requested information to the best of their ability.

6.   Upon receipt of a notification referred to in Article 12, the Member States are requested to inform the Commission, at the latest within the set period of time stipulated in the guidelines referred to in point 8, of the following—

(a)   whether the product has been marketed in their territory;
(b)   what measures concerning the product in question they may be adopting in the light of their own circumstances, stating the reasons, including any differing assessment of risk or any other special circumstance justifying their decision, in particular lack of action or of follow-up;
(c)   any relevant supplementary information they have obtained on the risk involved, including the results of any tests or analyses carried out.

The guidelines referred to in point 8 shall provide precise criteria for notifying measures limited to national territory and shall specify how to deal with notifications concerning risks which are considered by the Member State not to go beyond its territory.

7.   Member States shall immediately inform the Commission of any modification or lifting of the measure(s) or action(s) in question.

8.   The Commission shall prepare and regularly update, in accordance with the procedure laid down in Article 15(3), guidelines concerning the management of RAPEX by the Commission and the Member States.

9.   The Commission may inform the national contact points regarding products posing serious risks, imported into or exported from the Community and the European Economic Area.

10.   Responsibility for the information provided lies with the notifying Member State.

11.   The Commission shall ensure the proper functioning of the system, in particular classifying and indexing notifications according to the degree of urgency. Detailed procedures shall be laid down by the guidelines referred to in point 8.

[4423]

NOTES
[1]   OJ L147, 9.6.1975, p 13. Directive as last amended by Commission Directive 2000/38/EC (OJ L139, 10.6.2000, p 28).
[2]   OJ L317, 6.11.1981, p 1. Directive as last amended by Commission Directive 2000/37/EC (OJ L139, 10.6.2000, p 25).

³   OJ L84, 5.4.1993, p 1.
⁴   OJ 196, 16.8.1967, p 1/67. Directive as last amended by Commission Directive 2000/33/EC (OJ L136, 8.6.2000, p 90).

ANNEX III

PERIOD FOR THE TRANSPOSITION AND APPLICATION OF THE REPEALED DIRECTIVE

(REFERRED TO IN THE FIRST SUBPARAGRAPH OF ARTICLE 22)

Directive	Period for transposition	Period for bringing into application
Directive 92/59/EEC	29 June 1994	29 June 1994

[4424]

ANNEX IV

CORRELATION TABLE

(REFERRED TO IN THE SECOND SUBPARAGRAPH OF ARTICLE 22)

This Directive	Directive 92/59/EEC
Article 1	Article 1
Article 2	Article 2
Article 3	Article 4
Article 4	—
Article 5	Article 3
Article 6	Article 5
Article 7	Article 5(2)
Article 8	Article 6
Article 9	—
Article 10	—
Article 11	Article 7
Article 12	Article 8
Article 13	Article 9
Articles 14 and 15	Article 10
Article 16	Article 12
Article 17	Article 13
Article 18	Article 14
Article 19	Article 15
Article 20	—
Article 21	Article 17
Article 22	Article 18
Article 23	Article 19
Annex I	—
Annex II	Annex
Annex III	—
Annex IV	

DIRECTIVE OF THE EUROPEAN PARLIAMENT AND OF THE COUNCIL

of 23 September 2002

concerning the distance marketing of consumer financial services and amending Council Directive 90/619/EEC and Directives 97/7/EC and 98/27/EC

(2002/65/EC)

NOTES

Date of publication in OJ: OJ L271, 9.10.02, p 16.

This Directive has been implemented in the UK by the Financial Services (Distance Marketing) Regulations 2004, SI 2004/2095 at **[3413]** and the Consumer Credit (Disclosure of Information) Regulations 2010, SI 2010/1013 at **[3964]**.

THE EUROPEAN PARLIAMENT AND THE COUNCIL OF THE EUROPEAN UNION,

Having regard to the Treaty establishing the European Community, and in particular Article 47(2), Article 55 and

Article 95 thereof,

Having regard to the proposal from the Commission,[1]

Having regard to the opinion of the Economic and Social Committee,[2]

Acting in accordance with the procedure laid down in Article 251 of the Treaty,[3]

Whereas:—

(1) It is important, in the context of achieving the aims of the single market, to adopt measures designed to consolidate progressively this market and those measures must contribute to attaining a high level of consumer protection, in accordance with Articles 95 and 153 of the Treaty.

(2) Both for consumers and suppliers of financial services, the distance marketing of financial services will constitute one of the main tangible results of the completion of the internal market.

(3) Within the framework of the internal market, it is in the interest of consumers to have access without discrimination to the widest possible range of financial services available in the Community so that they can choose those that are best suited to their needs. In order to safeguard freedom of choice, which is an essential consumer right, a high degree of consumer protection is required in order to enhance consumer confidence in distance selling.

(4) It is essential to the smooth operation of the internal market for consumers to be able to negotiate and conclude contracts with a supplier established in other Member States, regardless of whether the supplier is also established in the Member State in which the consumer resides.

(5) Because of their intangible nature, financial services are particularly suited to distance selling and the establishment of a legal framework governing the distance marketing of financial services should increase consumer confidence in the use of new techniques for the distance marketing of financial services, such as electronic commerce.

(6) This Directive should be applied in conformity with the Treaty and with secondary law, including Directive 2000/31/EC[4] on electronic commerce, the latter being applicable solely to the transactions which it covers.

(7) This Directive aims to achieve the objectives set forth above without prejudice to Community or national law governing freedom to provide services or, where applicable, host Member State control and/or authorisation or supervision systems in the Member States where this is compatible with Community legislation.

(8) Moreover, this Directive, and in particular its provisions relating to information about any contractual clause on law applicable to the contract and/or on the competent court does not affect the applicability to the distance marketing of consumer financial services of Council Regulation (EC) No 44/2001 of 22 December 2000 on jurisdiction and the recognition and enforcement of judgements in civil and commercial matters[5] or of the 1980 Rome Convention on the law applicable to contractual obligations.

(9) The achievement of the objectives of the Financial Services Action Plan requires a higher level of consumer protection in certain areas. This implies a greater convergence, in particular, in non harmonised collective investment funds, rules of conduct applicable to investment services and consumer credits. Pending the achievement of the above convergence, a high level of consumer protection should be maintained.

(10) Directive 97/7/EC of the European Parliament and of the Council of 20 May 1997 on the protection of consumers in respect of distance contracts,[6] lays down the main rules applicable to distance contracts for goods or services concluded between a supplier and a consumer. However, that Directive does not cover financial services.

(11) In the context of the analysis conducted by the Commission with a view to ascertaining the need for specific measures in the field of financial services, the Commission invited all the interested parties to transmit their comments, notably in connection with the preparation of its Green Paper entitled "Financial Services – Meeting Consumers' Expectations". The consultations in this

context showed that there is a need to strengthen consumer protection in this area. The Commission therefore decided to present a specific proposal concerning the distance marketing of financial services.

(12) The adoption by the Member States of conflicting or different consumer protection rules governing the distance marketing of consumer financial services could impede the functioning of the internal market and competition between firms in the market. It is therefore necessary to enact common rules at Community level in this area, consistent with no reduction in overall consumer protection in the Member States.

(13) A high level of consumer protection should be guaranteed by this Directive, with a view to ensuring the free movement of financial services. Member States should not be able to adopt provisions other than those laid down in this Directive in the fields it harmonises, unless otherwise specifically indicated in it.

(14) This Directive covers all financial services liable to be provided at a distance. However, certain financial services are governed by specific provisions of Community legislation which continue to apply to those financial services. However, principles governing the distance marketing of such services should be laid down.

(15) Contracts negotiated at a distance involve the use of means of distance communication which are used as part of a distance sales or service-provision scheme not involving the simultaneous presence of the supplier and the consumer. The constant development of those means of communication requires principles to be defined that are valid even for those means which are not yet in widespread use. Therefore, distance contracts are those the offer, negotiation and conclusion of which are carried out at a distance.

(16) A single contract involving successive operations or separate operations of the same nature performed over time may be subject to different legal treatment in the different Member States, but it is important that this Directive be applied in the same way in all the Member States. To that end, it is appropriate that this Directive should be considered to apply to the first of a series of successive operations or separate operations of the same nature performed over time which may be considered as forming a whole, irrespective of whether that operation or series of operations is the subject of a single contract or several successive contracts.

(17) An "initial service agreement" may be considered to be for example the opening of a bank account, acquiring a credit card, concluding a portfolio management contract, and "operations" may be considered to be for example the deposit or withdrawal of funds to or from the bank account, payment by credit card, transactions made within the framework of a portfolio management contract. Adding new elements to an initial service agreement, such as a possibility to use an electronic payment instrument together with one's existing bank account, does not constitute an "operation" but an additional contract to which this Directive applies. The subscription to new units of the same collective investment fund is considered to be one of "successive operations of the same nature".

(18) By covering a service-provision scheme organised by the financial services provider, this Directive aims to exclude from its scope services provided on a strictly occasional basis and outside a commercial structure dedicated to the conclusion of distance contracts.

(19) The supplier is the person providing services at a distance. This Directive should however also apply when one of the marketing stages involves an intermediary. Having regard to the nature and degree of that involvement, the pertinent provisions of this Directive should apply to such an intermediary, irrespective of his or her legal status.

(20) Durable mediums include in particular floppy discs, CD-ROMs, DVDs and the hard drive of the consumer's computer on which the electronic mail is stored, but they do not include Internet websites unless they fulfil the criteria contained in the definition of a durable medium.

(21) The use of means of distance communications should not lead to an unwarranted restriction on the information provided to the client. In the interests of transparency this Directive lays down the requirements needed to ensure that an appropriate level of information is provided to the consumer both before and after conclusion of the contract. The consumer should receive, before conclusion of the contract, the prior information needed so as to properly appraise the financial service offered to him and hence make a well-informed choice. The supplier should specify how long his offer applies as it stands.

(22) Information items listed in this Directive cover information of a general nature applicable to all kinds of financial services. Other information requirements concerning a given financial service, such as the coverage of an insurance policy, are not solely specified in this Directive. This kind of information should be provided in accordance, where applicable, with relevant Community legislation or national legislation in conformity with Community law.

(23) With a view to optimum protection of the consumer, it is important that the consumer is adequately informed of the provisions of this Directive and of any codes of conduct existing in this area and that he has a right of withdrawal.

(24) When the right of withdrawal does not apply because the consumer has expressly requested the performance of a contract, the supplier should inform the consumer of this fact.

(25) Consumers should be protected against unsolicited services. Consumers should be exempt from any obligation in the case of unsolicited services, the absence of a reply not being construed as

signifying consent on their part. However, this rule should be without prejudice to the tacit renewal of contracts validly concluded between the parties whenever the law of the Member States permits such tacit renewal.

(26) Member States should take appropriate measures to protect effectively consumers who do not wish to be contacted through certain means of communication or at certain times. This Directive should be without prejudice to the particular safeguards available to consumers under Community legislation concerning the protection of personal data and privacy.

(27) With a view to protecting consumers, there is a need for suitable and effective complaint and redress procedures in the Member States with a view to settling potential disputes between suppliers and consumers, by using, where appropriate, existing procedures.

(28) Member States should encourage public or private bodies established with a view to settling disputes out of court to cooperate in resolving cross-border disputes. Such cooperation could in particular entail allowing consumers to submit to extra-judicial bodies in the Member State of their residence complaints concerning suppliers established in other Member States. The establishment of FIN-NET offers increased assistance to consumers when using cross-border services.

(29) This Directive is without prejudice to extension by Member States, in accordance with Community law, of the protection provided by this Directive to non-profit organisations and persons making use of financial services in order to become entrepreneurs.

(30) This Directive should also cover cases where the national legislation includes the concept of a consumer making a binding contractual statement.

(31) The provisions in this Directive on the supplier's choice of language should be without prejudice to provisions of national legislation, adopted in conformity with Community law governing the choice of language.

(32) The Community and the Member States have entered into commitments in the context of the General Agreement on Trade in Services (GATS) concerning the possibility for consumers to purchase banking and investment services abroad. The GATS entitles Member States to adopt measures for prudential reasons, including measures to protect investors, depositors, policy-holders and persons to whom a financial service is owed by the supplier of the financial service. Such measures should not impose restrictions going beyond what is required to ensure the protection of consumers.

(33) In view of the adoption of this Directive, the scope of Directive 97/7/EC and Directive 98/27/EC of the European Parliament and of the Council of 19 May 1998 on injunctions for the protection of consumers' interests[7] and the scope of the cancellation period in Council Directive 90/619/EEC of 8 November 1990 on the coordination of laws, regulations and administrative provisions relating to direct life assurance, laying down provisions to facilitate the effective exercise of freedom to provide services[8] should be adapted.

(34) Since the objectives of this Directive, namely the establishment of common rules on the distance marketing of consumer financial services cannot be sufficiently achieved by the Member States and can therefore be better achieved at Community level, the Community may adopt measures, in accordance with the principles of subsidiarity as set out in Article 5 of the Treaty. In accordance with the principle of proportionality, as set out in that Article, this Directive does not go beyond what is necessary to achieve that objective,

NOTES

[1] OJ C385, 11.12.1998, p 10 and OJ C177 E, 27.6.2000, p 21.
[2] OJ C169, 16.6.1999, p 43.
[3] Opinion of the European Parliament of 5 May 1999 (OJ C 279, 1.10.1999, p 207), Council Common Position of 19 December 2001 (OJ C58 E, 5.3.2002, p 32) and Decision of the European Parliament of 14 May 2002 (not yet published in the Official Journal). Council Decision of 26 June 2002 (not yet published in the Official Journal).
[4] OJ L178, 17.7.2000, p 1.
[5] OJ L12, 16.1.2001, p 1.
[6] OJ L144, 4.6.1997, p 19.
[7] OJ L166, 11.6.1998, p 51. Directive as last amended by Directive 2000/31/EC (OJ L178, 17.7.2001, p 1).
[8] OJ L330, 29.11.1990, p 50. Directive as last amended by Directive 92/96/EEC (OJ L360, 9.12.1992, p 1).

HAVE ADOPTED THIS DIRECTIVE—

Article 1
Object and scope

1. The object of this Directive is to approximate the laws, regulations and administrative provisions of the Member States concerning the distance marketing of consumer financial services.

2. In the case of contracts for financial services comprising an initial service agreement followed by successive operations or a series of separate operations of the same nature performed over time, the provisions of this Directive shall apply only to the initial agreement.

In case there is no initial service agreement but the successive operations or the separate operations of the same nature performed over time are performed between the same contractual parties, Articles 3 and 4 apply only when the first operation is performed. Where, however, no operation of the same nature is performed for more than one year, the next operation will be deemed to be the first in a new series of operations and, accordingly, Articles 3 and 4 shall apply.

[4426]

Article 2
Definitions

For the purposes of this Directive—

(a) 'distance contract' means any contract concerning financial services concluded between a supplier and a consumer under an organised distance sales or service-provision scheme run by the supplier, who, for the purpose of that contract, makes exclusive use of one or more means of distance communication up to and including the time at which the contract is concluded;

(b) 'financial service' means any service of a banking, credit, insurance, personal pension, investment or payment nature;

(c) 'supplier' means any natural or legal person, public or private, who, acting in his commercial or professional capacity, is the contractual provider of services subject to distance contracts;

(d) 'consumer' means any natural person who, in distance contracts covered by this Directive, is acting for purposes which are outside his trade, business or profession;

(e) 'means of distance communication' refers to any means which, without the simultaneous physical presence of the supplier and the consumer, may be used for the distance marketing of a service between those parties;

(f) 'durable medium' means any instrument which enables the consumer to store information addressed personally to him in a way accessible for future reference for a period of time adequate for the purposes of the information and which allows the unchanged reproduction of the information stored;

(g) 'operator or supplier of a means of distance communication' means any public or private, natural or legal person whose trade, business or profession involves making one or more means of distance communication available to suppliers.

[4427]

Article 3
Information to the consumer prior to the conclusion of the distance contract

1.   In good time before the consumer is bound by any distance contract or offer, he shall be provided with the following information concerning—

(1) the supplier

(a) the identity and the main business of the supplier, the geographical address at which the supplier is established and any other geographical address relevant for the customer's relations with the supplier;

(b) the identity of the representative of the supplier established in the consumer's Member State of residence and the geographical address relevant for the customer's relations with the representative, if such a representative exists;

(c) when the consumer's dealings are with any professional other than the supplier, the identity of this professional, the capacity in which he is acting vis-à-vis the consumer, and the geographical address relevant for the customer's relations with this professional;

(d) where the supplier is registered in a trade or similar public register, the trade register in which the supplier is entered and his registration number or an equivalent means of identification in that register;

(e) where the supplier's activity is subject to an authorisation scheme, the particulars of the relevant supervisory authority;

(2) the financial service

(a) a description of the main characteristics of the financial service;

(b) the total price to be paid by the consumer to the supplier for the financial service, including all related fees, charges and expenses, and all taxes paid via the supplier or, when an exact price cannot be indicated, the basis for the calculation of the price enabling the consumer to verify it;

(c) where relevant notice indicating that the financial service is related to instruments involving special risks related to their specific features or the operations to be executed or whose price depends on fluctuations in the financial markets outside the supplier's control and that historical performances are no indicators for future performances;

(d) notice of the possibility that other taxes and/or costs may exist that are not paid via the supplier or imposed by him;

(e) any limitations of the period for which the information provided is valid;

(f)   the arrangements for payment and for performance;

(g)   any specific additional cost for the consumer of using the means of distance communication, if such additional cost is charged;

(3)   the distance contract

    (a)   the existence or absence of a right of withdrawal in accordance with Article 6 and, where the right of withdrawal exists, its duration and the conditions for exercising it, including information on the amount which the consumer may be required to pay on the basis of Article 7(1), as well as the consequences of non-exercise of that right;

    (b)   the minimum duration of the distance contract in the case of financial services to be performed permanently or recurrently;

    (c)   information on any rights the parties may have to terminate the contract early or unilaterally by virtue of the terms of the distance contract, including any penalties imposed by the contract in such cases;

    (d)   practical instructions for exercising the right of withdrawal indicating, inter alia, the address to which the notification of a withdrawal should be sent;

    (e)   the Member State or States whose laws are taken by the supplier as a basis for the establishment of relations with the consumer prior to the conclusion of the distance contract;

    (f)   any contractual clause on law applicable to the distance contract and/or on competent court;

    (g)   in which language, or languages, the contractual terms and conditions, and the prior information referred to in this Article are supplied, and furthermore in which language, or languages, the supplier, with the agreement of the consumer, undertakes to communicate during the duration of this distance contract;

(4)   redress

    (a)   whether or not there is an out-of-court complaint and redress mechanism for the consumer that is party to the distance contract and, if so, the methods for having access to it;

    (b)   the existence of guarantee funds or other compensation arrangements, not covered by Directive 94/19/EC of the European Parliament and of the Council of 30 May 1994 on deposit guarantee schemes[1] and Directive 97/9/EC of the European Parliament and of the Council of 3 March 1997 on investor compensation schemes.[2]

2.   The information referred to in paragraph 1, the commercial purpose of which must be made clear, shall be provided in a clear and comprehensible manner in any way appropriate to the means of distance communication used, with due regard, in particular, to the principles of good faith in commercial transactions, and the principles governing the protection of those who are unable, pursuant to the legislation of the Member States, to give their consent, such as minors.

3.   In the case of voice telephony communications

    (a)   the identity of the supplier and the commercial purpose of the call initiated by the supplier shall be made explicitly clear at the beginning of any conversation with the consumer;

    (b)   subject to the explicit consent of the consumer only the following information needs to be given—

        — the identity of the person in contact with the consumer and his link with the supplier,

        — a description of the main characteristics of the financial service,

        — the total price to be paid by the consumer to the supplier for the financial service including all taxes paid via the supplier or, when an exact price cannot be indicated, the basis for the calculation of the price enabling the consumer to verify it,

        — notice of the possibility that other taxes and/or costs may exist that are not paid via the supplier or imposed by him,

        — the existence or absence of a right of withdrawal in accordance with Article 6 and, where the right of withdrawal exists, its duration and the conditions for exercising it, including information on the amount which the consumer may be required to pay on the basis of Article 7(1).

The supplier shall inform the consumer that other information is available on request and of what nature this information is. In any case the supplier shall provide the full information when he fulfils his obligations under Article 5.

4.   Information on contractual obligations, to be communicated to the consumer during the pre-contractual phase, shall be in conformity with the contractual obligations which would result from the law presumed to be applicable to the distance contract if the latter were concluded.

[4428]

NOTES
   1   OJ L135, 31.5.1994, p 5.
   2   OJ L84, 26.3.1997, p 22.

Article 4
Additional information requirements

1.   Where there are provisions in the Community legislation governing financial services which contain prior information requirements additional to those listed in Article 3(1), these requirements shall continue to apply.

2.   Pending further harmonisation, Member States may maintain or introduce more stringent provisions on prior information requirements when the provisions are in conformity with Community law.

3.   Member States shall communicate to the Commission national provisions on prior information requirements under paragraphs 1 and 2 of this Article when these requirements are additional to those listed in Article 3(1). The Commission shall take account of the communicated national provisions when drawing up the report referred to in Article 20(2).

4.   The Commission shall, with a view to creating a high level of transparency by all appropriate means, ensure that information, on the national provisions communicated to it, is made available to consumers and suppliers.

[5.   Where Directive 2007/64/EC of the European Parliament and of the Council of 13 November 2007 on payment services in the internal market[1] is also applicable, the information provisions under Article 3(1) of this Directive, with the exception of paragraphs (2)(c) to (g), (3)(a), (d) and (e), and (4)(b), shall be replaced with Articles 36, 37, 41 and 42 of that Directive.]

[4429]

NOTES
   Para 5: added by European Parliament and Council Directive 2007/64/EC, Art 90(1).
   1   OJ L319, 5.12.2007, p 1.

Article 5
Communication of the contractual terms and conditions and of the prior information

1.   The supplier shall communicate to the consumer all the contractual terms and conditions and the information referred to in Article 3(1) and Article 4 on paper or on another durable medium available and accessible to the consumer in good time before the consumer is bound by any distance contract or offer.

2.   The supplier shall fulfil his obligation under paragraph 1 immediately after the conclusion of the contract, if the contract has been concluded at the consumer's request using a means of distance communication which does not enable providing the contractual terms and conditions and the information in conformity with paragraph 1.

3.   At any time during the contractual relationship the consumer is entitled, at his request, to receive the contractual terms and conditions on paper. In addition, the consumer is entitled to change the means of distance communication used, unless this is incompatible with the contract concluded or the nature of the financial service provided.

[4430]

Article 6
Right of withdrawal

1.   The Member States shall ensure that the consumer shall have a period of 14 calendar days to withdraw from the contract without penalty and without giving any reason. However, this period shall be extended to 30 calendar days in distance contracts relating to life insurance covered by Directive 90/619/EEC and personal pension operations.

The period for withdrawal shall begin—
   —   either from the day of the conclusion of the distance contract, except in respect of the said life assurance, where the time limit will begin from the time when the consumer is informed that the distance contract has been concluded, or
   —   from the day on which the consumer receives the contractual terms and conditions and the information in accordance with Article 5(1) or (2), if that is later than the date referred to in the first indent.

Member States, in addition to the right of withdrawal, may provide that the enforceability of contracts relating to investment services is suspended for the same period provided for in this paragraph.

2.   The right of withdrawal shall not apply to—

   (a)   financial services whose price depends on fluctuations in the financial market outside the suppliers control, which may occur during the withdrawal period, such as services related to—
- foreign exchange,
- money market instruments,
- transferable securities,
- units in collective investment undertakings,
- financial-futures contracts, including equivalent cash-settled instruments,
- forward interest-rate agreements (FRAs),
- interest-rate, currency and equity swaps,
- options to acquire or dispose of any instruments referred to in this point including equivalent cash-settled instruments.

This category includes in particular options on currency and on interest rates;

   (b)   travel and baggage insurance policies or similar short-term insurance policies of less than one month's duration;

   (c)   contracts whose performance has been fully completed by both parties at the consumer's express request before the consumer exercises his right of withdrawal.

3.   Member States may provide that the right of withdrawal shall not apply to:

   (a)   any credit intended primarily for the purpose of acquiring or retaining property rights in land or in an existing or projected building, or for the purpose of renovating or improving a building, or

   (b)   any credit secured either by mortgage on immovable property or by a right related to immovable property, or

   (c)   declarations by consumers using the services of an official, provided that the official confirms that the consumer is guaranteed the rights under Article 5(1).

This paragraph shall be without prejudice to the right to a reflection time to the benefit of the consumers that are resident in those Member States where it exists, at the time of the adoption of this Directive.

4.   Member States making use of the possibility set out in paragraph 3 shall communicate it to the Commission.

5.   The Commission shall make available the information communicated by Member States to the European Parliament and the Council and shall ensure that it is also available to consumers and suppliers who request it.

6.   If the consumer exercises his right of withdrawal he shall, before the expiry of the relevant deadline, notify this following the practical instructions given to him in accordance with Article 3(1)(3)(d) by means which can be proved in accordance with national law. The deadline shall be deemed to have been observed if the notification, if it is on paper or on another durable medium available and accessible to the recipient, is dispatched before the deadline expires.

7.   This Article does not apply to credit agreements cancelled under the conditions of Article 6(4) of Directive 97/7/EC or Article 7 of Directive 94/47/EC of the European Parliament and of the Council of 26 October 1994 on the protection of purchasers in respect of certain aspects of contracts relating to the purchase of the right to use immovable properties on a timeshare basis.[1]

If to a distance contract of a given financial service another distance contract has been attached concerning services provided by the supplier or by a third party on the basis of an agreement between the third party and the supplier, this additional distance contract shall be cancelled, without any penalty, if the consumer exercises his right of withdrawal as provided for in Article 6(1).

8.   The provisions of this Article are without prejudice to the Member States' laws and regulations governing the cancellation or termination or non-enforceability of a distance contract or the right of a consumer to fulfil his contractual obligations before the time fixed in the distance contract. This applies irrespective of the conditions for and the legal effects of the winding-up of the contract.

[4431]

NOTES

[1]   OJ L280, 29.10.1994, p 83.

Article 7
Payment of the service provided before withdrawal

1.   When the consumer exercises his right of withdrawal under Article 6(1) he may only be required to pay, without any undue delay, for the service actually provided by the supplier in accordance with the contract. The performance of the contract may only begin after the consumer has given his approval. The amount payable shall not—
- exceed an amount which is in proportion to the extent of the service already provided in comparison with the full coverage of the contract,

—   in any case be such that it could be construed as a penalty.

2.   Member States may provide that the consumer cannot be required to pay any amount when withdrawing from an insurance contract.

3.   The supplier may not require the consumer to pay any amount on the basis of paragraph 1 unless he can prove that the consumer was duly informed about the amount payable, in conformity with Article 3(1)(3)(a). However, in no case may he require such payment if he has commenced the performance of the contract before the expiry of the withdrawal period provided for in Article 6(1) without the consumer's prior request.

4.   The supplier shall, without any undue delay and no later than within 30 calendar days, return to the consumer any sums he has received from him in accordance with the distance contract, except for the amount referred to in paragraph 1. This period shall begin from the day on which the supplier receives the notification of withdrawal.

5.   The consumer shall return to the supplier any sums and/or property he has received from the supplier without any undue delay and no later than within 30 calendar days. This period shall begin from the day on which the consumer dispatches the notification of withdrawal.

[4432]–[4433]

Article 8

(Repealed by European Parliament and Council Directive 2007/64/EC, Art 90(2).)

[Article 9

Given the prohibition of inertia selling practices laid down in Directive 2005/29/EC of 11 May 2005 of the European Parliament and of the Council concerning unfair business-to-consumer commercial practices in the internal market[1] and without prejudice to the provisions of Member States' legislation on the tacit renewal of distance contracts, when such rules permit tacit renewal, Member States shall take measures to exempt the consumer from any obligation in the event of unsolicited supplies, the absence of a reply not constituting consent.]

[4434]

NOTES

Substituted by European Parliament and Council Directive 2005/29/EC, Art 15(2).

[1]   OJ L149, 11.6.2005, p 22.

Article 10
Unsolicited communications

1.   The use by a supplier of the following distance communication techniques shall require the consumer's prior consent—

     (a)   automated calling systems without human intervention (automatic calling machines);

     (b)   fax machines.

2.   Member States shall ensure that means of distance communication other than those referred to in paragraph 1, when they allow individual communications:

     (a)   shall not be authorised unless the consent of the consumers concerned has been obtained, or

     (b)   may only be used if the consumer has not expressed his manifest objection.

3.   The measures referred to in paragraphs 1 and 2 shall not entail costs for consumers.

[4435]

Article 11
Sanctions

Member States shall provide for appropriate sanctions in the event of the supplier's failure to comply with national provisions adopted pursuant to this Directive.

They may provide for this purpose in particular that the consumer may cancel the contract at any time, free of charge and without penalty.

These sanctions must be effective, proportional and dissuasive.

[4436]

Article 12
Imperative nature of this Directive's provisions

1.   Consumers may not waive the rights conferred on them by this Directive.

2.   Member States shall take the measures needed to ensure that the consumer does not lose the protection granted by this Directive by virtue of the choice of the law of a non-member country as the law applicable to the contract, if this contract has a close link with the territory of one or more Member States.

[4437]

Article 13
Judicial and administrative redress

1. Member States shall ensure that adequate and effective means exist to ensure compliance with this Directive in the interests of consumers.

2. The means referred to in paragraph 1 shall include provisions whereby one or more of the following bodies, as determined by national law, may take action in accordance with national law before the courts or competent administrative bodies to ensure that the national provisions for the implementation of this Directive are applied—
    (a)   public bodies or their representatives;
    (b)   consumer organisations having a legitimate interest in protecting consumers;
    (c)   professional organisations having a legitimate interest in acting.

3. Member States shall take the measures necessary to ensure that operators and suppliers of means of distance communication put an end to practices that have been declared to be contrary to this Directive, on the basis of a judicial decision, an administrative decision or a decision issued by a supervisory authority notified to them, where those operators or suppliers are in a position to do so.

[4438]

Article 14
Out-of-court redress

1. Member States shall promote the setting up or development of adequate and effective out-of-court complaints and redress procedures for the settlement of consumer disputes concerning financial services provided at distance.

2. Member States shall, in particular, encourage the bodies responsible for out-of-court settlement of disputes to cooperate in the resolution of cross-border disputes concerning financial services provided at distance.

[4439]

Article 15
Burden of proof

Without prejudice to Article 7(3), Member States may stipulate that the burden of proof in respect of the supplier's obligations to inform the consumer and the consumer's consent to conclusion of the contract and, where appropriate, its performance, can be placed on the supplier.

Any contractual term or condition providing that the burden of proof of the respect by the supplier of all or part of the obligations incumbent on him pursuant to this Directive should lie with the consumer shall be an unfair term within the meaning of Council Directive 93/13/EEC of 5 April 1993 on unfair terms in consumer contracts.[1]

[4440]

NOTES
[1]   OJ L95, 21.4.1993, p 29.

Article 16
Transitional measures

Member States may impose national rules which are in conformity with this Directive on suppliers established in a Member State which has not yet transposed this Directive and whose law has no obligations corresponding to those provided for in this Directive.

[4441]

Articles 17–19

(*Art 17 amends Directive 90/619/EEC, Art 15(1); Art 18 amends Directive 97/7/EC, Art 3(1) at* [4307], *Annex II; Art 19 spent (amended Directive 98/27/EC, Annex (repealed)).*)

Article 20
Review

1. Following the implementation of this Directive, the Commission shall examine the functioning of the internal market in financial services in respect of the marketing of those services. It should seek to analyse and detail the difficulties that are, or might be faced by both consumers and suppliers, in particular arising from differences between national provisions regarding information and right of withdrawal.

2. Not later than 9 April 2006 the Commission shall report to the European Parliament and the Council on the problems facing both consumers and suppliers seeking to buy and sell financial

services, and shall submit, where appropriate, proposals to amend and/or further harmonise the information and right of withdrawal provisions in Community legislation concerning financial services and/or those covered in Article 3.

[4442]

Article 21
Transposition

1. Member States shall bring into force the laws, regulations and administrative provisions necessary to comply with this Directive not later than 9 October 2004. They shall forthwith inform the Commission thereof.

When Member States adopt these measures, they shall contain a reference to this Directive or shall be accompanied by such a reference on the occasion of their official publication. The methods of making such reference shall be laid down by Member States.

2. Member States shall communicate to the Commission the text of the main provisions of national law which they adopt in the field governed by this Directive together with a table showing how the provisions of this Directive correspond to the national provisions adopted.

[4443]

Article 22
Entry into force

This Directive shall enter into force on the day of its publication in the *Official Journal of the European Communities*.

[4444]

Article 23
Addressees

This Directive is addressed to the Member States.

[4445]

Done at Brussels, 23 September 2002.

DIRECTIVE OF THE EUROPEAN PARLIAMENT AND OF THE COUNCIL

of 11 May 2005

concerning unfair business-to-consumer commercial practices in the internal market and amending Council Directive 84/450/EEC, Directives 97/7/EC, 98/27/EC and 2002/65/EC of the European Parliament and of the Council and Regulation (EC) No 2006/2004 of the European Parliament and of the Council ("Unfair Commercial Practices Directive")

(2005/29/EC)

(Text with EEA relevance)

NOTE
Date of publication in OJ: OJ L149, 11.6.2005, p 22.
This Directive has been implemented in the UK by the Consumer Protection from Unfair Trading Regulations 2008, SI 2008/1277 at [3675].

THE EUROPEAN PARLIAMENT AND THE COUNCIL OF THE EUROPEAN UNION,
Having regard to the Treaty establishing the European Community, and in particular Article 95 thereof,
Having regard to the proposal from the Commission,
Having regard to the opinion of the European Economic and Social Committee[1],
Acting in accordance with the procedure laid down in Article 251 of the Treaty[2],
Whereas:
(1) Article 153(1) and (3)(a) of the Treaty provides that the Community is to contribute to the attainment of a high level of consumer protection by the measures it adopts pursuant to Article 95 thereof.
(2) In accordance with Article 14(2) of the Treaty, the internal market comprises an area without internal frontiers in which the free movement of goods and services and freedom of establishment are ensured. The development of fair commercial practices within the area without internal frontiers is vital for the promotion of the development of cross-border activities.

(3)   The laws of the Member States relating to unfair commercial practices show marked differences which can generate appreciable distortions of competition and obstacles to the smooth functioning of the internal market. In the field of advertising, Council Directive 84/450/EEC of 10 September 1984 concerning misleading and comparative advertising[3] establishes minimum criteria for harmonising legislation on misleading advertising, but does not prevent the Member States from retaining or adopting measures which provide more extensive protection for consumers. As a result, Member States' provisions on misleading advertising diverge significantly.

(4)   These disparities cause uncertainty as to which national rules apply to unfair commercial practices harming consumers' economic interests and create many barriers affecting business and consumers. These barriers increase the cost to business of exercising internal market freedoms, in particular when businesses wish to engage in cross border marketing, advertising campaigns and sales promotions. Such barriers also make consumers uncertain of their rights and undermine their confidence in the internal market.

(5)   In the absence of uniform rules at Community level, obstacles to the free movement of services and goods across borders or the freedom of establishment could be justified in the light of the case-law of the Court of Justice of the European Communities as long as they seek to protect recognised public interest objectives and are proportionate to those objectives. In view of the Community's objectives, as set out in the provisions of the Treaty and in secondary Community law relating to freedom of movement, and in accordance with the Commission's policy on commercial communications as indicated in the Communication from the Commission entitled "The follow-up to the Green Paper on Commercial Communications in the Internal Market", such obstacles should be eliminated. These obstacles can only be eliminated by establishing uniform rules at Community level which establish a high level of consumer protection and by clarifying certain legal concepts at Community level to the extent necessary for the proper functioning of the internal market and to meet the requirement of legal certainty.

(6)   This Directive therefore approximates the laws of the Member States on unfair commercial practices, including unfair advertising, which directly harm consumers' economic interests and thereby indirectly harm the economic interests of legitimate competitors. In line with the principle of proportionality, this Directive protects consumers from the consequences of such unfair commercial practices where they are material but recognises that in some cases the impact on consumers may be negligible. It neither covers nor affects the national laws on unfair commercial practices which harm only competitors' economic interests or which relate to a transaction between traders; taking full account of the principle of subsidiarity, Member States will continue to be able to regulate such practices, in conformity with Community law, if they choose to do so. Nor does this Directive cover or affect the provisions of Directive 84/450/EEC on advertising which misleads business but which is not misleading for consumers and on comparative advertising. Further, this Directive does not affect accepted advertising and marketing practices, such as legitimate product placement, brand differentiation or the offering of incentives which may legitimately affect consumers' perceptions of products and influence their behaviour without impairing the consumer's ability to make an informed decision.

(7)   This Directive addresses commercial practices directly related to influencing consumers' transactional decisions in relation to products. It does not address commercial practices carried out primarily for other purposes, including for example commercial communication aimed at investors, such as annual reports and corporate promotional literature. It does not address legal requirements related to taste and decency which vary widely among the Member States. Commercial practices such as, for example, commercial solicitation in the streets, may be undesirable in Member States for cultural reasons. Member States should accordingly be able to continue to ban commercial practices in their territory, in conformity with Community law, for reasons of taste and decency even where such practices do not limit consumers' freedom of choice. Full account should be taken of the context of the individual case concerned in applying this Directive, in particular the general clauses thereof.

(8)   This Directive directly protects consumer economic interests from unfair business-to-consumer commercial practices. Thereby, it also indirectly protects legitimate businesses from their competitors who do not play by the rules in this Directive and thus guarantees fair competition in fields coordinated by it. It is understood that there are other commercial practices which, although not harming consumers, may hurt competitors and business customers. The Commission should carefully examine the need for Community action in the field of unfair competition beyond the remit of this Directive and, if necessary, make a legislative proposal to cover these other aspects of unfair competition.

(9)   This Directive is without prejudice to individual actions brought by those who have been harmed by an unfair commercial practice. It is also without prejudice to Community and national rules on contract law, on intellectual property rights, on the health and safety aspects of products, on conditions of establishment and authorisation regimes, including those rules which, in conformity with Community law, relate to gambling activities, and to Community competition rules and the national provisions implementing them. The Member States will thus be able to retain or introduce restrictions and prohibitions of commercial practices on grounds of the protection of the health and safety of consumers in their territory wherever the trader is based, for example in relation to alcohol, tobacco or pharmaceuticals. Financial services and immovable property, by reason of their complexity and inherent serious risks, necessitate detailed requirements, including positive

obligations on traders. For this reason, in the field of financial services and immovable property, this Directive is without prejudice to the right of Member States to go beyond its provisions to protect the economic interests of consumers. It is not appropriate to regulate here the certification and indication of the standard of fineness of articles of precious metal.

(10) It is necessary to ensure that the relationship between this Directive and existing Community law is coherent, particularly where detailed provisions on unfair commercial practices apply to specific sectors. This Directive therefore amends Directive 84/450/EEC, Directive 97/7/EC of the European Parliament and of the Council of 20 May 1997 on the protection of consumers in respect of distance contracts[4] Directive 98/27/EC of the European Parliament and of the Council of 19 May 1998 on injunctions for the protection of consumers' interests[5] and Directive 2002/65/EC of the European Parliament and of the Council of 23 September 2002 concerning the distance marketing of consumer financial services[6]. This Directive accordingly applies only in so far as there are no specific Community law provisions regulating specific aspects of unfair commercial practices, such as information requirements and rules on the way the information is presented to the consumer. It provides protection for consumers where there is no specific sectoral legislation at Community level and prohibits traders from creating a false impression of the nature of products. This is particularly important for complex products with high levels of risk to consumers, such as certain financial services products. This Directive consequently complements the Community acquis, which is applicable to commercial practices harming consumers' economic interests.

(11) The high level of convergence achieved by the approximation of national provisions through this Directive creates a high common level of consumer protection. This Directive establishes a single general prohibition of those unfair commercial practices distorting consumers' economic behaviour. It also sets rules on aggressive commercial practices, which are currently not regulated at Community level.

(12) Harmonisation will considerably increase legal certainty for both consumers and business. Both consumers and business will be able to rely on a single regulatory framework based on clearly defined legal concepts regulating all aspects of unfair commercial practices across the EU. The effect will be to eliminate the barriers stemming from the fragmentation of the rules on unfair commercial practices harming consumer economic interests and to enable the internal market to be achieved in this area.

(13) In order to achieve the Community's objectives through the removal of internal market barriers, it is necessary to replace Member States' existing, divergent general clauses and legal principles. The single, common general prohibition established by this Directive therefore covers unfair commercial practices distorting consumers' economic behaviour. In order to support consumer confidence the general prohibition should apply equally to unfair commercial practices which occur outside any contractual relationship between a trader and a consumer or following the conclusion of a contract and during its execution. The general prohibition is elaborated by rules on the two types of commercial practices which are by far the most common, namely misleading commercial practices and aggressive commercial practices.

(14) It is desirable that misleading commercial practices cover those practices, including misleading advertising, which by deceiving the consumer prevent him from making an informed and thus efficient choice. In conformity with the laws and practices of Member States on misleading advertising, this Directive classifies misleading practices into misleading actions and misleading omissions. In respect of omissions, this Directive sets out a limited number of key items of information which the consumer needs to make an informed transactional decision. Such information will not have to be disclosed in all advertisements, but only where the trader makes an invitation to purchase, which is a concept clearly defined in this Directive. The full harmonisation approach adopted in this Directive does not preclude the Member States from specifying in national law the main characteristics of particular products such as, for example, collectors' items or electrical goods, the omission of which would be material when an invitation to purchase is made. It is not the intention of this Directive to reduce consumer choice by prohibiting the promotion of products which look similar to other products unless this similarity confuses consumers as to the commercial origin of the product and is therefore misleading. This Directive should be without prejudice to existing Community law which expressly affords Member States the choice between several regulatory options for the protection of consumers in the field of commercial practices. In particular, this Directive should be without prejudice to Article 13(3) of Directive 2002/58/EC of the European Parliament and of the Council of 12 July 2002 concerning the processing of personal data and the protection of privacy in the electronic communications sector[7].

(15) Where Community law sets out information requirements in relation to commercial communication, advertising and marketing that information is considered as material under this Directive. Member States will be able to retain or add information requirements relating to contract law and having contract law consequences where this is allowed by the minimum clauses in the existing Community law instruments. A non-exhaustive list of such information requirements in the acquis is contained in Annex II. Given the full harmonisation introduced by this Directive only the information required in Community law is considered as material for the purpose of Article 7(5) thereof. Where Member States have introduced information requirements over and above what is specified in Community law, on the basis of minimum clauses, the omission of that extra information will not constitute a misleading omission under this Directive. By contrast Member States will be able, when allowed by the minimum clauses in Community law, to maintain or

introduce more stringent provisions in conformity with Community law so as to ensure a higher level of protection of consumers' individual contractual rights.

(16) The provisions on aggressive commercial practices should cover those practices which significantly impair the consumer's freedom of choice. Those are practices using harassment, coercion, including the use of physical force, and undue influence.

(17) It is desirable that those commercial practices which are in all circumstances unfair be identified to provide greater legal certainty. Annex I therefore contains the full list of all such practices. These are the only commercial practices which can be deemed to be unfair without a case-by-case assessment against the provisions of Articles 5 to 9. The list may only be modified by revision of the Directive.

(18) It is appropriate to protect all consumers from unfair commercial practices; however the Court of Justice has found it necessary in adjudicating on advertising cases since the enactment of Directive 84/450/EEC to examine the effect on a notional, typical consumer. In line with the principle of proportionality, and to permit the effective application of the protections contained in it, this Directive takes as a benchmark the average consumer, who is reasonably well-informed and reasonably observant and circumspect, taking into account social, cultural and linguistic factors, as interpreted by the Court of Justice, but also contains provisions aimed at preventing the exploitation of consumers whose characteristics make them particularly vulnerable to unfair commercial practices. Where a commercial practice is specifically aimed at a particular group of consumers, such as children, it is desirable that the impact of the commercial practice be assessed from the perspective of the average member of that group. It is therefore appropriate to include in the list of practices which are in all circumstances unfair a provision which, without imposing an outright ban on advertising directed at children, protects them from direct exhortations to purchase. The average consumer test is not a statistical test. National courts and authorities will have to exercise their own faculty of judgement, having regard to the case-law of the Court of Justice, to determine the typical reaction of the average consumer in a given case.

(19) Where certain characteristics such as age, physical or mental infirmity or credulity make consumers particularly susceptible to a commercial practice or to the underlying product and the economic behaviour only of such consumers is likely to be distorted by the practice in a way that the trader can reasonably foresee, it is appropriate to ensure that they are adequately protected by assessing the practice from the perspective of the average member of that group.

(20) It is appropriate to provide a role for codes of conduct, which enable traders to apply the principles of this Directive effectively in specific economic fields. In sectors where there are specific mandatory requirements regulating the behaviour of traders, it is appropriate that these will also provide evidence as to the requirements of professional diligence in that sector. The control exercised by code owners at national or Community level to eliminate unfair commercial practices may avoid the need for recourse to administrative or judicial action and should therefore be encouraged. With the aim of pursuing a high level of consumer protection, consumers' organisations could be informed and involved in the drafting of codes of conduct.

(21) Persons or organisations regarded under national law as having a legitimate interest in the matter must have legal remedies for initiating proceedings against unfair commercial practices, either before a court or before an administrative authority which is competent to decide upon complaints or to initiate appropriate legal proceedings. While it is for national law to determine the burden of proof, it is appropriate to enable courts and administrative authorities to require traders to produce evidence as to the accuracy of factual claims they have made.

(22) It is necessary that Member States lay down penalties for infringements of the provisions of this Directive and they must ensure that these are enforced. The penalties must be effective, proportionate and dissuasive.

(23) Since the objectives of this Directive, namely to eliminate the barriers to the functioning of the internal market represented by national laws on unfair commercial practices and to provide a high common level of consumer protection, by approximating the laws, regulations and administrative provisions of the Member States on unfair commercial practices, cannot be sufficiently achieved by the Member States and can therefore be better achieved at Community level, the Community may adopt measures, in accordance with the principle of subsidiarity as set out in Article 5 of the Treaty. In accordance with the principle of proportionality, as set out in that Article, this Directive does not go beyond what is necessary in order to eliminate the internal market barriers and achieve a high common level of consumer protection.

(24) It is appropriate to review this Directive to ensure that barriers to the internal market have been addressed and a high level of consumer protection achieved. The review could lead to a Commission proposal to amend this Directive, which may include a limited extension to the derogation in Article 3(5), and/or amendments to other consumer protection legislation reflecting the Commission's Consumer Policy Strategy commitment to review the existing acquis in order to achieve a high, common level of consumer protection.

(25) This Directive respects the fundamental rights and observes the principles recognised in particular by the Charter of Fundamental Rights of the European Union,

HAVE ADOPTED THIS DIRECTIVE:

NOTES

1   OJ C108, 30.4.2004, p 81.
2   Opinion of the European Parliament of 20 April 2004 (OJ C104 E, 30.4.2004, p 260), Council Common Position of 15 November 2004 (OJ C38 E, 15.2.2005, p 1), Position of the European Parliament of 24 February 2005 (not yet published in the Official Journal) and Council Decision of 12 April 2005.
3   OJ L250, 19.9.1984, p 17. Directive as amended by Directive 97/55/EC of the European Parliament and of the Council (OJ L290, 23.10.1997, p 18).
4   OJ L144, 4.6.1997, p 19. Directive as amended by Directive 2002/65/EC (OJ L271, 9.10.2002, p 16).
5   OJ L166, 11.6.1998, p 51. Directive as last amended by Directive 2002/65/EC.
6   OJ L271, 9.10.2002, p 16.
7   OJ L201, 31.7.2002, p 37.

CHAPTER 1
GENERAL PROVISIONS

Article 1
Purpose

The purpose of this Directive is to contribute to the proper functioning of the internal market and achieve a high level of consumer protection by approximating the laws, regulations and administrative provisions of the Member States on unfair commercial practices harming consumers' economic interests.

[4446]

Article 2
Definitions

For the purposes of this Directive:

(a)   'consumer' means any natural person who, in commercial practices covered by this Directive, is acting for purposes which are outside his trade, business, craft or profession;

(b)   'trader' means any natural or legal person who, in commercial practices covered by this Directive, is acting for purposes relating to his trade, business, craft or profession and anyone acting in the name of or on behalf of a trader;

(c)   'product' means any goods or service including immovable property, rights and obligations;

(d)   'business-to-consumer commercial practices' (hereinafter also referred to as commercial practices) means any act, omission, course of conduct or representation, commercial communication including advertising and marketing, by a trader, directly connected with the promotion, sale or supply of a product to consumers;

(e)   'to materially distort the economic behaviour of consumers' means using a commercial practice to appreciably impair the consumer's ability to make an informed decision, thereby causing the consumer to take a transactional decision that he would not have taken otherwise;

(f)   'code of conduct' means an agreement or set of rules not imposed by law, regulation or administrative provision of a Member State which defines the behaviour of traders who undertake to be bound by the code in relation to one or more particular commercial practices or business sectors;

(g)   'code owner' means any entity, including a trader or group of traders, which is responsible for the formulation and revision of a code of conduct and/or for monitoring compliance with the code by those who have undertaken to be bound by it;

(h)   'professional diligence' means the standard of special skill and care which a trader may reasonably be expected to exercise towards consumers, commensurate with honest market practice and/or the general principle of good faith in the trader's field of activity;

(i)   'invitation to purchase' means a commercial communication which indicates characteristics of the product and the price in a way appropriate to the means of the commercial communication used and thereby enables the consumer to make a purchase;

(j)   'undue influence' means exploiting a position of power in relation to the consumer so as to apply pressure, even without using or threatening to use physical force, in a way which significantly limits the consumer's ability to make an informed decision;

(k)   'transactional decision' means any decision taken by a consumer concerning whether, how and on what terms to purchase, make payment in whole or in part for, retain or dispose of a product or to exercise a contractual right in relation to the product, whether the consumer decides to act or to refrain from acting;

(l)   'regulated profession' means a professional activity or a group of professional activities, access to which or the pursuit of which, or one of the modes of pursuing which, is conditional, directly or indirectly, upon possession of specific professional qualifications, pursuant to laws, regulations or administrative provisions.

[4447]

Article 3
Scope

1.   This Directive shall apply to unfair business-to-consumer commercial practices, as laid down in Article 5, before, during and after a commercial transaction in relation to a product.

2.   This Directive is without prejudice to contract law and, in particular, to the rules on the validity, formation or effect of a contract.

3.   This Directive is without prejudice to Community or national rules relating to the health and safety aspects of products.

4.   In the case of conflict between the provisions of this Directive and other Community rules regulating specific aspects of unfair commercial practices, the latter shall prevail and apply to those specific aspects.

5.   For a period of six years from 12 June 2007, Member States shall be able to continue to apply national provisions within the field approximated by this Directive which are more restrictive or prescriptive than this Directive and which implement directives containing minimum harmonisation clauses. These measures must be essential to ensure that consumers are adequately protected against unfair commercial practices and must be proportionate to the attainment of this objective. The review referred to in Article 18 may, if considered appropriate, include a proposal to prolong this derogation for a further limited period.

6.   Member States shall notify the Commission without delay of any national provisions applied on the basis of paragraph 5.

7.   This Directive is without prejudice to the rules determining the jurisdiction of the courts.

8.   This Directive is without prejudice to any conditions of establishment or of authorisation regimes, or to the deontological codes of conduct or other specific rules governing regulated professions in order to uphold high standards of integrity on the part of the professional, which Member States may, in conformity with Community law, impose on professionals.

9.   In relation to "financial services", as defined in Directive 2002/65/EC, and immovable property, Member States may impose requirements which are more restrictive or prescriptive than this Directive in the field which it approximates.

10.   This Directive shall not apply to the application of the laws, regulations and administrative provisions of Member States relating to the certification and indication of the standard of fineness of articles of precious metal.

[4448]

Article 4
Internal market

Member States shall neither restrict the freedom to provide services nor restrict the free movement of goods for reasons falling within the field approximated by this Directive.

[4449]

CHAPTER 2
UNFAIR COMMERCIAL PRACTICES

Article 5
Prohibition of unfair commercial practices

1.   Unfair commercial practices shall be prohibited.

2.   A commercial practice shall be unfair if:
   (a)   it is contrary to the requirements of professional diligence,
          and
   (b)   it materially distorts or is likely to materially distort the economic behaviour with regard to the product of the average consumer whom it reaches or to whom it is addressed, or of the average member of the group when a commercial practice is directed to a particular group of consumers.

3.   Commercial practices which are likely to materially distort the economic behaviour only of a clearly identifiable group of consumers who are particularly vulnerable to the practice or the underlying product because of their mental or physical infirmity, age or credulity in a way which the trader could reasonably be expected to foresee, shall be assessed from the perspective of the average member of that group. This is without prejudice to the common and legitimate advertising practice of making exaggerated statements or statements which are not meant to be taken literally.

4.   In particular, commercial practices shall be unfair which:
   (a)   are misleading as set out in Articles 6 and 7,
          or
   (b)   are aggressive as set out in Articles 8 and 9.

5.　Annex I contains the list of those commercial practices which shall in all circumstances be regarded as unfair. The same single list shall apply in all Member States and may only be modified by revision of this Directive.

[4450]

SECTION 1
MISLEADING COMMERCIAL PRACTICES

Article 6
Misleading actions

1.　A commercial practice shall be regarded as misleading if it contains false information and is therefore untruthful or in any way, including overall presentation, deceives or is likely to deceive the average consumer, even if the information is factually correct, in relation to one or more of the following elements, and in either case causes or is likely to cause him to take a transactional decision that he would not have taken otherwise:
    (a)　the existence or nature of the product;
    (b)　the main characteristics of the product, such as its availability, benefits, risks, execution, composition, accessories, after-sale customer assistance and complaint handling, method and date of manufacture or provision, delivery, fitness for purpose, usage, quantity, specification, geographical or commercial origin or the results to be expected from its use, or the results and material features of tests or checks carried out on the product;
    (c)　the extent of the trader's commitments, the motives for the commercial practice and the nature of the sales process, any statement or symbol in relation to direct or indirect sponsorship or approval of the trader or the product;
    (d)　the price or the manner in which the price is calculated, or the existence of a specific price advantage;
    (e)　the need for a service, part, replacement or repair;
    (f)　the nature, attributes and rights of the trader or his agent, such as his identity and assets, his qualifications, status, approval, affiliation or connection and ownership of industrial, commercial or intellectual property rights or his awards and distinctions;
    (g)　the consumer's rights, including the right to replacement or reimbursement under Directive 1999/44/EC of the European Parliament and of the Council of 25 May 1999 on certain aspects of the sale of consumer goods and associated guarantees[1], or the risks he may face.

2.　A commercial practice shall also be regarded as misleading if, in its factual context, taking account of all its features and circumstances, it causes or is likely to cause the average consumer to take a transactional decision that he would not have taken otherwise, and it involves:
    (a)　any marketing of a product, including comparative advertising, which creates confusion with any products, trade marks, trade names or other distinguishing marks of a competitor;
    (b)　non-compliance by the trader with commitments contained in codes of conduct by which the trader has undertaken to be bound, where:
        (i)　the commitment is not aspirational but is firm and is capable of being verified, and
        (ii)　the trader indicates in a commercial practice that he is bound by the code.

[4451]

NOTES
[1]　　OJ L171, 7.7.1999, p 12.

Article 7
Misleading omissions

1.　A commercial practice shall be regarded as misleading if, in its factual context, taking account of all its features and circumstances and the limitations of the communication medium, it omits material information that the average consumer needs, according to the context, to take an informed transactional decision and thereby causes or is likely to cause the average consumer to take a transactional decision that he would not have taken otherwise.

2.　It shall also be regarded as a misleading omission when, taking account of the matters described in paragraph 1, a trader hides or provides in an unclear, unintelligible, ambiguous or untimely manner such material information as referred to in that paragraph or fails to identify the commercial intent of the commercial practice if not already apparent from the context, and where, in either case, this causes or is likely to cause the average consumer to take a transactional decision that he would not have taken otherwise.

3.　Where the medium used to communicate the commercial practice imposes limitations of space or time, these limitations and any measures taken by the trader to make the information available to consumers by other means shall be taken into account in deciding whether information has been omitted.

4.   In the case of an invitation to purchase, the following information shall be regarded as material, if not already apparent from the context:

(a)   the main characteristics of the product, to an extent appropriate to the medium and the product;

(b)   the geographical address and the identity of the trader, such as his trading name and, where applicable, the geographical address and the identity of the trader on whose behalf he is acting;

(c)   the price inclusive of taxes, or where the nature of the product means that the price cannot reasonably be calculated in advance, the manner in which the price is calculated, as well as, where appropriate, all additional freight, delivery or postal charges or, where these charges cannot reasonably be calculated in advance, the fact that such additional charges may be payable;

(d)   the arrangements for payment, delivery, performance and the complaint handling policy, if they depart from the requirements of professional diligence;

(e)   for products and transactions involving a right of withdrawal or cancellation, the existence of such a right.

5.   Information requirements established by Community law in relation to commercial communication including advertising or marketing, a non-exhaustive list of which is contained in Annex II, shall be regarded as material.

[4452]

SECTION 2
AGGRESSIVE COMMERCIAL PRACTICES

Article 8
Aggressive commercial practices

A commercial practice shall be regarded as aggressive if, in its factual context, taking account of all its features and circumstances, by harassment, coercion, including the use of physical force, or undue influence, it significantly impairs or is likely to significantly impair the average consumer's freedom of choice or conduct with regard to the product and thereby causes him or is likely to cause him to take a transactional decision that he would not have taken otherwise.

[4453]

Article 9
Use of harassment, coercion and undue influence

In determining whether a commercial practice uses harassment, coercion, including the use of physical force, or undue influence, account shall be taken of:

(a)   its timing, location, nature or persistence;

(b)   the use of threatening or abusive language or behaviour;

(c)   the exploitation by the trader of any specific misfortune or circumstance of such gravity as to impair the consumer's judgement, of which the trader is aware, to influence the consumer's decision with regard to the product;

(d)   any onerous or disproportionate non-contractual barriers imposed by the trader where a consumer wishes to exercise rights under the contract, including rights to terminate a contract or to switch to another product or another trader;

(e)   any threat to take any action that cannot legally be taken.

[4454]

CHAPTER 3
CODES OF CONDUCT

Article 10
Codes of conduct

This Directive does not exclude the control, which Member States may encourage, of unfair commercial practices by code owners and recourse to such bodies by the persons or organisations referred to in Article 11 if proceedings before such bodies are in addition to the court or administrative proceedings referred to in that Article.

Recourse to such control bodies shall never be deemed the equivalent of foregoing a means of judicial or administrative recourse as provided for in Article 11.

[4455]

CHAPTER 4

FINAL PROVISIONS

Article 11
Enforcement

1.   Member States shall ensure that adequate and effective means exist to combat unfair commercial practices in order to enforce compliance with the provisions of this Directive in the interest of consumers.

Such means shall include legal provisions under which persons or organisations regarded under national law as having a legitimate interest in combating unfair commercial practices, including competitors, may:

  (a)   take legal action against such unfair commercial practices;
         and/or

  (b)   bring such unfair commercial practices before an administrative authority competent either to decide on complaints or to initiate appropriate legal proceedings.

It shall be for each Member State to decide which of these facilities shall be available and whether to enable the courts or administrative authorities to require prior recourse to other established means of dealing with complaints, including those referred to in Article 10. These facilities shall be available regardless of whether the consumers affected are in the territory of the Member State where the trader is located or in another Member State.

It shall be for each Member State to decide:

  (a)   whether these legal facilities may be directed separately or jointly against a number of traders from the same economic sector;
         and

  (b)   whether these legal facilities may be directed against a code owner where the relevant code promotes non-compliance with legal requirements.

2.   Under the legal provisions referred to in paragraph 1, Member States shall confer upon the courts or administrative authorities powers enabling them, in cases where they deem such measures to be necessary taking into account all the interests involved and in particular the public interest:

  (a)   to order the cessation of, or to institute appropriate legal proceedings for an order for the cessation of, unfair commercial practices;
         or

  (b)   if the unfair commercial practice has not yet been carried out but is imminent, to order the prohibition of the practice, or to institute appropriate legal proceedings for an order for the prohibition of the practice,

even without proof of actual loss or damage or of intention or negligence on the part of the trader.

Member States shall also make provision for the measures referred to in the first subparagraph to be taken under an accelerated procedure:

  —   either with interim effect,
         or

  —   with definitive effect,

on the understanding that it is for each Member State to decide which of the two options to select.

Furthermore, Member States may confer upon the courts or administrative authorities powers enabling them, with a view to eliminating the continuing effects of unfair commercial practices the cessation of which has been ordered by a final decision:

  (a)   to require publication of that decision in full or in part and in such form as they deem adequate;

  (b)   to require in addition the publication of a corrective statement.

3.   The administrative authorities referred to in paragraph 1 must:

  (a)   be composed so as not to cast doubt on their impartiality;

  (b)   have adequate powers, where they decide on complaints, to monitor and enforce the observance of their decisions effectively;

  (c)   normally give reasons for their decisions.

Where the powers referred to in paragraph 2 are exercised exclusively by an administrative authority, reasons for its decisions shall always be given. Furthermore, in this case, provision must be made for procedures whereby improper or unreasonable exercise of its powers by the administrative authority or improper or unreasonable failure to exercise the said powers can be the subject of judicial review.

[4456]

Article 12
Courts and administrative authorities: substantiation of claims

Member States shall confer upon the courts or administrative authorities powers enabling them in the civil or administrative proceedings provided for in Article 11:

  (a)   to require the trader to furnish evidence as to the accuracy of factual claims in relation to a commercial practice if, taking into account the legitimate interest of the trader and any

PART 3

EU AND INTERNATIONAL MATERIALS

other party to the proceedings, such a requirement appears appropriate on the basis of the circumstances of the particular case; and

(b)   to consider factual claims as inaccurate if the evidence demanded in accordance with (a) is not furnished or is deemed insufficient by the court or administrative authority.

[4457]

Article 13
Penalties

Member States shall lay down penalties for infringements of national provisions adopted in application of this Directive and shall take all necessary measures to ensure that these are enforced. These penalties must be effective, proportionate and dissuasive.

[4458]

Articles 14–16

(*Art 14 spent* (*amended Directive 84/450/EEC* (*repealed*)); *Art 15 substitutes Directive 97/7/EC, Art 9 at* **[4313]** *and Directive 2002/65/EC, Art 9 at* **[4434]***; Art 16 amended Directive 98/27/EC, Annex* (*repealed*) *and amends Regulation 2006/2004/EC.*)

Article 17
Information

Member States shall take appropriate measures to inform consumers of the national law transposing this Directive and shall, where appropriate, encourage traders and code owners to inform consumers of their codes of conduct.

[4459]

Article 18
Review

1.   By 12 June 2011 the Commission shall submit to the European Parliament and the Council a comprehensive report on the application of this Directive, in particular of Articles 3(9) and 4 and Annex I, on the scope for further harmonisation and simplification of Community law relating to consumer protection, and, having regard to Article 3(5), on any measures that need to be taken at Community level to ensure that appropriate levels of consumer protection are maintained. The report shall be accompanied, if necessary, by a proposal to revise this Directive or other relevant parts of Community law.

2.   The European Parliament and the Council shall endeavour to act, in accordance with the Treaty, within two years of the presentation by the Commission of any proposal submitted under paragraph 1.

[4460]

Article 19
Transposition

Member States shall adopt and publish the laws, regulations and administrative provisions necessary to comply with this Directive by 12 June 2007. They shall forthwith inform the Commission thereof and inform the Commission of any subsequent amendments without delay.

They shall apply those measures by 12 December 2007. When Member States adopt those measures, they shall contain a reference to this Directive or be accompanied by such a reference on the occasion of their official publication. Member States shall determine how such reference is to be made.

[4461]

Article 20
Entry into force

This Directive shall enter into force on the day following its publication in the *Official Journal of the European Union*.

[4462]

Article 21
Addressees

This Directive is addressed to the Member States.

[4463]

Done at Strasbourg, 11 May 2005.

ANNEX I

COMMERCIAL PRACTICES WHICH ARE IN ALL CIRCUMSTANCES CONSIDERED UNFAIR

Misleading commercial practices

1. Claiming to be a signatory to a code of conduct when the trader is not.

2. Displaying a trust mark, quality mark or equivalent without having obtained the necessary authorisation.

3. Claiming that a code of conduct has an endorsement from a public or other body which it does not have.

4. Claiming that a trader (including his commercial practices) or a product has been approved, endorsed or authorised by a public or private body when he/it has not or making such a claim without complying with the terms of the approval, endorsement or authorisation.

5. Making an invitation to purchase products at a specified price without disclosing the existence of any reasonable grounds the trader may have for believing that he will not be able to offer for supply or to procure another trader to supply, those products or equivalent products at that price for a period that is, and in quantities that are, reasonable having regard to the product, the scale of advertising of the product and the price offered (bait advertising).

6. Making an invitation to purchase products at a specified price and then:
    (a)   refusing to show the advertised item to consumers;
          or
    (b)   refusing to take orders for it or deliver it within a reasonable time;
          or
    (c)   demonstrating a defective sample of it,
with the intention of promoting a different product (bait and switch)

7. Falsely stating that a product will only be available for a very limited time, or that it will only be available on particular terms for a very limited time, in order to elicit an immediate decision and deprive consumers of sufficient opportunity or time to make an informed choice.

8. Undertaking to provide after-sales service to consumers with whom the trader has communicated prior to a transaction in a language which is not an official language of the Member State where the trader is located and then making such service available only in another language without clearly disclosing this to the consumer before the consumer is committed to the transaction.

9. Stating or otherwise creating the impression that a product can legally be sold when it cannot.

10. Presenting rights given to consumers in law as a distinctive feature of the trader's offer.

11. Using editorial content in the media to promote a product where a trader has paid for the promotion without making that clear in the content or by images or sounds clearly identifiable by the consumer (advertorial). This is without prejudice to Council Directive 89/552/EEC[1].

12. Making a materially inaccurate claim concerning the nature and extent of the risk to the personal security of the consumer or his family if the consumer does not purchase the product.

13. Promoting a product similar to a product made by a particular manufacturer in such a manner as deliberately to mislead the consumer into believing that the product is made by that same manufacturer when it is not.

14. Establishing, operating or promoting a pyramid promotional scheme where a consumer gives consideration for the opportunity to receive compensation that is derived primarily from the introduction of other consumers into the scheme rather than from the sale or consumption of products.

15. Claiming that the trader is about to cease trading or move premises when he is not.

16. Claiming that products are able to facilitate winning in games of chance.

17. Falsely claiming that a product is able to cure illnesses, dysfunction or malformations.

18. Passing on materially inaccurate information on market conditions or on the possibility of finding the product with the intention of inducing the consumer to acquire the product at conditions less favourable than normal market conditions.

19. Claiming in a commercial practice to offer a competition or prize promotion without awarding the prizes described or a reasonable equivalent.

20. Describing a product as "gratis", "free", "without charge" or similar if the consumer has to pay anything other than the unavoidable cost of responding to the commercial practice and collecting or paying for delivery of the item.

21.   Including in marketing material an invoice or similar document seeking payment which gives the consumer the impression that he has already ordered the marketed product when he has not.

22.   Falsely claiming or creating the impression that the trader is not acting for purposes relating to his trade, business, craft or profession, or falsely representing oneself as a consumer.

23.   Creating the false impression that after-sales service in relation to a product is available in a Member State other than the one in which the product is sold.

Aggressive commercial practices

24.   Creating the impression that the consumer cannot leave the premises until a contract is formed.

25.   Conducting personal visits to the consumer's home ignoring the consumer's request to leave or not to return except in circumstances and to the extent justified, under national law, to enforce a contractual obligation.

26.   Making persistent and unwanted solicitations by telephone, fax, e-mail or other remote media except in circumstances and to the extent justified under national law to enforce a contractual obligation. This is without prejudice to Article 10 of Directive 97/7/EC and Directives 95/46/EC[2] and 2002/58/EC.

27.   Requiring a consumer who wishes to claim on an insurance policy to produce documents which could not reasonably be considered relevant as to whether the claim was valid, or failing systematically to respond to pertinent correspondence, in order to dissuade a consumer from exercising his contractual rights.

28.   Including in an advertisement a direct exhortation to children to buy advertised products or persuade their parents or other adults to buy advertised products for them. This provision is without prejudice to Article 16 of Directive 89/552/EEC on television broadcasting.

29.   Demanding immediate or deferred payment for or the return or safekeeping of products supplied by the trader, but not solicited by the consumer except where the product is a substitute supplied in conformity with Article 7(3) of Directive 97/7/EC (inertia selling).

30.   Explicitly informing a consumer that if he does not buy the product or service, the trader's job or livelihood will be in jeopardy.

31.   Creating the false impression that the consumer has already won, will win, or will on doing a particular act win, a prize or other equivalent benefit, when in fact either:

    —   there is no prize or other equivalent benefit,

        or

    —   taking any action in relation to claiming the prize or other equivalent benefit is subject to the consumer paying money or incurring a cost.

[4464]

NOTES
[1]   Council Directive 89/552/EEC of 3 October 1989 on the coordination of certain provisions laid down by Law, Regulation or Administrative Action in Member States concerning the pursuit of television broadcasting activities (OJ L298, 17.10.1989, p 23). Directive as amended by Directive 97/36/EC of the European Parliament and of the Council (OJ L202, 30.7.1997, p 60).
[2]   Directive 95/46/EC of the European Parliament and of the Council of 24 October 1995 on the protection of individuals with regard to the processing of personal data and on the free movement of such data (OJ L281, 23.11.1995, p 31). Directive as amended by Regulation (EC) No 1882/2003 (OJ L284, 31.10.2003, p 1).

ANNEX II

COMMUNITY LAW PROVISIONS SETTING OUT RULES FOR ADVERTISING AND COMMERCIAL COMMUNICATION

Articles 4 and 5 of Directive 97/7/EC

Article 3 of Council Directive 90/314/EEC of 13 June 1990 on package travel, package holidays and package tours[1]

Article 3(3) of Directive 94/47/EC of the European Parliament and of the Council of 26 October 1994 on the protection of purchasers in respect of certain aspects of contracts relating to the purchase of a right to use immovable properties on a timeshare basis[2]

Article 3(4) of Directive 98/6/EC of the European Parliament and of the Council of 16 February 1998 on consumer protection in the indication of the prices of products offered to consumers[3]

Articles 86 to 100 of Directive 2001/83/EC of the European Parliament and of the Council of 6 November 2001 on the Community code relating to medicinal products for human use[4]

Articles 5 and 6 of Directive 2000/31/EC of the European Parliament and of the Council of 8 June 2000 on certain legal aspects of information society services, in particular electronic commerce, in the Internal Market (Directive on electronic commerce)[5]

Article 1(d) of Directive 98/7/EC of the European Parliament and of the Council of 16 February 1998 amending Council Directive 87/102/EEC for the approximation of the laws, regulations and administrative provisions of the Member States concerning consumer credit[6]

Articles 3 and 4 of Directive 2002/65/EC

Article 1(9) of Directive 2001/107/EC of the European Parliament and of the Council of 21 January 2002 amending Council Directive 85/611/EEC on the coordination of laws, regulations and administrative provisions relating to undertakings for collective investment in transferable securities (UCITS) with a view to regulating management companies and simplified prospectuses[7]

Articles 12 and 13 of Directive 2002/92/EC of the European Parliament and of the Council of 9 December 2002 on insurance mediation[8]

Article 36 of Directive 2002/83/EC of the European Parliament and of the Council of 5 November 2002 concerning life assurance[9]

Article 19 of Directive 2004/39/EC of the European Parliament and of the Council of 21 April 2004 on markets in financial instruments[10]

Articles 31 and 43 of Council Directive 92/49/EEC of 18 June 1992 on the coordination of laws, regulations and administrative provisions relating to direct insurance other than life assurance[11] (third non-life insurance Directive)

Articles 5, 7 and 8 of Directive 2003/71/EC of the European Parliament and of the Council of 4 November 2003 on the prospectus to be published when securities are offered to the public or admitted to trading[12]

[4465]

NOTES

[1]   OJ L158, 23.6.1990, p 59.
[2]   OJ L280, 29.10.1994, p 83.
[3]   OJ L80, 18.3.1998, p 27.
[4]   OJ L311, 28.11.2001, p 67. Directive as last amended by Directive 2004/27/EC (OJ L136, 30.4.2004, p 34).
[5]   OJ L178, 17.7.2000, p 1.
[6]   OJ L101, 1.4.1998, p 17.
[7]   OJ L41, 13.2.2002, p 20.
[8]   OJ L9, 15.1.2003, p 3.
[9]   OJ L345, 19.12.2002, p 1. Directive as amended by Council Directive 2004/66/EC. (OJ L168, 1.5.2004, p 35).
[10]   OJ L145, 30.4.2004, p 1.
[11]   OJ L228, 11.8.1992, p 1. Directive as last amended by Directive 2002/87/EC of the European Parliament and of the Council (OJ L35, 11.2.2003, p 1).
[12]   OJ L345, 31.12.2003, p 64.

DIRECTIVE OF THE EUROPEAN PARLIAMENT AND OF THE COUNCIL

of 26 October 2005

on the prevention of the use of the financial system for the purpose of money laundering and terrorist financing

(2005/60/EC)

(Text with EEA relevance)

NOTES

Date of publication in OJ: OJ L309, 25.11.2005, p 15.
This Directive has been implemented in the UK by the Money Laundering Regulations 2007, SI 2007/2157 (as amended) at **[3559]**, the Terrorism Act 2000 (as amended), and by the Proceeds of Crime Act 2002 (as amended) at **[1839]**.

THE EUROPEAN PARLIAMENT AND THE COUNCIL OF THE EUROPEAN UNION,
    Having regard to the Treaty establishing the European Community, and in particular Article 47(2), first and third sentences, and Article 95 thereof,
    Having regard to the proposal from the Commission,

Having regard to the opinion of the European Economic and Social Committee[1],
Having regard to the opinion of the European Central Bank[2],
Acting in accordance with the procedure laid down in Article 251 of the Treaty[3],
Whereas:

(1)   Massive flows of dirty money can damage the stability and reputation of the financial sector and threaten the single market, and terrorism shakes the very foundations of our society. In addition to the criminal law approach, a preventive effort via the financial system can produce results.

(2)   The soundness, integrity and stability of credit and financial institutions and confidence in the financial system as a whole could be seriously jeopardised by the efforts of criminals and their associates either to disguise the origin of criminal proceeds or to channel lawful or unlawful money for terrorist purposes. In order to avoid Member States' adopting measures to protect their financial systems which could be inconsistent with the functioning of the internal market and with the prescriptions of the rule of law and Community public policy, Community action in this area is necessary.

(3)   In order to facilitate their criminal activities, money launderers and terrorist financers could try to take advantage of the freedom of capital movements and the freedom to supply financial services which the integrated financial area entails, if certain coordinating measures are not adopted at Community level.

(4)   In order to respond to these concerns in the field of money laundering, Council Directive 91/308/EEC of 10 June 1991 on prevention of the use of the financial system for the purpose of money laundering[4] was adopted. It required Member States to prohibit money laundering and to oblige the financial sector, comprising credit institutions and a wide range of other financial institutions, to identify their customers, keep appropriate records, establish internal procedures to train staff and guard against money laundering and to report any indications of money laundering to the competent authorities.

(5)   Money laundering and terrorist financing are frequently carried out in an international context. Measures adopted solely at national or even Community level, without taking account of international coordination and cooperation, would have very limited effects. The measures adopted by the Community in this field should therefore be consistent with other action undertaken in other international fora. The Community action should continue to take particular account of the Recommendations of the Financial Action Task Force (hereinafter referred to as the FATF), which constitutes the foremost international body active in the fight against money laundering and terrorist financing. Since the FATF Recommendations were substantially revised and expanded in 2003, this Directive should be in line with that new international standard.

(6)   The General Agreement on Trade in Services (GATS) allows Members to adopt measures necessary to protect public morals and prevent fraud and adopt measures for prudential reasons, including for ensuring the stability and integrity of the financial system.

(7)   Although initially limited to drugs offences, there has been a trend in recent years towards a much wider definition of money laundering based on a broader range of predicate offences. A wider range of predicate offences facilitates the reporting of suspicious transactions and international cooperation in this area. Therefore, the definition of serious crime should be brought into line with the definition of serious crime in Council Framework Decision 2001/500/JHA of 26 June 2001 on money laundering, the identification, tracing, freezing, seizing and confiscation of instrumentalities and the proceeds of crime[5].

(8)   Furthermore, the misuse of the financial system to channel criminal or even clean money to terrorist purposes poses a clear risk to the integrity, proper functioning, reputation and stability of the financial system. Accordingly, the preventive measures of this Directive should cover not only the manipulation of money derived from crime but also the collection of money or property for terrorist purposes.

(9)   Directive 91/308/EEC, though imposing a customer identification obligation, contained relatively little detail on the relevant procedures. In view of the crucial importance of this aspect of the prevention of money laundering and terrorist financing, it is appropriate, in accordance with the new international standards, to introduce more specific and detailed provisions relating to the identification of the customer and of any beneficial owner and the verification of their identity. To that end a precise definition of "beneficial owner" is essential. Where the individual beneficiaries of a legal entity or arrangement such as a foundation or trust are yet to be determined, and it is therefore impossible to identify an individual as the beneficial owner, it would suffice to identify the class of persons intended to be the beneficiaries of the foundation or trust. This requirement should not include the identification of the individuals within that class of persons.

(10)   The institutions and persons covered by this Directive should, in conformity with this Directive, identify and verify the identity of the beneficial owner. To fulfil this requirement, it should be left to those institutions and persons whether they make use of public records of beneficial owners, ask their clients for relevant data or obtain the information otherwise, taking into account the fact that the extent of such customer due diligence measures relates to the risk of money laundering and terrorist financing, which depends on the type of customer, business relationship, product or transaction.

(11)   Credit agreements in which the credit account serves exclusively to settle the loan and the repayment of the loan is effected from an account which was opened in the name of the customer

with a credit institution covered by this Directive pursuant to Article 8(1)(a) to (c) should generally be considered as an example of types of less risky transactions.

(12) To the extent that the providers of the property of a legal entity or arrangement have significant control over the use of the property they should be identified as a beneficial owner.

(13) Trust relationships are widely used in commercial products as an internationally recognised feature of the comprehensively supervised wholesale financial markets. An obligation to identify the beneficial owner does not arise from the fact alone that there is a trust relationship in this particular case.

(14) This Directive should also apply to those activities of the institutions and persons covered hereunder which are performed on the Internet.

(15) As the tightening of controls in the financial sector has prompted money launderers and terrorist financers to seek alternative methods for concealing the origin of the proceeds of crime and as such channels can be used for terrorist financing, the anti-money laundering and anti-terrorist financing obligations should cover life insurance intermediaries and trust and company service providers.

(16) Entities already falling under the legal responsibility of an insurance undertaking, and therefore falling within the scope of this Directive, should not be included within the category of insurance intermediary.

(17) Acting as a company director or secretary does not of itself make someone a trust and company service provider. For that reason, the definition covers only those persons that act as a company director or secretary for a third party and by way of business.

(18) The use of large cash payments has repeatedly proven to be very vulnerable to money laundering and terrorist financing. Therefore, in those Member States that allow cash payments above the established threshold, all natural or legal persons trading in goods by way of business should be covered by this Directive when accepting such cash payments. Dealers in high-value goods, such as precious stones or metals, or works of art, and auctioneers are in any event covered by this Directive to the extent that payments to them are made in cash in an amount of EUR 15000 or more. To ensure effective monitoring of compliance with this Directive by that potentially wide group of institutions and persons, Member States may focus their monitoring activities in particular on those natural and legal persons trading in goods that are exposed to a relatively high risk of money laundering or terrorist financing, in accordance with the principle of risk-based supervision. In view of the different situations in the various Member States, Member States may decide to adopt stricter provisions, in order to properly address the risk involved with large cash payments.

(19) Directive 91/308/EEC brought notaries and other independent legal professionals within the scope of the Community anti-money laundering regime; this coverage should be maintained unchanged in this Directive; these legal professionals, as defined by the Member States, are subject to the provisions of this Directive when participating in financial or corporate transactions, including providing tax advice, where there is the greatest risk of the services of those legal professionals being misused for the purpose of laundering the proceeds of criminal activity or for the purpose of terrorist financing.

(20) Where independent members of professions providing legal advice which are legally recognised and controlled, such as lawyers, are ascertaining the legal position of a client or representing a client in legal proceedings, it would not be appropriate under this Directive to put those legal professionals in respect of these activities under an obligation to report suspicions of money laundering or terrorist financing. There must be exemptions from any obligation to report information obtained either before, during or after judicial proceedings, or in the course of ascertaining the legal position for a client. Thus, legal advice shall remain subject to the obligation of professional secrecy unless the legal counsellor is taking part in money laundering or terrorist financing, the legal advice is provided for money laundering or terrorist financing purposes or the lawyer knows that the client is seeking legal advice for money laundering or terrorist financing purposes.

(21) Directly comparable services need to be treated in the same manner when provided by any of the professionals covered by this Directive. In order to ensure the respect of the rights laid down in the European Convention for the Protection of Human Rights and Fundamental Freedoms and the Treaty on European Union, in the case of auditors, external accountants and tax advisors, who, in some Member States, may defend or represent a client in the context of judicial proceedings or ascertain a client's legal position, the information they obtain in the performance of those tasks should not be subject to the reporting obligations in accordance with this Directive.

(22) It should be recognised that the risk of money laundering and terrorist financing is not the same in every case. In line with a risk-based approach, the principle should be introduced into Community legislation that simplified customer due diligence is allowed in appropriate cases.

(23) The derogation concerning the identification of beneficial owners of pooled accounts held by notaries or other independent legal professionals should be without prejudice to the obligations that those notaries or other independent legal professionals have pursuant to this Directive. Those obligations include the need for such notaries or other independent legal professionals themselves to identify the beneficial owners of the pooled accounts held by them.

(24)   Equally, Community legislation should recognise that certain situations present a greater risk of money laundering or terrorist financing. Although the identity and business profile of all customers should be established, there are cases where particularly rigorous customer identification and verification procedures are required.

(25)   This is particularly true of business relationships with individuals holding, or having held, important public positions, particularly those from countries where corruption is widespread. Such relationships may expose the financial sector in particular to significant reputational and/or legal risks. The international effort to combat corruption also justifies the need to pay special attention to such cases and to apply the complete normal customer due diligence measures in respect of domestic politically exposed persons or enhanced customer due diligence measures in respect of politically exposed persons residing in another Member State or in a third country.

(26)   Obtaining approval from senior management for establishing business relationships should not imply obtaining approval from the board of directors but from the immediate higher level of the hierarchy of the person seeking such approval.

(27)   In order to avoid repeated customer identification procedures, leading to delays and inefficiency in business, it is appropriate, subject to suitable safeguards, to allow customers to be introduced whose identification has been carried out elsewhere. Where an institution or person covered by this Directive relies on a third party, the ultimate responsibility for the customer due diligence procedure remains with the institution or person to whom the customer is introduced. The third party, or introducer, also retains his own responsibility for all the requirements in this Directive, including the requirement to report suspicious transactions and maintain records, to the extent that he has a relationship with the customer that is covered by this Directive.

(28)   In the case of agency or outsourcing relationships on a contractual basis between institutions or persons covered by this Directive and external natural or legal persons not covered hereby, any anti-money laundering and anti-terrorist financing obligations for those agents or outsourcing service providers as part of the institutions or persons covered by this Directive, may only arise from contract and not from this Directive. The responsibility for complying with this Directive should remain with the institution or person covered hereby.

(29)   Suspicious transactions should be reported to the financial intelligence unit (FIU), which serves as a national centre for receiving, analysing and disseminating to the competent authorities suspicious transaction reports and other information regarding potential money laundering or terrorist financing. This should not compel Member States to change their existing reporting systems where the reporting is done through a public prosecutor or other law enforcement authorities, as long as the information is forwarded promptly and unfiltered to FIUs, allowing them to conduct their business properly, including international cooperation with other FIUs.

(30)   By way of derogation from the general prohibition on executing suspicious transactions, the institutions and persons covered by this Directive may execute suspicious transactions before informing the competent authorities, where refraining from the execution thereof is impossible or likely to frustrate efforts to pursue the beneficiaries of a suspected money laundering or terrorist financing operation. This, however, should be without prejudice to the international obligations accepted by the Member States to freeze without delay funds or other assets of terrorists, terrorist organisations or those who finance terrorism, in accordance with the relevant United Nations Security Council resolutions.

(31)   Where a Member State decides to make use of the exemptions provided for in Article 23(2), it may allow or require the self-regulatory body representing the persons referred to therein not to transmit to the FIU any information obtained from those persons in the circumstances referred to in that Article.

(32)   There has been a number of cases of employees who report their suspicions of money laundering being subjected to threats or hostile action. Although this Directive cannot interfere with Member States' judicial procedures, this is a crucial issue for the effectiveness of the anti-money laundering and anti-terrorist financing system. Member States should be aware of this problem and should do whatever they can to protect employees from such threats or hostile action.

(33)   Disclosure of information as referred to in Article 28 should be in accordance with the rules on transfer of personal data to third countries as laid down in Directive 95/46/EC of the European Parliament and of the Council of 24 October 1995 on the protection of individuals with regard to the processing of personal data and on the free movement of such data[6]. Moreover, Article 28 cannot interfere with national data protection and professional secrecy legislation.

(34)   Persons who merely convert paper documents into electronic data and are acting under a contract with a credit institution or a financial institution do not fall within the scope of this Directive, nor does any natural or legal person that provides credit or financial institutions solely with a message or other support systems for transmitting funds or with clearing and settlement systems.

(35)   Money laundering and terrorist financing are international problems and the effort to combat them should be global. Where Community credit and financial institutions have branches and subsidiaries located in third countries where the legislation in this area is deficient, they should, in order to avoid the application of very different standards within an institution or group of institutions, apply the Community standard or notify the competent authorities of the home Member State if this application is impossible.

(36) It is important that credit and financial institutions should be able to respond rapidly to requests for information on whether they maintain business relationships with named persons. For the purpose of identifying such business relationships in order to be able to provide that information quickly, credit and financial institutions should have effective systems in place which are commensurate with the size and nature of their business. In particular it would be appropriate for credit institutions and larger financial institutions to have electronic systems at their disposal. This provision is of particular importance in the context of procedures leading to measures such as the freezing or seizing of assets (including terrorist assets), pursuant to applicable national or Community legislation with a view to combating terrorism.

(37) This Directive establishes detailed rules for customer due diligence, including enhanced customer due diligence for high-risk customers or business relationships, such as appropriate procedures to determine whether a person is a politically exposed person, and certain additional, more detailed requirements, such as the existence of compliance management procedures and policies. All these requirements are to be met by each of the institutions and persons covered by this Directive, while Member States are expected to tailor the detailed implementation of those provisions to the particularities of the various professions and to the differences in scale and size of the institutions and persons covered by this Directive.

(38) In order to ensure that the institutions and others subject to Community legislation in this field remain committed, feedback should, where practicable, be made available to them on the usefulness and follow-up of the reports they present. To make this possible, and to be able to review the effectiveness of their systems to combat money laundering and terrorist financing Member States should keep and improve the relevant statistics.

(39) When registering or licensing a currency exchange office, a trust and company service provider or a casino nationally, competent authorities should ensure that the persons who effectively direct or will direct the business of such entities and the beneficial owners of such entities are fit and proper persons. The criteria for determining whether or not a person is fit and proper should be established in conformity with national law. As a minimum, such criteria should reflect the need to protect such entities from being misused by their managers or beneficial owners for criminal purposes.

(40) Taking into account the international character of money laundering and terrorist financing, coordination and cooperation between FIUs as referred to in Council Decision 2000/642/JHA of 17 October 2000 concerning arrangements for cooperation between financial intelligence units of the Member States in respect of exchanging information[7], including the establishment of an EU FIU-net, should be encouraged to the greatest possible extent. To that end, the Commission should lend such assistance as may be needed to facilitate such coordination, including financial assistance.

(41) The importance of combating money laundering and terrorist financing should lead Member States to lay down effective, proportionate and dissuasive penalties in national law for failure to respect the national provisions adopted pursuant to this Directive. Provision should be made for penalties in respect of natural and legal persons. Since legal persons are often involved in complex money laundering or terrorist financing operations, sanctions should also be adjusted in line with the activity carried on by legal persons.

(42) Natural persons exercising any of the activities referred to in Article 2(1)(3)(a) and (b) within the structure of a legal person, but on an independent basis, should be independently responsible for compliance with the provisions of this Directive, with the exception of Article 35.

(43) Clarification of the technical aspects of the rules laid down in this Directive may be necessary to ensure an effective and sufficiently consistent implementation of this Directive, taking into account the different financial instruments, professions and risks in the different Member States and the technical developments in the fight against money laundering and terrorist financing. The Commission should accordingly be empowered to adopt implementing measures, such as certain criteria for identifying low and high risk situations in which simplified due diligence could suffice or enhanced due diligence would be appropriate, provided that they do not modify the essential elements of this Directive and provided that the Commission acts in accordance with the principles set out herein, after consulting the Committee on the Prevention of Money Laundering and Terrorist Financing.

(44) The measures necessary for the implementation of this Directive should be adopted in accordance with Council Decision 1999/468/EC of 28 June 1999 laying down the procedures for the exercise of implementing powers conferred on the Commission[8]. To that end a new Committee on the Prevention of Money Laundering and Terrorist Financing, replacing the Money Laundering Contact Committee set up by Directive 91/308/EEC, should be established.

(45) In view of the very substantial amendments that would need to be made to Directive 91/308/EEC, it should be repealed for reasons of clarity.

(46) Since the objective of this Directive, namely the prevention of the use of the financial system for the purpose of money laundering and terrorist financing, cannot be sufficiently achieved by the Member States and can therefore, by reason of the scale and effects of the action, be better achieved at Community level, the Community may adopt measures, in accordance with the principle of subsidiarity as set out in Article 5 of the Treaty. In accordance with the principle of proportionality, as set out in that Article, this Directive does not go beyond what is necessary in order to achieve that objective.

(47)   In exercising its implementing powers in accordance with this Directive, the Commission should respect the following principles: the need for high levels of transparency and consultation with institutions and persons covered by this Directive and with the European Parliament and the Council; the need to ensure that competent authorities will be able to ensure compliance with the rules consistently; the balance of costs and benefits to institutions and persons covered by this Directive on a long-term basis in any implementing measures; the need to respect the necessary flexibility in the application of the implementing measures in accordance with a risk-sensitive approach; the need to ensure coherence with other Community legislation in this area; the need to protect the Community, its Member States and their citizens from the consequences of money laundering and terrorist financing.

(48)   This Directive respects the fundamental rights and observes the principles recognised in particular by the Charter of Fundamental Rights of the European Union. Nothing in this Directive should be interpreted or implemented in a manner that is inconsistent with the European Convention on Human Rights,

HAVE ADOPTED THIS DIRECTIVE:

NOTES

1   Opinion delivered on 11 May 2005 (not yet published in the Official Journal).
2   OJ C40, 17.2.2005, p 9.
3   Opinion of the European Parliament of 26 May 2005 (not yet published in the Official Journal) and Council Decision of 19 September 2005.
4   OJ L166, 28.6.1991, p 77. Directive as amended by Directive 2001/97/EC of the European Parliament and of the Council (OJ L344, 28.12.2001, p 76).
5   OJ L182, 5.7.2001, p 1.
6   OJ L281, 23.11.1995, p 31. Directive as amended by Regulation (EC) No 1882/2003 (OJ L284, 31.10.2003, p 1).
7   OJ L271, 24.10.2000, p 4.
8   OJ L184, 17.7.1999, p 23.

CHAPTER I
SUBJECT MATTER, SCOPE AND DEFINITIONS

Article 1

1.   Member States shall ensure that money laundering and terrorist financing are prohibited.

2.   For the purposes of this Directive, the following conduct, when committed intentionally, shall be regarded as money laundering:

(a)   the conversion or transfer of property, knowing that such property is derived from criminal activity or from an act of participation in such activity, for the purpose of concealing or disguising the illicit origin of the property or of assisting any person who is involved in the commission of such activity to evade the legal consequences of his action;

(b)   the concealment or disguise of the true nature, source, location, disposition, movement, rights with respect to, or ownership of property, knowing that such property is derived from criminal activity or from an act of participation in such activity;

(c)   the acquisition, possession or use of property, knowing, at the time of receipt, that such property was derived from criminal activity or from an act of participation in such activity;

(d)   participation in, association to commit, attempts to commit and aiding, abetting, facilitating and counselling the commission of any of the actions mentioned in the foregoing points.

3.   Money laundering shall be regarded as such even where the activities which generated the property to be laundered were carried out in the territory of another Member State or in that of a third country.

4.   For the purposes of this Directive, "terrorist financing" means the provision or collection of funds, by any means, directly or indirectly, with the intention that they should be used or in the knowledge that they are to be used, in full or in part, in order to carry out any of the offences within the meaning of Articles 1 to 4 of Council Framework Decision 2002/475/JHA of 13 June 2002 on combating terrorism[1].

5.   Knowledge, intent or purpose required as an element of the activities mentioned in paragraphs 2 and 4 may be inferred from objective factual circumstances.

[4466]

NOTES

1   OJ L164, 22.6.2002, p 3.

Article 2

1. This Directive shall apply to:
   (1) credit institutions;
   (2) financial institutions;
   (3) the following legal or natural persons acting in the exercise of their professional activities:
   (a) auditors, external accountants and tax advisors;
   (b) notaries and other independent legal professionals, when they participate, whether by acting on behalf of and for their client in any financial or real estate transaction, or by assisting in the planning or execution of transactions for their client concerning the:

   (i)   buying and selling of real property or business entities;

   (ii)   managing of client money, securities or other assets;

   (iii) opening or management of bank, savings or securities accounts;

   (iv)   organisation of contributions necessary for the creation, operation or management of companies;

   (v)   creation, operation or management of trusts, companies or similar structures;

   (c) trust or company service providers not already covered under points (a) or (b);
   (d) real estate agents;
   (e) other natural or legal persons trading in goods, only to the extent that payments are made in cash in an amount of EUR 15000 or more, whether the transaction is executed in a single operation or in several operations which appear to be linked;
   (f) casinos.

2. Member States may decide that legal and natural persons who engage in a financial activity on an occasional or very limited basis and where there is little risk of money laundering or terrorist financing occurring do not fall within the scope of Article 3(1) or (2).

[4467]

Article 3

For the purposes of this Directive the following definitions shall apply:
   (1) 'credit institution' means a credit institution, as defined in the first subparagraph of Article 1(1) of Directive 2000/12/EC of the European Parliament and of the Council of 20 March 2000 relating to the taking up and pursuit of the business of credit institutions[1], including branches within the meaning of Article 1(3) of that Directive located in the Community of credit institutions having their head offices inside or outside the Community;
   (2) 'financial institution' means:
   [(a) an undertaking, other than a credit institution, which carries out one or more of the operations included in points 2 to 12 and points 14 and 15 of Annex I to Directive 2006/48/EC, including the activities of currency exchange offices (bureaux de change);]
   (b) an insurance company duly authorised in accordance with Directive 2002/83/EC of the European Parliament and of the Council of 5 November 2002 concerning life assurance[2], insofar as it carries out activities covered by that Directive;
   (c) an investment firm as defined in point 1 of Article 4(1) of Directive 2004/39/EC of the European Parliament and of the Council of 21 April 2004 on markets in financial instruments[3];
   (d) a collective investment undertaking marketing its units or shares;
   (e) an insurance intermediary as defined in Article 2(5) of Directive 2002/92/EC of the European Parliament and of the Council of 9 December 2002 on insurance mediation[4], with the exception of intermediaries as mentioned in Article 2(7) of that Directive, when they act in respect of life insurance and other investment related services;
   (f) branches, when located in the Community, of financial institutions as referred to in points (a) to (e), whose head offices are inside or outside the Community;
   (3) 'property' means assets of every kind, whether corporeal or incorporeal, movable or immovable, tangible or intangible, and legal documents or instruments in any form including electronic or digital, evidencing title to or an interest in such assets;
   (4) 'criminal activity' means any kind of criminal involvement in the commission of a serious crime;
   (5) 'serious crimes' means, at least:
   (a) acts as defined in Articles 1 to 4 of Framework Decision 2002/475/JHA;
   (b) any of the offences defined in Article 3(1)(a) of the 1988 United Nations Convention against Illicit Traffic in Narcotic Drugs and Psychotropic Substances;
   (c) the activities of criminal organisations as defined in Article 1 of Council Joint

Action 98/733/JHA of 21 December 1998 on making it a criminal offence to participate in a criminal organisation in the Member States of the European Union[5];

(d) fraud, at least serious, as defined in Article 1(1) and Article 2 of the Convention on the Protection of the European Communities' Financial Interests[6];

(e) corruption;

(f) all offences which are punishable by deprivation of liberty or a detention order for a maximum of more than one year or, as regards those States which have a minimum threshold for offences in their legal system, all offences punishable by deprivation of liberty or a detention order for a minimum of more than six months;

(6) 'beneficial owner' means the natural person(s) who ultimately owns or controls the customer and/or the natural person on whose behalf a transaction or activity is being conducted. The beneficial owner shall at least include:

(a) in the case of corporate entities:

(i) the natural person(s) who ultimately owns or controls a legal entity through direct or indirect ownership or control over a sufficient percentage of the shares or voting rights in that legal entity, including through bearer share holdings, other than a company listed on a regulated market that is subject to disclosure requirements consistent with Community legislation or subject to equivalent international standards; a percentage of 25% plus one share shall be deemed sufficient to meet this criterion;

(ii) the natural person(s) who otherwise exercises control over the management of a legal entity:

(b) in the case of legal entities, such as foundations, and legal arrangements, such as trusts, which administer and distribute funds:

(i) where the future beneficiaries have already been determined, the natural person(s) who is the beneficiary of 25% or more of the property of a legal arrangement or entity;

(ii) where the individuals that benefit from the legal arrangement or entity have yet to be determined, the class of persons in whose main interest the legal arrangement or entity is set up or operates;

(iii) the natural person(s) who exercises control over 25% or more of the property of a legal arrangement or entity;

(7) 'trust and company service providers' means any natural or legal person which by way of business provides any of the following services to third parties:

(a) forming companies or other legal persons;

(b) acting as or arranging for another person to act as a director or secretary of a company, a partner of a partnership, or a similar position in relation to other legal persons;

(c) providing a registered office, business address, correspondence or administrative address and other related services for a company, a partnership or any other legal person or arrangement;

(d) acting as or arranging for another person to act as a trustee of an express trust or a similar legal arrangement;

(e) acting as or arranging for another person to act as a nominee shareholder for another person other than a company listed on a regulated market that is subject to disclosure requirements in conformity with Community legislation or subject to equivalent international standards;

(8) 'politically exposed persons' means natural persons who are or have been entrusted with prominent public functions and immediate family members, or persons known to be close associates, of such persons;

(9) 'business relationship' means a business, professional or commercial relationship which is connected with the professional activities of the institutions and persons covered by this Directive and which is expected, at the time when the contact is established, to have an element of duration;

(10) 'shell bank' means a credit institution, or an institution engaged in equivalent activities, incorporated in a jurisdiction in which it has no physical presence, involving meaningful mind and management, and which is unaffiliated with a regulated financial group.

[4468]

NOTES

Para 2: sub-para (a) substituted by European Parliament and Council Directive 2009/110/EC, Art 19(1).

[1] OJ L126, 26.5.2000, p 1. Directive as last amended by Directive 2005/1/EC (OJ L79, 24.3.2005, p 9).
[2] OJ L345, 19.12.2002, p 1. Directive as last amended by Directive 2005/1/EC.
[3] OJ L145, 30.4.2004, p 1.
[4] OJ L9, 15.1.2003, p 3.
[5] OJ L351, 29.12.1998, p 1.

⁶　　OJ C316, 27.11.1995, p 49.

Article 4

1.　Member States shall ensure that the provisions of this Directive are extended in whole or in part to professions and to categories of undertakings, other than the institutions and persons referred to in Article 2(1), which engage in activities which are particularly likely to be used for money laundering or terrorist financing purposes.

2.　Where a Member State decides to extend the provisions of this Directive to professions and to categories of undertakings other than those referred to in Article 2(1), it shall inform the Commission thereof.

[4469]

Article 5

The Member States may adopt or retain in force stricter provisions in the field covered by this Directive to prevent money laundering and terrorist financing.

[4470]

CHAPTER II
CUSTOMER DUE DILIGENCE

SECTION 1
General provisions

Article 6

Member States shall prohibit their credit and financial institutions from keeping anonymous accounts or anonymous passbooks. By way of derogation from Article 9(6), Member States shall in all cases require that the owners and beneficiaries of existing anonymous accounts or anonymous passbooks be made the subject of customer due diligence measures as soon as possible and in any event before such accounts or passbooks are used in any way.

[4471]

Article 7

The institutions and persons covered by this Directive shall apply customer due diligence measures in the following cases:
- (a)　when establishing a business relationship;
- (b)　when carrying out occasional transactions amounting to EUR 15000 or more, whether the transaction is carried out in a single operation or in several operations which appear to be linked;
- (c)　when there is a suspicion of money laundering or terrorist financing, regardless of any derogation, exemption or threshold;
- (d)　when there are doubts about the veracity or adequacy of previously obtained customer identification data.

[4472]

Article 8

1.　Customer due diligence measures shall comprise:
- (a)　identifying the customer and verifying the customer's identity on the basis of documents, data or information obtained from a reliable and independent source;
- (b)　identifying, where applicable, the beneficial owner and taking risk-based and adequate measures to verify his identity so that the institution or person covered by this Directive is satisfied that it knows who the beneficial owner is, including, as regards legal persons, trusts and similar legal arrangements, taking risk-based and adequate measures to understand the ownership and control structure of the customer;
- (c)　obtaining information on the purpose and intended nature of the business relationship;
- (d)　conducting ongoing monitoring of the business relationship including scrutiny of transactions undertaken throughout the course of that relationship to ensure that the transactions being conducted are consistent with the institution's or person's knowledge of the customer, the business and risk profile, including, where necessary, the source of funds and ensuring that the documents, data or information held are kept up-to-date.

2.　The institutions and persons covered by this Directive shall apply each of the customer due diligence requirements set out in paragraph 1, but may determine the extent of such measures on a risk-sensitive basis depending on the type of customer, business relationship, product or transaction. The institutions and persons covered by this Directive shall be able to demonstrate to the competent authorities mentioned in Article 37, including self-regulatory bodies, that the extent of the measures is appropriate in view of the risks of money laundering and terrorist financing.

[4473]

Article 9

1.   Member States shall require that the verification of the identity of the customer and the beneficial owner takes place before the establishment of a business relationship or the carrying-out of the transaction.

2.   By way of derogation from paragraph 1, Member States may allow the verification of the identity of the customer and the beneficial owner to be completed during the establishment of a business relationship if this is necessary not to interrupt the normal conduct of business and where there is little risk of money laundering or terrorist financing occurring. In such situations these procedures shall be completed as soon as practicable after the initial contact.

3.   By way of derogation from paragraphs 1 and 2, Member States may, in relation to life insurance business, allow the verification of the identity of the beneficiary under the policy to take place after the business relationship has been established. In that case, verification shall take place at or before the time of payout or at or before the time the beneficiary intends to exercise rights vested under the policy.

4.   By way of derogation from paragraphs 1 and 2, Member States may allow the opening of a bank account provided that there are adequate safeguards in place to ensure that transactions are not carried out by the customer or on its behalf until full compliance with the aforementioned provisions is obtained.

5.   Member States shall require that, where the institution or person concerned is unable to comply with points (a), (b) and (c) of Article 8(1), it may not carry out a transaction through a bank account, establish a business relationship or carry out the transaction, or shall terminate the business relationship, and shall consider making a report to the financial intelligence unit (FIU) in accordance with Article 22 in relation to the customer.

Member States shall not be obliged to apply the previous subparagraph in situations when notaries, independent legal professionals, auditors, external accountants and tax advisors are in the course of ascertaining the legal position for their client or performing their task of defending or representing that client in, or concerning judicial proceedings, including advice on instituting or avoiding proceedings.

6.   Member States shall require that institutions and persons covered by this Directive apply the customer due diligence procedures not only to all new customers but also at appropriate times to existing customers on a risk-sensitive basis.

[4474]

Article 10

1.   Member States shall require that all casino customers be identified and their identity verified if they purchase or exchange gambling chips with a value of EUR 2000 or more.

2.   Casinos subject to State supervision shall be deemed in any event to have satisfied the customer due diligence requirements if they register, identify and verify the identity of their customers immediately on or before entry, regardless of the amount of gambling chips purchased.

[4475]

SECTION 2

Simplified customer due diligence

Article 11

1.   By way of derogation from Articles 7(a), (b) and (d), 8 and 9(1), the institutions and persons covered by this Directive shall not be subject to the requirements provided for in those Articles where the customer is a credit or financial institution covered by this Directive, or a credit or financial institution situated in a third country which imposes requirements equivalent to those laid down in this Directive and supervised for compliance with those requirements.

2.   By way of derogation from Articles 7(a), (b) and (d), 8 and 9(1) Member States may allow the institutions and persons covered by this Directive not to apply customer due diligence in respect of:

(a)   listed companies whose securities are admitted to trading on a regulated market within the meaning of Directive 2004/39/EC in one or more Member States and listed companies from third countries which are subject to disclosure requirements consistent with Community legislation;

(b)   beneficial owners of pooled accounts held by notaries and other independent legal professionals from the Member States, or from third countries provided that they are subject to requirements to combat money laundering or terrorist financing consistent with international standards and are supervised for compliance with those requirements and provided that the information on the identity of the beneficial owner is available, on request, to the institutions that act as depository institutions for the pooled accounts;

(c)   domestic public authorities,

or in respect of any other customer representing a low risk of money laundering or terrorist financing which meets the technical criteria established in accordance with Article 40(1)(b).

3. In the cases mentioned in paragraphs 1 and 2, institutions and persons covered by this Directive shall in any case gather sufficient information to establish if the customer qualifies for an exemption as mentioned in these paragraphs.

4. The Member States shall inform each other and the Commission of cases where they consider that a third country meets the conditions laid down in paragraphs 1 or 2 or in other situations which meet the technical criteria established in accordance with Article 40(1)(b).

5. By way of derogation from Articles 7(a), (b) and (d), 8 and 9(1), Member States may allow the institutions and persons covered by this Directive not to apply customer due diligence in respect of:

    (a)   life insurance policies where the annual premium is no more than EUR 1000 or the single premium is no more than EUR 2500;

    (b)   insurance policies for pension schemes if there is no surrender clause and the policy cannot be used as collateral;

    (c)   a pension, superannuation or similar scheme that provides retirement benefits to employees, where contributions are made by way of deduction from wages and the scheme rules do not permit the assignment of a member's interest under the scheme;

    [(d)   electronic money, as defined in point 2 of Article 2 of Directive 2009/110/EC of the European Parliament and of the Council of 16 September 2009 on the taking up, pursuit and prudential supervision of the business of electronic money institutions[1] where, if it is not possible to recharge, the maximum amount stored electronically in the device is no more than EUR 250, or where, if it is possible to recharge, a limit of EUR 2 500 is imposed on the total amount transacted in a calendar year, except when an amount of EUR 1 000 or more is redeemed in that same calendar year upon the electronic money holder's request in accordance with Article 11 of Directive 2009/110/EC. As regards national payment transactions, Member States or their competent authorities may increase the amount of EUR 250 referred to in this point to a ceiling of EUR 500.]

or in respect of any other product or transaction representing a low risk of money laundering or terrorist financing which meets the technical criteria established in accordance with Article 40(1)(b).

[4476]

NOTES

Para 5: sub-para (d) substituted by European Parliament and Council Directive 2009/110/EC, Art 19(2).
  [1]   OJ L267, 10.10.2009, p 7.

Article 12

Where the Commission adopts a decision pursuant to Article 40(4), the Member States shall prohibit the institutions and persons covered by this Directive from applying simplified due diligence to credit and financial institutions or listed companies from the third country concerned or other entities following from situations which meet the technical criteria established in accordance with Article 40(1)(b).

[4477]

SECTION 3
Enhanced customer due diligence

Article 13

1. Member States shall require the institutions and persons covered by this Directive to apply, on a risk-sensitive basis, enhanced customer due diligence measures, in addition to the measures referred to in Articles 7, 8 and 9(6), in situations which by their nature can present a higher risk of money laundering or terrorist financing, and at least in the situations set out in paragraphs 2, 3, 4 and in other situations representing a high risk of money laundering or terrorist financing which meet the technical criteria established in accordance with Article 40(1)(c).

2. Where the customer has not been physically present for identification purposes, Member States shall require those institutions and persons to take specific and adequate measures to compensate for the higher risk, for example by applying one or more of the following measures:

    (a)   ensuring that the customer's identity is established by additional documents, data or information;

    (b)   supplementary measures to verify or certify the documents supplied, or requiring confirmatory certification by a credit or financial institution covered by this Directive;

    (c)   ensuring that the first payment of the operations is carried out through an account opened in the customer's name with a credit institution.

3. In respect of cross-frontier correspondent banking relationships with respondent institutions from third countries, Member States shall require their credit institutions to:

    (a)   gather sufficient information about a respondent institution to understand fully the nature of the respondent's business and to determine from publicly available information the reputation of the institution and the quality of supervision;

    (b)   assess the respondent institution's anti-money laundering and anti-terrorist financing controls;

    (c)   obtain approval from senior management before establishing new correspondent banking relationships;

    (d)   document the respective responsibilities of each institution;

    (e)   with respect to payable-through accounts, be satisfied that the respondent credit institution has verified the identity of and performed ongoing due diligence on the customers having direct access to accounts of the correspondent and that it is able to provide relevant customer due diligence data to the correspondent institution, upon request.

4.   In respect of transactions or business relationships with politically exposed persons residing in another Member State or in a third country, Member States shall require those institutions and persons covered by this Directive to:

    (a)   have appropriate risk-based procedures to determine whether the customer is a politically exposed person;

    (b)   have senior management approval for establishing business relationships with such customers;

    (c)   take adequate measures to establish the source of wealth and source of funds that are involved in the business relationship or transaction;

    (d)   conduct enhanced ongoing monitoring of the business relationship.

5.   Member States shall prohibit credit institutions from entering into or continuing a correspondent banking relationship with a shell bank and shall require that credit institutions take appropriate measures to ensure that they do not engage in or continue correspondent banking relationships with a bank that is known to permit its accounts to be used by a shell bank.

6.   Member States shall ensure that the institutions and persons covered by this Directive pay special attention to any money laundering or terrorist financing threat that may arise from products or transactions that might favour anonymity, and take measures, if needed, to prevent their use for money laundering or terrorist financing purposes.

[4478]

SECTION 4

Performance by third parties

Article 14

Member States may permit the institutions and persons covered by this Directive to rely on third parties to meet the requirements laid down in Article 8(1)(a) to (c). However, the ultimate responsibility for meeting those requirements shall remain with the institution or person covered by this Directive which relies on the third party.

[4479]

Article 15

[1.   Where a Member State permits credit and financial institutions referred to in Article 2(1)(1) or (2) situated in its territory to be relied on as a third party domestically, that Member State shall in any case permit institutions and persons referred to in Article 2(1) situated in its territory to recognise and accept, in accordance with Article 14, the outcome of the customer due diligence requirements laid down in Article 8(1)(a) to (c), carried out in accordance with this Directive by an institution referred to in Article 2 (1)(1) or (2) in another Member State, with the exception of currency exchange offices and payment institutions as defined in Article 4(4) of Directive 2007/64/EC of the European Parliament and of the Council of 13 November 2007 on payment services in the internal market[1], which mainly provide the payment service listed in point 6 of the Annex to that Directive, including natural and legal persons benefiting from a waiver under Article 26 of that Directive, and meeting the requirements laid down in Articles 16 and 18 of this Directive, even if the documents or data on which these requirements have been based are different to those required in the Member State to which the customer is being referred.

2.   Where a Member State permits currency exchange offices referred to in Article 3(2)(a) and payment institutions as defined in Article 4(4) of Directive 2007/64/EC, which mainly provide the payment service listed in point 6 of the Annex to that Directive, situated in its territory to be relied on as a third party domestically, that Member State shall in any case permit them to recognise and accept, in accordance with Article 14 of this Directive, the outcome of the customer due diligence requirements laid down in Article 8(1)(a) to (c), carried out in accordance with this Directive by the same category of institution in another Member State and meeting the requirements laid down in Articles 16 and 18 of this Directive, even if the documents or data on which these requirements have been based are different to those required in the Member State to which the customer is being referred.]

3. Where a Member State permits persons referred to in Article 2(1)(3)(a) to (c) situated in its territory to be relied on as a third party domestically, that Member State shall in any case permit them to recognise and accept, in accordance with Article 14, the outcome of the customer due diligence requirements laid down in Article 8(1)(a) to (c), carried out in accordance with this Directive by a person referred to in Article 2(1)(3)(a) to (c) in another Member State and meeting the requirements laid down in Articles 16 and 18, even if the documents or data on which these requirements have been based are different to those required in the Member State to which the customer is being referred.

[4480]

NOTES
Paras 1, 2: substituted by European Parliament and Council Directive 2007/64/EC, Art 91(2).
¹   OJ L319, 5.12.2007, p 1.

Article 16

1. For the purposes of this Section, 'third parties' shall mean institutions and persons who are listed in Article 2, or equivalent institutions and persons situated in a third country, who meet the following requirements:
   (a) they are subject to mandatory professional registration, recognised by law;
   (b) they apply customer due diligence requirements and record keeping requirements as laid down or equivalent to those laid down in this Directive and their compliance with the requirements of this Directive is supervised in accordance with Section 2 of Chapter V, or they are situated in a third country which imposes equivalent requirements to those laid down in this Directive.

2. Member States shall inform each other and the Commission of cases where they consider that a third country meets the conditions laid down in paragraph 1(b).

[4481]

Article 17

Where the Commission adopts a decision pursuant to Article 40(4), Member States shall prohibit the institutions and persons covered by this Directive from relying on third parties from the third country concerned to meet the requirements laid down in Article 8(1)(a) to (c).

[4482]

Article 18

1. Third parties shall make information requested in accordance with the requirements laid down in Article 8(1)(a) to (c) immediately available to the institution or person covered by this Directive to which the customer is being referred.

2. Relevant copies of identification and verification data and other relevant documentation on the identity of the customer or the beneficial owner shall immediately be forwarded, on request, by the third party to the institution or person covered by this Directive to which the customer is being referred.

[4483]

Article 19

This Section shall not apply to outsourcing or agency relationships where, on the basis of a contractual arrangement, the outsourcing service provider or agent is to be regarded as part of the institution or person covered by this Directive.

[4484]

CHAPTER III
REPORTING OBLIGATIONS

SECTION 1

General provisions

Article 20

Member States shall require that the institutions and persons covered by this Directive pay special attention to any activity which they regard as particularly likely, by its nature, to be related to money laundering or terrorist financing and in particular complex or unusually large transactions and all unusual patterns of transactions which have no apparent economic or visible lawful purpose.

[4485]

Article 21

1. Each Member State shall establish a FIU in order effectively to combat money laundering and terrorist financing.

2.   That FIU shall be established as a central national unit. It shall be responsible for receiving (and to the extent permitted, requesting), analysing and disseminating to the competent authorities, disclosures of information which concern potential money laundering, potential terrorist financing or are required by national legislation or regulation. It shall be provided with adequate resources in order to fulfil its tasks.

3.   Member States shall ensure that the FIU has access, directly or indirectly, on a timely basis, to the financial, administrative and law enforcement information that it requires to properly fulfil its tasks.

[4486]

Article 22

1.   Member States shall require the institutions and persons covered by this Directive, and where applicable their directors and employees, to cooperate fully:
    (a)   by promptly informing the FIU, on their own initiative, where the institution or person covered by this Directive knows, suspects or has reasonable grounds to suspect that money laundering or terrorist financing is being or has been committed or attempted;
    (b)   by promptly furnishing the FIU, at its request, with all necessary information, in accordance with the procedures established by the applicable legislation.

2.   The information referred to in paragraph 1 shall be forwarded to the FIU of the Member State in whose territory the institution or person forwarding the information is situated. The person or persons designated in accordance with the procedures provided for in Article 34 shall normally forward the information.

[4487]

Article 23

1.   By way of derogation from Article 22(1), Member States may, in the case of the persons referred to in Article 2(1)(3)(a) and (b), designate an appropriate self-regulatory body of the profession concerned as the authority to be informed in the first instance in place of the FIU. Without prejudice to paragraph 2, the designated self-regulatory body shall in such cases forward the information to the FIU promptly and unfiltered.

2.   Member States shall not be obliged to apply the obligations laid down in Article 22(1) to notaries, independent legal professionals, auditors, external accountants and tax advisors with regard to information they receive from or obtain on one of their clients, in the course of ascertaining the legal position for their client or performing their task of defending or representing that client in, or concerning judicial proceedings, including advice on instituting or avoiding proceedings, whether such information is received or obtained before, during or after such proceedings.

[4488]

Article 24

1.   Member States shall require the institutions and persons covered by this Directive to refrain from carrying out transactions which they know or suspect to be related to money laundering or terrorist financing until they have completed the necessary action in accordance with Article 22(1)(a). In conformity with the legislation of the Member States, instructions may be given not to carry out the transaction.

2.   Where such a transaction is suspected of giving rise to money laundering or terrorist financing and where to refrain in such manner is impossible or is likely to frustrate efforts to pursue the beneficiaries of a suspected money laundering or terrorist financing operation, the institutions and persons concerned shall inform the FIU immediately afterwards.

[4489]

Article 25

1.   Member States shall ensure that if, in the course of inspections carried out in the institutions and persons covered by this Directive by the competent authorities referred to in Article 37, or in any other way, those authorities discover facts that could be related to money laundering or terrorist financing, they shall promptly inform the FIU.

2.   Member States shall ensure that supervisory bodies empowered by law or regulation to oversee the stock, foreign exchange and financial derivatives markets inform the FIU if they discover facts that could be related to money laundering or terrorist financing.

[4490]

Article 26

The disclosure in good faith as foreseen in Articles 22(1) and 23 by an institution or person covered by this Directive or by an employee or director of such an institution or person of the information referred to in Articles 22 and 23 shall not constitute a breach of any restriction on disclosure of information imposed by contract or by any legislative, regulatory or administrative provision, and shall not involve the institution or person or its directors or employees in liability of any kind.

[4491]

Article 27

Member States shall take all appropriate measures in order to protect employees of the institutions or persons covered by this Directive who report suspicions of money laundering or terrorist financing either internally or to the FIU from being exposed to threats or hostile action.

[4492]

SECTION 2

Prohibition of disclosure

Article 28

1. The institutions and persons covered by this Directive and their directors and employees shall not disclose to the customer concerned or to other third persons the fact that information has been transmitted in accordance with Articles 22 and 23 or that a money laundering or terrorist financing investigation is being or may be carried out.

2. The prohibition laid down in paragraph 1 shall not include disclosure to the competent authorities referred to in Article 37, including the self-regulatory bodies, or disclosure for law enforcement purposes.

3. The prohibition laid down in paragraph 1 shall not prevent disclosure between institutions from Member States, or from third countries provided that they meet the conditions laid down in Article 11(1), belonging to the same group as defined by Article 2(12) of Directive 2002/87/EC of the European Parliament and of the Council of 16 December 2002 on the supplementary supervision of credit institutions, insurance undertakings and investment firms in a financial conglomerate[1].

4. The prohibition laid down in paragraph 1 shall not prevent disclosure between persons referred to in Article 2(1)(3)(a) and (b) from Member States, or from third countries which impose requirements equivalent to those laid down in this Directive, who perform their professional activities, whether as employees or not, within the same legal person or a network. For the purposes of this Article, a 'network' means the larger structure to which the person belongs and which shares common ownership, management or compliance control.

5. For institutions or persons referred to in Article 2(1)(1), (2) and (3)(a) and (b) in cases related to the same customer and the same transaction involving two or more institutions or persons, the prohibition laid down in paragraph 1 shall not prevent disclosure between the relevant institutions or persons provided that they are situated in a Member State, or in a third country which imposes requirements equivalent to those laid down in this Directive, and that they are from the same professional category and are subject to equivalent obligations as regards professional secrecy and personal data protection. The information exchanged shall be used exclusively for the purposes of the prevention of money laundering and terrorist financing.

6. Where the persons referred to in Article 2(1)(3)(a) and (b) seek to dissuade a client from engaging in illegal activity, this shall not constitute a disclosure within the meaning of the paragraph 1.

7. The Member States shall inform each other and the Commission of cases where they consider that a third country meets the conditions laid down in paragraphs 3, 4 or 5.

[4493]

NOTES
1   OJ L35, 11.2.2003, p 1.

Article 29

Where the Commission adopts a decision pursuant to Article 40(4), the Member States shall prohibit the disclosure between institutions and persons covered by this Directive and institutions and persons from the third country concerned.

[4494]

CHAPTER IV
RECORD KEEPING AND STATISTICAL DATA

Article 30

Member States shall require the institutions and persons covered by this Directive to keep the following documents and information for use in any investigation into, or analysis of, possible money laundering or terrorist financing by the FIU or by other competent authorities in accordance with national law:

   (a)   in the case of the customer due diligence, a copy or the references of the evidence required, for a period of at least five years after the business relationship with their customer has ended;

   (b)   in the case of business relationships and transactions, the supporting evidence and records, consisting of the original documents or copies admissible in court proceedings under the applicable national legislation for a period of at least five years following the carrying-out of the transactions or the end of the business relationship.

[4495]

Article 31

1. Member States shall require the credit and financial institutions covered by this Directive to apply, where applicable, in their branches and majority-owned subsidiaries located in third countries measures at least equivalent to those laid down in this Directive with regard to customer due diligence and record keeping.

Where the legislation of the third country does not permit application of such equivalent measures, the Member States shall require the credit and financial institutions concerned to inform the competent authorities of the relevant home Member State accordingly.

2. Member States and the Commission shall inform each other of cases where the legislation of the third country does not permit application of the measures required under the first subparagraph of paragraph 1 and coordinated action could be taken to pursue a solution.

3. Member States shall require that, where the legislation of the third country does not permit application of the measures required under the first subparagraph of paragraph 1, credit or financial institutions take additional measures to effectively handle the risk of money laundering or terrorist financing.

[4496]

Article 32

Member States shall require that their credit and financial institutions have systems in place that enable them to respond fully and rapidly to enquiries from the FIU, or from other authorities, in accordance with their national law, as to whether they maintain or have maintained during the previous five years a business relationship with specified natural or legal persons and on the nature of that relationship.

[4497]

Article 33

1. Member States shall ensure that they are able to review the effectiveness of their systems to combat money laundering or terrorist financing by maintaining comprehensive statistics on matters relevant to the effectiveness of such systems.

2. Such statistics shall as a minimum cover the number of suspicious transaction reports made to the FIU, the follow-up given to these reports and indicate on an annual basis the number of cases investigated, the number of persons prosecuted, the number of persons convicted for money laundering or terrorist financing offences and how much property has been frozen, seized or confiscated.

3. Member States shall ensure that a consolidated review of these statistical reports is published.

[4498]

CHAPTER V
ENFORCEMENT MEASURES

SECTION 1

Internal procedures, training and feedback

Article 34

1. Member States shall require that the institutions and persons covered by this Directive establish adequate and appropriate policies and procedures of customer due diligence, reporting, record keeping, internal control, risk assessment, risk management, compliance management and communication in order to forestall and prevent operations related to money laundering or terrorist financing.

2. Member States shall require that credit and financial institutions covered by this Directive communicate relevant policies and procedures where applicable to branches and majority-owned subsidiaries in third countries.

[4499]

Article 35

1. Member States shall require that the institutions and persons covered by this Directive take appropriate measures so that their relevant employees are aware of the provisions in force on the basis of this Directive.

These measures shall include participation of their relevant employees in special ongoing training programmes to help them recognise operations which may be related to money laundering or terrorist financing and to instruct them as to how to proceed in such cases.

Where a natural person falling within any of the categories listed in Article 2(1)(3) performs his professional activities as an employee of a legal person, the obligations in this Section shall apply to that legal person rather than to the natural person.

2. Member States shall ensure that the institutions and persons covered by this Directive have access to up-to-date information on the practices of money launderers and terrorist financers and on indications leading to the recognition of suspicious transactions.

3. Member States shall ensure that, wherever practicable, timely feedback on the effectiveness of and follow-up to reports of suspected money laundering or terrorist financing is provided.

[4500]

SECTION 2

Supervision

Article 36

1. Member States shall provide that currency exchange offices and trust and company service providers shall be licensed or registered and casinos be licensed in order to operate their business legally. ...

2. Member States shall require competent authorities to refuse licensing or registration of the entities referred to in paragraph 1 if they are not satisfied that the persons who effectively direct or will direct the business of such entities or the beneficial owners of such entities are fit and proper persons.

[4501]

NOTES

Para 1: words omitted repealed by European Parliament and Council Directive 2007/64/EC, Art 91(3).

Article 37

1. Member States shall require the competent authorities at least to effectively monitor and to take the necessary measures with a view to ensuring compliance with the requirements of this Directive by all the institutions and persons covered by this Directive.

2. Member States shall ensure that the competent authorities have adequate powers, including the power to compel the production of any information that is relevant to monitoring compliance and perform checks, and have adequate resources to perform their functions.

3. In the case of credit and financial institutions and casinos, competent authorities shall have enhanced supervisory powers, notably the possibility to conduct on-site inspections.

4. In the case of the natural and legal persons referred to in Article 2(1)(3)(a) to (e), Member States may allow the functions referred to in paragraph 1 to be performed on a risk-sensitive basis.

5. In the case of the persons referred to in Article 2(1)(3)(a) and (b), Member States may allow the functions referred to in paragraph 1 to be performed by self-regulatory bodies, provided that they comply with paragraph 2.

[4502]

SECTION 3

Cooperation

Article 38

The Commission shall lend such assistance as may be needed to facilitate coordination, including the exchange of information between FIUs within the Community.

[4503]

SECTION 4

Penalties

Article 39

1. Member States shall ensure that natural and legal persons covered by this Directive can be held liable for infringements of the national provisions adopted pursuant to this Directive. The penalties must be effective, proportionate and dissuasive.

2. Without prejudice to the right of Member States to impose criminal penalties, Member States shall ensure, in conformity with their national law, that the appropriate administrative measures can

be taken or administrative sanctions can be imposed against credit and financial institutions for infringements of the national provisions adopted pursuant to this Directive. Member States shall ensure that these measures or sanctions are effective, proportionate and dissuasive.

3.   In the case of legal persons, Member States shall ensure that at least they can be held liable for infringements referred to in paragraph 1 which are committed for their benefit by any person, acting either individually or as part of an organ of the legal person, who has a leading position within the legal person, based on:

   (a)   a power of representation of the legal person;

   (b)   an authority to take decisions on behalf of the legal person, or

   (c)   an authority to exercise control within the legal person.

4.   In addition to the cases already provided for in paragraph 3, Member States shall ensure that legal persons can be held liable where the lack of supervision or control by a person referred to in paragraph 3 has made possible the commission of the infringements referred to in paragraph 1 for the benefit of a legal person by a person under its authority.

[4504]

CHAPTER VI
IMPLEMENTING MEASURES

Article 40

1.   In order to take account of technical developments in the fight against money laundering or terrorist financing and to ensure uniform implementation of this Directive, the Commission may ... adopt the following implementing measures:

   (a)   clarification of the technical aspects of the definitions in Article 3(2)(a) and (d), (6), (7), (8), (9) and (10);

   (b)   establishment of technical criteria for assessing whether situations represent a low risk of money laundering or terrorist financing as referred to in Article 11(2) and (5);

   (c)   establishment of technical criteria for assessing whether situations represent a high risk of money laundering or terrorist financing as referred to in Article 13;

   (d)   establishment of technical criteria for assessing whether, in accordance with Article 2(2), it is justified not to apply this Directive to certain legal or natural persons carrying out a financial activity on an occasional or very limited basis.

[The measures referred to in the first subparagraph, designed to amend non-essential elements of this Directive, inter alia by supplementing it, shall be adopted in accordance with the regulatory procedure with scrutiny referred to in Article 41(2a).]

2.   In any event, the Commission shall adopt the first implementing measures to give effect to paragraphs 1(b) and 1(d) by 15 June 2006.

3.   The Commission shall ... adapt the amounts referred to in Articles 2(1)(3)(e), 7(b), 10(1) and 11(5)(a) and (d) taking into account Community legislation, economic developments and changes in international standards.

[The measures referred to in the first subparagraph, designed to amend non-essential elements of this Directive, shall be adopted in accordance with the regulatory procedure with scrutiny referred to in Article 41(2a).]

4.   Where the Commission finds that a third country does not meet the conditions laid down in Article 11(1) or (2), Article 28(3), (4) or (5), or in the measures established in accordance with paragraph 1(b) of this Article or in Article 16(1)(b), or that the legislation of that third country does not permit application of the measures required under the first subparagraph of Article 31(1), it shall adopt a decision so stating in accordance with the procedure referred to in Article 41(2).

[4505]

NOTES

   Paras 1, 3: words omitted repealed and words in square brackets added by European Parliament and Council Directive 2008/20/EC, Art 1(1), (2).

Article 41

1.   The Commission shall be assisted by a Committee on the Prevention of Money Laundering and Terrorist Financing, hereinafter 'the Committee'.

2.   Where reference is made to this paragraph, Articles 5 and 7 of Decision 1999/468/EC shall apply, having regard to the provisions of Article 8 thereof and provided that the implementing measures adopted in accordance with this procedure do not modify the essential provisions of this Directive.

The period laid down in Article 5(6) of Decision 1999/468/EC shall be set at three months.

[2a.   Where reference is made to this paragraph, Article 5a(1) to (4) and Article 7 of Decision 1999/468/EC shall apply, having regard to the provisions of Article 8 thereof.]

[3. By 31 December 2010, and thereafter at least every three years, the Commission shall review the provisions concerning its implementing powers and present a report to the European Parliament and to the Council on the functioning of those powers. The report shall examine, in particular, the need for the Commission to propose amendments to this Directive in order to ensure the appropriate scope of the implementing powers conferred on the Commission. The conclusion as to whether or not an amendment is necessary shall be accompanied by a detailed statement of reasons. If necessary, the report shall be accompanied by a legislative proposal to amend the provisions conferring implementing powers on the Commission.]

[4506]

NOTES
Para 2a: inserted by European Parliament and Council Directive 2008/20/EC, Art 1(3)(a).
Para 3: substituted, for original paras 3, 4, by European Parliament and Council Directive 2008/20/EC, Art 1(3)(b).

CHAPTER VII
FINAL PROVISIONS

Article 42
By 15 December 2009, and at least at three-yearly intervals thereafter, the Commission shall draw up a report on the implementation of this Directive and submit it to the European Parliament and the Council. For the first such report, the Commission shall include a specific examination of the treatment of lawyers and other independent legal professionals.

[4507]

Article 43
By 15 December 2010, the Commission shall present a report to the European Parliament and to the Council on the threshold percentages in Article 3(6), paying particular attention to the possible expediency and consequences of a reduction of the percentage in points (a)(i), (b)(i) and (b)(iii) of Article 3(6) from 25% to 20%. On the basis of the report the Commission may submit a proposal for amendments to this Directive.

[4508]

Article 44
Directive 91/308/EEC is hereby repealed.

References made to the repealed Directive shall be construed as being made to this Directive and should be read in accordance with the correlation table set out in the Annex.

[4509]

Article 45
1. Member States shall bring into force the laws, regulations and administrative provisions necessary to comply with this Directive by 15 December 2007. They shall forthwith communicate to the Commission the text of those provisions together with a table showing how the provisions of this Directive correspond to the national provisions adopted.

When Member States adopt those measures, they shall contain a reference to this Directive or be accompanied by such a reference on the occasion of their official publication. The methods of making such reference shall be laid down by Member States.

2. Member States shall communicate to the Commission the text of the main provisions of national law which they adopt in the field covered by this Directive.

[4510]

Article 46
This Directive shall enter into force on the 20th day after its publication in the *Official Journal of the European Union*.

[4511]

Article 47
This Directive is addressed to the Member States.

[4512]

Done at Strasbourg, 26 October 2005.

PART 3   EU AND INTERNATIONAL MATERIALS

ANNEX
CORRELATION TABLE

This Directive	Directive 91/308/EEC
Article 1(1)	Article 2
Article 1(2)	Article 1(C)
Article 1(2)(a)	Article 1(C) first point
Article 1(2)(b)	Article 1(C) second point
Article 1(2)(c)	Article 1(C) third point
Article 1(2)(d)	Article 1(C) fourth point
Article 1(3)	Article 1(C), third paragraph
Article 1(4)	
Article 1(5)	Article 1(C), second paragraph
Article 2(1)(1)	Article 2a(1)
Article 2(1)(2)	Article 2a(2)
Article 2(1)(3)(a), (b) and (d) to (f)	Article 2a(3) to (7)
Article 2(1)(3)(c)	
Article 2(2)	
Article 3(1)	Article 1(A)
Article 3(2)(a)	Article 1(B)(1)
Article 3(2)(b)	Article 1(B)(2)
Article 3(2)(c)	Article 1(B)(3)
Article 3(2)(d)	Article 1(B)(4)
Article 3(2)(e)	
Article 3(2)(f)	Article 1(B), second paragraph
Article 3(3)	Article 1(D)
Article 3(4)	Article 1(E), first paragraph
Article 3(5)	Article 1(E), second paragraph
Article 3(5)(a)	
Article 3(5)(b)	Article 1(E), first indent
Article 3(5)(c)	Article 1(E), second indent
Article 3(5)(d)	Article 1(E), third indent
Article 3(5)(e)	Article 1(E), fourth indent
Article 3(5)(f)	Article 1(E), fifth indent, and third paragraph
Article 3(6)	
Article 3(7)	
Article 3(8)	
Article 3(9)	
Article 3(10)	
Article 4	Article 12
Article 5	Article 15
Article 6	
Article 7(a)	Article 3(1)
Article 7(b)	Article 3(2)
Article 7(c)	Article 3(8)
Article 7(d)	Article 3(7)
Article 8(1)(a)	Article 3(1)

This Directive	Directive 91/308/EEC
Article 8(1)(b) to (d)	
Article 8(2)	
Article 9(1)	Article 3(1)
Article 9(2) to (6)	
Article 10	Article 3(5) and (6)
Article 11(1)	Article 3(9)
Article 11(2)	
Article 11(3) and (4)	
Article 11(5)(a)	Article 3(3)
Article 11(5)(b)	Article 3(4)
Article 11(5)(c)	Article 3(4)
Article 11(5)(d)	
Article 12	
Article 13(1) and (2)	Article 3(10) and (11)
Article 13(3) to (5)	
Article 13(6)	Article 5
Article 14	
Article 15	
Article 16	
Article 17	
Article 18	
Article 19	
Article 20	Article 5
Article 21	
Article 22	Article 6(1) and (2)
Article 23	Article 6(3)
Article 24	Article 7
Article 25	Article 10
Article 26	Article 9
Article 27	
Article 28(1)	Article 8(1)
Article 28(2) to (7)	
Article 29	
Article 30(a)	Article 4, first indent
Article 30(b)	Article 4, second indent
Article 31	
Article 32	
Article 33	
Article 34(1)	Article 11(1) (a)
Article 34(2)	
Article 35(1), first paragraph	Article 11(1)(b), first sentence
Article 35(1), second paragraph	Article 11(1)(b) second sentence
Article 35(1), third paragraph	Article 11(1), second paragraph
Article 35(2)	
Article 35(3)	

This Directive	Directive 91/308/EEC
Article 36	
Article 37	
Article 38	
Article 39(1)	Article 14
Article 39(2) to (4)	
Article 40	
Article 41	
Article 42	Article 17
Article 43	
Article 44	
Article 45	Article 16
Article 46	Article 16

[4513]

DIRECTIVE OF THE EUROPEAN PARLIAMENT AND OF THE COUNCIL

of 12 December 2006

concerning misleading and comparative advertising

(2006/114/EC)

(codified version)

(Text with EEA relevance)

NOTES
Date of publication in OJ: OJ L376, 27/12/2006, p 21.
This Directive has been implemented in the UK by the Business Protection from Misleading Marketing Regulations 2008, SI 2008/1276 at **[3646]**.

THE EUROPEAN PARLIAMENT AND THE COUNCIL OF THE EUROPEAN UNION,

Having regard to the Treaty establishing the European Community, and in particular Article 95 thereof,

Having regard to the proposal from the Commission,

Having regard to the opinion of the European Economic and Social Committee[1],

Acting in accordance with the procedure laid down in Article 251 of the Treaty[2],

Whereas:

(1) Council Directive 84/450/EEC of 10 September 1984 concerning misleading and comparative advertising[3] has been substantially amended several times[4]. In the interests of clarity and rationality the said Directive should be codified.

(2) The laws against misleading advertising in force in the Member States differ widely. Since advertising reaches beyond the frontiers of individual Member States, it has a direct effect on the smooth functioning of the internal market.

(3) Misleading and unlawful comparative advertising can lead to distortion of competition within the internal market.

(4) Advertising, whether or not it induces a contract, affects the economic welfare of consumers and traders.

(5) The differences between the laws of the Member States on advertising which misleads business hinder the execution of advertising campaigns beyond national boundaries and thus affect the free circulation of goods and provision of services.

(6) The completion of the internal market means a wide range of choice. Given that consumers and traders can and must make the best possible use of the internal market, and that advertising is a very important means of creating genuine outlets for all goods and services throughout the Community, the basic provisions governing the form and content of comparative advertising should be uniform and the conditions of the use of comparative advertising in the Member States should be harmonised. If these conditions are met, this will help demonstrate objectively the merits of the

various comparable products. Comparative advertising can also stimulate competition between suppliers of goods and services to the consumer's advantage.

(7)   Minimum and objective criteria for determining whether advertising is misleading should be established.

(8)   Comparative advertising, when it compares material, relevant, verifiable and representative features and is not misleading, may be a legitimate means of informing consumers of their advantage. It is desirable to provide a broad concept of comparative advertising to cover all modes of comparative advertising.

(9)   Conditions of permitted comparative advertising, as far as the comparison is concerned, should be established in order to determine which practices relating to comparative advertising may distort competition, be detrimental to competitors and have an adverse effect on consumer choice. Such conditions of permitted advertising should include criteria of objective comparison of the features of goods and services.

(10)   The international conventions on copyright as well as the national provisions on contractual and non-contractual liability should apply when the results of comparative tests carried out by third parties are referred to or reproduced in comparative advertising.

(11)   The conditions of comparative advertising should be cumulative and respected in their entirety. In accordance with the Treaty, the choice of forms and methods for the implementation of these conditions should be left to the Member States, insofar as those forms and methods are not already determined by this Directive.

(12)   These conditions should include, in particular, consideration of the provisions resulting from Council Regulation (EC) No 510/2006 of 20 March 2006 on the protection of geographical indications and designations of origin for agricultural products and foodstuffs[5], and in particular Article 13 thereof, and of the other Community provisions adopted in the agricultural sphere.

(13)   Article 5 of First Council Directive 89/104/EEC of 21 December 1988 to approximate the laws of the Member States relating to trade marks[6] confers exclusive rights on the proprietor of a registered trade mark, including the right to prevent all third parties from using, in the course of trade, any sign which is identical to, or similar to, the trade mark in relation to identical goods or services or even, where appropriate, other goods.

(14)   It may, however, be indispensable, in order to make comparative advertising effective, to identify the goods or services of a competitor, making reference to a trade mark or trade name of which the latter is the proprietor.

(15)   Such use of another's trade mark, trade name or other distinguishing marks does not breach this exclusive right in cases where it complies with the conditions laid down by this Directive, the intended target being solely to distinguish between them and thus to highlight differences objectively.

(16)   Persons or organisations regarded under national law as having a legitimate interest in the matter should have facilities for initiating proceedings against misleading and unlawful comparative advertising, either before a court or before an administrative authority which is competent to decide upon complaints or to initiate appropriate legal proceedings.

(17)   The courts or administrative authorities should have powers enabling them to order or obtain the cessation of misleading and unlawful comparative advertising. In certain cases it may be desirable to prohibit misleading and unlawful comparative advertising even before it is published. However, this in no way implies that Member States are under an obligation to introduce rules requiring the systematic prior vetting of advertising.

(18)   The voluntary control exercised by self-regulatory bodies to eliminate misleading or unlawful comparative advertising may avoid recourse to administrative or judicial action and ought therefore to be encouraged.

(19)   While it is for national law to determine the burden of proof, it is appropriate to enable courts and administrative authorities to require traders to produce evidence as to the accuracy of factual claims they have made.

(20)   Regulating comparative advertising is necessary for the smooth functioning of the internal market. Action at Community level is therefore required. The adoption of a Directive is the appropriate instrument because it lays down uniform general principles while allowing the Member States to choose the form and appropriate method by which to attain these objectives. It is in accordance with the principle of subsidiarity.

(21)   This Directive should be without prejudice to the obligations of the Member States relating to the time-limits for transposition into national law and application of the Directives as set out in Part B of Annex I,

HAVE ADOPTED THIS DIRECTIVE:

NOTES

1   Opinion of 26 October 2006 (not yet published in the Official Journal).

2   Opinion of the European Parliament of 12 October 2006 (not yet published in the Official Journal) and Council Decision of 30 November 2006.

3   OJ L250, 19.9.1984, p 17. Directive as last amended by Directive 2005/29/EC of the European Parliament and of the Council (OJ L149, 11.6.2005, p 22).

4   See Annex I, Part A.

5   OJ L93, 31.3.2006, p 12.
6   OJ L40, 11.2.1989, p 1. Directive as amended by Decision 92/10/EEC (OJ L6, 11.1.1992, p 35).

Article 1

The purpose of this Directive is to protect traders against misleading advertising and the unfair consequences thereof and to lay down the conditions under which comparative advertising is permitted.

[4514]

Article 2

For the purposes of this Directive:

(a)   'advertising' means the making of a representation in any form in connection with a trade, business, craft or profession in order to promote the supply of goods or services, including immovable property, rights and obligations;

(b)   'misleading advertising' means any advertising which in any way, including its presentation, deceives or is likely to deceive the persons to whom it is addressed or whom it reaches and which, by reason of its deceptive nature, is likely to affect their economic behaviour or which, for those reasons, injures or is likely to injure a competitor;

(c)   'comparative advertising' means any advertising which explicitly or by implication identifies a competitor or goods or services offered by a competitor;

(d)   'trader' means any natural or legal person who is acting for purposes relating to his trade, craft, business or profession and anyone acting in the name of or on behalf of a trader;

(e)   'code owner' means any entity, including a trader or group of traders, which is responsible for the formulation and revision of a code of conduct and/or for monitoring compliance with the code by those who have undertaken to be bound by it.

[4515]

Article 3

In determining whether advertising is misleading, account shall be taken of all its features, and in particular of any information it contains concerning:

(a)   the characteristics of goods or services, such as their availability, nature, execution, composition, method and date of manufacture or provision, fitness for purpose, uses, quantity, specification, geographical or commercial origin or the results to be expected from their use, or the results and material features of tests or checks carried out on the goods or services;

(b)   the price or the manner in which the price is calculated, and the conditions on which the goods are supplied or the services provided;

(c)   the nature, attributes and rights of the advertiser, such as his identity and assets, his qualifications and ownership of industrial, commercial or intellectual property rights or his awards and distinctions.

[4516]

Article 4

Comparative advertising shall, as far as the comparison is concerned, be permitted when the following conditions are met:

(a)   it is not misleading within the meaning of Articles 2(b), 3 and 8(1) of this Directive or Articles 6 and 7 of Directive 2005/29/EC of the European Parliament and of the Council of 11 May 2005 concerning unfair business-to-consumer commercial practices in the internal market ("Unfair Commercial Practices Directive")[1];

(b)   it compares goods or services meeting the same needs or intended for the same purpose;

(c)   it objectively compares one or more material, relevant, verifiable and representative features of those goods and services, which may include price;

(d)   it does not discredit or denigrate the trade marks, trade names, other distinguishing marks, goods, services, activities or circumstances of a competitor;

(e)   for products with designation of origin, it relates in each case to products with the same designation;

(f)   it does not take unfair advantage of the reputation of a trade mark, trade name or other distinguishing marks of a competitor or of the designation of origin of competing products;

(g)   it does not present goods or services as imitations or replicas of goods or services bearing a protected trade mark or trade name;

(h)   it does not create confusion among traders, between the advertiser and a competitor or between the advertiser's trade marks, trade names, other distinguishing marks, goods or services and those of a competitor.

[4517]

NOTES
¹   OJ L149, 11.6.2005, p 22.

Article 5

1.   Member States shall ensure that adequate and effective means exist to combat misleading advertising and enforce compliance with the provisions on comparative advertising in the interests of traders and competitors.

Such means shall include legal provisions under which persons or organisations regarded under national law as having a legitimate interest in combating misleading advertising or regulating comparative advertising may:
(a)   take legal action against such advertising; or
(b)   bring such advertising before an administrative authority competent either to decide on complaints or to initiate appropriate legal proceedings.

2.   It shall be for each Member State to decide which of the facilities referred to in the second subparagraph of paragraph 1 shall be available and whether to enable the courts or administrative authorities to require prior recourse to other established means of dealing with complaints, including those referred to in Article 6.

It shall be for each Member State to decide:
(a)   whether these legal facilities may be directed separately or jointly against a number of traders from the same economic sector; and
(b)   whether these legal facilities may be directed against a code owner where the relevant code promotes non-compliance with legal requirements.

3.   Under the provisions referred to in paragraphs 1 and 2, Member States shall confer upon the courts or administrative authorities powers enabling them, in cases where they deem such measures to be necessary taking into account all the interests involved and in particular the public interest:
(a)   to order the cessation of, or to institute appropriate legal proceedings for an order for the cessation of, misleading advertising or unlawful comparative advertising; or
(b)   if the misleading advertising or unlawful comparative advertising has not yet been published but publication is imminent, to order the prohibition of, or to institute appropriate legal proceedings for an order for the prohibition of, such publication.

The first subparagraph shall apply even where there is no proof of actual loss or damage or of intention or negligence on the part of the advertiser.

Member States shall make provision for the measures referred to in the first subparagraph to be taken under an accelerated procedure either with interim effect or with definitive effect, at the Member States' discretion.

4.   Member States may confer upon the courts or administrative authorities powers enabling them, with a view to eliminating the continuing effects of misleading advertising or unlawful comparative advertising, the cessation of which has been ordered by a final decision:
(a)   to require publication of that decision in full or in part and in such form as they deem adequate;
(b)   to require in addition the publication of a corrective statement.

5.   The administrative authorities referred to in point (b) of the second subparagraph of paragraph 1 must:
(a)   be composed so as not to cast doubt on their impartiality;
(b)   have adequate powers, where they decide on complaints, to monitor and enforce the observance of their decisions effectively;
(c)   normally give reasons for their decisions.

6.   Where the powers referred to in paragraphs 3 and 4 are exercised exclusively by an administrative authority, reasons for its decisions shall always be given. In this case, provision must be made for procedures whereby improper or unreasonable exercise of its powers by the administrative authority or improper or unreasonable failure to exercise the said powers can be the subject of judicial review.

[4518]

Article 6

This Directive does not exclude the voluntary control, which Member States may encourage, of misleading or comparative advertising by self-regulatory bodies and recourse to such bodies by the persons or organisations referred to in the second subparagraph of Article 5(1) on condition that proceedings before such bodies are additional to the court or administrative proceedings referred to in that Article.

[4519]

PART 3
EU AND INTERNATIONAL MATERIALS

Article 7

Member States shall confer upon the courts or administrative authorities powers enabling them in the civil or administrative proceedings referred to in Article 5:

(a)   to require the advertiser to furnish evidence as to the accuracy of factual claims in advertising if, taking into account the legitimate interest of the advertiser and any other party to the proceedings, such a requirement appears appropriate on the basis of the circumstances of the particular case and in the case of comparative advertising to require the advertiser to furnish such evidence in a short period of time; and

(b)   to consider factual claims as inaccurate if the evidence demanded in accordance with point (a) is not furnished or is deemed insufficient by the court or administrative authority.

[4520]

Article 8

1.   This Directive shall not preclude Member States from retaining or adopting provisions with a view to ensuring more extensive protection, with regard to misleading advertising, for traders and competitors.

The first subparagraph shall not apply to comparative advertising as far as the comparison is concerned.

2.   The provisions of this Directive shall apply without prejudice to Community provisions on advertising for specific products and/or services or to restrictions or prohibitions on advertising in particular media.

3.   The provisions of this Directive concerning comparative advertising shall not oblige Member States which, in compliance with the provisions of the Treaty, maintain or introduce advertising bans regarding certain goods or services, whether imposed directly or by a body or organisation responsible, under the law of the Member States, for regulating the exercise of a commercial, industrial, craft or professional activity, to permit comparative advertising regarding those goods or services. Where these bans are limited to particular media, this Directive shall apply to the media not covered by these bans.

4.   Nothing in this Directive shall prevent Member States, in compliance with the provisions of the Treaty, from maintaining or introducing bans or limitations on the use of comparisons in the advertising of professional services, whether imposed directly or by a body or organisation responsible, under the law of the Member States, for regulating the exercise of a professional activity.

[4521]

Article 9

Member States shall communicate to the Commission the text of the main provisions of national law which they adopt in the field covered by this Directive.

[4522]

Article 10

Directive 84/450/EEC is hereby repealed, without prejudice to the obligations of the Member States relating to the time-limits for transposition into national law and application of the Directives, as set out in Part B of Annex I.

References made to the repealed Directive shall be construed as being made to this Directive and should be read in accordance with the correlation table set out in Annex II.

[4523]

Article 11

This Directive shall enter into force on 12 December 2007.

[4524]

Article 12

This Directive is addressed to the Member States.

[4525]

Done at Strasbourg, 12 December 2006.

ANNEX I

PART A
REPEALED DIRECTIVE WITH ITS SUCCESSIVE AMENDMENTS

Council Directive 84/450/EEC (OJ L250, 19.9.1984, p 17)	
Directive 97/55/EC of the European Parliament and of the Council (OJ L290, 23.10.1997, p 18)	
Directive 2005/29/EC of the European Parliament and of the Council (OJ L149, 11.6.2005, p 22)	only Article 14

[4526]

PART B
LIST OF TIME-LIMITS FOR TRANSPOSITION INTO NATIONAL LAW AND APPLICATION
(referred to in Article 10)

Directive	*Time-limit for transposition*	*Date of application*
84/450/EEC	1 October 1986	—
97/55/EC	23 April 2000	—
2005/29/EC	12 June 2007	12 December 2007

[4527]

ANNEX II
CORRELATION TABLE

Directive 84/450/EEC	*This Directive*
Article 1	Article 1
Article 2, introductory words	Article 2, introductory words
Article 2, point 1	Article 2(a)
Article 2, point 2	Article 2(b)
Article 2, point 2a	Article 2(c)
Article 2, point 3	Article 2(d)
Article 2, point 4	Article 2(e)
Article 3	Article 3
Article 3a(1)	Article 4
Article 4(1), first subparagraph, first sentence	Article 5(1), first subparagraph
Article 4(1), first subparagraph, second sentence	Article 5(1), second subparagraph
Article 4(1), second subparagraph	Article 5(2), first subparagraph
Article 4(1), third subparagraph	Article 5(2), second subparagraph
Article 4(2), first subparagraph, introductory words	Article 5(3), first subparagraph, introductory words
Article 4(2), first subparagraph, first indent	Article 5(3), first subparagraph, point (a)
Article 4(2), first subparagraph, second indent	Article 5(3), first subparagraph, point (b)
Article 4(2), first subparagraph, final words	Article 5(3), second subparagraph
Article 4(2), second subparagraph, introductory words	Article 5(3), third subparagraph
Article 4(2), second subparagraph, first indent	Article 5(3), third subparagraph

PART 3

EU AND INTERNATIONAL MATERIALS

Directive 84/450/EEC	This Directive
Article 4(2), second subparagraph, second indent	Article 5(3), third subparagraph
Article 4(2), second subparagraph, final words	Article 5(3), third subparagraph
Article 4(2), third subparagraph, introductory words	Article 5(4), introductory words
Article 4(2), third subparagraph, first indent	Article 5(4), point (a)
Article 4(2), third subparagraph, second indent	Article 5(4), point (b)
Article 4(3), first subparagraph	Article 5(5)
Article 4(3), second subparagraph	Article 5(6)
Article 5	Article 6
Article 6	Article 7
Article 7(1)	Article 8(1), first subparagraph
Article 7(2)	Article 8(1), second subparagraph
Article 7(3)	Article 8(2)
Article 7(4)	Article 8(3)
Article 7(5)	Article 8(4)
Article 8, first subparagraph	—
Article 8, second subparagraph	Article 9
—	Article 10
—	Article 11
Article 9	Article 12
—	Annex I
—	Annex II

[4528]

DIRECTIVE OF THE EUROPEAN PARLIAMENT AND OF THE COUNCIL

of 23 April 2008

on credit agreements for consumers and repealing Council Directive 87/102/EEC

(2008/48/EC)

NOTES
Date of publication in OJ: OJ L133, 22.5.2008, p 66.
This Directive has been implemented in the UK by the Consumer Credit (EU Directive) Regulations 2010, SI 2010/1010 at **[3939]**, the Consumer Credit (Total Charge for Credit) Regulations 2010, SI 2010/1011 at **[3944]**, the Consumer Credit (Disclosure of Information) Regulations 2010, SI 2010/1013 at **[3964]**, the Consumer Credit (Agreements) Regulations 2010, SI 2010/1014 at **[3979]**, and the Consumer Credit (Advertisements) Regulations 2010, SI 2010/1970 at **[3991]**.

THE EUROPEAN PARLIAMENT AND THE COUNCIL OF THE EUROPEAN UNION,

Having regard to the Treaty establishing the European Economic Community, and in particular Article 100 thereof,

Having regard to the Treaty establishing the European Community, and in particular Article 95 thereof,

Having regard to the proposal from the Commission,

Having regard to the opinion of the European Economic and Social Committee,[1]

Acting in accordance with the procedure laid down in Article 251 of the Treaty,[2]

Whereas:

(1) Council Directive 87/102/EEC of 22 December 1986 for the approximation of the laws, regulations and administrative provisions of the Member States concerning consumer credit[3] lays down rules at Community level concerning consumer credit agreements.

(2) In 1995, the Commission presented a report on the operation of Directive 87/102/EEC and undertook a broad consultation of the interested parties. In 1997, the Commission presented a summary report of reactions to the 1995 report. A second report was produced in 1996 on the operation of Directive 87/102/EEC.

(3) Those reports and consultations revealed substantial differences between the laws of the various Member States in the field of credit for natural persons in general and consumer credit in particular. An analysis of the national laws transposing Directive 87/102/EEC shows that Member States use a variety of consumer protection mechanisms, in addition to Directive 87/102/EEC, on account of differences in the legal or economic situation at national level.

(4) The *de facto* and *de jure* situation resulting from those national differences in some cases leads to distortions of competition among creditors in the Community and creates obstacles to the internal market where Member States have adopted different mandatory provisions more stringent than those provided for in Directive 87/102/EEC. It restricts consumers' ability to make direct use of the gradually increasing availability of cross-border credit. Those distortions and restrictions may in turn have consequences in terms of the demand for goods and services.

(5) In recent years the types of credit offered to and used by consumers have evolved considerably. New credit instruments have appeared, and their use continues to develop. It is therefore necessary to amend existing provisions and to extend their scope, where appropriate.

(6) In accordance with the Treaty, the internal market comprises an area without internal frontiers in which the free movement of goods and services and freedom of establishment are ensured. The development of a more transparent and efficient credit market within the area without internal frontiers is vital in order to promote the development of cross-border activities.

(7) In order to facilitate the emergence of a well-functioning internal market in consumer credit, it is necessary to make provision for a harmonised Community framework in a number of core areas. In view of the continuously developing market in consumer credit and the increasing mobility of European citizens, forward-looking Community legislation which is able to adapt to future forms of credit and which allows Member States the appropriate degree of flexibility in their implementation should help to establish a modern body of law on consumer credit.

(8) It is important that the market should offer a sufficient degree of consumer protection to ensure consumer confidence. Thus, it should be possible for the free movement of credit offers to take place under optimum conditions for both those who offer credit and those who require it, with due regard to specific situations in the individual Member States.

(9) Full harmonisation is necessary in order to ensure that all consumers in the Community enjoy a high and equivalent level of protection of their interests and to create a genuine internal market. Member States should therefore not be allowed to maintain or introduce national provisions other than those laid down in this Directive. However, such restriction should only apply where there are provisions harmonised in this Directive. Where no such harmonised provisions exist, Member States should remain free to maintain or introduce national legislation. Accordingly, Member States may, for instance, maintain or introduce national provisions on joint and several liability of the seller or the service provider and the creditor. Another example of this possibility for Member States could be the maintenance or introduction of national provisions on the cancellation of a contract for the sale of goods or supply of services if the consumer exercises his right of withdrawal from the credit agreement. In this respect Member States, in the case of open-end credit agreements, should be allowed to fix a minimum period needing to elapse between the time when the creditor asks for reimbursement and the day on which the credit has to be reimbursed.

(10) The definitions contained in this Directive determine the scope of harmonisation. The obligation on Member States to implement the provisions of this Directive should therefore be limited to its scope as determined by those definitions. However, this Directive should be without prejudice to the application by Member States, in accordance with Community law, of the provisions of this Directive to areas not covered by its scope. A Member State could thereby maintain or introduce national legislation corresponding to the provisions of this Directive or certain of its provisions on credit agreements outside the scope of this Directive, for instance on credit agreements involving amounts less than EUR 200 or more than EUR 75 000. Furthermore, Member States could also apply the provisions of this Directive to linked credit which does not fall within the definition of a linked credit agreement as contained in this Directive. Thus, the provisions on linked credit agreements could be applied to credit agreements that serve only partially to finance a contract for the supply of goods or provision of a service.

(11) In the case of specific credit agreements to which only some provisions of this Directive are applicable, Member States should not be allowed to adopt national legislation implementing other provisions of this Directive. However, Member States should remain free to regulate, in their national legislation, such types of credit agreements as regards other aspects not harmonised by this Directive.

(12) Agreements for the provision on a continuing basis of services or for the supply of goods of the same kind, where the consumer pays for them for the duration of their provision by means of instalments, may differ considerably, in terms of the interests of the contractual parties involved, and the modalities and performance of the transactions, from credit agreements covered by this

Directive. Therefore, it should be clarified that such agreements are not regarded as credit agreements for the purposes of this Directive. Such types of agreement include, for example, an insurance contract where the insurance is paid for in monthly instalments.

(13) This Directive should not apply to certain types of credit agreement, such as deferred debit cards, under the terms of which the credit has to be repaid within three months and only insignificant charges are payable.

(14) Credit agreements covering the granting of credit secured by real estate should be excluded from the scope of this Directive. That type of credit is of a very specific nature. Also, credit agreements the purpose of which is to finance the acquisition or retention of property rights in land or in an existing or projected building should be excluded from the scope of this Directive. However, credit agreements should not be excluded from the scope of this Directive only because their purpose is the renovation or increase of value of an existing building.

(15) The provisions of this Directive apply irrespective of whether the creditor is a legal person or a natural person. However, this Directive does not affect the right of Member States to limit, in conformity with Community law, the provision of credit for consumers to legal persons only or to certain legal persons.

(16) Certain provisions of this Directive should apply to natural and legal persons (credit intermediaries) who, in the course of their trade, business or profession, for a fee, present or offer credit agreements to consumers, assist consumers by undertaking preparatory work in respect of credit agreements or conclude credit agreements with consumers on behalf of the creditor. Organisations which allow their identity to be used in promoting credit products, such as credit cards, and which may also recommend those products to their members should not be regarded as credit intermediaries for the purposes of this Directive.

(17) This Directive regulates only certain obligations of credit intermediaries in relation to consumers. Member States should therefore remain free to maintain or introduce additional obligations incumbent on credit intermediaries, including the conditions under which a credit intermediary may receive fees from a consumer who has requested his service.

(18) Consumers should be protected against unfair or misleading practices, in particular with respect to the disclosure of information by the creditor, in line with Directive 2005/29/ EC of the European Parliament and of the Council of 11 May 2005 concerning unfair business-to-consumer commercial practices in the internal market ('Unfair Commercial Practices' Directive).[4] However, this Directive should contain specific provisions on advertising concerning credit agreements as well as certain items of standard information to be provided to consumers in order to enable them, in particular, to compare different offers. Such information should be given in a clear, concise and prominent way by means of a representative example. A ceiling should be provided where it is not possible to indicate the total amount of credit as the total sums made available, in particular where a credit agreement gives the consumer freedom of drawdown with a limitation with regard to the amount. The ceiling should indicate the upper limit of credit which can be made available to the consumer. In addition, Member States should remain free to regulate information requirements in their national law regarding advertising which does not contain information on the cost of the credit.

(19) In order to enable consumers to make their decisions in full knowledge of the facts, they should receive adequate information, which the consumer may take away and consider, prior to the conclusion of the credit agreement, on the conditions and cost of the credit and on their obligations. To ensure the fullest possible transparency and comparability of offers, such information should, in particular, include the annual percentage rate of charge applicable to the credit, determined in the same way throughout the Community. As the annual percentage rate of charge can at this stage be indicated only through an example, such example should be representative. Therefore, it should correspond, for instance, to the average duration and total amount of credit granted for the type of credit agreement under consideration and, if applicable, to the goods purchased. When determining the representative example, the frequency of certain types of credit agreement in a specific market should also be taken into account. As regards the borrowing rate, the frequency of instalments and the capitalisation of interest, creditors should use their conventional method of calculation for the consumer credit concerned.

(20) The total cost of the credit to the consumer should comprise all the costs, including interest, commissions, taxes, fees for credit intermediaries and any other fees which the consumer has to pay in connection with the credit agreement, except for notarial costs. Creditors' actual knowledge of the costs should be assessed objectively, taking into account the requirements of professional diligence.

(21) Credit agreements in which a borrowing rate is periodically revised in line with changes occurring in a reference rate referred to in the credit agreement should not be regarded as credit agreements with a fixed borrowing rate.

(22) Member States should remain free to maintain or introduce national provisions prohibiting the creditor from requiring the consumer, in connection with the credit agreement, to open a bank account or conclude an agreement in respect of another ancillary service, or to pay the expenses or fees for such bank accounts or other ancillary services. In those Member States where such combined offers are allowed, consumers should be informed before the conclusion of the credit agreement about any ancillary services which are compulsory in order for the credit to be obtained in the first place or on the terms and conditions marketed. The costs payable in respect of those ancillary services should be included in the total cost of the credit; alternatively, if the amount of

such costs cannot be determined in advance, consumers should receive adequate information about the existence of costs at a pre-contractual stage. The creditor must be presumed to have knowledge of the costs of the ancillary services which he offers to the consumer himself, or on behalf of a third party, unless the price thereof depends on the specific characteristics or situation of the consumer.

(23)   For specific types of credit agreements, however, it is appropriate, in order to ensure an adequate level of consumer protection without placing an excessive burden on creditors or, where applicable, credit intermediaries, to restrict the pre-contractual information requirements of this Directive, taking into account the specific character of such types of agreements.

(24)   The consumer needs to be given comprehensive information before he concludes the credit agreement, regardless of whether or not a credit intermediary is involved in the marketing of the credit. Therefore, in general, the pre-contractual information requirements should also apply to credit intermediaries. However, where suppliers of goods and services act as credit intermediaries in an ancillary capacity, it is not appropriate to burden them with the legal obligation to provide the pre-contractual information in accordance with this Directive. Suppliers of goods and services may be deemed, for example, to be acting as credit intermediaries in an ancillary capacity if their activity as credit intermediaries is not the main purpose of their trade, business or profession. In those cases, a sufficient level of consumer protection is still achieved since the creditor is responsible for ensuring that the consumer receives the full pre-contractual information, either from the intermediary, if the creditor and the intermediary so agree, or in some other appropriate manner.

(25)   The potentially binding character of the information to be provided to the consumer prior to the conclusion of the credit agreement and the period of time during which the creditor is to be bound by it may be regulated by the Member States.

(26)   Member States should take appropriate measures to promote responsible practices during all phases of the credit relationship, taking into account the specific features of their credit market. Those measures may include, for instance, the provision of information to, and the education of, consumers, including warnings about the risks attaching to default on payment and to over-indebtedness. In the expanding credit market, in particular, it is important that creditors should not engage in irresponsible lending or give out credit without prior assessment of creditworthiness, and the Member States should carry out the necessary supervision to avoid such behaviour and should determine the necessary means to sanction creditors in the event of their doing so. Without prejudice to the credit risk provisions of Directive 2006/48/EC of the European Parliament and of the Council of 14 June 2006 relating to the taking up and pursuit of the business of credit institutions,[5] creditors should bear the responsibility of checking individually the creditworthiness of the consumer. To that end, they should be allowed to use information provided by the consumer not only during the preparation of the credit agreement in question, but also during a longstanding commercial relationship. The Member States' authorities could also give appropriate instructions and guidelines to creditors. Consumers should also act with prudence and respect their contractual obligations.

(27)   Despite the pre-contractual information to be provided, the consumer may still need additional assistance in order to decide which credit agreement, within the range of products proposed, is the most appropriate for his needs and financial situation. Therefore, Member States should ensure that creditors provide such assistance in relation to the credit products which they offer to the consumer. Where appropriate, the relevant pre-contractual information, as well as the essential characteristics of the products proposed, should be explained to the consumer in a personalised manner so that the consumer can understand the effects which they may have on his economic situation. Where applicable, this duty to assist the consumer should also apply to credit intermediaries. Member States could determine when and to what extent such explanations are to be given to the consumer, taking into account the particular circumstances in which the credit is offered, the consumer's need for assistance and the nature of individual credit products.

(28)   To assess the credit status of a consumer, the creditor should also consult relevant databases; the legal and actual circumstances may require that such consultations vary in scope. To prevent any distortion of competition among creditors, it should be ensured that creditors have access to private or public databases concerning consumers in a Member State where they are not established under non-discriminatory conditions compared with creditors in that Member State.

(29)   Where a decision to reject an application for credit is based on the consultation of a database, the creditor should inform the consumer of this fact and of the particulars of the database consulted. However, the creditor should not be obliged to give such information when this is prohibited by other Community legislation, for example legislation on money laundering or the financing of terrorism. Furthermore, such information should not be given if this would be contrary to objectives of public policy or public security, such as the prevention, investigation, detection or prosecution of criminal offences.

(30)   This Directive does not regulate contract law issues related to the validity of credit agreements. Therefore, in that area, the Member States may maintain or introduce national provisions which are in conformity with Community law. Member States may regulate the legal regime governing the offer to conclude the credit agreement, in particular when it is to be given and the period during which it is to be binding on the creditor. If such an offer is made at the same time as the pre-contractual information provided for by this Directive is given, it should, like any additional information the creditor may wish to give to the consumer, be provided in a separate document which may be annexed to the Standard European Consumer Credit Information.

(31)   In order to enable the consumer to know his rights and obligations under the credit agreement, it should contain all necessary information in a clear and concise manner.

(32)   In order to ensure full transparency, the consumer should be provided with information concerning the borrowing rate, both at a pre-contractual stage and when the credit agreement is concluded. During the contractual relationship, the consumer should further be informed of changes to the variable borrowing rate and changes to the payments caused thereby. This is without prejudice to provisions of national law not related to consumer information which lay down conditions for, or prescribe the consequences of, changes, other than changes concerning payments, in borrowing rates and other economic conditions governing the credit, for instance rules providing that the creditor may change the borrowing rate only where there is a valid reason for such change or that the consumer may terminate the contract should there be a change in the borrowing rate or in some other economic condition concerning the credit.

(33)   The contracting parties should have the right to effect a standard termination of an open-end credit agreement. In addition, if agreed in the credit agreement, the creditor should have the right to suspend the consumer's right to draw down on an open-end credit agreement for objectively justified reasons. Such reasons may include, for instance, suspicion of an unauthorised or fraudulent use of the credit or a significantly increased risk of the consumer being unable to fulfil his obligation to repay the credit. This Directive does not affect national law in the area of contract law regulating the rights of the contracting parties to terminate the credit agreement on the basis of a breach of contract.

(34)   In order to approximate the procedures for exercising the right of withdrawal in similar areas, it is necessary to make provision for a right of withdrawal without penalty and with no obligation to provide justification, under conditions similar to those provided for by Directive 2002/65/EC of the European Parliament and of the Council of 23 September 2002 concerning the distance marketing of consumer financial services.[6]

(35)   Where a consumer withdraws from a credit agreement in connection with which he has received goods, in particular from a purchase in instalments or from a hiring or leasing agreement providing for an obligation to purchase, this Directive should be without prejudice to any regulation by Member States of questions concerning the return of the goods or any related questions.

(36)   In some cases, national legislation already provides that funds cannot be made available to the consumer before the expiry of a specific deadline. In these cases, consumers may wish to ensure that they receive the goods or services purchased early. Therefore, in the case of linked credit agreements, Member States may exceptionally provide that, if the consumer explicitly wishes early receipt, the deadline for the exercise of the right of withdrawal could be reduced to the same deadline before which funds cannot be made available.

(37)   In the case of linked credit agreements, a relationship of interdependence exists between the purchase of goods or services and the credit agreement concluded for that purpose. Therefore, where the consumer exercises his right of withdrawal in respect of the purchase agreement, based on Community law, he should no longer be bound by the linked credit agreement. This should not affect national law applicable to linked credit agreements in cases where a purchase agreement has been voided or where the consumer has exercised his right of withdrawal based on national law. Nor should this affect the rights of consumers granted by national provisions according to which no commitment may be entered into between the consumer and a supplier of goods or services, nor any payment made between those persons, as long as the consumer has not signed the credit agreement to finance the purchase of the goods or services.

(38)   Under certain conditions, the consumer should be allowed to pursue remedies against the creditor in the event of problems related to the purchase agreement. However, Member States should determine to what extent and under what conditions the consumer is required to pursue his remedies against the supplier, in particular by bringing an action against the latter, before being in a position to pursue them against the creditor. This Directive should not deprive consumers of their rights under national provisions attaching joint and several liability to the seller or supplier of services and to the creditor.

(39)   The consumer should have the right to discharge his obligations before the date agreed in the credit agreement. In the case of early repayment, either in part or in full, the creditor should be entitled to compensation for the costs directly linked to the early repayment, taking into account also any savings thereby made by the creditor. However, in order to determine the method of calculating the compensation, it is important to respect several principles. The calculation of the compensation due to the creditor should be transparent and comprehensible to consumers already at the pre-contractual stage and in any case during the performance of the credit agreement. In addition, the calculation method should be easy for creditors to apply, and supervisory control of the compensation by the responsible authorities should be facilitated. Therefore, and due to the fact that consumer credit is, given its duration and volume, not financed by long-term funding mechanisms, the ceiling for the compensation should be fixed in terms of a flat-rate amount. This approach reflects the special nature of credits for consumers and should not prejudice the possibly different approach in respect of other products which are financed by long-term funding mechanisms, such as fixed-rate mortgage loans.

(40)   Member States should have the right to provide that compensation for early repayment may be claimed by the creditor only on condition that the amount repaid over a 12-month period

exceeds a threshold defined by Member States. When fixing that threshold, which should not exceed EUR 10 000, Member States should for instance take into account the average amount of consumer credits in their market.

(41) Assignment of the creditor's rights under a credit agreement should not have the effect of placing the consumer in a less favourable position. The consumer should also be properly informed when the credit agreement is assigned to a third party. However, where the initial creditor, in agreement with the assignee, continues to service the credit vis-à-vis the consumer, the consumer has no significant interest in being informed of the assignment. Therefore, a requirement at EU level that the consumer be informed of the assignment in such cases would be excessive.

(42) Member States should remain free to maintain or introduce national rules providing for collective forms of communication when this is necessary for purposes relating to the effectiveness of complex transactions such as securitisations or liquidation of assets that take place in the compulsory administrative liquidation of banks.

(43) In order to promote the establishment and functioning of the internal market and to ensure a high degree of protection for consumers throughout the Community, it is necessary to ensure the comparability of information relating to annual percentage rates of charge throughout the Community. Despite the uniform mathematical formula for its calculation, the annual percentage rate of charge provided for in Directive 87/102/EEC is not yet fully comparable throughout the Community. In individual Member States different cost factors are taken into account in the calculation thereof. This Directive should therefore clearly and comprehensively define the total cost of a credit to the consumer.

(44) In order to ensure market transparency and stability, and pending further harmonisation, Member States should ensure that appropriate measures for the regulation or supervision of creditors are in place.

(45) This Directive respects fundamental rights and observes the principles recognised in particular by the Charter of Fundamental Rights of the European Union. In particular, this Directive seeks to ensure full respect for the rules on protection of personal data, the right to property, non-discrimination, protection of family and professional life, and consumer protection pursuant to the Charter of Fundamental Rights of the European Union.

(46) Since the objective of this Directive, namely the establishment of common rules for certain aspects of the laws, regulations and administrative provisions of the Member States concerning consumer credit, cannot be sufficiently achieved by the Member States and can therefore be better achieved at Community level, the Community may adopt measures, in accordance with the principle of subsidiarity as set out in Article 5 of the Treaty. In accordance with the principle of proportionality, as set out in that Article, this Directive does not go beyond what is necessary in order to achieve that objective.

(47) Member States should lay down rules on penalties applicable to infringements of the national provisions adopted pursuant to this Directive and ensure that they are implemented. While the choice of penalties remains within the discretion of the Member States, the penalties provided for should be effective, proportionate and dissuasive.

(48) The measures necessary for the implementation of this Directive should be adopted in accordance with Council Decision 1999/468/EC of 28 June 1999 laying down the procedures for the exercise of implementing powers conferred on the Commission.[7]

(49) In particular, the Commission should be empowered to adopt additional assumptions for the calculation of the annual percentage rate of charge. Since those measures are of general scope and are designed to amend non-essential elements of this Directive, they must be adopted in accordance with the regulatory procedure with scrutiny provided for in Article 5a of Decision 1999/468/EC.

(50) In accordance with point 34 of the Interinstitutional Agreement on better law-making,[8] Member States are encouraged to draw up, for themselves and in the interests of the Community, their own tables illustrating, as far as possible, the correlation between this Directive and the transposition measures, and to make them public.

(51) Accordingly, taking account of the number of amendments that need to be made to Directive 87/102/EEC due to the evolution of the consumer credit sector and in the interests of the clarity of Community legislation, that Directive should be repealed and replaced by this Directive,

NOTES

[1] OJ C234, 30.9.2003, p 1.

[2] Opinion of the European Parliament of 20 April 2004 (OJ C104 E, 30.4.2004, p 233), Council common position of 20 September 2007 (OJ C270 E, 13.11.2007, p 1) and Position of the European Parliament of 16 January 2008 (not yet published in the Official Journal). Council Decision of 7 April 2008.

[3] OJ L42, 12.2.1987, p 48. Directive as last amended by Directive 98/7/EC of the European Parliament and of the Council (OJ L101, 1.4.1998, p 17).

[4] OJ L149, 11.6.2005, p 22.

[5] OJ L177, 30.6.2006, p 1. Directive as last amended by Directive 2008/24/EC (OJ L81, 20.3.2008, p 38).

[6] OJ L271, 9.10.2002, p 16. Directive as last amended by Directive 2007/64/EC (OJ L319, 5.12.2007, p 1).

⁷   OJ L184, 17.7.1999, p 23. Decision as amended by Decision 2006/512/EC (OJ L200, 22.7.2006, p 11).
⁸   OJ C321, 31.12.2003, p 1.

HAVE ADOPTED THIS DIRECTIVE—

CHAPTER I
SUBJECT MATTER, SCOPE AND DEFINITIONS

Article 1
Subject matter

The purpose of this Directive is to harmonise certain aspects of the laws, regulations and administrative provisions of the Member States concerning agreements covering credit for consumers.

[4529]

Article 2
Scope

1.   This Directive shall apply to credit agreements.

2.   This Directive shall not apply to the following—
   (a)   credit agreements which are secured either by a mortgage or by another comparable security commonly used in a Member State on immovable property or secured by a right related to immovable property;
   (b)   credit agreements the purpose of which is to acquire or retain property rights in land or in an existing or projected building;
   (c)   credit agreements involving a total amount of credit less than EUR 200 or more than EUR 75 000;
   (d)   hiring or leasing agreements where an obligation to purchase the object of the agreement is not laid down either by the agreement itself or by any separate agreement; such an obligation shall be deemed to exist if it is so decided unilaterally by the creditor;
   (e)   credit agreements in the form of an overdraft facility and where the credit has to be repaid within one month;
   (f)   credit agreements where the credit is granted free of interest and without any other charges and credit agreements under the terms of which the credit has to be repaid within three months and only insignificant charges are payable;
   (g)   credit agreements where the credit is granted by an employer to his employees as a secondary activity free of interest or at annual percentage rates of charge lower than those prevailing on the market and which are not offered to the public generally;
   (h)   credit agreements which are concluded with investment firms as defined in Article 4(1) of Directive 2004/39/EC of the European Parliament and of the Council of 21 April 2004 on markets in financial instruments¹ or with credit institutions as defined in Article 4 of Directive 2006/48/EC for the purposes of allowing an investor to carry out a transaction relating to one or more of the instruments listed in Section C of Annex I to Directive 2004/39/EC, where the investment firm or credit institution granting the credit is involved in such transaction;
   (i)   credit agreements which are the outcome of a settlement reached in court or before another statutory authority;
   (j)   credit agreements which relate to the deferred payment, free of charge, of an existing debt;
   (k)   credit agreements upon the conclusion of which the consumer is requested to deposit an item as security in the creditor's safe-keeping and where the liability of the consumer is strictly limited to that pledged item;
   (l)   credit agreements which relate to loans granted to a restricted public under a statutory provision with a general interest purpose, and at lower interest rates than those prevailing on the market or free of interest or on other terms which are more favourable to the consumer than those prevailing on the market and at interest rates not higher than those prevailing on the market.

3.   In the case of credit agreements in the form of an overdraft facility and where the credit has to be repaid on demand or within three months, only Articles 1 to 3, Article 4(1), Article 4(2)(a) to (c), Article 4(4), Articles 6 to 9, Article 10(1), Article 10(4), Article 10(5), Articles 12, 15, 17 and Articles 19 to 32 shall apply.

4.   In the case of credit agreements in the form of overrunning, only Articles 1 to 3, 18, 20 and 22 to 32 shall apply.

5.   Member States may determine that only Articles 1 to 4, 6, 7 and 9, Article 10(1), points (a) to (h) and (l) of Article 10(2), Article 10(4) and Articles 11, 13 and 16 to 32 shall apply to credit agreements which are concluded by an organisation which—
   (a)   is established for the mutual benefit of its members;
   (b)   does not make profits for any other person than its members;

(c)   fulfils a social purpose required by domestic legislation;

(d)   receives and manages the savings of, and provides sources of credit to, its members only; and

(e)   provides credit on the basis of an annual percentage rate of charge which is lower than that prevailing on the market or subject to a ceiling laid down by national law,

and whose membership is restricted to persons residing or employed in a particular location or employees and retired employees of a particular employer, or to persons meeting other qualifications laid down under national law as the basis for the existence of a common bond between the members.

Member States may exempt from the application of this Directive credit agreements concluded by such an organisation where the total value of all existing credit agreements entered into by the organisation is insignificant in relation to the total value of all existing credit agreements in the Member State in which the organisation is based and the total value of all existing credit agreements entered into by all such organisations in the Member State is less than 1% of the total value of all existing credit agreements entered into in that Member State.

Member States shall each year review whether the conditions for the application of any such exemption continue to exist and shall take action to withdraw the exemption where they consider that the conditions are no longer met.

6.   Member States may determine that only Articles 1 to 4, 6, 7, 9, Article 10(1), points (a) to (i), (l) and (r) of Article 10(2), Article 10(4), Articles 11, 13, 16 and Articles 18 to 32 shall apply to credit agreements which provide for arrangements to be agreed by the creditor and the consumer in respect of deferred payment or repayment methods, where the consumer is already in default on the initial credit agreement and where—

(a)   such arrangements would be likely to avert the possibility of legal proceedings concerning such default; and

(b)   the consumer would not thereby be subject to terms less favourable than those laid down in the initial credit agreement.

However, if the credit agreement falls within the scope of paragraph 3, only the provisions of that paragraph shall apply.

[4530]

NOTES

¹   OJ L145, 30.4.2004, p 1. Directive as last amended by Directive 2008/10/EC (OJ L76, 19.3.2008, p 33).

Article 3
Definitions

For the purposes of this Directive, the following definitions shall apply—

(a)   'consumer' means a natural person who, in transactions covered by this Directive, is acting for purposes which are outside his trade, business or profession;

(b)   'creditor' means a natural or legal person who grants or promises to grant credit in the course of his trade, business or profession;

(c)   'credit agreement' means an agreement whereby a creditor grants or promises to grant to a consumer credit in the form of a deferred payment, loan or other similar financial accommodation, except for agreements for the provision on a continuing basis of services or for the supply of goods of the same kind, where the consumer pays for such services or goods for the duration of their provision by means of instalments;

(d)   'overdraft facility' means an explicit credit agreement whereby a creditor makes available to a consumer funds which exceed the current balance in the consumer's current account;

(e)   'overrunning' means a tacitly accepted overdraft whereby a creditor makes available to a consumer funds which exceed the current balance in the consumer's current account or the agreed overdraft facility;

(f)   'credit intermediary' means a natural or legal person who is not acting as a creditor and who, in the course of his trade, business or profession, for a fee, which may take a pecuniary form or any other agreed form of financial consideration—

(i)   presents or offers credit agreements to consumers;

(ii) assists consumers by undertaking preparatory work in respect of credit agreements other than as referred to in (i); or

(iii) concludes credit agreements with consumers on behalf of the creditor;

(g)   'total cost of the credit to the consumer' means all the costs, including interest, commissions, taxes and any other kind of fees which the consumer is required to pay in connection with the credit agreement and which are known to the creditor, except for notarial costs; costs in respect of ancillary services relating to the credit agreement, in particular insurance premiums, are also included if, in addition, the conclusion of a service contract is compulsory in order to obtain the credit or to obtain it on the terms and conditions marketed;

(h)   'total amount payable by the consumer' means the sum of the total amount of the credit and the total cost of the credit to the consumer;

(i)   'annual percentage rate of charge' means the total cost of the credit to the consumer, expressed as an annual percentage of the total amount of credit, where applicable including the costs referred to in Article 19(2);

(j)   'borrowing rate' means the interest rate expressed as a fixed or variable percentage applied on an annual basis to the amount of credit drawn down;

(k)   'fixed borrowing rate' means that the creditor and the consumer agree in the credit agreement on one borrowing rate for the entire duration of the credit agreement or on several borrowing rates for partial periods using exclusively a fixed specific percentage. If not all borrowing rates are determined in the credit agreement, the borrowing rate shall be deemed to be fixed only for the partial periods for which the borrowing rates are determined exclusively by a fixed specific percentage agreed on the conclusion of the credit agreement;

(l)   'total amount of credit' means the ceiling or the total sums made available under a credit agreement;

(m)   'durable medium' means any instrument which enables the consumer to store information addressed personally to him in a way accessible for future reference for a period of time adequate for the purposes of the information and which allows the unchanged reproduction of the information stored;

(n)   'linked credit agreement' means a credit agreement where

  (i)   the credit in question serves exclusively to finance an agreement for the supply of specific goods or the provision of a specific service, and

  (ii)   those two agreements form, from an objective point of view, a commercial unit; a commercial unit shall be deemed to exist where the supplier or service provider himself finances the credit for the consumer or, if it is financed by a third party, where the creditor uses the services of the supplier or service provider in connection with the conclusion or preparation of the credit agreement, or where the specific goods or the provision of a specific service are explicitly specified in the credit agreement.

[4531]

CHAPTER II
INFORMATION AND PRACTICES PRELIMINARY TO THE CONCLUSION OF THE CREDIT AGREEMENT

Article 4
Standard information to be included in advertising

1.   Any advertising concerning credit agreements which indicates an interest rate or any figures relating to the cost of the credit to the consumer shall include standard information in accordance with this Article.

This obligation shall not apply where national legislation requires the indication of the annual percentage rate of charge in advertising concerning credit agreements which does not indicate an interest rate or any figures relating to any cost of credit to the consumer within the meaning of the first subparagraph.

2.   The standard information shall specify in a clear, concise and prominent way by means of a representative example—

(a)   the borrowing rate, fixed or variable or both, together with particulars of any charges included in the total cost of the credit to the consumer;

(b)   the total amount of credit;

(c)   the annual percentage rate of charge; in the case of a credit agreement of the kind referred to in Article 2(3), Member States may decide that the annual percentage rate of charge need not be provided;

(d)   if applicable, the duration of the credit agreement;

(e)   in the case of a credit in the form of deferred payment for a specific good or service, the cash price and the amount of any advance payment; and

(f)   if applicable, the total amount payable by the consumer and the amount of the instalments.

3.   Where the conclusion of a contract regarding an ancillary service relating to the credit agreement, in particular insurance, is compulsory in order to obtain the credit or to obtain it on the terms and conditions marketed, and the cost of that service cannot be determined in advance, the obligation to enter into that contract shall also be stated in a clear, concise and prominent way, together with the annual percentage rate of charge.

4.   This Article shall be without prejudice to Directive 2005/29/EC.

[4532]

Article 5
Pre-contractual information

1. In good time before the consumer is bound by any credit agreement or offer, the creditor and, where applicable, the credit intermediary shall, on the basis of the credit terms and conditions offered by the creditor and, if applicable, the preferences expressed and information supplied by the consumer, provide the consumer with the information needed to compare different offers in order to take an informed decision on whether to conclude a credit agreement. Such information, on paper or on another durable medium, shall be provided by means of the Standard European Consumer Credit Information form set out in Annex II. The creditor shall be deemed to have fulfilled the information requirements in this paragraph and in Article 3, paragraphs (1) and (2) of Directive 2002/65/EC if he has supplied the Standard European Consumer Credit Information.

The information in question shall specify—

(a) the type of credit;

(b) the identity and the geographical address of the creditor as well as, if applicable, the identity and geographical address of the credit intermediary involved;

(c) the total amount of credit and the conditions governing the drawdown;

(d) the duration of the credit agreement;

(e) in the case of a credit in the form of deferred payment for a specific good or service and linked credit agreements, that good or service and its cash price;

(f) the borrowing rate, the conditions governing the application of the borrowing rate and, where available, any index or reference rate applicable to the initial borrowing rate, as well as the periods, conditions and procedure for changing the borrowing rate; if different borrowing rates apply in different circumstances, the abovementioned information on all the applicable rates;

(g) the annual percentage rate of charge and the total amount payable by the consumer, illustrated by means of a representative example mentioning all the assumptions used in order to calculate that rate; where the consumer has informed the creditor of one or more components of his preferred credit, such as the duration of the credit agreement and the total amount of credit, the creditor shall take those components into account; if a credit agreement provides different ways of drawdown with different charges or borrowing rates and the creditor uses the assumption set out in point (b) of Part II of Annex I, he shall indicate that other drawdown mechanisms for this type of credit agreement may result in higher annual percentage rates of charge;

(h) the amount, number and frequency of payments to be made by the consumer and, where appropriate, the order in which payments will be allocated to different outstanding balances charged at different borrowing rates for the purposes of reimbursement;

(i) where applicable, the charges for maintaining one or several accounts recording both payment transactions and drawdowns, unless the opening of an account is optional, together with the charges for using a means of payment for both payment transactions and drawdowns, any other charges deriving from the credit agreement and the conditions under which those charges may be changed;

(j) where applicable, the existence of costs payable by the consumer to a notary on conclusion of the credit agreement;

(k) the obligation, if any, to enter into an ancillary service contract relating to the credit agreement, in particular an insurance policy, where the conclusion of such a contract is compulsory in order to obtain the credit or to obtain it on the terms and conditions marketed;

(l) the interest rate applicable in the case of late payments and the arrangements for its adjustment, and, where applicable, any charges payable for default;

(m) a warning regarding the consequences of missing payments;

(n) where applicable, the sureties required;

(o) the existence or absence of a right of withdrawal;

(p) the right of early repayment, and, where applicable, information concerning the creditor's right to compensation and the way in which that compensation will be determined in accordance with Article 16;

(q) the consumer's right to be informed immediately and free of charge, pursuant to Article 9(2), of the result of a database consultation carried out for the purposes of assessing his creditworthiness;

(r) the consumer's right to be supplied, on request and free of charge, with a copy of the draft credit agreement. This provision shall not apply if the creditor is at the time of the request unwilling to proceed to the conclusion of the credit agreement with the consumer; and

(s) if applicable, the period of time during which the creditor is bound by the pre-contractual information.

Any additional information which the creditor may provide to the consumer shall be given in a separate document which may be annexed to the Standard European Consumer Credit Information form.

2. However, in the case of voice telephony communications, as referred to in Article 3(3) of Directive 2002/65/EC, the description of the main characteristics of the financial service to be provided pursuant to the second indent of Article 3(3)(b) of that Directive shall include at least the items referred to in points (c), (d), (e), (f) and (h) of paragraph (1) of this Article, together with the annual percentage rate of charge illustrated by means of a representative example and the total amount payable by the consumer.

3. If the agreement has been concluded at the consumer's request using a means of distance communication which does not enable the information to be provided in accordance with paragraph 1, in particular in the case referred to in paragraph 2, the creditor shall provide the consumer with the full pre-contractual information using the Standard European Consumer Credit Information form immediately after the conclusion of the credit agreement.

4. Upon request, the consumer shall, in addition to receiving the Standard European Consumer Credit Information, be supplied free of charge with a copy of the draft credit agreement. This provision shall not apply if the creditor is at the time of the request unwilling to proceed to the conclusion of the credit agreement with the consumer.

5. In the case of a credit agreement under which payments made by the consumer do not give rise to an immediate corresponding amortisation of the total amount of credit, but are used to constitute capital during periods and under conditions laid down in the credit agreement or in an ancillary agreement, the pre-contractual information required under paragraph 1 shall include a clear and concise statement that such credit agreements do not provide for a guarantee of repayment of the total amount of credit drawn down under the credit agreement, unless such a guarantee is given.

6. Member States shall ensure that creditors and, where applicable, credit intermediaries provide adequate explanations to the consumer, in order to place the consumer in a position enabling him to assess whether the proposed credit agreement is adapted to his needs and to his financial situation, where appropriate by explaining the pre-contractual information to be provided in accordance with paragraph 1, the essential characteristics of the products proposed and the specific effects they may have on the consumer, including the consequences of default in payment by the consumer. Member States may adapt the manner by which and the extent to which such assistance is given, as well as by whom it is given, to the particular circumstances of the situation in which the credit agreement is offered, the person to whom it is offered and the type of credit offered.

[4533]

Article 6
Pre-contractual information requirements for certain credit agreements in the form of an overdraft facility and for certain specific credit agreements

1. In good time before the consumer becomes bound by any credit agreement or offer concerning a credit agreement as referred to in Article 2(3), (5) or (6), the creditor and, where applicable, the credit intermediary shall, on the basis of the credit terms and conditions offered by the creditor and, if applicable, the preferences expressed and information supplied by the consumer, provide the consumer with the information needed to compare different offers in order to take an informed decision on whether to conclude a credit agreement.

The information in question shall specify—
   (a)   the type of credit;
   (b)   the identity and geographical address of the creditor as well as, if applicable, the identity and geographical address of the credit intermediary involved;
   (c)   the total amount of credit;
   (d)   the duration of the credit agreement;
   (e)   the borrowing rate; the conditions governing the application of that rate, any index or reference rate applicable to the initial borrowing rate, the charges applicable from the time the credit agreement is concluded, and, where applicable, the conditions under which those charges may be changed;
   (f)   the annual percentage rate of charge, illustrated by means of representative examples mentioning all the assumptions used in order to calculate that rate;
   (g)   the conditions and procedure for terminating the credit agreement;
   (h)   in the case of credit agreements as referred to in Article 2(3), where applicable, an indication that the consumer may be requested to repay the amount of credit in full at any time;
   (i)   the interest rate applicable in the case of late payments and the arrangements for its adjustment, and, where applicable, any charges payable for default;
   (j)   the consumer's right to be informed immediately and free of charge, pursuant to Article 9(2), of the result of a database consultation carried out for the purposes of assessing his creditworthiness;
   (k)   in the case of credit agreements as referred to in Article 2(3), information about the charges applicable from the time such agreements are concluded and, if applicable, the conditions under which those charges may be changed;

(l)   if applicable, the period of time during which the creditor is bound by the pre-contractual information.

Such information shall be provided on paper or on another durable medium and all information shall be equally prominent. It may be provided by means of the European Consumer Credit Information form set out in Annex III. The creditor shall be deemed to have fulfilled the information requirements in this paragraph and in Article 3(1) and (2) of Directive 2002/65/EC if he has supplied the European Consumer Credit Information.

2.   In the case of a credit agreement of the kind referred to in Article 2(3), Member States may decide that the annual percentage rate of charge need not be provided.

3.   In the case of a credit agreement as referred to in Article 2(5) and (6), the information provided to the consumer in accordance with paragraph 1 of this Article shall also include—

(a)   the amount, number and frequency of payments to be made by the consumer and, where appropriate, the order in which payments will be allocated to different outstanding balances charged at different borrowing rates for the purposes of reimbursement; and

(b)   the right of early repayment, and, where applicable, information concerning the creditor's right to compensation and the way in which that compensation will be determined.

However, if the credit agreement falls within the scope of Article 2(3), only the provisions of paragraph 1 of this Article shall apply.

4.   However, in the case of voice telephony communications and where the consumer requests that the overdraft facility be made available with immediate effect, the description of the main characteristics of the financial service shall include at least the items referred to in points (c), (e), (f) and (h) of paragraph 1. In addition, in credit agreements of the kind referred to in paragraph 3, the description of the main characteristics shall include a specification of the duration of the credit agreement.

5.   Notwithstanding the exclusion provided for in Article 2(2)(e), the Member States shall apply at least the requirements of the first sentence of paragraph 4 of this Article to credit agreements in the form of an overdraft facility and where the credit has to be repaid within one month.

6.   Upon request, the consumer shall, in addition to receiving the information referred to in paragraphs 1 to 4, be supplied free of charge with a copy of the draft credit agreement containing the contractual information provided for by Article 10 insofar as that Article is applicable. This provision shall not apply if the creditor is at the time of the request unwilling to proceed to the conclusion of the credit agreement with the consumer.

7.   If the agreement has been concluded at the consumer's request using a means of distance communication which does not enable the information to be provided in accordance with paragraphs 1 and 3, including in the cases referred to in paragraph 4, the creditor shall immediately after the conclusion of the credit agreement fulfil his obligations under paragraphs 1 and 3 by providing the contractual information pursuant to Article 10 insofar as that Article is applicable.

[4534]

Article 7
Exemptions from the pre-contractual information requirements

Articles 5 and 6 shall not apply to suppliers of goods or services acting as credit intermediaries in an ancillary capacity. This is without prejudice to the creditor's obligation to ensure that the consumer receives the pre-contractual information referred to in those Articles.

[4535]

Article 8
Obligation to assess the creditworthiness of the consumer

1.   Member States shall ensure that, before the conclusion of the credit agreement, the creditor assesses the consumer's creditworthiness on the basis of sufficient information, where appropriate obtained from the consumer and, where necessary, on the basis of a consultation of the relevant database. Member States whose legislation requires creditors to assess the creditworthiness of consumers on the basis of a consultation of the relevant database may retain this requirement.

2.   Member States shall ensure that, if the parties agree to change the total amount of credit after the conclusion of the credit agreement, the creditor updates the financial information at his disposal concerning the consumer and assesses the consumer's creditworthiness before any significant increase in the total amount of credit.

[4536]

CHAPTER III
DATABASE ACCESS

Article 9
Database access

1. Each Member State shall in the case of cross-border credit ensure access for creditors from other Member States to databases used in that Member State for assessing the creditworthiness of consumers. The conditions for access shall be non-discriminatory.

2. If the credit application is rejected on the basis of consultation of a database, the creditor shall inform the consumer immediately and without charge of the result of such consultation and of the particulars of the database consulted.

3. The information shall be provided unless the provision of such information is prohibited by other Community legislation or is contrary to objectives of public policy or public security.

4. This Article shall be without prejudice to the application of Directive 95/46/EC of the European Parliament and of the Council of 24 October 1995 on the protection of individuals with regard to the processing of personal data and on the free movement of such data.[1]

[4537]

NOTES

[1]   OJ L 281, 23.11.1995, p 31. Directive as amended by Regulation (EC) No 1882/2003 (OJ L284, 31.10.2003, p 1).

CHAPTER IV
INFORMATION AND RIGHTS CONCERNING CREDIT AGREEMENTS

Article 10
Information to be included in credit agreements

1. Credit agreements shall be drawn up on paper or on another durable medium. All the contracting parties shall receive a copy of the credit agreement.

This Article shall be without prejudice to any national rules regarding the validity of the conclusion of credit agreements which are in conformity with Community law.

2. The credit agreement shall specify in a clear and concise manner—

    (a)   the type of credit;

    (b)   the identities and geographical addresses of the contracting parties as well as, if applicable, the identity and geographical address of the credit intermediary involved;

    (c)   the duration of the credit agreement;

    (d)   the total amount of credit and the conditions governing the drawdown;

    (e)   in case of a credit in the form of deferred payment for a specific good or service or in the case of linked credit agreements, that good or service and its cash price;

    (f)   the borrowing rate, the conditions governing the application of that rate and, where available, any index or reference rate applicable to the initial borrowing rate, as well as the periods, conditions and procedures for changing the borrowing rate and, if different borrowing rates apply in different circumstances, the abovementioned information in respect of all the applicable rates;

    (g)   the annual percentage rate of charge and the total amount payable by the consumer, calculated at the time the credit agreement is concluded; all the assumptions used in order to calculate that rate shall be mentioned;

    (h)   the amount, number and frequency of payments to be made by the consumer and, where appropriate, the order in which payments will be allocated to different outstanding balances charged at different borrowing rates for the purposes of reimbursement;

    (i)   where capital amortisation of a credit agreement with a fixed duration is involved, the right of the consumer to receive, on request and free of charge, at any time throughout the duration of the credit agreement, a statement of account in the form of an amortisation table.
The amortisation table shall indicate the payments owing and the periods and conditions relating to the payment of such amounts; the table shall contain a breakdown of each repayment showing capital amortisation, the interest calculated on the basis of the borrowing rate and, where applicable, any additional costs; where the interest rate is not fixed or the additional costs may be changed under the credit agreement, the amortisation table shall indicate, clearly and concisely, that the data contained in the table will remain valid only until such time as the borrowing rate or the additional costs are changed in accordance with the credit agreement;

    (j)   if charges and interest are to be paid without capital amortisation, a statement showing the periods and conditions for the payment of the interest and of any associated recurrent and non-recurrent charges;

    (k)   where applicable, the charges for maintaining one or several accounts recording both payment transactions and drawdowns, unless the opening of an account is optional, together with the charges for using a means of payment for both payment transactions and drawdowns, and any other charges deriving from the credit agreement and the conditions under which those charges may be changed;

(l) the interest rate applicable in the case of late payments as applicable at the time of the conclusion of the credit agreement and the arrangements for its adjustment and, where applicable, any charges payable for default;

(m) a warning regarding the consequences of missing payments;

(n) where applicable, a statement, that notarial fees will be payable;

(o) the sureties and insurance required, if any;

(p) the existence or absence of a right of withdrawal, the period during which that right may be exercised and other conditions governing the exercise thereof, including information concerning the obligation of the consumer to pay the capital drawn down and the interest in accordance with Article 14(3)(b) and the amount of interest payable per day;

(q) information concerning the rights resulting from Article 15 as well as the conditions for the exercise of those rights;

(r) the right of early repayment, the procedure for early repayment, as well as, where applicable, information concerning the creditor's right to compensation and the way in which that compensation will be determined;

(s) the procedure to be followed in exercising the right of termination of the credit agreement;

(t) whether or not there is an out-of-court complaint and redress mechanism for the consumer and, if so, the methods for having access to it;

(u) where applicable, other contractual terms and conditions;

(v) where applicable, the name and address of the competent supervisory authority.

3. Where paragraph 2(i) applies, the creditor shall make available to the consumer, free of charge and at any time throughout the duration of the credit agreement, a statement of account in the form of an amortisation table.

4. In the case of a credit agreement under which payments made by the consumer do not give rise to an immediate corresponding amortisation of the total amount of credit, but are used to constitute capital during periods and under conditions laid down in the credit agreement or in an ancillary agreement, the information required under paragraph 2 shall include a clear and concise statement that such credit agreements do not provide for a guarantee of repayment of the total amount of credit drawn down under the credit agreement, unless such a guarantee is given.

5. In the case of credit agreements in the form of overdraft facilities as referred to in Article 2(3), the following shall be specified in a clear and concise manner—

(a) the type of credit;

(b) the identities and geographical addresses of the contracting parties as well as, if applicable, the identity and geographical address of the credit intermediary involved;

(c) the duration of the credit agreement;

(d) the total amount of the credit and the conditions governing the drawdown;

(e) the borrowing rate, the conditions governing the application of the borrowing rate and, where available, any index or reference rate applicable to the initial borrowing rate, as well as the periods, conditions and procedure for changing the borrowing rate and, if different borrowing rates apply in different circumstances, the abovementioned information in respect of all the applicable rates;

(f) the annual percentage rate of charge and the total cost of the credit to the consumer, calculated at the time the credit agreement is concluded; all the assumptions used in order to calculate that rate as referred to in Article 19(2) in conjunction with Article 3(g) and (i) shall be mentioned; Member States may decide that the annual percentage rate of charge need not be provided;

(g) an indication that the consumer may be requested to repay the amount of credit in full on demand at any time;

(h) conditions governing the exercise of the right of withdrawal from the credit agreement; and

(i) information concerning the charges applicable from the time such agreements are concluded and, if applicable, the conditions under which those charges may be changed.

[4538]

Article 11
Information concerning the borrowing rate

1. Where applicable, the consumer shall be informed of any change in the borrowing rate, on paper or another durable medium, before the change enters into force. The information shall state the amount of the payments to be made after the entry into force of the new borrowing rate and, if the number or frequency of the payments changes, particulars thereof.

2. However, the parties may agree in the credit agreement that the information referred to in paragraph 1 is to be given to the consumer periodically in cases where the change in the borrowing

rate is caused by a change in a reference rate, the new reference rate is made publicly available by appropriate means and the information concerning the new reference rate is also kept available in the premises of the creditor.

[4539]

Article 12
Obligations in connection with credit agreement in the form of an overdraft facility

1. Where a credit agreement covers credit in the form of an overdraft facility, the consumer shall be kept regularly informed by means of a statement of account, on paper or on another durable medium, containing the following particulars—
   (a) the precise period to which the statement of account relates;
   (b) the amounts and dates of drawdowns;
   (c) the balance from the previous statement, and the date thereof;
   (d) the new balance;
   (e) the dates and amounts of payments made by the consumer;
   (f) the borrowing rate applied;
   (g) any charges that have been applied;
   (h) where applicable, the minimum amount to be paid.

2. In addition, the consumer shall be informed on paper or another durable medium of increases in the borrowing rate, or in any charges payable, before the change in question enters into force.

However, the parties may agree in the credit agreement that information concerning changes in the borrowing rate is to be given in the manner provided for in paragraph 1 in cases where the change in the borrowing rate is caused by a change in a reference rate, the new reference rate is made publicly available by appropriate means and the information concerning the new reference rate is also kept available in the premises of the creditor.

[4540]

Article 13
Open-end credit agreements

1. The consumer may effect standard termination of an open-end credit agreement free of charge at any time unless the parties have agreed on a period of notice. Such a period may not exceed one month.

If agreed in the credit agreement, the creditor may effect standard termination of an open-end credit agreement by giving the consumer at least two months' notice drawn up on paper or on another durable medium.

2. If agreed in the credit agreement, the creditor may, for objectively justified reasons, terminate the consumer's right to draw down on an open-end credit agreement. The creditor shall inform the consumer of the termination and the reasons for it on paper or on another durable medium, where possible before the termination and at the latest immediately thereafter, unless the provision of such information is prohibited by other Community legislation or is contrary to objectives of public policy or public security.

[4541]

Article 14
Right of withdrawal

1. The consumer shall have a period of 14 calendar days in which to withdraw from the credit agreement without giving any reason.

That period of withdrawal shall begin—
   (a) either from the day of the conclusion of the credit agreement, or
   (b) from the day on which the consumer receives the contractual terms and conditions and information in accordance with Article 10, if that day is later than the date referred to in point (a) of this subparagraph.

2. Where in the case of a linked credit agreement, as defined in Article 3(n), national legislation at the time of the entry into force of this Directive already provides that funds cannot be made available to the consumer before the expiry of a specific period, Member States may exceptionally provide that the period referred to in paragraph 1 of this Article may be reduced to this specific period at the explicit request of the consumer.

3. If the consumer exercises his right of withdrawal, he shall—
   (a) in order to give effect to the withdrawal before the expiry of the deadline referred to in paragraph 1, notify this to the creditor in line with the information given by the creditor pursuant to Article 10(2)(p) by means which can be proven in accordance with national law. The deadline shall be deemed to have been met if that notification, if it is on paper or on another durable medium that is available and accessible to the creditor, is dispatched before the deadline expires; and
   (b) pay to the creditor the capital and the interest accrued thereon from the date the credit was drawn down until the date the capital is repaid, without any undue delay and no later

than 30 calendar days after the despatch by him to the creditor of notification of the withdrawal. The interest shall be calculated on the basis of the agreed borrowing rate. The creditor shall not be entitled to any other compensation from the consumer in the event of withdrawal, except compensation for any non-returnable charges paid by the creditor to any public administrative body.

4. If an ancillary service relating to the credit agreement is provided by the creditor or by a third party on the basis of an agreement between the third party and the creditor, the consumer shall no longer be bound by the ancillary service contract if the consumer exercises his right of withdrawal from the credit agreement in accordance with this Article.

5. If the consumer has a right of withdrawal under paragraphs 1, 3 and 4, Articles 6 and 7 of Directive 2002/65/EC and Article 5 of Council Directive 85/577/EEC of 20 December 1985 to protect the consumer in respect of contracts negotiated away from business premises[1] shall not apply.

6. Member States may provide that paragraphs 1 to 4 of this Article shall not apply to credit agreements which by law are required to be concluded through the services of a notary, provided that the notary confirms that the consumer is guaranteed the rights provided for under Articles 5 and 10.

7. This Article shall be without prejudice to any rule of national law establishing a period of time during which the performance of the contract may not begin.

[4542]

NOTES

[1]   OJ L372, 31.12.1985, p 31.

Article 15
Linked credit agreements

1. Where the consumer has exercised a right of withdrawal, based on Community law, concerning a contract for the supply of goods or services, he shall no longer be bound by a linked credit agreement.

2. Where the goods or services covered by a linked credit agreement are not supplied, or are supplied only in part, or are not in conformity with the contract for the supply thereof, the consumer shall have the right to pursue remedies against the creditor if the consumer has pursued his remedies against the supplier but has failed to obtain the satisfaction to which he is entitled according to the law or the contract for the supply of goods or services. Member States shall determine to what extent and under what conditions those remedies shall be exercisable.

3. This Article shall be without prejudice to any national rules rendering the creditor jointly and severally liable in respect of any claim which the consumer may have against the supplier where the purchase of goods or services from the supplier has been financed by a credit agreement.

[4543]

Article 16
Early repayment

1. The consumer shall be entitled at any time to discharge fully or partially his obligations under a credit agreement. In such cases, he shall be entitled to a reduction in the total cost of the credit, such reduction consisting of the interest and the costs for the remaining duration of the contract.

2. In the event of early repayment of credit the creditor shall be entitled to fair and objectively justified compensation for possible costs directly linked to early repayment of credit provided that the early repayment falls within a period for which the borrowing rate is fixed.

Such compensation may not exceed 1% of the amount of credit repaid early, if the period of time between the early repayment and the agreed termination of the credit agreement exceeds one year. If the period does not exceed one year, the compensation may not exceed 0,5% of the amount of credit repaid early.

3. Compensation for early repayment shall not be claimed—
    (a)   if the repayment has been made under an insurance contract intended to provide a credit repayment guarantee;
    (b)   in the case of overdraft facilities; or
    (c)   if the repayment falls within a period for which the borrowing rate is not fixed.

4. Member States may provide that—
    (a)   such compensation may be claimed by the creditor only on condition that the amount of the early repayment exceeds the threshold defined by national law. That threshold shall not exceed EUR 10 000 within any period of 12 months;
    (b)   the creditor may exceptionally claim higher compensation if he can prove that the loss he suffered from early repayment exceeds the amount determined under paragraph 2.

If the compensation claimed by the creditor exceeds the loss actually suffered, the consumer may claim a corresponding reduction.

In this case, the loss shall consist of the difference between the initially agreed interest rate and the interest rate at which the creditor can lend out the amount repaid early on the market at the time of early repayment, and shall take into account the impact of early repayment on administrative costs.

5.   Any compensation shall not exceed the amount of interest the consumer would have paid during the period between the early repayment and the agreed date of termination of the credit agreement.

[4544]

Article 17
Assignment of rights

1.   In the event of assignment to a third party of the creditor's rights under a credit agreement or the agreement itself, the consumer shall be entitled to plead against the assignee any defence which was available to him against the original creditor, including set-off where the latter is permitted in the Member State concerned.

2.   The consumer shall be informed of the assignment referred to in paragraph 1 except where the original creditor, by agreement with the assignee, continues to service the credit vis-à-vis the consumer.

[4545]

Article 18
Overrunning

1.   In the case of an agreement to open a current account, where there is a possibility that the consumer is allowed an overrun, the agreement shall contain in addition the information referred to in Article 6(1)(e). The creditor shall in any case provide that information on paper or another durable medium on a regular basis.

2.   In the event of a significant overrunning exceeding a period of one month, the creditor shall inform the consumer without delay, on paper or on another durable medium,
   (a)   of the overrunning;
   (b)   of the amount involved;
   (c)   of the borrowing rate;
   (d)   of any penalties, charges or interest on arrears applicable.

3.   This Article shall be without prejudice to any rule of national law requiring the creditor to offer another kind of credit product when the duration of the overrunning is significant.

[4546]

CHAPTER V
ANNUAL PERCENTAGE RATE OF CHARGE

Article 19
Calculation of the annual percentage rate of charge

1.   The annual percentage rate of charge, equating, on an annual basis, to the present value of all commitments (drawdowns, repayments and charges), future or existing, agreed by the creditor and the consumer, shall be calculated in accordance with the mathematical formula set out in Part I of Annex I.

2.   For the purpose of calculating the annual percentage rate of charge, the total cost of the credit to the consumer shall be determined, with the exception of any charges payable by the consumer for non-compliance with any of his commitments laid down in the credit agreement and charges other than the purchase price which, for purchases of goods or services, he is obliged to pay whether the transaction is effected in cash or on credit.

The costs of maintaining an account recording both payment transactions and drawdowns, the costs of using a means of payment for both payment transactions and drawdowns, and other costs relating to payment transactions shall be included in the total cost of credit to the consumer unless the opening of the account is optional and the costs of the account have been clearly and separately shown in the credit agreement or in any other agreement concluded with the consumer.

3.   The calculation of the annual percentage rate of charge shall be based on the assumption that the credit agreement is to remain valid for the period agreed and that the creditor and the consumer will fulfil their obligations under the terms and by the dates specified in the credit agreement.

4.   In the case of credit agreements containing clauses allowing variations in the borrowing rate and, where applicable, charges contained in the annual percentage rate of charge but unquantifiable at the time of calculation, the annual percentage rate of charge shall be calculated on the assumption that the borrowing rate and other charges will remain fixed in relation to the initial level and will remain applicable until the end of the credit agreement.

5.   Where necessary, the additional assumptions set out in Annex I may be used in calculating the annual percentage rate of charge.

If the assumptions set out in this Article and in Part II of Annex I do not suffice to calculate the annual percentage rate of charge in a uniform manner or are not adapted any more to the commercial situation at the market, the Commission may determine the necessary additional assumptions for the calculation of the annual percentage rate of charge, or modify existing ones. These measures, designed to amend non-essential elements of this Directive, shall be adopted in accordance with the regulatory procedure with scrutiny referred to in Article 25(2).

[4547]

CHAPTER VI
CREDITORS AND CREDIT INTERMEDIARIES

Article 20
Regulation of creditors

Member States shall ensure that creditors are supervised by a body or authority independent from financial institutions, or regulated. This shall be without prejudice to Directive 2006/ 48/EC.

[4548]

Article 21
Certain obligations of credit intermediaries vis-à-vis consumers

Member States shall ensure that—
   (a)   a credit intermediary indicates in advertising and documentation intended for consumers the extent of his powers, in particular whether he works exclusively with one or more creditors or as an independent broker;
   (b)   the fee, if any, payable by the consumer to the credit intermediary for his services is disclosed to the consumer, and agreed between the consumer and the credit intermediary on paper or another durable medium before the conclusion of the credit agreement;
   (c)   the fee, if any, payable by the consumer to the credit intermediary for his services is communicated to the creditor by the credit intermediary, for the purpose of calculation of the annual percentage rate of charge.

[4549]

CHAPTER VII
IMPLEMENTING MEASURES

Article 22
Harmonisation and imperative nature of this Directive

1.   Insofar as this Directive contains harmonised provisions, Member States may not maintain or introduce in their national law provisions diverging from those laid down in this Directive.

2.   Member States shall ensure that consumers may not waive the rights conferred on them by the provisions of national law implementing or corresponding to this Directive.

3.   Member States shall further ensure that the provisions they adopt in implementation of this Directive cannot be circumvented as a result of the way in which agreements are formulated, in particular by integrating drawdowns or credit agreements falling within the scope of this Directive into credit agreements the character or purpose of which would make it possible to avoid its application.

4.   Member States shall take the necessary measures to ensure that consumers do not lose the protection granted by this Directive by virtue of the choice of the law of a third country as the law applicable to the credit agreement, if the credit agreement has a close link with the territory of one or more Member States.

[4550]

Article 23
Penalties

Member States shall lay down the rules on penalties applicable to infringements of the national provisions adopted pursuant to this Directive and shall take all measures necessary to ensure that they are implemented. The penalties provided for must be effective, proportionate and dissuasive.

[4551]

Article 24
Out-of-court dispute resolution

1.   Member States shall ensure that adequate and effective out-of-court dispute resolution procedures for the settlement of consumer disputes concerning credit agreements are put in place, using existing bodies where appropriate.

2. Member States shall encourage those bodies to cooperate in order to also resolve cross-border disputes concerning credit agreements.

[4552]

Article 25
Committee procedure

1. The Commission shall be assisted by a Committee.

2. Where reference is made to this paragraph, Article 5a(1) to (4) and Article 7 of Decision 1999/468/EC shall apply, having regard to the provisions of Article 8 thereof.

[4553]

Article 26
Information to be supplied to the Commission

Where a Member State makes use of any of the regulatory choices referred to in Article 2(5) and 2(6), Article 4(1), Article 4(2)(c), Article 6(2), Article 10(1), Article 10(2)(g), Article 14(2) and Article 16(4), it shall inform the Commission thereof as well as of any subsequent changes. The Commission shall make that information public on a website or in another easily accessible way. Member States shall take the appropriate measures to diffuse that information amongst national creditors and consumers.

[4554]

Article 27
Transposition

[1. Before 11 June 2010] Member States shall adopt and publish the provisions necessary to comply with this Directive. They shall forthwith inform the Commission thereof.

They shall apply those provisions [from 11 June 2010].

When Member States adopt these provisions, they shall contain a reference to this Directive or be accompanied by such reference on the occasion of their official publication. The methods of making such reference shall be laid down by Member States.

2. [The Commission shall undertake, every five years and for the first time 11 June 2013], a review of the thresholds laid down in this Directive and its annexes and the percentages used to calculate the compensation payable in the event of early repayment, assessing them in the light of economic trends in the Community and the situation of the market concerned. The Commission shall also monitor the effect of the existence of the regulatory choices referred to in Article 2(5) and 2(6), Article 4(1), Article 4(2)(c), Article 6(2), Article 10(1), Article 10(2)(g), Article 14(2) and Article 16(4) on the internal market and consumers. The results shall be made known to the European Parliament and the Council, accompanied where appropriate by a proposal to modify the thresholds and percentages as well as the abovementioned regulatory choices accordingly.

[4555]

NOTES
Words in square brackets substituted by Corrigendum (OJ L207, 11.8.2009, p 14).

Article 28
Conversion of amounts expressed in euro into national currency

1. For the purposes of this Directive, those Member States who convert the amounts expressed in euro into their national currency shall initially use in the conversion the exchange rate prevailing on the date of adoption of this Directive.

2. Member States may round off the amounts resulting from the conversion provided that such rounding off does not exceed EUR 10.

[4556]

CHAPTER VIII
TRANSITIONAL AND FINAL PROVISIONS

Article 29
Repeal

Directive 87/102/EEC shall be repealed [with effect from 11 June 2010].

[4557]

NOTES
Words in square brackets substituted by Corrigendum (OJ L207, 11.8.2009, p 14).

Article 30
Transitional measures

1.   This Directive shall not apply to credit agreements existing on the date when the national implementing measures enter into force.

2.   However, Member States shall ensure that Articles 11, 12, 13 and 17, the second sentence of Article 18(1), and Article 18(2) are applied also to open-end credit agreements existing on the date when the national implementing measures enter into force.

[4558]

Article 31
Entry into force

This Directive shall enter into force on the 20th day following its publication in the Official Journal of the European Union.

[4559]

Article 32
Addressees

This Directive is addressed to the Member States.

[4560]

Done at Strasbourg, 23 April 2008.

ANNEX I

I.   The basic equation expressing the equivalence of drawdowns on the one hand and repayments and charges on the other.

The basic equation, which establishes the annual percentage rate of charge (APR), equates, on an annual basis, the total present value of drawdowns on the one hand and the total present value of repayments and payments of charges on the other hand, ie:

$$\sum_{k=1}^{m} C_k (1+X)^{-t_k} = \sum_{l=1}^{m'} D_l (1+X)^{-S_l}$$

where:

—   X is the APR,

—   m is the number of the last drawdown,

—   k is the number of a drawdown, thus $1 \le k \le m$,

— C_k is the amount of drawdown k,

— t_k is the interval, expressed in years and fractions of a year, between the date of the first drawdown and the date of each subsequent drawdown, thus $t_{1 = 0}$,

—   m' is the number of the last repayment or payment of charges,

—   l is the number of a repayment or payment of charges,

— D_l is the amount of a repayment or payment of charges,

— s_l is the interval, expressed in years and fractions of a year, between the date of the first drawdown and the date of each repayment or payment of charges.

Remarks:

(a)   The amounts paid by both parties at different times shall not necessarily be equal and shall not necessarily be paid at equal intervals.

(b)   The starting date shall be that of the first drawdown.

(c)   Intervals between dates used in the calculations shall be expressed in years or in fractions of a year. A year is presumed to have 365 days (or 366 days for leap years), 52 weeks or 12 equal months. An equal month is presumed to have 30,41666 days (ie 365/12) regardless of whether or not it is a leap year.

(d)   The result of the calculation shall be expressed with an accuracy of at least one decimal place. If the figure at the following decimal place is greater than or equal to 5, the figure at that particular decimal place shall be increased by one.

(e)   The equation can be rewritten using a single sum and the concept of flows (A_k), which will be positive or negative, in other words either paid or received during periods 1 to k, expressed in years, ie:

$$S = \sum_{k=1}^{n} A_k (1+X)^{-t_k},$$

S being the present balance of flows. If the aim is to maintain the equivalence of flows, the value will be zero.

II.   Additional assumptions for the calculation of the annual percentage rate of charge

(a)   if a credit agreement gives the consumer freedom of drawdown, the total amount of credit shall be deemed to be drawn down immediately and in full;

(b)   if a credit agreement provides different ways of drawdown with different charges or borrowing rates, the total amount of credit shall be deemed to be drawn down at the highest charge and borrowing rate applied to the most common drawdown mechanism for this type of credit agreement;

(c) if a credit agreement gives the consumer freedom of drawdown in general but imposes, amongst the different ways of drawdown, a limitation with regard to the amount and period of time, the amount of credit shall be deemed to be drawn down on the earliest date provided for in the agreement and in accordance with those drawdown limits;

(d) if there is no fixed timetable for repayment, it shall be assumed:
   (i) that the credit is provided for a period of one year; and
   (ii) that the credit will be repaid in 12 equal instalments and at monthly intervals;

(e) if there is a fixed timetable for repayment but the amount of such repayments is flexible, the amount of each repayment shall be deemed to be the lowest for which the agreement provides;

(f) unless otherwise specified, where the credit agreement provides for more than one repayment date, the credit is to be made available and the repayments made on the earliest date provided for in the agreement;

(g) if the ceiling applicable to the credit has not yet been agreed, that ceiling is assumed to be EUR 1 500;

(h) in the case of an overdraft facility the total amount of credit shall be deemed to be drawn down in full and for the whole duration of the credit agreement. If the duration of the credit agreement is not known the annual percentage rate of charge shall be calculated on the assumption that the duration of the credit is three months;

(i) if different interest rates and charges are offered for a limited period or amount, the interest rate and the charges shall be deemed to be the highest rate for the whole duration of the credit agreement;

(j) for consumer credit agreements for which a fixed borrowing rate is agreed in relation to the initial period, at the end of which a new borrowing rate is determined and subsequently periodically adjusted according to an agreed indicator, the calculation of the annual percentage rate shall be based on the assumption that, at the end of the fixed borrowing rate period, the borrowing rate is the same as at the time of calculating the annual percentage rate, based on the value of the agreed indicator at that time.

[4561]

ANNEX II
STANDARD EUROPEAN CONSUMER CREDIT INFORMATION

1. Identity and contact details of the creditor/credit intermediary

Creditor Address Telephone number [*] E-mail address [*] Fax number [*] Web address [*]	[Identity] [Geographical address to be used by the consumer]
If applicable Credit intermediary Address Telephone number [*] E-mail address [*] Fax number [*] Web address [*]	[Identity] [Geographical address to be used by the consumer]
[*] This information is optional for the creditor.	

Wherever 'if applicable' is indicated, the creditor must fill in the box if the information is relevant to the credit product or delete the respective information or the entire row if the information is not relevant for the type of credit considered.

Indications between square brackets provide explanations for the creditor and must be replaced with the corresponding information.

2. Description of the main features of the credit product

The type of credit	
The total amount of credit *This means the ceiling or the total sums made available under the credit agreement.*	

The conditions governing the drawdown *This means how and when you will obtain the money.*	
The duration of the credit agreement	
Instalments and, where appropriate, the order in which instalments will be allocated	You will have to pay the following: [The amount, number and frequency of payments to be made by the consumer] Interest and/or charges will be payable in the following manner:
The total amount you will have to pay *This means the amount of borrowed capital plus interest and possible costs related to your credit.*	[Sum of total amount of credit and total cost of credit]
If applicable The credit is granted in the form of a deferred payment for a good or service or is linked to the supply of specific goods or the provision of a service Name of good/service Cash price	
If applicable Sureties required *This is a description of the security to be provided by you in relation to the credit agreement.*	[Kind of sureties]
If applicable *Repayments do not give rise to immediate amortisation of the capital.*	

3. Costs of the credit

The borrowing rate or, if applicable, different borrowing rates which apply to the credit agreement	[% —fixed or, —variable (with the index or reference rate applicable to the initial borrowing rate), —periods],
Annual Percentage Rate of Charge (APR) *This is the total cost expressed as an annual percentage of the total amount of credit.* *The APR is there to help you compare different offers.*	[% A representative example mentioning all the assumptions used for calculating the rate to be set out here]
Is it compulsory, in order to obtain the credit or to obtain it on the terms and conditions marketed, to take out —an insurance policy securing the credit, or —another ancillary service contract, *If the costs of these services are not known by the creditor they are not included in the APR.*	Yes/no [if yes, specify the kind of insurance] Yes/no [if yes, specify the kind of ancillary service]
Related costs	
If applicable Maintaining one or more accounts is required for recording both payment transactions and drawdowns	
If applicable Amount of costs for using a specific means of payment (e.g. a credit card)	
If applicable Any other costs deriving from the credit agreement	

If applicable Conditions under which the abovementioned costs related to the credit agreement can be changed	
If applicable Obligation to pay notarial fees	
Costs in the case of late payments *Missing payments could have severe consequences for you (e g forced sale) and make obtaining credit more difficult.*	You will be charged [...... (applicable interest rate and arrangements for its adjustment and, where applicable, default charges)] for missing payments.

4. Other important legal aspects

Right of withdrawal *You have the right to withdraw from the credit agreement within a period of 14 calendar days.*	Yes/no
Early repayment *You have the right to repay the credit early at any time in full or partially.*	
If applicable The creditor is entitled to compensation in the case of early repayment	[Determination of the compensation (calculation method) in accordance with the provisions implementing Article 16 of Directive 2008/48/EC]
Consultation of a database *The creditor must inform you immediately and without charge of the result of a consultation of a database, if a credit application is rejected on the basis of such a consultation. This does not apply if the provision of such information is prohibited by European Community law or is contrary to objectives of public policy or public security.*	
Right to a draft credit agreement *You have the right, upon request, to obtain a copy of the draft credit agreement free of charge. This provision does not apply if the creditor is at the time of the request unwilling to proceed to the conclusion of the credit agreement with you.*	
If applicable The period of time during which the creditor is bound by the pre-contractual information	This information is valid from ... until ...

If applicable

5. Additional information in the case of distance marketing of financial services

(a) concerning the creditor	
If applicable Representative of the creditor in your Member State of residence Address Telephone number [*] E-mail address [*] Fax number [*] Web address [*]	[Identity] [Geographical address to be used by the consumer]
If applicable Registration	[The trade register in which the creditor is entered and his registration number or an equivalent means of identification in that register]
If applicable The supervisory authority	

(b) concerning the credit agreement	
If applicable Exercise of the right of withdrawal	[Practical instructions for exercising the right of withdrawal indicating, inter alia, the period for exercising the right, the address to which notification of exercise of the right of withdrawal should be sent and the consequences of non-exercise of that right]
If applicable The law taken by the creditor as a basis for the establishment of relations with you before the conclusion of the credit contract	
If applicable Clause stipulating the governing law applicable to the credit agreement and/or the competent court	[Relevant clause to be set out here]
If applicable Language regime	Information and contractual terms will be supplied in [specific language]. With your consent, we intend to communicate in [specific language/languages] during the duration of the credit agreement.
(c) concerning redress	
Existence of and access to out-of-court complaint and redress mechanism	[Whether or not there is an out-of-court complaint and redress mechanism for the consumer who is party to the distance contract and, if so, the methods of access to it]
[*] This information is optional for the creditor.	

[4562]

ANNEX III
EUROPEAN CONSUMER CREDIT INFORMATION FOR (1) OVERDRAFTS (2) CONSUMER CREDIT OFFERED BY CERTAIN CREDIT ORGANISATIONS (ARTICLE 2(5) OF DIRECTIVE 2008/48/EC) (3) DEBT CONVERSION

1. Identity and contact details of the creditor/credit intermediary

Creditor Address Telephone number [*] E-mail address [*] Fax number [*] Web address [*]	[Identity] [Geographical address to be used by the consumer]
If applicable Credit intermediary Address Telephone number [*] E-mail address [*] Fax number [*] Web address [*]	[Identity] [Geographical address to be used by the consumer]
[*] This information is optional for the creditor.	

Wherever 'if applicable' is indicated, the creditor must fill in the box if the information is relevant to the credit product or delete the respective information or the entire row if the information is not relevant for the type of credit considered.

Indications between square brackets provide explanations for the creditor and must be replaced with the corresponding information.

PART 3

EU AND INTERNATIONAL MATERIALS

2. Description of the main features of the credit product

The type of credit	
The total amount of credit *This means the ceiling or the total sums made available under the credit agreement.*	
The duration of the credit agreement	
If applicable You may be requested to repay the amount of credit in full on demand at any time.	

3. Costs of the credit

The borrowing rate or, if applicable, different borrowing rates which apply to the credit agreement	[% —fixed or, —variable (with the index or reference rate applicable to the initial borrowing rate)]
If applicable The annual percentage rate of charge (APR) [*] *This is the total cost of credit expressed as an annual percentage of the total amount of credit. The APR is there to help you compare different offers.*	[% A representative example mentioning all the assumptions used for calculating the rate to be set out here]
If applicable Costs If applicable The conditions under which those costs may be changed	[The costs applicable from the time the credit agreement is concluded]
Costs in the case of late payments	You will be charged [...... (applicable interest rate and arrangements for its adjustment and, where applicable, default charges)] for missing payments.

[*] Not applicable to European Consumer Credit Information for overdrafts in those Member States which decide on the basis of Article 6(2) of Directive 2008/48/EC that the APR need not be provided for overdrafts.

4. Other important legal aspects

Termination of the credit agreement	[The conditions and procedure for terminating the credit agreement]
Consultation of a database *The creditor must inform you immediately and without charge of the result of a consultation of a database if a credit application is rejected on the basis of such a consultation. This does not apply if the provision of such information is prohibited by European Community law or is contrary to objectives of public policy or public security.*	
If applicable The period of time during which the creditor is bound by the pre-contractual information	This information is valid from ... until ...

If applicable

5. Additional information to be given where the pre-contractual information is provided by certain credit organisations (Article 2(5) of Directive 2008/48/EC or relates to a consumer credit for debt conversion

Instalments and, where appropriate, the order in which instalments will be allocated	You will have to pay the following: [Representative example of an instalment table including the amount, number and frequency of payments to be made by the consumer]
The total amount you will have to pay	
Early repayment *You have the right to repay the credit early at any time in full or partially.* If applicable The creditor is entitled to compensation in the case of early repayment	[Determination of the compensation (calculation method) in accordance with the provisions implementing Article 16 of Directive 2008/48/EC]

If applicable

6. Additional information to be given in the case of distance marketing of financial services

(a) concerning the creditor	
If applicable Representative of the creditor in your Member State of residence Address Telephone number [*] E-mail address [*] Fax number [*] Web address [*]	[Identity] [Geographical address to be used by the consumer]
If applicable Registration	[The trade register in which the creditor is entered and his registration number or an equivalent means of identification in that register]
If applicable The supervisory authority	
(b) concerning the credit agreement	
Right of withdrawal *You have the right to withdraw from the credit agreement within a period of 14 calendar days.* If applicable Exercise of the right of withdrawal	Yes/no [Practical instructions for exercising the right of withdrawal indicating, inter alia, the address to which notification of exercise of the right of withdrawal should be sent and the consequences of non-exercise of that right]
If applicable The law taken by the creditor as a basis for the establishment of relations with you before the conclusion of the credit contract	
If applicable Clause stipulating the law applicable to the credit agreement and/or the competent court	[Relevant clause to be set out here]
If applicable Language regime	Information and contractual terms will be supplied in [specific language]. With your consent, we intend to communicate in [specific language/languages] during the duration of the credit agreement.

(c) concerning redress	
Existence of and access to out-of-court complaint and redress mechanism	[Whether or not there is an out-of-court complaint and redress mechanism for the consumer who is party to the distance contract and, if so, the methods of access to it]

[*] This information is optional for the creditor.

[4563]

DIRECTIVE OF THE EUROPEAN PARLIAMENT AND OF THE COUNCIL

of 14 January 2009

on the protection of consumers in respect of certain aspects of timeshare, long-term holiday product, resale and exchange contracts

(2008/122/EC)

(Text with EEA relevance)

NOTE

Date of publication in OJ: OJ L33, 3.2.2009, p 10.
As at 29 July 2010 this Directive had not been implemented in the UK.

THE EUROPEAN PARLIAMENT AND THE COUNCIL OF THE EUROPEAN UNION,

Having regard to the Treaty establishing the European Community, and in particular Article 95 thereof,

Having regard to the proposal from the Commission,

Having regard to the opinion of the European Economic and Social Committee[1],

Acting in accordance with the procedure laid down in Article 251 of the Treaty[2],

Whereas:

(1) Since the adoption of Directive 94/47/EC of the European Parliament and of the Council of 26 October 1994 on the protection of purchasers in respect of certain aspects of contracts relating to the purchase of the right to use immovable properties on a timeshare basis[3], timeshare has evolved and new holiday products similar to it have appeared on the market. These new holiday products and certain transactions related to timeshare, such as resale contracts and exchange contracts, are not covered by Directive 94/47/EC. In addition, experience with the application of Directive 94/47/EC has shown that some subjects already covered need to be updated or clarified, in order to prevent the development of products aiming at circumventing this Directive.

(2) The existing regulatory gaps create appreciable distortions of competition and cause serious problems for consumers, thus hindering the smooth functioning of the internal market. Directive 94/47/EC should therefore be replaced by a new up-to-date directive. Since tourism plays an increasingly important role in the economies of the Member States, greater growth and productivity in the timeshare and long-term holiday product industries should be encouraged by adopting certain common rules.

(3) In order to enhance legal certainty and fully achieve the benefits of the internal market for consumers and businesses, the relevant laws of the Member States need to be approximated further. Therefore, certain aspects of the marketing, sale and resale of timeshares and long-term holiday products as well as the exchange of rights deriving from timeshare contracts should be fully harmonised. Member States should not be allowed to maintain or introduce in their national legislation provisions diverging from those laid down in this Directive. Where no such harmonised provisions exist, Member States should remain free to maintain or introduce national legislation in conformity with Community law. Thus, Member States should, for instance, be able to maintain or introduce provisions on the effects of exercising the right of withdrawal in legal relationships falling outside the scope of this Directive or provisions according to which no commitment may be entered into between a consumer and a trader of a timeshare or long-term holiday product, nor any payment made between those persons, as long as the consumer has not signed a credit agreement to finance the purchase of those services.

(4) This Directive should be without prejudice to the application by Member States, in accordance with Community law, of the provisions of this Directive to areas not within its scope. Member States could therefore maintain or introduce national legislation corresponding to the provisions of this Directive or certain of its provisions in relation to transactions that fall outside the scope of this Directive.

(5)   The different contracts covered by this Directive should be clearly defined in such a way as to preclude circumvention of its provisions.

(6)   For the purposes of this Directive, timeshare contracts should not be understood as covering multiple reservations of accommodation, including hotel rooms, in so far as multiple reservations do not imply rights and obligations beyond those arising from separate reservations. Nor should timeshare contracts be understood as covering ordinary lease contracts since the latter refer to one single continuous period of occupation and not to multiple periods.

(7)   For the purposes of this Directive, long-term holiday product contracts should not be understood as covering ordinary loyalty schemes which provide discounts on future stays in the hotels of a hotel chain, since membership in the scheme is not obtained for consideration nor is the consideration paid by the consumer primarily for the purpose of obtaining discounts or other benefits in respect of accommodation.

(8)   This Directive should not affect the provisions of Council Directive 90/314/EEC of 13 June 1990 on package travel, package holidays and package tours[4].

(9)   Directive 2005/29/EC of the European Parliament and of the Council of 11 May 2005 concerning unfair business-to-consumer commercial practices in the internal market (Unfair Commercial Practices Directive)[5] prohibits misleading, aggressive and other unfair commercial business-to-consumer practices. Given the nature of the products and the commercial practices related to timeshares, long-term holiday products, resale and exchange, it is appropriate to adopt more detailed and specific provisions regarding information requirements and sales events. The commercial purpose of invitations to sales events should be made clear to consumers. The provisions concerning pre-contractual information and the contract should be clarified and updated. In order to give consumers the possibility to acquaint themselves with the information before the conclusion of the contract, it should be provided by means which are easily accessible to them at that time.

(10)   Consumers should have the right, which should not be refused by traders, to be provided with pre-contractual information and the contract in a language, of their choice, with which they are familiar. In addition, in order to facilitate the execution and the enforcement of the contract, Member States should be allowed to determine that further language versions of the contract should be provided to consumers.

(11)   In order to provide consumers with the opportunity of fully understanding their rights and obligations under the contract, they should be allowed a period during which they may withdraw from the contract without having to justify the withdrawal and without bearing any cost. Currently the length of this period varies between Member States, and experience shows that the length prescribed in Directive 94/47/EC is not sufficiently long. The period should therefore be extended in order to achieve a high level of consumer protection and more clarity for consumers and traders. The length of the period, the modalities for and the effects of exercising the right of withdrawal should be harmonised.

(12)   Consumers should have effective remedies in the event that traders do not comply with the provisions regarding pre-contractual information or the contract, in particular those laying down that the contract should include all the information required and that the consumer should receive a copy of the contract at the time of its conclusion. In addition to the remedies existing under national law, consumers should benefit from an extended withdrawal period where information has not been provided by traders. The exercise of the right of withdrawal should remain free of charge during that extended period regardless of what services consumers may have enjoyed. The expiration of the withdrawal period does not preclude consumers from seeking remedies in accordance with national law for breaches of the information requirements.

(13)   Council Regulation (EEC, Euratom) No 1182/71 of 3 June 1971 determining the rules applicable to periods, dates and time limits[6] should apply to the calculation of the periods set out in this Directive.

(14)   The prohibition on advance payments to traders or any third party before the end of the withdrawal period should be clarified in order to improve consumer protection. For resale contracts, the prohibition of advance payment should apply until the actual sale takes place or the resale contract is terminated, but Member States should remain free to regulate the possibility and modalities of final payments to intermediaries where resale contracts are terminated.

(15)   For long-term holiday product contracts, the price to be paid in the context of a staggered payment schedule could take into consideration the possibility that subsequent amounts could be adjusted after the first year in order to ensure that the real value of those instalments is maintained, for instance to take account of inflation.

(16)   In the event of a consumer withdrawing from a contract where the price is entirely or partly covered by credit granted to the consumer by the trader or by a third party on the basis of an arrangement between that third party and the trader, the credit agreement should be terminated at no cost to the consumer. The same should apply to contracts for other related services provided by the trader or by a third party on the basis of an arrangement between that third party and the trader.

(17)   Consumers should not be deprived of the protection granted by this Directive where the law applicable to the contract is that of a Member State. The law applicable to a contract should be determined in accordance with the Community rules on private international law, in particular Regulation (EC) No 593/2008 of the European Parliament and of the Council of 17 June 2008 on the law applicable to contractual obligations (Rome I)[7]. Under that Regulation, the law of a third

country may be applicable, in particular where consumers are targeted by traders whilst on holiday in a country other than their country of residence. Given that such commercial practices are common in the area covered by this Directive and that the contracts involve considerable amounts of money, an additional safeguard should be provided in certain specific situations, in particular where the courts of any Member State have jurisdiction over the contract, to ensure that the consumer is not deprived of the protection granted by this Directive. This concept reflects the particular needs of consumer protection arising from the typical complexity, long-term nature and financial relevance of the contracts falling within the scope of this Directive.

(18)   It should be determined in accordance with Council Regulation (EC) No 44/2001 of 22 December 2000 on jurisdiction and the recognition and enforcement of judgments in civil and commercial matters[8] which courts have jurisdiction in proceedings which have as their object matters covered by this Directive.

(19)   In order to ensure that the protection afforded to consumers under this Directive is fully effective, in particular as regards compliance by traders with the information requirements both at the pre-contractual stage and in the contract, it is necessary that the Member States lay down effective, proportionate and dissuasive penalties for infringements of this Directive.

(20)   It is necessary to ensure that persons or organisations having, under national law, a legitimate interest in the matter have legal remedies for initiating proceedings against infringements of this Directive.

(21)   It is necessary to develop suitable and effective redress procedures in the Member States for settling disputes between consumers and traders. To this end, Member States should encourage the establishment of public or private bodies for settling disputes out of court.

(22)   Member States should ensure that consumers are effectively informed of the national provisions transposing this Directive and encourage traders and code owners to inform consumers about their codes of conduct in this field. With the aim of pursuing a high level of consumer protection, consumer organisations could be informed of, and involved in, the drafting of codes of conduct.

(23)   Since the objectives of this Directive cannot be sufficiently achieved by the Member States and can therefore be better achieved at Community level, the Community may adopt measures in accordance with the principle of subsidiarity as set out in Article 5 of the Treaty. In accordance with the principle of proportionality, as set out in that Article, this Directive does not go beyond what is necessary in order to eliminate the internal market barriers and achieve a high common level of consumer protection.

(24)   This Directive respects the fundamental rights and observes the principles recognised in particular by the European Convention on Human Rights and Fundamental Freedoms and the Charter of Fundamental Rights of the European Union.

(25)   In accordance with point 34 of the Interinstitutional agreement on better law-making[9], Member States are encouraged to draw up, for themselves and in the interests of the Community, their own tables, which will, as far as possible, illustrate the correlation between this Directive and the transposition measures, and to make them public,

NOTES

[1]   OJ C44, 16.2.2008, p 27.
[2]   Opinion of the European Parliament of 22 October 2008 (not yet published in the Official Journal) and Council Decision of 18 December 2008.
[3]   OJ L280, 29.10.1994, p 83.
[4]   OJ L158, 23.6.1990, p 59.
[5]   OJ L149, 11.6.2005, p 22.
[6]   OJ L124, 8.6.1971, p 1.
[7]   OJ L177, 4.7.2008, p 6.
[8]   OJ L12, 16.1.2001, p 1.
[9]   OJ C321, 31.12.2003, p 1.

HAVE ADOPTED THIS DIRECTIVE:

Article 1
Purpose and scope

1.   The purpose of this Directive is to contribute to the proper functioning of the internal market and to achieve a high level of consumer protection, by approximating the laws, regulations and administrative provisions of the Member States in respect of certain aspects of the marketing, sale and resale of timeshares and long-term holiday products as well as exchange contracts.

2.   This Directive applies to trader-to-consumer transactions.
This Directive is without prejudice to national legislation which:
   (a)   provides for general contract law remedies;
   (b)   relates to the registration of immovable or movable property and conveyance of immovable property;
   (c)   relates to conditions of establishment or authorisation regimes or licensing requirements; and

(d)   relates to the determination of the legal nature of the rights which are the subject of the contracts covered by this Directive.

[4564]

Article 2
Definitions

1.   For the purposes of this Directive, the following definitions shall apply:

(a)   "timeshare contract" means a contract of a duration of more than one year under which a consumer, for consideration, acquires the right to use one or more overnight accommodation for more than one period of occupation;

(b)   "long-term holiday product contract" means a contract of a duration of more than one year under which a consumer, for consideration, acquires primarily the right to obtain discounts or other benefits in respect of accommodation, in isolation or together with travel or other services;

(c)   "resale contract" means a contract under which a trader, for consideration, assists a consumer to sell or buy a timeshare or a long-term holiday product;

(d)   "exchange contract" means a contract under which a consumer, for consideration, joins an exchange system which allows that consumer access to overnight accommodation or other services in exchange for granting to other persons temporary access to the benefits of the rights deriving from that consumer's timeshare contract;

(e)   "trader" means a natural or legal person who is acting for purposes relating to that person's trade, business, craft or profession and anyone acting in the name of or on behalf of a trader;

(f)   "consumer" means a natural person who is acting for purposes which are outside that person's trade, business, craft or profession;

(g)   "ancillary contract" means a contract under which the consumer acquires services which are related to a timeshare contract or long-term holiday product contract and which are provided by the trader or a third party on the basis of an arrangement between that third party and the trader;

(h)   "durable medium" means any instrument which enables the consumer or the trader to store information addressed personally to him in a way which is accessible for future reference for a period of time adequate for the purposes of the information and which allows the unchanged reproduction of the information stored;

(i)   "code of conduct" means an agreement or set of rules not imposed by law, regulation or administrative provision of a Member State which defines the behaviour of traders who undertake to be bound by the code in relation to one or more particular commercial practices or business sectors;

(j)   "code owner" means any entity, including a trader or group of traders, which is responsible for the formulation and revision of a code of conduct and/or for monitoring compliance with the code by those who have undertaken to be bound by it.

2.   In calculating the duration of a timeshare contract or a long-term holiday product contract, as defined in points (a) and (b) of paragraph 1 respectively, any provision in the contract allowing for tacit renewal or prolongation shall be taken into account.

[4565]

Article 3
Advertising

1.   Member States shall ensure that any advertising specifies the possibility of obtaining the information referred to in Article 4(1) and indicates where it can be obtained.

2.   Where a timeshare, long-term holiday product, resale or exchange contract is to be offered to a consumer in person at a promotion or sales event, the trader shall clearly indicate in the invitation the commercial purpose and the nature of the event.

3.   The information referred to in Article 4(1) shall be available to the consumer at any time during the event.

4.   A timeshare or a long-term holiday product shall not be marketed or sold as an investment.

[4566]

Article 4
Pre-contractual information

1.   In good time before the consumer is bound by any contract or offer, the trader shall provide the consumer, in a clear and comprehensible manner, with accurate and sufficient information, as follows:

(a)   in the case of a timeshare contract: by means of the standard information form as set out in Annex I and information as listed in Part 3 of that form;

(b)   in the case of a long-term holiday product contract: by means of the standard information form as set out in Annex II and information as listed in Part 3 of that form;

(c)   in the case of a resale contract: by means of the standard information form as set out in Annex III and information as listed in Part 3 of that form;

    (d)   in the case of an exchange contract: by means of the standard information form as set out in Annex IV and information as listed in Part 3 of that form.

2.   The information referred to in paragraph 1 shall be provided, free of charge, by the trader on paper or on another durable medium which is easily accessible to the consumer.

3.   Member States shall ensure that the information referred to in paragraph 1 is drawn up in the language or one of the languages of the Member State in which the consumer is resident or a national, at the choice of the consumer, provided it is an official language of the Community.

[4567]

Article 5
The timeshare, long-term holiday product, resale or exchange contract

1.   Member States shall ensure that the contract is in writing, on paper or on another durable medium, and drawn up in the language or one of the languages of the Member State in which the consumer is resident or a national, at the choice of the consumer, provided it is an official language of the Community.

However, the Member State in which the consumer is resident may require that in addition:
    (a)   in every instance, the contract be provided to the consumer in the language or one of the languages of that Member State, provided it is an official language of the Community;
    (b)   in the case of a timeshare contract concerning one specific immovable property, the trader provide the consumer with a certified translation of the contract in the language or one of the languages of the Member State in which the property is situated, provided it is an official language of the Community.

The Member State on whose territory the trader carries out sale activities may require that, in every instance, the contract be provided to the consumer in the language or one of the languages of that Member State, provided it is an official language of the Community.

2.   The information referred to in Article 4(1) shall form an integral part of the contract and shall not be altered unless the parties expressly agree otherwise or the changes result from unusual and unforeseeable circumstances beyond the trader's control, the consequences of which could not have been avoided even if all due care had been exercised.

These changes shall be communicated to the consumer on paper or on another durable medium easily accessible to him, before the contract is concluded.

The contract shall expressly mention any such changes.

3.   In addition to the information referred to in Article 4(1), the contract shall include:
    (a)   the identity, place of residence and signature of each of the parties; and
    (b)   the date and place of the conclusion of the contract.

4.   Before the conclusion of the contract, the trader shall explicitly draw the consumer's attention to the existence of the right of withdrawal, the length of the withdrawal period referred to in Article 6, and the ban on advance payments during the withdrawal period referred to in Article 9.

The corresponding contractual clauses shall be signed separately by the consumer.

The contract shall include a separate standard withdrawal form, as set out in Annex V, intended to facilitate the exercise of the right of withdrawal in accordance with Article 6.

5.   The consumer shall receive a copy or copies of the contract at the time of its conclusion.

[4568]

Article 6
Right of withdrawal

1.   In addition to the remedies available to the consumer under national law in the event of breach of the provisions of this Directive, Member States shall ensure that the consumer is given a period of 14 calendar days to withdraw from the timeshare, long-term holiday product, resale or exchange contract, without giving any reason.

2.   The withdrawal period shall be calculated:
    (a)   from the day of the conclusion of the contract or of any binding preliminary contract; or
    (b)   from the day when the consumer receives the contract or any binding preliminary contract if it is later than the date referred to in point (a).

3.   The withdrawal period shall expire:
    (a)   after one year and 14 calendar days from the day referred to in paragraph 2 of this Article, where a separate standard withdrawal form as required by Article 5(4) has not been filled in by the trader and provided to the consumer in writing, on paper or on another durable medium;
    (b)   after three months and 14 calendar days from the day referred to in paragraph 2 of this Article, where the information referred to in Article 4(1), including the applicable standard information form set out in Annexes I to IV, has not been provided to the consumer in writing, on paper or on another durable medium.

In addition, Member States shall provide for appropriate penalties in accordance with Article 15, in particular in the event that, on expiry of the withdrawal period, the trader has failed to comply with the information requirements set out in this Directive.

4. Where a separate standard withdrawal form as required by Article 5(4) has been filled in by the trader and provided to the consumer in writing, on paper or on another durable medium, within one year from the day referred to in paragraph 2 of this Article, the withdrawal period shall start from the day the consumer receives that form. Similarly, where the information referred to in Article 4(1), including the applicable standard information form set out in Annexes I to IV, has been provided to the consumer in writing, on paper or on another durable medium, within three months from the day referred to in paragraph 2 of this Article, the withdrawal period shall start from the day the consumer receives such information.

5. In the event that the exchange contract is offered to the consumer together with and at the same time as the timeshare contract, only a single withdrawal period in accordance with paragraph 1 shall apply to both contracts. The withdrawal period for both contracts shall be calculated according to the provisions of paragraph 2 as they apply to the timeshare contract.

[4569]

Article 7
Modalities for exercising the right of withdrawal

Where the consumer intends to exercise the right of withdrawal the consumer shall, before the expiry of the withdrawal period, notify the trader on paper or on another durable medium of the decision to withdraw. The consumer may use the standard withdrawal form set out in Annex V and provided by the trader in accordance with Article 5(4). The deadline is met if the notification is sent before the withdrawal period has expired.

[4570]

Article 8
Effects of exercising the right of withdrawal

1. The exercise of the right of withdrawal by the consumer terminates the obligation of the parties to perform the contract.

2. Where the consumer exercises the right of withdrawal, the consumer shall neither bear any cost nor be liable for any value corresponding to the service which may have been performed before withdrawal.

[4571]

Article 9
Advance payment

1. Member States shall ensure that in relation to timeshare, long-term holiday product and exchange contracts any advance payment, provision of guarantees, reservation of money on accounts, explicit acknowledgement of debt or any other consideration to the trader or to any third party by the consumer before the end of the withdrawal period according to Article 6, is prohibited.

2. Member States shall ensure that in relation to resale contracts any advance payment, provision of guarantees, reservation of money on accounts, explicit acknowledgement of debt or any other consideration to the trader or to any third party by the consumer before the actual sale takes place or the resale contract is otherwise terminated, is prohibited.

[4572]

Article 10
Specific provisions relating to long-term holiday product contracts

1. For long-term holiday product contracts, payment shall be made according to a staggered payment schedule. Any payment of the price specified in the contract otherwise than in accordance with the staggered payment schedule shall be prohibited. The payments, including any membership fee, shall be divided into yearly instalments, each of which shall be of equal value. The trader shall send a written request for payment, on paper or on another durable medium, at least fourteen calendar days in advance of each due date.

2. From the second instalment payment onwards, the consumer may terminate the contract without incurring any penalty by giving notice to the trader within fourteen calendar days of receiving the request for payment of each instalment. This right shall not affect rights to terminate the contract under existing national legislation.

[4573]

Article 11
Termination of ancillary contracts

1. Member States shall ensure that, where the consumer exercises the right to withdraw from the timeshare or long-term holiday product contract, any exchange contract ancillary to it or any other ancillary contract is automatically terminated, at no cost to the consumer.

2. Without prejudice to Article 15 of Directive 2008/48/EC of the European Parliament and of the Council of 23 April 2008 on credit agreements for consumers[1], where the price is fully or partly covered by a credit granted to the consumer by the trader, or by a third party on the basis of an arrangement between the third party and the trader, the credit agreement shall be terminated, at no cost to the consumer, where the consumer exercises the right to withdraw from the timeshare, long-term holiday product, resale or exchange contract.

3. The Member States shall lay down detailed rules on the termination of such contracts.

[4574]

NOTES

¹ OJ L133, 22.5.2008, p 66.

Article 12
Imperative nature of the Directive and application in international cases

1. Member States shall ensure that, where the law applicable to the contract is the law of a Member State, consumers may not waive the rights conferred on them by this Directive.

2. Where the applicable law is that of a third country, consumers shall not be deprived of the protection granted by this Directive, as implemented in the Member State of the forum if:

— any of the immovable properties concerned is situated within the territory of a Member State, or,

— in the case of a contract not directly related to immovable property, the trader pursues commercial or professional activities in a Member State or, by any means, directs such activities to a Member State and the contract falls within the scope of such activities.

[4575]

Article 13
Judicial and administrative redress

1. Member States shall ensure that, in the interests of consumers, adequate and effective means exist to ensure compliance by traders with this Directive.

2. The means referred to in paragraph 1 shall include provisions whereby one or more of the following bodies, as determined by national law, shall be entitled to take action in accordance with national law before the courts or competent administrative bodies to ensure that the national provisions for implementing this Directive are applied:

(a) public bodies and authorities or their representatives;

(b) consumer organisations with a legitimate interest in protecting consumers;

(c) professional organisations with a legitimate interest in taking such action.

[4576]

Article 14
Consumer information and out-of-court redress

1. Member States shall take appropriate measures to inform consumers of the national law transposing this Directive and shall encourage, where appropriate, traders and code owners to inform consumers of their codes of conduct.

The Commission shall encourage the drawing up at Community level, particularly by professional bodies, organisations and associations, of codes of conduct aimed at facilitating the implementation of this Directive, in conformity with Community law. It shall also encourage traders and their branch organisations to inform consumers of any such codes, including, where appropriate, by means of a specific marking.

2. Member States shall encourage the setting up or development of adequate and effective out-of-court complaints and redress procedures for the settlement of consumer disputes under this Directive and shall, where appropriate, encourage traders and their branch organisations to inform consumers of the availability of such procedures.

[4577]

Article 15
Penalties

1. Member States shall provide for appropriate penalties in the event of a trader's failure to comply with the national provisions adopted pursuant to this Directive.

2. Those penalties shall be effective, proportionate and dissuasive.

[4578]

Article 16
Transposition

1. Member States shall adopt and publish, by 23 February 2011, the laws, regulations and administrative provisions necessary to comply with this Directive. They shall forthwith communicate to the Commission the text of those provisions.

They shall apply those provisions from 23 February 2011.

When Member States adopt those provisions, they shall contain a reference to this Directive or be accompanied by such a reference on the occasion of their official publication. Member States shall determine how such reference is to be made.

2. Member States shall communicate to the Commission the text of the main provisions of national law which they adopt in the field covered by this Directive.

[4579]

Article 17
Review

The Commission shall review this Directive and report to the European Parliament and the Council no later than 23 February 2014.

If necessary, it shall make further proposals to adapt it to developments in the area.

The Commission may request information from the Member States and the national regulatory authorities.

[4580]

Article 18
Repeal

Directive 94/47/EC shall be repealed.

References to the repealed Directive shall be construed as references to this Directive and shall be read in accordance with the correlation table in Annex VI.

[4581]

Article 19
Entry into force

This Directive shall enter into force on the 20th day following its publication in the *Official Journal of the European Union*.

[4582]

Article 20
Addressees

This Directive is addressed to the Member States.

[4583]

Done at Strasbourg, 14 January 2009.

ANNEX I
STANDARD INFORMATION FORM FOR TIMESHARE CONTRACTS
Part 1:

Identity, place of residence and legal status of the trader(s) which will be party to the contract:
Short description of the product (e g description of the immovable property):
Exact nature and content of the right(s):
Exact period within which the right which is the subject of the contract may be exercised and, if necessary, its duration:
Date on which the consumer may start to exercise the contractual right:
If the contract concerns a specific property under construction, date when the accommodation and services/facilities will be completed/available:
Price to be paid by the consumer for acquiring the right(s):
Outline of additional obligatory costs imposed under the contract; type of costs and indication of amounts (e g annual fees, other recurrent fees, special levies, local taxes):

A summary of key services available to the consumer (eg electricity, water, maintenance, refuse collection) and an indication of the amount to be paid by the consumer for such services:

A summary of facilities available to the consumer (eg swimming pool or sauna):

Are these facilities included in the costs indicated above?

If not, specify what is included and what has to be paid for:

Is it possible to join an exchange scheme?

If yes, specify the name of the exchange scheme:

Indication of costs for membership/exchange:

Has the trader signed a code/codes of conduct and, if yes, where can it/they be found?

Part 2:

General information:
— The consumer has the right to withdraw from this contract without giving any reason within 14 calendar days from the conclusion of the contract or any binding preliminary contract or receipt of those contracts if that takes place later.
— During this withdrawal period, any advance payment by the consumer is prohibited. The prohibition concerns any consideration, including payment, provision of guarantees, reservation of money on accounts, explicit acknowledgement of debt etc. It includes not only payment to the trader, but also to third parties.
— The consumer shall not bear any costs or obligations other than those specified in the contract.
— In accordance with international private law, the contract may be governed by a law other than the law of the Member State in which the consumer is resident or is habitually domiciled and possible disputes may be referred to courts other than those of the Member State in which the consumer is resident or is habitually domiciled.

Signature of the consumer:

Part 3:

Additional information to which the consumer is entitled and where it can be obtained specifically (for instance, under which chapter of a general brochure) if not provided below:

1. INFORMATION ABOUT THE RIGHTS ACQUIRED
— conditions governing the exercise of the right which is the subject of the contract within the territory of the Member States(s) in which the property or properties concerned are situated and information on whether those conditions have been fulfilled or, if they have not, what conditions remain to be fulfilled,
— where the contract provides rights to occupy accommodation to be selected from a pool of accommodation, information on restrictions on the consumer's ability to use any accommodation in the pool at any time.

2. INFORMATION ON THE PROPERTIES
— where the contract concerns a specific immovable property, an accurate and detailed description of that property and its location; where the contract concerns a number of properties (multi-resorts), an appropriate description of the properties and their location; where the contract concerns accommodation other than immovable property, an appropriate description of the accommodation and the facilities,

— the services (eg electricity, water, maintenance, refuse collection) to which the consumer has or will have access to and under what conditions,
— where applicable, the common facilities, such as swimming pool, sauna, etc, to which the consumer has or may have access and under what conditions.

3. ADDITIONAL REQUIREMENTS FOR ACCOMMODATION UNDER CONSTRUCTION (where applicable)
— the state of completion of the accommodation and of the services rendering the accommodation fully operational (gas, electricity, water and telephone connections) and any facilities to which the consumer will have access,
— the deadline for completion of the accommodation and of the services rendering it fully operational (gas, electricity, water and telephone connections) and a reasonable estimate of the deadline for the completion of any facilities to which the consumer will have access,
— the number of the building permit and the name(s) and full address(es) of the competent authority or authorities,
— a guarantee regarding completion of the accommodation or a guarantee regarding reimbursement of any payment made if the accommodation is not completed and, where appropriate, the conditions governing the operation of such guarantees.

4. INFORMATION ON THE COSTS
— an accurate and appropriate description of all costs associated with the timeshare contract; how these costs will be allocated to the consumer and how and when such costs may be increased; the method for the calculation of the amount of charges relating to occupation of the property, the mandatory statutory charges (for example, taxes and fees) and the administrative overheads (for example, management, maintenance and repairs),
— where applicable, information on whether there are any charges, mortgages, encumbrances or any other liens recorded against title to the accommodation.

5. INFORMATION ON TERMINATION OF THE CONTRACT
— where appropriate, information on the arrangements for the termination of ancillary contracts and the consequences of such termination,
— conditions for terminating the contract, the consequences of termination, and information on any liability of the consumer for any costs which might result from such termination.

6. ADDITIONAL INFORMATION
— information on how maintenance and repairs of the property and its administration and management are arranged, including whether and how consumers may influence and participate in the decisions regarding these issues,
— information on whether or not it is possible to join a system for the resale of the contractual rights, information about the relevant system and an indication of costs related to resale through this system,
— indication of the language(s) available for communication with the trader in relation to the contract, for instance in relation to management decisions, increase of costs and the handling of queries and complaints,
— where applicable, the possibility for out-of-court dispute resolution.

Acknowledgement of receipt of information:

Signature of the consumer:

[4584]

ANNEX II
STANDARD INFORMATION FORM FOR LONG-TERM HOLIDAY PRODUCT CONTRACTS
Part 1:

Identity, place of residence and legal status of the trader(s) which will be party to the contract:
Short description of the product:
Exact nature and content of the right(s):

Exact period within which the right which is the subject of the contract may be exercised and, if necessary, its duration:

Date on which the consumer may start to exercise the contractual right:

Price to be paid by the consumer for acquiring the right(s), including any recurring costs the consumer can expect to incur resulting from the right to obtain access to the accommodation, travel and any related products or services as specified:

The staggered payment schedule setting out equal amounts of instalments of this price for each year of the length of the contract and the dates on which they are due to be paid:

After year 1, subsequent amounts may be adjusted to ensure that the real value of those instalments is maintained, for instance to take account of inflation.

Outline of additional obligatory costs imposed under the contract; type of costs and indication of amounts (e g annual membership fees):

A summary of key services available to the consumer (e g discounted hotel stays and flights):

Are they included in the costs indicated above?

If not, specify what is included and what has to be paid for (e g three-night stay included in annual membership fee, all other accommodation must be paid for separately):

Has the trader signed a code/codes of conduct and, if yes, where can it/they be found?

Part 2:

General information:
— The consumer has the right to withdraw from this contract without giving any reason within 14 calendar days from the conclusion of the contract or any binding preliminary contract or receipt of those contracts if that takes place later.
— During this withdrawal period, any advance payment by the consumer is prohibited. The prohibition concerns any consideration, including payment, provision of guarantees, reservation of money on accounts, explicit acknowledgement of debt etc. It includes not only payment to the trader, but also to third parties.
— The consumer has the right to terminate the contract without incurring any penalty by giving notice to the trader within 14 calendar days of receiving the request for payment for each annual instalment.
— The consumer shall not bear any costs or obligations other than those specified in the contract.
— In accordance with international private law, the contract may be governed by a law other than the law of the Member State in which the consumer is resident or is habitually domiciled and possible disputes may be referred to courts other than those of the Member State in which the consumer is resident or is habitually domiciled.

Signature of the consumer:

Part 3:

Additional information to which the consumer is entitled and where it can be obtained specifically (for instance, under which chapter of a general brochure) if not provided below:
1. INFORMATION ABOUT THE RIGHTS ACQUIRED

— an appropriate and correct description of discounts available for future bookings, illustrated by a set of examples of recent offers,

— information on the restrictions on the consumer's ability to use the rights, such as limited availability or offers provided on a first-come-first-served basis, time limits on particular promotions and special discounts.

2. INFORMATION ON THE TERMINATION OF THE CONTRACT

— where appropriate, information on the arrangements for the termination of ancillary contracts and the consequences of such termination,

— conditions for terminating the contract, the consequences of termination, and information on any liability of the consumer for any costs which might result from such termination.

3. ADDITIONAL INFORMATION

— indication of the language(s) available for communication with the trader in relation to the contract, for instance in relation to the handling of queries and complaints,

— where applicable, the possibility for out-of-court dispute resolution.

Acknowledgement of receipt of information:

Signature of the consumer:

[4585]

ANNEX III
STANDARD INFORMATION FORM FOR RESALE CONTRACTS

Part 1:

Identity, place of residence and legal status of the trader(s) which will be party to the contract:
Short description of the services (e g marketing):
Duration of the contract:
Price to be paid by the consumer for acquiring the services:
Outline of additional obligatory costs imposed under the contract; type of costs and indication of amounts (e g local taxes, notary fees, cost of advertising):
Has the trader signed a code/codes of conduct and, if yes, where can it/they be found?

Part 2:

General information:

— The consumer has the right to withdraw from this contract without giving any reason within 14 calendar days from the conclusion of the contract or any binding preliminary contract or receipt of those contracts if that takes place later.

— Any advance payment by the consumer is prohibited until the actual sale has taken place or the resale contract otherwise is terminated. The prohibition concerns any consideration, including payment, provision of guarantees, reservation of money on accounts, explicit acknowledgement of debt etc. It includes not only payment to the trader, but also to third parties.

— The consumer shall not bear any costs or obligations other than those specified in the contract.

— In accordance with international private law, the contract may be governed by a law other than the law of the Member State in which the consumer is resident or is habitually domiciled and possible disputes may be referred to courts other than those of the Member State in which the consumer is resident or is habitually domiciled.

Signature of the consumer:

Part 3:

> Additional information to which the consumer is entitled and where it can be obtained specifically (for instance, under which chapter of a general brochure) if not provided below:
> — conditions for terminating the contract, the consequences of termination, and information on any liability of the consumer for any costs which might result from such termination,
> — indication of the language(s) available for communication with the trader in relation to the contract, for instance in relation to the handling of queries and complaints,
> — where applicable, the possibility for out-of-court dispute resolution.

Acknowledgement of receipt of information:

Signature of the consumer:

[4586]

ANNEX IV
STANDARD INFORMATION FORM FOR EXCHANGE CONTRACTS

Part 1:

Identity, place of residence and legal status of the trader(s) which will be party to the contract:
Short description of the product:
Exact nature and content of the right(s):
Exact period within which the right which is the subject of the contract may be exercised and, if necessary, its duration:
Date on which the consumer may start to exercise the contractual right:
Price to be paid by the consumer for the exchange membership fees:
Outline of additional obligatory costs imposed under the contract; type of costs and indication of amounts (e g renewal fees, other recurrent fees, special levies, local taxes):
A summary of key services available to the consumer:
Are they included in the costs indicated above?
If not, specify what is included and what has to be paid for (type of costs and indication of amounts; e g an estimate of the price to be paid for individual exchange transactions, including any additional charges):
Has the trader signed a code/codes of conduct and, if yes, where can it/they be found?

Part 2:

General information:

— The consumer has the right to withdraw from this contract without giving any reason within 14 calendar days from the conclusion of the contract or any binding preliminary contract or receipt of those contracts if that takes place later. In cases where the exchange contract is offered together with and at the same time as the timeshare contract, only a single withdrawal period shall apply to both contracts.

— During this withdrawal period, any advance payment by the consumer is prohibited. The prohibition concerns any consideration, including payment, provision of guarantees, reservation of money on accounts, explicit acknowledgement of debt etc. It includes not only payment to the trader, but also to third parties.

— The consumer shall not bear any costs or obligations other than those specified in the contract,

— In accordance with international private law, the contract may be governed by a law other than the law of the Member State in which the consumer is resident or is habitually domiciled and possible disputes may be referred to courts other than those of the Member State in which the consumer is resident or is habitually domiciled.

Signature of the consumer:

Part 3:

Additional information to which the consumer is entitled and where it can be obtained specifically (for instance, under which chapter of a general brochure) if not provided below:

1. INFORMATION ABOUT THE RIGHTS ACQUIRED

— explanation of how the exchange system works; the possibilities and modalities for exchange; an indication of the value allotted to the consumer's timeshare in the exchange system and a set of examples of concrete exchange possibilities,

— an indication of the number of resorts available and the number of members in the exchange system, including any limitations on the availability of particular accommodation selected by the consumer, for example, as the result of peak periods of demand, the potential need to book a long time in advance, and indications of any restrictions on the choice resulting from the timeshare rights deposited into the exchange system by the consumer.

2. INFORMATION ON THE PROPERTIES

— a brief and appropriate description of the properties and their location; where the contract concerns accommodation other than immovable property, an appropriate description of the accommodation and the facilities; description of where the consumer can obtain further information.

3. INFORMATION ON THE COSTS

— information on the obligation on the trader to provide details before an exchange is arranged, in respect of each proposed exchange, of any additional charges for which the consumer is liable in respect of the exchange.

4. INFORMATION ON THE TERMINATION OF THE CONTRACT

— where appropriate, information on the arrangements for the termination of ancillary contracts and the consequences of such termination,

— conditions for terminating the contract, the consequences of termination, and information on any liability of the consumer for any costs which might result from such termination.

5. ADDITIONAL INFORMATION

— indication of the language(s) available for communication with the trader in relation to the contract, for instance in relation to the handling of queries and complaints,

— where applicable, the possibility for out-of-court dispute resolution.

Acknowledgement of receipt of information:

Signature of the consumer:

ANNEX V
SEPARATE STANDARD WITHDRAWAL FORM TO FACILITATE THE RIGHT OF WITHDRAWAL

Right of withdrawal

The consumer has the right to withdraw from this contract within 14 calendar days without giving any reason.

The right of withdrawal starts from .... (to be filled in by the trader before providing the form to the consumer).

Where the consumer has not received this form, the withdrawal period starts when the consumer has received this form, but expires in any case after one year and 14 calendar days.

Where the consumer has not received all the required information, the withdrawal period starts when the consumer has received that information, but expires in any case after three months and 14 calendar days.

To exercise the right of withdrawal, the consumer shall notify the trader using the name and address indicated below by using a durable medium (e g written letter sent by post, e-mail). The consumer may use this form, but it is not obligatory.

Where the consumer exercises the right of withdrawal, the consumer shall not be liable for any costs.

In addition to the right of withdrawal, national contract law rules may provide for consumer rights, e g to terminate the contract in case of omission of information.

Ban on advance payment

During the withdrawal period any advance payment by the consumer is prohibited. The prohibition concerns any consideration, including payment, provision of guarantees, reservation of money on accounts, explicit acknowledgement of debt, etc.

It includes not only payment to the trader, but also to third parties.

Notice of withdrawal

— To (Name and address of the trader) (*):

— I/We (**) hereby give notice that I/We (**) withdraw from the contract,

— Date of conclusion of contract (*):

— Name(s) of consumer(s) (***):

— Address(es) of consumer(s) (***):

— Signature(s) of consumer(s) (only if this form is notified on paper) (***):

— Date (***):

(*) To be filled in by the trader before providing the form to the consumer.

(**) Delete as appropriate.

(***) To be filled in by the consumer(s) where this form is used to withdraw from the contract.

Acknowledgement of receipt of information:

Signature of the consumer:

[4588]

ANNEX VI
CORRELATION TABLE BETWEEN PROVISIONS OF THIS DIRECTIVE AND DIRECTIVE 94/47/EC

Directive 94/47/EC	*This Directive*
Article 1, first paragraph	Article 1(1) and Article 1(2), first subparagraph
Article 1, second paragraph	—
Article 1, third paragraph	Article 1(2), second subparagraph
Article 2, first indent	Article 2(1)(a)

Directive 94/47/EC	*This Directive*
—	Article 2(1)(b) (new)
—	Article 2(1)(c) (new)
—	Article 2(1)(d) (new)
Article 2, second indent	—
Article 2, third indent	Article 2(1)(e)
Article 2, fourth indent	Article 2(1)(f)
—	Article 2(1)(g) (new)
—	Article 2(1)(h) (new)
—	Article 2(1)(i) (new)
—	Article 2(1)(j) (new)
—	Article 2(2) (new)
Article 3(1)	Article 4(1)
Article 3(2)	Article 5(2)
Article 3(3)	Article 3(1)
—	Article 3(2) (new)
—	Article 3(3) (new)
—	Article 3(4) (new)
Article 4, first indent	Article 5(1), first subparagraph, and Article 5(2), first subparagraph
Article 4, second indent	Article 4(3) and Article 5(1)
—	Article 4(2) (new)
—	Article 5(4) (new)
—	Article 5(5) (new)
Article 5(1), introductory sentence	Article 6(1)
Article 5(1), first indent	Article 6(1) and Article 6(2)
Article 5(1), second indent	Article 6(3) and Article 6(4)
Article 5(1), third indent	Article 6(3)
—	Article 6(5) (new)
Article 5(2)	Article 7
—	Article 8(1) (new)
Article 5(3)	Article 8(2)
Article 5(4)	Article 8(2)
Article 6	Article 9(1)
—	Article 9(2) (new)
—	Article 10(1) (new)
—	Article 10(2) (new)
—	Article 11(1) (new)
Article 7, first paragraph	Article 11(2)
Article 7, second paragraph	Article 11(3)
Article 8	Article 12(1)
Article 9	Article 12(2)
Article 10	Articles 13 and 15
Article 11	—
—	Article 14(1) (new)
—	Article 14(2) (new)

Directive 94/47/EC	This Directive
Article 12	Article 16
—	Article 17 (new)
—	Article 18 (new)
—	Article 19 (new)
Article 13	Article 20
Annex	Annex I
Annex, point (a)	Article 5(3)(a), and Annex I, Part 1, first box
Annex, point (b)	Annex I, Part 1, third box, and Annex I, Part 3, point 1, first indent
Annex, point (c)	Annex I, Part 1, second box, and Annex I, Part 3, point 2, first indent
Annex, point (d)(1)	Annex I, Part 3, point 3, first indent
Annex, point (d)(2)	Annex I, Part 1, fourth box, and Annex I, Part 3, point 3, second indent
Annex, point (d)(3)	Annex I, Part 3, point 3, third indent
Annex, point (d)(4)	Annex I, Part 3, point 3, first indent
Annex, point (d)(5)	Annex I, Part 3, point 3, fourth indent
Annex, point (e)	Annex I, Part 1, sixth box, and Annex I, Part 3, point 2, second indent
Annex, point (f)	Annex I, Part 1, sixth box, and Annex I, Part 3, point 2, third indent
Annex, point (g)	Annex I, Part 3, point 6, first indent
Annex, point (h)	Annex I, Part 1, fourth box
Annex, point (i)	Annex I, Part 1, fifth and sixth boxes, and Annex I, Part 3, point 4, first indent
Annex, point (j)	Annex I, Part 2, third indent
Annex, point (k)	Annex I, Part 2, seventh box, and Annex I, Part 3, point 6, second indent
Annex, point (l)	Annex I, Part 2, first and third indents, Annex I, Part 3, point 5, first indent, and Annex V (new)
Annex, point (m)	Article 5(3)(b)
—	Annex I, Part 1, eighth box (new)
—	Annex I, Part 2, second indent (new)
—	Annex I, Part 2, fourth indent (new)
—	Annex I, Part 3, point 1, second indent (new)
—	Annex I, Part 3, point 4, second indent (new)
—	Annex I, Part 3, point 5, second indent (new)
—	Annex I, Part 3, point 6, third indent (new)
—	Annex I, Part 3, point 6, fourth indent (new)
—	Annexes II to V (new)

DIRECTIVE OF THE EUROPEAN PARLIAMENT AND OF THE COUNCIL

of 23 April 2009

on injunctions for the protection of consumers' interests
(Text with EEA relevance)

(2009/22/EC)

NOTE
Date of publication in OJ: OJ L110, 1.5.2009, p 30.
As at 29 July 2010 this Directive had not been implemented in the UK.

THE EUROPEAN PARLIAMENT AND THE COUNCIL OF THE EUROPEAN UNION,

Having regard to the Treaty establishing the European Community, and in particular Article 95 thereof,

Having regard to the proposal from the Commission,

Having regard to the opinion of the European Economic and Social Committee[1],

Acting in accordance with the procedure laid down in Article 251 of the Treaty[2],

Whereas:

(1)   Directive 98/27/EC of the European Parliament and of the Council of 19 May 1998 on injunctions for the protection of consumers' interests[3] has been substantially amended several times[4]. In the interests of clarity and rationality the said Directive should be codified.

(2)   Certain Directives, listed in Annex I to this Directive, lay down rules with regard to the protection of consumers' interests.

(3)   Current mechanisms available for ensuring compliance with those Directives, both at national and at Community level, do not always allow infringements harmful to the collective interests of consumers to be terminated in good time. Collective interests means interests which do not include the cumulation of interests of individuals who have been harmed by an infringement. This is without prejudice to individual actions brought by individuals who have been harmed by an infringement.

(4)   As far as the purpose of bringing about the cessation of practices that are unlawful under the national provisions applicable is concerned, the effectiveness of national measures transposing the Directives in question, including protective measures that go beyond the level required by those Directives, provided they are compatible with the Treaty and allowed by those Directives, may be thwarted where those practices produce effects in a Member State other than that in which they originate.

(5)   Those difficulties can disrupt the smooth functioning of the internal market, their consequence being that it is sufficient to move the source of an unlawful practice to another country in order to place it out of reach of all forms of enforcement. This constitutes a distortion of competition.

(6)   Those difficulties are likely to diminish consumer confidence in the internal market and may limit the scope for action by organisations representing the collective interests of consumers or independent public bodies responsible for protecting the collective interests of consumers, adversely affected by practices that infringe Community law.

(7)   Those practices often extend beyond the frontiers between the Member States. There is an urgent need for some degree of approximation of national provisions designed to enjoin the cessation of the unlawful practices irrespective of the Member State in which the unlawful practice has produced its effects. With regard to jurisdiction, this is without prejudice to the rules of private international law and the Conventions in force between Member States, while respecting the general obligations of the Member States deriving from the Treaty, in particular those related to the smooth functioning of the internal market.

(8)   The objective of the action envisaged can only be attained by the Community. It is therefore incumbent on the Community to act.

(9)   The third paragraph of Article 5 of the Treaty makes it incumbent on the Community not to go beyond what is necessary to achieve the objectives of the Treaty. In accordance with that Article, the specific features of national legal systems must be taken into account to every extent possible by leaving Member States free to choose between different options having equivalent effect. The courts or administrative authorities competent to rule on the proceedings referred to in this Directive should have the right to examine the effects of previous decisions.

(10)   One option should consist in requiring one or more independent public bodies, specifically responsible for the protection of the collective interests of consumers, to exercise the rights of action

PART 3

EU AND INTERNATIONAL MATERIALS

set out in this Directive. Another option should provide for the exercise of those rights by organisations whose purpose is to protect the collective interests of consumers, in accordance with criteria laid down by national law.

(11)   Member States should be able to choose between or combine these two options in designating at national level the bodies and/or organisations qualified for the purposes of this Directive.

(12)   For the purposes of intra-Community infringements the principle of mutual recognition should apply to these bodies and/or organisations. The Member States should, at the request of their national entities, communicate to the Commission the name and purpose of their national entities which are qualified to bring an action in their own country according to the provisions of this Directive.

(13)   It is the business of the Commission to ensure the publication of a list of these qualified entities in the *Official Journal of the European Union*. Until a statement to the contrary is published, a qualified entity is assumed to have legal capacity if its name is included in that list.

(14)   Member States should be able to require that a prior consultation be undertaken by the party that intends to bring an action for an injunction, in order to give the defendant an opportunity to bring the contested infringement to an end. Member States should be able to require that this prior consultation take place jointly with an independent public body designated by those Member States.

(15)   Where the Member States have established that there should be prior consultation, a deadline of two weeks after the request for consultation is received should be set after which, should the cessation of the infringement not be achieved, the applicant shall be entitled to bring an action, without any further delay, before the competent court or administrative authority.

(16)   It is appropriate that the Commission report on the functioning of this Directive and in particular on its scope and on the operation of prior consultation.

(17)   The application of this Directive should not prejudice the application of Community competition rules.

(18)   This Directive should be without prejudice to the obligations of the Member States concerning the time limits for transposition and application in national law of the Directives set out in Annex II, Part B,

NOTES

1	OJ C161, 13.7.2007, p 39.
2	Opinion of the European Parliament of 19 June 2007 (OJ C146 E, 12.6.2008, p 73) and Council Decision of 23 March 2009.
3	OJ L166, 11.6.1998, p 51.
4	See Annex II, Part A.

HAVE ADOPTED THIS DIRECTIVE:

Article 1
Scope

1.   The purpose of this Directive is to approximate the laws, regulations and administrative provisions of the Member States relating to actions for an injunction referred to in Article 2 aimed at the protection of the collective interests of consumers included in the Directives listed in Annex I, with a view to ensuring the smooth functioning of the internal market.

2.   For the purposes of this Directive, an infringement means any act contrary to the Directives listed in Annex I as transposed into the internal legal order of the Member States which harms the collective interests referred to in paragraph 1.

[4590]

Article 2
Actions for an injunction

1   Member States shall designate the courts or administrative authorities competent to rule on proceedings commenced by qualified entities within the meaning of Article 3 seeking:

(a)   an order with all due expediency, where appropriate by way of summary procedure, requiring the cessation or prohibition of any infringement;

(b)   where appropriate, measures such as the publication of the decision, in full or in part, in such form as deemed adequate and/or the publication of a corrective statement with a view to eliminating the continuing effects of the infringement;

(c)   in so far as the legal system of the Member State concerned so permits, an order against the losing defendant for payments into the public purse or to any beneficiary designated in or under national legislation, in the event of failure to comply with the decision within a time limit specified by the courts or administrative authorities, of a fixed amount for each day's delay or any other amount provided for in national legislation, with a view to ensuring compliance with the decisions.

2.   This Directive shall be without prejudice to the rules of private international law with respect to the applicable law, that is, normally, either the law of the Member State where the infringement originated or the law of the Member State where the infringement has its effects.

[4591]

Article 3
Entities qualified to bring an action

For the purposes of this Directive, a 'qualified entity' means any body or organisation which, being properly constituted according to the law of a Member State, has a legitimate interest in ensuring that the provisions referred to in Article 1 are complied with, in particular:
  (a)   one or more independent public bodies, specifically responsible for protecting the interests referred to in Article 1, in Member States in which such bodies exist; and/or
  (b)   organisations whose purpose is to protect the interests referred to in Article 1, in accordance with the criteria laid down by the national law.

[4592]

Article 4
Intra-Community infringements

1.   Each Member State shall take the measures necessary to ensure that, in the event of an infringement originating in that Member State, any qualified entity from another Member State where the interests protected by that qualified entity are affected by the infringement, may apply to the court or administrative authority referred to in Article 2, on presentation of the list provided for in paragraph 3 of this Article. The courts or administrative authorities shall accept this list as proof of the legal capacity of the qualified entity without prejudice to their right to examine whether the purpose of the qualified entity justifies its taking action in a specific case.

2.   For the purposes of intra-Community infringements, and without prejudice to the rights granted to other entities under national legislation, the Member States shall, at the request of their qualified entities, communicate to the Commission that these entities are qualified to bring an action under Article 2. The Member States shall inform the Commission of the name and purpose of these qualified entities.

3.   The Commission shall draw up a list of the qualified entities referred to in paragraph 2, with the specification of their purpose. This list shall be published in the *Official Journal of the European Union*; changes to this list shall be published without delay and the updated list shall be published every six months.

[4593]

Article 5
Prior consultation

1.   Member States may introduce or maintain in force provisions whereby the party that intends to seek an injunction can only start this procedure after it has tried to achieve the cessation of the infringement in consultation either with the defendant or with both the defendant and a qualified entity within the meaning of Article 3(a) of the Member State in which the injunction is sought. It shall be for the Member State to decide whether the party seeking the injunction must consult the qualified entity. If the cessation of the infringement is not achieved within two weeks after the request for consultation is received, the party concerned may bring an action for an injunction without any further delay.

2.   The rules governing prior consultation adopted by Member States shall be notified to the Commission and shall be published in the *Official Journal of the European Union*.

[4594]

Article 6
Reports

1.   Every three years and for the first time no later than 2 July 2003 the Commission shall submit to the European Parliament and to the Council a report on the application of this Directive.

2.   In its first report the Commission shall examine in particular:
  (a)   the scope of this Directive in relation to the protection of the collective interests of persons exercising a commercial, industrial, craft or professional activity;
  (b)   the scope of this Directive as determined by the Directives listed in Annex I;
  (c)   whether the prior consultation provided for in Article 5 has contributed to the effective protection of consumers.

Where appropriate, this report shall be accompanied by proposals with a view to amending this Directive.

[4595]

Article 7
Provisions for wider action

This Directive shall not prevent Member States from adopting or maintaining in force provisions designed to grant qualified entities and any other person concerned more extensive rights to bring action at national level.

[4596]

Article 8
Implementation

Member States shall communicate to the Commission the provisions of national law which they adopt in the field covered by this Directive.

[4597]

Article 9
Repeal

Directive 98/27/EC, as amended by the Directives set out in Annex II, Part A, is repealed, without prejudice to the obligations of the Member States concerning the time limits for transposition into national law and application of the Directives set out in Annex II, Part B.

References to the repealed Directive shall be construed as references to this Directive and shall be read in accordance with the correlation table in Annex III.

[4598]

Article 10
Entry into force

This Directive shall enter into force on 29 December 2009.

[4599]

Article 11
Addressees

This Directive is addressed to the Member States.

[4600]

Done at Strasbourg, 23 April 2009.

ANNEX I
LIST OF DIRECTIVES REFERRED TO IN ARTICLE 1[1]

1.   Council Directive 85/577/EEC of 20 December 1985 to protect the consumer in respect of contracts negotiated away from business premises (OJ L372, 31.12.1985, p 31).

2.   Council Directive 87/102/EEC of 22 December 1986 for the approximation of the laws, regulations and administrative provisions of the Member States concerning consumer credit (OJ L42, 12.2.1987, p 48)[2].

3.   Council Directive 89/552/EEC of 3 October 1989 on the coordination of certain provisions laid down by law, regulation or administrative action in Member States concerning the pursuit of television broadcasting activities: Articles 10 to 21 (OJ L298, 17.10.1989, p 23).

4.   Council Directive 90/314/EEC of 13 June 1990 on package travel, package holidays and package tours (OJ L158, 23.6.1990, p 59).

5.   Council Directive 93/13/EEC of 5 April 1993 on unfair terms in consumer contracts (OJ L95, 21.4.1993, p 29).

6.   Directive 97/7/EC of the European Parliament and of the Council of 20 May 1997 on the protection of consumers in respect of distance contracts (OJ L144, 4.6.1997, p 19).

7.   Directive 1999/44/EC of the European Parliament and of the Council of 25 May 1999 on certain aspects of the sale of consumer goods and associated guarantees (OJ L171, 7.7.1999, p 12).

8.   Directive 2000/31/EC of the European Parliament and of the Council of 8 June 2000 on certain legal aspects on information society services, in particular electronic commerce, in the internal market (Directive on electronic commerce) (OJ L178, 17.7.2000, p 1).

9.   Directive 2001/83/EC of the European Parliament and of the Council of 6 November 2001 on the Community code relating to medicinal products for human use: Articles 86 to 100 (OJ L311, 28.11.2001, p 67).

10.   Directive 2002/65/EC of the European Parliament and of the Council of 23 September 2002 concerning the distance marketing of consumer financial services (OJ L271, 9.10.2002, p 16).

11.   Directive 2005/29/EC of the European Parliament and of the Council of 11 May 2005 concerning unfair business-to-consumer commercial practices in the internal market (OJ L149, 11.6.2005, p 22).

12.   Directive 2006/123/EC of the European Parliament and of the Council of 12 December 2006 on services in the internal market (OJ L376, 27.12.2006, p 36).

13.   Directive 2008/122/EC of the European Parliament and of the Council of 14 January 2009 on the protection of consumers in respect of certain aspects of timeshare, long-term holiday product, resale and exchange contracts (OJ L33, 3.2.2009, p 10).

[4601]

NOTES

[1]   The Directives referred to in points 5, 6, 9 and 11 contain specific provisions concerning injunctions.

[2]   The said Directive was repealed and replaced, with effect from 12 May 2010, by Directive 2008/48/EC of the European Parliament and of the Council of 23 April 2008 on credit agreements for consumers (OJ L133, 22.5.2008, p 66).

ANNEX II

PART A

REPEALED DIRECTIVE AND ITS AMENDMENTS

(referred to in Article 9)

Directive 98/27/EC of the European Parliament and of the Council
(OJ L166, 11.6.1998, p 51).

Directive 1999/44/EC of the European Parliament and of the Council (OJ L171, 7.7.1999, p 12).	Article 10 only
Directive 2000/31/EC of the European Parliament and of the Council (OJ L178, 17.7.2000, p 1).	Article 18(2) only
Directive 2002/65/EC of the European Parliament and of the Council (OJ L271, 9.10.2002, p 16).	Article 19 only
Directive 2005/29/EC of the European Parliament and of the Council (OJ L149, 11.6.2005, p 22).	Article 16(1) only
Directive 2006/123/EC of the European Parliament and of the Council (OJ L376, 27.12.2006, p 36).	Article 42 only

[4602]

PART B

LIST OF TIME LIMITS FOR TRANSPOSITION INTO NATIONAL LAW AND APPLICATION

(referred to in Article 9)

Directive	*Time limit for transposition*	*Date of application*
98/27/EC	1 January 2001	—
1999/44/EC	1 January 2002	—
2000/31/EC	16 January 2002	—
2002/65/EC	9 October 2004	—
2005/29/EC	12 June 2007	12 December 2007
2006/123/EC	28 December 2009	—

[4603]

ANNEX III
CORRELATION TABLE

Directive 98/27/EC	*This Directive*
Articles 1 to 5	Articles 1 to 5
Article 6(1)	Article 6(1)
Article 6(2), first subparagraph, first indent	Article 6(2), first subparagraph, point (a)
Article 6(2), first subparagraph, second indent	Article 6(2), first subparagraph, point (b)
Article 6(2), first subparagraph, third indent	Article 6(2), first subparagraph, point (c)
Article 6(2), second subparagraph	Article 6(2), second subparagraph
Article 7	Article 7
Article 8(1)	—
Article 8(2)	Article 8
—	Article 9
Article 9	Article 10
Article 10	Article 11
Annex	Annex I
—	Annex II
—	Annex III

[4604]

APPENDIX
CCA 1974 (PRE CCA 2006)

CONSUMER CREDIT ACT 1974 (PRE CCA 2006)

(1974 c 39)

ARRANGEMENT OF SECTIONS

PART I
OFFICE OF FAIR TRADING

PART II
CREDIT AGREEMENTS, HIRE AGREEMENTS AND LINKED TRANSACTIONS

PART III
LICENSING OF CREDIT AND HIRE BUSINESSES

Licensing principles

Issue of licences

Renewal, variation, suspension and revocation of licences

Miscellaneous

PART IV
SEEKING BUSINESS

Advertising

An Act to establish for the protection of consumers a new system, administered by the Director General of Fair Trading, of licensing and other control of traders concerned with the provision of credit, or the supply of goods on hire or hire-purchase, and their transactions, in place of the present enactments regulating moneylenders, pawnbrokers and hire-purchase traders and their transactions, and for related matters

[31st July 1974]

NOTES
    The text of the Consumer Credit Act 1974 reproduced in this Appendix is as it had effect on 15 June 2006, prior to amendments made by the Consumer Credit Act 2006, and subsequent amendments. For the text of the 1974 Act as it has effect on 29 July 2010, with all amendments incorporated, see [651] et seq and the notes to individual provisions below.
    Substitution of references to the Director General of Fair Trading: the Enterprise Act 2002, s 2(1), at [1860], provides that, as from the coming into force of that section (on 1 April 2003, see the Enterprise Act 2002 (Commencement No 2, Transitional and Transitory Provisions) Order 2003, SI 2003/766), the functions of the Director General of Fair Trading, his property, rights and liabilities are transferred to the Office of Fair Trading. Accordingly, (by virtue of s 2(2), (3) of the 2002 Act) the office of the Director is abolished, and amendments are made to this Act by the 2002 Act to take account of this (see Sch 25, para 6). Consequently, throughout this Act, unless noted otherwise, the words "OFT", "OFT's", "it", "it" and "its" are substituted for the original words "Director", "Director's", "he", "him" and "his" respectively. For transitional provisions in connection with the transfer, see s 276(1) of, and Sch 24, para 6 to, the 2002 Act.

PART I
[OFFICE OF FAIR TRADING]

NOTES
    Part heading: words in square brackets substituted by the Enterprise Act 2002, s 278(1), Sch 25, para 6(1), (2), as from 1 April 2003.

1   General functions of [OFT]

    (1)   It is the duty of the [Office of Fair Trading ("the OFT")]—
        (a)   to administer the licensing system set up by this Act,
        (b)   to exercise the adjudicating functions conferred on [it] by this Act in relation to the issue, renewal, variation, suspension and revocation of licences, and other matters,
        (c)   generally to superintend the working and enforcement of this Act, and regulations made under it, and

    (d)   where necessary or expedient, [itself] to take steps to enforce this Act, and regulations so made.

    (2)   It is the duty of the [OFT], so far as appears to [it] to be practicable and having regard both to the national interest and the interests of persons carrying on businesses to which this Act applies and their customers, to keep under review and from time to time advise the Secretary of State about—

    (a)   social and commercial developments in the United Kingdom and elsewhere relating to the provision of credit or bailment or (in Scotland) hiring of goods to individuals, and related activities; and

    (b)   the working and enforcement of this Act and orders and regulations made under it.

        [A1]

NOTES

    This section is printed as it was in force on 15 June 2006, prior to amendments made by the Consumer Credit Act 2006 and subsequent amendments; for the text of this provision as it currently has effect, see [651].

    Sub-s (1): words in first pair of square brackets and words in square brackets in para (d) substituted by the Enterprise Act 2002, s 278(1), Sch 25, para 6(1), (2)(a)(i), (iii), as from 1 April 2003.

    References to the OFT, etc: as to the abolition of the office of the Director General of Fair Trading and the substitution of the original references to the Director (and related expressions), see the note preceding s 1 at [A1].

2 Powers of Secretary of State

    (1)   The Secretary of State may by order—

    (a)   confer on the [OFT] additional functions concerning the provision of credit or bailment or (in Scotland) hiring of goods to individuals, and related activities, and

    (b)   regulate the carrying out by the [OFT] of [its] functions under this Act.

    (2)   The Secretary of State may give general directions indicating considerations to which the [OFT] should have particular regard in carrying out [its] functions under this Act, and may give specific directions on any matter connected with the carrying out by the [OFT] of those functions.

    (3)   The Secretary of State, on giving any directions under subsection (2), shall arrange for them to be published in such manner as he thinks most suitable for drawing them to the attention of interested persons.

    (4)   With the approval of the Secretary of State and the Treasury, the [OFT] may charge, for any service or facility provided by [it] under this Act, a fee of an amount specified by general notice (the "specified fee").

    (5)   Provision may be made under subsection (4) for reduced fees, or no fees at all, to be paid for certain services or facilities by persons of a specified description, and references in this Act to the specified fee shall, in such cases, be construed accordingly.

    (6)   An order under subsection (1)(a) shall be made by statutory instrument and shall be of no effect unless a draft of the order has been laid before and approved by each House of Parliament.

    (7)   References in subsection (2) to the functions of the [OFT] under this Act do not include the making of a determination to which section 41 or 150 (appeals from [OFT] to the Secretary of State) applies.

        [A2]

NOTES

    This section is printed as it was in force on 15 June 2006, prior to amendments made by the Consumer Credit Act 2006 and subsequent amendments; for the text of this provision as it currently has effect, see [652].

    References to the OFT, etc: as to the abolition of the office of the Director General of Fair Trading and the substitution of the original references to the Director (and related expressions), see the note preceding s 1 at [A1].

    Order: the Consumer Credit Licensing (Representations) Order 1976, SI 1976/191.

3   *(Repealed by the Tribunals and Inquiries Act 1992, s 18(2), Sch 4, Pt I, as from 1 October 1992.)*

4 Dissemination of information and advice

The [OFT] shall arrange for the dissemination, in such form and manner as [it] considers appropriate, of such information and advice as it may appear to [it] expedient to give to the public in the United Kingdom about the operation of this Act, the credit facilities available to them, and other matters within the scope of [its] functions under this Act.

        [A3]

NOTES
This section is printed as it was in force on 15 June 2006, prior to amendments made by the Consumer Credit Act 2006 and subsequent amendments; for the text of this provision as it currently has effect, see [653].
References to the OFT, etc: as to the abolition of the office of the Director General of Fair Trading and the substitution of the original references to the Director (and related expressions), see the note preceding s 1 at [A1].

5 (*Repealed by the Enterprise Act 2002, s 278(2), Sch 26, as from 20 June 2003.*)

6 Form etc of application

(1) An application to the [OFT] under this Act is of no effect unless the requirements of this section are satisfied.

(2) The application must be in writing, and in such form, and accompanied by such particulars, as the [OFT] may specify by general notice, and must be accompanied by the specified fee.

(3) After giving preliminary consideration to an application, the [OFT] may by notice require the applicant to furnish [it] with such further information relevant to the application as may be described in the notice, and may require any information furnished by the applicant (whether at the time of the application or subsequently) to be verified in such manner as the [OFT] may stipulate.

(4) The [OFT] may by notice require the applicant to publish details of his application at a time or times and in a manner specified in the notice.

[A4]

NOTES
This section is printed as it was in force on 15 June 2006, prior to amendments made by the Consumer Credit Act 2006 and subsequent amendments; for the text of this provision as it currently has effect, see [654].
References to the OFT, etc: as to the abolition of the office of the Director General of Fair Trading and the substitution of the original references to the Director (and related expressions), see the note preceding s 1 at [A1].

7 Penalty for false information

A person who, in connection with any application or request to the [OFT] under this Act, or in response to any invitation or requirement of the [OFT] under this Act, knowingly or recklessly gives information to the [OFT] which, in a material particular, is false or misleading, commits an offence.

[A5]

NOTES
This section is printed as it was in force on 15 June 2006, prior to amendments made by the Consumer Credit Act 2006 and subsequent amendments; for the text of this provision as it currently has effect, see [655].
References to the OFT, etc: as to the abolition of the office of the Director General of Fair Trading and the substitution of the original references to the Director (and related expressions), see the note preceding s 1 at [A1].

PART II
CREDIT AGREEMENTS, HIRE AGREEMENTS AND LINKED TRANSACTIONS

8 Consumer credit agreements

(1) A personal credit agreement is an agreement between an individual ("the debtor") and any other person ("the creditor") by which the creditor provides the debtor with credit of any amount.

(2) A consumer credit agreement is a personal credit agreement by which the creditor provides the debtor with credit not exceeding [£25,000].

(3) A consumer credit agreement is a regulated agreement within the meaning of this Act if it is not an agreement (an "exempt agreement") specified in or under section 16.

[A6]

NOTES
This section is printed as it was in force on 15 June 2006, prior to amendments made by the Consumer Credit Act 2006 and subsequent amendments; for the text of this provision as it currently has effect, see [656].
Sub-s (2): sum in square brackets substituted by the Consumer Credit (Increase of Monetary Limits) Order 1983, SI 1983/1878, Schedule, Pt II (as amended by SI 1998/996, art 2), as from 1 May 1998.

9 Meaning of credit

(1) In this Act "credit" includes a cash loan, and any other form of financial accommodation.

(2)   Where credit is provided otherwise than in sterling, it shall be treated for the purposes of this Act as provided in sterling of an equivalent amount.

(3)   Without prejudice to the generality of subsection (1), the person by whom goods are bailed or (in Scotland) hired to an individual under a hire-purchase agreement shall be taken to provide him with fixed-sum credit to finance the transaction of an amount equal to the total price of the goods less the aggregate of the deposit (if any) and the total charge for credit.

(4)   For the purposes of this Act, an item entering into the total charge for credit shall not be treated as credit even though time is allowed for its payment.

[A7]

NOTES
   This section is printed as it was in force on 15 June 2006, prior to amendments made by the Consumer Credit Act 2006 and subsequent amendments; for the text of this provision as it currently has effect, see [657].

10   Running-account credit and fixed-sum credit

(1)   For the purposes of this Act—
   (a)   running-account credit is a facility under a personal credit agreement whereby the debtor is enabled to receive from time to time (whether in his own person, or by another person) from the creditor or a third party cash, goods and services (or any of them) to an amount or value such that, taking into account payments made by or to the credit of the debtor, the credit limit (if any) is not at any time exceeded; and
   (b)   fixed-sum credit is any other facility under a personal credit agreement whereby the debtor is enabled to receive credit (whether in one amount or by instalments).

(2)   In relation to running-account credit, "credit limit" means, as respects any period, the maximum debit balance which, under the credit agreement, is allowed to stand on the account during that period, disregarding any term of the agreement allowing that maximum to be exceeded merely temporarily.

(3)   For the purposes of section 8(2), running-account credit shall be taken not to exceed the amount specified in that subsection ("the specified amount") if—
   (a)   the credit limit does not exceed the specified amount; or
   (b)   whether or not there is a credit limit, and if there is, notwithstanding that it exceeds the specified amount,—
      (i)   the debtor is not enabled to draw at any one time an amount which, so far as (having regard to section 9(4)) it represents credit, exceeds the specified amount, or
      (ii)   the agreement provides that, if the debit balance rises above a given amount (not exceeding the specified amount), the rate of the total charge for credit increases or any other condition favouring the creditor or his associate comes into operation, or
      (iii)   at the time the agreement is made it is probable, having regard to the terms of the agreement and any other relevant considerations, that the debit balance will not at any time rise above the specified amount.

[A8]

NOTES
   This section is printed as it was in force on 15 June 2006, prior to amendments made by the Consumer Credit Act 2006 and subsequent amendments; for the text of this provision as it currently has effect, see [658].

11   Restricted-use credit and unrestricted-use credit

(1)   A restricted-use credit agreement is a regulated consumer credit agreement—
   (a)   to finance a transaction between the debtor and the creditor, whether forming part of that agreement or not, or
   (b)   to finance a transaction between the debtor and a person (the "supplier") other than the creditor, or
   (c)   to refinance any existing indebtedness of the debtor's, whether to the creditor or another person,
and "restricted-use credit" shall be construed accordingly.

(2)   An unrestricted-use credit agreement is a regulated consumer credit agreement not falling within subsection (1), and "unrestricted-use credit" shall be construed accordingly.

(3)   An agreement does not fall within subsection (1) if the credit is in fact provided in such a way as to leave the debtor free to use it as he chooses, even though certain uses would contravene that or any other agreement.

(4)   An agreement may fall within subsection (1)(b) although the identity of the supplier is unknown at the time the agreement is made.

[A9]

NOTES
   This section is printed as it was in force on 15 June 2006, prior to amendments made by the Consumer Credit Act 2006 and subsequent amendments; for the text of this provision as it currently has effect, see [659].

12   Debtor-creditor-supplier agreements

A debtor-creditor-supplier agreement is a regulated consumer credit agreement being—
- (a)   a restricted-use credit agreement which falls within section 11(1)(a), or
- (b)   a restricted-use credit agreement which falls within section 11(1)(b) and is made by the creditor under pre-existing arrangements, or in contemplation of future arrangements, between himself and the supplier, or
- (c)   an unrestricted-use credit agreement which is made by the creditor under pre-existing arrangements between himself and a person (the "supplier") other than the debtor in the knowledge that the credit is to be used to finance a transaction between the debtor and the supplier.

[A10]

NOTES
   This section is printed as it was in force on 15 June 2006, prior to amendments made by the Consumer Credit Act 2006 and subsequent amendments; for the text of this provision as it currently has effect, see [660].

13   Debtor-creditor agreements

A debtor-creditor agreement is a regulated consumer credit agreement being—
- (a)   a restricted-use credit agreement which falls within section 11(1)(b) but is not made by the creditor under pre-existing arrangements, or in contemplation of future arrangements, between himself and the supplier, or
- (b)   a restricted-use credit agreement which falls within section 11(1)(c), or
- (c)   an unrestricted-use credit agreement which is not made by the creditor under pre-existing arrangements between himself and a person (the "supplier") other than the debtor in the knowledge that the credit is to be used to finance a transaction between the debtor and the supplier.

[A11]

NOTES
   This section is printed as it was in force on 15 June 2006, prior to amendments made by the Consumer Credit Act 2006 and subsequent amendments; for the text of this provision as it currently has effect, see [661].

14   Credit-token agreements

(1)   A credit-token is a card, check, voucher, coupon, stamp, form, booklet or other document or thing given to an individual by a person carrying on a consumer credit business, who undertakes—
- (a)   that on the production of it (whether or not some other action is also required) he will supply cash, goods and services (or any of them) on credit, or
- (b)   that where, on the production of it to a third party (whether or not any other action is also required), the third party supplies cash, goods and services (or any of them), he will pay the third party for them (whether or not deducting any discount or commission), in return for payment to him by the individual.

(2)   A credit-token agreement is a regulated agreement for the provision of credit in connection with the use of a credit-token.

(3)   Without prejudice to the generality of section 9(1), the person who gives to an individual an undertaking falling within subsection (1)(b) shall be taken to provide him with credit drawn on whenever a third party supplies him with cash, goods or services.

(4)   For the purposes of subsection (1), use of an object to operate a machine provided by the person giving the object or a third party shall be treated as the production of the object to him.

[A12]

NOTES
   This section is printed as it was in force on 15 June 2006, prior to amendments made by the Consumer Credit Act 2006 and subsequent amendments; for the text of this provision as it currently has effect, see [662].

15 Consumer hire agreements

(1) A consumer hire agreement is an agreement made by a person with an individual (the "hirer") for the bailment or (in Scotland) the hiring of goods to the hirer, being an agreement which—

(a) is not a hire-purchase agreement, and

(b) is capable of subsisting for more than three months, and

(c) does not require the hirer to make payments exceeding [£25,000].

(2) A consumer hire agreement is a regulated agreement if it is not an exempt agreement.

[A13]

NOTES

This section is printed as it was in force on 15 June 2006, prior to amendments made by the Consumer Credit Act 2006 and subsequent amendments; for the text of this provision as it currently has effect, see [663].

Sub-s (1): sum in square brackets in para (c) substituted by the Consumer Credit (Increase of Monetary Limits) Order 1983, SI 1983/1878, Schedule, Pt II (as amended by SI 1998/996, art 2), as from 1 May 1998.

16 Exempt agreements

(1) This Act does not regulate a consumer credit agreement where the creditor is a local authority … , or a body specified, or of a description specified, in an order made by the Secretary of State, being—

[(a) an insurer,]

(b) a friendly society,

(c) an organisation of employers or organisation of workers,

(d) a charity,

(e) a land improvement company, …

(f) a body corporate named or specifically referred to in any public general Act

[(ff) a body corporate named or specifically referred to in an order made under—

section 156(4), *444(1)* or 447(2)(a) of the Housing Act 1985,

[section 156(4) of that Act as it has effect by virtue of section 17 of the Housing Act 1996 (the right to acquire),]

(*applies to Scotland only.*)

Article 154(1)(a) or 156AA of the Housing (Northern Ireland) Order 1981 or Article 10(6A) of the Housing (Northern Ireland) Order 1983; or]

[(g) a building society][, or

[(h) a deposit-taker]].

(2) Subsection (1) applies only where the agreement is—

(a) a debtor-creditor-supplier agreement financing—

(i) the purchase of land, or

(ii) the provision of dwellings on any land,

and secured by a land mortgage on that land, or

(b) a debtor-creditor agreement secured by any land mortgage; or

(c) a debtor-creditor-supplier agreement financing a transaction which is a linked transaction in relation to—

(i) an agreement falling within paragraph (a), or

(ii) an agreement falling within paragraph (b) financing—

(aa) the purchase of any land, or

(bb) the provision of dwellings on any land,

and secured by a land mortgage on the land referred to in paragraph (a) or, as the case may be, the land referred to in sub-paragraph (ii).

[(3) Before he makes, varies or revokes an order under subsection (1), the Secretary of State must undertake the necessary consultation.

(3A) The necessary consultation means consultation with the bodies mentioned in the following table in relation to the provision under which the order is to be made, varied or revoked:

Table

Provision of subsection (1)	Consultee
Paragraph (a) or (b)	The Financial Services Authority
Paragraph (d)	Charity Commissioners
Paragraph (e), (f) or (ff)	Any Minister of the Crown with responsibilities in relation to the body in question

Provision of subsection (1)	Consultee
Paragraph (g) or (h)	The Treasury and the Financial Services Authority]

(4)   An order under subsection (1) relating to a body may be limited so as to apply only to agreements by that body of a description specified in the order.

(5)   The Secretary of State may by order provide that this Act shall not regulate other consumer credit agreements where—
  (a)   the number of payments to be made by the debtor does not exceed the number specified for that purpose in the order, or
  (b)   the rate of the total charge for credit does not exceed the rate so specified, or
  (c)   an agreement has a connection with a country outside the United Kingdom.

(6)   The Secretary of State may by order provide that this Act shall not regulate consumer hire agreements of a description specified in the order where—
  (a)   the owner is a body corporate authorised by or under any enactment to supply electricity, gas or water, and
  (b)   the subject of the agreement is a meter or metering equipment,
[or where the owner is a [provider of a public electronic communications service who is specified in the order]].

[(6A)   This Act does not regulate a consumer credit agreement where the creditor is a housing authority and the agreement is secured by a land mortgage of a dwelling.

  (6B)   In subsection (6A) "housing authority" means—
  (a)   as regards England and Wales, [the Housing Corporation ... and] an authority or body within section 80(1) of the Housing Act 1985 (the landlord condition for secure tenancies), other than a housing association or a housing trust which is a charity;
  (b)   (*applies to Scotland only*);
  (c)   as regards Northern Ireland, the Northern Ireland Housing Executive.]

  [(6C)   This Act does not regulate a consumer credit agreement if—
  (a)   it is secured by a land mortgage; and
  (b)   entering into that agreement as lender is a regulated activity for the purposes of the Financial Services and Markets Act 2000.

  (6D)   But section 126, and any other provision so far as it relates to section 126, applies to an agreement which would (but for subsection (6C) be a regulated agreement.

  (6E)   Subsection (6C) must be read with—
  (a)   section 22 of the Financial Services and Markets Act 2000 (regulated activities: power to specify classes of activity and categories of investment);
  (b)   any order for the time being in force under that section; and
  (c)   Schedule 2 to that Act.]

(7)   Nothing in this section affects the application of sections 137 to 140 (extortionate credit bargains).

(8)   (*Applies to Scotland only.*)

(9)   In the application of this section to Northern Ireland [subsection (3A)] shall have effect as if any reference to a Minister of the Crown were a reference to a Northern Ireland department, ... and any reference to the Charity Commissioners were a reference to the Department of Finance for Northern Ireland.

  [(10)   In this section—
  (a)   "deposit-taker" means—
    (i)   a person who has permission under Part 4 of the Financial Services and Markets Act 2000 to accept deposits,
    (ii)   an EEA firm of the kind mentioned in paragraph 5(b) of Schedule 3 to that Act which has permission under paragraph 15 of that Schedule (as a result of qualifying for authorisation under paragraph 12 of that Schedule) to accept deposits,
    (iii)   any wholly owned subsidiary (within the meaning of the Companies Act 1985) of a person mentioned in sub-paragraph (i), or
    (iv)   any undertaking which, in relation to a person mentioned in sub-paragraph (ii), is a subsidiary undertaking within the meaning of any rule of law in force in the EEA State in question for purposes connected with the implementation of the European Council Seventh Company Law Directive of 13 June 1983 on consolidated accounts (No 83/349/EEC), and which has no members other than that person;
  (b)   "insurer" means—

      (i)   a person who has permission under Part 4 of the Financial Services and Markets
           Act 2000 to effect or carry out contracts of insurance, or

      (ii)   an EEA firm of the kind mentioned in paragraph 5(d) of Schedule 3 to that Act,
           which has permission under paragraph 15 of that Schedule (as a result of
           qualifying for authorisation under paragraph 12 of that Schedule) to effect or
           carry out contracts of insurance,

      but does not include a friendly society or an organisation of workers or of employers.

(11)   Subsection (10) must be read with—
   (a)   section 22 of the Financial Services and Markets Act 2000;
   (b)   any relevant order under that section; and
   (c)   Schedule 2 to that Act.]

                                                                   [A14]

NOTES

   This section is printed as it was in force on 15 June 2006, prior to amendments made by the Consumer Credit Act 2006 and subsequent amendments; for the text of this provision as it currently has effect, see [664].

   Sub-s (1): first words omitted repealed, and para (g) added, by the Building Societies Act 1986, s 120, Sch 18, Pt I, para 10(2), Sch 19, Pt I, as from 1 January 1987; para (a) substituted by the Financial Services and Markets Act 2000 (Consequential Amendments and Repeals) Order 2001, SI 2001/3649, art 165(1), (2)(a), as from 1 December 2001; para (ff) inserted by the Housing and Planning Act 1986, s 22(2), (4), as from 7 January 1987 with respect to agreements made after that date, number in italics repealed by the Housing Act 1996, s 227, Sch 19, Pt XIV, as from a day to be appointed, and words in square brackets inserted by the Housing Act 1996 (Consequential Amendments) (No 2) Order 1997, SI 1997/627, art 2, Schedule, para 2, as from 1 April 1997; para (h) added by the Banking Act 1987, s 88 as from 1 October 1987, and substituted by SI 2001/3649, art 165(1), (2)(b), as from 1 December 2001.

   Sub-ss (3), (3A): substituted for original sub-s (3), by SI 2001/3649, art 165(1), (3), as from 1 December 2001.

   Sub-s (6): words in first (outer) pair of square brackets substituted by the Telecommunications Act 1984, s 109, Sch 4, para 60(1), as from 5 August 1984; words in second (inner) pair of square brackets substituted by the Communications Act 2003, s 406(1), Sch 17, para 47, as from 29 December 2003.

   Sub-s (6A): inserted, together with sub-s (6B), by the Housing and Planning Act 1986, s 22(3), (4), as from 7 January 1987 with respect to agreements made after that date.

   Sub-s (6B): inserted as noted to sub-s (6A); words in square brackets inserted by the Housing Act 1988, s 140(1), Sch 17, Pt I, para 20, as from 15 January 1989; words omitted repealed, subject to transitional provisions, by the Government of Wales Act 1998, ss 141, 152, Sch 18, Pt VI, as from 1 November 1998.

   Sub-s (6C)–(6E): inserted by the Financial Services and Markets Act 2000 (Regulated Activities) Order 2001, SI 2001/544, art 90(1), (2), as from 31 October 2004.

   Sub-s (9): words in square brackets substituted, and words omitted repealed, by SI 2001/3649, art 165(1), (5), as from 1 December 2001.

   Sub-ss (10), (11): added by SI 2001/3649, art 165(1), (6), as from 1 December 2001.

   Order: the Consumer Credit (Exempt Agreements) Order 1989, SI 1989/869 at **[3080]**.

---

17 Small agreements

(1)   A small agreement is—
   (a)   a regulated consumer credit agreement for credit not exceeding [£50], other than a
       hire-purchase or conditional sale agreement; or
   (b)   a regulated consumer hire agreement which does not require the hirer to make payments
       exceeding [£50],

being an agreement which is either unsecured or secured by a guarantee or indemnity only (whether or not the guarantee or indemnity is itself secured).

(2)   Section 10(3)(a) applies for the purposes of subsection (1) as it applies for the purposes of section 8(2).

(3)   Where—
   (a)   two or more small agreements are made at or about the same time between the same
       parties, and
   (b)   it appears probable that they would instead have been made as a single agreement but for
       the desire to avoid the operation of provisions of this Act which would have applied to
       that single agreement but, apart from this subsection, are not applicable to the small
       agreements,

this Act applies to the small agreements as if they were regulated agreements other than small agreements.

(4)   If, apart from this subsection, subsection (3) does not apply to any agreements but would apply if, for any party or parties to any of the agreements, there were substituted an associate of that party, or associates of each of those parties, as the case may be, then subsection (3) shall apply to the agreements.

                                                                   [A15]

NOTES
   This section is printed as it was in force on 15 June 2006, prior to amendments made by the Consumer Credit Act 2006 and subsequent amendments; for the text of this provision as it currently has effect, see [665].
   Sub-s (1): sums in square brackets substituted by the Consumer Credit (Increase of Monetary Limits) Order 1983, SI 1983/1878, art 3, Schedule, Pt I, as from 1 May 1998.

18   Multiple agreements

(1)   This section applies to an agreement (a "multiple agreement") if its terms are such as—
   (a)   to place a part of it within one category of agreement mentioned in this Act, and another part of it within a different category of agreements so mentioned, or within a category of agreement not so mentioned, or
   (b)   to place it, or a part of it, within two or more categories of agreement so mentioned.

(2)   Where a part of an agreement falls within subsection (1), that part shall be treated for the purposes of this Act as a separate agreement.

(3)   Where an agreement falls within subsection (1)(b), it shall be treated as an agreement in each of the categories in question, and this Act shall apply to it accordingly.

(4)   Where under subsection (2) a part of a multiple agreement is to be treated as a separate agreement, the multiple agreement shall (with any necessary modifications) be construed accordingly; and any sum payable under the multiple agreement, if not apportioned by the parties, shall for the purposes of proceedings in any court relating to the multiple agreement be apportioned by the court as may be requisite.

(5)   In the case of an agreement for running-account credit, a term of the agreement allowing the credit limit to be exceeded merely temporarily shall not be treated as a separate agreement or as providing fixed-sum credit in respect of the excess.

(6)   This Act does not apply to a multiple agreement so far as the agreement relates to goods if under the agreement payments are to be made in respect of the goods in the form of rent (other than a rent-charge) issuing out of land.

[A16]

NOTES
   This section is printed as it was in force on 15 June 2006, prior to amendments made by the Consumer Credit Act 2006 and subsequent amendments; for the text of this provision as it currently has effect, see [666].

19   Linked transactions

(1)   A transaction entered into by the debtor or hirer, or a relative of his, with any other person ("the other party"), except one for the provision of security, is a linked transaction in relation to an actual or prospective regulated agreement (the "principal agreement") of which it does not form part if—
   (a)   the transaction is entered into in compliance with a term of the principal agreement; or
   (b)   the principal agreement is a debtor-creditor-supplier agreement and the transaction is financed, or to be financed, by the principal agreement; or
   (c)   the other party is a person mentioned in subsection (2), and a person so mentioned initiated the transaction by suggesting it to the debtor or hirer, or his relative, who enters into it—
       (i)   to induce the creditor or owner to enter into the principal agreement, or
       (ii)   for another purpose related to the principal agreement, or
       (iii) where the principal agreement is a restricted-use credit agreement, for a purpose related to a transaction financed, or to be financed, by the principal agreement.

(2)   The persons referred to in subsection (1)(c) are—
   (a)   the creditor or owner, or his associate;
   (b)   a person who, in the negotiation of the transaction, is represented by a credit-broker who is also a negotiator in antecedent negotiations for the principal agreement;
   (c)   a person who, at the time the transaction is initiated, knows that the principal agreement has been made or contemplates that it might be made.

(3)   A linked transaction entered into before the making of the principal agreement has no effect until such time (if any) as that agreement is made.

(4)   Regulations may exclude linked transactions of the prescribed description from the operation of subsection (3).

[A17]

NOTES
   This section is printed as it was in force on 15 June 2006, prior to amendments made by the Consumer Credit Act 2006 and subsequent amendments; for the text of this provision as it currently has effect, see [667].
   Regulations: the Consumer Credit (Linked Transactions) (Exemptions) Regulations 1983, SI 1983/1560 at [3031].

20 Total charge for credit

   (1)   The Secretary of State shall make regulations containing such provisions as appear to him appropriate for determining the true cost to the debtor of the credit provided or to be provided under an actual or prospective consumer credit agreement (the "total charge for credit"), and regulations so made shall prescribe—
   (a)   what items are to be treated as entering into the total charge for credit, and how their amount is to be ascertained;
   (b)   the method of calculating the rate of the total charge for credit.

   (2)   Regulations under subsection (1) may provide for the whole or part of the amount payable by the debtor or his relative under any linked transaction to be included in the total charge for credit, whether or not the creditor is a party to the transaction or derives benefit from it.

[A18]

NOTES
   This section is printed as it was in force on 15 June 2006, prior to amendments made by the Consumer Credit Act 2006 and subsequent amendments; for the text of this provision as it currently has effect, see [668].
   Regulations: the Consumer Credit (Total Charge for Credit) Regulations 1980, SI 1980/51 at [3010].

PART III

LICENSING OF CREDIT AND HIRE BUSINESSES

Licensing principles

21 Businesses needing a licence

   (1)   Subject to this section, a licence is required to carry on a consumer credit business or consumer hire business.

   (2)   A local authority does not need a licence to carry on a business.

   (3)   A body corporate empowered by a public general Act naming it to carry on a business does not need a licence to do so.

[A19]

NOTES
   This section is printed as it was in force on 15 June 2006, prior to amendments made by the Consumer Credit Act 2006 and subsequent amendments; for the text of this provision as it currently has effect, see [669].

22 Standard and group licences

   (1)   A licence may be—
   (a)   a standard licence, that is a licence, issued by the [OFT] to a person named in the licence on an application made by him, which, during the prescribed period, covers such activities as are described in the licence, or
   (b)   a group licence, that is a licence, issued by the [OFT] (whether on the application of any person or of [its] own motion), which, during such period as the [OFT] thinks fit or, if [it] thinks fit, indefinitely, covers such persons and activities as are described in the licence.

   (2)   A licence is not assignable or, subject to section 37, transmissible on death or in any other way.

   (3)   Except in the case of a partnership or an unincorporated body of persons, a standard licence shall not be issued to more than one person.

   (4)   A standard licence issued to a partnership or an unincorporated body of persons shall be issued in the name of the partnership or body.

   (5)   The [OFT] may issue a group licence only if it appears to [it] that the public interest is better served by doing so than by obliging the persons concerned to apply separately for standard licences.

   (6)   The persons covered by a group licence may be described by general words, whether or not coupled with the exclusion of named persons, or in any other way the [OFT] thinks fit.

(7)   The fact that a person is covered by a group licence in respect of certain activities does not prevent a standard licence being issued to him in respect of those activities or any of them.

(8)   A group licence issued on the application of any person shall be issued to that person, and general notice shall be given of the issue of any group licence (whether on application or not).

[(9)   Subsection (10) applies if a standard licence is issued to an EEA consumer credit firm.

(10)   The activities described in the licence are not to include an activity for which the firm has, or could obtain, permission under paragraph 15 of Schedule 3 to the Financial Services and Markets Act 2000.]

[A20]

NOTES

     This section is printed as it was in force on 15 June 2006, prior to amendments made by the Consumer Credit Act 2006 and subsequent amendments; for the text of this provision as it currently has effect, see [670].

     Sub-ss (9), (10): added by the Financial Services and Markets Act 2000 (Consequential Amendments and Repeals) Order 2001, SI 2001/3649, art 166, as from 1 December 2001.

     References to the OFT, etc: as to the abolition of the office of the Director General of Fair Trading and the substitution of the original references to the Director (and related expressions), see the note preceding s 1 at [A1].

     Regulations: the Consumer Credit (Termination of Licences) Regulations 1976, SI 1976/1002.

23   Authorisation of specific activities

(1)   Subject to this section, a licence to carry on a business covers all lawful activities done in the course of that business, whether by the licensee or other persons on his behalf.

(2)   A licence may limit the activities it covers, whether by authorising the licensee to enter into certain types of agreement only, or in any other way.

(3)   A licence covers the canvassing off trade premises of debtor-creditor-supplier agreements or regulated consumer hire agreements only if, and to the extent that, the licence specifically so provides; and such provision shall not be included in a group licence.

(4)   Regulations may be made specifying other activities which, if engaged in by or on behalf of the person carrying on a business, require to be covered by an express term in his licence.

[A21]

NOTES

     This section is printed as it was in force on 15 June 2006, prior to amendments made by the Consumer Credit Act 2006 and subsequent amendments; for the text of this provision as it currently has effect, see [671].

24   Control of name of business

A standard licence authorises the licensee to carry on a business under the name or names specified in the licence, but not under any other name.

[A22]

NOTES

     This section is printed as it was in force on 15 June 2006, prior to amendments made by the Consumer Credit Act 2006 and subsequent amendments; for the text of this provision as it currently has effect, see [672].

25   Licensee to be a fit person

(1)   A standard licence shall be granted on the application of any person if he satisfies the [OFT] that—

     (a)   he is a fit person to engage in activities covered by the licence, and

     (b)   the name or names under which he applies to be licensed is or are not misleading or otherwise undesirable.

[(1A)   The [OFT] shall refuse an application for the grant of standard licence made by a consumer credit EEA firm if all of the activities described in the licence are activities for which the firm has permission, or could obtain permission, under paragraph 15 of Schedule 3 to the Financial Services and Markets Act 2000.

(1B)   If an application for the grant of a standard licence—

     (a)   is made by a person with permission under Part 4 of the Financial Services and Markets Act 2000 to accept deposits, and

     (b)   relates to a listed activity,

the Financial Services Authority may, if it considers that the [OFT] ought to refuse the application, notify him of that fact.

(1C)   In subsection (1B) "listed activity" means an activity listed in Annex 1 to the banking consolidation directive (2000/12/EC) or in the Annex to the investment services directive (93/22/EEC) and references to deposits and to their acceptance must be read with—
   (a)   section 22 of the Financial Services and Markets Act 2000;
   (b)   any relevant order under that section; and
   (c)   Schedule 2 to that Act.]

(2)   In determining whether an applicant for a standard licence is a fit person to engage in any activities, the [OFT] shall have regard to any circumstances appearing to [it] to be relevant, and in particular any evidence tending to show that the applicant, or any of the applicant's employees, agents or associates (whether past or present) or, where the applicant is a body corporate, any person appearing to the [OFT] to be a controller of the body corporate or an associate of any such person, has—
   (a)   committed any offence involving fraud or other dishonesty, or violence,
   (b)   contravened any provision made by or under this Act, or by or under any other enactment regulating the provision of credit to individuals or other transactions with individuals,
   [(bb)   contravened any provision in force in an EEA State which corresponds to a provision of the kind mentioned in paragraph (b);]
   (c)   practised discrimination on grounds of sex, colour, race or ethnic or national origins in, or in connection with, the carrying on of any business, or
   (d)   engaged in business practices appearing to the [OFT] to be deceitful or oppressive, or otherwise unfair or improper (whether unlawful or not).

(3)   In subsection (2), "associate", in addition to the persons specified in section 184, includes a business associate.

[A23]

NOTES
   This section is printed as it was in force on 15 June 2006, prior to amendments made by the Consumer Credit Act 2006 and subsequent amendments; for the text of this provision as it currently has effect, see **[673]**.
   Sub-s (1A)–(1C): inserted by the Financial Services and Markets Act 2000 (Consequential Amendments and Repeals) Order 2001, SI 2001/3649, art 167(1), (2), as from 1 December 2001.
   Sub-s (2): para (bb) inserted by SI 2001/3649, art 167(1), (3), as from 1 December 2001.
   References to the OFT, etc: as to the abolition of the office of the Director General of Fair Trading and the substitution of the original references to the Director (and related expressions), see the note preceding s 1 at **[A1]**.

[26   Conduct of business

(1)   Regulations may be made as to—
   (a)   the conduct by a licensee of his business; and
   (b)   the conduct by a consumer credit EEA firm of its business in the United Kingdom.

(2)   The regulations may in particular specify—
   (a)   the books or other records to be kept by any person to whom the regulations apply;
   (b)   the information to be furnished by such a person to those persons with whom—
       (i)   that person does business, or
       (ii)   that person seeks to do business,
       and the way in which that information is to be furnished.]

[A24]

NOTES
   This section is printed as it was in force on 15 June 2006, prior to amendments made by the Consumer Credit Act 2006 and subsequent amendments; for the text of this provision as it currently has effect, see **[674]**.
   Substituted by the Financial Services and Markets Act 2000 (Consequential Amendments and Repeals) Order 2001, SI 2001/3649, art 168, as from 1 December 2001.
   Regulations: the Consumer Credit (Conduct of Business) (Credit References) Regulations 1977, SI 1977/330; the Consumer Credit (Conduct of Business) (Pawn Records) Regulations 1983, SI 1983/1565.

Issue of licences

27   Determination of applications

(1)   Unless the [OFT] determines to issue a licence in accordance with an application [it] shall, before determining the application, by notice—
   (a)   inform the applicant, giving [its] reasons, that, as the case may be, [it] is minded to refuse the application, or to grant it in terms different from those applied for, describing them, and
   (b)   invite the applicant to submit to the [OFT] representations in support of his application in accordance with section 34.

(2)   If the [OFT] grants the application in terms different from those applied for then, whether or not the applicant appeals, the [OFT] shall issue the licence in the terms approved by [it] unless the applicant by notice informs [it] that he does not desire a licence in those terms.

[A25]

NOTES
   This section is printed as it was in force on 15 June 2006, prior to amendments made by the Consumer Credit Act 2006 and subsequent amendments; for the text of this provision as it currently has effect, see **[675]**.
   References to the OFT, etc: as to the abolition of the office of the Director General of Fair Trading and the substitution of the original references to the Director (and related expressions), see the note preceding s 1 at **[A1]**.

28   Exclusion from group licence

Where the [OFT] is minded to issue a group licence (whether on the application of any person or not), and in doing so to exclude any person from the group by name, [it] shall, before determining the matter,—

   (a)   give notice of that fact to the person proposed to be excluded, giving [its] reasons, and
   (b)   invite that person to submit to the [OFT] representations against his exclusion in accordance with section 34.

[A26]

NOTES
   This section is printed as it was in force on 15 June 2006, prior to amendments made by the Consumer Credit Act 2006 and subsequent amendments; for the text of this provision as it currently has effect, see **[676]**.
   References to the OFT, etc: as to the abolition of the office of the Director General of Fair Trading and the substitution of the original references to the Director (and related expressions), see the note preceding s 1 at **[A1]**.

Renewal, variation, suspension and revocation of licences

29   Renewal

   (1)   If the licensee under a standard licence, or the original applicant for, or any licensee under, a group licence of limited duration, wishes the [OFT] to renew the licence, whether on the same terms (except as to expiry) or on varied terms, he must, during the period specified by the [OFT] by general notice or such longer period as the [OFT] may allow, make an application to the [OFT] for its renewal.

   (2)   The [OFT] may of [its] own motion renew any group licence.

   (3)   The preceding provisions of this Part apply to the renewal of a licence as they apply to the issue of a licence, except that section 28 does not apply to a person who was already excluded in the licence up for renewal.

   (4)   Until the determination of an application under subsection (1) and, where an appeal lies from the determination, until the end of the appeal period, the licence shall continue in force, notwithstanding that apart from this subsection it would expire earlier.

   (5)   On the refusal of an application under this section, the [OFT] may give directions authorising a licensee to carry into effect agreements made by him before the expiry of the licence.

   (6)   General notice shall be given of the renewal of a group licence.

[A27]

NOTES
   This section is printed as it was in force on 15 June 2006, prior to amendments made by the Consumer Credit Act 2006 and subsequent amendments; for the text of this provision as it currently has effect, see **[677]**.
   References to the OFT, etc: as to the abolition of the office of the Director General of Fair Trading and the substitution of the original references to the Director (and related expressions), see the note preceding s 1 at **[A1]**.

30   Variation by request

   (1)   On an application made by the licensee, the [OFT] may if [it] thinks fit by notice to the licensee vary a standard licence in accordance with the application.

   (2)   In the case of a group licence issued on the application of any person, the [OFT], on an application made by that person, may if [it] thinks fit by notice to that person vary the terms of the licence in accordance with the application; but the [OFT] shall not vary a group licence under this subsection by excluding a named person, other than the person making the request, unless that named person consents in writing to his exclusion.

(3)   In the case of a group licence from which (whether by name or description) a person is excluded, the [OFT], on an application made by that person, may if [it] thinks fit, by notice to that person, vary the terms of the licence so as to remove the exclusion.

(4)   Unless the [OFT] determines to vary a licence in accordance with an application [it] shall, before determining the application, by notice—

(a)   inform the applicant, giving [its] reasons, that [it] is minded to refuse the application, and

(b)   invite the applicant to submit to the [OFT] representations in support of his application in accordance with section 34.

(5)   General notice shall be given that a variation of a group licence has been made under this section.

[A28]

NOTES

This section is printed as it was in force on 15 June 2006, prior to amendments made by the Consumer Credit Act 2006 and subsequent amendments; for the text of this provision as it currently has effect, see [678].

References to the OFT, etc: as to the abolition of the office of the Director General of Fair Trading and the substitution of the original references to the Director (and related expressions), see the note preceding s 1 at [A1].

31   Compulsory variation

(1)   Where at a time during the currency of a licence the [OFT] is of the opinion that, if the licence had expired at that time, [it] would, on an application for its renewal or further renewal on the same terms (except as to expiry), have been minded to grant the application but on different terms, and that therefore the licence should be varied, [it] shall proceed as follows.

(2)   In the case of a standard licence the [OFT] shall, by notice—

(a)   inform the licensee of the variations the [OFT] is minded to make in the terms of the licence, stating [its] reasons, and

(b)   invite him to submit to the [OFT] representations as to the proposed variations in accordance with section 34.

(3)   In the case of a group licence the [OFT] shall—

(a)   give general notice of the variations [it] is minded to make in the terms of the licence, stating [its] reasons, and

(b)   in the notice invite any licensee to submit to [it] representations as to the proposed variations in accordance with section 34.

(4)   In the case of a group licence issued on application the [OFT] shall also—

(a)   inform the original applicant of the variations the [OFT] is minded to make in the terms of the licence, stating [its] reasons, and

(b)   invite him to submit to the [OFT] representations as to the proposed variations in accordance with section 34.

(5)   If the [OFT] is minded to vary a group licence by excluding any person (other than the original applicant) from the group by name the [OFT] shall, in addition, take the like steps under section 28 as are required in the case mentioned in that section.

(6)   General notice shall be given that a variation of any group licence has been made under this section.

(7)   A variation under this section shall not take effect before the end of the appeal period.

[A29]

NOTES

This section is printed as it was in force on 15 June 2006, prior to amendments made by the Consumer Credit Act 2006 and subsequent amendments; for the text of this provision as it currently has effect, see [679].

References to the OFT, etc: as to the abolition of the office of the Director General of Fair Trading and the substitution of the original references to the Director (and related expressions), see the note preceding s 1 at [A1].

32   Suspension and revocation

(1)   Where at a time during the currency of a licence the [OFT] is of the opinion that if the licence had expired at that time [it] would have been minded not to renew it, and that therefore it should be revoked or suspended, [it] shall proceed as follows.

(2)   In the case of a standard licence the [OFT] shall, by notice—

(a)   inform the licensee that, as the case may be, the [OFT] is minded to revoke the licence, or suspend it until a specified date or indefinitely, stating [its] reasons, and

   (b)   invite him to submit representations as to the proposed revocation or suspension in accordance with section 34.

  (3)   In the case of a group licence the [OFT] shall—

   (a)   give general notice that, as the case may be, [it] is minded to revoke the licence, or suspend it until a specified date or indefinitely, stating [its] reasons, and

   (b)   in the notice invite any licensee to submit to [it] representations as to the proposed revocation or suspension in accordance with section 34.

  (4)   In the case of a group licence issued on application the [OFT] shall also—

   (a)   inform the original applicant that, as the case may be, the [OFT] is minded to revoke the licence, or suspend it until a specified date or indefinitely, stating [its] reasons, and

   (b)   invite him to submit representations as to the proposed revocation or suspension in accordance with section 34.

  (5)   If [it] revokes or suspends the licence, the [OFT] may give directions authorising a licensee to carry into effect agreements made by him before the revocation or suspension.

  (6)   General notice shall be given of the revocation or suspension of a group licence.

  (7)   A revocation or suspension under this section shall not take effect before the end of the appeal period.

  (8)   Except for the purposes of section 29, a licensee under a suspended licence shall be treated, in respect of the period of suspension, as if the licence had not been issued; and where the suspension is not expressed to end on a specified date it may, if the [OFT] thinks fit, be ended by notice given by [it] to the licensee or, in the case of a group licence, by general notice.

[A30]

NOTES

  This section is printed as it was in force on 15 June 2006, prior to amendments made by the Consumer Credit Act 2006 and subsequent amendments; for the text of this provision as it currently has effect, see **[680]**.

  References to the OFT, etc: as to the abolition of the office of the Director General of Fair Trading and the substitution of the original references to the Director (and related expressions), see the note preceding s 1 at **[A1]**.

33 Application to end suspension

  (1)   On an application made by a licensee the [OFT] may, if [it] thinks fit, by notice to the licensee end the suspension of a licence, whether the suspension was for a fixed or indefinite period.

  (2)   Unless the [OFT] determines to end the suspension in accordance with the application [it] shall, before determining the application, by notice—

   (a)   inform the applicant, giving [its] reasons, that [it] is minded to refuse the application, and

   (b)   invite the applicant to submit to the [OFT] representations in support of his application in accordance with section 34.

  (3)   General notice shall be given that a suspension of a group licence has been ended under this section.

  (4)   In the case of a group licence issued on application—

   (a)   the references in subsection (1) to a licensee include the original applicant;

   (b)   the [OFT] shall inform the original applicant that a suspension of a group licence has been ended under this section.

[A31]

NOTES

  This section is printed as it was in force on 15 June 2006, prior to amendments made by the Consumer Credit Act 2006 and subsequent amendments; for the text of this provision as it currently has effect, see **[681]**.

  References to the OFT, etc: as to the abolition of the office of the Director General of Fair Trading and the substitution of the original references to the Director (and related expressions), see the note preceding s 1 at **[A1]**.

Miscellaneous

34 Representations to [OFT]

  (1)   Where this section applies to an invitation by the [OFT] to any person to submit representations, the [OFT] shall invite that person, within 21 days after the notice containing the invitation is given to him or published, or such longer period as the [OFT] may allow,—

   (a)   to submit his representations in writing to the [OFT], and

   (b)   to give notice to the [OFT], if he thinks fit, that he wishes to make representations orally, and where notice is given under paragraph (b) the [OFT] shall arrange for the oral representations to be heard.

(2)   In reaching [its] determination the [OFT] shall take into account any representations submitted or made under this section.

(3)   The [OFT] shall give notice of [its] determination to the persons who were required to be invited to submit representations about it or, where the invitation to submit representations was required to be given by general notice, shall give general notice of the determination.

[A32]

NOTES
   This section is printed as it was in force on 15 June 2006, prior to amendments made by the Consumer Credit Act 2006 and subsequent amendments; for the text of this provision as it currently has effect, see [682].
   References to the OFT, etc: as to the abolition of the office of the Director General of Fair Trading and the substitution of the original references to the Director (and related expressions), see the note preceding s 1 at [A1].

35   The register

(1)   The [OFT] shall establish and maintain a register, in which [it] shall cause to be kept particulars of—
  (a)   applications not yet determined for the issue, variation or renewal of licences, or for ending the suspension of a licence;
  (b)   licences which are in force, or have at any time been suspended or revoked, with details of any variation of the terms of a licence;
  (c)   decisions given by [it] under this Act, and any appeal from those decisions; and
  (d)   such other matters (if any) as [it] thinks fit.

[(1A)   The [OFT] shall also cause to be kept in the register any copy of any notice or other document relating to a consumer credit EEA firm which is given to the [OFT] by the Financial Services Authority for inclusion in the register.]

(2)   The [OFT] shall give general notice of the various matters required to be entered in the register, and of any change in them made under subsection (1)(d).

(3)   Any person shall be entitled, on payment of the specified fee—
  (a)   to inspect the register during ordinary office hours and take copies of any entry, or
  (b)   to obtain from the [OFT] a copy, certified by the [OFT] to be correct, of any entry in the register.

(4)   The [OFT] may, if [it] thinks fit, determine that the right conferred by subsection (3)(a) shall be exercisable in relation to a copy of the register instead of, or in addition to, the original.

(5)   The [OFT] shall give general notice of the place or places where, and times when, the register or a copy of it may be inspected.

[A33]

NOTES
   This section is printed as it was in force on 15 June 2006, prior to amendments made by the Consumer Credit Act 2006 and subsequent amendments; for the text of this provision as it currently has effect, see [683].
   Sub-s (1A): inserted by the Financial Services and Markets Act 2000 (Consequential Amendments and Repeals) Order 2001, SI 2001/3649, art 169, as from 1 December 2001.
   References to the OFT, etc: as to the abolition of the office of the Director General of Fair Trading and the substitution of the original references to the Director (and related expressions), see the note preceding s 1 at [A1].

36   Duty to notify changes

(1)   Within 21 working days after a change takes place in any particulars entered in the register in respect of a standard licence or the licensee under section 35(1)(d) (not being a change resulting from action taken by the [OFT]), the licensee shall give the [OFT] notice of the change; and the [OFT] shall cause any necessary amendment to be made in the register.

(2)   Within 21 working days after—
  (a)   any change takes place in the officers of—
    (i)   a body corporate, or an unincorporated body of persons, which is the licensee under a standard licence, or
    (ii)   a body corporate which is a controller of a body corporate which is such a licensee, or
  (b)   a body corporate which is such a licensee becomes aware that a person has become or ceased to be a controller of the body corporate, or
  (c)   any change takes place in the members of a partnership which is such a licensee

(including a change on the amalgamation of the partnership with another firm, or a change whereby the number of partners is reduced to one),

the licensee shall give the [OFT] notice of the change.

(3) Within 14 working days after any change takes place in the officers of a body corporate which is a controller of another body corporate which is a licensee under a standard licence, the controller shall give the licensee notice of the change.

(4) Within 14 working days after a person becomes or ceases to be a controller of a body corporate which is a licensee under a standard licence, that person shall give the licensee notice of the fact.

(5) Where a change in a partnership has the result that the business ceases be carried on under the name, or any of the names, specified in a standard licence the licence shall cease to have effect.

(6) Where the [OFT] is given notice under subsection (1) or (2) of any change, and subsection (5) does not apply, the [OFT] may by notice require the licensee to furnish [it] with such information, verified in such manner, as the [OFT] may stipulate.

[A34]

NOTES
This section is printed as it was in force on 15 June 2006, prior to amendments made by the Consumer Credit Act 2006 and subsequent amendments; for the text of this provision as it currently has effect, see [684].
References to the OFT, etc: as to the abolition of the office of the Director General of Fair Trading and the substitution of the original references to the Director (and related expressions), see the note preceding s 1 at [A1].

37 Death, bankruptcy etc of licensee

(1) A licence held by one individual terminates if he—
   (a)   dies, or
   (b)   is adjudged bankrupt, or
   (c)   becomes a patient within the meaning of Part VIII of the Mental Health Act 1959.

(2) In relation to a licence held by one individual, or a partnership or other unincorporated body of persons, or a body corporate, regulations may specify other events relating to the licensee on the occurrence of which the licence is to terminate.

(3) Regulations may—
   (a)   provide for the termination of a licence by subsection (1), or under subsection (2), to be deferred for a period not exceeding 12 months, and
   (b)   authorise the business of the licensee to be carried on under the licence by some other person during the period of deferment, subject to such conditions as may be prescribed.

(4) This section does not apply to group licences.

[A35]

NOTES
This section is printed as it was in force on 15 June 2006, prior to amendments made by the Consumer Credit Act 2006 and subsequent amendments; for the text of this provision as it currently has effect, see [685].
Regulations: the Consumer Credit (Termination of Licences) Regulations 1976, SI 1976/1002.

38   (*Application of s 37 to Northern Ireland and Scotland; outside the scope of this work.*)

39 Offences against Part III

(1) A person who engages in any activities for which a licence is required when he is not a licensee under a licence covering those activities commits an offence.

(2) A licensee under a standard licence who carries on business under a name not specified in the licence commits an offence.

(3) A person who fails to give the [OFT] or a licensee notice under section 36 within the period required commits an offence.

[A36]

NOTES
This section is printed as it was in force on 15 June 2006, prior to amendments made by the Consumer Credit Act 2006 and subsequent amendments; for the text of this provision as it currently has effect, see [686].
References to the OFT, etc: as to the abolition of the office of the Director General of Fair Trading and the substitution of the original references to the Director (and related expressions), see the note preceding s 1 at [A1].

40 Enforcement of agreements made by unlicensed trader

(1) A regulated agreement, other than a non-commercial agreement, if made when the creditor or owner was unlicensed, is enforceable against the debtor or hirer only where the [OFT] has made an order under this section which applies to the agreement.

(2) Where during any period an unlicensed person (the "trader") was carrying on a consumer credit business or consumer hire business, he or his successor in title may apply to the [OFT] for an order that regulated agreements made by the trader during that period are to be treated as if he had been licensed.

(3) Unless the [OFT] determines to make an order under subsection (2) in accordance with the application, [it] shall, before determining the application, by notice—

    (a) inform the applicant, giving his reasons, that, as the case may be, [it] is minded to refuse the application, or to grant it in terms different from those applied for, describing them, and

    (b) invite the applicant to submit to the [OFT] representations in support of [its] application in accordance with section 34.

(4) In determining whether or not to make an order under subsection (2) in respect of any period the [OFT] shall consider, in addition to any other relevant factors—

    (a) how far, if at all, debtors or hirers under regulated agreements made by the trader during that period were prejudiced by the trader's conduct,

    (b) whether or not the [OFT] would have been likely to grant a licence covering that period on an application by the trader, and

    (c) the degree of culpability for the failure to obtain a licence.

(5) If the [OFT] thinks fit, [it] may in an order under subsection (2)—

    (a) limit the order to specified agreements, or agreements of a specified description or made at a specified time;

    (b) make the order conditional on the doing of specified acts by the applicant.

[(6) This section does not apply to a regulated agreement, other than a non-commercial agreement, made by a consumer credit EEA firm unless at the time it was made that firm was precluded from entering into it as a result of

    (a) a consumer credit prohibition imposed under section 203 of the Financial Services and Markets Act 2000; or

    (b) a restriction imposed on the firm under section 204 of that Act.]

[A37]

NOTES

This section is printed as it was in force on 15 June 2006, prior to amendments made by the Consumer Credit Act 2006 and subsequent amendments; for the text of this provision as it currently has effect, see [687].

Sub-s (6): added by the Financial Services and Markets Act 2000 (Consequential Amendments and Repeals) Order 2001, SI 2001/3649, art 170, as from 1 December 2001.

References to the OFT, etc: as to the abolition of the office of the Director General of Fair Trading and the substitution of the original references to the Director (and related expressions), see the note preceding s 1 at [A1].

41 Appeals to Secretary of State under Part III

(1) If, in the case of a determination by the [OFT] such as is mentioned in column 1 of the table set out at the end of this section, a person mentioned in relation to that determination in column 2 of the table is aggrieved by the determination he may, within the prescribed period, and in the prescribed manner, appeal to the Secretary of State.

(2) Regulations may make provision as to the persons by whom (on behalf of the Secretary of State) appeals under this section are to be heard, the manner in which they are to be conducted, and any other matter connected with such appeals.

(3) On an appeal under this section, the Secretary of State may give such directions for disposing of the appeal as he thinks just, including a direction for the payment of costs by any party to the appeal.

(4) A direction under subsection (3) for payment of costs may be made a rule of the High Court on the application of the party in whose favour it is given.

(5) *(Applies to Scotland only.)*

Table

Determination	Appellant
Refusal to issue, renew or vary licence in accordance with terms of application.	The applicant.
Exclusion of person from group licence.	The person excluded.
Refusal to give directions in respect of a licensee under section 29(5) or 32(5)	The licensee.
Compulsory variation, or suspension or revocation, of standard licence.	The licensee.
Compulsory variation, or suspension or revocation, of group licence.	The original applicant or any licensee.
Refusal to end suspension of licence in accordance with terms of application.	The applicant.
Refusal to make order under section 40(2) in accordance with terms of application.	The applicant.
[Imposition of, or refusal to withdraw, consumer credit prohibition under section 203 of the Financial Services and Markets Act 2000.	The consumer credit EEA firm concerned.
Imposition of, or refusal to withdraw, a restriction under section 204 of the Financial Services and Markets Act 2000.	The consumer credit EEA firm concerned.]

[A38]

NOTES

This section is printed as it was in force on 15 June 2006, prior to amendments made by the Consumer Credit Act 2006 and subsequent amendments; for the text of this provision as it currently has effect, see [688].

References to the OFT, etc: as to the abolition of the office of the Director General of Fair Trading and the substitution of the original references to the Director (and related expressions), see the note preceding s 1 at [A1].

Table: entries relating to the Financial Services and Markets Act 2000, ss 203, 204 added by the Financial Services and Markets Act 2000 (Consequential Amendments and Repeals) Order 2001, SI 2001/3649, art 171, as from 1 December 2001.

Regulations: the Consumer Credit Licensing (Appeals) Regulations 1998, SI 1998/1203.

42   (*Repealed by the Tribunals and Inquiries Act 1992, s 18(2), Sch 4, Pt I, as from 1 October 1992.*)

PART IV
SEEKING BUSINESS

Advertising

43   Advertisements to which Part IV applies

(1)   This Part applies to any advertisement, published for the purposes of a business carried on by the advertiser, indicating that he is willing—

     (a)   to provide credit, or

     (b)   to enter into an agreement for the bailment or (in Scotland) the hiring of goods by him.

(2)   An advertisement does not fall within subsection (1) if the advertiser does not carry on—

     (a)   a consumer credit business or consumer hire business, or

     (b)   a business in the course of which he provides credit to individuals secured on land, or

     (c)   a business which comprises or relates to unregulated agreements where—

         (i)   the [law applicable to] the agreement is the law of a country outside the United Kingdom, and

         (ii)   if the [law applicable to] the agreement were the law of a part of the United Kingdom it would be a regulated agreement.

(3)   An advertisement does not fall within subsection (1)(a) if it indicates—

     (a)   that the credit must exceed [£25,000], and that no security is required, or the security is to consist of property other than land, or

(b)   that the credit is available only to a body corporate.

[(3A)   An advertisement does not fall within subsection (1)(a) in so far as it is a communication of an invitation or inducement to engage in investment activity within the meaning of section 21 of the Financial Services and Markets Act 2000, other than an exempt generic communication.

(3B)   An "exempt generic communication" is a communication to which subsection (1) of section 21 of the Financial Services and Markets Act 2000 does not apply, as a result of an order under subsection (5) of that section, because it does not identify a person as providing an investment or as carrying on an activity to which the communication relates.]

(4)   An advertisement does not fall within subsection (1)(b) if it indicates that the advertiser is not willing to enter into a consumer hire agreement.

(5)   The Secretary of State may by order provide that this Part shall not apply to other advertisements of a description specified in the order.

[A39]

NOTES
    This section is printed as it was in force on 15 June 2006, prior to amendments made by the Consumer Credit Act 2006 and subsequent amendments; for the text of this provision as it currently has effect, see [689].
    Sub-s (2): words in square brackets substituted by the Contracts (Applicable Law) Act 1990, s 5, Sch 4, para 2, as from 1 April 1991.
    Sub-s (3): sum in square brackets in para (a) substituted by the Consumer Credit (Increase of Monetary Limits) Order 1983, SI 1983/1878, Schedule, Pt II (as amended by SI 1998/996, art 2, as from 1 May 1998.
    Sub-ss (3A), (3B): inserted by the Financial Services and Markets Act 2000 (Regulated Activities) Order 2001, SI 2001/544, art 90(1), (3), as from 31 October 2004.
    Order: the Consumer Credit (Exempt Advertisements) Order 1985, SI 1985/621.

44   Form and content of advertisements

(1)   The Secretary of State shall make regulations as to the form and content of advertisements to which this Part applies, and the regulations shall contain such provisions as appear to him appropriate with a view to ensuring that, having regard to its subject-matter and the amount of detail included in it, an advertisement conveys a fair and reasonably comprehensive indication of the nature of the credit or hire facilities offered by the advertiser and of their true cost to persons using them.

(2)   Regulations under subsection (1) may in particular—
    (a)   require specified information to be included in the prescribed manner in advertisements, and other specified material to be excluded;
    (b)   contain requirements to ensure that specified information is clearly brought to the attention of persons to whom advertisements are directed, and that one part of an advertisement is not given insufficient or excessive prominence compared with another.

[A40]

NOTES
    This section is printed as it was in force on 15 June 2006, prior to amendments made by the Consumer Credit Act 2006 and subsequent amendments; for the text of this provision as it currently has effect, see [690].
    Regulations: the Consumer Credit (Advertisements) Regulations 2004, SI 2004/1484 at [3400].

45   Prohibition of advertisement where goods etc not sold for cash

If an advertisement to which this Part applies indicates that the advertiser is willing to provide credit under a restricted-use credit agreement relating to goods or services to be supplied by any person, but at the time when the advertisement is published that person is not holding himself out as prepared to sell the goods or provide the services (as the case may be) for cash, the advertiser commits an offence.

[A41]

NOTES
    This section is printed as it was in force on 15 June 2006, prior to amendments made by the Consumer Credit Act 2006 and subsequent amendments; for the text of this provision as it currently has effect, see [691].

46   False or misleading advertisements

(1)   If an advertisement to which this Part applies conveys information which in a material respect is false or misleading the advertiser commits an offence.

(2)   Information stating or implying an intention on the advertiser's part which he has not got is false.

[A42]

47 Advertising infringements

(1) Where an advertiser commits an offence against regulations made under section 44 or against section 45 or 46, or would be taken to commit such an offence but for the defence provided by section 168, a like offence is committed by—

    (a)   the publisher of the advertisement, and

    (b)   any person who, in the course of a business carried on by him, devised the advertisement, or a part of it relevant to the first-mentioned offence, and

    (c)   where the advertiser did not procure the publication of the advertisement, the person who did procure it.

(2) In proceedings for an offence under subsection (1)(a) it is a defence for the person charged to prove that—

    (a)   the advertisement was published in the course of a business carried on by him, and

    (b)   he received the advertisement in the course of that business, and did not know and had no reason to suspect that its publication would be an offence under this Part.

[A43]

Canvassing etc

48 Definition of canvassing off trade premises (regulated agreements)

(1) An individual (the "canvasser") canvasses a regulated agreement off trade premises if he solicits the entry (as debtor or hirer) of another individual (the "consumer") into the agreement by making oral representations to the consumer, or any other individual, during a visit by the canvasser to any place (not excluded by subsection (2)) where the consumer, or that other individual, as the case may be, is, being a visit—

    (a)   carried out for the purpose of making such oral representations to individuals who are at that place, but

    (b)   not carried out in response to a request made on a previous occasion.

(2) A place is excluded from subsection (1) if it is a place where a business is carried on (whether on a permanent or temporary basis) by—

    (a)   the creditor or owner, or

    (b)   a supplier, or

    (c)   the canvasser, or the person whose employee or agent the canvasser is, or

    (d)   the consumer.

[A44]

49 Prohibition of canvassing debtor-creditor agreements off trade premises

(1) It is an offence to canvass debtor-creditor agreements off trade premises.

(2) It is also an offence to solicit the entry of an individual (as debtor) into a debtor-creditor agreement during a visit carried out in response to a request made on a previous occasion, where—

    (a)   the request was not in writing signed by or on behalf of the person making it, and

    (b)   if no request for the visit had been made, the soliciting would have constituted the canvassing of a debtor-creditor agreement off trade premises.

(3) Subsections (1) and (2) do not apply to any soliciting for an agreement enabling the debtor to overdraw on a current account of any description kept with the creditor, where—

    (a)   the [OFT] has determined that current accounts of that description kept with the creditor are excluded from subsections (1) and (2), and

    (b)   the debtor already keeps an account with the creditor (whether a current account or not).

(4) A determination under subsection (3)(a)—

    (a)   may be made subject to such conditions as the [OFT] thinks fit, and

(b)   shall be made only where the [OFT] is of opinion that it is not against the interests of debtors.

(5)   If soliciting is done in breach of a condition imposed under subsection (4)(a), the determination under subsection (3)(a) does not apply to it.

[A45]

NOTES
   This section is printed as it was in force on 15 June 2006, prior to amendments made by the Consumer Credit Act 2006 and subsequent amendments; for the text of this provision as it currently has effect, see [695].
   References to the OFT, etc: as to the abolition of the office of the Director General of Fair Trading and the substitution of the original references to the Director (and related expressions), see the note preceding s 1 at [A1].

50   Circulars to minors

(1)   A person commits an offence who, with a view to financial gain, sends to a minor any document inviting him to—
   (a)   borrow money, or
   (b)   obtain goods on credit or hire, or
   (c)   obtain services on credit, or
   (d)   apply for information or advice on borrowing money or otherwise obtaining credit, or hiring goods.

(2)   In proceedings under subsection (1) in respect of the sending of a document to a minor, it is a defence for the person charged to prove that he did not know, and had no reasonable cause to suspect, that he was a minor.

(3)   Where a document is received by a minor at any school or educational establishment for minors, a person sending it to him at that establishment knowing or suspecting it to be such an establishment shall be taken to have reasonable cause to suspect that he is a minor.

[A46]

NOTES
   This section is printed as it was in force on 15 June 2006, prior to amendments made by the Consumer Credit Act 2006 and subsequent amendments; for the text of this provision as it currently has effect, see [696].

51   Prohibition of unsolicited credit-tokens

(1)   It is an offence to give a person a credit-token if he has not asked for it.

(2)   To comply with subsection (1) a request must be contained in a document signed by the person making the request, unless the credit-token agreement is a small debtor-creditor-supplier agreement.

(3)   Subsection (1) does not apply to the giving of a credit-token to a person—
   (a)   for use under a credit-token agreement already made, or
   (b)   in renewal or replacement of a credit-token previously accepted by him under a credit-token agreement which continues in force, whether or not varied.

[A47]

NOTES
   This section is printed as it was in force on 15 June 2006, prior to amendments made by the Consumer Credit Act 2006 and subsequent amendments; for the text of this provision as it currently has effect, see [697].

Miscellaneous

52   Quotations

(1)   Regulations may be made—
   (a)   as to the form and content of any document (a "quotation") by which a person who carries on a consumer credit business or consumer hire business, or a business in the course of which he provides credit to individuals secured on land, gives prospective customers information about the terms on which he is prepared to do business;
   (b)   requiring a person carrying on such a business to provide quotations to such persons and in such circumstances as are prescribed.

(2)   Regulations under subsection (1)(a) may in particular contain provisions relating to quotations such as are set out in relation to advertisements in section 44.

[(3)   In this section, "quotation" does not include—

(a)   any document which is a communication of an invitation or inducement to engage in investment activity within the meaning of section 21 of the Financial Services and Markets Act 2000; or

(b)   any document (other than one falling within paragraph (a)) provided by an authorised person (within the meaning of that Act) in connection with an agreement which would or might be an exempt agreement as a result of section 16(6C).]

[A48]

NOTES
This section is printed as it was in force on 15 June 2006, prior to amendments made by the Consumer Credit Act 2006 and subsequent amendments; for the text of this provision as it currently has effect, see [698].
Sub-s (3): added by the Financial Services and Markets Act 2000 (Regulated Activities) Order 2001, SI 2001/544, art 90(1), (4), as from 31 October 2004.
Regulations: the Consumer Credit (Quotations) (Revocation) Regulations 1997, SI 1997/211.

53 Duty to display information

Regulations may require a person who carries on a consumer credit business or consumer hire business, or a business in the course of which he provides credit to individuals secured on land [(other than credit provided under an agreement which is an exempt agreement as a result of section 16(6C))], to display in the prescribed manner, at any premises where the business is carried on to which the public have access, prescribed information about the business.

[A49]

NOTES
This section is printed as it was in force on 15 June 2006, prior to amendments made by the Consumer Credit Act 2006 and subsequent amendments; for the text of this provision as it currently has effect, see [699].
Words in square brackets inserted by the Financial Services and Markets Act 2000 (Regulated Activities) Order 2001, SI 2001/544, art 90(1), (5), as from 31 October 2004.

54 Conduct of business regulations

Without prejudice to the generality of section 26, regulations under that section may include provisions further regulating the seeking of business by [a person to whom the regulations apply] who carries on a consumer credit business or a consumer hire business.

[A50]

NOTES
This section is printed as it was in force on 15 June 2006, prior to amendments made by the Consumer Credit Act 2006 and subsequent amendments; for the text of this provision as it currently has effect, see [700].
Words in square brackets substituted by the Financial Services and Markets Act 2000 (Consequential Amendments and Repeals) Order 2001, SI 2001/3649, art 172, as from 1 December 2001.

PART V
ENTRY INTO CREDIT OR HIRE AGREEMENTS

Preliminary matters

55 Disclosure of information

(1)   Regulations may require specified information to be disclosed in the prescribed manner to the debtor or hirer before a regulated agreement is made.

(2)   A regulated agreement is not properly executed unless regulations under subsection (1) were complied with before the making of the agreement.

[A51]

NOTES
This section is printed as it was in force on 15 June 2006, prior to amendments made by the Consumer Credit Act 2006 and subsequent amendments; for the text of this provision as it currently has effect, see [701].
Regulations: the Consumer Credit (Disclosure of Information) Regulations 2004, SI 2004/1481 at **[3385]**.

56 Antecedent negotiations

(1)   In this Act "antecedent negotiations" means any negotiations with the debtor or hirer—
   (a)   conducted by the creditor or owner in relation to the making of any regulated agreement, or

(b)   conducted by a credit-broker in relation to goods sold or proposed to be sold by the credit-broker to the creditor before forming the subject-matter of a debtor-creditor-supplier agreement within section 12(a), or

(c)   conducted by the supplier in relation to a transaction financed or proposed to be financed by a debtor-creditor-supplier agreement within section 12(b) or (c),

and "negotiator" means the person by whom negotiations are so conducted with the debtor or hirer.

(2)   Negotiations with the debtor in a case falling within subsection (1)(b) or (c) shall be deemed to be conducted by the negotiator in the capacity of agent of the creditor as well as in his actual capacity.

(3)   An agreement is void if, and to the extent that, it purports in relation to an actual or prospective regulated agreement—

(a)   to provide that a person acting as, or on behalf of, a negotiator is to be treated as the agent of the debtor or hirer, or

(b)   to relieve a person from liability for acts or omissions of any person acting as, or on behalf of, a negotiator.

(4)   For the purposes of this Act, antecedent negotiations shall be taken to begin when the negotiator and the debtor or hirer first enter into communication (including communication by advertisement), and to include any representations made by the negotiator to the debtor or hirer and any other dealings between them.

[A52]

NOTES

This section is printed as it was in force on 15 June 2006, prior to amendments made by the Consumer Credit Act 2006 and subsequent amendments; for the text of this provision as it currently has effect, see [702].

57 Withdrawal from prospective agreement

(1)   The withdrawal of a party from a prospective regulated agreement shall operate to apply this Part to the agreement, any linked transaction and any other thing done in anticipation of the making of the agreement as it would apply if the agreement were made and then cancelled under section 69.

(2)   The giving to a party of a written or oral notice which, however expressed, indicates the intention of the other party to withdraw from a prospective regulated agreement operates as a withdrawal from it.

(3)   Each of the following shall be deemed to be the agent of the creditor or owner for the purpose of receiving a notice under subsection (2)—

(a)   a credit-broker or supplier who is the negotiator in antecedent negotiations, and

(b)   any person who, in the course of a business carried on by him, acts on behalf of the debtor or hirer in any negotiations for the agreement.

(4)   Where the agreement, if made, would not be a cancellable agreement, subsection (1) shall nevertheless apply as if the contrary were the case.

[A53]

NOTES

This section is printed as it was in force on 15 June 2006, prior to amendments made by the Consumer Credit Act 2006 and subsequent amendments; for the text of this provision as it currently has effect, see [703].

Regulations: the Consumer Credit (Repayment of Credit on Cancellation) Regulations 1983, SI 1983/1559.

58 Opportunity for withdrawal from prospective land mortgage

(1)   Before sending to the debtor or hirer, for his signature, an unexecuted agreement in a case where the prospective regulated agreement is to be secured on land (the "mortgaged land"), the creditor or owner shall give the debtor or hirer a copy of the unexecuted agreement which contains a notice in the prescribed form indicating the right of the debtor or hirer to withdraw from the prospective agreement, and how and when the right is exercisable, together with a copy of any other document referred to in the unexecuted agreement.

(2)   Subsection (1) does not apply to—

(a)   a restricted-use credit agreement to finance the purchase of the mortgaged land, or

(b)   an agreement for a bridging loan in connection with the purchase of the mortgaged land or other land.

[A54]

NOTES
This section is printed as it was in force on 15 June 2006, prior to amendments made by the Consumer Credit Act 2006 and subsequent amendments; for the text of this provision as it currently has effect, see [704].
Regulations: the Consumer Credit (Cancellation Notices and Copies of Documents) Regulations 1983, SI 1983/1557.

59 Agreement to enter future agreement void

(1) An agreement is void if, and to the extent that, it purports to bind a person to enter as debtor or hirer into a prospective regulated agreement.

(2) Regulations may exclude from the operation of subsection (1) agreements such as are described in the regulations.

[A55]

NOTES
This section is printed as it was in force on 15 June 2006, prior to amendments made by the Consumer Credit Act 2006 and subsequent amendments; for the text of this provision as it currently has effect, see [705].
Regulations: the Consumer Credit (Agreements to Enter Prospective Agreements) (Exemptions) Regulations 1983, SI 1983/1552.

Making the agreement

60 Form and content of agreements

(1) The Secretary of State shall make regulations as to the form and content of documents embodying regulated agreements, and the regulations shall contain such provisions as appear to him appropriate with a view to ensuring that the debtor or hirer is made aware of—

    (a) the rights and duties conferred or imposed on him by the agreement,

    (b) the amount and rate of the total charge for credit (in the case of a consumer credit agreement),

    (c) the protection and remedies available to him under this Act, and

    (d) any other matters which, in the opinion of the Secretary of State, it is desirable for him to know about in connection with the agreement.

(2) Regulations under subsection (1) may in particular—

    (a) require specified information to be included in the prescribed manner in documents, and other specified material to be excluded;

    (b) contain requirements to ensure that specified information is clearly brought to the attention of the debtor or hirer, and that one part of a document is not given insufficient or excessive prominence compared with another.

(3) If, on an application made to the [OFT] by a person carrying on a consumer credit business or a consumer hire business, it appears to the [OFT] impracticable for the applicant to comply with any requirement of regulations under subsection (1) in a particular case, [it] may, by notice to the applicant, direct that that requirement be waived or varied in relation to such agreements, and subject to such conditions (if any), as [it] may specify, and this Act and the regulations shall have effect accordingly.

(4) The [OFT] shall give a notice under subsection (3) only if [it] is satisfied that to do so would not prejudice the interests of debtors or hirers.

[A56]

NOTES
This section is printed as it was in force on 15 June 2006, prior to amendments made by the Consumer Credit Act 2006 and subsequent amendments; for the text of this provision as it currently has effect, see [706].
References to the OFT, etc: as to the abolition of the office of the Director General of Fair Trading and the substitution of the original references to the Director (and related expressions), see the note preceding s 1 at [A1].
Regulations: the Consumer Credit (Agreements) Regulations 1983, SI 1983/1553.

61 Signing of agreement

(1) A regulated agreement is not properly executed unless—

    (a) a document in the prescribed form itself containing all the prescribed terms and conforming to regulations under section 60(1) is signed in the prescribed manner both by the debtor or hirer and by or on behalf of the creditor or owner, and

    (b) the document embodies all the terms of the agreement, other than implied terms, and

    (c) the document is, when presented or sent to the debtor or hirer for signature, in such a state that all its terms are readily legible.

(2)   In addition, where the agreement is one to which section 58(1) applies, it is not properly executed unless—

(a)   the requirements of section 58(1) were complied with, and

(b)   the unexecuted agreement was sent, for his signature, to the debtor or hirer [by an appropriate method] not less than seven days after a copy of it was given to him under section 58(1), and

(c)   during the consideration period, the creditor or owner refrained from approaching the debtor or hirer (whether in person, by telephone or letter, or in any other way) except in response to a specific request made by the debtor or hirer after the beginning of the consideration period, and

(d)   no notice of withdrawal by the debtor or hirer was received by the creditor or owner before the sending of the unexecuted agreement.

(3)   In subsection (2)(c), "the consideration period" means the period beginning with the giving of the copy under section 58(1) and ending—

(a)   at the expiry of seven days after the day on which the unexecuted agreement is sent, for his signature, to the debtor or hirer, or

(b)   on its return by the debtor or hirer after signature by him,

whichever first occurs.

(4)   Where the debtor or hirer is a partnership or an unincorporated body of persons, subsection (1)(a) shall apply with the substitution for "by the debtor or hirer" of "by or on behalf of the debtor or hirer".

[A57]

NOTES

This section is printed as it was in force on 15 June 2006, prior to amendments made by the Consumer Credit Act 2006 and subsequent amendments; for the text of this provision as it currently has effect, see [707].

Sub-s (2): in para (b) words in square brackets substituted by the Consumer Credit Act 1974 (Electronic Communications) Order 2004, SI 2004/3236, art 2(1), (2), as from 31 December 2004.

Regulations: the Consumer Credit (Agreements) Regulations 1983, SI 1983/1553.

62 Duty to supply copy of unexecuted agreement

(1)   If the unexecuted agreement is presented personally to the debtor or hirer for his signature, but on the occasion when he signs it the document does not become an executed agreement, a copy of it, and of any other document referred to in it, must be there and then delivered to him.

(2)   If the unexecuted agreement is sent to the debtor or hirer for his signature, a copy of it, and of any other document referred to in it, must be sent to him at the same time.

(3)   A regulated agreement is not properly executed if the requirements of this section are not observed.

[A58]

NOTES

This section is printed as it was in force on 15 June 2006, prior to amendments made by the Consumer Credit Act 2006 and subsequent amendments; for the text of this provision as it currently has effect, see [708].

63 Duty to supply copy of executed agreement

(1)   If the unexecuted agreement is presented personally to the debtor or hirer for his signature, and on the occasion when he signs it the document becomes an executed agreement, a copy of the executed agreement, and of any other document referred to in it, must be there and then delivered to him.

(2)   A copy of the executed agreement, and of any other document referred to in it, must be given to the debtor or hirer within the seven days following the making of the agreement unless—

(a)   subsection (1) applies, or

(b)   the unexecuted agreement was sent to the debtor or hirer for his signature and, on the occasion of his signing it, the document became an executed agreement.

(3)   In the case of a cancellable agreement, a copy under subsection (2) must be sent [by an appropriate method].

(4)   In the case of a credit-token agreement, a copy under subsection (2) need not be given within the seven days following the making of the agreement if it is given before or at the time when the credit-token is given to the debtor.

(5)   A regulated agreement is not properly executed if the requirements of this section are not observed.

[A59]

NOTES
This section is printed as it was in force on 15 June 2006, prior to amendments made by the Consumer Credit Act 2006 and subsequent amendments; for the text of this provision as it currently has effect, see [709].
Sub-s (3): words in square brackets substituted by the Consumer Credit Act 1974 (Electronic Communications) Order 2004, SI 2004/3236, art 2(1), (3), as from 31 December 2004.

64 Duty to give notice of cancellation rights

(1) In the case of a cancellable agreement, a notice in the prescribed form indicating the right of the debtor or hirer to cancel the agreement, how and when that right is exercisable, and the name and address of a person to whom notice of cancellation may be given,—

(a) must be included in every copy given to the debtor or hirer under section 62 or 63, and

(b) except where section 63(2) applied, must also be sent [by an appropriate method] to the debtor or hirer within the seven days following the making of the agreement.

(2) In the case of a credit-token agreement, a notice under subsection (1)(b) need not be sent [by an appropriate method] within the seven days following the making of the agreement if either—

(a) it is sent [by an appropriate method] to the debtor or hirer before the credit-token is given to him, or

(b) it is sent [by an appropriate method] to him together with the credit-token.

(3) Regulations may provide that except where section 63(2) applied a notice sent under subsection (1)(b) shall be accompanied by a further copy of the executed agreement, and of any other document referred to in it.

(4) Regulations may provide that subsection (1)(b) is not to apply in the case of agreements such as are described in the regulations, being agreements made by a particular person, if—

(a) on an application by that person to the [OFT], the [OFT] has determined that, having regard to—

(i) the manner in which antecedent negotiations for agreements with the applicant of that description are conducted, and

(ii) the information provided to debtors or hirers before such agreements are made, the requirement imposed by subsection (1)(b) can be dispensed with without prejudicing the interests of debtors or hirers; and

(b) any conditions imposed by the [OFT] in making the determination are complied with.

(5) A cancellable agreement is not properly executed if the requirements of this section are not observed.

[A60]

NOTES
This section is printed as it was in force on 15 June 2006, prior to amendments made by the Consumer Credit Act 2006 and subsequent amendments; for the text of this provision as it currently has effect, see [710].
Sub-ss (1), (2): words in square brackets substituted by the Consumer Credit Act 1974 (Electronic Communications) Order 2004, SI 2004/3236, art 2(1), (4), as from 31 December 2004.
References to the OFT, etc: as to the abolition of the office of the Director General of Fair Trading and the substitution of the original references to the Director (and related expressions), see the note preceding s 1 at [A1].
Regulations: the Consumer Credit (Cancellation Notices and Copies of Documents) Regulations 1983, SI 1983/1557; the Consumer Credit (Notice of Cancellation Rights) (Exemptions) Regulations 1983, SI 1983/1558.

65 Consequences of improper execution

(1) An improperly-executed regulated agreement is enforceable against the debtor or hirer on an order of the court only.

(2) A retaking of goods or land to which a regulated agreement relates is an enforcement of the agreement.

[A61]

NOTES
This section is printed as it was in force on 15 June 2006, prior to amendments made by the Consumer Credit Act 2006 and subsequent amendments; for the text of this provision as it currently has effect, see [711].

66 Acceptance of credit-tokens

(1) The debtor shall not be liable under a credit-token agreement for use made of the credit-token by any person unless the debtor had previously accepted the credit-token, or the use constituted an acceptance of it by him.

(2) The debtor accepts a credit-token when—

(a)　it is signed, or

(b)　a receipt for it is signed, or

(c)　it is first used,

either by the debtor himself or by a person who, pursuant to the agreement, is authorised by him to use it.

[A62]

NOTES

This section is printed as it was in force on 15 June 2006, prior to amendments made by the Consumer Credit Act 2006 and subsequent amendments; for the text of this provision as it currently has effect, see [712].

Cancellation of certain agreements within cooling-off period

67　Cancellable agreements

A regulated agreement may be cancelled by the debtor or hirer in accordance with this Part if the antecedent negotiations included oral representations made when in the presence of the debtor or hirer by an individual acting as, or on behalf of, the negotiator, unless—

(a)　the agreement is secured on land, or is a restricted-use credit agreement to finance the purchase of land or is an agreement for a bridging loan in connection with the purchase of land, or

(b)　the unexecuted agreement is signed by the debtor or hirer at premises at which any of the following is carrying on any business (whether on a permanent or temporary basis)—

　　(i)　the creditor or owner;

　　(ii)　any party to a linked transaction (other than the debtor or hirer or a relative of his);

　　(iii)　the negotiator in any antecedent negotiations.

[A63]

NOTES

This section is printed as it was in force on 15 June 2006, prior to amendments made by the Consumer Credit Act 2006 and subsequent amendments; for the text of this provision as it currently has effect, see [713].

68　Cooling-off period

The debtor or hirer may serve notice of cancellation of a cancellable agreement between his signing of the unexecuted agreement and—

(a)　the end of the fifth day following the day on which he received a copy under section 63(2) or a notice under section 64(1)(b), or

(b)　if (by virtue of regulations made under section 64(4)) section 64(1)(b) does not apply, the end of the fourteenth day following the day on which he signed the unexecuted agreement.

[A64]

NOTES

This section is printed as it was in force on 15 June 2006, prior to amendments made by the Consumer Credit Act 2006 and subsequent amendments; for the text of this provision as it currently has effect, see [714].

69　Notice of cancellation

(1)　If within the period specified in section 68 the debtor or hirer under a cancellable agreement serves on—

(a)　the creditor or owner, or

(b)　the person specified in the notice under section 64(1), or

(c)　a person who (whether by virtue of subsection (6) or otherwise) is the agent of the creditor or owner,

a notice (a "notice of cancellation") which, however expressed and whether or not conforming to the notice given under section 64(1), indicates the intention of the debtor or hirer to withdraw from the agreement, the notice shall operate—

　　(i)　to cancel the agreement, and any linked transaction, and

　　(ii)　to withdraw any offer by the debtor or hirer, or his relative, to enter into a linked transaction.

(2)　In the case of a debtor-creditor-supplier agreement for restricted-use credit financing—

(a)　the doing of work or supply of goods to meet an emergency, or

(b)　the supply of goods which, before service of the notice of cancellation, had by the act of the debtor or his relative become incorporated in any land or thing not comprised in the agreement or any linked transaction, subsection (1) shall apply with the substitution of the following for paragraph (i)—

"(i) to cancel only such provisions of the agreement and any linked transaction as—

(aa) relate to the provision of credit, or

(bb) require the debtor to pay an item in the total charge for credit, or

(cc) subject the debtor to any obligation other than to pay for the doing of the said work, or the supply of the said goods".

(3) Except so far as is otherwise provided, references in this Act to the cancellation of an agreement or transaction do not include a case within subsection (2).

(4) Except as otherwise provided by or under this Act, an agreement or transaction cancelled under subsection (1) shall be treated as if it had never been entered into.

(5) Regulations may exclude linked transactions of the prescribed description from subsection (1)(i) or (ii).

(6) Each of the following shall be deemed to be the agent of the creditor or owner for the purpose of receiving a notice of cancellation—

(a) a credit-broker or supplier who is the negotiator in antecedent negotiations, and

(b) any person who, in the course of a business carried on by him, acts on behalf of the debtor or hirer in any negotiations for the agreement.

[(7) Whether or not it is actually received by him, a notice of cancellation sent to a person shall be deemed to be served on him—.

(a) in the case of a notice sent by post, at the time of posting, and

(b) in the case of a notice transmitted in the form of an electronic communication in accordance with section 176A(1), at the time of the transmission.]

[A65]

NOTES

This section is printed as it was in force on 15 June 2006, prior to amendments made by the Consumer Credit Act 2006 and subsequent amendments; for the text of this provision as it currently has effect, see **[715]**.

Sub-s (7): substituted by the Consumer Credit Act 1974 (Electronic Communications) Order 2004, SI 2004/3236, art 2(1), (5), as from 31 December 2004.

Regulations: the Consumer Credit (Linked Transactions) (Exemptions) Regulations 1983, SI 1983/1560 at **[3031]**.

70 Cancellation: recovery of money paid by debtor or hirer

(1) On the cancellation of a regulated agreement, and of any linked transaction,—

(a) any sum paid by the debtor or hirer, or his relative, under or in contemplation of the agreement or transaction, including any item in the total charge for credit, shall become repayable, and

(b) any sum, including any item in the total charge for credit, which but for the cancellation is, or would or might become, payable by the debtor or hirer, or his relative, under the agreement or transaction shall cease to be, or shall not become, so payable, and

(c) in the case of a debtor-creditor-supplier agreement falling within section 12(b) any sum paid on the debtor's behalf by the creditor to the supplier shall become repayable to the creditor.

(2) If, under the terms of a cancelled agreement or transaction, the debtor or hirer, or his relative, is in possession of any goods, he shall have a lien on them for any sum repayable to him under subsection (1) in respect of that agreement or transaction, or any other linked transaction.

(3) A sum repayable under subsection (1) is repayable by the person to whom it was originally paid, but in the case of a debtor-creditor-supplier agreement falling within section 12(b) the creditor and the supplier shall be under a joint and several liability to repay sums paid by the debtor, or his relative, under the agreement or under a linked transaction falling within section 19(1)(b) and accordingly, in such a case, the creditor shall be entitled, in accordance with rules of court, to have the supplier made a party to any proceedings brought against the creditor to recover any such sums.

(4) Subject to any agreement between them, the creditor shall be entitled to be indemnified by the supplier for loss suffered by the creditor in satisfying his liability under subsection (3), including costs reasonably incurred by him in defending proceedings instituted by the debtor.

(5) Subsection (1) does not apply to any sum which, if not paid by a debtor, would be payable by virtue of section 71, and applies to a sum paid or payable by a debtor for the issue of a credit-token only where the credit-token has been returned to the creditor or surrendered to a supplier.

(6) If the total charge for credit includes an item in respect of a fee or commission charged by a credit-broker, the amount repayable under subsection (1) in respect of that item shall be the excess over [£5] of the fee or commission.

(7)   If the total charge for credit includes any sum payable or paid by the debtor to a credit-broker otherwise than in respect of a fee or commission charged by him, that sum shall for the purposes of subsection (6) be treated as if it were such a fee or commission.

(8)   So far only as is necessary to give effect to section 69(2), this section applies to an agreement or transaction within that subsection as it applies to a cancelled agreement or transaction.

[A66]

NOTES
This section is printed as it was in force on 15 June 2006, prior to amendments made by the Consumer Credit Act 2006 and subsequent amendments; for the text of this provision as it currently has effect, see [716].
Sub-s (6): sum in square brackets substituted by the Consumer Credit (Further Increase of Monetary Amounts) Order 1998, SI 1998/997, art 3, Schedule, as from 1 May 1998.

71   Cancellation: repayment of credit

(1)   Notwithstanding the cancellation of a regulated consumer credit agreement, other than a debtor-creditor-supplier agreement for restricted-use credit, the agreement shall continue in force so far as it relates to repayment of credit and payment of interest.

(2)   If, following the cancellation of a regulated consumer credit agreement, the debtor repays the whole or a portion of a credit—
  (a)   before the expiry of one month following service of the notice of cancellation, or
  (b)   in the case of a credit repayable by instalments, before the date on which the first instalment is due,
no interest shall be payable on the amount repaid.

(3)   If the whole of a credit repayable by instalments is not repaid on or before the date specified in subsection (2) (b), the debtor shall not be liable to repay any of the credit except on receipt of a request in writing in the prescribed form, signed by or on behalf of the creditor, stating the amounts of the remaining instalments (recalculated by the creditor as nearly as may be in accordance with the agreement and without extending the repayment period), but excluding any sum other than principal and interest.

(4)   Repayment of a credit, or payment of interest, under a cancelled agreement shall be treated as duly made if it is made to any person on whom, under section 69, a notice of cancellation could have been served, other than a person referred to in section 69(6)(b).

[A67]

NOTES
This section is printed as it was in force on 15 June 2006, prior to amendments made by the Consumer Credit Act 2006 and subsequent amendments; for the text of this provision as it currently has effect, see [717].
Regulations: the Consumer Credit (Repayment of Credit on Cancellation) Regulations 1983, SI 1983/1559.

72   Cancellation: return of goods

(1)   This section applies where any agreement or transaction relating to goods, being—
  (a)   a restricted-use debtor-creditor-supplier agreement, a consumer hire agreement, or a linked transaction to which the debtor or hirer under any regulated agreement is a party, or
  (b)   a linked transaction to which a relative of the debtor or hirer under any regulated agreement is a party,
is cancelled after the debtor or hirer (in a case within paragraph (a)) or the relative (in a case within paragraph (b)) has acquired possession of the goods by virtue of the agreement or transaction.

(2)   In this section—
  (a)   "the possessor" means the person who has acquired possession of the goods as mentioned in subsection (1),
  (b)   "the other party" means the person from whom the possessor acquired possession, and
  (c)   "the pre-cancellation period" means the period beginning when the possessor acquired possession and ending with the cancellation.

(3)   The possessor shall be treated as having been under a duty throughout the pre-cancellation period—
  (a)   to retain possession of the goods, and
  (b)   to take reasonable care of them.

(4)   On the cancellation, the possessor shall be under a duty, subject to any lien, to restore the goods to the other party in accordance with this section, and meanwhile to retain possession of the goods and take reasonable care of them.

(5)   The possessor shall not be under any duty to deliver the goods except at his own premises and in pursuance of a request in writing signed by or on behalf of the other party and served on the possessor either before, or at the time when, the goods are collected from those premises.

(6)   If the possessor—
    (a)   delivers the goods (whether at his own premises or elsewhere) to any person on whom, under section 69, a notice of cancellation could have been served (other than a person referred to in section 69(6)(b)), or
    (b)   sends the goods at his own expense to such a person,
he shall be discharged from any duty to retain the goods or deliver them to any person.

(7)   Where the possessor delivers the goods as mentioned in subsection (6)(a) his obligation to take care of the goods shall cease; and if he sends the goods as mentioned in subsection (6)(b), he shall be under a duty to take reasonable care to see that they are received by the other party and not damaged in transit, but in other respects his duty to take care of the goods shall cease.

(8)   Where, at any time during the period of 21 days following the cancellation, the possessor receives such a request as is mentioned in subsection (5), and unreasonably refuses or unreasonably fails to comply with it, his duty to take reasonable care of the goods shall continue until he delivers or sends the goods as mentioned in subsection (6), but if within that period he does not receive such a request his duty to take reasonable care of the goods shall cease at the end of that period.

(9)   The preceding provisions of this section do not apply to—
    (a)   perishable goods, or
    (b)   goods which by their nature are consumed by use and which, before the cancellation, were so consumed, or
    (c)   goods supplied to meet an emergency, or
    (d)   goods which, before the cancellation, had become incorporated in any land or thing not comprised in the cancelled agreement or a linked transaction.

(10)   Where the address of the possessor is specified in the executed agreement, references in this section to his own premises are to that address and no other.

(11)   Breach of a duty imposed by this section is actionable as a breach of statutory duty.
                                                                     [A68]

NOTES
   This section is printed as it was in force on 15 June 2006, prior to amendments made by the Consumer Credit Act 2006 and subsequent amendments; for the text of this provision as it currently has effect, see [718].

73   Cancellation: goods given in part-exchange

(1)   This section applies on the cancellation of a regulated agreement where, in antecedent negotiations, the negotiator agreed to take goods in part-exchange (the "part-exchange goods") and those goods have been delivered to him.

(2)   Unless, before the end of the period of ten days beginning with the date of cancellation, the part-exchange goods are returned to the debtor or hirer in a condition substantially as good as when they were delivered to the negotiator, the debtor or hirer shall be entitled to recover from the negotiator a sum equal to the part-exchange allowance (as defined in subsection (7)(b)).

(3)   In the case of a debtor-creditor-supplier agreement within section 12(b), the negotiator and the creditor shall be under a joint and several liability to pay to the debtor a sum recoverable under subsection (2).

(4)   Subject to any agreement between them, the creditor shall be entitled to be indemnified by the negotiator for loss suffered by the creditor in satisfying his liability under subsection (3), including costs reasonably incurred by him in defending proceedings instituted by the debtor.

(5)   During the period of ten days beginning with the date of cancellation, the debtor or hirer, if he is in possession of goods to which the cancelled agreement relates, shall have a lien on them for—
    (a)   delivery of the part-exchange goods, in a condition substantially as good as when they were delivered to the negotiator, or
    (b)   a sum equal to the part-exchange allowance;
and if the lien continues to the end of that period it shall thereafter subsist only as a lien for a sum equal to the part-exchange allowance.

(6)   Where the debtor or hirer recovers from the negotiator or creditor, or both of them jointly, a sum equal to the part-exchange allowance, then, if the title of the debtor or hirer to the part-exchange goods has not vested in the negotiator, it shall so vest on the recovery of that sum.

(7)   For the purposes of this section—
    (a)   the negotiator shall be treated as having agreed to take goods in part-exchange if,   in

pursuance of the antecedent negotiations, he either purchased or agreed to purchase those goods or accepted or agreed to accept them as part of the consideration for the cancelled agreement, and

(b) the part-exchange allowance shall be the sum agreed as such in the antecedent negotiations or, if no such agreement was arrived at, such sum as it would have been reasonable to allow in respect of the part-exchange goods if no notice of cancellation had been served.

(8) In an action brought against the creditor for a sum recoverable under subsection (2), he shall be entitled, in accordance with rules of court, to have the negotiator made a party to the proceedings.

[A69]

NOTES

This section is printed as it was in force on 15 June 2006, prior to amendments made by the Consumer Credit Act 2006 and subsequent amendments; for the text of this provision as it currently has effect, see [719].

Exclusion of certain agreements from Part V

74 Exclusion of certain agreements from Part V

(1) This Part (except section 56) does not apply to—

(a) a non-commercial agreement, or

(b) a debtor-creditor agreement enabling the debtor to overdraw on a current account, or

(c) a debtor-creditor agreement to finance the making of such payments arising on, or connected with, the death of a person as may be prescribed.

(2) This Part (except sections 55 and 56) does not apply to a small debtor-creditor-supplier agreement for restricted-use credit.

[(2A) In the case of an agreement to which the Consumer Protection (Cancellation of Contracts Concluded away from Business Premises) Regulations 1987 apply the reference in subsection (2) to a small agreement shall be construed as if in section 17(1)(a) and (b) "£35" were substituted for "£50".]

(3) Subsection (1)(b) or (c) applies only where the [OFT] so determines, and such a determination—

(a) may be made subject to such conditions as the [OFT] thinks fit, and

(b) shall be made only if the [OFT] is of opinion that it is not against the interests of debtors.

[(3A) Notwithstanding anything in subsection (3)(b) above, in relation to a debtor-creditor agreement under which the creditor is the Bank of England or a bank within the meaning of the Bankers' Books Evidence Act 1879, the [OFT] shall make a determination that subsection (1)(b) above applies unless [it] considers that it would be against the public interest to do so.]

(4) If any term of an agreement falling within subsection [(1)(c)] or (2) is expressed in writing, regulations under section 60(1) shall apply to that term (subject to section 60(3)) as if the agreement was a regulated agreement not falling within subsection [(1)(c)] or (2).

[A70]

NOTES

This section is printed as it was in force on 15 June 2006, prior to amendments made by the Consumer Credit Act 2006 and subsequent amendments; for the text of this provision as it currently has effect, see [720].

Sub-s (2A): inserted by the Consumer Protection (Cancellation of Contracts Concluded away from Business Premises) Regulations 1987, SI 1987/2117, reg 9, as from 1 July 1988.

Sub-s (3A): added by the Banking Act 1979, s 38(1), as from 1 October 1979.

Sub-s (4): words in square brackets substituted by the Banking Act 1979, s 38(1), as from 1 October 1979.

References to the OFT, etc: as to the abolition of the office of the Director General of Fair Trading and the substitution of the original references to the Director (and related expressions), see the note preceding s 1 at [A1].

Regulations: the Consumer Credit (Payments Arising on Death) Regulations 1983, SI 1983/1554.

PART VI

MATTERS ARISING DURING CURRENCY OF CREDIT OR HIRE AGREEMENTS

75 Liability of creditor for breaches by supplier

(1) If the debtor under a debtor-creditor-supplier agreement falling within section 12(b) or (c) has, in relation to a transaction financed by the agreement, any claim against the supplier in respect of a misrepresentation or breach of contract, he shall have a like claim against the creditor, who, with the supplier, shall accordingly be jointly and severally liable to the debtor.

(2)   Subject to any agreement between them, the creditor shall be entitled to be indemnified by the supplier for loss suffered by the creditor in satisfying his liability under subsection (1), including costs reasonably incurred by him in defending proceedings instituted by the debtor.

(3)   Subsection (1) does not apply to a claim—

(a)   under a non-commercial agreement, or

(b)   so far as the claim relates to any single item to which the supplier has attached a cash price not exceeding [£100] or more than [£30,000].

(4)   This section applies notwithstanding that the debtor, in entering into the transaction, exceeded the credit limit or otherwise contravened any term of the agreement.

(5)   In an action brought against the creditor under subsection (1) he shall be entitled, in accordance with rules of court, to have the supplier made a party to the proceedings.

[A71]

NOTES

This section is printed as it was in force on 15 June 2006, prior to amendments made by the Consumer Credit Act 2006 and subsequent amendments; for the text of this provision as it currently has effect, see [721].

Sub-s (3): sums in first and second pairs of square brackets in para (b) substituted by the Consumer Credit (Increase of Monetary Limits) Order 1983, SI 1983/1878, arts 3, 4, Schedule, Pts I, II, as from 1 May 1998.

76   Duty to give notice before taking certain action

(1)   The creditor or owner is not entitled to enforce a term of a regulated agreement by—

(a)   demanding earlier payment of any sum, or

(b)   recovering possession of any goods or land, or

(c)   treating any right conferred on the debtor or hirer by the agreement as terminated, restricted or deferred,

except by or after giving the debtor or hirer not less than seven days' notice of intention to do so.

(2)   Subsection (1) applies only where—

(a)   a period for the duration of the agreement is specified in the agreement, and

(b)   that period has not ended when the creditor or owner does an act mentioned in subsection (1),

but so applies notwithstanding that, under the agreement, any party is entitled to terminate it before the end of the period so specified.

(3)   A notice under subsection (1) is ineffective if not in the prescribed form.

(4)   Subsection (1) does not prevent a creditor from treating the right to draw on any credit as restricted or deferred and taking such steps as may be necessary to make the restriction or deferment effective.

(5)   Regulations may provide that subsection (1) is not to apply to agreements described by the regulations.

(6)   Subsection (1) does not apply to a right of enforcement arising by reason of any breach by the debtor or hirer of the regulated agreement.

[A72]

NOTES

This section is printed as it was in force on 15 June 2006, prior to amendments made by the Consumer Credit Act 2006 and subsequent amendments; for the text of this provision as it currently has effect, see [722].

Regulations: the Consumer Credit (Enforcement, Default and Termination Notices) Regulations 1983, SI 1983/1561.

77   Duty to give information to debtor under fixed-sum credit agreement

(1)   The creditor under a regulated agreement for fixed-sum credit, within the prescribed period after receiving a request in writing to that effect from the debtor and payment of a fee of [£1], shall give the debtor a copy of the executed agreement (if any) and of any other document referred to in it, together with a statement signed by or on behalf of the creditor showing, according to the information to which it is practicable for him to refer,—

(a)   the total sum paid under the agreement by the debtor;

(b)   the total sum which has become payable under the agreement by the debtor but remains unpaid, and the various amounts comprised in that total sum, with the date when each became due; and

(c)   the total sum which is to become payable under the agreement by the debtor, and the various amounts comprised in that total sum, with the date, or mode of determining the date, when each becomes due.

(2) If the creditor possesses insufficient information to enable him to ascertain the amounts and dates mentioned in subsection (1)(c), he shall be taken to comply with that paragraph if his statement under subsection (1) gives the basis on which, under the regulated agreement, they would fall to be ascertained.

(3) Subsection (1) does not apply to—
    (a) an agreement under which no sum is, or will or may become, payable by the debtor, or
    (b) a request made less than one month after a previous request under that subsection relating to the same agreement was complied with.

(4) If the creditor under an agreement fails to comply with subsection (1)—
    (a) he is not entitled, while the default continues, to enforce the agreement; …
    (b) …

(5) This section does not apply to a non-commercial agreement.

[A73]

NOTES

This section is printed as it was in force on 15 June 2006, prior to amendments made by the Consumer Credit Act 2006 and subsequent amendments; for the text of this provision as it currently has effect, see [723].

Sub-s (1): sum in square brackets substituted by the Consumer Credit (Further Increase in Monetary Amounts) Order 1998, SI 1998/997, art 3, Schedule, as from 1 May 1998.

Sub-s (4): words omitted repealed by the Consumer Protection from Unfair Trading Regulations 2008, SI 2008/1277, reg 30(1), (3), Sch 2, Pt 1, paras 17, 19, Sch 4, as from 26 May 2008.

Regulations: the Consumer Credit (Prescribed Periods for Giving Information) Regulations 1983, SI 1983/1569.

78 Duty to give information to debtor under running-account credit agreement

(1) The creditor under a regulated agreement for running-account credit, within the prescribed period after receiving a request in writing to that effect from the debtor and payment of a fee of [£1], shall give the debtor a copy of the executed agreement (if any) and of any other document referred to in it, together with a statement signed by or on behalf of the creditor showing, according to the information to which it is practicable for him to refer,—
    (a) the state of the account, and
    (b) the amount, if any, currently payable under the agreement by the debtor to the creditor, and
    (c) the amounts and due dates of any payments which, if the debtor does not draw further on the account, will later become payable under the agreement by the debtor to the creditor.

(2) If the creditor possesses insufficient information to enable him to ascertain the amounts and dates mentioned in subsection (1)(c), he shall be taken to comply with that paragraph if his statement under subsection (1) gives the basis on which, under the regulated agreement, they would fall to be ascertained.

(3) Subsection (1) does not apply to—
    (a) an agreement under which no sum is, or will or may become, payable by the debtor, or
    (b) a request made less than one month after a previous request under that subsection relating to the same agreement was complied with.

(4) Where running-account credit is provided under a regulated agreement, the creditor shall give the debtor statements in the prescribed form, and with the prescribed contents—
    (a) showing according to the information to which it is practicable for him to refer, the state of the account at regular intervals of not more than twelve months, and
    (b) where the agreement provides, in relation to specified periods, for the making of payments by the debtor, or the charging against him of interest or any other sum, showing according to the information to which it is practicable for him to refer the state of the account at the end of each of those periods during which there is any movement in the account.

(5) A statement under subsection (4) shall be given within the prescribed period after the end of the period to which the statement relates.

(6) If the creditor under an agreement fails to comply with subsection (1)—
    (a) he is not entitled, while the default continues, to enforce the agreement; and
    (b) if the default continues for one month he commits an offence.

(7) This section does not apply to a non-commercial agreement, and subsections (4) and (5) do not apply to a small agreement.

[A74]

NOTES

This section is printed as it was in force on 15 June 2006, prior to amendments made by the Consumer Credit Act 2006 and subsequent amendments; for the text of this provision as it currently has effect, see [724].

Sub-s (1): sum in square brackets substituted by the Consumer Credit (Further Increase in Monetary Amounts) Order 1998, SI 1998/997, art 3, Schedule, as from 1 May 1998.

Regulations: the Consumer Credit (Prescribed Periods for Giving Information) Regulations 1983, SI 1983/1569; the Consumer Credit (Running-Account Credit) Information Regulations 1983, SI 1983/1570.

79 Duty to give hirer information

(1)   The owner under a regulated consumer hire agreement, within the prescribed period after receiving a request in writing to that effect from the hirer and payment of a fee of [£1], shall give to the hirer a copy of the executed agreement and of any other document referred to in it, together with a statement signed by or on behalf of the owner showing, according to the information to which it is practicable for him to refer, the total sum which has become payable under the agreement by the hirer but remains unpaid and the various amounts comprised in that total sum, with the date when each became due.

(2)   Subsection (1) does not apply to—

(a)   an agreement under which no sum is, or will or may become, payable by the hirer, or

(b)   a request made less than one month after a previous request under that subsection relating to the same agreement was complied with.

(3)   If the owner under an agreement fails to comply with subsection (1)—

(a)   he is not entitled, while the default continues, to enforce the agreement; and

(b)   if the default continues for one month he commits an offence.

(4)   This section does not apply to a non-commercial agreement.

[A75]

NOTES

This section is printed as it was in force on 15 June 2006, prior to amendments made by the Consumer Credit Act 2006 and subsequent amendments; for the text of this provision as it currently has effect, see [725].

Sub-s (1): sum in square brackets substituted by the Consumer Credit (Further Increase in Monetary Amounts) Order 1998, SI 1998/997, art 3, Schedule, as from 1 May 1998.

Regulations: the Consumer Credit (Prescribed Periods for Giving Information) Regulations 1983, SI 1983/1569.

80 Debtor or hirer to give information about goods

(1)   Where a regulated agreement, other than a non-commercial agreement, requires the debtor or hirer to keep goods to which the agreement relates in his possession or control, he shall, within seven working days after he has received a request in writing to that effect from the creditor or owner, tell the creditor or owner where the goods are.

(2)   If the debtor or hirer fails to comply with subsection (1), and the default continues for 14 days, he commits an offence.

[A76]

NOTES

This section is printed as it was in force on 15 June 2006, prior to amendments made by the Consumer Credit Act 2006 and subsequent amendments; for the text of this provision as it currently has effect, see [726].

81 Appropriation of payments

(1)   Where a debtor or hirer is liable to make to the same person payments in respect of two or more regulated agreements, he shall be entitled, on making any payment in respect of the agreements which is not sufficient to discharge the total amount then due under all the agreements, to appropriate the sum so paid by him—

(a)   in or towards the satisfaction of the sum due under any one of the agreements, or

(b)   in or towards the satisfaction of the sums due under any two or more of the agreements in such proportions as he thinks fit.

(2)   If the debtor or hirer fails to make any such appropriation where one or more of the agreements is—

(a)   a hire-purchase agreement or conditional sale agreement, or

(b)   a consumer hire agreement, or

(c)   an agreement in relation to which any security is provided,

the payment shall be appropriated towards the satisfaction of the sums due under the several agreements respectively in the proportions which those sums bear to one another.

[A77]

NOTES
This section is printed as it was in force on 15 June 2006, prior to amendments made by the Consumer Credit Act 2006 and subsequent amendments; for the text of this provision as it currently has effect, see [727].

82 Variation of agreements

(1)   Where, under a power contained in a regulated agreement, the creditor or owner varies the agreement, the variation shall not take effect before notice of it is given to the debtor or hirer in the prescribed manner.

(2)   Where an agreement (a "modifying agreement") varies or supplements an earlier agreement, the modifying agreement shall for the purposes of this Act be treated as—
(a)   revoking the earlier agreement, and
(b)   containing provisions reproducing the combined effect of the two agreements,
and obligations outstanding in relation to the earlier agreement shall accordingly be treated as outstanding instead in relation to the modifying agreement.

[(2A)   Subsection (2) does not apply if the modifying agreement is an exempt agreement as a result of section 16(6C).]

(3)   If the earlier agreement is a regulated agreement but (apart from this subsection) the modifying agreement is not then, [unless the modifying agreement is—
(a)   for running account credit; or
(b)   an exempt agreement as a result of section 16(6C),
it shall be treated as a regulated agreement.]

(4)   If the earlier agreement is a regulated agreement for running-account credit, and by the modifying agreement the creditor allows the credit limit to be exceeded but intends the excess to be merely temporary, Part V (except section 56) shall not apply to the modifying agreement.

(5)   If—
(a)   the earlier agreement is a cancellable agreement, and
(b)   the modifying agreement is made within the period applicable under section 68 to the earlier agreement,
then, whether or not the modifying agreement would, apart from this subsection, be a cancellable agreement, it shall be treated as a cancellable agreement in respect of which a notice may be served under section 68 not later than the end of the period applicable under that section to the earlier agreement.

[(5A)   Subsection (5) does not apply where the modifying agreement is an exempt agreement as a result of section 16(6C).]

(6)   Except under subsection (5), a modifying agreement shall not be treated as a cancellable agreement.

(7)   This section does not apply to a non-commercial agreement.

[A78]

NOTES
This section is printed as it was in force on 15 June 2006, prior to amendments made by the Consumer Credit Act 2006 and subsequent amendments; for the text of this provision as it currently has effect, see [728].
Sub-s (2A): inserted by the Financial Services and Markets Act 2000 (Consequential Amendments) Order 2005, SI 2005/2967, art 2(1), (2), as from 16 November 2005.
Sub-s (3): words in square brackets substituted by SI 2005/2967, art 2(1), (3), as from 16 November 2005.
Sub-s (5A): inserted by SI 2005/2967, art 2(1), (4), as from 16 November 2005.
Regulations: the Consumer Credit (Notice of Variation of Agreements) Regulations 1977, SI 1977/328.

83 Liability for misuse of credit facilities

(1)   The debtor under a regulated consumer credit agreement shall not be liable to the creditor for any loss arising from use of the credit facility by another person not acting, or to be treated as acting, as the debtor's agent.

(2)   This section does not apply to a non-commercial agreement, or to any loss in so far as it arises from misuse of an instrument to which section 4 of the Cheques Act 1957 applies.

[A79]

NOTES
This section is printed as it was in force on 15 June 2006, prior to amendments made by the Consumer Credit Act 2006 and subsequent amendments; for the text of this provision as it currently has effect, see [729].

84   Misuse of credit-tokens

(1)   Section 83 does not prevent the debtor under a credit-token agreement from being made liable to the extent of [£50] (or the credit limit if lower) for loss to the creditor arising from use of the credit-token by other persons during a period beginning when the credit-token ceases to be in the possession of any authorised person and ending when the credit-token is once more in the possession of an authorised person.

(2)   Section 83 does not prevent the debtor under a credit-token agreement from being made liable to any extent for loss to the creditor from use of the credit-token by a person who acquired possession of it with the debtor's consent.

(3)   Subsections (1) and (2) shall not apply to any use of the credit-token after the creditor has been given oral or written notice that it is lost or stolen, or is for any other reason liable to misuse.

[(3A)   Subsections (1) and (2) shall not apply to any use, in connection with a distance contract (other than an excepted contract), of a card which is a credit-token.

(3B)   In subsection (3A), "distance contract" and "excepted contract" have the meanings given in the Consumer Protection (Distance Selling) Regulations 2000.]

[(3C)   Subsections (1) and (2) shall not apply to any use, in connection with a distance contract within the meaning of the Financial Services (Distance Marketing) Regulations 2004, of a card which is a credit-token.]

(4)   Subsections (1) and (2) shall not apply unless there are contained in the credit-token agreement in the prescribed manner particulars of the name, address and telephone number of a person stated to be the person to whom notice is to be given under subsection (3).

(5)   Notice under subsection (3) takes effect when received, but where it is given orally, and the agreement so requires, it shall be treated as not taking effect if not confirmed in writing within seven days.

(6)   Any sum paid by the debtor for the issue of the credit-token, to the extent (if any) that it has not been previously offset by use made of the credit token, shall be treated as paid towards satisfaction of any liability under subsection (1) or (2).

(7)   The debtor, the creditor, and any person authorised by the debtor to use the credit-token, shall be authorised persons for the purposes of subsection (1).

(8)   Where two or more credit-tokens are given under one credit-token agreement, the preceding provisions of this section apply to each credit-token separately.

[A80]

NOTES
     This section is printed as it was in force on 15 June 2006, prior to amendments made by the Consumer Credit Act 2006 and subsequent amendments; for the text of this provision as it currently has effect, see [730].
     Sub-s (1): sum in square brackets substituted by the Consumer Credit (Further Increase in Monetary Amounts) Order 1998, SI 1998/997, art 3, Schedule, as from 1 May 1998.
     Sub-ss (3A), (3B): inserted by the Consumer Protection (Distance Selling) Regulations 2000, SI 2000/2334, reg 21(5), as from 31 October 2000.
     Sub-s (3C): inserted by the Financial Services (Distance Marketing) Regulations 2004, SI 2004/2095, reg 14(4), as from 31 October 2004 (in relation to distance contracts made on or after that date).
     Regulations: the Consumer Credit (Credit-Token Agreements) Regulations 1983, SI 1983/1555.

85   Duty on issue of new credit-tokens

(1)   Whenever, in connection with a credit-token agreement, a credit-token (other than the first) is given by the creditor to the debtor, the creditor shall give the debtor a copy of the executed agreement (if any) and of any other document referred to in it.

(2)   If the creditor fails to comply with this section—
     (a)   he is not entitled, while the default continues, to enforce the agreement; and
     (b)   if the default continues for one month he commits an offence.

(3)   This section does not apply to a small agreement.

[A81]

NOTES
     This section is printed as it was in force on 15 June 2006, prior to amendments made by the Consumer Credit Act 2006 and subsequent amendments; for the text of this provision as it currently has effect, see [731].

86   Death of debtor or hirer

(1)   The creditor or owner under a regulated agreement is not entitled, by reason of the death of the debtor or hirer, to do an act specified in paragraphs (a) to (e) of section 87(1) if at the death the agreement is fully secured.

(2)   If at the death of the debtor or hirer a regulated agreement is only partly secured or is unsecured, the creditor or owner is entitled, by reason of the death of the debtor or hirer, to do an act specified in paragraphs (a) to (e) of section 87(1) on an order of the court only.

(3)   This section applies in relation to the termination of an agreement only where—
    (a)   a period for its duration is specified in the agreement, and
    (b)   that period has not ended when the creditor or owner purports to terminate the agreement,
but so applies notwithstanding that, under the agreement, any party is entitled to terminate it before the end of the period so specified.

(4)   This section does not prevent the creditor from treating the right to draw on any credit as restricted or deferred, and taking such steps as may be necessary to make the restriction or deferment effective.

(5)   This section does not affect the operation of any agreement providing for payment of sums—
    (a)   due under the regulated agreement, or
    (b)   becoming due under it on the death of the debtor or hirer,
out of the proceeds of a policy of assurance on his life.

(6)   For the purposes of this section an act is done by reason of the death of the debtor or hirer if it is done under a power conferred by the agreement which is—
    (a)   exercisable on his death, or
    (b)   exercisable at will and exercised at any time after his death.

[A82]

NOTES
This section is printed as it was in force on 15 June 2006, prior to amendments made by the Consumer Credit Act 2006 and subsequent amendments; for the text of this provision as it currently has effect, see [732].

PART VII
DEFAULT AND TERMINATION
Default notices

87   Need for default notice

(1)   Service of a notice on the debtor or hirer in accordance with section 88 (a "default notice") is necessary before the creditor or owner can become entitled, by reason of any breach by the debtor or hirer of a regulated agreement,—
    (a)   to terminate the agreement, or
    (b)   to demand earlier payment of any sum, or
    (c)   to recover possession of any goods or land, or
    (d)   to treat any right conferred on the debtor or hirer by the agreement as terminated, restricted or deferred, or
    (e)   to enforce any security.

(2)   Subsection (1) does not prevent the creditor from treating the right to draw upon any credit as restricted or deferred, and taking such steps as may be necessary to make the restriction or deferment effective.

(3)   The doing of an act by which a floating charge becomes fixed is not enforcement of a security.

(4)   Regulations may provide that subsection (1) is not to apply to agreements described by the regulations.

[A83]

NOTES
This section is printed as it was in force on 15 June 2006, prior to amendments made by the Consumer Credit Act 2006 and subsequent amendments; for the text of this provision as it currently has effect, see [733].
Regulations: the Consumer Credit (Enforcement, Default and Termination Notices) Regulations 1983, SI 1983/1561.

88   Contents and effect of default notice

(1)   The default notice must be in the prescribed form and specify—
    (a)   the nature of the alleged breach;
    (b)   if the breach is capable of remedy, what action is required to remedy it and the date before which that action is to be taken;

(c) if the breach is not capable of remedy, the sum (if any) required to be paid as compensation for the breach, and the date before which it is to be paid.

(2) A date specified under subsection (1) must not be less than seven days after the date of service of the default notice, and the creditor or owner shall not take action such as is mentioned in section 87(1) before the date so specified or (if no requirement is made under subsection (1)) before those seven days have elapsed.

(3) The default notice must not treat as a breach failure to comply with a provision of the agreement which becomes operative only on breach of some other provision, but if the breach of that other provision is not duly remedied or compensation demanded under subsection (1) is not duly paid, or (where no requirement is made under subsection (1)) if the seven days mentioned in subsection (2) have elapsed, the creditor or owner may treat the failure as a breach and section 87(1) shall not apply to it.

(4) The default notice must contain information in the prescribed terms about the consequences of failure to comply with it.

(5) A default notice making a requirement under subsection (1) may include a provision for the taking of action such as is mentioned in section 87(1) at any time after the restriction imposed by subsection (2) will cease, together with a statement that the provision will be ineffective if the breach is duly remedied or the compensation duly paid.

[A84]

NOTES
  This section is printed as it was in force on 15 June 2006, prior to amendments made by the Consumer Credit Act 2006 and subsequent amendments; for the text of this provision as it currently has effect, see [734].
  Regulations: the Consumer Credit (Enforcement, Default and Termination Notices) Regulations 1983, SI 1983/1561.

89 Compliance with default notice

If before the date specified for that purpose in the default notice the debtor or hirer takes the action specified under section 88(1)(b) or (c) the breach shall be treated as not having occurred.

[A85]

NOTES
  This section is printed as it was in force on 15 June 2006, prior to amendments made by the Consumer Credit Act 2006 and subsequent amendments; for the text of this provision as it currently has effect, see [735].

Further restriction of remedies for default

90 Retaking of protected hire-purchase etc goods

  (1) At any time when—
    (a) the debtor is in breach of a regulated hire-purchase or a regulated conditional sale agreement relating to goods, and
    (b) the debtor has paid to the creditor one-third or more of the total price of the goods, and
    (c) the property in the goods remains in the creditor,
the creditor is not entitled to recover possession of the goods from the debtor except on an order of the court.

  (2) Where under a hire-purchase or conditional sale agreement the creditor is required to carry out any installation and the agreement specifies, as part of the total price, the amount to be paid in respect of the installation (the "installation charge") the reference in subsection (1)(b) to one third of the total price shall be construed as a reference to the aggregate of the installation charge and one third of the remainder of the total price.

  (3) In a case where—
    (a) subsection (1)(a) is satisfied, but not subsection (1)(b), and
    (b) subsection (1)(b) was satisfied on a previous occasion in relation to an earlier agreement, being a regulated hire-purchase or regulated conditional sale agreement, between the same parties, and relating to any of the goods comprised in the later agreement (whether or not other goods were also included),
subsection (1) shall apply to the later agreement with the omission of paragraph (b).

  (4) If the later agreement is a modifying agreement, subsection (3) shall apply with the substitution, for the second reference to the later agreement, of a reference to the modifying agreement.

  (5) Subsection (1) shall not apply, or shall cease to apply, to an agreement if the debtor has terminated, or terminates, the agreement.

APPENDIX
CCA 1974 (PRE CCA 2006)

(6) Where subsection (1) applies to an agreement at the death of the debtor, it shall continue to apply (in relation to the possessor of the goods) until the grant of probate or administration, or (in Scotland) confirmation (on which the personal representative would fall to be treated as the debtor).

(7) Goods falling within this section are in this Act referred to as "protected goods".

[A86]

NOTES
   This section is printed as it was in force on 15 June 2006, prior to amendments made by the Consumer Credit Act 2006 and subsequent amendments; for the text of this provision as it currently has effect, see [736].

91   Consequences of breach of s 90

If goods are recovered by the creditor in contravention of section 90—
   (a)   the regulated agreement, if not previously terminated, shall terminate, and
   (b)   the debtor shall be released from all liability under the agreement, and shall be entitled to recover from the creditor all sums paid by the debtor under the agreement.

[A87]

NOTES
   This section is printed as it was in force on 15 June 2006, prior to amendments made by the Consumer Credit Act 2006 and subsequent amendments; for the text of this provision as it currently has effect, see [737].

92   Recovery of possession of goods or land

(1) Except under an order of the court, the creditor or owner shall not be entitled to enter any premises to take possession of goods subject to a regulated hire-purchase agreement, regulated conditional sale agreement or regulated consumer hire agreement.

(2) At any time when the debtor is in breach of a regulated conditional sale agreement relating to land, the creditor is entitled to recover possession of the land from the debtor, or any person claiming under him, on an order of the court only.

(3) An entry in contravention of subsection (1) or (2) is actionable as a breach of statutory duty.

[A88]

NOTES
   This section is printed as it was in force on 15 June 2006, prior to amendments made by the Consumer Credit Act 2006 and subsequent amendments; for the text of this provision as it currently has effect, see [738].

93   Interest not to be increased on default

The debtor under a regulated consumer credit agreement shall not be obliged to pay interest on sums which, in breach of the agreement, are unpaid by him at a rate—
   (a)   where the total charge for credit includes an item in respect of interest, exceeding the rate of that interest, or
   (b)   in any other case, exceeding what would be the rate of the total charge for credit if any items included in the total charge for credit by virtue of section 20(2) were disregarded.

[A89]

NOTES
   This section is printed as it was in force on 15 June 2006, prior to amendments made by the Consumer Credit Act 2006 and subsequent amendments; for the text of this provision as it currently has effect, see [739].

93A   *(Applies to Scotland only.)*

Early payment by debtor

94   Right to complete payments ahead of time

(1) The debtor under a regulated consumer credit agreement is entitled at any time, by notice to the creditor and the payment to the creditor of all amounts payable by the debtor to him under the agreement (less any rebate allowable under section 95), to discharge the debtor's indebtedness under the agreement.

(2) A notice under subsection (1) may embody the exercise by the debtor of any option to purchase goods conferred on him by the agreement, and deal with any other matter arising on, or in relation to, the termination of the agreement.

[A90]

NOTES
   This section is printed as it was in force on 15 June 2006, prior to amendments made by the Consumer Credit Act 2006 and subsequent amendments; for the text of this provision as it currently has effect, see **[740]**.

95 Rebate on early settlement

   (1)   Regulations may provide for the allowance of a rebate of charges for credit to the debtor under a regulated consumer credit agreement where, under section 94, on refinancing, on breach of the agreement, or for any other reason, his indebtedness is discharged or becomes payable before the time fixed by the agreement, or any sum becomes payable by him before the time so fixed.

   (2)   Regulations under subsection (1) may provide for calculation of the rebate by reference to any sums paid or payable by the debtor or his relative under or in connection with the agreement (whether to the creditor or some other person), including sums under linked transactions and other items in the total charge for credit.

[A91]

NOTES
   This section is printed as it was in force on 15 June 2006, prior to amendments made by the Consumer Credit Act 2006 and subsequent amendments; for the text of this provision as it currently has effect, see **[741]**.
   Regulations: the Consumer Credit (Early Settlement) Regulations 2004, SI 2004/1483 at **[3389]**.

96 Effect on linked transactions

   (1)   Where for any reason the indebtedness of the debtor under a regulated consumer credit agreement is discharged before the time fixed by the agreement, he, and any relative of his, shall at the same time be discharged from any liability under a linked transaction, other than a debt which has already become payable.

   (2)   Subsection (1) does not apply to a linked transaction which is itself an agreement providing the debtor or his relative with credit.

   (3)   Regulations may exclude linked transactions of the prescribed description from the operation of subsection (1).

[A92]

NOTES
   This section is printed as it was in force on 15 June 2006, prior to amendments made by the Consumer Credit Act 2006 and subsequent amendments; for the text of this provision as it currently has effect, see **[742]**.
   Regulations: the Consumer Credit (Enforcement, Default and Termination Notices) Regulations 1983, SI 1983/1561.

97 Duty to give information

   (1)   The creditor under a regulated consumer credit agreement, within the prescribed period after he has received a request in writing to that effect from the debtor, shall give the debtor a statement in the prescribed form indicating, according to the information to which it is practicable for him to refer, the amount of the payment required to discharge the debtor's indebtedness under the agreement, together with the prescribed particulars showing how the amount is arrived at.

   (2)   Subsection (1) does not apply to a request made less than one month after a previous request under that subsection relating to the same agreement was complied with.

   (3)   If the creditor fails to comply with subsection (1)—
   (a)   he is not entitled, while the default continues, to enforce the agreement; and
   (b)   if the default continues for one month he commits an offence.

[A93]

NOTES
   This section is printed as it was in force on 15 June 2006, prior to amendments made by the Consumer Credit Act 2006 and subsequent amendments; for the text of this provision as it currently has effect, see **[743]**.
   Regulations: the Consumer Credit (Settlement Information) Regulations 1983, SI 1983/1564; the Consumer Credit (Early Settlement) Regulations 2004, SI 2004/1483 at **[3389]**.

Termination of agreements

98 Duty to give notice of termination (non-default cases)

   (1)   The creditor or owner is not entitled to terminate a regulated agreement except by or after giving the debtor or hirer not less than seven days' notice of the termination.

(2) Subsection (1) applies only where—

    (a) a period for the duration of the agreement is specified in the agreement, and

    (b) that period has not ended when the creditor or owner does an act mentioned in subsection (1),

but so applies notwithstanding that, under the agreement, any party is entitled to terminate it before the end of the period so specified.

(3) A notice under subsection (1) is ineffective if not in the prescribed form.

(4) Subsection (1) does not prevent a creditor from treating the right to draw on any credit as restricted or deferred and taking such steps as may be necessary to make the restriction or deferment effective.

(5) Regulations may provide that subsection (1) is not to apply to agreements described by the regulations.

(6) Subsection (1) does not apply to the termination of a regulated agreement by reason of any breach by the debtor or hirer of the agreement.

[A94]

NOTES

This section is printed as it was in force on 15 June 2006, prior to amendments made by the Consumer Credit Act 2006 and subsequent amendments; for the text of this provision as it currently has effect, see [744].

Regulations: the Consumer Credit (Enforcement, Default and Termination Notices) Regulations 1983, SI 1983/1561.

99 Right to terminate hire-purchase etc agreements

(1) At any time before the final payment by the debtor under a regulated hire-purchase or regulated conditional sale agreement falls due, the debtor shall be entitled to terminate the agreement by giving notice to any person entitled or authorised to receive the sums payable under the agreement.

(2) Termination of an agreement under subsection (1) does not affect any liability under the agreement which has accrued before the termination.

(3) Subsection (1) does not apply to a conditional sale agreement relating to land after the title to the land has passed to the debtor.

(4) In the case of a conditional sale agreement relating to goods, where the property in the goods, having become vested in the debtor, is transferred to a person who does not become the debtor under the agreement, the debtor shall not thereafter be entitled to terminate the agreement under subsection (1).

(5) Subject to subsection (4), where a debtor under a conditional sale agreement relating to goods, terminates the agreement under this section after the property in the goods has become vested in him, the property in the goods shall thereupon vest in the person (the "previous owner") in whom it was vested immediately before it became vested in the debtor:

Provided that if the previous owner has died, or any other event has occurred whereby that property, if vested in him immediately before that event, would thereupon have vested in some other person, the property shall be treated as having devolved as if it had been vested in the previous owner immediately before his death or immediately before that event, as the case may be.

[A95]

NOTES

This section is printed as it was in force on 15 June 2006, prior to amendments made by the Consumer Credit Act 2006 and subsequent amendments; for the text of this provision as it currently has effect, see [745].

100 Liability of debtor on termination of hire-purchase etc agreement

(1) Where a regulated hire-purchase or regulated conditional sale agreement is terminated under section 99 the debtor shall be liable, unless the agreement provides for a smaller payment, or does not provide for any payment, to pay to the creditor the amount (if any) by which one-half of the total price exceeds the aggregate of the sums paid and the sums due in respect of the total price immediately before the termination.

(2) Where under a hire-purchase or conditional sale agreement the creditor is required to carry out any installation and the agreement specifies, as part of the total price, the amount to be paid in respect of the installation (the "installation charge") the reference in subsection (1) to one-half of the total price shall be construed as a reference to the aggregate of the installation charge and one-half of the remainder of the total price.

(3) If in any action the court is satisfied that a sum less than the amount specified in subsection (1) would be equal to the loss sustained by the creditor in consequence of the termination of the agreement by the debtor, the court may make an order for the payment of that sum in lieu of the amount specified in subsection (1).

(4) If the debtor has contravened an obligation to take reasonable care of the goods or land, the amount arrived at under subsection (1) shall be increased by the sum required to recompense the creditor for that contravention, and subsection (2) shall have effect accordingly.

(5) Where the debtor, on the termination of the agreement, wrongfully retains possession of goods to which the agreement relates, then, in any action brought by the creditor to recover possession of the goods from the debtor, the court, unless it is satisfied that having regard to the circumstances it would not be just to do so, shall order the goods to be delivered to the creditor without giving the debtor an option to pay the value of the goods.

[A96]

NOTES

This section is printed as it was in force on 15 June 2006, prior to amendments made by the Consumer Credit Act 2006 and subsequent amendments; for the text of this provision as it currently has effect, see [746].

101 Right to terminate hire agreement

(1) The hirer under a regulated consumer hire agreement is entitled to terminate the agreement by giving notice to any person entitled or authorised to receive the sums payable under the agreement.

(2) Termination of an agreement under subsection (1) does not affect any liability under the agreement which has accrued before the termination.

(3) A notice under subsection (1) shall not expire earlier than eighteen months after the making of the agreement, but apart from that the minimum period of notice to be given under subsection (1), unless the agreement provides for a shorter period, is as follows.

(4) If the agreement provides for the making of payments by the hirer to the owner at equal intervals, the minimum period of notice is the length of one interval or three months, whichever is less.

(5) If the agreement provides for the making of such payments at differing intervals, the minimum period of notice is the length of the shortest interval or three months, whichever is less.

(6) In any other case, the minimum period of notice is three months.

(7) This section does not apply to—
    (a) any agreement which provides for the making by the hirer of payments which in total (and without breach of the agreement) exceed [£1,500] in any year, or
    (b) any agreement where—
        (i) goods are bailed or (in Scotland) hired to the hirer for the purposes of a business carried on by him, or the hirer holds himself out as requiring the goods for those purposes, and
        (ii) the goods are selected by the hirer, and acquired by the owner for the purposes of the agreement at the request of the hirer from any person other than the owner's associate, or
    (c) any agreement where the hirer requires, or holds himself out as requiring, the goods for the purpose of bailing or hiring them to other persons in the course of a business carried on by him.

(8) If, on an application made to the [OFT] by a person carrying on a consumer hire business, it appears to the [OFT] that it would be in the interest of hirers to do so, [it] may by notice to the applicant direct that this section shall not apply to consumer hire agreements made by the applicant, and subject to such conditions (if any) as the [OFT] may specify, this Act shall have effect accordingly.

(9) In the case of a modifying agreement subsection (3) shall apply with the substitution, for "the making of the agreement" of "the making of the original agreement".

[A97]

NOTES

This section is printed as it was in force on 15 June 2006, prior to amendments made by the Consumer Credit Act 2006 and subsequent amendments; for the text of this provision as it currently has effect, see [747].

References to the OFT, etc: as to the abolition of the office of the Director General of Fair Trading and the substitution of the original references to the Director (and related expressions), see the note preceding s 1 at [A1].

Sub-s (7): sum in square brackets substituted by the Consumer Credit (Further Increase in Monetary Amounts) Order 1998, SI 1998/997, art 3, Schedule, as from 1 May 1998.

102 Agency for receiving notice of rescission

(1)   Where the debtor or hirer under a regulated agreement claims to have a right to rescind the agreement, each of the following shall be deemed to be the agent of the creditor or owner for the purpose of receiving any notice rescinding the agreement which is served by the debtor or hirer—
- (a)   a credit-broker or supplier who was the negotiator in antecedent negotiations, and
- (b)   any person who, in the course of a business carried on by him, acted on behalf of the debtor or hirer in any negotiations for the agreement.

(2)   In subsection (1) "rescind" does not include—
- (a)   service of a notice of cancellation, or
- (b)   termination of an agreement under section 99 or 101, or by the exercise of a right or power in that behalf expressly conferred by the agreement.

[A98]

NOTES
This section is printed as it was in force on 15 June 2006, prior to amendments made by the Consumer Credit Act 2006 and subsequent amendments; for the text of this provision as it currently has effect, see [748].

103 Termination statements

(1)   If an individual (the "customer") serves on any person (the "trader") a notice—
- (a)   stating that—
  - (i)   the customer was the debtor or hirer under a regulated agreement described in the notice, and the trader was the creditor or owner under the agreement, and
  - (ii)   the customer has discharged his indebtedness to the trader under the agreement, and
  - (iii)   the agreement has ceased to have any operation; and
- (b)   requiring the trader to give the customer a notice, signed by or on behalf of the trader, confirming that those statements are correct,

the trader shall, within the prescribed period after receiving the notice, either comply with it or serve on the customer a counter-notice stating that, as the case may be, he disputes the correctness of the notice or asserts that the customer is not indebted to him under the agreement.

(2)   Where the trader disputes the correctness of the notice he shall give particulars of the way in which he alleges it to be wrong.

(3)   Subsection (1) does not apply in relation to any agreement if the trader has previously complied with that subsection on the service of a notice under it with respect to that agreement.

(4)   Subsection (1) does not apply to a non-commercial agreement.

(5)   If the trader fails to comply with subsection (1), and the default continues for one month, he commits an offence.

[A99]

NOTES
This section is printed as it was in force on 15 June 2006, prior to amendments made by the Consumer Credit Act 2006 and subsequent amendments; for the text of this provision as it currently has effect, see [749].
Regulations: the Consumer Credit (Prescribed Periods for Giving Information) Regulations 1983, SI 1983/1569.

104   *(Applies to Scotland only.)*

PART VIII
SECURITY

General

105   Form and content of securities

(1)   Any security provided in relation to a regulated agreement shall be expressed in writing.

(2)   Regulations may prescribe the form and content of documents ("security instruments") to be made in compliance with subsection (1).

(3)   Regulations under subsection (2) may in particular—
- (a)   require specified information to be included in the prescribed manner in documents, and other specified material to be excluded;
- (b)   contain requirements to ensure that specified information is clearly brought to the attention of the surety, and that one part of a document is not given insufficient or excessive prominence compared with another.

(4)   A security instrument is not properly executed unless—

(a)   a document in the prescribed form, itself containing all the prescribed terms and conforming to regulations under subsection (2), is signed in the prescribed manner by or on behalf of the surety, and

(b)   the document embodies all the terms of the security, other than implied terms, and

(c)   the document, when presented or sent for the purpose of being signed by or on behalf of the surety, is in such a state that its terms are readily legible, and

(d)   when the document is presented or sent for the purpose of being signed by or on behalf of the surety there is also presented or sent a copy of the document.

(5)   A security instrument is not properly executed unless—

(a)   where the security is provided after, or at the time when, the regulated agreement is made, a copy of the executed agreement, together with a copy of any other document referred to in it, is given to the surety at the time the security is provided, or

(b)   where the security is provided before the regulated agreement is made, a copy of the executed agreement, together with a copy of any other document referred to in it, is given to the surety within seven days after the regulated agreement is made.

(6)   Subsection (1) does not apply to a security provided by the debtor or hirer.

(7)   If—

(a)   in contravention of subsection (1) a security is not expressed in writing, or

(b)   a security instrument is improperly executed,

the security (so far as provided in relation to a regulated agreement) is enforceable against the surety on an order of the court only.

(8)   If an application for an order under subsection (7) is dismissed (except on technical grounds only) section 106 (ineffective securities) shall apply to the security.

(9)   Regulations under section 60(1) shall include provision requiring documents embodying regulated agreements also to embody any security provided in relation to a regulated agreement by the debtor or hirer.

[A100]

NOTES
   This section is printed as it was in force on 15 June 2006, prior to amendments made by the Consumer Credit Act 2006 and subsequent amendments; for the text of this provision as it currently has effect, see [750].
   Regulations: the Consumer Credit (Agreements) Regulations 1983, SI 1983/1553; the Consumer Credit (Guarantees and Indemnities) Regulations 1983, SI 1983/1556.

106   Ineffective securities

Where, under any provision of this Act, this section is applied to any security provided in relation to a regulated agreement, then, subject to section 177 (saving for registered charges),—

(a)   the security, so far as it is so provided, shall be treated as never having effect;

(b)   any property lodged with the creditor or owner solely for the purposes of the security as so provided shall be returned by him forthwith;

(c)   the creditor or owner shall take any necessary action to remove or cancel an entry in any register, so far as the entry relates to the security as so provided; and

(d)   any amount received by the creditor or owner on realisation of the security shall, so far as it is referable to the agreement, be repaid to the surety.

[A101]

NOTES
   This section is printed as it was in force on 15 June 2006, prior to amendments made by the Consumer Credit Act 2006 and subsequent amendments; for the text of this provision as it currently has effect, see [751].

107   Duty to give information to surety under fixed-sum credit agreement

(1)   The creditor under a regulated agreement for fixed-sum credit in relation to which security is provided, within the prescribed period after receiving a request in writing to that effect from the surety and payment of a fee of [£1], shall give to the surety (if a different person from the debtor)—

(a)   a copy of the executed agreement (if any) and of any other document referred to in it;

(b)   a copy of the security instrument (if any); and

(c)   a statement signed by or on behalf of the creditor showing, according to the information to which it is practicable for him to refer,—

   (i)   the total sum paid under the agreement by the debtor,

   (ii)   the total sum which has become payable under the agreement by the debtor but remains unpaid, and the various amounts comprised in that total sum, with the date when each became due, and

   (iii)   the total sum which is to become payable under the agreement by the debtor, and the various amounts comprised in that total sum, with the date, or mode of determining the date, when each becomes due.

(2) If the creditor possesses insufficient information to enable him to ascertain the amount and dates mentioned in subsection (1)(c) (iii), he shall be taken to comply with that sub-paragraph if his statement under subsection (1)(c) gives the basis on which, under the regulated agreement, they would fall to be ascertained.

(3) Subsection (1) does not apply to—
    (a) an agreement under which no sum is, or will or may become, payable by the debtor, or
    (b) a request made less than one month after a previous request under that subsection relating to the same agreement was complied with.

(4) If the creditor under an agreement fails to comply with subsection (1)—
    (a) he is not entitled, while the default continues, to enforce the security, so far as provided in relation to the agreement; and
    (b) if the default continues for one month he commits an offence.

(5) This section does not apply to a non-commercial agreement.

[A102]

NOTES

This section is printed as it was in force on 15 June 2006, prior to amendments made by the Consumer Credit Act 2006 and subsequent amendments; for the text of this provision as it currently has effect, see [752].

Sub-s (1): sum in square brackets substituted by the Consumer Credit (Further Increase in Monetary Amounts) Order 1998, SI 1998/997, art 3, Schedule, as from 1 May 1998.

Regulations: the Consumer Credit (Prescribed Periods for Giving Information) Regulations 1983, SI 1983/1569.

108 Duty to give information to surety under running-account credit agreement

(1) The creditor under a regulated agreement for running-account credit in relation to which security is provided, within the prescribed period after receiving a request in writing to that effect from the surety and payment of a fee of [£1], shall give to the surety (if a different person from the debtor)—
    (a) a copy of the executed agreement (if any) and of any other document referred to in it;
    (b) a copy of the security instrument (if any); and
    (c) a statement signed by or on behalf of the creditor showing, according to the information to which it is practicable for him to refer,—
        (i) the state of the account, and
        (ii) the amount, if any, currently payable under the agreement by the debtor to the creditor, and
        (iii) the amounts and due dates of any payments which, if the debtor does not draw further on the account, will later become payable under the agreement by the debtor to the creditor.

(2) If the creditor possesses insufficient information to enable him to ascertain the amounts and dates mentioned in subsection (1)(c)(iii), he shall be taken to comply with that sub-paragraph if his statement under subsection (1)(c) gives basis on which, under the regulated agreement, they would fall to be ascertained.

(3) Subsection (1) does not apply to—
    (a) an agreement under which no sum is, or will or may become, payable by the debtor, or
    (b) a request made less than one month after a previous request under that subsection relating to the same agreement was complied with.

(4) If the creditor under an agreement fails to comply with subsection (1)—
    (a) he is not entitled, while the default continues, to enforce the security, so far as provided in relation to the agreement; and
    (b) if the default continues for one month he commits an offence.

(5) This section does not apply to a non-commercial agreement.

[A103]

NOTES

This section is printed as it was in force on 15 June 2006, prior to amendments made by the Consumer Credit Act 2006 and subsequent amendments; for the text of this provision as it currently has effect, see [753].

Sub-s (1): sum in square brackets substituted by the Consumer Credit (Further Increase in Monetary Amounts) Order 1998, SI 1998/997, art 3, Schedule, as from 1 May 1998.

Regulations: the Consumer Credit (Prescribed Periods for Giving Information) Regulations 1983, SI 1983/1569.

109 Duty to give information to surety under consumer hire agreement

(1) The owner under a regulated consumer hire agreement in relation to which security is provided, within the prescribed period after receiving a request in writing to that effect from the surety and payment of a fee of [£1], shall give to the surety (if a different person from the hirer)—

(a) a copy of the executed agreement and of any other document referred to in it;

(b) a copy of the security instrument (if any); and

(c) a statement signed by or on behalf of the owner showing, according to the information to which it is practicable for him to refer, the total sum which has become payable under the agreement by the hirer but remains unpaid and the various amounts comprised in that total sum, with the date when each became due.

(2) Subsection (1) does not apply to—

(a) an agreement under which no sum is, or will or may become, payable by the hirer, or

(b) a request made less than one month after a previous request under that subsection relating to the same agreement was complied with.

(3) If the owner under an agreement fails to comply with subsection (1)—

(a) he is not entitled, while the default continues, to enforce the security, so far as provided in relation to the agreement; and

(b) if the default continues for one month he commits an offence.

(4) This section does not apply to a non-commercial agreement.

[A104]

NOTES

This section is printed as it was in force on 15 June 2006, prior to amendments made by the Consumer Credit Act 2006 and subsequent amendments; for the text of this provision as it currently has effect, see [754].

Sub-s (1): sum in square brackets substituted by the Consumer Credit (Further Increase in Monetary Amounts) Order 1998, SI 1998/997, art 3, Schedule, as from 1 May 1998.

Regulations: the Consumer Credit (Prescribed Periods for Giving Information) Regulations 1983, SI 1983/1569.

110 Duty to give information to debtor or hirer

(1) The creditor or owner under a regulated agreement, within the prescribed period after receiving a request in writing to that effect from the debtor or hirer and payment of a fee of [£1], shall give the debtor or hirer a copy of any security instrument executed in relation to the agreement after the making of the agreement.

(2) Subsection (1) does not apply to—

(a) a non-commercial agreement, or

(b) an agreement under which no sum is, or will or may become, payable by the debtor or hirer, or

(c) a request made less than one month after a previous request under subsection (1) relating to the same agreement was complied with.

(3) If the creditor or owner under an agreement fails to comply with subsection (1)—

(a) he is not entitled, while the default continues, to enforce the security (so far as provided in relation to the agreement); ...

(b) ...

[A105]

NOTES

This section is printed as it was in force on 15 June 2006, prior to amendments made by the Consumer Credit Act 2006 and subsequent amendments; for the text of this provision as it currently has effect, see [755].

Sub-s (1): sum in square brackets substituted by the Consumer Credit (Further Increase in Monetary Amounts) Order 1998, SI 1998/997, art 3, Schedule, as from 1 May 1998.

Sub-s (3): words omitted repealed by the Consumer Protection from Unfair Trading Regulations 2008, SI 2008/1277, reg 30(1), (3), Sch 2, Pt 1, paras 17, 28, Sch 4, as from 26 May 2008.

Regulations: the Consumer Credit (Prescribed Periods for Giving Information) Regulations 1983, SI 1983/1569.

111 Duty to give surety copy of default etc notice

(1) When a default notice or a notice under section 76(1) or 98(1) is served on a debtor or hirer, a copy of the notice shall be served by the creditor or owner on any surety (if a different person from the debtor or hirer).

(2) If the creditor or owner fails to comply with subsection (1) in the case of any surety, the security is enforceable against the surety (in respect of the breach or other matter to which the notice relates) on an order of the court only.

[A106]

APPENDIX

CCA 1974 (PRE CCA 2006)

NOTES
This section is printed as it was in force on 15 June 2006, prior to amendments made by the Consumer Credit Act 2006 and subsequent amendments; for the text of this provision as it currently has effect, see [756].

112 Realisation of securities

Subject to section 121, regulations may provide for any matters relating to the sale or other realisation, by the creditor or owner, of property over which any right has been provided by way of security in relation to an actual or prospective regulated agreement, other than a non-commercial agreement.

[A107]

NOTES
This section is printed as it was in force on 15 June 2006, prior to amendments made by the Consumer Credit Act 2006 and subsequent amendments; for the text of this provision as it currently has effect, see [757].

113 Act not to be evaded by use of security

(1)   Where a security is provided in relation to an actual or prospective regulated agreement, the security shall not be enforced so as to benefit the creditor or owner, directly or indirectly, to an extent greater (whether as respects the amount of any payment or the time or manner of its being made) than would be the case if the security were not provided and any obligations of the debtor or hirer, or his relative, under or in relation to the agreement were carried out to the extent (if any) to which they would be enforced under this Act.

(2)   In accordance with subsection (1), where a regulated agreement is enforceable on an order of the court or the [OFT] only, any security provided in relation to the agreement is enforceable (so far as provided in relation to the agreement) where such an order has been made in relation to the agreement, but not otherwise.

(3)   Where—
    (a)   a regulated agreement is cancelled under section 69(1) or becomes subject to section 69(2), or
    (b)   a regulated agreement is terminated under section 91, or
    (c)   in relation to any agreement an application for an order under section 40(2), 65(1), 124(1) or 149(2) is dismissed (except on technical grounds only), or
    (d)   a declaration is made by the court under section 142(1) (refusal of enforcement order) as respects any regulated agreement,
section 106 shall apply to any security provided in relation to the agreement.

(4)   Where subsection (3)(d) applies and the declaration relates to a part only of the regulated agreement, section 106 shall apply to the security only so far as it concerns that part.

(5)   In the case of a cancelled agreement, the duty imposed on the debtor or hirer by section 71 or 72 shall not be enforceable before the creditor or owner has discharged any duty imposed on him by section 106 (as applied by subsection (3)(a)).

(6)   If the security is provided in relation to a prospective agreement or transaction, the security shall be enforceable in relation to the agreement or transaction only after the time (if any) when the agreement is made; and until that time the person providing the security shall be entitled, by notice to the creditor or owner, to require that section 106 shall thereupon apply to the security.

(7)   Where an indemnity [or guarantee] is given in a case where the debtor or hirer is a minor, or [an indemnity is given in a case where he] is otherwise not of full capacity, the reference in subsection (1) to the extent to which his obligations would be enforced shall be read in relation to the indemnity [or guarantee] as a reference to the extent to which [those obligations] would be enforced if he were of full capacity.

(8)   Subsections (1) to (3) also apply where a security is provided in relation to an actual or prospective linked transaction, and in that case—
    (a)   references to the agreement shall be read as references to the linked transaction, and
    (b)   references to the creditor or owner shall be read as references to any person (other than the debtor or hirer, or his relative) who is a party, or prospective party, to the linked transaction.

[A108]

NOTES
This section is printed as it was in force on 15 June 2006, prior to amendments made by the Consumer Credit Act 2006 and subsequent amendments; for the text of this provision as it currently has effect, see [758].
Sub-s (7): words in square brackets inserted or substituted by the Minors' Contracts Act 1987, s 4(1), as from 9 June 1987.

References to the OFT, etc: as to the abolition of the office of the Director General of Fair Trading and the substitution of the original references to the Director (and related expressions), see the note preceding s 1 at [A1].

Pledges

114 Pawn-receipts

(1) At the time he receives the article, a person who takes any article in pawn under a regulated agreement shall give to the person from whom he receives it a receipt in the prescribed form (a "pawn-receipt").

(2) A person who takes any article in pawn from an individual whom he knows to be, or who appears to be and is, a minor commits an offence.

(3) This section and sections 115 to 122 do not apply to—
    (a)   a pledge of documents of title [or of bearer bonds], or
    (b)   a non-commercial agreement.

[A109]

NOTES
  This section is printed as it was in force on 15 June 2006, prior to amendments made by the Consumer Credit Act 2006 and subsequent amendments; for the text of this provision as it currently has effect, see [759].
  Sub-s (3): words in square brackets inserted by the Banking Act 1979, s 38(2), as from 1 October 1979.
  Regulations: the Consumer Credit (Agreements) Regulations 1983, SI 1983/1553; the Consumer Credit (Pawn Receipts) Regulations 1983, SI 1983/1566.

115 Penalty for failure to supply copies of pledge agreement, etc

If the creditor under a regulated agreement to take any article in pawn fails to observe the requirements of sections 62 to 64 or 114(1) in relation to the agreement he commits an offence.

[A110]

NOTES
  This section is printed as it was in force on 15 June 2006, prior to amendments made by the Consumer Credit Act 2006 and subsequent amendments; for the text of this provision as it currently has effect, see [760].

116 Redemption period

(1) A pawn is redeemable at any time within six months after it was taken.

(2) Subject to subsection (1), the period within which a pawn is redeemable shall be the same as the period fixed by the parties for the duration of the credit secured by the pledge, or such longer period as they may agree.

(3) If the pawn is not redeemed by the end of the period laid down by subsections (1) and (2) (the "redemption period"), it nevertheless remains redeemable until it is realised by the pawnee under section 121, except where under section 120(1)(a) the property in it passes to the pawnee.

(4) No special charge shall be made for redemption of a pawn after the end of the redemption period, and charges in respect of the safe keeping of the pawn shall not be at a higher rate after the end of the redemption period than before.

[A111]

NOTES
  This section is printed as it was in force on 15 June 2006, prior to amendments made by the Consumer Credit Act 2006 and subsequent amendments; for the text of this provision as it currently has effect, see [761].

117 Redemption procedure

(1) On surrender of the pawn-receipt, and payment of the amount owing, at any time when the pawn is redeemable, the pawnee shall deliver the pawn to the bearer of the pawn-receipt.

(2) Subsection (1) does not apply if the pawnee knows or has reasonable cause to suspect that the bearer of the pawn-receipt is neither the owner of the pawn nor authorised by the owner to redeem it.

(3) The pawnee is not liable to any person in tort or delict for delivering the pawn where subsection (1) applies, or refusing to deliver it where the person demanding delivery does not comply with subsection (1) or, by reason of subsection (2), subsection (1) does not apply.

[A112]

118   Loss etc of pawn-receipt

(1)   A person (the "claimant") who is not in possession of the pawn-receipt but claims to be the owner of the pawn, or to be otherwise entitled or authorised to redeem it, may do so at any time when it is redeemable by tendering to the pawnee in place of the pawn-receipt—

(a)   a statutory declaration made by the claimant in the prescribed form, and with the prescribed contents, or

(b)   where the pawn is security for fixed-sum credit not exceeding [£75] or running-account credit on which the credit limit does not exceed [£75], and the pawnee agrees, a statement in writing in the prescribed form, and with the prescribed contents, signed by the claimant.

(2)   On compliance by the claimant with subsection (1), section 117 shall apply as if the declaration or statement were the pawn-receipt, and the pawn-receipt itself shall become inoperative for the purposes of section 117.

[A113]

119   Unreasonable refusal to deliver pawn

(1)   If a person who has taken a pawn under a regulated agreement refuses without reasonable cause to allow the pawn to be redeemed, he commits an offence.

(2)   On the conviction in England or Wales of a pawnee under subsection (1) where the offence does not amount to theft, [section 148 of the Powers of Criminal Courts (Sentencing) Act 2000 (restitution orders)] shall apply as if the pawnee had been convicted of stealing the pawn.

(3)   On the conviction in Northern Ireland of a pawnee under subsection (1) where the offence does not amount to theft, section 27 (orders for restitution) of the Theft Act (Northern Ireland) 1969, and any provision of the Theft Act (Northern Ireland) 1969 relating to that section, shall apply as if the pawnee had been convicted of stealing the pawn.

[A114]

120   Consequence of failure to redeem

(1)   If at the end of the redemption period the pawn has not been redeemed—

(a)   notwithstanding anything in section 113, the property in the pawn passes to the pawnee where the redemption period is six months and the pawn is security for fixed-sum credit not exceeding [£75] or running-account credit on which the credit limit does not exceed [£75]; or

(b)   in any other case the pawn becomes realisable by the pawnee.

(2)   Where the debtor or hirer is entitled to apply to the court for a time order under section 129, subsection (1) shall apply with the substitution, for "at the end of the redemption period" of "after the expiry of five days following the end of the redemption period".

[A115]

121   Realisation of pawn

(1)   When a pawn has become realisable by him, the pawnee may sell it, after giving to the pawnor (except in such cases as may be prescribed) not less than the prescribed period of notice of the intention to sell, indicating in the notice the asking price and such other particulars as may be prescribed.

(2)   Within the prescribed period after the sale takes place, the pawnee shall give the pawnor the prescribed information in writing as to the sale, its proceeds and expenses.

(3)   Where the net proceeds of sale are not less than the sum which, if the pawn had been redeemed on the date of the sale, would have been payable for its redemption, the debt secured by the pawn is discharged and any surplus shall be paid by the pawnee to the pawnor.

(4)   Where subsection (3) does not apply, the debt shall be treated as from the date of sale as equal to the amount by which the net proceeds of sale fall short of the sum which would have been payable for the redemption of the pawn on that date.

(5)   In this section the "net proceeds of sale" is the amount realised (the "gross amount") less the expenses (if any) of the sale.

(6)   If the pawnor alleges that the gross amount is less than the true market value of the pawn on the date of sale, it is for the pawnee to prove that he and any agents employed by him in the sale used reasonable care to ensure that the true market value was obtained, and if he fails to do so subsections (3) and (4) shall have effect as if the reference in subsection (5) to the gross amount were a reference to the true market value.

(7)   If the pawnor alleges that the expenses of the sale were unreasonably high, it is for the pawnee to prove that they were reasonable, and if he fails to do so subsections (3) and (4) shall have effect as if the reference in subsection (5) to expenses were a reference to reasonable expenses.

[A116]

NOTES
   This section is printed as it was in force on 15 June 2006, prior to amendments made by the Consumer Credit Act 2006 and subsequent amendments; for the text of this provision as it currently has effect, see [766].
   Regulations: the Consumer Credit (Realisation of Pawn) Regulations 1983, SI 1983/1568.

122   (*Applies to Scotland only.*)

Negotiable instruments

123   Restrictions on taking and negotiating instruments

(1)   A creditor or owner shall not take a negotiable instrument, other than a bank note or cheque, in discharge of any sum payable—
   (a)   by the debtor or hirer under a regulated agreement, or
   (b)   by any person as surety in relation to the agreement.

(2)   The creditor or owner shall not negotiate a cheque taken by him in discharge of a sum payable as mentioned in subsection (1), except to a banker (within the meaning of the Bills of Exchange Act 1882).

(3)   The creditor or owner shall not take a negotiable instrument as security for the discharge of any sum payable as mentioned in subsection (1).

(4)   A person takes a negotiable instrument as security for the discharge of a sum if the sum is intended to be paid in some other way, and the negotiable instrument is to be presented for payment only if the sum is not paid in that way.

(5)   This section does not apply where the regulated agreement is a non-commercial agreement.

(6)   The Secretary of State may by order provide that this section shall not apply where the regulated agreement has a connection with a country outside the United Kingdom.

[A117]

NOTES
   This section is printed as it was in force on 15 June 2006, prior to amendments made by the Consumer Credit Act 2006 and subsequent amendments; for the text of this provision as it currently has effect, see [767].
   Order: the Consumer Credit (Negotiable Instruments) (Exemption) Order 1984, SI 1984/435.

124   Consequences of breach of s 123

(1)   After any contravention of section 123 has occurred in relation to a sum payable as mentioned in section 123(1)(a), the agreement under which the sum is payable is enforceable against the debtor or hirer on an order of the court only.

(2)   After any contravention of section 123 has occurred in relation to a sum payable by any surety, the security is enforceable on an order of the court only.

(3)   Where an application for an order under subsection (2) is dismissed (except on technical grounds only) section 106 shall apply to the security.

[A118]

NOTES
   This section is printed as it was in force on 15 June 2006, prior to amendments made by the Consumer Credit Act 2006 and subsequent amendments; for the text of this provision as it currently has effect, see **[768]**.

125   Holders in due course

(1)   A person who takes a negotiable instrument in contravention of section 123(1) or (3) is not a holder in due course, and is not entitled to enforce the instrument.

(2)   Where a person negotiates a cheque in contravention of section 123(2), his doing so constitutes a defect in his title within the meaning of the Bills of Exchange Act 1882.

(3)   If a person mentioned in section 123(1)(a) or (b) ("the protected person") becomes liable to a holder in due course of an instrument taken from the protected person in contravention of section 123(1) or (3), or taken from the protected person and negotiated in contravention of section 123(2), the creditor or owner shall indemnify the protected person in respect of that liability.

(4)   Nothing in this Act affects the rights of the holder in due course of any negotiable instrument.

[A119]

NOTES
   This section is printed as it was in force on 15 June 2006, prior to amendments made by the Consumer Credit Act 2006 and subsequent amendments; for the text of this provision as it currently has effect, see **[769]**.

Land mortgages

126   Enforcement of land mortgages

A land mortgage securing a regulated agreement is enforceable (so far as provided in relation to the agreement) on an order of the court only.

[A120]

NOTES
   This section is printed as it was in force on 15 June 2006, prior to amendments made by the Consumer Credit Act 2006 and subsequent amendments; for the text of this provision as it currently has effect, see **[770]**.

PART IX
JUDICIAL CONTROL
Enforcement of certain regulated agreements and securities

127   Enforcement orders in cases of infringement

(1)   In the case of an application for an enforcement order under—
   (a)   section 65(1) (improperly executed agreements), or
   (b)   section 105(7)(a) or (b) (improperly executed security instruments), or
   (c)   section 111(2) (failure to serve copy of notice on surety), or
   (d)   section 124(1) or (2) (taking of negotiable instrument in contravention of section 123),
the court shall dismiss the application if, but (subject to subsections (3) and (4)) only if, it considers it just to do so having regard to—
   (i)   prejudice caused to any person by the contravention in question, and the degree of culpability for it; and
   (ii)   the powers conferred on the court by subsection (2) and sections 135 and 136.

(2)   If it appears to the court just to do so, it may in an enforcement order reduce or discharge any sum payable by the debtor or hirer, or any surety, so as to compensate him for prejudice suffered as a result of the contravention in question.

(3)   The court shall not make an enforcement order under section 65(1) if section 61(1)(a) (signing of agreements) was not complied with unless a document (whether or not in the prescribed form and complying with regulations under section 60(1)) itself containing all the prescribed terms of the agreement was signed by the debtor or hirer (whether or not in the prescribed manner).

(4)   The court shall not make an enforcement order under section 65(1) in the case of a cancellable agreement if—

(a)   a provision of section 62 or 63 was not complied with, and the creditor or owner did not give a copy of the executed agreement, and of any other document referred to in it, to the debtor or hirer before the commencement of the proceedings in which the order is sought, or

(b)   section 64(1) was not complied with.

(5)   Where an enforcement order is made in a case to which subsection (3) applies, the order may direct that the regulated agreement is to have effect as if it did not include a term omitted from the document signed by the debtor or hirer.

[A121]

NOTES

   This section is printed as it was in force on 15 June 2006, prior to amendments made by the Consumer Credit Act 2006 and subsequent amendments; for the text of this provision as it currently has effect, see **[771]**.

   Regulations: the Consumer Credit (Agreements) Regulations 1983, SI 1983/1553.

128   Enforcement orders on death of debtor or hirer

The court shall make an order under section 86(2) if, but only if, the creditor or owner proves that he has been unable to satisfy himself that the present and future obligations of the debtor or hirer under the agreement are likely to be discharged.

[A122]

NOTES

   This section is printed as it was in force on 15 June 2006, prior to amendments made by the Consumer Credit Act 2006 and subsequent amendments; for the text of this provision as it currently has effect, see **[772]**.

Extension of time

129   Time orders

(1)   [Subject to subsection (3) below,] if it appears to the court just to do so—

(a)   on an application for an enforcement order; or

(b)   on an application made by a debtor or hirer under this paragraph after service on him of—

       (i)   a default notice, or

       (ii)   a notice under section 76(1) or 98(1); or

(c)   in an action brought by a creditor or owner to enforce a regulated agreement or any security, or recover possession of any goods or land to which a regulated agreement relates,

the court may make an order under this section (a "time order").

(2)   A time order shall provide for one or both of the following, as the court considers just—

(a)   the payment by the debtor or hirer or any surety of any sum owed under a regulated agreement or a security by such instalments, payable at such times, as the court, having regard to the means of the debtor or hirer and any surety, considers reasonable;

(b)   the remedying by the debtor or hirer of any breach of a regulated agreement (other than the non-payment of money) within such period as the court may specify.

[(3)   (*Applies to Scotland only.*)]

[A123]

NOTES

   This section is printed as it was in force on 15 June 2006, prior to amendments made by the Consumer Credit Act 2006 and subsequent amendments; for the text of this provision as it currently has effect, see **[773]**.

   Sub-s (1): words in square brackets inserted by Debtors (Scotland) Act 1987, s 108(1), Sch 6, para 17, in relation to Scotland only.

130   Supplemental provisions about time orders

(1)   Where in accordance with rules of court an offer to pay any sum by instalments is made by the debtor or hirer and accepted by the creditor or owner, the court may in accordance with rules of court make a time order under section 129(2)(a) giving effect to the offer without hearing evidence of means.

(2)   In the case of a hire-purchase or conditional sale agreement only, a time order under section 129(2)(a) may deal with sums which, although not payable by the debtor at the time the order is made, would if the agreement continued in force become payable under it subsequently.

(3) A time order under section 129(2)(a) shall not be made where the regulated agreement is secured by a pledge if, by virtue of regulations made under section 76(5), 87(4) or 98(5), service of a notice is not necessary for enforcement of the pledge.

(4) Where, following the making of a time order in relation to a regulated hire-purchase or conditional sale agreement or a regulated consumer hire agreement, the debtor or hirer is in possession of the goods, he shall be treated (except in the case of a debtor to whom the creditor's title has passed) as a bailee or (in Scotland) a custodier of the goods under the terms of the agreement, notwithstanding that the agreement has been terminated.

(5) Without prejudice to anything done by the creditor or owner before the commencement of the period specified in a time order made under section 129(2)(b) ("the relevant period"),—

    (a)   he shall not while the relevant period subsists take in relation to the agreement any action such as is mentioned in section 87(1);

    (b)   where—

        (i)   a provision of the agreement ("the secondary provision") becomes operative only on breach of another provision of the agreement ("the primary provision"), and

        (ii)   the time order provides for the remedying of such a breach of the primary provision within the relevant period,

       he shall not treat the secondary provision as operative before the end of that period;

    (c)   if while the relevant period subsists the breach to which the order relates is remedied it shall be treated as not having occurred.

(6) On the application of any person affected by a time order, the court may vary or revoke the order.

[A124]

NOTES

  This section is printed as it was in force on 15 June 2006, prior to amendments made by the Consumer Credit Act 2006 and subsequent amendments; for the text of this provision as it currently has effect, see [774].

Protection of property pending proceedings

131 Protection orders

The court, on the application of the creditor or owner under a regulated agreement, may make such orders as it thinks just for protecting any property of the creditor or owner, or property subject to any security, from damage or depreciation pending the determination of any proceedings under this Act, including orders restricting or prohibiting use of the property or giving directions as to its custody.

[A125]

NOTES

  This section is printed as it was in force on 15 June 2006, prior to amendments made by the Consumer Credit Act 2006 and subsequent amendments; for the text of this provision as it currently has effect, see [775].

Hire and hire-purchase etc agreements

132 Financial relief for hirer

(1) Where the owner under a regulated consumer hire agreement recovers possession of goods to which the agreement relates otherwise than by action, the hirer may apply to the court for an order that—

    (a)   the whole or part of any sum paid by the hirer to the owner in respect of the goods shall be repaid, and

    (b)   the obligation to pay the whole or part of any sum owed by the hirer to the owner in respect of the goods shall cease,

and if it appears to the court just to do so, having regard to the extent of the enjoyment of the goods by the hirer, the court shall grant the application in full or in part.

(2) Where in proceedings relating to a regulated consumer hire agreement the court makes an order for the delivery to the owner of goods to which the agreement relates the court may include in the order the like provision as may be made in an order under subsection (1).

[A126]

NOTES

  This section is printed as it was in force on 15 June 2006, prior to amendments made by the Consumer Credit Act 2006 and subsequent amendments; for the text of this provision as it currently has effect, see [776].

133   Hire-purchase etc agreements: special powers of court

(1)   If, in relation to a regulated hire-purchase or conditional sale agreement, it appears to the court just to do so—

    (a)   on an application for an enforcement order or time order; or

    (b)   in an action brought by the creditor to recover possession of goods to which the agreement relates,

the court may—

    (i)   make an order (a "return order") for the return to the creditor of goods to which the agreement relates,

    (ii)   make an order (a "transfer order") for the transfer to the debtor of the creditor's title to certain goods to which the agreement relates ("the transferred goods"), and the return to the creditor of the remainder of the goods.

(2)   In determining for the purposes of this section how much of the total price has been paid ("the paid-up sum"), the court may—

    (a)   treat any sum paid by the debtor, or owed by the creditor, in relation to the goods as part of the paid-up sum;

    (b)   deduct any sum owed by the debtor in relation to the goods (otherwise than as part of the total price) from the paid-up sum,

and make corresponding reductions in amounts so owed.

(3)   Where a transfer order is made, the transferred goods shall be such of the goods to which the agreement relates as the court thinks just; but a transfer order shall be made only where the paid-up sum exceeds the part of the total price referable to the transferred goods by an amount equal to at least one-third of the unpaid balance of the total price.

(4)   Notwithstanding the making of a return order or transfer order, the debtor may at any time before the goods enter the possession of the creditor, on payment of the balance of the total price and the fulfilment of any other necessary conditions, claim the goods ordered to be returned to the creditor.

(5)   When, in pursuance of a time order or under this section, the total price of goods under a regulated hire-purchase agreement or regulated conditional sale agreement is paid and any other necessary conditions are fulfilled, the creditor's title to the goods vests in the debtor.

(6)   If, in contravention of a return order or transfer order, any goods to which the order relates are not returned to the creditor, the court, on the application of the creditor, may—

    (a)   revoke so much of the order as relates to those goods, and

    (b)   order the debtor to pay the creditor the unpaid portion of so much of the total price as is referable to those goods.

(7)   For the purposes of this section, the part of the total price referable to any goods is the part assigned to those goods by the agreement or (if no such assignment is made) the part determined by the court to be reasonable.

[A127]

NOTES

This section is printed as it was in force on 15 June 2006, prior to amendments made by the Consumer Credit Act 2006 and subsequent amendments; for the text of this provision as it currently has effect, see [777].

---

134   Evidence of adverse detention in hire-purchase etc cases

(1)   Where goods are comprised in a regulated hire-purchase agreement, regulated conditional sale agreement or regulated consumer hire agreement, and the creditor or owner—

    (a)   brings an action or makes an application to enforce a right to recover possession of the goods from the debtor or hirer, and

    (b)   proves that a demand for the delivery of the goods was included in the default notice under section 88(5), or that, after the right to recover possession of the goods accrued but before the action was begun or the application was made, he made a request in writing to the debtor or hirer to surrender the goods,

then, for the purposes of the claim of the creditor or owner to recover possession of the goods, the possession of them by the debtor or hirer shall be deemed to be adverse to the creditor or owner.

(2)   In subsection (1) "the debtor or hirer" includes a person in possession of the goods at any time between the debtor's or hirer's death and the grant of probate or administration, or (in Scotland) confirmation.

(3)   Nothing in this section affects a claim for damages for conversion or (in Scotland) for delict.

[A128]

Supplemental provisions as to orders

135 Power to impose conditions, or suspend operation of order

(1) If it considers it just to do so, the court may in an order made by it in relation to a regulated agreement include provisions—
- (a) making the operation of any term of the order conditional on the doing of specified acts by any party to the proceedings;
- (b) suspending the operation of any term of the order either—
  - (i) until such time as the court subsequently directs, or
  - (ii) until the occurrence of a specified act or omission.

(2) The court shall not suspend the operation of a term requiring the delivery up of goods by any person unless satisfied that the goods are in his possession or control.

(3) In the case of a consumer hire agreement, the court shall not so use its powers under subsection (1)(b) as to extend the period for which, under the terms of the agreement, the hirer is entitled to possession of the goods to which the agreement relates.

(4) On the application of any person affected by a provision included under subsection (1), the court may vary the provision.

[A129]

136 Power to vary agreements and securities

The court may in an order made by it under this Act include such provision as it considers just for amending any agreement or security in consequence of a term of the order.

[A130]

Extortionate credit bargains

137 Extortionate credit bargains

(1) If the court finds a credit bargain extortionate it may reopen the credit agreement so as to do justice between the parties.

(2) In this section and sections 138 to 140—
- (a) "credit agreement" means any agreement [(other than an agreement which is an exempt agreement as a result of section 16(6C))] between an individual (the "debtor") and any other person (the "creditor") by which the creditor provides the debtor with credit of any amount, and
- (b) "credit bargain"—
  - (i) where no transaction other than the credit agreement is to be taken into account in computing the total charge for credit, means the credit agreement, or
  - (ii) where one or more other transactions are to be so taken into account, means the credit agreement and those other transactions, taken together.

[A131]

138 When bargains are extortionate

(1) A credit bargain is extortionate if it—

(a)   requires the debtor or a relative of his to make payments (whether unconditionally, or on certain contingencies) which are grossly exorbitant, or

(b)   otherwise grossly contravenes ordinary principles of fair dealing.

(2)   In determining whether a credit bargain is extortionate, regard shall be had to such evidence as is adduced concerning—

(a)   interest rates prevailing at the time it was made,

(b)   the factors mentioned in subsections (3) to (5), and

(c)   any other relevant considerations.

(3)   Factors applicable under subsection (2) in relation to the debtor include—

(a)   his age, experience, business capacity and state of health; and

(b)   the degree to which, at the time of making the credit bargain, he was under financial pressure, and the nature of that pressure.

(4)   Factors applicable under subsection (2) in relation to the creditor include—

(a)   the degree of risk accepted by him, having regard to the value of any security provided;

(b)   his relationship to the debtor; and

(c)   whether or not a colourable cash price was quoted for any goods or services included in the credit bargain.

(5)   Factors applicable under subsection (2) in relation to a linked transaction include the question how far the transaction was reasonably required for the protection of debtor or creditor, or was in the interest of the debtor.

[A132]

NOTES

This section is printed as it was in force on 15 June 2006, prior to amendments made by the Consumer Credit Act 2006 and subsequent amendments. It has subsequently been repealed (see the note following [780]).

139   Reopening of extortionate agreements

(1)   A credit agreement may, if the court thinks just, be reopened on the ground that the credit bargain is extortionate—

(a)   on an application for the purpose made by the debtor or any surety to the High Court, county court or sheriff court; or

(b)   at the instance of the debtor or a surety in any proceedings to which the debtor and creditor are parties, being proceedings to enforce the agreement, any security relating to it, or any linked transaction; or

(c)   at the instance of the debtor or a surety in other proceedings in any court where the amount paid or payable under the credit agreement is relevant.

(2)   In reopening the agreement, the court may, for the purpose of relieving the debtor or a surety from payment of any sum in excess of that fairly due and reasonable, by order—

(a)   direct accounts to be taken, or (in Scotland) an accounting to be made, between any persons,

(b)   set aside the whole or part of any obligation imposed on the debtor or surety by the credit bargain or any related agreement,

(c)   require the creditor to repay the whole or part of any sum paid under the credit bargain or any related agreement by the debtor or a surety, whether paid to the creditor or any other person,

(d)   direct the return to the surety of any property provided for the purposes of the security, or

(e)   alter the terms of the credit agreement or any security instrument.

(3)   An order may be made under subsection (2) notwithstanding that its effect is to place a burden on the creditor in respect of an advantage unfairly enjoyed by another person who is a party to a linked transaction.

(4)   An order under subsection (2) shall not alter the effect of any judgment.

(5)   In England and Wales, an application under subsection (1)(a) shall be brought only in the county court in the case of—

(a)   a regulated agreement, or

(b)   an agreement (not being a regulated agreement) under which the creditor provides the debtor with fixed-sum credit ... or running-account credit ...

[(5A)   ...]

(6)   (*Applies to Scotland only.*)

(7)   In Northern Ireland an application under subsection (1)(a) may be brought in the county court in the case of—

(a)   a regulated agreement, or

(b)   an agreement (not being a regulated agreement) under which the creditor provides the debtor with fixed-sum credit not exceeding [£105,000] or running-account credit on which the credit limit does not exceed [£105,000].

[A133]

NOTES

This section is printed as it was in force on 15 June 2006, prior to amendments made by the Consumer Credit Act 2006 and subsequent amendments. It has subsequently been repealed (see the note following [780]).

Sub-s (5): words omitted repealed by the High Court and County Courts Jurisdiction Order 1991, SI 1991/724, art 2(1), (8), Schedule, Pt I, as from 1 July 1991.

Sub-s (5A): inserted by the Administration of Justice Act 1982, s 37, Sch 3, Pt II, para 4; repealed by SI 1991/724, art 2(1), (8), Schedule, Pt I, as from 1 July 1991.

Sub-s (7): sums in square brackets substituted by virtue of the County Courts (Financial Limits) Order (Northern Ireland) 1993, SR 1993/282, art 2, Schedule, as from 1 September 1993.

140 Interpretation of sections 137 to 139

Where the credit agreement is not a regulated agreement, expressions used in sections 137 to 139 which, apart from this section, apply only to regulated agreements, shall be construed as nearly as may be as if the credit agreement were a regulated agreement.

[A134]

NOTES

This section is printed as it was in force on 15 June 2006, prior to amendments made by the Consumer Credit Act 2006 and subsequent amendments. It has subsequently been repealed (see the note following [780]).

Miscellaneous

141 Jurisdiction and parties

(1) In England and Wales, the county court shall have jurisdiction to hear and determine—

    (a) any action by the creditor or owner to enforce a regulated agreement or any security relating to it;

    (b) any action to enforce any linked transaction against the debtor or hirer or his relative;

and such an action shall not be brought in any other court.

(2) Where an action or application is brought in the High Court which, by virtue of this Act, ought to have been brought in the county court it shall not be treated as improperly brought, but shall be transferred to the county court.

(3)–(3B) *(Apply to Scotland only.)*

(4) In Northern Ireland the county court shall have jurisdiction to hear and determine any action or application falling within subsection (1).

(5) Except as may be provided by rules of court, all the parties to a regulated agreement, and any surety, shall be made parties to any proceedings relating to the agreement.

[A135]

NOTES

This section is printed as it was in force on 15 June 2006, prior to amendments made by the Consumer Credit Act 2006 and subsequent amendments; for the text of this provision as it currently has effect, see [785].

142 Power to declare rights of parties

(1) Where under any provision of this Act a thing can be done by a creditor or owner on an enforcement order only, and either—

    (a) the court dismisses (except on technical grounds only) an application for an enforcement order, or

    (b) where no such application has been made or such an application has been dismissed on technical grounds only, an interested party applies to the court for a declaration under this subsection,

the court may if it thinks just make a declaration that the creditor or owner is not entitled to do that thing, and thereafter no application for an enforcement order in respect of it shall be entertained.

(2) Where—

    (a) a regulated agreement or linked transaction is cancelled under section 69(1), or becomes subject to section 69(2), or

    (b) a regulated agreement is terminated under section 91, and an interested party applies to the court for a declaration under this subsection, the court may make a declaration to that effect.

[A136]

NOTES
  This section is printed as it was in force on 15 June 2006, prior to amendments made by the Consumer Credit Act 2006 and subsequent amendments; for the text of this provision as it currently has effect, see [786].

143, 144   (*Apply to Northern Ireland only.*)

PART X

ANCILLARY CREDIT BUSINESS

Definitions

145   Types of ancillary credit business

(1)   An ancillary credit business is any business so far as it comprises or relates to—
  (a)   credit brokerage,
  (b)   debt-adjusting,
  (c)   debt-counselling,
  (d)   debt-collecting, or
  (e)   the operation of a credit reference agency.

(2)   Subject to section 146(5) [and (5A)], credit brokerage is the effecting of introductions—
  (a)   of individuals desiring to obtain credit—
      (i)   to persons carrying on businesses to which this sub-paragraph applies, or
      (ii)   in the case of an individual desiring to obtain credit to finance the acquisition or provision of a dwelling occupied or to be occupied by himself or his relative, to any person carrying on a business in the course of which he provides credit secured on land, or
  (b)   of individuals desiring to obtain goods on hire to persons carrying on businesses to which this paragraph applies, or
  (c)   of individuals desiring to obtain credit, or to obtain goods on hire, to other credit-brokers.

(3)   Subsection (2)(a)(i) applies to—
  (a)   a consumer credit business;
  (b)   a business which comprises or relates to consumer credit agreements being, otherwise than by virtue of section 16(5)(a), exempt agreements;
  (c)   a business which comprises or relates to unregulated agreements where—
      (i)   the [law applicable to] the agreement is the law of a country outside the United Kingdom, and
      (ii)   if the [law applicable to] the agreement were the law of a part of the United Kingdom it would be a regulated consumer credit agreement.

(4)   Subsection (2)(b) applies to—
  (a)   a consumer hire business;
  (b)   a business which comprises or relates to unregulated agreements where—
      (i)   the [law applicable to] the agreement is the law of a country outside the United Kingdom, and
      (ii)   if the [law applicable to] the agreement were the law of a part of the United Kingdom it would be a regulated consumer hire agreement.

(5)   Subject to [section 146(5B) and (6)], debt-adjusting is, in relation to debts due under consumer credit agreements or consumer hire agreements,—
  (a)   negotiating with the creditor or owner, on behalf of the debtor or hirer, terms for the discharge of a debt, or
  (b)   taking over, in return for payments by the debtor or hirer, his obligation to discharge a debt, or
  (c)   any similar activity concerned with the liquidation of a debt.

(6)   Subject to [section 146(5C) and (6)], debt-counselling is the giving of advice to debtors or hirers about the liquidation of debts due under consumer credit agreements or consumer hire agreements.

(7)   Subject to section 146(6), debt-collecting is the taking of steps to procure payment of debts due under consumer credit agreements or consumer hire agreements.

(8)   A credit reference agency is a person carrying on a business comprising the furnishing of persons with information relevant to the financial standing of individuals, being information collected by the agency for that purpose.

[A137]

146 Exceptions from section 145

(1)   A barrister or advocate acting in that capacity is not to be treated as doing so in the course of any ancillary credit business.

(2)   A solicitor engaging in contentious business (as defined in [section 87(1) of the Solicitors Act 1974]) is not to be treated as doing so in the course of any ancillary credit business.

(3)   (*Applies to Scotland only.*)

(4)   A solicitor in Northern Ireland engaging in [contentious business (as defined in Article 3(2) of the Solicitors (Northern Ireland) Order 1976], is not to be treated as doing so in the course of any ancillary credit business.

(5)   For the purposes of section 145(2), introductions effected by an individual by canvassing off trade premises either debtor-creditor-supplier agreements falling within section 12(a) or regulated consumer hire agreements shall be disregarded if—
  (a)   the introductions are not effected by him in the capacity of an employee, and
  (b)   he does not by any other method effect introductions falling within section 145(2).

[(5A)   It is not credit brokerage for a person to effect the introduction of an individual desiring to obtain credit if the introduction is made—
  (a)   to an authorised person, within the meaning of the 2000 Act, who has permission under that Act to enter as lender into relevant agreements; or
  (b)   to a qualifying broker, with a view to that individual obtaining credit under a relevant agreement.

(5B)   It is not debt-adjusting for a person to carry on an activity mentioned in paragraph (a), (b) or (c) of section 145(5) if—
  (a)   the debt in question is due under a relevant agreement; and
  (b)   that activity is a regulated activity for the purposes of the 2000 Act.

(5C)   It is not debt-counselling for a person to give advice to debtors about the liquidation of debts if—
  (a)   the debt in question is due under a relevant agreement; and
  (b)   giving that advice is a regulated activity for the purposes of the 2000 Act.

(5D)   In this section—
  "the 2000 Act" means the Financial Services and Markets Act 2000;
  "relevant agreement" means [an] agreement which is secured by a land mortgage, where entering into that agreement as lender is a regulated activity for the purposes of the 2000 Act;
  "qualifying broker" means a person who may effect introductions of the kind mentioned in subsection (5A) without contravening the general prohibition, within the meaning of section 19 of the 2000 Act,
and references to "regulated activities" and the definition of "qualifying broker" must be read with—
  (a)   section 22 of the 2000 Act (regulated activities: power to specify classes of activity and categories of investment);
  (b)   any order for the time being in force under that section; and
  (c)   Schedule 2 to that Act.]

(6)   It is not debt-adjusting, debt-counselling or debt-collecting for a person to do anything in relation to a debt arising under an agreement if—
  (a)   he is the creditor or owner under the agreement, otherwise than by virtue of an assignment, or
  (b)   he is the creditor or owner under the agreement by virtue of an assignment made in connection with the transfer to the assignee of any business other than a debt-collecting business, or
  (c)   he is the supplier in relation to the agreement, or

(d) he is a credit-broker who has acquired the business of the person who was the supplier in relation to the agreement, or

(e) he is a person prevented by subsection (5) from being treated as a credit-broker, and the agreement was made in consequence of an introduction (whether made by him or another person) which, under subsection (5), is to be disregarded.

[A138]

NOTES

This section is printed as it was in force on 15 June 2006, prior to amendments made by the Consumer Credit Act 2006 and subsequent amendments; for the text of this provision as it currently has effect, see [788].

Sub-ss (2), (4): words in square brackets substituted by the Arbitration Act 1996, s 107(1), Sch 3, para 28, as from 31 January 1997.

Sub-ss (5A)–(5C): inserted, together with sub-s (5D), by the Financial Services and Markets Act 2000 (Regulated Activities) (Amendment) (No 1) Order 2003, SI 2003/1475, art 21(2), as from 31 October 2004.

Sub-s (5D): inserted as noted above; in definition "relevant agreement" word in square brackets substituted by the Financial Services and Markets Act 2000 (Consequential Amendments) Order 2005, SI 2005/2967, art 3, as from 16 November 2005.

Solicitors: references to solicitors are modified so as to include references to recognised bodies within the meaning of the Administration of Justice Act 1985, s 9, by the Solicitors' Incorporated Practices Order 1991, SI 1991/2684, arts 3–5, Sch 1.

Licensing

147 Application of Part III

(1) The provisions of Part III (except section 40) apply to an ancillary credit business as they apply to a consumer credit business.

(2) Without prejudice to the generality of section 26, regulations under that section (as applied by subsection (1)) may include provisions regulating the collection and dissemination of information by credit reference agencies.

[A139]

NOTES

This section is printed as it was in force on 15 June 2006, prior to amendments made by the Consumer Credit Act 2006 and subsequent amendments; for the text of this provision as it currently has effect, see [789].

Regulations: the Consumer Credit (Termination of Licences) Regulations 1976, SI 1976/1002; the Consumer Credit (Conduct of Business) (Credit References) Regulations 1977, SI 1977/330; the Consumer Credit Licensing (Appeals) Regulations 1998, SI 1998/1203.

148 Agreement for services of unlicensed trader

(1) An agreement for the services of a person carrying on an ancillary credit business (the "trader"), if made when the trader was unlicensed, is enforceable against the other party (the "customer") only where the [OFT] has made an order under subsection (2) which applies to the agreement.

(2) The trader or his successor in title may apply to the [OFT] for an order that agreements within subsection (1) are to be treated as if made when the trader was licensed.

(3) Unless the [OFT] determines to make an order under subsection (2) in accordance with the application, [it] shall, before determining the application, by notice—

(a) inform the trader, giving [its] reasons, that, as the case may be, [it] is minded to refuse the application, or to grant it in terms different from those applied for, describing them, and

(b) invite the trader to submit to the [OFT] representations in support of his application in accordance with section 34.

(4) In determining whether or not to make an order under subsection (2) in respect of any period the [OFT] shall consider, in addition to any other relevant factors,—

(a) how far, if at all, customers under agreements made by the trader during that period were prejudiced by the trader's conduct,

(b) whether or not the [OFT] would have been likely to grant a licence covering that period on an application by the trader, and

(c) the degree of culpability for the failure to obtain a licence.

(5) If the [OFT] thinks fit, [it] may in an order under subsection (2)—

(a) limit the order to specified agreements, or agreements of a specified description or made at a specified time;

(b) make the order conditional on the doing of specified acts by the trader.

[(6) This section does not apply to an agreement made by a consumer credit EEA firm unless at the time it was made that firm was precluded from entering into it as a result of—

    (a)   a consumer credit prohibition imposed under section 203 of the Financial Services and Markets Act 2000; or

    (b)   a restriction imposed on the firm under section 204 of that Act.]

[A140]

___

NOTES

This section is printed as it was in force on 15 June 2006, prior to amendments made by the Consumer Credit Act 2006 and subsequent amendments; for the text of this provision as it currently has effect, see [790].

Sub-s (6): added by the Financial Services and Markets Act 2000 (Consequential Amendments and Repeals) Order 2001, SI 2001/3649, art 173, as from 1 December 2001.

References to the OFT, etc; as to the abolition of the office of the Director General of Fair Trading and the substitution of the original references to the Director (and related expressions), see the note preceding s 1 at [A1].

149 Regulated agreements made on introductions by unlicensed credit-broker

(1)   A regulated agreement made by a debtor or hirer who, for the purpose of making that agreement, was introduced to the creditor or owner by an unlicensed credit-broker is enforceable against the debtor or hirer only where—

    (a)   on the application of the credit-broker, the [OFT] has made an order under section 148(2) in respect of a period including the time when the introduction was made, and the order does not (whether in general terms or specifically) exclude the application of this paragraph to the regulated agreement, or

    (b)   the [OFT] has made an order under subsection (2) which applies to the agreement.

(2)   Where during any period individuals were introduced to a person carrying on a consumer credit business or consumer hire business by an unlicensed credit-broker for the purpose of making regulated agreements with the person carrying on that business, that person or his successor in title may apply to the [OFT] for an order that regulated agreements so made are to be treated as if the credit-broker had been licensed at the time of the introduction.

(3)   Unless the [OFT] determines to make an order under subsection (2) in accordance with the application, [it] shall, before determining the application, by notice—

    (a)   inform the applicant, giving [its] reasons, that, as the case may be, [it] is minded to refuse the application, or to grant it in terms different from those applied for, describing them, and

    (b)   invite the applicant to submit to the [OFT] representations in support of his application in accordance with section 34.

(4)   In determining whether or not to make an order under subsection (2) the [OFT] shall consider, in addition to any other relevant factors—

    (a)   how far, if at all, debtors or hirers under regulated agreements to which the application relates were prejudiced by the credit-broker's conduct, and

    (b)   the degree of culpability of the applicant in facilitating the carrying on by the credit-broker of his business when unlicensed.

(5)   If the [OFT] thinks fit, [it] may in an order under subsection (2)—

    (a)   limit the order to specified agreements, or agreements of a specified description or made at a specified time;

    (b)   make the order conditional on the doing of specified acts by the applicant.

[(6)   For the purposes of this section, "unlicensed credit-broker" does not include a consumer credit EEA firm unless at the time the introduction was made that firm was precluded from making it as a result of—

    (a)   a consumer credit prohibition imposed under section 203 of the Financial Services and Markets Act 2000; or

    (b)   a restriction imposed on the firm under section 204 of that Act.]

[A141]

___

NOTES

This section is printed as it was in force on 15 June 2006, prior to amendments made by the Consumer Credit Act 2006 and subsequent amendments; for the text of this provision as it currently has effect, see [791].

Sub-s (6): added by the Financial Services and Markets Act 2000 (Consequential Amendments and Repeals) Order 2001, SI 2001/3649, art 174, as from 1 December 2001.

References to the OFT, etc: as to the abolition of the office of the Director General of Fair Trading and the substitution of the original references to the Director (and related expressions), see the note preceding s 1 at [A1].

150 Appeals to Secretary of State against licensing decisions

Section 41 (as applied by section 147(1)) shall have effect as if the following entry were included in the table set out at the end—

Determination	Appellant
Refusal to make order under section 148(2) or 149(2) in accordance with terms of application	The applicant

[A142]

NOTES
This section is printed as it was in force on 15 June 2006, prior to amendments made by the Consumer Credit Act 2006 and subsequent amendments. It has subsequently been repealed (see the note following [791]).

Seeking business

151 Advertisements

(1) Sections 44 to 47 apply to an advertisement published for the purposes of a business of credit brokerage carried on by any person, whether it advertises the services of that person or the services of persons to whom he effects introductions, as they apply to an advertisement to which Part IV applies.

(2) Sections 44, 46 and 47 apply to an advertisement, published for the purposes of a business carried on by the advertiser, indicating that he is willing to advise on debts, or engage in transactions concerned with the liquidation of debts, as they apply to an advertisement to which Part IV applies.

[(2A) An advertisement does not fall within subsection (1) or (2) in so far as it is a communication of an invitation or inducement to engage in investment activity within the meaning of section 21 of the Financial Services and Markets Act 2000, other than an exempt generic communication (as defined in section 43(3B)).]

(3) The Secretary of State may by order provide that an advertisement published for the purposes of a business of credit brokerage, debt-adjusting or debt-counselling shall not fall within subsection (1) or (2) if it is of a description specified in the order.

(4) An advertisement does not fall within subsection (2) if it indicates that the advertiser is not willing to act in relation to consumer credit agreements and consumer hire agreements.

(5) In subsections (1) and (3) "credit brokerage" includes the effecting of introductions of individuals desiring to obtain credit to any person carrying on a business in the course of which he provides credit secured on land.

[A143]

NOTES
This section is printed as it was in force on 15 June 2006, prior to amendments made by the Consumer Credit Act 2006 and subsequent amendments; for the text of this provision as it currently has effect, see [793].
Sub-s (2A): inserted by the Financial Services and Markets Act 2000 (Regulated Activities) Order 2001, SI 2001/544, art 90(1), (7), as from 31 October 2004.
Regulations: the Consumer Credit (Advertisements) Regulations 2004, SI 2004/1484 at [3400].

152 Application of sections 52 to 54 to credit brokerage etc

(1) Sections 52 to 54 apply to a business of credit brokerage, debt-adjusting or debt-counselling as they apply to a consumer credit business.

(2) In their application to a business of credit brokerage, sections 52 and 53 shall apply to the giving of quotations and information about the business of any person to whom the credit-broker effects introductions as well as to the giving of quotations and information about his own business.

[A144]

NOTES
This section is printed as it was in force on 15 June 2006, prior to amendments made by the Consumer Credit Act 2006 and subsequent amendments; for the text of this provision as it currently has effect, see [794].

153 Definition of canvassing off trade premises (agreements for ancillary credit services)

(1) An individual (the "canvasser") canvasses off trade premises the services of a person carrying on an ancillary credit business if he solicits the entry of another individual (the "consumer") into an agreement for the provision to the consumer of those services by making oral representations to the consumer, or any other individual, during a visit by the canvasser to any place (not excluded by subsection (2)) where the consumer, or that other individual, as the case may be, is, being a visit—

(a)　carried out for the purpose of making such oral representations to individuals who are at that place, but

(b)　not carried out in response to a request made on a previous occasion.

(2)　A place is excluded from subsection (1) if it is a place where (whether on a permanent or temporary basis)—

(a)　the ancillary credit business is carried on, or

(b)　any business is carried on by the canvasser or the person whose employee or agent the canvasser is, or by the consumer.

[A145]

NOTES

　This section is printed as it was in force on 15 June 2006, prior to amendments made by the Consumer Credit Act 2006 and subsequent amendments; for the text of this provision as it currently has effect, see [795].

154　Prohibition of canvassing certain ancillary credit services off trade premises

It is an offence to canvass off trade premises the services of a person carrying on a business of credit brokerage, debt-adjusting or debt-counselling.

[A146]

NOTES

　This section is printed as it was in force on 15 June 2006, prior to amendments made by the Consumer Credit Act 2006 and subsequent amendments; for the text of this provision as it currently has effect, see [796].

155　Right to recover brokerage fees

(1)　[Subject to subsection (2A),] the excess over [£5] of a fee or commission for his services charged by a credit-broker to an individual to whom this subsection applies shall cease to be payable or, as the case may be, shall be recoverable by the individual if the introduction does not result in his entering into a relevant agreement within the six months following the introduction (disregarding any agreement which is cancelled under section 69(1) or becomes subject to section 69(2)).

(2)　Subsection (1) applies to an individual who sought an introduction for a purpose which would have been fulfilled by his entry into—

(a)　a regulated agreement, or

(b)　in the case of an individual such as is referred to in section 145(2)(a)(ii), an agreement for credit secured on land, or

(c)　an agreement such as is referred to in section 145(3)(b) or (c) or (4)(b).

[(2A)　But subsection (1) does not apply where—

(a)　the fee or commission relates to the effecting of an introduction of a kind mentioned in section 146(5A); and

(b)　the person charging that fee or commission is an authorised person or an appointed representative, within the meaning of the Financial Services and Markets Act 2000.]

(3)　An agreement is a relevant agreement for the purposes of subsection (1) in relation to an individual if it is an agreement such as is referred to in subsection (2) in relation to that individual.

(4)　In the case of an individual desiring to obtain credit under a consumer credit agreement, any sum payable or paid by him to a credit-broker otherwise than as a fee or commission for the credit-broker's services shall for the purposes of subsection (1) be treated as such a fee or commission if it enters, or would enter, into the total charge for credit.

[A147]

NOTES

　This section is printed as it was in force on 15 June 2006, prior to amendments made by the Consumer Credit Act 2006 and subsequent amendments; for the text of this provision as it currently has effect, see [797].

　Sub-s (1): words in first pair of square brackets inserted by the Financial Services and Markets Act 2000 (Regulated Activities) (Amendment) (No 1) Order 2003, SI 2003/1475, art 22(1), (2), as from 31 October 2004; sum in square brackets substituted by the Consumer Credit (Further Increase in Monetary Amounts) Order 1998, SI 1998/997, art 3, Schedule, as from 1 May 1998.

　Sub-s (2A): inserted by SI 2003/1475, art 22(1), (3), as from 31 October 2004.

Entry into agreements

156　Entry into agreements

Regulations may make provision, in relation to agreements entered into in the course of a business of credit brokerage, debt-adjusting or debt-counselling, corresponding, with such modifications as the Secretary of State thinks fit, to the provision which is or may be made by or under sections 55, 60, 61, 62, 63, 65, 127, 179 or 180 in relation to agreements to which those sections apply.

[A148]

NOTES
This section is printed as it was in force on 15 June 2006, prior to amendments made by the Consumer Credit Act 2006 and subsequent amendments; for the text of this provision as it currently has effect, see [798].

Credit reference agencies

157 Duty to disclose name etc of agency

(1) A creditor, owner or negotiator, within the prescribed period after receiving a request in writing to that effect from the debtor or hirer, shall give him notice of the name and address of any credit reference agency from which the creditor, owner or negotiator has, during the antecedent negotiations, applied for information about his financial standing.

(2) Subsection (1) does not apply to a request received more than 28 days after the termination of the antecedent negotiations, whether on the making of the regulated agreement or otherwise.

(3) If the creditor, owner or negotiator fails to comply with subsection (1) he commits an offence.

[A149]

NOTES
This section is printed as it was in force on 15 June 2006, prior to amendments made by the Consumer Credit Act 2006 and subsequent amendments; for the text of this provision as it currently has effect, see [799].
Regulations: the Consumer Credit (Credit Reference Agency) Regulations 2000, SI 2000/290.

158 Duty of agency to disclose filed information

(1) A credit reference agency, within the prescribed period after receiving,
  (a) a request in writing to that effect from any individual [partnership or other unincorporated body of persons not consisting entirely of bodies corporate] (the "consumer") and
  (b) such particulars as the agency may reasonably require to enable them to identify the file, and
  (c) a fee of [£2],
shall give the consumer a copy of the file relating to [it] kept by the agency.

(2) When giving a copy of the file under subsection (1), the agency shall also give the consumer a statement in the prescribed form of [the consumer's] rights under section 159.

(3) If the agency does not keep a file relating to the consumer it shall give [the consumer] notice of that fact, but need not return any money paid.

(4) If the agency contravenes any provision of this section it commits an offence.

(5) In this Act "file", in relation to an individual, means all the information about him kept by a credit reference agency, regardless of how the information is stored and "copy of the file", as respects information not in plain English, means a transcript reduced into plain English.

[A150]

NOTES
This section is printed as it was in force on 15 June 2006, prior to amendments made by the Consumer Credit Act 2006 and subsequent amendments; for the text of this provision as it currently has effect, see [800].
Sub-s (1): words in first and third pairs of square brackets substituted by the Data Protection Act 1998, s 62(1)(a), as from 1 March 2000, subject to savings in Sch 14, para 20 to that Act; sum in square brackets in para (c) substituted by the Consumer Credit (Further Increase of Monetary Amounts) Order 1998, SI 1998/997, Schedule, para 3, as from 1 May 1998.
Sub-s (2), (3): words in square brackets substituted by the Data Protection Act 1998, s 62(1)(b), (c), as from 1 March 2000, subject to savings in Sch 14, para 20 to that Act.
Regulations: the Consumer Credit (Credit Reference Agency) Regulations 2000, SI 2000/290.

159 Correction of wrong information

[(1) Any individual (the "objector") given—
  (a) information under section 7 of the Data Protection Act 1998 by a credit reference agency, or
  (b) information under section 158,

who considers that an entry in his file is incorrect, and that if it is not corrected he is likely to be prejudiced, may give notice to the agency requiring it either to remove the entry from the file or amend it.]

(2)   Within 28 days after receiving a notice under subsection (1), the agency shall by notice inform the [objector] that it has—

(a)   removed the entry from the file, or

(b)   amended the entry, or

(c)   taken no action,

and if the notice states that the agency has amended the entry it shall include a copy of the file so far as it comprises the amended entry.

(3)   Within 28 days after receiving a notice under subsection (2) or, where no such notice was given, within 28 days after the expiry of the period mentioned in subsection (2), the [objector] may, unless he has been informed by the agency that it has removed the entry from his file, serve a further notice on the agency requiring it to add to the file an accompanying notice of correction (not exceeding 200 words) drawn up by the [objector] and include a copy of it when furnishing information included in or based on that entry.

(4)   Within 28 days after receiving a notice under subsection (3), the agency, unless it intends to apply to the [the relevant authority] under subsection (5), shall by notice inform the [objector] that it has received the notice under subsection (3) and intends to comply with it.

(5)   If—

(a)   the [objector] has not received a notice under subsection (4) within the time required, or

(b)   it appears to the agency that it would be improper for it to publish a notice of correction because it is incorrect, or unjustly defames any person, or is frivolous or scandalous, or is for any other reason unsuitable,

the [objector] or, as the case may be, the agency may, in the prescribed manner and on payment of the specified fee, apply to the [the relevant authority], who may make such order on the application as he thinks fit.

(6)   If a person to whom an order under this section is directed fails to comply with it within the period specified in the order he commits an offence.

[(7)   The [Information Commissioner] may vary or revoke any order made by him under this section.

(8)   In this section "the relevant authority" means—

(a)   where the objector is a partnership or other unincorporated body of persons, the [OFT], and

(b)   in any other case, the [Information Commissioner].]

[A151]

NOTES

   This section is printed as it was in force on **15 June 2006, prior to amendments made by the Consumer Credit Act 2006 and subsequent amendments; for the text of this provision as it currently has effect, see [801].**

   Sub-s (1): substituted by the Data Protection Act 1998, s 62(1), (2), as from 1 March 2000; for savings see Sch 14, para 20 to that Act and the Data Protection Act 1998 (Commencement) Order 2000, SI 2000/183, art 2(2).

   Sub-ss (2)–(5): words in square brackets substituted by the Data Protection Act 1998, s 62(3), as from 1 March 2000; for savings see Sch 14, para 20 thereto and SI 2000/183, art 2(2).

   Sub-s (7): added, together with sub-s (8), by the Data Protection Act 1998, s 62(4), as from 1 March 2000 (for savings see Sch 14, para 20 thereto and SI 2000/183, art 2(2)); words in square brackets substituted by the Freedom of Information Act 2000, s 18(4), Sch 2, Pt I, para 7, as from 30 January 2001.

   Sub-s (8): added as noted to sub-s (7) above; words final pair of in square brackets substituted by the Freedom of Information Act 2000, s 18(4), Sch 2, Pt I, para 7, as from 30 January 2001.

   References to the OFT, etc: as to the abolition of the office of the Director General of Fair Trading and the substitution of the original references to the Director (and related expressions), see the note preceding s 1 at [A1].

   Regulations: the Consumer Credit (Credit Reference Agency) Regulations 2000, SI 2000/290.

160   Alternative procedure for business consumers

(1)   The [OFT], on an application made by a credit reference agency, may direct that this section shall apply to the agency if [it] is satisfied—

(a)   that compliance with section 158 in the case of consumers who carry on a business would adversely affect the service provided to its customers by the agency, and

(b)   that, having regard to the methods employed by the agency and to any other relevant factors, it is probable that consumers carrying on a business would not be prejudiced by the making of the direction.

(2)   Where an agency to which this section applies receives a request, particulars and a fee under section 158(1) from a consumer who carries on a business, and section 158(3) does not apply, the agency, instead of complying with section 158, may elect to deal with the matter under the following subsections.

(3)   Instead of giving the consumer a copy of the file, the agency shall within the prescribed period give notice to the consumer that it is proceeding under this section, and by notice give the consumer such information included in or based on entries in the file as the [OFT] may direct, together with a statement in the prescribed form of the consumer's rights under subsections (4) and (5).

(4)   If within 28 days after receiving the information given [to the consumer] under subsection (3), or such longer period as the [OFT] may allow, the consumer—

    (a)   gives notice to the [OFT] that [the consumer] is dissatisfied with the information, and

    (b)   satisfies the [OFT] that [the consumer] has taken such steps in relation to the agency as may be reasonable with a view to removing the cause of [the consumer's] dissatisfaction, and

    (c)   pays the [OFT] the specified fee,

the [OFT] may direct the agency to give the [OFT] a copy of the file, and the [OFT] may disclose to the consumer such of the information on the file as the [OFT] thinks fit.

(5)   Section 159 applies with any necessary modifications to information given to the consumer under this section as it applies to information given under section 158.

(6)   If an agency making an election under subsection (2) fails to comply with subsection (3) or (4) it commits an offence.

[(7)   In this section "consumer" has the same meaning as in section 158.]

[A152]

NOTES

This section is printed as it was in force on 15 June 2006, prior to amendments made by the Consumer Credit Act 2006 and subsequent amendments; for the text of this provision as it currently has effect, see [802].

Sub-s (4): words in first, fourth, sixth and seventh pairs of square brackets substituted by the Data Protection Act 1998, s 62(5)(a), as from 1 March 2000; for savings see Sch 14, para 20 to that Act and the Data Protection Act 1998 (Commencement) Order 2000, SI 2000/183, art 2(2).

Sub-s (7): added by the Data Protection Act 1998, s 62(5)(b), as from 1 March 2000; for savings see Sch 14, para 20 thereto and SI 2000/183, art 2(2).

References to the OFT, etc: as to the abolition of the office of the Director General of Fair Trading and the substitution of the original references to the Director (and related expressions), see the note preceding s 1 at [A1].

Regulations: the Consumer Credit (Credit Reference Agency) Regulations 2000, SI 2000/290.

PART XI

ENFORCEMENT OF ACT

161   Enforcement authorities

(1)   The following authorities ("enforcement authorities") have a duty to enforce this Act and regulations made under it—

    (a)   the [OFT],

    (b)   in Great Britain, the local weights and measures authority,

    (c)   in Northern Ireland, the Department of Commerce for Northern Ireland.

(2)   ...

(3)   Every local weights and measures authority shall, whenever the [OFT] requires, report to [it] in such form and with such particulars as [it] requires on the exercise of their functions under this Act.

(4)–(6)   ...

[A153]

NOTES

This section is printed as it was in force on 15 June 2006, prior to amendments made by the Consumer Credit Act 2006 and subsequent amendments; for the text of this provision as it currently has effect, see [803].

Sub-s (2): repealed by the Enterprise Act 2002, s 278, Sch 25, para 6(1), (32)(b), Sch 26, as from 1 April 2003.

Sub-ss (4)–(6): repealed by the Local Government, Planning and Land Act 1980, ss 1(4), 194, Sch 4, para 10, Sch 34, Pt IV, as from 13 November 1980.

References to the OFT, etc: as to the abolition of the office of the Director General of Fair Trading and the substitution of the original references to the Director (and related expressions), see the note preceding s 1 at [A1].

APPENDIX
CCA 1974 (PRE CCA 2006)

162 Powers of entry and inspection

(1)   A duly authorised officer of an enforcement authority, at all reasonable hours and on production, if required, of his credentials, may—

    (a)   in order to ascertain whether a breach of any provision of or under this Act has been committed, inspect any goods and enter any premises (other than premises used only as a dwelling);

    (b)   if he has reasonable cause to suspect that a breach of any provision of or under this Act has been committed, in order to ascertain whether it has been committed, require any person—

        (i)   carrying on, or employed in connection with, a business to produce any books or documents relating to it; or

        (ii) having control of any information relating to a business recorded otherwise than in a legible form to provide a document containing a legible reproduction of the whole or any part of the information,

        and take copies of, or of any entry in, the books or documents;

    (c)   if he has reasonable cause to believe that a breach of any provision of or under this Act has been committed, seize and detain any goods in order to ascertain (by testing or otherwise) whether such a breach has been committed;

    (d)   seize and detain any goods, books or documents which he has reason to believe may be required as evidence in proceedings for an offence under this Act;

    (e)   for the purpose of exercising his powers under this subsection to seize goods, books or documents, but only if and to the extent that it is reasonably necessary for securing that the provisions of this Act and of any regulations made under it are duly observed, require any person having authority to do so to break open any container and, if that person does not comply, break it open himself.

(2)   An officer seizing goods, books or documents in exercise of his powers under this section shall not do so without informing the person he seizes them from.

(3)   If a justice of the peace, on sworn information in writing, or, in Scotland, a sheriff or a magistrate or justice of the peace, on evidence on oath,—

    (a)   is satisfied that there is reasonable ground to believe either—

        (i)   that any goods, books or documents which a duly authorised officer has power to inspect under this section are on any premises and their inspection is likely to disclose evidence of a breach of any provision of or under this Act; or

        (ii) that a breach of any provision of or under this Act has been, is being or is about to be committed on any premises; and

    (b)   is also satisfied either—

        (i)   that admission to the premises has been or is likely to be refused and that notice of intention to apply for a warrant under this subsection has been given to the occupier; or

        (ii) that an application for admission, or the giving of such a notice, would defeat the object of the entry or that the premises are unoccupied or that the occupier is temporarily absent and it might defeat the object of the entry to wait for his return,

the justice or, as the case may be, the sheriff or magistrate may by warrant under his hand, which shall continue in force for a period of one month, authorise an officer of an enforcement authority to enter the premises (by force if need be).

(4)   An officer entering premises by virtue of this section may take such other persons and equipment with him as he thinks necessary; and on leaving premises entered by virtue of a warrant under subsection (3) shall, if they are unoccupied or the occupier is temporarily absent, leave them as effectively secured against trespassers as he found them.

(5)   Regulations may provide that, in cases described by the regulations, an officer of a local weights and measures authority is not to be taken to be duly authorised for the purposes of this section unless he is authorised by the [OFT].

(6)   A person who is not a duly authorised officer of an enforcement authority, but purports to act as such under this section, commits an offence.

(7)   Nothing in this section compels a barrister, advocate or solicitor to produce a document containing a privileged communication made by or to him in that capacity or authorises the seizing of any such document in his possession.

[A154]

NOTES

   This section is printed as it was in force on 15 June 2006, prior to amendments made by the Consumer Credit Act 2006 and subsequent amendments; for the text of this provision as it currently has effect, see [804].

References to the OFT, etc: as to the abolition of the office of the Director General of Fair Trading and the substitution of the original references to the Director (and related expressions), see the note preceding s 1 at [A1].

Seize and detain goods, etc: the powers of seizure conferred by sub-s (1)(c), (d) are powers to which the Criminal Justice and Police Act 2001, s 50 apply (additional powers of seizure from premises); see s 50 of, and Sch 1, Pt 1, para 19 to, that Act.

Regulations: the Consumer Credit (Entry and Inspection) Regulations 1977, SI 1977/331.

163   Compensation for loss

(1) Where, in exercising his powers under section 162, an officer of an enforcement authority seizes and detains goods and their owner suffers loss by reason of—

    (a)   that seizure, or

    (b)   the loss, damage or deterioration of the goods during detention,

then, unless the owner is convicted of an offence under this Act committed in relation to the goods, the authority shall compensate him for the loss so suffered.

(2) Any dispute as to the right to or amount of any compensation under subsection (1) shall be determined by arbitration.

[A155]

NOTES

This section is printed as it was in force on 15 June 2006, prior to amendments made by the Consumer Credit Act 2006 and subsequent amendments; for the text of this provision as it currently has effect, see [805].

164   Power to make test purchases etc

(1) An enforcement authority may—

    (a)   make, or authorise any of their officers to make on their behalf, such purchases of goods; and

    (b)   authorise any of their officers to procure the provision of such services or facilities or to enter into such agreements or other transactions,

as may appear to them expedient for determining whether any provisions made by or under this Act are being complied with.

(2) Any act done by an officer authorised to do it under subsection (1) shall be treated for the purposes of this Act as done by him as an individual on his own behalf.

(3) Any goods seized by an officer under this Act may be tested, and in the event of such a test he shall inform the person mentioned in section 162(2) of the test results.

(4) Where any test leads to proceedings under this Act, the enforcement authority shall—

    (a)   if the goods were purchased, inform the person they were purchased from of the test results, and

    (b)   allow any person against whom the proceedings are taken to have the goods tested on his behalf if it is reasonably practicable to do so.

[A156]

NOTES

This section is printed as it was in force on 15 June 2006, prior to amendments made by the Consumer Credit Act 2006 and subsequent amendments; for the text of this provision as it currently has effect, see [806].

165   Obstruction of authorised officers

(1) Any person who—

    (a)   wilfully obstructs an officer of an enforcement authority acting in pursuance of this Act; or

    (b)   wilfully fails to comply with any requirement properly made to him by such an officer under section 162; or

    (c)   without reasonable cause fails to give such an officer (so acting) other assistance or information he may reasonably require in performing his functions under this Act,

commits an offence.

(2) If any person, in giving such information as is mentioned in subsection (1)(c), makes any statement which he knows to be false, he commits an offence.

(3) Nothing in this section requires a person to answer any question or give any information if to do so might incriminate that person or (where that person is [married or a civil partner) the spouse or civil partner] of that person.

[A157]

166 Notification of convictions and judgments to [OFT]

Where a person is convicted of an offence or has a judgment given against him by or before any court in the United Kingdom and it appears to the court—

    (a)   having regard to the functions of the [OFT] under this Act, that the conviction or judgment should be brought to the [OFT's] attention, and

    (b)   that it may not be brought to [its] attention unless arrangements for that purpose are made by the court,

the court may make such arrangements notwithstanding that the proceedings have been finally disposed of.

[A158]

167 Penalties

(1)   An offence under a provision of this Act specified in column 1 of Schedule 1 is triable in the mode or modes indicated in column 3, and on conviction is punishable as indicated in column 4 (where a period of time indicates the maximum term of imprisonment, and a monetary amount indicates the maximum fine, for the offence in question).

(2)   A person who contravenes any regulations made under section 44, 52, 53, or 112, or made under section 26 by virtue of section 54, commits an offence.

[A159]

168 Defences

(1)   In any proceedings for an offence under this Act it is a defence for the person charged to prove—

    (a)   that his act or omission was due to a mistake, or to reliance on information supplied to him, or to an act or omission by another person, or to an accident or some other cause beyond his control, and

    (b)   that he took all reasonable precautions and exercised all due diligence to avoid such an act or omission by himself or any person under his control.

(2)   If in any case the defence provided by subsection (1) involves the allegation that the act or omission was due to an act or omission by another person or to reliance on information supplied by another person, the person charged shall not, without leave of the court, be entitled to rely on that defence unless, within a period ending seven clear days before the hearing, he has served on the prosecutor a notice giving such information identifying or assisting in the identification of that other person as was then in his possession.

[A160]

169 Offences by bodies corporate

Where at any time a body corporate commits an offence under this Act with the consent or connivance of, or because of neglect by, any individual, the individual commits the like offence if at that time—

    (a)   he is a director, manager, secretary or similar officer of the body corporate, or

(b)   he is purporting to act as such an officer, or
(c)   the body corporate is managed by its members, of whom he is one.

[A161]

NOTES
   This section is printed as it was in force on 15 June 2006, prior to amendments made by the Consumer Credit Act 2006 and subsequent amendments; for the text of this provision as it currently has effect, see **[811]**.

170   No further sanctions for breach of Act

   (1)   A breach of any requirement made (otherwise than by any court) by or under this Act shall incur no civil or criminal sanction as being such a breach, except to the extent (if any) expressly provided by or under this Act.

   (2)   In exercising [its] functions under this Act the [OFT] may take account of any matter appearing to [it] to constitute a breach of a requirement made by or under this Act, whether or not any sanction for that breach is provided by or under this Act and, if it is so provided, whether or not proceedings have been brought in respect of the breach.

   (3)   Subsection (1) does not prevent the grant of an injunction, or the making of an order of certiorari, mandamus or prohibition or as respects Scotland the grant of an interdict or of an order under section 91 of the Court of Session Act 1868 (order for specific performance of statutory duty).

[A162]

NOTES
   This section is printed as it was in force on 15 June 2006, prior to amendments made by the Consumer Credit Act 2006 and subsequent amendments; for the text of this provision as it currently has effect, see **[812]**.
   References to the OFT, etc: as to the abolition of the office of the Director General of Fair Trading and the substitution of the original references to the Director (and related expressions), see the note preceding s 1 at **[A1]**.
   Court of Session Act 1868, s 91: repealed by the Court of Session Act 1988.

171   Onus of proof in various proceedings

   (1)   If an agreement contains a term signifying that in the opinion of the parties section 10(3)(b)(iii) does not apply to the agreement, it shall be taken not to apply unless the contrary is proved.

   (2)   It shall be assumed in any proceedings, unless the contrary is proved, that when a person initiated a transaction as mentioned in section 19(1)(c) he knew the principal agreement had been made, or contemplated that it might be made.

   (3)   Regulations under section 44 or 52 may make provision as to the onus of proof in any proceedings to enforce the regulations.

   (4)   In proceedings brought by the creditor under a credit-token agreement—
      (a)   it is for the creditor to prove that the credit-token was lawfully supplied to the debtor, and was accepted by him, and
      (b)   if the debtor alleges that any use made of the credit-token was not authorised by him, it is for the creditor to prove either—
         (i)   that the use was so authorised, or
         (ii)   that the use occurred before the creditor had been given notice under section 84(3).

   (5)   In proceedings under section 50(1) in respect of a document received by a minor at any school or other educational establishment for minors, it is for the person sending it to him at that establishment to prove that he did not know or suspect it to be such an establishment.

   (6)   In proceedings under section 119(1) it is for the pawnee to prove that he had reasonable cause to refuse to allow the pawn to be redeemed.

   (7)   If, in proceedings referred to in section 139(1), the debtor or any surety alleges that the credit bargain is extortionate it is for the creditor to prove the contrary.

[A163]

NOTES
   This section is printed as it was in force on 15 June 2006, prior to amendments made by the Consumer Credit Act 2006 and subsequent amendments; for the text of this provision as it currently has effect, see **[813]**.

172   Statements by creditor or owner to be binding

   (1)   A statement by a creditor or owner is binding on him if given under—
      section 77(1),

section 78(1),
section 79(1),
section 97(1),
section 107(1)(c),
section 108(1)(c), or
section 109(1)(c).

(2)   Where a trader—
    (a)   gives a customer a notice in compliance with section 103(1)(b), or
    (b)   gives a customer a notice under section 103(1) asserting that the customer is not indebted to him under an agreement,

the notice is binding on the trader.

(3)   Where in proceedings before any court—
    (a)   it is sought to rely on a statement or notice given as mentioned in subsection (1) or (2), and
    (b)   the statement or notice is shown to be incorrect,

the court may direct such relief (if any) to be given to the creditor or owner from the operation of subsection (1) or (2) as appears to the court to be just.

[A164]

NOTES
This section is printed as it was in force on 15 June 2006, prior to amendments made by the Consumer Credit Act 2006 and subsequent amendments; for the text of this provision as it currently has effect, see [814].

173   Contracting-out forbidden

(1)   A term contained in a regulated agreement or linked transaction, or in any other agreement relating to an actual or prospective regulated agreement or linked transaction, is void if, and to the extent that, it is inconsistent with a provision for the protection of the debtor or hirer or his relative or any surety contained in this Act or in any regulation made under this Act.

(2)   Where a provision specifies the duty or liability of the debtor or hirer or his relative or any surety in certain circumstances, a term is inconsistent with that provision if it purports to impose, directly or indirectly, an additional duty or liability on him in those circumstances.

(3)   Notwithstanding subsection (1), a provision of this Act under which a thing may be done in relation to any person on an order of the court or the [OFT] only shall not be taken to prevent its being done at any time with that person's consent given at that time, but the refusal of such consent shall not give rise to any liability.

[A165]

NOTES
This section is printed as it was in force on 15 June 2006, prior to amendments made by the Consumer Credit Act 2006 and subsequent amendments; for the text of this provision as it currently has effect, see [815].
References to the OFT, etc: as to the abolition of the office of the Director General of Fair Trading and the substitution of the original references to the Director (and related expressions), see the note preceding s 1 at [A1].

PART XII
SUPPLEMENTAL
General

174   (*Repealed by the Enterprise Act 2002, ss 247(d), 278(2), Sch 26, as from 20 June 2003.*)

175   Duty of persons deemed to be agents

Where under this Act a person is deemed to receive a notice or payment as agent of the creditor or owner under a regulated agreement, he shall be deemed to be under a contractual duty to the creditor or owner to transmit the notice, or remit the payment, to him forthwith.

[A166]

NOTES
This section is printed as it was in force on 15 June 2006, prior to amendments made by the Consumer Credit Act 2006 and subsequent amendments; for the text of this provision as it currently has effect, see [817].

176   Service of documents

(1)   A document to be served under this Act by one person ("the server") on another person ("the subject") is to be treated as properly served on the subject if dealt with as mentioned in the following subsections.

(2)   The document may be delivered or sent [by an appropriate method] to the subject, or addressed to him by name and left at his proper address.

(3)   For the purposes of this Act, a document sent by post to, or left at, the address last known to the server as the address of a person shall be treated as sent by post to, or left at, his proper address.

(4)   Where the document is to be served on the subject as being the person having any interest in land, and it is not practicable after reasonable inquiry to ascertain the subject's name or address, the document may be served by—
  (a)   addressing it to the subject by the description of the person having that interest in the land (naming it), and
  (b)   delivering the document to some responsible person on the land or affixing it, or a copy of it, in a conspicuous position on the land.

(5)   Where a document to be served on the subject as being a debtor, hirer or surety, or as having any other capacity relevant for the purposes of this Act, is served at any time on another person who—
  (a)   is the person last known to the server as having that capacity, but
  (b)   before that time had ceased to have it,
the document shall be treated as having been served at that time on the subject.

(6)   Anything done to a document in relation to a person who (whether to the knowledge of the server or not) has died shall be treated for the purposes of subsection (5) as service of the document on that person if it would have been so treated had he not died.

[(7)   The following enactments shall not be construed as authorising service on the Public Trustee (in England and Wales) or the Probate Judge (in Northern Ireland) of any document which is to be served under this Act—
  section 9 of the Administration of Estates Act 1925;
  section 3 of the Administration of Estates Act (Northern Ireland) 1955.]

(8)   References in the preceding subsections to the serving of a document on a person include the giving of the document to that person.

                                                                          [A167]

___

NOTES
   This section is printed as it was in force on 15 June 2006, prior to amendments made by the Consumer Credit Act 2006 and subsequent amendments; for the text of this provision as it currently has effect, see [818].
   Sub-s (2): words in square brackets substituted by the Consumer Credit Act 1974 (Electronic Communications) Order 2004, SI 2004/3236, art 2(1), (6), as from 31 December 2004.
   Sub-s (7): substituted by the Law of Property (Miscellaneous Provisions) Act 1994, s 21(1), Sch 1, para 6, as from 1 July 1995.

___

[176A   Electronic transmission of documents

(1)   A document is transmitted in accordance with this subsection if—
  (a)   the person to whom it is transmitted agrees that it may be delivered to him by being transmitted to a particular electronic address in a particular electronic form,
  (b)   it is transmitted to that address in that form, and
  (c)   the form in which the document is transmitted is such that any information in the document which is addressed to the person to whom the document is transmitted is capable of being stored for future reference for an appropriate period in a way which allows the information to be reproduced without change.

(2)   A document transmitted in accordance with subsection (1) shall, unless the contrary is proved, be treated for the purposes of this Act, except section 69, as having been delivered on the working day immediately following the day on which it is transmitted.

(3)   In this section, "electronic address" includes any number or address used for the purposes of receiving electronic communications.]

                                                                          [A168]

___

NOTES
   This section is printed as it was in force on 15 June 2006, prior to amendments made by the Consumer Credit Act 2006 and subsequent amendments; for the text of this provision as it currently has effect, see [818A].
   Inserted by the Consumer Credit Act 1974 (Electronic Communications) Order 2004, SI 2004/3236, art 2(1), (7), as from 31 December 2004.

___

177 Saving for registered charges

(1) Nothing in this Act affects the rights of a proprietor of a registered charge (within the meaning of the [Land Registration Act 2002]), who—
    (a) became the proprietor under a transfer for valuable consideration without notice of any defect in the title arising (apart from this section) by virtue of this Act, or
    (b) derives title from such a proprietor.

(2) Nothing in this Act affects the operation of section 104 of the Law of Property Act 1925 (protection of purchaser where mortgagee exercises power of sale).

(3) Subsection (1) does not apply to a proprietor carrying on a business of debt-collecting.

(4) Where, by virtue of subsection (1), a land mortgage is enforced which apart from this section would be treated as never having effect, the original creditor or owner shall be liable to indemnify the debtor or hirer against any loss thereby suffered by him.

(5) *(Applies to Scotland only.)*

(6) In the application of this section to Northern Ireland—
    (a) any reference to the proprietor of a registered charge (within the meaning of the [Land Registration Act 2002]) shall be construed as a reference to the registered owner of a charge under the Local Registration of Title (Ireland) Act 1891 or Part IV of the Land Registration Act (Northern Ireland) 1970, and
    (b) for the reference to section 104 of the Law of Property Act 1925 there shall be substituted a reference to section 21 of the Conveyancing and Law of Property Act 1881 and section 5 of the Conveyancing Act 1911.

[A169]

NOTES
This section is printed as it was in force on 15 June 2006, prior to amendments made by the Consumer Credit Act 2006 and subsequent amendments; for the text of this provision as it currently has effect, see [819].
Sub-ss (1), (6): words in square brackets substituted by the Land Registration Act 2002, s 133, Sch 11, para 11, as from 13 October 2003.
Conveyancing and Law of Property Act 1881, s 21: repealed by the Law of Property Act 1925, s 207, Sch 7.
Conveyancing Act 1911: repealed by the Settled Land Act 1925, the Trustee Act 1925 and the Law of Property Act 1925.

178 Local Acts

The Secretary of State or the Department of Commerce for Northern Ireland may by order make such amendments or repeals of any provision of any local Act as appears to the Secretary of State or, as the case may be, the Department, necessary or expedient in consequence of the replacement by this Act of the enactments relating to pawnbrokers and moneylenders.

[A170]

NOTES
This section is printed as it was in force on 15 June 2006, prior to amendments made by the Consumer Credit Act 2006 and subsequent amendments; for the text of this provision as it currently has effect, see [820].
Order: the Consumer Credit (Local Acts) Order 1984, SI 1984/1107.

Regulations, orders, etc

179 Power to prescribe form etc of secondary documents

(1) Regulations may be made as to the form and content of credit-cards, trading-checks, receipts, vouchers and other documents or things issued by creditors, owners or suppliers under or in connection with regulated agreements or by other persons in connection with linked transactions, and may in particular—
    (a) require specified information to be included in the prescribed manner in documents, and other specified material to be excluded;
    (b) contain requirements to ensure that specified information is clearly brought to the attention of the debtor or hirer, or his relative, and that one part of a document is not given insufficient or excessive prominence compared with another.

(2) If a person issues any document or thing in contravention of regulations under subsection (1) then, as from the time of the contravention but without prejudice to anything done before it, this Act shall apply as if the regulated agreement had been improperly executed by reason of a contravention of regulations under section 60(1).

[A171]

NOTES

This section is printed as it was in force on 15 June 2006, prior to amendments made by the Consumer Credit Act 2006 and subsequent amendments; for the text of this provision as it currently has effect, see [821].

180 Power to prescribe form etc of copies

(1) Regulations may be made as to the form and content of documents to be issued as copies of any executed agreement, security instrument or other document referred to in this Act, and may in particular—

    (a) require specified information to be included in the prescribed manner in any copy, and contain requirements to ensure that such information is clearly brought to the attention of a reader of the copy;

    (b) authorise the omission from a copy of certain material contained in the original, or the inclusion of such material in condensed form.

(2) A duty imposed by any provision of this Act (except section 35) to supply a copy of any document—

    (a) is not satisfied unless the copy supplied is in the prescribed form and conforms to the prescribed requirements;

    (b) is not infringed by the omission of any material, or its inclusion in condensed form, if that is authorised by regulations;

and references in this Act to copies shall be construed accordingly.

(3) Regulations may provide that a duty imposed by this Act to supply a copy of a document referred to in an unexecuted agreement or an executed agreement shall not apply to documents of a kind specified in the regulations.

[A172]

NOTES

This section is printed as it was in force on 15 June 2006, prior to amendments made by the Consumer Credit Act 2006 and subsequent amendments; for the text of this provision as it currently has effect, see [822].

Regulations: the Consumer Credit (Cancellation Notices and Copies of Documents) Regulations 1983, SI 1983/1557.

181 Power to alter monetary limits etc

(1) The Secretary of State may by order made by statutory instrument amend, or further amend, any of the following provisions of this Act so as to reduce or increase a sum mentioned in that provision, namely, sections 8(2), 15(1)(c), 17(1), 43(3)(a), 70(6), 75(3)(b), 77(1), 78(1), 79(1), 84(1), 101(7)(a), 107(1), 108(1), 109(1), 110(1), 118(1)(b), 120(1)(a), 139(5) and (7), 155(1) and 158(1).

(2) An order under subsection (1) amending section 8(2), 15(1)(c), 17(1), 43(3)(a), 75(3)(b) or 139(5) and (7) shall be of no effect unless a draft of the order has been laid before and approved by each House of Parliament.

[A173]

NOTES

This section is printed as it was in force on 15 June 2006, prior to amendments made by the Consumer Credit Act 2006 and subsequent amendments; for the text of this provision as it currently has effect, see [823].

Orders: the Consumer Credit (Increase of Monetary Limits) Order 1983, SI 1983/1878; the Consumer Credit (Further Increase of Monetary Amounts) Order 1998, SI 1998/997.

182 Regulations and orders

(1) Any power of the Secretary of State to make regulations or orders under this Act, except the power conferred by sections 2(1)(a), 181 and 192, shall be exercisable by statutory instrument subject to annulment in pursuance of a resolution of either House of Parliament.

(2) Where a power to make regulations or orders is exercisable by the Secretary of State by virtue of this Act, regulations or orders made in the exercise of that power may—

    (a) make different provision in relation to different cases or classes of case, and

    (b) exclude certain cases or classes of case, and

    (c) contain such transitional provisions as the Secretary of State thinks fit.

(3) Regulations may provide that specified expressions, when used as described by the regulations, are to be given the prescribed meaning, notwithstanding that another meaning is intended by the person using them.

(4)   Any power conferred on the Secretary of State by this Act to make orders includes power to vary or revoke an order so made.

[A174]

NOTES
This section is printed as it was in force on 15 June 2006, prior to amendments made by the Consumer Credit Act 2006 and subsequent amendments; for the text of this provision as it currently has effect, see [824].

183   Determinations etc by [OFT]

The [OFT] may vary or revoke any determination or direction made or given by [it] under this Act (other than Part III, or Part III as applied by section 147).

[A175]

NOTES
This section is printed as it was in force on 15 June 2006, prior to amendments made by the Consumer Credit Act 2006 and subsequent amendments; for the text of this provision as it currently has effect, see [825].
References to the OFT, etc: as to the abolition of the office of the Director General of Fair Trading and the substitution of the original references to the Director (and related expressions), see the note preceding s 1 at [A1].

Interpretation

184   Associates

[(1)   A person is an associate of an individual if that person is—
  (a)   the individual's husband or wife or civil partner,
  (b)   a relative of—
    (i)   the individual, or
    (ii)   the individual's husband or wife or civil partner, or
  (c)   the husband or wife or civil partner of a relative of—
    (i)   the individual, or
    (ii)   the individual's husband or wife or civil partner.]

(2)   A person is an associate of any person with whom he is in partnership, and of the husband or wife [or civil partner] or a relative of any individual with whom he is in partnership.

(3)   A body corporate is an associate of another body corporate—
  (a)   if the same person is a controller of both, or a person is a controller of one and persons who are his associates, or he and persons who are his associates, are the controllers of the other; or
  (b)   if a group of two or more persons is a controller of each company, and the groups either consist of the same persons or could be regarded as consisting of the same persons by treating (in one or more cases) a member of either group as replaced by a person of whom he is an associate.

(4)   A body corporate is an associate of another person if that person is a controller of it or if that person and persons who are his associates together are controllers of it.

(5)   In this section "relative" means brother, sister, uncle, aunt, nephew, niece, lineal ancestor or lineal descendant, … references to a husband or wife include a former husband or wife and a reputed husband [or wife, and references to a civil partner include a former civil partner] [and a reputed civil partner]; and for the purposes of this subsection a relationship shall be established as if any illegitimate child, step-child or adopted child of a person [were the legitimate child of the relationship in question].

[A176]

NOTES
This section is printed as it was in force on 15 June 2006, prior to amendments made by the Consumer Credit Act 2006 and subsequent amendments; for the text of this provision as it currently has effect, see [826].
Sub-s (1): substituted by the Civil Partnership Act 2004, s 261(1), Sch 27, para 51(1), (2), as from 5 December 2005.
Sub-s (2): words in square brackets inserted by the Civil Partnership Act 2004, s 261(1), Sch 27, para 51(1), (3), as from 5 December 2005.
Sub-s (5): word omitted repealed and words in first and third pairs of square brackets substituted by the Civil Partnership Act 2004, s 261(1), (4), Sch 27, para 51(1), (4), Sch 30; words in second pair of square brackets inserted by the Civil Partnership Act 2004 (Overseas Relationships and Consequential, etc Amendments) Order 2005, SI 2005/3129, art 4(4), Sch 4, para 2, as from 5 December 2005.

185 Agreement with more than one debtor or hirer

(1) Where an actual or prospective regulated agreement has two or more debtors or hirers (not being a partnership or an unincorporated body of persons)—

(a) anything required by or under this Act to be done to or in relation to the debtor or hirer shall be done to or in relation to each of them; and

(b) anything done under this Act by or on behalf of one of them shall have effect as if done by or on behalf of all of them.

(2) Notwithstanding subsection (1)(a), where running-account credit is provided to two or more debtors jointly, any of them may by a notice signed by him (a "dispensing notice") authorise the creditor not to comply in his case with section 78(4) (giving of periodical statement of account); and the dispensing notice shall have effect accordingly until revoked by a further notice given by the debtor to the creditor:

Provided that:

(a) a dispensing notice shall not take effect if previous dispensing notices are operative in the case of the other debtor, or each of the other debtors, as the case may be;

(b) any dispensing notices operative in relation to an agreement shall cease to have effect if any of the debtors dies.

(3) Subsection (1)(b) does not apply for the purposes of section 61(1)(a) or 127(3).

(4) Where a regulated agreement has two or more debtors or hirers (not being a partnership or an unincorporated body of persons), section 86 applies to the death of any of them.

(5) An agreement for the provision of credit, or the bailment or (in Scotland) the hiring of goods, to two or more persons jointly where—

(a) one or more of those persons is an individual, and

(b) one or more of them is a body corporate,

is a consumer credit agreement or consumer hire agreement if it would have been one had they all been individuals; and the body corporate or bodies corporate shall accordingly be included among the debtors or hirers under the agreement.

(6) Where subsection (5) applies, references in this Act to the signing of any document by the debtor or hirer shall be construed in relation to a body corporate as referring to a signing on behalf of the body corporate.

[A177]

NOTES

This section is printed as it was in force on 15 June 2006, prior to amendments made by the Consumer Credit Act 2006 and subsequent amendments; for the text of this provision as it currently has effect, see **[827]**.

186 Agreement with more than one creditor or owner

Where an actual or prospective regulated agreement has two or more creditors or owners, anything required by or under this Act to be done to, or in relation to, or by, the creditor or owner shall be effective if done to, or in relation to, or by, any one of them.

[A178]

NOTES

This section is printed as it was in force on 15 June 2006, prior to amendments made by the Consumer Credit Act 2006 and subsequent amendments; for the text of this provision as it currently has effect, see **[828]**.

187 Arrangements between creditor and supplier

(1) A consumer credit agreement shall be treated as entered into under pre-existing arrangements between a creditor and a supplier if it is entered into in accordance with, or in furtherance of, arrangements previously made between persons mentioned in subsection (4)(a), (b) or (c).

(2) A consumer credit agreement shall be treated as entered into in contemplation of future arrangements between a creditor and a supplier if it is entered into in the expectation that arrangements will subsequently be made between persons mentioned in subsection (4)(a), (b) or (c) for the supply of cash, goods and services (or any of them) to be financed by the consumer credit agreement.

(3) Arrangements shall be disregarded for the purposes of subsection (1) or (2) if—

(a) they are arrangements for the making, in specified circumstances, of payments to the supplier by the creditor, and

(b) the creditor holds himself out as willing to make, in such circumstances, payments of the kind to suppliers generally.

[(3A)   Arrangements shall also be disregarded for the purposes of subsections (1) and (2) if they are arrangements for the electronic transfer of funds from a current account at a bank within the meaning of the Bankers' Books Evidence Act 1879.]

(4)   The persons referred to in subsections (1) and (2) are—
   (a)   the creditor and the supplier;
   (b)   one of them and an associate of the other's;
   (c)   an associate of one and an associate of the other's.

(5)   Where the creditor is an associate of the supplier's, the consumer credit agreement shall be treated, unless the contrary is proved, as entered into under pre-existing arrangements between the creditor and the supplier.

[A179]

NOTES
   This section is printed as it was in force on 15 June 2006, prior to amendments made by the Consumer Credit Act 2006 and subsequent amendments; for the text of this provision as it currently has effect, see [829].
   Sub-s (3A): inserted by the Banking Act 1987, s 89, as from 1 October 1987.

188   Examples of use of new terminology

(1)   Schedule 2 shall have effect for illustrating the use of terminology employed in this Act.

(2)   The examples given in Schedule 2 are not exhaustive.

(3)   In the case of conflict between Schedule 2 and any other provision of this Act, that other provision shall prevail.

(4)   The Secretary of State may by order amend Schedule 2 by adding further examples or in any other way.

[A180]

NOTES
   This section is printed as it was in force on 15 June 2006, prior to amendments made by the Consumer Credit Act 2006 and subsequent amendments; for the text of this provision as it currently has effect, see [830].

189   Definitions

(1)   In this Act, unless the context otherwise requires—
   "advertisement" includes every form of advertising, whether in a publication, by television or radio, by display of notices, signs, labels, showcards or goods, by distribution of samples, circulars, catalogues, price lists or other material, by exhibition of pictures, models or films, or in any other way, and references to the publishing of advertisements shall be construed accordingly;
   "advertiser" in relation to an advertisement, means any person indicated by the advertisement as willing to enter into transactions to which the advertisement relates;
   "ancillary credit business" has the meaning given by section 145(1);
   "antecedent negotiations" has the meaning given by section 56;
   "appeal period" means the period beginning on the first day on which an appeal to the Secretary of State may be brought and ending on the last day on which it may be brought or, if it is brought, ending on its final determination, or abandonment;
   ["appropriate method" means–
      (a)   post, or
      (b)   transmission in the form of an electronic communication in accordance with section 176A(1);]
   "assignment", in relation to Scotland, means assignation;
   "associate" shall be construed in accordance with section 184;
      [......]
   "bill of sale" has the meaning given by section 4 of the Bills of Sale Act 1878 or, for Northern Ireland, by section 4 of the Bills of Sale (Ireland) Act 1879;
   ["building society" means a building society within the meaning of the Building Societies Act 1986;]
   "business" includes profession or trade, and references to a business apply subject to subsection (2);
   "cancellable agreement" means a regulated agreement which, by virtue of section 67, may be cancelled by the debtor or hirer;
   "canvass" shall be construed in accordance with sections 48 and 153;
   "cash" includes money in any form;
   "charity" means as respects England and Wales a charity registered under [the Charities Act 1993] or an exempt charity (within the meaning of that Act), [as respects] Northern Ireland an institution or other organisation established for charitable purposes only

("organisation" including any persons administering a trust and "charitable" being construed in the same way as if it were contained in the Income Tax Acts) [and as respects Scotland a body entered in the Scottish Charity Register];

"conditional sale agreement" means an agreement for the sale of goods or land under which the purchase price or part of it is payable by instalments, and the property in the goods or land is to remain in the seller (notwithstanding that the buyer is to be in possession of the goods or land) until such conditions as to the payment of instalments or otherwise as may be specified in the agreement are fulfilled;

"consumer credit agreement" has the meaning given by section 8, and includes a consumer credit agreement which is cancelled under section 69(1), or becomes subject to section 69(2), so far as the agreement remains in force;

"consumer credit business" means any business so far as it comprises or relates to the provision of credit under regulated consumer credit agreements;

"consumer hire agreement" has the meaning given by section 15;

"consumer hire business" means any business so far as it comprises or relates to the bailment or (in Scotland) the hiring of goods under regulated consumer hire agreements;

"controller", in relation to a body corporate, means a person—

    (a)   in accordance with whose directions or instructions the directors of the body corporate or of another body corporate which is its controller (or any of them) are accustomed to act, or

    (b)   who, either alone or with any associate or associates, is entitled to exercise or control the exercise of, one third or more of the voting power at any general meeting of the body corporate or of another body corporate which is its controller;

"copy" shall be construed in accordance with section 180;

"costs", in relation to Scotland, means expenses;

"court" means in relation to England and Wales the county court, in relation to Scotland the sheriff court and in relation to Northern Ireland the High Court or the county court;

"credit" shall be construed in accordance with section 9;

"credit-broker" means a person carrying on a business of credit brokerage;

"credit brokerage" has the meaning given by section 145(2);

"credit limit" has the meaning given by section 10(2);

"creditor" means the person providing credit under a consumer credit agreement or the person to whom his rights and duties under the agreement have passed by assignment or operation of law, and in relation to a prospective consumer credit agreement, includes the prospective creditor;

"credit reference agency" has the meaning given by section 145(8);

"credit-sale agreement" means an agreement for the sale of goods, under which the purchase price or part of it is payable by instalments, but which is not a conditional sale agreement;

"credit-token" has the meaning given by section 14(1);

"credit-token agreement" means a regulated agreement for the provision of credit in connection with the use of a credit-token;

"debt-adjusting" has the meaning given by section 145(5);

"debt-collecting" has the meaning given by section 145(7);

"debt-counselling" has the meaning given by section 145(6);

"debtor" means the individual receiving credit under a consumer credit agreement or the person to whom his rights and duties under the agreement have passed by assignment or operation of law, and in relation to a prospective consumer credit agreement includes the prospective debtor;

"debtor-creditor agreement" has the meaning given by section 13;

"debtor-creditor-supplier agreement" has the meaning given by section 12;

"default notice" has the meaning given by section 87(1);

"deposit" means [(except in section 16(10) and 25(1B))] any sum payable by a debtor or hirer by way of deposit or down-payment, or credited or to be credited to him on account of any deposit or down-payment, whether the sum is to be or has been paid to the creditor or owner or any other person, or is to be or has been discharged by a payment of money or a transfer or delivery of goods or by any other means;

"electric line" has the meaning given by [the Electricity Act 1989] or, for Northern Ireland, [the Electricity (Northern Ireland) Order 1992];

["electronic communication" means an electronic communication within the meaning of the Electronic Communications Act 2000 (c 7);]

"embodies" and related words shall be construed in accordance with subsection (4);

"enforcement authority" has the meaning given by section 161(1);

"enforcement order" means an order under section 65(1), 105(7)(a) or (b), 111(2) or 124(1) or (2);

"executed agreement" means a document, signed by or on behalf of the parties, embodying the terms of a regulated agreement, or such of them as have been reduced to writing;

"exempt agreement" means an agreement specified in or under section 16;

"finance" means to finance wholly or partly and "financed" and "refinanced" shall be construed accordingly;

"file" and "copy of the file" have the meanings given by section 158(5);

"fixed-sum credit" has the meaning given by section 10(1)(b);

"friendly society" means a society registered [or treated as registered under the Friendly Societies Act 1974 or the Friendly Societies Act 1992] ... ;

"future arrangements" shall be construed in accordance with section 187;

"general notice" means a notice published by the [OFT] at a time and in a manner appearing to [it] suitable for securing that the notice is seen within a reasonable time by persons likely to be affected by it;

"give", means, deliver or send [by an appropriate method] to;

"goods" has the meaning given by [section 61(1) of the Sale of Goods Act 1979];

"group licence" has the meaning given by section 22(1)(b);

"High Court" means Her Majesty's High Court of Justice, or the Court of Session in Scotland or the High Court of Justice in Northern Ireland;

"hire-purchase agreement" means an agreement, other than a conditional sale agreement, under which—

    (a)   goods are bailed or (in Scotland) hired in return for periodical payments by the person to whom they are bailed or hired, and

    (b)   the property in the goods will pass to that person if the terms of the agreement are complied with and one or more of the following occurs—

        (i)   the exercise of an option to purchase by that person,

        (ii)   the doing of any other specified act by any party to the agreement,

        (iii)   the happening of any other specified event;

"hirer" means the individual to whom goods are bailed or (in Scotland) hired under a consumer hire agreement, or the person to whom his rights and duties under the agreement have passed by assignment or operation of law, and in relation to a prospective consumer hire agreement includes the prospective hirer;

"individual" includes a partnership or other unincorporated body of persons not consisting entirely of bodies corporate;

"installation" means—

    (a)   the installing of any electric line or any gas or water pipe,

    (b)   the fixing of goods to the premises where they are to be used, and the alteration of premises to enable goods to be used on them,

    (c)   where it is reasonably necessary that goods should be constructed or erected on the premises where they are to be used, any work carried out for the purpose of constructing or erecting them on those premises;

"judgment" includes an order or decree made by any court;

"land", includes an interest in land, and in relation to Scotland includes heritable subjects of whatever description;

"land improvement company" means an improvement company as defined by section 7 of the Improvement of Land Act 1899;

"land mortgage" includes any security charged on land;

"licence" means a licence under Part III (including that Part as applied to ancillary credit businesses by section 147);

"licensed", in relation to any act, means authorised by a licence to do the act or cause or permit another person to do it;

"licensee", in the case of a group licence, includes any person covered by the licence;

"linked transaction" has the meaning given by section 19(1);

"local authority", in relation to England ..., means ... a county council, a London borough council, a district council, the Common Council of the City of London, or the Council of Isles of Scilly, [in relation to Wales means a county council or a county borough council,] and in relation to Scotland, means a [council constituted under section 2 of the Local Government etc (Scotland) Act 1994], and, in relation to Northern Ireland, means a district council;

"modifying agreement" has the meaning given by section 82(2);

"mortgage", in relation to Scotland, includes any heritable security;

"multiple agreement" has the meaning given by section 18(1);

"negotiator" has the meaning given by section 56(1);

"non-commercial agreement" means a consumer credit agreement or a consumer hire agreement not made by the creditor or owner in the course of a business carried on by him;

"notice" means notice in writing;

"notice of cancellation" has the meaning given by section 69(1);

["OFT" means the Office of Fair Trading;]

"owner" means a person who bails or (in Scotland) hires out goods under a consumer hire agreement or the person to whom his rights and duties under the agreement have passed by assignment or operation of law, and in relation to a prospective consumer hire agreement, includes the prospective bailor or persons from whom the goods are to be hired;

"pawn" means any article subject to a pledge;

"pawn-receipt" has the meaning given by section 114;

"pawnee" and "pawnor" include any person to whom the rights and duties of the original pawnee or the original pawnor, as the case may be, have passed by assignment or operation of law;

"payment" includes tender;

"personal credit agreement" has the meaning given by section 8(1);

"pledge" means the pawnee's rights over an article taken in pawn;

"prescribed" means prescribed by regulations made by the Secretary of State;

"pre-existing arrangements" shall be construed in accordance with section 187;

"principal agreement" has the meaning given by section 19(1);

"protected goods" has the meaning given by section 90(7);

"quotation" has the meaning given by section 52(1)(a);

"redemption period" has the meaning given by section 116(3);

"register" means the register kept by the [OFT] under section 35;

"regulated agreement" means a consumer credit agreement, or consumer hire agreement, other than an exempt agreement, and "regulated" and "unregulated" shall be construed accordingly;

"regulations" means regulations made by the Secretary of State;

"relative", except in section 184, means a person who is an associate by virtue of section 184(1);

"representation" includes any condition or warranty, and any other statement or undertaking, whether oral or in writing;

"restricted-use credit agreement" and "restricted-use credit" have the meanings given by section 11(1);

"rules of court", in relation to Northern Ireland means, in relation to the High Court, rules made under section 7 of the Northern Ireland Act 1962, and, in relation to any other court, rules made by the authority having for the time being power to make rules regulating the practice and procedure in that court;

"running-account credit" shall be construed in accordance with section 10;

"security", in relation to an actual or prospective consumer credit agreement or consumer hire agreement, or any linked transaction, means a mortgage, charge, pledge, bond, debenture, indemnity, guarantee, bill, note or other right provided by the debtor or hirer, or at his request (express or implied), to secure the carrying out of the obligations of the debtor or hirer under the agreement;

"security instrument" has the meaning given by section 105(2);

"serve on" means deliver or send [by an appropriate method] to;

"signed" shall be construed in accordance with subsection (3);

"small agreement" has the meaning given by section 17(1), and "small" in relation to an agreement within any category shall be construed accordingly;

"specified fee" shall be construed in accordance with section 2(4) and (5);

"standard licence" has the meaning given by section 22(1)(a);

"supplier" has the meaning given by section 11(1)(b) or 12(c) or 13(c) or, in relation to an agreement falling within section 11(1)(a), means the creditor, and includes a person to whom the rights and duties of a supplier (as so defined) have passed by assignment or operation of law, or (in relation to a prospective agreement) the prospective supplier;

"surety" means the person by whom any security is provided, or the person to whom his rights and duties in relation to the security have passed by assignment or operation of law;

"technical grounds" shall be construed in accordance with subsection (5);

"time order" has the meaning given by section 129(1);

"total charge for credit" means a sum calculated in accordance with regulations under section 20(1);

"total price" means the total sum payable by the debtor under a hire-purchase agreement or a conditional sale agreement, including any sum payable on the exercise of an option to purchase, but excluding any sum payable as a penalty or as compensation or damages for a breach of the agreement;

      .....

"unexecuted agreement" means a document embodying the terms of a prospective regulated agreement, or such of them as it is intended to reduce to writing;

"unlicensed" means without a licence but applies only in relation to acts for which a licence is required;

"unrestricted-use credit agreement" and "unrestricted-use credit" have the meanings given by section 11(2);

"working day" means any day other than—

(a)   Saturday or Sunday,

(b)   Christmas Day or Good Friday,

(c)   a bank holiday within the meaning given by section 1 of the Banking and Financial Dealings Act 1971.

(2)   A person is not to be treated as carrying on a particular type of business merely because occasionally he enters into transactions belonging to a business of that type.

(3)   Any provision of this Act requiring a document to be signed is complied with by a body corporate if the document is sealed by that body.

This subsection does not apply to Scotland.

(4)   A document embodies a provision if the provision is set out either in the document itself or in another document referred to in it.

(5)   An application dismissed by the court or the [OFT] shall, if the court or the [OFT] (as the case may be) so certifies, be taken to be dismissed on technical grounds only.

(6)   Except in so far as the context otherwise requires, any reference in this Act to an enactment shall be construed as a reference to that enactment as amended by or under any other enactment, including this Act.

(7)   In this Act, except where otherwise indicated—

(a)   a reference to a numbered Part, section or Schedule is a reference to the Part or section of, or the Schedule to, this Act so numbered, and

(b)   a reference in a section to a numbered subsection is a reference to the subsection of that section so numbered, and

(c)   a reference in a section, subsection or Schedule to a numbered paragraph is a reference to the paragraph of that section, subsection or Schedule so numbered.

[A181]

NOTES

This section is printed as it was in force on 15 June 2006, prior to amendments made by the Consumer Credit Act 2006 and subsequent amendments; for the text of this provision as it currently has effect, see [831].

Sub-s (1) is amended as follows:

definitions "appropriate method", "electronic communication" inserted and in definitions "give" and "serve on", words in square brackets substituted by the Consumer Credit Act 1974 (Electronic Communications) Order 2004, SI 2004/3236, art 2(1), (8), (9), as from 31 December 2004;

definition "authorised institution" inserted by the Banking Act 1987, s 88, as from 1 October 1987, and repealed by the Financial Services and Markets Act 2000 (Consequential Amendments and Repeals) Order 2001, SI 2001/3649, art 176(a), as from 1 December 2001;

definition "building society" substituted by the Building Societies Act 1986, s 120, Sch 18, Pt I, para 10(4), as from 1 January 1987;

in definition "charity" words in first pair of square brackets substituted by the Charities Act 1993, s 98(1), Sch 6, para 30, as from 1 March 1996, words in second pair of square brackets substituted and words in third pair of square brackets added by the Charities and Trustee Investment (Scotland) Act 2005 (Consequential Provisions and Modifications) Order 2006, SI 2006/242, art 5, Schedule, Pt 1, para 1, as from 1 April 2006;

in definition "deposit" words in square brackets inserted by SI 2001/3649, art 176(b), as from 1 December 2001;

definition "Director" (omitted) repealed by the Enterprise Act 2002, s 278, Sch 25, para 6(1), (38)(a)(i), Sch 26, as from 1 April 2003;

in definition "electric line" words in first pair of square brackets substituted by the Electricity Act 1989, s 112(1), Sch 16, para 17(1), (3), as from 31 March 1990, words in second pair of square brackets substituted by the Electricity (Northern Ireland) Order 1992, SI 1992/231, art 95(1), Sch 12, para 15;

in definition "friendly society" words in square brackets substituted by SI 2001/3649, art 176(c), as from 1 December 2001, words omitted repealed by the Friendly Societies Act 1992, s 120, Sch 22, Pt I, as from 1 January 1994;

in definition "goods" words in square brackets substituted by the Sale of Goods Act 1979, s 63, Sch 2, para 18, as from 1 January 1980;

definition "insurance company" (omitted) repealed by SI 2001/3649, art 176(a), as from 1 December 2001;

in definition "local authority" words omitted in the first place repealed, and words in first pair of square brackets inserted, by the Local Government (Wales) Act 1994, s 66(6), (8), Sch 16, para 45, Sch 18, as from 1 April 1996, words omitted in the second place repealed by the Local Government Act 1985, s 102, Sch 17, as from 16 July 1985, and words in second pair of square brackets substituted by the Local Government etc (Scotland) Act 1994, s 180(1), Sch 13, para 94, as from 1 April 1996;

definition "minor" (omitted) repealed by the Age of Legal Capacity (Scotland) Act 1991, s 10, Sch 2; and definition "OFT" inserted by the Enterprise Act 2002, s 278(1), Sch 25, para 6(1), (38)(a)(iii), as from 1 April 2003;

References to the OFT, etc: as to the abolition of the office of the Director General of Fair Trading and the substitution of the original references to the Director (and related expressions), see the note preceding s 1 at **[A1]**.

[189A   Meaning of "consumer credit EEA firm"

In this Act "consumer credit EEA firm" means an EEA firm falling within sub-paragraph (a), (b) or (c) of paragraph 5 of Schedule 3 to the Financial Services and Markets Act 2000 carrying on, or seeking to carry on, consumer credit business, consumer hire business or ancillary credit business for which a licence would be required under this Act but for paragraph 15(3) of Schedule 3 to the Financial Services and Markets Act 2000.]

[A182]

NOTES
This section is printed as it was in force on 15 June 2006, prior to amendments made by the Consumer Credit Act 2006 and subsequent amendments; for the text of this provision as it currently has effect, see [832].
Inserted by the Financial Services and Markets Act 2000 (Consequential Amendments and Repeals) Order 2001, SI 2001/3649, art 177, as from 1 December 2001.

Miscellaneous

190   Financial provisions

(1)   There shall be defrayed out of money provided by Parliament—
   (a)   all expenses incurred by the Secretary of State in consequence of the provisions of this Act;
   (b)   any expenses incurred in consequence of those provisions by any other Minister of the Crown or Government department;
   (c)   any increase attributable to this Act in the sums payable out of money so provided under the Superannuation Act 1972 or the Fair Trading Act 1973.

(2)   Any fees received by the [OFT] under this Act shall be paid into the Consolidated Fund.

[A183]

NOTES
This section is printed as it was in force on 15 June 2006, prior to amendments made by the Consumer Credit Act 2006 and subsequent amendments; for the text of this provision as it currently has effect, see [833].
References to the OFT, etc: as to the abolition of the office of the Director General of Fair Trading and the substitution of the original references to the Director (and related expressions), see the note preceding s 1 at **[A1]**.

191   (*Applies to Northern Ireland only.*)

192   Transitional and commencement provisions, amendments and repeals

(1)   The provisions of Schedule 3 shall have effect for the purposes of this Act.

(2)   The appointment of a day for the purposes of any provision of Schedule 3 shall be effected by an order of the Secretary of State made by statutory instrument; and any such order shall include a provision amending Schedule 3 so as to insert an express reference to the day appointed.

(3)   Subject to subsection (4)—
   (a)   the enactments specified in Schedule 4 shall have effect subject to the amendments specified in that Schedule (being minor amendments or amendments consequential on the preceding provisions of this Act), and
   (b)   the enactments specified in Schedule 5 are hereby repealed to the extent shown in column 3 of that Schedule.

(4)   The Secretary of State shall by order made by statutory instrument provide for the coming into operation of the amendments contained in Schedule 4 and the repeals contained in Schedule 5, and those amendments and repeals shall have effect only as provided by an order so made.

[A184]

NOTES
This section is printed as it was in force on 15 June 2006, prior to amendments made by the Consumer Credit Act 2006 and subsequent amendments; for the text of this provision as it currently has effect, see [834].
Orders: the Consumer Credit Act 1974 (Commencement No 1) Order 1975, SI 1975/2123; the Consumer Credit Act 1974 (Commencement No 2) Order 1977, SI 1977/325; the Consumer Credit Act 1974 (Commencement No 3) Order 1977, SI 1977/802; the Consumer Credit Act 1974 (Commencement No 4) Order 1977, SI 1977/2163; the Consumer Credit Act 1974 (Commencement No 5) Order 1979, SI 1979/1685; the Consumer Credit Act 1974 (Commencement No 6) Order 1980, SI 1980/50; the Consumer Credit Act 1974 (Commencement No 7) Order 1981, SI 1981/280; the Consumer Credit Act 1974 (Commencement No 8) Order 1983, SI 1983/1551; the Consumer Credit Act 1974 (Commencement No 9) Order 1984, SI 1984/436; the Consumer Credit Act 1974 (Commencement No 10) Order 1989, SI 1989/1128

193 Short title and extent

(1) This Act may be cited as the Consumer Credit Act 1974.

(2) This Act extends to Northern Ireland.

[A185]

NOTES

This section is printed as it was in force on 15 June 2006, prior to amendments made by the Consumer Credit Act 2006 and subsequent amendments; for the text of this provision as it currently has effect, see [835].

SCHEDULES

SCHEDULE 1
PROSECUTION AND PUNISHMENT OF OFFENCES

Section 167

1 Section	*2* Offence	*3* Mode of prosecution	*4* Imprisonment or fine
7	Knowingly or recklessly giving false information to [OFT].	(a) Summarily. (b) On indictment.	[The prescribed sum]. 2 years or a fine or both.
39(1)	Engaging in activities requiring a licence when not a licensee.	(a) Summarily. (b) On indictment.	[The prescribed sum]. 2 years or a fine or both.
39(2)	Carrying on business under a name not specified in licence.	(a) Summarily. (b) On indictment.	[The prescribed sum]. 2 years or a fine or both.
39(3)	Failure to notify changes in registered particulars.	(a) Summarily. (b) On indictment.	[The prescribed sum]. 2 years or a fine or both.
45	Advertising credit where goods etc not available for cash.	(a) Summarily. (b) On indictment.	[The prescribed sum]. 2 years or a fine or both.
46(1)	False or misleading advertisements.	(a) Summarily. (b) On indictment.	[The prescribed sum]. 2 years or a fine or both.
47(1)	Advertising infringements.	(a) Summarily. (b) On indictment.	[The prescribed sum]. 2 years or a fine or both.
49(1)	Canvassing debtor-creditor agreements off trade premises.	(a) Summarily. (b) On indictment.	[The prescribed sum]. 1 year or a fine or both.
49(2)	Soliciting debtor-creditor agreements during visits made in response to previous oral requests.	(a) Summarily. (b) On indictment.	[The prescribed sum]. 1 year or a fine or both.
50(1)	Sending circulars to minors.	(a) Summarily. (b) On indictment.	[The prescribed sum]. 1 year or a fine or both.
51(1)	Supplying unsolicited credit-tokens.	(a) Summarily. (b) On indictment.	[The prescribed sum]. 2 years or a fine or both.

1 Section	2 Offence	3 Mode of prosecution	4 Imprisonment or fine
77(4)	Failure of creditor under fixed-sum credit agreement to supply copies of documents etc.	Summarily.	[Level 4 on the standard scale].
78(6)	Failure of creditor under running-account credit agreement to supply copies of documents etc.	Summarily.	[Level 4 on the standard scale].
79(3)	Failure of owner under consumer hire agreement to supply copies of documents etc.	Summarily.	[Level 4 on the standard scale].
80(2)	Failure to tell creditor or owner whereabouts of goods.	Summarily.	[Level 3 on the standard scale].
85(2)	Failure of creditor to supply copy of credit-token agreement.	Summarily.	[Level 4 on the standard scale.].
97(3)	Failure to supply debtor with statement of amount required to discharge agreement.	Summarily.	[Level 3 on the standard scale].
103(5)	Failure to deliver notice relating to discharge of agreements.	Summarily.	[Level 3 on the standard scale].
107(4)	Failure of creditor to give information to surety under fixed-sum credit agreement.	Summarily.	[Level 4 on the standard scale].
108(4)	Failure of creditor to give information to surety under running-account credit agreement.	Summarily.	[Level 4 on the standard scale].
109(3)	Failure of owner to give information to surety under consumer hire agreement.	Summarily.	[Level 4 on the standard scale].
110(3)	Failure of creditor or owner to supply a copy of any security instrument to debtor or hirer.	Summarily.	[Level 4 on the standard scale].
114(2)	Taking pledges from minors.	(a) Summarily. (b) On indictment.	[The prescribed sum]. 1 year or a fine or both.
115	Failure to supply copies of a pledge agreement or pawn-receipt.	Summarily.	[Level 4 on the standard scale.]
119(1)	Unreasonable refusal to allow pawn to be redeemed.	Summarily.	[Level 4 on the standard scale.]

1 Section	2 Offence	3 Mode of prosecution	4 Imprisonment or fine
154	Canvassing ancillary credit services off trade premises.	(a) Summarily.	[The prescribed sum].
		(b) On indictment.	1 year or a fine or both.
157(3)	Refusal to give name etc of credit reference agency.	Summarily.	[Level 4 on the standard scale.]
158(4)	Failure of credit reference agency to disclose filed information.	Summarily.	[Level 4 on the standard scale.]
159(6)	Failure of credit reference agency to correct information.	Summarily.	[Level 4 on the standard scale.]
160(6)	Failure of credit reference agency to comply with section 160(3) or (4).	Summarily.	[Level 4 on the standard scale.]
162(6)	Impersonation of enforcement authority officers.	(a) Summarily.	[The prescribed sum].
		(b) On indictment.	2 years or a fine or both.
165(1)	Obstruction of enforcement authority officers.	Summarily.	[Level 4 on the standard scale.]
165(2)	Giving false information to enforcement authority officers.	(a) Summarily.	[The prescribed sum].
		(b) On indictment.	2 years or a fine or both.
167(2)	Contravention of regulations under section 44, 52, 53, 54 or 112.	(a) Summarily.	[The prescribed sum].
		(b) On indictment.	2 years or a fine or both.
174(5)	Wrongful disclosure of information.	(a) Summarily.	[The prescribed sum].
		(b) On indictment.	2 years or a fine or both.

[A186]

NOTES

This Schedule is printed as it was in force on 15 June 2006, prior to amendments made by the Consumer Credit Act 2006 and subsequent amendments; for the text of this provision as it currently has effect, see [836].

References to the prescribed sum substituted by virtue of the Magistrates' Courts Act 1980, s 32(2).

References to a level on the standard scale substituted by virtue of the Criminal Justice Act 1982, ss 38, 46.

References to the OFT, etc: as to the abolition of the office of the Director General of Fair Trading and the substitution of the original references to the Director (and related expressions), see the note preceding s 1 at [A1].

SCHEDULE 2
EXAMPLES OF USE OF NEW TERMINOLOGY

Section 188(1)

PART I
LIST OF TERMS

Term	Defined in section	Illustrated by example(s)
Advertisement	189(1)	2
Advertiser	189(1)	2
Antecedent negotiations	56	1, 2, 3, 4
Cancellable agreement	67	4
Consumer credit agreement	8	5, 6, 7, 15, 19, 21
Consumer hire agreement	15	20, 24
Credit	9	16, 19, 21
Credit-broker	189(1)	2
Credit limit	10(2)	6, 7, 19, 22, 23
Creditor	189(1)	1, 2, 3, 4
Credit-sale agreement	189(1)	5
Credit-token	14	3, 14, 16
Credit-token agreement	14	3, 14, 16, 22
Debtor-creditor agreement	13	8, 16, 17, 18
Debtor-creditor-supplier agreement	12	8, 16
Fixed-sum credit	10	9, 10, 17, 23
Hire-purchase agreement	189(1)	10
Individual	189(1)	19, 24
Linked transaction	19	11
Modifying agreement	82(2)	24
Multiple agreement	18	16, 18
Negotiator	56(1)	1, 2, 3, 4
Personal credit agreement	8(1)	19
Pre-existing arrangements	187	8, 21
Restricted-use credit	11	10, 12, 13, 14, 16
Running-account credit	10	15, 16, 18, 23
Small agreement	17	16, 17, 22
Supplier	189(1)	3, 14
Total charge for credit	20	5, 10
Total price	189(1)	10
Unrestricted-use credit	11	8, 12, 16, 17, 18

[A187]

NOTES
 This Schedule is printed as it was in force on 15 June 2006, prior to amendments made by the Consumer Credit Act 2006 and subsequent amendments; for the text of this provision as it currently has effect, see [837].

PART II
EXAMPLES

EXAMPLE 1

Facts. Correspondence passes between an employee of a moneylending company (writing on behalf of the company) and an individual about the terms on which the company would grant him a loan under a regulated agreement.

Analysis. The correspondence constitutes antecedent negotiations falling within section 56(1)(a), the moneylending company being both creditor and negotiator.

EXAMPLE 2

Facts. Representations are made about goods in a poster displayed by a shopkeeper near the goods, the goods being selected by a customer who has read the poster and then sold by the shopkeeper to a finance company introduced by him (with whom he has a business relationship). The goods are disposed of by the finance company to the customer under a regulated hire-purchase agreement.

Analysis. The representations in the poster constitute antecedent negotiations falling within section 56(1)(b), the shopkeeper being the credit-broker and negotiator and the finance company being the creditor. The poster is an advertisement and the shopkeeper is the advertiser.

EXAMPLE 3

Facts. Discussions take place between a shopkeeper and a customer about goods the customer wishes to buy using a credit-card issued by the D Bank under a regulated agreement.

Analysis. The discussions constitute antecedent negotiations falling within section 56(1)(c), the shopkeeper being the supplier and negotiator and the D Bank the creditor. The credit-card is a credit-token as defined in section 14(1), and the regulated agreement under which it was issued is a credit-token agreement as defined in section 14(2).

EXAMPLE 4

Facts. Discussions take place and correspondence passes between a secondhand car dealer and a customer about a car, which is then sold by the dealer to the customer under a regulated conditional sale agreement. Subsequently, on a revocation of that agreement by consent, the car is resold by the dealer to a finance company introduced by him (with whom he has a business relationship), who in turn dispose of it to the same customer under a regulated hire-purchase agreement.

Analysis. The discussions and correspondence constitute antecedent negotiations in relation both to the conditional sale agreement and the hire-purchase agreement. They fall under section 56(1)(a) in relation to the conditional sale agreement, the dealer being the creditor and the negotiator. In relation to the hire-purchase agreement they fall within section 56(1)(b), the dealer continuing to be treated as the negotiator but the finance company now being the creditor. Both agreements are cancellable if the discussions took place when the individual conducting the negotiations (whether the "negotiator" or his employee or agent) was in the presence of the debtor, unless the unexecuted agreement was signed by the debtor at trade premises (as defined in section 67(b)). If the discussions all took place by telephone however, or the unexecuted agreement was signed by the debtor on trade premises (as so defined) the agreements are not cancellable.

EXAMPLE 5

Facts. E agrees to sell to F (an individual) an item of furniture in return for 24 monthly instalments of £10 payable in arrears. The property in the goods passes to F immediately.

Analysis. This is a credit-sale agreement (see definition of "credit-sale agreement" in section 189(1)). The credit provided amounts to £240 less the amount which, according to regulations made under section 20(1), constitutes the total charge for credit. (This amount is required to be deducted by section 9(4)). Accordingly the agreement falls within section 8(2) and is a consumer credit agreement.

EXAMPLE 6

Facts. The G Bank grants H (an individual) an unlimited overdraft, with an increased rate of interest on so much of any debit balance as exceeds £2,000.

Analysis. Although the overdraft purports to be unlimited, the stipulation for increased interest above £2,000 brings the agreement within section 10(3)(b)(ii) and it is a consumer credit agreement.

EXAMPLE 7

Facts. J is an individual who owns a small shop which usually carries a stock worth about £1,000. K makes a stocking agreement under which he undertakes to provide on short-term credit the stock needed from time to time by J without any specified limit.

Analysis. Although the agreement appears to provide unlimited credit, it is probable, having regard to the stock usually carried by J, that his indebtedness to K will not at any time rise above £5,000. Accordingly the agreement falls within section 10(3)(b)(iii) and is a consumer credit agreement.

EXAMPLE 8

Facts. U, a moneylender, lends £500 to V (an individual) knowing he intends to use it to buy office equipment from W. W introduced V to U, it being his practice to introduce customers needing finance to him. Sometimes U gives W a commission for this and sometimes not. U pays the £500 direct to V.

Analysis. Although this appears to fall under section 11(1)(b), it is excluded by section 11(3) and is therefore (by section 11(2)) an unrestricted-use credit agreement. Whether it is a debtor-creditor agreement (by section 13(c)) or a debtor-creditor-supplier agreement (by section 12(c)) depends on whether the previous dealings between U and W amount to "pre-existing arrangements", that is whether the agreement can be taken to have been entered into "in accordance with, or in furtherance of" arrangements previously made between U and W, as laid down in section 187(1).

EXAMPLE 9

Facts. A agrees to lend B (an individual) £4,500 in nine monthly instalments of £500.

Analysis. This is a cash loan and is a form of credit (see section 9 and definition of "cash" in section 189(1)). Accordingly it falls within section 10(1)(b) and is fixed-sum credit amounting to £4,500.

EXAMPLE 10

Facts. C (in England) agrees to bail goods to D (an individual) in return for periodical payments. The agreement provides for the property in the goods to pass to D on payment of a total of £7,500 and the exercise by D of an option to purchase. The sum of £7,500 includes a down-payment of £1,000. It also includes an amount which, according to regulations made under section 20(1), constitutes a total charge for credit of £1,500.

Analysis. This is a hire-purchase agreement with a deposit of £1,000 and a total price of £7,500 (see definitions of "hire-purchase agreement", "deposit" and "total price" in section 189(1)). By section 9(3), it is taken to provide credit amounting to £7,500 – (£1,500 + £1,000), which equals £5,000. Under section 8(2), the agreement is therefore a consumer credit agreement, and under sections 9(3) and 11(1) it is a restricted-use credit agreement for fixed-sum credit. A similar result would follow if the agreement by C had been a hiring agreement in Scotland.

EXAMPLE 11

Facts. X (an individual) borrows £500 from Y (Finance). As a condition of the granting of the loan X is required—
    (a)   to execute a second mortgage on his house in favour of Y (Finance), and
    (b)   to take out a policy of insurance on his life with Y (Insurances).

In accordance with the loan agreement, the policy is charged to Y (Finance) as collateral security for the loan. The two companies are associates within the meaning of section 184(3).

Analysis. The second mortgage is a transaction for the provision of security and accordingly does not fall within section 19(1), but the taking out of the insurance policy is a linked transaction falling within section 19(1)(a). The charging of the policy is a separate transaction (made between different parties) for the provision of security and again is excluded from section 19(1). The only linked transaction is therefore the taking out of the insurance policy. If X had not been required by the loan agreement to take out the policy, but it had been done at the suggestion of Y (Finance) to induce them to enter into the loan agreement, it would have been a linked transaction under section 19(1)(c)(i) by virtue of section 19(2)(a).

EXAMPLE 12

Facts. The N Bank agrees to lend O (an individual) £2,000 to buy a car from P. To make sure the loan is used as intended, the N Bank stipulates that the money must be paid by it direct to P.

Analysis. The agreement is a consumer credit agreement by virtue of section 8(2). Since it falls within section 11(1)(b), it is a restricted-use credit agreement, P being the supplier. If the N Bank had not stipulated for direct payment to the supplier, section 11(3) would have operated and made the agreement into one for unrestricted-use credit.

EXAMPLE 13

Facts. Q, a debt-adjuster, agrees to pay off debts owed by R (an individual) to various moneylenders. For this purpose the agreement provides for the making of a loan by Q to R in return for R's agreeing to repay the loan by instalments with interest. The loan money is not paid over to R but retained by Q and used to pay off the moneylenders.

Analysis. This is an agreement to refinance existing indebtedness of the debtor's, and if the loan by Q does not exceed £5,000 is a restricted-use credit agreement falling within section 11(1)(c).

EXAMPLE 14

Facts. On payment of £1, S issues to T (an individual) a trading check under which T can spend up to £20 at any shop which has agreed, or in future agrees, to accept S's trading checks.

Analysis. The trading check is a credit-token falling within section 14(1)(b). The credit-token agreement is a restricted-use credit agreement within section 11(1)(b), any shop in which the credit-token is used being the "supplier". The fact that further shops may be added after the issue of the credit-token is irrelevant in view of section 11(4).

EXAMPLE 15

Facts. A retailer, L, agrees with M (an individual) to open an account in M's name and, in return for M's promise to pay a specified minimum sum into the account each month and to pay a monthly charge for credit, agrees to allow to be debited to the account, in respect of purchases made by M from L, such sums as will not increase the debit balance at any time beyond the credit limit, defined in the agreement as a given multiple of the specified minimum sum.

Analysis. This arrangement provides credit falling within the definition of running-account credit in section 10(1)(a). Provided the credit limit is not over £5,000, the agreement falls within section 8(2) and is a consumer credit agreement for running-account credit.

EXAMPLE 16

Facts. Under an unsecured agreement, A (Credit), an associate of the A Bank, issues to B (an individual) a credit-card for use in obtaining cash on credit from A (Credit), to be paid by branches of the A Bank (acting as agent of A (Credit)), or goods or cash from suppliers or banks who have agreed to honour credit-cards issued by A (Credit). The credit limit is £30.

Analysis. This is a credit-token agreement falling within section 14(1)(a) and (b). It is a regulated consumer credit agreement for running-account credit. Since the credit limit does not exceed £30, the agreement is a small agreement. So far as the agreement relates to goods it is a debtor-creditor-supplier agreement within section 12(b), since it provides restricted-use credit under section 11(1)(b). So far as it relates to cash it is a debtor-creditor agreement within section 13(c) and the credit it provides is unrestricted-use credit. This is therefore a multiple agreement. In that the whole agreement falls within several of the categories of agreement mentioned in this Act, it is, by section 18(3), to be treated as an agreement in each of those categories. So far as it is a debtor-creditor-supplier agreement providing restricted-use credit it is, by section 18(2), to be treated as a separate agreement; and similarly so far as it is a debtor-creditor agreement providing unrestricted-used credit. (See also Example 22.)

EXAMPLE 17

Facts. The manager of the C Bank agrees orally with D (an individual) to open a current account in D's name. Nothing is said about overdraft facilities. After maintaining the account in credit for some weeks, D draws a cheque in favour of E for an amount exceeding D's credit balance by £20. E presents the cheque and the Bank pay it.

Analysis. In drawing the cheque D, by implication, requests the Bank to grant him an overdraft of £20 on its usual terms as to interest and other charges. In deciding to honour the cheque, the Bank by implication accepts the offer. This constitutes a regulated small consumer credit agreement for unrestricted-use, fixed-sum credit. It is a debtor-creditor agreement, and falls within section 74(1)(b) if covered by a determination under section 74(3). (Compare Example 18.)

EXAMPLE 18

Facts. F (an individual) has had a current account with the G Bank for many years. Although usually in credit, the account has been allowed by the Bank to become overdrawn from time to time. The maximum such overdraft has been is about £1,000. No explicit agreement has ever been made about overdraft facilities. Now, with a credit balance of £500, F draws a cheque for £1,300.

Analysis. It might well be held that the agreement with F (express or implied) under which the Bank operate his account includes an implied term giving him the right to overdraft facilities up to say £1,000. If so, the agreement is a regulated consumer credit agreement for unrestricted-use, running-account credit. It is a debtor-creditor agreement, and falls within section 74(1)(b) if covered by a direction under section 74(3). It is also a multiple agreement, part of which (i.e. the part not dealing with the overdraft), as referred to in section 18(1)(a), falls within a category of agreement not mentioned in this Act. (Compare Example 17.)

EXAMPLE 19

Facts. H (a finance house) agrees with J (a partnership of individuals) to open an unsecured loan account in J's name on which the debit balance is not to exceed £7,000 (having regard to payments into the account made from time to time by J). Interest is to be payable in advance on this sum, with provision for yearly adjustments. H is entitled to debit the account with interest, a "setting-up" charge, and other charges. Before J has an opportunity to draw on the account it is initially debited with £2,250 for advance interest and other charges.

Analysis. This is a personal running-account credit agreement (see sections 8(1) and 10(1)(a), and definition of "individual" in section 189(1)). By section 10(2) the credit limit is £7,000. By section 9(4) however the initial debit of £2,250, and any other charges later debited to the account by H, are not to be treated as credit even though time is allowed for their payment. Effect is given to this by section 10(3). Although the credit limit of £7,000 exceeds the amount (£5,000) specified in section 8(2) as the maximum for a consumer credit agreement, so that the agreement is not within section 10(3)(a), it is caught by section 10(3)(b)(i). At the beginning J can effectively draw (as credit) no more than £4,750, so the agreement is a consumer credit agreement.

EXAMPLE 20

Facts. K (in England) agrees with L (an individual) to bail goods to L for a period of three years certain at £2,000 a year, payable quarterly. The agreement contains no provision for the passing of the property in the goods to L.

Analysis. This is not a hire-purchase agreement (see paragraph (b) of the definition of that term in section 189(1)) and is capable of subsisting for more than three months. Paragraphs (a) and (b) of section 15(1) are therefore satisfied, but paragraph (c) is not. The payments by L must exceed £5,000 if he conforms to the agreement. It is true that under section 101 L has a right to terminate the agreement on giving K three months' notice expiring not earlier than eighteen months after the making of the agreement, but that section applies only where the agreement is a regulated consumer hire agreement apart from the section (see subsection (1)). So the agreement is not a consumer hire agreement, though it would be if the hire charge were say £1,500 a year, or there were a "break" clause in it operable by either party before the hire charges exceeded £5,000. A similar result would follow if the agreement by K had been a hiring agreement in Scotland.

EXAMPLE 21

Facts. The P Bank decides to issue cheque cards to its customers under a scheme whereby the Bank undertakes to honour cheques of up to £30 in every case where the payee has taken the cheque in reliance on the cheque card, whether the customer has funds in his account or not. The P Bank writes to the major retailers advising them of this scheme and also publicises it by advertising. The Bank issues a cheque card to Q (an individual), who uses it to pay by cheque for goods costing £20 bought by Q from R, a major retailer. At the time, Q has £500 in his account at the P Bank.

Analysis. The agreement under which the cheque card is issued to Q is a consumer credit agreement even though at all relevant times Q has more than £30 in his account. This is because Q is free to draw out his whole balance and then use the cheque card, in which case the Bank has bound itself to honour the cheque. In other words the cheque card agreement provides Q with credit, whether he avails himself of it or not. Since the amount of the credit is not subject to any express limit, the cheque card can be used any number of times. It may be presumed however that section 10(3)(b)(iii) will apply. The agreement is an unrestricted-use debtor-creditor agreement (by section 13(c)). Although the P Bank wrote to R informing R of the P Bank's willingness to honour any cheque taken by R in reliance on a cheque card, this does not constitute pre-existing arrangements as mentioned in section 13(c) because section 187(3) operates to prevent it. The agreement is not a credit-token agreement within section 14(1)(b) because payment by the P Bank to R, would be a payment of the cheque and not a payment for the goods.

EXAMPLE 22

Facts. The facts are as in Example 16. On one occasion B uses the credit-card in a way which increases his debit balance with A (Credit) to £40. A (Credit) writes to B agreeing to allow the excess on that occasion only, but stating that it must be paid off within one month.

Analysis. In exceeding his credit limit B, by implication, requests A (Credit) to allow him a temporary excess (compare Example 17). A (Credit) is thus faced by B's action with the choice of treating it as a breach of contract or granting his implied request. He does the latter. If he had done the former, B would be treated as taking credit to which he was not entitled (section 14(3)) and, subject to the terms of his contract with A (Credit), would be liable to damages for breach of contract. As it is, the agreement to allow the excess varies the original credit-token agreement by adding a new term. Under section 10(2), the new term is to be disregarded in arriving at the credit limit, so that the credit-token agreement at no time ceases to be a small agreement. By section 82(2) the later agreement is deemed to revoke the original agreement and contain provisions reproducing the combined effect of the two agreements. By section 82(4), this later agreement is exempted from Part V (except section 56).

EXAMPLE 23

Facts. Under an oral agreement made on 10th January, X (an individual) has an overdraft on his current account at the Y Bank with a credit limit of £100. On 15th February, when his overdraft standards at £90, X draws a cheque for £25. It is the first time that X has exceeded his credit limit, and on 16th February the bank honours the cheque.

Analysis. The agreement of 10th January is a consumer credit agreement for running-account credit. The agreement of 15th–16th February varies the earlier agreement by adding a term allowing the credit limit to be exceeded merely temporarily. By section 82(2) the later agreement is deemed to revoke the earlier agreement and reproduce the combined effect of the two agreements. By section 82(4), Part V of this Act (except section 56) does not apply to the later agreement. By section 18(5), a term allowing a merely temporary excess over the credit limit is not to be treated as a separate agreement, or as providing fixed-sum credit. The whole of the £115 owed to the Bank by X on 16th February is therefore running-account credit.

EXAMPLE 24

Facts. On 1st March 1975 Z (in England) enters into an agreement with A (an unincorporated body of persons) to bail to A equipment consisting of two components (component P and component Q). The agreement is not a hire-purchase agreement and is for a fixed term of 3 years, so paragraphs (a) and (b) of section 15(1) are both satisfied. The rental is payable monthly at a rate of £2,400 a year, but the agreement provides that this is to be reduced to £1,200 a year for the remainder of the agreement if at any time during its currency A returns component Q to the owner Z. On 5th May 1976 A is incorporated as A Ltd., taking over A's assets and liabilities. On 1st March 1977, A Ltd. returns component Q. On 1st January 1978, Z and A Ltd. agree to extend the earlier agreement by one year, increasing the rental for the final year by £250 to £1,450.

Analysis. When entered into on 1st March 1975, the agreement is a consumer hire agreement. A falls within the definition of "individual" in section 189(1) and if A returns component Q before 1st May 1976 the total rental will not exceed £5,000 (see section 15(1)(c)). When this date is passed without component Q having been returned it is obvious that the total rental must now exceed £5,000. Does this mean that the agreement then ceases to be a consumer hire agreement? The answer is no, because there has been no change in the terms of the agreement, and without such a change the agreement cannot move from one category to the other. Similarly, the fact that A's rights and duties under the agreement pass to a body corporate on 5th May 1976 does not cause the agreement to cease to be a consumer hire agreement (see the definition of "hirer" in section 189(1)).

The effect of the modifying agreement of 1st January 1978 is governed by section 82(2), which requires it to be treated as containing provisions reproducing the combined effect of the two actual agreements, that is to say as providing that—

(a) obligations outstanding on 1st January 1978 are to be treated as outstanding under the modifying agreement;

(b) the modifying agreement applies at the old rate of hire for the months of January and February 1978, and

(c) for the year beginning 1st March 1978 A Ltd. will be the bailee of component P at a rental of £1,450.

The total rental under the modifying agreement is £1,850. Accordingly the modifying agreement is a regulated agreement. Even if the total rental under the modifying agreement exceeded £5,000 it would still be regulated because of the provisions of section 82(3).

[A188]

NOTES

This Schedule is printed as it was in force on 15 June 2006, prior to amendments made by the Consumer Credit Act 2006 and subsequent amendments; for the text of this provision as it currently has effect, see [838].

(Sch 3 (Transitional and Commencement Provisions), Sch 4 (Minor and Consequential Amendments) outside the scope of this work.)

Index